AF694489

JONES & SUFRIN'S
EU COMPETITION LAW

JONES AND SUFRIN'S EU COMPETITION LAW

Text, Cases, and Materials

EIGHTH EDITION

Alison Jones

Solicitor, Professor of Law, King's College London

Brenda Sufrin

Solicitor, Emeritus Professor of Law, University of Bristol

Niamh Dunne

Solicitor, Associate Professor of Law, London School of Economics

OXFORD
UNIVERSITY PRESS

OXFORD
UNIVERSITY PRESS

Great Clarendon Street, Oxford, OX2 6DP,
United Kingdom

Oxford University Press is a department of the University of Oxford.
It furthers the University's objective of excellence in research, scholarship, and education by publishing worldwide. Oxford is a registered trade mark of Oxford University Press in the UK and in certain other countries

© Alison Jones, Brenda Sufrin, and Niamh Dunne 2023

The moral rights of the authors have been asserted

Fifth edition 2014
Sixth edition 2016
Seventh edition 2019

All rights reserved. No part of this publication may be reproduced, stored in a retrieval system, or transmitted, in any form or by any means, without the prior permission in writing of Oxford University Press, or as expressly permitted by law, by licence or under terms agreed with the appropriate reprographics rights organization. Enquiries concerning reproduction outside the scope of the above should be sent to the Rights Department, Oxford University Press, at the address above

You must not circulate this work in any other form
and you must impose this same condition on any acquirer

Public sector information reproduced under Open Government Licence v3.0
(http://www.nationalarchives.gov.uk/doc/open-government-licence/open-government-licence.htm)

Published in the United States of America by Oxford University Press
198 Madison Avenue, New York, NY 10016, United States of America

British Library Cataloguing in Publication Data

Data available

Library of Congress Control Number: 2023933630

ISBN 978–0–19–285501–5

Printed in the UK by
Bell & Bain Ltd., Glasgow

Links to third party websites are provided by Oxford in good faith and for information only. Oxford disclaims any responsibility for the materials contained in any third party website referenced in this work.

The manufacturer's authorised representative in the EU for product safety is Oxford University Press España S.A. of El Parque Empresarial San Fernando de Henares, Avenida de Castilla, 2 – 28830 Madrid (www.oup.es/en or product.safety@oup.com). OUP España S.A. also acts as importer into Spain of products made by the manufacturer.

PREFACE

Every new edition we comment on the breathtaking number of developments in EU competition law that have taken place since the previous one. This edition is no exception. On the contrary, not only has the breadth and pace of development in the last four years been even more remarkable than for the past editions, but it has taken place against a background of growing change, and instability, across the world. Indeed, an increasing numbers of States have been, and are, facing crises of governance, embracing populist and protectionist policies, and at the same time are having to grapple with some of the greatest challenges that they have faced in decades, including the management of the Covid-19 pandemic and its consequences, and dealing with climate change, war, energy, and cost-of-living crises, and the rising power of big corporations, especially the Big Tech companies.

Although a well-functioning economy and EU internal market, protected by rigorous enforcement of competition law (refined and reformed to meet market developments), may help a country to meet some of these challenges, the crises combined with waning trust in governments and markets to deliver good outcomes for citizens, has intensified the debate as to whether broader public policy objectives should be folded into competition law appraisal. Indeed, consideration of the question of what the objectives of EU competition law are, or should be, still continues and underpins much discussion in the book as to how the competition laws should be interpreted and applied. Different views on this matter have divided commentators, including in relation to the question of whether, and if so how, competition law should appraise conduct designed to achieve sustainability objectives, to protect workers or EU firms, and tackle issues arising in the digital age, especially in the sphere of defining markets and assessing market power, and in the application of Article 102 and EU merger control. These issues have provoked discussion not only in the EU but across the globe. In the US, for example, the leaders of the federal enforcement agencies appointed during the Biden administration have been seeking to redress alleged competition law shortcomings of the past, and to deal with problems arising from market failures, increasing concentration, and inequality, and the power of large tech firms. Although there has also been discussion in the US about new legislation to deal with these issues, so far none has been forthcoming.

In the EU, however, the perceived difficulties of applying ordinary competition law effectively in the digital economy culminated in the signing into law in September 2022 of a new Digital Markets Act, which regulates the activities of gatekeepers that provide core platform services and seeks to ensure contestable and fair markets in the digital economy. Indeed, the intense focus in the EU on competition law in the digital economy has led us to dedicate an entirely new chapter in this edition to EU competition law and policy in this sphere (Chapter 16). The need to accommodate issues including ecosystem competition, potential competition, and zero-price products has also been at the forefront in the Commission's efforts to devise a new Market Definition Notice. The revised Notice is due for publication in the third quarter of 2023; in this edition, we have worked primarily from the draft revised Notice, published in November 2022.

The debate over the objectives of EU competition law, and how they may be achieved, continues to fuel consideration of the question of how restrictions of competition within the meaning of Article 101 can be identified and balanced against offsetting benefits. A number of cases before the EU Courts, explored in Chapters 5 and 9–12, continue to raise the question of when restraints incorporated within agreements can be said to be restrictive of competition by object (including the Court of Justice's judgments in *Generics* and *Lundbeck*), how competition law can identify, prevent, deter, and punish cartel activity, how sustainability agreements and collective bargaining arrangements involving the self-employed should be appraised under Article 101, how existing principles should be applied in digital markets, and how competition policy should be balanced against broader single market objectives, especially in relation to e-commerce and against the backdrop of the Commission's broader Digital Single Market Initiative. Chapters 10 and 11 analyse the impact of the Commission's review of the horizontal cooperation and verticals regimes. The new Verticals Regime came into force on 1 June 2022, following adoption of a new Verticals Block Exemption Regulation and Guidelines in May 2022. Although the new Horizontal Cooperation Regime was due to be finalised in December 2022, the decision to delay this timetable and to extend the block exemptions until the end of June 2023 meant that we have had to work principally from the draft block exemptions and guidelines, published for consultation in March 2022 and then to incorporate the final versions, first published on 1 June 2023, as best we could at proof stage. In November 2022, the Commission also launched a review of the regime governing technology transfer agreements, which is discussed in Chapter 12.

With reference to Article 102, Chapters 6 and 7 consider the implications of numerous judgments of the EU Courts. These include the General Court's significant rulings in *Google (Shopping)* on self-preferencing conduct, *Intel (RENV)*, *Qualcomm*, and *Google (Android)*, in relation to rebates, and the Court of Justice's judgments in *Slovak Telekom*, on margin squeeze and refusal to supply, and in *Unilever* on exclusive dealing. They also consider the Commission's enforcement activity, including its investigations, infringement, and commitments decisions in diverse sectors including in the digital economy (*Amazon*, *Apple*, *Google*, and *Meta*), the pharmaceutical sector (*Aspen* and *Teva*), and energy (*Romanian Gas*). The Amendments to the Commission's Guidance Paper issued in March 2023 took us, and indeed many in the competition law community, by surprise, but we were fortunate to be able to reflect these changes at the copyediting stage.

In relation to mergers, Chapter 15 discusses developments, together with the debates, on jurisdictional gaps (including the judgments in *Illumina* and *Towercast*) the appropriate burden and standard of proof in merger cases (including the proceedings before the EU Courts in *CK Telecoms*), the role of public policy, foreign direct investment, and State subsidies, in merger control, and how EU merger rules can permit adequate scrutiny of mergers in digital markets and mergers which impact on consumers' privacy or on innovation, especially in relation to acquisitions of start-ups or emerging competitors.

New Chapter 16 focuses more specifically on how Articles 101, 102, and the EUMR have been applied to conduct and new practices emerging in the digital economy. It scrutinises some of the more ambitious theories of harm that have been advanced, and the extent to which the emergence of 'big data' may create distinct antitrust problems. It also considers the rationale for, and the provisions of, the Digital Markets Act and how it is likely to work alongside, and complement, competition law in the future.

The Commission's continuing focus on the energy, pharmaceutical, and financial sectors, as well as the digital economy, has generated a number of new cases and argument as to how competition law should: deal with issues arising in these sectors; interact with regulatory rules, liberalisation programmes, data protection, and intellectual property law; and evolve to deal with online practices and practices arising on multi-sided markets or platforms. Chapters 7, 11, 12, and 16 in particular, have to grapple with a number of these matters, including: (a) whether and if so how Article 102 can control the behaviour of firms that are vertically integrated or which operate in ecosystems; (b) whether Article 102 can limit the exercise of intellectual property rights (especially the conduct of owners of standard essential patents); (c) how Articles 101 and 102 apply to a host of distribution and other practices on online markets and platforms and patent settlement agreements; and (d) the optimal role of competition law for the digital market and how the Digital Markets Act will complement and interact with it. Further, Chapters 5, 9, and 10 consider how Article 101 has been applied to a number of agreements occurring in the financial and insurance sectors.

It is now nearly 19 years since the 'modernisation' of the enforcement of Articles 101 and 102, and the Commission has been considering the working of the competition enforcement system and whether further changes and adjustments to it are required, including whether it should be willing to grant 'comfort letters' to firms as to the compatibility of their agreements with Article 101. Although the Commission has still not made use of its powers to make a finding of inapplicability pursuant to Article 10 of Regulation 1/2003, during the Covid crisis, the Commission issued some comfort letters (see, for example, *Medicines for Europe*) and in October 2022 it adopted a more flexible antitrust Informal Guidance Notice. It has continued to use its powers to issue commitments decisions (for example, *Aspen* involving allegations of excessive pricing in the pharmaceutical sector) and to adopt settlements in cartel cases, and has also made increasing use of informal settlements under Article 7 of Regulation 1/2003 in non-cartel cases. The EU Courts have handed down some important issues on matters of practice, procedure, and enforcement. In particular, in *Sped-Pro*, competition law met the EU rule of law debate, when the General Court held that the Commission may be obliged to investigate complaints relating to practices occurring in a single Member State, if there is a risk that they may not be impartially investigated by authorities at the national level; compliance with the rule of law is a relevant factor which the Commission must take into account when determining which competition authority in the EU is best placed to act. The Court of Justice has also given judgments on the principle of *ne bis idem* (including *Slovak Telekom*, *bpost*, and *Nordzucker*), and whether private damages actions can be brought against the subsidiary of a company fined by the Commission for breaching Article 101 (*Sumal*).

Each edition has also charted the growth, encouraged by the European Commission, of enforcement of Articles 101 and 102 at the national level—both by national competition authorities, many of whom have been very active in the area of vertical agreements and digital economy sphere, and in national courts. Indeed, the trajectory of increased private enforcement has continued over the last four years and, following the introduction of the Damages Directive, in a broadening group of Member States. These actions are providing a rich line of new references to the Court of Justice (including *Sumal*, and the Court of Justice's judgment in *Paccar* on the Damages Directive concept of discoverable evidence).

These and other developments, encapsulated in a host of judgments, decisions, acts, and other measures of the Court of Justice, the Commission, the EU legislature, the national courts, and national competition authorities of the Member States, together with reports, policy debate, and commentary, have required substantial reconsideration of, and changes to, almost every chapter of this book. In some cases, the developments that have occurred have necessitated the significant restructuring, or rewriting, of a chapter as well as the introduction of the new chapter on EU competition law and policy in the digital economy.

We have attempted to process these changes and to consider their wider implications for the development of EU competition law and policy fully, whilst endeavouring to keep the book manageable. Our aim with this edition is, as ever, to provide students, and all others interested in competition law, with as comprehensive as possible a package of text, commentary, and materials given the confines of space. That task becomes more difficult with each edition, given not only the ever-expanding body of the law but also the ever-increasing body of literature and commentary on it. The last four years have seen a wealth of new literature, including the publication of a number of scholarly monographs, practitioner volumes, books combining law and economics, and articles in law journals. This is evidence of the continuing dynamism, excitement, and commercial importance of this area of law and its inter-disciplinary nature which sits at the interface of law and economics. As always, some things we would have liked to have included have been left on the cutting-room floor but we have attempted to give readers at least a flavour of the main debates and ideas, and to provide references and further reading indicating where these may be pursued.

We would like to extend our thanks to everyone who has assisted us in the preparation of this edition, in particular, Andrea Usai, the amazing King's College London 2022 competition law moot team (Leonardo Antonelli, Elena Micheli, Draga Petrovic, and Ilia Sigarev), and Isaac Cui for their research assistance, and the Dickson Poon School of Law at King's College London and the School of Law at the London School of Economics for their generous research funding. We also owe a debt of gratitude to Sera Singh, Emily Hoyland, and their colleagues at OUP, and our copy-editor Joy Ruskin-Tompkins, for their helpfulness and efficiency as always.

Our intention was to state the law as at 26 November 2022. With the cooperation of OUP, however, we have been able to include a note at least of some later developments including the adoption of the new Horizontal Cooperation Regime in June 2023.

The authors would like to dedicate this edition to Jack, Matilda, and Holly Keen; Maya Rae Lowe, and Madoc and Mostyn John; and Ailbhe Carozzi.

Alison Jones
Brenda Sufrin
Niamh Dunne
26 November 2022

ACKNOWLEDGEMENTS

Grateful acknowledgement is made to all the authors and publishers of copyright material that appear in this book, and in particular to the following for permission to reprint material from the sources indicated:

Extracts from the reports of the European Court of Justice and Court of First Instance (ECR) are taken from www.curia.europa.eu. These are unauthenticated reports and are reproduced free of charge. The definitive versions are published in Reports of Cases before the Court of Justice or the Official Journal of the European Union.

Extracts from Scalia, A. & Supreme Court Of The United States. (2003) U.S. Reports: Verizon Communications Inc. v. Law Offices of Curtis V. Trinko, LLP, 540 U.S. 398. [Periodical] Retrieved from the Library of Congress, https://www.loc.gov/item/usrep540398/; and Breyer, S. G. & Supreme Court Of The United States. (2003) U.S. Reports: F. Hoffmann-La Roche Ltd. et al. v. Empagran S. A. et al., 542 U.S. 155. [Periodical] Retrieved from the Library of Congress, https://www.loc.gov/item/usrep542155/, are in the public domain and have been reproduced free of charge.

Cambridge University Press: extracts from A. Jones and R. Nazzini, 'The Effect of Competition Law on Patent Remedies' in B Biddle, J.L. Contreras, B.J. Love, and N.V. Siebrasse, eds. Patent Remedies and Complex Products: Toward a Global Consensus (Cambridge University Press, 2019). Reproduced with permission of Cambridge University Press through PLSclear.

Columbia Business Law Review: extracts from William E. Kovacic, 'The Intellectual DNA of Modern U.S. Competition Law For Dominant Firm Conduct: The Chicago/Harvard Double Helix' [2007] 1(1) Columbia Business LR 8-10.

Hart Publishing, an imprint of Bloomsbury Publishing Plc.: extracts from G. Amato: Antitrust and the Bounds of Power (Hart, 1997). © G. Amato 1997.

Harvard Law Review Association: extracts from W. S. Comanor: 'Vertical price-fixing, vertical market restrictions, and the new antitrust policy', 98 Harvard LR 983 (1985), copyright © 1985 The Harvard Law Review Association.

Herbert Hovenkamp: extracts from H. Hovenkamp, 'Antitrust Policy After Chicago', 84 Mich LR 213 (1985).

Oxford University Press: extracts from S. D. Anderman and J. Kallaugher, Technology Transfer and the New EU Competition Rules: Intellectual Property Licensing after Modernization (OUP, 2006); J. Faull and A. Nikpay (eds.), The EU Law of Competition (3rd edn, OUP, 2014); C. Harding and J. Joshua, Regulating Cartels in Europe (2nd edn, OUP, 2010); reproduced with permission of Oxford University Press through PLSclear. Also extracts from J.L.da Cruz Vilaça, 'The Intensity of Judicial Review in Complex Economic Matters – Recent Competition Law Judgments of the Court of Justice of the EU' (2018) 6 J of Antitrust Enforcement 173, and the Journal of European Competition Law and Practice, B. Meyring, 'T-Mobile: Further confusion on information exchanges between competitors: Case C-8/08 T-Mobile Netherlands and others [2009] ECR I-4529', JECLAP 30 (2010).

RELX (UK) Limited, trading as LexisNexis: W. Allan, M. Furse, and B. Sufrin (eds.) Butterworths Competition Law.

Sweet & Maxwell Ltd: extracts from S. Bishop and M. Walker, The Economics of EC Competition Law: Concepts, Application and Measurement (3rd edn, Sweet & Maxwell, 2010); extracts from European Law Review, P. Nebbia, 'Damages Actions for the Infringement of EC Competition Law: Compensation or Deterrence?', ELRev (2008); extracts from R. Nazzini, 'The Objective of Private Remedies in EU Competition Law', Global Competition Litigation Review (2011); extracts from R. J. Van den Bergh and P. D. Camesasca, European Competition Law and Economics: A Comparative Perspective (2nd edn, Sweet & Maxwell, 2006); and extracts from Common Market Law Reports (CMLR). Reproduced with permission of Sweet & Maxwell Ltd through PLSclear.

West Academic: extracts from H. Hovenkamp, Federal Antitrust Policy: The Law of Competition and its Practice (4th edn, West, 2011) and H. Hovenkamp, Federal Antitrust Policy: The Law of Competition and its Practice (5th edn, West, 2016).

Wolters Kluwer Law & Business: extracts from Common Market Law Review, Giorgio Monti, 'Article 81 EC and Public Policy', CMLRev (2002) 1057, 'The Scope of Collective Dominance under Article 82C', 38 CMLRev (2001) 131; and extracts from L. Peeperkorn, 'IP Licences and Competition Rules: Striking the Right Balance', 26 World Competition (2003) 527; Case IV/34.174, Sealink/B&I Holyhead: Interim Measures [1992] 5 CMLR 255, G. Monti, 'Restraints on Selective Distribution Agreements' (2013) World Competition 36(4) 489.

Every effort has been made to trace and contact copyright holders prior to publication but this has not been possible in every case. If notified, the publisher will undertake to rectify any errors or omissions at the earliest opportunity.

OUTLINE CONTENTS

OUTLINE CONTENTS

CONTENTS

TABLE OF EUROPEAN CASES

COMMISSION DECISIONS

GENERAL COURT (ALPHABETICAL TABLE)

GENERAL COURT (NUMERICAL TABLE)

COURT OF JUSTICE (ALPHABETICAL TABLE)

COURT OF JUSTICE (NUMERICAL TABLE)

TABLE OF INTERNATIONAL CASES

TABLE OF LEGISLATION

EUROPEAN SECONDARY LEGISLATION

Regulations

Directives

Decisions

Notices Etc.

TABLE OF EUROPEAN AND INTERNATIONAL TREATIES, CONVENTIONS, AND CHARTERS

BIBLIOGRAPHY

The following are general works on EU competition law which cover the material dealt with in this book. Specialised reading is listed at the end of each chapter in the 'Further Reading' section.

AMATO, G., and EHLERMANN, C.-D., *EC Competition Law: A Critical Assessment* (Hart Publishing, 2007)

BELLAMY, G., and CHILD, G. (D. Bailey and L. John, eds.), *European Union Law of Competition* (8th edn, Oxford University Press, 2018)

BISHOP, S., and WALKER, M., *The Economics of EC Competition Law* (3rd edn, Sweet & Maxwell, 2010)

FAULL, J., and NIKPAY, A. (eds.), *The EU Law of Competition* (3rd edn, Oxford University Press, 2014)

FOX, E.M., and GERARD, D., *EU Competition Law* (2nd edn., Edward Elgar, 2023)

GOYDER, J., and ALBORS-LLORENS, A., *Goyder's EC Competition Law* (5th edn, Oxford University Press, 2009)

MONTI, G., *EC Competition Law* (Cambridge University Press, 2007)

MOTTA, M., *Competition Policy: Theory and Practice* (Cambridge University Press, 2004)

VAN BAEL, I., and BELLIS, J.-F., *Competition Law of the European Community* (6th edn, Wolters Kluwer, 2021)

VAN DE GRONDEN, J. W., and RUSU, C. S., *Competition Law in the EU* (Edward Elgar, 2021)

WHISH, R., and BAILEY, D., *Competition Law* (9th edn, Oxford University Press, 2018)

Blogs

Chilling' Competition <http://chillingcompetition.com> (Alfonso Lamadrid de Pablo and Pablo Ibáñez Colomo)

The Platform Law Blog <https://the platformlaw.blog> (Geradin Partners)

LIST OF ABBREVIATIONS

AAC	average avoidable cost
AEC	as efficient competitor
AFG	Bundesanstalt für Arbeit (Federal Office for Employment, the Bundesanstalt, Germany)
AI	artificial intelligence
AIC	average incremental cost
AJIL	*American Journal of International Law*
All ER	All England Law Reports
Am Econ Rev	*American Economic Review*
Ant Bull	*Antitrust Bulletin*
APPA	Across Platform Parity Agreement
ATC	average total cost
ATP	absolute territorial protection
AVC	average variable cost
Bell J Econ	*Bell Journal of Economics*
BER	block exemption regulation
BYIL	*British Yearbook of International Law*
CAP	Common Agricultural Policy
CAT	Competition Appeal Tribunal
CFI	Court of First Instance (renamed as General Court (GC) by the Treaty of Lisbon)
Charter	Charter of Fundamental Rights of the European Union
CISAC	International Confederation of Societies of Authors and Composers
CJ	Court of Justice
CJEU	Court of Justice of the European Union
CLI	*Competition Law Insight*
CLJ	*Cambridge Law Journal*
CLP	*Current Legal Problems*
CLPD	*Competition Law & Policy Debate*
CMA	Competition and Markets Authority (UK)
CMLR	Common Market Law Reports
CMLRev	*Common Market Law Review*
CMO	Common Organisation of Agricultural Markets
CompAR	Competition Appeal Reports
Comp Law	*Competition Law Journal*
Cowp	Cowper's King's Bench Report
CPS	core platform services
CYELS	*Cambridge Yearbook of European Legal Studies*
DG Comp	European Commission Competition Directorate-General
DMA	Digital Markets Act
DOJ	Department of Justice (US)

EAGCP	European Advisory Group on Competition Policy
EBU	European Broadcasting Union
EC	European Community
ECC	European Commercial Cases
ECHR	European Convention for the Protection of Human Rights
ECJ	European Court of Justice
ECLR	*European Competition Law Review*
ECN	European Competition Network
ECR	European Court Reports
ECSC	European Coal and Steel Community
ECtHR	European Court of Human Rights
EEA	European Economic Area
EEC	European Economic Community
EFTA	European Free Trade Area
EGD	European Green Deal
EGLR	Estates Gazette Law Reports
EHRLR	*European Human Right Law Review*
EHRR	European Human Rights Reports
EIPR	*European Intellectual Property Review*
ELRev	*European Law Review*
ESA	EFTA Surveillance Authority
EStAL	*European State Aid Law Quarterly*
ETSI	European Telecommunications Standards Institute
EU	European Union
EUConst	*European Constitutional Law Review*
EUMR	European Union Merger Regulation (Reg. 139/2004)
Euratom	European Atomic Energy Community
EVP	Executive Vice-President
EWCA Civ	England and Wales Court of Appeal (Civil)
EWHC	England and Wales High Court
FCO	Federal Cartel Office (Bundeskartellamt, Germany)
FDI	foreign direct investment
FIFA	International Federation of Association Football
Fla LR	*Florida Law Review*
Fordham Corp L Inst	*Fordham Corporate Law Institute*
Fordham Int'l LJ	*Fordham International Law Journal*
FRAND	fair, reasonable, and non-discriminatory
FTAIA	Foreign Trade Antitrust Improvements Act (US)
FTC	Federal Trade Commission (US)
GAFAM	Google, Apple, Facebook, Amazon, Microsoft
GC	General Court (formerly the Court of First Instance)
Geo LJ	*Georgetown Law Review*
GUPPI	gross upward pricing pressure index
HBERs	Horizontal Block Exemption Regulations

HHI	Herfindahl–Hirschman index
HMG	Horizontal Merger Guidelines
HMT	hypothetical monopolist test
HO	Hearing Officer
ICLQ	*International and Comparative Law Quarterly*
ICN	International Competition Network
Indus & Corp Change	*Industrial and Corporate Change*
IOC	International Olympic Committee
IP	intellectual property
IPR	intellectual property right
J	*Journal*
JBL	*Journal of Business Law*
JECLAP	*Journal of European Competition Law and Practice*
JIEL	*Journal of International Economic Law*
JO	Journal Officiel
JV	joint venture
LIEI	*Legal Issues in European Integration/Legal Issues in Economic Integration*
LJ	*Law Journal*
LPP	legal professional privilege
LR	*Law Review*
LRAIC	long-run average incremental cost
MES	minimum efficient scale
MFN	most favoured nation
Mich LR	*Michigan Law Review*
MIF	multilateral interchange fee
MLP	Model Leniency Programme
MLR	*Modern Law Review*
NBS	New (or Neo) Brandeis School
NCAs	national competition authorities
New York Univ LR	*New York University Law Review*
NHMG	Non-Horizontal Merger Guidelines
NJECL	*New Journal of European Criminal Law*
NRA	national regulatory authority
OECD	Organisation for Economic Co-operation and Development
OFT	Office of Fair Trading (UK)
OJ	Official Journal
OPEC	Organization of the Petroleum Exporting Countries
OS	operating system
P & I	protection and indemnity
P2B	platform-to-business
PPLR	*Public Procurement Law Review*
PSO	public service obligation
Quart J of Econ	*Quarterly Journal of Economics*
R&D	research and development

RdC	Recueil des Cours de l'Académie de droit international de La Haye
RPM	resale price maintenance
RRC	raising rivals' costs
SCI	single continuing infringement
SDS	selective distribution system
SEP	standard-essential patent
SGEI	service of general economic interest
SGI	service of general interest
SIEC	significant impediment to effective competition
SLC	substantial lessening of competition
SMEs	small and medium-sized enterprises
SMP	substantial market power
SO	statement of objections
SRMC	short-run marginal cost
SSNDQ	Small but Significant Non-transitory Deterioration of the Quality
SSNIP	Small but Significant Non-transitory Increase in Price
Stan LR	*Stanford Law Review*
TEU	Treaty on European Union
TFEU	Treaty on the Functioning of the European
Union	Technology Transfer Block Exemption
TTBER	Regulation (Reg. 772/2004) (or BER)
UNCTAD	United Nations Conference on Trade and Development
Univ Chic LR	*University of Chicago Law Review*
U Pa LR	*University of Pennsylvania Law Review*
UPP	upward pricing pressure
USO	universal service obligation
VBER	Vertical Block Exemption Regulation (Reg. 2022/720)
Wash Univ LR	*University of Washington Law Review*
WD	working day
WTO	World Trade Organization
YEL	*Yearbook of European Law*

1

INTRODUCTION TO COMPETITION LAW

1. CENTRAL ISSUES

1. Competition law is concerned with ensuring that firms operating in the free market economy do not prevent the market from functioning optimally by acting anti-competitively.
2. Over the last few decades, the world economy has become globalised and this has brought disadvantages as well as benefits. The world at present is dealing with a number of crises: the aftermath of Covid-19, climate change, and war in Europe in the shape of the Russian invasion of Ukraine. In digitisation, it is going through a fourth industrial revolution. Competition law has to be viewed against this background.
3. This chapter explains the economic theory that holds that competition amongst undertakings produces the best outcomes for society. The theory employs models of perfect competition and monopoly, and concepts of welfare and efficiency.
4. Competition law is concerned with preventing restrictive agreements between firms, dealing with oligopolistic markets, preventing anti-competitive behaviour by firms with market power, and preventing anti-competitive mergers. Competition law in the EU is also concerned with State aid, whereby Member States give favourable treatment to particular undertakings.
5. Competition law's function is to make markets work well. However, there are differing views about what exactly this means. It is possible for systems of competition law to simply pursue the economic objectives of welfare and efficiency. Whether competition law should do this, or should pursue other objectives, is a matter of ongoing controversy. Ordoliberalism, a school of political theory originating in Germany, includes ideas about competition which have been influential in the EU. Since the 1970s the views of the Chicago School, which holds that the sole aim of competition law should be efficiency and welfare, have been in the ascendant, but recently there has been a resurgence of the belief that competition law should serve a wider range of socio-political goals.
6. Competition law is embedded in the EU's economic constitution. The imperative of the integration of the single market is a fundamental and unique aspect of EU competition law.
7. From the 1990s onwards, EU competition law underwent a process of 'modernisation' in which the EU Commission directed the application of the competition rules to the objective of consumer welfare. The attitude of the EU Courts was more ambivalent. 'Fairness' has featured prominently in the rhetoric of the Competition Commi8.ssioner since 2014. In March 2023, the Commission announced a revised policy towards exclusionary abuse of dominance cases.
8. The development of digital markets and the rise of Big Tech present particular challenges for competition law.

2. INTRODUCTION

A. GENERAL

Modern competition policy is concerned with ensuring that firms operating in a free market economy do not, by acting anti-competitively, prevent the market from functioning optimally.[1] The terms competition *policy* and competition *law* are often used synonymously but for present purposes competition law can be described as the means by which competition policy is implemented. A market economy is one in which the allocation of resources is determined by supply and demand in free markets. There are different models of market economy but the basis of a free market is competition between firms, with industry and commerce in private hands. A social market economy combines a capitalist free market with government regulation and a social welfare system.

The foundation of free market theory is usually located in the eighteenth-century work of Adam Smith.[2] He considered that governments should remove artificial obstacles to the operation of free markets, such as price controls, and allow competition to flourish. Individuals pursuing their own self-interest competing in the marketplace would be led by the 'invisible hand' to achieve the general good:

> Every individual necessarily labours to render the annual revenue of the society as great as he can. He generally neither intends to promote the public interest, nor knows how much he is promoting it . . . He intends only his own gain, and he is in this, as in many other cases, led by an invisible hand to promote an end which was no part of his intention. Nor is it always the worse for society that it was no part of his intention. By pursuing his own interest he frequently promotes that of the society more effectually than when he really intends to promote it. I have never known much good done by those who affected to trade for the public good.[3]

From this developed the concept of the market as an efficient and self-regulating mechanism. Faith in the market was shaken by the Great Depression of the 1930s, but it recovered to become by the second half of the twentieth century the organising principle of western economies, exported around the world. For some three decades after the Second World War, free market capitalism was tempered, under the influence of the ideas of John Maynard Keynes,[4] by government intervention in the economy, regulated markets, substantial social welfare programmes, and high taxes on business and the wealthy. This consensus was challenged in the 1970s (which saw a number of economic calamities such as the oil crisis, rising unemployment, and runaway inflation) by the 'neoliberal' ideology of

[1] For a historical survey of pre-modern rules in respect, inter alia, of monopolies, restrictive practices, and high prices dating back to the ancient world, see N. Green, 'From Rome to Rome: The Evolution of Competition Law into a Twenty-first Century Religion' [2010] *Comp Law* 7; B. Hawk, *Antitrust and Competition Laws* (Juris Publishing, 2020), Chap. 2.

[2] See Adam Smith, *An Inquiry into the Nature and Causes of the Wealth of Nations* (1776, reprinted Penguin, 1999).

[3] Ibid., Book IV. The phrase 'the invisible hand' also appears in *The Theory of Moral Sentiments* (1759, reprinted Penguin Classics, 2010), Part IV, Chap. 1, in which Smith argues that the rich benefit the poor through their investment and employment and that 'they are led by an invisible hand to make nearly the same distribution of the necessaries of life, which would have been made, had the earth been divided into equal proportions among all its inhabitants, and thus without intending it, without knowing it, advance the interest of the society, and afford means to the multiplication of the species'. For the argument that Smith has been wrongly misrepresented as a market fundamentalist and an apologist for inequality and human selfishness, see J. Norman, *Adam Smith: What He Thought and Why it Matters* (Allen Lane, 2018).

[4] (1883–1946); J. M. Keynes, *The General Theory of Employment, Interest and Money* (Macmillan, 1936).

economists and political theorists such as Friedrich von Hayek,[5] Milton Friedman,[6] and other adherents of 'Chicago School economics'.[7] Neoliberalism advocates the deregulation of national economies, privatisation, downsizing government, tax cutting, and the liberalisation of international trade to create a single global market.[8] These policies were put into practice in the 1980s by the UK government of Margaret Thatcher and in the US by Ronald Reagan. They became the new orthodoxy around the world, driven by the international financial institutions (the IMF and the World Bank) imposing the 'Washington Consensus' on their client governments by conditioning aid on the implementation of neoliberal policies.[9]

The fall of the Communist regimes of the Soviet Union and Eastern Europe in 1990 was celebrated as the triumph of free market capitalism over central planning. However, the financial crisis of 2008 shattered any belief that markets are omniscient.[10] In contrast to the caution which Adam Smith displayed towards banks,[11] from the 1960s onwards financial economists developed theories such as the efficient-market hypothesis[12] and rational expectations theory[13] which posited financial markets as rational, self-correcting organisms. Financial trading was globalised, financial markets were deregulated, and new and highly complex securitisation instruments were developed. When the whole edifice came crashing down, affecting the non-financial as well as the financial economy (at least in the West), governments embarked on huge interventions in order to rescue their financial institutions. The crisis led to a widespread loss of faith in the robustness of the market and a rejection of some of the wilder excesses of free market capitalism.

The consequences of the austerity policies with which many western governments responded to the financial crisis after the bail-out of the banks fuelled popular disenchantment with globalisation. Globalisation is the increasing inter-connectedness of the world economically, culturally, socially, and politically. It has accelerated to an enormous degree since 1970, driven by the neoliberal vision of a single free global market, and by the international economic institutions, the vastly increased number of transnational corporations, and latterly by the development of digital technology which has revolutionised communications and flows of capital across the world. The benefits of globalisation, however, have been unevenly spread, and globalisation has engendered vast inequalities of wealth and prosperity, both between countries and within them[14] while markets have become more concentrated. The resulting discontent contributed to the populism which helped to propel Trump,

[5] (1899–1992), see *The Road to Serfdom* (Routledge, 1944).

[6] (1912–2006), see *Capitalism and Freedom* (1962, 40th anniversary edn, Chicago University Press, 2002).

[7] Called after the university where many of its originators did their work. For Chicago School antitrust, see Section 5.A.iii.

[8] See D. Harvey, *A Brief History of Neoliberalism* (Oxford University Press, 2005).

[9] The 'consensus' being that between the US Treasury, the IMF, and the World Bank. The policies include fiscal discipline, reduction in public expenditure, financial liberalisation, privatisation of State enterprises, deregulation of the economy, and promotion of foreign direct investment. Ironically, the IMF, which emerged from the 1944 Bretton Woods Conference, was the child of Maynard Keynes.

[10] For a general overview of the financial crisis and the relevant theories of the economics of financial markets, see J. Cassidy, *How Markets Fail: The Logic of Economic Calamities* (Allen Lane, 2009); A. Tooze, *Crashed: How a Decade of Financial Crises Changed the World* (Allen Lane, 2018).

[11] *An Inquiry into the Nature and Causes of the Wealth of Nations*, n. 2, 402.

[12] Efficient-market hypothesis is particularly associated with Professor Eugene Fama, see e.g. E. Fama, 'Efficient Capital Markets: A Review of Theory and Empirical Work' (1970) 25 *J of Finance* 383–441.

[13] See J. Muth, 'Rational Expectations and the Theory of Price Movements' (1961) 29 *Econometrica* 315–333; R. Lucas, 'Expectations and the Neutrality of Money' (1972) 4 *J of Econ Theory* 103–112.

[14] See T. Piketty, *Capital in the Twenty-first Century* (Harvard University Press, 2014); J. Stiglitz, *The Price of Inequality* (Penguin, 2013); A. Atkinson, *Inequality: What Can Be Done?* (Harvard University Press, 2015, reprinted 2018). For the argument that it is the disastrous *mismanagement* of globalisation which has failed, see J. Stiglitz, *Globalization and its Discontents: Anti-Globalization in the Era of Trump* (Penguin, 2017).

with his promise of national protectionism, to the White House, contributed to the 'leave' vote in the UK's EU referendum, and changed the political landscape in many European countries.

The 2008 financial crisis was followed in 2010 by the Eurozone debt crisis.[15] Then, in 2020, came the Covid-19 pandemic. The response of governments throughout the world was to shut down economic, educational, and social activity and, abandoning any idea that everything could be left to the market, to undertake massive interventions in the economy to support businesses and citizens—loans, guarantees, bail-outs, subsidies, tax cuts, furlough schemes, and so on. By November 2021, governments were estimated to have spent $17 trillion coping with the fall-out from the pandemic.[16]

By the time the pandemic broke out, climate change (discussed in Section 2.B) had finally been recognised by the global community, albeit belatedly, as an existential threat to life as we know it. Covid-19—a zoonotic mutation—glaringly illustrated how the exploitation and misuse of the earth's resources had already brought calamity, and the pandemic has been described as 'a comprehensive crisis of the neoliberal era'[17] by a scholar who says:

> The historic force that finally burst the dykes of the neoliberal order was not radical populism or the revival of class struggle—it was a plague unleashed by heedless global growth and the massive flywheel of financial accumulation.[18]

This does not mean that the belief that competition in free markets produces optimal outcomes for society has suddenly been replaced by faith in central planning or wholesale government intervention in consumer markets. Rather, it means that there is a renewed questioning of the place of competition in the economy and of the role and goals of competition policies.[19] The EU, for example, considers that competition is central to its economic recovery from the pandemic and its attempts to transform its economy in response to the climate change crisis.[20]

Along with the pandemic and the climate change crisis, another phenomenon which is changing the world is digitisation and the rise of the Big Tech firms with unprecedented power. This is discussed in Section 12 of this chapter, Chapter 16, and in context throughout the book. Finally, Russia's invasion of Ukraine in February 2022 resulted in a severe and ongoing shock to the global economy, particularly in Europe with its heavy reliance on Russia's energy supplies and Ukrainian food production.

B. CLIMATE CHANGE AND SUSTAINABILITY

(i) General

Climate change is the greatest problem facing humanity.[21] This generation must tackle the environmental crisis before it is engulfed by it and the EU is at the forefront of international efforts to limit global warming by decarbonising the world economy by mid-century. This is now the absolute

[15] Which had particularly severe effects on Portugal, Ireland, Italy, Greece, and Spain.

[16] *The Economist*, 18 November 2021, 13.

[17] A. Tooze, *Shutdown: How COVID-19 Shook the World's Economy* (Allen Lane, 2021), 22.

[18] A. Tooze, 'COVID-19 and the Crisis of Neoliberalism', *The Observer*, 2 September 2021.

[19] For the argument that too much competition is not a good thing, see M. E. Stucke, 'Is Competition Always Good?' (2013) 1(1) *J of Antitrust Enforcement* 162; M. Stucke and A. Ezrachi, *Competition Overdose: How Free Market Mythology Transformed Us From Citizen Kings to Market Servants* (HarperBus, 2020).

[20] See <https://ec.europa.eu/competition-policy/policy/green-gazette_en>.

[21] See IPCC, *Climate Change 2021: The Physical Science Basis, Contribution of Working Group 1 to the Sixth Assessment Report of the Intergovernmental Panel on Climate Change* (V. Masson-Delmotte et al. (eds.), Cambridge University Press, 2021). The IPCC (Intergovernmental Panel on Climate Change) is the UN body which assesses science related to climate change; J. R. McNeil and P. Engelke, *The Great Acceleration: An Environmental History of the Anthropocene Since 1945* (Harvard University Press, 2016).

priority of the European Commission, which recognises that climate change and environmental degradation 'present an existential threat to Europe and the world'.[22]

The EU is a signatory to the 2016 Paris Agreement, as are the individual Member States. The Paris Agreement is a legally binding international treaty on climate change which had, as at February 2023, been ratified or acceded to by 194 States (plus the EU) who are parties to the United Nations Framework Convention on Climate Change (UNFCCC).[23] The goal of the Paris Agreement is to limit global warming to below 2 degrees Celsius, and preferably to 1.5 degrees, compared to pre-industrial levels. This requires the parties to reduce their greenhouse gas emissions as soon as possible in order to achieve a climate-neutral world by mid-century. In fact, in the light of the alarming findings of the 2021 IPCC report,[24] the Paris Agreement timeframe may need reviewing and the 'mid-century' target brought forward, although little progress was made at COP27 in November 2022. The achievement of climate neutrality requires the transformation of the world's economies.

Sustainable development is 'development that meets the needs of the present without compromising the ability of future generations to meet their own needs'.[25] This obviously covers the climate but the concept of sustainability is broader than this and encompasses 'three pillars'—economics, society (or 'social equity'), and the environment.[26] All these intertwined elements must be taken into account. The 2015 UN resolution on the 2030 Agenda for Sustainable Development set out 17 sustainable development goals including—as well as taking urgent action to combat climate change and its impacts—ending poverty in all forms everywhere, ending hunger, reducing inequality within and among countries, ensuring healthy lives, and promoting well-being for all at all ages.[27]

(ii) The European Green Deal

The European Green Deal (EGD) is the EU's strategy for tackling climate change and achieving sustainability. The EGD has the goal of making Europe the first climate-neutral continent by 2050. The EGD was originally unveiled by the Commission in December 2019,[28] but in December 2020 the Council endorsed a new binding EU target for a net domestic reduction in greenhouse gas emissions of at least 55 per cent, compared to 1990 levels, by 2030. The EU's commitment to climate neutrality and to the intermediate '55 per cent by 2030' target are enshrined in the European Climate Law.[29] In July 2021, the Commission adopted a package of legislative proposals and initiatives to make the EU's

[22] Commission Press Release, 11 December 2019, IP/19/6691.

[23] The UNFCCC entered into force on 21 March 1994. See <https://UNFCCC.int/>. The Paris Agreement was adopted at COP21 (the 21st Conference of the Parties to the UNFCCC) in Paris on 12 December 2015. It entered into force on 4 December 2016. The US left the Agreement in November 2020, but rejoined again at the beginning of President Biden's presidency in 2021.

[24] See n. 21.

[25] The definition adopted by the United Nations World Commission on Environment and Development (WCED), previously the Brundtland Commission, in its seminal 1987 report, 'Our Common Future'.

[26] See OECD, 'Sustainability and Competition', OECD Competition Committee Discussion Paper (Julian Norway), (2020) <www.oecd.org/daf/competition/sustainability-and-competition-2020.pdf>, prepared for the OECD best practice roundtable in December 2020, <www.oecd.org/daf/competition/sustainability-and-competition.htm>.

[27] UN, 'Transforming our world: the 2030 Agenda for Sustainable Development', <https://sdgs.un.org>.

[28] Communication from the Commission to the European Parliament, the European Council, the Council, the Economic and Social Committee and the Committee of the Regions, 'The European Green Deal', COM(2019) 640 final, 11 December 2019 (Communications from the Commission to the other EU institutions are subsequently referred to as 'Communication from the Commission').

[29] Council Reg. 2021/1119 on establishing the framework for achieving climate neutrality (European Climate Law) [2021] OJ L243/1, see Press Release 562/21, <www.consilium.europa.eu/en/press/press-releases/2021/06/28/council-adopts-european-climate-law/pdf>; <https://climate.ec.europa.eu/eu-action/european-green-deal_en>.

climate, energy, land use, transport, and taxation policies fit for achieving the 55 per cent reduction.[30] It had already published its Biodiversity[31] and Farm to Fork[32] strategies. The Commission sees the Green Deal as 'our lifeline out of the Covid-19 pandemic'[33] and as fundamentally transforming 'our economy and society for a fair, green and prosperous future'.[34]

(iii) Competition Law, Climate Change, and Sustainability

Action to combat climate change and promote sustainability primarily involves government initiatives, public regulation, and the enactment of legislation but this alone is not enough. The mobilisation of the private sector is crucial as the low carbon transition is impossible without innovation from the players on the market developing the green products, systems, and services which are needed to replace those which are destroying the environment. The question therefore arises as to how competition law, which deals with the practices and transactions of private firms competing on the market, could or should respond to the need for sustainability and take environmental factors into account. There is much debate about this, which is the continuation of arguments about public policy factors in competition law which have gone on for decades.[35] If sustainability is to be taken into account (called the 'greening' of competition law[36]), there may need to be a rethinking of basic concepts such as consumer welfare and efficiency[37] and a significant reorientation of the law in many jurisdictions. How such reorientation can be done within any particular jurisdiction depends on the position of competition law within the constitutional, legal, and administrative structure of that state.[38]

We examine these issues in respect of EU competition law in the relevant places throughout this book.

3. THE PURPOSE OF COMPETITION LAW

Competition law seeks to deal with market imperfections and failures. It strengthens the workings of the market by prohibiting anti-competitive behaviour by firms acting alone or in concert. A firm which is a monopolist or is in what in EU law is called a 'dominant position' may face no constraints

[30] Communication from the Commission, 'Fit for 55: delivering the EU's 2030 Climate Target on the way to climate neutrality', COM(2021) 550 final, 14 July 2021; 'European Green Deal: Commission proposes transformation of EU economy and society to meet climate ambitions', IP/21/3541.

[31] Communication from the Commission, 'EU Biodiversity Strategy for 2030, Bringing nature back into our lives', COM(2020) 380 final, 20 May 2020.

[32] Communication from the Commission, 'A Farm to Fork Strategy for a fair, healthy and environmentally-friendly food system', COM(2020) 381 final, 20 May 2020. Its objective is to have at least 25% of the EU's agricultural land under organic farming by 2030 and a significant increase in organic aquaculture.

[33] <https://commission.europa.eu/strategy-and-policy/priorities-2019-2024/european-green-deal_en>.

[34] IP/21/354.

[35] See, in particular, the discussion in Section 7 on the goals of competition law, Section 9.B on the objectives of EU competition law, Chap. 5 on the substantive appraisal of Art. 101 TFEU and Chap. 15 on mergers.

[36] See Executive Vice-President M. Vestager, 'The Green Deal and Competition Policy', Renew Webinar, 22 September 2020, <https://ec.europa.eu/commission/commissioners/2019-2024/vestager/announcements/green-deal-and-competition-policy_en>, referring to 'our debate on greening competition policy' and, e.g., S. Kingston, *Greening EU Competition Law and Policy* (Cambridge University Press, 2011); G. Monti, 'Four Options for a Greener Competition Law' (2020) 11(3)–(4) *JECLAP* 124; S. Holmes, D. Middelschulte, and M. Snoep (eds.), *Competition Law, Climate Change and Environmental Sustainability* (Concurrences, 2021); S. Holmes, *Climate Change, Sustainability and Competition Law* (2020) 8 *J of Antitrust Enforcement* 354; cf. C. Veljanovski, 'The Case Against Green Antitrust' (2022) 18 *European Competition Journal*, available at <https://ssrn.com/abstract=3955340>.

[37] See Section 4.F.

[38] See OECD, 'Sustainability and Competition', OECD Competition Committee Discussion Paper (2020).

on its exercise of 'market power'. Market power, a concept which is discussed in Chapter 3, basically means in neoclassical economics the ability to keep prices high over a period of time, but also to prejudicially affect the other 'parameters of competition' by restricting output or innovation, lowering quality, or limiting choice, for example. However, firms in markets with many players, if left alone to determine their own conduct, are likely to combine or collude in ways which restrict competition and allow them collectively to exercise market power. Adam Smith himself described the tendency of those operating within the same trade to conspire to fix prices,[39] in what we now call cartels. On markets where only a few firms operate without any one of them dominating (called an oligopoly) they may be able to behave as monopolists by acting together without conspiring. Positions of market power may also be created by firms merging with one another. Competition laws may therefore be framed:

(a) to prevent restrictive agreements between firms;

(b) to deal with anti-competitive behaviour by dominant firms;

(c) to deal with the anti-competitive consequences of oligopolistic markets; and

(d) to prevent mergers which lead to concentrations with market power.

The widespread recognition of the need to have some form of such rules means that the great majority of countries now have competition law regimes and over 120 jurisdictions are members of the International Competition Network (ICN), the virtual network of competition authorities discussed in Chapter 17.

The rise of the Big Tech firms of the digital economy is presenting competition law with new challenges and leading to a rethinking of the nature and shape of competition rules.[40] One problem is that the traditional concept of market power is insufficient to deal with zero-price markets, where consumers are given services for free in exchange for surrendering their personal data. Moreover, the concern is not just that Big Tech firms have *market* power in the traditional sense but that they also have *economic* power—the excess influence owners of large businesses can exert over political and commercial markets. In the case of Big Tech, it extends to a power of influence or control over every aspect of life including political and democratic processes. Another problem is that the digital economy is characterised by competition between ecosystems rather than single products and services. An ecosystem is a web of complementary goods and services designed to work together, where innovation and evolution is coordinated across different firms, markets, and industries 'whose individual business activities share in some large measure the fate of the whole community'.[41]

Competition can also be distorted by the actions of the State in the form, for example, of legislative, administrative, or regulatory provisions. In Chapter 8, we discuss this in respect of EU competition law. Furthermore, the EU has a large body of rules on 'State aid' which specifically concern aid, such as financial advantages, given by Member States to particular firms. This book does not deal comprehensively with State aid (otherwise it would be twice the size) but Section 13 of this chapter describes the State aid regime in outline.

[39] *An Inquiry into the Nature and Causes of the Wealth of Nations*, n. 2.

[40] See I. Lianos and B. Carballa Smichowski, 'Economic Power and New Business Models in Competition Law and Economics: Ontology and New Metrics' (15 March 2021), available at <https://ssrn.com/abstract=3818943>; V. H. S. E. Robertson, 'Antitrust, Big Tech, and Democracy: A Research Agenda' (2022) 67(2) *Ant Bull* 259; I. Lianos, 'Reorienting Competition Law' (2022) 10 *J of Antitrust Enforcement* 1; and generally Chap. 16.

[41] J. F. Moore, 'Business Ecosystems and the View from the Firm' (2006) 51(1) *Ant Bull* 31, 33; Lianos and Carballa Smichowski, n. 40.

In respect of terminology, it should be noted that competition law is often called by its American name, 'antitrust' or 'antitrust law'. However, the European Commission (the EU competition authority of which DG Comp is the Competition Directorate) uses the term 'antitrust' to denote the areas of competition law other than merger control and State aid. The reader will find, nevertheless, that many of the sources quoted in this book use 'antitrust' in its more general meaning.

4. THE ECONOMICS OF COMPETITION LAW

In this section, we set out some basic concepts of neoclassical welfare economics and explain why competition is considered to achieve efficiency and produce the greatest benefits to society in the form of welfare.[42]

A. BASIC CONCEPTS

(i) Demand Curves and Consumer and Producer Surplus

Consumers place different values on things, have different preferences and different incomes, and will consequently be willing to pay different prices for a particular product. The maximum amount a consumer is willing to pay for a product is their reservation price. Suppliers might wish to charge each consumer their individual reservation price but in practice this is not usually possible (although it is becoming more so in some online markets where sellers can exploit customers' data to tailor prices to the individual). The supplier must therefore consider the relationship between the consumer's willingness to pay and the quantity which will be bought on the market as a whole. If only buyers with very high reservation prices are supplied, the quantity produced will be smaller than if buyers with lower reservation prices are supplied. Conversely, if greater quantities are produced the price will have to fall to incorporate buyers with lower reservation prices. The relationship between price and supply is represented by the market demand curve. The demand curve normally slopes downwards from left to right.

Assuming a market price of £50, we see that some consumers will be paying £50 for a product for which they would have paid more. This results in what is known as *consumer surplus* and is shown by the hatched area in Fig. 1.1. It is the difference between the buyers' reservation price and the market price.[43]

The supply curve shows the marginal cost of production. In Fig. 1.1 we see that the producer is selling the output for more than it costs to produce. This results in what is known as *producer surplus* and is shown by the shaded area in Fig. 1.1.

(ii) Elasticity of Demand (Own Price Elasticity)

The amount by which the quantity demanded increases as price reduces (and vice versa) depends on the elasticity of demand for the product.

[42] See D. Geradin, A. Layne-Farrar, and N. Petit, *EU Competition Law and Economics* (Oxford University Press, 2012), 2.10–2.34; J. Faull and A. Nikpay (eds.), *The EU Law of Competition* (3rd edn, Oxford University Press, 2014) (Faull and Nikpay), Chap. 1, 1.21–1.119. Many of the team who write Faull and Nikpay are past or present European Commission officials.

[43] The concept of consumer surplus was first described by Alfred Marshall, *Principles of Economics* (8th edn, Macmillan, 1920).

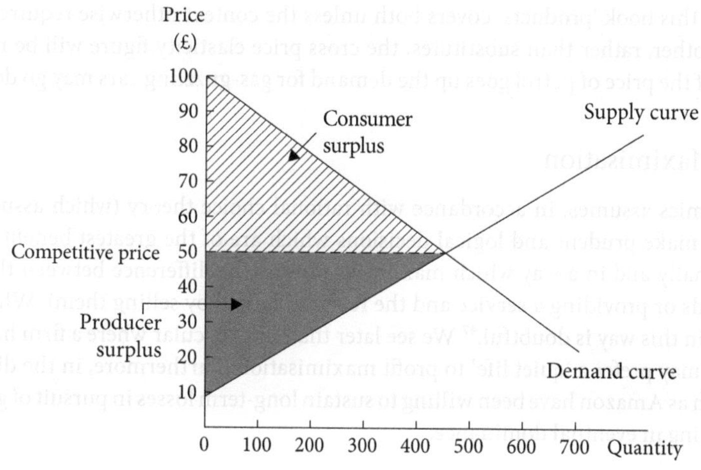

Figure 1.1 Demand curve and consumer and producer surplus

Price elasticity of demand measures the sensitivity of the quantity demanded to the price. Demand is said to be *inelastic* if an increase in price leads to an insignificant fall in demand. Conversely, demand is *elastic* if an increase in price leads to a significant fall in demand.

Technically, price elasticity of demand is the percentage change in the quantity of a product demanded divided by the corresponding percentage change in its price. The result is a negative figure as the fall in demand is expressed as a negative figure from the starting point. If demand for widgets[44] falls by 2 per cent as a result of a 1 per cent price increase, the change in demand will be expressed as –2 per cent. The demand elasticity is then –2 divided by 1 (the price increase), which is –2.[45] Typically, elasticity falls as one moves down the demand curve, so that at higher prices demand is more elastic. Economic theory puts the dividing line between elastic and inelastic demand at –1. Demand is elastic at a figure below, or more negative, than –1. It is inelastic between –1 and 0. In markets where demand is inelastic, shortages will lead to higher prices. So a bad harvest may be better for food producers than a good one. The position of an individual firm is different from that of producers on the market as a whole. Even if the demand for a product is inelastic, the price for any individual brand may not be.

(iii) Cross-elasticity of Demand

Cross price elasticity of demand measures how much the demand for one product (A) increases when the price of *another* (B) goes up. It is measured by the percentage change in the quantity demanded of product A divided by the percentage increase in the price of B. Cross-elasticity of demand is crucial to market definition.[46]

Cross price elasticity is positive if the price increase in B leads to an increase in demand for A, and this suggests that A and B are substitutes. There may be cross price elasticity in one direction and not in the other. Coffee drinkers may not drink tea when the price of coffee increases, but this does not mean that tea drinkers would not turn to coffee in response to a similar price rise in tea. If products

[44] A widget is a mythical product with no specific characteristics used in competition law examples.

[45] This figure is often expressed without the minus (as it is always negative). The bigger the negative number, the 'higher' the elasticity, e.g. elasticity of –5 is higher than elasticity of –1.

[46] See Chap. 3, Section 4.

(or services, in this book 'products' covers both unless the context otherwise requires) are complements of each other, rather than substitutes, the cross price elasticity figure will be negative rather than positive. If the price of petrol goes up the demand for gas-guzzling cars may go down.

(iv) Profit Maximisation

Welfare economics assumes, in accordance with rational choice theory (which assumes that individuals always make prudent and logical decisions which are of the greatest benefit to them), that firms act rationally and in a way which maximises profits (the difference between the total cost of producing goods or providing a service and the revenue earned by selling them). Whether firms do always behave in this way is doubtful.[47] We see later that, in particular where a firm has a monopoly, that managers may prefer a 'quiet life' to profit maximisation. Furthermore, in the digital economy companies such as Amazon have been willing to sustain long-term losses in pursuit of gains in market share culminating in eventual dominance.

(v) Economies of Scale and Scope

Economies of scale occur when the average cost of producing a commodity falls as more is produced. If a widget factory produces only one widget that one widget must bear the whole cost of establishing and running the factory. If it produces 100,000 widgets, however, the costs are spread over 100,000 widgets. Some costs (variable costs) may increase with production (energy and labour for example, although they may not increase proportionately to the number of extra units). However, some costs may not increase at all: for example, the driver of a delivery lorry will be paid the same whether the lorry is full or half empty.

Economies of scale result where efficiency in production is achieved as output is increased but there comes a point when the average cost ceases to fall and economies of scale can no longer be reaped. That point is called the minimum efficient scale (MES). MES has important repercussions for market structure. Where the MES is very large in relation to the market, i.e. a producer has to supply a large quantity of products on the market before the MES is reached, only a few firms, possibly just one, will be able to operate efficiently on the market. This gives rise to a 'natural monopoly' where it is less costly for just one firm to serve the market than for the market to be divided between more players. On a competitive market, however, the MES is low in comparison to overall demand so that numerous firms can operate efficiently on the market.

Economies of scope occur where it is cheaper to produce two different products jointly than each separately. This may result from factors such as shared assembly lines or shared personnel which enable the firm to make costs savings by producing a range of goods rather than the individual products on their own. Economies of scope may mean that a multi-product firm has lower unit costs than a single-product firm. They are a significant feature of digital ecosystems.

[47] Behavioural economics (see Section 5.D) has cast doubt on rational choice theory; see H. A. Simon, 'Theories of Decision-making in Economic and Behavioral Sciences' (1959) 49 *Am Econ Rev* 253; R. Van den Bergh, 'Behavioural Antitrust: Not Ready for the Main Stage' (2013) 9(1) *J of Competition Law and Economics* 203; S. Bhattacharya and R. Van den Bergh, 'The Contribution of Management Studies to Understanding Firm Behaviour and Competition Law' (2014) 37 *World Competition* 517. Furthermore, the seminal work of A. A. Berle and G. C. Means, *The Modern Corporation and Private Property* (revised edn 1968, Harcourt Brace and World, 1932) explored the consequences of the separation of ownership from control in all but the smallest companies. In the layers of complex organisation which make up modern businesses, decisions may be made by managers and executives with their own particular agendas. See also J. E. Parkinson, *Corporate Power and Responsibility* (Oxford University Press, 1993), particularly Chaps. 2–4.

(vi) Externalities

Externalities are costs or benefits of an activity which are experienced by third parties, or by society as a whole. They may be negative or positive.

Negative externalities are uncompensated production (or consumption) costs imposed on third parties to their disadvantage. For example, a factory which discharges pollutants degrades the environment for all. Negative externalities are an important factor in competition law because they distort the true costs and price of products and services but they are usually not taken into account. This may need to change as competition law faces the challenges of sustainability.[48]

Positive externalities are benefits enjoyed by those who have not paid for them. For example, commuters by train save others from the pollution they would cause if they drove. *Positive network externalities* are where the value of a product or service to a user increases as the number of other users increases. They are an important feature of digital markets.

B. PERFECT COMPETITION AND EFFICIENCY

(i) Perfect Competition

The theory of perfect competition presents a model of a market in which efficiency is maximised and cannot, therefore, be improved by the application of competition rules.

In a perfectly competitive market, there are a large number of buyers and sellers (firms with very small market shares can operate at minimal costs since the MES is small in comparison to the size of the market); the product is homogeneous; all buyers and sellers have perfect information;[49] there are no barriers to entry or exit so that sellers can come on to, and leave, the market freely;[50] there are no transaction costs (buyers and sellers do not incur costs or fees to participate in the market); and there are no externalities (firms bear the full cost of their production processes). The result is that each seller is insignificant in relation to the market as a whole and has no influence on the product's price. Consequently, sellers are price-takers, not price-makers.

In a perfectly competitive market, the price does not exceed marginal cost. Marginal cost is the cost of producing one extra unit. So if it costs £100 to produce ten widgets but £105 to produce 11, the marginal cost is £5. On such a market the firm will always be able to add to profit where the marginal cost of producing a unit is less than the price. The producer will therefore increase production until the price obtained per unit equals marginal cost. If the price is below marginal cost the firm will have to respond by reducing output. In other words, in a perfectly competitive market a firm's marginal revenue (the rise in what the firm earns by one extra unit of output) equals marginal cost.[51]

Where the price charged for a product is at marginal cost the firm makes only a 'normal' profit, that is a rate of profit just sufficient to keep the firm in the industry. All the factors of production used to make the product must be taken into account when computing the cost, including the capital.

[48] The European Commission recognises this in paras. 545–546 of the Draft Horizontal Cooperation Guidelines, [2022] OJ C164/2.

[49] Buyers and sellers know of every change in price or demand and so respond immediately to such changes.

[50] For a discussion of barriers to entry, see Chap. 3, Section 5.

[51] The reason for this is that although the *industry's* demand curve is downward sloping, the demand curve for *each individual firm* is horizontal, which means that however much it sells it will get the market price. For further explanation of this, see D. W. Carlton and J. M. Perloff, *Modern Industrial Organization* (4th edn, Pearson Addison Wesley, 2005), Chap. 3.

The firm has to make enough of a return on the capital employed in the business to make it worthwhile staying on the market. In economics, 'zero profits' means that there is no profit above the 'normal' level, which is assessed in relation to the 'opportunity cost'. Opportunity costs are the value of what has to be given up to do something else. The capital employed in the business must therefore reap a profit to compensate the business for the profit which would come from a different outlay.

The relationship between marginal and average cost is significant. The average cost is the costs of the firm evened out over all the units produced. When the marginal cost of the next unit exceeds the average cost of the existing units, producing the next unit raises average costs. In that case, the firm can decrease costs by reducing supply. If, on the other hand, the marginal cost of the next unit is less than the average cost of the existing units, an extra unit reduces average costs. In that case, the firm can decrease costs by increasing supply. So the producer will produce at the point at which the average cost curve and the marginal cost curve intersect.

(ii) Allocative Efficiency

The fact that on a perfectly competitive market the market price equals the marginal cost is said to lead to *allocative efficiency*.

Allocative efficiency results from the fact that goods are produced in the quantities valued by society. The supplier will expand production to the point where market price and marginal cost coincide. The supplier will not make more but neither, if it is acting rationally to maximise profits, will it make less. Everyone who is willing and able to purchase the product at its cost of production is able to do so. The result is a market which is in equilibrium. Allocative efficiency is a state in which none of the players, sellers or buyers, could be made better off without someone being made worse off. It is sometimes known as Pareto optimal after the Italian economist, Vilfredo Pareto (1848–1923), who first developed the theory.

(iii) Productive Efficiency

Productive (or technical) efficiency also results from perfectly competitive markets. Goods are produced at the lowest possible cost. Every firm must produce at minimum cost or lose its custom to others, make losses, and eventually be obliged to leave the market. Given the perfect information in the market any cost-cutting techniques will be copied by the other firms and the market price will be lowered generally. There is therefore downward pressure on costs and cost reductions are passed on to customers because of the competitive pressure from other suppliers.

(iv) Dynamic Efficiency

Dynamic efficiency is a third type of efficiency. Allocative and productive efficiency describe static situations, but dynamic efficiency is concerned with how well a market delivers innovation and technological progress. Innovation can be defined as new combinations of new or existing knowledge, resources, equipment, and other factors, carried out for commercial purposes within the economic sphere[52] and is currently considered vital to the fight against climate change. Dynamic efficiency is arguably the most important kind of efficiency for maximising 'welfare', a concept explained in Section 4.F, as innovation is the key driver of economic growth. For the debate about whether innovation is better delivered by competitive or monopolistic markets, see Section 4.G.

[52] See F. Schumpeter, *The Theory of Economic Development* (Harvard University Press, 1934).

C. MONOPOLY

At the opposite end of the spectrum to perfect competition lies monopoly. A monopoly is a market where there is only one producer. This may be because there are barriers which prevent other firms from entering the market or because there is a natural monopoly.

Theory predicts that a firm unconstrained by competitors will price as high as possible. The monopoly price will be above the competitive market price. The price that the monopolist charges is, however, still affected by demand and is constrained to some extent by products from outside the market. As the price rises some potential customers will not purchase the product but will use their resources to purchase something else instead. The firm usually faces a downward-sloping demand curve, so the higher the price it charges the lower the demand for its product.[53]

A monopolist selling just one unit may receive a very high price for that unit but that price is unlikely to cover its costs. The monopolist wishing to sell more units must lower the price in order to attract customers with lower reservation prices. Unless the monopolist can price discriminate between customers (which we have already noted is increasingly possible in digital markets), the monopolist must lower the price on all units, not just the extra ones. The producer's marginal revenue is the extra amount the monopolist obtains from selling the extra unit, but because it involves lowering the price across the board the marginal revenue is less than the selling price. This means that the monopolist will sell units only up to the point at which the marginal revenue equals the marginal cost. A monopolist's marginal revenue is below the market price. This in turn means that the quantity supplied of the product will be less than that which would be supplied on a competitive market. Thus prices are higher than those resulting on a competitive market and output is restricted. This is illustrated in Fig. 1.2.

Figure 1.2 shows that, in the absence of price discrimination, the marginal revenue curve is always under the demand curve.[54] Because price is above the competitive price the monopolist makes abnormal profits but some consumers who would have paid the competitive (marginal cost) price are deprived of the product. Some of the consumer surplus identified in Fig. 1.1 is therefore transferred to the producer as monopoly profit but some is lost altogether. The horizontally hatched triangle in Fig. 1.2 shows this *deadweight loss of monopoly*, the loss of consumer surplus which is not turned into profit for the producer.

According to this theory, therefore, the main distinction between perfect competition and pure monopoly is that the monopolist's price exceeds marginal cost, while the price on a perfectly competitive market equals marginal cost. This monopoly pricing leads to a transfer of wealth from consumer to producer (the vertically hatched area in Fig. 1.2). This is why firms operating on a competitive market may wish to emulate the effect of monopoly by colluding, for example, to set their prices at above the competitive level and by reducing output. The transfer of wealth to the monopolist or colluding firms does not simply lead to a redistribution of income but also results in the misallocation in resources and a deadweight loss. This loss to efficiency as a whole is of great concern.

> This seeming technicality, so trivial at first glance, is the basis of the economist's most general condemnation of monopoly: it leads to an allocation of resources that is inefficient in the sense of failing to satisfy consumer wants as completely as possible.[55]

[53] This is not true of many luxury goods markets.

[54] If the monopolist is able to practise perfect price discrimination, i.e. charge each customer his reservation price, the marginal revenue curve and the demand curve are the same.

[55] F. M. Scherer and D. Ross, *Industrial Market Structure and Economic Performance* (3rd edn, Houghton Mifflin, 1990), 23.

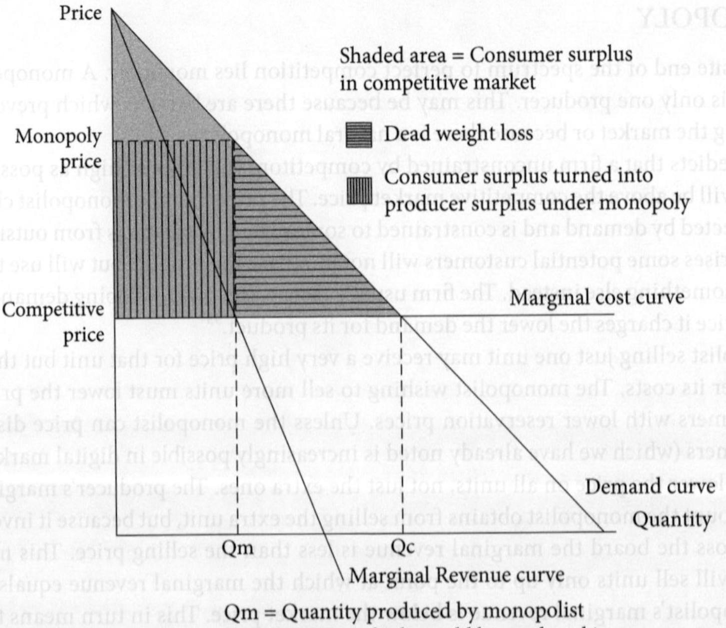

Figure 1.2 The deadweight loss due to monopoly

The objection to monopoly is therefore that it is inefficient.[56] Consumers who would have bought the product at the competitive price will spend their money on other things and welfare is not maximised as allocative inefficiency results.[57]

Another objection to monopoly is that a monopolist may not have the same pressure as firms operating on a competitive market to reduce its costs. This 'X-inefficiency' was identified by Leibenstein. It describes internal inefficiencies and rising costs due, for example, to high salaries, excessive perks, overmanning, and the lack of need to minimise the cost of production.[58] A monopolist may also waste resources defending its monopoly position, for example by maintaining excess capacity or indulging in excessive product differentiation.[59] These inefficiencies will be reflected in higher prices. For whether or not a monopolist not subject to competitive pressures has less incentive to innovate and to improve its production methods, see Section 4.G.

A monopoly on the buying side is called a monopony. There are currently particular concerns about monopsonies in labour markets.[60]

[56] Economists have sought to quantify the deadweight loss. The starting point was Harberger's article in 1954 in which he calculated the loss in the US as less than 0.1% of national income: see A. C. Harberger, 'Monopoly and Resource Allocation' (1954) 44 *Am Econ Rev* 77–87. In a mass of further studies this was been found to be a great underestimate (for the literature on this, see Scherer and Ross, n. 55, 661–667). Cowling and Mueller calculated it as 7%: see K. Cowling and D. C. Mueller, 'The Social Costs of Monopoly Power' (1978) 88 *Economic Journal* 724–748, although Scherer and Ross, n. 55, describe these results as 'exaggerated'. In this, as in much else in economics, there are wide differences in views.

[57] Moreover, the redistribution of benefits to producers from consumers who buy at above the competitive price may itself be a form of inefficiency—distributive inefficiency: see Geradin, Layne-Farrar, and Petit, n. 42, 2.29.

[58] H. Leibenstein, 'Allocative Efficiency vs. "X-efficiency"' (1966) 56 *Am Econ Rev* 392–415.

[59] See e.g. R. Posner, 'The Social Costs of Monopoly and Regulation' (1975) *J of Political Economy* 83.

[60] The OECD held an Open Day on labour markets in February 2020, see <www.oecd.org/daf/competition/competition-concerns-in-labour-markets.htm>.

D. OLIGOPOLY

Oligopoly is a market structure lying between perfect competition and monopoly on the spectrum in which the market (or most of it) is shared by only a few firms, so that the market is 'concentrated' without any single firm dominating it. Given their small number, the firms know each other's identities and recognise that they are affected by the output and pricing decisions of the others. This mutual awareness may lead to tacit (understood or implied without being stated) collusion between them. It may also lead them to collude expressly. Many markets are oligopolistic and present market power concerns for competition law similar to those arising on monopolistic markets. The mainstream explanations of oligopolistic behaviour and the ways in which EU competition law deals with oligopolistic markets are described in Chapter 9.

E. 'IMPERFECT' OR 'MONOPOLISTIC' COMPETITION

Monopolies may be created and maintained by State regulation and/or may be natural. Pure monopoly is relatively rare outside these circumstances but on some markets which are not 100 per cent monopolised a dominant firm may hold a very large share of the market and exercise market power.

Outside economic theory, perfectly competitive markets hardly ever exist. Rather, the model of perfect competition is just that—a model. It is a useful starting point because it demonstrates the concepts of productive and allocative efficiency. In reality, however, markets very rarely possess all the characteristics of perfect competition. It is unlikely that an infinite number of firms will be operating at identical costs levels, that producers will not benefit from economies of scale, and that sellers *and* buyers have perfect information across an atomistic market (on the contrary, in many digital markets there are vast information asymmetries). In particular, in most markets economies of scale make perfect competition impossible and some markets are 'natural' monopolies because of the MES or because of 'winner-takes-all' features.

Most markets therefore lie somewhere between perfect competition and monopoly, in a state of what is called 'imperfect' or 'monopolistic' competition where firms make differentiated or heterogeneous products which consumers regard as imperfect substitutes, so that each firm has some degree of market power in that it can raise its prices without losing all its customers. The model of perfect competition serves as a benchmark against which to measure the competitiveness of real markets, as the difference between perfectly competitive and monopolistic markets focuses attention on the crucial question of whether the firm has sufficient market power to raise prices above the competitive level and keep them there. It is important, however, to design competition laws to reflect the real-world phenomenon of imperfect competition.[61]

F. THE CONCEPT OF WELFARE: TOTAL (SOCIAL) WELFARE, CONSUMER WELFARE, AND EFFICIENCY

In neoclassical welfare economics theory, a perfectly competitive market maximises welfare because it leads to efficiency. However, there are different concepts of welfare.

We have already seen that producer surplus is the profit a producer makes by selling goods above the cost of production. Consumer surplus is the difference between what consumers would be prepared to

[61] One criticism made of the Chicago School (see Section 5.A.iii) is that for a long time it did not take account of monopolistic competition but rather based its models on perfect competition: see H. Hovenkamp and F. Scott Morton, 'Framing the Chicago School of Antitrust Analysis' (2020) 168 *U Pa LR* 1843.

pay for goods and what they do pay. Total surplus is the sum of these two surpluses. *Total welfare* can for present purposes be equated to total surplus. The objection to monopoly, it will be recalled, is that it does not just transfer some consumer surplus to producers but that some surplus (the deadweight) is totally lost to the market. That is a loss to total welfare. Total welfare is sometimes called *social welfare*. It is also sometimes used synonymously with *general welfare* which more accurately describes the surplus enjoyed not only by producers and consumers but also by all others affected by the practice under consideration. In this book, we use the expression 'total welfare' unless the context otherwise requires, as the most significant distinction in competition law is between total/social/general welfare and *consumer* welfare.

Consumer welfare is a concept whose meaning is not always clear. The term was popularised by the American, Robert Bork, whose contribution to competition law theory is discussed in Section 5.A, but whose use of the term, as we see there, has caused confusion.[62] 'Consumer welfare' in economics means the buyer's well-being in the form of the benefits derived from consuming goods and services, but that is not a useable standard for competition law. 'Consumer welfare' in competition law, on the other hand, is often equated with consumer surplus (the aggregate measure of the surplus of all consumers).[63] A competition policy concerned with consumer welfare rather than with total welfare is inimical to the transfer of surplus from consumers to producers even though total welfare may be maximised by such a transfer. Conduct and transactions which reduce consumer welfare will therefore be prohibited even if they would create efficiency gains which would maximise total welfare. In contrast, a competition policy which pursues total welfare as an objective is concerned only with the loss of efficiency represented by the deadweight 'triangle' and is not concerned about the redistributive effects. Total welfare therefore allows practices which raise consumer prices (and the corollary, reduced output) if they lead to efficiencies. A further consideration is that allocative efficiency, to which theory accords prime position, may conflict with the goals of productive or dynamic efficiency. Improving overall efficiency may therefore require a trade-off between different types of efficiencies.[64] So long as where there are both winners and losers, the winners win more than the losers lose (what is known in economics as a 'Kaldor-Hicks' or 'potential Pareto' improvement) total welfare is not prejudiced.[65] That, however, does not satisfy the consumer welfare test if it is consumers who lose. In a perfectly competitive market, there is no difference between total and consumer welfare, but competition law is there to deal with *imperfect* markets. In fact, in reality the difference

[62] See e.g. B. Orbach, 'The Antitrust Consumer Welfare Paradox' (2011) 7(1) *J of Competition Law and Economics* 133–164; Arizona Legal Studies Discussion Paper No. 10-07, <https://ssrn.com/abstract=1553226>; L. Kaplow, 'On the Choice of Welfare Standards in Competition Law', Harvard Law and Economics Discussion Paper No. 693 (1 May 2011), <https://ssrn.com/abstract=1873432>; S. Salop, 'Question: What is the Real and Proper Antitrust Welfare Standard? Answer: The *True* Consumer Welfare Standard' (2014) 22 *Loyola Consumer LR* 336; H. Hovenkamp, 'Is Antitrust's Consumer Welfare Principle Imperiled?', University of Pennsylvania Law School, Institute for Law and Economics Research Paper No. 18-15, <https://ssrn.com/abstract=3197329>, 3–4; H. Hovenkamp, 'On the Meaning of Antitrust's Consumer Welfare Principle', *Concurrentialiste* (17 January 2020), <https://leconcurrentialiste.com/herbert-hovenkamp-meaning-consumer-welfare/?mc_cid=05eddf4e53&mc_eid=34790440cd>. For the argument that both the total and consumer welfare standards are theoretically flawed and unsuitable to be used in competition policy, see M. Glick, 'The Unsound Theory Behind the Consumer (and Total) Welfare Goal in Antitrust' (2018) 63(4) *Ant Bull* 455.

[63] See Orbach, n. 62, 137–140.

[64] The classic text on efficiency trade-offs is O. E.Williamson, 'Economies as an Antitrust Defense: The Welfare Tradeoffs' (1968) 58 *Am Econ Rev* 18. For the relevance of this in EU merger control, see Chap. 15, Section 5.D.vi.

[65] See R. J. Van den Bergh and P. D. Camesasca, *European Competition Law and Economics: A Comparative Perspective* (2nd edn, Sweet & Maxwell, 2006), 29–30, 51–52.

between applying the total welfare or consumer welfare test in any particular case usually makes very little difference.[66]

There is also a broader conception of consumer welfare for the purposes of competition law which embraces, as well as the low prices and higher output caught by the consumer surplus standard, factors such as quality, choice, and innovation (known as 'qualitative efficiencies') which may be important to consumers. This is discussed in Section 7 where we look at the possible goals of competition law, and in Section 9 on EU law.

G. DYNAMIC COMPETITION AND SCHUMPETERIAN RIVALRY

The trade-off between different types of efficiencies already mentioned is particularly difficult when dynamic efficiencies are considered. There is a long-standing argument as to whether or not monopolists have fewer incentives to innovate than firms in competitive markets or whether substantial market power is an incentive to innovate.[67] The view of the Austrian economist Joseph Schumpeter was that monopoly is the better spur to innovation because a monopolist, motivated by the prospect of monopoly profits, may be more willing to bear the risks and costs involved.[68] Moreover, Schumpeter argued that competition in innovation is more important than price competition because it is a more effective means of obtaining a competitive advantage. This is known as 'Schumpeterian rivalry', where firms compete in a constant race to bring new products on to the market in 'gales of creative destruction', competition is dynamic, and positions of market power are short term because further innovation hands the advantage to another player. Short-term positions of substantial market power may arise but that this is not necessarily inimical to consumer welfare.[69] The view of the Nobel Laureate Kenneth Arrow, however, was that monopoly is a disincentive to innovation.[70] It is now generally recognised that the optimal incentives for innovation result from a complex mixture of factors

[66] See S. Bishop and M. Walker, *The Economics of EC Competition Law* (3rd edn, Sweet & Maxwell, 2010), 31–32; H. Hovenkamp, 'Antitrust Policy and Inequality of Wealth', *CPI Antitrust Chronicle* October 2017, <http://ssrn.com/abstract=2998220>, 4–5; E. Fox, 'Is Efficiency All That Counts'? in R. Pitofsky, *How Chicago Overshot the Mark: The Effect of Conservative Economic Analysis on US Antitrust* (Oxford University Press, 2008), 78. It is often claimed that it may make a difference in respect of horizontal mergers where economies of scale lead to lower output, but Hovenkamp says these are very rare (and can find no US example). L. Kaplow, 'On the Choice of Welfare Standards in Competition Law', Harvard Law and Economics Discussion Paper No. 693 (1 May 2011), <http://ssrn.com/abstract=1873432>, Chap. 3 in D. Zimmer (ed.), *The Goals of Competition Law* (Edward Elgar, 2012), also identifies a difference in cases of price-fixing and exclusionary conduct by dominant firms according to whether the baseline price is already elevated or not. For a Canadian case where, applying the total welfare approach, a merger which reduced prices and lowered output was allowed because these negative effects were outweighed by efficiency gains, see *Commissioner of Competition v Superior Propane Inc* (2003) 23 CPR (4th) 316 (FCA).

[67] See e.g. H. First, 'Digital Platforms and Competition Policy in Developing Countries' [2021] 2 *Concurrences* l, and in N. Charbit and S. Gachot, (eds.), *Eleanor M. Fox: Antitrust Ambassador to the World—Liber Amicorum* (Concurrences, 2021); G. Frederico, 'Horizontal Mergers, Innovation and the Competitive Process' (2017) 8 *JECLAP* 668; Giulio Federico, Fiona Scott Morton, and Carl Shapiro, 'Antitrust and Innovation: Welcoming and Protecting Disruption' (2020) 20 *Innovation Policy and the Economy* 125.

[68] J. A. Schumpeter, *Capitalism, Socialism and Democracy* (Harper, 1942).

[69] See D. Hildebrand, 'The European School in EC Competition Law' (2002) 25 *World Competition* 3.

[70] K. Arrow, 'Economic Welfare and the Allocation of Resources to Invention' in *The Rate and Direction of Inventive Activity: Economic and Social Factors* (NBER, 1962), 609; and see C. Shapiro, 'Did Arrow Hit the Bull's Eye' in J. Lerner and S. Stern (eds.), *The Rate and Direction of Inventive Activity Revisited* (University of Chicago Press, 2012), 361, and the research by P. Aghion, N. Bloom, R. Blundell, R. Griffith, and P. Howitt, 'Competition and Innovation: An Inverted-U Relationship' (2005) 120 *Quart J of Econ* 701, seeking to demonstrate that monopolies and tight oligopolies are less conducive to innovation than less concentrated markets.

and that the effect of the degree of concentration will vary depending on the nature of the market.[71] The concepts of dynamic efficiency, dynamic competition, and Schumpeterian rivalry are particularly relevant to high technology markets in the digital economy where the winner takes all, and positions of dominance are not eroded by competition but rather displaced by innovation and new products. Schumpeter's 'creative destruction' is also seen in the rise of 'disrupter' digital companies which attack established market models.[72]

5. SCHOOLS OF COMPETITION ANALYSIS AND THEORIES AND CONCEPTS RELEVANT TO COMPETITION LAW

A. HARVARD, CHICAGO, AND POST CHICAGO

(i) Introduction

The US was the first jurisdiction to adopt a 'modern' system of competition law. It enacted the Sherman Act in 1890[73] and important 'schools' of thinking about the law and economics of what Americans call antitrust have emerged from there over the years. In this section, we outline the Harvard, Chicago, and Post-Chicago schools.

(ii) The Harvard School

The original 'Harvard School' stemmed mainly from the work of economists working at Harvard University from the 1930s onwards, particularly Edward Mason and Joseph Bain.[74] They contributed significantly to the formulation of what is called the Structure → Conduct → Performance (S→C→P) paradigm. This was developed through empirical studies of American industries rather than from theoretical models. It holds that the structure of the market determines the firm's conduct and that conduct determines market performance (such as profitability, efficiency, technical progress, and growth). In other words, certain industry structures lead to certain types of conduct and, in particular, high concentration leads to reduced output and monopoly prices.

The conclusion that market structure dictates performance (structuralism) led to a belief that competition law should be concerned with structural rather than behavioural remedies. Bain considered that most industries were more concentrated than was necessary (economies of scale were not substantial in most industries); that because barriers to entry were widespread and high, new firms were prevented from entering markets; and that the monopoly pricing associated with oligopolies began to occur at relatively low levels of concentration.

[71] R. J.Gilbert, *Innovation Matters: Competition Policy for the High-Technology Economy* (MIT Press, 2020); C. Shapiro, 'Did Arrow Hit the Bull's Eye' in J. Lerner and S. Stern (eds.), *The Rate and Direction of Inventive Activity Revisited* (University of Chicago Press, 2012), 361; G. Frederico, 'Horizontal Mergers, Innovation and the Competitive Process' (2017) 8 *JECLAP* 668.

[72] For the Competition Commissioner's approval of 'creative destruction', see EVP Vestager, Speech for the Acceptance of the Schumpeter Award: 'Creative Renewal: defending competition in the face of disruption', 19 May 2022, <https://ec.europa.eu/commission/presscorner/detail/en/SPEECH_22_3215>.

[73] Canada passed the Act for the Prevention and Suppression of Combinations Formed in Restraint of Trade, in 1889, which was limited to agreements and conspiracies in restraint of trade and was incorporated in to the Criminal Code two years later.

[74] See E. S. Mason, *Economic Concentration and the Monopoly Problem* (Harvard University Press, 1957); J. S. Bain, *Barriers to New Competition* (Harvard University Press, 1956) and *Industrial Organization* (2nd edn, Wiley, 1968). In fact, Bain spent the last 35 years of his career at the University of California, Berkeley.

Adherence to the S→C→P paradigm, with its correlation between market concentration and market power and the assumption that firms with market power would act anti-competitively, led Harvard School scholars to presume the illegality of mergers at relatively low market share levels, and to condemn practices by which firms obtained, exercised, or enhanced market power even if they benefited consumers by, for example, lowering prices. Harvard held that firms could leverage market power in one market to gain market power in another, took a strict view of vertical mergers and vertical restraints, and made heavy use of presumptions of illegality. Harvard therefore favoured interventionist competition law policies.

Critics of the Bainian analysis, led by the Chicago School,[75] argued that the conclusions drawn from the empirical studies were flawed, that it wrongly found barriers to entry to be pervasive, and wrongly found economies of scale to be rare. The equating of concentration with anti-competitive outcomes was argued to be misconceived, with undue interventions resulting in prejudice to innovation.[76] As a result, the tide turned against structuralism as the foundation of antitrust analysis and mainstream antitrust no longer holds that structure dictates performance.[77]

The Harvard School approach has fundamentally evolved since the heyday of structuralism and began to converge with the Chicago School in the late 1960s and 1970s. The 'New' or 'Modern' Harvard School as it is called is, for instance, less reliant on presumptions, less concerned with barriers to entry, more relaxed about mergers and vertical restraints, and less interventionist than the original Harvard.[78] It embraces the use of price theory, recognises the complexity of markets, and has more confidence in the ability of markets to correct themselves.[79] Harvard scholars were instrumental in the development by the US Supreme Court of the 'rule of reason' doctrine.[80] Today, Harvard shares with the Chicago School the belief that competition law should focus on the economic effects on consumers and that the rightful goal of antitrust is consumer welfare, but its prescriptions tend be more 'moderate' than those of Chicago.[81]

(iii) The Chicago School

'Chicago' antitrust theory is part of what is known as Chicago economics, the school of neoclassical, libertarian, free-market economics which we noted in Section 2.

Even as the S→C→P paradigm was becoming established as the dominant ideology of the day, Chicago scholars were developing an alternative model based on neoclassical price theory.[82] This

[75] Discussed in Section 5.A.iii.

[76] See H. Demesetz, 'Industry Structure, Market Rivalry, and Public Policy' (1973) 16 *J of L & Econ* 1–3; H. Demesetz, 'Two Systems of Belief About Monopoly' in H. J. Goldschmidt et al. (eds.), *Industrial Concentration: The New Learning* (Little Brown, 1974).

[77] See the account in H. Hovenkamp, *Federal Antitrust Policy: The Law of Competition and its Practice* (6th edn, West, 2020), Chap. 1.

[78] See H. Hovenkamp, *The Antitrust Enterprise, Principle and Execution* (Harvard University Press, 2005), 35–38; T. A. Piraino Jr, 'Reconciling the Harvard and Chicago Schools: A New Antitrust Approach for the 21st Century' (2007) 82 *Indiana LJ* 345.

[79] The first three volumes of the major treatise on US antitrust law, P. Areeda and D. Turner, *Antitrust Law: An Analysis of Antitrust Principles and their Application*, which exemplifies modern Harvard thinking and has been cited by the Supreme Court more than 50 times, were first published in 1978 (it is now Areeda and H. Hovenkamp (Wolters Kluwer).

[80] See Chap. 5, Section 2.D.

[81] For the influence of the Harvard School in US antitrust law, see Section 8 and C. S. Yoo, 'Herbert Hovenkamp as Antitrust Oracle: Appreciating the Overlooked Contributions of the New Harvard School' in N. Charbit and S. Gachot (eds.), *Herbert Hovenkamp: The Dean of American Antitrust Law, Liber Amicorum* (Concurrences, 2021), 3.

[82] See generally R. Posner, 'The Chicago School of Antitrust Analysis' (1979) 127 *U Pa LR* 925. He says at p 926 that 'These ideas did not, I believe, emerge from a full-blown philosophy of antitrust. Rather, they were the product of pondering specific questions raised by antitrust cases, and only in retrospect did it become clear that they constituted the basis of a general theory of the proper scope of antitrust policy.' Leading proponents of Chicago antitrust, besides Posner, include Aaron Director, George Stigler, Harold Demsetz, Yale Brozen, Robert Bork, and Judge Frank Easterbrook.

produced a 'revolution' in competition thinking in the US and has had a significant influence throughout the world, including Europe.[83] Chicago antitrust is not monolithic, and 'enjoys considerable heterogeneity in both economic approaches and policy prescriptions'.[84] However, it is possible to summarise its essentials. Put simply, Chicago antitrust holds (in accordance with rational choice theory) that people are rational, that markets work and are self-correcting, and that in most situations intervention in markets makes matters worse rather than better. Chicago has an ideological bias against intervention. The fundamental Chicago view is that the pursuit of economic efficiency[85] should be the sole goal of competition law and so the test for Chicago is whether the impugned practice leads to higher prices and reduced output, thereby harming consumer welfare. Competition cases should therefore be decided purely on the economic evidence of the effects of a particular transaction or conduct on consumers. The consumer welfare standard produces 'technical' competition law, reducing it 'to an elegant and precise formula that ostensibly could be applied with consistency, accountability, and scientific rigor'.[86]

Chicago is not sentimental towards small businesses but rather places trust in the market. The identity of the winners or losers among competitors is irrelevant so long as efficiency is achieved. Since Chicago holds that there are few barriers to entry, that industries frequently benefit from economies of scale, and that businesses are profit-maximisers, it has faith in the ability of the market to correct itself and achieve efficiency without intervention from governments in the form of competition laws. Hovenkamp set out the basic tenets of the Chicago School in 1985.

H. Hovenkamp, 'Antitrust Policy After Chicago' (1985) 84 *Mich LR* 213, 226–229

(1) Economic efficiency, the pursuit of which should be the exclusive goal of the antitrust laws, consists of two relevant parts: allocative efficiency and productive efficiency . . . Occasionally practices that increase a firm's productive efficiency reduce the market's allocative efficiency. For example, construction of a large plant and acquisition of large market share may increase a firm's productive efficiency by enabling it to achieve economies of scale; however, these actions may simultaneously reduce allocative efficiency by facilitating monopoly pricing. A properly defined antitrust policy will attempt to maximize net efficiency gains . . .

(2) Most markets are competitive, even if they contain a relatively small number of sellers. Furthermore, product differentiation tends to undermine competition far less than was formerly presumed. As a result, neither high market concentration nor product differentiation are the anti-competitive problems earlier oligopoly theorists believed them to be . . .

(3) Monopoly, when it exists, tends to be self-correcting; that is, the monopolist's higher profits generally attract new entry into the monopolist's market, with the result that the monopolist's position is quickly eroded. About the best that the judicial process can do is hasten the correction process . . .

[83] For the view that Chicago has had a more limited effect on competition laws internationally than is sometimes assumed, see A. Bradford, A. Chilton and F. Lancieri, 'The Chicago School's Limited Influence on International Antitrust' (2020) 87 *Univ Chic LR* 297 and further, Chap. 17.

[84] J. Wright, 'Abandoning Antitrust's Chicago Obsession: The Case for Evidence-Based Antitrust' (2012) 78 *Antitrust LJ* 241, 244.

[85] See Section 4.B.

[86] D. A. Crane, 'The Tempting of Antitrust: Robert Bork and the Goals of Antitrust Policy' (2014) 79 *Antitrust LJ* 835, 835. For a discussion of the scholarship which preceded Chicago, see T. Muris and J. Nuechterlein, 'Chicago and Its Discontents' (2020) 87(2) *Univ Chic LR* 495, 495, 502 ff.

(4) 'Natural' barriers to entry are more imagined than real. As a general rule investment will flow into any market where the rate of return is high. The one significant exception consists of barriers to entry that are not natural—that is, barriers that are created by government itself. In most markets the government would be best off if it left entry and exit unregulated . . .

(5) Economies of scale are far more pervasive than economists once believed, largely because earlier economists looked only at intra-plant or production economics, and neglected economies of distribution. As a result, many more industries than were formerly thought may operate most economically only at fairly high concentration levels . . .

(6) Business firms are profit-maximizers. That is, their managers generally make decisions that they anticipate will make the firm more profitable than any alternative decision would. The model would not be undermined, however, if it should turn out that many firms are not profit maximizers, but are motivated by some alternative goal, such as revenue maximization, sales maximization, or 'satisficing.' . . .[87] The integrity of the market efficiency model requires only that a few firms be profit-maximizers. In that case, the profits and market shares of these firms will grow at the expense of other firms in the market . . .

(7) Antitrust enforcement should be designed in such a way as to penalize conduct precisely to the point that it is inefficient, but to tolerate or encourage it when it is efficient . . .

(8) The decision to make the neoclassical market efficiency model the exclusive guide for antitrust policy is nonpolitical.

To these should be added (9) that virtually all instances of vertical integration, including tying arrangements, resale price maintenance, and vertical non-price restraints are efficient and (10) that even if markets are imperfect and prone to anti-competitive outcomes, intervention is justified only if the result is an improvement, taking the costs of intervention into account.[88] This 'costs of intervention' or 'error–cost' framework is a crucial feature of Chicago. It presumes that the social costs of false findings of anti-competitive practices (false positives) are greater than the costs of false acquittals (false negatives) because in the long run markets move towards more competition or 'work themselves pure' anyway.[89] The error–cost framework therefore tends to lead to sparing application of the competition rules, other than in cases of horizontal price-fixing and market division, and horizontal mergers to monopoly or duopoly.[90]

The argument that competition law should be concerned only with economic efficiency was set out in Robert Bork's celebrated Chicago polemic, *The Antitrust Paradox*.[91] The second of the following extracts, the Epilogue, was added when the book was reprinted in 1993 and is a riposte to those who argued that the law should also take into account other matters (as US antitrust had done previously, as discussed in Section 8).

[87] 'Satisficing' is when management adopts certain goals for profits, sales, etc. and tries to meet, but not necessarily exceed, them. See Simon, n. 47.

[88] Hovenkamp, *Federal Antitrust Policy*, n. 77, para. 2.2b.

[89] See F. Easterbrook, 'The Limits of Antitrust'(1984) 63 *Tex LR* 1; for a recent criticism of this famous article, see H. Hovenkamp, 'Antitrust Error Costs' (2021) *Faculty Scholarship at Penn Law* 2742, <https://scholarship.law.upenn.edu/faculty_scholarship/2742>, available at <https://ssrn.com/abstract=3853282>.

[90] See J. B. Baker, 'Taking the Error out of 'Error Cost' Analysis: What's Wrong with Antitrust's Right' (2015) 80 *Antitrust Law Journal* 8, <https://ssrn.com/abstract=2333736>.

[91] For the argument that the Chicago approach set out in Bork did not represent an abrupt break from prior academic analysis of antitrust law but that it was a logical continuation of the antitrust analysis developed over the preceding decades, see T. Muris and J. Nuechterlein, 'Chicago and Its Discontents' (2020) 87(2) *Univ Chic LR* 495.

R. H. Bork, *The Antitrust Paradox: A Policy at War with Itself* (Basic Books, 1978, reprinted with a new Introduction and Epilogue, 1993), 90–91

Antitrust is about the effects of business behavior on consumers. An understanding of the relationship of that behavior to consumer well-being can be gained only through basic economic theory. The economic models involved are essential to all antitrust analysis, but they are simple and require no previous acquaintance with economics to be comprehended. Indeed, since we can hardly expect legislators, judges, and lawyers to be sophisticated economists as well, it is only the fact that the simple ideas of economics are powerful and entirely adequate to this field that makes it conceivable for the law to frame and implement useful policy.

Consumer welfare is greatest when society's economic resources are allocated so that consumers are able to satisfy their wants as fully as technological constraints permit. Consumer welfare, in this sense, is merely another term for the wealth of the nation. Antitrust thus has a built-in preference for material prosperity, but it has nothing to say about the ways prosperity is distributed or used. Those are matters for other laws. Consumer welfare, as the term is used in antitrust, has no sumptuary or ethical component, but permits consumers to define by their expression of wants in the marketplace what things they regard as wealth. Antitrust litigation is not a process for deciding who should be rich or poor, nor can it decide how much wealth should be expended to reduce pollution or undertake to mitigate the anguish of the cross-country skier at the desecration wrought by snowmobiles. It can only increase collective wealth by requiring that many lawful products, whether skis or snowmobiles, be produced and sold under conditions most favorable to consumers.

The role of the antitrust laws, then, lies at that stage of the economic process in which production and distribution of goods and services are organized in accordance with the scale of values that consumers choose by their relative willingness to purchase. The law's mission is to preserve, improve, and reinforce the powerful economic mechanisms that compel businesses to respond to consumers. 'From a social point of view,' as Frank H. Knight puts it, 'this process may be viewed under two aspects, (a) the assignment or allocation of the available productive forces and materials among the various lines of industry, and (b) the effective *co-ordination* of the various means of production in each industry into such groupings as will produce the greatest result.' . . .

These two factors may conveniently be called *allocative efficiency* and *productive efficiency* . . . These two types of efficiency make up the overall efficiency that determines the level of our society's wealth, or consumer welfare. The whole task of antitrust can be summed up as the effort to improve allocative efficiency without impairing productive efficiency so greatly as to produce either no gain or a net loss in consumer welfare. That task must be guided by basic economic analysis, otherwise the law acts blindly upon forces it does not understand and produces results it does not intend.

R. H. Bork, *The Antitrust Paradox: A Policy at War with Itself* (Basic Books, 1978, reprinted with a new Introduction and Epilogue, 1993), 426–429

Of the two, the issue of the goals of antitrust seems to have fared somewhat better than the law's capacity to deal with economics. Fifteen years ago, the question of what goals antitrust serves, and hence what factors a judge may properly consider in deciding an antitrust case, had not been addressed in any systemic fashion. The answers given by courts and commentators were hardly more than slogans of a more or less appealing variety, depending on your taste for populist rhetoric. Though the preservation of competition was often cited as the aim of the law, there seemed no agreed definition of what, for the purposes of antitrust, competition is.

'Competition,' the courts assured us, meant the preservation or comfort of small businesses, the advancement of first amendment values, the preservation of political democracy, the preservation of local ownership, and so on ad infinitum. Judges could and did choose among the items they had invented and placed in this grab bag in order to legislate freely. Cornucopias have their attractions but, when it comes to finding and applying a policy to guide adjudication, horns of plenty make anything resembling a rule of law impossible.

The argument of this book, of course, is that competition must be understood as the maximization of consumer welfare or, if you prefer, economic efficiency. That requires economic reasoning because courts must balance, when they conflict, possible losses of efficiency in the allocation of resources with possible gains in the productive use of those resources. In a word, the goal is maximum economic efficiency to make us as wealthy as possible. The distribution of that wealth or the accomplishment of noneconomic goals are the proper subjects of other laws and not within the competence of judges deciding antitrust cases.

By and large, with some ambiguity at times, the more recent cases have adopted a consumer welfare model. Aside from some explicit statements to that effect, the best evidence for the proposition is that courts now customarily speak the language of economics rather than pop sociology and political philosophy. If the conversion from a multi-goal jurisprudence is not complete, it is nevertheless very substantial. Explicit opposition to the consumer welfare thesis comes less from judges than from the academics. The objections are generally of two kinds: denial that an exclusive consumer welfare focus is to be found in the various antitrust statutes; and insistence that such a policy is not desirable . . . .

A different line of attack comes from those who observe, quite correctly, that people value things other than consumer welfare, and, therefore, quite incorrectly, that antitrust ought not be confined to advancing that goal. As non sequiturs go, that one is world class. There may be someone identified with the Chicago School who thinks all human activity can be analyzed in terms of economics and efficiency, but that is not true of most Chicagoans and certainly constitutes no part of my argument. No one body of law can protect everything that people value. If antitrust could, we would need no other statutes. If we trace the implications of the proposition, it results in judges deciding cases as if the Sherman Act said: 'A restraint of trade shall consist of any contract, combination, or conspiracy that fails to produce, in the eyes of the court, the optimum mix of consumer welfare and other good things that Americans want.' That is inevitably the result of bringing into judicial consideration an open-ended list of attractive-sounding goals to be weighed against consumer welfare.

Nor is there any force to the argument that the consumer welfare cannot be the exclusive mission of antitrust since that mission will be rendered less effective unless all other government policies pursue the same goal. Of course, antitrust will be less effective in promoting consumer welfare if government simultaneously subsidizes small business. A tariff policy designed to keep American companies viable will be less effective if government allows foreign competitors to set up manufacturing operations in the United States. That fact does not state a reason for a judge to alter the way he construes the tariff laws or other laws that apply to foreign companies' operations here. Many statutory policies conflict to some degree with other statutory policies. Whether or not they should do so, and to what degree, is a subject for legislation rather than adjudication.

In any event, no matter what policy goals or combination of goals one attributes to antitrust, the effectiveness of the law in forwarding those policies will be diminished by other public policies. That fact tells us nothing about how judges should go about deciding cases under the antitrust statutes.

As the conditions for Pareto-efficiency can rarely be fulfilled, Chicago usually uses 'potential' Pareto-efficiency as the guide, which means a policy whereby the total gains of all those who gain should be greater than the total losses of all those who lose.[92] Most crucially, it should be noted from the second paragraph of the first extract that Bork equates 'consumer welfare' with the 'wealth of the

[92] See Section 4.F.

nation'. His conception of 'consumer welfare' is therefore what is usually called 'general' welfare[93] although despite the reference to the 'wealth of the nation' he is mainly concerned with producer and consumer surplus only, which equates to total welfare rather than general welfare.[94] The confusion arising from Bork's terminology should be borne in mind when reading Chicago School sources.[95] In the application of Chicago principles in the US, 'consumer welfare' has generally been given the meaning of consumer surplus.

The adoption of economic efficiency and consumer welfare as the sole goal of competition laws entails excluding non-economic values from any place in competition policy, as seen in the second extract from Bork. The Chicago School (see the Hovenkamp extract) claims that this stance is non-political. The essential argument is that since competition policy is dictated only by microeconomics it is ideology-free. However, others argue that the adoption of such a policy is itself ideological in that it fosters certain outcomes which affect the distribution of resources and allows business practices which other approaches would disallow.[96] Moreover, Chicago is essentially libertarian, reflecting an inbuilt bias against 'government', i.e. competition law intervention.

The argument between Chicago and those who believe that competition policy should encompass other values, such as the protection of small businesses, the dispersal of economic power, the distribution or redistribution of wealth, fairness, equity, the impact on employment, or other 'public interest' considerations, has been called 'the battle for the soul of antitrust'.[97]

Even those who share the Chicago view that non-economic factors should be excluded from consideration have questioned many of the foundations on which the Chicago concept of efficiency was built and challenge its faith in the ability of the market to correct itself.[98] Criticisms have been made of the belief that barriers to entry are rare outside government regulation, that potential competition polices the market as well as existing competitors (because in the absence of barriers to entry monopolists will be challenged by new entrants if they reap monopoly profits), that oligopolies are fragile and that most markets are competitive. The Chicago model is criticised for placing too much emphasis on the perfect competition model rather than allowing for imperfect or monopolistic competition, for being 'static' and taking insufficient account of dynamic efficiency, and for failing to allow for differences in markets, industries, and firms and, rather, treating them as all alike, in accordance with price theory.[99] It is argued that the neoclassical market efficiency model of Chicago is too simple to account for or predict business behaviour in the real world.

[93] Ibid.

[94] See e.g. H. Hovenkamp, 'Is Antitrust's Consumer Welfare Principle Imperiled?', University of Pennsylvania Law School, Institute for Law and Economics Research Paper No. 18-15, <https://ssrn.com/abstract=3197329>, 3; S. Salop, 'Question: What is the Real and Proper Antitrust Welfare Standard? Answer: The *True* Consumer Welfare Standard' (2014) 22 *Loyola Consumer LR* 336; B. Orbach, 'The Antitrust Consumer Welfare Paradox' (2011) 7(1) *J of Competition Law and Economics* 133–164; Arizona Legal Studies Discussion Paper No. 10-07, <https://ssrn.com/abstract=1553226>; L. Kaplow, 'On the Choice of Welfare Standards in Competition Law', Harvard Law and Economics Discussion Paper No. 693 (1 May 2011), <https://ssrn.com/abstract=1873432>; G. Werden, 'Antitrust's Rule of Reason: Only Competition Matter' (2014) 79 *Antitrust LJ* 713, Part I; M. Glick, 'How Chicago Economics Distorts "Consumer Welfare" in Antitrust' (2019) 64(4) *Ant Bull* 495. For a defence of Bork's use of the terminology, see D. Crane, 'The Tempting of Antitrust: Robert Bork and the Goals of Antitrust Policy' (2014) 79 *Antitrust LJ* 835, 845–847.

[95] See K. Cseres, *Competition Law and Consumer Protection* (Kluwer Law International, 2005), 331–332; P. Akman, 'Consumer versus "Customer": The Devil in the Detail' (2010) 37 *J of L & Soc* 315.

[96] See e.g. A. Katz, 'The Chicago School and the Forgotten Political Dimension of Antitrust Law' (2020) 87(2) *Univ Chic LR* 413, 416.

[97] E. Fox, 'The Battle for the Soul of Antitrust' (1987) 75 *Cal LR* 917; E. Fox and L. Sullivan, 'Antitrust—Retrospective and Prospective: Where Are We Coming From? Where Are We Going?' (1987) 62 *New York Univ LR* 936, 956. Compare this with the argument set out in Posner's seminal book first published in 1976, R. A. Posner, *Antitrust Law* (2nd edn, University of Chicago Press, 2001); and see now the rise of the Neo-Brandeisians (Section 5.B and Section 8) and e.g. D. Gerard and I. Lianos (eds.), '*Reconciling Efficiency and Equity*' (Cambridge University Press, 2019).

[98] See H. Hovenkamp and F. Scott Morton, 'Framing the Chicago School of Antitrust Analysis' (2020) 168 *U Pa LR* 1843.

[99] For a general criticism of Chicago, see H. Hovenkamp and F. Scott Morton, 'Framing the Chicago School of Antitrust Analysis' (2020) 168 *U. PA. L. Rev.* 1843.

'Neo-Chicago' describes a 'school' which is faithful to the core tenets of Chicago but takes on board criticisms made of it. A Neo-Chicago approach '(a) accepts the Chicago tenet that legal rules can and should be assessed on their consequences in terms of efficiency, and (b) makes use of Chicago and Post-Chicago insights in designing these rules' (Post-Chicago is discussed in the following section).[100] One scholar has said that the success of the Neo-Chicago school 'depends critically on replenishing Chicago's intellectual stock, providing empirical support for Chicago School theories, and renewing the case for Chicago's "articles of faith"'.[101] However, it is doubtful whether Neo-Chicago is a new 'school' at all, as Chicago has refined its principles and taken on board new insights, and it is unclear what differentiates Neo-Chicago from evolved Chicago thinking.[102]

(iv) Post-Chicago

The 'Post-Chicago School'[103] shares Chicago's belief in efficiency and the maximisation of consumer welfare as the goal of competition, and in rational choice theory, but holds that Chicago has relied on simplified assumptions about markets which led in the US to excessive under-enforcement,[104] especially in the area of exclusionary behaviour, and particularly in the light of raising rivals' costs (RRC) theory.[105] Post-Chicago recognises the effect that the strategic conduct of firms can have in different market situations and uses game theoretic approaches[106] to examine how firms may indulge in strategic entry deterrence. Post-Chicago competition scholarship therefore admits of more complexities than the orthodox Chicago approach and 'helps observers understand why conduct thought benign in light of Chicago School teaching might in fact lessen competition'.[107] It also incorporates the importance of dynamic competition. However, Post-Chicago analysis is heavily theoretical and makes greater demands on competition authorities and decision-makers because of the very wealth of models and theories that fall to be considered, and it is criticised for offering little by way of empirical verification and therefore as being of limited practical utility.[108] Post-Chicago literature has been described as 'a collection of what we call "possibility theorems"' whose limited value arises from the data critical to deciding whether reality fits the models being typically unavailable.[109]

[100] D. Evans and A. Jorge Padilla, 'Designing Antitrust Rules for Assessing Unilateral Practices: A Neo-Chicago Approach' (2005) 72 *Univ Chic LR* 73, 75; D. Crane, 'Chicago, Post-Chicago and Neo-Chicago' (2009) 76 *Univ Chic LR* 1911.

[101] Crane, ibid., 1929.

[102] See e.g. J. D. Wright, 'Abandoning Antitrust's Chicago Obsession: The Case for Evidence-Based Antitrust' (2012) 78 *Antitrust LJ* 241, 250–253; D. Crane, 'A Neo-Chicago Perspective on Antitrust Institutions' (2012) 78 *Antitrust LJ* 43 (the whole of (2012) 78 *Antitrust LJ* is devoted to a symposium on Neo-Chicago).

[103] See H. Hovenkamp, 'Post-Chicago Antitrust: A Review and Critique' (2001) *Colum Bus LR* 257; C. S. Yoo, 'The Post-Chicago Antitrust Revolution: A Retrospective' (2020) 168 *U Pa LR* 2145. The term 'Post-Chicago' first seems to have been used in Hovenkamp's 1985 article extracted in the previous section at pp. 217 and 225.

[104] For the development of US antitrust generally, see Section 8.

[105] For raising rivals' costs, see Section 5.E.

[106] See Section 5.C.

[107] E. Gellhorn, W. Kovacic, and S. Calkins, *Antitrust Law and Economics* (5th edn, West, 2004), 97; see further A. Cucinotta, R. Pardolesi, and R. Van den Bergh, *Post-Chicago Developments in Antitrust Law* (Edward Elgar, 2002).

[108] See D. Crane, 'Chicago, Post-Chicago and Neo-Chicago' (2009) 76 *Univ Chicago LR* 1911; J. D. Wright, 'Abandoning Antitrust's Chicago Obsession: The Case for Evidence-Based Antitrust' (2012) 78 *Antitrust LJ* 241, 244; B. Kobayashi and T. Muris, 'Chicago, Post-Chicago, and Beyond: Time to Let Go of the 20th Century' (2012) 78 *Antitrust LJ* 147; H. Hovenkamp, *The Antitrust Enterprise* (Harvard University Press, 2005) 38–39; cf. D. Rubenfield, 'On the Foundations of Antitrust Law and Economics' in R. Pitofsky (ed.), *How Chicago Overshot the Mark: The Effect of Conservative Economic Analysis on US Antitrust* (Oxford University Press, 2008), 51, 55.

[109] D. Evans and A. Jorge Padilla, 'Designing Antitrust Rules for Assessing Unilateral Practices: A Neo-Chicago Approach' (2005) 72 *Univ Chic LR* 73, 79–80.

(v) Conclusion

The Chicago School focuses competition law on the issue of economic efficiency to the exclusion of all other considerations. It concentrates on one question, the impact on consumer welfare and it claims that this can be identified by rigorous economic analysis.

It has been persuasively argued that the Chicago/Post-Chicago/Neo-Chicago labels are unhelpful and should be abandoned, as an 'excessive focus on the label "Chicago" School and its various iterations now threatens to undermine the empirical rigor Chicago School economists pioneered'[110] and that 'frequently-voiced suggestions that the Chicago School and the Post-Chicago School are antonyms overlooks important connections between them'.[111] The source of that second quotation, a leading American scholar and former chairman of the Federal Trade Commission (FTC) also counsels caution against depicting Chicago School advocates as extremists, close-minded fanatics, or mere 'ideologues'.[112]

Whatever criticisms can be and have been made of it, Chicago undeniably changed competition law thinking profoundly. The impact of Harvard and Chicago on US antitrust is discussed in Section 8. For EU competition law, what is important is not the labels and the politics, but the ideas, theories, and insights which this rich American discourse provides and which is reflected in many of the debates over the EU rules, as discussed in the subsequent chapters of this book. In the third decade of the twenty-first century, Harvard, Chicago, and Post-Chicago all hold to the economic efficiency/consumer welfare goal and the arguments between them centre on what tests, presumptions, and economic models should be used to determine where consumer welfare lies in any particular case. The crucial divide is that between adherents to the consumer welfare standard and those who advocate that competition law should not just pursue efficiency goals but rather incorporate wider social and public interest concerns. This argument is a current issue in the EU too (albeit one conducted with less partisan passion than in the US).

B. THE NEO-BRANDEISIAN SCHOOL

The Neo-Brandeisian School[113] (pejoratively called 'hipster antitrust' by its critics) is a contemporary movement in the US advocating that antitrust abandon the goal of economic efficiency in favour of public interest goals. It is motivated in a large part by concerns about the Big Tech companies but also by the concentration of global economic power more generally. We discuss the Neo-Brandeisians in

[110] J. D. Wright, 'Abandoning Antitrust's Chicago Obsession: The Case for Evidence-Based Antitrust' (2012) 78 *Antitrust LJ* 241, 270–271; see also T. Muris and J. Nuechterlein, 'Chicago and Its Discontents' (2020) 87(2) *Univ Chic LR* 495.

[111] W. Kovacic, 'The Intellectual DNA of Modern US Competition Law for Dominant Firm Conduct: The Chicago/Harvard Double Helix' (2007) 1(1) *Colum Bus LR* 8–10 ('Many Post-Chicago School scholars build upon theoretical or empirical propositions advanced by Chicago School exponents . . . Some Chicago scholars appear to acknowledge the value of Post-Chicago ideas, at least so far as finding similarities between the modern Post-Chicago scholarship and early Chicago School views on antitrust policy . . . '); see also J. Soven, 'Afterword: Does Antitrust Need More Schools' (2012) 78 *Antitrust LJ* 273.

[112] Kovacic, 'The Intellectual DNA of Modern US Competition Law', n. 111, 10; see also W. Kovacic, 'The Chicago Obsession in the Interpretation of US Antitrust History' (2020) 87 *Univ Chic LR* 459. A book critical of Chicago and its influence on US antitrust, edited by Robert Pitofsky (chair of the FTC in the Clinton administration), *How Chicago Overshot the Mark: The Effect of Conservative Economic Analysis on US Antitrust* (Oxford University Press, 2008) provoked a fierce defence from those who considered that it misrepresented Chicago as an extremist conservative ideology.

[113] After Supreme Court Justice (1916–1939) Louis Brandeis, who was much concerned with the concentration of economic power in the hands of corporate monopolies in the US in the first half of the 20th century, and who wrote *The Curse of Bigness* (Viking Press) in 1934. See L. M. Khan, 'The New Brandeis Movement' (2018) 9 *J of European Comp L & Practice* 131; D. Crane, 'How Much Brandeis Do the Neo-Brandeisians Want?' (2019) 64(4) *Ant Bull* 531.

the context of US law in Section 8, but the description 'Neo-Brandeisian' is now being attached to views about wider objectives for competition laws outside the US as well, including in the EU.

C. GAME THEORY

Game theory is central to much modern industrial organisation theory and stems from work done in the 1940s by von Neumann and Morgenstern.[114] It models strategic interactions between firms, with their conflict and cooperation, as games in which each firm plans its own strategy, for example with regard to pricing or output, in the light of assumptions about strategy which will be adopted by its competitors. Game theory is a particularly important tool in analysing the conduct of oligopolies and is discussed further in that context in Chapter 9.

D. BEHAVIOURAL ANTITRUST

Behavioural antitrust is an approach to competition law based on behavioural economics.[115] Behavioural economics centres 'on the insight that ordinary consumers do not behave as the so-called perfectly rational consumer of neoclassical economics'.[116] Rather, 'real people' differ from the 'homo economicus' on which the neoclassical model is based by displaying three important 'bounds' on human behaviour.[117] 'Bounded rationality' recognises that the ability of an individual to be rational is limited by intellectual and cognitive constraints and the time available for making the relevant decision,[118] and that when making choices individuals are affected by a whole range of instincts and impulses, such as heuristics (rules of thumb), biases (including bias towards the status quo), loss aversion, endowment effects,[119] risk aversion, self-control (and lack of it), herd instinct, and myopia.[120] As far as firms are concerned, large corporations are considered more likely to act rationally than individual consumers, but small businesses may act like individuals. 'Bounded willpower' refers to the

[114] J. von Neumann and O. Morgenstern, *The Theory of Games and Economic Behaviour* (Princeton University Press, 1944).

[115] Behavioural antitrust was first discussed by Avishalom Tor in his article 'The Fable of Entry: Bounded Rationality, Market Discipline, and Legal Policy' (2002) 101 *Mich LR* 482; see also A. P. Reeves and M. E. Stucke, 'Behavioural Antitrust' (2011) 86 *Indiana LJ* 1527.

[116] D. Currie, 'Homo Economicus and Homo Sapiens: The CMA Experience of Behavioural Economics', Speech, 21 April 2015, <www.gov.uk/government/speeches/david-currie-speaks-about-the-cma-experience-of-behavioural-economics>.

[117] See C. Jolls, C. Sunstein, and R. Thaler, 'A Behavioral Approach to Law and Economics' (1998) 50(5) *Stan LR* 1471; R. Thaler, *Misbehaving: The Making of Behavioural Economics* (W. W. Norton, 2015, Penguin Books, 2016).

[118] See H. Simon, *Models of Man, Social and Rational: Mathematical Essays on Rational Human Behaviour in a Social Setting* (Wiley, 1957).

[119] The endowment effect is that individuals value things they already own (their 'endowment') more highly than things that they do not yet own but are available and could become part of their endowment.

[120] See e.g. A. Tversky and D. Kahneman, 'Judgment Under Uncertainty: Heuristics and Biases' (1974) *Science* 185, no. 4157:1124; D. Kahneman and A. Tversky, 'Prospect Theory: An Analysis of Decision Under Risk' (1979) 47 *Econometrica* 263; R. Thaler, 'Towards a Positive Theory of Consumer Choice' (1980) 1(1) *J of Econ Behaviour & Organization* 39; D. Kahneman, 'Anomalies: The Endowment Effect, Loss Aversion, and Status Quo Bias' (1991) 5(1) *J of Econ Perspectives* 193; R. Thaler, *The Winner's Curse: Paradoxes and Anomalies of Economic Life* (Princeton University Press, 1992); R. Thaler, A. Tversky, D. Kahneman, and A. Schwartz, 'The Effect of Myopia and Loss Aversion on Risk Taking: An Experimental Test' (1997) 112(2) *Quart J of Econ* 647. Adam Smith recognised the limits of individuals' rationality in both *The Theory of Moral Sentiments* (1759) and *An Inquiry into the Nature and Causes of the Wealth of Nations* (1776) and has been called 'the father of behavioural economics' (in J. Norman, *Adam Smith: What He Thought and Why it Matters* (Allen Lane, 2018), 199).

tendency of people to give way to temptation and to make choices which they know are against their own long-term interests.[121] 'Bounded self-interest' recognises that people often behave altruistically, rather than in their own material self-interest.[122] One problem with behavioural economics is that it has been largely based on surveys and experiments[123] and its critics claim that it depends too heavily on anecdotal evidence and that it assumes permanent irrationality on the part of incumbent firms but rationality on the part of new entrants, or else vice versa.

Behavioural antitrust suggests that as consumers are shown by behavioural economics to take actions that are not necessarily in their wealth-maximising self-interest, competition law policy-makers and decision-takers should take that into account and reflect a more realistic view of conduct in the marketplace and in their analyses of what competition is and how it works.[124] Behavioural economists have produced economic models which can be used to do this.

E. RAISING RIVALS' COSTS

Raising rivals' costs (RRC) describes the strategic behaviour of a firm which is designed to raise the marginal costs of its rivals relative to its own and so lead the rivals to reduce their output.[125] It normally requires some degree of market power (or, for some strategies, political power or influence). It includes interfering with the production or selling methods of rivals, lobbying for or supporting government regulation which has a differential impact on the rivals' costs, raising the price of inputs, tying, raising switching costs (so that customers find it difficult or expensive to change to the rival's goods or services), and indulging in rapid product innovation in primary markets.[126] Some behaviour which raises rivals' costs may also increase welfare and whether competition law should sanction or allow it often depends on the particular circumstance of the case. In the following chapters of this book, we will come across many examples of behaviour which can raise rivals' costs. RRC is usually associated with the Post-Chicago school but it is also recognised as having its roots in Chicago.[127]

[121] See Jolls, Sunstein, and Thaler, n. 117, 1479. [122] Ibid.

[123] Often conducted using university students.

[124] D. Currie, the then chair of the UK Competition and Markets Authority suggested (see n. 116) that behavioural insights indicate that standard competition remedies of removing barriers to entry to enhance competition, and increasing transparency and consumer information, may not be adequate; see also M. Walker, 'Behavioural Economics: The Lessons for Regulators' (2017) 13(1) *European Competition Journal* 1. There is an ongoing debate, particularly in the US, between advocates of behavioural antitrust and those who still hold to rational choice theory. See M. E. Stucke, 'Reconsidering Competition' (2011) 81 *Mississippi LJ* 107, <https://ssrn.com/abstract=1646151>; J. D. Wright and J. Stone, 'Misbehavioural Economics: The Case Against Behavioural Antitrust' (2012) 33 *Cardozo LR* 1517. M. Huffman, 'Marrying Neo-Chicago with Behavioural Antitrust' (2012) 78 *Antitrust LJ* 105, <https://ssrn.com/abstract=2079329>, proposes 'a possible synthesis of Neo-Chicago with Behavioral Antitrust into an enterprise of "economically informed antitrust"'; A. Tor, 'Should Antitrust Survive Behavioural Economics?' (2019) *CPI Antitrust Chronicle* 1 considers that antitrust and behavioural economics can coexist, see also A. Tor, 'Justifying Competition Law in the Face of Consumers' Bounded Rationality' in K. Mathis and A. Tor (eds.), *New Developments in Competition Law and Economics* (Springer, 2018).

[125] T. Krattenmaker and S. Salop, 'Anti-competitive Exclusion: Raising Rivals' Costs to Achieve Power Over Price' (1986) 96 *Yale LJ* 209; D. Scheffman and R. Higgins, 'Raising Rivals' Costs' in R. Blair and D. Sokol (eds.), *The Oxford Handbook of International Antitrust Economics, Vol. 2* (Oxford University Press, 2014).

[126] See Carlton and Perloff, n. 51, 371–379.

[127] See S. Salop, 'Economic Analysis of Exclusionary Vertical Conduct: Where Chicago Has Overshot the Mark' in Pitofsky, n. 112, 142–144.

F. TRANSACTION COST ECONOMICS

Transaction cost economics is based on the theory developed by Ronald Coase in *The Nature of the Firm*.[128] Transaction costs are the costs a firm incurs by trading with other parties. Coase's argument was that a firm can choose to organise its activities by doing things itself (so internalising the costs) or by using other parties to do them (i.e. using the market). A firm may have a choice between producing the inputs necessary for production itself or obtaining them from other parties. Similarly it may have a choice between doing its own distribution or using independent distributors. The first of these options in each case involves vertical integration while the second involves agreements with others. Which is preferable will depend on its comparative efficiency. The insight from transaction cost economics for competition law is that competition law should not be designed so as to force firms to take less efficient options for doctrinaire reasons of promoting more competitive markets.

> Transaction cost research has identified efficiency reasons for which firms use various forms of internal organization and has underscored the importance of contractual techniques in curbing opportunistic behavior that, if left unchecked, undermines business arrangements that increase efficiency. By showing that the main purpose of many forms of economic organization—for example, joint ventures, vertical integration, and restrictive distribution contracts—often is to reduce costs, transaction costs scholars have spurred a reevaluation of antitrust doctrines that have treated such arrangements with hostility.[129]

Transaction cost economics was taken on board by the Post-Chicago School, but in contrast to other ideas adopted by Post-Chicago, such as the anti-competitive effects of strategic behaviour, transaction cost economics points to a *less* expansive application of competition rules.

G. WORKABLE COMPETITION

The theory of 'workable competition' was developed by J. M. Clark in the 1940s.[130] It holds that as perfect competition is usually impossible to attain, competition policy should aim to produce the best competitive arrangement practically attainable. The criteria by which workability can be assessed may be divided into structure, conduct, and performance criteria but it may be hard to assess whether or not they have been satisfied in any particular industry; and if some are satisfied and some not, it may be difficult to decide whether workability has been attained without making subjective value judgments.[131]

The Court of Justice (CJ) referred to workable competition in 1977 in *Metro I*, equating it with 'the degree of competition necessary to ensure the observance of the basic requirements and the attainment of the objectives of the EEC Treaty'.[132]

[128] (1937) 4 *Economica* 38. See also the work of Oliver E. Williamson, particularly 'Transaction Cost Economics' in R. Schmalensee and R. Willig (eds.), *Handbook of Industrial Organization, Vol. 1* (North-Holland, 1989), 135 and 'Transaction Cost Economics: An Introduction', <http:www.economics-ejournal.org/economics/discussionpapers/2007-3/file>. H. Hovenkamp, 'Antitrust and the Costs of Movement' (2012) 78 *ALJ* 67 argues that as well as transaction costs, competition policy should take into account the costs of moving resources.

[129] Gellhorn, Kovacic, and Calkins, n. 107, 101. See also Van den Bergh and Camesasca, n. 65, 94–98; P. L. Joskow, 'The Role of Transaction Cost Economics in Antitrust and Public Utility Regulatory Policies' (1991) 7 *J of Law, Economics & Organization* 53.

[130] J. M. Clark, 'Towards a Concept of Workable Competition' (1940) 30 *Am Econ Rev* 241–256; J. M.Clark, '*Competition as a Dynamic Process*' (Brookings Institution, 1961); see also S. Sosnick, 'A Critique of Concepts of Workable Competition' (1958) 72 *Quart J of Econ* 380–423.

[131] See further Scherer and Ross, n. 55, 52–55.

[132] Case 26/76, *Metro v Commission (Metro I)* EU:C:1977:167, para. 20.

H. CONTESTABLE MARKETS

Contestable markets theory[133] places the main emphasis on freedom of entry to, and exit from, a market. It attaches importance not to the structure of the market but to its contestability. So long as 'hit-and-run' entry by competitors is possible, the behaviour of firms operating on the market will be constrained and they will perform efficiently and price competitively. The minimum conditions for a contestable market are instantaneous entry and costless exit and, crucially, the inability of the incumbent to respond to entry by another competitor by lowering its prices. This last point is vital because otherwise the incumbent firm can keep its prices at monopoly level and only lower them when it needs to respond to competition. In reality, again, the conditions for perfect contestability are rarely found.[134] However, the term 'contestable market', meaning one with low barriers to entry and exit where the threat of entry does significantly constrain the incumbent, is used more loosely and is often found in competition law discourse.[135] The Commission looked at the contestability of the market and therefore approved a merger despite a highly concentrated market and high market shares in its *Syniverse/MACH* decision.[136] The EU Competition Commissioner speaking in May 2022 of the importance of innovation in the EU's Recovery and Resilience Plans, said that the main role of the Commission is to help the process of creative destruction by preserving contestable markets.[137] Contestable markets are a major concept in the EU's 2022 Digital Markets Act, the title of which is 'Regulation 2022/1925 on contestable and fair markets in the digital sector'.[138]

I. THE AUSTRIAN SCHOOL

The Austrian School embraces a theory of dynamic competition which goes beyond that advanced by Schumpeter.[139] As with Chicago, the Austrian School's conception of competition policy is just one facet of a wider school of economic theory,[140] one of whose leading figures was von Hayek.[141] Von Hayek's conception of competition was that it is a 'discovery process'. He considered that the market is only discovered through the rivalry of firms competing for consumers' custom, as information about what consumers want only becomes known as they respond to firms' efforts to do better than their competitors. This is in contrast to the theory of a perfectly competitive market, which posits that both consumers and competitors have perfect information. The logical conclusion of von Hayek's view is that competition laws should not interfere with rivalrous competitive behaviour at all, not even by prohibiting cartels, because such intervention distorts the discovery process.[142]

[133] W. J. Baumol, J. Panzar, and R. Willig, *Contestable Markets and the Theory of Industry Structure* (Harcourt Brace Jovanovich, 1982); W. J. Baumol, 'Contestable Markets: An Uprising in the Theory of Industry Structure' (1982) 72 *Am Econ Rev* 1.

[134] Sunk costs, for example, will be a hindering factor, see Chap. 3, Section 5.B.

[135] S. Bishop and M. Walker, *The Economics of EC Competition Law* (3rd edn, Sweet & Maxwell, 2010), 3.35.

[136] M.6690, *Syniverse/MACH* [2014] OJ C60/7, 29 May 2013; see G. Goeteyn and S. Ashall, 'Away From Market Shares? The Increasing Importance of Contestability in EU Competition Law Case' (2015) 6 *JECLAP* 197.

[137] EVP Vestager, Speech for the Acceptance of the Schumpeter Award, 'Creative Renewal: defending competition in the face of disruption', 19 May 2022, <https://ec.europa.eu/commission/presscorner/detail/en/SPEECH_22_3215>.

[138] Digital Markets Act [2022] OJ L265/1.

[139] See Section 4.G.

[140] Originating with Carl Menger, Professor of Economics at the University of Vienna, 1873–1903.

[141] Von Hayek's most famous work is *The Road to Serfdom* (Routledge, 1944).

[142] See further F. von Hayek, *Law, Legislation and Liberty* (reprinted Routledge, 2013); Van den Bergh and Camesasca, n. 65, 88.

J. EFFECTIVE COMPETITION

The concept of effective competition is an important feature in EU competition law, as seen in Section 9.B.i. What is meant by effective competition is discussed in the following passage, which explains that it is outcome-based.

S. Bishop and M. Walker, *The Economics of EC Competition Law* (3rd edn, Sweet & Maxwell, 2010), 20–21

2-008 . . . The economic goal of EC competition law is the protection and promotion of effective competition. But this is a goal only because of the benefits that it delivers to European consumers. What matters therefore are the outcomes for consumers that competition in a particular market delivers—not the particular form that the competition process takes. Whether a market is characterized by effective competition or not therefore depends on the outcomes it produces.

This raises the question of what outcomes are produced by effective competition and how can they be distinguished from those produced by less than effective competition. The practical application of competition law ought to be interested less in outcomes that are desirable in some theoretical, abstract sense and more in outcomes that are feasible for regulatory intervention to achieve . . . To draw this distinction requires consideration of the various economic models of competition and the implications each type of model has for consumer welfare.

6. ORDOLIBERALISM

Ordoliberalism is a school of thought[143] which originated in Germany in the 1930s and was nurtured at the University of Freiburg during the Nazi era.[144] It became a key element of post-war thinking in Germany, where the concentrated economic power enjoyed by monopolies had facilitated Hitler's consolidation of political power and shown how monopoly can undermine democracy, and it provided the theoretical foundations for the German social market economy.[145] Ordoliberalism has been developed over the years by succeeding generations of adherents.[146] It advocates an 'economic

[143] Or perhaps more accurately a 'family of ideas', see M. Marquis, 'Introduction, Summary, Remarks' in C.-D. Ehlermann and M. Marquis (eds.), *European Competition Law Annual 2007: A Reformed Approach to Article 82* (Hart Publishing, 2008), xxxi. It should be noted that the term 'Ordoliberal' is sometimes tossed around to denote any approach (especially in Europe) which is not based on economic efficiency. However, as we see in this section, the principles of Ordoliberalism are more precise.

[144] The leading Ordoliberal theorists were the economist Walter Eucken (see W. Eucken, 'Die Wettbewerbsordnung und ihre Verwirklichung' (1949) 2 ORDO—*Jahrbuch für die Ordnung der Wirtschaft und Gesellschaft* 1–99, reprinted and translated in (2006) 2(2) *Competition Policy International* 219 (C. Ahlborn and C. Grave), and the lawyers Franz Böhm and Hans Grossmann-Doerth. See further D. Gerber, 'Constitutionalizing the Economy: German Neo-liberalism, Competition Law and the "New Europe" ' (1994) 42 *Am J of Comparative L* 25; V. Vanberg, 'The Freiburg School: Walter Eucken and Ordoliberalism', Freiburg Discussion Papers on Constitutional Economics, No. 04/11 (2004), <www.econstor.eu/bitstream/10419/4343/1/04_11bw.pdf>; C. Ahlborn and C. Grave, 'Walter Eucken and Ordoliberalism: An Introduction from a Consumer Welfare Perspective' (2006) 2(2) *Competition Policy International* 197; G. Schnyder and M. Siems, 'The Ordoliberal Variety of Neoliberalism' in S. J. Konzelmann and M. Fovargue-Davies (eds.), *Banking Systems in the Crisis: The Faces of Liberal Capitalism* (Routledge, 2013), 250; available at <http://ssrn.com/abstract=2142529>.

[145] See W. Eucken, *The Foundations of Economics* (William Hodge, 1951).

[146] It is therefore erroneous to represent it by reference only to its initial form: see P. Behrens, 'The Ordoliberal Concept of "Abuse" of a Dominant Position and its Impact on Article 102 TFEU', <http://ssrn.com/abstract=2658045>, who criticises D. Gerber, *Law and Competition in Twentieth Century Europe* (Oxford University Press, 1998), for doing this.

constitution' whereby competition and economic freedom are embedded into the law so that there is neither unconstrained private power nor discretionary government intervention in the economy.[147] Competition principles are therefore basic constitutional principles binding both private actors and the State. For Ordoliberals, a competitive market is 'a system of decentralized economic planning based on individual economic freedom legally protected by the system of private law of property and contract' and it is the role of competition law 'to protect competition *as a system* within which individuals are free to make their choices on the market'.[148] Ordoliberalism therefore conceives 'the competitive process as a process resulting from the exercise of individual economic liberties'[149] and competition laws as the 'rules of the game'.

The constituent elements of Ordoliberalism have been summarised as follows:

- Competition results from individual freedom of producers to choose what they want to offer and of consumers to choose what they want to buy;
- Competition is understood as a dynamic system (process) of interaction between choice-making individuals who by making their choices reveal their preferences and produce the kind of information that other individuals need to make their choices;
- It is the fundamental role of the system of private law to provide individuals with legal rights the unrestricted use of which forms the basis of competitive rivalry among producers and of consumers' freedom of choice among alternative sources of supply;
- It is the task of the state to provide laws against restraints of such competitive rivalry and to enforce them as rules of the game with which market participants have to comply.[150]

7. THE POSSIBLE GOALS AND VALUES OF COMPETITION LAW

A. GENERAL

There is much disagreement about exactly what competition laws should seek to achieve. One scholar describes competition law as having 'sponge-like' characteristics which make it 'inherently predisposed to a wide range of values and considerations'.[151] Here we briefly set out the main candidates for the aims of competition law, some of which overlap or are intertwined.[152] There is at the present time an urgent debate about the objectives of competition laws, driven by the current problems in the world economy including the economic and political power of the Big Tech companies, the recovery from Covid-19, the need to confront climate change, and the effects of the war in Ukraine, as we outlined in Sections 2 and 3.

[147] W. Möschel, 'Competition Policy from an Ordo Point of View' in A. Peacock and H. Willgerodt (eds.), *German Neo-liberals and the Social Market Economy* (Macmillan, 1989), 142.

[148] Behrens, n. 146, 11.

[149] H. Schweitzer, 'The History, Interpretation and Underlying Principles of Section 2 Sherman Act and Article 82 EC' at <http://cadmus.eui.eu/bitstream/handle/1814/7626/LAW-2007-32.pdf>, p. 41.

[150] Behrens, n. 146, 12.

[151] A. Ezrachi, 'Sponge' (2017) 5 *J of Antitrust Enforcement* 49, 50.

[152] See further e.g. G. Monti, *EC Competition Law* (Cambridge University Press, 2007), Chap. 2; K. Coates, *Competition Law and Regulation of Technology Markets* (Oxford University Press, 2011), Chap. 2; R. Nazzini, *The Foundations of European Union Competition Law: The Objectives and Principles of Article 102* (Oxford University Press, 2011), Chap. 2; Geradin, Layne-Farrar, and Petit, n. 42, 1.61–1.69; D. Zimmer (ed.), *The Goals of Competition Law* (Edward Elgar, 2012) I. Lianos, 'Polycentric Competition Law' (*CLP*, 2018); available at: https://ssrn.com/abstract=3257296.

B. ECONOMIC EFFICIENCY AND WELFARE

The welfarist approach holds that the aim of competition law is to maximise welfare by promoting economic efficiency, as explained in Section 4. This is an economic aim which is associated with the Chicago School.

If the objective of a competition regime is economic efficiency, the first question is whether the welfare standard is consumer welfare or total welfare.[153] The latter standard, it will be recalled, permits practices which lead to higher prices and thus consumer harm if they create efficiencies which increase overall wealth. Most systems of competition law with an economic efficiency goal have converged towards the consumer welfare standard (in the usual rather than the Borkian sense) by which it is consumers who must benefit. There are a number of reasons for this. One is that consumer welfare is 'a politically acceptable way of arguing for an economic approach to competition law' and 'a politically acceptable way to disguise a non-interventionist agenda'.[154] Moreover, the consumer welfare standard addresses inequality through redistributive effects from producer to consumer,[155] has less tolerance of significant amounts of market power in the economy,[156] and is usually easier to apply than total welfare because under the latter consumer losses must be offset against efficiency gains that accrue to producers, which is a more complex and difficult task except in the most simple and straightforward cases.[157]

However, it is arguable that despite the widespread preference for the consumer welfare standard amongst competition law regimes, it is inferior to a total welfare standard, and is widely adopted only for the kind of 'political economy-oriented' reasons just mentioned. [158] Arguments in favour of the total welfare test also include the fact that producers may have institutional shareholders such as pension funds and life assurance firms, although given that shareholders as a class are wealthier than consumers as a class, and shareholdings are disproportionately held by the rich, 'a dollar plucked from the consumer class and deposited into the hands of the shareholder class in proportion to their equity entails an increase in the Gini coefficient'.[159] However, as we have already noted, the reality is that in most cases the outcome will be much the same whether a consumer welfare or total welfare standard is applied.

The second question is what 'price' the consumer welfare standard uses. This is a pressing matter in the face of sustainability concerns. It may be that the consumer welfare standard is inadequate if price externalities are ignored, and that the true price, which includes unpaid external costs, should be used instead. That would entail trying to factor in pollution costs, the most pressing externality of all.[160]

[153] See Section 4.F.

[154] R. Nazzini, *The Foundations of European Union Competition Law: The Objectives and Principles of Article 102* (Oxford University Press, 2011), 45.

[155] See J. B. Baker and S. Salop, 'Antitrust, Competition Policy, and Inequality' (2015) 104 Geo LJ 1–28, <http://scholarship.law.georgetown.edu/facpub/1462> and <http://ssrn.com/abstract=2567767>, 16–17.

[156] Hovenkamp, 'Is Antitrust's Consumer Welfare Principle Imperiled?', n. 94; Baker and Salop, n. 155, 16–18, <https://ssrn.com/abstract=3197329>, 8.

[157] H. Hovenkamp, 'Antitrust Policy and Inequality of Wealth', *CPI Antitrust Chronicle* October 2017, <http://ssrn.com/abstract=2998220>, 4–5.

[158] See M. Trebilcock and F. Ducci, 'The Multifaceted Nature of Fairness in Competition Policy', *CPI Antitrust Chronicle* October 2017, <www.competitionpolicyinternational.com/wp-content/uploads/2017/10/CPI-Trebilcock-Ducci.pdf>.

[159] D. Crane, 'Further Reflections of Antitrust and Wealth Inequality', *CPI Antitrust Chronicle* October 2017, 14. The Gini coefficient is a statistical measure of income inequality amongst a state's residents.

[160] See M. Dolmans, 'Sustainable Competition Policy' (2020) 6(1) *Competition Law and Policy Debate* 4, <https://ssrn.com/abstract=3608023>; S. Holmes, *Climate Change, Sustainability and Competition Law* (2020) 8 *Journal of Antitrust Enforcement* 354; and Section 4.A.vi.

The third question is what the 'consumer welfare standard' comprises, i.e. what efficiencies does it include? The 'narrow' interpretation of consumer welfare equates it with consumer surplus.[161] The question for competition authorities working with this version of the consumer welfare standard is therefore whether the effect of the agreement, transaction, or practice under consideration is to raise consumer prices/reduce output. There may be further issues such as whether this is to be judged over the short or long term, but one of the greatest virtues of this standard, according to its advocates, is that it is capable of objective econometric measurement.

A broader conception of consumer welfare embraces 'qualitative efficiencies' such as quality, choice, and innovation, which also concern consumers, and may need to be balanced against lower prices. Taking these kinds of efficiencies into account may make the tests and measurements more difficult, but it is a still a standard which is concerned with the effects on *consumers*. Competition law regimes which work to a consumer welfare standard differ in the extent to which they accord qualitative efficiencies as much weight as consumer prices and output restrictions.[162]

The climate crisis has made the question of the content of the consumer welfare standard an urgent one. Competition law regimes which hold that competition policy should promote only consumer welfare (rather than wider public interest or socio-political goals) are faced with the question of whether there is any room in that standard for sustainability benefits. For example, an agreement between competitors to abandon certain polluting inputs may raise consumer prices and restrict consumer choice but benefit the environment. There are powerful arguments that environmental benefits and costs can be quantified and should be incorporated as efficiencies into the broader concept of consumer welfare.[163]

The use of the consumer welfare standard raises the fundamental question of who is a 'consumer'.[164] The general meaning of 'consumer' is a private final end-user who purchases for their own consumption but some systems of competition law (including that of the EU[165]) conflate 'consumer' with 'customer' and include within the definition intermediate customers who purchase in order to sell on (in which case the consumer welfare standard favours the buying *firm* over the selling one).[166]

Furthermore, it is argued that competition law should recognise that the identity of a 'consumer' is increasingly complex and multifaceted and goes beyond being a 'chooser' whose choices drive the market economy.[167] For example, 'consumer-citizens' may make consumption choices which, rather than being rooted in self-interest, are motivated by political, social, or moral concerns such as making environmentally responsible choices, boycotting goods produced unethically, and actively seeking out products which reflect their values;[168] and 'consumer-workers' actively co-create online

[161] See Section 4.F.

[162] For the European Commission's latest approach to this, see the Horizontal Cooperation Guidelines, 17 July 2023, discussed in Chap. 10.

[163] See e.g. Dolmans, n. 160.

[164] See e.g. Orbach, n. 94, 138–140; Hovenkamp, 'Is Antitrust's Consumer Welfare Principle Imperiled', n. 94, 13–14 ('what we really want is a name for some class of actors who is injured by either the higher buying price or the lower selling price that attends a monopolistic output reduction').

[165] See Section 9.B.v.

[166] See J. Farrell and M. L. Katz, 'The Economics of Welfare Standards in Antitrust' (2006) 2(2) *Competition Policy International* 3; K. Cseres, *Competition Law and Consumer Protection* (Kluwer Law International, 2005), 331–332; P. Akman, 'Consumer versus "Customer": The Devil in the Detail' (2010) 37 *J of L & Soc* 315. For a discussion of the concept of 'consumer' in EU competition law generally, see A. Jones and A. Albors-Llorens, 'The Images of the "Consumer" in EU Competition Law' (2016), <http://papers.ssrn.com/sol3/papers.cfm?abstract_id=2750922>.

[167] C. Beaton-Wells, 'Antitrust's Neglected Question: Who Is "The Consumer"?' (2020) 65(1) *Ant Bull* 173.

[168] Such consumer behaviour is recognised in the European Commission's Horizontal Cooperation Guidelines, 17 July 2023, Chap. 9 on Sustainability Agreements, paras. 575–581, see Chap. 10, which introduces the concept of 'individual non-use value benefits'.

content by browsing, searching, interacting, and sharing online, thereby generating wealth for the firms which exploit their data.[169]

A further issue is whether the 'consumers' with whom the standard is concerned are only those presently within the relevant market[170] or can also encompass those outside the market who are affected by negative or positive externalities, and/or future consumers. Again, this long-standing question is specially pertinent in the light of the climate crisis and, in the EU, to the building of the resilience of the single market.[171] A focus on short-term advantages for present consumers within the market may not be adequate. For example, a choice between dependence on importing into the EU cheap(er) solar panels from China or manufacturing more expensive ones in Europe may need to be taken on wider grounds than cost.[172]

C. PROTECTING THE COMPETITIVE PROCESS OR PROTECTING COMPETITION

Competition law can be primarily concerned with protecting the process of competition. The law then focuses on securing an environment favourable to vigorous competition, it being presumed that such an environment is most conducive to the good of society.[173] The objective is therefore to protect a *process* rather than an outcome, and to value that process as a good in itself. Protecting the competitive *process* and protecting *competition* are often used interchangeably[174] because 'competition is a process that results in the wealth of society being put to its highest uses rather than dictating a specific outcome, while competition law is concerned with protecting this process'.[175] This approach to competition law is often referred to as protecting 'competition as such'.

Ordoliberals advocate the protection of the process of competition as the goal of competition as a way of protecting the right of individuals to participate in economic life, as explained in Section D.

D. PROTECTION OF ECONOMIC FREEDOM, PROTECTING COMPETITORS, AND THE DISPERSAL OF ECONOMIC POWER

Competition law aimed at securing economic freedom is concerned not with direct effects on consumers but with the maintenance of a system which protects individual economic freedom of action and enables all citizens to participate in the market. Competition law therefore protects market

[169] Beaton-Wells, n. 167, 183–186.

[170] For the concept of the relevant market, see Chap. 3. And for EU law, see the discussion of Art. 101(3) in Chap. 5, Section 4.D.

[171] Communication from the Commission, 'Updating the 2020 New Industrial Strategy: Building a Stronger Single Market for Europe's Recovery', COM(2021)350 final.

[172] This example was discussed at the European Commission's Conference on 'Making Markets Work for People' on 27 October 2022, see <www.youtube.com/watch?v=ZqGrnjm_Xs0>.

[173] See the discussion in N. Dunne, *Competition Law and Economic Regulation* (Cambridge University Press, 2015), 28–30 and the critique of the competitive process approach in N. Petit, '*Intel*, Leveraging Rebates and the Goals of Article 102', <http://ssrn.com/abstract=2567628>, 24–28; E. Fox, 'The Modernization of Antitrust: A New Equilibrium' (1981) 66 *Cornell LR* 1140, 1191.

[174] See e.g. T. Wu, 'After Consumer Welfare, Now What? The "Protection of Competition" Standard in Practice', *CPI Antitrust Chronicle* April 2018, who says at p. 7 that protecting the competitive process is like asking 'enforcers and judges to act like referees [in American football], calling out fouls and penalties, with the goal of ultimately protecting the quality of play, which in this case means an economy that does not allow size, market power, or anticompetitive agreements to be used as weapons, and instead seeks to reward the firms with better products'.

[175] Dunne, n. 173, 29.

participants from the undue economic power of others. The 'economic freedom' theory is associated in Europe with Ordoliberalism, discussed in Section 6, where we see that Ordoliberals mandate the State to protect the process of competition as part of the protection of economic freedom. The economic freedom conception may lead to competition law protecting competitors rather than competition. It may, for example, protect small firms from the dominant firm's (efficient) low pricing, or force a dominant firm to give access to its resources to a smaller firm in order to allow the latter to compete with it. In some circumstances it may be necessary to protect particular competitors in order to prevent a welfare loss. However, there is a difference between, on the one hand, protecting competitors as a means of protecting competition and economic welfare and, on the other hand, protecting particular competitors for their own sake or for the sake of maintaining a particular market structure as a matter of principle.

The protection of inefficient competitors normally takes wealth from consumers and leads to a loss in welfare. On the other hand, a policy which protects competitors for their own sakes may enable a government to nurture small businesses, to combat 'big' firms, and to promote a society in which citizens are encouraged to be their own boss, run their own business, and behave in an entrepreneurial manner. By combating 'big' firms, it leads to the dispersal of economic power and, in line with Ordoliberal thinking, that upholds liberal democracy because economic power can lead to political power and undermine democratic institutions.[176] The protection of competitors from 'big' firms became unfashionable after the ascendancy of the economic efficiency/consumer welfare prescription and has often been derided as 'populist'[177] but it is an idea which has come to the fore again because of current concerns over the rising levels of concentration and monopoly and the economic power of Big Tech.

Economic freedom and the dispersal of economic power are aspects of the 'public interest' and are entwined with the issues of fairness, redistribution, and equality we discuss in the next section.[178]

E. THE PUBLIC INTEREST, FAIRNESS, EQUALITY (ECONOMIC EQUITY), AND REDISTRIBUTION

Competition law can be understood generally as a type of public interest law.[179] Beyond this, however, there is the question of whether competition law could or should be used to pursue *specific* public interest goals. 'Public interest goals' is a nebulous concept but is used here to encompass objectives which embrace values that go beyond purely economic efficiency.[180] Some of the goals already discussed, such as dispersing economic power and protecting competitors, can be described as an application of competition law in the public interest.

[176] For an interesting argument that the monopoly power of the German chemical firm I. G. Farben, which supported and facilitated the aggression of the Nazi regime, could have been prevented by the application of consumer welfare-orientated competition law rather than needing laws specifically designed to uphold political liberalism, see D. Crane, 'Antitrust and Democracy: A Case Study from German Fascism', University of Michigan Law and Economic Research Paper No. 18-009, University of Michigan Public Law Research Paper No. 595 (April 2018), <https://ssrn.com/abstract=3164467>.

[177] E.g. Posner, *Antitrust Law*, n. 97, 25.

[178] Although there is disagreement about the extent to which Ordoliberalism is concerned with fairness as an objective of competition law, see Behrens, n. 146; cf. P. Akman, *The Concept of Abuse in EU Competition Law* (Hart Publishing, 2012), 151.

[179] See N. Dunne, 'Public Interest and EU Competition Law' (2020) 65(2) *Ant Bull* 256, 256.

[180] Ibid., 258.

Fairness is a possible public interest goal.[181] 'Fairness', however, is also a nebulous concept and raises the question 'fairness for whom?'. For example, the protection of smaller competitors on grounds of fairness may result in inefficiency and so lead to the 'unfairness' of consumers paying higher prices than necessary. Competition laws concerned with fairness should be clear about whom fairness protects. Trebilcock and Ducci[182] identify four possible notions of fairness in competition policy: horizontal fairness on the demand side (i.e. between consumers), horizontal fairness on the supply side (i.e. between producers), vertical fairness (i.e. between producers and consumers), and procedural fairness (i.e. in due process in both public and private enforcement). Unsurprisingly, they consider procedural fairness a rightful concern of competition law. Horizontal fairness on the demand side is reflected in provisions and cases prohibiting price discrimination and other discriminatory practices by dominant firms[183] and in concerns about platform markets and behavioural discrimination.[184] On the supply side, concern with fairness is reflected in the law which targets anti-competitive exclusionary conduct by dominant firms and barriers to entry which deter the entry of equally efficient competitors.[185] The issue of vertical fairness takes us back to the question of the choice of welfare standard. The consumer welfare standard can be seen as a policy of fairness towards consumers, but conversely favouring consumers at the expense of producers can be considered unfair to the latter.[186] Vertical fairness is also reflected in competition laws which intervene against monopoly prices.[187] There is a specific example of fairness in the FRAND (fair, reasonable, and non-discriminatory) concept used by the European Commission in respect of standard essential patents and standardisation agreements[188] and fairness is a major concept in the EU's 2022 Digital Markets Act, whose purpose is to ensure 'contestable and fair markets in the digital sector'.[189] Fairness can mean that all market participants should have equal opportunities to compete on a level playing field (a matter which can also been seen as one of economic freedom and of protecting competition).[190]

While fairness as a general consideration in competition law is still an anathema to many of those who hold to efficiency and welfare as the sole goal, others see fairness as an integral part of the concept of protecting competition and a value which can and should live alongside efficiency considerations.

[181] Competition laws concerned with fairness should be distinguished from laws against unfair trading practices such as deceptive, fraudulent, or unethical behaviour. The latter are best dealt with by specific legislation, including consumer protection legislation outlawing conduct such as misleading advertising and aggressive marketing techniques; see e.g. EU Dir. on Unfair Commercial Practices, 2005/29/EC [2005] OJ L149/22. However, misrepresentations made to public authorities were dealt with under the EU competition rules in Case C-457/10 P, *AstraZeneca AB and AstraZeneca plc v Commission* EU:C:2012:770, see Chap. 7, Section 14.C.

[182] M. Trebilcock and F. Ducci, 'The Multifaceted Nature of Fairness in Competition Policy', *CPI Antitrust Chronicle* October 2017, <www.competitionpolicyinternational.com/wp-content/uploads/2017/10/CPI-Trebilcock-Ducci.pdf>.

[183] See Chap. 7, for the relevant EU law.

[184] Although Trebilcock and Ducci see no compelling justification for accounting for the dimension of fairness on the demand side insofar as the source of differential treatment among consumers is in their demand conditions.

[185] See Chap. 7.

[186] Trebilcock and Ducci disapprove of the consumer welfare standard on those grounds. Cf. F. Jenny (Chairman, OECD Competition Committee), 'Populism, Fairness and Competition: Should We Care and What Could We Do?', 30 October 2018, <https://ssrn.com/abstract=3476227>.

[187] For the EU provisions, see Chap. 7.

[188] See Chap. 10. Section 8, and the Horizontal Cooperation Guidelines, 17 July 2023, Chap. 7.

[189] Digital Markets Act, Reg. 2022/1925 [2022] OJ L265/1, Art. 1(1); see Section 12 and Chap. 16.

[190] The General Court said in Case T-612/17, *Google and Alphabet v Commission (Google Shopping)* EU:T:2021:763, para. 180, on appeal Case C-48/22 P, judgment pending, that 'a system of undistorted competition can be guaranteed only if equality of opportunity is secured as between the various economic operators . . . '.

A. Lamadrid de Pablo, 'Competition Law as Fairness' (2017) 8 *JECLAP* 147

In this sense, competition law should not—and does not need to—be diverted to pursue fairness because it is already about fairness. The very notion of merit-based competition carries implicit in it a sense of fairness, understood as equality of opportunity, for what is the sense of a competition if the game is rigged, if some enjoy advantages over others, if not all have a chance?

Fairness, in other words, is not an abstract standalone goal liable to divert or distort a correct enforcement of the law, but rather its natural outcome.

Protecting the competitive process will naturally benefit all participants in the process, consumers, counterparties, employees, and society overall. The sound application of competition law will often result in a more efficient economy, but this is not the point of the discipline; what ultimately matters is that the application of competition law has a good chance of resulting in a fairer society.

Connecting 'fairness' to competition law is therefore not a way to divorce the discipline from economics but to reconcile it with society, showing the wider public that it can contribute to their well-being. It is not about introducing populism, but about resisting populist drives. There is no harm in acknowledging, and no reason to reject, the beneficial effects and, in the end, the moral underpinning of competition law. It is about telling a true story in terms that are more understandable and, especially, more appealing.[191]

The general concept of fairness and competition law is significant in the context of contemporary concerns about the ever-increasing wealth and income inequality which poses a threat to the existing political and social order across the globe[192] and which is explicable by a number of factors (such as globalisation, financialisation, the drop in real wage values, the waning of collective bargaining, unfair labour, and tax systems etc)[193] but there is strong evidence that inequality is also related to the exercise of market power and the persistence of high monopoly profits.[194] Some of the blame for the increasing level of economic concentration and incidence of corporate market power in the last 30 years or so has been laid at the door of the allegedly lax enforcement of competition law and of its preoccupation with the consumer welfare standard and low prices, particularly in the US;[195] whereas a competition policy directed at dispersing economic power would be redistributive. The case is therefore often made for framing and enforcing competition law with the goal of maximising economic

[191] See also D. Gerard, 'Fairness in EU Competition Policy: Significance and Implications' (2018) 9(4) *JECLAP* 211.

[192] See Section 2. The October 2017 issue of the *CPI Antitrust Chronicle* was devoted to competition law and inequality, see particularly H. Hovenkamp, 'Antitrust Policy and Inequality of Wealth', *CPI Antitrust Chronicle* October 2017, <http://ssrn.com/abstract=2998220>, 7 and D. Crane, 'Further Reflections of Antitrust and Wealth Inequality', *CPI Antitrust Chronicle* October 2017, 14.

[193] See I. Lianos, 'Competition Law as a Form of Social Regulation' (2020) 65(1) *Ant Bull* 3.

[194] OECD, S. Ennis and Y. Kim, 'Market Power and Wealth Distribution' in *A Step Ahead: Competition Policy for Shared Prosperity and Inclusive Growth* (OECD Publishing, Paris/World Bank Group, 2017), <https://doi.org/10.1787/9781464809460-1-en>; see also J. Stiglitz, 'Monopoly's New Era', <www.project-syndicate.org/commentary/high-monopoly-profits-persist-in-markets-by-joseph-e--stiglitz-2016-05>; B. Milanovic, *Global Inequality: A New Approach For The Age Of Globalisation* (Harvard University Press, 2016); I. Lianos, 'The Poverty of Competition Law' in D. Gerard and I. Lianos (eds.), *Reconciling Efficiency and Equity* (Cambridge University Press, 2019).

[195] E.g. L. Khan and S. Vaheesan, 'Market Power and Inequality: The Antitrust Counterrevolution and Its Discontents' (2017) 11 *Harvard L and Policy Rev* 135, <https://ssrn.com/abstract=2769132>; B. Lynn, *Cornered, The New Monopoly Capitalism and the Economics of Destruction* (Wiley, 2010); M. Steinbaum and M. E. Stucke, 'The Effective Competition Standard: A New Standard for Antitrust' (2020) 87(2) *Univ Chic LR* 595; T. Wu, *The Curse of Bigness* (Columbia Global Reports, 2018, Atlantic Books, 2020); J. Tepper with D. Hearn, '*The Myth of Capitalism*' (Wiley, 2018).

equity, thereby protecting the social contract which underpins the organisation of society, rather than continuing to pursue economic *efficiency*.[196]

Against the use of competition law to combat inequality are the arguments[197] that greater competition and economic rivalry tend to more rather than less inequality, so that aggressive enforcement can lead to a *regressive* redistribution of wealth; that the call for greater competition law enforcement against market power rests on simplistic assumptions; and that 'the wealth distribution effects of antitrust enforcement and monopoly are almost impossible to know systematically or to generalize'.[198] The goal of economic equity has inevitably been condemned as 'populist' and subject to the criticism of bringing uncertainty into the law. Nevertheless, the advocacy of fairness and equality in competition law is currently undergoing a great resurgence.[199]

F. PUBLIC POLICIES

One aspect of the public interest is the use of competition law to service specific governmental policies such as social, employment, industrial, environmental, and regional policy (for example, by prohibiting mergers which will cause job losses, or allowing restrictive agreements which will prolong the life of declining industries). Currently, for example, there is the question of employing competition law to protect privacy[200] and the major issue of how, and to what extent, climate change and sustainability could or should be taken into account in the formulation and application of competition law. In the EU, there is a new public policy imperative in the form of 'resilience'.[201]

In some countries, socio-political objectives are set out in the competition legislation, or the competition rules are embedded in other provisions.[202] In the EU, competition law has a special dimension in the imperative of the integration of the single market. This is discussed in Section 9.B.iii.

G. CONCLUSION

It is often claimed that a major advantage of economic efficiency as the sole goal of competition law is that it provides certainty, clarity, and consistency. There are, as we see throughout this book, differences of opinion as to *how* it is to be determined whether a certain practice maximises or undermines welfare, as to the tests that should be applied, the presumptions which should be used, and so on, but at least the goal towards which the competition authorities and courts are working is clear. The consumer welfare standard, it is argued, is a 'legalist' test, based on an objective standard and economic

[196] See D. Gerard and I. Lianos (eds.), *Competition Law: Between Equity and Efficiency* (Cambridge University Press, 2019), passim; D. Waked, 'Antitrust as Public Interest Law: Redistribution, Equity, and Social Justice' (2020) 65(1) *Ant Bull* 87; C. Beaton-Wells and J. Paul-Taylor, 'Efficiency and Fairness: Interdependent Discourses in Supermarket Supplier Relations' in I. Lianos, A. Ivanov, and D. Davis (eds.), *Global Food Value Chains and Competition Law* (Cambridge University Press, 2021).

[197] See D. Crane, 'Antitrust and Wealth Inequality' (2016) 101 *Cornell LR* 1171, <https://ssrn.com/abstract=2648541>.

[198] D. Crane, 'Further Reflections of Antitrust and Wealth Inequality', *CPI Antitrust Chronicle* October 2017, 14, 18.

[199] It never went away, as can be seen, inter alia, from the lifetime work of Eleanor Fox, author of 'The Battle for the Soul of Antitrust' (1987) 75(3) *California LR* 917, who is celebrated in N. Charbit and S. Gachot, (eds.), *Eleanor M. Fox: Antitrust Ambassador to the World—Liber Amicorum* (Concurrences, 2021) and see also the essays in D. Gerard and I. Lianos (eds.), *Reconciling Efficiency and Equity* (Cambridge University Press, 2019), including E. Fox, 'Competition Policy at the Intersection of Equity and Efficiency: The Developed and Developing Worlds' at 441–445.

[200] See e.g. the Symposium on competition law and privacy in (2018) 8(3) *International Data Privacy Law*.

[201] See Sections 9.A and B.viii. [202] See Chap. 17.

analysis whereas the disadvantage of any other goal or consideration is that it necessarily involves discretion on the part of competition authorities and courts.[203]

The advocates of economic efficiency alone as the goal of competition law do not thereby (necessarily) reject the need for other policies but consider that competition law should deal only with well-defined economic questions rather than employ some kind of value-based and discretionary public interest test[204] and that excluding social and political objectives gives intellectual coherence and predictability to the law.[205] In the 1970s, that view became in the ascendant in the US[206] and then spread across the globe.

Recently the tide has begun to turn, and the idea that 'making markets work well' should encompass more than efficiency has regained traction. This development has been prompted by the political and economic developments we have already mentioned, such as increasing inequality, concentration, and populism, and also by the rise of Big Tech which poses particular problems for competition law.[207] However, it should not be left to competition authorities to decide on the hierarchy of priorities and complex trade-offs between multifaceted objectives. It should be for legislatures to establish the framework of values within which the decisions are made. Furthermore, it is arguable that however attractive it might be to take advantage of established agencies with powerful enforcement tools, competition authorities and competition law cannot do everything and solve every problem.[208]

8. US ANTITRUST LAW

It is difficult to discuss EU competition law without some reference to US antitrust law because of the influence which those working within that system have had on competition law thinking, as is apparent from Section 6.

The Sherman Act was enacted in 1890[209] and is still in force. Section 1[210] deals with agreements between firms. It states:

> Every contract, combination in the form of trust or otherwise, or conspiracy, in restraint of trade or commerce among the several States, or with foreign nations, is hereby declared to be illegal. Every person who shall make any contract or engage in any combination or conspiracy hereby declared to be illegal shall be deemed guilty of a felony . . .

[203] One scholar therefore describes the debate about goals as really being between legalists and discretionalists, see P. P. Ibáñez Colomo, <https://chillingcompetition.com/2018/05/28/discretionalists-vs-legalists-the-true-divide-in-the-competition-law-community/>. The consumer welfare test has been described in respect of the US as 'bringing the rule of law to antitrust', see E. Dorsey, J. Rybnicek, and J. D. Wright, 'Hipster Antitrust Meets Public Choice Economics: The Consumer Welfare Standard, Rule of Law, and Rent Seeking', *CPI Antitrust Chronicle* April 2018, who argue that that replacing the consumer welfare test with some form of public interest test allows for the regulatory capture of competition agencies by corporate bodies and for political influence over them.

[204] See e.g. J. Pecman, 'Populism, Public Interest and Competition', <www.canada.ca/en/competition-bureau/news/2018/05/john-pecman-commissioner-of-competition---populism-public-interest-and-competition.html> (at the time Pecman was the Commissioner of Competition in Canada).

[205] J. D. Wright and D. Ginsburg, 'The Goals of Antitrust: Welfare Trumps Choice' (2013) 81 *Fordham L Rev* 2405.

[206] See Section 8. [207] See Section 12 and Chap. 16.

[208] As the US judge Frank Easterbrook said, there must be 'limits of antitrust': 'The Limits of Antitrust'(1984) 63 *Texas LR* 1.

[209] 'An Act to protect trade and commerce against unlawful restraints and monopolies', 15 USC, 2 July 1890. Some US states had already adopted competition laws in the late 1880s.

[210] Discussed in Chap. 5, Section 2.D.

Section 2 deals with the acts of single firms by creating the offence of 'monopolization'. It states:

> Every person who shall monopolize, or attempt to monopolize, or combine or conspire with any other person or persons, to monopolize any part of the trade or commerce among several States, or with foreign nations, shall be deemed guilty of a felony . . .

None of the expressions used in the Sherman Act, such as 'in restraint of trade' or 'monopolize', were defined. The Act was intended to be interpreted in accordance with the normal common law tradition,[211] although the Supreme Court has also referred to it as a 'charter of freedom'[212] and a 'comprehensive charter of economic liberty',[213] according it quasi-constitutional status.[214] It has been supplemented by subsequent statutes, particularly the Clayton Act 1914 (amended by the Celler–Kefauver Act 1950) which, inter alia, prohibits mergers whose effect may be substantially to lessen competition or to tend to create a monopoly.[215] The federal antitrust laws are enforced by the Department of Justice (DOJ) Antitrust Division and by the FTC[216] bringing actions before the ordinary federal courts. As violations of the Sherman Act are felonies, the DOJ may bring criminal as well as civil proceedings. Prosecutions may also be brought by state governments, and companies and individuals may bring private actions (under the Clayton Act, s. 4, private parties may sue for treble damages). Private actions are a major element of US antitrust and are discussed further in Chapter 14, Section 3. We see there how the problems of enforcement through private actions has had a profound effect on the development of the law.

The Sherman Act arose from concern in late nineteenth-century US about widespread cartelisation and about the rise of large monopolistic firms often created by mergers and acquisitions. It was particularly directed at the 'trusts', especially those in the railroad industry. The trust in this context was a device by which stock owners in competing companies transferred their holdings to trustees who then controlled the activities of those competitors, removing competition between them and enabling the trust to behave as one enterprise (thus 'antitrust' law). The Sherman Act was therefore an assault on the growth of corporate power, although there remains much dispute about the exact legislative intent of Congress (and about whether the legislative intent matters) in the sense of what (if any) economic theory it espoused.[217] Robert Bork argued that it was passed to preserve economic efficiency, [218] despite the fact that the theories of efficiency and welfare had not been published at the time of the Act's passage.[219]

[211] Although from early on it was not interpreted in accordance with *existing* common law.

[212] *Sugar Institute, Inc v United States*, 297 US 553 (1936).

[213] *Northern Pacific Railway Co v United States*, 356 US 1 (1958).

[214] See B. Hawk, *Antitrust and Competition Laws* (Juris Publishing, 2020), 98–99.

[215] See also the Federal Trade Commission Act 1914, the Robinson–Patman Act (1936), dealing with price discrimination, and the Hart–Scott–Rodino Antitrust Improvements Act 1976.

[216] Established by the Federal Trade Commission Act 1914.

[217] See E. T. Sullivan (ed.), *The Political Economy of the Sherman Act* (Oxford University Press, 1991) for a collection of essays written between 1959 and 1989 on the Sherman Act, published to mark its centenary. The articles display the wide divergence of views on the genesis of the Act between some of the most eminent names in antitrust thinking, as well as historians and DOJ officials. See also Gellhorn, Kovacic, and Calkins, n. 107, 22–36; Hawk, *Antitrust and Competition Laws*, n. 214, Chap. 3, 85–95; W. Kovacic and C. Shapiro, 'Antitrust Policy: A Century of Economic and Legal Thinking' (2000) 14 *J of Econ Perspective* 43.

[218] For Robert Bork's view of the intention of Congress, see R. H. Bork, *The Antitrust Paradox: A Policy at War with Itself* (Basic Books, 1978, reprinted with a new Introduction and Epilogue, 1993), Chap. 2; R. Bork, 'Legislative Intent and the Policy of the Sherman Act' (1966) 9 *J of L & Econ* 7.

[219] Marshall's *Principles of Economics*, n. 43, was first published in 1890 and Pareto published his theory in 1909.

In the half-century following the passing of the Sherman Act, US law developed in a series of judicial decisions[220] which reflected the experiences of the American economy as it went through an industrial revolution, the Depression (when antitrust enforcement was relaxed),[221] and the New Deal.[222] From 1937 until the late 1970s, now referred to as the 'expansionary' or 'egalitarian' phase,[223] the US agencies, backed by a Supreme Court concerned with social and political effects, pursued a policy of aggressive antitrust enforcement, driven by the belief, inter alia, that without intervention market power would endure, that small firms were desirable in themselves and should be protected from large ones, that markets were too concentrated, and that, in the light of the S→C→P paradigm, concentration was harmful. This resulted in the prohibition of, or tough restrictions on, many horizontal and non-horizontal mergers, some involving very small market shares; in findings of s. 2 monopolisation;[224] and in the classification of a large number of restraints in vertical agreements as 'per se' illegal.[225] These features of antitrust enforcement coincided with the general trend in US Congressional policies which sought to protect small businesses and which were suspicious of business expansion. Interventionist antitrust was particularly marked in the 1960s decisions of the Supreme Court under Chief Justice Earl Warren.[226]

However, in the late 1970s Chicago School thinking[227] became increasingly influential and led to a fundamental change of direction in the application and enforcement of antitrust law[228] and to the beginning of what has been called the 'inhospitality era'.[229] This was not solely due to Chicago, as it was complemented by the New Harvard School, particularly because of the publication of the initial parts of the definitive Areeda and Turner treatise in 1978.[230]

220 Note in particular *United States v Addyston Pipe and Steel* Co, 85 Fed 271 (1898), *aff'd* 175 US 211 (the relationship between the Sherman Act and the common law, and the per se nature of 'naked' restraints) and the divestitures in *Standard Oil Co of New Jersey v United States*, 221 US 1 (1911) and *United States v American Tobacco Co*, 221 US 106 (1911) as a remedy for s. 2 monopolization offences.

221 For the claim that this prolonged the Depression, see J. D. Harkrider, 'Lessons from the Great Depression' (2009) 23 *Antitrust* 6.

222 The federal policy begun under President Roosevelt in 1933 to aid those thrown out of employment in the Depression. Collusion between competitors was first encouraged and then prosecuted.

223 1937 was the start of Roosevelt's second term. The expansionary phase was interrupted by the Second World War (1941 in the US). For a historical analysis of US antitrust laws in the 20th century, see M. Glick, *Antitrust and Economic History: The Historic Failure of the Chicago School of Antitrust* (2020) 64(3) *Ant Bull* 295.

224 See particularly *United States v Aluminum Co of America*, 148 F.2d. 416 (2d Cir. 1945) (*Alcoa*), a famous judgment by Judge Learned Hand; and *United States v United Shoe Machinery Corp*, 347 US 521, 74 S.Ct 699 (1954).

225 See Chap. 5, Section 2.D.

226 E.g. *Brown Shoe Co v United States*, 370 US 294, 82 S.Ct 1502 (1962) (condemnation of a horizontal merger because the post-merger firm would be able to undercut its smaller competitors); *FTC v Consolidated Foods Corp*, 380 US 592, 85 S.Ct 1220 (1965) (condemnation of a conglomerate merger on the grounds that it facilitated reciprocal buying); *FTC v Procter & Gamble Co*, 386 US 568, 87 S.Ct 1224 (1967) (condemnation of a horizontal merger on the ground, inter alia, that the post-merger firm could take advantage of volume discounts in advertising and undercut its competitors in some products); *United States v Arnold, Schwinn & Co*, 388 US 365, 87 S.Ct 1856 (1967) (per se illegality of customer and territorial restraints in vertical agreements).

227 Discussed in Section 5.A. Developments in the Harvard School were also influential, see W. Kovacic, 'The Chicago Obsession in the Interpretation of US Antitrust History' (2020) 87 *Univ Chic LR* 459.

228 See generally Pitofsky, n. 112; D. Crane, 'Chicago, Post-Chicago and Neo-Chicago' (2009) 76 *Univ Chic LR* 1911 (a review of the Pitofsky book); C. E. Mueller, 'Antitrust Economics and the "The Flying Dutchman": How Economists Ruined Antitrust in Reagan's 1980s' (2008) 32 *Antitrust L and Econ Rev* 1; H. Hovenkamp and F. Scott Morton, 'Framing the Chicago School of Antitrust Analysis' (2020) 168 *U Pa LR* 1843.

229 Hawk, *Antitrust and Competition Laws*, n. 214, 126–153.

230 Areeda and Turner, n. 79. See W. Kovacic, 'The Chicago Obsession in the Interpretation of US Antitrust History' (2020) 87 *Univ Chic LR* 459 (2020) (arguing that the contribution of Harvard to the development of US antitrust is often overlooked); T. Muris and J. Nuechterlein, 'Chicago and Its Discontents' (2020) 87 *Univ Chic LR* 495.

The change saw the Supreme Court describe the antitrust rules as 'a consumer welfare prescription'[231] and deliver a number of landmark Chicago-inspired judgments, beginning with *Sylvania* in 1977 which overruled the per se rule against non-price intra-brand vertical restraints.[232] The Court proceeded, inter alia, to overrule the per se rule against maximum resale price maintenance (RPM)[233] and the per se rule against fixed and minimum RPM,[234] adopt a standard for proving predatory pricing which makes it extremely difficult for plaintiffs to succeed,[235] increase the threshold for pleading conspiracy under s. 1,[236] and show itself inimical to claims of refusal to supply.[237]

In the 40 plus years following *Sylvania*, US antitrust was solely concerned with economic efficiency, applying a 'consumer welfare' prescription which only addressed effects on consumers. Driven by the reluctance to intervene in the working of the market and preoccupied by concerns about administrability and the costs of litigation (particularly in the light of private damages actions[238]), antitrust became increasingly narrow and technical, reduced to econometric tests for proving anti-competitive effects. An 'anti-enforcement bias' became built into the system through the application of the 'error–cost framework' which holds that false findings of harm to competition are more prejudicial to the economy than false findings of no harm.[239] Efficiencies were assumed without proof, whereas anti-competitive effects had to be precisely proved by plaintiffs carrying a heavy burden of proof.[240]

By the end of the second decade of the twenty-first century, US antitrust was in the main concerned only with cartels involving anti-competitive horizontal price-fixing and market division, and with horizontal mergers which led to monopoly or duopoly with provable effects on consumers. It was generally not concerned with discrimination, exclusionary conduct,[241] or vertical mergers. Corporate size and concentration were not of themselves considered problematic. The implications of this limitation of antitrust law, which is seen to reflect a triumph of the conservative right, have been extensively debated.[242]

[231] *Reiter v Sonotone Corp*, 442 US 339, 343 (1979), quoting Bork, *The Antitrust Paradox*, n. 218, 66.

[232] *Continental TV, Inc v GTE Sylvania*, 433 US 36 (1977).

[233] *State Oil v Khan*, 522 US 3 (1997).

[234] *Leegin Creative Leather Products Inc v PSKS, Inc*, 551 US 887 (2007).

[235] *Brooke Group Ltd v Brown and Williamson Tobacco Corp*, 509 US 209 (1993); *Matsushita Elec. Indus. Co v Zenith Radio Corp*, 475 US 574 (1986). However, the standard adopted, the 'Areeda–Turner' rule, discussed in Chap. 7, was the product of the new Harvard School, and less absolutist than the Chicago approach. Bork's view was that predatory pricing could not exist as an offence as low prices were always good for consumers.

[236] *Bell Atl. Corp v Twombly*, 550 US 544 (2007).

[237] *Verizon Communications Inc v Trinko LLP*, 540 US 398, 124 S.Ct 872 (2004).

[238] See Chap. 14, Section 3.

[239] For a critique of the application of error–cost analysis in US law, see J. B. Baker, 'Taking the Error out of "Error Cost" Analysis: What's Wrong with Antitrust's Right' (2015) 80 *Antitrust LJ* 8, <https://ssrn.com/abstract=2333736>; H. Hovenkamp, 'Antitrust Error Costs', U Pa J of Bus L, University of Pennsylvania, Institute for Law & Economics Research Paper No. 21-32 (29 January 2022), available at <https://ssrn.com/abstract=3853282>.

[240] The US 'rule of reason', discussed in the introduction to EU law on restrictive agreements in Chap. 5, Section D, which applies when practices are neither per se legal or illegal, requires the plaintiff to prove that the challenged restraint has substantial anti-competitive effects. If they succeed, the burden then shifts to the defendant to show a pro-competitive rationale for the restraint. If the defendant does that successfully, the burden shifts back to the plaintiff to demonstrate that the pro-competitive efficiencies could reasonably be achieved through less anti-competitive means. In the last 45 years, nearly all rule of reasons cases have been disposed of by the plaintiff failing at the first hurdle: see the Supreme Court in *NCAA v Alston*, 594 US (2021).

[241] *US v Microsoft Corp*, 253 F.3d 34 (CADC 2001) was an exception. Microsoft was charged by the DOJ and a number of states with violations of s. 2 of the Sherman Act. The District Court found against Microsoft and ordered its break-up (into one part producing the operating system and the other producing software). The Court of Appeals upheld the judge's findings of fact but overturned his rulings against Microsoft. Ultimately the case was concluded by a settlement between Microsoft and the DOJ in November 2001.

[242] See e.g. A. Jones and W. Kovacic, 'Antitrust's Implementation Blindside': Challenges to Major Expansion of US Competition Policy (2020) 65(2) *Ant Bull* 227, 231–234.

The last 45 years of antitrust policy stand accused of contributing significantly to the creation and entrenchment of market power in many economic sectors (particularly the digital economy[243]), to increased concentration,[244] and to reduced competition.[245] Many mainstream scholars and commentators, including some of the leading figures in US antitrust,[246] are critical of the position reached and advocate change. Broadly, they variously suggest that US antitrust should be as concerned with under-enforcement as with over-enforcement, and should scrutinise a far wider range of exclusionary or collusive practices, and mergers.[247] Crucially, however, many of these critics do not favour abandoning the consumer welfare standard. They hold to the view that antitrust should be concerned only with economic welfare and should use rigorous econometrics to quantify anti-competitive effects of challenged practices.[248] Other policies should directly address ills such as income inequality and the political power of large corporations.[249] Some critics consider that although antitrust law should continue to have only an economic standard, this should cease to be consumer welfare.[250]

Another group of critics goes further than this. Blaming the shortcomings in the antitrust system for contributing to many of America's economic and socio-political problems, they advocate a fundamental change of direction. From the mid to late 2010s, this view was set out in a number of high-profile publications, including Tim Wu's 2018 book *The Curse of Bigness*,[251] and Lina Khan's 2017 article on the rise of Amazon.[252] These critics wish to replace the consumer welfare standard and the pursuit of efficiency with a broad standard that encompasses a wide range of public interest concerns such as the diffusion of private and political power, the reduction of inequality, the preservation of democracy, the protection of the interests of workers and small businesses, and the promotion of opportunity for individuals.

[243] Including the failure to prevent the takeovers of start-ups and waving through controversial mergers, such as Facebook's acquisition of WhatsApp and Instagram, Google's acquisition of Waze and DoubleClick, and Microsoft's acquisition of GitHub and LinkedIn. See further K. Bryant and E. Hovenkamp, 'Startup Acquisitions, Error Costs, and Antitrust Policy' (2020) 87(2) *Univ Chic LR* 331.

[244] See e.g. J. B. Baker, *The Antitrust Paradigm—Restoring a Competitive Economy* (Harvard University Press, 2019).

[245] See M. Glick, 'Antitrust and Economic History: The Historic Failure of the Chicago School of Antitrust' (2020) 64(3) *Ant Bull* 295.

[246] See, for example, H. Hovenkamp, 'Whatever *Did* Happen to the Antitrust Movement' (2018) 94 *Notre Dame LR* 583.

[247] A. Douglas Melamed, 'Antitrust Law and Its Critics' (2020) 83(1) *Antitrust LJ* 269, Jones and Kovacic, n. 242; H. Hovenkamp, 'Antitrust Error Costs' (2021) *Faculty Scholarship at Penn Law* 2742, <https://scholarship.law.upenn.edu/faculty_scholarship/2742>; Baker, *The Antitrust Paradigm*, n. 244; H. Hovenkamp, 'Whatever *Did* Happen to the Antitrust Movement' (2018) 94 *Notre Dame LR* 583.

[248] See Muris and Nuechterlein, 'Chicago and Its Discontents', n. 230; H. Hovenkamp, 'Whatever *Did* Happen to the Antitrust Movement' (2018) 94 *Notre Dame LR* 583. The consumer welfare standard has also come under attack from the 'right', from those who advocate moving to a total welfare standard which, as explained in Section 4.F, allows practices which are efficient even where they lead to higher prices and consumer harm, and is not concerned with how the efficiency gains are distributed, see Hovenkamp, Antitrust Policy and Inequality of Wealth', n. 192.

[249] See, for example, C. Shapiro, 'Antitrust in a Time of Populism' (2018) 61 *Int'l J of Industrial Org* 714.

[250] See M. Steinbaum and M. E. Stucke, 'The Effective Competition Standard: A New Standard for Antitrust' (2020) 87(2) *Univ Chic LR* 595, who suggest the goal of 'effective competition'.

[251] T. Wu, *The Curse of Bigness in the Gilded Age: How Corporate Giants Came to Rule the World* (Columbia Global Reports, 2018), reviewed by Lina Khan under the title 'The End of Antitrust History Revisited' in (2020 133 *Harvard LR* 1655.

[252] L. M. Khan, 'Amazon's Antitrust Paradox' (2017) 126 *Yale LJ* 710. See also Z. Teachout and L. M. Khan, 'Market Structure and Political Law: A Taxonomy of Power' (2014) 9 *Duke J of Const L & Pub Policy* 38; S. Vaheesan, 'The Twilight of the Technocrats' Monopoly on Antitrust?' (2018) 127 *Yale LJ Forum* 980, <www.yalelawjournal.org/forum/the-twilight-of-the-technocrats-monopoly-on-antitrust>; L. M. Khan and S. Vaheesan, 'Market Power and Inequality: The Antitrust Counterrevolution and Its Discontents' (2017) 11 *Harvard L and Policy Rev* 135; S. Vaheesan, 'The Profound Nonsense of Consumer Welfare Antitrust' (2019) 64(4) *Ant Bull* 479.

This 'progressive' movement which is often described as 'populist' antitrust and even more pejoratively by those who disagree with it, as 'Hipster Antitrust',[253] calls itself the 'new (or Neo) Brandeis School' (NBS).[254] Politically, the division between those defending the consumer welfare standard and the Neo-Brandesians advocating a wider set of goals can be seen as one between the right and the left. However, not all US antitrust scholars who hold to consumer welfare can be described as 'right-wing'. Rather, they are 'non-populists' believing in the restriction of antitrust to economic efficiency considerations, although often now advocating for changes to enforcement and application, as already noted. Furthermore, although Republicans are inimical to populist antitrust, many are equally opposed to Big Tech which they condemn as a liberal elite which censors conservative views. A change in the political mood led to notable development in antitrust enforcement from the end of 2018 when, under popular as well as political pressure, antitrust finally turned to deal with the Big Tech companies, and a raft of s. 2 cases were begun both at federal and state level, along with a number of private damages actions.[255] This was a remarkable change, given the paucity of monopolisation cases in the past three decades.[256] The FTC also launched a study of the acquisitions by the Big Tech companies between 2010 and 2019 which had not required notification.[257]

The NBS movement has incurred vociferous criticism[258] but was taken up by the Democratic Party in the 2020 election. After his victory, President Biden appointed Tim Wu to the National Economic Council as a Special Assistant to the President for Technology and Competition Policy, Linda Khan as chair of the FTC, and Jonathan Kanter, a well-known critic of Google, as Assistant Attorney General for the Antitrust Division of the DOJ.[259]

On 9 July 2021, President Biden, referring to 'the misguided philosophy of people like Robert Bork' and a failed 40-year 'experiment',[260] signed an Executive Order on Promoting Competition in the American Economy containing 72 initiatives, which says in s. 1:

> This order affirms that it is the policy of my Administration to enforce the antitrust laws to combat the excessive concentration of industry, the abuses of market power, and the harmful effects of monopoly and monopsony—especially as these issues arise in labor markets, agricultural markets, Internet platform industries, healthcare markets (including insurance, hospital, and prescription drug markets), repair markets, and United States markets directly affected by foreign cartel activity.

[253] K. Medvedovsky, 'Hipster Antitrust—A Brief Fling or Something More?', *CPI Antitrust Chronicle* April 2018. The phrase was originally credited to Joshua Wright of George Mason University, a former Republican FTC Commissioner.

[254] L. M. Khan, 'The New Brandeis Movement' (2018) 9 *J of European Comp L & Practice* 131.

[255] See G. Priest, 'The Antitrust Attack on Big Tech', *CPI Antitrust Chronicle* March 2021. The DOJ opened an investigation into Google's practices in ensuring Google Search is the default search engine on Apple and Android devices in 2019, and a slew of other cases followed: three lawsuits were filed against Google in the last two months of 2020 alone and another in July 2021. The FTC and 48 states started an action against Facebook for alleged illegal monopolisation of the social networking market in December 2020, and Epic Games sued Apple about the restrictions on in-app purchasing methods: *Epic Games Inc v Apple Inc* No.21-16506(9th Cir.2023).

[256] Although note *US v Microsoft Corp*, 253 F.3d 34 (CADC 2001), see n. 241.

[257] FTC Press Release, 11 February 2020, <www.ftc.gov/news-events/press-release/2020/02/ftc-examine-past-acquisitions-large-technology-companies?utm_source+slider>.

[258] See e.g. Hovenkamp, 'Is Antitrust's Consumer Welfare Principle Imperiled?', n. 94; Dorsey, Rybnicek, and Wright, n. 253, 1; J. Coniglio, 'Why the "New Brandeis Movement" Gets Antitrust Wrong' (24 April 2018), <https://ssrn.com/abstract=3166286>; J. Wright, E. Dorsey, J. Klick, and J. Rybnicek, 'Requiem for a Paradox: The Dubious Rise and Inevitable Fall of Hipster Antitrust', George Mason Law and Economics Research Paper (14 September 2018), <https://ssrn.com/abstract=3249524>; Remarks by Judge Douglas Ginsburg on the Consumer Welfare Standard on the Occasion of Receiving the 2020 Sherman Award <www.justice.gov/opa/speech/honorable-douglas-h-ginsburg-delivers-remarks-consumer-welfare-standard-occasion>.

[259] See the remarks of Jonathan Kanter at the New York City Bar Association's Milton Handler Lecture, 18 May 2022, <www.justice.gov/opa/speech/assistant-attorney-general-jonathan-kanter-delivers-remarks-new-york-city-bar-association>.

[260] <www.whitehouse.gov/briefing-room/speeches-remarks/2021/07/09/remarks-by-president-biden-at-signing-of-an-executive-order-promoting-competition-in-the-american-economy/>.

> It is also the policy of my Administration to enforce the antitrust laws to meet the challenges posed by new industries and technologies, including the rise of the dominant Internet platforms, especially as they stem from serial mergers, the acquisition of nascent competitors, the aggregation of data, unfair competition in attention markets, the surveillance of users, and the presence of network effects.[261]

In January 2022, the FTC and DOJ launched a joint review of the Merger Guidelines.[262]

Even with a Democratic majority on the FTC and 'progressives' in charge of the DOJ antitrust division and the FTC, reform of the application of the law is likely to be difficult because of the institutional and constitutional complexities of the American system.[263] Ultimately, the power to alter the direction of the law lies with the courts. Given the current complexion of the Supreme Court, the numerous conservative judges on the federal bench, and the continued hostility of part of the antitrust establishment, the road ahead is likely to be rocky. Moreover, a Republican victory in 2024 would be likely to see another change in policy. As far as the big platforms are concerned, however, there has been some bipartisan cooperation in bringing forward bills in Congress to curtail their power. A Congressional investigation into Amazon, Apple, Google, and Facebook produced a highly critical report in October 2020.[264] It led to five bills being introduced, one of which, the American Choice and Innovation Online Act,[265] aimed to prevent 'self-preferencing'[266] which is also a target of the EU's Digital Markets Act[267] and has already been the subject of action by the European Commission.[268] In the end, only two measures passed through the House in September 2022. One gives state attorneys general more ability to stop companies moving federal antitrust lawsuits to jurisdictions they perceive as more favourable[269] and the other allows the DOJ and FTC to raise filing fees for large mergers in order to fund more anttitrust activity without additional cost to the taxpayer.[270]

9. EU COMPETITION LAW

A. THE OBJECTIVES OF THE EU AND THE ROLE OF THE COMPETITION RULES

The EU competition provisions do not exist in a vacuum. In this section, we look at the aims and objectives of the EU in order to understand the context within which the competition rules are set.[271]

[261] Ibid.

[262] <www.ftc.gov/news-events/news/press-releases/2022/01/federal-trade-commission-justice-department-seek-strengthen-enforcement-against-illegal-mergers>.

[263] See Jones and Kovacic, n. 242; G. Werden and L. Froeb, 'Can the FTC Turn Back the Clock?', *Antitrust Magazine Online* (ABA), October 2021; D. Crane (ed.), *Rulemaking Authority of the US Federal Trade Commission* (Concurrences, 2022).

[264] Subcommittee on Antitrust, Commercial and Administrative Law of the Committee on the Judiciary, *Investigation of Competition in Digital Markets. Majority Staff Report and Recommendations* (2020), <https://judiciary.house.gov/uploadedfiles/competition_in_digital_markets.pdf>.

[265] The others being the Platform Competition and Opportunity Act, the Ending Platform Monopolies Act, the Augmenting Compatibility and Competition by Enabling Switching Act, and the Merger Filing Fee Modernization Act.

[266] See Chaps. 7 and 16.

[267] Reg. 2022/1925 on contestable and fair markets in the digital sector (Digital Markets Act) [2022] OJ L265/1. See Section 12 and Chap. 16.

[268] Case T-612/17, *Google and Alphabet v Commission (Google Shopping)* EU:T:2021:763, on appeal Case C-48/22 P, *Google and Alphabet v Commission*, judgment pending, see Chaps. 7 and 16.

[269] The State Antitrust Enforcement Venue Act. The Big Tech companies would prefer cases to be heard in Northern California.

[270] The Merger Filing Fee Modernization Act.

[271] For a historical analysis of the foundational phase of EU competition law, see K. K. Patel and H. Schweitzer (eds.), *The Historical Foundations of EU Competition Law* (Oxford University Press, 2013).

The fourth Preamble to the Treaty of Rome, which established the EEC (later the EC[272]) recognised that:

> the removal of existing obstacles calls for concerted action in order to guarantee steady expansion, balanced trade and fair competition.

The objectives of the EEC were set out in Article 2 of the Treaty of Rome, which in its final form[273] stated:

> The Community shall have as its task, by establishing a common market and an economic and monetary union and by implementing the common policies or activities referred to in Articles 3 and 4, to promote throughout the Community a harmonious, balanced and sustained development of economic activities, a high level of employment and of social protection, equality between men and women, sustainable and non-inflationary growth, a high degree of competitiveness and convergence of economic performance, a high level of protection and improvement of the quality of the environment, the raising of the standard of living and quality of life, and economic and social cohesion and solidarity among Member States.

The Community therefore sought to achieve a number of wide-ranging and aspirational goals through economic integration. The common market was not an end in itself, but one means of pursuing the matters listed in Article 2. The 'common market' is an area where direct and indirect barriers to trade and movement between Member States are removed to create an 'internal market' and a common import and export policy for commercial transactions is adopted towards the outside world.

Article 3 of the Treaty of Rome set out a broad range of Community 'activities' necessary to achieve the purposes in Article 2. Article 3(1)(g) (originally Article 3(f))[274] stated that the activities should include:

> a system ensuring that competition in the internal market is not distorted.

Article 3(1)(g) was of great importance because it embedded the principle of undistorted competition in the fundamental provisions of the Treaty. The Court considered it the foundation for the specific competition rules and referred to it in interpreting those rules in the seminal *Continental Can* case.[275]

The Treaty of Lisbon subsumed the EC into the EU and amended both the Treaty on European Union (TEU) and the EC Treaty, which was renamed the Treaty on the Functioning of the European Union (TFEU), as from 1 December 2009.[276]

[272] After the Treaty of Maastricht, 1992. [273] After the Treaty of Amsterdam came into effect in 1999.

[274] And then Art. 3(g). The renumbering was brought about by the Treaties of Maastricht (the TEU) and Amsterdam in 1993 and 1999, respectively. In this book the provision is referred to as 'Art. 3(1)(g)' throughout, unless otherwise indicated. Until the 1993 amendments it read: '*the institution of* a system ensuring that competition in the common market is not distorted' (emphasis added).

[275] Case 6/72, *Continental Can* EU:C:1973:22, discussed further in Chaps. 6 and 7. See also Case C-68/94, *French Republic v Commission* EU:C:1998:148.

[276] The specific competition provisions (Arts. 101–106) remained unchanged by Lisbon, other than minor amendments such as replacing 'common market' with 'internal market' and an addition to one of the procedural articles, Art. 105.

The fourth Preamble to the Treaty of Rome, with its recognition of the need for 'fair competition' is repeated as the fourth Preamble to the TFEU. The objectives of the EU are now set out in Article 3(1) TEU:

> The Union's aim is to promote peace, its values and the well-being of its peoples.

The reference to 'values' relates to Article 2 TEU which lists these as respect for human dignity, freedom, democracy, equality, the rule of law, and respect for human rights.

Article 3(3) TEU makes it clear that the EU is founded on a social market economy[277] and provides for the establishment of the internal market:

> The Union shall establish an internal market. It shall work for the sustainable development of Europe based on balanced economic growth and price stability, a highly competitive social market economy, aiming at full employment and social progress, and a high level of protection and improvement of the quality of the environment. It shall promote scientific and technological advance . . .

'Internal market' is defined in Article 26 TFEU:[278]

> The internal market shall comprise an area without internal frontiers in which the free movement of goods, persons, services and capital is ensured in accordance with the provisions of these Treaties.[279]

Articles 119 and 120 TFEU refer to the Member States and the EU adopting, and acting in accordance with, 'an open market economy with free competition'. However, neither the TEU or the TFEU replicates Article 3(1)(g). Article 3(3) TEU, the provision on the establishment of the internal market, contains nothing about undistorted competition.[280] Instead, the principle appears in a Protocol annexed to and forming 'an integral part'[281] of the Treaties. Protocol No. 27 on the Internal Market and Competition states that the High Contracting Parties,

> Considering that the internal market as set out in Article 3 of the Treaty on European Union includes a system ensuring that competition is not distorted, Have agreed that: To this end, the Union shall, if necessary, take action under the provisions of the Treaties, including under Article 352 of the Treaty on the Functioning of the European Union.

Moreover, Article 3(1)(b) TFEU states that one of the areas in which the Union has exclusive competence is:

> The establishing of the competition rules necessary for the functioning of the internal market.

[277] See R. Claassen, A. Gerbrandy, S. Princen, and M. Segers, 'Rethinking the European Social Market Economy' (2019) 57(1) *J of Common Market Studies* 3.

[278] Previously Art. 14(2) of the Treaty of Rome (ex Art. 7a). The concept of the 'internal market' was first formally enshrined in the Treaty by the Single European Act 1986 (SEA).

[279] 'These Treaties' refers to the TFEU and the Treaty on European Union (TEU).

[280] The removal of the reference to free and undistorted competition from the body of the Treaties is attributed to President Sarkozy of France. The provision disappeared on the night of 21 June 2007 during the final last-minute negotiations on the Treaty of Lisbon. President Sarkozy was reported as saying at the time, 'Competition as an ideology, as a dogma: what has it done for Europe?', *Financial Times*, 26 June 2007, p. 12.

[281] Art. 51 TEU.

The CJ confirmed in *TeliaSonera*, concerning the interpretation of one of the competition articles, Article 102, that notwithstanding this change in the provisions the position in respect of 'undistorted competition' remains the same.[282]

Case C-52/09, *Konkurrensverket v TeliaSonera Sverige AB* EU:C:2011:83

Court of Justice

20. In order to answer those questions, it must be observed at the outset that Article 3(3) TEU states that the European Union is to establish an internal market, which, in accordance with Protocol No 27 on the internal market and competition, annexed to the Treaty of Lisbon (OJ 2010 C 83, p. 309), is to include a system ensuring that competition is not distorted.

21. Article 102 TFEU is one of the competition rules referred to in Article 3(1)(b) TFEU which are necessary for the functioning of that internal market.

Furthermore, in its Opinion on the draft agreement on the accession of the EU to the ECHR, the CJ placed competition policy among the fundamental provisions to which the pursuit of the EU's objectives were entrusted:

The pursuit of the EU's objectives, as set out in Article 3 TEU, is entrusted to a series of fundamental provisions, such as those providing for the free movement of goods, services, capital and persons, citizenship of the Union, the area of freedom, security and justice, and competition policy. Those provisions, which are part of the framework of a system that is specific to the EU, are structured in such a way as to contribute—each within its specific field and with its own particular characteristics—to the implementation of the process of integration that is the *raison d'être* of the EU itself.[283]

This Opinion also reflects Article 7 TFEU, which demands consistency between all the EU's policies:

The Union shall ensure consistency between its policies and activities, taking all of its objectives into account and in accordance with the principle of conferral of powers.

Articles 9, 10, and 12 TFEU, respectively, stipulate that in defining and implementing its policies and activities the EU should take into account employment, social protection,[284] education, training, human health,[285] combating discrimination,[286] and consumer protection.[287] Article 11 requires the integration of environmental concerns (EU environmental policy is set out in Title XX, Articles 191–193 TFEU). It is therefore impossible for EU competition law, as part of the EU's economic constitution, to operate in isolation.

[282] See also Case C-377/20, *Servizio Elettrico Nazionale and Others v Autorità Garante della Concorrenza e del Mercato e.a* EU:C:2022:379, paras. 41–43. When the Lisbon Treaty was agreed the Commission issued a press release declaring that it would carry on enforcing competition policy as before, MEMO 07/250, 23 June 2007.

[283] *Opinion 2/13* EU:C:2014:2454, para. 172.

[284] Promotion of a high level of employment, adequate social protection; and the fight against social exclusion.

[285] Art. 9 TFEU. The health of animals is dealt with in Art. 13. [286] Art. 10 TFEU. [287] Art. 12 TFEU.

In March 2020, the Commission adopted 'A New Industrial Strategy for Europe'[288] which set out the EU's twin policy priorities, the green transition and the digital transition. The green transition was already the subject of the Green Deal, adopted by the Commission in December 2019.[289] The digital transition, setting out a strategy for Europe retaining its technological and digital sovereignty and being the global digital leader, was first adopted by the Commission in 2020.[290] Its aims were rendered more urgent by the war in Ukraine, and EVP (and Competition Commissioner) Vestager[291] spoke in October 2022 of how digital technologies were being used as a powerful weapon for destabilisation and how the Kremlin was using 'every available technology to infiltrate or disrupt networks, to misinform and spread toxic propaganda, attacking our democracies and the core values of Europe. As such, digital technologies are now at the core of geopolitics.'[292]

The Commission took the lead in the EU's response to the Covid-19 crisis.[293] In March 2021, after a year of the crisis, the Commission adopted another Communication, 'Updating the 2020 New Industrial Strategy: Building a Stronger Single Market for Europe's Recovery',[294] which outlined new measures to support the green and digital transitions and set out a third priority: strengthening the resilience of the single market in the light of the weaknesses revealed by the disruption in supply chains, border closures, and economic slowdown arising from Covid-19. Resilience is now a major plank of EU policy, its crucial importance having been reinforced by the consequences of Russia's invasion of Ukraine, the resulting energy crisis, and the rise in the cost of living and inflation across Europe.

B. THE OBJECTIVES OF EU COMPETITION LAW

(i) General

It is clear from Protocol 27, as from Article 3(1)(g) before it, that the function of EU competition law is to ensure that competition in the internal market is not distorted, in order to achieve the objectives of the EU. This was restated by Commission in 2021.

Communication from the Commission to the European Parliament, the Council, the EESC and the Committee of the Regions, 'A Competition Policy Fit For New Challenges', COM (2021) 713 final, 6

The Union's prosperity is deeply rooted in its commitment to the principles of a social market economy as enshrined in the Treaty of Lisbon. Competition policy is part of a broad regulatory and enforcement toolbox to ensure that the markets work to the benefit of customers and consumers. By keeping

[288] Communication from the Commission, 'A New Industrial Strategy for Europe', COM (2020) 102 final.

[289] Communication from the Commission, 'The European Green Deal', COM(2019) 640 final, discussed in Section 2.B.ii.

[290] Communication from the Commission, 'Strategy on Shaping Europe's Digital Future', COM(2020) 67 final; Communication from the Commission, '2030 Digital Compass: The European Way for the Digital Decade', COM(2021)118 final, 9 March 2021, <https://ec.europa.eu/info/strategy/priorities-2019-2024/europe-fit-digital-age_en>. The Digital Strategy has given rise, inter alia, to the Digital Services Act, Reg. 2022/2065 [2022] OJ L277/1 and the Digital Markets Act, Reg. 2022/[2022] OJ L265/1, see Section 12 and Chap. 16.

[291] In 2019, Competition Commissioner Margrethe Vestager was also appointed Executive Vice-President (EVP) of the Commission in charge of the 'Europe Fit for the Digital Age' policy.

[292] Remarks of EVP Vestager at the Annual Conference of the EU Heads of Delegation Brussels, 11 October 2022, Speech/22/6115, <https://ec.europa.eu/commission/presscorner/detail/en/SPEECH_22_6115>.

[293] For the details, see <https://ec.europa.eu/info/live-work-travel-eu/coronavirus-response/overview-commissions-response_en>.

[294] COM(2021) 350 final.

> markets open and competitive and ensuring a level playing field, competition policy helps achieving the Union's wider priorities as set in its regulatory policies.
>
> More concretely, the purpose of competition policy is to prevent and remedy market distortions through effective public intervention.

The question of the precise policy which should be pursued in fulfilment of that function of preventing and remedying market distortions is what concerns us here.[295]

The basic concept is 'effective competition'. A dominant position is defined for the purposes of Article 102 TFEU[296] as involving an undertaking's power to 'prevent effective competition being maintained on the relevant market'[297] and under the EU Merger Regulation (EUMR) the grounds for the prohibition of a merger are that it would 'significantly impede effective competition'.[298] In *Continental Can* in 1974, the Court said that the competition provisions, Articles 101 and 102, both seek to achieve the same aim, '*viz.* the maintenance of effective competition'.[299] The Commission uses the concept of effective competition in a number of instruments[300] and the General Court (GC) said in *GlaxoSmithKline* that 'the competition referred to in Article 3(1)(g) EC[301] and Article [101 TFEU] is taken to mean effective competition, that is to say, the degree of competition necessary to ensure the attainment of the objectives of the Treaty'.[302] In the Horizontal Cooperation Guidelines, the Commission states:[303]

> 518. Competition law enforcement contributes to sustainable development by ensuring effective competition, which spurs innovation, increases the quality and choice of products, ensures an efficient allocation of resources, reduces the costs of production, and thereby contributes to consumer welfare.

That still leaves open exactly what effective competition entails.

[295] See generally e.g. C.-D. Ehlermann and L. Laudati (eds.), *European Competition Law Annual 1997: Objectives of Competition Policy* (Hart Publishing, 1998); L. Parret, 'The Objectives of EU Competition Law and Policy' (2010) 6 *European Competition Journal* 339; R. Nazzini, *The Foundations of European Union Competition Law: The Objectives and Principles of Article 102* (Oxford University Press, 2011); P. Akman, *The Concept of Abuse in EU Competition Law* (Hart Publishing, 2012); P. Akman, 'The Role of "Freedom" in EU Competition Law' (2014) 34 *Legal Studies* 183; Geradin, Layne-Farrar, and Petit, n. 42, 1.61–1.80. For the history of the EU competition rules, see D. Gerber, 'Constitutionalizing the Economy: German Neo-liberalism, Competition Law and the "New Europe"' (1994) 42 *Am J of Comparative L* 25; D. Gerber, *Law and Competition in Twentieth Century Europe* (Oxford University Press, 1998); A. Weitbrecht, 'From Freiburg to Chicago and Beyond—The First 50 Years of European Competition Law' [2008] *ECLR* 81; Patel and Schweitzer, n. 271.

[296] One of the two main EU competition law articles. See Chaps. 6–7.

[297] Case 27/76, *United Brands v Commission* EU:C:1978:22, para. 65; Case 85/76, *Hoffmann-La Roche & Co AG v Commission* EU:C:1979:36, para. 38.

[298] Council Reg. 139/2004 [2004] OJ L124/1, Art. 2(3); see Chap. 15.

[299] Case 6/72, *Europemballage Corp and Continental Can Co Inc v Commission* EU:C:1973:22, para. 25.

[300] See Guidance on the Commission's Enforcement Priorities in Applying Article 82 of the EC Treaty to Abusive Exclusionary Conduct by Dominant Undertakings [2009] OJ C45/2 (the Guidance Paper), paras. 5, 6, and 19 (as amended); Commission Guidelines on vertical restraints [2022] OJ C248/01, para. 295; see also Framework Directive on Electronic Communications, 2002/21 [2002] OJ 108/33, recital 27.

[301] For Art. 3(1)(g), see Section 8.A.

[302] Case T-168/01, *GlaxoSmithKline Services Unlimited v Commission* EU:T:2006:265, para. 109; see also Case T-321/05, *AstraZeneca* v. *Commission* EU:T:2010:266.

[303] 17 July 2023, para. 518.

(ii) The Competition Provisions

The substantive antitrust provisions, Articles 101, 102, and 106,[304] do not expressly articulate any particular policy. However, there is a reference to fairness and to consumers in the exemption provision in Article 101(3) (a 'fair share' of benefit to consumers), a prohibition in Article 102(a) on dominant firms imposing unfair prices and unfair trading conditions, and a prohibition on dominant firms limiting production, markets, or technical development to the prejudice of consumers in Article 102(b). As regards consumers, they must therefore be relevant to all abuses covered by Article 102,[305] and to Article 101 as a whole, given that Articles 101 and 102 serve the same end.[306] That is not the same as saying that the aim of the provisions is consumer welfare in the technical sense.

(iii) The Single Market

As we have seen, competition policy was embedded in the Treaty of Rome in 1958 as part of a set of wide policy instruments oriented towards the objective of European economic integration. Competition policy was necessary to underpin the internal market aspect of the common market because there was no point in dismantling, by means of the free movement provisions, State measures which divided the Community territorially and compartmentalised the market if private undertakings could erect and maintain barriers to trade between Member States by carving up markets between them and indulging in anti-competitive practices. Economic integration is therefore promoted both by free movement and by competition. Commissioner Vestager said in 2015:

> The founding fathers of Europe understood that there would be no genuine integration without a Single Market—and no functioning Single Market without a strong competition policy enforced by a central competition authority.
>
> Six decades later, here we are. The Single Market has been—and still is—a powerful engine of European integration in the economic sphere and beyond. And this will continue into the future.[307]

The role of competition law as an instrument of single market integration remains a dominant theme in EU competition law and differentiates EU law from any other system of competition law. This is seen most strikingly in respect of the law on vertical restraints.[308] Both the EU Courts and the Commission have repeatedly stressed the fundamental nature of the competition rules in achieving the single market.[309] In *GlaxoSmithKline*, the CJ confirmed that agreements limiting parallel imports have the object of restricting competition contrary to Article 101(1), referring to 'the Treaty's objective of achieving the integration of national markets through the establishment of a single market'.[310] In *Sot. Lélos*, the CJ held a dominant undertaking's refusal to supply in order to prevent parallel trade

[304] Art. 106 deals with the application of the rules to public undertakings and those granted special rights, see Chap. 8.

[305] The abuses listed in Art. 102 are not an exhaustive list of the ways in which Art. 102 can be infringed, see Chap. 7.

[306] Case 6/72, *Continental Can* EU:C:1973:22, para. 25.

[307] M. Vestager, 'The Values of Competition Policy' (13 October 2015), <https://ec.europa.eu/commission/commissioners/2014-2019/vestager/announcements/values-competition-policy_en>.

[308] From Cases 56 and 58/64, *Etablissements Consten SA & Grundig-Verkaufs-GmbH v Commission* EU:C:1965:55 onwards; see Chap. 11.

[309] See Case C-126/97, *Eco Swiss China Time Ltd v Benetton International NV* EU:C:1999:269, para. 36; Case C-453/99, *Courage Ltd v Crehan* EU:C:2001:465, para. 20; Case T-168/01, *GlaxoSmithKline Services* EU:T:2006:265, para. 11 ('indispensable for the achievement of the missions entrusted to the Community'); Commission Guidelines on the application of Article 81(3) of the Treaty [2004] OJ C101/97, para. 13; Commission Guidelines on vertical restraints [2022] OJ C248/1, para. 5.

[310] Case C-501/06 P, *GlaxoSmithKline* EU:C:2009:610, paras. 59–62, disapproving on this point the judgment of the GC, see Chap. 5.

between Member States is prima facie an abuse under Article 102 for that reason alone (although capable of objective justification);[311] *Pierre Fabre* was driven by the wish to stop contractual provisions (*in casu* selling over the internet) from preventing inter-Member State trade;[312] and the finding in *Football Association Premier League* that the arrangements for selling Premier League TV rights contravened Article 101 as well as the free movement of services provisions was because they resulted in the artificial partitioning of the single market.[313] Further, in the 2008 Guidance on Article 102 enforcement priorities[314] the Commission says that in addition to exclusionary abuses (the subject of the Guidance) it may intervene in relation to 'certain behaviour that undermines the efforts to achieve an integrated internal market'. In the *Swedish Connectors* case, the Commission's reason for intervening in the anti-congestion arrangements of the Swedish electricity transmission operator was that they segmented the internal market.[315] In September 2015,[316] Commissioner Vestager stressed the importance of the Commission's e-commerce inquiry[317] in revealing and removing barriers to the single market and contributing to the EU's Digital Single Market strategy.[318]

(iv) The Early Development of the Law

There is some argument about the influence of Ordoliberalism on the drafting of the EEC competition provisions in 1956–1957 and their subsequent development.[319] The main debate during the drafting was certainly between the French and German delegations, but their positions appear to have been more nuanced and complex than has sometimes been supposed.[320] It has been persuasively concluded that:

> The EC Treaty was indeed a collective work, moulded by various influences, all of which are reflected in the various provisions referring to competition policy. In other words, the Treaty's commitment to 'undistorted competition' enshrines a multi-faceted concept.[321]

[311] Cases C-468–478/06, *Sot. Lélos kai Sia EE and others v GlaxoSmithKline AEVE Farmakeftikon Proionton* EU:C:2008:504, see Chap. 7.

[312] Case C-439/09, *Pierre Fabre Dermo-Cosmétique SAS v Président de l'Autorité de la Concurrence* EU:C:2011:649 (complete prohibition of online selling by selective distributors not allowed, see further Chap. 11).

[313] Case C-403/08, *Football Association Premier League* EU:C:2011:631; see the comments of the Commissioner on this in the speech 'Competition—What's in it for Consumers?', European Competition and Consumer Day, Poznan, 24 November 2011, SPEECH/11/803.

[314] Guidance on the Commission's Enforcement Priorities in Applying Article 82 of the EC Treaty to Abusive Exclusionary Conduct by Dominant Undertakings [2009] OJ C45/2 (the Guidance Paper), amended by Communication from the Commission and Annex, C(2023)1923 final, 27 March 2023 (the Guidance Paper Amendments), para. 7.

[315] COMP/39.351, *Swedish Interconnectors* [2010] OJ C142/28.

[316] IP/15/4921, see Chap. 11, Section 3.C.iii.

[317] The final report, COM(2017) 229 final, was published in May 2017, <http://ec.europa.eu/competition/antitrust/sector_inquiry_final_report_en.pdf>.

[318] The Digital Single Market strategy, launched in 2015, is intended to remove virtual borders, boost digital connectivity, and make it easier for consumers to access cross-border online content, <https://ec.europa.eu/commission/priorities/digital-single-market_en>.

[319] See Gerber, n. 295; P. Akman, 'Searching for the Long-Lost Soul of Article 82EC' (2009) 29 *OJLS* 267; Akman, *The Concept of Abuse in EU Competition Law*, n. 295; Behrens, n. 146; H. Schweitzer, 'The History, Interpretation and Underlying Principles of Section 2 Sherman Act and Article 82 EC' in Ehlermann and Marquis, n. 143, 119; P. Ibáñez Colomo, *The Shaping of EU Competition Law* (Cambridge University Press, 2018), 279–280.

[320] Particularly in respect of what is now Art. 102. The French legislation on agreements between undertakings strongly influenced the wording of what is now Art. 101, see L. F. Pace and K. Seidel, 'The Drafting and Role of Regulation 17: A Hard-Fought Compromise' in Patel and Schweitzer, n. 271, 54, 59. There was also an American influence. The ECSC competition provisions, which were the pattern for the later EEC ones, were based on a draft prepared at the behest of Jean Monnet by the Harvard antitrust lawyer Robert Bowie, who was an adviser to John McCloy, the US High Commissioner for Germany and a close ally of Monnet.

[321] Geradin, Layne-Farrar, and Petit, n. 42, 1.70.

There was an important German influence in the competition Directorate General (then DG IV) at the outset because of the powerful presence of German officials[322] and the drafting of Regulation 17, the provision which implemented the competition rules, was greatly influenced by the external experts, who were all German.[323] Although those concerned were not necessarily Ordoliberals, Ordoliberalism provided the intellectual and theoretical framework for the development of the law but Ordoliberalism is not a static body of ideas and it developed and changed over the relevant period.

In *Continental Can*, the first judgment on Article 102 in 1973, the Court said:

> Article [102] is not only aimed at practices which may cause damage to consumers directly, but also at those which are detrimental to them through their impact on an effective competition structure such as is mentioned in Article [3(1)(g)] . . .[324]

This looks to the protection of consumers, but not just at immediate direct effects on them. It looks also to the protection of the market structure because of possible long-term effects. As Articles 101 and 102 have the same aim this applies to both provisions. As we see in the cases discussed in this book, the rules have sometimes been applied in an interventionist way, to protect competitors rather than competition, to favour small or medium-sized enterprises, and to keep markets open. Although not couched expressly in 'freedom' terms some of the decisional practice and judgments, particularly on Article 102, have reflected Ordoliberal principles. A previous Director-General of Competition acknowledged:

> The case-law of the EU Courts and also the decisional practice of the Commission were initially influenced by ordoliberal thought which has its origin in the so-called Freiburg School . . . The protection of individual economic freedom—as a value in itself—was regarded as the primary objective of competition policy.[325]

(v) 'Modernisation' and the Policy of the Commission

'Modernisation' is a term used to describe the major reform in the enforcement procedures in respect of the non-merger provisions of EU competition law which took place in 2004 when Regulation 1/2003 came into force.[326] However, it should be understood in a wider sense. During the 1990s, the Commission began a move towards a realignment of competition law in line with the economic thinking on economic efficiency and consumer welfare which had been developed by the Chicago School and taken root in the US.[327] Furthermore, the Commission moved to an 'effects' approach in

[322] E.g. Hans von der Groeben from the German Economics Ministry, who was one of the authors of the Spaak Report (the report by an intergovernmental committee of the six Member States of the ECSC which formed the basis for what became the EEC and Euratom) was the chairman of the group who drafted the competition articles during the Treaty negotiations. He became the first Commissioner for Competition, 1958–1967. E.-J. Mestmäcker, an Ordoliberal (see his paper 'Wettsbewerbsfreiheit und Wohlfahrt' (Freedom of Competition and Welfare), Max Planck Law Research Paper No. 12/2, 2012, <http://ssrn.com/abstract=1983193>) was special adviser to DGIV, 1960–1970.

[323] Pace and Seidel, n. 320, 72. [324] Case 6/72, *Continental Can* EU:C:1973:22, para. 12.

[325] P. Lowe, 'Consumer Welfare and Efficiency—New Guiding Principles of Competition Policy?', 13th International Competition and 14th European Competition Day, Munich, 27 March 2007, <http://ec.europa.eu/competition/speeches/index_2007.html>.

[326] Council Reg. 1/2003 [2003] OJ L1/1 and the accompanying secondary legislation and Notices, discussed in Chaps. 2 and 13.

[327] See Sections 5.A and 8.

applying the law.[328] 'Modernisation' therefore also encompasses the gradual revolution in the interpretation and application of the substantive law which took place both in the lead up to 2004[329] and afterwards. This is often called the 'more economic' approach, meaning an approach which makes greater use of economic theories and methods, adopts economic objectives (particularly the consumer welfare objective), and is effects-based.[330]

As modernisation progressed the instruments and pronouncements emanating from the Commission proclaimed the latter's conversion to the efficiency/consumer welfare standard.[331] In a highly significant speech in July 2001, Commissioner Monti said:

> . . . the goal of competition policy, in all its aspects, is to protect consumer welfare by maintaining a high degree of competition in the common market. Competition should lead to lower prices, a wider choice of goods, and technological innovation, all in the interest of the consumer.[332]

The policy continued under successive Competition Commissioners. For example, Commissioner Kroes said in 2005:

> Consumer welfare is now well established as the standard the Commission applies when assessing mergers and infringements of the Treaty rules on cartels and monopolies. Our aim is simple: to protect competition in the market as a means of enhancing consumer welfare and ensuring an efficient allocation of resources. An effects-based approach, grounded in solid economics, ensures that citizens enjoy the benefits of a competitive, dynamic market economy.[333]

By choosing the consumer, rather than total, welfare standard the Commission showed its concern with distributive effects. This accords with Article 101(3) TFEU which demands that a 'fair share' of the efficiency gains resulting from anti-competitive agreements must be passed on to consumers.[334]

It will be noted from the Commissioners' speeches above that consumer welfare is to be achieved by maintaining or protecting competition. So the initial objective of the law is to protect competition/the competitive process because that is the way to protect consumer welfare. This objective has been

[328] See Section 10.A.

[329] This could first be discerned in the approach to the assessment of mergers under the regime which came into operation in 1990 (Council Reg. 4064/89 [1990] OJ L257/13, see Chap. 15). See also the Market Definition Notice [1997] OJ C372/5; the Green Paper on vertical restraints, COM (96) 721 final, paving the way for the reform of the Commission's much-criticised policy towards vertical restraints in 1999 (Commission Reg. 2790/99 [1999] OJ L336/21 and the Guidelines on vertical restraints [2000] OJ C291/1), see Chap. 11; and the legislation and guidelines on horizontal cooperation in 2000 (see Chap. 10).

[330] See H. Schweitzer and K. K. Patel, 'EU Competition Law in Historical Context: Continuity and Change' in Patel and Schweitzer (eds.), *The Historical Foundations of EU Competition Law* (Oxford University Press, 2013), 207, 220; L. Lovdahl Gormesen, 'The Conflict between Economic Freedom and Consumer Welfare in the Modernisation of Article 82' (2007) 3 *European Competition Journal* 329.

[331] Particularly after the appointment of an economist, Mario Monti, as Competition Commissioner in 1999, see e.g. M. Monti, 'European Competition Policy for the 21st Century', SPEECH/00/389, 20 October 2000, <www.ec.europa.eu./competition/speeches/> and in [2000] *Fordham Corp L Inst*, Chap. 15.

[332] M. Monti, 'The Future for Competition Policy in the European Union', London, 9 July 2001, SPEECH/01/340, <www.ec.europa.eu/competition/speeches/>.

[333] 'Delivering Better Markets and Better Choices', European Consumer and Competition Day, London, 15 September 2005, SPEECH/05/512, <http://ec.europa.eu/competition/speeches/>.

[334] See Chap. 5.

continually repeated in Commission Notices and other soft law instruments. The Commission's 2004 Guidelines on Article 101(3) state that:

> [t]he objective of Article [101] is to protect competition on the market as a means of enhancing consumer welfare and of ensuring an efficient allocation of resources.[335]

Subsequent Guidelines and similar documents take a similar stance.[336] The 2008 Guidance Paper on Article 102 states that the Commission will focus on those types of conduct that are most harmful to consumers[337] and adopts 'anti-competitive foreclosure' as the standard for intervention.[338] It says that the emphasis of the Commission's enforcement activity in relation to exclusionary conduct is on safeguarding the effective competitive process (and not on protecting competitors).[339] The 2023 Horizontal Guidelines, as already noted, state:

> Competition law enforcement contributes to sustainable development by ensuring effective competition, which spurs innovation, increases the quality and choice of products, ensures an efficient allocation of resources, reduces the costs of production, and thereby contributes to consumer welfare.[340]

The word 'consumers' appears twice in the substantive competition provisions of the TFEU, in Article 101(3) and in Article 102(b), as already mentioned. It also appears in Article 2(1)(b) of the EUMR where it is expressly said that 'consumers' means all direct and indirect users and not just private end-users, i.e. it includes intermediate customers as well[341] and this is the interpretation of 'consumer' throughout EU competition law[342] unless the qualification 'final' is added.[343]

The concept of the consumer welfare standard in EU competition law is broader than that usually applied in the US where, as we saw in Section 7, 'consumer welfare' has tended to be construed narrowly and associated with (short-term) low prices. In the EU, consumer welfare means that the

335 Guidelines on the application of Article 81(3) [now Article 101(3)] of the Treaty [2004] OJ C101/97, para. 13 (the Article 101(3) Guidelines).

336 Such as Guidelines on the assessment of horizontal mergers [2004] OJ C31/03, para. 8; Guidelines on the assessment of non-horizontal mergers [2008] OJ C265/7, para. 10; Guidelines on technology transfer agreements [2014] OJ L89/3, para. 5. The 2022 Guidelines on Vertical Restraints [2022] OJ C248/1, para. 5 state that 'the objective of Art. 101 is to ensure that undertakings do not use agreements to prevent, restrict or distort competition to the detriment of consumers'.

337 The Guidance Paper, as amended, n. 314, para. 5.

338 Ibid., para. 19. The content of the anti-competitive foreclosure concept was changed by the 2023 amendments, see further Chap. 7.

339 Ibid., para. 6. 340 Commission's Horizontal Cooperation Guidelines, 17 July 2023, para. 518.

341 EUMR, Reg. 139/2004 [2004] OJ L124/1, Art. 2(1)(b) provides that in appraising a merger the Commission shall take into account, inter alia, 'the interests of the intermediate and ultimate consumers, and the development of technical and economic progress provided that it is to consumers' advantage and does not form an obstacle to competition'. See the EUMR. For a discussion of the concept of 'consumer' in EU competition law generally, see A. Jones and A. Albors-Llorens, 'The Images of the "Consumer" in EU Competition Law' (2016), <http://papers.ssrn.com/sol3/papers.cfm?abstract_id=2750922>. In appraising a merger, the Commission shall take into account, inter alia, 'the interests of the intermediate and ultimate consumers, and the development of technical and economic progress provided that it is to consumers' advantage and does not form an obstacle to competition', EUMR, Art. 2(1)(b).

342 See Case C-377/20, *Servizio Elettrico Nazionale and Others v Autorità Garante della Concorrenza e del Mercato e.a* EU:C:2022:379, para. 46.

343 See e.g. the Article 101(3) Guidelines, n. 335, para. 84; Guidance Paper on Article 102, as amended, para. 19, fn. 2; Guidelines on vertical restraints [2022] OJ C248/01, para. 3. A. Jones and A. Albors-Llorens, 'The Images of the "Consumer" in EU Competition Law' (2016), <http://papers.ssrn.com/sol3/papers.cfm?abstract_id=2750922>; P. Akman, '"Consumer" versus "Customer": the Devil in the Detail' (2010) 37 *J of Law and Society* 315.

Commission seeks to apply the competition rules to deliver to consumers lower prices, greater output, greater choice, higher quality, and more innovation in products and services. In the Guidance Paper, the Commission refers to these matters as 'the parameters of competition' and says it uses 'prices' as shorthand for all of them.[344] There is therefore an expressly dynamic aspect to consumer welfare in the EU, and the Commission has never been simply fixated on low prices and no output restrictions.[345] This EU conception of consumer welfare is sometimes known as 'consumer sovereignty'.[346]

The rhetoric of the Commission in its press releases, speeches, policy documents, reports, social media, and other publications has been to stress that its activities are for the benefit of European consumers. However, it has often strayed into speaking of the benefits that the enforcement of the competition rules has for individual *citizens*. This is understandable—the average European probably tends not to think of themself as a 'consumer' separate from their other identities. In the 2021 Report on Competition Policy, the Commission referred to its 'work to make markets work better for citizens and businesses of all sizes by enforcing the EU competition rules . . .'[347] and, in October 2022, the Commission organised a conference on 'making markets work for people'[348] where the difficulty of isolating 'consumers' was again apparent.

The EU Treaties contain specific references to fairness as explained in Section 9,[349] and after Competition Commissioner Vestager took office in 2014 she put 'fairness', particularly in respect of consumers, at the heart of EU competition policy. For example:

> Like any of the other rules that govern our world, we have competition rules because we believe they make our society a better place to live. That they make our markets work more fairly for consumers.[350]

The Commissioner's emphasis on fairness alarmed some critics who consider it a subjective concept at odds with the technical consumer welfare standard,[351] although the Commissioner also made it clear that the job of the Commission is to 'defend competition—not competitors'.[352] The then Director-General said that 'fairness has always been a value underpinning EU competition law and its enforcement' and described it as a 'guiding principle' which does not detract from the Commission's task in looking for evidence, conducting rigorous economic analysis, and checking findings against the law and guidance provided by the EU Courts.[353] Another senior official described fairness as

[344] Guidance Paper, n. 314, para. 11. See also Commissioner Monti's 2001 speech, 'The Future for Competition Policy in the European Union', n. 332.

[345] See the speech by the Director-General, Johannes Laitenberger, 'EU Competition Law: Relevance Anchored in Empiricism', 5 December 2018, <http://ec.europa.eu/competition/speeches/index_speeches_by_the_dg.html> ('We must take an empirically driven view of consumer welfare and recognise that some consumer harm is not readily visible in price and output effects', p. 2).

[346] See e.g. N. Economides and I. Lianos, 'The Elusive Antitrust Standard on Bundling in Europe and in the United States in the Aftermath of the Microsoft Cases' (2009) 76 *Antitrust LJ* 483.

[347] 'Commission Report on Competition Policy 2021', COM(2022)337 final, 14 July 2022, para. 1.

[348] 27 October 2022, Brussels, <www.youtube.com/watch?v=ZqGrnjm_Xs0>.

[349] And 'fair competition' is mentioned in the Preamble to the TFEU, see Section 9.B.ii.

[350] Commissioner Vestager, 'Fairness and Competition', 25 January 2018, <https://ec.europa.eu/commission/commissioners/2014-2019/vestager/announcements/fairness-and-competition_en>; see also Commissioner Vestager, 'Protecting consumers from exploitation', 21 November 2016, <https://ec.europa.eu/commission/commissioners/2014-2019/vestager/announcements/protecting-consumers-exploitation_en>.

[351] See e.g. 'Vestager's 'fairness' mantra rattles through EU competition law', <https://mlexmarketinsight.com/insights-center/editors-picks/antitrust/europe/vestagers-fairness-mantra-rattles-through-eu-competition-law>, where the Commissioner's concern with fairness isascribed in part to her being the daughter of two Lutheran pastors.

[352] Vestager, 'Protecting consumers from exploitation', n. 350.

[353] J. Laitenberger, 'Fairness in EU Competition Law Enforcement', 20 June 2018, <http://ec.europa.eu/competition/speeches/text/sp2018_10_en.pdf>.

a consequence rather than a goal of competition enforcement analysis, and said that EU concepts such as 'abuse', 'competition on the merits', and 'exploitative abuse' are 'words very much tied to fairness'.[354] 'Fairness' continues to feature prominently during the Commissioner's second mandate.[355]

In a speech in October 2022 EVP Vestager described the competition rules as having multiple goals which include fairness and consumer welfare but also encompass guaranteeing plurality and democracy[356] echoing the GC in the *Google Android* judgment five weeks earlier.[357] This speech was referred to in the Commission's Policy Brief explanation of its Guidance Paper amendments in March 2023, discussed below.[358]

(vi) The Case Law of the EU Courts

The EU Courts never unequivocally embraced the consumer welfare standard. It will be recalled that in *Continental Can* in 1973 the CJ said that the competition provisions were aimed at practices which were detrimental to consumers through their impact on an effective competition structure as well as those causing damage to them directly.[359] The EU Courts have repeated this in many subsequent cases, including *TeliaSonera* in 2011[360] and *Post Danmark I* in 2012.[361] In *TeliaSonera*, the CJ said that the competition provisions had to be interpreted in this way because the 'function of those rules is precisely to prevent competition from being distorted to the detriment of the public interest, individual undertakings and consumers, thereby ensuring the well-being of the European Union'.[362] The phrase 'well-being of the Union' is a clear reference to the aims of the EU set out in Article 3(1) TEU ('well-being of its peoples').[363] In 2013, the CJ said in *Protimonopolný úrad Slovenskej republiky* that 'Article 101 TFEU is intended to protect not only the interests of competitors or consumers but also the structure of the market and thus competition as such'.[364]

[354] Brice Allibert, Deputy Head of Unit, Antitrust, DG Competition, European Commission, speaking in a personal capacity at GCR 7th Annual Telecoms, Media and Technology Conference in London, 21 May 2018, <https://globalcompetitionreview.com/article/1169803/dg-comp-official-fairness-is-a-consequence-not-a-%20goal>. 'Fairness' has been described as 'expeditious shorthand to explain to EU citizens what the dark arts of competition law do for them', see 'Vestager's "fairness" mantra rattles through EU competition law', <https://mlexmarketinsight.com/insights-center/editors-picks/antitrust/europe/vestagers-fairness-mantra-rattles-through-eu-competition-law>. The Commission's vigorous enforcement efforts within the digital economy can be seen as showing how the 'fairness' concept plays out in practice, see Chaps. 7 and 16 and, further, N. Dunne, 'Public Interest and EU Competition Law' (2020) 65(2) *Ant Bull* 256, 275–280.

[355] See e. g. EVP Vestager, Keynote Speech at the European Competition Day 2022 in Prague, 'Fairness and Competition Policy', Speech/22/6067, <https://ec.europa.eu/commission/presscorner/detail/en/SPEECH_22_6067>.

[356] EVP Vestager, 'A Principles Based Approach to Competition Policy' Competition Law Tuesdays, 25 October 2022, Speech/22/6393, <https://ec.europa.eu/commission/presscorner/detail/en/speech_22_6393>.

[357] Case T-604/18, *Google and Alphabet v Commission (Google Android)* EU:T:2022:541, para. 1028.

[358] In Section 9.B.vii. [359] Case 6/72, *Continental Can* EU:C:1973:22, para. 26.

[360] Case C-52/09, *Konkurrensverket v TeliaSonera Sverige AB* EU:C:2011:83, para. 24.

[361] Case C-209/10, Post Danmark A/S v Konkurrencerådet (Post Danmark I) EU:C:2012:172, para. 20. See also Case C-23/14, Post Danmark A/S v Konkurrencerådet (Post Danmark II) EU:C:2015:651, para. 69, Case C-680/20, *Unilever Italia Mkt. Operations Srl* EU:C:2023:33, para. 36, and also, in the GC, Case T-851/14 Slovak Telekom v Commission EU:T:2018:929, para. 110 ('Article 102 TFEU covers not only those practices that directly cause harm to consumers but also practices that cause consumers harm by interfering with the free play of competition').

[362] Case C-52/09, *Konkurrensverket v TeliaSonera Sverige AB* EU:C:2011:83, para. 22.

[363] See Section 9.A.

[364] Case C-68/12, *Protimonopolný úrad Slovenskej republiky v Slovenská sporiteľňa as* EU:C:2013:71, para. 18, repeating and citing Case C-501/06 P, *GlaxoSmithKline Services* EU:C:2009:610, para. 63. In *GlaxoSmithKline*, this had led to the CJ concluding that 'for a finding that an agreement has an anti-competitive object, it is not necessary that final consumers be deprived of the advantages of effective competition in terms of supply or price' (para. 63), thereby overturning the GC, Case T-168/01, *GlaxoSmithKline Services* EU:T:2006:265; see further Chap. 5, Section 3.B. See also Case C-8/08, *T-Mobile Netherlands BV v Raad van bestuur van de Nederlandse Mededingingsautoriteit* EU:C:2009:343, para. 38.

In *Servizio Elettrico*,[365] the Italian court specifically asked the CJ about the purpose of Article 102:

> Is the purpose of the concept of abuse to maximise the well-being of consumers, with the court being responsible for determining whether that well-being has been (or could be) reduced, or does the concept of an infringement of competition law have the function of preserving in itself the competitive structure of the market, in order to avoid the creation of economic power groupings that are, in any case, considered harmful for the community?[366]

The CJ replied to this by reiterating that direct negative effects on consumers were not required. A competition authority could find a practice of a dominant undertaking to infringe Article 102 if it could impair 'an effective competition structure, without it being necessary for that authority to prove that the practice may also cause direct harm to consumers' unless the harm was counterbalanced or outweighed by positive effects for consumers.[367]

In *Google Android*, the GC condemned as abusive practices restricting consumer choice and depriving consumers of features of benefit to them, which 'were also necessary in order to ensure plurality in a democratic society'.[368] These words were quoted by the Commission in its Policy Brief on its revised approach to abuse of dominance, discussed in Section viii.

(vii) 'A Competition Policy Fit For New Challenges'

We noted in Section 9.A that the EU is engaged with three major priorities, the green transition,[369] the digital transition,[370] and strengthening the resilience of the single market. The Industrial Strategy Communications dealing with these priorities make it clear that competition policy has a crucial role to play in relation to these initiatives.

During the Covid-19 crisis, the Commission, the national competition authorities, and the EFTA Surveillance Authority issued a joint statement on the application of the EU competition rules during the pandemic, explaining how the authorities could help companies deal with the crisis.[371] It also issued a Temporary Framework Communication on cooperation projects to address shortages of essentials,[372] sent the first 'comfort letter' since 2003 to Medicines for Europe about coordination in the pharmaceutical industry,[373] and resurrected the 'informal guidance' procedure.[374]

In November 2021, the Commission adopted a Communication, 'A Competition Policy Fit For New Challenges',[375] setting out the need for 'strong and effective competition policy and enforcement

[365] Case C-377/20, *Servizio Elettrico Nazionale and Others v Autorità Garante della Concorrenza e del Mercato e.a* EU:C:2022:379.

[366] Ibid., para. 27(2). [367] Ibid., para. 47.

[368] Case T-604/18, *Google and Alphabet v Commission (Google Android)* EU:T:2022:541, para. 1028, on appeal Case C-738/22 P, judgment pending.

[369] Communication from the Commission, 'The European Green Deal', COM(2019) 640 final, 11 December 2019.

[370] Communication from the Commission, '2030 Digital Compass: The European Way for the Digital Decade', COM(2021)118 final, 9 March 2021.

[371] <https://competition-policy.ec.europa.eu/system/files/2021-03/202003_joint-statement_ecn_corona-crisis.pdf>, 8 April 2020.

[372] [2020] OJ C1/7. It was withdrawn on 3 October 2022. For further procedural adjustments during the pandemic, see Chap. 13.

[373] For further procedural adjustments during the pandemic, see Chap. 13.

[374] [2022] OJ C381/9, see Chap. 13.

[375] Communication from the Commission, 'A Competition Policy Fit for New Challenges', COM (2021) 713 final, <https://competition-policy.ec.europa.eu/policy/competition-policy-fit-new-challenges_en>; Remarks by EVP Vestager, 18 November 2021, Speech/21/6115, <https://ec.europa.eu/commission/presscorner/detail/en/speech_21_6115>.

to give the European economy the agility to mount the recovery path and meet its twin green and digital ambitions in a sustainable, socially and territorially inclusive manner'[376] and to foster the resilience of the single market. The action to be taken includes continuing the Commission's review of its competition rules and guidelines to ensure that they are all 'fit for purpose' and deal properly with contemporary circumstances.[377] This also encompasses a review of the crisis measures in the State aid field, discussed in Section 14. Shortly after the adoption of the Communication, the economies of the EU and its Member States were thrown into further disarray by Russia's invasion of Ukraine, in particular by its effects on energy markets. The Commission is faced with unprecedented turmoil on every front, including war in Europe, and appreciates that competition policy needs to rapidly evolve to meet the new challenges. In the 2023 Guidelines on Horizontal Cooperation the Commission has an extensive section on the application of Article 101 to sustainability agreements, which it wishes to encourage in line with the EU's Green Deal policy.[378]

(viii) The Revision of the Commission's Policy towards Article 102

On 27 March 2023, the Commission announced a revision of its approach to abuse of dominance cases under Article 102.[379] It launched a Call for Evidence seeking feedback on the adoption of new Guidelines on exclusionary abuses[380] and adopted a Communication and Annex amending its 2008 Guidance on enforcement priorities in applying Article 82 in the meantime.[381] At the same time, the Commission published a Competition Policy Brief setting out its revised approach to abuse cases (and more particularly, exclusionary abuses) and discussing the amendments to the 2008 Guidance.[382]

Article 102 has hitherto been the major area of competition law without Guidelines setting out the Commission's view of the law. The Guidance was, rather, a statement of the Commission's *priorities in enforcing* the law[383] embodying the 'more economic approach'. The Commission explains in the Policy Brief that the Guidance has successfully helped to move the enforcement of Article 102 away from a formalistic approach to an effects-based approach.[384] However, since 2008 there had been 32 decisions of the EU Courts on Article 102, with significant developments in the case law,[385] and also significant developments in the global and European economies, including increased market concentration and the growing importance of the fast-moving digital economy. Hence the desirability of finally adopting a set of Guidelines on Article 102 and of amending the Guidance in the interim.

The Policy Brief is remarkable in that it expressly moves away from the 'more economic'/consumer welfare approach to one directed to a broader range of goals, quoting the reference by the GC in *Google Android* to democracy and pluralism.

[376] Communication from the Commission, COM (2021) 713 final, 2.

[377] For example, the Verticals Regulation, Reg. 2022/720 [2022] OJ L134/4 and the Guidelines on vertical restraints [2022] OJ C248/01, take on board online sales and the online platform economy, see Chap. 11, and the Horizontal Cooperation Guidelines, 17 July 2023, OJ C164/2 deal with sustainability agreement, see Chap. 10.

[378] See Chap. 10.

[379] Abuse of a dominant position is discussed in Chap. 7.

[380] IP/23/1911. The Commission intends to publish a draft of the new Guidelines for public consultation in mid-2024, and adopt the final version in 2025.

[381] Communication from the Commission, 'Amendments to the Communication from the Commission on Guidance on the Commission's enforcement priorities in applying Article 82 of the EC Treaty to abusive exclusionary conduct by dominant undertakings', and Annex, C(2023)1923 final, 27 March 2023 (the Guidance Amendments), see further Chap. 7.

[382] Commission, 'A dynamic and workable effects-based approach to the abuse of dominance' [2023] 1 *Competition Policy Brief*, <https://competition-policy.ec.europa.eu/document/40413680-4eda-4ba0-96b1-e3e9d4e22106_en>.

[383] See Chap. 7, Section 4 for a discussion of the effect of the Guidance.

[384] See Section 10.

[385] Where the EU Courts had often differed from the Commission's approach, see Chap. 7.

Commission, 'A Dynamic and Workable Effects-based Approach to the Abuse of Dominance' [2023] 1 *Competition Policy Brief*

The enforcement of competition rules also contributes to achieving objectives that go beyond consumer welfare, at least when the latter is defined strictly in economic terms. As stated by Executive Vice President Vestager: 'By basing our policy intent and action on principles that stem directly from the Treaties, EU competition policy is able to pursue multiple goals, such as fairness and level-playing field, market integration, preserving competitive processes, consumer welfare, efficiency and innovation, and ultimately plurality and democracy.'[386] The case law has also confirmed that competition law can achieve broader objectives, as ensuring consumer choice is a means to ultimately guarantee plurality in a democratic society.[387] It is therefore of the utmost importance that the Union's competition rules are applied vigorously and effectively. This is all the more necessary in times of economic hardship, and in the presence of a growing body of evidence of market concentration in various industries.

The amendments to the Guidance detailed in the Annex to the Communication, concerning matters such as the notion of anti-competitive foreclosure, as-efficient competitors, and the use of the as efficient competitor test all indicate the Commission moving away from the more economic approach. However, how or whether the embrace of broader goals will be applied by the Commission to Article 101 and (particularly importantly) to mergers is not immediately clear, although it is difficult to conceive EU competition law having different goals depending on the provision being applied. There is also the question of what will happen to the GC's judgment in the *Google Android* appeal to the CJ.

(ix) Public Policy Considerations and EU Competition Law

Prior to modernisation in 2004, there were a number of Article 101 cases in which the Commission applied the exemption provision, Article 101(3), in a way which took account of public policy considerations,[388] but the 2004 Guidelines[389] limited this possibility, as explained in Chapter 5. Even if a consumer welfare standard is being applied, however, there are various ways in which non-competition public interest concerns can be accommodated in EU competition law.[390]

First, a matter may be excluded from the scope of competition law altogether. Instances of this are the exclusion by Article 346 TFEU of the trade in arms where a Member State can take protective measures in the interests of national security, and the CJ's exclusion of collective bargaining agreements between employer and employees on the ground that such arrangements fall within the ambit of social policy.[391] Further, Article 106(2) TFEU contains a partial derogation for undertakings entrusted with services of general economic interest.[392] Secondly, the law applies only to 'undertakings' carrying on 'economic activities'. Despite the broad interpretation given to these terms, there are

[386] This is a passage from the EVP's speech of 25 October 2022, referred to in Section 9.B.v at n. 356 and accompanying text.

[387] The Commission here refers to the *Google Android* case, para. 1023, see Section 9.B.vi at n. 368 and accompanying text.

[388] Including COMP/36.718, *CECD* [2000] OJ L187/47, see Chap. 5. In 2020, the case was scathingly described by the US judge Douglas Ginsburg as a time when the Commission 'fell off a stool', <www.justice.gov/opa/speech/honorable-douglas-h-ginsburg-delivers-remarks-consumer-welfare-standard-occasion>. And see G. Monti, 'Article 81 EC and Public Policy' (2002) 30 *CMLRev* 1057.

[389] Guidelines on the application of Article 81(3) [now Article 101(3)]of the Treaty [2004] OJ C101/97.

[390] See A. C. Witt, 'Public Policy Goals under EU Competition Law' (2012) 8 *European Competition Journal* 443.

[391] Case C-67/96, *Albany International BV v Stichting Bedrijfspensioenfonds Textielindustrie* EU:C:1999:430: see Chap. 4.

[392] See Chap. 8.

many cases finding that an entity is not an 'undertaking' because its activities are not 'economic' and its agreements or conduct therefore not subject to the competition rules.[393] These include cases related to social welfare and concerning 'social solidarity', and those found to involve the exercise of 'official authority' or public power.[394]

The CJ found in *Wouters*, discussed in Chapter 5, that in certain limited circumstances the public interest objectives of an agreement (*in casu* the proper regulation of the legal profession) could be balanced against a restriction of competition so that the agreement did not infringe the competition rules[395] but in general the CJ has hitherto been unwilling to excuse anti-competitive conduct which is claimed to pursue broader public interest considerations.[396]

The EUMR enables Member States to take account of certain public policy considerations (including media plurality) in respect of mergers to which the Regulation applies.[397] Apart from this, the Commission has judged mergers only from a competition perspective, as was shown in the *Bayer/Monsanto* merger in 2017, when the Commission came under enormous pressure to forbid the merger on food safety, environmental, and climate grounds. The Commission acknowledged that these concerns were of great importance but refused to take them into account as they could not form the basis of a merger assessment which had to be based on competition grounds only.[398] In 2019, the Commission prohibited the cross-border Franco-German *Siemens/Alstom* trains and signalling merger on competition grounds despite intense lobbying from Member States (including France and Germany) urging it to allow the creation of a 'European Champion', to compete in particular with Chinese suppliers.[399] The Commission, however, was determined to maintain effective competition in the EU for the benefit of European consumers.[400] *Bayer/Monsanto* and *Siemens/Alstom* led to calls for the overhaul of the competition rules from many Member States and from the European Parliament. Although competition is at the heart of the EU's industrial policy, Commissioner Vestager said in 2015 (notably before the crises engulfing Europe since 2019) that 'decision-making in individual competition cases cannot be bent to political priorities' and competition enforcement 'follows its own principles and rules—and they are cast in stone'.[401]

It is possible for the Commission to pursue broader public interest concerns by concentrating enforcement in particular areas or in pursuit of particular objectives.[402] This has notably been done in

[393] E.g. Case C-205/03 P, *Federación Nacional de Empresas de Instrumentación Científica, Médica, Técnica y Dental (FENIN) v Commission* EU:C:2006:453; Cases C-264, 306, 354, and 355/01, *AOK Bundesverband and others v Ichtyol-Gesellschaft Cordes and others* EU:C:2004:150, and the cases discussed in Chap. 4, Section 4.

[394] See Chap. 4, Section 4.

[395] Case C-309/99, *Wouters v Algemene Raad van de Nederlandse Orde van Advocaten* EU:C:2002 98. For the position of sporting rules, see Chap. 2, Section 7.F.

[396] See, for example, Case C-209/07, *Beef Industry Development Society (BIDS)* EU:C:2008:643 (where the impugned agreement furthered Irish industrial policy objectives); Case C-501/06 P etc, *Commission v GlaxoSmithKline Services Unlimited* [2009] ECR I-610; Case C-68/12, *Protimonopolný úrad Slovenskej republiky v Slovenská sporiteľňa a.s.* EU:C:2013:71; Case C-280/08 P, *Deutsche Telekom v Commission* EU:C:2010:603.

[397] Council Reg. 139/2004 [2004] OJ L124/1, Art. 21(4); see Chap. 15.

[398] M.8084, Press Release of 21 March 2018, IP/18/2282. See also Commissioner Vestager's reply to the petitioners on 22 August 2017, <http://ec.europa.eu/competition/mergers/cases/additional_data/m8084_4719_6.pdf>.

[399] M.8677, Decision of 6 February 2019, IP/19/881.

[400] See Vestager, speeches, 'Hitting the sweet spot in antitrust enforcement', 25 September 2018, <https://ec.europa.eu/commission/presscorner/detail/en/speech_18_3906>, and 'The Champions Europe Needs', 9 January 2019, <https://ec.europa.eu/commission/presscorner/detail/en/speech_19_6872>.

[401] Speech, 'The Values of Competition Law', 13 October 2015, <http://ec.europa.eu/commission/2014-2019/vestager/announcements/values-competition-policy_en>.

[402] See N. Dunne, 'Public Interest and EU Competition Law' (2020) 65(2) *Ant Bull* 256.

the pharmaceutical sector,[403] the digital economy,[404] and in support of EU-level liberalisation policies in the telecommunications and energy sectors.[405] EU competition law is founded on the belief that open and competitive markets, integrated across the Union, are the best means to pursue broader public interest concerns and by 'making markets work well' it seeks to advance the single market and contribute to the other objectives of the EU discussed in Section 9.A. However, at present, EU competition law faces two particular issues. The first is how to react generally to the change in the zeitgeist which has seen the consensus around economic efficiency and consumer welfare fractured by increased calls for a progressive rethinking of the role of competition laws. The second is the role of competition law in the EU's battle with the greatest period of instability and crisis since the Second World War. The Commission's new approach to exclusionary abuses described in Section viii shows one response to these challenges.

10. THE APPLICATION OF EU COMPETITION LAW

A. FORM, EFFECTS, PRESUMPTIONS, AND THEORIES OF HARM

The EU competition provisions are drafted in broad terms. Article 101 TFEU prohibits restrictive agreements,[406] Article 102 TFEU prohibits abuse of a dominant position, and the EUMR is designed to preclude mergers which would significantly impede effective competition.

The Commission and the EU Courts were criticised in the past for failing to take a sufficiently economically rigorous approach to the application of the provisions and for instead adopting a 'form-based' approach. This means simply prohibiting certain types of agreements or practices as a matter of course, because they are presumed to be anti-competitive, without examining their actual or likely effects in the particular case. 'Modernisation' included moving towards the application of a proper 'effects-based' approach whereby agreements and practices are judged not by their form but by assessing their actual or likely effects on competition in all the circumstances in the light of an analysis of market dynamics . This is one aspect of the 'more economic approach' discussed in Section 9.B.v. One way of describing the difference between matters judged by their form and those judged by effects is to categorise them as those subject to rules and those subject to standards.[407]

It will be seen in Chapter 5 that in respect of Article 101 the EU Courts took the lead in moving away from a form-based approach to a more effects-based analysis.[408] The Commission then took the effects-based approach in the Article 101(3) Guidelines which it issued in 2004 to accompany Regulation 1/2003[409] and in all the Guidelines it has published since in respect of the application of Article 101

[403] Where the problems are in respect of the patent system, see the 'pay-for-delay' cases, such as Case C-591/16 P, *Lundbeck v Commission* EU:C:2021: 243 and Case T-691/14, *Servier v Commission* EU:T:2018:922, on appeal Case C-201/19 P, judgment pending, discussed in Chap. 5 and the regulatory gaming cases, Case C-457/10 P, *AstraZeneca v Commission* EU:C:2012:770 and Case T-691/14, *Servier*, discussed in Chap. 7.

[404] The large number of cases in the digital economy include Case T-201/04, *Microsoft v Commission* EU:T:2007:289, the *Intel* litigation originating in Commission decision COMP/C-3/37.990, *Intel* [2009] OJ C227/13; Case T-612/17, *Google and Alphabet v Commission (Google Shopping)* EU:T:2021:763, 10, on appeal Case C-48/22 P, judgment pending, and Case T-604/18, *Google and Alphabet v Commission (Google Android)* EU:T:2022:541; see further Chaps. 7 and 16.

[405] See the cases discussed in Chap. 7.

[406] And decisions of associations of undertakings, and concerted practices.

[407] See P. Ibáñez Colomo, *The Shaping of EU Competition Law* (Cambridge University Press, 2018), 29–44; D. Crane, 'Rules Versus Standards in Antitrust Adjudication' (2007) *Washington & Lee LR* 49.

[408] Case C-234/89, *Delimitis v Henninger Bräu AG* EU:C:1991:91 was of particular significance in this regard.

[409] See n. 335.

to particular types of agreement and to particular types of mergers.[410] In respect of Article 102, the Commission Guidance on Article 102 enforcement priorities[411] adopted an effects-based approach, However, in respect of Article 102 the EU Courts continued to eschew this in respect of some of the most heavily contested areas of Article 102. This changed with the CJ's judgment in *Intel* in 2017[412] discussed in Chapter 7, and the EU Courts have now endorsed and confirmed the effects-based approach.

The effects-based approach does not mean that EU competition law does not make use of presumptions. It does, and the way in which these are used in particular contexts is discussed throughout this book.[413] For example, Article 101 prohibits agreements which have as their 'object or effect' the restriction of competition and there is therefore a presumption that horizontal price-fixing cartels between competitors infringe by object.[414]

Two points should be noted in respect of the effects-based approach. First, adopting a consumer welfare objective and following an effects-based approach are not synonymous, although they were both part of the 'modernisation' and are often both described as 'more economic'. It is possible to apply a consumer welfare standard while using form-based rules and vice versa.[415] Secondly, there is a need for legal certainty in the application of competition law. As it is unacceptable to have a system of competition law in which it is impossible for firms to tell in advance whether their agreements or arrangements are compliant, an effects-based approach should contain the elements which make such judgments possible. The application of competition rules prohibiting agreements, conduct, or mergers should require the party alleging that the competition rules have been infringed to spell out a convincing *theory of harm*. This means explaining in exactly what way the agreement, practice, or merger is, or is capable of being, anti-competitive. In the following extract, two economists set out the characteristics of a well-developed theory of harm.

H. Zenger and M. Walker, 'Theories of Harm in European Competition Law: A Progress Report' in J. Bourgeois and D. Waelbrock (eds.), *Ten Years of Effects-based Approach in EU Competition Law* (Bruylant, 2012), 185 and available at <http://ssrn.com/abstract=2009296>

The requirement to present a theory of harm imposes a logically consistent approach to the assessment of anti-competitive behaviour. If the theory of harm is made explicit by competition authorities, then this makes it much harder for internally inconsistent or speculative competition concerns to survive the process of assessment.

A well-developed theory of harm has the following characteristics:

- it should articulate how competition, and, ultimately, consumers will be harmed relative to an appropriately defined counter-factual;
- it should be internally logically consistent;
- it should be consistent with the incentives that the various parties face; and
- it should be consistent with (or at least not inconsistent with) the available empirical evidence.

410 See Chaps. 9–11 and 15. 411 The Guidance Paper, n. 314.

412 Case C-413/14 P, *Intel Corporation v Commission* EU:C:2017:632.

413 And see A. Witt, 'The European Court of Justice and the More Economic Approach to EU Competition Law—Is the Tide Turning?' (2019) 64(2) *Ant Bull* 172.

414 See the discussion in Chap. 5, Section 3.B.

415 Although the pursuit of broader objectives through an effects-based approacht might be more difficult, see further C. Ahlborn and D. Piccinin, 'The *Intel* Judgment and Consumer Welfare—A Response to Wouter Wils' (2015)1 *CLPD* 60, 61.

The Commission has been particularly active recently in developing new theories of harm, such as self-preferencing,[416] to deal with new phenomena and practices in the digital economy, and has been supported in this by the GC.[417]

An effects-based approach entails identifying the relevant threshold of anti-competitive effects. The EU Courts have established that it is not necessary to find actual effects, but neither can they be purely hypothetical. The EU Courts have variously referred, inter alia, to 'capable of', 'potential', 'probable', and 'likely' anti-competitive effects, as we see in the cases discussed in the following chapters of this book.[418]

B. OVER- AND UNDER-ENFORCEMENT: TYPE 1 AND TYPE 2 ERRORS

One reason for using effects-based analysis is to achieve an optimal level of enforcement of the competition rules. 'Error cost analysis' means choosing an approach to enforcement which minimises the costs of error. Ideally EU law should avoid both over- and under-enforcement. Over-enforcement means prohibiting agreements, conduct, or mergers where there is no actual or likely anti-competitive harm. These are called Type 1 errors, or 'false positives'. Under-enforcement means failing to prohibit such things where there *is* anti-competitive harm. These are called Type 2 errors, or 'false negatives'. In line with Chicago theory, the generally prevailing view in the EU for the last 30 or so years[419] has been that Type 1 errors are the more harmful because preventing practices, conduct, and mergers which are in reality not anti-competitive chills pro-competitive activity and stunts innovation.[420] Whether a competition law system is equally, or more, worried about Type 1 or Type 2 errors is fundamental to its operation. We saw in Section 8.A that fear of false positives is a major element in US antitrust law and a major factor leading to the minimal level of enforcement there in recent years. It is now suggested that the costs of false positives have been systemically overstated and those of false negatives understated, and that this is particularly relevant in digital markets.[421] In the EU, the 2019 Commission Report on Competition Policy for the Digital Era proposed that in respect of digital markets competition law should err on the side of disallowing potentially anti-competitive conduct by incumbents, because the characteristics of many digital markets have arguably changed the balance of error cost and implementation costs, such that some modifications of the established tests, including allocation of the burden of proof and definition of the standard of proof, should be made[422] In the March 2023 Competition Policy Brief, the Commission, too, is concerned about the damage that can be inflicted where the threshold for intervention in an effects-based approach is set too high:

> While a form-based approach may carry the risk of capturing false positives, an overly rigid implementation of the effects-based approach could set the bar for intervention at a level that would render enforcement against practices that restrict competition unduly burdensome or even impossible, with serious negative consequences for consumers, the EU economy and society at large.[423]

416 See Chaps. 7 and 16.

417 AT.39740, *Google Search (Shopping)* Decision of 27 June 2017, on appeal Case T-612/17, *Google and Alphabet v Commission (Google Shopping)* EU:T:2021:763, 10 November 2021, on appeal Case C-48/22 P, *Google and Alphabet v Commission*, judgment pending.

418 And see also Commission [2023] 1 *Competition Policy Brief*, n. 382, p. 2.

419 See H. Schweitzer and R. Welker, 'Competition Policy for the Digital Era', *CPI Antitrust Chronicle* December 2019, 3.

420 See e.g. the discussion by L. Peeperkorn, 'Coherence in the Application of Articles 101 and 102: A Realistic Prospect or an Elusive Goal?' (2016) 39 *World Competition* 389, 407–409.

421 D. Geradin and D. Katsifis, 'Strengthening Effective Antitrust Enforcement in Digital Platform Markets' (2022) 18(2) *European Competition Journal*, 356, 376.

422 'Competition Policy for the Digital Era', report by J. Crémer, Y.-A. de Montjoye, and H. Schweitzer (2019), <https://ec.europa.eu/competition/publications/reports/kd0419345enn.pdf>, (the CDPE report), Chap. 1, p. 4 and Chap. 3.IV, p. 50 ff.; and see in the US, Stigler Committee on Digital Platforms, Final Report, September 2019, <www.chicagobooth.edu/research/stigler/news-and-media/committee-on-digital-platforms-final-report>.

423 Commission [2023] 1 *Competition Policy Brief*, n. 382, p. 4.

C. THE USE OF ECONOMIC ANALYSIS

Both the consumer welfare standard and the effects-based approach involve extensive use of economic analysis[424] and undertakings involved in competition issues make heavy use of economists.[425] Economic analysis, however, does not necessarily tell the competition authority what the outcome of any given agreement or conduct will be. Economics employs assumptions and models, economists commonly come to different conclusions on any given matter, and economics does not provide the answer to every question. The economic view that monopoly is inefficient and that the exercise of market power leads to prices above the competitive level is only the starting point to the application of the law in any particular case. Furthermore, even if there is agreement that competition law should be about consumer welfare, there can be disagreement about how allocative, productive, and dynamic efficiencies should be weighed against one another, what are the welfare implications of certain practices, or whether the protection of competitors in the short term is necessary to protect competition, and thus consumer welfare, in the longer term. We see these debates played out in the cases discussed throughout this book. Merger control, for example, discussed in Chapter 15, involves predicting the future effects of transactions that have not yet taken place.

It is seen in this chapter that there are fashions in economic theory and schools of antitrust analysis, and that today's orthodoxy may be overtaken by new ideas. Nevertheless, given that competition policy is concerned with economic structures, conduct, and effects, its application should be as economically sound as possible. Faull and Nikpay explain the advantages and limitations of economic analysis in competition cases.[426]

J. Faull and A. Nikpay (eds.), *The EU Law of Competition* (3rd edn, Oxford University Press, 2014), 3–4

1.03 Economic theories and models are built on and around assumptions. This approach has the benefit of making explicit the various elements relied upon in arriving at a particular conclusion or insight. At the same time, these assumptions by definition do not cover (all) real world situations. In addition, when the assumptions are changed the outcomes of the models may look very different. It is for these reasons that the application of economic theories may not always be able to give a clear and definitive answer, for example as to what will happen in a market when companies merge, or when companies try to collude or engage in specific types of conduct.

1.04 The best that the application of economic principles can do in general is to provide a coherent framework of analysis, to provide relevant lines of reasoning, to identify the main issues to be checked in the context of certain theories of competitive harm, and possibly to exclude certain outcomes. The application of empirical methods may further help to test the relevance of theories of harm. In this way, economics helps to tell the most plausible story. In individual cases, it will be necessary first to find the concepts and the model that best fit the actual market conditions of the case and then to proceed with the analysis of the actual or possible competition consequences. Economic insights can also be useful in the formulation of policy rules, indicating under what conditions anti-competitive outcomes are very unlikely, very likely, or rather likely, and helping to devise safe harbours.

[424] See D. Neven, 'Competition Economics and Antitrust in Europe' (2006) 21(48) *Oxford Rev of Economic Policy* 742.

[425] For a highly critical view of this, see W. Wils, 'The Judgment of the EU General Court in *Intel* and the So-called "More Economic Approach" to Abuse of Dominance' (2014) 37 *World Competition* 405.

[426] See also J. Briones, 'A Balance of the Impact of Economic Analysis on the EU Competition Policy' (2009) 32 *World Competition* 27; S. Bishop, 'Snake-oil with Mathematics is Still Snake-oil: Why Recent Trends in the Application of So-called "Sophisticated" Economics is Hindering Good Competition Enforcement' (2013) 9 *European Competition Journal* 67.

11. EU COMPETITION LAW AND REGULATION

Competition law is one method of dealing with market failures. Another is economic regulation.[427] Regulation generally involves a State-directed, positive, coercive alteration or derogation from the operation of the free market in a particular sector,[428] i.e. it 'consists of public interventions which affect the operation of markets through command and control'.[429] Since the last quarter of the twentieth century, many State-owned, and often vertically integrated, monopolies throughout Europe have been wholly or partly privatised.

Sectors previously monopolised by State enterprises legally protected from competition have been opened up, a process known as liberalisation. The EU has pursued a far-reaching programme of liberalisation and harmonisation in respect of the transport, postal services, energy, and telecommunications (electronic communications) markets.[430] However liberalisation can lead to private monopolies replacing public ones. There are particular problems in sectors where the provision of services depends on the use of network infrastructures (such as railway lines or telephone lines) which cannot feasibly be duplicated and where control of the network may create a 'bottleneck' monopoly which hinders downstream competitors. Moreover, some services—such as the supply of water, sewage, and basic postal services—may need to be the subject of a public service obligation such as 'universal service' (USO). As the market does not provide satisfactory outcomes to these problems the liberalised sectors are often subject to regulation.

Regulation typically involves setting up a regulatory body which implements controls on prices and quality, fixes terms of contracts, mandates and polices access by downstream competitors, and oversees the obligations of the undertaking such as the USO.[431] There are at present no EU-wide regulators as such[432] other than under the 2022 Digital Markets Act where regulatory powers are exercised by the Commission.[433] In other sectors, EU law provides for a regulatory regime in Member States through regulations and directives. The relevant EU sector legislation may require the establishment of an independent national regulatory authority (NRA) and specify in detail the powers and duties it must possess. Under the European Electronic Communications Code, for example,[434] the Commission may become closely involved in regulatory remedies chosen by the NRAs.

Although it has been persuasively argued that competition law is 'conceptually very similar' to some types of regulation, namely the type of regulation that encourages or promotes competitive markets, rather than that which pursues public policy objectives (some regulation pursues both),[435] there are differences between regulation and competition law.[436]

[427] See N. Dunne, *Competition Law and Economic Regulation* (Cambridge University Press, 2015).

[428] Ibid., 3. [429] T. Prosser, *Law and the Regulators* (Oxford University Press, 1997), 4.

[430] It has been pursued through directives adopted under the special procedure laid down in Art. 106(3) TFEU and through Council harmonisation directives under Art. 114 TFEU.

[431] Prosser, n. 429, 5–6. The functions of the regulators differ between sectors and different States organise regulation differently.

[432] Though note that the expression 'regulator' is often used loosely to mean 'competition authority'. As far as EU-wide sector regulators are concerned, the Commission proposed an EU-wide authority for electronic communications during negotiations on the reform of the electronic communications legislation. As the Member States did not accept this, a new body, the Body of European Regulators for Electronic Communications (BEREC) consisting of the heads of the Member States' NCAs, was created in 2009. This is now governed by Reg. 2018/1971 [2018] OJ L321/1.

[433] Reg. 2022/1925 on contestable and fair markets in the digital sector (Digital Markets Act) [2022] OJ L265/1.

[434] Dir. (EU) 2018/1972 establishing the European Electronic Communications Code.

[435] Coates, n. 152, 2.03–2.04; Dunne, n. 427, 43–48.

[436] P.-A. Buigues and R. Klotz, 'Margin Squeeze in Regulated Industries: The CFI Judgment in the *Deutsche Telekom* Case' (2008) *GCP* (July (1)) 1, 17; J. C. Laguna de Paz, 'Regulation and Competition Law' [2012] *ECLR* 77; R. O'Donoghue and A. J. Padilla, *The Law and Economics of Article 102* (3rd edn, Hart Publishing, 2013), 45–47; N. Dunne, 'Between Competition Law and Regulation: Hybridised Approaches to Market Control' (2014) 2 *J of Antitrust Enforcement* 225.

First, regulation normally acts *ex ante* (in advance) whereas competition law (other than merger control) normally acts *ex post* (reacting to conduct which is taking place or has taken place).[437] Where prices are concerned, for example, a regulator sets out in advance what the undertaking may charge while a competition authority will step in only if and when it appears that an undertaking's pricing infringes the competition rules. On the other hand, the desire of undertakings to comply with competition laws means that in practice competition law does have considerable *ex ante* effect.[438]

Secondly, competition law is applicable across all markets while regulation is enacted on a sector-by-sector basis. Regulatory agencies usually possess more extensive and technical expertise on their sector and more detailed information about the whole industry and the wider issues affecting the market than do competition authorities. The position of a regulator may be affected by its closeness to the market players and to the government (despite liberalisation, many States retain a financial stake in former State-owned monopolies).

Thirdly, competition law prohibits certain categories of conduct and competition authorities generally try to avoid behavioural remedies, whereas sector regulators provide detailed rules on matters such as prices and conditions which require close monitoring. Regulation is more *dirigiste* than competition law.

Fourthly, regulation may have redistributive and social goals written into its mandate and may tolerate inefficiency in a trade-off for other, socially important, goals, such as USO obligations which force some consumers to subsidise others.

Fifthly, competition law is a more dynamic tool than regulation. Regulation defines the market problems in advance, for example identifying structural or distributional issues that cannot self-correct, and provides solutions. It may be difficult for the regulator to respond to changes in the economic environment.

Competition laws can apply to regulated sectors concurrently with the regulatory regime.[439] The fact that a sector is regulated does not usually remove all ordinary competitive dynamics and anti-competitive conduct can therefore still arise, although it is possible for regulation to endow an entity with special powers that make it akin to a public body, or take it outside the scope of 'economic activity' so that the competition rules do not apply.[440] Where they do apply, the fact that an undertaking was encouraged or facilitated in its anti-competitive conduct by the regulatory framework will not exempt it from liability although the regulated context will be taken into account, for as we see in subsequent chapters, it is long established that conduct has to be judged within the legal and economic context in which it occurs.[441]

The relationship between sector-specific regulation and competition law has been considered in a number of cases, including *Deutsche Telekom*[442] in which the CJ held that an undertaking could

[437] Monopoly control is generally *ex post*, and so, in the current regime under Reg. 1/2003, is the control of anti-competitive agreements (although there is the possibility of interim measures or injunctions). Merger control is *ex ante* (the EU merger regime requires prior notification of mergers with a 'Community dimension', see Chap. 15).

[438] Coates, n. 152, 2.2.17–2.2.19.

[439] See G. Monti, 'Managing the Intersection of Utilities Regulation and EC Competition Law' (2008) 4 *Competition Law Review* 121. Member States vary as to whether its NRAs may apply competition rules as well as regulatory rules, or whether competition law can be applied only by competition authorities.

[440] See the discussion in Chap. 4, Section 4.

[441] Case 56/65, *Société La Technique Minière v Maschinenbau Ulm GmbH* EU:C:1966:38; Case C-228/18, *Gazdasági Versenyhivatal v Budapest Bank Nyrt. and others* EU:C:2020:265.

[442] Case C-280/08 P, *Deutsche Telekom* EU:C:2010:603. See D. Geradin and R. O'Donoghue, 'The Concurrent Application of Competition Law and Regulation: The Case of Margin Squeeze Abuses in the Telecommunications Sector' (2005) 1 *J of Competition Law and Economics* 355, GCLC Working Paper 04/05, 51–65; Case T-336/07, *Telefónica* EU:T:2012:172, *aff'd* Case C-295/12 P, *Telefónica* EU:C:2014:2062; Case T-398/07, *Spain v Commission* EU:T:2012:173. See also COMP/39.525, *Telekomunikacja Polska* 22 June 2011; Case T-486/11, *Orange Polska SA v Commission* EU:T:2015:1002, *aff'd* Case C-123/16, *Orange Polska SA v Commission* EU:C:2018:590; D. Kamiński, A. Rogozińska, and B. Sasinowska, '*Telekomunikacja Polska* Decision: Competition Law Enforcement in Regulated Markets' (2011) 3 *Competition Policy Newsletter* 3.

infringe Article 102 by applying a pricing policy which constituted an abusive 'margin squeeze' even though the prices had been approved by the national telecommunications regulator, as the competition rules supplemented by *ex post* review the legislative framework adopted by the Union legislator for *ex ante* regulation of the telecommunications market.[443] It was held that regulatory approval does not remove an undertaking's liability for infringing the competition rules unless the restrictive effects of its conduct are caused wholly by the national law and the undertaking has no room for manoeuvre.[444] The Commission cannot be bound by a decision taken by a national body[445] which, although bound to respect the Treaty provisions, operates under national law which might have different sectoral objectives to Union law.[446]

There are a number of cases, discussed in Chapter 7, which concern the relationship between mandated access to facilities under a regulatory regime and 'refusal to deal' in competition law.[447]

The position is different in the US where the Supreme Court has declined to apply ordinary competition law (s. 2 of the Sherman Act) to conduct in the regulated telecommunications sector on the grounds that it is the regulatory regime which is designed to deter and remedy anti-competitive harm.[448] The US has a federal sector regulation regime[449] so the dynamics of the relationship with federal antitrust law are different from those of the relationship between EU competition law and national regulation in the Member States.

The EU regulation of Big Tech, in the form of the Digital Markets Act of 2022[450] is noted in Section 12 and discussed fully in Chapter 16.

12. THE DIGITAL ECONOMY

The digital economy and EU competition law is discussed fully in Chapter 16. In this section, we introduce the basic outlines of the topic.

The digital economy[451] is the global network of economic activities and commercial transactions enabled by information and communication technologies.[452] In the space of 20 years, it has grown into a vast tech universe and brought about a new industrial revolution. Online platforms—defined

443 Case C-280/08 P, *Deutsche Telekom* EU:C:2010:603, para. 92. See further Chap. 7.

444 Ibid., paras. 80–89.

445 Ibid., para. 90.

446 Case T-271/03, *Deutsche Telekom* [2008] ECR II-477, para. 113.

447 See COMP/39.525, *Telekomunikacja Polska* 22 June 2011, upheld on appeal Case T-486/11, *Orange Polska SA v Commission* EU:T:2015:1002, *aff'd* Case C-123/16, *Orange Polska SA v Commission* EU:C:2018:590; discussed in D. Kamiński, A. Rogozińska, and B. Sasinowska, '*Telekomunikacja Polska* Decision: Competition Law Enforcement in Regulated Markets' (2011) 3 *Competition Policy Newsletter* 3; Case C-165/19 P, *Slovak Telekom a.s. v Commission* EU:C:2021:239; Case T-814/17 *Lietuvos geležinkeliai* EU:T:2020:545, on appeal Case C-42/21 P, EU:C:2023:12.

448 *Verizon Communications Inc v Trinko LLP*, 540 US 398, 124 S.Ct 872 (2004), see Chap. 7.

449 See Hovenkamp, *Federal Antitrust Policy*, n. 77, Chap. 19.

450 Reg. (EU) 2022/1925 of the European Parliament and of the Council of 19 October 2022 on contestable and fair markets in the digital sector (Digital Markets Act) [2022] OJ L265/1. The Regulation differs from traditional sector-specific regulation, see further B. Beems, 'The DMA in the Broader Regulatory Landscape of the EU: An Institutional Perspective' (2023) 19(1) *European Comp J*, 1, and Chap. 16.

451 The expression was first used by Dan Tapscott in *The Digital Economy: Promise and Perils in the Age of Networked Intelligence* (McGraw-Hill, 1994); see also Don Trapscott, *Rethinking the Digital Economy: Promise and Perils in the Age of Networked Intelligence: Anniversary Edition* (McGraw Hill, 2014).

452 See generally A. Ezrachi and M. E. Stucke, *Virtual Competition: The Promise and Perils of the Algorithm-Driven Economy* (Harvard University Press, 2016); M. Moore and D. Tambini (eds.), *Digital Dominance: The Power of Google, Amazon, Facebook, and Apple* (Oxford University Press, 2018); N. Srnicek, *Platform Capitalism* (Polity Press, 2017); D. S. Evans, A. Fels, and C. Tucker, *The Evolution of Antitrust in the Digital Era* (Competition Policy International, 2020).

as digital services that facilitate interactions between two or more distinct but independent sets of users (whether firms or individuals) who interact through the service via the internet[453]—are a major feature of the digital economy and in competition law the term 'digital economy' is often used as a synonym for the platform economy. The giants of the platform economy, known as 'Big Tech' or GAFA (Google, Apple, Facebook, Amazon, or GAFAM if Microsoft is included[454]) have achieved positions of enormous global market power. This was increased by Covid-19, when even more of the world's economic and social activity moved online and governments and their agencies became dependent on social media and apps to engage with their citizens in their management of the pandemic.

Data is central to the digital economy. The data which is produced in great volume, variety, and velocity by every transaction, interaction, and social media exchange online is known as 'Big Data' and forms the basis of much of the digital economy in a business model developed by Google and Facebook which involves 'collecting and monetizing user data, which are aggregated, refined, and sold to third parties in order to facilitate the precise targeting of advertisements [and other messages] at users'.[455] This has been described as 'surveillance capitalism'[456] whereby customers pay for what is ostensibly a 'free' service by surrendering their personal information which then is crawled over by increasingly sophisticated algorithms.[457] Digital platforms can therefore exploit consumers' behavioural biases.[458] Data is both a raw material and a currency[459] and the possession of Big Data by incumbent firms is a high barrier to entry. Other characteristics of the digital economy which present problems for competition law[460] are extreme and increasing returns to scale, network externalities and effects, multi-sidedness, 'winner takes all' (tipping) dynamics, significant economies of scope, and the control by firms such as Apple and Google over entire ecosystems of complementary products and services connected to each other and accessible only from products and services within the same system.[461]

Many of the usual tests and concepts in competition law which we discuss at various places throughout this book are difficult to apply to digital markets.[462] These include the definition of the

[453] OECD, 'An Introduction to Online Platforms and their Role in the Digital Transformation', 2019, <www.oecd-ilibrary.org/science-and-technology/an-introduction-to-online-platforms-and-their-role-in-the-digital-transformation_53e5f593-en>.

[454] Google now has a parent company, Alphabet, and Facebook is Meta, but the acronym remains.

[455] J. Naughton, 'Platform Power and Responsibility in the Attention Economy' in M. Moore and D. Tambini (eds.), *Digital Dominance: The Power of Google, Amazon, Facebook, and Apple* (Oxford University Press, 2018), 372 (words in brackets added).

[456] S. Zuboff, 'Big Other: Surveillance Capitalism and the Prospects of an Information Civilization' (2015) 30 *J of Information Technology* 75–89, <https://ssrn.com/abstract=2594754; S. Zuboff, *The Age of Surveillance Capitalism: The Fight for a Human Future at the New Frontier of Power* (Profile Books, 2019).

[457] A. Moazed and N. L. Johnson, *Modern Monopolies: What IT Takes to Dominate the 21st Century Economy* (St Martin's Press, 2016), 71. All summed up in the saying 'if you're not paying, you're the product'.

[458] For behavioural economics, see Section 5.D.

[459] The EU Competition Commissioner remarked, 'These incredibly powerful tools, like search engines and social media, are available for free. In many cases, that's because we as consumers have a new currency that we can use to pay for them—our data.' Commissioner Vestager, 'Competition in a Big Data World', Speech, 18 January 2016, <http://ec.europa.eu/commission/2014-2019/vestager/announcements/competition-big-data-world_en>. Data is a raw material in the sense that it needs to be processed by algorithms in order to be truly useful.

[460] See Crémer, de Montjoye, and Schweitzer, n. 422, Chap. 2.I.A, p. 20 ff.

[461] Ibid., Chap. 2.II.A, p. 34; M. Jacobides and I. Lianos, 'Ecosystems and Competition Law in Theory and Practice', <www.ucl.ac.uk/cles/sites/cles/files/cles-1-2021.pdf>; D. Geradin and D. Katsifis, 'Strengthening Effective Antitrust Enforcement in Digital Platform Markets' (2022) 18(2) *European Comp J* 356; F. Jenny, 'Competition Law Enforcement and Regulation for Digital Ecosystems: Understanding the Issues, Facing Challenges and Moving Forward' [2021] 3 *Concurrences* 38.

[462] See D. Sokol and J. Ma, 'Understanding Online Markets and Antitrust Analysis' (2017) 15 *Northwestern J of Technology and Intellectual Property* 43, University of Florida Levin College of Law Research Paper No. 17-22, <https://ssrn.com/abstract=2813855>.

relevant market,[463] the HMT/SSNIP test,[464] and the concept of market power as relating to the ability of an undertaking to raise prices. The thresholds for the application of merger control[465] make it difficult to deal with platforms buying up nascent competitors (so-called 'killer acquisitions')[466] and the widespread use of algorithms clouds the distinction between collusion and legal parallel conduct arising from reaction to competitors' behaviour, and may facilitate or strengthen explicit and tacit collusion.[467]

The power and influence of Big Tech 'becoming the owners of the infrastructures of society'[468] troubles governments across the world. There is much concern that digital platforms can use data on individuals to undermine democratic processes.[469] The question that concerns us in this book is how competition law can and/or should respond to the shape and reach of the digital economy.[470] One view is that the developments in the digital economy, and particularly the rise of the super-platforms and the power that they exercise, are unprecedented phenomena which threaten the fabric of economic, social, and political life and with which competition law, which has evolved to deal with market capitalism not surveillance capitalism, is not equipped to deal. The other view is that the existing principles of competition law do not need to fundamentally change to cope with digital markets, given the capacity of the law to continually grow, adapt, and reinvent itself, and that there is no need for special rules to cover Big Tech.[471]

In the EU, the Commission has enforced, and continues to enforce, the existing competition rules in a number of high-profile and contentious cases,[472] making creative use of the existing provisions, particularly Article 102 TFEU, against the practices of online platforms, and developing new theories of harm which have been upheld by the EU Courts,[473] as discussed in Chapters 7 and 16. In 2018, the

[463] See Chap. 3, Section 4.

[464] The hypothetical monopolist/Small but Significant Non-transitory Increase in Price test, see Chap. 3, Section 4.E. In AT.39740, *Google Search (Shopping)* Decision of 27 June 2017, upheld in the main Case T-612/17, *Google and Alphabet v Commission* EU:T:2021:763, on appeal Case C-48/22 P, *Google and Alphabet v Commission*, judgment pending, the Commission held that there can be a market where services are free of charge.

[465] In the EU Merger Regulation, Reg. 139/2004 [2004] OJ L124/1, these are set out in Art. 1.

[466] See Chaps. 15 and 16. In March 2021, the Commission took steps to deal with this by a creative use of EUMR, Art. 22, see Chap. 15.

[467] See OECD Roundtable, 'Algorithms and Collusion: Competition policy in the digital age', (2017), <www.oecd.org/daf/competition/cartels/algorithms-collusion-competition-policy-in-the-digital-age.htm>; A. Ezrachi and M. E. Stucke, *Virtual Competition: The Promise and Perils of the Algorithm-Driven Economy* (Harvard University Press, 2016); P. G. Picht and B. Freund, 'Competition (Law) in the Era of Algorithms' [2018] *ECLR* 403 (CIPO workshop); and further, Chap. 9, Section 3.B.iv.

[468] See N. Srnicek, *Platform Capitalism* (Polity Press, 2017), 92.

[469] See e.g. V. Robertson, 'Antitrust, Big, Tech, and Democracy: A Research Agenda' (2022) 67(2) *Ant Bull* 259.

[470] See e.g. M. Stucke and A. Grunes, 'No Mistake About It: The Important Role of Antitrust in the Era of Big Data', University of Tennessee College of Law, Research Paper No. 269, <http://ssrn.com/abstract=2600051>; M. Botta and K. Wiedemann, 'EU Competition Law Enforcement vis-à-vis Exploitative Conducts in the Data Economy, Exploring the Terra Incognita', Max Planck Institute for Innovation and Competition Research Paper No. 18-08, <http://ssrn.com/abstract=3184119>.

[471] See P. Ibáñez Colomo and G. De Stefano, *JELAP* Editorial, 'The Challenge of Digital Markets: First, Let Us Not Forget the Lessons Learnt Over the Years', <https://academic.oup.com/jeclap/article/9/8/485/5102579>; and more generally R. D. Atkinson and J. Kennedy, 'The Antitrust "Challenge" of Digital Platforms: How a Fixation on Size Threatens Productivity and Innovation' in D. S. Evans, A. Fels, and C. Tucker, *The Evolution of Antitrust in the Digital Era*, vol. 1 (Competition Policy International, 2020).

[472] Such as AT.40099, *Google Android* decision of 18 July 2018, on appeal Case T-604/18, *Google and Alphabet v Commission* EU:T:2022:541; AT.40411, *Google Search (AdSense)* decision of 20 March 2019; IP/19/1770, on appeal Case T-334/19, *Google and Alphabet v European Commission*, judgment pending; AT.40743, *Amazon—Buy Box*, proceedings opened 10 November 2020, IP/20/2077; AT40703, *Apple—App Store Practices (music streaming)*, proceedings opened 16 June 2020, IP/20/1073, Statement of Objections sent 30 April 2021, IP/21/2061; AT40652, *Apple—App Store Practices (e-books/audiobooks)*, proceedings opened 16 June 2020, IP/20/1073.

[473] AT.39740, *Google Search (Shopping)* Decision of 27 June 2017, on appeal Case T-612/17, *Google and Alphabet v Commission (Google Shopping)* EU:T:2021:763, on appeal Case C-48/22 P, *Google and Alphabet v Commission*, judgment pending.

Competition Commissioner appointed a panel of three experts 'to look into the implications of the digital era for competition policy'[474] and their report was published in April 2019.[475]

In 2020, the Commission started exploring the possibility of adopting a new competition tool (NCT) in the form of a market investigation procedure.[476] The NCT would have complemented the existing competition tools in order to deal with structural competition problems across markets which could not be tackled or addressed in the most effective manner on the basis of the current provisions. In the end, the Commission dropped this in favour of a proposal for a new regime confined to the digital sector, which became the 2022 Digital Markets Act[477] (the proposal for a broader NCT may be revived in the future). The Act was adopted alongside the Digital Services Act[478] which deals with the responsibilities and obligations of digital services to their customers and users, covering matters such as the liability of online intermediaries for third party content, safety of users online, and asymmetric due diligence obligations.

The Digital Markets Act (DMA), which is discussed in Chapter 16, introduces into EU law an *ex ante* regulation system in the digital sector to operate alongside the competition law regime of Articles 101 and 102 TFEU. It provides for a provider of 'core platform services' (CPS) meeting certain criteria to be designated as a 'gatekeeper'. 'Gatekeepers'[479] are subject to a list of obligations.[480] The DMA eschews the use of the concepts developed in EU competition law over the last 60 years, such as dominance, abuse, and market definition, in favour of describing as a gatekeeper a core platform provider which has a significant impact on the internal market, operates a core platform service which serves as an important gateway for business users to reach end users, and enjoys an entrenched and durable position in its operations or will foreseeably enjoy such a position in the near future.

13. COMPETITION LAW AND THE INTERNATIONAL CONTEXT

The effects of anti-competitive practices and the exercise of market power can be felt in States far away from that in which the undertaking concerned is located. Many undertakings in today's globalised economy are truly 'multinational' in the sense that they have a presence throughout the world. One of the most important issues in competition law is international application and enforcement and there is much international cooperation in competition matters. States throughout the world, including many developing countries, have systems of competition law. The international aspects of competition law arise throughout this book, but are discussed as a whole in Chapter 17.

[474] Speech by Commissioner Vestager in Vienna, 24 September 2018, <https://ec.europa.eu/commission/commissioners/2014-2019/vestager/announcements/helping-digital-economy-keep-its-promises_en>.

[475] Crémer, de Montjoye, and Schweitzer, n. 413.

[476] Press Release IP/20/977, 2 June 2020; <https://ec.europa.eu/competition/consultations/2020_new_comp_tool/new_comp_tool_inception_impact_assessment.pdfV>; Speech, Commissioner Vestager, 'Competition in a Digital Age: Changing Enforcement for Challenging Times', ASCOLA Annual Conference, 26 June 2020, <https://ec.europa.eu/commission/commissioners/2019-2024/vestager/announcements/competition-digital-age-changing-enforcement-changing-times_en>.

[477] Reg. 2022/1925 on contestable and fair markets in the digital sector (Digital Markets Act) [2022] OJ L265/1.

[478] Reg. 2022/2065 on a Single Market for Digital Services [2022] OJ L277/1. It came into force on 1 November 2022, IP/22/6423. It builds on and amends Dir. 2000/31/EC on electronic commerce, OJ [2000] L178/1 (e-Commerce Directive).

[479] According to the criteria laid down in Art. 3 of the DMA.

[480] Ibid., Arts. 5 and 6.

14. STATE AID

The State aid provisions, Articles 107–109 TFEU, deal with favourable treatment given to undertakings by a Member State. By controlling such aid, EU law makes serious inroads into the freedom of the Member States to act unilaterally in the realm of industrial and economic policy. The Commission adopted a major initiative in 2012, the State Aid Modernisation (SAM)[481] which resulted in a extensive overhauling of the State aid rules and a large number of new and/or revised Commission measures.

Article 107 states the basic principle that aid which distorts or threatens to distort competition and affects trade between Member States is incompatible with the internal market (Article 107(1)). It contains an exception for three kinds of aid that *are* compatible with the internal market (Article 107(2)) and an exception for four kinds of aid that *may be* compatible (Article 107(3)).

Article 107 TFEU

1. Save as otherwise provided in the Treaties, any aid granted by a Member State or through State resources in any form whatsoever which distorts or threatens to distort competition by favouring certain undertakings or the production of certain goods shall, in so far as it affects trade between Member States, be incompatible with the internal market.
2. The following shall be compatible with the internal market:
   (a) aid having a social character, granted to individual consumers, provided that such aid is granted without discrimination related to the origin of the products concerned;
   (b) aid to make good the damage caused by natural disasters or exceptional occurrences;
   (c) aid granted to the economy of certain areas of the Federal Republic of Germany affected by the division of Germany, in so far as such aid is required in order to compensate for the economic disadvantages caused by that division. Five years after the entry into force of the Treaty of Lisbon, the Council, acting on a proposal from the Commission, may adopt a decision repealing this point.
3. The following may be considered to be compatible with the internal market:
   (a) aid to promote the economic development of areas where the standard of living is abnormally low or where there is serious underemployment, and of the regions referred to in Article 349, in view of their structural, economic and social situation;
   (b) aid to promote the execution of an important project of common European interest or to remedy a serious disturbance in the economy of a Member State;
   (c) aid to facilitate the development of certain economic activities or of certain economic areas, where such aid does not adversely affect trading conditions to an extent contrary to the common interest;
   (d) aid to promote culture and heritage conservation where such aid does not affect trading conditions and competition in the Union to an extent that is contrary to the common interest;
   (e) such other categories of aid as may be specified by decision of the Council on a proposal from the Commission.

The constitutive elements of State aid are therefore the existence of a recipient undertaking,[482] financing through State resources and the imputability of the measure to the State, the grant of a

[481] State Aid Modernisation Communication, COM(2012) 209 final. It supplemented the earlier State Aid Action Plan, COM(2005) 107 final.

[482] 'Undertaking' is given the same meaning here as for the purposes of Arts. 101 and 102.

selective advantage, and an effect on competition and on trade in the internal market. The notion of an 'aid' prohibited by Article 107(1) is very wide and the subject of an extensive body of case law. It is an objective legal concept.

The Commission published a Notice on the Notion of State aid in 2016.[483] Case law has established that to constitute State aid the measure must confer on the recipient undertaking an economic advantage that it could not have obtained under normal market conditions from a private economic operator acting in the light of normal commercial considerations (the market operator or MEO principle). The advantage must be selective, so that it constitutes an advantage for certain undertakings in comparison with others which are in a comparable legal and factual situation. From 2013, the Commission embarked upon a policy of employing the State aid rules against tax deals made by Member States with multinational companies but this attempt to use the rules to remedy the lack of a harmonised EU tax regime has in general not been successful.[484]

By Article 108(3), Member States have to inform the Commission of any plans to grant or alter aid which falls within Article 107(1). They may not put any such plan into effect unless and until the Commission has authorised it (the stand-still provision). The Commission procedure for examining and investigating aid is a matter between the Member State concerned and the Commission, and the recipient/beneficiary undertaking, and the competitors of that undertaking, have only limited rights in the procedure.

The three types of aid listed in Article 107(2) are automatically exempt. Aid claimed to be within one of these categories still has to be notified to the Commission under Article 108(3), but the Commission's function is limited to deciding whether or not it does fall within a category. Once it has assessed the aid as falling within Article 107(2), the Commission has no further discretion to exercise in that respect,[485] although it remains under a continuing duty to ensure that the operation of the aid keeps within the bounds of the provision.

In respect of the categories of aid which may be compatible with the internal market under Article 107(3), the power to decide on that is given to the Commission by Article 108. The Commission decides, first, whether the aid falls within one of the listed categories and, secondly, whether it is compatible with the internal market. As Article 107(3) provides a derogation from the general principle contained in Article 107(1), it has to be strictly interpreted.[486] The Commission has power under Council Regulation 2015/1589 (the 'Procedural Regulation')[487] to adopt decisions containing conditions subject to which an aid may be considered compatible with the internal market. It has issued a large number of instruments such as Guidelines and Frameworks setting out its policy on some of the forms which aid falling within these exceptions may take. The General Block Exemption Regulation (GBER)[488] exempts many aid measures without notification to the Commission where they meet the conditions laid down and are below certain thresholds. There are major 'horizontal' provisions such as those on Regional Aid,[489] Research and Development and Innovation,[490]

[483] Commission Notice on the notion of State aid as referred to in Article 107(1) TFEU [2016] OJ C262/1.

[484] See e.g. Cases T-778/16 and T-892/16, *Ireland v Commission* EU:T:2020:338, on appeal Case C-465/20 P, judgment pending; Case C-885/19 P, *Luxembourg v Commission* EU:C:2022:859.

[485] A decision by the Commission as to whether or not aid falls within Art. 107(2) can be appealed to the GC under Art. 263 TFEU.

[486] Case C-277/00, *Germany v Commission* [2004] ECR I-3925, para. 20; Case T-461/13 *Spain v Commission* EU:T:2015:891, para. 97.

[487] [2015] OJ L248/9, replacing Reg. 659/1999.

[488] Commission Reg. (EU) 651/2014 of 17 June 2014 declaring certain categories of aid compatible with the internal market [2014] OJ L187/1.

[489] Communication from the Commission, 'Guidelines on regional State aid' [2021] OJ C153/1 (for 2022–2027).

[490] Communication from the Commission, 'Framework for State aid for Research and Development and Innovation' [2022] OJ C414/2.

and Important Projects of Common European Interest,[491] and particular provisions for certain sectors of the economy.[492] There is special guidance on compensation paid to undertakings providing services of general economic interest.[493]

Unauthorised State aid is unlawful and illegal aid must be recovered by the Member State concerned. If a Member State does not does not comply within the stated time with a Commission decision stating that aid must be abolished or altered, the Commission may take the State before the CJ under Article 108(2)(ii). The prohibition against implementing non-notified aid (the stand-still provision) is directly effective and must be applied by national courts.

State aid became of crucial importance during the financial and economic crisis of 2008 when Member States' governments intervened in the market to support and assist their financial institutions. The crisis presented the Commission with an unprecedented challenge from which it emerged as a leading player in the reconstruction of the European financial sector. It put into place a special regime to tackle the crisis which was extended twice.[494] The Banking Communication of 2013 developed it further.[495] Between 1 October 2008 and the end of 2014, the Commission issued over 400 decisions authorising State aid measures to the financial sector and approved aid totalling €4,884.1 billion.[496]

Since 2019, the Commission has been faced with two further crises. First Covid-19 and then the war in Ukraine. Both have led to Member States needing to provide massive financial interventions. In respect of Covid-19, the Commission put into place a Temporary Framework 'to enable Member States to use the full flexibility foreseen under State aid rules to support the economy in the context of the coronavirus outbreak'.[497] The Ukraine war led to the Commission putting in place a Temporary Framework in March 2022, since amended.[498]

A regulation of the Council and the Parliament of 14 December 2022, the Foreign Subsidies Regulation,[499] removes the long-standing anomaly whereby EU Member States' subsidies to their industries are subject to the close scrutiny of the State aid rules while foreign subsidies to undertakings in the EU go unchecked thereby providing the recipients with unfair advantages. The regulation gives the Commission power to investigate financial contributions granted by non-EU governments to companies active in the EU and to impose measures to remedy any distortive effects it finds.

[491] Communication from the Commission, 'Criteria for the analysis of the compatibility with the internal market of State aid to promote the execution of important projects of common European interest' [2021] OJ C528/10.

[492] Available on the Commission website at <https://competition-policy.ec.europa.eu/sectors_en>.

[493] See Chap. 8 Section 7, and <https://competition-policy.ec.europa.eu/state-aid/legislation/sgei_en>.

[494] Communication from the Commission on the application after 1 January 2011 of State aid rules to support measures in favour of banks in the context of the financial crisis [2010] OJ C329/7 and Communication from the Commission on the application from 1 January 2012 of State aid rules to support measures in favour of banks in the context of the financial crisis [2010] OJ C356/7.

[495] Communication from the Commission on the application from 1 August 2013 of State aid rules to support measures in favour of banks in the context of the financial crisis, Press Release IP/13/672, 10 July 2013.

[496] Commission State Aid Scoreboard 2015. Of this, €1934.9 billion had been used.

[497] Communication from the Commission, 'Temporary Framework for State aid measures to support the economy in the current COVID-19 outbreak' [2020] OJ C911/1, 20 March 2020. It generally expired on 30 June 2022, but with some extensions and transitional provisions, see <https://competition-policy.ec.europa.eu/state-aid/coronavirus/temporary-framework_en>.

[498] On 11 June 2023, the latest version was that of 9 March 2023, Communication from the Commission, 'Temporary Crisis Framework for State Aid measures to support the economy following the aggression against Ukraine by Russia' [2023] OJ C101/3, which fostered support measures in sectors key for the transition to the net-zero economy. See also Communication from the Commission, 'REPowerEU: Joint European Action for more affordable, secure and sustainable energy', COM(2022) 108 final, 8 March 2022, and <https://competition-policy.ec.europa.eu/state-aid/ukraine_en>.

[499] Reg. 2022/2560 of 14 December 2022 on foreign subsidies distorting the internal market [2022] OJ L330/1.

15. CONCLUSIONS

1. Competition law upholds the workings of the free market economy by policing the conduct of firms as they compete in the market. The belief that competition produces the best outcomes for society is based on neoclassical economic theory. This holds that in competitive markets prices are kept down, and other benefits, such as quality, choice, and innovation, flow to consumers, whereas in markets which are monopolised output is reduced, prices rise, and consumers are deprived of these benefits. In the twenty-first century, belief in the beneficial effects of free markets has been questioned by those who consider that neoliberal economic policies have led to unacceptable global inequalities and insecurities.

2. Competition laws can be applied to pursue a variety of goals. The belief that competition law should be concerned only with the goal of consumer welfare and economic efficiency, and not with socio-political and public interest issues, largely originated in Chicago School economics and held sway in the US for 40 years. It became the mainstream economic consensus in Europe and other developed jurisdictions. That is now changing. Matters which were considered by much of the competition law establishment to have been settled long ago are wide open for discussion again. There are arguments that inadequacies in competition laws and/or their enforcement have contributed to the deleterious consequences of globalisation and to the unhindered rise of Big Tech. In the US, proponents of the view that competition law should embrace socio-political and public interest issues again are in charge of the federal authorities, at least until 2024.

3. In the current age of multiple crises, inequalities and insecurities have contributed to the rise of right-wing populism, including within the EU. In digitisation, the world is going through a fourth industrial revolution which has thrown up undertakings with unprecedented power and reach. Climate change threatens our very existence and makes (or should make) sustainability feature in all other policies. The effects of Covid-19's devastating impact on the global economy are likely to last for a long time. War has returned to Europe on the very frontiers of the EU, adding to inflationary pressures and creating an energy crisis which prejudices the attainment of climate goals.

4. All this suggests that competition law needs some reorientation in order to carry on with its mission of protecting free markets. The old arguments about the place of socio-political goals in competition law have become revitalised but there is also the possibility of re-imagining the concepts of efficiency and consumer welfare to incorporate sustainability and inequality concerns, for example.

5. EU competition law is part of the EU economic constitution and plays a pivotal role in the integration of the single market. It never embraced the hard-line version of the consumer welfare standard that has applied in the US and the European Courts have continued to speak of protecting the competitive structure. With its 'A Competition Policy Fit For New Challenges' policy, the Commission has embraced the role of competition law in the Union's green transition, digital transition, and resilience policies. In March 2023, the Commission announced a revised policy to Article 102 cases which moves away from the consumer welfare standard towards broader objectives.

16. FURTHER READING

A. Books

AKMAN, P., *The Concept of Abuse in EU Competition Law* (Hart Publishing, 2012), Chap. 1

AMATO, G., *Antitrust and the Bounds of Power* (Hart Publishing, 1997)

ATKINSON, A., *Inequality: What Can Be Done?* (Harvard University Press, 2015, reprint 2018)

BAIN, J. S., *Barriers to New Competition* (Harvard University Press, 1956)

BAIN, J. S., *Industrial Organization* (2nd edn, John Wiley, 1968)

BAKER, J. B., *The Antitrust Paradigm: Restoring a Competitive Economy* (Harvard University Press, 2019)

BAQUERO CRUZ, J., *Between Competition and Free Movement* (Hart Publishing, 2002)

BEGG, D., VERNASCA, G., FISCHER, S., and DORNBUSCH, R., *Economics* (12th edn, McGraw-Hill, 2020)

BELLAMY and CHILD (D. Bailey and L. John, eds.), *European Union Law of Competition* (8th edn, Oxford University Press, 2018), Chap. 4

BISHOP, S., and WALKER, M., *The Economics of EC Competition Law: Concepts, Application and Measurement* (3rd edn, Sweet & Maxwell, 2010)

BOURGEOIS, J., and WAELBROCK, D. (eds.), *Ten Years of Effects-based Approach in EU Competition Law* (Bruylant, 2012)

BORK, R. H., *The Antitrust Paradox: A Policy at War with Itself* (Basic Books, 1978, reprinted with a new Introduction and Epilogue, 1993)

CARLTON, D. W., and PERLOFF, J. M., *Modern Industrial Organization* (4th edn, Pearson Addison Wesley, 2015)

CASSIDY, J., *How Markets Fail: The Logic of Economic Calamities* (Allen Lane, 2009)

CHARBIT, N., and GACHOT, S., *Eleanor M. Fox, Antitrust Ambassador to the World—Liber Amicorum* (Concurrences, 2021)

COATES, K., *EC Competition Law in Technology Markets* (Oxford University Press, 2010), Chap. 2

CRANE, D., and HOVENKAMP, H., *The Making of Competition Policy: Legal and Economic Sources* (Oxford University Press, 2013)

CSERES, K., *Competition Law and Consumer Protection* (Kluwer Law International, 2005), 331–332

CUCINOTTA, A., PARDOLESI, R., and VAN DEN BERGH, R., *Post-Chicago Developments in Antitrust Law* (Edward Elgar, 2002)

DAVIDSON, A., FINCK, M., and INFRANCA, J. (eds.), *Cambridge Handbook on Law and Regulation of the Sharing Economy* (Cambridge University Press, 2018)

DUNNE, N., *Competition Law and Economic Regulation* (Cambridge University Press, 2015)

EBENSTEIN, A., *Hayek's Journey: The Mind of Friedrick Hayek* (Palgrave Macmillan, 2003)

ELHAUGE, E., and GERADIN, D., *Global Competition Law and Economics* (2nd edn, Hart Publishing, 2011), Chap. 1

EPSTEIN, G., *Financialization and the World Economy* (Edward Elgar, 2005), available at <https://peri.umass.edu/fileadmin/pdf/programs/globalization/financialization/chapter1.pdf>

EZRACHI, A., and STUCKE, M. E., *Virtual Competition: The Promise and Perils of the Algorithm-Driven Economy* (Harvard University Press, 2016)

FATUR, A., *EU Competition Law and the Information and Communication Technology Network Industries* (Hart Publishing, 2012)

FAULL, J., and NIKPAY, A. (eds.), *The EU Law of Competition* (3rd edn, Oxford University Press, 2014), Chap. 1

FOX, E.M., and GERARD, D., *EU Competition Law* (2nd edn, Edward Elgar, 2023)

FRIEDMAN, M., *Capitalism and Freedom* (1962, 40th anniversary edn, Chicago University Press, 2002)

GAL, M. S., *Competition Policy for Small Market Economies* (Harvard University Press, 2003)

GAVIL, A., KOVACIC, W., BAKER, J., and WRIGHT, J., *Antitrust Law in Perspective: Cases, Concepts and Problems in Competition Policy* (3rd edn, West, 2017)

GELLHORN, E., KOVACIC, W., and CALKINS, S., *Antitrust Law and Economics* (5th edn, West, 2004)

GERADIN, D., LAYNE-FARRAR, A., and PETIT, N., *EU Competition Law and Economics* (Oxford University Press, 2012)

GERADIN, D., ZENGER, H., and STEPHAN, A., *EU Cartel Law and Economics* (Oxford University Press, 2016)

GERARD, D., and LIANOS, I., (eds.), *Reconciling Efficiency and Equity* (Cambridge University Press, 2019)

GERBER, D., *Law and Competition in Twentieth Century Europe: Protecting Prometheus* (Oxford University Press, 1998)

GIFFORD, D. J., and KUDRLE, R. T., *The Atlantic Divide in Antitrust: An Examination of US and EU Competition Policy* (University of Chicago Press, 2015)

HARVEY, D., *A Brief History of Neoliberalism* (Oxford University Press, 2005)

HAWK, B.E., *Antitrust and Competition Laws* (Juris Publishing, 2020)

VON HAYEK, F., *The Road to Serfdom* (Routledge, 1944)

HILDEBRAND, D., *The Role of Economics Analysis in the EC Competition Rules* (Kluwer Law International, 2002)

HOLMES, S., MIDDELSCHULTE, D., and SNOEP, M. (eds.), *Competition Law, Climate Change and Environmental Sustainability* (Concurrences, 2021)

HOVENKAMP, H., *The Antitrust Enterprise, Principle and Execution* (Harvard University Press, 2005)

HOVENKAMP, H., *Federal Antitrust Policy: The Law of Competition and its Practice* (6th edn, West, 2020)

HYLTON, K. N., *Antitrust Law and Economics* (Edward Elgar, 2010)

IBÁÑEZ COLOMO, P., *The Shaping of EU Competition Law* (Cambridge University Press, 2018)

KAPLOW, L., and SHAVELL, S., *Fairness versus Welfare* (Harvard University Press, 2006)

KINGSTON, S., *Greening EU Competition Law and Policy* (Cambridge University Press, 2011)

LIANOS, I., and SOKOL, D., *The Global Limits of Competition Law* (Stanford University Press, 2012)

LYON, B., *Cornered: The New Monopoly Capitalism and the Economics of Destruction* (John Wiley, 2010)

MATEUS, A. M., and MOIREIRA, T., *Competition Law and Economics* (Edward Elgar, 2010)

MERCURO, N., and MEDEMA, S. G., *Economics and the Law: From Posner to Post-Modernism* (Princeton University Press, 1999)

MOAZED, A., and JOHNSON, N. L., *Modern Monopolies: What It Takes to Dominate the 21st Century Economy* (St Martin's Press, 2016)

MOORE, M., and TAMBINI, D., *Digital Dominance: The Power of Google, Amazon, Facebook, and Apple* (Oxford University Press, 2018)

MOTTA, M., *Competition Policy* (Cambridge University Press, 2004)

NAZZINI, R., *The Foundations of European Union Competition Law: The Objectives and Principles of Article 102* (Oxford University Press, 2011), Chap. 2

NIELS, G., JENKINS, H., and KAVANAGH, J., *Economics for Competition Lawyers* (2nd edn, Oxford University Press, 2016)

NORMAN, J., *Adam Smith: What He Thought and Why it Matters* (Allen Lane, 2018)

ODUDU, O., *The Boundaries of EC Competition Law* (Oxford University Press, 2006), Chap. 2

PATEL, K. K., and SCHWEITZER, H., *The Historical Foundations of EU Competition Law* (Oxford University Press, 2013)

PITOFSKY, R. (ed.), *How Chicago Overshot the Mark: The Effect of Conservative Economic Analysis on US Antitrust* (Oxford University Press, 2008)

POSNER, R. A., *Antitrust Law* (2nd edn, University of Chicago Press, 2001)

POSNER, R. A., *A Failure of Capitalism* (Harvard University Press, 2009)

POSNER, R. A., *The Crisis of Capitalist Democracy* (Harvard University Press, 2010)

SAUTER, W., *Competition Law and Industrial Policy in the EU* (Oxford University Press, 1997)

SCHERER, F. M., and ROSS, D., *Industrial Market Structure and Economic Performance* (3rd edn, Houghton Mifflin, 1990), Chaps. 1, 2, and 4

SCHUMPETER, F., *The Theory of Economic Development* (Harvard University Press, 1934)

SHAH, R., GAO, Z., and MITTAL, H., *Innovation, Entrepreneurship and the Economy in the US, China and India* (Academic Press, 2015)

SKIDELSKY, R., *Keynes: The Return of the Master* (Public Affairs, 2010)

SMITH, A., *The Theory of Moral Sentiments* (1759, reprinted Penguin Classics, 2010)

SMITH, A., *An Inquiry into the Nature and Causes of the Wealth of Nations* (1776, reprinted Penguin, 1999)

SRNICEK, N., *Platform Capitalism* (Polity Press, 2017)

STIGLER, G. J., *The Organization of Industry* (Irwin, 1968)

STIGLITZ, J., *Freefall: Free Markets and the Sinking of the Global Economy* (Penguin, 2010)

STIGLITZ, J., *The Price of Inequality* (Penguin, 2013)

STIGLITZ, J., *Globalization and Its Discontents Revisited* (Penguin, 2017)

STUCKE, M., and GRUNES, A., *Big Data and Competition Policy* (Oxford University Press, 2016)

STUCKE, M., and EZRACHI, A., *Competition Overdose: How Free Market Mythology Transformed Us From Citizen Kings to Market Servants* (HarperBus, 2020)

THALER, R., *The Winner's Curse: Paradoxes and Anomalies of Economic Life* (Princeton University Press, 1992)

TIROLE, J., *The Theory of Industrial Organization* (MIT Press, 1988)

TOOZE, A., *Crashed: How a Decade of Financial Crises Shook the World* (Allen Lane, 2018)

TOOZE, A., *Shutdown: How Covid Shook the World's Economy* (Allen Lane, 2021)

TOWNLEY, C., *Article 81 EC and Public Policy* (Hart Publishing, 2009)

VAN DEN BERGH, R. J., and CAMESASCA, P. D., *European Competition Law and Economics: A Comparative Perspective* (2nd edn, Sweet & Maxwell, 2006)

VIVES, X. (ed.), *Competition Policy in the EU: Fifty Years on from the Treaty of Rome* (Oxford University Press, 2009)

WAPSHOTT, N., *Keynes Hayek: The Clash that Defined Modern Economics* (W. W.Norton, 2012)

WU, T., *The Curse of Bigness* (Columbia Global Reports, 2018; Atlantic Books, 2020)

ZIMMER, D. (ed.), *The Goals of Competition Law* (Edward Elgar, 2012)

ZUBOFF, S., *The Age of Surveillance Capitalism* (Profile Books, 2019)

B. Chapters in Books

Dunne, N., 'Competition Law (and Its Limits) in the Sharing Economy' in N. Davidson, M. Finck, and J. Infranca (eds.), *Cambridge Handbook on Law and Regulation of the Sharing Economy* (Cambridge University Press, 2018)

Lianos, I., Minssen, T., and Kollmar, C., 'Tackling Grand Challenges with Competition Law: Lessons from the Pandemic' in W. Sauter, M. Canoy, and J. Mulder (eds.), *EU Competition Law and Pharmaceuticals* (Edward Elgar, 2022), available at <https://ssrn.com/abstract=3985344>

Möschel, W., 'Competition Policy from an Ordo Point of View' in A. Peacock and H. Willgerodt (eds.), *German Neo-liberals and the Social Market Economics* (Macmillan, 1989), 142

Scheffman, D., and Higgins, R., 'Raising Rivals' Costs' in R. Blair and D. Sokol (eds.), *The Oxford Handbook of International Antitrust Economics, Vol. 2* (Oxford University Press, 2014)

Schnyder, G., and Siems, M., 'The Ordoliberal Variety of Neoliberalism' in S. J. Konzelmann and M. Fovargue-Davies (eds.), *Banking Systems in the Crisis: The Faces of Liberal Capitalism* (Routledge, 2013) 250, available at <http://ssrn.com/abstract=2142529>

Schweitzer, H., 'The History, Interpretation and Underlying Principles of Section 2 Sherman Act and Article 82 EC' in C.-D. Ehlermann and M. Marquis (eds.), *European Competition Law Annual 2007: A Reformed Approach to Article 82* (Hart Publishing, 2008), 119

Schweitzer, H., and Patel, K. K., 'EU Competition Law in Historical Context: Continuity and Change' in Patel and Schweitzer (eds.), *The Historical Foundations of EU Competition Law* (Oxford University Press, 2013), 207

Zenger, H., and Walker, M., 'Theories of Harm in European Competition Law: A Progress Report', <http://ssrn.com/abstract=2009296> in J. Bourgeois and D. Waelbrock (eds.), *Ten Years of Effects-based Approach in EU Competition Law* (Bruylant, 2012), 185

C. Articles

Akman, P., 'Searching for the Long-lost Soul of Article 82' (2009) 29 *OJLS* 267

Akman, P., '"Consumer" versus "Customer": The Devil in the Detail' (2010) 37 *J of Law and Society* 315

Akman, P., 'The Role of Freedom in EU Competition Law' (2014) 34(2) *Legal Studies* 183

Andriychuk, O., 'The Dialectics of Competition Law: Sketching the Ordo-Austrian Approach to Antitrust' (2012) 35 *World Competition* 355

Ashall, S., 'Away From Market Shares? The Increasing Importance of Contestability in EU Competition Law Case' (2015) 6 *JECLAP* 197

Averitt, N. W., and Lande, R., H., 'Using the "Consumer Choice" Approach to Antitrust Law' (2007) 74 *Antitrust LJ* 175

Bain, J. S., 'Economies of Scale, Concentration, and the Condition of Entry in Twenty Manufacturing Industries' (1954) 44 *Am Econ Rev* 15

Baker, J. B., 'Taking the Error out of "Error Cost" Analysis: What's Wrong with Antitrust's Right' (2015) 80 *Antitrust Law Journal* 8

Baker, J. B., and Salop, S., 'Antitrust, Competition Policy, and Inequality' (2015) 104 *Geo LJ* 1

Beaton-Wells, C., 'Antitrust's Neglected Question: Who Is "The Consumer"?' (2020) 65(1) *Antitrust Bull* 173

Behrens, P., 'The Ordoliberal Concept of "Abuse" of a Dominant Position and its Impact on Article 102 TFEU', <http://ssrn.com/abstract=2658045>

BISHOP, S., 'Snake-oil with Mathematics is Still Snake-oil: Why Recent Trends in the Application of So-called "Sophisticated" Economics is Hindering Good Competition Enforcement' (2013) 9 *European Competition Journal* 67

BLOCKX, J., 'Competition law in an era of deglobalization' [2022] 4 *Concurrences* 108953

BOTTA, M., and WIEDEMANN, K., 'EU Competition Law Enforcement Vis-à-Vis Exploitative Conducts in the Data Economy, Exploring the Terra Incognita', Max Planck Institute for Innovation & Competition Research Paper No. 18-08 (24 May 2018), <https://ssrn.com/abstract=3184119>

BRIONES, J., 'A Balance of the Impact of Economic Analysis on the EU Competition Policy' (2009) 32 *World Competition* 27

CAILLAUD, B., and JULIEN, B., 'Chicken and Egg: Competition Among Intermediation Service Providers' (2003) 34(2) *RAND J of Economics* 309

CARLTON, D. W., and KEATING, B., 'Rethinking Antitrust in the Presence of Transaction Costs: Coasian Implications' (2015) 46 *Rev of Industrial Organization* 307, available at <http://ssrn.com/abstract=2561783>

CHIRITA, A., 'Competition Policy's Social Paradox: Are We Losing Sight of the Wood for the Trees?' (2018) 14(2)–(3) *European Competition Journal* 367

CLAASSEN, R. GERBRANDY, A., PRINCEN, S., and SEGERS, M., 'Rethinking the European Social Market Economy' (2019) 57(1) *J of Common Market Studies* 3

COATES, K., and MIDDELSCHULTE, D., 'Getting Consumer Welfare Right: The Competition Law Implications of Market-Driven Sustainability Initiatives' (2019) 15(2)–(3) *European Competition Journal* 318

COLANGELO, G., and MAGGIOLINI, M., 'Big Data as Misleading Facilities' (2017) 13 *European Competition Journal* 249

CRANE, D., 'Chicago, Post-Chicago and Neo-Chicago' (2009) 76 *Univ Chic LR* 1911

CRANE, D., 'The Tempting of Antitrust: Robert Bork and the Goals of Antitrust Policy' (2014) 79 *Antitrust LJ* 835

CRANE, D., 'Antitrust and Wealth Inequality' (2016) 101 *Cornell LR* 1171, available at<https://ssrn.com/abstract=2648541>

CRANE, D., 'Further Reflections of Antitrust and Wealth Inequality', *CPI Antitrust Chronicle* October 2017, 14

CRANE, D., 'Antitrust and Democracy: A Case Study from German Fascism', University of Michigan Law and Economic Research Paper No. 18-009, University of Michigan Public Law Research Paper No. 595 (April 2018), <https://ssrn.com/abstract=3164467>

CRANE, D., 'How Much Brandeis Do the Neo-Brandeisians Want?' (2019) 64(4) *Ant Bull* 531

DALY, A., 'Beyond "Hipster Antitrust": A Critical Perspective on the European Commission's Google Decision' (2017) 1(3) *Eur Comp & Regulation LR* 188

DOLMANS, M., 'Sustainable Competition Policy' (2020) 5(4) and 6(1) *Competition Law and Policy Debate*, <https://ssrn.com/abstract=3608023>

DORSEY, E., RYBNICEK, J., and WRIGHT, J. D., 'Hipster Antitrust Meets Public Choice Economics: The Consumer Welfare Standard, Rule of Law, and Rent-Seeking', *CPI Antitrust Chronicle* April 2018

DUNNE, N., 'Between Competition Law and Regulation: Hybridised Approaches to Market Control' (2014) 2 *J of Antitrust Enforcement* 225

DUNNE, N., 'Public Interest and EU Competition Law' (2020) 65(2) *Ant Bull* 256

EASTERBROOK, F. H., 'The Limits of Antitrust' (1984) 63(6) *Texas LR* 1

EDELMAN, B., and GERADIN, D., 'Efficiencies and Regulatory Shortcuts: How Should We Regulate Companies Like Airbnb and Uber' (2016) 19 *Stan Tech LR* 293

EVANS, D. S., and SCHMALENSEE, R., 'Why Winner-Take-All Thinking Doesn't Apply to the Platform Economy', *Harvard Business Rev* (4 May 2016), available at <https://hbr.org/2016/05/why-winner-takes-all-thinking-doesnt-apply-to-silicon-valley>

EZRACHI, A., 'Sponge' (2017) 5 *J of Antitrust Enforcement* 49

FARRELL, J., and KATZ, M. L., 'The Economics of Welfare Standards in Antitrust' (2006) 2(2) *Competition Policy International* 3

FEDERICO, G., SCOTT MORTON, F., and SHAPIRO, C., 'Antitrust and Innovation: Welcoming and Protecting Disruption' (2020) 20 *Innovation Policy and the Economy* 126

FOX, E. M., 'The New American Competition Policy: From Antitrust to Pro-efficiency?' [1981] *ECLR* 439

FOX, E. M., 'The Modernisation of Antitrust: A New Equilibrium' (1981) 66 *Cornell LR* 1140

FOX, E. M., 'Consumer Beware Chicago' (1984–1985) 84 *Mich LR* 1714

FOX, E. M., 'The Battle for the Soul of Antitrust' (1987) 75(3) *California LR* 917

FOX, E. M., 'What is Harm to Competition? Exclusionary Practices and Anti-competitive Effect' (2002) 70 *ALJ* 371

FOX, E. M., and SULLIVAN, L. A., 'Antitrust—Retrospective and Prospective: Where Are We Coming From? Where Are We Going?' (1987) 62 *New York Univ LR* 936

GASSLER, M., 'Sustainability, the Green Deal, and Article 101 TFEU: Where We Are and Where We Could Go' (2021) 12(6) *JECLAP* 430

GERBRANDY, A., 'Rethinking Competition Law within the European Economic Constitution' (2019) 57(1) *J of Common Market Studies* 127

GERARD, D., 'Fairness in EU Competition Policy: Significance and Implications' (2018) 9(4) *JECLAP* 211

GERBER, D., 'Constitutionalizing the Economy: German Neo-liberalism, Competition Law and the "New Europe" ' (1994) 42 *Am J of Comparative L* 25

GIFFORD, D. J., and KUDRLE, R., T., 'Antitrust Goals, Procedures, and Policies in the U.S. and the EU' (2017) 62(2) *Ant Bull* 239

GLICK, M., 'The Unsound Theory Behind the Consumer (and Total) Welfare Goal in Antitrust' (2018) 63(4) *Ant Bull* 455

GLICK, M., 'Antitrust and Economic History: The Historic Failure of the Chicago School of Antitrust' (2020) 64(3) *Ant Bull* 295

GREEN, N., 'From Rome to Rome: The Evolution of Competition Law into a Twenty-first Century Religion' [2010] *Comp Law* 25

GRUNES, A. P., and STUCKE, M. E., 'No Mistake About It: The Important Role of Antitrust in the Era of Big Data', *Antitrust Source* (April 2015), University of Tennessee Legal Studies Research Paper No. 269, <https://ssrn.com/abstract=2600051>

HILDEBRAND, D., 'The European School in EC Competition Law' (2002) 25 *World Competition* 3

HOLMES, S., 'Climate Change, Sustainability and Competition Law' (2020) 8 *J of Antitrust Enforcement* 354

HOVENKAMP, H., 'Antitrust after Chicago' (1984–1985) 84 *Mich LR* 213

HOVENKAMP, H., 'Is Antitrust's Consumer Welfare Principle Imperiled?', University of Pennsylvania Law School, Institute for Law and Economics Research Paper No. 18-15 (2015)

Hovenkamp, H., 'Antitrust Policy and Inequality of Wealth', *CPI Antitrust Chronicle* October 2017, 7

Hovenkamp, H., 'On the Meaning of Antitrust's Consumer Welfare Principle' *Concurrentialiste* (17 January 2020), <https://leconcurrentialiste.com/herbert-hovenkamp-meaning-consumer-welfare/?mc_cid=05eddf4e53&mc_eid=34790440cd>

Hovenkamp, H., 'Antitrust Error Costs' (2021) *Faculty Scholarship at Penn Law* 2742, <https://scholarship.law.upenn.edu/faculty_scholarship/2742>

Hovenkamp, H., and Scott Morton, F., 'Framing the Chicago School of Antitrust Analysis' (2020) 168 *U.Pa.L.R.* 1843

Hovenkamp, H., 'Antitrust and Platform Monopoly' (2021) 130 *Yale LJ* 1952

Huffman, M., 'Marrying Neo-Chicago with Behavioural Antitrust' (2012) 78(1) *Antitrust LJ* 105

Hüschelrath, K., 'The Costs and Benefits of Antitrust Enforcement: Identification and Measurement' (2012) 35 *World Competition* 121

Ibáñez Colomo, P., 'Discretionalists vs Legalists: the true divide in the competition law community' (2018), <https://chillingcompetition.com/2018/05/28/discretionalists-vs-legalists-the-true-divide-in-the-competition-law-community/>

Jolls, C., Sunstein, C., and Thaler, R., 'A Behavioural Approach to Law and Economics' (1998) 50(5) *Stan LR* 1471

Jones, A., and Albors-Llorens, A., 'The Images of the "Consumer" in EU Competition Law' (2016), <http://papers.ssrn.com/sol3/papers.cfm?abstract_id=2750922>

Jones, A., and Kovacic, W., 'Antitrust's Implementation Blindside: Challenges to Major Expansion of US Competition Policy' (2020) 65(2) *Ant Bull* 227

Katz, A., 'The Chicago School and the Forgotten Political Dimension of Antitrust Law' (2020) 87(2) *Univ Chic LR* 413

Kaplow, L., 'On the Choice of Welfare Standards in Competition Law', Harvard Law and Economics Discussion Paper No. 693 (1 May 2011), <http://ssrn.com/abstract=1873432>

Khan, L., 'Amazon's Antitrust Paradox' (2017) 126 *Yale LJ* 710

Khan, L., 'The New Brandeis Movement' (2018) 9 *J of European Comp L & Practice* 131

Khan, L., and Vaheesan, S., 'Market Power and Inequality: The Antitrust Counterrevolution and its Discontents' (2017) 11 *Harvard L & Policy Rev* 235, available at <https://ssrn.com/abstract=2769132>

Khan, L., 'The End of Antitrust History Revisited' (2020) 133 *Harvard LR* 1655

Kovacic, W., 'The Intellectual DNA of Modern U.S. Competition Law For Dominant Firm Conduct: The Chicago/Harvard Double Helix' (2007) 1 *Colum Business LR* 1

Lamadrid de Pablo, A., 'Competition Law as Fairness' (2017) 8(3) *JECLAP* 147

Leibenstein, H., 'Allocative Efficiency vs. "X-efficiency"' (1966) 56 *Am Econ Rev* 392

Lianos, I., 'Polycentric Competition Law' *CLP* 2018, available at SSRN:https://ssrn.com/abstract=3257296

Lianos, I., 'Reorienting Competition Law' (2022) 10 *J of Antitrust Enforcement* 1

Lovdahl Gormesen, L., 'The Conflict between Economic Freedom and Consumer Welfare in the Modernisation of Article 82' (2007) 3 *European Competition Journal* 329

Lowe, P., 'The Design of Competition Policy Institutions for the 21st Century—The Experience of the European Commission and DG Competition' (2008) 3 *Competition Policy Newsletter* 1

Manne, G. A., and Wright, J. D., 'Innovation and the Limits of Antitrust' (2010) 1 *J of Competition Law and Economics*, Special Issue, 'The Limits of Antitrust Revisited'

Marsden, P., and Whelan, P., 'Consumer Detriment and its Application in EC and UK Competition Law' [2006] *ECLR* 569

Medvedovsky, K., 'Hipster Antitrust—A Brief Fling or Something More?', *CPI Antitrust Chronicle* April 2018, available at <www.competitionpolicyinternational.com/wpcontent/uploads/2018/04/CPI-Medvedovsky.pdf>

Melamed, A. D., 'Antitrust Law and Its Critics' (2020) 83(1) *Antitrust LJ 269*

Monti, G., 'Four Options for a Greener Competition Law' (2020) 11 *JECLAP* 124

Mueller, C. E., 'Antitrust Economics and the "The Flying Dutchman": How Economists Ruined Antitrust in Reagan's 1980s' (2008) 34(2) *Antitrust L& Econ Rev* 1

Muris, T., and Nuechterlein, J., 'Chicago and Its Discontents' (2020) 87(2) *Univ Chic LR* 495

Orbach, B., 'The Antitrust Consumer Welfare Paradox' (2011) 7(1) *J of Competition Law and Economics* 133

Parret, L., 'The Objectives of EU Competition Law and Policy' (2010) 6 *European Competition Journal* 339

Petit, N., and Neyrinck, N., 'Industrial Policy and Competition Enforcement: Is There, Could There and Should There Be a Nexus?', <http://ssrn.com/abstract=2225903>

Piraino, T. A. Jr. (2007), 'Reconciling the Harvard and Chicago Schools: A New Antitrust Approach for the 21st Century' (2007) 82(2) *Indiana LJ*, article 4, available at <www.repository.law.indiana.edu/ilj/vol82/iss2/4>

Picht, P. G., and Freund, B., 'Competition (Law) in the Era of Algorithms' [2018] *ECLR* 403

Posner, R. A., 'The Social Costs of Monopoly and Regulation' [1975] *J of Political Economy* 83

Posner, R. A., 'The Chicago School of Antitrust Analysis' (1979) 127 *U Pa LR* 925

Ritter, C., 'Presumptions in EU Competition Law' (2018) 6 *J of Antitrust Enforcement* 189

Salop, S., 'Question: What is the Real and Proper Antitrust Welfare Standard? Answer: The *True* Consumer Welfare Standard' (2014) 22 *Loyola Consumer LR* 336

Sivinski, G., Okuliar, A., and Kjolbye, L., 'Is Big Data a Big Deal? A Competition Law Approach to Big Gata' (2017) 13(2)–(3) *European Competition Journal* 199

Sokol, D., and Ma, J., 'Understanding Online and Antitrust Analysis' (2017) 15 *Nw J of Tech & Intell Prop* 43

Steinbaum, M., and Stucke, M., 'The Effective Competition Standard: A New Standard for Antitrust' (2020) 87(2) *Univ Chic LR* 595

Stucke, M., 'Reconsidering Competition' (2011) 81 *Mississippi LJ* 107, available at <https://ssrn.com/abstract=1646151>

Stucke, M. E., 'Is Competition Always Good?' (2013) 1(1) *J of Antitrust Enforcement* 162

Teachout, Z., and Khan, L., 'Market Structure and Political Law: A Taxonomy of Power' (2014) 9 *Duke J of Const L & Pub Policy* 38

Townley, C., 'Which Goals Count in Article 101 TFEU?: Public Policy and its Discontents' [2011] *ECLR* 441

Townley, C., Morrison, E., and Yeung, K., 'Big Data and Personalised Price Discrimination in EU Competition Law' (2017) 36 *YEL* 683

Trebilcock, M., and Ducci, F., 'The Multifaceted Nature of Fairness in Competition Policy', *CPI Antitrust Chronicle* October 2017

Vaheesan, S., 'The Twilight of the Technocrats' Monopoly on Antitrust?'(2017–2018) 127 *Yale LJ Forum* 980

Vaheesan, S., 'The Profound Nonsense of Consumer Welfare Antitrust' (2019) 64(4) *Ant Bull* 479

Vanberg, V., 'The Freiburg School: Walter Eucken and Ordoliberalism', Freiburg Discussion Papers on Constitutional Economics, No. 04/11 (2004), <www.econstor.eu/bitstream/10419/4343/1/04_11bw.pdf>

Walker, M., 'Behavioural Economics: The Lessons for Regulators' (2017) 13(1) *European Competition Journal* 1

Weitbrecht, A., 'From Freiburg to Chicago and Beyond—The First 50 Years of European Competition Law' [2008] *ECLR* 81

Werden, G., and Froeb, L., 'Can the FTC Turn Back the Clock?' *Antitrust Magazine Online* (ABA, October 2021)

White, L., 'The Dead Hand of Cellophane and the Federal Google and Facebook Antitrust Cases: Market Delineation Will Be Crucial' (2022) 67(1) *Ant Bull* 113

Witt, A. C., 'Public Policy Goals under EU Competition Law' (2012) 8 *European Competition Journal* 443

Witt, A. C., 'The European Court of Justice and the More Economic Approach to EU Competition Law—Is the Tide Turning?' (2019) 64(2) *Ant Bull* 172

Wright, J. D., 'Abandoning Antitrust's Chicago Obsession: The Case for Evidence-Based Antitrust' (2012) 78 *Antitrust LJ* 241, 244

Wright, J. D., and Stone, J., 'Misbehavioral Economics: The Case Against Behavioral Antitrust' (2012) 33(4) *Cardozo LR* 1517, available at <https://ssrn.com/abstract=1686389>

Wright, J. D., Dorsey, E., Klick, J., and Rybnicek, J. M., 'Requiem for a Paradox: The Dubious Rise and Inevitable Fall of Hipster Antitrust', George Mason Law and Economics Research Paper (14 September 2018), <https://ssrn.com/abstract=3249524>

Yoo, C. S., 'The Post-Chicago Antitrust Revolution: A Retrospective' (2020) 168 *U Pa LR* 2145

D. Blogs

Informa Connect <https://knect365.com/complaw-blog/>

Chillin'Competition <https://chillingcompetition.com>

2

THE COMPETITION LAW AND INSTITUTIONS OF THE EUROPEAN UNION

1. CENTRAL ISSUES

1. The European Union (EU) was originally the European Economic Community (EEC), established in 1957. The EEC later became the European Community (EC). On 1 December 2009 the Treaty of Lisbon came into force and the EU replaced and succeeded the EC.
2. The Treaties governing the EU are the Treaty on European Union (TEU), the Treaty on the Functioning of the European Union (TFEU), and the Charter of Fundamental Rights of the European Union (the Charter). Until 1 December 2009 the competition rules were in the E(E)C Treaty and are now in the TFEU.
3. The Council plays a relatively minor role in competition law. In 1962, Council Regulation 17 gave wide powers to enforce and apply the competition rules to the Commission. Regulation 17 was replaced by Regulation 1/2003.
4. The Commission is divided into Directorates-General. One, the Directorate-General for Competition (DG Comp), is responsible for competition policy under the direction of the Commissioner who holds the competition portfolio.
5. The national competition authorities (NCAs) of the Member States and the national courts share with the Commission the responsibility for the application and enforcement of the EU competition rules. Together the Commission and the NCAs form the European Competition Network (ECN).
6. The Court of Justice of the European Union (CJEU) includes the Court of Justice (CJ) and the General Court (GC), previously the Court of First Instance (CFI). These are together referred to in this book as 'the EU Courts'. In the field of competition law, they hear actions for judicial review of Commission decisions and the CJ hears preliminary references from national courts of the Member States.
7. The general principles of EU law and fundamental human rights are important in competition law, which entails the imposition of penalties and sanctions upon legal persons.
8. Three provisions, Articles 101, 102 and 106 TFEU, contain the substantive antitrust rules. The European Merger Regulation (EUMR) provides for merger control. These are amplified by rafts of delegated legislation, Notices and other instruments, Commission decisions in individual cases, and by the case law of the EU Courts.
9. The EU and three other States form the European Economic Area (EEA) and in effect the EU competition rules apply throughout the EEA.

2. INTRODUCTION

In this chapter, we describe the EU institutions concerned with competition law. We set out the competition provisions and briefly explain the way in which those rules are applied and enforced.[1] This chapter discusses the legal provisions and the powers of the institutions with regard only to antitrust and mergers, not to State aid, and the words 'competition law' should be understood in this sense unless the context otherwise requires.

3. INTRODUCTION TO THE EUROPEAN UNION

A. THE HISTORY OF THE EUROPEAN UNION

The EU has its foundation in the EEC. After the Second World War three European Communities were created: the European Coal and Steel Community (ECSC), 1951; the European Atomic Energy Community (Euratom), 1957; and the EEC, created by the Treaty of Rome, 1957. The ECSC Treaty was concluded for 25 years and expired on 23 July 2002. Euratom is under the control of the EU but is a legally distinct entity.[2]

The Treaty of Rome governing the EEC was amended several times, including by the Treaty of Amsterdam in 1999 which renumbered the Treaty Articles. The Treaty on European Union (TEU)[3] which entered into force on 1 November 1993 created a new entity, the European Union (EU). Inter alia it expanded the ambit of the EEC and renamed it the European Community (EC).

The Treaty of Lisbon, which came into force on 1 December 2009, amended both the TEU and the EC Treaty. The EC was subsumed into the EU.[4] On 1 December 2009, therefore, EC competition law became EU competition law. The amended EC Treaty was renamed the Treaty on the Functioning of the Union (TFEU).[5] The TEU and the TFEU, which have the 'same legal value',[6] are together referred to in this book as 'the Treaties'.

The Charter of Fundamental Rights, which had been 'solemnly proclaimed' in 2000,[7] was rendered legally binding by the amendments to Article 6 TEU made by the Treaty of Lisbon. Article 6 states that it has the 'same legal value' as the TEU and TFEU.[8]

Following the departure of the UK on 31 January 2020 (Brexit), the EU comprises 27 Member States, ten of which entered in 2004.[9] The 2004 enlargement was one of the reasons for the 'decentralisation' of enforcement of EU competition law in Regulation 1/2003.

B. THE EU TREATIES

The TEU establishes the EU, states its values and objectives, sets out the respective competences of the EU and the Member States, and provides for the EU institutions and for the Common Defence and Security policy. The TFEU contains more detailed provisions and the rules of substantive law.

[1] Public and private enforcement are examined in Chaps. 13 and 14 and merger procedure in Chap. 15.

[2] See further <http://ec.europa.eu//euratom/index.html>.

[3] 'Maastricht'.

[4] Art. 1 TEU, as amended by the Treaty of Lisbon.

[5] For the full consolidated texts of the TEU, as amended, and the TFEU, see [2008] OJ C115/1.

[6] Art. 1 TEU.

[7] By the Council, Parliament, and Commission. It was politically approved by the Member States at the Nice European Council summit in December 2000: [2000] OJ C364/1.

[8] See also Declaration 1 to the Treaties. The UK, Poland, and the Czech Republic were granted a partial opt-out from the Charter, Protocol 30 to the Treaties.

[9] Cyprus, the Czech Republic, Estonia, Hungary, Latvia, Lithuania, Malta, Poland, Slovakia, and Slovenia.

The competition rules, including the State aid rules, are set out in Articles 101–109 TFEU. The aims and objectives of the EC Treaty, and now the TEU and the TFEU, have provided the context for the application of the competition rules. In particular, the single market objective influences the way in which the competition rules are interpreted and applied, as explained in Chapter 1.[10]

C. THE NON-JUDICIAL EU INSTITUTIONS

(i) General

The Treaties establish the EU's autonomous institutions and the rules governing them. They confer legislative, executive, and judicial powers upon the institutions to enable the achievement of the EU's tasks. The main institutions of the EU are the European Council, the Council, the European Parliament, the Commission, the Court of Justice of the European Union, the European Central Bank, and the Court of Auditors. In this section, we consider the roles of the Council, the Parliament, and the Commission in respect of EU competition law, and note also the Advisory Committees provided for by Regulation 1/2003 and Regulation 139/2004, and the Ombudsman. The EU Courts are considered in Section 3.E.

(ii) The European Council

The European Council, consisting of the heads of government presided over by its elected President, 'shall provide the Union with the necessary impetus for its development and shall define the general political directions and priorities thereof' (Article 15 TEU). It deals with matters such as institutional changes, constitutional initiatives, policy strategies, external relations, and new accessions. It has no legislative powers and normally plays no role in competition policy.

(iii) The Council of the European Union

The Council, which is comprised of representatives of each Member State, takes the final step in passing primary EU legislation, now often under the co-decision procedure with the European Parliament.[11] It concludes agreements with foreign countries and plays a key role in the EU budget. In the sphere of EU competition law, it does not play a role on a day-to-day basis. Nonetheless, it has been responsible for the adoption of a number of important legislative acts in respect of competition law. In particular, by Regulation 17 and Regulation 1/2003 the Council conferred power on the Commission to enforce the competition rules.[12] It has also given the Commission power to adopt regulations exempting groups of agreements from the application of the competition rules (block exemptions),[13] and it adopted the European Merger Regulation (EUMR) conferring power on the Commission to rule on the compatibility with the internal market of certain mergers.[14]

The delegation to the Commission of the routine enforcement of the competition rules has largely protected the development and enforcement of competition law from the delays and compromises encountered in other areas of EU activity. Where the Council plays a significant role, progress is dependent on the political will of the Member States, reflecting their differing views and interests. Notably, the original Merger Regulation[15] took 16 years to enact.

[10] See Chap. 1, Section 9.B.iii.

[11] See Arts. 294–296 TFEU. Legislation passed by the co-decision procedure is often cited in this book as 'Council Regulation' for convenience.

[12] And, in Council Reg. 1/2003, on the NCAs of the Member States. [13] See Chap. 4.

[14] Reg. 139/2004 [2004] OJ L24/1, replacing Reg. 4064/89 [1989] OJ L395/1.

[15] Art. 352 (then Art. 308 EC), one basis for the Merger Regulation, requires unanimous approval in the Council.

(iv) The European Parliament

The European Parliament has co-decision powers with the Council in the sphere of the internal market, including competition. Otherwise, its role in competition policy is mainly a consultative one. Nonetheless, it is influential. Each year it adopts its own-initiative report on EU competition policy.[16] The report for 2021 wanted an active role for Parliament in the political debate on competition policy and greater involvement as an observer in the International Competition Network (ICN) and the OECD.[17]

(v) The European Commission and DG Comp

The Commission is the key enforcer of the competition rules at EU level.[18] It has power, for example, to take decisions which find an infringement of the competition rules and impose remedies and fines on those responsible, and may prohibit mergers above certain thresholds. EU competition law is therefore primarily applied at EU level through a 'public' enforcement system, by an administrative body acting in the public interest, rather than through private litigation in national courts (although the latter is actively encouraged). Competition law is exceptional in giving the Commission power to directly enforce the law through decisions addressed to private persons. For 60 years, the Commission has both enforced the competition rules and played the central role, subject only to the oversight of the EU Courts, in developing the law.[19] The Commission's ability to shape the law is underpinned by its power to set its own priorities and to choose the cases it wishes to pursue. Moreover, under the TEU's usual legislative procedures the Commission has the sole power to initiate legislation. If it wishes the Council to take action in the competition field it may therefore make a proposal.[20]

One of the Commissioners holds the competition portfolio.[21] Administratively the European Commission is divided into Directorates-General, one of which, the Competition Directorate-General, known as DG Comp, deals with competition.[22] Below the Competition Commissioner it is headed by a Director-General. Deputy Directors-General each head one of the Directorates respectively dealing with antitrust, mergers, and State aid. A special unit may deal with the Digital Markets Act.[23] DG Comp also has a Chief Competition Economist.

Although one Commissioner is responsible for the competition portfolio, formal decisions taken by the Commission must be adopted by the College of Commissioners as a whole,[24] subject to some delegation of investigatory and procedural matters. The significance of DG Comp being part of the Commission as a whole was explained by the then Director-General in the following passage.[25]

16 Available at <www.europarl.europa.eu/doceo/document>.

17 Para. 82, <www.europarl.europa.eu/doceo/document/TA-9-2022-0202_EN.html>, May 2022. For the ICN and OECD, see Chap. 17.

18 The Commission is 'required to ensure the application of the principles' laid down in the competition Articles, Case T-99/04, *AC-Treuhand AG v Commission* EU:T:2008:256, para. 163; Cases C-189, 202, 208, and 213/02 P, *Dansk Rørindustri A/S and others v Commission* EU:C:2005:408, para. 170; Cases 100–103/80, *Musique Diffusion Française SA v Commission (Pioneer)* EU:C:1983:158, para. 105.

19 For the way in which the Commission adopted a 'more economic' or 'consumer welfare' approach, and how that may now be changing, see Chap. 1, Section 9.B.

20 Art. 17(2) TEU; Art. 294 TFEU.

21 Since 2014, the Danish Commissioner, Executive Vice-President Margrethe Vestager.

22 Before 1999, the Directorate-General dealing with competition was known as DG IV.

23 Reg. 2022/1925 [2022] OJ L265/1; see Chap. 1, Section 12 and Chap. 16.

24 Decisions may be passed by a simple majority: Art. 219 TFEU.

25 For a critical American view of the Commission's position, see D. J. Gifford and R. T. Kudrle, 'Antitrust Goals, Procedures, and Policies in the US and the EU' (2017) 62(2) *Ant Bull* 239.

P. Lowe, 'The Design of Competition Policy Institutions for the 21st Century—The Experience of the European Commission and DG Competition' (2008) 3 *Competition Policy Newsletter* 1, 6

The European Commission finds itself in a substantially different position to a national authority. In the first place, its institutional independence should not be in question. As reflected in the EU treaties, its independence from national and political interests is fundamental to its mission of promoting the 'common interest' of the European Union as a whole.

Secondly, the Commission has delegated fully its powers to investigate a case, and manage the due process, to DG Competition. The Commissioner for Competition is in addition empowered to take decisions on cases and problems which raise no significant policy issue. These arrangements offer a solid guarantee of the integrity and impartiality of investigations and their conclusions, while reserving all key decisions on cases and policy for the college of Commissioners as a whole.

Thirdly, a competition authority certainly needs to be independent and impartial. But it should not be isolated or uninformed. It needs to be fully aware of the market and the regulatory environment around competition law enforcement. And it needs to be in a position to influence legislators and regulators, particularly when competition problems can be better addressed by new or amended regulation. This only underlines the advantage of EU competition policy of having the work of the Competition Commissioner and DG Competition fully embedded within the Commission. Finally, it is worth underlining again that the Commission as an institution, and not just DG Competition, retains the role of Europe's competition authority.

Particularly since 2008, when DG Comp became concerned with the application of the State aid rules during the financial crisis, it has worked in close cooperation with the Directorates-General for Financial Markets and for Economic and Monetary Affairs. The position of DG Comp within the Commission has been crucially important in the Covid-19 and Ukraine crises. The fact that final decisions are taken by the College as a whole raises the possibility that the Competition Commissioner may be overridden by Commissioners advancing or defending other interests. This is thought to have happened infrequently, but there are instances of problematic merger cases, discussed in Chapter 15.[26]

The office of Chief Competition Economist[27] was created in 2003, mainly in response to a series of judgments annulling Commission merger decisions[28] which convinced the Commission that its decisions should be subjected to a more rigorous internal regime of economic oversight, particularly as competition cases are highly fact-specific. The role of the Chief Competition Economist and their team is to give independent guidance on methodological issues of economics and econometrics in the application of the competition rules; to contribute to individual competition cases, in particular those involving complex economic issues and quantitative analysis; to contribute to the development of general policy instruments; and to assist with cases before the EU Courts.[29] He or she is responsible

[26] Chap. 15, Section 5.D.

[27] <https://competition-policy.ec.europa.eu/chief-competition-economist_en>.

[28] Case T-342/99, *Airtours plc v Commission* EU:T:2002:146; Case T-310/01, *Schneider Electric SA v Commission* EU:T:2002:254; Case T-5/02, *Tetra Laval BV v Commission* EU:T:2002:264, *aff'd* Case C-12/03 P, *Commission v Tetra Laval* EU:C:2005:87. See Chap. 15.

[29] <https://competition-policy.ec.europa.eu/chief-competition-economist_en>.

for coordinating the activities of the Economic Advisory Group on Competition Policy (EAGCP)[30] and acts as a focus for economics debates within DG Comp.

Details of DG Comp, its Directorates, and staff are on its website.[31] The website is crucial for those practising or studying EU competition law. For example, relevant legislation, Commission decisions, daily news, weekly updates, press releases, speeches, articles, proposals, public consultations, and Commission publications such as the *Competition Policy Brief*, the *Competition Merger Brief*, the Annual Reports, and evaluations of the outcomes of the Commission's activity[32] can be found there. The site also provides links to the sites of the Member States' NCAs, the European Competition Network (ECN), the International Competition Network (ICN), and other international organisations concerned with competition policy.[33]

Under the regime brought into effect on 1 May 2004 by Council Regulation 1/2003[34] to modernise the enforcement of the rules, the NCAs and national courts of the Member States share the enforcement of the competition rules with the Commission. Every Member State is required to have an NCA and empower it to enforce the rules. The ECN was created by the Commission and NCAs to achieve, amongst other things, a harmonious and consistent application of the competition rules. More enforcement is now carried out at national level by NCAs than by the Commission.[35] The relationship between the Commission and the NCAs and the national courts is discussed in Chapter 13.

The Legal Service of the Commission is not part of any Directorate General. It advises the Commission and represents it before the EU Courts. It checks the legality of DG Comp's decisions.

(vi) The Advisory Committee on Restrictive Practices and Dominant Positions and the Advisory Committee on Concentrations

Regulation 1/2003 provides for an Advisory Committee on Restrictive Practices and Dominant Positions.[36] It is 'the forum where experts from the various [national] competition authorities discuss individual cases and general issues of Community competition law'.[37] The role and powers of the Advisory Committee were strengthened by Regulation 1/2003. A similar Advisory Committee on Concentrations has functions under the EU Merger Regulation.[38]

[30] EAGCP (<https://competition-policy.ec.europa.eu/chief-competition-economist/eagcp_en>) is a group of academic industrial organisation economists whose members represent different fields of research and academic research centres in Europe. Members are nominated by the Commissioner on the proposal of the Chief Economist. EAGCP's role is to support DG Comp's economic reasoning in competition policy analysis, see <http://ec.europa.eu/dgs/competition/economist/eagcp.html>. The Commissioner or the Director-General may also ask EAGCP members on an ad hoc basis to provide economic advice on particular issues: see e.g. EAGCP's July 2005 opinion on the reform of Art. 102, <https://competition-policy.ec.europa.eu/system/files/2021-07/eagcp-opinion_economic_approach_to_article82.pdf>, and its evaluation of the proposal for a New Competition Tool, <https://op.europa.eu/en/publication-detail/-/publication/f4f0013b-35e3-11eb-b27b-01aa75ed71a1>.

[31] <https://competition-policy.ec.europa.eu/index_en>. An organisational chart is available at <http://ec.europa.eu/dgs/competition/directory/organi_en.pdf>.

[32] E.g. <https://competition-policy.ec.europa.eu/system/files/2022-03/kdaq22001enn_macroeconomic_impact_of_competition_policy_2021.pdf>.

[33] See Chap. 17, Section 6.C. [34] [2003] OJ L1/1: see Chap. 13.

[35] The enforcement powers of the NCAs were augmented by the ECN/+ Directive, Dir. (EU) 2019/1 to empower the competition authorities of the Member States to be more effective enforcers and to ensure the proper functioning of the internal market [2019] OJ C11/3.

[36] Art. 14.

[37] Commission Notice on cooperation within the Network of Competition Authorities [2004] OJ C101/43, para. 58.

[38] Reg. 139/2004, Art. 19.

(vii) The European Ombudsman

Article 228 TFEU provides for a European Ombudsman, elected by the European Parliament, who is empowered to deal with complaints in respect of maladministration by EU institutions (other than the CJEU acting in a judicial capacity).[39] This includes complaints against the Commission in its enforcement of the competition rules.[40]

D. EU LEGISLATIVE AND OTHER ACTS

EU acts adopted by the autonomous EU institutions (the Council, the Commission, and the European Parliament), such as regulations, directives, decisions, recommendations, and opinions, flesh out the basic principles set out in the Treaties.[41] Most general legislative acts, intended to apply in all of the Member States, are adopted by regulation or directive.

It has already been seen that a number of regulations have been adopted by the Council to enable the European competition rules to be applied and enforced. In the field of competition, the Commission has adopted a number of regulations under powers delegated to it by the Council and applies the competition rules to undertakings by means of decisions.[42] Decisions contain a statement of reasons (grounds) and an operative part which is formulated in Articles. The grounds and the operative part must be consistent with one another.[43]

E. THE EU COURTS

The Court of Justice of the European Union (CJEU) includes the Court of Justice (CJ) and the General Court (GC).[44] They are together referred to in this book as 'the EU Courts'.[45] The GC, previously called the Court of First Instance (CFI),[46] was established in 1989.

In the context of EU competition law, the EU Courts hear two main types of action. First, there are direct actions. Article 263 TFEU provides for the review of the legality of acts adopted by the EU institutions, i.e. for judicial review. This includes challenging the legality of the Commission's competition decisions and of a number of other administrative acts of the Commission in the competition field which are capable of affecting the interests of individuals. Challenges are normally made in the first instance to the GC.[47] In addition, Article 261 TFEU gives the EU Courts 'unlimited jurisdiction' to

[39] <www.ombudsman.europa.eu/en/home>.

[40] The first decision on such a complaint was issued on 30 September 2008, Case 1881/2006/JF.

[41] Art. 288 TFEU defines the main characteristics of each of these measures. Other *sui generis* acts adopted by one of the EU institutions may also be capable of producing legal effects: Case 22/70, *Commission v Council (ERTA)* EU:C:1971:32. Under the TFEU there is a distinction between 'legislative' and 'non-legislative' acts: see Arts. 289–290.

[42] The Commission also has powers under Art. 106(3) TFEU, which deals with public undertakings and those to whom Member States grant special or exclusive rights, to adopt directives (addressed to Member States) without the participation of the Council: see Chap. 8.

[43] In Cases T-9/11 etc., *Air Canada v Commission* EU:T:2015:994 the Commission decision in the *Air Freight* cartel decision, 9 November 2010, was annulled for inconsistency between the two parts; see Chap. 13, Section 7.A.v.

[44] The CJEU 'shall ensure that in the interpretation and application of the Treaties the law is observed': Art. 17 TEU. For the EU Courts generally, see A. Arnull, *The European Union and its Court of Justice* (2nd edn, Oxford University Press, 2006).

[45] In 2003, provision was made for specialist courts to be attached to the GC and this is now contained in Art. 257 TFEU. No specialist court has yet been established except for the Civil Service Tribunal (2005) which was dissolved in 2016 and its jurisdiction transferred to the GC by Council Reg. 2016/1192 [2016] OJ L200/137.

[46] The name was changed by the Treaty of Lisbon.

[47] For the derogations, see Art. 256(1) TFEU and the Protocol on the Statute of the CJEU, Art. 51.

review fines or periodic penalties imposed by the Commission, Article 265 TFEU provides an action for failure to act, and Article 340 TFEU provides for damages for non-contractual liability.

Competition cases form a significant part of the GC's work and the GC has considerable competition law expertise. The intensity (or lack of it) with which the GC reviews Commission competition decisions is a major issue in the enforcement of EU competition law[48] and one which has human rights implications.[49] Appeals on points of law can be made from the GC to the CJ[50] but it is often necessary to look at the GC judgment rather than that of the CJ to find a full account of all the issues.

Secondly, the national courts apply Articles 101 and 102, which are directly applicable. Article 267 TFEU provides a procedure whereby a national court or tribunal may (and in some circumstances must) request the CJ to give a preliminary ruling on a question on the interpretation or validity of EU law where a decision on the question is necessary to enable that court or tribunal to give judgment.[51] At present these references must be made directly to the CJ.[52] The CJ refuses to give a ruling on a reference from a body that does not constitute a 'court or tribunal' within the criteria laid down in the case law. On these grounds it refused to rule on a reference from the Greek competition authority on an important point concerning the application of Article 102 but accepted a reference on the same issue from a Greek court.[53]

Cases before national courts which give rise to preliminary references include not only private litigation arising from the direct applicability of the competition Articles but also cases involving NCAs applying the EU rules within their national jurisdiction. Furthermore, the CJ sometimes gives rulings on points of EU law which are crucial to the interpretation of domestic law in the case before the referring court. This is important in competition law as most Member States have domestic laws which deliberately mirror the EU rules and are interpreted in line with them. Leading rulings in EU competition law have been given in such cases.[54]

The judgments in the EU Courts in judicial review actions are limited by the grounds of appeal and the way that the parties argue the case. In preliminary rulings, the CJ is freer, because it is answering questions on the interpretation of the law. The EU Courts do not operate under a system of binding precedent, but they usually shift their position only incrementally, and even when in effect departing from their previous case law, may not expressly admit it. A striking recent example of this is the matter of exclusionary rebates in the *Intel* case,[55] discussed in Chapter 7. The *modus operandi* of the CJ is described by a long-standing former member of the Court in the following extract.[56]

[48] For criticism of the GC by the CJ for its review, see e.g. Case C-67/13 P, *Groupement des Cartes Bancaires v Commission* EU:C:2014:2204 and Case C-413/14 P, *Intel Corpn v Commission* EU:C:2017:632.

[49] See Chap. 13. [50] Protocol on the Statute of the Court of Justice, Art. 51.

[51] Final courts must refer. See P. Craig and G. de Búrca, *EU Law: Text, Cases, and Materials* (6th edn, Oxford University Press, 2015), Chap. 13.

[52] Art. 256 TFEU provides that the GC shall have jurisdiction to give preliminary rulings 'in specific areas laid down by the Statute'. The Statute of the Court does not yet lay down any such areas and all preliminary rulings continue to go to the CJ.

[53] Case C-53/03, *Synetairismos Farmakopoion Aitolias & Akarnanias (Syfait) v GlaxoSmithKline* EU:C:2005:333 (reference refused); Cases C-468–478/06, *Sot. Lélos kai Sia and others EE v GlaxoSmithKline AEVE Farmakeftikon Proionton* EU:C:2008:504 (preliminary ruling given).

[54] E.g. the refusal to supply case, Case C-7/97, *Oscar Bronner GmbH & Co KG v Mediaprint* EU:C:1998:569.

[55] Case C-413/14 P, *Intel Corporation v Commission* EU:C:2017:632. For a rare instance of the CJ expressly departing from its previous ruling, see Case 10/89, *SA CNL-SUCAL NV v HAG GF AG* EU:C:1990:359, overruling Case 192/93, *Van Zuylen Frères v Hag AG* EU:C:1974:72.

[56] See also P. Ibáñez Colomo, *The Shaping of EU Competition Law* (Cambridge University Press, 2018), Chap. 6.

J. L. da Cruz Vilaça, 'The Intensity of Judicial Review in Complex Economic Matters—Recent Competition Law Judgments of the Court of Justice of the EU' (2018) 6 *J of Antitrust Enforcement* 173

It is true that the Court of Justice (and the General Court as regards its own case-law) rarely makes a clear break from its previous line of case-law. But, in our system, past decisions are authoritative as a model and source of inspiration that guarantees a line of continuity and coherence indispensable for legal certainty.

However, the Court takes each case on its own merits and does not purport to lay down a rule to be followed inexorably by other judgment formations of the same size and level in future cases. In particular, every composition of the Grand Chamber retains its autonomy to make a decision on the basis of the legal and factual circumstances of the case and the assessment carried out by its members.

The Court is a judicial body whose mission consists in interpreting EU law and dispensing justice when required by a national court or by an applicant entitled to bring an action, be it a Member State, an EU institution or a private person.

The Court does not set its own agenda and, in fact, it does not have a political or ideological agenda to promote.

The case-law is therefore arrived at step by step, according to the merits of each specific case.

The way the Court necessarily operates helps to explain why one may sometimes feel that the Court did not always follow an unambiguous line of reasoning in judgments concerning the same field of competition law. It may simply happen that time have not yet come for certain developments.

The collegiate and confidential process of decision-making contributes to ensuring the independence of the judicial body, at the same time as it guarantees that different conceptions are confronted.

Therefore, do not expect to find in the Court's case-law a monolithic body of jurisprudence obeying a single pattern of decision-making or a unique conception of the law.

Admittedly, the Court is able to rely on a wealth of case-law that serves as a guide and beacon: any departure from a well-established line of case-law must be transparent, duly motivated, well-reasoned, and respectful of legitimate expectations.

But in a fast moving world, judges must also permanently listen to changes in the social, economic, technical, and political environment. How could it be different in the digital age, in a time of globalization and in a knowledge and information-based society?

The same holds true as regards the evolution of economics as applied to competition law and policy. Nobody can deny the progress made in the economic analysis of competition matters in the last forty years!

The EU Courts' volume of work can cause severe delays for litigants despite the existence of an expedited procedure.[57] There have been calls for the creation of a specialist competition court to remedy the delay problem, but despite the provision for the setting up of specialist courts in Article 257 TFEU this has not been done. Instead, the number of GC judges was increased[58] and since September 2019 there are in effect two from each Member State. The issue of whether the judicial architecture should be reformed to encompass a specialist competition court also arises in the context of the debate about whether the current arrangements for judicial review of Commission proceedings is adequate and in particular whether it satisfies the requirements of the ECHR.[59]

[57] Rules of Procedure of the General Court [2015] OJ L105/1, Art. 151. For the problems of the GC, see D. Hadroušek and M. Smolek, 'Solving the European Union's General Court' (2015) 40 *ELRev* 188 and Chap. 13, Section 8.A.ix.

[58] Council Reg. 2015/2422 [2015] OJ L341/14, amending Protocol No. 3 on the Statute of the CJEU.

[59] See Chap. 13, Sections 5 and 7.

F. GENERAL PRINCIPLES OF EU LAW AND FUNDAMENTAL (HUMAN) RIGHTS

We saw in Section 3.A that the EU has its own Charter of Fundamental Rights which is of 'equal value' to the TEU and TFEU. Prior to the Charter the EU Courts had already developed a body of law known as the general principles of law and fundamental (or 'human') rights, based on national laws of Member States and international treaties to which the Member States are signatories, particularly the European Convention on Human Rights (ECHR). The Charter can 'perhaps best be described as a creative distillation of the rights contained in the various European and international agreements and national constitutions on which the ECJ had for some years already drawn'.[60]

There are three overlapping sources of fundamental rights in EU law. Article 6(1) TEU provides for the recognition of the rights, freedoms, and principles set out in the Charter and Article 6(3) TEU provides for fundamental rights derived from (a) the ECHR and (b) the constitutional traditions common to the Member States, to constitute general principles of EU law. Many of the Charter's provisions directly correspond to those in the ECHR. Article 6(2) TEU provides that the EU will accede to the ECHR, but until that happens the EU is not formally bound by the ECHR.[61] Nevertheless, Article 6(3) ensures that the special significance of the ECHR for the EU continues, and Article 52(3) of the Charter provides for its provisions to be interpreted in accordance with the ECHR.

General principles of law and fundamental rights are of great importance in respect of the enforcement of EU law, as seen in Chapter 13. However, they are also relevant to the substantive law, as in *Google Shopping* where the GC applied the 'general principle of equal treatment' in holding Google to have infringed Article 102 by favouring its own downstream services over those of its competitors.[62]

4. THE COMPETITION PROVISIONS

A. GENERAL

By Article 3(1)(b) TFEU, 'the establishing of the competition rules necessary for the functioning of the internal market' is an area of exclusive Union competence. The EU competition rules apply only to agreements and practices when they affect trade between Member States or, usually, to mergers that have an EU dimension. Matters that do not have such effect or dimension are of national concern only as they do not concern the functioning of the internal market, except for mergers subject to Article 22 of the Merger Regulation.[63]

[60] P. Craig and G. de Búrca, *EU Law: Text, Cases, and Materials* (6th edn, Oxford University Press, 2015), 396. The Charter has been applied or referred to in a number of competition cases, including Case T-286/09, *Intel v Commission* EU:T:2014:547, para. 63.

[61] Case C-501/11 P, *Schindler v European Commission* EU:C:2013:522, para. 32. A draft accession agreement between the EU and the Council of Europe was held by the CJ to be incompatible with EU law, Opinion C-2/13, EU:C:2014:2454: the relationship between the ECHR and EU law is described in paras. 37–45. See also P. Gragl, *The Accession of the European Union to the ECHR* (Hart Publishing, 2013).

[62] Case T-612/17, *Google and Alphabet v Commission (Google Shopping)* EU:T:2021:763, para. 155, on appeal Case C-48/22 P, *Google and Alphabet v Commission*, judgment pending, citing Case C-127/07, *Arcelor Atlantique et Lorraine and Others* EU:C:2008:728, para. 23.

[63] EUMR, Reg. 139/2004 [2004] OJ L124/1.

(i) Article 3(1)(g) of the EC Treaty

The omission of an equivalent provision in the body of the TEU or TFEU to Article 3(1)(g) of the EC Treaty is discussed in Chapter 1.[64] As explained there, the relegation of the words 'a system ensuring that competition is not distorted' to a Protocol is of no significance.[65] When examining the way in which the EU Courts have hitherto interpreted the competition provisions it is impossible to ignore Article 3(1)(g). Article 3(1)(g) was crucial to the judgment in *Continental Can*, the seminal competition case in 1973 on what is now Article 102 TFEU.[66] The words of Article 3(1)(g), now in Protocol 27, must therefore always be borne in mind when looking at the provisions which set out the competition rules in greater detail.

(ii) The Main Treaty Provisions and the Merger Regulation

The main competition rules are contained in Chapter 1 of Title VII of the TFEU. Section 1 (Articles 101–106) deals with rules applying to undertakings.[67] Section 2 (Articles 107–109) deals with State aid. Merger control has never been expressly contained in any Treaty provision. It is provided for in Council Regulation 139/2004.[68]

B. THE SUBSTANTIVE COMPETITION PROVISIONS OF THE TFEU

The substantive competition provisions of the TFEU are summarised here.[69] The provisions are dealt with fully in later chapters.

(i) Article 101 TFEU

Article 101 is in three parts: Article 101(1) prohibits agreements, decisions of associations of undertakings, and concerted practices which have as their object or effect the prevention, restriction, or distortion of competition and which may affect trade between Member States. Article 101(2) states that such agreements are void. Article 101(3) provides that Article 101(1) may be 'declared inapplicable' in respect of agreements, decisions, or concerted practices or of categories of such agreements which are on balance beneficial as they satisfy the criteria set out in that provision. The analysis of the agreement is split, therefore, between Article 101(1) and Article 101(3).

The wording in Article 101(3) that Article 101(1) 'may . . . be declared inapplicable' to certain agreements left open, deliberately perhaps, the question of how and by whom this declaration was to be made. The Council in 1962 conferred exclusive power on the Commission to exempt agreements from the prohibition of Article 101(1),[70] and later enabled it to adopt 'block exemption' regulations exempting categories of agreements from the prohibition. The system of individual notification and exemption was abolished by Council Regulation 1/2003[71] and from 1 May 2004 Article 101(3) has had direct effect and is applied directly by the Commission, national courts, and NCAs as an exception to the Article 101(1) prohibition.

[64] See Chap. 1, Section 9.B.

[65] Case C-52/09, *Konkurrensverket v TeliaSonera Sverige AB* EU:C:2011:83, paras. 20–22.

[66] Case 6/72, *Europemballage Corp and Continental Can Co Inc v Commission* EU:C:1973:22, para. 23. See Chaps. 6 and 7. See also Case C-68/94, *French Republic v Commission* EU:C:1998:148.

[67] Broadly, any entity engaged in commercial activities: see Chap. 4.

[68] [2004] OJ L24/1, replacing Council Reg. 4064/89 [1989] OJ L395/1, as amended by Council Reg. 1310/97 [1997] OJ L180/1.

[69] In these Articles the Treaty of Lisbon replaced the words 'common market' in the EC Treaty with 'internal market'. This makes no substantive difference.

[70] Reg. 17 [1959–62] OJ Spec. Ed. 87, Art. 9.

[71] [2003] OJ L1/1.

(ii) Article 102 TFEU

Article 102 prohibits an undertaking which holds a dominant position in the internal market, or a substantial part of it, from abusing that position insofar as it may affect inter-Member State trade. It contains no express provision for exception or exemption.

(iii) Article 106

Article 106 deals with the application of the competition rules (and other rules of the Treaties) to public undertakings and undertakings given special or exclusive rights by Member States. It contains a limited derogation (Article 106(2)) from the Treaty rules for undertakings entrusted with services of general economic interest.

(iv) Article 37 TFEU

Article 37[72] is situated in the part of the TFEU concerned with the free movement of goods. It requires Member States which have State monopolies of a commercial character to eliminate discrimination between nationals of Member States regarding the conditions under which goods are procured and marketed.

C. THE PROCEDURAL PROVISIONS

(i) Article 103 TFEU

Article 103[73] confers a general power on the Council to adopt secondary legislation to give effect to the principles laid down in Articles 101 and 102. It provides:

> 1. The appropriate regulations or directives to give effect to the principles set out in Articles 101 and 102 shall be laid down by the Council on a proposal from the Commission and after consulting the European Parliament.
> 2. The regulations or directives referred to in paragraph 1 shall be designed, in particular:
>   (a) to ensure compliance with the prohibitions laid down in Article 101(1) and in Article 102 by making provision for fines and periodic penalty payments;
>   (b) to lay down detailed rules for the application of Article 101(3), taking into account the need to ensure effective supervision on the one hand, and to simplify administration to the greatest possible extent on the other;
>   (c) to define, if need be, in the various branches of the economy, the scope of the provisions of Articles 101 and 102;
>   (d) to define the respective functions of the Commission and of the Court of Justice of the European Union in applying the provisions laid down in this paragraph;
>   (e) to determine the relationship between national laws and the provisions contained in this Section or adopted pursuant to this Article.

[72] Art. 37.

[73] For the constitutional implications of Art. 103, particularly as regard the relationship between the Commission and the NCAs, see C. Townley and A. Türk, 'The Constitutional Limits of EU Competition Law—United in Diversity' (2019) 64(2) *Ant Bull* 235.

a. Implementing Legislation

The Council has adopted regulations pursuant to Article 103 implementing Articles 101 and 102. The most important of these is Regulation 1/2003, which replaced Regulation 17 of 1962 on 1 May 2004. Regulation 1/2003 confers power to enforce the competition rules on the Commission and on the NCAs of the Member States.

b. Block Exemptions

The Council has adopted regulations delegating power to the Commission to adopt regulations granting block exemptions, by which Article 101(1) is declared to be inapplicable to specified types of agreements.[74] The Commission has issued a number of block exemptions under these delegated powers. The majority are general (such as those on vertical restraints[75]) but some relate only to particular sectors (for example, maritime transport[76]).

c. Other Regulations and Measures Adopted by the Commission

The Commission has also adopted secondary legislation which implements Council Regulation 1/2003. For example, Regulation 773/2004[77] governs proceedings by the Commission, covering matters such as the Commission's powers in carrying out investigations under Regulation 1/2003, the handling of complaints[78] by the Commission, and the hearings which Regulation 1/2003 requires the Commission to carry out. Directives are not often used in areas of substantive competition law,[79] but there are important ones about private enforcement[80] and the ECN.[81] Unusually, the *Commission* has power under Article 106 to issue directives in order to ensure the application of that Article.[82]

(ii) Article 104 TFEU

Article 104[83] confers power on 'authorities in Member States' to apply the competition rules prior to the Council's adoption of implementing rules.[84] Article 104 was designed as a transitional provision but it remained significant in conferring power on the NCAs to act whenever EU implementing legislation did not apply. All sectors of the economy are now subject to Regulation 1/2003 and Article 104 is therefore without practical purpose.

[74] See Chap. 5. [75] Commission Reg. 2022/720 [2022] OJ L134/4.

[76] Commission Reg. 906/2009 [2009] OJ L256/31, adopted pursuant to Council Reg. 246/2009 [2009] OJ L79/1.

[77] [2004] OJ L123/18.

[78] Complaints to the Commission that undertakings have infringed the competition rules.

[79] But see e.g. in the sector of electronic communications, Dir. (EU) 2018/1972 establishing the European Electronic Communications Code [2028] OJ L321/36 (made under Art. 114 TFEU).

[80] Dir. 2014/104/EU [2014] OJ L349/1 on certain rules governing actions for damages under national law for infringements of the competition rules of the Member States and of the European Union (the Damages Dir.).

[81] Dir. (EU) 2019/1 to empower the competition authorities of the Member States to be more effective enforcers and to ensure the proper functioning of the internal market (the ECN/+ Directive) [2019] OJ L11/3.

[82] See Chap. 8. [83] Ex Art. 84 EC, ex Art. 88 EC.

[84] See Cases 209–213/84, *Ministère Public v Lucas Asjes (Nouvelles Frontières)* EU:C:1986:188.

(iii) Article 105 TFEU

Article 105 imposes a general duty on the Commission to ensure compliance with the competition rules:

> 1. Without prejudice to Article 104, the Commission shall ensure the application of the principles laid down in Articles 101 and 102. On application by a Member State or on its own initiative, and in co-operation with the competent authorities in the Member States, who shall give it their assistance, the Commission shall investigate cases of suspected infringement of these principles. If it finds that there has been an infringement, it shall propose appropriate measures to bring it to an end.
> 2. If the infringement is not brought to an end, the Commission shall record such infringement of the principles in a reasoned decision. The Commission may publish its decision and authorise Member States to take the measures, the conditions and details of which it shall determine, needed to remedy the situation.
> 3. The Commission may adopt regulations relating to the categories of agreement in respect of which the Council has adopted a regulation or a directive pursuant to Article 103(2)(b).

Article 105 originally included the words 'as soon as it takes up its duties' between the words 'shall' and 'ensure' in the first line. This suggested that it was merely a transitional provision enabling the Commission to enforce Articles 101 and 102 prior to the adoption of implementing legislation.[85] The change of wording (effected by the Treaty of Amsterdam) recognises that it is not a temporary measure, but confers on the Commission a permanent residual power to intervene.

D. THE EUROPEAN MERGER REGULATION (EUMR)

The current European Merger Regulation (EUMR), 139/2004,[86] was adopted by the Council pursuant to what are now Article 103 and Article 352 TFEU. It replaced, with effect from 1 May 2004, Regulation 4064/89.[87] The EUMR applies to concentrations with a 'Community [now EU] dimension'.

E. OTHER RELEVANT TREATY PROVISIONS

Other provisions of the TFEU may interact with the competition provisions. For example, the provisions relating to the free movement of goods, Articles 34–36, and relating to the free movement of services, Articles 56–62. There is a significant interface between the free movement rules and the competition provisions. The free movement rules are of particular importance when dealing with intellectual property rights.

Articles 114 and 115 TFEU permit the EU institutions to adopt measures to achieve the approximation of national rules which affect the establishment and functioning of an internal market. Article 114 is the legal base of the Digital Markets Act[88] and one base of the Damages Directive and the ECN+ Directive.[89]

[85] The Commission asserted jurisdiction under Art. 105 over a proposed alliance between British Airways and American Airlines at the time when air transport between a Community airport and a non-Member State was not covered by the relevant legislation: Commission Notice concerning the Alliance Agreement between British Airways and American Airlines [1996] OJ C288/4.

[86] [2004] OJ L24/1. [87] [1989] OJ L395/1, as amended by Council Reg. 1310/97 [1997] OJ L180/1, see Chap. 15.

[88] Reg. 2022/1925 on contestable and fair markets in the digital sector (Digital Markets Act) [2022] OJ L265/1, see Chap. 16.

[89] See n. 80 and n. 81.

Article 352 TFEU is the residual legislative power, providing for the Council, acting unanimously on a proposal from the Commission and with the consent of Parliament, to take action necessary to attain one of the objectives of the Treaties where the Treaties have not provided the necessary powers. It was used as one of the bases for both the original and current Merger Regulations as it was thought that, on its own, Article 103 was an inadequate basis for legislation to control mergers.[90]

5. COMMUNICATIONS AND NOTICES

The Commission issues a wide variety of Communications and Notices (some of which are called 'Guidelines') which play a significant role in EU competition law. Notices are statements of how the Commission deals with certain matters and are essential to an understanding of how the competition rules are applied in practice. Some Notices state the Commission's view of the substantive law and explain the approach the Commission takes to particular kinds of agreements, practices, or mergers[91] and some set out the principles by which the Commission exercises its powers and administrative discretion.[92] A number of Notices were issued to accompany Regulation 1/2003 and its flanking legislation in order to flesh out the details of the new enforcement system.[93] The Notices are crucial to an overall picture of the competition rules and in practice they influence the way in which firms conduct business. Notices do not have legislative force and are sometimes referred to as 'soft law'.[94] However, the CJ has held that they may form rules of practice from which the Commission cannot depart in an individual case without giving reasons that are compatible with the principles of equal treatment and legitimate expectation.[95] We see throughout this book instances in which cases before the EU Courts are fought on the issue of whether the Commission did or did not properly follow or apply one or more of its Notices.[96] The Notices are not binding on the courts or NCAs of the Member States.[97]

[90] Previous to the Lisbon Treaty, Art. 352 (then Art. 308) did not require the consent of Parliament, only that it be consulted.

[91] Such as the Guidelines on vertical restraints [2022] OJ C248/01; and Guidelines on the assessment of horizontal mergers [2004] OJ C31/5. In some cases, the EU Courts have in effect adopted the position set out in a Notice, see e.g. the 'efficiency defence' in respect of Art. 102, discussed in Chap. 7, Section 5.D.

[92] Such as the Guidelines on the method of setting fines imposed pursuant to Article 23(2)(a) of Regulation No. 1/2003 [2006] OJ C210/2 (the Fining Guidelines) and Commission Notice on Immunity from Fines and Reduction of Fines in Cartel Cases [2006] OJ C298/17 (the Leniency Notice).

[93] The Notice on informal guidance relating to novel questions [2004] OJ C101/78 was replaced by [2022] OJ C381/9, see Chap.13, Section 4.

[94] L. Senden, *Soft Law in European Community Law* (Hart Publishing, 2004); S. Lefevre, 'Interpretative Communications and the Implementation of Community Law at National Level' (2004) 29 *ELRev* 808; H. A. Cosma and R. Whish, 'Soft Law in the Field of EU Competition Policy' (2003) 14 *European Business LR* 25; N. Petit and M. Rato, 'From Hard to Soft Enforcement of EC Competition Law—A Bestiary of "Sunshine" Enforcement Instruments', <http://ssrn.com/abstract=1270109>; O. Stefan, *Soft Law in Court: Competition Law, State Aid and the Court of Justice of the European Union* (Kluwer, 2013). The European Parliament was extremely critical in 2007 of the widespread use of 'soft law', see European Parliament Resolution of 4 September 2007 on institutional and legal implications of the use of 'soft law' instruments (2007/2028(INI)).

[95] Cases C-189, 202, 208, and 213/02 P, *Dansk Rørindustri A/S and Others v Commission* EU:C:2005:408, paras. 209–213; Case C-397/03 P, *Archer Daniels Midland Co v Commission* EU:C:2006:328, para. 91; Case C-226/11, *Expedia Inc v Autorité de la Concurrence* EU:C:2012:795, para. 28; Case T-446/05, *Amann & Söhne GmbH & Co KG v Commission* EU:T:2010:165, paras. 137–139; Case C-439/11 P, *Ziegler SA v Commission* EU:C:2013:513, para. 60; H. C. H. Hofmann, 'Negotiated and Non-negotiated Administrative Rule-making: The Example of EC Competition Policy' (2006) 43 *CMLRev* 153; Senden, n. 94.

[96] Particularly in respect of the Fining Guidelines (currently [2006] OJ C210/2) and the Leniency Notice (currently [2006] OJ C298/17).

[97] Case C-360/09, *Pfleiderer AG v Bundeskartellamt* [2011] ECR I-5161; Case C-226/11, *Expedia Inc v Autorité de la Concurrence* EU:C:2012:795; Case C-23/14, *Post Danmark A/S v Konkurrencerådet (Post Danmark II)* EU:C:2015:651, para. 52.

6. REGULATION 1/2003 AND MODERNISATION

As already noted, on 1 May 2004 Council Regulation 1/2003[98] brought in a new era in EU competition law. Regulation 1/2003 was a decentralising measure whereby a greater role than previously is given to the NCAs and national courts of the Member States to share with the Commission the enforcement and application of the competition rules. In June 2022, the Commission embarked on an evaluation of Regulation 1/2003 to see whether, in the light of 20 years of practice and experience and of the changes in the economic landscape that have taken place in that time, it needs amending,[99] This is part of the Commission's review of its rules and guidelines pursuant to the 'Competition Policy Fit for New Challenges' programme, discussed in Chapter 1, Section 9.

Regulation 1/2003 did not, in itself, change the substantive law but, as will be seen throughout this book, the mechanisms for enforcement and application have impacted on the development of the substantive law and an appreciation of how the law is, and has been, enforced is necessary to a proper understanding of it. Some of the cases discussed in this book were decided under the previous enforcement system. That system is described, where the context requires, when the present system is examined. Since modernisation, the linchpin of which was rendering Article 101(3) directly applicable and abolishing the previous system of prior notification,[100] the cases handled by the Commission have predominantly been cartels, mergers, and Article 102 cases on abuse of a dominant position (particularly, latterly, in the digital economy).

Regulation 1/2003 effected the voluntary surrender by the European Commission of some of its monopoly powers. It contained measures of decentralisation of enforcement to the NCAs and to national courts and created the European Competition Network (ECN), comprising the Commission and the NCAs. Nevertheless, it must be stressed that despite the changes brought into effect by Regulation 1/2003 the Commission remains at the heart of the system, at the centre of the development and application of EU competition law and policy, as it has been since 1962. Indeed, the modernisation can be seen as *increasing* the Commission's powers by strengthening its ability to dictate policy.[101]

7. PARTICULAR SECTORS

The basic position is that the competition rules cover all areas of the economy. However, the following should be noted about the position of certain sectors.

A. COAL AND STEEL

Coal and steel passed into the scope of the EC Treaty and thence into that of the TEU and TFEU upon the expiry of the ECSC Treaty on 23 July 2002.[102]

[98] [2003] OJ L1/1.

[99] IP/22/4194, and see W. Wils, 'Regulation 1/2003, An Assessment After Twenty Years' (2023) 46(1) *World Competition*, <http://ssrn.com/author=456087>. See also C. Townley and A. Türk, 'The Constitutional Limits of EU Competition Law—United in Diversity' (2019) 64(2) *Ant Bull* 235.

[100] See Chaps. 5 and 13.

[101] The Commission has been described as executing a 'strategic coup', by marginalising national laws and in effect centralising rather than decentralising control of the application of the competition rules: see S. Wilkes, 'Agency Escape: Decentralization or Dominance of the European Commission in the Modernisation of Competition Policy' (2005) 18 *Governance* 431; see also G. Monti, *EU Competition Law* (Cambridge University Press, 2008), 438–439.

[102] The Commission issued a Communication in June 2002 explaining how the EC rules would in future apply to coal and steel: [2002] OJ C152/5.

B. ATOMIC ENERGY

The Euratom Treaty 1957 established the European Atomic Energy Community in respect of the non-military use of nuclear energy. Article 305(2) EC provided that the EC competition provisions applied to nuclear energy insofar as they did not derogate from the Euratom Treaty. That article was repealed by the Treaty of Lisbon. The Commission has taken a number of decisions on horizontal co-operation agreements in the industry, including the commitments decision *Siemens/Areva* in 2012[103] dealing with non-compete obligations in a joint venture agreement.

C. AGRICULTURE

The Common Agricultural Policy (CAP) is set out in Articles 38–44 TFEU. Its objectives are set out in Article 39.[104] In December 2021, the Council adopted the CAP for 2023–2027, paving the way 'for a fairer, greener and more performance-based CAP'[105] as part of the drive to sustainability reflected in the Green Deal,[106] and the 'Farm to Fork' strategy, intended to shift the EU food system towards a sustainable model.[107]

Article 42 TFEU provides that the competition rules apply to the production of and trade in agricultural products (listed in Annex 1) only to the extent determined by the European Parliament and the Council. This means that the CAP takes precedence over the objectives of the Treaty in the field of competition and also recognises the EU legislature's power to decide to what extent the rules on competition are to be applied in the agricultural sector.[108] However, the maintenance of effective competition on the markets for agricultural products is one of the objectives of the CAP[109] and it is not a 'competition free zone'.[110]

The CAP was reformed in 2013 and set out in four Council regulations.[111] One of these, the 'Common Market Organisation (CMO) Regulation', as amended[112] contains the competition rules applicable to agriculture. Article 206 thereof states that the standard competition rules apply to agricultural products, save for the exclusions set out in the Regulation. These now include, in Article 210A, agreements aimed at achieving sustainability objectives by applying standards higher that what is mandatory under EU and/or national laws.[113]

In respect of fisheries and aquaculture products, the competition rules are set out in Regulation 1379/2013.[114] As with agricultural products, the standard competition rules apply subject to some derogations.

[103] COMP/39.736, OJ C280/8.

[104] Increase agricultural productivity, ensure a fair standard of living for agricultural community, stabilise markets, assure availability of supply, and ensure reasonable prices for consumers.

[105] <www.consilium.europa.eu/en/press/press-releases/2021/12/02/council-adopts-fairer-greener-and-more-performance-based-farming-policy-for-2023-2027/>.

[106] Communication from the Commission, 'The European Green Deal', COM(2019) 640 final, see Chap. 1, Section 2.B.ii.

[107] Communication from the Commission, 'A Farm to Fork Strategy for a fair, healthy and environmentally-friendly food system', COM(2020) 381 final, <www.consilium.europa.eu/en/policies/from-farm-to-fork/>.

[108] Case C-671/15, *President of the Autorité de la Concurrence v Association des Producteurs Vendeurs d'Endives (APVE) and others* (the *Endives Cartel*) EU:C:2017:860, para. 37, citing Case C-280/93, *Germany v Council* EU:C:1994:367, para. 61, and Case C-456/00, *France v Commission* EU:C:2002:753, para. 33.

[109] Case C-137/00, *Milk Marque and National Farmers' Union* EU:C:2003:429, paras. 57 and 58; Case C-671/15, *APVE*, n. 108, para. 48.

[110] Case C-137/00, *Milk Marque and National Farmers' Union*, n. 109, para. 61; Case C-671/15, *APVE*, n. 108, para. 47.

[111] Reg. 1305/2013 [2013] OJ L347/487, Reg. 1306/2013 [2013] OJ L347/549, Reg. 1307/2013 [2013] OJ L347/608, and Reg. 1308/2013 [2013] OJ L347/671; there was also a transitional Regulation, Council Reg. 1310/2013 [2013] OJ L347/865.

[112] Reg. 1308/2013 as amended by the 'Omnibus Regulation' Reg. 2017/2393 [2017] OJ L350/15 and further by Council Reg. 2021/2117 [2021] OJ L435/262.

[113] In January 2023, the Commission published draft Guidelines on how to design sustainability agreements in the field of agriculture, using this exclusion, and launched a public consultation, IP/23/102.

[114] [2013] OJ L354/1, Art. 40. In July 2022, the Council approved the Strategic Guidelines for more sustainable and competitive EU aquaculture, COM/2021/236 final, Council Press Release 680/22.

D. TRANSPORT

The transport sector, once characterised by national legal monopolies in respect of rail and air transport, has since 2000 gradually been liberalised and brought within the general competition regime from which it was originally excluded by Regulation 141.[115] Council Regulation 487/2009[116] provides for block exemptions in the air transport sector but currently there are no such exemptions in force. The maritime transport sector was previously subject to an especially generous regime but now only a block exemption for shipping consortia providing international liner shipping services from or to one or more EU ports remains.[117] In respect of inland transport, there remains a limited block exemption, applicable to rail, road, and inland waterways, for technical agreements, and agreements of groups of small and medium-sized undertakings (SMEs).[118] In the rail sector, freight was fully liberalised from 1 January 2007 and international passenger services as from 1 January 2010.[119] The Single European Railway Area was provided for in Directive 2012/34[120] and the 'Fourth Railway Package' of 2016 was a set of six legislative texts designed to complete it.[121]

E. OTHER SECTORS SUBJECT TO LIBERALISATION

The EU embarked on programmes of liberalisation and/or harmonisation of the energy, telecommunications, broadcasting, and financial services sectors with the aim of opening them up to greater competition. The relationship between competition law and the specific regulatory regimes which apply to these sectors is discussed in Chapter 1.[122] There has been little sympathy for the claims that these sectors should receive favourable treatment and should be protected from the competitive process and there has been a plethora of competition decisions concerning them.[123] The Commission is also concerned with the application of the competition rules to professional services.[124]

[115] (1959–62) OJ Spec. Ed. 291. The EU provisions on transport generally are set out in Arts. 90–100 TFEU. The exclusion of certain maritime transport services from Reg. 1/2003 by Art. 32 was removed by Council Reg. 1419/2006 [2006] OJ L269/1. Until Reg. 411/2004 [2004] OJ L68/1, the competition rules did not apply to aviation between the EU and third countries. Reg. 1/2003 now applies to the enforcement of the competition rules in the transport sector. See L. Ortiz Blanco and B. Van Houtte (eds.), *EU Competition Law and Regulation in the Transport Sector* (2nd edn, Oxford University Press, 2017).

[116] [2009] OJ L148/1.

[117] Council Reg. 246/2009 [2009] OJ L79/1 gives the Commission power to adopt block exemptions in respect of international liner consortia. Pursuant to this the Commission adopted Reg. 906/2009 [2009] OJ L256/31, currently extended by Reg. 2020/436 [2020] OJ L90/1 to 25 April 2024. The Commission Guidelines on the application of Art. 101 to maritime transport services, [2008] OJ C245/2 were not renewed upon their expiry in 2013. In 2022, the Commission embarked on an evaluation of Reg. 906/2009, to decide whether or not to renew or replace it.

[118] Council Reg. 169/2009 [2009] OJ L61/1.

[119] Dir. 2007/58/EC [2007] OJ L315/44; IP/09/2001. [120] [2012] OJ L343/32.

[121] Council Reg. 2016/796 [2016] OJ L138/1; Dir. 2016/797 [2016] OJ L138/44; Dir. 2016/798 [2016] OJ L138/102; Council Reg. 2016/2337 [2016] OJ L352/20; Council Reg. 2016/2338 [2016] OJ L352/22; and Dir. 2016/2370 [2016] OJ L352/1, <https://ec.europa.eu/transport/modes/rail/packages/2013_en>.

[122] See Chap. 1, Section 11.

[123] See Chap. 7. The Commission undertook a sector inquiry under Reg. 1/2003, Art. 17 in respect of the energy sector, see Chap. 9. Art. 102 is rigorously applied to the energy sector in order to make liberalisation effective. See P. Cameron, *Competition in Energy Markets* (2nd edn, Oxford University Press, 2007). For 'universal service' obligations, see further Chap. 8.

[124] The Commission produced two reports: 'Report on Competition in Professional Services', COM/2004/0083 final, February 2004; and 'Professional Services—Scope for More Reform', COM/2005/0405 final, in September 2005. As a follow-up the European Parliament passed a resolution in December 2006 supporting the Commission's moves to rid the professional services sector of overly restrictive regulation (often put in place, or maintained, by the actions of Member States). For the regulation of the legal profession, see the discussion of Case C-309/99, *Wouters v Algemene Raad van de Nederlandse Orde van Advocaten* [2002] ECR I-1577 in Chaps. 4 and 5. See further I. E. Wendt, *EU Competition Law and Liberal Professions: An Uneasy Relationship?* (Martinus Nijhoff, 2012).

F. SPORT

By Article 165 TFEU, the EU 'shall contribute to the promotion of European sporting issues . . .'. However, sport is not immune from the EU competition rules[125] as was made clear by the CJ in *Meca-Medina*.[126]

Early cases on EU law and sport concerned the application of the free movement provisions to sporting rules. The CJ established that the practice of sport was subject to Community law insofar as it constituted an economic activity.[127] Competition law is therefore applied to the commercial aspects of sport[128] which have huge economic impact in the EU.[129] The Commission has at times been particularly concerned with the joint sale and acquisition of media rights to sporting events[130] and with ticketing arrangements (including exclusivity deals concerning the sponsors' credit cards).[131] Furthermore, cases on the commercial aspects of sport have reached the CJ from national courts.[132]

A governing body of some sort is essential in organised competitive sport. There have to be rules and conditions and competitions need to be coordinated and regulated.[133] Sports governing bodies may be an association of undertakings for the purposes of Article 101[134] or be in a dominant[135] or collectively dominant[136] position for the purposes of Article 102.

[125] <https://competition-policy.ec.europa.eu/sectors/sports_en>. See generally Annex 1 to the Staff Working Document accompanying the Commission White Paper on Sport of July 2007, 'The EU and Sport: Background and Context', SEC(2007)935, accompanying the White Paper, COM(2007) 391 final; P. Kienapfel and A. Stein, 'The Application of Articles 81 and 82 EC in the Sports Sector' (2007) 3 *Competition Policy Newsletter* 6; E. Szyszcak, 'Competition and Sport' (2007) 32 *ELRev* 95; S. Van den Bogaert and A. Vermeersch, 'Sport and the EC Treaty: A Tale of Uneasy Bedfellows?' (2006) 31 *ELRev* 821; O. Budzinski and S. Szymanski, 'Are Restrictions of Competition by Sports Associations Horizontal or Vertical in Nature?' (2015) 11 *J of Competition Law and Economics* 409; P. Ibáñez Colomo, 'Competition Law and Sports Governance: Disentangling a Complex Relationship' (2022) 45(3) *World Competition* 321, <https://papers.ssrn.com/sol3/papers.cfm?abstract_id=4130043>; B. Keane and B. Foster, 'Survey on Competition Policy Developments in the Sports Sector 2018–2021' (2021) 12(8) *JECLAP* 655.

[126] Case C-519/04, *Meca-Medina and Majcen v Commission* EU:C:2006:492.

[127] Case 36/74, *Walrave and Koch v Association Union Cycliste Internationale* EU:C:1974:140; Case 13/76, *Donà v Mantero* EU:C:1976:115. The free movement rules were applied to the transfer system in professional football in Case C-415/93, *URBSFA v Bosman* EU:C:1995:463.

[128] See section 3 of Annex 1 to the Commission Staff Working Document, n. 125.

[129] The Commission found that in 2012 sport-related GDP in the EU was €279.7 bn, or 2.12% of the total GDP, and that 5.67 million employees could be attributed to sport, a share of 2.72%: Commission, DG for Education, Youth, Sport and Culture, *Study on the economic impact of sport through sport satellite accounts* (Publications Office, 2018), <https://data.europa.eu/doi/10.2766/156532>.

[130] COMP/37.398, *Joint selling of the commercial rights of the UEFA Champions League* [2003] OJ L291/25; COMP/37.214, *Deutsche Bundesliga* [2005] OJ L134/46; COMP/38.173, *FA Premier League* 22 March 2006; and Annex 1 to the Commission Staff Working Document, n. 125, section 3; Cases T-528, 542, 543, and 546/93, *Métropole Télévision SA v Commission* EU:T: 1996:99; Case T-206/99, *Métropole Télévision SA v Commission* EU:T:2001:101; Cases T-185, 216, 299, and 300/00, *Métropole Télévision SA (M6) v Commission* EU:T:2002:242, *aff'd* Case C-470/02 P, EU:C:2004:565. For the sale of media rights, see also T. Toft, 'Developments in European Law', Speech to the Sports and Law Congress, Berlin, 28 April 2006, <http://ec.europa.eu/competition/speeches/text/sp2006_003_en.pdf>.

[131] COMP/33.384 and COMP/33.378, *FIFA World Cup 1990* [1992] OJ L326/31; COMP/36.888, *1998 Football World Cup* [2000] OJ L5/55; COMP/39.177, *Which?/DFB, Mastercard and FIFA*, IP/05/519.

[132] Such as Cases C-403 and 429/08, *Football Association Premier League v QC Leisure* and *Karen Murphy v Media Protection Services Ltd* EU:C:2011:631 (broadcasting of FAPL matches in the UK using unauthorised non-UK decoder): the cases also concerned the free movement of services.

[133] See Ibáñez Colomo, n. 125.

[134] As in COMP/40.208, *International Skater's Union Eligibility Rules (ISU)*, discussed later, where the ISU was found to be an association composed of individual national ice-skating associations which administered skating and conducted economic activity in respect of skating at the national level.

[135] See e.g. Case C-49/07, *Motosykletistiki Omospondia Ellados NPID (MOTOE) v Elliniko Dimosio* EU:C:2008:376 (Greek Motorcycling Federation).

[136] See Case T-193/02, *Laurent Piau v Commission* EU:T:2005:22 (FIFA).

Meca-Medina concerned the International Olympic Committee's (IOC's) doping rules for swimming. The CJ held that the competition rules do not apply to matters which are of a 'purely sporting interest and, as such, have nothing to do with economic activity'[137] but recognised 'the difficulty of severing the economic aspects from the sporting aspects of a sport'.[138] It said:

> . . . it is apparent that the mere fact that a rule is purely sporting in nature does not have the effect of removing from the scope of the Treaty the person engaging in the activity governed by that rule or the body which has laid it down.
>
> If the sporting activity in question falls within the scope of the Treaty, the conditions for engaging in it are subject to all the obligations which result from the various provisions of the Treaty . . .[139]

In *Meca-Medina*, the Court accepted that governing bodies may have rules which are necessary for regulating sporting activity even if they limit competition, because such a limitation is 'inherent in the organisation and proper conduct of competitive sport and its very purpose is to ensure healthy rivalry between athletes'.[140] Nevertheless, EU law must be the judge of whether the restrictive rules are compatible with the competition rules, which means that they must pursue a legitimate objective and that the restrictions must be inherent and proportionate to reaching that objective.[141] In *Meca-Medina*, the Court found the Commission to be justified in considering that the IOC doping rules were legitimate and that the penalties imposed (exclusion for two years) were compatible with the competition rules.[142]

The Commission does not, therefore, intervene in what it considers to be pure sporting issues, and cooperates with sporting bodies in trying to reach a consensus on regulatory and organisational matters with economic implications.[143] In *Laurent Piau*, it upheld the Commission's rejection of a complaint about UEFA's rules on licensing football agents[144] and it dismissed three appeals against Commission rejections of complaints, one of which concerned the sanctions imposed on Juventus in the Italian match-rigging scandal.[145]

Governing bodies are facing increasing attempts by independent sports operators to mount breakaway events outside the established structures. In *ISU*,[146] the Commission found that the

137 Case C-519/04, *Meca-Medina* EU:C:2006:492, para. 25. 138 Ibid., para. 26.

139 Ibid., paras. 27–28. 140 Ibid., para. 45. 141 Ibid., para. 42.

142 The CJ set aside the GC's judgment (Case T-313/02, EU:T:2004:282) which had granted sporting rules a more extensive 'safe harbour' from the competition provisions (the outcome for the appellants was the same).

143 See COMP/39.732, *BRV/FIA, FIM and others* 4 August 2011 (Commission rejected a complaint re FIA regulations on Formula 1 engine specifications); COMP/36.583, *FGTB/FIFA/Ligue Football/SETCA/URBSFA* 28 May 2002 (FIFA adopted international player transfer rules acceptable to the Commission); COMP/35.163, *FIA*; COMP/36.638, *FIA/FOA*; and COMP/36.776, *GTR/FIA* [2001] OJ C169/5, IP/01/1523 (FIFA, in order to prevent conflicts of interest, agreed to limit its regulatory role and to remove certain restrictions on the parties' commercial activities); COMP/36.851, *UEFA* [1999] OJ C363/2 (Commission rejected a complaint against UEFA's 'home and away' rule that each club must play its home matches at its own ground, IP/99/965); COMP/37.362, *UEFA* (Commission closed investigation into UEFA's rule precluding more than one club belonging to the same owner from taking part in the same competition as it was justified by the need to guarantee the integrity of competitions, IP/02/942).

144 Case T-193/02, *Laurent Piau v Commission* EU:T:2005:22.

145 Case T-273/09, *Associazione 'Giùlemanidallajuve' v Commission* EU:T:2012:129; the decision was COMP/39.464, *Supporters Juventus Turin—FIGC-CONI-UEFA-FIFA*. The other two cases were Case T-508/09, *Cañas v Commission* EU:T:2012:152, upheld Case C-269/12 P, *Cañas v Commission* EU:C:2013:415 (anti-doping sanctions in tennis) and Case T-341/10, *F91 Diddeleng* EU:T:2012:183 (rules of the Luxembourg FA).

146 COMP/40.208, *International Skater's Union Eligibility Rules (ISU)*. Case C-49/07, *MOTOE v Elliniko Dimosio* EU:C:2008:376 also concerned breakaway sports events, but in the context of administrative powers given to a sports body by the State, and it is therefore discussed in Chap. 8.

'Eligibility Rules' of the International Skating Union (ISU), which imposed a lifetime ban from all ISU-mandated competitions on athletes participating in non-ISU-mandated events, infringed Article 101 by both object and effect.[147] The complaint to the Commission was triggered by the ISU's refusal to authorise a 'Dubai Grand Prix' event.[148] The Commission found that at the time there was no formal authorisation procedure in place for recognising third party commercial events[149] and that the 'Eligibility Rules' were designed to exclude competitors. The GC upheld the finding of the existence of a restriction of competition by object and did not therefore examine whether there was a restriction by effect,[150] but said that governing bodies *are* entitled to have a pre-authorisation system in place, to protect common standards, fairness, and physical and ethical integrity.[151] The ISU's problem was that its eligibility rules contained only vague expressions that did not meet the GC's criteria.

In April 2021, the formation of a European football 'Super League' was announced.[152] UEFA and FIFA refused permission for the League, pursuant to their prior authorisation rules, and announced sanctions which included threats to exclude participating clubs from any other football competition at domestic, European, or world level and denying their players the opportunity to represent national teams. Although nine of the 12 founder members withdrew, the Super League company sued UEFA and FIFA in Spain, claiming infringement of Articles 101 and 102. The Madrid court made a reference to the CJ.[153]

In December 2022, Advocate General Rantos gave Opinions in the *ISU* and *Super League* cases on the same day. In *ISU*, he disagreed that there was a restriction by object and recommended setting aside the GC's judgment and referring the case back to the GC for consideration as to whether there was a restriction by effect. In *Super League*, he considered that the restrictive effects arising from the prior authorisation scheme appeared inherent in, and proportionate for achieving, the legitimate objectives pursued by UEFA and FIFA which are related to the specific nature of sport. Sanctions involving exclusion targeted at players who have no involvement in the project were, however, disproportionate.[154]

G. SECURITY CONNECTED WITH MILITARY EQUIPMENT

Article 346(1)(b) provides that the Treaty shall not preclude any Member State from taking 'such measures as it considers necessary for the protection of the essential interests of its security which are connected with the production of or trade in arms, munitions and war material; such measures shall not adversely affect the conditions of competition in the internal market regarding products which are not intended for specifically military purposes'. This provision has, for example, been used by Member States to retain jurisdiction over mergers with a military significance.[155] A list of the

[147] For the distinction between restrictions by object and restrictions by effect, see Chap. 5, Section 3.

[148] Organised by a Korean undertaking which planned to organise events at which people could bet, although there would not be any betting at the test event in Dubai. The ISU objected to betting.

[149] COMP/40.208, *ISU*, para. 175.

[150] Case T-93/18, *International Skating Union v Commission* EU:T:2020:610, on appeal Case C-124/21 P, judgment pending.

[151] Ibid., para. 108; see Keane and Foster, n. 125, 655–658.

[152] Certain elite European football clubs would form a closed league to play each other in a format which did not provide for relegation or promotion, instead of participating in UEFA's Champions League.

[153] Case C-333/21, *European Super League Company v UEFA and FIFA*, judgment pending.

[154] *ISU* Opinion, EU:C:2022:988; *Super League* Opinion, EU:C:2022:993.

[155] See Chap. 15. For Art. 346 TFEU generally, see P. Koutrakos, *Trade, Foreign Policy and Defence in EU Constitutional Law* (Hart Publishing, 2001).

products covered by Article 346(1)(b) is contained in a Council decision of 1958.[156] The provision is interpreted strictly and a Member State relying on it must prove that it is necessary to have recourse to it in order to protect its essential security interests.[157]

8. THE COMPETITION RULES AND THE EUROPEAN ECONOMIC AREA

The agreement establishing the European Economic Area (EEA) came into force on 1 January 1994. The EEA creates a free trade area between the EU and the European Free Trade Area (EFTA) countries except Switzerland.[158] The EEA competition rules are modelled on those in the EC Treaty (now the TFEU). References to trade between the contracting parties replace references to trade between Member States. The agreement effectively extends to the territory of the relevant EFTA States the EU competition rules and all the rules governing the internal market, including intellectual property.

Article 53 EEA is modelled on Article 101 TFEU, Article 54 EEA is modelled on Article 2, Article 59 EEA is modelled on Article 106, and Article 57 EEA effectively applies the rules set out in the EUMR to the EEA.

The EFTA Surveillance Authority (ESA) is entrusted, together with the Commission, with the enforcement of the EEA competition rules. The EEA Agreement sets out when the ESA or the Commission has jurisdiction over a particular case. Essentially the ESA has jurisdiction where:

(a) only trade between the EFTA States is affected; or

(b) trade between one or more EFTA States and the EU is affected and the turnover of the undertakings concerned in the EFTA States is one-third or more of the total turnover of those undertakings in the EEA as a whole.[159] Where, however, trade in the EU is affected to an appreciable extent the Commission and not the ESA has jurisdiction.[160] The Commission has jurisdiction in all other cases.

The EEA Agreement also established an EFTA Court. It has jurisdiction in competition matters to deal with appeals from the ESA, infringement actions brought by the ESA against EFTA States, and the settlement of disputes between two or more EFTA States.[161]

9. CONCLUSIONS

1. The EU competition rules are primarily contained in Chapter 1 of Title VII of the TFEU.

2. The two main competition Articles are Article 101TFEU which applies to agreements between undertakings and Article 102 which applies to the conduct of undertakings in a 'dominant position'.

3. Articles 101 and 102 are supplemented by Article 106 (public undertakings, undertakings with special or exclusive rights, and those entrusted with services of general economic interest) and by procedural Articles (Articles 103, 104 and 105).

[156] Council Decision 255/58. [157] Case C-284/05, *Commission v Finland* EU:C:2009:778, paras. 46–49.

[158] Switzerland did not join the EEA after membership was rejected in a referendum. As Austria, Finland, and Sweden joined the EU on 1 January 1995, the only States which are in the EEA and not also in the EU, as at 25 November 2022, are Liechtenstein, Iceland, and Norway. Switzerland has special bilateral arrangements with the EU.

[159] EEA Agreement, Art. 56(1)(a) and (b). [160] Ibid., Art. 56(1)(c) and (3). [161] Ibid., Art. 108(2).

4. The competition Articles were held by the CJ to be a specific working out of Article 3(1)(g) EC, now in effect Protocol 27 to the TEU and TFEU.

5. The control of mergers is governed by Council Regulation 139/2004 (the EUMR).

6. The EU competition rules are primarily enforced by administrative bodies by way of 'public' enforcement. This has affected the development of the law because the Commission has chosen which cases to bring and has been able to prioritise.

7. The European Commission enforces the EU competition rules through DG Comp, the Competition Directorate-General. However, the modernisation embodied in Regulation 1/2003 decentralised enforcement to the NCAs of the Member States which form, together with the Commission, the European Competition Network (ECN). The Commission inaugurated a review of Regulation 1/2003 in 2022.

8. The competition rules are directly applicable and can be enforced in national courts.

9. The enforcement and application of the competition rules must be seen in the context of the EU legal order as whole.

10. FURTHER READING

A. Books

Bellamy and Child (D. Bailey and L. John, eds.), *European Union Law of Competition* (8th edn, Oxford University Press, 2018), 1.001–1.081

Castillo de la Torre, F., and Gippini Fournier, E., *Evidence, Proof and Judicial Review in EU Competition Law* (Edward Elgar, 2017)

Craig, P., and De Búrca, G., *EU Law: Text, Cases, and Materials* (6th edn, Oxford University Press, 2015), Chaps. 1, 2, 4, 11

Hartley, T. C., *The Foundations of European Community Law* (8th edn, Oxford University Press, 2014)

Ibáñez Colomo, P., *The Shaping of EU Competition Law* (Cambridge University Press, 2018), Chaps. 1 and 2

Stefan, O., *Soft Law in Court: Competition Law, State Aid and the Court of Justice of the European Union* (Kluwer, 2013)

de Vries, S., Bernitz, U., and Weatherill, S., (eds.), *The Protection of Fundamental Rights in the EU after Lisbon* (Hart Publishing, 2013)

de Vries, S., Bernitz, U., and Weatherill, S. (eds.), *The EU Charter of Fundamental Rights as a Binding Instrument* (Hart Publishing, 2015)

B. Articles

Budzinski, O., and Szymanski, S., 'Are Restrictions of Competition by Sports Associations Horizontal or Vertical in Nature?' (2015) 11 *J of Competition Law and Economics* 409

Cosma, H. A., and Whish, R., 'Soft Law in the Field of EU Competition Policy' (2003) 14 *European Business Law Review* 25

Da Cruz Vilaça, J. L. 'The Intensity of Judicial Review in Complex Economic Matters—Recent Competition Law Judgments of the Court of Justice of the EU' (2018) 6 *J of Antitrust Enforcement* 173

Garcia, B., Vermeersch, A., and Wetherill, S., 'New Horizons in European Sports Law: The Application of the EU State Aid Rules Meets the Specific Nature of Sport' (2017) 13(1) *European Competition Journal* 28

Hadroušek, D., and Smolek, M., 'Solving the European Union's General Court' (2015) 40 *ELRev* 188

Ibáñez Colomo, P., 'Competition Law and Sports Governance: Disentangling a Complex Relationship' (2022) 45(3) *World Competition* 321, available at <https://papers.ssrn.com/sol3/papers.cfm?abstract_id=4130043>

Keane, B., and Foster, B., 'Survey on Competition Policy Developments in the Sports Sector 2018–2021' (2021) 12(8) *JECLAP* 655

Lefevre, S., 'Interpretative Communications and the Implementation of Community Law at National Level' (2004) 29 *ELRev* 808

Robertson, A., 'Agriculture and Competition Law: Some Recent Developments' [2018] *ECLR* 293

Townley, C., and Türk, A., 'The Constitutional Limits of EU Competition Law—United in Diversity' (2019) 64(2) *Ant Bull* 235

3

MARKET POWER, MARKET DEFINITION, AND BARRIERS TO ENTRY

1. CENTRAL ISSUES

1. Market power is the central concept of competition law.
2. Market power can be assessed by the direct or indirect method. EU competition law, like most systems of competition law, employs the indirect method.
3. The indirect method involves first identifying the 'relevant market', so that market shares can be assessed, and then identifying what barriers exist to entry on to, or exit from, that market.
4. The first step, identifying the relevant market, entails an exercise in market definition. The purpose of market definition is to identify which goods or services are such close substitutes that they exert competitive pressure on the behaviour of the suppliers of those goods or services. Substitutability has two aspects, demand substitutability and supply substitutability. Potential competition is also important but normally taken into account at a later stage of the analysis.
5. The relevant market has both a product and a geographic aspect and both must be defined.
6. The market may be identified by using qualitative or quantitative criteria. In 1997, the Commission adopted a Notice on the Definition of the Relevant Market. The Notice favoured the use of quantitative criteria, in particular the Hypothetical Monopolist, or Small but Significant Non-transitory Increase in Price, Test (HMT and SSNIP). This postulates a small but significant increase in the price of one product and looks at the effect on the demand for another. Customers who will change in the event of a price rise are called marginal customers.
7. There are problems in applying the HMT/SSNIP test. One of these, in non-merger cases, is the 'cellophane fallacy' which arises because the test cannot identify whether or not the current price from which the rise is postulated is already a monopoly price. Another is its unsuitability in zero-price markets.
8. The digital economy presents significant challenges for market definition. In particular, digital platforms are multi-sided markets where all sides of the market have to be taken into account in the definition exercise, zero-prices are a feature, and competition is not just between products but between ecosystems.
9. The Commission embarked on a revision of the Market Definition Notice in 2020 and published a draft of a new notice in

November 2022. The draft draws on the case law of the EU Courts and the Commission's cases in the intervening 25 years. It concentrates less on price-based tests and more on the other parameters of competition. It engages with the issues in the digital economy.

10. There are a number of particular issues which can arise in defining markets, apart from those in the digital economy. These include differentiated products and chains of substitution, aftermarkets, markets for inputs, pharmaceutical markets and markets in highly innovative industries.
11. High market shares may not be significant in competition terms if other firms can enter the market. The factors which prevent firms from entering, or expanding on, a market are known as barriers to entry.
12. Barriers to entry include sunk costs, structural barriers, and strategic behaviour by incumbents. Structural barriers include economies of scale and network effects.

2. INTRODUCTION

In Chapter 1, we explained that the central concern of competition law is with market power. In this chapter, we discuss generally how market power is assessed in EU competition law. The case law and the relevant Commission decisions in specific contexts are described in subsequent chapters.

3. MARKET POWER

Economists usually define market power as the ability to price above short-run marginal cost and, in the long run, above average total cost.[1] Therefore firms that, individually or collectively, are able to restrict output, increase prices above the competitive level, and earn monopoly profits are said to have market power. Concomitantly, they can influence the variety or quality of goods or services, innovation, and the other parameters of competition.[2] Most firms have some market power in the short term (for instance, customers and competitors need time to react to a price increase) but it is 'substantial' market power which endures for a significant period of time that matters.[3] In this chapter, we introduce the concepts of market definition and barriers to entry which are central to the assessment of market power in EU competition law and to the discussion throughout this book.

In 1981, a seminal paper by William Landes and Richard Posner triggered a continuing debate about the assessment of market power and the point at which the degree of market power warrants antitrust proceedings.[4] Landes and Posner advocated the use of the Lerner index to assess market

[1] See D. W. Carlton and J. M. Perloff, *Modern Industrial Organization* (4th edn, Pearson Addison Wesley, 2005), 642; S. Bishop and M. Walker, *The Economics of EC Competition Law*, (3rd edn, Sweet & Maxwell, 2010), 3–002; J. Faull and A. Nikpay, *The EU Law of Competition* (3rd edn, Oxford University Press, 2014), 1.22. For market power in EU competition law generally, see L. Ortiz Blanco, *Market Power in EU Antitrust Law* (Hart Publishing, 2012).

[2] Guidance on the Commission's Enforcement Priorities in Applying Article 82 of the EC Treaty to Abusive Exclusionary Conduct by Dominant Undertakings [2009] OJ C45/2 (the Guidance Paper), para. 11.

[3] There are other concepts of market power, such as the power to exclude competitors, which are also relevant to competition law; G. Monti, *EC Competition Law* (Cambridge University Press, 2007), 124–127; Bishop and Walker, n. 1, 3–041; and see Chap. 6.

[4] W. M. Landes and R. A. Posner, 'Market Power in Antitrust Cases' (1981) 94 *Harvard LR* 937. See the discussion in J. Vickers, 'Market Power in Competition Cases' (2006) 2 *European Competition Journal* 3.

power.[5] This expresses the concept of market power 'as the setting of price in excess of marginal cost by measuring the proportional deviation of price at the firm's profit-maximizing output from the firm's marginal costs at that output'.[6]

There are two ways of measuring a firm's market power, 'direct' and 'indirect'. The 'direct' method involves estimating market power by using econometric methods, particularly the residual demand curve (the demand curve facing a single firm).[7] This requires data which is often not available and even if it is the estimation of market power in this way may prove problematic, but it has considerable support amongst economists.[8] The 'indirect' method involves a structural approach. First the 'relevant market' is defined and then the power on that market of the undertaking under review is assessed using market share and 'barriers to entry' analysis. Barriers to entry are vital to the determination of market power by this method since it is these which enable a firm already in the market to earn monopoly profits without attracting entry by other firms. The 'indirect' method is the one most commonly used by competition authorities throughout the world.[9] It is used by the European Commission[10]and has the imprimatur of the CJ.[11]

The size of a firm's market share, both in absolute terms and relative to those of its competitors, is the usual starting point for assessing market power.[12] It is normally insufficient on its own for, as already noted, a more detailed analysis of the economic features of the market, such as barriers to entry, will also be required in order to determine the competitive constraints to which the firm is subject. However, in some areas of EU competition law market share stands proxy for market power. The current thinking of the Commission, in line with mainstream economic theory, is that many agreements between undertakings are not anti-competitive unless a degree of market power is present, although that degree may be less than that required to put an undertaking into a 'dominant position' for the purpose of Article 102. Block exemption regulations, which exempt categories of agreements from

[5] A. P. Lerner, 'The Concept of Monopoly and the Measurement of Monopoly Power' (1934) *Review of Economic Studies* 157.

[6] R. J. Van den Bergh and P. D. Camesasca, *European Competition Law and Economics: A Comparative Perspective* (2nd edn, Sweet & Maxwell, 2006), 110, give the simplest formulation as L = (P – MC)/P. See also Vickers, n. 4, 4–6.

[7] Called 'residual' as it is demand not met by other firms in the market: see Carlton and Perloff, n. 1, 66–69.

[8] For the arguments, see M. Motta, *Competition Policy* (Cambridge University Press, 2004), 116–117; J. Vickers, 'Market Power in Competition Cases' (2006) 2 *European Competition Journal* 3, 7. See also J. B. Baker and T. F. Bresnahan, 'Estimating the Residual Demand Curve Facing a Single Firm' (1988) 6 *International J of Industrial Organization* 283; J. A. Keyte and N. R. Stoll, 'Markets? We Don't Need No Stinking Markets! The FTC and Market Definition' (2004) 49 *Ant Bull* 593; S. Bhattacharya and R. Van den Bergh, 'The Contribution of Management Studies to Understanding Firm Behaviour and Competition Law' (2014) 37 *World Competition* 517, 533–535; L. Kaplow, 'Why (Ever) Define Markets?' (2010) 124 *Harvard LR* 437 (in which the author argues that 'the market definition process is incoherent as a matter of basic economic principle and hence should be abandoned entirely') and see the discussion of this article in *Antitrust Bulletin* Special Issue: L. Kaplow, 'Why (Ever) Define Markets?' (2012) 57(4) *Ant Bull* 915; D. Crane, 'Market Power Without Market Definition' (2014) 90(1) *Notre Dame LR* 31. The argument that in some cases market power can be deduced directly by observing the demand responses to price changes was put forward in the US case, *Ohio v American Express Co*, 138 S.Ct. 2274 (2018) but rejected in that case by the Supreme Court; see the criticism of this in H. Hovenkamp and F. Scott Morton, 'Framing the Chicago School of Antitrust Analysis' (2020) 168 *U Pa LR* 1843, 1872–1873.

[9] Including all the EEA countries, Australia, Brazil, Canada, Japan, South Korea, the UK, and the US, see Commission Staff Working Document, Evaluation of the Commission Notice on the definition of relevant market for the purposes of Community competition law of 9 December 1997, SWD(2021) 199 final, 12 July 2021, fn. 2. However, some competition agencies now supplement or substitute the traditional indirect analysis beginning with market definition with tools such as pricing pressure indices, particularly for mergers in differentiated product markets: see the discussion in Chap. 15, Section 5.E.ii.

[10] See Section 4.C.

[11] Case 6/72, *Europemballage Corp and Continental Can (Continental Can)* [1973] ECR 215, para. 32 and subsequent case law, including Case C-307/18, *Generics (UK) Ltd v CMA* EU:C:2020:52, para. 127.

[12] See the Guidance Paper, n. 2, para. 13 and Chap. 6.

the prohibition in Article 101(1) TFEU, are therefore drafted to apply only to situations in which the undertakings' market shares are below certain thresholds.[13] This approximation of market share with market power is simplistic but considered the most practicable way of enabling the block exemptions to be applied. The use of market share as the sole determinant is likely to overestimate rather than underestimate the market power of the undertakings concerned.

4. MARKET DEFINITION AND EU COMPETITION LAW

A. THE PURPOSE OF MARKET DEFINITION

Defining the relevant market is the first step in assessing a firm's market power by the 'indirect' method.[14] The purpose of defining the relevant market (which may include markets where goods or services are provided free of charge)[15] is to identify which products (or services or technologies)[16] are such close substitutes for one another that they exert immediate competitive constraints on the behaviour of the suppliers of those products.[17] Suppose, for example, you are suspicious that Y, the only producer of yellow widgets, is exercising market power and engaging in monopoly pricing. The preliminary question is whether or not the product has substitutes to which customers could easily turn. If it does, then if Y raises prices it will lose customers. If customers can buy blue widgets, which are perfect substitutes, from other firms a rise in the price of yellow widgets will lead customers to buy (cheaper) blue ones instead. Saying that Y has a 'monopoly' or 'market power' over the sale of yellow widgets is meaningless in economic terms. Similarly, suppose Y is the sole manufacturer of all colours of widgets. Y will still not be able to raise prices without losing customers if blodgets, which are made by other firms which can expand output, are perfect substitutes for widgets. However, it is often difficult to determine which products or services are in the same market. It is obvious, for example, that steel beams and chewing-gum are not in the same market, but what about coffee and tea, vodka and whisky, bananas and apples, Eurostar and cross-Channel ferries, comparison shopping services and merchant platforms?

It is important to remember that market definition is not an end in itself. Rather, it is a means to an end, a tool used for identifying and defining the boundaries of competition between undertakings.[18] Defining the relevant market is often a complex exercise entailing a variety of quantitative and qualitative evidence. There may be a range of possible and plausible definitions. Moreover, defining a

[13] So below the threshold there is a 'safe harbour'. See e.g. Commission Reg. 2022/720 [2022] OJ L134/4 on vertical restraints, discussed in Chap. 11 and the block exemptions on horizontal cooperation agreements discussed in Chap. 10.

[14] For market definition generally, see OECD Policy Roundtable on market definition, DAF/COMP(2012)19, <www.oecd.org/daf/competition/Marketdefinition2012.pdf>; Bellamy and Child (D. Bailey and L. John, eds.), *European Union Law of Competition* (8th edn, Oxford University Press, 2018), Chap. 4; R. O'Donoghue and A. J. Padilla, *The Law and Economics of Article 102* (2nd edn, Hart Publishing, 2013), Chap. 3; G. Niels, H. Jenkins, and J. Kavanagh, *Economics for Competition Lawyers* (2nd edn, Oxford University Press, 2016), Chap. 2; M. S. Ferro, *Market Definition in EU Competition Law* (Edward Elgar, 2019).

[15] AT.39740, *Google Search (Shopping)* Decision of 27 June 2017, mainly *aff'd* Case T-612/17, *Google and Alphabet v Commission (Google Shopping)* EU:T:2021:763, on appeal Case C-48/22 P, *Google and Alphabet v Commission*, judgment pending; and see further J. Newman, 'Antitrust in Zero-Price Markets: Applications' (2016) 94 *Wash Univ LR* 49.

[16] In this chapter, 'product(s)' is used to include services and technologies as well, unless the context otherwise requires, and similarly 'production' covers the supply of services or technologies.

[17] Draft Commission Notice on the definition of the relevant market for the purposes of Union competition law, 8 November 2022, <https://competition-policy.ec.europa.eu/public-consultations/2022-market-definition-notice_en>, (the Draft Notice), para. 5.

[18] Ibid.

relevant market does not mean that there are no competitive constraints from outside the market. The Commission has said of market definition:

> Market definition is not a policy statement. The Commission doesn't define markets, markets define themselves. A market definition is based on business reality: it is a factual and empirical exercise undertaken on a case-by-case basis.[19]

We now consider how the relevant market has been defined for the purposes of EU competition law and outline the way in which the EU institutions go about, or should go about, determining what the relevant market is in any given case.[20] The specific application of market definition in respect of Article 101, Article 102, and merger control, is discussed in context in subsequent chapters.[21]

B. THE DEFINITION OF THE RELEVANT MARKET

The definition of the relevant market is relevant in EU competition law in respect of the following:

- the application of Article 101 TFEU, where the determination of the market is ordinarily necessary before it can be determined whether or not an agreement appreciably prevents, restricts, or distorts competition;[22] however, in some cases of restriction of competition 'by object', such as horizontal price-fixing cartels, it may be unnecessary to define the market precisely as the Commission is entitled to use as the relevant market the group of products over which the undertakings have colluded;[23]
- the determination of whether or not an agreement *appreciably* restricts inter-Member State trade;[24]
- the determination of whether or not an agreement substantially eliminates competition in the internal market for the purposes of Article 101(3);
- the determination of whether a block exemption is applicable or not, because of the market share thresholds;
- establishing a breach of Article 102 TFEU prohibiting the abuse of a dominant position[25] as the application of the Article requires the existence of a dominant position in a given market 'which presupposes that such a market has already been defined';[26]

[19] Commission, 'Market Definition in a Globalised World' [2015] 2 *Competition Policy Brief*, <http://ec.europa.eu/competition/publications/cpb/2015/002_en.pdf>.

[20] See further Faull and Nikpay, n. 1, 1.134–1.189; O'Donoghue and Padilla, n. 14, Chap. 3.

[21] See particularly Chaps. 5, 6, 11, 12, and 15.

[22] Cases T-374, 375, 384, and 388/94, *European Night Services v Commission* EU:T:1998:198, paras. 93–95 and 105; Case T-62/98, *Volkswagen AG v Commission* EU:T:2000:180, para. 230.

[23] E.g. Cases T-71, 74, 87, and 93/03, *Tokai Carbon Co Ltd v Commission* [2005] ECR II-10, para. 90; Cases T-259–264 and 271/02, *Raiffeisen Zentralbank Österreich and Others v Commission* (the *Lombard Club* case) EU:T:2006:396 (*aff'd* on appeal, Cases C-125, 113, 135, and 137/07 P, *Erste Group Bank AG v Commission* EU:C:2009:576, paras. 62–63); but cf. Case T-61/99, *Adriatica di Navigazione v Commission* EU:T:2003:335 where the GC said that the relevant market could affect various issues such as the scope of the cartel and the role of particular participants.

[24] See Case C-439/11 P, *Ziegler SA v Commission* EU:C:2013:513.

[25] Case 6/72, *Continental Can* EU:C:1973:22, para. 32. On the other hand, if the conduct complained of would not amount to an abuse even if the undertaking concerned *was* in a dominant position, it may not be necessary to define the market.

[26] Case T-62/98, *Volkswagen* EU:T:2000:180, para. 230; Case T-111/08, *MasterCard Inc and Others v Commission* EU:T:2012:260, para. 171.

- the application of the Merger Regulation (EUMR), as the test is whether a merger would significantly impede effective competition in the common market, in particular by creating or strengthening a dominant position;[27]
- in the enforcement of the equivalent competition provisions of the EEA Agreement;[28]
- occasionally, the enforcement of the State aid rules[29] may require a market definition although normally the assessment is not concerned with the competitive constraints faced by the aid recipient;[30]
- occasionally, when Article 106 TFEU cases concerning public undertakings and those granted special or exclusive rights raise issues of market power.[31]

The EU Courts define the relevant market in terms of interchangeability (or 'substitutability'). The CJ has adopted a definition of a relevant market which describes the market as consisting of products[32] which are interchangeable with each other but not (or only to a limited extent) interchangeable with those outside it. This interchangeability may be with other products (blodgets as substitutes for widgets) or with the same products from elsewhere (widgets from France as substitutes for widgets from Germany). The relevant market therefore has both a product aspect (the product market) and a geographic aspect (the geographic market).

In *Continental Can*, the CJ said of the *relevant product market*:

> . . . the definition of the relevant market is of essential significance, for the possibilities of competition can only be judged in relation to those characteristics of the products in question by virtue of which those products are particularly apt to satisfy an inelastic need and are only to a limited extent interchangeable with other products.[33]

In *Generics* in 2020, the Court elaborated on this:

> . . . it is clear from settled case-law that the concept of the relevant market implies that there can be effective competition between the products or services which form part of it, and this presupposes that there is a sufficient degree of interchangeability between all the products or services forming part of the same market in so far as a specific use of such products or services is concerned. That interchangeability or substitutability is not assessed solely in relation to the objective characteristics of the products and services at issue. There must also be taken into consideration the conditions of competition and the structure of supply and demand on the market.[34]

In *Generics*, the Court expressly acknowledged the dynamism of product markets, saying that the 'interchangeability or substitutability of products are naturally dynamic, in that a new supply of products may alter the conception of the products considered to be interchangeable with a product already

[27] EUMR, Reg, 139/2004 [2004] OJ L24/1, Art. 2(2) and (3). See further Chap. 15. In merger cases the definition of the market may be left open if none of the plausible candidates would lead to concerns of a significant impediment.

[28] See Chap. 2. Section 6.

[29] For State aid, see Chap. 1, Section 14.

[30] Draft Notice, n. 17, fn. 5.

[31] Ibid.

[32] Services or technologies, see n. 16.

[33] Case 6/72, *Continental Can* EU:C:1973:22, para. 32; and similarly Case 85/76, *Hoffmann-La Roche* EU:C:1979:36, para. 28; Case 322/81, *Nederlandsche Banden-Industrie Michelin v Commission (Michelin 1)* EU:C:1983:313, para. 37; Case C-179/16, *F. Hoffmann-La Roche and ors* EU:C:2018.25, para. 51.

[34] Case C-307/18, *Generics (UK) Ltd v CMA* EU:C:2020:52, para. 129.

present on the market or as substitutable for that product and, in that way, justify a new definition of the parameters of the relevant market'.[35]

Assessing interchangeability by the 'qualitative' criteria of characteristics, price, and use can be challenging. For some products, good substitutes may be readily identifiable on this basis 'but more often than not these factors are unlikely to provide a clear basis for deciding which products should be part of the relevant market'.[36] Take, for example, the question which arose in the *Nestlé/Perrier* merger case[37] of whether sparkling mineral water is in the same market as still mineral water, tap water, orange juice, or tonic water, all of which have similar characteristics and uses. In particular, if the market is not determined scientifically too much subjectivity may be introduced into the determination, leading to the delineation of overly narrow markets. The most famous example of this was *United Brands where* the CJ upheld the Commission's finding that bananas were in a separate market from other fruit.[38]

The concept of the *relevant geographic market* was originally defined by the CJ in *United Brands*:

> The opportunities for competition under Article [102 TFEU] must be considered having regard to the particular features of the product in question and with reference to a clearly defined geographic area in which it is marketed and where the conditions of competition are sufficiently homogeneous for the effect of the economic power of the undertaking concerned to be able to be evaluated. . . . The conditions for the application of Article [102] to an undertaking in a dominant position presuppose the clear delimitation of the substantial part of the Common Market in which it may be able to engage in abuses which hinder effective competition and this is an area where the objective conditions of competition applying to the product in question must be the same for all traders.[39]

In some cases, there may also be a temporal aspect to the market, although this is usually considered as a feature of the product and therefore part of the delineation of the product market.[40]

The EU Courts recognise the degree of discretion afforded to the Commission concerning the task of market definition, which involves 'complex economic assessments'.[41] Nevertheless, the Commission's evidence must substantiate its conclusions and the Courts do occasionally overrule the Commission's definition of the relevant market, as in the first case on Article 102, *Continental Can*,[42] and the 2018 case of *Servier*,[43] in both of which rejecting the Commission's definition meant that the finding of abuse of a dominant position was annulled.

[35] Ibid., para. 130, approving the Opinion of Advocate Kokott, EU:C:2020:28, para. 222.

[36] Faull and Nikpay, n. 1, 1.143.

[37] M.190 [1992] OJ L356/1, discussed in Chap. 15.

[38] Case 27/76, *United Brands* EU:C:1978:22; see Chap. 6. Section 8.A.

[39] Case 27/76, *United Brands* EU:C:1978:22, paras. 11 and 44, see further Chap. 6, Section 8.A.

[40] However, see Draft Notice, para. 22, noted in Section 4.C.iii. However, temporal factors may come into play where there are peak/off-peak hours or seasons involved, such as the merger cases M.5467 *RWE/Essent* (generation and supply of electricity) and M.8869 *Ryanair/Laudamotion* (air passenger transport in summer as opposed to winter), see Draft Notice, para. 22.

[41] Case T-201/04, *Microsoft v Commission* EU:T:2007:289, paras. 87–89; Case T-699/14 *Topps Europe Ltd v Commission* EU:T:2017:2, para. 80.

[42] Case 6/72, *Europemballage Corp and Continental Can Co Inc v Commission* EU:C:1973:22.

[43] Case T-691/14, *Servier SAS v Commission* EU:T:2018:922, on appeal Cases C-176 and 201/19 P, judgment pending.

C. THE COMMISSION NOTICES ON THE DEFINITION OF THE RELEVANT MARKET FOR THE PURPOSES OF EU COMPETITION LAW

(i) The 1997 Notice

In 1997, the Commission published a Notice on the definition of the relevant market for the purposes of Community competition law (the 1997 Notice)[44] to 'provide guidance as to how the Commission applies the concept of relevant product and geographic market in its ongoing enforcement of Community competition law'.[45] The Commission had previously been criticised for taking an approach to market definition in Article 101 and Article 102 cases which was insufficiently economically rigorous and the Notice provided a 'modernised' framework for determining the relevant market on economic principles. It reflected the new practice the Commission had developed in the area of merger control after the EUMR came into force in 1990.[46]

The Commission stated that market definition is a tool to identify and define the boundaries of competition between firms and serves to establish the framework within which the Commission applies competition policy (para. 2). By publishing the Notice the Commission sought to increase transparency in respect of the procedures it followed and the evidence upon which it relied in reaching decisions on market definition, and thus assist undertakings in their decision-making.[47] As in respect of other Notices, by adopting and publishing its rules of conduct the Commission had imposed a limit on the exercise of its discretion from which it could not depart without being liable to be found in breach of fundamental principles of law such as equal treatment or protection of legitimate expectations.[48]

(ii) The New Notice on the Definition of the Relevant Market

In March 2020, the Commission launched an evaluation of the functioning of the 1997 Market Definition Notice and opened a public consultation exercise to gather contributions from stakeholders. The evaluation was published in June 2021.[49] In November 2022, the Commission published a draft of a new Notice and opened a further public consultation.[50]

The Commission embarked upon the reassessment of the 1997 Notice because in the intervening 23 years, during which the Commission had acquired a wealth of experience in defining markets,[51] there had been major developments in best practices in market definition. Moreover, the revolution in

[44] Commission Notice on the Definition of the Relevant Market for the Purposes of Community Competition Law [1997] OJ C372/5.

[45] Ibid., para. 1. [46] See Chap. 15.

[47] Market Definition Notice, paras. 4 and 5. The GC confirmed this role of the Notice in Case T-446/05, *Amann & Söhne GmbH & Co KG v Commission* EU:T:2010:168, paras. 137–139.

[48] Case T-446/05, *Amann & Söhne* EU:T:2010:165, para. 137, following Cases C-189, 202, 208, and 213/02 P, *Dansk Rørindustri A/S and Others v Commission* EU:C:2005:408, paras. 209–211.

[49] Press release, 'Commission publishes findings of evaluation of Market Definition Notice', 12 July 2021, IP/21/3585; Commission Staff Working Document, Evaluation of the Commission Notice on the definition of relevant market for the purposes of Community competition law of 9 December 1997, SWD(2021) 199 final, 12 July 2021. This was accompanied, inter alia, by a commissioned external support study.

[50] Commission Press Release, 'Competition: Commission seeks feedback on draft revised Market Definition Notice', 8 November 2022, <https://ec.europa.eu/commission/presscorner/detail/en/ip_22_6528>. The consultation closed on 13 January 2023.

[51] Particularly from merger cases. There were 8,738 notifications of mergers between 1990, when the EUMR first came into force, and December 2022.

markets which had taken place, above all with the evolution of the digital economy and increased globalisation, required that the Notice be updated to reflect current phenomena. In particular, the main quantitative technique adopted in the 1997 Notice, the Small but Significant Non-transitory Increase in Price (SSNIP) test, is not appropriate in zero-price digital markets. The updating of the Notice is part of the programme of reappraisal of all its competition law instruments which the Commission is carrying out in accordance with its 'A Competition Policy Fit For New Challenges' initiative,[52] discussed in Chapter 1.

The discussion in this chapter focuses on the November 2022 Draft Notice. It is a more extensive document than the 1997 Notice, gives detailed guidance derived from the recent case law of the EU Courts and the cases dealt with by the Commission, and engages with the digital economy. It focuses less on price and more on the non-price parameters of competition. It is not anticipated that the final version will differ from the Draft Notice on these major matters of principle but there may well be significant adjustments to some of the detailed provisions.

(iii) The Definition of the Relevant Market in the Notices

The definition of the relevant product market adopted by the Commission in the 1997 Notice was based on the case law going back to *Continental Can* and *Hoffmann La Roche*:

> . . . A relevant product market comprises all those products and/or services which are regarded as interchangeable or substitutable by the consumer, by reason of the products' characteristics, their prices and their intended use.[53]

The definition in the Draft Notice reflects and cites the longer one in *Generics*.[54] The definition of the geographic market is the same as that in the 1997 Notice, except for minor linguistic differences.

> **Draft Commission Notice on the Definition of the Relevant Market for the Purposes of Union Competition Law (8 November 2022)**
>
> (20) The relevant product market comprises all those products that customers regard as interchangeable or substitutable to the product(s) of the undertaking(s) involved, based on the products' characteristics, their prices and their intended use, taking into consideration the conditions of competition and the structure of supply and demand on the market . . . .
>
> (21) The relevant geographic market comprises the area in which the undertaking(s) involved supply or demand relevant products, in which the conditions of competition are sufficiently homogeneous and which can be distinguished from neighbouring areas, in particular because the conditions of competition are appreciably different in those areas . . .

There is no definition of a temporal market in the Draft Notice, but paragraph 22 says that temporal factors may come into play where there are peak/off-peak hours or seasons involved, such as in the merger cases M.5467 *RWE/Essent* (generation and supply of electricity) and M.8869 *Ryanair/Laudamotion* (air passenger transport in summer as opposed to winter).

[52] COM (2021) 713 final.

[53] 1997 Notice, para. 7, cited by GC in Case T-427/08, *Confédération européenne des associations d'horlogers-réparateurs (CEAHR) v Commission* EU:T:2010:517, para. 68.

[54] See n. 34 and accompanying text.

(iv) The General Principles of Market Definition

In the Draft Notice, the Commission sets out eight particular general principles it applies to market definition.[55] These are:

- market definition is based on the facts of the case, and the Commission is not bound to apply the definition of a relevant market in past decisions in future cases;[56]
- the definition of the relevant market includes both product and geographic markets. Market definition takes account of all the parameters of competition that customers consider relevant in the area and period assessed. These include not only price but also innovation, quality (which covers e.g. durability, sustainability, value and variety of uses, image conveyed, or security and privacy protection afforded), and availability (including lead-times, supply chain resilience, supply reliability, and transport costs). Notably, there was no reference to privacy (a concern with digital markets) or sustainability in the 1997 Notice;
- market definition is only one step in the Commission's competitive assessment and does not prejudge that assessment;
- market definition allows for the inclusion of only immediate competitive constraints in the relevant market, whereas all competitive constraints are accounted for in the (later) competitive assessment, e.g. there is a distinction between supply-side substitutes and potential competition;[57]
- when the same economic activity in terms of products and geography is concerned, the markets defined are often the same across cases and assessments, but may differ in the light of different parameters of competition, the particular undertakings involved, and the time period under consideration;
- the Commission may take into account expected transitions in the structure of the market when the case concerns a forward-looking assessment. Structural market conditions are those which affect the general dynamics of demand and supply in a market rather than only individual undertakings or consumers. In product markets, this covers the probability of new products about to come onto the market,[58] and in geographic markets it includes the trend towards internationalization;
- the concept of the 'relevant market' is unique to competition law and market definitions used in other areas of law cannot be extrapolated to competition;[59]
- the Commission need not reach a definitive conclusion on the precise relevant market where the outcome of its assessment would not change under different plausible market definitions.

D. DEMAND AND SUPPLY SUBSTITUTION

We have seen that the relevant market depends on the determination of which products in which geographic areas are substitutes for one another. If a product has perfect substitutes the sole producer of the product has no market power because if the producer tries to exploit its monopoly by raising the

[55] Draft Notice, paras. 11–18.

[56] Case T-151/05, *NVV v Commission* EU:T:209:144, para. 136.

[57] See Section 4.F.

[58] This is particularly relevant in medicinal product markets, as in Case C-307/18, *Generics (UK) Ltd v CMA* EU:C:2020:52, see n. 89 and accompanying text, and Chap. 6, Section 8.A. See also Section 4.F.ix for paras. 89–93 of the Draft Notice.

[59] Draft Notice, para. 17; the Commission specifically says that the concept of a market in the area of electronic communications is not decisive for competition law purposes.

price its customers will turn to the substitutes. There are two aspects to substitutability. *Demand substitution* is concerned with the ability of users of the product to switch to substitute products. *Supply substitution* is concerned with the ability of producers of similar products to switch to producing the relevant product. *Potential competition* is important as the behaviour of an undertaking on a market will be constrained if competitors are easily able to enter the market. Potential competition is, however, ordinarily taken into account not at the stage of market definition but further on, in the competitive assessment stage, when an undertaking's position on the already defined market is considered.[60]

When defining the relevant market both demand and supply substitutability have to be considered.[61] The 1997 Notice indicated, however, that the Commission mainly focuses on demand-side substitution,[62] and this is repeated in the new Draft Notice.

Draft Commission Notice on the Definition of the Relevant Market for the Purposes of Union Competition Law (8 November 2022)

(25) Undertakings are subject to three main sources of competitive constraints: demand substitution, supply substitution and potential competition. Demand substitution constitutes the most immediate and effective disciplinary force on the suppliers of a given product . . . An undertaking's influence over prevailing conditions of sale, such as prices, depends on the extent to which its customers can switch easily to available products that the customers consider as substitutes. . . . Supply substitution can also be relevant for the definition of the relevant market in some cases, namely when it is as immediate and effective as demand substitution. By contrast, more remote competitive constraints that do not meet the criteria of supply substitution in terms of immediacy and effectiveness require an analysis of additional factors, including the circumstances related to the conditions of entry, and are taken into account during the competitive assessment as constraints arising from potential competition. . . .

(26) The assessment of demand and supply substitution helps identify the products in the relevant market, and hence the suppliers active in the market. To provide a useful framework for the competitive assessment, market definition must also identify the customers that are likely to face similar effects of the conduct or concentration in question. Accordingly, the Commission focuses on the degree to which customers face similar or differing conditions of competition when it decides on which customers are included in the relevant market. This is relevant from a geographic perspective, where the Commission includes those areas in the relevant geographic market in which customers face sufficiently homogenous conditions of competition. The Commission may also distinguish between customer groups that face materially different conditions of competition in differing contexts, for example when there is price discrimination between different customer groups . . .

E. DEMAND SUBSTITUTION

(i) Measuring Demand Substitution in Product Markets

Demand substitution identifies which products a consumer considers to be substitutes. Unless products are totally homogeneous there will be no perfect substitutes. However, most products have imperfect substitutes. Whether or not products are substitutes for one another is dependent on a number

[60] See Chap. 6.

[61] The Commission lost the *Continental Can* case (Case 6/72, EU:C:1973:22) on the issue of demand substitution, see Chap. 6.

[62] 1997 Notice, paras. 13 and 14. Paragraph 13 was approved by the GC in Case T-177/04, *easyJet v Commission* EU:T:2006:187, para. 99.

of factors, particularly customer preference, whether customers can switch immediately or need time to adapt, whether there is similarity in quality or price, and whether the substitutes are available. The matter may be complicated if some customers can switch to substitutes but others cannot or if a product has several uses and there are substitutes for some of those uses but not for others. Products may be substitutes in one direction and not in the other (asymmetrical substitution). For example, in *Microsoft*[63] the Commission found that while a streaming media player was a substitute for a media player which delivered less functionality, substitution the other way round was not readily available as less powerful media players did not satisfy consumer demand for features such as streaming or video playback.

(ii) The SSNIP Test

In the 1997 Notice, the Commission adopted a more economically rigorous approach to market definition, favouring quantitative techniques, and particularly the hypothetical monopolist test (HMT) which is put into effect by the SSNIP test, as its preferred means of measuring cross-elasticity.

SSNIP stands for a Small but Significant Non-transitory Increase in Price.[64] The test[65] was set out in paragraphs 15–17 of the 1997 Notice. The test is as follows: a small (5–10 per cent) rise in the price of widgets is assumed. It is then asked whether this price increase would cause widget customers to purchase blodgets, or to purchase widgets from another area, to such an extent that the price rise is unprofitable (customers who are able and willing to switch are called 'marginal' customers). If the answer is yes, then blodgets and/or widgets from the other area form part of the same market. The test is then repeated for that bigger bundle of products until the point is reached when the price rise would be profitable.[66]

The EU Courts have approved the use of the SSNIP test. For example, in *AstraZeneca* the GC said, '[i]n order to evaluate the merits of the applicants' arguments, both in principle and in the specific circumstances of this case, it is necessary to place them in the theoretical framework adopted by the Commission in the Notice on market definition for the purposes of determining competitive constraints' and referred to paragraphs 15–19 of the Notice.[67] However, in paragraph 15 of the 1997 Notice the Commission described the SSNIP test as being 'one way' of determining the relevant market, not *the* way. In *Topps Europe*,[68] which concerned alleged anti-competitive practices by the well-known manufacturer of sporting collectibles, Panini, the GC considered the increasingly central role played by the SSNIP test in contemporary competition analysis. It recognised the degree of discretion afforded to the Commission concerning the task of market definition, which involves complex economic assessments and clarified that although the SSNIP test now constitutes a 'recognised

[63] COMP/37.792, [2007] OJ L32/23, para. 415, on appeal Case T-201/04, *Microsoft* [2007] ECR II-3601; see also Case T-340/03, *France Télécom SA v Commission* [2007] ECR II-107, paras. 88–90; Case T-321/05, *AstraZeneca v Commission* [2010] ECR II-2805, paras. 89–107.

[64] Note that where buying (procurement) markets are concerned, the test may involve a postulated *reduction* in price, as in the merger case, Case T-151/05, *Nederlandse Vakbond Varkenshouders (NVV) v Commission* EU:T:2009:144 where in defining the geographic market the question arose as to whether a reduction in the prices paid for pigs by slaughterhouses in some areas would lead to pig farmers exporting their pigs to slaughterhouses in other areas.

[65] Or rather 'conceptual framework'; see Draft Notice, para. 33 and Van den Bergh and Camesasca, n. 6, 131: 'The so-called SSNIP test is not a test in itself but a conceptual framework, within which several quantitative tests can be employed to address the market delineation question.'

[66] The equivalent analysis can be done in respect of purchasing markets, where the starting point is to analyse switching reactions is the supplier, see Draft Notice, fn. 45.

[67] Case T-321/05, *AstraZeneca v Commission* EU:T:2010:266, paras. 86–87. See also Case T-151/05, *NVV v Commission* EU:T:2009:144.

[68] Case T-699/14, *Topps Europe Ltd v Commission* EU:T:2017:2.

method' for market definition, it is not an indispensable one. Although it might be expected that the Commission will perform a SSNIP test as a matter of routine where the necessary data exists, it is *not* obliged to do so where the test would not prove helpful.

Case T-699/14, *Topps Europe Ltd v Commission* EU:T:2017:2

General Court

80. In that regard, it is to be noted that the Commission has a certain discretion concerning the definition of the relevant market, in so far as that definition involves complex economic assessments (see judgment of 15 December 2010, *CEAHR* v *Commission*, T-427/08, . . ., paragraph 66 and the case-law cited).

81. The concept of the relevant market in fact implies that there can be effective competition between the products or services which form part of it and this presupposes that there is a sufficient degree of interchangeability between all the products or services forming part of the same market in so far as a specific use of such products or services is concerned. The interchangeability or substitutability is not assessed solely in relation to the objective characteristics of the products and services at issue, but the competitive conditions and the structure of supply and demand on the market must also be taken into consideration (see judgment of 15 December 2010, *CEAHR* v *Commission*, T-427/08, . . . paragraph 67 and the case-law cited).

82 . . . . [A]lthough that type of economic test is indeed a recognised method for defining the market at issue, it is not the only method available to the Commission. It may also take into account other tools for the purposes of defining the relevant market, such as market studies or an assessment of consumers' and other competitors' points of view. The SSNIP test may also prove unsuitable in certain cases, for example in the presence of the 'cellophane fallacy', that is, the situation where the undertaking concerned already holds a virtual monopoly and the market prices are already at a supra-competitive level, or where there are free goods or goods the cost of which is not borne by those determining the demand. It is also apparent from point 25 of the Commission notice on the definition of relevant market for the purposes of Community competition law (OJ 1997 C 372, p. 5) that the definition of the relevant market does not require the Commission to follow a rigid hierarchy of different sources of information or types of evidence. The Commission did not, therefore, commit a manifest error of assessment in basing its conclusions on the relevant market on its assessment of the evidence gathered without having recourse to an SSNIP test.

The GC, moreover, emphasised that the fact that a portion of the relevant demand was inelastic was not determinative of the market definition, but rather the question was whether a sufficiently significant portion would switch in response to a price rise. Thus, the fact that some children would never consider switching from Panini stickers (and thus would not view alternative collectibles as substitutes) did not preclude a finding of a wider market for collectibles if a sufficient number would do so.[69] The Commission repeated that it is not obliged to apply the SSNIP test in its *Google Search (Shopping)* decision.[70]

[69] Ibid., para. 91.

[70] AT.39740, *Google Search (Shopping)* Decision of 27 June 2017, para. 243; on appeal Case T-612/17, *Google and Alphabet v Commission* EU:T:2021:763.

(iii) Problems with the SSNIP test

Because the SSNIP test is only concerned with price there are some contexts in which it cannot be applied, or cannot be applied satisfactorily, and which therefore seriously limit its utility. These include the 'cellophane fallacy', zero-priced markets, and multi-sided markets in the digital economy,[71] bidding markets (where firms bid for contracts through a tendering process), markets in which prices are subject to regulation, and any market in which the undertakings do not compete on price.

a. *The Cellophane Fallacy*

The problem of the 'cellophane fallacy', was mentioned by the GC in *Topps*.[72] Paragraph 19 of the 1997 Notice recognised the difficulties it presents for the SSNIP test (although without naming it). The fallacy arises because the SSNIP test cannot identify whether the current price from which the price rise is postulated is *already* a monopoly price resulting from the exercise of market power. It is named after the subject matter of a US case in which the Supreme Court erroneously accepted Du Pont's argument that cellophane was not a separate relevant market but competed directly and closely with other flexible packaging materials such as aluminium foil, polythene, and wax paper.[73]

The difficulty is that a profit-maximising firm will price as high as possible. If X is the sole supplier of widgets, it will normally set the price of widgets at a level where other products constrain it. If the marginal cost of a widget is €5 but blodgets, which perform the same function as widgets, are sold at their marginal cost of €10, X will sell widgets at just under £10. That way X still makes a supra-normal profit and does not lose out to the blodget manufacturers. At the price of €10 blodgets and widgets are substitutes, and X can argue, as Du Pont did in *Cellophane*, that since it cannot raise the price without losing sales it must be operating on a competitive market. Yet X is already making a monopoly profit. In the *Cellophane* case, the US Supreme Court found that the market was that for all flexible wrapping materials as other materials competed with cellophane at its current price. It did not ask, however, whether or not cross-elasticity between cellophane and other materials was only high *because Du Pont was already exercising market power*. The 1997 Notice recognises this difficulty and states that using the prevailing market price as the base figure from which to hypothesise the 5–10 per cent price rise of the SSNIP test may be inappropriate where that price has been determined in the absence of competition. This means that great care will have to be exercised in using the SSNIP test to determine whether or not an incumbent on a market has a 'dominant position' for the purposes of Article 102. Recognition of the cellophane fallacy prevented the Commission using the SSNIP test in the Article 101 case *MasterCard*.[74]

In contrast, in merger cases it has only to be decided whether or not the merger will create or increase market power. The SSNIP test is thus much more reliable since the prevailing market price is the appropriate starting point from which to assess the effects of the merger. The cellophane fallacy is a great problem because in very many markets prices do reflect some degree of market power and the failings of the SSNIP test in dealing with these is a serious limitation on its utility in non-merger cases.[75] Furthermore, it is not just an issue where prices are already set above the competitive level, but

[71] See AT.39740, *Google Search (Shopping)* Decision of 27 June 2017 and the discussion in Sections 4.I.viii and ix.

[72] Case T-699/14, *Topps Europe Ltd v Commission* EU:T:2017:2, para. 82.

[73] *United States v EI du Pont de Nemours & Co*, 351 US 377 (1956).

[74] COMP/34.579, *MasterCard* 19 December 2007, on appeal Case T-111/08, *MasterCard Inc v Commission* EU:T:2012:260 and Case C-382/12 P, *MasterCard Inc v Commission* EU:C:2014:2201.

[75] The SSNIP was pioneered by the US Department of Justice in 1982 and in the US is usually used only in merger cases; see the US 2010 Horizontal Merger Guidelines, section 4, <www.justice.gov/atr/horizontal-merger-guidelines-08192010>. And see L. White, 'The Dead Hand of Cellophane and the Federal Google and Facebook Antitrust Cases: Market Delineation Will Be Crucial' (2022) 67(1) *Ant Bull* 113 and D. Geradin, A. Layne-Farrar, and N. Petit, *EU Competition Law and Economics* (Oxford University Press, 2012), 185–186.

also where the prevailing price is too low.[76] In its *Slovak Telekom* decision in 2014, the Commission said that because of the cellophane fallacy it did not normally rely on the SSNIP test in cases based on Article 102.[77] In the Draft Notice, the Commission says that it may apply the test starting from a counterfactual price that would prevail under (more) effective competition, or may rely on other evidence.[78]

b. Zero-price Markets

Multi-sided technology markets in the digital economy[79] often feature zero-price products for which consumers on one-side do not pay in conventional monetary terms. Rather, they are subsidised by users on the other side and the service provider makes its revenue from selling advertising. In reality, consumers pay for their use of the service by their attention to the advertising and/or by giving up their personal data. However, it is not possible in such markets to satisfactorily apply the SSNIP test, relying as it does on consumers' anticipated responses to price rises.[80] In *Google Android*,[81] the Commission applied instead the test which postulates a Small but Significant Non-transitory *Decrease in Quality* (SSNDQ). The GC endorsed this.[82] In the Draft Notice, which refers to *Google Android*, the Commission describes the SSNDQ test as 'a conceptual framework for a qualitative assessment of competitive restraints' but says it does not normally engage in a quantitative application of it as it is subject to several difficulties including in respect of the quantification of quality.[83]

(iv) The SSNIP test in the Draft Notice

A great deal of the Commission's attention is now focused on digital markets and the shortcomings of the SSNIP test in that context, as well as the ongoing problems of the cellophane fallacy, have resulted in the Commission downplaying the SSNP test as a tool for identifying the relevant market. It says in paragraph 33 of the Draft Notice that other types of evidence are equally valid.

Draft Commission Notice on the Definition of the Relevant Market for the Purposes of Union Competition Law (8 November 2022)

(31) The theoretical criterion used to determine whether all sufficiently close substitutes have been identified is whether a hypothetical monopolist in the candidate market could exercise market power. This question can be assessed by asking whether a hypothetical monopolist in the candidate market would find it profitable to implement a small but significant non-transitory increase in price (the 'SSNIP test'). If such a price increase is unprofitable for the hypothetical monopolist, the process of adding additional substitutes to the candidate market continues with the addition of the next closest substitute. If the price increase is profitable for the hypothetical monopolist, the process stops and the products in the candidate market constitute a relevant market.

(32) When undertakings compete on parameters other than price, such as quality or level of innovation, this makes the application of the SSNIP test difficult, in particular in the context of zero monetary

[76] See P. Crocioni, 'The Hypothetical Monopolist Test: What It Can and Cannot Tell You' [2002] *ECLR* 355.

[77] AT.39523 *Slovak Telekom*, 15 October 2014, para. 158.

[78] Draft Notice, fn 48. [79] See Section 4.G **.

[80] See further Chap. 6, Section 8. [81] AT.40099, *Google Android* 18 July 2018.

[82] Case T-604/18, *Google Android* EU:T:2022:541, paras. 177 and 180, on appeal, Case C-738/22 P, judgment pending.

[83] Draft Notice, fn. 47.

> price products (footnote 47) and highly innovative industries. Further difficulties arise depending on the type of assessment carried out. When the assessment focuses on the change in market power of the undertaking(s) involved, such as for the analysis of concentrations involving horizontal overlaps, the SSNIP test can generally be applied at the prevailing market price. However, this may not be the case where the focus is on the assessment of the existing market power of the undertaking(s) involved, such as when defining markets in the context of assessing the existence of dominance under Article 102 TFEU (footnote 48). Moreover, practical constraints can make it difficult to apply the SSNIP test empirically when defining the relevant product market in real-life cases. For example, it may not be possible to gather reliable information on the amount of losses a hypothetical monopolist would incur when implementing a SSNIP.
>
> (33) Therefore, while the Commission may rely on the principles of the SSNIP test in its assessment of the relevant market, there is no obligation on the Commission to apply the SSNIP test empirically, and other types of evidence are equally valid to inform the market definition, as further described in section 3. . . . In fact, in many cases the SSNIP test serves only as a conceptual framework for the interpretation of available qualitative evidence.

Footnote 47 deals with the SSNDQ test and *Google Android.* Footnote 48 is a long account of the cellophane fallacy difficulty and suggests that the Commission would apply the test using a counterfactual price.

F. SUPPLY SUBSTITUTION IN PRODUCT MARKETS

In *Continental Can*,[84] the CJ held that the market must be defined by reference both to supply-side and demand-side substitutability. If most manufacturers of one product can readily switch production to another, related, product then both products may be in the same market.[85] The difficulty is distinguishing supply-side substitution from potential competition which is taken into account at the stage of the competitive assessment. The Draft Notice, paragraph 35,[86] indicates that supply substitution is relevant only where four conditions are fulfilled:

(a) most, if not all, suppliers are able to switch production;
(b) they will incur only insignificant additional sunk costs or risks in doing so;
(c) they have the incentive to do so when relative prices or demand conditions change; and
(c) they can market the products effectively in the short term.

Production which does not satisfy these conditions is not relevant at the stage of market definition, but may be important when assessing market power as if a producer can enter the market then it is a potential competitor whose existence may have a constraining effect on those operating on the market. Supply substitution is likely to be possible only where producers make products which, while not substitutes for one another from the consumer's perspective, are nonetheless similar. *Continental Can* itself concerned different types of can. An example given by the Commission in its 1997 Notice was markets for paper.

[84] Case 6/72, *Continental Can* EU:C:1973:22.

[85] The SSNIP test can be applied to supply-side substitution by postulating whether the price increase would be rendered unprofitable by other suppliers moving to produce the product; see G. Niels, 'The SSNIP Test: Some Common Misconceptions' (2004) *Comp Law* 267; Bellamy and Child, n. 14, 4.055–4.062.

[86] In the 1997 Notice supply substitution was dealt with in paras. 20–23.

Draft Commission Notice on the Definition of the Relevant Market for the Purposes of Union Competition Law (8 November 2022)

(34) The Commission may also take into account the substitutability of products from the perspective of suppliers (supply substitution). Supply substitution can be relevant when defining the relevant market where suppliers use the same assets and processes to produce related products that are not substitutes for customers, and where this leads to similar conditions of competition across the range of such related products. In such cases, it may be appropriate to include such related products in the relevant product market, provided the constraining effect of supply substitution across the range of products is equivalent to that of demand substitution in terms of effectiveness and immediacy.

(35) The necessary conditions for the market to be broadened based on supply substitution are that most, if not all, suppliers are able to switch production between products in the range of related products, while incurring only insignificant additional sunk costs or risks, have the incentive to do so when relative prices or demand conditions change, and can market them effectively in the short term.

(36) Situations of sufficiently strong supply substitution may arise typically when undertakings market a range of qualities or grades of one product. An example of the approach to supply substitution is the Commission's past assessment of the market for stainless steel slabs. In that case, the Commission found that, from a demand point of view, customers could not use different grades or families of grades for the same purpose. However, it was possible to switch from the production of one family of grades to another in a short time-frame and using the same equipment with limited additional costs. In the absence of particular difficulties in distribution, stainless steel manufacturers were able, therefore, to compete for orders of the various grades. The Commission therefore included the various grades of stainless steel in the same relevant market.

(37) Supply substitution can also be relevant for market definition when customers purchase bespoke products, for example, when customers issue tenders for construction projects or the procurement of trains or gas turbines. In such cases, there may be no or limited demand substitution between the bespoke products for different customers. Instead, the competitive constraint derives from the ability of other suppliers to produce the specific product that fits the needs of the customer. When the same suppliers can and generally do respond with offers to the specifications of different customers, the bespoke products can be included in the same relevant product market.

(38) When only some of the suppliers meet the above conditions for supply substitution, it is not appropriate to include the product range in the same relevant market. When carrying out the competitive assessment, the Commission nevertheless takes into account the competitive constraint exercised by those suppliers that meet the conditions, including whether they are likely to expand their sales of the relevant products in the future when the case calls for a forward-looking assessment. An example of this approach is the Commission's past assessment of the market for metallic coated steel. . . . The Commission did not accept supply substitution regarding tinplate and electrolytically coated chromium steel in that case because only one competing supplier was able to produce these products on the same production line and because producing both products on 'swing lines' capable of switching did not play a material role in the market. However, the Commission took into account the constraint exercised by the supplier that was able to produce tinplate and electrolytically coated chromium steel on 'swing lines' in its competitive assessment.

(39) Similarly, when supply substitution would entail the need to significantly adjust existing tangible and intangible assets outside the regular course of business, to incur more than insignificant additional investments, sunk costs or risks, to take strategic decisions of a lasting nature or to incur time delays, the Commission does not widen the relevant market based on supply substitution. This can arise even if producers are already involved in production across the range of related products. For example, although producers of cheese may in principle produce different types of cheese, there may be significant costs and lead times involved before a producer of a certain type of cheese could switch production and start selling a different type of cheese . . . In these cases, the Commission examines the effects of such switching in the competitive assessment as constraints from potential competition.

Whether or not supply-side issues are taken into account at the market definition stage is of utmost importance in cases where the only issue is market share and there is no 'competitive assessment' as referred to at the end of paragraph 39 of the Draft Notice. As already explained, a feature of current block exemption regulations is that they apply only to agreements where the parties have market shares below a particular threshold.[87] Supply-side substitution taken into account at the market definition stage may widen the market and enable the parties concerned to take advantage of the block exemption, although they would have too large a share of a narrower market. Furthermore, in cases where the question is whether an undertaking is in a dominant position, too little emphasis on supply-side substitutability may lead to over-narrow definitions of the market, a matter which is not necessarily remedied by taking into account potential competition at the stage of the competitive assessment. In particular, in effect a presumption of dominance for the purposes of Article 102 is triggered at a market share of 50 per cent so the dynamics of the assessment may be skewed by omitting supply-side substitutability.[88]

Supply-side substitutability has become an important element in cases in the pharmaceutical sector concerning entry on to the market by generic manufacturers when patent protection on the originator medicine is about to expire. The question, which was at issue in *Generics*,[89] is whether these potential competitors should be included in the relevant market. The matter is discussed in Chapter 6.[90]

G. EVIDENCE USED IN DEFINING MARKETS

(i) General

In paragraphs 46–82 of the Draft Notice, which correspond to paragraphs 25–52 of the original 1997 Notice, the Commission sets out its general approach in practice to defining markets, the evidence it uses, and the ways in which that evidence is gathered and evaluated. The Commission says that it can often identify the most plausible relevant market on readily available information, past Commission decisions, and information supplied by the undertakings concerned. This can then be adjusted in the light of evidence gained in the investigation.[91] The Commission relies on both qualitative and quantitative information and has an open approach to empirical evidence.[92] The GC has confirmed that the Commission is not required to follow a rigid hierarchy of evidence and the Commission bases its decisions on a number of factors (see later) depending on the product, industry, and circumstances.

(ii) Product Markets and Demand Substitution

The Draft Notice describes six types of evidence that may be relevant to defining the product market. Evidence used in the definition of geographic markets is described in Section H. The types of evidence in respect of product markets are characteristics, price, use, and general customer preferences; past substitution; hypothetical substitution; competitive constraints based on industry views; barriers to substitution and switching costs; and the SSNIP test.

[87] See further Chap. 5, Section 4.E.iv. The Notice on agreements of minor importance [2014] OJ C291/1, also uses market share thresholds.

[88] For a more detailed discussion, see Chap. 6.

[89] Case C-307/18, *Generics (UK) Ltd v CMA* EU:C:2020:52.

[90] Chap. 6, Section 8.A.xiv.

[91] Draft Notice, para. 46.

[92] Ibid., para. 76.

a. Characteristics, Price, and Intended Use

The factors of characteristics, price, and use have been part of the concept of the relevant market since the judgment in *Continental Can*,[93] and the case law of the EU Courts and the decisions of the Commission discussed in this book are replete with considerations of those factors in market definition.[94] However, as the Commission said in the 1997 Notice:

> . . . product characteristics and intended use are insufficient to show whether two products are demand substitutes. Functional interchangeability or similarity in characteristics may not, in themselves, provide sufficient criteria, because the responsiveness of customers to relative price changes may be determined by other considerations as well. For example, there may be different competitive constraints in the original equipment market for car components and in spare parts, thereby leading to a separate delineation of two relevant markets. Conversely, differences in product characteristics are not in themselves sufficient to exclude demand substitutability, since this will depend to a large extent on how customers value different characteristics.[95]

In the Notice, the Commission therefore described an analysis of product characteristics and intended use as 'a first step, to limit the field of investigation of possible substitutes'[96] and focused on the SSNIP test, as explained earlier.[97] After the publication of the Notice, the Commission continued to use characteristics, price, and use where appropriate, in particular where there was insufficient data to apply the SSNIP test, as was often the case,[98] and where the cellophane fallacy hindered its use in non-merger cases. In its *Michelin II* decision of 2001,[99] the Commission held, without mentioning the SSNIP test, that the market for new replacement tyres for lorries and buses was separate to that for retreads. It took into account the 'analysis of their specific characteristics and their uses by final consumers'[100] based on surveys of those consumers (the haulier firms). In the Article 102 decisions, *Microsoft*,[101] *Wanadoo*,[102] and *Clearstream*,[103] the Commission relied heavily on qualitative analysis, although in *Wanadoo* it also referred to the SSNIP test.[104] In short, the examination of characteristics and use was often not in practice confined to the 'first step' as suggested in paragraph 36 of the Notice. In *Google Search (Shopping)*,[105] the Commission relied on the features of various online services to draw distinctions between services that were functionally similar. It therefore distinguished between general search and special search, between search

[93] Case 6/72, *Continental Can* EU:C:1972: 22, para. 32, see Section 4.B, p. 115. [94] See particularly Chap. 6.

[95] 1997 Notice, para. 36. [96] Ibid. [97] Section 4.E.ii.

[98] See e.g. *Van den Bergh Foods Ltd* [1998] OJ L246/1, particularly paras. 130–138, where the Commission held that impulse ice-cream (bought as individual portions in shops for immediate consumption) and take-home ice-cream (multi-packs of single items designed for storage and consumption at home) were in different markets (it also distinguished catering ice-cream, sold in bulk to catering establishments, from impulse and take-home ice-cream, and it distinguished between the markets for industrial (produced for wide-scale distribution) and 'artisan' (produced, distributed, and consumed locally on a small scale) ice-cream). The decision was upheld in Case T-65/98, *Van den Bergh Foods Ltd v Commission* EU:T:2003:281, where the GC said that the 'distinction on the basis of the consumer's intended purpose in purchasing the ice cream in turn determines the differences in characteristics and price between impulse and take-home products' (para. 132).

[99] COMP/36.041 [2002] OJ L143/1, upheld Case T-203/01, *Michelin v Commission (Michelin II)* EU:T:2003:250: see further Chap. 6.

[100] Case T-203/01, *Michelin II* EU:T:2003:250, para. 116. [101] COMP/37.792, *Microsoft* [2007] OJ L32/23.

[102] COMP/38.233, 16 July 2003, upheld Case T-340/03, *France Télécom* EU:T:2007:22.

[103] COMP/38.096, 2 June 2004, upheld Case T-301/04, *Clearstream Banking v Commission* EU:T:2009:317.

[104] See further Chap. 6. [105] AT.39740, *Google Search (Shopping)* Decision of 27 June 2017.

engines and social networking sites, and between comparison shopping services and both special search and online marketplaces.[106]

The 2019 Report on Competition Policy for the Digital Era recognised that the difficulties in applying the SSNIP test in digital economy cases had caused the Commission to turn instead to assessing functionalities and accepted that although they lack 'the same degree of theoretical rigour that the SSNIP test has introduced', they 'may well be all we have in the case of multi-sided platforms'.[107]

The price of products may affect whether or not they are in the same market. Price may be a reflection of a product's characteristics. This is so with products which are available in cheap utility and in luxury versions, such as pens, watches, cosmetics, and perfume, where the price difference relates to characteristics which do not necessarily affect use and function. In such cases, the utility and luxury versions may be in separate product markets. In *CEAHR*, the GC accepted the Commission's distinction between cheap watches and luxury/prestige watches costing 60 to 160 times as much.[108] However, cheap and luxury products may also be part of a continuous chain of substitution in which a rise in the price of the cheapest model may lead consumers to switch to the next cheapest, and so on.[109] The switching may be one way, however, so that there are two markets, one for lower quality and higher quality versions, and one for higher quality alone.[110] In *Microsoft*, the Commission held that higher level operating systems and basic workgroup server systems were in different markets because it would be 'extremely cost inefficient' for a customer to buy a (more expensive) higher level system just to fulfil basic workgroup functions.[111] The observable fact that the prices of different products move together over time (co-movement, which can be analysed by quantitative techniques such as price correlation and stationarity tests) does not necessarily denote substitutability as it may be due to factors unrelated to demand. On the other hand, as the Commission says in a footnote to paragraph 50 below, an *absence* of co-movement indicates that the products are unlikely to be demand substitutes.

In the Draft Notice, the Commission says as follows about characteristics, price and use.

Draft Commission Notice on the Definition of the Relevant Market for the Purposes of Union Competition Law (8 November 2022)

(49) *Product characteristics, prices, intended use and general customer preferences.* Evidence on elements such as product characteristics (also including product quality or level of innovation), prices and intended use, which is often readily available, is generally useful to identify the range of possible substitutes that are available to the customers of the undertaking(s) involved.

(50) However, an assessment of whether products are similar along observable characteristics, whether their prices are comparable . . . or whether the products serve the same intended

[106] See the discussion of the decision and the appeal in Chap. 6, Section 8.A.v. See there also a discussion of AT40153, *E-book MFNs (Amazon)* Decision of 4 May 2017, in which the Commission distinguished between e-books and print books and put them into different markets.

[107] Expert report on *Competition Policy for the Digital Era* (CPDE report), prepared for the European Commission by J. Crémer, Y.-A. de Montjoye, and H. Schweitzer (2019), <http://ec.europa.eu/competition/publications/reports/kd0419345enn.pdf>, Chap. 3.D, p. 45.

[108] Case T-427/08, *CEAHR* EU:T:2010:517, paras. 73–74. The phrase 'luxury/prestige' was the Commission's interpretation of the description 'watches worth repairing' contained in the complaint whose rejection was the subject of the case.

[109] For chains of substitution, see Section 4.G.i, p. 135.

[110] COMP/38.233, *Wanadoo*; and see O'Donoghue and Padilla, n. 14, 132–133.

[111] COMP/37.792, *Microsoft* [2007] OJ L32/23, para. 376.

use may be insufficient to determine whether two products are demand substitutes. This is because such considerations may not accurately reflect the customers' value of the product attributes and how customers would react to changes in relative supply conditions such as a price increase. Conversely, differences in product characteristics, prices and intended use may not always, in themselves, be sufficient to determine that two products belong to different product markets . . .

(51) The Commission therefore assesses the underlying reasons why customers would substitute one product with another or not by seeking to identify the parameters that are most relevant for the choices of customers. A variety of parameters can drive customers' choices in addition to the product's price, such as, for example, its level of innovation or its quality in various ways, as set out in paragraph (12). Differences between distribution channels, including online and offline channels . . ., or the regulatory framework . . . can also be relevant. Identifying those parameters that are most relevant for customers' choice allows the Commission to compare the products along those parameters, which is informative to assess the degree of substitutability between them.

b. Past Substitution

Evidence of past actual substitution between products as a result of structural changes, events, or shocks in the market ('shock analysis') is 'informative' as the Commission puts it in the Draft Notice.[112] The Commission prefers evidence from substitution caused by exogenous shifts in relative supply conditions (i.e. unexpected events that have no direct effect on demand). Evidence may also be derived from new product launches, reactions to a supplier's exit from the market, or (temporary) unavailability of a product. The Commission may be able to apply quantitative tests and techniques where there is sufficient data on past substitution.[113]

c. Hypothetical substitution

As the Commission admits, evidence of hypothetical substitution—how customers are likely to react to hypothetical changes in relative conditions, gleaned from surveys and questionnaires etc.—is less reliable than evidence of actual past substitution.[114] Hypothetical demand substitution has no actual consequences for the respondents.[115] The reliability, completeness, and accuracy of this type of evidence will vary from case to case. In 'rapidly evolving industries, especially those characterised by fast technological progress, the Commission may take into account the expected changes in substitution possibilities resulting from the change in competitive dynamics'.[116]

[112] Draft Notice, para.52.

[113] Such as deriving diversion ratios or estimating own-price or cross-price elasticities, Draft Notice, para. 53.

[114] Draft Notice, para. 54.

[115] Where consumers are concerned, it is widely recognised that asking hypothetical questions may lead to biased results and that interviewees may behave in practice differently from how they answer survey questions, see M. Hughes and N. Beale, 'Customer Surveys in UK Merger Cases—The Art and Science of Asking the Right People the Right Questions' [2005] *ECLR* 297. Research on consumer behaviour has led economists to favour 'conjoint analysis' whereby the 'trade-offs' which consumers make when confronted with different products (between, e.g., price and quality, reliability and trendiness) can be built into the analysis. See B. Dunbow, 'Understanding Consumers: The Value of Stated Preferences in Antitrust Proceedings' [2003] *ECLR* 141; D. Hildebrand, 'Using Conjoint Analysis for Market Definition: Application of Modern Market Research Tools to Implement the Hypothetical Monopolist Test' (2006) 29 *World Competition* 315.

[116] Draft Notice, para. 55.

d. Evidence on Competitive Constraints Based on Industry Views

Useful information may be derived from the usual monitoring of competition that undertakings typically carry out in the normal course of business, as well as monitoring by industry associations or experts.[117]

e. Barriers and Costs from Switching

Switching costs are the price which customers pay for changing to another product. They may be financial but cover inconvenience and a range of other problems as well, as the Commission explains in the Draft Notice. They include direct and indirect network effects, which are a major concern in high-tech markets. The significance of switching costs for market definition is that they may render substitution so difficult that what might appear to be substitute products are in fact in different markets.

> There are various potential barriers to substitution and switching costs. These barriers and costs may have a wide range of origins, such as contractual obligations, costs of searching for alternative products, uncertainty about the quality and reputation of alternative products, the costs of learning to use other products or of adapting own production processes, brand recognition, regulatory barriers or other forms of state intervention, the existence of direct and indirect networks effects . . ., the costs of data portability or the degree of interoperability . . . with other products.

Barriers to switching may also arise from the inability of customers to switch between different sales channels.[118] Switching costs may act as barriers to entry[119] and may be created or increased by incumbent firms as an exclusionary tactic.[120]

f. The SSNIP Test

In paragraph 59 of the Draft Notice, the Commission considers the implementation of the SSNIP test, saying that '[i]n some cases, it may be possible to determine the boundaries of the relevant market also by assessing quantitatively whether a SSNIP would be profitable for a hypothetical monopolist'. It says that a 'critical loss analysis' is an example of an implementation of the SSNIP test. Critical loss analysis seeks to identify the smallest percentage of sales which, if lost, would make a SSNIP unprofitable, i.e. 'the critical loss is the point where the two opposing effects of a price increase offset each other so that the net effect in profits is nil'.[121] If the critical loss is greater than the likely actual loss, a SSNIP would be profitable, indicating that the products form a relevant market.[122]

(iii) Product Markets and Supply Substitution

In assessing whether the market should be widened on the supply side, the best evidence is past substitution in response to exogenous changes in supply or demand conditions. In the absence of past substitution, the Commission is less inclined to consider supply substitution equivalent to substitution on the demand side. The Commission takes into account a range of factors which may constitute barriers to switching or present incentives or disincentives.

[117] Ibid., para. 56. [118] Ibid., para. 58. [119] See Section 5.

[120] Draft Notice, para. 57. Switching costs were dealt with in para. 42 of the 1997 Notice.

[121] O'Donoghue and Padilla, n. 14, 110. [122] Draft Notice, para. 59.

Draft Commission Notice on the Definition of the Relevant Market for the Purposes of Union Competition Law (8 November 2022)

(60) *Evidence of past substitution.* When assessing supply substitution, the Commission may consider evidence from undertakings about the existence of overcapacity and their ability and incentive to redeploy production and supply in the short term. Evidence of past redeployment of production or supply to the products in question in response to exogenous changes in supply or demand conditions is particularly relevant. By contrast, absent evidence of past supply substitution, the Commission may consider it less likely that the effect of such substitution would be equivalent to that of demand substitution in terms of effectiveness and immediacy.

(61) *Barriers and costs associated with switching supply.* The Commission considers several barriers and costs when assessing the possibility of widening the market based on supply substitution. For example, it considers whether, to switch their production or supply, undertakings need to incur specific capital investments or specific investments in production processes, learning and human capital, establishment of brand or name recognition, access to data, retooling costs or other investments. Information on the existence of legal or administrative obstacles, such as the necessity of holding a particular licence, or obstacles of a strategic nature that may affect the switch of production or supply, such as contractual ties or exclusivity agreements, can also be relevant. The Commission also analyses the incentives of undertakings to switch their production or supply, including whether such a switch would lead to a loss in sales of other products, and their willingness to switch. As explained in paragraph (39), when any such barriers or costs are not insignificant, the Commission takes into account the competitive constraints (if any) exercised by such undertakings as part of the competitive assessment rather than by expanding the relevant market.

(iv) Gathering Evidence

Evidence used by the Commission should be reliable, so it is particularly useful when it comes from public authorities, or is supported by multiple sources, including by market participants with conflicting interests. Evidence is of higher probative value if it predates the Commission's investigation (including discussions of a merger) and so could not have been influenced by it.[123] The Commission may seek the views of the main customers and competitors in the industry, trade and customer associations, companies in upstream or related markets, and other stakeholders.[124] It may request information from the relevant entities, especially the undertakings involved, including business plans and other strategic documents, marketing studies, customer surveys, and data on purchasing patterns etc. Documentation prepared in the ordinary course of business is more relevant than that prepared in view of or during the Commission's investigation.[125] The Commission may conduct or commission a survey of its own,[126] and rely on public information, reports, and, where relevant, the data and views of sector regulators.[127] It may carry out visits or formal inspections at the premises of the parties and/or their customers and competitors.[128]

[123] Ibid., para. 77. [124] Ibid., para. 78. [125] Ibid., para. 79.
[126] Ibid., para. 80. [127] Ibid., para.81. [128] Ibid., para. 82.

H. THE GEOGRAPHIC MARKET

(i) General

The CJ in *United Brands* stressed the importance of defining the market from a geographic perspective.[129] As relevant markets are determined by reference to substitutability even firms producing identical products will not operate in the same market if they operate within mutually exclusive geographic areas. However where, for example, a customer in Germany may be able to substitute French widgets for German ones, the German producer will not have market power if a small but significant price rise causes its customers to purchase French widgets instead. Whether or not the geographic market in a particular product is global, regional, national, or local depends on a number of factors, including the cost of transport, the nature of the product, legal regulation and barriers (including intellectual property rights), language, and customer preferences. These factors may result in the definition of narrow markets, particularly in transport cases where markets (which are in effect both product and geographic markets) consisting of individual airports, rail routes, and ferry routes have been defined.[130]

It will be recalled that in paragraph 21 of the Draft Notice, as in paragraph 8 of the original 1997 Notice, the Commission describes the geographic market as comprising an area 'in which the conditions of competition are sufficiently homogeneous and which can be distinguished from neighbouring areas, in particular because the conditions of competition are appreciably different in those areas', faithfully following the CJ's definition in *United Brands*.[131] In *Deutsche Bahn*, the GC held that 'the definition of the geographical market does not require the objective conditions of competition between traders to be perfectly homogenous. It is sufficient if they are "similar" or "sufficiently homogeneous" and accordingly, only areas in which the objective conditions of competition are "heterogeneous" may not be considered to constitute a uniform market.'[132]

(ii) Evidence for Defining Geographic Markets

The Draft Notice says that the usual starting point for analysis is the location of the customers who would be likely to be affected by the relevant conduct or concentration.[133] It then examines a variety of evidence. The gathering and evaluation of evidence is the same as for product markets.

Draft Commission Notice on the Definition of the Relevant Market for the Purposes of Union Competition Law (8 November 2022)

(41) The Commission carries out its assessment of the conditions of competition by examining a variety of evidence. Such evidence includes, depending on the requirements and particularities of each case: the presence of different or the same suppliers across geographic areas; similarities or differences in their market shares and prices; similarities or differences in customer preferences and purchasing

[129] Case 27/76, *United Brands* EU:C:1978:22.

[130] See Chap. 6, Section 8.B, which also discusses the notable *Michelin I* case on the tyre market in the Netherlands, Case 322/81, *NV Nederlandsche Banden-Industrie Michelin v Commission* EU:C:1983:313.

[131] Case 27/76, *United Brands* EU:C:1978:22, para. 11.See also e.g. Case T-151/05, *NVV and others v Commission* EU:T:2009:144, para. 52; Case 380/17, *HeidelbergCement v Commission* EU:T:2020:471, para. 294.

[132] Case T-229/94, *Deutsche Bahn AG v Commission* EU:T:1997:155, para. 92; see also Case T-51/89, *Tetra Pak Rausing SA v Commission (Tetra Pak I)* EU:T:1990:41, paras. 91 and 92.

[133] Draft Notice, para. 40.

behaviour; barriers and costs associated with supplying customers in a different area; distance related factors affecting costs, quantities available or reliability of supply; and trade flows and patterns of shipments . . .

(42) When defining relevant geographic markets, the Commission usually also analyses demand substitution patterns—such as switching to imports—to identify the alternative supply options available to customers . . . When customers in two areas consider mostly the same suppliers as alternatives and can readily switch purchase volumes between them, this may indicate, together with other factors, that conditions of competition between both areas are sufficiently homogeneous and thus that the two areas should be part of the same relevant geographic market. Conversely, when customers in two areas regard different suppliers as alternatives or when the volumes that can and are switched to imports is limited, for instance because of customer preferences or because of limits in the import volumes available, this indicates that conditions of competition in the two areas are not sufficiently homogeneous . . .

As far as imports are concerned, the fact that products are imported from one country to another does not put the two countries into the same geographic market. There may be very different conditions of competition in the country of export to those in the country of import. However, the Commission does take account of imports into the relevant geographic market in its calculation of market shares, and in its competitive assessment at the next stage of determining market power.[134]

(iii) Categories of Evidence

The categories of evidence upon which the Commission relies include those in the following section.[135] See Chapter 6 for a discussion of the application of these in practice in Article 102 cases, and Chapter 15 in respect of mergers.

a. The Identity of Available Suppliers, Market Shares, and Prices

If customers in different geographic areas have access to the same actual and potential suppliers and the suppliers have similar market shares in different areas, it is a first indication of sufficient homogeneity for the identification of the same geographic market. Pricing and price differences are also evidence. However, there may be particular reasons for similarities or differences in market shares and prices, so further exploration is always necessary.[136]

b. Customer Preferences and Purchasing Behaviour

The Commission recognises that differences 'in culture, language, life style, demographics or socio-economic background can lead to local, national or regional preferences for specific products or brands'.[137] Good examples of this include the 1992 *Nestlé/Perrier* merger case[138] in which the Commission accepted that consumers in France simply would not buy non-French mineral water

[134] Ibid., paras. 43 and 44. This is illustrated (para. 45) by reference to the merger case M.8444 *ArcelorMittal/Ilva* where the relevant geographic market for carbon steel products was limited to the EEA because across the rest of the world market structures differed, sourcing occurred at regional level, and pricing differed.

[135] Draft Notice, paras. 64–67. [136] Ibid., paras. 64–66. [137] Ibid., para. 68.

[138] M.190 [1992] OJ L356/1, discussed in Chap. 15.

and, more recently, *Google Search (Shopping)*[139] in which the Commission found a series of national markets for general search services as the search results were tailored to each jurisdiction and provided in the local language.[140]

c. *Barriers and Costs Associated with Supplying in Different Areas*

There may be barriers and costs which render it impossible or unattractive for a supplier to competitively serve a new area. These include the whole gamut of regulatory rules imposed by the State[141] as well as customer preferences for suppliers with a local presence. At the EU level, regulatory barriers to trade are greatly reduced and even at global level there may be some harmonisation. This leads the Commission to consider that geographic markets are likely to become wider.[142]

d. *Distance-related Factors, Transport Costs, and Catchment Areas*

If transport costs are high relative to the value of the product as, for example, in the case of paving slabs, a geographic market may be small, perhaps even local, as suppliers further away will be at a significant competitive disadvantage. In paragraph 73 of the Draft Notice, the Commission gives 'sustainability considerations' as another factor—along with perishability, security of supply, and accessibility—that may have a similar effect. The Commission may define geographic markets in terms of catchment areas, often drawn around supplier locations. Catchment areas are generally measured either in terms of customers' travel distance or time (isochrones) or in terms of delivery distance or time around a location, The typical starting point is a catchment area covering 80 per cent of sales or customers.[143]

e. *Trade Flows and Pattern of Shipments*

The Commission analyses the pattern and evolution of trade flows and shipments. However, these may not be enough to show the required sufficiency of homogeneity for establishing a geographic market and the Commission may instead take imports into account at the competitive assessment stage.[144]

I. PARTICULAR ISSUES IN MARKET DEFINITION

(i) Chains of Substitution and Differentiated Products

Demand-side substitutability can be complicated by the existence of a 'chain of substitution', where B is a substitute for A and C is a substitute for B, etc. This can occur in geographic as well as product markets. In product markets, chains of substitution can arise from products with multiple uses or from versions of products sold at different prices. The leading case is *Hoffmann-La Roche*,[145] discussed in Chapter 6, which concerned a vitamin with two uses, for one of which there was no substitute while for the other there was. The 1997 Market Definition Notice discussed the chain of substitution

[139] AT.39740, 27 June 2017, paras. 252–255. [140] See further Chap. 6, Section 8.

[141] Such as tariffs and quotas, public procurement, public subsidies, price regulation, technical standards, licences and permits, linguistic requirements, and legal monopolies, see Draft Notice, para. 71.

[142] Ibid., para. 72. [143] Ibid., para. 74. [144] Ibid., para. 75.

[145] Case 85/76, *Hoffmann-La Roche & Co AG v Commission* EU:C:1979:36.

problem and concluded that the real question was how far the existence of substitutes has a constraining influence on an undertaking's pricing policy.[146]

In the Draft Notice, there is a section on differentiated products,[147] i.e. the situation where there is a range of products with different attributes which may affect customers' choices (design, brand image, service level, etc.). Depending on the facts, the Commission may define separate relevant markets within the continuum of differentiated products or one relatively broad market that includes differentiated ones. In the presence of differentiated products, the Notice says that market shares are a less important indicator of market power. That reduces the importance of market definition and puts more emphasis on the competitive assessment. In paragraph 87 on chains of substitution at the end of this section, the Commission says that it will not usually define a market where the products or areas at the extremes of the market are not directly substitutable.

(ii) Distinct Groups of Customers and Price Discrimination

Customers as a whole have different preferences and priorities but some customers may be able to turn to a substitute in response to a price rise (marginal customers) while for others it is impossible (infra-marginal customers). The most (in)famous case on this in EU law is *United Brands*[148] in which the CJ confirmed the Commission's finding that there was a market for bananas separate from that for other fruit partly on the grounds that for some consumers (the very young, the old, and the sick) bananas were a uniquely suitable fruit (they can be mashed for babies, are easily digestible, are easy to handle, and can be eaten by people with no teeth). This reasoning, however, is incorrect. The fact that bananas satisfy a unique need of a particular class of customers does not mean that bananas constitute a separate market if the average customer is not so limited in their choice and can respond to a price rise in bananas by buying other fruit. If it is impossible to discriminate against the 'infra-marginal' customers who cannot switch—the young, old, and sick—by charging them a higher price, then the behaviour of marginal customers (who are able to switch) must be taken into account.[149] It is the marginal customers who affect a supplier's pricing decisions and whose behaviour is, consequently, crucial in the determination of the market. One group of customers which has a particular need for the product is difficult to exploit unless it can somehow be kept separate from other customers and the other customers can be prevented from making sales on to the special class (arbitrage) or the profits from the special class outweigh the loss of the marginal customers.

In the 1997 Notice, the Commission recognised (despite *United Brands*) that a distinct group of customers are relevant to market definition only where they constitute a separate market and price discrimination between the different groups of customers is possible.[150]

The Draft Notice has a section on market definition in the presence of price discrimination.[151] It says that there can be distinct groups of customers constituting a narrower, distinct market, where they are charged different prices for the same product. However, three conditions must normally be met for this: (a) identification of the customer as a member of the group at the moment of sale;

[146] So a chain of substitution can place a series of products into a single market if a SSNIP in respect of products in one part of the chain would be unprofitable because customers would switch to products elsewhere in the chain, 1997 Notice, paras. 57 and 58.

[147] Draft Notice, paras. 84–87.

[148] Case 27/76, *United Brands* EU:C:1978:22, discussed further in Chap. 6.

[149] But note that the ability of suppliers to discriminate between customers is being transformed by digital technology, at least in online sales.

[150] 1997 Notice, para. 43.

[151] Draft Notice, para. 88.

(b) trade among customers or third party arbitrage is unlikely; and (c) the price discrimination is of a lasting nature. Price discrimination based on customers' location is likely to be a matter of geographic market definition.

(iii) The Structure of Supply and Demand

The structure of supply and demand may be important in determining the relevant market and may cause identical products to fall into different markets because the dynamics of the transactions concerning them differ. The structure of supply and demand may also create 'sub-markets'. This is seen further in Chapter 6.

(iv) Bundles, Aftermarkets, and Ecosystems

a. One Market or Two?

Special problems of market definition arise where products are connected with one another but are not substitutes. Demand substitutability does not help with the issue of determining whether certain products are one whole product (or 'system') or whether they are separate. One aspect of this is 'aftermarkets'. In other situations, the products may be supplied at the same time, or may be part of a range sold together. What, for instance, about size 38 and size 42 shoes (they are not substitutes for one another, so are there separate product markets for each size of shoe?).[152] Is a pair of shoes one product or two (a right and left shoe are not substitutes for one another)? What about the shoes and the laces (again, they are not substitutes for one another)? The division of products into separate markets can be crucial in Article 102 abuse cases concerning allegations of leveraging (such as tying, bundling, and 'self-preferencing'). Leveraging consists of an undertaking making strategic use of its strength in one market to increase its market power in another, discrete (though typically related) market.[153] For example, the cases the Commission has brought against Google[154] involve leveraging abuses. In *Microsoft*, a case on tying and the first case in which the Commission took on Big Tech, the GC held that the criterion for assessing the distinctiveness of products in Article 102 cases is consumer demand.[155]

b. Aftermarkets

An 'aftermarket' is a market comprising complementary ('secondary') products or services that are purchased after another ('primary') product to which they relate. Many durable goods, such as cars, need compatible spare parts and some need a constant supply of 'consumables' (vacuum cleaners and bags, photocopiers and toner cartridges, and so on). Furthermore, durables (such as cars) need servicing and repair. The customer may be 'locked in'—once a particular durable is purchased, the owner needs spare parts which fit that make and model. The CJ established in *Hugin* in 1978[156] that

[152] See the definition of the tyre market in Case 322/81, *NV Nederlandsche Banden-Industrie Michelin v Commission (Michelin I)* EU:C:1983:313, discussed in Chap. 6.

[153] See further Chap. 7, Section 6.

[154] See AT.39740, *Google Search (Shopping)* 27 June 2017, mainly *aff'd* Case T-612/17, *Google and Alphabet v Commission (Google Shopping)* EU:T:2021:763, on appeal Case C-48/22 P, *Google and Alphabet v Commission*, judgment pending; AT.40099, *Google Android*, 18 July 2018, mainly *aff'd* Case T-604/18, *Google and Alphabet v Commission (Google Android)* EU:T:2022:541, on appeal Case C-738/22 P, judgment pending, see further Chaps. 7 and 16.

[155] Case T-201/04, *Microsoft* EU:T:2002:289, para. 917. A much earlier proceeding against IBM was concluded by an informal settlement, see [1984] 3 CMLR 147.

[156] Case 22/78, *Hugin v Commission* EU:C: 1979:138; see also in particular Case T-427/08, *CEAHR* EU:T:2010:517.

one brand of spare parts may constitute a market separate from the primary product to which it relates. However, it may not be a relevant market for the purposes of market definition because if customers can see the costs they will incur in the aftermarket when buying the primary product (i.e. they can estimate the 'whole-life' cost of the primary and secondary products together), the decision as to which brand of primary product to purchase may be influenced by those costs. In such a case, the primary and secondary products comprise one single unified 'system' market and the competition is between the 'systems'. The case law on aftermarkets is discussed in Chapter 6.[157] The position as the Commission sees it is set out in the Draft Notice and is more extensive than the equivalent provision in the 1997 Notice.

Draft Commission Notice on the Definition of the Relevant Market for the Purposes of Union Competition Law (8 November 2022)

(100) There are generally three possible ways to define relevant product markets in the case of primary and secondary products, namely: (i) as a system market comprising both the primary and the secondary product . . . ; (ii) as multiple markets, namely a market for the primary product and separate markets for the secondary products associated with each brand of the primary product . . . or (iii) as dual markets, namely the market for the primary product on the one hand and the market for the secondary product on the other hand. . . .

(101) The definition of a system market may be more appropriate: (i) the more likely it is that customers take the whole-life costs into account when purchasing the primary product; (ii) the higher the expenditure on (or the value of) the secondary product(s) compared to the expenditure on (or the value of) the primary product; (iii) the higher the degree of substitutability between primary products and the lower the switching costs between primary products; and (iv) when there are no or few suppliers specialised only in the secondary product(s). . . . When these circumstances are less likely to be met, it may be more appropriate to define dual markets or multiple markets, depending primarily on the degree of substitutability between the secondary products of the various suppliers. For instance, if secondary products from different suppliers are compatible with all or most of the primary products the definition of dual markets may be more appropriate, whereas if customers of the primary product are locked-in to using only a restricted set of secondary products, the definition of multiple markets may be more appropriate.

(102) In other circumstances, although the consumption of one or more products is not dependent on a primary product, customers may still prefer to consume several products together as a bundle. In these circumstances, the Commission may examine whether the bundle constitutes a relevant product market distinct from the individual products . . .

c. *Digital Ecosystems*

An ecosystem is a web of complementary goods and services designed to work together, Digital ecosystems, described by the OECD as bringing together 'a broad range of products, often centred around a multi-sided platform'[158] are a major feature of the digital economy, and are discussed in Chapter 16. In an ecosystem, competition may be between ecosystems rather than between individual products, although there may also be competition between undertakings offering potentially

[157] See Chap. 6, Section 8.A.

[158] OECD, *OECD Handbook on Competition in the Digital Age* (2022), <www.oecd.org/daf/competition-policy-in-the-digital-age>, p. 23. For further definitions, see Chap. 16, Section 5.A.i.

substitute products within the same ecosystem, and competition between the orchestrator of the ecosystem and other suppliers operating within the platform.[159]

Customers may be locked in to ecosystems and the 2019 CPDE Report suggested that where firms' lock-in strategies are successful, and consumers are drawn into ecosystems which they find difficult to leave, ecosystem-specific aftermarkets may need to be defined.[160]

In *Google Android*,[161] which is discussed in Chapters 6 and 16, the GC recognised the concept of a digital ecosystem. Referring to that judgment, the Draft Notice says:

> (103) Digital ecosystems can in certain circumstances be thought of as consisting of a primary core product and several secondary (digital) products whose consumption is connected to the core product, for instance, by technological links or interoperability. . . . When considering digital ecosystems, the Commission may thus apply similar principles to the ones applied to after markets to define the relevant product market(s) . . . When the secondary (digital) products are offered as a bundle, the Commission may also assess the possibility of that bundle constituting a relevant market on its own. Although not all digital ecosystems fit an after market or bundle market approach, the Commission may in any event take into account elements such as network effects, switching costs and (single and/or multi)-homing decisions for the purpose of defining the relevant product market(s).

In footnote 123, the Commission quotes paragraph 116 of the *Google Android* judgment where the GC says that the products or services which form part of the relevant markets within the ecosystem may overlap or be connected to each other on the basis of their horizontal or vertical complementarity.[162]

(v) Multi-sided Markets and Zero-prices

A multi-sided market is one where the firms have to compete simultaneously for more than one group of customers. It can be described as a market in which a firm acts as a platform and sells different products to different groups of customers, while recognising that the demand from one group of customers depends on the demand from the other group(s).[163] Multi-sided markets are not new, and businesses such as newspapers (readers and advertisers) and estate agents (buyers and sellers) are examples of multi-sided platform markets and even in such conventional markets it may be necessary to subsidise customers on one side or even provide the product or service for free. Multi-sided markets are problematic for market definition.[164] One question is whether there is one market, comprising all sides of the platform (which may be part of a wider relevant market) or two or more separate markets. If there are separate markets and one side is being subsidised or provided with free services, the application of the SSNIP test will be likely to lead to incorrect, particularly over-narrow, definitions.

The rise of the power and importance of platforms in the digital economy have made the question of market definition in multi-sided markets one of the greatest problems in contemporary competition law. Digital platforms typically offer their product to one side at zero-price, so that using a search

[159] See M. Jacobides and I. Lianos, 'Ecosystems and Competition Law in Theory and Practice' (2021) 30 *Industrial and Corporate Change* 1199, 1201. Competition between the orchestrator and other suppliers in the ecosystem is the subject of the *Google Search (Shopping)* case.

[160] Expert report on *Competition Policy for the Digital Era* (CPDE report), see n. 107, Chap. 3.III.F, p. 48.

[161] Case T-604/18, *Google and Alphabet v Commission (Google Android)*, n. 154.

[162] See the further discussion of *Google Android* in Chap. 6, Section 8 and Chap. 16, Section 5.A.i.

[163] See OECD, *Rethinking Antitrust Tools for Multi-Sided Platforms* (2018), p. 10 (C. Pike), DAF/COMP(2012)19, <www.oecd.org/daf/competition/Marketdefinition2012.pdf>.

[164] See D. S. Evans and M. D. Noel, 'Defining Antitrust Markets When Firms Operate Two-sided Platforms' (2005) 3 *Colum Bus LR* 557.

engine or social media is 'free' (paid for in reality by what is learned about the users) and the absence of a price which can be used as a factor in market definition is a major problem. Much has been written about the complexities of market definition in respect of digital platforms,[165] and we pursue these issues in Chapters 6 and 16. One reason for the downplaying of the SSNIP test by the Commission, which we have already seen in this chapter, is its limited utility in digital platform markets. This followed the recommendations of the 2019 Expert's Report on Competition Policy for the Digital Era (the CPDE Report)[166] which highlighted the problems for market definition and identifying and measuring market power in digital markets because, inter alia, of network effects, zero-prices, increasing returns to scale, data, and the dynamic nature of these markets.

Market definition in multi-sided markets was an issue in *MasterCard MIF*,[167] which concerned MasterCard's multilateral interchange fees for cross-border payment card transactions. The two sides were an upstream market where the different card schemes competed in persuading financial institutions to join their schemes and where they provided services to those institutions, and a downstream market where the financial institutions competed for acquiring services, i.e. contracting with merchants (such as retailers) so that they would accept payments by card. The Commission recognised the two-sided nature of the market and the indirect network effects, and held that the relevant market was the downstream one for acquiring payment cards.[168] In *Google Search (Shopping)*, the Commission did not apply the SSNIP test, stating that it would not have been appropriate because Google provides its search services for free to users.[169]

The Draft Notice contains a section on multi-sided markets. It was written in the light of the *Google Android* judgment and refers to the SSNDQ test.[170]

Draft Commission Notice on the Definition of the Relevant Market for the Purposes of Union Competition Law (8 November 2022)

(95) In the presence of multi-sided platforms, the Commission may define a relevant product market for the products offered by a platform as a whole, in a way that encompasses all (or multiple) user groups . . ., or it may define separate relevant product markets for the products offered on each side

[165] See e.g. A. Lamadrid de Pablo, 'The Double Duality of Two-sided Markets' [2015] *Comp Law* 5; D. Auer and N. Petit, 'Two-sided Markets and the Challenge of Turning Economic Theory into Antitrust Policy', <http://ssrn.com/abstract=2552337>; D. S. Evans and R. Schmalensee, *Matchmakers: The New Economics of Multisided Markets* (Harvard Business Review Press, 2016); L. Filistrucchi, D. Geradin, E. van Damme, and P. Affeldt, 'Market Definition in Two-sided Markets: Theory and Practice' (2014) 10(2) *J of Competition Law and Economics* 293; F. Thépot, 'Market Power in Online Search and Social Networking: A Matter of Two-sided Markets' (2013) 36 *World Competition* 195; S. Broos and J. M. Ramos, '*Google, Google Shopping* and *Amazon*: The Importance of Competing Business Models and Two-sided Intermediaries in Defining Relevant Markets' (2017) 62(2) *Ant Bull* 382, <https://ssrn.com/abstract=2696045>; P. Ward, 'Testing for Multisided Platform Effects in Antitrust Market Definition' (2017) 84 *Univ Chic LR* 2059; S. Wismer, C. Bongard, and A. Rasek, 'Multi-sided Economics in Competition Law Enforcement' (2017) 8(4) *JECLAP* 257; L. Filistrucchi, 'Market Definition in Multi-Sided Markets' in OECD, *Rethinking Antitrust Tools for Multi-Sided Markets* (2018), 37–54; J. Franck and M. Peitz, 'Market Definition in the Platform Economy' (2021) 23 *CYELS* 91; M. Eben and V. Robertson, 'Digital Market Definition in the European Union, United States, and Brazil: Past, Present, and Future' (2021) 18 *J of Competition Law and Economics* 417.

[166] Expert report on *Competition Policy for the Digital Era* (CPDE report), n. 107, Chap. 3.III.G, p. 48.

[167] COMP/34.579, *MasterCard* 19 December 2007.

[168] Ibid., para. 316 (the market definition point was not raised on appeal, Case T-111/08, *MasterCard Inc v Commission* EU:T:2012:260, *aff'd* Case C-382/12 P, *MasterCard Inc v Commission* EU:C:2014:2201); Case C-67/13 P, *Groupement des Cartes Bancaires v Commission* EU:C:2014:2022. *Mastercard* should be compared to *Ohio v American Express Co*, 138 S.Ct. 2274 (2018), see n. 8, where in similar circumstances the Supreme Court held that both sides of the platform constituted a single market.

[169] AT.39740, *Google Search (Shopping)* Decision of 27 June 2017, para. 243; on appeal, Case T-612/17, *Google and Alphabet v Commission* EU:T:2021:763.

[170] See Section 4.E, text at n.82.

of the platform. . . . Depending on the facts of the case, it may be more appropriate to define separate markets where there are significant differences in the substitution possibilities on the different sides of the platform. To assess if such differences exist, the Commission may take into account factors such as whether the undertakings offering substitutable products for each user group differ, the degree of product differentiation on each side (or each user group's perception thereof), behavioural factors such as the homing decisions . . . of each user group and the nature of the platform (for instance whether it is a transaction or a matching platform). Where separate markets have been defined for the products offered on each side of the platform, network effects and constraints from the other side of the platform may still be taken into account in the competitive assessment.

(96) In practice, the presence of indirect network effects may render the assessment of demand substitution and, in particular, the application of the SSNIP test more challenging than in situations where no such demand interdependence between user groups exists.

(97) Multi-sided platforms often supply a product at a zero monetary price to a user group in order to attract users to products offered on the other sides of the platform and monetise their products on those sides. Zero monetary prices are an integral part of multi-sided platforms' business strategy, so the fact that a product is supplied at a zero monetary price does not imply that there is no relevant market for that product.

(98) In such cases, non-price elements are particularly relevant for the assessment of substitution. The Commission focuses on elements such as product functionalities . . ., intended use . . ., evidence on hypothetical substitution and on competitive constraints based on industry views . . ., barriers or costs of switching such as interoperability with other products and licensing features. . . . The Commission may also consider alternatives to the SSNIP framework, namely by assessing the switching behaviour of customers in response to a small but significant non-transitory decrease of quality ('SSNDQ') . . .

(vi) Markets for Raw Materials and 'Inputs'

A raw material may constitute a separate product market even though the derivative product made from it forms part of a wide product market which has a number of substitutes. This was established in *Commercial Solvents*.[171] There may also be a market consisting of a resource or facility which an undertaking does not market to third parties but uses solely for its own production purposes. The EU Courts have held that this 'input' may constitute a potential or hypothetical market separate from that for the product or service in which it is used.[172] The point is important in cases of refusal to supply under Article 102 where the existence of two markets, rather than one, is crucial.[173]

(vii) Markets Created by State Regulation

A relevant market may be affected by State regulation. Legislation may, for example, define a statutory market. Such regulation may mean that no substitutes are permitted for a particular product or service. In *General Motors*[174] and *British Leyland*,[175] national regulations required conformity or type-approval certificates from importers of motor vehicles and provided that they could only be issued by the vehicle manufacturer. In both cases, the CJ held that the provision of the certificates was a separate market and not part of the motor car market.

[171] Cases 6 and 7/73, *Istituto Chemioterapico Italiano Spa & Commercial Solvents v Commission* EU:C:1974:18.

[172] Case C-418/01, *IMS Health GmbH & Co OHG v NDC Health GmbH & Co KG* EU:C:2004:257, paras. 43–45; Case T-201/04, *Microsoft* EU:T:2007:289, para. 335; Case T-301/04, *Clearstream* EU:T:2009:317, paras. 65–66.

[173] See Chap. 7. [174] Case 26/75, *General Motors v Commission* EU:C:1975:150.

[175] Case 226/84, *British Leyland v Commission* EU:C:1986:421.

(viii) Markets in the Pharmaceutical Sector

The Commission defines markets in the pharmaceutical sector by reference to the third level of the WHO/EphMRA Anatomical Therapeutical Chemical (ATC) classification which groups medicines in terms of therapeutic indications, i.e. intended use. Where appropriate in the circumstances of the case, however, an analysis may be carried out at another level, such as four (mode of action) or five (individual active substances).[176] The GC in *AstraZeneca* approved the Commission's approach.[177] *AstraZeneca* also established that pharmaceutical markets can be narrowly delineated by reference to the *means* by which the treatment is effected, rather than to the condition being treated. Furthermore *AstraZeneca* shows that the general principles of market definition apply in the pharmaceutical sector and that they are not excluded by regulation in the sector or by reimbursement of the cost of medicine by national health systems. However, in *Servier*[178] the GC recognised that the particular features of the pharmaceutical sector mean that price pressures do not apply in the same way as they do in other markets. The demand for prescription medicines is determined for the most part not by the ultimate consumers but by the prescribing doctors who are primarily guided by therapeutic use rather than cost. The Commission had found a relevant market consisting of one particular ACE inhibitor drug, périndopril,[179] but the GC held that the Commission had under-estimated the non-price competitive pressure from other medicines in the same therapeutic class and attributed excessive importance to the price factor in analysing the competitive constraints. It therefore annulled the finding of an Article 102 abuse as the erroneous market definition invalidated the finding of a dominant position. The Advocate General recommended setting aside the GC judgment for lack of adequate reasoning.

The issue of supply-side substitutability arising from the presence of generic manufacturers poised to enter the market on the expiry of pharmaceutical patents arose in *Generics* and is discussed in Section F and in Chapters 6 and 12.

(ix) Markets in Highly Innovative Industries

There is a new section in the Draft Notice (paragraphs 89–93) on highly innovative industries characterised by frequent and significant investments in research and development (R&D). The Draft Notice says that where there are 'pipeline products' in the R&D process which are visible enough to establish to which market they are likely to belong, the Commission may find that they belong to an existing relevant product and geographic market or to a new market limited by the pipeline products and their substitutes. Where the R&D process is not closely related to any specific product but is at an earlier stage of research which may serve multiple purposes, it may still be possible to identify the boundaries within which undertakings compete in such earlier innovation efforts. The Commission has already used this concept of an 'innovation' space in some merger cases, including *Dow/Dupont*[180] where it took into account innovation competition in crop protection. In paragraph 93, the Commission stresses that innovation is a key parameter of competition.

[176] COMP/37.507/F3, *AstraZeneca* 15 June 2005, para. 3.

[177] Case T-321/05, *AstraZeneca v Commission* EU:T:2010:266; *aff'd* Case C-457/10 P, *AstraZeneca* EU:C:2012:770. See J. Westin, 'Defining Relevant Market in the Pharmaceutical Sector in the Light of the *Losec* Case—Just How Different is the Pharmaceutical Market?' [2011] *ECLR* 57.

[178] Case T-691/14, *Servier SAS v Commission* EU:T:2018:922, on appeal Case C-176/19, judgment pending, Opinion of Kokott AG, EU:C:2022:576.

[179] COMP/39.612, *Périndopril (Servier)* 9 July 2014, IP14/799.

[180] M.7932, 12 October 2017; see also M.8084, *Bayer/Monsanto*.

(x) Markets on the Buying Side (Procurement Markets)

The previous discussion is predicated on markets defined on the supply side. However, it is also possible to define markets on the demand side, that is, in terms of what is being bought. This is illustrated in the *British Airways* case, discussed in Chapters 6 and 7.[181] A number of merger cases have involved buying markets, for example *NewsCorp/Telepiù*[182] and *NVV v Commission*.[183] The SSNIP test is applied by postulating a 5–10 per cent *reduction* in price in buying markets.

J. THE CALCULATION OF MARKET SHARES

At the end of the Draft Notice, the Commission has a brief section on the calculation of market shares. This is discussed in Chapter 6, Section 9.B.

5. BARRIERS TO ENTRY AND EXPANSION

A. THE ROLE OF BARRIERS TO ENTRY

A firm with a 100 per cent share of a market may not, in economic terms, have a monopoly. Market shares tell us nothing about why the firm has such a high market share or about potential competition. It tells us only about the current state of competition. A firm will not be able to charge monopoly prices if other firms can freely enter the market and compete with it. Excessive prices indicate to others that the market is profitable. Whether or not a firm really does have market power is, therefore, dependent on how vulnerable it is to new entrants. Such vulnerability to new entrants is dependent upon 'barriers to entry'. A firm can exercise market power for a significant time only if barriers to entry exist. As Bork states:[184] '[t]he concept of barriers to entry is crucial to antitrust debate ... The ubiquity and potency of the concept are undeniable.'

It is difficult to give any definition of 'barriers to entry' without taking sides in a long-standing debate. To put it as neutrally as possible, however, a barrier to entry is something which prevents or hinders the emergence of potential competition which would otherwise constrain the incumbent undertaking. A barrier to expansion is something which prevents or hinders an existing competitor from expanding output. The term 'barriers to entry' is used in the present discussion to include both barriers to entry and barriers to expansion, unless the context otherwise requires. However, it should be noted that barriers to entry may be high although barriers to expansion are low.[185] The height of barriers to entry, as well as their existence, must always be taken into account.

[181] Case C-95/04 P, *British Airways* EU:C:2007:166. [182] M.2876 [2004] OJ L110/73 (broadcasting rights).

[183] Case T-151/05, *Nederlandse Vakbond Varkenshoudes (NVV) v Commission* EU:C:2009:144, the appeal from M.3605, *Sovion/HMG* (purchase of pigs by slaughterhouses).

[184] R. H. Bork, *The Antitrust Paradox: A Policy at War with Itself* (Basic Books, 1978, reprinted with a new Introduction and Epilogue, 1993), 310–311.

[185] See Geradin, Layne-Farrar, and Petit, n. 75, 4.69; e.g. entry may require large capital investment while expansion of existing plant does not.

(i) The Definition of a Barrier to Entry

The seminal work on barriers to entry was that of J. S. Bain who belonged to the Harvard School.[186] Bain described barriers to entry as:

> the extent to which, in the long run, established firms can elevate their selling prices above the minimal average costs of production and distribution . . . without inducing potential entrants to enter the industry.[187]

This defines barriers to entry in an effects-based way. In contrast, Stigler, a leading exponent of the Chicago School,[188] adopted a narrower definition, focusing on the differences in demand and cost conditions suffered by incumbent firms and potential entrants, respectively. He defined a barrier to entry as:

> a cost of producing (at some or every rate of output) which must be borne by a firm which seeks to enter the industry but is not borne by firms already in the industry.[189]

Gilbert's definition follows Bain but emphasises 'first-mover advantages' (the advantages the firm derives simply from being on the market before its potential competitors) rather than absolute costs advantages:

> a barrier to entry is a rent that is derived from incumbency. It is the additional profit that a firm can earn as a sole consequence of being established in an industry.[190]

The essential debate remains whether the definition of Bain or of Stigler and the Chicago School is the more appropriate. The Bain approach results in many things being identified as barriers. Conversely, the definition adopted by Stigler means that very few things constitute barriers to entry.[191] For example, Bain's approach, unlike Stigler's, accepts that market conduct may operate as a barrier to entry because the definition is effects-based.[192] Further, Bain's definition admits that economies of scale

[186] See Chap. 1, Section 5.A.

[187] J. S. Bain, *Industrial Organization* (2nd edn, John Wiley, 1968), 242. See also J. S. Bain, 'Economies of Scale, Concentration, and the Condition of Entry in Twenty Manufacturing Industries' (1954) 44 *Am Econ Rev* 15, and J. S. Bain, *Barriers to New Competition* (Harvard University Press, 1956).

[188] See Chap. 1, Section 5.B.

[189] G. J. Stigler, *The Organization of Industry* (Irwin, 1968), 67; see also W. Baumol and R. Willig, 'Fixed Costs, Sunk Costs, Entry Barriers and Sustainability of Monopoly' (1981) 95 *Quart J of Econ* 405, 408, and C. von Weizsäcker, 'A Welfare Analysis of Barriers to Entry' (1980) 11 *Bell J Econ* 399, 400. D. Carlton, 'Why Barriers to Entry are Barriers to Understanding' (2004) 94(2) *Am Econ Rev* 466, 468, says that 'Although Stigler's definition of "barrier" as a differential cost is concise and unambiguous, it does raise the question of why it should be called a "barrier". Why not call it "differential cost advantage?" This may seem overly pedantic, but introduction of unnatural use of language can lead to confusion. Consider, for example, an industry where the government restricts the numbers of firms to 100. It issues 100 licences to operate that are then sold in an open market. The entry restriction is likely to be inefficient, but as long as all firms have access to the (artificially) scarce license at the market-clearing price, there is no entry barrier according to Stigler's definition. All firms earn a normal rate of return. Yet there is a restriction to entry. It seems to mangle the English language to refuse to call this entry restriction a "barrier to entry".'

[190] R. Gilbert, 'Mobility Barriers and the Value of Incumbency' in R. Schmalensee and R. Willig (eds.), *Handbook of Industrial Organization, Vol. 1* (North-Holland, 1989), 478. For absolute costs advantages, see Section 5.B.ii, p. x.

[191] All Stiglerian entry barriers are Bainian entry barriers as well, but not vice versa.

[192] R. P. McAfee, H. M. Mialon, and M. A. Williams, 'What is a Barrier to Entry?' (2004) 94(2) *Am Econ Rev* 461, 462 comment that 'Bain's definition is flawed in that it builds the consequences of the definition into the definition itself'.

may operate as a barrier to entry, since they deter new entrants and so allow prices to remain above minimum unit cost. Stigler's definition does not, however, accept that economies of scale operate as a barrier since both incumbents and new competitors have to face them at the time they enter the market.[193] There is therefore a lack of the asymmetry which the Stigler definition demands.

It is the Bain approach which today has the greatest influence in industrial economics and which is ordinarily used in competition law decisions in both the EU and the US.[194] The various definitions of barriers to entry are summed up in the OECD's Roundtable report of 2005.[195]

The proper identification of barriers to entry is vital to the determination of market power. If factors are too readily identified as entry barriers, a firm may be wrongly found to have market power and its legitimate conduct then constrained by competition laws. Similarly a merger between two firms may be prohibited although it would not lead to the merged firm acquiring market power. On the other hand, if the possibility of entry barriers is too easily dismissed, undertakings which do have market power may escape the prohibitions of competition law and mergers which create or strengthen market power may be allowed.

B. TYPES OF BARRIER TO ENTRY

Post-Chicago and modern industrial organisation theory stresses the strategic conduct of undertakings, looking to the effect which conduct has on structure, rather than vice versa. Whether a new entrant will enter a market will depend, at least in part, on the conditions of competition it will face post-entry. Thus predatory behaviour by the incumbent firm may constitute a barrier to entry.

The list of barriers to entry considered in Sections (i)–(iii) follows that in the OECD report.[196] The OECD divides barriers to entry into two types, structural and strategic, but notes that '[s]ome arguably spill over from one category to the other, and none of them should be viewed in isolation because they can interact with and magnify each other'.[197] The report considers sunk costs separately, because they 'permeate the whole discussion'. [198]

(i) Sunk Costs

Sunk costs[199] can generally affect entry in two ways. First, because the money has already gone an incumbent undertaking can rationally ignore sunk costs when making pricing decisions so they may deter some entrants that are equally, and maybe even more, efficient. Secondly, sunk costs make entry more risky as if entry turns out to be a failure the sunk costs will be irrecoverable. Examples of sunk costs are:[200]

- start-up phase losses;
- investments in human capital such as recruiting and training costs;

[193] McAfee, Mialon, and Williams, ibid., say that the present tense 'is' in Stigler's definition is confusing as '[l]iterally, the definition implies that a cost that only entrants (not incumbents) have to bear today is an entry barrier, even if incumbents had to bear it in the past (when they entered the market)'.

[194] See the US Horizontal Merger Guidelines 2010 (<www.justice.gov/atr/horizontal-merger-guidelines-08192010>).

[195] OECD Policy Roundtable on barriers to entry, DAF/COMP(2005)42, <www.oecd.org/daf/competition/abuse/36344429.pdf>, section 2.2.

[196] See also the 'slightly adapted version' of the list in D. Geradin, A. Layne-Farrar, and N. Petit, *EU Competition Law and Economics* (Oxford University Press, 2012), 2.104–2.124.

[197] OECD Roundtable, n. 195, section 3.

[198] Ibid., section 3.1.

[199] See R. Schmalensee, 'Sunk Costs and Antitrust Barriers to Entry' (2004) 94(2) *Am Econ Rev* 471.

[200] OECD Roundtable, n. 195, section 3.1.

- investments in highly specialised equipment or buildings with limited resale value;
- advertising and promotion costs;
- R&D that does not yield results with alternative uses;
- expenses of complying with government regulations.

(ii) Structural Barriers

Structural barriers[201] arise from the basic conditions in the industry and are normally factors out of the incumbents' direct control or originating from their general efforts to compete and not from specific entry-deterring strategies. They include:

- *Absolute costs advantages*,[202] which are advantages which the incumbent enjoys but which are not available to entrants, such as exclusive access to necessary resources or technology.[203]
- *Economies of scale and scope.*[204] In the absence of sunk costs, economies of scale and scope do not normally deter or prevent entry, although economies of scope are significant in digital ecosystems.
- *High capital costs.* The OECD says that 'high' has two meanings: absolute and relative.[205] Whether high capital costs constitute a barrier to entry is a matter of debate. Bain considered that capital requirements could give rise to barriers to entry because of the amount a new entrant would need to enter the market at an efficient scale.[206] However, in Bork's view:

> Capital requirements exist and certainly inhibit entry—just as talent requirements for playing professional football exist and inhibit entry. Neither barrier is in any sense artificial or the proper subject of special concern for antitrust policy.[207]

The Commission explained in the Discussion Paper on Article 102 that:

> in some cases [financial strength] may be one of the factors that contribute to a finding of a dominant position, in particular in those cases where (i) finance is relevant to the competitive process in the industry under review; (ii) there are significant asymmetries between competitors in terms of their internal financing capabilities; and (iii) particular features of the industry make it difficult for firms to attract external funds.[208]

[201] Ibid., section 3.2. [202] Ibid., section 3.2.1.

[203] They have been described as arising 'if some factor of production is denied to the potential entrant and, but for this omitted factor, the latter firm would be as efficient as the incumbent firm', Van den Bergh and Camesasca, n. 6, 142, referring to R. J. Gilbert, 'Mobility Barriers and the Value of Incumbency' in Schmalensee and Willig, n. 190. Cost advantages may not endure in high-tech markets with a rapid rate of innovation, and in those markets the timescale of change will be important.

[204] OECD Roundtable, n. 195, sections 3.2.2 and 3.2.3. For economies of scale and scope, see Chap. 1, Section 4.A.v, p. x.

[205] OECD Roundtable, n. 195, section 3.2.4.

[206] J. S. Bain, *Barriers to New Competition* (Harvard University Press, 1956), where he reported on a survey of 20 US industries. Capital requirements are therefore linked to economies of scale.

[207] Bork, n. 184, 320.

[208] Commission Staff Discussion Paper on the application of Article 82 to exclusionary abuses, Brussels, 9 December 2005, para. 40.

The OECD says that it is probably most useful to think about how capital costs affect a potential entrant's decision.[209] The Commission found high investment costs to be barriers to entry in both *Google Search (Shopping)*[210] and *Amazon*.[211]

- *Reputational effects* whereby the incumbent has a strong reputation for reliability or quality. The effects will be greater where customers will incur significant risk, inconvenience, or expense in trying new products.[212]
- *Network effects* (network externalities).[213] Direct network effects (or network externalities) occur when a product becomes more valuable and attractive to users the more users it has, as with social media sites, where an increased number of users means more people with whom to interact. Indirect network effects arise in multi-sided markets and mean that increased usage of one product increases the value of complementary ones. They have been described as 'among the determinants of the conditions of entry in many industries, and they can create a truly formidable entry obstacle, sufficient to permit prices to persist above competitive level[s] for a substantial period of time without attracting entry'.[214] Indirect network effects are of crucial importance in respect of the digital economy. The majority view is that they constitute serious barriers to entry in digital markets, where they are reinforced by the Big Data which is also a characteristic of those markets. The more data which is collected, the better the algorithms can target customers and users, which then attracts additional users, reinforcing the incumbent's power.[215]
- *Data.* Apart from reinforcing network effects, data may constitute, of itself, a barrier to entry[216] if a firm has exclusive control over it and access is required by entrants.[217] The fact that product improvement in general search services required access to a critical mass of search query data, which gave incumbent operators like Google a significant advantage, was treated as a barrier to entry by the Commission in *Google Search (Shopping)*.[218] Would-be entrants argued that obtaining the large quantity of data necessary to develop the algorithms required for a rival search engine[219] would be a significant barrier to entry.[220]
- *Legal and regulatory barriers*[221] include all kinds of rules, restrictions, externalities, and conditions imposed by governments on entry on to or operation within a market. The Chicago School

[209] OECD Roundtable, n. 195, section 3.2.4, citing Schmalensee's 'pragmatic approach' in R. Schmalensee, 'Horizontal Merger Policy: Problems and Changes' (1987) 1 *Economic Perspectives* 4, that if business people think the cost of capital is a barrier to entry, then that will affect their decisions about entry and become a *de facto* barrier.

[210] AT.39740, *Google Search (Shopping)* Decision of 27 June 2017, paras. 286 and 291.

[211] AT40153, *E-book MFNs and related matters (Amazon)*, Decision of 4 May 2017, para. 65. See also AT39813, *Baltic Rail* Decision of 2 October 2017, paras. 162–167.

[212] OECD Roundtable, n. 195, section 3.2.5. [213] Ibid., section 3.2.6.

[214] G. J. Werden, 'Network Effects and Conditions of Entry: Lessons from the Microsoft Case' (2001) 69 *ALJ* 8 (discussing the US case).

[215] See e.g. A. Ezrachi and M. E. Stucke, *Virtual Competition: The Promise and Perils of the Algorithm-Driven Economy* (Harvard University Press, 2016), 237–239; N.-P. Schepp and A. Wambach, 'On Big Data and Its Relevance for Market Power Assessment' (2016) 7(2) *JECLAP* 120; but cf. D. S. Evans and R. Schmalensee, 'Debunking the 'Network Effects' Bogeyman' (2017) 40 *Regulation* 36 and D. S. Evans and R. Schmalensee, *Matchmakers: The New Economics of Multisided Platforms* (Harvard Business Review Press, 2016).

[216] R. Mahnke, 'Big Data as a Barrier to Entry' 2 *CPI Antitrust Chronicle* May 2015.

[217] N. Newman, 'Search, Antitrust and the Economics of the Control of User Data' (2014) 31(2) *Yale J on Regulation* 401.

[218] AT.39740, *Google Search (Shopping)* Decision of 27 June 2017, on appeal, Case T-612/17, *Google and Alphabet v Commission* EU:T:2021:763.

[219] Ibid., paras. 286–289. [220] See further Chap. 6. [221] OECD Roundtable, n. 195, section 3.2.7.

views them as the most substantial barriers to entry. If legal and regulatory barriers are manipulated by incumbents they can be seen as strategic barriers too.[222] Intellectual property rights (IPRs) can also be included here, but are not necessarily an absolute barrier to entry, since it may be open to potential competitors to challenge them. In *Generics*, the CJ considered that a generic version of an originator medicine should be included in the market despite the latter's protection by a process patent whose validity was disputed.[223]

- *Barriers to exit.*[224] The costs of exiting a market may deter undertakings from entering it in the first place. High costs of exit (including sunk costs) make entry riskier. The OECD report points out that high barriers to exit may make incumbents respond more aggressively to entrants, thus creating more barriers to entry.
- *First-mover advantages*[225] are the advantages that the incumbent derives from being the first in the market and which mean that subsequent entrants cannot compete on equal terms. First-mover advantages include some of the barriers to entry already mentioned, such as network effects, reputation, and IPRs.
- *Vertical integration* means that an undertaking operates at more than one stage of the production and distribution chain.[226] It may be difficult for an entrant to enter at only one stage and the vertical integration may endow the incumbent with advantages that can be replicated only by a similarly integrated entrant. It can be argued, however, that when vertical integration takes place barriers to entry are only added up and are not multiplied. Vertical integration may therefore accompany monopoly but is not an indicator of it.[227] Vertically integrated firms may discriminate in favour of their own downstream operations, which becomes a strategic barrier, as in the case of margin squeeze, discussed in Chapter 7 and of 'self-preferencing' which is the theory of harm applied in *Google Search (Shopping)*.

(iii) Strategic Behaviour by Incumbents

Strategies which deter entry may be intentionally created or enhanced for that purpose.[228] Strategic behaviour may be used to pre-empt entry or to retaliate against entry that has already occurred. Threats are an effective deterrent if (and only if) they are credible. Some of the practices below are discussed in Chapter 7 as they constitute conduct which can amount to an abuse of a dominant position for the purposes of Article 102 insofar as they 'foreclose' the market, i.e. have exclusionary effects.

- *Predatory pricing*[229] is where an incumbent prices below cost to deter entrants or drive out competitors.
- *Limit pricing* is where the incumbent does not price below cost but deliberately fails to maximise short-term profit, so that it leaves too little residual demand for entry to be profitable. It normally works only if there are economies of scale or scope, because it depends on the entrant being

[222] See e.g. Case C-457/10 P, *AstraZeneca* EU:C:2012:770, discussed in Chap. 7.

[223] Case C-307/18, *Generics (UK) Ltd v CMA* EU:C:2020:52, see Section 4.F and Chap. 6, Section 8.

[224] OECD Roundtable, n. 195, section 3.2.8. [225] Ibid., section 3.2.9. [226] Ibid., section 3.2.10.

[227] See C. Baden Fuller, 'Art. 86 EEC: Economic Analysis of the Existence of a Dominant Position' (1979) 4 *ELRev* 423, 440 and the economic literature cited there; D. Harbord and T. Hoehn, 'Barriers to Entry and Exit in European Competition Policy' (1994) 14 *International Review of Law and Economics* 411, 419; V. Korah, 'Concept of a Dominant Position Within The Meaning of Art. 86' (1980) 17 *CMLRev* 395, 408.

[228] OECD Roundtable, n. 195, section 3.3. [229] Ibid., section 3.3.1.

unable to operate efficiently at the available level of demand.[230] The potential entrants also need to believe that the incumbent will maintain that level of output whether or not the new entry occurs.

- *Intentional over-investment in capacity and sunk costs.*[231] An incumbent undertaking may over-invest in sunk assets so that it operates with significant spare capacity. The threat of this spare capacity being used may deter a potential entrant, as the incumbent may be able to manufacture large quantities of the product using that spare capacity at a very low unit cost.
- *Fidelity (loyalty) and bundled rebates*[232] comprise pricing practices whereby undertakings give discounts and rebates to customers in exchange for the customers' loyalty in not buying elsewhere or for buying certain amounts.
- *Product differentiation and advertising.*[233] There is an extensive economics literature about the extent to which advertising, reputation, and goodwill may operate as barriers to entry. There can be economies of scale in advertising and advertising expenditures will usually be sunk costs.[234] Bain considered advertising a barrier to entry.[235] Advertising builds up goodwill and reputation, and the first brand in the market may enjoy a classic first-mover advantage which will operate as a barrier to entry to later entrants.[236] Stigler's view, however, was that advertising is not a barrier to entry: it reduces consumer search costs and is pro-competitive.[237] Advertising and brand reputation may contribute to rendering the undertaking's product a 'must-stock' item, which can in turn make the undertaking an 'unavoidable trading partner'. There is also a significant literature on brand proliferation and product differentiation as barriers to entry.[238] Van den Bergh and Camesasca explain that the insights of modern industrial organisation theory show that advertising and product differentiation can reduce consumer welfare in some circumstances.

R. J. Van den Bergh and P. D. Camesasca, *European Competition Law and Economics: A Comparative Perspective* (2nd edn, Sweet & Maxwell, 2006), 145–146

Recent work in modern industrial organisation has further contributed to our understanding of product differentiation and advertising as entry barriers. It now appears that a cautious approach is warranted. Product differentiation and advertising can, under certain conditions, reduce consumer welfare. Advertising may be used either to increase the objective knowledge of products or to create consumers' preferences for a particular brand, thereby making the demand for those products less elastic and market entry by newcomers more difficult. However, to qualify as an entry barrier and not just as

[230] Ibid., section 3.3.2.

[231] Ibid., section 3.3.3, which cites A. M. Spence, 'Entry, Capacity, Investment and Oligopolistic Pricing' (1977) 8 *Bell J Econ* 53 and A. Dixit, 'The Role of Investment in Entry Deterrence' (1980) 90 *Economic Journal* 9 on the theory of this strategy.

[232] OECD Roundtable, n. 195, section 3.3.4. [233] Ibid., section 3.3.5.

[234] Although a brand image built up by advertising might be deployable in a separate market, e.g. the name Virgin is applied to many different products and services. The Commission described advertising and promotion as sunk costs in the merger decision *Nestlé/Perrier* [1992] OJ L356/1, para. 97.

[235] Bain, n. 206. See also M. Spence, 'Notes on Advertising, Economies of Scale and Entry Barriers' (1980) 95 *Quart J of Econ* 493; J. Sutton, *Sunk Costs and Market Structure: Price Competition, Advertising, and the Evolution of Concentration* (MIT Press, 1991).

[236] See R. Schmalensee, 'Entry Deterrence in the Ready-to-eat Breakfast Cereal Industry' (1978) 9 *Bell J Econ* 305.

[237] G. Stigler, 'The Economics of Information' (1961) 69 *J of Political Economy* 213; see Van den Bergh and Camesasca, n. 6, 144–145.

[238] See Bain, n. 206; R. Schmalensee, 'Product Differentiation Advantages of Pioneering Brands' (1981) 72 *Am Econ Rev* 349. Bain, unlike the Chicago School, considered product differentiation a barrier to entry.

an entry impediment, the effects of advertising must last sufficiently long to enable incumbent firms to earn super-normal profits persistently. On the latter point the relevant empirical evidence is mixed: some researchers found that the effects of advertising lasted for several years, whereas others found that advertising effects are gone within a year . . . Modern industrial organisation stresses the importance of sunk costs in assessing whether advertising may function as a barrier to entry. Sunk costs are central to the calculations of potential entrants: advertising costs to build consumer loyalty are normally sunk costs unless an exiting firm could either sell its brand name or use it somewhere else without a loss. The higher advertising and promotion expenditures that cannot be recovered on exiting a particular market, the more entry will be deterred. . . . Recent literature in industrial organisation on product differentiation also includes the view that it may be used as an instrument to obstruct market entry. To deter entrants looking for unfulfilled product design or brand image niches, established sellers might seek to crowd product space with enough brands (brand proliferation) so that no room for profitable new entry remains. . . .

The Commission Staff Discussion Paper said:[239]

it may be difficult to enter an industry where experience or reputation is necessary to compete effectively, both of which may be difficult to obtain as an entrant. Factors such as consumer loyalty to a particular brand, the closeness of relationships between suppliers and customers, the importance of promotion or advertising, or other reputation advantages will be taken into account. Advertising and other investments in reputation are often sunk costs which cannot be recovered in the case of exit and which therefore make entry more risky.

- *Tying.*[240] Tying and bundling are types of leveraging whereby a dominant undertaking makes the purchase of one product conditional on the purchase of another, or 'bundles' them together.
- *Exclusive dealing arrangements*[241] are vertical arrangements whereby customers contract with an incumbent undertaking to purchase all their requirements of the relevant product from that undertaking. They raise similar issues to fidelity rebates, which may have the same effect. The OECD report notes that an incumbent undertaking operating on a market where it is necessary to use distributors may sign exclusive contracts with enough of the available distributors (rather than directly with the customers) to mean that new entrants would need in effect to vertically integrate, a requirement that would render entry riskier and therefore less likely.
- *Patent hoarding.*[242] Although IPRs can be structural barriers (both as legal and regulatory barriers and as first-mover advantages) the way in which they are used by their holders can also be strategic barriers. The OECD mentions the practice of 'patent hoarding' whereby an undertaking acquires numerous patents that block the feasible methods of competing and thereby builds a 'fortress' around its market position. These may be patents that the undertaking has no intention of exploiting commercially, but are simply deterrents to entry.[243]

Although not specifically listed in the OECD Roundtable document, switching costs, discussed earlier in respect of their possible effect on market definition, can also constitute barriers to entry.

[239] Commission Staff Discussion Paper, n. 207, para. 40.

[240] OECD Roundtable, n. 195, section 3.3.6. [241] Ibid., section 3.3.7.

[242] Ibid., section 3.3.8. The practice is also addressed in the OECD Roundtable report *Intellectual Property Rights*, DAF(2004)24, <www.oecd.org/daf/competition/34306055.pdf>.

[243] The abuse of IPRs is discussed in Chaps. 7 and 12.

Switching costs are structural barriers but can also be exploited by undertakings and so form strategic barriers. Furthermore, opportunity costs can act as barriers. Opportunity costs, the value of what has to be given up to do something else,[244] can be classed as an absolute cost advantage for the incumbent.

The Commission sets out the forms that barriers to entry can take in the 2004 Horizontal Merger Guidelines, which are discussed in Chapter 15.[245] In the Guidelines, the Commission takes a broad view of barriers to entry, considering that they can comprise legal or technical advantages or may exist because of the established position of the incumbent firms on the market. The Commission also deals with barriers to entry in the Guidance Paper, as discussed in Chapter 6 where the decisional practice of the Commission and the case law in respect of Article 102 are considered.

6. CONCLUSIONS

1. 'Market power' is the central concept of competition law. Market power is usually defined as the ability to profitably raise prices above the competitive level for a significant period of time.

2. In EU competition law, market power is normally assessed by defining the relevant product and geographic market, calculating the market shares of the undertaking concerned, and then engaging in a competitive assessment to determine what degree of competitive constraint the undertaking faces. Market definition is therefore the first step in assessing market power by this 'indirect method'.

3. The EU Courts define the relevant product market as all those products considered by the consumer as substitutable or interchangeable by reason of their characteristics, price, and intended use. This involves both demand and supply substitution. The geographic market is defined in terms of an area where the conditions of competition are 'sufficiently homogeneous'.

4. In 1997, the Commission adopted a Notice on Market Definition which saw the Commission set out a more economically rigorous approach than it had sometimes employed hitherto, favouring quantitative rather than qualitative methods and in particular adopting the methodology of the 'hypothetical monopolist' or SSNIP test.

5. There are certain situations in which the SSNIP test is unsuitable. It is a test which hypothesises price changes but, although that may work for merger assessments, it may not be useful in Article 102 cases where the prices may already be at monopoly level.

6. The 25 years since the Notice have seen the development of the digital economy and in particular the rise of the powerful digital platforms and digital ecosystems. There are significant difficulties of market definition in respect of digital platforms, stemming in particular from their multi-sided nature and the fact that they feature zero-prices, which makes reliance on price-based tests impracticable.

7. The Commission has embarked upon a review of the Market Definition Notice and a draft was published in November 2022. The final version is expected in 2023. The Draft Notice gives more detailed guidance than the 1997 Notice on many issues and focuses more attention on non-price elements of competition, downplaying the SSNIP test. It engages fully with the digital economy.

8. Market shares alone are not determinative of market power. Barriers to entry must be taken into account when assessing the competitive constraints to which firms are subject. Network effects can be a barrier to entry and are of great significance in digital markets. Big Data is a new phenomenon and the way in which, and the extent to which, its ownership acts as a barrier to entry has to be confronted.

[244] See Chap. 1, Section 3.B.i, p. 8.

[245] [2004] OJ C31/5. See also the Commission Guidelines on the application of Article 81(3) of the Treaty [2004] C 101/97, paras. 114–115.

9. There are difficulties involved in defining markets and identifying barriers to entry. This should be borne in mind in all cases where the application of competition rules is being considered. If markets are wrongly defined and barriers to entry imagined, the application of the competition rules can prohibit conduct which might otherwise be welfare-enhancing. Conversely, wrong market definitions and ignoring real barriers to entry may leave undertakings with market power free to act anti-competitively.

7. FURTHER READING

A. Books

BAIN, J. S., *Barriers to New Competition* (Harvard University Press, 1956)

BEGG, D., VERNASCA, G., FISCHER, S., and DORNBUSCH, R., *Economics* (10th edn, McGraw-Hill, 2011)

BELLAMY and CHILD (D. Bailey and L. John, eds.), *European Union Law of Competition* (8th edn, Oxford University Press, 2018), Chap. 4

BISHOP, S., and WALKER, M., *The Economics of EC Competition Law: Concepts, Application and Measurement* (3rd edn, Sweet & Maxwell, 2010)

CARLTON, D. W., and PERLOFF, J. M., *Modern Industrial Organization* (4th edn, Pearson Addison Wesley, 2005)

COATES, K., *EC Competition Law in Technology Markets* (Oxford University Press, 2010), Chap. 2

EVANS, D. S., and SCHMALENSEE, R., *Matchmakers: The New Economics of Multisided Platforms* (Harvard Business Review Press, 2016)

EZRACHI, A., and STUCKE, M. E., *Virtual Competition: The Promise and Perils of the Algorithm-Driven Economy* (Harvard University Press, 2016)

FATUR, A., *EU Competition Law and the Information and Communication Technology Network Industries* (Hart Publishing, 2012)

FAULL, J., and NIKPAY, A. (eds.), *The EU Law of Competition* (3rd edn, Oxford University Press, 2014), Chap. 1

FERRO, M. S., *Market Definition in EU Competition Law* (Edward Elgar, 2019)

GERADIN, D., LAYNE-FARRAR, A., and PETIT, N., *EU Competition Law and Economics* (Oxford University Press, 2012)

GERADIN, D., ZENGER, H., and STEPHAN, A., *EU Cartel Law and Economics* (Oxford University Press, 2016)

HILDEBRAND, D., *The Role of Economics Analysis in the EC Competition Rules* (Kluwer Law International, 2002)

HOVENKAMP, H., *Federal Antitrust Policy: The Law of Competition and its Practice* (6th edn, West, 2020)

MATEUS, A. M., and MOIREIRA, T., *Competition Law and Economics* (Edward Elgar, 2010)

MERCURO, N., and MEDEMA, S. G., *Economics and the Law: From Posner to Post-Modernism* (Princeton University Press, 1999)

MOTTA, M., *Competition Policy* (Cambridge University Press, 2004)

NIELS, G., JENKINS, H., and KAVANAGH, J., *Economics for Competition Lawyers* (2nd edn, Oxford University Press, 2016)

ORTIZ BLANCO, L., *Market Power in EU Antitrust Law* (Hart Publishing, 2012)

VAN DEN BERGH, R. J., and CAMESASCA, P. D., *European Competition Law and Economics: A Comparative Perspective* (2nd edn, Sweet & Maxwell, 2006)

B. Chapters in Books

FILISTRUCCHI, L., 'Market Definition in Multi-Sided Markets' in OECD (ed.), *Rethinking Antitrust Tools for Multi-Sided Markets* (OECD, 2008), 37

C. Articles

ANTITRUST BULLETIN SPECIAL ISSUE: KAPLOW, L., 'Why (Ever) Define Markets?' (2012) 57(4) *Ant Bull* 915

ASHALL, S., 'Away From Market Shares? The Increasing Importance of Contestability in EU Competition Law Case' (2015) 6 *JECLAP* 197

AUER, D., and PETIT, N., 'Two-sided Markets and the Challenge of Turning Economic Theory into Antitrust Policy', <http://ssrn.com/abstract=2552337>

COATE, M. B., and FISCHER, J. H., 'Is Market Definition Still Needed After All These Years' (2014) 2(2) *J of Antitrust Enforcement* 422

COLITTI, K., 'Countervailing Buyer Power and its Role in Competition Analysis' (2016) 12(2)–(3) *European Competition Journal* 361

CROCIONI, P., 'The Hypothetical Monopolist Test: What it Can and Cannot Tell You' [2002] *ECLR* 355

DUNBOW, B., 'Understanding Consumers: The Value of Stated Preferences in Antitrust Proceedings' [2003] *ECLR* 141

EVANS, D. S., and SCHMALENSEE, R., 'Debunking the "Network Effects" Bogeyman' (2017) 40 *Regulation* 36

FILISTRUCCHI, L., GERADIN, D., VAN DAMME, E., and AFFELDT, P., 'Market Definition in Two-sided Markets: Theory and Practice' (2014) 10(2) *J of Competition Law and Economics* 293

GRAEF, I., 'Market Definition and Market Power in Data: The Case of Online Platforms' (2015) 38 *World Competition* 473

HARBORD, D., and HOEHN, T., 'Barriers to Entry and Exit in European Competition Policy' (1994) 14 *International Review of Law and Economics* 41

HOVENKAMP, H., 'Platforms and the Rule of Reason: The *American Express* Case' [2019] *Colum Bus LR* 35

HOVENKAMP, H., 'Antitrust and Platform Monopoly' (2021) 130 *Yale LJ* 1952

HÜSCHELRATH, K., 'Critical Loss Analysis in Market Definition and Merger Control' (2009) 3 *European Competition Journal* 757

JACOBIDES, M., and LIANOS, I., 'Ecosystems and Competition Law in Theory and Practice' (2021) 30 *Industrial and Corporate Change* 1199, 1201

JONES, A., and ALBORS-LLORENS, A., 'The Images of the "Consumer" in EU Competition Law' (2016), University of Cambridge Faculty of Law Research Paper No. 17/2016 <http://papers.ssrn.com/sol3/papers.cfm?abstract_id=2750922>

KAPLOW, L., 'Why (Ever) Define Markets?' (2010) 124 *Harvard LR* 437

KAPLOW, L., 'On the Relevance of Market Power' (2017) 130 *Harvard LR* 1303

Katz, M., and Sallet, J., 'Multisided Platforms and Antitrust Enforcement' (2018) 127 *Yale LJ* 2142

Lamadrid de Pablo, A., 'The Double Duality of Two-sided Markets' [2015] *Comp Law* 5

Lancieri, F., and Morita Sakowski, P., 'Competition in Digital Markets: A Review of Expert Reports' (2021) 26 *Stanford J of Law, Business & Finance* 65

Landes, W. M., and Posner, R. A., 'Market Power in Antitrust Cases' (1981) 94 *Harvard LR* 937

Mahnke, R., 'Big Data as a Barrier to Entry' (2015) 2 *CPI Antitrust Chronicle* 2

Rochet, J.-C., and Tirole, J., 'Two-sided Markets: A Progress Report' (2006) 35(3) *RAND J of Economics* 645

Schepp, N.-P., and Wambach, A., 'On Big Data and Its Relevance for Market Power Assessment' (2016) 7(2) *JECLAP* 120

Thépot, F., 'Market Power in Online Search and Social Networking: A Matter of Two-sided Markets' (2013) 36 *World Competition* 195

Ward, P., 'Testing for Multisided Platform Effects in Antitrust Market Definition' (2017) 84 *Univ Chic LR* 2059

Veljanovski, C., 'Markets without Substitutes: Substitution versus Constraints as the Key to Market Definition' [2010] *ECLR* 122

4

ARTICLE 101 TFEU: THE ELEMENTS

1. CENTRAL ISSUES

1. This chapter, together with Chapter 5, sets out and introduces the core elements of Article 101. The way in which Article 101 applies to specific types of business agreements (e.g. cartels, horizontal cooperation agreements, distribution agreements, and intellectual property licensing agreements) is explored more fully in later chapters, especially Chapters 9–12.
2. Article 101(1) prohibits agreements and concerted practices between two or more independent undertakings and decisions by associations of undertakings which have as their object or effect the prevention, restriction, or distortion of competition and which affect trade between Member States.
3. The CJ has held that Article 101(1) applies only to agreements that appreciably affect competition and trade.
4. Article 101(3) provides that the Article 101(1) prohibition may be declared inapplicable to agreements which restrict competition but which fulfil its four criteria, broadly where the agreement produces countervailing beneficial effects.
5. This chapter focuses on the following issues:
   (a) *who* Article 101 applies to, i.e. which entities constitute an 'undertaking' and are consequently bound to comply with the competition rules;
   (b) what constitutes *joint* conduct (an agreement, decision, or concerted practice) caught by Article 101(1) and how this is distinguished from unilateral conduct falling outside its scope; and
   (c) when an agreement appreciably *affects trade* between Member States and so falls within the jurisdictional scope of Article 101(1).
6. Chapter 5 focuses on the question of *which* agreements are prohibited by Article 101. In particular:
   (a) when an agreement appreciably 'restricts' competition (by object or effect) for the purposes of Article 101(1); and
   (b) when the beneficial aspects of the agreement enable it to satisfy the conditions of Article 101(3) and offset the restriction of competition identified under Article 101(1).

2. INTRODUCTION

This chapter introduces the scheme of Article 101 and some of the key elements of Article 101(1). Chapter 5 focuses on the substantive question of which agreements are prohibited by Article 101 and the relationship between Article 101(1) and Article 101(3).

How the elements of Article 101 are interpreted and applied depends upon the policy objectives being pursued in its enforcement. It has been seen in Chapter 1 that the answer to the question 'what are the goals of Article 101?' is not entirely straightforward. The view set out by the Commission in its current guidelines, including the Guidelines on the application of Article 81(3) [now Article 101(3)] (the 'Article 101(3) Guidelines'), is that:[1]

> [t]he objective of Article [101] is to protect competition on the market as a means of enhancing consumer welfare and of ensuring an efficient allocation of resources. Competition and market integration serve these ends since the creation and preservation of an open single market promotes an efficient allocation of resources throughout the Community for the benefit of consumers.[2]

Court judgments, however, although placing emphasis on consumer welfare as a goal,[3] also stress the importance of the internal market imperative and the structure of competition. Indeed, in *GlaxoSmithKline Services Unlimited v Commission* the CJ held that the competition rules are designed 'to achieve the Treaty's objective of achieving the integration of national markets through the establishment of a single market',[4] and aim 'to protect not only the interests of competitors or of consumers, but also the structure of the market and, in so doing, competition as such'.[5] Further, concerns about climate change, economic and wealth inequality, the well-being of national and EU industries, the benefits of international trade, and the mounting power of the Big Tech companies have reignited the debate as to whether competition law should pursue a purist, efficiency-based goal, or whether it can or should embrace broader objectives, including sustainability goals and environmental protection. In this and other chapters, it will be seen that although Article 101 analysis is principally focused on the impact of the agreement on competition and consumers, 'non-competition' factors have on some occasions been influential in its interpretation.

3. THE TEXT AND SCHEME OF ARTICLE 101

A. THE THREE PARAGRAPHS

(i) The Text

Article 101 is in three parts, encompassing a prohibition of certain restrictive agreements etc. (Article 101(1)), setting out one of the consequences of infringing the prohibition (Article 101(2)), and providing a legal exception to the Article 101(1) prohibition (Article 101(3)).

[1] [2004] OJ C101/97, para. 13. [2] Ibid.

[3] See e.g. Case C-377/20, *Servizio Elettrico Nazionale* EU:C:2022:379 and Chap. 1.

[4] Cases C-501, 513, 515, and 519/06 P, EU:C:2008:738, para. 61.

[5] Ibid., para. 63. See also Case C-8/08, *T-Mobile Netherlands BV v Raad van Bestuur van de Nederlandse Mededingingsautoriteit* EU:C:2009:343, para. 38.

1. The following shall be prohibited as incompatible with the common market: all agreements between undertakings, decisions by associations of undertakings and concerted practices which may affect trade between Member States and which have as their object or effect the prevention, restriction or distortion of competition within the common market, and in particular those which:
   (a) directly or indirectly fix purchase or selling prices or any other trading conditions;
   (b) limit or control production, markets, technical development, or investment;
   (c) share markets or sources of supply;
   (d) apply dissimilar conditions to equivalent transactions with other trading parties, thereby placing them at a competitive disadvantage;
   (e) make the conclusion of contracts subject to acceptance by the other parties of supplementary obligations which, by their nature or according to commercial usage, have no connection with the subject of such contracts.
2. Any agreements or decisions prohibited pursuant to this Article shall be automatically void.
3. The provisions of paragraph 1 may, however, be declared inapplicable in the cases of:
   — any agreement or category of agreements between undertakings;
   — any decision or category of decisions by associations of undertakings;
   — any concerted practice or category of concerted practices,

   which contributes to improving the production or distribution of goods or to promoting technical or economic progress, while allowing consumers a fair share of the resulting benefit, and which does not:
   (a) impose on the undertakings concerned restrictions which are not indispensable to the attainment of these objectives;
   (b) afford such undertakings the possibility of eliminating competition in respect of a substantial part of the products in question.

(ii) The Article 101(1) Prohibition

For the prohibition in Article 101(1) to apply the following must be established:

(a) collusion or joint conduct—in the form of an agreement or concerted practice between two or more undertakings or a decision by an association of undertakings;

(b) collusion which appreciably[6] restricts competition, whether by object or effect. An illustrative, but not exhaustive, list of examples of such restrictions is set out; and

(c) an appreciable effect on trade between Member States.

(iii) Nullity

Article 102(2) sets out one of the consequences of infringing Article 101 (but see further Section 3.B). Although it states that an agreement, decision, or concerted practice prohibited by Article 101(1) is automatically void, the CJ has held that the nullity affects *only* the clauses in the agreement prohibited by the provision (see further Section 5).[7]

[6] The appreciability requirement has been added by the CJ, see Sections 4.D and 4.E.

[7] Case 56/65, *Société Technique Minière (STM) v Maschinenbau Ulm GmbH* EU:C:1966:38. See Section 5 and Chap. 14.

(iv) Article 101(3)—Legal Exception

The Article 101(1) prohibition may be declared inapplicable to an agreement, etc.,[8] which fulfils the four criteria (two positive and two negative) set out in Article 101(3). Between 1962 and 2004, agreements could benefit from Article 101(3) only if they were specifically 'exempted' from the Article 101(1) prohibition by virtue of either: an *individual exemption* granted by the Commission following notification of the agreement to it (it had *sole* power under Regulation 17 of 1962 to declare Article 101(1) inapplicable to individual agreements pursuant to Article 101(3)[9]); or a *block exemption*, granted by EU regulation to certain categories of agreement.

From 1 May 2004, however, it has not been possible to gain an individual exemption for an agreement from the Commission (although block exemptions remain), and the Commission's exclusive competence to apply Article 101(3) has been removed. Regulation 1/2003[10] makes it clear that the Commission, the national competition authorities (NCAs), and national courts may apply Article 101(3) individually to agreements whenever an agreement's compatibility with the provision is questioned. Further, in exceptional circumstances, the Commission may be willing to grant 'comfort letters' to firms as to the compatibility of their agreements with Article 101.[11]

B. THE CONSEQUENCES OF INFRINGEMENT

Apart from the nullity provided for in Article 101(2), other severe consequences may result for parties to an agreement which contravenes Article 101. The provision may be enforced both:

- publicly by the Commission and NCAs—which may investigate a violation of the rules and seek, or impose, fines or other sanctions on undertakings found to be in breach (and/or, in some Member States, on executives or employees working within them[12]); and
- privately by litigants bringing tortious or other proceedings against an infringing undertaking before a national court.

Public and private enforcement are considered in detail in Chapters 13 and 14, respectively.

C. BURDEN AND STANDARD OF PROOF

The burden of proving an infringement of Article 101(1) is on the Commission, or other person alleging the same—the claimant must put forward the facts and, where necessary, related evidence.[13] Once this is established, the burden shifts on to the undertakings claiming the benefit of Article 101(3) to establish that the agreement meets its criteria.[14]

[8] Unless the context otherwise requires, or the discussion is specifically about one or other category of collusion, the word 'agreement' is used as shorthand to cover agreements, decisions, and concerted practices.

[9] Reg. 17 [1959–1962] OJ Spec. Ed. 87, Art. 9(1), see Chaps. 2, 5, and 13.

[10] [2003] OJ L1/1, see Chaps. 2 and 13.

[11] See e.g. Commission adopts a more flexible antitrust Informal Guidance Notice; withdraws Antitrust COVD Temporary Framework, 3 October 2022, discussed in Chap. 13. During the Covid crisis, the Commission issued some comfort letters, see e.g. Medicines for Europe, 8 April 2020, IP/20/618. The Commission also has power to adopt non-infringement decisions, see Chap. 13.

[12] See further Chaps. 9 and 13 and Dir. 2019/1 to empower the competition authorities of the Member States to be more effective enforcers and to ensure the proper functioning of the internal market [2019] OJ L11/3.

[13] See Kokott AG in Case C-8/08, *T-Mobile Netherlands and Others* EU:C:2009:110.

[14] See Reg. 1/2003, Art. 2. Cases C-204, 205, 211, 213, 217, and 219/00 P, *Aalborg Portland A/S v Commission (Cement)* EU:C:2004:6, para. 78, A. Kalintiri, 'The Allocation of the Legal Burden of Proof in Article 101 TFEU Cases: A "Clear" Rule with Not-So-Clear Implications' (2015) 34(1) *Yearbook of European Law* 232 and Chap. 13.

The standard of proof—the standard to which facts have to be proven—depends upon the forum of the proceedings.[15] Antitrust proceedings brought by the Commission are characterised as administrative. Nonetheless, they may culminate in non-negligible stigma for the legal or natural persons involved and the imposition of punitive fines by the Commission, which are treated as *de facto* criminal charges for the purposes of Article 6(1) of the European Convention on Human Rights (ECHR). This has important consequences for the procedures carried out by the Commission and the standard of review of its decisions that must be conducted by the EU Courts.[16] In particular, the CJ has confirmed that 'the presumption of innocence resulting in particular from Article 6(2) of the ECHR . . . applies to the procedures relating to infringements of the competition rules applicable to undertakings that may result in the imposition of fines or periodic penalties payments'.[17] Consequently, the Commission must establish 'sufficiently precise and coherent proof'[18] of an infringement (and its scope and duration)—it must provide 'a firm, precise and consistent body of evidence' to justify its view[19] and all the facts enabling the conclusion to be drawn that an undertaking participated in an infringement; 'any doubt of the Court must benefit the undertaking' to which an infringement decision is addressed.[20] Although '[t]he Court cannot therefore conclude that the Commission has established the existence of the infringement at issue to the requisite legal standard if it still entertains doubts on that point, in particular in proceedings for the annulment of a decision imposing a fine',[21] it appears that proof beyond reasonable doubt is not required.[22]

It will be seen, nonetheless, that in certain circumstances the Commission (or another claimant) can, without undermining the presumption of innocence, rely on inferences drawn from the evidence, coincidences, and indicia and reasonable presumptions to provide evidence of an infringement of Article 101(1) (for example, it is presumed that an undertaking which attended a meeting at which an anti-competitive agreement was concluded subscribed to the anti-competitive initiative unless it is able to establish that it publicly distanced itself from the illegal scheme[23]). An important difference thus exists between the legal burden of proof and the burden of providing evidence—the evidential burden.[24]

4. THE INTERPRETATION AND APPLICATION OF ARTICLE 101(1)

A. 'UNDERTAKING' AND 'ASSOCIATIONS OF UNDERTAKINGS'

(i) Every Entity Engaged in an Economic Activity

Article 101 applies to agreements and concerted practices between undertakings and decisions by associations of undertakings. Although not defined in the Treaty, it has become settled that the term undertaking 'encompasses every entity engaged in an economic activity, regardless of the legal status

[15] Case C-74/14, *'Eturas' UAB v Lietuvos Respublikos konkurencijos taryba* EU:C:2016:42, see n. 328 and text.

[16] See further Chap. 13. [17] Case C-199/92 P, *Hüls AG v Commission* EU:C:1999:358, paras. 149–150.

[18] Cases 29 and 30/83, *Compagnie Royale Asturienne des Mines SA and Rheinzink GmbH v Commission* EU:C:1984:130. The standard of proof in national proceedings will be a matter for national law (subject to any constraints imposed by EU law), see Chaps. 13 and 14.

[19] Cases C-89, 104, 114, 116, 117, and 125–129/85, *Ahlström Osakeyhtiö and Others v Commission (Woodpulp)* EU:C:1993:120, para. 127.

[20] Case T-442/08, *International Confederation of Societies of Authors and Composers (CISAC) v Commission* EU:T:2013:188, para. 92.

[21] Case T-348/08, *Aragonesas Industrias y Energía, SAU v Commission* EU:T:2011:621, paras. 92–93.

[22] Case T-53/03, *BPB v Commission* EU:T:2008:254, paras. 61–64.

[23] See Section 4.B.iii.d. Where enough has been done to comply with the standard of proof, the burden will be discharged unless the parties produce counter-evidence capable of discrediting the charge.

[24] See e.g. Kalintiri, n. 14; M. Abenhaïm, 'Public Distancing and Liability in Cartel Cases: Does Distance Lend Enchantment?' (2016) 39(3) *World Competition* 413, 419; and K. Khoo, 'Regulating the Inferential Process in Alleged Article 101 Infringements' (2017) 13(1) *J of Competition Law and Economics* 45.

of the entity and the way in which it is financed'.[25] Undertaking has the same meaning for the purposes of both Article 101 and Article 102[26] so the concept determines 'the categories of actors to which the competition rules apply'.[27] Entities which are not engaged in economic activity, but perform tasks in the public interest or exercise public powers or official authority, fall outside the scope of the rules.[28] The critical question, therefore, is what constitutes 'economic activity'.

(ii) The Legal Status or Form or the Entity Is Immaterial

Because the notion of an undertaking focuses on the nature of the activity carried out by the entity concerned (a functional approach is adopted),[29] the legal personality of the entity is not decisive. The notion may encompass natural persons, legal persons, and/or State and public bodies (even if they do not have an independent legal personality but form part of a State's general administration,[30] they supply public services, or they are subject to a public service obligation (see further Chapter 8)). As well as companies and partnerships, therefore, individuals,[31] trade associations,[32] agricultural co-operatives,[33] medical aid organisations,[34] collecting societies,[35] and professional bodies[36] have been found to be undertakings for the purposes of the rules. The fact that the business occupation of a body is viewed as a liberal profession is not inconsistent with the fact that it may be an undertaking or an association of undertakings engaged in an economic activity.[37] In *Wouters v Algemene Raad van de Nederlandse Orde van Advocaten*,[38] for example, the CJ made it clear that members of the Bar which

[25] Case C-41/90, *Höfner and Elser v Macrotron GmbH* EU:C:1991:161, para. 21. See also e.g. Case 364/92, *SAT Fluggesellschaft mbH v Eurocontrol* EU:C:1994:7, para. 18; and Case C-138/11, *Compass-Datenbank GmbH v Republik Österreich* EU:C:2012:449, para. 35.

[26] See Cases T-68, 77, and 78/89, *Società Italiana Vetro SpA v Commission* EU:T:1992:38, para. 358. Many of the cases discussed in this chapter concern Art. 102, not Art. 101. It also has the same meaning in the context of EU merger control and State aid.

[27] Case C-67/96, *Albany International BV (Albany) v Stichting Bedrijfspensioenfonds Textielindustrie* EU:C:1999:430, Jacobs AG, para. 206.

[28] For the view that the Treaty contains a public/private divide and that the different treatment of these entities is 'justified by a presumption underlying the rules of the private sphere that its occupants are self-interested and the presumption underlying rules of the public sphere that its occupants operate in pursuit of the public interest', see O. Odudu, *The Boundaries of EC Competition Law: The Scope of Article 81* (Oxford University Press, 2006), 45–56.

[29] See O. Odudu, 'The Meaning of Undertaking within Article 101' (2005) 7 *Cambridge Yearbook of European Legal Studies* 211, 212 citing A. Deringer, *The Competition Law of the European Economic Community: A Commentary on the EEC Rules of Competition (Articles 85 to 90) Including the Implementing Regulations and Directives* (Commerce Clearing House, 1968), 5.

[30] COMP/26.870, *Aluminium Products* [1985] OJ L92/1 at part II para. 9.2. See also Case 118/85, *Commission v Italy* EU:C:1987:283, para. 16.

[31] COMP/29.559, *RAI/UNITEL* [1978] OJ L157/39, COMP/38.279, *French Beef* [2003] OJ L209/12, *aff'd* (but fines reduced) in Cases T-217 and 245/03, *FNSEA v Commission* EU:T:2006:391, Cases C-101 and 110/07, *Coop de France bétail et viande v Commission*, Case C-110/07, *FNSEA v Commission* EU:C:2007:219, but not, it seems, employees, see Section 4.A.v.

[32] Case 96/82, *NV IAZ International Belgium v Commission* EU:C:1983:310.

[33] See Case C-250/92, *Gøttrup-Klim e.a. Grovvareforeninger and Others v Dansk Landbrugs Grovvareselskab AmbA* EU:C:1994:413.

[34] Case C-475/99, *Firma Ambulanz Glöckner v Landkreis Südwestpfalz* EU:C:2001:577.

[35] Which engage in the commercial provision of services, see e.g. Case 127/73, *Belgische Radio en Televisie v SV SABAM* EU:C:1974:25.

[36] See generally M. Monti, 'Competition in Professional Services: New Light and New Challenges', Speech to the German Federal Bar Association (Bundesanwaltskammer), 21 March 2003.

[37] COMP/33.407, *AICIA v CNSD* [1993] OJ L203/27, para. 40.

[38] Case C-309/99, EU:C:2002:98.

offered, for a fee, services in the form of legal assistance carried out an economic activity and so were undertakings for the purposes of the rules. Neither the complex and technical nature of the services provided, nor the fact that the profession was regulated altered this conclusion.[39]

Although in some circumstances it may be inappropriate to apply competition rules to functions carried out by sporting bodies,[40] such bodies will be found to be undertakings when carrying out economic activities.[41] In a case concerning the 1990 World Cup, for example, the Commission held that the international football federation (FIFA), the Italian FA (FIGC), and the local organising committee, which carried out economic activities were all undertakings within the meaning of Article 101(1).[42] Further, in *Motosykletistiki Omospondia Ellados NPID (MOTOE) v Ellinkio Dimosio*,[43] the CJ held that a legal (non-profit-making) entity which organised motorcycling events and entered into sponsorship, advertising, and insurance contracts designed to exploit those events commercially was an undertaking, even though it was also vested with public powers (authorising the organisation of motorcycling events) which were not of an economic nature.

(iii) Distinguishing Economic Activity from Functions Which Are Not Economic

a. *Characterising Economic Activity*

The case law indicates that the characteristic features of 'economic activity' are (a) the offering of goods or services on the market,[44] (b) where that activity 'could, at least in principle, be carried on by a private undertaking in order to make profits'.[45] It is economic if it could be carried out in a market by a private undertaking[46] or if offered in competition with other operators which do seek to make a profit, even if the offering entity itself does not, or does not seek to, make a profit,[47] or is not set up

[39] Case C-309/99, *Wouters* EU:C:2002:98, paras. 46–49, 64. See also Case C-1/12, *Ordem dos Técnicos Oficiais de Contas v Autoridade da Concorrência* EU:C:2013:127 (chartered accountants, who offer accounting services for remuneration and assume the financial risks related to the exercise of those activities, are undertakings) and Cases C-180–184/98, *Pavlov* EU:C:2000:428 (specialist medical doctors in private practice are undertakings).

[40] See Chap. 2.

[41] COMP/33.384 and COMP/33.378, *The Distribution of Package Tours During the 1990 World Cup* [1992] OJ L326/31, especially paras. 44–60.

[42] Ibid. See also COMP/36.888, *1998 World Cup Finals* [2000] OJ L5/55. See also Case C-333/21, *European Super League v FIFA and UEFA* EU:C:2022:993, Rantos AG, paras. 56–59, judgment of the CJ pending.

[43] Case C-49/07, *MOTOE* EU:C:2008:376. See also Case C-519/04 P, *Meca-Medina v Commission* EU:C:2006:492 and Case COMP/40.208, *ISU* 8 December 2017 (international sport associations which have as their members national sport associations 'are undertakings to the extent they themselves carry out activities of an economic nature (such as the organisation and commercial exploitation of sport events)). International sport associations may also be associations of undertakings if their members carry out activities of an economic nature, regardless of whether the international sport associations themselves carry out such activities', para. 137, *aff'd* Case T-93/18, EU:T:2020:610, on appeal Case C-124/21 P, judgment pending. See further Chap. 5.

[44] See e.g. Case C-475/99, *Firma Ambulanz Glöckner v Landkreis Südwestpfalz* EU:C:2001:577, para. 19, Case C-35/96 *Commission v Italy* EU:C:1998:303, para. 36, and Case C-205/03 P, *FENIN v Commission* EU:C:2006:453, para. 25.

[45] Case C-67/96, *Albany* EU:C:1999:430, Jacobs AG, para. 311. See also Cases C-180–184/98, *Pavlov* EU:C:2000:428, para. 117.

[46] Cases C-264, 306, 354, and 355/01, *AOK Bundesverband v Ichthyol-Gesellschaft Cordes, Hermani & Co* EU:C:2004:150, Jacobs AG, para. 28 ('If there were no possibility of a private undertaking carrying on a given activity, there would be no purpose in applying the competition rules to it'). See also Case C-475/99, *Firma Ambulanz Glöckner v Landkreis Südwestpfalz* EU:C:2001:577.

[47] Case C-67/96, *Albany* EU:C:1999:430; Case C-475/99, *Firma Ambulanz Glöckner v Landkreis Südwestpfalz* EU:C:2001:577; Cases C-262 and 271/18 P, *Dôvera zdravotnápoist'ovňa, a.s. v Commission* EU:C:2020:450.

for an economic purpose.[48] Such 'economic' activities are distinguished from the exercise of 'official authority' or 'public powers'.[49]

It is not always easy to distinguish economic activity from the performance of public tasks. In the important case of *Höfner and Elser v Macrotron*, the CJ focused on the responsibilities of the relevant entity, holding that employment procurement activities were economic in nature, since they had not always been, and are not necessarily, carried out by public entities (even if they were often entrusted to public agencies). Neither the fact that the procurement office had a legal monopoly over employment procurement of higher staff, nor that it provided such services without charge altered the conclusion.

Case C-41/90, *Höfner and Elser v Macrotron* [1991] ECR I-1979

Under German law on the promotion of employment (the AFG), the Bundesanstalt für Arbeit (Federal Office for Employment, the Bundesanstalt), a public agency financed principally through employer and employee contributions, had a monopoly in employment recruitment. Nevertheless, it tolerated private agencies dealing with the recruitment of business executives. This case concerned a contractual dispute which arose in the German courts. A private recruitment agency sought to recover fees from a company for which it had provided recruitment services (in breach of the Bundesanstalt's exclusive right). The German courts took the view that the claim should fail on the ground that the contract had been concluded in breach of German law and was void. The Oberlandesgericht München referred a number of questions to the CJ under Article 267 TFEU, including whether the Bundesanstalt had committed an abuse of a dominant position. This necessitated consideration of whether the Bundesanstalt was an undertaking for the purposes of the competition rules.

Court of Justice

21. It must be observed, in the context of competition law, first that the concept of an undertaking encompasses every entity engaged in an economic activity, regardless of the legal status of the entity and the way in which it is financed and, secondly, that employment procurement is an economic activity.

22. The fact that employment procurement activities are normally entrusted to public agencies cannot affect the economic nature of such activities. Employment procurement has not always been, and is not necessarily, carried out by public entities. That finding applies in particular to executive recruitment.

23. It follows that an entity such as a public employment agency engaged in the business of employment procurement may be classified as an undertaking for the purpose of applying the Community competition rules.

[48] Case 155/73, *Italy v Sacchi* EU:C:1974:40. See also cases dealing with sporting associations, nn. 40–43 and text.

[49] But see e.g. Case C-67/96, *Albany* EU:C:1999:430; Case C-309/99, *Wouters v Algemene Raad van de Nederlandse Orde van Advocaten* EU:C:2002:98; and Art. 106(2) (undertakings entrusted with the operation of services of general economic interest or having the character of a revenue-producing monopoly are subject to the competition rules only insofar as the application of the rules does not obstruct the performance of the tasks assigned to them). Art. 106(2), like all derogations from the main Treaty objectives, is construed narrowly, see Chap. 8. A finding that an entity is not an undertaking obviates the need for reliance on Art. 106(2).

b. Exercise of Public Powers in the Public Interest or Exercise of Official Authority

Although *Höfner* suggests a broad approach to the concept of economic activity (potentially bringing within it many State services),[50] the CJ has held that the rules do not apply to the exercise of sovereign powers of the State, tasks performed in the public interest (essential functions of the State), or administrative functions.[51] In *SAT Fluggesellschaft mbH v Eurocontrol*,[52] for example, the CJ indicated that Eurocontrol (European Organisation for the Safety of Air Navigation), which performed tasks which were in the public interest[53] (maintaining and improving air navigation safety) at the request of Contracting States, was not an undertaking even though it collected route charges (which were set not by it but by the Contracting States). The supervision of airspace was a duty typically reserved to public authorities. In a later case, the CJ confirmed that Eurocontrol would not act as an undertaking even when conducting economic activities if those activities were connected with, and inseparable from, the exercise of its public powers.[54]

In *Diego Calì*,[55] the CJ referred to *Eurocontrol* when dealing with a case concerning anti-pollution surveillance and intervention entrusted by the national port authority at Genoa to a *private* limited company, SEPG. A port user, Diego Calì, challenged charges levied on it by SEPG in respect of services provided on the grounds that SEPG had abused its dominant position contrary to Article 102. The CJ found that SEPG was not an undertaking since it carried out services relating to the protection of the environment which were not of an economic nature but which were essential functions of the State. The purpose of the activity was to guarantee safety, to protect the port environment, and to ensure public assets were properly protected in the interest of the State and citizens.[56]

> 22. The anti-pollution surveillance for which SEPG was responsible in the oil port of Genoa is a task in the public interest which forms part of the essential functions of the State as regards protection of the environment in maritime areas.
>
> 23. Such surveillance is connected by its nature, its aim and the rules to which it is subject with the exercise of powers relating to the protection of the environment which are typically those of a public authority. It is not of an economic nature justifying the application of the Treaty rules on competition . . .
>
> 24. The levying of a charge by SEPG for preventive anti-pollution surveillance is an integral part of its surveillance activity in the maritime area of the port and cannot affect the legal status of that activity (Case C-364/92 *SAT Fluggesellschaft v Eurocontrol* . . . paragraph 28). Moreover, as stated in paragraph 8 of this judgment, the tariffs applied by SEPG have been approved by the public authorities.

The outcome of *Eurocontrol* and *Diego Calì* thus turned upon the CJ's assessment that these tasks, in contrast to those carried out in *Höfner and Elser*, could only be performed by or on behalf of a public body (the task would not have been performed without State intervention).[57] These cases made it clear

[50] See E. Kloosterhuis, 'Defining Non-economic Activities in Competition Law' (2017) 13(1) *European Competition Journal* 117.

[51] Case 30/87, *Corinne Bodson v SA Pompes funèbres des régions libérées* EU:C:1988:225 (the competition rules are not applicable to communes acting in their capacity as public authorities and entrusted with the 'operation of a public service', e.g. carrying out an administrative duty, granting concessions for funeral services, para. 18).

[52] Case C-364/92, EU:C:1994:7.

[53] See also Case C-74/16, *Congregación de Escuelas Pías Provincia Betania v Ayuntamiento de Getafe* EU:C:2017:496.

[54] Case C-113/07, *SELEX Sistemi Integrati SpA (SELEX Sistemi) v Commission* EU:C:2009:191, see n. 85 and text.

[55] Case C-343/95, *Diego Calì e Figli Srl v SEPG* EU:C:1997:160. [56] Ibid., Cosmas AG, paras. 44–46.

[57] 'Both *Eurocontrol* and *Diego Calì* show recognition that effective provision of a public good is impossible absent the coercive power of the state', Odudu, n. 28, 42–45 (identifying the two characteristics of public goods that make profit impossible: they are non-rivalrous in consumption (once produced, an infinite number of consumers can enjoy them without increased production cost or diminished enjoyment by others); and the benefits are non-excludable (it is not possible to prevent people from enjoying the benefits once the good is produced)).

that the fact that a product or a service supplied by a public entity is provided in return for remuneration, or even by a private entity, will not necessarily lead to the activity being classified as economic, especially if the price is not independently set by the entity. Similarly, in *Compass-Datenbank GmbH v Republik Österreich*,[58] the CJ held that a public authority which stored data 'in relation to undertakings, on the basis of a statutory obligation on those undertakings to disclose the data and power of enforcement related thereto' exercised 'public powers'[59] even though it charged those who wished to search that data and/or provided print-outs for it:

> 42. With regard to the fact that the making available to interested persons of the data in such a database is remunerated, it should be noted that . . . to the extent that the fees or payments due for the making available to the public of such information are not laid down directly or indirectly by the entity concerned but are provided for by law, the charging of such remuneration can be regarded as inseparable from that making available of data. Thus, the charging by the Republik Österreich of fees or payments due for the making available to the public of that information cannot change the legal classification of that activity, meaning that it does not constitute an economic activity.

c. Social Security Schemes, Healthcare, and Social Services: Activities Fulfilling an Exclusively Social Function

A line of cases concerning pension funds and social security schemes (for example, relating to healthcare or accident insurance) make it clear that EU law does not detract from the powers of the Member States to organise their social security systems.[60] However, a distinction has been drawn between:

(a) entities fulfilling an exclusively social function, that is which:

  (i) carry out an activity based on the principle of solidarity—'the redistribution of income between those who are better off and those who, in view of their resources . . . would be deprived'[61] or 'the inherently uncommercial act of involuntary subsidization of one social group by another'[62]—or which involves an element of cross-subsidy (for example, because benefits paid or the scope of coverage are not proportionate to contributions, contributions are not proportionate to risk, benefits may be payable even though contributions due have not been paid), and

  (ii) are subject to State supervision as to how the scheme functions

—which are not classified as undertakings (even if they are for-profit[63]);[64] and

(b) entities operating in the same way as, or in competition with, ordinary commercial enterprises in the same sector—which are undertakings even if the scheme has a social objective.

[58] Case C-138/11, EU:C:2012:449. [59] Ibid., para. 40.

[60] Case C-218/00, *Cisal di Battistello Venanzio & Co v Istituto nazionale per l'assicurazione contro gli infortuni sul lavoro (INAIL)* EU:C:2002:36, para. 31 (relying in particular on Case C-158/96, *Kohl* EU:C:1998:171, para. 17).

[61] Cases C-159–160/91, *Poucet et Pistre v Assurances Générales de France* EU:C:1993:63, para. 10.

[62] Case C-70/95, *Sodemare SA v Regione Lombardia* EU:C:1997:301, Fennelly AG, para. 29. See also Odudu, n. 28, 39–42.

[63] See Cases C-262 and 271/18 P, *Dôvera zdravotná poisťovňa, a.s. v Commission* EU:C:2020:450 (confirming that even if some entities within a compulsory health insurance scheme are undertakings, those pursuing a social objective and applying the principle of solidarity under State supervision are not (even if for-profit companies governed by private law) and setting aside Case T-216/15, EU:T:2018:64).

[64] See Case C-350/07, *Kattner Stahlbau GmbH v Maschinenbau- und Metall- Berufsgenossenschaft* EU:C:2009:127 (a body to which firms in an industry must be affiliated in respect of insurance against accidents at work and occupational diseases is not an undertaking but fulfils a social function where such a body operates within the framework of a scheme which applies the principle of solidarity and is subject to State supervision), and Case C-437/09, *AG2R Prévoyance v Beaudout Père et Fils SARL* EU:C:2011:112, paras. 53–65.

Thus, in *Poucet et Pistre*,[65] a French body running a compulsory social security scheme was held not to be an undertaking—benefits received under the scheme administered were not proportionate to contributions and contributions made were proportionate to income (there was an element of cross-subsidy); similarly in *AOK Bundesverband v Ichthyol-Gesellschaft Cordes, Hermani & Co Bundesverband*,[66] the CJ held that sickness funds fulfilled 'an exclusively social function, which is founded on the principle of national solidarity and is entirely non-profit making'.[67] In particular, the funds were obliged to offer benefits to members which were not dependent upon the amount of contributions, and an equalisation of costs and risks was operated between the funds. This conclusion was not affected by the fact that latitude was available to the funds when setting their contribution rate and that some competition with one another did exist.

In contrast:

- in *Fédération Française des Sociétés d'Assurance*,[68] a non-profit-making body operating a pension scheme was found to be an undertaking—the entity operated in the same way as other insurance companies, the rules were like those of private schemes, and there was no mutuality or cross-subsidy between the beneficiaries;
- in *Albany International BV v Stichting Bedrijfspensioenfonds Textielindustrie*,[69] a supplementary pension fund (affiliation to which was compulsory in the textile industry) was found to be an undertaking even though the supplementary pension scheme was designed to top up an extremely limited statutory pension, the sectoral pension fund was non-profit-making, and the pension fund was obliged to accept all workers without a medical examination.[70] The CJ accepted that the social objectives which the pension fund was required to pursue might make the service it provided less competitive than those offered by other insurance companies. These factors did not, however, detract from the fact that the activities it engaged in were economic ones. The pension fund determined the amount of contributions made and benefits received (the latter were dependent upon the results of the investments made by it) and it could, in certain circumstances, grant exemption from affiliation to the fund. The social objectives were relevant, however, to the CJ's finding that the public authority could nonetheless confer on a pension fund the exclusive right to manage a supplementary pension scheme in a given sector.[71]

d. *Purchasing of Goods and Services by an Entity Not Engaged in Economic Activity*

In *Federación Nacional de Empresas de Instrumentación Científica, Médica, Técnica y Dental (FENIN) v Commission*,[72] the EU Courts confirmed that an organisation managing a national health system and providing services free of charge on the basis of universal cover, is not an undertaking. It also

[65] Cases C-159–160/91, EU:C:1993:63.

[66] Cases C-264, 306, 354, and 355/01, EU:C:2004:150. See also Case C-218/00, *Cisal di Battistello Venanzio & Co v Istituto nazionale per l'assicurazione contro gli infortuni sul lavoro (INAIL)* EU:C:2002:36 (an institution providing compulsory insurance against accidents at work and occupational diseases applied the principle of solidarity and did not carry out an economic activity: contributions were not systematically set at a rate proportionate to the risk of insurance; the amount of benefits paid was not necessarily proportionate to earnings (there was no direct link between the contributions paid and the benefits granted, which were rather, in the last resort, fixed by the State; and affiliation of the scheme was compulsory and essential to its financial balance and for the application of the principle of solidarity, paras. 31–46, Jacobs AG, paras. 71–82)).

[67] *AOK-Bundesverband* ibid., para. 51. Contrast the view of Jacobs AG in his Opinion, para. 43.

[68] Case C-244/94, *Fédération Française des Sociétés d'Assurance and Others v Ministère de l'Agriculture et de la Pêche* EU:C:1995:392.

[69] Case C-67/96, EU:C:1999:430. The case concerned a dispute between the fund and Albany, a textile business, which wished to be exempted from the affiliation.

[70] Ibid., paras. 77–87. See also Cases C-180–184, *Pavlov* EU:C:2000:428.

[71] See further Chap. 8.

[72] Case C-205/03 P, *FENIN v Commission* EU:C:2006:453; Case T-319/99, EU:T:2003:50.

had to be considered, however, when 'purchasing' of goods and services by a public entity that discharges social functions might constitute economic activity. In this case, an association of the undertakings which marketed medical goods and equipment to bodies forming part of the Spanish Health Service (SNS) complained to the Commission that SNS organisations were guilty of an abuse of a dominant position, in particular because they systematically took an average of 300 days to pay their debts. The Commission rejected the complaint on the ground that the organisations in question were not undertakings. The GC affirmed. Bodies forming part of the SNS, and funded from social security contributions and other State funding, did not act as an undertaking when *purchasing* medical goods and equipment for the purpose of using them for activities of a purely social nature—to provide free health services to SNS members on the basis of universal cover—by which it operated according to the principle of solidarity.[73] The Court stressed that it was the *supply* function—the offering of goods and services on a market—of the entity that was important when determining whether economic activity was carried out and not the purchasing function.[74] If the activity for which the entity purchased goods was not an economic one, it made no difference that the entity might wield very considerable economic power, even giving rise to a monopsony.[75] The GC did not consider whether the fact that SNS did charge some patients, those not covered by SNS, for care would alter the conclusion on the undertaking question. Although this point was raised on appeal, the Court held that as it had not been put to the Commission, it was not relevant for the purposes of reviewing the legality of its decision.[76] The CJ[77] upheld the decision of the GC.

Case C-205/03, *Federación Nacional de Empresas de Instrumentación Científica, Médica, Técnica y Dental (FENIN) v Commission* EU:C:2006:453

Court of Justice

23. In support of the first part of its plea, FENIN argues that the [GC] adopted a definition of economic activity which is too narrow, holding that that activity necessarily consists of the offer of goods or services on a given market and excluding all purchasing activity from that definition. FENIN submits that the approach of the [GC] would enable many bodies to avoid the competition rules of the Treaty, even though competition is affected by the conduct of such bodies.

24. The Commission submits that it is precisely the act of placing goods or services on a given market which characterises the concept of economic activity and not purchasing activity as such. Accordingly, there is no need to dissociate the purchase from the use to which the purchased goods are put.

Findings of the Court

25. The [GC] rightly held, in paragraph 35 of the judgment under appeal, that in Community competition law the definition of an 'undertaking' covers any entity engaged in an economic activity, regardless of the legal status of that entity and the way in which it is financed (Case C-41/90 *Höfner and Elser* . . ., paragraph 21, and Joined Cases C-264/01, C-306/01, C-354/01, and C-355/01 *AOK-Bundesverband* . . ., paragraph 46). In accordance with the case-law of the Court of Justice, the [GC] also stated, in paragraph 36 of the judgment under appeal, that it is the activity consisting in offering goods and services on a given market that is the characteristic feature of an economic activity (Case C-35/96 *Commission v Italy* . . ., paragraph 36).

[73] See also Cases C-264, 306, 354, and 355/01, *AOK Bundesverband v Ichthyol-Gesellschaft Cordes, Hermani & Co* EU:C:2004:150.

[74] Case T-319/99, EU:T:2003:50, para. 36. [75] Ibid., para. 37. [76] Ibid., paras. 40–43.

[77] Case C-205/03 P, *FENIN v Commission* EU:C:2006:453.

> 26. The [GC] rightly deduced, in paragraph 36 of the judgment under appeal, that there is no need to dissociate the activity of purchasing goods from the subsequent use to which they are put in order to determine the nature of that purchasing activity, and that the nature of the purchasing activity must be determined according to whether or not the subsequent use of the purchased goods amounts to an economic activity.
>
> 27. It follows that the first part of the single plea raised by FENIN in support of its appeal, that the purchasing activity of the SNS management bodies constitutes an economic activity in itself, dissociable from the service subsequently provided and which, as such, should have been examined separately by the [GC], must be dismissed as unfounded.

The judgment in *FENIN* thus holds that *purchasing* for consumption is not economic activity unless the goods and services acquired are subsequently used as an input for an economic activity. This means that public bodies, even if wielding substantial purchasing power, will escape the reach of competition law unless the goods or services are bought in order to conduct economic activity. Although the view could be taken that economic activity should depend equally on buyers and sellers so that there is no reason why the concept of an undertaking should apply only to one side of the equation,[78] the Court was perhaps mindful of the 'dangerous territory' it enters in this area and felt it needed to find a balance between the protection of undistorted competition, on the one hand, 'and respect for the power of the Member States', on the other.[79] The judgment also leaves open some difficult issues for resolution, such as when purchasing is sufficiently closely linked to the provision of goods or services by a purchaser to constitute economic activity, and how purchasing should be treated when only some or a small proportion of the goods acquired are used in connection with an economic activity.

(iv) The Notion of an Undertaking Is a Relative Concept

As the notion of undertaking focuses on the nature of the activity carried out by the entity concerned, it is 'a relative concept in the sense that a given entity might be regarded as an undertaking for one part of its activities while the rest fall outside the competition rules'.[80] Thus 'the fact that, for the exercise of part of its activities, an entity is vested with public powers does not, in itself, prevent it from being classified as an undertaking . . . in respect of the remainder of its economic activities'.[81] For example, in *SELEX Sistemi Integrati SpA (SELEX Sistemi) v Commission*,[82] which concerned the Commission finding that (relying on previous proceedings concerning Eurocontrol[83]) Eurocontrol was not an undertaking, the EU Courts stressed the need to review each of Eurocontrol's individual activities.[84] The CJ held that Eurocontrol would be subject to competition law insofar as it

[78] Contrast the (prior) conclusion reached by the UK's Competition Appeal Tribunal in *Bettercare Group Ltd v DGFT* [2002] CAT 7 (the conclusion by a public entity of commercial contracts with private sector bodies was an economic activity whether it acted as purchaser, or supplier, of the services) and see e.g. J. Skilbeck, 'The EC Judgment in *AOK*: Can a Major Public Sector Purchaser Control the Prices It Pays or Is It Subject to Competition Act?' (2004) 44 *PPLR* NA95–97 and L. Montana and J. Jellis, 'The Concept of Undertakings in EC Competition Law and its Application to Public Bodies: Can You Buy Your Way into Article 82?' [2003] *Comp Law* 110 (arguably this means that suppliers will be made to make sacrifices in the name of the principle of solidarity) and Chap. 8.

[79] Case C-205/03 P, *FENIN v Commission* EU:C:2006:453, Maduro AG, para. 26.

[80] Case C-475/99, *Firma Ambulanz Glöckner v Landkreis Südwestpfalz* EU:C:2001:577, Jacobs AG, para. 72.

[81] Case C-49/07, *MOTOE* EU:C:2008:376, para. 25.

[82] Case T-155/04, EU:T:2006:387; Case C-113/07 P, EU:C:2009:191.

[83] Case C-364/92, *SAT Fluggesellschaft mbH v Eurocontrol* EU:C:1994:7, para. 30, see n. 52 and text.

[84] Case T-155/04, *SELEX Sistemi* EU:T:2006:387, paras. 50–94.

engaged in economic activities which are not connected with the exercise of public powers.[85] Only activities ancillary to non-economic activity would fall outside its scope. As the activity at issue in this case, of assisting the national administrations, was connected with (and inseparable from) the exercise of public powers, the organisation was not, in carrying out that activity, acting as an undertaking.[86] In *MOTOE*,[87] in contrast, the CJ held that a legal (non-profit-making) person that organised motorcycling events and entered into sponsorship, advertising, and insurance contracts designed to exploit those events commercially, *was* an undertaking. These activities were not ancillary or connected to its non-economic public powers (authorising the organisation of motorcycling events). Similarly, in *Aéroports de Paris v Commission*,[88] the CJ held that ADP's administrative and supervisory activities, such as air traffic control (not economic activity), were distinct from its provision of airport services in return for fees fixed on a commercial basis (in respect of which it was an undertaking).

(v) Employees and Trade Unions

Although self-employed individuals may act as independent economic actors and constitute undertakings,[89] individual employees who do not bear the financial risks of the business but perform work for and under the direction of their employers, do not 'in themselves constitute "undertakings"'.[90]

In *Albany*, Advocate General Jacobs[91] clearly set out his view that the competition rules were not structured to be applicable to employees who did not perform the 'functions' of undertakings. Rather, he considered work and labour to be distinct from the provision of goods or services. Consequently, trade unions would not be characterised as undertakings, or associations of undertakings, insofar as they act as agents for their members (employees).[92]

The line between workers/employees and self-employed undertakings in EU competition law is difficult to draw. The CJ has held that a service provider will not constitute an independent undertaking if it does not determine independently its own conduct on the market, but is dependent on a principal because it does not bear the financial or commercial risks arising out of the principal's business (and so operates an auxiliary organ within it).[93] It may not, therefore, be easy to determine whether,

[85] Case C-113/07 P, *SELEX Sistemi* EU:C:2009:191 (the GC erred in law in finding it an undertaking).

[86] Ibid. [87] Case C-49/07, EU:C:2008:376. [88] Case C-82/01 P, EU:C:2002:617.

[89] See n. 31 and text.

[90] Case C-22/98, *Criminal Proceedings Against Becu* EU:C:1999:419, para. 26 (the employees form part of the undertaking within which they work, see further nn. 102 and 227 and text). Whether or not agreements relating to self-employed workers fall outside Art. 101 depends on whether the worker 'acts under the direction of his employer as regards, in particular, his freedom to choose the time, place and content of his work . . . does not share in the employer's commercial risks . . . and . . . forms an integral part of that employer's undertaking', Case C-413/13, *FNV v Netherlands* EU:C:2014:2411, para. 36, see also nn. 340–341 and text.

[91] The CJ did not rule specifically on this issue as it held that collective agreements concluded between trade unions and employers relating to conditions of employment and working conditions fell outside Art. 101(1) altogether, see n. 247 and text.

[92] If the employee does not constitute an undertaking, the trade union could not constitute an association of undertakings. But see S. Bradshaw, 'Is a Trade Union an Undertaking under EU Competition Law?' (2016) 12(2)–(3) *European Competition Journal* 320.

[93] See Case C-413/13, *FNV Kunsten* EU:C:2014:2411, especially paras. 32–37 and e.g. M. J. Schmidt-Kessen, C. Bergqvist, C. Jacqueson, Y. Lind, and M. Huffman, '"I'll call my Union", said the driver—Collective bargaining of gig workers under EU competition rules' Copenhagen Business School Law Research Paper Series No. 20-43 (2020) (concluding that the two main criteria determining whether a person is a worker/employee or self-employed/undertaking are: (a) subordination; and (b) the allocation of economic risk between the parties).

for example, workers in the gig economy constitute self-employed independent undertakings[94] or whether they form part of the entity to which they provide services.[95]

(vi) Summary

The different strands of the EU cases described are not entirely easy to rationalise. The following guidance and considerations on the meaning of an undertaking can be extracted, however:[96]

(a) A functional approach is adopted: where a body carries out several activities, it is necessary to consider each discrete function separately.

(b) Where the activity carried out by a body (public or private) is a core function of the State connected with the exercise of official authority, derived directly from legislation, or exercised on behalf of the State, it will not be an undertaking.

(c) Where the charges levied by a body are determined not by it, but by a public authority, that may indicate that it is not an undertaking.

(d) If a social security scheme is based on the principle of solidarity and subject to State control, no economic activities are involved.

(e) The fact that a body does not operate for profit is relevant but not decisive.

(vii) Single Economic Units

a. *The Undertaking as a Single Economic Unit—Natural Persons, Legal Persons, Principal–Agent and Parent–Subsidiary Relationships*

The previous section explains that the legal form of an entity is irrelevant to its characterisation as an undertaking; what is important is whether it conducts economic activity. It has also been held that the term undertaking[97] is not necessarily synonymous with natural or legal personality[98] but denotes 'an economic unit . . . even if in law that economic unit consists of several persons, natural or legal'.[99] The concept thus captures economic units 'which consist of a unitary organization of personal, tangible and intangible elements which pursues a specific economic aim on a long-term basis and can contribute to the commission of an infringement'.[100] Consequently, it may be comprised of, for example:

- an individual sole trader (a natural person);[101]
- a legal person, such as a company or partnership, made up of a collection of individual persons. In this context, the cases do not look behind the legal personality; individuals working within

[94] Such workers are frequently not given employment contracts and so in many jurisdictions are treated as self-employed and unable to receive protection under labour laws. National classification does not affect characterisation under EU competition law, however.

[95] Where they do constitute independent undertakings, an important question which has arisen is whether collective arrangements designed to improve their working conditions (through collective bargaining) are compatible with Art. 101, see n. 251 and text.

[96] See J. W. van de Gronden, 'Services of General Interest and the Concept of Undertaking: Does EU Competition Law Apply?' (2018) 41(2) *World Competition* 197 and UK case, Case 1258/5/7/16, *UKRS Training Ltd v NSAR Ltd* [2017] CAT 14.

[97] See further W. Wils, 'The Undertaking as Subject of E.C. Competition Law and the Imputation of Infringements to Natural or Legal Persons' (2000) 25 *ELRev* 99 and A. Jones, 'The Boundaries of an Undertaking in EU Competition Law' (2012) 8 *European Competition Journal* 301.

[98] COMP/35.691, *Pre-insulated Pipe Cartel* [1999] OJ L24/1, para. 154.

[99] Case 170/83, *Hydrotherm Gerätebau GmbH v Compact de Dott Ing Mario Adredi & CSAS* EU:C:1984:271, para. 11; Case C-97/08 P, *Akzo Nobel v Commission* EU:C:2009:536, para. 55.

[100] Case T-11/89, *Shell International Chemical Co v Commission* EU:T:1992:33, para. 311.

[101] See n. 31 and text.

the legal person and not accepting individual risk are treated as constituent elements of it. Thus, in *Becu*, the CJ held that dock workers, performing work for and under the direction of their employers, were to be viewed as being incorporated into the undertaking concerned and forming part of the 'economic unit';[102]

- principal and agent. The close economic links which exist in many agency relationships have led the CJ to recognise that an independently owned agent may lose its character as an independent trader and, in certain situations, operate instead as an auxiliary organ 'forming an integral part of the principal's undertaking'.[103] This is likely to be the case where the agent does not take on any (or only a negligible portion of) financial and commercial risk linked to sales of goods to third parties on behalf of the principal (see further Chapter 11);[104]
- parent and subsidiary(ies). Such entities will constitute an economic unit if the subsidiary 'enjoys no economic independence',[105] or if the entities 'form an economic unit within which the subsidiary has no real freedom to determine its course of action on the market'[106] but carries out the instructions issued by the parent company controlling it. The formal separation of those entities resulting from distinct legal identity is not, therefore, decisive. The relevant question is whether they behave together as a single unit on the market (see further Section 4.A.vii.c).[107]

b. Consequences of the Single Economic Unit Doctrine

The economic unit doctrine has a number of important consequences.

First, it affects the substantive reach of Article 101: agreements and concerted practices between the parent and subsidiary (or other entities) forming part of the same economic unit, and concerned merely with the internal allocation of tasks between them, fall outside Article 101[108] ('substantive reach cases'). In *Viho*,[109] the CJ confirmed that the Commission had been correct to reject a complaint that Parker's distribution agreements concluded with its 100 per cent owned subsidiaries infringed Article 101. Parker controlled the sales, advertising, and marketing policy of its subsidiaries which had no real autonomy to determine their course of action. Consequently, agreements and arrangements between these companies constituted internal allocation of functions of a single enterprise (unilateral behaviour) and not collusive action triggering the application of Article 101.[110]

[102] See nn. 90–92 and discussion of workers in the gig economy, n. 93 and text. There is thus a difficult line to be drawn between legal entities, economic units, and cartels. Entities such as partnerships inevitably eliminate competition and result in price-fixing and market-sharing competition between individuals within them. Characterisation of a partnership as an undertaking renders such arrangements per se legal under Art. 101, see e.g. H. Hovenkamp and C. R. Leslie, 'The Firm as Cartel Manager' (2011) 64(3) *Vanderbilt LR* 813, 818 ('[t]he lines between firms, cartels and joint ventures are notoriously indistinct'); M. Anderson and M. Huffman, 'The Sharing Economy Meets the Sherman Act: Is Uber a Firm, a Cartel, or Something in Between?' (2018) 2 *Columbia Business LR* 859 and J. Nowag, 'When Sharing Platforms Fix Sellers' Prices' (2018) 6 *J of Antitrust Enforcement* 382.

[103] Case C-266/93, *Bundeskartellamt v Volkswagen and VAG Leasing GmbH* EU:C:1995:345, paras. 18–19.

[104] Case C-279/06, *CEPSA* EU:C:2008:485, para. 36.

[105] Case 22/71, *Béguelin Import Co v SAGL Import Export* EU:C:1971:113, para. 8.

[106] Case 15/74, *Centrafarm BV and Adriaan De Peijper v Sterling Drug Inc* EU:C:1974:114, para. 41.

[107] Case T-325/01, *DaimlerChrysler AG v Commission* EU:T:2005:322, para. 85.

[108] See n. 102 and text and Case 15/74, *Centrafarm BV and Adriaan De Peijper v Sterling Drug Inc* EU:C:1974:114, para. 41. See also Case 170/83, *Hydrotherm Gerätebau GmbH v Compact de Dott. Ing. Mario Adreoli* EU:C:1984:271, para. 11 and Case 30/87, *Bodson v Pompes Funèbres* EU:C:1988:225, para. 19.

[109] Case C-73/95 P, *Viho Europe BV v Commission* EU:C:1996:405.

[110] In contrast, the arrangements between Parker and its *independent distributors*, i.e. firms which were not connected to Parker by any type of ownership or control, infringed Art. 101(1), see Case T-66/92, *Herlitz AG v Commission* EU:T:1994:84 and Case T-77/92, *Parker Pen Ltd v Commission* EU:T:1994:85.

Case C-73/95 P, *Viho Europe BV v Commission* EU:C:1996:405

In this case a Dutch company, Viho, an office-equipment wholesaler, complained to the Commission that distribution agreements between Parker Pen (producer of writing utensils) and its 100 per cent-owned subsidiary companies infringed Article 101(1). The Commission rejected the complaint, finding that as Parker's subsidiary companies were wholly dependent on it and enjoyed no real autonomy, the distribution system did not go beyond the normal allocation of tasks within a group. The EU Courts[111] affirmed.

Court of Justice

13. The appellant claims that the fact that the conduct in question occurs within a group of companies does not preclude the application of Article [101(1)], since the division of responsibilities between the companies in the Parker group aims to maintain and partition national markets by means of absolute territorial protection. The evaluation of such conduct, which has harmful effects on competition, should not therefore depend on whether it takes place within a group or between Parker and its independent distributors. The appellant points out that such territorial protection prevents third parties such as itself from obtaining supplies freely within the Community from the subsidiary which offers the best commercial terms, so as to be able to pass such benefits on to the customer.

14. Consequently, the appellant considers that Article [101(1)] . . . must apply, since the referral policy in question goes far beyond a mere internal allocation of tasks within the Parker group.

15. It should be noted, first of all, that it is established that Parker holds 100 per cent of the shares of its subsidiaries in Germany, Belgium, Spain, France and the Netherlands and that the sales and marketing activities of its subsidiaries are directed by an area team appointed by the parent company and which controls, in particular, sales targets, gross margins, sales costs, cash flow and stocks. The area team also lays down the range of products to be sold, monitors advertising and issues directives concerning prices and discounts.

16. Parker and its subsidiaries thus form a single economic unit within which the subsidiaries do not enjoy real autonomy in determining their course of action in the market, but carry out the instructions issued to them by the parent company controlling them (Case 48/69, *ICI v E.C. Commission* . . . ; Case 15/74, *Centrafarm v Sterling Drug* . . . ; Case 16/74, *Centrafarm v Winthrop* . . . ; Case 30/87, *Bodson v Pompes Funèbres* . . . ; and Case 66/86, *Ahmed Saeed Flugreisen and Others v Zentrale zur Bekämpfung unlauteren Wettbewerbs* . . .).

17. In those circumstances, the fact that Parker's policy of referral, which consists essentially in dividing various national markets between its subsidiaries, might produce effects outside the ambit of the Parker group which are capable of affecting the competitive position of third parties cannot make Article [101(1)] applicable . . . On the other hand, such unilateral conduct could fall under Article [102] if the conditions for its application, as laid down in that article[,] were fulfilled.

18. The [GC] was therefore fully entitled to base its decision solely on the existence of a single economic unit in order to rule out the application of Article [101(1)] to the Parker group.

[111] Case T-102/92, EU:T:1995:3 (Art. 101(1) referred only to relations between economic entities which were capable of competing with one another).

In *Hydrotherm Gerätebau GmbH v Compact del Dott Ing Mario Andreoli & C Sas*,[112] the CJ also confirmed that a natural person, a limited partnership, and another firm constituted (and so counted as) a single economic unit when they were all controlled by the same natural person.[113]

Although the rationale underpinning this line of judgments has not been made explicit, in *Hydrotherm* the CJ stated that where entities form part of the same economic unit, competition between the parties is impossible.[114] The Court thus seems to consider that the arrangements between such entities resemble the internal workings of the firm and that the unity of purpose that they pursue renders meaningless the application of Article 101 to agreements between them (there is no competition to be protected[115]). If the subsidiary's strategy is determined by the parent, the parent and subsidiary will pursue a common course irrespective of the existence of any agreement between them: 'the unified conduct on the market of the parent company and its subsidiaries takes precedence over the formal separation between those companies as a result of their separate legal personalities'.[116]

Secondly, and more controversially, the doctrine has been relied on as a mechanism for attributing liability and responsibility to one entity in an economic unit for an infringement of the competition law rules committed by another entity within it ('attribution of liability' cases).[117] Where an undertaking intentionally or negligently infringes competition rules, the Commission is empowered to impose fines on it;[118] 'it falls, according to the principle of personal responsibility, to that entity to answer for that infringement'.[119] As, however, decisions cannot be addressed to an undertaking, they must be addressed, and liability imputed, to a legal person (or persons) on whom fines may be imposed. The economic entity doctrine has been utilised to allow a fine to be imposed not only on the legal entity which has actually infringed the competition rules but also on other entities within the corporate group, especially a parent of an infringing subsidiary,[120] 'without having to establish the personal involvement of the latter in the infringement'.[121] The Commission's approach has been to use this concept to shift liability upwards to parents of the infringing entity. Although early cases suggested

[112] Case 170/83, EU:C:1984:271.

[113] Confusingly perhaps, the judgment refers to the partnership and the firm as undertakings and concludes that the block exemption regulation can be applied 'even if several legally independent undertakings participate in the agreement as one contracting party provided that those undertakings constitute an economic unit for the purposes of the agreement', para. 12. This suggests an economic unit is comprised of a number of undertakings, which are natural or legal persons engaged in economic activity, see also Case 15/74, *Centrafarm BV and Adriaan De Peijper v Sterling Drug Inc* EU:C:1974:114, para. 41 and Case T-102/92, *Viho Europe BV v Commission* EU:T:1995:3, paras. 47–53.

[114] Case 170/83, EU:C:1984:271, para. 11, see also n. 111. See also the opinion of the US Supreme Court in *Copperweld Corp v Independence Tube Corp*, 467 US 752 (1984) (since a parent and a wholly owned subsidiary have a complete unity of interest and because a parent can assert full control at any moment if a subsidiary fails to act in a parent's interest, the parent and subsidiary have a unity of purpose or common design that belies the existence of an agreement for antitrust purposes).

[115] For an interesting account of the cases dealing with this issue and the principles underpinning them, see Lenz AG in Case C-73/95 P, *Viho Europe BV v Commission* EU:C:1996:405, paras. 31–73, especially para. 67.

[116] Case T-102/92, *Viho Europe BV v Commission* EU:T:1995:3, para. 50. See also Case T-9/99, *HFB Holdings v Commission* EU:T:2002:70, paras. 54–68 and Case C-97/08 P, *Akzo Nobel v Commission* EU:C:2009:536, para. 55.

[117] See e.g. J. Joshua, Y. Botteman, and L. Atlee, '"You Can't Beat the Percentage"—The Parental Liability Presumption in EU Cartel Enforcement' in *Global Competition Review—The European Antitrust Review 2012*, 3; S. Thomas, 'Guilty of a Fault that One has not Committed: The Limits of the Group-Based Sanction Policy Carried out by the Commission and the European Courts in EU-Antitrust Law' (2012) 3 *JECLAP* 11; K. Hofstetter and M. Ludescher, 'Fines against Parent Companies in EU Antitrust Law: Setting Incentives for "Best Practice Compliance"' (2010) 33 *World Competition* 55; and S. Daly and A. Jones, 'The Undertaking and Single Economic Entity Concepts in EU and UK Competition Law: Proposals for a Refined Approach' in F. Thépot and A. Tzanaki (eds.), *Research Handbook on Competition and Corporate Law* (Edward Elgar, Forthcoming).

[118] Reg. 1/2003, Art. 23(2) and Chap. 13.

[119] Case C-97/08 P, *Akzo Nobel v Commission* EU:C:2009:536, para. 56. Case C-434/13 P *Commission v Parker Hannifin Manufacturing and Parker-Hannifin* EU:C:2014:2456, para. 39.

[120] See Case 48/69, *Imperial Chemical Industries v Commission (Dyestuffs)* EU:C:1972:70, paras. 131–140.

[121] Case C-97/08 P, *Akzo Nobel v Commission* EU:C:2009:536, paras. 58–59.

a need for a connection between the parent and the infringement before imposing a fine,[122] subsequently the Commission's policy in cartel cases has been to hold, wherever possible, parent companies (and top group holding companies[123]) jointly and severally liable with their (infringing) subsidiaries within the same economic unit irrespective of any connection or knowledge of, or personal involvement in, the infringement,[124] and even if the parent company is not actively involved in economic activity but is just a non-operational holding company,[125] or there is an intermediary company between the parent and the offending subsidiary.[126]

This approach has been upheld by the EU Courts which have affirmed that parental liability is not based on the fault of the entity to which liability is being imputed, but derives from the personal responsibility of the undertaking, and that the Commission may freely choose which legal entity belonging to an undertaking that participated in an infringement to hold liable for it.[127] Further, in *Sumal*[128] the Grand Chamber of the CJ held that because the rationale for liability is not the decisive influence exercised by the parent but the personal responsibility attached to the economic unit, a subsidiary can be held liable (in that case in the context of private damages litigation) for the (infringing) conduct of its parent company. The Court held, however, that liability could only be imposed on a subsidiary where it engages in activities connected or linked to the subject matter of the infringement.

This policy of personal responsibility for the undertaking as a whole is aimed at having a strong deterrent effect, maximising the total level of fines by augmenting the level of fines which can be imposed (the cap is 10 per cent of the turnover of the undertaking as a whole[129]), enhancing the risk of an uplift in the fine for recidivism,[130] and strengthening the working of the EU competition laws by punishing anti-competitive behaviour (Chapter 13 discusses fining policy more fully).[131] It also maximises the chance of recovery, in case one of the legal entities is unable to pay any fine imposed and enables liability to be imposed on a parent company which operated the agreement, and concocted the breach, outside the EU.[132] Although endorsed by the CJ on numerous occasions, the economic unit doctrine has been strongly contested as a mechanism for attributing liability (see further Section 4.A.vii.d).

[122] See e.g. Cases 48, 49, and 51–57/69, *ICI v Commission (Dyestuffs)* EU:C:1972:70 and A. Kalintiri, 'Revisiting Parental Liability in EU Competition Law' (2018) 43 *ELRev* 145.

[123] '[T]he existence of intermediary companies between the subsidiary and the parent company does not affect the possibility of applying the presumption that the parent company in fact exercises decisive influence over the subsidiary', Case T-343/06, *Shell Petroleum v Commission* EU:T:2012:478, para. 52. See also Case C-90/09 P, *General Química SA v Commission* EU:C:2011:21, paras. 88–89.

[124] Case C-97/08 P, *Akzo Nobel NV v Commission* EU:C:2009:536, paras. 58–59.

[125] Case C-440/11 P, *Commission v Stichting Administratiekantoor Portielje and Gosselin Group NV* EU:C:2013:514.

[126] Case T-343/06, *Shell Petroleum v Commission* EU:T:2012:478, para. 52. See also Case C-90/09 P, *General Química SA v Commission* EU:C:2011:21, [2011] ECR I-001, paras. 88–89.

[127] Case C-882/19, *Sumal, SL v Mercedes Benz Trucks España, SL* EU:C:2021:800, para. 63. See also Cases C-231–233/11, *Commission v Siemens AG Österreich* EU:C:2014:256 (the Commission only determines joint and several liability from an external perspective and does not have power to determine the shares to be paid by the legal persons that make up that undertaking from the perspective of their internal relationship).

[128] Ibid., paras. 42–51 (see also the Opinion of Pitruzzella AG, EU:C:2021:293). See also Case C-425/22, *MOL Magyar Olaj-és Gázipari Nyrt v Mercedes-Benz Group AG* judgment pending (concerning an action brought by a parent company in respect of anti-competitive conduct by another company, which harmed its subsidiary).

[129] See Reg. 1/2003 [2003] OJ L1/1, Art. 23(2) and Chap. 13.

[130] See e.g. Case T-341/18, *NEC v Commission* EU T:2021:634, where the GC held that the fine imposed on a parent for the infringement of its subsidiary could be increased for recidivism in circumstances where the parent (but not the subsidiary) had been involved in a prior cartel.

[131] Joshua, Botteman, and Atlee, n. 117, 3–4. Case C-882/19, *Sumal, SL v Mercedes Benz Trucks España, SL* EU:C:2021:800, paras. 35–38.

[132] Cases 48, 49, and 51–57/69, *ICI v Commission (Dyestuffs)* EU:C:1972:70, paras. 125–146. The use of the single economic entity doctrine in this way allows the extraterritorial application of EU competition law without recourse to the more controversial 'implementation' or 'effects' doctrines, see Chap. 17 and in the UK, Case 1574/10/12/22, *BMW AG and VW AG v Competition and Markets Authority* [2023] CAT 7.

Thirdly, the single economic unit doctrine has also been relied upon in private litigation to anchor an action in a particular jurisdiction[133] and by an injured entity seeking damages[134] in respect of loss suffered in consequence of an antitrust infringement by an undertaking, for example in proceedings against a parent in relation to an infringement by its subsidiary,[135] or in proceedings against a subsidiary of a parent named in a Commission infringement decision.[136] In *Sumal SL v Mercedes Benz Trucks España*,[137] the CJ confirmed that as the concept of an undertaking has the same scope and meaning in the context of an action for damages brought before a national court as it does in relation to a case concerning the imposition of fines by the Commission, it can also be relied on to attribute liability for damages caused by an infringement to any legal entity forming part of the economic unit at the time of the infringement.[138]

Finally, a similar concept is utilised in a number of EU Regulations and Commission Notices. For example, most of the block exemptions[139] and the Commission's Notice on agreements of minor importance[140] apply only to situations where the parties to the agreement do not exceed specified market shares. These provisions require that, when calculating market shares, the shares of all undertakings closely 'connected' (as defined therein) to the entity that actually entered into the agreement must be taken into account.[141] Similarly, the activities of the group must be considered when determining whether or not the parties to the agreement are competing undertakings[142] or when calculating an undertaking's turnover.[143] Although the definition of connected entities in these provisions is designed to provide legal certainty, some of the language used within them is confusing, as it suggests an approach to the concept of undertaking which is not evidently consistent with the notion of an undertaking as defined by the EU Courts.[144] Indeed, if the conduct of a single economic entity is viewed as unilateral (not joint) conduct of an undertaking, substantive competition analysis should automatically reflect the true market power of such undertaking(s), as a whole. Assessment of market shares, market power, and dominance should therefore automatically take account of the position of all entities within the economic unit.

The question of whether the concept of an economic entity does, or should, have the same meaning and should be interpreted in exactly the same way in each of the distinct scenarios described, in particular in substantive reach and in attribution of liability cases, is explored in the following sections.

c. *The Boundaries of the Economic Unit: Parent and Subsidiary*

Given the significant consequences that flow from the acceptance of the single economic unit doctrine, a critical issue is exactly how broadly the concept of an economic unit extends and, in particular,

[133] For example, claimants before English courts sought to anchor damages actions in the UK by bringing them against a member of the economic unit domiciled in the UK (a UK subsidiary), where another member of that unit (for example, a non-UK parent) has committed the violation of the competition law rules, see Chap. 14 and e.g. *Provimi v Aventis* [2003] EWHC 961 (Comm), *Cooper Tire & Rubber v Shell Chemicals* [2009] EWHC 2609 (Comm), [2010] EWCA Civ 864 (appeal dismissed) and *Toshiba Carrier UK Ltd v KME Yorkshire Ltd* [2012] EWCA Civ 1190.

[134] Many actions are now being based on the EU Damages Directive, Dir. 2014/104/EU on certain rules governing actions for damages under national law for infringements of the competition law provisions of the Member States and of the European Union [2014] OJ L349/1 (requiring Member States to ensure full compensation to those harmed by an antitrust infringement by an undertaking, Art. 1), see Chap. 14.

[135] See Case C-724/17, *Skanska Industrial Solutions* EU:C:2019:204 (recognising that the same principles are to be applied in private proceedings as those governing economic units and dealing with economic continuity in EU cases concerning penalty payments) and Chap. 14.

[136] Case C-882/19, *Sumal, SL v Mercedes Benz Trucks España, SL* EU:C:2021:800.

[137] Ibid., but see n. 128 and text. [138] Ibid., paras. 38–63. [139] See Chap. 5.

[140] Commission Notice on agreements of minor importance which do not appreciably restrict competition under Article 101(1) [2014] OJ C291/1.

[141] See e.g. ibid., para. 16. [142] See e.g. Chap. 10.

[143] See Chap. 15 (and discussion of EU dimension in EU merger control). [144] See Jones, n. 97.

exactly when parents and subsidiaries may be said to form part of the same unit. Although there is relatively little case law which deals with the question of when an agreement falls outside the ambit of Article 101 on this basis (and so when the concept of an undertaking affects the substantive reach of Article 101[145]), there are a significant number of 'attribution of liability' cases, especially in the last decade, which shed light on the question. These cases clarify that the parent (even where the parent is a 'financial investor'[146]) may be held jointly and severally liable for the conduct of its subsidiary[147] where the parent is able to, and does actually, exercise decisive influence over the policy and direct the conduct of its subsidiary, so that the subsidiary does not enjoy real autonomy or independence in determining its course of action in the market.[148] In particular, that:

(i) where a parent holds all or almost all of the capital in a subsidiary, a 100 per cent shareholding or a de minimis amount less than 100 per cent, or holds 100 per cent of the voting rights,[149] there is a rebuttable presumption that the parent does in fact exercise decisive influence over the commercial policy and conduct of its subsidiary applies (no indicia relating to the actual exercise of influence is required). This was established in *Akzo Nobel*.[150]

Case C-97/08 P, *Akzo Nobel NV and Others v Commission* [2009] ECR I-8237

Court of Justice

58. It is clear from settled case-law that the conduct of a subsidiary may be imputed to the parent company in particular where, although having a separate legal personality, that subsidiary does not decide independently upon its own conduct on the market, but carries out, in all material respects, the instructions given to it by the parent company (see, to that effect, *Imperial Chemical Industries v Commission*, paragraphs 132 and 133; *Geigy v Commission*, paragraph 44; Case 6/72 *Europemballage and Continental Can v Commission* . . ., paragraph 15; and *Stora*, paragraph 26),

[145] But see also Case C-531/16, *Ecoservices projektai in the 'Specializuotas transportas* EU:C:2018:324 where the CJ confirmed that where entities forming part of a single economic unit (a matter to be determined by the referring court in that case) submit coordinated, but separate, bids in a public tender process, no collusive bidding arrangement is formed for the purposes of Art. 101. The CJ did hold, nonetheless, that the conduct might infringe public procurement rules set out in EU procurement directives if autonomous and independent tenders had not been submitted.

[146] See e.g. COMP/39.610, *Power Cables* 2 April 2014 (Goldman Sachs was held liable as the (indirect) parent company of Prysmian SpA and its wholly owned subsidiary, which had participated in the power cables cartel. Initially it held 100% of the shares—although that holding decreased between 2005–2007, it retained 100% of the voting rights), *aff'd* Case T-419/14, *The Goldman Sachs Group, Inc v Commission* EU:T:2018:445, Case C-595/18 EU:C:2021:73. But see Case T-24/05, *Alliance One International v Commission* EU:T:2010:453, especially paras. 195–197, on appeal Case C-14/11 P, EU:C:2012:479 (liability can be avoided if the nature of ownership is purely financial and no decisive influence is exercised).

[147] Also that the acts of an agent can be imputed to a principal where the agent must be treated as an auxiliary body forming an integral part of the principal's business who must carry out the principal's instructions and, like a commercial employee, forms an economic unit within that undertaking, see COMP/39.406, *Marine Hoses* 28 January 2009, para. 330 and Case T-66/99, *Minoan Lines v Commission* EU:T:2003:337, paras. 121–129, appeal dismissed Case C-121/04 P, EU:C:2005:695. Principal and agent relationships are discussed further in Chap. 11.

[148] Case 48/69, *Imperial Chemical Industries v Commission (Dyestuffs)* EU:C:1972:70, paras. 125–146.

[149] See e.g. Case T-299/08, *Elf Aquitaine v Commission* EU:T:2011:217 (*aff'd* Case C-404/11 P, EU:C:2012:56); Case C-508/11, *Eni SpA v Commission* EU:C:2013:289; and Case C-595/18, *The Goldman Sachs Group, Inc v Commission* EU:C:2021:73.

[150] Case C-97/08 P, *Akzo Nobel NV v Commission* EU:C:2009:536, para. 60. See also Case C-286/98 P, *Stora Kopparbergs Bergslags AB v Commission* EU:C:2000:630, para. 29; Cases C-201 and 216/09 P, *ArcelorMittal Luxembourg SA v Commission* EU:C:2011:190; and Case C- 155/14 P, *Evonik Degussa and Alzchem v Commission* EU:C:2016:446.

having regard in particular to the economic, organisational and legal links between those two legal entities (see, by analogy, *Dansk Rørindustri and Others v Commission*, paragraph 117, and *ETI and Others*, paragraph 49).

59. That is the case because, in such a situation, the parent company and its subsidiary form a single economic unit and therefore form a single undertaking . . . Thus, the fact that a parent company and its subsidiary constitute a single undertaking within the meaning of Article [101] enables the Commission to address a decision imposing fines to the parent company, without having to establish the personal involvement of the latter in the infringement.

60. In the specific case where a parent company has a 100% shareholding in a subsidiary which has infringed the Community competition rules, first, the parent company can exercise a decisive influence over the conduct of the subsidiary (see, to that effect, *Imperial Chemical Industries v Commission*, paragraphs 136 and 137) and, second, there is a rebuttable presumption that the parent company does in fact exercise a decisive influence over the conduct of its subsidiary (see, to that effect, *AEG-Telefunken v Commission*, paragraph 50, and *Stora*, paragraph 29).

61. In those circumstances, it is sufficient for the Commission to prove that the subsidiary is wholly owned by the parent company in order to presume that the parent exercises a decisive influence over the commercial policy of the subsidiary. The Commission will be able to regard the parent company as jointly and severally liable for the payment of the fine imposed on its subsidiary, unless the parent company, which has the burden of rebutting that presumption, adduces sufficient evidence to show that its subsidiary acts independently on the market (see, to that effect, *Stora*, paragraph 29).

In such cases, joint and several liability for the parent firm follows unless it adduces sufficient evidence to show that the subsidiary acted independently.[151] The fact that a subsidiary does not comply with an express instruction given by its parent company is not sufficient, by itself, to establish the absence of actual exercise of decisive influence by the parent over the subsidiary; it is not necessary for the subsidiary to carry out all the parent company's instructions to demonstrate decisive influence, as long as the failure to carry out those instructions is not the norm.[152] A contested issue is exactly when the presumption can be rebutted in practice.[153] However, the CJ has held that 'the fact that it is difficult to adduce the evidence necessary to rebut a presumption of actual exercise of decisive influence does not in itself mean that that presumption is in fact irrebuttable, especially where the entities against which the presumption operates are those best placed to seek that evidence within their own sphere of activity'.[154]

[151] See Case C-595/18 P, *The Goldman Sachs Group, Inc v Commission* EU:C:2021:73, para. 32. The GC made it clear that a pure financial investor, an investor who holds shares in a company in order to make a profit, who refrains from any involvement in its management and in its control, may be able to rebut any presumption of actual exercise of decisive influence over its subsidiary, Case T-419/14, EU:T:2018:445, para. 151. The CJ held that the GC did not err in law in finding that the appellant had not succeeded in rebutting the presumption in this case. See also n. 146.

[152] Case C-155/14 P, *Evonik Degussa and Alzchem v Commission* EU:C:2016:446, para. 40 (the arguments raised did not show the absence of the parents' actual exercise of decisive influence over the subsidiary and thus were not sufficient to rebut the shareholding presumption), relying on Cases C-93 and 123/13 P, *Commission v Versalis* EU:C:2015:150, paras. 42 and 43.

[153] See Joshua, Botteman, and Atlee, n. 117, 3 and R. Burnley, 'Group Liability for Antitrust Infringements: Responsibility and Accountability' (2010) 33 *World Competition* 595. The Commission is obliged to consider the rebuttal evidence and if it fails to do so its decision will be overturned, see e.g. Case T-185/06, *L'Air liquide SA v Commission* EU:T:2011:275; Case T-517/09, *Alstom v Commission* EU:T:2014:999; and Case C-446/11 P, *Commission v Edison SpA* EU:C:2013:798.

[154] Cases C-93 and 123/13 P, *Commission v Versalis*, EU:C:2015:150, para. 46.

(ii) the ability to, and actual, exercise of decisive influence can be ascertained in other situations 'on the basis of a body of factual evidence, including, in particular, any management power exercised by the parent company or companies over their subsidiary'. In such cases 'account must be taken of all the relevant factors relating to the economic, organisational and legal links which tie the subsidiary to its parent company and, therefore, of economic reality' and 'the exercise of decisive influence may be inferred from a body of consistent evidence, even if some of that evidence, taken in isolation, is insufficient to establish the existence of such influence . . . '.[155] For example, decisive influence may be found where the parent holds a majority interest in a subsidiary[156] or a minority interest which is allied to rights greater than those normally granted to minority shareholders.[157] Although negative control over a subsidiary may generally be insufficient to establish decisive influence, two or more parents of a joint venture (JV)[158] which cooperate to determine the JV's commercial policy—that is, in situations where the parents have the power to exercise, and have actually exercised, *joint control* over a JV—may be responsible for the conduct of the JV. In *Dow*,[159] both the CJ and the GC upheld the Commission's finding that Dow (and the other parent EI Du Pont) was jointly and severally liable for the participation of its JV in a cartel and formed part of the same economic unit with it.

Relying amongst other things[160] on the fact that the Commission had found that they had acquired joint control of the JV when appraising it on its creation under the EU Merger Regulation (EUMR),[161] the EU Courts accepted that the parents had been found to have the power to jointly control their JV and further that, in the light of all the economic, legal, and organisational links, control had actually been exercised. It was not therefore accepted that the parents could not be liable as they merely exercised joint negative control over the JV and only had a right of veto over its commercial strategy (and did not have the power to exercise decisive influence over its day-to-day management). 'Even if parent companies are not able to impose decisions on their joint venture, they are able to prevent their joint venture from taking certain decisions and thereby exercise decisive influence over its business strategy . . . The "negative" nature of the control that the applicant held over [JV] did not therefore prevent it from exercising over [JV] sufficient decisive influence to enable the Commission to impute to it the unlawful conduct of that joint venture.'[162]

155 Cases C-293 and 294/13 P, *Fresh Del Monte Produce Inc v Commission* EU:C:2015:416, paras. 76–77.

156 Case T-141/89, *Tréfileurope Sales SARL v Commission* EU:T:1995:62. See also Cases 6 and 7/73, *Istituto Chemioterapico Italiano SpA and Commercial Solvents Corp v Commission* EU:C:1974:18 (parent and subsidiary in which the parent held a 51% shareholding were to be treated as an economic unit).

157 Case T-132/07, *Fuji Electric System Co Ltd v Commission* EU:T:2011:344, para. 183.

158 The term JV can be used to describe a wide spectrum of commercial arrangements between firms. In competition law, it is frequently used to describe an entity which (a) constitutes a separate business entity, and (b) is jointly controlled by at least two parents.

159 Case T-77/08, *The Dow Chemical Co v Commission* EU:T:2012:47; Case C-179/12 P, *The Dow Chemical Co v Commission* EU:C:2013:605. See also Case C-623/15, *Toshiba Corp v Commission* EU:C:2017:21 (liability attributed where parent had 35.5% share and joint control).

160 E.g. the facts that each had the right to participate on a Members' Committee which approved certain matters pertaining to the strategic direction of the JV, that they had both withdrawn from the chloroprene rubber market and participated on it only through their JV. Net profits or losses of the JV were allocated in equal proportions to the two parents.

161 M.663, 21 February 1996. The operational autonomy required of full-function JVs under the EUMR, however, does not 'mean that the joint venture enjoys autonomy as regards the adoption of its strategic decisions (and that it is not therefore under the decisive influence exercised by its parent companies for the purposes of the application of Article [101])', Case T-77/08, *The Dow Chemical Co v Commission* EU:T:2012:47, para. 93, *aff'd* Case C-179/12 P, EU:C:2013:605, para. 65.

162 Case T-77/08, ibid., para. 92.

In *Fresh Del Monte Produce Inc v Commission*,[163] the CJ also held that the exercise of joint control, by two parents, of their subsidiary did not preclude a finding of the existence of an economic unit comprising one of those parent companies and the subsidiary, and in some cases the GC has even gone so far as to hold that where two companies are placed in a position analogous to that in which a single company owns the entire share capital of its subsidiary, it is possible to apply the *presumption* that a parent company in fact exercises decisive influence over its subsidiary. Thus in *Avebe*, it held that a JV, on the one hand, and its parents, on the other 'do form an economic unit . . . in the context of which the unlawful conduct of the subsidiary may be imputed to the parent companies, who become liable by virtue of the fact that they in reality control its marketing policy'.[164] Further, in *Shell Petroleum NV v Commission*[165] the GC endorsed the Commission's view that the situation (notwithstanding the coexistence of two legal parent entities) was analogous to that in which a single parent company controls fully its subsidiary, so entitling the Commission to rely on the *Akzo* presumption. In this case, the parents jointly appointed the members of the board of directors of the subsidiaries, had equal representation in two supervisory committees, and a body coordinated the operational activity and governed all the group companies.

In *Sumal*,[166] the CJ held that where liability in administrative or civil proceedings is to be attributed to a subsidiary for the infringement of another legal entity within the economic unit (rather than to a controlling parent), an additional requirement must be established. Not only do the requisite economic, organisational, and legal links need to exist, but a link must also be established between the economic activity of the legal entity targeted and the subject matter of the infringement.[167] Although therefore the parent is liable whenever it is able to, and does actually, exercise decisive influence over its subsidiary, the subsidiary cannot be held liable for a parent's (or presumably a sibling's) infringement if it was in no way involved in the infringement and the infringement was in an economic field entirely unconnected with its own activity. This means that the 'same parent company may be part of several economic units made up, depending on the economic activity in question, of itself and of different combinations of its subsidiaries all belonging to the same group of companies. If that were not the case, a subsidiary within such a group could be held liable for infringements committed in the context of economic activities entirely unconnected to its own activity and in which they were in no way involved, even indirectly.'[168]

d. The Boundaries of an Economic Unit: A Single Concept and Proper Basis for Parental Liability?

An important question is whether the concept of an undertaking developed in these different lines of cases are the same; in particular, whether the concept developed in the attribution of liability line of cases is, or should be, identical to that developed in the substantive reach and other cases.

Logically, a coherent approach and system would suggest that the term undertaking should be applied uniformly in the context of the EU competition laws and support can be found for that view. Not only do the cases all hinge on the interpretation of the term 'undertaking', without any explicit suggestion that the concept should be considered differently in differing scenarios, but:

(a) in *Flat Glass*,[169] the GC clarified that the term 'undertaking' has the same meaning in Article 102 as the one given to it in the context of Article 101;

(b) in *Hydrotherm*,[170] the CJ held that 'in competition law, the term "undertaking" must be understood as designating an economic unit . . .'; and

[163] Cases C-293 and 294/13 P, EU:C:2015:416, paras. 76–100.

[164] Case T-314/01, *Avebe v Commission* EU:T:2006:266, para. 141.

[165] Case T-343/06, EU:T:2012:478, Case C-585/12 P, EU:C:2013:236 (appeal withdrawn).

[166] Case C-882/19, EU:C:2021:800. [167] Ibid., paras. 45–52. [168] Ibid., para. 47.

[169] Cases T-68 and 77–78/89, *Società Italiano Vetro SpA v Commission* EU:T:1992:38, paras. 357–358.

[170] Case 170/83, *Hydrotherm Gerätebau GmbH v Compact de Dott Ing Mario Adredi & CSAS* EU:C:1984:271, para. 11.

(c) in *Sumal*,[171] the CJ stressed that the concept of undertaking constituted an autonomous concept of EU law, which cannot have a different scope with regard to the imposition of fines by the Commission as compared to actions for damages for infringements of the competition rules. Further, in both *Dyestuffs*[172] and *Viho*,[173] the CJ held that the consequence of the economic doctrine was both that Article 101(1) was inapplicable to arrangements between entities within the economic unit and that the actions of the subsidiary could be attributed to the parent company.[174] In some instances, there has also been cross-referral between the lines of cases.[175]

If this is correct, the consequences are far-reaching and the doctrine potentially excludes a relatively wide spectrum of behaviour from Article 101(1), in particular, agreements between:

i. persons bound together by a contractual relationship which results in one person working for and under the direction of another and so being integrated within that other (for example, an employment or agency contract) or one person controlling the behaviour of another;[176]
ii. a parent and a subsidiary, where the latter has no freedom to determine its course of action or economic independence as the parent has sufficient rights to exercise, and does actually exercise, positive control over its behaviour;
iii. a parent and a subsidiary, where the former has sufficient rights to veto strategic decisions of the latter, and actually exercises such negative control over its behaviour;
iv. subsidiaries/sibling companies[177] which are controlled (within the meaning set out earlier) by the same parent; and
v. a JV and its parent(s) or between parents which have the power to, and do actually, exercise jointly control and decisive influence over the JV's behaviour.

Because of the functional approach taken to the concept of an undertaking, however, it would seem that even if such a broad exclusion from Article 101 applies, it would relate only to conduct which concerns the internal working of, or the internal allocation of responsibilities within, the economic unit. In the context of a JV, for example, this would suggest that only conduct inherent to the working and operation of the JV would fall outside Article 101 and that Article 101 could apply to agreements outside its scope. Indeed, in its Horizontal Cooperation Guidelines, the Commission states that although

[171] Case C-882/19, EU:C:2021:800, para. 38.

[172] Case 48/69, *Imperial Chemical Industries v Commission (Dyestuffs)* EU:C:1972:70, paras. 132–136.

[173] Case C-73/95 P, *Viho Europe BV v Commission* EU:C:1996:405, para. 16. In Case T-102/92, *Viho Europe BV v Commission* EU:T:1995:3 the GC relied on cases concerning parental liability in its judgment upholding the Commission's conclusion that agreements between Parker Pen and its subsidiaries fell outside Art. 101(1). Indeed, it concluded that the Commission had been correct in finding that because the subsidiaries' conduct could be *imputed* to the parent the integrated distribution system fell outside Art. 101.

[174] See also Kokott AG in Case C-440/11 P, *Commission v Stichting Administratiekantoor Portielje and Gosselin Group NV* EU:C:2012:763, para. 31 and Bot AG in Cases C-201 and 216/09 P, *ArcelorMittal Luxembourg SA v Commission* EU:C:2010:634, para. 178.

[175] See e.g. Case T-112/05, *Akzo Nobel v Commission* EU:T:2007:381, paras. 63–64, *aff'd* Case C-97/08 P, *Akzo Nobel v Commission* EU:C:2009:536, paras. 72–78 and Case T-132/07, *Fuji Electric System Co Ltd v Commission* EU:T:2011:344, para. 180.

[176] See also e.g. Commission Consolidated Jurisdictional Notice under Council Regulation (EC) No. 139/2004 on the control of concentrations between undertakings [2008] OJ C95/1, para. 20, and the Commission's decision in COMP/39.188, *Bananas*, 15 October 2008, where the Commission found that the combination of a partnership, capital links, and a distribution agreement was sufficient to give Del Monte the possibility to exercise decisive influence on the way Weichert ran its business and that Del Monte did exercise such influence, paras. 383–385, *aff'd* Case T-587/08, *Del Monte* EU:T:2013:129 and Cases C-293 and 294/13 P, EU:C:2015:416.

[177] Guidelines on the applicability of Article 101 of the Treaty on the Functioning of the European Union to horizontal co-operation agreements, 17 July 2023, para. 11 ('Companies that form part of the same undertaking are not considered to be competitors for the purposes of these Guidelines, even if they are both active on the same relevant . . . markets').

it will typically not apply Article 101(1) to arrangements concerning the activity where the JV is active, it will apply it to agreements between the parents to create or alter the scope of the JV, between the parents and the JV concerning products of geographies in which the JV is not active, and between the parents, without the involvement of the JV.[178] If correct, the question of whether the entities are acting as a single undertaking would thus appear to turn on the complex question of whether the conduct limits competition among the parents and the JV outside its scope.

Nonetheless, it is arguable that a more nuanced and context-specific approach to the concept of an economic unit/undertaking (rather than a single one) should be adopted, which reflects the different objectives underpinning the distinct lines of cases.

In substantive reach cases, the policy is to take outside the scope of Article 101 only arrangements which resemble the internal workings of a firm and/or arrangements between entities which are in any event bound to pursue a common policy on a market. This could suggest a narrower concept of an undertaking, for example in the parent/subsidiary context confined to scenarios where a subsidiary has no freedom to determine its course of action as the parent has sufficient rights to exercise, and does actually exercise, positive control over its behaviour. Indeed, it must be questioned whether, in particular, negative control over a subsidiary or JV should be sufficient to ensure that a parent and that subsidiary/JV pursue a common course of conduct and so to justify the conduct escaping scrutiny under Article 101.[179]

In contrast, in attribution of liability cases the issue is the effectiveness of EU competition law (strengthening the working of the rules by discouraging infringements[180]) and when it is appropriate, or efficient,[181] to ignore the legal personality of the entity that committed the infringement and to impose liability for that infringement on another entity within the corporate group—in other words, when can the latter be said to have 'personal responsibility' for the violation (and liability imputed to it).[182] Reflecting this purpose, the CJ has adopted a different approach, depending upon whether liability is being imputed upwards or downwards within the corporate group. Where liability is being imposed on a parent, the EU Courts have focused on the question of whether the parent has control and has exercised decisive influence over the infringing entity. In contrast, the CJ held that liability cannot be attached to a non-infringing subsidiary (controlled by an infringing parent) unless, in addition, its economic activities are linked to those of the infringing entity.

It is not surprising, therefore, to find some support in the case law and commentary for a context-specific approach. For example, in *Dow*[183] the CJ specifically confined its comments about the

[178] Ibid., para. 12.

[179] Such an interpretation would also seem to conflict with decisions adopted by the Commission in cases which specifically dealt with the application of Art. 101 to arrangements between parent and JV, see for example, COMP/32.732, *IJsselcentrale* [1991] OJ L28/32, COMP/32.186, *Gosmé/Martell-DMP* [1991] OJ L185/23 and with jurisprudence dealing with 'associations of undertakings' which have generally interpreted this concept broadly to encompass entities used as an institutionalised mechanism for coordinating the members/shareholders' conduct (see Section 3.A.viii.a).

[180] Case C-882/19, *Sumal, SL v Mercedes Benz Trucks España, SL* EU:C:2021:800, paras. 35–36.

[181] See C. Koenig, 'An Economic Analysis of the Single Economic Entity Doctrine in EU Competition Law' (2017) 13(2) *J of Competition Law and Economics* 281.

[182] See Case T-587/08, *Del Monte* EU:T:2013:129, para. 151 (when determining whether the conduct of one firm (Weichert) could be imputed to another (Del Monte), the applicant's reference to *Suiker Unie* and *BMW* were irrelevant 'since those judgments concern legal issues and have factual backgrounds that differ from those of the present case. . . . In neither of those decisions was the Court required to examine and determine the question whether the conditions for the imputation to one undertaking of an infringement committed by another were satisfied'). In the appeal, the CJ discussed imputation of liability without referring to the other line of cases, Cases C-293 and 294/13 P, EU:C:2015:416.

[183] Case C-179/12 P, EU:C:2013:605, para. 58 ('Where two parent companies each have a 50% shareholding in the joint venture which committed an infringement of the rules of competition law, *it is only for the purposes of establishing liability for participation in the infringement of that law* and only in so far as the Commission has demonstrated, on the basis of factual evidence, that both parent companies did in fact exercise decisive influence over the joint venture, that those three entities can be considered to form a single economic unit and therefore form a single undertaking for the purposes of Article [101 TFEU].' (Emphasis added.)

single economic unit and undertaking concept to circumstances in which imputation of liability was at issue and in *Sumal* the Court focused attention on the notion of an undertaking as a perpetrator of an infringement and as a unit responsible for that infringement—whether in public enforcement proceedings by the Commission or in private proceedings for damages.

Even if this is correct, an important question is whether the use of the concept of an economic unit in all of these ways is appropriate. Although a carefully confined economic unit doctrine might make good sense as a means for excluding what is essentially *unilateral*—the internal workings of a firm—and not *joint* conduct from the scope of Article 101 and ensuring that market power assessments reflect the power of the economic unit as a whole, arguably the doctrine does not provide a convincing basis for holding parents liable for the conduct of their subsidiaries (or vice versa).[184] Rather, it sits uncomfortably with principles of personal responsibility (by ignoring involvement in, or control over, the infringement), company law (e.g. by disregarding rules of separate legal personality), and the presumption of innocence,[185] and could be abandoned in favour of another, more appropriate, foundation for, and theory of, parental liability—such as failure to exercise vigilance, negligence[186]—or by reserving liability for situations where the parent or subsidiary is also found to be part of the unlawful conspiracy.[187]

Such a solution would, however, require a change in direction by the EU Courts. Indeed, in 2021 the CJ stressed in *Sumal* the importance of the concept of an undertaking to the working of the EU rules and discouraging infringements of them, and that the Treaty had chosen 'the concept of an undertaking to designate the perpetrator of an infringement of competition law, who is liable to be punished by application of that provision, rather than other concepts such as those of "company" or "legal person"'.[188] The Court thus reiterated prior rulings holding that it is for the economic unit, in accordance with the principle of personal responsibility, to answer for the infringement of any legal entity within it.

e. *The Boundaries of the Economic Unit on a Dynamic Basis*

The constitution of an undertaking may change over time, especially following a corporate reorganisation or a sale of the responsible entity to another or its absorption into another entity. This may be relevant, for example, where the Commission wishes to impose a fine on responsible persons within the economic unit. '[R]eorganisations, disposals of undertakings and other changes can lead to the situation in which at the time a cartel offence is penalised the person who conducts an undertaking which participated in the cartel is not the person who conducted the undertaking at the time of the infringement.'[189]

The general rule flowing from the principle of personal responsibility[190] is that liability should attach to the legal entity (even if it has changed form or name) or original operator managing the undertaking in question at the time the infringement was committed; responsibility is personal in nature and cannot be avoided by transferring relevant business activities to another.[191] An infringing undertaking (which is still in existence) must therefore ordinarily answer itself for its unlawful

[184] Kalintiri, n. 122. [185] See articles cited in n. 117.

[186] See e.g. Kalintiri, n. 122 and discussion of *Remonts*, n. 340 and text.

[187] See e.g. the discussion of the case of *Remonts*, n. 340 and text and Case C-680/20, *Unilever Italia Mkt, Operations Srl v Autorità Garante della Concorrenza e del Mercato* EU:C:2023:33.

[188] Case C-882/19, *Sumal, SL v Mercedes Benz Trucks España, SL* EU:C:2021:800, para. 39.

[189] Case C-280/06, *ETI and Others* EU:C:2007:775, Kokott AG, para. 73.

[190] Ibid., para. 71. ('Personal responsibility means that in principle a cartel offence is to be attributed to the natural or legal person who operates the undertaking who participates in the cartel.')

[191] Case C-49/92 P, *Commission v Anic Partecipazioni* EU:C:1999:356.

activity and remains, subject to the limitation rules, liable for its past infringements even if it sells the subsidiary or assets that were the vehicle of the infringement.[192] Conversely, subsequent purchasers or transferees are not normally held responsible for prior breaches but only in respect of continuous, repeat, or new infringements by the entity committed after the date of transfer.[193] In exceptional circumstances, however, in order to ensure that liability for an infringement is not avoided through means of organisational change (for example, where the transferor ceases to exist, and has been absorbed within the new operator, or is left as an empty shell), liability may be transferred to a new operator which, in economic terms, can be regarded as the successor of the original operation or which continues the undertaking which participated in the cartel (the 'economic continuity' test is satisfied). In *Parker-Hannifin v Commission*,[194] the CJ explained:

> 40. The Court has noted that, when an entity that has committed an infringement of the competition rules is subject to a legal or organisational change, this change does not necessarily create a new undertaking free of liability for the conduct of its predecessor that infringed the competition rules, when, from an economic point of view, the two entities are identical. If undertakings could escape penalties by simply changing their identity through restructurings, sales or other legal or organisational changes, the objective of suppressing conduct that infringes the competition rules and preventing its reoccurrence by means of deterrent penalties would be jeopardised (judgment in *ETI and Other*, . . ., paragraphs 41 and 42 . . .).
>
> 41. The Court has thus held that where two entities constitute one economic entity, the fact that the entity that committed the infringement still exists does not as such preclude imposing a penalty on the entity to which its economic activities were transferred. In particular, applying penalties in this way is permissible where those entities have been under the control of the same person and have therefore, given the close economic and organisational links between them, carried out, in all material respects, the same commercial instructions (judgments in *ETI and Others*, . . ., paragraphs 48 and 49 . . ., and *Versalis v Commission*, . . ., paragraph 52).

Liability under the economic continuity principle may thus be transferred to a new operator where, for example:

(a) the responsible legal entity has ceased to exist in law and is absorbed into the business of a new owner.[195] The change in the legal form and/or name does not create a new undertaking free of liability for the conduct of its predecessor when from 'an economic point of view the two are

[192] COMP/37.027, *Zinc Phosphate* [2003] OJ L153/1, para. 238. See Case C-263/16 P, *Schenker v Commission*, EU:C:2018:58, paras. 47–52 (the Commission has a discretion concerning the choice of legal entities on which it can impose a penalty for an infringement of EU competition law. The fact that it holds a parent company liable for the conduct of its subsidiary which participated directly in the infringement does not imply in any way that it is also under the obligation to hold the earlier parent company of that subsidiary liable or jointly liable (e.g. if such an expansion of proceedings would add considerably to the work involved and so long as it has regard to fundamental rights such as the principle of equal treatment)).

[193] Assuming that, in the case of a transfer of a legal entity, the parental liability conditions are satisfied. If not, the acquiring entity cannot be held liable—only the acquired, infringing entity will attract liability.

[194] Case C-434/13, *Commission v Parker Hannifin Manufacturing Srl and Parker-Hannifin Corp* EU:C:2014:2456. See Case T-146/09 RENV, *Parker Hannifin Manufacturing Srl v Commission* EU:T:2016:411.

[195] See e.g. Cases T-259–264 and 271/02, *Raiffeisen Zentralbank Österreich v Commission* EU:T:2006:396; Case T-349/08, *Uralita v Commission* EU:T:2011:622; and Case T-194/06, *SNIA v Commission* EU:T:2011:279, *aff'd* Case C-448/11 P, EU:C:201:801. But contrast Case C-49/92, *Commission v Anic Partecipazioni* EU:C:1999:356, para. 145 (where the legal person responsible for running the undertaking had not ceased to exist in law) and Case T-9/99 *HFB and Others v Commission* EU:T:2002:70, para. 104.

identical'.[196] The Commission may identify the 'combination of physical and human elements which contributed to the commission of the infringement' and then impose liability on the legal person which has become responsible for their operation;[197] or

(b) the legal person that committed the infringement still exists but no longer carries on an economic activity in the relevant market and there are close structural links between the original and new operators which are under the control of the same person.[198] In such circumstances, the existence of the structural links between the original and new operators justifies the imposition of liability on both (the new operator being jointly and severally liable for the fine).[199] In *ETI*, for example, the CJ held that responsibility for past antitrust infringements committed by AAMS, an organ of the State, on the cigarette market, could be attributed to its successor company, ETI. AAMS's tobacco business (manufacture and sales) had been transferred in 1999 by the Italian Government to ETI which, at that time, was also owned by the Italian Ministry of Economy and Finance. In 2003, ETI was privatised and acquired by British American Tobacco. The CJ held that liability could be imposed on ETI in respect of infringements committed by AAMS if it, and AAMS, constituted one economic entity—if they answered to, and were owned and subject to control by, the same public entity. Applying penalties in this way 'is permissible where those entities have been subject to control by the same person within the group and have therefore given the close economic and organisational links between them carried out, in all material respects, the same commercial instructions'.[200]

Although in *Hoechst* the GC held that the principle of personal liability cannot 'be called into question by the principle of economic continuity in cases where . . . an undertaking involved in the cartel has transferred a part of its business to an independent third party and there is no structural link between the initial operator and the new operator (see, to that effect, Opinion of Advocate General Kokott in *ETI and Others*, paragraph 82)',[201] in *Parker-Hannifin* the CJ clarified that where an infringing business had been transferred into a new subsidiary simply for the purpose of transferring that business to a third party, the economic continuity principle may apply. '[F]or the purpose of establishing the existence of economic continuity, the relevant date for assessing whether the transfer of activities is within a group or between independent undertakings must be that of the transfer itself'; the economic links need therefore to exist only *at the time of* the acquisition and two distinct transactions, an internal transaction, and a subsequent transfer to a third party cannot be treated as one.

In *ETI*, Advocate General Kokott indicated that, although the criterion of economic continuity is not intended to substitute for the principle of personal responsibility, new circumstances of 'economic continuity' might be recognisable where the effective enforcement of competition law requires a derogation from the principle of personal responsibility in order to ensure that an offence is punished effectively according to fault; for example, where organisational changes are made 'abusively' in an attempt to circumvent liability to pay a fine.[202]

[196] Cases 29 and 30/83, *CRAM and Rheinzink v Commission* EU:C:1984:130, para. 9. Case C-280/06 *ETI and Others* EU:C:2007:775, Kokott AG ('having regard to economic continuity ensures that legal persons cannot escape their responsibility under antitrust law merely by changing their legal form or their name. The same must be true for example in respect of a merger in which the original operator of the undertaking which participated in the cartel surrenders its legal personality to another legal person which is its successor in law', para. 78).

[197] Case T-6/89, *Enichem v Commission* EU:T:1991:74, 237.

[198] Cases C-204/00 P etc., *Aalborg Portland and Others v Commission* EU:C:2004:6, para. 359 and Case C-280/06, *ETI and Others* EU:C:2007:775, paras. 41 and 48.

[199] Case T-405/06, *ArcelorMittal v Commission* EU:T:2009:90, paras. 112–117.

[200] Case C-280/06, *ETI and Others* EU:C:2007:775, para. 49.

[201] Case T-161/05, *Hoechst v Commission* EU:T:2009:366, para. 61.

[202] Case C-280/06, *ETI and Others* EU:C:2007:775, Kokott AG, para. 82.

(viii) Associations of Undertakings

a. *Institutionalised Forms of Cooperation*

Article 101(1) applies not only to agreements and concerted practices between undertakings but to decisions by associations of undertakings. In *Wouters*,[203] Advocate General Léger stated that the concept:

> seeks to prevent undertakings from being able to evade the rules on competition on account simply of the form in which they coordinate their conduct on the market. To ensure that this principle is effective, Article [101(1)] covers not only direct methods of coordinating conduct between undertakings (agreements and concerted practices) but also institutionalised forms of cooperation, that is to say, situations in which economic operators act through a collective structure or a common body.[204]

An association of undertakings 'consists of undertakings of the same general type and makes itself responsible for representing and defending their common interests vis-à-vis other economic operators, government bodies and the public in general'.[205] It is thus widely construed to cover bodies formed to represent the commercial interests of its member undertakings and has been found to apply to: trade associations (which may provide a forum for competitors in a particular industry to get together and to discuss matters which may be to their mutual interest); agricultural cooperatives;[206] associations of collecting societies;[207] bodies set up by statute and with public functions if they represent the trading interests of the members;[208] and professional associations (even if governed by a public law statute).[209] It has also been found that *Visa*[210] and *MasterCard*[211] are associations of undertakings. Such a categorisation means that their recommendations, rules, and other unilateral acts may constitute decisions which are brought within Article 101 (without separate proof of a concerted practice or agreement between the individual members of the association, see further Section 4.B).

b. *The Relationship between Associations of Undertakings and Undertakings*

In some cases, an entity has sometimes been found to be acting both jointly with its parents/members (as an association of undertakings) and unilaterally as a single undertaking at the same time. In *Laurent Piau*,[212] for example, the GC held that although a sporting association constituted an

[203] Case C-309/99, EU:C:2002:98. [204] Ibid., Léger AG, para. 62. [205] Ibid., para. 61.

[206] Case C-250/92, *Gøttrup-Klim e.a. Grovvareforeninger and Others v Dansk Landbrugs Grovvareselskab AmbA* EU:C:1994:413.

[207] See COMP/38.698, *CISAC Agreement* 16 July 2008, partially annulled on appeal, Case T-442/08, *International Confederation of Societies of Authors and Composers (CISAC) v Commission* EU:T:2013:188, see Chap. 9.

[208] Case 123/83, *BNIC v Clair* EU:C:1985:33.

[209] See Case C-35/96, *Commission v Italy* EU:C:1998:303, paras. 36–38 (dealing with a professional association of custom agents); Cases C-180–184/98, *Pavlov* EU:C:2000:428, paras. 73–77; and Case C-309/99, *Wouters* EU:C:2002:98, para. 65.

[210] E.g. COMP/29.373, *Visa International* [2002] OJ L318/17.

[211] See COMP/34.579, *Europay (Eurocard-MasterCard)* 19 December 2007 (rejecting MasterCard's argument that its public listing on the New York Stock Exchange had changed the organisation's governance so fundamentally that any decision of its board no longer qualified as a decision of an association (an institutionalised form of coordination of the banks' conduct) but rather constituted a 'unilateral' act by which each member bank bilaterally agrees to abide), *aff'd* Case T-111/08, *MasterCard Inc v Commission* EU:T:2012:260, paras. 241–260 and Case C-382/12 P, EU:C:2014:2201, paras. 62–77 (the banks still participated in the decision-making process and shared a commonality of interest with MasterCard).

[212] Case T-193/02, *Piau v Commission* EU:T:2005:22, para. 69, see nn. 41–43 and text and e.g. Case C-333/21, *European Super League v FIFA and UEFA* EU:C:2022:993, Rantos AG, paras. 56–59, judgment of the CJ pending.

association of undertakings, it also constituted an undertaking insofar as it engaged in economic activity in a market itself.[213]

A further question arising is whether an association of undertakings which carries out non-economic activity should be subject to the competition rules. It would seem that such non-economic activity should not be caught as, in essence, the conduct of the association is treated as the joint conduct of its members/shareholders (whose actions are not caught unless they are economic in nature).[214] Indeed, in *Wouters*,[215] the CJ suggests that a functional approach should be adopted to the concept of an association of undertakings in the same way as it applies to the concept of an undertaking. In that case, it was argued that the Bar of the Netherlands, a body governed by public law, should not constitute an association of undertakings when exercising regulatory powers in order to perform a task of public interest. The CJ held that the 'rules of competition do not apply to activity which, by its nature, its aim and the rules to which it is subject does not belong to the sphere of economic activity . . . or which is connected with the exercise of the powers of a public authority . . . '.[216] It held, however, that in adopting the regulatory rules the association was neither fulfilling a social function based on the principle of solidarity, nor exercising powers which are typically those of a public authority. Rather, it was acting as the regulatory body of a profession, the practice of which constitutes an economic activity. It thus concluded that the Bar of the Netherlands must be regarded as an association of undertakings within the meaning of Article 101(1) when adopting a regulation such as one which prohibited certain multidisciplinary partnerships. 'Such a regulation constitutes the expression of the intention of the delegates of the members of a profession that they should act in a particular manner in carrying on their economic activity.'[217]

Similarly, in *Ordem dos Técnicos Oficiais de Contas (OTOC) v Autoridade da Concorrência*,[218] the CJ held that a professional association of chartered accountants was to be regarded as an association of undertakings when it adopted a regulation providing that certain compulsory training to be undertaken by chartered accountants could be provided only by OTOC. Even though OTOC was regulated by public law and required to adopt binding rules putting in place a system of compulsory training for its members and to ensure a quality service, it could not be regarded, when adopting the rules, as exercising powers which are typically those of a public authority. The rules belonged to the sphere of economic activity (they had a direct impact on the market for compulsory training for chartered accountants[219]). The CJ also held that it was immaterial that OTOC did not seek to make a profit: 'that does not prevent an entity which carries out operations on the market from being considered an undertaking, where the corresponding offer of services exists in competition with that of other operators which do seek to make a profit'.[220]

[213] This reasoning, is not entirely easy. If the association is an undertaking, the parents/members form part of that economic unit. But if the parents are not undertakings, the sporting association cannot be an association of undertakings.

[214] But see Odudu, n. 28, 52–53. See also Cases 209–215 and 218/78, *Van Landewyck and Others v Commission* EU:C:1980:248, paras. 87–88; Cases 96–102, 104, 105, 108, and 110/82, *NV IAZ International Belgium SA v Commission* EU:C:1983:310, paras. 19–20; and Cases T-25, 26, 30–32, 34–39, 42–46, 48, 50–71, 87, 88, 103, and 104/95, *Cimenteries CBR v Commission* EU:T:2000:77, para. 1320.

[215] Case C-309/99, EU:C:2002:98.

[216] Ibid., para. 57.

[217] Ibid., para. 64 (finding that: (a) the governing body of the Bar was composed exclusively of members of the Bar elected solely by members of the profession; (b) when adopting regulatory measures the Bar was not required to be guided by reference to specified public-interest criteria; and (c) the regulation influenced the conduct of the members of the Bar on the market in legal services).

[218] Case C-1/12, EU:C:2013:127.

[219] Ibid., para. 45 (it did not matter that it did not affect competition on the market on which the members practised their profession).

[220] Ibid., para. 57.

B. THE MEANING OF 'AGREEMENT', 'DECISION', AND 'CONCERTED PRACTICE'

(i) Introduction

Article 101 applies to 'agreements between undertakings, decisions by associations of undertakings and concerted practices'—some 'collusion' or 'cooperation' between independent undertakings is required. Although these three terms are distinguishable from each other by their intensity and the forms in which they manifest themselves, the precise characterisation of the cooperation does not alter the legal analysis to be conducted.[221] Rather, their aim is to catch different forms of coordination and collusion, which extend well beyond the conclusion of formal contracts,[222] and, collectively, to draw a critical dividing line between joint conduct caught by Article 101[223] and independent behaviour falling outside its scope. The importance is not, therefore, the distinction between, for example, an agreement and a concerted practice—conduct may present elements of both—but to ascertain and define the minimum degree or loosest form of interaction necessary between undertakings for it to be shown that they have acted jointly rather than unilaterally.[224]

In many Article 101 cases, the existence of an agreement is not in doubt. There may be doubt, however, as to the precise terms of the agreement and/or as to whether the terms can be said to restrict competition. In other cases, frequently where it is suspected that a serious violation of the EU competition rules has been committed (e.g. horizontal or vertical price-fixing), evidence that independent undertakings agreed or concerted (e.g. to fix prices) will, effectively, prove a violation of Article 101(1)[225] and result in severe consequences for those involved in the infringement (see Section 3.B and Chapters 13 and 14). In such cases, the parties who have been 'colluding' are more likely to do so in an amorphous way and/or to try and conceal its existence rather than attempt to try to defend its legitimacy. The challenge for the competition authorities in such cases is to uncover such covert operations and to determine whether or not the behaviour on the market results from prohibited collusion. Proof of collusion may be founded upon either direct evidence, which may be difficult to uncover,[226] or indirect or circumstantial evidence from which such conduct may be inferred.

(ii) Collusion Orchestrated by Employees

Collusion arises from the actions of individuals. Where an employee has entered into secret arrangements to rig markets, EU law holds that the undertaking will be liable for the actions of its employees even if they were not authorised or instructed to act in that way by senior management—personal conduct on the part of, or the assent of, a representative authorised under the undertaking's constitution

[221] For the view that the agreement concept encompasses concerted practices and decisions (and tacit collusion, see further Chap. 9) rendering the trichotomy of arrangements under Art. 101 unnecessary, see K. Kwok, 'The Concept of "Agreement" under Article 101 TFEU: A Question of EU Treaty Interpretation' (2019) 44(2) *ELRev* 196.

[222] Case C-238/05, *Asnef-Equifax, Servicios de Información sobre Solvencia y Crédito, SL v Asociación de Usuarios de Servicios Bancarios (Ausbanc)* EU:C:2006:734.

[223] Case C-49/92 P, *Commission v Anic* EU:C:1999:356, paras. 112 and 131. The different forms are to be understood in the light of the concept inherent in the competition rules that each economic operator must determine independently the policy that it intends to adopt.

[224] COMP/31.149, *Polypropylene* [1986] OJ L230/1, para. 87 ('The importance of the concept of a concerted practice does not thus result so much from the distinction between it and an agreement as from the distinction between forms of collusion falling under Article [101(1)] and mere parallel behaviour with no element of concertation').

[225] If the agreement has as its 'object' the restriction of competition, its anti-competitive 'effect' does not need to be demonstrated, see Chap. 5.

[226] I.e. smoking-gun evidence (written or parol), which does not require inferences to establish the agreement or other collusion alleged. see further Chaps. 9 and 13.

is not required. In *Protimonopolný úrad Slovenskej republiky v Slovenská sporiteľňa a.s,*[227] the CJ thus clarified that:

> it is not necessary for there to have been action by, or even knowledge on the part of, the partners or principal managers of the undertaking concerned; action by a person who is authorised to act on behalf of the undertaking suffices.

Undertakings should, therefore, have in place, and should enforce, a compliance programme to prevent breaches of the competition rules.[228] Although EU law does not provide sanctions (disqualification, fines, and/or imprisonment) for individual employees, such sanctions are available in some EU Member States.

(iii) Agreement

a. A Concurrence of Wills

The term 'agreement' has been given a liberal construction. In *Bayer AG v Commission,*[229] the GC held that proof of an agreement must be founded upon 'the existence of the subjective element that characterises the very concept of the agreement, that is to say a concurrence of wills between economic operators on the implementation of a policy, the pursuit of an objective, or the adoption of a given line of conduct on the market'.[230] It is 'clear from the case-law that in order for there to be an agreement . . . it is sufficient that the undertakings in question should have expressed their joint intention to conduct themselves on the market in a specific way'.[231]

So long as there is a concurrence of wills, constituting the faithful expression of the parties' intention,[232] its form is unimportant. Therefore, an agreement may be found whether or not the conduct amounts to a contract under national law or is intended to be legally binding, whether or not sanctions are provided for a breach, and whether it is in writing or oral.[233] It covers 'gentlemen's agreements',[234] standard conditions of sale,[235] trade association rules (which are treated as an agreement between the members to abide by the rules),[236] and agreements entered into to settle disputes.[237] An agreement exists once the parties agree on 'good neighbour rules' or 'establish practice and ethics' or 'certain rules of the game which it is in the interests of all of us to follow'.[238] Even if an agreement has been terminated (formally), it may be caught by Article 101(1) if it continues to have effects.[239] It is also

[227] Case C-68/12, EU:C:2013:71, para. 25. See also Case C-542/14, *VM Remonts* EU:C:2016:578, paras. 23–27 (an undertaking's control over a contractor may operate as a disguised employment relationship) and discussion n. 340 and text (the position is different where a truly independent service provider is concerned) and see n. 152 and text (concerning a parent's liability for a subsidiary that disregards express instructions).

[228] See further Chap. 13.

[229] Case T-41/96, EU:T:2000:242, *aff'd* on appeal Cases C-2 and 3/01 P, EU:C:2004:2.

[230] Ibid.

[231] Ibid., para. 67, relying on e.g. Case 41/69, *ACF Chemiefarma NV v Commission* EU:C:1970:71, para. 112. See also Case C-49/92, *Commission v Anic Partecipazioni* EU:C:1999:356, paras. 79 and 122.

[232] Case T-41/96, ibid., para. 69. See also Case T-62/98, *Volkswagen AG v Commission* EU:T:2000:180, *aff'd* Case C-338/00 P, *Volkswagen AG v Commission* EU:C:2003:473.

[233] See e.g. Case 28/77, *Tepea BV v Commission* EU:C:1978:133.

[234] Case 41/69, *ACF Chemiefarma NV v Commission* EU:C:1970:71 (an export cartel was extended within the EU through a gentlemen's agreement. So long as the parties had declared themselves willing to abide by it that was sufficient).

[235] Case C-277/87, *Sandoz prodotti farmaceutici SpA v Commission* EU:C:1989:363.

[236] COMP/30.804, *Nuovo Cegam* [1984] OJ L99/29.

[237] See Chap. 12.

[238] Cases 209–215 and 218/78, *Van Landewyck v Commission* EU:C:1980:248, paras. 85 and 86.

[239] Case T-7/89, *SA Hercules Chemicals NV v Commission* EU:T:1991:75.

immaterial that an undertaking was bullied into concluding the agreement,[240] or that an undertaking had cheated or never intended to implement or to adhere to the terms of the agreement. 'The notion of "agreement" is objective in nature. The actual motives (and hidden intentions) which underlay the behaviour adopted are irrelevant.'[241]

b. Agreements between Undertakings Operating at Different Levels of the Economy or in Separate Markets

Article 101(1) applies to agreements concluded between two or more undertakings (bilateral or multilateral agreements), whether or not they are actual or potential competitors. Even though Article 101 is not applicable to agreements concluded between companies forming part of a single economic entity, such as a parent and subsidiary/distributor,[242] in the foundational case of *Consten and Grundig v Commission*,[243] the CJ confirmed that it applied to agreements concluded between undertakings operating at different levels of the economy—i.e. to vertical arrangements (the agreement in this case had not been concluded between a manufacturer and an entity integrated within it but had been concluded between independent undertakings). The wording of Article 101 did not suggest that a distinction between horizontal (between actual or potential competitors operating at the same level of the economy) and vertical agreements (between parties operating at different levels of the economy, for example, an agreement between a manufacturer and its distributor) should be drawn. Rather, it applied to all agreements between undertakings which had the potential to distort competition within the common market.

Cases 56 and 58/64, Établissements Consten SA and Grundig-Verkaufs-GmbH v Commission EU:C:1966:41

In 1957, Grundig, a German manufacturer of radios, tape recorders, dictaphones, and televisions, appointed Consten as its exclusive agent for France. Consten agreed, amongst other things, not to handle any competing products, to order a minimum quantity of Grundig products, to stock accessories and spare parts, and to provide after-sales services. In return, Grundig agreed not to deliver the product for sale in France and imposed export and re-export restrictions on all distributors in other Member States. The Grundig trade mark, Gint, was registered in France in Consten's name. Under the agreements Consten, therefore, had absolute territorial protection. No one else was entitled to sell Grundig products in France either actively or passively. When UNEF and Leissner started importing and selling Grundig products at more favourable prices in France, Consten thus commenced proceedings in the French courts claiming, amongst other things, unfair competition and trade mark infringement. UNEF complained to the Commission and, in 1963, the agreement was notified to the Commission for examination. The French court adjourned its proceedings to await the Commission's decision.

The Commission concluded that the agreements did infringe Article 101(1) and could not be individually exempted under Article 101(3). Consten and Grundig appealed to the Court of Justice. One of their pleas, supported by the Italian Government, was that Article 101(1) applied only to 'horizontal' and not 'vertical' agreements.

[240] Case T-25/95, *Cimenteries CBR SA v Commission* EU:T:2000:77, para. 2557.

[241] See e.g. COMP/36.700, *Industrial and Medical Gases* [2003] OJ L84/1 (the Commission rejected the arguments of Air Liquide and Westfalen, that they had not actually taken part in the agreements or ever intended to implement them), *aff'd* on appeal Case T-304/02, *Hoek Loos NV v Commission* EU:T:2006:184.

[242] See Section 4.A.vii.

[243] Cases 56 and 58/64, *Consten and Grundig* EU:C:1966:41.

Court of Justice

The complaints concerning the applicability of Article [101(1)] to sole distributorship contracts

The applicants submit that the prohibition in Article [101(1)] applies only to so-called horizontal agreements. The Italian Government submits furthermore that sole distributorship contracts do not constitute 'agreements between undertakings' within the meaning of that provision, since the parties are not on a footing of equality. With regard to these contracts, freedom of competition may only be protected by virtue of Article [102] of the Treaty.

Neither the wording of Article [101] nor that of Article [102] gives any ground for holding that distinct areas of application are to be assigned to each of the two Articles according to the level in the economy at which the contracting parties operate. Article [101] refers in a general way to all agreements which distort competition within the Common Market and does not lay down any distinction between those agreements based on whether they are made between competitors operating at the same level in the economic process or between non-competing persons operating at different levels. In principle, no distinction can be made where the Treaty does not make any distinction.

Furthermore, the possible application of Article [101] to a sole distributorship contract cannot be excluded merely because the grantor and the concessionnaire [*sic*] are not competitors *inter se* and not on a footing of equality. Competition may be distorted within the meaning of Article [101(1)] not only by agreements which limit it as between the parties but also by agreements which prevent or restrict the competition which might take place between one of them and third parties. For this purpose, it is irrelevant whether the parties to the agreement are or are not on a footing of equality as regards their position and function in the economy. This applies all the more, since, by such an agreement, the parties might seek, by preventing or limiting the competition of third parties in respect of the products, to create or guarantee for their benefit an unjustified advantage at the expense of the consumer or user, contrary to the general aims of Article [101].

It is thus possible that, without involving an abuse of a dominant position, an agreement between economic operators at different levels may affect trade between Member States and at the same time have as its object or effect the prevention, restriction or distortion of competition, thus falling under the prohibition of Article [101(1)].

In addition, it is pointless to compare on the one hand the situation, to which Article [101] applies, of a producer bound by a sole distributorship agreement to the distributor of his products with on the other hand that of a producer who includes within his undertaking the distribution of his own products by some means, for example, by commercial representatives, to which Article [101] does not apply. These situations are distinct in law and, moreover, need to be assessed differently, since two marketing organizations, one of which is [i]ntegrated into the manufacturer's undertaking whilst the other is not, may not necessarily have the same efficiency. The wording of Article [101] causes the prohibition to apply, provided that the other conditions are met, to an agreement between several undertakings. Thus it does not apply where a sole undertaking integrates its own distribution network into its business organization. It does not thereby follow, however, that the contractual situation based on an agreement between a manufacturing and a distributing undertaking is rendered legally acceptable by a simple process of economic analogy—which is in any case incomplete and in contradiction with the said Article. Furthermore, although in the first case the Treaty intended in Article [101] to leave untouched the internal organization of an undertaking and to render it liable to be called in question, by means of Article [102], only in cases where it reaches such a degree of seriousness as to amount to an abuse of a dominant position, the same reservation could not apply when the impediments to competition result from agreement between two different undertakings which then as a general rule simply require to be prohibited.

Finally, an agreement between producer and distributor which might tend to restore the national divisions in trade between Member States might be such as to frustrate the most fundamental objectives of the Community. The Treaty, whose preamble and content aim at abolishing the barriers between States, and which in several provisions gives evidence of a stern attitude with regard to their reappearance, could not allow undertakings to reconstruct such barriers. Article [101(1)] is designed to pursue this aim, even in the case of agreements between undertakings placed at different levels in the economic process.

The submissions set out above are consequently unfounded.

In *AC-Treuhand AG v Commission*,[244] the CJ also made it clear that Article 101(1) catches agreements between undertakings even where the purpose of the agreement is to restrict competition on a market on which one of the undertakings is not active. Accordingly, the CJ confirmed that a consultancy firm may be party to an agreement infringing Article 101(1) where it actively contributes to the implementation and continuation of an unlawful agreement among competing producers (for example, through organising meetings, collecting and supplying sales data, and moderating disputes between parties in return for remuneration), even if it does not itself operate on the affected market. The terms agreement and concerted practice do not presuppose 'a mutual restriction of freedom of action on one and the same market on which all the parties are present'; rather, it applies generally to all collusion which distorts competition 'irrespective of the market on which the parties operate'.[245] An intermediary assisting or facilitating an agreement is liable if, as in *Treuhand* itself, it intended to contribute to the common objectives pursued by the participants, was aware of the actual conduct planned in pursuit of the objectives, or could reasonably have foreseen it, and was prepared to take the risk.[246] The CJ reiterated that the main objective of Article 101(1) is to ensure that competition remains undistorted, so it had to be possible to put a stop to a restriction of competition even if the conduct does not relate to an economic activity forming part of the relevant market on which the restriction came about (or was intended to come about).

c. Collective Bargaining Agreements

In *Albany*,[247] the CJ held that collective agreements concluded by representatives of employers and workers in a sector fall outside the scope of Article 101(1) insofar as they relate to the improvement of conditions of work and employment; application of Article 101 would thwart/undermine the Treaty's

[244] Case C-194/14 P, EU:C:2015:717, paras. 26–47 (but contrast Wahl AG in his Opinion in this case, EU:C:2015:350, para.34), affirming Case T-27/10, *AC-Treuhand AG v Commission* EU:T:2014:59 (see also Case T-99/04, *AC-Treuhand AG v Commission* EU:T:2008:256). In 2017, the GC, although upholding the principle that third party facilitators can be liable for a cartel, annulled a fine imposed by the Commission (COMP/39.861, Yen Interest Rate Derivatives (YIRD) IP/15/1404) on ICAP, a broker that it alleged had facilitated several cartels in the sector of Yen interest rate derivatives, Case T-180/15 P, *ICAP v Commission* EU:T:2017:795. It also annulled one of the six infringements found (and four in part), stressing that firm and precise evidence was necessary to establish that the facilitator intended to contribute to the objectives of the cartel participants and was aware of the conduct planned, or could reasonably have foreseen such action and was prepared to take the risk. The Commission's appeal was dismissed, Case C-39/18 P, EU:C:2019:584.

[245] Ibid., paras. 33–35.

[246] Ibid., para. 30 (it had not just carried out peripheral services unconnected with the restrictive arrangements) and see n. 382 and text. For the view that Art. 101 prohibits conduct that facilitates an Art. 101 infringement and that this would be a preferable way for sanctioning such conduct (rather than extending the principle of an agreement), see L. M. Baudenbacher and A. Weitbrecht, 'Facilitation of Infringements of EU Competition Law and General Principles Common to the Law of Member States' (2018) *ECLR* 1.

[247] Case C-67/96, EU:C:1999:430, see especially paras. 46–64. See also Cases C-115–117/97, *Brentjens' Handelsonderneming BV v Stichting Bedrijfspensioenfonds voor de Handel in Bouwmaterialen* EU:C:1999:434 para. 57; Cases C-180–184/98, *Pavlov* EU:C:2000:428, para. 67; and Case C-437/09, *AG2R Prévoyance v Beaudout Père et Fils SARL* EU:C:2011:112, paras. 28–36. See also nn. 91–93 and text.

objective to achieve a high level of employment and social protection.[248] In *Holship Norge*,[249] the EFTA Court considered the *Albany* exemption to be a narrow one and not applicable to a collective agreement which goes beyond the improvement of work and employment conditions (construed broadly to cover agreements in relation to wages, working hours, other working conditions and possibly safety, the workplace environment, holidays, training, continuing education, and consultation and co-determination between workers and management). Moreover, an agreement which requires a port user to engage dockworkers employed by an administrative office (AO) to unload or load cargo from or to their ships, unless the latter decides that it has insufficient capacity to take on an assignment, appeared not to be limited to the establishment or improvement of working conditions of the workers of the AO and so to go beyond the core object and elements of collective bargaining.

Collective bargaining arrangements that are not between employer and employees/workers, for example involving self-employed undertakings, cannot benefit from the *Albany* exception (unless they qualify as 'false self-employed').[250] The Commission has nonetheless been keen to ensure that competition law should not stand in the way of agreements designed to improve the working conditions of the self-employed, especially those operating in the 'gig' economy. In October 2022, it adopted Guidelines[251] setting out guidance on the compatibility with Article 101 of agreements relating to working conditions negotiated between counterparties (undertakings to which solo self-employed persons provide their services) and solo self-employed people who have little influence over their working conditions (because they are in a situation comparable to workers[252] or are in a weak negotiating position[253]). They 'clarify: (a) that collective agreements by solo self-employed persons who are in a situation comparable to that of workers fall outside the scope of Article 101 TFEU; and (b) that the Commission will not intervene against collective agreements of solo self-employed persons who experience an imbalance in bargaining power vis-à-vis their counterparty/-ies'.[254] A difficulty with the latter solution is they might not provide sufficient comfort to the self-employed given that action at the national level will remain possible, including through private litigation,[255] and they do not contain guidance on how substantive assessment of such agreements is to be conducted and when they may not infringe Article 101(1).[256]

[248] TEU, Art. 3(3) states that the EU shall promote a highly competitive social market economy, aiming at full employment and social progress and the importance of social dialogue and collective bargaining is recognised both in TFEU, Art. 153 and the EU Charter, Art. 28.

[249] Case E-14/15, *Holship Norge AS v Norsk Transportarbeiderforbund* 19 April 2016.

[250] See Case C-413/13, *FNV Kunsten Informatie en Media v Staat der Nederlanden* EU:C:2014:2411.

[251] See Communication from the Commission, Guidelines on the application of Union competition law to collective agreements regarding the working conditions of solo self-employed persons [2022] OJ C374/2 and V. Daskalova, 'The Competition Law Framework and Collective Bargaining Agreements for Self-Employed: Analysing Restrictions and Mapping Exemption Opportunities' in B. Waas, and C. Hießl (eds.), *Collective Barning for Self-employed Workers in Europe: Approaches to Reconcile Competition Law and Labour Rights* (Kluwer Law International, 2021), e.g. HIVA-KU Leuven, 'Study to Gather Evidence on the Working Conditions of Platform Workers', December 2019 (noting that competition law is perceived to be an obstacle to collective bargaining by platform workers) and G. Monti, 'Collective Labour Agreements and EU Competition Law: Five Configurations' (2021) 17(3) *European Competition Journal* 714.

[252] E.g. who provide the same or similar tasks side-by-side with workers or provide services to or through a digital labour platform.

[253] E.g. when providing services to counterparties of a certain economic strength or where bargaining collectively pursuant to national or EU legislation.

[254] Guidelines on the application of Union competition law to collective agreements regarding the working conditions of solo self-employed persons [2022] OJ C374/2, para. 9.

[255] Some Member States have legislation protecting such agreements from competition law, see V. Daskalova, 'Rethinking Collective Bargaining for the Self-employed: European Commission publishes Guidelines on Exemption and Non-Enforcement', Kluwer Competition Law blog, 7 October 2022.

[256] But see Daskalova, n. 251 and Monti, n. 251.

d. Participation in Meetings—Passive Participation in an Agreement

In *Anic*,[257] the CJ confirmed that the GC was entitled to hold, without unduly reversing the burden of proof, that since the Commission had established that Anic had participated in meetings at which price initiatives had been decided on, planned, and monitored, it was for Anic to adduce evidence that it had not subscribed to those initiatives. Indeed, it is now established that a participant in a meeting at which an anti-competitive agreement is concluded will be presumed to have taken part in it, and to have tacitly approved or accepted it, if it does not publicly distance itself from the agreement[258] or report it to the administrative authorities, even if it did not go to the meeting with an anti-competitive intent and did not put the initiatives into effect. '[I]t is sufficient for the Commission to show that the undertaking concerned participated in meetings at which anticompetitive agreements were concluded, without manifestly opposing them, to prove to the requisite standard that the undertaking participated in a cartel' (*Aalborg Portland*).[259]

By being at a meeting without publicly distancing itself from what is discussed, an undertaking passively partakes in the infringement, leads the other participants to believe that it subscribes to what was decided there and will comply with it, and effectively encourages the continuation of the agreement and compromises its discovery.[260] Evidence of prices or other behaviour not reflecting those discussed at the meeting are not, therefore, sufficient to prove that it had not participated in the scheme.[261] Cases establish that it is very hard for an undertaking to establish that it has publicly distanced itself from cartel discussions in practice and, in particular, that to be successful it must leave the participating undertakings in no doubt about its public distancing from the conduct.[262]

e. Vertical Agreements and Unilateral Conduct

It is clear that the word 'agreement' catches terms and conditions even if imposed by one party on another. If the terms are accepted, the fact that one of the parties was unwilling to accept them does not prevent the agreement from being formed (although fines may be reserved for the principal beneficiaries of the activity involved).[263] In *BMW*,[264] an agreement was found to have been concluded which incorporated export bans imposed on reluctant BMW dealers.

A further related issue is the extent to which the term agreement can encompass what, at first sight at least, appears to be a purely unilateral policy or unilateral conduct pursued by one of its parties. The question of when behaviour is truly unilateral (where the aims can be achieved without the participation of another) and when unilateral behaviour is merely *apparent* (receiving explicit or tacit acquiescence by another) is an important and difficult one which has provoked considerable litigation. The former, even if restrictive of competition or hindering parallel imports, falls outside Article 101.

[257] Case C-49/92 P, *Commission v Anic* EU:C:1999:356, para. 96.

[258] Such an intention must be expressed firmly and unambiguously, so other participants fully understand the undertaking's intention.

[259] Cases C-204, 205, 211, 213, 217, and 219/00 P, *Aalborg Portland AS v Commission* EU:C:2004:6, paras. 81–87.

[260] Ibid.

[261] Case T-3/89, *Atochem v Commission* EU:T:1991:58, para. 100 and Case T-53/03, *British Plasterboard v Commission* EU:T:2008:254, para. 85.

[262] For a review of all (unsuccessful) attempts to do so until 2016, see Abenhaïm, n. 24 and for a criticism of the over-inclusive nature of the presumption, see Khoo, n. 24.

[263] The Commission may decline to impose a fine on a party that has acted unwillingly, against its own economic interest, or under duress, see e.g. COMP/35.733, *Volkswagen* [1998] OJ L124/60, on appeal Case T-62/98, *Volkswagen AG v Commission* EU:T:2000:180, Case C-338/00 P, *Volkswagen AG v Commission* EU:C:2003:473. See Chap. 13 for a discussion of the Commission's fining policy.

[264] Cases 32 and 36–82/78 *BMW v Commission* EU:C:1979:191.

Take, for example, a vertical agreement between a supplier and a dealer.[265] In the EU, such agreements are unlikely to incorporate explicit provisions imposing resale price maintenance (RPM) or incorporating an export ban as these generally constitute clear restrictions of competition.[266] What would be the position, however, if a supplier unilaterally announces that it will not deal with dealers that do not adhere to minimum recommended prices *or* who sell outside their allotted territory or if it is understood that if dealers do not adhere to minimum recommended prices and/or if they sell outside their allotted territory, they will not be supplied? Can an agreement to adhere to minimum resale prices or an export ban between the supplier and dealers be established and/or can a dealer that continues to accept supply be said to have 'tacitly' acquiesced in the supplier's policy and to have agreed to adhere to the anti-competitive terms? Does it make any difference whether or not the dealers do in fact adhere to the terms or whether they price cut or make sales outside their territory and/or whether the policy manifests itself before or after the agreement was concluded?

The Commission has been prepared to find the existence of an agreement based on seemingly unilateral conduct. For example, in *AEG*, AEG-Telefunken (a developer and manufacturer of consumer electronic products) notified its selective distribution system to the Commission;[267] the Commission indicated that it did not infringe Article 101(1). Subsequently, however, the Commission received complaints alleging that AEG had refused to supply certain resellers which would not adhere to a policy of charging minimum prices.[268] AEG argued that the acts complained of were not part of its agreement with resellers but were decisions that it had taken unilaterally. Both the Commission and the Court rejected this argument. The CJ held that this behaviour:

> on the part of the manufacturer does not constitute, on the part of the undertaking, unilateral conduct which, as AEG claims, would be exempt from the prohibition contained in Article [101(1)]. On the contrary, it forms part of the contractual relations between the undertaking and resellers. Indeed, in the case of the admission of a distributor, approval is based on the acceptance, tacit or express, by the contracting parties of the policy pursued by AEG which requires *inter alia* the exclusion from the network of all distributors who are qualified for admission but are not prepared to adhere to that policy.[269]

The Court thus found that the resellers' admission to the network was dependent upon their acceptance, express or tacit, of AEG's policy.

A similar approach has been adopted in other cases, many involving export bans imposed on distributors. In *Ford*,[270] the Commission concluded that Ford's decision to cease supply of right-hand-drive cars to German dealers formed an integral part of the agreements with the dealers. The CJ upheld its finding that admission to the Ford AG dealer network implied acceptance by the contracting parties of the policy pursued by Ford with regard to the models delivered to the German market. In *Sandoz*,[271] the CJ also affirmed the Commission's view that Sandoz's policy of sending invoices to customers with the words 'export prohibited' upon them did not constitute unilateral conduct, but, on the contrary, formed part of the general framework of commercial relations which

[265] See Chap. 11.

[266] Such agreements are generally assumed to restrict competition (Art. 101(1)) and not to meet the conditions of Art. 101(3), see further Chaps. 5 and 11.

[267] A selective distribution system is one where the supplier limits the number or, more usually, the type of outlets that sell its products, see Chap. 11.

[268] See Chap. 11. [269] Case 107/82, *AEG-Telefunken v Commission* EU:C:1983:293, para. 38.

[270] Cases 228 and 229/82, *Ford Werke AG and Ford of Europe Inc v Commission* EU:C:1984:80. See also Case C-279/87, *Tipp-Ex GmbH v Commission* EU:C:1990:57.

[271] Case C-277/87, *Sandoz prodotti farmaceutici SpA v Commission* EU:C:1990:6.

the undertaking maintained with its customers. The Court stressed the uniform and systematic repetition of this practice noting that customers:

> were sent the same standard invoice after each individual order . . . The repeated orders of the products and the successive payments without protest by the customer of the prices indicated on the invoice bearing the words 'export prohibited', constituted a tacit acquiescence on the part of the latter in the clauses stipulated in the invoice.[272]

In each of these cases, the apparently unilateral conduct was read into the agreement even though, in the export ban cases at least, it did not operate to the dealer's advantage.[273] In both *Bayer AG v Commission*[274] and *Volkswagen v Commission*,[275] however, the GC annulled Commission decisions which had wrongly concluded that unilateral conduct formed part of the agreement in question.[276] In *Bayer AG v Commission*,[277] the EU Courts made it clear that the Commission had pushed the concept of an agreement too far and stressed that a finding of an agreement will not be upheld in the absence of evidence of a concurrence of wills between the undertakings.

In *Bayer*, the Commission[278] had imposed a fine of €3 million on Bayer AG for taking action to prevent parallel imports in the pharmaceutical market. Bayer reduced the volumes of the drug supplied to its French and Spanish distributors. As these dealers had obligations to supply their home markets' requirements, this curbed their ability to engage in parallel trade and sales of the drug Adalat into the UK. The Commission found that the export ban was an integral element in the continuous commercial relations between Bayer and its wholesalers (which were aware of Bayer's policy and continued to place and renew orders for the product).

On appeal, the GC[279] considered that the Commission erred when deciding that the wholesalers' continuation of commercial relations with Bayer amounted to their acquiescence in its restrictive supply policy. In fact, their actual conduct was contrary to that policy—a concurrence of wills between Bayer and the wholesalers, designed to prevent or limit exports of Adalat, had not been established. The GC drew a distinction between cases in which a genuinely unilateral measure had been adopted (without express or implied participation of another) and those in which the unilateral character of the measure was merely apparent, receiving at least the tacit acquiescence of the dealers.[280] It also held that the Commission could not rely on case law precedents, in which a concurrence of wills had been found, to call into question the Court's conclusion that neither agreement nor acquiescence in Bayer's policy had been established. In distinguishing *AEG* and *Ford*, the GC stressed that the practices of the manufacturers in those cases, refusing to approve distributors who satisfied the qualitative criteria,

[272] Ibid., paras. 7–12.

[273] See e.g. H. Lidgard, 'Unilateral Refusal to Supply: An Agreement in Disguise?' [1997] *ECLR* 354.

[274] Case T-41/96, *Bayer AG v Commission* EU:T:2000:242, *aff'd* Cases C-2 and 3/01 P, EU:C:2004:2.

[275] Case T-208/01, *Volkswagen v Commission* EU:T:2003:326, *aff'd* Case C-74/04 P, EU:C:2006:460.

[276] See also Case T-368/00, *General Motors Nederland BV and Opel Nederland BV v Commission* EU:T:2003:275 (annulling a finding of the Commission that Opel and dealers in the Netherlands had agreed to a policy of preventing exports), *aff'd* Case C-551/03 P, *General Motors BV v Commission* EU:C:2006:229 and Case T-67/01, *JCB Service v Commission* EU:T:2004:3, *aff'd* Case C-167/04, *JCB Service v Commission* EU:C:2006:594 (annulling a finding of an agreement to fix retail prices and discounts).

[277] Case T-41/96, EU:T:2000:242, and Cases C-2 and 3/01 P, EU:C:2004:2.

[278] COMP/34.279 [1996] OJ L201/1. See also discussion of Cases C-501, 513, 515, and 519/06 P, *GlaxoSmithKline Services v Commission* EU:C:2009:610, Chap. 5, and Case C-468–478/06, *Sot. Lélos kai Sia EE v GlaxoSmithKline AEVE* EU:C:2008:504, Chap. 7.

[279] Case T-41/96, EU:T:2000:242, *aff'd* Cases C-2 and 3/01 P, EU:C:2004:2.

[280] Case T-41/96, ibid., paras. 66–71.

were not unilateral but part of the contractual relations between the manufacturers and resellers since *admission* to the selective distribution networks in those cases was based on the acceptance, tacit or express, by the contracting parties, of the policy pursued by the supplier.[281]

Case T-41/96, *Bayer AG v Commission* EU:T:2000:242

General Court

B. The concept of an agreement within the meaning of Article [101(1)]

66. The case-law shows that, where a decision on the part of a manufacturer constitutes unilateral conduct of the undertaking, that decision escapes the prohibition in Article [101(1)] (Case 107/82 *AEG v Commission*..., paragraph 38; Joined Cases 25/84 and 26/84 *Ford and Ford Europe v Commission*..., paragraph 21; Case T-43/92 *Dunlop Slazenger v Commission*..., paragraph 56).

67. It is also clear from the case-law that in order for there to be an agreement within the meaning of Article [101(1)] it is sufficient that the undertakings in question should have expressed their joint intention to conduct themselves on the market in a specific way (Case 41/69 *ACF Chemiefarma v Commission*..., paragraph 112; Joined Cases 209/78 to 215/78 and 218/78 *Van Landewyck and Others v Commission*..., paragraph 86; Case T-7/89 *Hercules Chemicals v Commission*..., paragraph 256).

68. As regards the form in which that common intention is expressed, it is sufficient for a stipulation to be the expression of the parties' intention to behave on the market in accordance with its terms (see, in particular, *ACF Chemiefarma*, paragraph 112, and *Van Landewyck*, paragraph 86), without its having to constitute a valid and binding contract under national law (*Sandoz*, paragraph 13).

69. It follows that the concept of an agreement within the meaning of Article [101(1)], as interpreted by the case-law, centres around the existence of a concurrence of wills between at least two parties, the form in which it is manifested being unimportant so long as it constitutes the faithful expression of the parties' intention.

70. In certain circumstances, measures adopted or imposed in an apparently unilateral manner by a manufacturer in the context of his continuing relations with his distributors have been regarded as constituting an agreement within the meaning of Article [101(1)] (Joined Cases 32/78, 36/78 to 82/78 *BMW Belgium and Others v Commission*..., paragraphs 28 to 30; *AEG*, paragraph 38; *Ford and Ford Europe*, paragraph 21;... *Metro II*..., paragraphs 72 and 73; *Sandoz*, paragraphs 7 to 12; Case C-70/93 *BMW v ALD*..., paragraphs 16 and 17).

71. That case-law shows that a distinction should be drawn between cases in which an undertaking has adopted a genuinely unilateral measure, and thus without the express or implied participation of another undertaking, and those in which the unilateral character of the measure is merely apparent. Whilst the former do not fall within Article [101(1)], the latter must be regarded as revealing an agreement between undertakings and may therefore fall within the scope of that article. That is the case, in particular, with practices and measures in restraint of competition which, though apparently adopted unilaterally by the manufacturer in the context of its contractual relations with its dealers, nevertheless receive at least the tacit acquiescence of those dealers.

72. It is also clear from that case-law that the Commission cannot hold that apparently unilateral conduct on the part of a manufacturer, adopted in the context of the contractual relations which he maintains with his dealers, in reality forms the basis of an agreement between undertakings within the

[281] See further Case 107/82, *AEG-Telefunken AG v Commission* EU:C:1983:293 (in a selective distribution system, admission to the network may be based on acceptance by the distributors of the policy pursued by the producers).

meaning of Article [101(1)] if it does not establish the existence of an acquiescence by the other partners, express or implied, in the attitude adopted by the manufacturer (*BMW Belgium*, paragraphs 28 to 30; *AEG*, paragraph 38; *Ford and Ford Europe*, paragraph 21; *Metro II*, paragraphs 72 and 73; *Sandoz*, paragraphs 7 to 12; *BMW v ALD*, paragraphs 16 and 17).

In addition, the GC held that the Commission had *not* shown that Bayer had sought to obtain agreement or acquiescence from its wholesalers to adhere to its policy or that the wholesalers had acquiesced, explicitly or implicitly, in the policy. Rather, the evidence demonstrated that they had sought to circumvent the policy.[282] It was not 'open to the Commission to achieve a result, such as the harmonization of prices in the medicinal products markets, by enlarging or straining the scope' of the Treaty rules.[283]

The GC's judgment was upheld by the CJ. The CJ started by stating that its judgment was confined to the question of whether there was an agreement within the meaning of Article 101. 'It should be made clear, therefore, that neither the possible application of other aspects of Article [101], nor Article [102] . . . , nor any other possible definitions of the relevant market are at issue in these proceedings.'[284] The CJ did not therefore deny that Article 102 proceedings might have been possible, if a position of dominance had been established.[285] Like the GC, the CJ stressed that the Commission could not assume that the expression of a unilateral policy by one of the parties established an agreement. It also distinguished cases such as *AEG* and *Ford* on the basis that admission to the network in those cases was based on adherence to the manufacturer's policy.

Cases C-2 and 3/01 P, *Bundesverband der Arzneimittel-Importeure EV and Commission v Bayer* AG EU:C:2004:2

Court of Justice

102. For an agreement within the meaning of Article [101(1)] to be capable of being regarded as having been concluded by tacit acceptance, it is necessary that the manifestation of the wish of one of the contracting parties to achieve an anti-competitive goal constitute an invitation to the other party, whether express or implied, to fulfil that goal jointly, and that applies all the more where, as in this case, such an agreement is not at first sight in the interests of the other party, namely the wholesalers.

103. Therefore, the [GC] was right to examine whether Bayer's conduct supported the conclusion that the latter had required of the wholesalers, as a condition of their future contractual relations, that they should comply with its new commercial policy.

. . .

141. . . . [I]t is important to note that this case raises the question of the existence of an agreement prohibited by Article [101(1)]. The mere concomitant existence of an agreement which is in itself neutral and a measure restricting competition that has been imposed unilaterally does not amount to an agreement prohibited by that provision. Thus, the mere fact that a measure adopted by a manufacturer, which has the object or effect of restricting competition, falls within the context of continuous business

[282] Case T-41/96, *Bayer AG v Commission* EU:T:2000:242, paras. 151–157.
[283] Ibid., para. 179. [284] Cases C-2 and 3/01 P, EU:C:2004:2, para. 42.
[285] See discussion of refusal to deal in Chap. 7.

relations between the manufacturer and its wholesalers is not sufficient for a finding that such an agreement exists.

142. The case of *Sandoz* concerned an export ban imposed by a manufacturer in the context of continuous business relations with wholesalers. The Court of Justice held that there was an agreement prohibited by Article [101(1)]. However, as the [GC] points out in paragraphs 161 and 162 of the judgment under appeal, that conclusion was based upon the existence of an export ban imposed by the manufacturer which had been tacitly accepted by the wholesalers. In that regard, at paragraph 11 of the *Sandoz* judgment, the Court of Justice held that [t]he repeated orders of the products and the successive payments without protest by the customer of the prices indicated on the invoices, bearing the words export prohibited, constituted a tacit acquiescence on the part of the latter in the clauses stipulated in the invoice and the type of commercial relations underlying the business relations between Sandoz PF and its clientele. The existence of a prohibited agreement in that case therefore rested not on the simple fact that the wholesalers continued to obtain supplies from a manufacturer which had shown its intention to prevent exports, but on the fact that an export ban had been imposed by the manufacturer and tacitly accepted by the wholesalers. Therefore, the appellants cannot usefully rely on the *Sandoz* judgment in support of their plea that the [GC] erred in law by requiring acquiescence of the wholesalers in the measures imposed by the manufacturer.

143. Nor can the appellants rely on *AEG, Ford* and *BMW Belgium*, arguing that business relations in the wholesale trade in pharmaceutical products are comparable to a selective distribution system such as that which was at issue in those cases. As has been stated in paragraph 141 of this judgment, the relevant question is that of the existence of an agreement within the meaning of Article [101(1)].

144. As has been stated in paragraph 106 of this judgment, in the *AEG* and *Ford* judgments the need to demonstrate the existence of an agreement within the meaning of Article [101(1)] was not at issue. The existence of an agreement capable of infringing that provision having already been established, the question raised was whether the measures adopted by the manufacturer formed part of that agreement and therefore had to be taken into account when examining the compatibility of that agreement with Article [101(1)]. In that regard, the [GC] rightly pointed out that, in those judgments, the Court of Justice had held that, at the time of a distributor's admission, its authorisation was based on its adherence to the policy pursued by the manufacturer . . .

145. A similar analysis must be drawn from the judgment in *BMW Belgium*, in which the question was whether Article [101(1)] of the [EC] Treaty must be interpreted as [prohibiting] a motor vehicle manufacturer which sells its vehicles through a selective distribution system from agreeing with its authorised dealers that they are not to supply vehicles to independent leasing companies where, without granting an option to purchase, those companies make them available to lessees residing or having their seat outside the contract territory of the authorised dealer in question, or from calling on such dealers to act in such a way (paragraph 14).

In *Volkswagen v Commission*,[286] the GC also annulled a Commission decision[287] in which the Commission had found that VW had set the selling price of the VW Passat in Germany in an agreement with its dealers;[288] unilateral calls by the manufacturer, intended to influence the dealers,[289] did not provide sufficient evidence of an agreement between them. 'In doing so, the Commission is seeking to impose a new legal approach which not only enlarges the meaning of agreement, but also

[286] Case T-208/01, EU:T:2003:326, *aff'd* Case C-74/04 P, EU:C:2006:460.

[287] COMP/36.693 [2001] OJ L262/14 (imposing a fine of €30.96 million on Volkswagen).

[288] Case T-208/01, EU:T:2003:326, paras. 30–35, *aff'd* Case C-74/04 P, EU:C:2006:460.

[289] The calls were intended to influence the dealer in the performance of the contract, Case T-208/01, ibid., paras. 30–57.

changes the rules on the burden of proof in its favour.'[290] The EU Courts rejected the Commission's argument that acquiescence in the supplier's policy could be inferred simply from the dealer being part of a selective distribution network and that signature of an agreement which complies with competition law implied tacit acceptance of *future* unlawful variations of the agreement.[291] Rather, acquiescence and the existence of an agreement had to be established.[292] A request by a manufacturer did not relieve the Commission of its obligation to prove that there was a concurrence of wills on the part of the parties to the dealership agreement (established either from the clauses of the dealership agreement or from the conduct of the parties, in particular from tacit acquiescence by the dealers in the manufacturer's request).[293]

The EU Courts in both *Bayer* and *Volkswagen* thus admonished the Commission for too easily finding an agreement where none existed. It is now apparent that simply continuing to participate in a selective distribution system or accepting supplies under the terms of a distribution agreement will be insufficient to establish liability. A dealer that signs up to a distribution agreement or selective distribution network in no way binds itself to accept future variations in the way the agreement is operated. Where, however, the dealer knows of the supplier's policy at the time it enters contractual relations, it may then be concluded that the contract was dependent upon the dealer accepting that policy.

In the absence of any direct documentary evidence of a written agreement incorporating the allegedly unilateral policy, the Commission (or other person trying to prove a violation) will have to adduce to the requisite legal standard proof sufficient to establish a concurrence of wills. In *Activision Blizzard Germany GmbH v Commission*,[294] the CJ expressly clarified that the standard of proof required for the purposes of establishing an anti-competitive agreement is the same whether in the framework of a vertical or a horizontal relationship.[295] Although an important difference is that in the framework of a vertical relationship between a manufacturer and a distribution a certain measure of contact between the parties is lawful, in each case it is still necessary to ask whether an agreement can be inferred from all the evidence having regard to all the relevant factors, and the economic and legal context specific to the case.[296] The cases demonstrate, nonetheless, that great care will need to be exercised by firms in this area and that this requirement does not provide a mechanism for parties to avoid the application of Article 101 by operating an agreement informally—if it can be established that an invitation to pursue the policy has been accepted, at least tacitly, or acquiesced in by the other party to the contract, the actions may be found to have spilled over into an agreement.

f. Hub and Spoke Arrangements

Anti-competitive agreements (or concerted practices) may have both horizontal and vertical elements. For example, collusion between retailers (the spokes) as to the price at which they will sell a particular product could be achieved, directly, or indirectly, through the intermediary of a supplier

[290] Ibid., para. 19. See also e.g. Case T-67/01, *JCB Service v Commission* EU:T:2004:3 (the GC annulled a Commission finding that a supplier's policy of drawing up lists of recommended retail prices amounted to RPM maintenance, see especially paras. 121–133. This finding was not challenged before the CJ, Case C-167/04, *JCB Service v Commission* EU:C:2006:594).

[291] The Commission's case amounted to a claim that a dealer who signed a dealership which complies with competition law is deemed to have accepted in advance a later unlawful variation of the contract.

[292] In contrast in COMP/35.733, *Volkswagen* [1998] OJ L124/60 (*aff'd* Case T-62/98, *Volkswagen AG v Commission* EU:T:2000:180, Case C-338/00 P, *Volkswagen AG v Commission* EU:C:2003:473), acquiescence in, or acceptance of, the policy had been established, see further Chap. 11.

[293] In this case, the Commission had not attempted to show that the dealers had tacitly acquiesced in the manufacturer's request but had argued that the concurrence was part of the dealership agreement.

[294] Case C-260/09 P, EU:C:2011:62. [295] Ibid., para. 71. [296] Ibid., para. 72.

(a hub). In such a case, it could be critical to determine both whether a vertical price-fixing agreement exists (between the supplier and the relevant retailers) and/or whether there is an agreement, or a concerted practice, between the supplier and retailers to fix the retail prices of the product. Where the violation also has a horizontal element, it may become a more serious infringement.[297] Hub and spoke arrangements are discussed further in the section on concerted practices below.[298]

g. *Recommendations by Bodies Constituted under Statutory Powers*

Several cases have raised the question of whether there is an 'agreement' where undertakings are represented on a body constituted under statutory powers to make recommendations in respect of a certain industry, etc. The CJ has held that there is not an agreement even when the trade representatives are in the majority on the committee, provided that the public authorities have not delegated their power of decision and that the matters to be fixed (e.g. tariffs) are fixed with due regard for public-interest criteria.[299]

(iv) Concerted Practices

a. *Description of a Concerted Practice*

It has been seen that Article 101(1) is aimed at explicit collusion, whether occurring through a formal agreement or more informal arrangements. The term 'concerted practice'[300] aims to forestall the possibility of undertakings evading the application of Article 101 by colluding in a manner falling short of an agreement. Classic descriptions of a concerted practice are set out by the CJ in *ICI v Commission (Dyestuffs)*[301] and *Suiker Unie*.[302] In *Dyestuffs*, it held that the purpose of the term was to preclude:

> co-ordination between undertakings which, without having reached the stage where an agreement, properly so called, has been concluded, knowingly substitutes practical co-operation between them for the risks of competition.[303]

In *Suiker Unie*, the Court held that the concept does not require 'the working out of an actual plan',[304] but precludes:

> any direct or indirect contact between such operators, the object or effect whereof is either to influence the conduct on the market of an actual or potential competitor or to disclose to such a competitor the course of conduct which they themselves have decided to adopt or contemplate adopting on the market.[305]

[297] See e.g. discussion of Case 1022/1/1/03, *JJB Sports plc v Office of Fair Trading* [2004] CAT 17, *aff'd* [2006] EWCA Civ 1318 at n. 335 and text. But see R. Amore, 'Three (or More) is a Magic Number: Hub & Spoke Collusion as a Way to Reduce Downstream Competition' (2016) 12(1) *European Competition Journal* 28.

[298] See Section 4.A.iv.d, especially nn. 334–338 and text.

[299] See e.g. Cases C-184 etc./13, *API-Anonima* EU:C:2014:2147 and Chap. 8. See also the discussion of association of undertakings in Section 4.A.viii.

[300] The concept is explored further in Chap. 9.

[301] Cases 48, 49, and 51–57/69, *ICI v Commission* EU:C:1972:70.

[302] Cases 40–48, 50, 54–56, 111, and 113–114/73, *Re the European Sugar Cartel; Coöperatieve Vereniging 'Suiker Unie' UA v Commission* EU:C:1975:174.

[303] Cases 48, 49, and 51–57/69, *ICI v Commission* EU:C:1972:70, paras. 64 and 65.

[304] Cases 40–48, 50, 54–56, 111, and 113–114/73, *Suiker Unie* EU:C:1975:174, para. 173.

[305] Ibid., para. 174.

It thus requires *reciprocal* cooperation between the parties, a 'meeting of the minds'[306] or a joint intention to conduct themselves in a specific way, disclosed through direct or indirect contact, designed to influence the conduct of an actual or potential competitor, to reveal to them the course of conduct that it will or may adopt on the market, or to remove strategic uncertainty about each other's future conduct on the market:

> [T]he criteria of coordination and cooperation necessary for determining the existence of concerted practice are understood in the light of the notion inherent in the Treaty provisions on competition, according to which an economic operator must determine independently the policy which he intends to adopt on the common market (judgment in *T-Mobile Netherlands and Others*, C-8/08 . . ., paragraph 32).[307]

However, it 'does not deprive economic operators of a right to adapt intelligently to the existing and anticipated conduct of their competitors'.[308]

b. The Need for Concertation, Conduct (Implementation), and a Relationship of Cause and Effect between the Two

One important difference between the concept of an agreement (a consensual act) and the concept of a concerted practice is that the latter term implies a requirement that the concertation should be practised, or implemented, on the market. In the appeals from the Commission's decision in *Polypropylene*,[309] the CJ accepted this difference and that both concertation and conduct, as well as a causal connection between the two, is required for a concerted practice to be established.[310] The CJ clarified, however, that undertakings taking part in the concerted action and remaining active on the market are presumed to take account of the information exchanged with competitors in determining their conduct on the market.[311] This is true whether the undertakings concert together on a regular basis over a long period, or whether the concerted practice stems from a single meeting.[312] It is, therefore, for the undertaking to establish that concertation had not been followed by conduct on the market.

The following are examples of the type of behaviour which might be used to establish that the parties involved have engaged in a 'concerted practice'.

[306] Case T-587/08, *Del Monte* EU:T:2013:129 ('the intervener's complaint that the contested decision does not mention a meeting of minds between it and Dole or the existence of a common course of conduct is irrelevant, since the conduct in question falls within the specific legal classification of a concerted practice and not of an anti-competitive agreement'), the appeal to the CJ on substantive grounds was dismissed, Cases C-293 and 294/13 P, EU:C:2015:416.

[307] Case C-286/13 P, *Dole Food and Dole Fresh Fruit Europe v Commission* EU:C:2015:184, para. 199.

[308] Case C-89/85, *Woodpulp* EU:C:1993:120, para. 71.

[309] COMP/31.149, *Polypropylene* [1986] OJ L230/1, appeals substantially dismissed by both the GC and the CJ: see e.g. Case C-51/92 P, *SA Hercules Chemicals NV v Commission* EU:C:1999:357, and Case C-199/92 P, *Hüls AG v Commission* EU:C:1999:358 (some parties argued that there would be no concerted *practice* if the parties only *plotted* to coordinate their behaviour but did not carry it out, see Opinion of AG Vesterdorf (appointed following the order of the CJ referring this and other cases to the GC soon after its establishment), see Case T-9/89, EU:T:1992:31).

[310] Case C-199/92 P, *Hüls AG* ibid., paras. 158–167. See also Case C-286/13 P, *Dole* EU:C:2015:184, paras. 125–126. But see Case C-74/14, *'Eturas' UAB v Lietuvos Respublikos konkurencijos taryba* EU:C:2016:42, n. 328 and text.

[311] Case C-199/92 P, *Hüls AG* ibid., para. 162 and Case C-49/92 P, *Commission v Anic Partecipazioni* EU:C:1999:356, para. 121 (the question whether or not the parties had engaged in a concerted practice is distinct from the question whether or not that concertation had restricted competition. But where the object of the concerted practice is to restrict competition, a restriction of competition is also assumed, see Chap. 5).

[312] Case C-8/08, *T-Mobile Netherlands BV v Raad van bestuur van de Nederlandse Mededingingsautoriteit* EU:C:2009:343.

c. Direct Contact—Frequent or Isolated Exchanges, or Disclosure, of Information

The cases establish that even if undertakings do not agree to fix prices or share markets, etc., the reciprocal exchange of strategic information may constitute a mechanism for concerting. A simple exchange of price information may, therefore, constitute a concerted practice where the behaviour of the undertakings eliminates 'the risks of competition and the hazards of competitors' spontaneous reactions . . .'[313] In *Suiker Unie*,[314] documents established that the parties had contacted each other and that they pursued the aim of removing in advance any uncertainty about the future conduct of their competitors. In *Belgian Brewers*,[315] the Commission took the view that, in respect of one of the cartels it found to be operating on the Belgian market—the private label cartel—it could not establish an agreement from available evidence, but that a concerted practice was proven. Meetings between the brewers had clearly served to influence the market behaviour of the competitors and to report on market behaviour to competitors.

> At the meetings not only was information exchanged but prices and customers were discussed. From statements . . . it is clear that the aim of the meetings was, firstly, to prevent a price war and adopt a position on prices and, secondly, to share out customers by not making (real) offers to the customers of other brewers.[316]

In *Polypropylene*,[317] although the Commission had concluded that an agreement existed between the undertakings, the GC[318] confirmed that the Commission had been correct to classify the meetings in the alternative as a concerted practice. The clear purpose of the competing undertakings participating in meetings, during which information was exchanged about, for example, prices and sales volumes, was to disclose to each other the course of conduct which each of the producers itself contemplated adopting on the market.[319] Participants clearly had the aim of eliminating any uncertainty about the future conduct of their competitors. They were bound to take into account the course of conduct upon which other participants had decided.

Further, in *T-Mobile Netherlands BV v Raad van bestuur van de Nederlandse Mededingingsautoriteit*,[320] the CJ confirmed that a concerted practice could result not only from meetings which occurred on a regular basis over a long period but from an isolated exchange of information. In this case, competing mobile telephone network operators had only met on a single occasion and discussed the reduction of certain standard dealer remunerations for post-paid subscriptions (packages whereby customers pay a fixed subscription charge and are invoiced subsequently for the number of minutes called). Article 101 precluded contact between firms which, however frequent and in whatever form, might influence the conduct on the market of competitors or disclose to them its decisions or

[313] Cases 48, 49, and 51–57/69, *ICI v Commission (Dyestuffs)* EU:C:1972:70, para. 119. But such conduct may be hard to distinguish from a unilateral decision, for example to send a price list to the press for publication or to make price announcements in advance, see discussion in Chap. 9.

[314] Cases 40–48, 50, 54–56, 111, and 113–114/73, *Suiker Unie* EU:C:1975:174.

[315] COMP/37.614 [2003] OJ L200/1. [316] Ibid., para. 254.

[317] COMP/31.149, *Polypropylene* [1986] OJ L230/1.

[318] The judgments of the CJ focused mainly on procedural arguments, but see e.g. Case C-199/92 P, *Hüls AG v Commission* EU:C:1999:358, para. 157.

[319] E.g. Case T-7/89, *SA Hercules Chemicals NV v Commission* EU:T:1991:75, para. 259, see Case C-199/92 P, *Hüls v Commission* EU:C:1999:358, para. 155; Case C-49/92 P, *Commission v Anic* EU:C:1999:356, para. 96; Case C-291/98 P, *Sarrió SA v Commission* EU:C:2000:631, para. 50.

[320] Case C-8/08, EU:C:2009:343.

intentions concerning its own conduct on the market.[321] The CJ also confirmed that the presumption that a concerted practice would influence the conduct of the undertakings participating in the practice where they remain active on that market was an integral part of EU law which had to be applied by a national court.[322]

Case C-8/08, *T-Mobile Netherlands BV v Raad van bestuur van de Nederlandse Mededingingsautoriteit* EU:C:2009:343

Court of Justice

59. Depending on the structure of the market, the possibility cannot be ruled out that a meeting on a single occasion between competitors . . . may, in principle, constitute a sufficient basis for the participating undertakings to concert their market conduct and thus successfully substitute practical cooperation between them for competition and the risks that that entails . . .

60. . . . [T]he number, frequency, and form of meetings between competitors needed to concert their market conduct depend on both the subject-matter of that concerted action and the particular market conditions. If the undertakings concerned establish a cartel with a complex system of concerted actions in relation to a multiplicity of aspects of their market conduct, regular meetings over a long period may be necessary. If, on the other hand . . . the objective of the exercise is only to concert action on a selective basis in relation to a one-off alteration in market conduct with reference simply to one parameter of competition, a single meeting between competitors may constitute a sufficient basis on which to implement the anti-competitive object which the participating undertakings aim to achieve.

61. In those circumstances, what matters is not so much the number of meetings held between the participating undertakings as whether the meeting or meetings which took place afforded them the opportunity to take account of the information exchanged with their competitors in order to determine their conduct on the market in question and knowingly substitute practical cooperation between them for the risks of competition. Where it can be established that such undertakings successfully concerted with one another and remained active on the market, they may justifiably be called upon to adduce evidence that that concerted action did not have any effect on their conduct on the market in question.

In *Bananas*,[323] the Commission also found that three banana importers—Chiquita, Dole, and Weichert, which had engaged in direct bilateral pre-pricing communications (prior to setting their weekly quotation prices)—had taken part in a concerted practice to coordinate quotation prices for bananas. They repeatedly communicated over a two-year period in relation to price-setting factors (factors relevant for setting of quotation prices) before quotation prices were set. As the communications were about future pricing policies, the participants could not have failed to take that information into account when determining the policy which they intended to pursue on the market. Further, the Commission held that the bilateral exchange of quotation prices after they had been set provided a monitoring mechanism for the pre-pricing communications. It thus considered that it had demonstrated cooperation (that the parties had knowingly adopted or adhered to collusive devices which facilitated the coordination of their commercial behaviour) and subsequent conduct on the market sufficient to establish the existence of a concerted practice: 'the exchange of information between

[321] Ibid., paras. 32–35. [322] Ibid., para. 52.

[323] COMP/39.188, 15 October 2008, *aff'd* Cases T-587/08, *Del Monte* EU:T:2013:129 and T-588/08 P, *Dole* EU:T:2013:130 and Cases C-293 and 294/13 P, *Del Monte* EU:C:2015:416 and Case C-286/13 P, *Dole* EU:C:2015:184. Weichert's appeal, Case T-2/09, *Internationale Fruchtimport Gesellschaft Weichert v Commission* EU:T:2009:478 was dismissed as it was lodged out of time, *aff'd* Case C-73/10 P, *Internationale Fruchtimport Gesellschaft Weichert GmbH & Co. KG v European Commission* EU:C:2010:684.

competitors is liable to be incompatible with the competition rules if it reduces or removes the degree of uncertainty as to the operation of the market in question, with the result that competition between undertakings is restricted . . .'[324]

The concept of a concerted practice may also encompass a disclosure of strategic information by one undertaking to a competitor (whether by, for example, mail, email, phone call, or orally at a meeting) where the recipient requests the information or accepts it.[325] As is the case, therefore, for those who participate in meetings where agreements are concluded, a recipient of strategic information is presumed to have accepted information tendered to it and to have altered its conduct accordingly, unless it publicly distances itself from and clearly states that it does not wish to receive it.[326]

For example, participation in a meeting . . . where one undertaking discloses its pricing plans to its competitors – without those competitors publicly distancing themselves – is likely to be caught by Article 101(1), even in the absence of an explicit agreement to raise prices . . .[327]

An issue which may also arise is when concerted practices may occur through communications online and, if so, what firms must do to distance themselves publicly from such communications (see further Chapter 9). In *'Eturas' UAB v Lietuvos Respublikos konkurencijos taryba*,[328] the CJ set out detailed guidance as to how the existence of a concerted practice can be proved in the context of an online travel system, and how an alleged conspirator can publicly distance itself from concertation instigated through an electronic communication. In this case, the question arose as to whether travel agents which participated in the online system engaged in a concerted practice when the administrator sent messages, via a personal electronic mailbox, to members relating to the capping of the level of online discounts that travel agents could grant. Some of travel agents alleged that as they had not opened and read the message, they could not be presumed to have been aware of the message and so could not have engaged in a concerted practice. The competition authority, in contrast, alleged that, in the absence of any opposition on the part of the agents, they could be presumed to have participated in the concerted practice.

On a reference to it from the Lithuanian Supreme Administrative Court, the CJ held, stressing the obligation of economic operators to determine their policy on the market independently, that although passive modes of participation in an infringement (such as presence at meetings at which anti-competitive agreements were concluded without that undertaking opposing them) were indicative of collusion, the question of whether a dispatch of a message constituted sufficient evidence to establish that its addressees were aware, or ought to have been aware, was a question which had to be determined in the national proceedings following an assessment of evidence.[329] Although the concerted practice could be established not only from direct evidence but also through indicia (provided that they were objective and consistent), the presumption of innocence precludes the referring court from inferring that the travel agencies concerned ought to have been aware of the content of that message simply from the mere dispatch of the message at issue in the main proceedings; it could be inferred, however, from the dispatch of the message together with other objective and consistent indicia, so

324 Case C-286/13 P, *Dole* EU:C:2015:184, para. 121.

325 See e.g. Cases T-25/95 etc., *Cimenteries CBR SA v Commission* EU:T:2000:77; Cases T-202/98 etc., *Tate & Lyle, Napier Brown and British Sugar* EU:T:2001:185, *aff'd* Case C-359/01 P, *British Sugar* EU:C:2004:255.

326 See n. 258 and text.

327 Horizontal Cooperation Guidelines, para. 397, relying on Cases T-202/98 etc., *Tate & Lyle* EU:T:2001:185, para, 54.

328 Case C-74/14, EU:C:2016:42.

329 Ibid., paras. 26–38.

long as the travel agencies had the ability to rebut it (for example, by proving that they did not receive that message, that they did not look at the section in question or did not look at it until some time had passed since that dispatch). A travel agency could also rebut a presumption that it had concerted by showing that it had publicly distanced itself from the concertation, reporting it to authorities or establishing that it had systematically not adhered to the cap.[330]

Case C-74/14, *'Eturas' UAB v Lietuvos Respublikos konkurencijos taryba* EU:C:2016:42

Court of Justice

43. Secondly, it must be pointed out that the case at issue in the main proceedings, as presented by the referring court, is characterised by the fact that the administrator of the information system at issue sent a message concerning a common anticompetitive action to the travel agencies participating in that system, a message which could only be consulted in the 'Notices' section of the information system in question and to which those agencies did not expressly respond. Following the dispatch of that message, a technical restriction was implemented which limited the discounts that could be applied to bookings made via that system to 3%. Although that restriction did not prevent the travel agencies concerned from granting discounts greater than 3% to their customers, it nevertheless required them to take additional technical steps in order to do so.

44. Those circumstances are capable of justifying a finding of a concertation between the travel agencies which were aware of the content of the message at issue in the main proceedings, which could be regarded as having tacitly assented to a common anticompetitive practice, provided that the two other elements constituting a concerted practice, noted in paragraph 42 above, are also present. Depending on the referring court's assessment of the evidence, a travel agency may be presumed to have participated in that concertation if it was aware of the content of that message.

45. However, if it cannot be established that a travel agency was aware of that message, its participation in a concertation cannot be inferred from the mere existence of a technical restriction implemented in the system at issue in the main proceedings, unless it is established on the basis of other objective and consistent indicia that it tacitly assented to an anticompetitive action.

46. In the third place, it must be pointed out that a travel agency may rebut the presumption that it participated in a concerted practice by proving that it publically [*sic*] distanced itself from that practice or reported it to the administrative authorities. In addition, according to the case-law of the Court, in a case such as that at issue in the main proceedings, which does not concern an anticompetitive meeting, public distancing or reporting to the administrative authorities are not the only means of rebutting the presumption that a company has participated in an infringement; other evidence may also be adduced with a view to rebutting that presumption (see, to that effect, judgment in Total Marketing Services v Commission . . ., paragraphs 23 and 24).

47. As regards the examination of whether the travel agencies concerned publicly distanced themselves from the concertation at issue in the main proceedings, it must be noted that, in particular circumstances such as those at issue in the main proceedings, it cannot be required that the declaration by a travel agency of its intention to distance itself be made to all of the competitors which were the addressees of the message at issue in the main proceedings, since that agency is not in fact in a position to know who those addressees are.

48. In that situation, the referring court may accept that a clear and express objection sent to the administrator of the E-TURAS system is capable of rebutting that presumption.

[330] Ibid., paras. 39–49. The latter statement, that the presumption of a causal connection between the concertation and the market conduct of the undertakings participating in the practice, could be rebutted by evidence of a systematic application of a discount exceeding the cap in question is not easy to reconcile with prior case law.

> 49. As regards the possibility of rebutting the presumption of participation in a concerted practice by means other than public distancing or reporting it to the administrative authorities, it must be held that, in circumstances such as those at issue in the main proceedings, the presumption of a causal connection between the concertation and the market conduct of the undertakings participating in the practice, referred to in paragraph 33 of the present judgment, could be rebutted by evidence of a systematic application of a discount exceeding the cap in question.

d. Indirect Contact/Sharing of Information and Hub and Spoke Arrangements

More difficult to categorise are situations where undertakings do not directly pass information to each other but disclose information which is nonetheless received by competitors, for example because the information was published publicly by an undertaking (perhaps on a website or to investors[331]), or because the information was received and published or transferred by an intermediary (such as a newspaper or trade journal, an independent consultant, a trade association, or a mutual customer or supplier). In such situations, it is necessary to assess carefully on the facts whether or not the undertakings have acted independently, adapting their conduct to that of their competitors, or whether they have engaged in indirect contact designed to influence the conduct of their competitors.

> While it is correct to say that this requirement of independence does not deprive economic operators of the right to adapt themselves intelligently to the existing or anticipated conduct of their competitors, it does, none the less, strictly preclude any direct or indirect contact between such operators by which an undertaking may influence the conduct on the market of its actual or potential competitors or disclose to them its decisions or intentions concerning its own conduct on the market where the object or effect of such contact is to create conditions of competition which do not correspond to the normal conditions of the market in question, regard being had to the nature of the products or services offered, the size and number of the undertakings involved and the volume of that market . . .[332]

In *Wood Pulp*,[333] for example, the CJ found that despite the undertakings announcing their price increases in advance and the information being rapidly transferred between both buyers and sellers by means of publication in the trade press, no collusion had been established.

Where exchanges of information between competitors (A and C) take place through the intermediary of a common customer or supplier (B) a concern is that B might act as a 'hub' collating and distributing competitively sensitive information relating to its retailers (A and C, the 'spokes'). Information exchanged in this way may be of a type which reduces the uncertainty over the pricing intentions or output of rival retailers; for example, it may reveal future pricing intentions. The question of exactly when a vertical information exchange (a frequent and often necessary practice in many supplier/customer relationships) may also support the existence of a concerted practice involving competitors at the upstream or downstream level is complex.[334] Although an agreement or concerted practice can be presumed where a competitor discloses strategic information directly to

[331] E.g. earnings calls with industry analysts are often monitored by competitors.

[332] Case C-8/08, *T-Mobile* EU:C:2009:343, para. 33.

[333] Cases C-89, 104, 114, 116–117, and 125–129/85, *Re Wood Pulp Cartel: Ahlström Osakeyhtiö v Commission (Wood Pulp II)* EU:C:1993:120, see further Chap. 9.

[334] See e.g. P. J. G. Van Cayseele, 'Hub-and-spoke Collusion: Some Nagging Questions Raised by Economists' (2014) 5 *JECLAP* 164, see further Chaps. 9 and 11. For proposals on improvements to the system in the US, see B. Klein, 'Inferring Agreement in Hub-and-Spoke Conspiracies' (2020) 83(1) *Antitrust LJ* 127.

another competitor and the latter accepts it (and does not publicly distance itself from it), such a presumption should, arguably, not be made simply because A passed strategic information (for example about its intended retail pricing) to B, who then passed the information to C, as there may have been valid business justification for A sharing this information with B.

Hub and spoke agreements have been examined and condemned in some Member States.[335] For example, the Belgian competition authority imposed fines on 18 companies (distributors and manufacturers) for hub and spoke arrangements in personal care and hygiene products and the Netherlands Authority for Consumers and Markets (the Dutch competition authority) fined four cigarette manufactures for exchanging information through wholesalers.[336] Further, the Court of Appeal (England & Wales) held in *JJB Sports plc v Office of Fair Trading*[337] that a concerted practice may be established where retailer A intended that the information be passed on by B and that retailer C knew that the information had been provided by A to B and used that information in setting its prices. Where a horizontal conspiracy is found, the intermediary may also be held to be part of the cartel, having facilitated it if it intended to contribute to it and was aware of actual conduct planned or if it could reasonably have foreseen it and was prepared to take the risk.[338]

The EU authorites have not yet had to rule expressly on the question of what is required to establish hub and spoke collusion between competitors via the intermediary of a supplier or distributor. However, in *e-books*[339] it accepted commitments before terminating proceedings investigating whether five principal publishers had engaged, with Apple in a concerted practice to raise the retail prices of electronic books. Further, in *VM Remonts v Konkurences padome; Konkurences padome v Pārtikas*,[340] the CJ, in a preliminary ruling, provided guidance on the question of whether a company, Pārtikas, could be held liable for collusion when a subcontractor (an independent service provider) it had engaged to prepare a bid for a public tender had, without its knowledge, used its price information to set the price for tenders made by two of its competitors. The CJ held that although employees' actions are automatically attributable to their employers, an undertaking which engaged an independent service provider is liable for its conduct only if:

- the provider is not genuinely independent and acts under the control of the undertaking—where its notional independence disguises an employment relationship or where control might be inferred from organisational, economic, and legal links between the undertaking and the service provider;[341] or
- the undertaking engaging the provider was aware of the anti-competitive objectives being pursued by its competitors and the provider, and intended to contribute to them; or where it could reasonably have foreseen the anti-competitive acts, and was prepared to accept that risk.

Consequently, it appears that a concerted practice could be attributed to an undertaking (or spoke) where, for example, it intended, through the intermediary of its service provider, to disclose

[335] For the argument that hub and spoke collusion can sometimes improve consumer welfare, see N. Sahuguet and A. Walckiers, 'A Theory of Hub-and-spoke Collusion' (2017) 53 *International J of Industrial Organization* 353.

[336] See Decisions of 22 June 2015, and 29 September 2020, respectively, see <www.acm.nl/en/publications/four-cigarette-manufacturers-fined-82-million-euros-distorting-competition>. And discussion of national cases in Van Cayseele, n. 334.

[337] [2006] EWCA Civ 1318.

[338] See n. 244 and accompanying text and Amore, n. 297.

[339] COMP/39.847 (the proceedings were terminated when, in December 2012 and July 2013, the companies offered a number of commitments, which addressed the Commission's concerns, see further Chap. 11).

[340] Case C-542/14, EU:C:2016:578. See also discussion of Case C-74/14, *'Eturas' UAB v Lietuvos Respublikos konkurencijos taryba* EU:C:2016:42, n. 328 and text.

[341] Ibid., para. 27. See also nn. 187 and 227 and text and I. Apostolakis, 'Antitrust Liability in Cases of Indirect Contacts Between Competitors: *VM Remonts*' (2017) 54 *CMLRev* 605, 615–619.

commercially sensitive information to its competitors, or when it expressly or tacitly consented to the provider sharing that commercially sensitive information with them but *not* when a service provider had, without informing the undertaking using its services, used the undertaking's commercially sensitive information to complete competitors' tenders:[342]

> The concerted practice at issue may also be attributed to the undertaking using those services if the latter could reasonably have foreseen that the service provider retained by it would share its commercial information with its competitors and if it was prepared to accept the risk which that entailed.[343]

This reasonable foreseeability test set out by the CJ, which also governs the liability of the other spoke(s) and the hub (facilitator), is less demanding than the standard imposed by the Court of Appeal in England & Wales.[344]

e. Parallel Behaviour, Price Signalling, and Online Exchanges

Market data may show that undertakings have acted in parallel (for example, that competing undertakings increased prices at the same moment, offered the same discounts and/or terms and conditions to customers, etc.). In the context of Article 101, a crucial question is whether such parallel behaviour results from independent or concerted action, as Article 101 does not prohibit 'mere parallel behaviour with no element of concertation'.[345] The question of whether parallel behaviour results from a concerted practice or furnishes proof of a concerted practice, and the CJ's important judgment in *Ahlström Osakeyhtiö v Commission (Wood Pulp)*[346] on this issue, is examined in Chapter 9. Chapter 9 also explores further the circumstances in which exchanges of information (direct or indirect, public or private) between undertakings may constitute an infringement of the rules.

f. Concerted Practice and Vertical Arrangements

A concerted practice may be operated horizontally between colluding competitors but also vertically between a manufacturer and its distributors. In *Pioneer*,[347] for example, the Commission found that Pioneer and its European exclusive distributors had engaged in concerted practices to prevent the parallel import of Pioneer products from the UK and Germany into France.

(v) Decisions by Associations of Undertakings

a. Medium for a Cartel

Trade and other associations perform a plethora of legitimate functions that promote the competitiveness of the industry as a whole. However, membership of an association, particularly a trade association, may also tempt the undertakings meeting within its auspices to collude together and to

[342] Ibid., para. 30. [343] Ibid., para. 31.

[344] See also Horizontal Cooperation Guidelines, 6.2.4.2. The Court of Appeal approach thus seems incompatible with EU law, see P. A. Perinetto, 'Hub-and-spoke Arrangements: Future Challenges within Article 101 TFEU Assessment' (2019) 15(2)–(3) *European Competition Journal* 281.

[345] COMP/31.149, *Polypropylene* [1986] OJ L230/1, para. 87.

[346] Case C-89/85, *Woodpulp* EU:C:1993:120.

[347] COMP/29.595 [1980] OJ L60/21, *aff'd* Cases 100–103/80, *SA Musique Diffusion française SA v Commission* EU:C:1983:158, especially paras. 75–76. See also Case 86/82, *Hasselblad (GB) Ltd v Commission* EU:C:1984:65, paras. 24–29 and Case T-43/92, *Dunlop Slazenger International Ltd v Commission* EU:T:1994:79 and, in the UK, Case 1022/1/1/03, *JJB Sports plc v Office of Fair Trading* [2004] CAT 17, paras. 150–163, 637–670, *aff'd* [2006] EWCA Civ 1318.

coordinate their action. Indeed, studies have shown that where there are a relatively large number of players on the market, coordination through a trade association or some other vehicle may be critical to successful collusion.

> Trade associations can play a particularly important role when [a] cartel involves a large number of firms. Hay and Delley (1974) found that trade associations were involved in more than 80 per cent of the cartels they studied that had more than 15 members, and in 100 per cent of cartels with more than 25 members. Levenstein and Suslow (2006) found that 29 per cent of the cartels in their sample involved trade associations. In 2003 the Commission found Treuhand AG, a Swiss consultancy, guilty of cartel behaviour because it facilitated a cartel even though it did not itself produce or sell the relevant product. The actual cartel was for organic peroxides and included Akzo Group, Atofina SA and Peroxid Chemic GmbH. The Commission found that AC-Treuhand had actively organised the cartel and provided support to it, such as organising meetings, providing and sharing information and storing contracts.[348]

In *Re Belgian Roofing Felt Cartel*,[349] an agreement was discovered between members of Belasco (Société Coopérative des Asphalteurs Belges) to adopt a common price list and minimum selling prices for roofing felt, to set quotas for sales on the Belgian market, and to advertise jointly their 'Belasco' products. The agreement was implemented by resolutions passed at the general meeting of Belasco. Belasco actively participated in the operations in a number of ways: in particular, it employed an accountant to monitor compliance with quotas (penalties were levied on members that had exceeded them). Further, it financed the joint advertising of the 'Belasco' trade mark which fostered users' impression of a homogeneous product.

It may be that in many situations the conduct adopted by the members of an association may be characterised as an agreement or a concerted practice. However, the prohibition of decisions may facilitate the proof and prohibition of collusive devices operated through associations. The concept has been interpreted broadly to catch conduct designed to coordinate the conduct of the members contrary to Article 101(1),[350] whether engaged in through resolutions, recommendations, the operation of certification schemes, or through the association's constitution itself.

b. *Trade Association Recommendations*

A recommendation by an association to its members will constitute a decision, even if it has no binding effect, if in reality it is intended to determine, or is likely to have the effect of determining, the members' conduct. In *IAZ*,[351] a recommendation made by an association of water-supply undertakings that its members should not connect 'unauthorised' appliances (without a conformity label supplied by another Belgian trade association) to the mains systems was held to be a binding decision capable of restricting competition within the meaning of Article 101(1). The practice discriminated against non-Belgian producers of the appliances. Similarly, in *FENEX*,[352] the Commission held that the recommendation of tariffs by a Dutch association to its member forwarding companies constituted a decision by an association of undertakings within the meaning of Article 101(1). Although the tariffs merely took the form of recommendations, the procedure for drawing up and circulating the tariffs was a habitual activity of the association and was accompanied by circulars drafted in more

[348] S. Bishop and M. Walker, *The Economics of EC Competition Law: Concepts, Application and Measurement* (3rd edn, Sweet & Maxwell, 2010), para. 5.016, see also n. 244 and text and Chap. 9.

[349] Case 246/86, *Re Roofing Felt Cartel: S.C. Belasco v Commission* EU:C:1989:301.

[350] Cases 96–102, 104, 105, 108, and 110//82, *NV IAZ International Belgium v Commission* EU:C:1983:310, para. 20.

[351] COMP/29.995, *Anseau* [1982] OJ L167/39, on appeal Case 96/82, ibid.

[352] COMP/34.983, [1996] OJ L181/28.

mandatory terms. The Commission concluded that the circulation of the tariffs had to be interpreted as a faithful reflection of the association's resolve to coordinate the conduct of its members on the relevant market.

c. *Medium for Exchange of Information*

More subtly, the association may simply collect and disseminate sensitive information and facilitate its exchange between competitors. Were the association to be used, for example, as a vehicle for exchanging information on the prices that the members intended to charge for their products, etc., the parties are likely to be found to be operating a concerted practice.[353]

d. *Certification Schemes*

Certification schemes operated by members of an association may, in reality, be designed to exclude non-members from business opportunities, or to preclude foreign undertakings from penetrating the domestic market of the association's members.[354] The word 'decision', in addition to catching acts of the association which are binding on its members, may also catch these types of more informal methods of coordinating members' actions. In *Stichting Certificatie Kraanverhuurbedrijf and the Federatie van Nederlandse Kraanbedrijven v Commission*,[355] the Commission fined both FNK and SCK after an examination of agreements that they had notified.[356] Not only were the rules of FNK providing for the charging of 'reasonable' rates by its members caught by Article 101(1), but SCK's rules on the certification of the crane-hire trade were also caught. The prohibition on the certificate holders from hiring cranes from non-affiliated firms without valid certification plates (and not affiliated to SCK) restricted competition between affiliated firms and substantially restricted access to the market by other firms.

e. *The Trade Association's Constitution*

The constitution and rules of a trade association may themselves qualify as a decision (and an agreement) within Article 101(1).[357]

(vi) Complex Arrangements and Single Infringements

a. *The Concept of a Single Infringement and its Implications*

A cartel operated through an agreement or concerted practice can consist of a whole complex set of arrangements affecting a number of products and be spread out over a number of different countries and over a lengthy period of time. Where a cartel operates, for example, on a global basis, it may also involve a number of sub-agreements affecting different products/services operated in different

[353] See Cases 40–48, 50, 54–56, 111, and 113–114/73, *Suiker Unie* EU:C:1975:174. See also COMP/31.370 and COMP/31.446, *UK Agricultural Tractor Exchange* [1992] OJ L68/19, upheld on appeal, Case T-34/92, *Fiatagri and Ford New Holland v Commission* EU:T:1994:258 and Case T-35/92, *John Deere Ltd v Commission* EU:T:1994:259, on appeal to the CJ Case C-7/95 P, *John Deere Ltd v Commission* EU:C:1998:256, see Chap. 9.

[354] As in *Anseau*, n. 351. See also Case 8/72, *Vereeniging van Cementhandelaren v Commission* EU:C:1972:84.

[355] COMP/34.179, *Stichting Certificatie Kraanverhuurbedrijf and Federatie van Nederlandse Kraanbedrijven* [1995] OJ L312/79; on appeal Cases T-213/95 and 18/96, *Stichting Certificatie Kraanverhuurbedrijf and Federatie van Nederlandse Kraanbedrijven v Commission* EU:T:1997:157.

[356] After a preliminary examination of the agreements ([1994] OJ L117/30), the Commission suspended the parties' immunity from fines that arose on the notification of an agreement to the Commission (Reg. 17 [1959–1962] OJ Spec. Ed. 87, Art. 15(6)).

[357] COMP/27.958, *National Sulphuric Acid* [1980] OJ L260/24.

countries, some firms may leave and others may join during its tenure, and some firms may play full and others more subsidiary roles (some may participate in only parts of the arrangements). In such, cases it is necessary to determine the scope of the cartel (in terms of product and geographical reach), the time period over which it operated and its members—for example, whether the arrangements are sufficiently linked that it can be said that there is one single and continuous cartel or whether there are a number of smaller cartels.

The concept of a single continuing infringement (SCI) is '[d]esigned to capture the dynamic of one and the same cartel under Article [101]'[358] operated over a period of time (as opposed to multiple separate cartel agreements). The Commission summarised the nature of the concept in the *Shrimp*[359] case:

> 378. . . . The notion of a single infringement covers precisely a situation in which several undertakings participated in an infringement in which continuous conduct in pursuit of a single economic aim was intended to distort competition and where individual infringements were linked to one another by the same object (elements as a whole sharing the same aim) and the same subjects (same undertakings who are aware that they are participating towards the same object). The existence of synergies and the complementarity between the different lines of conduct are objective indicia of the existence of such an overall plan.

In such circumstances, 'it would be artificial to split up such continuous conduct, characterised by a single purpose, by treating it as consisting of several separate infringements, when what was involved was a single infringement which progressively would manifest itself in both agreements and concerted practices'.[360]

Where a single and continuous cartel infringement can be established, meaningful consequences follow. For example, responsibility for the infringement may be attributed to those undertakings that participate in the whole infringement and to an undertaking who participated directly only in one or some of the constituent elements of that cartel if it intended to contribute to it and was either aware of the conduct of the other participants or it could reasonably have foreseen it and it was prepared to take the risk[361] (responsibility is, however, limited to the period of the undertaking's participation in the infringements[362]). Although the Commission may take account of the extent of an undertaking's participation in setting the level of the fine, the finding relating to the scope of the infringement is binding on national courts, meaning that an undertaking which has participated only in constituent parts may be jointly and severally liable for the harm resulting from the infringement as a whole.[363]

[358] J. Joshua, 'Single Continuous Infringement of Article 81 EC: Has the Commission Stretched the Concept Beyond the Limit of its Logic?' (2009) 5 *European Competition Journal* 451, 451. See also D. Bailey, 'Single, Overall Agreement in EU Competition Law' (2010) 47 *CMLRev* 473.

[359] COMP/39.633, *Shrimps* 27 November 2013.

[360] COMP/39.579, *Consumer Detergents* 13 April 2011 [2011] OJ C193/14, paras. 36–37.

[361] See Case C-614/13 P, *Masco Corp v Commission* EU:C:2017:63, para. 23; 39.633, *Shrimps*, 27 November 2013, para. 380, citing Cases T-147/89 etc., *Buchmann v Commission* EU:T:1995:67; Case T-9/99 *HFB and Others v Commission* EU:T:2002:70, para. 231; Cases T-101/05 etc., *BASF and UCB v Commission* EU:T:2007:380, para. 160. But see Case T-68/09, *Soliver NV v Commission* EU:T:2014:867 (where the GC found that the Commission had failed to establish that Soliver, a fringe player, should be held responsible for the wider cartel agreement participated in by the three larger car glass producers. The Commission had not established that Soliver was aware, or should have been aware, of the cartel as a whole and that the contacts it had with its competitors were implementations of a wider cartel).

[362] Case C-614/13 P, *Masco Corp* ibid., para. 23.

[363] See further Chap. 14 and M. J. Frese, 'Civil Liability for Single and Continuous Infringements' (2018) 41(2) *World Competition* 179 (arguing that evidentiary rules—including the SCI doctrine—combine to make civil litigation too claimant-friendly—making limiting principles on the doctrine crucial).

Further, a finding that old conduct forms part of an agreement which has endured over a long period may also avoid the applicability of the five-year limitation period.[364] The fact that there is just one infringement, however, means that only a single fine is imposed. Harding and Joshua note the significance of the concept.

C. Harding and J. Joshua, *Regulating Cartels in Europe* (2nd edn, Oxford University Press, 2010), 175–177

Aggregation into a single infringement may well increase the size of the market and extent of trade affected, increase the number of participants, and perhaps extend the duration, all of which would add to the gravity of the infringement and justify higher fines. For the participants, there may be exposure to additional legal risks, notably prosecution in other jurisdictions, the transfer of the liability of core players to minor actors, and increased exposure to consequent civil liability claims. Time bars may be removed in relation to earlier activities, now joined to more recent cartel operations. The only possible consolation for cartel participants would be the capping of penalties in terms of the maximum which might be imposed for a single infringement . . .

On the other hand, the consequences of disaggregation or decortications into multiple separate cartels are various. On the whole it is likely to increase prosecution effort and costs, it may multiply the involvement of different enforcement agencies, and complicate the legal process, especially the management of leniency applications . . . There is likely to be a larger number of smaller fines, which may or may not in aggregate match the larger single fine resulting from the single infringement. On the other hand, there may be a prosecutorial advantage in disaggregation, if this allows large corporate structures to be broken down, so that different companies within the same group may be dealt with in relation to separate cartels according to their different involvement in the same market.

Such considerations confirm the significance of the criteria for cartel definition and deciding whether there may be a single or multiple cartels.

b. A Single Infringement—Elements

The concept of a single and continuing infringement was first used in *Polypropylene*,[365] a case concerning a long-lasting cartel in the petrochemical industry. Fifteen firms were held by the Commission to have infringed the competition rules by participating in a framework agreement to fix prices and sales volumes. The Commission considered that the cartel, which was based on an overall framework agreement or a common and detailed plan manifested in a series of more detailed sub-agreements worked out from time to time, constituted a single continuing agreement for the purpose of Article 101(1). Some firms claimed they were not liable, as they had not participated in all aspects of the arrangements. The GC held that the Commission was justified in treating the entire course of the collusion as one single agreement. For there to be an 'agreement' for the purposes of Article 101(1) it was sufficient for the undertakings to have 'expressed their joint intention to conduct themselves on the

[364] See further Chap. 13. But see Cases T-101/05 etc., *BASF and UCB v Commission* EU:T:2007:380 where the Commission's finding of SCI was not upheld (and the decision found to be time-barred). See also e.g. Case T-655/11, *FSL Holdings v Commission* EU:T:2015:383 and Case T-104/13, *Toshiba v Commission* EU:T:2015:610. Occasionally, fines may be maximised by finding not a single cartel but a series of cartels over a number of different markets, see n. 377 and text and Chap. 13.

[365] COMP/31.149, *Polypropylene* [1986] OJ L230/1; on appeal Cases T-1, 2, 3, 6, and 7/89, *SA Hercules Chemicals NV v Commission* EU:T:1991:75, appeals broadly dismissed: see e.g. Case C-49/92 P, *Commission v Anic Partecipazioni* EU:C:1999:356.

market in a specific way'.[366] In this case, the undertakings had, throughout the whole course of the arrangements, pursued the single economic aim of distorting the polypropylene market.

The CJ in *Anic* stressed the core of the concept: an agreement or concerted practice sharing the same anti-competitive object or effect and pursuing a single purpose (a common objective). Further, it clarified that an undertaking may be responsible for the infringement where it intended to contribute to the common objective and was either aware of the conduct of the other participants or it could reasonably have foreseen it and it was prepared to take the risk.[367]

Case C-49/92 P, *Commission v Anic Partecipazioni* EU:C:1999:356

Court of Justice

77. The Commission states that characterisation as a single infringement involves no legal concept but consists of a characterisation of the facts, which presupposes the finding of a link between various lines of concerted conduct having a single objective in a specific economic situation. It cannot be excluded in the abstract that certain facts may be characterised as a single infringement. The Commission and [General Court] could therefore have committed at most an error in characterising the facts, but certainly not an error of law. This kind of characterisation does not run counter to the principle of the personal nature of criminal responsibility, assuming that this could be applicable by analogy in this case.

78. On this question the Court must observe, first of all, that, given the nature of the infringements in question and the nature and degree of severity of the ensuing penalties, responsibility for committing those infringements is personal in nature.

79. Secondly, the agreements and concerted practices referred to in Article [101(1)] necessarily result from collaboration by several undertakings, who are all co-perpetrators of the infringement but whose participation can take different forms according, in particular, to the characteristics of the market concerned and the position of each undertaking on that market, the aims pursued and the means of implementation chosen or envisaged.

80. However, the mere fact that each undertaking takes part in the infringement in ways particular to it does not suffice to exclude its responsibility for the entire infringement, including conduct put into effect by other participating undertakings but sharing the same anti-competitive object or effect.

81. Thirdly, it must be remembered that [Article 101] prohibits agreements between undertakings and decisions by associations of undertakings, including conduct which constitutes the implementation of those agreements or decisions, and concerted practices when they may affect intra-Community trade and have an anti-competitive object or effect. It follows that infringement of that article may result not only from an isolated act but also from a series of acts or from continuous conduct. That interpretation cannot be challenged on the ground that one or several elements of that series of acts or continuous conduct could also constitute in themselves an infringement of [Article 101].

82. In the present case the [GC] held, at paragraph 204 of the judgment, that, because of their identical object, the agreements and concerted practices found to exist, formed part of systems of regular meetings, target-price fixing and quota-fixing, and that those schemes were part of a series of efforts made by the undertakings in question in pursuit of a single economic aim, namely to distort the normal movement of prices. It considered that it would be artificial to split up such continuous conduct,

[366] See especially Case T-1/89, *Rhône-Poulenc v Commission* EU:T:1991:56, para. 120, relying on Case 41/69, *ACF Chemiefarma NV v Commission* EU:C:1970:71, para. 112.

[367] The awareness condition guards against overly expansive SCI findings. An undertaking must be aware of the general scope and characteristics of the cartel; specific awareness is required and awareness of rumours is insufficient, see e.g. Frese, n. 363, 190, Case T-59/06, *Low & Bonar v Commission* EU:T:2011:669.

characterised by a single purpose, by treating it as consisting of several separate infringements, when what was involved was a single infringement which progressively manifested itself in both agreements and concerted practices.

83. In such circumstances, the [GC] was entitled to consider that an undertaking that had taken part in such an infringement through conduct of its own which formed an agreement or concerted practice having an anti-competitive object for the purposes of [Article 101(1)] and which was intended to help bring about the infringement as a whole was also responsible, throughout the entire period of its participation in that infringement, for conduct put into effect by other undertakings in the context of the same infringement. That is the case where it is established that the undertaking in question was aware of the offending conduct of the other participants or that it could reasonably have foreseen it and that it was prepared to take the risk.

84. Contrary to Anic's submission, such a conclusion is not contrary to the principle that responsibility for such infringements is personal in nature. It fits in with widespread conception in the legal orders of the Member State concerning the attribution of responsibility for infringements committed by several perpetrators according to their participation in the infringement as a whole, which is not regarded in those legal systems as contrary to the personal nature of responsibility.

85. Nor does such an interpretation neglect individual analysis of the evidence adduced against an undertaking, in disregard of the applicable rules of evidence, or infringe the rights of defence of the undertakings involved.

86. Where there is a dispute as to the existence of an infringement of the competition rules, it is incumbent on the Commission to prove the infringements which it has found and to adduce evidence capable of demonstrating to the requisite legal standard the existence of circumstances constituting an infringement (Case C-185/95 P *Baustahlgewebe* v *Commission* . . ., paragraph 58). In doing this, the Commission must establish in particular all the facts enabling the conclusion to be drawn that an undertaking participated in such an infringement and that it was responsible for the various aspects of it.

87. When, as in the present case, the infringement involves anti-competitive agreements and concerted practices, the Commission must, in particular, show that the undertaking intended to contribute by its own conduct to the common objectives pursued by all the participants and that it was aware of the actual conduct planned or put into effect by other undertakings in pursuit of the same objectives or that it could reasonably have foreseen it and that it was prepared to take the risk.

88. The [GC] found, at paragraph 204, cited above, that all the efforts of the participating undertakings were in pursuit of a common anti-competitive aim. It is clear from all the findings of fact made by the [GC], at paragraphs 63 to 178 of the contested judgment, with regard to the various aspects of the infringement, that it reached the finding that Anic had participated in each of those aspects only on the basis of Anic's own conduct, the contribution it thus intended to make towards those aspects and of its knowledge of the conduct planned or put into effect by other undertakings gained through its participation in the regular meetings of polypropylene producers. In those circumstances, the [GC] was entitled to consider that Anic's participation, through its own conduct, in the infringement rendered it co-responsible for the entire infringement committed during its participation.

89. Secondly, the undertakings concerned are able to exercise their rights of defence both in regard to the charge that they actually participated in the infringement and in regard to the actual conduct of which other undertakings are accused but which relates to the same infringement. In the case of agreements or concerted practices having anti-competitive object, they will also be able to exercise those rights in respect of the existence of a common objective, their intention to contribute to the infringement as a whole by their own conduct and their knowledge of the conduct of other participants or its foreseeability and the acceptance of the related risk.

90. The fact that an undertaking has not taken part in all aspects of an anti-competitive scheme or that it played only a minor role in the aspects in which it did participate must be taken into consideration when the gravity of the infringement is assessed and if and when it comes to determining the fine.

Since then, the Commission has frequently relied on the concept which has facilitated the application of Article 101 to cartels 'which are "not born fully grown" but develop organically as the members conceive ever more sophisticated ways to achieve their objectives while reducing the risk of detection'.[368] In *Aalborg Portland*,[369] the CJ confirmed that an undertaking can participate in the implementation of a single agreement passively, including by tacitly approving the unlawful initiative (for example, by participating in meetings and not publicly distancing itself from the scheme), if it was aware of the conduct planned or could reasonably have foreseen it and was prepared to take the risk.

c. *A Single Infringement or Separate Infringements?*

To establish a single infringement the Commission, or other claimant, must demonstrate that the conduct at issue is linked by a shared common objective. This requires a careful analysis of all the evidence establishing, or casting doubt, on such a link (for example, whether geographically disparate collusion pursues a common objective of controlling the market[370]).

C. Harding and J. Joshua, *Regulating Cartels in Europe* (2nd edn, Oxford University Press, 2010), 175–177

In . . . reviewing the activities of alleged cartel participants, the [GC] has used a vocabulary of 'complementary' action as descriptive of single infringement and cartel: the acts must be 'closely linked', an 'integrated set of arrangements', 'interwoven and uninterrupted', or be bound together by a 'sufficient definite and decisive causal link'. Evidence of such complementarity would include, in the Court's view, the period of application, the objective, and the content, including the methods used. More specifically, the Commission in its decisions on cartels has identified a number of 'objective elements' as indicia of a single infringement: common objective; similarity of products or services; similarity of behaviour in different geographical areas, commonality of membership, modus operandi, personnel, and the nature of meetings. But the factual complexities of and variations as between actual cases may render the organization of such criteria for purposes of overall assessment a difficult matter. As Joshua has commented:

> . . . rarely does the Commission explain how the components are interlinked or what degree of knowledge is required. No doubt the Commission often reaches the 'right' solution intuitively. The danger is that if the exercise becomes a mere recitation, it fuels accusation that the result is 'political'. It also does not help that, to the extent the Commission has developed and articulated any principled test, its application on the ground is not entirely consistent . . . if the distinction between a single and many conspiracies is clear enough conceptually, its empirical application is beset with difficulty.

Part of the problem is the organizational complexity of some cartels, which may have core and minor memberships, national or regional subsets, and an overarching or 'global' coordination, all of which may be matters of evidential difficulty. Some cartels may resemble 'hub and spoke' conspiracies, with which there may be little awareness on the spoke of the main or core conspiracy at the hub. It may be necessary for regulators and courts to master a complex factual scenario in order to define the limits of a cartel and thus the extent of liability.

It may be argued that a convincing and reliable test may be based on elements of interdependence and knowledge. 'Interdependence' describes well the idea of a chain of activities which all contribute in a necessary and decisive way to the goals of the cartel organization—the resulting network of activity of linked but crucial actions defines the infrastructure and scope of the cartel. But it is also necessary for

368 Joshua, n. 358, 459.

369 Cases C-204, 205, 211, 213, 217, and 219/00 P, *Aalborg Portland A/S v Commission (Cement)* EU:C:2004:6.

370 See e.g. Case T-21/99, *Dansk Rørindustri v Commission* EU:T:2002:74, *aff'd* Case C-189/02 P, EU:C:2005:408.

this interdependent activity to be performed with knowledge of its purpose and significance, an awareness which characterizes the action and also supplies a justifiable mental element as a basis for liability. Thus in the *Treuhand* case, the consultancy firm was aware that its servicing of the cartel's activities was a necessary part of the success of those activities. On the other hand, in the *Choline Chloride Cartel* . . . [t]he earlier involvement of the American and Canadian companies was not necessary or decisive for the later operation of the cartel in Europe. A *knowing interdependence* may therefore be put forward as a test of cartel scope and perpetrator liability, separating 'core' involvement from acts of ancillary, unknowing, and uninformed support for minor actors who are thus outside the cartel and not liable in a significant way for the cartel's activity.

Cartel identification and definition is thus an issue of some complexity, but one that must be mastered, since the existence and identify of the cartel must first be proven for the offence or infringement to be properly prosecuted. A crucial problem would seem to be that of sorting the peripheral accessory players and their activities from the essential participation.

In *Bananas*,[371] the GC and CJ affirmed a Commission decision finding that three competitors were party to a single and continuous infringement which had as its object the restriction of competition. Bilateral communications took place between Dole and Chiquita and Dole and Weichert, and Chiquita knew, or at least foresaw, that Dole communicated with Weichert.

Cases C-293 and 294/13 P, *Fresh Del Monte Produce Inc v Commission* EU:C:2015:416

Court of Justice

156. According to settled case-law, an infringement of Article [101(1)] can result not only from an isolated act, but also from a series of acts or from continuous conduct, even if one or more aspects of that series of acts or continuous conduct could also, in themselves and taken in isolation, constitute an infringement of that provision. Accordingly, if the different actions form part of an 'overall plan' because their identical object distorts competition within the common market, the Commission is entitled to impute responsibility for those actions on the basis of participation in the infringement considered as a whole (judgment in *Commission v Verhuizingen Coppens* . . . , paragraph 41 . . .).

157. An undertaking which has participated in such a single and complex infringement, by its own conduct, which meets the definition of an agreement or concerted practice having an anti-competitive object within the meaning of Article [101(1)] and was intended to help bring about the infringement as a whole, may also be responsible for the conduct of other undertakings in the context of the same infringement throughout the period of its participation in the infringement. That is the position where it is shown that the undertaking intended, through its own conduct, to contribute to the common objectives pursued by all the participants and that it was aware of the offending conduct planned or put into effect by other undertakings in pursuit of the same objectives or that it could reasonably have foreseen it and was prepared to take the risk (judgment in *Commission v Verhuizingen Coppens* . . . , paragraph 42 . . .).

158. An undertaking may thus have participated directly in all the forms of anti-competitive conduct comprising the single and continuous infringement, in which case the Commission is entitled to attribute liability to it in relation to that conduct as a whole and, therefore, in relation to the infringement

[371] COMP/39.188, 15 October 2008, *aff'd* Cases T-587/08, *Fresh Del Monte Produce v Commission* EU:T:2013:129 and T-588/08 P, *Dole Food and Dole Germany v Commission* EU:T:2013:130 and Cases C-293 and 294/13 P, *Fresh Del Monte v Commission* EU:C:2015:416 and Case C-286/13 P, *Dole Food Company Inc v Commission* EU:C:2015:184. Contrast Case T-655/11, *FSL Holdings v Commission* EU:T:2015:383.

as a whole. Equally, the undertaking may have participated directly in only some of the forms of anti-competitive conduct comprising the single and continuous infringement, but have been aware of all the other unlawful conduct planned or put into effect by the other participants in the cartel in pursuit of the same objectives, or could reasonably have foreseen that conduct and have been prepared to take the risk. In such cases, the Commission is also entitled to attribute liability to that undertaking in relation to all the forms of anti-competitive conduct comprising such an infringement and, accordingly, in relation to the infringement as a whole (judgment in *Commission v Verhuizingen Coppens* . . ., paragraph 43).

159. On the other hand, if an undertaking has directly taken part in one or more of the forms of anti-competitive conduct comprising a single and continuous infringement, but it has not been shown that that undertaking intended, through its own conduct, to contribute to all the common objectives pursued by the other participants in the cartel and that it was aware of all the other offending conduct planned or put into effect by those other participants in pursuit of the same objectives, or that it could reasonably have foreseen all that conduct and was prepared to take the risk, the Commission is entitled to attribute to that undertaking liability only for the conduct in which it had participated directly and for the conduct planned or put into effect by the other participants, in pursuit of the same objectives as those pursued by the undertaking itself, where it has been shown that the undertaking was aware of that conduct or was able reasonably to foresee it and prepared to take the risk (judgment in *Commission v Verhuizingen Coppens* . . ., paragraph 44).

Similarly, in the *Smart Card Chip* cartel[372] the Commission found a single and continuous infringement carried out through bilateral exchanges of sensitive information between competitors, concluding that there were objective grounds to assume the single anti-competitive aim of the participants in the collusive contacts and their common pattern of behaviour.[373]

In *Trelleborg Industrie v Commission*,[374] an appeal from the Commission's *Marine Hoses* decision, the GC explained that, as in cases of serious infringements of the competition rules the existence of an infringement frequently had to be pieced together from fragmentary evidence (see further Chapter 9), coincidences and indicia might be relied on to provide information not only about the mere existence of anti-competitive practices or agreements but also about their duration or the period of application. Thus, the Commission might be entitled to support a finding of a single infringement by relying on evidence that actions formed part of an overall plan—for example, establishing the identical nature of the objectives of the practices at issue, the identical nature of the undertakings which participated in the infringement, the identical nature of the detailed rules for its implementation, the fact that the natural persons involved on behalf of the undertakings and/or the geographical scope of the practices are identical—even if evidence of the infringement has not been produced in relation to all specific periods.[375]

[372] AT39574, 3 September 2014.

[373] Case T-758/14, *Infineon Technologies AG v Commission* EU:T:2016:737, para. 29 (relying on: the fact that the collusive practices in question had the same economic aim; the common characteristics of the contacts, the identity of the people participating in the contacts, the timing of the contacts or their proximity in time, confirming that those collusive contacts were linked and complementary in nature and contributed to the realisation of the set of anti-competitive effects).

[374] Cases T-147 and 148/09, EU:T:2013:259.

[375] Ibid., paras. 50–71.

Cases T-147 and 148/09 *Trelleborg Industrie v Commission* EU:T:2013:259

General Court

– The existence of a continuous infringement

57. It should be borne in mind that, in most cases, the existence of an anti-competitive practice or agreement must be inferred from a number of coincidences and indicia which, taken together, may, in the absence of another plausible explanation, constitute evidence of an infringement of the competition rules. Such coincidences and indicia, when evaluated overall, may provide information not just about the mere existence of anti-competitive practices or agreements, but also about the duration of continuous anti-competitive practices or the period of application of anti-competitive agreements (see, to that effect, *Aalborg Portland and Others v Commission*, paragraph 52 above, paragraph 57, and Case C-105/04 P *Nederlandse Federatieve Vereniging voor de Groothandel op Elektrotechnisch Gebied* v *Commission* . . ., paragraphs 94 to 96 . . .).

58. Furthermore, such an infringement may be the consequence not only of an isolated act but also of a series of acts or indeed of continuous conduct. That interpretation cannot be challenged on the ground that one or more elements of that series of acts or of that continuous conduct might also constitute in themselves, and taken in isolation, an infringement of the competition rules. Where the various actions form part of an 'overall plan', owing to their identical object, which distorts competition within the common market, the Commission is entitled to impute liability for those actions according to participation in the infringement considered as a whole (see *Aalborg Portland and Others v Commission*, . . . paragraph 258 and *Nederlandse Federatieve Vereniging voor de Groothandel op Elektrotechnisch Gebied v Commission*, . . . paragraph 110).

59. As regards the lack of evidence that there was an agreement during certain specific periods or, at least, the lack of evidence of its implementation by an undertaking during a given period, it should be recalled that the fact that evidence of the infringement has not been produced in relation to certain specific periods does not preclude the infringement from being regarded as established during a longer overall period than those periods, provided that such a finding is supported by objective and consistent indicia. In the context of an infringement extending over a number of years, the fact that a cartel is shown to have applied during different periods, which may be separated by longer or shorter periods, has no effect on the existence of the cartel, provided that the various actions which form part of the infringement pursue a single purpose and fall within the framework of a single and continuous infringement (*Nederlandse Federatieve Vereniging voor de Groothandel op Elektrotechnisch Gebied v Commission*, . . . paragraphs 97 and 98; see also, to that effect, *Aalborg Portland and Others v Commission*, . . . paragraph 260).

60. In that regard, several criteria have been identified by the case-law as relevant for assessing whether there is a single infringement, namely the identical nature of the objectives of the practices at issue (Case T-21/99 *Dansk Rørindustri v Commission* . . . paragraph 67; see also, to that effect, Case C-113/04 P *Technische Unie v Commission* . . . paragraphs 170 and 171; and Case T-43/02 *Jungbunzlauer v Commission* . . . paragraph 312), the identical nature of the goods or services concerned (see, to that effect, judgment of 15 June 2005 in Joined Cases T-71/03, T-74/03, T-87/03 and T-91/03 *Tokai Carbon and Others v Commission*, . . . paragraphs 118, 119 and 124, and *Jungbunzlauer v Commission*, paragraph 312), the identical nature of the undertakings which participated in the infringement (*Jungbunzlauer v Commission*, paragraph 312), and the identical nature of the detailed rules for its implementation (*Dansk Rørindustri v Commission*, paragraph 68). Furthermore, whether the natural persons involved on behalf of the undertakings are identical and whether the geographical scope of the practices at issue is identical are also factors which may be taken into consideration for the purposes of that examination.

61. The case-law therefore permits the Commission to assume that the infringement—or the participation of an undertaking in the infringement—has not been interrupted, even if it has no evidence

of the infringement in relation to certain specific periods, provided that the various actions which form part of the infringement pursue a single purpose and are capable of falling within the framework of a single and continuous infringement; such a finding must be supported by objective and consistent indicia showing that an overall plan exists.

62. If those conditions are satisfied, the concept of continuous infringement . . . allows the Commission to impose a fine in respect of the whole of the period of infringement taken into consideration and establishes the date on which the limitation period begins to run, namely the date on which the continuous infringement ceased.

63. However, the undertakings accused of collusion may attempt to rebut that presumption by submitting indicia and evidence proving that, on the contrary, the infringement—or their participation in it—did not continue during those same periods.

Nonetheless, a finding of a single and continuous infringement must be made sufficiently clearly and precisely. In *Airfreight*,[376] for example, the GC annulled fines imposed by the Commission on 13 companies it found to have participated in the airfreight cartel. The GC held that although the Commission had described a single and continuous agreement in its statement of reasons, that finding was not clearly reflected in the operative part of the decision. Contradictions and inconsistencies in the decision infringed rights of defence and precluded review by the Court.

In *Treuhand*,[377] the applicant, in contrast to the cases described earlier, challenged the Commission's decision finding two parallel but similar cartels (and imposing two separate fines)—the applicant contended that they formed one single infringement and so there had been an infringement of Regulation 1/2003 (Article 23(2)), as the fines imposed on it related to the same infringement but together exceeded 10 per cent of its total turnover (the maximum fine permitted under the Regulation). The GC rejected this argument. Recalling that the notion of a single infringement covers a situation in which undertakings participate in continuous, complementary conduct in pursuit of a single economic aim, it was necessary to take into account circumstances capable of establishing that link, or of casting doubt upon it, such as the period of implementation the content and the objectives of the various acts. On the facts, it found that the Commission had been correct to find that there was not a single continuous infringement and the members of the two cartels did not have a common project nor a common objective: the parties of the two cartels were not all the same; the products did not form part of the same market and were not complementary; the cartels did not have the same duration; and indeed some of the undertakings in one cartel were buyers in the other cartel market.

d. Who Are the Participants in the Single Infringement?

Even if the Commission establishes that the agreements or concerted practices at issue form part of an overall plan knowingly implemented by undertakings in question with a view to achieving a single anti-competitive objective (through objective indicia of an overall plan), participation of co-perpetrators can take different forms.[378] It has been seen in *Bananas*[379] that where there is a single infringement, the Commission is entitled to attribute liability on the basis of participation in the infringement as a whole. Undertakings which directly participated in only one of some of

[376] Cases T-9/11 etc., *Air Canada v Commission* EU:T:2015:994 (the Commission readopted the decision in 2017, AT/39.258, 17 March 2017).

[377] Case T-27/10, *AC-Treuhand v Commission* EU:T:2014:59, *aff'd* Case C-194/14 P, EU:C:2015:717.

[378] This might also be reflected in the level of the fines impose, see Chap. 13.

[379] Cases C-293 and 294/13 P, EU:C:2015:416, n. 371 and text.

the constituent elements of the infringement will, however, only be liable for the whole if they intended to contribute by their own conduct to the common objectives pursued by all the participants and were either aware of the actual conduct planned or put into effect by the other undertakings in pursuit of the same objectives (even if not aware of all the details of the communications) or could reasonably have foreseen it and that it was prepared to take the risk. In *Bananas*, therefore, although Chiquita and Dole were held responsible for the entire single and continuous infringement, Weichert was held responsible only for the part of the infringement relating to the collusive agreements with Dole. Similarly, in *Infineon*,[380] the GC confirmed that the Commission was not entitled to hold Infineon liable for the Smarts Card infringement as a whole, since it had participated in collusive practices only with Samsung and Renesas and not with Philips, and there was no evidence that it had contacts with Philips or that it had the subjective impression of participating in the whole of the infringement at issue.

> [I]t is only if the undertaking knew or should have known when it participated in an agreement that in doing so it was joining in the cartel as a whole that its participation in the agreement concerned can constitute the expression of its accession to that cartel . . . In other words, the Commission must show that the undertaking intended to contribute by its own conduct to the common objectives pursued by all the participants and that it was aware of the unlawful conduct planned or put into effect by other undertakings in pursuit of the same objectives or that it could reasonably have foreseen it and that it was prepared to take the risk. The undertaking concerned must therefore be aware of the general scope and the essential characteristics of the cartel as a whole.[381]

e. *Facilitators and Liability for Independent Service Providers*

It has been seen earlier in this chapter that 'facilitators' can be found to be part of an agreement or concerted practice pursued by a number of other undertakings, and that an undertaking can be liable for anti-competitive arrangements between an independent service provider it engaged, on the one hand, and its competitors, on the other. In these cases, the EU Courts have applied the same principles to establish liability as those applicable in cases dealing with single continuous infringements. Thus in *Treuhand*,[382] the CJ confirmed, relying on *Anic*, that Treuhand could be found to have participated in an infringement and liable for all of its elements if it intended to contribute 'by its own conduct to the common objectives pursued by all the participants and that it was aware of the actual conduct planned or put into effect by other undertakings in pursuit of the same objectives or that it could reasonably have foreseen it and that it was prepared to take the risk'. Further, that passive modes of participation (such as the presence of an undertaking in meetings at which anti-competitive agreements were concluded, without the undertaking clearly opposing them) are sufficient. '[A] party which tacitly approves of an unlawful initiative, without publicly distancing itself from its content or reporting it to the administrative authorities, encourages the continuation of the infringement and compromises its discovery.'[383] Similarly, in *VM Remonts*[384] the CJ held that an undertaking could be held responsible for an anti-competitive arrangement pursued by an independent service provider and competitors if the undertaking engaging the provider was aware of the anti-competitive objectives being pursued and intended to contribute to them by its own conduct or where it could reasonably have foreseen the anti-competitive acts and was prepared to accept that risk.

[380] See Case T-758/14, *Infineon Technologies AG v Commission* EU:T:2016:737. [381] Ibid., paras. 221–223.
[382] Case C-194/14 P, EU:C:2015:717, para. 30, see n. 244 and text.
[383] Ibid., para. 31. [384] Case C-542/14, EU:C:2016:578.

C. OBJECT OR EFFECT OF THE PREVENTION, RESTRICTION, OR DISTORTION OF COMPETITION

Agreements and other collusive practices are not prohibited unless they have as their object or effect the prevention, restriction, or distortion of competition. The way in which this phrase is interpreted determines the types of agreements which are prohibited by Article 101(1) and the role of the legal exception to the prohibition set out in Article 101(3). The interpretation, relationship, and interaction of these two paragraphs is fully explored in Chapter 5.

D. AN APPRECIABLE EFFECT ON COMPETITION AND TRADE

The CJ has held that 'in order to come within the prohibition imposed by Article [101], the agreement must affect trade between Member States and the free play of competition to an appreciable extent'.[385] The concept of appreciability was introduced in *Völk v Vervaecke*.

Case 5/69, *Völk v SPRL Ets J. Vervaecke* EU:C:1969:35

The case concerned an exclusive distribution agreement concluded between Mr Völk, the owner of a company, Erd & Co, which manufactured washing machines, and Vervaecke, a Belgian company which distributed household electrical appliances. Under the agreement, Vervaecke had the exclusive right to sell Völk's products in Belgium and Luxembourg. According to the Commission, Erd & Co had only 0.08 per cent of the market for the production of washing machines EU-wide, 0.2 per cent of the market in Germany, and 0.6 per cent of the market in Belgium and Luxembourg. Following a dispute which raised the validity of the agreement before the German courts, the Oberlandesgericht in Munich made an Article 234 reference to the EU Courts. In particular, it asked the CJ whether, in considering if an agreement fell within Article 101(1), regard had to be had to the proportion of the market that the grantor had.

Court of Justice

If an agreement is to be capable of affecting trade between Member States it must be possible to foresee with a sufficient degree of probability on the basis of a set of objective factors of law or of fact that the agreement in question may have an influence, direct or indirect, actual or potential, on the pattern of trade between Member States in such a way that it might hinder the attainment of the objectives of a single market between States. Moreover the prohibition in Article [101(1)] is applicable only if the agreement in question also has as its object or effect the prevention, restriction or distortion of competition within the common market. Those conditions must be understood by reference to the actual circumstances of the agreement. Consequently an agreement falls outside the prohibition in Article [101] when it has only an insignificant effect on the markets, taking into account the weak position which the persons concerned have on the market of the product in question. Thus an exclusive dealing agreement, even with absolute territorial protection, may, having regard to the weak position of the persons concerned on the market in the products in question in the area covered by the absolute protection, escape the prohibition laid down in Article [101(1)].

[385] Case 22/71, *Béguelin Import Co v SAGL Import Export* EU:C:1971:113, para. 16.

This case clarifies that EU law is not concerned with agreements concluded between parties that hold a weak position on the market and which have an insignificant effect on intra-Community trade and/or on competition. The insignificant position held by the undertakings means the agreement does not threaten the EU objectives.[386] Because the concept of appreciability is of huge practical importance to undertakings, particularly small and medium-sized ones, the Commission has, over the years, issued a series of Notices indicating when, in its view, an agreement is likely to fall outside Article 101 on this ground. The Commission's interpretation of appreciability is now fleshed out in two separate Notices—one dealing with the effect on trade concept and one dealing with agreements of minor importance which do not appreciably restrict competition. The former Notice is dealt with in the section below, whilst the latter is dealt with in Chapter 5.

E. AN APPRECIABLE EFFECT ON TRADE BETWEEN MEMBER STATES

(i) Jurisdictional Limit

The concept of an effect on trade between Member States sets out a jurisdictional limit to the prohibition laid down in Article 101 (it is also a requirement that any abuse of a dominant position should affect trade for the purposes of Article 102). The criterion confines the scope of the application of Articles 101 and 102 to agreements having a minimum level of cross-border effects within the EU, hence the practices must *appreciably* affect trade between Member States.[387] It has been interpreted broadly, although it is accepted that the EU has no jurisdiction over conduct whose effect is confined to one Member State.[388] The meaning of an effect on trade has been clarified in the case law. The Commission has also prepared a Notice on the concept of effect on trade between Member States[389] which seeks to describe the principles developed by the Court and to spell out when agreements and conduct may 'appreciably' affect trade between Member States. It aims 'to set out the methodology for the application of the effect on trade concept and to provide guidance on its application in frequently occurring situations'.[390] In paragraphs 58–109 of the Guidelines, it applies the general principles set out in the cases to common types of agreements and abuses, for example: different types of agreements and abuse covering or implemented in several Member States; agreements and abuses covering a single or only part of a Member State; agreements and abuses involving imports and exports with undertakings located in third countries; and agreements and practices involving undertakings located in third countries. The interpretation of the concept in the Guidelines is without prejudice to the interpretation given to the concept by the EU Courts.[391]

(ii) The Tests

The Commission's Notice stresses, relying on case-law of the Court,[392] that '[t]he concept of "trade" is not limited to traditional exchanges of goods and services across borders. It is a wider concept, covering all cross-border economic activity, including establishment. This interpretation

[386] Rather, it is more appropriate that they should be examined, if at all, within the framework of national competition legislation.

[387] Guidelines on the effect on trade concept contained in Articles 81 and 82 of the Treaty (Guidelines on the effect on trade concept) [2004] OJ C101/81, para. 13.

[388] Case 22/78, *Hugin v Commission* EU:C:1979:138.

[389] [2004] OJ C101/81.

[390] Guidelines on the effect on trade concept, para. 3.

[391] Ibid., para. 5.

[392] See e.g. Case 172/80, *Züchner v Bayerische Vereinsbank AG* EU:C:1981:178, para. 18; Case C-309/99, *Wouters v Algemene Raad van de Nederlandse Orde van Advocaten* EU:C:2002:98; Case C-41/90, *Höfner and Elser v Macrotron* EU:C:1991:161.

is consistent with the fundamental objective of the Treaty to promote free movement of goods, services, persons and capital.'[393] An agreement will be found to 'affect trade' if it interferes with the pattern of trade between Member States.[394] There must be an impact on the flow of goods and services or other relevant economic activities involving at least two Member States. An agreement or practice may also be found to affect trade if it is liable to interfere with the structure of competition in the common market, for example where it eliminates or threatens to eliminate competitors operating within the Union. This latter structural test is more commonly used in the context of Article 102 than Article 101.[395]

(iii) Pattern of Trade Test

In *Société Technique Minière v Maschinenbau Ulm*,[396] the CJ set out a broad interpretation of the requirement that an agreement should affect trade so that it is easily satisfied. All that is necessary is that 'it must be possible to foresee with a sufficient degree of probability on the basis of a set of objective factors of law or of fact that the agreement in question may have an influence, direct or indirect, actual or potential, on the pattern of trade between Member States . . .'[397]

The test requires the following to be shown:

(a) a sufficient degree of probability on the basis of a set of objective factors of law of fact;[398]
(b) an influence on the pattern of trade between Member States;[399]
(c) a direct or indirect, actual or potential influence on the pattern of trade.[400]

An agreement will, therefore, be caught even if it cannot be established that it will affect the pattern of trade if it can be shown that it is *capable* of having such an effect,[401] for example if it is anticipated that it will affect the pattern of trade in the future. As it is only a jurisdictional criterion, it is not necessary to establish that the agreement actually has cross-border effects. Relevant factors to the determination will be: the nature of the agreement and practice; the nature of the products; and the position and importance of the undertakings involved.

The fact that the influence on trade need only be direct, indirect, actual, or potential means that a broad range of agreements will be caught, including for example agreements affecting goods or services that are not traded, but which are used in the supply of a final product, which is traded;[402] and agreements which do not actually affect trade but which, taking account of foreseeable market developments, may affect trade in the future. In *AEG v Commission*,[403] the CJ held that the fact that there was little inter-State trade did not mean that Article 101(1) was inapplicable if it could reasonably be expected that the patterns of trade in the future might change. The Commission states, however, that the inclusion of indirect and potential effects in the analysis of effects on trade between Member States does not mean that the analysis can be based on remote, hypothetical, or speculative effects.

[393] Guidelines on the effect on trade concept, para. 19. [394] Case 56/65, *STM* EU:C:1966:38.

[395] See Case 6–7/73, *Istituto Chemioterapico Italiano SpA and Commercial Solvents Corp v Commission* EU:C:1974:18, especially paras. 5 and 30–35, and Chap. 5.

[396] Case 56/65, EU:C:1966:38. [397] Ibid., 249, and Case 5/69, *Völk v Vervaecke* EU:C:1969:35, 302.

[398] Guidelines on the effect on trade concept, paras. 25–32. [399] Ibid., paras. 33–35.

[400] Ibid., paras. 36–43. [401] Ibid., para. 26.

[402] Case 123/83, *BNIC v Clair* EU:C:1985:33, para. 29.

[403] Case 107/82, EU:C:1983:293, para. 60; see also *AEI/Reyrolle Parsons re Vacuum Interrupters* [1977] OJ L48/32.

[404] Guidelines on the effect on trade concept, para. 43.

> For instance, an agreement that raises the prices of a product which is not tradable reduces the disposable income of consumers. As consumers have less money to spend they may purchase fewer products imported from other Member States. However, the link between such income effects and trade between Member States is generally in itself too remote to establish [EU] law jurisdiction.[404]

(iv) An Increase in Trade

In *Consten and Grundig*,[405] the parties argued before the CJ that their distribution agreement did not produce an effect on trade within the meaning of Article 101(1) since it increased trade between Member States (in the absence of the agreement, Grundig products might not have been sold in France at all). This argument was partially supported by a textual analysis of the Treaty since, in at least one language (Italian), the text suggested that the effect on trade should be a harmful or prejudicial one. The CJ[406] rejected this argument, ruling that 'the fact that an agreement encourages an increase, even a large one, in the volume of trade between states is not sufficient to exclude the possibility that the agreement may "affect" such trade . . .'.[407] Rather, it considered that the contract, which precluded anyone other than Consten from importing Grundig products into France, and prohibited Consten from re-exporting the products into other Member States, 'indisputably' affected trade between Member States. Instead of a literal interpretation, the CJ adopted one which respected the aims and spirit of the Treaty. The aim of the Treaty was not to increase trade as an end in itself, but to create a system of undistorted competition. It was important that agreements, such as the exclusive distribution agreement at issue in that case, should be capable of being scrutinised under the provisions.

The CJ concluded that Article 101 applied to any agreement which might threaten the freedom of trade between Member States in a manner which might harm the attainment of the single market. The term pattern of trade is neutral, it is not a condition that trade is restricted or reduced.

(v) Partitioning of the Internal Market

Vertical and IP licensing agreements may incorporate territorial restrictions restricting the territory into which the buyer or licensee can sell the goods. In *Consten and Grundig*, the CJ found that the nature of the territorial restrictions in that case was to affect trade.[408] Similarly, other agreements concerning imports or exports and containing provisions sharing markets between a manufacturer and its distributor or between distributors *inter se* are capable of affecting trade between Member States.[409]

Even an agreement covering third countries and undertakings located in third countries may appreciably affect trade between Member States where it is capable of affecting cross-border economic activity inside the Union, for example an agreement preventing a distributor appointed for a territory outside the EU from making sales outside its contractual territory (and, consequently, into the EU).

[405] Cases 56 and 58/64, *Consten and Grundig* EU:C:1966:41.

[406] The argument was, however, supported by Roemer AG. He took the view that the effect on trade would have to be an unfavourable one before the prohibition applied.

[407] Cases 56 and 58/64, *Consten and Grundig* EU:C:1966:41, 341.

[408] See n. 405 and text.

[409] Case 161/84, *Pronuptia de Paris GmbH v Pronuptia de Paris Irmgard Schillgallis* EU:C:1986:41, para. 27.

If, in the absence of the agreement, resale to the EU would be both possible and likely, it may be capable of affecting patterns of trade inside the EU.[410] Whether or not an agreement with an undertaking outside the EU will affect trade will depend on factors such as the object of the agreement (whether the object of the agreement is to restrict competition within the EU), the prices for the contractual products charged in the EU and those charged outside the EU, the level of customs duties, and transport costs. Further, the product volumes exported compared to the total market for those products in the territory of the common market must not be insignificant.[411]

It is also possible that an agreement may have an effect on trade even if it does not appear to do so at first sight. The impact on inter-State trade may be revealed on a closer examination of the agreement. In *Delimitis v Henninger Bräu*,[412] for example, a beer-supply agreement between a German brewer and a German café proprietor imposed an obligation on the latter to purchase beer only from the brewer. In derogation from this obligation, however, it included an access clause permitting the café proprietor to purchase competing beer from suppliers in other Member States. The CJ ruled that the national court would have to examine the agreement in greater detail. It was critical to determine whether or not this 'access' clause was hypothetical or real. The contract obliged the café proprietor to purchase a specific quantity of the brewer's beer each year. It had to be determined, therefore, whether or not this clause stipulating the minimum quantity of the brewer's beer to be purchased in reality left the café proprietor with a real opportunity to purchase beer from brewers in other Member States. If it did not, the agreement would produce an effect on inter-State trade, despite the access clause. On the other hand, if the agreement left a real possibility for foreign brewers to supply the outlet, the agreement was not in principle capable of affecting trade between Member States.

(vi) Agreements Operating in One Member State

It tends to be assumed that an agreement between parties situated in different Member States affects trade between Member States.[413] It can be seen from *Delimitis* that an agreement which operates in only one Member State is also quite capable of affecting trade between Member States.

Similarly, national cartels, especially those dominating the whole or a large part of a market, tend to reinforce compartmentalisation and make it more difficult for undertakings from other Member States to penetrate the market.[414] The CJ has consistently held that the fact that a cartel relates only to the marketing of products in a single Member State is not sufficient to exclude the possibility that trade between Member States might be affected.[415] Indeed, the cartel is likely to be successful only if the members can defend themselves against foreign competition. If they do not, and the product covered by the agreement is tradable, the cartel is likely to be undermined by competition from undertakings in other Member States. The agreement in *Belasco*,[416] for example, specifically provided for protective and defensive measures to be taken against foreign undertakings. Where the relevant product or service affected by the cartel is easily transmissible across borders it is likely that an effect on trade will be found. A Dutch cartel agreement which operated in order to restrict competition in the market for mobile cranes was held to have an effect on intra-Union trade. Since the cranes could travel at speeds

[410] Case C-306/96, *Javico International and Javico AF v Yves Saint Laurent Parfums SA* EU:C:1998:173, paras. 15–28.
[411] Ibid., para.16.
[412] Case C-234/89, EU:C:1991:91.
[413] See e.g. Guidelines on the effect on trade concept, paras. 61–72.
[414] Case 8/72, *Vereeniging van Cementhandelaren v Commission* EU:C:1972:84. But see Cases C-215 and 216/96, *Bagnasco v Banca Popolare di Novara (BPN) and Cassa di Risparmio di Genova e Imperia SpA (Carige)* EU:C:1999:12, paras. 38–53, n. 419 and text.
[415] Case C-246/86, *S.C. Belasco v Commission* EU:C:1989:301, para. 33.
[416] Ibid., paras. 35–38.

of between 63 and 78 kph, the agreement was likely to affect German and Belgian firms operating near the Dutch border.[417] The Commission reached a similar conclusion in *Luxembourg Brewers*[418] in respect of a cartel designed to insulate the Luxembourg market against imports of beer from other Member States.

In *Carlo Bagnasco v BPN*[419] and *Dutch Banks*,[420] the CJ and Commission respectively concluded that purely national banking agreements were not capable of affecting trade between Member States. *Bagnasco*, for example, concerned retail banking services (guarantees for current account credit facilities), and the CJ considered that trade was not capable of being *appreciably* affected because the potential for trade in the products was very limited. The market was not particularly susceptible to imports and retail banking services were not an important factor affecting the choice made by undertakings from other Member States when determining whether or not to establish themselves in another Member State. Although somewhat out of line with other case law and decisions setting out extensive EU jurisdiction, the cases may be explicable by virtue of a reluctance at the time to apply EU law to cases which essentially have a national impact and so can be dealt with at a national level. Since 2004, however, such cases may be appraised by the appropriate NCA under Article 101 (if an effect on trade is found) as well as domestic law.[421]

(vii) Restrictions on Competition and Restrictions on Trade

It is clear that so long as the agreement as a whole affects trade between Member States, it is immaterial that the clause (or clauses) which restricts competition does not itself affect trade.[422]

(viii) Agreements Which Appreciably Affect Trade between Member States

The Commission's Notice dealing with the effect on trade concept also deals with the quantitative element of the criterion, the question of when an agreement will appreciably affect trade between Member States.[423] It states that EU law limits jurisdiction to agreements and practices capable of having effects on trade of a certain magnitude. In particular, appreciability can be appraised by reference to the position and importance of the undertakings on the relevant market. The Commission considers that appreciability can be measured both in absolute terms (turnover) and in relative terms, comparing the position of the relevant undertakings with others on the market (market share).[424] In paragraphs 50–57, the Commission seeks to quantify appreciability, stressing that the assessment depends on the circumstances of each individual case. The Notice does, however, set out a negative rebuttable presumption, defining the absence of an appreciable effect on trade between Member States (the NAAT-rule). In contrast to the Notice on agreements of minor importance, it states that the rule applies to *all* agreements irrespective of the restrictions contained within them (i.e. it applies even to agreements containing object (or hardcore) restraints, see further Chapter 5).[425] Agreements which do not fall within its negative definition of appreciability do not, however, necessarily appreciably affect trade.

[417] COMP/34.179, *Stichting Certificatie Kraanverhuurbedrijf and Federatie van Nederlandse Kraanbedrijven* [1995] OJ L312/79.
[418] COMP/37.800 [2002] OJ L253/21, paras. 77–81.
[419] Case C-215/96, EU:C:1999:12. See also Guidelines on the effect on trade concept, para. 60.
[420] COMP/31.499 [1989] OJ L253/1.
[421] But see discussion of Reg. 1/2003, Art. 3 in Chap. 13.
[422] See Case 193/83, *Windsurfing International Inc v Commission* EU:C:1986:75.
[423] Commission Guidelines on the effect on trade concept, paras. 44–57.
[424] Ibid., para. 46.
[425] Ibid., para. 50. See also Case T-254/12, *Kühne + Nagel International AG v Commission* EU:T:2016:114 , *aff'd* Case C-261/16 EU:C:2018:56.

At paragraph 52, the Commission states its view that 'in principle agreements are not capable of appreciably affecting trade between Member States when the following *cumulative* conditions are met' (emphasis added):[426]

> (a) The aggregate market share of the parties on any relevant market within the Community affected by the agreement does not exceed 5 per cent,[427] and
>
> (b) In the case of horizontal agreements, the aggregate annual Community turnover of the undertakings concerned in the products covered by the agreement does not exceed 40 million Euro.[428] In case of agreements concerning joint buying of products, the relevant turnover shall be the parties' combined purchases of the products covered by the agreement.
>
> In the case of vertical agreements, the aggregate annual Community turnover of the supplier in the products covered by the agreement does not exceed 40 million Euro. In the case of licence agreements, the relevant turnover shall be the aggregate turnover of the licensees in the products incorporating the licensed technology and the licensor's own turnover in such products. In cases involving agreements concluded between a buyer and several suppliers, the relevant turnover shall be the buyer's combined purchase of the products covered by the agreement.

Paragraph 52 also provides marginal relief for those that outgrow the Notice in two successive calendar years. In cases where the presumption applies, the Commission will not normally institute proceedings. Further, where undertakings assumed in good faith that an agreement is covered by the negative presumption, the Commission will not impose fines.[429]

In contrast, paragraph 53 states that for agreements that, by their very nature, are capable of affecting trade between Member States, such as agreements concerning imports and exports or covering several Member States, there is a *rebuttable positive presumption* that the effects on trade are appreciable when the turnover of the parties exceeds €40 million. It may also often be presumed that effects are appreciable where the 5 per cent threshold is exceeded. These rebuttable presumptions will obviously be of central importance when these issues are litigated before national courts.

(ix) The Relationship between EU and National Law

The breadth of the effect on trade criterion affects the scope of Article 3 of Regulation 1/2003, which determines the relationship between Articles 101 and 102 and national law. The effect on trade criterion can therefore have a substantive outcome. Essentially, Article 3 provides that whenever an NCA or national court applies national competition laws to an agreement or practice that affects trade between Member States, it must also apply Articles 101 and 102. The application of national competition law may not, however, lead to the prohibition of agreements which affect trade between Member States but which do not restrict competition within the meaning of Article 101(1), or which fulfil the conditions of Article 101(3), or which are covered by an EU block exemption. Further, a national authority cannot authorise an agreement prohibited by EU law. The relationship between EU and national law is dealt with more fully in Chapter 13.

426 The NAAT-rule does not apply in emerging markets. In such cases appreciability may have to be assessed on the basis of the position of the parties on related product markets or their strength in technologies relating to the agreement, ibid.

427 See Case C-439/11 P, *Ziegler SA v Commission* EU:C:2013:513.

428 The turnover threshold is calculated on the basis of total EU sales excluding tax during the last financial year by the undertakings concerned. Sales between entities that form part of the same undertaking are excluded, Commission Guidelines on the effect on trade concept, para. 54.

429 Commission Guidelines on the effect on trade concept, para. 50.

F. AGREEMENTS REQUIRED BY NATIONAL LEGISLATION OR ENCOURAGED BY NATIONAL GOVERNMENTS

National law or national regulatory regimes may affect competition in a market. Case law makes it clear that Article 101 is not applicable to the anti-competitive activities of a firm if the restrictive effects on competition originate solely from the implementation of national law, for example where national law requires an agreement or creates a framework eliminating any possible competitive conduct.[430] In such a case, the anti-competitive effect results not from the autonomous conduct of the firms but from the national law.[431] Article 101 is concerned with the conduct of undertakings and not with laws or regulations of Member States.[432]

Agreements may be caught by Article 101, however, if national law leaves room for, and does not preclude, competition even if they are encouraged or approved by national law[433] or entered into after consultation with the national authorities.[434] In both *Competition Authority v Beef Industry Development Society Ltd (BIDS)*[435] and *Coop de France bétail et viande v Commission*,[436] undertakings were found to have violated Article 101, even though national governments had some knowledge of, or involvement with, the relevant agreements concluded.[437]

Similarly, in *Telefónica v Commission*[438] the GC rejected the applicant's argument that, in concluding the terms of an agreement, it had been so influenced by the Portuguese Government that it had 'lost autonomy' over its conduct (which should consequently be removed from the scope of Article 101(1)). The GC reiterated that in the absence of any binding regulatory provision imposing the anti-competitive conduct, or the conduct being imposed on the traders by the national authorities through the exercise of irresistible pressures sufficient to deprive the traders concerned of any autonomy,[439] the fact that anti-competitive conduct was favoured or encouraged by the public authorities has no impact on the applicability of Article 101. On the facts, the GC concluded that the applicant 'cannot claim that the alleged actions of the Portuguese Government caused it to lose all autonomy. It is apparent from the file . . . that the final agreement is the outcome of a joint arrangement between the parties. Nor is there any evidence to show that those provisions were imposed unilaterally by the Portuguese Government.'

[430] Where a Member State takes measures which lead to an infringement of the antitrust rules by a firm, the Commission may be able to issue an infringement decision against that State, see Chap. 8.

[431] In such cases, a Member State may violate EU obligations, see e.g. Cases C-94 and 202/04, *Cipolla v Fazari* EU:C:2006:758, para. 47, cf. Case C-446/05, *Criminal Proceedings against Doulamis* EU:C:2008:157, paras. 19–22 and Chap. 8. A national authority is duty-bound to disapply national legislation which violates EU law, see Case C-198/01, *Consorzio Industrie Fiammiferi (CIF) v Autorità Garante della Concorrenza e del Mercato* EU:C:2003:430 and Chap. 13.

[432] See Cases C-94 and 202/04 and Cases T-191 and 212–214/98, *Atlantic Container Line v Commission* EU:T:2003:245, para. 1130.

[433] See Cases 43 and 63/82, *VBVB & VBBB v Commission* EU:C:1984:9; COMP/26.870, *Aluminium Imports from Eastern Europe* [1985] OJ L92/1; COMP/29.525 and COMP/30.000, COMP/29.883 *AROW/BNIC* [1982] OJ L379/1.

[434] Cases 240–242, 261, and 262/82, *SSI v Commission* EU:C:1985:488. For the position where the State *requires* or encourages undertakings to enter into anti-competitive agreements, see Section 5.F and Chap. 8.

[435] Case C-209/07, EU:C:2008:643. [436] Cases C-101 and 110/07 P, EU:C:2008:741.

[437] Governments, or their agencies, may put forward or encourage firms to conclude voluntary agreements to achieve important health, environmental, or other policy objectives, or be sympathetic to, and encourage, arrangements put together by entities operating in an industry in crisis. Such action may undermine compliance with competition law by sending mixed signals to businesses as to what is permitted and what is prohibited. Competition agencies thus increasingly engage in advocacy with government departments providing advice on the effects of, and alternatives to, restrictions of competition in any aspect of the law or a proposed change to it.

[438] Case T-216/13, EU:T:2016:369, paras. 111–116.

[439] Such as the threat to adopt State measures likely to cause them to sustain substantial losses.

G. COMMISSION NOTICES

The Commission has issued a number of Notices/Guidelines which provide useful guidance on the interpretation of Article 101 generally, including the elements discussed in this chapter.[440] Even though they are not rules of law, they nevertheless form rules of practice from which the Commission itself may not depart without giving reasons that are compatible with the principle of equal treatment.[441] Many will be examined in subsequent chapters of this book including, especially:

- Guidelines on the application of Article 101 to Vertical Restraints;[442]
- Guidelines on the application of Article 101 to horizontal cooperation agreements;[443]
- Guidelines on the application of Article 101 to technology transfer agreements;[444]
- Commission Notice on agreements which do not appreciably restrict competition under Article 101(1) of the Treaty on the Functioning of the European Union (De Minimis Notice);[445]
- Guidelines on the application of Article 81(3) of the Treaty [now Article 101(3)].[446]

H. EXTRATERRITORIALITY

The question of when and in what circumstances the competition rules may be applied to the acts (which appreciably effect trade between Member States) of overseas undertakings (which are not established in the EU) is controversial and politically sensitive and is explored in Chapter 17.

5. ARTICLE 101(2)

It has been seen that despite the clear wording of Article 101(2), the nullity provided for in that provision applies only to individual *clauses* in the agreement affected by the Article 101(1) prohibition. In *Société Technique Minière v Maschinenbau Ulm GmbH*,[447] the CJ held that the agreement as a whole is void only where those clauses are not severable from the remaining terms of the agreement;[448] the question of severability is matter of national, not EU, law.[449] Each national court will, therefore, have to apply its own national rules on severance to determine the impact of Article 101(2) on the arrangements before it.[450]

The nullity resulting from Article 101(2) is automatic and is not dependent upon any prior decision to that effect.[451] The English Court of Appeal took the view that the nullity imposed is not absolute, but only has the same temporaneous or transient effect as the prohibition in Article 101(1) (an agreement will cease to be void if the agreement itself ceases to restrict competition or to affect trade within the meaning of Article 101(1)).[452]

[440] These are discussed further in subsequent chapters, especially Chaps. 5 and 9–12.
[441] See Chap. 2, Section 5. [442] [2022] OJ C248/1.
[443] Adopted on 17 July 2023 (see also Draft Guidelines, C(2022) 1159 final). [444] [2014] OJ C89/03.
[445] [2014] OJ C291/01. [446] [2004] OJ C101/97. [447] Case 56/65, EU:C:1966:38, 250.
[448] It thus interpreted Art. 101(2) with reference only to its purpose in EU law and to ensure compliance with the Treaty.
[449] See also Case 319/82, *Société de Vente de Ciments et Bétons de l'Est v Kerpen & Kerpen GmbH & Co KG* EU:C:1983:374, para. 11. See Chap. 14.
[450] See further Chap. 14 and e.g. C. Cauffman, 'The Impact of Voidness for Infringements of Article 101 TFEU on Related Contracts' (2012) 8 *European Competition Journal* 95.
[451] See Reg. 1/2003, Art. 1. [452] *Passmore v Morland plc* [1999] 3 All ER 1005, see further Chap. 14.

6. EXCLUSIONS

Article 101 does not refer to any express exclusions. Nonetheless, in practice a number of agreements are excluded from its scope. For example, the scheme of the EU Merger Regulation is such that, with certain limited exceptions, merger transactions that constitute a 'concentration' are assessed either under any applicable national competition legislation, or, where the transaction has an EU dimension, under the provisions of the Merger Regulation itself. The idea is that concentrations, which include certain joint venture agreements, should not generally be appraised under Article 101.[453] In addition, exclusions/derogations apply in relation to certain agricultural agreements,[454] and Article 106(2) TFEU provides that the competition rules do not apply to some activities of public bodies or bodies entrusted with public services. In interpreting the elements of Article 101(1), the CJ has also excluded from its ambit agreements belonging to the realm of social policy, agreements concluded by firms carrying out tasks of a public or social nature, agreements between entities which form part of the same economic unit, agreements required by national legislation, and matters which are of a purely sporting interest and, as such, have nothing to do with economic activity.

7. CONCLUSIONS

1. Article 101 applies to a broad range of collusive arrangements between undertakings which appreciably affect trade between Member States.

2. The elements of Article 101(1) have been interpreted expansively to catch an array of joint, or coordinated, conduct between undertakings, whether or not actual or potential competitors, and to hold firms liable, in certain circumstances, for the conduct of their subsidiaries, agents, independent service providers, and co-conspirators, even if they were not aware, or fully aware of the extent, of their anti-competitive arrangements.

3. The discussion in this chapter has, however, established that the following agreements (or conduct) will fall outside Article 101(1) and escape the prohibition altogether:

- agreements which are not concluded by two or more entities engaged in economic activity;
- agreements between entities which are part of the same economic unit, for example certain parent and subsidiary or principal and agent relationships;
- collective agreements between employers and workers or solo self-employed persons who are in a situation comparable to workers;
- unilateral conduct not explicitly or tacitly accepted by another or by another party to a contract;
- agreements which relate to the production of, or trade in, certain agricultural products;
- agreements which do not appreciably affect trade between Member States (although such agreements may be subject to national competition law);

[453] For discussion of the complicated question of which transactions fall to be assessed within the procedure of the Merger Reg., Council Reg. 139/2004 [2004] OJ L24/1, and not under Art. 101, see Chaps. 10 and 15.

[454] See e.g. Reg. 1184/2006 [2006] OJ L214/7, Reg. 1308/2013 [2013] OJ L347/671 (amended by Reg. 2017/2393 [2017] OJ L350/15, Reg. 2020/593 [2020] OJ L140/13, Reg. 2020/594 [2020] OJ L140/17, and Reg. 2020/599 [2020] OJ L140/37). However, the derogations are construed strictly, see Case C-671/15, *Authorité de la Concurrence v APVE* EU:C:2017:860, para. 46. See also J. Blockx and J. Vandenberghe, 'Balancing Commercial Relations Along the Food Supply Chain: The Agricultural Exemption from EU Competition Law after Regulation 1308/2013' (2014) 10 *European Competition Journal* 387. For discussion of whether a similar system could be introduced for collective bargaining of the self-employed, see Daskalova, n. 251.

- agreements which are necessary for the performance of a task of general economic interest entrusted to them by a Member State (see Article 106(2));
- agreements required by national law; and
- agreements which are truly extraterritorial.

4. In Chapter 5, it is seen that agreements between undertakings which appreciably affect trade also escape the Article 101(1) prohibition if they do not appreciably restrict competition or are excepted, or exempted, from the prohibition under Article 101(3).

8. FURTHER READING

A. Books

Harding, C., and Joshua, J., *Regulating Cartels in Europe* (2nd edn, Oxford University Press, 2010)

B. Chapters in Books

Daly, S., and Jones, A., 'The Undertaking and Single Economic Entity Concepts in EU and UK Competition Law: Proposals for a Refined Approach' in F. Thépot and A. Tzanaki (eds.), Research Handbook on Competition and Corporate Law (Edward Elgar, Forthcoming)

Daskalova, V., 'The Competition Law Framework and Collective Bargaining Agreements for Self-Employed: Analysing Restrictions and Mapping Exemption Opportunities' in B. Waas and C. Hießl (eds.), *Collective Barning for Self-employed Workers in Europe: Approaches to Reconcile Competition Law and Labour Rights* (Kluwer Law International, 2021)

C. Articles

Abenhaïm, M., 'Public Distancing and Liability in Cartel Cases: Does Distance Lend Enchantment?' (2016) 39(3) *World Competition* 413

Jones, A., 'The Boundaries of an Undertaking in EU Competition Law' (2012) 8 *European Competition Journal* 301

Joshua, J., 'Single Continuous Infringement of Article 81 EC: Has the Commission Stretched the Concept Beyond the Limit of its Logic?' (2009) 5 *European Competition Journal* 451

Kalintiri, A., 'Revisiting Parental Liability in EU Competition Law' (2018) 43 *ELRev* 145

Koenig, C., 'An Economic Analysis of the Single Economic Entity Doctrine in EU Competition Law' (2017) 13(2) *J of Competition Law and Economics* 281

Schmidt-Kessen, M. J., Bergqvist, C., Jacqueson, C., Lind, Y., and Huffman, M., '"I'll call my Union", said the driver—Collective bargaining of gig workers under EU competition rules', Copenhagen Business School Law Research Paper Series No. 20-43 (2020).

Wils, W., 'The Undertaking as Subject of EC Competition Law and the Imputation of Infringements to Natural or Legal Persons' (2000) 25 *ELRev* 99

5

ARTICLE 101 TFEU: SUBSTANTIVE APPRAISAL

1. CENTRAL ISSUES

1. Chapter 4 examines the scheme and structure of Article 101.
2. This chapter explores the relationship between Article 101(1) and Article 101(3), focusing on the substantive question of *which* agreements contravene the objectives of Article 101 and so should be prohibited; that is, which agreements appreciably restrict competition (by object or effect) within the meaning of Article 101(1) and which restrictive agreements satisfy the conditions of Article 101(3).
3. The Commission states that it takes an economic approach to Article 101 based on a consumer welfare objective. Article 101(1) is about identifying the anti-competitive object or effect of an agreement, whilst Article 101(3) allows the balancing of offsetting efficiencies against these restrictive effects. Not all of the case law of the EU Courts is easy to reconcile with this approach, however.

2. INTRODUCTION AND BACKGROUND

A. ARTICLE 101(1) AND ARTICLE 101(3)

This chapter focuses on the question of which agreements, etc. falling within the scope of Article 101 (which appreciably affect trade between Member States), contravene the objectives of Article 101 and are prohibited by it. Substantive analysis under Article 101 is conducted in two parts. First, an agreement has to be scrutinised to determine whether it infringes Article 101(1), i.e. whether it appreciably restricts[1] competition (by object or effect). If it does not, that is the end of the story. If it does, it must, secondly, be determined whether or not the agreement meets the criteria set out in Article 101(3); whether it provides specified benefits (broadly, it improves the production or distribution of goods or services or promotes technical or economic progress), allows consumers a fair share of the benefit, does not contain any indispensable restrictions, and does not eliminate competition in a substantial part of the products in question.

[1] The words 'prevention, restriction, or distortion' are intended to cover any interference with competition, and are synonymous. The term 'restriction' is used as shorthand in this text to cover all three.

This section starts by examining possible ways of reconciling the two parts of Article 101 and how they have been balanced over time. Section 3 then scrutinises more closely how agreements are analysed under Article 101(1), whilst Section 4 considers the analysis required under Article 101(3). The chapter concludes that the jurisprudence in this sphere is not all easy to reconcile and some rationalisation is required.

B. POSSIBLE WAYS OF RECONCILING ARTICLE 101(1) AND ARTICLE 101(3)

The bifurcated structure of Article 101 has, to some extent, complicated its interpretation and led to uncertainty as to the correct role for, and analysis to be conducted under, each part. Key questions arising are which objectives influence the interpretation of Article 101 and what factors are taken into account at each stage, i.e.: (a) when identifying a restriction of competition for the purposes of Article 101(1); and (b) when determining what are Article 101(3) benefits which can trump an Article 101(1) restriction? Finding the right balance between the application of Article 101(1) and Article 101(3) has proved difficult.

The wording of Article 101(1) and Article 101(3) itself does not define their relationship. A number of different approaches may be adopted, or advocated, as to how they should be reconciled. For example:

(1) One way of reconciling the two parts is to adopt a literal or broad interpretation of Article 101(1), bringing many agreements within its net, and conducting a more detailed analysis of the anti-competitive, pro-competitive, and other aspects of the agreement within the more structured framework of Article 101(3). In this scenario, the requirement that the agreement restricts competition serves a jurisdictional function (bringing within its ambit all potentially problematic agreements). The rigorous substantive assessment is then completed under Article 101(3).

(2) A second approach is to conduct a more detailed analysis when determining whether an agreement restricts competition (Article 101(1)) and to thereby confine the role of Article 101(3). For example, an assessment of an assumed (in object cases), actual, potential, or likely (in effect cases) adverse impact on consumer welfare is made when determining whether it restricts competition. Article 101(3) then plays a more limited role, excepting agreements assumed to restrict competition *and*, perhaps, allowing other demonstrable public policy benefits (such as benefits to environment, health, industry, culture, or employment) to be balanced against identified anti-competitive effects.

(3) A third approach is to divide the substantive appraisal more evenly between the two parts. There are a number of ways in which this division could be effected, but one method could be to use Article 101(1) to identify presumed, actual, potential, or likely anti-competitive effects and Article 101(3) to enable the parties to establish that the agreement achieves offsetting efficiencies or pro-competitive effects (the analysis as a whole would thus determine whether the agreement adversely impacts on consumer welfare). For example, Article 101(1) could become concerned with allocative efficiency (and, essentially, deadweight loss resulting from contrived restrictions of output) whilst Article 101(3) could become a productive and dynamic efficiency inquiry, available to allow the parties to demonstrate that the restraints in the agreement are necessary to achieve efficiencies which will be passed on to consumers and compensate them for the resulting allocative inefficiencies.[2] An important issue would be whether public policy factors should also be relevant to the assessment and, if so, whether they are relevant at the Article 101(1) or Article 101(3) stage of the analysis (or both).

[2] See e.g. O. Odudu, *The Boundaries of EC Competition Law: The Scope of Article 81* (Oxford University Press, 2006), Chaps. 5–7.

The discussion in Sections 2.C–2.E establishes that the Commission initially adopted an approach close to (1) but that many commentators urged it to take an approach closer to (2) (which it was argued would be in line with the jurisprudence of the EU Courts). Further, that although neither the EU Courts' nor the Commission's current approach equates *exactly* to any of those outlined, the modernised approach most closely resembles (3).

C. THE INTERPRETATION OF 'OBJECT OR EFFECT IS THE PREVENTION, RESTRICTION, OR DISTORTION OF COMPETITION'—THE EARLY APPROACH

Following the setting up of the notification and exemption system by Regulation 17, the Commission was able to play an extremely influential role in the interpretation of Article 101. One of the most strident criticisms made of the Commission's application of the competition rules until the 1990s was its failure to adopt a sufficiently realistic economic interpretation of Article 101(1), in particular, when determining whether or not an agreement restricts competition. In short, it was complained that the Commission found many agreements were caught within the widely cast net of Article 101(1) but subsequently completed its analysis, by utilising its exclusive power to authorise (or exempt) many agreements, using Article 101(3)[3] (the analysis thus resembled approach (1) set out in Section 2.B).

This approach seems to have been motivated both by ideology and practicalities. Arguably, the Commission employed Article 101, in accordance with the ordoliberal philosophy, to limit restrictions on conduct (restraints on economic freedom), to promote rivalry between undertakings operating on a market,[4] as well as to prevent interferences with the single market project.[5] Further, a broad, more jurisdictional, interpretation of Article 101(1) cemented the Commission's central role in the moulding and shaping of EU competition policy since it had the exclusive right to apply Article 101(3) through the system of 'notification and exemption'.[6]

This approach raised both conceptual and practical difficulties. First, businesses found it hard to understand why their agreement was characterised as restrictive of competition, simply because it imposed restrictions on the conduct of one of the parties. Secondly, until 1 May 2004 when Regulation 1/2003 came into force, negative procedural consequences resulted from this approach. Parties fearful that their agreement might infringe Article 101(1) had either to notify their agreement to the Commission (which although having the sole right to grant individual exemptions had limited resources to give them in practice)[7] or draft it to fall within a block exemption (discussed in Section 4.E). The Commission's monopoly over Article 101(3) also made it hard for national courts and national competition authorities (NCAs) to participate fully in the enforcement process.

[3] See e.g. COMP/23.013, *Goodyear Italiana-Euram* [1975] OJ L38/10, COMP/28.173, *Campari* [1978] OJ L70/69, para. 7, part IIA, COMP/27.442; *Vacuum Interrupters* [1977] OJ L48/32, COMP/27.093; *De Laval-Stork* [1977] OJ L215/11, para. 6; and COMP/28.796, *Beecham/Parke, Davis* [1979] OJ L70/11.

[4] See J. Faull and A. Nikpay (eds.), *The EU Law of Competition* (3rd edn, Oxford University Press, 2014), 3.160–3.166.

[5] See Chap. 1 and e.g. Faull and Nikpay, ibid.

[6] See Reg. 17 [1959–1962] OJ Spec. Ed. 87, Arts. 9(1) and 4 (enabling it to influence the form and way in which agreements were operated through its application of Art. 101(3)). In contrast, had it adopted a narrower, more effects-based approach to Art. 101(1), greater enforcement of agreements would have been delegated to the national level and the uniform interpretation of the competition rules might have been compromised.

[7] Reg. 17 [1959–1962] OJ Spec. Ed. 87, Art. 9(1). Notification was a time- and cost-consuming exercise and in reality the Commission could not grant more than a few individual exemptions each year (see e.g. Case T-67/01, *JCB Service v Commission* EU:T:2004:3 (*aff'd* Case C-167/04, EU:C:2006:594) concerning an agreement notified to the Commission in 1973 but not dealt with until 2000).

The Commission was subjected to significant criticism for this approach[8] and it was argued that a more sophisticated approach to Article 101(1) was required because:

- the legal rules followed by the Commission under Article 101(1) were overbroad (wrongly favouring the freedom of individual traders over consumer welfare) and did not provide sufficiently transparent, precise, and operable criteria to determine which agreements restricted competition;[9]
- the approach adopted led to the condemnation under Article 101(1) of innocuous agreements which did not in fact restrict competition through anti-competitive effects.[10] Because of the unlikelihood of gaining an exemption, pro-competitive agreements were being deterred resulting in Type 1 errors;
- if a consideration of anti- and pro-competitive effects was conducted under Article 101(1), many of the procedural problems experienced in consequence of the notification and exemption system would fall away; and critically
- the advocated approach was necessitated by the case law of the EU Courts which had not interpreted the concept of a restriction of competition under Article 101(1) so broadly as the Commission. Although it has been clear since the CJ's judgment in *Établissements Consten SàRL and Grundig-Verkaufs-GmbH v Commission*[11] that there is no need to take account of the effects of an agreement if its *object* is to restrict competition, it was maintained that in other, 'effect', cases, a series of judgments commencing with *Société Technique Minière v Maschinenbau Ulm GmbH (STM)*[12] (and including cases such as *Nungesser v Commission*,[13] *Erauw-Jacquéry Sprl v La Hesbignonne Société Coopérative*,[14] *Remia BV and NV Verenigde Bedrijven Nutricia v Commission*,[15] *Pronuptia de Paris GmbH v Pronuptia de Paris Irmgard Schillgallis*,[16] *Brasserie de Haecht (No. 1)*,[17] *Gøttrup-Klim Grovvareforeninger and Others v Dansk Landbrugs Grovvareselskab AmbA*,[18] and *Delimitis v Henninger Bräu*)[19] required the drawing up of a competition balance sheet and a weighing of anti- and pro-competitive effects under Article 101(1).[20]

D. SECTION 1 OF THE SHERMAN ACT

During the debate, reference was frequently made to the need for greater economic analysis under Article 101(1), similar perhaps to 'rule of reason' analysis conducted in the US under s. 1 of the Sherman Act 1890 (the US equivalent of Article 101).

[8] See e.g. R. Joliet, *The Rule of Reason in Antitrust Law* (Nijhoff, 1967); I. Forrester and C. Norall, 'The Laïcization of Community Law: Self-help and the Rule of Reason: How Competition is and Could be Applied' (1984) 21 *CMLRev* 11; V. Korah, 'EEC Competition Policy—Legal Form or Economic Efficiency?' (1986) 39 *CLP* 85; B. E. Hawk, 'System Failure: Vertical Restraints and EC Competition Law' (1995) 32 *CMLRev* 973; R. Whish and B. Sufrin, 'Article 85 and the Rule of Reason' (1987) 7 *YEL* 1. See also A. Jones, 'Analysis of Agreements under US and EC Antitrust Law—Convergence or Divergence?' (2006) 51 *Ant Bull* 691.

[9] See e.g. Hawk, ibid.

[10] Since many of the agreements prohibited created or increased competition they should not have required authorisation under Art. 101(3), see e.g. Roemer AG in his Opinion in Cases 56 and 58/64, *Établissements Consten S.à.R.L and Grundig-Verkaufs-GmbH v Commission* EU:C:1966:19.

[11] Ibid. [12] Case 56/65, EU:C:1966:38. [13] Case 258/78, EU:C:1982:211.

[14] Case 27/87, EU:C:1988:183. [15] Case 42/84, EU:C:1985:327. [16] Case 161/84, EU:C:1986:41.

[17] Case 23/67, EU:C:1967:54. [18] Case C-250/92, EU:C:1994:413. [19] Case C-234/89, EU:C:1991:91.

[20] See Section 3.

Section 1 provides that '[e]very contract, combination in the form of a trust or otherwise, or conspiracy, in restraint of trade or commerce among the several States, or with foreign nations, is declared to be illegal . . . ' but contains no legal exception to the prohibition. Since the main objective of a contract is to restrain the conduct of the parties to it, the US Supreme Court soon recognised that a literal interpretation of the section might result in many agreements being held to be illegal.[21] 'Every agreement concerning trade, every regulation of trade, restrains. To bind, to restrain, is of their very essence.'[22] The US courts thus construed the section to mean that contracts must not restrain trade unreasonably.[23] Since the end of the 1970s, the US Supreme Court has held that this constitutes an inquiry into the competitive significance of the restraint.[24]

In determining whether or not an agreement does restrain competition unreasonably, the courts traditionally adopted two categories of analysis—per se and fuller rule of reason.[25] Some agreements, such as naked 'cartel' arrangements among competitors to fix price, restrict output, share markets, or rig bids,[26] are considered to be so likely to be anti-competitive that the court will not waste time or resources requiring that anti-competitive effects must be proved and/or hearing justifications for the agreement, they are illegal per se. This bright-line rule focuses on whether the conduct took place, not on its effect.

> There are certain agreements or practices which because of their pernicious effect on competition and lack of any redeeming virtue are conclusively presumed to be unreasonable and therefore illegal without elaborate inquiries as to the precise harm they have caused or the business excuse for their use.[27]

In the 1960s a relatively large number of restraints were categorised as illegal per se (for the sake of business certainty and litigation efficiency, the courts were prepared to tolerate the invalidation of some agreements that might not have been proved to be unreasonable following a fuller analysis[28]). However, from the end of the 1970s the Supreme Court has gradually retreated from this position. Not only does a rigorous categorisation process now take place before classifying an agreement as illegal per se,[29] but the Court has held that the presumptive and prevailing standard is the 'rule of reason'[30]—the per se rule is reserved for agreements which theory and experience show to have, or almost always have, harmful effects. Under the fuller rule of reason analysis, agreements are not assumed to restrain trade unreasonably but are assessed in their legal and economic context to determine:

> whether the restraint imposed is such as merely regulates and perhaps thereby promotes competition or whether it is such as may suppress or even destroy competition. To determine that question the

[21] But see the approach adopted in *United States v Trans-Missouri Freight Ass'n*, 166 US 290 (1897).

[22] *Chicago Board of Trade v United States*, 246 US 231, 238 (1918), per Brandeis J.

[23] *Standard Oil Co of New Jersey v United States*, 221 US 1 (1911); *United States v American Tobacco Co*, 221 US 106 (1911), but see Chap. 1.

[24] *National Society of Professional Engineers v United States*, 435 US 679 (1978).

[25] As the law has developed, however, the boundary between the two categories has become increasingly blurred so that 'there is often no bright line separating per se from Rule of Reason analysis', *NCAA v Board of Regents of University of Oklahoma*, 468 US 85, 104 (1984). This has led some courts to conclude that there has been a move away from fixed categories to a continuum, *Polygram Holding, Inc v Federal Trade Commission*, 416 F.3d 29, 35 (DC Cir. 2005) and Jones, n. 8.

[26] *United States v Socony-Vacuum Oil Co*, 310 US 150 (1940) and see further Chap. 9.

[27] *Northern Pac R Co v United States*, 356 US 1, 5 (1958).

[28] *Arizona v Maricopa County Medical Society*, 457 US 332, 344 (1982).

[29] *Broadcast Music, Inc (BMI) v Columbia Broadcasting System, Inc*, 441 US 1 (1979), see n. 136 and text.

[30] *Continental TV, Inc v GTE Slyvania Inc*, 433 US 36 (1977).

> court must ordinarily consider the facts peculiar to the business to which the restraint is applied; its condition before and after the restraint was imposed; the nature of the restraint and its effect, actual or probable.[31]

Although a number of different means of applying the fuller rule of reason appraisal now exist, in each case the anti- and pro-competitive effects of the agreement are assessed through a burden-shifting structure and, where both are demonstrated, weighed before an agreement is condemned as illegal (there has thus been a shift away from a dichotomous approach to one based on a continuum).[32]

Not all commentators agreed that EU case law supported an approach identical or similar to the US rule of reason under Article 101(1).[33] Nonetheless, the core message was simple—a more economic approach in tune with the objectives underlying Article 101 was required, especially under Article 101(1).

E. MODERNISATION

(i) Substantive Analysis and Procedural Steps

Eventually, the Commission recognised that the status quo was no longer tenable: the notification system was failing and some change was obligatory. Not only did it set about reformulating its interpretation of Article 101, reviewing and rethinking its analysis over a number of years,[34] but it resolved the procedural problems arising by proposing that its monopoly over Article 101(3) should be revoked. On 1 May 2004, Council Regulation 1/2003 abolished the Commission's exclusive right to rule on the compatibility of an agreement with Article 101(3), paving the way for Article 101(3) to be rendered directly applicable as a legal exception to Article 101(1)[35] by the Commission, the NCAs, and the national courts.[36]

The Commission's current framework for analysis of agreements is set out in its Guidelines on the application of Article 81(3) [now Article 101(3)] of the Treaty (the Article 101(3) Guidelines),[37] which is elucidated further in specific Guidelines dealing with horizontal cooperation, vertical agreements, and technology transfer agreements, respectively.[38] These Guidelines state that consumer welfare should be the benchmark against which agreements are tested under Article 101 and that substantive appraisal should be divided between, and conducted at both, the Article 101(1) and 101(3) stages; a

[31] *Chicago Board of Trade v United States*, 246 US 231, 238 (1918), per Brandeis J.

[32] The rule of reason analysis is not easy to apply in practice and there is limited guidance from the Supreme Court on this issue, but see *Ohio v. American Express Co*, 138 SCt 2274 (2018) and *NCAA v Alston*, 141 SCt 2141 (2021). The circuit courts have developed approaches, tailoring the extent of the inquiry to the suspect conduct in each case, see e.g. *Polygram Holding, Inc v FTC*, 416 F.3d 29, 33–34 (DC Cir. 2005). Few cases, however, actually deal with the question of how competing effects are weighed, see e.g. R. H. Allensworth, 'The Commensurability Myth in Antitrust' (2016) 69(1) *Vand LR* 1 and D. C. Fundakowski, 'The Rule of Reason: From Balancing to Burden Shifting' (2013) 1 *Perspectives in Antitrust* 1.

[33] See e.g. Whish and Sufrin, n. 8.

[34] It reviewed and overhauled the working of Art. 101 between 1996 and 2004. See further Chaps. 9–12.

[35] Reg. 1/2003, Art. 1 provides that agreements which are caught by Art. 101(1) and which do not satisfy the conditions of Art. 101(3) are prohibited, no prior decision to that effect being required. Further that agreements which are caught by Art. 101(1), but which satisfy the conditions of Art. 101(3), are not prohibited, no prior decision to that effect being required.

[36] Reg. 1/2003, Arts. 7–10, 5, and 3. The Commission is seeking to encourage greater 'private' enforcement of EU competition law, see Chap. 14.

[37] See Guidelines on the application of Article 81(3) [now Article 101(3)] of the Treaty (the Article 101(3) Guidelines) [2004] OJ C101/97.

[38] Discussed in Chaps. 9–12.

'rule of reason' style analysis, balancing anti- and pro-competitive should *not* therefore be conducted at the Article 101(1) stage. Rather, Article 101(1) is about identifying restrictions on inter- or intra-brand competition and it is Article 101(3), not Article 101(1), which provides the appropriate forum for weighing the restrictions identified at this stage against the economic benefits and efficiencies created by the agreement.[39] Otherwise, Article 101(3) would be rendered virtually redundant.

Although it will be seen that the EU cases on this issue are difficult to reconcile, some judgments of the GC, including *Métropole Télévision (M6) v Commission*,[40] support the view of the Commission that Article 101(3) provides the main forum for weighing anti- and pro-competitive aspects of an agreement.

M6 concerned an appeal from a Commission decision holding that the creation of the joint venture, Télévision par Satellite (TPS), did not infringe Article 101(1) but that certain clauses in the notified agreements did and could be exempted under Article 101(3) *only* for a period of three years. Amongst other things, the applicants argued that the Commission had been wrong to exempt the clauses. Rather, the reasoning adopted by the Commission indicated that these clauses *favoured* competition and did not restrict it. Had the Commission, therefore, correctly applied Article 101(1) using the rule of reason, weighing the pro- and anti-competitive effects of the agreement, the Commission should have found that the agreement did not restrict competition.[41]

The GC did not accept the parties' argument, observing that, contrary to the applicants' assertions, the existence of such a rule had not been confirmed by the EU Courts. Echoing the view of the Commission, that such an interpretation would be difficult to reconcile with the rules prescribed by Article 101, it stated that Article 101(3) provided the correct forum for weighing the pro- and anti-competitive aspects of the agreement. The Court recognised that some EU cases, such as *STM*,[42] favoured a 'more flexible' interpretation of the Article 101(1) prohibition,[43] but held that they did not establish the existence of a rule of reason. Rather, such a rule had not been confirmed by the Courts and the cases simply formed part of a broader trend in the case law according to which it is not necessary to hold, wholly abstractly, that any agreement restricting the freedom of action of one or more of the parties is necessarily caught by Article 101(1).[44]

Case T-112/99, *Métropole Télévision (M6) v Commission* EU:T:2001:215

General Court

72. According to the applicants, as a consequence of the existence of a rule of reason in [EU] competition law, when Article [101(1)] is applied it is necessary to weigh the pro and anti-competitive effects of an agreement in order to determine whether it is caught by the prohibition laid down in that article.

[39] See White Paper on the Modernisation of the Rules Implementing Articles 85 and 86 of the EC Treaty [now Articles 101 and 102 TFEU] [1999] OJ C132/1, paras. 56–57.

[40] Case T-112/99, *Métropole Télévision SA (M6) v Commission* EU:T:2001:215. See also Case T-65/98, *Van den Bergh Foods* EU:T:2003:281, *aff'd* Case C-552/03 P, *Unilever Bestfoods v Commission* EU:C:2006:607; Case T-328/03, *O2 (Germany) GmbH & Co OHG v Commission* EU:T:2006:116.

[41] Case T-112/99, *M6* ibid., para. 69.

[42] Case 56/65, EU:C:1966:38, 249. See also Case 258/78, *Nungesser and Eisele v Commission* EU:C:1982:211; Case 161/84, *Pronuptia de Paris GmbH v Pronuptia de Paris Irmgard Schillgallis* EU:C:1986:41; Cases T-374, 375, 384, and 388/94, *European Night Services v Commission* EU:T:1998:198; and Case C-250/92, *Gøttrup-Klim Grovvareforening and Others v Dansk Landbrugs Grovvareselskab AmbA* EU:C:1994:413, paras. 31–35.

[43] Case T-112/99, *M6* EU:T:2001:215, para. 75.

[44] For the argument (rejected) that Art. 101(1) could not apply as the agreement did *not* restrain the freedom of action of one of the parties to the agreement, see discussion of Case C-194/14 P, *AC-Treuhand AG* EU:C:2015:717 in Chap. 4.

It should, however, be observed, first of all, that contrary to the applicants' assertions the existence of such a rule has not, as such, been confirmed by the [EU] courts. Quite to the contrary, in various judgments the Court of Justice and the [GC] have been at pains to indicate that the existence of a rule of reason in [EU] competition law is doubtful (see Case C-235/92 P *Montecatini v Commission* . . . paragraph 133 (. . . even if the rule of reason did have a place in the context of Article [101(1)]of the Treaty), and Case T-14/89 *Montedipe v Commission* . . . paragraph 265, and in Case T-148/89 *Tréfilunion v Commission* . . . paragraph 109).

73. Next, it must be observed that an interpretation of Article [101(1)], in the form suggested by the applicants, is difficult to reconcile with the rules prescribed by that provision.

74. Article [101] expressly provides, in its third paragraph, for the possibility of exempting agreements that restrict competition where they satisfy a number of conditions, in particular where they are indispensable to the attainment of certain objectives and do not afford undertakings the possibility of eliminating competition in respect of a substantial part of the products in question. It is only in the precise framework of that provision that the pro and anti-competitive aspects of a restriction may be weighed (see, to that effect, Case 161/84 *Pronuptia* . . . paragraph 24, and Case T-17/93 *Matra Hachette v Commission* . . . paragraph 48, and *European Night Services and Others v Commission* . . . paragraph 136). Article [101(3)] would lose much of its effectiveness if such an examination had to be carried out already under Article [101(1)].

75. It is true that in a number of judgments the Court of Justice and the [GC] have favoured a more flexible interpretation of the prohibition laid down in Article [101(1)] (see, in particular, *Société technique minière* and *Oude Luttikhuis and Others* . . . *Nungesser and Eisele v Commission* and *Coditel and Others* . . . *Pronuptia* . . . and *European Night Services and Others v Commission* . . . as well as the judgment in Case C-250/92 *DLG* . . . paragraphs 31 to 35).

76. Those judgments cannot, however, be interpreted as establishing the existence of a rule of reason in [EU] competition law. They are, rather, part of a broader trend in the case-law according to which it is not necessary to hold, wholly abstractly and without drawing any distinction, that any agreement restricting the freedom of action of one or more of the parties is necessarily caught by the prohibition laid down in Article [101(1)]. In assessing the applicability of Article [101(1)] to an agreement, account should be taken of the actual conditions in which it functions, in particular the economic context in which the undertakings operate, the products or services covered by the agreement and the actual structure of the market concerned (see, in particular, *European Night Services and Others v Commission* . . . paragraph 136, *Oude Luttikhuis* . . . paragraph 10, and *VGB and Others v Commission* . . . paragraph 140, as well as the judgment in Case C-234/89 *Delimitis* . . . paragraph 31).

77. That interpretation, while observing the substantive scheme of Article [101] and, in particular, preserving the effectiveness of Article [101(3)], makes it possible to prevent the prohibition in Article [101(1)] from extending wholly abstractly and without distinction to all agreements whose effect is to restrict the freedom of action of one or more of the parties. It must, however, be emphasised that such an approach does not mean that it is necessary to weigh the pro and anti-competitive effects of an agreement when determining whether the prohibition laid down in Article [101(1)] applies.

In *M6*, the GC appears, therefore, to reject both the first two of the possible approaches set out in Section 2.B and to favour the third (one which divides the substantive appraisal between Article 101(1) and 101(3)).

This supposition leads to two further questions. Was the GC correct to interpret previous case law this way? If so, exactly how is the envisaged division in analysis made in practice: in particular, what constitutes a restriction of competition for the purpose of Article 101(1) and what 'pro-competitive' 'aspects of a restriction' can be weighed against them under Article 101(3)? In seeking to answer these questions, the discussion in Sections 3 and 4 indicates that, unfortunately, the position does not seem to be quite as clear as the GC in *M6* suggests.

(ii) Identifying Anti-competitive Agreements: Clear Rules or More Complex Standards?

Even if it is correct that the goal of Article 101 is to identify agreements that harm consumer welfare and that the analysis should be divided between Article 101(1) and Article 101(3), it still leaves the conundrum of how exactly this is to be done. How can rules or standards to identify such conduct be constructed which can be applied in a timely manner and at minimum cost and which will be both sufficiently:

(a) clear—so as to enable firms to comply with them and courts or other decision-makers to administer them; and

(b) accurate—identifying and prohibiting conduct which harms the objectives of the Article whilst permitting those that may promote competition?

Although at first sight it might appear necessary to ensure accuracy that in each individual case actual or likely anti-competitive effects should be rigorously assessed under Article 101(1) and balanced under Article 101(3) against any pro-competitive benefits raised, such an approach is likely to impose too high a burden on firms (especially small ones), competition agencies (and other claimants), and courts, creating a risk both that pro-competitive agreements will be deterred and too little enforcement/condemnation of harmful agreements will occur.

Most competition systems thus accept that a trade-off needs to be made between the application of more complex standards, requiring detailed economic analysis of an agreement in the context in which it occurs, which are more difficult and costly to apply, and simpler bright-line rules prohibiting or exonerating specific arrangements, which may be less accurate but which are easier and less costly to apply (they require less sophisticated analysis and less emphasis on expert economic evidence) and which provide greater clarity and legal certainty (and in the case of prohibitory rules, a patent deterrent to the practice at issue).[45] The difference between rules and standards is a matter of degree, and the line between them can be fine. In seeking to balance accuracy (based on widely accepted economic principles), consistency, predictability, administrability, timeliness, and cost minimisation,[46] competition law systems frequently utilise a continuum of tests—a mix of rules, standards, and hybrid approaches in between—to identify anti-competitive agreements. For example, categorical rules that condemn[47] or exculpate certain conduct; standards that test conduct with a more complex, multi-faceted analysis of the restrictive and pro-competitive effects of each agreement, accounting for the context in which the behaviour took place and the situation that would occur without the agreement; and/or intermediate types of analysis developed, such as a rule which requires the weighing or balancing of certain factors before it is applied, the application of rebuttable presumptions of legality or illegality, or a structured standard which requires a series of specified factors to be taken into account.

[45] See A. Jones and W. E. Kovacic, 'Identifying Anticompetitive Agreements in the United States and the European Union: Developing a Coherent Antitrust Analytical Framework' (2017) 62(2) *Ant Bull* 254.

[46] See e.g. OECD Policy Roundtables: Resale Price Maintenance (2008), <www.oecd.org/daf/competition/43835526.pdf>.

[47] These may arguably be favoured by competition agencies, concerned about their reputation and public image, see Y. Katsoulacos, S. Avdasheva, and S. Golovanova, 'Legal Standards and the Role of Economics in Competition Law Enforcement' (2016) 12 *European Competition Journal* 277.

In relation to agreements, this may mean that different degrees of analysis are required depending on the degree of risk to competition that they pose. For example, a number of jurisdictions:

- apply rules against agreements which are very likely to cause anti-competitive effects and unlikely to have offsetting benefits (such agreements may be prohibited per se (as in the US) or *presumed* to be incompatible with the competition law rules);
- apply rules in favour of agreements which are very unlikely to cause anti-competitive effects—in some systems, such agreements may benefit from a safe harbour or a presumption of compatibility with the rules; and
- reserve more detailed and complex analysis in relation to agreements whose effects are more ambiguous—which require closer individual scrutiny of anti-competitive and pro-competitive effects.

The question of how any such categories are to be drawn, how flexibly they are applied, and which agreements fall within each category is generally controversial. Where courts conclude that antitrust chiefly seeks to promote economic efficiency, economics will guide the answer to these questions[48] (here a central focus of analysis is to assess how likely it is that the conduct at issue will permit the relevant firm(s) to exercise market power and interfere with the competitive process, and deny consumers the products and/or services which offer the best value for money). It may also be necessary to consider whether an approach which may sometimes condemn legitimate business practices (false positives or 'Type 1' errors) and so potentially chill pro-competitive conduct, is a lesser or greater evil than one which may sometimes allow anti-competitive practices to escape antitrust prohibitions (false negatives or 'Type 2' errors).[49]

In the EU, the Treaty itself supports the use of different degrees of competition analysis, as it distinguishes between agreements that are restrictive by object and restrictive by effect and envisions the use of group, or block, exemptions. Four different types of analysis have developed in the assessment of agreements (see further Fig. 5.1):

(a) agreements found to have as their object the restriction of competition are assumed to restrict competition appreciably within the meaning of Article 101(1). Such agreements are not illegal per se, as they are justifiable under Article 101(3). In practice, however, the object category has close parallels with the per se rule in the US. The Commission has developed a view that such restraints are presumed *not* to satisfy the conditions of Article 101(3)—it equates them with 'hardcore' restraints which preclude the safe harbour of a block exemption from applying (see point (c)) and make it most unlikely that the agreement will individually satisfy the Article 101(3) criteria.[50] 'It is the low potential and/or likelihood of creating efficiencies that justifies applying the two negative presumptions to agreements containing by object restrictions.'[51] As guidance

[48] Economic decision theory has frequently been used to explain how and when rules or standards should be applied, see especially I. Ehrlich and R. A. Posner, 'An Economic Analysis of Rulemaking' (1974) 3 *J Legal Stud* 257 and more recently e.g. S. Salop, 'An Enquiry Meet for the Case: Decision Theory, Presumptions, and Evidentiary Burdens in Formulating Antitrust Legal Standards' (2017) *Scholarship@Georgetown Law.*

[49] See Chap. 1 and R. A. Woodcock, 'Per Se In Itself: How Bans Reduce Error in Antitrust' (2017), <https://ssrn.com/abstract=2896453> (concluding that a strong per se rule is an essential component of error cost minimization for those who believe that possible under-enforcement harm is large).

[50] It considers agreements of this nature (a) generally fail to create objective economic benefits, (b) do not benefit consumers, and/or (c) are unlikely to be considered indispensable to the attainment of any efficiencies created by the agreement in question (efficiencies generated can generally be achieved by less restrictive means), see e.g. Art. 101(3) Guidelines, paras. 46, 79, 105 and L. Peeperkorn, 'Coherence in the Application of Articles 101 and 102: A Realistic Prospect or an Elusive Goal?' (2016) 39(3) *World Competition* 389, 398–400.

[51] Peeperkorn, ibid., 400.

as to when agreements found to restrict competition by object may satisfy the four onerous conditions of Article 101(3) is sparse (and unlikely to emerge),[52] and there is a risk of fines being imposed on parties to such agreements, firms generally perceive this conduct to be prohibited or at least extremely risky to pursue;

(b) agreements between undertaking which have a weak position on the market fall outside the scope of Article 101(1) where they do not have a significant, or appreciable, effect on competition;

(c) agreements between undertakings which satisfy conditions set out in an EU block exemption are assumed to satisfy the conditions of Article 101(3) and to be compatible with Article 101. The block exemptions operate as a safe harbour for agreements and their benefit can only be withdrawn prospectively;

(d) other agreements are analysed individually to determine whether they have as their effect the restriction of competition (Article 101(1)) and, if so, whether the agreement satisfies the four conditions of Article 101(3).

The question of determining how a particular agreement is to be assessed is explored in the remainder of this chapter and subsequently in Chapters 9–12.

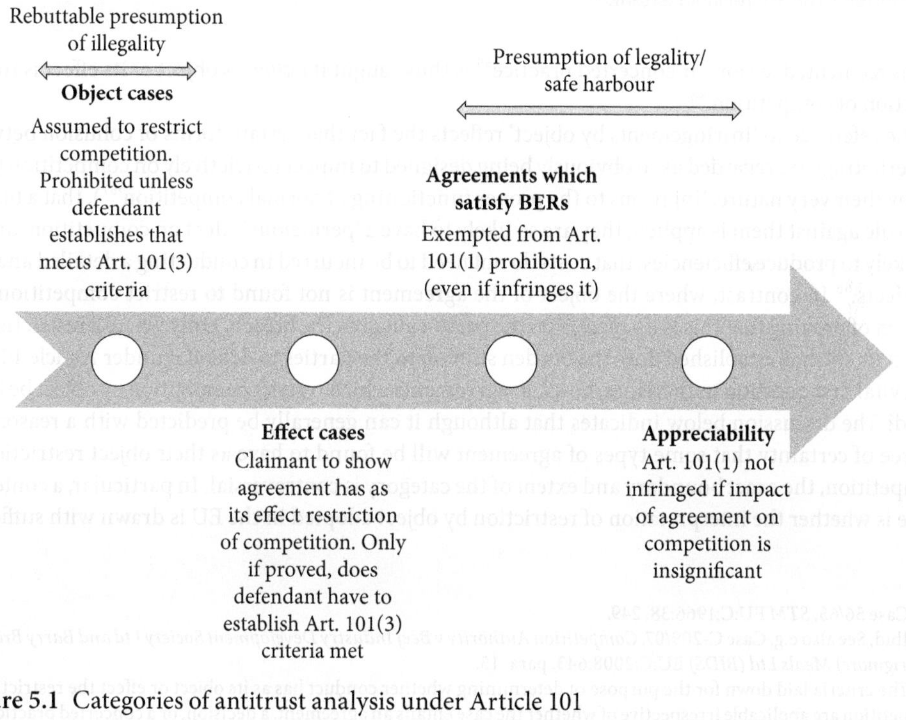

Figure 5.1 Categories of antitrust analysis under Article 101

[52] Indeed, most cases pursued by the Commission under Art. 101 have been object cases and it seems improbable that the Commission will wish, or be able, to dedicate resources to adopting this kind of decision (NCAs are not permitted to adopt non-infringement decisions (see Case C-375/09, *Tele2Polska* EU:C:2011:270)). In practice, competition agencies may be more likely to deal with object restraints that they consider to be 'unproblematic' from a competition perspective by deciding not to prioritise them for enforcement.

3. ARTICLE 101(1), AGREEMENTS WHICH HAVE AS THEIR OBJECT OR EFFECT THE PREVENTION, RESTRICTION, OR DISTORTION OF COMPETITION

A. OBJECT OR EFFECT

In *STM*,[53] the CJ clarified that the words 'object or effect' in Article 101(1) are not cumulative but are alternative conditions.

> [F]or the agreement at issue to be caught by the prohibition contained in Article [101(1)] it must have as its 'object or effect the prevention, restriction or distortion of competition . . .'.
>
> The fact that these are not cumulative but alternative requirements, indicated by the conjunction 'or', leads first to the need to consider the precise purpose of the agreement, in the economic context in which it is to be applied. This interference with competition referred to in Article [101(1)] must result from all or some of the clauses of the agreement itself. Where, however, an analysis of the said clauses does not reveal the effect on competition to be sufficiently deleterious, the consequences of the agreement should then be considered and for it to be caught by the prohibition it is then necessary to find that those factors are present which show that competition has in fact been prevented or restricted or distorted to an appreciable extent.[54]

An agreement, decision, or concerted practice[55] is thus caught if *either* its object *or* its effect is the restriction of competition.[56]

The reference to 'infringements by object' reflects the fact that certain forms of collusion between undertakings are regarded as so obviously being designed to impact restrictively on competition (they are by their very nature, 'injurious to the proper functioning of normal competition'[57]), that a bright-line rule against them is applied; they are so likely to have a 'pernicious' effect on competition, and so unlikely to produce efficiencies, that costs do not need to be incurred in conducting a detailed analysis of effects.[58] In contrast, where the object of the agreement is not found to restrict competition, the burden of proving that this is its *effect* is on the person alleging the breach. Only where a restriction by object or effect is established does the burden shift on to the parties to defend it under Article 101(3).

A vital first question is, therefore, how can agreements which restrict competition by object be identified? The discussion below indicates that although it can generally be predicted with a reasonable degree of certainty that some types of agreement will be found to have as their object restriction of competition, the exact boundary and extent of the category is controversial. In particular, a contested issue is whether the interpretation of restriction by object adopted in the EU is drawn with sufficient

[53] Case 56/65, *STM* EU:C:1966:38, 249.

[54] Ibid. See also e.g. Case C-209/07, *Competition Authority v Beef Industry Development Society Ltd and Barry Brothers (Carrigmore) Meals Ltd (BIDS)* EU:C:2008:643, para. 15.

[55] The criteria laid down for the purpose of determining whether conduct has as its object or effect the restriction of competition are applicable irrespective of whether the case entails an agreement, a decision, or a concerted practice, see Case C-8/08, *T-Mobile* EU:C:2009:343.

[56] Case 56/65, *STM* EU:C:1966:38, 249. See also Case C-234/89, *Delimitis v Henninger Bräu* EU:C:1991:91, para. 13 and Cases T-374, 375, 384, and 388/94, *European Night Services v Commission* EU:T:1998:198, para. 136. In Case C-228/18, *Gazdasági Versenyhivatal v Budapest Bank Nyrt and others (Budapest Bank)*, EU:C:2020:265, the CJ held that an agreement can have as its object and effect the restriction of competition as long as each are established separately (although a finding of a restriction of competition by object relieves the competent authority or court of the need to examine the effects of that restriction, it does not mean that the authority or court cannot make such an examination).

[57] Case C-209/07, *BIDS* EU:C:2008:643, para. 17.

[58] See Case C-8/08, *T-Mobile* EU:C:2009:110, Kokott AG, para. 43. The approach has some similarities to the rule of per se illegality adopted in the US, but see n. 50 and text.

clarity and in accordance with the objectives underpinning the rules and so as to yield minimal error costs and to preclude the application of an over-inclusive presumption of illegality.[59]

B. AGREEMENTS THAT RESTRICT COMPETITION BY OBJECT: RESTRAINTS WHICH REVEAL A SUFFICIENTLY DELETERIOUS IMPACT ON COMPETITION

(i) Identifying Restrictions by Object—Content, Objectives, and Context

In *STM*,[60] the CJ held that agreements are restrictive of competition by object where an analysis of the purpose of the agreement, taking account of its clauses and the economic context in which it operates, reveals a sufficiently deleterious impact on competition; the category encompasses coordination revealing 'in itself a sufficient degree of harm to competition law'.[61]

In accordance with *STM*, case law consistently reiterates that to identify agreements incorporating object restrictions, 'regard must be had inter alia to the content of its provisions, the objectives it seeks to ascertain and the economic and legal context of which it forms part'.[62] It is the case law of the EU Courts, therefore (rather than the Treaty itself[63]), which sheds light on the question of which clauses are likely to be problematic and how much analysis of the clauses in the context in which they are operated is required.[64]

When assessing the objective or purpose of the agreement, closer regard in the cases is 'paid to the wording of its provision and to the objectives which it is intended to attain'[65] than to the subjective intention of the parties. Although the parties' intention is not a necessary condition to a finding of a restrictive purpose, it can be taken into account, for example to corroborate or supplement the finding of an anti-competitive aim:[66]

> [T]he anti-competitive object of an agreement may be deduced not only from the content of its clauses but also from the intention of the parties as it arises from the 'genesis' of the agreement and/or manifests itself in the 'circumstances in which it was implemented' and in the 'conduct' of the companies concerned.[67]

[59] See Case C-67/13 P, *Groupement des Cartes Bancaires (CB) v Commission* EU:C:2014:2204, Wahl AG.

[60] Case 56/65, *STM* EU:C:1966:38, 249.

[61] Case C-67/13P, *CB* EU:C:2014:2204, para. 57. See generally e.g. A. Jones, 'Left Behind by Modernisation? Restrictions by Object under Article 101(1)' (2010) 6 *European Competition Journal* 649; L. Peeperkorn, 'Defining "By Object" Restrictions' [2015] 3 *Concurrences* 40; and P. Ibáñez Colomo and A. Lamadrid, 'On the Notion of Restriction of Competition: What we Know and What We Don't Know we Know' in D. Gerard, M. Merola, and B. Meyring (eds.), *The Notion of Restriction of Competition: Revisiting the Foundations of Antitrust Enforcement in Europe* (Bruylant, 2017).

[62] Case C-501/06 P, *GlaxoSmithKline Services Unlimited (GSK) v Commission* EU:C:2009:610, para. 58.

[63] Although in Case C-8/08, *T-Mobile* EU:C:2009:343, para. 37 the CJ held that 'it is apparent from Article [101(1)(a)] that concerted practices may have an anti-competitive object if they "directly or indirectly fix purchase or selling prices or any other trading conditions"' it has never been suggested that tying or price discrimination (listed in Art. 101 (1)(c) and (d)) should be restrictive by object. See also MEMO/14/440, 25 June 2014, Commission's Staff Working Document, Guidance on restrictions of competition 'by object' for the purposes of defining which agreements may benefit from the *De Minimis* Notice, SWD(2014) 198 final.

[64] Object categorisation is not affected by the fact that an undertaking adversely affected and complaining about the agreement is operating illegally on the relevant market: Case C-68/12, *Protimonopolný úrad Slovenskej republiky v Slovenská sporitelňa a.s.* EU:C:2013:71, paras. 14–21.

[65] Case C-209/07, *BIDS* EU:C:2008:643, para. 21.

[66] See e.g. Case C-8/08, *T-Mobile* EU:C:2009:343, para. 27, Case 96/82, *IAZ International Belgium v Commission* EU:C:1983:310, paras. 23–25 and Saugmandsgaard Øe AG in Case C-279/16, *F Hoffmann-La Roche and Novartis* EU C:2017:714.

[67] COMP/40.208, *International Skating Union Eligibility Rules (ISU)* 8 December 2017, para. 156, on appeal the GC found there was no need to rule on the applicants' arguments concerning the Commission's conclusions relating to intention as the existence of a restriction of competition had been sufficiently substantiated by the examination of content, objectives of the eligibility rules, and their context, Case T-93/18, EU:T:2020:610, para. 121, Case C-124/21 P, judgment pending.

In addition, the fact that the parties did not intend to restrict competition and infringe Article 101 cannot be relied upon to exculpate restrictive conduct. In *Competition Authority v Beef Industry Development Society Ltd (BIDS)*,[68] for example, the CJ rejected the parties' argument that by acting to reduce capacity on the Irish beef market they had not acted with an anti-competitive purpose or an intention to injure competition and the welfare of consumers, but with the intention of rationalising the beef industry and so making it more competitive by reducing, but not eliminating, production overcapacity.

> [T]o determine whether an agreement comes within the prohibition laid down in Article [101(1)], close regard must be paid to the wording of its provisions and to the objectives which it is intended to attain. In that regard, even supposing it to be established that the parties to an agreement acted without any subjective intention of restricting competition, but with the object of remedying the effects of a crisis in their sector, such considerations are irrelevant for the purposes of applying that provision.[69]

The CJ noted this 'type of arrangement conflicts patently with the concept inherent in the [TFEU] provisions relating to competition, according to which each economic operator must determine independently the policy which it intends to adopt on the common market',[70] and indicated clearly that it is not generally legitimate to argue that competition itself is bad and will lead to ruinous or unfair outcomes. In this case, the arrangements were intended to change appreciably the structure of the market through the withdrawal of competitors, and so was principally premised on the basis that competition itself was unsustainable.

(ii) Content—Restrictive Clauses in the Agreement

Although there is no fixed list of object restraints, [71] jurisprudence has, over the years, clarified that agreements containing certain 'established' restrictions have a high potential of being found to pursue a restrictive objective. When identifying whether such restraints have been incorporated into an agreement, it may be necessary to consider the behaviour of the parties as the way in which the parties behave or in which 'an agreement is actually implemented may reveal a restriction of competition by object even where the formal agreement does not contain an express provision to that effect'.[72]

In particular, horizontal arrangements between actual or potential competitors are liable to restrict competition by object if they:

(a) fix prices, limit output, share markets (see *European Night Services v Commission*[73] and *Toshiba Corporation v Commission*[74]) or rig bids;
(b) reduce capacity (see *BIDS*[75]);

[68] Case C-209/07, *BIDS* EU:C:2008:643. [69] Ibid., para. 21.

[70] Case C-209/07, *BIDS* EU:C:2008:643, para. 34. An 'agreement may be regarded as having a restrictive object even if it does not have the restriction of competition as its sole aim but also pursues other legitimate objectives . . . It is only in connection with Article [101(3)] that matters such as those relied upon by BIDS may, if appropriate, be taken into consideration for the purposes of obtaining an exemption from the prohibition laid down in Article [101(1)]', para. 21.

[71] See Case C-439/09, *Pierre Fabre* EU:C:2011:649 and Mazák AG in his Opinion in this case, EU:C:2011:113, para. 29 (the fact that the Commission has categorised it as a hardcore restraint does not necessarily mean that it has the object or effect of restricting competition).

[72] Article 101(3) Guidelines, para. 22. See also discussion of agreements and unilateral conduct in Chap. 4.

[73] Cases T-374, 375, 384, and 388/94, EU:T:1998:198, para. 136 and see further Chap. 9.

[74] Case C-373/14 P, EU:C:2016:26 (rejecting the argument raised that as the parties to the alleged market-sharing agreement operated in different geographic markets, they were not actual or potential competitors, so the agreement was not restrictive of competition by object, see nn. 120 and 126 and text).

[75] Case C-209/07, EU:C:2008:643.

(c) are designed, directly or indirectly, to fix purchase or selling prices through exchanges of information (see *T-Mobile Netherlands BV v Raad van bestuur van de Nederlandse Mededingingsautoriteit*);[76] and/or

(d) boycott a competitor (collective exclusive dealing).[77]

As there is broad international acceptance that '*naked*' cartel activity (secret agreements between competitors which seek to constrain competition without producing any objective countervailing benefits) poses a serious threat to economies and consumers,[78] an assumption that, in principle, horizontal agreements to fix prices, reduce output, or share markets are liable to restrict competition is justified. Parties to cartels deliberately set out to interfere with fundamental parameters of competition, to contradict the principles of the free market economy, and to act instead to protect the prosperity of the participants as a whole. In *Groupement des Cartes Bancaires (CB) v Commission*,[79] the CJ recognised that since horizontal price-fixing by cartels, are 'so likely to have negative effects, in particular on the price, quantity or quality of the goods and services, . . . it may be considered redundant, for the purposes of applying Article [101(1)], to prove that they have actual effects on the market . . . '[80]

The extent to which the object category should be utilised more broadly than this, however, is contentious (especially given the difficulty of justifying restrictions of object under Article 101(3)). One controversy in the EU is that it has consistently been held that certain restraints in vertical agreements constitute, in principle, restrictions by object even though they are not made between competitors, but between providers of complementary goods and services, and may provide scope for efficiencies, for example arrangements:[81]

(a) involving vertical price-fixing (resale price maintenance);[82] and

(b) conferring absolute territorial protection (ATP) on a distributor or otherwise aimed at partitioning national markets according to national borders or limiting parallel trade;[83] and (arguably)

(c) certain selective distribution agreements.[84]

These cases are explored in greater detail in Chapter 11. However, a few comments are made about the cases governing ATP here. Ever since *Consten and Grundig*[85] in 1966, it has been held that distribution agreements which provide a distributor with an exclusive sales territory and protection from

[76] Case C-8/08, EU:C:2009:343, paras. 36–43.

[77] See COMP/33.884, *Nederlandse Federatieve Vereniging voor de Groothandel op Elektrotechnisch Gebied and Technische Unie* [2000] OJ L39/1 (collective exclusive dealing arrangements by association intended to prevent supplies to undertakings not belonging to that association, *aff'd* Cases T-5 and 6/00, *Nederlandse Federatieve Vereniging voor de Groothandel op Elektrotechnisch Gebied v Commission* EU:T:2003:342 and Case C-105/04 P, EU:C:2006:592), Case C-68/12, *Protimonopolný* EU:C:2013:71 and Staff Working Document, n. 63, 2.5.

[78] See Chap. 9. [79] Case C-67/13 P, EU:C:2014:2204. [80] Ibid., para. 51.

[81] Restrictions in intellectual property licensing agreements (between non-competitors) on the determination of prices for the licensed products or providing ATP for the licensee, also ordinarily have as their *object* the restriction of competition within the meaning of Art. 101(1), see Chap. 12 and e.g. Cases C-403 and 429/08, *Football Association Premier League Ltd and Others v QC Leisure and Others and Karen Murphy v Media Protection Services Ltd (Murphy)* EU:C:2011:631 (contrast e.g. Case 62/79, *Coditel v Ciné Vog Films (Coditel I)* EU:C:1980:84).

[82] See e.g. Case 26/76, *Metro-SB-Grossmärkte GmbH v Commission (Metro I)* EU:C:1977:167 and Chap. 11. See also Case C-211/22, *Super Bock Bebidas* (judgment pending).

[83] See especially Cases 56 and 58/64, *Consten and Grundig* EU:C:1966:41.

[84] Case C-439/09, *Pierre Fabre v Président de l'Autorité de la concurrence* EU:C:2011:649 but see Case C-230/16, *Coty* EU:C:2017:941 and Chap. 11.

[85] Cases 56 and 58/64, EU:C:1966:41. It has been reiterated in a series of cases since then, see e.g. Case C-501/06 P, *GSK* EU:C:2009:610, para. 61 and Chap. 11.

sales by others within the territory (creating ATP) are liable to have as their object the restriction of competition. This case (examined in Chapter 4) concerned an exclusive distribution agreement concluded between Grundig, a German manufacturer of electronic products, and Consten, imposing obligations on Consten but granting Consten ATP. To reinforce Consten's territorial protection Grundig assigned to Consten the rights to the Grundig trademark, GINT, in France. The Commission held that the agreement was designed to restrict competition and an exemption was refused. The exclusive contract and ancillary arrangements (in particular, in relation to the trademark) had the object of relieving Consten of the competition of other undertakings insofar as it involved the import or wholesale trade in Grundig products in France.

The parties appealed, challenging the Commission's decision on several grounds. In particular, they vigorously denied that the arrangements restricted competition and complained that the Commission had erred in its application of Article 101(1) since it had failed to base itself on the 'rule of reason'. Broadly, their argument hinged on the fact that the provisions had been essential to enable Grundig to penetrate the French market. The Commission had wrongly considered the transaction with hindsight, *ex post*, when matters had turned out well. If, however, it had taken account of the market at the time that the agreement was entered into, *ex ante*, when matters looked risky and uncertain, it would have been apparent that the exclusivity was crucial to encourage the distributor to take on an uncertain new venture and invest resources in promoting the new product on the French market. Such a distributor would have to persuade French consumers to purchase Grundig products instead of other competing brands of electrical products available and established on the French market and would have demanded that other distributors be prevented from taking a 'free ride'[86] on its promotional and investment efforts by importing the products more cheaply from Germany[87] (this was, in fact, exactly what UNEF, a Parisian company, and Leissner in Strasbourg had done).

The parties thus argued that despite the fact that the agreement resulted in the existence of only one distributor of Grundig products in France (there was a restriction on *intra-brand competition*), the agreement led to an increase in competition for electrical products in France (there was an increase in *inter-brand competition*). French consumers wishing to purchase such products now also had the option to purchase Grundig products in addition to those of the other manufacturers on the market. Consequently, the Commission should instead have considered the effects of the disputed contract upon competition between Grundig and its competitors' products.

The notion that the Commission's decision should have been marked with greater market analysis was supported by Advocate-General Roemer[88] who agreed that Article 101(1) required a consideration of the effects of the agreement on the market. This could not be established without looking at the market *in concreto* and without taking account of competition between similar products and making a comparison between two market situations: that after making the agreement and that which would have arisen had there been no agreement. If Grundig would not have found an outlet for its products in the absence of supplying a sole concessionaire, the exclusive distribution agreement clearly promoted competition and Article 101(1) should not be applied. It would have been necessary for Grundig to gain access to or penetrate the new market.

In this case, the CJ did not agree with its Advocate-General but upheld the Commission's decision.[89] It held that as the agreement giving Consten a monopoly over the sale of Grundig products in France (ATP) had as its *object* the restriction of competition, an assessment of its *effect* was unnecessary.

[86] For a more detailed discussion of the free-rider arguments, see Chap. 11.
[87] The German distributors would not have to engage in such high levels of promotion and investment.
[88] Cases 56 and 58/64, *Consten and Grundig* EU:C:1966:41. [89] Ibid.

Cases 56 and 58/64, *Établissements Consten SàRL and Grundig-Verkaufs-GmbH v Commission* EU:C:1966:41, 342–343

Court of Justice

The complaints concerning the criterion of restriction on competition

The applicants and the German Government maintain that since the Commission restricted its examination solely to Grundig products the decision was based upon a false concept of competition and of the rules on prohibition contained in Article [101(1)], since this concept applies particularly to competition between similar products of different makes; the Commission, before declaring Article [101(1)] to be applicable, should, by basing itself upon the 'rule of reason', have considered the economic effects of the disputed contract upon competition between the different makes. There is a presumption that vertical sole distributorship agreements are not harmful to competition and in the present case there is nothing to invalidate that presumption. On the contrary, the contract in question has increased the competition between similar products of different makes. The principle of freedom of competition concerns the various stages and manifestations of competition. Although competition between producers is generally more noticeable than that between distributors of products of the same make, it does not thereby follow that an agreement tending to restrict the latter kind of competition should escape the prohibition of Article [101(1)] merely because it might increase the former.

Besides, for the purpose of applying Article [101(1)], there is no need to take account of the concrete effects of an agreement once it appears that it has as its object the prevention, restriction or distortion of competition.

Therefore the absence in the contested decision of any analysis of the effects of the agreement on competition between similar products of different makes does not, of itself, constitute a defect in the decision.

It thus remains to consider whether the contested decision was right in founding the prohibition of the disputed agreement under Article [101(1)] on the restriction on competition created by the agreement in the sphere of the distribution of Grundig products alone. The infringement which was found to exist by the contested decision results from the absolute territorial protection created [by] the said contract in favour of Consten on the basis of French law. The applicants thus wished to eliminate any possibility of competition at the wholesale level in Grundig products in the territory specified in the contra[c]t essentially by two methods.

First, Grundig undertook not to deliver even indirectly to third parties products intended for the area covered by the contract. The restrictive nature of that undertaking is obvious if it is considered in the light of the prohibition on exporting which was imposed not only on Consten but also on all the other sole concessionnaires [*sic*] of Grundig, as well as the German wholesalers.

Secondly, the registration in France by Consten of the GINT trademark, which Grundig affixes to all its products, is intended to increase the protection inherent in the disputed agreement, against the risk of parallel imports into France of Grundig products, by adding the protection deriving from the law on industrial property rights. Thus no third party could import Grundig products from other Member States of the [Union] for resale in France without running serious risks.

The defendant properly took into account the whole distribution system thus set up by Grundig. In order to arrive at a true representation of the contractual position, the contract must be placed in the economic and legal context in the light of which it was concluded by the parties. Such a procedure is not to be regarded as an unwarrantable interference in legal transactions or circumstances which were not the subject of the proceedings before the Commission.

The situation as ascertained above results in the isolation of the French market and makes it possible to charge for the products in question prices which are sheltered from all effective competition. In addition, the more producers succeed in their efforts to render their own makes of product individually distinct in the eyes of the consumer, the more the effectiveness of competition between producers tend[s] to diminish. Because of the considerable impact of distribution costs on the aggregate cost price, it seems important that competition between dealers should also be stimulated. The efforts of the dealer are stimulated by competition between distributors of products of the same make. Since the agreement thus aims at isolating the French market for Grundig products and maintaining artificially, for products of a very well-known brand, separate national markets within the [EU], it is therefore such as to distort competition in the Common Market.

It was therefore proper for the contested decision to hold that the agreement constitutes an infringement of Article [101(1)]. No further considerations, whether of economic data (price differences between France and Germany, representative character of the type of appliance considered, level of overheads borne by Consten) or of the corrections of the criteria upon which the Commission relied in its comparisons between the situations of the French and German markets, and no possible favourable effects of the agreement in other respects, can in any way lead, in the face of above-mentioned restrictions, to a different solution under Article [101(1)].

In its judgment, the CJ, although recognising the importance of competition between producers (inter-brand competition), held that agreements which restricted competition between distributors (intra-brand competition) could also restrict competition for the purposes of Article 101(1). It was important that competition between dealers should be stimulated, and intra-brand as well as inter-brand competition maintained. In particular, restrictions on intra-brand competition might facilitate brand differentiation and diminish competition between producers. The agreement in question eliminated any possibility of competition between distributors of Grundig products and led to the isolation of the French market and so distorted competition and infringed Article 101(1). The Commission had not, therefore, erred by failing to consider the effects of the agreement for the purposes of Article 101(1).

There seems little doubt that the Court in *Consten and Grundig* was concerned not only about the agreement's impact on competition but also by its effects from the internal market perspective. Whatever the economic justifications for the agreement, the affront in this case to the market integration goal, through the erection of barriers to cross-border trade, was too severe.[90] Arguably, it was this 'higher' factor that played a central part in the categorisation of the agreement. The object of the agreement was to grant ATP, to isolate the French market, and shelter the French distributor from all effective (intra-brand) competition. The Court sent out a clear message: agreements which divide up the internal market and re-erect barriers to trade in the contract product will not be tolerated.

G. Amato, *Antitrust and the Bounds of Power* (Hart Publishing, 1997), 48–49

In the leading case in this area, *Consten and Grundig*, of 1966 . . . the Commission challenged the exclusive agreement for France that Grundig had given to Consten and had strengthened by barring its wholesale distributors in Germany and other countries from selling to France, where the price of Grundig products was kept higher than elsewhere, net of French tax. The parties maintained, first before the Commission itself and then before the Court of Justice, that Article [101] referred primarily to inter-brand competition, and that as far as intra-brand restrictions went, one had to presume efficiency in promoting inter-brand competition failing proof of the contrary. This argument copied word-for-word

90 See Chap. 1.

approaches of the Chicago School, which in fact at the time the American courts themselves had rejected, in the name of protection (dropped later in the *Sylvania* case) for the right of each distributor or retailer to exercise freedom of trade without restraint. Our court did not accept the arguments either, but for very different reasons. It accepted that inter-brand competition was the most relevant for the purposes of prohibition under Article [101], but added that this did not *a priori* exempt intra-brand restrictions, with the consequence—inconceivable today (and perhaps in earlier times too) for an American court—that the fact that the Commission was not concerned to ascertain the size of inter-brand competition was irrelevant. On this basis, the absolute territorial protection by which the exclusivity for France was guaranteed was illegitimate. It is indeed true, said the Court, that imports have an effect on the supply planning that Consten may engage in and on the organization of services it may offer customers. But a margin of risk is inherent in commercial activity, and in any case 'the more manufacturers isolate themselves from each other in consumers' eyes, the more competition among them is reduced. Moreover, competition among wholesale distributors of products of one and the same brand enlivens the downstream market of sales to final consumers'.

As we can see, these are very important assertions of principle that bring the decision close to the American ones of the 1960s. But there are two important differences, one explicit and the other implicit. The explicit one is that the need for intra-brand competition is based on protection not of an individual right (freedom of trade) but of a general and objective principle (competitiveness of the market in all its segments). The implicit one is that such a pervasive and rigorous principle is asserted to the extent that it serves to protect another principle, a higher one in 1966, that of market integration. For the territory protected by Consten's rigid exclusivity coincided with that of the French State, and both the Commission and the Court saw this protection as persistence of the segmentation of economic activities along national frontiers, violating the 'Grundnorm' of the whole [EU] system.

The question of whether this strict stance taken towards vertical territorial (and price) restraints was, or remains, appropriate is much debated and considered in greater detail in Chapter 11.[91] The position is complex, however, and the EU Courts, which generally strive for consistency in their case law,[92] have not to date shown an inclination to deviate from the starting point that these vertical price and severe territorial restrictions are in principle restrictive of competition.

(iii) The Importance of Context in Identifying the Purpose or Objective of the Agreement

a. *A Risk of Over-expansion of the Object Category*

Although a list of 'established' restraints liable to restrict competition by object has emerged, the role that 'context' plays in the characterisation process, and the question of how contextual analysis differs from that required to demonstrate restrictive effect, has been less apparent.[93] For a while, there was concern that insufficient attention to context was leading to an over-expansion of the object

[91] In the US, the category of agreements considered illegal per se has, to prevent false positives, and to reflect changes in ideology and economic thinking changed over time, see e.g. A. Jones, 'Completion of the Revolution in Antitrust Doctrine on Restricted Distribution: *Leegin* and its Implications for EC Competition Law' (2008) 53 *Ant Bull* 903, 918–920.

[92] Case 4/73, *Nold v Commission* EU:C:1974:51. See also A. Arnull, 'Owning Up to Fallibility: Precedent and the Court of Justice' (1993) 30 *CMLRev* 247.

[93] Since the 1960s, the CJ has stressed the need to examine an agreement which did not have as its object the restriction of competition in its market context to determine its effect, see Section 3.C.

category. For example, in some cases those relying on the object category were criticised for focusing too heavily on the existence of an established restraint without adequate consideration of the context of the case.[94] In others, claimants and courts were criticised for improperly relying on context to expand the object category to 'new' restraints that have not been classified as object restrictions in past case law, for example multilateral interchange fees (MIFs);[95] most favoured nation clauses;[96] patent settlement agreements involving reverse payments;[97] agreements relating to the dissemination of information regarding marketed pharmaceutical products;[98] eligibility rules for participating in a sporting association's activities;[99] or no-poach agreements—agreements between competitors not to solicit or hire each other's employees.[100] This created concern that the category was continually being expanded to incorporate conduct which, in some cases, was found only to be likely, or to have the potential, to produce, or to be capable of producing, negative effects of competition (without demonstrating why they evidently restrict competition).[101]

In *T-Mobile*,[102] for example, the CJ, although considering a case in which the practice at issue indirectly facilitated the fixing of prices between competing mobile operators in the Netherlands, made some expansive statements, particularly in paragraphs 31 and 43, about the concept of an object restraint.

> 31. With regard to the assessment as to whether a concerted practice, such as that at issue in the main proceedings, pursues an anti-competitive object, it should be noted, first, as pointed out by the Advocate General at point 46 of her Opinion, that in order for a concerted practice to be regarded as having an anti-competitive object, it is sufficient that it has the potential to have a negative impact on competition. In other words, the concerted practice must simply be capable in an individual case, having regard to the specific legal and economic context, of resulting in the prevention, restriction or distortion of competition within the common market. Whether and to what extent, in fact, such anti-competitive effects result can only be of relevance for determining the amount of any fine and assessing any claim for damages.
>
> . . .
>
> 43. In the light of all the foregoing considerations, the answer to the first question must be that a concerted practice pursues an anti-competitive object for the purpose of Article [101(1)] where, according to its content and objectives and having regard to its legal and economic context, it is capable in an individual case of resulting in the prevention, restriction or distortion of competition within the common market. It is not necessary for there to be actual prevention, restriction or distortion of competition or a direct link between the concerted practice and consumer prices. An exchange of information between competitors is tainted with an anti-competitive object if the exchange is capable of removing uncertainties concerning the intended conduct of the participating undertakings.

[94] See e.g. Case C-228/18, *Budapest Bank* EU:C:2020:265. [95] See Chap. 9. [96] See Chap. 11.

[97] See Chap. 12 and especially Case C-307/18, *Generics (UK) Ltd v Competition and Markets Authority (Generics)* EU:C:2020:52, and Case T-472/13, *H Lundbeck A/S v Commission* EU:T:2016:449, *aff'd* Case C-591/16 P, EU:C:2021:243.

[98] See Chap. 12 and Case C-179/16, *Hoffmann-La Roche and Novartis v AGCM* EU:C:2018:25.

[99] Case COMP/40.208, *ISU* 8 December 2017, *aff'd* Case T-93/18, *International Skating Union v Commission* EU:T:2020:610, Case C-124/21 P, judgment pending.

[100] See Chap. 9.

[101] A view which was fuelled by the Commission's publication, in June 2014, of a Staff Working Document on 'restrictions of competition "by object"', SWD(2014) 198 final, adopting a liberal approach to the issue—but which was revised in its final form in 2015, see n. 63, with some of the more expansive statements removed.

[102] Case C-8/08, EU:C:2009:343.

This judgment led to complaints that the CJ had gone further than required for the case and adopted too broad an interpretation of a restriction of competition by object. In particular that, as noted in the extract below, the statement that object restraints should only have the potential to have a negative effect on competition and the test of capability referred to, set the threshold for finding infringements by object too low and extended the category of object restraints to a somewhat unclear extent.

B. Meyring, 'T-Mobile: Further Confusion on Information Exchanges Between Competitors' (2010) 1 *JECLAP* 30

Even though this seems to be what point 31 says ('*it is sufficient*'), it would be wrong to conclude that any potential to have a negative impact is sufficient to establish that a practice is a restriction by object. First, this would do away with restrictions by effect altogether because practices that are not even capable of having anti-competitive effects will not produce such effects in any event—and all other restrictions would be restrictions by object. Second, the concept of a violation by object is a narrow one. As the Court notes in point 29, restrictions by object are only the severest forms of collusion that '*can be regarded, by their very nature, as being injurious to the proper functioning of normal competition*'....

Practices outside this category may or may not affect competition, depending on their economic context. They merit and require a careful analysis as to their effects on competition. It would be inappropriate to circumvent this requirement by simply classifying them as restrictions by object.

Although a narrow interpretation of the CJ's ruling in *T-Mobile* was possible—that the CJ simply made it clear that a finding of an anti-competitive object for obvious restraints does not depend upon an assessment of its actual impact on competition so long as the restraints are clearly capable of restricting competition in the circumstances of the case—in *Allianz Hungária Biztosító Zrt, Generali-Providencia Biztosító Zrt v Gazdasági Versenyhivatal*[103] the CJ, when asked to consider the question of whether a number of bilateral agreements concluded between insurance companies and car repairers were restrictive of competition by object, also used broad language stating that:[104]

agreements would . . . amount to a restriction of competition by object in the event that the referring court found that it is likely that, having regard to the economic context, competition on that market would be eliminated or seriously weakened following the conclusion of those agreements. In order to determine the likelihood of such a result, that court should in particular take into consideration the structure of that market, the existence of alternative distribution channels and their respective importance and the market power of the companies concerned.

Two difficulties arose from these judgments. First, such broad statements about the concept of a restriction by object appeared to be out of tune with the objectives underpinning the rules and liable to expand the category well beyond agreements that are obviously liable to harm competition and consumer welfare. Secondly, the suggestion that an abbreviated analysis of market structure and market

[103] Case C-32/11, EU:C:2013:160.

[104] Ibid., para. 48 (these agreements did not contain any 'established' restraints. The concern about the restrictions arose, however, because of the market power of the insurers involved and the concentrated structure of the market). In Case C-439/09, *Pierre Fabre* EU:C:2011:649, the CJ also cast doubt on the traditional view that selective distribution agreements require some form of analysis of the restrictive effects of the agreement, stating that they necessarily affect competition and 'are to be considered, in the absence of objective justification, as "restrictions by object"', see further Chap. 11.

power is required inappropriately blurs the analysis required in object and effects cases respectively; the whole purpose of the category is to sidestep detailed market analysis in the case of obvious restraints.[105] Indeed, the proposition that any agreement which, following an abbreviated market analysis, can be shown to have the potential, or to be likely, to have a negative impact on competition is restrictive by object could, at its most far-reaching construction, have done away with the need for effects analysis completely and lowered the threshold for demonstration of a restriction of competition, so shifting the burden to the parties to defend their agreement under Article 101(3).

b. Clarification of the Role of Context and the Restrictive Nature of the Object Category

In a series of judgments of the EU Courts, starting with *CB*,[106] the CJ has clarified how object restraints are to be identified and the role of context.

First, these judgments have stressed that, as recognised by the CJ in *STM*, the category of object restrictions is a *restrictive* one, reserved exclusively for agreements which inherently reveal a sufficient degree of harm to competition—it is only then that the Commission (or other claimant) may be exempted from demonstrating actual anti-competitive effects.

Secondly, that to ensure Article 101 analysis is in tune with the objectives underpinning it and the risk of Type I errors is minimised, 'context' forms an essential part of the characterisation exercise.

Thirdly, although contextual analysis is vital, it is limited in the characterisation setting and confined 'to what is strictly necessary . . . to establish the existence of a restriction of competition by object'.[107] Although fact- and context-specific, the assessment required is not therefore as in-depth as that required to identify actual or likely restrictive effects and does not generally demand a detailed assessment of the relevant market or counterfactual scenario.[108]

Fourthly, the need to assess context means both that:

(a) even 'established' restraints may not restrict competition by object if contextual evidence casts reasonable doubt[109] on the conclusion that the agreement by its very nature harms competition.[110] In this setting, abbreviated contextual analysis provides a reality check to the assessment. As explained by Advocate General Bobek in *Gazdasági Versenyhivatal v Budapest Bank Nyrt (Budapest Bank)*,[111] the yardstick is whether a 'reasonable' countervailing hypothesis exists which is plausible enough to warrant further examination (it does not need to be fully established, argued, and proven) and challenges, in the context of the individual case, the general conventional wisdom;[112] and

(b) in spite of its narrow nature, the category of object restraints can encompass new agreements (beyond those established in past cases) where sufficient and consistent experience and evidence exists of the inherently harmful nature of the type of agreement,[113] or where it is equivalent to a price-fixing, output, or capacity-limiting, market-sharing, or other obviously anti-competitive agreement.[114] Where established, it is no defence that, at the time an agreement was concluded,

[105] See Peeperkorn, n. 50.

[106] Case C-67/13 P, EU:C:2014:2204. See also Case C-228/18, *Budapest Bank* EU:C:2020:265, para. 54.

[107] Case C-373/14 P, *Toshiba Corp v Commission* EU:C:2016:26, para. 29.

[108] Case C-591/16 P, *H Lundbeck v Commission* EU:C:2021:243, para. 140.

[109] A mere unsubstantiated assertion concerning procompetitive effects is insufficient *Lundbeck*, ibid., para. 137.

[110] Case C-228/18, *Budapest Bank* EU:C:2019:678, paras. 82–83 (e.g. because it reveals that the agreement pursues a credible, pro-competitive commercial objective or was designed to prevent upward pressure on prices).

[111] Ibid., para. 79. [112] Ibid. [113] See n. *** and text.

[114] See e.g. Case C-179/16, *Hoffmann-La Roche and Novartis v AGCM* EU:C:2018:25.

there were doubts as to whether it could be found to be restrictive of competition by object—'all that matters are the specific characteristics of that agreement'.[115] Object categorisation is not, however, appropriate for agreements involving complex measures,[116] or where experience with the restraint is limited or insufficiently reliable and robust to justify an assumption that competition is restricted.[117] If there is a need to conduct a detailed market analysis to assess the impact of the agreement, it should not constitute an object restriction.

c. *Contextual Analysis in the Cases*

Crucial issues when examining the legal and economic context are likely to include whether the parties are actual or potential competitors (and so whether a horizontal agreement exists), whether experience and evidence establishes the inherently harmful nature of the type of agreement, or whether established or other severe restraints seem plausibly necessary to a pro-competitive venture or an efficiency-enhancing cooperation arrangement between the parties[118]—there is another credible explanation for the agreement other than the commercial interest of the parties not to compete or to restrict competition[119] (see further Chapters 9–12).

For example, in *Toshiba Corp v Commission*,[120] it was argued that a market-sharing agreement involving Japanese and EEA producers should not have been found to be restrictive of competition by object, as it has not been ascertained (by the Commission or GC) whether entry by Japanese producers into the EEA market was an economically viable strategy for them (and consequently whether they were potential competitors in the EEA). The CJ held, however, that as the GC had examined, and ruled out, Toshiba's argument that it could not restrict competition because the Japanese and EEA producers were not competitors, the GC had carried out correct sufficient analysis of the context.[121] The question of whether or not parties to an agreement are competitors has also been important in a series of cases in which, in the context of a patent infringement dispute, generic producers of pharmaceutical products have agreed with the manufacturer of an originator product not to enter a market, in return for payment. In its judgments in both *Lundbeck*[122] and *Generics*[123] (discussed in Chapter 12), the CJ has made it clear that a generic producer of pharmaceutical products that is not present in a market may be a potential competitor of an originator in a market where there are real and concrete possibilities of the former entering the market sufficiently quickly and competing with the latter.[124]

[115] Case C-591/16 P, *H Lundbeck v Commission* EU:C:2021:243, para. 131.

[116] In that case it was argued that the horizontal cooperation was designed to ensure the success of the carte bleu system, in particular through combating free-riding and balancing issuing/acquisition activities. The Court considered that, given the complex nature of the market and the efficiency justifications raised, negative effects could not be considered so likely to make assessment of effects redundant.

[117] Case C-67/13 P, *CB* EU:C:2014:2204, para. 51. See also Case C-286/13 P, *Dole Food Co Inc and Dole Fresh Fruit Europe v Commission (Dole)* EU:C:2015:184, para. 115, Wathelet AG in Case C-373/14, *Toshiba Corp v Commission* EU:C:2015:427, Case C-228/18, *Budapest Bank* EU:C:2020:265, paras. 76–79k and Bobek AG in Case C-228/18, *Budapest Bank* 2019:678, para. 72 (suggesting that there must be sufficient consensus among economists of the inherently anti-competitive nature of the agreement).

[118] See nn. 109–112 and text.

[119] Case C-307/18, *Generics* EU:C:2020:52, para. 111, Case C-228/18, *Budapest Bank* EU:C:2020:265, paras. 71–75, Wahl AG in Case C-67/13, *CB* EU:2014:1958, para. 56 and see further Chaps. 9 and 10.

[120] Case C-373/14 P, EU:C:2016:26M. See also Cases T-208 and 216/13, *Portugal Telecom* and *Telefónica SA v Commission* EU:T:2016:369, *aff'd* Case C-487/16 P, *Telefónica SA v Commission* EU:C:2017:961.

[121] Ibid., paras. 31–34. See also Case C-331/21, *Autoridade da Concorrência and EDP* EU:C:2023:153, Opinion of Rantos AG, paras. 35–85 and 114–120.

[122] Case C-591/16 P, *H Lundbeck A/S v Commission* EU:C:2021:243.

[123] Case C-307/18, *Generics* EU:C:2020:52.

[124] Ibid., para. 36.

Although therefore hypothetical possibility of entry is not sufficient to demonstrate potential competition, the ability to enter (successfully) does not have to be demonstrated with certainty.[125] Further, in general, the Court takes the view that the conclusion of a market-sharing agreement between undertakings operating at the same level in the production chain constitutes a strong indication that a competitive relationship exists between those undertakings even where some have no presence in the market concerned.[126]

In contrast, in *CB* the CJ held that the GC had erred in affirming a Commission decision finding that a number of measures designed to achieve interoperability within a system for payment and withdrawal by bank cards were restrictive of competition by object. It criticised the GC for:

- ruling that the concept of restriction of competition by 'object' was not to be interpreted 'restrictively';
- not explaining why the measures were by their very nature harmful to the proper functioning of normal competition rather than just being capable of restricting competition (on the contrary, the CJ considered that as the GC had conducted an assessment of the potential effects of the measures, it has thereby make it clear that they did not reveal a sufficient degree of harm to competition);[127] and
- taking insufficient account of the fact that restraints had been incorporated to ensure the success of the system, in particular through combating free-riding and balancing issuing/acquisition activities. In contrast to *BIDS*, the purpose of the agreement was not simply to reduce overcapacity, but was to achieve a given ratio between the issuing and acquisition activities of the member of the grouping in order to develop the CB system.[128]

Case C-67/13 P, *Groupement des Cartes Bancaires (CB) v Commission* EU:C:2014:2204

Court of Justice

–Examination of whether there is a restriction of competition by 'object' within the meaning of Article [101(1)]

48. It must be recalled that, to come within the prohibition laid down in Article [101(1)], an agreement, a decision by an association of undertakings or a concerted practice must have 'as [its] object or effect' the prevention, restriction or distortion of competition in the internal market.

49. In that regard, it is apparent from the Court's case-law that certain types of coordination between undertakings reveal a sufficient degree of harm to competition that it may be found that there is no need to examine their effects (see, to that effect, judgment in *LTM*, 56/65 . . ., paragraphs 359 and 360; judgment in *BIDS*, paragraph 15, and judgment in *Allianz Hungária Biztosító and Others*, C-32/11 . . ., paragraph 34 . . .).

125 Ibid., para. 38.

126 Ibid., para. 55, relying on Case C-373/14 P, *Toshiba Corp v Commission* EU:C:2016:26, paras. 33–34.

127 See also Case C-345/14, *SIA 'Maxima Latvija' v Konkurences padome* EU:C:2015:784 where the CJ also stressed the restrictive nature of the by object category and that it should only be expanded outside the established category of restraints where the agreement 'reveals in itself a sufficient degree of harm to competition for it to be considered that it is not appropriate to assess its effects'. In that case, a commercial lease incorporating a clause giving the tenant the right to oppose the lease of commercial premises in the shopping centre to other tenants was not 'among the agreements which it is accepted may be considered, by their very nature, to be harmful to the proper functioning of competition', the agreement had to be assessed in the economic and legal context in which it occurred to determine its effects, paras. 20–21.

128 The CJ referred the matter back to the GC to determine whether the Commission had established that the agreement had as its effect the restriction of competition.

50. That case-law arises from the fact that certain types of coordination between undertakings can be regarded, by their very nature, as being harmful to the proper functioning of normal competition (see, to that effect, in particular, judgment in *Allianz Hungária Biztosító and Others* . . . paragraph 35 . . .).

51. Consequently, it is established that certain collusive behaviour, such as that leading to horizontal price-fixing by cartels, may be considered so likely to have negative effects, in particular on the price, quantity or quality of the goods and services, that it may be considered redundant, for the purposes of applying Article [101(1)], to prove that they have actual effects on the market (see, to that effect, in particular, judgment in *Clair*, 123/83, . . ., paragraph 22). Experience shows that such behaviour leads to falls in production and price increases, resulting in poor allocation of resources to the detriment, in particular, of consumers.

52. Where the analysis of a type of coordination between undertakings does not reveal a sufficient degree of harm to competition, the effects of the coordination should, on the other hand, be considered and, for it to be caught by the prohibition, it is necessary to find that factors are present which show that competition has in fact been prevented, restricted or distorted to an appreciable extent (judgment in *Allianz Hungária Biztosító* . . ., paragraph . . .).

53. According to the case-law of the Court, in order to determine whether an agreement between undertakings or a decision by an association of undertakings reveals a sufficient degree of harm to competition that it may be considered a restriction of competition 'by object' within the meaning of Article [101(1)], regard must be had to the content of its provisions, its objectives and the economic and legal context of which it forms a part. When determining that context, it is also necessary to take into consideration the nature of the goods or services affected, as well as the real conditions of the functioning and structure of the market or markets in question (see, to that effect, judgment in *Allianz Hungária Biztosító and Others* . . ., paragraph 36 . . .).

54. In addition, although the parties' intention is not a necessary factor in determining whether an agreement between undertakings is restrictive, there is nothing prohibiting the competition authorities, the national courts or the Courts of the European Union from taking that factor into account (see judgment in *Allianz Hungária Biztosító and Others* . . ., paragraph 37 . . .).

55. In the present case, it must be noted that, when the General Court defined in the judgment under appeal the relevant legal criteria to be taken into account in order to ascertain whether there was, in the present case, a restriction of competition by 'object' within the meaning of Article [101(1)], it reasoned as follows, in paragraphs 124 and 125 of that judgment:

> 124. According to the case-law, the types of agreement covered by Article [101(1)(a) to (e) . . .] do not constitute an exhaustive list of prohibited collusion and, accordingly, the concept of infringement by object should not be given a strict interpretation (see, to that effect, [judgment in *BIDS*], paragraphs 22 and 23).
>
> 125. In order to assess the anti-competitive nature of an agreement or a decision by an association of undertakings, regard must be had *inter alia* to the content of its provisions, its objectives and the economic and legal context of which it forms a part. In that regard, it is sufficient that the agreement or the decision of an association of undertakings has the potential to have a negative impact on competition. In other words, the agreement or decision must simply be capable in the particular case, having regard to the specific legal and economic context, of preventing, restricting or distorting competition within the common market. It is not necessary for there to be actual prevention, restriction or distortion of competition or a direct link between [that agreement or decision] and consumer prices. In addition, although the parties' intention is not a necessary factor in determining whether an agreement is restrictive, there is nothing prohibiting the Commission or the Community judicature from taking it into account (see, to that effect, [judgment in *T-Mobile* . . .], paragraphs 31, 39 and 43, and [judgment in *GlaxoSmithKline* . . .] paragraph 58 . . .).

56. It must be held that, in so reasoning, the General Court in part failed to have regard to the case-law of the Court of Justice and, therefore, erred in law with regard to the definition of the relevant legal criteria in order to assess whether there was a restriction of competition by 'object' within the meaning of Article [101(1)].

57. First, in paragraph 125 of the judgment under appeal, when the General Court defined the concept of the restriction of competition 'by object' within the meaning of that provision, it did not refer to the settled case-law of the Court of Justice mentioned in paragraphs 49 to 52 of the present judgment, thereby failing to have regard to the fact that the essential legal criterion for ascertaining whether coordination between undertakings involves such a restriction of competition 'by object' is the finding that such coordination reveals in itself a sufficient degree of harm to competition.

58. Secondly, in the light of that case-law, the General Court erred in finding, in paragraph 124 of the judgment under appeal, and then in paragraph 146 of that judgment, that the concept of restriction of competition by 'object' must not be interpreted 'restrictively'. The concept of restriction of competition 'by object' can be applied only to certain types of coordination between undertakings which reveal a sufficient degree of harm to competition that it may be found that there is no need to examine their effects, otherwise the Commission would be exempted from the obligation to prove the actual effects on the market of agreements which are in no way established to be, by their very nature, harmful to the proper functioning of normal competition. The fact that the types of agreements covered by Article [101(1)] do not constitute an exhaustive list of prohibited collusion is, in that regard, irrelevant.

59. It is, however, necessary to examine whether those errors of law were capable of vitiating the General Court's analysis as regards the characterisation of the measures at issue in the light of Article [101(1)].

. . .

65. Although it is apparent from the judgment under appeal that the General Court took the view that the restrictive object of the measures at issue could be inferred from their wording alone, the fact remains that it did not at any point explain, in the context of its review of the lawfulness of the decision at issue, in what respect that wording could be considered to reveal the existence of a restriction of competition 'by object' within the meaning of Article [101(1)].

. . .

69. However, although the General Court thereby set out the reasons why the measures at issue, in view of their formulas, are capable of restricting competition and, consequently, of falling within the scope of the prohibition laid down in Article [101(1)], it in no way explained—contrary to the requirements of the case-law referred to in paragraphs 49 and 50 above—in what respect that restriction of competition reveals a sufficient degree of harm in order to be characterised as a restriction 'by object' within the meaning of that provision, there being no analysis of that point in the judgment under appeal.

70. Although, as the General Court correctly found in paragraphs 76 and 140 to 144 of the judgment under appeal, the fact that the measures at issue pursue the legitimate objective of combatting free-riding does not preclude their being regarded as having an object restrictive of competition, the fact remains that that restrictive object must be established.

71. It follows that the General Court, in its characterisation of the measures at issue, not only vitiated the judgment under appeal by defective reasoning, but also misinterpreted and misapplied Article [101(1)].

72. It is indeed clear, in particular, from paragraphs 204 and 247 of the judgment under appeal, that the General Court rejected on several occasions the appellant's claim that it was apparent from formulas prescribed for the measures at issue that the latter sought to develop the acquisition activities of the members in order to achieve an optimal rate of balance between issuing and acquisition activities. On the other hand, it is not disputed—as is apparent, in particular, from paragraphs 198, 199, 245, 247 and 327 of the judgment under appeal—that those formulas encouraged the members of the Grouping, in order to avoid the payment of fees introduced by those measures, not to exceed a certain

volume of CB card issuing that enabled them to achieve a given ratio between the issuing and acquisition activities of the Grouping.

73. After stating, in paragraph 83 of the judgment under appeal, that the Grouping is active on the 'payment systems market', the General Court found, in paragraph 102 of that judgment, in its assessment of the facts—which is not subject to appeal and is not challenged in these proceedings—that, in the present case, in a card payment system that is by nature two-sided, such as that of the Grouping, the issuing and acquisition activities are 'essential' to one another and to the operation of that system: first, traders would not agree to join the CB card payment system if the number of cardholders was insufficient and, secondly, consumers would not wish to hold a card if it could not be used with a sufficient number of traders.

74. Having therefore found, in paragraph 104 of the judgment under appeal, that there were 'interactions' between the issuing and acquisition activities of a payment system and that those activities produced 'indirect network effects', since the extent of merchants' acceptance of cards and the number of cards in circulation each affects the other, the General Court could not, without erring in law, conclude that the measures at issue had as their object the restriction of competition within the meaning of Article [101(1)].

75. Having acknowledged that the formulas for those measures sought to establish a certain ratio between the issuing and acquisition activities of the members of the Grouping, the General Court was entitled at the most to infer from this that those measures had as their object the imposition of a financial contribution on the members of the Grouping which benefit from the efforts of other members for the purposes of developing the acquisition activities of the system. Such an object cannot be regarded as being, by its very nature, harmful to the proper functioning of normal competition, the General Court itself moreover having found, in particular in paragraphs 76 and 77 of the judgment under appeal, that combatting free-riding in the CB system was a legitimate objective.

76. In that regard, as the Advocate General observed at point 149 of his Opinion, the General Court wrongly held, in paragraph 105 of the judgment under appeal, that the analysis of the requirements of balance between issuing and acquisition activities within the payment system could not be carried out in the context of Article [101(1)] on the ground that the relevant market was not that of payment systems in France but the market, situated downstream for the issue of payment cards in that Member State.

77. In so doing, the General Court confused the issue of the definition of the relevant market and that of the context which must be taken into account in order to ascertain whether the content of an agreement or a decision by an association of undertakings reveals the existence of a restriction of competition 'by object' within the meaning of Article [101(1)].

78. In order to assess whether coordination between undertakings is by nature harmful to the proper functioning of normal competition, it is necessary, in accordance with the case-law referred to in paragraph 53 above, to take into consideration all relevant aspects—having regard, in particular, to the nature of the services at issue, as well as the real conditions of the functioning and structure of the markets—of the economic or legal context in which that coordination takes place, it being immaterial whether or not such an aspect relates to the relevant market.

79. That must be the case, in particular, when that aspect is the taking into account of interactions between the relevant market and a different related market (see, by analogy, judgment in *Delimitis*, . . ., paragraphs 17 to 23, and judgment in *Allianz Hungária Biztosító and Others* . . ., paragraph 42) and, all the more so, when, as in the present case, there are interactions between the two facets of a two-sided system.

80. Admittedly, it cannot be ruled out that the measures at issue, as the General Court found in paragraphs 198, 227 and 234 of the judgment under appeal, hinder competition from new entrants—in the light of the difficulty which those measures create for the expansion of their acquisition activity—and even lead to their exclusion from the system, on the basis, as BPCE argued at the hearing, of the level of fees charged pursuant to those measures.

81. However, as the Advocate General observed in point 131 of his Opinion, such a finding falls within the examination of the effects of those measures on competition and not of their object.

82. It must therefore be found that, while purporting to examine, in paragraphs 161 to 193 of the judgment under appeal, the 'options' left open to the members of the Grouping by the measures at issue—at the end of which it concluded, in paragraph 194 of that judgment, that 'in practice MERFA left two options open to the banks subject to it: payment of a fee or limiting the issue of CB cards'—the General Court in fact assessed the potential effects of those measures, analysing the difficulties for the banks of developing acquisition activity on the basis of market data, statements made by certain banks and documents seized during the inspections, and thereby indicating itself that the measures at issue cannot be considered 'by their very nature' harmful to the proper functioning of normal competition.

83. In that regard, the General Court erred, in paragraphs 197 and 198 of the judgment under appeal, in finding that the measures at issue could be regarded as being analogous to those examined by the Court of Justice in the *BIDS* judgment, in which the Court of Justice held that the arrangements referred to ('the BIDS arrangements'), concluded between the ten principal beef and veal processors in Ireland, members of BIDS . . ., had as their object the restriction of competition within the meaning of Article [101(1)].

84. By providing for a reduction of the order of 25% in processing capacity, the BIDS arrangements were intended, essentially, as their own wording makes clear, to enable several undertakings to implement a common policy which had as its object the encouragement of some of them to withdraw from the market and the reduction, as a consequence, of the overcapacity which affects their profitability by preventing them from achieving economies of scale. The object of the BIDS arrangements was therefore to change, appreciably, the structure of the market through a mechanism intended to encourage the withdrawal of competitors in order, first, to increase the degree of concentration in the sector concerned by reducing significantly the number of undertakings supplying processing services and, secondly, to eliminate almost 75% of excess production capacity (*BIDS* judgment, paragraphs 31 to 33).

85. In the judgment under appeal, the General Court made no such finding, nor indeed was it argued before it that the measures at issue, like the BIDS arrangements, were intended to change appreciably the structure of the market concerned through a mechanism intended to encourage the withdrawal of competitors and, accordingly, that those measures revealed a degree of harm such as that of the BIDS arrangements.

86. Although the General Court found, in paragraph 198 of the judgment under appeal, that the measures at issue encouraged the members of the Grouping not to exceed a certain volume of CB card issuing, the objective of such encouragement was, according to its own findings in paragraphs 245, 247 and 327 of that judgment, not to reduce possible overcapacity on the market for the issue of payment cards in France, but to achieve a given ratio between the issuing and acquisition activities of the members of the Grouping in order to develop the CB system further.

87. It follows that the General Court could not, without erring in law, characterise the measures at issue as restrictions of competition 'by object' within the meaning of Article [101(1)].

. . .

92. In the light of all the foregoing, it must be found that, in holding that the measures at issue had as their object a restriction of competition within the meaning of Article [101(1)], the General Court erred in law and failed to observe the standard of review required under the case-law.

This judgment makes it clear that, if a contextual analysis reveals that the agreement containing established restraints cannot be said to pose an obvious risk to competition or have an obviously restrictive purpose, it should not be assumed to restrict competition and should be condemned only if found to restrict competition in fact.

Similarly, CJ judgments in *Budapest Bank*,[129] *Generics*,[130] and *Lundbeck*,[131] establish that horizontal agreements involving some form of price-fixing or market-sharing will not restrict competition by object if required to achieve a plausible pro-competitive objective, or efficiency-enhancing cooperation agreement.[132] The category is not intended to extend to horizontal cooperation arrangements which have the potential for mixed effects on competition. Rather, it appears confined to restrictions that 'generally have net negative effects'—a high potential to create negative effects whilst being highly unlikely to be used to create efficiencies.[133] Although it has always been clear that by object restrictions may benefit from the Article 101(3) exception, this approach means that where efficiency stories are successfully proffered at the Article 101(1) stage, the claimant will be required to demonstrate actual or likely anti-competitive effects before these arguments are tested fully under Article 101(3). It also ensures that Article 101 analysis is in line with the objectives underpinning it and merger analysis (see further Chapters 9–12 and 15).[134]

d. Context, Characterisation, and Ancillary Restraints

This description of how object restraints are to be identified bears resemblance to the '*characterisation*' mechanism utilised in the US to distinguish per se restraints from restraints which have to be analysed under the rule of reason (referred to in the US as the 'ancillary restraints' doctrine). In *Broadcast Music, Inc ('BMI') v Columbia Broadcasting System Inc*,[135] the US Supreme Court, warning that 'easy labels do not always supply ready answers', drew a distinction between:

- practices between competitors which facially appear to be one that would always or almost always tend to restrict competition and decrease output—such as naked price-fixing and market-sharing agreements with no purpose except stifling competition which are illegal per se; and
- practices designed to increase economic efficiency and render markets more, rather than less, competitive—such as agreements where price-fixing and market division are 'ancillary' to co-operative productive activity engaged in by the agreeing parties, which must be analysed under the rule of reason.

Thus, the blanket copyright licence at issue in that case, concluded by BMI and ASCAP, although literally constituting 'price fixing', was not to be summarily condemned as illegal per se. Rather it has to be analysed under the rule of reason as it had the potential to achieve efficiencies by eliminating the costs of individual negotiation.[136]

[129] Case C-228/18, EU:C:2020:265. [130] Case C-307/18, EU:C:2020:52.

[131] Case C-591/16 P, EU:C:2021:243.

[132] Case C-307/18, *Generics* EU:C:2020:52, para. 111, see also Case C-228/18, *Budapest Bank* EU:C:2020:265, paras. 71–75, Wahl AG in Case C-67/13, *CB* EU:2014:1958, para. 56. In relation to vertical agreements, see Case 262/81, *Coditel v Ciné Vog Films (Coditel II)* [1982] ECR 3381, Cases C-403 and 429/08, *Murphy* EU:C:2011:631, and Case C-439/09, *Pierre Fabre v Président de l'Autorité de la concurrence* EU:C:2011:649 and discussion in Chaps. 11 and 12.

[133] Peeperkorn, n. 50, 399–400.

[134] See Chap. 10, Commission Staff Working Document, n. 63, pp. 5–6, C. E. Mosso, 'The Contribution of Merger Control to the Definition of Harm to Competition', GCLC Conference, Brussels, February 2016 (object restrictions have no equivalent in merger analysis, rather each merger is analysed to determine its likely impact on the main market parameters of competition).

[135] *BMI*, n. 29. See e.g. K. Kwok, 'Re-conceptualizing "Object" Analysis under Article 101 TFEU: Theoretical and Comparative Perspectives' (2018) *Journal of Competition Law and Economics* 467.

[136] Under this approach, the initial inquiry as to whether the restraint is ancillary is distinct from the substantive rule of reason analysis conducted; the fact that it is ancillary to legitimate joint activity is not enough to establish as a matter of law that the agreement does not unreasonably restrain trade and so falls outside s. 1 of the Sherman Act, only that per se analysis is not to be applied.

Finally, in some judgments the CJ has accepted that arrangements which at first sight are patently restrictive, do not restrict competition by object (or effect) where necessary to achieve a legitimate pro-competitive, public policy, or regulatory objective, for example 'the proper practice of the legal profession'[137] or the organisation and proper conduct of competitive sport[138] (see further the discussion in Sections 3.D and 3.E).

(iv) Object Restraints and Actual or Likely Effects

Once an agreement has been characterised as restrictive of competition by object, the agreement is simply assumed to restrict competition. It is not a presumption of illegality which can be rebutted,[139] for example by showing that the agreement does not, or is not likely to, have an actual restrictive effect (whether on prices or other parameters of competition),[140] perhaps because it failed to achieve its purpose on account of the fact that the parties did not have sufficient market power or because of other specific features of the market. Although therefore some contextual market analysis is required to ascertain the true purpose of the agreement and that it is capable of having anti-competitive effects, an analysis of the actual or likely effects of an agreement has no place in object cases. Rather, a core purpose of this approach is to ensure that full, complex effects analysis is sidestepped. This seems to be the reason why the CJ, in *GlaxoSmithKline Services Unlimited (GSK) v Commission*,[141] overturned the GC's ruling in relation to Article 101(1).[142]

The case concerned the general sales conditions for the supply of certain pharmaceuticals products to Spanish wholesalers which GSK had notified to the Commission (under the pre-2004 notification and exemption system), seeking confirmation that the agreement did not infringe Article 101. The arrangements incorporated (in clause 4) a dual pricing system which resulted in Spanish wholesalers being charged a higher price for drugs resold in other Member States than for those resold in Spain. The purpose of this provision was to restrict parallel trade, but GSK argued that parallel trade benefited only the intermediaries (the parallel importers and exporters). In contrast, the restriction on parallel trade benefited final consumers as it provided GSK with additional resources for investment in the research and development (R&D) of new medicines. The Commission rejected these arguments, concluding both that (a) the general sales conditions infringed Article 101(1)—they had as their object and effect the restriction of competition; and (b) they did not merit an exemption as GSK had not proved its case under Article 101(3).

At first instance the GC annulled the Commission's decision insofar as it had rejected GSK's exemption application.[143] Further, although upholding the finding that Article 101(1) was infringed (it had a restrictive effect), it held that the Commission had been wrong to characterise the agreement as

[137] Case C-309/99, *Wouters v Algemene Raad van de Nederlandse Orde van Advocaten* EU:C:2002:98, at paras. 106–110.

[138] Case C-519/04 P, *Meca-Medina v Commission* EU:C:2006:492, paras. 45–47.

[139] See Kokott AG in Case C-307/18, *Generics* EU:C:2020:28, para. 162. But contrast the approach of the CJ in Case C-413/14 P, *Intel v Commission* EU:C:2017:632, paras. 136–139, applying a presumption that exclusivity clauses and loyalty rebates are abusive, unless the defendant can produce evidence indicating a lack of anti-competitive effects or countervailing efficiencies (a rebuttable presumption of illegality), see Chap. 8.

[140] 'Accordingly, . . . there is no need to consider the effects of a concerted practice where its anti-competitive object is established', Case C-8/08, *T-Mobile* EU:C:2009:343, para. 31.

[141] Case C-501/06 P [2009] ECR I-9291 and Case T-168/01 [2006] ECR II-2969.

[142] See also Cases C-101 and 110/07 P, *Coop de France bétail et viande v Commission* [2008] ECR I-10193 ('since the [GC] concluded that it was established that the object of the Agreement . . . was anti-competitive, it correctly ruled . . . that the Commission was not bound to research the actual effects on competition of the measure', para. 88).

[143] The GC held that the Commission had not adequately refuted GSK's evidence of efficiencies, see further Section 4.

restrictive by object. Although an agreement intended to prevent parallel trade unfavourably had, in principle, to be regarded as having its object the restriction of competition, an abridged (contextual) analysis was also required to determine whether the agreement restricted competition, to the detriment of final consumers. The GC concluded that, in this case, the specific characteristics of the pharmaceutical sector, which led to prices of medicine being largely shielded from the free play of supply and demand by regulation, meant that no assumption could be made that parallel trade would reduce prices and increase the welfare of final consumers.

As the conclusion drawn by the GC seemed potentially to open the possibility for effects analysis to brought into object cases, the Commission appealed. The CJ upheld the Commission's finding that the agreement was restrictive by object.[144] In principle, agreements aimed at prohibiting or limiting parallel trade have as their object the prevention of competition,[145] even if they could not be presumed to deprive final consumers of the advantages of effective competition in terms of price.[146] An agreement tending to restore national divisions in trade between Member States might be such as to frustrate the Treaty's single market objective.

(v) Object Cases and Appreciability

In the preceding discussion, it has been seen that restrictions of competition by object are assumed to constitute a threat to the attainment of the Treaty's objectives, irrespective of their actual effects. The person alleging the infringement is not, therefore, generally required to demonstrate the relevant market, the existence of market power, or actual or likely harm to competition or consumers and an assumption cannot be rebutted by a demonstration that restrictive effects are not likely.

In order to come within the prohibition imposed by Article 101(1), however, 'the agreement must affect trade between Member States and the free play of competition to an appreciable extent' (see Chapter 4).[147] EU law is not concerned with agreements which have an 'insignificant effect on the market, taking into account the weak position which the persons concerned have on the market of the product in question' (*Völk*).[148] An important question, therefore, is whether a market analysis is required in object cases to demonstrate appreciable effects on competition.

Although in 1969 in *Völk* the CJ indicated that even object restraints may fall outside Article 101(1) on de minimis grounds (in that case the agreement conferred ATP on the distributor but the parties had an exceptionally small market shares of less than 1 per cent), in *Expedia Inc v Authorité de la Concurrence*,[149] the CJ implicitly (but not perhaps as clearly as it could have done)[150] overruled *Völk* on this point. The Court stated at paragraph 37 that 'an agreement that may affect trade between Member States and that has an anti-competitive object constitutes, by its nature and independently of any concrete effect that it may have, an appreciable restriction on competition.'

[144] Case C-501/06 P, *GlaxoSmithKline Services v Commission* EU:C:2009:610.

[145] Ibid., paras. 58–61.

[146] Ibid., paras. 62–64.

[147] Case 22/71, *Béguelin Import Co v GL Import-Export SA* [1971] ECR 949.

[148] Case 5/69, *Völk v Vervaecke* EU:C:1969:35, 302.

[149] Case C-226/11, EU:C:2012:795.

[150] If it did intend to overrule *Völk*, it did not do so as clearly as it could have. In particular, it relies on *Völk* both as authority for the settled position that an agreement falls outside Art. 101(1) if it has only an insignificant effect on the market and also as a case in which it was found 'that an exclusive dealing agreement, even with absolute territorial protection, has only an insignificant effect on the market . . . taking into account the weak position which the persons concerned have in that market'. Further, it concludes that an NCA can only apply Art. 101(1) to an agreement, stated by the national court to be restrictive by object, 'provided that that agreement constitutes an appreciable restriction of competition', ibid., paras. 22 and 38.

The case has been widely interpreted as deciding that in object cases an appreciable restriction of competition is assumed and the Commission's view that agreements which have as their object the restriction of competition always appreciably restrict competition is clearly set out in paragraph 13 of its Notice on agreements of minor importance (De Minimis Notice), published in 2014.[151] This provides that the usual market share thresholds used to quantify which agreements are, in the Commission's view, *not* likely to constitute an appreciable restriction, do *not* apply to agreements which have as their object the restriction of competition (this was why the Commission published an accompanying Staff Working Document setting out guidance on what it considers to constitute a restriction by object):

Notice on agreements of minor importance which do not appreciably restrict competition under Article 101(1) of the Treaty on the Functioning of the European Union (De Minimis Notice) [2014] OJ C291/01

2. The Court of Justice has also clarified that an agreement which may affect trade between Member States and which has as its object the prevention, restriction or distortion of competition within the internal market constitutes, by its nature and independently of any concrete effects that it may have, an appreciable restriction of competition. This Notice therefore does not cover agreements which have as their object the prevention, restriction or distortion of competition within the internal market.

. . .

13. In view of the clarification of the Court of Justice referred to in point 2, this Notice does not cover agreements which have as their object the prevention, restriction or distortion of competition within the internal market. The Commission will thus not apply the safe harbour created by the market share thresholds set out in points 8, 9, 10 and 11 to such agreements. For instance, as regards agreements between competitors, the Commission will not apply the principles set out in this Notice to, in particular, agreements containing restrictions which, directly or indirectly, have as their object: a) the fixing of prices when selling products to third parties; b) the limitation of output or sales; or c) the allocation of markets or customers. Likewise, the Commission will not apply the safe harbour created by those market share thresholds to agreements containing any of the restrictions that are listed as hardcore restrictions in any current or future Commission block exemption regulation, which are considered by the Commission to generally constitute restrictions by object.

In *Ziegler SA v Commission*,[152] the EU Courts had to deal with the argument that the Commission had failed to define the relevant market for the purposes of determining whether the agreement had an appreciable effect on trade.[153] The CJ held that the Commission did have to define the market if it chose to apply its Notice on the effect on trade concept. Nonetheless it rejected Ziegler's argument on the facts as the GC had found that the Commission had provided a sufficiently detailed description of the relevant sector, including supply, demand, and scope, to allow the Court to verify the Commission's basic assertions that the combined market share far exceeded the 5 per cent threshold set out in that Notice.[154]

[151] Notice on agreements of minor importance which do not appreciably restrict competition under Article 101(1) of the Treaty on the Functioning of the European Union (De Minimis Notice) [2014] OJ C291/01. The previous notice was set out in [2001] OJ C368/13.

[152] Case C-439/11 P, EU:C:2013:513. See also Case T-254/12, *Kühne + Nagel International AG v Commission* EU:T:2016:114, *aff'd* Case C-261/16 EU:C:2018:56.

[153] See Chap. 4, Section 4.E.

[154] Case C-439/11 P, EU:C:2013:513, paras. 57–89.

(vi) Restrictions by Object and 'Hardcore' Restraints

The previous discussion sets out the types of contractual provisions that have caused a finding that an agreement has as its object the restriction of competition. These established, object restraints broadly correspond with a list of 'hardcore' restraints, identified by the Commission in its Notices, Guidelines, and block exemptions, as agreements highly likely to restrict competition by object and infringe Article 101(1) and highly unlikely to satisfy the Article 101(3) criteria.[155] Indeed, in the previous section, it was seen that the Commission equates 'hardcore' with object restrictions in paragraph 13 of its De Minimis Notice.

Caution needs to be adopted to this approach, however. First, as a matter of law, it has been seen that an agreement only restricts competition by object if its precise purpose can be said to restrict competition (a list of object restraints cannot be codified).[156] Secondly, the Commission has sought to create the impression that agreements incorporating object or hardcore restrictions are most unlikely to satisfy the conditions of Article 101(3)—so bringing EU law on object restraints more closely in line with the US per se rule, where a conclusive presumption of unreasonableness is applied. All agreements are, however, capable of satisfying the conditions of Article 101(3) even those incorporating object restraints (see further Section 4).

C. ESTABLISHING RESTRICTIVE EFFECTS

(i) General

Where the object of an agreement cannot be said to restrict competition, an analysis of its *effect* becomes crucial.

> Where . . . an analysis of the said clauses does not reveal the effect on competition to be sufficiently deleterious, the consequence of the agreement should then be considered and for it to be caught by the prohibition it is then necessary to find that those factors are present that show that competition has in fact been prevented or restricted or distorted to an appreciable extent. The competition in question must be understood within the actual context in which it would occur in the absence of the agreement in dispute.[157]

Because of significant reliance on both the category of object restraints (by claimants) and the de minimis principle and BERs (by firms), the question of how antitrust analysis is conducted in effects cases has arisen relatively rarely before the EU courts and so is under-explored. Indeed, despite modernisation there has been no steady flow of cases emerging before the EU courts (whether from Commission decisions[158] or from national courts or tribunals), which has allowed the case law in this area to be developed and honed. However, given recent judgments reinforcing the narrow role of the object category, competition agencies/claimants may more frequently be required to demonstrate restrictive effects in Article 101 cases.

[155] Article 101(3) Guidelines, para. 23. See also e.g. COMP/39.579, *Consumer Detergents* [2011] OJ C193/14, 13 April 2011, paras. 53–54.

[156] See n. 71 and text. [157] Case 56/65, *STM* EU:C:1966:38, 249.

[158] See e.g. A. Witt, 'The Enforcement of Article 101 TFEU: What Has Happened to the Effects Analysis?' (2018) 55 *CMLRev* 417 (noting at 419 that there has been next to no effects analysis in the Commission's decisional practice on Art. 101 since the last set of Art. 101 guidelines in 2004—rather it has based prohibition decisions almost exclusively on object restrictions).

The Commission's view is that consumer welfare should be the benchmark against which agreements are tested.[159] Further, that to identify anti-competitive effects under Article 101(1), the likely impact of the agreement on inter- or intra-brand competition must be determined and two counterfactuals used:

- one to determine whether the agreement restricts inter-brand competition—whether the agreement restricts actual or potential competition that would have existed without the agreement;[160] and
- one to determine whether it restricts intra-brand competition (whether the agreement restricts actual or potential competition that would have existed in the absence of the contractual restraints).

This requires a theory of harm, proof that the agreement either (a) affects 'actual or potential competition to such an extent that on the relevant market negative effects on prices, output, innovation or the variety or quality of goods and services can be expected with a reasonable degree of probability'[161] or (b) restricts a supplier's distributors from competing with each other, since potential competition that could have existed between the distributors absent the restraint is restricted. If, following these principles, it is concluded that the transaction is not restrictive of competition, the Commission states that restraints 'ancillary' to the main non-restrictive transaction also fall outside Article 101(1).[162] Where a restriction is identified, restrictive effects are weighed against the economic benefits and efficiencies established within the forum of Article 101(3).

The case law that does exist in this area (explored further later and in subsequent chapters) sets out some important starting principles relevant for Article 101(1) analysis, for example, that: Article 101 is concerned both with restrictions of competition between the parties and between a party and third parties; it is necessary to examine an agreement in its market context to determine its effects (whether alone or in combination with other agreements); the analysis should be conducted in the light of the competition which would occur if the agreement in question had not been made (against a counterfactual); and even where an assessment is being made *ex post*, demonstration of actual or potential effects is sufficient.

(ii) Appraisal of an Agreement in its Legal and Economic Context

Since the 1960s and the cases of *STM*[163] and *Brasserie de Haecht v Wilkin (No. 1)*,[164] the CJ has stressed the need to examine an agreement which did not have as its object the restriction of competition in its market context to determine its effect. In *STM*, the CJ dealt with an exclusive distribution agreement which, in contrast to that concerned in *Consten and Grundig*, did not confer ATP (or a complete monopoly over the right to distribute in France) on the distributor; the contractual arrangements admitted the possibility of parallel imports from distributors in other Member States. In this case, the CJ did not hold that the object of the agreement was to restrict

[159] See White Paper on the Modernisation of the Rules Implementing Articles 85 and 86 of the EC Treaty [now Articles 101 and 102 TFEU] [1999] OJ C132/1, paras. 56–57.

[160] The need to consider the impact of the agreement as against the counterfactual—the position which would have existed in the absence of the agreement—has been stressed in a number of cases, see e.g. Case 56/65, *STM* EU:C:1966:38.

[161] Article 101(3) Guidelines, para. 24. This could be because the agreement restricts actual or potential competition between the parties or between any one of the parties and third parties that could have existed absent the agreement, ibid, paras. 25–26.

[162] Ibid., paras. 28–31.

[163] Case 56/65, *STM* EU:C:1966:38.

[164] Case 23/67, EU:C:1967:54.

competition. Rather, accepting similar arguments to those raised by the parties (but rejected by the Court) in *Consten and Grundig*, it indicated that an exclusive distribution agreement would not restrict competition if the appointment of an exclusive distributor was necessary in order to enable a manufacturer to penetrate a new market.[165] Before it could be determined whether the agreement restricted competition, the agreement should be examined in the light of the competition which would occur if the agreement in question were not or had not been made. In this case, it seemed that the economic justifications for the agreement might outweigh the territorial restrictions inherent in the agreement.

Case 56/65, *Société Technique Minière v Maschinenbau Ulm GmbH* EU:C:1966, 249-250

The parties entered into an agreement by which a French company was given exclusive rights to distribute the equipment (levelling machines) of a German manufacturer in France. The French company was free to re-export the equipment outside France. In litigation in the French courts, the question arose whether the agreement infringed Article 101(1) and was void (Article 101(2)). The Cour d'Appel Paris asked how it should assess the compatibility of this type of agreement with Article 101(1).

Court of Justice

The effects of the agreement on competition

. . . The competition in question must be understood within the actual context in which it would occur in the absence of the agreement in dispute. In particular it may be doubted whether there is an interference with competition if the said agreement seems really necessary for the penetration of a new area by an undertaking. Therefore, in order to decide whether an agreement containing a clause 'granting an exclusive right of sale' is to be considered as prohibited by reason of its object or of its effect, it is appropriate to take into account in particular the nature and quantity, limited or otherwise, of the products covered by the agreement, the position and importance of the grantor and the concessionnaire [*sic*] on the market for the products concerned, the isolated nature of the disputed agreement or, alternatively, its position in series of agreements, the severity of the clauses intended to protect the exclusive dealership or, alternatively, the opportunities allowed for other commercial competitors in the same products by way of parallel re-exportation and importation.

Brasserie de Haecht concerned the compatibility of a beer-supply agreement, containing a beer tie, with Article 101(1). In many Member States, brewers conclude agreements with outlets such as public houses, which, in return for certain benefits from the brewer, oblige the outlet to purchase beer (and perhaps other drinks) exclusively from the brewer (or another named supplier). The CJ held that in considering whether there was a restriction of competition, it was necessary to take account of the whole market context in which the beer-supply agreement operated, including the simultaneous existence of similar contracts.

[165] In line with *STM*, the CJ has also held that where exclusivity provisions do not give a licensee of intellectual property (IP) rights ATP, restrictions in a licensing agreement may fall outside Art. 101(1) if necessary to protect the investment of the licensee, see Chap. 12.

(iii) Does the Agreement Enable the Parties to Exercise Market Power?

The CJ built upon the foundations of *Brasserie de Haecht* in another case involving a beer-supply agreement, *Delimitis v Henninger Bräu*.[166] This judgment supports the view that the Article 101(1) effects inquiry focuses on the important question of whether or not the agreement, alone or in conjunction with a network of similar agreements, has an appreciable impact on the parameters of competition (such as price, quantity, or quality) on an identified market through allowing the parties to exercise market power—in that case through a restriction of inter-brand competition.

In *Delimitis*, the CJ held that as the object of a commitment to purchase beer and other drinks exclusively from named suppliers was not to restrict competition (on the contrary, benefits flowed from such an agreement, for example: the guarantee for a supplier of an outlet for its product; the assurance that the retailer would concentrate its sales efforts on the distribution of the contract goods; the ability of the retailer to gain access to the market on favourable terms; and the guarantee for the retailer of supply of products), the agreement would only be prohibited by Article 101(1) if this was its effect. In determining the effect, it is first necessary to define the relevant market. It must then be ascertained whether there is a concrete possibility for new competitors to penetrate the market or existing competitors to expand taking account of the number and size of producers operating on the market, the existence of networks of agreements, the saturation of the market, and brand loyalty, etc. If analysis shows that there is no denial of access to the market, an agreement cannot be found to restrict competition. Conversely, if access is inhibited it must then be assessed whether the agreement in question (which is taken to mean the agreements of that particular producer or brewer) contributes appreciably to that situation.

Case C-234/89, *Delimitis v Henninger Bräu* EU:C:1991:91

Delimitis and a brewer concluded an agreement in which the brewer let a public house to Delimitis. In return, Delimitis undertook to obtain beer and soft drinks from the brewer or its subsidiaries. On the termination of the agreement a dispute arose as to the agreement's compatibility with Article 101. On a preliminary reference the Court of Justice set out guidelines in order to enable the national court to assess the compatibility of the agreement with Article 101. The extract below deals with Article 101(1).

Court of Justice

The compatibility of beer supply agreements with Article [101(1)]

10. Under the terms of beer supply agreements, the supplier generally affords the reseller certain economic and financial benefits, such as the grant of loans on favourable terms, the letting of premises for the operation of a public house and the provision of technical installations, furniture and other equipment necessary for its operation. In consideration for those benefits, the reseller normally undertakes, for a predetermined period, to obtain supplies of the products covered by the contract only from the supplier. That exclusive purchasing obligation is generally backed by a prohibition on selling competing products in the public house let by the supplier.

11. Such contracts entail for the supplier the advantage of guaranteed outlets, since, as a result of his exclusive purchasing obligation and the prohibition on competition, the reseller concentrates his

[166] Case C-234/89, EU:C:1991:91.

sales efforts on the distribution of the contract goods. The supply agreements, moreover, lead to co-operation with the reseller, allowing the supplier to plan his sales over the duration of the agreement and to organize production and distribution effectively.

12. Beer supply agreements also have advantages for the reseller, inasmuch as they enable him to gain access under favourable conditions and with the guarantee of supplies to the beer distribution market. The reseller's and supplier's shared interest in promoting sales of the contract goods likewise secures for the reseller the benefit of the supplier's assistance in guaranteeing product quality and customer service.

13. If such agreements do not have the object of restricting competition within the meaning of Article [101(1)], it is nevertheless necessary to ascertain whether they have the effect of preventing, restricting or distorting competition.

14. In its judgment in Case 23/67 *Brasserie De Haecht v Wilkin . . .*, the Court held that the effects of such an agreement had to be assessed in the context in which they occur and where they might combine with others to have a cumulative effect on competition. It also follows from that judgment that the cumulative effect of several similar agreements constitutes one factor amongst others in ascertaining whether, by way of a possible alteration of competition, trade between Member States is capable of being affected.

15. Consequently, in the present case it is necessary to analyse the effects of a beer supply agreement, taken together with other contracts of the same type, on the opportunities of national competitors or those from other Member States, to gain access to the market for beer consumption or to increase their market share and, accordingly, the effects on the range of products offered to consumers.

16. In making that analysis, the relevant market must first be determined. The relevant market is primarily defined on the basis of the nature of the economic activity in question, in this case the sale of beer. Beer is sold through both retail channels and premises for the sale and consumption of drinks. From the consumer's point of view, the latter sector, comprising in particular public houses and restaurants, may be distinguished from the retail sector on the grounds that the sale of beer in public houses does not solely consist of the purchase of a product but is also linked with the provision of services, and that beer consumption in public houses is not essentially dependent on economic considerations. The specific nature of the public house trade is borne out by the fact that the breweries organize specific distribution systems for this sector which require special installations, and that the prices charged in that sector are generally higher than retail prices.

17. It follows that in the present case the reference market is that for the distribution of beer in premises for the sale and consumption of drinks. That finding is not affected by the fact that there is a certain overlap between the two distribution networks, namely inasmuch as retail sales allow new competitors to make their brands known and to use their reputation in order to gain access to the market constituted by premises for the sale and consumption of drinks.

18. Secondly, the relevant market is delimited from a geographical point of view. It should be noted that most beer supply agreements are still entered into at a national level. It follows that, in applying the [EU] competition rules, account is to be taken of the national market for beer distribution in premises for the sale and consumption of drinks.

19. In order to assess whether the existence of several beer supply agreements impedes access to the market as so defined, it is further necessary to examine the nature and extent of those agreements in their totality, comprising all similar contracts tying a large number of points of sale to several national producers (judgment in Case 43/69 *Bilger v Jehle . . .*). The effect of those networks of contracts on access to the market depends specifically on the number of outlets thus tied to national producers in relation to the number of public houses which are not so tied, the duration of the commitments entered into, the quantities of beer to which those commitments relate, and on the proportion between those quantities and the quantities sold by free distributors.

20. The existence of a bundle of similar contracts, even if it has a considerable effect on the opportunities for gaining access to the market, is not, however, sufficient in itself to support a finding that the relevant market is inaccessible, inasmuch as it is only one factor, amongst others, pertaining to the economic and legal context in which an agreement must be appraised (Case 23/67 *Brasserie De Haecht*, cited above). The other factors to be taken into account are, in the first instance, those also relating to opportunities for access.

21. In that connection it is necessary to examine whether there are real concrete possibilities for a new competitor to penetrate the bundle of contracts by acquiring a brewery already established on the market together with its network of sales outlets, or to circumvent the bundle of contracts by opening new public houses. For that purpose it is necessary to have regard to the legal rules and agreements on the acquisition of companies and the establishment of outlets, and to the minimum number of outlets necessary for the economic operation of a distribution system. The presence of beer wholesalers not tied to producers who are active on the market is also a factor capable of facilitating a new producer's access to that market since he can make use of those wholesalers' sales networks to distribute his own beer.

22. Secondly, account must be taken of the conditions under which competitive forces operate on the relevant market. In that connection it is necessary to know not only the number and the size of producers present on the market, but also the degree of saturation of that market and customer fidelity to existing brands, for it is generally more difficult to penetrate a saturated market in which customers are loyal to a small number of large producers than a market in full expansion in which a large number of small producers are operating without any strong brand names. The trend in beer sales in the retail trade provides useful information on the development of demand and thus an indication of the degree of saturation of the beer market as a whole. The analysis of that trend is, moreover, of interest in evaluating brand loyalty. A steady increase in sales of beer under new brand names may confer on the owners of those brand names a reputation which they may turn to account in gaining access to the public-house market.

23. If an examination of all similar contracts entered into on the relevant market and the other factors relevant to the economic and legal context in which the contract must be examined shows that those agreements do not have the cumulative effect of denying access to that market to new national and foreign competitors, the individual agreements comprising the bundle of agreements cannot be held to restrict competition within the meaning of Article [101(1)]. They do not, therefore, fall under the prohibition laid down in that provision.

24. If, on the other hand, such examination reveals that it is difficult to gain access to the relevant market, it is necessary to assess the extent to which the agreements entered into by the brewery in question contribute to the cumulative effect produced in that respect by the totality of the similar contracts found on that market. Under the [EU] rules on competition, responsibility for such an effect of closing off the market must be attributed to the breweries which make an appreciable contribution thereto. Beer supply agreements entered into by breweries whose contribution to the cumulative effect is insignificant do not therefore fall under the prohibition under Article [101(1)].

25. In order to assess the extent of the contribution of the beer supply agreements entered into by a brewery to the cumulative sealing-off effect mentioned above, the market position of the contracting parties must be taken into consideration. That position is not determined solely by the market share held by the brewery and any group, to which it may belong, but also by the number of outlets tied to it or to its group, in relation to the total number of premises for the sale and consumption of drinks found in the relevant market.

26. The contribution of the individual contracts entered into by a brewery to the sealing-off of that market also depends on their duration. If the duration is manifestly excessive in relation to the average duration of beer supply agreements generally entered into on the relevant market, the individual

contract falls under the prohibition under Article [101(1)]. A brewery with a relatively small market share which ties its sales outlets for many years may make a significant contribution to a sealing-off of the market as a brewery in a relatively strong market position which regularly releases sales outlets at shorter intervals.

27. The reply to be given to the first three questions is therefore that a beer supply agreement is prohibited by Article [101(1)], if two cumulative conditions are met. The first is that, having regard to the economic and legal context of the agreement at issue, it is difficult for competitors who could enter the market or increase their market share to gain access to the national market for the distribution of beer in premises for the sales and consumption of drinks. The fact that, in that market, the agreement in issue is one of a number of similar agreements having a cumulative effect on competition constitutes only one factor amongst others in assessing whether access to that market is indeed difficult. The second condition is that the agreement in question must make a significant contribution to the sealing-off effect brought about by the totality of those agreements in their economic and legal context. The extent of the contribution made by the individual agreement depends on the position of the contracting parties in the relevant market and on the duration of the agreement.

The analysis required by the CJ in this case highlights the importance of looking at the contractual restraint, not in isolation or abstractly as a restraint, but under existing conditions to assess prevailing market forces and entry conditions. It is only by examining it in the context in which it operates that its effect can be determined. Irrespective of the fact that the judgment in *Delimitis* dealt only with beer-supply agreements, it affirmed the general need for an economic approach when determining the compatibility of an agreement with Article 101(1) and an assessment of the impact of the agreement on inter-brand competition. In *SIA 'Maxima Latvija' v Konkurences padome*,[167] the CJ held the same approach applied to assess the compatibility of a commercial lease incorporating a clause giving the tenant the right to oppose the lease of commercial premises in the shopping centre to other tenants with Article 101(1). The agreement was not restrictive of competition by object[168] so it had to be considered whether, assessed in the economic and legal context in which it occurs, it has as its effect the restriction of competition. This requires an analysis of (a) factors which determine access to the relevant market (and assessing whether there are real concrete possibilities for a new competitor to establish itself),[169] and (b) the conditions under which competitive forces operate on the relevant market, including the number and size of operators present on the market, the degree of concentration and customer fidelity to existing brands, and consumer habits.[170]

It is only if, after a thorough analysis of the economic and legal context in which the agreements at issue in the main proceedings occur and the specificities of the relevant market, it is found that access to that market is made difficult by all the similar agreements found on the market, that it will then be necessary to analyse to what extent they contribute to any closing-off of that market, on the basis that only agreements which make an appreciable contribution to that closing-off are prohibited . . . To assess the extent of the contribution of each of the agreements at issue in the main proceedings to the cumulative closing-off effect, the position of the contracting parties on the market in question and the duration of the agreements must be taken into consideration.[171]

[167] Case C-345/14, EU:C:2015:784, see n. 127 and text. [168] Ibid. [169] Ibid., para. 27.
[170] Ibid., para. 28. [171] Ibid., para. 29.

The need for a similar assessment has been stressed in the context of some horizontal agreements where actual or potential competitors cooperate. For example, parties may create a joint venture[172] to pool their resources, perhaps to facilitate or speed up new entry into a market, to share financial risks, to achieve cost savings, or even to enable entry into a new market (each undertaking individually may not have the necessary skills or technology to make entry feasible). Although such agreements may raise competition concerns,[173] in *European Night Services*[174] the GC emphasised that where such an agreement does not incorporate obvious restrictions of competition, the actual conditions in which an agreement functions must be taken into account when considering whether or not it has the effect of restricting competition. In particular, account has to be taken of 'the economic context in which the undertakings operate, the products or services covered by the agreement and the actual structure of the market concerned'.[175] The importance of examining the conditions of competition, including existing and *potential* competition, was stressed. This was necessary:

> in order to ascertain whether, in the light of the structure of the market and the economic and legal context within which it functions, there are real concrete possibilities for the undertakings concerned to compete among themselves or for a new competitor to penetrate the relevant market and compete with the undertakings already established.[176]

Similarly in *O2 (Germany) GmbH & Co OHG v Commission*[177] the GC held that:

> 71. The examination required in the light of Article [101(1)] consists essentially in taking account of the impact of the agreement on existing and potential competition (see, to that effect, Case C-234/89, *Delimitis* . . .) and the competition situation in the absence of the agreement (*Société minière et technique* . . .), those two factors being intrinsically linked.
>
> 72. The examination of competition in the absence of an agreement appears to be particularly necessary as regards markets undergoing liberalization or emerging markets . . . where effective competition may be problematic owing, for example, to the presence of a dominant operator, the concentrated nature of the market structure or the existence of significant barriers to entry—factors referred to, in the present case, in the Decision.[178]

The Commission relies in its Guidelines on cases such as *Delimitis, European Night Services*, and *O2* to support its statement that a restriction of competition may be established by proof that anti-competitive effects (e.g. a reduction in output or an increase in price) are the expected consequence of a restriction.[179] This does not mean that 'an assessment of the positive and negative effects of the agreement from the point of view of competition must be carried out at the stage of Article [101(1)]',[180] but that Article 101(1) is about determining actual or potential anti-competitive effects through an examination of whether the parties individually or jointly have some degree of market power and, if so, whether the agreement contributes to the creation, maintenance, or strengthening of that market

[172] In some circumstances, the establishment of a joint venture amounts to a concentration for the purposes of the EU Merger Reg., Council Reg. 139/2004 [2004] OJ L24/1, discussed further in Chaps. 10 and 15.

[173] See Chap. 10. [174] Cases T-374, 375, and 388/94, EU:T:1998:198. [175] Ibid., para. 136.

[176] Ibid. For joint ventures generally, see Chap. 10. [177] Case T-328/03 [2006] ECR II-1231.

[178] Ibid., paras. 71–72. In this case, the GC found that the Commission had not carried out an economic analysis of the effect of the agreement on the competitive situation.

[179] Ibid., paras. 18 and 24 and Case T-328/03, *O2 (Germany) GmbH & Co OHG v Commission* [2006] ECR II-1231, para. 68.

[180] Ibid., paras. 69–71.

power or allows the parties to exploit it.[181] Where the parties have no such market power, the agreement cannot have anti-competitive effects, and, therefore, cannot be said to restrict competition.

The scarcity of the case law and economically reasoned Commission decisions in this area make it difficult to draw conclusions as to the *degree* of market power required to establish anti-competitive effects. The Article 101(3) Guidelines state only that the requisite degree is 'less than the degree of market power required for a finding of dominance under Article [102]'.[182] This, combined with the moderately low market share thresholds, of 20–30 per cent, that are set out in the block exemptions,[183] which *exempt* agreements from the Article 101(1) prohibition, may cause firms to be concerned that market power issues will arise under Article 101(1) where relatively low market share thresholds are exceeded (10–20 per cent for agreements between competitors and 15–30 per cent for agreements between non-competitors).

(iv) Restraints on Competition between a Supplier's Distributors (Intra-brand Competition)

In a line of cases (explored more fully in Chapters 11 and 12) dealing with vertical and IP licensing agreements, the Court has tended to assume that restraints on a supplier's distributors/licensees competing with each other (restraints on intra-brand competition) are restrictive of competition unless objectively necessary to achieve some identified, legitimate purpose or for the existence of an agreement of that type or nature, for example: to facilitate the penetration of a new market by an undertaking through the prevention of free riding on a dealer's marketing and promotion efforts (see, in particular, *STM*); to encourage investment by a licensee; or to encourage non-price competition between dealers in a SDS (see, in particular, *Metro-SB-Grossmärkte GmbH v Commission (Metro 1)*[184]). This approach potentially brings many vertical and IP licensing agreements within the ambit of Article 101 whether or not the parties have market power and/or the ability to affect prices or output on the market, for example by foreclosing access to supply or distribution channels to competitors.

(v) Appreciability

Where an agreement does not contain object or 'hardcore' restraints, the Commission's De Minimis Notice provides that the agreement is not likely to restrict competition appreciably if the aggregate market share held by the parties to the agreement does not exceed certain thresholds—10 per cent (for competitors) or 15 per cent (for non-competitors). Where it is difficult to classify the agreement, the 10 per cent threshold applies and where competition in a market is restricted by the cumulative effect of agreements entered into by different suppliers and distributors, the threshold is reduced to 5 per cent.[185]

When calculating market shares, the market shares of 'connected undertakings' are included. The Notice also contains provisions governing the situation where undertakings meet the thresholds, but subsequently outgrow them.

[181] Article 101(3) Guidelines, paras. 17–27. [182] Ibid., para. 26. [183] See Section 4.E.

[184] Case 26/76, EU:C:1977:167, see also discussion of franchising and *Pronuptia*, n. 188 and text.

[185] Access to a market is unlikely to be foreclosed by the cumulative effect of parallel networks of agreements, however, where they cover less than 30% of the market. This provision is particularly important in the context of distribution agreements, for example beer-supply agreements, which operate in a similar way to other agreements on the market. Beer-supply agreements will not restrict competition at all, however, if they do not significantly contribute to a cumulative effect caused by the network on the market, see Case 234/89, *Delimitis* EU:C:1991:91, paras. 24–26, discussed in Section 3.C.iii.

Notice on agreements of minor importance which do not appreciably restrict competition under Article 101(1) of the Treaty on the Functioning of the European Union (De Minimis Notice) [2014] OJ C291/01

I.

3. In this Notice the Commission indicates, with the help of market share thresholds, the circumstances in which it considers that agreements which may have as their effect the prevention, restriction or distortion of competition within the internal market do not constitute an appreciable restriction of competition under Article 101 of the Treaty. This negative definition of appreciability does not imply that agreements between undertakings which exceed the thresholds set out in this Notice constitute an appreciable restriction of competition. Such agreements may still have only a negligible effect on competition and may therefore not be prohibited by Article 101(1) of the Treaty.

4. Agreements may also fall outside Article 101(1) of the Treaty because they are not capable of appreciably affecting trade between Member States. This Notice does not indicate what constitutes an appreciable effect on trade between Member States. Guidance to that effect is to be found in the Commission's Notice on effect on trade, in which the Commission quantifies, with the help of the combination of a 5 % market share threshold and a EUR 40 million turnover threshold, which agreements are in principle not capable of appreciably affecting trade between Member States. Such agreements normally fall outside Article 101(1) of the Treaty even if they have as their object the prevention, restriction or distortion of competition.

5. In cases covered by this Notice, the Commission will not institute proceedings either upon a complaint or on its own initiative. In addition, where the Commission has instituted proceedings but undertakings can demonstrate that they have assumed in good faith that the market shares mentioned in points 8, 9, 10 and 11 were not exceeded, the Commission will not impose fines. Although not binding on them, this Notice is also intended to give guidance to the courts and competition authorities of the Member States in their application of Article 101 of the Treaty.

6. The principles set out in this Notice also apply to decisions by associations of undertakings and to concerted practices.

7. This Notice is without prejudice to any interpretation of Article 101 of the Treaty which may be given by the Court of Justice of the European Union.

II.

8. The Commission holds the view that agreements between undertakings which may affect trade between Member States and which may have as their effect the prevention, restriction or distortion of competition within the internal market, do not appreciably restrict competition within the meaning of Article 101(1) of the Treaty:

(a) if the aggregate market share held by the parties to the agreement does not exceed 10 % on any of the relevant markets affected by the agreement, where the agreement is made between undertakings which are actual or potential competitors on any of those markets (agreements between competitors); or

(b) if the market share held by each of the parties to the agreement does not exceed 15 % on any of the relevant markets affected by the agreement, where the agreement is made between undertakings which are not actual or potential competitors on any of those markets (agreements between non-competitors).9. In cases where it is difficult to classify the agreement as either an agreement between competitors or an agreement between non-competitors the 10 % threshold is applicable.

10. Where, in a relevant market, competition is restricted by the cumulative effect of agreements for the sale of goods or services entered into by different suppliers or distributors (cumulative foreclosure effect of parallel networks of agreements having similar effects on the market), the market share thresholds set out in point 8 and 9 are reduced to 5 %, both for agreements between competitors and for agreements between non-competitors. Individual suppliers or distributors with a market share not exceeding 5 %, are in general not considered to contribute significantly to a cumulative foreclosure effect. A cumulative foreclosure effect is unlikely to exist if less than 30 % of the relevant market is covered by parallel (networks of) agreements having similar effects.

11. The Commission also holds the view that agreements do not appreciably restrict competition if the market shares of the parties to the agreement do not exceed the thresholds of respectively 10 %, 15 % and 5 % set out in points 8, 9 and 10 during two successive calendar years by more than 2 percentage points.

12. In order to calculate the market share, it is necessary to determine the relevant market. This consists of the relevant product market and the relevant geographic market. When defining the relevant market, reference should be had to the Notice on the definition of the relevant market. The market shares are to be calculated on the basis of sales value data or, where appropriate, purchase value data. If value data are not available, estimates based on other reliable market information, including volume data, may be used.

. . .

14. The safe harbour created by the market share thresholds set out in points 8, 9, 10 and 11 is particularly relevant for categories of agreements not covered by any Commission block exemption regulation. The safe harbour is also relevant for agreements covered by a Commission block exemption regulation to the extent that those agreements contain a so-called excluded restriction, that is a restriction not listed as a hardcore restriction but nonetheless not covered by the Commission block exemption regulation.

15. For the purpose of this Notice, the terms 'undertaking', 'party to the agreement', 'distributor' and 'supplier' include their respective connected undertakings.

16. For the purpose of the Notice 'connected undertakings' are:

(a) undertakings in which a party to the agreement, directly or indirectly:
   i. has the power to exercise more than half the voting rights, or
   ii. has the power to appoint more than half the members of the supervisory board, board of management or bodies legally representing the undertaking, or
   iii. has the right to manage the undertaking's affairs;

(b) undertakings which directly or indirectly have, over a party to the agreement, the rights or powers listed in (a);

(c) undertakings in which an undertaking referred to in (b) has, directly or indirectly, the rights or powers listed in (a);

(d) undertakings in which a party to the agreement together with one or more of the undertakings referred to in (a), (b) or (c), or in which two or more of the latter undertakings, jointly have the rights or powers listed in (a);

(e) undertakings in which the rights or the powers listed in (a) are jointly held by:
   i. parties to the agreement or their respective connected undertakings referred to in (a) to (d), or
   ii. one or more of the parties to the agreement or one or more of their connected undertakings referred to in (a) to (d) and one or more third parties.17. For the purposes of point € in point 16, the market share held by these jointly held undertakings is apportioned equally to each undertaking having the rights or the powers listed in point (a) in point 16.

D. ANCILLARY, OR OBJECTIVELY NECESSARY, RESTRAINTS

The Commission states in its Guidelines that restraints which are ancillary to the implementation of a non-restrictive agreement do not restrict competition within the meaning of Article 101(1). Thus, for example:

(i) Remia and Nutricia

In *Remia and Nutricia*,[186] the CJ recognised that a non-compete clause on the sale of a business was likely to be an essential part of an agreement to sell a business. Viewed *ex post*, a non-compete clause may appear to restrict competition between the parties. However, when assessed *ex ante* it may become clear that competition is not restricted. No undertaking would be willing to purchase the business without an assurance from the vendor that it will not remain in business in such a way that it would still be able to exploit the goodwill and the customers of the business sold. Nonetheless, the Court held that the non-compete clause must be limited to what is necessary to make the transaction viable. If it is broader than required for the sale, for example if it precludes the vendor from setting up any business within a wide geographic area for an indefinite period of time, it will restrict competition within the meaning of Article 101(1).[187]

> 17. It should be stated at the outset that the Commission has rightly submitted . . . that the fact that noncompetition clauses are included in an agreement for the sale of an undertaking is not of itself sufficient to remove such clauses from the scope of Article [101(1)].
>
> 18. In order to determine whether or not such clauses come within the prohibition in Article [101(1)], it is necessary to examine what would be the state of competition if those clauses did not exist.
>
> 19. If that were the case, and should the vendor and the purchaser remain competitors after the transfer, it is clear that the agreement for the transfer of the undertaking could not be given effect. The vendor, with his particularly detailed knowledge of the transferred undertaking, would still be in a position to win back his former customers immediately after the transfer and thereby drive the undertaking out of business. Against that background non-competition clauses incorporated in an agreement for the transfer of an undertaking in principle have the merit of ensuring that the transfer has the effect intended. By virtue of that very fact they contribute to the promotion of competition because they lead to an increase in the number of undertakings in the market in question.
>
> 20. Nevertheless, in order to have that beneficial effect on competition, such clauses must be necessary to the transfer of the undertaking concerned and their duration and scope must be strictly limited to that purpose. The Commission was therefore right in holding that where those conditions are satisfied such clauses are free of the prohibition laid down in Article [101(1)].

(ii) Pronuptia

In *Pronuptia de Paris GmbH v Pronuptia de Paris Irmgard Schillgallis*,[188] the CJ set out guidelines for a national court ruling on the compatibility of a distribution franchising agreement with Article 101(1). It held that restrictions objectively necessary to the successful operation of a distribution franchise agreement, which provided a means for an undertaking to derive financial benefit from its expertise without investing its own capital and a means for traders who do not have expertise to benefit from the franchisor's experience and reputation, would not restrict competition and fall outside of Article

[186] Case 42/84, EU:C:1985:327. Merger transactions now generally fall for appraisal under the EU Merger Reg. rather than Art. 101, see Chap. 15.

[187] Ibid., paras. 17–36.

[188] Case 161/84, EU:C:1986:41.

101(1). For example, the franchisor should be able to communicate know-how without running the risk that it would be used to benefit competitors and to take measures necessary to maintain the identity and reputation of the network.[189] In contrast, provisions which were not 'necessary for the protection of the know-how provided or the maintenance of the network's identity and reputation', such as provisions sharing markets between the franchisor and/or franchisees or preventing franchisees from engaging in price competition with each other, would restrict competition.[190]

(iii) Gøttrup-Klim

In *Gøttrup-Klim Grovvareforening and Others v Dansk Landbrugs Grovvareselskab AmbA*,[191] the CJ was asked by a Danish court whether a clause in the statutes of Dansk Landbrugs Grovvareselskab AmbA (a Danish cooperative association distributing farm supplies (DLG)) restricted competition within the meaning of Article 101(1). The object of DLG was to provide its members with farm supplies (such as fertiliser) at the lowest possible prices and to offer its members other services, particularly in the area of finance. In 1988, the statutes of DLG were changed, because of increasing competition, to preclude some of DLG's members from holding membership of, or any other kind of participation in, associations, societies, or other forms of cooperative organisation in competition with DLG, with regard to the purchase and sale of fertilisers and plant-protection products. Members which infringed this rule could be excluded from DLG (and some members were in fact excluded).[192]

DLG contended that the aim of the clause was not to restrict competition. On the contrary it (a) enabled the members to stand up to a few very large multinational producers of fertilisers and plant-protection products in order to obtain lower purchase prices for Danish farmers, and (b) prevented competitors' representatives from taking part in the association's management bodies (shareholders' committee and board of directors) in which business secrets were discussed. The claimants challenged the compatibility of the provision with Article 101 and sought compensation and damages in respect of the loss sustained from their exclusion from DLG. The CJ held that a provision in the statutes of a commercial cooperative society excluding members that participated in a cooperative organisation which competed would not be contrary to Article 101(1) so long as the provision was restricted to what was necessary to ensure that the cooperative functioned properly and maintained its contractual power in relation to producers.

(iv) MasterCard

Arguments relating to ancillary restraints were also important in *MasterCard, Inc v Commission*.[193] The CJ summarised the core of the Commission's decision which led to the appeals:

[189] Ibid., paras. 16–17, see also Chap. 10. [190] Ibid., para. 23.

[191] Case C-250/92, *Gøttrup-Klim* EU:C:1994:413.

[192] DLG had notified the amendment to the Commission for negative clearance or exemption, but at the time of the proceedings had not received an answer. In the proceedings, the Commission stated its view that the amendment to the statutes did not infringe Art. 101(1).

[193] Case C-382/12 P, EU:C:2014:2201 (before the GC, Case T-111/08, *MasterCard, Inc v Commission* EU:T:2012:260). See also e.g. Case T-360/09, *E.ON Ruhrgas* EU:T:2012:332 (a side letter providing for market sharing is not ancillary to an agreement for the construction and operation of a gas pipe line, paras. 60–82) and Case T-112/99, *M6* EU:T:2001:215, paras. 103–117 (the GC rejected the parties' argument that two clauses—an exclusivity clause granting TPS the exclusive right to broadcast general-interest channels and a clause essentially granting TPS the right of first refusal with regard to special-interest channels produced by the parties—were 'ancillary' to the operation of the non-restrictive joint venture; it found that the clauses were not objectively necessary for the operation of the joint venture and, even if they were, the Commission had not committed a manifest error in concluding that the restrictions were not proportionate to, or exceeded what was necessary for, the creation of the joint venture).

11. By the decision at issue, the Commission found that the appellants had infringed Article [101 TFEU] and Article 53 of the Agreement on the European Economic Area. That decision includes the considerations set out below:

- Interchange fees concern the relationship between issuing and acquiring banks on settlement of card transactions and correspond to a sum deducted in favour of the issuing bank. These fees must be distinguished from the costs charged to merchants by the acquiring bank (merchant service charges; 'MSC'). The decision at issue relates only to the MIF, and not to the interchange fees agreed bilaterally between issuing and acquiring banks or the interchange fees set collectively at national level.
- It is necessary to distinguish between three different product markets in the sphere of open bank card systems: first of all, the 'inter-systems market', in which the various card systems compete; then the 'issuing market', in which the issuing banks compete for the business of the cardholders; and, lastly, the 'acquiring market', in which the acquiring banks compete for the merchants' business. The relevant market for the purposes of the decision at issue is made up of the national acquiring markets in the Member States of the EEA.
- The appellants' decisions in relation to the setting of the MIF constitute decisions by an association of undertakings within the meaning of Article [101(1) TFEU], notwithstanding the changes in MasterCard's structure and governance arising from the IPO.
- The MIF have the effect of inflating the base of the MSC, while the latter could be lower if there were no MIF and if there were a prohibition of unilateral pricing *a posteriori* of transactions by the issuing banks, that is to say, a rule prohibiting issuing and acquiring banks from defining the amount of the interchange fees after a purchase has been made by one of the issuing bank's cardholders from one of the acquiring bank's merchants and the transaction has been submitted for payment ('prohibition of *ex post* pricing'). The MIF therefore lead to a restriction of price competition between acquiring banks to the detriment of merchants and their customers.
- MIF cannot be regarded as 'ancillary restrictions' in so far as they are not objectively necessary for the operation of an open payment card scheme. The scheme could function simply on the basis of the remuneration of issuing banks by cardholders, of acquiring banks by merchants, and of the owner of the scheme by the fees paid by the issuing and acquiring banks. Unlike restrictions which are necessary for implementing a main operation, restrictions which are merely desirable for the commercial success of that operation, or which offer greater efficiency, can be examined only within the framework of Article [101(3)] EC.
- With regard to the impact of the requirement, in the context of the MasterCard system, that all Maestro or MasterCard cards should be accepted irrespective of the issuing bank (the 'Honour All Cards Rule'), the elimination of the MIF would not mean that the issuing banks could freely and unilaterally set interchange fees, since that risk could be avoided by a rule having effects less restrictive of competition, such as the prohibition of *ex post* pricing.
- As regards Article [101(3)], the economic arguments put forward by the appellants in relation to the role of the MIF in the balancing of the MasterCard system and its maximisation are inadequate for the purposes of establishing that the MIF generate objective advantages. The appellants notably did not produce evidence to show that any objective advantages counterbalanced the disadvantages of the MIF for merchants and their customers.

MasterCard sought annulment of the decision. One argument was that the setting of the MIF in the payment system operated by MasterCard did not produce restrictive effects and/or was objectively necessary to the operation of the payment card system (without it the acquiring banks would be at the mercy of the issuing banks so the main operation would be difficult or even impossible to implement in its absence). On appeal, the CJ held that the GC had been correct to uphold the Commission's findings that MIFs were not objectively necessary, and so were not ancillary restrictions. In determining if a restriction is objectively necessary, it held that the correct test was whether MasterCard could function without a MIF—whether the operation would be impossible to carry out in the absence of the restriction in question—and not whether or not the absence of the restriction would have adverse consequences on MasterCard's business. The CJ confirmed that in testing the counterfactual in an ancillary restraints analysis, the Commission can rely on the existence of realistic alternatives that are less restrictive of competition; it is not limited to postulating simply the absence of the restriction, but may also consider other possible developments that may realistically occur. In so ruling, the CJ explored the meaning of an ancillary restriction and how the concept relates to the rule of reason debate and the analysis required under Article 101(3).

Case C-382/12 P, *MasterCard, Inc v Commission* EU:C:2014:2201

Court of Justice

89. It is apparent from the case-law of the Court of Justice that if a given operation or activity is not covered by the prohibition rule laid down in Article [101(1)], owing to its neutrality or positive effect in terms of competition, a restriction of the commercial autonomy of one or more of the participants in that operation or activity is not covered by that prohibition rule either if that restriction is objectively necessary to the implementation of that operation or that activity and proportionate to the objectives of one or the other (see to that effect, in particular, judgments in *Remia and Others* v *Commission*, . . . paragraphs 19 and 20; *Pronuptia de Paris*, . . . paragraphs 15 to 17; *DLG*, . . . paragraph 35, and *Oude Luttikhuis and Others*, . . . paragraphs 12 to 15).

90. Where it is not possible to dissociate such a restriction from the main operation or activity without jeopardising its existence and aims, it is necessary to examine the compatibility of that restriction with Article [101] in conjunction with the compatibility of the main operation or activity to which it is ancillary, even though, taken in isolation, such a restriction may appear on the face of it to be covered by the prohibition rule in Article [101(1)].

91. Where it is a matter of determining whether an anti-competitive restriction can escape the prohibition laid down in Article [101(1)] because it is ancillary to a main operation that is not anti-competitive in nature, it is necessary to inquire whether that operation would be impossible to carry out in the absence of the restriction in question. Contrary to what the appellants claim, the fact that that operation is simply more difficult to implement or even less profitable without the restriction concerned cannot be deemed to give that restriction the 'objective necessity' required in order for it to be classified as ancillary. Such an interpretation would effectively extend that concept to restrictions which are not strictly indispensable to the implementation of the main operation. Such an outcome would undermine the effectiveness of the prohibition laid down in Article [101(1)].

92. However, that interpretation does not mean that there has been an amalgamation of, on the one hand, the conditions laid down by the case-law for the classification—for the purposes of the application of Article [101(1)]—of a restriction as ancillary, and, on the other hand, the criterion of the indispensability required under Article [101(3)] in order for a prohibited restriction to be exempted.

93. In that regard, suffice it to note that those two provisions have different objectives and that the latter criterion relates to the issue whether coordination between undertakings that is liable to have an appreciable adverse impact on the parameters of competition, such as the price, the quantity and quality of the goods or services, which is therefore covered by the prohibition rule laid down in Article [101(1)], can none the less, in the context of Article [101(3)], be considered indispensable to the improvement of production or distribution or to the promotion of technical or economic progress, while allowing consumers a fair share of the resulting benefits. By contrast, as is apparent from paragraphs 89 and 90 of the present judgment, the objective necessity test referred to in those paragraphs concerns the question whether, in the absence of a given restriction of commercial autonomy, a main operation

or activity which is not caught by the prohibition laid down in Article [101(1)] and to which that restriction is secondary, is likely not to be implemented or not to proceed.

94. In ruling, in paragraph 89 of the judgment under appeal, that '[o]nly those restrictions which are necessary in order for the main operation to be able to function in any event may be regarded as falling within the scope of the theory of ancillary restrictions', and in concluding, in paragraph 90 of the judgment under appeal, that 'the fact that the absence of the MIF may have adverse consequences for the functioning of the MasterCard system does not, in itself, mean that the MIF must be regarded as being objectively necessary, if it is apparent from an examination of the MasterCard system in its economic and legal context that it is still capable of functioning without it', the General Court did not, therefore, err in law.

. . .

106. . . . [A]s is apparent from paragraphs 96 and 97 of the present judgment, the appellants are critical of the fact that the General Court relied on the premiss of a prohibition of *ex post* pricing—a scenario which, in their view, would not occur, in the absence of MIF, without a regulatory intervention, and which in any event would not differ from that resulting from the existence of the MIF—in order to conclude in paragraph 96 of the judgment under appeal that '[t]he fact that there are default transaction settlement procedures less restrictive of competition than the MIF precludes the latter from being regarded as objectively necessary for the operation of the MasterCard system'.

107. It must be noted in that regard that, as is apparent from paragraphs 89 and 90 of the present judgment, in the context of the assessment, for the purposes of the application of Article [101(1)], of the ancillary nature of a given restriction of commercial autonomy in relation to a main operation or activity, it is necessary to consider not only whether that restriction is necessary for the implementation of the main operation or activity, but also whether that restriction is proportionate to the underlying objectives of that operation or activity.

108. It should be pointed out that, irrespective of the context or aim in relation to which a counterfactual hypothesis is used, it is important that that hypothesis is appropriate to the issue it is supposed to clarify and that the assumption on which it is based is not unrealistic.

109. Accordingly, in order to contest the ancillary nature of a restriction, as referred to in paragraphs 89 and 90 of the present judgment, the Commission may rely on the existence of realistic alternatives that are less restrictive of competition than the restriction at issue.

110. In that regard, as is apparent from paragraph 97 of the present judgment, the appellants also submit, in essence, that the General Court wrongly failed to penalise the Commission for not having tried, in the decision at issue, to understand how competition would function in the absence both of the MIF and of the prohibition of *ex post* pricing, a prohibition which the appellants would not have chosen to adopt without a regulatory intervention.

111. However, the alternatives on which the Commission may rely in the context of the assessment of the objective necessity of a restriction are not limited to the situation that would arise in the absence of the restriction in question but may also extend to other counterfactual hypotheses based, inter alia, on realistic situations that might arise in the absence of that restriction. The General Court was therefore correct in concluding, in paragraph 99 of the judgment under appeal, that the counterfactual hypothesis put forward by the Commission could be taken into account in the examination of the objective necessity of the MIF in so far as it was realistic and enabled the MasterCard system to be economically viable.

Arguments that restraints were ancillary to a pro-competitive agreement, venture or objective were also raised, but rejected by the Commission and EU Courts in both *Telefónica SA v Commission*[194]

[194] Cases T-208 and 216/13, *Portugal Telecom* and *Telefónica SA v Commission* EU:T:2016:369, *aff'd* Case C-487/16 P, *Telefónica SA v Commission* EU:C:2017:961.

and *Lundbeck* (discussed in Chapter 12).[195] In *Telefónica*, it was not accepted that a non-compete clause between Telefónica and Portugal Telecom affecting the Iberian market was ancillary to a transaction concerning a venture whose activity was confined to Brazil (the clause was also not saved from illegality by the stipulation that it applied only 'to the extent permitted by the law').

The doctrine of ancillary restraints is not without difficulties. Not only can it be difficult to separate a main transaction from its ancillary restraints, but it is by no means easy to identify whether or not a particular restraint is 'ancillary' to the operation of that agreement or what the counterfactual is. Further, as explored further below, its relationship to other analysis required under Article 101 is not entirely clear.

E. RESTRAINTS INHERENT IN THE PURSUIT OF A LEGITIMATE (PUBLIC POLICY?) OBJECTIVE: *WOUTERS* AND *MECA-MEDINA*

In *Wouters v Algemene Raad van de Nederlandse Orde van Advocaten*,[196] the CJ considered the compatibility with Article 101(1) of rules[197] adopted in the Netherlands which prohibited members of the Bar practising in full partnership with accountants. It held that although the rules had an adverse effect on competition and limited production and technical development within the meaning of Article 101(1)(b) (partnerships of lawyers and accountants would, for example, be able to offer a wider range of services and result in economies of scale), account had to be taken of the objectives of the restrictions and the overall context in which they were adopted. Not every agreement that restricted the freedom of action of the parties necessarily fell within the prohibition of Article 101(1).

Case C-309/99, *Wouters v Algemene Raad van de Nederlandse Orde van Advocaten* EU:C:2002:98

Court of Justice

73. By its second question the national court seeks, essentially, to ascertain whether a regulation such as the 1993 Regulation which, in order to guarantee the independence and loyalty to the client of members of the Bar who provide legal assistance in conjunction with members of other liberal professions, adopts universally binding rules governing the formation of multi-disciplinary partnerships, has the object or effect of restricting competition within the common market and is likely to affect trade between Member States.

. . .

86. It appears to the Court that the national legislation in issue in the main proceedings has an adverse effect on competition and may affect trade between Member States.

87. As regards the adverse effect on competition, the areas of expertise of members of the Bar and of accountants may be complementary. Since legal services, especially in business law, more and more frequently require recourse to an accountant, a multi-disciplinary partnership of members of the Bar and accountants would make it possible to offer a wider range of services, and indeed to propose new ones. Clients would thus be able to turn to a single structure for a large part of the services necessary for the organisation, management and operation of their business (the 'one-stop shop' advantage).

[195] Case T-472/13, *H Lundbeck A/S v Commission* EU:T:2016:449, *aff'd* Case C-591/16 P, *H Lundbeck A/S v Commission* EU:C:2021:243.

[196] Case C-309/99, EU:C:2002:98.

[197] The Bar was created by legislation which imposed an obligation on it to ensure the proper practice of the profession and power to adopt measures to contribute to that end.

88. Furthermore, a multi-disciplinary partnership of members of the Bar and accountants would be capable of satisfying the needs created by the increasing interpenetration of national markets and the consequent necessity for continuous adaptation to national and international legislation.

89. Nor, finally, is it inconceivable that the economies of scale resulting from such multi-disciplinary partnerships might have positive effects on the cost of services.

90. A prohibition of multi-disciplinary partnerships of members of the Bar and accountants, such as that laid down in the 1993 Regulation, is therefore liable to limit production and technical development within the meaning of Article [101(1)(b)].

. . .

97. However, not every agreement between undertakings or every decision of an association of undertakings which restricts the freedom of action of the parties or of one of them necessarily falls within the prohibition laid down in Article [101(1)]. For the purposes of application of that provision to a particular case, account must first of all be taken of the overall context in which the decision of the association of undertakings was taken or produces its effects. More particularly, account must be taken of its objectives, which are here connected with the need to make rules relating to organisation, qualifications, professional ethics, supervision and liability, in order to ensure that the ultimate consumers of legal services and the sound administration of justice are provided with the necessary guarantees in relation to integrity and experience (see, to that effect, Case C-3/95 *Reisebüro Broede* . . . paragraph 38). It has then to be considered whether the consequential effects restrictive of competition are inherent in the pursuit of those objectives.

98. Account must be taken of the legal framework applicable in the Netherlands, on the one hand, to members of the Bar and to the Bar of the Netherlands, which comprises all the registered members of the Bar in that Member State, and on the other hand, to accountants.

99. As regards members of the Bar, it has consistently been held that, in the absence of specific Community rules in the field, each Member State is in principle free to regulate the exercise of the legal profession in its territory (Case 107/83 *Klopp* . . . paragraph 17, and *Reisebüro*, paragraph 37). For that reason, the rules applicable to that profession may differ greatly from one Member State to another.

100. The current approach of the Netherlands, where Article 28 of the Advocatenwet entrusts the Bar of the Netherlands with responsibility for adopting regulations designed to ensure the proper practice of the profession, is that the essential rules adopted for that purpose are, in particular, the duty to act for clients in complete independence and in their sole interest, the duty, mentioned above, to avoid all risk of conflict of interest and the duty to observe strict professional secrecy.

101. Those obligations of professional conduct have not inconsiderable implications for the structure of the market in legal services, and more particularly for the possibilities for the practice of law jointly with other liberal professions which are active on that market.

102. Thus, they require of members of the Bar that they should be in a situation of independence *vis-à-vis* the public authorities, other operators and third parties, by whom they must never be influenced. They must furnish, in that respect, guarantees that all steps taken in a case are taken in the sole interest of the client.

103. By contrast, the profession of accountant is not subject, in general, and more particularly, in the Netherlands, to comparable requirements of professional conduct.

104. As the Advocate General has rightly pointed out in paragraphs 185 and 186 of his Opinion, there may be a degree of incompatibility between the 'advisory' activities carried out by a member of the Bar and the 'supervisory' activities carried out by an accountant. The written observations submitted by the respondent in the main proceedings show that accountants in the Netherlands perform a task of certification of accounts. They undertake an objective examination and audit of their clients' accounts, so as to be able to impart to interested third parties their personal opinion concerning the reliability of those accounts. It follows that in the Member State concerned accountants are not bound by a rule of professional secrecy comparable to that of members of the Bar, unlike the position under German law, for example.

105. The aim of the 1993 Regulation is therefore to ensure that, in the Member State concerned, the rules of professional conduct for members of the Bar are complied with, having regard to the prevailing perceptions of the profession in that State. The Bar of the Netherlands was entitled to consider that members of the Bar might no longer be in a position to advise and represent their clients independently and in the observance of strict professional secrecy if they belonged to an organisation which is also responsible for producing an account of the financial results of the transactions in respect of which their services were called upon and for certifying those accounts.

106. Moreover, the concurrent pursuit of the activities of statutory auditor and of adviser, in particular legal adviser, also raises questions within the accountancy profession itself, as may be seen from the Commission Green Paper 96/C/321/01 'The role, the position and the liability of the statutory auditor within the European Union' (OJ 1996 C 321, p. 1; see, in particular, paragraphs 4.12 to 4.14).

107. A regulation such as the 1993 Regulation could therefore reasonably be considered to be necessary in order to ensure the proper practice of the legal profession, as it is organised in the Member State concerned.

108. Furthermore, the fact that different rules may be applicable in another Member State does not mean that the rules in force in the former State are incompatible with [EU] law (see, to that effect, Case C-108/96 *Mac Quen and Others* . . . paragraph 33). Even if multi-disciplinary partnerships of lawyers and accountants are allowed in some Member States, the Bar of the Netherlands is entitled to consider that the objectives pursued by the 1993 Regulation cannot, having regard in particular to the legal regimes by which members of the Bar and accountants are respectively governed in the Netherlands, be attained by less restrictive means (see, to that effect, with regard to a law reserving judicial debt-recovery activity to lawyers, *Reisebüro*, paragraph 41).

109. In light of those considerations, it does not appear that the effects restrictive of competition such as those resulting for members of the Bar practising in the Netherlands from a regulation such as the 1993 Regulation go beyond what is necessary in order to ensure the proper practice of the legal profession (see, to that effect, Case C-250/92 *DLG* . . . paragraph 35).

110. Having regard to all the foregoing considerations, the answer to be given to the second question must be that a national regulation such as the 1993 Regulation adopted by a body such as the Bar of the Netherlands does not infringe Article [101(1)], since that body could reasonably have considered that that regulation, despite the effects restrictive of competition that are inherent in it, is necessary for the proper practice of the legal profession, as organised in the Member State concerned.

The reasoning in this case is not easy. Despite appearing to find that the conduct had 'an adverse effect on competition', in terms of services that could be offered and economies of scope, and was liable to limit production and technical development, the CJ indicated that the regulation at issue did not infringe Article 101(1) (by object or effect)[198] 'since the association could reasonably have considered that, despite its inherent restrictive effect on competition, it was necessary for the proper practice of the legal profession as organized in the Member States concerned'.[199] The objective of the rules was to ensure that the ultimate consumers of legal services and the sound administration of justice were provided with the necessary guarantees in relation to integrity and experience. For example, members of the Bar might not be in a position to advise and represent clients independently if they belonged to an organisation which was also responsible for producing an account for the financial results of the transactions in respect of which their services were called upon and for certifying those

[198] The CJ had after all made it clear that the rules might have negative effects on prices, innovation, and/or the variety or quality of goods and services that could be expected.

[199] Case C-309/99, EU:C:2002:98, at paras. 106–110. Contrast Léger AG in this case (the rule of reason in EU competition law was strictly confined to a 'purely competitive balance-sheet of the effects of the agreement' and social concerns, and considerations connected with the pursuit of the public interest, were relevant only to the Art. 101(3) appraisal, paras. 104–105).

accounts. As the agreement did not infringe Article 101(1), it did not have to be determined whether the rules of ethics could have been exempted through the application of Article 101(3).[200] In so ruling, the CJ did not appear, as it had done with respect to collective bargaining agreements in *Albany*,[201] to hold that reasonable rules relating to the regulation of the provision of professional services should fall outside Article 101(1) altogether. Rather, in determining whether Article 101(1) was infringed it seemed to weigh the anti-competitive effects of the agreement against benefits which were *not* economic efficiency benefits.

The approach taken in *Wouters* is not easy to reconcile with all of the jurisprudence, for example *BIDS* or the GC's (subsequent) judgment in *Laurent Piau*.[202] In the latter case, the GC held, distinguishing *Wouters*, that the actual principle of a licence, required by FIFA (a private body which was not acting according to power delegated by a public authority) as a condition for carrying on the occupation of players' agent, constituted a 'barrier to access to that economic activity and therefore necessarily affects competition' which could be accepted 'only in so far as the conditions set out in Article [101(3)] are satisfied'.[203]

Further, if the approach in *M6* and the Commission's analytical framework is correct, it might have been expected that the CJ in *Wouters* would (in line with the approach taken in *Piau* and *BIDS*) have found that the agreement restricted competition (in terms of the services that could be offered and economies of scope)[204] and held that the justifications raised by the parties could then only have been appraised when determining whether the rules of ethics could be excepted through the application of Article 101(3). The CJ did not, however, take this course. Had it done so, the referring national court, which did not, at this time, have jurisdiction to rule on the compatibility of the agreement with Article 101(3), would have been compelled to rule that the regulations, or at least the restrictive rules within them, were void. This has led some to argue that, because the CJ considered that the Bar Association had not been unreasonable in considering that the restrictive rules were warranted by reference to the objective pursued, it conflated and operated Article 101(1) and Article 101(3) as if they were a single provision in order to avoid this consequence.[205] Even if, however, this explains *why* the Court might have decided to adopt this course of action, the case still stands for authority (applied in subsequent cases) that some balancing of the restriction(s) identified against *other* legitimate objectives can take place under Article 101(1) and that restraints proportionate to such legitimate objectives fall outside of its scope entirely. Indeed, the *Wouters* exception has subsequently been invoked in a number of cases,[206]

[200] Or, perhaps through Art. 106(2) on the grounds that the rules were necessary to the task entrusted by statute to the Dutch Bar Council. The CJ considered, however, that it was precluded from applying Art. 106(2) as the Bar Council was not an entrusted undertaking or group of undertakings within the meaning of Art. 106, Case C-309/99, EU:C:2002:98, paras. 111–116. Contrast e.g. Léger AG, paras. 114 and 201, see Chap. 8.

[201] Case C-67/96, *Albany International BV v Stichting Bedrijfspensioenfonds Textielindustrie* EU:C:1999:430, discussed in Chap. 4.

[202] Case T-193/02, *Laurent Piau v Commission* EU:T:2005:22.

[203] Ibid., para. 101. The regulations, or at least the restrictive rules within them, would thus have been void as they had not been notified to the Commission for exemption, see Reg. 17 [1959–1962] OJ Spec. Ed. 87, Art. 4.

[204] See n. 198.

[205] See J. Goyder and A. Albors-Llorens, *Goyder's EC Competition Law* (5th edn, Oxford University Press, 2009), 115–116. For the view that *Wouters* is explicable by the fact that the rule was promulgated not by an undertaking but by an association of undertakings, see Odudu, n. 2, 53.

[206] Albeit unsuccessfully in many cases, e.g. Case C-1/12, *Ordem dos Técnicos Oficiais de Contas (OTOC) v Autoridade da Concorrência* EU:C:2013:127 (the CJ held that rules adopted by a professional association of chartered accountants providing that certain compulsory training to be undertaken by chartered accountants could be provided only by OTOC was not necessary to achieve a legitimate objective (in that case to guarantee the quality of the services offered by chartered accountants). The rules eliminated all competition rather than putting in place criteria to ensure training bodies equal access to the market); Case T-90/11, *Ordre national des pharmaciens v Commission* EU:T:2014:1049 (the GC upheld the Commission's decision fining three French pharmacists' trade bodies for various decisions: (a) setting minimum prices for certain medical analyses through restrictions on rebates; and (b) restricting the development of laboratory groups which competed with pharmacists, and rejecting justifications for the conduct based on *Wouters*); Cases C-184/13 etc., *API v Ministero delle Infrastrutture e dei Trasporti* EU:C:2014:2147 and Case 136/12, *Consiglio nazionale dei geologi v AGCM* EU:C:2013:489.

including *Meca-Medina*,[207] where the Court held that restraints on freedom of action resulting from anti-doping rules do not constitute a restriction of competition[208] if inherent in, and justified by, a legitimate objective, in that case the organisation and proper conduct of competitive sport (such rules relating to the organisation of competitive sport fall outside the application of Article 101(1)).[209]

The question of when sporting rules are compatible with Article 101 is also central to the pending appeals before the Court of Justice in the *International Skating Union (ISU)* and the *European Super League* cases.[210] The former raises the question of whether ISU eligibility rules—broadly, enabling skaters participating in certain competitor events to be sanctioned with a life-time ban from skating in ISU events—restrict competition by object or effect or are justified by the objective of protecting the integrity of speed skating, whilst the latter raises the question of whether UEFA/FIFA's refusal to authorise a new European Super League under their prior authorisation schemes is compatible with Article 101. On 15 December 2022, Advocate General Rantos delivered his opinions in the separate cases, proposing a framework of analysis for determining whether the eligibility and authorisation rules respectively restrict competition by object or effect (for example, by unduly denying third parties access to the market), and whether potential restraints may be ancillary, and proportionate, to pursuit of a non-commercial objective (and so take precedence over any restriction).[211]

The question of how widely the *Wouters* exception applies has been much debated—Monti, for example, argues that pursuing a free movement-style analysis in the competition sphere allows an association of undertakings to pursue, in a non-discriminatory and proportionate way, an objective in the public interest which could not be achieved by other less restrictive measures (so allowing the Court to take account of non-competition factors relating to domestic interests).[212]

G. Monti, 'Article 81 EC and Public Policy' (2002) 30 *CMLRev* 1057, 1087–1088

This is a remarkable *ratio decidendi* for the Court intertwines principles of competition law and free movement . . . In simple terms, the line of reasoning followed is this: we know from *Cassis de Dijon* that an indistinctly applicable domestic rule which is an obstacle to the free movement of goods does not fall under the prohibition in Article [34] if it is necessary to satisfy a mandatory requirement relating to, for example, fairness of commercial transactions or the defence of the consumer. The same approach has been applied in relation to other freedoms. In *Wouters*, the Court relies on this line of case-law, specifically referring to *Reisbüro Vroede*, a case in relation to the regulation of the legal profession in the context of Article [56] (freedom to provide services) where it held that a non-discriminatory rule of German law which infringed Article [56] might be justified in the public interest. The Court then holds that the principle created by this case-law (labelled by many commentators a 'rule of reason') applies *mutatis mutandis* to Article [101]. Having transposed a rule from the free movement case-law into the competition case-law, the Court was free to say that the prohibition in Article [101] could not apply. This reasoning incorporates the rule of reason deployed in the free movement area as a mechanism

[207] Case C-519/04 P, *Meca-Medina v Commission* EU:C:2006:492.

[208] '[T]he penal nature of the anti-doping rules . . . are capable of producing adverse effects on competition because they could, if penalties were ultimately to prove unjustified, result in an athlete's unwarranted exclusion from sporting events', ibid., para. 47.

[209] Ibid., paras. 45–47. The CJ set aside the judgment of the GC which had held that the sporting rules had nothing to do with economic activity and so fell outside the scope of Art. 101, Case T-313/02, EU:T:2004:282.

[210] Case C-124/21 P EU:C:2022:988 (Opinion of Rantos AG, judgment pending (relating to COMP/40.208, *ISU* 8 December 2017 (finding that the *Meca-Medina* criteria were not met), *aff'd* Case T-93/18, EU:T:2020:610) and Case C-333/21, *European Super League Company, S.L. v Union of European Football Associations (UEFA) and Fédération Internationale de Football Association (FIFA)* EU:C:2022:993 Opinion of Rantos AG, judgment pending.

[211] Case C-124/21 P, EU:C:2022:988 and Case C-333/21, EU:C:2022:993.

[212] See also G. Monti, *EC Competition Law* (Cambridge University Press, 2007), 110–113.

> for justifying an agreement otherwise unlawful under Article [101(1)]. It is ironic that while the Court (most explicitly in *Métropole*) has regularly refused to adopt an *American-style* rule of reason in Article [101] (whereby the legality of an agreement would depend upon whether, on balance it increased consumer welfare) it has in *Wouters* given strong indications that what I shall call the *European-style rule of reason*, developed in the free movement field, can apply to competition cases so that an anti-competitive agreement necessary to preserve a domestic mandatory requirement of public policy is allowed to escape the application of Article [101]. Thus *Wouters* is another in a line of cases that exemplifies what Mortelmans[213] labelled a 'convergence' in the application of the rules on free movement and competition. The purpose of convergence in this case is to allow the Court to take into account non-competition factors which relate to *domestic* interests.

Although in some cases where the *Wouters* exception has not been successfully invoked a restriction of competition by object has been found, the Court's approach is different to that adopted in the traditional line of cases dealing with object restraints such as *CB* and *Generics*. First, in conducting contextual analysis the Court goes beyond looking for evidence which casts reasonable doubt on a conclusion that the agreement at issue reveals sufficient harm, testing not only if the restraints pursue the legitimate objective but also whether they are inherent, necessary, and proportionate to them.[214] Secondly, if the restraints are found to be inherent in, and proportionate to, a legitimate objective, they fall outside the scope of Article 101(1) entirely—it does not have to be determined whether their effect is the restriction of competition. Public policy justifications thus remove practices from the scope of Article 101(1) altogether, whilst the pro-competitive justifications referred to in *Generics* only remove practices from the by object category. The appeals in *ISU* and *European Super Leagues* provides an opportunity for the Court of Justice to clarify the relationship between these strands of case law as well as the scope of the *Wouters* exception. In the latter case, Advocate General Rantos sets out his view that the *Wouters* analysis is distinct from object (or effects) analysis. Consequently, it is only if the practice potentially restricts competition that it is to be considered whether the restriction(s) are inherent in the pursuit of legitimate objectives and proportionate to them.

F. CONCLUSIONS AND REFLECTIONS ON ARTICLE 101(1) ANALYSIS

The previous sections highlight the crucial distinction that Article 101 draws between agreements which restrict competition by object or effect.

Object restraints are, on account of their injurious nature, assumed to produce anti-competitive effects and to restrict competition appreciably within the meaning of Article 101(1). This assumption cannot be rebutted by proving that anti-competitive effects did not in fact result from the agreement (as long as it is capable of producing such effects). The parties may, however, seek to justify such an agreement by establishing that it meets the conditions of Article 101(3). Although sidestepping individual economic analysis, the assumption of anti-competitive effects in object cases is justified, *so long as* the category is based on economic principles and is designed to eradicate the need to prove, at cost, the adverse consequences of agreements which are in practice highly likely to harm competition and are highly unlikely to have any redeeming justification. The controversial issue is not therefore the existence of the object category, but the question of which agreements fall within it.

[213] K. Mortelmans, 'Towards Convergence in the Application of the Rules on Free Movement and on Competition' (2001) 38 *CMLRev* 613.

[214] The approach undoubtedly has conceptual similarities to, and parallels with, other cases in which the courts have accepted that restraints which are objectively necessary to the operation of a pro-competitive commercial transaction may fall outside Art. 101(1), see Section 3.D.

The jurisprudence of the EU Courts makes it clear that the content, objective, and context of an agreement are all crucial factors in determining whether it has a restrictive object. Although it can be predicted that certain 'established' restraints will be found, in principle, to have a restrictive purpose, there is no definitive list of object restraints as an abbreviated analysis of 'context', as well as content, forms part of the characterisation exercise. Indeed, not only have competition agencies and claimants sought to extend the category beyond these established restraints, but defendants have sought to argue that in some contexts even these seemingly severe restraints should not be held to be of their very nature injurious to competition. Recent cases have stressed the narrow nature of the category of object restraints. If contractual measures do not reveal a sufficiently injurious impact in the context which they operate, for example because they may be ancillary to a legitimate, pro-competitive objective pursued by the parties, a fuller examination of the effects of the agreement is required. 'Restrictions by object' and 'restrictions by effect' are not therefore separate analytical approaches but are joined by unifying concepts. In each case, the analysis (the decision to place an agreement in the object category or the appraisal of restrictive effects) must be referable to a theory of harm and, in particular, to the question of whether the agreement can be expected to restrict competition.[215] In object cases, EU decision-takers must, to ensure that the category is not over-inclusive, be clear how experience, theory, and context justifies a conclusion that competitive harm is highly likely[216] (likely, potential, or a capability of, anti-competitive effects is insufficient). The difference between object and effect analysis is thus 'more of degree and depth than of kind. The two types of analysis are simply different ways, in the light of the knowledge and experience acquired by the authority, to answer one and the same question: whether the agreement at issue may prevent, restrict or distort competition in the internal market.'[217]

Where there is no restriction by object, a claimant is required to demonstrate restrictive effects before the parties to the agreement can be required to provide a robust justification of its efficiencies within the Article 101(3) forum. This requires a detailed analysis of the effects of the agreement in the context in which operates taking account of the position that would have occurred in the absence of the agreement. It has been seen that the cases in this sphere are not all entirely easy to reconcile with each other or a purely consumer welfare objective. Thus whilst some cases hold that restrictive effects may be demonstrated by establishing that the agreement affects actual or potential competition to such an extent that on the relevant market negative effects on prices, output, innovation, or the variety or quality of goods and services can be expected (it will allow the parties to create, maintain, strengthen, or exploit market power (e.g. *Delimitis, European Night Services, M6*, and *O2*)), others focus more closely on the objective necessity of the restraints to a pro-competitive agreement (for example, certain vertical restraints on intra-brand competition).

Two other lines of cases also hold that agreements incorporating restraints which are objectively necessary to the implementation of a main non-restrictive operation (which would be impossible to implement without the restriction—frequently described as ancillary restraints cases) or other legitimate objective (e.g., *Wouters*)[218] fall outside Article 101(1). These latter strands of cases, developed

[215] See M. de la Mano and A. Jones, 'Vertical Agreements under EU Competition Law: Proposals for Pushing Article 101 Analysis, and the Modernization Process, to a Logical Conclusion' in D. Healey, M. Jacobs and R. L. Smith (eds.), *Research Handbook on Methods and Models of Competition Law* (Edward Elgar, 2020).

[216] Wahl AG in Case C-67/13, *CB* EU:2014:1958, para. 8.

[217] See Bobek AG in Case C-228/18, *Budapest Bank* EU:C:2019:678, para. 32.

[218] But see the view of Léger AG in Case C-309/99, *Wouters v Algemene Raad van de Nederlandse Orde van Advocaten* EU:C:2002:390, para. 103 ('Confronted with certain classes of agreement . . . [the CJ] has drawn up a competition balance-sheet and, where the balance is positive, has held that the clauses necessary to perform the agreement fell outside the prohibition laid down by Article [101(1)]'). See also Case 1035/1/1/04, *The Racecourse Association (the 'RCA') v OFT* [2005] CAT 29, where the UK's Competition Appeal Tribunal (CAT) confessed to having 'some difficulty in reconciling' the approach in *Gøttrup-Klim* and *Wouters* with that in *M6*. It considered that the analysis required under Art. 101(1) by the CJ in *Gøttrup-Klim* and *Wouters* was a rather more flexible exercise than the GC had been willing to appreciate in *M6*.

from early jurisprudence (prior to modernisation), do not fit neatly within either the object of effect categories of analysis, and display slightly different nuances, without fully clarifying their relationship with each other and/or other Article 101(1) and Article 101(3) analysis more generally.

In the vertical objective necessity and *Wouters* line of cases, the assessment adopted seems to operate as a form of truncated Article 101(1) analysis, involving balancing, and consideration, of the benefits raised by the defendant against harms (analysis that seems very close to that required under Article 101(3) and which is reminiscent of the European-style rule of reason analysis conducted in internal market case law). If the restraints seem necessary, and proportionate, to the legitimate agreement or objective pursued, they do not restrict competition (by object or effect) and fall outside of Article 101(1)—it seems to be assumed that the legitimate objective pursued outweighs any restrictions which flow from the restraints identified (e.g. *STM*, *Pronuptia*, *Metro*, *Wouters*). If they are not necessary and proportionate, however in *Pierre Fabre* and *ISU* (General Court) it was held that the arrangements would be restrictive of competition (and in those cases, it held restrictive of competition by object). This analysis does not, however, exactly mirror that conducted in other by object cases (in conducting contextual analysis the Court goes beyond looking for evidence which casts reasonable doubt on a conclusion that the agreement at issue reveals sufficient harm, testing not only if the restraints pursue the legitimate objective but also whether they are inherent, necessary, and proportionate to them) or by effect cases (requiring an assessment of the agreement's effects on competition or the extent to which a negative effect on prices, output, innovation, or the variety or quality of goods and services can be expected). Avoiding this difficulty, Advocate General Rantos in the *European Super League* case, sets out his view that the ancillary restraints appraisal laid down for the first time in *Wouters* is distinct from object (or effects) analysis. Consequently, it must be determined whether the agreement, concerted practice, or decision restricts competition by object or effect. Even if there is a restriction of competition, however, restrictions inherent in the pursuit of legitimate objectives and proportionate to those objectives, escape the Article 101(1) prohibition—that is where they allow the legitimate objectives pursued to be achieved without going beyond what is necessary for their achievement.

The approach adopted by Advocate General Rantos accords more closely with that adopted in the commercial ancillary restraints cases, where the appraisal of necessity and proportionality seems to function both as a form of truncated Article 101(1) analysis and a characterisation mechanism. If they are necessary and proportionate to a legitimate objective, they (as previously) fall outside Article 101(1). If they are not, however, it must be determined whether the agreement as a whole restricts competition by object and so is assumed to infringe Article 101(1) (see e.g. *Telefónica*), or whether its effect is to restrict competition (see e.g. *MasterCard*).

It is submitted that although these latter lines of cases may have made sense in the pre-modernised era (and when getting an Article 101(3) exemption for an agreement was frequently impractical) and make sense as characterisation mechanisms (determining whether object or effects analysis should be applied), their use as method for truncated analysis is more problematic to the scheme of Article 101 envisaged by the Commission and the GC in *M6*. Not only do the cases seem to miss some important steps in the competition analysis (they do not fully analyse the restrictive impact of the relevant restraints), but they appear to demand inquiries under Article 101(1) which duplicate or overlap with analysis required in the process of applying Article 101(3). The law in this area would thus benefit from development and refinement. Greater use of the EU administrative framework could provide the flexible forum for Article 101(1) effects analysis (rather than just the limits of the by object category) to be advanced and clarified.[219]

[219] See Jones and Kovacic, n. 45.

4. ARTICLE 101(3)

A. APPLICATION OF ARTICLE 101(3)

Although a number of block exemptions exempt certain categories of agreement from Article 101(3) (see Section 4.E) and in exceptional circumstances comfort letters may be granted by the Commission, it has not been possible, since 2004, to notify an individual agreement to the Commission seeking an exemption decision from the Commission—it is thus generally for parties to self-assess the compatibility of their agreements with Article 101(3). Article 101(3) is only applied individually, when raised in proceedings before the Commission, NCAs or national courts. As since 'modernisation' there have been very few cases dealing with the application of Article 101(3) to an agreement (most cases brought by the Commission/NCAs relate to object infringements and provide limited scope for Article 101(3) arguments to be raised), little light has been shed by the jurisprudence on the question of how the complex balancing of pro- and anti-competitive effects, including quantitative and qualitative measures of consumer welfare (price, output, quality, choice, and variety), is to be conducted.

B. BURDEN AND STANDARD OF PROOF

Agreements meeting the conditions of a block exemption are assumed to meet the Article 101(3) criteria and are automatically exempted from Article 101(1) (the benefit of a block exemption can only be withdrawn prospectively). In an individual case, however, those claiming the benefit of Article 101(3) have the burden[220] of establishing, by means of convincing argument and evidence, that *all* four[221] Article 101(3) criteria are satisfied:[222] (1) that the agreement achieves the specified benefits; (2) that a fair share of those benefits are passed on to consumers; (3) that the agreement does not contain any indispensable restraints; and (4) that it does not eliminate competition in respect of a substantial part of the products in question. The exception rule applies only for as long as the four conditions are met.[223]

Once undertakings have submitted evidence to support an argument that Article 101(3) is satisfied, it is for the fact-finder to examine whether, on the balance of probabilities,[224] the agreement meets these criteria. The Commission's view is that efficiencies achieved by the agreement must be demonstrated to outweigh negative effects, so that the agreement is on balance pro-competitive.[225]

> Agreements that restrict competition may at the same time have pro-competitive effects by way of efficiency gains. Efficiencies may create additional value by lowering the cost of producing an output, improving the quality of the product or creating a new product. When the pro-competitive effects of an agreement outweigh its anti-competitive effects the agreement is on balance pro-competitive and compatible with the objectives of the [EU] competition rules. The net effect of such agreements is to promote the very essence of the competitive process, namely to win customers by offering better products or better prices than those offered by rivals.[226]

[220] Reg. 1/2003, Art. 2.

[221] The requirements are cumulative, see Case T-528/93, *Métropole Télévision SA v Commission* EU:T:1996:99, para. 93 and Case C-68/12, *Protimonopolný* EU:C:2013:71, paras. 31–34.

[222] Case T-168/01, *GSK* EU:T:2006:265, para. 235.

[223] It ceases to apply when that is no longer the case, Article 101(3) Guidelines, para. 44. Under the old notification system an exemption was granted to an agreement for a specified period of time.

[224] See Case C-501/06 P, *GSK* EU:C:2009:610, paras. 93–95 (indicating that parties need to demonstrate that it is more likely than not that the agreement satisfies the Art. 101(3) conditions).

[225] The Article 101(3) Guidelines increased the bar for those seeking to justify their agreement under Art. 101(3), in terms of the level and sophistication of evidence required. The Horizontal, Vertical, and Technology Transfer Guidelines provide more specific guidance on how the Commission considers the Art. 101(3) criteria apply to those agreements, see Chaps. 10–12.

[226] Article 101(3) Guidelines, para. 33.

It is frequently complained that the Commission has, post-modernisation, imposed an excessively high burden of proof on those seeking to establish that the conditions of Article 101(3) are met.[227] Further, that the system of judicial review makes challenging a finding that the conditions of Article 101(3) are not met very difficult (see further Chapter 13). In *MasterCard*, however, the GC rejected the parties' argument that the Commission had imposed an excessively high standard of proof and had not adequately examined their arguments and evidence in relation to Article 101(3). It had properly concluded that Article 101(3)'s conditions were not fulfilled.[228]

C. ANY AGREEMENT MAY IN PRINCIPLE BENEFIT FROM ARTICLE 101(3)

Any agreement may in principle benefit from Article 101(3) (including agreements containing object restraints); fact-finders must therefore examine arguments presented in relation to Article 101(3) whatever the nature of the agreement. Indeed, in *GSK*,[229] the GC[230] annulled a Commission decision on the basis that it had not adequately discharged its burden of examining the Article 101(3) arguments put forward by the parties in respect of an agreement designed to prevent parallel trade in its pharmaceutical products, and refuting them by means of substantiated evidence.[231]

Case T-168/01, *GlaxoSmithKline Services Unlimited v Commission* [2006] ECR II-2969

General Court

233. Any agreement which restricts competition, whether by its effects or by its object, may in principle benefit from an exemption (*Consten and Grundig v Commission* . . . 342, 343 and 347, and Case T-17/93 *Matra Hachette v Commission* . . . paragraph 85), as the Commission, moreover, observed at recital 153 to the Decision and at the hearing.

234. The application of that provision is subject to certain conditions, satisfaction of which is both necessary and sufficient (*Remia and Others v Commission* . . . paragraph 38, and *Matra Hachette v Commission* . . . paragraph 104). First, the agreement concerned must contribute to improving the production or distribution of the goods in question, or to promoting technical or economic progress; second, consumers must be allowed a fair share of the resulting benefit; third, it must not impose on the participating undertakings any restrictions which are not indispensable; and, fourth, it must not afford them the possibility of eliminating competition in respect of a substantial part of the products in question.

235. Consequently, a person who relies on Article [101(3)] must demonstrate that those conditions are satisfied, by means of convincing arguments and evidence (Joined Cases 43/82 and 63/82 *VBVB and VBBB v Commission* . . . paragraph 52, and *Aalborg Portland and Others v Commission* . . . paragraph 78).

236. The Commission, for its part, must adequately examine those arguments and that evidence (*Consten and Grundig v Commission* . . . 347), that is to say, it must determine whether they demonstrate that the conditions for the application of Article [101(3)] are satisfied. In certain cases, those arguments and that evidence may be of such a kind as to require the Commission to provide an explanation or justification, failing which it is permissible to conclude that the burden of proof borne by the person who relies on Article [101(3)] has been discharged (*Aalborg Portland and Others v Commission*, paragraph 55 above, paragraph 79). As the Commission agrees in its written submissions, in such a case it must refute those arguments and that evidence.

[227] See e.g. Case T-111/08, *MasterCard Inc v Commission* EU:T:2012:260, para. 194.

[228] Ibid., paras. 194–237, *aff'd* Case C-382/12 P, *MasterCard and Others v Commission* EU:C:2014:2201.

[229] Case T-168/01, EU:T:2006:265, paras. 247–252, this aspect of the judgment was *aff'd* Cases C-501 and 513, 515, and 519/06 P. See also Case T-17/93, *Matra Hachette v Commission* EU:T:1994:89, para. 85.

[230] The CJ upheld the GC's ruling with regard to Art. 101(3), Case C-501/06 P, EU:C:2009:610.

[231] In some respects, the GC held that the Commission had sought to reject the arguments on the basis of evidence which was, to say the least, fragmentary and of limited relevance or value.

Given a dearth of guidance on when agreements containing object restraints might satisfy the Article 101(3) criteria, undertakings nonetheless remain reluctant in practice to incorporate such restraints within their agreements.

D. THE ARTICLE 101(3) CRITERIA

(i) Criterion 1: The Agreement Must Lead to an Improvement in the Production or Distribution of Goods or the Promotion of Technical or Economic Progress

a. *Article 101(3) Benefits*

Criterion 1 requires that the agreement: (1) lead to an improvement in the production of goods or services;[232] (2) lead to an improvement in the distribution of goods or services; (3) promote technical progress; and/or (4) promote economic progress. The benefits referred to are not subjective ones that result to the parties to the agreement (for example, from the exercise of market power) and must be derived from empirical data and facts not just economic theory. The CJ has stressed that the improvement must 'show appreciable objective advantages of such a character as to compensate for the disadvantages which they cause in the field of competition'[233] and that improvement within the meaning of Article 101(3) 'cannot be identified with all the advantages which the parties obtain from the agreement in their production or distribution activities';[234] consequently it will not apply if the parties are 'primary beneficiaries' of the benefits flowing from the arrangement.

b. *Efficiency Gains*

This first limb permits the parties to establish that, despite the fact that the agreement restricts competition, efficiency gains, cost efficiencies,[235] and qualitative efficiencies, creating value in the form of new or improved products (dynamic efficiencies),[236] will result from the economic activity that forms the object of the agreement (there must be a causal link between the agreement and the claimed efficiencies).[237] The Commission's Article 101(3) Guidelines state that parties must substantiate efficiency claims by showing the nature of the claimed efficiencies, the link between the agreement and the efficiencies, the likelihood and magnitude of each claimed efficiency, and how and when each claimed efficiency would be achieved.[238]

Parties may, therefore, establish that the agreement will improve production or distribution or promote technical or economic progress, for example through cost reduction (such as those originating from: development of new production technologies and methods; synergies resulting from an integration of existing assets; economies of scale or scope; or better production planning)[239] and/or through improvement in the quality and choice of goods and services.[240]

A number of joint venture agreements have succeeded on the grounds that new or better products will be produced and that the cooperation permitted the parties to do so more quickly or cheaply and/or through the sharing of risk or cost, through the pooling of technical expertise and/or by making

[232] Although Art. 101(3) does not make specific reference to services, services are covered by analogy: see e.g. COMP/30.373, *P & I Clubs* [1985] OJ L376/2 and Article 101(3) Guidelines, para. 48.

[233] Cases 56 and 58/64, *Consten and Grundig* EU:C:1966:41.

[234] Case C-382/12 P, *MasterCard Inc v Commission* EU:C:2014:2201, para. 234.

[235] Article 101(3) Guidelines, paras. 64–68. [236] Ibid., paras. 69–72. [237] Ibid., para. 45.

[238] Ibid., paras. 51 and 52–59. Examples of different types of efficiencies are given at paras. 59–72.

[239] Ibid., paras. 64–68.

[240] The enhancing potential of the agreement may not therefore be cost reduction but quality improvement resulting from technical and technological advance. R&D, technology licensing, joint production, and distribution agreements may all be capable of realising these qualitative efficiencies, ibid., paras. 69–72.

the venture financially viable.[241] In *Ford/Volkswagen*,[242] for example, the Commission held that the parties' creation of a joint venture company to develop and produce a multi-purpose vehicle (MPV) in Portugal would improve the production of goods and promote technical development. It would rationalise product development and manufacturing and establish a new and modern manufacturing plant which would be using the latest production technology. In addition, the parties' pooling of technical knowledge would be converted into a significantly improved and innovative MPV.

In the context of vertical and intellectual property licensing agreements, the Commission has taken account of the fact that the agreement will improve production and distribution of products through, for example, permitting an increase in production capacity, conferring incentives to promote a product, and conferring incentives to concentrate sales efforts, and/or through reduction in transaction costs.[243] In *GSK*,[244] Glaxo argued that the territorial restraints in the distribution agreements were necessary to stimulate and support costly and risky global R&D in a market where inter-brand competition was driven by innovation not price and where in many Member States the prices were controlled by public authorities. The agreement would thus encourage competition upstream by encouraging innovation and, on the market itself, by optimising the distribution of medicines. In particular, it was stressed that the strong competitive pressure to innovate would ensure that any additional profits made would be ploughed into investment in R&D. The GC considered that the Commission had been wrong to reject the evidence raised, which appeared 'relevant, reliable and credible' and, to some extent, to be corroborated by Commission documents.[245]

c. *Non-competition Factors*

A controversial issue is whether the first head of Article 101(3) permits the parties to rely on broader public policy benefits achieved by the agreement,[246] including public sustainability objectives. Some argue that it should, otherwise competition law might lead to a 'sustainability deficit';[247] the prohibition and hindering of agreements between competitors that have animal-welfare, social,[248] environmental, or sustainability aims. Further, that a narrow efficiency-focused interpretation of Article 101 requires a

[241] See e.g. COMP/28.796, *Beecham/Parke, Davis* [1979] OJ L70/11 (R&D agreement would promote 'technical progress' by creating a product for the prevention or treatment of an impairment for which there was no known marketed compound and where the pooling of research capacities was a major factor in providing a reasonable likelihood of success); COMP/27.093, *De Laval-Stork* [1977] OJ L215/11 (R&D agreement would enable the parties to penetrate a market more easily and quickly, reach optimal size, work at greater capacity, and share the latest technical advances) and Chap. 10.

[242] COMP/33.814 [1993] OJ L20/14.

[243] See e.g. COMP/23.013, *Goodyear Italiana-Euram* [1975] OJ L38/10; COMP/171, 856, 172, 117, and 28.173, *Campari* [1978] OJ L70/69.

[244] Case T-168/01 [2006] ECR II-2969.

[245] Ibid., paras. 233–307, Cases C-501, 513, 515, and 519/06 P, EU:C:2009:610 (finding the GC had not erred in law in finding that the Commission had failed to take into account certain facts highlighted by GSK).

[246] This question was of importance in the modernisation debate. A concern was that an acceptance that Art. 101(3) permitted a balancing of conflicting policies might have militated against the proposals; requiring this task to be delegated to a multiplicity of bodies, including national courts.

[247] See e.g. A. Gerbrandy, 'Solving a Sustainability-Deficit in European Competition Law' (2017) 40(4) *World Competition* 539 (discussing tensions that have arisen between EU competition law principles and sustainability-focused agreements in the Netherlands and proposing solutions to the sustainability deficit), S. Holmes, 'Climate Change, Sustainability, and Competition Law' (2020) 8 *J of Antitrust Enforcement* 354. Sustainability, the European Green Deal, and climate change are discussed in Chap. 1.

[248] For a discussion of whether Art. 101(3) can be 'reimagined' to except collective bargaining arrangements for the self-employed, see V. Daskalova, 'The Competition Law Framework and Collective Bargaining Agreements for Self-Employed: Analysing Restrictions and Mapping Exemption Opportunities' in B. Waas and C. Hießl (eds.), *Collective Barning for Self-Employed Workers in Europe: Approaches to Reconcile Competition Law and Labour Rights* (Kluwer Law International, 2021). See also discussion in Chap. 4.

strained interpretation of past judgments and decisional practice which allow for Article 101(3) to be interpreted broadly against the backdrop of the wider EU aims and objectives, and taking account of certain 'policy-linking' clauses, such as environmental protection, employment, culture, health, consumer protection, industrial policy, and/or the elimination of regional disparities (see Article 7 TFEU).[249]

Indeed, in *Metro I*,[250] the CJ held that the fact that an agreement might lead to stability in the labour market was a matter which could be taken into account within the first criterion of Article 101(3). The agreement in question constituted 'a stabilizing factor with regard to the provision of employment which, since it improves the general conditions of production, especially when market conditions are unfavourable, comes within the framework of the objective to which reference may be had pursuant to Article [101(3)]'.[251] Further, in *Métropole Télévision SA v Commission*[252] the GC stated that 'the Commission is entitled to base itself on considerations connected with the pursuit of the public interest in order to grant exemption under Article [101(3)]'.[253] Although these judgments related to the position pre-modernisation when the Commission had a monopoly over the application of Article 101(3), in 2011, in *Premier League Ltd v QC Leisure* and *Murphy v Media Protection Services Ltd*,[254] the CJ referred to the applicant's argument that an agreement was justifiable under Article 101(3) on the grounds that the restraints were necessary to ensure that the intellectual property rights holder was appropriately remunerated and to encourage the public to attend football stadiums. It rejected the arguments on the facts, but without explicitly stating whether such arguments were cognisable under Article 101(3) at all.

Prior to 2004, the Commission took a number of decisions which, arguably, took at least some account of public policy goals under Article 101(3). For example, although the Commission did not take a benevolent approach to crisis cartels following the 2008 financial and economic crisis, in a series of decisions in the 1980s, the Commission exempted agreements concluded between competitors designed to ensure an orderly reduction of capacity between the undertakings which were operating in an industry in crisis (see further Chapter 9).[255]

In *Exxon/Shell*,[256] the Commission held that a reduction in pollution would lead to a technological improvement for the purposes of Article 101(3). Further, in *European Council of Manufacturers of Domestic Appliances (CECED)*[257] it exempted an agreement concluded between 95 per cent of the producers and importers of washing machines operating on the EU market. The agreement was

[249] Art. 101(3) could therefore be construed to permit authorisation of agreements which provide benefits, e.g. from a regional, social, environmental, cultural, and/or industrial perspective. E.g. a key objective of the EU is an internal market that works for sustainable development and a high level of protection and improvement of the quality of the environment (TEU, Art. 3(3)): see Chap. 1 (and discussion of Arts. 8–13 TFEU); C. Townley, *Article 101 and Public Policy* (Hart Publishing, 2009); Odudu, n. 2, 161; and A. C. Witt, 'Public Policy Goals under EU Competition Law: Now is the Time to Set the House in Order' (2012) 8(3) *European Competition Journal* 443.

[250] Case 26/76, *Metro I* EU:C:1977:167. [251] Ibid., para. 43.

[252] Cases T-528, 542, 543, and 546/93, EU:T:1996:99. See also Case T-193/02, *Laurent Piau v Commission* EU:T:2005:22, para. 103 (a licence system for players' agents required by FIFA resulted in a qualitative selection, appropriate for the attainment of the objective of raising professional standards for the occupation of players' agents rather than a quantitative restriction on access to that occupation).

[253] Cases T-528, 542, 543, and 546/93, EU:T:1996:99, para. 118.

[254] Cases C-403 and 429/08, EU:C:2011:43.

[255] See e.g. COMP/30.810, *Synthetic Fibres* [1984] OJ L207/17, paras. 30–38 (in authorising an agreement between competitors to reduce capacity, the Commission accepted that the agreement provided the needed structural adjustment that the market had failed to provide, would also improve technical efficiency by enabling the undertakings to specialise, and eventually raise profitability and restore competitiveness and make it easier to 'cushion the social effects of the restructuring by making suitable arrangements for the retraining and redeployment of workers made redundant'). See also COMP/34.456, *Stichting Baksteen* [1994] OJ L131/15, especially paras. 27–28

[256] COMP/33.640 [1994] OJ L144/20.

[257] COMP/36.718 [2000] OJ L187/47. See also COMP/39.579, *Consumer Detergents* [2011] OJ C193/14, paras. 53–54; COMP/34.950 and Chap. 10.

found to restrict competition, as it restricted the parties' autonomy to produce or import the least energy-efficient washing machines, had the object of controlling one important product characteristic on which there was competition, thereby restricting competition between the parties and reducing consumer choice. Nonetheless, the Commission considered that the agreement satisfied Article 101(3). It would reduce the potential energy consumption of new machines (so lowering electricity and water costs) and consequently lessen pollution, create more technically efficient machines, and focus future R&D on furthering energy efficiency.[258] It also seems that the production of a product which increases safety for a consumer may constitute a technical improvement.[259]

In contrast, others take the view that Article 101(3) should not be expanded to include benefits beyond efficiency ones. Indeed, in its White Paper on Modernisation, the Commission stated that Article 101(3) is intended 'to provide a legal framework for the economic assessment of restrictive practices and not to allow the application of the competition rules to be set aside because of political considerations'.[260] In its Article 101(3) Guidelines, the discussion of the first condition of Article 101(3) is headed 'Efficiency gains' and *only* efficiency gains are discussed within suggesting that goals pursued by other Treaty provisions can only be taken into account 'superogatorily', on condition that they can be subsumed under the four conditions of Article 101(3);[261] the public policy considerations thus supplement the economic benefits.

Case T-17/93, *Matra Hachette v Commission* [1994] ECR II-595

General Court

139. As regards the argument based on the reference to 'exceptional circumstances', the Court observes that, although the Commission refers to them, in particular in paragraphs 23 and 28, and in paragraph 36, in which the Decision concludes its examination of the condition under review and considers the project's impact on public infrastructures and on employment, and its impact on European integration, the latter paragraph ends with the following sentence: 'This would not be enough to make an exemption possible unless the conditions of Article [101(3)] were fulfilled, but it is an element which the Commission has taken into account'. The Court considers that it is clear from the latter sentence that the 'exceptional circumstances' thus referred to in the Decision were taken into consideration by the Commission only supererogatorily. In other words, it is sufficiently established that, if those circumstances had not been referred to, the operative part of the decision adopted would have been exactly the same as that of the contested Decision. It follows that the applicant's argument that, on the contrary, the individual exemption decision granted for the project in question was adopted only on the basis of the 'exceptional circumstances' surrounding the project must be rejected.

[258] See IP/00/148 (the decision illustrates the principle that environmental concerns are in no way contradictory with competition policy 'provided that restrictions of competition are proportionate and necessary to achieving the environmental objectives aimed at, to the benefit of current and future generations' (then) Commissioner Monti).

[259] COMP/29.146, *BMW Belgium NV and Belgian BMW Dealers* [1978] OJ L46/33. See also COMP/34.493, *DSD* [2001] OJ L319/1.

[260] [1999] OJ C132/1, para. 56. See e.g. C.-D. Ehlermann in C.-D. Ehlermann and L. Laudati (eds.), *European Competition Law Annual 1997: Objectives of Competition Policy* (Hart Publishing, 1998), 480; R. Wesseling, 'The Commission White Paper on Modernisation of EC Antitrust Law: Unspoken Consequences and Incomplete Treatment of Alternative Options' [1999] *ECLR* 420.

[261] Article 101(3) Guidelines, para. 42. See Faull and Nikpay, n. 4, 3.458–3.459. Thus although in COMP/33.814, *Ford/Volkswagen* [1993] OJ L20/14 the Commission noted, in exempting a joint venture, that it would lead to the creation of a number of jobs and substantial foreign investment in one of the poorest regions of the EU—it would promote harmonious development, reduce regional disparities, and contribute to the integration of the European market—both the Commission and the GC, on appeal, emphasised that these broader factors would not have caused the agreement to merit an exemption had the other conditions of Art. 101(3) not been fulfilled, ibid., para. 36 and see Case T-17/93, *Matra Hachette v Commission* EU:T:1994:89, para. 139.

This issue and the scope of Article 101(3) is crucial to the debate as to whether, and if so how, competition, European Green Deal[262] and sustainability[263] policies can work together (see further Chapter 1). Although sustainability agreements (e.g. agreements to phase out or withdraw non-sustainable products and processes) may not infringe Article 101(1) at all in certain circumstances,[264] where they do so the question of whether and if so when such agreements might satisfy the conditions of Article 101(3) is crucial.[265]

Some NCAs, especially the Netherlands Authority for Consumers & Markets (ACM), have actively supported the view that, because of market failures (individual decisions can have negative effects on the environment as these effects are not taken into account by undertakings or consumers that cause them) and regulatory failures (environmental rules are not being enacted quickly enough to deal with climate change) competition law should not stand in the way of private sustainability initiatives, including collective actions designed to cure or mitigate negative externalities. Indeed, the ACM prepared guidance indicating that such agreements can, within carefully crafted parameters, satisfy the Article 101(3) conditions when delivering quantified benefits to consumers (especially through reducing environmental damage which causes negative externalities to citizens), which cannot be achieved by the firms individually.[266] However, other NCAs take the view that sustainability and other public policy benefits are too complex for competition agencies, or other decision-takers, to quantify and weigh against anti-competitive effects and that there other, better and more direct, mechanisms which can be used to achieve these objectives[267] and, further, that competition provides a stronger incentive for firms to invest in greener technologies.

Although the Commission does not support such a broad view of Article 101(3) as the ACM, it does take the view that sustainability benefits are often manifested in the form of broad qualitative or cost efficiencies (e.g. cleaner production or distribution technologies or less pollution) that benefit consumers and outweigh the increase in cost of more sustainable processes, see further Chapter 10.[268]

[262] See <https://ec.europa.eu/competition/information/green_deal/index_en.html>, Commission, 'The European Green Deal', COM (2019) 640 final, Speech of Executive Vice-President Vestager, ' 'The Green Deal and competition policy', 22 September 2020 (public consultation) and a conference, 4 February 2021, considering how EU competition policies can support green policies.

[263] The topic of sustainability was raised by numerous respondents in the Commission's public consultation on the review of the horizontal cooperation block exemptions, see e.g. 'Factual summary of the contributions received during the public consultation on the evaluation of the two block exemption regulations and the guidelines on horizontal cooperation agreements', <https://ec.europa.eu/competition-policy/system/files/2021-03/HBERs_consultation_summary.pdf> and is now dealt with in the Guidelines on the applicability of Article 101 of the Treaty on the Functioning of the European Union to horizontal co-operation agreements, 17 July 2023, see Chap. 10.

[264] E.g. because they fall outside Art. 101(1) under the *Wouters* exception (see Section 3.E) or following Case C-67/96, *Albany* EU:C:1999:430 (see Chap. 4), or because they do not restrict competition at all, see further Chap. 10 and e.g. M. Gassler, 'Sustainability, the Green Deal and Art. 101 TFEU: Where We Are and Where We Could Go' (2021) 9(1) *JECLAP* 1, but see Horizontal Cooperation Guidelines, ibid., para. 521.

[265] See e.g. K. Coates and D. Middelschulte, 'Getting Consumer Welfare Right: The Competition Law Implications of Market-driven Sustainability Initiatives' (2019) 15(2)–(3) *European Competition Journal* 318.

[266] See 'Second draft version: Guidelines on Sustainability Agreements—Opportunities within competition law', 26 January, 2021. See also the Hellenic Competition Commission, 'Staff Discussion Paper on Sustainability Issues and Competition Law' (2000). See also ACM's 'Guideline Regarding Tariff Agreements Between Solo Self-Employed' (2020) and Hellenic Competition Commission Staff Working Paper, 'Sustainability Issues and Competition Law', 16 September 2020, available at <www.epant.gr>.

[267] See e.g. E. Loozen, 'Strict Competition Enforcement and Welfare: A Constitutional Perspective Based on Article 101 TFEU and Sustainability' (2019) 56 *CMLRev* 1265 and F. Gomez-Martinez, S. Ondeistal, and M. P. Schinkel, 'Can Collusion Promote Corporate Social Responsibility? Evidence from the Lab', Amsterdam Law School Research Paper No. 2019-13, available at <http://ssrn.com/abstract=3372917>. See also O. Brook, 'Struggling with Article 101(3) TFEU: Diverging Approaches of the Commission, EU Courts, and Five Competition Authorities' (2019) 56 *CMLRev* 56.

[268] Horizontal Co-operation Guidelines, 1 June 2023, especially 9.4.

(ii) Criterion 2: Allowing Consumers a Fair Share of the Resulting Benefit

The second criterion of Article 101(3) requires that the agreement allows consumers a fair share of the benefit. In the Article 101(3) Guidelines, the Commission states that this condition should be considered only after it has been determined that the restrictions incorporated in the agreement are indispensable (see Criterion 3) as it 'implies a balancing of pro-competitive and anti-competitive effects. This balancing exercise should not include restrictions that in any event are unnecessary to achieve the efficiencies.'[269]

The Article 101(3) Guidelines states that this requirement is to be satisfied by showing that there is a pass-on of the cost and quality efficiencies to consumers.[270] This accords with the Commission's view that the objective of Article 101 is consumer not total welfare.[271]

Consumer is interpreted broadly to include final consumers (end-users) and intermediate consumers, including wholesalers and retailers, that purchase products in the course of their trade or business, and whether legal persons or private individuals.[272] In its Article 101(3) Guidelines, the Commission states that:

> 85. The concept of 'fair share' implies that the pass-on of benefits must at least compensate consumers for any actual or likely negative impact caused to them by the restriction of competition found under Article [101(1)]. In line with the overall objective of Article [101] to prevent anti-competitive agreements, the net effect of the agreement must at least be neutral from the point of view of those consumers directly or likely affected by the agreement. If such consumers are worse off following the agreement, the second condition of Article [101(3)] is not fulfilled. The positive effects of an agreement must be balanced against and compensate for its negative effects on consumers. When that is the case consumers are not harmed by the agreement. Moreover, society as a whole benefits because the efficiencies lead either to fewer resources being used to produce the output consumed or to the production of more valuable products and thus to a more efficient allocation of resources.

Further, that it is *not* necessary that consumers receive a share of each and every efficiency gain identified under the first condition, nor that the pass-on must occur immediately or within a specified period of time.[273]

Two important issues are: (a) whether the benefits must result to the same consumers in the same market as those suffering anti-competitive effects; and (b) to what extent it is possible to take account of the fact that future consumers will benefit if current consumers will be hurt by the arrangement. These questions are of particular relevance to the sustainability debate, as the benefits of such agreements may accrue more generally to citizens or society at large in the future (for example, by reducing environmental harm) rather than to, or just to, the consumers of the relevant products or services that suffer harm.[274] Some take the view that a 'net benefit' test can, and should, be applied, weighing the total sum of costs and benefits (even those accruing out of market).

The Article 101(3) Guidelines suggest that the benefits must be felt by consumers (as a whole[275]) in the same market(s) as that in which the anti-competitive effects take place.[276] Although in

[269] Faull and Nikpay, n. 4, 3.489. [270] Article 101(3) Guidelines, paras. 83–104. [271] See Chap. 1.

[272] COMP/21.353, *Kabel und Metallwerke Neumeyer AG and Etablissements Luchaire SA Agreement* [1975] OJ L222/34.

[273] Article 101(3) Guidelines, paras. 86–89. [274] See ACM Draft Guidelines, n. 266.

[275] '[I]t is the beneficial nature of the effect on all consumers in the relevant markets that must be taken into consideration, not the effect on each member of that category of consumers', Case C-238/05, *Asnef-Equifax v Asociación de Usuarios de Servicios Bancarios (Ausbanc)* EU:C:2006:734, para. 70.

[276] The group of consumers affected by the restriction and benefiting from the efficiency gains on a different market should at least substantially be the same, Article 101(3) Guidelines, para. 43. Higher prices for consumers can be compensated through other benefits, e.g. increased quality, ibid., paras. 103–104. See also Case T-111/08, *MasterCard v Commission* EU:T:2012:260, para. 228 (if an agreement harms two groups of consumers, a fair share of benefits must flow to both groups).

MasterCard[277] the CJ held that it is necessary to take into account the objective advantages flowing from the measure not only on the market in which the restriction has been established but also in other markets, that case concerned a two-sided system, with an undisputed interaction between the two sides. Further, the CJ held that some advantage must flow to the side of the market where the restrictive measures are felt, if the consumers on the affected markets are not substantially the same.[278]

Future consumer benefits should be relevant, so long as some benefit to consumers affected by the restriction can be established. Such an interpretation would also be compatible with the approach adopted under Article 102 where both the short-term and longer-term effects of a strategy may be relevant to the assessment. Clearly, however, even if future benefits to future consumers are relevant, it may be extremely difficult for the parties to provide convincing evidence that such benefits will result.[279]

This approach suggests that where consumers are forced to pay a higher price without attaining other benefits from the agreement, this fair share criterion will not be satisfied and such a shortcoming cannot be made up by, for example, benefits including to citizens who are not active in the market (e.g. from a reduction of externalities[280]). Thus in *VBBB and VBVB*,[281] the Commission found Article 101(3) not to be satisfied as consumers would not benefit from the parties' agreement to fix the retail prices of books. On the contrary, they would be deprived of the opportunity to pay lower prices. In section 9 of its Horizontal Cooperation Guidelines,[282] however, the Commission states that harmed consumers can benefit from a sustainability agreement in a variety of different ways, through: individual use value benefits (e.g. from the qualitative improvements in the product); individual non-use value benefits (e.g. from their appreciation of the impact of their sustainable consumption on others); and collective benefits (as part of a larger group of beneficiaries).

(iii) Criterion 3: Indispensable Restrictions

To satisfy Article 101(3), an agreement must only contain restrictions which are indispensable to the achievement of the benefits shown to result from it. Such restrictions may be indispensable only for a period of time.

The Commission distinguishes this inquiry from that made under the doctrine of ancillary restraints by asking whether the restrictive agreement and restrictions make it possible to perform the activity in question more efficiently, i.e. 'if its absence would eliminate or significantly reduce the

[277] Case C-382/12 P, EU:C:2014:2201.

[278] As in that case no advantages were found to flow from the MIF to the merchants (affected by the restriction), it was not necessary to examine the advantages flowing to cardholders since these could not by themselves be of such a character to compensate for the disadvantages resulting from those fees, ibid., paras. 242–243. See also Case T-86/95, *Compagnie Générale Maritime v Commission* EU:T:2002:50, para. 343 and the approach of the UK Supreme Court in *Sainsbury's v Mastercard* [2020] UKSC 24.

[279] See C. Townley, 'Inter-generational Impacts in Competition Law: Remembering Those Not Yet Born' [2011] *ECLR* 580.

[280] See Expert advice prepared for the Commission on the assessment of sustainability benefits in the context of the review of the Commission Guidelines on horizontal cooperation agreements, R. Inderst, 'Incorporating Sustainability into an Effects-Analysis of Horizontal Agreements' (2022).

[281] COMP/428, *VBBB and VBVB* [1982] OJ L54/36, *aff'd* in Cases C-43 and 63/82, *VBVB and VBBB v Commission* EU:C:1984:9. Similarly in Case T-29/92, *SPO and others v Commission* EU:T1995:34 the Commission refused an exemption to a Dutch building association which had entered into an agreement to protect members from ruinous competition. The GC upheld the Commission's decision, stating that 'by taking action to counteract what they regard as ruinous competition, the applicants necessarily restrict competition and therefore deprive consumers of its benefits', para. 294. In contrast in COMP/30.810, *Synthetic Fibres* [1984] OJ L207/17 the Commission concluded that consumers would benefit from an agreement between competitors on a market to reduce capacity. Although prices might rise initially, the agreement would result in a healthier, more competitive industry in the long run, paras. 39–41.

[282] 17 July 2023, 9.4.3 and see further Chap. 10.

efficiencies that follow from the agreement or make it significantly less likely that they will materialize'.[283] In *MasterCard* the CJ also stressed the separate nature of the ancillary restraints and indispensability requirements and their different objectives. The indispensability criterion 'relates to the issue whether coordination between undertakings that is liable to have an appreciable adverse impact on the parameters of competition . . . can none the less, in the context of Article [101(3)], be considered indispensable to the improvement of production or distribution or to the promotion of technical or economic progress, while allowing consumers a fair share of the resulting benefits. By contrast . . . the objective necessity test . . . concerns the question whether, in the absence of a given restriction of commercial autonomy, a main operation or activity which is not caught by the prohibition laid down in Article [101(1)] and to which that restriction is secondary, is likely not to be implemented or not to proceed.'[284] On the facts the CJ held that the GC had not erred in rejecting both the argument that the MIF was objectively necessary for the operation of the MasterCard system and that the MIF had contributed to increasing the output of the system.[285]

The Commission states that this condition, an application of the EU principle of proportionality,[286] implies a twofold test.

Guidelines on the application of Article 81(3) [now Article 101(3)] of the Treaty (the Article 101(3) Guidelines) [2004] OJ C101/97

73. According to the third condition of Article [101(3)] the restrictive agreement must not impose restrictions, which are not indispensable to the attainment of the efficiencies created by the agreement in question. This condition implies a two-fold test. First, the restrictive agreement as such must be reasonably necessary in order to achieve the efficiencies. Secondly, the individual restrictions of competition that flow from the agreement must also be reasonably necessary for the attainment of the efficiencies.

74. In the context of the third condition of Article [101(3)] the decisive factor is whether or not the restrictive agreement and individual restrictions make it possible to perform the activity in question more efficiently than would have been the case in the absence of the agreement or the restriction concerned. The question is not whether in the absence of the restriction the agreement would not have been concluded, but whether more efficiencies are produced with the agreement or restriction than in the absence of the agreement.[[287]]

Restrictions will not therefore be indispensable if the efficiencies specific to the agreement can be achieved by other practicable and less restrictive means, or if individual restrictions are not reasonably

[283] Article 101(3) Guidelines, para. 79 (and not whether the restraint is necessary to the implementation of the agreement). But see Case C-1/12, *OTOC* EU:C:2013:127, where the CJ relies on the same factors to state both that the agreement went beyond what was necessary to achieve a legitimate objective (and so did not fall outside Art. 101(1)) and that the restrictions could not be regarded as essential for the purposes of Art. 101(3). In COMP/36.253, *P&O Stena Line* [1999] OJ L163/61 the Commission granted an exemption to a joint venture which combined the parties' services on a particular ferry route. It accepted the argument that less restrictive alternatives, such as joint scheduling, or pooling, would not enable the parties to achieve the benefits, such as cost savings and increased frequency in service, of their joint venture.

[284] Case C-382/12 P, *MasterCard and Others v Commission* EU:C:2014:2201, para. 93.

[285] Ibid., paras. 232–234.

[286] The principle of proportionality essentially requires that an action (whether of the EU or of a State or, in this case, parties to an agreement) should be suitable and necessary to achieve its end and should not be excessive in relation to the objective sought, see e.g., P. Craig and G. de Búrca, *EU Law: Text, Cases, and Materials* (7th edn, Oxford University Press, 2020), 604.

[287] See Article 101(3) Guidelines, para. 18.

necessary to produce the efficiencies. In *Protimonopolný úrad Slovenskej republiky v Slovenská sporiteľňa as*,[288] for example, the CJ rejected an argument that an anti-competitive agreement was required to eliminate undertakings operating illegally on the market. The CJ stressed that even if some efficiency could be demonstrated by the parties from forcing those undertakings to comply with national law (for example, from protecting the conditions for healthy competition and so seeking to promote economic progress on the market), less restrictive measures could have been adopted. In particular, rather than taking steps to eliminate the undertaking themselves, the parties could have lodged a complaint with competent authorities.

The Commission's view is that restrictions by object and hardcore restraints are generally *not* indispensable.[289] The list of 'hardcore' restraints in the block exemptions thus provide useful guidance on the types of provisions that the Commission considers are not essential to achieving the benefits produced by a particular type of agreement.

J. Faull and A. Nikpay (eds.), *The EU Law of Competition* (3rd edn, Oxford University Press, 2014)

3.494 . . . Once it is found that the agreement in question is necessary in order to produce the efficiencies the indispensability of each restriction of competition flowing from the agreement must be assessed. A restriction is indispensable if its absence would eliminate or significantly reduce the efficiencies achieved by the agreement or make it significantly less likely that they will materialize. The assessment of alternative solutions must take into account the actual and potential improvement in competition by the elimination of a particular restriction or the application of a less restrictive alternative. The third condition of Article 101(3) thus incorporates a sliding scale. The more restrictive the restraint, the stricter the test under the third condition. Restrictions that are identified as hardcore restrictions in Commission block exemption regulations or guidelines and notices are unlikely to be considered indispensable.

It is reiterated, however, that *every* agreement is potentially capable of exemption and the Commission has since the publication of these Guidelines been prepared to concede that even hardcore restraints may sometimes satisfy the Article 101(3) criteria; examples are given of some such cases in later chapters.[290]

(iv) Criterion 4: The Agreement Must Not Afford the Parties the Possibility of Eliminating Competition

The last requirement is that the agreement as a whole must not lead to the elimination of competition. This criterion appears to reflect the view that short-term efficiency gains must not be outweighed by longer-term losses stemming from the elimination of competition.

The Commission states in the Article 101(3) Guidelines that '[u]ltimately the protection of rivalry and the competitive process is given priority over potentially pro-competitive efficiency gains which could result from restrictive agreements'.[291] Further, it sets out its view that rivalry between undertakings on the market should be preserved since rivalry is the essential driver of economic efficiency, including dynamic efficiency.

[288] Case C-68/12, EU:C:2013:71.

[289] See e.g. Article 101(3) Guidelines, para. 46 (these types of restraints are unlikely to satisfy the first two conditions of Art. 101(3) since they neither create objective economic benefits nor benefit consumers).

[290] See e.g. Chaps. 9 and 11.

[291] Article 101(3) Guidelines, para. 105.

When competition is eliminated the competitive process is brought to an end and short-term efficiency gains are outweighed by longer-term losses stemming *inter alia* from expenditures incurred by the incumbent to maintain its position (rent seeking), misallocation of resources, reduced innovation and higher prices.[292]

This criterion thus requires an analysis of the competitive restraints imposed on the parties, the degree of competition existing prior to the agreement, and the impact of the agreement on competition. Sources of competition, through actual and potential competitors, must be analysed along with the impact of the agreement on these competitive constraints.

The Commission considers, in its assessment, the market shares of the parties, the incentives for actual competitors to compete, the impact of the agreement on the various parameters of competition, the actual market conduct of the parties (where the agreement has been implemented), past competitive interaction, the closeness of competition previously existing between the competitors, and the scope of potential competition.

When assessing barriers to entry the Commission stresses that it takes into account the real possibility for new entry into the market.[293] At paragraph 116 of the Guidelines the Commission sets out some hypothetical examples of how this fourth condition is applied.

The Guidelines also explore the relationship between this requirement (and Article 101(3) more generally) with Article 102.[294] The following principles are set out:

(a) the application of Article 101(3) does not prevent the application of Article 102;
(b) conduct which is abusive should not be permitted under Article 101(3).[295] Article 101(3) could however be used to authorise an agreement concluded by a dominant undertaking which does not constitute an abuse of a dominant position;[296]
(c) not all agreements infringing Article 101 constitute an abuse of a dominant position.

E. BLOCK EXEMPTIONS

(i) General

A number of EU regulations[297] grant exemption to categories of agreements that satisfy their conditions. They are adopted for a specified period of time and kept under review during that period. In *Pierre Fabre*,[298] the CJ held, when interpreting the block exemption applicable to vertical agreements, that as undertakings have the option of asserting that Article 101(3) applies on an individual basis to their agreement, it is not necessary to adopt a broad interpretation of the block exemption provisions.

(ii) Current Block Exemptions

Some block exemptions pertain to specific sectors. Others, however, apply more generally to vertical, horizontal, and technology transfer agreements respectively. The latter block exemptions are discussed in further detail in Chapters 10–12. Table 5.1 sets out the block exemptions currently in force.

[292] Ibid. [293] Ibid., para. 115 and see Chap. 1. [294] Ibid., para. 106.

[295] Ibid. In COMP/34.395 and COMP/35.436, *Van den Bergh Foods* [1998] OJ L264/1, upheld on appeal Case T-65/98, *Van den Bergh Foods* EU:T:2003:281, *aff'd* Case C-552/03 P, *Unilever Bestfoods v Commission* EU:C:2006:607, the Commission declined to grant an exemption to conduct found to contravene Art. 102. The finding of dominance influenced the Commission's decision that the agreement would substantially eliminate competition within the meaning of Art. 101(3), see paras. 242–246.

[296] Article 101(3) Guidelines, para. 106.

[297] Although some have been adopted by the Council, a majority have been adopted by the Commission following authorisation from the Council.

[298] Case C-439/09, EU:C: 2011:649.

Table 5.1 Block exemptions currently in force

Regulation	Categories of agreements covered	Enabling legislation (Council Regulation)[299] (where relevant)
Commission Regulation 316/2014[300]	Technology transfer agreements	Regulation 19/65[301] (amended by Council Regulation 1215/99 and 1216/2000)[302]
Commission Regulation 2022/720[303]	Vertical agreements	
Commission Regulation 461/2010[304]	Vertical agreements and concerted practices in the motor vehicle sector	
Commission Regulation 2023/1067[305]	Specialisation agreements	Regulation 2821/71[306]
Commission Regulation 2023/1066[307]	R&D agreements	
Commission Regulation 906/2009[308]	Liner shipping consortia	Council Regulation 246/2009[309]
Council Regulation 169/2009[310]	Rail, road, and inland waterway sectors	

[299] Council Reg. 487/2009 [2009] OJ L148/1 authorises the granting of block exemptions in the air transport sector, but none have been adopted. Further, Council Reg. 1534/91 [1991] OJ L143/1 authorises the granting of block exemptions in the insurance sector. Commission Reg. 267/2010 [2010] OJ L83/1 was adopted under it but expired at the end of March 2017 following a Commission report published on its functioning and considering whether an industry-specific block exemption was still required or appropriate (March 2016).

[300] [2014] OJ L93/17 (as the Reg. expires on 30 April 2026, the Commission launched an evaluation of the regime governing technology transfer agreements on 25 November 2022).

[301] [1965–1966] OJ Spec. Ed. 35. [302] [1999] OJ L148/1 and [1999] OJ L148/5. [303] [2022] OJ L134/4.

[304] [2010] OJ L129/52, currently under review but prolonged until 31 May 2028, see Chap. 11.

[305] [2023] OJ L143/20, replacing Reg. 1217/2010 [2010] OJ L335/43 (the duration of the 2010 block exemption was prolonged to 30 June 2023. The 2023 block exemption, took effect on 1 July 2023).

[306] [1971] OJ Spec. Ed. 1032.

[307] [2023] OJ L143/9, replacing Reg. 1218/2010 [2010] OJ L335/36 (the duration of the 2010 block exemption was prolonged to 30 June 2023. The 2023 block exemption, took effect on 1 July 2023).

[308] [2009] OJ L256/31 (amended and extended by Reg. 697/2014 [2014] OJ L184/3 and extended again until 25 April 2024 by Reg. 2020/436 [2020] OJ L90/1). The Commission has now launched an initiative to evaluate how the BER has functioned since it was extended in 2020, <https://ec.europa.eu/info/law/better-regulation/have-your-say/initiatives/13519-EU-competition-law-evaluation-of-the-Consortia-Block-Exemption-Regulation_en>.

[309] [2009] OJ L79/1. [310] [2009] OJ L61/1.

(iii) Direct Applicability

As regulations are directly applicable (Article 288 TFEU), agreements falling within the ambit of one of the block exemptions are automatically exempt from the Article 101(1) prohibition and the national courts are, and always have been, free to apply them. If an agreement does not fall precisely within the scope of a block exemption the national court may not extend it to cover the agreement, see further Chapters 10–12.[311]

(iv) Market Share Thresholds

The new block exemptions, adopted since 1999, have generally sought to reflect the economic objective underpinning the competition law rules by providing a rule of thumb that agreements concluded by undertakings which do not exceed specified market share thresholds (and so the parties are unlikely to have sufficient market power to harm competition) are unlikely to raise competition problems (so long as the other conditions of the block exemption are satisfied). For example, Regulation 330/2010, relating to vertical agreements, applies only where the relevant undertakings' market shares do not exceed 30 per cent, Regulation 316/2014, the technology transfer block exemption, applies only where the parties' market shares do not exceed 20 or 30 per cent of the market (depending upon whether the parties are competitors or non-competitors), and the R&D and specialisation block exemptions apply only provided the parties do not exceed market share thresholds of 25 and 20 per cent respectively.[312]

(v) 'Hardcore' Restraints

Most block exemptions also contain a list of hardcore restraints which, if included within the agreement, preclude the application, and safe harbour, of the block exemption.[313] These are severe restraints which the Commission considers are, in most cases restrictive of competition by object, and which are unlikely to satisfy the Article 101(3) conditions, and so cannot benefit from a block exemption.

(vi) Withdrawal of Block Exemptions

Regulation 1/2003 provides that the Commission may withdraw prospectively the benefit of any Commission block exemption when 'it finds that in any particular case an agreement, decision or concerted practice to which the exemption Regulation applies has certain effects which are incompatible with Article [101(3)]'.[314] Withdrawal was threatened on several occasions under some of the old regulations[315] and actually occurred in *Langnese-Iglo*.[316] Some block exemptions also provide for the Commission to withdraw their benefit to specified categories of agreements (rather than individual agreements) by regulation.[317]

[311] See also n. 298 and text.

[312] Above those market shares, however, the restraints may pose competition problems on account of the market power so an individual assessment is required, see especially Chaps. 10–12.

[313] They are distinct from 'excluded restraints' included in some block exemptions which do not themselves benefit from the block exemption but do not necessarily prevent the remaining provisions of the agreement benefiting from it, see Chaps. 10–12.

[314] Reg. 1/2003 [2003] OJ L1/1, Art. 29(1).

[315] See e.g. *Tetra Pak/BTG* [1988] OJ L272/27.

[316] COMP/34.072 [1993] OJ L183/19, *aff'd* Case T-7/93, *Langnese-Iglo GmbH v Commission* EU:T:1995:98 and Case C-279/95, EU:C:1998:447.

[317] See e.g. Chap. 11.

Regulation 1/2003 also provides NCAs with power to withdraw the benefit of any Commission block exemption where the agreement, to which the regulation applies, has 'effects which are incompatible with Article [101(1)] in the territory of a Member State, or in a part thereof, which has all the characteristics of a distinct geographic market'.[318]

(vii) Safe Harbours and Relationship with Article 101(1)

The block exemptions are designed to provide legal certainty for undertakings. Undertakings know that agreements satisfying their conditions are valid and compatible with Article 101. Although the introduction of market share thresholds detracts somewhat from this objective, their incorporation goes hand in hand with the desire that they reflect the economic goals underpinning Article 101.

Initially, the block exemptions were adopted as an essential response to the broad interpretation given to Article 101(1). Exemption under Article 101(3) was vital to the validity of many agreements. The block exemptions still operate as important safe harbours for firms, exempting agreements in case they infringe Article 101(1) and providing welcome legal certainty. They do nonetheless result in attention continuing to be concentrated on Article 101(3) and, arguably, contribute to the lack of clarity surrounding the question of how Article 101(1) analysis is to be conducted (especially as in some cases agreements satisfying their conditions appear unlikely to restrict actual or potential competition to such an extent that a negative effect on prices, output, innovation, or the variety or quality of goods and services can be expected on the market).

F. UNILATERAL ACTION AND ARTICLE 101(3)

In certain circumstances, seemingly unilateral conduct of one party to a contract might form part of the contractual arrangements between it and a co-contractor, for example where it has been explicitly or tacitly accepted by the latter. In many cases, the Commission has relied on such behaviour to find a breach of Article 101(1) (see Chapter 4). Similarly, in *Ford Werke AG v Commission*[319] the Commission relied both on the terms of the agreement and on the way in which it was operated by Ford when it issued a decision refusing Ford an exemption for its selective distribution system. The CJ held that the Commission was entitled, when considering the terms of the agreement, to take account not only of the written terms of the agreement but also of the way the agreement was operated. In this case, Ford had essentially refused to supply right-hand-drive cars to its German dealers in order to protect the higher prices which the distributors charged in the UK. That apparently unilateral decision was, in this case, found to form part of the contractual arrangements since admission to the network involved implicit acceptance by the dealers of the terms imposed by Ford.

5. CONCLUSIONS

1. The challenge for a system of competition law is to design a set of transparent and predictable rules which can be used to determine as accurately as possible, and at a tolerable cost, which agreements harm competition and should be prohibited and deterred. It has been seen in this chapter that this challenge has been rendered particularly difficult in the EU both by the lack of clarity over Article 101's objectives and its bifurcated structure.

[318] Reg. 1/2003 [2003] OJ L1/1, Art. 29(2).

[319] Cases 228 and 229/82, EU:C:1984:80.

2. The Commission has moved away from its broad, jurisdictional approach to Article 101(1) which created an expansive role for Article 101(3) and (at the time) a pressing need for block exemptions. It now seeks to adopt a more realistic approach to Article 101(1) and Article 101(3) based on a consumer welfare objective.

3. In modernising its approach to Article 101, the Commission has not accepted that Article 101(1) provides the correct forum for weighing pro- and anti-competitive effects on the basis that this approach would result in Article 101(3) being 'cast aside'. Rather, the Commission considers that Article 101(1) is about identifying restrictions on competition (assumed (in object cases), actual or likely (in effect cases)), whilst Article 101(3) provides the forum determining whether demonstrated counteracting benefits or efficiencies resulting from the agreement outweigh the effect of those restrictions.[320]

4. The difficulty with this structure is that it requires a strained view of some of the jurisprudence. A number of judgments of the CJ, relying on principles developed in the pre-modernisation era, support the view that some balancing of pro- and anti-competitive aspects of an agreement should be conducted within the framework of Article 101(1) (restrictions of competition necessary and proportionate to a legitimate objective fall outside Article 101(1)). Further, precedent indicates that public policy objectives may, in certain circumstances, be taken into account.

6. FURTHER READING

A. Books

AMATO, G., *Antitrust and the Bounds of Power* (Hart Publishing, 1997), Chap. 4

ODUDU, O., *The Boundaries of EC Competition Law: The Scope of Article 81* (Oxford University Press, 2006)

TOWNLEY, C., *Article 81 EC and Public Policy* (Hart Publishing, 2009)

B. Articles

HAWK, B. E., 'System Failure: Vertical Restraints and EC Competition Law' (1995) 32 *CMLRev* 973

JONES, A., 'Left Behind by Modernisation? Restrictions by Object under Article 101(1)' (2010) 6 *European Competition Journal* 649

JONES, A., and KOVACIC, W., 'Identifying Anticompetitive Agreements in the United States and the European Union: Developing a Coherent Antitrust Analytical Framework (2017) 62(2) *Ant Bull* 254

PEEPERKORN, L., 'Defining "By Object" Restrictions' [2015] 3 *Concurrences* 40

SUFRIN, B., 'The Evolution of Article 81(3) of the EC Treaty' (2006) 51 *Ant Bull* 915

WHISH, R., and SUFRIN, B., 'Article 85 and the Rule of Reason' (1987) 7 *YEL* 1

[320] The weighing is conducted therefore within the framework of Art. 101(3) rather than under Art. 101(1).

6

ARTICLE 102 TFEU: INTRODUCTION AND DOMINANT POSITION

1. CENTRAL ISSUES

1. Article 102 TFEU (previously Article 82 EC) addresses the unilateral conduct of undertakings in a 'dominant position'.

2. Article 102 prohibits one or more undertakings which hold a dominant position in the internal market or a substantial part thereof from abusing that position insofar as it may affect inter-Member State trade. For an infringement be established, five cumulative elements must be established.

3. 'Undertaking' has the same meaning as under Article 101. 'One or more undertakings' means that several independent undertakings may together hold a 'collective' dominant position. The meaning of an effect on inter-Member State trade is set out in the Commission Guidelines on the effect on trade concept, which explain the case law.

4. The elements of 'dominant position' and 'abuse' are difficult both to define and to establish. The holding of a 'dominant position' is not prohibited, only its 'abuse'. Article 102 does not apply to conduct whereby non-dominant firms achieve dominance.

5. The way in which the Commission and the EU Courts have interpreted Article 102 has been controversial. Article 102 is mainly applied to 'exclusionary abuses', i.e. to conduct which impedes effective competition by excluding (foreclosing) competitors. In the past, it was often applied in a formalistic way, with presumptions drawn from the form of the impugned conduct, rather than an analysis of actual effects on the market. Further, it has sometimes been applied to protect competitors rather than to protect the competitive process for the benefit of consumers.

6. The Commission sought to 'modernise' the application of Article 102, by taking an effects-based approach directed to the objective of consumer welfare. Key to this process was the publication, in 2009, of Guidance on the Commission's enforcement priorities in applying Article 102 to exclusionary conduct (the Guidance Paper). This document set out the principles which were to guide the Commission in deciding when to intervene, with an overarching objective of preventing anti-competitive foreclosure. Subsequent enforcement activity did not, however, adhere rigidly to its prescriptions, and in 2023 the Commission amended the Guidance Paper to make it easier to intervene under Article 102 in certain circumstances.

7. The EU Courts were slower to depart from the established case law. Certain subsequent judgments demonstrated a stronger

attachment to the form-based approach than that advocated in the Commission's Guidance Paper. The rulings in cases including *Post Danmark (I)*, *Intel*, and *Unilever*, however, suggest greater acceptance of a more economic approach under Article 102.

8. Article 102 only applies to undertakings which, singly or collectively, hold a 'dominant position'. This is defined by the Court of Justice in terms of an undertaking's independence and ability to prevent effective competition. This is normally equated with substantial market power, which is the ability to profitably raise prices above the competitive level for a significant period.

9. Dominance can be measured 'directly' or 'indirectly'. EU law measures it indirectly for the purposes of Article 102 by defining the market and then assessing the undertaking's degree of power on that market.

10. Once the market is defined, the case law places heavy reliance on market shares in order to assess the degree of market power. In particular, once an undertaking has 50 per cent of the market there is a presumption of dominance. Conversely, the cases do not establish a figure below which dominance cannot be found. In the Guidance Paper, the Commission states that market shares provide a 'useful first indication' of the market structure and the relative importance of the undertakings active on it.

11. Barriers to entry (and expansion) are also taken into account, and the lower the market share, the greater the importance attached to them. A wide range of potential barriers to entry and other factors indicating dominance is recognised in the case law.

2. INTRODUCTION

Article 102 addresses monopoly and substantial market power. In contrast to Article 101, which focuses on agreements *between* undertakings, Article 102 addresses unilateral conduct by undertakings which hold a 'dominant position'. It seeks to constrain the behaviour of undertakings which are not sufficiently restrained by other competitors, by prohibiting the 'abuse' of market dominance. The concept of abuse encompasses both conduct that exploits consumers directly, for example unfairly high prices, and conduct by which a dominant undertaking excludes actual or potential competitors from the market.[1] Article 102 applies only to the conduct of undertakings which are already dominant, and so does not apply to anti-competitive conduct by which an undertaking *achieves* dominance, or to unilateral conduct by a non-dominant firm which nonetheless harms consumers.[2]

The application of Article 102 by the Commission and the EU Courts has often been controversial. This is principally due to:

- questionable findings that an undertaking holds a dominant position;
- an emphasis on the *form* that the behaviour of a dominant undertaking takes, rather than on its *effects*;

[1] See Case 6/72, *Europemballage Corp and Continental Can Co Inc v Commission* EU:C:1973:22 and Chap. 7.

[2] For comments on this 'enforcement gap', see L.-H. Roeller, 'Exploitative Abuses' in C.-D. Ehlermann and M. Marquis (eds.), *European Competition Law Annual 2007: A Reformed Approach to Article 82* (Hart Publishing, 2008); I. Kokkoris, 'Are We Underenforcing Article 102 TFEU' in F. Etro and I. Kokkoris (eds.), *Competition Law and the Enforcement of Article 102* (Oxford University Press, 2010), Chap. 9.

- an absence of coherent and consistent principles or a clear analytical framework of analysis in the approach to Article 102;[3] and
- the effect that the imperative of single market integration has played.

Partly in response to such criticism, from the mid-2000s onwards the Commission sought to pursue a 'more economic approach' to the application of Article 102, similar to what had occurred in relation to Article 101 and merger control. The modernisation of Article 102 has proven contentious, however, both because of an early reluctance of the part of the EU Courts to fully embrace a more economic understanding of the prohibition, and because of inconsistencies in the Commission's own approach. These issues are discussed throughout this chapter and the next.

3. THE TEXT AND SCHEME OF ARTICLE 102

A. THE PROHIBITION

Article 102 comprises a single paragraph which sets out its prohibition:[4]

> Any abuse by one or more undertakings of a dominant position within the internal market or in a substantial part of it shall be prohibited as incompatible with the internal market insofar as it may affect trade between Member States. Such abuse may, in particular, consist in:
>
> (a) directly or indirectly imposing unfair purchase or selling prices or other unfair trading conditions;
>
> (b) limiting production, markets or technical development to the prejudice of consumers;
>
> (c) applying dissimilar conditions to equivalent transactions with other trading parties, thereby placing them at a competitive disadvantage;
>
> (d) making the conclusion of contracts subject to acceptance by the other parties of supplementary obligations which, by their nature or according to commercial usage, have no connection with the subject of such contracts.

Article 102 prohibits undertakings from committing an abuse of a dominant position held within the internal market or a substantial part of it where that abuse may have an effect on trade between Member States. The provision does not establish a separate procedure for declaring an undertaking to be dominant and thus subject to Article 102.[5] An undertaking is dominant simply when it satisfies the criteria for dominance, and its conduct then becomes potentially subject to the prohibition. Although sub-paragraphs (a)–(d) set out examples of abuses, they do not provide an exhaustive list of types of prohibited conduct.[6]

Article 102 contains no express exception provision equivalent to Article 101(3). It is, however, open to a dominant undertaking to plead that its conduct is 'objectively justified'.[7] Further, although it must

[3] See e.g. J. Temple Lang and R. O'Donoghue, 'Defining Legitimate Competition: How to Clarify Pricing Abuses under Article 82EC' (2002) 26 *Fordham Int'l LJ* 83, 84.

[4] The wording of Art. 102 TFEU is unchanged from that of Art. 82 EC, other than the substitution of the phrase 'internal market' for 'common market'.

[5] This contrasts with the approach of the Digital Markets Act, discussed in Chap. 16, according to which undertakings are designated *ex ante* as digital 'gatekeepers', at which point they become subject to the obligations contained in the regulation.

[6] See Case 6/72, *Continental Can* EU:C:1973:22; Case C-333/94 P, *Tetra Pak International v Commission* EU:C:1996:436 (*Tetra Pak II*), para. 37; Case C-95/04 P, *British Airways v Commission* EU:C:2007:166, para. 57; Case T-201/04, *Microsoft v Commission* EU:T:2007:289, para. 860; Case C-280/08 P, *Deutsche Telekom v Commission* EU:C:2010:603, para. 173.

[7] See Chap. 7, Section 5.

be established that the dominant position is held 'in a substantial part of the internal market' and that there is an *appreciable* effect on inter-Member State trade, there is no de minimis threshold equivalent to that adopted in respect of restrictions of competition under Article 101(1).[8]

The burden of proving an infringement of Article 102 rests on the party or authority alleging the infringement.[9] The burden where objective justification is pleaded is discussed in Chapter 7.[10]

Five elements must be established before the prohibition applies. They are:

(a) one or more undertakings;

(b) a dominant position;

(c) the dominant position must be held within the internal market or a substantial part of it;

(d) an abuse; and

(e) an effect on inter-State trade.

It is often difficult to determine whether these criteria are satisfied, in particular whether an undertaking holds a 'dominant position', and/or whether it has committed an 'abuse' of that dominant position.

The question of dominance requires the definition of the 'relevant market' on which the undertaking is alleged to be dominant.[11] The undertaking's position on the market is then assessed. It is not an offence to hold a dominant position, as Article 102 does not prohibit dominance but only its abuse.[12] However, behaviour which is considered unproblematic from a competition perspective when engaged in by an undertaking on a competitive market may be prohibited when engaged in by dominant undertakings. Dominant and non-dominant firms are thus in crucially different positions. An incorrect finding of dominance may consequently lead to an erroneous ruling that an undertaking's pro-competitive behaviour is abusive (a Type 1 'false positive' error).

In addition, if the concept of an abuse is held to encompass an unjustifiably wide spectrum of behaviour, Article 102 may come perilously close to forbidding dominance itself. The question of what amounts to an 'abuse' is a vexed one. It requires a delimitation of what conduct can and what conduct cannot legitimately be carried out by dominant undertakings. This, of course, depends partly upon the purposes of the provision. It has often been unclear, however, what objectives are to be pursued in the enforcement of Article 102.

This chapter, after setting out the consequences of infringing Article 102, examines the five elements of Article 102 in turn, and deals with general issues concerning their scope, interpretation, and application. It then considers in detail how it is ascertained whether an undertaking holds a dominant position. Chapter 7 addresses the types of conduct that may constitute abuse of a dominant position. It is important to appreciate that the different elements of Article 102 cannot always be considered separately. In particular, the questions whether an undertaking is dominant and whether it has committed an abuse may be interrelated and intertwined.[13] As we shall see, it has even been argued that there should be no need to establish a preliminary and separate assessment of dominance, but that the analysis of dominance and abuse should be integrated.[14]

[8] Case C-23/14, *Post Danmark A/S v Konkurrencerådet (Post Danmark II)* EU:C:2015:651, paras. 72–74. For the appreciability of the effect on inter-Member State trade, see Section 4.E. See Chap. 4 for de minimis in respect of Art. 101.

[9] Reg. 1/2003, Art. 2. [10] Chap. 7, Section 5. [11] Case 6/72, *Continental Can* EU:C:1973:22.

[12] This point was reiterated in Case C-209/10, *Post Danmark I* EU:C:2012:172, paras. 21–22.

[13] See T. Eilmansberger, 'Dominance—The Lost Child? How the Effects-based Rules Could and Should Change Dominance Analysis' (2006) 2 *European Law Journal* 15.

[14] Report by EAGCP, July 2005; see Section 5.B.

B. THE ENFORCEMENT OF ARTICLE 102

(i) Complaints to Competition Authorities

Under Regulation 1/2003, both the Commission and the national competition authorities (NCAs) are empowered to enforce Article 102.[15] The great majority of Article 102 cases arise from complaints. Both the Commission and NCAs inaugurate cases after receiving complaints, and the latter may ultimately come before the CJ in an Article 267 reference. Complaints are usually made by competitors, not customers, and Article 102 has sometimes been deployed as a weapon in the commercial struggle between market rivals.

(ii) Infringement Decisions, Fines, and Other Remedies

The Commission investigates undertakings that it suspects have breached Article 102. Where the Commission finds that an infringement has been committed, it can issue a decision ordering the undertaking to put an end to the abuse, impose behavioural or structural remedies,[16] and impose substantial fines. The difficulties involved in determining whether an infringement of Article 102 has been committed, and the controversy surrounding many of the Commission's decisions under Article 102, have rendered its willingness to impose heavy fines contentious. Moreover, behavioural remedies—such as ordering an undertaking to supply or to cease tying products—may be more significant for the defendant than a large fine.[17]

Regulation 1/2003, Article 5, provides that the NCAs shall similarly have powers to take infringement and fining decisions, alongside acceptance of commitments (discussed below).[18]

(iii) Commitments Decisions

Under Regulation 1/2003, Article 9, the Commission can alternatively take 'commitments decisions',[19] whereby it accepts binding commitments from undertakings under investigation rather than proceeding to a final prohibition decision. Following introduction of this instrument in 2004, the Commission made enthusiastic use of Article 9 in Article 102 cases. Yet the termination of cases by commitments can have serious implications for the development of Article 102 jurisprudence, as such decisions do not involve a formal finding of infringement, and do not amount to formal statements about the parameters of Article 102. Article 9 cases rarely come before the EU Courts, thus diluting the control of the Commission by the Courts. More recent enforcement practice suggests a greater willingness on the part of the Commission to take formal infringement decisions in Article 102 investigations,[20] in some cases using an informal procedure combining settlement with a finding of breach and fines.[21]

[15] See Chap. 13. [16] Reg. 1/2003, Art. 7. See Chap. 13. [17] As in Case T-201/04, *Microsoft* EU:T:2007:289.

[18] See also Arts. 12 (commitments) and 13–16 (fines) of the ECN+ Directive.

[19] See Chap. 13, Section 6.E.iii. See e.g. AT.40462, *Amazon Marketplace and AT.40703, Amazon Buy Box* 20 December 2022.

[20] Most notably, in cases involving undertakings operating in the digital economy: see, e.g., AT.39740, *Google Search (Shopping)* 27 June 2017, AT.40099, *Google Android* 18 July 2018, AT.40411, *Google Search (AdSense)* 20 March 2019, AT.40220, *Qualcomm (Exclusivity payments)* 24 January 2018 (overturned on appeal in Case T-235/18, *Qualcomm Inc.* EU:T:2022:358); and AT.39711, *Qualcomm (Predation)* 18 July 2019.

[21] AT.39759, *ARA Foreclosure* 20 September 2016, and AT.40134, *AB InBev beer trade restrictions* 12 May 2019.

(iv) Judicial Review in Article 102 Cases

The standard and intensity of the judicial review of the Commission's decisions in competition cases is discussed in Chapter 13.[22] A few preliminary points can be made here. Article 102 cases are highly fact-specific. Many of the Commission's decisions are disputed, and the extent to which they are subject to review has been of concern in the past. In principle, the EU Courts decline to substitute their own assessment of 'complex economic matters' for that of the Commission. Reflecting the growing importance of fundamental rights within the EU judicial system, however, the CJ increasingly stresses that the GC conducts an 'in-depth review' of Article 102 cases.[23] Appeals lie from the GC to the CJ on points of law only. There may, however, be an indistinct line between points of fact and points of law in practice.[24] Historically, it was rare for the Commission to lose Article 102 cases on the substance: indeed, it had a success rate described as 'staggering'.[25] More recent jurisprudence, however, suggest a greater willingness on the part of the EU Courts to scrutinise and, where necessary, correct the Commission's decision-making in this area.[26]

(v) Private Actions in National Courts and Article 267 References

Article 102, like Article 101, is directly effective.[27] It is possible, therefore, for an entity injured by a breach of Article 102 to bring proceedings before a national court seeking an injunction or damages in respect of loss resulting from the breach.[28] Further, a party to a contract concluded with a dominant undertaking may claim that clauses within it are prohibited by Article 102, and consequently void or unenforceable.[29] That party may also bring proceedings to recover benefits conferred under a prohibited provision.

National courts before which Article 102 is raised may make references to the CJ for preliminary rulings under Article 267. Many leading cases on Article 102 have come before the CJ in this way.[30] The use of commitments decisions by the Commission, and the consequent paucity of appeals to the EU Courts, make the Article 267 route significant for the development of the law.

[22] Chap. 13, Section 7.

[23] For example, Case T-321/05, *AstraZeneca v Commission* EU:T:2010:266.

[24] See, e.g., Case C-95/04 P, *British Airways v Commission* EU:C:2007:166, for a frustrating example of the CJ's classification of a plea as inadmissible on the basis that it concerned a point of fact not law.

[25] R. O'Donoghue and A. J. Padilla, *The Law and Economics of Article 102* (3nd edn, Hart Publishing, 2020), 94, quoting, inter alia, research by the former Chief Competition Economist which showed the Commission's success rate in defending challenges to its decisions as 98%. See D. Neven, 'Competition Economics and Antitrust in Europe' (2006) 21(48) *Economic Policy* 742; and C. Ahlborn and D. S. Evans, 'The *Microsoft* Judgment and its Implications for Competition Policy Towards Dominant Firms in Europe' (2008–2009) 75 *Antitrust LJ* 887.

[26] See, e.g., Cases C-413/14 P, *Intel v Commission* EU:C:2017:632 (remitted to GC for scrutiny of foreclosure capacity of loyalty rebates, subsequently annulled in T-286/09 RENV, *Intel* EU:T:2022:19), T-851/14, *Slovak Telekom v Commission* EU:T:2018:929 (infringement decision annulled in part with respect to finding of margin squeeze), T-691/14, *Servier and Others v Commission* EU:T:2018:922 (finding of dominance annulled due to erroneous market definition), and T-235/18, *Qualcomm* EU:T:2022:358 (finding of abusive loyalty rebates annulled on both substantive and procedural grounds; Commission has chosen not to appeal the judgment).

[27] See Case 127/73, *SABAM* EU:C:1974:25. [28] See Chap. 14.

[29] For an example, see the national litigation that preceded the preliminary ruling in Case C-595/17, *Apple Sales International* EU:C:2018:854. For an example see, e.g., *English Welsh and Scottish Railway Ltd v E.ON UK plc* [2007] EWHC 599 (Comm).

[30] Such as Case 311/84, *Télémarketing* EU:C:1985:394; Case C-7/97, *Oscar Bronner* EU:C:1998:569; Case C-418/01, *IMS Health* EU:C:2004:257; Cases C-468–478/06, *Sot. Lélos kai Sia* EU:C:2008:504; Case C-525/16, *MEO* EU:C:2018:270; Case C-307/18, *Generics (UK)* EU:C:2020:52; Case C-680/20, *Unilever Italia* EU:C:2023:33.

4. OVERVIEW OF ARTICLE 102

A. THE MEANING OF ONE OR MORE UNDERTAKINGS

(i) General

'Undertaking' is interpreted in the same way for the purpose of Article 102 as for Article 101. It is construed broadly and 'encompasses every entity engaged in an economic activity'.[31] Two points of particular importance arise when considering the meaning of the term 'undertaking' within the context of Article 102. First, since State regulation is a frequent source of an entity's market power, it is crucial to know to what extent public bodies or bodies with a special connection with the State may be characterised as undertakings and so subject to Article 102. Secondly, it must be considered what is meant by the reference to 'one or more undertakings' within the text of Article 102, and specifically, the extent to which the provision covers the collective conduct of one or more *independent* undertakings?

(ii) Public Bodies and Bodies Performing Public Functions

The term 'undertaking' applies to any entity engaged in commercial activities whether or not it is a State entity, even if it has no identity separate from that of the State.[32] The fact that an undertaking's market power has been created by State action provides no defence under Article 102, unless the narrow exception set out in Article 106(2) TFEU applies. That provision states that '[u]ndertakings entrusted with the operation of services of general economic interest or having the character of a revenue-producing monopoly' are subject to the competition rules unless those rules 'obstruct the performance, in law or in fact, of the particular tasks assigned to them'. This topic is discussed in Chapter 8.

(iii) Collective Dominance

Initially, it was believed that the term 'one or more undertakings' referred only to bodies which were part of the same economic entity, meaning that the purpose of the term was to ensure that the conduct of all bodies within a corporate group was taken into account when assessing whether a breach of Article 102 had occurred. In that understanding, the term referred principally to circumstances, such as those in *Continental Can*[33] and *Commercial Solvents*,[34] in which the market position and conduct of both a parent company and its subsidiary were relevant to the existence of abuse of dominance. That view also found support in a statement of the CJ in *Hoffmann La-Roche*.[35]

Such an interpretation would, however, have meant that the term 'undertaking' in Article 102 had a different meaning from Article 101. In Chapter 4, it was explained that the term 'undertaking' applies to *all* bodies which form part of the *same* economic entity. Legally distinct bodies within the same corporate group are treated as a single undertaking if the bodies 'form an economic unit within which the subsidiary has no real freedom to determine its course of action on the market, and if the agreements or practices are concerned merely with the internal allocation of tasks'.[36] If the same

[31] Case C-41/90, *Höfner and Elser v Macrotron* EU:C:1991:161, para. 21; see also Chap. 4.

[32] See Chaps. 4 and 8. For two important CJ judgments concerning the status of undertakings exercising certain public powers, see Case C-113/07, *SELEX Systemi Integrati SpA v Commission* EU:C:2009:191 and Case C-49/07, *Motosykletistiki Omospondia Ellados NPID (MOTOE) v Ellinkio Dimosi* EU:C:2008:376.

[33] Case 6/72, *Continental Can* EU:C:1973:22.

[34] Cases 6 and 7/73, *Commercial Solvents* EU:C:1974:18.

[35] Case 85/76, *Hoffmann-La Roche* EU:C:1979:36, para. 39.

[36] Case 15/74, *Centrafarm BV and Adriaan De Peijper v Sterling Drug Inc* EU:C:1974:114, para. 41, repeated in Case 30/87, *Bodson v Pompes funèbres des régions libérées SA* EU:C:1988:225, para. 19.

interpretation was applicable under Article 102, it would render the reference to 'one or more undertakings' within the text of prohibition largely unnecessary.

Instead, it is now accepted that the phrase refers to legally independent undertakings which together hold a 'collective dominant position' on the market. Article 102 applies both to dominant positions held by single firms *and* to those held collectively. The issue of what constitutes a collective (or 'joint') dominant position is considered in Section 10. The concept has had a somewhat tortuous evolution, and its interpretation involves not only Article 102 but also the EU Merger Regulation (EUMR).[37] It also important not to overstate the importance of the collective dominance concept in practice. Perhaps due to the demanding legal requirements to demonstrate either oligopolistic[38] or non-oligopolistic collective dominance,[39] the concept of collective dominance has had a very limited presence in the Commission's enforcement practice in recent years.[40]

B. A DOMINANT POSITION

The definition of a dominant position is established in the case law of the CJ. The meaning of 'dominant position', and the way to determine whether an undertaking holds such a position, are considered later in this chapter. One important point should be noted at this juncture. Although many undertakings found to infringe Article 102 are large multinational firms, dominance relates to an undertaking's power on a defined 'relevant market', rather than its economic power more broadly. Markets can be defined narrowly[41]—for example, Boosey & Hawkes was found to be dominant in the market for brass instruments for British-style brass bands[42]—meaning that small firms can be dominant. If such a firm commits an abuse of that position, however, it may not have an appreciable effect on inter-Member State trade, in which case its conduct might be subject only to national competition provisions. Even if the other elements of Article 102 *are* satisfied, the Commission may be unlikely to bring proceedings. NCAs also apply Article 102, however, and the provision can be enforced in private litigation. Conversely, the mere fact that a firm is large, profitable, and globally prominent does not itself justify a finding of dominance, where it nonetheless faces significant competitive constraints on a particular market. The concept of a 'gatekeeper' within the meaning of the Digital Markets Act, discussed in Chapter 16, has been introduced precisely to address the problem that even very large and powerful Big Tech firms may not fall so easily within the somewhat technical definition of dominance for the purposes of Article 102.

C. A DOMINANT POSITION WITHIN A SUBSTANTIAL PART OF THE INTERNAL MARKET

(i) Purpose of the Requirement

The dominant position must be held within the internal market or a substantial part of it. The purpose of this requirement is to exclude from the Article's scope purely localised monopoly situations in which there is no Union interest. Together with the necessity that the abuse of dominance must have an effect on trade between Member States, this determines the limit of the EU's jurisdiction.

[37] See Chap. 15. For collective dominance generally, see G. Monti, 'The Scope of Collective Dominance Under Article 82 EC' (2001) 38 *CMLRev* 131.

[38] Case T-342/99, *Airtours v Commission* EU:T:2002:146.

[39] Cases C-395 and 396/96 P, *Compagnie Maritime Belge* EU:C:2000:132.

[40] A rare example is the commitments decision in COMP/39.388, *German Electricity Wholesale Market* and COMP/39.389, *German Electricity Balancing Market* 26 November 2008, paras. 13–24.

[41] For the principles of market definition, see Chap. 3.

[42] *BBI/Boosey & Hawkes* [1987] OJ L286/36.

(ii) Meaning of a Substantial Part of the Internal Market

A 'substantial part' does not simply mean substantial in geographic terms. It is not a matter of counting hectares. In *Suiker Unie*, the CJ stated that:

> [f]or the purpose of determining whether a specific territory is large enough to amount to a 'substantial part of the [internal] market' within the meaning of Article [102 TFEU] the pattern and volume of the production and consumption of the said product as well as the habits and economic opportunities of vendors and purchasers must be considered.[43]

(iii) Relevance of Volume of Production

In *Suiker Unie*, the CJ compared the volume of sugar production in Belgium, Luxembourg, and southern Germany to that of Union production overall. It held that each of those markets was a substantial part of the internal market. The CJ has never specified whether there is a particular percentage of the EU market which could automatically be said to satisfy the 'substantial' criterion. However, Advocate General Warner, in the *ABG Oil* case, considered that the Dutch petrol market, which was approximately 4.6 per cent of the overall Union market at the time, was substantial. He stated that:

> [t]here is . . . in my opinion, in this kind of field, a danger in focusing attention exclusively on percentages. The opposite of 'substantial' is 'negligible', and what may seem negligible when looked at in the terms of a percentage may seem otherwise when looked at in absolute terms. The population of Luxembourg is, I believe, about 0.23 per cent of the population of the whole [Union]. I would however shrink from saying that one who had a monopoly, or near monopoly, of the Luxembourg market for a particular product was exempt from the application of Article [102].[44]

(iv) A Member State is Likely to be a Substantial Part of the Internal Market

In a number of cases, individual Member States have constituted a 'substantial part'[45] of the internal market, as have parts of Member States.[46] As the EU is enlarged, the concept of what is a 'substantial part' may alter, with previously substantial parts becoming less significant, so that older cases may no longer be a reliable guide. For reasons of political sensitivity, it is difficult to imagine that a single Member State would be held not to constitute a substantial part of the internal market, even in an EU of more than 27 Member States. If and when the EU expands further, however, the delineation of geographic markets may become broader, and it may become rarer for a position of dominance to be found in a single Member State other than in cases of statutory monopoly.

(v) Transport Cases

What constitutes a 'substantial part' of the internal market may depend on the nature of the market. There have been a number of transport cases, in particular, in which small areas have been found to

[43] Cases 40/73 etc., *Coöperatieve Vereniging 'Suiker Unie' UA v Commission* EU:C:1975:174, para. 371.

[44] Case 77/77, *Benzine en Petroleum Handelsmaatschappij* EU:C:1978:141, 1537. The CJ, held that the undertaking's conduct could not constitute an abuse and did not address the dominance issue.

[45] For instance, Belgium was held to be a substantial part of the internal market in Cases 127/73, *SABAM* EU:C:1974:25 and 26/75, *General Motors* EU:C:1975:150.

[46] For instance, the south-east of the UK in Case 22/78, *Hugin* EU:C:1979:138. A number of local markets in a Member State may be aggregated to form a 'substantial part', as in Case C-323/93, *Crespelle* EU:C:1994:368, where there was a series of local statutory monopolies in bovine insemination services which together covered the whole of France. See also Case 30/87, *Bodson v Pompes Funèbres des Régions Libérées* EU:C:1988:225.

be substantial. In *Sealink/B&I Holyhead: Interim Measures*[47] and *Sea Containers Ltd/Stena Sealink Ports*,[48] Holyhead Harbour in Wales was held to be a substantial part of the internal market. In the former case, the Commission stated:

> 40. . . . The port of Holyhead constitutes a substantial part of the [Internal] Market because it is a port providing one of the main links between two member-States; more especially, it provides the direct link between Great Britain and the capital city of Ireland. It should also be noted that this is, at least for passengers and cars, the most popular ferry route between Ireland and Great Britain.

In *Port of Roscoff*,[49] the Commission emphasised the importance that might be played by the catchment area served by a port. In *Merci Convenzionali*, the CJ looked to the volume of traffic handled by the port of Genoa. After stressing its importance in relation to the overall volume of imports and exports by sea to and from Italy, the Court held that the market 'may be regarded as constituting a substantial part of the [internal] market'.[50] The Commission has also found activities at the port of Rødby[51] and various airports[52] to involve substantial parts of the internal market.

The transport cases suggest that, once it has been established that the routes or traffic concerned are significant in anything other than a purely domestic context, the 'substantial part' criterion is satisfied.[53] Indeed, the full application of Article 102 to maritime and air transport would be impossible in the absence of such an interpretation.

D. ABUSE

As with 'dominant position', the meaning of 'abuse' derives from the case law of the CJ. The definition of abuse, and the issue of what conduct can amount to an abuse, is the subject of Chapter 7. The concept hinges on the harmful *behaviour* of the dominant undertaking, and not merely the fact that it holds significant market power. A basic distinction is drawn between 'exploitative' and 'exclusionary' abuses. An *exploitative* abuse involves conduct whereby the dominant undertaking takes advantage of its market power to exploit its customers. An *exclusionary* abuse involves conduct which impedes effective competition by excluding (foreclosing) competitors. The application of Article 102 is mainly concerned with exclusionary abuses. The Commission Guidance Paper on enforcement priorities, discussed in Section 5.C, addresses only exclusionary abuses.

E. AN EFFECT ON TRADE BETWEEN MEMBER STATES

(i) General

Article 102 applies only if the abuse of a dominant position *appreciably* affects trade between Member States. As in the context of Article 101, this requirement marks the jurisdictional divide between

[47] [1992] 5 CMLR 255, Commission's *XXIInd Annual Report on Competition Policy* (1992), point 219.

[48] [1994] OJ L15/8.

[49] Reported as *Irish Continental Group v CCI Morlaix* [1995] 5 CMLR 177, para. 58.

[50] Case C-179/90, *Merci Convenzionali Porto di Genova* EU:C:1991:464, para. 15; see also Case C-266/96, *Corsica Ferries* EU:C:1998:306, para. 38.

[51] *Port of Rødby* [1994] OJ L55/52.

[52] E.g., *FAG-Flughafen Frankfurt/Main AG* [1998] OJ L72/30; *Alpha Flight Services/Aéroports de Paris* [1998] OJ L230/10; *Portuguese Airports* [1999] OJ L69/31, on appeal Case C-163/99, *Portugal v Commission* EU:C:2001:189; *Ilmailulaitos/Luftfartsverket* [1999] OJ L69/24; *Spanish Airports* [2000] OJ L208/36.

[53] See Case 66/86, *Ahmed Saeed* EU:C:1989:140; *British Midland v Aer Lingus* [1992] OJ L96/34, 596.

EU and national law. The concept of an effect on trade is interpreted in the same way under both Articles 101 and 102.[54] Thus an agreement or conduct will affect trade if it interferes with the pattern of trade between Member States or if it interferes with the effective competitive structure in the internal market even if there is no alteration to the flow of goods or services between Member States. The latter test was first adopted in *Commercial Solvents*.[55] The approach is particularly relevant to Article 102 cases in which abusive conduct might result in a competitor leaving the market, as occurred in *Commercial Solvents*. Here, Zoja, an Italian pharmaceutical company, claimed it was being driven out of the market for a certain type of anti-TB drug by the conduct of the dominant supplier of the necessary raw material. At the time there was an insignificant incidence of TB in Europe, and Zoja was principally manufacturing for export to the developing world. The CJ said that whether or not there was trade between Member States in the drug was immaterial:

> 33. The [Union] authorities must therefore consider all the consequences of the conduct complained of for the competitive structure in the [internal] market without distinguishing between production intended for sale within the market and that intended for export. When an undertaking in a dominant position with[in] the [internal] market abuses its position in such a way that a competitor in the [internal] market is likely to be eliminated, it does not matter whether the conduct relates to the latter's exports or its trade within the [internal] market, once it has been established that this elimination will have repercussions on the competitive structure within the [internal] market.[56]

In judging the effect on trade, it is necessary to look at the conduct as a whole, and not at individual transactions in isolation.[57] In *Intel*, the GC said that the concept applied not only to eliminating a competitor but also to weakening one.[58]

Hugin,[59] however, shows that not every alteration in the competitive structure may affect trade. The case concerned the supply of cash register spare parts by a Swedish undertaking to a servicing and repair firm in the UK, prior to Sweden's accession to the EU. The servicing firm's activities were confined to the London area and there was no inter-State trade in spare parts. The CJ quashed the Commission's decision, on the ground that there was no effect on trade between Member States. The alteration in the competitive structure if the firm went out of business would not be felt outside one part of the UK. The CJ stated:

> 17. . . . The interpretation and application of the condition relating to effects on trade between Member States contained in Articles [101 and 102 TFEU] must be based on the purpose of that condition which is to define, in the context of the law governing competition, the boundary between the areas respectively covered by [Union] law and the law of the Member States. Thus [Union] law covers any agreement or any practice which is capable of constituting a threat to freedom of trade between Member States in a manner which might harm the attainment of the objectives of a single market between the Member States, in particular by partitioning the national markets or by affecting the structure of competition within the [internal] market. On the other hand conduct the effects of which are confined to the territory of a single Member State is governed by the national legal order.

[54] See Chap. 4. [55] Cases 6 and 7/73, *Commercial Solvents* EU:C:1974:18.

[56] Ibid., para. 33. This paragraph does not say '*effective* competitive structure' but the phrase appears elsewhere in the judgment (e.g. para. 32) and in subsequent cases, see Case 22/79, *Greenwich Film Production v SACEM* EU:C:1979:245, para. 11 and Case T-286/09, *Intel* EU:T:2014:547, para. 275.

[57] Case T-286/09, *Intel* EU:T:2014:547, para. 269.

[58] Ibid., para. 275. The competitor concerned was Intel's 'sole significant competitor at the worldwide level' and was being foreclosed from 'the most important sales channels'.

[59] Case 22/78, *Hugin Kassaregister AB and Hugin Cash Registers Ltd v Commission* EU:C:1979:138.

Accordingly, before trade between Member States can be affected, the alteration in the effective competitive structure must have repercussions beyond the borders of a single Member State.

The meaning of an appreciable effect on inter-Member State trade for the purposes of Article 102 is now set out in the Commission Guidelines on the effect on trade concept, which was adopted as part of the modernisation programme. The Guidelines explain how Article 102 applies where the dominant undertaking is pursuing several practices in an overall strategy, not all of which have an effect on inter-Member State trade.

Commission Guidelines on the Effect of Trade Concept Contained in Articles 81 and 82 of the Treaty [2004] OJ C101/81

17. In the case of Article [102] it is the abuse that must affect trade between Member States. This does not imply, however, that each element of the behaviour must be assessed in isolation. Conduct that forms part of an overall strategy pursued by the dominant undertaking must be assessed in terms of its overall impact. Where a dominant undertaking adopts various practices in pursuit of the same aim, for instance practices that aim at eliminating or foreclosing competitors, in order for Article [102] to be applicable to all the practices forming part of this overall strategy, it is sufficient that at least one of these practices is capable of affecting trade between Member States.

The Guidelines address four potential situations of abuse of a dominant position: abuses covering several Member States; covering a single Member State; covering only part of a Member State; and involving trade with third countries or practices involving undertakings in third countries. The principles in the Notice basically summarise the case law.

(ii) Abuse of a Dominant Position Covering Several Member States

Both exclusionary and exploitative abuses in which a dominant undertaking engages in more than one Member State are normally, by their very nature, capable of affecting trade between Member States.[60]

(iii) Abuse of a Dominant Position Covering a Single Member State

Where an undertaking has a dominant position which covers the whole of a Member State, the Guidelines distinguish between exclusionary and exploitative abuses. Where exclusionary abuses are concerned, trade between Member States is normally capable of being affected, because the abuse will generally make it more difficult for competitors from other Member States to penetrate the market.[61] A number of cases illustrate this.[62] In *Greek Lignite and Electricity Markets*,[63] for example, a State-owned electricity company in Greece had a near-monopoly of the exploitation rights of an important raw material. The Commission held that this discouraged potential new market entrants from exercising their right of establishment in Greece.[64] Exclusionary abuses may also affect the competitive structure in a Member State in a way that affects inter-Member State trade. The Guidelines explain:

[60] Guidelines on the effect on trade concept, paras. 73–76. [61] Ibid., para. 93.

[62] E.g. Case 322/81, *Michelin I* EU:C:1983:313; Case T-65/89, *BPB Industries* EU:T:1993:31.

[63] COMP/38.700, *Greek Lignite and Electricity Markets* 5 March 2008, upheld Case C-554/12 P, *Commission v DEI* EU:C:2014:2085.

[64] COMP/38.700, *Greek Lignite and Electricity Markets* Decision of 5 March 2008, para. 244.

> 94. Exclusionary abuses that affect the competitive market structure inside a Member State, for instance by eliminating or threatening to eliminate a competitor, may also be capable of affecting trade between Member States. Where the undertaking that risks being eliminated only operates in a single Member State, the abuse will normally not affect trade between Member States. However, trade between Member States is capable of being affected where the targeted undertaking exports to or imports from other Member States . . . and where it also operates in other Member States. . . . An effect on trade may arise from the dissuasive impact of the abuse on other competitors. If through repeated conduct the dominant undertaking has acquired a reputation for adopting exclusionary practices towards competitors that attempt to engage in direct competition, competitors from other Member States are likely to compete less aggressively, in which case trade may be affected, even if the victim in the case at hand is not from another Member State.

In the case of exploitative abuses, such as price discrimination and excessive pricing, there will normally be no inter-Member State trade effect if only domestic customers are affected. But the Guidelines explain how, nevertheless, there may be:

> 95. However, it may do so if the buyers are engaged in export activities and are disadvantaged by the discriminatory pricing or if this practice is used to prevent imports . . . Practices consisting of offering lower prices to customers that are the most likely to import products from other Member States may make it more difficult for competitors from other Member States to enter the market. In such cases trade between Member States is capable of being affected.

Once the undertaking's *dominant position* covers a whole Member State, it will normally not matter whether the *abuse* affects only some of the territory or some customers.[65]

(iv) Abuse of a Dominant Position Covering only Part of a Member State

If a dominant position is held in only part of a Member State, there will, first, be a question of whether that part is a 'substantial part of the internal market'. If so, then it is a matter of deciding whether access by competitors from other Member States is made more difficult. If it is, inter-Member State trade must normally be considered as being appreciably affected.[66]

(v) Abuses Involving Trade with Third Countries

Abuses involving trade outside the EU will be caught by Article 102 if they are implemented in the EU.[67] If the conduct relates to imports or exports to and from the EU, there may be an effect on cross-border activity. Imports into one Member State may affect the conditions of competition there, which may have a knock-on effect in others.[68] Where the object is to restrict competition inside the EU, the requisite effect on inter-Member State trade is more readily established than when it is predominantly to restrict competition outside it.[69] A more detailed analysis is necessary where the practice is not aimed at competition inside the EU, to identify how, if at all, patterns of trade between Member States may be affected.[70] Thus, the conduct of liner conferences operating on routes between European ports and third countries was held to affect inter-Member State trade, in that it obstructed the activities of competitors operating from ports in other Member States, limited the choice of services available to shippers in various Member States, and disturbed normal trade patterns in the internal market.[71]

[65] Guidelines on the effect on trade concept, para. 96.
[66] Ibid., para. 90.
[67] See Chap. 17.
[68] Guidelines on the effect on trade concept, para. 101.
[69] Ibid., para. 103.
[70] Ibid., paras. 106–109.
[71] See e.g. *CEWAL* [1993] OJ L34/20.

(vi) Regulation 1/2003, Article 3

The question of whether an effect on inter-Member State trade exists acquired added significance after 1 May 2004. Regulation 1/2003, Article 3 provides that, where an NCA applies national competition law to an abuse prohibited by Article 102, it must also apply Article 102. Accordingly, if there is an effect on inter-Member State trade, the NCA cannot address conduct which meets the other criteria of Article 102 under national law alone. Article 3(2) nevertheless allows stricter national laws to be applied to unilateral conduct which affects inter-Member State trade, while Article 3(3) permits national provisions which predominantly pursue an aim different from Article 102.[72] The judgment in *Tele2 Polska*,[73] to the effect that NCAs may not make findings that there has been no infringement of Article 102, reinforced the significance of the inter-Member State trade condition.

5. ARTICLE 102 AND THE 'MORE ECONOMIC APPROACH'

A. THE REVIEW OF ARTICLE 102

The optimal approach to Article 102, and in particular what sorts of behaviour by dominant firms ought to be considered abusive, is a contentious question. In 2003, DG Comp initiated a major internal review of its policy on Article 102, following similar exercises in relation to Article 101 and merger control. This was considered desirable, in particular, in the light of the introduction of Regulation 1/2003, which gave the NCAs 'parallel competence' to apply Article 102. The Commission considered that 'a policy which is clear on the substantive interpretation of the Article is essential to make the system work', and that a 'credible policy on abusive conduct must be compatible with mainstream economics'.[74] However, whereas the more economic approach to Article 101 had been largely initiated and endorsed by the EU Courts,[75] a more conservative judicial attitude was visible initially in relation to Article 102.[76]

B. THE STAFF DISCUSSION PAPER

The review was informed, first, by a report commissioned by DG Comp's Chief Economist from EAGCP, the Economic Advisory Group on Competition Policy, published in July 2005 (the EAGCP report).[77] The EAGCP report advocated strongly for '[a]n economics-based approach' to Article 102, that would require 'a careful examination of how competition works in each particular market in order to evaluate how specific company strategies affect consumer welfare'.[78] It argued that there were two clear benefits to such an approach: 'it ensures that anti-competitive behaviour does not outwit legal provisions', and 'guarantees that the statutory provisions do not unduly thwart pro-competitive strategies'.[79]

[72] See further Chap. 13, Section 9. [73] Case C-375/09, *Tele2 Polska* EU:C:2011:270.

[74] Speech by then Director-General of DG Comp, Philip Lowe, at Fordham Corporate Law Institute 30th Annual Conference on International Antitrust Law and Policy, 23 October 2003 [2003] *Fordham Corp L Inst* 163.

[75] See Chap. 5.

[76] As shown by two GC judgments in 2003, Case T-203/01, *Michelin II* EU:T:2003:250 and Case T-219/99, *British Airways* EU:T:2003:343.

[77] The EAGCP report is available at <http://ec.europa.eu/dgs/competition/economist/eagcp_july_21_05.pdf>.

[78] Ibid., p. 2. [79] Ibid.

This was followed, in December 2005, by a DG Comp Staff Discussion Paper on the application of the Article to exclusionary abuses (the Discussion Paper).[80] The Discussion Paper considered only the application of Article 102 to *exclusionary* abuses, defined as behaviour by a dominant undertaking which is likely to have a foreclosure effect on the market.[81] The thrust of the Discussion Paper was to reorientate the application of Article 102 in exclusionary abuse cases to the recommended 'effects-based' analysis and the consumer welfare standard. It stated that the objective of Article 102 with regard to exclusionary abuses was 'the protection of competition on the market as a means of enhancing consumer welfare and of ensuring an efficient allocation of resources'.[82]

The Discussion Paper was put out for public consultation and stimulated wide-ranging debate. While the direction was welcomed, broadly speaking, there was disagreement about specific proposals and concern about the impact on legal certainty.[83] The outcome of the consultation was expected to be the publication of guidelines, similar to those provided on Article 101(3).[84] There was a considerable problem, however, as to how any guidelines embodying a reform in the law could be reconciled with the existing case law, unless the EU Courts changed their approach.

C. THE GUIDANCE PAPER

(i) The Road to the Guidance Paper

Two months after the publication of the Discussion Paper, Advocate General Kokott made oblique reference to the proposed reform in her Opinion in the *British Airways* appeal, emphasising that the Commission would nonetheless remain bound by the existing Article 102 case law:

> . . . even if its administrative practice were to change, the Commission would still have to act within the framework prescribed for it by Article [102] as interpreted by the Court of Justice.[85]

The subsequent judgment of the CJ took a conservative and formalistic approach to Article 102, showing little regard for likely impact on consumers. Its treatment of rebates was at odds with the effects-based and consumer welfare analysis suggested in the Discussion Paper.[86] The GC judgment in *Microsoft* several months later likewise concentrated on competitors and market structure rather than consumers.[87] Whereas the *British Airways* judgment was an appeal against a 1999 Commission decision, taken before the Article 102 review had been initiated, in its *Microsoft* decision the Commission had purported to apply a 'more economic approach', which included an effects analysis and examination of consumer welfare aspects.[88]

[80] Brussels, December 2005, available at <http://ec.europa.eu//competition/antitrust/art82/discpaper2005.pdf>.

[81] Discussion Paper, para. 1. [82] Ibid., para. 4.

[83] '. . . [T]he upswing is good but the downswing and the follow-through needs a lot of work', as the Director General said in Brussels, 14 June 2006, summing up the responses to the Discussion Paper.

[84] The Discussion Paper described its contents as 'possible principles for the Commission's application of Article 82' (para. 1) and was written in a similar format to the Article 101(3) Guidelines.

[85] Case C-95/04 P, *British Airways* EU:C:2006:133, Kokott AG, para. 28. The AG made the same point in a post-Guidance Paper case, Case C-109/10 P, *Solvay* EU:C:2011:256 , para. 21 of her Opinion.

[86] Cf. Discussion Paper, paras. 134–176. The case is discussed in Chap. 7.

[87] Case T-201/04, *Microsoft* EU:T:2007:289; see also Case T-271/03, *Deutsche Telekom v Commission* EU:T:2008:101 and Cases C-468–478/06, *Sot. Lélos* EU:C:2008:504.

[88] COMP/37.792, *Microsoft* 24 March 2004, see Chap. 7.

As one commentator remarked:

> Cynics might point out that the European courts' interpretation of Article [102] has been guided to a large extent by the Commission's historic approach, which was formalistic in nature. Subsequently, the Commission's creative leeway is restricted by its own historic analysis which was approved by the European courts. Having been embedded in the European case law, this structured analysis cannot easily be changed.[89]

The Commission was thus faced with an unreceptive attitude from the EU Courts, alongside the practical difficulty of drafting guidelines in an area so rife with disagreements even among advocates of effects-based analysis. When it finally adopted a formal Notice in February 2009, this document was explicitly styled, not as 'guidelines', but merely 'guidance' on the Commission's *own* enforcement priorities in applying Article 102 to abusive exclusionary conduct (the Guidance Paper).[90]

(ii) The Content of the Guidance Paper

The Guidance Paper specifically states that it is not intended to be a statement of the law and that it is without prejudice to the interpretation of Article 102 by the EU Courts.[91] Rather, it sets out the enforcement priorities that will guide the Commission's enforcement activity,[92] by identifying what kinds of conduct it considers egregious enough to warrant expending resources on intervention. It focuses on 'those types of conduct that are most harmful to consumers'.[93] It makes it clear that it is concerned, not with protecting competitors, but with protecting an effective competitive process, because of the resulting benefits that will arise for consumers.

> **Guidance on the Commission's Enforcement Priorities in Applying Article 82 of the EC Treaty to Abusive Exclusionary Conduct by Dominant Undertakings [2009] OJ C45/2**
>
> 5. In applying Article [102] to exclusionary conduct by dominant undertakings, the Commission will focus on those types of conduct that are most harmful to consumers. Consumers benefit from competition through lower prices, better quality and a wider choice of new or improved goods and services. The Commission, therefore, will direct its enforcement to ensuring that markets function properly and that consumers benefit from the efficiency and productivity which result from effective competition between undertakings.
>
> 6. The emphasis of the Commission's enforcement activity in relation to exclusionary conduct is on safeguarding the competitive process in the internal market and ensuring that undertakings which hold a dominant position do not exclude their competitors by other means than competing on the merits of the products or services they provide. In doing so the Commission is mindful that what really matters is protecting an effective competitive process and not simply protecting competitors. This may well mean that competitors who deliver less to consumers in terms of price, choice, quality and innovation will leave the market.

[89] A. Ezrachi, 'The Commission's Guidance on Article 82 EC and the Effects Based Approach—Legal and Practical Challenges' in A. Ezrachi (ed.), *Article 82 EC: Reflections on its Recent Evolution* (Hart Publishing, 2009), 51, 56. Or, as Hamlet put it, 'hoist with one's own petard'.

[90] Guidance on the Commission's Enforcement Priorities in Applying Article 82 of the EC Treaty to Abusive Exclusionary Conduct by Dominant Undertakings [2009] OJ C45/2. See generally P. Akman, 'The European Commission's Guidance on Article 102 TFEU: From *Inferno* to *Paradiso*?' (2010) 73 *MLR* 605; D. Geradin, 'Is the Guidance Paper on the Commission's Enforcement Priorities in Applying Article 102 TFEU to Abusive Exclusionary Conduct Useful?', <http://ssrn.com/abstract=1569502>.

[91] Guidance Paper, para. 3. [92] Ibid., para. 2. [93] Ibid., para. 5.

The Guidance Paper does not address exploitative abuses,[94] discrimination,[95] or abuses by undertakings in a collective dominant position. It contains an introductory section setting out the purpose of the Guidance;[96] an explanation of its general approach to exclusionary conduct, including a section on market power and dominance and another on price-based exclusionary conduct generally;[97] and a part applying that approach to specific forms of exclusionary conduct.[98] These are exclusive dealing; tying and bundling; predation; and some exclusionary refusals to supply. It also does not cover the many 'new' types of abusive conduct with which the Commission has become concerned since publication of the Guidance Paper, such as denial of access to standard essential patents[99] or self-preferencing.[100] In this regard, it could be argued that the original iteration of the Guidance Paper began to age rather rapidly.

Throughout the Guidance Paper, the Commission sets out a general rule as to its 'normal' approach, but leaves 'wriggle room' by adding a proviso to cover situations where it may wish to take enforcement action because of particular circumstances. It thus retains a wide degree of administrative discretion. This has been criticised in legal certainty terms, although the Guidance Paper maintains that its publication should 'help undertakings better assess whether certain behaviour is *likely* to result in intervention by the Commission'.[101]

The decision to issue a document on its enforcement priorities rather than fully fledged Guidelines met with a mixed response. It was said that:

> In a world where the European Courts cling to old case law like castaways to a wreckage, guidelines for the Commission's enforcement priorities may be the best that can be achieved at present. The inability of the European Courts to provide intellectual leadership regarding the modernisation of these rules is all the more surprising as they have been at the forefront of modernisation in the areas of restrictive agreements and [EU] merger control.[102]

The substantive provisions of the Guidance Paper are discussed further throughout this chapter and the next.

(iii) The Effect of the Guidance Paper

No Guidelines or Guidance can override the existing case law of the EU Courts.[103] Such a document could, however, potentially influence the way that the EU Courts approach the interpretation of Article 102 in future. Following issuance of the Guidance Paper, the question was the extent to which the Courts too would embrace the 'more economic approach', whether by expressly adopting or implicitly following its prescriptions.

To the extent that the EU Courts have considered *directly* the relevance of the Guidance Paper in terms of shaping the jurisprudence going forward, a rather conservative approach has sometimes been taken. In *Tomra*[104] and *Intel*,[105] both appeals from Commission decisions taken pursuant to proceedings initiated before publication of the Guidance Paper, the CJ and GC respectively held that it was essentially irrelevant. The Courts instead applied only the existing case law, eschewing an effects-based

[94] Guidance Paper, para. 7. [95] In the sense discussed in Chap. 7, Section 7.B.
[96] Guidance Paper, paras. 1–8. [97] Ibid., paras. 9–31. [98] Ibid., paras. 32–90.
[99] See Chap. 7, Section 7.C. [100] See Chap. 7, Section 13. [101] Guidance Paper, para. 2 (emphasis added).
[102] Linklaters Press Release, 2 December 2008.
[103] See L. Lovdahl Gormesen, 'Why the European Commission's Enforcement Priorities on Article 82 Should Be Withdrawn' [2010] *ECLR* 45, who argued accordingly that the Commission should withdraw the Guidance Paper.
[104] Case C-549/10 P, *Tomra* EU:C:2012:221. [105] Case T-286/09, *Intel* EU:T:2014:547.

approach and focusing on competitors rather than consumers.[106] More explicitly, in *Post Danmark II*, an Article 267 reference which also concerned rebates, the CJ stated that the Guidance Paper:

> . . . merely sets out the Commission's approach as to the choice of cases that it intends to pursue as a matter of priority; accordingly, the administrative practice followed by the Commission is not binding on national competition authorities and courts.[107]

Outside the context of rebates, the CJ in *Deutsche Telekom* similarly diverged from the Commission's indicated approach in relation to margin squeeze.[108] In *TeliaSonera*, Advocate General Mazák described the Guidance Paper as 'a useful point of reference',[109] and considered margin squeeze as a type of refusal to supply, in line with the Commission in the Guidance Paper. The CJ however held, contrary to the Guidance Paper but without referring to it, that margin squeeze is a separate abuse.[110]

One should not conclude, however, that the EU Courts are uninfluenced by the Guidance Paper. Of particular significance is the ruling in *Post Danmark I*.[111] Here, the CJ applied the as efficient competitor (AEC) test and incremental cost standards in predatory pricing,[112] formulated an efficiencies defence in line with paragraph 30 of the Guidance Paper, inserted a reference to consumers into the definition of an abuse from *Hoffmann-La Roche*,[113] and generally took a robust and economics-based attitude to the application of Article 102. Despite dismissing the Guidance Paper as 'administrative practice', *Post Danmark II* similarly took a less rigid, more effects-focused attitude than previous cases.[114] Subsequently, in *Intel*, the CJ 'clarified' its earlier formalistic treatment of loyalty rebates, embracing instead an approach premised squarely upon foreclosure of equally efficient competitors. This was obviously in line with, though made no express reference to, the approach of the Guidance Paper.[115] Most remarkably, in *Android*, where the Commission relied upon third party data to conduct its AEC test contrary to the approach advocated in the Guidance Paper, the GC treated the prescribed methodology as essentially determinative of the correct manner in which to perform the AEC analysis. Accordingly, the Commission's failure to follow its Guidance Paper meant that it had 'failed to conduct an appropriate examination of the costs',[116] which raised doubts as to 'the correctness and validity of the AEC test carried out'.[117] Finally, in *Unilever*, the CJ referenced the Guidance Paper to support its holding that contractual exclusivity clauses should not be treated as 'automatic' abusive behaviour.[118] Accordingly, although the EU Courts have denied that they are *legally* bound by the positions espoused by the Commission in the Guidance Paper, in practice the Courts' jurisprudence increasingly recognises the relevance and merits of the 'more economic approach'. The result is that the case law and Guidance Paper have become more closely aligned, at least in certain areas.

[106] The cases are discussed in Chap. 7, Section 10.
[107] Case C-23/14, *Post Danmark II* EU:C:2015:651, para. 52.
[108] Case C-280/08 P, *Deutsche Telekom* EU:C:2010:603.
[109] Case C-52/09, *TeliaSonera* EU:C:2010:483, fn. 21 of the Opinion.
[110] Case C-52/09, *TeliaSonera* EU:C:2011:83, paras. 55–56, followed in Case T-336/07, *Telefónica* EU:T:2012:172, *aff'd* Case C-295/12 P, *Telefónica SA* EU:C:2014:2062.
[111] Case C-209/10, *Post Danmark I* EU:C:2012:172; see E. Rousseva and M. Marquis, 'Hell Freezes Over: A Climate Change for Assessing Exclusionary Conduct under Article 102 TFEU' (2012) 4 *JECLAP* 32.
[112] Following its earlier *de facto* adoption in Case C-62/86, *AKZO* EU:C:1991:286.
[113] Case C-209/10, *Post Danmark I* EU:C:2012:172, para. 24; see Chap. 7.
[114] Case C-23/14, *Post Danmark II* EU:C:2015:651, paras. 28–50, see Chap. 7.
[115] Case C-413/14 P, *Intel* EU:C:2017:632; see also Case T-604/18, *Google Android* EU:T:2022:541, paras. 643–644, where the GC explicitly acknowledged the AEC test's origins in the Guidance Paper.
[116] Case T-604/18, *Google Android* EU:T:2022:541, para. 746. [117] Ibid., para. 752.
[118] Case C-680/20, *Unilever Italia* EU:C:2023:33, para. 51.

One curious feature of the judicial reception of the Guidance Paper was an apparent disjuncture between the positions advocated by the Commission within the Guidance Paper itself, and those advanced or defended by the Commission's Legal Service before the EU Courts.[119] In the latter, the Commission revealed more conservative tendencies. Yet the explanation for this disconnect perhaps reflects not so much the merits of the respective legal positions, but an institutional disagreement within the Commission itself. Writing a year before the important judgment of the CJ in *Intel*, one prominent practitioner and economist explained the position as follows:

J. Padilla, 'Whither Article 102 TFEU: A Comment on Akman and Crane' (2016) 81 *Antitrust LJ* 223, 229

The Commission's Guidance is the result of a difficult compromise between various interest groups: the Commission's legal service, the CET [Chief Economist Team], DG Comp's hierarchy, and the EU Member States. It is not a secret that the Commission's legal service does not like the Guidance. The EU courts' rulings, with the exception perhaps of the European Court of Justice's ruling in *Post Danmark [I]* have strengthened the position of the legal service on Article 102 at the expense of the supporters of the Guidance. The legal service is focused on winning cases. For as long as the EU courts endorse the formalistic approach adopted in the Commission's decisions and dismiss the economic analyses that are appended to those decisions, the formalistic approach constitutes a powerful litigation tool, which the legal service is understandably not willing to surrender. Obviously, it is much more difficult to overturn a prohibition decision on appeal, when the conduct at stake is regarded as quasi-per se illegal, than when it is recognized that it can produce both procompetitive and anticompetitive effects and thus must be assessed under the rule of reason.

The impact of the Guidance Paper extends beyond the Commission itself. Undertakings obviously look at the Guidance Paper for enlightenment as to what conduct the Commission views as particularly problematic under Article 102, and thus likely candidates for future enforcement activity. The degree to which the Guidance Paper is riddled with caveats and exceptions, however, would make it difficult for any undertaking to challenge Commission enforcement action on the ground that the conduct falls outside the identified 'priorities', and thus breaches the defendant's legitimate expectations.[120] The *Treuhand*[121] judgments also made it clear that the principle of legitimate expectations cannot hinder the Commission's duty to enforce the competition rules. National courts applying Article 102 are bound by the case law, and must look to that rather than to Notices from the Commission, as the CJ emphasised in *Post Danmark II*. NCAs must also follow the case law, and should they fail to do so, are liable to be overturned by national courts. NCAs may, however, be influenced by the Commission in the cases that they prioritise for enforcement, and the effects-based approach has trickled down to the enforcement activities of certain NCAs under both Article 102 and domestic equivalents.

[119] This disjuncture is not limited to Art. 102 cases: see e.g. the GC's radical judgment on 'by object' restrictions under Art. 101(1) in Case T-168/01, *GlaxoSmithKline* EU:T:2006:265 against which the Commission similarly appealed. The judgment subsequently was disapproved on this point by the CJ in Cases C-501/06 P etc., *GlaxoSmithKline* EU:C:2009:610.

[120] The precise legal status of the Guidance is unclear, see further O'Donoghue and Padilla, n. 25, 96-97. See Chap. 2 for the status of 'Guidelines', described by the CJ in Cases C-189/02 P etc., *Dansk Rørindustri* EU:C:2005:408, para. 209, as rules of practice rather than rules of law.

[121] Case T-99/04, *AC-Treuhand* EU:T:2008:256, para. 163.

(iv) The Amendments to the Guidance Paper

The authors of the EAGCP report had insisted that the economics-based approach to Article 102 'is not a question of having more or less intervention, but of *more effective* intervention'.[122] Nonetheless, it is unarguable that the approach espoused by the Commission in the Guidance Paper would generally result in fewer findings of abuse than a more formalistic one. This can be applauded to the extent that it leads to fewer erroneous findings of infringement in circumstances where the dominant firm's behaviour does not harm effective competition within the market (i.e. Type I errors). Yet to the extent that an economics-based approach significantly increases the burden that the Commission itself must discharge to successfully prosecute abusive behaviour, it is more controversial. The argument that an economics-based approach poses unnecessary and illegitimate hurdles to intervention against harmful exercises of monopoly power has also been a prominent theme in the New Brandeisian critique of contemporary antitrust enforcement in the United States.[123]

It was noted earlier that the Guidance Paper appeared to be ageing poorly. This was partly because the EU Courts did not always agree subsequently with the approach set out in the Guidance Paper,[124] and partly because the focus of the Commission's enforcement activity under Article 102 had shifted beyond the traditional categories of abuses addressed by the Guidance Paper. But it was also because the Commission itself appeared to have lost some of its earlier enthusiasm for economics-based analysis.[125] A divide thus emerged, between the rigorous and somewhat restrictive approach advocated in the Guidance Paper, and what the Commission was actually doing in Article 102 cases. This gap between the Commission's prescriptions and its practice troubled some commentators, and it was argued that it should either adhere to the Guidance Paper or formally withdraw it.[126]

The Commission, for its part, initially maintained that an efficiency-focused approach could be reconciled with the pursuit of other social values such as fairness through competition enforcement.[127] In March 2023, however, without prior warning (or public consultation), the Commission issued a series of Amendments to the Guidance Paper, annexed to a brief Communication setting out the rationale for the changes.

Amendments to the Guidance on the Commission's enforcement priorities in applying Article 82 of the EC Treaty to abusive exclusionary conduct by dominant undertakings C(2023) 1923 final

7. The Commission's enforcement priorities have evolved over time, thanks to the experience gained through the Commission's practice which took into account the evolution of the case law of the Union Courts, as well as market developments. Notably, the case law of the Union Courts has confirmed an effects-based approach to Article 102 TFEU as well as clarified the meaning and scope of certain concepts included in the Guidance on enforcement priorities.

8. In light of those developments, this Communication amends parts of the Guidance on enforcement priorities that no longer reflect the Commission's approach in determining whether to pursue certain cases as a matter of priority. The amendments are done in accordance with the principle of good administration and with a view to enhancing transparency on the principles underpinning the Commission's enforcement action.

[122] EAGCP report, p. 4 (emphasis added). [123] See Chap. 1, Section 5.B.

[124] See, for instance, the differing approaches to margin squeeze and constructive refusal to deal, discussed in Chap. 7, Sections 9 and 12, respectively.

[125] Discussing the movement away from the 'more economic approach' in the Commission's enforcement practice, see P. Ibáñez Colomo, 'Whatever Happened to the "More Economics-Based Approach"?' (2020) 11 *JECLAP* 473 and N. Dunne, 'Fairness and the Challenge of Making Markets Work Better' (2021) 84 *MLR* 230.

[126] See e.g. N. Petit, 'Rebates and Article 102 TFEU: The European Commission's Duty to Apply the Guidance Paper' (2016) 2 *Competition Law & Policy Debates* 4.

[127] See e.g. Speech of Commissioner Vestager, 'Fairness and Competition Policy', Keynote speech at the European Competition Day 2022 in Prague, 10 October 2022.

The amendments encompass five broad revisions to the text of the original Guidance Paper. Two of these follow directly from the jurisprudence of the EU Courts: namely, removing the requirement to establish indispensability as part of the legal tests for margin squeeze and constructive refusal to deal. The other three changes are by no means required by the evolving case law, however, and instead indicate an unmistakable desire on the part of the Commission to move away from the strictures of the more economic approach. These involve changing the definition of anti-competitive foreclosure; de-emphasising the relevance of *as efficient* competitors when considering whether allegedly behaviour generates harmful effects; and softening the requirement to conduct an AEC test to analyse price-based exclusionary conduct. In an accompanying Policy Brief nominally written by numerous DG Comp officials in their personal capacity, the Commission justified these changes with explicit reference to concerns about Type II errors and under-enforcement:

> The move towards an effects-based enforcement of Article 102 TFEU raises the question of whether the heightened substantive legal standard that the Union Courts have accorded to it may inadvertently lead to undesirable outcomes. While a form-based approach may carry the risk of capturing false positives, an overly rigid implementation of the effects-based approach could set the bar for intervention at a level that would render enforcement against practices that restrict competition unduly burdensome or even impossible, with serious negative consequences for consumers, the EU economy, and society at large.[128]

The substantive implications of each of the Amendments is considered further in Chapter 7.

Alongside the publication of the Amendments, the Commission announced a renewed intention to issue more concrete guidelines on the application of Article 102, in lieu of the existing Guidance Paper.[129] It issued a wide-ranging 'call for evidence' to aid the preparation of draft guidelines, with an aim to enact formal guidelines by 2025.[130] It is also assisted in this task, according to the Commission, by the development of a 'sufficiently detailed and comprehensive' body of Article 102 case law since it last attempted to enact guidelines in the mid-2000s.[131] As shall be seen in Chapter 7, however, much of this jurisprudence is equivocal in nature, some of it is rather contradictory, and an increasingly large chunk of it appears to endorse a more rigorously economic s-based approach than the Commission itself would seem to be comfortable with today.

6. THE RELATIONSHIP BETWEEN ARTICLE 102 AND ARTICLE 101

Articles 101 and 102 are not mutually exclusive, and they serve the same aim.[132] Yet the provisions pursue different objectives in terms of the *specific* types of behaviour that each regulates.[133] It is for this reason that the same practice may give rise to violations of Articles 101 and 102 in tandem. This point was established in *Hoffmann-La Roche*,[134] where the CJ confirmed that both prohibitions may apply to the same

[128] L. McCallum, I. Bernaerts, M. Kadar, J. Holzwarth, D. Kovo, M. Lagrue, E. Leduc, L. Manigrassi, J. Marcos Ramos, I. Pereira Alves, V. Pozzato, and P. Stamou, 'A Dynamic and Workable Effects-based Approach to Abuse of Dominance' [2023] 1 *Competition Policy Brief* 4.

[129] Commission, 'Antitrust: Commission announces Guidelines on exclusionary abuses and amends Guidance on enforcement priorities', 27 March 2023.

[130] Ibid.

[131] Commission, 'Call for Evidence for an Initiative: EU competition law—guidelines on exclusionary abuses by dominant undertakings', Ares(2023)2189183, 27 March 2023.

[132] Case 6/72, *Continental Can* EU:C:1973:22, para. 25.

[133] Case C-307/18, *Generics (UK)* EU:C:2020:52, para. 146, following the approach in the Opinion of Kokott AG in Case C-307/18, EU:C:2020:28, paras. 245–247.

[134] Case 85/76, *Hoffmann-La Roche* EU:C:1979:36. See also Cases C-395 and 396/96 P, *Compagnie Maritime Belge* EU:C:2000:132, para. 33.

contractual arrangements. The rationale for permitting the parallel application of both provisions is that Article 102 is 'expressly aimed in fact at situations which clearly originate in contractual relations',[135] by virtue of the examples listed in Article 102(a)–(d). Naturally, such arrangements typically also fall within the scope of Article 101. This point was reaffirmed in *Generics*, where the CJ emphasised that a 'contract-oriented strategy' may fall within the scope of Article 102, in particular, on the basis of 'the possible additional damage that strategy may cause to the competitive structure of a market in which, because of the dominance in that market of that manufacturer of originator medicines, the degree of competition is already weakened'.[136] When dealing with an exclusive requirements contract concluded by a dominant undertaking, for instance, the Commission may proceed under either Article 101 or Article 102, or indeed both to the extent that the individual requirements for each Article are made out on the facts.[137]

The fact that both Articles can be applied to the same agreements or practices arguably provides an argument for aligning the approach to the two provisions. Nonetheless, an agreement involving a dominant undertaking may infringe Article 102 even where it complies with Article 101.[138] This includes an agreement which benefits from a block exemption and is therefore exempt from Article 101 by virtue of Article 101(3). In *Tetra Pak I*,[139] the Commission found that Tetra Pak had breached Article 102 when it acquired an undertaking which held an exclusive patent licence, which itself fell under a block exemption. The GC confirmed that an undertaking could commit an abuse of dominance by operating an agreement which was exempted under a block exemption. Otherwise, the exception provided by Article 101(3) would also operate as an exemption from Article 102.[140]

Where the individual application of Article 101(3) by NCAs or national courts is at issue, the Notice on the application of Article 101(3) states that the concept of the elimination of competition in respect of a substantial part of the products in question, which precludes the exemption of an agreement from the Article 101(1) prohibition, is an 'autonomous [Union] law concept specific to Article 101(3)'.[141] This is narrower than 'dominance' under Article 102.[142] The Notice makes it clear that Article 101(3) cannot be applied to permit an agreement that constitutes an *abuse* of a dominant position.[143] Not all restrictive agreements entered into by dominant firms will, however, constitute an abuse. The Notice gives the example of a dominant firm's participation in a non-full-function joint venture.

It has been argued that it would be preferable if only Article 101 were applicable to the vertical arrangements of dominant undertakings, leaving Article 102 to deal with abusive unilateral conduct falling outside Article 101.[144] Complications which arise from the applicability of both Articles to the same conduct include the difference in the position as regards the burden of proof,[145] and the fact that arrangements such as exclusive dealing were previously subject to less rigorous economic analysis under Article 102 than under Article 101.[146] The counter-argument, emphasised in Advocate General Kokott's Opinion in *Generics*, is that Article 102 addresses contract-oriented abusive strategies that

135 Case 85/76, *Hoffmann-La Roche* EU:C:1979:36, para. 116.

136 Case C-307/18, *Generics (UK)* EU:C:2020:52, para. 147.

137 As in *Van den Bergh (Irish Ice Cream)* [1998] OJ L246/1, and the subsequent appeals, and exclusive dealing generally, Chap. 7, Section 10.

138 Reaffirmed in Case T-712/14, *CEAHR* EU:T:2017:748, para. 94.

139 [1988] OJ L272/27; confirmed on appeal in Case T-51/89, *Tetra Pak Rausing v Commission (Tetra Pak I)* EU:T:1990:41.

140 Such a situation is unlikely to reoccur today, as block exemptions now typically include market share thresholds above which the exemption is inapplicable.

141 [2004] OJ C101/97, para. 106. 142 See Case T-395/94, *Atlantic Container Line* EU:T:2002:49, para. 330.

143 Notice on the application of Article 101(3), para. 106.

144 See E. Rousseva, 'Modernising by Eradicating: How the Commission's New Approach to Article 81 EC Dispenses with the Need to Apply Article 82 to Vertical Restraints' (2005) 42 *CMLRev* 587; E. Rousseva, *Rethinking Exclusionary Abuses in EU Competition Law* (Hart Publishing, 2010), 460–473.

145 See also I. Lianos, 'Categorical Thinking in Competition Law and the "Effects-based Approach" in Article 82' in A. Ezrachi (ed.), *Article 82 EC: Reflections on its Recent Evolution* (Hart Publishing, 2009), 19, 26–30.

146 See discussion in Chap. 7, Section 10.

cause harm to competition precisely as a result of the dominant undertaking's presence in the market and the existing absence of structural competition that this implies.[147] Limiting the application of Article 102 only to behaviour not already regulated by Article 101 might artificially and unhelpfully constrain the scope of the abuse of dominance provision, given the significant overlap in practice in terms of the conduct covered by each.

The relationship between Article 101 and Article 102 is also relevant to the question of collective dominance under Article 102.[148] Both provisions may apply to the conduct of such undertakings. It is possible that an agreement between the parties will infringe Article 101, and that behaviour conducted in consequence of that agreement will amount to an abuse of a collective dominant position. Moreover, a collective dominant position may arise from agreements between the parties.

7. THE CONCEPT OF DOMINANCE

Article 102 only applies to undertakings in a dominant position. Whether or not an undertaking holds a 'dominant position' is therefore of central importance.[149] The reason for limiting scrutiny under Article 102 to the activities of dominant undertakings is that such undertakings are otherwise insufficiently constrained by market forces. A non-dominant undertaking that acts in a way that is disadvantageous to consumer welfare—for instance, by raising its prices significantly—is likely to find such behaviour unprofitable, because it will lose a critical mass of customers to its competitors. Instead, if it wishes to exercise the necessary degree of market power to charge supra-competitive prices in future, the non-dominant undertaking needs to increase its market share, and it can typically do so only through effective competition on the merits.[150] Conversely, an undertaking that *already* holds a dominant position benefits from a substantial degree of 'freedom of action which is the special feature of a dominant position'.[151] Because the dominant undertaking's behaviour is not adequately constrained by market forces, this provides a regulatory rationale for supplementing the supervision of its market activities using competition law.

Clearly the notion of dominance is not intended only to refer to a complete monopolist, meaning a single undertaking which occupies a relevant market. It also encompasses undertakings which have a certain degree of market power.[152] The difficulty is to determine what degree of market power is necessary for Article 102 to apply.

> Perfect competition is rarely encountered outside textbooks; almost all firms have some market power, though most have very little. Accordingly, the relevant question in antitrust cases is not whether market power is present, but whether it is important.[153]

The initial problem is to identify with sufficient clarity the point at which an undertaking becomes, and can *know* it becomes, dominant, and so potentially subject to the prohibition. This is at some point on the spectrum of market power. Economists usually describe *substantial* market power (SMP) as the ability of a firm to raise prices above the competitive level without attracting new entrants and

[147] Opinion in Case C-307/18, *Generics (UK)* EU:C:2020:28, paras. 245–251. [148] See Section 10.

[149] The concept of a 'dominant position' is also employed in the EU Merger Reg. (the EUMR), Council Reg. 139/2004 [2004] OJ L24/1, see Chap. 15.

[150] For discussion of the reasons for exempting the unilateral behaviour of non-dominant undertakings from the ambit of competition law, see the US Supreme Court judgment of *Copperweld v Independence Tube*, 467 US 752, 774–776 (1984).

[151] Case 85/76, *Hoffmann-La Roche* EU:C:1979:36, para. 41.

[152] Although the terms 'monopoly' and 'monopolist' are sometimes used as a shorthand for both here.

[153] R. Schmalensee, 'Another Look at Market Power' (1981–1982) 95 *Harvard LR* 1789, 1790.

losing sales to competitors so rapidly that the price increase becomes unprofitable.[154] Another way of looking at SMP is to relate it to the power to exclude competitors, although this can be problematic.[155] In US law, monopoly power for the purposes of s. 2 of the Sherman Act has been defined as 'the power to control prices or to exclude competition'.[156] In the remainder of this chapter, we consider how 'dominant position' has been defined and interpreted by the EU Courts and the Commission.

A. THE DEFINITION OF A DOMINANT POSITION IN THE CASE LAW

The CJ defines dominance in terms of an undertaking's 'economic strength' and its ability to act independently on the market. Two important early cases establish the parameters of the concept of dominance: *United Brands* and *Hoffmann-La Roche*.[157]

In *United Brands*, the CJ said that an undertaking would hold a dominant position where it could prevent effective competition being maintained by virtue of its ability to behave independently of the usual competitive constraints facing market operators.[158]

Case 27/76, *United Brands v Commission* EU:C:1978:22

Court of Justice

65. The dominant position referred to in this Article relates to a position of economic strength enjoyed by an undertaking which enables it to prevent effective competition being maintained on the relevant market by giving it the power to behave to an appreciable extent independently of its competitors, customers and ultimately of its consumers.

66. In general a dominant position derives from a combination of several factors which, taken separately, are not necessarily determinative.

In *Hoffmann-La Roche*, the CJ elaborated on this definition. It emphasised that a position of dominance did not preclude some competition, and particularly focused on the ability of the undertaking to influence the conditions of competition on the market.

Case 85/76, *Hoffmann-La Roche & Co AG v Commission* EU:C:1979:36, paras. 38–39

Court of Justice

39. [A dominant] position does not preclude some competition, which it does where there is a monopoly or quasi-monopoly, but enables the undertaking which profits by it, if not to determine, at least to have an appreciable influence on the conditions under which that competition will develop, and in any case to act largely in disregard of it so long as such conduct does not operate to its detriment.

[154] See W. Landes and R. Posner, 'Market Power in Antitrust Cases' (1980–1981) 94 *Harvard LR* 937, and Chap. 1.

[155] S. Bishop and M. Walker, *The Economics of EC Competition Law* (3rd edn, Sweet & Maxwell, 2010), 3-041; D. Geradin, A. Layne-Farrar, and N. Petit, *EU Competition Law and Economics* (Oxford University Press, 2012), 4.57; R. Nazzini, *The Foundations of European Union Competition Law: The Objectives and Principles of Article 102* (Oxford University Press, 2011), 335–342.

[156] See *Standard Oil Co of New Jersey v United States*, 221 US 1 (1911); *United States v E I du Pont de Nemours & Co*, 351 US 377 (1956); *United States v Grinnell Corp*, 384 US 563 (1966).

[157] See recently Case C-52/09, *TeliaSonera* EU:C:2011:83, para. 23, Case C-457/10 P, *AstraZeneca* EU:C:2012:770, para. 175.

[158] See also *Continental Can* [1972] JO L7/25, para. 3, where the Commission described dominance in terms of independence and power over price. On appeal, Case 6/72, *Continental Can* EU:C:1973:22, the CJ did not expressly comment on the formulation of dominance, but it was approved by Roemer AG at EU:C:1972:101, 257 and implicitly by the Court.

The definition presupposes a dominant supplier. However, it is clear that the dominant position may be on the buying, rather than the selling, side (what is sometimes referred to as 'monopsony' power). In the latter case, the issue will be one of the independence of the undertaking from its suppliers. *British Airways*, for example, concerned the position of BA as a dominant buyer of air travel agency services.[159]

The formulation of dominance in *United Brands* and *Hoffmann-La* Roche is contentious. The test uses the concept of 'independence', which is more nebulous than power over price. Because such independence must exist only 'to an appreciable extent' and is compatible with continuing competition on the market, it brings uncertainty to the operation of Article 102. Commentators have questioned whether the reference both to the ability of the undertaking to impede effective competition—which implies the power to exclude competitors—and to behave independently are separate elements.[160] In subsequent cases, however, the EU Courts 'have never drawn any distinction between them'.[161]

The 'act independently' criterion has been criticised on the basis that it does not satisfactorily distinguish between dominant and non-dominant firms. No successful firm, it is said,[162] can act to an appreciable extent independently of its consumers, unless it is a monopolist operating in a market protected by insurmountable barriers to entry and facing completely inelastic demand.[163] It really amounts to a matter of appreciable independence from *competitors*, which comes back to the ability to sustain an above competitive level price rise. Moreover, the 'independence' referred to in *Hoffmann-La Roche*, it has been argued, is not the ability to set price independently of demand, but the ability to behave, to an appreciable extent, unconstrained by competitive pressure and demand discipline.[164] The GC equated 'independence' with the ability to maintain high prices in *AstraZeneca*:

> . . . [A] finding of market power, that is to say the ability of an undertaking to behave to an appreciable extent independently of its competitors, its customers and, ultimately, consumers, in the sense that it is in particular able to maintain prices at a higher level while retaining a much higher market share than those of its competitors . . .[165]

The 'position of economic strength' enabling the undertaking 'to prevent effective competition' element in *Hoffmann-La Roche* implies a power to exclude. The problem is the chicken-and-egg conundrum, as exclusionary behaviour is one form of abuse of dominance forbidden by Article 102.[166] Faull and Nikpay conclude that this merely requires that the ability to harm competition must derive from the position of economic strength which is the hallmark of dominance, namely SMP.[167]

B. DOMINANT POSITION IN THE GUIDANCE PAPER

In the Guidance Paper, the Commission has a short section on 'market power'.[168] It starts with the *United Brands/Hoffmann-La Roche* definition. It relates 'independence' to the degree of competitive

[159] Case C-95/04 P, *British Airways* EU:C:2007:166. See also e.g. *Re Eurofima* [1973] CMLR D217; Case 298/83, *CICCE* EU:C:1985:150.

[160] T. Eilmansberger, 'Dominance—The Lost Child? How the Effects-based Rules Could and Should Change Dominance Analysis' (2006) 2 *European Law Journal* Special Issue 15, 16.

[161] Geradin, Layne-Farrar, and Petit, n. 155, 4.51.

[162] See e.g. J. P. Azevedo and M. Walker, 'Dominance: Meaning and Measurement' [2002] *ECLR* 363, 364. The authors suggest that a better test would be 'the ability to restrict output substantially in the market-place'.

[163] O'Donoghue and Padilla, n. 25, 186.

[164] J. Faull and A. Nikpay (eds.), *The EU Law of Competition* (3rd edn, Oxford University Press, 2014), 4.125.

[165] Case T-321/05, *AstraZeneca* EU:T:2010:266, para. 267. On appeal, the CJ affirmed the relevant passage without commenting on it directly, Case C-457/10 P, *AstraZeneca* EU:C:2012:770, paras. 177–181.

[166] See further Geradin, Layne-Farrar, and Petit, n. 155, 4.57. [167] Faull and Nikpay, n. 164, 4.126.

[168] Guidance on the Commission's Enforcement Priorities in Applying Article 82 of the EC Treaty to Abusive Exclusionary Conduct by Dominant Undertakings [2009] OJ C45/2, paras. 9–15.

constraint upon an undertaking. Dominance entails insufficiently effective competitive constraints, so that the undertaking has SMP over a period of time. An undertaking that can sustain price rises above the competitive level can generally be regarded as dominant.

Guidance on the Commission's Enforcement Priorities in Applying Article 82 of the EC Treaty to Abusive Exclusionary Conduct by Dominant Undertakings [2009] OJ C45/2

9. The assessment of whether an undertaking is in a dominant position and of the degree of market power it holds is a first step in the application of Article [102]. According to the case-law, holding a dominant position confers a special responsibility on the undertaking concerned, the scope of which must be considered in the light of the specific circumstances of each case . . .

10. Dominance has been defined under Community law as a position of economic strength enjoyed by an undertaking, which enables it to prevent effective competition being maintained on a relevant market, by affording it the power to behave to an appreciable extent independently of its competitors, its customers and ultimately of consumers . . . This notion of independence is related to the degree of competitive constraint exerted on the undertaking in question. Dominance entails that these competitive constraints are not sufficiently effective and hence that the undertaking in question enjoys substantial market power over a period of time. This means that the undertaking's decisions are largely insensitive to the actions and reactions of competitors, customers and, ultimately, consumers. The Commission may consider that effective competitive constraints are absent even if some actual or potential competition remains . . . In general, a dominant position derives from a combination of several factors which, taken separately, are not necessarily determinative . . .

11. The Commission considers that an undertaking which is capable of profitably increasing prices above the competitive level for a significant period of time does not face sufficiently effective competitive constraints and can thus generally be regarded as dominant . . . In this Communication, the expression 'increase prices' includes the power to maintain prices above the competitive level and is used as shorthand for the various ways in which the parameters of competition—such as prices, output, innovation, the variety or quality of goods or services—can be influenced to the advantage of the dominant undertaking and to the detriment of consumers . . .

Notably, the Commission equates dominance with power over price. However, it makes the important point that the power to maintain supra-competitive prices is not the only hallmark of SMP. It also includes the power to artificially limit output or innovation, or the production of poor quality and/or choice of goods or services,[169] meaning that 'increase prices' is employed as an umbrella term.

Faull and Nikpay explain that the Guidance Paper is consistent with the case law.[170]

J. Faull and A. Nikpay (eds.), *The EU Law of Competition* (3rd edn, Oxford University Press, 2014), 4.133–4.134

4.133 The question then is whether dominance requires more than the possession of substantial and durable market power. The case law appears to place emphasis on the dominant undertaking's ability to harm competition rather than on its ability to raise price substantially above the competitive level for

[169] See Azevedo and Walker, n. 162.

[170] See similarly L. Ortiz Blanco, *Market Power in EU Antitrust Law* (Hart Publishing, 2012), 47: 'in effect, the traditional definition of a dominant position, based on the concept of independence, and the more modern one, which requires the capacity to maintain supra-competitive prices, basically refer to the same thing. In a market economy that focuses on profit, independence can only lead to price increases, and, at the same time, improvements in the results or the positions of the companies'. See also Geradin, Layne-Farrar, and Petit, n. 155, 4.52.

a significant period of time . . . It could be argued that there is a tension between a structural definition of dominance as substantial and durable market power, adopted by the Commission in its guidance, and a behavioural definition of dominance as ability to harm competition, adopted by the EU Courts.

4.134 This tension may be more apparent than real and can be reconciled. The ability of a dominant undertaking to harm competition presupposes substantial and durable market power. If a firm is subject to effective competitive pressure and, therefore, has no substantial market power it is unlikely to be able to harm competition within the meaning of Article 102 because competitors and customers will generally be able to neutralise any potentially anti-competitive behaviour of the firm in question. The application of a prohibition of abusive unilateral conduct to such firms would give rise to a high risk of error that would not be counterbalanced by the magnitude and likelihood of the harm that they can inflict on the economy. It can be concluded therefore, that the definition of dominance in the case law and that in the Guidance on Article 102 are coextensive and both equally consistent with the text and purpose of Article 102.

C. EFFECTS-BASED ANALYSIS AND THE CONCEPT OF DOMINANCE

As explained, the modernisation of Article 102 centred on the idea that an effects-based analysis which is concerned primarily with consumer welfare should be adopted. It might thus be argued that, if a rigorous economic approach is taken to determining whether the conduct of an undertaking harms consumers, the preliminary question of whether that undertaking is in a dominant position need not be separately answered.[171] This approach was urged by the EAGCP, in its report which preceded publication of the Discussion Paper.[172] The EAGCP did not advocate an approach premised upon 'abuse, *ergo* dominance', but argued for an *integrated* examination of the issues.[173]

Report by the EAGCP, 'An Economic Approach to Article 102', Brussels, 14–15 July 2005

In proposing to reduce the role of separate assessments of dominance and to integrate the substantive assessment of dominance with the procedure for establishing competitive harm itself, we depart from the tradition of case law concerning Art. [102], but *not*, we believe, from the legal norm itself. Art. [102] is concerned not just with dominance as such, but with abuses of dominance. The case law tradition of having separate assessments of dominance and of abusiveness of behaviour simplifies procedures, but this simplification involves a loss of precision in the implementation of the legal norm. The structural indicators which traditionally serve as proxies for 'dominance' provide an appropriate measure of power in some markets, but not in others. In a market in which these indicators do not properly measure the firm's ability to impose abusive behaviour on others, the competition authority's intervention under traditional modes of procedure is likely to be inappropriate, too harsh in some cases and too lenient in others. Given that the Treaty itself does not provide a separate definition of dominance, let alone call for any of the traditionally used indicators as such, it seems more appropriate to have the implementation of the Treaty itself focus on the abuses and to treat the assessment of dominance in this context.

Lawyers are likely to be more troubled than economists by the inconvenient fact that, from *Continental Can* onwards,[174] the EU Courts have said that when applying Article 102 dominance must first be established, and then the conduct under review judged abusive or not. Commentators

[171] See *Eastman Kodak Co v Image Technical Services Inc*, 504 US 451, 112 S.Ct 2072 (1992) for this approach in the US.
[172] See Section 5.B.
[173] J. Vickers, 'Market Power in Competition Cases' (2006) 2 *European Competition Journal* Special Issue 3, 11.
[174] See Case 6/72, *Continental Can* EU:C:1973:22.

have also disagreed with the EAGCP's suggestion for other reasons, arguing in particular that it *is* possible for anti-competitive effects to be caused by the conduct of non-dominant undertakings,[175] that a dominance 'screen' is desirable for administrative reasons to avoid Type 1 'false positive errors', and that a threshold requirement of dominance provides a 'safe harbour', freeing the vast majority of undertakings from a fear of accusations of abuse.[176]

Nonetheless, the suggestion has received renewed attention in the light of the particular problems of identifying dominance within the digital economy. Thus, an expert report commissioned at Member State level concluded that:

> Digital markets—and markets characterized by digital platforms in particular—pose new challenges to competition law when it comes to market definition. Hence, there are good arguments for more flexibility in the assessment of dominance. Instead of requiring competition authorities and courts to always define markets first, as is currently the case, it can make sense, in some cases, to simply infer dominance if it can be established that some unilateral conduct is not sufficiently disciplined by competition and this practice has an exclusionary effect. However, such an evolution of Art. 102 TFEU is to be left to the Union courts.[177]

The Commission's 2019 Report on Competition Policy for the Digital Era similarly highlighted the complexities of defining and measuring market power in digital markets, including issues raised by network effects, 'zero-price' products, and the dynamic and fast-moving nature of such sectors. It stopped short of advocating for its wholesale abandonment, however, arguing instead for a careful context-specific assessment of market power on a case-by-case basis.[178]

Notably, the Digital Markets Act (DMA),[179] discussed in Chapter 16, deliberately dispenses with the market definition and market power requirements, aiming instead at the activities of large digital 'gatekeepers'. This is a novel concept which focuses on an undertaking's 'significant impact on the internal market', its role as 'an important gateway for business users to reach end users', and the fact that it 'enjoys an entrenched and durable position, in its operations'.[180] Not uncontroversially, the DMA also deploys quantitative criteria related to the undertaking's annual turnover, market capitalisation, and the number of active end-users and business users, which function as a proxy to establish gatekeeper status.[181]

D. ESTABLISHING DOMINANCE: A TWO-STAGE APPROACH

We now consider how the existence of a 'dominant position' is established for the purposes of Article 102.

In *Continental Can*, the CJ stressed that dominance exists only in relation to a particular market and not in the abstract. It held that 'the definition of the relevant market is of essential

[175] See e.g. G. Monti, 'The Concept of Dominance in Article 82' (2006) 2 *European Competition Journal* 31, 45–46, discussing predatory pricing; I. Kokkoris, *A Gap in the Enforcement of Article 82* (BIICL, 2009).

[176] Vickers, n. 173, 11–12; G. J. Werden, 'Competition Policy on Exclusionary Conduct: Towards an Effects-based Analysis' (2006) 2 *European Competition Journal* 53, 55–57; Faull and Nikpay, n. 164, 4.137–4.138.

[177] H. Schweitzer, J. Haucap, W. Kerber, and R. Welker, 'Modernising the law on abuse of market power, Report for the Federal Ministry for Economic Affairs and Energy (Germany)' [English language summary], 4 September 2018, <https://papers.ssrn.com/sol3/papers.cfm?abstract_id=3250742>, para. 1.

[178] J. Crémer, Y.-A. de Montjoye, and H. Schweitzer, Report on Competition Policy for the Digital Era, European Commission, 4 April 2019, in particular pp. 42–50.

[179] Reg. (EU) 2022/1925 of the European Parliament and of the Council of 14 September 2022 on contestable and fair markets in the digital sector and amending Dirs. (EU) 2019/1937 and (EU) 2020/1828 (Digital Markets Act) [2022] OJ L265/1.

[180] Art. 3(1), DMA. [181] Art. 3(2), DMA. See further discussion in Chap. 16, Section 6.C.

significance'[182] in determining whether an undertaking is dominant. Commission decisions applying Article 102 will be quashed if the market is not properly defined.[183] The Commission follows a two-stage procedure: first, identification of the relevant market and, second, examination of the undertaking's position on that market and analysis of the competitive constraints which it faces. The Commission does this by considering the market share of the undertaking concerned and 'other factors indicating dominance', including barriers to entry and expansion.

The two-stage procedure can be problematic. Not only are markets notoriously difficult to define,[184] but the process of market definition may be hard to separate from the supposed second step, namely assessing the undertaking's power on that market. It can be difficult to determine which factors should be taken into account when defining markets and which factors should be taken into account when considering the undertaking's market position. For example, it may be challenging to decide whether account should be taken of the presence of a producer which can switch its production when defining the market (supply-side substitutability) or when assessing the competitive constraints that the allegedly dominant undertaking faces (potential competition). In addition, as noted, the question whether an undertaking is dominant can be hard to disentangle from the question whether or not it has committed an abuse of dominance.

In its earlier enforcement practice, the Commission was often criticised for finding that an undertaking occupied a 'dominant position' where, in reality, it had little market power. Specifically, it was criticised for defining markets too narrowly, for being too ready to find that an undertaking was dominant by relying heavily on market shares, for finding dominance at comparatively low market shares, and/or for taking an insufficiently rigorous view of barriers to entry. This approach, coupled with the wide interpretation given to the concept of 'abuse', created a perception that the Commission played a decidedly interventionist role through its application of Article 102. With a focus on enforcement against Big Tech more recently, the concern that the Commission may be erroneously targeting its efforts at undertakings that obviously lack market power is arguably less compelling.

8. MARKET DEFINITION IN ARTICLE 102 CASES

A. GENERAL

Chapter 3 explained that the purpose of defining the relevant market is to identify those products and services that are such close substitutes for the product or service under consideration that they operate as a competitive constraint on the behaviour of suppliers of the latter. Here, we focus on the approach in Article 102 cases, always remembering that market definition is not an end in itself. Rather, it is a preliminary step and a tool necessary to answer the real question: does this firm occupy a dominant position for the purposes of Article 102? Occasionally, therefore, the Commission has left open the precise definition of the market, where it would make no difference to question of dominance either way.[185] As discussed in Chapter 3, the Commission has opted to update its long-standing

[182] Case 6/72, *Continental Can* EU:C:1973:22, para. 32. See also Case C-7/97, *Oscar Bronner* EU:C:1998:569, para. 32; Case C-52/07, *Kanal 5* EU:C:2008:703, para. 19.

[183] In *Continental Can* itself, the CJ quashed the Commission's decision due to its failure to define adequately the market from the supply side. More recently, see Case T-691/14, *Servier* EU:T:2018:922.

[184] See Chap. 3, Section 4.

[185] See e.g. COMP/37.990, *Intel* 13 May 2009, in which the Commission left open the question of whether there was one relevant market (CPUs for all computers) or three separate markets (CPUs for desktops, laptops, and servers). See also AT40153, *E-book MFNs and related matters (Amazon)* 4 May 2017.

Market Definition Notice,[186] issuing a 'draft revised Market Definition Notice'[187] in November 2022. This discussion draws on both documents as appropriate.

The market must be defined anew, and a fresh analysis of the conditions of competition made, each time Article 102 is applied. The approach to market definition in prior decisional practice 'can give only an indication' of the appropriate factors to be taken into account in later cases, 'insofar as the facts of those cases are not the same'.[188] The Commission cannot rely on findings of dominance in previous cases,[189] although it is entitled to take such assessments into account as a relevant factor among others, where there is nothing to indicate that the conditions of competition have changed significantly.[190]

In most Article 102 cases, the defendant undertaking will argue that the market at issue is a wide one—for example, all fruit, rather than just bananas—on the basis that, the broader the market, the less likely the finding of dominance.[191] The assessment of the relevant market is therefore crucial. If defined too narrowly, an undertaking's position will be exaggerated, and a finding of dominance becomes more likely. Furthermore, there may be a question as to whether a 'market' exists at all.[192]

In its Market Definition Notice, the Commission identified three main competitive constraints to which firms are subject: demand substitutability, supply substitutability, and potential competition.[193] Demand and, to a more limited extent, supply substitutability are relevant to the determination of the market. Potential competition is relevant when considering the allegedly dominant undertaking's position on the market once defined, although potential competitors may in certain circumstances be considered supply substitutes.[194]

(i) Substitutability

In determining demand substitutability, the original Market Definition Notice preferred quantitative methods over qualitative methods which take account of characteristics, price, and intended use. Specifically, it adopted the SSNIP test, which asks whether a small (5–10 per cent) but non-transitory increase in price of one product will cause purchasers to purchase sufficient of another product instead to make the price increase unsustainable.[195] The use of the SSNIP test in Article 102 cases is, however, complicated by the 'cellophane fallacy'.[196]

A key impetus behind the Commission's decision to revise the existing Market Definition Notice was a general acknowledgement of the limitations of the SSNIP test. This is because the test is difficult to carry out in practice, and because the existing Notice provided no guidance on how it could or should be applied in markets where price is not the only parameter of competition.[197] This is a particular

[186] Commission Notice on the Definition of the Relevant Market for the Purposes of Community Competition Law [1997] OJ C372/5 (hereafter Market Definition Notice).

[187] Commission Press Release, 'Competition: Commission seeks feedback on draft revised Market Definition Notice', 8 November 2022, <https://ec.europa.eu/commission/presscorner/detail/en/ip_22_6528>, which provides access to the text (hereafter Draft Notice).

[188] Case T-604/18, *Google Android* EU:T:2022:541, para. 164.

[189] Cases T-125/97 etc., *Coca-Cola* EU:T:2000:84, para. 82.

[190] Case T-699/14, *Topps Europe* EU:T:2017:2, para. 93.

[191] More unusually, the undertaking may argue for a narrow definition: e.g. in Case C-62/86, *AKZO* EU:C:1991:286, the undertaking argued for a narrow market definition as in the narrow niche market it was relatively weak, but in the wider market as a whole it had a large share.

[192] See the discussion on 'input' markets in Section 8.B, and Case T-219/99, *British Airways* EU:T:2003:343, *aff'd* Case C-95/04 P, *British Airways* EU:C:2007:166.

[193] Market Definition Notice, para. 13. This approach is retained in the Draft Notice, para. 25.

[194] Chap. 3, Section 4.

[195] Market Definition Notice, paras. 15–19. [196] See Chap. 3, Section 4.E.iii.a.

[197] Commission Staff Working Document, 'Evaluation of the Commission Notice on the definition of relevant market for the purposes of Community competition law of 9 December 1997', SWD(2021) 199 final, 12 July 2021, p. 37.

concern with respect to zero-price products, which arise with frequency in the digital economy where the Commission has focused much of its Article 102 enforcement in recent years.[198] The revised Draft Notice thus clarifies that the 'there is no obligation on the Commission to apply the SSNIP test empirically, and other types of evidence are equally valid to inform the market definition'.[199]

The problems of identification using characteristics, price, and intended use are illustrated by two leading early Article 102 cases, *United Brands* and *Michelin I*.[200] These extracts are followed by two more recent cases involving the digital economy, *Wanadoo* (*France Télécom*), which employed both a qualitative assessment and the SSNIP test, and *Google Shopping*, which concerned a multi-sided market.

(ii) The *United Brands* Case

In *United Brands*, the defendant (a banana producer) challenged the Commission's finding that a separate relevant market existed for bananas, arguing instead that bananas formed part of a wider fresh fruit market. The CJ thus considered why people eat bananas, and whether or not consumers treat bananas as reasonably interchangeable with other fresh fruits. It decided that there was only a small degree of substitutability with other fruit, partly because of the unique appearance, taste, softness, seedlessness, and easy handling nature of the banana.

Case 27/76, *United Brands v Commission* EU:C:1978:22

Court of Justice

12. As far as the product market is concerned it is first of all necessary to ascertain whether, as the applicant maintains, bananas are an integral part of the fresh fruit market, because they are reasonably interchangeable by consumers with other kinds of fresh fruit such as apples, oranges, grapes, peaches, strawberries, etc. or whether the relevant market consists solely of the banana and is a market sufficiently homogeneous and distinct from the market of other fresh fruit.

13. The applicant submits in support of its argument that bananas compete with other fresh fruit in the same shops, on the same shelves, at prices which can be compared, satisfying the same needs: consumption as a dessert or between meals.

14. The statistics produced show that consumer expenditure on the purchase of bananas is at its lowest between June and December when there is a plentiful supply of domestic fresh fruit on the market.

15. Studies carried out by the Food and Agriculture Organization . . . confirm that banana prices are relatively weak during the summer months and that the price of apples for example has a statistically appreciable impact on the consumption of bananas in the Federal Republic of Germany.

16. Again according to these studies some easing of prices is noticeable at the end of the year during the 'orange season'.

17. The seasonal peak periods when there is a plentiful supply of other fresh fruit exert an influence not only on the prices but also on the volume of sales of bananas and consequently on the volume of imports thereof.

18. The applicant concludes from these findings that bananas and other fresh fruit form only one market and that UBC's operations should have been examined in this context for the purpose of any application of Article [102].

[198] See, generally, Chap. 16. [199] Draft Notice, para. 33.

[200] Case 27/76, *United Brands v Commission* EU:C:1978:22; Case 322/81, *NV Nederlandsche Banden-Industrie Michelin v Commission (Michelin I)* EU:C:1983:313.

19. The Commission maintains that there is a demand for bananas which is distinct from the demand for other fresh fruit especially as the banana is a very important part of the diet of certain sections of the community.

20. The specific qualities of the banana influence customer preference and induce him not to readily accept other fruits as a substitute.

21. The Commission draws the conclusion from the studies quoted by the applicant that the influence of the prices and availability of other types of fruit on the prices and availability of bananas on the relevant market is very ineffective and that these effects are too brief and too spasmodic for such other fruit to be regarded as forming part of the same market as bananas or as a substitute therefor.

22. For the banana to be regarded as forming a market which is sufficiently differentiated from other fruit markets it must be possible for it to be singled out by such special features distinguishing it from other fruits that it is only to a limited extent interchangeable with them and is only exposed to their competition in a way that is hardly perceptible.

23. The ripening of bananas takes place the whole year round without any season having to be taken into account.

24. Throughout the year production exceeds demand and can satisfy it at any time.

25. Owing to this particular feature the banana is a privileged fruit and its production and marketing can be adapted to the seasonal fluctuations of other fresh fruit which are known and can be computed.

26. There is no unavoidable seasonal substitution since the consumer can obtain this fruit all the year round.

27. Since the banana is a fruit which is always available in sufficient quantities the question whether it can be replaced by other fruits must be determined over the whole of the year for the purpose of ascertaining the degree of competition between it and other fresh fruit.

28. The studies of the banana market on the Court's file show that on the latter market there is no significant long term cross-elasticity any more than—as has been mentioned—there is any seasonal substitutability in general between the banana and all the seasonal fruits, as this only exists between the banana and two fruits (peaches and table grapes) in one of the countries (West Germany) of the relevant geographic market.

29. As far as concerns the two fruits available throughout the year (oranges and apples) the first are not interchangeable and in the case of the second there is only a relative degree of substitutability.

30. This small degree of substitutability is accounted for by the specific features of the banana and all the factors which influence consumer choice.

31. The banana has certain characteristics, appearance, taste, softness, seedlessness, easy handling, a constant level of production which enable it to satisfy the constant needs of an important section of the population consisting of the very young, the old and the sick.

32. As far as prices are concerned two FAO studies show that the banana is only affected by the prices—falling prices—of other fruits (and only of peaches and table grapes) during the summer months and mainly in July and then by an amount not exceeding 20 per cent.

33. Although it cannot be denied that during these months and some weeks at the end of the year this product is exposed to competition from other fruits, the flexible way in which the volume of imports and their marketing on the relevant geographic market is adjusted means that the conditions of competition are extremely limited and that its price adapts without any serious difficulties to this situation where supplies of fruit are plentiful.

34. It follows from all these considerations that a very large number of consumers having a constant need for bananas are not noticeably or even appreciably enticed away from the consumption of this product by the arrival of other fresh fruit on the market and that even the personal peak periods only affect it for a limited period of time and to a very limited extent from the point of view of substitutability.

35. Consequently, the banana market is a market which is sufficiently distinct from the other fresh fruit markets.

Here, the CJ was concerned with the question of whether the banana could be singled out by special features that distinguished it from other fruits from a demand perspective. The 'special features' it identified were, first, that the banana was a 'privileged fruit'[201] in that it was not seasonal and, secondly, that it had 'certain characteristics' making it suitable for the very young, the old, and the sick.[202] These characteristics, apart from constant availability, were appearance, taste, softness, seedlessness, and easy handling. This is a strange list. Softness, seedlessness, and easy handling may make bananas suitable for the young, old, and sick, but it is difficult to see why their appearance does and it is never explained what is so special about their taste. Moreover, it is wrong to conclude from the dependence of one group of customers that a product forms a separate market unless it is possible to price discriminate at the point of sale and to prevent arbitrage. This is recognised in the Market Definition Notice.[203] It may be that, if the question arose again, bananas would still be held to constitute a separate market, but it is unlikely that this would be on the basis of their 'special suitability' for certain customers. Rather, evidence would be sought from technology such as supermarket scanners, which would enable own-price and cross-price elasticities to be measured.[204]

(iii) The *Michelin* Case

In *Michelin I*, the Commission found that Michelin had abused a dominant position on the market for new replacement tyres for lorries, buses, and similar vehicles.[205] Michelin claimed, inter alia, that the Commission's definition of the market was narrow and arbitrary, and that there was instead a wider tyre market in which Michelin did not hold a dominant position.[206] The CJ had to determine whether the Commission had correctly defined the market. A number of facts were taken into account: that lorries and buses need larger tyres than cars and vans; that there are different sizes of lorry and bus tyres; that tyre manufacturers supply their tyres separately to new lorry and bus manufacturers *and* to dealers who fit tyres on lorries and buses as replacements; and that tyre dealers also fit retreaded or remoulded tyres to vehicles whose owners do not want new replacement tyres. Which, if any, of these tyres were substitutes so that they formed part of the same product market?

Case 322/81, *Nederlandsche Banden-Industrie Michelin v Commission* EU:C:1983:313

Court of Justice

The market in replacement tyres for heavy vehicles

37. [F]or the purposes of investigating the possibly dominant position of an undertaking on a given market . . . an examination limited to the objective characteristics only of the relevant products cannot be sufficient: the competitive conditions and the structure of supply and demand on the market must also be taken into consideration.

38. Moreover, it was for that reason that the Commission and Michelin NV agreed that new, original-equipment tyres should not be taken into consideration in the assessment of market shares. Owing to the particular structure of demand for such tyres characterized by direct orders from car manufacturers, competition in this sphere is in fact governed by completely different factors and rules.

39. As far as replacement tyres are concerned, the first point which must be made is that at the user level there is no interchangeability between car and van tyres on the one hand and heavy-vehicle

[201] Ibid., para. 25. [202] Ibid., para. 31. [203] Para. 43; see also Draft Notice, para. 88.
[204] See O'Donoghue and Padilla, n. 25, 124. [205] [1981] OJ L353/33.
[206] Michelin also challenged the definition of the geographic market as being the Netherlands. See Section 8.C.

tyres on the other. Car and van tyres therefore have no influence at all on competition on the market in heavy-vehicle tyres.

40. Furthermore, the structure of demand for each of those groups of products is different. Most buyers of heavy-vehicle tyres are trade users, particularly haulage undertakings, for whom, as the Commission explained, the purchase of replacement tyres represents an item of considerable expenditure and who constantly ask their tyre dealers for advice and long-term specialized services adapted to their specific needs. On the other hand, for the average buyer of car or van tyres the purchase of tyres is an occasional event and even if the buyer operates a business he does not expect such specialized advice and service adapted to specific needs. Hence the sale of heavy-vehicle tyres requires a particularly specialized distribution network which is not the case with the distribution of car and van tyres.

. . .

42. The Commission rightly examined the structure of the market and demand primarily at the level of dealers to whom Michelin NV applied the practice in question. Michelin NV has itself stated . . . that it was compelled to change its discount system to take account of the tendency towards specialization amongst its dealers, some of whom, such as garage owners, no longer sold tyres for heavy vehicles and vans. This confirms the differences existing in the structure of demand between different groups of dealers. Nor has Michelin NV disputed that the distinction drawn between tyres for heavy vehicles, vans and cars is also applied by all its competitors, especially as regards discount terms, even if in the case of certain types of tyre the distinctions drawn by different manufacturers may vary in detail.

43. Nevertheless, it cannot be deduced from the fact that the conduct to which exception is taken in this case affects dealers that Michelin NV's position ought to be assessed on the basis of the proportion of Michelin heavy-vehicle tyres in the dealers' total turnover. Since it is a question of investigating whether Michelin NV holds a dominant position in the case of certain products, it is unimportant that the dealers also deal in other products if there is no competition between those products and the products in question.

44. On the other hand, in deciding whether a dominant position exists, neither the absence of elasticity of supply between different types and dimensions of tyres for heavy vehicles, which is due to differences in the conditions of production, nor the absence of interchangeability and elasticity of demand between those types and dimensions of tyre from the point of view of the specific needs of the user allow a number of smaller markets, reflecting those types and dimensions, to be distinguished, as Michelin NV suggests. Those differences between different types and dimensions of tyre are not vitally important for dealers, who must meet demand from customers for the whole range of heavy-vehicle tyres. Furthermore, in the absence of any specialization on the part of the undertakings concerned, such differences in the type and dimensions of a product are not a crucial factor in the assessment of an undertaking's market position because in view of their similarity and the manner in which they complement one another at the technical level, the conditions of competition on the market are the same for all the types and dimensions of the product.

45. In establishing that Michelin NV has a dominant position the Commission was therefore right to assess its market share with reference to replacement tyres for lorries, buses and similar vehicles and to exclude consideration of car and van tyres.

The taking into consideration of competition from retreads

. . .

48. . .. [A]lthough the existence of a competitive relationship between two products does not presuppose complete interchangeability for a specific purpose, it is not a pre-condition for a finding that a dominant position exists in the case of a given product that there should be a complete absence of competition from other partially interchangeable products as long as such competition does not affect the undertaking's ability to influence appreciably the conditions in which that competition may be exerted

or at any rate to conduct itself to a large extent without having to take account of that competition and without suffering any adverse effects as a result of its attitude.

49. It is clear from the facts . . . that it cannot be denied that new tyres and retreads are interchangeable to some degree but only to a limited extent and not for all purposes. Although Michelin NV has produced calculations to show that the price and quality of retreads are comparable to those of new tyres and that a number of users do in fact consider the two groups of products interchangeable for their purposes; it has nevertheless admitted that in terms of safety and reliability a retread's value may be less than that of new tyre and, what is more, the Commission has shown that a number of users have certain reservations, which may or may not be justified, regarding the use of a retread, particularly on a vehicle's front axle.

50. In order to assess the effect of this limited competition from retreads on Michelin NV's market position it must be borne in mind that at least some retreads are not put on sale but are produced to order for the user as some transport undertakings attach importance to having their own tyre carcasses retreaded in order to be sure of not receiving damaged carcasses. . . . [A] proportion of retreads reaching the consumer stage are not in competition with new tyres because they involve a service provided directly by the retreading firms to the users.

51. Furthermore, in assessing the size of Michelin NV's market share in relation to its competitors' it must not be overlooked that the market in renovated tyres is a secondary market which depends on supply and prices on the market in new tyres since every retread is made from a tyre which was originally a new tyre and there is a limit to the number of occasions on which a tyre may be retreaded. Consequently a considerable proportion of demand will inevitably always be satisfied by new tyres. In such circumstances the possession by an undertaking of a dominant position in new tyres gives it a privileged position as regards competition from retreading undertakings and this enables it to conduct itself with greater independence on the market than would be possible for a retreading undertaking.

52. It is clear from the considerations set out above that the partial competition to which manufacturers of new tyres are exposed from retreading undertakings is not sufficient to deprive a manufacturer of new tyres of the economic power which he possesses by virtue of his dominant position on the market in new tyres. In assessing Michelin NV's position in relation to the strength and number of its competitors the Commission was therefore right to take into consideration a market share [of] 57 to 65 per cent on the market in new replacement tyres for heavy vehicles. Compared with the market shares of Michelin NV's main competitors amounting to 4 to 8 per cent, that market share constitutes a valid indication of Michelin NV's preponderant strength in relation to its competitors, even when allowance is made for some competition from retreads.

The CJ thus upheld the Commission's decision.[207] The CJ considered that, in the context of finding a dominant position, it is unnecessary that products be completely interchangeable: partial interchangeability is enough. The issue is whether the other product exerts a competitive restraint.[208]

(iv) The *France Télécom* Case

In *Wanadoo*,[209] the Commission defined the relevant market as the French market for high-speed internet access for residential customers.[210] The Commission examined the differences in performance

[207] [1981] OJ L353/33. [208] See also Case T-301/04, *Clearstream Banking v Commission* EU:T:2009:317, para. 64.

[209] COMP/38.233, 16 July 2003.

[210] Asynchronous Digital Subscriber Line, which allows broadband services to be provided over traditional telephone copper wires.

between high- and low-speed internet access, and concluded that these were clearly perceived by consumers, and that an analysis of price differences showed that consumers were prepared to pay a premium for the extra performance and convenience of high speed.[211] On appeal, France Télécom (WIN) pleaded, inter alia, that the Commission should have considered the market as comprising both high-speed and low-speed access.[212]

Case T-340/03, *France Télécom SA v Commission* EU:T:2007:22

General Court

79. If a product could be used for different purposes and if these different uses are in accordance with economic needs, which are themselves also different, there are good grounds for accepting that this product may, according to the circumstances, belong to separate markets which may present specific features which differ from the standpoint both of the structure and of the conditions of competition. However, this finding does not justify the conclusion that such a product, together with all the other products which can replace it as far as concerns the various uses to which it may be put and with which it may compete, forms one single market.

80. The concept of the relevant market in fact implies that there can be effective competition between the products which form part of it and this presupposes that there is a sufficient degree of interchangeability between all the products forming part of the same market in so far as a specific use of such products is concerned (Case 85/76 *Hoffmann-La Roche* v *Commission* . . . paragraph 28).

. . .

82. It must be stated that there is not a mere difference in comfort or quality between high- and low-speed access. It is clear from the evidence provided by the Commission . . . that some applications available with high-speed access are simply not feasible with low-speed access, including, for example, the downloading of very voluminous video files or interactive network games. WIN also confirmed . . . that there are 'audiovisual/multimedia activities . . . more specific to ADSL'. In addition, the study undertaken by the . . . Research Centre for the Study and Monitoring of Living Standards[] (Crédoc) on behalf of WIN . . . also describes new uses developed on the internet by the eXtense service and which are specific to high-speed access, that is, playing network games, listening to radio online, watching a video online and shopping online. According to that study, moreover, the subscriber with high-speed access goes online far more often and, on average, for considerably longer than the low-speed access user.

83. As regards the differences in technical features and performances, it is clear from the Commission's contentions . . . that an important technical feature of high-speed internet access is the specific nature of the modems used. A high-speed internet access modem cannot be used for low-speed internet access and vice versa . . . In addition, in the case of high-speed access, the connection is always on and the telephone line always available for making calls.

84. In addition, in the case of the French market, it should be pointed out that, for the period investigated, the offers of high-speed access involved download speeds in the region of 512 kbits/s . . . The offers of traditional low-speed access (limited to 56 kbits/s) and of ISDN (integrated services digital network) (64 or 128 kbits/s) only allowed speeds of 4 to 10 times less. The ADSL offers with download speeds of 128 kbits/s, which, according to the applicant, bear witness to the continuity between low-speed and high-speed, only became available at the end of the period covered by the decision. In addition, even in the case of an offer of 128 kbits/s, the difference between low-speed and high-speed access is considerable. The difference in performance was therefore considerable during the period investigated.

85. In addition to the differences in use, features and performances, there is a significant price differential between low-speed and high-speed access . . .

[211] COMP/38.233, para. 187.

[212] On appeal to the CJ, Case C-202/07 P, *France Télécom SA v Commission* EU:C:2009:214, the market definition was not challenged.

...

87. According to [the Market Definition Notice], the assessment of demand substitution entails a determination of the range of products which are viewed as substitutes by the consumer. One way of making this determination can be viewed as a speculative experiment, postulating a hypothetical small but lasting change in relative prices and evaluating the likely reactions of customers to that increase. In paragraph 17 of the notice, the Commission states '[t]he question to be answered is whether the parties' customers would switch to readily available substitutes . . . in response to a hypothetical small (in the range 5 to 10%) but permanent relative price increase in the products and areas being considered'.

88. . .. [T]he Commission admits that low-speed and high-speed access indeed present some degree of substitutability. It adds . . . however, that the operation of such substitutability is extremely asymmetrical, the migrations of customers from offers of high-speed to low-speed access being negligible compared with the migrations in the other direction. However, according to the Commission, if the products were perfectly substitutable from the point of view of demand, the rates of migration should be identical or at least comparable.

89. It should be pointed out, in this respect, that, first of all, . . . the migration rates of high-speed subscribers to integral low-speed offers were very low during the period covered, in spite of the difference in price between those services, which should have prompted numerous internet users to turn to low-speed access. This large discrepancy in the rates of migration between low-speed and high-speed access and between high-speed and low-speed access does not lend credence to the argument that those services are interchangeable in the eyes of consumers. In the application, WIN also failed to adduce any evidence to cast doubt on that analysis.

90. Secondly, it transpires that, according to a survey carried out on behalf of the Commission and presented by WIN in an annex to its application, 80% of subscribers would maintain their subscription in response to a price increase in the range 5 to 10%. According to paragraph 17 of the Notice on the definition of the relevant market for the purposes of Community competition law . . . this high percentage of subscribers who would not abandon high-speed access in response to a price increase of 5 to 10% provides a strong indication of the absence of demand-side substitution.

91. Consequently, on the basis of all the foregoing, it should be held that the Commission was right to find that a sufficient degree of substitutability between high-speed and low-speed access did not exist and to define the market in question as that of high-speed internet access for residential customers.

Notably, the GC cited both the case law of the CJ on identifying substitute products by reference to characteristics and use, and the Market Definition Notice and the SSNIP test. In particular, it cited a survey showing that 80 per cent of subscribers to the high-speed service would be impervious to a 5–10 per cent price increase. The GC concluded that this 'provides a strong indication' of the absence of demand-side substitution.[213] The relevant market definition was not raised before the CJ on further appeal.[214]

(v) Market Definition in Multi-sided Markets: The *Google Shopping* Case

The concept of market multi-sidedness was introduced in Chapter 1. *Google Shopping*[215] illustrates the potential complexity of market definition where there are two or more interrelated sources of

[213] It may not have needed SSNIP tests to convince the Court that low-speed internet access is no substitute for high-speed.

[214] Case C-202/07 P, *France Télécom v Commission* EU:C:2009:214.

[215] AT.39740, *Google Search (Shopping)* 27 June 2017, essentially upheld on appeal in Case T-612/17 *Google Shopping* EU:T:2021:763.

demand. The case concerned self-preferencing,[216] a leveraging abuse[217] that is premised upon two distinct albeit complementary markets: here, these were general online search services and comparison shopping services. Google was held to be dominant on various national markets for general online search, which it did not dispute on appeal.[218] More contentious, however, was the finding that comparison shopping constituted a distinct product market, in respect of which Google had attempted to *extend* its dominance.

The Commission found that comparison shopping is distinct from other specialised search services, as each focus on providing different information to users. It is also distinct from online search advertising which is, essentially, a form of quid pro quo for the free services that users receive. The Commission further distinguished the services provided by online retailers and merchant platforms (online marketplaces). Online retailers rarely link to other e-commerce sites, whereas comparison shopping sites operate precisely as intermediaries, linking users and different retailers, thus allowing comparisons across multiple retailers. Conversely, while comparison shopping services and online marketplaces each aggregate offers from different sellers, such platforms have limited substitutability, because marketplaces enable buyers and sellers to meet *and* to conclude sales, whereas comparison shopping sites merely allow buyers to 'shop around'. Finally, comparison shopping sites are distinguished from offline comparison shopping tools: online tools provide greater levels of information, they usually link directly to e-commerce sites, and the business models differ.

Google challenged the choice to exclude merchant platforms from the definition of the relevant market, which it argued had led the Commission to overstate the anticipated anti-competitive effects.[219] The GC noted the two-sided nature of the market. Accordingly, it was necessary to consider whether comparison shopping services could be differentiated from merchant platforms by 'particular characteristics' from a demand perspective with respect to both internet users (i.e. would-be shoppers) *and* online sellers.[220]

Case T-612/17, *Google and Alphabet v European Commission (Google Shopping)* EU:T:2021:763

General Court

473. At issue . . . is a two-sided market, that is to say, a market in which suppliers simultaneously respond to two distinct demands from different types of service user: on the one hand, the demand of internet users wishing to compare features and prices of products before ultimately making a purchase, and, on the other, the demand of those wishing to sell their products who feed information about those products into suppliers' databases for the purposes of such comparisons with a view to their products being purchased by internet users, although any transaction between buyer and seller will take place, if at all, on a different market. In the present case, the suppliers in respect of whom a determination must be made as to whether they are participants in the same comparison shopping services market fall into two categories, that of 'pure' comparison shopping services and that of merchant platforms, while those who seek their services are, on one side of the two-sided market, internet users, and, on the other side of that market, online sellers.

474. The Court notes that . . . the Commission did not reduce the relevant market for comparison shopping services to the side that is of interest to internet users only . . . The Commission's arguments

[216] See Chap. 7, Section 13. [217] See Chap. 7, Section 6.

[218] Case T-612/17, *Google Shopping* EU:T:2021:763, para. 469.

[219] Ibid., paras. 469–470. [220] Ibid., para. 472.

in defining the contours of that market include . . . not only an analysis in the contested decision of the characteristics of demand from the point of view of internet users, but also an analysis of the characteristics of demand from the point of view of online sellers.

475. For example . . . when the Commission considers whether comparison shopping services and other specialised search services are substitutable, it refers to the commercial workforce necessary in order to enter into agreements with online sellers of the products or services that will ultimately be sold, which shows that it is also taking account of that side of the market on which those specialised search services are the suppliers, and online sellers represent the demand for their services. Similarly . . . when the Commission considers whether comparison shopping services and advertising services are substitutable, it explains that those services are not substitutable, from the perspective of both internet users and online sellers. As regards the substitutability of comparison shopping services and merchant platforms, the Commission first examines substitutability from the point of view of demand from internet users . . ., then of demand from online sellers . . . Next, it analyses the characteristics of the service offered by comparison shopping services and merchant platforms to internet users . . . and to online sellers. . . Lastly, the Commission rejects Google's arguments in favour of the substitutability of comparison shopping services and merchant platforms, which concern the side of the market that is of interest to internet users as well as the side that is of interest to online sellers . . .

476. Both sides of the market at issue were therefore examined by the Commission, leading it in particular to conclude that merchant platforms were not participating in the same market for comparison shopping services as comparison shopping service providers. Consequently, the Commission did not reduce the market to just one of its sides.

477. Yet . . . the fact that, in order to meet demand on one side of a two-sided market, the services of two categories of supplier may be largely interchangeable does not necessarily mean that that is the case on the other side of that market with regard to the other demand that is expressed there. On a two-sided market, since demand does not emanate from the same source on each side of the market, it cannot be assumed that the issue of the substitutability of services will be resolved in the same way for each side.

478. It is therefore necessary to ascertain whether, in respect of one or other of the two sides of the market for comparison shopping services, the Commission demonstrated to the requisite standard . . . that the services offered by comparison shopping service providers had particular characteristics that so differentiate them from the comparison shopping services offered by merchant platforms, or vice versa, that they are only to a small degree interchangeable with each other and competition between them is insignificant.

479. In the contested decision the Commission indicated . . . that while comparison shopping service providers and merchant platforms both offered comparison shopping services, they served a different purpose for internet users and for online sellers.

480. As regards demand from internet users, the Commission noted . . . that comparison shopping services acted as intermediaries between internet users and individual sellers or merchant platforms, allowing users to compare different product offers; that they did not offer internet users the possibility of making purchases on their own websites, but referred them to sellers' websites; that they did not offer after-sales support or product return options; and that they listed offers only for new products. Merchant platforms, on the other hand, allowed purchases to be made on their own websites, including of third-party products, and sometimes of second-hand products sold by non-professionals; were perceived as multi-brand retailers, that is to say, as places where users can buy products; and offered after-sales support, product return and even, in some cases, indemnification against a problem. The Commission relied in that regard on numerous statements from undertakings that participated in the procedure, and stated moreover . . . that a majority of the comparison shopping services questioned considered merchant platforms to be business partners, not competitors, and vice versa . . . [T]he contested decision indicate[s] that internal Google documents show that Google does not equate one category of player with the other.

481. Admittedly, as Google submits, the fact that merchant platforms provide far more functions than comparison shopping services and are their customers does not in itself prove that, in relation only to comparison shopping services offered to internet users, the services offered by both categories of player are only to a small degree interchangeable with each other and competition between them is insignificant, in other words, that they serve different purposes.

482. Nevertheless, the contested decision contains other material that substantiates this.

483. It is apparent from the information set out in paragraph 480 above that, for internet users, merchant platforms appear primarily to be places where goods can be purchased and which provide all the traditional sales functions, including in some cases operating as a sales counter for non-professionals, while the primary function of comparison shopping services is to provide information.

484. In that regard, the Commission states . . . that comparison shopping services generally display a wider range of offers than merchant platforms, which specifically includes offers from merchant platforms. Therefore, while there is a certain overlap between the databases of merchant platforms and those of comparison shopping services, the latter appear to be a much more powerful search tool in terms of search range than the comparison shopping services of merchant platforms, which are limited to their own offers and those of only those sellers that have decided to entrust the marketing of all or some of their products to a merchant platform.

. . .

486. The use of one search tool or another, from the perspective of internet users, appears to differ therefore. Users would consult a comparison shopping service in order to obtain a selection of product offers from the entire market, but would consult the comparison shopping service of a merchant platform only in order to obtain a selection of offers from that platform alone, albeit with the option of proceeding immediately, within that selection, to purchase the product sought.

. . .

492 As regards the side of the market of interest to online sellers . . . the Commission explained . . . that comparison shopping services tended to list offers from larger online retailers who wanted to retain control over the marketing of their products, whereas merchant platforms tended to list offers from small and medium-sized retailers, and possibly non-professional sellers, who were unwilling or unable to engage in online selling themselves. That shows in essence that comparison shopping services and merchant platforms have broadly different customer bases and are therefore in different markets with regard to online sellers. The Commission substantiates that assertion with the replies of comparison shopping services and merchant platforms to its questions . . .

. . .

494. The Commission must therefore be considered to have demonstrated that, for those sellers, the services of comparison shopping services and those of merchant platforms were also only to a small degree interchangeable and that competition between them was insignificant.

Surveying the available evidence, the GC rejected the argument that the Commission had drawn unduly narrow distinctions between functionally equivalent products from a demand perspective.[221] Both comparison shopping sites and merchant platforms, broadly speaking, enable internet users to find and compare products offered for sale by online sellers. Yet the manner in which both groups actually *use* those services demonstrated that each satisfies quite different needs from a consumer perspective. The Commission did not conduct a SSNIP analysis, an omission disputed by Google during the administrative procedure but not challenged on appeal.[222]

[221] A point developed further in S. Broos and J. Marcos Ramos, 'Competing Business Models and Two-Sidedness: An Application to the Google Shopping Case' (2017) 62 *Ant Bull* 382.

[222] Case T-612/17, *Google Shopping* EU:T:2021:763, para. 493.

(vi) Demand Substitution in Zero-price Markets

Zero-price products are a common feature of multi-sided technology markets, where one user group may subsidise others. The general search services and comparison shopping services in *Google Shopping* each fall into this category,[223] as both are accessed by users at zero-price because the service provider makes its revenue in online advertising sales. Zero-price products pose problems for market definition to the extent that this is conventionally conceived as a quantitative exercise that focuses on consumers' presumed responses to small but significant increases in price.[224] Yet in most zero-price markets, although the product may be *price*-less, it is not *free*: rather, consumers exchange something of value—typically, attention to advertising or personal data—in order to access the product.[225]

In *Google Shopping*, the Commission noted that the fact that a product is provided free of charge does not prevent its provision from constituting an economic activity and thus a relevant product market (although this might be significant in assessing dominance).[226] Although consumers do not pay monetary consideration for online search services, they contribute to its monetisation by providing data with each query.[227] Moreover, while online search engines do not compete on price, they compete on other parameters of competition, such as relevance of results, the speed at which results are provided, the attractiveness of the user interface, and the depth of indexing of the web.[228] Finally, the Commission pointed to the multi-sided nature of search platforms: although services are free of charge to end-users, multi-sided platforms nonetheless earn significant revenues from online advertisements. Since the success of its advertising business is dependent upon attracting sufficient end-users—competition for customer 'eyeballs'—the two sources of demand are distinct but interdependent.[229]

In *Google Android*,[230] each of the products affected by the anti-competitive practices[231] could be installed on smartphones by device manufacturers free-of-charge: namely, Google's open source mobile operating system (OS), Android, and its proprietary apps (Play Store, Google Search, and Chrome). When defining the relevant markets, the Commission considered the hypothetical impact of a 'small but significant non-transitory deterioration of the quality' (SSNDQ) of the Android OS and the various apps. The GC endorsed the use of the SSNDQ test in such circumstances.

> 177. In the case of a product that was very unlikely to lend itself to the classic hypothetical monopolist test aimed at verifying the market's response to a small but significant and non-transitory increase in the price of an asset (Small but Significant and Non-Transitory Increase in Price), the SSNDQ test, which envisages the quality degradation of the product at issue, did constitute relevant evidence for the purpose of defining the relevant market. Competition between undertakings can indeed take place in terms of price, but also in terms of quality and innovation.
>
> ...
>
> 180. [D]efining a precise quantitative standard of degradation of quality of the target product cannot be a prerequisite for the application of the SSNDQ test. The hypothesis of a small deterioration in the

[223] AT.39740, *Google Search (Shopping)* 27 June 2017; essentially upheld on appeal in Case T-612/17, *Google Shopping* EU:T:2021:763.

[224] M. Sousa Ferro, '*De Gratis Non Curat Lex*: Abuse of Dominance in Online Free Services' (2017) 12 *Competition Law Review* 153.

[225] J. Newman, 'Antitrust in Zero-price Markets: Applications' (2016) 94 *Wash Univ LR* 49; M. Gal and D. Rubinfeld, 'The Hidden Costs of Free Goods: Implications for Antitrust Enforcement' (2016) 80 *Antitrust LJ* 401.

[226] AT.39740, *Google Search (Shopping)* 27 June 2017, para. 152.

[227] Ibid., para. 158. [228] Ibid., para. 160. [229] Ibid., para. 159.

[230] AT.40099, *Google Android* 18 July 2018.

[231] In essence, tying and exclusivity payments, although only the former were upheld on appeal in Case T-604/18, *Google Android* EU:T:2022:541. See Chap. 7, Sections 10 and 11.

> quality of Android did not require—as in the case of the classic hypothetical monopolist test for which a small but significant and non-transitory increase in price can be more easily quantified—a precise standard of degradation to be set beforehand. All that matters is that the quality degradation remains small, albeit significant and non-transitory.[232]

This approach is replicated in the Draft Notice, which cites paragraphs 177 and 180 of *Google Android*.[233] The Draft Notice notes that the Commission does not usually engage in a quantitative application of the SSNDQ test.[234]

(vii) Chains of Substitution and Products with Multiple Applications

Hoffmann-La Roche[235] demonstrates the chain of substitution problem discussed in Chapter 3, Section 4.I.i. Hoffmann-La Roche (HLR) challenged the Commission's finding that it had committed a number of abuses of dominant positions held on several separate vitamin markets. Two of the vitamins had two distinct uses: each had a bio-nutritive use, for which there were no substitutes, and an antioxidant use, for which multiple vitamins could act as substitutes. HLR claimed that the two vitamins were in the same market for antioxidants together with these other products. The CJ, concentrating on the bio-nutritive use, upheld the finding that the vitamins each constituted a separate market. The reasoning was not entirely satisfactory, however, as the CJ failed to take due account of the distinct uses. If HLR could not profitably increase the price to customers in the bio-nutritive market without also losing customers in the antioxidant market, then arguably they should have formed part of the same market.

AKZO[236] shows how the circumstances of a case can influence the market definition where there are chains of substitution. AKZO produced organic peroxides, which had multiple uses: they were used both in polymer manufacturing, where there were limited substitutes; and, additionally, the main organic perozide, benzoyl peroxide, could be used as a bleaching agent in flour-milling. AKZO argued that the relevant market was that for flour additives, where its market share was low. The Commission, instead, found that the relevant market was for organic peroxides as a whole, in which AKZO held a 50 per cent share. The CJ upheld the Commission's market definition, because AKZO's conduct—lowering its prices in the flour-milling sector to protect its position in the polymer sector—as well as its internal documentation, showed that the undertaking itself treated the market as a single one.

In the extract from *France Télécom*,[237] it was seen at paragraph 79 that the GC explained that a product used for separate purposes may belong to separate markets, and that this does not mean that the product, along with all its replacements for the different uses, can be placed in one single market.

The original Market Definition Notice recognised that practical problems may arise in determining both geographic and product markets where chains of substitution exist.[238] The Draft Notice observes that, in practice, the Commission's analysis usually leads it to reject wider market definitions on this basis due to breaks in the chain of substitution.[239]

[232] Ibid. [233] Draft Notice, fn. 47. [234] Ibid.
[235] Case 85/76, *Hoffmann-La Roche* EU:C:1979:36, paras. 28–30.
[236] Case C-62/86, *AKZO* EU:C:1991:286. [237] Section 8.B.i.d. [238] Market Definition Notice, para. 57.
[239] Draft Notice, para. 87.

(viii) The Structure of Supply and Demand

The importance of the structure of supply and demand in market definition was first identified in *Michelin I*, paragraph 37.[240] The *Michelin* cases show that the structure of supply and demand may cause identical products to fall into different markets. It was seen in the extract that the CJ upheld the Commission finding that identical new heavy-vehicle tyres and retreads formed two separate product markets, and that the market for the supply of heavy-vehicle tyres to vehicle manufacturers as original equipment was distinct from the market for the supply to dealers to be fitted as replacements. In both cases, the EU Courts stressed the difference in the dynamics of the transactions.[241] Conversely, different types of heavy-vehicle tyres, although not substitutes, were in the same market. This was because dealers had to stock all tyres and the conditions of competition were the same for all types and dimensions.

Similarly, in *Van den Bergh Foods* the Commission emphasised the structure of supply and demand in finding that the markets for single-wrapped, individual ice-cream and individual portions of soft ice-cream were distinct. Although the consumer might perceive the two types of ice-cream to be reasonably interchangeable, the competitive conditions under which they were offered to the retail trade were different. Soft ice-cream, for example, had to be processed by the retailer and so required the installation of special processing and dispensing machines; it was not self-service and was not normally branded. Similarly, single wrapped ice-cream was distinct from multiple packs of ice-cream sold in supermarkets.

> The consumer's point of view is . . . not in every instance the sole criterion in the determination of a product market; nor is an examination limited only to the objective characteristics of the products in question sufficient. The competitive conditions and the structure of supply and demand on the market must also be taken into consideration.[242]

The latter consideration was stressed in *France Télécom*,[243] and *Clearstream*.[244] In *AB Inbev*, beer sold via the off-trade channel (where end consumers purchase the product in stores for consumption outside those premises) was held to constitute a different product market from the same beer brands sold via the on-trade channel (where the customer resells to final consumers for consumption of their premises, e.g. in bars and restaurants). This was due to 'differences in, inter alia, the consumption pattern, the distribution system, the price level, the product assortment, the packaging, promotions and the accompanying experience or services in the on-trade channel' compared with off-trade sales.[245]

(ix) One Product Market or Two

In cases that involve a claimed 'leveraging' of market power from one product market to another,[246] an issue may arise as to whether the different market segments are sufficiently distinct. A paradigmatic example of the sometimes-fuzzy line between products that can be considered a single whole

[240] See Section 8.B.i.c. [241] See also Case C-333/94 P, *Tetra Pak II* EU:C:1996:436, para. 13.

[242] [1998] OJ L246/1, para. 133. Upheld on appeal, Case T-65/98, *Van den Bergh Foods* EU:T:2003:281, *aff'd* Case C-552/03 P, *Unilever Bestfoods* EU:C:2006:607, where the definition of the market was not challenged.

[243] Case T-340/03, *France Télécom* EU:T:2007:22, para. 78.

[244] Case T-301/04, *Clearstream Banking* EU:T:2009:317, para. 65.

[245] AT.40134, *AB Inbev beer trade restrictions* 13 May 2019, para. 50. [246] See Chap. 7, Section 6.

or as a number of separate products is illustrated by *Microsoft*.[247] Here, the Commission pursued Microsoft for infringing Article 102 by engaging in technical tying, in that it supplied its Windows desktop operating system with its Windows Media Player pre-installed. Microsoft, for its part, insisted that it sold a single integrated product, and so the alleged abusive tying was simply part of the product design. The GC agreed with the Commission,[248] but somewhat notoriously, customers appeared to agree with the defendant, as there was almost no consumer demand for the unbundled product subsequently made available. As the issue of whether products are distinct is inextricably bound up with that of the abuse of tying, this is discussed further in Chapter 7.[249]

Google Shopping[250] similarly involved a leveraging abuse, whereby Google was held to have favoured its own comparison shopping service in the results provided by its general search engine. In identifying the product market in which Google was dominant, the Commission distinguished *general* online search from *specialised* search products, a wide-ranging category which included comparison shopping services. The Commission noted that general search covers the entire internet, whereas specialised search addresses a limited subset of relevant (and often, more readily specialisable) information; that the services are distinguished by their technical characteristics and the data utilised; that Google maintained both stand-alone and distinct commercial activities; and that, although the results provided by each may overlap, the two services function as complements rather than substitutes.[251] Search services can also be distinguished from social networks: while the latter often include search functionality, the primary purpose is different.[252] Google did not challenge this product market definition before the GC.[253]

(x) Primary and Secondary Markets (Aftermarkets)

Microsoft concerned complementary products. An 'aftermarket' is a particular instance of complementary products. Aftermarkets comprise products or services which follow on from adjacent markets, such as spare parts,[254] consumables, or maintenance services. Competition issues can arise when the supplier of the original (primary) product or equipment also supplies the secondary product or service in the aftermarket. Indeed, in some markets the producer may make more money from the sale of consumables than the original product. There are two possible scenarios.

First, the supplier may not be the only source of products or services in the aftermarket, as the primary product is compatible with different brands.[255] Here, the supplier may try to ensure that its customers obtain the aftermarket goods or services from itself rather than competitors. Where the supplier is dominant on the market for the primary product, the steps it takes to this end may constitute the abuse of 'tying' or 'bundling'.[256] The dominant manufacturer of the primary product may seek to present itself as supplying an indivisible 'system' consisting of the durable primary product and, for example, an ongoing supply of the consumable or provision of a maintenance and repair service. Conversely, if there is only one product, consisting of the 'system', then tying or bundling is unproblematic.

Secondly, the supplier may be the only source of products or services in the aftermarket which are compatible with the primary product. Here there are two further possibilities, depending upon whether the supplier is dominant or not on the market for the primary product.

247 COMP/37.792, *Microsoft* 24 March 2004. 248 Case T-201/04, *Microsoft* EU:T:2007:289.

249 See Chap. 7, Section 11. 250 AT.39740, *Google Search (Shopping)* 27 June 2017.

251 Ibid., paras. 166–177. 252 Ibid., paras. 178–183.

253 Case T-612/17, *Google Shopping* EU:T:2021:763, para. 469.

254 A replacement for an integral part of the original product, produced by the supplier of that product and/or by independent manufacturers. Motor vehicle tyres have never been considered 'spare parts' in this sense.

255 This means that the primary product producer does not have intellectual property rights (IPRs) which prevent competitors making compatible spare parts or consumables. For refusal to license as an abuse, see Chap. 7, Section 12.

256 See, e.g., Cases T-30/89, *Hilti* EU:T:1991:70 and T-83/91, *Tetra Pak II* EU:T:1994:246.

In the first case on spare parts and aftermarkets, *Hugin*,[257] the undertaking was not dominant on the primary market. The Commission defined the aftermarket narrowly, finding that the spare parts constituted a separate market from the original equipment supplied. The justification was that original equipment and its spare parts or consumables were not substitutes. The result is that, where only the supplier's brand in the aftermarket is compatible with the primary product, an undertaking with a small share of the original equipment market may be held dominant in the aftermarket.

Hugin was a Swedish producer of cash registers and their spare parts. It had approximately 12 per cent of the Union cash register market. Hugin decided to cease supplying its machines and spare parts to Liptons, a small British firm which serviced cash registers, including Hugin machines. Without the spare parts, Liptons could not continue servicing Hugin machines. The Commission held that the relevant product market consisted of Hugin spare parts required by the independent undertakings which maintained and repaired its cash registers. Since Hugin was the sole supplier, it was dominant on that market, and had abused its dominance by refusing to continue supply. The CJ upheld the finding on the relevant market and dominance.[258]

The finding that the market was defined, not as the market for spare parts needed by the owners of Hugin machines, but by the needs of general repairers and servicers of the machines, is problematic.[259] If the focus of the case was the independent repairer, an analysis was needed of the feasibility of their shifting their business to dealing with other brands. Moreover, the interests of the ultimate consumer—the owners of Hugin machines—were not considered. Nevertheless, the principle established in *Hugin*, namely that one brand of spare parts can constitute a separate product market under Article 102, has been applied subsequently, including in *Volvo*[260] and *Renault*.[261]

The *Hugin* principle was applied to consumables in *Hilti*. Hilti was dominant in the market for nail guns for the construction industry. Nails compatible with Hilti guns were made both by Hilti and by independent firms, who complained that Hilti was engaging in practices designed to ensure that purchasers of its guns bought only Hilti's own nails. The Commission held that these practices violated Article 102.[262] Hilti argued that the consumables were useless without the nail guns, and that the guns and consumables formed a 'powder-actuated fastening system', which was in the same market as other construction fastening systems. Since the nail guns, cartridges, and nails were not distinct but formed one indivisible product, it claimed, its conduct in 'tying' the sales could not constitute an abuse. These arguments were rejected by the GC.[263]

Case T-30/89, *Hilti AG v Commission* EU:T:1991:70

General Court

66. The Court takes the view that nail guns, cartridge strips and nails constitute three specific markets. Since cartridge strips and nails are specifically manufactured, and purchased by users, for a single brand of gun, it must be concluded that there are separate markets for Hilti-compatible cartridge strips and nails, as the Commission found in its decision (paragraph 55).

67. With particular regard to the nails whose use in Hilti tools is an essential element of the dispute, it is common ground that since the 1960s there have been independent producers, including the

[257] [1978] OJ L22/23, on appeal Case 22/78, *Hugin* EU:C:1979:138.

[258] The CJ quashed the Commission finding of abuse on the basis of an absence of effect on inter-Member State trade, see Section 4.E.

[259] C. W. Baden Fuller, 'Article 86: Economic Analysis of the Existence of a Dominant Position' (1979) 4 *ELRev* 423, 423.

[260] Case 238/87, *AB Volvo v Erik Veng* EU:C:1988:477.

[261] Case 53/87, *CICCRA v Renault* EU:C:1988:472.

[262] *Eurofix-Bauco v Hilti* [1988] OJ L65/19.

[263] *Aff'd* Case C-53/92 P, *Hilti AG v Commission* EU:C:1994:77.

interveners, making nails intended for use in nail guns. Some of those producers are specialized and produce only nails, and indeed some make only nails specifically designed for Hilti tools. That fact in itself is sound evidence that there is a specific market for Hilti-compatible nails.

68. Hilti's contention that guns, cartridge strips and nails should be regarded as forming an indivisible whole, 'a powder-actuated fastening system' is in practice tantamount to permitting producers of nail guns to exclude the use of consumables other than their own branded products in their tools. However, in the absence of general and binding statements or rules, any independent producer is quite free, as far as [Union] competition law is concerned, to manufacture consumables intended for use in equipment manufactured by others, unless in doing so it infringes a patent or some other industrial or intellectual property right. Even on the assumption that, as the applicant has argued, components of different makes cannot be interchanged without the system characteristics being influenced, the solution should lie in the adoption of appropriate laws and regulations, not in unilateral measures taken by nail gun producers which have the effect of preventing independent producers from pursuing the bulk of their business.

In paragraph 68, the GC stated that independent producers are free, under competition law, to manufacture consumables. This statement thus reveals the policy behind the narrow market definition adopted in some of the cases. It is not, as the wording suggests, that competition law *allows* independents to operate in the relevant aftermarket, but that Article 102 may preclude the producer of original equipment from foreclosing others from the market.[264]

In *Tetra Pak II*,[265] the Commission refused to accept that Tetra Pak supplied 'systems' and held rather that it operated on four separate product markets. The following extract is from the judgment of the GC, which was confirmed by the CJ.

Case T-83/91, *Tetra Pak Rausing v Commission* EU:T:1994:246

Tetra Pak produced aseptic cartons for packaging ultra-heat treated milk, and machines for processing the milk and filling the cartons. It also produced non-aseptic cartons for pasteurised (non-aseptic) milk, and machines for pasteurising the milk and filling those cartons. The Courts confirmed the Commission's finding that there were four product markets concerned: aseptic packaging machines, aseptic cartons, non-aseptic machines, and non-aseptic cartons.

General Court

82. First . . . consideration of commercial usage does not support the conclusion that the machinery for packaging a product is indivisible from the cartons. For a considerable time there have been independent manufacturers who specialize in the manufacture of non-aseptic cartons designed for use in machines manufactured by other concerns and who do not manufacture machinery themselves. It is apparent in particular from the Decision . . . until 1987, Elopak, which was set up in 1957, manufactured only cartons and accessory equipment, for example handling equipment. Moreover, also according to the Decision . . . approximately 12 per cent of the non-aseptic carton sector was

[264] See Chap. 7.

[265] *Elopak Italia/Tetra Pak* [1991] OJ L72/1, upheld Case T-83/91, *Tetra Pak International SA v Commission* EU:T:1994:246, *aff'd* Case C-333/94 P, *Tetra Pak II* EU:C:1996:436.

shared in 1985 between three companies manufacturing their own cartons, generally under licence and acting, for machinery, only as distributors. In those circumstances, tied sales of machinery and cartons cannot be considered to be in accordance with commercial usage, given that such sales were not the general rule of the non-aseptic sector and that there were only two manufacturers in the aseptic sector, Tetra Pak and PKL.

83. Furthermore, the applicant's argument as to the requirements for the protection of public health and its interests and those of its customers cannot be accepted. It is not for the manufacturers of complete systems to decide that, in order to satisfy requirements in the public interest, consumable products such as cartons constitute, with the machines with which they are intended to be used, an inseparable integrated system. According to settled case-law, in the absence of general and binding standards or rules, any independent producer is quite free, as far as [Union] competition law is concerned, to manufacture consumables intended for use in equipment manufactured by others, unless in doing so it infringes a competitor's intellectual property right: see Case T-30/89, *Hilti* v. *EC Commission* . . . and Case C-53/92P, *Hilti* v. *EC Commission*. . .

84. In those circumstances, whatever the complexity in this case of aseptic filling processes, the protection of public health may be guaranteed by other means, in particular by notifying machine users of the technical specifications with which cartons must comply in order to be compatible with those machines, without infringing manufacturers' intellectual property rights. Moreover, even on the assumption, shared by the applicant, that machinery and cartons from various sources cannot be used together without the characteristics of the system being affected thereby, the remedy must lie in appropriate legislation or regulations, and not in rules adopted unilaterally by manufacturers, which would amount to prohibiting independent manufacturers from conducting the essential part of their business.

85. It follows that the applicant's argument that the markets in machinery for packaging a product and those in packaging cartons are inseparable cannot be accepted.

Nonetheless, it is possible that the interaction between the primary market and the aftermarket may be such that the primary and secondary products form a single 'system' market, and competition is between the 'systems' as a whole. Whether this is so depends on the likely reactions of customers to moderate price increases in the aftermarket. A separate aftermarket consisting of the secondary products or services of one brand of primary product will be a relevant market only if (a) switching to other brands of secondary products is not possible, and (b) there are high switching costs for the primary product.[266] In *Pelikan/Kyocera*,[267] the Commission held that Kyocera was not dominant in the aftermarket for its own brand of printer cartridges, because customers made purchasing decisions based on whole-life costs and commonly used the 'total cost per page' when choosing a printer. Printers are a product where the long-term costs in the aftermarket significantly exceed those for the primary product. The Commission did not expressly state that this was a 'systems' market, but did find that intense competition on the primary market restrained Kyocera's behaviour on the aftermarket to the extent that it could not be dominant on the latter. This amounted to the same thing.[268] The Commission applied these principles in *EFIM*, in which it rejected a complaint alleging that the conduct of four manufacturers of inkjet printers had illegally excluded competitors from the aftermarket

[266] See Case T-427/08, *CEAHR* EU:T:2010:517; F. Domanico and M. Angeli, 'An Analysis of the IBM Commitment Decision concerning the Aftermarket for IBM Mainframe Computers' (2012) 1 *Competition Policy Newsletter*.

[267] *Pelikan/Kyocera*, see Commission's *XXVth Report on Competition Policy* (1995), pp. 41–42.

[268] See also *Info-Lab/Ricoh*, Case IV/36.431.

for cartridges. Since the primary market was intensely competitive, 'even if' each of the various markets for cartridges constituted separate relevant markets, the manufacturers were not dominant on their respective aftermarkets.[269]

More recently, in *CEAHR*, the Commission identified various relevant product markets: a primary market for 'prestige watches' costing more than €1,000; an aftermarket for repair and maintenance services for each prestige brand, given limited substitutability across brands; and an aftermarket for spare parts, again for each brand, insofar as consumers preferred original parts in order to prevent the value of their watches from depreciating.[270] Notably, however, the Commission rejected a complaint from independent watch repairers alleging restrictive conditions in the supply of spare parts by prestige watch manufacturers, while the GC asserted, in upholding this rejection, that '[t]he need to preserve undistorted competition . . . does not entail a need to protect the existence of independent repairers *as such*.'[271]

An open question is the extent to which 'aftermarkets' related to the control and processing of machine usage data might arise in the context of the digital economy. The Commission's expert Report on Competition Policy for the Digital Era provides a thoughtful treatment. While acknowledging a general contemporary scepticism towards the aftermarkets doctrine, the report argued that 'the specificities of data could imply that the competition policy treatment of data should be different from that of standard aftermarkets: in the data economy, the aftermarkets doctrine may need an update, and may be up for a revival.'[272] Specifically, the report highlighted the extent to which data from one machine user may affect the aftermarket opportunities of other users, for instance through use of a predictive artificial intelligence (AI) algorithm, and the possibility that it may prevent switching at the time of replacement of the machine, as competing machines may have less information on which to base their offers to consumers. The report noted, however, the absence of available economic analysis, which rendered the identified concerns 'very preliminary'.[273]

(xi) Ecosystems

The potential for ecosystem competition is again a particular consideration in the digital economy.[274] According to the OECD, '[d]igital product ecosystems bring together a broad range of products, often centred around a multi-sided platform'.[275] In principle, the discrete products or services provided through the platform could each constitute different relevant markets for competition law purposes. As the GC in *Google Android* acknowledged, however, 'mere segmentation into markets' may fail to capture fully the competitive constraints within digital ecosystems or the extent to which market power arises.[276] Accordingly,

> in a digital 'ecosystem', which brings together several categories of supplier, customer and consumer and causes them to interact within a platform, the products or services which form part of the relevant markets that make up that ecosystem may overlap or be connected to each other on the basis of their horizontal or vertical complementarity. Taken together, the relevant markets may also have a

[269] COMP/39.391, *EFIM* rejection decision 20 May 2009; upheld Case T-296/09, *EFIM* EU:T:2011:693, *aff'd* Case C-59/12 P, *EFIM* EU:C:2013:575.

[270] Case T-712/14, *CEAHR* EU:T:2017:748, paras. 10–15.

[271] Ibid., para. 112 (emphasis added).

[272] Crémer, de Montjoye, and Schweitzer, n. 178, p. 90.

[273] Ibid.

[274] See also the discussion in Chap. 16, Section 5.A.i.

[275] OECD, *OECD Handbook on Competition in the Digital Age* (2022), <www.oecd.org/daf/competition-policy-in-the-digital-age>, p. 23.

[276] Case C-604/18, *Google Android* EU:T:2022:541, para. 114.

global dimension in the light of the system that brings its components together and of any competitive constraints within that system or from other systems.[277]

The Commission suggests that, for market definition purposes, digital ecosystems can sometimes be thought of as consisting of a primary core product and several secondary products whose consumption is connected to the core product. It argues, therefore, that the principles regarding aftermarkets may, in appropriate circumstances, be applied to identify the relevant market(s). Alternatively, to the extent that the secondary products are offered as a bundle, the bundle may constitute a relevant market on its own. The Commission furthermore notes that, when dealing with digital ecosystems, it is necessary to take account of factors such as network effects, switching costs, and multi-homing decisions when identifying the relevant product market.[278]

In the *Google Android* case, the Commission defined a relevant product market for Android app stores, as distinct inter alia from app stores for other smart mobile operating systems (OSs), whether licensable or non-licensable. It found that Google, with its Play Store, was dominant in this market. On appeal, Google argued that the Commission had understated the competitive constraints imposed on it by Apple and in particular, Apple's App Store. The GC rejected this argument, holding that the Play Store and App Store could not be dissociated from their relevant ecosystems, namely the Android OS and Apple iOS, respectively. To the extent that the Commission had found, correctly, that iOS did not impose an effective competitive constraint on Android, the same logic supported its conclusion that the App Store did not impose an effective competitive constraint on the Play Store. This point is explained in the extract below.

Case C-604/18 *Google Android* EU:T:2022:541

General Court

246. As regards the examination of the competitive constraint from the App Store . . . [u]nlike Android, iOS had only one app store and could not, for that reason alone, be dissociated from it. In that sense, the Play Store and the App Store were both competing through the system to which those stores belonged, Android and iOS respectively.

247. Faced with the Apple system, and for the purposes of assessing the competitive constraint exercised by the App Store, the Play Store likewise cannot be dissociated from Android, particularly because Google makes access to the Play Store conditional on the conclusion of an [restrictive anti-fragmentation agreement], which enables the Play Store to be associated only with versions of Android that satisfy Google's compatibility test.

248. It follows from the foregoing that to assess, as regards users and app developers, the competitive constraint exerted by the App Store on the Play Store is effectively to take into account the competitive constraint exerted by iOS on Android . . .

249. The competitive constraint exerted by the App Store on the Play Store depended on that exerted by iOS on Android. In addition to the fact that the OS is a prerequisite for the functioning of a mobile device, the proper functioning and variety of available apps also depend on its quality.

250. That fact, which leads to an assessment of competition between systems, is confirmed on reading the contested decision. The Commission found . . . that the App Store did not exercise a sufficient competitive constraint on the Play Store, referring in particular to Section 9.3.4, at the end of

[277] Ibid., para. 116. See also the discussion of this aspect of the *Android* judgment in Chap. 16, Section 5.A.i.

[278] Draft Notice, para. 103.

which it found that iOS did not exercise a sufficient competitive constraint on Android from the point of view of users.

251. Similarly, from the point of view of app developers, the Commission relied on essentially identical grounds . . . in concluding that iOS exercised an insufficient competitive constraint on Android and that the App Store exercised the same level of constraint on the Play Store . . .

252. Thus, the merits of the second part of the first plea depend on the merits of the first part, by which Google claims that the Commission disregarded the competitive constraint exercised by iOS on Android as regards users and app developers. Logically, it is not possible that a competitive constraint exercised by the App Store on the Play Store would differ in intensity from that exercised by iOS on Android. In both cases, the data taken into account in order to assess the intensity of the competitive constraint are the same.

Since Google had failed to persuade the GC that the Apple iOS exerted effective competitive pressure on the Android OS then, almost inevitably, its arguments regarding the alleged pressure exerted by the App Store on the Play Store would similarly fail, given the indissociable nature of the relationship between the constituent elements of the relevant ecosystems.

(xii) Markets for Raw Materials and Inputs

A raw material or other input may, in appropriate circumstances, constitute its own product market. This was the case in *Commercial Solvents*, where aminobutanol, used to produce ethambutol, an anti-TB drug, constituted a distinct product market.[279] Zoja manufactured ethambutol from aminobutanol, which had been manufactured by Commercial Solvents. Other, non-ethambutol-based, anti-TB drugs were also available. The CJ held that the relevant market was not the market for the derivatives (the drugs), but instead the market for the raw material. There may have been substitute drugs to combat TB, but a manufacturer of ethambutol could not operate without aminobutanol.

The concept developed in *Commercial Solvents*, that an input may be distinguished from its derivative(s), has proved of great importance under Article 102. The raw material in *Commercial Solvents* was an input into a production process and had been previously sold to Zoja. The question has arisen, however, whether there can be a market in an 'input' which its producer uses only for its own purposes. In *Magill*,[280] the CJ upheld a market in 'television listings', although the broadcasting companies did not sell them for publication. In *Bronner*,[281] it accepted that there could be a market in schemes for the home delivery of newspapers, even though the undertaking concerned had developed its scheme solely to distribute its own newspapers. Again, in *IMS*,[282] the CJ said that there could be a 'potential' or 'hypothetical' market in inputs which a dominant undertaking did not market independently. All that is needed is that two distinct stages of production can be identified. In *Microsoft*, the 'input' was the IPRs over its Windows technology.[283] The point can be of great importance where the alleged abuse is a refusal to supply—as *Magill, Bronner, IMS*, and *Microsoft* each involved—because, generally, there can be such an abuse only where two markets are involved and the defendant is dominant upstream.[284]

[279] Cases 6 and 7/73, *Commercial Solvents* EU:C:1974:18.

[280] Cases C-241–242/91 P, *Magill* EU:C:1995:98.

[281] Case C-7/97, *Oscar Bronner* EU:C:1998:569.

[282] Case C-418/01, *IMS Health* EU:C:2004:257, paras. 43–44.

[283] Case T-201/04, *Microsoft* EU:T:2007:289, para. 335.

[284] See Chap. 7, Section 12.

(xiii) Markets on the Buying Side (Procurement Markets)

It is possible for a buyer to be dominant (sometimes referred to as a monopsonist). The complications of market definition in such situations are illustrated by a case which concerned BA's system of rewards to travel agents. BA was a supplier of services: namely, air travel. Like other suppliers, however, it also *purchased* goods and services as inputs. The Commission held that travel agents supplied a service to BA by selling tickets for BA flights.[285] That service, 'air travel agency services' in the UK, was a relevant market. The Commission found that BA was the dominant buyer here, and that it had abused its dominance. BA argued that the market identified did not exist and that, even if it did, it was not the relevant market to consider. It claimed that the Commission should have looked instead at its position on the market for the provision of air transport services to passengers. The GC upheld the Commission's market definition.[286]

Case T-219/99, *British Airways plc v Commission* EU:T:2003:343

General Court

92. It is clear from BA's pleadings that it itself acknowledges the existence of an independent market for air travel agency services, since it states . . . that travel agents themselves operate in a competitive market, competing with each other to provide the best possible service to their customers.

93. In that regard, although travel agents act on behalf of the airlines, which assume all the risks and advantages connected with the transport service itself and which conclude contracts for transport directly with travellers, they nevertheless constitute independent intermediaries carrying on an independent business of providing services. . .

94. . .. [T]hat specific business of travel agents consists, on the one hand, in advising potential travellers, reserving and issuing airline tickets, (and) collecting the price of the transport and remitting it to the airlines, and, on the other hand, in providing those airlines with advertising and commercial promotion services.

95. In that regard, BA itself states that travel agents are and will remain, in the short term at least, a vital distribution channel for airlines, allowing them efficiently to sell seats on the flights they offer, and that there is a mutual dependence between travel agents and airlines which are not in themselves in a position to market their air transport services effectively.

96. As BA has also stated, travel agents offer a wider range of air routes, departure times and arrival times than any airline could. Travel agents filter information concerning various flights for the benefit of travellers faced with the proliferation of different air transport fare structures, which arise from the real-time pricing systems operated by airlines.

97. BA has further recognised that the role which travel agents play in the distribution of airline tickets explains why airlines seek to offer them advantages so that they sell seats on their flights. The irreplaceable nature of the services which travel agents provide to airlines is thus borne out by all the payments which the airlines make to them.

98. Finally, BA has itself emphasised that major travel agents individually negotiate agreements for the distribution of air tickets and that they are thus in a position to set the airlines in competition.

99. That specific nature of the services provided to airlines by travel agents, without any serious possibility of the airlines substituting themselves for the agents in order to carry out the same services

[285] COMP/34.780 *Virgin/BA* [2000] OJ L30/1.

[286] The GC's judgment was affirmed in Case C-95/04 P, *British Airways* EU:C:2007:166, where the market definition point was not appealed.

themselves, is corroborated by the fact that, at the time of the events of which complaint is made, 85 per cent of air tickets sold in the territory of the United Kingdom were sold through the intermediary of travel agents.

100. The Court therefore considers that the services of air travel agencies represent an economic activity for which, at the time of the contested decision, airlines could not substitute another form of distribution of their tickets, and that they therefore constitute a market for services distinct from the air transport market.

101. With regard to the fact that the restrictions on competition which the Commission imputes to BA's performance reward schemes arise from the position which BA holds in its capacity not as supplier but as purchaser of air travel agency services, this is irrelevant having regard to the definition of the market in question. Article [102] applies both to undertakings whose possible dominant position is established, as in this case, in relation to their suppliers and to those which are capable of being in the same position in relation to their customers.

102. BA itself acknowledged at the hearing, moreover, that it is possible both for a seller and for a purchaser to hold a dominant position within the meaning of Article [102].

103. BA cannot therefore validly argue that, in order to define the product market in question, with a view to assessing the effects on competition of the financial advantages which it allows to travel agents established in the United Kingdom, it is necessary to determine whether a single supplier of air transportation services on a particular route can profitably increase its prices.

104. Such a parameter, which might be relevant in relation to each airline, is not of such a kind as to enable measurement of BA's economic strength in its capacity not as provider of air transport services but as purchaser of travel agency services, on all routes to and from United Kingdom airports, either in relation to all other airlines regarded in the same capacity as purchasers of air travel agency services or in relation to travel agents established in the United Kingdom.

105. BA's objections to the relevance of the product market adopted by the Commission, based on the possible marginalisation of the distribution of airline tickets through the intermediary of travel agents, on the exclusive specialisation of airlines by geographical destinations, and on the independent behaviour of an airline in a monopoly situation on certain routes, therefore have no bearing.

106. Those arguments are based on situations which are either hypothetical or foreign to the conditions of competition operating in the product market in question constituted by air travel agency services, both between the agents providing those services and between the airlines using them.

107. The Commission did not therefore make any error of assessment in defining the relevant product market as that for services provided by travel agents in favour of airlines, for the purposes of establishing whether BA holds a dominant position on that market in its capacity as bidder for those services.

(xiv) Supply Substitution

In *Continental Can*, the CJ held that the market must be defined from the supply side as well as the demand side. There, the Commission found three separate markets consisting of different types of metal containers for food packaging: for canned meat products, for canned fish products, and metal closures for the food packing industry. The Court found that the Commission had not explained why these products were in separate markets and not instead part of a larger light metal container market. In particular, it had not explained why competitors could not enter the identified markets simply by adapting their production facilities. Consequently, 'a dominant position on the market for light metal containers for meat and fish cannot be decisive, as long as it has not been proved that competitors from other sectors of the market for light metal containers are not in a position to enter this market, by a simple adaptation, with sufficient strength to create a serious counterweight'.[287] The CJ also held that the Commission should not have dismissed the possibility of customers themselves commencing manufacture of their own cans.[288]

Subsequent to *Continental Can*, it is common for supply-side substitution to be considered. In *Michelin*,[289] the CJ held that there was no elasticity of supply between tyres for heavy vehicles and car tyres 'owing to significant differences in production techniques and in the plant and tools needed for their manufacture. The fact that time and considerable investment were required in order to modify production plant for the manufacture of light-vehicle tyres instead of heavy-vehicle tyres or vice versa meant that there was no discernible relationship between the two categories of tyre enabling production to be adapted to demand on the market.' Similarly, in *Tetra Pak I*,[290] the Commission dismissed the feasibility of supply-side substitution. Manufacturers of other types of milk-packaging machinery were not readily able to switch to producing aseptic packaging machinery and cartons.

The *Generics* preliminary ruling nonetheless reasserts the relevance of supply substitutability in appropriate circumstances. The case concerned an originator pharmaceutical company, GSK, which was approaching the end of patent protection for its blockbuster antidepressant drug, paroxetine. GSK allegedly engaged in restrictive practices intended to delay generic entry, which the NCA construed as contrary to both Articles 101 and 102. One of the questions before the CJ was whether the potential generic competitors, poised to enter the market but not yet competing directly against GSK, should be included in the definition of the relevant market for the purposes of finding dominance under Article 102. This possibility was complicated by the fact that GSK claimed to hold valid process patents that could prevent lawful generic entry even after the active ingredient patent had expired. Yet the CJ in *Generics* held that this did not pose an insurmountable obstacle to including these potential competitors within the relevant market.

C-307/18 *Generics (UK) Ltd and Others v Competition and Markets Authority* EU:C:2020:52

Court of Justice

126. [The question is] whether Article 102 TFEU must be interpreted as meaning that, in a situation where a manufacturer of originator medicines containing an active ingredient which is in the public domain, but the process of manufacturing which is covered by a process patent, the validity of which is uncertain, impedes, on that basis, the market entry of generic versions of that medicine, there should be taken into consideration for the definition of the product market concerned not only the originator version of that medicine but also its generic versions, although the latter would not be able legally to enter the market before the expiry of that process patent.

...

129. As regards the product market, which is the only point at issue in this question, it is clear from settled case-law that the concept of the relevant market implies that there can be effective competition between the products or services which form part of it, and this presupposes that there is a sufficient degree of interchangeability between all the products or services forming part of the same market in so far as a specific use of such products or services is concerned. That interchangeability

[287] Case 6/72, *Europemballage Corp and Continental Can Co Inc v Commission* EU:C:1973:22, para. 33.

[288] Case 6/72, *Continental Can* EU:C:1973:22, para. 36.

[289] Case 322/81, *Michelin I* EU:C:1983:313, para. 41. The issue of supply substitutability was not addressed in the decision [1981] OJ L353/33.

[290] *TetraPak (BTG Licence)* [1988] OJ L272/27, paras. 36–38, upheld Case T-51/89, *Tetra Pak Rausing SA v Commission (Tetra Pak I)* EU:T:1990:41 where the market definition was not challenged.

or substitutability is not assessed solely in relation to the objective characteristics of the products and services at issue. There must also be taken into consideration the conditions of competition and the structure of supply and demand on the market (. . . *F. Hoffmann-La Roche and Others*, C-179/16, EU:C:2018:25, paragraph 51 . . .).

130. In that context . . . the interchangeability or substitutability of products are naturally dynamic, in that a new supply of products may alter the conception of the products considered to be interchangeable with a product already present on the market or as substitutable for that product and, in that way, justify a new definition of the parameters of the relevant market.

131. As regards, in particular, the definition of the product market to which, for the possible application of Article 102 TFEU, an originator medicine belongs such as, . . . it is clear from the point made in the preceding paragraph of the present judgment that a supply of generic medicines containing the same active ingredient, in this case paroxetine, could lead to a situation where the originator medicine is considered, in the professional circles concerned, to be interchangeable only with those generic medicines and, consequently, to belong to a specific market, limited exclusively to medicines which contain that active ingredient.

132. Such a finding presupposes, however . . . that there is a sufficient degree of interchangeability between the originator medicine and the generic medicines concerned.

133. Such is the case if the manufacturers concerned of generic medicines are in a position to present themselves within a short period on the market concerned with sufficient strength to constitute a serious counterbalance to the manufacturer of the originator medicine already on the market (. . . *Continental Can* v *Commission*, 6/72, EU:C:1973:22, paragraph 34).

134. That is accordingly true where, on the expiry of the patent relating to the active ingredient concerned, or of the data exclusivity period of that active ingredient, those manufacturers of generic medicines are in a position to enter the market immediately or within a short period, particularly where those parties have formed a prior effective strategy for market entry, have taken the steps necessary to achieve it, such as, for example, the lodging of an MA application or the obtaining of such an MA, or have concluded supply contracts with third-party distributors.

135. In that regard, . . . evidence of the perception, by the manufacturer of originator medicines, of the immediacy of the threat of market entry by the manufacturers of generic medicines might also be taken into account in order to assess the significance of the competitive constraints imposed by the latter.

136. The fact that the manufacturer of originator medicines relies on an intellectual property right over the process of manufacturing the active ingredient concerned as capable of possibly impeding the market entry of generic versions of the originator medicine containing that active ingredient cannot be sufficient ground for any other finding.

137. While, admittedly, . . . Directive 2004/48 and Article 17(2) of the Charter of Fundamental Rights ensure a high level of protection of intellectual property in the internal market, the fact remains that the process patent on which a manufacturer of originator medicines is likely to rely in order to impede the placing on the market of a generic version of a medicine containing an active ingredient that is in the public domain does not offer any certainty to the manufacturer of the originator medicine concerned that the generic medicine containing that active ingredient may not lawfully be placed on the market or that that patent is safe from any challenge, as was moreover the case in the main proceedings . . .

138. Consequently, and provided that the conditions set out in paragraphs 133 and 134 of the present judgment are satisfied, the generic versions of an originator medicine containing an active ingredient which is in the public domain, but the process of manufacturing which is protected by a patent, the validity of which remains uncertain, must be taken into account for the purposes of definition of the relevant market, if due regard is to be given to the case-law cited in paragraph 129 of the present judgment, which requires the taking into consideration of the conditions of competition and the structure of supply and demand in the market concerned.

The difficulty is to distinguish supply-side substitution from potential competition, which is considered at the stage of assessing market power. In her Opinion in *Generics*, Advocate General Kokott acknowledged that questions of potential competition and supply-side substitutability overlap in part. Yet they differ insofar as the latter requires, in essence, a possibility of *immediate* new entry by the prospective competitor, whereas potential competition can exist and function as a relevant competitive constraint even if it fails to materialise in the short term.[291]

In Chapter 3, it was seen that in the Draft Notice, the Commission indicates that supply substitution is relevant only where most, if not all, suppliers: (a) are able to switch production between products in the range of related products; while (b) incurring only insignificant additional sunk costs or risks; (c) have the incentive to do so when relative prices or demand conditions change; and (d) can market them effectively in the short term.[292]

B. THE GEOGRAPHIC MARKET

We saw in Chapter 3 that the relevant market has a geographic as well as a product dimension. The Market Definition Notice, and now the Draft Notice, explain at length how the geographic market is determined.

Legal regulation may create national markets, as in the type-approval certificate cases.[293] In some instances, an undertaking has a statutory monopoly. In *AKZO*,[294] the geographic market was defined by the fact that the UK and Ireland were the only Member States which permitted the use of bleaching agents in flour. In *ARA Foreclosure*, it was dictated by the underlying national legislation, which required that exemption systems for packaging waste recycling be equipped to collect waste in the whole of the territory of Austria.[295] In *Aspen*, disparate national rules for public reimbursement of medicines and the different prescribing practices of doctors similarly resulted in a series of Member State-wide markets.[296] Narrow geographic markets may be created through factors including EU regulation,[297] high transport costs, language,[298] marketing infrastructures, consumer preference,[299] national or local regulations,[300] or even 'the fact that sense of humour and other sensibilities may vary from country to country'.[301] In cases involving transport services, narrow geographic markets have frequently been accepted (here, the geographic and product markets may in effect be the same). The Commission has, for example, defined as separate markets the air route between Dublin and Heathrow,[302] the ferry route between Holyhead and Dun Laoghaire,[303] and the rail routes between a large oil refinery and the three nearest seaports capable of handling oil exports.[304]

[291] Opinion in C-307/18, *Generics (UK)* EU:C:2020:52, para. 234.

[292] Draft Notice, para. 35. See also Chap. 3, Section 4.F.

[293] Case 26/75, *General Motors* EU:C:1975:150; Case 226/84, *British Leyland* EU:C:1986:421.

[294] Case C-62/86, *AKZO* EU:C:1991:286. [295] AT39759, *ARA Foreclosure* 20 September 2016, para. 56.

[296] AT.40394, *Aspen* 10 February 2021, para. 60.

[297] As was the case with sugar: see *Napier Brown-British Sugar* [1988] OJ L284/41; *Irish Sugar* [1997] OJ L258/1.

[298] AT40153, *E-book MFNs and related matters (Amazon)* 4 May 2017.

[299] In the merger case *Nestlé/Perrier* [1992] OJ L356/1 (see Chap. 15), for example, the Commission found that the relevant geographic market for mineral water was limited to France. Irrespective of European integration, French consumers continued to prefer local products.

[300] As in Case C-385/07 P, *Der Grüne Punkt* EU:C:2009:456, which concerned the German recycling regime. In Case 27/76, *United Brands* EU:C:1978:22 the geographic market was held not to include France, the UK, or Italy, because of their special import regimes for bananas, stemming in the case of the first two from former colonial ties.

[301] AT.40411, *Google AdSense* 20 March 2019, para. 214, justifying a series of national markets for online search advertising services.

[302] *British Midland v Aer Lingus* [1992] OJ L96/34.

[303] IV/34.174, *Sealink/B&I Holyhead: Interim Measures* 11 June 1992.

[304] AT39813, *Baltic Rail* 2 October 2017, paras. 115–158.

One of the most notorious cases on the geographic market is *Michelin I*, where the CJ upheld the Commission's finding that there was a separate market for heavy-vehicle new replacement tyres in the Netherlands.

Case 322/81, *Nederlandsche Banden-Industrie Michelin v Commission* EU:C:1983:313

Court of Justice

23. The applicant[] challenges the Commission's finding that the substantial part of the [internal] market on which it holds a dominant position is the Netherlands. Michelin NV maintains that this geographical definition of the market is too narrow. It is contradicted by the fact that the Commission itself based its decision on factors concerning the Michelin group as a whole such as its technological lead and financial strength which, in the applicant's view, relate to a much wider market or even the world market. The activities of Michelin NV's main competitors are world-wide too.

24. The Commission maintains that this objection concerns less the definition of the market than the criteria used to establish the existence of a dominant position. Since tyre manufacturers have on the whole chosen to sell their products on the various national markets through the intermediary of national subsidiaries, the competition faced by Michelin NV is on the Netherlands market.

25. The point to be made in this regard is that the Commission addressed its decision not to the Michelin group as a whole but only to its Netherlands subsidiary whose activities are concentrated on the Netherlands market. It has not been disputed that Michelin NV's main competitors also carry on their activities in the Netherlands through Netherlands subsidiaries of their respective groups.

26. The Commission's allegation concerns Michelin NV's conduct towards tyre dealers and more particularly its discount policy. In this regard the commercial policy of the various subsidiaries of the groups competing at the European or even the world level is generally adapted to the specific conditions existing on each market. In practice dealers established in the Netherlands obtain their supplies only from suppliers operating in the Netherlands. The Commission was therefore right to take the view that the competition facing Michelin NV is mainly on the Netherlands market and that it is at that level that the objective conditions of competition are alike for traders.

27. This finding is not related to the question whether in such circumstances factors relating to the position of the Michelin group and its competitors as a whole and to a much wider market may enter into consideration in the adoption of a decision as to whether a dominant position exists on the relevant product market.

28. Hence the relevant substantial part of the [internal] market in this case is the Netherlands and it is at the level of the Netherlands market that Michelin NV's position must be assessed.

The question whether or not customers could easily have bought Michelin or other tyres outside the Netherlands was not asked. Rather, the geographic market was confined to the area in which the Commission found that the abuse had been committed.[305]

The Commission pursued a second investigation against Michelin 20 years later, which challenged Michelin's discount and rebate system as an abuse of its dominant position. In *Michelin II*,[306] the Commission concluded that new replacement tyres for trucks and buses in France and retreaded

[305] Bishop and Walker, n. 155, para. 4.70. See also the criticism in V. Korah, 'The Michelin Decision of the Commission' (1982) 7 *ELRev* 130.

[306] COMP/36.041, *Michelin* [2002] OJ L143/1 (*Michelin II*).

tyres for trucks and buses in France were two separate markets, and that Michelin was dominant on both.[307] The decision devoted considerable attention to the geographic market. Taking into account the CJ's judgment of 1983, the company argued that the new replacement tyre market had become international in the intervening years, as 'the main players ... compete on a world scale'.[308] The Commission disagreed, maintaining that what mattered was 'the real capacity of dealers to obtain supplies from outside their national territory and the similarities or differences in the supply structure'.[309] The Commission took into account the fact that large manufacturers still organised their distribution and sales along national lines;[310] that there were considerable differences in their market shares from country to country;[311] and that there were appreciable price differences.[312] It rejected the argument that hauliers could easily purchase their tyres from abroad if they wished: among the reasons was the structure of the road haulage industry in France, which was composed mainly of small firms without the resources to surmount the linguistic obstacles to intra-Union trade.[313] As far as the retread market was concerned, the Commission held that since this was a market for the provision of *services* rather than goods, 'it is a national market and therefore at most of national dimension'. Moreover, there were differences in the structure of demand which set the French market apart, including the fact that in France the predominant method of retreading was 'mould-cure' and custom retreading, rather than 'precure' treading.[314]

A geographic market may be broader than the confines of one Member State. Inherent in the notion of the internal market is the assumption that, eventually, the conditions of competition across the Member States will be sufficiently homogeneous to constitute a single geographic territory. This ambition underpins efforts to facilitate in particular the emergence of the Digital Single Market, allowing technology companies, service providers, and online retailers to sell across national boundaries.[315] In *Google AdSense*, the market for online search advertising intermediation was found to be EEA-wide in scope: the main providers offered their services in a variety of European languages, and large publishers typically entered into supply agreements that enabled them to tailor the service provided to the IP address of the reader.[316] In *Microsoft*,[317] *Intel*,[318] and *Broadcom*,[319] moreover, the relevant geographic market was held to be worldwide in scope. In *Broadcom*, this was despite the fact that significant price differentials existed between sales made in Europe and the US, compared to the rest of the world. Instead, the Commission found that these price differentials represented a differentiated *product* market, as higher specification products were typically required by European and US customers.

Yet the mere fact that a technology company provides essentially the same product on a worldwide basis will not necessarily prompt a worldwide market definition. In *Google Shopping*, for instance, the Commission identified a series of *national* markets for general search and comparison shopping services across the EEA. Although general search services were accessible worldwide, the Commission emphasised that the main providers had different national sites for each country within the EEA. Search results were tailored to each jurisdiction, and provided in the local language. While

[307] On appeal, Case T-203/01, *Michelin II* EU:T:2003:250, neither the market definition nor the finding of dominance were challenged.

[308] Ibid., para. 121. [309] Ibid., para. 124. [310] Ibid., paras. 125–131. [311] Ibid., para. 133.

[312] Ibid., paras. 134–141. [313] Ibid., para. 144. [314] Ibid., para. 157.

[315] European Commission, A Digital Single Market Strategy for Europe, COM(2015) 192 final.

[316] AT.40411, *Google AdSense* 20 March 2019, paras. 218–221.

[317] Case T-201/04, *Microsoft* EU:T:2007:289, para. 29. [318] Case T-286/09, *Intel* EU:T:2014:547, para. 24.

[319] AT.40608, *Broadcom* 7 October 2020, confirming the approach in the interim measures decision of 16 October 2019.

it was technically possible to provide general search services which covered several jurisdictions at once, there were prohibitively high costs associated with doing so, even from the perspective of large technology companies.[320] Language and tailoring to local markets was also relevant in informing a series of national geographic markets for comparison shopping services. Moreover, the Commission noted that commercial agreements between shopping services and retailers were typically concluded on a national basis, and that there were often barriers to selling goods offered for sale in one jurisdiction across national borders.[321]

In its *E-book MFNs (Amazon)* decision, the Commission left open the question whether the geographic market was national, linguistic, or EEA-wide in scope, because Amazon had sufficiently high market shares to sustain a finding of dominance regardless. It noted, nonetheless, that geo-blocking practices at the national level by retailers could support a national market definition, since customers are either precluded or dissuaded from purchasing digital goods from other countries. Conversely, linguistic preferences might inform a wider-than-national definition, in particular because online retailers often operate stores that target a particular language, e.g. UK and Irish customers purchasing in English, German and Austrian customers purchasing in German.[322]

Finally, it is conceivable that the existence of the allegedly abusive behaviour might inform the geographic market definition, particularly if the defendant engages in practices which inhibit market interpenetration. This was the case in *Gazprom*, where the very fact that the defendant included territorial restrictions in its gas supply contracts meant that there were little or no cross-border flows of gas across Central and Eastern Europe. Therefore, the geographic scope of each market was national.[323]

Again, the difficulty involved in defining the geographic market, as when defining product markets, can be tempered if competition from outside the market is considered when assessing market power. If this is taken into account subsequently, then overly narrow market definitions, and the rather artificial distinction between market definition and market power assessment, are less misleading. However, the size, financial strength, and degree of diversification of competitors at a worldwide level does not necessarily deprive an undertaking of dominance in a relevant geographical market.

C. THE TEMPORAL MARKET

The temporal dimension of the market—whereby the conditions of demand or supply may fluctuate over time—is often ignored. The original Market Definition Notice did not refer to it, and it is mentioned only in passing in the revised Draft Notice. This is because most markets do not have a temporal dimension.[324] It can nonetheless be relevant when considering transport markets, for example,[325] where peak and off-peak markets may differ.[326] In such markets, the temporal dimension may be an inherent part of the definition of the product market.

Seasonality is another potential way in which temporal considerations may be relevant to market definition, and is listed as such in the Draft Notice.[327] In *United Brands*,[328] for instance, there was evidence that demand for bananas fluctuated from season to season, depending on the availability of other fruits. This suggested that there were different seasonal markets, and that, in summer, bananas were part of a wider fruit market. The Commission disregarded this evidence, and defined a single year-round market consisting only of bananas. The CJ did not pursue the issue.

[320] AT.39740, *Google Search (Shopping)* 27 June 2017, paras. 252–255. [321] Ibid., paras. 256–262.
[322] AT40153, *E-book MFNs and related matters (Amazon)* 4 May 2017, paras. 48–51.
[323] AT39816, *Upstream gas supplies in Central and Eastern Europe (Gazprom)* 24 May 2018, para. 32.
[324] Case 322/81, *Michelin I* EU:C:1983:313, para. 59.
[325] See Cases T-374 etc., *European Night Services* EU:T:1998:198. [326] Draft Notice, para. 22.
[327] Draft Notice, para. 22. [328] Case 27/76, *United Brands* EU:C:1978:22.

In *ABG Oil*,[329] the Commission looked at the oil market just in the period of the OPEC crisis in the 1970s.

9. ASSESSING MARKET POWER

A. GENERAL

Once the market has been defined, the power which the undertaking has on that market must be assessed in order to determine whether it is 'dominant'.[330] As explained, the concept of dominance is not equivalent to monopoly—that is, it does not anticipate that the defendant is the *only* undertaking operating on the relevant market—but instead requires, in effect, a demonstration that the undertaking concerned holds substantial market power.

It is possible, although rare in the absence of a statutory monopoly, for an undertaking to have 100 per cent of a market. Even an undertaking with a 100 per cent market share does not necessarily possess substantial market power, however. Market shares do not tell us why the undertaking has 100 per cent of the market, or about potential competition. They do not explain, for example, whether the undertaking has a high market share because it produces the best products most efficiently, or because the minimum efficient scale of production means that it is a 'natural' monopoly. Nor do they indicate whether the undertaking is vulnerable to market entry. The vulnerability of an undertaking to entry is dependent upon whether or not there are 'barriers to entry' to the market. This is why barriers to entry is such a central concept.

We saw in Chapter 1 that there has been a long-running debate about what constitutes a barrier to entry or expansion (hereafter, unless the context otherwise requires, 'barriers to entry'), and even about how the term should be defined. It has also been argued that the disciplining effect of potential, as distinct from existing, competitors can be exaggerated.[331]

EU law on barriers to entry does not follow the minimalist approach advocated by Stigler.[332] In the past, a wide variety of factors have been found to constitute barriers to entry or, in the terminology used by the EU Courts, 'other factors indicating dominance'.[333] Account is also taken of evidence of actual competition on the market, for example how undertakings have been affected (or not) in periods of economic downturn.[334]

Sections 9.B–9.E set out the approach of the EU Courts and the Commission when determining whether an undertaking is dominant on a particular market. Reliance is placed first on the market shares of the undertakings concerned, and then on barriers to entry and other factors indicating dominance. One recurrent criticism of the case law under Article 102 has been a tendency to place too great an emphasis on market shares and a failure, at least previously, to display rigorous economic

[329] [1977] OJ L117/1 (the decision was annulled on appeal on the abuse issue: Case 77/77, *Benzine Petroleum Handelsmaatschappij* EU:C:1978:141).

[330] See Landes and Posner, n. 154; Schmalensee, n. 153.

[331] See E. M. Fox and L. A. Sullivan, 'Antitrust—Retrospective and Prospective: Where Are We Coming From? Where Are We Going?' (1987) 62 *New York Univ LR* 936, 975: 'Potential competition is not an existing alternative source of supply; it does not satisfy buyers' desires for choice or the opportunity for buyers to play one seller against another; and it is normally an inconsequential source of pressure to innovate.'

[332] G. J. Stigler, *The Organization of Industry* (Irwin, 1968), discussed in Chap. 3, Section 5.

[333] 'Other' meaning factors other than market share. The Commission now uses the term 'barriers to entry': see e.g. Commission Guidelines on the assessment of horizontal mergers under the Council Regulation on the control of concentrations between undertakings [2004] OJ C31/5 and the Guidance Paper.

[334] See O'Donoghue and Padilla, n. 25, 220–222.

analysis. When combined with the tendency to define markets narrowly, the importance attached to market shares and the broad approach to barriers to entry mean that an undertaking's market power may be exaggerated. Undertakings which do not in reality have market power may be precluded or deterred from engaging in conduct which is pro-competitive or at least neutral from a competition perspective (Type 1 errors). Competition law may then have the perverse effect of inhibiting the competitive process.

The Commission has not issued a general Notice on market power analogous to that on market definition. However, the matter is considered in the Guidance Paper, paragraphs 9–18. In paragraph 12, the Commission says that the assessment of dominance will take into account the competitive structure of the market, and in particular:

- the market position of the dominant undertaking and its competitors (i.e. current market shares);
- constraints imposed by credible threats of expansion or entry (barriers to expansion or entry); and
- countervailing buyer power.

The Commission is committed to an economically rigorous approach to the assessment of dominance.[335]

B. MARKET SHARES

(i) General

Market share relates to the first indent in paragraph 12 of the Guidance Paper. Market shares reflect the *present* state of competition in the market.

If an undertaking has a statutory monopoly over a relevant market, that concludes the matter. It holds a dominant position.[336] In the absence of statutory monopoly, it has been settled case law since *Hoffmann-La Roche*[337] that the starting point for the assessment of dominance is market share.

The EU Courts place great reliance on market shares, although, as explained, economic theory suggests that, in the absence of barriers to entry, high market shares are not themselves indicative of dominance. Critics thus argue, inter alia, that reliance upon market shares depends on the uncertain art of market definition and that market definition is an 'in or out' (zero-one fallacy) game, whereas in reality products are often imperfect substitutes and undertakings may be constrained by the existence of products outside the defined market. One suggestion is that it may be possible to devise a 'weighted market share' approach, 'to take account of the fact that substitutability is a matter of degree in market power assessment'. This would involve taking into account imperfect substitutes when calculating the market share of a product but with a lesser weight than if it were a more perfect substitute.[338] Another potential problem with reliance on market share is that market share analysis is essentially 'static', and thus ill-suited for application to dynamically competitive markets such as those in the digital economy.

[335] See Faull and Nikpay, n. 164, 4.122–4.217.

[336] An example is AT.40335, *Romanian gas interconnectors* 6 March 2020, paras. 23–25, where the defendant held an exclusive concession to manage and operate the Romanian natural gas transmission network and was considered to be dominant on that basis.

[337] Case 85/76, *Hoffmann-La Roche* EU:C:1979:36.

[338] Vickers, n. 173, 8–10.

(ii) The Calculation of Market Shares

The calculation of market shares is addressed in the Market Definition Notice and Draft Notice. The original Market Definition Notice took as its starting point, for each supplier, their sales of the relevant products in the relevant area.[339] It nonetheless accepted that, in some industries, sales figures may not be the most appropriate basis for the calculation.[340] The Draft Notice elaborates on the alternative bases that may be available.

Draft Commission Notice on the Definition of the Relevant Market for the Purposes of Union Competition Law (8 November 2022)

106. The Commission usually relies on market shares based on sales. Conversely, in procurement markets, the Commission usually relies on market shares based on purchases. Generally, both the value of sales or purchases and the volume of sales or purchases provide useful information.

107. In addition to sales or purchases, depending on the specific products or on the specific industry in question, other metrics can offer complementary or more useful information to determine market shares. These may include: capacity or production volumes (in particular for markets characterised by the strategic importance of capacity); the number of suppliers (in particular in markets with formal tenders or in situations where innovative products are at the development stage); the number of tenders awarded; usage metrics such as the number of (active) users, the number of visits, time spent or audience numbers, the number of downloads and updates, the number of interactions or volume or value of transactions concluded over a platform (in particular where access to products is provided mainly for free, as can be the case for instance in digital markets, or more generally in the case of multi-sided platforms); units of fleet, seat capacity, number of trips or access rights such as slots at specific airports (for instance in transport markets); and/or reserves held (for instance in the mining sector). In markets where there are frequent and significant investments in R&D, the level of R&D expenditure or the number of patents or patent citations may be used as relevant metrics to assess the relative competitive position of companies.

108. In markets characterised by a significant degree of product differentiation, market shares measured in sales value and sales volume can be significantly different. In these circumstances, the Commission usually considers sales values to better reflect the heterogeneity between the different products. Sales volumes complement sales value and may in some instances better reflect the competitive strength of undertakings. For example, in the case of a concentration involving two undertakings offering a product at a much lower price than others, but capturing a significant share of customers, sales value alone may underestimate the competitive importance and interactions of those undertakings.

Market share has, for example, been calculated using the number of subscribers signed up to a high-speed internet service;[341] the number of units shipped;[342] the units sold and size of the installed base (i.e. the number of machines installed in a given market);[343] the number of retail telecommunications lines and by revenues;[344] and the volume of user traffic in general search services.[345]

339 Market Definition Notice, para. 53.
340 Ibid., para. 54.
341 COMP/38.233, *Wanadoo* 16 July 2003.
342 Case T-201/04, *Microsoft* EU:T:2007:289, paras. 555–585 and 1038.
343 COMP/38.113, *Prokent/Tomra* 29 March 2006, para. 59. The point was not pursued on appeal, Case T-155/06, *Tomra Systems* EU:T:2010:370.
344 COMP/39.525, *Telekomunikacja Polska* 22 June 2011, upheld Case T-486/11, *Orange Polska* EU:T:2015:1002 where the market definition was unchallenged, and C-123/16 P, *Orange Polska* EU:C:2018:590.
345 AT.39740, *Google Search (Shopping)* 27 June 2017, para. 273. Google did not challenge its finding of dominance in general search markets on appeal in Case T-612/17 *Google Shopping* EU:T:2021:763.

(iii) High Market Shares

The higher the market share, the more likely a finding of dominance. In *Hoffmann-La Roche*,[346] the CJ, although recognising that the significance of market shares may vary between markets, and acknowledging the relevance of other factors, held that 'very large shares' held over 'some time' are in themselves indicative of dominance, absent 'exceptional circumstances'.[347]

Case 85/76, *Hoffmann-La Roche & Co AG v Commission* EU:C:1979:36

Court of Justice

39. . . . The existence of a dominant position may derive from several factors which, taken separately, are not necessarily determinative but among these factors a highly important one is the existence of very large market shares.

40. A substantial market share as evidence of the existence of a dominant position is not a constant factor and its importance varies from market to market according to the structure of these markets, especially as far as production, supply and demand are concerned. . .

41. Furthermore although the importance of the market shares may vary from one market to another the view may legitimately be taken that very large shares are in themselves, and save in exceptional circumstances, evidence of the existence of a dominant position. An undertaking which has a very large market share and holds it for some time, by means of the volume of production and the scale of the supply which it stands for—without those having much smaller market shares being able to meet rapidly the demand from those who would like to break away from the undertaking which has the largest market share—is by virtue of that share in a position of strength which makes it an unavoidable trading partner and which, already because of this secures for it, at the very least during relatively long periods, that freedom of action which is the special feature of a dominant position.

In *AKZO*, the CJ explained what was meant by a 'very high market share' within the meaning of the test set out in *Hoffmann-La Roche*. It interpreted it as 50 per cent of the market:

With regard to market shares the Court has held that very large shares are in themselves, and save in exceptional circumstances, evidence of the existence of a dominant position: Case 85/76 *Hoffmann-La Roche* v. *EC Commission*. That is the situation where there is a market share of 50 per cent such as that found to exist in this case.[348]

The CJ confirmed this in *AstraZeneca*.[349]

The outcome of *Hoffmann-La Roche* and *AKZO* is generally interpreted as providing a presumption of dominance at 50 per cent of the market, although Faull and Nikpay argue that it is not a legal presumption but rather a permissible inference on the facts of individual cases.[350] If it is a presumption, it is a rebuttable one, and weaker at 50 per cent than above 70 per cent. Even when dealing with firms with very high market shares, the EU Courts refer to evidence of other indications of dominance which show that the 'exceptional circumstances' referred to in *Hoffmann-La Roche* are

[346] Case 85/76, *Hoffmann-La Roche* EU:C:1979:36, para. 41.
[347] See also Case C-457/10 P, *AstraZeneca* EU:C:2012:770, para. 176.
[348] Case C-62/86, *AKZO* EU:C:1991:286, para. 60. [349] Case C-457/10 P, *AstraZeneca* EU:C:2012:770, para. 176.
[350] Faull and Nikpay, n. 164, 4.158–4.160.

not present. In *AKZO* itself, the CJ said that the Commission had 'rightly pointed out that other factors confirmed AKZO's predominance in the market'.[351] In *Hilti*[352] and *Tetra Pak II*,[353] the GC held, citing *Hoffmann-La Roche*, that market shares, respectively, of 70–80 per cent and 90 per cent were in themselves evidence of a dominant position, but further noted that barriers to entry were high.[354] In *AstraZeneca*, where the market shares in some Member States were in the 80–90 per cent region, the GC said approvingly that the Commission 'did not base its examination exclusively on AZ's market share, but took care to conduct an in-depth analysis of competitive conditions by taking into account various factors . . .'[355] It is Commission practice to examine whether 'exceptional circumstances' are present even when dealing with undertakings with extremely high market shares. This was so in *Microsoft*, where it examined barriers to entry (in particular network effects), even though Microsoft had a market share of over 90 per cent;[356] in *Intel*, where there were market shares of over 70 and 80 per cent in the relevant markets;[357] and in *Google Shopping*, where Google's share of user traffic in general search services was 90 per cent or higher in most EEA countries.[358]

There is also a question of what holding a very large market share 'for some time' in *Hoffmann-La Roche* means. In *AstraZeneca*, the CJ interpreted this as 'a long period'.[359] Bellamy and Child suggest that a high and stable market share for 'a period of five years would probably afford sufficient evidence while any period of less than three years, especially in a dynamic market, might be considered too short for a high market share to be an indicator of dominance'.[360]

(iv) Relative Market Shares

Market shares must be considered in relative as well as absolute terms, as recognised in paragraph 13 of the Guidance Paper. This means that, when considering the market shares of the undertaking under scrutiny, it is also necessary to consider the market shares of competitors. The CJ said in *Hoffmann-La Roche* that 'the relationship between the market shares of the undertaking concerned and of its competitors, especially those of the next largest' was a relevant factor.[361] The market power of an undertaking with a market share of 51 per cent will be considerably different depending on whether, for example, it has one competitor with a 49 per cent share of the market, three competitors which have 16, 16, and 17 per cent of the market, respectively, or 49 competitors each with 1 per cent of the market. The differentials in market share are extremely significant. A market where there are two undertakings, A with 51 per cent and B with 49 per cent, is a duopoly. It is not dominated by A, although there may be collective dominance with B.[362]

[351] Case C-62/86, *AKZO* EU:C:1991:286, para. 61.

[352] Case T-30/89, *Hilti* EU:T:1991:70, paras. 91–94, *aff'd* Case C-53/92 P, *Hilti AG* EU:C:1994:77.

[353] Case T-83/91, *Tetra Pak* EU:T:1994:246, paras. 109–110, *aff'd* Case C-333/94 P, *Tetra Pak II* EU:C:1996:436.

[354] See also Case T-395/94, *Atlantic Container Line* EU:T:2002:49, para. 328, and Case T-228/97, *Irish Sugar* EU:T:1999:246, paras. 71–104.

[355] Case T-321/05, *AstraZeneca* EU:T:2010:266, para. 244.

[356] COMP/37.792, *Microsoft* 24 March 2004, paras. 448–464 and 515–540.

[357] COMP/37.990, *Intel* 13 May 2009, paras. 853–912.

[358] AT.39740, *Google Search (Shopping)* 27 June 2017.

[359] Case C-457/10 P, *AstraZeneca* EU:C:2012:770, para. 176.

[360] Bellamy and Child (D. Bailey and L. John, eds.), *European Union Law of Competition* (8th edn, Oxford University Press, 2018), 10.026. In 'bidding markets' where contracts are awarded by a competitive tendering process and the 'winner takes all', market shares are not necessarily a useful indicator of dominance, see Bellamy and Child, 10.027.

[361] Case 85/76, *Hoffmann-La Roche* EU:C:1979:36, para. 48.

[362] For collective dominance in respect of Art. 102, see Section 10.

In *United Brands*,[363] UBC was held to be dominant although its market share was only 45 per cent. That was, however, almost twice as large as the share of its nearest competitor. The dispersed nature of the remaining competition was also a feature supporting the finding of dominance in *Michelin I*,[364] where the defendant had a 57–65 per cent market share, in *Michelin II*,[365] where the defendant's market share was taken to be over 50 per cent, and in *AB Inbev*,[366] where the defendant held around a 55 per cent market share. In *British Airways*,[367] BA's share was seven times greater than its nearest rival. The CJ in *AstraZeneca* thus agreed with the GC that the 'generally very large' market shares of AstraZeneca (AZ) indicated that its market power was 'out of all comparison to those of the other market players'.[368] Once an undertaking has a market share as large as 70 per cent, it is bound to have at least twice the share of its nearest competitor.[369] In these circumstances, it will be difficult for the undertaking to preclude a finding of dominance. It will therefore be appreciated why narrow market definitions may be fatal for undertakings, and how important it is to make a realistic determination of the market.

(v) Market Share and the Commission Guidance Paper

In the Guidance Paper, the Commission states that market shares simply provide a *useful first indication* of market structure,[370] thus downplaying the reliance on market share.

Guidance on the Commission's Enforcement Priorities in Applying Article 82 of the EC Treaty to Abusive Exclusionary Conduct by Dominant Undertakings [2009] OJ C45/2

13. Market shares provide a useful first indication for the Commission of the market structure and of the relative importance of the various undertakings active on the market . . . However, the Commission will interpret market shares in the light of the relevant market conditions, and in particular of the dynamics of the market and of the extent to which products are differentiated. The trend or development of market shares over time may also be taken into account in volatile or bidding markets.

. . .

15. Experience suggests that the higher the market share and the longer the period of time over which it is held, the more likely it is that it constitutes an important preliminary indication of the existence of a dominant position and, in certain circumstances, of possible serious effects of abusive conduct, justifying an intervention by the Commission under Article [102]. However, as a general rule, the Commission will not come to a final conclusion as to whether or not a case should be pursued without examining all the factors which may be sufficient to constrain the behaviour of the undertaking.

In the last sentence, the Commission does not completely preclude reaching a finding of dominance without looking at 'all the factors'. Nevertheless, in recent cases the Commission has examined all the factors carefully, and there is no case where it has reached a conclusion based on market share alone.

363 Case 27/76, *United Brands* EU:C:1978:22. 364 Case 322/81, *Michelin I* EU:C:1983:313.
365 *Michelin* [2001] OJ L143/1. 366 AT.40134, *AB Inbev beer trade restrictions* 13 May 2019, paras. 69–70.
367 Case T-219/99, *British Airways* EU:T:2003:343.
368 Case C-457/10 P, *AstraZeneca* EU:C:2012:770, para. 177, *aff'g* para. 253 of Case T-321/05, *AstraZeneca* EU:T:2010:266.
369 See also COMP/38.113, *Prokent Tomra* 29 March 2006, paras. 84–85, upheld Case T-155/06, *Tomra* EU:T:2010:370, *aff'd* Case C-549/10 P, *Tomra* EU:C:2012:221.
370 The same phrase appears in the Horizontal Merger Guidelines [2004] OJ C31/3, para. 14.

The Guidance Paper makes no reference to the significance of 50 per cent of the market, let alone to presumptions at that level.

(vi) Low Market Shares and Dominance

It is important to know the minimum market share at which an undertaking is likely to be held dominant. The crucial range is 40–50 per cent, for above that the market share is 'very high', and below that a finding of dominance is unlikely though possible. The lower the market share of the undertaking, the greater the significance which attaches to other factors indicating dominance. The lowest share at which an undertaking has been found dominant under Article 102 was 39.7 per cent in *British Airways*. The market definition aspect of *British Airways* has been considered already.[371] As is apparent from the following extract, there were a number of special circumstances which led the GC to uphold the Commission's finding that BA was dominant with such a low market share.

BA argued, inter alia, that the Commission should not have found it dominant as a buyer without taking into account the intense competition it faced as a supplier of air transport services; that the Commission had not explained how its dominance as a buyer of air travel agency services arose from its successful position in air transport; that its market share did not establish a position of dominance; that its market share was falling; that it was not an 'obligatory business partner' of travel agents; and finally, that if it *were* dominant, then it would not have had to spend substantial sums on improving its services.

Case T-219/99, *British Airways v Commission* EU:T:2003:343

General Court

197. For the purposes of establishing whether BA holds a dominant position on the United Kingdom market for air travel agency services, there is no need to assess its economic strength on that market by reference to the competition between airlines providing services on each of the routes served by BA and its competitors to and from United Kingdom airports.

198. . . . [T]hose various United Kingdom markets in air transport services are distinct from air travel agency services, including the distribution of air tickets in particular.

. . .

209. The Court still needs to examine whether the reasoning followed by the Commission in order to establish BA's dominant position, on the basis of the evidence which it thus lawfully used, might not be vitiated by errors of assessment.

210. In that respect, account must be taken of the highly significant indicator which is the fact that the undertaking in question holds large shares of the market and of the ratio between the market share held by the undertaking concerned and that of its nearest rivals (*Hoffmann-La Roche* . . . at paragraphs 39 and 48), particularly since the nearest rivals hold only marginal market shares (. . . *United Brands v. Commission* . . . paragraph 111).

211. . . . [N]ot only is BA's market share in the total of air ticket sales . . . to be regarded as large, but it invariably constitutes a multiple of the market shares of each of its five main competitors on the United Kingdom market for air travel agency services.. . .

212. The economic strength which BA derives from its market share is further reinforced by the world rank it occupies in terms of international scheduled passenger-kilometres flown, the extent of the range of its transport services and its hub network.

[371] See Section 8.A.xiii.

213. According to BA's own statements, its network operations allow it, in comparison with its five competitors, to offer a wider choice of routes and more frequent flights.

214. . . . [I]n 1995, it operated 92 of the 151 international routes from Heathrow Airport and 43 of the 92 routes in service at Gatwick, that is to say several times the number of routes served by each of its three or four nearest rivals (operating) from those two airports.

215. As a whole, the services operated by BA on routes to and from United Kingdom airports have the cumulative effect of generating the purchase by travellers of a preponderant number of BA air tickets through travel agents established in the United Kingdom, and, correspondingly, at least as many transactions between BA and those agents for the purposes of supplying air travel agency services, particularly in the distribution of BA air tickets.

216. It necessarily follows that those agents substantially depend on the income they receive from BA in consideration for their air travel agency services.

217. BA is therefore wrong to deny that it is an obligatory business partner of travel agents established in the United Kingdom and to maintain that those agents have no actual need to sell BA tickets. BA's arguments are not capable of calling into question the finding, in recital 93 of the contested decision, that BA enjoys a particularly powerful position in relation to its nearest rivals and the largest travel agents.

218. The facts of this case therefore show that BA was in a position, unilaterally by circular of 17 November 1997, to impose a reduction as from 1 January 1998 of its rates of commission in force up to that date and to extend its new performance reward scheme to all travel agents established in the United Kingdom.

219. In those circumstances, neither the possibly modest size of the share of BA ticket sales in the business of some of the main agencies, which has moreover merely been alleged, nor the alleged fluctuations of BA's share in the total figure of air ticket sales by travel agents established in the United Kingdom can call into question the Commission's finding that BA holds a dominant position on the United Kingdom market for air travel agency services.

220. Nor are the great dependence of United Kingdom travel agents upon BA and BA's corresponding freedom of manoeuvre in relation to other companies using the services of air travel agencies capable of being called into question by the fact that those agents do not normally hold stocks of air tickets.

221. Such a purely logistical circumstance is not of such a kind as to affect the dominant position which BA derives from its preponderant weight on the United Kingdom market for air travel agency services.

222. The argument that, as an undertaking in a dominant position, BA would have no interest in spending considerable sums improving its services so as to compete more effectively with its rivals is irrelevant in that it concerns the United Kingdom air transport markets and not the United Kingdom market for air travel agency services which the Commission took to establish the dominant position of BA.

223. Finally, for the same reason, neither the decline in the percentage of BA air ticket sales nor the advance in market share of certain rival companies is sufficiently large to call into question the existence of BA's dominant position on the United Kingdom market for air travel agency services.

224. In this case, the reduction in BA's market share cannot, in itself, constitute proof that there is no dominant position. The position which BA still occupies on the United Kingdom market for air travel agency services remains very largely preponderant. As the table in paragraph 211 above shows, a substantial gap remained, during the whole of the period of the infringement found by the Commission, between, on the one hand, BA's market share and, on the other, both the market share of its closest rival and the cumulative shares of its five main competitors on the United Kingdom market for air travel agency services.

225. The Commission was therefore right to hold that BA held a dominant position on the United Kingdom market for air travel agency services.

Furthermore, in *Gøttrup Klim*, the CJ did not dismiss the possibility of an undertaking with 36 and 32 per cent of two relevant markets being in a dominant position:

> While an undertaking which holds market shares of that size may, depending on the strength and number of its competitors, be considered to be in a dominant position, those market shares cannot on their own constitute conclusive evidence of the existence of a dominant position.[372]

As with the presumption of dominance at 50 per cent of the market, the fact that it is possible to have a dominant position, and thus be subject to Article 102, at a market share lower than 40 per cent is a striking feature of EU competition law. It is frequently argued[373] that there should be a 'safe harbour' for Article 102, similar to that provided by the block exemptions in respect of Article 101, whereby a finding of dominance would be ruled out at, say, below a 40 per cent market share. Such a 'dominance screen' could possibly allow some firms with market power to escape Article 102, but would, on the other hand, generate additional legal certainty for undertakings and could help to avoid Type 1 errors. The Commission, which had never ruled out the possibility of finding dominance at a market share of 20–40 per cent,[374] sets out a *qualified* safe harbour in the Guidance Paper.

> **Guidance on the Commission's Enforcement Priorities in Applying Article 82 of the EC Treaty to Abusive Exclusionary Conduct by Dominant Undertakings [2009] OJ C45/2**
>
> 14. The Commission considers that low market shares are generally a good proxy for the absence of substantial market power. The Commission's experience suggests that dominance is not likely if the undertaking's market share is below 40% in the relevant market. However, there may be specific cases below that threshold where competitors are not in a position to constrain effectively the conduct of a dominant undertaking, for example where they face serious capacity limitations. Such cases may also deserve attention on the part of the Commission.

The Guidance Paper was therefore a disappointment to those who argued for a real safe harbour. Dominance below 40 per cent is 'not likely', but the Commission reserves its position over certain 'specific cases'. In this, paragraph 14 is like many other places in the Guidance Paper, where the Commission sets out a general rule and then qualifies it.

(vii) Market Shares in the Digital Economy

The extent to which market shares offer an accurate proxy for existing levels of competition has been disputed in the context of the digital economy. Early on, it was argued that even quasi-monopolists in digital markets were 'under permanent threat from innovating competitors and they are only able to retain their position if they continue to innovate'. Thus contestability was considered to provide a better indicator of market power, to the extent that the threat of *potential* competition could act as an effective competitive constraint.[375] More recently, however, the Commission's expert Report on

[372] Case C-250/92, *Gøttrup Klim v KLG* EU:C:1994:413.

[373] See the comments received on the Commission Staff Discussion Paper, available at <http://ec.europa.eu/competition/antitrust/art82/contributions.html>. The Discussion Paper, para. 31, did not merely fail to rule out dominance below 40%, it expressly said that undertakings with market share below 25% were merely 'not likely' to enjoy a dominant position.

[374] See Commission's *Xth Report on Competition Policy* (1981), point 150.

[375] C. Ahlborn, D. Evans, and A. Padilla, 'Competition Policy in the New Economy: Is Competition Law Up to the Challenge?' [2001] ECLR 156, 162.

Competition Policy for the Digital Era has emphasised the extent to which market power might arise even in apparently fragmented digital marketplaces, due to inter alia the existence of multi-sided markets, network externalities, and access to data. It cautioned against over-reliance upon any single parameter as a measurement of market power, arguing instead for a case-specific assessment in every instance.[376]

In *France Télécom*,[377] the undertaking claimed that market shares were not a reliable indicator in the context of an emerging market. The GC said that the fact that this was a fast-growing market could not preclude application of the competition rules,[378] but it did examine the claimant's contention that the market should be looked at from a dynamic perspective by assessing potential as well as actual competition, and found that the Commission had taken proper account of this.[379]

What is notable about the Commission's more recent enforcement activity in digital markets is the high and stable market shares enjoyed by incumbents, which the Commission has frequently emphasised. In *Google Shopping*, this meant shares of around 90 per cent or higher in general search markets, held for almost a decade.[380] Similarly, Amazon's market share for the distribution of English language e-books across the EEA was estimated to be constantly around 80 to 100 per cent from 2011 to 2015.[381] Notably, the Commission in *Google Shopping* acknowledged that, in fast-growing sectors characterised by short innovation cycles, large market shares could turn out to be ephemeral, and not necessarily indicative of a dominant position. Yet, following the approach of the GC in *France Télécom*, it held that the mere fact that a market was characterised by rapid innovation did not preclude application of competition law, and certainly had not prevented Google from maintaining high and stable market shares.[382] In *Google AdSense*, the Commission noted that Google's share of national markets for online search advertising had increased progressively between 2006 and 2016, to the point where, by the end of the period of the infringement, few if any competitors to Google existed in most national markets.[383] In approving the commitments offered by Amazon to settle the *E-book MFNs* case, however, the Commission invoked the 'fast-moving' nature of the e-commerce sector to justify the relatively short duration of the agreed commitments.[384]

(viii) Market Shares in the Case of Collective Dominance

Most of the existing Article 102 cases finding collective dominance have involved undertakings with combined market shares above 90 per cent in a 'quasi-monopoly'.[385] In *Atlantic Container Line*,[386] however, a liner conference with market shares of 60–70 per cent on various markets was held to be collectively dominant, and the GC rejected the argument that a market share above 50 per cent could not suffice to found a presumption of a collective dominant position. In cases of 'oligopolistic'

[376] Crémer, de Montjoye, and Schweitzer, n. 178, pp. 48–50.

[377] Case T-340/03, *France Télécom* EU:T:2007:22, *aff'd* Case C-202/07 P, *France Télécom* EU:C:2009:214.

[378] Case T-340/03, *France Télécom* EU:T:2007:22, para. 10.

[379] Ibid., paras. 110–113.

[380] AT.39740, *Google Search (Shopping)* 27 June 2017.

[381] AT40153, *E-book MFNs and related matters (Amazon)* May 2017.

[382] AT.39740, *Google Search (Shopping)* June 2017, para. 267.

[383] AT.40411, *Google Search (AdSense)* 20 March 2019, para. 230.

[384] AT40153, *E-book MFNs and related matters (Amazon)* 4 May 2017, para. 193.

[385] Case T-228/97, *Irish Sugar plc v Commission* EU:T:1999:246, *aff'd*, Case C-497/99 P, *Irish Sugar plc v Commission* EU:C:2001:393; Cases C-395 and 396/96 P, *Compagnie Maritime Belge Transports SA v Commission* EU:C:2000:132, discussed in Chap. 9.

[386] Cases T-191/98 and 212–214/98, *Atlantic Container Line* EU:T:2003:245, paras. 931–935.

collective dominance, where undertakings can coordinate their behaviour without express collusion or structural links, the situation may be different because the significance of high market shares is not the same.[387]

C. OTHER FACTORS INDICATING DOMINANCE AND BARRIERS TO ENTRY

(i) General

A wide range of matters have been held by the EU Courts and the Commission to constitute 'other factors indicating dominance'. In *United Brands* and *Hoffmann-La Roche*, the CJ held that a dominant position derives from a combination of several factors which, taken separately, are not necessarily determinative.[388] The 'other factors indicating dominance' comprise both matters involving the undertaking itself, and barriers to entry and expansion.

(ii) Indications from the Undertaking

a. *The Undertaking's Own Assessment of its Position*

The EU Courts and the Commission have sometimes relied on an undertaking's own internal documentation to indicate its dominance. Such evidence was referred to in *BBI/Boosey & Hawkes* ('"automatic first choice" of all the top brass bands'),[389] *AKZO* ('AKZO regards itself as the world leader in the peroxides market'),[390] and *Broadcom* (where the Commission referenced an internal presentation describing Broadcom as 'dominant' and holding the '#1 market share').[391] The opinions of managers, however, are not incontrovertible evidence of their truth. Managers may try to 'talk up' the undertaking's position to convince themselves, others, or both.[392]

b. *Profits*

Since a monopolist can reap the benefits of its market power by earning monopoly profits, profit margins may provide a means of identifying market power. It has been argued, however, that no significant relationship between profit margins and market power exists.[393] Moreover, it may be difficult to determine whether an undertaking is in fact earning monopoly profits. Accordingly, profitability assessment has not been much used in EU cases to assist in the assessment of dominance, although in *Microsoft* the Commission was impressed by the fact that Microsoft operated on a profit margin of approximately 81 per cent.[394] Conversely, a lack of profits is not necessarily a contra-indication of dominance. In *United Brands*[395] and *Michelin I*,[396] the CJ held that an undertaking's economic strength is

[387] Monti, n. 37, 136–138; Ortiz Blanco, n. 170, 168–172. For oligopolistic collective dominance, see Chap. 9.

[388] Case 27/76, *United Brands* EU:C:1978:22, para. 66; Case 85/76, *Hoffmann-La Roche* EU:C:1979:36, para. 39.

[389] *BBI/Boosey & Hawkes* [1987] OJ L286/36, para. 18.

[390] Case C-62/86, *AKZO* EU:C:1991:286, para. 61.

[391] AT.40608, *Broadcom* 16 October 2019, paras. 132 and 151.

[392] The same problem with internal documentation arises when it is used to establish that an abuse has been committed: see Chap. 7.

[393] See R. Bork and J. Sidak, 'The Misuse of Profit Margins to Infer Market Power' (2013) 9 *J of Competition Law and Economics* 511.

[394] COMP/37.792, *Microsoft* 24 March 2004, para. 464.

[395] Case 27/76, *United Brands* EU:C:1978:22, paras. 126–128.

[396] Case 322/81, *Michelin I* EU:C:1983:313, para. 59.

not measured by profitability alone.[397] On the contrary, losses, at least if temporary, may demonstrate the economic strength of an undertaking with the ability to absorb them.[398]

c. *Performance Indicators and Price Levels*

An undertaking's economic performance can be an indicator of dominance. In *Hoffmann-La Roche*,[399] the CJ took spare manufacturing capacity into account as a factor indicating dominance, although it did not distinguish between idle and excess capacity. Capacity is idle when its use would be unprofitable because the market price is less than the cost of its use. It is found on both competitive and non-competitive markets. Excess capacity means that the undertaking is producing less than the optimal output that the plant is designed to produce, so that it could increase its output without its unit costs increasing.[400]

The technical definition of market power refers to the ability of an undertaking to profitably raise and maintain prices above the level that would prevail under competition.[401] Accordingly, the fact that an undertaking has in practice raised and maintained its prices at elevated levels has been taken into account as a factor indicating the presence of significant market power in certain cases. The ability of an undertaking to obtain premium prices was relevant in the early cases of *United Brands*[402] and *BBI/Boosey & Hawkes*,[403] and more recently in *AB Inbev*[404] and *Aspen*.[405] In *AstraZeneca*, it was relevant that AZ was able to maintain its prices at a higher level than those of its competitors while retaining a much higher market share. This was a consequence of the way in which public health systems operated in covering the cost of medicines and the resulting insensitivity of prescribing doctors and patients.[406]

d. *Overall Size and Strength and Range of Products (Portfolio Power)*

In its decision in *Hoffmann-La Roche*, the Commission took into account the undertaking's position as the world's largest vitamin producer and leading pharmaceuticals producer, and the wide range of vitamins it manufactured.[407] The CJ rejected the assertion that these factors were indicators of dominance, however. On the facts, each group of vitamins constituted a specific market, and the question whether Hoffmann-La Roche was dominant in one product category could not predetermine whether it was dominant in others.[408]

Yet although size is not per se an indicator of dominance on a particular market, it may be relevant. In *Michelin*, the CJ took into account the advantages Michelin NV derived from belonging to a multinational group of undertakings.[409] In *Soda Ash–Solvay*,[410] the Commission considered Solvay's manufacturing strength with plant in six other Member States to be part of the 'relevant

[397] See also COMP/39.985, *Motorola—Enforcement of GPRS Standard Essential Patents* 29 April 2014, para. 251, where the Commission cited *Michelin I* in dismissing Motorola's argument about its unprofitability/losses.

[398] For example, AT.40462, *Amazon Marketplace* and AT.40703, *Amazon Buy Box* 20 December 2022, para. 92.

[399] Case 85/76, *Hoffmann-La Roche* EU:C:1979:36, para. 48.

[400] Excess capacity can be used against potential competitors as a form of strategic entry deterrence.

[401] See discussion in Chap. 3. [402] Case 27/76, *United Brands* EU:C:1978:22, para. 91.

[403] *BBI/Boosey & Hawkes* [1987] OJ L286/36, para. 18.

[404] AT.40134, *AB Inbev beer trade restrictions* 13 May 2019, paras. 71–73.

[405] AT.40394, *Aspen* 10 February 2021, para. 71.

[406] Case T-321/05, *AstraZeneca* EU:T:2010:266, paras. 256–268, *aff'd* Case C-457/10 P, *AstraZeneca* EU:C:2012:770, paras. 178–180.

[407] Case IV/29.020, *Vitamins* [1976] OJ L223/27 at recitals 5, 6, and 21.

[408] Case 85/76, *Hoffmann-La Roche* EU:C:1979:36, paras. 45–47.

[409] Although without specifying what these were: Case 322/81, *Michelin I* EU:C:1983:313, para. 55.

[410] [2003] OJ L10/10, para. 138.

economic evidence' in assessing dominance. The geographical spread of an undertaking's operations may make it less vulnerable to natural disasters[411] and/or other fluctuations.[412] In *AstraZeneca*, the GC confirmed as 'relevant indicia' the fact that AZ's resources and performances outclassed those of its competitors, including its general financial solidity, R&D resources, and marketing resources. AZ's turnover, unlike its competitors', was derived almost exclusively from the sale of pharmaceutical products, and these superior resources were devoted to its pharmaceutical business.[413]

Moreover, operating successfully across a diversity of product markets may provide an undertaking with the practical ability to engage in abusive behaviour in certain circumstances. In *Tetra Pak II*,[414] the Commission held that such diversity 'allows it, if necessary, to make financial sacrifices on one or other of its products without affecting the overall profitability of its operations'. This is a polite way of saying that 'deep pockets' can facilitate practices such as predatory pricing.[415]

(iii) Barriers to Entry and Expansion

The second indent in paragraph 12 of the Guidance Paper refers to the constraints imposed on an undertaking by credible threats of future entry or expansion. Barriers to entry and expansion are important because, where they exist, rivals cannot enter or expand on the market, in order to compete away the incumbent's market share. The Commission explains the importance of potential expansion by existing competitors or potential entry by new ones in paragraph 16 of the Guidance Paper. It considers that such entry or expansion is only a curb on the putatively dominant undertaking if it is 'likely, timely and significant'. Small-scale or niche entry is insufficient. In paragraph 17, the Commission sets out the forms that barriers to entry or expansion can take. In the last sentence, the Commission says that persistently high market shares may indicate the existence of barriers to entry and expansion.

Guidance on the Commission's Enforcement Priorities in Applying Article 82 of the EC Treaty to Abusive Exclusionary Conduct by Dominant Undertakings [2009] OJ C45/2

16. Competition is a dynamic process and an assessment of the competitive constraints on an undertaking cannot be based solely on the existing market situation. The potential impact of expansion by actual competitors or entry by potential competitors, including the threat of such expansion or entry, is also relevant. An undertaking can be deterred from increasing prices if expansion or entry is likely, timely and sufficient. For the Commission to consider expansion or entry likely it must be sufficiently profitable for the competitor or entrant, taking into account factors such as the barriers to expansion or entry, the likely reactions of the allegedly dominant undertaking and other competitors, and the risks and costs of failure. For expansion or entry to be considered timely, it must be sufficiently swift to deter or defeat the exercise of substantial market power. For expansion or entry to be considered sufficient, it cannot be simply small-scale entry, for example into some market niche, but must be of such a magnitude as to be able to deter any attempt to increase prices by the putatively dominant undertaking in the relevant market.

17. Barriers to expansion or entry can take various forms. They may be legal barriers, such as tariffs or quotas, or they may take the form of advantages specifically enjoyed by the dominant undertaking,

411 As with the banana plantations in Case 27/76, *United Brands* EU:C:1978:22, para. 75.
412 See *Elopak Italia/Tetra Pak* [1991] OJ L72/1, para. 101.
413 Case T-321/05, *AstraZeneca* EU:T:2010:266, paras. 284–286.
414 *Elopak Italia/Tetra Pak* [1991] OJ L72/1, para. 101.
415 One of the abuses which was found in Case C-333/94 P, *Tetra Pak II* EU:C:1996:436: see Chap. 7.

> such as economies of scale and scope, privileged access to essential inputs or natural resources, important technologies . . . or an established distribution and sales network . . . They may also include costs and other impediments, for instance resulting from network effects, faced by customers in switching to a new supplier. The dominant undertaking's own conduct may also create barriers to entry, for example where it has made significant investments which entrants or competitors would have to match . . . or where it has concluded long-term contracts with its customers that have appreciable foreclosing effects. Persistently high market shares may be indicative of the existence of barriers to entry and expansion.

(iv) Summary of Barriers to Entry for the Purposes of Article 102

This section discusses the main barriers to entry which have been held to indicate dominance in Article 102 cases, which are summarised in paragraph 17 of the Guidance Paper.[416] This section should be read in the light of the section on barriers to entry in Chapter 3.[417]

a. Economies of Scale and Scope and Sunk Costs

In *United Brands*, the CJ recognised that economies of scale 'from which newcomers to the market cannot derive any immediate benefit' can operate as a barrier to entry. It also referred to sunk costs when it spoke of 'costs which are irrecoverable if the attempt fails'.[418] Whether or not competitors can enter a market on a small scale depends on the characteristics of the market. In *Intel*, the Commission found that in respect of the x86CPU market there were (a) significant sunk costs in R&D, (b) significant sunk costs in plant production, and (c) resulting significant economies of scale which meant that the minimum efficient scale was high relative to overall market demand. Accordingly, entry barriers were significant. Furthermore, once entry had occurred, expanding output would require additional sunk investment into new property, plant, and equipment and several years' lead time.[419] The Commission explained the link between economies of scale, sunk investments, and high fixed costs:

> In general, a high share of fixed costs is indicative of significant barriers to entry and expansion. These barriers to entry give rise to market power, which in turn enables a firm to set prices above marginal costs. In the presence of fixed costs, pricing above marginal cost is necessary for a firm to generate profits and thus remain viable. As long as barriers to entry remain moderate, new entrants could be expected to compete away any supra-competitive profits, leading to more or less comparable levels of net profits across companies (after accounting for risk). The higher the proportion of fixed costs in a given industry, the more concentrated it is likely to be, because higher mark-ups are necessary for firms to remain profitable.[420]

In *Telefónica*, the Commission noted the significant sunk costs for new operators, and the fact that the incumbent benefited from economies of scale and scope, whereas new operators would have to secure a sufficient number of customers while facing higher unit costs.[421]

[416] See Section 9.C.iii. [417] Chap. 3, Section 5.

[418] Case 27/76, *United Brands* EU:C:1978:22, para. 122. [419] COMP/37.990, *Intel* 13 May 2009, para. 866.

[420] Ibid., para. 878.

[421] COMP/38.784, *Wanadoo España v Telefónica*, 4 July 2007, paras. 224–226, upheld Case T-336/07, *Telefónica* EU:T:2012:172, para. 154, *aff'd* Case C-295/12 P, *Telefónica* EU:C:2014:2062.

b. Access to Key Inputs or Facilities

New entrants may be unable to enter the market because of lack of access to key inputs. This includes raw materials, intangible property covered by IPRs, or items such as airport slots. In *BPB*,[422] any new entrant would have needed access to the relevant raw material, gypsum. There was no availability for this in the UK without opening new mines, so that the only alternative was import, which would incur additional cost and risk. In *E-book MFNs (Amazon)*, the fact that potential new e-book retailers would need to secure the rights to a sufficient catalogue of available e-books was similarly treated as a barrier to entry.[423]

An increasing concern, particularly in markets related to the digital economy, is the extent to which access to valuable consumer data might constitute a barrier to entry.[424] Although the point is disputed,[425] in *Google Shopping* the Commission treated as a barrier to entry the fact that product improvement in general search services (i.e. refinement of search results) required access to a critical mass of search query data, which gave incumbent operators like Google a significant advantage.[426] As discussed in Chapter 16, the DMA now contains several obligations which require designated digital gatekeepers to provide access to certain categories of (non-personal) data.

Where key inputs are unavailable to new entrants, refusals to supply can amount to strategic entry-deterring behaviour by the incumbent undertaking and may in certain circumstances amount to an abuse of dominance.[427] Access to facilities is a particular problem in network industries, where it is often addressed by sector regulation.

c. Access to Financial Resources and the Need for Investment

In *United Brands*[428] and *Hoffmann-La Roche*,[429] the CJ considered that the need for large-scale capital investment constituted a barrier to entry. In *Continental Can*,[430] the Commission similarly treated the undertaking's access to international capital markets as an indicator of its dominance. High investment costs were cited as barriers to entry in more recent cases involving the technology giants, Google[431] and Amazon,[432] both in terms of the level of investment required to establish viable online platforms and, in the case of Google, the need for continuing investment in order constantly to improve its product offering.

[422] *BPB Industries* [1989] OJ L10/50, para. 120.

[423] AT40153, *E-book MFNs and related matters (Amazon)* 4 May 2017.

[424] Compare e.g. R. Mahnke, 'Big Data as a Barrier to Entry', *CPI Antitrust Chronicle* May 2015; I. Graef, 'Market Definition and Market Power in Data: The Case of Online Platforms' (2015) 38 *World Competition* 473; N. Schepp and A. Wambach, 'On Big Data and Its Relevance for Market Power Assessment' (2016) 7 *JECLAP* 120; G. Lougher and S. Kalmanowicz, 'EU Competition Law in the Sharing Economy' (2016) 7 *JECLAP* 87, 98; D. Sokol and R. Comerford, 'Antitrust and Regulating Big Data' (2016) 23 *George Mason LR* 119; G. Colangelo and M. Maggiolino, 'Big Data as Misleading Facilities' (2017) 13 *European Competition Journal* 249; and D. Rubinfeld and M. Gal, 'Access Barriers to Big Data' (2017) 59 *Arizona LR* 339. The competition issues raised by data more generally are considered in Crémer, de Montjoye, and Schweitzer, n. 178, Chap. 5.

[425] See, in particular, G. Manne and B. Sperry, 'The Problems and Perils of Bootstrapping Privacy and Data into an Antitrust Framework', *CPI Antitrust Chronicle*, May 2015.

[426] AT.39740, *Google Search (Shopping)* 27 June 2017, paras. 287–290.

[427] See the case law on refusal to supply and the essential facilities doctrine, discussed in Chap. 7.

[428] Case 27/76, *United Brands* EU:C:1978:22, para. 122.

[429] Case 85/76, *Hoffmann-La Roche* EU:C:1979:36, para. 49.

[430] *Continental Can* [1972] JO L7/25, para. 13.

[431] AT.39740, *Google Search (Shopping)* 27 June 2017, paras. 286 and 291.

[432] AT40153, *E-book MFNs and related matters (Amazon)* 4 May 2017, para. 65.

d. Legal and Regulatory Barriers and Intellectual Property Rights

State or regulatory measures which subject a market to licensing requirements, or which grant to a particular undertaking a statutory monopoly (such as that held by the State-owned rail company in *Baltic Rail* for management of railway infrastructure[433]), an exclusive concession (such as in the provision of undertaking services in *Bodson*[434]), or exclusive access to finite resources (such as radio frequencies in *Decca Navigator*[435] or airport slots in *British Midland–Aer Lingus*[436]), are obvious barriers to entry. Most legal and regulatory barriers to entry can be classified as absolute costs advantages.[437] They are structural factors inherent in the market, and they may impact differently on new entrants than on incumbents.[438] The EU Courts and the Commission have frequently held such measures to be factors indicating dominance and many cases on Article 102 concern statutory monopolists.[439]

Although not legal regulation as such, it was found in *AstraZeneca*[440] that the organisation and dynamics of the health and social security systems in Member States made it difficult for competitors to gain market share. This gave AZ first-mover advantages.

IPRs are a particular type of legal right granted by national (or European) law. The CJ has consistently held that the mere possession of IPRs does not *necessarily* confer a dominant position.[441] The legal monopoly may not equate to an economic monopoly if the relevant market is wider than the protected product. The issue is how far possession of the IPR enables the holder to prevent effective competition. The fact that access to a market is protected by IPRs may be relevant as a barrier to entry. IPRs can be classified both as absolute cost advantages and first-mover advantages. IPRs constituted barriers to entry in *Hugin*,[442] *Eurofix-Bauco v Hilti*,[443] and *Tetra Pak II*.[444] In *Intel*, the Commission remarked on the 'significant intellectual property-related barriers that any new entrant would have to overcome'.[445] Similarly, the strength of the patent protection enjoyed by AZ, and its rigorous enforcement of its rights, contributed to the finding of dominance in *AstraZeneca*.[446] Cases on refusal to license copyrights arise because, without access to the copyright-protected material, the competitor cannot enter the market.[447]

The Commission has also been concerned about standard-essential patents (SEPs), where an undertaking holds a patent which is necessary to the technical standard adopted by an industry for a particular product or process.[448] Again, mere ownership of a SEP does not necessarily confer dominance. Whether a dominant position arises also depends on other factors such as whether compliance with the standard is necessary to enter a market and whether competition from other technologies is possible.[449] In its first Article 102 decision on SEPs,[450] the Commission found that it was indispensable

[433] AT39813, *Baltic Rail* 2 October 2017, paras. 162–167.

[434] Case 30/87, *Bodson v Pompes Funèbres des Régions Libérées* EU:C:1988:225.

[435] [1989] OJ L43/7.

[436] [1992] OJ L96/34.

[437] See D. Harbord and T. Hoehn, 'Barriers to Entry and Exit in European Competition Policy' (1994) 14 *International Review of Law and Economics* 411.

[438] Faull and Nikpay, n. 164, 4.189.

[439] E.g. Case 311/84, *Télémarketing* EU:C:1985:394; Cases C-241–242/91 P, *Magill* EU:C:1995:98; Case 226/84, *British Leyland* EU:C:1986:421; IV/34.174 *Sealink/B&I Holyhead: Interim Measures* 11 June 1992, and other transport cases; Case C-23/14, *Post Danmark II* EU:C:2015:651.

[440] Case C-457/10 P, *AstraZeneca* EU:C:2012:770.

[441] Case 24/67, *Parke Davis v Probel* EU:C:1968:11; Cases C-241–242/91 P, *Magill* EU:C:1995:98.

[442] Case 22/78, *Hugin* EU:C:1979:138.

[443] [1988] OJ L65/19.

[444] Case C-333/94 P, *Tetra Pak II* EU:C:1996:436.

[445] COMP/37.990, *Intel* 13 May 2009, para. 858.

[446] Case T-321/05, *AstraZeneca* EU:T:2010:266, paras. 270–275, *aff'd* Case C-457/10 P, *AstraZeneca* EU:C:2012:770, paras. 186–188.

[447] Case C-418/01, *IMS Health* EU:C:2004:257; Cases C-241–242/91 P, *Magill* EU:C:1995:98.

[448] For SEPs, see further Chap. 7, Section 14.C.

[449] See further the discussion in O'Donoghue and Padilla, n. 25, 851.

[450] COMP/39.985, *Motorola—Enforcement of GPRS Standard Essential Patents* 29 April 2014, MEMO/14/322.

for manufacturers of mobile devices to comply with the GPRS standard owned by Motorola. The first (and hitherto only) competition case to reach the EU Courts on SEPs, *Huawei*, considered only the issue of abuse, not dominance.[451]

e. *Superior Technology*

A more contentious group of potential barriers to entry arise from the successful operation of the putatively dominant undertaking's own business, whether it deploys better technology, or it benefits from more efficient internal or external organisation. Such structural advantages may indeed make it more difficult for new entrants to compete successfully against the incumbent. Yet it may be difficult to maintain, as a matter of competition policy, that the fact that an undertaking is a particularly successful competitor is an appropriate ground for attracting antitrust scrutiny. The CJ's approach to structural advantages as a barrier to entry is illustrated in this extract from *United Brands*, in which, it will be recalled, the Court was called upon to determine whether UBC had a dominant position on the market for bananas as distinct from other fresh fruit:

Case 27/76, United Brands v Commission EU:C:1978:22

Court of Justice

. . . The structure of UBC

69. It is advisable to examine in turn UBC's resources for and methods of producing, packaging, transporting, selling and displaying its product.

70. UBC is an undertaking vertically integrated to a high degree.

71. This integration is evident at each of the stages from the plantation to the loading on wagons or lorries in the ports of delivery and after those stages, as far as ripening and sale prices are concerned, UBC even extends its control to ripener/distributors and wholesalers by setting up a complete network of agents.

72. At the production stage UBC owns large plantations in Central and South America.

73. In so far as UBC's own production does not meet its requirements it can obtain supplies without any difficulty from independent planters since it is an established fact that unless circumstances are exceptional there is a production surplus.

74. Furthermore several independent producers have links with UBC through contracts for the growing of bananas which have caused them to grow the varieties of bananas which UBC has advised them to adopt.

75. The effects of natural disasters which could jeopardize supplies are greatly reduced by the fact that the plantations are spread over a wide geographic area and by the selection of varieties not very susceptible to diseases.

76. This situation was born out by the way in which UBC was able to react to the consequences of hurricane 'Fifi' in 1974.

77. At the production stage UBC therefore knows that it can comply with all the requests which it receives.

78. At the stage of packaging and presentation on its premises UBC has at its disposal factories, manpower, plant and material which enable it to handle the goods independently.

79. The bananas are carried from the place of production to the port of shipment by its own means of transport including railways.

[451] Case C-170/13, *Huawei Technologies v ZTE* EU:C:2015:477.

80. At the carriage by sea stage it has been acknowledged that UBC is the only undertaking of its kind which is capable of carrying two thirds of its exports by means of its own banana fleet.

81. Thus UBC knows that it is able to transport regularly, without running the risk of its own ships not being used and whatever the market situation may be, two thirds of its average volume of sales and is alone able to ensure that three regular consignments reach Europe each week, and all this guarantees it commercial stability and well being.

82. In the field of technical knowledge and as a result of continual research UBC keeps on improving the productivity and yield of its plantations by improving the draining system, making good soil deficiencies and combating effectively plant disease.

83. It has perfected new ripening methods in which its technicians instruct the distributor/ripeners of the Chiquita banana.

84. That is another factor to be borne in mind when considering UBC's position since competing firms cannot develop research at a comparable level and are in this respect at a disadvantage compared with the applicant.

From this discussion it can be identified that the superior technology of an undertaking may be treated as a factor indicating dominance. This factor was also relevant in, inter alia, *Hoffmann-La Roche, Michelin, Eurofix-Bauco v Hilti*, and *Tetra Pak*. It is, however, questionable from an economic perspective to treat an undertaking's technological superiority as a barrier to entry per se. It is true that expenditure on technological development can be a sunk cost of entry, but it is equally true that a new entrant may not have to spend the same resources on R&D as the incumbent: there is no need to reinvent the wheel.[452] Superior technology does not operate as a barrier to entry, according to Stigler,[453] since it does not represent a cost to the new entrant which was not borne by the incumbent.

In *Michelin (I)* the CJ was faced with the argument that taking account of an undertaking's superior technology would amount to penalising it for its success. Rejecting this claim, the CJ reiterated that dominance itself is not prohibited by Article 102, but merely its abuse. More controversially, the CJ then articulated its 'special responsibility' doctrine, which plays an important role in shaping the existence of abuses of dominance, considered further in Chapter 7.

Case 322/81, *Nederlandsche Banden-Industrie Michelin v Commission* EU:C:1983:313

Court of Justice

55. . .. [I]n order to assess the relative economic strength of Michelin NV and its competitors on the Netherlands market the advantages which those undertakings may derive from belonging to groups of undertakings operating throughout Europe or even the world must be taken into consideration. Amongst those advantages, the lead which the Michelin group has over its competitors in the matters of investment and research and the special extent of its range of products, to which the Commission referred in its decision, have not been denied. In fact in the case of certain types of tyres the Michelin group is the only supplier on the market to offer them in its range.

[452] See V. Korah, 'Concept of a Dominant Position Within The Meaning of Art. 86' (1980) 17 *CMLRev* 395, 408, and 410; Harbord and Hoehn, n. 434, 411, 419; Baden Fuller, n. 256, 423, 437.

[453] See Chap. 3, Section 5.

> 56. That situation ensures that on the Netherlands market a large number of users of heavy-vehicle tyres have a strong preference for Michelin tyres. As the purchase of tyres represents a considerable investment for a transport undertaking and since much time is required in order to ascertain in practice the cost-effectiveness of a type or brand of tyre, Michelin NV therefore enjoys a position which renders it largely immune to competition. As a result, a dealer established in the Netherlands normally cannot afford not to sell Michelin tyres.
>
> 57. It is not possible to uphold the objections . . . that Michelin NV is thus penalized for the quality of its products and services. A finding that an undertaking has a dominant position is not in itself a recrimination but simply means that, irrespective of the reasons for which it has such a dominant position, the undertaking concerned has a special responsibility not to allow its conduct to impair genuine undistorted competition on the [internal] market.

f. Established Distribution and Sales Networks

Similarly, the overall efficacy of the undertaking's commercial arrangements has been held to contribute to its dominant position in several cases. The approach of the CJ in *Michelin (I)* provides a clear illustration:

> 58. Due weight must also be attached to the importance of Michelin NV's network of commercial representatives, which gives it direct access to tyre users at all times. Michelin NV has not disputed the fact that in absolute terms its network is considerably larger than those of its competitors or challenged the description, in the decision at issue, of the services performed by its network whose efficiency and quality of service are unquestioned. The direct access to users and the standard of service which the network can give them enables Michelin NV to maintain and strengthen its position on the market and to protect itself more effectively against competition.

In *Eurofix-Bauco v Hilti*, the Commission likewise placed emphasis on the fact that 'Hilti has a strong and well-organised distribution system—in the EEC it has subsidiaries and independent dealers integrated into its selling network who deal mostly direct with customers', which served to 'reinforce and maintain its position in the nail gun market'.[454] This is particularly marked in *United Brands*, which was also a case of vertical integration.[455] These older judgments can, however, be criticised for failing to explain *why* a new entrant could not replicate these arrangements. Otherwise, again, the authorities appear simply to be penalising the undertaking for its efficiency, despite the CJ's protestations to the contrary in *Michelin (I)*.[456] In the Discussion Paper, the Commission identified 'a highly developed distribution and sales network' as potential barriers to entry and expansion, and stated that 'the allegedly dominant undertaking may have its own dense outlet network, established distribution logistics or wide geographical coverage that would be difficult for rivals to replicate'.[457] In the Guidance Paper, paragraph 17, they are listed without comment, with a reference to *Hoffmann-La Roche*.

g. Vertical Integration

Vertical integration may be considered a barrier to entry. Once again, this might appear to condemn an undertaking in respect of its efficiency. Further, it can be argued that, when vertical integration occurs, the barriers to entry are only added up and are not multiplied. Vertical integration may therefore

[454] *Eurofix-Bauco v Hilti* [1988] OJ L65/19, para. 69.

[455] Case 27/76, *United Brands* EU:C:1978:22, paras. 75–95.

[456] Case 322/81, *Michelin I* EU:C:1983:313, para. 57.

[457] Discussion Paper, para. 40.

accompany monopoly but is not an indicator of it.[458] Nonetheless, in *United Brands* vertical integration was an important factor in the finding of dominance. In the context of the growing and marketing of highly perishable bananas, vertical integration played an important part in UBC's ability to distribute its bananas as quickly as possible. It is quite another thing, however, to hold that such vertical integration constituted a barrier to entry. There was no explanation of why, or even if, vertical integration was regarded as an entry barrier.[459] In a number of telecommunication cases, however, it has been found that the benefits to a vertically integrated undertaking of operating on both upstream and downstream markets gave it a competitive advantage over competitors operating at only one level of the market.[460] Similarly, the fact that Amazon operated its own e-book self-publishing imprint strengthened its position in the downstream market for e-books retailing, given that potential retail entrants needed access to a sufficient catalogue of e-books to compete effectively.[461] The discrimination of a vertically integrated undertaking in favour of its own downstream operations may both constitute a strategic barrier to entry and amount to an abuse.[462]

h. Advertising, Reputation, Product Differentiation

Advertising and other promotional efforts may raise barriers to entry where these serve to generate particularly strong consumer preferences. This can be illustrated, once again, by the findings of the CJ in *United Brands*, which dedicated close attention to the marketing strategies pursued by the defendant in respect of its branded Chiquita bananas.[463]

> 91. UBC has made this product distinctive by large-scale repeated advertising and promotion campaigns which have induced the consumer to show a preference for it in spite of the difference between the price of labelled and unlabelled bananas (in the region of 30 to 40 per cent) and also of Chiquita bananas and those which have been labelled with another brand name (in the region of 7 to 10 per cent).
>
> 92. It was the first to take full advantage of the opportunities presented by labelling in the tropics for the purpose of large-scale advertising and this, to use UBC's own words, has 'revolutionized the commercial exploitation of the banana' . . .
>
> 93. It has thus attained a privileged position by making Chiquita the premier banana brand name on the relevant market with the result that the distributor cannot afford not to offer it to the consumer.

The Court did not contemplate the possibility that consumers might have been swayed by the quality of the product rather than by advertising. It concluded that, among the barriers faced by new competitors, would be 'the mounting of very large-scale advertising campaigns'.[464] Similarly, in the merger case of *Nestlé/Perrier*,[465] the Commission considered it relevant to the existence of dominance that any new entrant would face formidable advertising and promotion requirements. The Commission considered the difficulty of access to distribution outlets in a brand-crowded market, and referred to the problem of shelf-space in retail stores. In *BBI/Boosey & Hawkes*,[466] the Commission relied on the

[458] See Baden Fuller, n. 256, 423, 440 and the economic literature cited there; Harbord and Hoehn, n. 434, 411, 419; Korah, n. 449, 395, 408.

[459] See also *Soda Ash–Solvay* [2003] OJ L10/10, where the Commission treated Solvay's production of the raw material as a factor indicating its dominance.

[460] See Case T-340/03, *France Télécom* EU:T:2007:22; COMP/38.784, *Telefónica* 4 July 2007; COMP/39.525, *Telekomunikacja Polska* 22 June 2011, upheld Case T-486/11, *Orange Polska* EU:T:2015:1002.

[461] AT40153, *E-book MFNs and related matters (Amazon)* 4 May 2017, para. 65.

[462] As in the margin squeeze cases: see Chap. 7, Section 9.

[463] Case 27/76, *United Brands* EU:C:1978:22, para. 91.

[464] Ibid., para. 122.

[465] [1992] OJ L356/1, at recital 97. See Chap. 15.

[466] *BBI/Boosey & Hawkes* [1987] OJ L286/36, para. 18.

goodwill and reputation enjoyed by Boosey & Hawkes, listing among 'other factors which tend . . . to support a preliminary finding of dominance' the 'strong buyer preference for B&H instruments' and 'its close identification with the brass band movement'. In *Intel*, its extensive advertising campaigns and product differentiation constituted barriers.[467]

i. Opportunity Costs

Opportunity costs are something of value which must be given up in order to achieve or acquire something else. These can be classified as an absolute cost advantage for the incumbent. In *British Midland–Aer Lingus*,[468] the Commission considered as a barrier to entry to the Heathrow–Dublin air route the opportunity costs involved in an airline having to divert its Heathrow airport slots, currently employed for other (profitable) routes, to service the less profitable Irish destination.

j. Switching Costs

Switching costs are costs which a customer must bear if it moves its business to a competitor. These include a need to invest in new infrastructure, staff training or procedures, or sacrificing advantages obtained from the existing supplier (such as frequent flyer programmes).[469] Switching costs constitute first-mover advantages.

The costs to customers in switching supplier were taken into account in, inter alia, *Tetra Pak I*,[470] *IMS/NDC*,[471] and *Microsoft*.[472] In *E-book MFNs (Amazon)*, the Commission identified as a barrier to entry the potential for consumer 'lock-in' through the 'walled garden' of the Amazon Kindle e-reader ecosystem, although it noted that e-book users tended to multi-home in practice.[473] Conversely, in *Google Shopping*, although there were few if any *technical* barriers to switching between providers of general search services, few users multi-homed *in practice*, which the Commission treated as further evidence of market power on Google's part.[474] Switching costs arising from, for example, the loss of rebates or privileges attached to long-term or exclusive supply contracts may be strategic behaviour on the part of a dominant firm which constitutes an abuse.

k. Network Effects and Multi-sided Markets

Network effects and the complications posed by two- or multi-sided markets were discussed in Chapter 3. In the context of Article 102, these issues arise most frequently in relation to the digital economy, where such characteristics are common.[475] Multi-sided markets, as discussed, involve two or more distinct though interrelated sources of demand. Network effects arise where a product becomes more valuable from a consumer perspective as the number of other users increases: whether directly, through interactions between consumers in the same market, or indirectly, through interactions between different

[467] COMP/37.990, *Intel* 13 May 2009, paras. 867–870. [468] *British Midland–Aer Lingus* [1992] OJ L96/34.

[469] See R. J. Van den Bergh and P. D. Camesasca, *European Competition Law and Economics: A Comparative Perspective* (2nd edn, Sweet & Maxwell, 2006), 146.

[470] [1988] OJ L272/37. [471] *NDC Health/IMS: Interim Measures* [2002] OJ L59/18.

[472] COMP/37.792, *Microsoft* 24 March 2004.

[473] AT40153, *E-book MFNs and related matters (Amazon)* 4 May 2017, para. 65. There is a distinction between 'single-homing' (the customer accesses only one network/platform/facility) and 'multi-homing' (the user is connected to a number of networks).

[474] AT.39740, *Google Search (Shopping)* 27 June 2017, paras. 306–315.

[475] See e.g. D. Teece and M. Coleman, 'The Meaning of Monopoly: Antitrust Analysis in High-technology Industries' [1998] *Ant Bull* 801, 853–857; and H. Hovenkamp, 'Antitrust and Information Technologies' (2016) 68 *Fla LR* 419.

groups of consumers across a multi-sided market.[476] Network effects are associated with so-called 'tipping', whereby the underlying effects become so great that the market may tip into dominance or even monopoly.[477] Moreover, particularly in markets for online intermediation services—such a ride-hailing platforms like Uber or e-commerce marketplaces like eBay—network effects can help to generate the 'thick' market conditions necessary to help match supply and demand more effectively.[478]

The extent to which network effects, or the multi-sided nature of many digital markets, may operate as a barrier to entry is disputed.[479] Although, in some markets, consumers may be better served by one network, in others there is room for several, and the critical question is whether they interconnect. Moreover, it is not necessarily true that once a network has 'won', it cannot be dislodged: think, for instance, of the social network Facebook displacing its rival Myspace, once the most visited website in the US. If a new product offers superior benefits, consumers may be prepared to bear the switching costs, and there are always *new* consumers coming on stream.

Competition authorities need to be sensitive to the special characteristics of digital markets, and to refrain from moving against apparent dominance which may be transitory.[480] On the other hand, positions of durable market power clearly can arise in multi-sided markets. In *Microsoft*, the Commission examined the network effects carefully, and concluded that the barriers to entry were such that the dominant position was far from transitory:

> In industries exhibiting strong network effects, consumer demand depends critically on expectations about future purchases. If consumers expect a firm with a strong reputation in the current (product) generation to succeed in the next generation, this will tend to be self-fulfilling as the consumers direct their purchases to the product that they believe will yield the greatest network gains.[481]

Similarly, in *Google Shopping*, the Commission treated as a barrier to entry the existence of positive feedback effects on both sides of the two-sided platform formed by the general search and online advertising sectors. Direct network effects arose in the form of the significant minority of search engine users who valued the presence of paid-for search results within the platform. Indirect network effects arose because the existence of greater numbers of users on the search side of the platform made it more attractive to advertisers, which generated greater revenues. This, in turn, allowed Google to invest in and fine-tune its search product, attracting ever greater levels of users.[482]

l. Conduct

An undertaking's ability to act in a certain way may indicate that it is dominant. Moreover, its conduct may itself constitute a barrier to entry.

[476] Generally M. Katz and C. Shapiro, 'Network Externalities, Competition, and Compatibility' (1985) 75 *Am Econ Rev* 424.

[477] Discussed in OECD, The Digital Economy, DAF/COMP(2012)22 (2012).

[478] G. Lougher and S. Kalmanowicz, 'EU Competition Law in the Sharing Economy' (2016) 7 *JECLAP* 87, 96.

[479] See e.g. C. Veljanovski, 'Antitrust in the New Economy: Is the European Commission's View of the Network Economy Right?' [2001] *ECLR* 115; D. Evans and R. Schmalensee, 'Debunking the "Network Effects" Bogeyman' (2017) 40 *Regulation* 36; and S. Broos and J. Marcos Ramos, 'Competing Business Models and Two-sidedness: An Application to the Google Shopping Case' (2017) 62 *Ant Bull* 382.

[480] Teece and Coleman, n. 472, 801; C. Ahlborn, D. S. Evans, and A. J. Padilla, 'Competition Policy in the New Economy: Is European Competition Law up to the Challenge?' [2001] *ECLR* 156; R. Lind and P. Muysert, 'Innovation and Competition Policy: Challenges for the New Millennium' [2003] *ECLR* 87.

[481] COMP/37.792, *Microsoft*, para. 438, upheld Case T-201/04, *Microsoft* EU:T:2007:289. The Commission noted (para. 520) that the easier it is to find technicians to service a product, the more customers will buy it, and the more customers buy it, the more technicians will learn to service it, thus making it even more popular with customers, and so on.

[482] AT.39740, *Google Search (Shopping)* 27 June 2017, paras. 292–296. Google did not challenge the finding of dominance in the general search services market in Case T-612/17, *Google Shopping* EU:T:2021:763, although the GC referenced network effects in confirming that Google's behaviour constituted an abuse (see paras. 178 and 226).

In *United Brands*, the Commission considered that the undertaking's geographical price discrimination and export bans were evidence of its dominance, and the CJ said that its economic strength had 'enabled it to adopt a flexible overall strategy directed against new competitors'.[483] In *Eurofix-Bauco*, the Commission said that the undertaking's behaviour was 'witness to its ability to act independently of, and without due regard to, either competitors or customers . . . This behaviour and its economic consequences would not normally be seen where a company was facing real competitive pressure.'[484]

This reasoning causes some concern on account of its circularity: the conduct leads to finding dominance, which leads to finding the conduct is an abuse because the undertaking is dominant. It may be justified, however, so long as caution is exercised. First, some conduct *is* impossible without market power. Secondly, some conduct may operate as a strategic entry barrier.[485] If the conditions of post-entry competition are an important factor in undertakings' decisions about entering markets, predatory behaviour may deter entry, and practices such as exclusive dealing, tying, and refusals to supply may foreclose markets to new entrants.[486] Industrial organisation theory, by emphasising the analysis of strategic competition, makes the incumbent undertakings' conduct a major consideration in assessing dominance. Giving a prime place to conduct in the assessment of market power is one reason why the issues of identifying dominance and of deciding whether such dominance has been abused cannot be neatly separated. The Guidance Paper states that the fact that the undertaking has made significant investments which entrants or competitors would have to match can constitute a barrier (citing in a footnote *United Brands*).[487]

m. An Unavoidable Trading Partner

The fact that an undertaking constitutes an 'unavoidable trading' partner for its customers, in the sense that customers must deal with that undertaking in order to source the required quantity or quality of a particular product within the marketplace, is recognised as a further barrier to entry.[488] In *Deutsche Bahn*, railway operators were described as being in a position of 'economic dependence' on the supplier of rail services.[489] The very large gas reserves held by Gazprom rendered it an unavoidable trading partner for large parts of domestic consumption in Central and East European countries.[490] In *British Airways*, the GC confirmed the Commission's finding that BA was an 'obligatory business partner' for travel agents.[491] Given BA's leading position on the UK air transport market, it was imperative that travel agents could offer their customers BA tickets. An undertaking can therefore be an unavoidable trading partner, not because there is no other source of its product or service, but because it has become a 'must-stock' product, perhaps as the result of advertising, marketing, and/or product differentiation, as was found in *Intel*.[492]

[483] Case 27/76, *United Brands* EU:C:1978:22, para. 121.
[484] [1988] OJ L65/19 at recital 71. See similarly *ECS/AKZO* [1985] OJ L374/1 at recital 56, upheld in Case C-62/86, *AKZO* EU:C:1991:286, para. 61. [485] See Chap. 3, Section 5.B.
[486] For discussion of these practices as abuses, see Chap. 7. [487] Guidance Paper, para. 17.
[488] Case 85/76, *Hoffmann-La Roche* EU:C:1979:36, para. 41.
[489] Case T-229/94, *Deutsche Bahn* EU:T:1997:155, para. 57.
[490] AT39816, *Upstream gas supplies in Central and Eastern Europe (Gazprom)* 24 May 2018, para. 34.
[491] Case T-219/99, *British Airways* EU:T:2003:343, para. 217, upholding *Virgin/BA* [2000] OJ L30/1, para. 92.
[492] COMP/37.990, *Intel* 13 May 2009.

D. COUNTERVAILING BUYER POWER

Countervailing buyer power is mentioned in the third indent of paragraph 12 of the Guidance Paper.[493] As the essence of dominance is defined as the independence of an undertaking from, inter alia, its customers,[494] it follows that an undertaking constrained by a powerful buyer may not be dominant.[495] However, it is not enough that powerful buyers extract favourable terms from the supplier *for themselves*. In order to counter a finding of dominance, they must be able to protect *the market*, by defeating any price increase through paving the way for new entry or leading existing competitors to expand production. This is possible, for example, where the buying side is highly concentrated.[496] It is possible that powerful buyers who are able to get a good deal for themselves could constitute a market for market definition purposes separate from that of other customers.[497] The Guidance Paper says of countervailing buyer power:

> 18. Competitive constraints may be exerted not only by actual or potential competitors but also by customers. Even an undertaking with a high market share may not be able to act to an appreciable extent independently of customers with sufficient bargaining strength. . .. Such countervailing buying power may result from the customers' size or their commercial significance for the dominant undertaking, and their ability to switch quickly to competing suppliers, to promote new entry or to vertically integrate, and to credibly threaten to do so. If countervailing power is of a sufficient magnitude, it may deter or defeat an attempt by the undertaking to profitably increase prices. Buyer power may not, however, be considered a sufficiently effective constraint if it only ensures that a particular or limited segment of customers is shielded from the market power of the dominant undertaking.

In *Prokent/Tomra*,[498] a supplier of reverse vending machines with over 70 per cent of the relevant markets argued that it was constrained by the power of its customers, the supermarkets, and other retail outlets. The Commission said that concentration on the demand side was much lower than on the supply side.

> **COMP/38.113, *Prokent Tomra* 29 March 2006**
>
> Commission
>
> 89. The existence of buyer power on the demand side requires that there are either credible alternative suppliers to which the customers could turn, or that customers are able to sponsor new entrants. However, in the absence of established competitors which achieve significant and stable market

[493] On the role of buyer power in market power analysis generally, see I. Herrera Anchustegui, *Buyer Power in EU Competition Law* (Institute of Competition Law, 2017).

[494] Case 85/76, *Hoffmann-La Roche* EU:C:1979:36, para. 38.

[495] See Case T-228/97, *Irish Sugar* EU:T:1999:246, paras. 97–104.

[496] As e.g. in the merger cases, M/1225, *Enso/Stora*; M.495, *Behringwerke/Armour Pharmaceutical*. In *Irish Sugar* [1997] OJ L258/1, paras. 97–98, however, the GC held that where a supplier controls over 90% of a market, the presence of one or more large customers is not capable of affecting the dominant position of the supplier where there are a number of customers who are not equally strong and whose demand cannot be aggregated.

[497] Discussion Paper, para. 42. The Notice on the definition of the relevant market, para. 43, acknowledges that the ability of an undertaking to price discriminate may put customers in different markets. For the technique of market definition where there is market power on the demand side, see I. Kokkoris, 'Buyer Power Assessment in Competition Law: A Boon or a Menace?' (2006) 29 *World Competition* 139.

[498] On appeal, Case T-155/06, *Tomra* EU:T:2010:370, the dominance point was not argued.

> shares, there cannot be a credible threat of even the largest customers moving all or a very large proportion of their requirements away from Tomra, by way of a bidding process or otherwise. Procurement of reverse vending equipment is not part of the core activities of retail groups. The circumstances of the case do not suggest that they are likely to act in a strategic manner in order to subsidise and actively build up competing suppliers to which large parts of the demand could be diverted. There is no evidence for any such behaviour of sponsoring new entry in the period under investigation. Moreover, such behaviour would have been prone to free riding, as building up a competitor would have resulted in a public good. Therefore, there was no substantial countervailing buyer power which would have been able to challenge Tomra's dominance in any of the markets concerned.

Nonetheless, even a monopoly buyer (monopsonist) may be unable to constrain effectively the behaviour of a dominant firm. This is notably so in respect of pharmaceutical companies and national health services.[499] In *AstraZeneca*, the argument that AZ was constrained by the public authorities which paid for the drugs was dismissed after analysis of the way in which AZ's first-mover advantages enabled it to maintain both high prices and high market share.[500] Conversely, the fact that the seller is itself a monopolist does not necessarily prevent effective countervailing buyer power from emerging. In *MEO*, Advocate General Wahl doubted whether the defendant—a collecting society with a *de facto* but no legal monopoly in Portugal—actually held a dominant position, in the light of factual evidence which indicated that its large customers exercised significant negotiating power in setting tariffs.[501]

In *Motorola*, the Commission distinguished countervailing buyer power from *bargaining* power. The SEP case against Motorola was initiated by a complaint from Apple, a would-be licensee, and Motorola claimed there was therefore countervailing buyer power. The Commission dismissed this, saying that 'Motorola's interpretation of countervailing buyer power would mean that it would be impossible to establish the existence of a dominant position in cases where the conduct is directed against a purchaser that is economically strong on a market for a product the dominant undertaking needs access to for its own activities'.[502] It is possible for both seller and buyer to be dominant within the meaning of Article 102.[503]

10. COLLECTIVE DOMINANCE

It was noted earlier that the reference to 'one or more undertakings' within Article 102 gives rise to the possibility that a position of dominance may be held (and abused) collectively by two or more otherwise independent undertakings. The concept of collective dominance initially arose in respect of undertakings which were linked by licences or agreements. However, in the first case in which the

[499] In the UK case *Genzyme*, where there was only one drug efficacious in treating a rare disease, the CAT described the monopoly buyer, the NHS, as being in a 'relatively weak' bargaining position, *Genzyme Ltd v OFT* [2004] CAT 4, para. 250. There was no alternative to Genzyme's Cerezyme for treating Gaucher's Disease patients, and without it they would die. A similar approach was taken by the CAT subsequently in Cases 1275–1276/1/12/17, *Flynn and Pfizer* [2018] CAT 11.

[500] COMP/37.507, *Generics/AstraZeneca* 15 June 2005, upheld Case T-321/05, *AstraZeneca* EU:T:2010:266, paras. 256–268, *aff'd* Case C-457/10 P, *AstraZeneca* EU:C:2012:770, paras. 178–180.

[501] Case C-525/16, *MEO* EU:C:2017:1020, Wahl AG, paras. 50–52. The point was not addressed by the CJ in its preliminary ruling, EU:C:2018:942.

[502] COMP/39.985, *Motorola—Enforcement of GPRS Standard Essential Patents* 29 April 2014, para. 246.

[503] Ibid., citing Case T-219/99, *British Airways* EU:T:2003:343, para. 102.

concept was accepted, *Flat Glass*,[504] the GC spoke, broadly, of entities 'united by such *economic links* that . . . together they hold a dominant position vis-à-vis the other operators on the same market'.[505] This raised the possibility that a collective dominant position could be held by legally independent undertakings which operate on an oligopolistic market. Oligopolies present great problems for competition laws. As explained in Chapter 9, undertakings on oligopolistic markets may act in parallel without expressly colluding but, rather, recognising their 'interdependence', instead 'tacitly' collude. Such tacit collusion is not caught by Article 101. Therefore, if 'economic links' include the interdependence of undertakings on an oligopolistic market, Article 102 might provide a way to address the 'oligopoly problem'.

The issue of oligopolies also arises in merger control. The concept of a 'dominant position' appears not only in Article 102 but also in the EUMR.[506] It was important to know whether the concept in the EUMR covered collective as well as single dominance. If it did, the EUMR covered the creation and strengthening of a collective dominant position, and thus could be applied to prevent anti-competitive oligopolistic market structures from being created or strengthened.[507]

Following the *Flat Glass* judgment, there was a stream of cases both on Article 102 and the EUMR. The EU Courts have cited their merger judgments in Article 102 cases and vice versa, so the development of collective dominance in the both contexts is inextricably intertwined. The case law, which must be read as a whole, establishes that collective dominance comprises two principal types.

- 'Non-oligopolistic'[508] or 'expressly or pure collusive' ('traditional')[509] collective dominance, involving contractual, commercial, or structural links between the parties, or direct or indirect contact. The parties may operate on an oligopolistic market, but their collusion is express rather than tacit.
- 'Oligopolistic' collective dominance, which arises on tightly oligopolistic markets where the undertakings can coordinate their behaviour without express collusion and have the incentive to do so.

Given the importance of the concept of oligopolistic collective dominance in respect of tacit collusion and of mergers, the relevant case law is discussed in Chapters 9 and 15. We set out here some points about non-oligopolistic collective dominance. The starting point is *Flat Glass*, in which the Commission found that three Italian glass producers infringed Article 101(1) by concluding agreements to, inter alia, fix prices and sales quotas, and also infringed Article 102 by abusing a collective dominant position. The Commission did not, however, adduce additional evidence to establish the latter infringement beyond that relied on under Article 101.[510] On appeal, the GC quashed the finding of breach of Article 102, on the grounds that it was insufficient simply to recycle the Article 101 infringement in order to establish abuse of collective dominance. Nevertheless, the GC indicated that

[504] Cases T-68, 77, and 78/89, *Società Italiano Vetro SpA v Commission* EU:T:1992:38 (the *Italian Flat Glass Cartel* appeal), paras. 357–358; Cases C-395 and 396/96 P, *Compagnie Maritime Belge Transports* EU:C:2000:132; Cases T-191 and 212–214/98, *Atlantic Container Line* EU:T:2003:245, para. 595.

[505] Cases T-68, 77, and 78/89, *Società Italiano Vetro* EU:T:1992:38, para. 358 (emphasis added).

[506] Council Reg. 139/2004 [2004] OJ L124/1, on the control of concentrations between undertakings, Art. 2(2) and (3), previously Council Reg. 4064/89 [1989] OJ L395/1.

[507] The Commission's stretching of the collective dominance concept to deal with the situation where a merger has anti-competitive effects without creating or strengthening a single dominant position was the subject of Case T-342/99, *Airtours* EU:T:2002:146. The importance of dominance in respect of the EUMR was lessened by the changes made in Art. 2(2) and (3) by Reg. 139/2004, see further Chaps. 9 and 15.

[508] See R. Nazzini, *The Foundations of European Union Competition Law: The Objectives and Principles of Article 102* (Oxford University Press, 2011), Chap. 11; Faull and Nikpay, n. 164, 4.220–4.240.

[509] See Ortiz Blanco, n. 170, Chap. 10.

[510] *Flat Glass* [1989] OJ L33/44.

Article 102 *could* in principle apply to the collective conduct of independent undertakings, and so was not confined merely to undertakings within the same corporate group.

In a series of decisions involving shipowners that were members of liner conferences, the Commission applied the concept of collective dominance to undertakings bound by contractual links. In *French-West African Shipowners' Committees*, the Commission imposed fines on shipowners that participated in cargo-sharing systems on international routes. The Committees monitored the quota systems and penalised members that exceeded the quotas without approval. The Commission found that these agreements infringed Article 101(1),[511] and could not be exempted under Article 101(3) or the existing block exemption for liner conferences.[512] In addition, it held that the shipowners had infringed Article 102. As a result of the conference, the shipowners presented a united front to shippers, so that their position on the market had to be assessed collectively. Since the Committees had been set up by a group of shipowners covering virtually the entire market, the agreement resulted in the creation of collective dominance. Their practices, which endeavoured to eliminate effective competition for non-Committee shipping lines, constituted an abuse within the meaning of Article 102(b), by limiting the supply of liner services available.

Similarly, in *CEWAL*[513] and *TACA*,[514] the Commission found that members of a liner conference were collectively dominant on certain international shipping routes from Northern Europe. Again, the agreements enabled the undertakings to present a united front to customers. Although it was not strictly necessary to use Article 102 since Article 101 was applicable, the cases fitted neatly within the formulation in *Flat Glass* as the parties were united by 'economic links'. The GC in the *TACA* appeal held that these links (a common tariff, enforcement provisions and penalties, a secretariat, and annual business plans) were 'capable of justifying a collective assessment of the position on the relevant market of the members of that conference for the purposes of the application of Article [102], insofar as those links are such as to allow them to adopt together, as a single entity which presents itself as such on the market vis-à-vis users and competitors, the same line of conduct on that market'.[515] It furthermore stated that it was not a necessary requirement, in order to establish the existence of a collective dominant position, that the elimination of effective competition, as stipulated in *Airtours*,[516] must result in the elimination of *all* competition between the undertakings concerned.[517]

The concept of collective dominance was extended in *Irish Sugar*,[518] in which the Commission found Irish Sugar to be collectively dominant with one of its distributors. Here, the producer and distributor were linked *vertically* by agreements and other factors (such as close management relationships), which created a clear parallelism of interest, including a significant equity holding by Irish Sugar in the distributor. The links between the companies were very strong, and only just failed to satisfy the requirements for a single economic entity.[519] Collective dominance was similarly found to exist in *Almelo*, which involved Dutch regional electricity distributors.[520]

[511] The object and effect of the agreements was to share markets amongst the members and to limit the supply of transport services available, contrary to Art. 101(1)(c) and (b), respectively.

[512] Reg. 4056/86. [513] [1993] OJ L34/20.

[514] [1999] OJ L95/1. The finding of collective dominance was upheld on appeal, but the finding of abuse and fines were annulled, see Cases T-191 and 214–216/98, *Atlantic Container Line* EU:T:2003:245, but see the Commission's revised decision [2003] OJ L26/53.

[515] Cases T-191 and 214–216/98, *Atlantic Container Line* EU:T:2003:245, para. 602.

[516] Case T-342/99, *Airtours* EU:T:2002:146, para. 63.

[517] Cases T-191 and 212–214/98, *Atlantic Container Line* EU:T:2003:245, para. 130.

[518] [1997] OJ L25/1. The GC upheld the finding of collective dominance: Case T-228/97, *Irish Sugar* EU:T:1999:246.

[519] Case T-228/97, *Irish Sugar* EU:T:1999:246, para. 28.

[520] Case C-393/92, *Almelo* EU:C:1994:171, para. 42. See also Case C-140/94, *DIP v Comune di Bassano del Grappa* EU:C:1995:330, para. 27.

The most significant statement of what constitutes a position of collective dominance under Article 102 is *Compagnie Maritime Belge*,[521] the appeal from the *CEWAL* decision. Here, the CJ said that a collective dominant position could be held by undertakings which 'present themselves or act together on a particular market as a collective entity',[522] which is established by examining the economic links or factors which give rise to a connection between them.[523] It must then be decided whether that collective entity holds a dominant position.[524] Although the undertakings involved in the CEWAL liner conference were linked by express agreements, the CJ said that the existence of such agreements or other links in law was not indispensable to a finding of collective dominance.[525] Because of its importance in developing the application of collective dominance to tacit collusion, the judgment is discussed further in Chapter 9.

Sports organisations may hold a collective dominant position. In *Laurent Piau*, the GC said that it was 'unrealistic' to claim that FIFA could not be in a collective dominant position in respect of the market for football players' agents' services. It was irrelevant that FIFA was not itself an economic operator buying such services, as it was the emanation of the national associations and the clubs, which did.[526]

Finally, difficult cases arise where allegations of a collective dominant position follow from national legislation or regulation. These have typically been rejected by the CJ, mainly because the measures concerned did not cause the undertakings to cease to compete with one another.[527]

11. CONCLUSIONS

1. Article 102 is a powerful regulatory tool. Its application has suffered, however, from the lack of a proper theoretical framework and from confused policy goals. Protecting competitors for their own sake, or even to protect the competitive process, can lead to consumer detriment by penalising efficient conduct. The more economic approach to enforcing Article 102 aims to avoid the danger of too many 'false positive' errors, i.e. over-enforcement which chills competition and harms consumers. Yet an undue focus on hard-to-satisfy economic standards may conversely result in under-enforcement against dominant firm behaviour.

2. The Commission had initially intended to publish Guidelines on Article 102, similar to those published in respect of Article 101 and of mergers, setting out its concept of an abuse in a consumer welfare-focused manner and using effects-based analysis. Instead, it limited itself, at first, to 'Guidance' as to its 'enforcement priorities'. Although the Guidance Paper states that it is not a statement of the law, it is difficult not to read the document as an explanation of what the Commission understands the concept of abuse to constitute.

3. The approach taken by the Guidance Paper received a mixed reception in the EU Courts. Some cases decided since its publication have taken a notably different approach, but there are issues on which the EU Courts and the Commission agree. Generally, it seems that the Courts are increasingly persuaded of the merits of the 'more economic approach' to Article 102.

[521] Cases C-395 and 396/96 P, *Compagnie Maritime Belge* EU:C:2000:132. [522] Ibid., para. 36.
[523] Ibid., para. 41. [524] Ibid., para. 39. [525] Ibid., para. 45.
[526] Case T-193/02, *Laurent Piau* EU:T:2005:22, paras. 112–116. This was a case, like *Atlantic Container Line*, where, although dealing with a situation where there were express agreements between the parties concerned, the GC made important statements which relate to tacit collusion and oligopolistic collective dominance.
[527] See Case C-96/94, *Centro Servizi Spediporto v Spedizioni Marritima del Golfo* EU:C:1995:308; Case C-140/94, *DIP v Comune di Bassano del Grappa* EU:C:1995:330; and Case C-70/95, *Sodemare v Regione Lombardia* EU:C:1997:301.

4. Reflecting concerns about under-enforcement, in 2023 the Commission unexpectedly issued Amendments to its Guidance Paper. Although some of the changes merely reflect the jurisprudence, others clearly indicate that the more economic approach has fallen out of favour with the Commission. Moreover, the Commission is once again hoping to issue Guidelines on Article 102, with the intention to have these in place by 2025.

5. The definition in the case law of what constitutes a 'dominant position' is usually interpreted as substantial market power which enables the undertaking concerned to profitably raise prices above the competitive level over a significant period of time.

6. The way that dominance is assessed under Article 102 puts great emphasis on market shares. However, market definition is an inexact science, which places products either in a market or outside it, whereas in reality there are degrees of substitution. Further, market shares are a static measurement that does not reflect dynamic developments in the market and potential competition.

7. The situation is exacerbated by the broad approach taken to barriers to entry and expansion.

8. There is a risk that undertakings may be found to be in a dominant position when in reality they do not have significant market power.

9. Dominance has been found in EU law at market shares of 40 per cent. Moreover, the EU Courts and the Commission have not ruled out finding dominance below that point. There are good arguments for a dominance 'screen' or 'safe harbour', whereby undertakings with market shares below a certain point would have the legal certainty of knowing they were not subject to Article 102.

10. The collective dominance concept permits the application of Article 102 to the activities of two or more otherwise independent undertakings that commit an abuse collectively. Its requirements are difficult to satisfy, however, and the concept plays a very limited role in contemporary Article 102 jurisprudence.

12. FURTHER READING

A. Books

Akman, P., *The Concept of Abuse in EU Competition Law* (Hart Publishing, 2012), Chap. 2

Ehlermann, C.-D., and Marquis, M. (eds.), *European Competition Law Annual 2007: A Reformed Approach to Article 82* (Hart Publishing, 2008)

Faull, J., and Nikpay, A. (eds.), *The EU Law of Competition* (3rd edn, Oxford University Press, 2014), Chap. 4

Herrera Anchustegui, I., *Buyer Power in EU Competition Law* (Institute of Competition Law, 2017)

Ibáñez Colomo, P., *The Shaping of EU Competition Law* (Cambridge University Press, 2018), Chap. 4

Joliet, R., *Monopolization and Abuse of Dominant Position* (Nijhoff, 1970)

Kokkoris, I., *A Gap in the Enforcement of Article 82* (BIICL, 2009)

Nazzini, R., *The Foundations of European Union Competition Law: The Objectives and Principles of Article 102* (Oxford University Press, 2011), Chaps. 4 and 11

O'Donoghue, R., and Padilla, A. J., *The Law and Economics of Article 102* (3rd edn, Hart Publishing, 2020), Chaps. 1 and 2

Ortiz Blanco, L., *Market Power in EU Antitrust Law* (Hart Publishing, 2012), Chap. 10

Pace, L. F. (ed.), *European Competition Law: The Impact of the Commission's Guidance on Article 102* (Edward Elgar, 2011)

ROUSSEVA, E., *Rethinking Exclusionary Abuses in EU Competition Law* (Hart Publishing, 2010), Chap. 1

VAN DEN BERGH, R. J., *Comparative Competition Law and Economics* (Edward Elgar, 2017), Chap. 7

B. Chapters in Books

LIANOS, I., 'Categorical Thinking in Competition Law and the Effects-based Approach in Article 82' in A. Ezrachi (ed.), *Article 82 EC: Reflections on its Recent Evolution* (Hart Publishing, 2009), 19

MESTMÄCKER, E.-J., 'The Development of German and European Competition Law with Special Reference to the EU Commission's Article 82 Guidelines of 2008' in L. F. Pace (ed.), *European Competition Law: The Impact of the Commission's Guidance on Article 102* (Edward Elgar, 2011), 43

C. Articles

AHLBORN, C., EVANS, D. S., and PADILLA, A. J., 'Competition Policy in the New Economy: Is European Competition Law up to the Challenge?' [2001] *ECLR* 156

AKMAN, P., 'The European Commission's Guidance on Article 102 TFEU: From *Inferno* to *Paradiso*' (2010) 73 *MLR* 605

ALLAN, B., 'Article 102: A Commentary on DG Competition's Discussion Paper' [2006] *Competition Policy International* 43

AZEVEDO, J. P., and WALKER, M., 'Dominance: Meaning and Measurement' [2002] *ECLR* 363

BABAYEV, R., 'Duality of Economic Freedom Protection in the Interplay of Article 16 CFR and Article 102 TFEU' (2020) 45 *ELRev* 694

BADEN FULLER, C. W., 'Article 86 EEC: Economic Analysis of the Existence of a Dominant Position' (1979) 4 *ELRev* 423

BAILEY, D., 'The New Frontiers of Article 102 TFEU: Antitrust Imperialism or Judicious Intervention?' (2018) 6 *J of Antitrust Enforcement* 25

BISHOP, W., and CAFFARRA, C., 'Editorial, Dynamic Competition and Aftermarkets' [1998] *ECLR* 265

BORK, R. H., and SIDAK, J. G., 'The Misuse of Profit Margins to Infer Market Power' (2013) 9 *J of Competition Law and Economics* 511

EILMANSBERGER, T., 'Dominance—The Lost Child? How the Effects-Based Rules Could and Should Change Dominance Analysis' (2006) 2 *European Law Journal* Special Issue 15

FJELL, K., and SØRGARD, L., 'How to Test for Abuse of Dominance?' (2006) 2 *European Law Journal* 69

GERADIN, D., 'Is the Guidance Paper on the Commission's Enforcement Priorities in Applying Article 102 TFEU to Abusive Exclusionary Conduct Useful?', <http://ssrn.com/abstract=1569502>

HARBORD, D., and HOEHN, T., 'Barriers to Entry and Exit in European Competition Policy' (1994) 14 *International Review of Law and Economics* 411

HARTMAN, R., TEECE, D., MITCHELL, W., and JORDE, T., 'Assessing Market Power in Regimes of Rapid Technological Change' (1993) 2 *Indus & Corp Change* 317

IBÁÑEZ COLOMO, P., 'Beyond the "More Economics-Based Approach": A Legal Perspective on Article 102 TFEU Case Law' (2016) 53 *CMLRev* 709

Ide, E., Montero, J.-P., and Figueroa, N., 'Discounts as a Barrier to Entry' (2016) 106 *Am Econ Rev* 1849

Kaplow, L., 'Market Definition, Market Power' (2015) 43 *International J of Industrial Organization* 148

Kellerbauer, M., 'The Commission's New Enforcement Priorities in Applying Article 82 EC to Dominant Companies' Exclusionary Conduct: A Shift Towards a More Economic Approach?' [2010] *ECLR* 175

Kokkoris, I., 'Buyer Power Assessment in Competition Law: A Boon or A Menace?' (2006) 29 *World Competition* 139

Kroes, N., 'Tackling Exclusionary Practices to Avoid Exploitation of Market Power: Some Preliminary Thoughts on the Policy Review of Article 82' [2005] *Fordham Corp L Inst* 381

Landes, D., and Posner, R. A., 'Market Power in Antitrust Cases' (1981) 94 *Harvard LR* 937

Lianos, I., and Motchenkova, E., 'Market Dominance and Search Quality in the Search Engine Market' (2013) 9 *J of Competition Law and Economics* 419

Lovdahl Gormesen, L., 'Why the European Commission's Enforcement Priorities on Article 82 Should Be Withdrawn' [2010] *ECLR* 45

Monti, G., 'The Concept of Dominance in Article 82' (2006) 2 *European Competition Journal* 31

Möschel, W., 'Market Definition with Branded Goods and Private Label Products' [2014] *ECLR* 29

Nazzini, R., 'The Wood Began to Move: An Essay on Consumer Welfare, Evidence and Burden of Proof in Article 82 EC Cases' (2006) 31 *ELRev* 518

Newman, J., 'Antitrust in Zero-price Markets: Applications' (2016) 94 *Wash Univ LR* 49

Niels, G., and Ralston, H., 'Two-sided Market Definition: Some Common Understandings' (2021) 17 *European Competition Journal* 118

Petit, N., 'From Formalism to Effects—The Commission's Communication on Enforcement Priorities in Applying Article 82 EC' (2009) 32 *World Competition* 485

Robertson, V., 'The Relevant Market in Competition Law: A Legal Concept' (2019) 7 *J of Antitrust Enforcement* 158

Schepp, N.-P., and Wambach, A., 'On Big Data and Its Relevance for Market Power Assessment' (2016) 7 *JECLAP* 120

Schmalensee, R., 'Entry Deterrence in the Ready-to-eat Breakfast Cereal Industry' (1978) 9 *Bell J Econ* 305

Schmalensee, R., 'Product Differentiation Advantages of Pioneering Brands' (1981) 72 *Am Econ Rev* 349

Schmalensee, R., 'Another Look at Market Power' (1981–1982) 95 *Harvard LR* 1789

Schmalensee, R., 'Ease of Entry: Has the Concept Been Applied too Readily?' (1987) 56 *Antitrust LJ* 41

Shapiro, C., 'Aftermarkets and Consumer Welfare: Making Sense of *Kodak*' (1995) 63 *Antitrust LJ* 483

Sher, B., 'The Last of the Steam-powered Trains: Modernising Article 82' [2004] *ECLR* 243

Solek, L., 'Need to Revise or Apply the Concept of Market Definition with a View to "Zero-price" and Overarching Markets' (2021) 12 *JECLAP* 593

Spence, M., 'Notes on Advertising, Economies of Scale and Entry Barriers' (1980) 95 *Quart J of Econ* 493

Stucke, M., and Ezrachi, A., 'When Competition Fails to Optimise Quality: A Look at Search Engines' (2016) 18 *Yale J of L & Tech* 70

Teece, D., and Coleman, M., 'The Meaning of Monopoly: Antitrust Analysis in High-technology Industries' [1998] *Ant Bull* 801

Temple Lang, J., 'Monopolisation and the Definition of "Abuse" of a Dominant Position under Article 86 EEC Treaty' (1979) 16 *CMLRev* 345

Vickers, J., 'Market Power in Competition Cases' (2006) 2 *European Competition Journal* Special Issue 3

Werden, G. J., 'Competition Policy on Exclusionary Conduct: Towards an Effects-based Analysis' (2006) 2 *European Competition Journal* 53

Westin, J., 'Defining Relevant Market in the Pharmaceutical Sector in the Light of the *Losec* Case—Just How Different is the Pharmaceutical Market?' [2011] *ECLR* 57

7

ARTICLE 102 TFEU: CONDUCT WHICH CAN BE AN ABUSE

1. CENTRAL ISSUES

1. The main concern of the Commission in applying Article 102 has been with 'exclusionary' rather than 'exploitative' abuses. The definition of exclusionary abuse, laid down in *Hoffmann-La Roche*, involves a difficult distinction between 'competition on the merits' and conduct which is abusive.
2. The EU Courts have held that dominant undertakings have a 'special responsibility' to protect the competitive process. That principle has impacted significantly on the type of conduct which has been held to be abusive.
3. The Guidance on the Commission's Enforcement Priorities in Applying Article 102 addresses only exclusionary abuses, covering in detail the main categories: predatory pricing, exclusive dealing, discounts and rebates, tying, and refusal to supply.
4. The Guidance Paper adopts a concept of *anti-competitive foreclosure* to identify those cases which are an enforcement priority for the Commission. This has two elements, exclusion of competitors and harm to consumers.
5. The Guidance Paper adopts the 'as efficient competitor' (AEC) test in respect of pricing abuses. The CJ has adopted the AEC test for predatory pricing and margin squeeze, and considers it one tool amongst others in respect of rebates.
6. The EU predatory pricing rules centre on the AEC test. The Guidance Paper adopts a 'sacrifice' test for predatory pricing.
7. The conduct of dominant undertakings may infringe Article 102 even where it has been approved by national sector regulators. This has been shown in cases on 'margin squeeze' in the telecommunications sector.
8. Initially, the application of Article 102 to exclusive dealing and rebates treated some of these practices as virtually per se abuses ('by object' abuses) and others as requiring a capability of restricting competition. The Guidance Paper considers their likely or actual effects rather than their form. This is also the approach following the *Intel* and *Unilever* cases, which suggest a more economic approach to exclusive dealing.
9. Tying and bundling practices aim to leverage power from the dominated market into adjacent sectors for complementary products or services. Recent cases have focused on technical tying in digital markets, whereby two elements were integrated into the product sold to the consumer.

10. The idea that it can be an abuse for a dominant undertaking to refuse to supply another party clashes with fundamental notions of freedom of contract. There is also a danger that it may be harmful to consumer welfare as it may discourage innovation and investment. Nevertheless, the case law establishes that in certain situations it can be an abuse for a dominant undertaking to refuse to supply. These mainly concern competitors on downstream markets. There is a special problem over vertically integrated undertakings and the licensing of intellectual property rights (IPRs).
11. Self-preferencing arises where a dominant platform operator gives preferential treatment to its own products or services when these are in competition with products and services provided by other entities using the platform. It has emerged as a leading theory of harm in digital markets.
12. The Commission has paid less attention to exploitative abuses. The paradigmatic exploitative abuse is the charging of unfair prices. There is great difficulty in assessing whether a price is excessive. It is a question of assessing whether the price is excessive in relation to the 'economic value' of the product in issue.
13. Article 102(c) specifically prohibits discrimination which puts the other trading parties at a competitive disadvantage. Price discrimination may be welfare-enhancing or otherwise, depending on the circumstances of the case.
13. Refusals to supply, and certain other practices, may be abusive simply on the grounds that they prevent or hinder parallel trade between Member States. This theory of harm links to EU competition law's role in promoting market integration in the EU.
14. In principle, even a prima facie abuse of dominance can be defended by reference to valid objective justifications. Two main categories are recognised: claims of objective necessity, and of countervailing efficiencies. In practice, however, defendants face a high hurdle to justify ostensibly abusive conduct.

2. INTRODUCTION

In this chapter, we consider the meaning of 'abuse' in Article 102 and examine the types of conduct which may constitute an abuse.[1] This must be seen in the context of the objectives of EU competition law in general and of Article 102 in particular, as discussed in Chapters 1 and 6.

In Chapter 6, we explained that, from the mid-2000s, the Commission embarked upon a review of Article 102 aimed at 'modernising' its application. This culminated in the Guidance Paper on enforcement priorities in respect of exclusionary abuses.[2] The motivation was a belief that Article 102 should be applied to pursue a consumer welfare objective rather than to protect competition and particular competitors for their own sakes. The Commission advocated an effects-based, rather than a form-based, approach to the application of Article 102. However, a series of Amendments to the Guidance

[1] See generally Bellamy and Child (D. Bailey and L. John, eds.), *European Union Law of Competition* (8th edn, Oxford University Press, 2018), Chap. 10; J. Faull and A. Nikpay (eds.), *The EU Law of Competition* (3rd edn, Oxford University Press, 2014), Chap. 4; R. O'Donoghue and A. J. Padilla, *The Law and Economics of Article 102* (3rd edn, Hart Publishing, 2020).

[2] Guidance on the Commission's Enforcement Priorities in Applying Article 82 of the EC Treaty to Abusive Exclusionary Conduct by Dominant Undertakings [2009] OJ C45/2 (the Guidance Paper).

Paper, adopted in 2023, suggest a more recent movement away from an economics-oriented approach to enforcement.[3] The extent to which the effects-based approach is reflected in past and present enforcement practice under Article 102 will be considered throughout this chapter.

The enforcement of Article 102 has seen, and continues to provide the context for, some of the most hotly disputed cases in the realm of EU competition law. Most obviously, we see here the greatest disparity with the interpretation of the equivalent provision of US antitrust law governing unilateral conduct, namely s. 2 of the Sherman Act.[4] In this regard, it should be acknowledged that there has been considerable criticism of the narrowness of the contemporary application of s. 2, suggesting that the root of the division does not lie solely on this side of the Atlantic.[5] The Commission's ambitious application of Article 102 to novel forms of abuse, often within markets already subject to considerable *ex ante* regulation, or within the highly dynamic digital economy, has prompted claims of 'antitrust imperialism'.[6] As we shall see, the EU Courts historically have been reluctant to constrain the enforcement powers of the Commission under Article 102, yet they are increasingly receptive to a more exacting 'more economic approach' to its application.

3. THE MEANING OF ABUSE

A. GENERAL

Article 102 does not forbid the holding of a dominant position, but only the abuse thereof.[7] Even a dominant undertaking is permitted to compete vigorously and effectively, provided that it does so using what is referred to as 'competition on the merits'.[8] It has been said of the equivalent provision regulating unilateral conduct under the US Sherman Act that it requires 'monopoly power coupled not with building the better mousetrap, but monopoly power coupled with some impropriety'.[9] In this context, the meaning of 'abuse' is of vital importance. Although the term is not defined, Article 102 sets out what it 'may, in particular, consist in':

(a) directly or indirectly imposing unfair purchase or selling prices or other unfair trading conditions;

(b) limiting production, markets or technical development to the prejudice of consumers;

(c) applying dissimilar conditions to equivalent transactions with other trading parties, thereby placing them at a competitive disadvantage;

[3] Amendments to the Commission Guidance on the Commission's enforcement priorities in applying Article 82 of the EC Treaty to abusive exclusionary conduct by dominant undertakings, C(2023) 1923 final (Amendments to the Guidance Paper).

[4] An exploration is P. Larouche and M. P. Schinkel, 'Continental Drift in the Treatment of Dominant Firms: Article 102 TFEU in Contrast to §2 Sherman Act', TILEC Discussion Paper No. 2013-020.

[5] See e.g. J. Baker, J. Sallet, and F. Scott Morton, 'Unlocking Antitrust Enforcement' (2018) 127 *Yale LJ* 1916, and L. Khan and S. Vaheesan, 'Market Power and Inequality: The Antitrust Counterrevolution and its Discontents' (2017) 11 *Harvard L & Policy Rev* 235.

[6] D. Bailey, 'The New Frontiers of Article 102 TFEU: Antitrust Imperialism or Judicious Intervention?' (2018) 6 *J of Antitrust Enforcement* 25.

[7] Reiterated in Case C-209/10, *Post Danmark A/S v Konkurrencerådet (Post Danmark I)* EU:C:2012:172, para. 21; see also Case C-23/14, *Post Danmark A/S v Konkurrencerådet (Post Danmark II)* EU:C:2015:651, para. 67. In Case C-52/09, *TeliaSonera* EU:C:2011:83, para. 24, the CJ said, 'Whilst Article 102 TFEU does not prohibit an undertaking from acquiring, *on its own merits*, [emphasis added] the dominant position in a market', which could suggest that where the dominant position has been acquired otherwise, such as by the past conferment of a legal monopoly, special considerations might apply, and see E. Rousseva and M. Marquis, 'Hell Freezes Over: A Climate Change for Assessing Exclusionary Conduct under Article 102 TFEU' (2013) 4 *JECLAP* 32.

[8] See Section 3.E.

[9] P. Areeda, 'Essential Facilities: An Epithet in Need of Limiting Principles' (1989) 58 *Antitrust LJ* 841, 846.

(d) making the conclusion of contracts subject to acceptance by the other parties of supplementary obligations which, by their nature or according to commercial usage, have no connection with the subject of such contracts.

Unlike Article 101, there is no reference to conduct having as its 'object or effect the restriction of competition',[10] which could help to clarify why particular behaviour might constitute an abuse. Article 102 does not, therefore, indicate what 'theory of harm' it embodies.

B. TYPES OF ABUSE COVERED BY ARTICLE 102 TFEU

(i) Categories of Abuse

The principal categories of abuse are exploitation and exclusion. *Exploitative* abuses involve conduct whereby the dominant undertaking takes advantage of its market power to exploit its trading partners (customers or suppliers). *Exclusionary* abuses involve conduct whereby the dominant undertaking prevents or hinders competition on the market. In *Post Danmark I*, the CJ classified exclusionary abuses as 'practices that *cause consumers harm* through their impact on competition'.[11] *Discrimination* abuses, whereby the dominant undertaking applies discriminatory prices or conditions to its customers or suppliers, thereby creating a 'competitive disadvantage', are covered by Article 102(c). Conduct which inhibits *integration within the internal market* has occasionally been held abusive.[12] Finally, causing harm to *innovation*, without necessarily excluding competitors, arguably constitutes a stand-alone type of abuse.[13]

These categories—exploitative, exclusionary, discriminatory, and market integration-oriented abuses—are not mutually exclusive. The same conduct may be exploitative *and* may make it more difficult for a competitor to access the market, or may be exclusionary *and* discriminatory. For example, discriminatory prices offered to customers may also exclude competitors by charging lower prices to customers who might otherwise purchase from the competitor.[14] Limiting production and tying practices can simultaneously exploit customers and exclude competitors. Conduct aimed at dividing the internal market may be exclusionary where it excludes a competing distributor,[15] or exploitative where the object is to charge higher prices to consumers.[16]

C. ARTICLE 102 COVERS EXPLOITATIVE AND EXCLUSIONARY ABUSES

(i) The Continental Can Case

Article 102 clearly covers abusive exploitation and discrimination, as these are expressly provided for in Article 102(a) and Article 102(c), respectively. It was initially unclear, however, whether 'abuse'[17]

[10] An omission noted explicitly by the GC in Case T-612/17, *Google Shopping* EU:T:2021:763, para. 435.

[11] Case C-209/10, *Post Danmark I* EU:C:2012:172, para. 20 (emphasis added).

[12] See Cases C-468–478/06, *Sot. Lélos* EU:C:2008:504 and AT.40134, *AB InBev beer trade restrictions* 13 May 2019.

[13] See P. Ibáñez Colomo, 'Restrictions on Innovation in EU Competition Law' (2016) 41 *ELRev* 201. See e.g. Case T-201/04, *Microsoft* EU:T:2007:289, and aspects of Case T-612/17, *Google Shopping* EU:T:2021:763 and Case T-604/18, *Google Android* EU:T:2022:541.

[14] See e.g. Case C-95/04 P, *British Airways* EU:C:2007:166.

[15] As in Cases C-468–478/06, *Sot. Lélos* EU:C:2008:504.

[16] Case 226/84, *British Leyland* EU:C:1986:421, and more recently, AT.40703, *Amazon Buy Box* 20 December 2022.

[17] '. . . d'exploiter de façon abusive' in French; '*mibbräuchliche Ausnutzung*' in German.

went beyond this and covered conduct which had structural effects on competition by excluding or disadvantaging competitors, i.e. exclusionary abuses.[18] The argument was exemplified by an early debate between the scholars René Joliet and E.-J. Mestmäcker. Joliet argued that the prohibition of conduct because of its structural effects would be tantamount to the prohibition of a dominant position in itself, which was not the purpose of Article 102. Rather, its purpose was solely to control the abusive exploitation of existing power.[19] Mestmäcker, an Ordoliberal, argued that abuse could also involve conduct restricting the competition remaining on the dominated market, by preventing or hindering current or potential competition.[20]

The Commission, for its part, agreed that Article 102 *could* be applied to prohibit conduct affecting the structure of the market.[21] In 1972—before the Commission had a tailor-made system of merger control[22]—it issued its decision in *Continental Can*, finding that merger involving a dominant undertaking breached Article 102.[23] On appeal, the CJ confirmed this broad view of abuse.[24]

Case 6/72, *Europemballage Corp and Continental Can Co Inc v Commission* EU:C:1973:22

Continental Can manufactured metal packaging. It acquired an 85.8 per cent share in a metal can manufacturer, SLW. Through SLW, it formed a wholly owned subsidiary, Europemballage, through which it acquired TDV, another can manufacturer. The Commission adopted a decision holding that this was contrary to Article 86 (now Article 102). It held that, through SLW, Continental Can had dominant positions in several markets for light packaging, and that, by the purchase of a majority shareholding in TDV, Continental Can had abused this dominance by practically eliminating competition in the relevant market.

Court of Justice

20. Article 86(1) of the Treaty says, 'Any abuse by one or more undertakings of a dominant position within the common market or in a substantial part of it shall be prohibited as incompatible with the common market in so far as it may affect trade between Member States'. The question is whether the word 'abuse' in Article 86 refers only to practices of undertakings which may directly affect the market and are detrimental to production or sales, to purchasers or consumers, or whether this word refers also to changes in the structure of an undertaking, which lead to competition being seriously disturbed in a substantial part of the Common Market.

21. The distinction between measures which concern the structure of the undertaking and practices which affect the market cannot be decisive, for any structural measure may influence market conditions, if it increases the size and the economic power of the undertaking.

[18] See the debate about the origins of Art. 102 in e.g. P. Behrens, 'The Ordoliberal Concept of "Abuse" of a Dominant Position and its Impact on Article 102 TFEU', <http://ssrn.com/abstract=2658045>; H. Schweitzer, 'The History, Interpretation and Underlying Principles of Section 2 Sherman Act and Article 82 EC' in C.-D. Ehlermann and M. Marquis (eds.), *European Competition Law Annual 2007: A Reformed Approach to Article 82* (Hart Publishing, 2008), 119; P. Akman, 'Searching for the Long-lost Soul of Article 82EC' (2009) 29 *OJLS* 267; and P. Akman, *The Concept of Abuse in EU Competition Law* (Hart Publishing, 2012).

[19] See R. Joliet, *Monopolization and Abuse of Dominant Position* (Nijhoff, 1970).

[20] See E.-J. Mestmäcker, 'Wettsbewerbsfreiheit und Wohlfahrt' (Freedom of Competition and Welfare), Max Planck Law Research Paper No. 12/2 (2012), <http://ssrn.com/abstract=1983193>.

[21] *Le Problème de la Concentration dans le Marché Commun*, Etudes CEE, Série Concurrence No. 3, 1966, particularly paras. 25–27.

[22] See Chap. 15. [23] *Continental Can* [1972] OJ L7/25. [24] Case 6/72, *Continental Can* EU:C:1973:22.

22. In order to answer this question, one has to go back to the spirit, general scheme and wording of Article 86, as well as to the system and objectives of the Treaty. . . .

23. Article 86 is part of the chapter devoted to the common rules on the Community's policy in the field of competition. This policy is based on Article 3(f) of the Treaty according to which the Community's activity shall include the institution of a system ensuring that competition in the Common Market is not distorted. The applicants' argument that this provision merely contains a general programme devoid of legal effect, ignores the fact that Article 3 considers the pursuit of the objectives which it lays down to be indispensable for the achievement of the Community's tasks. As regards in particular the aim mentioned in 3(f), the Treaty in several provisions contains more detailed regulations for the interpretation of which this aim is decisive.

24. But if Article 3(f) provides for the institution of a system ensuring that competition in the Common Market is not distorted, then it requires a fortiori that competition must not be eliminated. This requirement is so essential that without it numerous provisions of the Treaty would be pointless. Moreover, it corresponds to the precept of Article 2 of the Treaty according to which one of the tasks of the Community is 'to promote throughout the Community a harmonious development of economic activities'. Thus the restraints on competition which the Treaty allows under certain conditions because of the need to harmonize the various objectives of the Treaty, are limited by the requirements of Articles 2 and 3. Going beyond this limit involves the risk that the weakening of competition would conflict with the aims of the Common Market.

25. With a view to safeguarding the principles and attaining the objectives set out in Articles 2 and 3 of the Treaty, Articles 85 to 90 have laid down general rules applicable to undertakings. Article 85 concerns agreements between undertakings, decisions of associations of undertakings and concerted practices, while Article 86 concerns unilateral activity of one or more undertakings. Articles 85 and 86 seek to achieve the same aim on different levels, *viz.* the maintenance of effective competition within the Common Market. The restraint of competition which is prohibited if it is the result of behaviour falling under Article 85, cannot become permissible by the fact that such behaviour succeeds under the influence of a dominant undertaking and results in the merger of the undertakings concerned. In the absence of explicit provisions, one cannot assume that the Treaty, which prohibits in Article 85 certain decisions of ordinary associations of undertakings restricting competition without eliminating it, permits in Article 86 that undertakings, after merging into an organic unity, should reach such a dominant position that any serious chance of competition is practically rendered impossible. Such a diverse legal treatment would make a breach in the entire competition law which could jeopardize the proper functioning of the Common Market. If, in order to avoid the prohibitions in Article 85, it sufficed to establish such close connections between the undertakings that they escaped the prohibition of Article 85 without coming within the scope of that of Article 86, then, in contradiction to the basic principles of the Common Market, the partitioning of a substantial part of this market would be allowed. The endeavour of the authors of the Treaty to maintain in the market real or potential competition even in cases in which restraints on competition are permitted, was explicitly laid down in Article 85(3)(b) of the Treaty. Article 86 does not contain the same explicit provisions, but this can be explained by the fact that the system fixed there for dominant positions, unlike Article 85(3), does not recognize any exemption from the prohibition. With such a system the obligation to observe the basic objectives of the Treaty, in particular that of Article 3(f), results from the obligatory force of these objectives. In any case Articles 85 and 86 cannot be interpreted in such a way that they contradict each other, because they serve to achieve the same aim.

26. It is in the light of these considerations that the condition imposed by Article 86 is to be interpreted whereby in order to come within the prohibition a dominant position must have been abused. The provision states a certain number of abusive practices which it prohibits. The list merely gives examples, not an exhaustive enumeration of the sort of abuses of a dominant position prohibited by the Treaty. As may further be seen from letters I and (d) of Article 86(2), the provision is aimed not only at practices which may cause damage to consumers directly but also at those which are detrimental to

them through their impact on an effective competition structure, such as is mentioned in Article 3(f) of the Treaty. Abuse may therefore occur if an undertaking in a dominant position strengthens such position in such a way that the degree of dominance reached substantially fetters competition, i.e., that only undertakings remain in the market whose behaviour depends on the dominant one.

27. Such being the meaning and the scope of Article 86, of the EEC Treaty the question of the link of causality raised by the applicants which in their opinion has to exist between the dominant position and its abuse, is of no consequence, for the strengthening of the position of an undertaking may be an abuse and prohibited under Article 86 of the Treaty, regardless of the means and procedure by which it is achieved, if it has the effects mentioned above.

Continental Can is the foundational judgment on Article 102. First, it clarified that Article 102 does not set out an exhaustive list of prohibited conduct. This important principle has been repeated many times.[25] However, it has been argued that although it is 'very difficult to think of unilateral conduct that falls outside these four clauses of Article 102 TFEU and which should be subject to competition law', if there *was*, the principle of legal certainty would prevent the application of Article 102.[26] Rather, the salient point is that there is no limit to the *specific* forms of conduct which fall within the provisions. Article 102(a) is wide enough to encompass all exploitative behaviour, Article 102(b) can cover all exclusionary abuses,[27] Article 102(c) contains a wide non-discrimination principle, and Article 102(d) addresses tying and bundling.

Secondly, the CJ established that the object of Article 102 is not merely to protect consumers directly from the exploitation of market power, but also to protect them from conduct which, through its impact on the structure of competition, is detrimental indirectly. Therefore, Article 102 applies to exclusionary, as well as to exploitative, abuses. Paragraph 26 of *Continental Can* is one of the most important passages in EU competition law.

Thirdly, a merger could be prohibited irrespective of the fact that the dominant undertaking had not exploited, or otherwise used, its market power in concluding the transaction. Thus, conduct by a dominant undertaking may constitute an abuse even without use of market power.[28]

Fourthly, the *way* in which the CJ interpreted Article 102 was significant. In determining the scope of the provision, the Court looked to the basic objectives of the (then) Community, and construed Article 102 as a specific application of Article 3(f).[29] This 'teleological' reasoning was an early indication of how the competition rules would be interpreted.[30]

(ii) Application of Article 102 after *Continental Can*

Since *Continental Can*, the story of Article 102 has predominantly been one of action against exclusionary abuses. There have been relatively few cases in which an undertaking's exploitation of its

[25] E.g. Case C-333/94 P, *Tetra Pak II* EU:C:1996:436, para. 37; Cases C-395 and 396/96 P, *Compagnie Maritime Belge* EU:C:2000:132, para. 112; Case C-95/04 P, *British Airways* EU:C:2007:166, paras. 57–58; Case T-201/04, *Microsoft* EU:T:2007:289, paras. 860–861 (Art. 102 must be interpreted as a whole); Case C-280/08, *Deutsche Telekom* EU:C:2010:603, para. 173.

[26] O'Donoghue and Padilla, n. 1, 314–315.

[27] See J. Temple Lang, 'How Can the Problems of Exclusionary Abuses under Article 102 TFEU Be Resolved?' (2012) 37 *ELRev* 136.

[28] The *Continental Can* judgment preceded the adoption of a merger control framework at EU level. In Case C-449/21, *Towercast* EU:C:2023:207, the CJ confirmed that this aspect of the judgment essentially remains good law; see discussion at Section 14.F.

[29] Later Art. 3(1)(g), now Protocol 27.

[30] E.g. Cases 6 and 7/73, *Commercial Solvents* EU:C:1974:18, para. 32.

dominant position has been prohibited.[31] This is partly because a dominant undertaking's ability to exploit its customers for a significant period indicates that there is something wrong with the market. For example, the ability to reap supra-competitive profits by charging excessive prices should, in theory, act as a spur to attract new competitors. In markets in which this cannot happen, such as those with high barriers to entry, the solution may be to impose price controls through sector regulation. In situations other than this, the Commission prefers to take action against any anti-competitive practices which prevent entry and cause the market failure, rather than to tackle the high prices directly. The Commission has made it clear, however, that there is no question of Article 102 being applied *only* to exclusionary abuses: 'Article 102 can properly be applied, where appropriate, to situations in which a dominant undertaking's behaviour directly prejudices the interests of consumers, notwithstanding the absence of any effect on the structure of competition.'[32] As a Commission official put it: 'the [EU] Founding Fathers' faith in competition as a process of rivalry between competitors was not strong enough to tolerate customer/consumer exploitation in the short run'.[33]

The prohibition of exclusionary behaviour may benefit consumers by protecting the competitive structure. Indeed, the view that consumer welfare is the objective of competition law holds that consumer benefit is the *only* reason for this prohibition. Such a prohibition also *directly* benefits competitors, by preventing their exclusion from the market. The prohibition of exclusionary behaviour may, therefore, allow competition authorities to go beyond the objective of protecting competition as a way of benefiting consumers. We see cases in this chapter where Article 102 has been applied to protect particular *competitors* rather than *competition*, and where it was questionable whether preventing exclusion of competitors in fact benefited consumers.[34]

D. THE BROAD NATURE OF THE CONCEPT OF ABUSE

(i) The Definition of 'Abuse'

In *Hoffmann La-Roche*, the CJ gave a definition of the concept of an (exclusionary) abuse which has been the foundation of the jurisprudence ever since.[35]

Case 85/76, *Hoffmann-La Roche & Co AG v Commission* EU:C:1979:36

Court of Justice

91. For the purpose of rejecting the finding that there has been an abuse of a dominant position the interpretation suggested by the applicant that an abuse implies that the use of the economic power bestowed by a dominant position is the means whereby the abuse has been brought about cannot be accepted. The concept of abuse is an objective concept relating to the behaviour of an undertaking in a dominant position which is such as to influence the structure of a market where, as a result of the very

[31] See Section 16. [32] *1998 World Cup* [2000] OJ L5/55, para. 100.

[33] L. Gyselen, 'Rebates: Competition on the Merits or Exclusionary Practice?' in C.- D. Ehlermann and I. Atanasiu (eds.), *European Competition Law Annual 2003: What is an Abuse of a Dominant Position?* (Hart Publishing, 2006), 287, 290. This contrasts with the US Sherman Act, s. 2, which is not applied to exploitative conduct.

[34] See e.g. Cases 6 and 7/73, *Commercial Solvents* EU:C:1974:18; Case 22/78, *Hugin* EU:C:1979:138; Case T-201/04, *Microsoft* EU:T:2007:289. In Case C-280/08 P, *Deutsche Telekom* EU:C:2010:603, the application of Art. 102 was to the short-term *detriment* to consumers in the form of higher prices.

[35] See e.g. Case C-62/86, *AKZO Chemie* EU:C:1991:286, para. 69; Case C-202/07 P, *France Télécom* EU:C:2009:214, para. 104; Case C-280/08 P, *Deutsche Telekom* EU:C:2010:603, para. 174; Case C-52/09, *TeliaSonera* EU:C:2011:83, para. 27.

> presence of the undertaking in question, the degree of competition is weakened and which, through recourse to methods different from those which condition normal competition in products or services on the basis of the transactions of commercial operators, has the effect of hindering the maintenance of the degree of competition still existing in the market or the growth of that competition.

The concept of abuse relates to the behaviour of the dominant undertaking and the (actual or anticipated) impact of this conduct on the market concerned. Accordingly, holding a dominant position 'is not in itself a recrimination':[36] the undertaking concerned must in some way *mis*use its market power through its conduct. In *Hoffmann-La Roche*, the CJ related the notion of abuse to the weakening of the structure of competition, in a passage which has been important in recent cases:[37]

> **Case 85/76, *Hoffmann-La Roche & Co AG v Commission* EU:C:1979:36**
>
> **Court of Justice**
>
> 123. . . . Since the course of conduct under consideration is that of an undertaking occupying a dominant position on a market where for this reason the structure of competition has already been weakened, within the field of application of Article [102] any further weakening of the structure of competition may constitute an abuse of a dominant position.

The crux of the notion of abuse of dominance is thus the harm that the undertaking's behaviour may cause in a market situation where there is already a structural absence of competition, due to the defendant's very presence on the market. In *Hoffmann-La Roche*, the CJ construed the notion of harm primarily in terms of additional damage to the structure of competition within the market. In *Post Danmark I*, the CJ (Grand Chamber) added an express requirement of consumer detriment, prefacing this with 'applies in particular':

> . . . Article [102] applies, in particular, to the conduct of a dominant undertaking that, through recourse to methods different from those governing normal competition on the basis of the performance of commercial operators, has the effect, to the detriment of consumers, of hindering the maintenance of the degree of competition existing in the market or the growth of that competition.[38]

Although some subsequent cases returned to the *Hoffmann-La Roche* formulation,[39] the emphasis upon protection of consumer welfare was forcefully reaffirmed by the CJ in *Intel*.[40]

[36] Case 322/81, *Michelin I* EU:C:1983:313, para. 57. See also e.g. Case T-228/97, *Irish Sugar* EU:T:1999:246, para. 112; Case T-201/04, *Microsoft* EU:T:2007:289, para. 229; Case C-202/07 P, *France Télécom* EU:C:2009:214, para. 105; Case C-52/09, *TeliaSonera* EU:C:2011:83, para. 24; Case C-457/10 P, *AstraZeneca* EU:C:2012:770, para. 134. See further K. McMahon, 'A Reformed Approach to Article 82 and the Special Responsibility Not to Distort Competition' in A. Ezrachi (ed.), *Article 82 EC: Reflections on Its Recent Evolution* (Hart Publishing, 2009), 121.

[37] E.g. Case C-23/14, *Post Danmark II* EU:C:2015:651, para. 72; and Case C-307/18, *Generics (UK)* EU:C:2020:52, para. 147.

[38] Case C-209/10, *Post Danmark I* EU:C:2012:172, para. 24.

[39] Case C-549/10 P, *Tomra* EU:C:2012:221, para. 17; and Case C-457/10 P, *AstraZeneca* EU:C:2012:770, para. 74.

[40] Case C-413/14 P *Intel* EU:C:2017:632.

Most recently, the CJ has defined the concept of abuse to encompass 'any practice capable of adversely affecting, by way of resources other than those which govern normal competition, an *effective competition structure*'.[41] In doing so, however, the CJ has linked the notion of an 'effective competition structure' directly to the protection of *efficient* competitive constraints,[42] a point developed further in Section 2.E.

One consequence of placing the emphasis so squarely upon the behaviour of dominant undertakings is that Article 102 does not catch attempted abuses of dominance. The CJ has thus held that 'a practice cannot be characterised as abusive if it remained at the project stage without having been implemented'.[43]

(ii) Market Power Does Not Need to be Used for an Abuse to be Committed

As noted, *Continental Can* established that the dominant undertaking does not need to *use* its dominance to commit an abuse.[44] Instead, it is the very fact of dominance that renders the undertaking's behaviour abusive. Such dominance means that the behaviour has anti-competitive effects which conduct of a non-dominant undertaking could not have. Since a dominant undertaking may be prohibited from some conduct even though it is not using its market power, some business strategies permitted by non-dominant firms will be prohibited, such as below-cost pricing. Thus, the dominant undertaking may abuse its position by engaging in conduct which is acceptable when carried out by its competitors, and irrespective of any intention to commit an abuse.[45]

(iii) Abuse as an Objective Concept

In *Hoffmann-La Roche*,[46] the CJ said that the notion of an abuse is an 'objective concept'. This reinforces the point that it is not essential to a finding of abuse that the dominant undertaking has used its dominant position.[47] Further, it means that the characterisation of a dominant undertaking's conduct as abusive does not imply fault,[48] and does not depend on the undertaking's subjective intent to exclude competitors or weaken competition. In *Clearstream*, for example, the GC stated that the defendant's argument that it had not pursued an anti-competitive objective was irrelevant to the legal characterisation of the facts.[49] Similarly, in *Tomra*, the CJ held that evidence of the defendant's subjective intention to compete on the merits could not prove the absence of abuse.[50]

Conduct may be considered abusive even if the dominant undertaking obtains no advantage, either financial or competitive, for itself. The discriminatory distribution of tickets by the French body which organised the 1998 World Cup was condemned as abusive although it was accepted that the body had

[41] Case C-377/20, *Servizio Elettrico Nazionale* EU:C:2022:379, para. 68. See also Case C-680/20, *Unilever Italia* EU:C:2023:33, para. 36, which refers to 'conduct of a dominant undertaking which . . . adversely affects an effective competition structure'.

[42] Case C-680/20, *Unilever Italia* EU:C:2023:33, paras. 37–39 in particular.

[43] Case C-377/20, *Servizio Elettrico Nazionale* EU:C:2022:379, para. 70.

[44] Case 6/72, *Continental Can* EU:C:1973:22, particularly paras. 26–27.

[45] Case T-111/96, *ITT Promedia* EU:T:1998:183, para. 139, and see the case law throughout this chapter.

[46] Case 85/76, *Hoffmann-La Roche* EU:C:1979:36, para. 91.

[47] See Kirschner AG in Case T-51/89, *Tetra Pak I* EU:T:1990:15, para. 64.

[48] See e.g. Case C-280/08 P, *Deutsche Telekom*, EU:C:2010:603, para. 89.

[49] Case T-301/04, *Clearstream* EU:T:2009:317, paras. 142–144, citing Case T-65/89, *BPB Industries Plc and British Gypsum Ltd* EU:T:1993:31, para. 70.

[50] Case C-549/10 P, *Tomra* EU:C:2012:221, paras. 16–22.

not gained any commercial or other advantage from its actions.[51] In the *Swedish Interconnectors*[52] and *DE/DK Interconnector*[53] commitments decisions, the defendant Transmission System Operators (TSOs)[54] were alleged to have limited cross-border electricity transmission capacity in order to manipulate energy prices, in circumstances where the beneficiaries were electricity consumers and electricity companies, respectively, within the defendants' home jurisdictions.

Conversely, the presence of an anti-competitive objective may 'reinforce' the conclusion that there is an abuse of a dominant position even though it is not a necessary condition for such a finding.[55] As seen later in this chapter, there are some types of abusive conduct where the undertaking's intent is of particular relevance, for example predatory pricing[56] and 'vexatious litigation'.[57]

Finally, the question of whether a dominant undertaking's behaviour was objectively 'intended to drive its competitors from the market concerned' is assessed by reference to the facts as these existed at time of the alleged abuse, 'irrespective of whether such practice has proved successful' subsequently.[58] A more complicated issue, however, is whether an absence of actual anti-competitive effects may challenge the presumption that behaviour had the capacity to foreclose competition.[59]

(iv) The 'Special Responsibility' of Dominant Undertakings

The EU Courts have consistently stressed that, although dominance as such is not prohibited under Article 102, dominant firms have a 'special responsibility' towards the competitive process. This idea was first expressed in *Michelin I*:

> A finding that an undertaking has a dominant position is not in itself a recrimination but simply means that, irrespective of the reasons for which it has such a dominant position, the undertaking concerned has a special responsibility not to allow its conduct to impair genuine undistorted competition on the common market.[60]

The concept has largely evaded elaboration in subsequent case law. It has been described simply as a duty to 'take care' not to infringe (in the sense of engage in conduct contrary to) Article 102.[61] Yet, as noted, liability under Article 102 does not depend upon demonstrating anti-competitive intention on the part of dominant undertakings. While prudent undertakings in possession of evident market power might reasonably be expected to take precautions to ensure that their behaviour does

[51] *1998 World Cup* [2000] OJ L5/55, para. 102; cf. Case T-155/04, *SELEX Sistemi Integrati* EU:T:2006:387, para. 108.

[52] COMP/39.351, *Swedish Interconnectors* 4 April 2010. [53] AT.40461, *DE/DK Interconnector* 7 December 2018.

[54] TSOs, a concept established in EU energy law, are entities entrusted with the operation of energy transport infrastructure. They are essentially natural monopolies, and thus the defendants in these cases faced no competition within their home jurisdictions.

[55] Case T-301/04, *Clearstream* EU:T:2009:317, para. 142; Case T-321/05, *AstraZeneca* EU:T:2010:266, para. 359.

[56] See Case C-62/86, *AKZO* EU:C:1991:286. [57] Case T-111/96, *ITT Promedia* EU:T:1998:183.

[58] Case C-377/20, *Servizio Elettrico Nazionale* EU:C:2022:379, para. 53.

[59] While evidence of an absence of actual anti-competitive effects 'cannot rule out the possibility' that an abuse has occurred, it 'may constitute evidence that the conduct in question was not capable of producing the alleged exclusionary effects': Case C-377/20, *Servizio Elettrico Nazionale* EU:C:2022, paras. 54–56.

[60] Case 322/81, *Michelin I* EU:C:1983:313, para. 57. See also e.g. Case T-228/97, *Irish Sugar plc v Commission* EU:T:1999:246, para. 112; Case T-201/04, *Microsoft* EU:T:2007:289, para. 229; Case C-202/07 P, *France Télécom* EU:C:2009:214, para. 105; Case C-52/09, *TeliaSonera* EU:C:2011:83, para. 24; Case C-457/10 P, *AstraZeneca* EU:C:2012:770, para. 134.

[61] W. Sauter, 'A Duty of Care to Prevent Online Exploitation of Consumers? Digital Dominance and Special Responsibility in EU Competition Caw' (2020) 8 *J of Antitrust Enforcement* 406, 409.

not infringe Article 102—'to be mindful'[62]—the special responsibility does not alter the objective nature of the notion of 'abuse'.

The crux of the concept instead appears to be that with 'great power comes great responsibility'. As discussed in Chapter 6, the concept of dominance hinges upon an undertaking's ability to escape, to an appreciable extent, the competitive constraints that ordinarily would be exerted by customers and competitors.[63] By definition, dominant undertakings enjoy a degree of freedom—in particular, the ability to engage in harmful behaviour largely unconstrained by market forces—that non-dominant undertakings do not possess. In that sense, dominance poses a particular challenge to the effective operation of the market mechanism. The special responsibility has thus been described as a requirement for any dominant firm 'to act in a manner proportionate to its economic strength'.[64] The doctrine implies that dominant firms cannot act merely as self-interested, profit-maximising actors, but must consider the effect of their actions on the presumed proper functioning of the market. While Article 102 does not guarantee a right for inefficient competitors to remain in the market, protecting competition 'as such' may require abstaining from certain aggressive actions against competitors.[65]

The special responsibility arises irrespective of the reasons for which the undertaking has its dominant position. In *Post Danmark I*, nonetheless, the CJ accorded particular importance to the origin of the dominant position in a legal monopoly:

> . . . [A] dominant undertaking has a special responsibility not to allow its behaviour to impair genuine, undistorted competition on the internal market . . . When the existence of a dominant position has its origins in a former legal monopoly, that fact has to be taken into account.[66]

This is significant in respect of dominant undertakings in liberalised markets, where the incumbents often continue to reap the advantages of their previous legal monopoly.[67]

The principle that dominant firms have a 'special responsibility' towards the competitive process is a key element in the application of Article 102.[68] It imposes what is, in effect, an affirmative duty on the dominant undertaking to act in certain ways. The consequences of this special responsibility will be seen throughout this chapter.

(v) Super-dominance

The link drawn between the scope of the special responsibility and the degree of economic strength possessed by the dominant undertaking coincides with the notion of 'super-dominance'. The idea first appeared in *Tetra Pak II*,[69] where the CJ approved the GC's statement that '[t]he actual scope of the special responsibility imposed on an undertaking in a dominant position must therefore be

[62] P. Alexiadis and A. de Streel, 'Designing an EU Intervention Standard for Digital Platforms', EUI Working Papers RSCAS 2020/14, p. 2.

[63] *United Brands*, para.65.

[64] K. McMahon, 'A Reformed Approach to Article 82 and the Special Responsibility Not to Distort Competition' in A. Ezrachi (ed.), *Article 82 EC: Reflections on its Recent Evolution* (Hart Publishing, 2009), 123.

[65] The tension is nicely explored in *Intel*, paras. 133–136.

[66] Case C-209/10, *Post Danmark I* EU:C:2012:172, para. 23.

[67] See Case T-486/11, *Orange Polska SA* EU:T:2015:1002, paras. 177–178 where, citing *Post Danmark I*, the GC took the former legal monopoly into account when setting the fine. See further Rousseva and Marquis, n. 7, 32; and see the discussion of the exceptions the Commission makes to its position on refusal to supply in the Guidance Paper, para. 82, in Section 12.G.

[68] See e.g. Case C-457/10 P, *AstraZeneca* EU:C:2012:770, paras. 134 and 149.

[69] Case C-333/94 P, *Tetra Pak II* EU:C:1996:436, para. 24.

considered in the light of the specific circumstances of the case'.[70] The 'special circumstances' in that instance included the undertaking's 'quasi-monopoly'.[71] In *Compagnie Maritime Belge*, Advocate General Fennelly spoke of the 'super-dominance' of monopolists and quasi-monopolists, and of the 'particularly onerous special responsibility' upon undertakings enjoying 'a position of dominance approaching a monopoly'.[72] While not expressly endorsing this, the CJ stated that the scope of the special responsibility was affected by the circumstances of the case. In particular, it indicated that an undertaking with a very large market share and only one competitor would be more likely to be found to have abused its dominance than a dominant undertaking with a lesser degree of market power.[73] In *Google Shopping*, the GC repeatedly referenced Google's super-dominant position in the context of explaining how its self-preferencing behaviour constituted an abuse.[74]

The concept of super-dominance has been criticised as lacking economic or legal foundation.[75] In *TeliaSonera*, the referring court asked, inter alia, whether the degree of dominance held by the undertaking was relevant to establishing whether the impugned pricing practice was abusive. Advocate General Mazák recommended that the answer should be 'no', as Article 102 'makes no reference to a 'super-dominant" position'.[76] The CJ agreed.

Case C-52/09, *Konkurrensverket v TeliaSonera Sverige* AB EU:C:2011:83

Court of Justice

79. . . . [T]he dominant position referred to in Article 102 TFEU relates to a position of economic strength enjoyed by an undertaking which enables it to prevent effective competition being maintained on the relevant market by affording it the power to behave to an appreciable extent independently of its competitors, its customers and ultimately of consumers.

80. Accordingly, that provision . . . does not envisage any variation in form or degree in the concept of a dominant position. Where an undertaking has an economic strength such as that required by Article 102 TFEU to establish that it holds a dominant position in a particular market, its conduct must be assessed in the light of that provision.

81. Of course, that does not mean that an undertaking's strength is not relevant to the assessment of the lawfulness of the conduct in the market of such an undertaking in the light of Article 102 TFEU. The Court itself has based its analyses on the fact that an undertaking enjoyed a position of super-dominance or a quasi-monopoly (. . . Case C-333/94 P *Tetra Pak* v *Commission* . . . paragraph 31, and *Compagnie maritime belge transports and Others* v *Commission*, paragraph 119). Nonetheless the degree of market strength is, as a general rule, significant in relation to the extent of the effects of the conduct of the undertaking concerned rather than in relation to the question of whether the abuse as such exists.

The CJ followed this approach in *Tomra*.[77]

As a general rule, therefore, the degree of market power held by a dominant undertaking is irrelevant to whether its conduct constitutes an abuse. Rather, it is relevant only to the *extent of the effects* of

[70] Case T-83/91, *Tetra Pak International SA v Commission* EU:T:1994:246, para. 115. [71] Ibid., para. 31.

[72] Cases C-395 and 396/96 P, *Compagnie Maritime Belge* EU:C:1998:518, Fennelly AG, para. 137. This is the source of the term 'super-dominance'.

[73] Ibid., paras. 112–119.

[74] Case T-604/18, *Google Android* EU:T:2022:541, paras. 182–183. See also A. D'Amico and B. Balasingham, 'Super-Dominant and Super-Problematic? The Degree of Dominance in the *Google Shopping* Judgment' (2022) 18 *European Competition Journal* 614.

[75] See L. Ortiz Blanco, *Market Power in EU Antitrust Law* (Hart Publishing, 2012), 49–50.

[76] Opinion in Case C-52/09, *TeliaSonera* EU:C:2011:83, para. 41.

[77] Case C-549/10 P, *Tomra Systems ASA v Commission* EU:C:2012:221, para. 39.

the conduct. As usual, the CJ in *TeliaSonera* entered the caveat 'as a general rule'. One cannot, therefore, say that super-dominance is completely irrelevant in the assessment of abuse. Moreover, the CJ in *Post Danmark* said, apropos the special responsibility, that the fact that the existence of a dominant position has its origins in a legal monopoly is of relevance.[78] Previous legal monopoly may therefore, in some cases, substitute for 'super-dominance'.

E. EXCLUSIONARY ABUSES: DISTINGUISHING ABUSIVE CONDUCTS FROM 'COMPETITION ON THE MERITS'

There is a problem inherent in the *Hoffmann-La Roche* definition of abusive exclusionary conduct. The principle that a dominant undertaking has a special responsibility to the competitive process, and that any conduct which strengthens the dominant position or further weakens the competitive structure may be an abuse, potentially brings within Article 102 an indefinite spectrum of conduct. The difficulty is that anything done by a dominant undertaking may improve its market position in comparison to those of its competitors. New and attractive products, improved quality, better service, effective advertising, and low prices may all attract custom from competitors. Should improving market share as a result of the dominant undertaking's increased efficiency and unbeatable products be forbidden? Obviously, such a finding would be absurd.

The key to distinguishing between illegitimate and legitimate conduct lies in the judgments in *Hoffmann-La Roche* and *Michelin I*.[79] In these cases, the CJ spoke of recourse to methods different from those which condition normal competition, respectively, 'on the basis of the transactions of commercial operators' and 'based on traders' performance'.[80] The Court thus distinguished anti-competitive behaviour from competition based on superior performance. A dominant undertaking that provides a better product at a low price which reflects its costs, competes on performance.[81] Its conduct is not prohibited even though its competitors, producing inferior products at less attractive prices, may lose customers. This is the natural operation of the market. In contrast, a dominant undertaking which, for example, practically gives away its products below cost in order to steal customers from its competitors, acts anti-competitively. The term most often used to denote what *Hoffmann-La Roche* refers to 'as normal competition in products or services on the basis of the transactions of commercial operators' is competition 'on the merits'.[82]

The enduring difficulty is how the line is drawn between anti-competitive conduct and competition on the merits. Prohibiting conduct that is pro-competitive (Type 1 errors) may be detrimental to consumers and to social welfare, stifling innovation and hindering dynamic competition. Moreover,

[78] Case C-209/10, *Post Danmark I* EU:C:2012:172, para. 23.

[79] Discussed, specifically in the context of exclusive dealing, in Section 10.

[80] The phraseology in English of *Hoffmann-La Roche* and *Michelin* is ungainly and unhelpful. For an explanation of the source of the original German in *Hoffmann-La Roche* and its translation see J. Kallaugher and B. Sher, 'Rebates Revisited: Anti-competitive Effects and Exclusionary Abuse Under Article 82' [2004] *ECLR* 263.

[81] 'Examples of competition on the merits . . . would include conduct which reduces the costs of the dominant undertaking by increasing efficiency in some way and which has the effect of broadening consumer choice by putting new goods on the market or by increasing the quantity or quality of the goods already on offer.' See Opinion of Rantos AG in Case C-377/20, *Servizio Elettrico Nazionale* EU:C:2021:998, para. 62.

[82] E.g. Case C-202/07 P, *France Télécom* EU:C:2009:214, para. 106; Case C-549/10 P, *Tomra* EU:C:2012:221, para. 42; Case C-209/10, *Post Danmark I* EU:C:2012:172, para. 22; Case 457/10 P, *AstraZeneca* EU:C:2012:770, paras. 93 and 134; Case C-413/14 P, *Intel* EU:C:2017:632, para. 136; Case C-307/18, *Generics (UK)* EU:C:2020:52, para. 152; Case T-612/17, *Google Shopping* EU:T:2021:763, para. 152; Case C-377/20, *Servizio Elettrico Nazionale* EU:C:2022:379, para. 75; and Case T-604/18, *Google Android* EU:T:2022:541, para. 276. See also the Guidance Paper, paras. 1 and 6.

companies must be able to pursue business strategies in the knowledge that they are behaving legally, meaning that there must be a sufficient degree of legal certainty in the interpretation and application of Article 102.[83] As Advocate General Rantos acknowledged in *Servizio Elettrico Nazionale*, 'formulating rules which allow conduct that is harmful to competition, and therefore abusive, to be clearly distinguished is neither easy nor intuitive. That complexity is linked, inevitably, to the objective difficulty of distinguishing in advance conduct which reveals aggressive, but lawful competitiveness from anticompetitive conduct.'[84]

One crucial implication of the notion of 'competition on the merits' is that it is not the role of Article 102 to keep inefficient competitors on the market. Thus rivals that are excluded through the 'normal' operation of the (often dog-eat-dog) market process are not protected. This chimes with the goal of modernising the application of Article 102, which put the interests of consumers at its centre.[85] Almost all exclusionary abuse cases originate, not from complaints by customers or consumers—who often are perfectly happy with low prices arising from predation, margin squeeze, or bundling practices—but rather from complaints or other legal action by rivals. Competition on the merits frequently hurts competitors. The CJ made an important statement in *Post Danmark*, however, clarifying that it is not the function of Article 102 to protect inefficient competitors, and that excluding competitors is not necessarily detrimental to competition.

Case C-209/10, *Post Danmark A/S v Konkurrencerådet* EU:C:2012:172

Court of Justice

21. It is settled case-law that a finding that an undertaking has such a dominant position is not in itself a ground of criticism of the undertaking concerned (Case 322/81 *Nederlandsche Banden-Industrie-Michelin* v *Commission* . . . paragraph 57, and Joined Cases C-395/96 P and C-396/96 P *Compagnie maritime belge transports and Others* v *Commission* . . . paragraph 37). It is in no way the purpose of Article [102] to prevent an undertaking from acquiring, on its own merits, the dominant position on a market (see, inter alia, *TeliaSonera Sverige*, paragraph 24). Nor does that provision seek to ensure that competitors less efficient than the undertaking with the dominant position should remain on the market.

22. Thus, not every exclusionary effect is necessarily detrimental to competition (see, by analogy, *TeliaSonera Sverige*, paragraph 43). Competition on the merits may, by definition, lead to the departure from the market or the marginalisation of competitors that are less efficient and so less attractive to consumers from the point of view of, among other things, price, choice, quality or innovation.

The principle set out in paragraph 22 of *Post Danmark I* has been reiterated by the GC[86] and CJ[87] on multiple occasions subsequently. It also informs the logic of the 'as efficient competitor' test, which has been used in the application of Article 102 in price-based abuse cases, and is discussed at Section 7.D.

[83] J. Temple Lang and R. O'Donoghue, 'Defining Legitimate Competition: How to Clarify Pricing Abuses under Article 82EC' (2002) 26 *Fordham Int'l LJ* 83, 83–84.

[84] Opinion of Rantos AG in Case C-377/20, *Servizio Elettrico Nazionale* EU:C:2021:998, para. 53.

[85] See also the then Commissioner Neelie Kroes: 'I like aggressive competition—including by dominant companies—and I don't care if it may hurt competitors—as long as it ultimately benefits consumers. That is because the main and ultimate objective of Article 102 is to protect consumers, and this does, of course, require the protection of an undistorted competitive process on the market', 'Preliminary Thoughts on Policy Review of Article 102', Fordham Corporate Law Institute, SPEECH/05/537, 23 September 2005.

[86] See e.g. Case T-612/17, *Google Shopping* EU:T:2021:763, para. 157; Case T-235/18, *Qualcomm* EU:T:2022:358, para. 351; and Case T-604/18, *Google Android* EU:T:2022:541, para. 278.

[87] See e.g. Case C-413/14 P, *Intel* EU:C:2017:632, para. 134; and Case C-377/20, *Servizio Elettrico Nazionale* EU:C:2022:379, para. 73.

F. FORM- AND EFFECTS-BASED ANALYSIS

It was explained earlier that, unlike Article 101(1), the Article 102 prohibition on abuse of dominance makes no reference to abuses arising 'by object' or 'by effect'. In the case law, it is nonetheless possible to identify certain categories of behaviour which have been prohibited under Article 102 essentially 'by object' (i.e. because the dominant undertaking engages in a business practice which is proscribed as such) and others which are prohibited 'by effect' (i.e. because it is demonstrated that the behaviour has, or is likely to have, anti-competitive effects). Given that there is always the theoretical possibility, however unlikely in practice, of the conduct being objectively justified,[88] no behaviour is irredeemably 'per se' illegal under Article 102.

Characterising certain forms of unilateral conduct as intrinsically anti-competitive, and thus meriting 'by object' condemnation, is a controversial proposition. A first concern is whether, from a competition policy perspective, it makes sense to prevent dominant undertakings *a priori* from engaging in any—even outwardly exclusionary—types of behaviour, without requiring a showing of related harmful effects. The most obvious argument for having a 'by object' category of abuses is to provide 'a clear and easy-to-apply general prohibition rule', which lays the burden of showing any possible objective justification upon the dominant undertaking which 'has the best access to all relevant information, and has a stronger risk-bearing capacity than its smaller competitors'.[89] Conversely, where a practice can be understood as a plausible form of competition on the merits, the EU Courts have been more reluctant to consider such conduct as abusive by its very nature.[90]

Yet the apparent simplicity of this distinction is disputed, not least because even overtly exclusionary conduct, when judged from the perspective of *competitors*, does not necessary translate into harm from the perspective of *consumers*. This returns us to the question of why exclusionary abuses are prohibited. If the competition rules only protect competition as a means of protecting consumers, then exclusion which does not harm consumers should be permitted.[91] In the following extract, taken from his Opinion in an important case exploring the use of 'by object' prohibitions under Article 102, Advocate General Wahl argues that demonstrating anti-competitive effects should be a necessary element of the concept of abuse.

Case C-413/14 P, *Intel v Commission*, Opinion of Advocate General Wahl EU:C:2016:788

Court of Justice

41. From the outset, EU competition rules have aimed to put in place a system of undistorted competition, as part of the internal market established by the EU. In that regard, it cannot be overemphasised that protection under EU competition rules is afforded to the competitive process as such, and not, for example, to competitors. In the same vein, competitors that are forced to exit the market due to fierce competition, rather than anticompetitive behaviour, are not protected. Therefore, not every exit from the market is necessarily a sign of abusive conduct, but rather a sign of aggressive, yet healthy

[88] For objective justification, see Section 5.

[89] W. Wils, 'The Judgment of the EU General Court in *Intel* and the So-called "More Economic Approach" to Abuse of Dominance' (2014) 4 *World Competition* 405.

[90] P. Ibáñez Colomo, 'Beyond the "More Economics-based Approach": A Legal Perspective on Article 102 TFEU Case Law' (2016) 53 *CMLRev* 709, 724–725.

[91] For a full discussion of the effects issue, see Akman, *The Concept of Abuse in EU Competition Law*, n. 18, 130–143.

> and permissible, competition. This is because, given its economic character, competition law aims, in the final analysis, to enhance efficiency. The importance placed on efficiency is also in my view clearly reflected in the case-law of the EU Courts.
>
> 42. From that emphasis it naturally follows that dominance as such is not considered to be at variance with Article 102 TFEU. Rather, only behaviour which constitutes an expression of market power to the detriment of competition and, thus, to consumers is prohibited and accordingly sanctioned as an abuse of dominance.
>
> 43. A logical corollary to the objective of enhanced efficiency is that the anticompetitive effects of a particular practice assume crucial importance. Irrespective of whether we are dealing with an enforcement shortcut such as that offered by the concept of 'restriction by object' in the context of Article 101 TFEU, or with single firm conduct falling within the scope of Article 102 TFEU, EU competition rules seek to capture behaviour that has anticompetitive effects. To date, the form of a particular practice has not been deemed important.
>
> . . .
>
> 78. As I see it, the analysis of 'context'—or 'all the circumstances', as it is termed in the Court's case-law—aims simply but crucially to ascertain that it has been established, to the requisite legal standard, that an undertaking has abused its dominant position. Even in the case of seemingly evident exclusionary behaviour, such as pricing below cost, context cannot be overlooked. Otherwise, conduct which, on occasion, is simply not capable of restricting competition would be caught by a blanket prohibition. Such a blanket prohibition would also risk catching and penalising pro-competitive conduct.
>
> . . .
>
> 103. It goes without saying that it is of the utmost importance that legal tests applied to one category of conduct are coherent with those applied to comparable practices. Sound and coherent legal categorisation benefits not only undertakings in terms of increased legal certainty, but also assists competition authorities in the enforcement of competition law. Arbitrary categorisation does not.

The final paragraph alludes to a second concern regarding the use of 'by object' prohibitions under Article 102. Even if it is accepted that certain forms of unilateral behaviour are so intrinsically harmful, or at least risky, in competition terms so as to merit 'by object' condemnation, there remains an open question about the desirability and/or necessity of securing coherence with the treatment of equivalent practices under Article 101.[92] Notably, the description in *Cartes Bancaires* of 'by object' restrictions under Article 101 as those that 'may be considered so likely to have negative effects . . . that it may be considered redundant, . . . to prove that they have actual effects on the market . . .'[93] also applies to unilateral conduct which is condemned as abusive because it is presumed to have anticompetitive effects. Accordingly, if for example contractual exclusivity obligations are not treated as 'by object' restrictions under Article 101, on the basis that such practices may generate significant efficiencies, does it make sense to prohibit exclusivity as a 'by object' abuse in the presence of dominance? In its defence of the 'by object' prohibition of exclusivity in *Intel*, the GC invoked the language of the 'by object' category developed under Article 101, characterising such practices as potentially harmful to competition 'by their very nature'.[94] Yet it argued for a fundamentally different approach

[92] See e.g. L. Peeperkorn, 'Coherence in the Application of Articles 101 and 102: A Realistic Prospect or an Elusive Goal?' (2016) 39 *World Competition* 389, and P. Ibáñez Colomo, 'Beyond the "More Economics-based Approach": A Legal Perspective on Article 102 TFEU Case Law' (2016) 53 *CMLRev* 709.

[93] Case C-67/13 P *CB* EU:C:2014:2204, para. 51.

[94] Case T-286/09, *Intel Corp* EU:T:2014:547, para. 85, echoing the approach in Case C-67/13 P, *CB* EU:C:2014:2204, para. 50.

to classifying practices as abusive 'by object' under Article 102, maintaining that the very presence of dominance—and the concomitant structural absence of competition—justifies a stricter treatment.[95] In the following extract, the author (a senior DG Competition official writing in a personal capacity) explains his disagreement with this perspective:

L. Peeperkorn, 'Coherence in the Application of Articles 101 and 102: A Realistic Prospect or an Elusive Goal?' (2016) 39 *World Competition* 389, 407–409

While it is generally recognized that negative effects can only arise where one or more of the firms involved has a degree of market power, it does not promote coherence . . . to create a category of restrictions or conduct which is considered to be by effect below the level of dominance but by object once one of the parties is dominant.

On the one hand, if a particular restriction or conduct is truly by object ('normally having a net negative effect on consumers'), treating it as by object only in cases of dominance will lead to under-enforcement and unnecessary complexity and enforcement costs. . . . [I]f a particular type of agreement or conduct normally produces net negative effects, it is because it is unlikely to be used to create efficiencies. In that case, there is no reason to expect that the negative effects will only materialize where one of the parties is dominant. Having to prove that the threshold of dominance has been reached will thus lead to unnecessary enforcement costs and indeed under-enforcement.

On the other hand, if a restriction or conduct is of the by effect type, i.e. a restriction or conduct that can and regularly is used to create efficiencies, treating it as by object as soon as one of the parties is above the dominance threshold leads to over-enforcement and unnecessary legal uncertainty for firms. The main reasons are, first, that the likelihood of efficiencies is generally not negatively correlated with holding market power. In other words, restrictions which are by effect below the dominance threshold do not generally suddenly change their character and start producing net negative effects above that threshold. Even though the firm in question is dominant, the restriction or conduct may very well still be used to create efficiencies. Second, a related point is that it is evidently wrong to consider that the effects will be very different depending on whether the firm in question is just over or just under the dominance threshold. In other words, introducing a sharp break in the assessment ('by effect' below the threshold and 'by object' above the threshold) is not justified. Lastly, making the by object classification dependent on the existence of dominance will create significant legal uncertainty, as the threshold itself is not necessarily clear and predictable in all cases. Applying the classification in this way will thus also have an impact on the behaviour of non-dominant firms, whose incentives to grant rebates or enter into exclusive arrangements will be undermined, leading in many cases to a loss of competition and consumer welfare.

This debate is not new. Using a market power filter or a dominance filter, including the use of a market share threshold as a proxy, is not the appropriate tool to distinguish between by object and by effect restrictions. Using such a threshold to distinguish 'good' from 'bad' will place undue importance on defining and applying the parameters of the threshold. If a market share threshold is used, one is likely to get into unhelpful disputes about the exact boundaries of the relevant market, about market share data, whether to use volume or turnover data, etc. As regards a dominance threshold, the focus will unfortunately shift to proving and prohibiting a dominant position, instead of assessing the allegedly abusive conduct and its effects.

[95] Case T-286/09, *Intel* EU:T:2014:547, paras. 89–90, discussed in detail in Section 10.

The question whether dominant firm behaviour should be prohibited due to its overtly anti-competitive form, or whether instead a demonstration of anti-competitive effects should be required, is a critical question within the Article 102 case law. It was explained in Chapter 6 that the Guidance Paper represented an enthusiastic (though not unqualified) endorsement of effects-based analysis by the Commission, while the later Amendments to the Guidance Paper suggest a movement away from this approach. The CJ too, in its more recent case law, has shown itself 'to be open to a less formal approach' to Article 102.[96] Crucially, in *Intel* in 2017, a case discussed in Section 10, a Grand Chamber sitting of the CJ took a notable step towards adopting an effects-based approach to exclusionary abuses in general under Article 102.[97] The *Intel* Court 'clarified' that even behaviour that might be presumed to be abusive by virtue of its restrictive form or object, can only be prohibited under Article 102 if it is actually capable of restricting competition in the circumstances.[98] In *Google Shopping*, the GC thus concluded that a 'practice cannot be categorised as abuse of a dominant position unless it is demonstrated that there is an anti-competitive effect, or at the very least a potential anti-competitive effect'.[99]

Yet this shift within the case law, though notable, leaves a number of questions unanswered. The first is what must be demonstrated to establish that conduct in fact has a 'capacity to foreclose'[100] or 'a potential anticompetitive effect'.[101] The more abstract or theoretical the possibility of such effects arising in practice, the less consequential this shift is likely to prove (though the theory of harm cannot be 'purely hypothetical')[102]. The case law establishes that it is unnecessary to demonstrate 'concrete' anti-competitive effects,[103] nor is it necessary to show that harm to the structure of the market 'may also cause direct harm to consumers'.[104] Despite holding that the concept of exclusionary abuse entails a demonstration of at least a potential anti-competitive effect, the GC in *Google Shopping* expressly stated that this did not require 'the existence of a foreclosure effect, namely that [the defendant's] conduct would give rise to the elimination of all competition'.[105] On the other hand, 'positive effects for consumers' would appear to preclude a finding of abuse of dominance.[106] Surveying the existing case law, the Commission has suggested that '[t]he wording that appears to be most suitable to capture [the applicable legal] standard is that of "potential effects", given that this term allows for sufficient differentiation between this type of effects on the one hand and merely hypothetical or actual effects on the other'.[107]

Secondly, it remains to be seen whether *all* exclusionary practices are now subject to an effects-based assessment, or whether pockets of 'by object' liability remain, for instance in 'classical' tying cases.[108] These questions are explored further later in this chapter.

[96] Opinion of Rantos AG in Case C-377/20, *Servizio Elettrico Nazionale* EU:C:2021:998, para. 6.

[97] Case C-413/14 P, *Intel* EU:C:2017:632. [98] Ibid., paras. 138–140.

[99] Case T-612/17, *Google Shopping* EU:T:2021:763, para. 438.

[100] Case C-413/14 P, *Intel* EU:C:2017:632, para. 140.

[101] Case T-612/17, *Google Shopping* EU:T:2021:763, para. 438.

[102] Case C-23/14, *Post Danmark II* EU:C:2015:651, para. 65; Case C-377/20, *Servizio Elettrico Nazionale* EU:C:2022:379, para. 70; and Case T-235/18, *Qualcomm* EU:T:2022:358, para. 397.

[103] Case C-23/14, *Post Danmark II* EU:C:2015:651, para. 66.

[104] Case C-377/20, *Servizio Elettrico Nazionale* EU:C:2022:379, para. 47.

[105] Case T-612/17, *Google Shopping* EU:T:2021:763, para. 523.

[106] Case C-377/20, *Servizio Elettrico Nazionale* EU:C:2022:379, para. 47.

[107] L. McCallum, I. Bernaerts, M. Kadar, J. Holzwarth, D. Kovo, M. Lagrue, E. Leduc, L. Manigrassi, J. Marcos Ramos, I. Pereira Alves, V. Pozzato, and P. Stamou, 'A Dynamic and Workable Effects-based Approach to Abuse of Dominance' [2023] 2 *Competition Policy Brief* 3. Note that, although nominally written by DG Comp officials in their personal capacity, this article was issued by the Commission alongside the Amendments to the Guidance Paper. The proposed standard has been criticised, however, on the basis that it appears to conflate the likelihood of such effects arising with their temporal dimension: see P. Ibáñez Colomo, 'From Guidance to Guidelines: Article 102 TFEU and the new EU competition law', *Chillin' Competition Blog*, 27 March 2023, <https://chillingcompetition.com/2023/03/27/from-guidance-to-guidelines-article-102-tfeu-and-the-new-eu-competition-law/>.

[108] E.g. AT.40009, *Google Android* 18 July 2018, para. 749; see also discussion at Section 11.

G. APPRECIABILITY

There is no appreciability threshold or de minimis doctrine in respect of abusive conduct under Article 102.[109] This was confirmed in *Post Danmark II*.[110] The CJ based the lack of an appreciability threshold on paragraph 123 of *Hoffmann-La Roche*, which established that *any* further weakening of the competitive structure of a market on which there is a dominant firm may constitute an abuse.[111] The Court concluded that an anti-competitive practice by the dominant undertaking is *by its very nature* liable to give rise to restrictions which are significant.[112] The approach in *Post Danmark II* had been prefigured by the judgment of the GC in *Intel*,[113] and was followed subsequently in *MEO*.[114]

While it would not make sense to have an appreciability threshold under Article 102 predicated on market share as in the Commission's de minimis Notice applicable to Article 101,[115] the dismissal of *any* concept of appreciability in respect of abusive conduct is striking.[116] It would be of importance mainly as regards conduct which may be considered abusive by object. By contrast, to the extent that conduct is judged by its probable effects in the light of 'all the circumstances', the issue of appreciability may be subsumed into the general analysis. Moreover, the Commission and national competition authorities (NCAs) might be expected to refrain from enforcement in the absence of significant anti-competitive effects, although private litigants may not.

4. THE COMMISSION'S APPROACH TO EXCLUSIONARY ABUSES IN THE GUIDANCE PAPER: THE 'ANTI-COMPETITIVE FORECLOSURE' CONCEPT

The Commission's Guidance Paper and its subsequent Amendments were discussed in Chapter 6.[117] In the Guidance Paper, the Commission adopted the concept of 'anti-competitive foreclosure' as the normal standard for intervention.[118] Importantly, this entails not mere 'foreclosure,' meaning exclusion of existing or potential competitors, but rather '*anti-competitive* foreclosure', which furthermore implies a degree of consumer harm arising from the exclusionary behaviour.

The original version of the Guidance Paper defined consumer harm as 'a situation where *effective access of actual or potential competitors to supplies or markets* is hampered or eliminated as a result of the conduct of the dominant undertaking whereby the dominant undertaking is likely to be in a position to *profitably* increase prices to the detriment of consumers'.[119] The term 'increase prices' was used broadly, as shorthand for multiple parameters of competition, including influencing output,

[109] Generally P. Ibáñez Colomo, 'Appreciability and *De Minimis* in Article 102 TFEU' (2016) 7 *JECLAP* 651.

[110] Case C-23/14, *Post Danmark II* EU:C:2015:651. [111] Ibid., para. 72. [112] Ibid., para. 73.

[113] Which was similarly premised upon para.123 of *Hoffmann-La Roche*, see Case T-286/09, *Intel* EU:T:2014:547, para. 116.

[114] Case C-295/17, *MEO* EU:C:2018:942, para. 29.

[115] Notice on agreements of minor importance [2014] OJ C57/1, see Chap. 3.

[116] The only exception of sorts lies with respective to excessive pricing: see Case C-177/16, *AKKA/LAA* EU:C:2017:689, discussed in Section 16.A.

[117] See Chap. 6, Section 5.

[118] For general commentary on the Guidance Paper, see N. Petit, 'From Formalism to Effects? The Commission's Communication on Enforcement Priorities in Applying Article 82' (2009) 32 *World Competition* 485; P. Akman, 'The European Commission's Guidance on Article 102 TFEU: From *Inferno* to *Paradiso*?' (2010) 73 *MLR* 605; L. Lovdahl Gormesen, 'Why the European Commission's Enforcement Priorities on Article 82 Should Be Withdrawn' [2010] *ECLR* 45; and L. F. Pace (ed.), *European Competition Law: The Impact of the Commission's Guidance on Article 102* (Edward Elgar, 2011).

[119] Guidance Paper, para. 19 (emphases added).

innovation, variety, and quality.[120] Nonetheless, the Commission subsequently took the view that this understanding of consumer harm was unduly narrow, in two dimensions. First, the notion of 'effective access of . . . competitors to supplies or markets' arguably failed to capture behaviour that weakened the effectiveness of the competitive structure, without resulting in exclusion of competitors as such. Secondly, the reference to profitability was considered to be at odds with the fact that it is unnecessary to demonstrate actual anti-competitive effects to establish an abuse: that is, behaviour can still be deemed abusive even if the dominant undertaking did not succeed in increasing its market power as a result.[121] The Amendments to the Guidance Paper thus modify the definition of anti-competitive foreclosure,[122] contained in paragraph 19 of the next extract, citing the *Unilever*[123] and *Android*[124] judgments to support the Commission's interpretation of the Article 102 jurisprudence.

Guidance on the Commission's Enforcement Priorities in Applying Article 82 of the EC Treaty to Abusive Exclusionary Conduct by Dominant Undertakings [2009] OJ C45/2 (as amended by C(2023) 1923 final)

19. The aim of the Commission's enforcement activity in relation to exclusionary conduct is to ensure that dominant undertakings do not impair effective competition by foreclosing their competitors in an anti-competitive way, thus having an adverse impact on consumer welfare, whether in the form of higher price levels than would have otherwise prevailed or in some other form such as limiting quality or reducing consumer choice. In this document the term 'anti-competitive foreclosure' is used to describe a situation where the conduct of the dominant undertaking adversely impacts an effective competitive structure thus allowing the dominant undertaking to negatively influence, to its own advantage and to the detriment of consumers, the various parameters of competition, such as price, production, innovation, variety or quality of goods or services. The identification of likely consumer harm can rely on qualitative and, where possible and appropriate, quantitative evidence. The Commission will address such anti-competitive foreclosure either at the intermediate level or at the level of final consumers, or at both levels.[[125]]

20. The Commission will normally intervene under Article [102] where, on the basis of cogent and convincing evidence, the allegedly abusive conduct is likely to lead to anti-competitive foreclosure. The Commission considers the following factors to be generally relevant to such an assessment:

— the position of the dominant undertaking: in general, the stronger the dominant position, the higher the likelihood that conduct protecting that position leads to anti-competitive foreclosure,

— the conditions on the relevant market: this includes the conditions of entry and expansion, such as the existence of economies of scale and/or scope and network effects. Economies of scale mean that competitors are less likely to enter or stay in the market if the dominant undertaking forecloses a significant part of the relevant market. Similarly, the conduct may allow the dominant undertaking to 'tip' a market characterised by network effects in its favour or to further entrench its position on such a market. Likewise, if entry barriers in the upstream and/or downstream market are significant, this means that it may be costly for competitors to overcome possible foreclosure through vertical integration,

— the position of the dominant undertaking's competitors: this includes the importance of competitors for the maintenance of effective competition. A specific competitor may play a significant

120 Ibid., para. 11, see Chap. 6, Section 5.
121 These elements are explained by McCallum et al., n. 107, p. 4.
122 Amendments to the Guidance Paper, Annex, para. 1.
123 Case C-680/20, *Unilever Italia* EU:C:2023:33, para. 36.
124 Case T-604/18, *Google Android* EU:T:2022:541, para. 281.
125 For the footnote at this point of the Guidance, see text accompanying n. 126.

competitive role even if it only holds a small market share compared to other competitors. It may, for example, be the closest competitor to the dominant undertaking, be a particularly innovative competitor, or have the reputation of systematically cutting prices. In its assessment, the Commission may also consider in appropriate cases, on the basis of information available, whether there are realistic, effective and timely counterstrategies that competitors would be likely to deploy,

— the position of the customers or input suppliers: this may include consideration of the possible selectivity of the conduct in question. The dominant undertaking may apply the practice only to selected customers or input suppliers who may be of particular importance for the entry or expansion of competitors, thereby enhancing the likelihood of anti-competitive foreclosure . . . In the case of customers, they may, for example, be the ones most likely to respond to offers from alternative suppliers, they may represent a particular means of distributing the product that would be suitable for a new entrant, they may be situated in a geographic area well suited to new entry or they may be likely to influence the behaviour of other customers. In the case of input suppliers, those with whom the dominant undertaking has concluded exclusive supply arrangements may be the ones most likely to respond to requests by customers who are competitors of the dominant undertaking in a downstream market, or may produce a grade of the product—or produce at a location—particularly suitable for a new entrant. Any strategies at the disposal of the customers or input suppliers which could help to counter the conduct of the dominant undertaking will also be considered,

— the extent of the allegedly abusive conduct: in general, the higher the percentage of total sales in the relevant market affected by the conduct, the longer its duration, and the more regularly it has been applied, the greater is the likely foreclosure effect,

— possible evidence of actual foreclosure: if the conduct has been in place for a sufficient period of time, the market performance of the dominant undertaking and its competitors may provide direct evidence of anti-competitive foreclosure. For reasons attributable to the allegedly abusive conduct, the market share of the dominant undertaking may have risen or a decline in market share may have been slowed. For similar reasons, actual competitors may have been marginalised or may have exited, or potential competitors may have tried to enter and failed,

— direct evidence of any exclusionary strategy: this includes internal documents which contain direct evidence of a strategy to exclude competitors, such as a detailed plan to engage in certain conduct in order to exclude a competitor, to prevent entry or to pre-empt the emergence of a market, or evidence of concrete threats of exclusionary action. Such direct evidence may be helpful in interpreting the dominant undertaking's conduct.

21. When pursuing a case the Commission will develop the analysis of the general factors mentioned in paragraph 20, together with the more specific factors described in the sections dealing with certain types of exclusionary conduct, and any other factors which it may consider to be appropriate. This assessment will usually be made by comparing the actual or likely future situation in the relevant market (with the dominant undertaking's conduct in place) with an appropriate counterfactual, such as the simple absence of the conduct in question or with another realistic alternative scenario, having regard to established business practices.

Many of the factors listed in paragraph 20 concern the structure of the market, and are factors the Commission customarily takes into account in both antitrust and merger analysis. These concern the 'foreclosure' element of the test. The Commission also takes other appropriate factors into account, including those that are conduct-specific. Paragraph 21 states that the Commission will base its assessment on an appropriate 'counterfactual', meaning a 'but for' analysis, in which it tries to determine what would be the situation in the absence of the impugned conduct. The assessment of consumer harm is mainly reflected in the last sentence of paragraph 19, which survived the Amendments to the Guidance Paper unscathed.

Paragraph 19 has an important footnote, which says that '"consumers" encompasses all direct and indirect users, including intermediate producers'.[126] That is the established interpretation of 'consumer' in EU competition law.[127] The footnote also states, however, that 'where intermediate users are actual or potential competitors of the dominant undertaking, the assessment focuses on the effects of the conduct on users *further downstream*'.[128] In such situations, emphasis on the effects on those competitor-customers may distort the analysis of the effects on final consumers and thus the overall assessment of harm.

Paragraph 22 turns away from effects-based analysis, and says that there may be conduct which is so egregious that its anti-competitive effect can be inferred.

> There may be circumstances where it is not necessary for the Commission to carry out a detailed assessment before concluding that the conduct in question is likely to result in consumer harm. If it appears that the conduct can only raise obstacles to competition and that it creates no efficiencies, its anti-competitive effect may be inferred. This could be the case, for instance, if the dominant undertaking prevents its customers from testing the products of competitors or provides financial incentives to its customers on condition that they do not test such products, or pays a distributor or a customer to delay the introduction of a competitor's product.

Although paragraph 22 was left untouched by the Amendments to the Guidance Paper, the principle that it states surely must be qualified by the *Intel* and *Unilever* judgments, which emphasise that it remains open to dominant undertakings to argue that their behaviour lacks the capacity to foreclose competition, even if it is superficially restrictive on its face.[129]

5. OBJECTIVE JUSTIFICATION, EFFICIENCIES, AND OTHER DEFENCES

A. GENERAL

Although Article 102 does not contain an exemption similar to the Article 101(3) exception rule, the EU Courts have developed the concept of 'objective justification' by which otherwise abusive conduct may escape infringing Article 102. There are two principal categories of potential objective justifications: claims of objective necessity, and countervailing efficiencies. The defence of objective justification means that there are no 'per se' abuses under Article 102. Conduct which is often described as per se abusive, because it is presumptively abusive or abusive 'by object',[130] nonetheless remains open to the possibility of justification.

The extent to which the possibility of objective justification provides a meaningful defence for dominant firms is contested. Almost inevitably, the subset of cases that come to public attention is heavily skewed towards those in which the justifications offered are weak or insufficient. Conversely, more plausible claims are likely to result in enforcement action being dropped prior to adoption of

[126] This is relevant to the assertion in para. 19 that *foreclosure* may arise at either the intermediate or final consumer levels.
[127] See Chap. 1. [128] Emphasis added.
[129] Case C-413/14 P, *Intel* EU:C:2017:632, paras. 138–139; Case C-680/20, *Unilever Italia* EU:C:2023:33, paras. 50–54.
[130] See Section 3.F.

any infringement decision. Since few undertakings would be inclined to appeal against a decision *not* to find them in violation of Article 102, inevitably it is the weaker cases which come before the EU Courts. This may reinforce the perception that the possibility of invoking an objective justification successfully under Article 102 is more theoretical than real. An interesting counter-example arose in *CEAHR*, which involved an appeal by complainants against a rejection decision of the Commission, denying their complaints against various prestige watch manufacturers for, inter alia, refusal to supply. The rejection decision took the view that any prima facie refusal could be explained by objective justifications and the pursuit of productivity gains, specifically the preservation of brand image and the quality of products, the prevention of counterfeiting, and the increased technical complexity of mechanical watches which necessitated high-quality repair. The GC accepted the Commission's approach in this regard.[131] The continuing possibility of objective justification received strong endorsement from the Grand Chamber of the CJ in *Intel* in 2017, which made clear that it functions as a defence in the sense that it 'saves' otherwise abusive conduct which fulfils the requirements for prohibition under Article 102.[132] Yet the limited weight given by the Commission to the proffered objective justifications in the *Google Shopping* and *Google Android* decisions[133] demonstrates that the hurdle to save prima facie abusive behaviour may indeed be high.

B. OBJECTIVE JUSTIFICATION IN *POST DANMARK I*

In *Post Danmark I*, in 2012 the CJ stated that conduct with anti-competitive effects may be justified and set out the conditions that a successful efficiencies defence must fulfil.[134]

Case C-209/10, *Post Danmark A/S v Konkurrencerådet* EU:C:2012:172

Court of Justice

40. . . . [I]t is open to a dominant undertaking to provide justification for behaviour that is liable to be caught by the prohibition under Article [102] (. . . Case 27/76 *United Brands and United Brands Continentaal* v *Commission* . . . paragraph 184; Joined Cases C-241/91 P and C-242/91 P *RTE and ITP* v *Commission* . . . paragraphs 54 and 55; and *TeliaSonera Sverige*, paragraphs 31 and 75).

41. In particular, such an undertaking may demonstrate, for that purpose, either that its conduct is objectively necessary (. . . Case 311/84 *CBEM* . . . paragraph 27), or that the exclusionary effect produced may be counterbalanced, outweighed even, by advantages in terms of efficiency that also benefit consumers (Case C-95/04 P *British Airways* v *Commission* . . . paragraph 86, and *TeliaSonera Sverige*, paragraph 76).

42. In that last regard, it is for the dominant undertaking to show that the efficiency gains likely to result from the conduct under consideration counteract any likely negative effects on competition and consumer welfare in the affected markets, that those gains have been, or are likely to be, brought about as a result of that conduct, that such conduct is necessary for the achievement of those gains in efficiency and that it does not eliminate effective competition, by removing all or most existing sources of actual or potential competition.

131 Case T-712/14, *CEAHR* EU:T:2017:748.

132 Case C-413/14 P, *Intel* EU:C:2017:632, para. 140.

133 Discussed in Sections 13 and 11.E, respectively.

134 Whether *Post Danmark I* means that 'objective necessity' is a synonym for 'objective justification' and that 'efficiency' is a separate defence, is a moot point. Rousseva and Marquis, n. 7, 32 consider that they are separate. In COMP/39.525, *Telekomunikacja Polska* 22 June 2011, paras. 873–874, upheld Case T-486/11, *Orange Polska* EU:T:2015:1002, the Commission referred to a dominant undertaking providing an objective justification *or* demonstrating that its conduct produces efficiencies.

In paragraphs 41 and 42, the CJ identifies two grounds of justification: (a) objective necessity and (b) efficiencies. By prefacing this with 'in particular', the CJ did not however rule out the existence of other grounds of justification.

C. OBJECTIVE NECESSITY

Post Danmark I did not elaborate on the meaning of 'objective necessity'. In *Google Shopping*, the GC identified two main categories of objective necessity, which can arise 'from legitimate commercial considerations, for example to protect against unfair competition or to take account of negotiations with customers . . ., but equally from technical justifications, for example linked to maintaining product or service performance or to improving performance'.[135] Conduct necessary to protect legitimate public-interest objectives could, in principle, be objectively justified,[136] and this could include the health and safety of consumers. In both *Hilti*[137] and *Tetra Pak II*,[138] however, claims that tie-ins were justified in order to ensure public safety were rejected on the grounds that safety was ensured by public authorities enforcing safety regulations and not by private undertakings indulging in exclusionary practices.[139] While the Commission in *Baltic Rail* accepted that, in theory, passenger safety considerations could provide a valid objective justification, the egregious facts of that case meant that a credible defence was not established.[140] Similarly, in *AstraZeneca*, the CJ said that pharmacovigilance obligations could constitute objective justification for deregistering a marketing authorisation, although it was not so in that case.[141] In *FAG-Flughafen-Frankfurt/Main*,[142] the undertaking argued that the refusal to allow independent ramp-handling and self-handling services at an airport was objectively justified by space and capacity restraints, and the Commission only rejected this after carefully considering technical reports.

In the Guidance Paper, the Commission states that the abusive conduct must be both 'objective necessary and proportionate' to achieve the legitimate aim sought.[143] It relates objective necessity to 'factors external to the undertaking'.[144] The only examples given are health and safety reasons, and it repeats what was said in *Hilti* and *Tetra Pak II* about the default role of public authorities in setting and enforcing healthy and safety standards.[145]

The limitation to 'external factors' is seen in the Commission's decisional practice. In *Telekomunikacja Polska*,[146] the Commission referred to 'allegedly abusive conduct that is actually necessary on the basis of factors external to the dominant undertaking and is proportionate'. The plea of the Romanian Power Exchange in *OPCOM/Romanian Power Exchange*, that its discriminatory treatment of power exchanges from other Member States was justified by the need to avoid an unlawful

[135] Case T-612/17, *Google Shopping* EU:T:2021:763, para. 552. See also Case 311/84, *Télémarketing* EU:C:1985:394, paras. 26–27.

[136] See P. Lowe, 'DG Competition's Review of the Policy on Abuse of Dominance' [2004] *Fordham Corp L Inst* 163 (the author was then Director-General of DG Comp).

[137] Case T-30/89, *Hilti* EU:T:1991:70, para. 118. [138] Case C-333/94 P, *Tetra Pak II* EU:C:1996:436.

[139] R. Nazzini, *The Foundations of European Union Competition Law: The Objectives and Principles of Article 102* (Oxford University Press, 2011), 317–320, describes this as a 'social welfare' defence.

[140] AT39813, *Baltic Rail* 2 October 2017, paras. 325–328. The decision was confirmed on appeal, Case T-814/17, *Lietuvos geležinkeliai* EU:T:2020:545, in a judgment in which the GC did not dispute the Commission's treatment of the claimed objective justification.

[141] Case C-457/10 P, *AstraZeneca* EU:C:2012:770, para. 135. The argument was raised for the first time before the GC.

[142] [1998] L72/30. [143] Guidance Paper, para. 29. [144] Ibid. [145] Ibid.

[146] COMP/39.525, *Telekomunikacja Polska* 22 June 2011, para. 874, upheld Case T-486/11, *Orange Polska* EU:T:2015:1002.

mismatch in VAT payments, was dismissed on the grounds that creating this barrier to entry was neither proportionate nor necessary.[147] Faull and Nikpay point out that the objective necessity defence 'does not require any balancing between the negative effects on competition of the conduct and its benefits . . . as long as the conduct is necessary to the achievement of the objective and proportionate to it, an objective necessity defence is made out'.[148]

D. EFFICIENCIES

In setting out the conditions for an 'efficiency defence', the CJ in *Post Danmark I* referred to its judgment in *British Airways*, repeated in *TeliaSonera*,[149] where it accepted that the dominant undertaking's conduct could be justified by efficiencies:

> It has to be determined whether the exclusionary effect arising from such a system, which is disadvantageous for competition, may be counterbalanced, or outweighed, by advantages in terms of efficiency which also benefit the consumer. If the exclusionary effect of that system bears no relation to advantages for the market and consumers, or if it goes beyond what is necessary in order to attain those advantages, that system must be regarded as an abuse.[150]

The rationale for recognising an efficiency defence thus relates to the concept of competition on the merits and, in particular, the assumption that consumers benefit from meritorious competitive market behaviour:

> [T]he concept of competition on the merits covers, in principle, a competitive situation in which consumers benefit from lower prices, better quality and a wider choice of new or improved goods and services. Thus . . . conduct which has the effect of broadening consumer choice by putting new goods on the market or by increasing the quantity or quality of the goods already on offer must, inter alia, be considered to come within the scope of competition on the merits.[151]

Despite the Court's reference to *British Airways* and *TeliaSonera*, the efficiency defence set out in paragraph 42 of *Post Danmark I* is stricter. The dominant undertaking must show:

- the likely efficiency gains counteract any likely negative effects on competition and consumer welfare;
- the gains have been, or are likely to be, brought about as a result of the conduct;
- the conduct is necessary for the achievement of the efficiency gains; *and*
- the conduct does not eliminate effective competition, by removing all or most existing sources of actual or potential competition.

Paragraphs 41–42 of *Post Danmark I* in effect adopt the efficiency test from paragraph 30 of the Guidance Paper. Paragraph 30 is similar to the efficiencies section in the Horizontal Merger Guidelines.[152]

[147] [2014] OJ C314/7, IP/14/214, STATEMENT/14/48. The Commission noted that no other European power exchange faced with a similar situation imposed such measures.

[148] Faull and Nikpay, n. 1, 4.291.

[149] Case C-52/09, *TeliaSonera* EU:C:2011:83, para. 76.

[150] Case C-95/04, *British Airways* EU:C:2007:166, para. 69.

[151] Case C-377/20, *Servizio Elettrico Nazionale* EU:C:2022, para. 85.

[152] Horizontal Merger Guidelines [2004] OJ C31/5, paras. 76–88, see Chap. 15.

Guidance on the Commission's Enforcement Priorities in Applying Article 82 of the EC Treaty to Abusive Exclusionary Conduct by Dominant Undertakings [2009] OJ C45/2

30. The Commission considers that a dominant undertaking may also justify conduct leading to foreclosure of competitors on the ground of efficiencies that are sufficient to guarantee that no net harm to consumers is likely to arise. In this context, the dominant undertaking will generally be expected to demonstrate, with a sufficient degree of probability, and on the basis of verifiable evidence, that the following cumulative conditions are fulfilled:[[153]]

— the efficiencies have been, or are likely to be, realised as a result of the conduct. They may, for example, include technical improvements in the quality of goods, or a reduction in the cost of production or distribution,

— the conduct is indispensable to the realisation of those efficiencies: there must be no less anti-competitive alternatives to the conduct that are capable of producing the same efficiencies,

— the likely efficiencies brought about by the conduct outweigh any likely negative effects on competition and consumer welfare in the affected markets,

— the conduct does not eliminate effective competition, by removing all or most existing sources of actual or potential competition. Rivalry between undertakings is an essential driver of economic efficiency, including dynamic efficiencies in the form of innovation. In its absence the dominant undertaking will lack adequate incentives to continue to create and pass on efficiency gains. Where there is no residual competition and no foreseeable threat of entry, the protection of rivalry and the competitive process outweighs possible efficiency gains. In the Commission's view, exclusionary conduct which maintains, creates or strengthens a market position approaching that of a monopoly can normally not be justified on the grounds that it also creates efficiency gains.

31. It is incumbent upon the dominant undertaking to provide all the evidence necessary to demonstrate that the conduct concerned is objectively justified. It then falls to the Commission to make the ultimate assessment of whether the conduct concerned is not objectively necessary and, based on a weighing-up of any apparent anti-competitive effects against any advanced and substantiated efficiencies, is likely to result in consumer harm.

The CJ in *Intel* described this assessment as the 'balancing of the favourable and unfavourable effects of the practice in question on competition'.[154] In *Generics (UK)*, the CJ added that this balancing exercise 'requires objective analysis of its effects on the market'.[155] The approach advocated in *Post Danmark I* has been described as amounting to 'a true Article 102(3) defence'.[156] It may be unsurprising, therefore, that the EU Courts are generally as sceptical of claims of objective justification under Article 102 as they have been to the exemption rule under Article 101(3).[157] The objectivity

[153] The Commission's footnote here refers to the Article 101(3) Guidelines.

[154] Case C-413/14 P, *Intel* EU:C:2017:632, para. 140.

[155] Case C-307/18, *Generics (UK)* EU:C:2020:52, para. 167.

[156] L. Peeperkorn, 'Coherence in the Application of Articles 101 and 102: A Realistic Prospect or an Elusive Goal?' (2016) 39 *World Competition* 389, 407.

[157] See Chap. 5, Section 3.

of the efficiency defence has one benefit for dominant undertakings, however: it is unnecessary to demonstrate that the defendant deliberately sought to achieve the efficiency benefits generated by the practice *ex ante*. It suffices even if these are 'only fortuitous or accidental'.[158]

In *Microsoft*, the GC considered the burden of proof in claims of objective justification. Paragraph 31 of the Guidance Paper reflects these parts of *Microsoft*.

Case T-201/04, *Microsoft v Commission* EU:T:2007:289

General Court

688. . . . [A]lthough the burden of proof of the existence of the circumstances that constitute an infringement of Article [102] is borne by the Commission, it is for the dominant undertaking concerned, and not for the Commission, before the end of the administrative procedure, to raise any plea of objective justification and to support it with arguments and evidence. It then falls to the Commission, where it proposes to make a finding of an abuse of a dominant position, to show that the arguments and evidence relied on by the undertaking cannot prevail and, accordingly, that the justification put forward cannot be accepted.

It appears from this, and from paragraph 42 of *Post Danmark*, that the evidential burden in respect of objective justification is on the dominant undertaking, meaning that once an abuse has been prima facie established, it is for the undertaking to adduce evidence and arguments that its conduct was justified. Accordingly, there is no requirement for the Commission or the other party alleging the infringement to demonstrate the *absence* of a valid objective justification at the outset. The rationale is that, generally speaking, 'the undertaking concerned is alone aware of that objective justification or is naturally better placed than the Commission to disclose its existence and demonstrate its relevance'.[159] In this regard, the approach to justifications under Article 102 is similar to the approach under Article 101(3).[160] Yet, as the prosecutor bears the ultimate burden of proof under Article 2 of Regulation 1/2003, it is for that party to show that the conduct was not objectively justified in the light of the evidence advanced.[161]

As noted, it has been argued that the possibility of succeeding under the efficiency defence is more theoretical than real. Efficiency claims are often dismissed with little discussion, as is shown in the cases discussed throughout this chapter. There are a number of problems with the defence.[162]

First, the requirements are stringent. The dominant undertaking must ensure no net harm to competition and consumer welfare. That balancing exercise is notoriously difficult, and the undertaking must make this assessment before it implements its commercial policy.

[158] Case C-307/18, *Generics (UK)* EU:C:2020:52, para. 168.

[159] Case T-321/05, *AstraZeneca* EU:T:2010:266, para. 686; Case T-612/17, *Google Shopping* EU:T:2021:763, para. 577.

[160] See Chap. 4, Section 4.

[161] See also R. Nazzini, 'The Wood Began to Move: An Essay on Consumer Welfare, Evidence and Burden of Proof in Article 102 EC Cases' (2006) 31 *ELRev* 518, 535: 'The analysis of the jurisprudence on objective justification demonstrates that this concept is not technically a defence. Rather it is used to explain the shifting of the evidential burden to the dominant undertaking once a prima facie case of abuse has been established', and further, Nazzini, n. 139, 289–294. See also C-53/03, *Syfait* EU:C:2004:673, Jacobs AG, para. 72.

[162] O'Donoghue and Padilla, n. 1, 351, note that it has been suggested that the Commission only pursues cases in which there are no offsetting efficiencies to the anti-competitive harm, but comment that this is difficult to reconcile with the Commission rejecting so few complaints on efficiency grounds.

Secondly, the requirements are subject to a high standard of proof. The Guidance Paper demands that the satisfaction of the conditions is demonstrated 'with a sufficient degree of probability, and on the basis of verifiable [i.e. quantifiable] evidence'. In *Post Danmark I*, the CJ talked of taking efficiency gains into account where 'their actual existence and their extent have been established . . . '.[163] In *Generics (UK)*, the CJ emphasised that an undertaking 'has to do more than put forward vague, general and theoretical arguments'.[164] This standard of proof contrasts with much of the case law, which allows the abusive conduct itself to be found by reference merely to 'likely' anti-competitive effects.

Thirdly, the final condition in *Post Danmark I*, i.e. that the conduct does not eliminate effective competition, is problematic when applied to the exclusionary conduct of a dominant undertaking. For example, in refusal to supply cases the refusal would not be a prima facie abuse in the first place without the (likely) elimination of effective competition in the downstream market.[165] It has been suggested that the requirement of 'effective' competition needs, therefore, to be read as 'existing' competition.[166] The danger is that the 'elimination of competition' condition means that consumers are deprived of the benefits of efficiencies because of the degree of dominance of the supplier.

Fourthly, the formulation of the efficiency defence appears to be narrow, and focused on the specific transaction. In *Michelin II*, for example, the GC dismissed claims about economies of scale,[167] and in *British Airways* it dismissed arguments about high fixed costs.[168]

Post Danmark and the Guidance Paper, in effect, import Article 101(3) into Article 102. However, there are cogent reasons for arguing that a provision designed as an exemption for negotiated agreements between independent undertakings which restrict competition is not suitable for application *ex post* to the unilateral actions of dominant undertakings where the theory of harm is far more difficult.[169] The question is not the desirability of taking efficiencies into account before finding an infringement of Article 102, but rather the stage of analysis at which they should be considered and the conditions that must be fulfilled.

E. PROTECTING THE UNDERTAKING'S OWN COMMERCIAL INTERESTS OR MEETING COMPETITION

'Protection of the undertaking's own commercial interests' as a defence was first accepted in *United Brands*, where the undertaking cut off supplies to a distributor to discipline it for participating in a rival's promotion. The fact that *United Brands* is cited in paragraph 40 of *Post Danmark I* suggests that the CJ considered it to be merely a category of objective justification, although *AstraZeneca* distinguished the two types of defences.[170] A 'commercial interest' has been described as 'an interest

[163] Case C-209/10, *Post Danmark I* EU:C:2012:172, para. 43.

[164] Case C-307/18, *Generics (UK)* EU:C:2020:52, para. 166.

[165] See e.g. Case C-7/97, *Oscar Bronner* EU:C:1998:569; Case C-418/01, *IMS Health* EU:C:2004:257; Case T-201/04, *Microsoft* EU:T:2007:289.

[166] Faull and Nikpay, n. 1, 4.296. [167] Case T-203/01, *Michelin II* EU:T:2003:250, para. 108.

[168] Case T-219/99, *British Airways* EU:T:2003:343, paras. 284–285.

[169] See further P. Akman, *The Concept of Abuse in EU Competition Law*, n. 18, 280–284; Nazzini, n. 139, 304–309; D. Walbroeck, 'The Assessment of Efficiencies under Article 102 TFEU and the Commission's Guidance Paper' in F. Etro and I. Kokkoris (eds.), *Competition Law and the Enforcement of Article 102* (Oxford University Press, 2010), 115.

[170] Case C-457/10 P, *AstraZeneca* EU:C:2012:770, para. 134.

consistent with the rational profit-maximizing behaviour of a non-dominant undertaking'.[171] The CJ said in *United Brands*:

> 189. Although it is true, as the applicant points out, that the fact that an undertaking is in a dominant position cannot disentitle it from protecting its own commercial interests if they are attacked, and that such an undertaking must be conceded the right to take such reasonable steps as it deems appropriate to protect its said interests, such behaviour cannot be countenanced if its actual purpose is to strengthen this dominant position and abuse it.
>
> 190. Even if the possibility of a counter-attack is acceptable that attack must still be proportionate to the threat taking into account the economic strength of the undertakings confronting each other.[172]

The CJ thus established that Article 102 does not prevent an undertaking from protecting its own commercial interests when they are attacked. However, this principle does not apply if the undertaking's 'actual purpose is to strengthen this dominant position and abuse it', i.e. if the undertaking has an anti-competitive intent. Furthermore, the undertaking's response must be 'reasonable' and 'proportionate'. In *Tetra Pak I*, Advocate General Kirschner said of proportionality:

> Applied to the conduct of an undertaking in a dominant position, that principle has the following meaning: the undertaking in a dominant position may act in a profit-oriented way, strive through its efforts to improve its market position and pursue its legitimate interests. But in so doing it may employ only such methods as are necessary to pursue those legitimate aims. In particular it may not act in a way which, foreseeably, will limit competition more than is necessary.[173]

The EU Courts and the Commission have relied on *United Brands* many times when considering a claim that the undertaking was merely protecting its own commercial interests.[174] In *BBI/Boosey & Hawkes*, another case in which a dominant undertaking cut off an existing customer,[175] the undertaking's *immediate* withdrawal of supplies was deemed unacceptable, as it was disproportionate to the threat faced. In *Generics (UK)*, which concerned allegedly abusive reverse-payment settlements in the pharmaceutical sector, the CJ said that dominant patent-holders are not prohibited as such from concluding patent litigation through settlements that have the effect of excluding generic competitors.[176] However, the patent-holder's legitimate commercial interests do not extend to settlements that are 'intended to deprive parties demonstrated as potential competitors of effective access to a market'.[177] The defence of protecting legitimate commercial interests has particularly been raised in cases of refusal to supply.[178] It played an important part in *Sot. Lélos*.[179] The CJ said that the

[171] Nazzini, n. 139, 300. [172] Case 27/76, *United Brands* EU:C:1978:22.

[173] Case T-51/89, *Tetra Pak I* EU:T:1990:15, para. 68 of the Opinion.

[174] See e.g. Case T-65/89, *BPB Industries and British Gypsum* EU:T:1993:31, para. 69; Cases T-24–26 and 28/93, *Compagnie Maritime Belge* EU:T:1996:139, para. 107; Case T-228/97, *Irish Sugar* EU:T:1999:246, para. 112; Cases T-191 and 212–214/98, *Atlantic Container Line* EU:T:2003:245, paras. 1113–1114, in which the GC said that objective justification applied only to practices reasonably taken to protect the undertaking's commercial interests; Case T-203/01, *Michelin II* EU:T:2003:250, para. 55; Cases C-468–478/06, *Sot. Lélos* EU:C:2008:504, para. 39; Case T-301/04, *Clearstream* EU:T:2009:317, para. 132.

[175] *BBI/Boosey & Hawkes: Interim Measures* [1987] OJ L282/36, para. 19. The customer began competing against the supplier.

[176] Case C-307/18, *Generics (UK)* EU:C:2020:52, paras. 149–150. [177] Ibid., para. 151.

[178] As in Case 27/76, *United Brands* EU:C:1978:22 and *BBI/Boosey & Hawkes* [1987] OJ L282/36.

[179] Cases C-468–478/06, *Sot. Lélos* EU:C:2008:504.

competition rules are incapable of being interpreted in such a way that, in order to defend its own commercial interests, the undertaking has no choice but to leave a particular market altogether.[180] There is little doubt that conduct protecting the dominant undertaking's interests would be justified if it consisted of legitimate business practices such as cutting off supplies to a bad debtor.[181]

The 'meeting competition defence' is a plea that the dominant undertaking is merely reacting to competition in a proportionate and reasonable way.[182] It is an aspect of the 'protecting legitimate commercial interests' defence,[183] and most relevant to pricing or margin squeeze cases where the dominant undertaking's prices are alleged to be predatory,[184] and/or exclusionary of equally efficient competitors.[185] The 'meeting competition' defence cannot save predatory pricing from constituting an abuse, as there is no absolute right for a dominant undertaking to align its prices with those of its competitors.

6. DOMINANCE AND ABUSE ON DIFFERENT MARKETS: 'LEVERAGING' OF MARKET POWER AS A THEORY OF HARM

Under Article 102, the dominant position may be held on a different market from that where the effects of the abuse are felt. In such cases, the crux of the abuse is typically the 'leveraging' of power from the dominant to the non-dominated market. The dominant undertaking, accordingly, attempts to make strategic use of its strength in one segment to increase its market power in a discrete (though typically related) market segment, whether upstream, downstream, or ancillary. Leveraging strategies can be *offensive*—that is, intended to enhance market power in the related segment in order to increase the dominant undertaking's profits in that market—or *defensive*—that is, intended to prevent entry into the core market.[186]

It is established, since the earliest cases under (now) Article 102,[187] that conduct that involves the leveraging of market power can constitute an abuse. However, the 'mere' fact that a dominant undertaking has been able subsequently to increase its share in an adjacent market segment is not, in itself, evidence that that undertaking has engaged in behaviour that can be characterised as abusive. This point was stated clearly by the GC in its *Google Shopping* judgment.[188]

Case T-612/17, *Google and Alphabet v Commission (Google Shopping)* EU:T:2021:763

General Court

162. The mere extension of an undertaking's dominant position to a neighbouring market cannot in itself constitute proof of conduct that departs from normal competition, even if that extension leads to the disappearance or marginalisation of competitors (. . . *Post Danmark*, C-209/10, EU:C:2012:172, paragraph 22, and . . . *Intel v Commission*, C-413/14 P, EU:C:2017:632, paragraph 134).

[180] Ibid., para. 68. [181] See *BBI/Boosey & Hawkes* [1987] OJ L282/36.

[182] See generally C. Simpson, 'Dominant Firms and Selective Discounting in the EU: When is "Meeting Competition" a Defence?' (2016) 12 *European Competition Journal* 1.

[183] See COMP/38.784, *Wanadoo España v Telefónica* 4 July 2007, para. 638. [184] See Sections 8 and 9.

[185] As in margin squeeze cases, see COMP/38.784, *Wanadoo España v Telefónica* 4 July 2007, para. 639.

[186] J. Crémer, Y.-A. de Montjoye, and H. Schweitzer, *Report on Competition Policy for the Digital Era*, European Commission, 4 April 2019, p. 65.

[187] Including Cases 6 and 7/73, *Commercial Solvents* EU:C:1974:18; Case 311/84, *Télémarketing* EU:C:1985:394; and Case C-260/89, *Elliniki Radiophonia Tileorasi (ERT) v DEP* EU:C:1991:254.

[188] See also para. 610 of that judgment: 'The possibility of identifying, possibly on the basis of Article 102 TFEU, an abuse on a market other than that on which the dominant position is held does not mean that every practice by which an undertaking uses its dominant position on a market to expand into another market is necessarily anticompetitive.'

> 163. . . . [A]s is apparent in essence from . . . *Tetra Laval v Commission* (T-5/02, EU:T:2002:264, paragraphs 156, 158 and 217), leveraging is a generic term in relation to the impact which a practice identified on one market may have on another market. The term may designate several different practices that are capable of being abusive, such as, in particular, tied sales as in . . . *Microsoft v Commission* (T-201/04, EU:T:2007:289), margin squeeze practices as in . . . *Telefónica and Telefónica de España v Commission* (T-336/07, EU:T:2012:172), or loyalty rebates as in . . . *Michelin v Commission* (T-203/01, EU:T:2003:250).
>
> 164. It must be noted that, while the leveraging practices of a dominant undertaking are not prohibited as such by Article 102 TFEU, the fact remains that that article is applicable to such practices. Thus . . . as indicated in paragraph 163 above, . . . several kinds of leveraging have previously been found to be contrary to Article 102 TFEU. In particular, in . . . *Microsoft v Commission* (T-201/04, EU:T:2007:289, paragraph 1344), the Court considered that the practices at issue, namely bundling and the refusal to supply interoperability information, formed part of a leveraging infringement, consisting in Microsoft's use of its dominant position on the client personal computer (PC) operating systems market to extend that dominant position to two adjacent markets.

To support the contention that leveraging as such is not prohibited, the GC cited the *Post Danmark I* and *Intel* judgments. In both cases, the CJ emphasised that exclusion of inefficient competitors as a result of effective competition on the merits by a dominant undertaking is not prohibited by Article 102, because 'not every exclusionary effect is necessarily detrimental to competition'.[189] Accordingly, the mere fact that an undertaking, initially dominant in market A, subsequently increases its market share in market B, tells us little about the reasons behind this change. There are many possible explanations of why the undertaking's share of market B might increase that are wholly compatible with competition on the merits: product improvements, a more attractive pricing policy, consumers shifting away from rival suppliers for reasons unrelated to the dominant undertaking, etc. In such circumstances, the dominant undertaking's share of the adjacent segment increases, and probably its market power too, but the reasons for this change cannot be considered abusive.

On the other hand, there are also numerous well-recognised types of abuse under Article 102 that involve precisely an effort to enhance the dominant undertaking's position in market B, by taking advantage of market power that it already enjoys in market A. What distinguishes the latter from the 'mere extension' of dominance is the fact that the dominant undertaking has proactively engaged in certain behaviour, other than 'on the merits', that is designed objectively to enhance its share of market B. The GC in *Google Shopping* identified several established examples of leveraging that may be abusive—tying and bundling, margin squeeze, loyalty rebates, and refusal to supply—and, on the facts of that case, it accepted that the Commission had correctly established another leveraging abuse involving artificial manipulation of an online search algorithm to discriminate in favour of the dominant undertaking's own service.[190]

In *Tetra Pak II*, the CJ confirmed that Article 102 can apply where abusive conduct occurs on a non-dominated market which is unrelated vertically to the dominated one, in order to gain an advantage in the former. Because, however, 'application of Article [102] presupposes a link between the dominant position and the alleged abusive conduct, which is normally not present where conduct

[189] Cases C-209/10, *Post Danmark I* EU:C:2012:172, para. 22, and C-413/14 P, *Intel* EU:C:2017:632, para. 134.

[190] See discussion in Section 13.

on a market distinct from the dominated market produces effects on that distinct market', the CJ held that it is necessary to demonstrate the existence of 'special circumstances' which justify the use of Article 102.[191] *Tetra Pak II* involved two separate and distinct carton markets—aseptic and non-aseptic[192]—with alleged predatory (i.e. below cost) pricing in the non-aseptic market. While the dominant undertaking did not directly use its dominance to commit the abuse, the dominance facilitated cross-subsidisation (i.e. Tetra Pak could fund the below-cost pricing campaign with profits from the dominant market). The special circumstances justifying the application of Article 102 were 'close associative links' between the two markets (including a large group of common customers for both products), the quasi-monopolistic position of Tetra Pak on the dominated market, and its leading position on the non-dominated market. Its powerful position on the dominated market meant that Tetra Pak could concentrate its efforts on the associated market, where it enjoyed greater freedom of action than its competitors. It was thus in a position comparable to that of holding a dominant position on the two markets as a whole.

Tetra Pak II does not establish that dominance on one market can always be abused by conduct on another distinct market. Rather, this is a possibility if particular circumstances mean that the undertaking's dominance gives it significant advantages on the second market. The special circumstances requirement was reiterated by the CJ in *TeliaSonera*, a margin squeeze case, where the Court emphasised that 'Article 102 TFEU gives no explicit guidance as to what is required in relation to where on the product markets the abuse took place'.[193]

7. GENERAL ISSUES IN RESPECT OF ABUSES CONCERNING PRICES

A. EXPLOITATIVE AND EXCLUSIONARY PRICING POLICIES

Many Article 102 cases concern the pricing policies of dominant firms. One of the most serious consequences of a firm being found to be dominant is that its pricing policies may become suspect. Some pricing practices, such as excessive pricing, are impossible or very unlikely in the absence of market power. Yet others, such as discriminatory pricing in the form of discount and rebate schemes, can be practised by any firm, and in non-dominated markets may be applauded as lively competition. Competition on price is the most basic form of competition but, where dominant firms are concerned, the Court has constantly reiterated that not all competition by means of price can be regarded as legitimate.[194]

For convenience, this chapter deals with pricing abuses under various headings and the sections on exclusionary price-based abuses largely follow the categorisation used in the Commission's Guidance Paper. It must be appreciated, however, that many of these abuses are interrelated, and that pricing policies may be characterised under more than one heading and may arise in combination. Exploitative pricing abuses are discussed in Section 16.A.

[191] Case C-333/94 P, *Tetra Pak II* EU:C:1996:436, para. 27.

[192] For market definition in the case, see Chap. 6, Section 8.

[193] Case C-52/09, *TeliaSonera* EU:C:2011:83, para. 84.

[194] See e.g. Case C-62/86, *AKZO* EU:C:1991:286, para. 70; Case C-209/10, *Post Danmark I* EU:C:2012:172, para. 25; and Case C-413/14 P, *Intel* EU:C:2017:632, para. 136.

B. PRICE DISCRIMINATION

(i) What is Price Discrimination?

Price discrimination[195] occurs where the same commodity is sold at different prices to different customers despite identical costs, i.e. the sales have different ratios of price to marginal cost. It also covers sales at the same price despite different costs. Price discrimination refers to a wide range of practices. Predatory pricing and rebate policies, for example, may involve price discrimination.

Price discrimination is 'persistent' when a supplier maintains a policy of obtaining a higher rate of return from some customers than from others. The ability to practise persistent price discrimination is a characteristic of market power. In a competitive market, customers who are charged higher prices typically can take their custom elsewhere. Persistent discrimination against some customers shows that it is difficult or impossible for them to switch suppliers. Price discrimination may occur in competitive markets, but it tends to be sporadic, i.e. it changes frequently, and customers may be in a favoured group today and disfavoured tomorrow.

All customers have a 'reservation price', namely the maximum price they will pay for the product.[196] In *perfect (first-degree) discrimination*, the supplier charges each customer his reservation price. This is often impossible in real life, meaning that a supplier can only practise *imperfect (second-degree)* discrimination, whereby he identifies different groups of customers with similar reservation prices and charges each group accordingly. He does this by offering various 'deals', in the form of goods or services in different packages, allowing customers to 'self-select' by choosing their preferred deal. In *third-degree discrimination*, the supplier sorts and targets different groups of customers by reference to some easily observable or ascertainable characteristic, such as old-age pensioners or students.[197] With the emergence of the digital economy and the advent of 'Big Data', personalised consumer price discrimination has become more straightforward and prevalent, particularly in e-commerce markets.[198]

Price discrimination works only if arbitrage is infeasible. Arbitrage occurs where customers trade amongst themselves, so that those customers charged the lowest prices sell on to those charged more. Arbitrage is not always possible, however. In *United Brands*,[199] for example, it was difficult to transport bananas, a highly delicate and perishable product, between Member States.

The general consensus among economists is that price discrimination is welfare-enhancing if it increases output.[200] Price discrimination may be pro-competitive in industries with high fixed (or sunk) costs and low marginal costs if an undertaking can charge above marginal cost to customers willing to pay, in order to recover some fixed costs, while charging lower near-marginal prices, to others.[201] This may in particular be a feature of high tech markets. However, it is possible for price

[195] See F. M. Scherer and D. Ross, *Industrial Market Structure and Economic Performance* (3rd edn, Houghton & Mifflin, 1990), Chap. 13; L. Philips, *The Economics of Price Discrimination* (Cambridge University Press, 1983); H. Varian, 'Price Discrimination' in R. Schmalensee and R. Willig (eds.), *Handbook of Industrial Organisation, Vol. 1* (North-Holland, 1989), Chap. 10; D. Geradin, A. Layne-Farrar, and N. Petit, *EU Competition Law and Economics* (Oxford University Press, 2012), 4.452–4.452; O'Donoghue and Padilla, n. 1, 959–967.

[196] See Chap. 1, Section 4.A. [197] M. Motta, *Competition Policy* (Cambridge University Press, 2004), 492.

[198] See e.g. C. Townley, E. Morrison, and K. Yeung, 'Big Data and Personalised Price Discrimination in EU Competition Law' (2017) 36 *YEL* 683.

[199] Case 27/76, *United Brands* EU:C:1978:22.

[200] There is a large literature on the economics of price discrimination, but see in particular R. Schmalensee, 'Output and Welfare Implications of Third Degree Price Discrimination' (1981) 71 *Am Econ Rev* 242; H. R. Varian, 'Price Discrimination and Social Welfare' (1985) 75 *Am Econ Rev* 870.

[201] See D. Ridyard, 'Exclusionary Pricing and Price Discrimination Abuses under Article 102—An Economic Analysis' [2002] *ECLR* 286, 287–278; J. Temple Lang and R. O'Donoghue, 'Defining Legitimate Competition: How to Clarify Pricing Abuses under Article 102EC' (2002) 26 *Fordham Int'l LJ* 83, 89–90.

discrimination to be anti-competitive and produce inefficient effects. It depends on the facts of the case. The challenge for competition law is to distinguish between those situations in which price discrimination is welfare-enhancing, and those in which it is not. In *Post Danmark I*, the CJ clarified that the fact that a practice is described as 'price discrimination' cannot of itself suggest that an exclusionary abuse exists.[202]

(ii) Primary Line and Secondary Line Injury

Price discrimination may involve primary or secondary line injury. Primary line injury prejudices the supplier's competitors, typically through foreclosure effects. In *Irish Sugar*[203] and *Compagnie Maritime Belge*,[204] for example, the dominant undertakings pursued selective (and therefore discriminatory) low pricing policies in order to exclude their competitors. Secondary line injury impacts upon the undertaking's customers. If a supplier sells a product to X more cheaply than to Y, and X and Y are competing manufacturers who need the product as an input, then X's costs will be lower than Y's. The supplier *may* distort competition between them as a result. The situation is more complex, however, if the supplier competes with the customer downstream.

Primary and secondary line injury may arise from the same scenario. In *British Airways*,[205] differential rebates given to travel agents were held to have an *exclusionary* effect on BA's competitor airlines (primary line injury), and a *distortive* effect on competition between travel agents (secondary line injury).

Primary line injury through exclusionary price discrimination is a major concern in EU competition law. Secondary line injury through discriminatory pricing is expressly listed as an abuse in Article 102(c).[206]

C. COST LEVELS

When looking at pricing abuses, it is necessary to understand costs terminology.[207]

(a) *Total cost* The total costs of production.

(b) *Average Total Cost (ATC)* The total costs involved in the production of one unit of output (i.e. total cost divided by the number of units produced).

(c) Total costs are of two kinds:

  (i) *Fixed costs*, which do not change with output over a given time period.

  (ii) *Variable costs*, which change with output.

(d) *Average Variable Cost (AVC)* The variable costs involved in the production of one unit (i.e. the variable costs added up and divided by the number of units produced).

(e) *Marginal Cost* The increase in total costs of a firm caused by increasing its output by one extra unit.

(f) *Short-run Marginal Cost (SRMC)* The marginal cost based on a firm's existing plant and equipment, rather than that which would be the most efficient.

[202] Case C-209/10, *Post Danmark I* EU:C:2012:172, para. 30.
[203] Case T-228/97, *Irish Sugar plc* EU:T:1999:246.
[204] Cases C-395 and 396/96 P, *Compagnie Maritime Belge* EU:C:2000:132.
[205] Case C-95/04 P, *British Airways* EU:C:2007:166.
[206] See Section 15.
[207] See also Chap. 3.

(g) *Avoidable Costs* The costs that will not be incurred if an undertaking ceases a particular operation. They are variable costs plus any fixed costs that are incurred during the period under examination (they cannot include sunk costs which have already been spent and cannot be recovered).

(h) *Average Avoidable Cost (AAC)* The average of the costs that could have been avoided if the undertaking had not produced a discrete amount of extra output.[208]

(i) *(Long-run) Average Incremental Cost ((LR)AIC)* The average of the (variable and fixed) costs that an undertaking incurs to produce a particular product.[209] This standard is useful in industries where there are large fixed costs but low, or even negligible, variable costs (because, e.g., the main cost is the provision of a network, as in telecommunications). LRAIC includes product-specific fixed costs made before the period under examination, and is useful in the case of multi-product undertakings where there are fixed costs common to a number of different activities carried on resulting in economies of scope. The Guidance Paper says that LRAIC and ATC are good proxies for one another and are the same in respect of a single product undertaking.[210]

D. THE 'AS EFFICIENT COMPETITOR' (AEC) TEST

It was explained earlier that the concept of competition 'on the merit' raises the difficult question of how one can draw the line, objectively, between meritorious (i.e. permissible) and unmeritorious (i.e. abusive) market conduct. Article 102 does not prohibit behaviour that leads to 'mere' exclusion of competitors,[211] but rather only where it can be demonstrated that exclusion translates into 'at the very least a potential anticompetitive effect'.[212] The 'as efficient competitor' (AEC) or 'equally efficient competitor' test is an analytical tool, which aims to identify situations where exclusion might be deemed anti-competitive on the basis that it is likely to result in the loss of efficient sources of supply from the market. It is a cost–price test, which asks whether a 'hypothetical competitor having the same costs as the dominant company'[213] would be able to operate profitably in the relevant market given the available profit margins when the effects of the dominant undertaking's (allegedly abusive) pricing practices are factored in. In *Google Shopping*, the GC explained the AEC test as follows.

Case T-612/17, *Google and Alphabet v Commission (Google Shopping)* EU:T:2021:763

General Court

538. . . . The use of the as-efficient-competitor test is warranted in the case of pricing practices (predatory pricing or a margin squeeze, for example), in order, in essence, to assess whether a competitor that is as efficient as the dominant undertaking allegedly responsible for those pricing practices, and which, in order not to be driven immediately from the market, would charge its customers the same prices as those charged by that undertaking, would have to do so at a loss and accentuating that loss, causing it to leave the market in the longer term (. . . *Post Danmark*, C-23/14, EU:C:2015:651, paragraphs 53 to 55 and the case-law cited). . . .

208 The definition of average avoidable cost given in the Guidance Paper, para. 26, fn. 2.

209 The definition of LRAIC given in the Guidance Paper, para. 26, fn. 2.

210 See Guidance Paper, para. 26, fn. 2.

211 Case T-612/17, *Google Shopping* EU:T:2021:763, para. 610.

212 Ibid., para. 438.

213 OECD Policy Brief, 'What is Competition on the Merits?' (2006), <www.oecd.org/competition/mergers/37082099.pdf>, 4.

> 539. . . . [I]n principle, the 'as-efficient competitor' is a hypothetical competitor, which is therefore presumed to charge its customers the same prices as the dominant undertaking, but is faced with the same costs as the dominant undertaking bears or makes its competitors bear if it sells them an input for the end product (. . . *TeliaSonera Sverige*, C-52/09, EU:C:2011:83, paragraphs 40 to 44). The use of the as-efficient-competitor test is intended to show that even a competitor as efficient as the undertaking that established the pricing practice at issue would be unable to withstand it in the long term by adopting the same pricing, since it would not be able to rely on the power conferred by the dominant position. That competitor is not therefore in principle an actual competitor whose actual efficiency would be assessed . . .
>
> 540. Furthermore, assuming it is possible for a competition authority such as the Commission to compare the actual efficiency of several undertakings by studying in depth the various parameters of their business, such an exercise could produce objective results only if the conditions of competition were not in fact distorted by anticompetitive behaviour. Consequently, such an exercise could not in itself serve to determine whether such conduct had been established.

The logic behind the AEC test is that conduct should be considered unlawful only if it is capable of excluding as efficient competitors, because it is only in such circumstances that we can be confident that the exclusion is the result of anti-competitive conduct rather than a by-product of permissible competition on the merits.[214] In loyalty rebate cases, for instance, the question is whether hypothetically efficient competitors would still be able to turn a profit, even after dropping their prices to compensate customers for loss of the exclusivity discounts offered by the dominant undertaking.[215] The AEC test has drawbacks, however, in allowing the exclusion of less efficient new competitors which could in time have become as efficient. Additionally, certain conduct caught by the test might nevertheless enhance consumer welfare, and it is unhelpful in situations where the efficiency of competitors is not an issue.[216]

The Commission's Guidance Paper originally adopted the AEC test as the standard by which pricing policies were 'normally' to be assessed, [217] with exceptions. Reflecting growing scepticism of the value of complicated economics-based tools in competition law assessment, however, the Amendments to the Guidance Paper have softened the recommendation as to whether and when an AEC test is likely to prove useful,[218] as set out in the next extract. While the Commission maintains that, 'generally', an AEC test will be conducted where alleged price-based abuses are at issue, 'at the same time' it now recognises that valuable competitive constraints can nonetheless be exerted by less efficient competitors.[219] Moreover, whereas the original Guidance Paper essentially used the AEC test as a filter by which to identify obviously unproblematic behaviour, the amended Guidance Paper suggests that the results should be considered as part of a 'general assessment of anti-competitive foreclosure, taking into account other relevant quantitative and/or qualitative evidence'.[220] Accordingly, the outcome of any AEC test should not be treated as determinative of whether a violation of Article 102 exists.

[214] See also Case C-377/20, *Servizio Elettrico Nazionale* EU:C:2022:379, para. 82, arguing that the AEC test provides a proxy for competition on the merits.

[215] See Section 10 for discussion of loyalty rebates and the role of the AEC test in this context.

[216] E.g. Case C-457/10 P, *AstraZeneca* EU:C:2012:770, where the undertaking was held to have misused the patent system to exclude competitors.

[217] Guidance Paper, para. 23 (original wording).

[218] In particular, while the original Guidance Paper, para. 25, stated that the Commission 'will' conduct an AEC test, the revised version merely states that it 'may' do so: see Amendments to the Guidance Paper, Annex, para. 3(b).

[219] Ibid., para. 2.

[220] Ibid., para. 3(b).

Guidance on the Commission's Enforcement Priorities in Applying Article 82 of the EC Treaty to Abusive Exclusionary Conduct by Dominant Undertakings [2009] OJ C45/2 (as amended by C(2023) 1923 final)

C. Price-based Exclusionary Conduct

23. The considerations in paragraphs 23 to 27 apply to price-based exclusionary conduct. Vigorous price competition is generally beneficial to consumers. With a view to preventing anti-competitive foreclosure, the Commission will generally intervene where the conduct concerned has already been or is capable of hampering competition from competitors which are considered to be as efficient as the dominant undertaking.

24. At the same time, the Commission recognises that in certain circumstances a less efficient competitor may also exert a constraint which should be taken into account when considering whether particular price-based conduct leads to anti-competitive foreclosure. The Commission will take a dynamic view of that constraint, given that in the absence of an abusive practice such a competitor may benefit from demand-related advantages, such as network and learning effects, which will tend to enhance its efficiency.

25. In order to determine whether even a hypothetical competitor as efficient as the dominant undertaking would be likely to be foreclosed by the conduct in question, the Commission may examine economic data relating to cost and sales prices, and in particular whether the dominant undertaking is engaging in below-cost pricing. This will require that sufficiently reliable data be available. Where available, the Commission will use information on the costs of the dominant undertaking itself. If reliable information on those costs is not available, the Commission may decide to use the cost data of competitors or other comparable reliable data.

26. The cost benchmarks that the Commission is likely to use are average avoidable cost (AAC) and long-run average incremental cost (LRAIC) . . . Failure to cover AAC indicates that the dominant undertaking is sacrificing profits in the short term and that an equally efficient competitor cannot serve the targeted customers without incurring a loss. LRAIC is usually above AAC because, in contrast to AAC (which only includes fixed costs if incurred during the period under examination), LRAIC includes product specific fixed costs made before the period in which allegedly abusive conduct took place. Failure to cover LRAIC indicates that the dominant undertaking is not recovering all the (attributable) fixed costs of producing the good or service in question and that an equally efficient competitor could be foreclosed from the market . . .

27. When analysing data to assess whether an equally efficient competitor can competeeffectively with the pricing conduct of the dominant undertaking, the Commissionwill integrate this analysis in the general assessment of anti-competitive foreclosure . . . taking into account other relevant quantitative and/orqualitative evidence.

The AEC test aligns with the Commission's declared focus on preventing anti-competitive foreclosure, insofar as the test recommends intervention where the conduct is, or is capable of, hampering competition from 'as efficient' competitors. The Commission has always, however, maintained a proviso that, 'in certain circumstances', competitive constraints exerted by *less* efficient competitors should be taken into account. The example given is of a competitor which, in the absence of abusive conduct, might benefit from demand-led advantages such as network and learning effects which could enhance its efficiency.[221] In the amended Guidance Paper, the Commission appears to put the

[221] Ibid., para. 24.

pressure that may be exerted by less efficient competitors on an almost equal footing to the constraints imposed by as efficient competitors, in appropriate circumstances.[222] While doing so gives the Commission greater scope to consider potential competition and dynamic efficiencies, it very clearly comes at the expense of legal certainty. The Commission will assess whether a competitor is 'as efficient' by examining the costs and sales price data of the dominant undertaking itself, but if this information is unavailable, the Commission may use that of competitors. Use of a competitor's data alone, however, cannot tell the Commission whether a competitor is 'as efficient'.[223]

The AEC test is recognised in, but typically not required by, the jurisprudence of the Union Courts: generally speaking, 'the competition authorities cannot be under a legal obligation to use the "as efficient competitor test" in order to find that a practice is abusive'.[224] The CJ in effect applied the AEC principle in the 1991 predatory pricing case of *AKZO*, where it established that whether low prices amount to an abuse depends on their relationship to the dominant undertaking's costs.[225] Since then, it has endorsed the AEC test as the legal standard for predatory pricing,[226] selective low pricing,[227] and margin squeeze cases.[228] The Union Courts have also recognised the utility of the AEC test in the context of price-based exclusivity practices, but do not mandate its application.[229] In *Google Android*, the GC emphasised that where the test *is* performed by the Commission to assist its analysis, 'it must be conducted rigorously'.[230]

The underlying inference of the AEC test—that, generally speaking, only efficient competitors deserve to be protected from the potentially exclusionary effects of the dominant undertaking's market activity—can also be seen in other areas of the Article 102 jurisprudence, such as the approach to the concept of indispensability in the *Bronner* case on refusal to deal.[231] In *Google Shopping*, the GC had suggested that 'the use of that test, which involves comparing prices and costs, did not . . . make sense', *unless* 'the competition issue identified was . . . one of pricing'.[232] The CJ in *Unilever* subsequently agreed that the AEC test 'may be inappropriate in particular in the case of certain non-pricing practices'.[233] It nonetheless held that 'even in the case of non-pricing practices, the relevance of such a test cannot be ruled out', in particular 'where the consequences of the practice in question can be quantified.'[234] In doing so, the *Unilever* Court appears to be more persuaded by the logic of the AEC test than the Commission in its amended Guidance Paper.[235]

In *Post Danmark II*, the CJ described the AEC test as merely 'one tool amongst others,'[236] and certainly other economics-based standards exist to guide competition law intervention. In the context of predatory pricing, for instance, the Guidance Paper advocates a *profit sacrifice* test as the usual

[222] Less efficient competitors can provide consumers with choice that some may value. See Case T-201/04, *Microsoft* EU:T:2007:289, para. 652; N. Petit, 'From Formalism to Effects? The Commission's Communication on Enforcement Priorities in Applying Article 82' (2009) 32 *World Competition* 485, 491.

[223] A practitioner has suggested that given the Commission's extensive powers of investigation and of sanctioning non-cooperation (see Chap. 13), it may merely be warning dominant undertakings to produce the data required: L. Kjølbe, 'Rebates Under Article 82EC: Navigating Uncertain Waters' [2010] *ECLR* 66, 74.

[224] Case C-680/20, *Unilever Italia* EU:C:2023:33, para. 58. [225] Case C-62/86, *AKZO* EU:C:1991:286.

[226] Ibid. [227] Case C-209/10, *Post Danmark I* EU:C:2012:172.

[228] Case C-280/08 P, *Deutsche Telekom* EU:C:2010:603; Case C-52/09, *TeliaSonera* EU:C:2011:83.

[229] Case C-413/14 P, *Intel* EU:C:2017:632, in particular paras. 133, 139, and 142–143.

[230] Case T-604/18, *Google Android* EU:T:2022:541, para. 664.

[231] Case C-7/97, *Oscar Bronner* EU:C:1998:569. [232] Case T-612/17, *Google Shopping* EU:T:2021:763, para. 539.

[233] Case C-680/20, *Unilever Italia* EU:C:2023:33, para. 57. [234] Ibid., para. 59.

[235] In the Amendments to the Guidance Paper, Annex, fn. 1, the Commission notably cites paras. 57–58 of *Unilever*, which emphasise the circumstances where the test may be 'inappropriate', but omits references to paras. 59–61, where the CJ emphasised the 'relevance' of the test.

[236] Case C-23/14, *Post Danmark II* EU:C:2015:651, para. 61.

standard.[237] This examines the dominant undertaking's conduct to see if it involves sacrificing profits in circumstances where it would only be rational to do so if the undertaking was thereby able to exclude competitors. A 'no economic sense' test has been used by the US Department of Justice (DOJ) when arguing certain cases under s. 2 of the Sherman Act.[238] It states that conduct should be considered abusive only if it makes no economic sense except for its tendency to lessen or exclude competition. The various versions of the 'consumer welfare balancing' test involve balancing the positive and negative effects of the conduct on consumer welfare. As the OECD says, such tests have 'a degree of intuitive appeal because they attempt to use consumer welfare effects themselves, rather than indirect factors such as profit sacrifice, as the gauge of dominant firm conduct'.[239] This is, however, perhaps easier to describe in theory than to execute in practice.[240] Finally, the 'own efficiency' test[241] asks whether the monopolist has improved its own efficiency by the conduct under review—which would be permitted—or whether it has impaired a competitor's efficiency—which would be prohibited. This test is most suitable where the exclusionary conduct is a 'refusal to deal'.[242]

8. PREDATORY PRICING

A. GENERAL

Predatory pricing is the practice whereby an undertaking sets its prices so low that rivals cannot compete effectively and are driven from the market.[243] Once competitors are excluded, the theory of predatory pricing assumes that the undertaking will increase its prices to monopoly levels, in order to recoup its losses. Such a strategy is anti-competitive because, although it generates low prices in the short term, its effects are to strengthen the power of the dominant undertaking to the prejudice of consumers. Predatory pricing has thus been described as 'a war of attrition, with its outcome determined by the combatants' relative losses and reserves'.[244] Predation can exclude firms which are *equally efficient* as the predator, yet which have shallower pockets.

The intractable problem for competition authorities is to identify where robust price competition ends and predation begins: '[p]redatory pricing is one of the most daunting subjects confronting nations with competition policies'.[245] At least initially, predatory pricing represents a boon for consumers, who benefit from aggressively low prices. As the US Supreme Court emphasised in its leading judgment of *Brooke Group*, an unsuccessful predation scheme therefore enhances consumer welfare in aggregate, insofar as it generates lower prices without a concomitant increase in market power.[246]

[237] Guidance Paper, paras. 64–65.

[238] E.g. in its briefs in *Microsoft*, <www.justice.gov/atr/case/us-v-microsoft-corporation-licensing>; *United States v AMR Corp*, 335 F.3d 1109 (10th Cir. 2005) (*American Airlines*); *United States v Dentsply International Inc*, 399 F.3d 181 (3d Cir. 2005).

[239] OECD Policy Brief (2006), 5. [240] Ibid.

[241] See E. Elhauge, 'Defining Better Monopolisation Standards' (2003–2004) 56 *Stan LR* 253.

[242] See Section 12.

[243] See generally P. L. Joskow and A. K. Klevorick, 'A Framework for Analyzing Predatory Pricing Policy' (1979) 89 *Yale LJ* 213; S. Bishop and M. Walker, *The Economics of EC Competition Law* (3rd edn, Sweet & Maxwell, 2010), 6.084–6.112; O'Donoghue and Padilla, n. 1, Chap. 6. Conduct, other than low pricing, designed to drive competitors out of the market can also be described as 'predatory'.

[244] R. Bork, *The Antitrust Paradox* (Basic Books, 1978, reprinted with new Introduction and Epilogue, Free Press, Macmillan, 1993), 147.

[245] E. Fox, 'Price Predation—US and EEC: Economics and Values' [1989] *Fordham Corp L Inst* 687, 687.

[246] *Brooke Group Ltd v Brown & Williamson Tobacco Corp*, 509 US 209, 224 (1993).

Moreover, to the extent that securing low prices represents a core concern of competition law, it may be considered counter-productive to deter firms from engaging in price-cutting behaviour through over-vigorous application of the antitrust rules.[247] While false positives (Type 1 errors) and false negatives (Type 2 errors) are both prejudicial to consumer welfare, many commentators argue that, particularly in respect of predatory pricing, the avoidance of Type 1 errors should be the priority.

Opinions differ as to how often predatory pricing occurs. The strategy of the predator is to sacrifice profit-maximisation in the short term, in order to reap monopoly profits in the long term. The conventional Chicago School view is that below-cost pricing is hardly ever a rational business strategy, and thus rare. This view was famously advanced by Bork: '[i]t seems unwise . . . to construct rules about a phenomenon that probably does not exist or which, should it exist in very rare cases, the courts would have grave difficulty in distinguishing from competitive price behavior'.[248] Losses incurred by the predator are suffered *today*, and may be heavy; any supra-competitive profits will be earned *tomorrow*, only if and when the predation strategy succeeds, and are inherently uncertain. In exiting the market, moreover, the entrant may dispose of its assets to other remaining competitors, thus prolonging the period of predation. A further difficulty is that predation is often a strategy to *gain* dominance, rather than a means to abuse *existing* dominance, yet EU law prohibits only the latter.[249] For this reason, the 'monopolisation' provision contained in s. 2 of the Sherman Act is arguably a better fit.

The mainstream view, however, is that predatory pricing can occur, and is contrary to Article 102, in certain circumstances.[250] The rationality of predatory pricing is conditioned upon the existence of barriers to entry. Otherwise, after one competitor is knocked out, others will enter when the incumbent raises its prices. The incumbent would thus be unable to enjoy the fruits of its predation. Crucially, predatory pricing may itself constitute a barrier to entry, where the presence of a known predator is a disincentive to entry. In this way, predatory pricing not only drives out existing competitors but repels potential competition. It may be easier to deter potential competitors than to expel existing ones, as incumbents may have incurred sunk costs and thus have an incentive to continue. Further, it is unlikely that all market actors have perfect information. A predatory price may give potential entrants erroneous signals about price levels in the market, which will deter entry as it appears unprofitable.

Predatory pricing is considered most feasible where firms operate multi-market, because, where the firm operates in only one market, it is more rational to absorb new entrants or to accommodate them, rather than to incur losses by undercutting. Where a firm is multi-market, it can potentially offset losses on one market with profits on another. A firm which establishes a reputation for aggressive reaction to competition may deter entry into other markets, meaning that one episode of predation may protect multiple markets. The firm may be multi-market in a geographical rather than a product sense, so that a reputation for predation in one geographic area may deter entrants elsewhere.[251]

[247] Ibid., 226–227. See also D. Crane, 'The Paradox of Predatory Pricing' (2005) 91 *Cornell LR* 1, for an emphatic argument in favour of under-enforcement against predatory pricing to avoid over-deterrence.

[248] Bork, n. 244, 154. The robustness of the economic evidence relied upon by Bork is subject to scathing critique in R. T. Rapp, 'Predatory Pricing and Entry Deterring Strategies: The Economics of *AKZO*' [1986] *ECLR* 233, fn. 1.

[249] M. Funk and C. Jaag, 'The More Economic Approach to Predatory Pricing' (2018) 14 *J of Competition Law and Economics* 292, 298.

[250] Discussing the circumstances in which predatory pricing may be a rational and profitable strategy, see R. van den Bergh, *Comparative Competition Law and Economics* (Edward Elgar, 2017), 334–340.

[251] Contrast, however, R. Selten, 'The Chain Store Paradox' (1978) 9 *Theory and Decision* 127–159.

The current consensus can be summed up as saying that predatory pricing can be a rational strategy where the conditions are right. In particular, it may be rational in digital markets, although the characteristics of the digital economy render application of the ordinary legal standard problematic. The Commission and the EU Courts consider that it can and does occur, and that it infringes Article 102 in such cases. The problem is to identify when abusive predation is present.

B. THE AREEDA–TURNER TEST

The legal test for predatory pricing found in both EU and US competition law has its origins in a *Harvard Law Review* article from 1975, written by Areeda and Turner, in which the authors advanced a costs-based test to identify predatory pricing.[252] Under this test, a price lower than reasonably anticipated short-run marginal cost (SRMC) would be considered predatory, on the basis that no rational dominant undertaking would voluntarily incur such losses unless for an anti-competitive purpose. Conversely, a price equal to or higher than reasonably anticipated SRMC should not be considered predatory, on the basis that each sale at least makes some contribution towards the firm's fixed costs.[253] SRMC is, however, almost impossible to compute in practice. The Areeda–Turner test therefore uses average variable cost (AVC) as a proxy for SRMC. The test is stated as follows:

- a price at or above reasonably anticipated AVC should be conclusively presumed lawful;
- a price below reasonably anticipated AVC should be conclusively presumed unlawful.

Despite criticisms of its shortcomings, the Areeda–Turner test has been highly influential in antitrust thinking.[254] In particular, it formed the basis of the argument in *AKZO*, in which the Commission first considered predatory pricing.[255]

C. THE TEST LAID DOWN IN *AKZO*

(i) The *AKZO* Case

ECS was a small UK firm which produced benzoyl peroxide, a catalyst used in plastics production and also (in the UK and Ireland) as a bleaching agent in flour-milling. ECS concentrated on the flour sector, where its major customer was Allied Mills. AKZO, a multinational chemicals company, produced benzoyl peroxide but concentrated on the plastics sector. ECS subsequently expanded its operations in the plastics sector, capturing one of AKZO's largest customers, which prompted AKZO to retaliate by threatening to attack ECS's flour sector business by reducing prices. It then supplied benzoyl peroxide at low prices, offering large discounts to ECS's best customers. The Commission subsequently held that AKZO had abused a dominant position contrary to Article 102.[256]

[252] P. Areeda and D. Turner, 'Predatory Pricing and Related Practices Under Section 2 of the Sherman Act' (1975) 88 *Harvard LR* 697.

[253] 'Reasonably anticipated' means that a firm's conduct is not judged *ex post facto*. The marginal cost is judged by what seemed reasonable at the time. If the SRMC turned out to be higher than anticipated, the firm should not be condemned for predatory pricing.

[254] See J. Brodley and D. Hay, 'Predatory Pricing: Competing Economic Theories and the Evolution of Legal Standards' (1981) 66 *Cornell LR* 738; J. Hurwitz and W. Kovacic, 'Judicial Analysis of Predation: The Emerging Trends' (1982) 35 *Vanderbilt LR* 63; E. Elhauge and D. Geradin, *Global Competition Law and Economics* (2nd edn, Hart Publishing, 2011), 353–368; H. Hovenkamp, *Federal Antitrust Policy* (5th edn, West, 2016), 457–485.

[255] *ECS/AKZO* [1985] OJ L374/1; upheld Case C-62/86, *AKZO* EU:C:1991:286.

[256] [1985] OJ L374/1.

The Commission found that AKZO was dominant in the organic peroxides market as a whole,[257] and had pursued a course of predation against ECS designed to drive it from the plastics sector. The finding of predation focused on AKZO's threats and its eliminatory intent. The decision did not lay down specific rules about the point at which low prices become predatory and suggested that even prices above ATC could be predatory.[258]

On appeal, AKZO argued that, since it had not reduced its prices below AVC, under the Areeda–Turner test its prices were not predatory. The CJ confirmed the Commission's market definition and finding of dominance. While it accepted AKZO's argument that some costs which the Commission had classified as variable were, in fact, fixed, it confirmed that AKZO was guilty of predatory pricing.[259] The CJ, however, set out a more structured, costs-based test to identify predation.

Case C-62/86, *AKZO Chemie BV v Commission* EU:C:1991:286

Court of Justice

69. . . . [A]s the Court held in Case 85/76, *Hoffmann-La Roche* . . ., the concept of abuse is an objective concept relating to the behaviour of an undertaking in a dominant position which is such as to influence the structure of a market where, as a result of the very presence of the undertaking in question, the degree of competition is weakened and through recourse to methods which, different from those which condition normal competition in products or services on the basis of the transactions of commercial operations, has the effect of hindering the maintenance of the degree of competition still existing in the market or the growth of that competition.

70. It follows that Article [102] prohibits a dominant undertaking from eliminating a competitor and thereby strengthening its position by using methods other than those which come within the scope of competition on the basis of quality. From that point of view, however, not all competition by means of price can be regarded as legitimate.

71. Prices below average variable costs (that is to say, those which vary depending on the quantities produced) by means of which a dominant undertaking seeks to eliminate a competitor must be regarded as abusive. A dominant undertaking has no interest in applying such prices except that of eliminating competitors so as to enable it subsequently to raise its prices by taking advantage of its monopolistic position, since each sale generates a loss, namely the total amount of the fixed costs (that is to say, those which remain constant regardless of the quantities produced) and, at least, part of the variable costs relating to the unit produced.

72. Moreover, prices below average total costs, that is to say, fixed costs plus variable costs, but above average variable costs, must be regarded as abusive if they are determined as part of a plan for eliminating a competitor. Such prices can drive from the market undertakings which are perhaps as efficient as the dominant undertakings but which, because of their smaller financial resources, are incapable of withstanding the competition waged against them.

73. These are the criteria that must be applied to the situation in the present case.

Following the logic of the Areeda–Turner test, the *AKZO* judgment states that prices below AVC 'must be regarded as abusive', because there is no profit-maximising reason for them. The only explanation is that they are intended to eliminate competitors. This establishes a strong presumption that pricing below AVC is abusive. Eliminatory intent is presumed. The CJ furthermore held that above AVC but

[257] See Chap. 6 for the market definition aspects of the case. [258] *ECS/AKZO* [1985] OJ L374/1, para. 79.
[259] Although it annulled the Commission's decision in respect of one customer and reduced the fine.

below ATC prices can also be abusive where they are part of a plan to eliminate competitors. In the latter case, there is no presumption as to the undertaking's intention, so the onus is on the Commission, or other party alleging abuse, to establish such intent in fact. Here, the Court departed from the Areeda–Turner test, which treats pricing above AVC as conclusively lawful. Sufficient eliminatory intent was found on the facts of *AKZO* from the direct threats and price cuts.

The CJ did not consider the situation where prices are at or above ATC. Nor did it say anything *expressly* about the dominant undertaking's possibility of recouping its losses, although arguably that it is implicit in paragraph 71.[260]

The test in *AKZO* is therefore:

- prices below AVC are presumed to be predatory;
- prices above AVC but below ATC (the 'grey' area) are not *presumed* predatory but are predatory if proven to be part of a plan to eliminate a competitor.

The *AKZO* test was reaffirmed in *Tetra Pak II*[261] and *France Télécom*.[262] It was further developed in *Post Danmark I*.[263]

(ii) The Criteria Laid Down in *AKZO*

a. *Problems with Costs-based Tests*

Costs-based criteria for predatory pricing have inherent limitations. Most basically, the logic of the Areeda–Turner test, which presumes that pricing below AVC provides adequate evidence of both exclusionary intent and impact, does not always hold true. Thus, it is argued that 'below-cost pricing is neither necessary nor sufficient for successful predation'.[264] A dominant firm can exclude through pricing practices that remain above cost, while below-cost pricing may fail to foreclose competition where, for instance, the expectations of rivals as to the future development of the market diverge from those of the predator.[265]

Secondly, even if one accepts the virtues of costs-based standard, AVC is a clumsy substitute for SRMC, because the AVC cost curve tends to be U-shaped and gives the undertaking a lot of room for manoeuvre. Marginal cost rises and falls more dramatically than AVC, because AVC averages out the cost of one additional unit over the entire output. The assumption that SRMC and AVC are equivalent holds good only in the long run.[266]

Thirdly, it is difficult to draw a rigid demarcation between fixed and variable costs. Classification is dependent upon the industry and the time period in issue. The longer the time period, the more costs become variable. In *AKZO*, the Court stated that 'an item of cost is not fixed or variable by nature'. It accordingly overruled the Commission's classification of labour costs as variable, as there was no direct correlation with quantities produced.[267] In *Wanadoo*,[268] the Commission classified the advertising of the undertaking's residential broadband services as a variable rather than a fixed cost, which the undertaking disputed.[269] Areeda and Turner recognised the problem of classification, and

[260] As suggested by Fennelly AG in his Opinion in Cases C-395 and 396/96 P, *Compagnie Maritime Belge* EU:C:1998:518.
[261] Case C-333/94 P, *Tetra Pak II* EU:C:1996:436. [262] Case C-202/07 P, *France Télécom* EU:C:2009:214.
[263] Case C-209/10, *Post Danmark I* EU:C:2012:172.
[264] P. Rey, Y. Spiegel, and K. Stahl, 'A Dynamic Model of Predation', CESifo Working Papers 9819 (2022), <www.cesifo.org/DocDL/cesifo1_wp9819.pdf>.
[265] Ibid. [266] Bishop and Walker, n. 243, 6.097. [267] *ECS/AKZO* [1985] OJ L374/1, para. 95.
[268] COMP/38.233, 16 July 2003.
[269] The GC dismissed the appeal on this point in Case T-340/03, *France Télécom* EU:T:2007:22 on procedural grounds, and likewise the plea that the Commission had calculated its recovery of costs incorrectly.

proposed that certain costs should always be treated as fixed (interest on debt, depreciation, taxes which do not vary with output).[270]

Fourthly, cost-based tests are unsatisfactory in markets in which AVC (or SRMC) is minimal, such as digital markets. Although this problem may be mitigated 'if one is careful to consider all (and only) costs that are variable during the period of alleged predation', equivalent difficulties may arise 'if the alleged predatory price is timed after the predator has incurred a fixed or sunk cost that the rival must decide whether to incur in the future'.[271]

In *AKZO*, the CJ gave no guidance as to the allocation of costs in multi-product/service firms. This situation was addressed in *Deutsche Post*, where the Commission applied the LRAIC standard when dealing with a statutory monopolist which was also active on a competitive market.[272] LRAIC was similarly applied in *Qualcomm*, where the various products concerned were different generations of chipsets, developed as part of an ongoing (and expensive) R&D process.[273] In calculating LRAIC, the Commission rejected the defendant's argument that all sunk costs should be excluded. To do so, '[i]n an industry like the semiconductor industry, which is characterised by low variable costs and high fixed costs that are mostly sunk by the time the products are commercialized . . . would make it very difficult, if not impossible, to detect any such foreclosure of an equally efficient competitor in a price-cost test'.[274]

b. *Rational Reasons for Below AVC Pricing*

The Areeda–Turner test presumes, conclusively, that pricing below cost is inherently irrational and thus anti-competitive. Yet there can be rational, non-predatory reasons for pricing under AVC: for example, to launch new lines, clear obsolete stock, or make continuous use of production facilities. In such circumstances, it may be preferable to sell temporarily at a loss and make some return, rather than none at all. Under the logic of Article 102, however, a defendant undertaking would be required to establish a valid objective justification or efficiency defence, which may be difficult in practice.[275] Multi-sided markets[276] present a particular problem, as undertakings may choose to price by charging only one side of the market or charging very low prices on one side. Such a strategy may be perfectly rational, and not anti-competitive.[277] The Guidance Paper recognises that, in multi-sided markets, it may be necessary to look at revenues and costs of both sides at the same time.[278]

c. *Ascertaining Intention Between AVC and ATC*

Under the *AKZO* test, the intention of the undertaking becomes a crucial factor when prices are in the 'grey' area between AVC and ATC. The test accepts that pricing at that level can be a rational, non-predatory strategy in certain circumstances, because the undertaking is covering its variable costs and at least some of its fixed costs on every unit sold. Accordingly, the undertaking may be seen as mitigating those costs that it will unavoidably incur, which is why Areeda and Turner viewed such pricing as conclusively lawful. Under the *AKZO* test, however, this benign explanation for pricing below ATC may be swept away by actual (rather than presumed) evidence of eliminatory intent. Evidence of anti-competitive intent thus 'serves to separate the wheat from the chaff, i.e. to clarify the purpose of a conduct that displays ambiguous welfare effects'.[279]

[270] P. Areeda and D. Turner, *Antitrust Law* (Little Brown, 1978), para. 715c.

[271] E. Elhauge, 'Why Above-cost Price Cuts to Drive Out Entrants Are Not Predatory—And the Implications for Defining Costs and Market Power' (2003) 112 *Yale LJ* 681, 710–711.

[272] *Deutsche Post* [2001] OJ L125/27.

[273] AT.39711, *Qualcomm (Predation)* 18 July 2019, paras. 780–796.

[274] Ibid., para. 787.

[275] See e.g. the scepticism expressed by the Commission in its Guidance Paper, para. 74.

[276] See Chap. 3, Section 4.I.

[277] See Geradin, Layne-Farrar, and Petit, n. 195, 4.527.

[278] Guidance Paper, para. 26, fn. 2. For the issue of low prices in the digital economy, see Section 8.H.

[279] N. Zingales, 'Antitrust intent in an age of algorithmic nudging' 7 *J of Antitrust Enforcement* 386 (2019), 392.

Intent is a slippery concept in the context of competition law. All undertakings might be said to *intend* to eliminate their competitors simply by their participation in the struggle for custom in the marketplace. The Court therefore means intention to eliminate competitors by resort to competitive methods that are not 'on the merits', and therefore not, in the words of *Hoffmann-La Roche*, 'normal' competition. Yet the distinction between 'normal' price competition and predatory pricing is precisely what the costs-based test aims to identify. 'Determined as part of a plan' seems to denote some degree of systematic and deliberate strategy, and the EU Courts treat 'plan' to eliminate and 'intent' to eliminate as synonymous.[280]

A finding of intention to eliminate must be established 'on the basis of sound and consistent evidence',[281] which may be 'direct' or 'indirect'.[282] Documentary evidence from the allegedly predating undertaking is 'direct evidence' of intention. In *AKZO*, eliminatory intention was derived partly from company documentation. Words may be open to different interpretations, however, and what seemed like an exhortationary address to the troops in the sales department at the time may read like threats of ruthless predatory intent subsequently.[283] Moreover, apparently blatant evidence of anti-competitive intention can mask the fact that an exclusionary outcome is highly unlikely to materialise in the circumstances.[284]

Nevertheless, in *Wanadoo*, the Commission relied, inter alia, upon internal documents to show that the defendant, WIN, had dropped its price for retail broadband access in order to 'pre-empt' the developing market. WIN disputed the significance of the documents, alleging that some were informal or impromptu. The GC noted that some of the incriminating words and phrases came from management-level staff, and were expressed in the context of formal presentations for the taking of a decision or of a very detailed framework letter.[285] It considered that the phrase, 'our pre-emption of the ASDL market is imperative', could not be read as anything other than a strategy to 'pre-empt'.[286] WIN claimed on appeal that this amounted to the GC finding a plan of predation on 'subjective' instead of 'objective' factors. The CJ rejected this, holding that the GC had deduced a 'strategy to pre-empt' from 'objective factors such as that of the undertaking's internal documents'.[287]

The ubiquity of email today may make the task of gathering evidence of anti-competitive intention more straightforward. In *Qualcomm*, the Commission placed heavy reliance on internal email correspondence between sales, marketing, and management-level staff to trace the evolving parameters of the dominant undertaking's exclusionary strategy.[288]

It has been said that, despite the GC's suggestions in *France Télécom* about the sufficiency of direct evidence such as internal documents, in practice the Commission always relies on 'indirect' corroborative evidence as well.[289] The type of indirect evidence used is illustrated by *Tetra Pak II*, where factors such as the duration and scale of the losses, and the tactic of specially importing the products into Italy in order to sell them at a loss, were taken into account in identifying a predatory strategy. The defendant in *Qualcomm*, apparently mindful of the antitrust prohibition on below-cost pricing, made several one-off payments to large customers in order to reduce the effective price they paid for

[280] Case T-83/91, *Tetra Pak II* EU:T:1994:246, para. 151; Case T-340/03, *France Télécom* EU:T:2007:22, para. 197.

[281] Case T-83/91, *Tetra Pak II* EU:T:1994:246, para. 151.

[282] For a discussion of the required evidence generally see Geradin, Layne-Farrar, and Petit, n. 195, 4.272–4.278.

[283] See e.g. *Napier Brown/British Sugar* [1988] OJ L284/41, where an internal memo which said, '[i]f we are to succeed in seeing off the Whitworths threat, we MUST attack on all fronts. It is time to get nasty!' did not go down well with the Commission.

[284] Zingales, n. 279, 387. [285] Case T-340/03, *France Télécom* EU:T:2007:22, para. 202.

[286] Ibid., para. 206. [287] Ibid., para. 98.

[288] AT.39711, *Qualcomm (Predation)* 18 July 2019, paras. 1121–1137. [289] Rousseva and Marquis, n. 7, 32.

the targeted product lines, which were formally recorded as payments against other chipsets. This was treated as indirect evidence of exclusionary intent.[290]

d. *Selective Below-cost Pricing*

A predatory pricing strategy may incorporate an element of price discrimination in order to make it more sustainable. As the Commission acknowledges in its Guidance Paper, '[i]t may be easier for the dominant undertaking to engage in predatory conduct if it selectively targets specific customers with low prices, as this will limit the losses incurred'.[291] This is, in essence, a type of intra-market cross-subsidisation, whereby the losses suffered in selling below-cost to the target customers are subsidised, in whole or part, by the profits earned from customers paying full whack.

The 'targeted and selective nature' of the below-cost pricing policy was a key element of the theory of harm in the *Qualcomm* decision.[292] Here, the defendant aimed its price cuts, strategically, at what it perceived to be the two most important customers for UMTS chipsets, Huawei and ZTE. It was thus able to minimise losses by confining its pricing policy to a subset of sales, while still denying its up-and-coming competitor, Icera, access to the customer base necessary to secure its success. The strategic targeting and selectivity of Qualcomm's pricing conduct was also invoked as *indirect* evidence of exclusionary intent where its prices were in the 'grey' area above ATC.[293]

Claims of predation are common in transport markets, where a dominant undertaking may operate on multiple routes and engage in predatory behaviour on one or a small number of these.[294] Somewhat unexpectedly, the Commission in 2022 dropped a high-profile investigation into predatory pricing in the provision of rail passenger transport services on the Prague–Ostrava rail route,[295] two years after issuing a Statement of Objections.[296]

D. THE *POST DANMARK I* CASE

Post Danmark I[297] developed the *AKZO* jurisprudence in respect both of the costs benchmarks which can be used and the position where prices are between ATC and AVC but no intent to eliminate competitors is shown. The case was a preliminary reference in respect of the pricing practices of Post Danmark (PD) on the liberalised unaddressed mail market in Denmark. PD had a statutory monopoly for addressed mail under a certain weight. For this purpose, it had a country-wide network, which it also used for its unaddressed mail business. A competitor on the latter market claimed that PD was enticing away its biggest customers through selective price reductions. The Konkurrencerådet (Danish competition authority) could not establish that PD had intentionally sought to eliminate competition. Examining its costs by reference to the concept of average incremental cost (AIC) in order to take account of the shared infrastructure, the Konkurrencerådet found that in two cases, PD's prices were above ATC, and in one, they were below ATC but above AIC. As it found no intention to eliminate, the Konkurrencerådet, following *AKZO*, held that PD had not engaged in predatory

[290] AT.39711, *Qualcomm (Predation)* 18 July 2019, para. 1142. [291] Guidance Paper, para. 72.

[292] AT.39711, *Qualcomm (Predation)* 18 July 2019, paras. 399–406. [293] Ibid., para. 1139.

[294] C. Hemphill and P. Weiser, 'Beyond *Brooke Group*: Bringing Reality to the Law of Predatory Pricing' (2018) 128 *Yale LJ* 2048, 2064–2073.

[295] The Commission issued a terse statement on 29 September 2022, stating merely that it had 'decided to close antitrust proceedings case in AT.40156—*Czech Rail*'.

[296] Commission Press Release, 'Antitrust: The Commission sends Statement of Objections to České dráhy for alleged predatory pricing', 30 October 2020.

[297] Case C-209/10, *Post Danmark I* EU:C:2012:172.

pricing. Instead, however, it had abused its dominance through a policy of selective price reductions which amounted to price discrimination.

On appeal, the national court considered it necessary to make a reference to the CJ under Article 267. The CJ took a different tack, holding that price discrimination cannot of itself suggest that there is an exclusionary abuse; that prices above ATC could not be considered to have anti-competitive effects; and that selective low prices do not amount to an exclusionary abuse merely because the price is lower than ATC but above AIC.

Case C-209/10, *Post Danmark A/S v Konkurrencerådet* EU:C:2012:172

Court of Justice

35. . . . [I]t was found, among other things, that the price offered to the Coop group did not enable Post Danmark to cover the average total costs attributed to the activity of unaddressed mail distribution taken as a whole, but did enable it to cover the average incremental costs pertaining to that activity, as estimated by the Danish competition authorities.

36. Moreover, it is common ground that, in the present case, the prices offered to the Spar and SuperBest groups were assessed as being at a higher level than those average total costs, as estimated by those authorities. In those circumstances, it cannot be considered that such prices have anti-competitive effects.

37. As regards the prices charged the Coop group, a pricing policy such as that in issue in the main proceedings cannot be considered to amount to an exclusionary abuse simply because the price charged to a single customer by a dominant undertaking is lower than the average total costs attributed to the activity concerned, but higher than the average incremental costs pertaining to the latter, as respectively estimated in the case in the main proceedings.

38. Indeed, to the extent that a dominant undertaking sets its prices at a level covering the great bulk of the costs attributable to the supply of the goods or services in question, it will, as a general rule, be possible for a competitor as efficient as that undertaking to compete with those prices without suffering losses that are unsustainable in the long term.

39. It is for the court making the reference to assess the relevant circumstances of the case in the main proceedings in the light of the finding made in the previous paragraph. In any event, it is worth noting that it appears from the documents before the Court that Forbruger-Kontakt managed to maintain its distribution network despite losing the volume of mail related to the three customers involved and managed, in 2007, to win back the Coop group's custom and, since then, that of the Spar group.

40. If the court making the reference, after carrying out that assessment, should nevertheless make a finding of anti-competitive effects due to Post Danmark's actions, it should be recalled that it is open to a dominant undertaking to provide justification for behaviour that is liable to be caught by the prohibition under Article [102] (see, to this effect, Case 27/76 *United Brands and United Brands Continentaal* v *Commission* . . . paragraph 184; Joined Cases C-241/91 P and C-242/91 P *RTE and ITP* v *Commission* . . . paragraphs 54 and 55; and *TeliaSonera Sverige*, paragraphs 31 and 75).

. . .

45. . . . Article [102] must be interpreted as meaning that a policy by which a dominant undertaking charges low prices to certain major customers of a competitor may not be considered to amount to an exclusionary abuse merely because the price that undertaking charges one of those customers is lower than the average total costs attributed to the activity concerned, but higher than the average incremental costs pertaining to that activity, as estimated in the procedure giving rise to the case in the main proceedings. In order to assess the existence of anti-competitive effects in circumstances such as those of that case, it is necessary to consider whether that pricing policy, without objective justification, produces an actual or likely exclusionary effect, to the detriment of competition and, thereby, of consumers' interests.

Although the Konkurrencerådet had used incremental costs rather than the variable costs concept found in the *AKZO* case law,[298] the CJ accepted use of the ATC and AIC benchmarks. The CJ did, however, suggest that the methodology applied to calculate AIC may have attributed an unduly large portion of common costs to the unaddressed mail activity.[299] As AIC is lower than ATC but always higher than AVC, some of the prices fell within the 'grey' area where intent to eliminate is necessary to establish abuse. PD's intention to eliminate had not been proved so, under *AKZO*, strictly speaking the prices were not abusive. The CJ left it open to the national court, however, to find that the pricing was abusive *if it made a finding of anti-competitive effects*.[300] The CJ considered this unlikely, because if, as here, the dominant undertaking set its prices at a level covering the bulk of its attributable costs, *as a general rule* an equally efficient competitor could compete without suffering unsustainable losses.[301] On the facts, moreover, the competitor had remained on the market and won back some of its customers.[302] Although the CJ specifically referred to prices below ATC charged to a *single customer*, it made a general point about the ability of equally efficient competitors to compete, i.e. it applied the AEC test. It is clear from paragraph 37 that mere selectivity alone does not make a price below ATC abusive.

A plain-meaning reading of the judgment would suggest that the CJ augmented the *AKZO* test in providing that anti-competitive effects may suffice as an alternative to eliminatory intent where prices are between ATC and AIC. The question then arises as to whether such effects also function as an alternative where prices are between AIC and AVC;[303] there is no logical reason why they should not. In its *Qualcomm* decision, however, the Commission disregarded the apparent modification effected in *Post Danmark I*. It relied instead on the *AKZO* orthodoxy, purely 'based on comparisons of the prices concerned and certain costs incurred by the dominant undertaking, as well as on the latter's strategy'.[304] It cited *AKZO*, *France Télécom*, and *Tetra Pak II* in setting out the relevant legal principles, but not *Post Danmark I*.[305] The exact status of this area of the jurisprudence is thus unclear. The *Qualcomm* decision has been appealed to the GC.[306]

E. THE 'MEETING COMPETITION' DEFENCE AND PREDATORY PRICING

It was noted earlier that one consequence of the heightened 'special responsibility' of dominant firms, and the fact that the concept of abuse does not require *use* of the defendant's market power, is that dominant undertakings may be prohibited from practices that are perfectly lawful for non-dominant firms. This includes below-cost pricing. In *France Télécom*,[307] the CJ confirmed that the prohibition on predatory prices extends to circumstances where the dominant undertaking's competitors set their own market prices at loss-making levels. Here, the defendant claimed that, in pricing below cost, it was merely 'meeting competition' and that it had the right to 'align' its prices with its rivals. The CJ upheld the GC[308] in finding that dominant undertakings do not have an *absolute* right to align. The problem in pleading a meeting competition defence in predatory pricing cases is that *AKZO* is

[298] Ibid., para. 31. [299] Ibid., para. 34. [300] Ibid., para. 40. [301] Ibid., para. 38.
[302] The Danish Supreme Court subsequently overturned the Konkurrencerådet's decision.
[303] See the discussion in Faull and Nikpay, n. 1, 4.342. [304] AT.39711, *Qualcomm (Predation)* 18 July 2019, para. 329.
[305] Ibid., paras. 329–332. [306] Case T-671/19, *Qualcomm v Commission*, pending.
[307] Case C-202/07 P, *France Télécom* EU:C:2009:214, paras. 35–45 in particular.
[308] Case T-340/03, *France Télécom* EU:T:2007:22.

formulated in intent terms. If the undertaking is pricing below cost and intent is presumed (below AVC), or has been proved (in the 'grey area'), then that concludes the matter. The 'right to align' is removed by the fact of the undertaking's dominance, which imposes on it 'specific obligations'[309] which, as the GC said, deprive it 'of the right to adopt a course of conduct or take measures which are not in themselves abuses and which would even be unobjectionable if adopted or taken by non-dominant undertakings'.[310] The GC rejected the plea that below-cost pricing could be justified by efficiencies garnered through economies of scale.[311]

F. RECOUPMENT

(i) The Possibility of Recoupment

The concept of predatory pricing rests on the assumption that the predator sacrifices short-term profits for future gains. It hinges on the possibility that the predator can recoup its losses, i.e. that short-term loss is more than compensated for in the long term when, after the competitor's exit, the undertaking can raise prices to monopoly level. In the absence of barriers to entry, the undertaking cannot recoup if it continually must price low in order to fight off new competitors (although predation may constitute a barrier to entry). The economics literature emphasises that ability to recoup is central to recognising predatory pricing as a plausible anti-competitive strategy. It is another matter, however, to say that demonstrating recoupment is possible or likely should be a *necessary* element of the legal test to establish predatory pricing as an abuse of dominance.

In the US, the courts do not recognise predatory pricing as a form of monopolisation *unless* the plaintiff demonstrates that the alleged predator had a dangerous probability of recouping its investment in below-cost prices.[312] Even if the plaintiff can show below-cost prices and anti-competitive intent, there will be no antitrust violation absent recoupment. The result is that it is very difficult for predatory pricing actions to succeed in the US courts.[313] The US position reflects the view that enhancing consumer welfare is the sole objective of s. 2 of the Sherman Act. There are good arguments against making feasibility of recoupment part of the legal test, however. For example, there are problems wherever the burden of proof is placed, predicting recoupment is difficult, and the 'recoupment' sought by the firm may, for example, consist of deterring entrants in other markets, which is impossible to measure.[314] The appropriateness of a mandatory recoupment requirement within the legal test for predatory pricing continues to be disputed,[315] and the US House Judiciary Committee has recommended that it should be removed through legislation overriding the Supreme Court precedent on the issue.[316]

[309] Case C-202/07 P, *France Télécom* EU:C:2009:214, para. 46.

[310] Ibid., para. 186. [311] Ibid., para. 217.

[312] *Brooke Group Ltd v Brown & Williamson Tobacco Corp*, 509 US 209 (1993).

[313] See e.g. C. Hemphill, 'The Role of Recoupment in Predatory Pricing Analyses' (2001) 53 *Stan LR* 1581.

[314] See Temple Lang and O'Donoghue, n. 201, 144–145.

[315] Compare e.g. Hemphill and Weiser, n. 294, and L. Kaplow, 'Recoupment, Market Power, and Predatory Pricing' (2018) 82 *Antitrust LJ* 167.

[316] House Committee on the Judiciary, Subcommittee on Antitrust, Commercial and Administrative Law, *Investigation of Competition in Digital Markets. Majority Staff Report and Recommendations* (October 2020), 397. Though the subject matter of the report is digital competition specifically, its recommendations with respect to predatory pricing appear to be of more general application.

(ii) The EU Case Law

EU law differs from US law. In *AKZO*, the CJ did not expressly consider whether recoupment made predation a plausible strategy, but this was arguably implicit in paragraph 71.[317] The question of whether a possibility of recoupment is part of the test for predatory pricing was raised in *Tetra Pak II* and answered in the negative; at least in that case, where the principles laid down in *AKZO* were confirmed and developed.[318]

In *Tetra Pak II*, the defendant's share of the dominated market was over 90 per cent. The abuse occurred on the unrelated non-dominated (non-aseptic carton) market, where Tetra Pak was found to have engaged in predatory pricing. The CJ held that the Commission did not have to prove that Tetra Pak could recoup to establish the abuse. The pivotal factor in the determination of predation is, instead, whether 'there is a risk that competitors will be eliminated'.[319] The CJ did not say that it would *never* be necessary to show the feasibility of recoupment, but only that it would be inappropriate *in the circumstances of that case*. That included Tetra Pak's quasi-monopoly and the possibility of cross-subsidisation between markets. Further, there was evidence that Tetra Pak was pursuing a deliberate strategy of eliminating competitors.

In *Compagnie Maritime Belge*, Advocate General Fennelly considered that the possibility of recoupment should be an essential part of the test for predatory pricing,[320] but the CJ did not address the point. In *France Télécom*, however, the GC ruled that proof of recoupment was *not* a precondition to a finding of predatory pricing.[321] On appeal, Advocate General Mazák argued that, in the light of the particular language of *Tetra Pak II*—no need '*in the circumstances of the present case*'—proof of the possibility of recoupment should be required, as without that possibility 'consumers and their interests should, in principle not be harmed'.[322] Yet the CJ upheld the GC in trenchant terms.

Case C-202/07 P, *France Télécom SA v Commission* EU:C:2009:214

Court of Justice

106. . . . Article [102] prohibits a dominant undertaking from eliminating a competitor and thereby strengthening its position by using methods other than those which come within the scope of competition on the basis of quality. From that point of view, not all competition by means of price can be regarded as legitimate (*AKZO v Commission*, paragraph 70).

107. In particular, it must be found that an undertaking abuses its dominant position where, in a market the competition structure of which is already weakened by reason precisely of the presence of that undertaking, it operates a pricing policy the sole economic objective of which is to eliminate its competitors with a view, subsequently, to profiting from the reduction of the degree of competition still existing in the market.

108. In order to assess the lawfulness of the pricing policy applied by a dominant undertaking, the Court, in paragraph 74 of *AKZO v Commission*, relied on pricing criteria based on the costs incurred by the dominant undertaking and on its strategy.

317 See Cases C-395 and 396/96 P, *Compagnie Maritime Belge*, Fennelly AG, para. 136.

318 Case C-333/94 P, *Tetra Pak II* EU:C:1996:436.

319 *Tetra Pak II*, para. 44.

320 Para. 136 of his Opinion in Cases C-395 and 396/96 P *Compagnie Maritime Belge* EU:C:1998:518.

321 Case T-340/03, *France Télécom* EU:T:2007:22. Both above and below AVC pricing were involved.

322 Case C-202/07 P, *France Télécom* EU:C:2009:214, paras. 73–74 of the Opinion.

109. Thus, the Court of Justice has held, first, that prices below average variable costs must be considered prima facie abusive inasmuch as, in applying such prices, an undertaking in a dominant position is presumed to pursue no other economic objective save that of eliminating its competitors. Secondly, prices below average total costs but above average variable costs are to be considered abusive only where they are fixed in the context of a plan having the purpose of eliminating a competitor (see *AKZO v Commission*, paragraphs 70 and 71, and *Tetra Pak v Commission*, paragraph 41).

110. Accordingly, contrary to what the appellant claims, it does not follow from the case-law of the Court that proof of the possibility of recoupment of losses suffered by the application, by an undertaking in a dominant position, of prices lower than a certain level of costs constitutes a necessary precondition to establishing that such a pricing policy is abusive. In particular, the Court has taken the opportunity to dispense with such proof in circumstances where the eliminatory intent of the undertaking at issue could be presumed in view of that undertaking's application of prices lower than average variable costs (see, to that effect, *Tetra Pak v Commission*, paragraph 44).

111. That interpretation does not, of course, preclude the Commission from finding such a possibility of recoupment of losses to be a relevant factor in assessing whether or not the practice concerned is abusive, in that it may, for example where prices lower than average variable costs are applied, assist in excluding economic justifications other than the elimination of a competitor, or, where prices below average total costs but above average variable costs are applied, assist in establishing that a plan to eliminate a competitor exists.

112. Moreover, the lack of any possibility of recoupment of losses is not sufficient to prevent the undertaking concerned reinforcing its dominant position, in particular, following the withdrawal from the market of one or a number of its competitors, so that the degree of competition existing on the market, already weakened precisely because of the presence of the undertaking concerned, is further reduced and customers suffer loss as a result of the limitation of the choices available to them.

Importantly, although the CJ did not consider a possibility of recoupment to constitute a 'necessary precondition' to establishing predatory pricing contrary to Article 102, such a possibility is not wholly irrelevant. As the CJ acknowledged, the feasibility of recouping an undertaking's 'investment' in below-cost pricing may thus be taken into consideration when assessing the existence of predatory intent where prices are above AVC but below ATC, or in examining claims of objective justification.

G. PREDATORY PRICING IN THE GUIDANCE PAPER AND THE 'SACRIFICE' PRINCIPLE

The Guidance Paper adopts the 'sacrifice' principle as the lynchpin of predatory pricing enforcement. The question is whether the undertaking deliberately incurs losses or foregoes profits in the short term, so as to foreclose actual or potential competitors with a view to maintaining or strengthening market power thereby causing consumer harm.[323] The Guidance Paper reflects the *AKZO* test, but the Commission states that it will use AAC and LRAIC rather than AVC and ATC to assess sacrifice. Pricing below AAC is clear evidence of sacrifice.[324] Where sufficiently reliable data exist, the Commission states that it will apply the AEC test to determine whether the conduct is capable of harming consumers.[325] The Guidance Paper notes that, '[n]ormally only pricing below LRAIC is

[323] Guidance Paper, para. 63. [324] Ibid., paras. 64–65. [325] Ibid., para. 67.

capable of foreclosing as efficient competitors from the market'.[326] LRAIC and ATC are the same in single-product undertakings, but LRAIC may be lower in the case of multi-product undertakings. Subsequent to the Guidance Paper, the CJ accepted the use of LRAIC in *Post Danmark I*, as discussed. The Commission does not rule out justification by efficiencies, but considers that possibility 'unlikely' in practice.[327]

The Guidance Paper does not mention 'recoupment'. The Commission nevertheless says that consumers are most likely to be harmed if the dominant undertaking can reasonably expect an increase in market power after its conduct has ended.[328] An increase in market power, however, does not necessarily denote an ability to recoup, which will depend on the circumstances.[329] The Commission will intervene not only if prices can be increased again but also if the conduct could prevent or delay a lowering of prices.[330]

In a footnote, the Commission states that it may pursue predatory practices by dominant undertakings on secondary markets on which they are not yet dominant.[331] This may particularly be so where a dominant undertaking on a market protected by a legal monopoly uses its profits to cross-subsidise activities in another market. Cross-subsidisation has never been held to be an abuse *in itself*. It is the below-cost prices on the subsidised market, or other abusive practices, which may infringe Article 102.[332]

H. PREDATORY PRICING IN HIGH TECH AND DIGITAL MARKETS

The particular characteristics of high tech and digital markets have been introduced in Chapter 1, and are discussed further in Chapter 16. One of these is the 'tipping' effect, whereby the successful competitor takes most (or all) of the market because its product or service becomes the standard. Predatory pricing may be a rational strategy in such markets: low pricing can achieve the critical mass of customers which results in the undertaking winning the competition 'for' the market. Further, high tech markets commonly have very high fixed costs and very low variable costs which may distort predatory pricing tests based on AVC.

France Télécom concerned a digital market, WIN's ADSL retail broadband services.[333] WIN was a majority-owned subsidiary of France Télécom, which controlled almost 100 per cent of the wholesale market for ADSL services. The Commission found that the undertaking deliberately pursued a loss-making retail pricing policy, 'designed to take the lion's share of a booming market at the expense of other competitors'.[334] WIN claimed that its conduct was rational: its pricing attracted new customers who would be profitable in under five years. The Commission, however, saw this reasoning as demonstrating that the pricing *was* predatory: 'the recoupment of initial losses over a certain period of time is in the most common settings the very objective of a predatory pricing behaviour'.[335] The Commission also disagreed that it was inappropriate to intervene at a nascent stage. This refusal to take a 'hands off' approach while the market developed was upheld on appeal.[336]

More recently, in *Qualcomm*,[337] the Commission condemned predatory pricing by a technology company which used selective below-cost pricing of certain categories of UMTS chipsets to prevent

[326] Ibid. [327] Ibid., para. 74. [328] Ibid., para. 70.

[329] See E. Rousseva, *Rethinking Exclusionary Abuses in EU Competition Law* (Hart Publishing, 2010), 408.

[330] Guidance Paper, para. 71. [331] Ibid., para. 63.

[332] See *Deutsche Post* [2001] OJ L125/27; Case C-333/94 P, *Tetra Pak II* EU:C:1996:436.

[333] COMP/38.233, *Wanadoo Interactive*, 16 July 2003. See R. Klotz and J. Fehrenbach (2003) 3 *Competition Policy Newsletter* 10.

[334] Ibid., 11. [335] Ibid., 12.

[336] Case T-340/03, *France Télécom* EU:T:2007:22 and Case C-202/07 P, *France Télécom* EU:C:2009:214.

[337] AT.39711, *Qualcomm (Predation)* 18 July 2019.

a new competitor from gaining a sufficient foothold in the semiconductor sector. *Qualcomm* illustrates what can be the extreme complexity of executing a price–cost test in high tech markets. The Commission grappled with a multi-product firm, high R&D costs albeit spread across multiple product lines, otherwise low variable costs, and the strategic use of reverse payments made by the *seller* to its customers which, as we shall see in Section 10, has become something of a hallmark of digital markets. The upshot was a complex and disputed set of calculations to determine the LRAIC and to 'reconstruct' the effective selling price. It also resulted in a drawn-out investigation process, with the infringement decision coming a decade after Icera's first complaint to the Commission.

The issue becomes even more complicated when multi-sided markets are a stake, increasing the likelihood that Type I or Type II errors may arise if standard predatory pricing rules are applied.[338] Here, cross-subsidies between user groups are commonplace, and the 'price' charged on one side of the market may be zero.[339] Yet 'the fact that no price is charged to consumers does not mean that no price is charged at all, or that none of the dominant firm's costs are recouped'.[340] Often customers can use a basic service for free, but are charged when they move to premium services with added features.[341] Alternatively, providers may make money from customers in other ways, such as commodification of their personal data.[342] The Commission, which conducted an initial investigation into alleged predatory pricing by Google in distributing its Android system for free, did not pursue this claim when it opened formal proceedings in the *Android* case.[343] Similarly, the Paris Court of Appeal, in a private damages claim, found that Google had not engaged in predatory pricing with respect to its free-to-use Google Maps product, because Google was not pricing below its costs once advertising revenues earned on interlinked markets were considered.[344] It may be unsurprising that calls for more muscular enforcement against low pricing by digital economy firms have been premised, primarily, upon the need to *dispense with* existing antitrust standards, and not merely apply them in the digital context.[345]

I. SELECTIVE ABOVE-COST PRICING

Predatory pricing may involve not just low prices across the board, but selective targeting of below-cost prices to certain customers.[346] In a strand of earlier case law, the EU Courts held that certain selective *above*-cost prices—i.e. which were *not* below costs, and thus did not involve absolute losses—nonetheless infringed Article 102. These cases—*Hilti*,[347] *Compagnie Maritime Belge*,[348] and *Irish Sugar*[349]—each had special features, and subsequently in *Post Danmark I*[350] the CJ held that prices

[338] See e.g. A. Fletcher, 'Predatory Pricing in Two-sided Markets: A Brief Comment' (2007) 3 *Competition Policy International* 221.

[339] In Chap. 1, Section 10.

[340] M. Rato and N. Petit, 'Abuse of Dominance in Technology-enabled Markets: Established Standards Reconsidered?' (2013) 9 *European Competition Journal* 1, 50.

[341] Ibid., para. 51. [342] See J. Newman, 'Antitrust in Zero-price Markets: Foundations' (2015) 164 *U Pa LR* 149.

[343] IP/15/4780; MEMO/15/4782; IP/16/1492; MEMO/16/1484.

[344] Discussed in A. Sibony, 'Predatory Pricing: The Paris Court of Appeal upholds the French Competition Authority's Decision Considering that No Predation can be Established on the French Market for Map APIs (*Google/Evermaps*)' [2016] 1 *Concurrences* 101–103.

[345] See e.g. L. Khan, 'Amazon's Antitrust Paradox' (2017) 126 *Yale LJ* 710.

[346] As in AT.39711, *Qualcomm (Predation)* 18 July 2019, and recognised in the Guidance Paper, para. 72.

[347] Case C-53/92 P, *Hilti* EU:C:1994:77.

[348] Cases C-395 and 396/96 P, *Compagnie Maritime Belge* EU:C:2000:132.

[349] Case T-228/97, *Irish Sugar* EU:T:1999:246. [350] Case C-209/10, *Post Danmark I* EU:C:2012:172.

above AIC are presumed to be legal. Thus, a 'health warning' must be attached about the continued reliability of the jurisprudence described in this section.[351]

Hilti involved a dominant undertaking that offered lower, but above-cost, prices to competitors' customers as part of a tying strategy.[352] In *Compagnie Maritime Belge*, undertakings in a collective dominant position engaged in selective low pricing targeted at a competitor's customers.[353] The undertakings were parties to a liner conference[354] (CEWAL), which faced competition from an independent shipping line (G&C). Among the practices it adopted in response were 'fighting ships', specially designated vessels whose sailing dates mirrored those of G&C and on which CEWAL dropped its rates to match G&C. The prices caused some revenue losses, but were not below CEWAL members' total costs. The Commission found this an abuse of CEWAL's collective dominant position.[355]

The GC upheld the Commission, focusing on CEWAL's intent to eliminate G&C and the possible effect of its actions.[356] It rejected the argument that CEWAL was trying to *meet* rather than *beat* competition, saying that its response was not reasonable or proportionate.[357] Advocate General Fennelly saw this as a case of a 'super-dominant' entity aiming to exclude a competitor. In such a situation, targeted selective price cuts designed to eliminate would be abusive regardless of the price–cost relationship.[358] The CJ held that the prices charged were abusive,[359] but its judgment was couched in narrower terms than the Advocate General's Opinion. It concentrated on the specifics of the case.

Cases C-395 and 396/96 P, *Compagnie Maritime Belge and Others v Commission* EU:C:2000:132

Court of Justice

112. It is settled case-law that the list of abusive practices contained in Article [102] of the Treaty is not an exhaustive enumeration of the abuses of a dominant position prohibited by the Treaty (Case 6/72 *Europemballage and Continental Can* v. *Commission* . . . paragraph 26).

113. It is, moreover, established that, in certain circumstances, abuse may occur if an undertaking in a dominant position strengthens that position in such a way that the degree of dominance reached substantially fetters competition (*Europemballage and Continental Can*, paragraph 26).

114. Furthermore, the actual scope of the special responsibility imposed on a dominant undertaking must be considered in the light of the specific circumstances of each case which show that competition has been weakened (Case C-333/94 P *Tetra Pak* v. *Commission* . . ., paragraph 24).

. . .

118. It is not necessary, in the present case, to rule generally on the circumstances in which a liner conference may legitimately, on a case-by-case basis, adopt lower prices than those of its advertised tariff in order to compete with a competitor who quotes lower prices . . .

[351] Although, more recently, the GC in Case T-612/17, *Google Shopping* EU:T:2021:763, paras. 155 and 239, cited *Irish Sugar* repeatedly to support its contention that violations of the general principle of equal treatment can amount to abuse of dominance in certain circumstances.

[352] See further Section 11.

[353] *CEWAL* [1993] OJ L34/20.

[354] A 'liner conference' is a group of two or more vessel-operators providing international services for carrying cargo on a particular route or routes within specified geographical limits, which has an agreement within the framework of which they operate under uniform or common freight rates and other agreed conditions.

[355] For the collective dominance aspects of the case, see Chap. 6.

[356] Cases T-24–26 and 28/93, *Compagnie Maritime Belge* EU:T:1996:139.

[357] Ibid., para. 148.

[358] Cases C-395 and 396/96 P, *Compagnie Maritime Belge* EU:C:1998:518, Fennelly AG, para. 137.

[359] The fines on the shipping lines were, however, annulled for procedural reasons as the Commission had not stated in its statement of objections that it intended to impose fines on the individual members. They were reimposed, *Compagnie Maritime Belge* [2005] OJ L171/28, appeal dismissed Case T-276/04, *Compagnie Maritime Belge* EU:T:2008:237.

> 119. It is sufficient to recall that the conduct at issue here is that of a conference having a share of over 90 per cent of the market in question and only one competitor. The appellants have, moreover, never seriously disputed, and indeed admitted at the hearing, that the purpose of the conduct complained of was to eliminate G & C from the market.
>
> 120. The [GC] did not, therefore, err in law, in holding that the Commission's objections to the effect that the practice known as 'fighting ships', as applied against G&C, constituted an abuse of a dominant position were justified. It should also be noted that there is no question at all in this case of there having been a new definition of an abusive practice.

The CJ reiterated that the 'special responsibility' of dominant undertakings must be considered in the light of the circumstances in each case, and confined its remarks thereafter to the particular facts. The CJ declined to say when a liner conference *could* legitimately drop its prices in order to compete. The pointed reference to the fact that the conference had a market share over 90 per cent, and its comments about liner conferences,[360] read with the reference to *Tetra Pak II*, suggest that undertakings in a monopolistic or quasi-monopolistic position have a heavy responsibility towards the competitive process.[361]

In *Irish Sugar*,[362] Irish Sugar was the sole producer of sugar beet in Ireland and Northern Ireland. It reacted to increasing imports from other Member States by a variety of practices.[363] This included dropping its prices to customers identified as most vulnerable to the imports, although the reductions did not take prices below total cost. As in *CEWAL*, the Commission held that the conduct was abusive because of the intent to exclude competition, and the selective, targeted nature of the price cuts. The appeal to the GC, on the grounds that it was merely defending its market position, was rejected. In particular, the GC stated that:

> [E]ven if the existence of a dominant position does not deprive an undertaking placed in that position of the right to protect its own commercial interests when they are threatened . . . the protection of the commercial position of an undertaking in a dominant position with the characteristics of that of the applicant at the time in question must, at the very least, in order to be lawful, be based on criteria of economic efficiency and consistent with the interests of consumers. In this case, the applicant has not shown that those conditions were fulfilled.[364]

Compagnie Maritime Belge and *Irish Sugar* have several common features:

- collectively held dominance;
- a market position amounting to 'super-dominance' or quasi-monopoly;
- clear evidence of exclusionary intent; *and*
- in both cases, the undertakings engaged in a range of exclusionary practices with cumulative anti-competitive effects.

In both cases, the Courts emphasised that the finding of abuse was informed by the market circumstances and the characteristics of the defendant(s).

[360] Cases C-395 and 396/96 P, *Compagnie Maritime Belge* EU:C:2000:132, paras. 115–117.

[361] Nazzini sees the CJ in *Compagnie Maritime Belge* as applying a dynamic AEC efficient competitor test: Nazzini, n. 139, 242–243.

[362] [1997] OJ L258/1.

[363] Including target rebates, export rebates, and product swaps.

[364] Case T-228/97, *Irish Sugar* EU:T:1999:246, para. 189.

The question is whether these distinctive features are sufficient to distinguish the earlier cases from *Post Danmark I*.[365] In that judgment, the CJ ruled that discriminatory pricing was not of itself abusive, and that selective low prices do not amount to an exclusionary abuse merely because the price is lower than ATC but higher than AIC. PD had also offered prices which were above its own ATC to two customers. The CJ said in respect of this:

> In those circumstances, it cannot be considered that such prices have anti-competitive effects.[366]

This is a significant statement. In the judgment the CJ mentioned *Compagnie Maritime Belge* only in support of the principle of the special responsibility of dominant undertakings, and ignored *Irish Sugar*. Advocate General Mengozzi had discussed both cases, however, and concluded that they were only 'marginally relevant': first, because in those cases there was evidence of intention to exclude; secondly, they concerned undertakings in near monopoly positions; and, thirdly, the pricing was one of a series of abusive practices.[367] Given the words '[i]n those circumstances', it cannot be concluded that above-ATC pricing could *never* be an abuse, although normally it will not be so as it does not exclude equally efficient competitors.

The Guidance Paper does not rule out intervention against above-cost selective pricing. It does not specifically deal with the issue, although it says in paragraph 72 that it is easier to engage in predatory conduct if the dominant undertaking selectively targets specific customers. Paragraph 63 nonetheless defines 'sacrifice' to include '*foregoing profits*' as well as incurring losses, and in paragraph 24 the Commission contemplates intervening to protect less efficient competitors in some situations. Article 102 might therefore still be enforced against such pricing exceptionally.

9. MARGIN SQUEEZE

A. GENERAL

Margin squeeze occurs where a vertically integrated undertaking which is dominant on the upstream market for an input sets its prices at such a level that its downstream competitors cannot compete for the supply of products or services to customers.[368] The dominant undertaking can apply a margin squeeze by setting a high price for the input, by charging low prices on the downstream market, or through a combination of the two. Margin squeeze occurs in regulated and non-regulated sectors, but it emerged as a particular issue in the EU following the liberalisation of the telecommunications sector which was intended to bring about retail competition.

The crux of margin squeeze is vertical integration. The dominant undertaking operates on two vertically related markets, typically facing competition in at least the downstream sector. Margin

[365] Case C-209/10, *Post Danmark I* EU:C:2012:172, see Section 8.D. [366] Ibid., para. 37.

[367] Ibid., Mengozzi AG, paras. 91–94.

[368] See e.g. R. Downing and A. Jones, 'Margin Squeezes in Telecommunications Markets' in S. Anderman and A. Ezrachi (eds.), *Intellectual Property and Competition Law: New Frontiers* (Oxford University Press, 2011); N. Dunne, 'Margin Squeeze: Theory, Practice, Policy', Parts I and II [2012] *ECLR* 29 and 61; D. W. Carlton, 'Should "Price Squeeze" be a Recognized Form of Anti-competitive Conduct?' (2008) 4 *J of Competition Law and Economics* 271; J. G. Sidak, 'Abolishing the Price Squeeze as a Theory of Antitrust Liability' (2008) 4 *J of Competition Law and Economics* 279; A. M. Panner, 'Are Price Squeezes Anti-competitive?' (2009) 1 *Global Competition Policy*; H. Hovenkamp and E. Hovenkamp, 'The Viability of Antitrust Price Squeeze Claims' (2009) 51 *Arizona LR* 273; O'Donoghue and Padilla, n. 1, Chap. 7; Bishop and Walker, n. 243, 6.119–6.139; G. Faella and R. Pardolesi, 'Squeezing Price Squeeze under EC Antitrust Law' (2010) 6 *European Competition Journal* 255; Faull and Nikpay, n. 1, 4.638–4.693.

squeeze is premised upon the dominant undertaking's ability to manipulate the profit margins that may be earned by rivals downstream. Thus, the integrated dominant firm can influence both the *costs* that competitors must cover (directly, in its capacity as wholesale supplier) and the *profits* that competitors may earn (indirectly, insofar as the dominant undertaking's own retail price influences the maximum price that can be charged by rivals). Vertical integration also explains why the dominant undertaking can endure the low profits generated in the retail market: since it is also active on the wholesale market where comparatively higher profits may be earned, the dominant undertaking may choose simply to take its profits upstream.

Like predatory pricing, margin squeeze is a contentious theory of harm.[369] One critic has described it as 'an antitrust rule that punishes a firm for failing to ensure its competitors' profitability'.[370] Objections include a concern that prohibitions on margin squeeze simply lead to wealth transfers from vertically integrated undertakings to their smaller rivals, without generating benefits for consumers; that the 'one monopoly profit' theory makes margin squeeze implausible, insofar as any increase in customer numbers at the retail level comes at the expense of business at the wholesale level, making such a strategy unprofitable overall; and that margin squeeze represents a 'moving target', requiring competition enforcers to police interaction between wholesale and retail prices. Yet a successfully executed margin squeeze has the potential to foreclose competition at the retail level, thus reducing consumer choice; to limit rivals' incentives to innovate downstream, thus inhibiting the emergence of more efficient retail markets; and to prevent rivals from subsequently climbing the 'ladder of investment', thereby foreclosing the possibility of competition at the wholesale level in the longer term.

Margin squeeze is an area where we see a sharp divergence between EU and US competition law. In *linkLine*,[371] the US Supreme Court held that prices which 'squeeze' the margin for efficient competitors downstream are not an antitrust offence contrary to s. 2 of the Sherman Act, *unless* there is a refusal to supply on the upstream market,[372] or a predatory retail price downstream.[373] Absent evidence of abuse at either the wholesale or retail levels individually, however, 'then a firm is certainly not required to price both of these services in a manner that preserves its rivals' profit margins'.[374]

Conversely, margin squeeze is recognised as a stand-alone theory of harm under Article 102. In its first decision on margin squeeze, *National Carbonizing*, the Commission stated that an 'enterprise in a dominant position may have an obligation to arrange its prices so as to allow a *reasonably efficient* manufacturer of the derivatives a margin sufficient to enable it to survive in the long term'.[375] Next came *Napier Brown/British Sugar*,[376] where the Commission found that British Sugar (BS) abused its dominant position in the industrial sugar market by maintaining a price for its own retail sugar which did not reflect its repackaging and selling costs. The Commission said that, if BS maintained its reduced margin, any company *equally efficient* in repackaging as BS but without a self-produced source of industrial sugar, would have to leave the market.[377] The concept was subsequently acknowledged by the GC in *Industrie des poudres sphériques*, couched in terms of denying rivals 'a sufficient profit margin'.[378]

[369] See generally OECD, *Margin Squeeze* DAF/COMP(2009)36.

[370] J. G. Sidak, 'Abolishing the Price Squeeze as a Theory of Antitrust Liability' (2008) 4 *J of Competition Law and Economics* 279, 294.

[371] *Pacific Bell Telephone Co v linkLine Communications Inc*, 129 S.Ct. 1109 (2009); see F. Enrique González Díaz and J. Padilla, 'The *linkLine* Judgment—A European Perspective' (2009) 1 *Global Competition Policy*.

[372] Which, following *Verizon Communications Inc v Trinko LLP*, 540 US 398, 124 S.Ct 872 (2004) is highly unlikely; see Section 12.

[373] *Brooke Group Ltd v Brown & Williamson Tobacco Corp*, 509 US 209 (1993).

[374] *linkLine*, Roberts CJ.

[375] *National Coal Board, National Smokeless Fuels Ltd and the National Carbonizing Company Ltd*, 79/185/ECSC [1976] OJ L35/6 at 7 (emphasis added).

[376] [1988] OJ L284/41.

[377] *Napier Brown* [1988] OJ L284/41, para. 66.

[378] Case T-5/97, *Industrie des poudres sphériques v Commission* EU:T:2000:278, para. 178.

The current law on margin squeeze has been established in several cases in the telecommunications sector: *Deutsche Telekom*,[379] *TeliaSonera*,[380] *Telefónica*,[381] and *Slovak Telekom*.[382] In short, a margin squeeze contrary to Article 102 arises where a dominant firm (a) maintains an 'unfair' (i.e. negative or insufficient) spread between its wholesale and retail prices, which (b) has an exclusionary effect on equally efficient competitors. The meaning of these elements, and the scope and limits of margin squeeze as a category of abuse, are explained in the following extracts.

B. THE CASE LAW

(i) Deutsche Telekom

In *Deutsche Telekom*[383] the Commission found that Deutsche Telekom (DT) had effected a margin squeeze by charging its competitors on the retail market in Germany a higher price for access to the 'local loop',[384] to which it was obliged to offer access pursuant to the EU telecommunications regime,[385] than it charged its own retail end-user customers. Competitors could not offer competitive retail prices unless they found efficiency gains elsewhere. Although DT's prices were approved by the German telecommunications regulator (RegTP), the Commission found that its pricing practices comprised a margin squeeze, because:[386]

> . . . the difference between the retail prices charged by a dominant undertaking and the wholesale prices it charges its competitors for comparable services is negative, or insufficient to cover the product-specific costs to the dominant operator of providing its own retail services on the downstream market.

Although the Commission analysed the likely exclusionary effects of DT's prices, it maintained that this was unnecessary to assess its effects, as by proving the existence of a margin squeeze the Commission considered that it had established the existence of an abuse.[387]

The GC dismissed DT's arguments that it could not have infringed Article 102 as its prices had been approved by RegTP,[388] and that DT had been left insufficient scope to adjust its retail prices to avoid the margin squeeze.[389] The GC said the Commission had correctly identified the abuse as consisting of the unfair 'spread' between the wholesale and resale prices,[390] thus treating margin squeeze as a separate abuse, independent from predatory pricing. It also upheld the Commission's adoption of the AEC test as the relevant costs benchmark.[391] This was required on grounds of legal certainty, as a dominant undertaking cannot be expected to make commercial decisions on the basis of the unknown costs of its competitors, and also on the principle of 'equality of opportunity'. The GC did not, however, agree that proof of a margin squeeze alone was sufficient to establish an abuse. Rather, the

[379] Case C-280/08 P, *Deutsche Telekom* EU:C:2010:603.

[380] Case C-52/09, *TeliaSonera* EU:C:2011:83; Case note, W. Wurmnest (2012) 49 *CMLRev* 721.

[381] Case C-295/12 P, *Telefónica SA v Commission* EU:C:2014:2062.

[382] Case T-851/14, *Slovak Telekom v Commission* EU:T:2018:929.

[383] COMP/37.451, 37.578, and 37.579, *Deutsche Telekom AG* [2003] OJ L263/9.

[384] The physical circuit connecting the network termination point at a subscriber's premises to the main distribution frame or equivalent facility in the fixed public telephone network: Case T-271/03, *Deutsche Telekom* EU:T:2008:101, para. 3.

[385] Decision No. 223a of the Federal Ministry of Post and Telecommunications of 28 May 1997, pursuant to the EU legislative regime for the telecommunications sector (since amended).

[386] [2003] OJ L263/9, para. 107.

[387] Ibid., paras. 179–180.

[388] Case T-271/03, *Deutsche Telekom* EU:T:2008:101, paras. 106–120.

[389] Ibid., paras. 121–151.

[390] Ibid., para. 167.

[391] Ibid., paras. 194 and 237.

Commission was required to demonstrate anti-competitive effects related to the barriers to entry that the pricing practices *could have created*.[392] The CJ upheld the GC's judgment.

Case C-280/08 P, *Deutsche Telekom v Commission* EU:C:2010:603

Court of Justice

176. Article [102] refers not only to practices which may cause damage to consumers directly, but also to those which are detrimental to them through their impact on competition . . .

177. It follows . . . that Article [102] prohibits a dominant undertaking from, inter alia, adopting pricing practices which have an exclusionary effect on its equally efficient actual or potential competitors, that is to say practices which are capable of making market entry very difficult or impossible for such competitors, and of making it more difficult or impossible for its co-contractors to choose between various sources of supply or commercial partners, thereby strengthening its dominant position by using methods other than those which come within the scope of competition on the merits. From that point of view, therefore, not all competition by means of price can be regarded as legitimate (see, to that effect, *Nederlandsche Banden-Industrie-Michelin* v *Commission*, paragraph 73; *AKZO* v *Commission*, paragraph 70; and *British Airways* v *Commission*, paragraph 68).

. . .

182. By further reducing the degree of competition existing on a market—the end-user access services market—already weakened precisely because of the presence of the appellant, thereby strengthening its dominant position on that market, the margin squeeze also has the effect that consumers suffer detriment as a result of the limitation of the choices available to them and, therefore, of the prospect of a longer-term reduction of retail prices as a result of competition exerted by competitors who are at least as efficient in that market (see, to that effect, *France Télécom* v *Commission*, paragraph 112).

183. In those circumstances, in so far as the appellant has scope to reduce or end such a margin squeeze . . . by increasing its retail prices for end-user access services, . . . that margin squeeze is capable, in itself, of constituting an abuse within the meaning of Article [102] in view of the exclusionary effect that it can create for competitors who are at least as efficient as the appellant. The General Court was not, therefore, obliged to establish, additionally, that the wholesale prices for local loop access services or retail prices for end-user access services were in themselves abusive on account of their excessive or predatory nature, as the case may be.

. . .

196. . . . [T]he as-efficient-competitor test used by the General Court in the judgment under appeal consists in considering whether the pricing practices of a dominant undertaking could drive an equally efficient economic operator from the market, relying solely on the dominant undertaking's charges and costs, instead of on the particular situation of its actual or potential competitors.

197. In the present case . . . the appellant's costs were taken into account by the General Court in order to establish the abusive nature of the appellant's pricing practices where the spread between its wholesale prices for local loop access services and its retail prices for end-user access services was positive. In such circumstances, the General Court considered that the Commission was entitled to regard those pricing practices as unfair within the meaning of Article [102], where that spread was insufficient to cover the appellant's product-specific costs of providing its own services.

198. In that regard, it must be borne in mind that the Court has already held that, in order to assess whether the pricing practices of a dominant undertaking are likely to eliminate a competitor contrary to

[392] Ibid., para. 235.

Article [102], it is necessary to adopt a test based on the costs and the strategy of the dominant undertaking itself (see *AKZO* v *Commission*, paragraph 74, and *France Télécom* v *Commission*, paragraph 108).

199. The Court pointed out, inter alia, in that regard that a dominant undertaking cannot drive from the market undertakings which are perhaps as efficient as the dominant undertaking but which, because of their smaller financial resources, are incapable of withstanding the competition waged against them (see *AKZO* v *Commission*, paragraph 72).

200. In the present case, since . . . the abusive nature of the pricing practices at issue in the judgment under appeal stems in the same way from their exclusionary effect on the appellant's competitors, the General Court did not err in law when it held . . . that the Commission had been correct to analyse the abusive nature of the appellant's pricing practices solely on the basis of the appellant's charges and costs.

201. . . . [S]ince such a test can establish whether the appellant would itself have been able to offer its retail services to end-users otherwise than at a loss if it had first been obliged to pay its own wholesale prices for local loop access services, it was suitable for determining whether the appellant's pricing practices had an exclusionary effect on competitors by squeezing their margins.

202. Such an approach is particularly justified because . . . it is also consistent with the general principle of legal certainty in so far as the account taken of the costs of the dominant undertaking allows that undertaking, in the light of its special responsibility under Article [102], to assess the lawfulness of its own conduct. While a dominant undertaking knows what its own costs and charges are, it does not, as a general rule, know what its competitors' costs and charges are.

. . .

252. . . . [T]he anti-competitive effect which the Commission is required to demonstrate, as regards pricing practices of a dominant undertaking resulting in a margin squeeze of its equally efficient competitors, relates to the possible barriers which the appellant's pricing practices could have created for the growth of products on the retail market in end-user access services and, therefore, on the degree of competition in that market.

253. . . . [A] pricing practice such as that at issue . . . constitutes an abuse within the meaning of Article [102] if it has an exclusionary effect on competitors who are at least as efficient as the dominant undertaking itself by squeezing their margins and is capable of making market entry more difficult or impossible for those competitors, and thus of strengthening its dominant position on that market to the detriment of consumers' interests.

254. Admittedly, where a dominant undertaking actually implements a pricing practice resulting in a margin squeeze of its equally efficient competitors, with the purpose of driving them from the relevant market, the fact that the desired result is not ultimately achieved does not alter its categorisation as abuse within the meaning of Article [102]. However, in the absence of any effect on the competitive situation of competitors, a pricing practice such as that at issue cannot be classified as exclusionary if it does not make their market penetration any more difficult.

The CJ in *Deutsche Telekom* confirmed the status of margin squeeze as a stand-alone abuse, independent of excessive pricing of the input or predatory pricing downstream. The essence, instead, is the unfairness of the spread between the defendant's wholesale and retail prices.[393] To identify whether unfairness exists, the CJ endorsed the AEC test, asking whether the dominant undertaking's downstream operation could trade profitably if subject to the same pricing regime as downstream competitors.[394] Yet it agreed that the mere existence of an apparently unfair spread is insufficient for an abuse to arise: in addition, there must be anti-competitive effects in the form of exclusionary effects on as efficient competitors. The question is whether the pricing is *capable* of making market entry more

[393] Ibid., paras. 157, 159, and 183. [394] Ibid., paras. 198–203.

difficult or impossible, and thus of strengthening the dominant position to the detriment of consumers' interests.[395] The CJ also confirmed several more anomalous aspects of the case. First, DT was obliged to avoid the margin squeeze even if it meant *raising* its retail prices to consumers.[396] Secondly, the fact that the pricing scheme was approved by the national regulator did not exempt those prices from scrutiny. A dominant undertaking can escape liability only if the anti-competitive conduct is *required* by national legislation or if the national framework *eliminates any possibility of competitive activity*; an exacting standard not met on the facts.[397]

(ii) TeliaSonera

In *TeliaSonera*, an Article 267 reference, the CJ clarified and elaborated upon these principles. TeliaSonera was in an analogous position to DT: a vertically integrated former State monopolist which retained ownership of the local loop. TeliaSonera offered local loop access to operators supplying broadband to end-users, and broadband connection services directly to end-users. Unlike DT, however, it had no statutory obligation to grant wholesale access, and there were several alternative technologies available.[398] Nevertheless, the Konkurrensverket (Swedish competition authority) alleged that TeliaSonera had abused its dominant position by applying a margin squeeze, insofar as the spread between its wholesale and retail prices was insufficient to cover the costs which it incurred in supplying its services to end-users. The following extracts deal with two key questions: the role of any regulatory obligation to supply within margin squeeze analysis, and the requirements of the effects limb of the legal test.

Case C-52/09, *Konkurrensverket v TeliaSonera Sverige* AB EU:C:2011:83

Court of Justice

The absence of any regulatory obligation to supply

47. . . . TeliaSonera . . . was not under any regulatory obligation to supply ADSL input services to operators.

. . .

54. TeliaSonera maintains, in that regard, that, in order specifically to protect the economic initiative of dominant undertakings, they should remain free to fix their terms of trade, unless those terms are so disadvantageous for those entering into contracts with them that those terms may be regarded, in the light of the relevant criteria set out in Case C-7/97 *Bronner* . . . as entailing a refusal to supply.

55. Such an interpretation is based on a misunderstanding of that judgment. In particular, it cannot be inferred from paragraphs 48 and 49 of that judgment that the conditions to be met in order to establish that a refusal to supply is abusive must necessarily also apply when assessing the abusive nature of conduct which consists in supplying services or selling goods on conditions which are disadvantageous or on which there might be no purchaser.

56. Such conduct may, in itself, constitute an independent form of abuse distinct from that of refusal to supply.

. . .

[395] Ibid., paras. 252–255. [396] Ibid., para. 181.

[397] Case C-280/08, *Deutsche Telekom* EU:C:2010:603, paras. 80–90.

[398] Case C-52/09, *TeliaSonera* EU:C:2010:483, Mazák AG, para. 20; this was why the referring court specifically asked whether the input had to be indispensable for there to be an abuse.

58. . . . [I]f *Bronner* were to be interpreted otherwise, in the way advocated by TeliaSonera, that would, as submitted by the European Commission, amount to a requirement that before any conduct of a dominant undertaking in relation to its terms of trade could be regarded as abusive the conditions to be met to establish that there was a refusal to supply would in every case have to be satisfied, and that would unduly reduce the effectiveness of Article 102 TFEU.

59. It follows that the absence of any regulatory obligation to supply the ADSL input services on the wholesale market has no effect on the question of whether the pricing practice at issue in the main proceedings is abusive.

Whether an anti-competitive effect is required and whether the product offered by the undertaking must be indispensable

61. . . . [T]he Court has ruled out the possibility that the very existence of a pricing practice of a dominant undertaking which leads to the margin squeeze of its equally efficient competitors can constitute an abuse within the meaning of Article 102 TFEU without it being necessary to demonstrate an anti-competitive effect (see, to that effect, *Deutsche Telekom* v *Commission*, paragraphs 250 and 251).

62. The case-law has furthermore made clear that the anti-competitive effect must relate to the possible barriers which such a pricing practice may create to the growth on the retail market of the services offered to end users and, therefore, on the degree of competition in that market (*Deutsche Telekom* v *Commission*, paragraph 252).

63. Accordingly, the practice in question, adopted by a dominant undertaking, constitutes an abuse within the meaning of Article 102 TFEU, where, given its effect of excluding competitors who are at least as efficient as itself by squeezing their margins, it is capable of making more difficult, or impossible, the entry of those competitors onto the market concerned (see, to that effect, *Deutsche Telekom* v *Commission*, paragraph 253).

64. It follows that, in order to establish whether such a practice is abusive, that practice must have an anti-competitive effect on the market, but the effect does not necessarily have to be concrete, and it is sufficient to demonstrate that there is an anti-competitive effect which may potentially exclude competitors who are at least as efficient as the dominant undertaking.

65. Where a dominant undertaking actually implements a pricing practice resulting in a margin squeeze on its equally efficient competitors, with the purpose of driving them from the relevant market, the fact that the desired result, namely the exclusion of those competitors, is not ultimately achieved does not alter its categorisation as abuse within the meaning of Article 102 TFEU.

66. However, in the absence of any effect on the competitive situation of competitors, a pricing practice such as that at issue in the main proceedings cannot be classified as an exclusionary practice where the penetration of those competitors in the market concerned is not made any more difficult by that practice (see, to that effect, *Deutsche Telekom* v *Commission*, paragraph 254).

67. In the present case, it is for the referring court to examine whether the effect of TeliaSonera's pricing practice was likely to hinder the ability of competitors at least as efficient as itself to trade on the retail market for broadband connection services to end users.

68. In that examination that court must take into consideration all the specific circumstances of the case.

69. In particular, the first matter to be analysed must be the functional relationship of the wholesale products to the retail products. Accordingly, when assessing the effects of the margin squeeze, the question whether the wholesale product is indispensable may be relevant.

70. Where access to the supply of the wholesale product is indispensable for the sale of the retail product, competitors who are at least as efficient as the undertaking which dominates the wholesale market and who are unable to operate on the retail market other than at a loss or, in any event, with reduced profitability suffer a competitive disadvantage on that market which is such as to prevent or

restrict their access to it or the growth of their activities on it (see, to that effect, *Deutsche Telekom* v *Commission*, paragraph 234).

71. In such circumstances, the at least potentially anti-competitive effect of a margin squeeze is probable.

72. However, taking into account the dominant position of the undertaking concerned in the wholesale market, the possibility cannot be ruled out that, by reason simply of the fact that the wholesale product is not indispensable for the supply of the retail product, a pricing practice which causes margin squeeze may not be able to produce any anti-competitive effect, even potentially. Accordingly, it is again for the referring court to satisfy itself that, even where the wholesale product is not indispensable, the practice may be capable of having anti-competitive effects on the markets concerned.

73. Secondly, it is necessary to determine the level of margin squeeze of competitors at least as efficient as the dominant undertaking. If the margin is negative, in other words if, in the present case, the wholesale price for the ADSL input services is higher than the retail price for services to end users, an effect which is at least potentially exclusionary is probable, taking into account the fact that, in such a situation, the competitors of the dominant undertaking, even if they are as efficient, or even more efficient, compared with it, would be compelled to sell at a loss.

74. If, on the other hand, such a margin remains positive, it must then be demonstrated that the application of that pricing practice was, by reason, for example, of reduced profitability, likely to have the consequence that it would be at least more difficult for the operators concerned to trade on the market concerned.

75. That said, it must be borne in mind that an undertaking remains at liberty to demonstrate that its pricing practice, albeit producing an exclusionary effect, is economically justified (. . . Case C-95/04 P *British Airways* v *Commission* . . . paragraph 69, and *France Télécom* v *Commission*, paragraph 111).

The above extracts establish two key points. The CJ reaffirmed margin squeeze as an independent form of abuse, clarifying that it is also distinct from refusal to supply. Thus the *Bronner* criteria, which as we shall see form the baseline test for establishing whether an abusive refusal to supply exists, are not determinative of whether a margin squeeze arises. In particular, there is no requirement that access to the wholesale-level input is 'indispensable' for competing downstream. Here, the CJ departed from the advice of its Advocate General, who contended that the restrictive logic of the *Bronner* case extends to margin squeeze, arguing that, '[i]f a dominant undertaking could lawfully have refused to provide the products in question, then it should not be reproached for providing those products at conditions which its competitors may consider not advantageous'.[399] The Commission's Guidance Paper too originally characterised margin squeeze as a sub-category of refusal to supply;[400] which made it all the more curious that the CJ's rejection of *Bronner* in *TeliaSonera* was apparently motivated by the Commission's submissions in the later case (paragraph 58). The expansive language by which CJ dismissed the relevance of the *Bronner* criteria in margin squeeze cases has moreover had a significant impact in the subsequent development of the case law on refusal to supply.[401]

Secondly, a margin squeeze exists where the spread between wholesale and retail prices is either negative or insufficient to cover the costs which the dominant undertaking incurs to supply its own retail services to end-users.[402] The CJ nonetheless reiterated that, to constitute an abuse contrary to Article 102, exclusionary effects on as efficient competitors must also be demonstrated. In ascertaining this, the relevant costs and prices are normally those of the defendant.[403] Yet, although it is

[399] Opinion of Mazák AG in Case C-52/09, *TeliaSonera Sverige* EU:C:2010:483, para. 21.
[400] See Section 12.G. [401] See Section 12.C. [402] Case C-52/09, *TeliaSonera* EU:C:2011:83, paras. 32–33.
[403] Ibid., para. 44.

necessary to demonstrate anti-competitive effects, those effects need not be concrete, but only *potentially* exclude competitors.[404] Where the input *is* indispensable, at least potentially anti-competitive effects are probable;[405] but an absence of indispensability does not preclude a pricing structure from being capable of having anti-competitive effects.[406] Where the spread is negative, i.e. the input price is higher than the dominant undertaking's retail price to end-users, an effect which is at least potentially exclusionary is probable. There may, nevertheless, be anti-competitive effects even if it remains positive.[407] Finally, the CJ confirmed that margin squeeze can be objectively justified on the basis of efficiencies.[408]

Furthermore, the *TeliaSonera* judgment established that the degree of dominance on the upstream market is irrelevant;[409] that a finding of a margin squeeze abuse does not require concomitant dominance on the downstream market;[410] and that 'the fact that the markets concerned are growing rapidly and involve new technology, requiring high levels of investment, is not, as a general rule, relevant to establishing whether the pricing practice at issue constitutes an abuse'.[411]

(iii) Margin Squeeze in Practice: Telecommunications and Beyond

Two later cases, *Telefónica* and *Slovak Telekom*, which again both involved former State-owned telecommunications monopolists, illustrate how these principles are to be interpreted and applied.

In 2007, the Commission fined Telefónica for abusing its dominant position for wholesale broadband in Spain.[412] It found that Telefónica had imposed a margin squeeze between its wholesale and retail prices, generating a margin that was insufficient to cover the costs that an equally efficient operator would incur. It assessed this based on Telefónica's downstream costs, using LRAIC as the appropriate standard. Under Spanish law, Telefónica had a regulatory duty to supply the wholesale product to downstream competitors. Telefónica argued that margin squeeze should be treated as a type of constructive refusal to supply and that the Commission could not deduce from the *regulatory* duty to supply that there was a duty to supply under Article 102.[413] As we have seen, the CJ subsequently rejected this characterisation of margin squeeze in *TeliaSonera*; so too did the Commission in *Telefónica*, albeit on slightly different grounds. The Commission held that the case was fundamentally different from *Bronner*, so that that legal test was inapplicable. First, the dominant undertaking had a regulatory duty to supply which had resulted from the balancing by public authorities of the incentives of Telefónica and its competitors to invest and innovate. Secondly, Telefónica's *ex ante* incentives to invest were not at stake because the infrastructure had been built at a time when Telefónica benefited from special or exclusive rights.[414] These circumstances, which have been called the '*Telefónica* exceptions',[415] were later repeated in the Guidance Paper.[416]

On appeal, both the GC[417] and CJ[418] followed the approach in *Deutsche Telekom* and *TeliaSonera*. The CJ clarified that the acknowledgement in *TeliaSonera* that indispensability might be relevant in identifying an abusive margin squeeze did not render this criterion a necessary precondition;[419] that potential anti-competitive effects could suffice to satisfy the effects limb of the test for margin squeeze;[420] and that the existence of *ex ante* sector-specific regulation neither precluded the later

[404] Ibid., para. 65. [405] Ibid., para. 71. [406] Ibid., para. 72. [407] Ibid., paras. 73–74.

[408] Ibid., paras. 31 and 75–76. [409] Ibid., paras. 78–82; see the discussion of 'super-dominance', see Section 3.D.

[410] Ibid., paras. 83–89. [411] Ibid., para. 104.

[412] COMP/38.784, *Wanadoo España v Telefónica* 4 July 2007. [413] Ibid., paras. 299–301.

[414] Ibid., paras. 303–304.

[415] D. Geradin, 'Refusal to Supply and Margin Squeeze: A Discussion of Why the "*Telefonica* Exceptions" are Wrong', TILEC Discussion Paper No. 2011-009, <http://papers.ssrn.com/sol3/papers.cfm?abstract_id=1762687>.

[416] Guidance Paper, para. 82, see Section 12.G. [417] Case T-336/07, *Telefónica* EU:T:2012:172.

[418] Case C-295/12 P, *Telefónica* EU:C:2014:2062. [419] Ibid., para. 118. [420] Ibid., para. 124.

application of Article 102 nor provided evidence that the regulated conduct complied with that provision.[421]

Slovak Telekom similarly focused on the efforts of the former Slovak telecommunications monopolist (ST), which aimed at 'keeping the life of [alternative operators] difficult' in the retail broadband sector.[422] Its strategy comprised both the imposing of unreasonable terms and conditions for access,[423] and a pricing policy which resulted in a margin squeeze of broadband access prices. The latter, again, was calculated by reference to the LRAIC standard. For a four-month period at the outset of its alleged campaign of margin squeeze, ST maintained a positive margin between wholesale and retail prices, while for the remainder the spread was negative. The Commission nonetheless found that the margin for the entire period was 'insufficient' under the case law.

On appeal, the GC accepted that a positive margin could still satisfy the requirement of the first limb of the test for margin squeeze, namely an *unfair spread* between prices.[424] Yet the GC held that the Commission had failed, in respect of the earlier time period, to discharge its burden of proof in respect of the second limb of the test, namely the need to establish *exclusionary effects*. In the absence of a negative margin, the Commission was required to do more than simply presume that low margins are harmful. The GC accordingly annulled the Commission decision finding abuse in respect of this initial period, and reduced the fine to reflect the shorter duration.[425] The judgment makes it clear that demonstrating exclusionary effects is a discrete requirement within the legal test for margin squeeze under Article 102, one of particular importance where the defendant maintains a positive (even if slim) margin and thus where anti-competitive effects cannot safely be presumed. The finding was not challenged by the Commission in the defendant's further appeal to the CJ.[426] The CJ confirmed, moreover, that the fact that a dominant undertaking is required to provide the Commission with data setting out its costs in order to allow the calculation of the spread in a margin squeeze case does not amount to a reversal of the burden of proof.[427]

Margin squeeze cases have arisen outside the telecommunications sector. The early cases of *National Carbonising, Napier Brown*, and *Industrie des poudres sphériques* were noted.[428] More recently, the Commission has settled investigations into alleged margin squeeze through commitment decisions.[429] In *RWE—Gas Foreclosure*, RWE, which controlled the gas transmission network in North Rhine-Westphalia, was alleged to have intentionally set its transmission tariffs at an artificially high level in order to squeeze the margins of its competitors on downstream gas supply markets. The commitment decision involved divestiture of RWE's transmission network.[430] In *Deutsche Bahn*, the German railway incumbent DB implemented a claimed squeeze through discounts on the purchasing of traction current which were available only to railway companies within the DB group. It offered a series of behavioural commitments, including a blanket reduction in price for traction current and permitting access to its network by third party providers of traction current.[431] The binding commitments were concluded early, following successful market entry of several alternative providers.[432]

[421] Ibid., paras. 128–135. [422] AT39523, *Slovak Telekom* 15 October 2014, para. 240.
[423] See discussion at Section *. [424] Case T-851/14, *Slovak Telekom* EU:T:2018:929.
[425] Ibid., paras. 447–448. [426] Case C-165/19 P, *Slovak Telekom* EU:C:2021:239. [427] Ibid., paras. 72–79.
[428] See Section 9.A. [429] See Chap. 13, Section 6.E.
[430] COMP/39.402, *RWE—Gas Foreclosure* Commitments 18 March 2009 [2009] OJ C133/10.
[431] AT39678/AT39731, *Deutsche Bahn I/II* 18 December 2013.
[432] Commission Press Release, 'Antitrust: successful market opening allows early termination of commitments in *Deutsche Bahn* case', 8 April 2016, IP/16/1322.

C. MARGIN SQUEEZE IN THE GUIDANCE PAPER

In its Guidance Paper, the Commission originally addressed margin squeeze as a category of refusal to supply. It construed the high price charged on the upstream market, when compared with the price that the dominant undertaking charged downstream, as effectively a constructive refusal to deal upstream on realistic terms.[433] To determine whether an abuse had occurred on this basis, the Commission advocated the use of the AEC test. As a sub-category of refusal to supply, however, the original Guidance Paper recommended intervention only where the indispensability criterion was satisfied.[434] The Guidance Paper nonetheless sets out some special circumstances where the Commission considers the normal criteria on refusal to supply do not apply,[435] which correspond to the '*Telefónica* exceptions' already mentioned.[436]

As we have seen, *TeliaSonera* and *Telefónica* subsequently established that margin squeeze is not dependent on the indispensability of the input or the other *Bronner* criteria. In the Amendments to the Guidance Paper, the Commission thus moves margin squeeze into its own distinct category of abuse, citing *TeliaSonera* in a footnote.[437] In a new subsection which consists of a single paragraph, the Commission commits, 'generally', to use of an AEC test based on the LRAIC of the dominant undertaking in the downstream market. The revised Guidance Paper makes no reference to anti-competitive effects, besides the general discussion of the anti-competitive foreclosure standard contained in the introductory sections.

> 90. A dominant undertaking may charge a price for the product on the upstreammarket which, compared to the price it charges on the downstream market, does not allow even an equally efficient competitor to trade profitably in the downstreammarket on a lasting basis (a so-called 'margin squeeze'). In margin squeeze cases the benchmark which the Commission will generally rely on to determine the costs of an equally efficient competitor are the LRAIC of the downstream division of the integrated dominant undertaking.

D. COMMENT

Treating margin squeeze as distinct from refusal to supply is difficult to rationalise.[438] Logic suggests that if there is no duty to supply, there can be no duty to supply at a particular price. EU law has reached the position, however, that an undertaking which does not infringe Article 102 if it expressly refuses to supply a rival,[439] can nevertheless infringe if it agrees to supply but does so at a price deemed to give rise to an abusive margin squeeze. This risks creating perverse incentives for vertically integrated dominant undertakings without any regulatory obligation to supply: it is safer to decide not to supply downstream competitors at all, which may be more anti-competitive and have detrimental welfare implications. The CJ's rationale for this state of affairs is that, were the established refusal to supply conditions applied in margin squeeze cases, it 'would unduly reduce the effectiveness of Article 102',[440] although it does not explain why this is so. This scepticism of the regulatory restraint implicit in the established refusal to supply case law has, furthermore, spilled over from the area of margin squeeze to prompt a loosening of requirements in refusal to deal cases, as discussed in Section 12. However, while the divorce of margin squeeze from refusal to supply means that the indispensability of the input to the downstream competitor is not a necessary condition for the pricing

[433] Guidance Paper, para. 80. [434] See Section 12.C. [435] Guidance Paper, para. 81 (renumbered).
[436] In Section 9.B.iii. [437] Amendments to the Guidance Paper, Annex, para. 5.
[438] See, specifically, Case C-52/09, *TeliaSonera* EU:C:2010:483, Mazák AG, paras. 21–23.
[439] Because the conditions in Case C-7/97, *Oscar Bronner* EU:C:1998:569 are not satisfied.
[440] Case C-52/09, *TeliaSonera* EU:C:2011:83, para. 58.

to constitute an abuse, it may be relevant to whether there are anti-competitive effects, as indispensability renders at least potential anti-competitive effects 'probable'.[441] In other words, the CJ's concern is with anti-competitive effects, not the indispensability of the input.

Similarly, the test for margin squeeze does not utilise a pure predatory pricing standard.[442] The focus on the unfairness of the 'spread' means that both upstream and downstream prices are considered, whereas, if the issue is whether prices downstream are predatory, only one market is relevant. Although the dismissal of the predatory pricing standard can be criticised as protecting competitors and risking consumer welfare,[443] the conceptualisation of margin squeeze as a stand-alone abuse has the advantage of being better able to reflect the realities of the situation and behaviour of a vertically integrated undertaking, in particular internal transfer pricing, cross-subsidies, and the leveraging of market power.[444]

Where the test for margin squeeze does align with predatory pricing is in application of the AEC standard, albeit the CJ in *TeliaSonera* considered that 'artificially reduced levels of profitability', and not merely a negative spread of prices, would indicate an abuse. By using the dominant undertaking's own costs as the benchmark, the AEC test is designed to ensure that the competition rules are applied only to prevent the anti-competitive foreclosure of those whose exclusion would be detrimental to welfare. It also has the advantages of enhancing the principle of legal certainty and enabling the dominant undertaking to assess the lawfulness of its own conduct. In *Deutsche Telekom*, the CJ endorsed the GC's finding that the AEC test chimed with principle of 'equality of opportunity' between economic operators, considered necessary to guarantee a system of undistorted competition.[445] However, the CJ left the door open to the use of downstream competitors' own costs in *TeliaSonera*, where it is impossible to use those of the dominant undertaking.[446] This 'reasonably efficient' competitor test risks depriving dominant undertakings of the legal certainty the CJ considers important, however. In practice, application of the AEC test can be problematic, as is seen in arguments about the methodology used to calculate the margin squeeze in *Deutsche Telekom*, *Telefónica*, and *Slovak Telekom*: specifically, the very fact of the vertical integration and the complications of regulated prices make carrying out the test difficult. It is important that opportunity costs are taken into account.[447]

The EU Courts have made it clear that it cannot be assumed that a margin squeeze harms consumers. Rather, it is necessary to consider the likely anti-competitive effects in either the upstream or downstream markets, and the impact of any ruling on innovation upstream. Concrete effects are not required, however, as it suffices to demonstrate an anti-competitive effect which may *potentially* exclude competitors.[448] There is, nonetheless, a need to demonstrate a coherent theory of harm relating

[441] Ibid., paras. 69–72.

[442] Arguing that a modified predatory pricing standard should be applied, see G. Gaudin and D. Mantzari, 'Margin Squeeze: An Above-cost Predatory Pricing Approach' (2016) 12 *J of Competition Law and Economics* 151.

[443] See Sidak, n. 370.

[444] See further Faella and Pardolesi, n. 368, 256–259; J. Meisel, 'The Law and Economics of Margin Squeezes in the US versus the EU' (2012) 8 *European Competition Journal* 383, 397–398.

[445] Case C-280/08 P, *Deutsche Telekom* EU:C:2010:603, para. 230, followed by the GC in Case T-336/07, *Telefónica* EU:T:2012:172, para. 204.

[446] Only the first example in para. 45, the non-identification of the dominant undertaking's own costs, can strictly be described as 'not possible'. The other examples are situations where the CJ does not consider it *acceptable* to use those costs and presumably it is in this sense that 'possible' must be construed.

[447] See further S. C. Salop, 'Refusals to Deal and Price Squeezes by an Unregulated Vertically Integrated Monopolist' (2010) 76 *Antitrust LJ* 709; Meisel, n. 444, 396–397; L. Colley and S. Burnside, 'Margin Squeeze Abuse' (2006) 2 *European Competition Journal*, Special Issue, 185, 193–195.

[448] Case C-52/09, *TeliaSonera* EU:C:2011:83, para. 64.

to entry barriers to the retail market and thus the degree of competition on that market.[449] The CJ accepted in *Deutsche Telekom* that it may be that the only way a dominant undertaking can avoid the margin squeeze is to increase its retail prices. This reaffirms that the concept of 'consumer welfare' in the EU law context encompasses more than short-term price effects; but it seems a slightly regrettable outcome. It can only be justified by the longer-term benefits to consumers in future which can be expected to arise through the maintenance of competition. This is consistent with the CJ's statement, in *TeliaSonera*, that the function of the competition rules is 'to prevent competition from being distorted to the detriment of the public interest, individual undertakings and consumers, thereby ensuring the well-being of the European Union'.[450]

Finally, the margin squeeze cases provide the fullest treatment yet of the relationship between regulation and Article 102, and the resulting situation is not a happy one.[451] The main reasons for finding that *ex ante* sector regulation does not preclude the application of the competition rules to the same conduct—that EU competition law cannot be excluded by decisions of national regulators, and that regulation and competition law pursue different objectives[452]—are understandable. Yet the result leaves dominant undertakings in a difficult position. The undertakings are subject to two separate sets of rules and can infringe Article 102 even though they have done everything required of them by a domestic regulator.[453] Moreover, the situation in which a vertically integrated dominant undertaking finds itself may have been largely created by the regulator. In *Deutsche Telekom*, the wholesale price was taken as having been fixed by the regulator and so, in respect of an abuse which was founded on the spread between two prices, the dominant undertaking had no power over one of them. DT was held to have 'scope' for remedying the margin squeeze because the 'State compulsion' defence was attenuated to the narrowest of circumstances, and it infringed Article 102 by failing to take the initiative and request an alteration to the retail price in favour of its competitors. In effect, the dominant undertaking is under a duty to help its competitor by taking positive action in a situation in which regulation has failed to achieve the best competitive outcome. Thus, there has been not merely market failure but a regulatory failure. It is doubtful, however, whether competition authorities should attempt to remedy defects in regulation by application of the competition rules or use competition law to achieve what are regulatory rather than competition objectives.[454] In both *Deutsche Telekom* and *Telefónica*, the argument that the Commission should have brought proceedings against the Member State under Article 258 for failure to properly implement the telecommunications Directives, instead of against the undertakings under Article 102, was dismissed.[455]

[449] W. Wurmnest, Case note on *TeliaSonera* (2012) 49 *CMLRev* 721.

[450] Case C-52/09, *TeliaSonera* EU:C:2011:83, para. 22.

[451] See in particular D. Geradin and R. O'Donoghue, 'The Concurrent Application of Competition Law and Regulation: The Case of Margin Squeeze Abuses in the Telecommunications Sector' (2005) *J of Competition Law and Economics* 355, GCLC Working Paper 04/05; N. Dunne, 'Margin Squeeze: Theory, Practice, Policy', Part II [2012] *ECLR* 61.

[452] See Chap. 1, Section 11.

[453] The GC dismissed claims that the principle of legitimate expectation had been breached, Case T-271/03, *Deutsche Telekom* EU:T:2008:101, paras. 267–269; the CJ held that the appeal against this was inadmissible, Case C-280/08, EU:C:2010:603, paras. 105–110.

[454] Geradin and O'Donoghue, n. 451, sections IV and V; Dunne, 'Margin Squeeze: Theory, Practice, Policy', n. 451, 63–66.

[455] Case T-271/03, *Deutsche Telekom* EU:T:2008:101, paras. 46–47; Case T-336/07, *Telefónica* EU:T:2012:172, para. 307; and see Dunne, 'Margin Squeeze: Theory, Practice, Policy', n. 451, 66.

10. EXCLUSIVE DEALING

A. GENERAL

The treatment of exclusive dealing under Article 102 has been perhaps the most contentious policy question relating to dominant firm conduct in recent years.[456] Exclusive dealing can arise through express contractual obligations, commercial practices which generate *de facto* exclusivity, discount/rebate policies, or outright exclusivity payments. The optimal method of identifying and condemning such practices reflects arguably the clearest divide between 'by object' versus 'by effect' approaches under Article 102. Should exclusivity be considered inherently problematic when implemented by a dominant undertaking and thus prohibited by its very nature, or should antitrust scrutiny require a positive determination that a specific practice is likely to generate actual harm to consumer welfare?

In the original Guidance Paper, the Commission strongly advocated for the latter 'more economic' approach. It recommended that exclusive dealing be subject to a rigorous effects-based analysis to demonstrate anti-competitive foreclosure and encouraged use of the 'as efficient competitor' standard where exclusivity results from a dominant undertaking's pricing policies.[457] As explained in Sections 4 and 7, the Amendments to the Guidance Paper soften the Commission's stance considerably with respect to effects-based analysis. Moreover, the EU Courts have, historically, been less convinced of the merits of a 'by effect' approach in this context. Adopting a formalistic reading of the CJ's judgment in *Hoffmann-La Roche*,[458] the Courts, in numerous cases decided *after* publication of the Guidance Paper, adhered to an apparent 'by object' condemnation of exclusivity.[459] This position also received support from the approach of the Commission's own Legal Service, which had a tendency to defend its cases on appeal addressing exclusivity solely from a 'by object' perspective.[460] A few judgments hinted at greater receptiveness towards the more economic approach, specifically in the area of loyalty-*inducing* rebates.[461] Yet it was not until the ruling of the Grand Chamber in *Intel* in 2017 that the CJ acknowledged the relevance of effects analysis within the treatment of exclusive dealing more generally. That judgment has precipitated a string of losses by the Commission before the GC in exclusive dealing cases subsequently.[462]

The term 'exclusive dealing' encompasses a broad spectrum of different commercial arrangements which seek to achieve the same ultimate objective[463]—namely, to secure for the dominant undertaking all or most of the business of its customers subject to the practice—but often through very different means. It is customary to distinguish between *exclusive purchasing*, whereby the customer commits to exclusivity obligations; *conditional discounts/rebates*, whereby the customer is incentivised to engage in exclusive purchasing through discount policies which reward single sourcing; and *exclusivity payments* (also referred to as *naked restrictions*) whereby the customer is paid a lump sum to source

[456] See e.g. W. Wils, 'The Judgment of the EU General Court in Intel and the So-called "More Economic Approach" to Abuse of Dominance' (2014) 37 *World Competition* 405; P. Rey and J. Venit, 'An Effects-based Approach to Article 102: A Response to Wouter Wils' (2015) 38 *World Competition* 3–29; D. Crane, 'Formalism and Functionalism in the Antitrust Treatment of Loyalty Rebates: A Comparative Perspective' (2016) 81 *Antitrust LJ* 209.

[457] Guidance Paper, paras. 32–46.

[458] Case C-85/76, *Hoffmann-La Roche* EU:C:1979:36.

[459] See e.g. Cases C-549/10 P *Tomra* EU:C:2012:221 and T-286/09 *Intel* EU:T:2014:547.

[460] See the discussion at Chap. 6, Section 5.C.

[461] See e.g. Case C-23/14, *Post Danmark II* EU:C:2015:651.

[462] In the remitted *Intel* case, Case T-286/09 RENV, EU:T:2022:19, in Case T-235/18, *Qualcomm* EU:T:2022:358, and the only portion of the Commission's *Android* decision which did not survive appeal, in Case T-604/18, *Google Android* EU:T:2022:541.

[463] The Commission in its Guidance Paper employed the term 'exclusive dealing' to encompass both exclusive purchasing (paras. 33–36) and conditional rebates (paras. 37–45), because such practices have similar effects.

exclusively from the dominant supplier. A complex jurisprudence developed regarding conditional rebate practices in particular, culminating in the identification by the GC in *Intel* of three distinct categories of rebates to which different rules each apply. Yet the subsequent approach of the CJ in the *Intel* and *Unilever* cases suggests that all exclusive dealing should now be treated as broadly equivalent under Article 102, regardless of the specific form which it takes. This section, first, considers the approach to exclusivity generally under Article 102, discussing the evolution from *Hoffmann-La Roche* to *Intel*. It then examines the treatment of discrete forms of exclusive dealing within the case law.

B. EXCLUSIVE DEALING: AN ABUSE 'BY OBJECT' OR 'BY EFFECT'?

At first glance, the anti-competitive potential of exclusivity is readily apparent: by securing all (or almost all) of its customers' business to itself, the dominant undertaking may foreclose rivals, not through competition on the merits but instead by strategically depriving competitors of access to a sufficiently large base of possible consumers. Exclusivity has the potential to drive efficient sources of supply from the market because, regardless of how effectively those undertakings might compete, there is simply an insufficient number of remaining customers available to allow rivals of the dominant undertaking to obtain a sustainable market share.

Yet, as the treatment of such arrangements under Article 101 demonstrates,[464] exclusivity practices are not unambiguously harmful to competition or consumer welfare. The Chicago School approach emphasises that customers typically give up their ability to 'shop around' only in exchange for some form of compensation (usually, lower prices), and, concomitantly, that suppliers only agree to pay such compensation where they achieve efficiencies as a result.[465] Potential pro-competitive efficiencies arising from exclusivity include: enabling manufacturers to increase sales stability and thus decrease inventory costs; generating economies of scale for either sellers and buyers; or incentivising promotional activity by retailers.[466] While such efficiency gains benefit suppliers, the lower prices that typically run alongside exclusivity may also benefit their customers and, in competitive markets, final consumers. Moreover, while even substantial advantages to *individual* customers cannot legitimate practices which harm the market *as a whole*, it is not inevitable that exclusivity practices affecting a portion of the available demand will exclude competition from the remainder (although rivals may be forced to 'raise their game' in order to compete successfully).

These ambiguities in terms of the effects of exclusive dealing practices—insofar as exclusivity is superficially anti-competitive, but potentially pro-competitive or at least neutral in practice—are reflected in the treatment of exclusivity under Article 102.

(i) *Hoffmann-La Roche*: The Abusive Nature of Exclusive Dealing

The starting point is *Hoffmann-La Roche*, decided by the CJ in 1979, which remains the foundation of the current law. Hoffmann-La Roche (HLR), a chemical company, was held by the Commission to occupy a dominant position in various markets for the wholesale-level supply of vitamins.[467] The undertaking was found to have abused that dominance by engaging in exclusivity practices which included: specific contractual commitments by its customers to obtain all or almost all of their required supplies from HLR, vaguer clauses articulating a 'preference' for doing so, and rebate policies which

[464] See Chap. 11. [465] O'Donoghue and Padilla, n. 1, 503–504.

[466] OECD, *Fidelity and Bundled Rebates and Discounts*, DAF/COMP(2008)29, p. 23.

[467] For the dominance aspects of this case, see Chap. 6.

rewarded certain customers for obtaining greater quantities of their requirements from HLR.[468] HLR appealed, prompting the CJ to consider whether and why such practices might violate Article 102.

Case 85/76, *Hoffmann-La Roche v Commission* EU:C:1979:36

Court of Justice

89. An undertaking which is in a dominant position on the market and ties purchasers—even if it does so at their request—by an obligation or promise on their part to obtain all or most of their requirements exclusively from the said undertaking abuses its dominant position within the meaning of Article [102], whether the obligation in question is stipulated without further qualification or whether it is undertaken in consideration of the grant of a rebate. The same applies if the said undertaking, without tying the purchasers by a formal obligation, applies, either under the terms of agreements concluded with these purchasers or unilaterally, a system of fidelity rebates, that is to say discounts conditional on the customer's obtaining all or most of its requirements—whether the quantity of its purchases be large or small—from the undertaking in a dominant position.

90. Obligations of this kind to obtain supplies exclusively from a particular undertaking, whether or not they are in consideration of rebates or of the granting of fidelity rebates intended to give the purchaser an incentive to obtain his supplies exclusively from the undertaking in a dominant position, are incompatible with the objective of undistorted competition within the [internal market], because—unless there are exceptional circumstances which may make an agreement between undertakings in the context of Article [101] and in particular of paragraph (3) of that Article, permissible—they are not based on an economic transaction which justifies this burden or benefit but are designed to deprive the purchaser of or restrict his possible choice of sources of supply and to deny other producers access to the market. The fidelity rebate, unlike quantity rebates exclusively linked with the volume of purchases from the producer concerned, is designed through the grant of a financial advantage to prevent customers from obtaining their supplies from competing producers. Furthermore, the effect of fidelity rebates is to apply dissimilar conditions to equivalent transactions with other trading parties in that two purchasers pay a different price for the same quantity of the same product depending on whether they obtain their supplies exclusively from the undertaking in a dominant position or have several sources of supply. Finally, these practices by an undertaking in a dominant position and especially on an expanding market tend to consolidate this position by means of a form of competition which is not based on the transactions effected and is therefore distorted.

In this famous passage, the CJ established a prohibition against dominant firms entering into exclusive purchasing agreements or operating rebate schemes which have the same effect: such practices are considered abusive by their very nature. The illegality does not depend on assessing the effects of the exclusivity practice on the market in the particular case. Instead, it is assumed that, if a dominant firm limits the ability or rewards its customers for not buying elsewhere, this is bound to have an exclusionary effect on competitors. Notably, there was no mention of the effect of the assumed foreclosure on *consumers*.

Later Courts interpreted *Hoffmann-La Roche* as establishing, in essence, a 'by object' prohibition of certain types of exclusive dealing under Article 102. Where behaviour by a dominant undertaking falling within a proscribed category could be identified, such conduct, simply by virtue of what it sought to achieve, would constitute a prima facie abuse. Moreover, given the difficulties of establishing a plausible objective justification, the 'by object' rule in *Hoffmann-La Roche* was taken

[468] Case 85/76, *Hoffmann-La Roche* EU:C:1979:36, paras. 83–87 in particular.

to amount, in effect, to a per se prohibition of exclusivity practices. Yet although such an approach is often described as 'form-based', the *Hoffmann-La Roche* Court adopted a functional view of what could be characterised as an exclusivity practice, encompassing explicit contractual obligations, rebates premised upon exclusivity, and—according to later courts—discount schemes which lead to *de facto* exclusive purchasing.

A number of not-insignificant objections could be raised against this seemingly straightforward legal outcome. First, and most fundamentally, 'by object' or outright condemnation of exclusivity failed to give any weight to the potentially welfare-enhancing aspects of such arrangements. Thus, the blanket ban on exclusivity under Article 102 generated a substantial risk of Type I errors, whereby efficient commercial behaviour would be prohibited. It also represented a significant incursion into the default freedom of businesses to identify and implement effective business practices.

Secondly, treating exclusivity as a 'by object' abuse contrasted markedly with the approach of equivalent practices under Article 101, where the significant potential for welfare-enhancing efficiencies led the CJ in *Delimitis* to determine that exclusivity should not be prohibited by object.[469] The *Hoffmann-La Roche* principle thus generated an internal inconsistency within the scheme of the EU competition provisions.[470] The overlapping application of Articles 101 and 102 was almost certainly a significant factor informing the approach in *Van den Bergh*, for instance, where the GC was called upon to review a Commission decision finding infringement of both provisions arising from exclusivity practices in the Irish impulse ice-cream market. It upheld the decision, but not before considering the effects of the agreements carefully, applying the principle in *Delimitis* in respect of Article 101.[471] When it came to Article 102, the GC did not simply treat the practices as inherently abusive, but instead held that they breached Article 102 because of their *effects* in preventing competitors gaining access to the market.[472] Yet in subsequent cases, where the potential for conflict between the two provisions was not so readily apparent, the EU Courts took a more absolutist view, interpreting and applying *Hoffmann-La Roche* as a 'by object' prohibition.

Thirdly, by extending the ambit of the 'by object' prohibition to exclusivity-*inducing* practices—in particular, to rebate policies with equivalent impact—the CJ initiated a complex and not always coherent jurisprudence which sought to distinguish permissible from automatically prohibited practices. The approach discernible in past case law involves narrow and arguably untenable distinctions between substantially similar pricing practices.[473] Yet the stakes are high: a rebate policy that falls on the wrong side of the legal line separating permissible from prohibited discounts or rebates would almost inevitably breach Article 102, where implemented by a dominant undertaking.

Fourthly, the unequivocal language of *Hoffmann-La Roche* appeared to conflict with what the Court had actually done in that case. Despite articulating a 'by object' approach, the CJ conducted an in-depth examination of the operation and impact of the impugned practices within their market context, which suggests that a purely formalistic prohibition was not what it had intended. This disjuncture between theory and practice particularly concerned Advocate General Wahl in *Intel*, who argued that a 'verbatim' approach to paragraph 89 of *Hoffmann-La Roche* was incompatible with the substance of the underlying judgment.[474]

[469] Case C-234/89, *Delimitis v Henninger Bräu* EU:C:1991:91, see also Chap. 11.

[470] See also Section 3.F. [471] Case C-234/89, *Delimitis v Henninger Bräu* EU:C:1991:91.

[472] Case T-65/98, *Van den Bergh Foods* EU:T:2003:281, para. 160.

[473] See also P. Ibáñez Colomo, 'AG Wahl in *Intel*, or the Value of Realism and Consistency in the Context of Article 102 TFEU' [2017] 1 *Concurrences* 16–35.

[474] See e.g. Opinion of AG Wahl in Case C-413/14 P *Intel* EU:C:2016:788, particularly paras. 66 and 70.

(ii) *Intel*: Revisiting the 'By Object' Condemnation of Exclusivity Practices

Debate about the optimal treatment of exclusivity under Article 102 found a focal point in the Commission's prosecution of Intel, which culminated in 2009 in the first-ever fine exceeding €1 billion to be imposed for abuse of dominance.[475] Intel was found to have given rebates on its x86 CPUs to computer manufacturers (OEMs) such as Dell and HP, which were conditional on the OEMs purchasing 80–100 per cent of their requirements from Intel.[476] The case also involved exclusivity payments, considered in Section 10.C.iv. In its infringement decision, the Commission adopted what might be termed a 'have your cake and eat it' approach to the assessment of these practices under Article 102. In line with the methodology advocated in its Guidance Paper, it engaged in a detailed context-specific assessment of the likely impact of the disputed conduct, applying the AEC test to arrive at an interim conclusion that Intel's conditional rebates were 'capable of causing or likely to cause anti-competitive foreclosure (which is likely to result in consumer harm)'.[477] Yet, in concluding that Intel had abused its dominance, the Commission maintained that, strictly as a matter of Article 102 jurisprudence, it was not required to demonstrate likely anti-competitive effects, but was entitled to rely upon the 'by object' prohibition of exclusivity practices emerging from *Hoffmann-La Roche*.[478]

The decision was subjected to considerable criticism, inter alia on the grounds that the theory of harm advanced in respect of the effect of the rebates on the OEM's purchasing strategy was speculative, that the analysis of the evidence was flawed, and that the consideration of 'harm to competition and consumers' was entirely theoretical.[479] The outcome of Intel's appeal to the GC was eagerly awaited as an opportunity to revisit the law regarding exclusivity practices in the light of the emerging 'more economic approach'. Nonetheless, the decision was upheld in its entirety.[480] In particular, the Commission's approach to the *Hoffmann-La Roche* precedent received full support from the GC, which endorsed in emphatic terms a 'by object' approach to the treatment of exclusive dealing under Article 102, subject only to the possibility of objective justification.

This embracing of form over substance drew trenchant criticism from Advocate General Wahl when the case was appealed to the CJ. The Advocate General emphasised the possible consumer benefits that exclusivity practices might generate, thus rendering them an inappropriate candidate for outright prohibition; and also the danger, in terms of both false positive *and* false negative findings, of condemning or permitting behaviour by reference to arbitrary categories which do not accurately reflect market impact.[481]

The CJ faced an apparently stark choice: to reaffirm the 'by object' prohibition from *Hoffmann-La Roche*, thus effectively rejecting modernisation within this area, or to abandon one of the longest-standing and most prominent, albeit contentious, rules within EU competition law. The CJ attempted to find a third way, nominally reaffirming the form-based rule, but also acknowledging the relevance of effects-based considerations.

The following extracts contrast the divergent approaches of the GC and CJ to the treatment of exclusivity practices. In the first, the GC sets out the rationale for the 'by object' condemnation of such

475 COMP/37.990, *Intel* 13 May 2009.

476 In Dell's case, for example, the rebate was conditional on 100% exclusivity. In HP's case it was 95%: when AMD offered HP one million CPUs *free*, it took only 160,000 of them in order to stay within Intel's limit (COMP/37.990, *Intel* 13 May 2009, paras. 956–957).

477 COMP/37.990, *Intel* 13 May 2009, para. 925.

478 Ibid., paras. 920–923. It also cited Case T-201/04, *Microsoft* EU:T:2007:289, as showing that the EU Courts do not look at the actual impact of the alleged anti-competitive conduct on the market.

479 D. Geradin, 'The Decision of the Commission of 13 May 2009 in the *Intel* Case: Where is the Foreclosure and Consumer Harm?' (2009) 2 *JECLAP* 9.

480 Case T-286/09, *Intel* EU:T:2014:547.

481 Opinion in Case C-413/14 P, *Intel* EU:C:2016:788.

conduct. Note that while the GC is primarily concerned with the treatment of rebates as distinct from other forms of exclusive dealing, the competition policy considerations it addresses are applicable to what the GC termed 'exclusivity conditions'[482] more broadly.

Case T-286/09, *Intel v Commission* EU:T:2014:547

General Court

85. . . . [E]xclusivity rebates granted by an undertaking in a dominant position are by their very nature capable of restricting competition.

86. The capability of tying customers to the undertaking in a dominant position is inherent in exclusivity rebates. The grant by an undertaking in a dominant position of a rebate in consideration of a customer's obtaining all or most of its requirements implies that the undertaking in a dominant position grants a financial advantage designed to prevent customers from obtaining their supplies from competing producers. It is therefore not necessary to examine the circumstances of the case in order to determine whether that rebate is designed to prevent customers from obtaining their supplies from competitors.

87. It should moreover be noted that exclusivity rebates granted by an undertaking in a dominant position are by their very nature capable of foreclosing competitors. A financial advantage granted for the purpose of inducing a customer to obtain all or most of its requirements from the undertaking in a dominant position means that that customer has an incentive not to obtain, in respect of the part of its requirements concerned by the exclusivity condition, supplies from competitors of the undertaking in a dominant position.

88. In that context, it should be observed that a foreclosure effect occurs not only where access to the market is made impossible for competitors, but also where that access is made more difficult (. . . *Michelin I*, . . . paragraph 85; Case C-52/09 *TeliaSonera Sverige* . . . , paragraph 63, and *Michelin II*, . . . paragraph 244). A financial incentive granted by an undertaking in a dominant position in order to induce a customer not to obtain, in respect of the part of its requirements concerned by the exclusivity condition, supplies from its competitors is by its very nature capable of making access to the market more difficult for those competitors.

89. Although exclusivity conditions may, in principle, have beneficial effects for competition, so that in a normal situation on a competitive market, it is necessary to assess their effects on the market in their specific context (. . . Case C-234/89 *Delimitis* . . ., paragraphs 14 to 27), those considerations cannot be accepted in the case of a market where, precisely because of the dominant position of one of the economic operators, competition is already restricted (. . . Case C-310/93 P *BPB Industries and British Gypsum* v *Commission*, paragraph 11 . . .).

90. That approach is justified by the special responsibility that an undertaking in a dominant position has not to allow its conduct to impair genuine undistorted competition in the common market and by the fact that, where an economic operator holds a strong position in the market, exclusive supply conditions in respect of a substantial proportion of purchases by a customer constitute an unacceptable obstacle to access to the market (. . . Case T-65/89 *BPB Industries and British Gypsum* . . ., paragraphs 65 to 68). In that case, the exclusivity of supply causes additional interference with the structure of competition on the market. Thus, the concept of abuse in principle includes any obligation to obtain supplies exclusively from an undertaking in a dominant position which benefits that undertaking (. . . *Hoffmann-La Roche*, . . . paragraphs 120, 121 and 123, Case C-310/93 P *BPB Industries and British Gypsum*, . . . paragraph 11, and the Opinion of Advocate General Léger in that case, . . . points 46 and 47).

[482] Case T-286/09, *Intel* EU:T:2014:547, para. 89.

91. Furthermore, it must also be stated that it is inherent in a strong dominant position, such as that occupied by the applicant, that, for a substantial part of the demand, there are no proper substitutes for the product supplied by the dominant undertaking. The supplier in a dominant position is thus, to a large extent, an unavoidable trading partner (. . . *Hoffmann-La Roche*, . . . paragraph 41; Case C-95/04 P *British Airways*, . . . paragraph 75; and Case T-155/06 *Tomra*, . . . paragraph 269). In the present case, the applicant does not contest the findings made in the contested decision that its position on the market during the period of the infringement found in this case was that of an unavoidable trading partner.

92. It follows from the position of unavoidable trading partner that customers will in any event obtain part of their requirements from the undertaking in a dominant position ('the non-contestable share'). The competitor of an undertaking in a dominant position is not therefore in a position to compete for the full supply of a customer, but only for the portion of the demand exceeding the non-contestable share ('the contestable share'). The contestable share is thus the portion of a customer's requirements which can realistically be switched to a competitor of the undertaking in a dominant position in any given period . . . The grant of exclusivity rebates by an undertaking in a dominant position makes it more difficult for a competitor to supply its own goods to customers of that dominant undertaking. If a customer of the undertaking in a dominant position obtains supplies from a competitor by failing to comply with the exclusivity or quasi-exclusivity condition, it risks losing not only the rebates for the units that it switched to that competitor, but the entire exclusivity rebate.

93. In order to submit an attractive offer, it is not therefore sufficient for the competitor of an undertaking in a dominant position to offer attractive conditions for the units that that competitor can itself supply to the customer; it must also offer that customer compensation for the loss of the exclusivity rebate. In order to submit an attractive offer, the competitor must therefore apportion the rebate that the undertaking in a dominant position grants in respect of all or almost all of the customer's requirements, including the non-contestable share, to the contestable share alone. Thus, the grant of an exclusivity rebate by an unavoidable trading partner makes it structurally more difficult for a competitor to submit an offer at an attractive price and thus gain access to the market. The grant of exclusivity rebates enables the undertaking in a dominant position to use its economic power on the non-contestable share of the demand of the customer as leverage to secure also the contestable share, thus making access to the market more difficult for a competitor.

Thus, the GC argued that exclusivity conditions should be considered *inherently* anti-competitive ('by their very nature'), therefore meriting 'by object' condemnation. In doing so, it expressly drew upon the special responsibility of dominant undertakings, suggesting that, since dominance implies a structural absence of competition, exclusivity poses unacceptable levels of risk to the remaining competitive dynamics. The GC noted that dominant undertakings typically represent 'unavoidable trading partners', in the sense that, practically speaking, customers must obtain at least a portion of their requirements from the dominant supplier. Exclusivity practices, accordingly, provide a means by which dominant undertakings may leverage their (inescapable) advantages in respect of the non-contestable portions of customer demand, in order to secure (unmerited) advantages in respect of the remainder of the market.

The GC acknowledged obliquely, and attempted to distinguish briefly, the markedly different approach to exclusivity under Article 101, where such practices are prohibited, if at all, only on a 'by effect' basis. Specifically, it argued that the assumption, implicit in cases like *Delimitis*, that exclusivity obligations are likely to have such mixed effects on competition that it is necessary to demonstrate actual anti-competitive effects to justify antitrust prohibition, could not be maintained where existing levels of competition are already so restricted by the presence of a dominant undertaking. As the Commission's Guidelines on Vertical Restraints recognise, the presence of market power at one or more levels of the value chain is the principal indication that a vertical agreement will generate competition concerns.[483] The 'by object' condemnation of exclusivity in the presence of dominance might be defended on the basis that, where *significant* market power exists, the substantial potential for actual anti-competitive effects to arise means that the balance of convenience lies in prohibiting such behaviour prima facie. It then falls to the dominant undertaking to make the case for why the impugned restraint is welfare-enhancing in substance.[484] The difficulty of this approach lies in the feebleness of the objective justification criterion as a vehicle by which to meaningfully counter any putative finding of abuse. The subsequent standpoint of the CJ in *Intel*, which attempts to incorporate both the 'by object' and 'by effect' standards, could nonetheless be understood as reflective of this logic—with, however, a notable attempt to strengthen the prospects for even dominant undertakings to excuse exclusivity obligations that do not generate negative effects on competition.

The judgment of the GC unleashed a storm of comment, most of it critical.[485] Amongst the most forthright objections came from the Advocate General in the subsequent further appeal. Advocate General Wahl was overtly critical of the GC's failure to consider the broader legal and economic context in which the exclusivity obligations operated, in order to determine whether the arrangements could result in anti-competitive foreclosure in practice.[486] In doing so, he attacked the use of 'by object' prohibitions under Article 102 generally, the salient passages of which were extracted earlier in this chapter.[487] This coincided with arguments advanced by Intel before the CJ, where it contended that 'neither the wording nor the structure of Article 102 TFEU suggests that some types of conduct, when undertaken by an undertaking in a dominant position, must be treated as inherently anti-competitive'.[488] Thus, although the case ostensibly concerned a relatively specific question regarding the treatment of conditional rebates, it also raised fundamental questions about the scope of the prohibition on abuse of dominance more broadly, to the extent that the Court might choose to engage with these issues.

[483] 2022 Verticals Guidelines, para. 11.

[484] A more sceptical viewpoint is P. Ibáñez Colomo, 'Beyond the "More Economics-based Approach": A Legal Perspective on Article 102 TFEU Case Law' (2016) 53 *CMLRev* 709, 736.

[485] See e.g. N. Petit, '*Intel*, Leveraging Rebates and the Goals of Article 102 TFEU' (2015) 11 *European Competition Journal* 26; L. Peeperkorn, 'Conditional Pricing: Why the General Court is Wrong in *Intel* and What the Court of Justice Can Do to Rebalance the Assessment of Rebates' [2015] 1 *Concurrences* 43; P. Ibáñez Colomo, '*Intel* and Article 102 TFEU Case Law: Making Sense of a Perpetual Controversy', LSE, Law, Society and Economy Working Papers 29/201; J. Venit, 'Case T-286/09, *Intel v Commission*—The Judgment of the General Court: All Steps Backward and No Steps Forward' (2014) 10 *European Competition Journal* 203; W. Wils, 'The Judgment of the EU General Court in *Intel* and the So-called "More Economic Approach" to Abuse of Dominance' (2014) 37 *World Competition* 405 (which approves the judgment); P. Rey and J. Venit, 'An Effects-based Approach to Article 102: A Response to Wouter Wils' (2015) 38 *World Competition* 3; R. Whish, '*Intel v Commission*: Keep Calm and Carry On!' (2015) 6 *JECLAP* 1; P. Nihoul, 'The Ruling of the General Court in *Intel*: Towards the End of an Effects-based Approach in European Competition Law?' (2014) 5 *JECLAP* 521; D. Geradin, 'Loyalty Rebates after *Intel*: Time for the European Court of Justice to Overrule *Hoffmann-La Roche*' (2015) 11 *J of Competition Law and Economics* 579; and the symposium in the first issue of *Competition Law and Policy Debate* [2015] 1 *CLPD* especially B. Allan, 'Loyalty and Fidelity Rebates: A Sense of Déjà Vu Again' [2015] 1 *CLPD* 50; C. Ahlborn and D. Piccinin, 'The *Intel* Judgment and Consumer Welfare—A Response to Wouter Wils' [2015] 1 *CLPD* 60; and M. Dolmans and T. Graf, 'Dealing with *Intel* Intelligently Delineating the Scope and Limits of the Court's Ruling' [2015] 1 *CLPD* 76.

[486] Opinion in Case C-413/14 P, *Intel v Commission* EU:C:2016:788.

[487] See Section 3.F.

[488] Case C-413/14 P, *Intel* EU:C:2016:788, para. 110.

Case C-413/14 P, *Intel v Commission* EU:C:2017:632

Court of Justice

129. In the first place . . . Intel . . . argues, in essence, that the General Court accepted that the practices at issue could be considered an abuse of a dominant position within the meaning of Article 102 TFEU without first examining all of the circumstances of the present case and without assessing the likelihood of that conduct restricting competition.

130. In the second place, . . . Intel criticises the General Court's analysis, carried out for the sake of completeness . . . concerning the capacity of the rebates and payments . . . to restrict competition in the circumstances of the case.

131. In that context, Intel challenges, inter alia, the General Court's assessment of the relevance of the AEC test applied by the Commission in the present case.

132. It submits, in particular, that, since the Commission applied that test, the General Court should have examined Intel's line of argument alleging that the application of that test was badly flawed and that, had it been correctly applied, it would have led to the conclusion contrary to that which the Commission reached, namely that the rebates at issue were not capable of restricting competition.

133. In that respect, it must be borne in mind that it is in no way the purpose of Article 102 TFEU to prevent an undertaking from acquiring, on its own merits, the dominant position on a market. Nor does that provision seek to ensure that competitors less efficient than the undertaking with the dominant position should remain on the market (. . . Post Danmark, C-209/10, paragraph 21 and the case-law cited).

134. Thus, not every exclusionary effect is necessarily detrimental to competition. Competition on the merits may, by definition, lead to the departure from the market or the marginalisation of competitors that are less efficient and so less attractive to consumers from the point of view of, among other things, price, choice, quality or innovation (. . . Post Danmark, C-209/10, paragraph 22 and the case-law cited).

135. However, a dominant undertaking has a special responsibility not to allow its behaviour to impair genuine, undistorted competition on the internal market (. . . Nederlandsche Banden-Industrie-Michelin v Commission, 322/81, paragraph 57, and . . . Post Danmark, C-209/10, paragraph 23 and the case-law cited).

136. That is why Article 102 TFEU prohibits a dominant undertaking from, among other things, adopting pricing practices that have an exclusionary effect on competitors considered to be as efficient as it is itself and strengthening its dominant position by using methods other than those that are part of competition on the merits. Accordingly, in that light, not all competition by means of price may be regarded as legitimate (. . . Post Danmark, C-209/10, paragraph 25).

137. In that regard, the Court has already held that an undertaking which is in a dominant position on a market and ties purchasers—even if it does so at their request—by an obligation or promise on their part to obtain all or most of their requirements exclusively from that undertaking abuses its dominant position within the meaning of Article 102 TFEU, whether the obligation is stipulated without further qualification or whether it is undertaken in consideration of the grant of a rebate. The same applies if the undertaking in question, without tying the purchasers by a formal obligation, applies, either under the terms of agreements concluded with these purchasers or unilaterally, a system of loyalty rebates, that is to say, discounts conditional on the customer's obtaining all or most of its requirements—whether the quantity of its purchases be large or small—from the undertaking in a dominant position (. . . Hoffmann-La Roche v Commission, 85/76, paragraph 89).

138. However, that case-law must be further clarified in the case where the undertaking concerned submits, during the administrative procedure, on the basis of supporting evidence, that its conduct was not capable of restricting competition and, in particular, of producing the alleged foreclosure effects.

> 139. In that case, the Commission is not only required to analyse, first, the extent of the undertaking's dominant position on the relevant market and, secondly, the share of the market covered by the challenged practice, as well as the conditions and arrangements for granting the rebates in question, their duration and their amount; it is also required to assess the possible existence of a strategy aiming to exclude competitors that are at least as efficient as the dominant undertaking from the market (. . . Post Danmark, C-209/10, paragraph 29).
>
> 140. The analysis of the capacity to foreclose is also relevant in assessing whether a system of rebates which, in principle, falls within the scope of the prohibition laid down in Article 102 TFEU, may be objectively justified. In addition, the exclusionary effect arising from such a system, which is disadvantageous for competition, may be counterbalanced, or outweighed, by advantages in terms of efficiency which also benefit the consumer (. . . British Airways v Commission, C-95/04 P, paragraph 86). That balancing of the favourable and unfavourable effects of the practice in question on competition can be carried out in the Commission's decision only after an analysis of the intrinsic capacity of that practice to foreclose competitors which are at least as efficient as the dominant undertaking.
>
> 141. If, in a decision finding a rebate scheme abusive, the Commission carries out such an analysis, the General Court must examine all of the applicant's arguments seeking to call into question the validity of the Commission's findings concerning the foreclosure capability of the rebate concerned.
>
> 142. In this case, while the Commission emphasised, in the decision at issue, that the rebates at issue were by their very nature capable of restricting competition such that an analysis of all the circumstances of the case and, in particular, an AEC test were not necessary in order to find an abuse of a dominant position . . ., it nevertheless carried out an in-depth examination of those circumstances, setting out . . . a very detailed analysis of the AEC test, which led it to conclude . . . that an as efficient competitor would have had to offer prices which would not have been viable and that, accordingly, the rebate scheme at issue was capable of having foreclosure effects on such a competitor.
>
> 143. It follows that, in the decision at issue, the AEC test played an important role in the Commission's assessment of whether the rebate scheme at issue was capable of having foreclosure effects on as efficient competitors.
>
> 144. In those circumstances, the General Court was required to examine all of Intel's arguments concerning that test.
>
> 145. It held, however . . . that it was not necessary to consider whether the Commission had carried out the AEC test in accordance with the applicable rules and without making any errors, and that it was also not necessary to examine the question whether the alternative calculations proposed by Intel had been carried out correctly.
>
> 146. In its examination of the circumstances of the case, carried out for the sake of completeness, the General Court therefore attached no importance . . . to the AEC test carried out by the Commission and, accordingly, did not address Intel's criticisms of that test.
>
> 147. Consequently . . . the judgment of the General Court must be set aside, since, in its analysis of whether the rebates at issue were capable of restricting competition, the General Court wrongly failed to take into consideration Intel's line of argument seeking to expose alleged errors committed by the Commission in the AEC test.

The CJ thus struggled to achieve the impossible in this judgment: it sought to reaffirm the formalistic *Hoffmann-La Roche* 'by object' prohibition of exclusivity, while simultaneously attempting to provide scope for greater 'by effect' assessment. It did so by stating in paragraph 138 that the former, though ostensibly still good law, 'must be further *clarified* in the case where the undertaking concerned submits . . . that its conduct was not capable of restricting competition'. In the latter circumstance, the Commission cannot rely upon the *Hoffmann-La Roche* prohibition alone. Additionally, it must consider 'the intrinsic capacity of that practice to foreclose competitors which are *at least as efficient* as the dominant undertaking' (paragraph 140, emphasis added), thus aligning the treatment of exclusive dealing with the jurisprudence which decouples mere exclusion of competitors from anti-competitive harm.[489] Moreover, the CJ emphasised that such a determination is distinct from the potential objective justification of prima facie abusive exclusivity obligations. Thus, dominant undertakings now have two opportunities to challenge a finding of abuse: first, by arguing that its conduct is incapable of restricting competition and, secondly, by arguing that any prima facie restriction is counterbalanced by efficiency gains.

(iii) Post-*Intel*: Where Do We Stand on Assessment of Exclusive Dealing?

The approach of the CJ contradicts the GC's defence of the treatment of exclusive dealing as a pure 'by object' restraint under Article 102. Yet the outcome was not as radical as either the Advocate General or defendant had endorsed.[490] In order to understand where the law on exclusivity stands after *Intel*, the following can be said.

a. *Scope of Application of the Intel Judgment to Exclusivity Practices*

Intel itself involved a specific form of exclusive dealing, namely conditional rebates. A first question is the extent to which the clarification contained in the judgment is applicable to other exclusivity obligations. On the one hand, the judgment refers to and would appear to be applicable to any exclusivity practice, regardless of the form these take. In reaffirming the *Hoffmann-La Roche* 'by object' prohibition, the CJ referenced both its limbs, encompassing exclusive purchasing obligations *and* loyalty rebates.[491] In the paragraph that immediately follows, which introduces the nominal clarification to that case law, the CJ speaks broadly of the defendant's 'conduct', making no reference to different forms of exclusive dealing.[492] Although the judgment subsequently focuses on how it might be demonstrated that rebate schemes specifically have a capacity to foreclose, the tenor and underlying logic of its approach is equally relevant across the whole spectrum of exclusivity.[493]

On the other hand, the extent to which the same legal test *should* apply to all exclusivity practices might be challenged.[494] For instance, evidence indicates that contractual exclusivity obligations agreed upfront have significantly greater potential for anti-competitive effects than rebate schemes which permit customers to determine the desirability of exclusivity during the course of the contract.[495] The Commission in its Guidance Paper addressed both exclusive purchasing and conditional rebates under the same heading—'exclusive dealing'—yet identified distinct methodologies to be applied to each.[496] The GC in *Intel* distinguished exclusivity obligations, including fidelity rebates, from other pricing practices, arguing with respect to the former that it is the conditionality of any rebate granted as opposed to its absolute level which violates Article 102.[497] Although the CJ in *Intel* did not address this contention directly, it drew a link between the nominal 'by object' prohibition from

[489] See e.g. Case C-209/10, *Post Danmark I* EU:C:2012:172 on price discrimination, and Case C-280/08 P, *Deutsche Telekom* EU:C:2010:603 on margin squeeze.

[490] See e.g. P. Déchamps and Gunnar Niels, 'The One Billion Euro Question for Intel: Moore's Law or Murphy's Law?' (2018) 9 *J of European Competition Law and Practice* 124.

[491] Case C-413/14 P, *Intel* EU:C:2017:632, para. 137.

[492] Ibid., para. 138.

[493] See R. Hajnovicova, N. Lang, and A. Usai, 'Exclusivity Agreements and the Role of the As-Efficient Competitor Test after *Intel*' (2019) 10 *JECLAP* 141, 149–150, offering further arguments why all exclusivity practices should be subject to the same legal treatment (although the authors themselves disagree with this position).

[494] See e.g. M. Kadar, 'Article 102 and Exclusivity Rebates in a Post-*Intel* World: Lessons from the Qualcomm and Google Android Cases' (2019) 10 *JECLAP* 439.

[495] E. Ide, J.-P. Montero, and N. Figueroa, 'Discounts as a Barrier to Entry' (2016) 106 *Am Econ Rev* 1849.

[496] Guidance Paper, paras. 33–45.

[497] Case C-413/14 P, *Intel* EU:C:2017:632, para. 99.

Hoffmann-La Roche and the broader statement of principle regarding exclusionary pricing practices confirmed in *Post Danmark I*.[498]

The Commission has addressed exclusivity practices in four decisions since the Grand Chamber judgment in *Intel*, as at the time of writing.[499] Two of these—*Qualcomm*[500] and *Google Android*[501]—involved exclusivity payments, and in each the Commission accepted that the *Intel* judgment required it to consider capacity to foreclose to establish sufficient evidence of the abuse. This approach was endorsed by the GC in both cases,[502] and indeed the language used by the GC is sufficiently expansive to envisage the application of the *Intel* 'clarification' to all exclusivity practices, including outright contractual exclusivity obligations. A further two Commission decisions—the *Google AdSense* infringement decision[503] and the *Broadcom* commitments decision[504]—concerned straightforward contractual exclusivity. In those cases, the Commission held that the clarification in *Intel* was irrelevant. It explained in *AdSense* that this is because, 'all other things being equal, an exclusive supply obligation constitutes a greater obstacle to access to the market than exclusivity rebates', insofar as it 'deprives a customer of the possibility to switch *any* of its requirements to a competitor of the dominant undertaking'.[505] Nonetheless, while maintaining that 'it is not legally required to do so',[506] the Commission hedged its bets in *AdSense* and *Broadcom* by considering the capacity of the relevant restraints to restrict competition.

The subsequent judgment of the CJ in the preliminary reference case of *Unilever* indicates, however, that the *Intel* 'clarification' now applies across the board for exclusive dealing practices. In *Unilever*, the CJ was asked inter alia whether and to what extent the assessment of contractual exclusivity under Article 102 now hinges on the impact of the relevant practice on equally efficient competitors. The CJ essentially transposed its reasoning in *Intel* to the context of contractual exclusivity. It began by recalling the established case law to the effect that Article 102 is intended neither to prevent the acquisition of dominance through competition on the merits nor to ensure that less efficient competitors remain in the marketplace; and that although it is unnecessary to establish actual anti-competitive effects in the context of an exclusionary abuse, the conduct in question must be at least capable of having such effects.[507] The CJ then turned its attention directly to the treatment of contractual exclusivity.

Case C-680/20, *Unilever Italia Mkt. Operations Srl v Autorità Garante della Concorrenza e del Mercato* EU:C:2023:33

Court of Justice

46. . . . [W]ith regard more specifically to exclusivity clauses, it is true that the Court has held that clauses by which contracting parties undertook to purchase all or a considerable part of their requirements from an undertaking in a dominant position, even if not accompanied by rebates, constituted, by their very nature, an exploitation of a dominant position and that the same was true of the loyalty rebates granted by such an undertaking (. . . *Hoffmann-La Roche* v *Commission*, 85/76, EU:C:1979:36, paragraph 89).

[498] Ibid., paras. 136–137. [499] As of April 2023.

[500] AT.40220, *Qualcomm (exclusivity payments)* 24 January 2018.

[501] AT.40099, *Google Android* 18 July 2018.

[502] Case T-604/18, *Google Android* EU:T:2022:541, para. 639; and Case T-235/18, *Qualcomm* EU:T:2022:358, paras. 354–356.

[503] AT.40411, *Google Search (AdSense)* 20 March 2019. [504] AT.40608, *Broadcom* 7 October 2020.

[505] AT.40411, *Google Search (AdSense)* 20 March 2019, para. 344.

[506] Ibid., para. 345. See also AT.40608, *Broadcom* 16 October 2019, para. 346, and AT.40608, *Broadcom* 7 October 2020, para. 61, where the Commission argued that exclusivity obligations 'may amount prima facie to an abuse of dominant position, without, in principle, it being necessary to conduct an analysis of their capability to restrict competition'.

[507] Case C-680/20 *Unilever Italia Mkt. Operations* EU:C:2023:33, paras. 36–42.

47. However, in . . . *Intel* v *Commission* (C-413/14 P, EU:C:2017:632, paragraph 138), the Court clarified, in the first place, that case-law in a situation where an undertaking in a dominant position submits, during the administrative procedure, with evidence in support of its claims, that its conduct was not capable of restricting competition and, in particular, of producing the alleged exclusionary effects.

48. In that regard, the Court stated that, in that situation, the competition authority is not only required to analyse, first, the extent of the undertaking's dominant position on the relevant market and, secondly, the share of the market covered by the challenged practice, as well as the conditions and arrangements for granting the rebates in question, their duration and their amount; it is also required to assess the possible existence of a strategy aiming to exclude competitors that are at least as efficient as the dominant undertaking from the market (. . . *Intel* v *Commission*, C-413/14 P, EU:C:2017:632, paragraph 139).

49. The Court added, in the second place, that the analysis of the capacity to foreclose is also relevant in assessing whether a system of rebates which, in principle, falls within the scope of the prohibition laid down in Article 102 TFEU, may be objectively justified. In addition, the exclusionary effect arising from such a system, which is disadvantageous for competition, may be counterbalanced, or outweighed, by advantages in terms of efficiency which also benefit the consumer. That balancing of the favourable and unfavourable effects of the practice in question on competition can be carried out only after an analysis of the intrinsic capacity of that practice to foreclose competitors which are at least as efficient as the dominant undertaking (. . . *Intel* v *Commission*, C-413/14 P, EU:C:2017:632, paragraph 140).

50. It is true that, in providing that second clarification, the Court referred only to rebate schemes. However, since both rebate practices and exclusivity clauses are capable of being objectively justified or of having the disadvantages which they generate counterbalanced, or even outweighed, by advantages in terms of efficiency which also benefit the consumer, such a clarification must be understood as applying to both of those practices.

51. Moreover, in addition to the fact that such an interpretation appears to be consistent with the first clarification provided by the Court in . . . *Intel* v *Commission* (C-413/14 P, EU:C:2017:632, paragraph 139), it must be held that, although, by reason of their nature, exclusivity clauses give rise to legitimate concerns of competition, their ability to exclude competitors is not automatic, as, moreover, is illustrated by the Communication from the Commission entitled 'Guidance on the Commission's enforcement priorities in applying Article [102 TFEU] to abusive exclusionary conduct by dominant undertakings (OJ 2009 C 45, p. 7, paragraph 36).

52. It follows that, first, where a competition authority suspects that an undertaking has infringed Article 102 TFEU by using exclusivity clauses, and where that undertaking disputes, during the procedure, the specific capacity of those clauses to exclude equally efficient competitors from the market, with supporting evidence, that authority must ensure, at the stage of classifying the infringement, that those clauses were, in the circumstances of the case, actually capable of excluding competitors as efficient as that undertaking from the market.

53. Secondly, the competition authority which initiated that procedure is also required to assess, specifically, the ability of those clauses to restrict competition where, during the administrative procedure, the undertaking which is under suspicion, without formally arguing that its conduct was incapable of restricting competition, maintains that there are justifications for its conduct.

b. *Relevance of the Hoffmann-La Roche Presumption Post-Intel*

This links to a second question, namely the extent to which the *Hoffmann-La Roche* presumption continues to have a meaningful role in the assessment of exclusivity practices post-*Intel*. By explicitly reaffirming *Hoffmann-La Roche* and making it incumbent upon dominant undertakings to raise the issue of capacity to foreclose, the judgment retains the possibility that, in certain instances, a defendant may be held to breach Article 102 merely by implementing exclusivity. In theory, that is, the 'by object' condemnation of exclusivity remains the default rule, absent intervention by the defendant. In reality, the likelihood of a dominant undertaking failing to raise a question of capacity to foreclose may be slim.[508] Given the 'escape route' identified by the CJ in *Intel*, any failure by the dominant undertaking's legal team to at least advance the point during the administrative procedure would surely amount to negligent lawyering. Moreover, if the Commission were to rely solely upon the 'by object' prohibition in future cases involving exclusivity, such an attitude may engender an unsympathetic response from the EU Courts.[509] When the GC reconsidered the *Intel* case in light of the 'clarified' principles articulated by the Grand Chamber, it stated unequivocally that 'what is involved is . . . a mere presumption and not a per se infringement of Article 102'.[510]

Uncertainty remains about the CJ's reference to the 'supporting evidence' which must be provided to underpin any claimed absence of capacity to foreclose.[511] The more rigorously this criterion is interpreted, the higher the hurdle faced by defendants seeking to overcome the presumed prohibition of exclusivity arrangements. Given that this requirement relates to the initial determination of whether behaviour *can* be abusive and not to the defendant's limited opportunity to defend prima facie abusive conduct, it would be unreasonable to subject the defendant to the same (exacting) standards of evidence that are necessary to establish an objective justification,[512] i.e. the burden of proof cannot shift to the defendant to disprove the Commission's case at this juncture. On the other hand, it has been argued that the *Hoffmann-La Roche* presumption would 'lack meaning if it only required a relatively low evidentiary standard to rebut the presumption under the facts of the given case'.[513] In *Android*, the GC accepted that the Commission was obliged to consider the anticipated effects of an exclusionary practice where the defendant 'claims . . . that its conduct was not capable of restricting competition'[514] or where that point is 'disputed',[515] without elaborating on the level of evidence necessary to back up any such claim. In *Servizio Elettrico Nazionale* and *Unilever*, the CJ moreover linked this obligation to the general EU law principle of the right to be heard.[516]

c. *'Capacity to Foreclosure' and the As Efficient Competitor Test*

Where a defendant can and does take advantage of the opportunity provided by *Intel* to rebut the *Hoffmann-La Roche* presumption, the burden shifts back to the Commission to consider the anticipated effects. The Grand Chamber in *Intel* described this variously as an assessment of the 'capacity to foreclose'[517] of the exclusivity practices, their 'foreclosure capability',[518] the question whether the defendant's conduct is 'capable of restricting competition',[519] and whether it is 'capable of having foreclosure effects on as efficient competitors'.[520] Here, conversely, the more strictly the criterion is

[508] See e.g. M. Friend, 'Loyalty Rebates and Abuse of Dominance' (2018) 77 *CLJ* 25, 28.

[509] J. da Cruz Vilaça, 'The Intensity of Judicial Review in Complex Economic Matters—Recent Competition Law Judgments of the Court of Justice of the EU' (2018) 6 *J of Antitrust Enforcement* 173, 183. The author, writing extrajudicially, acted as judge-rapporteur in the *Intel* case before the CJ.

[510] Case T-286/09 RENV, *Intel* EU:T:2022:19, para. 124.

[511] Case C-413/14 P, *Intel* EU:C:2017:632, para. 138. See also P. Ibáñez Colomo, 'The Future of Article 102 TFEU after *Intel*' (2018) 9 *JECLAP* 293, 302.

[512] Guidance Paper, paras. 28–31.

[513] Hajnovicova, Lang, and Usai, n. 493, 145, fn. 31. The authors, notably, are DG Comp officials albeit writing in a personal capacity.

[514] Case T-604/18, *Google Android* EU:T:2022:541, para. 639. [515] Ibid., para. 795.

[516] Case C-377/20, *Servizio Elettrico Nazionale and Others* EU:C:2022:379, para. 52, and Case C-680/20 *Unilever Italia Mkt. Operations* EU:C:2023, para. 54.

[517] Case C-413/14 P, *Intel* EU:C:2017:632, para. 140. [518] Ibid., para. 141. [519] Ibid., paras. 138 and 147.

[520] Ibid., para. 143.

interpreted, the more difficult it may become for the Commission to discharge its *own* burden of proof. In paragraph 139, the CJ identified five (presumably non-exhaustive[521]) factors relevant to the assessment of rebates specifically: the extent of the dominant position; the share of the market covered by the challenged practice; the conditions and arrangements for granting the discount; their duration and amount; and the possible existence of a strategy aiming to exclude competitors that are at least as efficient as the dominant undertaking.[522] What remains uncertain is how rigorously this requirement is to be interpreted so as to necessitate a demonstration of likely or even actual anti-competitive effects in order to sustain a finding of abuse.

The language of 'capacity to foreclose' is well established in the assessment of exclusivity practices under Article 102. Yet this standard has been applied primarily to determine whether discount policies that are not formally contingent on exclusivity might nonetheless be deemed 'loyalty-inducing' or functionally equivalent to fidelity rebates.[523] The bulk of the case law, epitomised by the *British Airways* judgment from 2007, takes a notably abstract approach, asking merely whether the suspect practice '*can* produce an exclusionary effect'[524] rather than whether it has or will do so in practice. A focus on the enhanced potential for or inherent ability of exclusivity obligations to harm competition is largely consistent with the rationale behind the GC's wholesale defence of a 'by object' condemnation of such arrangements in *Intel*. The judgment in the *Post Danmark II* preliminary reference case, decided just a couple of years before *Intel*, nonetheless suggested a greater receptiveness towards a requirement to demonstrate actual foreclosure effects. In *Qualcomm*, the GC invoked *Post Danmark II* to argue that 'since all the relevant circumstances surrounding the conduct complained of must be taken into account, the analysis of the anticompetitive capability of that conduct cannot be purely hypothetical'.[525]

The concept of capacity to foreclose was discussed by Advocate General Wahl in *Intel*, who, although rejecting the need for an outright effects analysis, argued for a demanding approach.

Case C-413/14 P, *Intel Corp v European Commission*, Opinion of Advocate General Wahl, delivered on 20 October 2016, EU:C:2016:788

114. Certainly, evidence of actual effects does not need to be presented. This is because it is sufficient, in relation to conduct that is presumptively unlawful, that the impugned conduct be capable of restricting competition. Importantly, however, that capability cannot merely be hypothetical or theoretically possible. Otherwise, there would be no need to consider all the circumstances in the first place.

115. True, there is some discrepancy in the case-law regarding the terminology employed. The case-law refers to capability and likelihood, sometimes even interchangeably. It is my understanding that those terms designate one and the same compulsory step in an analysis seeking to determine whether the use of loyalty rebates amounts to an abuse of a dominant position.

116. But what degree of probability of anticompetitive foreclosure is required? That question is at the core of the disagreement between the appellant and the Commission regarding the adequacy of the General Court's assessment of capability: whereas the Commission believes that the assessment was adequate, Intel claims that the General Court failed to verify that the appellant's conduct could, in the circumstances of the case, restrict competition.

[521] An assessment shared by Kadar, n. 494, 444, and Hajnovicova, Lang, and Usai, n. 493, 145.

[522] The GC in Case T-286/09 RENV, *Intel* EU:T:2022:19, paras. 119 and 125, grouped the criteria identified in para. 139 of the Grand Chamber judgment in this manner.

[523] See discussion in Section 10.C.iii.

[524] Case C-95/04 P, *British Airways* EU:C:2007:166, para. 68.

[525] Case T-235/18, *Qualcomm* EU:T:2022:358, para. 397.

> 117. The aim of the assessment of capability is to ascertain whether, in all likelihood, the impugned conduct has an anticompetitive foreclosure effect. For that reason, likelihood must be considerably more than a mere possibility that certain behaviour may restrict competition. Contrariwise, the fact that an exclusionary effect appears more likely than not is simply not enough.
>
> 118. Although it is certainly true that in its case-law the Court has consistently emphasised the special responsibility of dominant undertakings, that responsibility cannot be taken to mean that the threshold for the application of the prohibition of abuse laid down in Article 102 TFEU can be lowered to such an extent as to become virtually non-existent. That would be the case if the degree of likelihood required for ascertaining that the impugned conduct amounts to an abuse of a dominant position was nothing more than the mere theoretical possibility of an exclusionary effect, as seems to be suggested by the Commission. If such a low level of likelihood were accepted, one would have to accept that EU competition law sanctions form, not anticompetitive effects.
>
> 119. Clearly, that would considerably hamper the attainment of the objectives of EU competition law. To assume the existence of an abuse on the basis that, on balance, anticompetitive foreclosure seems more likely than not risks capturing not only isolated instances of practices, but a non-negligible number of practices that may, in reality, be pro-competitive. The cost of error of such an approach would be unacceptably high due to over-inclusion.
>
> 120. To avoid over-inclusion, the assessment of capability as concerns presumptively unlawful behaviour must be understood as seeking to ascertain that, having regard to all circumstances, the behaviour in question does not just have ambivalent effects on the market or only produce ancillary restrictive effects necessary for the performance of something which is pro-competitive, but that its presumed restrictive effects are in fact confirmed. Absent such a confirmation, a fully-fledged analysis has to be performed.

The difficulty with the suggested approach, however, is that although the Advocate General disclaimed the need for evidence of *actual* anti-competitive effects, it is hard to envisage how the presumed restrictive effects may be 'in fact confirmed' otherwise. This is precisely how some commentators interpreted the CJ's 'clarification' in *Intel*: as requiring, in practice, a 'full-fledged effects-based'[526] or even 'rule of reason'[527] assessment. Others were more cautious, suggesting that capability of foreclosure connotes a lower threshold of *plausibility*, requiring merely the demonstration that 'a restriction of competition is a conceivable—but not necessarily likely—outcome'.[528] Similarly, a 'balance of probabilities' approach has been suggested in order to better spread the risk between Type I errors, implicit in an unduly lenient interpretation of capacity to foreclose, and Type II errors, which might result from Advocate General Wahl's heightened requirements.[529] Writing extrajudicially, the judge-rapporteur before the CJ in *Intel* subsequently offered a fairly vague explanation of this element, albeit one falling considerably short of a rule of reason approach. He contended that 'the Court only requires that the conduct of the dominant undertaking is *capable of*, or *liable to*, or *tends to*, with a *sufficient degree of probability*, restrict or distort competition in the market and foreclose potential competitors or force actual competitors to leave the market place'.[530] He moreover suggested that the level of evidence and analysis required to demonstrate capacity to foreclose may differ depending upon the

[526] A. Komnimos, '*Intel*: The ECJ Finally Speaks—Time to Listen!' (2018) 4 *CLPD* 42.

[527] N. Petit, 'The Judgment of the EU Court of Justice in *Intel* and the Rule of Reason in Abuse of Dominance Cases' (2018) 43 *ELRev* 728.

[528] P. Ibáñez Colomo, 'The Future of Article 102 TFEU after *Intel*' (2018) 9 *JECLAP* 293, 299.

[529] J. Clarke, 'The Opinion of AG Wahl in the *Intel* Rebates Case: A Triumph of Substance over Form?' (2017) 40 *World Competition* 241, 263.

[530] Da Cruz Vilaça, n. 509, 185–186 (emphasis in original).

nature of the alleged restraint, insofar as certain practices—such as discounts or rebates explicitly conditioned upon exclusivity—have a more obvious inherent capacity to exclude rivals.[531] From this perspective, the presumption of abuse from *Hoffmann-La Roche* functions less as an irrebuttable 'by object' prohibition, and more as an indicator that an abridged assessment of capacity to foreclose may be permissible.

Notably, in outlining the factors to be considered when assessing the capacity of an exclusivity practice to foreclose competition, the CJ did not identify the AEC test as a *required* element. Although the position is not undisputed,[532] this approach was confirmed by the GC when *Intel* returned to the lower court.[533] In this regard, the CJ departed from the approach endorsed by the Commission in its Guidance Paper. It was nonetheless consistent with the judgment in *Post Danmark II*, where the CJ had acknowledged the aptness of the AEC test in assessing the anti-competitive potential of a rebate scheme, but stopped short of prescribing this costs-based methodology as the required means by which to identify abusive pricing practices. Instead, it described the AEC test as merely 'one tool amongst others' that may (but not *must*) be used to identify anti-competitive exclusivity practices.[534] The CJ in *Post Danmark II* did not dispute that the AEC test may provide an effective means of determining the likelihood of foreclosure in appropriate circumstances. Yet it rejected its mandatory application, taking the view, inter alia, that the metric was not an appropriate one by which to judge abusive behaviour in all cases. It is thus unsurprising that, in *Intel*, the CJ similarly declined to mandate the AEC test in exclusivity cases.

In *Unilever*, the CJ confirmed that the AEC test may prove useful to establish abusive exclusive dealing practices, but that it is not a necessary component of any such assessment. It moreover went further than both the *Intel* judgment and the Commission's Guidance Paper, in suggesting a potential role for the AEC test in the assessment of non-price-based exclusionary practices such as contractual exclusivity clauses. In doing so, the CJ also offered a strong endorsement of the *principle* underlying the AEC test.

Case C-680/20, *Unilever Italia Mkt. Operations Srl v Autorità Garante della Concorrenza e del Mercato* EU:C:2023:33

Court of Justice

56. As regards the 'as efficient competitor' test . . . it should be noted that that concept refers to various tests which have in common the aim of assessing the ability of a practice to produce anti-competitive exclusionary effects by reference to the ability of a hypothetical competitor of the undertaking in a dominant position, which is as efficient as the dominant undertaking in terms of cost structure, to offer customers a rate which is sufficiently advantageous to encourage them to switch supplier, despite the disadvantages caused, without that causing that competitor to incur losses. That ability is generally determined in the light of the cost structure of the undertaking in a dominant position itself.

57. A test of that nature may be inappropriate in particular in the case of certain non-pricing practices, such as a refusal to supply, or where the relevant market is protected by significant barriers. Moreover,

[531] Ibid., 185.

[532] In Case C-377/20, *Servizio Elettrico Nazionale* EU:C:2022:379, the CJ stated that loyalty rebates 'must be assessed, as a general rule, using the "as-efficient competitor" test' (para. 80), but then went on to hold that 'competition authorities do not have an obligation to rely always on that test in order to make a finding that a price-related practice is abusive' (para. 81).

[533] Case T-286/09 RENV, *Intel* EU:T:2022:19, para. 126: 'the Court of Justice did not hold that an AEC test necessarily had to be carried out in order to examine the foreclosure capability of all rebate systems'.

[534] Case C-23/14, *Post Danmark II* EU:C:2015:651, para. 61.

such a test is only one of a number of methods for assessing whether a practice is capable of producing exclusionary effects; moreover, that method takes into consideration only price competition. In particular, the use by a undertaking in a dominant position of resources other than those governing competition on the merits may be sufficient, in certain circumstances, to establish the existence of such an abuse (see . . . Servizio Elettrico Nazionale and Others, C-377/20, EU:C:2022:379, paragraph 78).

58. Consequently, the competition authorities cannot be under a legal obligation to use the 'as efficient competitor test' in order to find that a practice is abusive (see . . . Post Danmark, C-23/14, EU:C:2015:651, paragraph 57).

59. Nevertheless, even in the case of non-pricing practices, the relevance of such a test cannot be ruled out. A test of that type may prove useful where the consequences of the practice in question can be quantified. In particular, in the case of exclusivity clauses, such a test may theoretically serve to determine whether a hypothetical competitor with a cost structure similar to that of the undertaking in a dominant position would be able to offer its products or services otherwise than at a loss or with an insufficient margin if it had to bear the compensation which the distributors would have to pay in order to switch supplier, or the losses which they would suffer after such a change following the withdrawal of previously agreed discounts (see, by analogy . . . Slovak Telekom v Commission, C-165/19 P, EU:C:2021:239, paragraph 110).

60. Consequently, where an undertaking in a dominant position suspected of abuse provides a competition authority with an analysis based on an 'as efficient competitor test', that authority cannot disregard that evidence without even examining its probative value.

61. That fact is not called into question by the existence of a number of practices at issue. Even if the cumulative effects of those practices cannot be understood by such a test, the fact remains that the result of a test of that nature may nevertheless constitute an indication of the effects of some of those practices and, therefore, be relevant in order to determine whether certain classifications may be made with regard to the practices at issue.

In *Intel*, the CJ nonetheless took the view, in relation to the facts at issue, that because the Commission's own assessment of capacity to foreclose had granted an 'important role' to the AEC test, the GC ought to have examined all of the arguments advanced by the defendant concerning that test on appeal. The case was remitted back to the GC for further examination of the capacity to foreclose of the disputed practices.[535] The second time around, the GC engaged in a detailed and demanding assessment of the AEC test conducted with respect to the effects of rebates granted to five OEMs. Considering the factors identified in paragraph 139 of the Grand Chamber judgment, the GC identified errors with respect to the share of the market covered by the practices and their duration.[536] It concluded that the Commission had not established the 'foreclosure capability' of the rebate practices, and annulled the decision to the extent that it held that those rebates amounted to an abuse of dominance. It also cancelled the *entirety* of the fine imposed, including the portion relating to the 'naked restrictions', the illegality of which was not disputed.[537] The Commission has appealed the second GC judgment,[538] thus further prolonging a case that it has been working on since 2000.

[535] Case C-413/14 P, *Intel* EU:C:2017:632, paras. 143–150.

[536] Case T-286/09 RENV, *Intel* EU:T:2022:19, paras. 485–521.

[537] On the basis that, when the Commission imposed the fine of €1.06 billion, it had 'assessed the conduct in question as a whole and had come to the view that those infringements complemented and mutually reinforced one another': Case T-286/09 RENV, *Intel* EU:T:2022:19, para. 528.

[538] Case C-240/22 P, *Commission v Intel Corporation*, appeal pending.

The Commission's post-*Intel* decisional practice aimed to put its newly articulated[539] obligation to consider foreclosure capability into effect. In *Qualcomm, Android, AdSense*, and *Broadcom*, the Commission examined the foreclosure capacity of the disputed exclusivity practices. Consistent with the argument that the factors enumerated in *Intel* are indicative but not exhaustive, the Commission considered the impact of the practices on the purchasing/sourcing behaviour of customers, the impact on market/entry expansion by rival suppliers, the potential for the practices to harm innovation, and the coverage and duration of the practices. In doing so, it focused primarily on structural market features and qualitative evidence, with notable use of internal documents and other statements from defendants, their customers, and would-be rivals. Only in *Android* did the Commission conduct an AEC test. Instead, in these cases the Commission has concentrated on developing what it termed in *Qualcomm* 'a coherent story of harm to competition',[540] as evidenced by a variety of relevant market factors.

Unfortunately, in both *Qualcomm* and *Android*, the Commission's efforts have not withstood scrutiny on appeal. In *Qualcomm*, the GC held that the Commission failed to take account of all relevant market features while crafting its 'story of harm'. In particular, it overestimated the ability of the single affected customer (Apple) to switch to competing suppliers for both technical and logistical reasons. The qualitative evidence that the Commission had predominantly relied upon (emails, etc.) was further weakened by problems of inconsistency. The *Qualcomm* decision was also annulled because of serious breaches of the defendant's rights of defence,[541] and the Commission chose not to appeal the judgment.[542]

In *Android*, similarly, the GC annulled the Commission's finding that a revenue-sharing arrangement, which was conditional on exclusive pre-installation of Google's proprietary apps on mobile devices, amounted to an abusive exclusivity practice. The GC accepted that the practice could be characterised as an exclusivity payment.[543] Nonetheless, the Commission failed to discharge its burden of proving that the practice had foreclosure capacity. Since the practice covered less than 5 per cent of the market defined by the Commission, the share of the affected market could not be characterised as significant. The GC also identified numerous errors in the AEC analysis. First, the Commission had failed to obtain from Google all of the data necessary to conduct an accurate AEC test, relying instead on figures provided by a third party.[544] Secondly, the GC took issue with the Commission using as a starting point for assessment the existing low market shares of other operators in general search services markets, holding that this did not provide an appropriate benchmark by which to assess the impact on hypothetically as efficient competitors. It also identified errors in the Commission's assessment which rendered its analysis incomplete. Accordingly, the infringement decision was annulled to the extent that the payments in themselves had been held to constitute an abuse.[545]

d. Beyond Commission Enforcement

The *Intel* judgment referred only to the assessment of exclusive dealing in administrative procedures occurring before the Commission. Specifically, the CJ spoke in terms of the respective burdens of proof to be discharged by the Commission, on the one hand, and defendants, on the other. Yet it

[539] Although several Commission officials, writing in a personal capacity, have argued that *Intel* will have limited impact on the Commission's enforcement practice insofar as it has long considered the capacity to foreclose of suspect exclusivity practices alongside the *Hoffmann-La Roche* presumption: see Kadar, n. 494, 443, and Hajnovicova, Lang, and Usai, n. 493, 145.

[540] AT.40220, *Qualcomm (exclusivity payments)* 24 January 2018, para. 486.

[541] See discussion in Chap. 13, Section 6.

[542] Reuters, 'Win for Qualcomm as no EU appeal court ruling against $991 mln fine', 29 August 2022, <www.reuters.com/technology/exclusive-eu-will-not-appeal-court-ruling-against-991-mln-qualcomm-fine-sources-2022-08-29/>.

[543] Case T-604/18, *Google Android* EU:T:2022:541, paras. 651–657.

[544] Ibid., paras. 746–48.

[545] The GC also reduced the fine imposed by just over €200 million.

is inconceivable that the principles discussed therein would not have more general application. The judgment in *Unilever*, which was an Article 267 preliminary reference case from an Italian court, made reference to the obligations of 'competition authorities' more generally when assessment exclusive dealing practices. Going forward, *Intel* and *Unilever* should be treated as the authoritative statements of how the assessment of exclusivity is to be approached under Article 102, regardless of the identity of the enforcer, whether it is the Commission, an NCA, or indeed a private plaintiff.

C. CATEGORIES OF EXCLUSIVITY PRACTICES

The remainder of this section discusses the various categories of exclusive dealing that have been identified in the case law. Most of these cases predated *Intel*, and the earlier case law drew fine and sometimes unconvincing distinctions between the treatment of different categories. It is difficult to maintain, post-*Intel* and *Unilever*, that any types of exclusivity practices are prohibited conclusively 'by object'. Nonetheless, it remains useful to outline the conventional classifications, in order to understand both the earlier case law and the propensity of different arrangements to restrict competition in practice.

(i) Exclusive Purchasing

Exclusive purchasing—which can also be referred to as a requirements contract, an exclusive supply contract, exclusivity clauses, contractual exclusivity, or single branding—involves commercial arrangements whereby the customer must obtain all or most of its requirements for the relevant product from one supplier. In *Hoffmann-La Roche*, the CJ referred to an exclusive purchasing obligation covering 'all or most' of the customer's requirements.[546] Guidance as to what this means can be derived from the Verticals Regulation where a non-compete obligation is defined as including an obligation on a buyer to purchase at least 80 per cent of its requirements from one source.[547] In *Distrigaz*,[548] contractual obligations to purchase an annual minimum quantity of natural gas from the defendant were treated as exclusive purchasing obligations in a context where most customers had only one supplier.

To secure the commitment to exclusivity, the supplier may offer some form of incentive, often through lower prices. Contract-specific rewards may be provided, such as priority deliveries at times of shortage,[549] additional technical support, or early access to new products.[550] Unlike tying,[551] consumer coercion is not required to demonstrate abusive exclusivity obligations. In *Hoffmann-La Roche*, the CJ stated that exclusive dealing obligations could infringe Article 102 'even if' they were implemented at the request of the customer.[552] Thus in *Broadcom*, the defendant's claim that its contractual exclusivity obligations 'simply concretise[d] an already existing and entirely voluntary state of affairs'[553] not only failed to provide a good defence but was moreover taken as evidence that the

546 See also *Soda-Ash—ICI* [2003] OJ L10/33, para. 142.

547 Reg. 2022/720 [2022] OJ L134/4; Art.1(1)(f). See also Case T-286/09, *Intel* EU:T:2014:547, where the GC similarly suggested that exclusivity arrangements covering 80% of a customer's requirements in one (comparatively small) segment of its demand amounted to 'most' of its requirements.

548 COMP/337.966, 11 October 2007. See also COMP/39.386, *EDF—Long Term Electricity Contracts in France* 17 March 2010. Both cases involved long-term supply obligations in energy markets, and both were settled using the commitments decision procedure.

549 *BPB Industries* [1989] OJ L10/50, paras. 141–147, upheld in Case T-65/89, *BPB* EU:T:1993:31.

550 Both an additional perk of exclusive supply in AT.40608, *Broadcom* 7 October 2020, para. 59.

551 See Section 11.

552 Case C-85/76, *Hoffmann-La Roche* EU:C:1979:36, para. 89.

553 AT.40608, *Broadcom* 16 October 2019, para. 264.

arrangement served to preserve or even strengthen Broadcom's dominance by crystallising the status quo within the market.[554]

The abusive nature of exclusive purchasing is not removed by the presence of an 'English clause', whereby the customer can switch suppliers without penalty if the dominant undertaking cannot or will not match more favourable terms offered by other suppliers.[555] On the contrary, in *Hoffmann-La Roche* the CJ found that the presence of such a clause exacerbated the abuse, by enabling the dominant undertaking to learn of its competitors' offers.[556] This was followed in *AdSense*, where such a clause was held to enhance the 'capability' of exclusivity obligations to restrict competition.[557] The Verticals Guidelines say that even where there is no express exclusive purchasing arrangement, English clauses can 'be expected to have the same effect'.[558]

Article 102 applies to *de facto*, as well as contractual, exclusivity. *De facto* exclusivity occurs where there is no stipulation of exclusivity, but the arrangements are such that exclusivity results. *Van Den Bergh*,[559] the paradigm case, concerned an ice-cream manufacturer, HB, which provided retail outlets with freezers as part of its standard distribution practices. HB prohibited use of those freezers with other competing suppliers' ice-cream brands, leading to *de facto* exclusivity as it was generally impractical for retailers to accommodate a second freezer and they had few incentives to do so. The Commission found that the arrangements infringed Article 102 as well as Article 101. In *AdSense*,[560] the Commission condemned 'relaxed exclusivity'[561] obligations relating to the defendant's online search advertising intermediation service. While website publishers were permitted to run display adverts from rival brokers, they were obliged to display Google AdSense adverts in the most prominent (and thus most profitable) parts of their search result pages. Publishers also required permission from Google to alter the display of rival search adverts, giving the defendant control over the attractiveness of competing services. The Commission treated these obligations as analogous to formal exclusive dealing requirements. In *Broadcom*,[562] the Commission raised concerns about the 'quasi' exclusivity that resulted from contractual commitments made by Broadcom's customers, to submit bids for future work to their *own* customers specifying only Broadcom chipsets within the products to be provided.

As noted, the Commission's Guidance Paper deals with exclusive purchasing along with rebates in a section on 'exclusive dealing'.[563] Applying its effects-based approach, the Commission explains that it is not concerned solely with the effect on the customer who is party to the agreement, but rather with customers overall and with final consumers. It will be particularly troubled where consumers as a whole do not benefit, which is likely to be the case where the dominant firm has exclusive contracts with many customers meaning that competing undertakings are prevented from entering the market or expanding. In paragraph 36, the Commission explains that it will treat as an enforcement priority those cases where anti-competitive foreclosure is likely as the dominant undertaking is an 'unavoidable trading partner', because, for example, its brand is a 'must stock item' or the competitors are unable for reasons of capacity constraints to satisfy the entire demand of each individual customer. If competitors can compete equally for each customer's entire demand, exclusive purchasing obligations are unlikely to hamper effective competition. In general, the longer the duration of the obligation,

[554] Ibid., para. 282. [555] See also the discussion of 'most favoured nation' (MFN) clauses in Chap. 11.

[556] Case C-85/76, *Hoffmann-La Roche* EU:C:1979:36, paras. 107–108. The Commission objected to an English clause in *IRI/Nielsen, XXXVIth Report on Competition Policy* (1996), part 64.

[557] AT.40411, *Google AdSense* 20 March 2019, paras. 422–427.

[558] Verticals Guidelines [2022] OJ C248/1, para. 298.

[559] [1998] OJ L246/1, upheld Case T-65/98, *Van den Bergh Foods Ltd v Commission* EU:T:2003:281, *aff'd* Case C-552/03 P, *Unilever* EU:C:2006:607.

[560] AT.40411, *Google Search (AdSense)* 20 March 2019. [561] Ibid., para. 335.

[562] Described in the interim measures decision, AT.40608, *Broadcom* 16 October 2019. The case was settled by commitments decision a year later, AT.40608, *Broadcom* 7 October 2020.

[563] Guidance Paper, paras. 32–48.

the greater the likely foreclosure effect. If, however, the dominant undertaking is an unavoidable trading partner, even an exclusive purchasing obligation of short duration can cause anti-competitive foreclosure.

The Guidance Paper accepts that exclusive purchasing contracts could be justified by efficiencies: the Commission will consider evidence of advantages to particular customers if the exclusive dealing is necessary for the dominant undertaking to make relationship-specific investments.

(ii) Exclusive Distribution

Exclusive distribution, as discussed in Chapter 5, was the focus of some of the earliest judgments under Article 101. While there are few cases on exclusive distribution arrangements entered into by dominant undertakings, limiting customers' avenues of supply and thereby foreclosing competitors can constitute an abuse. *DeBeers/Alrosa*[564] concerned with an agreement between De Beers, the world's leading diamond mining company, and Alrosa, the world's second largest diamond producer. The agreement provided that Alrosa would distribute almost all its diamonds sold outside the former USSR through De Beers, which the Commission feared would generate de facto distribution exclusivity. De Beers committed to phase out purchases from Alrosa, and ultimately to cease purchasing entirely.

(iii) Exclusivity and Loyalty(-Inducing) Rebates

Granting discounts and rebates is a common commercial practice and a major way in which suppliers compete. Technically, a discount is a deduction from a price list and a rebate is a refund granted retrospectively, but in competition policy the terms are often used synonymously.[565] Here, we use the term rebate to refer broadly to both practices. Where undertakings are dominant, their rebate policies are constrained by Article 102, especially where such policies are premised upon explicit or de facto exclusivity. The concern centres on the exclusionary primary line injury that rebates may cause.[566] Anti-competitive effects arise mainly from the possibility of leverage: typically, the leveraging of market power from the non-contestable to the contestable portion of consumer demand. Yet even true fidelity rebates implemented by dominant undertakings may generate pro-competitive effects, including more efficient recovery of fixed costs, providing better incentives to retailers, reducing double marginalisation, and resolving 'hold-up' problems. The application of Article 102 to discounts and rebates has been one of the most contentious areas of EU competition law.[567] In brief, the criticisms have been

[564] Case COMP/B-2/38.381, *De Beers* [2006] OJ L205/24.

[565] For further discussion of terminology, see D. Ridyard, 'Exclusionary Pricing and Price Discrimination Abuses Under Article 102—An Economic Analysis' [2002] *ECLR* 286; Bishop and Walker, n. 243, 6.037–6.062.

[566] Thus they fall within Art. 102(b) in 'limiting production, markets or technical development to the prejudice of consumers', see Temple Lang and O'Donoghue, n. 201, 83; J. Temple Lang, 'How Can the Problems of Exclusionary Abuses under Article 102 TFEU be Resolved?' (2012) 37 *ELRev* 136. However, Art. 102(c) which should be applied to discrimination affecting downstream markets, has been expressly relied upon in some cases of primary line injury; see Geradin, Layne-Farrar, and Petit, n. 195, 4.499–4.505, and Section 15, where Art. 102(c) is discussed.

[567] See e.g. Temple Lang and O'Donoghue, n. 201; J. Kallaugher and B. Sher, 'Rebates Revisited: Anti-competitive Effects and Exclusionary Abuse under Article 82' [2004] *ECLR* 263; C. Ahlborn and D. Bailey, 'Discounts, Rebates and Selective Pricing by Dominant Firms: A Trans-Atlantic Comparison' (2006) 2 *European Competition Journal* 101; D. Spector, 'Loyalty Rebates: An Assessment of Competition Concerns and a Proposed Structured Rule of Reason' (2005) 1 *Competition Policy International* 89; Geradin, Layne-Farrar, and Petit, n. 195, 4.159–4.219; J. Temple Lang, 'How Can the Problems of Exclusionary Abuses under Article 102 TFEU be Resolved?' (2012) 37 *ELRev* 136; H. Zenger, 'Loyalty Rebates and the Competitive Process' (2012) 8 *J of Competition Law and Economics* 717, who says at 763 that there 'is no benefit in continuing to adhere to a delusive and antiquated theory of anticompetitive rebates that had no counterpart in economic reality even at the time when it was written down'; P. Ibáñez Colomo, '*Post Danmark II*, or the Quest for Administrability and Coherence in Article 102 TFEU', LSE, Law, Society and Economy Working Papers 15/2015, <http://ssrn.com/abstract=2636407>.

that the law distinguished between different types of discounts and rebates in a way that made no economic sense; that it was assumed that an exclusionary effect on competitors means consumer harm; and that insufficient account was taken of the reasons why undertakings adopt certain discounting and rebating practices and the fact that these might be pro-competitive. It was precisely such concerns, laid bare most notably in Advocate General Wahl's highly critical Opinion, which prompted the CJ's 'clarification' of the legal treatment of discounts and rebates in the pivotal *Intel* decision. Going forward, it appears that there are no categories of rebates which are conclusively presumed to violate Article 102 'by object', insofar as it remains open to dominant undertakings to argue that their practices lack the capacity to foreclose as efficient competitors.

The starting point to understand the earlier treatment of rebates under Article 102 is *Hoffmann-La Roche*, which drew a distinction between two categories: fidelity rebates and quantity rebates. **Fidelity rebates** are discounts which are granted conditional upon the customer obtaining all or most of its requirements from the dominant undertaking. Under *Hoffmann-La Roche*, fidelity rebates were treated as 'by object' infringements of Article 102, and thus prohibited unless objectively justified. The exclusivity condition need not be contained in a formal obligation, as 'it is sufficient that the undertaking in a dominant position indicates in a credible manner to its customer that the grant of a financial advantage depends on exclusive or quasi-exclusive supply'.[568] *Hoffmann-La Roche* was a paradigmatic fidelity rebate case, in which customers only received the maximum rebate level where they purchased the quantities of vitamins designed to reflect their individual 'capacity for absorption'.[569]

Quantity rebates, by contrast, are linked solely to the quantity of purchases made from the dominant undertaking.[570] Though the point was not stated explicitly in *Hoffmann-Law Roche*, quantity rebates are 'generally considered',[571] 'in principle',[572] to be compatible with Article 102. Such practices are thus presumptively lawful, meaning that, as Advocate General Wahl noted in *Intel*, '[a]ny investigation into the (un)lawfulness of such rebates necessarily requires a full examination of their actual or potential effects'.[573] The rationale is that quantity rebates are 'deemed to reflect gains in efficiency and economies of scale made by the undertaking in a dominant position'.[574]

The neat dichotomy of permissible and impermissible rebates identified in *Hoffmann-La Roche* does not, however, match the reality of the diverse types of discounting practices applied by firms. Accordingly, starting with *Michelin I*,[575] the CJ acknowledged that certain arrangements that were not, on their face, fidelity rebates might nonetheless be prohibited by Article 102 in appropriate circumstances. The GC in *Intel* in 2014 referred to rebates of this sort as **third category** rebates,[576] an approach that received oblique approval in *Post Danmark II*.[577] Third category rebates, even prior to the clarification from the Grand Chamber in *Intel*, were not presumed to be anti-competitive by their very nature, and thus were distinguished from fidelity rebates. Such practices could, however, have exclusionary effects, because they were 'loyalty-inducing'[578] or 'fidelity-building',[579] or had a 'suction effect' over the contestable portion of consumer demand.[580] Crucially, rebates within the third category required consideration of 'all the relevant circumstances' to determine whether the practice

568 Case C-85/76, *Hoffmann-La Roche* EU:C:1979:36, para. 106.

569 See also Case T-65/89, *BPB Industries* EU:T:1993:31, *aff'd* on appeal Case C-310/93 P, *BPB Industries* EU:C:1995:101.

570 Case C-85/76, *Hoffmann-La Roche* EU:C:1979:36, paras. 89 and 90.

571 Case T-286/09, *Intel* EU:T:2014:547, para. 75.

572 Case C-23/14, *Post Danmark II* EU:C:2015:651, para. 27.

573 Opinion in Case C-413/14 P, *Intel* EU:C:2016:788, para. 81.

574 Case T-286/09, *Intel* EU:T:2014:547, para. 75; see also Case T-203/01, *Michelin II* EU:T:2003:250, para. 58.

575 Case 322/81, *Michelin I* EU:C:1983:313.

576 Case T-286/09, *Intel* EU:T:2014:547, paras. 74–78.

577 Here, the CJ recognised that the rebate practice under scrutiny could not be characterised as either a fidelity or a quantity rebate: Case C-23/14, *Post Danmark II* EU:C:2015:651, para. 28.

578 [2002] OJ L143/1; upheld on appeal in Case T-203/01, *Michelin II* EU:T:2003:250.

579 Case T-286/09, *Intel* EU:T:2014:547, para. 78.

580 Case C-23/14, *Post Danmark II* EU:C:2015:651, para. 35.

violated Article 102. In particular, the concept was applied in cases involving target rebates[581] and standardised retroactive rebates.[582] The development of the law on third category rebates was one of the finickiest areas of the jurisprudence under Article 102, and a fuller account can be found in previous editions of this book.[583]

In the Guidance Paper, the Commission presented a different approach to that hitherto taken in the case law on rebates. It was the most radical part of the Guidance Paper and set out a new methodology for determining whether rebates are abusive.[584] The Guidance Paper broadly follows the Commission's proposals in the Staff Discussion Paper,[585] but is less complex.[586] Paragraphs 37–45 deal with what the Commission calls 'conditional rebates', defined as 'rebates granted to customers to reward them for a particular form of purchasing behaviour'. The Commission accepts that such rebates may stimulate demand and benefit consumers. However, they can also have foreclosure effects.[587]

The section on rebates must be read in conjunction with the general section on price-based exclusionary conduct.[588] The Commission is concerned with the anti-competitive foreclosure of as efficient competitors. However, the Commission notes that conditional rebates can have foreclosure effects without necessarily entailing a sacrifice for the dominant undertaking.[589] The question the Commission asks is what price a competitor would need to offer to compensate customers for the loss of the conditional rebate if the customer switched part of its demand away from the dominant undertaking.

The concepts used in the assessments are 'contestable' and 'non-contestable' portions of a customer's demand[590] and the 'relevant range'. A portion of demand may be 'non-contestable' because, for example, the dominant undertaking supplies a 'must-stock' product (due to brand loyalty) or because the competitors have capacity constraints and could not satisfy all the customer's demand. The Commission's concern is that the dominant undertaking may grant conditional rebates in order to use the non-contestable portion as leverage to decrease the price for the contestable portion.[591] The market may be significantly foreclosed if retroactive rebates make it less attractive for customers to switch small amounts of contestable demand. Therefore the Commission will try to estimate the price which a competitor would have to offer to compensate for the loss of the rebate if the customer were to switch part of its demand. The effective price the competitor has to match is the normal list price less the rebate lost by switching.[592] The Commission, using a method similar to the tests for predatory pricing, will apply costs levels to assess whether an as efficient competitor could compete profitably notwithstanding the rebate. If the effective price remains above the dominant undertaking's LRAIC,

[581] A target rebate is given to customers who buy more than a target (threshold) amount in a certain period. The target may be set according to the customer's perceived need for the good, and often requires the customer to buy a certain amount in excess of past purchases. See Case T-286/09, *Intel* EU:T:2014:547, para. 78; Case 322/81, *Michelin I* EU:C:1983:313; Case T-203/01, *Michelin II* EU:T:2003:250; and Case C-95/04 P, *British Airways* EU:C:2007:166.

[582] Standardised rebates are schemes where all customers get the same rebates on the same conditions. Retroactive rebates are awarded on all purchases once the customer reaches a certain threshold, as opposed to incremental rebates which are awarded only on additional purchases beyond the threshold. See Case C-23/14, *Post Danmark II* EU:C:2015:651, para. 28.

[583] See e.g. the 6th edition of this book (2016), pp. 445–471.

[584] See Faull and Nikpay, n. 1, 4.429–4.467, for a full discussion of the Guidance Paper treatment of rebates.

[585] Discussion Paper, paras. 151–169.

[586] See P. Marsden, 'Some Outstanding Issues from the European Commission's Guidance on Article 102 TFEU: Not-so-faint Echoes of Ordoliberalism' in F. Etro and I. Kokkoris (eds.), *Competition Law and the Enforcement of Article 102* (Oxford University Press, 2010), 64–66.

[587] Guidance Paper, para. 37. [588] See Section 7.

[589] Guidance Paper, para. 37. The assessment of conditional rebates is therefore different from that for predation which, according to paras. 64–66, always entails a sacrifice, para. 37, fn. 3.

[590] For the terminology, see Section 10.E.i. [591] Guidance Paper, para. 39. [592] Ibid., paras. 41–42.

the rebate is not 'normally' capable of anti-competitive foreclosure.[593] If it is below AAC 'as a general rule' it *is* capable of foreclosing as efficient competitors, whereas if it is between LRAIC and AAC the Commission 'will investigate whether other factors point to the conclusion that entry or expansion even by equally efficient competitors is likely to be affected'.[594] One important factor is whether the rebate is retroactive or incremental.[595] The Commission will consider efficiencies in respect of exclusive dealing in line with the principles laid out in the section of the Guidance Paper on objective necessities and efficiencies.[596] The Commission considers that transaction-related costs advantages are more likely with standardised volume targets than with individualised ones.[597]

(iv) Exclusivity Payments or 'Naked Restrictions'

Fidelity(-inducing) rebates provide discounts on purchases to customers who adhere to single sourcing from the dominant undertaking. Exclusivity payments similarly provide financial rewards for exclusivity, but typically take the form of discrete payments offered on the condition that the customer agrees to exclusive dealing.[598] Exclusivity payments arguably make the most sense as an exclusionary practice in circumstances where the customer would not benefit directly from discounting the price per unit of the relevant product, so that conventional fidelity rebates provide an insufficient incentive to single sourcing. This might be because the product is offered to the customer at a zero-price, as in *Google Android*.[599] Or it may be because the customer receiving the payment specifies the dominant undertaking as the supplier to a third party manufacturer, which uses the indicated product as an input for a finished product made for the customer, as in *Qualcomm*.[600] In *Intel*, the defendant made payments to customers to delay, restrict, or cancel the marketing of specific competing AMD-based products, a practice which the Commission described as 'naked restrictions'.[601]

The condemnation of naked restrictions was foreshadowed in paragraph 22 of the Guidance Paper, in which the Commission identified as one circumstance in which it may not be necessary to carry out a detailed assessment of potential consumer harm 'if the dominant undertaking . . . pays a distributor or a customer to delay the introduction of a competitor's product'. In *Intel*, the Commission found that the naked restrictions and fidelity rebates complemented each other as part of a single foreclosure strategy: the naked restrictions were 'tactical moves' to dissuade OEMs from producing specific AMD-based products, whereas conditional rebates were 'strategic devices to foreclose AMD from entire segments of OEMs' demand'.[602] The GC upheld the Commission. It rejected the plea that the use of the concept 'naked restriction' denoted a novel type of abuse. This aspect of the GC's judgment was not appealed by Intel.

Case T-286/09, *Intel v Commission* EU:T:2014:547

General Court

219. . . . [I]t is necessary to reject the applicant's argument that the use of the concept of 'naked restriction' constitutes a novel type of abuse. It must be stated that the legal characterisation of an abusive practice does not depend on the name given to it, but on the substantive criteria used in that

593 Ibid., para. 43. For LRAIC (long-run average incremental cost), see Section 7.C. 594 Ibid., para. 44.
595 Ibid., para. 45. 596 Ibid., para. 46, referring to paras. 28–31. 597 Ibid., para. 46.
598 See Hajnovicova, Lang, and Usai, n. 493, 142.
599 AT.40099, *Google Android*, 18 July 2018. Although OEMs did not pay to license Google's proprietary apps, they were granted a share of Google's advertising revenue where they agreed not to pre-install competing general search apps.
600 AT.40220, *Qualcomm (exclusivity payments)* 24 January 2018. 601 COMP/37.990, *Intel* 13 May 2009.
602 Ibid., para. 1642.

regard. Thus, the mere use of the concept of 'naked restriction' does not provide a sufficient basis on which to conclude that the substantive criteria applied are new. . . . [I]t is clear from the wording of point (b) of the second subparagraph of Article [102] that limiting markets constitutes an abuse. Moreover, it is not novel in competition law that a practice which clearly does not come within competition on the merits is regarded as unlawful (see, to that effect, *Hoffmann-La Roche*, . . . paragraph 91, and *AKZO* v *Commission* . . ., paragraph 70).

220. Lastly, even if the characterisation as abusive of the practices at issue were indeed 'novel', that would not call in question the Commission's power to prohibit them. Even in the area of the calculation of fines, the General Court has already held that the fact that conduct with the same features has not been examined in past decisions does not exonerate an undertaking (see, to that effect, *Michelin I*, . . . paragraph 107, and *AstraZeneca*, . . . paragraph 901).

In the post-*Intel* landscape, the Commission considers exclusivity payments to be less inherently anticompetitive than exclusive purchasing obligations. It thus accepts that the *Intel* clarification applies to exclusivity payments, so that it is necessary to demonstrate that such payments have the capacity to foreclose competition to establish a breach of Article 102.[603]

Exclusivity payments have been the subject of two Commission infringement decisions post-*Intel*. In *Qualcomm*, the defendant technology company made 'incentive payments' to one of its largest customers, Apple, on the condition that Apple specify Qualcomm as the baseband chipset supplier to be used by third party contract manufacturers producing certain iPhone and iPad products. These were held to be exclusivity payments despite the fact that they were formally presented as an option within the supply agreement, i.e. Apple could choose instead to source chipsets from rival suppliers and forego the payments, as it did in 2016.[604] In *Google Android*, the exclusivity payments comprised revenue-share arrangements between Google and mobile device manufacturers and mobile network operators (MNOs), agreed on the condition that the latter preinstall only the Google Search app on mobile devices.[605] It was pertinent that the payments were portfolio-based, meaning that if manufacturers/MNOs installed a competing search service on *any* device within an agreed portfolio, they lost the payment due for *all* devices within that group. It was explained earlier that the GC annulled both decisions on the basis that Commission had failed to establish foreclosure capacity.[606] The GC did not, however, challenge the characterisation of the relevant practices as potentially abusive exclusivity payments in either instance.

11. TYING AND BUNDLING

A. GENERAL

The concepts of tying and bundling encompass a range of business practices whereby a purchaser is required or incentivised to purchase two distinct (though typically complementary) goods or services together. Tying and bundling are common commercial practices, and can be implemented by non-dominant undertakings. In this section, we are concerned with the possibility that these practices

[603] See AT.40220, *Qualcomm (exclusivity payments)* 24 January 2018, paras. 382–383; AT.40099, *Google Android* 18 July 2018, paras. 1188–1189.

[604] AT.40220, *Qualcomm (exclusivity payments)* 24 January 2018, para. 402.

[605] AT.40099, *Google Android* 18 July 2018, paras. 1195–1196 and 2011–2014.

[606] See Section 10.B.iii.c.

might constitute an abuse under Article 102, in particular by enabling a dominant undertaking to leverage market power from one product market to another.

The concepts of tying and bundling are described in the Guidance Paper.[607]

> 48. 'Tying' usually refers to situations where customers that purchase one product (the tying product) are required also to purchase another product from the dominant undertaking (the tied product). Tying can take place on a technical or contractual basis . . . 'Bundling' usually refers to the way products are offered and priced by the dominant undertaking. In the case of pure bundling the products are only sold jointly in fixed proportions. In the case of mixed bundling, often referred to as a multi-product rebate, the products are also made available separately, but the sum of the prices when sold separately is higher than the bundled price.

Contractual tying, sometimes referred to as classical tying in the case law, 'occurs when the customer who purchases the tying product undertakes also to purchase the tied product (and not the alternatives offered by competitors)'.[608] Suppose X makes both widgets and blodgets. X is the monopoly supplier of widgets, but the blodget market is competitive. However, customers for widgets also require blodgets. If X refuses to supply widgets unless the customers buy its blodgets, that is a contractual tie. Contractual tying can also be effected through non-financial inducements, such as refusing to honour guarantees on the tying product if the tied product is not bought,[609] or offering priority delivery to customers who take both products.[610]

Pure bundling means that the products are only sold together, in fixed proportions, and the elements of the package are not supplied separately. The paradigmic example is a pair of shoes comprising a right shoe and a left shoe, which, strictly speaking, serve different demands. Nonetheless, a consumer that wishes to, for instance, replace a broken or mislaid right shoe is obliged to repurchase the whole pair, including the left shoe for which they have no need. Another example is where services are tied to products, meaning that the price for the product also includes subsequent services such as repair and maintenance. A customer who does not want the service will normally still have to pay the full price, or may be offered a reduction which does not reflect the true cost of the service element.

Technical tying occurs 'when the tying product is designed in such a way that it only works properly with the tied product (and not with the alternatives offered by competitors)'.[611] An example is the Apple Watch, which can only be used alongside Apple's iPhone product. Alternatively, the two products may be physically integrated so that they can only be sold together. The latter type is a form of *pure bundling*, and sometimes called *technical bundling*.[612] An example would be the Apple operating system, iOS, which is only available preinstalled within certain Apple devices, primarily iPhones.

Mixed bundling is also known as a multi-product rebate or economic tying. Instead of requiring the customer to obtain the tied product in order to be supplied with the tying product, or technically tying them together, the supplier offers a financially advantageous deal if the customer buys both. For example, if the normal unit price for widgets is €10 and the competitive unit price for blodgets is €5, the dominant widget supplier may offer both together for €13.

As the Commission explains in the Guidance Paper,[613] for Article 102 to apply, the undertaking must be dominant in the tying product market but not necessarily in the tied product market.

[607] See also the Non-Horizontal Merger Guidelines [2008] OJ C265/6, paras. 96–97; and Case T-210/01, *General Electric v Commission* [2005] EU:T:2005:456, para. 406.

[608] Guidance Paper, para. 48, fn. 2.

[609] See *Eurofix-Bauco v Hilti* [1988] OJ L65/19, para. 44.

[610] See Case T-65/89, *BPB Industries* EU:T:1993:31.

[611] Guidance Paper, para. 48, fn. 2.

[612] As in Case T-201/04, *Microsoft* EU:T:2007:289.

[613] Guidance Paper, para. 50, fn. 3.

In bundling cases, it must be dominant in one of the bundled markets. In the case of aftermarkets, the undertaking must be dominant in the tying and/or the tied market.

B. THE COMMERCIAL RATIONALE FOR TYING AND BUNDLING

Tying and bundling may make good commercial and economic sense for reasons which are not necessarily anti-competitive. They can be used as methods for obtaining royalties or fees for the use of a process or product, i.e. as a 'metering' device.[614] They can enable a supplier to spread the risk when trying to penetrate a new market. They can allow a supplier to achieve economies of scale, which are reflected in the price reduction offered to customers, or to offer a 'bundle' which is more attractive (and of greater value) to consumers than the sum of its parts. They can therefore have beneficial effects on consumer welfare. Suppliers may also tie products or services in order to ensure their optimal performance and maintain the supplier's reputation, or to ensure safety, although the EU Courts have not proved receptive to the latter justification.[615]

C. THE ECONOMIC ARGUMENTS OVER TYING AND BUNDLING

The basic objection to tying and bundling by dominant undertakings is that it enables leveraging of market power: the projection of dominance from one market to another.[616] The dominant undertaking thus uses its position on the market where it is dominant to foreclose competition on another market and acquire substantial market power ('offensive' leveraging). The fear is that, having thus extended its market power to the adjacent market segment, the dominant supplier can then extract two monopoly prices, one from the tying and one from the tied product. Such a concern has, historically, led competition laws to proscribe the practice as per se illegal.[617] Famously, however, the Chicago School argued that the extraction of two monopoly profits is impossible in this situation. This is because the inflated price for the package deal (comprising both the supra-competitively priced tying *and* tied products) becomes so unattractive to customers that the dominant firm loses a large number of sales. This would lead overall profits to fall below what it could achieve from pricing the tying product alone at the monopoly level and the tied product at the competitive level. Chicago School scholars thus advanced the 'single monopoly profit theorem' as a powerful riposte to the per se illegality position.

Post-Chicagoans, however, have argued that it *is* possible for tying to serve as a mechanism for leveraging market power, because the single monopoly profit theorem depends on certain assumptions.[618] The two products must be used in fixed proportions; the market for the tied

[614] E.g. *Vaassen/Moris* [1979] OJ L19/32, where the patentee of a device for filling *saucissons de Boulogne* supplied it royalty-free but on the condition that customers bought their sausage skins from him. This was an easy way of monitoring, and charging for, the use of the device (but found to be contrary to Art. 101(1)).

[615] As in the *Hilti* and *Tetra Pak II* cases, discussed in Section 11.E.

[616] For the economics of tying/bundling generally, see Bishop and Walker, n. 243, 6-063–6-083; Motta, n. 197, 7.3; R. J. Van den Bergh and P. D. Camesasca, *European Competition Law and Economics: A Comparative Perspective* (2nd edn, Sweet & Maxwell, 2006), 265–270; O'Donoghue and Padilla, n. 1, 700–711; Rousseva, n. 329, 239–245; Elhauge and Geradin, n. 254, 562–571.

[617] The US modified its previous absolute per se illegality rule in *Jefferson Parish Hospital District No. 2 v Hyde*, 466 US 2 (1984).

[618] The foundational article setting out the arguments against the Chicago position is M. Whinston, 'Tying, Foreclosure and Exclusion' (1990) 80 *Am Econ Rev* 837.

good must have a competitive, constant, returns-to-scale structure; and consumers need perfect information about prices. The economics of tying and bundling have generated a large and lively literature.[619] Ultimately, what this intellectual disagreement demonstrates most clearly is that these practices may have both pro- and anti-competitive effects. In short, everything depends on the facts of each case.

Leveraging can also be 'defensive'. The theory of defensive leveraging concentrates on the prolongation of power in the tying market. In this model, the dominant undertaking eliminates competitors on the tied market in order to prevent entry onto the tying market, or to make it more difficult, by depriving the entrant of access to the consumable. It may also be that the dominant undertaking wishes to exclude the competitor in the tied market where there is a possibility that the tied product may subsequently become a substitute for the tying product.[620] The *Google Android* case concerned an undertaking that was already dominant in *both* the tying and one of two tied product markets, and which engaged in technical tying in order to protect its market power in the latter. Google had initially developed its open-source Android mobile operating system (OS) precisely to preserve its monopoly in general search services.[621] In *Android*, the Commission condemned Google's practice of tying the Play Store app, which is essentially the gateway to the Android OS, to the Google Search and Chrome apps, in order to *defend* its existing market power in search.[622]

D. TYING AND BUNDLING AND ARTICLE 102

The Guidance Paper says:

> 49. Tying and bundling are common practices intended to provide customers with better products or offerings in more cost effective ways. However, an undertaking which is dominant in one product market (or more) of a tie or bundle (referred to as the tying market) can harm consumers through tying or bundling by foreclosing the market for the other products that are part of the tie or bundle (referred to as the tied market) and, indirectly, the tying market.

EU competition law is concerned with tying because of the leverage problem, which may result in the foreclosure of competitors. Tying can do this because the supplier is dominant in the market for the *tying* product, so the customer has difficulty going elsewhere, and therefore cannot or does not shop

[619] See e.g. J. Choi and C. Stefanadis, 'Tying, Investment and Dynamic Leverage Theory' (2001) 32 *RAND J of Economics* 52; K.-U. Kuhn, R. Stillman, and C. Caffarra, 'Economic Theories of Bundling and their Policy Implications in Abuse Cases' (2005) 1 *European Competition Journal* 85; D. Crane and J. Wright, 'Can Bundled Discounting Increase Consumer Prices Without Excluding Rivals?' (2009) 5 *Competition Policy International* 209; D. S. Evans and M. Salinger, 'Why Do Firms Bundle and Tie? Evidence from Competitive Markets and Implications for Tying Law' (2005) 22 *Yale J on Regulation* 37; B. Nabeluff, 'Exclusionary Bundling' (2005) 50 *Ant Bull* 321. An article published by E. Elhauge, 'Tying, Bundled Discounts, and the Death of the Single Monopoly Profit Theory' (2009) 123 *Harvard LR* 399 attracted much debate, see particularly P. Seabright, 'The Undead? A Comment on Professor Elhauge's Paper' (2009) 5 *Competition Policy International* 243; H. First, 'No Single Monopoly Profit, No Single Policy Prescription?' (2009) 5 *Competition Policy International* 199; and Elhauge's response, E. Elhauge, 'The Failed Resurrection of the Single Monopoly Profit Theory', Harvard Discussion Paper No. 664 (2010) 6 *Competition Policy International* 155.

[620] D. Carlton and M. Waldman, 'The Strategic Use of Tying to Preserve and Create Market Power in Evolving Industries' (2002) 33 *RAND J of Economics* 194; see generally P. Këllezi, 'Rhetoric or Reform: Does the Law of Tying and Bundling Reflect the Economic Theory' in Ezrachi, n. 36, 148, 152 ff.

[621] AT.40099, *Google Android* 18 July 2018, paras. 112–130.

[622] See Section 11.E.iv.

around for the *tied* product. Mixed bundling can have a foreclosure effect because it offers a price that competitors on the tied market cannot match. Article 102(d) specifically lists tying as a type of abuse:

> making the conclusion of contracts subject to acceptance by the other parties of supplementary obligations which, by their nature or according to commercial usage, have no connection with the subject of such contracts.

However, the case law shows that tying and bundling may infringe Article 102 even if it does not fit within that provision.

E. THE CASE LAW

(i) Contractual or 'Classical' Tying

Contractual tying is the 'classical' example of an abusive tying scenario.[623] The leading early cases are *Hilti* and *Tetra Pak II*, both of which concerned consumables in an aftermarket tied to a primary product. In each, the Commission found an abuse after minimal market analysis, and the EU Courts on appeal concentrated on the issues of market definition[624] and objective justification. In neither case did the Court require a demonstration of actual or potential anti-competitive effects.

Hilti involved the dominant supplier of nail guns for the construction industry. Hilti's nail guns and cartridge strips were protected by patents, but the nails themselves were not protected, and there were small, independent manufacturers of Hilti-compatible nails. Hilti sought to deny those independent manufacturers access to Hilti-compatible cartridge strips through various restrictive practices, including making the sale of patented cartridge strips conditional upon taking a corresponding complement of nails, reducing discounts on cartridges where the customer did not order nails, and refusing supplies of cartridges to customers who might re-sell to independent nail producers. The Commission held that the nail guns, cartridges, and nails constituted separate product markets and that Hilti was dominant in all of them. It found that Hilti had infringed Article 102 through these practices.

> ***Eurofix-Bauco/Hilti* [1988] OJ L65/19**
>
> **Commission**
>
> 74. Hilti has abused its dominant position in the EEC in the relevant market for nail guns and most importantly the markets for Hilti-compatible cartridge strips and nails . . . The different aspects of Hilti's commercial behaviour were designed to this effect and were aimed at preventing Hilti-compatible cartridge strips from being freely available. Without such availability of Hilti-compatible cartridge strips, . . . independent producers of Hilti-compatible nails have been severely restricted in their penetration of the market. Furthermore, customers have been obliged to rely on Hilti for both cartridges and nails for their Hilti nail guns. By limiting the effective competition from new entrants Hilti has been able to preserve its dominant position. The ability to carry out its illegal policies stems from its

[623] So described by the Commission in COMP/37.792, *Microsoft* 24 March 2004, para. 841 (and implicitly accepted by the GC, Case T-201/04, *Microsoft* EU:T:2007:289, para. 846) and AT.40099, *Google Android* 18 July 2018, para. 749 (again, accepted by the GC, Case T-604/18, *Google Android* EU:T:2022:541, paras. 287 and 290).

[624] See Chap. 6, Section 8.

power on the markets for Hilti-compatible cartridge strips and nail guns (where its market position is strongest and the barriers to entry are highest) and aims at reinforcing its dominance on the Hilti-compatible nail market (where it is potentially more vulnerable to new competition) . . .

75. Making the sale of patented cartridge strips conditional upon taking a corresponding complement of nails constitutes an abuse of a dominant position, as do reduced discounts and other discriminatory policies described above on cartridge-only orders. These policies leave the consumer with no choice over the source of his nails and as such abusively exploit him. In addition, these policies all have the object or effect of excluding independent nail makers who may threaten the dominant position Hilti holds . . .

The GC upheld the decision, dismissing pleas about the products forming a 'system' and refusing to accept that Hilti's conduct was justified by safety concerns.[625] The judgment was affirmed by the CJ.[626]

The facts of *Tetra Pak II* have already been given.[627] One of the abuses was tying the supply of non-aseptic packaging machines to the supply of cartons which the machines filled. Customers had to obtain the cartons, alongside all machine maintenance and repair services and spare parts, from Tetra Pak. The Commission held that this system of tied sales, 'which again limits outlets and makes contracts subject to acceptance of conditions (the purchase of cartons) which have no connection with their purpose (the sale of machines), constitutes a serious infringement of Article [102]'.[628] The GC upheld this, referring to the tied-sales clause intending to 'strengthen Tetra Pak's dominant position by reinforcing its customers' economic dependence on it'.[629] On appeal to the CJ, Tetra Pak claimed that Article 102(d) prohibited tying only where the supplementary obligations imposed had by their nature, or according to commercial usage, no connection with the subject of the contract, whereas its cartons and machines formed 'integrated distribution systems'.

Case C-333/94 P, *Tetra Pak International SA v Commission* EU:C:1996:436

Court of Justice

35. Tetra Pak interprets Article [102(d)] as prohibiting only the practice of making the conclusion of contracts dependent on acceptance of additional services which, by nature or according to commercial usage, have no link with the subject-matter of the contracts.

36. It must be noted, first, that the [GC] explicitly rejected the argument put forward by Tetra Pak to show the existence of a natural link between the machines and the cartons. . . . [I]t found: 'consideration of commercial usage does not support the conclusion that the machinery for packaging a product is indivisible from the cartons. For a considerable time there have been independent manufacturers who specialise in the manufacture of non-aseptic cartons designed for use in machines manufactured by other concerns and who do not manufacture machinery themselves'. That assessment, itself based on commercial usage, rules out the existence of the natural link claimed by Tetra Pak by stating that other manufacturers can produce cartons for use in Tetra Pak's machines. With regard to aseptic cartons, the [General Court] found . . . that 'any independent producer is quite free, as far as [Union] competition law is concerned, to manufacture consumables intended for use in equipment manufactured by others, unless in doing so it infringes a competitor's intellectual property right'. It also noted . . . rejecting the

625 Case T-30/89, *Hilti* EU:T:1991:70. 626 Case C-53/92 P, *Hilti* EU:C:1994:77.

627 Case C-333/94 P, *Tetra Pak II* EU:C:1996:436. See Section 6.

628 *Elopak Italia/Tetra Pak* [1991] OJ L72/1, para. 117. 629 Case T-83/91, *Tetra Pak* EU:T:1994:246, para. 140.

> argument based on the alleged natural link, that it was not for Tetra Pak to impose certain measures on its own initiative on the basis of technical considerations or considerations relating to product liability, protection of public health and protection of its reputation. Those factors, taken as a whole, show that the [GC] considered that Tetra Pak was not alone in being able to manufacture cartons for use in its machines.
>
> 37. It must, moreover, be stressed that the list of abusive practices set out in the second paragraph of Article [102] is not exhaustive. Consequently, even where tied sales of two products are in accordance with commercial usage or there is a natural link between the two products in question, such sales may still constitute abuse within the meaning of Article [102] unless they are objectively justified . . .

It is clear from *Tetra Pak II* that, once it is shown that the products or services tied together are distinct, a dominant undertaking cannot rely on the words about nature and commercial usage in Article 102(d). 'Commercial usage' may merely have been established by the dominant undertaking itself,[630] and the Court stressed the non-exhaustive character of the examples listed in Article 102(a)–(d). *Hilti* and *Tetra Pak II* were both driven by concerns about the structure of the market, not about the extraction of monopoly profits or the direct protection of consumers. In *Tetra Pak II*, the monopoly profit could have been extracted from the tying product (the machines), had Tetra Pak wished.[631]

The subsequent *Microsoft* decision on technical tying suggested that, in these 'classical' tying cases, 'the Commission and the Courts considered the foreclosure effect for competing vendors to be demonstrated by the bundling of a separate product with the dominant product'.[632] It was permissible therefore 'to assume without further analysis that [the practice] constitutes conduct which by its very nature is liable to foreclose competition'.[633] This view was essentially endorsed by the GC on appeal.[634] In the *Android* decision, the Commission was even more explicit about the absence of a foreclosure requirement in the 'classical' cases:

> Article 102 TFEU does not require demonstration of actual or potential anti-competitive effects in classical tying cases. Indeed, in *Hilti* and *Tetra Pak II*, it was sufficient to assume that the tying of a specific product has by its very nature a foreclosure effect. In *Microsoft*, however, the General Court explained that while it is true that Article 102 TFEU as a whole does not contain any reference to the anti-competitive effect of bundling, the fact remains that, in principle, conduct will be regarded as abusive only if it is capable of restricting competition . . . [T]he concept of abuse covers not only practices which may prejudice consumers directly but also those which may indirectly prejudice them by impairing an effective competitive structure.[635]

Again, the Commission's understanding of the *Hilti* and *Tetra Pak II* case law was not disputed by the GC.[636] As the discussion in Section 3.F explained, however, the *Intel* case suggests that even in classical tying cases, the presumption of capacity to foreclose is at most a rebuttable one. Accordingly, it should be open to a dominant undertaking to adduce evidence to challenge the presumption that its tying practice is in fact capable of foreclosing competition.

[630] See V. Korah, 'The Paucity of Economic Analysis in the EEC Decisions on Competition: *Tetra Pak II*' [1993] *CLP* 150; see also Case T-201/04, *Microsoft* EU:T:2007:289, para. 940.

[631] See Korah, ibid. [632] COMP/37.792, *Microsoft* 24 March 2004, para. 841.

[633] Ibid. [634] Case T-201/04, *Microsoft* EU:T:2007:289, paras. 846, 857, and 1035.

[635] AT.40099, *Google Android* 18 July 2018, para. 749.

[636] Case T-604/18, *Google Android* EU:T:2022:541, paras. 287 and 290.

(ii) Mixed Bundling

Several enforcement cases have involved mixed bundling, i.e. the use of financial incentives to prompt multi-product sales. Two such cases involved Coca-Cola. In *Coca-Cola Italia Undertaking* (1989),[637] the Commission alleged that Coca-Cola's practice of offering discounts to retailers based on a package of cola and non-cola was abusive. Coca-Cola committed not to make discounts for cola conditional on the retailers buying non-cola, and the case settled. In *Coca-Cola Undertaking* (2005),[638] Coca-Cola agreed, inter alia, to cease offering rebates to its customers that were conditional upon the customer buying other products together with Coca-Cola's best-selling products or reserving shelf space for the entire group of products.

In the aftermarket case, *Digital Undertaking*,[639] Digital, a computer supplier, offered a package of hardware maintenance services and software support services. The primary computer systems market was competitive, but the Commission alleged that, by offering customers a package in the aftermarket, Digital abused its dominant position on the software support market by making it uneconomic to buy the hardware maintenance from third parties. The Commission settled the proceedings when Digital undertook, inter alia, to offer hardware maintenance services on a stand-alone basis, and to price its package in a way which fell below the list prices of the individual component services only where the reduction reflected costs savings or other benefits stemming from efficient packaging.

(iii) Technical Tying and the *Microsoft* Case

Cases of technical tying under Article 102 have arisen most prominently in digital markets. The issue was first addressed by the Commission in 1984, when it reached a settlement with IBM[640] on foot of allegations that IBM had, inter alia, tied various computer products.[641] It returned to the issue two decades later in *Microsoft*.[642] The Commission held that Microsoft had abused its dominant position on the client PC operating systems market, where Microsoft's Windows system had over 90 per cent of the market, by supplying Windows to the computer manufacturers (OEMs) with its Windows Media Player (WMP) pre-installed. The Commission held that the Windows operating system and the WMP were two distinct products and that, by selling them together, Microsoft was leveraging its monopoly power on to the media player market where it faced greater competition. For tying to infringe Article 102, the Commission held that four elements must be present: two separate products; dominance in the tying market; coercion of customers who have no option to obtain the tying product alone; and foreclosure of competition as a result. It found that all four conditions were satisfied in the case. In this extract, the Commission explains the detrimental effects of Microsoft's practices.

[637] Commission's *XIXth Report on Competition Policy* (1989), para. 50.

[638] [2005] OJ L253/21.

[639] Commission Press Release IP/97/868. Cf. the *Pelikan/Kyocera* case, *XXVth Report on Competition Policy* (1995), part 87: see Chap. 6. See also D. Maldoom, 'The *Kodak* Case: Power in Aftermarkets' [1996] *ECLR* 473; M. Dolmans and V. Pickering, 'The 1997 Digital Undertaking' [1998] *ECLR* 108; P. Andrews, 'Aftermarket Power in the Computer Services Market: The Digital Undertaking' [1998] *ECLR* 176.

[640] See Commission, *XIVth Report on Competition Policy* (1984) paras. 94–95.

[641] This involved not offering central processing units (CPUs) without a capacity of main memory included in the price (memory bundling); and not offering CPUs without the basic software included in the price (software bundling). IBM did not admit its dominance or that it had committed an abuse, but nevertheless undertook to offer its CPUs in the EEC either without main memory or with only such capacity as was strictly required for testing.

[642] COMP/37.792, 24 March 2004. The case also concerned a refusal to supply, discussed in Section 12.E.

***Microsoft*, Commission Decision COMP/37.792, 24 March 2004**

Commission

(979) Through tying WMP with Windows, Microsoft uses Windows as a distribution channel to anti-competitively ensure for itself a significant competition advantage in the media player market. Competitors, due to Microsoft's tying, are *a priori* at a disadvantage irrespective of whether their products are potentially more attractive on the merits.

(980) Microsoft thus interferes with the normal competitive process which would benefit users in terms of quicker cycles of innovation due to unfettered competition on the merits. Tying of WMP increases the content and applications barrier to entry which protects Windows and it will facilitate the erection of such a barrier for WMP. A position of market strength achieved in a market characterised by network effects—such as the media player market—is sustainable, as once the network effects work in favour of a company which has gained a decisive momentum, they will amount to entry barriers for potential competitors . . .

(981) This shields Microsoft from effective competition from potentially more efficient media player vendors which could challenge its position. Microsoft thus reduces the talent and capital invested in innovation of media players, not least its own . . . and anti-competitively raises barriers to market entry. Microsoft's conduct affects a market which could be a hotbed for new and exciting products springing forth in a climate of undistorted competition.

(982) Moreover, tying of WMP allows Microsoft to anti-competitively expand its position in adjacent media-related software markets and weaken effective competition to the eventual detriment of consumers.

Notably, the Commission took a more 'effects-based' approach than it had done in *Hilti* or *Tetra Pak II*. Without calling into question the absence of a foreclosure requirement in those earlier cases, it held that, on the particular facts, there were 'good reasons not to assume without further analysis that tying WMP constitutes conduct which by its very nature is liable to foreclose competition'.[643] It thus carefully considered the harmful effects of Microsoft's tying practice. First, pre-installation provided a more efficient distribution system than was available to competitors and led to the 'ubiquity' of WMP.[644] That meant, secondly, that content providers and software developers increasingly used the WMP format to the detriment of the main competitors and their technologies.[645] That led, thirdly, to network effects which in the end would result in the market 'tipping' to WMP: it is unnecessary for a competition authority to wait until the tipping has occurred, by which time meaningful intervention would be too late.[646]

Microsoft was fined almost half a billion euro,[647] and the Commission ordered it to offer the OEMs a version of Windows without the WMP. The OEMs could choose between Windows alone and a 'package' of Windows plus the WMP. If they chose the former, they could install a rival media player. Consumers would therefore have a choice of media player when they bought their PC. Microsoft appealed to the GC.[648]

643 COMP/37.792, *Microsoft* 24 March 2004, para. 841. 644 Ibid., paras. 843–878.

645 Ibid., paras. 879–944. 646 Ibid., para. 946.

647 The fine also related to the other abuse investigated, refusal to supply interface information. This was not a case where the Commission refrained from imposing a fine because of the novelty of the case: it said that as regards the tying/bundling abuse it was not applying a new rule, but that *Hilti* and *Tetra Pak II* should have provided sufficient guidance to Microsoft to make it clear that its conduct infringed Art. 102: 'the software industry is not exempted from the application of competition law' (ibid., para. 1057).

648 Case T-201/04, *Microsoft* EU:T:2007:289; there was no further appeal to the CJ.

The Commission's decision raised several difficult and controversial issues. Among these was how far even dominant suppliers should be free to develop new versions of their products with 'built in' features. In the *Microsoft* appeal, the GC stuck closely to its brief of establishing that the Commission had provided adequate reasoning based on sufficient accurate, reliable, and consistent evidence. Crucially, it confirmed that the factors identified in the decision[649]—i.e. two products, dominance in the tying market, absence of choice, and foreclosure—were correct. The treatment of dominance was considered in Chapter 6. The three additional elements are considered in turn later.

The Commission's conclusions were premised on the existence of *two distinct products*, namely desktop operating systems and media players. Microsoft claimed that it did not supply two products but rather one single integrated one, so that it could not engage in tying or bundling. The GC upheld the finding of two products. It approved the Commission's approach of determining whether products are distinct for the purposes of Article 102 by reference 'consumer demand'.[650] The GC also looked at features of the market and at Microsoft's commercial practice.[651] It noted that operating systems and streaming media players had different functionality; distributors supplied media players separately from any supply of a PC client operating system; Microsoft distributed versions of the WMP designed to work with its competitors' operating systems; WMP could be downloaded independently from Microsoft's internet site; Microsoft engaged in WMP-specific promotion; Microsoft applied different licensing arrangements to Windows and to WMP; and that some consumers obtained media players from competitors, separately from their operating system.

The GC judgment followed three years after the infringement decision, by which time the unbundling remedy required by the Commission had had several years to take effect. Somewhat infamously, there had proven to be almost no demand from OEMs for the unbundled version of Windows.[652] (The remedy might have worked rather better had the Commission ordered Microsoft *not* to supply Windows with WMP.) On appeal, Microsoft invoked the evident lack of success of the unbundling remedy as further confirmation that, in reality, the technology concerned did not constitute two distinct products.[653] Yet the GC rejected the relevance of this *ex post facto* evidence, holding that 'any doubts as to the effectiveness of the remedy ordered by the Commission do not in themselves prove that its finding as to the existence of two separate products is wrong'.[654]

Microsoft further argued that there was no restriction of actual (rather than hypothetical) customer choice, i.e. there was no *'coercion'* involved. Consumers did not pay more for the WMP functionality of Windows, they did not have to use it, and they could install and use third party media players. The GC held all of this irrelevant. It was not necessarily true that the WMP was free just because there was no separate charge for it and, anyway, it was not required that consumers had to pay a certain price for the tied product.[655] Nor did Article 102(d), as could be seen from *Hilti*, require that the consumers be obliged to use the tied product.[656] Although both OEMs and consumers *could* install and/or use other media players, they had little incentive to do so.[657] This last point was vital for the issue of foreclosure.

The treatment of *foreclosure* is the most interesting part of the judgment.[658] Somewhat counter-intuitively, Microsoft first challenged the inclusion of a foreclosure element in the applicable

[649] COMP/37.792, *Microsoft*, Decision of 24 March 2004, para. 794.

[650] Case T-201/04, *Microsoft* EU:T:2007:289, paras. 917–918. [651] Ibid., paras. 927–932.

[652] According to C. Ahlborn and D. S. Evans, 'The *Microsoft* Judgment and its Implications for Competition Policy Towards Dominant Firms in Europe' (2008–2009) 75 *Antitrust LJ* 887 (who acted for Microsoft), between the date of the naked Windows being made available and the date of the oral hearing, no OEM in the world installed it. Retailers bought 11,787 copies of the naked Windows XP, less than 0.005% of those sold in Europe.

[653] Case T-201/04, *Microsoft* EU:T:2007:289, para. 943. [654] Ibid., para. 943. [655] Ibid., paras. 968–969.

[656] Ibid., para. 970. [657] Ibid., para. 971.

[658] For comment on this, see e.g. Ahlborn and Evans, n. 652, 252–255; L. Lovdahl Gormsen, 'Why the European Commission's Enforcement Priorities on Article 82 EC Should be Withdrawn' [2010] *ECLR* 45, 48; D. Howarth and K. McMahon, '"Windows has Performed an Illegal Operation": The Court of First Instance's Judgment in *Microsoft v Commission*' [2008] *ECLR* 117.

legal test, on the basis that this was not expressly required by Article 102(d).[659] The GC confirmed that the second paragraph of Article 102 is not exhaustive, and that the Commission's four factors, including the foreclosure requirement, 'can be deduced from the very concept of bundling and from the case law'.[660] Making reference to 'the specific circumstances of the present case', it accepted that the Commission 'could not merely assume, as it *normally* does in cases of abusive tying, that the tying . . . has by its nature a foreclosure effect'.[661] On the facts, the Commission was correct to consider 'more closely the *actual* effects which the bundling had'.[662] As noted earlier, however, the judgment pointedly did not embrace a foreclosure requirement for all tying/bundling cases.

Arguing in the alternative, Microsoft then claimed that the Commission had failed to prove that the integration of WMP with Windows involved foreclosure of competition. It argued that the Commission had applied a 'highly speculative theory, relying on a prospective analysis of the possible reactions of third parties, in order to reach the conclusion that the tying at issue was likely to foreclose competition'.[663] The GC rejected this too. It approached the question of foreclosure primarily in terms of the threat to the structure of competition. The court spoke of 'appreciably altering the balance of competition in favour of Microsoft',[664] and endorsed the Commission's finding that 'Microsoft interferes with the normal competitive process which would benefit users by ensuring quicker cycles of innovation as a consequence of unfettered competition on the merits'.[665] It moreover deduced from the first stage of the Commission's reasoning—that is, just its findings as to the ubiquity of WMP—that the Commission had demonstrated to the requisite legal standard that the bundling 'inevitably had significant consequences for the structure of competition'.[666] It was assumed that this advantage led to foreclosure.[667] The Commission thus discharged its burden of establishing foreclosure to the extent that it had established 'a reasonable likelihood that tying Windows and Windows Media Player would lead to a lessening of competition so that the maintenance of an effective competition structure would not be ensured in the foreseeable future'.[668] The GC considered it unnecessary to examine the further stages of the Commission's reasoning, i.e. the impact on the software developers and the evolution of the market,[669] although it did so for the sake of completeness. The emphasis was on the market structure, namely the fact that the ubiquity of WMP gave it an advantage unrelated to its 'intrinsic merits'.[670]

Microsoft argued that its behaviour was objectively justified. It defended its 'business model' as having benefits for software developers, OEMs, and consumers. The GC answered that some of the benefits could be achieved without integration and the fact that software developers and site creators found it convenient that WMP was present on nearly all client PCs worldwide was exactly why the integration led to foreclosure.[671] The GC dismissed the claim that the removal of WMP from Windows would lead to a degradation of the latter.[672] Above all, the GC stressed that the Commission had not ordered Microsoft to cease supplying Windows with WMP, but only to make Windows available without it. As noted, this remedy had proven to be practically quite useless.

In 2009, the Commission informed Microsoft of its concerns that it might have infringed Article 102 again by tying its Internet Explorer (IE) browser to Windows, which was only supplied with IE ready installed. The matter was concluded with a commitments decision whereby Microsoft undertook to provide users of Windows PCs with a browser 'Choice Screen' and to allow OEMs to choose which browser to install.[673] The 'Choice Screen' was made operational in March 2010. The commitments decision meant that the Commission did not have to produce a fully reasoned decision and

659 Case T-201/04, *Microsoft* EU:T:2007:289, paras. 845–847.
660 Ibid., para. 859.
661 Ibid., para. 868 (emphasis added).
662 Ibid., para. 868 (again, emphasis added).
663 Ibid., para. 1032.
664 Ibid., para. 1034.
665 Ibid., para. 1088.
666 Ibid., para. 1054.
667 Ibid., para. 1058.
668 Ibid., para. 1089.
669 Ibid., para. 1059.
670 Ibid., para. 1046.
671 Ibid., para. 1151.
672 Ibid., paras. 1164–1166.
673 AT.39530, *Microsoft (Tying)* 16 December 2009.

the possibility of the technical tying issue being re-examined in the GC did not arise. In March 2013, the Commission fined Microsoft €561 million for (allegedly inadvertent) failure to comply with its commitments.[674]

(iv) The *Google Android* Case

The latest evolution of the case law on tying is to be found in the Commission infringement decision against another tech giant, Google.[675] The case followed a year after the *Google Shopping* decision, discussed in Section 13. In addition to its pre-eminent position in online search markets, Google's ostensibly open-source Android mobile operating system (OS) runs on about 80 per cent of smart mobile devices in Europe. The Commission decision was premised upon Google holding a dominant position in at least three relevant markets: in national markets for general internet search services in the EEA, for licensable smart mobile OSs (worldwide excluding China), and for app stores for the Android mobile OS (again, worldwide excluding China).[676] The condemned behaviour related to restrictions imposed on Android device manufacturers and on mobile network operators, which the Commission held were intended to cement Google's dominant position in general internet search. The infringement decision identified three types of abusive restrictions, two of which it assessed under a tying analysis.[677] A record-breaking penalty of €4.34 billion was imposed as a result.

a. *Tying of Google's Proprietary Apps*

The first abuse was the tying of Google's proprietary apps, i.e. the tying of its Play Store app with its Google Search and Google Chrome apps. Although the source code for basic features of the Android OS is publicly available, any device manufacturer that wishes to include Google's proprietary apps and services must contract with Google, which imposed restrictions on licensing. Specifically, at the time Google required device manufacturers to license its mobile apps as a bundle, which included the Play Store, the Search app, and the Chrome browser. Any manufacturer which wanted to pre-install *any* of these products was required to pre-install *all* apps in the bundle. Since the Play Store constituted a 'must-have' app for device manufacturers (because users expect it to be pre-installed on their devices), the bundled licensing policy resulted in the tying of Google's search and browser products.

To assess the legality of the practice, the Commission started with the four-part test from *Microsoft*.[678] First, it emphasised the distinct functionalities that the three relevant apps provide to users, to conclude that each constituted a distinct product. Secondly, Google was dominant in the tying product markets, namely the Android app store and general search app markets.[679] Thirdly, its licensing policies amounted to coercion within the meaning of Article 102. Fourthly, those policies were 'capable of restricting competition'.

In regard to the final criterion, the decision moved away from the language of foreclosure, with the Commission instead favouring the more abstract formulation from *Michelin II*.[680] To establish a capability of restricting competition, the Commission found, first, that the tying practices provided Google with 'a significant competitive advantage' that competing general search services providers

[674] AT.39530, *Microsoft (Tying)* 6 March 2013. [675] AT.40099, *Google Android* 18 July 2018.

[676] Ibid., paras.439–727. [677] See Section 10 for analysis of the exclusive dealing elements.

[678] AT.40099, *Google Android*, 18 July 2018, para. 741.

[679] The decision comprised two separate findings of tying: that Google tied the Search app with its dominant Play Store app (Section 11.3 of the Decision) and that Google tied the Chrome browser app with its dominant Play Store *and* Search apps (Section 11.4 of the Decision).

[680] This had provided some of the initial impetus for the foreclosure requirement in *Microsoft*: see COMP/37.792, *Microsoft* 24 March 2004, para. 838.

and mobile web browsers could not offset.[681] Consistent with its approach in both *Microsoft* cases, the Commission focused on the '*status quo* bias'[682] that followed from mandatory pre-installation, which reduced the incentives of manufacturers to pre-install competing search and browser apps, and of users to download such apps. This, secondly, limited the ability of rivals in these markets to compete effectively with Google, deterred innovation, and was 'capable of harming, directly or indirectly, consumers who . . . may see less choice'.[683] Yet although the concept of consumer harm was forefront in the Commission's adoption of the more economic approach to Article 102, the concept was mentioned merely in passing in the decision rather than considered in-depth or established on the facts.[684]

The Commission quite straightforwardly rejected Google's claimed objective justifications.[685] Chief among these was the need to monetise Google's investment in Android, achieved through ensuring that mobile device users subsequently favoured its (revenue-generating) search and browser products. The counterfactual envisaged by Google was to charge OEMs to license the Play Store, which, Google argued, would ultimately increase the price of mobile devices for final consumers. In rejecting these claims, the Commission applied a test of strict necessity, pointing to the other revenue streams available to Google to cover its non-revenue-generating business activities. The rather blithe dismissal of Google's claims nonetheless raises an intriguing competition policy question. To what extent can and should competition enforcers dictate where dominant firms take their profits, where (at least some of) this revenue is then redeployed to develop and provide valuable free-to-use[686] products for consumers?

Google appealed to the GC, which upheld the Commission's findings on the first tying abuse. The extract below provides an overview of the GC's assessment, with emphasis on the foreclosure/capability of restricting competition requirement.

Case T-604/18, *Google and Alphabet v Commission (Google Android)* EU:T:2022:541

General Court

283. In the present case, the practices at issue . . . are instances of tying. This is a common practice in the course of trade which is normally intended to provide customers with better products or offerings in more cost-effective ways. Tying consists of a dominant undertaking making the sale of a specific product (the tying product) conditional upon the acquisition of another product (the tied product). It may have exclusionary effects on the tied market, the tying market or both at the same time. An undertaking which is dominant in one product market or more (market for the tying product) can harm consumers through that practice by foreclosing the market for the other products that are part of the tie (market for the tied product) and, indirectly, the tying market.

[681] AT.40099, *Google Android* 18 July 2018, paras. 773 and 896. [682] Ibid., paras. 812 and 851.

[683] Ibid., paras. 863 and 971.

[684] For each tying claim, the Commission dedicated a single paragraph (of 1,481 in total in the decision) to assert that the conduct was 'capable of harming, directly or indirectly, consumers' by diminishing choice (AT.40099, *Google Android* 18 July 2018, paras. 863 and 971).

[685] Ibid., para. 993.

[686] We use the word 'free' cautiously, acknowledging that products that are provided at zero-price in the digital economy context are rarely cost-less, insofar as users typically pay e.g. with their personal data, see, J. M. Newman, 'Antitrust in Zero-price Markets: Foundations' (2015) 164 *U Pa LR* 149.

284. In that regard, in order to assess the abusive nature of such practices, it has previously been held that the Commission was entitled to rely on the following factors (. . . *Microsoft v Commission*, T-201/04, EU:T:2007:289, paragraph 869):

— first, the tying and tied products are two separate products;

— second, the undertaking concerned is dominant in the market for the tying product;

— third, the undertaking concerned does not give customers a choice to obtain the tying product without the tied product;

— fourth, the practice in question 'forecloses competition';

— fifth, that practice is not objectively justified.

285. As regards, in particular, the fourth condition . . . relating to the foreclosure of competition, in . . . *Microsoft v Commission* (T-201/04, EU:T:2007:289), the Court recalled the substance of the earlier case-law according to which, 'in principle, conduct will be regarded as abusive only if it is capable of restricting competition'.

286. However, . . . the Court also noted that, in the decision that was contested in that case, 'the Commission [had] considered that, in light of the specific circumstances of the . . . case, it could not merely assume, as it normally [did] in cases of abusive tying, that the tying of a specific product and a dominant product [had] by its nature a foreclosure effect' and that, in such circumstances, 'the Commission [had] therefore examined more closely the actual effects which the bundling had already had on the [relevant] market and also the way in which that market was likely to evolve' (see, . . . *Microsoft v Commission*, T-201/04, EU:T:2007:289, paragraph 1035).

. . .

288. Consequently, . . . the Court considered that the question of the bundling had to be assessed by reference to the conditions set out in the decision that was contested in that case . . ., including the condition relating to the fact that the practice in question 'foreclose[d] competition'.

289. In the present case, . . . the Commission refers to . . . *Microsoft v Commission* (T-201/04, EU:T:2007:289), in setting out the conditions for characterising the first abuses . . .

290. In particular, regarding the fourth condition referred to in paragraph 284 above, the Commission, having indicated in the contested decision that . . . anticompetitive effects were not required to be demonstrated in 'classical tying cases', stated, in essence, that the fourth condition for establishing tying was, in principle, satisfied if the practice in question '[was] capable of restricting competition' (see recital 749 of the contested decision and footnote 813 thereto, which refers to . . . *Microsoft v Commission* (T-201/04, EU:T:2007:289, paragraph 867)).

291. In that regard, . . . it is apparent in the present case that, under the guise of applying a test formulated by reference to paragraph 867 of . . . *Microsoft v Commission* (T-201/04, EU:T:2007:289), as the 'capacity to restrict competition', the Commission was also careful to set out specifically in the contested decision the various factors which, in its view, made it possible to establish that the alleged exclusionary effects were real, in accordance with paragraph 868 of that judgment.

292. As Google has argued in the present case, it is easy for users to obtain general search or browser apps competing with those that are subject to tying. That fact is recognised by all parties, since what is at issue is not the possibility of users being readily able to download such apps but the incentives which they might have to do so . . .

293. In those circumstances, as was explained by the Court and confirmed by the parties at the hearing, it is indeed apparent from the contested decision that the Commission endeavoured to characterise a restriction of competition not only as 'potential' or 'possible' but also as 'actual' or 'concrete' with regard to some of its aspects. According to the Commission, from 2011 or August 2012 to July 2018, the practices at issue produced the exclusionary effects identified in the contested decision, which proved to be detrimental to competition on the merits.

> 294. By way of example, the Commission thus concludes that those practices had the effect, inter alia, of '[making] it harder' for competing search services to gain search queries and the revenues and data needed to improve their services . . ., that they 'increase[d] barriers to entry' by shielding Google from competition from other search services . . . and that they 'reduce[d] the incentives' for the innovations that competitors marketing specialised search services in a particular language or targeting a specific group of users wished to offer . . .
>
> 295. In the present case, the Commission therefore correctly found, as it did in the decision which gave rise to . . . *Microsoft v Commission* (T-201/04, EU:T:2007:289) (see paragraph 286 above), that close examination of the actual effects or further analysis, according to the terminology used in the past in that regard, was required before it could be concluded that the tying in question was harmful to competition. Such an examination, first, serves to reduce the risk that penalties may be imposed for conduct which is not actually detrimental to competition on the merits and, second, further to clarify the gravity of the conduct in question, which will facilitate determination of the appropriate level of any penalty.
>
> 296. Thus, given that the practices at issue took place over a long period and, according to the contested decision, had observable actual effects on the relevant markets, the benefit of a vaguer definition of 'restriction of competition' under the heading of its 'capacity to restrict competition' is less important than it might be in other circumstances.
>
> 297. It is not a question of the Commission carrying out a prospective analysis which would be based on effects that will arise in the light of assumptions that cannot yet be verified in practice, as might be the case in other circumstances (see . . . *Generics (UK) and Others*, C-307/18, EU:C:2020:52, paragraph 145).
>
> 298. Furthermore, where conduct has covered a number of years, the Commission may establish a restriction of competition by finding that those practices have eliminated or hampered sources of competition which would otherwise have taken place or developed. It is not, therefore, disputed that the actual and concrete effects of the practices at issue, effects which have arisen in the past, are to be assessed both in the light of the actual competition which the dominant undertaking had to face and in the light of the potential competition that could not arise because of the exclusionary practices.
>
> 299. Consequently, the difference between 'restriction of competition' and 'capacity to restrict competition' has no bearing on the requisite proof in cases where, as in this instance, the Commission has characterised the restriction of competition on the basis of the effects which the implementation of the practices at issue have had over a significant period of time, effects which may be observed and which enable the Commission to determine the nature and scope of the ensuing anticompetitive foreclosure, and the Court to review those findings.

The GC thus reaffirmed the four-fold criteria from *Microsoft* (plus an additional reference to the possibility of objective justification) as the appropriate legal test to be applied outside 'classical' tying cases. On the question of anti-competitive effects, the Court accepted the superficially less exacting standard of 'capacity to restrict competition' applied by the Commission. It cautioned, however, against putting too great an emphasis on the apparent difference between the language of 'restriction of competition' and 'capacity to restrict competition'. The GC noted that the Commission had, in the infringement decision, engaged in a close examination of the 'real', 'actual', 'concrete' effects of the practices, in order to conclude that these were 'harmful to competition'. This was important for two reasons, the GC argued: to reduce the likelihood of 'Type I' false positive errors occurring ('to reduce the risk that penalties may be imposed for conduct which is not actually detrimental to competition on the merits'[687]) and to determine the gravity of the breach, which would further determine the

[687] Case T-604/18, *Google Android* EU:T:2022:541, para. 295.

proportionate penalty that should be imposed. On the facts, the identified harmful effects hinged on the impact that the tying practices had on the incentives of device users to download competing apps.

The GC's review of Google's objective justification claims echoed the Commission's sceptical attitude. It confirmed that in order to defend the practices by reference to a claimed legitimate interest in monetising Android, Google was obliged to establish that the revenues generated as a result of the tying practice were *necessary* to achieve this. The GC demonstrated little sympathy for the argument that Google should be entitled to take its legitimate profits where it sees fit.[688] Moreover, the GC rejected the argument that the zero-price nature of the products concerned provided a valid reason to permit the tying practices, holding instead, perhaps counter-intuitively,[689] that paid licences might be preferable in some circumstances.[690]

To remedy the infringement (and alongside the record-breaking fine), the Commission had required Google to 'bring effectively to an end' the abusive practices identified.[691] To do so, Google introduced a new licensing option that enabled OEMs to pre-install the Play Store without the Search or Chrome apps, in exchange for a fee.[692] Additionally, for devices in which the full suite of proprietary apps continued to be pre-installed, Google agreed to implement a choice screen mirroring that of the *Microsoft Tying (II)* settlement, which was displayed during set-up and enabled users to pick a starting browser and search engine from a list of five options.[693] However, the effectiveness of the latter was heavily criticised by competing app developers, in particular because Google ran the choice screen as a 'pay-to-play' auction similar to its AdSense product.[694] In June 2021, Google announced significant changes that increased the number of competing options displayed in the choice screen and made participation free for eligible apps.[695] Nonetheless, the difficulties associated with implementing speedy and effective remedies in digital economy cases have been a significant motivating factor behind efforts to supplement (or arguably supersede) Article 102 enforcement in such markets through the Digital Markets Act, discussed in Chapter 16.

The scrutiny of tying/bundling practices in *Google (Android)* attracted much academic attention, raising questions of the extent to which the theory of harm continues to make sense within the digital economy. Supporters of the Commission's case have argued, inter alia, that tying and bundling offences are more prevalent and harmful in the digital environmental, thus meriting diligent intervention;[696] that the mere fact that Google operated in a two-sided market did not make a leverage theory of tying implausible;[697] and that under current competition law, the exclusionary nature and effects of

[688] Ibid., paras. 605–614.

[689] See also Case C-280/08 P, *Deutsche Telekom* EU:C:2010:603, to the effect that higher retail prices in the short term, in order to avert a margin squeeze, might ultimately benefit consumers in the longer term.

[690] Case T-604/18, *Google Android* EU:T:2022:541, paras. 615–618.

[691] AT.40099, *Google Android* 18 July 2018, Article 3.

[692] H. Lockheimer, 'Complying with the EC's Android decision', *Google in Europe Blog*, 16 October 2018, <www.blog.google/around-the-globe/google-europe/complying-ecs-android-decision/>.

[693] Described in R. Amadeo, 'Google to stop treating EU antitrust remedy as a "promotional opportunity"', *Ars Technica Blog*, 10 June 2021, <https://arstechnica.com/gadgets/2021/06/google-to-stop-treating-eu-antitrust-remedy-as-a-promotional-opportunity/>.

[694] N. Lomas, 'Google's EU Android choice screen isn't working say search rivals, calling for a joint process to devise a fair remedy', *TechCrunch Blog*, 27 October 2020, <https://techcrunch.com/2020/10/27/googles-eu-android-choice-screen-isnt-working-say-search-rivals-calling-for-a-joint-process-to-devise-a-fair-remedy/>.

[695] O. Bethell, 'Changes to the Android Choice Screen in Europe', *Google in Europe Blog*, 8 June 2021, <https://blog.google/around-the-globe/google-europe/changes-android-choice-screen-europe/>.

[696] S. Holzweber, 'Tying and Bundling in the Digital Era' (2018) 14 *European Competition Journal* 342.

[697] J. Choi and D. Jeon, 'A Leverage Theory of Tying in Two-sided Markets', CESifo Working Paper Series 6073 (2016); F. Etro and C. Caffarra, 'On the Economics of the *Android* Case' (2017) 13 *European Competition Journal* 282; and D. Mandrescu, 'Tying and Bundling by Online Platforms—Distinguishing Between Lawful Expansion Strategies and Anti-competitive Practices' (2021) 40 *Computer Law & Security Review* 105499.

its licensing policies could not be legitimised by the fact its products are (or were) provided for free.[698] Sceptics, conversely, argue that the traditional analysis adopted in the case ignores the benefits to consumers of the 'out-of-the-box' functionality provided by Google's bundle of apps;[699] that Google's practices represented a 'sensible' appropriability strategy, which enabled it as an innovator to capture an efficient share of the social benefits generated by its inventions through curation of the Android ecosystem;[700] that the standard of strict necessity to countervail the restrictive effects of the practice through an efficiencies claim is unrealistically (and inefficiently) demanding;[701] that the decision neglects the fact that the tying practice was originally implemented before Google had achieved dominance in the tying product market (though it was already dominant in the tied one);[702] and that the case marks a fundamental shift towards more intrusive antitrust intervention into, and thus greater second-guessing of, the product design and other business strategies of dominant firms.[703]

b. *'Anti-fragmentation' Licensing Obligations*

The *Android* decision also involved a second, less overt category of tying abuse. This practice aimed to prevent the emergence of Android 'forks', namely OSs that are based on the original Android source code, but which include modifications. The Commission found that Google viewed the emergence of Android forks as a 'credible competitive threat',[704] which might ultimately challenge Google's dominance in the smart mobile OS segment. To prevent this, Google included 'anti-fragmentation' clauses in its licensing agreements with device manufacturers. These required OEMs to commit not to sell *any* device that ran on an Android fork to order to be permitted to sell even a single device with the Play Store and Search apps pre-installed. The Commission treated these requirements as conditional 'supplementary obligations' under Article 102(d). Applying a modified version of the four-factor test established in *Microsoft* to identify technical tying,[705] the Commission found an abuse of dominance on the basis that: the supplementary obligations were unrelated to the subject of the licensing agreements; Google was dominant in the worldwide market (excluding China) for Android app stores and national markets for general search services; the obligations left OEMS with no choice to license the Play Store and Search apps other than by accepting the supplementary obligations; and they were capable of restricting competition.[706] To satisfy the fourth criterion, the Commission demonstrated that the anti-fragmentation requirements had allowed Google to actually exclude non-compatible forks, and that the exclusion was harmful as it had permitted Google to enhance its dominance on national general search services markets and had stifled innovation.

[698] B. Edelman and D. Geradin, 'Android and Competition Law: Exploring and Assessing Google's Practices in Mobile' (2016) 12 *European Competition Journal* 159.

[699] P. Todd, 'Out of the Box: Illegal Tying and Google's Suite of Apps for the Android OS' (2017) 13 *European Competition Journal* 62.

[700] D. Auer, 'Appropriability and the European Commission's Android Investigation' (2017) 23 *Columbia J of European Law* 647. On appropriability more generally, see J. Baker, 'Evaluating Appropriability Defenses for the Exclusionary Conduct of Dominant Firms in Innovative Industries' (2016) 80 *Antitrust LJ* 431.

[701] Q. Wu and N. Philipsen, 'The Law and Economics of Tying in Digital Platforms: Comparing *Tencent* and *Android*' (2022) *J of Competition Law & Economics*, forthcoming.

[702] P. Siciliani, 'On the Law & Economics of the *Android* Case' 10 *JECLAP* 638 (2020).

[703] P. Ibáñez Colomo, 'The Android decision is out: the exciting legal stuff beneath the noise', Chillin' Competition Blog, 18 July 2018, <https://chillingcompetition.com/2018/07/18/the-android-decision-is-out-the-exciting-legal-stuff-beneath-the-noise-by-pablo/>.

[704] AT.40099, *Google Android* 18 July 2018, para. 1038.

[705] Ibid., para. 1011.

[706] Ibid., paras. 1019–1154.

This additional finding of abuse was also upheld on appeal. Without addressing the precise nature of the abusive behaviour, the GC did not challenge the Commission's decision to assess the anti-fragmentation clauses by reference to 'the conditions under which it may be established that a bundle of products or obligations is abusive', as established in *Microsoft*.[707] Moreover, it disputed neither the 'material existence' of the anti-fragmentation obligations[708] nor, specifically with respect to devices on which Google's apps were not pre-installed, the fact that the restrictions were unrelated to the subject of the contract.[709] Instead, the GC's scrutiny focused on the question of whether the practice 'restricted competition, or at least was capable of doing so'.[710] First, relying primarily on Google's own statements, the GC confirmed 'the anticompetitive nature of the practice concerned',[711] namely that it 'was knowingly implemented with the aim of limiting market access of non-compatible Android forks'.[712] This phrasing suggests that Google's perceived anti-competitive intention was a decisive factor here. Secondly, the GC endorsed the Commission's approach to the restriction of competition criterion, concluding that:

> . . . the Commission has sufficiently established that the AFAs prohibited their signatories from providing markets for non-compatible Android forks. That impediment to Google's direct competitors on the OS market, the effects of which are, moreover, reinforced by Google's policy on the conditions for marketing its APIs and its other proprietary apps, also helped to strengthen Google's dominant position on the markets for general search services and additionally proved detrimental to end users.[713]

During the administrative proceeding, Google had defended its anti-fragmentation policies vigorously, by reference to objective justifications that encompassed both claims of objective necessity (concerning the harms that fragmentation would cause to the Android ecosystem) and countervailing efficiencies.[714] These were considered in depth by the Commission, but ultimately rejected.[715] The GC again confirmed the Commission's approach.[716] In particular, it noted the narrow scope of the abuse, which was limited to the application of the anti-fragmentation obligations specifically to devices on which Google's apps were not pre-installed. In such circumstances, the sweeping arguments invoked by Google which related to the need to preserve both the integrity and the consumer welfare-enhancing elements of the Android system could be considered, essentially, as pretextual. Contrary to the gist of Google's arguments, the GC concluded that '[p]reventing the development of non-compatible Android forks cannot be regarded as being indispensable per se to the setting of compatibility standards that are to be applied within the Android ecosystem'.[717] Even if preserving the integrity of the Android ecosystem was a legitimate interest, the blanket anti-fragmentation obligations were a *disproportionate* means to achieve this valuable goal. That being the case, moreover, the consumer benefits generated by the Android system could not be counterbalanced against the identified restrictions of competition, which related solely to the effects of the clause *outside* the Android ecosystem.

(v) Tying after *Google Android*: The *Facebook Marketplace* investigation

In December 2022, the Commission sent a statement of objections to Meta (Facebook's parent company), alleging inter alia tying of its dominant social network platform with its online classified ads service, Facebook Marketplace.[718] The case represents a further development of the law regulating

[707] Case T-604/18, *Google Android* EU:T:2022:541, para. 812.
[708] Ibid., para. 834. [709] Ibid., para. 811. [710] Ibid., para. 835. [711] Ibid., paras. 837–842.
[712] Ibid., para. 842. [713] Ibid., para. 863. [714] AT.40099, *Google Android* 18 July 2018, paras. 1155–1183.
[715] Ibid. [716] Case T-604/18, *Google Android* EU:T:2022:541, paras. 876–891. [717] Ibid., para. 891.
[718] Commission Press Release, 'Antitrust: Commission sends Statement of Objections to Meta over abusive practices benefiting Facebook Marketplace', 19 December 2022.

tying in the digital economy to potentially encompass on-platform tying, i.e. where the various services facilitated by an online platform are tied to each other.[719] Following the approach in *Google Shopping*,[720] it is plausible that social network services and marketplace services can be construed as distinct products in line with the *Microsoft* case law.[721] What is perhaps more contentious, however, is the argument that Facebook users are 'coerced' into obtaining the Facebook Marketplace service, even if they never click on the Marketplace tab from the Facebook homepage.[722]

F. TYING AND BUNDLING IN THE GUIDANCE PAPER

(i) General

The Commission deals with tying and bundling in paragraphs 47–74 of the Guidance Paper. It does 'not approach tying practices from a presumption of harm'.[723] Instead, it states that it will normally take action where an undertaking is dominant in the tying market and: (a) the tying and tied products are distinct products; and (b) the tying practice is likely to lead to anti-competitive foreclosure.[724] The Guidance Paper says nothing about the lack of choice/coercion condition that was endorsed in *Microsoft*. This is perhaps a sensible omission, given the complications of using coercion as a condition for identifying abuse as illustrated by the facts of *Microsoft* itself.[725]

(ii) The Tying and the Tied Goods are Two Separate Products

Both the case law and the Guidance Paper recognise that there must be distinct products involved. The problem is that almost any product can be broken down into smaller parts:

> A coat can be sold without its buttons, a desk without its drawers . . . The market would come to a standstill, however, if the antitrust laws gave every customer a legal right to atomize his purchases as much as he chose.[726]

In some cases, the separation is clear. This was so in *Télémarketing*,[727] where the television company tied the use of its own sales agents to the sale of its advertising slots, and in *Napier Brown/British Sugar*,[728] where the undertaking adopted a delivered pricing policy which, by only providing the product and the delivery together, excluded competition on the separate transport market. It is more difficult, however, when there is a possibility that the undertaking is supplying a 'system' consisting of several components, as in *Hilti* and *Tetra Pak II*.[729] The issue is even more difficult in IT markets.

The test for whether there are distinct products is 'consumer demand': is there actual or potential consumer demand for the products separately? However, there may be demand for only one of them on a stand-alone basis. In *Microsoft*, the GC approved the Commission's statement that there can be

[719] D. Mândrescu, 'On-platform Tying or Another Case of Leveraging—A Discussion on Facebook Marketplace', *Kluwer Competition Law Blog*, 4 January 2023, <https://competitionlawblog.kluwercompetitionlaw.com/2023/01/04/on-platform-tying-or-another-case-of-leveraging-a-discussion-on-facebook-marketplace/>.

[720] AT.39740, *Google Search (Shopping)* 27 June 2017. See the discussion of market definition issues in Chap. 6.

[721] Mândrescu, n. 719. [722] Ibid. [723] Faull and Nikpay, n. 1, 4.529. [724] Guidance Paper, para. 50.

[725] Case T-201/04, *Microsoft* EU:T:2007:289, where the GC accepted that coercion existed merely where the customer was forced to take the tied product alongside the tying product, even if the tied product was provided at zero-price and the customer was not obliged to use it.

[726] Hovenkamp, n. 254, 536.

[727] Case 311/84, *Télémarketing* EU:C:1985:394. The CJ treated this as a refusal to supply: see Section 12.

[728] [1988] OJ L284/41. [729] See also Case T-427/08, *CEAHR* EU:T:2010:517.

no abusive tying in the absence of independent demand for the allegedly *tied* product.[730] It rejected the relevance of Microsoft's arguments that there was no demand for the tying product separately. Nevertheless, the inconvenient fact in *Microsoft* was that there was no longer any such demand, and so it proved once the remedy was implemented.[731] Arguably the lack of demand for a 'naked' version of Windows should have led to the adoption of a different separate product test in the first place.

The Guidance Paper states:

> 51. Whether the products will be considered by the Commission to be distinct depends on customer demand. Two products are distinct if, in the absence of tying or bundling, a substantial number of customers would purchase or would have purchased the tying product without also buying the tied product from the same supplier, thereby allowing stand-alone production for both the tying and the tied product. Evidence that two products are distinct could include direct evidence that, when given a choice, customers purchase the tying and the tied products separately from different sources of supply, or indirect evidence, such as the presence on the market of undertakings specialised in the manufacture or sale of the tied product without the tying product or of each of the products bundled by the dominant undertaking, or evidence indicating that undertakings with little market power, particularly in competitive markets, tend not to tie or not to bundle such products.

It is clear from the second sentence that the test is whether, without the tie, a substantial number of customers would purchase the tied product *from the same supplier*. That is not the same as asking whether there would be a demand for the tying product *if the tied product did not exist*. In *Hilti* and *Tetra Pak II* the answer to that would be 'no' because the machinery was useless without the consumables.[732]

The Guidance Paper does not mention the 'commercial usage' test in Article 102(d) which the CJ dismissed as not decisive in *Tetra Pak II*.[733] Nevertheless, the last sentence of paragraph 51 contemplates using evidence of the practices of undertakings with little market power in competitive markets, if relevant.

Consumer demand can change, sometimes very quickly, and nowhere more so than in the digital economy.[734] New products brought on to the market may become commonly integrated into others, or products may be introduced which in time are broken down and the elements sold separately. Where new products are concerned, the 'commercial usage' test is again unhelpful. If the purpose of the rules on tying is the welfare of consumers, then the inquiry about distinct products is just part of the overall assessment of whether 'the efficiencies of tying outweighs the inherent reduction in choice for the consumer'.[735] Although there are usually consumers whose wants are different from those of the majority, the consumer welfare test has to ensure that *most* consumers are better off and that consumer gains exceed consumer losses.

(iii) Anti-competitive Foreclosure

The Guidance Paper adopts an effects-based approach to tying. This section of the Guidance Paper must be read in the light of the overall principle that the Commission's enforcement activity is focused

[730] Case T-201/04, *Microsoft* EU:T:2007:289, para. 918. [731] See n. 652.

[732] The GC relied on *Hilti* and *Tetra Pak II* in paras. 920–921 of the *Microsoft* judgment. See Ahlborn and Evans, n. 652.

[733] Case C-333/94 P, *Tetra Pak II* EU:C:1996:436, para. 37.

[734] The Court has to consider the position at the date of the adoption of the decision, Case T-201/04, *Microsoft* EU:T:2007:289, para. 943.

[735] See the comments of Linklaters on the Discussion Paper, available on DG Comp's website at <http://ec.europa.eu/competition/antitrust/art82/127.pdf>, 17.

on foreclosure which is 'anti-competitive', so it is the effects on consumers which are the issue. The Commission sets out various factors for identifying anti-competitive foreclosure,[736] including whether the dominant undertaking's strategy is a lasting one, for example through technical tying;[737] whether the undertaking is dominant in respect of more than one product in the bundle;[738] and whether there are insufficient customers who buy the tied product alone to sustain competitors, in which case those customers may face higher prices.[739] The Commission is also concerned with inputs to a production process where a dominant undertaking uses tying to prevent customers avoiding a rise in the price of the tying product:[740]

> 56. If the tying and the tied product can be used in variable proportions as inputs to a production process, customers may react to an increase in price for the tying product by increasing their demand for the tied product while decreasing their demand for the tying product. By tying the two products the dominant undertaking may seek to avoid this substitution and as a result be able to raise its prices.

The Commission furthermore highlights the situation where the tying product market is regulated so that, constrained in its pricing freedom in the tying market, the undertaking may use tying to raise prices in the tied market instead.[741]

The Guidance Paper recognises both 'offensive' and 'defensive' leverage,[742] and one of the factors the Commission will consider is the effect of tying in reducing the number of alternative tied product suppliers to the prejudice of those trying to enter the tying market alone.[743]

(iv) Multi-product Rebates (Mixed Bundling)

The Guidance Paper deals specifically with multi-product rebates.[744] The Commission's approach to multi-product rebates is similar to its approach to rebates generally, which was discussed in the context of exclusive dealing.[745] It would prefer to examine whether the incremental revenue covers the incremental costs for each product in the discounted bundle but, since that is not usually possible, the Commission will normally use the incremental price as a proxy. It will normally intervene only if the price of each product in the dominant undertaking's bundle falls below LRAIC. This is the application of the AEC test to what is in essence a pricing issue. Where both the dominant undertaking and its competitors are selling identical bundles[746] the Commission will examine whether the price of the *bundle* is predatory.[747]

(v) Efficiencies

If the conditions laid down in paragraph 30 of the Guidance Paper for the 'efficiency defence' are fulfilled, the Commission will consider efficiency claims.[748] It will look at claims of savings in production or distribution, reduced transaction costs for customers and suppliers, and enabling pass-on of efficiencies stemming from the supplier producing or purchasing large quantities of the tied product. It will also examine the possibility that combining two products into a single new one might 'enhance the ability to bring such a product to the market to the benefit of consumers'.

[736] Which should be read in conjunction with those in Guidance Paper, para. 20. [737] Ibid., para. 53.
[738] Ibid., para. 54. [739] Ibid., para. 55. [740] Ibid., para. 56. [741] Ibid., para. 57.
[742] Ibid., para. 52. For offensive and defensive leverage, see Section 11.C. [743] Ibid., para. 58.
[744] Ibid., paras. 59–61. [745] See Section 10.C.
[746] Or could do so in a timely way without being deterred by possible additional costs.
[747] Guidance Paper, para. 61. [748] Ibid., para. 62.

12. REFUSAL TO SUPPLY

A. GENERAL

A dominant undertaking may commit an abuse where it refuses to supply its goods/services or to grant access to its facilities to third parties. Refusal to supply (also known as refusal to deal) is an 'exceptional' abuse: even dominant undertakings have no absolute duty to supply all those who request it. This is because holding refusal to supply to be an abuse can conflict with deep-seated principles of freedom of contract and property, which establish that one should be free to deal with whomever one chooses and to dispose of one's property as one chooses.[749] Forced sharing may also threaten the dominant undertaking's incentives to invest and innovate, and indeed those of its rivals, which would harm dynamic efficiency and welfare. However, in certain situations a refusal to supply *may* constitute an abuse. EU law is mainly concerned with vertically integrated undertakings dominant in an upstream market that refuse to supply competitors downstream, which is the only scenario considered in the Guidance Paper.

Conduct which can be classified under some other heading of abuse, such as tying, can often be conceptualised, alternatively, as a refusal to supply. In *Télémarketing*,[750] a condition whereby advertisers could buy advertising time on television only if they used the television company's own sales agency was both a refusal to supply and a tying practice, as was the delivered pricing policy in *Napier Brown/British Sugar*.[751] Yet the law has developed different principles in respect of tying and refusal to supply. In the Guidance Paper, the Commission states that it will deal with refusals to supply customers who do not agree to tying arrangements under the principles on tying and bundling.[752]

Refusal to supply also raises the question of the appropriate remedy. Regulation 1/2003 and the ECN+ Directive empower the Commission and national competition authorities, respectively, to impose proportionate behavioural or structural remedies in response to violations of Article 102 where appropriate.[753] Given the nature of the abuse at issue in refusal to supply cases, imposing a mandatory duty to deal is often the logical conclusion. Yet competition authorities or courts sometimes baulk at the quasi-'regulatory' nature of such interventions.[754]

B. THE EXCLUSION OF COMPETITORS FROM DOWNSTREAM MARKETS

(i) The Commercial Solvents Case

Commercial Solvents was the first case in which a refusal to supply was held to be capable of infringing Article 102. It involved the archetypal scenario of a vertically integrated (or soon-to-be vertically integrated) undertaking opting to refuse wholesale-level supply to a downstream competitor, in order to favour its own activities in the same market.

[749] See Jacobs AG in Case C-7/97, *Oscar Bronner* EU:C:1998:264.

[750] Case 311/84, *Télémarketing* EU:C:1985:394.

[751] *Napier Brown/British Sugar* [1988] OJ L284/41.

[752] Guidance Paper, para. 77.

[753] Discussed in detail in Chap. 13.

[754] See, in particular, the extract from P. Areeda, 'Essential Facilities: An Epithet in Need of Limiting Principles' (1990) 58 *Antitrust LJ* 841, at Section 12.B.iii.

Cases 6 and 7/73, *Istituto Chemioterapico Italiano SpA and Commercial Solvents Corp v Commission* EU:C:1974:18

Commercial Solvents (CSC) supplied aminobutanol, a raw material from which a derivative, ethambutol, could be produced. CSC's Italian subsidiary, Istituto, resold aminobutanol to Zoja, a pharmaceutical company which made ethambutol-based anti-TB drugs. In 1970, Zoja cancelled its orders for aminobutanol from Istituto, as independent distributors were supplying it more cheaply. When this proved unsatisfactory, Zoja placed new orders with Istituto. However, CSC had decided no longer to supply aminobutanol but only an upgraded product, dextroaminobutanol, which Istituto would convert into ethambutol itself, manufacturing its own ethambutol-based drugs. Zoja was therefore refused supplies. Zoja could not obtain supplies elsewhere worldwide, so complained to the Commission. The Commission held that CSC was dominant in the market for aminobutanol and had abused its position by refusing to supply Zoja. CSC appealed to the CJ, which upheld the finding of dominance on the raw material market[755] and the finding of abuse.

Court of Justice

25. . . . [A]n undertaking being in a dominant position as regards the production of raw material and therefore able to control the supply to manufacturers of derivatives, cannot, just because it decides to start manufacturing these derivatives (in competition with its former customers) act in such a way as to eliminate their competition which in the case in question, would amount to eliminating one of the principal manufacturers of ethambutol in the [internal market]. Since such conduct is contrary to the objectives expressed in Article [3(1)(g)] of the Treaty and set out in greater detail in Articles [101 and 102], it follows that an undertaking which has a dominant position in the market in raw materials and which, with the object of reserving such raw materials for manufacturing its own derivatives, refuses to supply a customer, which is itself a manufacturer of these derivatives, and therefore risks eliminating all competition on the part of this customer, is abusing its dominant position within the meaning of Article [102]. In this context it does not matter that the undertaking ceased to supply in the spring of 1970 because of the cancellation of the purchases by Zoja, because it appears from the applicants' own statement that, when the supplies provided for in the contract had been completed, the sale of aminobutanol would have stopped in any case.

The salient factors leading to the finding of abuse were thus:

- CSC was using its dominant position on the raw material market to affect competition on the derivatives market;
- CSC was refusing to supply an existing customer[756] because it wanted to compete downstream; and
- the refusal risked eliminating the customer from the downstream market.

CSC had, in effect, decided to integrate vertically. The CJ did not consider whether this strategy might produce efficiencies, and there was no discussion about possible benefits to end-users, namely consumers.

[755] See Chap. 6, Section 8.

[756] It was immaterial that Zoja had previously cancelled its purchases from Istituto (see para. 25, last sentence).

(ii) Case Law After *Commercial Solvents*

The *Commercial Solvents* principle was applied to the deliberate removal of a downstream competitor in *Napier Brown/British Sugar*,[757] where the dominant supplier of industrial sugar, which itself produced the derivative retail sugar, refused to supply industrial sugar to a competitor who was an existing customer. In *Télémarketing*, the CJ applied the principle to *new* customers deprived of the provision of a *service*.[758]

Another early application of the *Commercial Solvents* principle involved the supply of spare parts. The CJ established in *Hugin*[759] that an undertaking which refuses to supply spare parts and services for its product may infringe Article 102, even though it is dominant only in the market for its own spare parts.[760] In *Hugin* the undertaking stopped supplying a customer which repaired and serviced its machines, because it wanted to integrate vertically. The Commission held that the refusal was an abuse, because it would lead to an existing customer being unable to carry out a line of business. It did not consider questions of efficiencies or the advantages of vertical integration for users of Hugin machines. While the CJ annulled the decision due to an absence of inter-State effect, it did not suggest that Hugin's conduct was legitimate.

The CJ dealt obliquely with refusal to supply spare parts in two cases concerning the licensing of IPRs covering car parts, *Renault*[761] and *Volvo*,[762] considered further later in this chapter. In *Renault*, the Court stated that a refusal by the manufacturer to license would constitute an abuse if it amounted to an 'arbitrary refusal to deliver spare parts to independent repairers'.[763] Similar issues arose in *IBM Maintenance Services*, where the Commission was concerned that IBM's dealings with third party maintenance service providers constituted a constructive refusal to supply spare parts.[764]

(iii) The 'Essential Facilities' Concept in EU law

The *Commercial Solvents* principle and its subsequent application[765] created scope to recognise a version of the 'essential facilities' concept in EU law. The concept originates in early US antitrust law,[766] though its later application has been contentious.[767] The phenomenon occurs where competitors downstream require access to something owned or controlled by a vertically integrated dominant undertaking in order to provide products or services to customers—what is sometimes referred to as a 'bottleneck monopoly'. The Commission first used the expression 'essential facility' in its *B&I/Sealink* decision.[768] Citing, inter alia, the judgment in *Commercial Solvents*, the Commission held:

> A dominant undertaking which both owns or controls and itself uses an essential facility, i.e., a facility or infrastructure without access to which competitors cannot provide services to their customers, and

[757] *Napier Brown/British Sugar* [1988] OJ L284/41.

[758] Case 311/84, *Télémarketing* EU:C:1985:394, paras. 25–27.

[759] Case 22/78, *Hugin* EU:C:1979:138.

[760] The CJ annulled the decision because it found no effect on inter-Member State trade, but it confirmed the finding of dominance. As discussed in Chap. 6, however, the spare parts of a particular brand do not always constitute a separate relevant market.

[761] Case 53/87, *CICCRA v Renault* EU:C:1988:472.

[762] Case 238/87, *AB Volvo v Erik Veng* EU:C:1988:477.

[763] Case 53/87, *CICCRA* EU:C:1988:472, para. 16.

[764] COMP/39.692, *IBM Maintenance Services* 13 December 2011. The case was concluded on the basis of commitments as to IBM's future practices and contractual conditions.

[765] Including the Commission Decisions in *London-European Sabena* [1988] OJ L317/47 and *British-Midland/Aer Lingus* [1992] OJ L96/34.

[766] First applied in *United States v Terminal Railroad Association*, 224 US 383 (1912). Other important Supreme Court decisions applying the doctrine include *Associated Press v United States*, 326 US 1 (1945), and *Lorain Journal Co v United States*, 342 US 143 (1951).

[767] See *Verizon v Trinko*, 540 US 398 (2004), discussed later in this subsection.

[768] IV/34.174, *Sealink/B&I Holyhead: Interim Measures* 11 June 1992.

> which refuses its competitors access to that facility or grants access to competitors only on terms less favourable than those which it gives its own services, thereby placing the competitors at a competitive disadvantage, infringes Article [102], if the other conditions of that Article are met . . .[769]

On the facts, this meant that the dominant defendant, which operated both a port and a ferry company, could not alter the sailing schedules of the latter to disadvantage other ferry companies using its port. The basic principle of a duty to provide non-discriminatory access to an essential facility was developed further in two additional port cases, *Sea Containers Ltd/Stena*[770] and *Port of Rødby*.[771]

The decision in *European Night Services*[772] was taken under Article 101 but raised similar issues. Several European railway undertakings formed a joint venture to provide overnight passenger rail services between the UK and continental Europe. The Commission granted an exemption conditional on the parent companies providing locomotives, train crews, and train paths to any other undertaking wishing to compete in the running of a similar service, on the same terms. The GC annulled the decision, inter alia,[773] in respect of the condition as regards the locomotives and train crews. It held that the Commission had not properly considered or explained why the requirement to supply was appropriate. The GC expressly referred to 'essential facilities'. It stressed that a facility can be essential only if there are no substitutes. Merely being advantageous for competitors is insufficient. This judgment showed a disinclination to apply the concept too widely, a disinclination vindicated by the CJ's *Bronner* judgment[774] two months later.

In adopting the language of essential facilities, the Commission drew an implicit link to the concept as it has developed in the US case law. Yet the precise parameters of the essential facilities doctrine remain disputed in the US. In the important *Trinko* case in 2004, the Supreme Court held, not entirely convincingly,[775] that it had 'never recognised such a doctrine'.[776] Unlike the GC,[777] the CJ too has not adopted the expression, deploying instead the term 'indispensable'. Much of the discourse on refusal to supply nonetheless continues to utilise the concept.[778] It is therefore a convenient expression in this context, provided that one does not accord it particular legal significance.

The reasons for the Supreme Court's ambivalence towards the essential facilities doctrine were touched upon in the introduction to this section. Defining a facility or infrastructure as 'essential' may result in the owner being forced to share with rivals. This is a severe interference with an undertaking's property rights, which can only be justified where there would otherwise be a serious detriment to competition irremediable by less intrusive measures. There must be some way of identifying assets to which access by competitors is truly 'essential', rather than merely desirable. Even when these are identified, there may be practical problems about access or sharing. Some facilities have limited capacity, and the question arises as to *which* competitors should receive access. The terms on which access is given may also raise problems. If the parties are left to settle their own terms, the

[769] Ibid., para. 41. [770] IV/34.689, *Sea Containers Ltd/Stena Sealink* [1994] OJ L15/8.

[771] *Port of Rødby (Euro-port) v Denmark* [1994] OJ L55/5. See also COMP/35.388, *Morlaix (Port of Roscoff)* [1995] 5 CMLR 177.

[772] [1994] OJ L259/20.

[773] Cases T-374–375, 384, and 388/94, *European Night Services* EU:T:1998:198. Other aspects of this case are dealt with in Chap. 5.

[774] Case C-7/97, *Bronner* EU:C:1998:569. [775] See the case law listed at n. *.

[776] *Verizon v Trinko*, 540 US 398 (2004).

[777] Cases T-374/94 etc., *European Night Services* EU:T:1998:198, para. 191, T-52/00, *Coe Clerici Logistics SpA* EU:T:2003:168, para. 62, and Case T-612/17 *Google Shopping* EU:T:2021:763, para. 215.

[778] See e.g. Crémer, de Montjoye, and Schweitzer, n. 186, 66, where the authors, somewhat perplexingly, use the concept in lieu of the legally recognised notion of indispensability.

owner of the facility may impose a price which is prohibitively high.[779] If the terms are to be set by the competition agency or court, it ends up acting as a price regulator.[780]

In largely rejecting the essential facilities doctrine, the Supreme Court in *Trinko* cited with approval an influential article by Areeda, which argued that it should be treated with the greatest circumspection, in particular because of the dangerous disincentive to innovation. The extract below sets out the conclusions of his critical survey, suggesting 'limiting principles' to keep the doctrine in check.

P. Areeda, 'Essential Facilities: An Epithet in Need of Limiting Principles' (1990) 58 *Antitrust LJ* 841, 852–853

I conclude by offering six principles that should limit application of the essential facilities concept.

(1) There is no general duty to share. Compulsory access, if it exists at all, is and should be very exceptional . . .

(2) A single firm's facility, as distinct from that of a combination, is 'essential' only when it is both critical to the plaintiff's competitive vitality and the plaintiff is essential for competition in the marketplace. 'Critical to the plaintiff's competitive vitality' means that the plaintiff cannot compete effectively without it and that duplication or practical alternatives are not available.

(3) No one should be forced to deal unless doing so is likely substantially to improve competition in the marketplace by reducing price or by increasing output or innovation. Such an improvement is unlikely (a) when it would chill desirable activity; (b) [when] the plaintiff is not an actual or potential competitor; (c) when the plaintiff merely substitutes itself for the monopolist or shares the monopolist's gains; or (d) when the monopolist already has the usual privilege of charging the monopoly price for its resources . . .

(4) Even when all these conditions are satisfied, denial of access is never per se unlawful; legitimate business purpose always saves the defendant. What constitutes legitimacy is a question of law for the courts. Although the defendant bears the burden of coming forward with a legitimate business purpose, the plaintiff bears the burden of persuading the tribunal that any such claim is unjustified.

(5) The defendant's intention is seldom illuminating, because every firm that denies its facilities to rivals does so to limit competition with itself and increase its profits. Any instruction on intention must ask whether the defendant had an intention to exclude by *improper* means. To get ahead in the marketplace is not, itself the kind of intention that contaminates conduct . . .

(6) No court should impose a duty to deal that it cannot explain or adequately and reasonably supervise. The problem should be deemed [irremediable] by antitrust law when compulsory access requires the court to assume the day-to-day controls characteristic of a regulatory agency. Remedies may be practical (a) when admission to a consortium is at stake, especially at the outset, (b) when divestiture is otherwise appropriate and effective, or (c) when . . . a regulatory agency already exists to control the terms of dealing. However, the availability of a remedy is not reason to grant one. Compulsory sharing should remain exceptional.

C. THE RISE AND FALL OF THE *BRONNER* CRITERIA

While *Commercial Solvents* was the starting point for the assessment of refusal to supply under Article 102, the 1998 judgment of the CJ in *Oscar Bronner* offered a more systematic appraisal of the

[779] See Case C-242/95, *GT-Link A/S v De Danske Statsbaner (DSB)* EU:C:1997:376, where the CJ held that excessive duties levied by a public undertaking on a ferry company in breach of Art. 106, in conjunction with Art. 102, had to be repaid.

[780] For the difficulty in settling the terms of supply, see Case T-167/08, *Microsoft* EU:T:2012:323.

circumstances in which access can be ordered. The '*Bronner* criteria'[781] or '*Bronner* conditions'[782] provide what was long seen as the default legal test for assessing refusal to deal cases. Yet recent case law increasingly paints it as 'a special case within the regulatory landscape of Article 102',[783] and its scope of application has been progressively narrowed. In this section, we discuss both the criteria and the increasingly broad range of exceptions to their application.

Bronner published a newspaper, *Der Standard*, which had a 3.6 per cent share of the daily newspaper market in Austria in terms of circulation and 6 per cent in terms of advertising revenue. Mediaprint published two daily newspapers in Austria, which together had a combined market share of 46.8 per cent of circulation and 42 per cent of advertising revenues. For the distribution of its newspapers, Mediaprint established a nationwide home-delivery scheme. Bronner wanted Mediaprint to include *Der Standard* in the scheme, but Mediaprint refused. Mediaprint delivered another newspaper that it did not publish, but it did both the printing *and* distribution for that paper. Bronner sought a court order requiring Mediaprint to include *Der Standard* in its home-delivery service in return for reasonable remuneration. It claimed that other methods of sale such as postal delivery were less advantageous, and that, given its small circulation, it would be unprofitable to organise its own home-delivery service. The Austrian court referred to the CJ two questions as to whether such conduct amounted to an abuse of dominance.[784]

Both the Advocate General and the CJ referenced the judgment in *Magill*,[785] which involved a refusal to license IPRs and is considered in Section 12.D. Briefly, *Magill* concerned an Irish publisher who wanted to publish a composite television listings magazine, but was refused access by broadcasters to the relevant programming schedules, which were protected by copyright under Irish and UK law. The CJ found that, in 'exceptional circumstances',[786] a refusal to supply copyrighted material could constitute an abuse, and it identified four cumulative circumstances that supported a finding of abuse on the facts. The approach in *Magill* subsequently informed the approach in *Bronner*.

Case C-7/97, *Oscar Bronner GmbH & Co KG v Mediaprint*

The Bronner case was notable, first, for the Opinion of Advocate General Jacobs, who urged that the essential facilities concept should be confined within strict limits. He emphasised that the primary purpose of Article 102 is to protect consumers, not competitors.

Advocate General Jacobs (EU:C:1998:264)

56. First, it is apparent that the right to choose one's trading partners and freely to dispose of one's property are generally recognized principles in the laws of the Member States, in some cases with constitutional status. Incursions on those rights require careful justification.

57. Secondly, the justification in terms of competition policy for interfering with a dominant undertaking's freedom to contract often requires a careful balancing of conflicting considerations. In the long term it is generally pro-competitive and in the interest of consumers to allow a company to

[781] So referred to by the Commission in AT.39740, *Google Search (Shopping)* 27 June 2017—where, however, the Commission refused to apply the relevant criteria to the abusive conduct. See also Case T-851/14 *Slovak Telekom* EU:T:2018:929, para. 114.

[782] AT.39849, *BEH Gas*, 17 December 2019, para. 445.

[783] Opinion in Case C-165/19 P, *Slovak Telekom* EU:C:2020:678, para. 55.

[784] Although there was no appreciable effect on inter-State trade, the reference was admissible insofar as the relevant Austrian competition rule mirrored Art. 102: see paras. 12–22 of the judgment.

[785] Cases C-241–242/91 P, *RTE & ITP v Commission* EU:C:1995:98, known as '*Magill*'.

[786] Ibid., para. 50.

retain for its own use facilities which it has developed for the purpose of its business. For example, if access to a production, purchasing or distribution facility were allowed too easily there would be no incentive for a competitor to develop competing facilities. Thus while competition was increased in the short term it would be reduced in the long term. Moreover, the incentive for a dominant undertaking to invest in efficient facilities would be reduced if its competitors were, upon request, able to share the benefits. Thus the mere fact that by retaining a facility for its own use a dominant undertaking retains an advantage over a competitor cannot justify requiring access to it.

58. Thirdly, in assessing this issue it is important not to lose sight of the fact that the primary purpose of Article [102] is to prevent distortion of competition—and in particular to safeguard the interests of consumers—rather than to protect the position of particular competitors. It may therefore, for example, be unsatisfactory, in a case in which a competitor demands access to a raw material in order to be able to compete with the dominant undertaking on a downstream market in a final product, to focus solely on the latter's market power on the upstream market and conclude that its conduct in reserving to itself the downstream market is automatically an abuse. Such conduct will not have an adverse impact on consumers unless the dominant undertaking's final product is sufficiently insulated from competition to give it market power.

Court of Justice (EU:C:1998:569)

38. Although in *Commercial Solvents* v. *Commission* and *CBEM*, cited above, the Court of Justice held the refusal by an undertaking holding a dominant position in a given market to supply an undertaking with which it was in competition in a neighbouring market with raw materials (*Commercial Solvents* v. *Commission*, paragraph 25) and services (*CBEM*, paragraph 26) respectively, which were indispensable to carrying on the rival's business, to constitute an abuse, it should be noted, first, that the Court did so to the extent that the conduct in question was likely to eliminate all competition on the part of that undertaking.

39. Secondly, in *Magill*, at paragraphs 49 and 50, the Court held that refusal by the owner of an intellectual property right to grant a licence, even if it is the act of an undertaking holding a dominant position, cannot in itself constitute abuse of a dominant position, but that the exercise of an exclusive right by the proprietor may, in exceptional circumstances, involve an abuse.

40. In *Magill*, the Court found such exceptional circumstances in the fact that the refusal in question concerned a product (information on the weekly schedules of certain television channels) the supply of which was indispensable for carrying on the business in question (the publishing of a general television guide), in that, without that information, the person wishing to produce such a guide would find it impossible to publish it and offer it for sale (paragraph 53), the fact that such refusal prevented the appearance of a new product for which there was a potential consumer demand (paragraph 54), the fact that it was not justified by objective considerations (paragraph 55), and that it was likely to exclude all competition in the secondary market of television guides (paragraph 56).

41. Therefore, even if that case-law on the exercise of an intellectual property right were applicable to the exercise of any property right whatever, it would still be necessary, for the *Magill* judgment to be effectively relied upon in order to plead the existence of an abuse within the meaning of Article [102] in a situation such as that which forms the subject-matter of the first question, not only that the refusal of the service comprised in home delivery be likely to eliminate all competition in the daily newspaper market on the part of the person requesting the service and that such refusal be incapable of being objectively justified, but also that the service in itself be indispensable to carrying on that person's business, inasmuch as there is no actual or potential substitute in existence for that home-delivery scheme.

42. That is certainly not the case even if, as in the case which is the subject of the main proceedings, there is only one nationwide home-delivery scheme in the territory of a Member State and, moreover,

> the owner of that scheme holds a dominant position in the market for services constituted by that scheme or of which it forms part.
>
> 43. In the first place, it is undisputed that other methods of distributing daily newspapers, such as by post and through sale in shops and at kiosks, even though they may be less advantageous for the distribution of certain newspapers, exist and are used by the publishers of those daily newspapers.
>
> 44. Moreover, it does not appear that there are any technical, legal or even economic obstacles capable of making it impossible, or even unreasonably difficult, for any other publisher of daily newspapers to establish, alone or in co-operation with other publishers, its own nationwide home-delivery scheme and use it to distribute its own daily newspapers.
>
> 45. It should be emphasised in that respect that, in order to demonstrate that the creation of such a system is not a realistic potential alternative and that access to the existing system is therefore indispensable, it is not enough to argue that it is not economically viable by reason of the small circulation of the daily newspaper or newspapers to be distributed.
>
> 46. For such access to be capable of being regarded as indispensable, it would be necessary at the very least to establish . . . that it is not economically viable to create a second home-delivery scheme for the distribution of daily newspapers with a circulation comparable to that of the daily newspapers distributed by the existing scheme.
>
> 47. In the light of the foregoing considerations, the answer to the first question must be that the refusal by a press undertaking which holds a very large share of the daily newspaper market in a Member State and operates the only nationwide newspaper home-delivery scheme in that Member State to allow the publisher of a rival newspaper, which by reason of its small circulation is unable either alone or in co-operation with other publishers to set up and operate its own home-delivery scheme in economically reasonable conditions, to have access to that scheme for appropriate remuneration does not constitute abuse of a dominant position within the meaning of Article [102].

In *Bronner*, the CJ took a restrictive view of the obligation to grant access under Article 102. It reiterated the 'exceptional circumstances' approach adopted in *Magill*.[787] It avoided using the term 'essential facilities', despite its use by the Advocate General, preferring instead the term 'indispensable'. Importantly, in paragraph 41, the CJ identified three key factors which must be present before the refusal could be an abuse:

- first, the refusal would have to be likely to eliminate all competition in the downstream market from the person requesting access;
- secondly, the refusal must be incapable of objective justification;
- thirdly, the access must be indispensable to carrying on the other person's business, meaning that there is no actual or potential substitute available.

These criteria were patently not fulfilled on the facts of *Bronner*.

Bronner was, arguably, an easy case. It concerned a facility developed by a private undertaking with its own resources and a situation in which the rival was operating satisfactorily on the downstream market without the requested access. If the CJ had considered this to be a situation suitable for application of the essential facilities doctrine, then all dominant firms owning or controlling a facility potentially useful to rivals might be at risk, and incentives to innovation would be seriously undermined. Nonetheless, the CJ made it clear that facilities should not be deemed 'indispensable' too

[787] Case C-7/97 *Bronner* EU:C:1998:569, paras. 39 and 40.

readily nor access required more generally too easily. The essential facilities doctrine was 'reined in' in *Bronner*,[788] where the CJ showed itself alive to the potential harm which can arise from an over-broad application of any antitrust duty to deal.

The *Bronner* criteria establish the conditions by which liability under Article 102 may arise based on a refusal to supply. They are not solely concerned with the remedy that may be imposed subsequently should breach be established. This point was disputed by the Commission in its *Google Shopping* decision, in which it argued that 'the *Bronner* criteria are irrelevant in a situation . . . where bringing to an end the infringement does not involve imposing a duty on the dominant undertaking to transfer an asset or enter into agreements with persons with whom it has not chosen to contract'.[789] On appeal, the GC rejected this contention, stating instead that '[t]here can be no automatic link between the criteria for the legal classification of the abuse and the corrective measures enabling it to be remedied'.[790]

Yet the *Bronner* judgment left many questions unanswered. The Court did not address problems about pricing, or how a facility owner should deal with competing claims for access, or the role of competition authorities in such scenarios. It did, however, emphasise that an obligation to grant access arises only exceptionally, and that the key issues are *indispensability* and the subsequent *elimination of competition*. Yet later case law and Commission practice has not always applied the criteria with the same rigour (and, perhaps, scepticism) as the *Bronner* Court itself. In what follows, the *Bronner* criteria are considered in turn, in order to understand their significance and how these elements have been interpreted and applied in practice. The increasingly broad array of circumstances in which the criteria have been deemed *not* to apply are similarly outlined and assessed.

(i) What Constitutes a 'Refusal' to Supply?

The concept of refusal to supply clearly encompasses outright refusals by a dominant undertaking to contract with third parties, whether to cease existing supply or to decline to supply a new customer. The facts of *Bronner* itself present an archetypal example. There is no need to demonstrate that the refusal is motivated by an anti-competitive objective (although, where established, this can be taken into account).[791] The mere fact that a dominant undertaking is not immediately receptive to a request for supply does not necessarily constitute a 'refusal', however. In *Topps*, the would-be competitor sent a pro forma letter to various sporting organisations seeking licensing rights to major sports events, and, having received no response, neglected to follow up for several months. In the circumstances, the GC held that those efforts could not 'reasonably be considered a serious effort to begin commercial negotiations', so that the organisations' failure to respond could not amount to a refusal which might constitute an abuse.[792]

Alternatively, a refusal to deal might arise in a 'constructive' sense, where the dominant firm nominally indicates willingness to contract with would-be customers, yet where the terms for access or the quality of supply delivered amount, in substance, to a refusal to do so. This possibility was acknowledged by the Commission in its original Guidance Paper, which stated that '[c]onstructive refusal could, for example, take the form of unduly delaying or otherwise degrading the supply of the product

[788] As the Commission recognised in IV/36.431, *Info-Lab* (1999), where Ricoh, a photocopier manufacturer, refused to supply a toner producer with empty cartridges compatible with its machines. The Commission held that Ricoh was not dominant, but that, even if it was, in the light of *Bronner* such forced cooperation could be envisaged only under exceptional circumstances.

[789] AT.39740, *Google Shopping*, 27 June 2017, para. 651.

[790] Case T-612/17 *Google Shopping* EU:T:2021:763, para. 244. For arguments defending this position, see N. Dunne, 'Dispensing with Indispensability' (2020) 16 *J of Competition Law and Economics* 74, 109–113.

[791] Case T-301/04, *Clearstream Banking v Commission* EU:T:2009:317, para. 142.

[792] Case T-699/14, *Topps Europe Ltd v Commission* EU:T:2017:2, para. 143.

or involve the imposition of unreasonable conditions in return for the supply'.[793] Constructive refusals to supply can cause longer-term harm to competition in the same manner and circumstances as explicit refusals, and antitrust intervention raises the same concerns from efficiency and equity perspectives.

It was previously understood that the refusal to deal concept encompassed both outright and constructive refusals, and that the *Bronner* criteria comprised the applicable legal standard in either circumstance. This was the approach adopted by the Commission's original Guidance Paper,[794] and in its earlier enforcement practice. An example is *Telekomunikacja Polska*, where the Commission found a constructive refusal, contrary to Article 102, where the defendant telecommunications company imposed unnecessary obstacles to the regulated wholesale-level supply of access to its broadband infrastructure. These included enforcing unreasonable supply conditions, artificially delaying negotiations, rejecting orders for unjustifiable reasons, and refusing to provide interconnection information in an accurate and usable format.[795] In *ARA Foreclosure*, an abusive refusal arose where the defendant did not reject outright requests for access to its infrastructure (for collection and recycling of packaging waste), but instead placed a positive obligation upon any would-be new entrant to prove the non-duplicability of that infrastructure on a region-by-region basis. The impracticality of this obligation meant that it constituted, in reality, implicit rejection of claims for access.[796] The constructive refusal to supply doctrine has been applied most expansively in the energy sector, where a broad array of strategic market conduct was conceptualised and prosecuted as implicit refusal to grant access to essential infrastructure.[797] Of note is *ENI*,[798] where the dominant natural gas company was alleged to have engaged in a three-pronged strategy for refusal to supply, which comprised: capacity-hoarding (managing and allocating capacity in a deliberately inefficient manner); capacity-degradation (intentionally providing access on a short-term basis to frustrate longer-term business planning by rivals); and the strategic limitation of investment in transport capacity (meaning that, years later, ENI had insufficient capacity available to meet the requirements of rivals). The latter theory of harm, in particular, has distinct regulatory undertones, and raises the question of the possible existence of a 'duty to invest' as well as a 'duty to supply' under Article 102.[799]

In these earlier constructive refusal to deal cases, and following the approach that it had advocated in its original Guidance Paper, the Commission analysed the acceptability of the dominant undertaking's behaviour through the lens of the *Bronner* criteria.[800] Yet bolstered by its success in persuading the CJ to decouple margin squeeze from refusal to supply in *TeliaSonera*,[801] the Commission began to argue that constructive refusals should be subject to a different, essentially less demanding legal standard than actual refusals.[802] In *TeliaSonera*, the CJ had held that 'it cannot be inferred from . . . [the *Bronner*] judgment that the conditions to be met in order to establish that a refusal to supply is abusive must necessarily also apply when assessing the abusive nature of conduct which consists in supplying services

[793] Guidance Paper, para.79. [794] Ibid., paras 79–81.

[795] COMP/39.525, *Telekomunikacja Polska* 22 June 2011; upheld on appeal in Cases T-486/11, *Orange Polska v Commission* EU:T:2015:1002, and C-123/16 P, *Orange Polska v Commission* EU:C:2018:590.

[796] AT39759, *ARA Foreclosure* 20 September 2016, para. 102.

[797] Including COMP/39.316, *Gaz de France* Decision of 3 December 2009; COMP/39.315, *ENI* Decision of 29 September 2010; COMP/39.402, *RWE—Gas Foreclosure* Commitments 18 March 2009 [2009] OJ C133/10; COMP/39.351, *Swedish Interconnectors* Decision of 4 April 2010; COMP/39.388 and 39.389, *German Electricity Markets* Decision of 26 November 2008; and COMP/39.317, *E.On Gas* Decision of 4 May 2010.

[798] COMP/39.315, *ENI* Decision of 29 September 2010.

[799] The commitments procedure is discussed in Chap. 13, Section 6.E.

[800] See COMP/39.525, *Telekomunikacja Polska* 22 June 2011, paras. 700–705; AT39759, *ARA Foreclosure* 20 September 2016, para. 76; and COMP/39.315, *ENI* 29 September 2010, paras. 39–44. [801] See Section 9.

[802] See e.g. AT39523, *Slovak Telekom* 15 October 2014 and AT.39849, *BEH Gas* 17 December 2019.

or selling goods on conditions which are disadvantageous or on which there might be no purchaser'.[803] The CJ then asserted that the latter 'may, in itself, constitute an independent form of abuse distinct from that of refusal to supply'.[804] As we saw in Section 9, the immediate relevance of this statement was that the CJ confirmed that margin squeeze is a stand-alone category of abuse, distinct from refusal to supply (unlike in the US), and subject to a specific legal test premised upon demonstrating likely exclusion of as efficient competitors and anti-competitive effects. Yet the Commission argued that the implications of the ruling went further, essentially restricting the relevance of the heightened *Bronner* criteria only to express refusals to supply. In *Slovak Telekom*, the CJ agreed.

Case C-165/19 P, *Slovak Telekom, a.s. v European Commission* EU:C:2021:239

ST was a formerly State-owned telecommunications incumbent. By infringement decision in 2014, the Commission found that it engaged both in a margin squeeze[805] and a constructive refusal to supply access to its unbundled local loops, the latter effected through a mesh of 'unfair'[806] and 'unacceptable'[807] terms and conditions. ST argued that the refusal to supply claim should be assessed under the *Bronner* criteria; the Commission rejected this on the basis that *TeliaSonera* restricted application of those conditions purely to cases of outright refusal.[808] On appeal, the GC agreed that the language of *TeliaSonera* 'suggests that the exclusionary practices to which reference was therefore made concerned not solely a margin squeeze, but also other business practices capable of producing unlawful exclusionary effects for current or potential competitors, like those classified by the Commission as an implicit refusal to supply'.[809] Yet having determined that the existence of a regulatory duty to supply rendered the *Bronner* criteria irrelevant, a point discussed in Section 12.B.iii, the GC's holding on the constructive refusal point had a tentative quality. ST appealed the GC's judgment to the CJ, which endorsed the Commission's reasoning in resounding terms.

Court of Justice

42. The examination of the abusive nature of a dominant undertaking's practice pursuant to Article 102 TFEU must be carried out by taking into consideration all the specific circumstances of the case (. . . *TeliaSonera*, paragraph 68; and . . . *Post Danmark*, C-23/14, EU:C:2015:651, paragraph 68, and . . . *MEO—Serviços de Comunicações e Multimédia*, C-525/16, EU:C:2018:270, paragraphs 27 and 28).

43. As follows from paragraph 37 of the judgment in *Bronner*, the case which gave rise to that judgment concerned the question whether the refusal of the owner of the only nationwide home-delivery scheme in the territory of a Member State, which uses that scheme to distribute its own daily newspapers, to allow the publisher of a rival newspaper access to it constituted an abuse of a dominant position, within the meaning of Article 102 TFEU, on the ground that such refusal deprives that competitor of a means of distribution judged essential for the sale of its products.

44. In response to that question, the Court found, in paragraph 41 of that judgment, that for that refusal to have constituted an abuse of a dominant position, it would have been necessary not only that the refusal of the service comprised in home delivery were likely to eliminate all competition in the daily newspaper market on the part of the person requesting the service and that such refusal were incapable of being objectively justified, but also that the service in itself were indispensable to carrying on that person's business, inasmuch as there was no actual or potential substitute in existence for that home-delivery scheme.

[803] Case C-52/09, *Konkurrensverket v TeliaSonera Sverige AB* EU:C:2011:83, para. 55. [804] Ibid., para. 56.
[805] The margin squeeze aspect of the case was discussed in Section 9.
[806] AT39523, *Slovak Telekom* 15 October 2014, para. 389. [807] Ibid., para. 820.
[808] Ibid., paras. 365–371. [809] Case T-851/14, *Slovak Telekom* EU:T:2018:929, para. 126.

45. The imposition of those conditions was justified by the specific circumstances of that case which consisted in a refusal by a dominant undertaking to give a competitor access to infrastructure that it had developed for the needs of its own business, to the exclusion of any other conduct.

46. In that regard . . . a finding that a dominant undertaking abused its position due to a refusal to conclude a contract with a competitor has the consequence of forcing that undertaking to conclude a contract with that competitor. Such an obligation is especially detrimental to the freedom of contract and the right to property of the dominant undertaking, since an undertaking, even if dominant, remains, in principle, free to refuse to conclude contracts and to use the infrastructure it has developed for its own needs (see, by analogy, . . . *Volvo*, 238/87, EU:C:1988:477, paragraph 8).

47. Furthermore, while, in the short term, an undertaking being held liable for having abused its dominant position due to a refusal to conclude a contract with a competitor has the consequence of encouraging competition, by contrast, in the long term, it is generally favourable to the development of competition and in the interest of consumers to allow a company to reserve for its own use the facilities that it has developed for the needs of its business. If access to a production, purchasing or distribution facility were allowed too easily, there would be no incentive for competitors to develop competing facilities. In addition, a dominant undertaking would be less inclined to invest in efficient facilities if it could be bound, at the mere request of its competitors, to share with them the benefits deriving from its own investments.

48. Consequently, where a dominant undertaking refuses to give access to an infrastructure that it has developed for the needs of its own business, the decision to oblige that undertaking to grant that access cannot be justified, at a competition policy level, unless the dominant undertaking has a genuinely tight grip on the market concerned.

49. The application, to a particular case, of . . . the condition relating to the indispensability of the access to the dominant undertaking's infrastructure, allows the competent authority or national court to determine whether that undertaking has a genuinely tight grip on the market by virtue of that infrastructure. Thus, that undertaking may be forced to give a competitor access to an infrastructure that it has developed for the needs of its own business only where such access is indispensable to the business of such a competitor, namely where there is no actual or potential substitute for that infrastructure.

50. By contrast, where a dominant undertaking gives access to its infrastructure but makes that access, provision of services or sale of products subject to unfair conditions, the conditions laid down . . . in *Bronner* do not apply. It is true that where access to such an infrastructure – or service or input – is indispensable in order to allow competitors of the dominant undertaking to operate profitably in a downstream market, this increases the likelihood that unfair practices on that market will have at least potentially anticompetitive effects and will constitute abuse within the meaning of Article 102 TFEU (. . . *Deutsche Telekom* v *Commission*, C-280/08 P, EU:C:2010:603, paragraph 234, and . . . *TeliaSonera*, paragraphs 70 and 71). Nevertheless, as regards practices other than a refusal of access, the absence of such an indispensability is not in itself decisive for the purposes of the examination of potentially abusive practices on the part of a dominant undertaking (. . . *TeliaSonera*, paragraph 72).

51. While such practices can constitute a form of abuse where they are able to give rise to at least potentially anticompetitive effects, or exclusionary effects, on the markets concerned, they cannot be equated to a simple refusal to allow a competitor access to the infrastructure, since the competent competition authority or national court will not have to force the dominant undertaking to give access to its infrastructure, as that access has already been granted. The measures that would be taken in such a context will thus be less detrimental to the freedom of contract of the dominant undertaking and to its right to property than forcing it to give access to its infrastructure where it has reserved that infrastructure for the needs of its own business.

52. To that effect, the Court of Justice has previously held, in . . . *Telefónica and Telefónica de España* v *Commission* (C-295/12 P, EU:C:2014:2062), that the conditions laid down by the Court of Justice in paragraph 41 of the judgment in *Bronner*, and in particular the condition relating to the indispensability

of the access, did not apply in the case of abuse in the form of a margin squeeze of competitor operators in a downstream market.

53. To the same effect, the Court of Justice held, in paragraph 58 of the judgment in *TeliaSonera*, in essence, that it cannot be required that the examination of the abusive nature of any type of conduct of a dominant undertaking towards its competitors be systematically carried out in the light of the conditions laid down by the Court of Justice in the judgment in *Bronner*, which concerned a refusal to provide a service. Therefore, the General Court was right to find, . . . that in paragraph 58 of the judgment in *TeliaSonera*, the Court of Justice was not referring only to the particular form of abuse constituted by a margin squeeze of competitor operators in a downstream market when it assessed the practices to which the conditions of the judgment in *Bronner* did not apply.

The CJ accordingly rejected the characterisation of constructive refusals to supply as *refusals* as such. It did not go as far as Advocate General Saugmandsgaard Øe, who had dismissed the 'spuriousness' of the notion of constructive or 'implicit' refusal,[810] and had chastised the Commission for its reluctance to disown the concept.[811] Yet in restricting the applicability of the *Bronner* criteria solely to situations where a finding of infringement might have 'the consequence of forcing that undertaking to conclude a contract with that competitor'[812] *only where this did not already exist*, the CJ effectively limited the category of 'refusal to supply' under Article 102 merely to cases involving a refusal in the most literal and explicit of senses. Anything less than an outright refusal should thus be treated merely as 'abusive commercial terms',[813] which can be scrutinised regardless of the competitor's necessity to gain access to the defendant's asset or service.

In doing so, the CJ maintained that it was simply following the legal path embarked upon in *TeliaSonera* to its logical conclusion. It reiterated the risk, raised by the Commission's Legal Service during their intervention in the *TeliaSonera* case,[814] that to hold otherwise would mean, in effect, 'that the examination of the abusive nature of any type of conduct of a dominant undertaking towards its competitors be systematically carried out in the light of the conditions laid down . . . in *Bronner*'.[815] The CJ also noted that concerns 'at a competition policy level' had motivated the heightened intervention standard in *Bronner*,[816] concerns that it evidently did not believe extend to constructive refusal cases. The Advocate General was even more unambiguous in seeing a zero-sum game whereby 'any extension of the scope of the *Bronner* case-law entails a reduction in the *effectiveness* of Article 102'.[817] Under the *Bronner* standard, the Commission is 'required to adduce significantly stronger evidence to establish the existence of abusive practices', which resulted in 'a weakening of the Commission's power to combat' such practices.[818] From this perspective the *Bronner* criteria are, in short, a millstone around the neck of Article 102 enforcement; and if the case cannot be overturned, then it should be confined to its own facts to the greatest extent possible.

There are, however, reasons for caution about any rigid segregation of actual and constructive refusals under Article 102. The inconsistency with the treatment of constructive refusals under the ordinary refusal to supply principles in earlier decisional practice, and with the Commission's approach in the original Guidance Paper, has already been discussed. As a matter of competition policy, the abandonment of the *Bronner* test also seems misjudged, suggesting as it does that the rationale behind the exacting criteria is less convincing where the refusal is constructive. Yet, as the GC acknowledged

[810] Opinion in Case C-165/19 P, *Slovak Telekom* EU:C:2020, para. 84. [811] Ibid., para. 83.
[812] Case C-165/19 P, *Slovak Telekom* EU:C:2021:239, para. 46.
[813] AT.39849, *BEH Ga*, 17 December 2018, para. 445. [814] See n. *.
[815] Case C-165/19 P, *Slovak Telekom* EU:C:2021:239, para. 53. [816] Ibid., para. 48.
[817] Opinion in Case C-165/19 P, *Slovak Telekom* EU:C:2020, para. 64 (emphasis added). [818] Ibid.

in *Slovak Telekom*, it is not the 'form' that a refusal takes, whether outright or constructive, that determines its seriousness from an antitrust perspective;[819] nor are questions of form determinative of the delicate balance between the risks of over- and under-intervention which are reflected in the *Bronner* criteria. Indeed, a logical response to the *Slovak Telekom* holding is that prudent dominant undertakings that are not obviously in control of an indispensable input may prefer to refuse outright to supply their downstream competitors, rather than risk having the terms and conditions of supply subject to exacting scrutiny under Article 102. This is a troublingly counterproductive outcome.

As a matter of competition *law*, it is far from clear that the judgment in *TeliaSonera* requires or even provides robust support for the outcome in *Slovak Telekom*. The fear that to subject constructive refusals to the *Bronner* criteria would, in effect, require a showing of indispensability in *all* Article 102 cases is misplaced.[820] It is true that many, for example, tying cases could also be construed as a constructive refusal to deal insofar as there is an implicit refusal to sell absent the tied sales. Yet, even if access to the tying or tied product is not indispensable, such behaviour would surely still amount to an abuse of dominance where there is evidence of customer coercion and resulting foreclosure.[821] The various legal tests developed under Article 102 are not mutually exclusive, but nor are they cumulative. This argument is well illustrated by the approach of the GC in *Google Shopping*, where the court emphasised that while leveraging as such is not prohibited under Article 102, '[t]he term may designate several different practices that are [each] capable of being abusive', including tying, margin squeeze, loyalty rebates, and refusal to supply.[822]

Moreover, the reliance on notions of 'unfair conditions'[823] and 'unfair practices'[824] in *Slovak Telekom* risks conflating exclusionary abuse (regulated under Article 102(b), and of which refusal to deal is typically considered a sub-category) and exploitative abuse (regulated under Article 102(a), which makes explicit reference to 'unfair . . . prices or other unfair trading conditions'). Both are prohibited, yet the competition policy considerations at play are different, and the legal treatment of these categories was historically quite distinct. The reason we might be concerned about the onerous terms and conditions applied by ST for wholesale-level local loop access is *not* because this amounts to exploitation of ST's wholesale customers in their capacity as intermediate consumers. It is because an effective denial of access on practicable terms is likely to inhibit retail-level competition, to the disadvantage of *final* consumers. This misunderstanding is particularly acute in the Opinion of the Advocate General, who supported his contention that *Bronner* cannot apply to 'unfair pricing' principally by citing a long line of case law applying the prohibition on *excessive* pricing under Article 102(a).[825] Contrary to the Advocate General's argument,[826] however, the concern in refusal to

[819] Case T-851/14, *Slovak Telekom* EU:T:2018:929, para. 133.

[820] The concern is that because such a wide range of behaviours could conceivably be construed as a constructive refusal to deal in some sense, recognising an indispensability requirement in such cases would effectively make it the default standard for *all* exclusionary abuse cases. Yet this approach neglects the fact that the Art. 102 case law recognises a variety of different 'plus factors', each of which may be sufficient to support the conclusion that the behaviour of a dominant firm amounts to something other than 'competition on the merits': from exclusive dealing obligations/incentives, to tied sales coupled with customer coercion, to maintaining an 'unfair' margin between wholesale and retail prices.

[821] See Section 11. [822] Case T-612/17, *Google Shopping* EU:T:2021:763, paras. 162–164.

[823] Case C-165/19 P, *Slovak Telekom* EU:C:2021:239, para. 50. [824] Ibid., paras. 50 and 51.

[825] Opinion in Case C-165/19 P, *Slovak Telekom* EU:C:2020, paras. 86–88, citing Cases C-26/75, *General Motors* EU:C:1975:150; C-226/84, *British Leyland* EU:C:1986:421; C-395/87, *Tournier* EU:C:1989:319; C-340/99, *TNT Traco* EU:C:2001:281; C-52/07, *Kanal 5* EU:C:2008:703; C-385/07 P, *Der Grüne Punkt—Duales System Deutschland* EU:C:2009:456; C-351/12m *OSA* EU:C:2014:110, and C-177/16, *AKKA* EU:C:2017:689. He also referenced the margin squeeze judgments in Cases C-52/09, *TeliaSonera* EU:C:2011:83 and C-295/12 P, *Telefonica* EU:C:2014:2062.

[826] See Opinion in *Slovak Telekom*, para. 85: 'One might, in extremis, ask whether *any* abusive practice does not in some way constitute an implicit refusal of access, since any disadvantage imposed by a dominant undertaking is liable to discourage potential customers from using the goods and services it offers.' (Emphasis in original.)

deal cases is not that the practice may dissuade customers from using the dominant undertaking's *own* product, but rather that it may have the ultimate effect of preventing potential customers from using those of the dominant undertaking's *competitor*(s).

Arguably, the real difficulty in *Slovak Telekom* stems from the fact that, by addressing a margin squeeze and refusal to deal in tandem, the logical inconsistency created by the absence of an indispensability requirement with respect to the former becomes more obvious, and jarring.[827] Yet, for the reasons discussed in Section 9, the more appropriate response may be to rethink the approach to margin squeeze, rather than distorting the case law on refusal to supply.

As discussed in Section 12.G, the Amendments to the Guidance Paper have removed the reference to 'constructive refusal' as a category of behaviour that is subject to assessment under the *Bronner* criteria.

(ii) Indispensability

The central concept emerging from *Bronner* is the indispensability requirement. The requested access must be *indispensable* to the competitive process, not merely desirable or convenient for the rival, and there must be no actual or potential substitute for the requested facility. The concept resembles that of a 'bottleneck monopoly',[828] a term which neatly illustrates the extent to which congestion at this level of the value chain can throttle competition further down. Such market characteristics arise infrequently, requiring the presence of a natural monopoly or at least very high economies of scale (e.g. an electricity or natural gas distribution network), or a legal monopoly (e.g. certain IPRs).[829] Because of the comparatively narrow range of circumstances in which indispensability might arise, the requirement has been described as 'a "peak" in the regulatory landscape of Article 102',[830] which 'translates into the prohibition only of "super abuse" of a dominant position'.[831]

What differentiates an *indispensable* input from wholesale markets in which the defendant simply has a very high market share is the consequences that arise downstream following a refusal to deal.[832] Denying access to an indispensable input essentially forecloses the possibility of competing downstream, and, where the defendant is vertically integrated, may enable it to leverage market power from one segment of the value chain to another.[833] It is therefore necessary to distinguish, as Advocate General Jacobs explained in *Bronner*, between circumstances where a dominant undertaking's market position upstream gives it merely a 'competitive advantage' downstream, and those where it allows it 'a genuine stranglehold on the related market'.[834] In the latter situation, the market power enjoyed by the defendant may enable it to achieve the 'permanent exclusion of competition on a related

[827] Although, as the Guidance Paper illustrates, every margin squeeze can be conceptualised as a constructive refusal to supply, not every constructive refusal takes the form of a margin squeeze. Thus, the complex constructive refusal to supply access to the defendant's local loop in *Slovak Telekom*, which comprised both price- and non-price-based exclusionary conduct, was nominally subject to assessment under two different legal standards.

[828] See, e.g., R. Crandall, 'The Remedy for the "Bottleneck Monopoly" in Telecom: Isolate It, Share It, or Ignore It?' (2005) 72 *Univ Chic LR* 3.

[829] O'Donoghue and Padilla, n. 1, 639–644. [830] Opinion in Case C-165/19 P, *Slovak Telekom* EU:C:2020, para. 63.

[831] Ibid., para. 65.

[832] Discussing the possible negative consequences of a refusal to deal, see H. Shelanski, 'Unilateral Refusals to Deal in Intellectual and Other Property' (2009) 76 *Antitrust LJ* 369, 370–373.

[833] The counter-argument, advanced in the EAGCP report, p. 27, is that 'there is a single final market and therefore only one profit to be reaped. And since the dominant firm can get this profit by exerting its market power over the bottleneck, it has no incentive to distort competition in the other markets'.

[834] Opinion in Case C-7/97, *Oscar Bronner* EU:C:1998:264, para. 65. This language was echoed, several decades later, by the CJ in Case C-165/19 P, *Slovak Telekom* EU:C:2021:239, paras. 48–49, which spoke of a 'genuinely tight grip' on the relevant market.

market'.[835] It is these oversized negative spill-over effects associated with blocking access that justify antitrust scrutiny of how the facility owner utilises its property.

The crux of the concept is that access upstream is a 'prerequisite for effective competition' downstream.[836] This requires an assessment that is highly context-specific,[837] but also rigorously objective. In *Bronner*, the rival claimed an entitlement to access on the basis that its small newspaper circulation figures meant that self-distribution would be 'entirely unprofitable', while the ordinary postal system presented a less advantageous alternative.[838] The CJ was unsympathetic, holding that the indispensability criterion would be satisfied only if it was not economically viable to create a home-delivery system for a newspaper *with a comparable circulation to that of the dominant firm*. It was insufficient to show it was unviable merely for a small-circulation paper. In *Servizio Elettrico Nazionale*, the CJ construed the indispensability criterion as essentially an application of the 'as efficient competitor' (AEC) test.[839] The Commission's Guidance Paper reiterates that the test is one of *objective*, rather than subjective, necessity.[840]

In *ARA Foreclosure*, for instance, the defendant refused to supply access to its Austria-wide collection infrastructure (recycling bins, etc.) for household packaging waste. That infrastructure was held to be 'non-duplicable', and thus indispensable, due to a combination of legal, practical, and economic obstacles. Under Austrian law, the construction of additional collection infrastructure required governmental approval. This was unlikely to be forthcoming from the environment ministry, on the basis that duplicate infrastructure raised environmental concerns and was likely to generate extra costs that would be borne by consumers.[841] The Commission also considered that any new entrant would face high start-up costs—approval would only be granted where the operator could service the entire country—and, at least initially, would have low turnover. On this basis, the Commission additionally found 'an economic obstacle capable of making it impossible, or at least unreasonably difficult, to set up an alternative household collection infrastructure'.[842]

The GC's judgment in *Google Shopping* provides a noteworthy assessment of indispensability. The question of whether access to equitable placement within the results generated by Google's online search engine could be considered 'indispensable' for providers of comparison shopping services was a much debated one, not least because there were multiple alternative (though undoubtedly suboptimal) ways by which potential customers could find comparison shopping websites.[843] The Commission, in its infringement decision, avoided the question by declining to consider the *Bronner* criteria at all, arguing instead that neither the theory of harm nor the remedy sought came within its scope.[844] The GC confirmed the Commission's characterisation of self-preferencing as an 'independent' form of abuse,[845] though it disputed its approach to the remedy point.[846] It nonetheless argued that the Commission's assessment had impliedly established the indispensable nature of access to Google's general search engine for comparison shopping services providers,[847] noting that 'Google's general results page had characteristics akin to those of an essential facility'.[848] This arose, in particular, as a result of very high barriers to entry into the general search services market, including the significant upfront investment required and network effects. It dismissed alternative routes to market for comparison shopping services providers as 'not economically viable'.[849]

[835] Opinion in Case C-7/97, *Oscar Bronner* EU:C:1998:264, para. 64. [836] Ibid., para. 33.
[837] M. Motta, *Competition Policy* (Cambridge University Press, 2004), 66.
[838] Case C-7/97, *Oscar Bronner* EU:C:1998:569, para. 8.
[839] Case C-377/20, *Servizio Elettrico Nazionale* EU:C:2022:379, para. 83. [840] Guidance Paper, para. 81.
[841] AT39759, *ARA Foreclosure* 20 September 2016, paras. 81–91. [842] Ibid., paras. 92–94.
[843] See e.g. P. Akman, 'The Theory of Abuse in *Google Search*: A Positive and Normative Assessment under EU Competition Law' [2017] *Univ Illinois J of Law, Technology & Policy* 301.
[844] AT.39740, *Google Search (Shopping)* 27 June 2017, paras. 650–651.
[845] Case T-612/17, *Google Shopping* EU:T:2021:763, para. 231. [846] Ibid., para. 244. [847] Ibid., para. 227.
[848] Ibid., para. 226. [849] Ibid., para. 226.

(iii) Refusal to Supply and the '*Telefónica* Exceptions'

The criterion of indispensability broadly coincides with the essential facilities concept, although, in *Bronner* the CJ seems to have opted deliberately against the language of the latter. The markets most ripe for application of the essential facilities doctrine are those concerning transport and utility infrastructures originally developed with public money. Where competition is introduced to markets which have previously been statutory monopolies, duplication of infrastructure such as networks may not be feasible.[850] Liberalisation therefore cannot be fully realised unless the new competitors have access to the incumbent's established facilities. Incumbents, however, have strong incentives to delay access and discriminate against downstream competitors.[851] The Commission has applied Article 102 against refusals to supply access to essential infrastructure in the transport,[852] energy,[853] and telecommunications[854] sectors.

What complicates the role for the essential facilities *antitrust* doctrine, however, is that, in each of those sectors, EU liberalisation rules impose parallel obligations on incumbent operators to grant access to defined categories of infrastructure. The boundaries of the mandatory access duties that arise under competition law and sector-specific regulation, respectively, are not entirely clear. In *Telekomunikacja Polska*, for instance, the abusive behaviour comprised, in essence, a failure to adhere to sector-specific regulatory duties to grant access.[855] The infrastructure owned by defendant undertakings, moreover, may have been developed when the dominant firm was in public ownership (i.e. using public money) and during a period when it benefited from a legal monopoly or other privileged market position.

We have already seen in the context of margin squeeze the '*Telefónica* exceptions', whereby the Commission argued, inter alia, that the pre-existence of regulatory supply duties negated an obligation to apply the *Bronner* criteria to find a violation of Article 102, in particular the requirement of indispensability.[856] Although the point was left open on appeal in *Telefónica*, the exceptions were replicated in the Commission's Guidance Paper, as indicating circumstances where an antitrust duty to supply would be 'manifestly not capable of having negative effects on . . . incentives to invest and innovate upstream, whether *ex ante* or *ex post*'.[857] This argument has now been confirmed in the *Slovak Telekom* and *Lithuanian Railways* judgments.

In *Slovak Telekom*, the defendant, ST, was similarly subject to mandatory obligations for local loop unbundling. It was found to have abused its dominant position in the upstream market by failing to provide effective access to its infrastructure. ST challenged the infringement finding, on the basis that the Commission had not established that access to its local loop was 'indispensable' as required by *Bronner*.[858] Besides disputing the characterisation of the conduct as a 'refusal' as such,[859] the Commission maintained that the existence of a regulatory duty to supply absolved it of any need to demonstrate an equivalent duty under competition law. In effect, the public regulation functioned as a proxy for the indispensable nature of the input, rendering redundant a parallel determination of whether indispensability in the *Bronner* sense arose in the same circumstances.[860]

[850] The facility may constitute a natural monopoly, for instance, or at least require unrealistically high levels of investment to replicate from scratch.

[851] See the discussion in DG Competition Report on Energy Sector Inquiry, SEC(2006) 1724, 10 January 2007.

[852] See e.g. *GVG/FS* [2004] OJ L11/17, where the Italian State-owned railway company (FS) abused its dominant position on the Italian passenger rail market by refusing to enter into an international grouping with a German railway company. FS gave undertakings to grant access.

[853] See the cases cited in n. 797.

[854] See e.g. Cases COMP/39.525, *Telekomunikacja Polska* 22 June 2011, and AT39523, *Slovak Telekom* 15 October 2014.

[855] COMP/39.525, *Telekomunikacja Polska* 22 June 2011.

[856] See Section 9.B.iii.

[857] Guidance Paper, para. 82.

[858] Case T-851/14, *Slovak Telekom v Commission* EU:T:2018:929, para. 114.

[859] See text accompanying n. 808.

[860] AT39523, *Slovak Telekom* 15 October 2014.

The GC agreed that the regulatory context rendered the latter unnecessary. The underlying framework for telecommunications regulation constituted 'a relevant factor in the application of Article 102',[861] and the regulatory regime existed 'in order to allow the emergence and development of effective competition'.[862] It upheld the Commission's decision not to require indispensability in the circumstances. The case was further appealed to the CJ, which took a more equivocal position on the impact of the regulatory framework within the Article 102 assessment.

Case C-165/19 P, *Slovak Telekom, a.s. v European Commission* EU:C:2021:239

54. In the present case, the appellant's situation was characterised in particular by the fact . . . that it was subject to a telecommunications regulatory obligation, in accordance with which it was required to give access to its local loop network. Following the decision of . . . [the Slovak telecommunications regulator] . . . the appellant was required to grant, in its capacity as operator with significant market power, all alternative operators' reasonable and justified requests for unbundling of its local loop, in order to enable those operators, on that basis, to offer their own services on the retail mass market for broadband services at a fixed location in Slovakia.

55. Such an obligation meets the objectives of development of effective competition on the telecommunications markets laid down by the EU legislature . . . [T]he imposition of such an access obligation is justified by the fact that, first, as operators with significant market power were able, over significant periods of time, to roll out their local access networks protected by exclusive rights and fund investment costs through monopoly rents, it would not be economically viable for new entrants to duplicate the incumbent's local access infrastructure and, second, alternative infrastructures do not constitute a viable substitute for those local access networks. Unbundled access to the local loop would therefore be such as to allow new entrants to compete with operators with significant market power . . .

. . .

57. By analogy with . . . *Deutsche Telekom* v *Commission* (C-280/08 P, EU:C:2010:603) . . . it should be considered that a regulatory obligation can be relevant for the assessment of abusive conduct, for the purposes of Article 102 TFEU, on the part of a dominant undertaking that is subject to sectoral rules. In the context of the present case, while the obligation imposed on the appellant to give access to the local loop cannot relieve the Commission of the requirement of establishing that there is abuse within the meaning of Article 102 TFEU, by taking account in particular of the applicable case-law, the imposition of that obligation has the consequence that, during the entire infringement period taken into account in the present case, the appellant could not and did not actually refuse to give access to its local loop network.

58. However, the appellant retained, during that period, decision-making autonomy, notwithstanding the abovementioned regulatory obligation, in respect of the conditions for such access. Apart from certain guiding principles, the mandatory content of the local loop unbundling reference offer . . . was not prescribed by the regulatory framework or by the decisions of the [regulator]. It was in accordance with that decision-making autonomy that the appellant adopted the practices at issue.

59. Nevertheless, as the practices at issue did not constitute refusal of access to the appellant's local loop but related to the conditions for such access, for the reasons referred to in paragraphs 45 to 51 of the present judgment, the conditions set out by the Court of Justice in paragraph 41 of the judgment in *Bronner*, referred to in paragraph 44 of the present judgment, did not apply in the present case.

60. Therefore, the General Court did not err in law when it considered . . . that the Commission was not required to demonstrate 'indispensability', for the purposes of the last condition set out in paragraph 41 of the judgment in *Bronner*, in order to find an abuse of a dominant position on the part of the appellant by virtue of the practices at issue.

[861] Case T-851/14, *Slovak Telekom* EU:T:2018:929, para. 117. [862] Ibid., para. 121.

The CJ thus confirmed that 'a regulatory obligation can be *relevant* for the assessment of abusive conduct', particularly where, as here, its presence meant that the defendant 'could not and did not actually refuse to give access to its local loop network'.[863] On the facts, however, the constructive nature of the refusal to supply was sufficient in itself to take the case outside the ambit of the *Bronner* criteria.[864] The CJ did not consider directly whether a binding regulatory duty might effectively substitute for indispensability in the face of an actual refusal to deal.

The implications of the '*Telefónica* exceptions' also arose in the appeal against the *Baltic Rail* infringement decision.[865] The case concerned the activities of LG, the Lithuanian railway undertaking and infrastructure manager. Following a dispute over rates, LG discovered that it was in danger of losing a long-standing freight customer to LDZ, the railway incumbent in neighbouring Latvia. To provide the services, LDZ required wholesale-level access to LG's track infrastructure, as provided for by EU rail liberalisation legislation. With this prospect in mind, LG announced that it had identified a 'deformation' on a 40m section of the required track, and ordered the suspension of all traffic. A month later, a *19km-long* stretch of the track was dismantled and removed. Although ostensibly pending renovation, the track had not been reinstated by the time of the infringement decision a decade later.

The Commission construed this deliberate act of removing existing infrastructure that could otherwise have been used by a competitor as recourse to 'methods different from those which condition normal competition',[866] and thus an abuse. It pointed to 'legal and factual circumstances'[867] which suggested that LG acted principally with anti-competitive intention: that it was aware that its customer was contemplating switching;[868] that the track was removed in great haste[869] and contrary to industry practice;[870] and that LG dissuaded the Lithuanian government from rebuilding.[871] This was complemented by a demonstration that the behaviour was 'capable of having anti-competitive effects in the downstream market for rail transport services'.[872]

On appeal,[873] the defendant argued that the case involved, in essence, a refusal to supply, so that the *Bronner* criteria were the applicable legal standard. Instead of focusing on the characterisation of the conduct, the GC instead offered a ringing endorsement of the '*Telefónica* exceptions', to explain why *Bronner* was inapplicable to an undertaking in the position of the defendant.[874] Given that the preceding Commission decision had made no reference to *Bronner* or its various claimed exceptions, the attention placed on the '*Telefónica* exceptions' in the appeal was somewhat curious. This is not least because the abuse at hand involved remarkably overt and deliberate efforts to suppress potential competition: what one commentator described as perhaps 'the most straightforward abuse case ever'.[875] Notably, the GC's holding in *Lithuanian Railways* was not referenced by the CJ in *Slovak Telekom*.[876]

On further appeal, the CJ upheld the finding of infringement, but did so primarily on the basis that the behaviour at issue could not be treated as a refusal to supply. Instead, the conduct was more readily characterised as 'destroying infrastructure', which differs from more straightforward cases of refusal to supply on the basis that, '[a]s a result of the destruction, the infrastructure inevitably becomes

[863] Ibid., para. 57 (emphasis added). [864] Ibid., para. 59. [865] AT39813, *Baltic Rail* 2 October 2017.
[866] Ibid., para. 178. [867] Ibid., para. 177. [868] Ibid., para. 183. [869] Ibid., paras. 184–193.
[870] Ibid., paras. 194–198. [871] Ibid., paras. 200–201. [872] Ibid., para. 202.
[873] Case T-814/17, *Lietuvos geležinkeliai* EU:T:2020:545. [874] Ibid., paras. 90–99.
[875] P. Ibáñez Colomo, 'Lithuanian Railways: the most straightforward abuse case ever?', *Chillin' Competition Blog*, 5 October 2017, available at: <https://chillingcompetition.com/2017/10/05/lithuanian-railways-the-most-straightforward-abuse-case-ever/>. See also V. Power, 'Lithuanian Railways: Ambitious European Commission Decision that Decommissioning Infrastructure can be an Abuse of Dominance' (2018) 39 *ECLR* 208, 211.
[876] The judgment of the CJ in *Slovak Telekom* was decided subsequent to the judgment of the GC in *Lithuanian Railways*, but prior to the judgment of the CJ in that case.

unusable by competitors but also by the dominant undertaking itself.'[877] The CJ nonetheless offered brief support for the '*Telefónica* exceptions' in the judgment.

Case C-42/21 P, *Lietuvos geležinkeliai AB v European Commission* EU:C:2023:12

86. . . . [I]t also follows from the Court's case-law that the criteria established in paragraph 41 of . . . *Bronner* (C-7/97, EU:C:1998:569), are intended to strike a fair balance between, on the one hand, the requirements of undistorted competition and, on the other hand, the freedom of contract and the right to property of the dominant undertaking. In that sense, those criteria are intended to be applicable in the event of refusal of access to infrastructure which the dominant undertaking owns and which it has developed for the needs of its own business by means of its own investments (see . . . *Bronner*, C-7/97, EU:C:1998:569, paragraph 37, and of 25 March 2021, *Deutsche Telekom* v *Commission*, C-152/19 P, EU:C:2021:238, paragraph 47).

87. Accordingly, the General Court did not err in law in holding, in essence, . . . that, having regard to their purpose, those criteria do not apply, in a situation such as that in the present case, where the infrastructure in question was financed by means not of investments specific to the dominant undertaking, but by means of public funds and that undertaking is not the owner of that infrastructure.

88. . . . [I]t is important to recall that the Court has already held that a regulatory obligation can be relevant for the assessment of abusive conduct, for the purposes of Article 102 TFEU. While the existence of a regulatory obligation on the dominant undertaking to grant access to the infrastructure in question cannot relieve the Commission of the requirement to establish the existence of an 'abuse' within the meaning of Article 102 TFEU, the fact remains that the imposition of such an obligation has the consequence that the dominant undertaking cannot actually refuse to give access to that infrastructure, without prejudice, as appropriate, to its decision-making autonomy in relation to the conditions for such access (see, to that effect, . . . *Deutsche Telekom* v *Commission*, C-152/19 P, EU:C:2021:238, paragraphs 57 and 58 and the case-law cited).

89. The General Court did not therefore err in law in holding . . . that the criteria established in . . . *Bronner* (C-7/97, EU:C:1998:569) are not applicable where the dominant undertaking is subject to an obligation to give access to its infrastructure.

The treatment of the '*Telefónica* exceptions' by the GC and CJ in *Slovak Telekom* essentially followed the approach of the Guidance Paper in viewing the indispensability criterion as hinging on the question of incentives. From a competition policy perspective, there is generally a reluctance to interfere with the use of private property too readily, to the extent that this may discourage beneficial investment or innovation by private market actors in future. The pragmatic logic of the regulated conduct exception is that incentives are already diminished by the prior existence of regulatory obligations, so there is, in effect, less to lose in such circumstances. Nonetheless, it may reasonably be questioned whether the public policy goals pursued by the various EU liberalisation regimes and the competition rules coincide precisely.[878] The link between incentives and the public monopoly/State resources exception is less obvious, particularly, as is often the case in Europe, where the entity concerned has been privatised subsequently. The exception has been criticised, moreover, on the basis that 'it is difficult to apply in practice and is likely to lead to unpredictable and erroneous results',[879] because how far the dominant undertaking's position has been developed in that way may not be

[877] Case C-42/21 P, *Lietuvos geležinkeliai AB v European Commission* EU:C:2023:12, para. 83.

[878] See e.g. G. Monti, 'Managing the Intersection of Utilities Regulation and EC Competition Law' (2008) 4 *Competition Law Review* 123.

[879] Geradin, Layne-Farrar, and Petit, n. 195, 4.354.

clear-cut and in particular which parts of the assets were paid for pre-liberalisation may be difficult to determine.[880] The GC in *Slovak Telekom*[881] made reference to paragraph 23 of *Post Danmark I*, recalling the special responsibility doctrine, which suggests perhaps that the true rationale is more an issue of legitimate expectations. An undertaking that has received public funding or been granted special rights within the marketplace can have less of an expectation of unfettered enjoyment of these privileges. In any event, the Commission 'still needs to prove an elimination of effective competition and consumer harm and these [exceptions] simply provide a (rebuttable) presumption that the indispensability condition is met'.[882]

(iv) Elimination of Competition

The CJ in *Bronner* stressed that the refusal must be likely to eliminate all competition from the undertaking requesting access, not merely make it harder for it to compete. This criterion has often been applied in a lax fashion, however. Following the judgment in *Microsoft*,[883] discussed in Section 12.E, the standard appears to have become one of elimination of 'effective competition'. In *Clearstream*, a case involving a refusal to supply access to essential services in the financial sector (clearing and settlement for securities), the GC interpreted the criterion as follows:

> With regard to the condition of elimination of all competition, it is not necessary, in order to establish an infringement of Article [102], to demonstrate that all competition on the market would be eliminated, but what matters is that the refusal at issue is liable to, or is likely to, eliminate all effective competition on the market. It is for the Commission to establish such a risk of the elimination of all effective competition.[884]

On the facts, it was sufficient that Clearstream had 'hindered' the capacity of its rival 'to provide comprehensive, pan-European and innovative services. That harmed innovation and competition in the provision of cross-border secondary clearing and settlement services, and ultimately consumers within the internal market.'[885] This approach was reiterated in *CEAHR*, which concerned the alleged refusal by several Swiss watch manufacturers to supply spare parts to independent repairers.[886] In determining that the criterion was not satisfied on the facts, the GC approved the Commission's decision to take account of, inter alia, the fact that the selective repair systems were compatible with Article 101;[887] that they allowed for the possibility of new entry, which exerted further competitive pressure;[888] and that competition continued to exist between existing selective repairers and the in-house repairers of the brands concerned.[889]

In *Telekomunikacja Polska*, the Commission established an elimination of competition on the basis that 'rivals are disadvantaged and consequently compete less aggressively'.[890] The Commission considered that it was of crucial importance to the competitors to obtain a minimum critical network size. TP's delaying tactics prevented competitors from reaching the critical customer size rapidly and

[880] See also Mazák AG in Case C-52/09, *TeliaSonera* EU:C:2010:483, para. 27 of the Opinion. The Commission is also criticised for ignoring the dominant undertaking's future incentives to invest, D. Geradin, 'Refusal to Supply and Margin Squeeze: A Discussion of Why the "*Telefonica* Exceptions" are Wrong', TILEC Discussion Paper No. 2011-009, <http://papers.ssrn.com/sol3/papers.cfm?abstract_id=1762687>.

[881] Case T-814/17, *Lietuvos geležinkeliai* EU:T:2020:545, para. 93. [882] Faull and Nikpay, n. 1, 4.690.

[883] Case T-210/04, *Microsoft* EU:T:2007.289. [884] Case T-301/04, *Clearstream* EU:T:2009:317, para. 148.

[885] Ibid., para. 149.

[886] Case T-712/14, *Confédération européenne des associations d'horlogers-réparateurs (CEAHR) v Commission* EU:T:2017:748, para. 91.

[887] Ibid., para. 108. [888] Ibid., para. 111. [889] Ibid., para. 109.

[890] COMP/39.525, *Telekomunikacja Polska* 22 June 2011, para. 815.

so prevented them from climbing the 'investment ladder'. In *ENI*, the Commission's preliminary view was that the elimination of competition limb was satisfied if the refusal was 'likely to lead either to the elimination or the prevention of the development of effective competition on the downstream market resulting in consumer harm'.[891] In *BEH Gas*, the Commission spoke of 'likely anticompetitive effects' arising from the practice.[892]

In *ARA Foreclosure*, moreover, the Commission took the view that the elimination of competition limb was satisfied from the mere fact of refusal to give access to non-duplicable infrastructure, thus eliding two formally distinct limbs of the *Bronner* test. The Commission explicitly disclaimed any obligation to establish causality between the defendant's refusal to grant access and the failure of any would-be competitors to enter the market. Thus it was irrelevant that, as the defendant claimed, there were other market circumstances that could explain the continuing lack of competition in the exemption system sector in Austria.[893] A generous reading of this analytically unsatisfactory approach may view it as a reiteration of the primary importance of the indispensability limb within the *Bronner* test. It thus emphasises that this central criterion must be applied in a sufficiently robust manner to also function as a proxy for anti-competitive effects.

(v) Absence of Objective Justification

As discussed in Section 5, in principle any prima facie abuse may be exempted from prohibition under Article 102 by reference to a defence of 'objective justification', the burden of establishing which lies with the defendant. It is notable that, in *Bronner*, the CJ made explicit and atypical reference to the *absence* of any objective justification when outlining the 'exceptional circumstances' that must be satisfied in order to establish that a refusal to supply constitutes an abuse of dominance.[894] This reiterates the default assumption that pervades *Bronner*, namely that refusals to supply are generally consistent with Article 102, on the basis either that the dominant undertaking is entitled to keep its property to itself or that it may have some legitimate reason for doing so. As the discussion in Section 5 revealed, however, the unreceptive attitude of the Commission and Courts towards claims of objective justification suggest that this is unlikely to be a substantial barrier to a successful claim of abusive refusal to supply in practice.

(vi) [The Absence of a] New Product Requirement

Finally, although the CJ in *Bronner* drew upon its *Magill* jurisprudence in order to identify the 'exceptional' circumstances in which a refusal to supply access to tangible property may similarly constitute an abuse, it (presumably deliberately) omitted one of the criteria identified in the earlier case: namely, that the 'refusal prevented the appearance of a new product . . . for which there was a potential consumer demand'.[895] The implications of the new product requirement in refusal to license cases are discussed in the next section. Implicitly, however, its omission from *Bronner* suggests a less demanding threshold to demonstrate abuse where the disputed property is not protected by a legal monopoly. The Guidance Paper, which merges the treatment of refusal to supply access to tangible and intangible property,[896] nonetheless incorporates a 'consumer harm' requirement, and lists as a potential example the fact that excluded rivals may be 'prevented from bringing innovative goods or services to market'.[897]

891 COMP/39.315, *ENI* 29 September 2010, para. 40. 892 AT.39849, *BEH Gas* 17 December 2018, para. 449.
893 AT.39759, *ARA Foreclosure* 20 September 2016, paras. 92–94 and 112.
894 Case C-7/97, *Bronner* EU:C:1998:569, para. 41.
895 Cases C-241 and 242/91 P, *RTE and ITP v Commission* EU:C:1995:98, para. 54.
896 Guidance Paper, para. 81. 897 Ibid., para. 87.

D. REFUSAL TO SUPPLY AND INTELLECTUAL PROPERTY RIGHTS

(i) General

Refusal to supply in respect of intellectual property rights (IPRs) is one aspect of the problematic interface between competition law and intellectual property law.[898] Criticisms centre around the fact that the law has already established a regime to deal with IPRs; that compulsory licensing may be a dangerous disincentive to innovation; and that, to date, the law has not properly explained why some situations are so 'exceptional' that the normal rights of an IPR owner should be eroded. The case law is nonetheless linked to the wider jurisprudence on refusal to supply, as the early leading case on IPRs, *Magill*,[899] featured significantly in *Bronner*,[900] which in turn was relied upon in the IPR case of *IMS*.[901]

Obviously, the existence of IPRs will prevent undertakings from competing on certain markets. Although the EU Courts have held that the ownership of IPRs does not necessarily mean that an undertaking holds a dominant position,[902] some rights nonetheless constitute a barrier to entry.[903] An undertaking cannot usually produce or use something protected by IPRs without the consent of the rights holder. IPRs owners frequently license their rights to others, and Chapter 12 deals with the application of Article 101 to such agreements. Article 102 may be relevant, however, when the rights holder is dominant and refuses to give licences in certain circumstances.

The question first came before the CJ in the car parts cases of *Volvo* and *Renault*.[904] In essence, the CJ was asked whether it is an abuse for a car manufacturer to refuse to license the design rights on its car parts to third parties wishing to manufacture and sell such parts[905] The CJ held that a refusal to license was not normally abusive, on the basis that the rights-holder's ability to deny access was inherent to 'the very subject-matter of his exclusive right'.[906] It might become so in certain circumstances, however, 'such as the arbitrary refusal to supply spare parts to independent repairers, the fixing of prices for spare parts at an unfair level or a decision no longer to produce spare parts for a particular model even though many cars of that model are still in circulation'.[907] In effect, the defendants in *Volvo* and *Renault* had a choice: either they could license third parties, or they could retain their monopoly but had to ensure that they did not arbitrarily refuse to supply independent repairers, did not charge unfairly, and continued to supply parts for old models. In this sense, an order to license might be seen as a *remedy* for other abuses.[908] The examples of abusive conduct are not unproblematic, however, including the issue of what constitutes an 'unfair' price.[909]

(ii) The *Magill* Case

Magill[910] concerned access to 'television listings' (television programme schedules), which, unusually, benefited from copyright protection for broadcasters under UK and Irish law. At the time,

[898] See also the issue of standard-essential patents, discussed in Section 14.C of this chapter, and Chap. 12 on the licensing of IPRs.

[899] Cases C-241–242/91 P, *Magill* EU:C:1995:98. [900] Case C-7/97, *Bronner* EU:C:1998:569.

[901] Case C-418/01, *IMS Health* EU:C:2004:257. [902] See Chap. 6, Section 9.C.iv.d.

[903] See Chap. 3, Section 5.

[904] Case 238/87, *AB Volvo v Erik Veng* EU:C:1988:477 and Case 53/87, *CICCRA and Maxicar v Renault* EU:C:1988:472, decided on the same day.

[905] The cases arose after the CJ had confirmed in Case 22/78, *Hugin* EU:C:1979:138 that an undertaking may be dominant on the market for its own spare parts even if the primary product market is competitive.

[906] Case 238/87, *Volvo* EU:C:1988:477, para. 8.

[907] Ibid., para. 9. See also Case 53/87, *Renault* EU:C:1988:472, para. 16.

[908] See the discussion in J. Temple Lang, 'Anti-competitive Non-Pricing Abuses under European and National Antitrust Law' [2003] *Fordham Corp L Inst* 235, 292–301.

[909] See Section 16.A.

[910] Cases C-241–242/91 P, *Magill* EU:C:1995:98, on appeal from Cases T-69–70/89, 76/89, *RTE, ITP, BBC (Magill) v Commission* EU:T:1991:39, on appeal from *Magill TV Guide* [1989] OJ L78/43.

the broadcaster RTE had a statutory monopoly over television broadcasting in Ireland, while the BBC and IBA had a statutory duopoly in the UK, including Northern Ireland. Most viewers in Ireland and Northern Ireland could receive the channels of all three broadcasters. The three broadcasters each published a weekly TV guide containing only their individual weekly programme listings. They also gave listings information to the press to be published according to strict licensing conditions. A publisher, Magill, started to publish a weekly TV guide giving details of all programmes available to viewers in Ireland and Northern Ireland, but the television companies obtained injunctions against it in national legal proceedings. Magill complained to the Commission that the broadcasters, by refusing to provide reliable advance listings information and protecting their listings by enforcing their copyright, infringed Article 102.

The EU Courts and the Commission appear to have been influenced by the fact that the UK and Ireland were alone among the Member States in affording copyright protection to TV listings, and that composite TV guides were published in other Member States, where they were popular.[911] The case became perceived as a battle between the protection of national IPRs and competition law, for if the TV companies' refusal to deal with Magill *was* an abuse, the only remedy was, in effect, to order them to license of their copyrights.

The Commission found that the television companies had infringed Article 102.[912] It held that each was dominant in the market for its weekly listings and that their restrictive licensing policies were driven by a desire to protect their own weekly guides in the downstream market. The GC upheld the Commission, relating the position under Article 102 to the case law on IPRs in the context of free movement.[913] On appeal, the CJ confirmed the finding of abuse, but its judgment was strikingly different to that of the GC. It concentrated on the specific scenario, and eschewed extended discussion about the nature of IPRs and their relationship to competition law. Rather, it treated the matter as a straightforward refusal to supply, and applied the principles laid down in existing Article 102 case law.

Cases C-241–242/91 P, *RTE & ITP v Commission* EU:C:1995:98 (*Magill*)

Court of Justice

48. With regard to the issue of abuse, the arguments of the appellants and IPO wrongly presuppose that where the conduct of an undertaking in a dominant position consists of the exercise of a right classified by national law as 'copyright', such conduct can never be reviewed in relation to Article [102].

49. Admittedly, in the absence of [Union] standardization or harmonization of laws, determination of the conditions and procedures for granting protection of an intellectual property right is a matter for national rules. Further, the exclusive right of reproduction forms part of the author's rights, so that refusal to grant a licence, even if it is the act of an undertaking holding a dominant position, cannot in itself constitute abuse of a dominant position (*Volvo* v. *Veng*, paragraphs 7 and 8).

50. However, it is also clear from that judgment . . . that the exercise of an exclusive right by the proprietor may, in exceptional circumstances, involve abusive conduct.

51. In the present case, the conduct objected to is the appellants' reliance on copyright conferred by national legislation so as to prevent Magill—or any other undertaking having the same intention—from publishing on a weekly basis information (channel, day, time and title of programmes) together with commentaries and pictures obtained independently of the appellants.

[911] See particularly the Commission's submissions to the GC, EU:T:1991:39, summarised in paras. 43–59 of the judgment, culminating in the Commission's statement in para. 59 that 'copyright should not subsist in compilations of banal information'.

[912] *Magill TV Guide* [1989] OJ L78/43.

[913] There were three separate judgments, but the crucial paras. are the same in all three.

52. Among the circumstances taken into account by the [GC] in concluding that such conduct was abusive was, first, the fact that there was, according to the findings of the [GC], no actual or potential substitute for a weekly television guide offering information on the programmes for the week ahead. On this point, the [GC] confirmed the Commission's finding that the complete lists of programmes for a 24-hour period—and for a 48-hour period at weekends and before public holidays—published in certain daily and Sunday newspapers, and the television sections of certain magazines covering, in addition, 'highlights' of the week's programmes, were only to a limited extent substitutable for advance information to viewers on all the week's programmes. Only weekly television guides containing comprehensive listings for the week ahead would enable users to decide in advance which programmes they wished to follow and arrange their leisure activities for the week accordingly. The [GC] also established that there was a specific, constant and regular potential demand on the part of consumers (see the *RTE* judgment, paragraph 62, and the *ITP* judgment, paragraph 48).

53. Thus the appellants—who were, by force of circumstance, the only sources of the basic information on programme scheduling which is the indispensable raw material for compiling a weekly television guide—gave viewers wishing to obtain information on the choice of programmes for the week ahead no choice but to buy the weekly guides for each station and draw from each of them the information they needed to make comparisons.

54. The appellants' refusal to provide basic information by relying on national copyright provisions thus prevented the appearance of a new product, a comprehensive weekly guide to television programmes, which the appellants did not offer and for which there was a potential consumer demand. Such refusal constitutes an abuse under heading (b) of the second paragraph of Article [102].

55. Second, there was no justification for such refusal either in the activity of television broadcasting or in that of publishing television magazines (*RTE* judgment, paragraph 73, and *ITP* judgment, paragraph 58).

56. Third, and finally, as the [GC] also held, the appellants, by their conduct, reserved to themselves the secondary market of weekly television guides by excluding competition on that market (*Commercial Solvents*, paragraph 25) since they denied access to the basic information which is the raw material indispensable for the compilation of such a guide.

57. In the light of all those circumstances, the [GC] did not err in law in holding that the appellants' conduct was an abuse of a dominant position within the meaning of Article [102].

Thus, while it is not true that the exercise of IRs can *never* be reviewed under Article 102, the CJ held that a refusal to grant a licence to reproduce cannot *in itself* constitute an abuse of a dominant position. It cited *Volvo* as establishing that a refusal might constitute an abuse *in exceptional circumstances*. In this case the exceptional circumstances were:

- there was no substitute for a composite weekly television guide, for which there was a specific, constant, and regular potential consumer demand;
- the appellants' refusal to supply prevented the appearance of a new product for which there was a potential consumer demand;[914]
- there was no justification for such refusal; and
- the appellants were reserving to themselves the secondary market of weekly television guides by excluding all competition.

[914] The AG on the other hand (paras. 93–102 of the Opinion) thought that the fact that the product Magill wanted to produce was new and would compete with the rights holders' own products was a reason to find that the refusal to supply was *not* abusive.

Refusal to license is *not* generally an abuse. Accordingly, the *Magill* judgment was less of an assault on IPRs than it was on the exploitation of information gained as a by-product of an undertaking's main business. It is also possible to see *Magill* as a limitation of the power wielded by statutory monopolists, insofar as the power of the television companies arose as a result of their privileged position on a broadcasting market with few channels. Notably, the CJ described the undertakings' conduct in terms of refusal to supply a raw material and referred to *Commercial Solvents*, approaching the case as an example of an established abuse of a dominant undertaking trying to exclude competition downstream. Unlike the car makers in *Volvo* and *Renault*, however, the broadcasters were not given a choice of how they could avoid committing an abuse. Although the judgment did not mention compulsory licensing, there was only one way in which the abuse could be remedied.

It was unclear, following *Magill*, whether the 'list' of exceptional circumstances identified was cumulative. In particular it was unclear whether the hindrance of a new product was a necessary, or a separate and sufficient, ground for holding the refusal to supply abusive. In *Tiercé Ladbroke*,[915] the GC read the 'exceptional circumstances' in *Magill* as alternative, rather than cumulative, criteria. The *IMS* case, however, established that they should be treated as cumulative.

(iii) The *IMS* Case

The case concerned a proprietary 'brick structure' for representing regional pharmaceutical sales data in Germany. It had been developed by IMS in collaboration with the pharmaceutical industry, and was the *de facto* industry standard. IMS's competitors attempted to develop similar systems, but IMS claimed that these infringed its copyright and it obtained interim injunctions to restrain their use. The competitors complained to the Commission that IMS's refusal to license the brick structure meant that it was impossible to provide pharmaceutical data services, as they could not present data in a manner acceptable to customers without infringing IMS's copyright, and there was no prospect of persuading customers to switch. The Commission found that the brick structure was indispensable to business in the relevant market; there was no actual or potential substitute; there was no objective justification for IMS's refusal to license; and there were 'exceptional circumstances' in the *Magill* sense. It ordered interim measures,[916] which were suspended pending the appeal.[917] In the meantime, domestic litigation between IMS and a competitor resulted in a preliminary reference to the CJ concerning the interpretation of Article 102 in the context of IMS's refusal to license. Although the Commission ultimately withdrew the interim measures,[918] the CJ ruled on the preliminary reference. In the extract below, the CJ considered the requirements of the *Magill/Bronner* case law.

Case C-418/01, *IMS Health GmbH & Co OHG v NDC Health GmbH & Co KG* EU:C:2004:257

Court of Justice

38. It is clear from [*Magill* and *Bronner*] that, in order for the refusal by an undertaking which owns a copyright to give access to a product or service indispensable for carrying on a particular business to be treated as abusive, it is sufficient that three cumulative conditions be satisfied, namely, that that

[915] Case T-504/93, *Tiercé Ladbroke SA v Commission* EU:T:1997:84.

[916] COMP/38.044, *NDC Health/IMS: Interim Measures* [2002] OJ L59/18. *IMS* was to give a licence on request and on a non-discriminatory basis to all undertakings on the German regional sales data services market.

[917] Case T-184/01 R, *IMS Health* EU:T:2001:200, para. 125, *aff'd* Case C-481/01 P(R), *IMS Health v Commission* EU:C:2002:223.

[918] In part, because NDC has begun to compete more effectively: Commission Decision 2003/741/EC [2003] OJ L268/69; IP/03/1159.

refusal is preventing the emergence of a new product for which there is a potential consumers demand, that it is unjustified and such as to exclude any competition on a secondary market.

. . .

The third condition, relating to the likelihood of excluding all competition on a secondary market

. . .

44. It appears . . . that . . . it is sufficient that a potential market or even hypothetical market can be identified. Such is the case where the products or services are indispensable in order to carry on a particular business and where there is an actual demand for them on the part of undertakings which seek to carry on the business for which they are indispensable.

45. Accordingly, it is determinative that two different stages of production may be identified and that they are interconnected, the upstream product is indispensable in as much as for supply of the downstream product.

46. Transposed to the facts of the case in the main proceedings, that approach prompts consideration as to whether the 1860 brick structure constitutes, upstream, an indispensable factor in the downstream supply of German regional sales data for pharmaceutical products.

47. It is for the national court to establish whether that is in fact the position, and, if so be the case, to examine whether the refusal by IMS to grant a licence to use the structure at issue is capable of excluding all competition on the market for the supply of German regional sales data on pharmaceutical products.

The first condition, relating to the emergence of a new product

48. . . . [T]hat condition relates to the consideration that, in the balancing of the interest in protection of copyright and the economic freedom of its owner, against the interest in protection of free competition the latter can prevail only where refusal to grant a licence prevents the development of the secondary market to the detriment of consumers.

49. Therefore, the refusal by an undertaking in a dominant position to allow access to a product protected by copyright, where that product is indispensable for operating on a secondary market, may be regarded as abusive only where the undertaking which requested the licence does not intend to limit itself essentially to duplicating the goods or services already offered on the secondary market by the owner of the copyright, but intends to produce new goods or services not offered by the owner of the right and for which there is a potential consumer demand.

50. It is for the national court to determine whether such is the case in the dispute in the main proceedings.

The second condition, relating to whether the refusal was unjustified

51. . . . [I]t is for the national court to examine, if appropriate, in light of the facts before it, whether the refusal of the request for a licence is justified by objective considerations.

Accordingly, three *cumulative* conditions made the refusal to license a copyright an abuse: a 'new product' was involved; access to the protected material was 'indispensable' so that the refusal would exclude any/all competition on a secondary market (and not merely, as in *Bronner*, all competition from the person requesting access); and the refusal was unjustified.

One view of the judgment is that the CJ came down firmly on the 'side' of the IPR holder, with a presumption *against* the mandatory licence. The CJ repeated that a refusal to grant a licence cannot in itself constitute an abuse, limiting the grant of compulsory licences only to 'exceptional circumstances'.

It incorporated into the exceptional circumstances the requirement of 'indispensability' in the *Bronner* sense, which sets a high bar, and it demanded that the party requiring the licence intends to offer new goods and services for which there is potential consumer demand.

On the other hand, the 'indispensability' and 'new product' requirements are such that everything will turn on the application of these conditions. In *IMS*, the CJ referred the case back to the national court without giving any indication as to whether the requirements were satisfied. Thus, there was room for argument about whether the competitor was providing a 'new product'.[919] In paragraph 48, the CJ said that the only situation in which free competition can override the rights of the copyright holder is where the refusal prevents the development of the secondary market to the detriment of consumers—in other words, limiting production to the detriment of consumers under Article 102(b). A licence should not be ordered to protect the competitor, but rather to protect consumers.

While the CJ required that the development of a secondary market be affected, it said that it is enough if a 'potential or even hypothetical' market can be identified upstream. It required only that 'two different stages of production' can be identified.[920] The question is how hypothetical the input market can be. The upstream market in *IMS* was decidedly artificial: IMS only developed the brick structure in order to produce its own sales reports. It was different in *Magill*, where the television listings existed as a by-product of the broadcasting activities and would have existed regardless of whether the broadcasters published their own magazines. As one commentator said (critically) of *IMS*, it was enough 'even if the input is a competitive advantage of a kind which has never previously been marketed or licensed by any company, and which it would not be economically rational to license to a direct competitor'.[921] There are few production processes that cannot be divided as in *IMS* if one thinks hard enough, and anything protected by an IPR can thus form an upstream market. One can compare *IMS* with the judgment of the US Supreme Court in *Trinko*,[922] where the fact that 'the services allegedly withheld are not otherwise marketed or available to the public' and existed 'only deep in the bowels of [the defendant]' was a factor in holding the refusal to deal lawful.[923]

The *IMS* ruling gave little flavour of the underlying factual situation. It is necessary to read the Commission decision to fully appreciate that *IMS*, like *Magill*, involved a 'weak' copyright. Indeed, the Commission seemed to consider that IMS had more or less hijacked the industry standard.[924] If *IMS* could be taken as turning on the particular facts of how the brick structure had been developed and the copyright acquired, it could be viewed as a response to a quirk of national law. Some commentators considered that the cases should be viewed in this light—as exceptional responses to unsatisfactory copyright laws—and argued that there was no reason to suppose that the same approach would be taken to strong patent rights.[925] However, *Magill* and *IMS* were relied upon by the GC in *Microsoft*, where any IPRs concerned were certainly not the product of quirks of copyright laws.

[919] Unlike *Bronner*, where the CJ made it clear that that the conditions were not satisfied.

[920] It can be argued that by saying that it was a matter of whether two *stages of production* can be identified the Court was abandoning the requirement of two *markets*: it is enough that there are two *products*. See J. Venit, 'The IP/Antitrust Interface After *IMS Health*' in Ehlermann and Atanasiu, n. 33, 609, 625.

[921] J. Temple Lang, 'Anti-competitive Non-pricing Abuses under European and National Antitrust Law' [2003] *Fordham Corp L Inst* 235, 307.

[922] 540 US 398, 124 S.Ct 872 (2004).

[923] Moreover *IMS* did not involve leveraging. IMS was not leveraging its dominance from the upstream to the downstream market: see Venit, n. 904.

[924] And see F. Fine, '*NDC/IMS*: A Logical Application of the Essential Facilities Doctrine' [2002] *ECLR* 457; F. Fine, '*NDC/IMS*: In Response to Professor Korah' (2002) 70 *Antitrust LJ* 247.

[925] See e.g. M. Delrahim, 'Forcing Firms to Share the Sandbox: Compulsory Licensing of Intellectual Property Rights and Antitrust', BIICL Conference, 10 May 2004, <www.justice.gov/atr/speech/forcing-firms-share-sandbox-compulsory-licensing-intellectual-property-rights-and>.

E. REFUSAL TO SUPPLY AND INTEROPERABILITY—THE *MICROSOFT* CASE

A particular kind of refusal to supply arises in digital markets in respect of interface information. Providers of software need to be able to make products which operate with other systems and programs. This is known as 'interoperability'. For this they require information about the systems and programs of other producers with which their products need to be compatible and usable. This information may be protected by IPRs (copyright). It may be obtainable by decompilation (reverse engineering), but this can be impossible or impractical or economically unfeasible.[926] Where there is a dominant undertaking on a software market, it may be essential to the competitive viability of other providers that their products are compatible with those of that undertaking.

The Commission first addressed this issue in 1984 when it dealt with a number of IBM's practices relating to its System/370.[927] In an informal settlement, IBM undertook to disclose sufficient interface information to enable competitors to attach hardware and software products of their own design to System/370.[928]

The *Microsoft* investigation began in 1998, following a complaint from Sun Microsystems. At the time, Microsoft had over 90 per cent of the PC operating systems market. The Commission described this as a near monopoly and Microsoft as being 'overwhelmingly dominant'.[929] Sun complained of Microsoft's refusal to disclose, to those who provided server operating systems, sufficient interface information to enable them to create 'workgroup server operating systems' (WGOS) that would operate satisfactorily with Microsoft's Windows desktop and server operating systems. Microsoft had previously supplied full interoperability information to server producers, but cut it back after entering that market itself. Five years and three statements of objections after the investigation began, the Commission held that Microsoft had committed an abuse by refusing to supply the interface information. Microsoft was fined €497,196,304,[930] and ordered to make the relevant information available to undertakings on the WGOS market within 120 days and to ensure that this information was updated in a timely manner.[931]

In the decision the Commission examined whether the *Bronner* and *Magill*[932] criteria were fulfilled, although it noted that it was 'of interest' that this was a case (unlike *Bronner* and *Magill*) of the disruption of previous levels of supply.[933] It held that the criteria were fulfilled. In doing so, the Commission followed the 'effects-based' approach which it set out the following year in its Discussion Paper. It examined the facts closely, identified effects on consumers, and considered the issues of incentives to innovation.

The Commission found that the information was indispensable by adopting a two-stage approach. First, it considered what degree of interoperability non-Microsoft WGOS required in order for competitors to be able to remain viably on the market. Secondly, it appraised whether the information that Microsoft refused to disclose was indispensable to attaining that. Based on customer surveys, the

[926] For the arguments about the possibilities of reverse engineering in *Microsoft*, see text at n. 934.

[927] For the tying aspects, see Section 11.E.iii.

[928] See Commission, *XIVth Report on Competition Policy* (1984) parts 94–95.

[929] COMP/37.792, *Microsoft* 24 March 2004, para. 435.

[930] The fine was also in respect of the tying abuse, see Section 11.E.iii.

[931] To be enforced by the appointment of a 'monitoring trustee' to ensure that the disclosures are complete and accurate. The dispute between the Commission and Microsoft as to whether Microsoft was complying with the obligation to supply the information on fair and reasonable terms led to the imposition of a periodic penalty payment, Case T-167/08, *Microsoft v Commission* EU:T:2012:323.

[932] The decision was adopted a month before the CJ's *IMS* ruling.

[933] Like e.g. *Commercial Solvents* and *Télémarketing*: COMP/37.792, *Microsoft* 24 March 2004, para. 556.

Commission found that, although the competitors' systems had features and functionalities which customers preferred over those of Microsoft, this was trumped by the attraction of full interoperability with Windows. It concluded that the competitors' systems had to interoperate with Windows on an equal footing with Microsoft's own systems if they were to compete viably, and that this was impossible without the information Microsoft refused to disclose. Microsoft argued, inter alia, that reverse engineering was a means of accessing the information, but the Commission held that this required 'considerable efforts with uncertain chances of success'.[934] Moreover, the viability of such products depended on Microsoft not breaking the compatibility, for instance by upgrading the operating system: '[r]everse engineering is therefore an unstable basis for a business model'.[935] With regard to the elimination of competition criterion, the Commission held that the refusal to supply put Microsoft's competitors 'at a strong competitive disadvantage',[936] which impacted on technical development to the prejudice of consumers.[937] Competitors were, at best, confined to niche existences with little scope for innovation,[938] while Microsoft's incentives to innovate were diminished by the disappearance of its competitors.[939] The Commission rejected Microsoft's claim that the refusal to supply was justified by the fact that the information was protected by IPRs and that forced disclosure would lessen those incentives to innovate. Even if there was such a disincentive, 'the possible negative impact of an order to supply on Microsoft's incentives to innovate is outweighed by its positive impact on the level of innovation of the whole industry (including Microsoft)'.[940]

The *Microsoft* decision stretched the *Magill* criteria. For example, the Commission held, not that the refusal prevented the appearance of a specific new product, but rather that 'technical development' would be limited. The Commission therefore hedged its bets. In case the Microsoft situation did not satisfy the principles within the previous cases, it argued that there was no 'exhaustive checklist' of exceptional circumstances and that it could have regard to other circumstances, i.e. that a refusal to supply should be examined on a case-by-case basis so that refusal that did not fit exactly within the *Bronner* or *Magill* criteria could still be abusive.[941]

On appeal, the GC applied the 'manifest error of assessment' standard of review,[942] which was significant insofar as the Commission was making predictions about the elimination of competition and the effects on innovation.[943] The GC examined first whether the Commission was justified in finding that the highest standard—the *Magill/IMS* exceptional circumstances test—was satisfied.[944] Having decided that it was, it upheld the Commission decision without expressly considering the position had it not been.[945] However, the GC had to give an expansive interpretation to the case law in order to do so, and it might have been preferable had it seized the opportunity to consider the case-specific circumstances put forward by the Commission.[946]

Setting out the applicable legal test, the GC endorsed the *Magill/IMS* criteria, which it held, 'in particular', denoted sufficiently 'exceptional' circumstances to merit liability under Article 102.[947] These required that the refusal: related to a product or service indispensable to the exercise of a

[934] COMP/37.792, *Microsoft* 24 March 2004, para. 685. [935] Ibid., para. 686. [936] Ibid., para. 589.

[937] Ibid., paras. 693–701. [938] Ibid., para. 700. [939] Ibid., para. 725. [940] Ibid., para. 783.

[941] Ibid., para. 555. In the Discussion Paper of 2005 the Commission reinforced this argument by placing interoperability in a separate category of refusal to supply. It said that 'it may not be appropriate to apply to such refusals to supply information the same high standards for intervention as those described in the previous subsections' (which set out the principles derived from the previous cases, by that time including *IMS*): Discussion Paper, paras. 271–272.

[942] Case T-210/04, *Microsoft* EU:T:2006:92, para. 87.

[943] For the recent cases on the standard of review, see Chap. 13, Section 7.A.

[944] Case T-210/04, *Microsoft* EU:T:2006:92, para. 336. [945] Ibid., para. 712.

[946] See P. Larouche, 'The European *Microsoft* Case at the Crossroads of Competition Policy and Innovation: Comment on Ahlborn and Evans' (2008–2009) 75 *Antitrust LJ* 933, 959. See also the discussion of special circumstances at COMP/37.792, *Microsoft* 24 March 2004, paras. 316–317.

[947] Case T-210/04, *Microsoft* EU:T:2006:92, para. 332.

particular activity on a neighbouring market; excluded any effective competition on that neighbouring market; prevented the appearance of a new product for which there is potential consumer demand;[948] and could not be objectively justified.[949] The GC examined the Commission's approach in the light of the conditions in this case law, and upheld the decision.

On the indispensability condition, the GC confirmed the Commission's approach to finding indispensability through the twofold test described, and its conclusion was that the test was satisfied.[950] The GC reiterated that, in order for a refusal to supply to be abusive on the grounds that it denies access to an indispensable product or service, two markets must be involved but the upstream market may merely be 'hypothetical'.[951] On the other conditions, it concluded as follows.

Case T-201/04, *Microsoft v Commission* EU:T:2007:289

General Court

Elimination of competition

560. In the contested decision, the Commission considered whether the refusal at issue gave rise to a 'risk' of the elimination of competition on the work group server operating systems market. . . . Microsoft contends that that criterion is not sufficiently strict, since according to the case-law on the exercise of an intellectual property right the Commission must demonstrate that the refusal to license an intellectual property right to a third party is 'likely to eliminate all competition', or, in other words, that there is a 'high probability' that the conduct in question will have such a result.

561. The Court finds that Microsoft's complaint is purely one of terminology and is wholly irrelevant. The expressions 'risk of elimination of competition' and 'likely to eliminate competition' are used without distinction by the [Union] judicature to reflect the same idea, namely that Article [102] does not apply only from the time when there is no more, or practically no more, competition on the market. If the Commission were required to wait until competitors were eliminated from the market, or until their elimination was sufficiently imminent, before being able to take action under Article [102], that would clearly run counter to the objective of that provision, which is to maintain undistorted competition in the common market and, in particular, to safeguard the competition that still exists on the relevant market.

562. In this case, the Commission had all the more reason to apply Article [102] before the elimination of competition on the work group server operating systems market had become a reality because that market is characterised by significant network effects and because the elimination of competition would therefore be difficult to reverse . . .

563. Nor is it necessary to demonstrate that all competition on the market would be eliminated. What matters, for the purpose of establishing an infringement of Article [102], is that the refusal at issue is liable to, or is likely to, eliminate all effective competition on the market. It must be made clear that the fact that the competitors of the dominant undertaking retain a marginal presence in certain niches on the market cannot suffice to substantiate the existence of such competition.

564. Last, it must be borne in mind that it is for the Commission to establish that the refusal to supply gives rise to a risk of the elimination of all effective competition. As already stated at paragraph 482 above, the Commission must base its assessment on accurate, reliable and coherent evidence which comprises all the relevant data that must be taken into consideration in order to assess a complex situation and which are capable of substantiating the conclusions drawn from them.

[948] Ibid. [949] Ibid., para. 333. [950] Case T-210/04, *Microsoft* EU:T:2007:289, paras. 369–436.
[951] Ibid., para. 335, citing Case C-418/01, *IMS* EU:C:2004:257, paras. 43–44.

New product

643. It must be emphasised that the fact that the applicant's conduct prevents the appearance of a new product on the market falls to be considered under Article [102(b)] . . . which prohibits abusive practices which consist in 'limiting production, markets or technical developments to the . . . prejudice of consumers'.

644. Thus, at paragraph 54 of *Magill* . . . the Court of Justice held that the refusal by the broadcasting companies concerned had to be characterised as abusive within the meaning of that provision because it prevented the appearance of a new product which the broadcasting companies did not offer and for which there was a potential consumer demand.

645. It is apparent from the decision at issue in that case that the Commission had, more specifically, considered that by their refusal, the broadcasting companies limited production or markets to the prejudice of consumers . . . The Commission had found that that refusal prevented publishers from producing and publishing a weekly television guide for consumers in Ireland and Northern Ireland, a type of guide not then available on that geographic market. Although each of the broadcasting companies concerned published a weekly television guide, each guide was devoted to that particular broadcaster's own programmes. In finding an abuse of a dominant position by those broadcasting companies, the Commission had emphasised the harm which the absence of a general weekly television guide on the market in Ireland and in Northern Ireland caused to consumers, who, if they wished to know what programmes were being offered in the coming week, had no alternative to buying the weekly guides of each channel and themselves extracting the relevant information in order to make comparisons.

646. In *IMS Health* . . . the Court of Justice, when assessing the circumstance relating to the appearance of a new product, also placed that circumstance in the context of the damage to the interests of consumers. Thus . . . the Court emphasised . . . that that circumstance related to the consideration that, in the balancing of the interest in protection of the intellectual property right and the economic freedom of its owner against the interest in protection of free competition, the latter can prevail only where refusal to grant a licence prevents the development of the secondary market, to the detriment of consumers.

647. The circumstance relating to the appearance of a new product . . . cannot be the only parameter which determines whether a refusal to license an intellectual property right is capable of causing prejudice to consumers within the meaning of Article [102(b)] . . . As that provision states, such prejudice may arise where there is a limitation not only of production or markets, but also of technical development.

648. It was on that last hypothesis that the Commission based its finding in the contested decision. Thus, the Commission considered that Microsoft's refusal to supply the relevant information limited technical development to the prejudice of consumers within the meaning of Article [102(b)] . . . and it rejected Microsoft's assertion that it had not been demonstrated that its refusal caused prejudice to consumers . . .

649. The Court finds that the Commission's findings . . . are not manifestly incorrect.

650. Thus, in the first place, the Commission was correct to observe, at recital 694 to the contested decision, that '[owing] to the lack of interoperability that competing work group server operating system products can achieve with the Windows domain architecture, an increasing number of consumers are locked into a homogeneous Windows solution at the level of work group server operating systems'.

651. It must be borne in mind that . . . Microsoft's refusal prevented its competitors from developing work group server operating systems capable of attaining a sufficient degree of interoperability with the Windows domain architecture, with the consequence that consumers' purchasing decisions in respect of work group server operating systems were channelled towards Microsoft's products . . .

652. The limitation thus placed on consumer choice is all the more damaging to consumers because . . . they consider that non-Microsoft work group server operating systems are better than Windows work group server operating systems with respect to a series of features to which they

attach great importance, such as 'reliability/availability of the . . . system' and 'security included with the server operating system'.

653. In the second place, the Commission was correct to consider that the artificial advantage in terms of interoperability that Microsoft retained by its refusal discouraged its competitors from developing and marketing work group server operating systems with innovative features, to the prejudice, notably, of consumers (see, to that effect, recital 694 to the contested decision). That refusal has the consequence that those competitors are placed at a disadvantage by comparison with Microsoft so far as the merits of their products are concerned, particularly with regard to parameters such as security, reliability, ease of use or operating performance speed (recital 699 to the contested decision).

. . .

658. Nor would Microsoft's competitors have any interest in merely reproducing Windows work group server operating systems. Once they are able to use the information communicated to them to develop systems that are sufficiently interoperable with the Windows domain architecture, they will have no other choice, if they wish to take advantage of a competitive advantage over Microsoft and maintain a profitable presence on the market, than to differentiate their products from Microsoft's products with respect to certain parameters and certain features . . .

659. Last, Microsoft's argument that it will have less incentive to develop a given technology if it is required to make that technology available to its competitors (see paragraph 627 above) is of no relevance to the examination of the circumstance relating to the new product, where the issue to be decided is the impact of the refusal to supply on the incentive for Microsoft's competitors to innovate and not on Microsoft's incentives to innovate. That is an issue which will be decided when the Court examines the circumstance relating to the absence of objective justification.

660. In the third place, the Commission is also correct to reject as unfounded Microsoft's assertion during the administrative procedure that it was not demonstrated that its refusal caused prejudice to consumers (recitals 702 to 708 to the contested decision).

661. . . . [C]ontrary to Microsoft's contention, consumers consider non-Microsoft work group server operating systems to be better than Windows work group server operating systems on a number of features to which they attach great importance.

. . .

. . . Article [102] . . . covers not only practices which may prejudice consumers directly but also those which indirectly prejudice them by impairing an effective competitive structure (Case 85/76 *Hoffmann-La Roche v Commission* . . . paragraph 125, and *Irish Sugar v Commission* . . . paragraph 232). In this case, Microsoft impaired the effective competitive structure on the work group server operating systems market by acquiring a significant market share on that market.

665. The Court concludes from all of the foregoing considerations that the Commission's finding to the effect that Microsoft's refusal limits technical development to the prejudice of consumers within the meaning of Article [102(b)] . . . is not manifestly incorrect. The Court therefore finds that the circumstance relating to the appearance of a new product is present in this case.

The GC upheld the Commission decision on the basis that exceptional circumstances were present. In doing so, the GC gave an elastic interpretation to those exceptional circumstances. Moreover, the GC did not confine its statements to copyrights. On the *indispensability* criterion, the GC upheld the Commission's finding that it was indispensable for the competitors' systems to work as seamlessly with Windows as Microsoft's own products,[952] even though a fringe of competitors continued to operate on the market. The interface information might have been greatly more convenient for the

[952] The Commission explained further at the hearing that this included a non-Windows WGOS being able to 'talk' to a Microsoft WGOS just as if it were itself a Microsoft WGOS: Case T-210/04, *Microsoft* EU:T:2007:289, para. 237.

competitors, but they could function without it. Indispensability thus did not mean exclusion from the market.[953]

On the *elimination of competition* criterion, the GC interpreted this as meaning the elimination of effective competition on the downstream market. The continued existence of fringe competitors in niche markets was irrelevant. The GC was content that the Commission could demonstrate merely a 'risk' of the elimination of effective competition and accepted that the Commission did not have to wait for actual elimination of competition before it could act. Unlike *Magill*, where the refusal to supply entirely excluded the potential entrant, the competitors in *Microsoft* were on the market but might leave it, or become marginalised, in future. This involved speculation as to how the—constantly evolving, high technology—market would develop. This is akin to the kind of prediction that is undertaken in merger cases, where the EU Courts hold the Commission to a rigorous standard of proof.[954] Yet in *Microsoft*, the GC was happy that the Commission had established a 'risk' based on accurate, reliable, and coherent evidence.[955] Furthermore, in Article 102 cases which may take years to reach the GC (over three in *Microsoft*), any 'risk' foreseen by the Commission at the time of the decision may or may not have materialised to a greater or lesser extent. The question is then how far the Court should employ the benefit of hindsight, given the limitations of judicial review.[956]

On the *new product* criterion, the GC said that the Commission had not made a manifest error in failing to identify a specific new product for which there was actual or potential consumer demand whose emergence was prevented by the refusal to supply. It was enough that the refusal limited 'technical developments to the prejudice of consumers'. Having noted that, in *IMS*, the CJ was concerned about refusals which prevented the development of the secondary market to the detriment of consumers,[957] the GC said that the appearance of a 'new product' was not the only relevant parameter. It noted that Article 102(b) applies to the limitation of technical development as well as production and markets. Accordingly, this criterion encompassed (as yet unspecified and unknown) products emerging from innovation by the competitors which would not occur if the competitors left the market and/or were unable to develop products fully compatible with Windows. The lack of interoperability meant that consumers were increasingly locked in to Windows WGOS. The GC agreed that competitors would not have any interest in just 'cloning' Microsoft's products but had every reason to develop differentiated products.[958] Notably, Microsoft's argument that it would have less incentive to develop new technology if it had to then divulge this to competitors was held to be irrelevant to the 'new product' condition which concerned only *competitors'* incentives to innovate, as Microsoft's incentives were considered an objective justification issue. The GC thus endorsed the Commission's view that a refusal to supply may be abusive not because it excludes competitors but because it is likely to hinder future innovation.

In dealing with Microsoft's plea of *objective justification*, the GC clarified how the defence works.[959] The case itself, however, demonstrates how difficult it is to separate objective justification from the finding of abuse.[960] The GC rejected Microsoft's plea that the fact that the information was covered by IPRs justified its refusal to disclose, on the grounds that it would lead to the conclusion that a refusal

[953] See D. Ridyard, 'Compulsory Access under EC Competition Law—A New Doctrine of "Convenient Facilities" and the Case for Price Regulation' [2004] *ECLR* 670.

[954] See D. Beard, '*Microsoft*: What Sort of Landmark?' (2008) 4 Competition Policy International 39, 42–43; for mergers, see Chap. 15.

[955] Case T-210/04, *Microsoft* EU:T:2007:289, paras. 564, 620.

[956] See further on this, Beard, n. 938, 47.

[957] Case C-418/01, *IMS* EU:C:2004:257, para. 48.

[958] It has been argued, however, that mere cloning could be profitable if they compete with Microsoft on price: see D. Howarth and K. McMahon, '"Windows has Performed an Illegal Operation": The Court of First Instance's Judgment in *Microsoft v Commission*' [2008] *ECLR* 117, 124.

[959] Case T-210/04, *Microsoft* EU:T:2007:289, para. 688.

[960] Ibid., in particular para. 659.

to license could never be an abuse. It also rejected Microsoft's pleas that disclosure would have a negative impact on its incentives to innovate, dismissing them as 'vague and theoretical arguments' which did not specify the technologies or products concerned.[961] The judgment suggests, therefore, that the defence might succeed if a greater level of detail were given. However, the GC put the burden of proof on the defendant to demonstrate that its incentives would be harmed by compulsory licensing,[962] and, especially where the evolution of high technology markets is involved, it is questionable whether it would ever be possible to discharge that burden. The GC's scepticism with respect to Microsoft's claimed objective justifications should also be contrasted to its willingness to accept, without similar specificity, the claims about 'technical development' being limited and its assumption that the refusal to deal would lead to consumer harm. One curious point is the GC's treatment of the Commission's statement that the positive impact on the industry as a whole outweighed the negative impact on Microsoft's incentives.[963] Microsoft argued that this introduced a new test into the application of Article 102,[964] and the GC's attempt to explain away the Commission's approach was unconvincing.[965] From an efficiencies perspective, it can be argued that the Commission was correct,[966] although it has also been said that balancing tests are 'an inherently unreliable and unpredictable method to address mandatory access'.[967]

As with the tying part of the judgment,[968] *Microsoft* is significant not only in respect of the substantive law on refusal to supply and IPRs but also in the context of the 'modernisation' of Article 102. First, the GC concentrated on the position of competitors, stressing the fall in their market share and the rise in Microsoft's. Secondly, it emphasised the disadvantage to the competitors and deduced consumer prejudice from that. Thirdly, the GC repeated that Article 102 is concerned with the impairment of the competitive structure, but said that Microsoft had done that by acquiring a significant market share and did not explain how it led to consumer detriment.

In May 2022, the Commission announced that it had sent a statement of objections to Apple, alleging abuse of dominance by virtue of limiting access to a standard technology, 'Near Field Communication' (NFC), used for contactless payments with mobile devices. The Commission claims that Apple prevents mobile wallets app developers from accessing the necessary hardware and software ('NFC input'). This is alleged to prevent the development of rival mobile wallet solutions on Apple's devices, to the advantage of its own payment solution, Apple Pay.[969]

F. REFUSAL TO SUPPLY IN SITUATIONS NOT INVOLVING UPSTREAM/DOWNSTREAM MARKETS

The cases discussed thus far have involved situations of vertical integration, where the competition policy concern is that the dominant defendant may seek to leverage its market power up or down the value chain. It is more unusual for the activities of non-vertically integrated undertakings to be scrutinised under the rubric of 'refusal to supply', insofar as such entities would normally have few

[961] Ibid., para. 698. [962] Ibid., para. 696. [963] COMP/37.792, *Microsoft* 24 March 2004, para. 783.

[964] Case T-210/04, *Microsoft* EU:T:2007:289, paras. 669–670. [965] Ibid., paras. 705–710.

[966] C. Ritter, 'Refusal to Deal and Essential Facilities: Does Intellectual Property Require Special Deference compared to Tangible Property?' (2005) 3 *World Competition* 281, 298.

[967] D. Geradin, 'Limiting the Scope of Article 82 EC: What Can the EU Learn from the Supreme Court's Judgment in *Trinko*, in the Wake of *Microsoft, IMS* and *Deutsche Telekom*?' (2004) 41 *CMLRev* 1526, 1542.

[968] See Section 11.E.iii.

[969] Commission Press Release, 'Antitrust: Commission sends Statement of Objections to Apple over practices regarding Apple Pay', 2 May 2022.

incentives to refuse to make sales in the market segment in which they take their profits. There are, nonetheless, several examples of refusal to supply in situations not involving upstream/downstream markets in the Article 102 jurisprudence. Such cases have mainly concerned the supply of products for distribution or resale and a dominant firm protecting its commercial interest.

Among the various abuses addressed in *United Brands*, the Commission held that UBC had abused its dominant position on the banana market by refusing to continue supplying its Chiquita bananas to its Danish ripener/distributor, Oelsen, in response to Oelsen taking part in an advertising and promotion campaign for rival 'Dole' bananas. Oelsen was not under an exclusive purchasing obligation, but UBC argued that Oelsen had sold fewer and fewer Chiquitas in comparison to Doles, and had taken less trouble in ripening them. Without contesting UBC's allegations, the CJ upheld the finding that the refusal to supply infringed Article 102. Whilst affirming that dominant undertakings are justified in acting to prevent attacks on their commercial interests,[970] the CJ judged UBC's response to be disproportionate despite recognising that it was in the midst of a 'banana war'.[971] It held that a dominant undertaking 'cannot stop supplying a long-standing customer who abides by regular commercial practice, if the orders placed by that customer are in no way out of the ordinary'.[972] Regrettably, the CJ failed to clarify what constitutes 'regular commercial practice', but that statement was subsequently relied upon in *Sot. Lélos* on a refusal to supply to prevent parallel trade.[973] The Guidance Paper says that exclusive dealing principles will be applied to the punishment of customers situation.[974]

In *Boosey & Hawkes*,[975] B&H, which was held to be dominant in the British-style brass band instrument market, refused to have further dealings with two firms, one a distributor of its instruments and the other a repairer, who had formed a company to manufacture and market competing instruments. The Commission took interim measures, ordering B&H to recommence supplies. Again, the Commission recognised the right of dominant undertakings to protect their interests, but refused to accept that B&H's conduct was justified and proportionate.

By contrast, *BP v Commission*[976] was a rare early case of the Commission losing an Article 102 case on the merits. The CJ held there was no duty to supply where, during the 1973 OPEC oil boycott, an oil supplier dealt with the shortage by supplying its regular, long-term rather than occasional customers. Contrary to the findings of the Commission, the CJ held that this strategy was reasonable in the circumstances and that the refusal to supply the complainant was justified.

Refusal to supply on grounds of nationality similarly may infringe Article 102.[977] The case law on the licensing of standard-essential patents might also be construed as a category of refusal to supply,[978] although these cases have not been treated as such by the Commission or Court.[979]

[970] For the protection of commercial interests as a defence, see Section 5.G.

[971] Case 27/76, *United Brands* EU:C:1978:22, para. 196. As discussed in Chap. 6, UBC was found dominant with 45% of a narrowly drawn market (bananas rather than fruit) despite evidence of what the Court itself called 'very lively competition'.

[972] Ibid., para. 182. [973] Cases C-468–478/06, *Sot. Lélos* EU:C:2008:504, see Section 17.

[974] Guidance Paper, para. 77.

[975] *BBI/Boosey & Hawkes* [1987] OJ L286/36. There were other alleged abuses by B&H, such as engaging in vexatious litigation (see Section 14.B).

[976] Case 77/77, *BP v Commission* EU:C:1978:141.

[977] See e.g. Case 7/82, *GVL v Commission* EU:C:1983:52, where the German collecting society refused to offer its services to artists established outside Germany unless they were of German nationality.

[978] As explained in N. Dunne, 'Dispensing with Indispensability' (2020) 16 *J of Competition Law and Economics* 74.

[979] See Section 14.C.

G. REFUSAL TO SUPPLY IN THE GUIDANCE PAPER

The Guidance Paper covers only situations where a vertically integrated dominant undertaking competes downstream with a buyer it refuses to supply (see paragraph 77). From the outset, the Guidance Paper takes a comparatively permissive approach: it states the basic principle of freedom to contract with whom one chooses, followed by the reasons for taking great care before competition law intervenes.

> 75. When setting its enforcement priorities, the Commission starts from the position that, generally speaking, any undertaking, whether dominant or not, should have the right to choose its trading partners and to dispose freely of its property. The Commission therefore considers that intervention on competition law grounds requires careful consideration where the application of Article [102] would lead to the imposition of an obligation to supply on the dominant undertaking . . . The existence of such an obligation—even for a fair remuneration—may undermine undertakings' incentives to invest and innovate and, thereby, possibly harm consumers. The knowledge that they may have a duty to supply against their will may lead dominant undertakings—or undertakings who anticipate that they may become dominant—not to invest, or to invest less, in the activity in question. Also, competitors may be tempted to free ride on investments made by the dominant undertaking instead of investing themselves. Neither of these consequences would, in the long run, be in the interest of consumers.

No distinction is made between refusal to license IPRs and other refusals. The Guidance Paper says that the concept of refusal to supply includes 'a broad range of practices' such as refusing to supply products to existing or new customers, refusal to license IPRs, including for purposes of interface information, or refusal to grant access to an essential facility or network.[980] The original Guidance Paper treated both 'constructive refusals'—such as undue delay, degradation of supply, or imposing unreasonable conditions[981]—and margin squeeze as types of refusal to supply,[982] although in this regard it was superseded by the approach of the CJ in *Slovak Telekom*[983] and *TeliaSonera*,[984] respectively. The Amendments to the Guidance Paper remove any reference to constructive refusals, and move margin squeeze into its own distinct category.[985]

The Guidance Paper sets out a test for when the Commission will consider it a priority to intervene. It comprises three cumulative conditions:

(a) the refusal relates to a product or service that is objectively necessary to compete on a downstream market;

(b) the refusal is likely to lead to the elimination of effective competition in the downstream market;

(c) the refusal is likely to lead to consumer harm.[986]

On condition (a), the objective necessity of the input (the term the Commission uses instead of 'indispensability'), the Commission relies on *Microsoft* to hold that this does not mean that without it no competitor could enter or survive on the downstream market.[987] The test is whether an alternative source of supply is capable of allowing competitors to exert a competitive constraint.

[980] Guidance Paper, para. 78. [981] Ibid., para. 79. [982] Ibid., para. 80.
[983] Case C-165/19 P, *Slovak Telekom* EU:C:2021:239, see Section 12.
[984] Case C-52/09, *TeliaSonera* EU:C:2011:83, see Section 9.
[985] Amendments to the Guidance Paper, Annex, paras. 4–5. See Section 9.C for discussion of the treatment of margin squeeze in the revised Guidance Paper.
[986] Guidance Paper, para. 80 (renumbered). [987] Ibid., para. 82 (renumbered).

On condition (b), the Commission states that if the objective necessity of the input is shown, the refusal to supply is generally liable to eliminate, immediately or over time, effective competition in the downstream market.[988] The requirement for elimination of *effective competition* comes from *Microsoft*, and the Commission has preferred this to the standard in the earlier non-IPR cases, *Commercial Solvents* and *Bronner*, which, as we have seen, required the elimination of competition from the person requesting access.[989]

On condition (c), the impact on consumer harm, the Commission says it will normally pursue the case if the likely negative effects of the refusal outweigh over time the negative effects of ordering supply. It then continues:[990]

> The Commission considers that consumer harm may, for instance, arise where the competitors that the dominant undertaking forecloses are, as a result of the refusal, prevented from bringing innovative goods or services to market and/or where follow-on innovation is likely to be stifled . . . This may be particularly the case if the undertaking which requests supply does not intend to limit itself essentially to duplicating the goods or services already offered by the dominant undertaking on the downstream market, but intends to produce new or improved goods or services for which there is a potential consumer demand or is likely to contribute to technical development . . .

The reference to innovation is not confined to IPR situations. Rather than distinguish between IPR and non-IPR cases, the Commission applies the need for 'consumer harm' to all cases. The concern with the stifling of innovation again reflects the *Microsoft* judgment.

The Commission says it will apply the enforcement priority criteria to both new and existing customers. However, the termination of existing supply is more likely to be found abusive. In such situations, the prior existence of a supply arrangement makes it less plausible for the dominant undertaking to argue that a mandatory supply obligation would result in inadequate compensation for its original investment. The customer itself is also more likely to have already made relationship-specific investments, which are dependent upon continued supply of the input from the dominant undertaking.[991]

The three conditions laid down for enforcement priority are subject to a proviso, the '*Telefónica* exceptions'.[992] In certain situations, such as where sector regulation has already provided for supply obligations or the upstream position of the dominant undertaking has been developed through State protection or State financing, the Commission's normal wariness about potential negative effects on investment and innovation incentives is eased. In such cases, the Commission will revert to its general enforcement standard set out in the Guidance Paper, i.e. likely anti-competitive foreclosure.

[988] Ibid., para. 84 (renumbered). Nazzini, n. 139, 267 takes issue with this, saying that proof of the effect of the refusal on downstream competition is a free-standing element of the test, and pointing out that the Commission itself in para. 84 sets out a number of factors which affect the likelihood of effective competition being eliminated. These include a high market share in the downstream market, the extent to which the dominant undertaking is comparatively capacity-constrained downstream, the substitutability between the dominant undertaking's output and that of its downstream competitors, and the proportion of downstream competitors affected by the refusal.

[989] Nazzini, n. 139, 267, argues that elimination of all competition and elimination of competition from the person requiring access amounts in reality to the same thing as indispensability is an objective concept so a refusal capable of excluding one competitor must be capable of excluding all.

[990] Guidance Paper, para. 86 (renumbered).

[991] Ibid., para. 83 (renumbered). There is no case law cited in support of this paragraph.

[992] COMP/38.784, *Wanadoo España v Telefónica* 4 July 2007, see Section 9.B.iii. See D. Geradin, 'Refusal to Supply and Margin Squeeze: A Discussion of Why the "*Telefonica* Exceptions" are Wrong', TILEC Discussion Paper No. 2011-009, <http://papers.ssrn.com/sol3/papers.cfm?abstract_id=1762687>.

As discussed in Section 12.C.iii, these criteria have now been endorsed, more or less, in *Slovak Telekom*[993] and *Lithuanian Railways*.[994]

The Guidance Paper states that the Commission will consider efficiencies claims, in a manner that reflects the kinds of arguments that were raised in *Microsoft*:

> The Commission will consider claims by the dominant undertaking that a refusal to supply is necessary to allow the dominant undertaking to realise an adequate return on the investments required to develop its input business, thus generating incentives to continue to invest in the future, taking the risk of failed projects into account. The Commission will also consider claims by the dominant undertaking that its own innovation will be negatively affected by the obligation to supply, or by the structural changes in the market conditions that imposing such an obligation will bring about, including the development of follow-on innovation by competitors.[995]

Citing *Microsoft*, the Guidance Paper says that it is for the dominant undertaking to demonstrate the negative impact of an obligation to supply on its own level of innovation.[996]

13. SELF-PREFERENCING

A. GENERAL

Self-preferencing is a theory of harm that has emerged as a pre-eminent competition concern in respect of the activities of dominant platforms operating in digital markets. It arises where the platform operator 'giv[es] preferential treatment to [their] own products or services when they are in competition with products and services provided by other entities using the platform'.[997] Self-preferencing is a kind of discriminatory leveraging.[998] It presupposes that the dominant platform operates in multiple complementary or vertically related markets, and that it provides products or services in one market to business customers against whom it competes in another market. Self-preferencing, to use the language of the Commission's press release announcing the *Google Shopping* decision, involves 'giving an illegal advantage'[999] to the dominant platform's product or service in the competitive market segment, by virtue of the privileges that it possesses as a result of operating multi-market. In this regard, the theory of harm might be considered to resemble refusal to deal or tying.[1000] The pivotal *Google Shopping* case, however, rejected this characterisation, establishing instead that self-preferencing constitutes an 'independent form of abuse falling outside the scope of competition on the merits'.[1001]

While leveraging as a broad category of abuse is 'well-established'[1002] within the Article 102 case law, the recognition of self-preferencing as a distinct *type* of abuse appears to be specific to digital platform markets. Most notably, the various cases taken to date by the Commission under this rubric

[993] Case C-165/19 P, *Slovak Telekom* EU:C:2021:239. [994] Case C-42/21 P, *Lietuvos geležinkeliai AB* EU:C:2023:12.
[995] Guidance Paper, para. 88 (renumbered). [996] Ibid., para. 89 (renumbered), citing para. 659 of *Microsoft*.
[997] Crémer, de Montjoye, and Schweitzer, n. 186, 7.
[998] B. Vesterdorf, 'Theories of Self-preferencing and Duty to Deal—Two Sides of the Same Coin?' (2015) 1 *CLPD* 4–9.
[999] Commission Press Release, 'Antitrust: Commission fines Google €2.42 billion for abusing dominance as search engine by giving illegal advantage to own comparison shopping service', Brussels, 27 June 2017.
[1000] See e.g. P. Akman, 'The Theory of Abuse in *Google Search*: A Positive and Normative Assessment under EU Competition Law' [2017] *Univ Illinois J of Law, Technology & Policy* 301; E. Iacobucci and F. Ducci, 'The *Google Search* Case in Europe: Tying and the Single Monopoly Profit Theorem in Two-sided Markets' (2019) 47 *European J of Law and Economics* 15 (2019).
[1001] AT.39740, *Google Search (Shopping)* 27 June 2017, para. 649. This approach was endorsed by the GC in Case T-612/17, *Google Shopping* EU:T:2021:763, para. 240.
[1002] AT.39740, *Google Search (Shopping)* 27 June 2017, para. 649.

have involved Big Tech actors.[1003] Self-preferencing has been identified and discussed as an obvious and urgent problem in many of the digital competition policy reports published worldwide in recent years, as discussed in Chapter 16. Moreover, certain types of self-preferencing, specifically by online platforms, have been the target of sector-specific legislation at EU level, namely the Regulation on Platform-to-Business (P2B) relations[1004] and the Digital Markets Act (DMA).[1005]

Digital platforms 'come in various shapes and sizes',[1006] ranging from the provision of payment systems or online search or advertising services, to app distribution, social media outlets, and connecting peer-to-peer users in the sharing economy. Yet platforms share certain characteristics, including operation as multi-sided markets, the centrality of network effects, and the ability to create new digital markets and monetise their functioning.[1007] Platforms are often described as digital intermediaries, the function of which is to 'bring together or facilitate transactions between third parties on the Internet'.[1008] There is also increased focus on the 'gatekeeper' role that platforms play, by controlling access to market segments or customers groups, and thus rendering them an unavoidable fixture within digital ecosystems.[1009] At the heart of self-preferencing is the question whether 'platforms implicitly promise unbiased treatment to all users',[1010] and in what circumstances a failure to live up to that promise violates competition law.

Yet the explicit focus of the P2B Regulation and the DMA is to ensure 'fair' outcomes for traders: a goal that, in the context of the DMA, is expressly stated to go beyond the existing scope of Articles 101 and 102.[1011] This hints at a concern that self-preferencing is a theory of harm that could draw EU competition law back towards its former much-criticised propensity for protecting competitors at the expense of consumer welfare more broadly. As we have seen, Article 102 does not prohibit dominance, nor does it guarantee 'less efficient' or 'less attractive' competitors any right to succeed or even remain in the market. In their 2019 report, the Commission's expert advisors on digital competition policy framed the dilemma of self-preferencing as follows:

> On the one hand, one could argue that giving its products or services preferential treatment is an appropriate reward for management of the platform. On the other hand, where a dominant platform engages in self-preferencing, the distortive effect on downstream markets may be substantial, such that self-preferencing ultimately constitutes a disproportionate form of reward.[1012]

Sceptics of self-preferencing argue that it is common and natural business behaviour for vertically integrated undertakings, and that it rarely results in consumer harm.[1013] This is, however, essentially

[1003] See discussion in Sections 13.B and 13.C.

[1004] Reg. 2019/1150 on promoting fairness and transparency for business users of online intermediation services [2019] OJ L186/57.

[1005] Reg. (EU) 2022/1925 of the European Parliament and of the Council of 14 September 2022 on contestable and fair markets in the digital sector and amending Dirs. (EU) 2019/1937 and (EU) 2020/1828 (DMA) [2022] OJ L265/1.

[1006] European Commission, 'Communication on Online Platforms and the Digital Single Market—Opportunities and Challenges for Europe', COM(2016) 288 final, p. 2.

[1007] Ibid., pp. 2–3.

[1008] OECD, *The Economic and Social Role of Internet Intermediaries* (April 2010), 9. The digital intermediary concept extends beyond platforms as such, however, to include e.g. internet service and web hosting providers.

[1009] See e.g. O. Lynskey, 'Regulating "Platform Power"', LSE Law, Society and Economy Working Papers 1/2017, 9, and I. Graef, 'Differentiated Treatment in Platform-to-Business Relations: EU Competition Law and Economic Dependence' (2019) 38 *YEL* 448, 486.

[1010] M. Salinger, 'Self-Preferencing,' in Global Antitrust Institute, *Report on the Digital Economy* (2020), 352.

[1011] See discussion at Chap. 16, Section 6.

[1012] Crémer, de Montjoye, and Schweitzer, n. 186, 66.

[1013] Se, e.g. Vesterdorf, n. 982; Salinger, n. 994; D. Hoffmann and G. Shinn, 'Self-preferencing and Antitrust: Harmful Solutions for an Improbable Problem', *CPI Antitrust Chronicle*, June 2021; and G. Colangelo, 'Antitrust Unchained: The EU's Case Against Self-preferencing', ICLE Working Paper No.2022-09-22 (2022), <https://papers.ssrn.com/sol3/papers.cfm?abstract_id=4227839>.

an empirical question.[1014] Self-preferencing is thus an inapposite candidate for 'by object' prohibition under Article 102.[1015] There is greater scope to develop a convincing theory of harm that hinges upon a demonstration of anti-competitive effects. Yet there is disagreement as to what should be required to establish an abuse of dominance on this basis. It has been suggested, for instance, that the evident pro-competitive potential of many of the behaviours that conceivably fall within the rubric of self-preferencing mean that a particularly 'robust' assessment of effects is required.[1016] Conversely, the Commission's expert advisors advocated a reverse burden of proof for any dominant digital platform that performs a 'regulatory'[1017] function: namely, that 'it should bear the burden of proving that self-preferencing has no long-run exclusionary effects on product markets. The dominant platform would then need to prove either the absence of adverse effects on competition or an overriding efficiency rationale.'[1018] The Commission's Guidance Paper predates the emergence of self-preferencing as a pre-eminent theory of harm in digital markets, and thus provides little guidance on how such cases should be analysed, beyond the general 'anti-competitive foreclosure' standard for intervention. Instead, we must turn to the case law.

B. THE *GOOGLE SHOPPING* CASE

Google Shopping was the first Commission decision to establish abusive self-preferencing by a dominant platform contrary to Article 102. A then-recording breaking fine of €2.42 billion accompanied the infringement decision,[1019] both of which were essentially upheld on appeal by the GC. As discussed in Chapter 6,[1020] the case involved two discrete services: Google's dominant general online search service, which enables users to find information across the internet; and its comparison shopping service, a specialised search engine which aggregates product offers from merchant websites, enabling users to compare e-commerce options. The disputed conduct comprised two interlinked practices: Google systematically demoted the results of competing comparison shopping products within its general search results pages; and granted more prominent placement to its own comparison shopping service compared with the 'organic' outcome if the ordinary search algorithm was applied. The rationale for doing so, the Commission argued, was Google's awareness of the limitations of its comparison shopping service, which would not rank highly within its general search results if subject to the same controls as rival comparison shopping products.[1021] The Commission construed this behaviour as abusive self-preferencing of Google's own comparison shopping product, by leveraging its dominance in the general online search market. The infringement decision required Google to cease and desist its abusive conduct, in a manner that would ensure that competing comparison shopping services were treated 'no less favourably than [Google's] own comparison shopping service within its general search results pages'.[1022]

In the extract below, the GC explains how the Commission constructed its theory of harm, and how this essentially novel type of abuse fits with established Article 102 jurisprudence prohibiting conduct that departs from 'competition on the merits'.

1014 P. Caro de Sousa, 'What Shall We Do About Self-preferencing?' *CPI Antitrust Chronicle*, June 2020.
1015 Crémer, de Montjoye, and Schweitzer, n. 186, 66.
1016 P. Ibáñez Colomo, 'Self-preferencing: Yet Another Epithet in Need of Limiting Principles' (2020) 43 *World Competition* 417, 446.
1017 Namely, 'setting up the rules and institutions through which their users interact,' see Crémer, de Montjoye, and Schweitzer, n. 186, 60.
1018 Ibid., 66–67. 1019 AT.39740, *Google Search (Shopping)* 27 June 2017.
1020 See Chap. 6, Section 8.A.v. 1021 AT.39740, *Google Search (Shopping)* 27 June 2017, para. 382.
1022 Ibid., para. 699.

Case T-612/17 *Google and Alphabet v Commission (Google Shopping)* EU:T:2021:763

General Court

167. The Commission considered that, through leveraging, Google was relying on its dominant position on the market for general search services in order to favour its own comparison shopping service on the market for specialised comparison shopping search services by promoting the positioning and display of that comparison shopping service and of its results on its general results pages, as compared to competing comparison shopping services, whose results, given their inherent characteristics, were prone to being demoted on those pages by adjustment algorithms.

168. The Commission observed . . . that while results from competing comparison shopping services could appear only as generic results, that is to say, simple blue links that were also prone to being demoted by adjustment algorithms, results from Google's own comparison shopping service were prominently positioned at the top of Google's general results pages, displayed in rich format and incapable of being demoted by those algorithms, resulting in a difference in treatment in the form of Google's favouring of its own comparison shopping service.

169. The Commission explained in particular that, on account of three specific circumstances—namely (i) the importance of traffic generated by Google's general search engine for comparison shopping services . . .; (ii) the behaviour of users when searching online . . .; and (iii) the fact that diverted traffic from Google's general results pages accounts for a large proportion of traffic to competing comparison shopping services and cannot be effectively replaced by other sources . . .—this favouring was liable to lead to a weakening of competition on the market.

. . .

175. It follows . . . that the Commission did not merely identify leveraging but, as required by the case-law, classified Google's accompanying practices in law on the basis of relevant criteria. Thus, if the favouring and its effects, identified in the light of the specific circumstances of the relevant markets, have been validly demonstrated by the Commission . . . the Commission will have been fully entitled to take the view that that favouring was a departure from competition on the merits.

176. It must be observed in that regard that, given the universal vocation of Google's general search engine, which . . . is designed to index results containing any possible content, the promotion on Google's general results pages of one type of specialised result—its own—over the specialised results of competitors involves a certain form of abnormality.

177. The infrastructure at issue, namely Google's general results pages which generate traffic to other websites, including those of competing comparison shopping services, is, in principle, open, which distinguishes it from other infrastructures referred to in the case-law, consisting of tangible or intangible assets (press distribution systems or intellectual property rights, respectively) whose value depends on the proprietor's ability to retain exclusive use of them.

178. Unlike the latter infrastructures, the rationale and value of a general search engine lie in its capacity to be open to results from external (third-party) sources and to display these multiple and diverse sources on its general results pages, sources which enrich and enhance the credibility of the search engine as far as the general public is concerned, and enable it to benefit from the network effects and economies of scale that are essential for its development and its subsistence in a market in which, by their very nature, few infrastructures of that kind can subsist, given those network effects. A very large number of users is needed to reach the critical mass capable of compensating for the service being free of charge on one side of the market and generating advertising income on its other side. Accordingly, for a search engine, limiting the scope of its results to its own entails an element of risk and is not necessarily rational, save in a situation, as in the present case, where the dominance and barriers to entry are such that no market entry within a sufficiently short period of time is possible in response to that limitation of internet users' choice.

> 179. Consequently, the fact . . . that Google favours its own specialised results over third-party results, which seems to be the converse of the economic model underpinning the initial success of its search engine, cannot but involve a certain form of abnormality. It . . . is for the person responsible for that difference in treatment to justify it in the light of competition law (. . . *Servier and Others v Commission*, T-691/14, under appeal, EU:T:2018:922, paragraph 1377 and the case-law cited).
>
> 180. It may be observed moreover, for the sake of completeness, that even in a situation that differs from that of the present case, the Court of Justice has ruled, with regard to internet access providers, that the EU legislature had intended, by Regulation (EU) 2015/2120 of the European Parliament and of the Council of 25 November 2015 laying down measures concerning open internet access . . . (OJ 2015 L 310, p. 1), to impose on those operators a general obligation of equal treatment, without discrimination, restriction or interference with traffic, from which derogation is not possible in any circumstances by means of commercial practices (. . . *Telenor Magyarország*, C-807/18 and C-39/19, EU:C:2020:708, paragraph 47). The fact that the legislature made that choice and the legal obligation of non-discrimination that follows from it for internet access providers on the upstream market cannot be disregarded when analysing the practices of an operator like Google on the downstream market, given the undisputed ultra-dominant position of Google on the market for general search services and its special responsibility not to allow its behaviour to impair genuine, undistorted competition in the internal market. It is of no relevance in that regard whether or not legislation calls, in general terms, for such non-discriminatory access to online search results, since, as is clear from the case-law, a system of undistorted competition can be guaranteed only if equality of opportunity is secured as between the various economic operators (. . . *Deutsche Telekom v Commission*, C-280/08 P, EU:C:2010:603, paragraph 230 and the case-law cited), which is consistent with the possibility that certain differences in treatment may be considered contrary to Article 102 TFEU when what is at issue are favouring practices established by operators in a dominant position in the internet sector.
>
> 181. Furthermore, . . . the deviation in relation to competition on the merits of the conduct at issue . . . is all the more obvious as it follows a change of conduct on the part of the dominant operator. Google did indeed change its conduct on the market for general search services.
>
> . . .
>
> 185. Accordingly . . . Google's conduct cannot, as such, constitute competition on the merits.

A number of observations can be made about the analysis here. First, the GC endorsed the Commission's recognition of self-preferencing as a stand-alone 'independent form of leveraging abuse'.[1023] It was explained earlier in the chapter[1024] that the GC rejected the contention that the 'mere' extension of market power from one segment to another constitutes an abuse in itself. It thus qualified the Commission's sweeping assertion in the infringement decision that 'conduct consisting in the use of a dominant position on one market to extend that dominant position to one or more adjacent markets can constitute an abuse'.[1025] The GC nonetheless accepted that, here, the leveraging practice took a plausibly abusive form, namely the artificial manipulation of the underlying general search algorithms, in a manner which was liable to result in a weakening of competition in comparison shopping markets. As discussed in Section 12, the GC was less dismissive than the Commission about the potential applicability of the *Bronner* criteria, and in particular the pivotal requirement of indispensability. Yet it was largely content to accept the Commission's analysis of this case as an example of discriminatory leveraging premised upon two key requirements: 'abnormal' business behaviour that resulted in the diversion of traffic away from Google's rivals, coupled with a capacity for anti-competitive effects.

[1023] Ibid., para. 649, language endorsed by the GC in Case T-612/12 *Google Shopping* EU:T:2021:763 at para. 240.
[1024] See Section 6.
[1025] AT.39740, *Google Search (Shopping)* 27 June 2017, para. 649.

The fact that the GC was apparently persuaded that access to Google's general search service is 'indispensable' to competing within the comparison shopping services market is nonetheless relevant to understanding its approach to 'normal' methods of competition here. The GC stated expressly that 'Google's general results page has characteristics akin to those of an essential facility',[1026] insofar as there is 'no viable alternative' for comparison shopping services providers to generate the necessary quantity of traffic to their websites.[1027] Likewise, it is the emphatically 'open' nature of Google's general search service that is key to its market-dominating business model.[1028] In principle, Google's search algorithms find and provide users with the most relevant responses to search queries, wherever these might be located across the internet.[1029] This is precisely why so many consumers use the Google search engine, to the point that Google holds a 'superdominant' position in the relevant national markets.[1030] Hence, it was Google's 'not necessarily rational'[1031] choice to prefer its own comparison shopping service in search results, *irrespective* of the service's intrinsic usefulness, which constituted a notable departure from its normal business behaviour. This, according to the GC, could be characterised as abnormal competition other than on the merits. The GC also emphasised that Google had changed its approach to ranking comparison shopping services only after it had itself started to compete in this adjacent market.

A question still arises as to why, if the obligation does not stem from the indispensability of access to its general search service in a legally binding sense, Google was nonetheless prohibited from favouring its own services. As critics of self-preferencing as a distinct category of abuse have observed, vertically integrated undertakings 'prefer' their own products or services all the time.[1032] This may be 'jolly inconvenient'[1033] for rivals of integrated dominant undertakings, but Article 102 does not prohibit dominant undertakings from being or becoming integrated. The holding in *Google Shopping* has thus been criticised for its 'sweeping interpretation' of the special responsibility doctrine for integrated dominant undertakings.[1034]

Contentiously, the GC invoked the general principle of equal treatment, which 'requires that comparable situations must not be treated differently and different situations must not be treated in the same way unless such treatment is objectively justified',[1035] to support its conclusion that Google could not engage in 'positive acts of discrimination' to favour its services or to disadvantage those of rivals.[1036] A general obligation of non-discrimination is difficult to reconcile with an understanding of Article 102 as an instrument to avoid *in*efficient foreclosure.[1037] It would also give insufficient weight both to the likely impact of such a duty on incentives to innovate[1038] and to the freedom to conduct a business guaranteed by Article 16 of the Charter. The judgment did not, therefore, articulate a general obligation, but instead focused on 'certain differences in treatment' which follow from 'favouring practices established by operators in a dominant position in the internet sector'.[1039] To the extent that the *Google Shopping* case establishes a duty under Article 102 not to engage in discriminatory self-preferencing, therefore, it arguably only applies (thus far at least) to the activities of dominant digital platforms.

[1026] Case T-612/17, *Google Shopping* EU:T:2021:763, para. 224. [1027] Ibid., para. 226.
[1028] Ibid., para. 177. [1029] Ibid., para. 178. [1030] Ibid., para. 182. [1031] Ibid., para. 178.
[1032] See e.g. Ibáñez Colomo, n. 1000.
[1033] D. Ridyard, 'Compulsory Access Under EC Competition Law—A New Doctrine of "Convenient Facilities" and the Case for Price Regulation' [2004] *ECLR* 669, 670.
[1034] E. Deutscher, '*Google Shopping* and the Quest for a Legal Test for Self-preferencing Under Article 102 TFEU' (2022) 6 *European Papers. European Forum*, Insight of 22 February 2022, 1345, 1353.
[1035] Case T-612/17, *Google Shopping* EU:T:2021:763, para. 155. [1036] Ibid., para. 240.
[1037] The GC at para. 162, notably, reiterated the orthodoxy on this point established in *Post Danmark I* and *Intel*.
[1038] The importance of which were recognised by the GC at para. 217.
[1039] Case T-612/17, *Google Shopping* EU:T:2021:763, para. 180.

Two aspects of the judgment support this more limited reading of its scope. First, the GC emphasised that what constitutes competition on the merits can only be understood by reference to 'the specific circumstances of the relevant markets' under scrutiny.[1040] A key aspect of general search services markets is that network effects mean that 'few infrastructures of that kind' can exist simultaneously.[1041] The GC also noted Google's 'superdominant' position and 'its role as a gateway to the internet' to support its holding that, accordingly, Google 'was under a stronger obligation not to allow its behaviour to impair genuine, undistorted competition on the related market for specialised comparison shopping search services'.[1042] Secondly, the GC drew a parallel to the EU net neutrality rules which impose a general obligation of equal treatment on internet access providers, arguing that this policy choice in the upstream market 'cannot be disregarded when analysing the practices of an operator like Google on the downstream market'.[1043] The principle of equal treatment was subsequently cited by the Commission in its commitments decision concerning various alleged self-preferencing practices by Amazon, which is considered in Section 13.C.[1044] As the case involved another Big Tech platform, however, it provides us with limited insight into the outer reaches of the principle in the sphere of Article 102.

Consistent with the movement towards a 'more economic approach', the Commission positioned self-preferencing as an effects-based theory of harm. Yet it rejected any need to demonstrate *actual* anti-competitive effects arising from the practice. Instead, the existence of an abuse was premised on the *capability* or *likelihood* of the disputed conduct to have anti-competitive effects in national markets for comparison shopping services.[1045] On this point, the GC was in complete agreement. As explained earlier in this chapter,[1046] the GC in *Google Shopping* expressly rejected the existence of 'by object'-type abuses under Article 102, holding instead that it is necessary to demonstrate that conduct has 'at the very least a potential anticompetitive effect'.[1047] As the extract below demonstrates, however, this can be satisfied merely by demonstrating that it results in a weakening of competition, with an assumption that consumer harm (e.g. less innovation, higher prices) is highly likely to follow. Demonstrating the existence of actual foreclosure effects is not required.[1048]

Case T-612/17, *Google and Alphabet v Commission (Google Shopping)* EU:T:2021:763

General Court

438. As regards exclusionary practices, . . . a practice cannot be categorised as abuse of a dominant position unless it is demonstrated that there is an anticompetitive effect, or at the very least a potential anticompetitive effect, although, in the absence of any effect on the competitive situation of competitors, an exclusionary practice cannot be classified as abusive vis-à-vis those competitors (see, . . . Deutsche Telekom v Commission, C-280/08 P, EU:C:2010:603, paragraphs 250 to 254; . . . TeliaSonera Sverige, C-52/09, EU:C:2011:83, paragraphs 61 to 66; and . . . Tomra Systems and Others v Commission, C-549/10 P, EU:C:2012:221, paragraph 68).

[1040] Ibid., para. 175. [1041] Ibid., para. 178. [1042] Ibid., para. 183.

[1043] Ibid., para. 180. This aspect of the GC's reasoning has been criticised for adding 'notable confusion', insofar as it appears to suggest that provisions of *primary* EU law (i.e. Art. 102, contained in the TFEU) can be interpreted against *secondary* law (the regulation on net neutrality): see C. Bergqvist, '*Google Shopping* and Self-favouring as a Separate Abuse' (2022) 43 *ECLR* 191, 194.

[1044] AT.40462, *Amazon Marketplace* and AT.40703, *Amazon Buy Box* 20 December 2022, para. 162.

[1045] Case T-612/17, *Google Shopping* EU:T:2021:763, para. 592. [1046] See Section 3.F.

[1047] Case T-612/17, *Google Shopping* EU:T:2021:763, para. 438. [1048] Ibid., para. 523.

439. In that context, even when conduct of dominant undertakings is in issue that is in principle anticompetitive, such as conduct designed to secure an exclusive or highly preferential purchasing relationship with customers, possibly by means of loyalty rebates (see, . . . Hoffmann-La Roche v Commission, 85/76, EU:C:1979:36, paragraph 89), if the dominant undertaking concerned disputes, with documented evidence, that its conduct was capable of restricting competition, the competition authority handling the case must analyse all the relevant circumstances in order to decide what the position is (see, . . . TeliaSonera Sverige, C-52/09, EU:C:2011:83, paragraph 68; . . . Post Danmark, C-23/14, EU:C:2015:651, paragraph 68; and . . . Intel v Commission, C-413/14 P, EU:C:2017:632, paragraphs 138 and 139).

440. In that regard, where the undertaking concerned maintains that its conduct was not capable of having—even potential—anticompetitive effects, and its case is supported by information about the actual development of the market, the competition authority is required to examine whether that information is such as to have an impact on its assessment of the existence of anticompetitive effects. In the case of practices that have actually been implemented and which are, as in this instance, complex, such information is capable of constituting relevant circumstances that may or may not corroborate the existence of an infringement of Article 102 TFEU.

441. It follows from the above that, in order to find that Google had abused its dominant position, the Commission had to demonstrate the—at least potential—effects attributable to the impugned conduct of restricting or eliminating competition on the relevant markets, taking into account all the relevant circumstances, particularly in the light of the arguments advanced by Google to contest the notion that its conduct had been capable of restricting competition.

442. However . . . the Commission was not required to identify actual exclusionary effects on the grounds that Google was allegedly not dominant on the national markets for comparison shopping services, that its conduct was part of improvements in its services for the benefit of consumers and online sellers and that that conduct had lasted for many years. Such a requirement of the Commission would be contrary to the principle, confirmed by the Courts of the European Union, that the categorisation of a practice as abuse within the meaning of Article 102 TFEU cannot be altered because the practice at issue has ultimately not achieved the desired result (see, . . . TeliaSonera Sverige, C-52/09, EU:C:2011:83, paragraphs 64 and 65, and, . . . Telefónica and Telefónica de España v Commission, T-336/07, EU:T:2012:172, paragraph 272).

443. Nor, a fortiori, was the Commission required to demonstrate that possible consequences of the elimination or restriction of competition actually manifested themselves, for example in the form of less innovation or price increases that could only be explained by the lack of competition. It is accepted in that regard that the weakening of competition is highly likely to have such consequences, as is explained in paragraphs 11 and 19 of the Guidance on the Commission's enforcement priorities in applying [Article 102 TFEU] to abusive exclusionary conduct by dominant undertakings.

On the facts, the GC held that the Commission 'had correctly established that Google's practices had had significant material effects on traffic from its general results page' and that the diverted traffic had represented 'a not insignificant share' of the markets for comparison shopping services. This was itself sufficient to support a finding of anti-competitive effects for the purposes of Article 102.[1049]

Finally, the possibility of invoking an objective justification to explain its behaviour was considered to be one of the stronger aspects of Google's defence. Yet the Commission gave short shrift to such claims, and the section on objective justifications is one of the briefest and most opaque in the infringement decision. On appeal, the GC agreed that Google had failed to discharge its burden of proving the existence of the claimed efficiencies and/or technical barriers to providing equal treatment.[1050]

[1049] Ibid., para. 527. [1050] Ibid., paras. 551–595.

C. SELF-PREFERENCING AFTER *GOOGLE SHOPPING*

The *Google Shopping* case addressed particular market circumstances and conduct, but it relied upon a broad and ambitious theory of harm. Following the decision, the Commission has pursued numerous additional investigations against large digital intermediaries under Article 102. While these later cases concern notably different business practices, each can be considered to fall within the broad definition of self-preferencing set out at the beginning of this section.

The *Amazon Marketplace* and *Amazon Buy Box* investigations, concluded by a commitments decision in late 2022,[1051] addressed the activities of the major online retail platform, Amazon. These cases hinged on Amazon's dual role as both a marketplace operator, through which third party retailers sold products directly to consumers, and as a direct retailer on the same marketplace, where it effectively competed against those third party retailers. In *Amazon Marketplace*, the Commission took issue with 'the systematic reliance by Amazon . . . on its online retail competitors' non-public data, obtained in the context of the provision of Amazon's dominant marketplace services to those sellers', which it used 'to optimise and calibrate [its own retail] operational decisions'.[1052] The Commission emphasised the richness of the data that was available to Amazon's retail operations by virtue of its role as marketplace operator,[1053] which, inter alia, enabled Amazon to identify products that were selling well for other retailers and to copy these, often undercutting the rival in the process.[1054] This practice has been described as a form of 'forced free-riding', which occurs 'when a platform appropriates innovation by other firms that depend on the platform for access to consumers'.[1055] The principal objection, from a competition perspective, is the extent to which the process of appropriating the developments of upstream or downstream rivals may dis-incentivise future innovation in these adjacent product segments.[1056] Alleged forced free-riding was also an element of the Commission's initial investigation of Google,[1057] though the claims were not pursued.[1058] In *Amazon Marketplace*, the Commission concluded that Amazon's strategic use of this sensitive information was likely to have provided it with a 'structural competitive advantage',[1059] although as the case was concluded by commitments it did not formally find a breach of Article 102.[1060] Ultimately, however, the instinctive objection may be less about exclusion and more about exploitation, a category of abuse discussed in

[1051] AT.40462, *Amazon Marketplace* and AT.40703, *Amazon Buy Box* 20 December 2022.

[1052] Ibid., paras. 169–170.

[1053] Ibid., para. 122. The Commission considered the volume, variety, granularity, and immediacy of the data, and its value in terms of informing Amazon's own retail decision-making.

[1054] This phenomenon was explored by L. Khan, 'Amazon's Antitrust Paradox' (2017) 126 *Yale LJ* 710, 780–783.

[1055] H. Shelanski, 'Information, Innovation and Competition Policy for the Internet' (2013) 161 *U Pa LR* 1663, 1699.

[1056] Ibid., 1700.

[1057] In the US, alleged content 'scraping' by Google—namely, that Google 'misappropriated the content of certain competing websites, passed this content off as its own, and then threatened to delist these rivals entirely from Google's search results when they protested the misappropriation of their content'—was investigated by the Federal Trade Commission, although the investigation was subsequently discontinued following prospective commitments by Google to refrain from such conduct: see 'Statement of the Federal Trade Commission Regarding Google's Search Practices In the Matter of Google Inc.', FTC File No. 111-0163, 3 January 2013, fn. 2.

[1058] See e.g. European Commission Press Release, 'Antitrust: Commission takes further steps in investigations alleging Google's comparison shopping and advertising-related practices breach EU rules', 14 July 2016, in which the Commission noted that 'it will continue to investigate . . . concerns with regard to copying of rivals' web content (known as "scraping")'. Also Reuters, 'EU's Vestager does not rule out action over Google scraping complaint', 14 October 2016.

[1059] AT.40462, *Amazon Marketplace* and AT.40703, *Amazon Buy Box* 20 December 2022, para. 171.

[1060] To resolve this aspect of the investigation, Amazon committed to putting in place a 'data-silo', which would prohibit it from making use of third party sellers' non-public data: ibid., para. 232. Considering the extent to which the theory of harm in *Amazon Marketplace* aligns with existing Art. 102 jurisprudence, see V. Reverdin, 'Abuse of Dominance in Digital Markets: Can Amazon's Collection and Use of Third-party Sellers' Data Constitute an Abuse of a Dominant Position Under the Legal Standards Developed by the European Courts for Article 102 TFEU?' (2021) 12 *JECLAP* 181.

Section 16: that is, the omniscient platform operator takes advantage of its superior knowledge and economic strength to exploit a smaller supplier, which had listed on its platform in good faith (in effect, a claim of 'unfair competition'[1061]).

The *Buy Box* investigation involved the more prominent positioning of certain products in the search results provided to customers using Amazon's marketplace. Specifically, the Commission found that Amazon had 'artificially favoured'[1062] both its own retail offers and products offered by marketplace sellers that also used Amazon's logistics and delivery services (referred to as 'FBA sellers') when it selected the most prominently displayed offer on the search results page (known as the 'Buy Box'). It also gave FBA sellers more favourable conditions of access to the Amazon loyalty programme, Prime. To the extent that the case concerned the favouring of Amazon's own retail operations, there are strong parallels to *Google Shopping*. To the extent that the conduct placed FBA sellers at a competitive advantage compared with third party sellers who did not purchase Amazon's logistics and delivery services, the abuse may be seen as an example of secondary line discrimination, discussed in Section 15.[1063] Again, this aspect of the case has also been resolved through commitments, inter alia 'to apply non-discriminatory conditions and criteria' both to products displayed in the Buy Box and for Prime eligibility,[1064] language which echoes the application of the principle of equal treatment by the GC in the *Google Shopping* appeal.

Both Apple and Google are facing Commission investigations into the rules for using the App Store[1065] and Play Store,[1066] respectively. Originally, both investigations combined issues of self-preferencing (in particular, the mandatory use of Apple/Google's proprietary payment technology for the distribution of paid digital content) with concerns about excessive pricing of commission fees.[1067] In early 2023, however, the Commission dropped key aspects of the Apple investigation, to focus only on Apple's 'anti-steering obligations' which prevent app developers from informing Apple device users of alternative (cheaper) music subscription services.[1068] Google is the subject of a further investigation into self-preferencing practices with respect to its 'ad tech' business.[1069] Alongside allegations of tying,[1070] the Commission has also claimed that Meta (the parent company of Facebook) has engaged in illegal leveraging through the imposition of 'unfair trading conditions' on providers of online classified ads services that advertise on Facebook.[1071] Specifically, the Commission alleges that 'the terms and conditions, which authorise Meta to use ads-related data derived from competitors for the benefit of Facebook Marketplace, are unjustified, disproportionate and not necessary', and 'impose a burden on competitors and only benefit Facebook Marketplace'.[1072]

1061 This was precisely the language used by Commissioner Vestager in a speech describing the Amazon Marketplace investigation: see 'Making the data revolution work for us', Mackenzie Stuart Lecture, Cambridge, 4 February 2019.

1062 AT.40462, *Amazon Marketplace* and AT.40703, *Amazon Buy Box* 20 December 2022, para. 97.

1063 The commitments decision, ibid., para. 164, cites Art. 102(c) and the key judgments in Cases C-525/16, *MEO* EU:C:2018:270 and C-95/04 P, *British Airways* EU:C:2007:166.

1064 AT.40462, *Amazon Marketplace* and AT.40703, *Amazon Buy Box* 20 December 2022, paras. 234 and 236.

1065 Commission Press Release, 'Antitrust: Commission sends Statement of Objections to Apple on App Store rules for music streaming providers', 30 April 2021.

1066 J. Masson, 'Google Confirms EU Play Store Investigation,' *Global Competition Review*, 28 October 2022, <https://globalcompetitionreview.com/article/google-confirms-eu-play-store-investigation>.

1067 J. Padilla, J. Perkins, and S. Piccolo, 'Self-preferencing in Markets with Vertically Integrated Gatekeeper Platforms' (2022) 70 *J of Industrial Economics* 371.

1068 Commission Press Release, 'Antitrust: Commission sends Statement of Objections to Apple clarifying concerns over App Store rules for music streaming providers', 28 February 2023.

1069 Commission Press Release, 'Antitrust: Commission sends Statement of Objections to Google over abusive practices in online advertising technology', 14 June 2023. The Commission anticipates that this investigation may result in structural remedies.

1070 See Section 11.E.v.

1071 Commission Press Release, 'Antitrust: Commission sends Statement of Objections to Meta over abusive practices benefiting Facebook Marketplace', 19 December 2022.

1072 Ibid.

D. COMMENT

Self-preferencing remains a contentious theory of harm. The principal objection to the approach in the initial *Google Shopping* decision was, arguably, the Commission's refusal to engage with its own novelty.[1073] Its insistence that self-preferencing as a theory of antitrust harm was already well established in the case law was not endorsed by the GC. The decision in *Google Shopping* therefore arguably represents a necessary evolution of EU competition law to address the sorts of competition problems that are likely to arise in digital markets. Yet even viewed from this perspective, the GC judgment has faced criticism for its failure to articulate a clear legal test to identify when self-preferencing may violate Article 102.[1074] Many years after the infringement decision, moreover, the effectiveness of Google's efforts to remedy the identified discrimination remains hotly disputed by competing comparison shopping service providers.[1075]

It is hard to argue that self-preferencing represents anything other than a substantive step away from the more economic approach towards a more holistic fairness-oriented assessment. Competition Commissioner Vestager recognised as much when she described self-preferencing as raising 'a broader issue for our societies, of whether we think it's right for companies like Google and others to have such control over the success or failure of other companies'.[1076] The Commissioner concluded that, ultimately, 'we may find that we need regulation' to address such concerns.[1077] The subsequent enactment of the DMA, with its focus on ensuring 'contestable and fair markets in the digital sector', reinforces the *Google Shopping* case's status as another example of competition enforcement pointing to the need for a more systematic legislative solution to emerging competition problems. Many of the mandatory obligations for designated gatekeepers in the DMA reflect a concern with self-preferencing, including explicit prohibitions on the behaviour that comprises the theory of harm in *Google Shopping*[1078] and the *Amazon Marketplace* investigation.[1079] The possibility of the concurrent application of the EU competition rules alongside the DMA is considered further in Chapter 16. Yet the very existence of the DMA, imposing *ex ante* prohibitions on self-preferencing by digital gatekeepers, raises a question of whether Article 102 remains a useful or necessary tool to police digital self-preferencing, at least by the very largest platforms.

14. OTHER EXCLUSIONARY PRACTICES

A. GENERAL

Any exclusionary conduct by a dominant undertaking may be capable of constituting an exclusionary abuse. Miscellaneous exclusionary conduct which has come before the EU Courts or Commission includes alleging to third parties that a competitor is a bad debtor;[1080] buying up a competitor's machines;[1081] monopolising the specialist advertising media;[1082] putting pressure on a shipping line to

[1073] Arguing that the decision thus raises concerns from a legal certainty perspective, see M. Eben, 'Fining Google: A Missed Opportunity for Legal Certainty?' (2018) 14 *European Competition Journal* 129.

[1074] See Deutscher, n. 1018.

[1075] In October 2022, more than 40 comparison shopping services wrote to the Commission, accusing Google of continued non-compliance with the obligations within the infringement decision: see N. Lomas, 'Google antitrust complainants call for EU to shutter its Shopping Ads Units', *TechCrunch*, 18 October 2022, <https://techcrunch.com/2022/10/18/eu-antitrust-complaint-google-shopping-units/>.

[1076] 'A digital future that works for Europeans', Speech of Commissioner Vestager, 27 August 2019.

[1077] Ibid. [1078] Art. 6(5), DMA. [1079] Art. 6(2), DMA.

[1080] *BBI/Boosey & Hawkes* [1987] OJ L282/36. [1081] *Elopak Italia/Tetra Pak* [1991] OJ L72/1, para. 165.

[1082] Ibid.

stop carrying the competitor's product by threatening to withdraw the dominant undertaking's own custom;[1083] 'inducing' a competitor shipping line to join a liner conference;[1084] and a liner conference pressurising the Zairian Government to observe the exclusive dealing provisions in their agreements and exclude rival carriers.[1085] In this section, we discuss several more niche exclusionary practices which have been held to infringe Article 102.

B. PURSUIT OF LEGAL PROCEEDINGS, VEXATIOUS LITIGATION, AND ENFORCING LEGAL RIGHTS

It may be an abuse for a dominant undertaking to pursue legal proceedings against a competitor. This was suggested by *BBI/Boosey & Hawkes*,[1086] but the Commission did not pursue the point, concentrating on the refusal to supply aspect.[1087] In *ITT Promedia*,[1088] Belgacom, the dominant supplier of voice telephony services in Belgium, was engaged in a dispute with Promedia about the publication of telephone directories. Promedia complained to the Commission that Belgacom was abusing its dominant position by pursuing national litigation against it. The Commission rejected the complaint on the grounds that the conduct of litigation by a dominant firm could be abusive only if two cumulative criteria, not present here, were met: (a) that the action could not reasonably be considered as an attempt to establish its rights and could therefore serve only to harass the opposite party; and (b) it was conceived in the framework of a plan whose goal was to eliminate competition. Promedia challenged the rejection, alleging that the Commission had applied the criteria incorrectly. The GC recognised the fundamental right, since enshrined in Article 47 of the Charter, of access to the courts. It said that it was unnecessary to rule on the correctness of the criteria,[1089] and confined itself to holding that they had been properly applied. The implication of the judgment, however, was that the criteria were indeed correct. This was confirmed in *Protégé International*.[1090] The following extract from *ITT* deals with the first criterion.

Case T-111/96, *ITT Promedia NV v EC Commission* EU:T:1998:183

General Court

60. . . . [A]s the Commission has rightly emphasised, the ability to assert one's rights through the courts and the judicial control which that entails, constitute the expression of a general principle of law which underlies the constitutional traditions common to the Member States and which is also laid down in Articles 6 and 13 of the European Convention for the Protection of Human Rights and Fundamental Freedoms of 4 November 1950 (see Case 222/84, *Johnson* v. *Chief Constable of the Royal Ulster Constabulary* . . .). As access to the Court is a fundamental right and a general principle ensuring the rule of law, it is only in wholly exceptional circumstances that the fact that legal proceedings are brought is capable of constituting an abuse of a dominant position within the meaning of Article [102].

[1083] *Irish Sugar* [1997] OJ L258/1, paras. 120–122, on appeal Case T–228/97, *Irish Sugar* EU:T:1999:246.

[1084] *Transatlantic Conference Agreement (TACA)* [1999] OJ L95/1. On appeal, Cases T-191 and 212–214/98, *Atlantic Container* EU:T:2003:245 the GC held that the Commission had not proved that the alleged 'inducement' had occurred so overturned the decision on that ground.

[1085] Cases C-395 and 396/96 P, *Compagnie Maritime Belge* EU:C:2000:132, paras. 80–88.

[1086] *BBI/Boosey & Hawkes* [1987] OJ L282/36. [1087] See Section 12.F.

[1088] Case T-111/96, *ITT Promedia* EU:T:1998:183. [1089] Ibid., para. 57.

[1090] Case T-119/09, *Protégé International* EU:T:2012:421.

> 61. Second, since the two cumulative criteria constitute an exception to the general principle of access to the courts, which ensures the rule of law, they must be construed and applied strictly, in the manner which does not defeat the application of the general rule (see, *inter alia*, Case T-105/95, *WWF UK* v. *E.C. Commission* . . .).
>
> . . .
>
> 72. According to the first of the two cumulative criteria set out by the Commission in the contested decision, legal proceedings can be characterised as an abuse, within the meaning of Article [102], only if they cannot reasonably be considered to be an attempt to assert the rights of the undertaking concerned and can therefore only serve to harass the opposing party. It is therefore the situation existing when the action in question is brought which must be taken into account in order to determine whether that criterion is satisfied.
>
> 73. Furthermore, when applying that criterion, it is not a question of determining whether the rights which the undertaking concerned was asserting when it brought its action actually existed or whether that action was well founded, but rather of determining whether such an action was intended to assert what that undertaking could, at that moment, reasonably consider to be its rights. According to the second part of that criterion, as worded, it is satisfied solely when the action did not have that aim, that being the sole case in which it may be assumed that such action could only serve to harass the opposing party.

The *ITT* test asks, not whether the rights claimed by the dominant undertaking exist, but whether the undertaking may reasonably consider that they do. The GC judgment therefore confirms that litigation *can* be an abuse, but only where it is, in effect, vexatious or 'sham'.[1091] Moreover, Belgacom was entitled to rely on its rights under national law unless and until it was ruled that the national law had been invalidated.[1092]

In *AstraZeneca*, the Commission considered whether a patent holder's defence to an action for a declaration of invalidity could be an abuse. The Commission differentiated between *defending* an action and *initiating* an action, but as it viewed the costs and delays at issue as having arisen from AZ's misrepresentations to the patent authorities rather than from its defence of legal proceedings, the question was not pursued.[1093]

In *Agria Polska*, the GC again emphasised the 'wholly exceptional' nature of manipulation of legal procedures as a theory of harm.[1094] The case concerned a Polish company involved in the parallel import of plant protection products in order, in essence, to engage in arbitrage between VAT rates in Member States. It was subject to various investigations by the tax authorities and other public bodies in Poland and Austria, and it complained to the Commission that these investigations had followed complaints by the companies which manufactured plant protection products, suggesting that this involved either a cartel or abuse of collective dominance. Its complaint was rejected, and in dismissing its subsequent appeal, the GC said that the necessary exceptional circumstances were unlikely to be satisfied on the facts, in particular because the public authorities to which the complaints had been issued had discretion to pursue or reject them, which was not the case in *ITT* or *AstraZeneca*.[1095]

1091 On the concept of 'sham' litigation under EU competition law more generally, see I. Lianos and P. Regibeau, '"Vexatious"/"Sham" Litigation in EU and US Antitrust Law: A Mechanism Design Approach' (2017) 62 *Ant Bull* 643.

1092 Case T-111/96, *ITT Promedia* EU:T:1998:183, paras. 93–95.

1093 COMP/.37.507, *Generics/AstraZeneca* 15 June 2005, paras. 736–739.

1094 Case T-480/15, *Agria Polska* EU:T:2017:339, para. 69; upheld on appeal in Case C-373/17 P, *Agria Polska* EU:C:2018:756.

1095 Case T-480/15, *Agria Polska* EU:T:2017:339, paras. 69–73.

The issue of bringing an injunction to protect IPRs arises in respect of standard-essential patents and is discussed in Section 14.C.

The GC also held in *ITT v Promedia* that a dominant undertaking which sought performance of a contract would commit an abuse only if the claim went beyond what it could reasonably expect from the contract.[1096] However, the CJ held that it was an abuse for the dominant liner conference in *Compagnie Maritime Belge*[1097] to insist on the (then) Zairean authorities keeping strictly to the terms of the exclusive contract they had signed. This meant that Zaire could not continue giving a small amount of trade to a new competitor.

C. 'REGULATORY GAMING'

'Regulatory gaming' refers to private market behaviour by undertakings that harnesses pro-competitive or neutral governmental regulations and uses them for exclusionary purposes.[1098] A number of recent Article 102 cases, particularly arising within the pharmaceutical sector,[1099] involve theories of harm which incorporate an element of regulatory gaming. Such cases bring to the fore the optimal relationship between competition law and other regulatory regimes. If a firm's behaviour is formally compliant with the 'letter' of a sectoral regime, yet has effects that are contrary to its perceived 'spirit', should competition law intervene to achieve a more competitive outcome?

(i) The *AstraZeneca* Case

AstraZeneca[1100] established that it can be an abuse for a dominant undertaking to make misrepresentations to regulatory authorities or to take steps with regard to regulatory procedures in order to exclude competitors.

Here, the Commission fined AstraZeneca (AZ) €60 million[1101] for (a) misrepresenting certain dates to national patent offices and national courts in order to obtain extra patent protection for its blockbuster drug, Losec;[1102] and (b) misusing marketing authorisation procedures by switching Losec from capsule to tablet form in order to hinder generic versions of the drug coming onto the market, and to hinder parallel imports. By deregistering the capsule marketing authorisation, AZ prevented generic manufacturers from making use of simplified marketing authorisation procedures which were available only where the original authorisation was still in force. The Commission found that depriving the generic manufacturers of the ability to use the faster and simpler procedure delayed the entry of the generic product.

a. *Misrepresentations to National Patent Offices and National Courts*

The GC[1103] upheld the Commission's finding that the presentation of the relevant dates which AZ made to the national patent offices and courts amounted to the provision of misleading information. Emphasising that abuse of dominance does not necessarily involve use by the dominant undertaking

[1096] Case T-111/96, *ITT Promedia* EU:T:1998:183, para. 129.
[1097] Cases C-395 and 396/96 P, *Compagnie Maritime Belge* EU:C:2000:132, paras. 72–88.
[1098] S. Dogan and M. Lemley, 'Antitrust Law and Regulatory Gaming' (2009) 87 *Texas LR* 685.
[1099] See e.g. L. Hancher and W. Sauter, 'A Dose of Competition: EU Antitrust Law in the Pharmaceuticals Sector' (2016) 4 *J of Antitrust Enforcement* 381.
[1100] Case C-457/10 P, *AstraZeneca v Commission* EU:C:2012:770.
[1101] COMP/37.507, *Generics/AstraZeneca* 15 June 2005.
[1102] An anti-ulcer medicine which is the main oral proton pump inhibitor. For the market definition and dominance aspects of the case, see Chap. 6, Sections 8 and 9.
[1103] Case T-321/05, *AstraZeneca* EU:T:2010:266.

of its economic power, the GC said that giving public authorities misleading information to secure the grant of an exclusive right to which it was not otherwise entitled constituted a practice falling outside the scope of competition on the merits. Here the public authorities had a limited discretion to verify the information provided to them, which was relevant in assessing whether the misrepresentations were liable to raise regulatory obstacles to competition. The GC referred to the special responsibility of a dominant undertaking which required it at least to inform the public authorities of any error made so that the matter could be rectified. As far as intention was concerned, the GC said that, although abuse is an objective concept and so does not require bad faith, nevertheless intention can constitute a relevant factor in support of the conclusion that an undertaking has abused its dominant position.

It was irrelevant whether or not the public authorities to whom misrepresentations were made were actually misled or not, and whether the exclusive rights obtained were afterwards revoked, as the abusive nature of the behaviour could not depend on the contingencies of third parties' reactions. Nor was it relevant whether the exclusive right obtained had actually been enforced, as mere possession of an IPR normally keeps competitors away.

Moreover, the GC held that finding that the unlawful acquisition of an exclusive right constituted an abuse did not depend on it having the effect of eliminating all competition. It was only necessary that the misrepresentations were *capable* of restricting competition. The ability of the practice to restrict competition could be *indirect*, provided that it could be shown that it was *actually liable* to do so. The existence of specific patent remedies did not mean that proof of anti-competitive effect was required. On appeal the CJ affirmed the judgment of the GC.

Case C-457/10 P, *AstraZeneca AB and AstraZeneca plc v Commission* EU:C:2012:770

Court of Justice

[The third ground of appeal, that the GC had taken a legally flawed approach to competition on the merits.]

98. [T]he third ground of appeal raised by them is tantamount to an argument that where an undertaking in a dominant position considers that it can, in accordance with a legally defensible interpretation, lay claim to a right, it may use any means to obtain that right, and even have recourse to highly misleading representations with the aim of leading public authorities into error. Such an approach is manifestly not consistent with competition on the merits and the specific responsibility on such an undertaking not to prejudice, by its conduct, effective and undistorted competition within the European Union.

99. . . . [T]he General Court did not hold that undertakings in a dominant position had to be infallible in their dealings with regulatory authorities and that each objectively wrong representation made by such an undertaking constituted an abuse of that position, even where the error was made unintentionally and immediately rectified. It is sufficient to note in this connection that, first, that example is radically different from AZ's conduct in the present case, and that, secondly, the General Court pointed out . . . that the assessment of whether representations made to public authorities for the purposes of improperly obtaining exclusive rights are misleading must be made *in concreto* and may vary according to the specific circumstances of each case. It thus cannot be inferred from that judgment that any patent application made by such an undertaking which is rejected on the ground that it does not satisfy the patentability criteria automatically gives rise to liability under Article [102].

[The fourth ground of appeal, that the GC erred in holding that the mere fact of applying for an SPC was sufficient to constitute an abuse.]

. . .

105. . . . [T]he General Court examined in the present case whether, in the light of the context in which the practice in question had been implemented, that practice was such as to lead the public

authorities wrongly to create regulatory obstacles to competition, for example by the unlawful grant of exclusive rights to the dominant undertaking. It held in this connection that the limited discretion of public authorities or the absence of any obligation on their part to verify the accuracy or veracity of the information provided could be relevant factors to be taken into consideration for the purposes of determining whether the practice in question was liable to raise regulatory obstacles to competition.

106. Contrary to what the appellants submit, that examination by the General Court is not in any way based on the assumption that the practice in question constitutes an 'abuse in itself', regardless of its anti-competitive effect. On the contrary, the General Court expressly pointed out . . . that representations designed to obtain exclusive rights unlawfully constitute an abuse only if it is established that, in view of the objective context in which they are made, those representations are actually liable to lead the public authorities to grant the exclusive right applied for.

. . .

111. So far as concerns the fact that the misleading representations did not enable AZ to obtain SPCs in Denmark and that in Ireland and the United Kingdom the SPCs were ultimately issued on the basis of the correct date, it must be stated that the General Court did not err in law in holding . . . that that fact does not mean that AZ's conduct in those countries was not abusive, since it is established that those representations were very likely to result in the issue of unlawful SPCs. In addition, as the Commission has pointed out, in so far as the impugned conduct forms part of an overall strategy seeking to unlawfully exclude manufacturers of generic products from the market by means of obtaining SPCs in breach of the regulatory framework which established them, the existence of an abuse is not affected by the fact that that strategy did not succeed in some countries.

112. Lastly, as regards the circumstances which, according to the appellants, must be present in order to be able to find that the misleading representations were such as to restrict competition, it is sufficient to note that in actual fact they amount to a requirement that current and certain anti-competitive effects be shown. However, it follows from the Court's case-law that, although the practice of an undertaking in a dominant position cannot be characterised as abusive in the absence of any anti-competitive effect on the market, such an effect does not necessarily have to be concrete, and it is sufficient to demonstrate that there is a potential anti-competitive effect (see, to that effect, *TeliaSonera Sverige*, paragraph 64).

b. *Withdrawal of the Marketing Authorisations*

In respect of the misuse of marketing authorisation procedures, the GC distinguished the situation from the 'essential facilities' cases, referring to *Bronner* and *Microsoft*. As a result of the EU scheme for marketing authorisations for generic products,[1104] AZ could not prevent national authorities from using the relevant data when giving authorisations under the abridged procedure. So this was not a 'refusal to supply' scenario.[1105] The GC rejected the argument that, as the undertaking was entitled to request the withdrawal of its marketing authorisations for Losec capsules, the deregistration could not constitute an abuse, because 'the illegality of abusive conduct under [Article 102] is unrelated to its compliance or non-compliance with other legal rules'.[1106] In cases of conduct by which regulatory procedures are used without any basis in competition on the merits, evidence that the conduct is *capable* of restricting competition is sufficient to classify it as an abuse.[1107] Although a dominant undertaking is under no obligation to protect the interests of its competitors, that does not make practices implemented solely to exclude competitors compatible with Article 102.[1108] Therefore, in the absence

[1104] Established by Dir. 65/65 [1965–1966] OJ Spec. Ed. 24, as amended.
[1105] Case T-321/05, *AstraZeneca* EU:T:2010:266, paras. 678–684. [1106] Ibid., para. 677.
[1107] Ibid., para. 824. [1108] Ibid., para. 816.

of objective justification, a dominant undertaking 'cannot use regulatory procedures solely in such a way as to prevent or make more difficult the entry of competitors on the market'.[1109] The CJ affirmed the judgment.

Case C-457/10 P, *AstraZeneca AB and AstraZeneca plc v Commission* EU:C:2012:770

[The fifth ground of appeal, that the GC had misinterpreted the concept of 'competition on the merits'.]

129. [T]he preparation by an undertaking, even in a dominant position, of a strategy whose object it is to minimise the erosion of its sales and to enable it to deal with competition from generic products is legitimate and is part of the normal competitive process, provided that the conduct envisaged does not depart from practices coming within the scope of competition on the merits, which is such as to benefit consumers.

130. However . . . conduct like that impugned in the context of the second abuse—consisting in the deregistration, without objective justification and after the expiry of the exclusive right to make use of the results of the pharmacological and toxicological tests and clinical trials granted by Directive 65/65, of the MAs for Losec capsules in Denmark, Sweden and Norway, by which AZ intended . . . to hinder the introduction of generic products and parallel imports—does not come within the scope of competition on the merits.

131. In this connection, it must in particular be stated that . . . after the expiry of the period of exclusivity referred to above, conduct designed, inter alia, to prevent manufacturers of generic products from making use of their right to benefit from those results was not based in any way on the legitimate protection of an investment which came within the scope of competition on the merits, precisely because, under Directive 65/65, AZ no longer had the exclusive right to make use of those results.

132. Furthermore, . . . the fact that under Directive 65/65 AZ was entitled to request the withdrawal of its MAs for Losec capsules in no way causes that conduct to escape the prohibition laid down in Article [102]. As [the GC] pointed out, the illegality of abusive conduct under Article [102] is unrelated to its compliance or non-compliance with other legal rules and, in the majority of cases, abuses of dominant positions consist of behaviour which is otherwise lawful under branches of law other than competition law.

133. Moreover . . . the primary purpose of Directive 65/65 is to safeguard public health while eliminating disparities between certain national provisions which hinder trade in medicinal products within the Union, and it therefore does not, as claimed by the appellants, pursue the same objectives as Article [102] in such a way that the application of the latter is no longer required for the purposes of ensuring effective and undistorted competition within the internal market.

134. It is important to point out, in this context, that an undertaking which holds a dominant position has a special responsibility in that latter regard (see Case C-202/07 P *France Télécom* v *Commission* . . . paragraph 105) and that . . . it cannot therefore use regulatory procedures in such a way as to prevent or make more difficult the entry of competitors on the market, in the absence of grounds relating to the defence of the legitimate interests of an undertaking engaged in competition on the merits or in the absence of objective justification.

. . .

[The sixth ground of appeal, that the GC erred in law in considering that the impugned conduct tended to restrict competition.]

148. . . . The situation which characterises the second abuse is not in any way comparable to a compulsory licence or to the situation which gave rise to the judgment in *IMS Health*, relied upon by the appellants, which concerned the refusal by an undertaking in a dominant position, which was the

[1109] Ibid., para. 817.

> owner of an intellectual property right in a 'brick structure', to grant its competitors a licence for the use of that structure.
>
> 149. In fact, the possibility provided for in Directive 65/65 of deregistering a MA is not equivalent to a property right. Consequently, the fact that, in the light of its special responsibility, an undertaking in a dominant position cannot make use of such a possibility in such a way as to prevent or render more difficult the entry of competitors on the market, unless it can, as an undertaking engaged in competition on the merits, rely on grounds relating to the defence of its legitimate interests or on objective justifications, does not constitute either an 'effective expropriation' of such a right or an obligation to grant a licence, but a straightforward restriction of the options available under European Union law.
>
> 150. The fact that the exercise of such options by an undertaking in a dominant position is limited or made subject to conditions in order to ensure that competition already weakened by the presence of that undertaking is not subsequently undermined is in no way an exceptional case and does not justify a derogation from Article [102], unlike a situation in which the unfettered exercise of an exclusive right awarded for the realisation of an investment or creation is limited.

In this highly significant judgment, the CJ concurred with the GC in widening the reach of Article 102. A dominant undertaking may commit an abuse even where it is exercising legal rights. This part of the judgment places severe limitations on the strategies adopted by dominant pharmaceutical companies for managing the life-cycle of their products and extracting the maximum return from their investments. Despite accepting that a dominant undertaking has no duty to protect its competitors, the EU Courts in effect imposed an obligation on AZ to maintain in force its marketing authorisations in order to assist competitors to enter the market. This was on the basis of the 'special responsibility' and a particular interpretation of 'competition on the merits'. Moreover, the requirement was merely premised upon evidence of the conduct's *capability* of anti-competitive effects rather than of actual or likely effects. AZ's intentions were accorded more importance than such effects, with no emphasis on consumers.

AstraZeneca must be seen in the context of the Commission's policy on generic drugs and the position of 'blockbuster' medicines,[1110] and it is fact-specific.[1111] It left pharmaceutical companies in a somewhat uncertain position in respect of what positive obligations can be imposed upon them and the extent of their freedom to pursue their own commercial interests.[1112] O'Donoghue and Padilla suggest five principles they might follow. First, assess the impact of the conduct on generic competition; secondly, consider whether the new replacement is advantageous relative to the replaced product; thirdly, if it is, ask whether there are legitimate reasons why they do not offer both new and old products; fourthly, ask whether the same decision would have been taken in the absence of generic competition; and, fifthly, think about internal evidence suggesting a subjective intention to reduce generic competition.[1113]

(ii) *Teva* and 'Divisionals Games'

In October 2022, the Commission announced that it had sent a statement of objections to the pharmaceutical company, Teva, alleging inter alia breach of Article 102 through use of divisional

[1110] See e.g. the Competition Commissioner's Press Release at the time of the decision, IP/05/737.

[1111] See also the subsequent Commission inquiry into the pharmaceutical sector, 8 July 2009, and IP/09/1098.

[1112] For a consideration of the issues, see F. Murphy and F. Liberatore, 'Abuse of Regulatory Procedures—the *Astra-Zeneca Case*' [2009] *ECLR* 223, 289, and 314 (in three parts, written before the GC judgment).

[1113] O'Donoghue and Padilla, n. 1, 778–780.

patent filings. Known as the 'divisionals game',[1114] this practice forces Teva's competitors to engage in multiple lengthy legal challenges in response. According to the Commission, '[t]his artificially prolongs legal uncertainty to the benefit of the patent holder, and can effectively block or delay entry of generic or generic-like medicines',[1115]

(iii) Pay-to-delay as Abuse of Dominance

The treatment of 'pay-to-delay' or patent settlement agreements as 'by object' restrictions contrary to Article 101(1) is discussed in Chapter 12. To the extent that the pharmaceutical company that produces the originator medicine also holds a dominant position within a relevant market, this behaviour may be alternatively or additionally conceptualised as an abuse of dominance.[1116]

This was the approach of the Commission in *Servier*, where the defendant concluded a series of 'pay-to-delay' agreements with several of the most advanced generic challengers anticipating entry into the market for hypertension drugs upon expiry of its patent protection. The Commission held that the individual settlements constituted anti-competitive agreements contrary to Article 101,[1117] an approach confirmed by the GC.[1118] Additionally, Servier engaged in practices intended to further protect its market position. These included the acquisition of various new technologies from third parties that had developed ways to produce the active pharmaceutical ingredient by means falling outside its patented processes, in order to remove those competing technologies from the market. Servier also developed a second-generation product, based on a new salt, for which it received patent protection, and to which it began switching patients, after which it withdrew its original product from the market in order to frustrate generic entry (along the lines of the abuse in *AstraZeneca*). In its infringement decision, the Commission construed these additional practices, taken with the patent settlements, as constituting a single continuous exclusionary strategy amounting to an abuse of dominance.

In a noteworthy passage, the Commission acknowledged the tension inherent in its enforcement activity relating to the application and protection of IPRs by dominant firms. However, it justified its efforts by explaining that such conduct only comes within the ambit of the competition rules where, as in *Servier* itself, the defendant goes beyond the legitimate exploitation of its property rights, in order artificially to prolong or extract further *il*legitimate rents.

Case AT.39612, *Perindopril (Servier)* Decision of 9 July 2014

Commission

2576. The fact that the Commission relies on the significant economic rents . . . and on the intellectual property rights in establishing Servier's dominant position should be viewed as natural in the context of the present case where Servier made recourse to the patent settlements and acquisitions to prolong its economic rents beyond the basic patent protection period. However, for the avoidance of doubt, the Commission wants to underline that neither enforcing the intellectual property rights nor

[1114] So described by the Commission in its Press Release announcing the investigation, 'Antitrust: Commission sends Statement of Objections to Teva over misuse of the patent system and disparagement of rival multiple sclerosis medicine', 10 October 2022. On 'divisional games' as an exclusionary strategy, see K. Foss-Solbrekk, 'The Divisional Game: Using Procedural Rights to Impede Generic/Biosimilar Market Entry' (2022) 53 *IIC* 1007.

[1115] Commission Press Release, 'Antitrust: Commission sends Statement of Objections to Teva over misuse of the patent system and disparagement of rival multiple sclerosis medicine', 10 October 2022.

[1116] On 'pay-to-delay' as an abuse of dominance generally, see S. Gallasch, 'A New Dimension to EU Pharma Antitrust Product Hopping and Unilateral Pay to Delay' (2016) 12 *European Competition Journal* 137.

[1117] Case AT.39612, *Perindopril (Servier)* 9 July 2014.

[1118] Case T-691/14, *Servier v Commission* EU:T:2018:922.

enjoying the high economic rents during the legitimate period of legal protection would have received its attention if not for Servier's practices that are the subject of this investigation.

2577. The position of market power is inherent in the system where innovation is rewarded by the exclusivity that intellectual property rights confer on the author of the innovation. The prospect of economic rents is precisely meant to give incentives for new innovation and so fuel the economic progress. However, if the commercial success of the protected product is prolonged through abusive practices, the holder of the rights may indeed be held liable for violation of Union competition law. The Commission wants to recall that the prohibition only concerns the abuse of a dominant position, not holding the position as such.

2578. The Commission regards dynamic competition in R&D as an important mechanism of economic growth. This mechanism requires that the market power needed to attract innovation is restricted in time and in scope as foreseen in the applicable legislative framework. These restrictions are necessary in order to keep incentives for the undertaking enjoying temporary market power to further develop through genuine innovation and avoid being overtaken by competitors. Prohibition of the abuse of a dominant position is only aimed at the attempts of circumventing the existing restrictions of market power that originate from the mechanism of dynamic competition and not at its exercise in terms of collecting the economic rents during the legitimate period of legal protection.

The GC annulled the finding of breach of Article 102 on the basis that the Commission had incorrectly (i.e. too narrowly) defined the relevant market, so that the finding of a dominant position held by Servier could not be sustained.[1119] The GC did not comment on the substance of the Commission's theory of harm in respect of the alleged abuse of dominance, nor on the relationship with Article 101 in such circumstances.[1120]

In its subsequent preliminary ruling in *Generics*, however, the CJ confirmed that pay-to-delay agreements can comprise behaviour amounting to abuse of dominance in appropriate circumstances. Moreover, Articles 101 and 102 can apply in parallel to the same conduct in such cases, provided that the specific requirements for each provision have been satisfied on the facts of the case. The CJ acknowledged the need for a degree of caution before prohibiting pay-to-delay agreements under the competition rules, on the basis that patent holders should be permitted to defend their legitimate commercial interests. The right to do so, however, is confined to the scope of competition on the merits, and so does not permit dominant undertakings to engage in contract-oriented strategies intended to keep viable potential competitors out of the relevant market.

Case C-307/18 *Generics (UK) Ltd and Others v Competition and Markets Authority* EU:C:2020:52

Court of Justice

146. In accordance with settled case-law, the same practice may give rise to an infringement of both Article 101 TFEU and Article 102 TFEU, even if the two provisions pursue distinct objectives (. . . *Hoffmann-La Roche v Commission*, 85/76, EU:C:1979:36, paragraph 116, and . . . *Compagnie maritime belge transports and Others v Commission*, C-395/96 P and C-396/96 P, EU:C:2000:132, paragraph 33).

[1119] Ibid.

[1120] The Commission has appealed the Art. 102 aspect of the GC's judgment: see pending Case C-176/19 P, *Commission v Servier*. AG Kokott has recommended that this aspect of the judgment be overturned: see Opinion in Case C-176/19 P, *Commission v Servier* EU:C:2022:576.

147. Accordingly, a contract-oriented strategy of a manufacturer of originator medicines holding a dominant position in a market may be penalised not only under Article 101 TFEU by reason of each agreement taken individually but also under Article 102 TFEU for the possible additional damage that strategy may cause to the competitive structure of a market in which, because of the dominance in that market of that manufacturer of originator medicines, the degree of competition is already weakened (. . . *Hoffmann-La Roche v Commission*, 85/76, EU:C:1979:36, paragraph 120).

. . .

149. However, the fact that an undertaking is in a dominant position does not disqualify it from protecting its own commercial interests if they are attacked, and it must be conceded the right to take such reasonable steps as it deems appropriate to protect its commercial interests (. . . *United Brands and United Brands Continentaal v Commission*, 27/76, EU:C:1978:22, paragraph 189).

150. More particularly, the exercise of an exclusive right linked to an intellectual property right, such as the conclusion of settlement agreements between the holder of a patent and parties allegedly infringing that patent in order to bring to an end litigation relating to that patent, is one of the rights of the holder of an intellectual property right, and consequently the exercise of such a right, even when done by a dominant undertaking, cannot in itself constitute an abuse of the dominant position (. . . *Huawei Technologies*, C-170/13, EU:C:2015:477 . . .).

151. However, such conduct cannot be accepted when its purpose is precisely to strengthen the dominant position of the party engaging in it and to abuse that position (. . . *United Brands and United Brands Continentaal v Commission*, 27/76, EU:C:1978:22, paragraph 189), as when such conduct is intended to deprive parties demonstrated to be potential competitors of effective access to a market, such as that of a medicine containing an active ingredient that is in the public domain.

152. Accordingly, when the intention of a manufacturer of originator medicines holding a dominant position is to protect its own commercial interests, in particular by defending its patents, and to guard itself against the competition of generic medicines, that alone does not justify resorting to practices that fall outside the scope of competition on the merits (see, by analogy . . . *Huawei Technologies*, C-170/13, EU:C:2015:477, paragraph 47 . . .).

153. A dominant undertaking has a special responsibility not to allow its behaviour to impair genuine, undistorted competition in the internal market (. . . *Intel v Commission*, C-413/14 P, EU:C:2017:632, paragraph 135 . . .).

154. From that perspective, it must, further, be observed that if such conduct is to be characterised as abusive, that presupposes that that conduct was capable of restricting competition and, in particular, producing the alleged exclusionary effects (. . . *TeliaSonera Sverige*, C-52/09, EU:C:2011:83, paragraphs 64 and 66, and . . . *Intel v Commission*, C-413/14 P, EU:C:2017:632, paragraph 138), and that assessment must be undertaken having regard to all the relevant facts surrounding that conduct (. . . *TeliaSonera Sverige*, C-52/09, EU:C:2011:83, paragraph 68).

155. In this case, the information contained in the documents available to the Court indicate that the [NCA] and the referring court considered that the set of settlement agreements concluded on the initiative of GSK were part of an overall strategy on the part of that manufacturer of originator medicines and had, if not as their object, at least the effect of delaying the market entry of generic medicines containing the active ingredient 'paroxetine' that had earlier entered the public domain and, therefore, of preventing a significant fall in the prices of the originator medicines containing that active ingredient and produced by GSK; the direct consequence of that entry would have been an appreciable reduction in GSK's market share and an equally appreciable reduction in the sale price of its originator medicine.

156. However, such a contract-oriented strategy, the actual nature of which it is for the referring court to determine having regard to the evidence available to it, constitutes, in principle, a practice that impedes, while adversely affecting at least the national health systems if not the final consumer, the growth of competition in the market of a medicine containing an active ingredient that is in the public domain.

157. The anticompetitive effects of such a contract-oriented strategy are liable to exceed the anticompetitive effects inherent in the conclusion of each of the agreements that are part of it. That strategy has a significant foreclosure effect on the market of the originator medicine containing the active ingredient at issue, depriving the consumer of the benefits of entry into that market of potential competitors manufacturing their own medicine and, therefore, reserving that market directly or indirectly to the manufacturer of the originator medicine concerned.

In the final paragraph of the extract, the CJ provided the rationale for pursuing pay-to-delay arrangements under Article 102 and not merely as restrictive agreements under Article 101: namely, that the cumulative effect of numerous agreements in parallel may have a greater exclusionary effect than if each is considered individually. Thus the sum of a pay-to-delay *strategy*, orchestrated by a dominant undertaking, may be greater (and more harmful to competition) than the mere sum of its parts.

(iv) Standard-essential Patents and Patent Ambushes

Standard-setting agreements are those whereby undertakings in a particular industry or market define technical or quality requirements with which current or future products, production processes, services, or methods may comply.[1121] This usually takes place through a standard-setting organization (SSO). Patents essential to the technology incorporated in such standards are known as standard-essential patents (SEPs).[1122] Negotiations prior to the adoption of the standard usually cover the use of SEPs, and the owners of such patents are normally required to commit themselves to licensing their rights to third parties on FRAND terms (fair, reasonable, and non-discriminatory).[1123]

Several disputes involving SEPs have come before the Commission and the Union Courts in the past decade or so. The overarching question in these cases is the extent to which Article 102 constrains a dominant patent holder's right to exercise its SEPs as it sees fit, either by refusing to license the technology or by imposing excessively high licensing fees. In this context, the decisional practice places considerable emphasis on the legitimate expectations generated by participation in a standard-setting process. This does not negate the patent holder's right to earn a fair reward for its successful innovation, but it implies that the technology will subsequently be available to all who would seek to use it on FRAND terms.[1124]

A 'patent ambush' arises where a party to a standard-setting agreement conceals that it has (typically, pending) patents relevant to the technology incorporated in the standard, and then attempts to enforce its rights. Where the undertaking concerned is dominant, a patent ambush can

[1121] See Chap. 10.

[1122] See D. Geradin and M. Rato, 'Can Standard-setting Lead to Exploitative Abuse? A Dissonant View of Patent Hold-up, Royalty-stacking and the Meaning of FRAND' (2007) 3 *European Competition Journal* 146; P. Chappatte, 'FRAND Commitments—The Case for Antitrust Intervention' (2009) 5 *European Competition Journal* 320; D. Geradin, 'Ten Years of DG Competition Effort to Provide Guidance on the Application of Competition Rules to the Licensing of Standard-essential Patents: Where Do We Stand?', <http://ssrn.com/abstract=2204359>; M. Rato and N. Petit, 'Abuse of Dominance in Technology-enabled Markets: Established Standards Reconsidered?' (2013) 9 *European Competition Journal* 1, 58–64; N. Petit, 'Injunctions for FRAND-pledged SEPs: The Quest for an Appropriate Test of Abuse under Article 102 TFEU' (2013) 9 *European Competition Journal* 677; A. Jones, 'Standard-essential Patents: FRAND Commitments, Injunctions and the Smartphone Wars' (2014) 10 *European Competition Journal* 1.

[1123] See Guidelines on horizontal co-operation agreements [2011] OJ C11/1, paras. 283–287. In the US, they are called RAND terms (the 'fair' is dropped).

[1124] Case C-170/13, *Huawei Technologies Co Ltd v ZTE Corp and ZTE Deutschland GmbH* EU:C:2015:477, para. 53. This aspect of the case law is explained further in N. Dunne, 'Dispensing with Indispensability' (2020) 16 *J of Competition Law and Economics* 74.

be an exclusionary abuse by which that undertaking may gain control over the standard, thereby excluding potentially competing technologies and raising barriers to entry.[1125] In *Rambus*,[1126] the Commission was concerned with the conduct of an undertaking it considered had engaged in a patent ambush in respect of the DRAM standard.[1127] Because Rambus was not in a dominant position during the standard-setting procedure, the Commission dealt with the matter as one of excessive pricing for the royalties charged subsequently for use of the patents, and adopted a commitments decision whereby Rambus agreed to cap the royalties.[1128]

Even without a deliberate manipulation of standard-setting processes, there can be disputes about the licensing of SEP-encumbered patents subsequently. In the mobile communications sector in particular, the SSOs failed to develop robust dispute resolution mechanisms capable of dealing with the contentious issues arising between the leading players,[1129] resulting in the so-called 'smartphone wars' involving global litigation between Big Tech firms including Google, Apple, Samsung, and Microsoft. In a number of actions before EU national courts, SEP holders have sued for patent infringement. In response, the Commission initiated proceedings against two SEP holders, on the basis that seeking an injunction can amount to an abuse of dominance. In *Motorola*,[1130] the Commission took a prohibition decision (without imposing a fine) against Motorola for pursuing an injunction against Apple for alleged infringement of the Electronic Telecommunications Standards Institute (ETSI) GPRS SEPs. Motorola had committed to licensing these on FRAND terms and Apple was a willing licensee, being prepared to take a licence on terms to be set by the national court. Moreover, Motorola had sought to prevent Apple challenging the validity of its patents. Therefore, said the Commission, the injunction action was an abuse. Such an action would not, however, be abusive if the SEP holder was taking reasonable steps to protect its own interests, for example where the potential licensee was financially distressed, its assets were in a jurisdiction that did not adequately provide for enforcement of damages, or it was unwilling to take a licence on FRAND terms.[1131] The Commission's action against Samsung alleged that Samsung had infringed Article 102 by seeking injunctions in various Member States to enforce its patents which were necessary to comply with the ETSI 3G UMTS standard, which Samsung had similarly agreed to license on FRAND terms. The case was settled by a commitments decision, in which Samsung undertook not to seek, for five years, an injunction in the EEA against potential licensees complying with the conditions set out in the decision.[1132]

Broadly speaking, the Commission's approach in *Motorola* and *Samsung* favours potential licensees, in that seeking an injunction is an abuse *unless* special conditions apply (the potential licensee's financial situation, etc.). In Germany, however, where a significant amount of the relevant litigation has taken place, the courts tended to be more favourable to patent holders.[1133] In the *Orange-Book-Standard* case,[1134] the Bundesgerichtshof held that a company would abuse its dominant position by seeking an injunction only in special circumstances.

The concept that a SEP holder abuses a dominant position by bringing an action for a prohibitory injunction (or recall of products) against an alleged infringer/potential licensee runs into two

[1125] See Commission MEMO/09/544. [1126] COMP/38.636, *Rambus* 9 December 2009.

[1127] Dynamic Random Access Memory chips. They are used to temporarily store data, particularly on PCs. At the time of the decision DRAMs compliant with the standard (the JEDEC standard) had approximately 95% of the (world) market and were used in nearly all PCs, see IP/09/1867.

[1128] See Section 16.A. [1129] Jones, n. 1106, 8.

[1130] COMP/39.985, *Motorola—Enforcement of GPRS Standard Essential Patents* 29 April 2014.

[1131] Ibid., para. 23. [1132] COMP/39.939, *Samsung—Enforcement of ETSI Standard Essential Patents* 29 April 2014.

[1133] This is partly because of the bifurcated nature of the court process in respect of patent cases, in that patent infringement cases come before specialist patent chambers of the Higher District Courts whereas challenges to the validity of patents are heard by the Federal Patent Court.

[1134] BGH, 6 May 2009, KZR 39/06, GRUR 2009, 694.

problems. The first is the familiar difficulties over the interface between IPRs and competition law.[1135] The second is that classifying legal proceedings as an abuse risks breaching the fundamental right of access to the courts, enshrined in Article 47 of the Charter, and the protection of intellectual property guaranteed by Article 17(2) of the Charter. We have seen in Section 14.B that, according to *ITT Promedia*, litigation can be an abuse only in 'wholly exceptional circumstances'.[1136]

The issue came before the CJ in *Huawei Technologies*,[1137] a preliminary reference from the Landgericht Düsseldorf, which was seised of a dispute in which a SEP holder alleged infringement of its patent. Aware of the difference between the Commission's approach and the *Orange-Book-Standard*, the German court referred a series of questions which the CJ summed up as asking, essentially:

> . . . in what circumstances the bringing of an action for infringement, by an undertaking in a dominant position and holding an SEP, which has given an undertaking to the standardisation body to grant licences to third parties on FRAND terms, seeking an injunction prohibiting the infringement of that SEP or seeking the recall of products for the manufacture of which the SEP has been used, is to be regarded as constituting an abuse contrary to Article 102 TFEU.[1138]

The CJ began by acknowledging that it was 'settled case law' that the exercise of an IPR by its proprietor may, exceptionally, involve abusive conduct contrary to Article 102.[1139] It cited *Volvo*, *Magill*, and *RTE*, but made it clear that the instant case had to be distinguished from refusal to supply cases.[1140] It proceeded to identify exceptional circumstances in the SEP situation which could lead to the exercise of an exclusive right linked to an IPR—in the form of bringing an action—being abusive, but it did not mention *ITT*. The circumstances are: (a) the fact that the patent at issue is essential to a standard established by a standardisation body,[1141] and (b) that the patent obtained SEP status only in return for the proprietor's irrevocable undertaking, given to the relevant standardisation body, that it is prepared to grant licences on FRAND terms.[1142] Given that these circumstances create legitimate expectations on the part of third parties, Article 102 may in principle provide a defence against actions by the SEP holder.[1143] The CJ recognised that the holder cannot in principle be deprived of the right to bring an action to enforce its exclusive rights, but stated that, in order to do so without infringing Article 102, 'specific requirements' must be met.[1144] These are that: (a) prior to bringing proceedings the holder must alert the alleged infringer to the alleged infringement;[1145] (b) after the alleged infringer has expressed willingness to take a licence on FRAND terms, the holder must present it with a specific written offer for a licence on FRAND terms;[1146] and (c) the alleged infringer must not have accepted the offer or promptly submitted a written counter-offer.[1147] Where no agreement is reached after the counter-offer, the parties 'may by common agreement' have the amount of the royalty independently determined.[1148] Furthermore, the alleged infringer 'cannot be criticised' for challenging the validity of the relevant patents,[1149] which presumably means that the alleged infringer may challenge without penalty. These conditions apply only to proceedings 'liable to prevent products complying with the

[1135] As in the refusal to supply cases involving two markets: *Magill*, *IMS*, and *Microsoft*, see Sections 12.D and 12.E.

[1136] Case T-111/96, *ITT Promedia* EU:T:1998:183, para. 60; Case T-119/09, *Protégé International Ltd v Commission* EU:T:2012:421.

[1137] Case C-170/13, *Huawei Technologies v ZTE* EU:C:2015:477; see N. Banasevic, 'Editorial: The Implications of the Court of Justice's *Huawei/ZTE* Judgment' (2015) 6 *JECLAP* 463.

[1138] *Huawei*, ibid., para. 44. [1139] Ibid., para. 47.

[1140] Ibid., para. 48. Critiquing this approach, however, see I. Marko Goikoetxea, '*Huawei v ZTE* Should Have Been Treated as a Refusal to Contract—to Grant SEP Licences—and Not as a New Category of Abuse' (2019) 40 *ECLR* 67.

[1141] Case C-170/13, *Huawei* EU:C:2015:477, paras. 49–50. [1142] Ibid., para. 51. [1143] Ibid., paras. 53–54.

[1144] Ibid., paras. 59–60. [1145] Ibid., paras. 60–61. [1146] Ibid., paras. 63–64. [1147] Ibid., paras. 65–67.

[1148] Ibid., para. 68. [1149] Ibid., para. 69.

standard in question manufactured by competitors from appearing or remaining on the market', and so do not apply to actions for the rendering of accounts or damages in respect of an alleged infringer's past use of the SEP.[1150]

The judgment gave no indication of what constitutes FRAND terms, beyond the reference to 'conditions which seek to ensure a fair balance between the interests concerned'.[1151] It is also unclear as to the position where the parties do not reach an agreement following the counter-offer. The judgment says that they 'may' by common agreement request a third party determination, but not that they 'must', and not what happens if common agreement is not forthcoming. Furthermore, as the judgment focuses on the impact in the market for the products implementing the standard, and on the legitimate expectations created by FRAND commitments, it is unclear that its reasoning would apply to an injunction action by a patent assertion entity,[1152] and/or to an undertaking to which the original SEP owner had sold the patent.

D. THE ACQUISITION OF INTELLECTUAL PROPERTY RIGHTS AND/OR COMPETING TECHNOLOGIES

It was seen in Chapter 6 that, in *Tetra Pak*,[1153] the acquisition by a dominant undertaking of an exclusive patent licence was held to be an abuse even though the licence agreement did not infringe Article 101 as it fell within the block exemption regulation.[1154] The GC said that, although the acquisition of an exclusive licence by a dominant undertaking is not an abuse per se, it *may* constitute an abuse, and was on the facts of this case. The principle in *Tetra Pak I* is a striking example of the onerous nature of the 'special responsibility' towards the competitive process imposed on dominant firms. In *Servier*, the Commission held that it was an abuse for a dominant pharmaceutical company to shut out a competing technology, inter alia by buying out a number of competitors which had developed competing medical processes.[1155]

E. VERTICAL AND HORIZONTAL INTEGRATION

It is not an infringement of Article 102 for a dominant undertaking to integrate vertically, but actions taken in pursuit of a policy of vertical integration may infringe. Many cases finding an abusive refusal to supply[1156] or tying[1157] involved actions taken by a dominant undertaking which would enable it to integrate vertically.

1150 Ibid., paras. 52–53 and 72–73. This was the CJ's response to a specific question put by the Landgericht.

1151 The difficulties of determining FRAND terms in practices are explored in G. Colangelo and G. Scaramuzzino, 'Unwired Planet Act 2: The Return of the FRAND Range' (2019) 40 *ECLR* 306; M. Botta, 'The Challenge of Sanctioning Unfair Royalty Rate by the SEP Holder: "When", "How" and "What"' (2021) 44 *World Competition* 3.

1152 An entity whose business is primarily to purchase and manage patents rather than produce products itself (also known as a non-practising entity, or more perjoratively a patent troll).

1153 Case T-51/89, *Tetra Pak Rausing v Commission (Tetra Pak I)* EU:T:1990:41.

1154 Reg. 2349/84 [1984] OJ L219/15 on patent licensing agreements (replaced by Reg. 240/96 [1996] OJ L31/2 on Technology Transfer Agreements and subsequently by Reg. 772/2004 [2004] OJ L123/11 (see Chap. 12)).

1155 COMP/39.612, *Périndopril (Servier)* 9 July 2014. The finding of infringement with respect to Art. 102 was annulled by the GC, however, on the basis that the Commission had incorrectly defined the relevant market: see Case T-691/14, *Servier* EU:T:2018:922.

1156 Such as Cases 6 and 7/73, *Commercial Solvents* EU:C:1974:18 and Case 22/78, *Hugin* EU:C:1979:138.

1157 E.g. the *Digital Undertaking*, IP/97/868.

In *Continental Can*,[1158] it was established that Article 102 could apply to mergers whereby an undertaking strengthened its dominant position. Since the EU Merger Regulation (EUMR) regime has been in force, the general rule is that it alone applies to mergers within its scope.[1159] In *Towercast*,[1160] half a century after the *Continental Can* judgment, the CJ nonetheless confirmed that Article 102 remains applicable to mergers involving dominant undertakings, at least in certain circumstances. The CJ recognised the EUMR as 'a specific procedural instrument intended to apply exclusively to concentrations of undertakings involving significant structural changes, the impact of which on the market goes beyond the national borders of any one Member State.' [1161] Yet although the EUMR 'must be applied as a matter of priority' to concentrations falling within its scope, 'that cannot, however, preclude the possibility for a competition authority to capture a concentration operation under Article 102 TFEU under certain conditions'.[1162] To support its position, the CJ emphasised both the directly effective nature of Article 102 as a provision of primary EU law and the need for a teleological approach to its interpretation.[1163] Adhering closely to the question referred by the national court, the CJ limited its precise response to situations where the relevant transaction is not notifiable under either the EUMR or a domestic merger control framework. In her Opinion in *Towercast*, Advocate General Kokott had argued that where a transaction has been scrutinised and approved *ex ante* under 'the more specific rules of merger control', the underlying concentration 'could not as such be qualified (any longer) as an abuse of a dominant position within the meaning of Article 102 TFEU, unless the undertaking concerned has engaged in conduct which goes beyond that and could be found to constitute such an abuse'.[1164] The somewhat more inscrutable language of the CJ arguably leaves open at least the possibility of applying Article 102 in tandem with *domestic* merger control rules, provided that this is not precluded by the national procedural framework.

The question of jurisdiction is, of course, only the first step to the use of Article 102 as an instrument of merger control. To actually establish an abuse of dominance arising from a concentration, it is necessary to demonstrate that the dominant merging undertaking:

> . . . has, by that conduct, substantially impeded competition on that market. In that regard, the mere finding that an undertaking's position has been strengthened is not sufficient for a finding of abuse, since it must be established that the degree of dominance thus reached would substantially impede competition, that is to say, that only undertakings whose behaviour depends on the dominant undertaking would remain in the market (see, to that effect . . . Europemballage and Continental Can v Commission, 6/72, EU:C:1973:22, paragraph 26, and . . . Compagnie maritime belge transports and Others v Commission, C-395/96 P and C-396/96 P, EU:C:2000:132, paragraph 113).[1165]

F. DISPARAGEMENT OF RIVALS

In October 2022, the Commission announced that it had sent a statement of objections to the pharmaceutical company Teva, alleging a so-called 'disparagement campaign' to discredit its closest competitor, contrary to Article 102. The behaviour comprised 'a systematic disparagement campaign targeting healthcare professionals and casting doubts about the safety and efficacy of a competing glatiramer acetate medicine and its therapeutic equivalence with Copaxone', Teva's blockbuster multiple sclerosis

[1158] Case 6/72, *Continental Can* EU:C:1973:22; see Section 3.C.i.
[1159] Council Reg. 139/2004 [2004] OJ L24/1, see Chap. 15.
[1160] Case C-449/21, *Towercast* EU:C:2023:207. For further discussion of this case, see Chap. 15, Section 3.E.ii.
[1161] Ibid., para. 37. [1162] Ibid., para. 40. [1163] Ibid., paras. 31 and 44. [1164] Ibid., para. 60.
[1165] Ibid., para. 52.

drug.[1166] Commercial disparagement is an issue that arises primarily in tort law; there is a relative absence of EU-level competition law precedent on the topic.[1167] In *BBI/Boosey & Hawkes*, the dominant undertaking was alleged to have made false representations about a new rival's creditworthiness.[1168] A parallel may be drawn to the Article 101 judgment in *Hoffmann-La Roche and Novartis*, whereby the defendants coordinated their lobbying efforts in order to persuade the EU authorities to issue an unfavourable opinion about the off-label use of a competing product.[1169] The Commission is also conducting a further investigation into abusive disparagement in the pharmaceutical sector.[1170]

15. SECONDARY LINE DISCRIMINATION

A. INTRODUCTION TO ARTICLE 102(C)

Many of the exclusionary practices discussed thus far, such as predatory pricing, margin squeezes, rebates, tying, and refusals to supply, involve discrimination in some form. The *Google Shopping* case, moreover, raises the prospect that a dominant firm might infringe Article 102 simply by favouring its own downstream operations, described earlier as 'self-preferencing'.[1171] What these practices have in common is that the abusive discrimination results in primary line injury,[1172] namely harm to *competitors* of the dominant undertaking. A more contentious question is the extent to which Article 102 should be concerned with discrimination resulting in secondary line injury, namely harm as between the *customers* of the dominant undertaking.

Discrimination between customers often presents, superficially, as an *unfair* practice. Different consumers may be charged notably different prices for exactly the same product, based on their perceived willingness to pay (often linked to how urgently they need the good), their ability to shop around, or even their susceptibility to manipulation or exploitation by sellers. Yet fairness and efficiency are hardly synonyms in competition law;[1173] and while the average consumer may consider price discrimination to be unconscionable, competition experts are much more ambivalent.[1174] The question from a competition policy perspective is whether and when discrimination should also be treated as an *anti-competitive* practice. Price discrimination has come within the ambit of Article 102, most typically, where the dominant firm operates further up the value chain and engages in discrimination between customers that are, themselves, also undertakings active in a relevant market. In such circumstances, price discrimination involving non-associated companies will, most likely, represent some form of efficient pricing.[1175] Moreover, as the CJ noted in *MEO*, a dominant firm that does not

[1166] Commission Press Release, 'Antitrust: Commission sends Statement of Objections to Teva over misuse of the patent system and disparagement of rival multiple sclerosis medicine', 10 October 2022.

[1167] A. Giraud, J. Raffaitin, and C. Dobelmann, 'Disparagement in the European Union and France' in W. Sauter, M. Canoy, and J. Mulder (eds.), *EU Competition Law and Pharmaceuticals* (Edward Elgar, 2022).

[1168] *BBI/Boosey & Hawkes* [1987] OJ L282/36.

[1169] Case C-179/16, EU:C:2018:25. Specifically, the defendants were held to have agreed 'to produce and disseminate opinions which could give rise to public concern regarding the safety of Avastin when used in ophthalmology and to downplay the value of scientific opinions to the contrary' (ibid., para. 32).

[1170] Commission Press Release, 'Antitrust: Commission opens investigation into possible anticompetitive disparagement by Vifor Pharma of iron medicine', 20 June 2022.

[1171] Case T-612/17, *Google Shopping* EU:T:2021:763.

[1172] See also Section 7.B.

[1173] The tension between efficiency and fairness in the treatment of price discrimination from a competition policy perspective is discussed by C. Townley, E. Morrison, and K. Yeung, 'Big Data and Personalised Price Discrimination in EU Competition Law' (2017) 36 *YEL* 683.

[1174] A. Ezrachi and M. Stucke, 'The Rise of Behavioural Discrimination' (2016) 37 *ECLR* 485, 491–492.

[1175] R. O'Donoghue, 'The Quiet Death of Secondary-Line Discrimination as an Abuse of Dominance: Case C-525/16 *MEO*' (2018) 9 *JECLAP* 443, 443.

operate itself in a downstream market generally has little interesting in harming the market position (and thus potentially excluding) a downstream trading partner.[1176]

Nonetheless, Article 102 expressly prohibits certain forms of discrimination in paragraph (c), which states that an abuse may, in particular, consist in:

> applying dissimilar conditions to equivalent transactions with other trading parties, thereby placing them at a competitive disadvantage.

The term, 'dissimilar conditions' is interpreted to include dissimilar prices. Article 102(c) has been applied in three types of situations, each of which raises distinct concerns: to exclusionary practices resulting in primary line injury; to discrimination premised on nationality, which both results in secondary line injury and raises internal market concerns; and to pure secondary line injury.

B. EXCLUSIONARY PRACTICES UNDER ARTICLE 102(C)

As noted, many established abusive practices involve a degree of discrimination in a literal sense: margin squeeze, for instance, involves a vertically integrated dominant undertaking engaging in price discrimination between its own downstream operation and its downstream competitors. Typically, however, such behaviour is conceptualised as an exclusionary abuse contrary to Article 102(b). In a number of older cases, however, Article 102(c) was applied to situations of primary line injury, where dissimilar prices or conditions were offered to different customers, in order to prejudice the supplier's competitors.

This can be traced back to *Hoffmann-La Roche*,[1177] and was a feature of *Michelin I*[1178] and *Irish Sugar*.[1179] In *British Airways*, the airline paid differing amounts of commission to travel agents depending on whether they had increased their BA ticket sales. The application of Article 102(c) was part of an action against BA for an exclusionary abuse against a competitor.[1180] It is notable that, in *Post Danmark II*, the CJ said that in principle a retroactive standardised rebate scheme did not result in the application of dissimilar conditions contrary to Article 102(c).[1181] In *Clearstream*,[1182] the undertaking had a role conferred by regulation,[1183] and charged higher prices to a competitor of its sister company. More recently, in the self-preferencing cases of *Google Shopping* and *Amazon Marketplace and Amazon Buy Box*, the GC and the Commission respectively invoked the general principle of equal treatment to bolster the conclusion that discriminatory behaviour by large digital platforms amounted to an exclusionary abuse.[1184]

[1176] Case C-525/16, *MEO* EU:C:2018:270, para. 35.

[1177] Case 85/76, *Hoffmann-La* EU:C:1979:36, para. 90, which does not actually mention Art. 102(c) but says that 'the effect of fidelity rebates is to apply dissimilar conditions to equivalent transactions with other trading parties . . .'. The Commission had characterised the rebates as contrary to Art. 102(c).

[1178] Case 322/81, *Michelin I* EU:C:1983:313, where, nevertheless, the CJ annulled the Commission's finding of discrimination contrary to Art. 102(c) on the facts (paras. 90–91).

[1179] Case T-228/97, *Irish Sugar* EU:T:1999:246, *aff'd* Case C-497/99 P, *Irish Sugar* EU:C:2001:393. See also Case T-65/89, *BPB Industries* EU:T:1993:31, *aff'd* Case C-310/93 P, *BPB Industries* EU:C:1995:101.

[1180] See Section 10.C.iii.

[1181] Case C-23/14, *Post Danmark II* EU:C:2015:651, para. 37.

[1182] Case T-301/04, *Clearstream* EU:T:2009:317.

[1183] It was the Central Securities Depository for securities issued under German law.

[1184] Case T-612/17, Google Shopping EU:T:2021:763 and AT.40462, *Amazon Marketplace* and AT.40703, *Amazon Buy Box* 20 December 2022, see Section 13.

The use of Article 102(c) in exclusionary situations has been widely criticised.[1185] One objection was that the standard of proof for 'competitive disadvantage' in Article 102(c) was, conventionally, interpreted in a less demanding manner than that pertaining to exclusionary abuses generally. Indeed, in his Opinion preceding the most recent statement of the CJ on the ambit of Article 102(c), *MEO*, Advocate General Wahl cast doubt on the continued relevance of this earlier jurisprudence, suggesting that such cases belonged to a bygone era which had been supplanted by the effects-focused approach accepted in, inter alia, *Intel*.[1186] In its Guidance Paper on the application of Article 102 to exclusionary abuses, the Commission made no reference to Article 102(c), concentrating on the most common categories of exclusionary abuses which it analysed in line with the 'anti-competitive foreclosure' standard. Moreover, in *MEO*, the CJ stated that 'the specific prohibition of discrimination under subparagraph (c) of the second paragraph of Article 102 TFEU is intended to ensure that competition is not distorted in the internal market. The commercial behaviour of the undertaking in a dominant position may not distort competition on an upstream or a downstream market, in other words, between *suppliers or customers of that undertaking*. Co-contractors of such undertakings must not be favoured or disfavoured in the area of the competition which they practise amongst themselves.'[1187] Although the CJ did not rule out application of Article 102(c) to exclusionary behaviour,[1188] the particular emphasis placed on the implications for co-contractors of the dominant firm—as opposed to rivals—suggests that, in future, application of this 'specific prohibition' should be confined to secondary line situations.

C. DISCRIMINATION ON GROUNDS OF NATIONALITY OR GEOGRAPHIC LOCATION

A second subset of cases under Article 102(c) involve discrimination premised upon the nationality or geographic location of customers of the dominant undertaking. Many such cases have involved a strict application of the Article 102(c) prohibition, akin perhaps to the 'by object' prohibition of contractual clauses granting absolute territorial protection or prohibiting parallel exports under Article 101(1).[1189] Price discrimination within this category need not be shown to be inefficient to fall foul of Article 102(c), therefore. Yet even proponents of a 'more economic approach' to Article 102(c) have defended the strict treatment of discriminatory policies in this context,[1190] *provided* that it is understood that such cases relate directly to development of the internal market and do *not* state a general rule against secondary line price discrimination as such.

A first group of cases involved discrimination premised on nationality. In the first *Corsica Ferries* case,[1191] the port operator in Genoa charged different prices for pilotage services depending on whether the vessels were sailing between two domestic (Italian) ports or were on an international route. In *Aéroports de Paris*,[1192] the airport authority at Orly and Charles de Gaulle in Paris charged different levels of fees to companies it licensed to provide ground-handling services. In none of these cases

[1185] See e.g. Temple Lang and O'Donoghue, n. 201; Rousseva, n. 329, 215–217; Nazzini, n. 139, 249–250; Geradin, Layne-Farrar, and Petit, n. 195, 4.475–4.505; Rousseva and Marquis, n. 7, 32.

[1186] Opinion of Wahl AG in Case C-525/16, *MEO* EU:C:2017:1020, paras. 91–92.

[1187] Case C-525/16, *MEO* EU:C:2018:270, para. 24 (emphasis added).

[1188] Instead, the CJ merely clarified that Art. 102(c) is not *necessarily* concerned with the impact of the discriminatory behaviour on the market position of the dominant undertaking: Case C-525/16, *MEO* EU:C:2018:270, para. 24.

[1189] See e.g. Cases C-56/64 *Consten and Grundig* EU:C:1966:41, C-501/06 P *GlaxoSmithKline* EU:C:2009:610, and C-439/09 *Pierre Fabre* EU:C:2011:649.

[1190] O'Donoghue, n. 1159. [1191] Case C-18/93, *Corsica Ferries* EU:C:1994:195.

[1192] Case T-128/98, *Aéroports de Paris* EU:T:2000:290, *aff'd* Case C-82/01, EU:C:2002:617.

was there found to be any objective justification for the differentials.[1193] Other cases include *Deutsche Post: Interception of Cross-Border Mail*,[1194] where the German postal authority discriminated without objective justification between different types of mail coming into Germany;[1195] *Deutsche Bahn*[1196] where a national rail operator applied different prices to traffic via German ports and via Belgian and Dutch ones; and *GT Link*[1197] where the State port authority discriminated in favour of its own ferry services.[1198] In *Portuguese Airports*, the airport authority applied a seemingly uniform system of quantity discounts which was so constructed that it gave larger discounts to Portuguese airlines than to others. This was found to infringe Article 102(c).[1199] The CJ said that, while it was inherent in any quantity discount system that the largest buyers obtained the highest reductions, nevertheless it could be discriminatory if the system included thresholds that only a few very large users could reach and which gave them disproportionate rewards.[1200] In *1998 World Cup*, organisers of the Football World Cup in France infringed Article 102 by setting up a ticket distribution system which indirectly discriminated against non-French residents/nationals.[1201] More recently, in *OPCOM/Romanian Power Exchange*,[1202] OPCOM, the Romanian power exchange, discriminated against electricity traders established in EU countries other than Romania by requiring them to obtain a Romanian VAT registration even though they were registered in their own country.

Article 102(c) has also been applied to geographical price discrimination. Such discrimination involves charging different prices for the same products or services in different geographical territories. Artificial price differences across the EU should be eliminated or reduced by arbitrage and parallel trade, and indeed the price differences should encourage parallel trade, but this may be impeded by other factors. In both leading cases on geographical price discrimination, *United Brands*[1203] and *Tetra Pak II*,[1204] Article 102(c) was applied to measures taken by a dominant undertaking to prevent parallel trade.

Case 27/76, *United Brands v Commission* EU:C:1978:22

United Brands shipped its bananas across the Atlantic, unloaded them at several European ports, and sold them to approved ripener/distributors from various Member States at different prices. The prices reflected the diverse prices in the retail markets across the Member States. The contractual conditions under which the bananas were sold contained a prohibition on the distributors reselling the bananas while they were still green (the 'green banana clause'). The Commission concluded that this clause was simply a tactic to reinforce the price differentials, because once the bananas had started to turn yellow they were so perishable that it was not possible to export them to other Member States. The Commission also found that United Brands' practice of supplying distributors with less than they ordered made them sell locally instead of in other markets. The Commission held that these practices infringed Article 102. United Brands appealed, inter alia on this issue.

[1193] See also *Brussels National Airport (Zaventem)* [1995] OJ L216/8; *Ilmailulaitos/Luftsfartverket (Finnish Airports)* [1999] OJ L69/24; *Spanish Airports* [2000] OJ L208/36.

[1194] [2002] OJ L331/40.

[1195] Statutory monopolists entrusted with a 'service of general economic interest' have a limited exemption from the competition rules under Art. 106(2) of the Treaty. This is discussed in Chap. 8.

[1196] *HOV SVZ/MCN* [1994] OJ L104/34, on appeal Case T-229/94, *Deutsche Bahn* EU:T:1997:155, *aff'd* Case C-436/97, *Deutsche Bahn* EU:C:1999:205.

[1197] Case C-242/95, *GT-Link A/S v DE Danske Statsbaner* EU:C:1997:376.

[1198] See also COMP/39.388 and 39.389, *German Electricity Markets (E.ON)* 26 November 2008, where the Commission considered that E.ON's discrimination in favour of its own production affiliate led it to discriminate between domestic balancing energy and imported balancing energy, contrary to Art. 12 TFEU.

[1199] Case C-163/99, *Portugal v Commission* EU:C:2001:189.

[1200] Ibid., paras. 50–53.

[1201] *1998 World Cup* [2000] OJ L5/55.

[1202] COMP/39.984, 5 March 2014.

[1203] Case 27/76, *United Brands* EU:C:1978:22.

[1204] Case C-333/94 P, *Tetra Pak II* EU:C:1996:436.

Court of Justice

227. Although the responsibility for establishing the single banana market does not lie with the applicant, it can only endeavour to take 'what the market can bear' provided that it complies with the rules for the regulation and co-ordination of the market laid down by the Treaty.

228. Once it can be grasped that differences in transport costs, taxation, customs duties, the wages of the labour force, the conditions of marketing, the differences in the parity of currencies, the density of competition may eventually culminate in different retail selling price levels according to the Member States, then it follows those differences are factors which UBC only has to take into account to a limited extent since it sells a product which is always the same and at the same place to ripener/distributors who—alone—bear the risks of the consumer's market.

229. The interplay of supply and demand should, owing to its nature, only be applied to each stage where it is really manifest.

230. The mechanisms of the market are adversely affected if the price is calculated by leaving out one stage of the market and taking into account the law of supply and demand as between the vendor and the ultimate consumer and not as between the vendor (UBC) and the purchaser (the ripener/distributor).

231. Thus, by reason of its dominant position UBC, fed with information by its local representatives, was in fact able to impose its selling price on the intermediate purchaser. This price and also the 'weekly quota allocated' is only fixed and notified to the customer four days before the vessel carrying the bananas berths.

232. These discriminatory prices, which varied according to the circumstances of the Member States, were just so many obstacles to the free movement of goods and their effect was intensified by the clause forbidding the resale of bananas while still green and by reducing the deliveries of the quantities ordered.

233. A rigid partitioning of national markets was thus created at price levels, which were artificially different, placing certain distributor/ripeners at a competitive disadvantage, since compared with what it should have been competition had thereby been distorted.

234. Consequently the policy of differing prices enabling UBC to apply dissimilar conditions to equivalent transactions with other trading parties, thereby placing them at a competitive disadvantage, was an abuse of a dominant position.

The reasoning in this part of the *United Brands* judgment was criticised.[1205] Criticisms included treating the law of supply and demand as normative or prescriptive ('to be applied') rather than descriptive; allowing an undertaking to take into account different retail conditions and taking what the market can bear only if it bears the risks of the consumer market, thus giving undertakings an incentive to vertically integrate; describing discriminatory prices as 'just so many obstacles to the free movement of goods' whereas differential pricing would normally stimulate parallel trade;[1206] and favouring profits going to distributors rather than producers. The real objection to the price discrimination in *United Brands* was of course that it offended against the concept of the single market.

[1205] W. Bishop, 'Price Discrimination under Article 86: Political Economy in the European Court' (1981) 44 *MLR* 282; L. Zanon, 'Price Discrimination under Article 102 of the EEC Treaty: A Comment on the *UBC* Case' (1982) 31 *ICLQ* 36; M. Siragusa, 'The Application of Article 86 to the Pricing Policy of Dominant Companies: Discriminatory and Unfair Prices' (1979) 16 *CMLRev* 179.

[1206] The problem in *United Brands* was rather the buttressing 'green banana' clause which did not intensify the effect of the differing prices but neutralised it.

In *Tetra Pak II*, the Commission found wide disparities in the prices that Tetra Pak charged for its milk packaging machinery and cartons in different Member States, despite the fact that the geographical market was EU-wide. It held these prices differences to be due to artificial partitioning of the market and not to objective market conditions.[1207] The decision was upheld by the GC, which found that 'those disparities in price could not be attributed to objective market conditions'.[1208]

In *Irish Sugar*,[1209] the dominant undertaking operated a system of 'sugar export rebates', granted on sales of industrial sugar to companies exporting to other Member States. The Commission found that this practice discriminated against customers of industrial sugar supplying the domestic Irish market. The GC upheld the Commission's finding that this was an abuse, holding that market mechanisms were distorted by pricing according to the location of the customers' buyers. *Post Danmark I*, as discussed, cast considerable doubt on *Irish Sugar* to the extent that the case dealt with selective though above-cost price-cutting.[1210] If treated as an instance of geographical price discrimination contrary to the development of the internal market, the holding may be more defensible even today.

Whether or not geographical price discrimination is an abuse in the absence of measures to partition the market is unclear. In *Tetra Pak II*, the GC reiterated that setting different prices could be justified by local conditions. In *United Brands*, however, local conditions did not justify variations in retail prices. This suggests that, once the Member States are in the same geographic market and costs are the same, objective justification for price discrimination will be hard to prove. In the absence of buttressing measures such as the 'green banana clause', however, the ability to maintain different prices in different geographical areas suggests that there are different geographic markets, and so Article 102(c) should not apply.[1211] Where there are buttressing measures, these are likely to be abusive themselves.

The abuse set out in Article 102(c) is the application of dissimilar conditions to equivalent transactions with other trading parties, 'thereby placing them at a competitive disadvantage'. In respect of the export rebates in *Irish Sugar*, the GC did not accept that the non-export customers suffered no competitive disadvantage.[1212] However, in *United Brands* the CJ applied Article 102(c) even though the ripener/distributors from different Member States did not compete, and greengrocers in Ireland certainly did not compete with those in Germany. Likewise, in *Corsica Ferries I*, the CJ applied Article 102(c) regardless of the fact that the domestic and international shipping lines were not competing.[1213] In *Deutsche Post: Interception of Cross-Border Mail*, the Commission rejected the argument that customers were not put at a competitive disadvantage by having to pay more than others for their cross-border mail, on the basis that the list of abuses in Article 102 is not exhaustive.[1214] Thus, directly damaging consumers may infringe Article 102, although of course consumers will usually not be 'in competition' with one another. Since Deutsche Post was a statutory monopolist the consumers had no alternative supplier: nor indeed did the shipping lines in *Corsica Ferries*. Moreover, given the implications for development of the internal market at issue in cases like *Deutsche Post*, *Corsica Ferries*, and *United Brands*, it is unsurprising that EU law disapproves of such discriminatory behaviour, although it is difficult to reconcile this with the precise wording of Article 102(c).

[1207] E.g. customers for the machines could purchase cartons only from Tetra Pak itself or a company designated by it, and so customers in high-price countries were not free to purchase from third parties in lower-price areas.

[1208] Case T-83/91, *Tetra Pak II* EU:T:1994:246, para. 170. See also Case T-168/01, *GlaxoSmithKline* EU:T:2006:265, para. 177.

[1209] [1997] OJ L258/1, [1997] 5 CMLR 666.

[1210] See e.g. Sections 8.D and 8.I.

[1211] See further Geradin, Layne-Farrar, and Petit, n. 195, 4.525–4.541.

[1212] Case T-228/97, *Irish Sugar* EU:T:1999:246, paras. 140–149.

[1213] Case C-18/93, *Corsica Ferries* EU:C:1994:195. The CJ did not mention the issue; the AG did, but considered that it did not matter, Van Gerven AG, para. 34.

[1214] [2002] OJ L331/40, para. 133.

D. SECONDARY LINE DISCRIMINATION AND 'COMPETITIVE DISADVANTAGE'

Outside the specific context of discrimination that inhibits development of the internal market, the concept of 'competitive disadvantage' is of renewed relevance and importance in relation to secondary line discrimination following the decision of the CJ in *MEO*. Prior to this judgment, the precise ambit of this requirement under Article 102(c) was unclear, at least in part due to a failure to distinguish 'ordinary' secondary line injury cases from those which implicated development of the internal market or which were mislabelled exclusionary abuses.[1215] Perhaps the leading case on 'competitive disadvantage' was the notorious decision in *British Airways*, in which the target bonus/commission scheme operated by British Airways was held to infringe Article 102 because of its capability to exclude competitors.[1216] It was also held to specifically infringe Article 102(c), because it discriminated between travel agents in giving different rewards to different agents for selling the same number of tickets. On appeal, the CJ restated the requirement that for discrimination to constitute an abuse under Article 102(c), there must be competitive disadvantage. However, it was assumed that the different financial arrangements that each agent had with BA automatically placed some at a competitive disadvantage, due to the different rebates they received. It was therefore necessary only to demonstrate that the behaviour of the dominant undertaking 'tends' to distort competition, and the CJ did not require proof of an actual quantifiable deterioration in the individual's competitive position.[1217] The standard of proof thus appeared to be lamentably low, as was demonstrated in *Clearstream*.[1218]

The Article 267 reference case of *MEO* therefore provided the CJ with an important opportunity to clarify the requirements to demonstrate anti-competitive secondary line discrimination contrary to Article 102(c). GDA was a collecting society that managed the rights of artists and performers in Portugal. Although without any legal monopoly, it was the only such agency in the country. MEO and NOS were television companies active in Portugal, and both contracted with GDA for the right to use its collectively managed content in television broadcasts. GDA charged various tariffs to customers, and was also covered by a national legal rule which provided for mandatory arbitration where GDA and its prospective customer were unable to reach an agreed tariff. MEO complained to the national competition authority that the tariff it was charged by GDA, which had been set through the arbitration process, was both excessively high and also discriminatory when compared with that enjoyed by NOS. Its complaint was rejected and MEO appealed to the relevant competition court, which made a reference asking, specifically, about the meaning of 'competitive disadvantage' within Article 102(c). The CJ's response was preceded by a characteristically bold Opinion from Advocate General Wahl. Regardless of the wording of Article 102(c), he insisted that 'discrimination, including discrimination in the charging of prices, is not in itself problematic from the point of view of competition law',[1219] but rather, '[i]t should only be possible to penalise price discrimination . . . if it creates an actual or potential anticompetitive effect'.[1220] To a large extent, this approach was adopted and reflected in the judgment of the CJ.

[1215] O'Donoghue, n. 1159, 443–444. [1216] *Virgin/British Airways* [2000] OJ L30/1.
[1217] Case C-95/04 P, *British Airways v* EU:C:2007:166, paras. 144–145.
[1218] Case T-301/04, *Clearstream* EU:T:2009:317; see also Case C-52/07, *Kanal 5* EU:C:2008:703.
[1219] Case C-525/16, *MEO* EU:C:2017:1020, Wahl AG, para. 61.
[1220] Ibid., para. 63.

Case C-525/16, *MEO–Serviços de Comunicações e Multimédia SA v Autoridade da Concorrência* EU:C:2018:270

Court of Justice

22. By its questions, which should be examined together, the referring court asks, in essence, whether the concept of 'competitive disadvantage', for the purposes of subparagraph (c) of the second paragraph of Article 102 TFEU, must be interpreted to the effect that it requires an analysis of the specific effects of differentiated prices being applied by an undertaking in a dominant position on the competitive situation of the undertaking affected and, as the case may be, whether the seriousness of those effects should be taken into account.

23. Under subparagraph (c) of the second paragraph of Article 102 TFEU, undertakings with a dominant position in the internal market, or in a substantial part of that market, are precluded from applying dissimilar conditions to equivalent transactions with other trading parties, thereby placing them at a competitive disadvantage, as trade between Member States may be affected.

24. In accordance with the case-law of the Court, the specific prohibition of discrimination under subparagraph (c) of the second paragraph of Article 102 TFEU is intended to ensure that competition is not distorted in the internal market. The commercial behaviour of the undertaking in a dominant position may not distort competition on an upstream or a downstream market, in other words, between suppliers or customers of that undertaking. Co-contractors of such undertakings must not be favoured or disfavoured in the area of the competition which they practise amongst themselves (. . . *British Airways v Commission*, C-95/04 P, EU:C:2007:166, paragraph 143). Thus, it is not necessary that the abusive conduct affects the competitive position of the dominant undertaking itself on the same market in which it operates, compared with its own potential competitors.

25. In order for the conditions for applying subparagraph (c) of the second paragraph of Article 102 TFEU to be met, there must be a finding, not only that the behaviour of an undertaking in a dominant market position is discriminatory, but also that it tends to distort that competitive relationship, in other words, to hinder the competitive position of some of the business partners of that undertaking in relation to the others (. . . *British Airways v Commission*, C-95/04 P, EU:C:2007:166, paragraph 144 and the case-law cited).

26. In order to establish whether the price discrimination on the part of an undertaking in a dominant position vis-à-vis its trade partners tends to distort competition on the downstream market, as the Advocate General submitted, in essence, in paragraph 63 of his Opinion, the mere presence of an immediate disadvantage affecting operators who were charged more, compared with the tariffs applied to their competitors for an equivalent service, does not, however, mean that competition is distorted or is capable of being distorted.

27. It is only if the behaviour of the undertaking in a dominant position tends, having regard to the whole of the circumstances of the case, to lead to a distortion of competition between those business partners that the discrimination between trade partners which are in a competitive relationship may be regarded as abusive. In such a situation, it cannot, however, be required in addition that proof be adduced of an actual, quantifiable deterioration in the competitive position of the business partners taken individually (. . . *British Airways v Commission*, C-95/04 P, EU:C:2007:166, paragraph 145).

28. Therefore, as the Advocate General submitted in paragraph 86 of his Opinion, it is necessary to examine all the relevant circumstances in order to determine whether price discrimination produces or is capable of producing a competitive disadvantage, for the purposes of subparagraph (c) of the second paragraph of Article 102 TFEU.

29. With regard to the issue whether, for the application of subparagraph (c) of the second paragraph of Article 102 TFEU, it is necessary to take into account the seriousness of a possible competitive disadvantage, it must be pointed out that fixing an appreciability (de minimis) threshold for the purposes of determining whether there is an abuse of a dominant position is not justified (. . . *Post Danmark*, C-23/14, EU:C:2015:651, paragraph 73).

30. However, in order for it to be capable of creating a competitive disadvantage, the price discrimination referred to in subparagraph (c) of the second paragraph of Article 102 TFEU must affect the interests of the operator which was charged higher tariffs compared with its competitors.

31. When it carries out the specific examination referred to in paragraph 28 above, the competition authority or the competent national court is required to take into account all the circumstances of the case submitted to it. It is open to such an authority or court to assess, in that context, the undertaking's dominant position, the negotiating power as regards the tariffs, the conditions and arrangements for charging those tariffs, their duration and their amount, and the possible existence of a strategy aiming to exclude from the downstream market one of its trade partners which is at least as efficient as its competitors (see, by analogy, . . . *Intel v Commission*, C-413/14 P, EU:C:2017:632, paragraph 139 and the case-law cited).

A number of aspects of the judgment are noteworthy. The CJ emphasised that Article 102(c) targets not discrimination *as such*, but only discrimination which tends to distort competition in the market concerned. Moreover, the notion of competitive disadvantage for these purposes cannot be equated to 'the mere presence of an immediate disadvantage' (e.g. higher costs) for traders affected negatively by the discrimination: additionally, it is necessary to show a distortion of *competition* stemming from that disparate treatment. Importantly, in order to demonstrate any likely distortion, the CJ referred to the much-debated 'all the relevant circumstances' standard, and identified a list of potentially significant considerations echoing those set out by the Grand Chamber in *Intel* just a few months previously, including mention of the AEC standard. Accordingly, the decision in *MEO* can be seen both as implicit confirmation of *Intel* and its reorientation of the substance of Article 102 generally towards an effects-based approach,[1221] and, more specifically, as a strong statement that Article 102(c) is concerned not with outwardly unfair or unequal behaviour, but rather only where such behaviour distorts competition within the market more broadly.[1222] The judgment has thus been described as representing a 'quiet death' for mere secondary line discrimination as a theory of harm under Article 102, as well as an effective (though characteristically non-explicit) reversal of the formalistic approach in *British Airways*.[1223]

16. EXPLOITATIVE ABUSES

A. UNFAIRLY HIGH OR LOW PRICING

(i) Unfairly High Prices

a. General

Article 102(a) provides that an abuse may consist in directly or indirectly imposing 'unfair purchase or selling prices or other unfair trading conditions'.[1224] We discussed unfairly *low* prices on the selling side in the sections on predatory pricing and other exclusionary pricing abuses. Here we

[1221] Arguing that *MEO* brings Art. 102(c) into line with the application of Art. 102 to exclusionary abuses more generally, see R. Horvath, L. Peeperkorn, and E. Rousseva, 'The Preliminary Ruling in MEO: Closing the Circle of Article 102 TFEU' (2020) 11 *JECLAP* 35.

[1222] For a more cautious reading of *MEO*, see C. Ritter, 'Price Discrimination as an Abuse of a Dominant Position under Article 102 TFEU: *MEO*' (2019) 56 *CMLRev* 259.

[1223] O'Donoghue, n. 1159.

[1224] See generally A. Svetlicinii and M. Botta, 'Article 102 TFEU as a Tool for Market Regulation' (2012) 8 *European Law Journal* 473; T. Ackermann, 'Excessive Pricing and the Goals of Competition Law' and J. P. Terhechte, 'Excessive Pricing and the Goals of Competition Law: An Enforcement Perspective—Comment on Ackermann' in D. Zimmer (ed.), *The Goals of Competition Law* (Edward Elgar, 2012), Chaps. 18 and 19, respectively; M. Furse, 'Excessive Prices, Unfair Prices and Economic Value' (2008) 4 *European Competition Journal* 59; Geradin, Layne-Farrar, and Petit, n. 195, 4.475–4.542.

look at unfairly *high* prices. 'Excessive pricing concerns, in essence, the extraction of excessive profits by a dominant undertaking by imposing particularly high and unfair prices on its customers, which cannot be explained by any legitimate considerations.'[1225]

Excessive pricing is the most obvious way in which a monopolist can exploit its position. We saw in Chapter 1 that monopoly prices are likely to be higher than those in competitive markets, and excessive prices match the popular conception of the evils of monopoly. Yet there is a remarkable reluctance in much competition law literature and practice to enforce the rules *directly* against high prices charged unilaterally by undertakings with significant market power. On the one hand, it has been argued that the free market economy needs the lure of monopoly pricing: '[t]he opportunity to charge monopoly prices—at least for a short period—is what attracts "business acumen" in the first place; it induces risk taking that produces innovation and economic growth'.[1226] Excessive prices may therefore be pro- rather than anti-competitive, where high prices and profits act as a signal to attract new competitors.[1227] On the other, even where high barriers to entry prevent markets from self-correcting, direct enforcement against high pricing raises the spectre of competition authorities acting as price regulators. Yet price regulation is the antithesis of the free market, and sensitive distributional questions may arise where agencies are required to arbitrate how profits ought to be shared out amongst market players. Under §2 of the Sherman Act, the position is thus that '[a] pristine monopolist . . . may charge as high a rate as the market will bear'.[1228] Accordingly, unless the position of significant market power has been acquired or maintained through anti-competitive behaviour, high pricing as such is per se legal in US antitrust law.

Despite the explicit authorisation reflected in Article 102(a), the Commission similarly has not much concerned itself with high prices.[1229] The Commission has long insisted that it 'is not and does not wish to act as a price regulator' in its enforcement activities under Article 102.[1230] It has often taken the view that interference with high prices and profits is a disincentive to innovation and investment, and considered it preferable to address problems of unfair pricing through action against exclusionary conduct whereby dominant firms seek to preserve their dominance.[1231] The motivation behind this orthodoxy was summed up by Advocate General Wahl in *AKKA/LAA*: 'there is simply no need to apply [the rule against excessive prices] in a free and competitive market: with no barriers to entry, high prices should normally attract new entrants. The market would accordingly self-correct.'[1232] As the Advocate General admitted, however, the orthodoxy does not hold true in all markets, particularly where insurmountable barriers to entry (e.g. the presence of legal monopoly) make new entry impossible.[1233] In such circumstances, and absent sector-specific regulatory intervention, competition enforcement may be necessary. A concern with excessive pricing also aligns with a renewed focus on 'fair' market outcomes as a goal of EU competition enforcement, as the Competition Commissioner explained in an ambitious speech in 2016.[1234]

1225 AT.40394, *Aspen* 10 February 2021, para. 76.

1226 *Verizon Communications Ltd v Trinko*, 540 US 398, 124 S.Ct 872, para. 2 (Scalia J).

1227 But against this view, see A. Ezrachi and D. Gilo, 'Are Excessive Prices Really Self-correcting?' (2009) 5 *J of Competition Law and Economics* 249, who argue that high prices alone are insufficient to persuade a new entrant to compete with the incumbent.

1228 *Berkey Photo, In. v Eastman Kodak Co*, 603 F.2d 263, 297 (2d Cir. 1979).

1229 As noted e.g. in Case-177/16, *AKKA/LAA* EU:C:2017:286, Wahl AG. para. 3.

1230 European Commission, *XXVIIth Report on Competition Policy* (1997), 29.

1231 See Commission, *XXIVth Report on Competition Policy* (1994), point 207.

1232 Case C-177/16, *AKKA/LAA* EU:C:2017:286, Wahl AG, para. 3.

1233 Ibid., para. 4.

1234 Commissioner Vestager, 'Protecting consumers from exploitation', Chillin' Competition Conference, Brussels, 21 November 2016, <https://ec.europa.eu/commission/commissioners/2014-2019/vestager/announcements/protecting-consumers-exploitation_en>.

b. Ascertaining What Constitutes an Unfairly High Price: The Concept of 'Economic Value'

The main legal problem in applying Article 102(a) is to identify what constitutes an 'unfair' price. The standard formulation comes from the *United Brands* judgment, although it arguably raises as many questions as it answers. Here, the Commission condemned UBC for charging excessive prices for Chiquita bananas in Germany, Denmark, and Benelux. It compared the prices with those for unbranded bananas, for competitors' bananas, and with the price of Chiquitas in Ireland, and it said that the prices were 'excessive in relation to the economic value of the product supplied'. On appeal, this aspect of the decision was annulled by the CJ, on the basis that the Commission had failed to present sufficient evidence of unfairness on the facts. However, the CJ accepted that 'excessive' prices can constitute an abuse in appropriate circumstances, and it considered how to identify when high prices might be abusive under Article 102.

Case 27/76, *United Brands v Commission* EU:C:1978:22

Court of Justice

248. The imposition by an undertaking in a dominant position directly or indirectly of unfair purchase or selling prices is an abuse to which exception can be taken under Article [102].

249. It is advisable therefore to ascertain whether the dominant undertaking has made use of the opportunities arising out of its dominant position in such a way as to reap trading benefits which it would not have reaped if there had been normal and sufficiently effective competition.

250. In this case charging a price which is excessive because it has no reasonable relation to the economic value of the product supplied would be such an abuse.

251. This excess could, *inter alia*, be determined objectively if it were possible for it to be calculated by making a comparison between the selling price of the product in question and its cost of production, which would disclose the amount of the profit margin; however the Commission has not done this since it has not analysed UBC's costs structure.

252. The questions therefore to be determined are whether the difference between the costs actually incurred and the price actually charged is excessive, and, if the answer to this question is in the affirmative, whether a price has been imposed which is either unfair in itself or when compared to competing products.

253. Other ways may be devised—and economic theorists have not failed to think up several—of selecting the rules for determining whether the price of a product is unfair.

The abuse of excessive pricing thus involves 'charging a price which . . . has no reasonable relation to the economic value of the product supplied'. This basic standard was reaffirmed by the CJ four decades later in *AKKA/LAA*.[1235] Yet the concept of 'economic value' is inherently vague: put simply, what is the economic value of a product, such as a banana, other than what customers are prepared to pay for it? The notion was first introduced in *General Motors*,[1236] where the defendant was a car manufacturer that charged high prices for the production of documentation without which car owners could not bring their cars into Belgium. The documentation was cheap to produce, but the 'value' to customers was great since, without the certificate, cars could not be imported. On the facts, the CJ accepted that no abuse had occurred,[1237] so the meaning of 'economic value' was not pursued.

[1235] Case C-177/16, *Biedrība 'Autortiesību un komunicçšanās konsultāciju aģentūra—Latvijas Autoru apvienība' Konkurences padome (AKKA/LAA)* EU:C:2017:689, para. 36.

[1236] Case 26/75, *General Motors v Commission* EU:C:1975:150.

[1237] Because the high price had been a temporary blip while national procedures were changed.

In *United Brands*, the CJ considered that excessiveness might be determined by comparing the selling and production costs (the 'cost\+ standard'), which would disclose the profit margin. It did not indicate, however, the level at which a profit margin would become excessive. In paragraph 252, the CJ clarified that finding a price is 'excessive' by these means is not the end of the matter: it must furthermore be determined whether the excessive price is, to use the language of Article 102(a), *unfair.* Accordingly, the CJ set out a two-stage test:

(a) is the price excessive; *and if it is*

(b) is the price either unfair in itself or when compared to competing products?

This means that prices cannot be deemed excessive simply because the dominant undertaking is earning a high profit margin compared with its costs: this is merely 'a screening exercise to assess whether the price charged is suspiciously high'.[1238] If this first limb of the test is satisfied, it is furthermore necessary to determine whether the price is unfair when compared either with a relevant competitive price benchmark—'when compared to competing products'—or, if no such benchmark price exists, by directly estimating the economic value of the product—'unfair in itself'.[1239] These are alternative requirements.[1240] The purpose of this second limb of the test is to examine 'whether there may be legitimate reasons underlying the excessive profits identified under Limb 1, in particular reasons not yet reflected in the costs analysis in Limb 1'.[1241] These might include superior efficiencies in the production or marketing of the product, or successful innovation by the dominant undertaking. While such factors do not necessarily legitimate high profit margins, they are relevant considerations in any assessment of potential *unfairness* of the price charged.[1242]

The implications of the 'economic value' standard are well illustrated by the *Scandlines* decision,[1243] in which the Commission rejected complaints of excessive pricing relating to the port fees charged at Helsingborg, Sweden, for services provided to ferry companies operating between Sweden and Denmark. The Commission adopted the two-stage methodology from *United Brands*, and confirmed that the stages are cumulative, not alternative. The Commission took the view that economic value had to be determined with regard to the circumstances and by taking into account non-cost-related factors, particularly demand-side aspects of the product or service. The demand side was relevant because 'customers are notably willing to pay more for something specific attached to the product/service that they consider valuable . . . [which] thereby increases the economic value'.[1244] Here, the fees charged at Helsingborg were acknowledged to be considerably higher than at competing ports. Yet the Commission was unable to conclude that the prices bore 'no reasonable relation' to the presumed economic value of the service, because the services provided at Helsingborg were highly valued by consumers.

Excessive pricing cases arise with particular frequency in markets that are protected by some form of legal monopoly.[1245] Where competition within the market is impossible, the comparison may be made with products in other geographic areas. In *Bodson,*[1246] which concerned funeral services in areas of France where there were monopoly concessions granted by local authorities, the CJ considered whether the price was 'fair' in comparison with prices in areas without such concessions. In *Gazprom*, the Commission compared the allegedly excessive wholesale gas prices charged in affected

[1238] AT39816, *Upstream gas supplies in Central and Eastern Europe* 24 May 2018, para. 65. [1239] Ibid.

[1240] Case C-159/08 P, *Scippacercola* EU:C:2009:188, para. 47.

[1241] AT.40394, *Aspen* 10 February 2021, para. 163. [1242] Ibid.

[1243] COMP/36.568, *Scandlines Sverige v Port of Helsingborg* 23 July 2004 and COMP/36.570, *Sundbesserne v Port of Helsingborg* 23 July 2004 (*Scandlines*).

[1244] *Scandlines*, para. 227. The complainants withdrew their appeal to the GC against the decision.

[1245] Case C-177/16, *AKKA/LAA* EU:C:2017:286, Wahl AG, para. 4.

[1246] Case 30/87 [1988] ECR 2479, para. 31.

countries to Gazprom's own long-term contract prices in Germany, and to European hub prices.[1247] The CJ in *Tournier* indeed suggested that where prices in one Member State 'are appreciably higher than those charged in other Member States and where a comparison of the fee levels has been made on a consistent basis, that difference must be regarded as indicative of an abuse of a dominant position'.[1248] Comparing the price of products across different Member States may be difficult, however, because of the different factors which might be affecting those prices, as demonstrated by *United Brands*.[1249] As Advocate General Wahl noted in *AKKA*/LAA, 'elements such as . . . domestic taxes, the particular characteristics of the national labour market and local consumers' preferences may significantly affect the final prices of the relevant product or service'.[1250] The CJ in *AKKA/LAA* therefore approved a two-pronged approach, involving, first, a direct comparison of prices in Latvia with those in two similarly situated Member States (Estonia and Lithuania) and, secondly, a comparison of prices charged in an additional 20 Member States, adjusted to take account of different purchasing power across these countries.[1251] By contrast, in *Deutsche Post*[1252] where the defendant, DPAG, had a statutory monopoly which made comparison with competitors impossible, the Commission compared the prices charged by DPAG for the forwarding and delivery of cross-border mail in Germany with the defendant's *own* domestic tariffs. The Commission held the former to be excessive as it had 'no sufficient or reasonable relationship to real costs or to the real value of the service provided'.[1253]

In cases concerning products covered by IPRs, the issue of a comparison with non-IPR-protected products has arisen. In *Parke, Davis*,[1254] the CJ said that the higher price of a patented compared with a non-patented product did not necessarily constitute an abuse. In *Renault*,[1255] however, it suggested that a car manufacturer which refused to license its IPRs in respect of its spare parts might commit an abuse if it charged 'unfair prices' for those parts. In *DSD*, the Commission condemned as excessive the fee charged for use of the defendant's trade-marked 'Green Dot' logo on consumer packaging, even where customers showed that they did not subsequently use DSD's system for packaging recycling.[1256] The idea that IPR owners may not extract the maximum return from their monopoly position raises difficult questions about the value of such rights. If cost-price comparisons are used to detect excessive pricing, the undertaking's past research costs, including research costs which do not result in commercially exploitable products, need to be taken into account in determining a 'fair' return. Conversely, in *Aspen*, where patent protection on the relevant products—six cancer medicines—had expired half a century previously, the Commission was understandably unsympathetic to the defendant's arguments premised upon commercial risk-taking, innovation, or investment.[1257] Yet IPRs constitute precisely the sorts of legal monopolies that may impose intractable barriers to entry and thus facilitate significant consumer exploitation, meaning that a blanket rule against the application of Article 102 cannot be justified.

In *AKKA/LAA*, while reaffirming the validity of the twofold *United Brands* test, the CJ clarified that it is not exhaustive: conceivably, 'there are other methods by which it can be determined whether a price may be excessive'.[1258] For more novel approaches, the CJ emphasised the need to used 'objective,

[1247] AT39816, *Upstream gas supplies in Central and Eastern Europe* 24 May 2018, paras. 62–78.

[1248] Case 395/87, EU:C:1989:319, para. 38. See also Case C-351/12, *OSA* EU:C:2014:110, para. 87; and Case C-177/16, *AKKA/LAA* EU:C:2017:689, para. 53.

[1249] See also Case C-159/08 P, *Scippacercola* EU:C:2009:188, where the complainants' attempts to compare the prices at Athens airports with those at airports in other Member States did not convince the Commission.

[1250] Case C-177/16, *AKKA/LAA* EU:C:2017:286, Wahl AG, para. 40. [1251] Ibid.

[1252] [2002] OJ L331/40. The case raised issues in respect of competition rules and undertakings granted monopoly rights by the State, and the application of Art. 106(2): see Chap. 8.

[1253] *Deutsche Post* [2001] OJ L125/27, paras. 159–167. [1254] Case 24/67, *Parke, Davis & Co v Probel* EU:C:1968:11.

[1255] Case 53/87, *Renault* EU:C:1988:472, para. 16, see Section 12.

[1256] COMP/34.493 etc., *DSD* 17 September 2001. [1257] AT.40394, *Aspen* 10 February 2021, para. 171.

[1258] Case C-177/16, *AKKA/LAA* EU:C:2017:689, para. 37.

appropriate and verifiable criteria',[1259] and for any comparisons to be made 'on a consistent basis'.[1260] Nonetheless, the approach adopted by the NCA in that case, involving comparisons between prices charged across different Member States for performing rights licences, can be reconciled with the 'competing products' limb of step (ii) of the *United Brands* criteria.

The *AKKA/LAA* Court also elaborated on the appreciability requirement. The CJ's starting point was the statement in *Tournier* that where 'appreciably higher' prices are charged in one Member State, that is in itself 'indicative' of abuse.[1261] Like many excessive pricing cases, *AKKA/LAA* involved the price policies of a collecting society with a national monopoly, located in this instance in Latvia. On the facts, the difference between the rates charged in Latvia and those in other Member States was not as large as the differences at issue in *Tournier*. Yet the CJ rejected the suggestion that the criterion of appreciability could be determined mechanically or in an *a priori* fashion:

> 55. . . . There is in fact no minimum threshold above which a rate must be regarded as 'appreciably higher', given that the circumstances specific to each case are decisive in that regard. Thus, a difference between rates may be qualified as 'appreciable' if it is both significant and persistent on the facts, with respect, in particular, to the market in question . . .
>
> 56. It should be emphasised in this regard that . . . the difference must be significant for the rates concerned to be regarded as 'abusive'. Furthermore, that difference must persist for a certain length of time and must not be temporary or episodic.

Accordingly, the key question to ask is whether the difference in prices is 'significant and persistent on the facts' (paragraph 55), thus measuring appreciability both in terms of magnitude and duration.

With its focus on the relationship between the price paid and economic value obtained by consumers, the *United Brands* test is, on its face, an objective one. In its *Aspen* commitment decision, however, the Commission invoked a range of more subjective factors to bolster its preliminary conclusion that the defendant's pricing policies infringed Article 102(a). *Aspen* involved not merely excessive pricing, but 'price gouging', whereby the dominant undertaking increased the prices that it charged for off-patent cancer medicines by up to several hundred per cent in a short period.[1262] The Commission pointed to internal documents, which indicated that Aspen had become 'conscious of the market power that it enjoyed, and decided to exploit it', resulting in 'a big push to increase the pricing'.[1263] It also noted efforts by the defendant to enforce its price rises through strategic threats to remove its products from several national reimbursement systems for medicines, and in some instance actual delisting,[1264] alongside attempts to 'game' the external price-referencing systems used to set reimbursement prices in various Member States.[1265]

Finally, it remains open for a defendant undertaking to objectively justify any perceived unfairness in the difference between the prices that it charges and any appropriately situated competing products or hypothetical benchmark price, by reference to 'objective dissimilarities' between the various products.[1266] In *AKKA/LAA*, for instance, the CJ suggested that a national law on fair remuneration, which required the defendant to secure higher profit margins, could perform such a role.[1267]

[1259] Ibid., para. 41. [1260] Ibid., para. 44.

[1261] Case C-177/16, *AKKA/LAA* EU:C:2017:689, para. 53, citing Case C-395/87, *Tournier* EU:C:1989:319, para. 38.

[1262] The term 'price gouging' was used explicitly by the Commission in the press release which announced the formal opening of an investigation into Aspen's behaviour (see Commission, 'Antitrust: Commission opens formal investigation into Aspen Pharma's pricing practices for cancer medicines', 15 May 2017), although it is not used in the final commitments decision.

[1263] AT.40394, *Aspen* 10 February 2021, para. 187. [1264] Ibid., paras. 90–96. [1265] Ibid., paras. 97–99.

[1266] Case C-395/87, *Tournier* EU:C:1989:319, para. 38; reaffirmed in Case C-177/16, *AKKA/LAA* EU:C:2017:689, para. 57.

[1267] Case C-177/16, *AKKA/LAA* EU:C:2017:689, para. 60.

c. The Future of the Excessive Pricing Under Article 102

Article 102 contrasts notably with s. 2 of the Sherman Act in its treatment of excessive pricing. Under US antitrust, the 'charging of monopoly prices' which follows from 'the mere possession of monopoly power'—i.e. which a dominant firm has acquired through competition on the merits—'is not only not unlawful; it is an important element of the free-market system'.[1268] From this perspective, the continuing European willingness to intervene directly against exploitative practices is perplexing.[1269] Yet exploitative abuse cases fit well with the muscular, interventionist vision of EU competition law that may be emerging as a rebuff to the more economic approach.[1270] The *Aspen* investigation is a good example, whereby the defendant undertaking was condemned not merely for its inefficiently high pricing practices, but also for acting 'without regard to health systems and patients'.[1271] The case also followed significant enforcement activity against excessive prices in the pharmaceutical sector by NCAs.[1272]

A notable feature of recent Commission decisions condemning excessive prices has been a tendency to conclude such cases under the commitments decision procedure provided by Article 9 of Regulation 1/2003.[1273] These include: *Standard & Poor's*,[1274] in which the Commission used an international standard, the ISO costs-recovery principle, as the benchmark to support its view that the charges of the ratings agency S&P for distributing US International Securities Identification Numbers (ISINs) were unfairly high; *Rambus*,[1275] in which the defendant undertook to cap (worldwide) for five years the royalty rates it charged for licences of its DRAM chips in the light of the Commission's concerns about a possible patent ambush;[1276] *Gazprom*, in which the excessive prices were facilitated by the defendant's concomitant contractual limitations imposed on wholesale gas customers which prevented them from reselling gas outside the national territory;[1277] and *Aspen* itself.[1278] The Article 9 instrument is, from one perspective, well suited to excessive pricing cases, insofar as defendant undertakings typically agree to pricing commitments that effectively eliminate the exploitative behaviour going forward. Yet the Commission's propensity to settle has been criticised on the basis that doing so relinquishes the opportunity to provide clearer and more detailed precedent in this still underdeveloped area of the case law.[1279] Because Article 9 cases rarely make it before the EU Courts, Article 267 has played an important role in developing the excessive pricing jurisprudence, including the cases of *Kanal*[1280] and *AKKA/LAA*.

1268 *Verizon v Trinko*, 540 US 398 (2004), Scalia J.

1269 G. Werden, 'Exploitative Abuse of a Dominant Position: A Bad Idea That Now Should be Abandoned' (2021) 17 *European Competition Journal* 682.

1270 See discussion in Chap. 1.

1271 AT.40394, *Aspen* 10 February 2021, para. 188.

1272 In the UK, see decision of the Competition and Markets Authority (CMA) in Case CE/9742-13, *Unfair pricing in respect of the supply of phenytoin sodium capsules in the UK*, 7 December 2016, overturned on appeal in Cases 1275–1276/1/12/17, *Flynn and Pfizer* [2018] CAT 11; for commentary see R. Bar-Isaac and M. Hughes, 'The Competition Appeal Tribunal's Judgment in *Pfizer/Flynn*—When is a High Price Unfair?' (2018) 39 *ECLR* 487. In Italy, see decision of the Autorità Garante della Concorrenza e del Mercato in Case A-480, *Aspen*, 29 September 2016; for commentary, see E. Lanza and P. Sfasciotti, 'Excessive Price Abuses: The Italian *Aspen* Case' (2018) 9 *JECLAP* 382. In Denmark, see decision of the Konkurrence- og Forbrugerstyrelsen in Case 14/08469, *CD Pharma's pricing of Syntocinon*, 31 January 2018. The OECD held a Roundtable on *Excessive Pricing in Pharmaceuticals* in November 2018: see <www.oecd.org/daf/competition/excessive-pricing-in-pharmaceuticals.htm>.

1273 Discussed in Chap. 13, Section 6.E.

1274 COMP/39.592, *S&P* 15 November 2011, paras. 26–30.

1275 COMP/38.636, *Rambus* 9 December 2009.

1276 See Section 14.C.iii.

1277 AT39816, *Upstream gas supplies in Central and Eastern Europe* 24 May 2018.

1278 AT.40394, *Aspen* 10 February 2021.

1279 B. Bär-Bouyssiere, A. Lacatus, Darach Connolly, and J. Borum, '*Aspen*: Quick Fix But Missed Opportunity', *Kluwer Competition Law Blog*, 23 October 2020.

1280 Case C-52/07, *Kanal* EU:C:2008:703.

(ii) Low Prices on the Buying Side

Although there is little case law, it is possible that unfairly low purchase prices may constitute an abuse where dominance lies on the buying side. *CICCE*[1281] concerned a complaint about allegedly low prices paid as licence fees for the showing of films on French television. The Commission dismissed the complaint on the ground of insufficient evidence, but did not deny that low prices could constitute an abuse. In *Trajektna Iuka Split*, where the complainant, a ferry terminal operator in the Port of Split, alleged that the maximum port fees that it could charge under a concession agreement were so prohibitively low as to violate Article 102, the Commission rejected the complaint on the basis that it had been dealt with by the relevant NCA.[1282]

B. IMPOSING UNFAIR TRADING CONDITIONS AND ENTERING INTO RESTRICTIVE AGREEMENTS

Article 102(a) expressly condemns unfair conditions, and Article 102(c) condemns discriminatory conditions. In a number of cases, conditions imposed by dominant undertakings on their customers have been condemned as abuses because they were unfair, and some have been addressed under other heads of abuse. In many, the unfair or discriminatory trading conditions were imposed in pursuit of a policy to exclude competitors. The Commission's 1994 investigation into Microsoft's licensing practices, for instance, concerned Microsoft's standard agreements for licensing its software to PC manufacturers, which discouraged the latter from using competitors' products. Microsoft used: 'per processor' licences which required payment of royalties on every computer either containing a particular processor type or belonging to a particular model series, whether or not the computer was shipped with Microsoft software pre-installed; 'minimum commitment' clauses which required licensees to pay for a minimum number of copies of a product regardless of actual use; and excessively long licence agreements. The Commission settled with Microsoft,[1283] which undertook not to enter licence contracts of more than one year's duration, and to abandon minimum commitment and per processor clauses.[1284]

In *Tetra Pak II*,[1285] the terms on which the dominant undertaking dealt with its customers were found to be unfairly onerous. They included placing limitations on the purchasers' use of its machines, binding purchasers to Tetra Pak's repair and maintenance services, and reserving to Tetra Pak the right to make surprise inspections. The rental payments were so high in comparison to sale prices that the supplier was considered to have relinquished its property rights to the hirer. Lease terms which exceeded the technological life of the machine were abusive. Further, clauses imposing penalties for breach of any of the terms of the agreements at Tetra Pak's discretion also infringed Article 102, as these were aimed at ensuring compliance with terms which were themselves abusive.

The terms on which DSD did business in respect of its 'Green Dot' logo in Germany were considered unfair in *Duales System Deutschland*, as DSD charged licence fees in circumstances where the trademark was not actually being used. This infringed Article 102(a) on the basis that '[u]nfair

1281 Case 298/83, *CICCE v Commission* EU:C:1985:150, upholding the Commission.

1282 Upheld by the GC in Case T-70/15 *Trajektna luka Split* EU:T:2016:592.

1283 *Microsoft*, IP/94/653 of 17 July 1994. The US FTC also reached a settlement with Microsoft.

1284 Per system clauses would be allowed if the licensees were given flexibility not to buy Microsoft products and not to have to pay for what they did not buy. See also Case C-310/93 P, *BPB Industries* EU:C:1995:101, where the company had applied dissimilar conditions to equivalent transactions on one market in order to strengthen its dominance on the other. Another example of customers (allegedly) suffering unfair conditions in pursuit of an exclusionary policy was the conditions imposed by IBM in Case COMP/39.692, *IBM Maintenance Services* 13 December 2011.

1285 Case C-333/94 P, *Tetra Pak II* EU:C:1996:436.

commercial terms exist where an undertaking in a dominant position fails to comply with the principle of proportionality'.[1286]

In *AAMS*[1287] the terms of the distribution agreements which the dominant wholesale distributor of cigarettes in Italy imposed on foreign producers were held to be unfair. They were also objectionable in that they limited the foreign producers' access to the Italian market, contrary to the imperative of the single market.[1288]

In a number of cases concerning performing rights societies the Commission has found the society to have committed abuses by virtue of the terms on which the society did business. For example, in *GEMA*[1289] the society wished to prevent members leaving it for direct relationships with undertakings such as record companies. Its rules took the rights to works even after the member's resignation, provided for long periods of withdrawal, and made payments to the social fund payable only to members of 20 years' standing. GEMA also discriminated on grounds of nationality.[1290]

A dominant undertaking entering into restrictive agreements may be caught by both Article 101 and Article 102. In *Ahmed Saeed*[1291] the CJ said that what appeared to be an agreement could really be the imposition on the other party of the dominant undertaking's will, the agreement simply constituting 'the formal measure setting the seal on an economic reality characterised by the fact that an undertaking in a dominant position has succeeded in having the tariffs in question applied by other undertakings'. Thus, while 'most favoured nations' (MFN) clauses have been assessed as potential violations of Article 101(1) by many NCAs,[1292] in *E-book MFNs (Amazon)*[1293] the Commission examined various parity clauses maintained by Amazon in its agreements with e-book suppliers under Article 102. These included a business model parity clause, which contractually obligated e-book suppliers to notify and offer to Amazon the terms for the distribution of e-books under a given business model; a selection parity clause, which required the supplier to make available to Amazon all e-book products (choice of titles, functionality, etc.) provided by that supplier to other retailers in the EEA; and various price parity clauses. The Commission considered that these parity clauses could potentially: reduce new entry into the market for e-book retailing, because new entrants would find it difficult to distinguish their offering insofar as e-book supplier would be obliged to offer the same terms and conditions to Amazon; reduce innovation in e-book retailing, insofar as new or existing suppliers or retailers might be more reluctant to invest in new products or business models, knowing that Amazon could potentially 'free-ride' by offering equivalent improvements; and soften price competition, insofar as e-book suppliers would be obliged to also offer any reduction in price to Amazon, thus making such reductions more expensive and less attractive. Amazon agreed to abandon the contractual requirements for five years, and the case was concluded under the commitments procedure without any finding of breach.

The dearth of cases and decisions on the imposition of unfair trading conditions can be explained by the prevalence of other legislative regimes, such as consumer protection and unfair competition and general contract and tort laws. Some of these rules have been enacted at EU level.[1294] Chapter 16 discusses the *German Facebook* case,[1295] in which a dominant undertaking was held to have breached the

[1286] [2001] OJ 1166/1, para. 112, *aff'd* on appeal, see also Section 16.A.i.b, on the excessive pricing finding.

[1287] Case T-139/98, *AAMS* EU:T:2001:272. [1288] See Section 17. [1289] [1971] OJ L134/15.

[1290] Contrary to Art. 18 TFEU; see also Case 7/82, *GVL* EU:C:1983:52. See also *1998 Football World Cup* [2000] OJ L5/55.

[1291] Case 66/86, *Ahmed Saeed* EU:C:1989:140. [1292] See Chap. 11.

[1293] AT40153, *E-book MFNs and related matters (Amazon)* 4 May 2017. Arguing persuasively that addressing such conduct under Art. 102 best reflects the competition concerns raised by such practices, see P. Akman, 'A Competition Law Assessment of Platform Most-favoured-customer Clauses' (2016) 12 *J of Competition Law and Economics* 781.

[1294] Such as Council Dir. 93/13/EEC [1993] OJ L95/29 on unfair contract terms.

[1295] Bundeskartellamt Decision of 6 February 2019, B6-22/16, *Facebook*.

German domestic equivalent of Article 102 through the imposition of unfair terms and conditions on its users, which involved breach of EU data protection rules. The behaviour was construed, in essence, as a qualitative exploitative abuse, whereby users were forced to consent to the excessive collection of personal data in order to use Facebook's social network. Although a competition law case, the theory of harm drew heavily from legal norms regulating both data privacy and unfair contract terms.[1296]

C. INEFFICIENCY AND LIMITING PRODUCTION

The Article 102(b) prohibition of 'limiting production, markets, or technical development to the prejudice of consumers' has been applied to dominant undertakings operating inefficiently and unable to meet demand, particularly public undertakings with statutory monopolies where Article 102 applies in conjunction with Article 106.[1297] In *Port of Genoa*,[1298] the Court held that an undertaking with the exclusive right to organise dock work at Genoa, which refused to use modern technology and thus raised costs and caused delays, breached Article 102. In *Höfner v Macrotron*, a State employment agency which was unable to meet the demand for its services was similarly considered to infringe Article 102.[1299] This type of abuse can, however, also be committed by private undertakings. In *P & I Clubs*,[1300] which concerned associations providing marine insurance, the Commission stated that it would intervene in situations only where there is 'clear and uncontroversial evidence that a very substantial share of the demand is being deprived of a service that it manifestly needs'.[1301] In the *E.ON* electricity case, where the Commission accepted commitments, one of the charges was that E.ON had limited its production of electricity in order to raise prices in the wholesale market.[1302]

17. CONDUCT HINDERING INTER-MEMBER STATE TRADE

Practices dividing markets or hindering trade between Member States may be abusive as contrary to single market integration.[1303] The excessive prices charged for the approval certificates in *British Leyland*[1304] were abusive because they both hindered parallel imports and exploited consumers. In *United Brands*[1305] the 'green banana clause' imposed on UBC's ripener/distributors, which prohibited them from reselling the bananas while they were still green, was treated as tantamount to an export ban which reinforced its policy of geographical price discrimination.[1306] The unfair distribution terms imposed in *AAMS*[1307] hindered the trade in cigarettes between Member States.

[1296] See discussion in Chap. 16, Section 5.B.ii.

[1297] See further Chap. 8. The issue often arises in cases in which the special or exclusive rights given to the undertaking are being challenged by a would-be entrant.

[1298] Case C-179/90, *Merci Convenzionali Porto di Genova* EU:C:1991:464.

[1299] Case C-41/90, *Höfner v Macrotron* EU:C:1991:161; see also Case C-55/96, *Job Centre Co-op arl* EU:C:1997:603; *Dutch Express Delivery Services* [1994] OJ L10/47; Case C-475/99, *Ambulanz Glöckner* EU:C:2001:577; Case T-556/08, *Slovenská Pošta* EU:C:2015:189.

[1300] [1999] OJ L125/12.

[1301] *P & I Clubs* [1999] OJ L125/12, para. 128. The undertakings, in a collective dominant position, offered only a single insurance product. They amended their arrangements so that there was no longer any question of an infringement of Art. 102.

[1302] COMP/39.388, *German Electricity Balancing Markets (E.ON)* 26 November 2008.

[1303] See e.g. Case 40/73, *Suiker Unie v EC Commission* EU:C:1975:174; *Eurofix-Bauco* [1988] OJ L65/19; Case C-333/94 P, *Tetra Pak II* EU:C:1996:436; Case T-65/89, *BPB Industries Plc and British Gypsum Ltd* EU:T:1993:31; Case T-228/97, *Irish Sugar* EU:T:1999:246.

[1304] Case 226/84, *British Leyland* EU:C:1986:421.

[1305] Case 27/76, *United Brands* EU:C:1978:22.

[1306] See Section 15.C.

[1307] Case T-139/98, *AAMS* EU:T:2001:272.

A more recent case is *AB Inbev*.[1308] Here, the Commission held that the dominant undertaking, a beer brewer, had abused Article 102 through a strategy to prevent supermarkets and wholesalers in Belgium from buying the beer brand Jupiler (the most popular beer in Belgium) at lower prices in the Netherlands, and from importing the product into Belgium. The challenged practices included changes to the packaging of cans sold in the Netherlands which made it harder to sell them in Belgium (e.g. by removing French text from cans sold in the Netherlands), and limiting the access of Dutch retailers to certain promotions where the defendant was concerned that the products might subsequently be resold in Belgium. While the abusive conduct, inter alia, enabled AB Inbev to maintain higher prices for beer in Belgium than in neighbouring countries,[1309] the Commission's investigation was aimed squarely at the market segmentation and thus hindrance to market interpenetration that the challenged practices entailed.[1310] A fine of more than €200 million was imposed for the infringement, and the defendant also committed to various food-labelling obligations for a period of five years following the decision.[1311]

Numerous commitment decisions in the energy sector reflect the Commission's preoccupation with developing an effective EU single market for energy,[1312] and its strategic deployment of competition law to assist that task. In *Swedish Interconnectors*,[1313] the Commission objected to the steps taken by the Swedish electricity network operator to reduce congestion on its grid by, in effect, limiting export to neighbouring countries. The operator gave commitments which bound it to remedy the problem by other means, which would not result in segmenting the internal market.[1314] A similar case alleging artificial limitations of electricity exports was pursued against a German transmission system operator, which offered commitments to increase cross-border transport capacity.[1315] In *Bulgarian Energy Holding*, the Commission was concerned that clauses in BEH's wholesale energy contracts contained territorial restrictions amounting to export bans.[1316] In *Romanian Gas Interconnectors*, the transmission system operator of the natural gas network in Romania was alleged to have created barriers to the cross-border flow of natural gas to other Member States. It achieved this through a combination of strategic under-investment in export infrastructure, excessively high export tariffs, and vexatious technical arguments which provided a pretext for restricting or delaying exports.[1317] Finally, in the politically sensitive *Gazprom* case, the Commission expressed concerns with territorial limitations contained in Gazprom's supply contracts for wholesale customers, which had the effect of preventing the resale of gas outside the national territory. In addition to segmenting the internal market, the policy also allegedly enabled Gazprom to pursue excessive pricing in five Member States which were particularly insulated from competitive supply alternatives.[1318]

The question of whether a refusal to supply in order to restrict parallel imports between Member States may be abusive on that ground alone arose in the context of the pharmaceutical sector.[1319]

[1308] AT.40134, *AB InBev beer trade restrictions*, 13 May 2019. [1309] Ibid., paras. 94–113.

[1310] For example, the section of the decision addressing the case law on abuse of dominance began by recalling Art. 3(3) TEU, which states that 'The Union shall establish an internal market' (ibid., para. 78).

[1311] See Chap. 13, Section 6.E for further discussion of settlement under Art. 7 of Reg. 1/2003.

[1312] See e.g. DG Competition Report on Energy Sector Inquiry, SEC(2006) 1724, 10 January 2007.

[1313] COMP/39.351, *Swedish Interconnectors* Decision of 4 April 2010; see M. Sadowska and B. Willems, 'Market Integration and Economic Efficiency at Conflict? Commitments in the *Swedish Interconnectors* Case' (2013) 36 *World Competition* 99.

[1314] By dividing the Swedish transmission market into bidding zones and building a new transmission line.

[1315] AT40461, *DK/DE Interconnector* 7 December 2018.

[1316] COMP/39.767, *Bulgarian Energy Holdings* 10 December 2015. The commitments involved a far-reaching industry restructuring.

[1317] AT.40335, *Romanian gas interconnectors* 6 March 2020.

[1318] AT39816, *Upstream gas supplies in Central and Eastern Europe* 24 May 2018.

[1319] Outside the pharmaceutical sector, see *Polaroid/SSI* where Polaroid allegedly refused to supply a customer with the quantities ordered because of concerns that it intended to export some of the products. Polaroid agreed to supply the full amount and the Commission closed its file: see *XIIIth Report on Competition Policy* (1983), point 157.

Greek pharmaceutical wholesalers were in dispute with GlaxoSmithKline, who they claimed had refused to fulfil their orders in respect of certain pharmaceuticals in order to prevent exportation to other Member States where prices were higher. The efforts of pharmaceutical companies to prevent such parallel trade had resulted in Article 101 proceedings, as seen in Chapters 4 and 5.[1320] The first case to reach the CJ on the application of Article 102 was *Syfait*,[1321] an Article 267 reference from the Greek Competition Commission. Recognising the special circumstances pertaining to trade in pharmaceuticals, Advocate General Jacobs considered that it was not necessarily an abuse to refuse to supply to prevent parallel trade.[1322] First, the price differentials between Member States were due to pervasive and diverse State intervention; secondly, EU and domestic regulation imposed obligations on pharmaceutical undertakings and wholesalers to ensure adequate stocks; thirdly, parallel trade could have potentially negative consequences on R&D incentives; and, fourthly, end consumers could not be assumed to benefit from parallel trade, given that parallel trade did not necessarily result in price competition. In those circumstances, a refusal to supply that aimed to limit parallel trade was capable of objective justification and thus of not constituting an abuse. The Advocate General emphasised that his conclusion was 'highly specific' to the peculiarities of the pharmaceutical market.[1323] The CJ refused to give judgment on the grounds that the reference was inadmissible.[1324] The Opinion, however, showed both a reluctance to widen the ambit of refusal to supply abuses simply on single market grounds, and a sympathetic stance towards the pharmaceutical industry.

The same matter involving the same parties came before the CJ again on a reference from a Greek court in *Sot. Lélos* (often known as *Glaxo Greece*).[1325] In the meantime the GC had delivered the Article 101 judgment, *GlaxoSmithKline* (or *Glaxo Spain*) in which the Advocate General's arguments in *Syfait* were largely accepted.[1326]

In *Sot. Lélos* the CJ reframed the questions it was asked as (i) whether there is an abuse contrary to Article 102 if a dominant pharmaceuticals company refused to meet orders sent to it by wholesalers on the basis that those wholesalers are involved in parallel exports of those products to other Member States;[1327] and (i) the relevance of factors such as the degree of national regulation to which the pharmaceuticals sector is subject, the impact of parallel trade on pharmaceuticals companies' revenues, and whether parallel trade is capable of generating financial benefits for the ultimate consumers of medicinal products.[1328] The CJ ruled that 'there can be no escape'[1329] from Article 102 for the practices of an undertaking in a dominant position which are aimed at avoiding all parallel exports. The peculiarities of the EU pharmaceutical sector did not alter this. However, the CJ accepted that the practices might be objectively justified by the undertaking's need to protect its own commercial interests and so it could refuse to meet orders which are out of the ordinary.

[1320] See Cases C-2 and 3/01 P, *Bayer* EU:C:2004:2, discussed in Chap. 5 (where it was held that there was no breach of Art. 101(1) as the refusal was a unilateral act and did not constitute an agreement: it was not claimed that Bayer was dominant) and Case C-501/06 P, *GlaxoSmithKline* EU:C:2009:610.

[1321] Case C-53/03, *Syfait* EU:C:2005:333.

[1322] Opinion in Case C-53/03, *Syfait* EU:C:2004:673, paras. 77–104.

[1323] Ibid., paras. 101–102.

[1324] The Greek Competition Commission did not constitute a 'court of tribunal of a Member State' with jurisdiction to make a reference under Art. 267.

[1325] See R. O'Donoghue and L. Macnab, 'Dominant Firms' Duties to Deal with Pharmaceutical Parallel Traders Following *Glaxo Greece*' (2009) 5 *Competition Policy International* 153; S. Kingston, 'Casenote on *Sot. Lélos*' (2009) 46 *CMLRev* 683.

[1326] The GC said that an agreement restricting parallel trade in the pharmaceutical sector was not restrictive by object because it could not be assumed that it reduced consumer welfare, Case T-168/01, *GlaxoSmithKline* EU:T:2006:265, see Chap. 5. A year after the *Sot. Lélos* ruling the CJ overruled the GC on that point, Case C-501/06 P, *GlaxoSmithKline* EU:C:2009:610.

[1327] Cases C-468–478/06, *Sot. Lélos* EU:C:2008:504, para. 28.

[1328] Ibid., para. 29.

[1329] Ibid., para. 66.

Cases C-468–478/06, *Sot. Lélos kai Sia EE v GlaxoSmithKline AEVE Farmakeftikon Proionton* EU:C:2008:504

Court of Justice

34. The established case-law of the Court shows that the refusal by an undertaking occupying a dominant position on the market of a given product to meet the orders of an existing customer constitutes abuse of that dominant position under Article [102] where, without any objective justification, that conduct is liable to eliminate a trading party as a competitor (. . . Joined Cases 6/73 and 7/73 *Istituto Chemioterapico Italiano and Commercial Solvents v Commission* . . . paragraph 25, and Case 27/76 *United Brands and United Brands Continentaal v Commission* . . . paragraph 183).

35. With regard to a refusal by an undertaking to deliver its products in one Member State to wholesalers which export those products to other Member States, such an effect on competition may exist not only if the refusal impedes the activities of those wholesalers in that first Member State, but equally if it leads to the elimination of effective competition from them in the distribution of the products on the markets of the other Member States.

. . .

49. It should be recalled that in paragraph 182 of its judgment in United Brands and *United Brands Continentaal v Commission* the Court held that an undertaking in a dominant position for the purpose of marketing a product—which cashes in on the reputation of a brand name known to and valued by consumers—cannot stop supplying a long-standing customer who abides by regular commercial practice, if the orders placed by that customer are in no way out of the ordinary. In paragraph 183 of the same judgment, the Court held that such conduct is inconsistent with the objectives laid down in [Article 3(1)(g) EC], which are set out in detail in Article [102] . . . since the refusal to sell would limit the markets to the prejudice of consumers and would amount to discrimination which might in the end eliminate a trading party from the relevant market.

50. In paragraph 189 of the judgment in *United Brands and United Brands Continentaal v Commission*, the Court stated that, although the fact that an undertaking is in a dominant position cannot deprive it of its right to protect its own commercial interests if they are attacked, and that such an undertaking must be conceded the right to take such reasonable steps as it deems appropriate to protect those interests, such behaviour cannot be accepted if its purpose is specifically to strengthen that dominant position and abuse it.

51. It must be examined in this context whether, as GSK AEVE claims, particular circumstances are present in the pharmaceuticals sector, by reason of which the refusal by an undertaking in a dominant position to supply clients in a given Member State who engage in parallel exports to other Member States where prices for medicines are higher does not, generally speaking, constitute an abuse.

The consequences of parallel trade for the ultimate consumers

52. The first thing to consider is GSK AEVE's argument that parallel trade in any event brings only few financial benefits to the ultimate consumers.

53. In that connection, it should be noted that parallel exports of medicinal products from a Member State where the prices are low to other Member States in which the prices are higher open up in principle an alternative source of supply to buyers of the medicinal products in those latter States, which necessarily brings some benefits to the final consumer of those products.

54. It is true, as GSK AEVE has pointed out, that, for medicines subject to parallel exports, the existence of price differences between the exporting and the importing Member States does not necessarily imply that the final consumer in the importing Member State will benefit from a price corresponding to the one prevailing in the exporting Member State, inasmuch as the wholesalers carrying out the exports will themselves make a profit from that parallel trade.

55. Nevertheless, the attraction of the other source of supply which arises from parallel trade in the importing Member State lies precisely in the fact that that trade is capable of offering the same products on the market of that Member State at lower prices than those applied on the same market by the pharmaceuticals companies.

56. As a result, even in the Member States where the prices of medicines are subject to State regulation, parallel trade is liable to exert pressure on prices and, consequently, to create financial benefits not only for the social health insurance funds, but equally for the patients concerned, for whom the proportion of the price of medicines for which they are responsible will be lower. At the same time, as the Commission notes, parallel trade in medicines from one Member State to another is likely to increase the choice available to entities in the latter Member State which obtain supplies of medicines by means of a public procurement procedure, in which the parallel importers can offer medicines at lower prices.

57. Accordingly, . . . it is clear that, in the circumstances of the main proceedings, such an undertaking cannot base its arguments on the premise that the parallel exports which it seeks to limit are of only minimal benefit to the final consumers.

The impact of state price and supply regulation in the pharmaceutical sector

. . .

64. On the other hand, it should be recalled that, where a medicine is protected by a patent which confers a temporary monopoly on its holder, the price competition which may exist between a producer and its distributors, or between parallel traders and national distributors, is, until the expiry of that patent, the only form of competition which can be envisaged.

65. In relation to the application of Article [101] the Court has held that an agreement between producer and distributor which might tend to restore the national divisions in trade between Member States might be such as to frustrate the objective of the Treaty to achieve the integration of national markets through the establishment of a single market. Thus on a number of occasions the Court has held agreements aimed at partitioning national markets according to national borders or making the interpenetration of national markets more difficult, in particular those aimed at preventing or restricting parallel exports, to be agreements whose object is to restrict competition within the meaning of that Treaty article (see, for example, Joined Cases 96/82 to 102/82, 104/82, 105/82, 108/82 and 110/82 IAZ International Belgium and Others v Commission . . . paragraphs 23 to 27; Case C-306/96 Javico . . . paragraphs 13 and 14; and Case C-551/03 P General Motors v Commission . . . paragraphs 67 to 69).

66. In the light of the abovementioned Treaty objective as well as that of ensuring that competition in the internal market is not distorted, there can be no escape from the prohibition laid down in Article [102] for the practices of an undertaking in a dominant position which are aimed at avoiding all parallel exports from a Member State to other Member States, practices which, by partitioning the national markets, neutralise the benefits of effective competition in terms of the supply and the prices that those exports would obtain for final consumers in the other Member States.

67. Although the degree of price regulation in the pharmaceuticals sector cannot therefore preclude the Community rules on competition from applying, the fact none the less remains that, when assessing, in the case of Member States with a system of price regulation, whether the refusal of a pharmaceuticals company to supply medicines to wholesalers involved in parallel exports constitutes abuse, it cannot be ignored that such State intervention is one of the factors liable to create opportunities for parallel trade.

68. Furthermore, in the light of the Treaty objectives to protect consumers by means of undistorted competition and the integration of national markets, the Community rules on competition are also incapable of being interpreted in such a way that, in order to defend its own commercial interests, the only choice left for a pharmaceuticals company in a dominant position is not to place its medicines on the market at all in a Member State where the prices of those products are set at a relatively low level.

69. It follows that, even if the degree of regulation regarding the price of medicines cannot prevent any refusal by a pharmaceuticals company in a dominant position to meet orders sent to it by wholesalers involved in parallel exports from constituting an abuse, such a company must nevertheless be in a position to take steps that are reasonable and in proportion to the need to protect its own commercial interests.

70. In that respect, and without it being necessary to examine the argument raised by GSK AEVE that it is necessary for pharmaceuticals companies to limit parallel exports in order to avoid the risk of a reduction in their investments in the research and development of medicines, it is sufficient to state that, in order to appraise whether the refusal by a pharmaceuticals company to supply wholesalers involved in parallel exports constitutes a reasonable and proportionate measure in relation to the threat that those exports represent to its legitimate commercial interests, it must be ascertained whether the orders of the wholesalers are out of the ordinary (see, to that effect, United Brands and United Brands Continentaal v Commission, paragraph 182).

71. Thus, although a pharmaceuticals company in a dominant position, in a Member State where prices are relatively low, cannot be allowed to cease to honour the ordinary orders of an existing customer for the sole reason that that customer, in addition to supplying the market in that Member State, exports part of the quantities ordered to other Member States with higher prices, it is none the less permissible for that company to counter in a reasonable and proportionate way the threat to its own commercial interests potentially posed by the activities of an undertaking which wishes to be supplied in the first Member State with significant quantities of products that are essentially destined for parallel export.

Thus, there is a different rule for refusals to supply to prevent parallel trade than for others. As the Commission recognises in the Guidance Paper, EU law normally starts from the position that 'any undertaking, whether dominant or not, should have the right to choose its trading partners'.[1330] That is why the 'exceptional circumstances' in the case law,[1331] which impose a duty to supply in derogation from this principle, are so important. In respect of parallel trade refusals, however, the position is that they are prima facie abusive, and can escape Article 102 only by objective justification.

In this regard, the CJ considered that final consumers and social security systems derived benefit from parallel trade and that an undertaking in GSK's position could not argue from the basis that the benefit to final consumers was minimal. It considered the effect of price controls by Member States, but stressed that for patented pharmaceuticals it is only parallel trade which can provide competition. Although the features of the pharmaceutical sector did not remove it from the normal competition rules against restrictions on parallel trade, the Court recognised the effect of national intervention. It accepted that the undertaking had a right to protect its own commercial interests and said that the competition rules could not be interpreted in such a way that it left an undertaking in Glaxo's position with no way to do this but to leave the market. The CJ therefore made the important concession that, although Glaxo could not cease honouring the 'ordinary orders of an existing customer', it *could* refuse orders which were 'out of the ordinary'. It was left to the national court to draw the difficult line between 'ordinary' and 'out of the ordinary' orders.[1332]

The ruling is notable for the way in which it treated Glaxo's arguments about the need to limit parallel trade in order to maintain profits for investment in R&D. In its formulation of the questions referred, the CJ referenced 'the pharmaceutical companies revenues', and in paragraph 70 it simply

[1330] Guidance Paper, para. 75. [1331] See Section 12.

[1332] This concept of 'ordinary' orders is found in *United Brands*, which the CJ cited. *United Brands* involved, however, a totally different scenario, namely a reprisal against customers dealing with a competitor, see Section 12.F.

treated their protection as a 'legitimate commercial interests' matter. It did not engage in any discussion about justifying the hindrance of parallel trade on 'efficiency' grounds, and specifically stated that it is unnecessary to examine the R&D question.

The judgment only dealt with the position of existing customers, which was the subject matter of the case. This does not mean that there is not also a duty to supply new customers, particularly given the prima facie nature of the abuse. Obviously different criteria for assessing the reasonable and proportionate nature of the refusal to protect legitimate commercial interests would need to be devised since there would be no 'ordinary' orders for comparison.

18. ABUSE AND COLLECTIVE DOMINANCE

It was explained in Chapter 6 that a 'dominant position' may be held by a single undertaking or by one or more independent undertakings which hold a collective dominant position. This concept and its application are explored in Chapter 9, in the context of cartels and oligopolies and the question of what can amount to the abuse of a collective dominance position is discussed there.[1333] In some of the cases discussed in this chapter, the dominant position being abused was a collective one.[1334] It should be noted here, however, that in *Irish Sugar* the GC said that it was not necessary for the collective dominant position to be *abused* collectively. It is possible that an undertaking may individually commit an abuse of a dominant position held collectively with other undertakings, at least insofar as the abuse is committed to protect the collective dominant position.[1335]

19. CONCLUSIONS

1. The matter of what conduct on the part of a dominant undertaking can constitute an infringement of Article 102 should be put on a sound and consistent economic footing. Conduct should be judged by its effects on the market, not on its form. However, theoretically sound, effects-based rules that are too complex or impractical are not a good basis on which to build a sound competition policy. Undertakings need legal certainty and they should be able to adopt commercial policies in the knowledge that their conduct is legal.

2. An abuse of a dominant position should only be found on the basis of a clearly articulated theory of harm.

3. In principle, the Guidance Paper was a welcome move which helped to clarify when certain types of conduct merit intervention by the Commission. According to the EU Courts the Guidance Paper is, however, only an administrative document setting out enforcement priorities, which does not bind either them, national courts, or NCAs. The EU Courts have not hesitated to diverge from their approach to topics such as loyalty rebates, margin squeeze, and the AEC test, and the Commission itself has issued Amendments which alter the Guidance Paper in certain important respects.

4. The EU Courts have not fully embraced the consumer welfare-focused approach to Article 102. They continue to hold that Article 102 is concerned, inter alia, with the impact of conduct on an effective competitive structure. However, the language of the Courts reflects more concern with effects

[1333] See Chap. 9, Section 5.B.ii.

[1334] See e.g. Cases C-395 and 396/96 P, *Compagnie Maritime Belge* EU:C:2000:132; Case T-193/02, *Laurent Piau* EU:T:2005:22.

[1335] Case T-228/97, *Irish Sugar* EU:T:1999:246, para. 66.

on consumers than it has in the past. The judgments are not always consistent, but *TeliaSonera, Post Danmark I, Intel*, and *Unilever* adopt a more effects-based approach.

5. The use of commitments decisions may have negative implications for the development of the law. Commitments negotiated between undertakings and the Commission do not result in a finding that (perhaps novel) conduct does indeed constitute an abuse and the questions at issue do not come before the EU Courts. The development of the jurisprudence on Article 102 is becoming more dependent on cases in national courts which reach the CJ under the preliminary reference procedure, but in such cases the Court is not called upon to apply the law to the facts.

6. There is a growing trend for Article 102 to be deployed a tool to regulate the digital economy, particularly since Article 102 is applied in a more interventionist way than s. 2 of the US Sherman Act. This is shown by the cases arising from the 'smartphone wars', and the *Google Shopping, Android, AdSense*, and *Amazon Marketplace* cases.

20. FURTHER READING

A. Books

Akman, P., *The Concept of Abuse in EU Competition Law* (Hart Publishing, 2012)

Bishop, S., and Walker, M., *The Economics of EC Competition Law: Concepts, Application and Measurement* (3rd edn, Sweet & Maxwell, 2010), Chap. 6

Bork, R., *The Antitrust Paradox* (Basic Books, 1978, reprinted with a new Introduction and Epilogue, 1993), Chap. 7

Ehlermann, C.-D., and Atanasiu, I. (eds.), *European Competition Law Annual 2003: What is Abuse of a Dominant Position?* (Hart Publishing, 2006)

Ehlermann, C.-D., and Atanasiu, I. (eds.), *European Competition Law Annual 2005: The Interaction Between Competition Law and Intellectual Property Law* (Hart Publishing, 2007)

Ehlermann, C.-D., and Marquis, M., *European Competition Law Annual 2007: A Reformed Approach to Article 82 EC* (Hart Publishing, 2008)

Etro, F., and Kokkoris, I. (eds.), *Competition Law and the Enforcement of Article 102* (Oxford University Press, 2010)

Ezrachi, A. (ed.), *Article 82 EC: Reflections on its Recent Evolution* (Hart Publishing, 2009)

Geradin, D., Layne-Farrar, A., and Petit, N., *EU Competition Law and Economics* (Oxford University Press, 2012), 4.131–4.542

Lovdhal Gormsen, L., *A Principled Approach to Abuse of Dominance in European Competition Law* (Cambridge University Press, 2010)

Motta, M., *Competition Policy* (Cambridge University Press, 2004), Chaps. 2 and 7

Nazzini, R., *The Foundations of European Union Competition Law: The Objectives and Principles of Article 102* (Oxford University Press, 2011)

O'Donoghue, R., and Padilla, A. J., *The Law and Economics of Article 102* (3rd edn, Hart Publishing, 2020), Chaps. 5–16

Petrovic, U., *Competition Law and Standard-essential Patents: A Transatlantic Perspective* (Kluwer Law International, 2014)

POSNER, R. A., *Antitrust Law* (2nd edn, University of Chicago Press, 2001), Chaps. 7 and 8

ROUSSEVA, E., *Rethinking Exclusionary Abuses in EU Competition Law* (Hart Publishing, 2010)

SCHMIDT, H., *Competition Law, Innovation and Antitrust* (Edward Elgar, 2009)

B. Chapters in Books

ACKERMANN, T., 'Excessive Pricing and the Goals of Competition Law' in D. Zimmer (ed.), *The Goals of Competition Law* (Edward Elgar, 2012), Chap. 18

FOX, E., 'Abuse of Dominance and Monopolisation: How to Protect Competition Without Protecting Competitors' in C.-D. Ehlermann and I. Atanasiu (eds.), *European Competition Law Annual 2003: What is Abuse of a Dominant Position?* (Hart Publishing, 2006), 69

HATZOPOULOS, V., 'The EC Essential Facilities Doctrine' in G. Amato and C.-D. Ehlermann (eds.), *EC Competition Law: A Critical Assessment* (Hart Publishing, 2007), 333

JONES, A., 'Refusal to Deal—EC and US Law Compared' in P. Marsden (ed.), *Handbook of Research in Trans-Atlantic Antitrust* (Edward Elgar, 2006), Chap. 8, 236–286

MARSDEN, P., 'Some Outstanding Issues from the European Commission's Guidance on Article 102 TFEU: Not-so-faint Echoes of Ordoliberalism' in F. Etro and I. Kokkoris (eds.), *Competition Law and the Enforcement of Article 102* (Oxford University Press, 2010), Chap. 3

VICKERS, J., 'How Does the Prohibition of Abuse of Dominance Fit with the Rest of Competition Policy?' in C.-D. Ehlermann and I. Atanasiu (eds.), *European Competition Law Annual 2003: What is Abuse of a Dominant Position?* (Hart Publishing, 2006), 147

VICKERS, J., 'Some Economics of Abuse of Dominance' in X. Vives (ed.), *Competition Policy in the EU: Fifty Years on from the Treaty of Rome* (Oxford University Press, 2009), 71

C. Articles

AHLBORN, C., and EVANS, D. S., 'The *Microsoft* Judgment and its Implications for Competition Policy Towards Dominant Firms in Europe' (2008–2009) 75 *Antitrust LJ* 887

AHLBORN, C. and PICCININ, D., 'The *Intel* Judgment and Consumer Welfare—A Response to Wouter Wils' [2015] 1 *CLPD* 60

AHLBORN, C., EVANS, D. S., and PADILLA, J., 'The Logic and Limits of Exceptional Circumstances Test in *Magill* and *IMS Health*' (2005) 28 *Fordham Int'l LJ* 1062

AKMAN, P., '"Consumer Welfare" and Article 82: Practice and Rhetoric' (2009) 32 *World Competition* 71

AKMAN, P., 'Searching for the Long-lost Soul of Article 82EC' (2009) 29 *OJLS* 267

AKMAN, P., 'The Reform of the Application of Article 102 TFEU: Mission Accomplished?' (2016) 81 *Antitrust LJ* 145

ALLAN, B., 'Article 102: A Commentary on DG Competition's Discussion Paper' (2006) 2 *Competition Policy International* 43

ANDREANGELI, A., 'Interoperability as an "Essential Facility" in the *Microsoft* Case—Encouraging Competition or Stifling Innovation' (2009) 34 *ELRev* 584

AREEDA, P., 'Essential Facilities: An Epithet in Need of Limiting Principles' (1990) 58 *Antitrust LJ* 841

AREEDA, P., and TURNER, D., 'Predatory Pricing and Related Practices under Section 2 of the Sherman Act' (1975) 88 *Harvard LR* 697

Baker, J., 'Exclusionary Conduct of Dominant Firms, R&D Competition, and Innovation' (2016) 48 *Rev Ind Organ* 269

Beard, D., '*Microsoft*: What Sort of Landmark?' (2008) 4 *Competition Policy International* 33

Bork., R., and Sidak, J. G., 'What Does the Chicago School Teach About Internet Search and the Antitrust Treatment of Google?' (2011) 8 *J of Competition Law and Economics* 663

Borlini, L., 'Methodological Issues of the "More Economic Approach" to Unilateral Exclusionary Conduct' (2009) 5 *European Competition Journal* 409

Botta, M., 'Nondiscrimination in Standard Essential Patents; ND Prong V. Art. 102(C) TFEU' (2021) 17 *J of Competition Law and Economics* 947

Botta, M., 'Sanctioning Unfair Pricing Under Article 102(a) TFEU: Yes, We Can!' (2021) 17 *European Competition Journal* 156

Brodley, J., and Hay, D., 'Predatory Pricing: Competing Economic Theories and the Evolution of Legal Standards' (1981) 66 *Cornell LR* 738

Bundeskartellamt, 'Competition Law Forum Debate on Reform of Article 102: A "Dialectic" on Competing Approaches' (2006) 2 *European Competition Journal* 211

Carlton, D., 'Should "Price Squeeze" be a Recognized Form of Anticompetitive Conduct?' (2008) 4 *J of Competition Law and Economics* 271

Carlton, D., and Waldman, W., 'The Strategic Use of Tying to Preserve and Create Market Power in Evolving Industries' (2002) 33 *RAND J of Economics* 194

Choi, J., and Stefanadis, C., 'Tying, Investment and Dynamic Leverage Theory' (2001) 32 *RAND J of Economics* 52

Colangelo, G., and Maggiolino, M., 'Big Data as Misleading Facilities' (2017) 13 *European Competition Journal* 249

Cole, M., 'Ordoliberalism and its Influence on EU Tying Law' [2015] *ECLR* 255

Crane, D., and Wright, J., 'Can Bundled Discounting Increase Consumer Prices Without Excluding Rivals?' (2009) 5 *Competition Policy International* 209

Crocioni, P., 'On the Relevant Cost Standards for Price-cost Test in Abuses of Dominance' (2018) 14 *J of Competition Law and Economics* 262

da Cruz Vilaca, J. L., 'The Intensity of Judicial Review in Complex Economic Matters—Recent Competition Law Judgments of the Court of Justice of the EU' (2018) 6 *J of Antitrust Enforcement* 173

Dolmans, M., and Graf, T., 'Dealing with *Intel* Intelligently: Delineating the Scope and Limits of the Court's Ruling' [2015] 1 *CLPD* 76

Dunne, N., 'Margin Squeeze: Theory, Practice, Policy', Parts I and II [2012] *ECLR* 29 and 61

Edelman, B., 'Does Google Leverage Market Power Through Tying and Bundling?' (2015) 11 *J of Competition Law and Economics* 365

Eilmansberger, T., 'How to Distinguish Good from Bad Competition under Article 102 EC: In Search of Clearer and More Coherent Standards for Anti-competitive Abuses' (2005) 42 *CMLRev* 129

Elhauge, E., 'Defining Better Monopolisation Standards' (2003–2004) 56 *Stan LR* 253

Elhauge, E., 'Tying, Bundled Discounts, and the Death of the Single Monopoly Profit Theory' (2009) 123 *Harvard LR* 399

Evans, D. S., and Salinger, M., 'Why Do Firms Bundle and Tie? Evidence from Competitive Markets and Implications for Tying Law' (2005) 22 *Yale J on Regulation* 37

Ezrachi, A., and Gilo, D., 'Are Excessive Prices Really Self-correcting?' (2009) 5 *J of Competition Law and Economics* 249

Faella, G., and Pardolesi, R., 'Squeezing Price Squeeze under EC Antitrust Law' (2010) 6 *European Competition Journal* 255

First, H., 'No Single Monopoly Profit, No Single Policy Prescription?' (2009) 5 *Competition Policy International* 199

Fjell, K., and Sørgard, L., 'How to Test for Abuse of Dominance?' (2006) 2 *European Competition Journal* 69

Fox, E., 'Price Predation—US and EEC: Economics and Values' [1989] *Fordham Corp L Inst* 687

Fox, E., 'What is Harm to Competition? Exclusionary Practices and Anti-competitive Effect' (2002) 70 *Antitrust LJ* 371

Fox, E., 'We Protect Competition, You Protect Competitors' (2003) 26 *World Competition* 149

Francis, D., 'Making Sense of Monopolization' (2022) 84 *Antitrust LJ* 779

Furse, M., 'Excessive Prices, Unfair Prices and Economic Value' (2008) 4 *European Competition Journal* 59

Geradin, D., 'Limiting the Scope of Article 82 EC: What Can the EU Learn from the Supreme Court's Judgment in *Trinko*, in the Wake of *Microsoft, IMS* and *Deutsche Telekom*?' (2004) 41 *CMLRev* 1526

Geradin, D., 'The Decision of the Commission of 13 May 2009 in the *Intel* Case: Where is the Foreclosure and Consumer Harm?' (2009) 2 *JECLAP* 9

Geradin, D., 'Is the Guidance Paper on the Commission's Enforcement Priorities in Applying Article 102 TFEU to Abusive Exclusionary Conduct Useful?' (2010), <http://ssrn.com/abstract=1569502>

Geradin, D., 'Refusal to Supply and Margin Squeeze: A Discussion of Why the "Telefonica Exceptions" are Wrong', TILEC Discussion Paper No. 2011-009, <http://ssrn.com/abstract=1750226>

Geradin, D., and O'Donoghue, R., 'The Concurrent Application of Competition Law and Regulation: The Case of Margin Squeeze Abuses in the Telecommunications Sector' (2005) 1 *J of Competition Law and Economics* 355

Geradin, D., and Rato, M., 'Can Standard-setting Lead to Exploitative Abuse? A Dissonant View of Patent Hold-up, Royalty-stacking and the Meaning of FRAND' (2007) 3 *European Competition Journal* 146

Hoppner, T., 'Competition Law in Intellectual Property Litigation: The Case for a Compulsory Licence Defence under Article 102 TFEU' (2011) 7 *European Competition Journal* 297

Howarth, D., and McMahon, K., '"Windows has performed an Illegal Operation": The Court of First Instance's Judgment in *Microsoft v Commission*' [2008] *ECLR* 117

Ibáñez Colomo, P., 'Exclusionary Discrimination under Article 102 TFEU' (2014) 51 *CMLRev* 141

Ibáñez Colomo, P., 'Appreciability and *De Minimis* in Article 102 TFEU' (2016) 7 *JECLAP* 651

Ibáñez Colomo, P., 'Legal Tests in EU Competition Law: Taxonomy and Operation' (2019) 10 *JECLAP* 424

Jones, A., 'Distinguishing Predatory Prices from Competitive Ones' [1995] *EIPR* 252

Jones, A., 'Standard-essential Patents: FRAND Commitments, Injunctions and the Smartphone Wars' (2014) 10 *European Competition Journal* 1

Kallaugher, J., and Sher, B., 'Rebates Revisited: Anti-competitive Effects and Exclusionary Abuse Under Article 82' [2004] *ECLR* 263

Kate, A., and Niels, G., 'On the Rationality of Predatory Pricing: The Debate between Chicago and Post-Chicago' (2002) 47 *Ant Bull* 1

Kellerbauer, M., 'The Commission's New Enforcement Priorities in Applying Article 82EC to Dominant Companies' Exclusionary Conduct: A Shift Towards a More Economic Approach?' [2010] *ECLR* 175

Khan, L., 'Amazon's Antitrust Paradox' (2017) 126 *Yale LJ* 710

Kjølbe, L., 'Rebates Under Article 82 EC: Navigating Uncertain Waters' [2010] *ECLR* 66

Kjølbe, L., 'Article 82 EC as Remedy to Patent System Imperfections: Fighting Fire with Fire?' (2009) 32 *World Competition* 163

Korah, V., 'The Interface between Intellectual Property and Antitrust: the European Experience' (2002) 69 *Antitrust LJ* 801

Kroes, N., 'Tackling Exclusionary Practices to Avoid Exploitation of Market Power: Some Preliminary Thoughts on the Policy Review of Article 82' [2005] *Fordham Corp L Inst* 381

Kuhn, K.-U., Stillman, R., and Caffarra, C., 'Economic Theories of Bundling and their Policy Implications in Abuse Cases' (2005) 1 *European Competition Journal* 85

Larouche, P., 'The European *Microsoft* Case at the Crossroads of Competition Policy and Innovation: Comment on Ahlborn and Evans' (2008) 75 *Antitrust LJ* 933

Lovdahl Gormesen, L., 'The Conflict between Economic Freedom and Consumer Welfare in the Modernisation of Article 82' (2007) 3 *European Competition Journal* 329

Lovdahl Gormesen, L., 'Why the European Commission's Enforcement Priorities on Article 82 Should Be Withdrawn' [2010] *ECLR* 45

Maier-Rigaud, F., 'Article 82 Rebates: Four Common Fallacies' (2006) 2 *European Competition Journal* 85

Manne, G., and Wright, J., '*Google* and the Limits of Antitrust: The Case Against the Case Against Google' (2011) 34 *Harvard J of Law & Public Policy* 171

Mateus, A., 'Predatory Pricing: A Proposed Structured Rule of Reason' (2011) 7 *European Competition Law* 243

Meisel, J., 'The Law and Economics of Margin Squeezes in the US versus the EU' (2012) 8 *European Competition Journal* 383

Monti, G., 'Rebates after the General Court's 2022 *Intel* Judgment' (2023) 60 *CMLRev* 107

Moore, D. W., and Wright, J. D., 'Conditional Discounts and the Law of Exclusive Dealing' (2015) 22 *George Mason LR* 1205

Mourade Silva, M., 'Predatory Pricing and the Recoupment Test: Do Not Go Gentle Into That Good Night' [2009] *ECLR* 61

Müller, U., and Rodenhausen, A., 'The Rise and Fall of the Essential Facilities Doctrine' [2008] *ECLR* 310

MURPHY, F., and LIBERATORE, F., 'Abuse of Regulatory Procedures—The *Astra-Zeneca* Case' [2009] *ECLR* 289 and 314

NAZZINI, R., '*Google* and the (Ever-stretching) Boundaries of Article 102 TFEU' (2015) 6 *JECLAP* 301

NIHOUL, P., 'The Ruling of the General Court in *Intel*: Towards the End of an Effects-based Approach in European Competition Law?' (2014) 5 *JECLAP* 521

O'DONOGHUE, R., and MACNAB, L., 'Dominant Firms' Duties to Deal with Pharmaceutical Parallel Traders Following *Glaxo Greece*' (2009) 5 *Competition Policy International* 153

PEEPERKORN, L., 'Conditional Pricing: Why the General Court is Wrong in *Intel* and What the Court of Justice Can Do to Rebalance the Assessment of Rebates' [2015] 1 *Concurrences* 43

PEEPERKORN, L., 'Coherence in the Application of Article 101 and 102: A Realistic Prospect or an Elusive Goal?' (2016) 39 *World Competition* 389

PEEPERKORN, L., and ROUSSEVA, E., 'Article 102 TFEU: Exclusive Dealing and Rebates' (2011) 2 *JECLAP* 36

PETIT, N., 'Injunctions for FRAND-pledged SEPs: The Quest for an Appropriate Test of Abuse under Article 102 TFEU' (2013) 9 *European Competition Journal* 677

PETIT, N., 'Theories of Self-preferencing under Article 102 TFEU: A Reply to Bo Vesterdorf' (2015), <http//:ssrn.com/abstract=2592253>

PETIT, N., 'The Judgment of the EU Court of Justice in Intel and the Rule of Reason in Abuse of Dominance Cases' (2018) *43 ELRev* 728.

PITOFSKY, R., PATTERSON, D., and HOOKS, J., 'The Essential Facilities Doctrine under US Antitrust Law' (2002) 70 *Antitrust LJ* 443

RAPP, R. T., 'Predatory Pricing and Entry Deterring Strategies: The Economics of *AKZO*' [1986] *ECLR* 233

RATO, M., and PETIT, N., 'Abuse of Dominance in Technology-enabled Markets: Established Standards Reconsidered?' (2013) 9 *European Competition Journal* 1

REY, P., and VENIT, J., 'An Effects-based Approach to Article 102: A Response to Wouter Wils' (2015) 38 *World Competition* 3

RIDYARD, D., 'Essential Facilities and the Obligation to Supply Competitors' [1996] *ECLR* 438

RIDYARD, D., 'Exclusionary Pricing and Price Discrimination Abuses under Article 102—An Economic Analysis' [2002] *ECLR* 286

RIDYARD, D., 'Compulsory Access under EC Competition Law—A New Doctrine of "Convenient Facilities" and the Case for Price Regulation' [2004] *ECLR* 670

RIDYARD, D., 'The Commission's Article 82 Guidelines: some Reflections on the Economic Issues' [2009] *ECLR* 230

RITTER, C., 'Refusal to Deal and Essential Facilities: Does Intellectual Property Require Special Deference compared to Tangible Property?' (2005) 3 *World Competition* 281

ROUSSEVA, E., 'Modernizing by Eradicating: How the Commission's New Approach to Article 81 EC Dispenses with the Need to Apply Article 82 EC to Vertical Restraints' (2005) 42 *CMLRev* 587

ROUSSEVA, E., and MARQUIS, M., 'Hell Freezes Over: A Climate Change for Assessing Exclusionary Conduct under Article 102 TFEU' (2012) 4 *JECLAP* 32

Schmalensee, R., 'Output and Welfare Implications of Third Degree Price Discrimination' (1981) 71 *Am Econ Rev* 242

Scott Hemphill, C., 'The Role of Recoupment in Predatory Pricing Analyses' (2001) 53 *Stan LR* 1581

Sher, B., 'The Last of the Steam-powered Trains: Modernising Article 82' [2004] *ECLR* 243

Sidak, J. G., 'Abolishing the Price Squeeze as a Theory of Antitrust Liability' (2008) 4 *J of Competition Law and Economics* 279

Sidak, J. G., and Teece, D. J., 'Dynamic Competition in Antitrust Law' (2009) 5 *J of Competition Law and Economics* 581

Spector, D., 'Loyalty Rebates: An Assessment of Competition Concerns and a Proposed Structured Rule of Reason' (2005) 1 *Competition Policy International* 89

Spector, D., 'From Harm to Competitors to Harm to Competition: One More Effort, Please!' (2006) 2 *European Competition Journal* 145

Subiotto, R., and Little, D., 'The Application of Article 102 TFEU by the European Commission and the European Courts' (2012) 3 *JECLAP* 175

Svetlicinii, A., and Botta, M., 'Article 102 TFEU as a Tool for Market Regulation' (2012) 8 *European Law Journal* 473

Temple Lang, J., 'The Principle of Essential Facilities in European Community Competition Law—The Position since *Bronner*' (2000) 1 *J of Network Industries* 375

Temple Lang, J., 'Reprisals and Overreaction by Dominant Companies as an Anti-competitive Abuse under Article 82(b)' [2008] *ECLR* 11

Temple Lang, J., 'How Can the Problems of Exclusionary Abuses under Article 102 TFEU be Resolved?' (2012) 37 *ELRev* 136

Temple Lang, J., 'Exclusionary Abuse, the Rule of Law, and the Effectiveness of the European Commission' (2016) 41 *ELRev* 243

Temple Lang, J., 'Comparing *Microsoft* and *Google*: The Concept of Exclusionary Abuse' (2016) 39 *World Competition* 5

Venit, J., 'Case T-286/09, *Intel v Commission*—The Judgment of the General Court: All Steps Backward and No Steps Forward' (2014) 10 *European Competition Journal* 203

Verhaert, J., 'The Challenges Involved with the Application of Article 102 TFEU to the New Economy: A Case Study of *Google*' [2014] *ECLR* 265

Vesterdorf, B., 'Theories of Self-preferencing and Duty to Deal—Two Sides of the Same Coin?' [2015] 1 *CLPD* 4

Vickers, J., 'Abuse of Market Power' (2005) 115 *Economic Journal* F244

Werden, G., 'Competition Policy on Exclusionary Analysis: Towards an Effects-based Analysis?' (2006) 2 *European Competition Journal* 53

Whinston, M., 'Tying, Foreclosure and Exclusion' (1990) 80 *Am Econ Rev* 837

Wils, W., 'The Judgment of the EU General Court in *Intel* and the So-called "More Economic Approach" to Abuse of Dominance' (2014) 37 *World Competition* 405

Zenger, H., 'Loyalty Rebates and the Competitive Process' (2012) 8 *J of Competition Law and Economics* 717

8

COMPETITION AND THE STATE: ARTICLE 106 TFEU

1. CENTRAL ISSUES

1. Article 4(3) TEU contains the principle of Union loyalty. Member States are required to take any appropriate measures to ensure fulfilment of their Union obligations, facilitate the achievement of the Union's tasks, and refrain from any measure that could jeopardise the attainment of the Union's objectives.
2. Article 106 TFEU addresses the application of the competition rules (and other rules of the Treaties) to State measures in respect of public undertakings and to undertakings granted special or exclusive rights, and to undertakings entrusted with services of general economic interest (SGEIs).
3. Article 106(1) is a prohibition addressed to Member States. Its object is to prevent Member States from depriving Treaty rules of their effectiveness by the measures they adopt in respect of public undertakings and those to which they grant special or exclusive rights.
4. The cases show that Article 106(1) is infringed if, in merely exercising the special or exclusive rights, the undertaking cannot avoid abusing its dominant position or if it is thereby led to abuse its dominant position. Some cases, however, have suggested that the very granting of special or exclusive rights is contrary to Article 106(1).
5. Services of general interest may be economic or non-economic. Non-economic services are not subject to the competition rules. SGEIs are subject to the competition rules. However, Article 106(2) provides a derogation from, inter alia, the competition rules for undertakings entrusted with SGEIs if otherwise they would be obstructed in the performance of their tasks.
6. It may be a crucial factor in the application of Article 106(2) that the undertaking has 'universal service' obligations (USO). Further, it may be important to shield an undertaking from competition so that it can cross-subsidise from profitable sectors to uneconomic ones and competitors cannot come in and 'cherry pick' the profitable parts of the operation.
7. Article 106(3) provides the Commission with special supervisory and policing powers to ensure the application of the Article. It can adopt directives as well as issue decisions.
8. Article 14 TFEU specifically deals with SGEIs. They are also the subject of an article in the Charter of Fundamental Rights and services of general interest are dealt with in a Protocol attached to the TEU and TFEU.

2. INTRODUCTION

In this chapter we discuss how competition law applies to the actions of the State when it intervenes in the market. We look at two matters: first, the obligation on Member States derived from Article 4(3) TEU not to adopt or maintain in force measures which could deprive the competition provisions of their effectiveness; and, secondly, the provisions of Article 106 which deal with public undertakings and those to which a Member State has granted special or exclusive rights, and with undertakings entrusted with services of general economic interest (SGEIs). State aid (Articles 107–109) is mentioned where it interacts with the issues discussed in this chapter, particularly in respect of SGEIs.

The State plays some part in the marketplace, directly or indirectly, in all the Member States, although the means and extent of this vary. The means and extent have also been transformed since the inception of the EEC. In 1957 there was widespread nationalisation. Since then there has been a move in Europe away from public ownership, and a revolution in the way that public services are delivered.[1] There has been increasing 'marketisation', whereby Member States have turned to the market to provide services to the public, and the distinction between public and private providers has been partly eroded. This is due to shifts in ideology and economic thinking, and to technological advances which mean that the arguments for publicly owned monopolies in sectors such as telecommunications and electricity-generation have fundamentally changed.[2] The EU has pursued a programme of liberalisation whereby sectors in which there were formerly State-owned monopolies have been opened up to competition and competition law is employed alongside the liberalising measures to make this effective. Liberalisation, which has been described as inspired as much by the desire to increase the integration of the market as by increasing competition (national monopolies tend to maintain the compartmentalisation of the internal market),[3] has been accompanied by the imposition of public service obligations (PSOs) such as universal service (USO) on undertakings operating on the liberalised market, and by the strengthening of consumer and user rights.[4]

Article 222 of the Treaty of Rome stated that the Treaty in no way prejudiced the rules in Member States governing the system of property ownership. That Article, now Article 345 TFEU, is unchanged although it is sometimes argued that the insertion by the TEU (Maastricht) of what is now Article 119 TFEU, saying that the activities of the Member States and the Union shall be conducted 'in accordance with the principle of an open market economy with free competition' represents a shift which favours private over public ownership.[5]

The question as to which, if any, areas of activity the normal principles of competition law should not apply, belongs in the political rather than the legal realm. The original Treaty of Rome contained nothing about public services, save for a provision about State aid in the inland transport sector in

[1] For the law in this area, see L. Hancher, 'Community, State and Market' in P. Craig and G. de Búrca (eds.), *The Evolution of EU Law* (Oxford University Press, 1999), 721 and E. Szyszczak, *The Regulation of the State in Competitive Markets in the EU* (Hart Publishing, 2007). And see generally J. Faull and A. Nikpay (eds.), *The EU Law of Competition* (3rd edn, Oxford University Press, 2014), Chap. 6 (J. L. Buendia Sierra); J. L. Buendia Sierra, *Exclusive Rights and State Monopolies in EC Law* (Oxford University Press, 1999); T. Prosser, *The Limits of Competition Law* (Oxford University Press, 2005); I. Van Bael and J.-F. Bellis, *Competition Law of the European Union* (6th edn, Wolters Kluwer, 2021), Chap. 9.

[2] See G. Amato, *Antitrust and the Bounds of Power: The Dilemma of Liberal Democracy in the History of the Market* (Hart Publishing, 1997), 88–89; E. Szyszczak, 'Public Service Provision in Competitive Markets' (2001) 20 *YEL* 35.

[3] See Hancher, n. 1, 722.

[4] See the Commission's comments on this in the Communication on 'Services of General Interest, including Social Services of General Interest: a New European Commitment' accompanying the Communication on 'A Single Market for 21st Century Europe', COM(2007) 725 final (the 2007 Communication), para. 2.2.

[5] See, however, e.g. the strong support for the traditional view of Art. 345 by the AG in Case C-367/98, *Commission v Portugal* EU:C:2002:369.

respect of 'certain obligations inherent in the concept of a public service' being permitted,[6] and the derogation in what is now Article 106(2) pertaining to 'services of general economic interest' (SGEIs). The 'services of general economic interest' concept was not defined and appeared nowhere else in the Treaty or in secondary legislation. Before 1990[7] the application of competition law to State-owned, State-controlled, or State-privileged undertakings was not a significant issue. It has become so because of technological, ideological, social, and economic changes, the increasing sophistication and reach of EU competition law, and the more aggressive enforcement of the law.

The debate about the relationship between competition law and public services resulted in the introduction into the Treaty of Rome by the Treaty of Amsterdam of what is now (with some modification) Article 14 TFEU,[8] and the inclusion in the Charter of Fundamental Rights of the European Union of Article 36, both of which proclaim the value and importance of 'services of general economic interest'.[9] Protocol No. 26 on 'services of general interest' is attached to the TEU and the TFEU by the Treaty of Lisbon.[10] The Commission has complemented these provisions with Communications.[11] There are two ways in which the application of EU competition law to public services can be limited. First, the activity can be found not to be 'economic', and therefore not subject to Articles 101 and 102 in the first place. Secondly, it can be found to be economic but allowed to take advantage of a derogation from the rules (in particular, the derogation provided in Article 106(2)).

Whether or not an activity is economic determines whether or not an entity is an 'undertaking' subject to the competition rules, as discussed in Chapter 4.[12] It will be recalled that 'undertaking' is a concept of EU law and that it is immaterial how the entity is regarded in national law. The question is whether it carries out commercial activities and not whether it is governed by public law or is non-profit-making.[13] It was also seen in Chapter 4 that bodies which exercise public powers which can be seen as part of the prerogatives of the State are not engaging in activities of an economic nature.[14] In determining the status of social security and health insurance funds, the EU Courts have used the concept of 'solidarity' to distinguish economic from non-economic activities.[15]

3. ARTICLE 4(3) TEU

Article 4(3) TEU contains the principle of Union loyalty. It requires Member States to take any appropriate measures to ensure fulfilment of their obligations under the Treaties or resulting from acts of the institutions; to facilitate the achievement of the Union's tasks; and to refrain from measures which could jeopardise the attainment of the Union's objectives. The CJ held in *INNO v ATAB* that pursuant

[6] Art. 73 EC, ex Art. 77. The Article was at issue in Case C-280/00, *Altmark Trans GmbH, Regierungspräsidium Magdeburg v Nahverkehrsgesellschaft Altmark GmbH* EU:C:2003:415 on whether compensation for services of general economic interest is a State aid: see Section 7.xx.

[7] The early 1990s saw the four major Art. 267 rulings, Case C-41/90, *Höfner v Macrotron* EU:C:1991:161; Case C-179/90, *Merci Convenzionali v Porto di Genova* EU:C:1991:464; Case C-260/89, *Elliniki Radiophonia Tileorasi (ERT) v DEP* EU:C:1991:254; and Case C-18/88, *RTT v GB-INNO-BM SA* EU:C:1991:474; and the telecommunications cases between the Commission and Member States, Case C-202/88, *France v Commission* EU:C:1991:120 (the *Telecommunications Equipment* case) and Cases C-271/90 etc., *Spain, Belgium & Italy v Commission* EU:C:1992:440 (the *Telecommunications Services* case).

[8] See Section 6.A.i, p. 631. [9] See Section 6.A.i, p. 632 ff. [10] See Section 6.A.i, p. 632 ff. [11] See Section 6.A. iii, p. 633. [12] Chap. 4, Section 4.A. [13] See Case C-41/90, *Höfner v Macrotron* EU:C:1991:161.

[14] See e.g. Case C-364/92, *SAT Fluggesellschaft v Eurocontrol* EU:C:1994:7; Case C-113/07, *SELEX Systemi Integrati SpA v Commission* EU:C:2009:191; Case C-343/95, *Diego Calì v SEPG* EU:C:1997:160; Case C-138/11, *Compass-Datenbank GmbH* EU:C:2012:449, para. 36.

[15] See Cases C-159–160/91, *Poucet and Pistre v Assurances Générales de France* EU:C:1993:63 and the other cases discussed in Chap. 4, Section 4.A.iii.

to this Member States are under a duty not to adopt or maintain in force measures which could deprive the competition provisions of their effectiveness.[16] This is the *effect utile* doctrine.

The effect of Article 4(3) together with Articles 101 and 102 is that a Member State may not require or favour the adoption of agreements, decisions, or concerted practices contrary to Article 101, or conduct contrary to Article 102, or reinforce their effects, and may not deprive its own legislation of its official character by delegating responsibility for taking decisions affecting the economic sphere to private traders.[17] We regard to the last point, we saw in Chapter 4 that where undertakings sit on statutory boards which simply make recommendations, there is no agreement between them within Article 101(1) and the ensuing rules retain their character as State measures.[18]

We also saw in Chapter 4 that Article 101 is not applicable to the anti-competitive activities of a firm if the restrictive effects on competition originate solely from the implementation of national law. Undertakings may therefore plead a 'State compulsion' defence and seek to show that their behaviour was not autonomous but dictated by national provisions. Such a plea will succeed only if the undertaking had no room for manoeuvre at all.[19] The same situation pertains to Article 102.[20]

4. ARTICLE 106

Article 106 deals with the application of EU rules to public undertakings and those granted special or exclusive rights.

Article 106

1. In the case of public undertakings and undertakings to which Member States grant special or exclusive rights, Member States shall neither enact nor maintain in force any measure contrary to the rules contained in the Treaties, in particular to those rules provided for in Article 18 and Articles 101 to 109.
2. Undertakings entrusted with the operation of services of general economic interest or having the character of a revenue-producing monopoly shall be subject to the rules contained in the Treaties, in particular to the rules on competition, in so far as the application of such rules does not obstruct the performance, in law or in fact, of the particular tasks assigned to them. The development of trade must not be affected to such an extent as would be contrary to the interests of the Union.
3. The Commission shall ensure the application of the provisions of this Article and shall, where necessary, address appropriate directives or decisions to Member States.

[16] Case 13/77, *NV GB-INNO-BM SA v ATAB* EU:C:1977:185, paras. 28–35.

[17] Case 267/86, *Van Eycke v ASPA NV* EU:C:1988:427, para. 16; Cases C-140–142/94, *DIP and Others v Commune di Bassano del Grappa* EU:C:1995:330, para. 15; Case C-266/96, *Corsica Ferries France SA v Gruppo Antichi Ormeggiatori del Porto di Genova* EU:C:1998:306, paras. 35, 36, and 49; Cases C-67/96 etc., *Albany International BV v Stichting Bedrijfspensioenfonds Textielindustrie* EU:C:1999:430, para. 65; Case C-94/04, *Cipolla and ors* EU:C:2006:758, para. 758; Case C-437/09, *AG2R Prévoyance v Beaudout* EU:C:2011:112, paras. 24 and 37. It was made clear in Case C-2/91, *Meng* EU:C:1993:885, para. 14, Case C-185/91, *Reiff* EU:C:1993:886, para. 14, and Case C-245/91, *Ohra* EU:C:1993:887 that Art. 4(3) applies in respect of competition only in combination with Art. 101 or Art. 102. See also Case C-327/12, *Ministero dello Sviluppo Economico v SOA Nazionale Costruttori—Organismo di Attestazione* EU:C:2013:827, para. 37.

[18] See Case C-96/94, *Centro Servizi Spediporto Srl v Spedizioni Marittima del Golfo Srl* EU:C:1995:308; Case C-184/13, *API-Anonima Petroli Italiana SpA v Ministero delle Infrastrutture e dei Trasporti* EU:C:2014:2147.

[19] See Cases C-359 and 379/95 P, *Commission and France v Ladbroke Racing* EU:C:1996:531 and the cases referred to in Chap. 4, Section 4.F.

[20] See e.g. Case C-280/08 P, *Deutsche Telekom v Commission* EU:C:2010:603, paras. 80–85, discussed in Chap. 7.

A. THE OBJECTIVES OF ARTICLE 106

Article 106 is applied in conjunction with another Article, since its function is to limit the ways in which State measures protecting certain undertakings hinder the operation of the Treaties. Article 106 does not deal only with competition, despite its position in the competition chapter of the TFEU. It deals with the application of *all* the Treaty rules, although it mentions in particular the competition rules (Articles 101–109 TFEU) and the prohibition on discrimination on the grounds of nationality (Article 18 TFEU). However, Article 106 has particular relevance to the competition provisions and especially Article 102, because public undertakings and undertakings granted special or exclusive rights frequently hold a dominant position.[21]

Article 106 is a specific manifestation of the duty of Union loyalty contained in Article 4(3) TEU.

B. THE FORMAT OF ARTICLE 106

Article 106 contains three interrelated provisions.

(i) Article 106(1): Prohibition Addressed to Member States

The prohibition in Article 106(1) is addressed to Member States. It prohibits Member States from enacting or maintaining in force any measures in relation to public undertakings and undertakings to which they have granted special or exclusive rights which are contrary to the Treaty rules. It is designed to prevent Member States from depriving the Treaty rules of their effectiveness through the measures they adopt in respect of public undertakings or through measures which enable private undertakings to escape the constraints of the competition provisions. The CJ confirmed in *DEI* that the provision is applicable to public undertakings on the one hand and to undertakings granted special or exclusive rights on the other. It is not necessary to show that the public undertaking has been granted special or exclusive rights.[22]

(ii) Article 106(2): Provision Addressed to Undertakings Providing for Limited Immunity from the Treaty Rules

Article 106(2) is addressed to undertakings. It gives a limited derogation from the Treaty rules to 'undertakings entrusted with the operation of services of general economic interest or having the character of a revenue producing monopoly' insofar as that is necessary for the carrying out of their tasks and subject to a proviso about affecting trade.

Despite being addressed to undertakings, Article 106(2) can be invoked by Member States in relation to special or exclusive rights they have granted.

(iii) Article 106(3): Policing and Legislative Powers of the Commission

Article 106(3) provides that the Commission may address decisions to Member States to ensure the observance of Article 106. This expedited enforcement mechanism does not have to comply with the procedures of the general enforcement provision, Article 258 TFEU, which provides for infraction proceedings brought by the Commission against Member States.

[21] Not inevitably: the usual criteria of dominance apply, and the exclusive right has to be over a relevant market: see Case 30/87, *Bodson v Pompes Funèbres des Régions Libérées* EU:C:1988:225, paras. 26–29.

[22] Case C-553/12 P, *Commission v Dimosia Epicheirisi Ilektrismou AE (DEI)* EU:C:2014:2083, paras. 56–58.

It also gives the Commission power to issue directives to Member States to ensure the application of the Article. The power need not be exercised within the detailed procedural framework ordinarily applicable to the adoption of directives set down in Articles 289–297 TFEU which involves other Union institutions.

5. ARTICLE 106(1)

A. DEFINITIONS

When considering Article 106(1) it is first necessary to determine the meaning of the concepts it employs, in particular the terms 'public undertakings', 'granted special or exclusive rights', and 'measures'.

(i) 'Public Undertakings'

Determining the meaning of 'public undertakings' means asking first, whether a particular body is an 'undertaking' and secondly, if it is, whether it is a 'public' undertaking.

What constitutes an undertaking, has already been considered in Chapters 4 and 6 and recalled in Section 2. The concept of a 'public' undertaking is a Union one[23] because Article 106(1) would be deprived of its effect if Member States were free to choose their own conception of 'public undertaking'. State participation in the ownership or running of undertakings comes in an almost indefinite range of guises and the Union concept must embrace them all.

The CJ in the *Transparency Directive* case[24] did not demur from the definition of a 'public undertaking' in Article 2(b) of the Transparency Directive:

> 'public undertakings' means any undertaking over which the public authorities may exercise directly or indirectly a dominant influence by virtue of their ownership of it, their financial participation therein or the rules which govern it. A dominant influence on the part of the public authorities shall be presumed when these authorities, directly or indirectly in relation to an undertaking:
>
> (i) hold the major part of the undertaking's subscribed capital: or
>
> (ii) control the majority of votes attaching to shares issued by the undertakings; or
>
> (iii) can appoint more than half of the members of the undertaking's administrative, managerial or supervisory body.[25]

The key is therefore control by the State. This can be through ownership or through some contractual, financial, structural, or other connection between the State and the undertaking which accords it a 'dominant influence'.

(ii) Undertakings Granted Special or Exclusive Rights

Special or exclusive rights may be granted in the whole of a national territory or in only part of it.[26] There are two categories of rights: 'special' and 'exclusive' are not synonymous. Entities with such rights may or may not be public undertakings.

[23] See Reischl AG in Cases 188–190/80, *France v Commission* EU:C:1982:134, para. 9.
[24] Cases 188–190/80, *France, Italy and the UK v Commission* EU:C:1982:257.
[25] Now Commission Dir. 2006/111/EC [2006] OJ L318/17.
[26] E.g. Case 30/87, *Bodson* EU:C:1988:225 (funeral services in particular French communes); Case C-179/90, *Merci Convenzionali* EU:C:1991:464 (the port of Genoa); Case C-323/93, *Société Civile Agricole du Centre d'Insémination de la Crespelle (Crespelle)* EU:C:1994:368 (defined areas of France).

Exclusive rights exist where a monopoly has been granted by the State to one entity to engage in a particular economic activity on an exclusive basis. They have been held to have been conferred, for example, upon broadcasting monopolies,[27] and upon undertakings granted the sole right to operate employment recruitment services,[28] the sole right to operate on a particular air route,[29] the sole right to supply unloading services at a port,[30] the sole right to provide bovine insemination services,[31] the exclusive right to receive and manage the contributions made under a compulsory social insurance scheme,[32] and the exclusive right to manage copyright relating to a certain category of works.[33] The rights granted to the television duopoly in the Greek television case, *ERT*,[34] were designated as 'special or exclusive'. Rather strangely, the CJ described the three firms entitled to collect waste for recycling in Copenhagen, as holding 'exclusive' rights.[35]

Exclusivity requires the creation of a closed class, and not merely the laying down of conditions of access.[36] Therefore the grant of intellectual property rights does not entail the granting of exclusive rights for the purposes of Article 106(1) because it involves laws laying down criteria which any undertaking is free to satisfy.

'Special rights' has been defined by the CJ in cases where Member States challenged directives issued by the Commission under Article 106(3) in pursuance of its objective to liberalise the telecommunications market. The liberalisation inevitably meant the removal of the protection hitherto given by Member States to national telecommunications operators.

France v Commission, the *Telecommunications Equipment* case,[37] concerned the challenge by France to Directive 88/301 on competition in the markets in telecommunications terminal equipment.[38] According to Article 2, Member States which had granted special or exclusive rights to undertakings for the importation, marketing, connection, bringing into service of telecommunications terminal equipment, and/or maintenance of such equipment were to ensure that those rights were withdrawn. The CJ held that Article 2 was void insofar as it concerned the withdrawal of *special* rights because:

> 45. . . . neither the provisions of the directive nor the preamble thereto specify the type of rights which are actually involved and in what respect the existence of such rights is contrary to the various provisions of the Treaty.
>
> 46. It follows that the Commission has failed to justify the obligation to withdraw special rights regarding the importation, marketing, connection, bringing into service and/or maintenance of telecommunications terminal equipment.

The *Telecommunications Services*[39] case concerned a similar challenge by Spain, Belgium, and Italy to Directive 90/388 on competition in the markets for telecommunications services.[40] Again the CJ annulled the provisions concerning the requirement to withdraw all special rights. In the directive, the

[27] Case 155/73, *Sacchi* EU:C:1974:40. [28] Case C-41/90, *Höfner v Macrotron* EU:C:1991:161.

[29] Case 66/86, *Ahmed Saeed Flugreisen and Silver Line Reisebüro GmbH v Zentrale zur Bekämpfung Unlauteren Wettwerbs eV* EU:C:1989:140; *Sterling Airways/SAS Denmark*, Commission's *Xth Report on Competition Policy* (1980), paras. 136–138.

[30] Case C-179/90, *Merci Convenzionali* EU:C:1991:464. [31] Case C-323/93, *Crespelle* EU:C:1994:368.

[32] Case C-437/09, *AG2R Prévoyance v Beaudout* EU:C:2011:112.

[33] Case C-351/12, *OSA—Ochranný svaz autorský pro práva k dílům hudebním o.s. v Léčebné lázně Mariánské Lázně a.s.* EU:C:2014:110, para. 82. [34] Case C-260/89, *ERT* EU:C:1991:254.

[35] Case C-209/98, *Entreprenørforeningens Affalds (FFAD), acting for Sydhavnens Sten and Grus ApS v Københavns Kommune (Sydhavnens)* EU:C:2000:279.

[36] See also Case C-327/12, *Ministero dello Sviluppo Economico v SOA Nazionale Costruttori—Organismo di Attestazione* EU:C:2013:827, where anybody who satisfied the relevant conditions could become a certification body.

[37] Case C-202/88, EU:C:1991:120. [38] [1988] OJ L131/73. [39] Cases C-271, 281, and 289/90, EU:C:1992:440.

[40] [1990] OJ L192/10.

Commission had defined 'special or exclusive rights' in Article 1 as being 'rights granted by a Member State or a public authority to one or more private or public bodies through any legal, regulatory or administrative instrument reserving them the right to provide a service or undertake an activity'. The CJ held that this was inadequate as it did not make it possible 'to determine the type of special rights with which the directive is concerned or in what respect the existence of those rights is contrary to the various provisions of the Treaty'.[41]

As a result of these cases, the Commission set out an extended definition of the meaning of 'special rights' in the field of telecommunications in the Preamble to Directive 94/46.[42] A special right is:

> granted by a Member State to a limited number of undertakings through any legislative, regulatory or administrative instruments which, within a given geographical area, limits to two or more, otherwise than according to objective, proportional and non-discriminatory criteria, the number of undertakings which are authorised to provide any such service, or designates, otherwise than according to such criteria, several competing undertakings, as those which are authorised to provide any such service, or confers on any undertaking or undertakings otherwise than according to such criteria, legal or regulatory advantages which substantially affect the ability of any other undertaking to provide that same telecommunications service in the same geographical area under substantially equivalent conditions.

This definition can be taken as generally applicable.[43] It identifies as 'special rights' those which are given by the State to a limited number of undertakings chosen in a subjective and discretionary manner.[44] In *Ambulanz Glöckner*, the CJ referred to a special or exclusive right existing where 'protection is conferred by a legislative measure on a limited number of undertakings which may substantially affect the ability of other undertakings to exercise the economic activity in question in the same geographical area under substantially equivalent conditions'.[45]

In *INNO v ATAB*, the CJ doubted whether special or exclusive rights could result from allowing manufacturers and importers of a particular product to impose resale price maintenance.[46] In *Banchero*,[47] it held that Italian laws on the distribution of tobacco did not entail special or exclusive rights as, although they governed access to the market, all undertakings were treated in the same way. Further, in *GEMA*[48] the Commission held that an authors' rights society did not enjoy special or exclusive rights even though legislation required authors to exercise their rights through such a society, because there was no limit on the number of rights societies which could exist. As with exclusive rights, special rights involve the creation of some sort of limited, closed class. In *FIFA*,[49] the GC dismissed the claim that the designation by the UK of the FIFA World Cup final stages as of major importance to society[50] meant that those broadcasters (BBC and ITV) who were prepared to take non-exclusive broadcasts were thereby given special or exclusive rights within Article 106(1). It was open to all broadcasters to acquire the rights and the reason that the pay-TV companies were uninterested in doing so was that their business model required exclusivity.

[41] EU:C:1992:440, para. 31. [42] Now Dir. 2002/77/EC [2002] OJ L249/21, Art. 1(6).

[43] There is a similar definition in Dir. 2006/111/EC, n. 25, Art. 2(g).

[44] See also the Commission's statement at the hearing in the *Telecommunications Services* case, Cases C-271, 281, and 289/90, EU:C:1992:440, quoted by Jacobs AG, para. 50.

[45] Case C-475/99, *Ambulanz Glöckner v Landkreis Südwestpfalz* EU:C:2001:577, para. 24; see also Case C-351/12, *OSA* EU:C:2014:110, para. 82.

[46] Case 13/77 [1977] ECR 2115: the point did not actually have to be answered because of the reply given to an earlier question.

[47] Case C-387/93, *Banchero* EU:C:1995:439. [48] [1971] OJ L134/15.

[49] Case T-68/08, *FIFA v Commission* EU:T:2011:44, *aff'd* Case C-201/11 P, *FIFA v Commission* EU:C:2013:478.

[50] Pursuant to Dir. 89/552/EEC [1989] OJ L298/23 as amended.

(iii) 'Measures'

The word 'measures' also appears in Article 4 TEU which obliges Member States to fulfil their Treaty obligations and not to jeopardise the objectives of the Treaties, and in Article 34 TFEU which prohibits, inter alia, measures having an equivalent effect to quantitative restrictions on imports between Member States.[51] 'Measures' must emanate from a branch of the public administration acting as a public authority. It does not include the actions of private undertakings, rather than the State actions which allow or authorise them, so that anti-competitive conduct engaged in by undertakings on their own initiative must be dealt with by Articles 101 and 102.[52] It is possible, however, that an exclusive or special right could be granted by a public authority through a private law contract which had a regulatory effect.[53]

B. MEASURES FORBIDDEN BY ARTICLE 106(1)

(i) Introduction

The wording of Article 106(1) seems to assume that Member States can confer special or exclusive rights on undertakings.[54] Moreover, in *Sacchi* in 1973, a case on broadcasting rights, the CJ accepted the legality of the granting of special or exclusive rights, saying:

> Nothing in the Treaty prevents Member States, for considerations of public interest, of a non-economic nature, from removing radio and television transmissions . . . from the field of competition by conferring on one or more establishments an exclusive right to conduct them.[55]

Sometimes, however, there is a clear violation of Article 106(1) in that some aspect of the State's arrangements inherently infringes a Treaty rule in itself. A good example not involving the competition rules is *Merci Convenzionali*,[56] where Italian laws reserved the loading and unloading of ships at an Italian port to certain dock-work companies whose worker-members had to be of Italian nationality. This infringed what is now Article 45 TFEU on the free movement of workers, which specifically applies the prohibition of nationality discrimination in situations governed by Union law.[57] In other cases, the measures taken by the Member State *result in* violations of the Treaties.

It was made clear in the *Telecommunications Equipment* case in 1991 that Member States do not have unassailable rights to create legal monopolies under any conditions they choose.

Case C-202/88, *France v Commission* EU:C:1991:120

France challenged the Telecommunications Terminal Equipment Directive, 88/301, inter alia, on the grounds that the Commission lacked competence to adopt it on the basis of Article 106(3). France claimed that Article 106 did not allow the Commission to interfere with the granting of special or

[51] See Dir. 70/50 [1970] OJ Spec. Ed. 17 on the abolition of measures which have an effect equivalent to quantitative restrictions on imports which defined measures as 'laws, regulations, administrative provisions, administrative practices, and all instruments issued from a public authority, including recommendations'.

[52] Case C-202/88, *France v Commission* EU:C:1991:120, para. 55.

[53] See Faull and Nikpay, n. 1, 6.34.

[54] See the discussion in Van Bael and Bellis, n. 1, p. 908.

[55] Case 155/73, *Sacchi* EU:C:1974:40, para. 14. However, the establishments remained subject to the discrimination prohibitions and fell under Art. 106.

[56] Case C-179/90, *Merci Convenzionali* EU:C:1991:464.

[57] Now Art. 18 TFEU.

exclusive rights by Member States because Article 106(1) presupposed the existence of special or exclusive rights so the granting of such rights could not itself constitute a 'measure' within the Article.

Court of Justice

21. . . . [I]t must be held in the first place that the supervisory power conferred on the Commission includes the possibility of specifying, pursuant to Article [106(3)], obligations arising under the Treaty. The extent of that power therefore depends on the scope of the rules with which compliance is to be ensured.

22. Next, it should be noted that even though that article presupposes the existence of undertakings which have certain special or exclusive rights, it does not follow that all the special or exclusive rights are necessarily compatible with the Treaty. That depends on different rules, to which Article [106(1)] refers.

. . .

51. It should be observed that a system of undistorted competition, as laid down in the Treaty, can be guaranteed only if equality of opportunity is secured as between the various economic operators. To entrust an undertaking which markets terminal equipment with the task of drawing up the specifications for such equipment, monitoring their application and granting type-approval in respect thereof is tantamount to conferring upon it the power to determine at will which terminal equipment may be connected to the public network, and thereby placing that undertaking at an obvious advantage over its competitors.

52. Consequently, the Commission was justified in seeking to entrust responsibility for drawing up technical specifications, monitoring their application and granting type-approval to a body independent of public or private undertakings offering competing goods and/or services in the telecommunications sector.

In this judgment, the CJ introduced the concept of 'equality of opportunity', which has played an important role in subsequent cases. This could not be guaranteed if the undertaking given the task of controlling specifications and issuing type approval certificates in respect of telecommunications equipment also marketed that equipment itself, in competition with the other suppliers it was overseeing.

As Edward and Hoskins[58] say:

It follows from *France* v. *Commission* that Member States have not retained complete sovereignty in relation to the creation of legal monopolies. Rather, the creation of such monopolies must be balanced with the principle of free competition.

It is therefore necessary to determine how that balance is struck. The basic principle is that there has to be some link between the State measures and the violation of the Treaties. The case law, however, is complex and sometimes inconsistent. In *Corbeau* in 1993,[59] there was some suggestion that despite *Sacchi* the very fact of granting monopoly rights may itself be a violation, although the CJ later retreated from that.[60]

[58] D. Edward and M. Hoskins, 'Art. 90: Deregulation and EC Law. Reflections Arising from the XVI FIDE Conference' (1995) 32 *CMLRev* 157, 160.

[59] Case C-320/91, *Corbeau* EU:C:1993:198.

[60] Case C-323/93, *La Crespelle* EU:C:1994:368.

In this section, we look first at the main cases chronologically, starting with four in 1991, to see how the law has developed and then consider what, if any, conclusions can be drawn from them.

(ii) *Höfner v Macrotron*

Case C-41/90, *Höfner v Macrotron* [1991] ECR I-1979

A company employed recruitment consultants. In a dispute about fees, the company claimed that the contract between the parties was void as it infringed the German law on the promotion of employment, the AFG. The AFG conferred on the Bundesanstalt, the Federal Office for Employment, the exclusive right to put prospective employees and employers in contact with one another. Nevertheless, to some extent the Bundesanstalt tolerated the existence and activities of independent recruitment consultants and it appeared that the Bundesanstalt was unable, on its own, to meet the demand for executive recruitment. The Court first held that the Bundesanstalt was an undertaking for the purposes of Articles 102 and 106.[61] It then considered the possible infringements.

Court of Justice

24. It must be pointed out that a public employment agency which is entrusted, under the legislation of a Member State, with the operation of services of general economic interest, such as those envisaged in Article 3 of the AFG, remains subject to the competition rules pursuant to Article [106(2)] unless and to the extent to which it is shown that their application is incompatible with the discharge of its duties (see judgment in Case 155/73 *Sacchi* . . .).

25. As regards the manner in which a public employment agency enjoying an exclusive right of employment procurement conducts itself in relation to executive recruitment undertaken by private recruitment consultancy companies, it must be stated that the application of Article [102] cannot obstruct the performance of the particular task assigned to that agency in so far as the latter is manifestly not in a position to satisfy demand in that area of the market and in fact allows its exclusive rights to be encroached on by those companies.

26. Whilst it is true that Article [102] concerns undertakings and may be applied within the limits laid down by Article [106(2)] to public undertakings or undertakings vested with exclusive rights, or specific rights, the fact nevertheless remains that the Treaty requires the Member States not to take or maintain in force measures which could destroy the effectiveness of that provision (see judgment in Case 13/77 *GB-INNO-BM* . . . paragraphs 31 and 32). Article [106(1)] in fact provides that the Member States are not to enact or maintain in force, in the case of public undertakings and the undertakings to which they grant special or exclusive rights, any measure contrary to the rules contained in the Treaty, in particular those provided for in Articles [101] to [109].

27. Consequently, any measure adopted by a Member State which maintains in force a statutory provision that creates a situation in which a public employment agency cannot avoid infringing Article [102] is incompatible with the rules of the Treaty.

28. It must be remembered, first, that an undertaking vested with a legal monopoly may be regarded as occupying a dominant position within the meaning of Article [102] of the Treaty (see judgment in Case 311/84 *CBEM*, . . .) and that the territory of a Member State, to which that monopoly extends, may constitute a substantial part of the common market (judgment in Case C 322/81 *Michelin* . . . paragraph 28).

[61] See Chap. 4, Section 4.A.iii.

> 29. Secondly, the simple fact of creating a dominant position of that kind by granting an exclusive right within the meaning of Article [106(1)] is not as such incompatible with Article [102] (see Case 311/84 *CBEM*, above, paragraph 17). A Member State is in breach of the prohibition contained in those two provisions only if the undertaking in question, merely by exercising the exclusive right granted to it, cannot avoid abusing its dominant position.
>
> 30. Pursuant to Article [102(b)], such an abuse may in particular consist in limiting the provision of a service, to the prejudice of those seeking to avail themselves of it.
>
> 31. A Member State creates a situation in which the provision of a service is limited when the undertaking to which it grants an exclusive right extending to executive recruitment activities is manifestly not in a position to satisfy the demand prevailing on the market for activities of that kind and when the effective pursuit of such activities by private companies is rendered impossible by the maintenance in force of a statutory provision under which such activities are prohibited and non-observance of that prohibition renders the contracts concerned void.
>
> 32. It must be observed, thirdly, that the responsibility imposed on a Member State by virtue of Articles [102 and 106(1)] is engaged only if the abusive conduct on the part of the agency concerned is liable to affect trade between Member States. That does not mean that the abusive conduct in question must actually have affected such trade. It is sufficient to establish that the conduct is capable of having such an effect (see Case 322/81 *Michelin*, above, paragraph 104).
>
> 33. A potential effect of that kind on trade between Member States arises in particular where executive recruitment by private companies may extend to the nationals or to the territory of other Member States.
>
> 34. In view of the foregoing considerations, it must be stated in reply to the fourth question that a public employment agency engaged in employment procurement activities is subject to the prohibition contained in Article [102], so long as the application of that provision does not obstruct the performance of the particular task assigned to it. A Member State which has conferred an exclusive right to carry on that activity upon the public employment agency is in breach of Article [106(1)] where it creates a situation in which that agency cannot avoid infringing Article [102]. That is the case, in particular, where the following conditions are satisfied.
>
> - the exclusive right extends to executive recruitment activities;
> - the public employment agency is manifestly incapable of satisfying demand prevailing on the market for such activities;
> - the actual pursuit of those activities by private recruitment consultants is rendered impossible by the maintenance in force of a statutory provision under which such activities are prohibited and non-observance of that prohibition renders the contracts concerned void;
> - the activities in question may extend to the nationals or to the territory of other Member States.

In *Höfner*, the CJ said (at paragraph 29) that the fact of creating a dominant position by granting exclusive rights is not as such incompatible with the Treaties. However, a Member State will infringe if the undertaking in question, *merely by exercising the exclusive right granted to it, cannot avoid* abusing its dominant position. In this case, the criterion was fulfilled as German law had given the undertaking a monopoly over services the demand for which it was incapable of satisfying. Such limitation of the service offered to customers constituted an abuse under Article 102(b), and so the Member State had created a situation in which the agency could not avoid infringing the Article.[62] This was reiterated in *Job Centre* where Italian law gave public placement offices a monopoly to act as employment

[62] See para. 27 of the judgment.

intermediaries. Again, the statutory monopolist was unlikely to be able to satisfy the demand on the employment market for recruitment services. The Member State had therefore created a situation in which the provision of a service was limited, contrary to Article 102(b).[63]

(iii) *ERT v DEP*

In its ruling in *ERT*, given eight weeks after that in *Höfner*, the Court did not talk of the abuse being unavoidable but of the exclusive rights being liable to create a situation where the undertaking is *led to infringe* Article 102.

Case C-260/89, *Elliniki Radiophonia Tileorassi Anonimi Etaira (ERT) v Dimotiki Etairia Pliroforissis (DEP)* EU:C:1991:254

The Greek Government granted exclusive rights in regard to the original broadcasting and retransmitting of programmes in Greece to ERT. Greek law prohibited any person from engaging in activities for which ERT had an exclusive right without ERT's authorisation. The Mayor of Thessaloniki and a municipal company, DEP, set up a television station and began broadcasting television programmes.

Court of Justice

10. In Case C-155/73 *Sacchi* . . . paragraph 14, the Court held that nothing in the Treaty prevents Member States, for considerations of a non-economic nature relating to the public interest, from removing radio and television broadcasts from the field of competition by conferring on one or more establishments an exclusive right to carry them out.

11. Nevertheless, it follows from Article [106(1) and (2)] that the manner in which the monopoly is organized or exercised may infringe the rules of the Treaty, in particular those relating to the free movement of goods, the freedom to provide services and the rules on competition.

12. The reply to the national court must therefore be that Community law does not prevent the granting of a television monopoly for considerations of a non-economic nature relating to the public interest. However, the manner in which such a monopoly is organized and exercised must not infringe the provisions of the Treaty on the free movement of goods and services or the rules on competition.

. . .

28. The independent conduct of an undertaking must be considered with regard to the provisions of the Treaty applicable to undertakings, such as, in particular, Articles [101], [102] and [106(2)].

29. As regards Article [101], it is sufficient to observe that it applies, according to its own terms, to agreements 'between undertakings'. There is nothing in the judgment making the reference to suggest the existence of any agreement between undertakings. There is therefore no need to interpret that provision.

30. Article [102] declares that any abuse of a dominant position within the common market or in any substantial part of it is prohibited as incompatible with the common market in so far as it may affect trade between Member States.

31. In that respect it should be borne in mind that an undertaking which has a statutory monopoly may be regarded as having a dominant position within the meaning of Article [102] (see the judgment in Case C-311/84 *CBEM* v. *CLT and IBP* . . . paragraph 16) and that the territory of a Member State over

[63] Case C-55/96, *Job Centre Coop arl* EU:C:1997:603. The Commission came to a similar conclusion in *Spanish Courier Services* [1990] OJ L233/19 (courier services reserved to Post Office which could not offer complete services). For inefficiency and the limitation of production and services as an abuse, see Chap. 7, Section 16.C.

which the monopoly extends may constitute a substantial part of the common market (see the judgment in Case C-322/81 *Michelin* v. *Commission* . . . paragraph 28).

32. Although Article [102] does not prohibit monopolies as such, it nevertheless prohibits their abuse. For that purpose Article [102] lists a number of abusive practices by way of example.

33. In that regard it should be observed that, according to Article [106(2)], undertakings entrusted with the operation of services of general economic interest are subject to the rules on competition so long as it is not shown that the application of those rules is incompatible with the performance of their particular task (see in particular, the judgment in *Sacchi*, cited above, paragraph 15).

34. Accordingly it is for the national court to determine whether the practices of such an undertaking are compatible with Article [102] and to verify whether those practices, if they are contrary to that provision, may be justified by the needs of the particular task with which the undertaking may have been entrusted.

35. As regards State measures, and more specifically the grant of exclusive rights, it should be pointed out that while Articles [101] and [102] are directed exclusively to undertakings, the Treaty none the less requires the Member States not to adopt or maintain in force any measure which could deprive those provisions of their effectiveness (see the judgment in Case C-13/77 *Inno* v. *ATAB* . . . paragraphs 31 and 32).

36. Article [106(1)] thus provides that, in the case of undertakings to which Member States grant special or exclusive rights, Member States are neither to enact nor to maintain in force any measure contrary to the rules contained in the Treaty.

37. In that respect it should be observed that Article [106(1)] prohibits the granting of an exclusive right to retransmit television broadcasts to an undertaking which has an exclusive right to transmit broadcasts, where those rights are liable to create a situation in which that undertaking is led to infringe Article [102] by virtue of a discriminatory broadcasting policy which favours its own programmes.

38. The reply to the national court must therefore be that Article [106(1)] prohibits the granting of an exclusive right to transmit and an exclusive right to retransmit television broadcasts to a single undertaking, where those rights are liable to create a situation in which that undertaking is led to infringe Article [102] by virtue of a discriminatory broadcasting policy which favours its own programmes, unless the application of Article [102] obstructs the performance of the particular tasks entrusted to it.

In this case, the CJ said that the Treaty did not prevent the granting of a monopoly but stressed, as it had in *INNO v ATAB*,[64] that Member States are prohibited from adopting measures which deprive the competition rules of their effectiveness. This means that the manner in which the monopoly is organised may infringe the competition rules (paragraph 11). The Court therefore concluded that the rules did prohibit the granting of an exclusive right to retransmit TV broadcasts to an undertaking which has exclusive rights to transmit broadcasts where those rights *are liable to create a situation in which that undertaking is led* to infringe Article 102 by virtue of a discriminatory broadcasting policy which favours its own programmes (paragraphs 37 and 38). In *ERT* the cumulation of rights in the hands of the monopolist did not result in an unavoidable infringement of Article 102, but did result in a situation where the monopolist was perceived as being led to infringe because it would inevitably discriminate in favour of retransmitting its own programmes rather than those of others. There was no evidence that ERT had done this. The Court was concerned with the possibility of an abuse.

[64] Case 13/77, *NV GB-INNO-BM SA v ATAB -BM* EU:C:1977:185.

(iv) *Merci Convenzionali*

In *Merci Convenzionali*, six months later, the Court talked of the exclusive rights *inducing* an abuse.

Case C-179/90, *Merci Convenzionali Porto di Genova v Siderurgica Gabrielli SpA* EU:C:1991:464

By Italian law Merci had the exclusive right to organise the loading, unloading, and other handling of goods within the Port of Genoa through a dock-work company. A delay in unloading Siderurgica's ship was caused in particular by a strike of the dock-work company's workers. The exclusive rights meant that the vessel's crew were not able to do the work themselves. Siderurgica demanded compensation and the reimbursement of the charges it had paid to Merci. The Tribunale di Genoa asked whether Article 106(1) in conjunction with Article 102 precluded the Italian rules. The CJ confirmed in paragraph 14 that an undertaking with a statutory monopoly over a substantial part of the common market could be regarded as having a dominant position within Article 102.

Court of Justice

16. It should next be stated that the simple fact of creating a dominant position by granting exclusive rights within the meaning of Article [106(1)] is not as such incompatible with Article [102].

17. However, the Court has had occasion to state, in this respect, that a Member State is in breach of the prohibitions contained in those two provisions if the undertaking in question, merely by exercising the exclusive rights granted to it, cannot avoid abusing its dominant position (see the judgment in Case C-41/90 *Höfner*, . . ., paragraph 29) or when such rights are liable to create a situation in which that undertaking is induced to commit such abuses (see the judgment in Case C-260/89 *ERT*, . . . , paragraph 37).

18. According to subparagraphs (a), (b) and (c) of the second paragraph of Article [102], such abuse may in particular consist in imposing on the persons requiring the services in question unfair purchase prices or other unfair trading conditions, in limiting technical development, to the prejudice of consumers, or in the application of dissimilar conditions to equivalent transactions with other trading parties.

19. In that respect it appears from the circumstances described by the national court and discussed before the Court of Justice that the undertakings enjoying exclusive rights in accordance with the procedures laid down by the national rules in question are, as a result, induced either to demand payment for services which have not been requested, to charge disproportionate prices, to refuse to have recourse to modern technology, which involves an increase in the cost of the operations and a prolongation of the time required for their performance, or to grant price reductions to certain consumers and at the same time to offset such reductions by an increase in the charges to other consumers.

20. In these circumstances it must be held that a Member State creates a situation contrary to Article [102] where it adopts rules of such a kind as those at issue before the national court, which are capable of affecting trade between Member States as in the case of the main proceedings, regard being had to the factors mentioned in paragraph 15 of this judgment relating to the importance of traffic in the Port of Genoa.

In this judgment, the CJ cited *ERT* for the proposition that a Member State infringes Article 102 where it grants rights which are liable to *induce* the undertaking to commit abuses (paragraphs 17 and 19). The abuses were unfair payment demands and prices (Article 102(a)), inefficiency (Article 102(b)), and discrimination between customers (Article 102(c)). So we reach the position that although, as the Court said in *Merci* (paragraph 16), the simple fact of creating a dominant position by granting exclusive rights is not incompatible with Article 106(1), the granting of rights which induce or lead to the undertakings committing abuses *is* incompatible.[65]

(v) *RTT v GB-INNO-BM*

The *GB-INNO-BM* ruling, three days after *Merci*, involved the cumulation of rights in the hands of one undertaking. This was similar to *ERT*.

Case C-18/88, *RTT v GB-INNO-BM SA* EU:C:1991:474

Under Belgian law RRT held a monopoly over the establishment and operation of the public telephone system. Only equipment supplied or approved by RTT could be connected to its network. GB-INNO sold telephones not approved by RTT. RTT sought an order that GB-INNO should not sell telephones without informing purchasers that they were not approved. The Italian Court asked, inter alia, whether a Member State was precluded from granting to the company operating the public telephone network the power to lay down the standards for telephone equipment and to check that economic operators meet those standards when it is competing with those operators on the market for terminals.

Court of Justice

15. Under Belgian law, the RTT holds a monopoly for the establishment and operation of the public telecommunications network. Moreover, only equipment supplied by the RTT or approved by it can be connected to the network. The RTT thus has the power to grant or withhold authorization to connect telephone equipment to the network, the power to lay down the technical standards to be met by that equipment, and the power to check whether the equipment not produced by it is in conformity with the specifications that it has laid down.

16. At the present stage of development of the Community, that monopoly, which is intended to make a public telephone network available to users, constitutes a service of general economic interest within the meaning of Article [106(2)].

17. The Court has consistently held that an undertaking vested with a legal monopoly may be regarded as occupying a dominant position within the meaning of Article [102] and that the territory of a Member State to which that monopoly extends may constitute a substantial part of the common market (judgments in Case C-41/90 *Höfner* . . . paragraph 28, and in Case C-260/89 *ERT* . . . paragraph 31).

18. The Court has also held that an abuse within the meaning of Article [102] is committed where, without any objective necessity, an undertaking holding a dominant position on a particular market reserves to itself an ancillary activity which might be carried out by another undertaking as part of its activities on a neighbouring but separate market, with the possibility of eliminating all competition from such undertaking (judgment in Case 311/84 *CBEM* . . .).

19. Therefore the fact that an undertaking holding a monopoly in the market for the establishment and operation of the network, without any objective necessity, reserves to itself a neighbouring but separate market, in this case the market for the importation, marketing, connection, commissioning and maintenance of equipment for connection to the said network, thereby eliminating all competition from other undertakings, constitutes an infringement of Article [102].

20. However, Article [102] applies only to anti-competitive conduct engaged in by undertakings on their own initiative (see judgment in Case C-202/88 *France* v. *Commission* 'Telecommunications

[65] See also Case C-18/93, *Corsica Ferries Italia Srl v Corpo dei Piloti del Porto di Genova* EU:C:1994:195.

terminals' . . .), not to measures adopted by States. As regards measures adopted by States, it is Article [106(1)] that applies. Under that provision, Member States must not, by laws, regulations or administrative measures, put public undertakings and undertakings to which they grant special or exclusive rights in a position which the said undertakings could not themselves attain by their own conduct without infringing Article [102].

21. Accordingly, where the extension of the dominant position of a public undertaking or undertaking to which the State has granted special or exclusive rights results from a State measure, such a measure constitutes an infringement of Article [106] in conjunction with Article [102].

22. The exclusion or the restriction of competition on the market in telephone equipment cannot be regarded as justified by a task of a public service of general economic interest within the meaning of Article [106(2)]. The production and sale of terminals, and in particular of telephones, is an activity that should be open to any undertaking. In order to ensure that the equipment meets the essential requirements of, in particular, the safety of users, the safety of those operating the network and the protection of public telecommunications networks against damage of any kind, it is sufficient to lay down specifications which the said equipment must meet and to establish a procedure for type-approval to check whether those specifications are met.

23. According to the RTT, there could be a finding of an infringement of Article [106(1)] only if the Member State had favoured an abuse that the RTT itself had in fact committed, for example by applying the provisions on type-approval in a discriminatory manner. It emphasizes, however, that the order for reference does not state that any abuse has actually taken place, and that the mere possibility of discriminatory application of those provisions by reason of the fact that the RTT is designated as the authority for granting approval and is competing with the undertakings that apply for approval cannot in itself amount to an abuse within the meaning of Article [102].

24. That argument cannot be accepted. It is sufficient to point out in this regard that it is the extension of the monopoly in the establishment and operation of the telephone network to the market in telephone equipment, without any objective justification, which is prohibited as such by Article [102], or by Article [106(1)] in conjunction with Article [102], where that extension results from a measure adopted by a State. As competition may not be eliminated in that manner, it may not be distorted either.

25. A system of undistorted competition, as laid down in the Treaty, can be guaranteed only if equality of opportunity is secured as between the various economic operators. To entrust an undertaking which markets terminal equipment with the task of drawing up the specifications for such equipment, monitoring their application and granting type-approval in respect thereof is tantamount to conferring upon it the power to determine at will which terminal equipment may be connected to the public network, and thereby placing that undertaking at an obvious advantage over its competitors (judgment in Case C-202/88, paragraph 51).

26. In those circumstances, the maintenance of effective competition and the guaranteeing of transparency require that the drawing up of technical specifications, the monitoring of their application, and the granting of type-approval must be carried out by a body which is independent of public or private undertakings offering competing goods or services in the telecommunications sector (judgment in Case C-202/88, paragraph 52).

27. Moreover, the provisions of the national regulations at issue in the main action may influence the imports of telephone equipment from other Member States, and hence may affect trade between Member States within the meaning of Article [102].

28. Accordingly, it must first be stated, in reply to the national court's questions, that Articles [3(1)(g) EC], [106] and [102] preclude a Member State from granting to the undertaking which operates the public telecommunications network the power to lay down standards for telephone equipment and to check that economic operators meet those standards when it is itself competing with those operators on the market for that equipment.

Here there was no allegation that RTT had actually behaved improperly. The objection was that the State measures in effect extended the monopoly position from one market to another, by giving the undertaking the authorisation power over its competitors, a situation which if brought about by the conduct of an undertaking rather than by State measures would have constituted an abuse (see paragraphs 18–20). In paragraph 25, the Court also referred to the principle of 'equality of opportunity' between economic operators which appeared in *France v Commission*.[66] The rights conferred on the undertakings in both *ERT* and *GB-INNO-BM SA* were also contrary to Article 106(1) by creating a conflict of interest in bundling together regulatory functions and commercial activities. This was also so in *Silvano Raso*[67] where an Italian law gave the exclusive right to supply temporary labour to other dock-work companies operating in a port to an undertaking which was also authorised to carry out dock-work itself. Again the CJ said that the company would have a conflict of interest.[68]

(vi) *Corbeau*

In *Corbeau*, the CJ appeared to suggest that the very granting of special or exclusive rights, even where the elements in the cases previously discussed are not present, might be contrary to Article 106(1).

Case C-320/91, *Corbeau* EU:C:1993:198

Belgian law conferred a monopoly on the Régie des Postes in respect of the collection, transporting, and delivery of various forms of correspondence. There were criminal sanctions for infringing the monopoly. Corbeau established a postal service in the Liège area, whereby personal collection was from the sender's premises and delivery made before noon next day in the same area, although deliveries outside the area were made by putting the items in the ordinary post. Corbeau was prosecuted for infringing the monopoly. The Liège court referred questions to the Court concerning the compatibility of the post office monopoly with Articles 101, 102, and 106, whether the monopoly should be modified to comply with Article 106(1), the application of Article 106(2), and whether the post office was in a dominant position. (The part of the judgment concerning Article 106(2) is reproduced in Section 6.E.iii.)

Court of Justice

7. With regard to the facts in the main proceedings, the questions referred to the Court must be understood as meaning that the national court is substantially concerned with the question whether Article [106] must be interpreted as meaning that it is contrary to that Article for the legislation of a Member State which confers on a body such as the Régie des Postes the exclusive right to collect, carry and distribute mail to prohibit an economic operator established in that State from offering, under threat of criminal penalties, certain specific services on that market.

8. To reply to that question, as thus reformulated, it should first be pointed out that a body such as the Régie des Postes, which has been granted exclusive rights as regards the collection, carriage and distribution of mail, must be regarded as an undertaking to which the Member State concerned has granted exclusive rights within the meaning of Article [106(1)].

[66] See Section 5.B.i, p. 612.

[67] Case C-163/96, *Silvano Raso* EU:C:1998:54.

[68] Ibid., para. 28. In Cases C-46/90 and C-93/91, *Laauche and Evrard* EU:C:1993:852 where the facts were similar to *GB-INNO-BM* but the undertaking had only a limited role in verifying the competitors' equipment, the Court referred to equality of opportunity but seemed to be satisfied that on the facts Art. 106(1) was not infringed.

> 9. Next it should be recalled that the Court has consistently held that an undertaking having a statutory monopoly over a substantial part of the Common Market may be regarded as having a dominant position within the meaning of Article [102] (see the judgments in Case C-179/90 *Merci Convenzionali Porto di Genova* . . . paragraph 14 and in Case C-18/88 *RTT* v. *GB-Inno-BM* . . . paragraph 17).
>
> 10. However, Article [102] applies only to anti-competitive conduct engaged in by undertakings on their own initiative, not to measures adopted by States (see the *RTT* v. *GB-Inno-BM* judgment . . . paragraph 20).
>
> 11. The Court has had occasion to state in this respect that although the mere fact that a Member State has created a dominant position by the grant of exclusive rights is not as such incompatible with Article [102], the Treaty none the less requires the Member States not to adopt or maintain in force any measure which might deprive those provisions of their effectiveness (see the judgment in Case C-260/89 *ERT* . . . paragraph 35).
>
> 12. Thus Article [106(1)] provides that in the case of public undertakings to which Member States grant special or exclusive rights, they are neither to enact nor to maintain in force any measure contrary to the rules contained in the Treaty with regard to competition.
>
> 13. That provision must be read in conjunction with Article [106(2)] which provides that undertakings entrusted with the operation of services of general economic interest are to be subject to the rules on competition in so far as the application of such rules does not obstruct the performance, in law or in fact, of the particular tasks assigned to them.
>
> 14. That latter provision thus permits the Member States to confer on undertakings to which they entrust the operation of services of general economic interest, exclusive rights which may hinder the application of the rules of the Treaty on competition in so far as restrictions on competition, or even the exclusion of all competition, by other economic operators are necessary to ensure the performance of the particular tasks assigned to the undertakings possessed of the exclusive rights.

There was no suggestion in *Corbeau* that the Régie des Postes had acted abusively. Corbeau's defence challenged the monopoly itself.[69] The CJ answered this in paragraphs 7–12 of the judgment. In paragraph 11, it said that the mere grant of exclusive rights was not in itself incompatible with the Treaty but also that Member States are not to adopt or maintain measures which may deprive the competition provisions of their effectiveness. It then quoted Article 106(1) and turned immediately to Article 106(2). It never clearly identified which, if any, features of the Belgian legislation were contrary to Article 106(1) and Article 102.[70] This case did not concern an undertaking accused of acting abusively, the extension of the monopoly into a neighbouring market, a conflict of interest, or the bundling of regulatory functions with entrepreneurial activities. It did, however, appear to suggest[71] that, in order to ensure the *effet utile* or effectiveness of Articles 106(1) and 102 and despite the Court's statement to the contrary at paragraph 11, the very existence of national rules conferring a dominant position on an undertaking is unacceptable unless the rights at issue can be justified under Article 106(2) (see paragraphs 13 and 14). In effect, it reversed the burden of proof: exclusive rights are not prima facie legal, but prima facie illegal unless they are objectively justified or fulfil the Article 106(2) criteria.[72]

[69] Since *Corbeau* the postal sector has been liberalised.

[70] As Jacobs AG pointed out in his Opinion in Cases C-67/96, 115–117/97, and 219/97, *Albany International BV v Stichting Bedrijfspensioenfonds Textielindustrie* EU:C:1999:28, para. 417.

[71] See L. Hancher, 'Casenote on *Corbeau*' (1994) 31 *CMLRev* 105, 111.

[72] See Faull and Nikpay, n. 1, 6.81, which says that in effect this brings the approach to Arts. 106(1) and 102 in line with the approach to the free movement of goods.

(vii) *La Crespelle*

The CJ did not pursue the line it took in *Corbeau* in the next case, *La Crespelle*,[73] where it again held that a Member State contravenes the Treaty only if, in merely exercising the exclusive right granted to it, the undertaking cannot avoid abusing its dominant position: it is not possible automatically to impute the abuse to the existence of the right. In this case, where the exclusive right concerned bovine insemination centres, there was nothing in the grant of exclusive rights which made the alleged abuse—excessive pricing—unavoidable. The same approach was followed in *Corsica Ferries*,[74] where the CJ held that the grant of the exclusive right to offer compulsory piloting services in a port was not in itself an infringement of Article 106(1) but the approval of the discriminatory tariffs, which were contrary to Article 102(c), *did* infringe. Similarly, in *Banchero* the CJ held that Article 106(1) was infringed only where the undertaking cannot avoid abusing its dominant position.[75]

(viii) *Albany*

Albany[76] concerned the Dutch pension regime whereby affiliation to a single sectoral pension fund was made compulsory for all undertakings in that sector. That provider both managed the sectoral scheme and was the authority responsible for deciding on the grant of exemptions from membership of it. Various undertakings brought proceedings in the Dutch courts challenging the compulsory affiliation on the grounds that they provided equivalent supplementary pension schemes themselves and arguing that the exclusive rights bestowed on the sectoral funds infringed Article 106(1).

The CJ said once again that the granting of exclusive rights is not contrary to the Treaty unless merely by exercising the right the undertaking is led to commit an abuse[77] or an abuse is unavoidable.[78] However, the Court did not proceed to consider whether the undertaking here *was* put in such a position, but instead turned to see whether the justification under Article 106(2) applied.[79] This can be contrasted with *Dusseldorp* where the CJ found the provision to be contrary to Article 106(1) in conjunction with Article 102 before turning to consider Article 106(2).[80] In *Albany*, the CJ, unlike Advocate General Jacobs in his Opinion,[81] was not concerned that the pension funds with the exclusive rights were also the authority able to grant exemptions from compulsory participation in them, considering this to be justified by the circumstances.[82]

[73] Case C-323/93, *La Crespelle* EU:C:1994:368.

[74] Case C-18/93, *Corsica Ferries Italia Srl v Corpo dei Piloti del Porto di Genova* EU:C:1994:195.

[75] Case C-387/93, *Banchero* EU:C:1995:439.

[76] Case C-67/96, *Albany International BV v Stichting Bedrijfspensioenfonds Textielindustrie* EU:C:1999:430. See also Cases C-115–117/97, *Brentjens' Handelsonderneming BV v Stichting Bedrijfspensioenfonds voor de Handel in Bouwmaterialen* EU:C:1999:434 and Case C-219/97, *Maatschappij Drijvende Bokken BV v Stichting Pensioenfonds voor de Vervoer-en Havenbedrijven* EU:C:1999:437, which raised the same issue. The cases also raised questions about the application of the competition rules to collective agreements between employers and employees, see Chap. 4. And see L. Gyselen, 'Case Note on *Albany, Brentjens'* and *Drijvende Bokken*' (2000) 37 *CMLRev* 425.

[77] Case C-67/96, *Albany*, para. 93.

[78] Ibid., para. 95.

[79] See L. Gyselen, 'Case Note on *Albany, Brentjens'* and *Drijvende Bokken*' (2000) 37 *CMLRev* 425. In Case C-209/98, *Sydhavnens* [2000] ECR I-3743 the CJ decided the exclusive right did *not* infringe Art. 106(1) but still proceeded to examine the application of Art. 106(2).

[80] Case C-203/96, *Chemische Afvalstoffen Dusseldorp BV v Minister van Volkshuisvesting, Ruimtelijke Ordening en Milieubeheer* EU:C:1998:316. The CJ held that a Dutch prohibition on a company exporting its waste oil filters for treatment in Germany amounted, in practice, to imposing an obligation on it to deliver the filters to the Dutch undertaking which held the exclusive right to incinerate dangerous waste. For the Art. 106(2) aspects of the case, see Section 6.E.iii.

[81] EU:C:1999:28, paras. 441–468.

[82] For the application of Art. 106(2) in *Albany*, see Section 6.E.iii, p. 645.

(ix) *Deutsche Post*

Deutsche Post[83] concerned a State monopoly (DP) with exclusive rights over certain categories of mail in Germany. It carried out the obligations flowing from the Universal Postal Convention (UPC). Under the UPC, States must forward and deliver international mail addressed to persons resident in their country which is passed to them by the postal services of other contracting parties. The receiving state may charge a fixed fee for the costs of the delivery (terminal dues). The Convention provides that where senders resident in country A cause mail addressed to addressees in country A to be posted in bulk in country B, country A is entitled to either charge its full internal rate or return the items to their origin. Various credit-card companies based in Germany electronically transmitted the data for their customers' bills to processing centres outside Germany (some in other Member States) which prepared the German customers' bills and posted them back to Germany. DP was merely paid the terminal dues. It demanded the full internal rate. The credit companies refused to pay. The German courts asked whether it was contrary to Article 106 and Article 102 for DP to exercise its Convention rights to charge the internal postage rate.

The CJ said that DP had been granted exclusive rights within the meaning of Article 106(1) and that the right under the UPC to treat international mail as internal mail did create a situation where 'it may be led, to the detriment of users of postal services, to abuse its dominant position'.[84] The CJ suggested that the abuse was a form of refusal to supply (because of the threat of non-delivery).[85] In paragraphs 40–41 of the ruling, it repeated paragraphs 12–13 of *Corbeau*, saying that Article 106(1) had to be read in conjunction with Article 106(2). It then turned to consider the application of that provision.[86]

(x) *Ambulanz Glöckner*

A similar approach to *Deutsche Post* was taken in *Ambulanz Glöckner*.[87]

Legislation in the Land of Rheinland-Pfalz of Germany governing the provision of the public ambulance service (the RettDG 1991) distinguished between 'emergency transport' and 'patient transport' (non-emergency). Emergency transport was entrusted to two medical aid organisations which also ran a non-emergency service. RettDG 1991 in effect provided that applications from other operators to run non-emergency services should be decided by the public authority in consultation with the medical aid organisations. Ambulanz Glöckner had previously provided a non-emergency service. When it applied to the relevant public authority for a renewal of its permit, the two medical aid organisations claimed that competition on the non-emergency market would affect their ability to provide the emergency service. As a result, the permit was refused.

The CJ said that the legislation was contrary to Article 106(1) as it allowed the holder of an exclusive right in one market to gain an advantage (and extend its dominant position) in another market on which an independent operator could have provided services (the urgent transport market and the patient transport market were held to be related but separate). This infringed Article 102(b).

> . . . it must be concluded that, in enacting Paragraph 18(3) of the RettDG 1991, the application of which involves prior consultation of the medical aid organisations in respect of any application for authorisation to provide non-emergency patient transport services submitted by an independent operator, the legislature of the Land of Rheinland-Pfalz gave an advantage to those organisations, which already

[83] Cases C-147–148/97, *Deutsche Post AG v Gesellschaft für Zahlungssysteme mbH (GZS) and Citicorp Kartenservice GmbH* EU:C:2000:74.

[84] Ibid., para. 48. [85] Ibid., para. 60. [86] See Section 6.E, p. 649.

[87] Case C-475/99, *Ambulanz Glöckner v Landkreis Südwestpfalz* EU:C:2001:577.

> had an exclusive right on the urgent transport market, by also allowing them to provide such services exclusively. The application of Paragraph 18(3) of the RettDG 1991 therefore has the effect of limiting markets . . . to the prejudice of consumers within the meaning of Article [102(b)], by reserving to those medical aid organisations an ancillary transport activity which could be carried on by independent operators.[88]

The CJ went on to consider whether Article 106(2) applied.[89]

(xi) *Connect Austria*

In *Connect Austria*,[90] the Austrian regulatory agency charged an applicant for a new standard digital mobile telecommunications licence fees that were greatly in excess of those it charged the incumbent public undertaking. This was likely to lead to the public undertaking extending or strengthening its dominant position, and the distorted competition 'would therefore result from a State measure which creates a situation where equality of opportunity for the various economic operators concerned cannot be ensured',[91] thus infringing Article 106(1) in conjunction with Article 102. The extension of the dominant position appeared to come from the State measure itself, not from any conduct by the undertaking. In paragraph 84, the CJ said:

> If inequality of opportunity between economic operators, and therefore distorted competition, results from a State measure, such a measure constitutes an infringement of Article [106(1)] in conjunction with Article [102].

(xii) *MOTOE*

In *MOTOE*, the reference concerned administrative powers given to a sports body which also competed in the market with those it authorised.[92]

> **Case C-49/07, *Motosykletistiki Omospondia Ellados NPID (MOTOE) v Ellinkio Dimosi* EU:C:2008:376**
>
> Greek legislation required ministerial authorisation for motorcycling competitions on public or private roads and spaces. Authorisation could only be given following the consent of ELPA, the Greek representative of the International Motorcycling Federation. ELPA, a non-profit-making association, organised motorcycling events in Greece and entered into sponsorship, advertising, and insurance contracts in that connection. MOTOE, another non-profit-making association, also organised motorcycling events in Greece. ELPA failed to consent to various proposed MOTOE events. One question asked by the Greek court concerned the authorisation power granted to ELPA in the situation where it also competed on the market with those it authorised.

[88] Ibid., para. 43. [89] For this aspect, see Section 6.E.iii, p. 647.

[90] Case C-462/99, *Connect Austria Gesellschaft für Telekommunikation GmbH v Telekom-Control-Kommission* EU:C:2003:297.

[91] Ibid., para. 87.

[92] See A. Veermersch, 'Casenote on Case C-49/07' (2009) 46 *CMLRev* 1327.

Court of Justice

48. . . . [I]t should be recalled that the mere creation or reinforcement of a dominant position through the grant of special or exclusive rights within the meaning of Article [106(1)] is not in itself incompatible with Article [102].

49. On the other hand, a Member State will be in breach of the prohibitions laid down by those two provisions if the undertaking in question, merely by exercising the special or exclusive rights conferred upon it, is led to abuse its dominant position or where such rights are liable to create a situation in which that undertaking is led to commit such abuses (*Höfner and Elser*, cited above, paragraph 29; *ERT*, cited above, paragraph 37; Case C-179/90 *Merci convenzionali porto di Genova* . . . paragraphs 16 and 17; and Case C-323/93 *Centre d'insémination de la Crespelle* . . . paragraph 18). In this respect, it is not necessary that any abuse should actually occur (see, to that effect, Case C-55/96 *Job Centre* . . . paragraph 36).

50. In any event, Articles [102 and 106(1)] are infringed where a measure imputable to a Member State, and in particular a measure by which a Member State confers special or exclusive rights within the meaning of Article [106(1)], gives rise to a risk of an abuse of a dominant position (see, to that effect, *ERT*, cited above, paragraph 37; *Merci convenzionali porto di Genova*, cited above, paragraph 17; and Case C-380/05 *Centro Europa 7* . . . paragraph 60).

51. A system of undistorted competition, such as that provided for by the Treaty, can be guaranteed only if equality of opportunity is secured as between the various economic operators. To entrust a legal person such as ELPA, which itself organises and commercially exploits motorcycling events, the task of giving the competent administration its consent to applications for authorisation to organise such events, is tantamount *de facto* to conferring upon it the power to designate the persons authorised to organise those events and to set the conditions in which those events are organised, thereby placing that entity at an obvious advantage over its competitors (see, by analogy, Case C-202/88 *France v Commission* . . . paragraph 51, and Case C-18/88 *GB Inno BM* . . . paragraph 25). Such a right may therefore lead the undertaking which possesses it to deny other operators access to the relevant market. That situation of unequal conditions of competition is also highlighted by the fact, confirmed at the hearing before the Court, that, when ELPA organises or participates in the organisation of motorcycling events, it is not required to obtain any consent in order that the competent administration grant it the required authorisation.

52. Furthermore, such a rule, which gives a legal person such as ELPA the power to give consent to applications for authorisation to organise motorcycling events without that power being made subject by that rule to restrictions, obligations and review, could lead the legal person entrusted with giving that consent to distort competition by favouring events which it organises or those in whose organisation it participates.

53. In the light of the foregoing, the answer to the questions referred must be that a legal person whose activities consist not only in taking part in administrative decisions authorising the organisation of motorcycling events, but also in organising such events itself and in entering, in that connection, into sponsorship, advertising and insurance contracts, falls within the scope of Articles [102 and 106]. . . .

One reason the CJ gave in *MOTOE* for finding that the national rule infringed Article 106(1) was that it created inequality of opportunity (paragraph 51), a concept already seen in *France v Commission*, *GB-INNO-BM*, and *Connect Austria*. It also, as in *GB-INNO-BM*, created a conflict of interest in giving ELPA regulatory powers over commercial activities in which it competed with others. Article 106(1) and Article 102 preclude a national rule which, inter alia, is liable to create a situation in which the undertaking is led to commit an abuse. However, it is not necessary that any abuse actually occurs (paragraph 49).

(xiii) *DEI*

The issues of equality of opportunity and the strengthening or extension of a dominant position over another market were explored in *Greek Lignite*. Lignite, a coal ore from which electricity can be produced, was the cheapest combustible for producing electricity in Greece, where the extensive lignite deposits are State-owned. The Greek Government gave PCC, the former monopoly generator of electricity in Greece prior to liberalisation (now a limited liability company in which the State had a controlling shareholding), rights to explore and exploit approximately half of the lignite deposits. No exploitation rights over the remaining deposits were granted to anyone. The Commission concluded that these arrangements infringed Article 106(1) in conjunction with Article 102[93] in that by granting and maintaining quasi-monopolistic lignite exploration rights in favour of PCC Greece had created inequality of opportunity between economic operators on the wholesale electricity market and thus distorted competition, thereby reinforcing the PCC's dominant position on that market.[94] *Greek Lignite* was an unusual case post-2000 in that it originated in an Article 106(3) infringement decision. The Commission's real problem in *Greek Lignite* was that it considered the situation in the Greek electricity market after liberalisation to be unsatisfactory. Unable to attack directly the Greek Government's failure to grant exploitation licences for the remaining deposits to PCC's competitors, it turned to the 'equality of opportunity' concept but did not identify what abuse PCC was being led to commit.

On appeal the GC annulled the decision.[95] It held that it was not enough to establish that a State measure simply distorted competition by creating inequality of opportunity. Rather, a breach of Article 106(1) in combination with Article 102 required an abuse to be identified. The GC distinguished the case from other cases discussed in this chapter because it considered that in those the way in which the undertaking was led, or would or could be led, to abuse its rights was identified. In this case, the Commission had held it was an infringement just to maintain PCC in a dominant position. However, the mere exercise of its licence could not amount to the undertaking extending its dominant position. On appeal by the Commission the CJ set aside the GC's judgment and referred the case back.[96] In the extract below, the Court deals first with the issue of inequality of opportunity and then with the issue of the extension of the dominant position. The undertaking had argued that the theory of the extension of the dominant position was governed by four conditions, which were not fulfilled here in that: (a) the State measure had not awarded DEI special or exclusive rights over a neighbouring and separate market; (b) DEI had no power to determine the activity of its competitors or impose costs upon them; (c) the Commission had not examined the impact on the interests of consumers; and (d) the Commission had defined lignite as an essential facility but had failed to show that it was in this case.

Case C-553/12 P, *Commission v Dimosia Epicheirisi Ilektrismou AE (DEI)* EU:C:2014:2083

Court of Justice

41. It should be noted that, according to the case-law, a Member State is in breach of the prohibitions laid down by Article [106(1)] in conjunction with Article [102] if it adopts any law, regulation or administrative provision that creates a situation in which a public undertaking or an undertaking on which it has

[93] COMP/38.700, *Greek Lignite* 5 March 2008.

[94] Ibid., paras. 190 and 238.

[95] Case T-169/08, *Dimosia Epicheirisi Ilektrismou AE (DEI) v Commission* EU:T:2012:448.

[96] Case T-169/08 RENV, *DEI v Commission* EU:T:2016:7333.

conferred special or exclusive rights, merely by exercising the preferential rights conferred upon it, is led to abuse its dominant position or when those rights are liable to create a situation in which that undertaking is led to commit such abuses (see, to that effect, the judgments in *Connect Austria*, . . ., paragraph 80, and *MOTOE*, . . . , paragraph 49 and the case-law cited). In that respect, it is not necessary that any abuse should actually occur (judgments in *GB-Inno-BM*, . . . , paragraphs 23 to 25; *Raso and Others*, . . ., paragraph 31; and *MOTOE*, . . . , paragraph 49).

42. Thus, a Member State will be in breach of those provisions where a measure imputable to a Member State gives rise to a risk of an abuse of a dominant position (see the judgment in *MOTOE*, . . ., paragraph 50 and the case-law cited).

43. It is clear from the Court's case-law that a system of undistorted competition, such as that provided for by the Treaty, can be guaranteed only if equality of opportunity is secured as between the various economic operators (see the judgments in *GB-Inno-BM*, . . . , paragraph 25; *MOTOE*, . . . , paragraph 51; and *Connect Austria*, . . . , paragraph 83 and case-law cited).

44. It follows that if inequality of opportunity between economic operators, and thus distorted competition, is the result of a State measure, such a measure constitutes an infringement of Article [106(1)] read together with Article [102] (see the judgment in *Connect Austria*, . . . , paragraph 84).

45. The Court has moreover had occasion to state in that regard that, although the mere fact that a Member State has created a dominant position by the grant of exclusive rights is not as such incompatible with Article [102], the EC Treaty none the less requires the Member States not to adopt or maintain in force any measure which might deprive that provision of its effectiveness (judgments in *ERT*, C-260/89, . . . , paragraph 35; *Corbeau*, C-320/91, . . . , paragraph 11; and *Deutsche Post*, C-147/97 and C-148/97, . . . , paragraph 39).

46. It follows from the matters addressed in paragraphs 41 to 45 above that, as the Advocate General states in point 55 of his Opinion, infringement of Article [106(1)] in conjunction with Article [102] may be established irrespective of whether any abuse actually exists. All that is necessary is for the Commission to identify a potential or actual anti-competitive consequence liable to result from the State measure at issue. Such an infringement may thus be established where the State measures at issue affect the structure of the market by creating unequal conditions of competition between companies, by allowing the public undertaking or the undertaking which was granted special or exclusive rights to maintain (for example by hindering new entrants to the market), strengthen or extend its dominant position over another market, thereby restricting competition, without it being necessary to prove the existence of actual abuse.

47. In those circumstances, it follows that, contrary to the General Court's analysis in paragraphs 105 and 118 of the judgment under appeal, it is sufficient to show that that potential or actual anti-competitive consequence is liable to result from the State measure at issue; it is not necessary to identify an abuse other than that which results from the situation brought about by the State measure at issue. It also follows that the General Court erred in law in holding that the Commission, by finding that DEI, a former monopolistic undertaking, continued to maintain a dominant position on the wholesale electricity market by virtue of the advantage conferred upon it by its privileged access to lignite and that that situation created inequality of opportunity on that market between the applicant and other undertakings, had neither identified nor established to a sufficient legal standard the abuse to which, within the meaning of Article [102], the State measure in question had led or could have led DEI.

. . .

65. In addition, the Court must disregard the claimed 'conditions of application' of the theory of the extension of a dominant position, which are summarised in paragraph 61 above and which, according to DEI, follow from the case-law of the Court.

66. It is settled case-law that practices by an undertaking in a dominant position which tend to extend that position to a neighbouring but separate market by distorting competition amount to abuse of a dominant position within the meaning of Article [102] (see, to that effect, the judgment in *Connect Austria*, . . . , paragraphs 81 and [102]and case-law cited).

67. Similarly, the Court has previously stated that the extension of a dominant position, without any objective justification, is prohibited 'as such' by Article [106(1)] in conjunction with Article [102], where that extension results from a State measure. As competition may not be eliminated in that manner, it may not be distorted either (see, to that effect, the judgments in *Spain and Others* v *Commission*, C-271/90, C-281/90 and C-289/90, . . . , paragraph 36, and *GB-Inno-BM*, . . . , paragraphs 21, 23 and 24).

68. It is therefore not necessary, as claimed by DEI, for the Commission to show, in every case, that the undertaking concerned enjoys a monopoly or that the State measure at issue awards it exclusive or special rights over a neighbouring and separate market, or that it has any regulatory powers. Having regard to the case-law referred to in paragraphs 41 to 44 above, the claim that there is an obligation on the Commission to show the impact of the infringement of the combined provisions of Articles [106(1)] and [102] on the interests of consumers must also be rejected; Article [102] may moreover cover practices which are harmful as a result of their impact on an effective competition structure (see, to that effect, the judgment in *Europemballage and Continental Can* v *Commission*, 6/72, . . . , paragraph 26). Finally, DEI's argument that the Commission defined lignite as an essential facility is based on a false premiss, as the Commission only referred to DEI's situation of 'quasi-monopoly' on the electricity wholesale market.

This judgment is highly significant. It establishes that inequality of opportunity 'and thus distorted competition' resulting from State measures constitutes an infringement of Article 106(1) in conjunction with Article 102 without any abuse occurring or existing. There needs simply to be identified 'a potential or actual anti-competitive consequence liable to result from the State measure'. An infringement can therefore be established where the measures affect the structure of the market by allowing the undertaking concerned to maintain, strengthen, or extend its dominant position over another market, without any necessity to identify any abuse other than that situation. Where the dominant position is extended as a result of the State measure, without any objective justification, it is prohibited 'as such'. Furthermore, there is no need to show an impact on the interests of consumers—the CJ referred back to *Continental Can*[97] in holding that Article 102 covers practices which are harmful to an effective competition structure.

(xiv) *Slovenská Pošta*

In *Slovakian Hybrid Mail Services*, another case involving a Commission decision, the delivery of hybrid mail[98] in Slovakia had been open to competition but by legislation in 2008 it was in effect 're-monopolised' and reserved to Slovenská Pošta, a State-owned undertaking. The service offered by Slovenská Pošta did not include many of the added features which the private operators had been offering and which customers valued.[99] The Commission held, on the basis of *Höfner*, that granting an exclusive right to an undertaking manifestly unable to satisfy the demand infringed Article 106 in conjunction with Article 102.[100] It was also a case of extending the public undertaking's monopoly—here from ordinary mail to hybrid mail. The decision was upheld.[101]

97 Case 6/72, *Europemballage Corp and Continental Can Co Inc v Commission* EU:C:1973:22, see Chap. 7.

98 Where the content is transferred electronically from the sender to the postal service operator who prints it out, puts it in envelopes, and sorts and delivers it.

99 Such as tracking services and seven days a week delivery.

100 COMP/39.562, 7 October 2008.

101 Case T-556/08, *Slovenská Pošta* EU:T:2015:189, *aff'd* by the CJ, Case C-293/15, EU:C:2016:511; see also Case C-437/09, *AG2R Prévoyance v Beaudout* EU:C:2011:112.

C. SUMMARY OF THE SITUATIONS WHICH INFRINGE ARTICLE 106(1) IN CONJUNCTION WITH ARTICLE 102

The cases discussed in the previous section variously establish that a Member State infringes Article 106(1) in conjunction with Article 102 if it creates a situation in which a public undertaking or one on which it has conferred special or exclusive rights cannot avoid committing an abuse, or is led to, or induced to, commit an abuse. This can be summed up as saying that a Member State infringes the provisions 'where a measure imputable to a Member State gives rise to a risk of an abuse of a dominant position'.[102] Measures may also infringe simply because they create inequality of opportunity and thus distorted competition. It is not possible to neatly categorise the case law and, even if it were, the categories would not be closed. However, looking at the cases already considered, and at others, one can identify the following.

(i) Inability to Meet Demand

Article 106(1) is infringed where a statutory monopoly is set up in such a way that it is incapable of meeting the demand in the reserved sector. This was the case in *Höfner v Macroton*,[103] *Job Centre Coop arl*,[104] *AG2R Prévoyance*,[105] and *Slovenská Pošta*.[106] *Merci Convenzionali* showed that Article 106(1) is infringed where the monopolist is enabled to behave inefficiently, exploit customers, and not modernise.[107] In *Ambulanz Glöckner*, the Advocate General discussed the possible causes for inefficiency or inability to meet demand. He considered that a Member State is only liable under Article 106(1) if the fault is in the system it has set up, and not where the only reason that an organisation is 'manifestly not able to satisfy demand' is inefficient management.[108] The CJ did not address this point in its judgment. Besides *Slovenská Pošta*, there are a number of other cases of this type in the postal[109] and telecommunications[110] sectors which have been the subject of Article 106(3) decisions. The abuses at issue under this head are violations of Article 102(b), 'limiting production, markets or technical development to the prejudice of consumers'.

(ii) The Cumulation of Rights Conferred on an Undertaking Create a Conflict of Interest

Cumulation of rights was an issue in *France v Commission*, *GB-INNO-BM*,[111] *ERT*,[112] *Raso*,[113] *Ambulanz Glöckner*,[114] and *MOTOE*[115] where some type of 'regulatory' function given to the monopoly would enable it to disadvantage competitors in a downstream market.

As already noted,[116] the CJ did not appear to find the dual role of the pension funds in *Albany* (as both managers of the scheme and the authority with power to grant exemptions whereby companies could be allowed to insure with other undertakings) to constitute a conflict of interest. The Court held the situation justified because '[e]xercise of that power of exemption involves an evaluation of

[102] Case 553/12 P, *DEI* EU:C:2014:2083, para. 42.
[103] See Section 5.B.ii. [104] Case C-55/96, EU:C:1997:603. [105] Case C-437/09, EU:C:2011:112.
[106] Case T-556/08, *Slovenská Pošta* EU:T:2015:189, *aff'd* Case C-293/15 P, EU:C:2016:511.
[107] See Section 5.B.iv.
[108] Case C-475/99, *Ambulanz Glöckner* EU:C:2001:284, Jacobs AG, para. 148.
[109] See *Dutch Express Delivery Services* [1994] OJ L10/47; *Spanish Express Courier Services* [1990] OJ L233/19.
[110] See *Italian GSM* [1995] OJ L280/49; *Spanish GSM* [1997] OJ L79/19.
[111] Case C-18/88, *RTT v GB-INNO-BM SA* EU:C:1991:474, see Section 5.B.v.
[112] Case C-260/89, *ERT* EU:C:1991:254, xx. [113] Case C-163/96, *Raso* EU:C:1998:54.
[114] Case C-475/99, *Ambulanz Glöckner* EU:C:2001:577. [115] Case C-49/07, *MOTOE* EU:C:2008:376, xx.
[116] See Section 5.B.viii.

complex data relating to the pension schemes involved and the financial equilibrium of the fund, which necessarily implies a wide margin of appreciation'.[117] It is unclear, however, whether the Court was applying Article 106(1) or Article 106(2) at this point.

(iii) The Extension of the Dominant Position

According to the CJ in *DEI* the extension of a dominant position, without any justification, is prohibited 'as such'.[118] As well as *DEI*, cases where Article 106(1) has been infringed by measures enabling an undertaking to extend its monopoly into neighbouring markets include *GB-INNO-BM* which can be classified under this head as well as head (ii) (cumulation of rights), as can *ERT*. The telecommunications case *France v Commission*[119] was also a matter of extension of rights as was *Connect Austria*.[120] In *Ambulanz Glöckner*, the consultation of the medical aid organisations by the authorities about the permit applications of other undertakings wishing to operate in the non-emergency market gave the aid organisations an advantage in the latter. The 'essential facilities' case, *Port of Rødby*,[121] concerned an infringement of Article 106(1) as the port authority was able to refuse access to the port it controlled, thus eliminating competition in a downstream market from a competitor ferry company.

(iv) Inequality of Opportunity and Distortion of Competition

Inequality of opportunity was an issue in a number of cases such as *France v Commission*, *GB-INNO-BM*, *Connect Austria*, and *MOTOE*. The CJ established in *DEI*[122] that a measure which creates inequality of opportunity and distorts competition thereby infringes Article 106(1) in conjunction with Article 102 without any need to identify any abuse. Rather, what needs to be shown is a potential or actual anti-competitive consequence. Inequality of opportunity concentrates on the duty of the Member State to fulfil its Treaty obligations rather than on the conduct of parties.[123]

(v) Pricing Abuses

Undertakings with exclusive rights may be enabled to commit pricing abuses. Price discrimination has featured in a number of cases concerning the conduct of undertakings given control over transport infrastructures.[124] *GT-Link*, where the port authority was guilty of price discrimination in waiving harbour duties in respect of its own ferry services and those of its partners but charging them to its competitors on the ferry market, is also a case of cumulation of rights and where the undertaking was extending its monopoly into a downstream market.[125] In *Silvano Raso*, the undertaking had imposed unduly high labour costs on its downstream competitors,[126] and Deutsche Post would have

[117] Case C-67/96, *Albany* EU:C:1999:430, para. 119. Jacobs AG was not so sanguine and considered that Art. 106(1) was infringed, see paras. 441–468 of EU:C:1999:28.

[118] Case C-553/12 P, *DEI* EU:C:2014:2083, see Section 5.B.xiii.

[119] Case C-202/88, *France v Commission* EU:C:1991:120, Section 5.B.i, p. 593.

[120] Case C-462/99, *Connect Austria* EU:C:2003:297.

[121] [1994] OJ L55/52, see Chap. 7.

[122] Case C-553/12 P, *DEI* EU:C:2014:2083.

[123] Van Bael and Bellis, n. 1, 921–922.

[124] See e.g. Case C-266/96, *Corsica Ferries France* EU:C:1998:306 (discussed in Section 6.E.iii, p. xx); Case C-163/99, *Portugal v Commission* EU:C:2001:189 (concerning landing fees at Portuguese airports); *Spanish Airports* [2000] OJ L208/36.

[125] Case C-242/95, *GT-Link A/S v Danske Statsbaner (DSB)* EU:C:1997:376 where the Court in effect imposed on undertakings in this position an obligation to maintain a transparent accounting system demonstrating that they did not favour their own operations. Otherwise they would not be able to avoid a finding of abuse.

[126] Case C-163/96, *Silvano Raso* EU:C:1998:54.

committed an abuse if it had charged both terminal dues and the full internal postage.[127] In *OSA*, the CJ held that excessive prices charged by a collecting society could be an abuse.[128]

(vi) Refusal to Supply

There may be a refusal to supply in cases involving an exclusive right to control 'essential facilities', as in *Port of Rødby* where the refusal was to enable an extension of the monopoly downstream.[129] The refusal to deliver incoming cross-border mail in *Deutsche Post*[130] unless extra payments were made was treated as a refusal to supply. The refusal of the exclusive rights holder in *Merci Convenzionali* to allow the vessel's crew to do the work themselves can also be seen as a type of refusal of access.[131]

(vii) 'Automatic' Abuse

In *Corbeau*,[132] the Court found an infringement without seeking to identify any abuse. It appeared to consider that a monopoly which was too wide infringed Article 106(1) for that reason alone and did not identify any abuse. Buendia Sierra calls it the 'automatic abuse doctrine'.[133] No other case is such a clear example of this, though Buendia Sierra detects the same approach in *Deutsche Post* and *Dusseldorp*. In all these cases, the Court was considering Article 106(1) en route to discussing the application of Article 106(2). In *Albany*,[134] the nature of the abuse was not clear, and the CJ concentrated on the application of Article 106(2). The Court did not however seem to be suggesting that the monopoly was too wide.

6. ARTICLE 106(2)

A. THE INSTITUTIONAL SETTING OF SERVICES OF GENERAL ECONOMIC INTEREST

(i) Article 14 TFEU and Protocols 26 and 29

The Treaty of Amsterdam added a new 'Principle', latterly Article 16, to the EC Treaty.[135] Article 16, expanded by the Treaty of Lisbon, is now Article 14 TFEU.

a. Article 14 TFEU

> Without prejudice to Article 4 of the Treaty on European Union or to Articles 93,[136] 106 and 107[137] of this Treaty, and given the place occupied by services of general economic interest in the shared values of the Union as well as their role in promoting social and territorial cohesion, the Union and the Member States, each within their respective powers and within the scope of application of the Treaties, shall take care that such services operate on the basis of

[127] Cases C-147–148/97, *Deutsche Post* EU:C:2000:74. [128] Case C-351/12, *OSA* EU:C:2014:110.
[129] [1994] OJ L55/52. [130] Cases C-147–148/97, *Deutsche Post* EU:C:2000:74. See Section 5.B.ix.
[131] Case C-179/90, *Merci Convenzionali* EU:C:1991:464.
[132] Case C-320/91, *Corbeau* EU:C:1993:198, Section 5.B.vi. [133] Buendia Sierra in Faull and Nikpay, n. 1, 6.77.
[134] Case C-67/96, *Albany* EU:C:1999:430, Section 5.B.viii.
[135] M. Ross, 'Art. 16 EC and Services of General Interest: From Derogation to Obligation?' (2000) 25 *ELRev* 22.
[136] Art. 93 TFEU is a specific provision dealing with State aid in the transport sector.
[137] Art. 107 TFEU is the general provision on State aid.

> principles and conditions, particularly economic and financial conditions, which enable them to fulfil their missions. The European Parliament and the Council, acting by means of regulations in accordance with the ordinary legislative procedure, shall establish these principles and set these conditions without prejudice to the competence of Member States, in compliance with the Treaties, to provide, to commission and to fund such services.

The two additions which did not appear in Article 16 EC are the phrase 'particularly economic and financial conditions' towards the end of the first sentence, and the whole of the second sentence.

Article 14 must be read in the context of the post-Lisbon Treaties as a whole. As explained in Chapter 1, according to Article 2 the Union is founded on values common to the Member States, which are 'respect for human dignity, freedom, democracy, equality, the rule of law and respect for human rights, including the rights of persons belonging to minorities', and Article 3 TEU states that the Union is working for the sustainable development of Europe based on a highly competitive *social market* economy.

b. Protocol (No. 26) on Services of General Interest

A Protocol on *services of general interest* (rather than just SGEIs) was attached to the TEU and TFEU by the Treaty of Lisbon.

> **Article 1**
>
> The shared values of the Union in respect of services of general economic interest within the meaning of Article 14 of the Treaty on the Functioning of the European Union include in particular:
>
> – the essential role and the wide discretion of national, regional and local authorities in providing, commissioning and organising services of general economic interest as closely as possible to the needs of the users;
>
> – the diversity between various services of general economic interest and the differences in the needs and preferences of users that may result from different geographical, social or cultural situations;
>
> – a high level of quality, safety and affordability, equal treatment and the promotion of universal access and of user rights.
>
> **Article 2**
>
> The provisions of the Treaties do not affect in any way the competence of Member States to provide, commission and organise non-economic services of general interest.

The Protocol therefore contains two Articles, one expanding on the meaning of Article 14 TFEU, and one which states that the Treaties do not in any way affect the competence of Member States in respect to non-economic services of *general interest.*

c. Protocol 29 on Public Broadcasting

Protocol 29 provides, subject to conditions, that the provisions of the Treaties are without prejudice to the competence of Member States to provide for the funding of public service broadcasting.

(ii) Article 36 of the Charter of Fundamental Rights

Article 36 of the Charter of Fundamental Rights of the European Union, entitled 'Access to Services of General Economic Interest', states:

> The Union recognises and respects access to services of general economic interest as provided for in national laws and practices, in accordance with the Treaties, in order to promote the social and territorial cohesion of the Union.

This provision is about *access to* SGEIs rather than to their content or establishment because the Charter is about *rights*. It appears in Chapter IV of the Charter, 'Solidarity', and elevates access to SGEIs to the status of a fundamental right.

(iii) Commission Communications on Services of General Economic Interest and Services of General Interest

The Commission has issued a number of Communications and other documents on SGEIs and services of general interest.[138] SGEIs are relevant to State aid as well as to the antitrust provisions (see Section 7) and a package of measures on SGEIs and State aid were adopted in 2012[139] to deal, inter alia, with the issues in the *Altmark* case,[140] and on SGEIs and public procurement.

B. THE CONCEPTS AND TERMINOLOGY OF 'SERVICES OF GENERAL ECONOMIC INTEREST' AND 'SERVICES OF GENERAL INTEREST'

The phrase '*services of general economic interest*' (SGEIs) has appeared in what is now Article 106(2) TFEU, since the inception of the EEC.[141] It has appeared in what is now Article 14 TFEU since 1999, as already explained. It now appears in Protocol 26 and Article 36 of the Charter as well. Article 106(2) gives a limited derogation from (inter alia) the competition rules to undertakings entrusted with such services, in certain circumstances. What amounts to an SGEI is the subject of a considerable body of case law. The phrase is an unhappy one because of the placing of the word 'economic'. It is the service to which the word 'economic' really applies, rather than the 'interest'. It also overlaps with the concept of a service of *general interest*. The words *service of general interest* appear only in Protocol 26.

In the 2011 Communication, the Commission set out what it understands by these 'dynamic and evolving' concepts.[142]

> Service of general interest (SGI): SGI are services that public authorities of the Member States classify as being of general interest and, therefore, subject to specific public service obligations (PSO). The term covers both economic activities (see the definition of SGEI below) and non-economic services. The latter are not subject to specific EU legislation and are not covered by the internal market and competition rules of the Treaty. Some aspects of how these services are organised may be subject to other general Treaty rules, such as the principle of non-discrimination.
>
> Service of general economic interest (SGEI): SGEI are economic activities which deliver outcomes in the overall public good that would not be supplied (or would be supplied under different conditions in terms of quality, safety, affordability, equal treatment or universal access) by the market without public intervention. The PSO is imposed on the provider by way of an entrustment and on the basis of a general interest criterion which ensures that the service is provided under conditions allowing it to fulfil its mission.

[138] See particularly Communication on Services of General Interest [2001] OJ C17/4 and Communication on 'A Quality Framework for Services of General Interest in Europe', COM(2011) 900 final. See also the 2007 Communication (COM(2007) 725 final), n. 4, which followed the Commission's Green and White Papers of 2003 and 2004, COM(2003) 270 final and COM(2004) 374, 12 May 2004, respectively.

[139] Including EU Framework for State aid in the form of public service compensation [2012] OJ C8/15 (the SGEI Framework).

[140] Case C-280/00, *Altmark Trans GmbH, Regierungspräsidium Magdeburg v Nahverkehrsgesellschaft Altmark GmbH* EU:C:2003:415, see Section 7.

[141] See A. Maziarz, 'Services of General Economic Interest: Towards Common Values?', *EStAL* 1/2016, 16, available at <https://ssrn.com/abstract=2663713>; M. Varju, 'Conflict and Complementarity: EU Obligations, Member State Interests and Services of General Interest' (2017) 23(2) *European Public Law* 347.

[142] Previously explained in the 2001 and 2007 Communications, see n. 138.

Social services of general interest (SSGI): these include social security schemes covering the main risks of life and a range of other essential services provided directly to the person that play a preventive and socially cohesive/inclusive role . . . While some social services (such as statutory social security schemes) are not considered by the European Court as being economic activities, the jurisprudence of the Court makes clear that the social nature of a service is not sufficient in itself to classify it as non-economic . . . The term social service of general interest consequently covers both economic and non-economic activities.

Universal service obligation (USO): USO are a type of PSO which sets the requirements designed to ensure that certain services are made available to all consumers and users in a Member State, regardless of their geographical location, at a specified quality and, taking account of specific national circumstances, at an affordable price. The definition of specific USO are set at European level as an essential component of market liberalization of service sectors, such as electronic communications, post and transport.

Public service: Public service is used in article 93 TFEU in the field of transport. However, outside this area, the term is sometimes used in an ambiguous way: it can relate to the fact that a service is offered to the general public and/or in the public interest, or it can be used for the activity of entities in public ownership. To avoid ambiguity, this Communication does not use the term but follows the terminology 'service of general interest' and 'service of general economic interest'.

The Commission therefore makes it clear that SGEIs are a subset of services of general interest (SGIs). SGIs comprise both non-economic (non-market) services to which the competition and internal market rules[143] do not apply in the first place, and SGEIs which supply economic (market) services. Whether a service falls into the category of 'economic' or 'non-economic' services depends on the application of the concept of an 'economic activity'. It is 'economic' services, SGEIs, which are the subject of Article 106(2).

C. THE PURPOSE OF ARTICLE 106(2)

Article 106(2) provides a limited derogation from the Treaty rules to deal with the activities of undertakings entrusted by the State with certain tasks.[144] It provides that the Treaty rules apply to two sorts of undertaking—revenue-producing monopolies and those entrusted with SGEIs—only insofar as that does not obstruct the performance of their tasks. It is subject to the proviso that the exception should not affect trade to an extent contrary to the interests of the Union. Unlike Article 106(1), Article 106(2) is addressed to undertakings and not to Member States, although Member States may rely on Article 106(2)[145] and, as we have seen, the two provisions may be applied together. As with Article 106(1), the competition rules are singled out for special mention and Article 106(2) is particularly important in relation to the application of Article 102. The purpose of Article 106(2) is to deal with market failures, i.e. SGEIs are services that the State considers should be provided but for which the market cannot adequately provide, as explained in the extract from the 2011 Communication set out earlier.[146]

143 Other EU rules, such as the principle of non-discrimination may, however, apply.

144 See generally J. M. Burke, *A Critical Account of Article 106(2) TFEU* (Hart Publishing, 2018). The text of Art. 106(2) is set out in Section 4.

145 See e.g. Case C-203/96, *Dusseldorp* EU:C:1998:316.

146 See A. M. Collins and M. Martínez Navarro, 'Economic Activity, Market Failure and Services of General Economic Interest: It Takes Two to Tango' (2021) 12 *JECLAP* 380.

D. UNDERTAKINGS HAVING THE CHARACTER OF A REVENUE-PRODUCING MONOPOLY

This is a reference to undertakings which exploit their exclusive rights to raise revenue for the State. They may constitute commercial monopolies and so be subject to the rules laid down in Article 37 TFEU. Article 37 applies to 'any body through which a Member State, in law or in fact, either directly or indirectly supervises, determines or appreciably influences imports or exports between Member States'. Article 37 appears among the free movement provisions, but the CJ has said that it aims to eliminate distortions in competition in the internal market as well as discrimination against the products and trade of other Member States.[147]

E. UNDERTAKINGS ENTRUSTED WITH THE OPERATION OF SERVICES OF GENERAL ECONOMIC INTEREST

(i) 'Undertakings Entrusted With . . . '

'Undertaking' has the meaning previously discussed.[148] The legal status of the undertaking in national law is immaterial. It can be a public or private undertaking, but the State must have assigned it certain tasks by a positive act conferring on it certain functions or by granting it a concession. Merely tolerating, approving, or endorsing its activities is insufficient. Therefore the Member States' approval of the Eurocheque system did not mean that Article 106(2) applied to the banks concerned.[149] The CJ has held that an authors' rights society was not within the provision merely because it was subject to obligations imposed on all monopolies by national law[150] but the Commission has left open the question of whether a rights society might be 'entrusted' if the Member State's legislation described the functions and status of the society in an appropriate way.[151] The CJ held that the collecting society in *OSA* was not within Article 106(2) as although it was given exclusive rights to manage certain copyrights the State had not assigned any tasks to it and it managed private interests (albeit intellectual property rights were protected by law).[152] In *Dusseldorp*, the Advocate General said that an undertaking is 'entrusted' with a service where 'certain obligations are imposed on it by the State in the general economic interest'.[153] In *Spain v Commission*, the CJ agreed with the GC requiring 'the presence of an act of a public authority entrusting SGEI tasks to the operators at issue and of the universal and compulsory nature of those tasks, together with a statement as to the nature and duration of the public service obligations, the undertakings and territory concerned'.[154]

'Entrustment' was considered at length by the GC in *BUPA*.[155] The Irish Government introduced a risk equalisation scheme in respect of private medical insurance (PMI) following the liberalisation of the sector. Under the scheme, insurers with a risk profile below the average were liable to pay a levy and those with a profile above the average were entitled to receive payments. The result of this was in effect to transfer funds from the private insurer, BUPA, to other operators. BUPA claimed that this amounted to illegal State aid. The question arose as to whether or not the PMI scheme adopted

[147] For a discussion of Art. 37 see Bellamy and Child (D. Bailey and L. John, eds.), *European Union Law of Competition* (8th edn, Oxford University Press, 2018), 11.037–11.046.

[148] See Chaps. 4 and 6. [149] *Uniform Eurocheques* [1985] OJ L35/43. [150] *GEMA* [1971] OJ L134/15.

[151] COMP/38.698, *CISAC Agreement*, on appeal decisions partially annulled on other grounds, Cases T-442/08 etc., *CISAC v Commission* EU:T:2013:188.

[152] Case C-351/12, *OSA* EU:C:2014:110, para. 81.

[153] Case C-203/96, *Dusseldorp* EU:C:1997:508, Jacobs AG, para. 103.

[154] Case C-114/17, *Spain v Commission* EU:C:2018:753, para. 87.

[155] Case T-289/03, *BUPA v Commission* EU:T:2008:29.

by Ireland had an SGEI mission. The question was relevant as compensation paid for the supply of SGEIs may not, in certain conditions, constitute State aid.[156] On appeal from the Commission decision holding that on these grounds the scheme did not constitute State aid, BUPA claimed that the insurers had not been 'entrusted' with an SGEI mission as required by Article 106(2). It argued that the existence of an SGEI was precluded because all PMI insurers were subject to certain obligations. The GC rejected this. Although it drew a distinction between a State imposing general regulatory rules on a sector and entrusting undertakings with an SGEI mission, it said that it did not follow that an SGEI could not be entrusted to a number of undertakings active on the same market.[157] Being entrusted with an SGEI did not necessarily mean that an undertaking had to be granted a special or exclusive right. It was therefore not required that each undertaking concerned had to be individually entrusted with the SGEI rather than just being subject to the scheme laid down by the State.[158]

(ii) Operation of Services of General Economic Interest

'Services' covers a wide spectrum of activities and is not limited to the meaning of the term as used in the free movement provisions. As we have already noted, 'services of general economic interest' denote activities that need to be carried out in the public interest.

In the *Telecommunications Equipment* case, the CJ explained that Article 106(2) reconciles the interests of Member States and the Union:[159]

> In allowing derogations to be made from the general rules of the Treaty in certain circumstances, that provision seeks to reconcile the Member States' interest in using certain undertakings, in particular in the public sector, as an instrument of economic or fiscal policy with the Community's interest in ensuring compliance with the rules on competition and the preservation of the unity of the common market.

Further, this passage refers to undertakings which are used as instruments of economic or fiscal policy. In *Albany International*, the CJ applied the same principle to social policy.[160] In *BUPA*, as seen in the next extract (paragraph 172), the GC stated that an SGEI has to satisfy certain minimum criteria derived from the case law. These are, in addition to the act of entrusting, that the mission has to be 'universal' and 'compulsory'. Within those criteria the Member States have a wide discretion. The standard of review of that discretion is whether the Member State has made a 'manifest error of assessment'.[161]

The EU Courts or the Commission have accepted as SGEIs, inter alia, the administration of major waterways;[162] the operation of non-economically viable air routes;[163] the operation of the electricity supply network;[164] the distribution of water;[165] the operation of the basic, as distinct from extra

[156] Case C-280/00, *Altmark* EU:C:2003:415, see Section 7, p. xx.

[157] Ibid., para. 179, expressly confirming paras. 14 and 15 of the 2001 Communication.

[158] Ibid., paras. 178–184.

[159] Case C-202/88, *France v Commission* EU:C:1991:120, para. 12; see also Case C-157/94, *Commission v Netherlands (Re Electricity Imports)* EU:C:1997:499, para. 39.

[160] Case C-67/96, *Albany* EU:C: 1999:430, paras. 103–105.

[161] The GC in para. 167 of *BUPA*, approved para. 22 of the Commission's 2001 Communication to this effect.

[162] Case 10/71, *Ministère Public of Luxembourg v Muller* EU:C:1971:85.

[163] Case 66/86, *Ahmed Saeed* EU:C:1989:140.

[164] Case C-393/92, *Gemeente Almelo* EU:C:1994:171; in Case C-157/94, *Commission v Netherlands (Re Electricity Imports)* EU:C:1997:499 the Commission did not contest that the monopoly electricity distributor in the Netherlands provided a service of general economic interest.

[165] *Navewa-Anseau* [1982] OJ L167/48.

'added-value', postal service;[166] the operation of public telecommunications networks;[167] television services;[168] employment recruitment;[169] mooring services in ports;[170] the treatment of waste;[171] regional development;[172] sectoral supplementary pension funds;[173] the performance of obligations flowing from the Universal Postal Convention;[174] the provision of emergency ambulance services;[175] and the provision of private medical insurance.[176] The CJ did not accept that commercial port operations are SGEIs[177] and it has sometimes left open the status of the services provided, and said that even if they were of general economic interest the other criteria in Article 106(2) were not fulfilled.[178]

Extracts from the judgments in the leading cases on what amounts to an SGEI are set out in Section 6.E.iii as they usually deal also with the question of whether non-compliance with the Treaty rules is essential to the fulfilment of the entrusted tasks. However, the following extract from *BUPA*, the facts of which have already been given, deals with the width of the Member States' discretion to define SGEIs and with what is meant by 'universal service'.

Case T-289/03, *BUPA v Commission* EU:T:2008:29

General Court

167. That prerogative of the Member State concerning the definition of SGEIs is confirmed by the absence of any competence specially attributed to the Commission and by the absence of a precise and complete definition of the concept of SGEI in Community law. The determination of the nature and scope of an SGEI mission in specific spheres of action which either do not fall within the powers of the Community, within the meaning of the first paragraph of Article [5 TEU], or are based on only limited or shared Community competence, within the meaning of the second paragraph of that article,[179] remains, in principle, within the competence of the Member States. As the defendant and Ireland maintain, the health sector falls almost exclusively within the competence of the Member States. In that sector, the Community can engage, under Article [168 TFEU] and [5 TEU], only in action which is not legally binding, while fully respecting the responsibilities of the Member States for the organisation and provision of health services and medical care. It follows that the determination of SGEI obligations in this context also falls primarily within the competence of the Member States. That division of powers is also reflected, generally, in Article [14 TFEU], which provides that, given the place occupied

[166] *Dutch Courier Services* [1990] OJ L10/47; *Spanish Courier Services* [1990] OJ L233/19; Case C-320/91, *Corbeau* EU:C:1993:198.

[167] Case 41/83, *Italy v Commission* EU:C:1985:120.

[168] Case 155/73, *Sacchi* EU:C:1974:40.

[169] Case 41/90, *Höfner* EU:C:1991:161.

[170] Case C-266/96, *Corsica Ferries France SA v Gruppo Antichi Ormeggiatori del Porto di Genova* EU:C:1998:306.

[171] Case C-209/98, *Sydhavnens* EU:C:2000:279.

[172] Case T-260/94, *Air Inter v Commission* EU:T:1994:265, para. 40, see Section 6.E.iii, p. 646.

[173] Case C-67/96, *Albany* EU:C:1999:430.

[174] Joined Cases C-147–148/97, *Deutsche Post* EU:C:2000:74.

[175] Case C-475/99, *Ambulanz Glöckner* EU:C:2001:577. Jacobs AG considered that non-emergency ambulance services were also services of general economic interest, see para. 175 of EU:C:2001:284.

[176] Case T-289/03, *BUPA* EU:T:2008:29; see M. G. Ross, 'A Healthy Approach to Services of General Economic Interest? The *BUPA* Judgment of the Court of First Instance' (2009) 34 *ELRev* 127.

[177] Case C-179/90, *Merci Convenzionali* EU:C:1991:464; Case C-242/95, *GT-Link v De Danske Statsbaner (DSB)* EU:C:1997:376.

[178] E.g. Case C-203/96, *Dusseldorp* EU:C:1998:316.

[179] Art. 5 TEU replaced Art. 5 EC to which this judgment actually refers. Both Articles deal with the competence of respectively the EU and the EC. Art. 5 TEU is more detailed and specific but does not alter the principle upon which the GC relied here.

by SGEIs in the shared values of the Union as well as their role in promoting social and territorial cohesion, the Community and the Member States, each within their respective powers and within the scope of application of the Treaty, are to take care that such services operate on the basis of principles and conditions which enable them to fulfil their missions.

168. In that regard, the applicants cannot validly rely on Case 41/83 *Italy v Commission*, paragraph 100 above (paragraph 30), to demonstrate the need for full and unrestricted control by the Community institutions of the existence of an SGEI mission in the health sector . . .

169. Consequently, the control which the Community institutions are authorised to exercise over the use of the discretion of the Member State in determining SGEIs is limited to ascertaining whether there is a manifest error of assessment. In the contested decision (recital 44), the Commission did in fact exercise that control by considering whether Ireland's assessment of the presence of an SGEI mission and of the characterisation of the PMI obligations as SGEI obligations was vitiated by a manifest error.

170. Accordingly, the complaint that the Commission unlawfully delegated to the Irish authorities the definition of the SGEIs in question and that it failed to exercise full and unrestricted control of the assessment made by those authorities with respect to a strict and objective definition of the SGEIs in Community law cannot be upheld.

iii) The existence of an SGEI mission in the present case

172. . . . In that regard, the Court notes at the outset that even though the Member State has a wide discretion when determining what it regards as an SGEI, that does not mean that it is not required, when it relies on the existence of and the need to protect an SGEI mission, to ensure that that mission satisfies certain minimum criteria common to every SGEI mission within the meaning of the EC Treaty, as explained in the case-law, and to demonstrate that those criteria are indeed satisfied in the particular case. These are, notably, the presence of an act of the public authority entrusting the operators in question with an SGEI mission and the universal and compulsory nature of that mission. Conversely, the lack of proof by the Member State that those criteria are satisfied, or failure on its part to observe them, may constitute a manifest error of assessment, in which case the Commission is required to make a finding to that effect, failing which the Commission itself makes a manifest error. Furthermore, it follows from the case-law on Article [106(2)] that the Member State must indicate the reasons why it considers that the service in question, because of its specific nature, deserves to be characterised as an SGEI and to be distinguished from other economic activities (see, to that effect, *Merci Convenzionali Porto di Genova*, paragraph 97 above, paragraph 27, and *Enirisorse*, paragraph 131 above, paragraphs 33 and 34). In the absence of such reasons, even a marginal review by the Community institutions . . . with respect to the existence of a manifest error by the Member State in the context of its discretion would not be possible.

173. It is in the light of those considerations that the Court will examine the complaints whereby the applicants seek to demonstrate that in this case the Commission was wrong to accept the existence of an SGEI mission.

. . .

4) The universal and compulsory nature of the services coming within the SGEI mission

General observations

186. As regards the universal nature of the PMI services, it must be noted at the outset that, contrary to the theory put forward by the applicants, it does not follow from Community law that, in order to be capable of being characterised as an SGEI, the service in question must constitute a universal service in the strict sense, such as the public social security scheme. In effect, the concept of universal service, within the meaning of Community law, does not mean that the service in question must respond to a need common to the whole population or be supplied throughout a territory (see, in that regard, *Ahmed Saeed Flugreisen*, paragraph 181 above, paragraph 55; *Corsica*

Ferries France, paragraph 97 above, paragraph 45; and *Olsen v Commission*, paragraph 166 above, paragraph 186 et seq.). As stated at recital 47 to the contested decision, with reference to paragraph 14 of the communication on SGEIs, although those characteristics correspond to the classical type of SGEI, and the one most widely encountered in Member States, that does not preclude the existence of other, equally lawful, types of SGEIs which the Member States may validly choose to create in the exercise of their discretion.

187. Accordingly, the fact that the SGEI obligations in question have only a limited territorial or material application or that the services concerned are enjoyed by only a relatively limited group of users does not necessarily call in question the universal nature of an SGEI mission within the meaning of Community law. It follows that the applicants' restrictive understanding of the universal nature of an SGEI, based on certain Commission reports or documents, the content of which, moreover, is not legally binding, is not compatible with the scope of the discretion which Member States have when defining an SGEI mission. Consequently, that argument must be rejected as unfounded.

188. As regards the argument that the PMI services represent only optional, indeed 'luxury', financial services, intended to provide complementary or supplementary cover by reference to the compulsory universal services provided for by the public health insurance system, the Court observes that the compulsory nature of the service in question is an essential condition of the existence of an SGEI mission within the meaning of Community law. That compulsory nature must be understood as meaning that the operators entrusted with the SGEI mission by an act of a public authority are, in principle, required to offer the service in question on the market in compliance with the SGEI obligations which govern the supply of that service. From the point of view of the operator entrusted with an SGEI mission, that compulsory nature—which in itself is contrary to business freedom and the principle of free competition—may consist, inter alia, particularly in the case of the grant of an exclusive or special right, in an obligation to exercise a certain commercial activity independently of the costs associated with that activity (see also, to that effect, paragraph 14 of the communication on SGEIs). In such a case, that obligation constitutes the counterpart of the protection of the SGEI mission and of the associated market position by the act which entrusted the mission. In the absence of an exclusive or special right, the compulsory nature of an SGEI mission may lie in the obligation borne by the operator in question, and provided for by an act of a public authority, to offer certain services to every citizen requesting them (see also, to that effect, paragraph 15 of the communication on SGEIs).

189. Contrary to the applicants' opinion, however, the binding nature of the SGEI mission does not presuppose that the public authorities impose on the operator concerned an obligation to provide a service having a clearly predetermined content . . . In effect, the compulsory nature of the SGEI mission does not preclude a certain latitude being left to the operator on the market, including in relation to the content and pricing of the services which it proposes to provide. In those circumstances, a minimum of freedom of action on the part of operators and, accordingly, of competition on the quality and content of the services in question is ensured, which is apt to limit, in the community interest, the scope of the restriction of competition which generally results from the attribution of an SGEI mission, without any effect on the objectives of that mission.

190. It follows that, in the absence of an exclusive or special right, it is sufficient, in order to conclude that a service is compulsory, that the operator entrusted with a particular mission is under an obligation to provide that service to any user requesting it. In other words, the compulsory nature of the service and, accordingly, the existence of an SGEI mission are established if the service-provider is obliged to contract, on consistent conditions, without being able to reject the other contracting party. That element makes it possible to distinguish a service forming part of an SGEI mission from any other service provided on the market and, accordingly, from any other activity carried out in complete freedom (see, to that effect, *GT-Link*, paragraph 97 above, paragraph 53, and *Merci Convenzionali Porto di Genova*, paragraph 97 above, paragraph 27).

The PMI scheme did therefore have an SGEI mission, despite it not being 'a universal service in the strict sense' of responding to a need common to the entire population or being supplied throughout a territory. It did not matter that there was a limited territorial or material application or that the services concerned were enjoyed by only a relatively limited group of users (paragraph 187). The important thing was the compulsory nature of the service and the fact that the service provider was obliged to contract, on consistent conditions, and could not refuse the other contracting party (paragraph 190). It is these features which define an SGEI.

(iii) Obstruct the Performance of the Particular Tasks Assigned to Them

Even if an activity is accepted as an SGEI it must still be shown that compliance with the Treaty rules would 'obstruct the performance' of the particular tasks assigned to the undertaking.

In *Höfner*, the CJ accepted that the Bundesanstalt had been entrusted with SGEIs but said that such an undertaking remained subject to the competition rules 'unless and to the extent to which it is shown that their application is *incompatible* with the discharge of its duties'[180] (emphasis added); in *Merci Convenzionali*[181] it said that even if SGEIs had been involved it would not have been necessary for the undertaking to infringe the Treaty rules; in *British Telecom*[182] it said that Italy had failed to establish that compliance by BT with the competition rules would obstruct it in carrying out its tasks; and in *GB-INNO-BM*[183] it did not accept that the undertaking entrusted with the public telephone network also needed power to lay down the standards for telephone equipment and to check rival equipment suppliers' compliance with them.[184]

From *Corbeau* in 1993[185] the EU Courts became more willing to accept that public service providers may need protection from the full rigours of competition and became more flexible in the way in which the criteria in Article 106(2) are applied. In *Corbeau*, the CJ recognised that Article 106(2) contains what is in effect a proportionality requirement in that the derogation from the competition rules applies only insofar as observance of the rules would obstruct the performance of the SGEI. Further, the Court recognised in *Corbeau* that the entrusted undertaking must have 'economically acceptable' conditions in which to perform its tasks. The lack of such conditions is likely to obstruct it. In the subsequent cases, we see that this has meant allowing cross-subsidisation, the maintenance of a satisfactory income-stream, and the prevention of cherry-picking/cream-skimming insofar as this satisfies the proportionality test.

In Section 5.B.vi, we saw that in *Corbeau* itself the CJ, in considering the Belgian postal monopoly, seemed to say that under Article 106(1) Member States may grant special or exclusive rights only insofar as they entrust undertakings with SGEIs and the criteria in Article 106(2) are fulfilled.[186] It then looked at the application of Article 106(2).

Case C-320/91, *Corbeau* EU:C:1993:198

Court of Justice

15. As regards the services at issue in the main proceedings, it cannot be disputed that the Régie des Postes is entrusted with a service of general economic interest consisting in the obligation to collect, carry and distribute mail on behalf of all users throughout the territory of the Member State

[180] Case C-41/90, *Höfner v Macrotron* EU:C:1991:161, para. 24.

[181] Case C-179/90, *Merci Convenzionali* EU:C:1991:464.

[182] Case 41/83, *Italy v Commission* EU:C:1985:120.

[183] Case C-18/88, *RTT v GB-INNO-BM SA* EU:C:1991:474.

[184] See also Case 66/86, *Ahmed Saeed* EU:C:1989:140; Commission Decision, *Dutch Courier Services* [1990] OJ L10/47.

[185] Case C-320/91, *Corbeau* EU:C:1993:198.

[186] Ibid., para. 14.

concerned, at uniform tariffs and on similar quality conditions, irrespective of the specific situations or the degree of economic profitability of each individual operation.

16. The question which falls to be considered is therefore the extent to which a restriction on competition or even the exclusion of all competition from other economic operators is necessary in order to allow the holder of the exclusive right to perform its task of general interest and in particular to have the benefit of economically acceptable conditions.

17. The starting point of such an examination must be the premise that the obligation on the part of the undertaking entrusted with that task to perform its services in conditions of economic equilibrium presupposes that it will be possible to offset less profitable sectors against the profitable sectors and hence justifies a restriction of competition from individual undertakings where the economically profitable sectors are concerned.

18. Indeed, to authorize individual undertakings to compete with the holder of the exclusive rights in the sectors of their choice corresponding to those rights would make it possible for them to concentrate on the economically profitable operations and to offer more advantageous tariffs than those adopted by the holders of the exclusive rights since, unlike the latter, they are not bound for economic reasons to offset losses in the unprofitable sectors against profits in the more profitable sectors.

19. However, the exclusion of competition is not justified as regards specific services dissociable from the service of general interest which meet special needs of economic operators and which call for certain additional services not offered by the traditional postal service, such as collection from the senders' address, greater speed or reliability of distribution or the possibility of changing the destination in the course of transit, in so far as such specific services, by their nature and the conditions in which they are offered, such as the geographical area in which they are provided, do not compromise the economic equilibrium of the service of general economic interest performed by the holder of the exclusive right.

20. It is for the national court to consider whether the services at issue in the dispute before it meet those criteria.

21. The answer to the questions referred to the Court by the Tribunal Correctionnel de Liège should therefore be that it is contrary to Article [106] for legislation of a Member State which confers on a body such as the Régie des Postes the exclusive right to collect, carry and distribute mail, to prohibit, under threat of criminal penalties, an economic operator established in that State from offering certain specific services dissociable from the service of general interest which meet the special needs of economic operators and call for certain additional services not offered by the traditional postal service, in so far as those services do not compromise the economic equilibrium of the service of general economic interest performed by the holder of the exclusive right. It is for the national court to consider whether the services in question in the main proceedings meet those criteria.

In this judgment, the Court accepted that the operation of a basic postal system providing a universal service is an SGEI and that the normal principles of competition law will not apply to the extent necessary to preserve it through cross-subsidy. The undertaking must have 'economically acceptable conditions' (paragraph 16) and be able to perform its task in 'conditions of economic equilibrium' (paragraph 17). If competitors are allowed to come in and 'cherry-pick' or 'cream-skim' the most profitable parts of the system the holder of the exclusive right required to operate the universal service cannot operate under economically acceptable conditions. The Court said, however, in paragraph 19 that this does not justify the exclusion of competition from additional services, separable from the basic public service, if these could be offered by other undertakings without compromising the economic viability of the latter. *Corbeau* is the high-water mark of hostility by the Court to the very existence of statutory monopoly in the context of Article 106(1) but the dawn of a more flexible and generous (to incumbents) interpretation of Article 106(2).

The CJ elaborated on the *Corbeau* ruling in *Commission v Netherlands*. It said again that the entrusted undertaking must be allowed 'economically acceptable conditions'. However, the undertaking does not have to prove that there is no other way but the impugned measure whereby it could carry out its task.[187]

Case 157/94, *Commission v Netherlands (Re Electricity Imports)* EU:C:1997:499

Court of Justice

52. . . . [I]t is not necessary, in order for the conditions for the application of Article [106(2)] to be fulfilled, that the financial balance or economic viability of the undertaking entrusted with the operation of a service of general economic interest should be threatened. It is sufficient that, in the absence of the rights at issue, it would not be possible for the undertaking to perform the particular tasks entrusted to it, defined by reference to the obligations and constraints to which it is subject.

53. Moreover, it follows from the *Corbeau* judgment . . . that the conditions for the application of Article [106(2)] are fulfilled in particular if maintenance of those rights is necessary to enable the holder of them to perform the tasks of general economic interest assigned to it under economically acceptable conditions.

. . .

58. Whilst it is true that it is incumbent upon a Member State which invokes Article [106(2)] to demonstrate that the conditions laid down by that provision are met, that burden of proof cannot be so extensive as to require the Member State, when setting out in detail the reasons for which, in the event of elimination of the contested measures, the performance, under economically acceptable conditions, of the tasks of general economic interest which it has entrusted to an undertaking would, in its view, be jeopardized, to go even further and prove, positively, that no other conceivable measure, which by definition would be hypothetical, could enable those tasks to be performed under the same conditions.

In *Corbeau*, the Court did not consider whether the universal service provision could be achieved by a less extreme measure than granting a monopoly. Universal service and cross-subsidisation are not inseparable: it is possible for the State to subsidise the universal service, for example. It will be noted that it was left (*Corbeau*, paragraph 21) to the national court actually to determine whether or not the additional services *were* severable and able to be operated by other undertakings without prejudicing the economic equilibrium of the traditional postal service. This left the national court with a difficult task involving extensive economic analysis. It had to decide the extent of the cross-subsidisation, and how far this was necessary to maintain the 'economic equilibrium'.[188] Cross-subsidisation is a problematic issue, particularly in respect of network monopolies.

Issues similar to those in *Corbeau* arose in *Almelo* where a Dutch court was dealing with litigation between regional and local electricity distributors concerning, inter alia, the legality of an exclusive purchasing clause.

[187] Cf. Darmon AG in Case C-393/92, *Almelo* EU:C:1994:258, on this point.

[188] See L. Hancher, 'Casenote on *Corbeau*' (1994) 31 *CMLRev* 105, 119–120.

Case C-393/92, *Gemeente Almelo and Others v Energiebedrijf Ijsselmij NV* EU:C:1994:171

Court of Justice

47. As regards the question whether an undertaking such as IJM has been entrusted with the operation of services of general interest, it should be borne in mind that it has been given the task, through the grant of a non-exclusive concession governed by public law, of ensuring the supply of electricity in part of the national territory.

48. Such an undertaking must ensure that throughout the territory in respect of which the concession is granted, all consumers, whether local distributors or end-users, receive uninterrupted supplies of electricity in sufficient quantities to meet demand at any given time, at uniform tariff rates and on terms which may not vary save in accordance with objective criteria applicable to all customers.

49. Restrictions on competition from other economic operators must be allowed so far as they are necessary in order to enable the undertaking entrusted with such a task of general interest to perform it. In that regard, it is necessary to take into consideration the economic conditions in which the undertaking operates, in particular the costs which it has to bear and the legislation, particularly concerning the environment, to which it is subject.

50. It is for the national court to consider whether an exclusive purchasing clause prohibiting local distributors from importing electricity is necessary in order to enable the regional distributor to perform its task of general interest.

Here again, the CJ accepted that the undertaking provided an SGEI and that Article 106(2) allows the restrictions of competition necessary for the performance of its universal service obligations (although it was for the national court to make the decision whether the actual restriction at issue in the case was necessary for that purpose). It has been argued that *Almelo*, reinforcing *Corbeau*, was a movement towards recognising the value of public service independently of its economic viability because 'it clearly indicated that the availability of the derogation was to be measured by a balancing exercise based upon competing priorities rather than inhibiting that choice by insisting upon narrow economic tests to be satisfied before the normal market rules can be disapplied'.[189]

In *Dusseldorp*,[190] concerning a monopoly over waste incineration, the Court reverted to a more stringent approach. It said that even if the task could constitute a task of general economic interest it was for the Dutch Government to show to the satisfaction of the national court that the objective could not be equally achieved by other means, and that Article 106(2) could apply only if it was shown that without the contested measure the undertaking could not carry out its entrusted task.[191]

In some references, unlike *Corbeau* and *Almelo*, the Court has not left the decision to the national court but has actually decided that the conditions in Article 106(2) were satisfied. This can be seen in *Corsica Ferries France*, *Albany*, and *Deutsche Post*.

Case C-266/96, *Corsica Ferries France SA v Gruppo Antichi Ormeggiatori del Porto di Genova Coop and Others* EU:C:1998:306

Under Italian law ships from other Member States were required to use the services of local mooring companies with exclusive concessions in each port. Corsica Ferries claimed that these companies were abusing their dominant positions by preventing shipping companies using their own staff to

[189] M. Ross, 'Art. 16 EC and Services of General Interest: From Derogation to Obligation', n. 135, 25.

[190] Case C-203/96, *Dusseldorp* EU:C:1998:316.

[191] Ibid., para. 67.

carry out mooring operations, in charging excessive prices which bore no relation to the actual cost of providing the service, and in fixing tariffs that varied from port to port for equivalent services. One question was whether the Treaty prohibited national measures which put the mooring companies in a position to act in this way.

Court of Justice

39. As far as the existence of exclusive rights is concerned, it is settled law that an undertaking having a statutory monopoly in a substantial part of the Common Market may be regarded as having a dominant position within the meaning of Article [102] of the Treaty (Case C-41/90, *Höfner and Elser* v. *Macrotron* . . . Case C-260/89, *ERT* v. *DEP* . . . *Merci Convenzionali Porto di Genova* . . . and *Raso and Others* . . .).

40. Next, it should be pointed out that although merely creating a dominant position by granting exclusive rights within the meaning of Article [106 (1)] is not in itself incompatible with Article [102], a Member State is in breach of the prohibitions contained in those two provisions if the undertaking in question, merely by exercising the exclusive rights granted to it, is led to abuse its dominant position or if such rights are liable to create a situation in which that undertaking is led to commit such abuses (Case C-41/90, *Höfner and Elser* v. *Macrotron* . . . Case C-260/89, *ERT* v. *DEP* . . . *Merci Convenzionali Porto di Genova* . . . Case C-323/93, *Centre d'Insemination de la Crespelle* . . . *Raso and others* . . .).

41. It follows that a Member State may, without infringing Article [102], grant exclusive rights for the supply of mooring services in its ports to local mooring groups provided those groups do not abuse their dominant position or are not led necessarily to commit such an abuse.

42. In order to rebut the existence of such abuse, the Genoa and La Spezia mooring groups rely on Article [106(2)], which provides that undertakings entrusted with the operation of services of general economic interest are to be subject to the competition rules contained in the Treaty only in so far as their application does not obstruct the performance, in law or in fact, of the particular tasks assigned to them. Article [106(2)] further provides that, in order for it to apply, the development of trade must not be affected to such an extent as would be contrary to the interests of the Community.

43. They maintain that the tariffs applied are indispensable if a universal mooring service is to be maintained. On the one hand, the tariffs include a component corresponding to the additional cost of providing a universal mooring service. On the other hand, the difference in the tariffs from one port to another, which, according to the file, result from account being taken, when the tariffs are calculated, of corrective factors reflecting the influence of local circumstances—which would tend to indicate that the services provided are not equivalent—are justified by the characteristics of the service and the need to ensure universal coverage.

44. It must therefore be considered whether the derogation from the rules of the Treaty provided for in Article [106(2)] may fall to be applied. To that end, it must be determined whether the mooring service can be regarded as a service of general economic interest within the meaning of that provision and, if so, first, whether performance of the particular tasks assigned to it can be achieved only through services for which the charge is higher than their actual cost and for which the tariff varies from one port to another, and secondly, whether the development of trade is not affected to such an extent as would be contrary to the interests of the Community (see, to that effect, Case C-157/94, *E.C. Commission* v. *Netherlands* . . .).

45. It is evident from the file on the case in the main proceedings that mooring operations are of general economic interest, such interest having special characteristics, in relation to those of other economic activities, which is capable of bringing them within the scope of Article [106(2)] Mooring groups are obliged to provide at any time and to any user a universal mooring service, for reasons of safety in port waters. At all events, Italy could properly have considered that it was necessary, on grounds of public security, to confer on local groups of operators the exclusive right to provide a universal mooring service.

46. In those circumstances it is not incompatible with Articles [102] and [106(1)] to include in the price of the service a component designed to cover the cost of maintaining the universal mooring service, inasmuch as it corresponds to the supplementary cost occasioned by the special characteristics of that service, and to lay down for that service different tariffs on the basis of the particular characteristics of each port.

47. Consequently, since the mooring groups have in fact been entrusted by the Member State with managing a service of general economic interest within the meaning of Article [106(2)], and the other conditions for applying the derogation from application of the Treaty rules which is laid down in that provision are satisfied, legislation such as that at issue does not constitute an infringement of Article [102], read in conjunction with Article [106(1)].

As in *Corbeau*, the CJ considered that the exclusive rights could escape the prohibition in Article 106(1) if they satisfied Article 106(2). However, the Court did not leave this determination to the national court, but said that the mooring operations were SGEIs provided on a universal basis and that it was, in the circumstances, not incompatible with the Treaty to include supplementary costs related to the running of that service and to charge varying tariffs (paragraph 46). There is no explanation of how the Court reached its conclusions in paragraph 46, or of how the supplementary costs arose or what cross-subsidisation was taking place.

The CJ also made a clear decision on the application of Article 106(2) in *Albany*, the case concerning the Dutch pensions regime.[192] The Court held that Article 106(2) applied because the scheme involved an SGEI which had to operate under 'economically acceptable conditions'.

Case C-67/96, *Albany International BV v Stichting Bedrijfspensioenfonds Textielindustrie* EU1999:430

Court of Justice

103. In allowing, in certain circumstances, derogations from the general rules of the Treaty, Article [106(2)] seeks to reconcile the Member States' interest in using certain undertakings, in particular in the public sector, as an instrument of economic or fiscal policy with the Community's interest in ensuring compliance with the rules on competition and preservation of the unity of the common market (Case C-202/88 *France* v. *Commission* . . . paragraph 12, and Case C-157/94 *Commission* v. *Netherlands* . . . paragraph 39).

104. In view of the interest of the Member States thus defined they cannot be precluded, when determining what services of general economic interest they entrust to certain undertakings, from taking account of objectives pertaining to their national policy or from endeavouring to attain them by means of obligations and constraints which they impose on such undertakings (*Commission v Netherlands*, cited above, paragraph 40).

105. The supplementary pension scheme at issue in the main proceedings fulfils an essential social function within the Netherlands pensions system by reason of the limited amount of the statutory pension, which is calculated on the basis of the minimum statutory wage.

[192] See Section 5.B.viii.

106. Moreover, the importance of the social function attributed to supplementary pensions has recently been recognised by the Community legislature's adoption of Council Directive 98/49/EC of 29 June 1998 on safeguarding the supplementary pension rights of employed and self-employed persons moving within the Community (OJ 1998 L209, p. 46).

107. Next, it is not necessary, in order for the conditions for the application of Article [106(2)] to be fulfilled, that the financial balance or economic viability of the undertaking entrusted with the operation of a service of general economic interest should be threatened. It is sufficient that, in the absence of the rights at issue, it would not be possible for the undertaking to perform the particular tasks entrusted to it, defined by reference to the obligations and constraints to which it is subject (*Commission v. Netherlands*, cited above, paragraph 52) or that maintenance of those rights is necessary to enable the holder of them to perform tasks of general economic interest which have been assigned to it under economically acceptable conditions (Case C-320/91 *Corbeau* . . . paragraphs 14 to 16, and *Commission v. Netherlands*, cited above, paragraph 53).

108. If the exclusive right of the fund to manage the supplementary pension scheme for all workers in a given sector were removed, undertakings with young employees in good health engaged in non-dangerous activities would seek more advantageous insurance terms from private insurers. The progressive departure of 'good' risks would leave the sectoral pension fund with responsibility for an increasing share of 'bad' risks, thereby increasing the cost of pensions for workers, particularly those in small and medium-sized undertakings with older employees engaged in dangerous activities, to which the fund could no longer offer pensions at an acceptable cost.

109. Such a situation would arise particularly in a case where, as in the main proceedings, the supplementary pension scheme managed exclusively by the Fund displays a high level of solidarity resulting, in particular, from the fact that contributions do not reflect the risk, from the obligation to accept all workers without a prior medical examination, the continuing accrual of pension rights despite exemption from the payment of contributions in the event of incapacity for work, the discharge by the Fund of arrears of contributions due from an employer in the event of insolvency and the indexing of the amount of pensions in order to maintain their value.

110. Such constraints, which render the service provided by the Fund less competitive than a comparable service provided by insurance companies, go towards justifying the exclusive right of the Fund to manage the supplementary pension scheme.

111. It follows that the removal of the exclusive right conferred on the Fund might make it impossible for it to perform the tasks of general economic interest entrusted to it under economically acceptable conditions and threaten its financial equilibrium.

123. The answer to the third question must therefore be that Articles [102] and [106] do not preclude the public authorities from conferring on a pension fund the exclusive right to manage a supplementary pension scheme in a given sector.

Again, the Court (paragraph 107) did not demand that the economic viability of the entrusted undertaking should be threatened without the exclusive right. Article 106(2) can apply where it is necessary to provide economically acceptable conditions.[193] Here again this meant preventing 'cherry-picking': without the exclusive rights other insurers would be able to offer a better deal to companies with predominantly young, healthy workforces.

However, the cross-subsidy argument failed in *Air Inter*[194] where the proportionality requirement was not satisfied. The Commission challenged the granting of exclusive rights on two internal French

[193] See also Case C-437/09, *AG2R Prévoyance v Beaudout* EU:C:2011:112, para. 76 and Case C-660/15 P, *Viasat Broadcasting UK Ltd v Commission* EU:C:2017:178, para. 30.

[194] Case T-260/94, *Air Inter v Commission* EU:T:1997:265.

air routes to Air Inter, which claimed that domestic air transport in France was based on cross-subsidy between profitable and unprofitable routes, in order to contribute to regional development. The GC said that Inter had not put a figure on the probable loss of revenue if other air carriers were allowed to compete with it on the routes in question, or shown that that loss of income would be so great that it would have to abandon certain routes. Moreover, the cross-subsidy system was merely the means the French authorities had chosen for developing the French regions but Air Inter had not argued or established that there was no appropriate alternative system for ensuring regional development and in particular of ensuring that loss-making routes continued to be financed.[195]

In *Ambulanz Glöckner*, the facts of which are given in Section B.x, the CJ again took an approach to the cross-subsidisation issue which favoured the incumbent. It identified the emergency ambulance service as being an SGEI subject to universal service and said that the extension of the provider's exclusive rights to the non-emergency market was justified so that it could subsidise the emergency from the non-emergency service.

Case C-475/99, *Ambulanz Glöckner v Landkreis Südwestpfalz* EU:C:2001:577

Court of Justice

55. With regard to those arguments, the medical aid organisations are incontestably entrusted with a task of general economic interest, consisting in the obligation to provide a permanent standby service of transporting sick or injured persons in emergencies throughout the territory concerned, at uniform rates and on similar quality conditions, without regard to the particular situations or to the degree of economic profitability of each individual operation.

56. However, Article [106(2)], read in conjunction with paragraph (1) of that provision, allows Member States to confer, on undertakings to which they entrust the operation of services of general economic interest, exclusive rights which may hinder the application of the rules of the Treaty on competition in so far as restrictions on competition, or even the exclusion of all competition, by other economic operators are necessary to ensure the performance of the particular tasks assigned to the undertakings holding the exclusive rights (Case C-320/91 *Corbeau* . . . paragraph 14).

57. The question to be determined, therefore, is whether the restriction of competition is necessary to enable the holder of an exclusive right to perform its task of general interest in economically acceptable conditions. The Court has held that the starting point in making that determination must be the premise that the obligation, on the part of the undertaking entrusted with such a task, to perform its services in conditions of economic equilibrium presupposes that it will be possible to offset less profitable sectors against the profitable sectors and hence justifies a restriction of competition from individual undertakings in economically profitable sectors (*Corbeau*, paragraphs 16 and 17).

58. In the case before the national court, . . . it appears that the system put in place by the RettDG 1991 is such as to enable the medical aid organisations to perform their task in economically acceptable conditions. In particular, the evidence placed before the Court shows that the revenue from non-emergency transport helps to cover the costs of providing the emergency transport service.

59. It is true that, in paragraph 19 of *Corbeau*, the Court held that the exclusion of competition is not justified in certain cases involving specific services, severable from the service of general interest in question, if those services do not compromise the economic equilibrium of the service of general economic interest performed by the holder of the exclusive rights.

[195] Ibid., paras. 139–140.

60. However, that is not the case with the two services now under consideration, for two reasons in particular. First, unlike the situation in *Corbeau*, the two types of service in question, traditionally assumed by the medical aid organisations, are so closely linked that it is difficult to sever the non-emergency transport services from the task of general economic interest constituted by the provision of the public ambulance service, with which they also have characteristics in common.

61. Second, the extension of the medical aid organisations' exclusive rights to the non-emergency transport sector does indeed enable them to discharge their general-interest task of providing emergency transport in conditions of economic equilibrium. The possibility which would be open to private operators to concentrate, in the non-emergency sector, on more profitable journeys could affect the degree of economic viability of the service provided by the medical aid organisations and, consequently, jeopardise the quality and reliability of that service.

62. However, as the Advocate General explains in point 188 of his Opinion, it is only if it were established that the medical aid organisations entrusted with the operation of the public ambulance service were manifestly unable to satisfy demand for emergency ambulance services and for patient transport at all times that the justification for extending their exclusive rights, based on the task of general interest, could not be accepted.

63. In this regard, Ambulanz Glöckner contends that Paragraph 18(3) of the RettDG 1991 does indeed promote the creation of a situation in which the medical aid organisations are not always able to satisfy all demand for patient transport services at acceptable prices (see, by analogy, Case C-41/90 *Höfner and Elser* . . . paragraph 31, and Case C-55/96 *Job Centre* . . . paragraph 35). On the other hand, the Landkreis and the ASB maintain that the public ambulance service is incontestably able to satisfy both demand for emergency transport and that for patient transport, even without private undertakings.

64. It is for [the] national court to determine whether the medical aid organisations which occupy a dominant position on the markets in question are in fact able to satisfy demand and to fulfil not only their statutory obligation to provide the public emergency ambulance services in all situations and 24 hours a day but also to offer efficient patient transport services.

65. Consequently, a provision such as Paragraph 18(3) of the RettDG 1991 is justified under Article [106(2)] provided that it does not bar the grant of an authorisation to independent operators where it is established that the medical aid organisations entrusted with the operation of the public ambulance service are manifestly unable to satisfy demand in the area of emergency transport and patient transport services.

In *Slovakian Hybrid Mail Services*,[196] the Commission stated that the presumption in the Postal Directive[197] of prima facie justification under Article 106(2) for services covered by the 'reserved area' as defined in that directive did not apply in that case because the hybrid service had previously been liberalised without endangering the public service. Therefore, extending the monopoly to cover hybrid mail again needed specific justification. Under the Postal Directive it is only possible to subsidise the universal service through extending or maintaining the reserved areas. It was not possible to finance any other type of service.[198] The decision was upheld.[199]

[196] COMP/39.562, 7 October 2008. [197] Dir. 97/67 [1998] OJ L15/14 as amended.

[198] COMP/39.562, *Slovakian Hybrid Mail* 7 October 2008, paras. 165–167. For the sectoral regime in the postal sector, see Bellamy and Child, n. 147, 12.157–12.170.

[199] Case T-556/08, *Slovenská Pošta v Commission* EU:T:2015:189, *aff'd* Case C-293/15 EU:C:2016:511.

We saw in Section 5.B.ix that in *Deutsche Post*[200] the CJ considered that a statutory monopolist's right stemming from an international convention (the UPC) to charge for international mail as though it were internal mail fell within Article 106(1) because it created a situation where the undertaking may be led to abuse its dominant position.[201] However, Article 106(1) had to be read in conjunction with Article 106(2). The UPC obligations were an SGEI.

Cases C-147–148/97, *Deutsche Post AG v Gesellschaft für Zahlungssysteme mbH (GZS) and Citicorp Kartenservice GmbH* EU:C:2000:74

Court of Justice

49. It is accordingly necessary to examine the extent to which exercise of such a right is necessary to enable a body of that kind to perform its task of general interest pursuant to the obligations flowing from the UPC and, in particular, to operate under economically acceptable conditions.

50. If a body such as Deutsche Post were obliged to forward and deliver to addressees resident in Germany mail posted in large quantities by senders resident in Germany using postal services of other Member States, without any provision allowing it to be financially compensated for all the costs occasioned by that obligation, the performance, in economically balanced conditions, of that task of general interest would be jeopardised.

51. The postal services of a Member State cannot simultaneously bear the costs entailed in the performance of the service of general economic interest of forwarding and delivering international items of mail, which is their responsibility by virtue of the UPC, and the loss of income resulting from the fact that bulk mailings are no longer posted with the postal services of the Member State in which the addressees are resident but with those of other Member States.

52. In such a case, it must be regarded as justified, for the purposes of the performance, in economically balanced conditions, of the task of general interest entrusted to Deutsche Post by the UPC, to treat cross-border mail as internal mail and, consequently, to charge internal postage.

. . .

54. Article [106(2)] therefore justifies, in the absence of an agreement between the postal services of the Member States concerned fixing terminal dues in relation to the actual costs of processing and delivering incoming trans-border mail, the grant by a Member State to its postal services of the statutory right to charge internal postage on items of mail where senders resident in that State post items, or cause them to be posted, in large quantities with the postal services of another Member State in order to send them to the first Member State.

. . .

56. On the other hand, in so far as part of the forwarding and delivery costs is offset by terminal dues paid by the postal services of other Member States, it is not necessary, in order for a body such as Deutsche Post to fulfil the obligations flowing from the UPC, that postage be charged at the full internal rate on items posted in large quantities with those services.

57. It is to be remembered that a body such as Deutsche Post which has a statutory monopoly over a substantial part of the common market may be regarded as holding a dominant position within the meaning of Article [102].

58. Thus, the exercise by such a body of the right to demand the full amount of the internal postage, where the costs relating to the forwarding and delivery of mail posted in large quantities with the postal services of a Member State other than the State in which both the senders and the addressees of that mail are resident are not offset by the terminal dues paid by those services, may be regarded as an abuse of a dominant position within the meaning of Article [102].

[200] Cases C-147–148/97, *Deutsche Post* EU:C:2000:74.

[201] Ibid., para. 48.

Here the Court stated without further explanation that levying the charges in issue was necessary to the performance of DP's task in 'economically balanced conditions'.[202] The assumption was that DP needed the income stream which it otherwise lost by what was in effect domestic mail being treated as international. It has been argued that this was very favourable treatment of Deutsche Post and that the need for cross-subsidisation should have been more closely examined.[203] In paragraph 58, the Court did say that it would be an abuse if DP did not offset the terminal dues against the internal postage rates, i.e. Article 106(2) did not justify collecting both. If there is no need to prevent cherry-picking or allow for cross-subsidisation etc., it is unlikely that Article 106(2) will apply. In *OTOC*,[204] which concerned the rules for training chartered accountants in Portugal there was no cross-subsidisation. The CJ doubted, on the documents before it, whether 'compulsory training of chartered accountants is of general economic interest exhibiting special characteristics as compared with that of other economic activities' but even if it was the CJ was doubtful that the restrictions on competition were necessary to the performance of OTOC's tasks and therefore the application of the competition rules would not obstruct it.[205]

F. NO EFFECT ON TRADE CONTRARY TO THE INTERESTS OF THE UNION

Article 106(2) contains a proviso that 'the development of trade must not be affected to such an extent as would be contrary to the interests of the Union'. Unlike the similar proviso to the free movement provisions in Article 36 TFEU, the tailpiece to Article 106(2) has not been of much importance. It was pleaded by the Commission in the electricity cases[206] but the CJ held that the Commission had provided no explanation to demonstrate such an effect on trade. The proviso must denote something different from 'affect trade between Member States' in Articles 101 and 102 because without such an effect on trade those Articles cannot apply at all. The EU Courts have confirmed that the tailpiece is a proportionality requirement. The GC said in the State aid case *DTS* that 'in order for an aid scheme for the benefit of an operator entrusted with a public service broadcasting mandate to be regarded as not fulfilling the condition laid down in Article 106(2) TFEU, it must affect trade and competition significantly and to an extent which is manifestly disproportionate to the objectives pursued by the Member States'.[207]

7. SERVICES OF GENERAL ECONOMIC INTEREST AND STATE AID

State aid is discussed in Chapter 1, Section 14.

There is an interface between State aid and Article 106(2) in respect of the financing of SGEIs. The question is whether, or in what circumstances, compensation for SGEIs is to be considered a State aid

[202] Ibid., para. 50.

[203] See A. Bartosch, 'Casenote on Cases C-147–148/97, *Deutsche Post AG . . .*' (2001) 38 *CMLRev* 195.

[204] Case C-1/12, *Ordem dos Técnicos Oficiais de Contas (OTOC) v Autoridade da Concorrência* EU:C:2013:81.

[205] Ibid., paras. 104–107. OTOC is the Portuguese Order of Chartered Accountants, empowered by statute to provide compulsory training schemes for members. OTOC adopted a regulation the effect of which was to impose stricter conditions on independent providers than on its own training operation.

[206] Case 157/94, *Commission v Netherlands (Re Electricity Imports)* EU:C:1997:499, paras. 66–72; Case C-159/94, *Commission v France (Re Electricity and Gas Imports)* EU:C:1997:501, paras. 109–116; see also COMP/37.859, *De Post-La Poste* [2002] OJ L61/32, paras. 80–81.

[207] Case T-533/10, *DTS Distribuidora de Televisión Digital SA v Commission* EU:T:2014:629, para. 155, *aff'd* Case C-449/14, EU:C:2016:848.

under Article 107. In *Altmark*,[208] the CJ established that compensation for the costs incurred in the discharge of public service obligations is not State aid[209] if four cumulative criteria ('the *Altmark* conditions') are satisfied.[210] They are:

> – first, the recipient undertaking is actually required to discharge public service obligations and those obligations have been clearly defined;
>
> – second, the parameters on the basis of which the compensation is calculated have been established beforehand in an objective and transparent manner;
>
> – third, the compensation does not exceed what is necessary to cover all or part of the costs incurred in discharging the public service obligations, taking into account the relevant receipts and a reasonable profit for discharging those obligations;
>
> – fourth, where the undertaking which is to discharge public service obligations is not chosen in a public procurement procedure, the level of compensation needed has been determined on the basis of an analysis of the costs which a typical undertaking, well run and adequately provided with means of transport so as to be able to meet the necessary public service requirements, would have incurred in discharging those obligations, taking into account the relevant receipts and a reasonable profit for discharging the obligations.[211]

Where these conditions are not all met, so that the measure constitutes State aid, the measure may nevertheless take advantage of the derogation in Article 106(2) and so be compatible with the internal market. Two of the *Altmark* conditions (one and three) correspond to the Article 106(2) conditions. The first is equivalent to the 'entrustment' of a defined task required by Article 106(2).[212] The third is similar to (but stricter than) the proportionality requirement under Article 106(2) developed in the case law.[213] The second has no direct counterpart in Article 106(2) but it reflects, although goes further than, the concern in the case law with overcompensation.

After *Altmark* the Commission adopted in 2005 a package of measures to provide guidance and legal certainty, which was replaced in 2011 by the 'Almunia package'. This includes a Framework setting out the principles on which the Commission bases its State aid assessment of public compensation for SGEIs under Article 106(2).[214] In *Viasat*, the EU Courts were faced, in effect, with the question of the relationship between Article 106(2), the Framework, and the *Altmark* criteria.[215] The GC said that three conditions must be fulfilled for Article 106(2) to apply: definition of the public service, entrustment, and proportionality.[216] The CJ, affirming the GC, made it clear that the second and fourth *Altmark* conditions do not apply in respect of Article 106(2).[217] In some respects, the post-*Altmark* package of measures takes a stricter attitude to the operation of Article 106(2) than the post-*Corbeau* case law.[218]

[208] Case C-280/00, *Altmark* EU:C:2003:415. See also Case C-442/21 P, *ITD and Danske Fragtmænd v Commission* EU:C:2022:872.

[209] And therefore does not require notification to the Commission under Art. 108(3).

[210] See S. Santamato and N. Pesaresi, 'Compensation for Services of General Economic Interest: Some Thoughts on the *Altmark* Ruling' (2004) 1 *Competition Policy Newsletter* 1.

[211] *Altmark*, para. 95 [212] See Section 6.E.i. [213] See Section 6.E.ii.

[214] EU Framework for State aid in the form of public service compensation [2012] OJ C8/15.

[215] See E. Szyszczak, 'Services of General Economic Interest, State Aid and State Measures Affecting Competition' (2017) 8 *JECLAP* 678.

[216] Case T-125/12, *Viasat Broadcasting UK Ltd v Commission* EU:T:2015:687, para. 61.

[217] Case C-660/15 P, *Viaset Broadcasting UK Ltd v Commission* EU:C:2017:178. See also Case T-561/18, *ITD, Brancheorganisation for den danske vejgodstransport A/S v Commission* EU:T:2021:240, *aff'd* Case C-442/21 P, *ITD and Danske Fragtmænd v Commission* EU:C:2022:872.

[218] See Burke, n. 144, 164–175.

8. THE DIRECT EFFECT OF ARTICLE 106(1) AND (2)

A. ARTICLE 106(1)

As Article 106(1) prohibits Member States from enacting or maintaining measures contrary to rules contained in the Treaties it applies only in conjunction with some other rule. Whether or not individuals may invoke Article 106(1) before a national court, i.e. whether Article 106(1) is directly effective, therefore depends on whether the rule infringed by the Member State is itself directly effective. In *Höfner*, for example, the litigant was able to claim in the German court that the German laws breached Article 106(1) because they led to an infringement of Article 102, which is directly effective.

B. ARTICLE 106(2)

There are four questions raised by Article 106(2): is the undertaking 'entrusted' with a task; is that task a 'service of general economic interest'; would the task be obstructed by complying with the Treaty rules; and would a derogation from the Treaty rules have an effect on trade contrary to the interests of the Union?

As far as the first two questions are concerned, the Court confirmed long ago that Article 106(2) is directly effective in that a national court may decide whether or not an undertaking has been entrusted with a service of general economic interest.[219]

As for the third question, whether the task would be obstructed, for a long time it appeared that the national courts were not competent to answer it and that only the Community institutions could decide the point in favour of the undertaking. [220]However, the CJ said in its *ERT* judgment[221] that it is for the national court to verify whether the application of the competition rules would obstruct the undertaking's task. The CJ also left this determination to the national court in, for example, *Corbeau* and *Almelo*.

The fourth question requires an assessment of whether the *interests of the Union* would be adversely affected. The issue seems more suited to a decision by the Commission than to a judgment by a national court. However, it may be that this is not an additional requirement at all, but part of the overall proportionality requirement to which the first sentence is subject.[222] If this is so Article 106(2) as a whole has direct effect. On the other hand, it can also be argued that only the first sentence of Article 106(2) has direct effect and that the Commission alone has competence to declare that the interest of the Union is being infringed. There is as yet no ruling of the EU Courts on the point.

9. ARTICLE 106(3)

A. THE AMBIT OF THE PROVISION

Article 106(3) provides that the Commission shall ensure the application of the Article[223] and gives it the supervisory and policing powers with which to do this. This is in addition to the powers conferred upon the Commission elsewhere in the Treaties. Under Article 106(3) the Commission can adopt

[219] Case 127/73, *BRT v SABAM* EU:C:1974:25.

[220] Case 10/71, *Ministère Public of Luxembourg v Muller* EU:C:1971:85; see also Case 155/73, *Sacchi* EU:C:1974:40; Case 172/82, *Syndicat National des Fabricants Raffineurs d'Huile de Graissage v Inter Huiles* EU:C:1983:69.

[221] Case C-260/89, *ERT* EU:C:1991:254, para. 34; see Section 5.B.iii; see also Case 66/86, *Ahmed Saeed* EU:C:1989:140, paras. 55–57.

[222] See Buendia Sierra in Faull and Nikpay, n. 1, 6.214.

[223] This is a specific manifestation of the Commission's general duty of enforcement and supervision under Art. 17 TEU.

two types of measure, decisions addressed to Member States (not to the undertakings themselves, in respect of whom the Commission must use its powers under Regulation 1/2003) and directives. The Commission may use these powers either to deal with some existing infringement of the Treaty rules or to take steps to prevent future infringements. The adoption of directives to deal with the latter has proved particularly contentious.

B. DECISIONS

The power to issue decisions addressed to Member States provides the Commission with an enforcement mechanism in respect of infringements of the Treaty in addition to the general power in Article 258 TFEU.[224] The Commission has to comply with the general principles of Union law, such as giving reasons and allowing the addressee to be heard, and failure to do so means that the decision can be quashed.[225] In *max.mobil*,[226] the GC held that the Commission was under an obligation to examine complaints based on Article 106 diligently and objectively. However, the CJ overruled the GC and held that the Commission's refusal to act under Article 106(3) is not susceptible to judicial review.[227] The Commission has adopted Article 106(3) decisions in a number of the cases discussed in this chapter and in Chapter 7, such as *Spanish Courier Services*,[228] *ANA*,[229] and the essential facilities case, *Port of Rødby*.[230] Most of the cases in this chapter were Article 267 references. Following the *Altmark* judgment the Commission issued a decision, now replaced with another, on State aid and public service compensation.[231]

C. DIRECTIVES

The adoption of directives under Article 106(3) can prove contentious because the Commission can thereby legislate alone, without going through the usual legislative procedures laid down in Articles 289–297. Although in practice it normally consults Parliament and the Member States the latter do not have any opportunity to vote against the measures in the Council and the Commission can act where there is no political consensus. This became an issue with regard to liberalisation where there is a thin line to be drawn between harmonisation under Articles 114 and 115 TFEU and what is 'appropriate' under Article 106(3). Directives adopted under Article 106(3) have been challenged by Member States claiming that the wrong legal base was used for their adoption. The Commission used its Article 106(3) powers for the first time in adopting the Transparency Directive[232] which was challenged by France, Italy, and the UK. The CJ confirmed that the Commission was entitled to proceed under Article 106(3) in adopting the Directive, a preventive measure which was aimed at creating greater transparency in the financial relationship between Member States and public undertakings, as it was necessary to its duty of surveillance under the Article.[233]

224 Cases C-48 and 66/90, *Netherlands and Koninklijke PTT Netherland v Commission* EU:C:1992:63.
225 Ibid. 226 Case T-54/99, *max.mobil* EU:T:2002:20. 227 Case C-141/02 P, *max.mobil* EU:C:2005:98.
228 [1990] OJ L233/19.
229 [1999] OJ L69/31, confirmed on appeal, Case C-163/99, *Portugal v Commission* EU:C:2001:189.
230 [1994] OJ L55/5. 231 See Section 7.
232 Dir. 80/723/EEC [1980] OJ L195/35, now Dir. 2006/111/EC [2006] OJ L318/17, see n. 25.
233 Cases 188–190/80, *France, Italy and the UK v Commission* EU:C:1982:257.

The Commission used Article 106(3) as the legal basis for two directives in the telecommunications sector, on telecommunications equipment[234] and telecommunications services,[235] both of which were challenged by Member States. In the *Telecommunications Equipment* case, the CJ held that Article 106(3) does not give the Commission a general legislative power, but a specific one to deal with State measures concerning legal monopolies.

Case C-202/88, *France v Commission (Telecommunications Equipment)* EU:C: 1991:120

Court of Justice

23. As regards the allegation that the Commission has encroached on the powers conferred on the Council by Articles [103 and 114 TFEU], those provisions have to be compared with Article [106], taking into account their respective subject-matter and purpose.

24. Article [114] is concerned with the adoption of measures for the approximation of the provisions laid down by law, regulation or administrative action in Member States which have as their object the establishment and functioning of the internal market. Article [103] is concerned with the adoption of any appropriate regulations or directives to give effect to the principles set out in Articles [101] and [102], that is to say the competition rules applicable to all undertakings. As for Article [106], it is concerned with measures adopted by the Member States in relation to undertakings with which they have specific links referred to in the provisions of that article. It is only with regard to such measures that Article [106] imposes on the Commission a duty of supervision which may, where necessary, be exercised through the adoption of directives and decisions addressed to the Member States.

25. It must therefore be held that the subject-matter of the power conferred on the Commission by Article [106(3)] is different from, and more specific than, that of the powers conferred on the Council by either Article [114] or Article [103].

26. It should also be noted that, as the Court held in Joined Cases 188 to 190/80 (*France, Italy and United Kingdom* v. *Commission* . . . paragraph 14), the possibility that rules containing provisions which impinge upon the specific sphere of Article [106] might be laid down by the Council by virtue of its general power under other articles of the Treaty does not preclude the exercise of the power which Article [106] confers on the Commission.

27. The plea in law alleging lack of powers on the part of the Commission must therefore be rejected.

In this case, although the CJ upheld the Commission's power to legislate over telecommunications equipment it did annul Article 7 of the Directive, which required Member States to ensure the telecommunications monopolies did not enter into certain types of long-term contracts. The Court said that 'anti-competitive conduct engaged in by undertakings on their own initiative' could be dealt with only by individual decisions adopted under Articles 101 and 102 and that Article 106(3) was not an appropriate basis. Likewise in the *Telecommunications Services* case[236] the CJ upheld the Commission's right to use Article 106(3) for measures which were necessary for its surveillance function.[237]

The Member States look jealously at the Commission's use of its Article 106(3) powers and the Commission strives to distinguish its surveillance and supervisory powers from other measures.

[234] Dir. 88/301/EEC [1988] OJ L131/73. [235] Dir. 90/388 [1990] OJ L192/10.

[236] Cases C-271, 281, and 289/90, *Spain, Belgium and Italy v Commission* EU:C:1992:440.

[237] Although Art. 8 was annulled on the same grounds as Art. 7 of the Equipment Dir., Dir. 88/301/EEC [1988] OJ L131/73 and the provisions on special rights were annulled for inadequacy of reasons.

The Open Network Provision Directive,[238] to which the Services Directive was an accompaniment, was adopted under Article 114 because it was a harmonisation measure, dealing with the conditions for access to, and use of, public networks and services.

The Constitutional Treaty of 2004, which never came into force,[239] would have amended Article 106(3) to read:

> The Commission shall ensure the application of this Article and shall, where necessary, adopt appropriate European regulations or decisions.

This would, in effect, have enacted the case law discussed earlier and clarified the limited extent of the Commission's powers.

10. CONCLUSIONS

1. Since 1990 the question of the relationship between competition law and public services has gone from being a side issue to a matter of central concern. This has largely been due to the programme of liberalisation in the EU which has introduced competition into sectors previously subject to statutory monopolies and thereby transformed the relationship between undertakings in those sectors and the State. The basic principle is that Member States may not do anything to undermine the *effet utile* of Articles 101 and 102, which are addressed to undertakings rather than to the States.

2. Article 106(1) is addressed to the Member States. The case law on Article 106(1) is inconsistent. The preponderance of the case law shows that Member States do not infringe the Treaties merely by maintaining public undertakings or granting undertakings special or exclusive rights. There will be an infringement, however, where the undertaking concerned, merely by exercising its rights, cannot avoid committing an abuse, or is led to, or induced to, commit an abuse. This situation has occurred where, for instance, the undertaking cannot meet demand, is given a cumulation of rights including regulatory functions, or is enabled to extend its dominant position, refuse access to facilities, or commit pricing abuses. Article 106(1) can be infringed by the creation of 'inequality of opportunity' even if no actual abuse is identified. There are cases where the very granting of the exclusive right seems to infringe but they are unclear because the Court has proceeded to the application of Article 106(2) without a proper conclusion on Article 106(1). Article 106(2) can justify measures which infringe Article 106(1).

3. Article 106(2) provides a derogation from the competition rules for SGEIs if compliance with the rules would obstruct the performance of their tasks. Article 106(2) therefore deals with market failure, in the sense that the market is unable to provide the necessary public services. The EU Courts have held that an undertaking cannot perform its SGEI tasks unless it has economically acceptable conditions. Producing such conditions may therefore mean allowing cross-subsidisation and preventing cherry-picking but the Courts have not required undertakings to demonstrate that there is no less restrictive means of maintaining the SGEI than the one they have chosen.

4. EU policy on the role of SGEIs has developed to the point where they are seen as a core unifying factor in the Union. Since the mid-nineties, the EU Courts have taken a more liberal attitude to Article 106(2) alongside their more hard-line approach to Article 106(1).

5. The case law on Article 106 reflects the tensions that exist within the EU and between Member States on the different choices that can be made in respect of the delivery of public services and to what extent they can be fully marketised.

[238] Council Dir. 90/387/EEC [1990] OJ L192/1.

[239] It was rejected by referenda in France and the Netherlands.

11. FURTHER READING

A. Books

BELLAMY and CHILD (D. Bailey and L. John, eds.), *European Union Law of Competition* (8th edn, Oxford University Press, 2018,) Chap. 11

BUENDIA SIERRA, J. L., *Exclusive Rights and State Monopolies in EC Law* (Oxford University Press, 2000)

BURKE, J. M., *A Critical Account of Article 106(2) TFEU* (Hart Publishing, 2018)

CREMONA, M. (ed.), *Market Integration and Public Service in the EU* (Oxford University Press, 2011)

FAULL, J., and NIKPAY, A., *The EU Law of Competition* (3rd edn, Oxford University Press, 2014), Chap. 6 (J. L. Buendia Sierra)

HANCHER, L., and SAUTER, W., *EU Competition and Internal Market Law in the Healthcare Sector* (Oxford University Press, 2012)

PROSSER, T., *The Limits of Competition Law* (Oxford University Press, 2005)

SAUTER, W., *Public Services in EU Law* (Cambridge University Press, 2014)

SZYSZCZAK, E., *The Regulation of the State in Competitive Markets in the European Union* (Hart Publishing, 2007)

VAN BAEL, I., and BELLIS, J.-F. (eds.), *Competition Law of the European Union* (6th edn, Wolters Kluwer, 2021), Chap. 9

B. Chapters in Books

BARNARD, C., 'EU Citizenship and the Principle of Solidarity' in M. Dougan and E. Spaventa (eds.), *Social Welfare and the Law* (Hart Publishing, 2005)

FLYNN, L., 'Competition Policy and Public Services in EC Law after the Maastricht and Amsterdam Treaties' in D. O'Keefe and P. Twomey (eds.), *Legal Issues of the Amsterdam Treaty* (Hart Publishing, 1999)

GARCIA, E. M., 'Public Service, Public Services, Public Functions, and Guarantees of the Rights of Citizens: Unchanging Needs in a Changed Context' in M. Freedland and S. Sciarra (eds.), *Public Services and Citizenship in European Law* (Clarendon Press, 1998)

HANCHER, L., 'Community, State and Market' in P. Craig and G. de Búrca (eds.), *The Evolution of EU Law* (Oxford University Press, 1999)

SAUTER, W., 'Universal Service Obligations and the Emergence of Citizens' Rights in European Telecommunications Liberalisation' in M. Freedland and S. Sciarra (eds.), *Public Services and Citizenship in European Law* (Clarendon Press, 1998)

SZYSZCZAK, E., 'Public Service and the Limits to Competition Law' in C. Graham and F. Smith (eds.), *Competition, Regulation and the New Economy* (Hart Publishing, 2004)

VAN MIERT, K., 'Liberalization of the Economy of the European Union: The Game is Not (Yet) Over' in D. Geradin (ed.), *The Liberalization of State Monopolies in the European Union and Beyond* (Kluwer, 2000)

C. Articles

BARTOSCH, A., 'Casenote on Cases C-147–8/97, *Deutsche Post AG v Gesellschaft für Zahlungssysteme mbH (GZS) and Citicorp Kartenservice GmbH*' (2001) 38 *CMLRev* 195

BOEGER, N., ' "New" Social Democracy before the Court of Justice' (2005–2006) 8 *Cambridge Yearbook of European Legal Studies* Chap. 5

BOEGER, N., 'Solidarity and EC Competition Law' (2007) 32 *ELRev* 319

COLLINS, A. M., and MARTÍNEZ NAVARRO, M., 'Economic Activity, Market Failure and Services of General Economic Interest: It Takes Two to Tango' (2021) 12 *JECLAP* 380

EDWARD, D., and HOSKINS, M., 'Article 90: Deregulation and EC Law. Reflections Arising from the XVI FIDE Conference' (1995) 32 *CMLRev* 157

GYSELEN, L., 'Case Note on *Albany, Brentjens'* and *Drijvende Bokken*' (2000) 37 *CMLRev* 425

HANCHER, L., 'Casenote on *Corbeau*' (1994) 31 *CMLRev* 105

HANCHER, L., and BUENDIA SIERRA, J. L., 'Cross-subsidization and EC Law' (1998) 35 *CMLRev* 901

MAZIARZ, A., 'Services of General Economic Interest: Towards Common Values?', *EStAL* 1/2016, 16

ØLYKKE, G. S., and MØLLGAARD, P., 'What is a Service of General Economic Interest?' (2016) 41 *European J of Law and Economics* 205

ROSS, M. G., 'Article 16 EC and Services of General Interest: From Derogation to Obligation?' (2000) 25 *ELRev* 22

ROSS, M. G., 'Promoting Solidarity: From Public Services to a European Model of Competition?' (2007) 44 *CMLRev* 1057

ROSS, M. G., 'A Healthy Approach to Services of General Economic Interest? The *BUPA* Judgment of the Court of First Instance' (2009) 34 *ELRev* 127

SANTAMATO, A., and PESARESI, N., 'Compensation for Services of General Economic Interest: Some Thoughts on the Altmark Ruling' (2004) 1 *Competition Policy Newsletter* 1

SAUTER, W., 'Casenote on Case T-289/03, *BUPA v Commission*' (2009) 46 *CMLRev* 269

SLOT, P. J., 'Applying the Competition Rules in the Healthcare Sector' [2003] *ECLR* 580

SZYSZCZAK, E., 'Public Service Provision in Competitive Markets' (2001) 20 *YEL* 35

SZYSZCZAK, E., 'Services of General Economic Interest, State Aid and State Measures Affecting Competition' (2017) 8 *JECLAP* 678

TESAURO, G., 'The Community's Internal Market in the Light of the Recent Case-law of the Court of Justice' (1995) 15 *YEL* 1

VAN DE GRONDEN, J. W., 'Purchasing Care: Economic Activity or Service of General Economic Interest?' [2004] *ECLR* 87

VARJU, M., 'Conflict and Complementarity: EU Obligations, Member State Interests and Services of General Interest' (2017) 23(2) *European Public Law* 347

VEERMERSCH, A., 'Casenote on Case C-49/07, *Motosykletistiki Omospondia Ellados NPID v Ellinkio Dimosi*' (2009) 46 *CMLRev* 1327

9

HORIZONTAL AGREEMENTS—CARTELS AND COLLUSION

1. CENTRAL ISSUES

1. This chapter deals with collusion, explicit and tacit, between actual or potential competitors. Oligopolistic markets, that is markets on which there are only a few suppliers, are particularly prone to collusion.

2. Firms may collude explicitly by concluding naked 'cartels'; joint arrangements to fix prices, restrict output, share markets, or rig bids. These are sometimes referred to as 'hardcore' cartels.

3. Cartels lead to higher prices (transferring wealth from consumers to the cartel), deadweight loss (allocative inefficiency), and reduced incentives for firms to keep costs low, to innovate, and to strive for efficiency. They are clearly prohibited by Article 101.

4. Since the end of the 1990s, the Commission has increasingly focused its resources on detecting and prohibiting cartels and fining undertakings involved in infringements. The number of cartel decisions adopted each year, and the fines imposed, have increased dramatically since 2000. In some Member States, as in the US, cartel activity constitutes a criminal offence.

5. Given the severe consequences that might result for those operating a cartel, most such arrangements are hidden. An acute problem is to detect and prove the existence of a cartel. A further difficulty is how to distinguish cartel behaviour from horizontal collaboration arrangements incorporating severe restraints but with a potential pro-competitive objective.

6. Consumer welfare is also harmed by tacit collusion or tacit coordination. This occurs where firms are able to coordinate their behaviour in a similar way to those operating a cartel, without express communication or explicitly colluding. Economic theory predicts that such conduct occurs on certain markets where players recognise that the profitability of what they do is dependent on the behaviour of other firms operating on the market, and that they are all better off if they charge higher prices and earn greater profits.

7. A challenge for competition law is how to deal with tacit collusion. Although the EU Merger Regulation can be used *ex ante* to prevent mergers likely to create conditions conducive to tacit (and explicit) collusion (see Chapter 15), this chapter examines whether, and if so when, competition law can prohibit or otherwise control the behaviour of firms actually engaged in tacit collusion, including conduct that may be facilitating or strengthening tacit collusion on a market. It also outlines other options that might be available deal with the problem of tacit collusion.

2. INTRODUCTION

A. GENERAL

This chapter considers how EU competition law applies to explicit collusion between undertakings operating cartels, other horizontal collaboration agreements that may appear to be akin to cartel conduct, and to tacit collusion or tacit coordination. It commences by examining what exactly cartel conduct is, the incentives for, and practical difficulties involved in, explicit collusion, and the difference between explicit and tacit collusion. It also considers how both practices may result in the reduction of consumer welfare, through the raising of prices, the restriction of output, productive inefficiency, or damaging variety and innovation.

Section 3 examines how cartels are analysed under Article 101, whilst Section 4 focuses on the analysis of horizontal agreements involving price or other severe restraints, but which are alleged to be related to the realisation of efficiencies. Section 4 also examines information-sharing agreements. Section 5 considers the problem of tacit collusion and whether, in particular, Articles 101 and 102 operate as effective mechanisms for dealing with it. It also outlines other options that might be available to prevent or control tacit collusion.

B. CARTELS AND COLLUSION—EXPLICIT AND TACIT

(i) Cartels—Explicit Collusion

a. Introduction

A Recommendation of the OECD Council Concerning Effective Action Against Hard Core Cartels, defines a 'hardcore' cartel as:

> an anti-competitive agreement, anti-competitive concerted practice, or anti-competitive arrangement by competitors to fix prices, make rigged bids (collusive tenders), establish output restrictions or quotas, or share or divide markets by allocating customers, suppliers, territories or lines of commerce.[1]

Of all agreements, cartels most contradict the principles of the free market economy as the operators specifically attempt to eliminate or limit the free play of competition. Further, they differ from other agreements considered in this book,[2] in that they are 'naked'—'[t]hey seek to restrict competition without producing any objective countervailing benefits'.[3] They lead to higher prices (transferring wealth from consumers to the cartel), deadweight loss (allocative inefficiency), and, ordinarily, productive inefficiency and dynamic harm resulting from reduced incentives to innovate and to strive for efficiency.

> A successful cartel raises price above the competitive level and reduces output. Consumers (which include businesses and governments) choose either not to pay the higher price for some or all of the cartelised product that they desire thus forgoing the product, or they pay the cartel price and thereby unknowingly transfer wealth to the cartel operators. Further, a cartel shelters its members from full exposure to market forces, reducing pressures on them to control costs and to innovate. All of these effects harm efficiency in a market economy.[4]

[1] OECD Publication C(98)35/FINAL, 25 March 1998. [2] See especially Chaps. 10–12.

[3] M. Monti, 'Fighting Cartels Why and How? Why Should We Be Concerned with Cartels and Collusive Behaviour?', 3rd Nordic Competition Policy Conference, Stockholm, 11–12 September 2000.

[4] OECD, 'Fighting Hard Core Cartels: Recent Progress and Challenges Ahead' (2003), and 'Hard Core Cartels—Harm and Effective Sanctions', OECD Policy Brief (May 2002), both available at <www.oecd.org>.

The costs of forming and enforcing the cartel are also welfare-reducing.[5]

Although assessing the harm caused by cartels is not easy, some competition agencies estimate that cartels charge at least 10 per cent over the competitive price.[6] A number of empirical studies suggest, however, that this figure may be conservative and that cartels 'lead to prices well in excess of 10 per cent, and sometimes in excess of 20 per cent, of competitive levels'.[7] For example, in his studies of US cartel decisions, John Connor concludes that the median cartel overcharge is closer to 25 per cent.[8] Further, the OECD, in *Hard Core Cartels*,[9] has estimated that cartels cost society billions and thwart the gains sought to be achieved through global market liberalisation. At the EU level, cartels may also frustrate attempts to liberalise and integrate European markets.

b. The Incentives for, and Complications Involved in, the Operation of a Cartel

In the 1940s, the work of von Neumann and Morgenstern[10] laid the foundation for the development of a new branch of economics, 'game theory', which deals with the strategic interaction of firms, and which is now highly developed. It is a helpful tool used to explain and predict the behaviour of firms on markets. Indeed, the 'prisoners' dilemma' model, explains the incentives that exist for firms operating on oligopolistic markets, where only a few players operate, to agree to coordinate their behaviour and to charge prices which are higher than those which would occur on a competitive market. It also exemplifies, through the Nash non-cooperative equilibrium, which arises 'when, given the behaviour of all other firms in the market, no firm wishes to change its behaviour (i.e. each firm maximises profit, given the behaviour of all the other firms)',[11] the practical difficulties involved in operating such an agreement.

In the extract, Bishop and Walker explain insights from game theory and the prisoners' dilemma.

S. Bishop and M. Walker, *The Economics of EC Competition Law: Concepts, Application and Measurement* (3rd edn, Sweet & Maxwell, 2010), 2.020–2.022

Oligopoly Models

2.020 Neither the paradigm of perfect competition nor that of monopoly provide adequate descriptions of competition in most industries. While the models of perfect competition and monopoly provide a good basis for understanding the basic economic principles, particularly in illustrating the detrimental welfare consequences of monopoly, neither model provides a solid framework on which to base policy

[5] R. Van den Bergh and P. Camesasca, *European Competition Law and Economics: A Comparative Perspective* (2nd edn, Sweet & Maxwell, 2006), 5.2.1.2.

[6] Monti, n. 3 ('The average increase from price fixing is estimated to amount to 10% of the selling price and the corresponding reduction of output to be as high as 20%. In some recent big cases prices have been increased by the cartel participants 30% (graphite electrodes) and 50% (citric acid)'). OECD, 'Guide for helping competition authorities assess the expected impact of their activities' (2014), <www.oecd.org/daf/competition/Guide-competition-impact-assessmentEN.pdf>.

[7] L. M. Froeb, R. A. Koyak, and G. J. Werden, 'What is the effect of bid rigging on prices' (1993) 42(4) *Economics Letters* 419.

[8] See e.g. J. M. Connor, *Price-fixing Overcharges*, (revised 3rd edn, 2014), available at <https://papers.ssrn.com/sol3/papers.cfm?abstract_id=2400780> (study of more than 700 economic studies and judicial decisions (and 2,041 quantitative estimates of overcharges), estimating a long-run median overcharge of 23% for all cartels, but with 25% lower mark-ups in bid rigging cases), but contrast M. Boyer and R. Kotchoni, 'How Much Do Cartel Overcharge?' *CIRANO*, 2015s-37; J. M. Connor and R. H. Lande, 'How High Do Cartels Raise Prices? Implications for Optimal Cartel Fines' (2005) 80 *Tulane LR* 513, M. C. Levenstein and V. Y. Suslow, 'What Determines Cartel Success?' (2006) 44 *J of Economic Literature* 43 and C. Beyer, K. von Blanckenburg and E. Kottmann, 'The Welfare Implications of the European Trucks Cartel' (2020) 55(2) *Intereconomics* 120 (estimating that the Truck Cartel inflicted a net welfare loss of up to €15.5 billion on the European economy and an overcharge of up to 7.6%).

[9] OECD, 'Fighting Hard Core Cartels', n. 4.

[10] J. von Neumann and O. Morgenstern, *The Theory of Games and Economic Behaviour* (Princeton University Press, 1944). See e.g. G. Stigler, 'A Theory of Oligopoly' (1964) 72 *J of Political Economy* 44 and J. Tirole, *The Theory of Industrial Organization* (MIT Press, 1988) and Chap. 1.

[11] S. Bishop and M. Walker, *The Economics of EC Competition Law: Concepts, Application and Measurement* (3rd edn, Sweet & Maxwell, 2010), 2.020.

prescriptions. These models ignore the interaction between firms and how this interaction may affect the outcomes of the competitive process. In the model of perfect competition, each firm is so small that it can put as much or as little for sale on the market without affecting the market price. For this reason, a firm in a competitive market has no reason to worry about what other firms will do when it makes its own plans. For example, a farmer selling his product in an international market does not consider whether his output will affect the market price but instead takes the market price as a given that he cannot affect. At the other extreme, the monopolist can directly set the market price as it has no rivals to worry about.

But in most markets, firms do need to take into account the commercial decisions of rivals when formulating their own commercial strategy. In most markets, firms recognise that changes in their own plans—*e.g.* prices, planned production and additions to capacity—may affect the decisions of other firms in the industry and will take this into account when making commercial decisions. When addressing what constitutes effective competition, these interactions between firms must be taken into account. This requires one to examine more realistic models of competition: models of oligopolistic behaviour. It is the outcomes produced by these models which should underpin our understanding of effective competition.

With advances in game theory, economic models of competition have become much more sophisticated and have started to take explicit account of the interactions between competing firms. Until the 1970s, the examination of oligopoly received little attention, reflecting the lack of analytical tools available in this area. But since that time, a new branch of economics—non-co-operative game theory—has grown up which addresses directly the strategic interactions between firms. Non-co-operative game theory sees competition between firms as each firm trying to do the best it can subject to the actions of its competitors. A key concept in this analysis is that of the Nash non-co-operative equilibrium. An equilibrium is a Nash non-co-operative equilibrium when, given the behaviour of all other firms in the market, no firm wishes to change its behaviour (i.e. each firm maximises profit given the behaviour of all the other firms).

2.021 The concept of a non-co-operative Nash equilibrium can be illustrated by reference to the following game, commonly known as the Prisoners' Dilemma. There are two firms, A and B, who must each decide whether to charge a high price or to charge a low price. There are therefore four possible outcomes: they could both charge high prices, both charge low prices, or one or other could charge a low price whilst the other charges a high price. The numbers in each box in Figure 2.4 denote the profits resulting from the outcome of the decisions of the two firms. The first number in each box shows the profits firm A makes whilst the second number shows the profits firm B makes. For example, if both firms choose a low price, each firm makes profits of 4 (see bottom right quadrant).

2.022 Considering the various outcomes, both firms would prefer an outcome in which both charged a high price to that in which they both charged a low price. In this case, both firms would earn profits of 10 (top left quadrant). But if firm A chooses a high price, what is the best action that firm B can take? With firm A choosing a high price, if firm B also chooses a high price it earns profits of 10 (top left).

		FIRM B	
		High	Low
FIRM A	High	10, 10	0, 30
	Low	30, 0	4, 4

Figure 2.4 Illustrating a Nash Equilibrium

But if firm B chooses a low price, it earns profits of 30 as a result of undercutting firm A (top right). Hence, given that firm A chooses a high price, firm B's best strategy is to charge a low price.

But if firm B charges a low price, what is the best course of action for firm A? With firm B charging a low price, if firm A charges a high price, it earns zero profits (top right) but if it charges a low price, firm A earns profits of 4 (bottom right quadrant). Hence, firm A will charge a low price if firm B charges a low price. This outcome (the shaded area) represents a Nash equilibrium: the best firm A can do if firm B charges a low price is also to choose a low price and vice versa. In this example, it is also the only Nash equilibrium. In each of the other three quadrants, at least one of the firms wishes to change its behaviour given the behaviour of the other firm. So in the top left quadrant both firms wish to change their behaviour, in the bottom left Firm B wants to change and in the top right Firm A wants to change.

This simple model shows that while both firms prefer a situation in which both firms charge a high price, the incentive to charge a low price while the rival firm charges a high price results in both firms charging a low price.

The model demonstrates that firms operating on a market realise that the profitability of what they do is dependent on the behaviour of other firms operating on the market. If firms compete vigorously with one another and charge low prices their overall profits will be considerably less than if they increase prices and increase profits. They are all better off if they coordinate their behaviour and charge higher prices—this illustrates why there is a strong collective *incentive* to collude explicitly on such markets. As Adam Smith noted in *The Wealth of Nations* (published in 1778):

people of the same trade seldom meet together, even for merriment and diversion, but the conversation ends in a conspiracy against the public, or in some contrivance to raise prices.

A player on the market nevertheless knows that if its competitor charges a high price, it will be better off if it charges a low price (and cheats on any cartel agreement). Further, that if its competitor charges a low price, it must also do so. The Nash equilibrium for a one-shot game is, therefore, for the two firms to lower prices: it is better for both firms to charge a low price, whatever decision the other takes. Where, however, the game is repeated, it may be possible, if certain conditions exist, that, through recurring market interaction, collusion at the high price may be sustained; repeated interaction and 'the shadow of the future' enables punishment and rewards that can lead to firms cooperating on a market.[12] Collusion can be sustained if the expected profit from colluding today outweighs the expected profit of deviating from the cooperative arrangement.

An understanding of how and when collusion may occur, and the market conditions likely to allow it, helps to build an understanding of how such conduct may be identified (which markets are most susceptible to collusion) and countered.

c. *Alignment, Detection, and Punishment of Deviation: Markets Prone to Explicit Collusion*

The prisoners' dilemma illustrates that achieving and sustaining a cartel or collusive strategy is not easy. The success of a cartel, and explicit collusion, are dependent upon the parties being able

[12] See P. Dal Bó and G. R. Fréchette, 'On the Determinants of Cooperation in Infinitely Repeated Games: A Survey' (2018) 56(1) *J of Economic Literature* 60. But see also D. Bernheim and E. Madsen, 'Price Cutting and Business Stealing in Imperfect Cartels' (2017) 107(2) *Am Econ Rev* 387 (deliberate cheating by cartelists which goes unpunished can in certain circumstances be critical to the healthy functioning of a cartel).

to interact over a period of time and to put in place pricing, allocation, and enforcement structures to:

(a) align their behaviour—the competitors must reach a common understanding on prices, output, or another factor of competition;
(b) monitor the market so that deviations from the collusive strategy (cheating), a key problem facing cartels, can quickly be detected (it is the fear of retaliation and punishment that makes the collusion sustainable) and cheaters punished (normally in the form of a promise of loss of profits once the collusion is uncovered, i.e. the other firms lower price and expand output so that prices revert to the non-collusive or competitive price, or through trying to exclude them from the market);
(c) counter external threats, especially from new entry or powerful buyers.

These requirements indicate that markets with the following characteristics are more likely to facilitate collusion.

Fewer firms and higher market concentration: the fewer the number of operators on the market, or controlling the market, the simpler it is to coordinate actions, the cheaper the costs of collusion, the easier it is to detect cheating, and the easier it is to keep the arrangement secret. Further, the larger the market share that each undertaking has the greater the potential profits to be earned from successful collusion (the bigger the share that each will receive of the collusive pie). The greater the anticipated rewards the more likely they are to outweigh the risks and costs of detection. In markets with larger numbers of players, trade associations may play a role in coordinating behaviour, policing the internal stability of a cartel (for example, through monitoring for reporting deviations from the cartel agreement) and so facilitating collusion.[13] Trade associations may also provide opportunities for communication and transfers between cartel members.

Barriers to entry: barriers to entry are important to the successful operation of a cartel. In the absence of barriers, an increase in price will attract new competitors into the market.

Homogeneous goods: it will be much easier for firms to collude where products are homogeneous/similar and where the main dimension of competition is price competition (competition is not multi-dimensional); the possibility for non-price competition through product differentiation and cost of collusion is reduced. Many of the Commission's decisions prohibiting the operation of a cartel have been taken against undertakings whose products offer little scope for differentiation, for example, steel tubes, vitamins, sugar, cement, cartonboard, PVC, soda ash, polypropylene. Where products are heterogeneous cartel members may take steps, e.g. through standardisation and joint advertising, to foster an impression in consumers that their products are homogeneous,[14] or may seek to find other mechanisms for successfully cooperating.[15]

Firms with similar cost structures or operating efficiencies and market shares: the more similar the cost structures, the easier it is for the firms to cooperate on prices to be charged. Otherwise, for example, lower-cost firms may seek lower prices than other cartel members.

Market transparency: the more transparent the market, the easier it will be for firms to monitor what their competitors are doing and to detect cheating on, or deviation from, any cartel arrangement.

[13] Levenstein and Suslow, n. 8 and 'Breaking Up is Hard to Do: Determinants of Cartel Duration' (2011) 54 *J of Law and Economics* 455.

[14] See e.g. Case 246/86, *Re Roofing Felt Cartel: BELASCO v Commission* EU:C:1989:301, n. 246 and text.

[15] See e.g. J. E. Harrington, 'Heterogeneous firms can always collude on a minimum price' (2016) 138 *Economic Letters* 46 (regardless of heterogeneity, there is always a minimum cartel price that will make all firms better off).

Cartel members may therefore develop preventive measures that make defection transparent to them and employ punishment strategies where cheating does occur.[16]

Mechanisms for coordination: to be successful cartels may need considerable coordination—to allow alignment of behaviour and to ensure the stability of the cartel. Internal enforcement mechanisms are time-consuming and expensive to operate, especially the larger the number of participants involved and the more complex the means of cooperation. The more elaborate the monitoring and enforcement devices, the more vulnerable the cartel is to detection. To make a cartel more robust, members may, in addition to price-fixing, agree to share markets and/or to adhere to quotas (restriction of output is ordinarily essential to sustain a price rise) which may be easier to implement and police.[17] Other agreements between firms may also facilitate collusion between them, for example by rendering the market more transparent through agreements to exchange information or vertical agreements containing provisions such as meeting competition clauses or resale price maintenance.[18]

Dispersed buyers with no controlling purchasing power: where buyers are numerous and dispersed it is difficult to advertise price-cuts or reductions and, consequently to cheat on the cartel, without it being brought to the attention of the other members. Further, it will be easier to operate a cartel where individual buyers do not have controlling purchasing power.

Demand patterns and depressed conditions: cyclical changes in demand and recession may incentivise the formation of a cartel but may also lead to its breakdown. Undertakings may find it difficult to determine whether a decline in demand for their products is due to recession, a reduction in demand as a whole or to another member cheating on the cartel. This uncertainty may cause the members to deviate from the terms of the cartel. Further, where large orders are put in for a product occasionally (rather than on a regular basis) there may be a greater temptation for cheating since the gains from cheating may exceed the anticipated gains from coordination.

Facilitators: as well as trade associations, cartels sometimes enlist the assistance of consultants to design and manage their operations. For example, the Commission found that Fides/AC Treuhand, an association-management company, helped guide the implementation of a number of chemical sector cartels.[19] In public procurement, corrupt government officials may also sometimes play a role in facilitating the operation of a bid rigging cartel.[20]

In a speech, the (then) Competition Commissioner Mario Monti emphasised that these types of factors are likely to lead to collusive arrangements between market operators. He recognised, however, that cartel agreements can also operate outside industries with these traditional characteristics.[21]

[16] See A. Bhaskarabhatla, C. Chatterjee, and B. Karreman, 'Hit Where it Hurts: Cartel Policing Using Targeted Sales and Supply Embargoes' (2016) 59 *J of Law and Economics* 805.

[17] See e.g. discussion of the global lysine cartel uncovered in the US, S. Hammond, 'Caught in the Act: Inside an International Cartel', Speech at OECD Competition Committee Working Party No. 3 Public Prosecutors Program, Paris, 18 October 2005.

[18] See further Chap. 11.

[19] See Chap. 4 and e.g. Case C-194/14 P, *AC-Treuhand AG v Commission* EU:C:2015:717, especially paras. 26–47 and see R. C. Marshall, 'Unobserved Collusion: Warning Signs and Concerns' (2017) 5 *J of Antitrust Enforcement* 329.

[20] See e.g. R. Anderson, A. Jones, and W. E. Kovacic, 'Preventing Corruption, Supplier Collusion and the Corrosion of Civic Trust: A Procompetitive Program to Improve the Effectiveness and Legitimacy of Public Procurement' (2019) 26(4) *George Mason LR* 1233.

[21] See also e.g. Harrington, n. 15 and M. Hellwig and K. Hüschelrath, 'Cartel Cases and the Cartel Enforcement Process in the European Union 2001–2015: A Quantitative Assessment' (2017) 62 *Ant Bull* 400.

M. Monti, 'Fighting Cartels Why and How? Why Should We Be Concerned with Cartels and Collusive Behaviour?', 3rd Nordic Competition Policy Conference, Stockholm, 11–12 September 2000

As we all know, cartels do not occur with the same frequency in all sectors. Indeed, some sectors have been particularly prone to cartelisation. These sectors are generally characterised by a relatively high degree of concentration, significant barriers to entry, homogeneous products, similar cost structures and mature technologies. In such stable sectors it is easier to reach consensus on the collusive outcome and to maintain it. The steel, cement and chemical industries can be mentioned as examples of sectors that fit this description and in which the Commission has in the past uncovered cartels.

However, our experience shows that cartel behaviour is not limited to such traditional industries. Recent investigations concerning the banking sector and the liberal professions demonstrate that we should certainly not lose sight of other sectors. In the case of the liberal professions collusion has generally involved the fixing of tariffs. In these sectors it is often quite difficult to assess with precision the level of quality. Price competition is therefore quite an important aspect of competition. It is also interesting to note that in these cases the cartels have virtually always been operated by a trade association. The involvement of an association is necessary due to the large number of operators. One study has found that trade associations were involved in most of the cases that involved more than 10 undertakings. Moreover, in the case of the liberal professions the rules of the association can be a very effective weapon in maintaining discipline.

d. *The Desire to Combat and Eliminate Cartels*

As consensus over the economic harm caused by cartels has taken hold, international initiatives[22] and greater multilateral and bilateral cooperation between competition authorities have significantly contributed to the dramatic shift in perceptions of, and attitudes towards, cartels and to the development of an international fight against them; '[a] truly global effort against hardcore cartels has emerged'.[23] Cartels have been described as 'the supreme evil of antitrust',[24] the most 'egregious' violation of competition law,[25] and as 'cancers on the open market economy'.[26]

It is sometimes argued that in the long run most cartels will break down without the intervention of any competition authority. The Commission (like other competition agencies) has however uncovered a number of cartels that have been operated successfully over long periods of time (the Animal Phosphates cartel, for example, was found to have lasted for 419 months—nearly 35 years).[27] In the meantime, loss to society as a whole is suffered. It is thus widely accepted that cartels should be summarily condemned when uncovered through the application of a per se rule, or a strong presumption

[22] The OECD has led an international effort to halt cartel conduct, see especially OECD, 'Recommendation of the Council Concerning Effective Action Against Hard Core Cartels', C(98)35/FINAL, May 1998, OECD, 'Fighting Hard Core Cartels—Harm, Effective Sanctions and Leniency Programmes' (2002) and OECD, 'Hard Core Cartels: Third Report on the Implementation of the 1998 Council Recommendation' (2005).

[23] ICN Cartels Working Group, 'Defining Hard Core Cartel Conduct, Effective Institutions, Effective Penalties' (2005), 5. International cooperation is discussed in Chap. 17.

[24] *Verizon Communications v Law Offices of Curtis V. Trinko*, 540 US 398, 408 (2004).

[25] 'Recommendation of the Council Concerning Effective action Against Hard Core Cartels', OECD Publication C(98)35/FINAL.

[26] Monti, n. 3.

[27] See Hellwig and Hüschelrath, n. 21 (finding that of the 113 cartels surveyed they lasted on average 87 months) and M. C. Levenstein and V. Y. Suslow, 'Price Fixing Hits Home: An Empirical Study of US Price-Fixing Conspiracies' (2016) 48 *Review of Industrial Organization* 361 (finding average cartel duration to be between five and six years).

of illegality[28] and attention has shifted to the questions of how the seriousness of cartel offences can best be reflected and how cartel activity can be prevented and deterred.

In the US, cartel activity is prosecuted criminally and, since the mid-1990s, the Department of Justice (DOJ) has concentrated its enforcement resources on international cartels that victimise American consumers and businesses. Huge fines are now imposed on corporations and executives, and executives are sent to prison for long periods, so providing a strong deterrent to cartel activity.[29] Further, firms in breach may be liable to treble damages to persons injured by the violation and may exceed any fine imposed.[30]

In the EU, the fight against cartels has also intensified since the end of the 1990s and become one of the principal concerns of the Commission;[31] it deploys significant resources to take effective action against them despite the major effort in terms of manpower and lengthy procedure that their identification and combating involves. This policy has not softened during the various financial, economic, and health crises since 2008 in order to allow firms to weather the storms.[32]

The Commission's commitment to fight cartels has been reflected by a number of initiatives designed to facilitate the detection and prohibition of cartels and to ensure their deterrence, for example:

- the creation of an entire cartel directorate (Comp.G) within DG Comp;
- the adoption of more cartel decisions since 2000;[33]
- the imposition of greater fines on cartel members (see Tables 9.1 and 9.2 and Chapter 13).

Table 9.1 Level of fines 1990 to 29 November 2022 (adjusted for Court judgments)*

Year	Amount in euros
1990–1994	344,282,550.00
1995–1999	270,963,500.00
2000–2004	3,157,348,710.00
2005–2009	7,863,307,786.50
2010–2014	7,598,728,479.00
2015–2019	8,187,380,159.00
2020–2022	2,222,928,000.00
Total	29,745,465,612.50

[28] See Section 3.

[29] See e.g. speech of S. D. Hammond, 'The Evolution of Criminal Antitrust Enforcement Over the Last Two Decades', 25 February 2010.

[30] See Chap. 14. [31] See Monti, n. 3.

[32] N. Kroes, 'Private and public enforcement of EU competition law—5 years on', Brussels, 12 March 2009 ('If we create the impression that it is OK to "turn a blind eye" to cartels or for an executive to fail to ask questions about suspicious behaviour, then we create only more trouble—not only in competition, but across all our markets. This sort of misbehaviour is infectious. They breed the sorts of complacent cultures that have generated our current financial and economic situation').

[33] See cartel statistics, available on DG Comp's website at: <http://ec.europa.eu/competition/cartels/statistics/statistics.pdf>, Hellwig and Hüschelrath, n. 21 (between 2001 and 2015 the Commission adopted 90 cartel decision, relating to 113 cartels) and A. Chapsal, P.Y. Cremieux, J. Freimark, and E. Frot, 'A Commissioners' History of Cartel Enforcement in Europe: Multidimensional Comparison of Administrations' (2020) 11 *JECLAP* 302. This was facilitated by the abolition of the notification and authorisation system in 2004.

Table 9.2 Highest cartel fines (adjusted for Court judgments) (to 8 July 2022)*

Commission Decision	Total fines (in €)
Trucks	3,807,022,000 (including a 1,008,766,000 fine for Daimler)
Forex	1,413,274,000
TV and Computer Monitor Tubes	1,409,588,000 (including a 705,296,000 fine for Philips)
Euro Interest Rate Derivatives (EIRD)	1,308,172,000 (including a 465,861,000 fine for Deutsche Bank)
Car Glass	1,185,500,000 (including a fine of 715,000,000 on Saint Gobain)
Automotive Bearings	953,306,000
Car Emissions	875,189,000 (including a fine of 502,362,000 for VW Group)
Elevators and Escalators	832,422,250
Vitamins	790,515,000
Airfreight (including re-adoption)	739,642,616

* See <http://ec.europa.eu/competition/cartels/cases/cases.html> and <http://ec.europa.eu/competition/cartels/statistics/statistics.pdf>.

Although these fines, imposed on undertakings following the Commission's administrative procedure,[34] are extremely high, some argue that they are not sufficient on their own to achieve deterrence and the view that other mechanisms to prevent and deter cartel conduct are necessary, including the punishment of *individuals* responsible for violation of cartel rules, is gaining traction.[35] A number of Member States have criminalised cartel activity, or certain types of it,[36] and/or impose civil sanctions on individuals.

Undertakings engaged in cartels may also be excluded from participation in public procurement processes.[37] In *Generali*,[38] the CJ ruled that an undertaking may be excluded by public authorities

[34] Reg. 1/2003 [2003] OJ L1/1, Art. 23(5) (which 'shall not be of a criminal law nature').

[35] See e.g. G. J. Werden and M. J. Simon, 'Why Price Fixers Should Go to Prison' (1987) 32 *Ant Bull* 917, C. Beaton-Wells and A. Ezrachi (eds.), *Criminalising Cartels: Critical Studies of an International Regulatory Movement* (Hart Publishing, 2011), P. Whelan, *The Criminalization of European Cartel Enforcement: Theoretical, Legal, and Practical Challenges* (Oxford University Press, 2014), but see e.g. A. Jones and R. Williams, 'The UK Response to the Global Effort Against Cartels: Is Criminalization Really the Solution? (2014) 2 *J of Antitrust Enforcement* 1, W. Wils, 'Does the Effective Enforcement of Articles 81 and 82 Require Not Only Fines on Undertakings but also Individual Penalties, in Particular Imprisonment?' in C.-D. Ehlermann (ed.), *European Competition Law Annual 2001: Effective Private Enforcement of EC Antitrust Law* (Hart Publishing, 2002).

[36] Some form of criminal regime exists in more than 30 jurisdictions including, e.g., Canada, US, Japan, France, Austria, Norway, South Korea, Iceland, Slovakia, Slovenia, Ireland, Romania, Denmark, Germany, UK, Estonia, Hungary, Czech Republic, South Africa, Mexico, and Australia. The more States that have criminal regimes, the harder it will be for an individual to avoid extradition where a criminal offence is committed, see Case C-191/16, *Pisciotti* EU:C:2018:222 (the extradition of Pisciotti from Germany to the US was not incompatible with EU law). See also J. E. Harrington, 'The Deterrence of Collusion by a Structural Remedy' (2017) 160 *Economic Letters* 78 (divestiture might operate as more of a deterrent, is more effective at compensating those consumers harmed, and is corrective by reducing the likelihood of recidivism and preventing post-cartel tacit collusion).

[37] See e.g. Council Dir. 2014/24/EU [2014] OJ L94/65, Art. 57 (contracting authorities may exclude, or be required by Member States to exclude, undertakings from procurement procedures where there are plausible grounds to conclude that they entered into agreements infringing Art. 101).

[38] Case C-470/13, EU:C:2014:2469.

from tendering for public contracts where it has committed an infringement of competition law, for which it was fined, even if the procurement procedure is not covered by the EU Procurement Directive.

Other factors that reflect the toughening attitude towards cartels include:

- the introduction in 1996 and refinement (in 2002 and 2006) of a leniency programme encouraging parties to confess to their participation in an illegal cartel in return for immunity from, or a reduction in, fines, the introduction in 2017 of a whistleblower tool, encouraging any individual to provide the Commission with information about cartel behaviour or other anti-competitive business practices,[39] and the Commission's introduction in 2008 of a settlement procedure for cartel cases (in return for a 10 per cent discount on fines),[40] see Chapter 13;
- increased international cooperation focused on the elimination of cartel activity, see Chapters 13 and 17; and
- the Commission's initiative to encourage greater private enforcement of the competition rules, see Chapter 14.

(ii) Tacit Collusion and the Oligopoly Problem

Economic pricing theories seeking to explain oligopolistic behaviour are numerous.[41] Game theory provides particularly important insights into the problems that may arise on an oligopolistic market and explains how 'virtually anything can happen'[42] on such markets. It challenges the view that concentrated markets always deliver poorer outcomes for consumers and higher profitability for firms, indicating that although on some oligopolistic markets players recognise that the price and output decisions they take are affected by the choices made by their rivals—i.e. that they are interdependent—and succeed in maintaining prices well above production costs for years, others gravitate towards price warfare.[43]

The prisoners' dilemma provides a framework for understanding when an oligopolistic market may be conducive to collusion. The model makes clear that, even without explicit collusion, where firms directly communicate with each other, oligopolists, which have heightened awareness of other firms' presence on the market and recognise their interdependence, understand that if they compete less vigorously they will be able to earn higher profits and that, conversely, cutting prices will simply lead to their rivals following suit; they may therefore coordinate and monitor actions without communication. As economists consider the outcome or effects to be similar to explicit collusion, they describe this behaviour as 'tacit collusion'.

For firms to be able to tacitly collude, however, certain conditions must hold. It is necessary for the firms: to realise their mutual interdependence; to be able successfully to engage in a common form of behaviour, i.e. to align their conduct (this is of course more difficult to achieve without explicit collusion); to monitor what their competitors are doing on the market and to realise that if they deviate from the common behaviour they will be punished or disciplined (with low prices and low profits); and to be

[39] See <http://ec.europa.eu/competition/cartels/overview/index_en.html>. In many Member States employees have been shown to be willing to engage in whistle-blowing, see e.g. the whistle-blowing survey carried out by Freshfields, Bruckhaus Deringer, <www.freshfields.com/en-gb/our-thinking/campaigns/whistleblowing/>.

[40] See <http://ec.europa.eu/competition/cartels/legislation/settlements.html> and IP/08/1056 (the procedure speeds up investigations, reduces the number of infringement decisions appealed, and so may free up Commission resources enabling it to handle more cartel cases).

[41] See e.g. Cournot's and Bertrand's oligopoly pricing model, discussed in e.g. S. Bishop and M. Walker, *The Economics of EC Competition Law: Concepts, Application and Measurement* (3rd edn, Sweet & Maxwell, 2010), 2.23–2.28.

[42] F. M. Scherer and D. Ross, *Industrial Market Structure and Economic Performance* (3rd edn, Houghton Mifflin, 1990), 199.

[43] Scherer and Ross, ibid. and Stigler, n. 10.

protected from external threats. These markets are likely to have similar characteristics to those which facilitate explicit collusion (and described earlier). For example, the market is likely to be transparent and characterised by high concentration, barriers to entry, homogenous products, firms with similar cost and demand structures and a common high valuation of future profits, some mechanism for alignment (for example, through either signalling[44] or a focal point[45]), and a mechanism for punishing those deviating from parallelism (perhaps through costly price wars or expansion of output). In contrast, coordination is liable to be difficult to sustain on markets characterised by differentiated products, volatile demand or demand booms, the existence of large and sophisticated buyers, and ease of entry or cost asymmetries.[46] Where tacit collusion is feasible, the incentives, and need, for explicit collusion may reduce. Explicit collusion may therefore be more likely in markets in which tacit collusion is difficult to sustain.[47]

C. COMPETITION LAW AND COLLUSION (EXPLICIT AND TACIT)

Explicit collusion in fixing prices, restricting output, and/or sharing markets through an agreement, decision, or concerted practice falls within the scope of, and is generally prohibited by, Article 101 (see Section 3). The difficulty with *tacit* collusion is that although the impact of such coordination on the market is the same as, or at least similar to, where it is explicit (and consumer welfare is harmed), the parties have not in fact *agreed* or otherwise explicitly communicated with each other to coordinate their behaviour. How then should the competition rules deal with tacit collusion?

In the EU, the European Commission can utilise the merger rules to try and prevent mergers between firms on an oligopolistic market, which would *create or strengthen* a market situation in which coordinated effects occur (collusion between the parties), so leading to a significant impediment to effective competition (see Chapter 15). But the question of what can be done about markets which are already concentrated and on which tacit collusion is, or may be, occurring is more difficult. In the US, in the 1960s, there was support for the view that this type of unreasonable market power should in itself be condemned and that there should be power to dissolve firms found to possess it.[48] Indeed, a White House Task Force on Antitrust Policy proposed legislation (never adopted) that would permit deconcentration of markets where four or fewer firms had a combined market share of 70 per cent or more *unless* the defendant could establish that such a step would reduce efficiency.[49] Although support for this kind of legislation was abandoned following 'post-1970s scepticism about ambitious governmental interventions in the economy',[50] concern about increasing market concentration and the power of large market players is remerging.[51]

[44] By signalling, e.g. making price announcements in advance, firms may be able to indicate what their future pricing policy will be. It will be a question of degree whether or not this type of conduct can be characterised as concerted behaviour contrary to Art. 101(1), see Section 3.B.iii.

[45] A practice of recommending prices can operate as a focal point and facilitate alignment of behaviour, see Chap. 11.

[46] See e.g. Van den Bergh and Camesasca, n. 5, 5.2.3 and N. Horstmann, J. Krämer, D. Schnurr, 'Number Effects and Tacit Collusion in Experimental Oligopolies' (2018) *J of Industrial Economics* 650.

[47] See L. Garrod and M. Olczak, 'Explicit vs Tacit Collusion: The Effects of Firm Numbers and Asymmetries' (2018) 56 *International J of Industrial Organization* 1.

[48] See e.g. C. Kaysen and D. Turner, *Antitrust Policy* (Harvard University Press, 1959), 110–119 and 266–272 and criticisms of these 'startling' conclusions set out in R. H. Bork, *The Antitrust Paradox* (Basic Books, 1978, reprinted with a new Introduction and Epilogue, 1993), 176.

[49] The White House Task Force Report on Antitrust Policy (the Neal Report), 1968 recommended adoption of this Concentrated Industries Act (it was endorsed by 11 of its 13 members) and reflected the beliefs of (then) the Harvard School, which subsequently were challenged and criticised, see e.g. H. Hovenkamp, 'The Neal Report and the Crisis in Antitrust', University of Iowa Legal Studies Research Paper No. 09-09 (March 2009).

[50] R. A. Posner, *Antitrust Law* (University of Chicago Press, 1976) and Hovenkamp, ibid. But see J. Baker and S. Salop, 'Antitrust, Competition Policy, and Inequality' (2015) *Geo LJ Online* 104.

[51] See Chap. 1, especially discussion of the Neo-Brandeis School.

In the EU, investigations into markets which do not appear to be operating effectively can be conducted, but generally the ability to impose sanctions and remedies is likely to depend upon a violation of the competition laws being established. An important question therefore is whether tacit collusion can be viewed as a problem stemming from the anti-competitive behaviour of the oligopolists which infringes Article 101 or Article 102. Since the effects of tacit collusion are similar to cases in which there is explicit collusion and the firms' decisions could be seen as not having been taken truly unilaterally (but rather taking into account the anticipated reaction of their competitors), it is arguable that parallel behaviour or conscious parallelism, without any proof of actual communication between the undertakings, can be prohibited as an illegal concerted practice under Article 101 or as an abuse of a collective dominant position under Article 102. In the US, for example, Richard Posner was at one time a proponent of the view that the concepts of contract, combination, or conspiracy in s. 1 of the Sherman Act 1890 were capable of reaching, and an appropriate mechanism for dealing with, tacit collusion.[52] This view has not, however, been accepted by the US Supreme Court.[53] or the CJ in the EU. Sections 3 to 5 consider the extent to which Article 101 or Article 102 may be applied as an effective tool against tacit collusion on a market or to prevent *other* behaviour of oligopolistic firms operating on the market, for example information-sharing practices which might lead to or encourage tacit collusion by rendering the market more transparent or discouraging or prohibiting deviation from a collusive strategy.

3. CARTELS

A. SUBSTANTIVE ANALYSIS UNDER ARTICLE 101

(i) Cartels Are Intrinsically Detrimental to the Competitive Process and Not Related to the Lawful Realisation of Efficiencies

Cartels, operated by fixing prices, bid rigging, imposing quotas on members, and/or sharing markets between them, are classic examples of joint conduct prohibited by Article 101. Indeed, Article 101(1) (a)–(c) specifically refers to restrictions of competition conducted through the fixing of purchase or selling prices, limiting or controlling production, markets, technical development, or investment or sharing markets or sources of supply.

In Chapters 4 and 5, it is seen that these types of 'naked' cartel activity have been found to have as their *object* the restriction of competition and are assumed to restrict competition[54] even if: the agreement has proved difficult to apply in practice (and may not, therefore, have had the effect of restricting competition); a participant always intended to ignore the terms of the agreement and that it did, in fact, cheat on the cartel (when cheating the undertaking inevitably relies on the existence of the agreement or concerted practice and will not gain unless the others adhere to its terms); the subjective motive of the parties to any such agreement may have been to deal with an industry crisis or overcapacity; and/or the parties had acted with the knowledge of, or with support from, a national government. Further, being naked, they have consistently been found to be incapable of satisfying

[52] On this debate, see e.g. R. Posner, 'Oligopoly and the Antitrust Laws: A Suggested Approach' (1969) 21 *Stan LR* 1562, but see now Posner, n. 50 and D. F. Turner, 'The Definition of Agreement under the Sherman Act: Conscious Parallelism and Refusals to Deal' (1962) 75 *Harvard LR* 655, L. Kaplow, 'Price-fixing policy' (2018) 61 *International J of Industrial Organization* 1 and K. Khoo, 'Regulating the Inferential Process in Alleged Article 101 Infringements' (2017) 13 *J of Competition Law and Economics* 45.

[53] See, in particular, *Theatre Enterprises v Paramount Film Distributing Corp*, 346 US 537 (1954).

[54] Case C-67/13 P, *Groupement des Cartes Bancaires v Commission* EU:C:2014:2204.

the conditions of Article 101(3). They are intrinsically detrimental to the competitive process and are not reasonably related to the lawful realisation of cost-reducing or output-enhancing efficiencies, so cannot be held lawful under Article 101.[55]

(ii) Price-fixing

From the earliest cases the CJ has stressed the importance of price competition between competitors. In *Dyestuffs*,[56] it stated:

> The function of price competition is to keep prices down to the lowest possible level . . . Although every producer is free to change his prices, taking into account in so doing the present or foreseeable conduct of his competitors, nevertheless it is contrary to the rules on competition contained in the Treaty for a producer to co-operate with his competitors, in any way whatsoever, in order to determine a co-ordinated course of action relating to a price increase and to ensure its success by prior elimination of all uncertainty as to each other's conduct regarding the essential elements of that action, such as the amount, subject-matter, date and place of the increases.[57]

Since then the Commission has condemned numerous cartels which directly or indirectly facilitate level pricing whether by suppliers or retailers concluding agreements, such as: to fix or prohibit discounts, rebates, or other financial concessions; to consult on price lists; to give warning of price increases to provide reassurance that a price war will not break out; to pursue a collaborative strategy of higher pricing; to exchange price information and price lists; and/or the discussion and implementation of target prices.[58] For example, it has condemned price coordination between undertakings selling: beef; aluminium fluoride; sodium chlorate; calcium carbide; magnesium-based reagents; concrete reinforcing bars; stainless steel; synthetic rubber; bleaching chemicals; acrylic glass; road bitumen; copper fittings; methylglucamine; Dutch industrial gases; zinc phosphates; carbonless paper; vitamin products; graphite electrodes; lysine; plasterboard; airfreight; LCD panels; washing powder; bananas; glass for cathode ray tubes; refrigeration compressors; mounting for windows and window doors; freight forwarders; water management products; TV and computer monitor tubes; automotive wire harnesses; shrimps; flexible polyurethane foam; car and truck bearings; steel abrasives; canned mushrooms; envelopes; parking heaters; retail food packaging; cargo block-train services; alternators and starters; trucks; rechargeable batteries; car battery recycling; thermal systems for cars; car lighting systems; car safety systems; spark plugs; car braking systems; maritime transport of vehicles; capacitors; car safety equipment; FOREX; canned vegetables; purchasers of ethylene; suppliers of closure systems for cars; European governments bonds; SSA bonds; and ethanol.[59]

[55] Monti, n. 3. In the US, cartel arrangements are illegal per se, see e.g. *Northern Pac R Co v United States*, 356 US 1, 5 (1958).

[56] Cases 48, 49, and 51–57/69, *ICI v Commission (Dyestuffs)* EU:C:1972:70.

[57] Ibid., paras. 115 and 118.

[58] See e.g. Case 311/85, *ASBL Vereniging van Vlaamse Reisbureaus v ASBL Sociale Dienst van de Plaatselijke en Gewestelijke Overheidsdiensten* EU:C:1987:418, COMP/33.708–33.711, *British Sugar plc, Tate & Lyle plc, Napier Brown & Co Ltd, James Budgett Sugars Ltd (British Sugar)* [1999] OJ L76/1, substantially upheld by the GC, Case T-202/98, *Tate & Lyle v Commission* EU:T:2001:185, on appeal Case C-359/01 P, EU:C:2004:255, COMP/37.152, *Plasterboard* [2005] OJ L166/8, see Case T-50/03, *Saint-Gobain Gyproc Belgium NV v Commission* EU:T:2008:252, Cases T-25/95 etc., *Cimenteries CBR SA v Commission* EU:T:2000:77, para. 1531 (at least where it underpins another anti-competitive agreement), broadly *aff'd* Cases C-204/00 P etc., *Aalborg Portland A/S v Commission* EU:C:2004:6, Case C-8/72, *Vereeniging van Cementhandelaren v Commission* EU:C:1972:84, para. 21. See also discussion of information exchange, Section 4.B.

[59] See <http://ec.europa.eu/competition/cartels/cases/cases.html>.

In many of the cases, the price-fixing has been supplemented by other restrictive operations such as measures designed: to limit imports; to allocate sales quotas; to share markets; to share customers; and/or to fix other trading conditions (such as transport costs).[60] In *Cartonboard*,[61] for example, the Commission fined 19 producers of cartonboard for, over a long period of time, planning and implementing uniform and regular price increases within the Union, planning and coordinating price initiatives in advance, freezing market shares, controlling output, and organising the exchange of confidential information.

A number of these cartels have been global ones. For example, the Commission's decision in *Vitamins*[62] followed criminal proceedings in the US.[63] The parties had agreed target and minimum prices, quotas (agreeing to maintain the status quo in respect of market shares), and provided for compensation payments to be paid in case quotas were exceeded. Elaborate provisions for monitoring and enforcing the agreements were also established and a formal structure and management was involved in the operation of the agreements, including at most senior levels of management.

Article 101(1) applies to price-fixing agreements in all economic sectors relating not only to goods but also to services. In *Fine Art Auction Houses*,[64] the Commission found that Christie's and Sotheby's had fixed commission fees and other trading conditions between 1993 and 2000, and cartels have been uncovered in the transport sector (for example, aviation and ferry services),[65] and in the financial sectors.[66] For example, the Commission imposed fines on banks in *German Banks*[67] and *Austrian Banks ('Lombard Club')*.[68] In the latter case, the Commission found that the Austrian banks had concluded agreements about interest rates and charges/fees and by meeting regularly had coordinated their conduct with respect to every essential factor of competition. In a series of cases, it has also imposed fines on undertakings (including a facilitator, ICAP) involved in manipulation of financial benchmarks such as London Interbank Offered Rate (LIBOR) and

[60] See e.g. COMP/38.279, *French Beef* [2003] OJ L209/12, *aff'd* (but fines reduced) in Cases T-217 and 245/03, *FNCBV v Commission* EU:T:2006:391, Cases C-101 and 110/07, *Coop de France Bétail, FNSEA and others v Commission* EU:C:2008:741, COMP/36.490, *Graphite Electrodes* [2002] OJ L100/1, on appeal Cases T-236/01, *Tokai Carbon v Commission* EU:T:2004:118 (some of the fines reduced on appeal), Cases C-301 and 308/04 P, *SGL v Commission* EU:C:2006:432 (fine increased on SGL), COMP/36.700, *Dutch Industrial Gases* [2003] OJ L84/1, *aff'd* Case T-303/02, *Westfalen Gassen Nederland v Commission* EU:T:2006:374, Case C-172/14, *ING Pensii v Consiliul Concuretnei* EU:C:2015:484, COMP/39.234, *Synthetic Rubber* [2007] OJ L182/31, Cases T-44 and 45/07 *Kaučuk v Commission* EU:T:2011:358, and Case T-304/02, *Hoek Loos NV v Commission* EU:T:2006:184.

[61] COMP/33.833 [1994] OJ L243/1, see on appeal e.g. Case T-334/94, *Sarrió SA v Commission* EU:T:1998:97, on appeal see e.g. Case C-286/98 P, *Stora Kopparbergs Bergslags AB v Commission* EU:C:2000:630.

[62] COMP/37.512 [2003] OJ L6/1, see Cases T-15 and 26/02, EU:T:2006:74 (reducing some of the fines) and Table 9.2.

[63] The defendants also agreed to pay US customers more than $1 billion in damages, see 'Status Report: An Overview of Recent Developments in the Antitrust Division's Criminal Enforcement Program', DOJ Antitrust Division, 25 February 2004.

[64] COMP/37.784 [2002] OJ L200/92 (a significant fine was imposed on Sotheby's, although Christie's escaped a fine in consequence of its cooperation with the Commission).

[65] See e.g. COMP/39.258, *Airfreight* [2014] OJ C371/57 (but fines annulled in Cases T-9/11 etc., *Air Canada v Commission* EU:T:2015:994) and COMP/37.444, *SAS/Maersk Air* [2001] OJ L265/15, *aff'd* Case T-241/01, *Scandinavian Airlines System AB v Commission* EU:T:2005:296.

[66] See also e.g. FOREX, European Governments Bonds, 20 May 2021.

[67] COMP/37.919 [2003] OJ L15/1, annulled Case T-44/02, *Dresdner Bank v Commission* EU:T:2006:271. See also COMP/30.717, *Eurocheque: Helsinki Agreement* [1992] OJ L95/50 (fines on French banks and Eurocheque for operating a scheme under which the same commission was charged for both Eurocheque transactions and the use of Carte Bleu), partially annulled and fines reduced on appeal, see Case T-39/92, *Groupement des Cartes Bancaires v Commission* EU:T:1994:20.

[68] COMP/36.571 [2004] OJ L56/1, *aff'd* (but fine reduced on Österreichische Postsparkasse AG) see Cases T-259–264 and 271/02, *Raiffeisen Zentralbank Österreich v Commission* EU:T:2006:396 and Case C-125/07 *Raiffeisen Zentralbank Österreich v Commission* EU:C:2009:576.

the Euro Interbank Offered Rate (EURIBOR) (including Swiss Franc, Euro, and Yen interest rate derivatives).[69]

The Commission has also been concerned that high levels of regulation (including State or self-regulation) within the sphere of professional services in Europe serve to restrict competition. Although some carefully targeted regulation may be necessary in the liberal professions to deal with specific issues arising, such as asymmetry of information between customers and service providers, externalities, and to ensure adequate and sufficient supply of these services, the Commission has been concerned that anti-competitive practices, such as the fixing of prices or recommended prices,[70] is widespread.[71] It has therefore adopted two reports on the subject, a 'Report on Competition in Professional Services'[72] and 'Professional Services—Scope for More Reform'[73] which have examined the question of whether the regulatory regimes existing for lawyers, notaries, accountants, architects, engineers, and pharmacies can be adapted or modernised to spur economic growth and value to consumers. In the first report, the Commission states that 'within an otherwise competitive market, price regulation is unlikely to ensure prices that are lower than competitive levels'.[74] Further, that price recommendations 'like fixed prices, may have a significant negative effect on competition. First, recommended prices may facilitate the coordination of prices between service providers. Secondly, they can mislead consumers about reasonable price levels.'[75]

Although the Commission called for restrictions to be reviewed and, where not objectively justified, removed or replaced by less restrictive rules[76] and for national competition authorities (NCAs) to deal with remaining restraints (since in most cases the professional rules have their origin and effect in a single Member State), the Commission has been prepared to take infringement procedures itself. In particular, it takes the view that rules relating to price are likely to constitute automatic violations of Article 101(1), even if in practice an increase in price may be very difficult to sustain in this sphere.[77] In *Belgian Architects*,[78] the Commission fined the Belgian Architects' Association in respect of its operation of a recommended minimum fee scale, laying down fees as a percentage of the value of

[69] The Commission e.g. imposed fines of €1.71 billion on 4 December 2013 in cartels in the Euro and Yen interest rate derivatives (EIRD and YIRD) markets, a fine of €14.9 million on 4 February 2015 on ICAP for participation in and facilitating several cartels in the YIRD sector, and in October 2014 fines of €61.6 million and €32.3 million on banks involved in cartels influencing Swiss Franc LIBOR and Swiss Franc interest derivatives, see <http://ec.europa.eu/competition/cartels/cases/cases.html>, Case T-180/15, *ICAP v Commission* EU:T:2017:795, P. J. F. Huizing, 'Parallel Enforcement of Rate Rigging: Lessons to be Learned from LIBOR' (2015) 3 *J of Antitrust Enforcement* 173 and A. K. Pascall, 'Tail Wagging the Dog: The Manipulation of Benchmark Rates—A Competitive Bone of Contention' (2016) 2 *World Competition* 162. See also €1.07 billion fines for foreign exchange spot trading, COMP/40.135, 16 May 2019.

[70] Communication from the Commission, Report on Competition in Professional Services, COM(2004) 83 final, 9 February 2004, <https://eur-lex.europa.eu/legal-content/EN/TXT/?uri=celex:52004DC0083>, Table 2 indicating that recommended prices existed in Austria, Belgium, Denmark, Greece, Ireland, Luxembourg, Portugal, and Spain. In 2018 the Cypriot Bar Association repealed rules which required lawyers to charge a minimum fee for their work rather than competing against each other on price following a Commission investigation triggered by a complaint lodged by Fairness in Fees Ltd, see <www.brickcourt.co.uk/news/detail/cyprus-lawyers-forced-to-abandon-minimum-fees>.

[71] Ibid., para. 1 (occupations requiring special training in the liberal arts or sciences, for example lawyers, notaries, accountants, architects, engineers, and pharmacists).

[72] Ibid., Table 1 (professions with fixed, minimum, or maximum prices exist in Austria, Belgium, France, Germany, Greece, Italy, Luxembourg, the Netherlands, and Spain).

[73] 'Professional Services—Scope for More Reform. Follow-up on Competition in Professional Services', SEC(2005) 1064.

[74] Ibid., para. 32. [75] Ibid., para. 37. [76] Ibid., para. 90.

[77] 'Since the number of practitioners in these markets is high, cartel discipline is difficult to maintain and cheating very attractive. The non-sustainability of price cartels under such circumstances is also confirmed by empirical evidence.' Van den Bergh and Camesasca, n. 5, 5.3.1.1. For an examination of developments in Ireland, see C. Boate and K. MacGuill, 'Regulating Competition in Professional Services—A Balancing Act' (2013) 9 *European Competition Journal* 105.

[78] COMP/38.549 [2005] OJ L004/10.

work realised. The practice had as its object the restriction of competition since it sought to coordinate the pricing behaviour of architects which was unnecessary for the proper practice of the profession. Rather, the architects should have been free to charge a fee commensurate with their skills, efficiency, costs, and reputation.[79]

(iii) Buyer Cartels, Wage-fixing, and No-poach Agreements

Price-fixing amongst buyers restricts the parties' freedom to negotiate buying prices for inputs and might increase buyer power and/or facilitate collusion in output markets. For example, agreement on the purchase price of a key raw material may facilitate the operation of the cartel at the downstream level.[80] In its Horizontal Cooperation Guidelines, the Commission describes buyer cartels as agreements or concerted practices between two or more purchasers which, without engaging in joint negotiations as to trading terms with a supplier, are: (a) aimed at coordinating the purchasers' competitive behaviour or influencing the relevant parameters of competition between them, for example, by fixing purchase prices or parts thereof (including agreements fixing wages or not to pay a price for a product) or other trading conditions, the allocation of purchase quotas, or the sharing of markets and suppliers; or (b) influencing those purchasers' individual negotiations with or individual purchases from suppliers.[81] A buyer cartel may also exist where purchasers agree to exchange commercially sensitive information about their purchasing intentions.[82] In both the Spanish and Italian raw tobacco cases,[83] the Commission imposed fines on companies active in raw tobacco processing for colluding on the prices paid to (as well as the quantities bought from) tobacco growers.

In *Car Battery Recycling*,[84] the Commission found that agreements and concerted practices fixing target purchase prices, maximum purchase prices, and fixed-amount price reductions, combined with the exchange of commercially sensitive information on future market conduct had as their object the restriction of competition. In so doing, it rejected the parties' arguments that the agreement could not give rise to a restriction of competition by object because the conduct led to price decreases and the parties continued to compete in the downstream market. Rather, it considered that instead of competing with each other as buyers, they had coordinated their pricing behaviour and did not determine their commercial behaviour independently.

Although the Commission has not yet concluded proceedings in relation to agreements relating to employees, for example as to salaries to be paid or no-poaching agreements (agreements restricting an undertaking from recruiting, soliciting, or hiring competitors' employees[85]), such arrangements seem liable to infringe Article 101. No-poaching agreements, for example, may constitute unlawful horizontal market allocation mechanisms for keeping wages down,

[79] For the view that specific problems may result from trying to introduce competition in markets for professional services in the ordinary way, Van den Bergh and Camesasca, n. 5, Box 5.3.

[80] See e.g. COMP/30.350, *Zinc Producer Group* [1984] OJ L220/7. It may also harm welfare by causing the input suppliers to reduce output.

[81] Guidelines on the applicability of Article 101 of the Treaty on the Functioning of the European Union to horizontal co-operation agreements, 17 July 2023, paras. 279–280.

[82] Ibid., para. 318. See also *Styrene Purchasers*, IP/22/7168.

[83] COMP/38.238, *Spanish Raw Tobacco* [2004] OJ L102/14, Cases T-37/05 etc., *World Wide Tobacco España v Commission* EU:T:2011:76, COMP/38.281, *Italian Raw Tobacco* [2005] OJ L353/45, Cases T-11–12/06, *Romana Tabacchi v Commission* EU:T:2011:560.

[84] AT/40018, 8 February 2017, *aff'd* Case T-222/17, *Recylex SA v Commission* EU:T:2019:3456, Case C-563/19 P, EU:C:2021:428. There have also been a number of buyer cartel cases at the national level, see European Commission Expert Report prepared by R. Whish and D. Bailey, 'Horizontal Guidelines on purchasing agreements: Delineation between by object and by effect restrictions' (2022), 39.

[85] But see the pending Art. 267 reference before the CJ, Case C-680/21, *Royal Antwerp FC v Royal Belgian FA* (a reference on the compatibility with Art. 101 of the 'home player' rule of the football association).

restricting competition for skilled employees, and limiting employees' job opportunities. In the US, the federal antitrust agencies have explained that 'competition among employers helps actual and potential employees through higher wages, better benefits, or other terms of employment. Consumers can also gain from competition among employers because a more competitive workforce may create more or better goods and services.'[86] They thus consider that these types of arrangement constitute serious, per se, infringements of US antitrust law that warrant criminal prosecution.[87] The Hong Kong Competition Commission has also published an advisory bulletin stressing that businesses should compete to hire the best employees and warning of the antitrust risk resulting from wage-fixing, no-poaching arrangements, and the sharing of information relating to hiring intentions.[88] In the EU, a number of NCAs have investigated and condemned wage-fixing under EU and national competition law,[89] in some cases where it has been part of a wider cartel agreement in the output market.[90]

(iv) Restrictions on Output or Production

A restriction of output automatically creates an imbalance between supply and demand and causes an increase in market prices.[91] A number of cartels involve sales quotas which are often easier to agree upon, enforce, and monitor than adherence to a pricing policy.

In *Quinine*,[92] the Commission fined undertakings for the operation of a cartel which raised prices by means of a limitation on production. In particular, certain French companies agreed not to manufacture synthetic quinidine. The Court dismissed the parties' contention that, in any event, the companies did not have either the expertise or the resources to manufacture it:

> The fact relied upon that, when the gentlemen's agreement was concluded, the French undertakings were not in a position to manufacture synthetic quinidine does not render lawful such a restriction which entirely precluded them from taking up this activity.[93]

[86] DOJ and FTC, 'Antitrust Guidance for Human Resource Professionals', October 2016.

[87] Although juries acquitted defendants charged by the DOJ for no-poach and wage-fixing agreements in *United States v DaVita Inc and Kent Thiry* (D. Colo., 15 April 2022) and *United States v Neeraj Jindal and John Rodger* (E.D. Tex., 9 December 2020), the DOJ secured a criminal no-poach conviction (following a guilty plea) against VDA, a healthcare staffing company (see *United States v VDA OC, LLC*, No. 2:21-cr-00098 (D. Nev. 27 Oct. 2022) and it has made it clear that it will continue to bring such cases. Previously, the DOJ also filed civil enforcement actions against the Arizona Hospital & Healthcare Association for acting on behalf of most hospitals in Arizona to set a uniform bill rate schedule that the hospitals would pay for temporary and per diem nurses and against technology companies and eBay and Intuit, Lucasfilm and Pixar, and Adobe, Apple, Google, Intel, Intuit, and Pixar, for entering into 'no-poach' agreements with competitors (agreeing not to cold call each other's employees) (follow-on damages claims in these cases led to settlements). The FTC has brought two cases relating to competition for employment, see ibid.

[88] <www.compcomm.hk/en/media/press/files/20180409_Competition_Commission_Advisory_Bulletin_Eng.pdf>.

[89] See e.g. Decision No. 97-D-52, 25 June 1997 (French Competition Council). Enforcement action has also occurred e.g. in Portugal (no-poach agreements in the sports sector, see Press Release 06/2022), and the Netherlands (see www.acm.nl/en/publications/acm-suspends-investigation-possible-wage-fixing-cartel-between-supermarkets-after-conclusion-collective-agreement). No-poach agreements may also violate other (non-competition) laws governing contracts.

[90] See e.g. Spanish NCA decisions in S/0120/98, *Freight Forwarding* and S/0086/08, *Professional Hairdressing.*

[91] Organization of the Petroleum Exporting Countries (OPEC), for example, is designed to coordinate and unify petroleum prices of Member Countries and to stabilise oil prices. In 1973 voluntary restrictions of outputs and adherence to quotas led to the world price of oil quadrupling within a year.

[92] COMP/26.623, *Quinine Cartel* [1969] OJ L192/5.

[93] Case 41/69, *ACF Chemiefarma NV v Commission* EU:C:1970:71.

In *Polypropylene*,[94] the EU Courts upheld the Commission's finding that the object of meetings to fix target prices and sale volume targets was anti-competitive and in *Zinc Phosphate*[95] market share quotas were found to constitute the central plank of the cartel. In this case, the parties calculated initial market shares and sales quotas were allocated at the European level on this basis. A monitoring system was set up and pressure brought to bear on those that did not comply. The parties also agreed on 'bottom' prices, and on some occasions, the allocation of customers. The cartel followed a prior period of low prices, aggressive price-cutting, and targeting of mutual customers.

A practice in the professions which can cause significant reductions in competition in the spectrum of services offered is the use of business structure regulations. In *Wouters v Algemene Raad van de Nederlandse Orde van Advocaten* (discussed in Chapter 5),[96] the CJ held that a professional rule that prevented lawyers from working in partnership with accountants, despite constituting a restriction on production and technical development within the meaning of Article 101(1)(b), did not restrict competition. Rather, it accepted that restrictions required to ensure the proper practice of the profession as organised in a Member State, and which did not go beyond what was necessary to ensure the proper practice of the legal profession, did not infringe Article 101(1). In a report on competition in professional services, however, the Commission sets out its view that such restrictions 'may have a negative economic impact',[97] particularly where collaboration is prevented between members of the same profession or between professions where there is no overriding need to protect independence or ethical standards.

(v) Market-sharing

Market-sharing agreements provide each cartelist with exclusivity in a particular geographical area, or over a particular customer group, which it is free to exploit. From the EU perspective, geographical market-sharing agreements, especially those based on the principle of mutual respect of national markets. also thwart the objective of integrating the single market and 'allows producers to pursue a commercial policy . . . which is insulated from the competition of other parties to the agreement in other Member States'.[98]

The Commission has acted against geographical market-sharing, for example agreements to limit sales to, and refrain from exporting from, home markets or agreements between EU and non-EU undertakings to protect the EU market from low-priced imports.[99]

In both *Cement*[100] and *Peroxygen Products*,[101] the Commission fined undertakings for operating agreements which included a 'home market' principle. In *Cement*, the parties made concerted efforts

[94] COMP/31.149, *Polypropylene* [1986] OJ 1230/1, appeals substantially dismissed by both the GC and the CJ: see e.g. Case C-51/92 P, *SA Hercules NV v Commission* EU:C:1999:357 and Case C-199/92 P, *Hüls AG v Commission (Polypropylene)* EU:C:1999:358. See also e.g. COMP/30.350, *Zinc Producer Group* [1984] OJ L220/27, COMP/36.545, *Amino Acid* [2001] OJ L152/24, appeal dismissed in part, Case T-224/00, *Archer Daniels Midlands Co and Archer Daniels Ingredients Ltd v Commission* EU:T:2003:195, *aff'd* Case C-397/03 P, *Archer Daniels Midlands Co and Archer Daniels Ingredients Ltd v Commission* EU:C:2006:328.

[95] COMP/37.027 [2003] OJ L153/1, see especially paras. 65–72.

[96] Case C-309/99, EU:C:2002:98.

[97] Communication from the Commission, Report on Competition in Professional Services, n. 70, paras. 59–64.

[98] Commission's *1st Report on Competition Policy* (1971), para. 2.

[99] See e.g. COMP/35.860, *Seamless Steel Tubes* [2003] OJ L140/1, on appeal Case T-44/00, *Mannesmannröhren-Werke AG v Commission* EU:T:2004:218 (fine reduced), Cases C-403/04 etc., *Sumitomo Metal Industries Ltd v Commission* EU:C:2007:52.

[100] COMP/33.126 and COMP/33.322 [1994] OJ L343/1, *aff'd* Cases T-25/95 etc., *Cimenteries CBR SA v Commission* EU:T:2000:77, broadly *aff'd* Cases C-204/00 P etc., *Aalborg Portland v Commission* EU:C:2004:6.

[101] COMP/30.907 [1985] OJ L35/1.

to stem cross-frontier flows and to reduce trade between Member States and a number of bilateral and multilateral agreements (relating to, for example, the exchange of sensitive price information) backed up the main agreement.

In *Soda Ash*,[102] the Commission imposed fines (of approximately €7 million) on ICI and Solvay, the two largest producers of synthetic soda ash in the Union, for the operation of an agreement under which ICI was exclusively to supply the UK and Ireland and Solvay was exclusively to supply continental Europe. Although the formal written agreement had been abandoned in 1972 (on the UK's accession to the EU) the Commission found that the agreement/concerted practice in fact continued unaltered.

In *SAS/Maersk*,[103] the Commission imposed fines of €52.5 million for market-sharing in the air transport sector. In this case, the parties had notified a cooperation agreement to the Commission, but following further investigations conducted at the parties' premises the Commission uncovered the market-sharing agreement. In *Gas*,[104] the Commission imposed very significant fines[105] on E.ON AG and GDF Suez SA (two of the largest players in the EU gas industry) for an agreement (in place since 1975) not to sell gas, transported through a jointly built and owned MEGAL pipeline, into each other's home markets. The market-sharing arrangement was maintained after the EU gas market was liberalised in 2000 and, by helping the parties to maintain their strong positions in the German and French gas markets, respectively, had thwarted the liberalisation process and deprived customers of choice. On appeal, the GC confirmed that an agreement between actual or potential competitors not to penetrate each other's home market was restrictive by object and upheld the Commission's decision.[106]

Market-sharing, through customer allocation, is also prohibited. In *Methylglucamine*,[107] for example, the parties sought to maintain the status quo of 50 per cent market share for both companies by trying to prevent switching by their respective customers from one to the other supplier and agreeing not to compete for each other's customers. In *Luxembourg Brewers*,[108] four Luxembourg brewers agreed (in signed writing)[109] not to supply beer, for an unlimited duration, to any customer tied to another by an exclusive purchasing commitment or beer tie.[110] When taking on a new customer, each would consult one another to check that a beer tie did not bind the customer to another. The parties also had measures in place that were designed to keep foreign brewers out of the market. Similarly, in *Belgian Brewers*[111] Interbrew and Danone shared out their distribution channels and pursued a policy of non-aggression.

[102] COMP/33.133 [1991] OJ L152/1, annulled on procedural grounds Case T-30/91, *Solvay SA v Commission* EU:T:1995:115 (see Chap. 13) but readopted COMP/33.133 [2003] OJ L10/1, see Case T-57/01, *Solvay v Commission* EU:T:2009:519.

[103] COMP/37.444, n. 65. But see discussion of airline alliances in Chap. 10.

[104] COMP/39.401, *Gas* [2009] OJ C248/5. [105] See Table 9.2.

[106] Case T-360/09, *E.ON Ruhrgas AG v Commission* EU:T:2012:332.

[107] COMP/37.978 [2004] OJ L38/18. See also e.g. COMP/39.234, *Synthetic Rubber* [2007] OJ L182/31, Cases T-44 and 45/07, *Kaučuk v Commission* EU:T:2011:358 and AT/40.330, *Rail Cargo* 20 April 2021 (fining three EU rail companies for a customer-allocation cartel).

[108] COMP/37.800 [2002] OJ L253/21, *aff'd* Case T-49/02, *Brasserie nationale SA v Commission* EU:T:2005:298.

[109] Interbrew disclosed details of the arrangement following an investigation into its practices on the Belgian beer market, see n. 111 and text.

[110] See discussion of single branding agreements in Chaps. 4 and 11.

[111] COMP/37.614 [2003] OJ L200/1, para. 247, *aff'd* Case T-38/02, *Groupe Danone v Commission* EU:T:2005:367 (small reduction in fine) and Case C-3/06 P, EU:C:2007:88. 'After the Commission, on its own initiative, uncovered a cartel on the Belgian beer market, InBev provided information under the auspices of the Commission's leniency policy that it was also involved in cartels in other European countries. This led to surprise inspections on brewers in France, Luxembourg, Italy, and the Netherlands. These investigations led to decisions condemning cartels in Belgium (see IP/01/1739 upheld by the [GC] and CJ, see CJE/07/13), France (see IP/04/1153, not appealed) and Luxembourg (see IP/01/1740, upheld by the CFI). The Italian investigation was closed without charges being brought' (IP/07/509). The Dutch cartel decision was adopted on 18 April 2007.

(vi) Collusive Tendering or Bid Rigging

Collusive tendering occurs where undertakings collaborate on responses to invitations to tender for the supply of goods and services (whether by public procurers or private bodies). Instead of competing to submit the lowest possible tender at the tightest possible margin, bid riggers thwart the essence of the tendering process—especially the ability to extract the most competitive, cost-effective bid for the products/services through tendering[112]—by limiting price competition or sharing markets between them. Well-documented techniques include bid suppression, cover, courtesy or complementary bidding, market or customer allocation, or bid rotation. In many cases, the collusion incorporates a mechanism to apportion and distribute profits among cartelists, for example through compensation or side payments or by having the winning bidder subcontract work to losing or non-tendering firms (such practices must be distinguished from joint bidding made openly and with the knowledge of the party seeking the tenders). Bid rigging automatically infringes Article 101(1).

> In a system of tendering, competition is of the essence. If the tenders submitted by those taking part are not the result of individual economic calculation, but of knowledge of the tenders by other participants or of concertation with them competition is prevented, or at least distorted and restricted.[113]

Numerous cases, studies, surveys, and articles document the pervasive nature of bid rigging, especially in government procurement cases[114] and the Commission has unearthed some cases.[115] In *Pre-Insulated Pipe Cartel*,[116] it imposed fines in excess of €92 million on ten undertakings it had found to be engaged in market-sharing, price-fixing, and bid rigging in the market for pipes used for district heating systems (contracts for the supply of pipes were almost all awarded on the basis of competitive tendering procedures). The parties had also tried to squeeze out of the market the only competitor that had refused to participate in the cartel and had deliberately flouted the EU Public Procurement Rules. In *Lifts and Escalators*,[117] the Commission imposed fines of €992 million on four firms for operating a number of bid rigging cartels for the installation and maintenance of lifts and escalators in Belgium, Germany, Luxembourg, and the Netherlands. The Commission was particularly incensed by this cartel since it affected a vast market for the sale, installation, maintenance, and modernisation of lifts and escalators (including in the buildings of the Commission itself and the courts in Luxembourg) and the cartel would have long-term effects because of the maintenance contracts which lasted decades. In *International Removals Services*,[118] the Commission reiterated the

[112] More efficient tenderers may also be excluded from the process, and incentives to improve quality and innovate are reduced.

[113] COMP/26.918, *Re The European Sugar Cartel* [1973] OJ L140/17, para. 42.

[114] See e.g., Anderson, Jones and Kovacic, n. 20.

[115] On 14 June 2022, the Commission confirmed that it was conducting inspections into suspected bid rigging in tenders involving EU funds for the construction of networks and treatment plants for drinking water and wastewater, see IP.22/3706. But only four of the 113 cartels identified by the Commission in its decisions between 2001–2015 related to bid rigging, see Hellwig and Hüschelrath, n. 21. Bid rigging has, however, been tackled by a number of NCAs and in a number of jurisdictions, including, e.g., Germany; it constitutes a criminal offence.

[116] COMP/35.691, *Pre-Insulated Pipe* [1999] OJ L24/1; decision substantially upheld on appeal (although some fines reduced) see e.g. Cases T-9/99 etc., *HFB Holdings v Commission* EU:T:2002:70, *aff'd* Cases C-189/02 P etc., *Dansk Rørindustri A/S* EU:C:2005:408. See also COMP/31.572 and COMP/32.571, *Building and Construction Industry in the Netherlands* [1992] OJ L92/1, *aff'd* Case T-29/92, *SPO v Commission* EU:T:1995:34, COMP/39.406, *Marine Hoses* [2009] OJ C168/6, see on appeal, e.g., Case T-146/09, *Parker-Hannifin* EU:T:2013:258, Case C-434/13, *Commission v Parker Hannifin Manufacturing Srl and Parker-Hannifin Corp* EU:C:2014:2456, COMP/38.899.

[117] COMP/38.823 [2007] OJ C75/19, Cases T-138/07 etc., *Schindler Holding v Commission* EU:T:2011:362.

[118] COMP/38.543 [2009] OJ C188/52.

serious nature of bid rigging when it condemned a cartel in which participants had agreed on prices, allocated removal contracts between themselves through bogus 'cover quotes', and benefited from a system of financial compensation called 'commissions'.

(vii) Bolstering Provisions and Restrictions on Non-price Trading Conditions or on Non-price Parameters of Competition

Provisions designed to reinforce or bolster the operation of a hardcore cartel, such as: measures designed to block imports;[119] refusals to supply or boycott customers who purchase from sellers outside the cartel; boycotts of competitors refusing to participate in the cartel arrangements;[120] collective exclusive dealing;[121] or information-sharing arrangements (see also Section 4.B)[122] are also likely to infringe Article 101(1).

Restraints on non-price trading conditions may also constitute, or reinforce, hardcore cartel activities. In *Fine Art Auction Houses*,[123] for example, Christie's and Sotheby's fixed not only the commissions that they charged but other conditions as well, such as payment conditions, guarantees, and advances.

Although in some circumstances it may be advantageous for undertakings to have access to suitably drafted terms and conditions and/or to adopt common quality or technical standards,[124] where the terms and conditions relate to 'important secondary aspects of competition',[125] that is, to any aspect of a supplier's offer which has economic value in the eyes of the customer (such as the loan of products or special delivery arrangements[126]), they may well infringe Article 101(1). In *Fabricants de Papiers Peints de Belgique*,[127] the Commission found that general conditions of sale concluded by Belgian manufacturers of wallpaper, which related to terms of delivery, returns policy, lengths of rolls, etc. infringed Article 101(1) and did not satisfy the conditions of Article 101(3).

The adoption of a common quality label (establishing that products meet a minimum quality standard) will not necessarily infringe Article 101(1), so long as the parties are free to market products of a different, inferior standard,[128] and it is not used to hinder technical development[129] or exclude competitors.

In *IAZ*,[130] a Belgian trade association agreed with Belgian manufacturers and sole importers for washing machines and dishwashers that only appliances with a 'conformity' label could be connected to the mains. To receive a conformity label the appliances had to comply with technical standards laid

[119] See e.g. COMP/31.204, *Meldoc* [1986] OJ L348/50, COMP/37.800, *Luxembourg Brewers* [2002] OJ L253/21, *aff'd* Case T-49/02, *Brasserie nationale SA v Commission* EU:T:2005:29.

[120] COMP/35.691, *Pre-Insulated Pipe* [1999] OJ L24/1; decision substantially upheld on appeal (although some fines reduced) Cases T-9/99 etc., *HFB Holdings v Commission* EU:T:2002:70, *aff'd* Case C-189/02 P, *Dansk Rørindustri A/S* EU:C:2005:408. See also COMP/31.572 and COMP/32.571, *Building and Construction Industry in the Netherlands* [1992] OJ L92/1, *aff'd* Case T-29/92, *SPO v Commission* EU:T:1995:34.

[121] See e.g. COMP/33.884, *Nederlandse Federative Vereniging voor de Groothandel op Elektrotechnisch Gebied and Technische Unie (FEG and TU)* [2000] OJ L39/1.

[122] Cases T-25/95 etc., *Cimenteries CBR SA v Commission* EU:T:2000:77, para. 1531, broadly *aff'd* Cases C-204/00 P etc., *Aalborg Portland A/S v Commission* EU:C:2004:6, COMP/400, *IFTRA Rules on Glass Containers* [1974] OJ L160/1.

[123] COMP/37.784 [2002] OJ L200/92.

[124] COMP/32.265, *Concordato Incendio* [1990] OJ L15/27.

[125] COMP/30.174, *Vimpoltu* [1983] OJ L200/44.

[126] See e.g. COMP/324, *VCH* [1972] OJ L13/34.

[127] COMP/426 [1974] OJ L237/3.

[128] COMP/32.202, *Belgian Association of Pharmacists* [1990] OJ L18/33. But see also *European Council of Manufacturers of Domestic Appliances* [2000] OJ L187/47, Chap. 4 and Case C-309/99, *Wouters v Algemene Raad van de Nederlandse Orde van Advocaten* EU:C:2002:98, Notice on Cooperation Agreements [1968] OJ C75/3, para. II(8).

[129] See e.g. COMP/29.151, *Video Cassette Recorders* [1978] OJ L47/42.

[130] COMP/29.995, *Anseau* [1982] OJ L167/39; on appeal Case 96/82, *IAZ International Belgium NV v Commission* EU:C:1983:310.

down by Belgian law. In fact, the label was available only to Belgian manufacturers or sole importers of products. Thus parallel imports of the appliances were made impossible in practice.

In *Car Emissions*,[131] the Commission fined EU car producers—Daimler, BMW, and Volkswagen Group (VW, Audi, and Porsche)—for colluding on technical development in the sphere of nitrogen oxide cleaning. Broadly, the companies, which met regularly to discuss technical standards and technology capable of eliminating harmful emissions, agreed not to compete in relation to technology they possessed to reduce such emissions beyond the legal requirements. The Commission found that the agreement restricted competition on technical development and product characteristics relevant for customers (contrary to Article 101(1)(b)).

B. PROVING A BREACH

(i) Establishing the Existence of an Agreement, Concerted Practice, or Decision

The previous sections demonstrate that naked cartel activity is liable to be found to restrict competition by object, not to satisfy the conditions of Article 101(3), and to result in significant fines (or other penalties) being imposed on those involved. This means that such activity tends to be hidden and/or that firms seek to find looser, more amorphous, mechanisms for coordinating their conduct on the market (for example, through signalling how they will behave in the future to their competitors).

The challenge for competition authorities, or other claimants, in cases where a cartel is suspected is therefore to establish that the undertakings involved have engaged in collusive activity prohibited by Article 101(1)[132]—through an agreement or concerted practice between undertakings or a decision by an association of undertakings. In Chapter 4, it was seen that these concepts are interpreted broadly to catch:

- formal and informal agreements;
- arrangements coordinated through the conduct of associations of undertakings (such as recommendations); and
- coordination between undertakings which, without having reached the stage where an agreement, properly so called, has been concluded, knowingly substitutes practical cooperation between them for the risks of competition (concerted practices). In particular, cooperation between undertakings which have not made an actual plan as to how they will behave on the market but who are not determining their conduct *independently* will be captured, for example, where competitors directly or indirectly share data/information through reciprocal exchanges or where 'one undertaking alone discloses commercially sensitive information to its competitors' so reducing strategic uncertainty as to the future operation of the market for those competitors and increasing the likelihood of limiting competition and of collusive behaviour.[133]

A challenge nonetheless is to define the exact boundary between joint conduct caught by Article 101(1) and unilateral conduct falling outside it and to demonstrate (through direct or circumstantial evidence) that the former has taken place. The following sections explore these issues and

[131] Case AT/40.178, 8 July 2021.

[132] The fact that a party has cheated on a cartel agreement cannot be used to demonstrate that it was not party to the arrangement. On the contrary, cheating may be part and parcel of ordinary cartel activity which may be characterised by sporadic price wars or outbreaks of conflict, see e.g. COMP/35.691, *Pre-Insulated Pipes* [1999] OJ L24/1, para. 132.

[133] Horizontal Cooperation Guidelines 17 July 2023, para. 396.

whether, and if so when, parallel conduct, unilateral price announcements, or online practices may indicate the existence of a concerted practice or other joint conduct caught by Article 101(1).

(ii) Parallel Conduct, Conscious Parallelism, and Collusion

An important question that has arisen is whether the concepts of agreement, decision, or concerted practice are broad enough to catch parallel conduct arising from tacit collusion on a market, where firms determine their strategy by taking account of the likely response of their competitors; in particular, whether tacit collusion constitutes a mechanism for substituting practical cooperation between undertakings (caught by Article 101(1)) or independent behaviour (outside its scope).[134] The judgment of the CJ in *Dyestuffs*[135] arguably left the position open. In this case, three general and uniform increases in the prices of dyestuffs had taken place within the EU over a period of years. The Commission concluded that the increases had occurred as a result of a concerted practice operating between ten producers (and in fact it had uncovered evidence of actual direct/indirect contact between the parties).[136] The CJ upheld the decision relying upon the facts that: price increases had been announced in advance (the announcements eliminating all uncertainty between them as regards their future conduct and the risk inherent in any independent change in conduct); the announcements rendered the market transparent as regards the rates of increase; and given the number of producers on the market, it did not consider that it was possible to say that the market was an oligopolistic one. It was not plausible, therefore, that the parallel conduct could have been brought into effect within a period of two to three days without prior concertation. The Court concluded that, taking into account the nature of the market in the products in question, the conduct of the undertakings was designed to replace both the risks of competition and the hazards of competitors' spontaneous reactions with cooperation.

Although there was some concern that the interpretation of the term 'concerted practice' in this case was broad enough to catch rational, and purely parallel, market behaviour,[137] the CJ did state that, although parallel conduct could provide 'strong evidence' of a concerted practice 'if it leads to conditions of competition which do not correspond to the normal conditions of the market, having regard to the nature of the products, the size and number of the undertakings, and the volume of the said market', it could 'not by itself be identified with a concerted practice'.[138] A producer is 'free to charge his prices, taking into account in so doing the present or foreseeable conduct of his competitors'.[139]

[134] In addition, if tacit collusion cannot be *equated* with a concerted practice, whether parallel conduct by firms operating on an oligopolistic market can ever be used as circumstantial evidence to justify a finding that an agreement or concerted practice existed between the undertakings.

[135] Case 48/69, *ICI v Commission* EU:C:1972:70.

[136] COMP/26.267, *Re Cartel in Aniline Dyes* [1969] OJ L195/11.

[137] See e.g. V. Korah, 'Concerted Practices' (1973) 36 *MLR* 260. Arguably, however, these concerns were overstated given that the Commission had, in this case, uncovered evidence of contact between the parties: similar orders sent by the producers to their subsidiaries or representatives on the various markets, to make the increases (sometime sent on the same day (at the same hour), and couched in similar terms); and records of meetings of the producers in Basel and London.

[138] Cases 48, 49, and 51–57/69, EU:C:1972:70, para. 66.

[139] Ibid., para. 118. The judgment was thus not so much worrying because of its definition of a concerted practice but more because it so easily assumed, without a detailed study of the market characteristics and without evidence of concertation, that parties had cooperated, G. Van Gerven and E. N. Varona, 'The *Wood Pulp* Case and the Future of Concerted Practices' (1994) 31 *CMLRev* 575, 590

Further, subsequent cases have now made it crystal clear that parallel conduct or tacit collusion is not in itself prohibited by Article 101(1). In *Suiker Unie*[140] and *Züchner*,[141] the CJ stressed that Article 101(1) did not prevent an undertaking from adapting its behaviour intelligently to the existing or anticipated conduct of competitors[142] and in *Re Wood Pulp Cartel: Ahlström Oy v Commission (Wood Pulp)*[143] the CJ delivered its clearest judgment on the relationship between conscious parallelism (or tacit collusion) and concerted practices. In this case, the Commission found that 43 pulp producers operating on the bleached sulphate wood pulp market had breached Article 101(1);[144] concertation between many of the Finnish, US, and Canadian undertakings with regard to both announced and transaction prices in the pulp market had led to prices which were both artificially high and rigid. It considered that the parallel behaviour was not explicable as rational behaviour.[145] It could not be explained as independently chosen parallel conduct in a narrow oligopolistic market (the market was characterised by a large number of producers, customers, and products; the market was not inherently transparent, but was only so as a result of the producers' deliberately chosen strategy of making price announcements in advance and there was no clear price leader, etc.).

The Court annulled much of the Commission's decision and many of the fines on substantive grounds. It made it clear that although parallel behaviour may furnish circumstantial proof of explicit collusion, it will not do so if the behaviour can be explained by the conditions of competition on the market, for example that the conditions have led to tacit collusion of the undertaking's behaviour (there is a plausible explanation for the conduct other than collusion).

Cases C-89, 104, 114, 116–117, and 125–129/85, *Re Wood Pulp Cartel: Ahlström Oy v Commission* [1993] ECR I-1307

Court of Justice

70. Since the Commission has no documents which directly establish the existence of concertation between the producers concerned, it is necessary to ascertain whether the system of quarterly price announcements, the simultaneity or near-simultaneity of the price announcements and the parallelism of price announcements as found during the period from 1975 to 1985 constitute a firm, precise and consistent body of evidence of prior concertation.

71. In determining the probative value of those different factors, it must be noted that parallel conduct cannot be regarded as furnishing proof of concertation unless concertation constitutes the only plausible explanation for such conduct. It is necessary to bear in mind that, although Article [101] . . . prohibits any form of collusion which distorts competition, it does not deprive economic operators of the right to adapt themselves intelligently to the existing and anticipated conduct of their competitors (see *Suiker Unie*, . . . paragraph 174).

[140] Cases 40/73 etc., *Re the European Sugar Cartel: Coöperatieve Vereniging 'Suiker Unie' UA v Commission* EU:C:1975:174.

[141] Case 172/80, *Züchner v Bayerische Vereinsbank* EU:C:1981:178.

[142] See COMP/30.350, *Zinc Producer Group* [1984] OJ L220/27, paras. 75–76 (parallel pricing behaviour in an oligopoly producing homogeneous goods is not in itself sufficient evidence of a concerted practice).

[143] Cases C-89, 104, 114, 116–117, and 125–129/85, EU:C:1993:120.

[144] COMP/29.725 [1985] OJ L85/1.

[145] Although the Commission relied on some documentary evidence to supplement its finding, this was excluded by the Court.

72. Accordingly, it is necessary in this case to ascertain whether the parallel conduct alleged by the Commission cannot, taking account of the nature of the products, the size and the number of the undertakings and the volume of the market in question, be explained otherwise than by concertation.

. . .

126. Following that analysis, it must be stated that, in this case, concertation is not the only plausible explanation for the parallel conduct. To begin with, the system of price announcements may be regarded as constituting a rational response to the fact that the pulp market constituted a long-term market and to the need felt by both buyers and sellers to limit commercial risks. Further, the similarity in the dates of price announcements may be regarded as a direct result of the high degree of market transparency, which does not have to be described as artificial. Finally, the parallelism of prices and the price trends may be satisfactorily explained by the oligopolistic tendencies of the market and by the specific circumstances prevailing in certain periods. Accordingly, the parallel conduct established by the Commission does not constitute evidence of concertation.

127. In the absence of a firm, precise and consistent body of evidence, it must be held that concertation regarding announced prices has not been established by the Commission. Article 1(1) of the contested decision must therefore be annulled.

In its judgment, the Court reiterated its previous holdings that parallel conduct will furnish proof of concertation only where it constitutes the only plausible explanation for such conduct. Further, it was not prepared to reject, as the Commission had done, the protestations that the undertakings' behaviour was a consequence, not of a concerted practice, but of non-collusive interdependence or conscious parallelism. It commissioned two independent reports from economic experts to analyse the wood pulp market and the evidence involved. The reports were extremely damaging to the Commission's case. On the facts, and relying on experts' reports, the Court found that the system of quarterly price announcements did not, of itself, amount to an infringement of Article 101(1)[146] and that this system and the parallelism of announced prices were not evidence of concertation. Further, it could not be said that the system of advance price announcements and parallel behaviour was not explicable otherwise than by concertation. The Commission had failed sufficiently to appreciate that the wood pulp market had oligopolistic tendencies, being characterised by oligopolies and oligopsonies (on the buying side) in particular pulp types. The market was also inherently transparent. Paper manufacturers were in constant touch with a number of pulp suppliers and exchanged price information amongst themselves and the transparency was reinforced both by a number of common agents that operated throughout the market and an active trade press.

The system of advanced announced prices was, therefore, explicable as a rational response to the fact that the pulp market was a long-term one and met a legitimate business concern of customers.

The judgment indicates, therefore, that the concept of a concerted practice demands *reciprocal* cooperation, through direct or indirect contact, designed to influence the conduct of an actual or potential competitor or to disclose to them the course of conduct that will or may be adopted on the market.[147] Where direct evidence of reciprocal cooperation is not available, parallel behaviour may furnish circumstantial proof of an agreement or concerted practice only if it is not the kind of

[146] Cases C-89, 104, 114, 116–117, and 125–129/85, EU:C:1993:120.

[147] See also Chap. 4 and, e.g., A. Albors-Llorens, 'Horizontal Agreements and Concerted Practices in EC Competition Law: Unlawful and Legitimate Contacts between Competitors' [2006] 51 *Ant Bull* 837 and A. Jones, '*Wood Pulp*: Concerted Practice and/or Conscious Parallelism' [1993] *ECLR* 273, 275–276.

behaviour which would be anticipated on the market involved (whether the parallel conduct alleged by the Commission cannot, taking into account the nature of the products, the size and number of the undertakings, and the volume of the market in question, be explained otherwise than by concertation) and if there is no other plausible explanation for the conduct. The number of undertakings on the market, the homogeneity of the product, and the transparency of the market will therefore be relevant to the analysis. The market structure may provide a plausible explanation for the behaviour. In *Wood Pulp*, the CJ's judgment describes the market characteristics in meticulous detail and makes it clear that explanations may be available even outside a tight oligopoly situation.

It is unclear whether, on the proof of parallel behaviour, the evidential burden shifts onto the accused to establish that there *is* a plausible explanation for the conduct. In *Wood Pulp*, the Advocate General considered that '[t]he burden of proof cannot be shifted simply by a finding of parallel conduct. Unless the Court can be satisfied by a set of presumptions having a solid basis, concertation is not established'.[148] It may thus be inadvisable for a claimant to try to rely solely on economic evidence (especially where a defence of oligopolistic interdependence might be raised), without corroborative evidence, to establish the existence of a cartel.[149] Where plausible explanations are raised by the accused each of those must be ruled out by the Commission. In *CISAC*,[150] for example, the GC annulled a Commission decision finding a concerted practice, as it had neither proven its existence by factors other than parallel conduct nor provided sufficient evidence to render implausible explanations of the undertakings for their parallel conduct.

(iii) Unilateral Public Price Announcements in Advance and Price Signalling

Like reciprocal exchanges of price information, public price announcements in advance on a market may signal to other players on the market what a firm's future price policy will be and may facilitate alignment of their behaviour and tacit collusion on an oligopolistic market. An important question, therefore, is whether, and if so when, public price announcements in advance might constitute indirect contact with a competitor sufficient to establish a concerted practice to fix prices. In *Dyestuffs*,[151] the CJ considered that advance price communications provided, in the circumstances, proof of a concerted practice. It held that the announcements rendered the market artificially transparent and eliminated all uncertainty between the operators as regards the rates of increase, future conduct, and the risks inherent in an independent change of conduct. The Court commented:

> . . . the undertakings taking the initiative . . . announced their intentions of making an increase some time in advance, which allowed the undertakings to observe each other's reactions on the different markets, and to adapt themselves accordingly. By means of these advance announcements the various undertakings eliminated all uncertainty between them as to their future conduct and, in doing so, also eliminated a large part of the risk usually inherent in any independent change of conduct on one or several markets. This was all the more the case since these announcements, which led to the fixing of

[148] EU:C:1993:120, Darmon AG, para. 195. This conclusion seems to be necessitated by the presumption of innocence that applies in competition law cases, see further Chap. 13.

[149] See e.g. COMP/33.833, *Cartonboard* [1994] OJ L243/1, para. 73. In 2015 the Commission closed an investigation into parallel pricing on cement and cement-related markets, COMP/39.520, *Cement* (initiated 6 December 2010). In a series of judgments, see e.g. Case C-247/14, *HeidelbergCement AG v Commission* EU:C:2016:149 the CJ annulled a Commission decision requesting information, broadly on the grounds that the Commission had not specified the purpose of the request and the alleged infringement precisely enough, see Chap. 13.

[150] Case T-442/08, *International Confederation of Societies of Authors and Composers (CISAC) v Commission* EU:T:2013:188.

[151] Cases 48, 49, and 51–57/69, *ICI v Commission (Dyestuffs)* EU:C:1972:70.

> general and equal increases in prices for the markets in dyestuffs, rendered the market transparent as regard the percentage rates of increase. Therefore, by the way in which they acted, the undertakings in question temporarily eliminated with respect to prices some of the preconditions for competition on the market which stood in the way of the achievement of parallel uniformity of conduct.[152]

This case must, however, be assessed in the light of its own particular facts and, now, the judgment of the CJ in *Wood Pulp*.[153] In the latter case, although the Commission found concertation in respect of both announced and actual transaction prices, the CJ held that price announcements in advance did not, in themselves, constitute an infringement of Article 101(1).

> 64. In this case, the communications arise from the price announcements made to users. They constitute in themselves market behaviour which does not lessen each undertaking's uncertainty as to the future attitude of its competitors. At the same time when each undertaking engages in such behaviour, it cannot be sure of the future conduct of the others.
>
> 65. Accordingly, the system of quarterly price announcements on the pulp market is not to be regarded as constituting in itself an infringement of Article [101](1).

Further, the Court held that it had not been established that the system amounted to a means of indirect communication between the competitors. The announcements served the need of customers desiring the information to plan the cost of their paper products. This provided a plausible or alternative explanation for the parallel behaviour.

G. van Gerven and E. N. Varona, 'The *Wood Pulp* Case and the Future of Concerted Practices' (1994) 31 *CMLRev* 575, 595

> It is clear that in deciding whether price signalling is illegal, one should not overlook the circumstances. In the *Wood Pulp* case, it was established that (i) there was a clear lawful business justification for advance price communications, since the price of wood pulp constituted a major proportion of the cost of paper and it was the paper producers themselves which had requested prior announcement; (ii) the announcements were made to customers. If, given the high transparency of the market, firms become aware of the prospective pricing of their competitors, so be it. If a rival adapts its pricing to the information it has obtained, it merely 'adapts intelligently to existing or anticipated conduct of its competitors' as allowed by the *Dyestuffs* and *Suiker Unie* judgments.
>
> Firstly, as Advocate Darmon pointed out in his opinion, if price signalling does not correspond to a legitimate business justification, such advance announcements may very well be considered as an illegal exchange of information. In the end, as so often in antitrust law, the decisive question in practice may be whether there is a valid business reason for the particular market conduct. In the *Wood pulp* judgment, the Court had no difficulty finding such a valid business reason for the price announcements and, therefore, it was easy and correct to conclude that the system of price announcements did not give rise to a concerted practice. However, price signalling, if not warranted by any legitimate explanation and clearly not in the individual (non-collusive) self-interest of the individual companies may constitute sufficient evidence of concertation.
>
> Secondly, in *Wood Pulp*, it appeared that the trade press was also very rapidly informed of the advance price announcements but the Court went out of its way to state that most of the wood pulp

[152] Ibid., paras. 100–103.

[153] Cases C-89, 104, 114, 116–117, and 125–129/85, *Wood Pulp* EU:C:1993:120.

producers did not send as a matter of course their announced prices to the trade press and that if, sporadically, this was done, such communications were made at the request of the press. Thus the Court implicitly rejected the Commission's claim that wood pulp producers had deliberately made the market transparent or increased transparency by talking to the press.

The Commission will inevitably be sensitive to attempts by firms, especially oligopolists, to make the market artificially more transparent than it otherwise would be. It is concerned that public announcements can constitute strategic ways of mutual communication which will restrict competition. Indeed, a case in this sphere which has caused controversy is *Container Shipping*[154] where the Commission examined:

regular public announcements of price increase intentions through press releases on [container shipping companies'] websites and in the specialised trade press. These announcements are made several times a year and contain the amount of increase and the date of implementation, which is generally similar for all announcing companies. The announcements are usually made by the companies successively a few weeks before the announced implementation date.

The Commission has concerns that this practice may allow the companies to signal future price intentions to each other and may harm competition and customers by raising prices . . .

The proceedings in this case were brought to an end when the 15 companies involved offered commitments (accepted by the Commission), including to change the way they make price announcements and not to make announcements more than 31 days before their entry into force (the parties voluntarily agreed to change their behaviour). Although no finding of infringement was made, the Commission stated[155] in the commitments decision that it was concerned that the future general rate increase announcements and price signalling in that case amounted to a strategy for reaching a common understanding about terms of coordination. The similar announcements constituted strategic responses of competitors to each other's public announcements. Its provisional conclusion was thus that as each party was able to take account of the information published in the others' announcements when determining its own conduct, it took part in a concerted practice by making announcements itself.[156] Further that the communications on future pricing intentions restricted competition by object and infringed Article 101(1). The case has caused concern that the provisional finding of a concerted practice, on the basis purely of unilateral public price communications: (a) expands the concept considerably beyond previous cases where a finding has been upheld; (b) unhelpfully blurs the line between a concerted practice operated through interaction between undertakings and lawful parallel behaviour and the intelligent adaption of behaviour to that of others on the market; and (c) may be used in the future as a basis to extend the concept of a concerted practice to unilateral conduct, even if it is very unlikely to operate as a focal point which produces and sustains collusion and where there

[154] COMP/39.850, 7 July 2016. See also COMP/39.520, *Cement* (proceedings closed 14 August 2015), on appeal Cases C-247, 248, 267, and 268/14 P, *Heidelberg Cement* (discussed in Chap. 13). NCAs have also been concerned about this type of conduct, see e.g. the Dutch mobile network operator investigation, Case 13.0612.53, 7 January 2014 and the order published following the UK Competition and Markets Authority into aggregates, cement, and ready-mixed concrete, 13 April 2016.

[155] COMP/39.850, 7 July 2016 (accepting that unilateral announcements which are genuinely public do not constitute a concerted practice).

[156] Ibid., paras. 45–47.

might be other plausible explanations for the conduct (an efficient tool to inform customers about rate changes).[157]

In its Horizontal Cooperation Guidelines,[158] the Commission states that although unilateral, public announcements generally do not constitute a concerted practice such a finding cannot be excluded, especially where they relate to future prices and do not commit the undertakings *vis-à-vis* its customers.

> 400. . . . *For example, a unilateral public announcement referring to intentions relating to future pricing (as opposed to communicating an actual decision to change prices as of a certain date in the near future) will not commit the undertaking making the announcement vis-à-vis its customers, but may give signals concerning an undertaking's intended strategy on the market to its competitors. This will be the case in particular if the information is sufficiently specific. Such announcements therefore generally do not create benefits for consumers and they may facilitate collusion.*
>
> *Unilateral public announcements may be indicative of an underlying anti-competitive agreement or concerted practice. For example, on a market where there are only a few competitors and with high barriers to entry, undertakings that continuously publish information that provides no apparent benefit for consumers (for instance, information on R&D costs, costs of adaptations to environmental requirements, etc.) may be engaged in restricting competition within the meaning of Article 101(1). The unilateral public announcements may be used to implement or monitor their collusive arrangements. Whether such a restriction is indeed found will depend on all the facts of the particular case.*

(iv) Collusion, Algorithms, and Online Practices

A matter which has been widely debated is whether, and if so when, online communications or practices operated, monitored, or facilitated by algorithms—decision-making software which turns digital inputs into digital outputs, which crawls the internet checking competitors' prices and which rapidly updates and makes pricing and output decisions without the need for human decision-making—can constitute concerted practices caught by Article 101. In contrast to the offline world, algorithms allow firms, almost in real time and at low cost, to monitor their competitors' and retailers' prices and so to rapidly adapt their own prices in response to them. The use of such algorithms is now widespread, and growing, and new generations of algorithms are powered by artificial intelligence. During the Commission's e-commerce sector inquiry, for example, 53 per cent of respondent retailers stated that they tracked online prices of competitors; of these, 67 per cent stated that they use automatic software programs to do so.[159]

Although algorithms may enhance competition by increasing price transparency, diminishing search costs, fostering choice, lowering prices, and making disruptive entry easier, there is also concern that the increase in online market transparency and information flows might in some circumstances facilitate or strengthen explicit and tacit collusion and lead to more effective cartels both by increasing the incentives and ability to align behaviour and decreasing the incentives to deviate from it. In particular, they may make it easier for firms to align behaviour, through repeated interaction or adhering to pre-agreed prices and, through price transparency and constant and perfect monitoring, to detect and punish deviations from the collusive scheme and to identify new entry. As they may also

[157] See e.g. P. D. Camesasca and L-A. Grelier, '"Close Your Eyes"? Navigating the Tortuous Waters of Conscious Parallelism and Signalling in the European Union' (2016) 7 *JECLAP* 599, but see I. Rabinovici, 'Public Exchange of Information After *Container Shipping*' (2017) 8 *JECLAP* 149.

[158] 17 July 2023.

[159] See Commission Staff Working Document accompanying the Final Report on the E-commerce Sector Inquiry, SWD(2017)154final, para. 149.

reduce the risk of irrational disruptive behaviour, the robo-seller may increase the power of oligopolists to charge supra-competitive prices and be a more skilful oligopolist than its human counterpart; given antitrust laws' weakness in dealing with oligopoly, the robo-seller may therefore be 'poised to strike powerfully at this weakness, to the detriment of consumers'.[160]

In some cases, competition agencies have uncovered scenarios where technology, or algorithms, has been used to assist in the implementation, monitoring, and/or policing of the explicit collusion concluded by humans. 'The computers . . . took over when it was time to put [the agreements] into practice.'[161] Agencies are making it clear that they will not tolerate anti-competitive conduct, whether or not it occurs in more traditional 'smoke-filled' rooms, or over the internet using complex pricing algorithms.[162] In cases involving the sale of posters online in the UK and the US, for example, an agreement between firms not to undercut each other on price was implemented through automated re-pricing software.[163] In a case such as this, the algorithm plays an ancillary enforcement role to the cartel arrangement, and may increase the parties' willingness to collude because they are able to distance themselves from its actual implementation.

Collusion can also be caught even if software actually makes an arrangement which is assented to by firms. In *Eturas' UAB v Lietuvos Respublikos konkurencijos taryba*,[164] discussed in Chapter 4, the Lithuanian competition agency condemned arrangements by travel agencies which used a common online travel booking system, in circumstances where the system administrator sent out an electronic message proposing to implement a software rule limiting the grant of discounts in the system. The CJ clarified that a concerted practice to eliminate discounts could be found if it could be established between travel agencies that were aware of the information sent out via the electronic mailbox and which had not publicly distanced themselves from the communications and the collusive scheme.

More difficult for competition law, however, would be a scenario where algorithms, especially self-learning[165] ones, 'collude' by reacting to each other and leading to alignment and maintenance of prices above the competitive level in concentrated markets without assistance from humans (decisions are made by machines not humans), for example where competitors adopt algorithms that: signal price announcements or communicate or exchange information with competitors which set prices at levels related to those of its competitors;[166] or which, even without such programming, learn means to optimise profit and sustain tacit collusion (the algorithms autonomously discover a profit-maximising price scheme).[167] Some commentators take the view that such algorithms pose a

[160] S. K. Mehra, 'Antitrust and the Robo-Seller: Competition in the time of Algorithms' (2016) 100 *Minnesota LR* 1323, 1340.

[161] Speech by Commissioner Vestager, Bundeskartellamt Conference on Competition, 16 March 2017.

[162] See e.g. speech of Commissioner Vestager, ibid., and US Department of Justice Press Release, 6 April 2015, <www.justice.gov/opa/pr/former-e-commerce-executive-charged-price-fixing-antitrust-divisions-first-online-marketplace>. For a discussion of when algorithms used by sharing economy platforms may be caught by, and infringe, Art. 101, see J. Nowag, 'When Sharing Platforms Fix Sellers' Prices' (2018) 6 *J of Antitrust Enforcement* 1.

[163] See e.g. UK competition authority decision in *Trod Ltd: posters and frames*, 21 July 2016 (horizontal agreement to restrict online selling prices implemented and policed through algorithms which enabled undertakings to see each others' prices; settlement led to fines and first director disqualification order under the UK Enterprise Act 2002) and criminal proceedings against David Tompkins in the US, US Department of Justice Press Release, 6 April 2015, n. 162. See also e.g. UK OFGEM decision, *Infringement by Economy Energy, E (Gas and Electricity) and Dyball Associates*, 26 July 2019.

[164] Case C-74/14, EU:C:2016:42.

[165] An algorithm amends its own decision-making to account for past experience.

[166] See C. Steiner, *Automate This: How Algorithms Came to Rule our World* (Portfolio, 2012) (discussing the example of the fruit-fly textbook where an algorithm led the price of the book to rise to $23.7 million).

[167] See e.g. M. Stucke and A. Ezrachi, 'Artificial Intelligence & Collusion: When Computers Inhibit Competition' (2017) 5 *Univ Illinois LR* 1775 and A. Ezrachi and M. E. Stucke, *Virtual Competition: The Problems and Promises of the Algorithm-driven Economy* (Harvard University Press, 2015).

significant risk to competition. For example, algorithms might solve some problems of colluding and, therefore, 'given the speed and enhanced transparency . . . expand the range of industries susceptible to collusion beyond duopolies to perhaps markets dominated by 5 or 6 players'.[168] It is possible therefore that price algorithms may change market dynamics and displace price competition between firms and make it easier for firms to collude.[169]

Although some consider this hypothesis to be exaggerated, with little evidence of real-world examples of such conduct yet occurring ('algorithmic collusive behaviour is not as likely or even unavoidable as some legal scholars seems to suspect'),[170] an important debate has been triggered as to whether, were such conduct to occur, it could be said to result from a concerted practice between firms or whether it constitutes tacit collusion falling outside Article 101's scope. If the latter, what other competition law solutions might remain?

Where an algorithm has been specifically chosen or programmed, and is being used, to exchange information between competitors, to signal future pricing intentions, or to engage in common or other collusive strategies it may be that a sufficient meeting of minds at the time of implementation of the computer system can be established which falls within the ambit of Article 101.[171] In such cases, pricing has been delegated to software with the object or effect of harmonising prices between competitors. Commissioner Vestager has stated:[172]

> Competition enforcers need to be suspicious of everyone who uses an automated system for pricing . . . What businesses need to know is that when they decide to use an automated system, they will be held responsible for what it does. So they had better know how that system works.

The Horizontal Cooperation Guidelines provide that where an undertaking discloses commercially sensitive information via an input in a shared algorithmic tool which is received by its competitors that may be sufficient to established a concerted practice: '*introducing a pricing rule in a shared algorithmic tool (for instance, a rule to match the lowest price on a particular online platform or shop +5 %, or to match the price of a particular competitor –5 %), is also likely to be caught by Article 101(1), even in the absence of an explicit agreement to align future pricing*'.[173] In principle, therefore, algorithms should be built to ensure that they do not collude. Further, hub-and-spoke collusion may be established if a platform operator or a third party provider of algorithmic software facilitates horizontal collusion between customers.[174]

[168] A. Ezrachi and M. Stucke, 'Algorithmic Collusion: Problems and Counter-measures', Note for OECD Roundtable on Algorithms and Collusion, 21–23 June 2017.

[169] See M. Gal, 'Limiting Algorithmic Cartels' (2023) 38(1) *Berkley J of Law and Technology* forthcoming (noting this consensus is built not only on theoretical studies but also on a growing body of experimental and empirical evidence). For a critique, see C. Veljanovski, 'What Do We Now Know about "Machine Collusion"' (2022) 13(1) *JECLAP* 47.

[170] See U. Schwalbe, 'Algorithms, Machine Learning, and Collusion' (2018) 14 *J of Competition Law and Economics* 568, 599. See also Veljanovski, n. 169 (reviewing the case for and evidence on algorithmic price collusion), A. Ittoo and N. Petit, 'Algorithmic Pricing Agents and Tacit Collusion: A Technological Perspective' <https://papers.ssrn.com/sol3/papers.cfm?abstract_id=3046405>, and J.E. Harrington, 'Developing Competition Law for Collusion by Autonomous Artificial Agents' (2019) 14 *JECLAP* 331, but contrast Gal, n. 169.

[171] A. Heinemann and A. Gebicka, 'Can Computers Form Cartels? About the Need for European Institutions to Revise the Concertation Doctrine in the Information Age' (2016) 7 *JECLAP* 431.

[172] Bundeskartellamt Conference on Competition, 16 March 2017.

[173] 17 July 2023, para. 397.

[174] See e.g. Hub-and-spoke arrangements—Note by the European Union for the OECD 132nd Competition Committee, 4 December 2019. See also Horizontal Cooperation Guidelines, ibid., para. 402.

It is, nonetheless, likely to present a challenge to a competition agency, given the complexity of algorithms and investigation, to demonstrate that there has been unlawful collusion rather than mere parallel conduct in these cases. It is not easy to know how algorithms work.

In contrast, it seems unlikely in situations where computers learn on their own, without human intervention, that a collusive strategy will maximise profits and that concertation can be established. Rather, it may be argued that there has been an intelligent reaction to market forces and the perceived strategy of competitors.[175] Thus 'algorithms achieving a tacitly collusive equilibrium without any need for contact between competitors or without putting in place any facilitating practice' are not likely to be covered by standard antitrust rules on cooperation between competitors, including Article 101; firms' actions become more interdependent without the need for explicit communication or interaction.[176] Some have argued that the concept of an agreement or concerted practice needs to be rethought or adapted to deal with the new environment created by technological developments.[177] Others have proposed that measures and countermeasures are necessary which expand beyond Article 101, such as market investigations and studies, enforcement of consumer and data protection laws, close scrutiny of mergers that may facilitate collusion in this way, or even regulation.[178]

(v) Uncovering Collusion

Even though the terms agreement, decision, and concerted practice have been interpreted broadly parties are likely to operate any offending cartel arrangements covertly in order to make detection difficult. A competition authority's task of proving the existence of the cartel is consequently an onerous one.

M. Monti, 'Fighting Cartels Why and How? Why Should We Be Concerned with Cartels and Collusive Behaviour?', 3rd Nordic Competition Policy Conference, Stockholm, 11–12 September 2000

Fighting cartels is not an easy business to be in. Companies operating cartels are of course very much aware of the illegality of their conduct under the antitrust laws. For that reason, cartels are typically operated in secrecy and considerable efforts are devoted by the participants to avoiding detection by the authorities. Meetings are held in exotic places around the globe. Incriminating documents are destroyed or stored outside the premises of the companies. Practices are arranged so as to simulate normal market behaviour and so on.

In order to be successful, a competition authority must be able to play a number of different cards. In particular, a successful fight against cartels presupposes an effective leniency programme, effective enforcement powers and sanctions, and close cooperation amongst competition authorities.

Because of the difficulty confronting the Commission in proving the existence of a breach, Regulation 1/2003 confers broad powers of investigation on the Commission to aid it in the task of gathering the evidence it requires to establish a breach (see further Chapter 13). Despite the existence

175 Increased transparency to aid competition may also provide a plausible justification for the conduct.

176 See e.g. Mehra, n. 160 and OECD, 'Algorithms and Collusion: Competition policy in the digital age' (2017).

177 See e.g. Heinemann and Gebicka, n. 171.

178 See e.g. Ezrachi and Stucke, nn. 167 and 168, and Mehra, n. 160, see further Section 5.C.

of these powers, it is difficult to uncover secretly operated cartels. More than 80 jurisdictions now encourage undertakings to cooperate with them prior to or during cartel investigations through the operation of 'leniency' regimes.[179] Leniency regimes have become a central part of policy in the fight against cartels. Authorities operating such schemes believe that the public interest in terminating and eradicating cartels outweighs the public interest in punishing those involved in the operation of cartels.[180]

The leniency regime in the US, for example, seems to have been successful for three reasons:[181] (a) it makes a genuinely good offer—complete immunity from a big penalty (fines and/or imprisonment) for the first to come forward; (b) it generates and exploits a nervousness that other cartel members may well be tempted by the same offer and win the race to obtain it; and (c) 'the ploy is reinforced by the general knowledge that only the first whistle-blower gets the big prize. It is thus reminiscent of the classical "Prisoner's Dilemma"—whether to play ball now, and quickly, or risk losing altogether. The strategy thus promotes within the cartel the sense of a higher risk, first, that somebody will blow the whistle and, secondly and consequently, of the other members being convicted. This serves to outweigh the previous benefits of solidarity, that is, of big profit from the offence plus a low risk of detection and conviction.'[182]

The Commission has operated a leniency regime since 1996, amending and improving it in 2002 and 2006.[183] Central to both the latter Notices is the provision that total immunity is available from Commission fines, but only to the *first* undertaking to submit evidence to the Commission (subject to other conditions also being satisfied). This provides a strong incentive for a cartel member to seek leniency prior to its co-collaborators and destabilises the game of collusion set up.[184] The regime is generally perceived to have operated successfully and firms have cooperated with the Commission in a high proportion of the cases occurring since 1996.[185] Its existence has had a marked effect on the nature of cartel decisions and appeals: in many cases the dispute now revolves not around the existence of an infringement but around the nature and duration of the infringement, which firms should be given what credit for cooperation under the relevant Leniency Notice, and other factors, such as the principle of equal treatment, which affect the level of the fine.

Although an effective tool, there is a growing view that antitrust authorities should not over rely 'on leniency applications to detect cartels'.[186] There is recognition that they may have their limits[187] and that: they may be ineffective in some industries or circumstances, especially where incentives for organising stable cartels exist; they may be most effective only where a cartel is in any event close to being discovered or breaking up (and less likely to be successful in identifying profitable and effective cartels);[188] they may be used by some larger multi-product firms operating a number of cartels as a

[179] See e.g. OECD, 'OECD Competition Trends' (2020), C. Harding and J. Joshua, *Regulating Cartels in Europe* (2nd edn, Oxford University Press, 2010), Chap. 8, and C. Beaton-Wells and C. Tan, *Anti-Cartel Enforcement in a Contemporary Age: Leniency Religion* (Hart Publishing, 2015).

[180] See OECD, 'Report on Leniency Programs to Fight Hard Core Cartels' (2001), and the 'Anti-Cartel Enforcement Manual' of the ICN's Cartel Working Group, April 2006, <www.internationalcompetitionnetwork.org/working-groups/>. See also the ECN Model Leniency Programme explained in Chap. 13.

[181] Harding and Joshua, n. 179, 235. [182] Ibid.

[183] Commission Notice on immunity from fines and reduction of fines in cartel cases [2006] OJ C298/17, see also 1996 and 2002 Notices, [1996] OJ C207/4 and [2002] OJ C45/3.

[184] Reductions in fines are also available to those who are not eligible for total immunity but who nevertheless provide the Commission with evidence that represents significant added value, see Chap. 13.

[185] But see e.g. A. Stephan, 'An Empirical Assessment of the European Leniency Notice' (2009) 5 *J of Competition Law and Economics* 537.

[186] C. Mena-Labarthe, 'Mexican Experience in Screens for Bid-Rigging', *CPI Antitrust Chronicle* March 2012.

[187] They also reward wrong-doers.

[188] J. E. Harrington, 'Detecting Cartels' in P. Buccirossi (ed.), *Handbook of Antitrust Economics* (MIT Press, 2008).

technique to prevent cheating and deviant conduct by smaller cartel members;[189] the increasing risk of individual sanctions, criminal prosecution, and/or private damages actions may be making persons more wary of submitting leniency applications;[190] and to be successful there must be a good track record of enforcement following the use of other detection techniques (without which, there will, of course, be no incentive to seek amnesty).[191] Indeed, evidence indicates that leniency applications may have been decreasing across the world, including in Europe.[192] Thus 'theory and practical experience seem to suggest that reliance on amnesty/leniency programmes alone may produce a sub-optimal probability of cartel detection, which in turn may have a negative effect on deterrence'.[193]

As a result, many competition enforcement agencies are now considering how to bolster and diversify their detection techniques and to collect evidence from a broader range of complainants including, competitors, customers, employees, or other whistle-blowers/informants capable of delivering credible evidence. In addition, internal proactive detection measures, including screens (both structural and behavioural) to adduce important prima facie evidence that collusion may have occurred or to identify early warning signs, are liable to produce 'positive externalities in terms of improving the efficacy of amnesty/leniency programmes';[194] they allow agencies to detect and prosecute conduct which would otherwise remain stable under a stand-alone amnesty/leniency regime. Public contract tenders are particularly suitable for the application of screening tools as the identification of a public tender market facilitates structural assessment and the data generated by the process facilitates subsequent behavioural assessments.[195]

In the EU, the Commission has sought to clarify that it will search for and find out about cartels whether or not one of the members seeks leniency.[196] It has developed a whistle-blowing tool encouraging any individual to provide it with information about cartel behaviour or other anti-competitive business practices[197] and uses proactive detection measures to help to uncover evidence. The Commission's investigative and enforcement powers and the leniency regime are dealt with fully in Chapter 13.

[189] R. C. Marshall, 'Unobserved Collusion: Warning Signs and Concerns' (2017) 5 *J of Antitrust Enforcement* 329.

[190] See e.g. O. Bodnar, M. Fremerey, H.-T. Normann, and J. Schad, 'The Effects of Private Damage Claims on Cartel Activity: Experimental Evidence' (2021) 39 *J of Law, Economics, and Organization* 27.

[191] D. C. Klawiter, 'Enhancing International Cartel Enforcement—Some Modest Suggestions', *CPI Antitrust Chronicle* September 2011 and D. C. Klawiter, 'Conspiracy Screens: Practical Defense Perspective', *CPI Antitrust Chronicle* March 2012.

[192] See OECD Competition Trends 2022, <www.oecd.org/daf/competition/oecd-competition-trends-2022.pdf>.

[193] OECD, 'Policy Roundtables: Ex Officio Cartel Investigations and the Use of Screens to Detect Cartels', DAF/COMP(2013)27.

[194] OECD, ibid.

[195] A burgeoning literature explores how screens, especially empirical screens based on economic and statistical analyses of variable data, including quantitative techniques (such as price variance analysis), can be applied to flag possible unlawful cartel behaviour and demonstrates that they are becoming increasingly important in the detection of conspiracies and manipulations. Because, however, they just flag indicators of possible collusion, and cannot distinguish explicit from tacit collusion, they ordinarily provide just one piece of evidence on which an investigation, or evidence of collusion, can be founded. See e.g. K. Hüschelrath and T. Veith, 'Cartel Detection in Procurement Markets', Discussion Paper No 11-066, Zentrum für Europäische Wirtschaftsforschung GmbH (2011) (monitoring procurement markets through screening tools has the potential to yield substantial cost reductions); R. Abrantes-Metz, L. Froeb, J. Geweke, and C. T. Taylor, 'A Variance Screen for Collusion' (2006) 4(3) *International J of Industrial Organization* 467–486; A. Deng, 'Cartel Detection and Monitoring: A Look Forward' (2017) 5 *J of Antitrust Enforcement* 488; D. Imhof, 'Detecting Bid-Rigging with Descriptive Statistics' (2020) 15(4) *J of Competition Law & Economics* 427.

[196] 'See e.g., N. Kroes, 'Flat Glass Cartel and Non-Horizontal Mergers', 28 November 2007.

[197] See European Commission, 'Cartels—Overview' (undated), <http://ec.europa.eu/competition/cartels/overview/index_en.html>.

4. CHARACTERISATION—IS IT A CARTEL?

A. HORIZONTAL AGREEMENTS INCORPORATING SEVERE RESTRAINTS ANCILLARY, OR NECESSARY, TO BENEFICIAL COLLABORATION

(i) General

Section 3 illustrates that agreements to fix prices, limit output, share markets, or rig bids ordinarily restrict competition by object and rarely satisfy the conditions of Article 101(3), because of the lack of consumer benefit. In the case of some horizontal collaboration, however, it may be argued that the agreement, even if containing price or output restraints, pursues a pro-competitive object (see further Chapter 10). The cases dealing with such scenarios, and discussed in the sections later, illustrate that they have not always found it easy to know how to deal with such arguments within the structure of Article 101.

In Chapter 5, however, it is seen that a recent line of cases, commencing with *Cartes Bancaires*,[198] indicates that the process in these types of case must start with a robust 'characterisation' mechanism to separate horizontal agreements which are obviously anti-competitive (which will always or almost always restrict competition and decrease output) and restrictive of competition by object, from those which do not have an obviously restrictive purpose—perhaps because it is not between competitors or because the venture and restraints are, plausibly, designed to achieve efficiency benefits (e.g. the creation of a new or better product or cost savings). In these latter cases, restrictive effects must be identified (rather than assumed) under Article 101(1), taking account of the broader context of the venture. Further, even where a restriction by object or effect is identified, the parties may seek to argue that the efficiencies generated by the agreement meet the conditions for exemption set out under Article 101(3).[199]

(ii) Price Restraints

A series of cases dealing with multilateral interchange fees (MIFs) set in card payment schemes (against MasterCard and Visa) illustrates some of the difficulties that have arisen in appraising these types of scenario. The Commission has been concerned that these practices may be anti-competitive, but a lack of clarity shrouded the question of how they are to be analysed under Articles 101(1) and 101(3). Thus, although in *Visa International-Multilateral Interchange Fee*[200] the Commission found, after Visa made certain reforms, that the arrangements met the Article 101(3) criteria,[201] in *MasterCard*[202] it held they did not—finding that no objective advantages under Article 101(3) had been demonstrated.[203] In a later case, it also imposed fines on

[198] Case C-67/13 P, *Groupement des cartes bancaires v Commission* EU:C:2014:2204.
[199] See discussion of *Broadcast Music, Inc v Columbia Broadcasting System, Inc*, 441 US 1 (1979) in Chap. 5.
[200] COMP/29.373, 9 August 2001. [201] See also discussion of the case in Chap. 5.
[202] COMP/34.579, 19 December 2007, *aff'd* Case T-111/08, EU:T:2012:260 and Case C-382/12 P, EU:C:2014:2201.
[203] See also COMP/39.398, *Visa Europe* IP/10/1684 (the Commission set out its preliminary view that the MIF set by Visa restricted competition between banks without benefiting consumers by contributing to technical and economic progress. The proceedings in relation to both Visa immediate debit card transactions and credit cards were resolved by commitments under Reg. 1/2003, Art. 9, decisions of 8 December 2010 and 26 February 2014) and a number of NCAs have brought similar actions, including in France, Germany, and Hungary (where fines of €1.75 million were imposed on both Visa and MasterCard), Italy, Poland, and the UK.

MasterCard[204] in relation to practices relating to inter-regional MIFs which led to higher prices for retailers and consumers and limited cross-border competition.

In the appeal from the 2007 *MasterCard* decision,[205] the EU Courts upheld the Commission's finding that the arrangements restricted competition[206] and did not meet the Article 101(3) criteria. In relation to the latter, the GC stated that even if it could be inferred from the evidence that the MIF contributed to increasing the output of the MasterCard system, that was not sufficient to establish that the first condition of Article 101(3) was satisfied; the primary beneficiaries of such an increase were the MasterCard payment organisation and participating banks. Case law specified that improvements had to display appreciable objective advantages so as to compensate for the disadvantages that they cause in the field of competition.[207] Although the Court did not rule on the question of whether the arrangements restricted competition by object, in *Gazdasági Versenyhivatal v Budapest Bank Nyrt*,[208] the CJ, in line with *Cartes Bancaires*, held that given: (a) the agreement on MIFs in the referred case did not set prices for final customers (rather it standardised one aspect of cost structure); and (b) the features of the case (including the two-sided nature of the market, the possible pro-competitive justification for the provisions, and the absence of experience demonstrating sufficient harm), the agreement could not be held to be restrictive by object unless the necessary degree of harm to competition was established by specific reference to the agreement's terms, objectives, and context.

A number of other horizontal collaboration cases have also involved an element of price-fixing. In *Reims II*,[209] the Commission found that although the fixing of terminal dues,[210] payable by post offices for the delivery of letters in other Member States, restricted competition, it led to an improvement in efficiency and eliminated cross-subsidy; the agreement would lead to a correlation between the terminal dues paid and cost and improve in the quality of service for cross-border mail. In *Uniform Eurocheques*,[211] the Commission also exempted, for a limited period, an agreement that fixed commissions for the cashing of Eurocheques. The Commission found that the agreement (a) improved payment methods and (b) benefited users (all currencies were available and interest-free credit was available whilst the cheques were being cleared). The restrictions were essential in the circumstances and did not lead to an elimination of competition.

The Commission has also considered whether joint distribution, joint selling, or collective licensing arrangements infringe Article 101. Although it is ordinarily hostile to joint selling or sales joint ventures as they effectively operate as horizontal price-fixing agreements,[212] the Commission has, particularly when dealing with copyright, or other neighbouring rights, sometimes been persuaded that joint selling or licensing may be beneficial and meet the criteria of Article 101(3).[213]

[204] COMP/400049, 22 January 2019. [205] Case T-111/08, EU:T:2012:260 and Case C-382/12 P, EU:C:2014:2201.

[206] See discussion of the case in Chap. 4.

[207] In relation to Art. 101(3). In 2015, the EU legislature adopted a regulation capping interchange fees, Reg. 2015/751 on interchange fees for card-based payment transactions [2015] OJ L123/1, see e.g. A. De Matteis and S. Giordano, 'Payment Cards and Permitted Multilateral Interchange Fees (MIFs): Will the European Commission Harm Consumers and the European Payment Industry?' (2015) 6 *JECLAP* 85. As this regulation does not deal with all the potential competition law issues arising, however, the Commission did not terminate all its investigations in this area.

[208] Case C-228/18, EU:C:2020:265.

[209] COMP/36.748 [1999] OJ L275/17, see also COMP/38.170 [2004] OJ L56/76.

[210] The remuneration that public postal operators (PPO) pay each other for the delivery of incoming cross-border mail. The receiving PPO is remunerated by the sending PPO for the delivery of the latter's mail.

[211] COMP/30.717 [1985] OJ L35/43. But see COMP/30.717-A, *Eurocheque: Helsinki Agreement* [1992] OJ L95/50, partially annulled and fines reduced on appeal, see Case T-39/92, *Groupement des Cartes Bancaires v Commission* EU:T:1994:20.

[212] But see Commission's Guidelines on joint selling of olive oil, beef and veal and arable crops, 27 November 2015 (providing guidance to farmers clarifying how they can, under certain conditions, cooperate to jointly sell these products without infringing Art. 101).

[213] See also the decision of the US Supreme Court, *Broadcast Music Inc v Columbia Broadcasting System Inc*, 441 US 1 (1979).

In *UIP*,[214] the Commission granted an exemption to agreements creating United International Pictures BV (UIP) a joint film distribution company established by Paramount Pictures Corp, Universal Studios Inc, and Metro-Goldwyn Mayer Inc. UIP distributed and licensed on an exclusive basis feature motion pictures, short subjects, and trailers produced by the parties for showing in cinemas. Following modifications to the agreement, the Commission accepted that the cooperation produced economic benefits for the production and distribution of motion pictures and for consumers, which could not be achieved in the absence of the joint venture and which outweighed its disadvantages.[215]

Broadcasting rights to sports matches or competitions are also frequently sold collectively on behalf of clubs or participants by sports associations. The agreements often involve exclusivity, leading to a concern that they will distort competition between broadcasters, encourage media concentration, and stifle the development of new products and services such as internet sports services and new generation mobile phones.[216] In *Joint selling of the commercial rights of the UEFA Champions League*,[217] the Commission, following revision of their terms, exempted regulations concerning the joint selling of the commercial rights to the UEFA Champions League on behalf of the clubs participating in the league (see further Chapter 10).

(iii) Joint Purchasing (Price-fixing Amongst Buyers)

Price-fixing amongst buyers may be designed to achieve lower prices for members, which may then be passed on to their customers (see further discussion of joint purchasing agreements in Chapter 10). The Commission thus recognises in its Horizontal Cooperation Guidelines[218] that although joint purchasing arrangements can restrict competition by object (where they serve as a tool to engage in a disguised buyer cartel), they will not do so if they truly concern a joint purchasing arrangement, 'namely where two or more purchasers jointly negotiate and conclude an agreement with a given supplier relating to one or more trading terms governing the supply of products to the cooperating purchasers'.[219] The Guidelines set out in paragraph 282 the factors that the Commission considers to be relevant in distinguishing purchasing agreements from buyer cartels, including whether it has been made clear to suppliers that the joint purchasing arrangement has been jointly negotiated and binds its members and whether the parties have defined the form of their cooperation, its scope, and operation in writing.

Similarly, in the context of employer agreements, it may be necessary to distinguish between naked wage-fixing or no-poach agreements among employers and those which are part of, and necessary for, a larger legitimate collaboration between them (for example, a research and development joint venture).

(iv) Output and Production Limitations

The Commission has been prepared to accept that agreements which limit output or production may not infringe Article 101. As with joint purchasing, where such restrictions are ancillary to a beneficial R&D, production, or specialisation agreement (and truly concern R&D, production or specialisation and do not serve simply as a tool to engage in a disguised cartel), the terms in such agreements are not

[214] COMP/30.566 [1989] OJ L226/35.

[215] See also IP/99/681 (comfort letter granted, subject to further amendments to the agreements, after the parties applied for an extension of the exemption) and COMP/38.014, *IFPI* [2003] OJ 107/46 (see Chap. 12).

[216] The Commission is concerned that exclusivity agreements do not lead to other broadcasters being excluded from the market altogether. Thus a long duration of exclusivity may be prohibited if there is a risk that a broadcaster might prevent its competitors gaining access.

[217] COMP/37.398 [2003] OJ L291/25. [218] 17 July 2023, at Chapter 4. [219] Ibid., para. 278.

liable to be found to be restrictive of competition by object and may satisfy the terms of Article 101(3) where restrictive effects are identified.[220]

Further, in the past at least, the Commission has exceptionally been sympathetic to parties that notified 'crisis cartels' for exemption (see further Chapter 5).[221] In these cases, it permitted undertakings operating in industries suffering severe difficulties to conclude cooperation agreements providing, for example, for an orderly reduction in overcapacity where the economic effect of the improved rationalisation outweighs the disadvantages of the reduced competition in the short term. However, it would not allow the restructuring to be achieved by unacceptable means such as price-fixing or market-sharing. Further, it would regard the restrictions as indispensable only if the agreement was concerned solely with the reduction of capacity and was limited from the outset to a period necessary for its setting up and implementation.[222]

These decisions are old ones, however, and more recently the Commission has indicated that it will not be willing to tolerate crisis cartels, at least where it can be expected that market forces will be able to remedy structural overcapacity.[223] For example, in 2009 during the financial and economic crisis (then) Competition Commissioner Neelie Kroes, indicated that not only would the Commission not turn a blind eye to cartels, but it would be vigilant for them, recognising that anti-competitive collaboration is a hugely tempting mechanism for firms to employ to shield themselves from ruinous competition in a climate of rising competition for a shrinking demand:

> If I may quickly mention the issue of so-called 'crisis-cartels' . . . There may be many temptations in 2009 to cut corners, but encouraging cartelists and others would be guaranteeing disaster. It would drag down recovery, increase consumer harm and create more cartel and cartel cases into the future. No-one wins—today's softness is tomorrow's nightmare.[224]

This stance has, however, raised some concern, especially in cases where, for example, governments may have endorsed or encouraged industry-wide measures to permit the weathering of an industry storm or even pressured industry members to adopt voluntary measures to achieve broader public policy objectives. This type of disquiet was perhaps experienced by the Irish courts, which had to adjudicate on the compatibility of a crisis cartel in the *BIDS* case (made with the knowledge of the Irish Government) with Article 101(3). In Chapter 5, it is seen that the CJ in *BIDS* held, following a reference to it from the Irish Supreme Court, that because an agreement to reduce capacity had as its object the restriction of competition, the fact that the parties did not intend to harm consumers but to benefit them through rationalisation of the industry was not relevant under Article 101(1). The objective pursued might, however, be relevant under Article 101(3). When the case returned to the Irish Supreme Court, the matter to be resolved, therefore, was whether or not the arrangements could benefit from Article 101(3). The Irish Supreme Court[225] felt that this issue should be remitted to the Irish High Court for decision, but nonetheless expressed a view on some general legal points that would be relevant to the assessment. In particular, it stressed that the case was far removed from

220 See Chap. 10.

221 One of the Commission's objectives was to ensure the elimination of overcapacity in an industry and to enable the industry to recover its profitability, Commission, *XX1st Report on Competition Policy* (1991), 207 ff.

222 See e.g. in COMP/31.055, *ENI/Montedison* [1987] OJ L5/13, for 15 years there was an agreement between two large petrochemical groups for rationalisation of their production capacities and transfer of certain businesses, leading to a *de facto* specialisation by each party.

223 But see B. Wardhaugh, 'Crisis Cartels: Non-economic Values, the Public Interest and Institutional Considerations' (2014) 10 *European Competition Journal* 311.

224 Speech by N. Kroes, 'Tackling cartels—a never-ending task', 8 October 2009.

225 *Competition Authority v Beef Industry Development Society Ltd* [2009] IESC 72.

a cartel scheme hatched in a smoke-filled room,[226] indicated (having regard to the Commission's previous decisions in *Synthetic Fibres* and *Dutch Bricks (Stichting Baksteen)*[227]) that the agreement was likely to realise substantial efficiencies (even if the value of those efficiencies could not be demonstrated), and pointed out that no consumers had complained and that powerful buyers (such as Tesco) were unlikely to tolerate the passing on of any price increases. The court noted further that restraints designed to prevent players who had been paid to leave the industry from re-entering and acquiring capacity seemed indispensable to the success of the arrangements.

Before the Irish High Court the Commission intervened in the case to submit observations on the application of Article 101(3) and setting out its view that it will only be in relatively rare circumstances that parties to an agreement involving a reduction in capacity will be able to demonstrate efficiencies, that the restrictive agreement is indispensable to achieve those efficiencies (and that they cannot be achieved by market forces), and that any benefits would be passed on to consumers.[228] In the end, however, the High Court did not have an opportunity to reach its decision on the application of Article 101(3), as BIDS withdrew its claim for exemption and agreed to pay a substantial proportion of the competition authority's costs. The Irish authority has now published a guidance note on agreements to reduce capacity which is based on its experience in the *BIDS* case.[229]

In another case, the Commission granted an exemption to an agreement which restricted the type of goods that the parties to the agreement could produce or import. In *European Council of Manufacturers of Domestic Appliances*,[230] the Commission exempted an agreement concluded between 95 per cent of the producers and importers of washing machines operating on the EU market that restricted their freedom to manufacture or import the least energy-efficient washing machines. The agreement was found to restrict competition within the meaning of Article 101(1).[231] Nonetheless, the Commission considered that the agreement met the criteria set out in Article 101(3) since it would reduce the potential energy consumption of new machines and consequently lessen pollution, create more technically efficient machines, and focus future R&D on furthering energy efficiency. Such economic and technical progress would benefit society and consumers. The Commission considered that the restrictions were indispensable to the agreement, which would not substantially eliminate competition.

These cases also reflect the current important debate, considered further in Chapters 5 and 10, as to whether, and if so when, broader public policy benefits, especially social or environmental sustainability objectives, can, or should, be subsumed within Article 101 analysis.

(v) Joint Tendering

It has been seen that bid rigging designed to thwart a pro-competitive tendering exercise is a classic example of cartel activity infringing Article 101. Joint tendering may, however, rather than collusive tendering, constitute a legitimate pro-competitive means of allowing firms to be able to tender at all[232] or to submit superior bids than those which could have been submitted individually and to produce efficiencies that outweigh the competition concerns.[233]

[226] Not only had the agreement been concluded with the knowledge of the Irish Government but it had been notified to the Irish competition authority. The latter felt it was anti-competitive, however, and for this reason brought proceedings before the Irish courts to have the agreement struck down.

[227] See Chap. 5.

[228] See <http://ec.europa.eu/competition/court/antitrust_amicus_curiae.html>.

[229] Notice on Agreements to Reduce Capacity, 16 June 2011.

[230] COMP/36.718 [2000] OJ L187/47.

[231] See Chap. 5, IP/01/1659 (where the Commission indicated its intention to take a similar approach to environmental agreements for water heaters and dishwashers) and contrast, e.g., COMP/39.579, *Consumer Detergents* [2011] OJ C193/14.

[232] See n. 238 and text.

[233] See e.g. C. Ritter, 'Joint Tendering under EU Competition Law' [2017] 2 *Concurrences* 60–69 and C. Thomas, 'Two Bids or not to Bid? An Exploration of the Legality of Joint Bidding and Subcontracting under EU Competition Law' (2015) 6 *JECLAP* 629.

There is no case in which the EU Courts have set out guidance on how joint tendering should be analysed. It has, however, been dealt with by the EFTA Court in a case involving a joint tender by two taxi companies to provide patient transport services to a hospital, *Ski Taxi SA v Konkurransetilsynet*.[234] In this case, the Court, stressing the CJ's requirement that object restraints 'must reveal a sufficient degree of harm to competition' and the importance of having regard to 'context' in the determination, held that object classification is appropriate only if the harmful nature of the agreement is easily identifiable. Thus, in determining whether joint bidding is restrictive of competition by object it has to be assessed, albeit in an abridged manner, whether its parties are actual or potential competitors and whether restraints might be ancillary. 'Whether the submission of joint bids by SFD on behalf of Ski Taxi and Follo Taxi in the two tender procedures is to be considered a restriction of competition by object is a matter of fact and as such for the referring court to assess.'[235]

In some pre-modernisation cases, the Commission did consider whether joint bidding might meet the Article 101(3) criteria.[236] In *FIEC/CEETB*,[237] the Commission indicated that it would take a favourable view of an agreement designed to standardise and reduce the cost of the tendering process between building contractors and subcontractors but which would not in any way limit either the firms who could tender or the prices at which they could tender. Chapter 5.4 of the Horizontal Cooperation Guidelines also provides guidance on how to distinguish collusive tendering which is restrictive by object and bidding consortia which do not infringe Article 101, for example where they allow the undertakings to participate in projects that they would not be able to undertake individually[238] (see also Chapter 10).

(vi) Market-sharing and Settlement Agreements

The important question of whether parties to an agreement are actual or potential competitors has also arisen in cases involving market-sharing and intellectual property (IP) settlements. In Chapter 5, it is seen that in *Toshiba Corp v Commission*[239] the CJ accepted that sufficient contextual analysis had been carried out (by the Commission and GC) to reject the parties' argument that their market-sharing agreement should not have been characterised as restrictive of competition by object as entry by Japanese producers into the EEA market was not economically viable (and so the parties were not actual or potential competitors). A similar approach was adopted in *Portugal Telecom* and *Telefónica v Commission*,[240] when an argument that non-competition clauses in an agreement between Portugal Telecom and Telefónica did not restrict competition by object was rejected. No detailed market analysis was necessary; the very existence of a non-compete clause, in the context of a liberalised market, provided a strong indication that the parties were at least potential competitors.

Chapter 12, which deals with IP agreements, also considers how settlement agreements, designed to resolve disputes concerning the validity or scope of IP especially in patent-intensive industries, are appraised under Article 101. It is seen that even though some such agreements may be beneficial, serving as a means to settle bona fide patent disputes, a concern is that some settlement agreements in pharmaceutical markets[241] may be designed to limit new entry by companies producing generic

[234] Case E-3/16, 22 December 2016, see I. Herrera Anchustegui, 'Joint Bidding and Object Restrictions of Competition: The EFTA Court's Take in the "Taxi Case"' (2017) 1(2) *European Competition and Regulatory LR* 1.

[235] Ibid., para. 94. [236] See e.g. COMP/30.064, *Cast Iron and Steel Rolls* [1983] OJ L317/1.

[237] COMP/31.014 [1988] OJ C52/2. [238] Horizontal Cooperation Guidelines, para. 352.

[239] Case C-373/14 P, EU:C:2016:26.

[240] Cases T-208 and 216/13, EU:T:2016:369, *aff'd* Case C-487/16 P, *Telefónica SA v Commission* EU:C:2017:961.

[241] Involving 'reverse' payments made by the patentee to the generics producer, rather than (as is normal in the settlement of a patent infringement case) by the alleged infringer to the patentee.

products (potential competitors) and operate as market-sharing or exclusion agreements which are restrictive of competition by object.[242]

(vii) Restrictions on Advertising

The advertising and promotion of a product may be an extremely important aspect of competition between undertakings. It may be a vital means of distinguishing the products, in the eyes of the consumer, from those of competitors and may draw attention to the different characteristics, prices, and qualities of the relevant products. It can also provide an important mechanism for entering a new market.

Restrictions on the ability of parties to an agreement to advertise are likely to be seen as a restriction on their competitive freedom and competition.[243] The Commission has shown particular concern about restrictions on advertising in the liberal professions.

Communication from the Commission, 'Report on Competition in Professional Services', COM(2004) 83 final (Brussels, 9 February 2004)

42. A large number of the EU professions are subject to sector-specific advertising regulation . . . in some cases advertising as such is prohibited. In others, specific media or advertising methods such as radio advertising, televisions advertising or 'cold calling' or specific types of advertising content are proscribed. In certain cases, there is a lack of clarity in existing advertising regulations which, in itself, may deter professions from employing certain advertising methods.

43. According to economic theory, advertising may facilitate competition by informing consumers about different products and allowing them to make better informed purchasing decisions. Advertising restrictions may thus reduce competition by increasing the costs of gaining information about different products, making it more difficult for consumers to search for the quality and price that best meets their needs. It is also widely recognised that advertising, and in particular comparative advertising, can be a crucial competitive tool for new firms entering the market and for existing firms to launch new products.

44. The proponents of advertising restrictions emphasise the asymmetry of information between practitioners and consumers of professional services. According to this argument, consumers find it difficult to assess information about professional services and therefore need particular protection from misleading or manipulative claims.

45. There is, however, an increasing body of empirical evidence which highlights the potentially negative effects of some advertising restrictions. This research suggests that restrictions may under certain circumstances increase the fees for professional services without having a positive effect on the quality of those services. The implication of these findings is that advertising restrictions as such do not, necessarily, provide an appropriate response to asymmetry of information in professional services. Conversely, truthful and objective advertising may actually help consumers to overcome the asymmetry and to make more informed purchasing decisions.

[242] See Chap. 12 and especially discussion of Case C-591/16 P, *H Lundbeck v Commission* EU:C:2021:243 and Case C-307/18, *Generics* EU:C:2020:52.

[243] See e.g. COMP/39.579, *Consumer Detergents* [2011] OJ C193/14 (restrictions on promotional activity treated as a form of price collusion).

In general, where parties agree jointly to advertise industry products or products of a common brand, there is no infringement of Article 101(1) so long as the parties are also free to advertise individually. The Commission has, therefore, sometimes accepted that it may be advantageous for undertakings to rationalise and coordinate their advertising efforts, particularly in the context of trade fairs.[244]

However, different rules may apply in an oligopolistic market where product differentiation and advertising may play a more vital role.

In *Milchförderungsfonds*,[245] the Commission held that a brand-advertising campaign by the German dairy industry restricted competition and artificially strengthened the position of German exporters abroad. Although generic advertising, which did not commend the products solely on the ground of their national origin and did not disparage foreign products, would have benefited all exporters, brand-oriented advertising appreciably reduced the possibility of sales for competing brands. Individual manufacturers benefited from the campaign without having to suffer a corresponding cost which otherwise would have been reflected in the sales price. In *BELASCO*,[246] it also prohibited joint advertising and promotion of competing products which were sold under a common trademark; the purpose of this standardisation was to reinforce the other provisions of the agreement which provided for a common price list and sales quotas. The fostering of an impression in consumers that their products were homogeneous limited the scope of competition by means of product differentiation.

B. INFORMATION-SHARING AGREEMENTS

(i) Exchange of Information Between Competitors

Another area where it is difficult to distinguish naked, restrictive, anti-competitive arrangements between competitors from ones which might be pursuing legitimate pro-competitive goals is in the realm of information exchange—the exchange of raw digital content, pre-processed data, manipulated data, or any other information, including non-digital information.[247] Where information exchange forms part of another type of horizontal cooperation agreement, for example a standardisation or an R&D agreement, or an acquisition process, it will need to be assessed against the backdrop of the wider arrangement (see Chapters 10 and 15). This section focuses on agreements, the main objective of which is information exchange.

The dissemination and exchange of information between competitors and the creation of a transparent market may be harmless or even highly beneficial to the competitive structure of the market.[248] In particular, the transparency created can produce significant efficiencies and benefits to both suppliers and customers. 'Many sectors of our economies now depend upon ready access to detailed information.'[249] Information exchange may allow suppliers to adapt their businesses, to improve commercial strategies, to improve effective allocation of resources, to increase internal efficiency (for example, by benchmarking their processes and performance against each other's best practices), to

[244] See e.g. COMP/28.775, *UNIDI* [1984] OJ L322/10.

[245] COMP/28.930 [1985] OJ L35/35.

[246] COMP/31.371, *BELASCO* [1986] OJ L232/15, Case 246/86, *Re Roofing Felt Cartel: BELASCO v Commission* EU:C:1989:301.

[247] Horizontal Cooperation Guidelines, para. 367.

[248] See e.g., M. Bennett and P. Collins, 'The Law and Economics of Information Sharing: The Good, the Bad and the Ugly' (2010) 6 *European Competition Journal* 311; K. U. Kühn and X. Vives, 'Information exchanges among firms and their impact on competition' (Office for Official Publications of the European Community, Luxembourg, 1995); OECD Roundtable on Information Exchange, DAF/COMP(2010)37; and V. Robertson, 'A Counterfactual on Information Sharing: The Commission's Horizontal Guidelines 2011 Applied to the Leading Cases' (2013) 36 *World Competition* 459.

[249] Bennett and Collins, ibid., 311.

promote innovation, to understand market trends and demand, to improve product positioning, to resolve information asymmetries, to inform decision-taking by enabling use of big data analytics and machine-learning techniques, and help to save costs.[250] From a consumer's perspective, it may increase transparency, reduce search costs, and help them fully to utilise their power of choice.[251]

Information exchanges may, however, also present the opportunity for competitors to coordinate their behaviour and to achieve and maintain a collusive equilibrium over time. First, they may be used to bolster or facilitate the operation of a cartel. Where the information is exchanged deliberately to support price-fixing or other hardcore cartel activity the Commission or other enforcing authority will take a dim view.[252]

Secondly, even if not ancillary to a cartel, exchanges of commercially sensitive information can '[b]y artificially increasing transparency between competitors in the market, . . . facilitate coordination of undertakings' behaviour and result in restrictions of competition'.[253] For example, information exchanged about firms' past, current, or future behaviour may provide a focal point facilitating competitors reaching a common understanding as to coordination of price or output levels on a market. It may also contribute to the internal and external stability of the collusive arrangement by enabling undertakings to determine quickly whether competitors are deviating from a coordinated strategy or whether new entrants may be threatening a collusive strategy, so enabling them to guard against them through retaliation or targeting new entrants. Information-sharing arrangements may also lead to anti-competitive foreclosure on the relevant, or a related, market, for example where competitors that are not part of an exchange of strategically important information are placed at a competitive disadvantage.[254]

A stand-alone information exchange may therefore in *itself* be sufficient to establish a violation of Article 101(1).[255]

(ii) Assessing the Competitive Effects of an Information-sharing Arrangement under Article 101(1) and Article 101(3)

a. Characterisation

In the EU, a narrow category of information exchange has been equated with cartel activity and considered to be restrictive by object. The majority of information agreements are, however, assessed individually in their market context to determine their actual or likely effects on competition. Apart from the de minimis principle, no safe harbour applies for the latter arrangements and there are relatively few bright lines or clear rules for business to adhere to in this area.

b. Object Restrictions

In *T-Mobile Netherlands BV v Raad van bestuur van de Nederlandse Mededingingsautoriteit*,[256] discussed in Chapter 5, the CJ clarified that a private[257] information exchange designed to facilitate the fixing

250 Horizontal Cooperation Guidelines 17 July 2023, para. 373.

251 Where information is available generally, consumers with complete knowledge of what is on offer may fully utilise their power of choice.

252 See e.g. COMP/31.572 and COMP/32.571, *Building and Construction Industry in the Netherlands* [1992] OJ L92/1, *aff'd* Case T-29/92, *SPO v Commission* EU:T:1995:34 and 'Commission fines the metal packaging producers Crown and Silgan €31.5 million in cartel settlement', IP/22/4483.

253 Horizontal Cooperation Guidelines, paras. 377–380.

254 Ibid., paras. 381–383.

255 See e.g. Case T-141/94, *Thyssen Stahl v Commission* EU:T:1999:48, paras. 379–392.

256 Case C-8/08, EU:C:2009:343, paras. 36–43.

257 For the view that public information exchanges relating to future (or current) prices are less likely to produce anti-competitive effects than private exchanges, see Bennett and Collins, n. 248, 334 and discussion of public announcements, Section 3.B.iii.

of prices between competitors falls within the category of restraints which are restrictive by object.[258] Further, in *Bananas*[259] the Commission fined three banana importers for engaging in a concerted practice concerning the fixing, development, and evolution of prices through a series of information exchanges. It found that the parties' regular pattern of communications relating to price-setting factors (such as the sales situation, supply and demand conditions liable to affect price levels for the coming weeks, and price trends and/or indications of quotation prices for the coming week) restricted competition by object; they were ultimately aimed at reducing or eliminating uncertainty as to the future pricing behaviour of the parties (the setting of quotation prices) and to maximise the price that they could individually and/or collectively obtain.[260] On appeal the argument was rejected that, as the pre-pricing communications were not able to remove uncertainty as to the setting of actual prices, they could not be considered to be restrictive by object. In particular, the CJ upheld the Commission's finding that the conduct could be regarded, by its very nature, to be harmful to the proper functioning of competition, reiterating (as in *T-Mobile*) that economic operators must determine their policy independently on the market and that conduct was liable to be incompatible with the competition law rules if it reduced or removed the degree of uncertainty as to the operation of the market in question.[261]

Case C-286/13 P, *Dole Food Co Inc v Commission* EU:C:2015:184

Court of Justice

122. In particular, an exchange of information which is capable of removing uncertainty between participants as regards the timing, extent and details of the modifications to be adopted by the undertakings concerned in their conduct on the market must be regarded as pursuing an anticompetitive object (see, to that effect, judgment in *T-Mobile* . . ., paragraph 41).

123. Moreover, a concerted practice may have an anticompetitive object even though there is no direct connection between that practice and consumer prices. Indeed, it is not possible on the basis of the wording of Article [101(1)] to conclude that only concerted practices which have a direct effect on the prices paid by end users are prohibited (see, to that effect, judgment in *T-Mobile* . . ., paragraph 36).

. . .

129. As observed by the Advocate General at points 115 and 116 of her Opinion, it is apparent from the extremely detailed findings of the General Court, first, that bilateral pre-pricing communications were exchanged between the Dole companies and other undertakings in the banana sector and, as part of those communications, the undertakings discussed their own quotation prices and certain price trends. Moreover, the Dole companies do not contest that finding.

130. Second, the General Court found, at paragraph 574 of the judgment under appeal, that quotation prices were relevant to the market concerned, since, on the one hand, market signals, market trends or indications as to the intended development of banana prices could be inferred from those quotation prices, which were important for the banana trade and the prices obtained and, on the other, in some transactions the actual prices were directly linked to the quotation prices.

[258] The same principles apply to the exchange of price information between distributors, see COMP/25.757, *Hasselblad* [1982] OJ L161/18, on appeal Case 86/82, *Hasselblad v Commission* EU:C:1984:65: where a market is not oligopolistic, the Commission has been prepared to accept that even the exchange of individual and confidential information concerning costs, sales volumes, and market shares may not infringe Art. 101: COMP/33.815, 35.842, *Eudim* [1996] OJ C111/8.

[259] Case COMP/39.188, *Bananas*, 15 October 2008, *aff'd* Cases T-587/08, *Fresh Del Monte Produce v Commission* EU:T:2013:129 and T-588/08 P, *Dole Food and Dole Germany v Commission* EU:T:2013:130 and Cases C-293 and 294/13 P, *Fresh Del Monte v Commission* EU:C:2015:416 and Case C-286/13 P, *Dole Food Co Inc v Commission* EU:C:2015:184.

[260] Ibid. [261] Case C-286/13 P, *Dole* EU:C:2015:184, paras. 119–121.

> 131. Third, at paragraph 580 of the judgment under appeal, the General Court found that the Dole employees involved in the pre-pricing communications participated in the internal pricing meetings.
>
> 132. Furthermore, those findings of the General Court are to a large extent based on statements made by Dole Food and the Dole companies have not alleged any form of distortion in that regard.
>
> 133. Accordingly, the General Court was entitled to take the view, without erring in law, that the conditions for the application of the presumption referred to at paragraph 127 above were fulfilled in the present case, with the result that the Dole companies' claims that that court infringed the principle governing the burden of proof and the presumption of innocence are unfounded.
>
> 134. It also follows that the General Court was entitled to take the view, as it did at paragraphs 553 and 585 of the judgment under appeal, without erring in law, that it was permissible for the Commission to conclude that, as they made it possible to reduce uncertainty for each of the participants as to the foreseeable conduct of competitors, the pre-pricing communications had the object of creating conditions of competition that do not correspond to the normal conditions on the market and therefore gave rise to a concerted practice having as its object the restriction of competition within the meaning of Article [101].

Although, as was the case in *T-Mobile*, the statements in this case seem potentially to extend the category of object restraints to a broad and somewhat uncertain group of information-exchange agreements, the statements were made in the context of a case in which the conduct at issue was found to be designed to facilitate the fixing of selling prices—the agreements thus inherently revealed a sufficient degree of harm to competition.

An approach closely in tune with economic effects suggests that only a narrow category of information-sharing agreements should be considered to be restrictive by object—the private sharing of disaggregated, confidential information relevant, or relating, to future pricing or output intentions between competitors.[262] The Horizontal Cooperation Guidelines state that an information exchange 'will be considered a restriction of competition by object where the information is commercially sensitive and the exchange is capable of removing uncertainty between participants as regards the timing, extent and details of the modifications to be adopted by the undertakings concerned in their conduct on the market'.[263] Further that an information exchange may be considered as a cartel if it is aimed at 'coordinating their competitive behaviour on the market or at influencing the relevant parameters of competition'.[264]

Private exchanges between competitors on their individualised intentions regarding future prices or quantities may thus be found to have the object of fixing prices or quantities and to infringe Article 101. In *Container Shipping*,[265] the Commission also took the provisional view that the public exchanges of information in that case constituted announcements of individualised future pricing intentions which restricted competition by object.

[262] See e.g. Bennett and Collins, n. 248, 329–331, Swedish Competition Authority, *The Pros and Cons of Information Sharing* (2006) and B. Meyring, 'T-Mobile: Further Confusion on Information Exchanges Between Competitors' (2010) 1 *JECLAP* 31. See also Case C-298/22, *Banco BPN/BIC Português* (judgment pending) Sharing of information by buyers could also be problematic, e.g. sharing of information with competitors about terms and conditions of employment (such as wage information), see DOJ and FTC, 'Antitrust Guidance for Human Resource Professionals', n. 86, Hong Kong CC Advisory Bulletin, n. 88.

[263] 17 July 2023, para. 413. [264] Ibid., para. 417.

[265] COMP/39.850, 7 July 2016, see nn. 154–155 and text.

c. *Analysing Other Information Exchanges*

Where an agreement is not found to have as its object the restriction of competition, it will need to be assessed individually in its market context to determine its actual or likely effect—in particular whether it is likely to facilitate collusion or result in anti-competitive foreclosure. 'For an information exchange to have restrictive effects on competition within the meaning of Article 101(1), it must be likely to have an appreciable adverse impact on one (or several) of the parameters of competition such as price, output, product quality, product variety or innovation.'[266] It has been seen that a particular concern is that information exchanges can facilitate interdependent behaviour by creating the conditions for it—by increasing transparency, reducing complexity, buffering instability, or compensating for asymmetry.[267] The CJ in *Asnef-Equifax, Servicios de Información sobre Solvencia y Crédito, SL v Asociación de Usuarios de Servicios Bancarios (Ausbanc)* stated:[268]

> the appraisal of the effects of agreements or practices . . . entails the need to take into consideration the actual context to which they belong, in particular the economic and legal context in which the undertakings concerned operate, the nature of the goods or services affected, as well as the real conditions of the functioning and the structure of the market or markets in question . . .
>
> Accordingly . . . the compatibility of an information exchange system . . . with the [EU] competition rules cannot be assessed in the abstract. It depends on the economic conditions on the relevant markets and on the specific characteristics of the system concerned, such as, in particular, its purpose and the conditions of access to it and participation in it, as well as the type of information exchanged—be that, for example, public or confidential, aggregated or detailed, historical or current—the periodicity of such information and its importance for the fixing of prices, volumes or conditions of service.

Relevant factors in conducting the assessment are the type/nature of the information exchanged, the specific characteristics of the exchange—its purpose, conditions of access, and participation—and the nature and economic conditions of the relevant market.

The type of information exchanged is of crucial importance to the appraisal.[269] Statistical information which enables undertakings to assess the level of demand and output in the market or the costs of its competitors may be beneficial and not of itself objectionable.[270] Similarly, exchange of technical or other information that does not restrict the parties' freedom to determine their market behaviour independently should not be objectionable. However, exchange of strategic or commercially sensitive data (that reduces strategic uncertainty in the market), such as information relating to prices, individual output or sales figures,[271] capacity increases,[272] costs,[273] demand, investment plans,[274] new technology and research projects, or other business secrets, may, even if not restrictive of competition by object, be liable to influence the commercial strategy of rivals, decrease the parties' incentive to compete, and increase opportunities for coordinated activity.

[266] Case C-286/13 P, *Dole* EU:C:2015:184, para. 75. [267] Ibid., para. 77.
[268] Case C-238/05, EU:C:2006:734, para. 54.
[269] Horizontal Cooperation Guidelines, 17 July 2023, 6.2.7.
[270] Case T-334/94, *Sarrió SA v Commission* EU:T:1998:97.
[271] See COMP/31.370 and 31.466, *UK Agricultural Tractor Registration Exchange* [1992] OJ L68/19.
[272] See e.g. COMP/243, 244, 245, *Re Cimbell* [1972] OJ L303/24.
[273] See e.g. COMP/400, *IFTRA Glass Containers* [1974] OJ L160/1; COMP/27.000, *IFTRA Aluminium* [1975] OJ L228/3.
[274] See e.g. COMP/30.350, *Zinc Producer Group* [1984] OJ L220/27.

The Horizontal Cooperation Guidelines recognise that the nature of the data, especially whether it is raw, individualized, or aggregated, is important as it affects the usefulness it has to competitors and its commercial sensitivity.

> 390. Whether information is commercially sensitive depends on its usefulness to competitors. In general, information that contains a lot of detail and enables the identification of the undertaking(s) that provided it will be more commercially sensitive. Exchanges of individualised information may facilitate a common understanding on the market and punishment strategies, by allowing coordinating undertakings to more easily single out a deviator or new entrant.
>
> 391. The exchange of aggregated information, where the attribution of information to particular undertakings is sufficiently difficult or uncertain, or where the data are aggregated across a range of different products, especially if the products have different characteristics or belong to different markets, is less likely to lead to a restriction of competition. . . . Nevertheless, the possibility cannot be excluded that even the exchange of aggregated information and data may facilitate a collusive outcome in markets with specific characteristics.

Further, if the information exchanged is old or 'historic' rather than current, the less likely it will facilitate the coordination of conduct on a market in the future.[275] In *Cobelpa/VNP*,[276] the Commission held that although there was nothing wrong in a trade association exchanging information on industry output and sales, in this case, where the information exchanged identified the output and sales of individual undertakings, the practice was prohibited. By exchanging information about matters normally regarded as confidential (especially where the information was not available to consumers) the parties were replacing practical cooperation for the normal risks of competition. It made no difference that the information could have been obtained from elsewhere.

Other factors, such as the frequency of the exchange, whether the information exchanged is in the public domain,[277] and whether the information exchange is public or private,[278] may also be relevant to the assessment. The core focus, nonetheless, is on the question of whether the information exchanged is commercially sensitive.[279]

In assessing information agreements, close attention also needs to be paid to the characteristics of the exchange (whether it is unilateral, genuinely public, reciprocal or indirect,[280] its frequency, and whether measures limit or control how data is used)[281] and the structure of the market.[282] Relevant market characteristics include the level of transparency, the number of undertakings present, the existence of barriers to entry, the homogenous nature of the product, service, and undertakings involved, and the stability of demand and supply conditions. It is easier to reach a common understanding on the terms of coordination and to monitor deviations from it where few undertakings are present. The improved knowledge of market conditions aimed at by information agreements strengthens the connection between the undertakings, in that they are enabled to react very efficiently to one another's actions, and thus lessens the intensity of competition. Information exchanges are

[275] See e.g. COMP/31.370 and COMP/31.466, *UK Agricultural Tractor Registration Exchange* [1992] OJ L68/19, and Bennett and Collins, n. 248, 331.

[276] COMP/312 and 366 [1977] OJ L242/10.

[277] Art. 101(1) may be infringed even if the information could have been obtained from other, less convenient, sources, see e.g. Case C-238/05, *Asnef-Equifax v Asociación Usuarios de Servicios Bancarios (Ausbanc)* EU:C:2006:734, para. 58.

[278] Any 'market transparency' attained may be offset by the fact that the information remains private to the undertakings concerned, see e.g. COMP/31.370 and 31.466, *UK Agricultural Tractor Registration Exchange* [1992] OJ L68/19.

[279] Horizontal Cooperation Guidelines, 6.2.3.

[280] Via a third party or a common agency, customer, or supplier.

[281] Horizontal Cooperation Guidelines, 6.2.4.

[282] Ibid., 6.2.5.

therefore more likely to be problematic on concentrated/oligopolistic markets which are conducive to interdependent coordinated behaviour, in particular, markets with a few players producing homogenous products which are sufficiently transparent, concentrated, stable, and symmetric. In contrast, where the market is fragmented, demand is volatile, or innovation is important, coordination may be more difficult.

In *UK Agricultural Tractor Registration Exchange*,[283] eight UK manufacturers and importers of agricultural tractors operated an information-exchange agreement that identified the volume of retail sales and market shares of each of the manufacturers individually. The Commission condemned the exchange taking account of the fact that:

(a) the market was highly concentrated (the eight manufacturers/importers had approximately 87–88 per cent of the relevant market);
(b) there were high barriers to entry into the market;
(c) there were insignificant extra-Union imports;
(d) the information exchanged was detailed and identified the exact retail sales and shares of the undertakings which were generally trade secrets between competitors; and
(e) the members met regularly.

First, the Commission held that the exchange of information prevented hidden competition by creating transparency on a market which was already highly concentrated, largely shielded from outside competition. Where demand was stable, a forecast of a competitor's future actions could be largely determined on the basis of past transactions. The forecast would be more effective the more accurate and recent the information was. The exchange of information could, however, truly be categorised as historic from a certain period of time (for example, if it was more than one year old).[284] Although the Commission recognised that there were benefits of transparency in a competitive market, in this case the concentration of the market was not low and the market transparency was not in any way directed towards the benefit of consumers. The information in this case enabled each participant accurately to establish its rivals' market position and to see immediately if a rival increased its market share (for example, by price reductions or other marketing incentives). It limited price competition since competitors would be able to react quickly to changes in market positions (this would, of course, mean that there was little incentive for a potential initiator to take steps to improve its position). Information would thus limit the possibility of surprise or secrecy if a rival received information disclosing sensitive information about its competitors. It would then be able to react quickly and eliminate any possible advantage to be gained by the initiator.

Secondly, the information would also be likely to increase barriers to entry since participants would know immediately of new market entrants and would be able to react accordingly.

The Commission's analysis was upheld by the EU Courts. In *John Deere Ltd v Commission*,[285] the GC accepted that a truly competitive market would benefit from transparency but that private exchanges (to the exclusion of other suppliers and customers) of precise information at short intervals on a highly concentrated market involving sufficiently homogenous products would be likely to impair competition existing between the traders; 'the sharing, on a regular and frequent basis, of information concerning the operation of the market has the effect of periodically revealing to all

[283] COMP/31.370 and 31.466 [1992] OJ L68/19, Case T-34/92, *Fiatagri & Ford New Holland v Commission* EU:T:1994:258 and Case T-35/92, *John Deere Ltd v Commission* EU:T:1994:259; Case C-7/95 P, *John Deere Ltd v Commission* EU:C:1998:256.

[284] See also COMP/34.936, *CEPI/Cartonboard* [1996] OJ C310/3.

[285] Case T-35/92, EU:T:1994:259, *aff'd* Case C-7/95 P, *John Deere Ltd v Commission* EU:C:1998:256.

the competitors the market positions and strategies of the various individual competitors'.[286] The arrangement allowed the parties to forecast more precisely the conduct of their competitors, so reducing or removing the degree of uncertainty which would have existed without the exchange. In addition, the information concerned 'which relates in particular to sales made in the territory of each of the dealerships in the distribution network, is in the nature of business secrets'.[287]

In *Eudim*,[288] in contrast, the Commission held that information sharing in a market that was competitive on both the purchasing and selling side did not infringe Article 101(1).

In *Asnef-Equifax, Servicios de Información sobre Solvencia y Crédito, SL v Asociación de Usuarios de Servicios Bancarios (Ausbanc)*,[289] Ausbanc challenged the exchange of information between financial institutions on the solvency of customers and borrower default. Following an Article 267 reference to it the CJ set out guidance for the referring court to determine the compatibility of the provisions for exchange with Article 101(1). With regard to the question of whether the agreement had as its effect the restriction of competition, the CJ stressed the importance of considering whether supply on the market was highly concentrated, whether information identified competitors individually, and whether access to the information was available in a non-discriminatory manner to all operators.

Case C-238/05, *Asnef-Equifax, Servicios de Información sobre Solvencia y Crédito, SL v Asociación de Usuarios de Servicios Bancarios (Ausbanc)* [2006] ECR I-11125

Court of Justice

55. As indicated at paragraph 47 of this judgment, registers such as the one at issue in the main proceedings, by reducing the rate of borrower default, are in principle capable of improving the functioning of the supply of credit. As the Advocate General observed, in substance, at point 54 of his Opinion, if, owing to a lack of information on the risk of borrower default, financial institutions are unable to distinguish those borrowers who are more likely to default, the risk thereby borne by such institutions will necessarily be increased and they will tend to factor it in when calculating the cost of credit for all borrowers, including those less likely to default, who will then have to bear a higher cost than they would if the institutions were in a position to evaluate the probability of repayment more precisely. In principle, registers such as that mentioned above are capable of reducing such a tendency.

56. Furthermore, by reducing the significance of the information held by financial institutions regarding their own customers, such registers appear, in principle, to be capable of increasing the mobility of consumers of credit. In addition, those registers are apt to make it easier for new competitors to enter the market.

57. None the less, whether or not there is in the main proceedings a restriction of competition within the meaning of Article [101(1) TFEU] depends on the economic and legal context in which the register exists, and in particular on the economic conditions of the market as well as the particular characteristics of the register.

58. In that regard, first of all, if supply on a market is highly concentrated, the exchange of certain information may, according in particular to the type of information exchanged, be liable to enable undertakings to be aware of the market position and commercial strategy of their competitors, thus distorting rivalry on the market and increasing the probability of collusion, or even facilitating it. On the other hand, if supply is fragmented, the dissemination and exchange of information between competitors may be neutral, or even positive, for the competitive nature of the market (see, to that effect, *Thyssen Stahl v*

[286] Case T-35/92, EU:T:1994:259, para. 51. [287] Ibid., para. 81.
[288] COMP/33.815 and 35.842 [1996] OJ C111/8.
[289] Case C-238/05, EU:C:2006:734. Contrast Case C-172/14, *ING Pensii v Consiliul Concuretnei* EU:C:2015:484.

> *Commission*, paragraphs 84 and 86). In the present case, it is common ground, as may be seen from paragraph 10 of this judgment, that the referring court premi[s]ed its reference for a preliminary ruling on the existence of 'a fragmented market', which it is for that court to verify.
>
> 59. Secondly, in order that registers such as that at issue in the main proceedings are not capable of revealing the market position or the commercial strategy of competitors, it is important that the identity of lenders is not revealed, directly or indirectly. In the present case, it is apparent from the decision for referral that the Tribunal de Defensa de la Competencia imposed on Asnef-Equifax, which accepted it, a condition that the information relating to lenders contained in the register not be disclosed.
>
> 60. Thirdly, it is also important that such registers be accessible in a non-discriminatory manner, in law and in fact, to all operators active in the relevant sphere. If such accessibility were not guaranteed, some of those operators would be placed at a disadvantage, since they would have less information for the purpose of risk assessment, which would also not facilitate the entry of new operators on to the market.
>
> 61. It follows that, provided that the relevant market or markets are not highly concentrated, that the system does not permit lenders to be identified and that the conditions of access and use by financial institutions are not discriminatory, an information exchange system such as the register is not, in principle, liable to have the effect of restricting competition within the meaning of Article [101(1) TFEU].
>
> 62. While in those conditions such systems are capable of reducing uncertainty as to the risk that applicants for credit will default, they are not, however, liable to reduce uncertainty as to the risks of competition. Thus, each operator could be expected to act independently and autonomously when adopting a given course of conduct, regard being had to the risks presented by applicants. Contrary to Ausbanc's contention, it cannot be inferred solely from the existence of such a credit information exchange that it might lead to collective anti-competitive conduct, such as a boycott of certain potential borrowers.
>
> 63. Furthermore, since, as the Advocate General observed, in substance, at point 56 of his Opinion, any possible issues relating to the sensitivity of personal data are not, as such, a matter for competition law, they may be resolved on the basis of the relevant provisions governing data protection. In the main proceedings, it is apparent from the documents before the Court that, under the rules applicable to the register, affected consumers may, in accordance with the Spanish legislation, check the information concerning them and, where necessary, have it corrected, or indeed deleted.

The CJ in *Asnef-Equifax* also recognised that the referring court might need to carry out an Article 101(3) assessment in order to resolve the dispute at issue.[290] For example, the court might be required to determine whether objective economic advantages, such as helping to prevent over-indebtedness for consumers of credit and leading to a greater overall availability of credit, might be such as to offset the disadvantages of any restriction of competition identified. The CJ stressed that in making the Article 101(3) determination, it was not necessary that all consumers should benefit from the system. Rather, it was not inconceivable that some applicants for credit would be faced with increased interest rates or refused credit. This circumstance was not in itself sufficient to prevent the condition that consumers be allowed a fair share of the benefit from being satisfied since 'it is the beneficial nature of the effect on all consumers in the relevant markets that must be taken into consideration, not the effect on each member of that category of consumers'.[291] Indeed, the exchange in this situation might be capable of leading to a greater overall availability of credit, including for applicants for whom interest rates might be excessive if lenders did not have appropriate knowledge of their personal system.

[290] See also Horizontal Cooperation Guidelines, 6.3.

[291] Case C-238/05, *Asnef-Equifax v Asociación Usuarios de Servicios Bancarios (Ausbanc)* EU:C:2006:734, para. 70.

d. *Business-to-Business (B2B) Exchanges*

B2B e-marketplaces, which allow industrial buyers and sellers to transact business online over the internet, have become common.[292] Although such marketplaces may create huge efficiency gains in purchasing and supply chain management there has also been a concern that such markets would create an ideal climate for collusion, due to increased communication and transparency in the market,[293] exchange of confidential information, and foreclosure. The Commission, however, recognises the clear advantages that may result from such marketplaces and has sought to develop a coherent approach to their assessment and has in many cases accepted that such agreements do not infringe Article 101(1) at all.[294] In *Covisint*,[295] for example, the Commission sent a comfort letter clearing the creation of the Covisint Automotive Internet Marketplace (the agreement did not infringe Article 101(1)). Six car manufacturers notified to the Commission a joint venture to serve the procurement needs of major car makers and suppliers and to reduce costs and improve efficiency in the supply chain. The Commission noted in its press release that in general B2B marketplaces should have pro-competitive effects by creating more transparency, integrating markets, and creating marketing efficiencies by reducing search and information costs and improving inventory management, leading ultimately to lower prices for the end consumer. In this case, the Commission was satisfied that potential competition concerns had been eliminated:

> Covisint is open to all firms in the industry on a non-discriminatory basis, is based on open standards, allows both shareholders and other users to participate in other B-2-B exchanges, does not allow joint purchasing between car manufacturers or for automotive-specific products, and provides for adequate data protection, including firewalls and security rules.

It has also sent negative clearance comfort letters in relation to B2B electronic marketplaces set up in other sectors.[296] In an article by a Commission official in the *Competition Policy Newsletter*, several guidelines are set out for companies considering setting up e-marketplaces.[297]

5. OLIGOPOLY AND THE PROBLEM OF TACIT COLLUSION

A. THE OLIGOPOLY PROBLEM AND ARTICLE 101

It has been seen in the previous sections that Article 101, which requires 'joint' conduct, does not reach tacit collusion. Competition agencies are, nonetheless, vigilant for cartel activity through agreements, concerted practices, or decisions on markets which are prone to collusion. Further, that agreements, such as information-sharing agreements, which may increase transparency or otherwise facilitate collusion, may be prohibited by Article 101. In Chapters 10 and 11, it will also be seen that horizontal

[292] J. Lüking, 'B2B e-Marketplaces and EU Competition Law: Where Do We Stand?' (2001) 3 *Competition Policy Newsletter* 14 and S. Stroux, 'B2B e-Market-places: The Emerging Competition Law Issues' (2001) 24 *World Competition* 125.

[293] OFT 308, 'E-Commerce and Its Implications for Competition Policy', para. 6.54.

[294] See e.g. M. Monti, 'European Competition Policy for the 21st Century' [2000] *Fordham Corp L Inst*, Chap. 15 and 'Competition in the New Economy', 10th International Conference on Competition of the Bundeskartellamt, Berlin, 21 May 2001.

[295] COMP/38.064, IP/01/1155 (a negative clearance comfort letter).

[296] See *Eutilia/Endorsial*, IP/01/1775; *Eurex*, IP/02/4; *Inreon*, IP/02/761; *Centradia*, IP 02/943; *Water Portal*, IP/02/956; and Lüking, n. 292.

[297] Lüking, n. 292.

cooperation and vertical agreements may be scrutinised particularly closely where there is a risk that they may facilitate collusion between undertakings.

B. OLIGOPOLY AND ARTICLE 102

Another question arising is whether Article 102 may control the behaviour of firms operating on an oligopolistic market. This depends on the question of whether the existence of a dominant position and an abuse of that dominant position can be established.

(i) 'One or More Undertakings'—Collective Dominance

A line of cases establishes that Article 102 applies to situations of collective dominance (see Chapter 6), as well as to situations of single-firm dominance. The starting point in that case law is *Flat Glass*[298] which clarified that two or more independent economic entities on a market may be united by such economic links that, by virtue of that fact, together they hold a dominant position on that market.

Cases T-68, 77, and 78/89, *Società Italiana Vetro SpA v Commission (Flat Glass)* [1992] ECR II-1403

General Court

357. The Court notes that the very words of the first paragraph of Article [102] provide that 'one or more undertakings' may abuse a dominant position. It has consistently been held, as indeed all the parties acknowledge, that the concept of agreement or concerted practice between undertakings does not cover agreements or concerted practices among undertakings belonging to the same group if the undertakings form an economic unit . . . It follows that when Article [101] refers to agreements or concerted practices between 'undertakings', it is referring to relations between two or more economic entities which are capable of competing with one another.

358. The Court considers that there is no legal or economic reason to suppose that the term 'undertaking' in Article [102] has a different meaning from the one given to it in the context of Article [101]. There is nothing in principle, to prevent two or more independent economic entities from being, on a specific market, united by such economic links that, by virtue of that fact, together they hold a dominant position *vis-à-vis* the other operators on the same market. This could be the case, for example, where two or more independent undertakings jointly have, through agreements or licences, a technological lead affording them the power to behave to an appreciable extent independently of their competitors, their customers and ultimately of their consumers (judgment of the Court in *Hoffmann-La Roche* . . ., paragraphs 38 and 48).

It was unclear after this judgment, however, exactly what economic links between undertakings were required for them to be found to hold a collective dominant position. The examples of links given by the Court in this case, of agreements or licences concluded between the undertakings, initially caused speculation that Article 102 might apply only to situations of 'non-oligopolistic' collective dominance.[299]

[298] Cases T-68 and 77–78/89, *Società Italiana Vetro SpA v Commission* EU:T:1992:38, paras. 357–358.

[299] This latter narrower view of the concept was supported by the Court's reliance in para. 359 on Art. 8(2) of Council Reg. 4056/86 [1986] OJ L378/1 and early decisions of the Commission which concerned cases of non-oligopolistic collective dominance.

Subsequent case law, developed both in the context of Article 102 and substantive assessment under the original EU Merger Regulation (EUMR) (which at that time centred around a dominance test),[300] has nonetheless confirmed that situations of 'oligopolistic' collective dominance—held by *independent* undertakings united by economic links derived from their economic interdependence on a market which dictates that they can, and have the incentive, to tacitly coordinate their behaviour without express collusion—are caught by Article 102 (and the EUMR). Thus: in *Almelo*,[301] the CJ clarified that 'in order for such a collective dominant position to exist, the undertakings in the group must be linked in such a way that they adopt the same conduct on the market';[302] in *Gencor*[303] the GC confirmed (in the context of the EUMR) that a 'relationship of interdependence existing between the parties to a tight oligopoly' which would make alignment of conduct likely, constituted a sufficient economic link on which to hinge a finding of collective dominance; and in *Airtours*[304] (again in the context of the EUMR) the GC stated that a collective dominant position would exist where each member of a dominant oligopoly would 'consider it possible, economically rational, and hence preferable, to adopt on a lasting basis a common policy on the market with the aim of selling at above competitive prices, without having to enter into an agreement or resort to a concerted practice within the meaning of Article 101 . . . '. It considered that a finding of collective dominance could be established if:

> first, each firm knew how other members were behaving (they could monitor the market to see if they were adopting the common policy);
>
> secondly, tacit co-ordination was sustainable over time, (i.e., there was not an incentive to depart from the common policy on the market); and
>
> thirdly, the foreseeable reactions of competitors (actual and potential) and customers would not jeopardize the results expected from the common policy.

In *Compagnie Maritime Belge*, the CJ also confirmed that the economic links necessary to establish the existence of a collective entity, 'could, but would not necessarily, be established by an agreement, decision, or concerted practice within the meaning of Article 101 concluded by the undertakings (the *CEWAL* agreement[305] did in fact provide such requisite links in that case). Rather, 'the existence of an agreement or of other links in law is not indispensable to a finding of a collective dominant position; such a finding may be based on other connecting factors and would depend on an economic assessment and, in particular, on an assessment of the structure of the market in question' (paragraph 45).

[300] Over time it has become clear that the concept of collective dominance is interpreted in the same way for the purposes of both the EUMR and Art. 102. Indeed, the judgments under the EUMR frequently rely on case law developed under Art. 102 and vice versa, see e.g. Case T-102/96, *Gencor Ltd v Commission* EU:T:1999:65, para. 273 and COMP/34.621 and COMP/35.059/F-3, *Irish Sugar* [1997] OJ L258/1, *aff'd* Case T-228/97, *Irish Sugar plc v Commission* EU:T:1999:246, para. 46, see also Chap. 15.

[301] Case C-393/92, *Almelo v NV Energiebedrijf Ijsselmij* EU:C:1994:171.

[302] Ibid., paras. 42–43, see also e.g. Case C-96/94, *Centro Servizi Spediporto Srl v Spedizioni Marittima de Golfo Srl* EU:C:1995:308, Case C-70/95, *Sodemare SA v Regione Lombardia* EU:C:1997:301, and Cases T-24/93 etc., *Compagnie Maritime Belge Transports SA v Commission* EU:T:1996:139.

[303] Case T-102/96, *Gencor Ltd v Commission* EU:T:1999:65.

[304] Case T-342/99, *Airtours v Commission* EU:T:2002:146. See also Case T-464/04, *Independent Music Publishers and Labels Association (Impala) v Commission* EU:T:2006:216. Although in the appeal from the GC's judgment in *Impala*, Case C-413/06 P, *Bertelsmann and Sony Corp v Commission* EU:C:2008:392, the CJ expressed the test in a slightly different way, the criteria it set out for establishing collective dominance are similar to and compatible with those set out by the GC, see Chap. 15.

[305] COMP/32.448 and COMP/32.450, *CEWAL* [1993] OJ L34/20.

Cases C-395 and 396/96 P, *Compagnie Maritime Belge Transports SA v Commission* [2000] ECR I-1365

Court of Justice

35. In terms of Article [102], a dominant position may be held by several 'undertakings'. The Court of Justice has held, on many occasions, that the concept of 'undertaking' in the chapter of the Treaty devoted to the rules on competition presupposes the economic independence of the entity concerned (see, in particular, Case 22/71 *Béguelin Import v G.L. Import Export* . . .).

36. It follows that the expression 'one or more undertakings', in Article [102] implies that a dominant position may be held by two or more economic entities legally independent of each other, provided that from an economic point of view they present themselves or act together on a particular market as a collective entity. That is how the expression 'collective dominant position', as used in the remainder of this judgment, should be understood.

37. However, a finding that an undertaking has a dominant position is not in itself a ground of criticism but simply means that, irrespective of the reasons for which it has such a dominant position, the undertaking concerned has a special responsibility not to allow its conduct to impair genuine undistorted competition on the common market (see *Michelin*, paragraph 57).

38. The same applies as regards undertakings which hold a collective dominant position. A finding that two or more undertakings hold a collective dominant position must, in principle, proceed upon an economic assessment of the position on the relevant market of the undertakings concerned, prior to any examination of the question whether those undertakings have abused their position on the market.

39. So, for the purposes of analysis under Article [102], it is necessary to consider whether the undertakings concerned together constitute a collective entity *vis-à-vis* their competitors, their trading partners and consumers on a particular market. It is only where that question is answered in the affirmative that it is appropriate to consider whether that collective entity actually holds a dominant position and whether its conduct constitutes abuse.

40. In the contested judgment, the [GC] was careful to examine separately those three elements, namely the collective position, the dominant position and the abuse of such a position.

41. In order to establish the existence of a collective entity as defined above, it is necessary to examine the economic links or factors which give rise to a connection between the undertakings concerned (see, *inter alia*, Case C-393/92 *Almelo* [1994] ECR I-1477, paragraph 43, and Joined Cases C-68/94 and C-30/95 *France and Others v Commission* . . . paragraph 221).

42. In particular, it must be ascertained whether economic links exist between the undertakings concerned which enable them to act together independently of their competitors, their customers and consumers (see *Michelin*).

43. The mere fact that two or more undertakings are linked by an agreement, a decision of associations of undertakings or a concerted practice within the meaning of Article [101(1)] of the Treaty does not, of itself, constitute a sufficient basis for such a finding.

44. On the other hand, an agreement, decision or concerted practice (whether or not covered by an exemption under Article [101(3)]) may undoubtedly, where it is implemented, result in the undertakings concerned being so linked as to their conduct on a particular market that they present themselves on that market as a collective entity *vis-à-vis* their competitors, their trading partners and consumers.

45. The existence of a collective dominant position may therefore flow from the nature and terms of an agreement, from the way in which it is implemented and, consequently, from the links or factors which give rise to a connection between undertakings which result from it. Nevertheless, the existence of an agreement or of other links in law is not indispensable to a finding of a collective dominant position; such a finding may be based on other connecting factors and would depend on an economic assessment and, in particular, on an assessment of the structure of the market in question.

It seems clear therefore that undertakings which are able to engage in a parallel manner on a market by tacitly coordinating their behaviour may be found collectively to hold a dominant position on a market. Indeed, in *Laurent Piau*[306] the GC stated that:

> [t]hree cumulative conditions must be met for a finding of collective dominance: first, each member of the dominant oligopoly must have the ability to know how the other members are behaving in order to monitor whether or not they are adopting the common policy; second, the situation of tacit coordination must be sustainable over time, that is to say, there must be an incentive not to depart from the common policy on the market; thirdly, the foreseeable reaction of current and future competitors, as well as of consumers, must not jeopardise the results expected from the common policy.

In conclusion, it is now established that:

(a) the concept of a collective dominant position is defined in the same way for the purposes of both the EUMR and Article 102 (although an important difference between the provisions is, of course, that in Article 102 cases a collective dominant position must exist as a threshold matter (it prohibits only abuses of a dominant or collective dominant position not abuses that may lead to the creation of a collective dominant position), whilst in merger cases the Commission may act to prevent mergers which lead to coordinated effects through the creation of a collective dominant position or to the strengthening of a pre-existing collective dominant position. This may affect the question of how proof of collective dominance is established);[307]

(b) independent economic entities may hold a collective dominant position provided that they are united by economic links which enable them to present themselves as a collective entity and to adopt the same conduct or a common policy on the market and are able to act to a considerable extent independent of their competitors, customers, and consumers;

(c) the economic links may be contractual, structural (such as cross-shareholdings or common directorships), or provided by the structure of the market which allows parallelism of behaviour or sustainable tacit collusion between firms (in particular, a high degree of transparency and no or little actual or potential competition);

(d) the existence of a collective dominant position depends not only on the establishment of the existence of a collective entity but also on it being established that the collective entity holds a dominant position.

(ii) Abuse of a Collective Dominant Position

The development of the concept of collective dominance in the context of the original EUMR ensured that the Commission had the power to prevent mergers which will, post-merger, lead to tacit collusion on a market.[308] The crucial issue in relation to Article 102, however, is what, if anything, can be done about firms that *are* already collectively dominant. Article 102 does not prohibit the holding of a dominant position, but only abuses of that position.[309] As the jurisprudence on the question of what

[306] Case T-193/02, *Laurent Piau v Commission* EU:T:2005:22, para. 111. See also Cases T-191 and 214–216/98, *Atlantic Container Line AB v Commission* EU:T:2003:245, paras. 595, 602, and 631.

[307] See Chap. 15.

[308] The fear that a merger might alternatively result in 'non-coordinated' effects but not dominance or collective dominance on the market led to alteration of the substantive test for appraisal of mergers, see Chap. 15.

[309] See e.g. P. Fernandez, 'Increasing Powers and Increasing Uncertainty: Collective Dominance and Pricing Abuses' (2000) 5 *ELRev* 645 and G. Monti, 'The Scope of Collective Dominance under Article 82' (2001) 38 *CMLRev* 131.

constitutes an abuse of a collective dominant position is relatively sparse, this section explores how the concept of abuse might, if there were a desire to do so, be developed or adapted to deal with specific problems which arise in the collective dominance context.

a. *Overlap with Article 101?*

In *Flat Glass*,[310] the Commission had concluded that the undertakings' communication of, for example, identical prices to customers and granting of identical discounts constituted abuses within the meaning of Article 102. However, the GC criticised the Commission for simply having recycled the facts of the Article 101 infringement to present an infringement of Article 102. Since then, the Commission has sought to spell out the relevant market for the purposes of Article 102, the position of the undertakings on the market, and the abuses in the context of the express provisions of Article 102. The conduct alleged to be abusive in *French-West African Shipowners' Committee, CEWAL*, and *TACA* was nonetheless broadly the same as that which the Commission had already held to infringe Article 101 (the attempt by the members of the committee to eliminate effective competition from non-committee shipowners).[311]

b. *Collective Abuses*

In Chapter 7, it was seen that Article 102 has been used to condemn a range of conduct. It prohibits both exploitative practices (such as excessive pricing or inertia) and anti-competitive, exclusionary practices (such as predatory or discriminatory pricing, tying, refusals to supply, etc.).

We have seen that, a key competition concern arising from tacit collusion is that undertakings do not engage in price competition, but set their prices at a level which produces supra-competitive profits and restricts output.[312] Although outside the scope of Article 101, could this behaviour constitute exploitative, 'unfair selling prices'?

(1) Exploitative Behaviour and Excessive Pricing

It is seen in Chapter 7 that Article 102 has, in fact, relatively rarely been used to condemn exploitative, unfairly high prices and cases based on purely exploitative, excessive, and unfair pricing generally prove controversial. Not only are there a number of conceptual[313] and practical problems in using Article 102 to prohibit excessive prices, but the Commission has generally sought to avoid acting as price regulator.[314] Even if theoretically possible, it seems unlikely therefore that Article 102 would be used to target the conduct of oligopolists that have engaged in parallel pricing at a level that the Commission considers to be unfair and excessive. It seems more likely therefore that if Article 102 is to be useful, it should be applied to prevent exclusionary conduct which is liable to strengthen the potential for tacit collusion on a market, for example by deterring deviation or excluding those that do not comply with the common policy.[315]

[310] Cases T-68, 77, and 78/89, *Società Italiana Vetro SpA v Commission* ('*Flat Glass*') EU:T:1992:38.

[311] Although the Commission couched its analysis in terms of Art. 102 and was careful not to recycle the facts, the fact remains that much of the conduct was anyway condemned under Art. 101.

[312] M/524, *Airtours/First Choice* [2000] OJ L93/1, annulled on appeal Case T-342/99, *Airtours plc v Commission* EU:T:2002:146.

[313] See R. Whish and B. Sufrin, 'Oligopolistic Markets and EC Competition Law' (1992) 12 *YEL* 59, 74–75. In condemning excessive prices of a monopolist, however, Art. 102 in the same sense also condemns natural or rational behaviour by a monopolist.

[314] See Chap. 7.

[315] See e.g. R. Gjendemsjø, E. J. Helmeng, and L. Sørgard, 'Abuse of Collective Dominance: The Need for a New Approach' (2013) 36 *World Competition* 355.

(2) Other Collective Abuses

In some liner conference cases, the Commission has condemned behaviour targeted at eliminating competitors seeking to compete outside the liner conference. In *Compagnie Maritime Belge*,[316] the CJ upheld the Commission's finding that the putting on of fighting ships by the undertakings was an abuse for the purposes of Article 102. In *TACA*,[317] the Commission found that the members had abused their dominant position by (a) agreeing to place restrictions on the availability and content of service contracts[318] and (b) altering the competitive structure of the market so as to reinforce TACA's dominant position (in particular, by trying to ensure that any potential competitor wishing to enter the market would do so only after it had become a party to the TACA). Although the existence of the first abuse was upheld on the appeal, the GC found that the Commission had failed to demonstrate that the members had induced potential competitors to join the TACA by the measures referred to in the decision.[319]

It is not easy to envisage what other exclusionary abuses may be committed by undertakings indulging in parallel behaviour. It might be difficult to explain parallel decisions refusing to supply an undertaking, or targeting or excluding a competitor or new entrant to the market, on the grounds of mutual interdependence. It could be argued, however, that an abuse will have been committed where: the undertakings are inefficient or refuse to innovate;[320] or where rivalry between the collectively dominant firms is dampened, the internal stability of the collusive arrangement is promoted and the collective dominant position strengthened, for example, where collectively dominant firms acquire minority shareholdings in competitors or incorporate vertical restraints into distribution arrangements (such as resale price maintenance, meeting competition, or parity clauses which reduce the profit to be gained from deviation and so may facilitate collusion).[321] Indeed, it has been argued that:

> Article 102 represents a still underdeveloped tool with regard to collective dominance in oligopolistic markets. This is so because no consistent theory or abusive behaviour in such market has been developed. . . . In our view the legal standard formulated by the [CJ] provides a sufficient legal basis for intervention against any conduct with the object or effect of strengthening the collective dominant position.
>
> It should be noted that this reading of Article 102 does not imply that tacit collusion is to be regarded as an independent abuse. On the contrary, tacit collusion is an unavoidable consequence of the market structure and must be regarded as a consequent of the right of every undertaking to adapt intelligently to the strategy or perceived strategy of its competitors. However, the practices targeted under the approach advocated here amount to conduct strengthening the dominant position and thereby restricting competition by altering the competitive structure. This concept should be easily distinguishable from competition on the merits and from tacit collusion as such.[322]

[316] Cases C-395 and 396/96 P, *Compagnie Maritime Belge Transports SA v Commission* EU:C:2000:132.

[317] COMP/35.134 [1999] OJ L95/1, on appeal, Case T-191/98, *Atlantic Container Line AB and Others v Commission* EU:T:2003:245.

[318] Contracts by which a shipper undertakes to provide a minimum quantity of cargo to be transported by the conference (conference service contracts) or by an individual carrier (individual service contracts) over a fixed period of time and the carrier or the conference commits to a certain rate or rate schedule as well as a defined service level.

[319] Cases T-191 and 212–214/98, *Atlantic Container Line v Commission* EU:T:2003:245.

[320] See Chap. 7.

[321] See Gjendemsjø, Helmeng, and Sørgard, n. 315. Such conduct may be likely to be caught by Art. 101(1) in any event, see Chaps. 5 and 11.

[322] Ibid., 371.

c. Abuse by One of the Collectively Dominant Undertakings

In *Irish Sugar plc v Commission*,[323] the GC held that an *individual* undertaking could engage in conduct which constitutes an abuse of its dominant position held collectively with one or more undertakings:

> Whilst the existence of a joint dominant position may be deduced from the position which the economic entities concerned together hold on the market in question, the abuse does not necessarily have to be the action of all the undertakings in question. It only has to be capable of being identified as one of the manifestations of such a joint dominant position being held. Therefore, undertakings occupying a joint dominant position may engage in joint or individual abusive conduct.[324]

This finding was made in the context of a dominant position held jointly by a dominant undertaking and its distributor (on a vertical level). In this case, Irish Sugar had such a close relationship with its distributor that it only narrowly failed to qualify as a single economic unit.[325] Had the Commission been able to make such a finding, it would of course have been unnecessary to invoke the concept of collective dominance.

The concept of an abuse has been principally developed in a line of cases dealing with the conduct of a single dominant undertaking and it seems likely that a different analysis may be required for identifying abusive conduct engaged in by one of a group of oligopolists. For example, although the grant of loyalty rebates by single dominant undertakings may unlawfully exclude competitors,[326] on an oligopolistic market, such conduct may indicate that price competition is in fact operating.[327]

The concept of an individual abuse of a dominant position might nonetheless be useful, for example, to preclude behaviour targeted by one of the members at another or a new entrant with the objective of protecting the internal or external stability of the collusive arrangement. If so, it could be used to prevent price cuts directed at a price-cutter that is destabilising tacit collusion on a tight oligopolistic market.[328] The implications of the *Irish Sugar* judgment are explored by G. Monti in an extract from his article.

G. Monti, 'The Scope of Collective Dominance under Article 82 EC' (2001) 38 *CMLRev* 131, 143

> This is an important conclusion, which could apply to a variety of situations, horizontal and vertical. On a horizontal level, it may be deployed to catch a scenario like this: say there are three companies that enjoy collective dominance (e.g. because of membership in an export cartel). Let us now say that a fourth competitor attempts to penetrate the market and one of the three engages in predatory pricing or other exclusionary tactics not forbidden by Article [101]. In this scenario, the Commission is now

[323] Case T-228/97, EU:T:1999:246.

[324] Ibid., para. 66. In the case these included seven individual abuses on the market in granulated sugar intended for retail sale and for industry in Ireland and some abuses of a collective dominant position held with a distributor.

[325] Case T-228/97, *Irish Sugar plc v Commission* EU:T:1999:246, para. 28.

[326] See discussion in Chap. 7 and e.g. Case 85/76, *Hoffmann-La Roche v Commission* EU:C:1979:36and Case C-680/20, *Unilever Italia Mkt, Operations Srl v Autorità Garante della Concorrenza e del Mercato* EU:C:2023:33 (it should be noted that in the light of Case C-209/10, *Post Danmark A/S v Konkurrencerådet* EU:C:2012:172, selective price-cutting which is not predatory is more likely to be an abuse if the dominant position is a collective one).

[327] See COMP/35.134, *TACA* [1999] OJ L95/6.

[328] In this case the predation may represent the 'punishment' mechanism which means that tacit collusion subsequently follows, see, e.g., the theory of harm alleged in *Brooke Group Ltd v Brown & Williamson Tobacco Corp*, 509 US 209 (1993).

empowered to find that undertaking liable under Article [102] for abusing the collective dominant position. It does not need to fine the other two undertakings. Moreover, and potentially more significantly, the *Irish Sugar* decision states that collective dominance can be held by undertakings in a vertical relationship, which entails that a non-dominant distributor who has sufficiently strong links with a dominant manufacturer has the same degree of responsibility not to hinder competition that the manufacturer has, thus any attempt to protect his market position (e.g. terminating a retailer who sells competing goods) may be found to be an abuse.

This vastly extends the jurisdiction of the Commission under Article [102]. While it is obviously a ruling which could be overturned by the CJ, it is submitted that the reasoning of the [GC] can be supported as consistent with well-established principles. Specifically, there is no need for a causal link between the dominant position and the abuse: the dominant position does not have to be used, so long as the conduct of a dominant firm has anti-competitive effects. This was established in *Continental Can* where the [CJ] said that 'the strengthening of the position of an undertaking may be an abuse and prohibited under Article [102], regardless of the means and procedure by which it is achieved' if it has anti-competitive effects. On this basis a contract clause that has an anti-competitive effects (e.g. SDL's product swap)[329] is a breach of Article [102] even if SDL is not individually dominant, because its effect was to consolidate the collective dominance by excluding potential competitors. This broad, effects-based application of Article [102] is in line with the 'special responsibility' imposed on dominant firms not to distort competition.

(iii) Conclusions

It appears that Article 102 applies to oligopolistic collective dominance. Even if Article 102 is applied to oligopolists linked only by their mutual interdependence, however, the concept of abuse, developed in relation to individually dominant firms, is not a mechanism ideally equipped to control the behaviour of oligopolists. It remains to be seen, however, whether the concept of individual or collective abuse might be further developed to prohibit practices which might facilitate collusion or contribute to the internal or external stability of a collusive strategy.

C. ALTERNATIVE METHODS FOR DEALING WITH OLIGOPOLISTIC MARKETS UNDER EU LAW

(i) Merger Regulation

Given that oligopolistic markets may not function as effectively as ones in which free competition operates, and given the difficulties involved in applying either Article 101 or Article 102 to the conduct of undertakings operating on such markets, it seems clear that the EUMR assumes importance in this area. The EUMR prohibits mergers which would significantly impede effective competition through either non-coordinated or coordinated effects on oligopolistic markets. Coordinated effects may arise where a merger facilitates collusion (explicit or tacit) on a market—even perhaps if the collusion may result because the merger is likely to increase algorithmic collusion. If mergers which cause market

[329] One of the abuses of a collective dominant position found by the Commission was that SDL, the distributor, had agreed with one retailer and one wholesaler to exchange its sugar for the sugar that the wholesaler and retailer had purchased from France.

imperfections are prohibited, there will be less need for *ex post* corrective measures under Article 101 or 102. It will be seen in Chapter 15, nonetheless, that, despite the importance of the EUMR in this context, it is not easy in practice for the Commission to demonstrate to the requisite standard that a merger is likely to lead to coordinated effects on a market.

(ii) Sector Inquiries and Broader Solutions

Since 1962 and the enactment of Regulation 17, the Commission has had wide discretion to conduct sector inquiries and to investigate markets that it considers to be malfunctioning. As Article 12(1) of that Regulation did not, however, give the Commission power to take action to remedy any defects identified following an investigation, Whish and Sufrin argued that the provision could, with reform, provide the basis of a proper investigative system.[330]

Article 17 of Regulation 1/2003 amended the Commission's powers but does not give it the broad basis called for.

Regulation 1/2003

Article 17 Investigations into sectors of the economy and into types of agreement

1. Where the trend of trade between Member States, the rigidity of prices or other circumstances suggest that competition may be restricted or distorted within the common market, the Commission may conduct its inquiry into a particular sector of the economy or into a particular type of [agreement] across various sectors. In the course of that inquiry, the Commission may request undertakings or associations of undertakings concerned to supply the information necessary for giving effect to Articles [101] and [102] of the Treaty.

   The Commission may in particular request the undertakings or associations of undertakings concerned to communicate to it all agreements, decisions and concerted practices.

   The Commission may publish a report on the results of its inquiry into particular sectors of the economy or of particular types of agreements across various sectors and invite comments from interested parties.

Article 17(1) thus provides the Commission with the powers to collect such information but does not confer power on the Commission to adopt remedies following such a report. Through such an inquiry, however, the Commission can obtain a broader view of the sector and examine more sector-wide practices than it would when concentrating on individual agreements concluded by firms operating on those markets. Having done this, it could then take further action, perhaps under the competition, or other Treaty, rules. The powers may be particularly useful for investigating suspicious pricing or other practices in oligopolistic markets where the presence of a small number of players may incite concerted practices or for scrutinising agreements being used on the market that may shape the future competitive environment. For example, inquires have been launched into: the sale of sports rights to internet companies and to providers of the third generation (3G) of mobile phones

[330] Whish and Sufrin, n. 313, 83.

services; roaming; leased lines; local loop; the energy, financial services and pharmaceutical sectors; and e-commerce.[331]

In 2020, the Commission consulted on the introduction of a New Competition Tool[332] aimed at addressing alleged gaps in the current EU competition rules and allowing for both investigation and timely and effective intervention against structural competition problems across markets, including where a market is not working well and not delivering outcomes due to its structure (e.g. oligopolistic market structure with an increased risk of tacit collusion). It appears, however, that the Commission does not intend to pursue the introduction of such a tool.[333]

The concern that competition law does not reach tacit coordination/collusion—which may now, because of algorithmic pricing, become more commonplace—has led some commentators to propose more innovative solutions. For example, Gal has proposed that the problem of algorithmic collusion can be dealt with through not only merger control but also by, for example, use of algorithms by consumers to breakdown and counteract some of the negative effects of algorithmic coordination, introduction of disruptive algorithms on the supply side, and freezing prices of one competitor.[334]

6. CONCLUSIONS

1. The Commission has wide investigative powers which it can use to unearth covertly operated cartels, explicit collusion between competitors to fix prices, restrict output, or share markets.

2. Cartels ordinarily infringe Article 101(1) automatically and are incapable of meeting the criteria of Article 101(3). In some cases, however, price or output restraints may be part of a wider beneficial collaborative arrangement between firms and require a fuller analysis to determine compatibility with Article 101 (see Chapter 10).

3. Where unlawful cartel activity is uncovered, heavy fines will be imposed by the Commission on the undertakings involved. Undertakings may also be excluded from future public procurement processes.

4. A number of Member States have criminalised cartel activity and/or set out criminal or civil sanctions for individuals involved in the conclusion of cartels.

5. The fight against cartels is a core priority of the Commission. Leniency applications and whistle-blowing are encouraged and repeat offenders are punished particularly severely.

6. The Commission also urges consumers harmed by cartels to seek compensation in the national courts from those engaged in hardcore cartel activity.

7. Article 101 prohibits joint conduct designed to supplement, or which facilitates, collusion between competitors (such as exchange of information, resale price maintenance, or meeting competition clauses).

8. Tacit collusion (or purely parallel behaviour) engaged in by firms operating on an oligopolistic market is not prohibited by Article 101(1). An agreement or some reciprocal contact, direct or indirect, between the undertakings operating on the market must be established.

9. Article 102 may apply to oligopolists which are found, collectively, to hold a dominant position on the market. Collective or individual actions designed to exclude new entrants into the market, or to deter or to punish deviations from a cooperative structure, might constitute abuses of a collective

331 See <http://ec.europa.eu/competition/antitrust/sector_inquiries.html>.

332 See <https://ec.europa.eu/info/law/better-regulation/have-your-say/initiatives/12416-Single-Market-new-complementary-tool-to-strengthen-competition-enforcement>.

333 Commission Press Release IP/20/2347, 15 December 2020 and see further Chap. 16.

334 Gal, n. 169.

dominant position. The EUMR also prohibits mergers which may lead to an increase in price through coordinated effects (collusion) on an oligopolistic market.

10. Article 17 of Regulation 1/2003 is an important mechanism for investigating concentrated markets or markets on which competition does not appear to be working well. The Commission uses it to identify problems on a market which can later be addressed through use of its powers under Articles 101, 102, 106, the EUMR, and/or the State aid rules.

11. Article 17 of Regulation 1/2003 does not provide such a broad basis for market investigation as does, for example, the UK's Enterprise Act, which provides for the investigation of markets where a feature or features of it appear to prevent, restrict, or distort competition. Where adverse effects on competition are identified in the UK following an investigation, remedies to deal with the problem may be imposed or recommended: for example, the total or partial termination of an agreement; that the prices to be charged for any specified goods or services on a market should be regulated; or that any business, or part of a business, be disposed of (by the sale of any part of an undertaking or assets or otherwise). In an investigation into aggregates, cement, and ready-mix concrete, for example, the UK competition authority required certain divestment remedies and said that it would implement remedy measures aimed at reducing transparency in the GB cement market, including a prohibition on generic cement price announcement letters to customers and restrictions on the disclosure and publication of GB cement market data.[335] It may also be suggested, or ordered, that measures should be taken by or against bodies other than the market players (for example, where it considers that the market rigidity has been caused, partly at least, by advertising restrictions or other legal or regulatory barriers). Although the Commission consulted on the introduction of a similar, new market-investigation competition tool in the EU, this proposal is not currently being pursued (see further Chapter 16).

12. Resort to such draconian remedies as price control and divestiture may not be a suitable means of dealing with the problems arising on oligopolistic markets. However, it can also be seen that a more flexible system may have advantages over one focusing exclusively on the abusive conduct, or the behaviour, of the undertakings on the market.

7. FURTHER READING

A. Books

Harding, C., and Joshua, J., *Regulating Cartels in Europe* (2nd edn, Oxford University Press, 2010)

B. Articles

Anderson, R., Jones, A., and Kovacic, W. E., 'Preventing Corruption, Supplier Collusion and the Corrosion of Civic Trust: A Procompetitive Program to Improve the Effectiveness and Legitimacy of Public Procurement' (2019) 26(4) *George Mason LR* 1233.

Franzosi, M., 'Oligopoly and the Prisoners' Dilemma: Concerted Practices and As If Behaviour' [1988] *ECLR* 385

Gal, M., 'Limiting Algorithmic Cartels' (2023) 38(1) *Berkley J of Law and Technology* forthcoming

[335] Competition Commission Report of 14 January 2014.

Heinemann, A., and Gebicka, A., 'Can Computers Form Cartels? About the Need for European Institutions to Revise the Concertation Doctrine in the Information Age' (2016) 7 *JECLAP* 431

Jones, A., '*Wood Pulp*: Concerted Practice and/or Conscious Parallelism' [1993] *ECLR* 273

OECD, 'Algorithms and Collusion: Competition policy in the digital age' (2017)

Van Gerven, G., and Varona, E. N., 'The *Wood Pulp* Case and the Future of Concerted Practices' (1994) 31 *CMLRev* 575

Werden, G. J., 'Sanctioning Cartel Activity: Let the Punishment Fit the Crime' (2009) 5 *European Competition Journal* 19

Whish, R., and Sufrin, B., 'Oligopolistic Markets and EC Competition Law' (1992) 12 *YEL* 59

10

HORIZONTAL COOPERATION AGREEMENTS

1. CENTRAL ISSUES

1. Horizontal cooperation agreements may bring benefits to consumers, by enabling firms to bring new products or services to the market and/or to penetrate new markets through, for example, sharing risk, pooling know-how, resources, and skills, saving cost, and/or achieving economies of scale.

2. Such arrangements may take a number of different forms ranging from loose cooperation arrangements, to the creation of a joint venture (JV) company. Although the form of cooperation does not generally affect the analysis of the conduct under Article 101, where the creation of a JV constitutes a 'concentration' with an EU dimension, the general rule is that the transaction is appraised under the EU Merger Regulation (EUMR), not Article 101. Over the years, the Commission has sought to ensure that the substantive assessment applicable to JVs under Article 101 and the EUMR, respectively, is broadly consistent.

3. The Commission's policy towards horizontal cooperation agreements under Article 101 has evolved significantly, from a time when a majority of such arrangements were found to infringe Article 101(1), but then more rigorously appraised, and where appropriate exempted, under Article 101(3), to the present position where a more economic approach is adopted and a fuller assessment is made of the agreement under both Article 101(1) and Article 101(3).

4. Since the abolition of the notification and exemption system in 2004, undertakings have ordinarily had to 'self-assess' to determine whether their horizontal cooperation agreements infringe Article 101. As there is relatively little case law and decisional practice in this area, the Commission's Guidelines on horizontal cooperation agreements (the Guidelines) are of practical importance. They provide both general guidance and specific guidance in relation to particular types of agreement: research and development (R&D), production (including specialisation), purchasing, commercialisation (including joint selling), information exchanges (examined in Chapter 9), standardisation, and (since 2023) sustainability agreements.

5. Since 2000, 'new generation' block exemption regulations on horizontal cooperation (HBERs) have covered R&D and specialisation agreements. They contain market share thresholds and lists of 'hardcore' restrictions and have been reformed and replaced twice (in 2010 and 2023, respectively). The 2010 BERs were due to expire

at the end of December 2022, but their duration was extended to 30 June 2023. New draft block exemptions (and accompanying Guidelines) were published for consultation in March 2022. Following extensive consultation, the final versions, taking effect from 1 July 2023, were first published on 1 June 2023.

2. INTRODUCTION

Horizontal cooperative arrangements (or arrangements between firms at the same level of the market) are extremely common. Such cooperation can take a variety of forms ranging from temporary arrangements at one level of activity, such as at the R&D stage, to the creation of a separate JV. Although the term JV could encompass a broad range of arrangements, it is normally used in the competition law context to describe an arrangement by which two or more undertakings (the 'parents'), in order to achieve a particular commercial goal, integrate part of their operations through the creation of an independent company or organisation, which they put under joint control. The parents also contribute resources into the enterprise, for example finance, intellectual property rights (IPRs), know-how, personnel, premises, or equipment. In the EU, the creation of certain JVs is subject to review under the EU merger rules rather than Article 101 (see Section 3).

Horizontal cooperation arrangements are not necessarily anti-competitive. On the contrary, in contrast to cartels discussed in Chapter 9, such cooperation may promote economic efficiency by, for example: facilitating the bringing of new products or services to the market (through enabling firms to share risk, pool know-how, resources, and skills, save cost, and/or achieve economies of scale); and/or enabling the penetration of new markets.[1] Without cooperation firms may simply not have the resources to invest in, or capabilities to embark on, such a venture, in particular, in rapidly developing markets such as telecommunications, information technology, and the media. Although, therefore, a competition law system will wish to remain steadfast against cartels, it will not wish to deter the conclusion of beneficial cooperation. In determining whether horizontal agreements do adversely impact on competition, competition authorities will be concerned not only with reductions of competition between the parties themselves but also with foreclosure effects on third parties and spill-over effects into other markets (in particular, other markets in which the parties to a JV compete).

This chapter commences in Section 3 by considering some general issues in respect of horizontal cooperation, in particular jurisdiction and the evolution of competition law and policy in this area. It is seen in this section that, as in other areas, EU competition policy towards horizontal cooperation has developed significantly over the years. Consequently, older decisions and policy statements of the Commission (prior to modernisation) must be approached with some caution. Indeed, following a review of its policy towards horizontal arrangements during the 1980s and 1990s,[2] the Commission adopted, in 2000, new-style block exemption regulations (BERs) (Regulation 2658/2000 on specialisation agreements[3] and Regulation 2659/2000 on R&D agreements[4]) and published a set of Guidelines on the applicability of Article 101 to horizontal cooperation[5] which reflected a 'modernised' interpretation of Article 101. These have now been updated and replaced

[1] See generally e.g., M. Hviid, 'The Treatment of Horizontal Agreements Aimed at Solving Incentive Problems' (2020) 65(3) *Ant Bull* 340.

[2] Commission, *XXVIIth Report on Competition Policy* (1997) paras. 46 and 47.

[3] [2000] OJ L304/3. [4] [2000] OJ L304/7. [5] [2001] OJ C3/2.

twice, first in 2010 (see Regulations 1217/2010[6] and 1218/2010[7] and accompanying Guidelines[8]) and subsequently in 2023, following extensive consultation. Although new draft block exemptions and Guidelines were published for consultation in March 2022, and the new regime was due to take effect on 1 January 2023, on 8 December 2022 the duration of the block exemptions was prolonged to 30 June 2023. The final horizontal BERs (HBERs) and Guidelines, taking effect from 1 July 2023, were initially published on 1 June 2023. This chapter discusses the 2023 R&D BER, Regulation 2023/1066,[9] Specialisation BER, Regulation 2023/1067,[10] and Guidelines.[11]

Sections 4–10 examine more specifically certain types of horizontal cooperation agreements, R&D, production (including specialisation), purchasing, commercialisation (including joint selling), standardisation, standard terms, and sustainability.

3. APPRAISAL OF HORIZONTAL COOPERATION AND JOINT VENTURES: EVOLUTION OF POLICY

A. APPRAISAL UNDER THE EU MERGER REGULATION OR ARTICLE 101?

Horizontal cooperation agreements and JVs fall for substantive assessment either under Article 101 or, since a system of EU merger control came into force in 1990, under the EU Merger Regulation (EUMR).[12] An important preliminary question, therefore, is which transactions, or JVs, fall for appraisal under Article 101 rather than the EUMR?

In Chapter 15, it is seen that the general scheme of the EUMR is that concentrations, which include jointly-controlled 'full-function' JVs ('performing on a lasting basis all the functions of an autonomous economic entity'[13]), with an EU dimension, are generally appraised exclusively by the Commission under the provisions of the EUMR, not Article 101. Such transactions have to be notified to the Commission and cannot be completed unless cleared, whether conditionally or unconditionally.

A number of advantages have arguably followed for transactions constituting a concentration. For example, not only do concentrations with an EU dimension generally benefit from a one-stop appraisal in the EU by the Commission completed within tight statutory timetables,[14] but, in the early days of the EUMR at least, concentrations benefited from a more lenient substantive assessment. Carles Esteva Mosso,[15] Deputy Director-General Mergers at DG Comp, explains the problem that arose.

[6] [2010] OJ L335/36.

[7] [2010] OJ L335/43. Reg. 267/2010 on the application of Article 101(3) to certain categories of agreements, decisions and concerted practices in the insurance sector [2010] OJ L83/1 has now expired.

[8] [2011] OJ C11/1.

[9] See [2023] OJ L143/9 and the previous draft, Annex to the Communication from the Commission: Approval of the content of a draft for a Commission Regulation on the application of Article 101(3) of the Treaty on the Functioning of the European Union to certain categories of research and development agreements, C(2022) 1161 final.

[10] See [2023] OJ L143/20 and the previous draft, Annex to the Communication from the Commission: Approval of the content of a draft for a Commission Regulation on the application of Article 101(3) of the Treaty on the Functioning of the European Union to certain categories of specialisation agreements, C(2022) 1160 final.

[11] Guidelines on the applicability of Article 101 of the Treaty on the Functioning of the European Union to horizontal co-operation agreements, 17 July 2023, see also the draft version published in [2022] OJ C164/2.

[12] Reg. 139/2004 [2004] OJ L24/1 (replacing Reg. 4064/89 [1989] OJ L395/1), see Chap. 15.

[13] EUMR, Art. 3(4).

[14] If such transactions meet the jurisdictional thresholds set out in the EUMR, they must ordinarily be notified to the Commission and cannot be completed until cleared by it.

[15] C. E. Mosso, 'The Contribution of Merger Control to the Definition of Harm to Competition', GCLC Conference, Brussels, February 2016.

Carles Esteva Mosso, 'The Contribution of Merger Control to the Definition of Harm to Competition', GCLC Conference, Brussels, February 2016

. . . [I]n the early years, the assessment of mergers was conceptually very different than the assessment under Article 101 of other types of agreements between undertakings, less structural in nature than mergers. Not only the substantive tests diverged: the 'creation or strengthening of a dominant position' was quite far apart from that of an agreement or practice 'having the object or effect of restricting competition'. Also the interpretation of both tests contributed further to the divergence of standards. In particular, under the previous, more form-based approach to the interpretation of 'restriction of competition', a large number of agreements were considered to be caught by the test of Article 101(1) and required exemption under Article 101(3), either by formal decision (rarely) or by comfort letter (more common). On the other hand, the dominance test in mergers was applied on the basis of the jurisprudence developed under Article 102 and found to be met in only a small proportion of the large number of mergers scrutinized by the Commission every year. Once dominance was found, no efficiency defence was considered to be available.

This divergence of standards, which in practice lead to a more lenient treatment of horizontal mergers than to collusive agreements between firms holding similar amounts of market power (also referred to as 'concentration privilege' 'Konzentrationsprivileg' in German), seems, with hindsight, difficult to explain.

It will be seen both in this chapter and Chapter 15 that the Commission has taken a series of steps to reform substantive assessment both under Article 101 and the EUMR, with the result that the assessment conducted under each has been brought more closely in line with the other.

Nonetheless, one remaining problem for parties whose transactions fall for assessment under Article 101, rather than the EUMR, is that it is rare to get 'clearance' or comfort that their transaction complies with Article 101. This may be problematic in relation to some transactions, such as partial-function production JVs, which 'require substantial investment and far reaching integration of operations, which makes it difficult to unravel them afterwards at the behest of a competition authority',[16] or in scenarios where it is less clear how Article 101 applies (for example, see discussion of sustainability agreements in Section 10). Although parties to agreements may seek informal guidance from the Commission,[17] and the Commission may adopt a decision finding that Article 101 is inapplicable to their agreement (see Regulation 1/2003, Article 10),[18] the latter has not yet been used. Further, even if the Commission is more willing to give informal guidance, in the majority of cases the parties will have no choice other than to 'self-assess' whether their agreement is compatible with Article 101. Given that there is relatively little modern jurisprudence in this sphere, the HBERs, the Guidelines,[19] and the general Article 101(3) Guidelines[20] play a central role in guiding that self-assessment.

[16] White Paper on modernisation of the rules implementing Articles 85 and 86 [now 101 and 82] of the EC Treaty [1999] OJ C132/1, para. 79. Although the Commission proposed bringing a broader category of JVs within the EUMR (paras. 80 and 101), this proposal was eventually dropped, see Chap. 15.

[17] See Commission adopts a more flexible antitrust Informal Guidance Notice; withdraws Antitrust COVD Temporary Framework, 3 October 2022 and Chap. 13.

[18] See Chap. 13.

[19] The Guidelines apply irrespective of the level of integration involved and do not deal with JVs as a separate species of agreement, but consider them according to their provisions and effects in the light of the principles set out therein.

[20] Guidelines on the application of Article 81(3) [now Article 101(3)] of the Treaty (the Article 101(3) Guidelines) [2004] OJ C101/97, see Chap. 5.

In some cases, post-2004, the Commission has also used commitments decisions[21] to close an investigation into a horizontal cooperation agreement. Indeed, the use of this procedure has arguably come close to replicating the functions previously performed under the old 'authorisation' system (enabling the Commission to influence the content of cooperation arrangements (for example, in the financial services and airlines sector))[22] and has some parallels with conditional clearances under the EUMR.

B. THE EVOLVING EU APPROACH TO HORIZONTAL COOPERATION

(i) General

Horizontal cooperation agreements between two or more undertakings[23] falling under Article 101 must be appraised to determine if they appreciably[24] restrict competition and, if so, whether they satisfy the conditions of Article 101(3).

Initially, the Commission took an interventionist approach to horizontal cooperation and JVs based on a fear of coordination between the parents and on the loss of potential competition. It took a broad view of what constituted a restriction of competition,[25] bringing many agreements within Article 101(1) and then assessing them under Article 101(3).[26] To deal with the practical difficulty of exempting all such agreements, in 1985 it adopted two block exemption regulations, Regulation 417/85 on specialisation agreements[27] and Regulation 418/85 on R&D agreements,[28] which were rigid and of limited utility in practice.

The wide interpretation the Commission adopted to the concept of a restriction of competition, and its concern about the loss of potential competition, is vividly illustrated by its decision in *Vacuum Interrupters*.[29] In this case, the Commission found that the formation of a JV for the development, production, and sale of a vacuum interrupter (to be incorporated into circuit-breakers) infringed Article 101(1) on the basis of the hypothetical possibility that the JV's parents (AEI and Reyrolle Parsons) might each have proceeded alone. In fact, each had been individually researching the development of the product for ten years, but its construction and operation was complex and difficult and neither had been able to bring the product to the market. As the Commission noted:

> Each of the companies found the cost of development was very substantial and each recognised that if vacuum interrupters were to be brought to commercial use at a price which would make them

[21] Reg. 1/2003, Art. 9, see Chap. 13.

[22] See N. Dunne, 'Commitment Decisions in EU Competition Law' (2014) 10 *J of Competition Law and Economics* 399, 406–410 and e.g. COMP 37.214, *DFB* 19 January 2005, COMP/38.173, *Joint Selling of the Media Rights to the FA Premier League* 22 March 2006, COMP 38.681, *Cannes Agreement* 4 October 2006, COMP/39.398, *Visa MIF* 26 February 2014, and COMP/39.595, *Star Alliance* 23 May 2013 (between Continental, United, Lufthansa, and Air Canada which was permitted subject to commitments), n. 49 and text.

[23] See Chap. 4.

[24] See Chap. 5 and the Notice on agreements of minor importance which do not appreciably restrict competition under Article 101(1) of the Treaty on the Functioning of the European Union (De Minimis Notice) [2014] OJ C291/01, providing that agreements between actual or potential competitors will not normally give rise to an appreciable restriction of competition where the parties' aggregate market share does not exceed 10%. Although the Notice does not normally apply to agreements incorporating hardcore restrictions, the Commission's guidance on by object sets out limited exceptions for certain joint purchasing, R&D, and specialisation agreements, see Staff Working Document on 'restrictions of competition "by object"', SWD(2014) 198 final, 2.1.2. See also Cases T-374–375, 384, and 388/94, *European Night Services v Commission* EU:T:1998:198, n. 35 and text.

[25] See especially Notice on cooperation agreements [1968] OJ C75/3 and Notice on the assessment of cooperative JVs pursuant to Article 101 [1993] OJ C43/2 (Notice on cooperative joint ventures).

[26] See further Chap. 5. [27] [1985] OJ L53/1. [28] [1985] OJ L53/5. [29] COMP/27.442 [1977] OJ L48/32.

competitive with the conventional forms of switchgear, a collaboration and pooling of the resources available was essential in order that the heavy expenditure involved by the individual companies would be reduced.[30]

However, as the Commission concluded that the JV had obvious advantages that would not have been achieved by either party individually, it did go on to find that the agreement satisfied the conditions of Article 101(3) and so merited an exemption.[31]

Decisions such as this were subject to significant criticism for finding restrictions of potential competition based on unrealistic assumptions. Further, the grant of an exemption seemed theoretically inconsistent with finding under Article 101(1). If the parents *were* able to enter the market independently, how could their coming together and the restrictions within the agreement be indispensable to the attainment of the agreement's (beneficial) objectives?

(ii) The Development of a More Economic Approach Towards the Application of Article 101 to Horizontal Cooperation

In Chapter 5 it is seen that the Commission, in light of criticism of its early approach to Article 101 and the case law of the EU Courts, has modernised its interpretation of Article 101. In the context of horizontal cooperation, this re-evaluation started, particularly in relation to its attitude towards potential competition, in 1983. The result of this was seen in *Optical Fibres*, involving an agreement between Corning Glass Works (a US company) and three European partners to develop, produce, and sell optical fibres and optical cables for use in the European telecommunications market. In this case, the Commission found that the individual JV agreement between Corning and its partners did not restrict competition as none were able to develop and put the JV product onto the market without the collaboration of the others. The Commission was concerned, however, by the setting up of a network of three JVs. Although it found that this aspect of the operation *did* infringe Article 101(1), it exempted the arrangements (for 15 years), following modifications to the agreements to ensure competition between the JVs and to reduce Corning's control over them.[32]

COMP/30.320, *Optical Fibres* [1986] OJ L236/30

Commission

46. The individual joint venture agreements do not as such restrict competition between Corning and its partners. When the agreements were concluded, the parties were not actual or potential competitors in the market for optical fibres or optical cables. The production of optical fibres and optical cables are different activities. Corning had no experience in cable manufacture, while Corning's partners had no experience in glass manufacture which could have led to an invention competitive with Corning's. In spite of the parties' considerable financial resources, the entry by Corning into the optical cables market or by Corning's partners into the optical fibres market was not a natural and reasonably foreseeable extension of their respective business activities. The cooperation between Corning and its partners is rather of a complementary nature which does not give rise to restriction or distortion of competition at the level of the cooperating parties. Moreover, the agreements do not foreclose market

[30] Ibid., para. 10. [31] Ibid., para. 22.

[32] See also COMP/31.340, *Mitchell Cotts/Solfitra* [1987] OJ L41/31 (parents neither actual nor potential competitors, but the distribution arrangements brought it within Art. 101(1) because they raised barriers to entry).

access by third parties or have any other foreseeable anti-competitive impact on their activities. The various amendments made to the original agreements ensure that competition is maintained and that third parties do not suffer from discrimination or market partitioning. In addition, by virtue of the conditions and obligations attached to this Decision, competition is safe-guarded and the Commission is in a position to monitor future developments.

47. There is neither restriction nor distortion of competition between the parents and the joint venture. The agreements provide that the parents are free to engage in independent R&D of optical fibres. Furthermore, the individual joint venture agreements do not contain obligations which go beyond what would be admitted in simple licensing agreements between non-competitors. Thus the parties are free to engage in independent R&D of optical fibres, although in practice they depend on a continuous transfer of technology from Corning. In addition, there is no obligation on the joint ventures to grant exclusive licenses to Corning in respect of improvements or innovations.

48. The principal restrictions and distortions of competition in this case are to be found rather in the relationship between the joint ventures. The joint ventures have substantially the same business activity, namely the production and marketing of optical fibres. These joint ventures are therefore directly competing companies. The agreements taken together give rise to the creation of a network of inter-related joint ventures with a common technology provider in an oligopolistic market. Corning is one of the major producers and distributors of optical fibres in the world. Its partners are cable makers with large market shares in their respective home countries. The joint ventures therefore bring together companies with strong positions in the optical fibres and cables markets. Although the joint ventures are free to make active and passive sales into each other's territories, only passive sales are permitted in territories where Corning has an exclusive licensee. Corning has interests, whether through joint ventures, subsidiaries or licensees, in several Member States. Its financial stake and key technical and financial personnel representation in the joint ventures, the success of which depends on rapid access to Corning's technology, ensure that Corning is in a position to influence and coordinate the joint venture's conduct.

Subsequently, in *ODIN*[33] the more liberal policy led to a negative clearance (a finding that the agreement did not infringe Article 101(1) at all). In this case, Metal Box (UK) and Elopak (Norway) set up a 50/50 jointly owned company called ODIN. Metal Box manufactured a range of metal, plastic, and polythene containers, bottles, and other packaging, and various closures and seals. Elopak's expertise was in cartons for the dairy and food industries. The JV was to develop a new form of paperboard-based package with a separate laminated metal lid to be used for UHT-treated foods with a long shelf-life. The parties were not existing competitors and neither of them had all the technology required for the new product or the technical knowledge to develop it separately. The agreement did not contain ancillary restrictions beyond those necessary to make the JV work.[34]

In *European Night Services*,[35] the GC stressed that the Commission was not at liberty to apply Article 101(3) as it had not shown why Article 101(1) applied to a JV between four railway companies to provide overnight passenger rail services between the UK and the continent through the Channel Tunnel. It had not identified the relevant market properly, or applied the appreciability criteria,

[33] COMP/32.009, *Metal Box/Elopak (ODIN)* [1990] OJ L209/15.

[34] See also COMP/32.668, *Konsortium ECR 900* [1990] OJ L228/31 (a JV between three undertakings for the development, manufacture, and distribution of a telecommunications system did not infringe Art. 101(1) as the undertakings could not have performed the tasks individually in the time demanded).

[35] Cases T-374–375, 384, and 388/94, *European Night Services v Commission* EU:T:1998:198; see further Chap. 5.

properly, and had demonstrated insufficient economic reasoning: for example, the holding that potential competition was restricted was based on 'a hypothesis unsupported by any evidence or any analysis of the structures of the relevant market from which it might be concluded that it represented a real, concrete possibility'.[36] Further, even if an exemption has been required, the exemption conditions were flawed as the Commission had applied the essential facilities concept inappropriately[37] and had granted the exemption for too short a time in view of the long-term investment required. Indeed, in a series of judgments the EU Courts have stressed the importance of careful analysis of horizontal cooperation agreements under Article 101(1) to determine if they restrict competition by object or effect.[38]

The Commission has consequently continued to define, and further refine, its policy.

(iii) The Horizontal Cooperation Guidelines

The Commission's evolving approach towards horizontal cooperation agreements has been reflected in a series of Guidelines. The Guidelines seek to provide legal certainty in the self-assessment of horizontal cooperation agreements concluded between actual competitors (active on the same market) or potential competitors.[39] According to the 2023 Horizontal Cooperation Guidelines (the Guidelines), a company is treated as a potential competitor of another company if:[40]

> 16. . . . in the absence of the agreement, it is likely that the former, within a short period of time . . . , would undertake the necessary additional investments or other necessary switching costs to enter the relevant market on which the latter is active. This assessment has to be based on realistic grounds; the mere theoretical possibility to enter a market is not sufficient. . . .

The Commission sets out its analytical framework for Article 101 assessment in Chapter 1 of the Guidelines, which is elaborated on more specifically in later sections dealing with particular types of agreement: R&D; production (including specialization and mobile infrastructure agreements); purchasing; commercialisation (including joint selling); information exchanges (examined in Chapter 9); standardization and standard terms; and sustainability agreements.[41]

The paragraphs start by outlining the main competition concerns relating to horizontal cooperation agreements (resulting from loss of competition, risk of collusion, or foreclosure), before briefly summarising how, in general, restrictions of competition—by object or effect—are identified and ancillary restraints analysed.

Later sections make it clear that horizontal cooperation agreements, which in some cases may contain price or output restraints, will not restrict competition by object if they truly concern horizontal cooperation. For example, paragraphs 222–223 state in relation to production agreements:

> 222. Generally, agreements which involve (a) price-fixing, (b) limiting output or (c) sharing markets or customers restrict competition by object.
>
> 223. However, in the context of production agreements, this does not apply where:

[36] Ibid., para. 142. [37] See Chap. 7.

[38] See Chap. 5, Sections 3.B and 3.C and e.g. Case C-228/18, *Budapest Bank* EU:C:2020:265, Case C-67/13 P, *Cartes Bancaires* EU:C:2014:2204.

[39] See, most recently, the 2023 Horizontal Cooperation Guidelines 17 July 2023, paras. 1–16.

[40] Ibid. See also Case C-373/14 P, *Toshiba Corp v Commission* EU:C:2016:26 and discussion of potential competitors in Chaps. 5 and 12.

[41] Although the 2000 Guidelines contained a specific chapter on environmental agreements, the 2010 Guidelines did not.

(a) the parties agree on the *output directly concerned by the production agreement* (for example, the capacity and production volume of a joint venture or the agreed amount of outsourced products), provided that competition on other parameters (for example, prices) is not eliminated; or

(b) a production agreement that also provides for the joint distribution of the jointly produced products provides for *joint setting of the sales prices* of those products, and only those products, provided that the restriction is objectively necessary for the implementation of the combined production and distribution agreement and proportionate to attain the objectives of that agreement.

This approach accords with the EU Courts' requirement that object classification should be used sparingly and only for coordination that reveals in itself a sufficient degree of harm to competition;[42] it is inappropriate, even if severe restraints are incorporated, where a reasonable countervailing hypothesis for the agreement exists (see Chapter 5).[43] An object restraint will be found, however, if the cooperation in fact serves as a tool to engage in a cartel or other object infringements.[44] For example, in *Telefónica/Portugal Telecom*,[45] the Commission imposed fines of €79 million on the parties for insertion of a non-compete clause in an agreement relating to a Brazilian JV, Vivo. As the non-compete provision applied in Spain and Portugal (not Brazil, the area in which the JV was active), the Commission considered that the agreement infringed Article 101(1) (it restricted competition by object and the restraints were not ancillary to the JV) and did not satisfy the conditions of Article 101(3).

Where the agreement does not in itself reveal a sufficient degree of harm to competition, it must be determined whether it has, or is likely to have, a restrictive effect. The Guidelines state:

30. A horizontal cooperation agreement that does not in itself reveal a sufficient degree of harm to competition may still have restrictive effects on competition. For a horizontal cooperation agreement to have restrictive effects on competition, it must have, or be likely to have, an appreciable adverse impact on at least one of the parameters of competition on the market, such as price, output, product quality, product variety or innovation. To establish whether this is the case, it is necessary to assess competition within the actual context in which it would occur if the agreement had not existed . . .

31. Agreements can have restrictive effects by appreciably reducing competition between the undertakings that are parties to the agreement or between any one of them and a third party. This means that the agreement must reduce the parties' decision-making independence . . .

32. In order to assess whether an agreement has restrictive effects, the following factors are relevant:

(a) the nature and content of the agreement;

(b) the actual context in which the cooperation occurs, in particular the economic and legal context in which the undertakings concerned operate, the nature of the goods or services affected, and the real conditions of the functioning and the structure of the market or markets in question . . . ;

[42] Case C-67/13 P, *Groupement des Cartes Bancaires v Commission* EU:C:2014:2204.

[43] It also aligns more closely with that adopted in merger cases, see also Mosso, n. 15 (restrictions of competition by object have no equivalent in merger control. Rather, a range of relevant factors, are analysed to determine the transaction's likely impact on the main parameters of competition (price, output, quality, innovation, etc.)).

[44] See Chaps. 5 and 9.

[45] COMP/39.839, 23 January 2013, *aff'd* Cases T-208 and 216/13, *Portugal Telecom and Telefónica SA v Commission* EU:T:2016:369, Case C-487/16 P, *Telefónica SA v Commission* EU:C:2017:961, see Chap. 5.

> (c) the extent to which the parties individually or jointly have or obtain some degree of market power . . . and the extent to which the agreement contributes to the creation, maintenance or strengthening of that market power or allows the parties to exploit such market power;
>
> (d) the restrictive effects on competition may be actual and potential, but they must, in any event, be sufficiently appreciable. . . .
>
> 33. In some cases, undertakings enter into horizontal cooperation agreements because, on the basis of objective factors, they would not be able to carry out the project or activity covered by the cooperation independently, for instance, due to their limited technical capabilities. Such horizontal cooperation agreements will generally not give rise to restrictive effects on competition within the meaning of Article 101(1), unless the parties could have carried out the project with less stringent restrictions. . . .

As in other areas of competition law, therefore, identification of relevant markets (see further Chapter 3) and the question of whether the undertakings concerned have market power plays a central role. Although there is no absolute threshold above which market power can be presumed to have been created or maintained in horizontal cooperation cases, the HBERs and Guidelines recognise that some types of cooperation are unlikely to infringe Article 101 (either because they do not infringe Article 101(1) or because they satisfy the conditions of Article 101(3)) if specified market share thresholds are not exceeded (these differ depending on the type of cooperation at issue, see Sections 4–9). In cases where agreements appear to span two or more of the categories, it may thus be important to identify the 'centre of gravity' of an agreement[46] so relevant thresholds can be identified.

The Commission's methodology in its assessment of horizontal cooperation agreements is now more closely aligned to that adopted in relation to its appraisal of horizontal mergers. Indeed, as Mosso recognised:

> both require a balancing of potential anti-competitive effects with likely efficiencies. While the fact that one of these tests is applied ex ante and the other normally ex post may undoubtedly be of practical relevance, it should have no bearing on the more conceptual question of whether or not both standards have actually converged.[47]

In the speech, Mosso identified, as examples, three cases in which the effects of airline alliances were analysed by the Commission.

> For instance, when assessing the Oneworld, Star Alliance and Skyteam airline alliances under Article 101 TFEU, the Commission looked at closeness of competition between the parties, their combined market shares and barriers to entry and carried out a price concentration analysis based on economic data. It also analysed foreclosure effects potentially resulting from the parties restricting access to connecting traffic. All these elements, in turn, formed a decisive part as well of the analysis conducted by the Commission in airline mergers cases such as Lufthansa/Austrian, Ryanair/Aer Lingus or British Airways/Iberia.[48]

In the airline alliance cases referred to, the Commission investigated revenue-sharing JVs between airlines for extensive cooperation on pricing, capacity, scheduling, and revenue-management coordination and designed to achieve efficiencies. For example, in *Star Alliance: Continental/United/*

[46] Guidelines, paras. 6–7. [47] Mosso, n. 15, 7–8. [48] Ibid.

Lufthansa/Air Canada[49] although the Commission's preliminary conclusion that the agreement restricted competition by object may not be easy to justify, the Commission did, as Mosso describes, go on to make a detailed analysis of the likely effects of the agreement, before concluding that the agreement would appreciably restrict competition. The Commission also examined Article 101(3), accepting that the agreement would produce both in-market and out-of-market efficiencies, but concluded that the level was insufficient to outweigh the likely significant negative effects resulting from the elimination of competition. It thus accepted commitments (including, amongst other things, the release of landing and take-off slots) which the Commission concluded addressed the concerns set out in its preliminary assessment.

Even where a restriction of competition under Article 101(1) is identified, Article 101(3) must be considered. The Guidelines thus provide guidance on the application of the block exemptions (the R&D and Specialisation BERs are based on the premise that the combination of complementary skills or assets can be the source of substantial efficiencies) and the Article 101(3) criteria individually. They make it clear that there is no presumption that cooperation agreements falling outside the scope of the BERs fall within Article 101(1) or fail to satisfy the conditions of Article 101(3).

4. RESEARCH AND DEVELOPMENT AGREEMENTS

A. THE APPLICATION OF ARTICLE 101(1)

R&D is crucial to the competitiveness of the EU.[50] R&D agreements can take many forms, as the Guidelines note:

> 52. R&D agreements vary in form and scope. They include agreements under which one party finances R&D carried out by another party . . . ; agreements covering the joint improvement of existing products and technologies, and agreements concerning the development of products and technologies that would create an entirely new demand. The R&D cooperation may take the form of a cooperation agreement or a joint venture, namely a jointly controlled company. . . . Undertakings may also cooperate in looser forms, such as technical cooperation in working groups.

In assessing the impact of cooperation, the Guidelines recognise that R&D arrangements may affect competition not only in existing product or technology markets but also in relation to innovation (R&D efforts for new products and/or technologies that create their own markets).[51] As far as assessment under Article 101(1) is concerned, the Guidelines state that R&D agreements restrict competition by object only if they are really a tool for a disguised cartel or other by object infringement (such as price fixing, output limitation, market allocation, or restrictions of technical development). In true R&D cases, therefore, a detailed analysis of effects, and a consideration of the relevant markets, the products or technologies capable of being improved, substituted, or replaced by the contract products or technologies, will be required as a preliminary matter.[52] The main competition concerns are that R&D agreements will directly limit competition between the parties, lead to anti-competitive foreclosure of third parties, or to a collusive outcome on the market.[53]

[49] COMP/39.595, 23 May 2013.

[50] Recital 2 of the R&D BER mentions Art. 179(2) TFEU which provides for the EU to encourage undertakings, including SMEs, in R&D and to support their cooperation efforts.

[51] Guidelines, para. 54.

[52] See also R&D BER, Art. 1, para. 1(16) and (17).

[53] Guidelines, para. 135.

The Guidelines provide that certain agreements are unlikely to infringe Article 101(1), those which: are entered into between non-competitors, for example because the parties' assets, technologies or skills are complementary (they would not be capable of carrying out the R&D on their own within a short period of time); involve outsourcing of R&D to specialised undertakings (which are not involved in the exploitation of the results); or relate to basic research (experimental or theoretical work undertaken primarily to acquire new knowledge).[54]

In other cases, a core issue in the appraisal is the market power of the parties; the stronger the combined position of the parties on existing markets and/or the lower the number of competing R&D efforts in addition to and comparable to those of the parties, the more likely it is that the agreement will have restrictive effects.[55] Thus R&D agreements seeking to improve existing products or technologies are only likely to produce restrictive effects if the parties have a strong position, entry is difficult, and there are only a few other remaining rivals capable of constraining the parties' behaviour. If the R&D is directed at the substitution or replacement of an existing product or technology, the assessment will focus on the question of whether the agreement will delay the development of the replacing product or technology, for example where the parties are the only ones that engage in such R&D or where a major player in an existing market cooperates with a potential competitor about to emerge. Agreements providing for joint exploitation have greater potential to restrict competition.[56]

The Guidelines also provide advice for the assessment of R&D efforts which impact on innovation relating to entirely new products and early innovation efforts.[57] Such agreements require an assessment of possible restrictions on innovation efforts (the quality and variety of possible future products or technologies or the speed or level of innovation) and the impact on the parties' independent research efforts.[58]

B. THE APPLICATION OF ARTICLE 101(3)

(i) The R&D Block Exemption

Even where there is concern that an agreement infringes Article 101(1), the R&D BER may apply. In summary: the R&D BER starts by defining R&D agreements and other core terms (Article 1); Article 2 provides the main exemption for R&D agreements; Articles 3–7 out the conditions for exemption, including satisfaction of the market share thresholds and the duration of the exemption; Article 8 deals with hardcore restrictions, the inclusion of which prevent the exemption applying, and Article 9 lists 'excluded restrictions', contractual provisions which cannot be block exempted but which do not necessarily prevent the block exemption from applying to the remaining provisions of the agreement (an excluded restraint will only take the rest of the agreement outside the protection of the Regulation if it violates Article 101 and is *not* severable from the remaining provisions of the agreement); Articles 10 and 11 clarify the withdrawal procedure and that the BER's benefit can be withdrawn, under Article 29(1)(2) of Regulation 1/2003, from an agreement which infringes Article 101, either by the Commission, or by a designated national competition authority (NCA) where the relevant geographic market constitutes the territory of that Member State, or a part thereof;[59] and Articles 12 and 13 contain final provisions, dealing with transitional periods and providing an expiry date of 30 June 2035.

[54] Ibid., 2.3.3. [55] Ibid., 2.3.5. [56] Ibid., 2.3.5.2, paras. 147–149 [57] Ibid., 2.3.5.3.
[58] Ibid. [59] Ibid., 2.2.6.

Articles 1 and 2 thus clarify the scope of the exemption for R&D agreements. The list of definitions in Article 1 is expansive, including definitions of not only R&D agreements but contract products and technologies, R&D, joint R&D and paid-for R&D, and the concept of exploitation of the results. Article 1(2) also clarifies that the terms 'undertaking' or 'party' includes their respective connected undertakings. Article 2 states that the exemption includes provisions on the assignment or licensing of intellectual property rights which are ancillary to the R&D agreement.

Article 1—Definitions

1. For the purposes of this Regulation, the following definitions shall apply:

    (1) 'research and development agreement' means an agreement entered into between two or more parties which relates to the conditions under which those parties pursue any of the following:

    (a) joint research and development of contract products or contract technologies which:

    (i) does not include joint exploitation of the results of that research and development, or

    (ii) includes joint exploitation of the results of that research and development;

    (b) paid-for research and development of contract products or contract technologies which:

    (i) does not include joint exploitation of the results of that research and development, or

    (ii) includes joint exploitation of the results of that research and development;

    (c) joint exploitation of the results of research and development of contract products or contract technologies carried out pursuant to a prior agreement falling under point (a) between the same parties; or

    (d) joint exploitation of the results of research and development of contract products or contract technologies carried out pursuant to a prior agreement falling under point (b) between the same parties;

    . . .

    (3) 'research and development' (means activities aimed at acquiring know-how relating to existing or new products, technologies or processes, the carrying out of theoretical analysis, systematic study or experimentation, including experimental and demonstrator production, technical testing of products or processes, the establishment of the necessary facilities up to demonstrator scale and the obtaining of intellectual property rights for the results;

    . . .

    (7) 'exploitation of the results' means the production or distribution of the contract products or the application of the contract technologies or the assignment or licensing of intellectual property rights or the communication of know-how required for such production, distribution or application;

    . . .

    (15) 'competing undertaking' means an actual or a potential competitor:

    (a) 'actual competitor' means an undertaking that is supplying a product, technology or process capable of being improved, substituted or replaced by the contract product or the contract technology on the relevant geographic market;

    (b) 'potential competitor' means an undertaking that, in the absence of the research and development agreement would, on realistic grounds and not just as a mere theoretical possibility, be likely to undertake, within not more than 3 years, the necessary additional investments or incur the necessary costs to supply a product, technology or process capable of being improved, substituted or replaced by the contract product or contract technology on the relevant geographic market;

(16) 'relevant product market' means the relevant market for the products capable of being improved, substituted or replaced by the contract products;

(17)'relevant technology market' means the relevant market for the technologies or processes capable of being improved, substituted or replaced by the contract technologies;

. . .

Article 2—Exemption

1. Pursuant to Article 101(3) of the Treaty and subject to the provisions of this Regulation, Article 101(1) of the Treaty shall not apply to research and development agreements.
2. The exemption provided for in paragraph 1 shall apply to the extent that research and development agreements contain restrictions of competition falling within the scope of Article 101(1) of the Treaty.
3. The exemption provided for in paragraph 1 shall also apply to research and development agreements which include provisions on the assignment or licensing of intellectual property rights to one or more of the parties or to an entity the parties establish to carry out the joint or paid-for research and development or joint exploitation, provided that those provisions are directly related to and necessary for the implementation of the agreement and do not constitute the primary object of the agreement.

In order to be covered by the block exemption, the R&D agreement must fulfil a number of conditions. Very broadly, this requires all parties to have full access to the final results of the R&D (subject to limited exceptions, Article 3) and to have access to pre-existing know-how in certain circumstances (in relation to agreements that exclude joint exploitation of R&D, Article 4), and the agreement to meet criteria as to when joint exploitation of the R&D is permitted (Article 5).[60] Crucially, Article 6 sets out market share thresholds and duration of the exemption. Although the BER applies irrespective of market shares where parties to a R&D agreement are not competing undertakings (Article 6(1)), in the case of agreements between actual or potential competitors, a 25 per cent market share threshold applies. A presumption is thus applied that below a certain level of market power the positive effects of R&D agreements will outweigh any negative effects on competition. Article 7 clarifies how market shares are to be calculated.

Article 6—Market share thresholds and duration of exemption

1. Where two or more of the parties are competing undertakings within the meaning of Article 1(1), point (15), the exemption established in Article 2 shall apply for the duration of the research and development if, at the time the agreement is entered into:
   (a) for the research and development agreements referred to in Article 1(1), points (1) (a) and (c), the combined market share of the parties to the agreement does not exceed 25 % on the relevant product and technology markets;
   (b) for the research and development agreements referred to in Article 1(1), points (1) (b) and (d), the combined market share of the financing party and all the parties with which the financing party has entered into research and development agreements with regard to the same contract products or contract technologies does not exceed 25 % on the relevant product and technology markets.

[60] See also ibid., 2.51–2.53.

2. Where the parties are not competing undertakings within the meaning of Article 1(1), point (15), the exemption established in Article 2 shall apply for the duration of the research and development.
3. For research and development agreements where the results are jointly exploited, the exemption established in Article 2 shall continue to apply for 7 years from the time the contract products or contract technologies are first put on the market within the internal market, if the conditions provided for in paragraphs 1 or 2 of this Article are satisfied at the time the agreement referred to in Article 1(1), point (1) (a) or (b) is entered into. For the research and development agreements referred to in Article 1(1), point (1) (c) and (d) to benefit from such a continued exemption, the conditions provided for in paragraphs 1 or 2 of this Article must be satisfied at the time the prior agreement referred to in Article 1(1), point (1) (a) or (b) was entered into.
4. After the end of the 7 year period referred to in paragraph 3 of this Article, the exemption established in Article 2 shall continue to apply as long as:
   (a) for the research and development agreements referred to in Article 1(1), points (1) (a) and (c), the combined market share of the parties to the agreement does not exceed 25 % on the relevant markets to which the contract products or contract technologies belong;
   (b) for the research and development agreements referred to in Article 1(1), points (1) (b) and (d), the combined market share of the financing party and all the parties with which the financing party has entered into research and development agreements relating to the same contract products or contract technologies does not exceed 25 % on the relevant markets to which the contract products or contract technologies belong.
5. If the combined market share of the relevant parties does not exceed the relevant threshold referred to in paragraph 4 at the end of the 7 year period referred to in paragraph 3, but subsequently rises above that threshold, the exemption established in Article 2 shall continue to apply for a period of 2 consecutive calendar years following the year in which the relevant market share threshold was first exceeded.

Article 8 contains the list of hardcore restrictions, which includes certain: restrictions on the freedom of the parties to carry out certain R&D independently, or in conjunction with third parties; limitations on output or sales or fixing prices (subject to important exceptions, for example where joint exploitation is involved); or territorial restrictions.

Article 8—Hardcore restrictions

The exemption established in Article 2 shall not apply to research and development agreements which, directly or indirectly, in isolation or in combination with other factors under the control of the parties, have as their object any of the following restrictions:

(a) the restriction of the freedom of the parties to carry out research and development independently or in cooperation with third parties:
   (i) in a field unconnected with that to which the research and development agreement relates; or
   (ii) after the completion of the joint or paid-for research and development, in the field to which the research and development agreement relates or in a connected field;

(b) the limitation of output or sales, with the exception of:
   (i) the setting of production targets, where the joint exploitation of the results includes the joint production of the contract products;
   (ii) the setting of sales targets, where the joint exploitation of the results:

(1) includes the joint distribution of the contract products or the joint licensing of the contract technologies, and

(2) is carried out by a joint team, organisation or undertaking, or is jointly entrusted to a third party;

(iii) practices constituting specialisation in the context of exploitation;

(iv) the restriction of the freedom of the parties to produce, sell, assign or license products, technologies or processes which compete with the contract products or contract technologies during the period for which the parties have agreed to jointly exploit the results;

(c) the fixing of prices when selling the contract products or licensing the contract technologies to third parties, with the exception of the fixing of prices charged to immediate customers or the fixing of licence fees charged to immediate licensees where the joint exploitation of the results:

(i) includes the joint distribution of the contract products or the joint licensing of the contract technologies, and

(ii) is carried out by a joint team, organisation or undertaking, or is jointly entrusted to a third party;

(d) the restriction of the territory in which, or of the customers to whom, the parties may passively sell the contract products or license the contract technologies, with the exception of the requirement to exclusively license the results of the research and development to another party;

(e) the restriction of active sales of the contract products or contract technologies in territories or to customers which have not been exclusively allocated to one of the parties by way of specialisation in the context of exploitation;

(f) the requirement to refuse to meet demand from customers in the parties' respective territories, or from customers otherwise allocated between the parties by way of specialisation in the context of exploitation, where such customers would market the contract products in other territories within the internal market;

(g) the requirement to make it difficult for users or resellers to obtain the contract products from other resellers within the internal market.

Article 9 sets out 'Excluded restrictions'. It deals with no-challenge clauses and licensing to third parties.

Article 9—Excluded restrictions

1. The exemption established in Article 2 shall not apply to the following obligations in research and development agreements:

(a) the obligation not to challenge:

(i) after completion of the research and development, the validity of intellectual property rights which:

(1) the parties hold in the internal market, and

(2) are relevant to the research and development; or

(ii) after the expiry of the research and development agreement, the validity of intellectual property rights which:

(1) the parties hold in the internal market, and

(2) protect the results of the research and development.

(b) the obligation not to grant licences to third parties to produce the contract products or to apply the contract technologies unless the agreement provides for the exploitation of the results of the joint or paid-for research and development by one or more of the parties and such exploitation takes place in the internal market vis-à-vis third parties.

2. Paragraph 1, point (a), is without prejudice to the possibility to provide for the termination of the research and development agreement in the event that one of the parties challenges the validity of the intellectual property rights referred to in paragraph 1, points (a) (i) and (ii).

3. If the research and development agreement includes any of the excluded restrictions referred to in paragraph 1 of this Article, the exemption established in Article 2 shall continue to apply to the remaining part of the research and development agreement, provided that the excluded restrictions can be severed from that remaining part and provided that the other conditions of this Regulation are met.

(ii) The Individual Application of Article 101(3)

Recognising that many R&D agreements will lead to efficiency gains by combining the undertakings' complementary skills and assets, thus resulting in improved or new products and technologies being developed and marketed more rapidly, or by leading to a wider dissemination of knowledge, triggering further innovation, the Guidelines note that R&D agreements may satisfy the conditions of Article 101(3) even where the BER does not apply (Chapter 2.4). Nonetheless, a careful look will be required at the efficiency justifications proffered, and whether a fair share of the benefits is passed on to consumers;[61] in particular, whether the benefits outweigh any price increases or other restrictive effects on competition. Hardcore restrictions are unlikely to fulfil the 'indispensability' criterion in Article 101(3).

The Guidelines also discuss the time of assessment. Although Article 101(3) ceases to apply if the criteria were once fulfilled but no longer are, the Commission will take into account the time needed for the parties to recoup sunk investments.[62] 'The risk facing the parties and the sunk investment that must be made to implement the agreement can thus lead to the agreement falling outside Article 101(1) or fulfilling the conditions of Article 101(3), as the case may be, for the period of time needed to recoup the investment.'[63] The Commission also accepts that some R&D agreements are irreversible events in that once the agreement has been implemented, the *ex ante* situation cannot be re-established. 'In such cases the assessment must be made exclusively on the basis of the facts pertaining at the time of implementation.'[64]

Chapter 2.6 sets out some worked examples of how Article 101 applies to R&D agreements.

5. PRODUCTION AGREEMENTS

A. THE APPLICATION OF ARTICLE 101(1)

Production agreements cover a number of scenarios, including: production (the manufacture of goods or the preparation of services) carried out by one of the parties; joint production (for example, through a jointly controlled JV); or subcontracting (where one party entrusts the other with production of

[61] See e.g. COMP/32.173, *Continental/Michelin* [1998] OJ L305/33, COMP/34.776, *Pasteur Mérieux-Merck* [1994] OJ L309/1, and COMP/33.863, *Asahi/Saint Gobain* [1994] OJ L354/87.

[62] Guidelines, 2.5. [63] Ibid., para. 164. [64] Ibid., para. 165.

certain goods). In unilateral specialisation, one or more parties cease production altogether and agree to purchase from the other(s), whereas in reciprocal specialisation two or more parties agree to give up manufacturing certain products and leaves it to the other(s) (and to purchase from/supply those others).[65] If subcontracting is between parties at different stages of the market, and not between parties operating in the same product market, it is not covered by the horizontal cooperation regime but may be covered by the verticals system or the Notice on subcontracting agreements.[66]

In Section 3.B.iii it is seen that production agreements, even those involving price-fixing, limiting production, or sharing markets or customers, will not restrict competition by object unless it operates as a disguised cartel. Nonetheless, production agreements can restrict competition by creating conditions which make it likely that competition between the parties will be limited, the parties will be able to coordinate their competitive behaviour as suppliers (facilitated because the agreement increases the commonality of costs or provides for exchanges of information), or that third parties will be anticompetitively foreclosed in spill-over markets (for example, downstream).

In Chapter 3.4.3, the Guidelines consider when a production agreement is likely to have restrictive effects, taking account of the characteristics of the market, the nature and market coverage of the cooperation, and the products concerned by the cooperation. Important factors include the parties' combined market shares, the degree of concentration in the market, whether the market is dynamic, the number of links between the parties, customer's ability to switch, and whether competitors may increase supply if prices increase.[67] Production agreements which also involve commercialisation functions, such as joint distribution or marketing, carry a higher risk of restrictive effects than pure joint production agreements, i.e. the closer to the consumer, the greater the risk for competition.[68]

Restrictive effects are unlikely if the parties are not competitors, if the production agreement gives rise to a new market (enabling the parties to launch a new product) or if the parties do not have market power in the market on which a restriction of competition is assessed (taking account of the individual and combined market share of the parties, the concentration ratio and number of players in the market, and dynamic and other factors affecting the market).[69]

B. THE APPLICATION OF ARTICLE 101(3)

(i) The Block Exemption for Specialisation Agreements

The Specialisation BER provides a safe harbour for three types of specialisation agreement. It is a less complex block exemption than the R&D BER, and does not contain 'conditions' or 'excluded restrictions'. In summary: Article 1 contains definitions; Article 2 sets out the core exemption for specialisation agreements; Articles 3 and 4 deal with market share thresholds; Article 5 contains the list of hardcore restraints; Articles 6 and 7 clarify that, as with the R&D BER, withdrawal of the benefit of the BER is possible pursuant to Article 29 of Regulation 1/2003; and Articles 8 and 9 contain final provisions (transitional periods and the duration of BER, until 30 June 2035).

[65] Ibid., 3.1. See e.g. COMP/26.437, *Jaz/Peter* [1969] OJ L195/5. Both parties manufactured clocks. Under the agreement, Jaz in France was to continue making only electric clocks and domestic alarm clocks and Peter in Germany was to make large mechanical alarm clocks. They agreed that they would each supply the other with their products and spare parts, that they could both sell the whole range of the products in their respective territories, and that they would not buy the products covered by the agreement from third parties. See also COMP/30.863, *ICI/BP* [1984] OJ L212/1.

[66] [1979] OJ C1/2, and Chap. 11.

[67] Similar factors are also relevant in the appraisal of horizontal mergers, see Chap. 15.

[68] Guidelines, para. 239.

[69] Ibid., para. 227.

Articles 1 and 2 make it clear that the block exemption covers agreements concerning the manufacture of goods or the preparation of services: unilateral specialisation agreements, reciprocal specialisation agreements, and joint production agreements. Further that the terms undertaking and party include their relevant connected undertakings (Article 1(2)). The block exemption only applies to unilateral and reciprocal specialisation agreements which include obligations on the non-producing party to purchase the products from the other (unilateral) and on both parties to purchase from each other (reciprocal). IPR licensing and assignment provisions are covered by the exemption, but only to the extent that they are ancillary to a specialisation agreement. If they are the primary object then the regime governing technology transfer, not specialisation, applies.[70] The exemption also applies where the purchase or supply obligations are exclusive and where the agreement provides for joint distribution.

Article 1—Definitions

1. For the purposes of this Regulation, the following definitions shall apply:

(1) 'specialisation agreement' means a unilateral specialisation agreement, a reciprocal specialisation agreement or a joint production agreement;

(a) 'unilateral specialisation agreement' means an agreement between two or more parties which are active on the same product market and under which one or more parties agree to fully or partly cease production of certain products or to refrain from producing those products and to purchase them from another party or parties, which agree to produce and supply them;

(b) 'reciprocal specialisation agreement' means an agreement between two or more parties which are active on the same product market and under which two or more parties, on a reciprocal basis, agree to fully or partly cease or refrain from producing certain but different products and to purchase those products from one or more of the other parties, which agree to produce and supply them;

(c) 'joint production agreement' means an agreement by virtue of which two or more parties agree to produce certain products jointly;

. . .

(4) 'production' means the manufacture of goods or the preparation of services, including by way of subcontracting;

(5) 'preparation of services' means activities carried out upstream of the provision of services to customers;

(6) 'specialisation product' means a product which is produced under a specialisation agreement;

(7) 'downstream product' means a product for which a specialisation product is used as an input by one or more of the parties and which is sold by those parties on the market;

(8) 'relevant market' means the relevant product and geographic market to which the specialisation products belong, and, in addition, where the specialisation products are intermediary products that are fully or partly used captively by one or more of the parties as inputs for the production of downstream products, the relevant product and geographic market to which the downstream products belong ;

[70] See Chap. 12.

(9) 'competing undertaking' means an actual or potential competitor:

(a) 'actual competitor' means an undertaking that is active on the same relevant market;

(b) 'potential competitor' means an undertaking that, in the absence of the specialisation agreement, would, on realistic grounds and not just as a mere theoretical possibility, be likely to undertake, within not more than 3 years, the necessary additional investments or other necessary costs to enter the relevant market;

. . .

Article 2—Exemption

1. Pursuant to Article 101(3) of the Treaty, and subject to the provisions of this Regulation, Article 101(1) of the Treaty shall not apply to specialisation agreements.
2. The exemption provided for in paragraph 1 shall apply to the extent that such agreements contain restrictions of competition falling within the scope of Article 101(1) of the Treaty.
3. The exemption provided for in paragraph 1 shall also apply to specialisation agreements which include provisions on the assignment or licensing of intellectual property rights to one or more of the parties, provided that those provisions are directly related to and necessary for the implementation of the agreement and do not constitute the primary object of the agreement.
4. The exemption provided for in paragraph 1 shall also apply to specialisation agreements whereby:

   (a) the parties accept an exclusive purchase or an exclusive supply obligation, or

   (b) the parties jointly distribute the specialisation products.

Article 3 sets the market share threshold at 20 per cent, Article 4 provides guidance on assessing market shares, and Article 5 prohibits certain hardcore restraints: price-fixing and limiting sales or output, subject to exceptions, and market or customer allocation.

Article 3—Market share threshold

1. The exemption provided for in Article 2 shall apply on condition that the combined market share of the parties does not exceed 20 % on the relevant market(s) to which the specialisation products belong.
2. Where the specialisation products are intermediary products that are fully or partly used captively by one or more of the parties as inputs for the production of downstream products, which they also sell, the exemption established in Article 2 shall only apply if both of the following conditions are fulfilled:

   (a) the parties' combined market share does not exceed 20 % on the relevant market(s) to which the specialisation products belong, and

   (b) the parties' combined market share does not exceed 20 % on the relevant market(s) to which the downstream products belong.

. . .

Article 5—Hardcore Restrictions

The exemption provided for in Article 2 shall not apply to specialisation agreements which, directly or indirectly, in isolation or in combination with other factors under the control of the parties, have as their object any of the following:

(a) the fixing of prices when selling the specialisation products to third parties, with the exception of the fixing of prices charged to immediate customers in the context of joint distribution;

(b) the limitation of output or sales, with the exception of:

(i) provisions on the agreed amount of products in the context of unilateral or reciprocal specialisation agreements;

(ii) provisions on setting capacity and production volumes in the context of a joint production agreement;

(iii) the setting of sales targets in the context of joint distribution;

(c) the allocation of markets or customers.

(ii) The Individual Application of Article 101(3)

Production agreements can provide efficiency gains in the form of costs savings or better production technologies by: enabling the undertakings to improve product quality, increase product variety, improve production techniques, launch new products (including sustainable ones), produce at, and pass on, lower costs; and incentivising and enabling undertakings to adapt their production capacities to a sudden change in demand and to address shortages and disruptions in the supply chain in critical sectors of the economy.[71] They may therefore satisfy the conditions of Article 101(3) even if the BER does not apply. However, restrictions on the parties' competitive conduct outside the cooperation and joint setting of prices (in relation to agreements which does not involve joint commercialisation) are not normally considered indispensable.[72]

The elimination of competition must be considered not only in respect of a substantial part of the products in question but also in relation to any possible spill-over markets.[73] High market shares are not necessarily a bar to Article 101(3) exemption, see, for example, *BPCL/ICI*,[74] *Philips/Osram*,[75] and *GEAE/P&W*.[76]

The Guidelines also provide additional guidance on mobile infrastructure-sharing agreements and illustrate the possible application of Article 101 to production agreements in a series of examples.[77]

6. PURCHASING AGREEMENTS

A. ANALYSIS OF JOINT PURCHASING UNDER ARTICLE 101

Joint purchasing agreements, involving the pooling of purchasing, carried out through a jointly controlled or owned company, a cooperative, or a contractual or other looser forms of cooperation, are found in a variety of economic sectors. They may also provide for additional activities, such as joint transport, quality control, and warehousing, and are generally aimed at creating buying power

[71] Guidelines, 3.5. [72] Ibid., 3.5.2. [73] Ibid., 3.5.4.

[74] COMP/30.863 [1984] OJ L212/1 (petroleum plastics). [75] COMP/34.252 [1994] OJ L378/37 (lead glass).

[76] COMP/36.213 [2000] OJ L58/16 (aircraft engines).

[77] Guidelines, 3.6 and 3.7 and e.g. AT.40.305, *Network sharing between O2 CZ/CETIN and T-Mobile CZ in the Czech Republic*.

vis-à-vis large suppliers.[78] They can lead to lower prices or more variety or better-quality products being passed on to consumers and avoid disruption in the supply chain. Not only does the joint purchasing agreement itself have to be appraised for compatibility with Article 101, but vertical agreements concluded by the joint purchasers both with their suppliers and the individual members must also be scrutinised.[79]

Joint purchasing agreements may affect two markets, both the market(s) on which the joint purchasers buy (the purchasing, or procurement, market) and the downstream market(s) on which they sell. Markets must thus be defined for purchasing (where substitutability has to be defined from the supply side) and for downstream selling market (if the joint purchasers are competitors there).[80]

It is seen in Chapter 9 that joint purchasing arrangements are to be distinguished from buyer cartels which restrict competition by object. Although this leaves a difficult, and arguably indistinct, line to be drawn between unlawful purchasing cartels and potentially beneficial purchasing cooperation agreements,[81] the actual or likely effects of the latter must ordinarily be assessed. The arrangements are less likely to give rise to anti-competitive effects in the purchasing or selling markets when the parties do not have market power and the restraints are limited to what is objectively necessary to ensure the arrangement's proper functioning.[82] Indeed, the Guidelines state that a restriction on competition is unlikely where the parties do not exceed a combined 15 per cent market share on the purchasing market(s) as well as a combined market share of 15 per cent on the selling market(s). These are not absolute thresholds and market shares above these will not necessarily mean a restriction of competition will be found.[83]

Where parties have buyer power, there is a risk that their agreement may harm competition upstream and, ultimately, cause competitive harm to consumers further downstream, foreclose competing purchase from the purchasing market by limiting their access to efficient suppliers, or reduce competition downstream (if they are competitors in the downstream market) through facilitating collusion.[84]

Although there is no block exemption in respect of joint purchasing, Chapter 4.3 of the Guidelines discusses the application of Article 101(3) to joint purchasing arrangements before providing specific examples of how Article 101 applies to certain agreements (Chapter 4.4). The Guidelines recognise that such agreements give rise to significant scope for efficiency gains, for example through cost saving (from lower purchase prices), economies of scale (from reduced transaction, transportation, and storage costs), and facilitating qualitative efficiency gains (by encouraging suppliers to innovate and introduce new or improved products), which may be passed on to consumers (perhaps through lower selling prices). The Guidelines recognise that in exceptional circumstances an obligation to purchase exclusively through cooperation may be indispensable to realise economies of scale.

B. CASES ON JOINT PURCHASING

Gøttrup-Klim,[85] discussed in Chapter 5, concerned joint purchasing of farming supplies such as fertilisers by a Danish cooperative association (DLG) on behalf of its members. The case arose following a challenge to DLG's rules, which precluded its members from belonging to any competing cooperative. The CJ held that the rules were not caught by Article 101(1) if they were necessary to ensure the proper functioning of the cooperative as a significant counterweight to the large multinational suppliers.

[78] Guidelines, 4.1, see further Chap. 9. [79] Ibid. and see Chap. 11. [80] Ibid., 4.2.3.

[81] See Chap. 9 and e.g. T. Kuhn and M. Rust, 'New Horizontal Guidelines and Block Exemptions—Four Chances for Improved Guidance' (2021) 42(5) *ECLR* 239, 241–243 (arguing that, especially given Commission and NCA willingness to pursue purchasing cartels, greater guidance on the distinction needs to be provided and e.g. questioning whether a secrecy requirement is really relevant to the assessment).

[82] Guidelines, 4.2.3. [83] Ibid., paras. 291–292. [84] Ibid., 4.2.3.2 and 4.2.3.3.

[85] Case C-250/92, EU:C:1994:413.

In *Métropole Télévision*,[86] the Commission dealt with a joint purchasing agreement in respect of television rights to sporting events. It concerned the European Broadcasting Union (EBU), an association of radio and television organisations established in 1950, which exchanged programmes amongst members through Eurovision. To become an active member, a broadcasting organisation had to satisfy certain conditions, inter alia, as to its national coverage and the nature and financing of programmes. Métropole applied to become a member six times but its application was rejected each time. This battle between Métropole and the EBU surfaced several times before the EU Courts. In this case, Métropole complained about EBU practices concerning the acquisition of TV rights to sporting events and challenged the Commission's exemption of its rules.[87] The GC annulled the decision on the ground that the Commission had not established that the final condition of Article 101(3) was satisfied.[88]

Cases T-185, 216, 299, and 300/00, *Métropole Télévision SA (M6) and others v Commission* [2002] ECR II-3805

The rules in question concerned granting access to Eurovision rights for pay-TV. The rules provided a 'sub-licensing scheme' which granted access to Eurovision rights to major sporting events to third parties who were competitors of EBU members. The Commission exempted EBU's rules for the sharing of jointly acquired sports TV rights on the grounds that the sub-licensing scheme guaranteed access to competitors and therefore avoided the elimination of competition in the market. The Commission did not settle on an exact definition of the market but contended that even on the basis of the narrowest possible definition (the acquisition of rights for a specific event such as the Football World Cup or the Summer Olympics) there was no elimination of competition. The GC accepted that the Commission's assertion that the market could consist entirely of major sporting events did not affect the analysis of whether Article 101(3) was satisfied. It then turned to consider whether in making that analysis the Commission had made a manifest error of assessment.

General Court

63. As regards the effects of the Eurovision system on competition, the contested decision shows (paragraphs 71 to 80) that there are two types of restrictions. First, the joint acquisition of television rights to sporting events, their sharing and the exchange of signal restricts or even eliminates competition among EBU members which are competitors on both the upstream market, for the acquisition of rights, and for the downstream market, for televised transmission of sporting events. In addition, that system gives rise to restrictions on competition as regards third parties since those rights, as set

[86] COMP/32.150 [2000] OJ L151/18 and Cases T-185, 216, 299, and 300/00, *Métropole Télévision SA (M6) and others v Commission* EU:T:2002:242.

[87] COMP/32.150 [2000] OJ L151/18. It had successfully challenged exemption of the preceding EBU rules, COMP/32.150 [1993] OJ L179/23 and Cases T-528, 542, 543, and 546/93, *Métropole Télévision SA v Commission* EU:T:1996:99.

[88] Other cases and decisions on joint purchasing include *National Sulphuric Acid Association* [1980] OJ L260/24 (Art. 101(3) applied after agreement amended) and COMP/27.958, *National Sulphuric Acid Association* [1989] OJ L190/22; Case 61/80, *Coöperatieve Stremsel- en Kleursfabriek v Commission* EU:C:1981:75 (the appeal from COMP/29.011, *Rennet* 5 December 1979) where the obligation of a group of over 90% of Dutch dairy producers to buy rennet exclusively from a cooperative was held to infringe Art. 101(1) and not satisfy Art. 101(3). See also Chap. 9.

out in paragraph 75 of the contested decision, are generally sold on an exclusive basis, so that EBU non-members would not in principle have access to them.

64. While it is true that the purchase of televised transmission rights for an event is not in itself a restriction on competition likely to fall under Article [101(1)] and may be justified by particular characteristics of the product and the market in question, the exercise of those rights in a specific legal and economic context may none the less lead to such a restriction (see, by analogy, Case 262/101 *Coditel v Ciné-Vog Films* . . . paragraphs 15 to 17).

65. In that vein, the Commission states, in paragraph 45 of the contested decision, that 'the acquisition of exclusive TV rights to certain major sporting events has a strong impact on the downstream television markets in which the sporting events are broadcast'.

66. In addition, it appears from the analysis of the documents in the case and the arguments of the parties that the acquisition of transmission rights to a major international sporting event such as the Olympics or the football World Cup cannot fail to affect strongly the market in sponsorship and advertising, which is the main source of revenue for television channels which broadcast free-to-air, since those programmes attract a very wide audience.

67. Moreover, as pointed out by SIC, the effects which restrict competition for third parties as a result of the Eurovision system are accentuated, first, by the level of vertical integration of the EBU and its members, which are not merely purchasers of rights but also television operators which broadcast the rights purchased, and second, by the geographic extent of the EBU, whose members broadcast in all the countries of the European Union. As a result, when the EBU acquires transmission rights for an international sporting event, the access to that event is in principle automatically precluded for all non-member operators. By contrast, the situation appears to be different when the transmission rights for sporting events are acquired by an agency which buys those rights in order to resell them, or when they are bought by a media group which only has operators in certain Member States, since that group will tend to enter into negotiations with operators in other Member States in order to sell those rights. In that case, despite the exclusive purchase of the rights, other operators still have the opportunity to negotiate their acquisition for their respective markets.

68. In light of those facts—that is, the structure of the market, the position of the EBU in the market for certain international sporting events and the level of vertical integration of the EBU and its members—there is reason to determine whether the scheme for third-party access to the Eurovision system makes it possible to counterbalance the restrictions on competition affecting those third parties and thus to avoid their exclusion from competition.

. . .

73. However, even if it proves necessary, for reasons linked to exclusive transmission rights for sporting events and the guarantee of their economic value (see paragraph 60 above), for EBU members to reserve for themselves live transmission of the programmes acquired by the EBU, none of these reasons justifies their being able to extend that right to all the competitions which are part of the same event, even when they do not intend to broadcast all those competitions live.

. . .

83. All the information provided to the [General Court] thus goes to show that, contrary to what the Commission concludes in the contested decision, the sub-licensing scheme does not guarantee competitors of EBU members sufficient access to rights to transmit sporting events held by the latter on the basis of their participation in that purchasing association. Apart from a few exceptions, nothing in the rules or mode of implementation of the scheme enables competitors of EBU members to obtain sub-licences for the live broadcast of unused Eurovision rights. In reality, the scheme merely permits the acquisition of sub-licences to transmit roundups of competitions under extremely restrictive conditions.

7. COMMERCIALISATION AGREEMENTS

Although there is limited jurisprudence on commercialisation agreements, involving cooperation between competitors in the selling, distribution, or promotion of their substitute products, Chapter 5 of the Guidelines sets out how the Commission analyses them under Article 101. Such agreements cover a wide spectrum of agreements, from joint selling agreements to more limited agreements addressing one specific commercialisation function, such as distribution (covered by the verticals regime unless between competitors), after-sales service, or advertising.[89] Where the commercialisation is related to another type of cooperation upstream, for example joint production or purchasing, the centre of gravity of the agreement must be determined and the analysis conducted accordingly.[90]

The main competition concerns relating to commercialisation agreements are that they may: lead to price-fixing or output limitations; allow the parties to allocate markets or customers; or facilitate collusion (for example, if they increase the parties' commonality of variable costs or involve the exchange of sensitive commercial information, such as in relation to marketing strategy or pricing). In particular, commercialisation agreements may restrict competition by object where they involve price-fixing, output limitations, or market partitioning (for example, price-fixing may result from commercialisation agreements purely limited to joint selling, see further Chapter 9).[91]

In other cases, restrictive effects will need to be appraised. Of particular importance to that assessment is the competitive relationship between the parties in relevant markets directly concerned by the agreement and in neighbouring (horizontally or vertically-related) markets. As with other horizontal cooperation agreements, anti-competitive effects are more likely where the parties have some degree of market power.[92] 'In addition, under a commercialisation agreement, the parties pool (part of) their market-related activities, namely activities that have a direct impact on their customers. This direct impact on customers increases the risk that commercialisation agreements may lead to anti-competitive effects.'[93] An agreement may not, however, give rise to competition concerns if market power is lacking (unlikely if the parties to the agreement have a combined market share not exceeding 15 per cent in the market in which they jointly commercialise the contractual products).[94]

As with joint purchasing, there is no block exemption on commercialisation. The Guidelines[95] recognise, however, that commercialisation may generate efficiency gains which may be passed on to consumers in the form of lower prices or better product quality or variety, for example through cost savings resulting from integration of economic activities,[96] integration of marketing functions, or economies of scale or scope. 'However, if the joint commercialisation consists of no more than a sales agency without any investment, it is unlikely to fulfil the conditions of Article 101(3).'[97] 'The question of indispensability is especially important for agreements that involve price fixing or market partitioning, which can only under exceptional circumstances be considered indispensable.'[98]

[89] Guidelines, 5.1. [90] See n. 46 and text. [91] Guidelines, 5.2.1–5.2.2. [92] Ibid., 5.2.3.
[93] Ibid., para. 335. [94] Ibid., paras. 339–340. [95] Ibid., 5.3.1–5.3.2.
[96] Ibid., para. 381 (the efficiency gains must not be savings which result only from the elimination of costs that are inherently part of competition, but must result from the integration of economic activities. A reduction of transport cost which is only a result of customer allocation without any integration of the logistical system can therefore not be regarded as an efficiency gain within the meaning of Art. 101(3)).
[97] Ibid., para. 343. [98] Ibid., para. 344.

Joint selling is often used in relation to media rights to sporting events and in respect of rights to music and films.[99] Indeed, the Commission has examined cases involving the joint selling of commercial rights[100] to sporting events, particularly the collective selling of media rights by a football association or league on behalf of individual member football clubs. Broadly, in the latter situation it accepts that joint selling[101] may be beneficial in principle, especially to ensure the principle of solidarity in sport. The Commission generally accepts joint selling, however, only so long as certain conditions are satisfied (for example, that there is an open and transparent tender process, licences are granted for a limited duration, and the rights are broken into several packages to allow several competitors to acquire the rights, the so-called single buyer rule). The single buyer condition, however, has the result that viewers of sports channels often have to subscribe to more than one broadcaster in order to watch all the available matches in a particular league. In particular, in a decision concerning the sale of media rights to the UEFA[102] Champions League, the Commission stressed how valuable rights to screen football matches are.

> In most countries football is not only the driving force for the development of pay-TV services but is also an essential programme item for free-TV broadcasters. Joint selling of free-TV and pay-TV rights combined with wide exclusive terms therefore has significant effects on the structure of the TV broadcasting markets as it can enhance media concentration and hamper competition between broadcasters. If one broadcaster holds all or most of the relevant football TV rights in a Member State, it is extremely difficult for competing broadcasters to establish themselves successfully in that market.[103]

The Commission only exempted the arrangements following a lengthy negotiation and an agreement by UEFA to amend aspects of the arrangements.

Subsequently, the Commission adopted a commitments decision in respect of the German Bundesliga's joint selling of broadcasting rights,[104] which permitted joint selling on similar terms to those agreed in the *UEFA* case. The Bundesliga was to make several packages available to broadcasters and exclusivity was not to last longer than three years at a time. This was the first commitments decision taken under Article 9 of Regulation 1/2003.[105]

The Guidelines also contain a specific section on bidding consortia (as distinct from bid-rigging agreements, see further Chapter 9),[106] which recognises that such arrangements are unlikely to

[99] See e.g. COMP/30.566, *UIP* [1989] OJ L226/25 (discussed in Chap. 9) and COMP/38.698, *CISAC* 16 July 2008, largely annulled, Case T-442/08, *International Confederation of Societies of Authors and Composers (CISAC) v Commission* EU:T:2013:188, discussed in Chaps. 5, 9, and 12.

[100] Media rights (radio, television, internet, and UMTS), sponsorship, suppliership, licensing, and IPRs, see e.g. J. Faull and A. Nikpay (eds.), *The EU Law of Competition* (3rd edn, Oxford University Press, 2014), 14.63–14.69. It has also been concerned with the arrangements for selling tickets for sporting events, see e.g. cases relating to, respectively, tickets sales for the 1990, 1998, and 2006 World Cups, e.g. COMP/33.384 and COMP/33.378, *The Distribution of Package Tours During the 1990 World Cup* [1992] OJ L326/31, COMP/36.888, *1998 World Cup Finals* [2000] OJ L5/55, and COMP/39.177, *Which?/DFB/+Mastercard/+FIFA*, IP/05/519.

[101] The consequences of football media rights being sold by individual clubs can be seen by looking at the position in Spain, where the rights are not sold collectively, and La Liga is dominated by two clubs. This is not to suggest that money is the only reason for Barcelona's success.

[102] An association of national football associations and the regulatory authority of European football.

[103] *Joint selling of the commercial rights of the UEFA Champions League* [2003] OJ L291/25, para. 20.

[104] COMP/37.214, *DFB* 19 January 2005. See also COMP/38.173, *Joint Selling of the Media Rights to the FA Premier League* 22 March 2006.

[105] See further Chap. 13.

[106] Guidelines, 5.4.

restrict competition if they allow the undertakings to participate in projects that they would not be able to undertake individually (where the parties are not competitors for the tender).[107] Chapter 5.5 sets out examples of how joint commercialisation agreements are to be analysed.

8. STANDARDISATION AGREEMENTS AND STANDARD-SETTING

Standardisation agreements, which 'have as their primary objective the definition of technical or quality requirements, with which current or future products, production processes, value chain due diligence processes, services or methods may comply'[108] are dealt with in Chapter 7 of the Guidelines. Sustainability standards, although having similarities, are discussed in a separate section on sustainability agreements.

Four relevant markets may be affected by a standardisation agreement: (a) that for the product(s) or service(s) to which the standard(s) relate; (b) the relevant technology market, if the standard-setting involves the selection of technology and IPRs are marketed separately from the products to which they relate; (c) the market for standard development (if different standard development organisations (SDOs) or agreements exist); and (d) a distinct market for testing and certification.[109]

Standardisation agreements usually have positive economic effects, promoting economic interpenetration on the internal market, encouraging the development of new and improved products and competition, and improved supply conditions.[110] They may be completed between producers of complementary goods or services and/or competitors and frequently involve intellectual property rights (IPRs). For example, standards involving IPRs are usually developed by undertakings that develop and market technologies, undertakings that manufacture products or services based on developed technologies, and integrated undertakings that both develop technology protected by IPR and sell products based on it (for which they would need a licence).

Where between competitors, standard-setting arrangements may reduce price competition, or limit or control production, markets, innovation, or technical development, for example, through foreclosing innovate technologies or by preventing certain undertakings from gaining effective access to the standard (whether they are prevented from obtaining access entirely or granted access only on prohibitive of discriminatory terms).[111]

Standard-setting arrangements may restrict competition by object if used as part of a broader restrictive agreement aimed at excluding actual or potential competitors or technologies,[112] or if they influence prices charged to customers.[113]

In other cases, an analysis of actual or likely effects is required. Restrictive effects are unlikely where market power is absent, for example because there is competition between a number of voluntary standards. In *EMC v Commission*,[114] the GC also affirmed the principle that a standard-setting

[107] Ibid., and Chap. 9.

[108] Ibid., para. 436. Standardisation can range from the adoption of consensus standards by the recognised European or national standards bodies, through consortia or fora, to agreements between independent companies (ibid., fn. 306).

[109] Ibid., para. 438. [110] Ibid., 7.3.1. [111] Ibid.

[112] As in COMP/35.691, *Pre-Insulated Pipe Cartel* [1999] OJ L24/1, para. 147. In Cases 96/82 etc., *IAZ v Commission* EU:C:1983:310 it was held that the agreement between Belgian water companies and Belgian washing-machine and dishwasher manufacturers in respect of conformity standards partitioned the market in excluding imports.

[113] Guidelines, 7.3.2.

[114] Case T-432/05, EU:T:2010:189, appeal dismissed by Order, Case C-367/10, EU:C:2011:203.

agreement would not infringe Article 101(1) if the standard-setting was non-discriminatory, open, and transparent. Thus, even where the standard development agreement risks creating market power, the Commission states that it will normally fall outside Article 101(1) where certain conditions set out in paragraphs 451–457 of the Guidelines are satisfied.

Horizontal Cooperation Guidelines

451. Where participation in standard development is unrestricted and the procedure for adopting the standard in question is transparent, standardisation agreements which contain no obligation to comply[322] with the standard and which provide effective access to the standard on FRAND terms will generally not restrict competition within the meaning of Article 101(1).

452. In particular, to ensure unrestricted participation, the rules of the SDO should provide that all competitors in the market or markets affected by the standard can participate in the process leading to the selection of the standard.[323] The SDO should also provide objective and non-discriminatory procedures for allocating voting rights, as well as, if relevant, objective criteria for selecting the technology to be included in the standard.

453. With respect to transparency, the relevant SDO should have procedures which allow stakeholders to effectively inform themselves of upcoming, on-going and finalised standardisation work in good time at each stage of the development of the standard.

454. Furthermore, the SDO's rules should ensure effective access to the standard on FRAND terms.[324]

455. Where an SDO develops standards involving IPR, a clear and balanced IPR policy,[325] adapted to the particular industry and the needs of the organisation in question, increases the likelihood that the implementers of the standards will be granted effective access.

456. In order to ensure effective access to the standard, the IPR policy should require participants wishing to have their IPR included in the standard to provide an irrevocable commitment in writing to offer to license their essential IPR to all third parties on FRAND terms ('FRAND commitment').[326] That commitment should be given prior to the adoption of the standard. At the same time, the IPR policy should allow IPR holders to exclude specified technology from the standard development process and thereby from the FRAND commitment, provided that exclusion takes place at an early stage in the development of the standard. To ensure the effectiveness of the FRAND commitment, there should also be a requirement for all participating IPR holders who provide such a commitment to ensure that any undertaking to which the IPR owner transfers its IPR (including the right to license that IPR) is bound by that commitment, for example through a contractual clause between buyer and seller. It should be noted that FRAND can also cover royalty-free licensing.

457. Moreover, the IPR policy should require good faith disclosure by participants of their IPR that may be essential for the implementation of the standard under development.[327] This is relevant to (a) enable the industry to make an informed choice of the technology to be included in a standard[328] and (b) achieve the goal of effective access to the standard. As the standard develops, the disclosure could be updated based on reasonable endeavours to identify IPR reading on the (future) standard. With respect to patents, the IPR disclosure should include at least the patent number or patent application number. If this information is not yet publicly available, then it is also sufficient if the participant declares that it is likely to have IPR claims over a particular technology, without identifying specific IPR claims or applications for IPR (so-called blanket disclosure).[329] Participants should also be encouraged to update their disclosures at the time of adoption of a standard, in particular if there are any changes which may have an impact on the essentiality or validity of their IPRs. Since the risks relating to effective access

are not the same in the case of an SDO with a royalty-free standards policy,[330] IPR disclosure would not be relevant in that context.

322. See also paragraph 464 in this regard.

323. Unrestricted participation should cover participation in all the steps of the process, including participation in the preparatory phase to the standardisation process within the SDO, such as in the context of SDO specific special interest groups.

324. For example, effective access should be granted to the specification of the standard.

325. As specified in paragraphs 456 and 457. See also the Communication from the Commission to the European Parliament, the Council and the European Economic and Social Committee Setting out the EU approach to Standard Essential Patents ('Communication on Standard Essential Patents') (COM/2017/0712 final).

326. See judgment of 16 July 2015, *Huawei Technologies Co. Ltd v ZTE Corp. and ZTE Deutschland GmbH*, C-170/13, EU:C:2015:477, paragraph 53: ' . . . See also Commission Decision in Case AT.39985 - *Motorola - Enforcement of GPRS standard essential patents*, paragraph 417: *'In view of the standardisation process that led to the adoption of the GPRS standard and Motorola's voluntary commitment to license the Cudak SEP on FRAND terms and conditions, implementers of the GPRS standard have a legitimate expectation that Motorola will grant them a licence over that SEP, provided they are not unwilling to enter into a licence on FRAND terms and conditions'.*

327. To obtain the desired result, good faith disclosure does not need to go as far as to require participants to compare their IPR against the potential standard and issue a statement positively concluding that they have no IPR reading on the potential standard.

328. Conversely, a 'patent ambush' occurs when an undertaking taking part in the standard-development process intentionally hides the fact that it holds essential patents over the standard being developed, and starts asserting such patents only after the standard has been agreed and other undertakings are therefore "locked in" to using it. When a 'patent ambush' occurs during the standard development process, this undermines confidence in the process, given that an effective standard development process is a precondition to technical development and the development of the market in general to the benefit of consumers. See, for example, Commission Decision of 9 December 2009 in Case COMP/38.636 – *RAMBUS*, OJ C 30, 6.2.2010, p. 17.

329. Participants should be encouraged to complete their earlier blanket disclosure with the patent number and/or patent application numbers when that information becomes publicly available.

330. The same would apply where the organisation applies a licensing policy based on a one-off nominal fee.

FRAND commitments are thus designed to ensure that standard-essential technology is available to users on FRAND terms, although compliance with Article 101 is not dependent on proof of compliance with the FRAND commitment by members. In Chapter 7, however, it is seen that the establishment of a standard can, in certain circumstances, increase the market power of IPR holders. Where a dominant position is held, IPR holders will have to ensure not only that their conduct complies with the standard-setting agreement but also that the conduct does not constitute an abuse of its dominant position. Chapter 7 considers the extent to which the holder of a standard-essential patent may abuse a dominant position through, for example. Patent ambushes, seeking injunctions, or licensing terms.[115]

Agreements which do not comply with the principles outlined in the Guidelines, do not necessarily infringe Article 101. Rather, a self-assessment is required to establish whether they do fall within Article 101(1) and, if so, whether Article 101(3) is satisfied.[116] The following considerations are likely to be relevant to the Article 101(1) appraisal: the market shares in relation to the goods, services, or technologies based on the standard and whether: the standard is voluntary (and what its scope is); access to the standard is available to all members or third parties; there is open participation in the

[115] See also Guidelines, paras. 458–461.

[116] Ibid., para. 450.

development of the standard; the standard development agreement discriminates against any participating or potential members; and there is *ex ante* disclosure of royalty rates.[117]

Although there is no block exemption for standardisation agreements, Chapter 7.4 of the Guidelines recognises their considerable scope to achieve efficiencies to the benefit of consumers[118] through, for example: the creation of Union-wide standards which may facilitate market integration and allow companies to market their goods and services in all Member States; increasing consumer choice and decreasing prices; establishing technical interoperability and compatibility; reducing transaction costs for sellers and buyers; facilitating consumer choice and increasing product quality; reducing the time taken to bring a new technology to the market; and facilitating innovation by allowing companies to build on top of agreed solutions.[119] The Guidelines set out important information relating to the indispensability requirement:

> 481. Participation in standard development should generally be open to all competitors in the market or markets affected by the standard unless such participation would generate significant inefficiencies . . .
>
> 482. As a general rule standardisation agreements should cover no more than what is necessary to ensure their aims, whether this is technical interoperability and compatibility or a certain level of quality. In cases where having only one technological solution would benefit consumers or the economy at large, that standard should be set on a non-discriminatory basis. Technology-neutral standards can, in certain circumstances, lead to larger efficiency gains. Including substitute IPR . . . as essential parts of a standard while at the same time forcing the users of the standard to pay for more IPR than technically necessary would go beyond what is necessary to achieve any identified efficiency gains. In the same vein, including substitute IPR as essential parts of a standard and limiting the use of that technology to that particular standard (that is to say, exclusive use) could limit inter-technology competition and would not be necessary to achieve the efficiencies identified.
>
> 483. Restrictions in a standardisation agreement making a standard binding and obligatory for the industry are in principle not indispensable.
>
> 484. In a similar vein, standardisation agreements that entrust certain bodies with the exclusive right to test compliance with the standard go beyond the primary objective of defining the standard and may also restrict competition. The exclusivity can, however, be justified for a certain period of time, for example by the need to recoup significant start-up costs . . . The standardisation agreement should in that case include adequate safeguards to mitigate possible risks to competition resulting from exclusivity. This concerns, among others, the certification fee, which should be reasonable and proportionate to the cost of the compliance testing.

9. STANDARD TERMS

Chapter 8 of the Guidelines discusses standard terms and conditions of sale or purchase, which set conditions of sale or purchase between competitors and consumers and are frequently used in some industries (for example, banking). The effects of standard terms are felt on the downstream market where the companies using them compete for customers and may restrict prices, limit product choice and innovation, or affect commercial conditions.[120] Where access to the standard terms is not open for anyone to use, they may also foreclose new entrants.

[117] Ibid., 7.3.3.2.

[118] Ibid., para. 485 ('where standards facilitate technical interoperability and compatibility or competition between new and already existing products, services and processes, it can be presumed that the standard will benefit consumers').

[119] Ibid., para. 475. [120] Ibid., 8.1–8.3.

It is seen in Chapter 9 that standard terms may restrict competition by object where they reinforce cartel activities, influence prices charged to customers, or relate to important secondary aspects of competition with economic value. They may also restrict competition by object, where aimed at excluding competitors.[121]

In other cases, the Guidelines indicate that restrictive effects are unlikely if participation in the establishment of standard terms is unrestricted and the terms are non-binding and effectively accessible for anyone.[122] The position may be different, however, if the terms define the scope of the product sold (creating a risk of limiting product choice) or where they become a *de facto* standard.

As far as the application of Article 101(3) is concerned, the Commission view is that such agreements can entail economic benefits for consumers[123] through: making it easier for customers to compare the conditions offered and thus facilitating switching between companies; leading to savings in transaction costs; facilitating entry; and increasing legal certainty for the contract parties.[124] 'The higher the number of competitors on the market, the greater the efficiency gain of facilitating the comparison of conditions offered.'[125] The Guidelines stress that agreements which make standard terms binding and obligatory are, generally, not indispensable to the achievement of efficiency gains. Given that the risk of restrictive effects on competition and the likelihood of efficiency gains increase with the companies' market shares and the extent to which the standard terms are used, the Guidelines states that it is not possible to provide any general 'safe harbour' for standard agreements 'within which there is no risk of restrictive effects on competition or which would allow the presumption that efficiency gains will be passed on to consumers to an extent that outweighs the restrictive effects on competition.'[126]

10. SUSTAINABILITY AGREEMENTS

It is seen in previous chapters that an important debate surrounds the question of how EU competition, sustainability, and Green Deal policies interact and the extent to which competition law can address market, and regulatory, failures and complement regulation in this sphere.[127] Indeed, in the context of Article 101, increasing attention has been focused on the question of whether, and if so when, agreements between competitors pursuing one or more sustainability objective (such as reducing greenhouse gas emissions, eliminating pollution, reducing waste, or ensuring animal welfare[128]) are compatible with Article 101. The 2010 Horizontal Cooperation Guidelines provided limited guidance on this matter, leading to complaints that the lack of clarity was discouraging businesses from concluding beneficial sustainability agreements, which are urgently required.[129] To address this gap, the Guidelines now devote an entire chapter (Chapter 9) to the appraisal of sustainability agreements and some worked examples of how Article 101 applies in different scenarios.

[121] See COMP/29.995, *Anseau* [1982] OJ L167/39; on appeal Case 96/82, *IAZ International Belgium NV v Commission* EU:C:1983:310 and ibid., 8.3.2.

[122] Ibid., para. 499. [123] Ibid., 8.4. [124] Ibid. [125] Ibid., para. 507. [126] Ibid., para. 509.

[127] See especially Chaps. 1 and 5 and e.g. E. Loozen, 'Strict Competition Enforcement and Welfare: A Constitutional Perspective Based on Article 101 TFEU and Sustainability' (2019) 56 *CMLRev* 1265 and [2021] 3 *Competition Policy Brief* (Special Issue, Young Experts' Views on Greening of Competition Policy).

[128] The parties may e.g. agree to phase out, withdraw, or replace non-sustainable products and processes with sustainable ones, harmonise sustainable packing methods, or agree to adopt or to comply with sustainability standards, Guidelines, 9.3.2.1.

[129] Jurisprudence on this matter is limited, but see COMP/36.718, *CECED* [2000] OJ L187/47 (discussed in Chap. 5), COMP/34.493 *DSD* [2001] OJ L319/1, and *Eco-Emballages* [2001] OJ L233/37 and see Kuhn and Rust, n. 81. But see C. Veljanovski, 'The Case Against Green Antitrust' (2022) 18(3) *European Competition Journal* 501 and M. P. Schinkel and L. Treuren, 'Corporate Social Responsibility by Joint Agreement', Tinbergen Institute Discussion Paper TF 2001-063/VII (2021).

The Guidelines recognise that sustainability agreements may take a variety of different forms corresponding to those discussed in other chapters of the Guidelines (R&D, production, purchasing, standardisation, etc.).[130] Further, that although competition law generally contributes to sustainable development by driving competition and spurring innovation, horizontal cooperation may sometimes be required to overcome market and regulatory failures.[131]

Horizontal Cooperation Guidelines

518 Competition law enforcement contributes to sustainable development by ensuring effective competition, which spurs innovation, increases the quality and choice of products, ensures an efficient allocation of resources, reduces the costs of production, and thereby contributes to consumer welfare.

519. However, one concern related to sustainable development is that individual production and consumption decisions can have negative effects ('negative externalities'), for example on the environment, that are not sufficiently taken into account by the economic operators or consumers that cause them. This type of market failure can be mitigated or cured by collective action, primarily through public policies or (sector-specific) regulation, and secondarily through cooperation agreements between undertakings that promote sustainable production or consumption.

520. Where such market failures are addressed by appropriate regulation, for example, mandatory Union pollution standards, pricing mechanisms, such as the Unions Emissions Trading System ('ETS'), or taxes, additional measures by undertakings, for example through cooperation agreements, may be unnecessary. However, cooperation agreements may address residual market failures that are not or not fully addressed by public policies and regulations.

The Guidelines thus go on to try and clarify when sustainability agreements may be compatible with Article 101. They start by explaining that agreements will not raise competition concerns under Article 101 if they do not affect the main parameters of competition, for example because they do not relate to the economic activity of competitors but to their internal corporate conduct. Agreements on the creation of databases about suppliers or distributors with good sustainability practices (but which does not require dealing with them) or on the organisation of awareness campaigns are also unlikely to affect competition.[132]

In considering how Article 101(1) applies to other agreements, the Commission takes the view that, even though arguments have been raised to the contrary, agreements cannot escape the Article 101(1) prohibition solely because they are necessary to pursue a sustainability objective.[133] The Guidelines also clarify that in general Article 101(1) assessment should follow that relevant to the type of cooperation concerned (whether R&D or joint production, etc.), so, although the sustainability objective must be

[130] Companies may therefore collaborate to: establish an industry self-control; invest in joint development of sustainable technology or systems; or agree to replace or introduce new more sustainable products, for example by setting product standards or not producing unsustainable products, see Kuhn and Rust, n. 81. On 10 January 2023, the Commission also launched a public consultation on a draft proposal for guidelines on sustainability agreements in the agriculture sector pursuant to Art. 210a of Reg. 1308/2013 as amended by Reg. 2021/2117 (with the intention that the guidelines should be in place by 8 December 2023).

[131] See also discussion of Art. 101(3) in Chap. 5, Section 4. [132] Guidelines, 9.2.

[133] Ibid., para. 521, and see discussion in footnote 366 of e.g. the judgments in Case C-309/99, *Wouters v Algemene Raad van de Nederlandse Orde van Advocaten* EU:C:2002:98 and Case C-519/04 P, *Meca-Medina v Commission* EU:C:2006:492 and discussion on the cases in Chap. 5 and Kuhn and Rust, n. 81. See also [2021] 3 *Competition Policy Brief* (Special Issue, Young Experts' Views on Greening of Competition Policy), pp. 57–58 (why *Albany* should cover sustainability agreements).

taken into account in that assessment,[134] no distinct methodology for analysis applies. Nonetheless, Chapter 9 does contain some detailed discussion of sustainability standardisation agreements,[135] when they may restrict competition by object, how appreciable restrictive effects on competition are to be identified and when they may satisfy the Article 101(3) criteria. It also provides a soft safe harbour for agreements meeting certai conditions:

Horizontal Cooperation Guidelines, para. 549

First, the procedure for developing the sustainability standard must be transparent,and all interested competitors must be able to participate in the process leading to the selection of the standard . . .

Second, the sustainability standard must not impose on undertakings that do not wish to participate in the standard any direct or indirect obligation to comply with the standard . . .

Third, in order to ensure compliance with the standard, binding requirements can be imposed on the participating undertakings, but they must remain free to apply higher sustainability standards.

Fourth, the parties to the sustainability standard must not exchange commercially sensitive information that is not objectively necessary and proportionate for the development, implementation, adoption or modification of the standard.

Fifth, effective and non-discriminatory access to the outcome of the standard-setting process must be ensured. This includes allowing effective and non-discriminatory access to the requirements and conditions for using the agreed label, logo or brand name, and allowing undertakings that have not participated in the process of developing the standard to adopt the standard at a later stage. . . .

Sixth, the sustainability standard must satisfy at least one of the following two conditions:

(a) The standard must not lead to a significant increase in the price . . . or a significant reduction in the quality of the products concerned;

(b) The combined market share of the participating undertakings . . . must not exceed 20 % on any relevant market affected by the standard. . . .

If these conditions are not met, it must still be assessed whether the agreement appreciably restricts competition. However, given the risk of sustainability standardisation agreements infringing Article 101(1), a principal focus of the Guidelines is how Article 101(3) applies to sustainability agreements. It is seen in Chapter 5 that this is a controversial and contested issue—in particular, different approaches have been proposed as to how efficiencies are to be demonstrated and weighed (given that sustainable development is generally more expensive), and which consumers must benefit from a pass-on of those benefits.[136] It is also seen that although the Commission does not take as expansive approach to Article 101(3) as some NCAs, it recognises that sustainability benefits are often manifested in the form of broad qualitative or cost efficiencies.

558. Examples of efficiencies that can be generated by sustainability agreements include the use of less polluting production or distribution technologies, improved conditions of production and distribution, more resilient infrastructure, better quality products. Sustainability agreements can also reduce supply chain disruptions, shorten the time it takes to bring sustainable products to the market and enable consumers to make informed purchasing decisions by facilitating the comparison of products. These efficiency gains can contribute to a resilient internal market.

[134] Competition authorities in the EU will no doubt be vigilant for cartels masquerading as sustainability agreements and have brought proceedings against firms that have colluded in a way which harms sustainability goals, see Chap. 9.

[135] See n. 130.

[136] See especially, Chap. 5, Section 4.D, see also e.g. K. Coates and D. Middelschulte, 'Getting Consumer Welfare Right: The Competition Law Implications of Market-driven Sustainability Initiatives' (2019) 15(2)–(3) *European Competition Journal* 318.

559. Such efficiencies cannot simply be assumed; they must be capable of being substantiated. . . . They also need to be objective, concrete and verifiable. . . . For instance, if the claimed efficiency consists of a product improvement, the parties must be able to demonstrate the exact characteristics of the product improvement. If the claimed efficiency is the reduction of water contamination, the parties must be able to explain how exactly the agreement contributes to the reduction of water contamination and provide an estimate of the magnitude of the claimed benefit. . . .

Further, the Commission accepts that sustainability agreements may be indispensable to overcome negative externalities, reach a sustainability goal in a more cost-efficient way, or to overcome market failures, and deals with the difficult question of which consumers must receive a fair share of the claimed benefits. Importantly, the Commission sets out its view that consumers can benefit from a sustainability agreement not only through individual use value benefits (from the qualitative improvements in the product) but also through individual non-use value benefits (from their appreciation of the impact of their sustainable consumption on others); and collective benefits (as part of a larger group of beneficiaries). Thus, although insisting that consumers affected by the restriction of competition must benefit from the efficiencies, the Commission recognises that those benefits can be manifested in different ways. The Guidelines clarify what is meant by individual non-use value benefits and collective benefits.

Horizontal Cooperation Guidelines

9.4.3.2. Individual non-use value benefits

575. Consumer benefits from sustainability agreements may consist not only of direct benefits from the use of a sustainable product but also indirect benefits resulting from consumers' appreciation of the impact of their sustainable consumption on others. In particular, some consumers may value their consumption of a sustainable product more highly than the consumption of a non-sustainable product because the sustainable product has less negative impact on others.

576. For example, consumers may opt for a particular washing liquid not because it cleans better but because it contaminates the water less. Similarly, consumers may be willing to pay a higher price for furniture made from wood that is grown sustainably, not because of the better quality of the furniture but because they want to stop de-forestation and the loss of natural habitats. Likewise, drivers may opt to use more expensive fuel not because it is of higher quality and better for their vehicles, but because it pollutes less.

577. In these cases, the consumer's experience of the product is not directly improved. Nevertheless, consumers may be willing to pay a higher price for a sustainable product or to limit their choice of products (by not buying non-sustainable variants) in order to benefit society or future generations. Hence, indirect, non-use value benefits accrue to consumers within the relevant market via their individual valuation of the effect on others, including on non-users outside the relevant market.

. . .

9.4.3.3. Collective benefits

582. Section 9.4.3.2 refers to individual non-use value benefits that are limited to voluntary (altruistic) choices by individual consumers. However, not all negative externalities can be cured through voluntary, individual consumer actions. As the sustainability impact from individual consumption accrues not necessarily to the consuming individual but to a larger group, a joint initiative, such as a cooperation agreement, may be needed to internalise negative externalities and bring about sustainability benefits for a wider section of society.[405] For example, consumers may be unwilling to pay a higher

price for a product produced with a green but costly technology. To ensure that the benefits derived from the use of that technology materialise, an agreement to phase out the polluting technology may be necessary. These benefits are referred to as 'collective benefits', as they occur irrespective of the consumers' individual appreciation of the product and accrue to a wider section of society than just consumers in the relevant market.

583. Although the weighing of the positive and negative effects of the restrictive agreements is normally done within the relevant market to which the agreement relates, where two markets are related, efficiencies generated on separate markets can be taken into account, provided that the group of consumers that is affected by the restriction and that benefits from the efficiencies is substantially the same. . . .

584. By analogy, where consumers in the relevant market substantially overlap with, or form part of the group of beneficiaries outside the relevant market, the collective benefits to the consumers in the relevant market that occur outside that market can be taken into account if they are significant enough to compensate the consumers in the relevant market for the harm that they suffer. . . .

585. For example, drivers purchasing less polluting fuel are also citizens who would benefit from cleaner air, if less polluting fuel were used. To the extent that a substantial overlap of consumers (the drivers in this example) and the wider beneficiaries (citizens) can be established, the sustainability benefits of cleaner air can be taken into account, provided that they compensate the consumers in the relevant market for the harm suffered. Conversely, consumers may buy clothing made of sustainable cotton that reduces the use of fertilisers and water on the land where the cotton is cultivated. Such environmental benefits could in principle be taken into account as collective benefits. However, in this case there is unlikely to be any substantial overlap between the consumers of the clothing and the beneficiaries of the environmental benefits, as these occur only in the area where the cotton is grown. Therefore, it is unlikely that these collective benefits would accrue to the consumers in the relevant market. They could therefore only be taken into account if and to the extent that consumers of the clothing are willing to pay more for clothing that is made of sustainably grown cotton (individual non-value benefit, see Section 9.4.3.2).

586. For collective benefits to materialise, the market coverage of the agreement will often need to be significant. If, for example, only two out of ten washing machine producers agree to abandon their more polluting models, then it is unlikely that the agreement will be able to prevent free-riding (by washing machine producers continuing to offer more polluting models) and hence will be unlikely to sufficiently reduce pollution, since self-interested consumers could switch to polluting models produced by the remaining suppliers.[408]

587. For collective benefits to be taken into account, the parties to the agreement must be able to:

(a) describe clearly the claimed benefits and provide evidence that they have already occurred or are likely to occur;[409]

(b) define clearly the beneficiaries;

(c) demonstrate that the consumers in the relevant market substantially overlap with the beneficiaries or form part of them . . . ; and

(d) demonstrate that the share of the collective benefits that accrues to the consumers in the relevant market, possibly together with individual use and non-use value benefits accruing to those consumers, outweighs the harm suffered by those consumers as a result of the restriction.

588. Evidence for collective benefits contained in public authorities' reports or in reports prepared by recognized academic organisations may be of particular value for this assessment.

589. Where there is no available data that allows for a quantitative analysis of the benefits of the agreement, other evidence may be considered, provided that it shows a clearly identifiable positive impact on consumers in the relevant market, not a marginal one. As there is currently little experience with measuring and quantifying collective benefits, the Commission aims to provide more guidance on this issue when it has gained sufficient experience of dealing with concrete cases, which may enable it to develop methodologies of assessment.

11. CONCLUSIONS

1. The Commission's policy towards horizontal cooperation agreements, as reflected in the modernised Guidelines, is to take a realistic view, based on an economic analysis, of whether an agreement infringes Article 101. A consideration of market power is central to the inquiry. Analysis of horizontal cooperation agreements has now been brought more closely into line with that adopted in merger cases.

2. Given relatively limited jurisprudence in this sphere, the Guidelines are designed to provide clarity to undertakings that must generally self-assess their horizontal cooperation agreements for compatibility with Article 101. This is especially important in respect of operations where the scale of the overall cooperation and the resources involved may be very large and in relation to sustainability agreements where other guidance is very limited.

3. The Commission has sought, in the Guidelines, to ensure that EU competition, sustainability, and Green Deal policies work together and do not stand in the way of agreements pursuing sustainability objectives and which will produce efficiencies that are passed on to consumers.

12. FURTHER READING

A. Articles

BRODLEY, J., 'Joint Ventures and Antitrust Policy' (1982) 95 *Harvard LR* 1521

GERADIN, D., LAYNE-FARRAR, A., and PADILLA, A. J., 'Competing Away Market Power? An Economic Assessment of *Ex Ante* Auctions in Standard Setting' (2008) 4 *European Competition Journal* 443

KITCH, E., 'The Antitrust Economics of Joint Ventures' (1987) 54 *Antitrust LJ* 957

KUHN, T. and RUST, M., 'New Horizontal Guidelines and Block Exemptions—Four Chances for Improved Guidance' (2021) 42(5) *ECLR* 239

LOOZEN, E., 'Strict Competition Enforcement and Welfare: A Constitutional Perspective Based on Article 101 TFEU and Sustainability' (2019) 56 *CMLRev* 1265

SCHINKEL, M. P., and TREUREN, L., 'Corporate Social Responsibility by Joint Agreement', Tinbergen Institute Discussion Paper TF 2001-063/VII (2021)

VELJANOVSKI, C., 'The Case Against Green Antitrust' (2022) 18(3) *European Competition Journal* 501

WILBERT, S., 'Joint Selling of Bundesliga Media Rights—First Commission Decision Pursuant to Article 9 of Regulation 1/2003' (2005) 2 *Competition Policy Newsletter* 44

11

VERTICAL AGREEMENTS

1. CENTRAL ISSUES

1. Vertical agreements are concluded between firms which operate at different levels of the production and supply chain. The parties thus produce complementary, not competing, products or services.
2. In 1999, after consultation and debate, the Commission overhauled and modernised its approach to, and the EU competition law regime governing, vertical agreements. Accepting that vertical restraints are generally less harmful than horizontal ones and are unlikely to give rise to competition concerns unless there is insufficient competition at one or more levels of trade, it adopted a broad block exemption for vertical agreements (the VBER) and published accompanying Guidelines. Since then, the VBER and Guidelines have been extensively reviewed and replaced twice, first in 2010 and, again, in 2022.
3. The current VBER, which entered into force on 1 June 2022, provides a safe harbour for many vertical agreements subject to certain conditions, in particular that the parties' market shares do not exceed 30 per cent and that the agreement does not contain specified 'hardcore' restraints.
4. Agreements containing 'hardcore' restraints, set out in the VBER, are considered to constitute serious restrictions of competition which are unlikely to be compatible with Article 101.
5. Where the VBER does not apply, individual assessment of a vertical agreement is required to determine whether or not it infringes Article 101(1) and, if so, whether it satisfies the conditions of Article 101(3).
6. Relatively little modern guidance has emerged on how Article 101 analysis should be conducted in individual cases, especially in relation to distribution practices, which have developed as online selling has advanced. Following the launch of an e-commerce sector inquiry in 2015, the Commission has, however, now conducted some investigations into online distribution practices and, in 2022, adapted the VBER and Guidelines to provide clearer direction on how such practices are treated and analysed under Article 101.
7. On 3 December 2018, Regulation 2018/302, on geo-blocking, came into force. This Regulation addresses the problem of unjustified geo-blocking, and other forms of discrimination based on customers' nationality, place of residence or establishment, which results in some customers being unable to buy goods and services from traders in a different Member State. It tackles a broad set of practices (which expand beyond restraints in vertical agreements) and forms part of wider set of EU measures aimed at boosting e-commerce and cross-border online sales within the single market.

2. INTRODUCTION

A. GENERAL

A manufacturer of a product (or a supplier of a service) is not solely concerned with manufacturing. If it does not itself use that product as an input, it must also plan for its distribution. Generally, the manufacturer will wish to minimise the costs of distribution and to ensure that its products are distributed to customers in the most efficient manner. Broadly, this may be achieved either by distributing the product itself or by delegating the task to a third party (for example, an independent distributor or an agent). Similarly, a supplier of a service will need to decide how best to distribute its services.

This chapter starts by outlining the choices available to a supplier when deciding how best to market and sell its products or services to customers and the impact that the competition rules may have on its choice. The discussion focuses, however, on distribution agreements concluded between vertically related firms, for example a manufacturer and an independent wholesaler or retailer[1] (the terms supplier and distributor or dealer will generally be used to describe the upstream and downstream parties respectively in this chapter), and the competition law problems that such agreements raise under Article 101.[2] These issues differ significantly from those raised in relation to horizontal agreements considered in prior chapters since the agreements are not usually concluded by competitors (actual or potential), but by suppliers of complementary products or services cooperating to enable the distribution of products and services to consumers. Consequently, 'normally (when neither have market power) their self-interested action leads to greater welfare to society. That is to say, when a manufacturer "restrains" its distributors, it normally does this because it expects that as a result sales will increase, and such an effect benefits manufacturer and distributor, and also consumers.'[3]

Section 3 then goes on to chart the evolution in policy towards vertical restraints, including the modernised approach heralded by the adoption in 1999 of a generic block exemption on vertical restraints,[4] together with accompanying Guidelines,[5] and their subsequent extensive review and replacement first in 2010, by Regulation 330/2010[6] and its accompanying Guidelines on Vertical Restraints,[7] and then in 2022, by Regulation 2022/720[8] (the VBER) and its accompanying Vertical Guidelines (the Guidelines)[9] (following the launch and completion of an E-Commerce Sector Inquiry[10]). In Sections 4 and 5, the application of Article 101, and the VBER, to vertical agreements is assessed. In Sections 6 and 7, subcontracting agreements and the possible application of Article 102 to distribution agreements are outlined. Section 8 concludes that some problems remain with the verticals regime. For example, although it has been developed and updated to reflect market developments, the legal framework is complex. Further, it continues to rely significantly on safe harbours and presumptions of illegality, meaning that a fully transparent, and modernised structure for analysing and balancing the competitive harms and benefits of other vertical arrangements is yet to emerge.

[1] An agreement between a manufacturer of a component and a producer of a product that uses that component is also a vertical agreement.

[2] Vertical restraints incorporated in contracts concluded by a dominant supplier are dealt with in Chap. 7.

[3] G. Monti, 'Restraints on Selective Distribution Agreements' (2013) 36 *World Competition* 489, 490.

[4] Reg. 2790/1999 [1999] OJ L336/21. [5] [2000] OJ C291/1. [6] [2010] OJ L102/1.

[7] [2010] OJ C130/1. [8] [2022] OJ L134/4. [9] [2022] OJ C248/1.

[10] The inquiry was launched in May 2015. The Commission published a Staff Working Document Preliminary Report (Preliminary Report) on 15 September 2016, SWD(2016) 312 final, and a Final Report and accompanying Staff Working Document on 10 May 2017, SWD(2017) 154 final ('the Final Report', which summarises the main findings of the e-commerce sector inquiry and incorporates comments submitted by stakeholders during the public consultation).

B. METHODS OF DISTRIBUTION

(i) Factors Affecting Choice

Essentially a supplier has the choice of distributing its product itself (through employees or a subsidiary), through the market, using an independent distributor, or through a hybrid model, using an agent or other intermediary. The method of distribution selected by a supplier is likely to be determined after consideration of a wide range of factors, including the relative costs of organising distribution internally compared with the costs of using the market or an agent, the nature of the product or service, the nature of the market, the size and resources of the supplier, and any tax or legal implications.

(ii) Vertical Integration

Whatever mode is selected, a supplier is likely to want to keep some control over how its products are distributed. It is likely to be able to retain maximum control by taking charge of distribution itself. The supplier may set up a distribution arm (internal growth) or may acquire an undertaking that is already in the distribution business (external growth).

A decision to move into distribution may, however, not always be practical and/or an efficient use of a firm's resources. A supplier may, therefore, prefer to leave distribution to entities that are experienced in retailing or local distributors who know more about the markets and customers to be targeted.

> Retailers commonly secure economies of scope by offering the consumer under one roof dozens or even thousands of products, often gathered together from a diversity of manufacturers. It would be prohibitively costly for the manufacturer of paper towels, crescent wrenches, or antibiotics to establish its own retail distribution facilities in order to control the conditions under which its product is resold to consumers. And even when there is a reasonably close fit between manufacturer product line and retail outlets' scope, as in automobiles, major appliances, or photo supplies, the two stages require quite different skills, attitudes, and spans of managerial focus, and the advantages of specialization typically require that retailers be kept separate organizationally from their primary suppliers.[11]

The fast growth of e-commerce, accelerated by the Covid-19 pandemic, has however enabled many more manufacturers to integrate vertically and to sell online, via their own websites. Dual distribution arrangements, where a manufacturer sells both through its own distribution arm and independent distributors, are becoming more commonplace.

(iii) Agency and Other Intermediaries

Whether or not a supplier decides to appoint a commercial agent or an independent distributor may depend on the independence it wishes the third party to be given, the risk it wishes to bear, and the responsibilities of the supplier on the termination of the relationship. Ordinarily, the functions of an agent are restricted and limited to negotiating sales or purchasing agreements on behalf of a principal. Indeed, the Commission defines an agent as 'a legal or natural person entrusted with the power to negotiate and/or conclude contracts on behalf of another person ("the principal"), either in the agent's

[11] F. M. Scherer and D. Ross, *Industrial Market Structure and Economic Performance* (3rd edn, Houghton Mifflin, 1990), 542.

own name or in the name of the principal, for the purchase of goods or services by the principal, or the sale of goods or services supplied by the principal'.[12] It thus typically operates as a marketing resource for the principal and bears little responsibility for the products it negotiates to sell. Agents usually receive either a commission based on the sales they make or a fixed salary.[13]

As the internet and online distribution has taken off, many suppliers now sell with the aid of online platforms or providers of online intermediation services (OIS providers), for example online marketplaces, app stores, social media services, or price comparison tools, which allow undertakings to offer goods and services to other undertakings or final consumers with a view to facilitating direct transactions between them.[14] Although often characterised commercially as agency relationships, a controversial issue is how these business practices should be analysed under Article 101.

(iv) Distribution through Independent Distributors

Alternatively, distribution may be left to independent distributors/dealers or buyers that will sell, or use, the goods or supply the services. Where an independent undertaking is chosen, a distribution agreement will be necessary. A supplier may simply wish to ensure that its products or services are distributed through as many outlets as possible. Alternatively, or additionally, restrictions and obligations limiting the number or type of distributors, or restricting the conduct of the parties, may be considered necessary to make the distribution agreement commercially viable and/or acceptable. Such restraints may be imposed with the objective of minimising distribution costs, of bringing a product or service to market in an efficient and effective manner, and of enhancing sales of the supplier's product.[15]

For example, a supplier may wish to encourage consumers to purchase its product by requiring its distributors to provide specific services, to contribute to the creation of a brand image for the contract product or service, and/or to concentrate their selling efforts on the supplier's products.[16] A distributor may, however, be unwilling to incur the costs involved in providing specific services unless other distributors, who are not subject to similar promotional, servicing, and/or stocking obligation, are prevented from taking a free-ride on its promotional or other efforts (free-riders). The supplier may, therefore, only be able to influence the level of services furnished by its distributors by selecting or limiting the number of dealers it appoints and/or by limiting competition between them—vertical agreements may therefore limit intra-brand competition (competition between distributors of the supplier's product or service) with the goal of increasing inter-brand competition (competition between the supplier and producers of competing products). The supplier may achieve this, for example, through:

- allocating an exclusive sales territory or exclusive customer group to a distributor/buyer, a limited number of buyers, or itself (exclusive distribution system[17]). Where the supplier is obliged or

[12] Guidelines, para. 29.

[13] If any agent appointed satisfies the definition of a 'commercial agent' set out in Council Dir. 86/653 on the coordination of the laws of the Member States relating to self-employed commercial agents [1986] OJ L382/17 ('a self-employed intermediary who has continuing authority to negotiate the sale or purchase of goods on behalf of another person (his principal) or to negotiate and conclude such transactions on behalf of and in the name of the principal'), that Directive contains provisions relating, for example, to the remuneration payable to it during the term of the agreement and as to indemnification or compensation on the termination or expiration of the agency contract, see Arts. 1(2) and 19, see J. Goyder, *EU Distribution Law* (5th edn, Hart Publishing, 2011), 6.3.

[14] See also VBER, Art. 1(1)(e) and Section 5.C.ii.

[15] See further Section 2.C.iii.b.

[16] Additionally, the supplier may wish to conclude an agreement which allows it to exploit economies of scale in distribution.

[17] See VBER, Art. 1(1)(h) ('a distribution system where the supplier allocates a territory or group of customers exclusively to itself or to a maximum of five buyers and restricts all its other buyers from actively selling into the exclusive territory or to the exclusive customer group') and Section 5.C.ii.

induced to sell the contract products only or mainly to one single buyer, there is an exclusive supply arrangement.[18] Exclusive distribution is sometimes combined with exclusive sourcing, where a buyer is obliged, or has incentives, to purchase a specific brand of product exclusively from the supplier.[19] Upfront access payments,[20] fixed fees that suppliers pay to distributors in order to get access to their distribution networks and remunerate services provided to the suppliers by the retailers (such as slotting allowances, 'pay to stay' fees, payments to have access to promotion campaigns), may induce a supplier to sell through only one distributor, or a limited number of distributors and so may operate like an exclusive supply agreement;

- specifying the price at which the products may be resold, for example a fixed or a minimum resale price (resale price maintenance (RPM)), or a maximum resale price (maximum RPM), and restricting the buyer's ability to determine its sale price;
- selecting through qualitative or quantitative criteria, the type or number of outlets in which the supplier's products are sold and where distributors undertake not to sell to unauthorised distributors outside the network (selective distribution system (SDS));[21]
- territorial or customer restraints. Exclusive, selective, and other forms of distribution agreements may incorporate restraints on the territories into which, or the customers to whom, the buyers, and the supplier itself, may sell the contract products or services (whether through active selling efforts or passively in response to unsolicited requests[22]). In the EU, a ban on internet selling is generally treated as a territorial or customer restraint as it prevents a dealer from selling to a broader audience. Other restraints may limit only certain forms of online selling, such as restrictions on the use by retailers of online marketplaces to sell their products, whether absolutely (marketplace or platform bans) or in specified circumstances, for example where those marketplaces do not fulfil certain quality criteria. Marketplace restrictions may be designed to: (a) protect the suppliers' brand image and reputation (which might be damaged by certain marketplaces especially where the supplier has no direct relationship with it and cannot control the presentation of its products on it); (b) combat the sale of counterfeit products; (c) ensure the provision of sufficient pre-sales services by retailers (including brick and mortar shops) and to prevent free-riding on them, (as marketplaces tend to focus on the price of the product rather than the quality of the product and services provided); or (d) protect direct customer relationships.[23] Similarly, a number of manufacturers seek to prevent retailers using price comparison tools (or certain sites), which they think might negatively impact on the suppliers' brand image (even if the products are not actually bought on the price comparison website) and the provision of services by specialised retailers (both online and offline). 'While price comparison tools may therefore increase sales in the short term, they may reduce incentives of specialised retailers to invest in quality and services and lead to a reduced number of retailers in the long run.'[24]
- parity obligations (sometimes referred to as Across Platform Parity Agreements (APPAs) or most favoured nation clauses (MFNs)), require a supplier of goods or services to offer them to another

[18] Guidelines, para. 321.

[19] This eliminates arbitrage between distributors, see ibid., para. 129. They may also be combined with a non-compete obligation, a prohibition on selling competing products: see e.g. Case C-234/89, *Delimitis v Henninger Bräu* EU:C:1991:91, para. 10.

[20] Guidelines, para. 379.

[21] See also VBER, Art. 1(1)(g) and Section 5.C.ii.

[22] See also ibid., Art. 1(1)(m) and discussion in Sections 5.C.ii and 5.C.v.

[23] See A. Jones, 'Expert report prepared for the Commission on the Review of the EU Verticals Block Exemption Regulation on Cases dealing with online sales, and online advertising, restrictions at EU and national level' (2021), <https://ec.europa.eu/competition-policy/system/files/2021-06/kd0921156enn_VBER_online_sales.pdf>.

[24] E-commerce SWD Final Report, n. 10, para. 537.

party on conditions that are no less favourable than the conditions offered by the supplier to certain other parties or on other channels (whether direct channels offered by the supplier or indirect channels operated by third parties).[25] In the VBER and Guidelines, a distinction is drawn between:

- across-platform retail parity obligations imposed by OIS providers which cause buyers of such services not to offer, sell, or resell goods or services to end-users under more favourable conditions using competing OIS providers;[26] and
- all other types of parity obligations, including narrow retail parity obligations relating to the direct sales channels of buyers of online intermediation services, obligations relating to the conditions under which goods or services are offered to undertakings that are not end-users, and obligations relating to the conditions under which manufacturers, wholesalers, or retailers purchase goods or services as inputs (most favoured customer obligations).[27]

In addition, and in order to ensure security of supply, purchase price and/or focused selling efforts, a vertical agreement may incorporate restraints which limit competition between the supplier and other producers of competing goods and services and hence, more directly, inter-brand competition. It may preclude or deter dealers from manufacturing, buying, marketing, or selling products which compete with the contract goods or services (through non-competition provisions, quantity forcing, or requirements contracts). For example:

- the buyer may be obliged or incentivised to purchase all (or a significant proportion) of its requirements on a particular market from only one supplier and not to manufacture, buy, resell, or incorporate competing goods or services, i.e. non-compete obligations,[28] or required or incentivised to concentrate its purchases to a large extent with one supplier (e.g. minimum purchase or stocking requirements, or conditional rebates, quantity forcing, or requirements contracts).[29] The Commission describes agreements in which a buyer is induced to concentrate orders for a type of product with one supplier as single branding agreements.[30] Upfront access payments may operate like single branding provisions if widespread use of such payments creates barriers to entry for small entrants. Further, category management agreements, by which the distributor entrusts the supplier (the category captain) with the marketing of a category of products (including the suppliers' and its competitors' products), may foreclose other suppliers and operate like single branding agreements if the category captain is able to influence the marketing decisions of the distributor or to limit or disadvantage the distribution of products of competing suppliers (e.g. through influencing product placement, promotion, or selection);[31]
- the distributor may be required to purchase a second distinct (tied) product as a condition of purchasing the first (tying) product (tying);[32]
- distributors may be required not to open a competing business for a certain period after the distribution agreement has been terminated. Such an obligation may be of particular importance in, for example, a franchising agreement where a supplier, a franchisor, grants the right to a distributor, a franchisee, to exploit a franchise and to set up a business marketing specified goods or services as part of a uniform business network established by the franchisor. The franchising

[25] Guidelines, para. 356. In other price relationship agreements, a supplier may require a reseller to set the resale price of its product at a price related to the price set for a competitor's product or offer a price match guarantee by which the price paid by the buyer is related to a price charged by a competitor for competing products.

[26] Ibid., paras. 253 and 360 and see Section 5.C.vi. [27] Ibid., para. 254.

[28] See VBER, Art. 1(1)(f) and Section 5.C.ii. [29] Guidelines, para. 298. [30] Ibid.

[31] Ibid., para. 385. [32] Ibid., para. 389.

agreement will ordinarily authorise the use of intellectual and industrial property rights, such as trademarks and know-how, to enable and to aid the franchisee to resell the goods and services. In addition, the franchisor usually provides the franchisee with commercial or technical assistance during the life of the agreement and requires a franchise fee for the use of the business method.[33]

Single branding and tying arrangements may create especially significant competition law problems where the firm imposing the provision is dominant (see Chapter 7).

(v) Distribution and E-commerce

The growth of e-commerce has led to significant changes in manufacturers' distribution strategies and vertical agreements. For example:

(a) many manufacturers have integrated vertically into online distribution. This means that manufacturers now more often compete with their independent distributors downstream;

(b) more manufacturers seek to control distribution, and to ensure its high quality, through the operation of SDSs allowing them, in particular to: (i) maintain a coherent brand image across all offline and online sales channels; (ii) limit free-riding between the two channels (given the greater opportunity for free-riding created by increased price transparency); and (iii) offer a certain degree of protection against the sale of counterfeit products;

(c) many manufacturers seek to use restraints that allow for a greater control over the distribution of their products, for example through pricing, dual-pricing, territorial and/or cross-border sales restrictions, marketplace (platform) bans, restrictions on the use of price comparison tools, and the exclusion of pure online players from distribution networks;

(d) manufacturers frequently pursue a multi-channel strategy, using both offline and online distribution mechanisms;

(e) sellers may sell, and purchasers may buy, through brick and mortar stores (occupying physical space), manufacturer or retailer websites, third party platforms or marketplaces (such as Amazon or eBay), and/or display on price comparison websites; and

(f) undertakings active in the online platform economy are playing increasingly prominent roles in the distribution of goods and services through intermediating between sellers of goods and services and customers.[34]

C. COMPETITION RULES AND DISTRIBUTION

(i) The Impact of the Competition Rules on Methods of Distribution

The following discussion establishes that a decision to distribute products through an independent distributor raises most problems from an EU competition law perspective; competition law may therefore constitute a relevant factor when a business is deciding how to distribute its products or services. Arguably, this should not be the case. Rather, 'businessmen should be left to select the most cost effective method with as little distortion as possible induced by the competition rules',[35]

[33] Ibid., paras. 165–169.

[34] These arrangements arguably confound the traditional supplier and distributor concepts, see Section 5.C.iii.b and nn. 264–265 and text.

[35] V. Korah and D. O'Sullivan, *Distribution Agreements Under the EC Competition Rules* (Hart Publishing, 2002), 1.1. See also discussion of transaction cost economics and Coase theory in Chap. 1.

otherwise there is a danger that competition policy might accelerate the trend towards vertical integration of the distribution process.[36]

(ii) Intra-undertaking Arrangements: Vertical Integration and Agency Agreements

a. *Parent–Subsidiary Arrangements*

In Chapter 4, it is seen that Article 101(1) does not apply to agreements concluded between entities forming part of the same economic unit (such as a parent supplier and its subsidiary distributor).[37] A supplier that sets up its own distribution arm is therefore unlikely to encounter difficulties with EU competition law unless (a) the integration is through external growth and the acquisition transaction is problematic under the EU merger rules (which, in the context of vertical mergers, is relatively rare);[38] and/or (b) Article 102 applies, because the undertaking is dominant on a relevant market.

b. *Agency Agreements*

The CJ has also held that the close economic links existing in an agency relationship mean that in some circumstances an agent is so closely interrelated with its principal that, as with the relationship between a parent and its subsidiary or employer and employee, the agent forms an integral part of the principal's business and the relationship is characterised by 'economic unity' (i.e. the agent no longer acts as an independent economic operator in the context of the sale or purchase of the goods or services[39]). Thus, under EU competition law:

- some agents operate as an 'auxiliary organ' 'forming an integral part of the principal's undertaking'[40] (an agent);
- whilst others operate as an independent economic operator so that the agency agreement is, like other vertical agreements, subject to Article 101(1).[41]

The jurisprudence makes it clear that it is not the parties' description of the arrangement (the form) which is determinative to the question of whether or not the agency agreement is governed by Article 101 but the economic reality.[42] Indeed, in a number of cases no 'genuine' agency agreement (as the Commission used to describe those falling outside Article 101(1)) has been found to exist, despite it being characterised as such by the parties.[43] It is for the Commission, or other person

[36] In the US, the Supreme Court recognised that 'the *per se* illegality of vertical restraints would create a perverse incentive for manufacturers to integrate vertically into distribution', *Business Electronics Corp v Sharp Electronics Corp*, 485 US 717, 725, per Scalia J (1988).

[37] See discussion of Case C-73/95 P, *Viho Europe BV v Commission* EU:C:1996:405 in Chap. 4, Section 4.A.vii.

[38] See Chap. 15.

[39] Guidelines, para. 30.

[40] See Case 311/85, *ASBL Vereniging van Vlaamse Reisbureaus v ASBL Sociale Dienst van de Plaatselijke en Gewestelijke Overheidsdiensten* EU:C:1987:418, paras. 19–20 and Case C-266/93, *Bundeskartellamt v Volkswagen AG and VAG Leasing GmbH* EU:C:1995:345, para. 19.

[41] Guidelines, para. 30.

[42] Case C-279/06, *CEPSA* EU:C:2008:485, para. 36.

[43] See COMP/26.894, 26.876, and 26.892, *Pittsburgh Corning* [1972] OJ L272/35 (although an agency agreement had been selected for tax purposes the Commission decided that the parties were not in a relationship of economic dependency); Joined Cases 40–48, 50, 54–56, 111, 113, and 114/73, *Suiker Unie v Commission* EU:C:1975:174, paras. 539–542 (parties, although technically commercial agents under German law, were found in fact to be powerful intermediaries which accepted the financial risks of the sales or of the performance of the contracts and operated at arm's length from their notional principals, and worked simultaneously as independent dealers for several undertakings); Case C-266/93, *Bundeskartellamt v Volkswagen AG and VAG Leasing GmbH* EU:C:1995:345, paras. 18–19 (the CJ rejected Volkswagen AG and VAG Leasing's argument that the German VAG dealers, as intermediaries of VAG Leasing, constituted exclusive agency agreements as the dealers bore some of the risks of leasing the contract vehicles. 'Representatives can lose their character as independent traders only if they do not bear any of the risks resulting from the contracts negotiated on behalf of the principal and they operate as auxiliary organs forming an integral part of the principal's undertaking').

trying to prove a violation of Article 101(1), however, to establish whether an entity is in fact acting as an independent operator.[44]

In *Confederación Española de Empresarios de Estaciones de Servicio v Compañia Española de Petróleos (CEES)*[45] and *CEPSA Estaciones de Servicio SA v LV Tobar e Hojos SL (CEPSA)*,[46] the CJ provided guidance on factors relevant to the assessment (in both cases the compatibility with Article 101(1) of motor fuel agreements concluded with operators of Spanish service stations had arisen before the Spanish courts). The CJ held that:[47]

- vertical agreements are covered by Article 101 only where the operator is regarded as an independent economic operator and there is, consequently, an agreement between two undertakings;
- '[t]he decisive factor for the purposes of determining whether [an entity] is an independent economic operator is to be found in the agreement concluded with the principal and, in particular, in the clauses of that agreement, implied or express, relating to the assumption of the financial and commercial risks linked to sales of goods to third parties.'[48]
- Article 101 is not applicable where the operator bears only a negligible proportion of the relevant risk.[49]

Relevant 'risks' are:

- risks which are directly related to the contracts concluded and/or negotiated by the agent on behalf of the principal. An important factor therefore is whether the 'agent' takes possession or acquires property of goods prior to selling them to a third party, assumes costs linked to distribution of goods, such as transport costs, maintains stocks at its own cost or risk, takes responsibility for customers' non-performance of the contract, assumes responsibility for any damage resulting from the supply of the goods, or bears the financial risk linked to the goods;[50]
- risks related to market-specific investments. These are investments specifically required for the type of activity for which the agent has been appointed by the principal and so to enable the agent to conclude and/or negotiate this type of contract. These include investments in premises, equipment, training of personnel, or advertising. Such investments are frequently sunk;[51]
- risks related to other activities required by the principal to be undertaken in the same product market.[52]

Broadly, therefore arrangements will fall outside the scope of the rules where the agent forms an integrated part of the principal's sales strategy and the principal both remains owner of the contract products[53] and bears all contract-specific risks, market-specific investments, and/or other risks resulting from the agents' activities.

In contrast, risks accepted by the agent on another market (separate from the goods sold on behalf of the principal) will not affect agency status. Thus in *Mercedes-Benz*,[54] the GC held that German dealers were agents[55] because Mercedes-Benz bore the risk associated with the contract and the purchase of

[44] Case T-325/01, *DaimlerChrysler v Commission* EU:T:2005:322, paras. 201 and 218.

[45] Case C-217/05, EU:C:2006:784. See also Guidelines, paras. 12–21. [46] Case C-279/06, EU:C:2008:485.

[47] Ibid., paras. 33–44, Case C-217/05, *CEES* EU:C:2006:784, paras. 38–63.

[48] *CEPSA*, para. 36, *CEES*, para. 46. See also Case C-331/21, *Autoridade da Concorrência and EDP* EU:C:2023:153, Opinion of Rantos AG, paras. 91–96.

[49] *CEPSA*, para. 40, *CEES*, para. 61. [50] *CEPSA*, para. 38, *CEES*, paras. 50–61, Guidelines, para. 31(a).

[51] Which means that upon leaving that particular field of activity the investment cannot be used for other activities or sold other than at a significant loss, Guidelines, para. 31(b).

[52] Ibid., para. 31(c). [53] But see ibid., para. 33(a). [54] COMP/36.264 [2002] OJ L257/1.

[55] Case T-325/01, *DaimlerChrysler v Commission* EU:T:2005:322 (annulling the Commission's findings on this matter).

new cars, not the commercial agents. Title in the cars passed directly from Mercedes-Benz to the customer and the agent had no authority to negotiate rebates except out of its own commission.[56] The fact that the agents bore responsibility for some activities and financial obligations on separate markets (such as transportation of the cars, purchase of demonstration cars, and provision of after-sales guarantee services) did not detract from this conclusion.

Although some older cases indicate that agents can lose their character as independent traders only if they operate as auxiliary organs forming an integral part of the principal's undertaking (see, for example, *VZW Vereniging van Vlaamse Reisbureaus v VZW Sociale Dienst van de Plaatselijke en Gewestelijke Overheidsdiensten*[57]), the focus on risk set out in the more recent cases appears to suggest that the appraisal is not so affected by the question of whether the agent acts only for one, or for several, principals; the same agent may form part of the same economic unit as one or more principals (and indeed it has been held that clauses preventing agents from acting for other principals may have to be assessed for their compatibility with Article 101(1)[58]).

The Commission summarises the relevance of risks in its Guidelines:

Guidelines on Vertical Restraints

(33) In light of the above, an agreement will generally be categorised as an agency agreement that falls outside the scope of Article 101(1) of the Treaty where all of the following conditions apply:

(a) the agent does not acquire the property in the goods bought or sold under the agency agreement and does not itself supply the services bought or sold under the agency agreement. The fact that the agent may temporarily, for a very brief period of time, acquire the property in the contract goods while selling them on behalf of the principal, does not preclude the existence of an agency agreement that falls outside the scope of Article 101(1) of the Treaty, provided that the agent does not incur any costs or risks in relation to the transfer of property;

(b) the agent does not contribute to the costs relating to the supply or purchase of the contract goods or services, including the costs of transporting the goods. This does not preclude the agent from carrying out the transport service, provided that the costs are covered by the principal;

(c) the agent does not maintain at its own cost or risk stocks of the contract goods, including the cost of financing the stock and the cost of lost stock. The agent should be able to return unsold goods to the principal without charge, unless the agent is at fault, for example, because it fails to comply with reasonable security or anti-theft measures to avoid stock losses;

(d) the agent does not take responsibility for the customers' non-performance of the contract, with the exception of the loss of the agent's commission, unless the agent is at fault (for example, failing to comply with reasonable security or anti-theft measures or failing to comply with reasonable measures to report theft to the principal or the police or to communicate to the principal all necessary information available to it on the customer's financial reliability);

(e) the agent does not assume responsibility towards customers or other third parties for loss or damage resulting from the supply of the contract goods or services, unless the agent is at fault;

[56] Ibid., paras. 93 and 94.

[57] Case 311/85, *VZW Vereniging van Vlaamse Reisbureaus v VZW Sociale Dienst van de Plaatselijke en Gewestelijke Overheidsdiensten* EU:C:1987:418 (the CJ held that Flemish travel agents which observed travel prices set by tour operators and acted on behalf of a large number of tour operators could not be regarded as an auxiliary part of the tour operators even though they contracted in the name of and on behalf of them). See also n. 43 and text.

[58] See nn. 61–62 and text.

(f) the agent is not, directly or indirectly, obliged to invest in sales promotion, including through contributions to the advertising budget of the principal or to advertising or promotional activities specifically relating to the contract goods or services, unless such costs are fully reimbursed by the principal;

(g) the agent does not make market-specific investments in equipment, premises, training of personnel or advertising, such as the petrol storage tank in the case of petrol retailing, specific software to sell insurance policies in the case of insurance agents, or advertising relating to routes or destinations in the case of travel agents selling flights or hotel accommodation, unless such costs are fully reimbursed by the principal;

(h) the agent does not undertake other activities within the same product market required by the principal under the agency relationship (for example, the delivery of the goods), unless those activities are fully reimbursed by the principal.

Even if a relationship between a supplier and its distributor is characterised as one of agency, a functional approach is taken to the concept of an undertaking. It is therefore only with regard to the market on which the agent offers its principal's goods or services to potential customers and obligations delineating the scope of that relationship that the principal and agent are considered to be acting unilaterally:[59] consequently, limitations of the territory into which, customers to whom, or prices and conditions at which the agent sells the goods or services and, possibly, exclusive agency provisions (i.e. provisions preventing the principal from appointing other agents in respect of a given type of transaction, customer, or territory) may fall outside Article 101(1).

In contrast, the agent is normally regarded as an independent operator with regard to the market on which the agent offers its agency services to potential principals.[60] Thus terms within an agency agreement may fall within the scope of Article 101 if they prevent the agent from acting as an agent or distributor of undertakings which compete with the principal (non-compete provisions) and so foreclose or lock up the relevant market, or where they facilitate collusion.[61] In *CEES*, the CJ held that:[62]

only the obligations imposed on the intermediary in the context of the sale of the goods to third parties on behalf of the principal fall outside the scope of that article. As the Commission submitted, an agency contract may contain clauses concerning the relationship between the agent and the principal to which that article applies, such as exclusivity and non-competition clauses. In that connection it must be considered that, in the context of such relationships, agents are, in principle, independent economic operators and such clauses are capable of infringing the competition rules in so far as they entail locking up the market concerned.

c. *Agency and Online Platforms*

The criteria set out in the agency cases, although developed in relation to offline scenarios, suggest that the agency principle could extend to situations where suppliers sell online, via platforms and

[59] Guidelines, paras. 41–45

[60] See Case C-279/06, *CEPSA* EU:C:2008:485, para. 41; Case C-217/05, *CEES* EU:C:2006:784, paras. 62–63; Guidelines, 3.2.2, paras. 41–45.

[61] E.g. when a number of principals use the same agents and collectively exclude others from using them, or when they use the agents to collude on marketing strategy or to exchange sensitive market information between the principals, Guidelines, para. 20.

[62] Case C-217/05, *CEES* EU:C:2006:784, para. 62.

following an agency model where, for example, ownership of the products/services is not passed to the platform (the platform does not buy products from suppliers for resale), contracts concluded are formed between the supplier and customer, and the platform does not bear any of the financial or commercial risks related to the sale or provision of the goods or services, but simply receives a commission or remuneration for concluded contracts.[63] The Commission's view, however, reflected in the 2022 Guidelines, is that agreements entered into by undertakings active in the online platform economy do not generally satisfy the conditions.[64]

Guidelines on Vertical Restraints

(46) Agreements entered into by undertakings active in the online platform economy generally do not meet the conditions to be categorised as agency agreements that fall outside the scope of Article 101(1) of the Treaty. Such undertakings generally act as independent economic operators and not as part of the undertakings for which they provide services. In particular, undertakings active in the online platform economy often serve a very large number of sellers, which prevents them from effectively becoming part of any of the sellers' undertakings. In addition, strong network effects and other features of the online platform economy can contribute to a significant imbalance in the size and bargaining power of the contracting parties. This can result in a situation where the conditions under which goods or services are sold and the commercial strategy are determined by the undertaking active in the online platform economy rather than by the sellers of the goods or services. In addition, undertakings active in the online platform economy typically make significant market-specific investments, for example, in software, advertising and after-sales services, indicating that those undertakings bear significant financial or commercial risks associated with the transactions that they intermediate.

Rather, the VBER and Guidelines instead treat some undertakings active in the online platform economy as 'suppliers' of online intermediation services to buyers/purchasers of those services (suppliers of goods or services), which act as intermediaries between such suppliers and end customers.[65]

The approach to agency and the online platform economy is not entirely easy to square with the principles developed in the cases, which are complex and not easy to navigate. This has led some to call for a more modified approach to be taken, which is more in tune with the economic nature or commercial realities of the agency arrangement.[66]

(iii) Vertical Agreements

a. Restraints on Conduct and Restrictions of Competition—The Problem

It has already been seen that vertical agreements concluded between suppliers and independent distributors operating at different levels of the supply chain ordinarily contain restraints on the conduct or commercial freedom of one or more of the parties. The issue for EU competition law is whether or not these restraints restrict competition for the purposes of Article 101(1) and/or generate efficiencies

[63] P. Akman, 'Online Platforms, Agency, and Competition Law: Mind the Gap' (2019) 43(2) *Fordham Int'l LJ* 209.

[64] In contrast, the 2010 Guidelines, para. 13 considered it to be immaterial whether an agent acts for one or several principals.

[65] VBER, Art. 1(1)(d) and (e).

[66] See e.g. A. H. Zhang, 'Toward an Economic Approach to Agency Agreements' (2013) 9 *J of Competition Law and Economics* 553 and Akman, n. 63.

cognisable under Article 101(3). Although economic theory supports a suspicion of horizontal agreements, the effects of vertical restraints are more complex as they may either increase or decrease efficiency depending on the context of the agreement.[67]

b. *The Positive Effects of Vertical Restraints*

In the 1960s, many commentators argued that competition law should rarely be troubled by vertical restraints which lead to increased sales and to the minimisation of distribution costs.

Main arguments in relation to intra-brand restraints are that they are frequently necessary to enable a supplier to protect its distributors from free-riders and to encourage inter-brand competition. For example, vertical agreements imposing RPM, awarding a distributor an exclusive distribution territory, or restricting supplies to selected retailers may be essential to encourage distributors to provide additional services necessary to boost sales and to persuade consumers to purchase more of the supplier's product. In the absence of such restraints, distributors might be unwilling to incur the cost of providing additional services since other distributors would be able to take a 'free-ride' on their investment.[68]

Bork went further, arguing that not only was the rationale for the imposition of such vertical restraints[69] obvious, but a supplier would only ever impose vertical restraints in order to achieve distributive efficiency and to increase its output. If it wrongly required distributors to provide services that customers did not want, or did not consider to be worth the increase in price, those consumers would purchase rival products instead. Where inter-brand competition is robust, the market itself will provide retribution for a supplier's mistaken belief that a vertical restraint is desirable.

Comanor explains these free-rider and distributive efficiency arguments more fully.

W. S. Comanor, 'Vertical Price-fixing, Vertical Market Restrictions, and the New Antitrust Policy' (1985) 98 *Harvard LR* 983, 986–990

Building on earlier studies . . . Lester Telser offered a detailed explanation of why manufacturers benefit from resale price maintenance [L. Telser, 'Why Should Manufacturers Want Fair Trade? (1960) 3 J of Law and Economics 86]. As he observed, because the quantity sold of a manufacturer's product depends on the final price paid by consumers, the manufacturer normally stands to gain from competition among dealers that limits the distribution margin. Only if other factors intervene can the manufacturer benefit from restraints on competition among his dealers. . . .

Telser's primary explanation centered on the distributor's role in furnishing 'services' along with the manufactured product. By 'services,' Telser referred not only to delivery, credit, and repair, but also to selling, advertising, and promotional activities . . . In short . . . all factors supplied by the distributor that may influence demand for the manufacturer's product. The provision of these services benefits the manufacturer as long as the positive effect on demand outweighs the depressing effect of the accompanying rise in price.

The manufacturer, however, can influence the level of services furnished only by limiting competition among his distributors. He cannot simply lower his price in the hope that distributors will use

[67] J. Tirole, *The Theory of Industrial Organisation* (MIT Press, 1988), 186.

[68] See especially L. Telser, 'Why Should Manufacturers Want Fair Trade?' (1960) 3 *J of Law and Economics* 86; L. Telser, 'Why Should Manufacturers Want Fair Trade II?' (1990) 33 *J of Law and Economics* 409; R. A. Posner, 'The Next Step in the Antitrust Treatment of Restricted Distribution: Per Se Legality' (1981) 48 *Univ Chic LR* 6; F. H. Easterbrook, 'Vertical Arrangements and the Rule of Reason' (1984) 53 *Antitrust LJ* 135.

[69] See R. H. Bork, 'The Rule of Reason and the Per Se Concept: Price Fixing and Market Division Part I' (1965) 74 *Yale LJ* 775; R. H. Bork, 'The Rule of Reason and the Per Se Concept: Price Fixing and Market Division Part II' (1966) 75 *Yale LJ* 373.

their increased revenues to finance the appropriate services. Even if some distributors will do so—recognizing that greater sales result from providing services jointly with the product—others will not, and might compete by setting a lower price. The result is the classic 'free rider' problem:

> Sales are diverted from the retailers who do provide the special services at the higher price to the retailers who do not provide the special services and offer to sell the product at the lower price. The mechanism is simple. A customer, because of the special services provided by one retailer, is persuaded to buy the product. But he purchases the product from another paying the latter a lower price. In this way the retailers who do not provide the special services get a free ride at the expense of those who have convinced consumers to buy the product.

In order to remain competitive with free riders, other distributors will cease to provide the requisite services . . . Thus, fewer services will be offered and total sales of the product will be lower than they would be otherwise . . . The solution, according to Telser, is for manufacturers to establish minimum retail prices, forcing retailers 'to compete by providing special services,' . . . and thereby eliminating the free-rider problem. . . .

Telser's analysis explains why manufacturers would wish to impose vertical restraints. What it does not do, nor claim to do, is answer the question whether dealers' provision of additional services is efficient—that is, whether the additional services justify the higher price charged for the product . . .

Judge Bork wrote the first article directly addressing the implications of vertical restraints for economic efficiency [R. H. Bork, 'The Rule of Reason and the per se Concept: Price Fixing and Market Division (pt. 2)' (1966) 75 *Yale LJ* 373]. His test was simple: restrictions on output are anti-competitive, and increases in output are pro-competitive. . . .

According to Bork, because a manufacturer will impose vertical restraints only if they lead to increased output and, in turn, to increased profits, such restraints must be pro-competitive . . . his position assumes that the interests of manufacturers and consumers fully coincide.

The reasoning behind Bork's theory, which appears to have gained acceptance among both lawyers and economists, is that manufacturers will not find it profitable to impose vertical restraints when customers do not find the value of the new services exceeds their incremental cost. Otherwise a rival manufacturer would surely offer the product without the additional services and lure customers away.

Inter-brand restraints limiting a purchaser's freedom to buy products from sources other than the seller or another specified supplier, such as exclusive dealing obligations, quantity-forcing provisions, requirements contracts, and tying arrangements, are also common practices, often with pro-competitive effect.[70] Single branding obligations, for example, may induce the dealer to concentrate its selling efforts on the promotion of the supplier's products, allow the seller to overcome free-rider issues (and give the seller an incentive to give dealers more support), reduce transaction costs, afford protection to the parties against price fluctuations, enable both parties to engage in long-term planning, and ensure a steady supply for the buyer and steady sales for the seller. Further, tying may assure product quality,[71] achieve cost saving, prevent excessive charges for the tied product (avoiding the double marginalisation problem),[72] or facilitate innovation, by incorporating new features into products, or enabling beneficial price discrimination between buyers by, for example, metering.

[70] See further Chap. 7.

[71] Ensuring that its product is not used with another that will impair its performance and/or quality.

[72] See B. Nalebuff, 'Bundling, Tying, and Portfolio Effects: Part 1: Conceptual Issues', DTI Economics Paper No. 1 (2003).

Restraints within a supply chain thus provide the opportunity to eliminate production or distribution inefficiencies and to align complementary activities and suppliers' and retailers' incentives; suppliers may consequently use them to ensure dealers take actions that will expand demand for their product and steal customers from their competitors (so promoting inter-brand competition). Arguably, the importance of vertical restraints as a means for aligning incentives has increased in the internet age, where numerous products are sold online or through platforms and where price comparison websites exist to facilitate consumers' buying choices. Even though therefore the growth of e-commerce has facilitated market access, increased price transparency, and lowered search costs, enabling customers instantaneously to obtain and compare product and price information online, e-commerce creates new challenges, especially where consumers continue to rely on retail services—for example, in the case of complex products, experience goods, or one-off purchases of durable goods. In such circumstances, e-commerce may exacerbate the risk of free-riding and create difficulties for manufacturers wishing to ensure that they control the image, reputation, and positioning of their brand and seeking to maintain a consistent quality of pre- and after-sales service.

The Commission is fully aware of the benefits that vertical restraints may bring and recognises that:

> vertical agreements between undertakings operating at different levels of the production or distribution chain are generally less harmful than horizontal agreements between competing undertakings supplying substitutable goods or services . . . In principle, this is due to the complementary nature of the activities carried out by the parties to a vertical agreement, which generally implies that pro-competitive actions by one party to the agreement will benefit the other party to the agreement and will ultimately benefit consumers. By contrast to horizontal agreements, the parties to a vertical agreement therefore tend to have an incentive to agree on lower prices and higher levels of service, which also benefit consumers. Similarly, a party to a vertical agreement usually has an incentive to oppose actions by the other party that may harm consumers, as such actions will typically also reduce the demand for the goods or services supplied by the first party. Moreover, the complementary nature of the activities of the parties to a vertical agreement in putting goods or services on the market also implies that vertical restraints provide greater scope for efficiencies, for example by optimising manufacturing and distribution processes and services.[73]

It thus accepts that vertical restraints may be essential to deal with externalities (vertical and horizontal),[74] to the realisation of positive effects, efficiencies, and the development of new markets, and to ensure the optimal level of investment and sales, lower prices, promotion of non-price competition, and improvement to the quality of service. Vertical agreements may be used to internalise externalities and increase the joint profit of the vertical supply and distribution chain. The Guidelines recognise a number of justifications for the use of vertical restraints (a listing which does not purport to be complete or exhaustive), especially when relating to the introduction of new and complex goods or services or when designed to protect relationship-specific investments. In particular:[75]

(a) the 'vertical externality issue'; the manufacturer may wish to ensure that retailers are not pricing too high or making too little sales efforts as increased sales also benefits manufacturers by bestowing a positive externality on it (if its wholesale price exceeds its marginal production

[73] Guidelines, para. 10.

[74] Ibid., para. 12 ('Simple contractual arrangements between a supplier and a buyer which determine only the price and the quantity of a transaction can often lead to sub-optimal levels of investments and sales, as they do not take into account externalities arising from the complementary nature of the activities of the supplier and its distributors').

[75] Ibid., para. 16.

costs). The negative externality of too high pricing by the retailer is sometimes called the 'double marginalisation problem' and it can be avoided by imposing a maximum resale price on the retailer. To increase retailers' sales efforts, selective or exclusive distribution or similar restrictions may be used;

(b) the 'free-rider problem'; the manufacturer may wish to prevent free-riding (at wholesale or retail level) on a distributor's pre-sales services, for example through the allocation of an exclusive territory to a distributor, especially in relation to goods and services that are relatively new, technically complex, dependent on reputation, or of a high value. Non-compete restrictions may help to overcome free-riding between suppliers;

(c) the need to 'open up or enter new markets'; a manufacturer may wish to induce a distributor to engage in sufficient (often sunk) investment to enable it to enter a new geographic market, for example through the allocation of an exclusive territory to a distributor;

(d) the 'certification free-rider issue'; a manufacturer may wish to introduce a product (and especially a new product) on a market particularly by selling through retailers that have a reputation for selling only 'quality' products, for example by appointing an exclusive distributor or establishing a SDS;

(e) the 'hold-up problem'; a manufacturer may wish to encourage client-specific investment and innovation, for example by conferring exclusivity on a distributor in order to allow it to contribute to the cost of developing the manufacturer's new product;

(f) the 'specific hold-up problem' that may arise where there is a transfer of substantial know-how; a manufacturer may wish to protect know-how transferred under a distribution agreement, for example through the imposition of non-compete restrictions;

(g) 'economies of scale in distribution'; a manufacture may seek to realise lower prices, for example by concentrating on resale and using exclusive or selective distribution systems or quantity-forcing provisions;[76]

(h) 'uniformity and quality standardisation'; a manufacturer may seek to increase sales by creating a brand image and increasing the attractiveness of a product to the final consumer, for example through the use of a SDS or franchising agreement;

(i) 'capital imperfections'; a manufacturer may wish to provide security in respect of loans made in the terms of the agreement, for example through the use of exclusivity provisions.

The Guidelines recognise that the same inefficiency problem may be addressed through different, substitutable, vertical restraints. However, they also note that the negative effects on competition of each type of restraint may differ—a factor that is relevant to the overall Article 101 appraisal.[77]

c. *Potential Anti-competitive Effects of Vertical Restraints*

Although vertical restraints might promote competition, economists are unwilling 'to make sweeping generalisations' and to regard them 'as *per se* beneficial for competition'.[78]

[76] The limitation of the number of distributors within the system will reduce the costs of distribution and of monitoring any promotional efforts required of distributors.

[77] Guidelines, para. 17 and see Section 5.E.ii.

[78] European Commission, Green Paper on Vertical Restraints in EC Competition Policy, COM(96)0721, para. 54 (emphasis added). See Scherer and Ross, n. 11, 541, W. S. Comanor, 'Vertical Price-fixing, Vertical Market Restrictions, and the New Antitrust Policy' (1985) 98 *Harvard LR* 983, and J. J. Flynn, 'The "Is" and "Ought" of Vertical Restraints After *Monsanto Co v Spray-Rite Service Corp*' (1985–1986) 71 *Cornell LR* 1095.

Comanor, for example, criticised Bork's assumption that restraints would always lead to the most efficient result and for failing to attach sufficient importance to the different preferences of consumers for extra dealer-provided services and to distinguish between marginal and infra-marginal consumers. The 'marginal consumer' is one whose valuation of the product approximates to its current price. This consumer is, therefore, sensitive to improvements leading to an increase in the market price of a product. This consumer will purchase more of the product only if the improvement in service or quality of the product is considered to be worth the increase in its price (otherwise they will purchase less). In contrast, 'infra-marginal consumers', who place a value on the product substantially higher than the original price, are relatively insensitive to increases in price. They will, therefore, not refrain from purchasing the product on an increase in price even if, in their view, the improvement in the quality of the products did not merit that increase in price.[79] In the view of Comanor, 'societal gains or losses from changes in the product depend on the preferences of *all* consumers, not merely those at the margin. To the extent that such alterations fail to reflect the preferences of infra-marginal consumers, the interests of consumers in general may not be served.'[80] Vertical restraints which are profitable to a manufacturer may thus not always achieve economic efficiency. In particular, vertical restraints imposed to promote the sale of established products may induce distributors to supply an excessive level of information services. In contrast, where consumers must be persuaded to purchase new products vertical restraints are less likely to harm consumer welfare. Consumers will require more information to entice them to purchase the products.

In the EU, the Commission is concerned that vertical restraints in distribution agreements may harm competition to the detriment of consumers through foreclosure of rivals, collusion, or softening or dampening competition between suppliers or distributors. A particular anxiety is also that vertical agreements may create obstacles to market integration by allowing firms to re-erect barriers to trade between Member States.[81]

Green Paper on Vertical Restraints in Competition Policy, COM(96)0721

70. The ongoing integration process of the Single Market adds an extra dimension to the analysis of vertical restraints. The 1992 programme was the result of a widely held conviction that the failure to achieve a single market has been costing European industry millions in unnecessary costs and lost opportunities. The exact title of the Cecchini Report, 'The cost of Non-Europe' . . . is a clear reflection of this. The efforts made since the entry into force of the EEC Treaty in 1958 had not exhausted by the mid-1980's all the potential gains to be expected from the full economic integration of the economies of the Member States. Now that more steps have been taken to eliminate the remaining obstacles to the free movement of goods, services and factors of production, it is still apparent that further efforts are necessary to achieve the maximum possible level of integration. . . .

78. The EC experience shows that the removal of non-tariff barriers is not sufficient for the full development of parallel trade, arbitrage and changes in distribution across Europe. For the complete success of economic integration it is necessary that producers, distributors and consumers, find it profitable to move towards the new market situation and do not take actions to avoid or counteract the effects of the Single Market measures. The elimination of barriers to trade may not achieve its objectives if producers and/or distributors introduce practices contrary to integration. Unfortunately in many cases it is likely that they have strong incentives to do so.

[79] Comanor, ibid., 991. [80] Ibid., 911.

[81] See also Chap. 1, and e.g. L. Gyselen, 'Vertical Restraints in the Distribution Process: Strength and Weakness of the Free Rider Rationale under EEC Competition Law' (1984) 21 *CMLRev* 647.

The Commission summarises the different negative effects in its Guidelines.

Guidelines on Vertical Restraints

(18) The negative effects on the market which can result from vertical restraints and which Union competition law aims to prevent are, in particular, the following:

(a) anti-competitive foreclosure of other suppliers or other buyers by raising barriers to entry or expansion;

(b) softening of competition between the supplier and its competitors and/or the facilitation of explicit or tacit collusion among competing suppliers, often referred to as the reduction of inter-brand competition;

(c) softening of competition between the buyer and its competitors and/or the facilitation of explicit or tacit collusion among competing buyers, often referred to as the reduction of intra-brand competition where it concerns distributors of the goods or services of the same supplier;

(iv) the creation of obstacles to market integration, including, in particular, limitations on consumer's choice to purchase goods or services in any Member State.

(19) Foreclosure, softening of competition and collusion at the supplier level may harm consumers, in particular by:

(a) increasing the prices charged to buyers of goods or services, which may in turn lead to higher retail prices;

(b) limiting the choice of goods or services;

(c) lowering the quality of goods or services;

(d) reducing innovation or service at the supplier level.

(20) Foreclosure, softening of competition and collusion at the distributor level may harm consumers, in particular by:

(a) increasing the retail prices of goods or services;

(b) limiting the choice of price-service combinations and distribution formats;

(c) lowering the availability and quality of retail services;

(d) reducing the level of innovation at the distribution level.

(21) A reduction of intra-brand competition (i.e. competition between distributors of the goods or services of the same supplier) is by itself unlikely to lead to negative effects for consumers if inter-brand competition (i.e. competition between distributors of the goods or services of different suppliers) is strong. In particular, in markets where individual retailers distribute the brand(s) of only one supplier, a reduction of competition between the distributors of the same brand will lead to a reduction of intra-brand competition between these distributors, but may not have a negative effect on competition between distributors in general.

(22) The possible negative effects of vertical restraints are reinforced where several suppliers and their buyers organise their trade in a similar way, leading to so-called cumulative effects.

Antitrust analysis of vertical restraints thus needs to focus on their ability to produce both positive and negative effects. For example, economic concerns about the impact of RPM derive from its ability to facilitate collusion—either at supplier or dealer level[82]—or to foreclose suppliers[83] or innovative and discounting retailers.[84]

Guidelines on Vertical Restraints

(196) RPM can restrict intra-brand and/or inter-brand competition in various ways:

(a) RPM may facilitate collusion between suppliers, by enhancing price transparency in the market, thereby making it easier to detect whether a supplier is deviating from the collusive equilibrium by cutting its price. This negative effect is more likely in markets prone to collusive outcomes, for example, where suppliers form a tight oligopoly and a significant share of the market is covered by RPM agreements;

(b) RPM may facilitate collusion between buyers at the distribution level, in particular where it is driven by the buyers. Strong or well organised buyers may be able to force or convince one or more of their suppliers to fix their resale price above the competitive level, thereby helping the buyers reach or stabilise a collusive equilibrium. RPM serves as a commitment device for retailers not to deviate from the collusive equilibrium through discounting prices;

(c) in some cases, RPM may also soften competition between manufacturers and/or between retailers, in particular when manufacturers use the same distributors to distribute their products and RPM is applied by all or many of them;

(d) RPM may reduce the pressure on the supplier's margin, in particular where a manufacturer has a commitment problem, that is, where it has an interest in lowering the price charged to subsequent distributors. In that situation, the manufacturer may prefer to agree to RPM, to help it to commit not to lower the price for subsequent distributors, and to reduce the pressure on its own margin;

(e) by preventing price competition between distributors, RPM may prevent or hinder the entry and expansion of new or more efficient distribution formats, thus reducing innovation at the distribution level;

(f) RPM may be implemented by a supplier with market power to foreclose smaller rivals. The increased margin that RPM may offer distributors may incentivise them to favour the supplier's brand over rival brands when advising customers, even where such advice is not in the customer's interest, or not to sell the rival brands at all;

(g) the direct effect of RPM is the elimination of intra-brand price competition, by preventing some or all distributors from lowering their sale price for the brand concerned, thus resulting in a price increase for that brand.

[82] E.g. it may make manufacturer collusion more stable by making it easier to detect deviations from a collusive strategy and reducing incentives for deviation. In other scenarios, retailers may induce a manufacturer to 'impose' RPM, to support their collusion, and to prevent deviations from the strategy.

[83] E.g. a supplier may use RPM to exclude competitors from the market by offering retailers a higher margin as a 'payment' for their willingness not to deal with competitors.

[84] E.g. a retailer may demand RPM from its supplier(s) to exclude discounting competitors or new entrants from their market

Similarly, territorial restraints or restraints on online selling may have anti-competitive consequences through exclusion or collusion at the supplier or distributor level, through restricting cross-border trade within the EU, or depriving consumers of the benefits of e-commerce.[85] A principal objective of the launch, as a complement to other initiatives pursued within the framework of the Digital Single Market strategy,[86] of the e-commerce sector inquiry was to identify barriers erected by companies to cross-border online trade and to analyse their impact on competition and consumers. The Final E-Commerce Report indicated that although e-commerce is an important driver of price transparency and price competition, certain online practices or restraints relating to online selling may raise competition concerns.[87] For example, the Commission noted that price-tracking software, which is becoming more prevalent and sophisticated, allows both retailers and manufactures to track online retail prices, creating a possible risk that the software can be used as a mechanism for facilitating or strengthening collusion between retailers or enabling manufacturers to monitor and enforce retailers' compliance with their particular pricing policies (especially if manufacturers have integrated into retailing).[88] As a result, the Commission has investigated a number of online restraints, including online RPM,[89] MFNs,[90] restraints on cross-border competition, and instances of 'geo-blocking'.[91]

3. THE EU APPROACH TO VERTICAL AGREEMENTS—AN OVERVIEW

A. BACKGROUND: THE EARLY APPROACH

The pro- and anti-competitive effects outlined earlier have caused many competition lawyers and economists to disagree vigorously over the years about when and/or how often the different types of vertical restraint cause anti-competitive harm, how any such harm should be reconciled with the efficiencies that vertical restraints may generate, and how legal rules or standards should be constructed to reflect, identify and weigh the competing effects.

The Commission's early approach to Article 101,[92] interpreting the concept of a restriction of competition set out in Article 101(1) broadly, led to conceptual and practical problems. It also created a central role both for Article 101(3) in the Article 101 framework and the Commission in its enforcement (national courts and NCAs could not apply Article 101(3)). As Carles Esteva Mosso, Deputy Director-General in DG Competition at the Commission, explains, under this:

> previous, more form-based approach to the interpretation of 'restriction of competition', a large number of agreements were considered to be caught by the test of Article 101(1) and required exemption under Article 101(3) . . .[93]

[85] See e.g. G. Accardo, 'Vertical Antitrust Enforcement: Transatlantic Perspectives on Restrictions of Online Distribution under EU and US Competition Law' (2013) 9 *European Competition Journal* 225, especially 261–263.

[86] A core priority of the Commission, <http://ec.europa.eu/priorities/digital-single-market/index_en.htm>. The Commission wishes to ensure that there is better access to online goods and services in the EU and is examining a broad range of barriers to cross-border e-commerce.

[87] E-commerce SWD Final Report, n. 10, e.g. para. 608

[88] Ibid., paras. 991 and 992.

[89] See Commission Press Release IP/18/460 and n. 110 and text (proceedings against Asus, Denon & Marantz, Philips, and Pioneer).

[90] See COMP/39.847, *E-books* [2013] OJ C378/25, n. 180 and text.

[91] See e.g. AT/40.428, *Guess* 17 December 2018 (€40 million fine for geo-blocking).

[92] See Chap. 5.

[93] C. Esteva Mosso, 'The Contribution of Merger Control to the Definition of Harm to Competition', Brussels, GCLC Conference, February 2016, 2.

Further, because the Commission adopted a strict and formalistic approach when applying the Article 101(3) criteria and the block exemption regulations (BERs) prior to 1999 were rigid and prescriptive, it intensely regulated the content of vertical agreements and imposed a significant and, arguably, unnecessary burden on firms.[94]

The Commission received sustained criticism for this approach. For example, Hawk, in a seminal article,[95] fiercely complained about: the overbroad application and anaemic economic analysis under Article 101(1) which was inconsistent with Court judgments (based on an incoherent rationale—notably the economic freedom notion, the market integration objective, and the desire to protect small and medium-sized enterprises); the extraordinary legal uncertainty this approach generated; and the fact that it led to a proliferation of BERs and legal formalisms, analysis of agreements by categories, and a de-emphasis on or lack of substantive economic analysis. The approach, he contended, ultimately had led to the failure of the notification system and eliminated 'what should be the heart of the matter: and antitrust (i.e. economics/law) substantive analysis of a particular agreement or practice, i.e. its competitive harms and benefits'.[96] This article is perceived to have been influential in finally convincing the Commission that its approach to vertical restraints had to change.

B. THE APPROACH SINCE 1999: THE BLOCK EXEMPTION AND REFORM

The Commission's modernisation programme commenced in January 1997, with its adoption of a Green Paper on Vertical Restraints. The Green Paper's conclusions, and the debate it triggered, led to a new regime centred around a more economic, flexible, overarching BER covering all vertical restraints concerning intermediate and final goods and services that met its requirements (1999)[97] and the publication of accompanying Guidelines[98] on the appraisal of vertical agreements, setting out a more coherent approach to analysis under Article 101 based on the economic objective underpinning it. Although the VBER and Guidelines have been revised and replaced twice since 1999, first in 2010 and subsequently in 2022, following comprehensive and lengthy evaluation processes and impact assessments,[99] the scheme of the 1999 system has broadly been preserved. On both occasions, however, modifications have been introduced to deal with legal developments and market changes, especially increased retailer power and the growth of e-commerce. Further, in the review leading up to the 2022 VBER the Commission considered that the VBER required fine-tuning to ensure that it did not create either false positives (by exempting new practices with potentially anti-competitive effect) or false negatives (by taking an overly restrictive view of certain restraints).

The changes since 1999 marked a major shift in Commission policy. The VBER provides a safe harbour for many vertical agreements, broadly those satisfying its market share thresholds and which do

[94] It meant that in practice firms would often have to seek an individual exemption for their agreement or, only a limited number of such decisions being rendered each year, more realistically, rely on a comfort letter: Green Paper, n. 78, 30.

[95] See e.g. B. E. Hawk, 'System Failure: Vertical Restraints and EC Competition Law' (1995) 32 *CMLRev* 973, 985.

[96] Ibid., section 2.5.

[97] [1999] OJ L336/21. [98] [2000] OJ C291/1.

[99] The consultation strategy document for the evaluation of the 2010 VBER was published in 2018, <https://competition-policy.ec.europa.eu/public-consultations/2018-vber_en> and followed by an evaluation phase with public consultation (see e.g. Staff Working Document and its annexes summarising the results of the evaluation of the VBER, published on 7 October 2020), an impact assessment phase with further public consultation and the publication of a draft revised block exemption and Guidelines for comment.

not contain hardcore restrictions, and the Guidelines promise more realistic analysis of other agreements under Article 101 based on a consumer welfare (and internal market) objective.

C. METHODOLOGY

The Commission's modernised approach signals that many vertical agreements may not infringe Article 101(1) at all, but even if they do, the VBER may provide a safe harbour for the agreement.

Logically, the first question that should be addressed in a verticals case is, does this agreement between undertakings infringe Article 101(1) at all? Practically, however, where an agreement appears to affect trade and restrict competition appreciably,[100] the parties are likely to prefer to rely on the 'safe haven' of the VBER rather than going through the complex analysis required to determine whether or not the agreement restricts competition. Indeed, paragraph 7 of the Guidelines recognises that although there is no mandatory sequence for the assessment of vertical agreements, it generally involves the following steps.

(a) first, the undertakings involved need to establish the market shares of the supplier and the buyer on the relevant market where they respectively sell and purchase the contract goods or services;

(b) if neither the market share of the supplier nor that of the buyer exceeds the 30 per cent market share threshold set out in Article 3 VBER, the vertical agreement is covered by the safe harbour established by the Regulation, provided that the agreement does not contain hardcore restrictions within the meaning of Article 4 or any excluded restrictions within the meaning of Article 5 of the Regulation that cannot be severed from the rest of the agreement;

(c) if the relevant market share of the supplier or the buyer exceeds the 30 per cent threshold or the agreement contains one or more hardcore restrictions or non-severable excluded restrictions, it is necessary to assess whether the vertical agreement falls within the scope of Article 101(1) of the Treaty;

(d) if the vertical agreement falls within the scope of Article 101(1) of the Treaty, it is necessary to examine whether it fulfils the conditions of the exception provided by Article 101(3) of the Treaty.

This approach clearly represents sensible and pragmatic advice as the VBER provides precious legal certainty for firms. The methodology does, however, preserve the emphasis of Article 101(3) in the system, over the question of whether the agreement infringes Article 101(1). Although this chapter starts with the question of whether the agreement infringes Article 101(1), before going on to consider the terms of the VBER and Article 101(3), it is recognised that in practice businesses will generally seek to sidestep complex Article 101(1) analysis, which is not always easy to navigate, and to start with the question: is this agreement covered by the VBER and so exempted from Article 101(1) if within it?

When considering the application of Article 101, an important point is that a fundamentally different approach applies depending upon whether the agreement contains object restraints or restraints identified as hardcore restraints in the VBER (see also Chapter 5 and Fig. 11.1). A hardcore restraint is likely to infringe Article 101(1) (many are liable in principle to restrict competition by object[101]) and is unlikely to fulfil the conditions of Article 101(3) (the VBER does not apply). In contrast, many other vertical agreements are likely to be compatible with Article 101, either because they do not appreciably restrict competition or because they satisfy the conditions of the VBER.

[100] See Chaps. 4 (discussing an appreciable effect on trade) and 5 (discussing appreciable restriction of competition).
[101] See further Chap. 5.

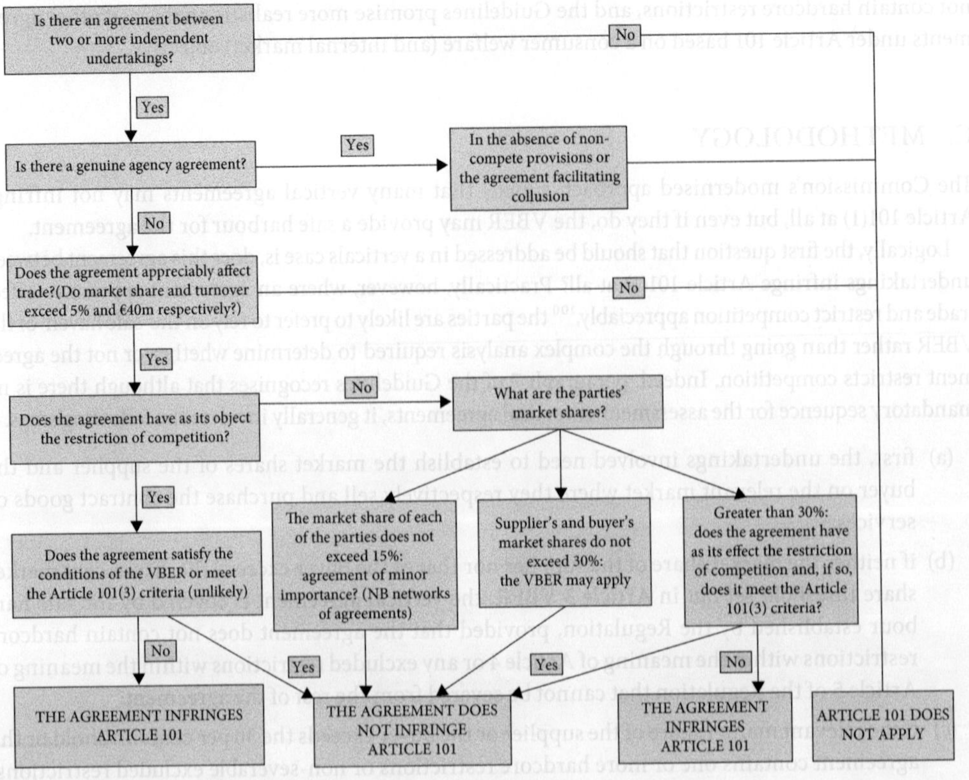

Figure 11.1 Analysis of vertical agreements under Article 101

4. VERTICAL AGREEMENTS AND ARTICLE 101(1)

A. RESTRICTIONS BY OBJECT

(i) Identifying Object Restraints

It was seen in Chapter 5 that in order to determine whether restraints are restrictive by object, 'regard must be had inter alia to the content of its provisions, the objectives it seeks to ascertain and the economic and legal context of which it forms a part'.[102] Further, that the following 'vertical' restraints are liable in principle to be restrictive by object:

- RPM provisions;
- restraints conferring absolute territorial protection (ATP) on a distributor or otherwise aimed at prohibiting or limiting parallel trade;
- certain SDSs;

unless the context and purpose of the agreement suggests otherwise.

[102] Case C-501/06 P, *GlaxoSmithKline Services Unlimited v Commission* EU:C:2009:610, para. 58.

(ii) Resale Price Maintenance, ATP, Export, and Online Sales Bans

A number of cases hold that, where an agreement between the supplier and distributor can be established,[103] a provision fixing minimum resale prices to be charged by distributors (or indirectly operating as an RPM provision) will be found to be by its very nature injurious to competition. In *Pronuptia de Paris v Schillgallis*, the CJ, in setting out guidelines on the compatibility of distribution franchises with Article 101(1), held that 'provisions which impair the franchisee's freedom to determine his own prices are restrictive of competition'[104] and in *SA Binon & Cie v SA Agence et Messageries de la Presse* it held that 'provisions which fix the prices to be observed in contracts with third parties constitute, of themselves, a restriction on competition within the meaning of Article [101(1)]'.[105] Further, although the cases recognise that a SDS, in which 'price competition is not generally emphasized either as an exclusive or indeed as a principal factor',[106] may be compatible with Article 101(1), in *Metro-SB-Grossmärkte GmbH v Commission (Metro I)*, the CJ stressed that price competition 'can never be eliminated'.[107]

In 2018,[108] the Commission condemned, in four separate settlement decisions, strategies pursued individually by four consumer electronics manufacturers to ensure retailers within SDSs, selling online, adhered to resale prices. These arrangements were designed to stabilise or increase the price of their products. The suppliers watched prices through price monitoring and adjustment software programs and, following their own investigations or complaints by other retailers, took retaliatory measures and issued threats against low-pricing retailers. Relying on *Binon* and *Groupement des Cartes Bancaires (CB) v Commission*,[109] the Commission held that RPM 'may be considered so likely to have negative effects, in particular on the price, choice, quantity or quality of the goods and services, that it may be considered redundant, for the purposes of applying Article 101(1) . . . to prove that they have actual effects on the market'; the conduct by its very nature, restricts competition.[110] The close monitoring of retailers' resale prices through software meant that the manufacturers could avoid price erosion across, potentially, their entire (online) retail network.

In contrast, providing dealers 'with price guidelines, so long as there is no concerted practice between the [parties] for the actual application of such prices'[111] and maximum price setting may not infringe Article 101(1) so long as these practices do not operate as a 'focal point for resellers', which will be followed by all or most of them, or soften competition and facilitate collusion.[112]

Ever since *Société Technique Minière v Maschinenbau Ulm GmbH (STM)*[113] and *Établissements Consten SàRL & Grundig-Verkaufs-GmbH v Commission (Consten and Grundig)*[114] it has been clear that although appointing an exclusive distributor for a specific sales territory might not infringe

[103] Case T-208/01, *Volkswagen v Commission* EU:T:2003:326, *aff'd* Case C-74/04 P, EU:C:2006:460 (the GC quashed a Commission decision condemning RPM on the ground that the Commission had failed to establish that the distributors had agreed to or acquiesced in the supplier's policy of RPM, see Chap. 5). But see reference made in Case C-211/22, *Super Bock Bebidas* (judgment pending) (asking whether RPM in itself constitutes an infringement by object).

[104] Case 161/84, EU:C:1986:41, para. 25. [105] Case 243/83, EU:C:1985:284, para. 44.

[106] Case 26/76, *Metro-SB-Grossmärkte GmbH v Commission (Metro I)* EU:C:1977:167, para. 21.

[107] Ibid. [108] See e.g. AT.40465, *Asus* 24 July 2018, Commission Press Release IP/18/4601.

[109] C-67/13 P, EU:C:2014:2204. [110] AT.40465, *Asus* 24 July 2018, paras. 105–107.

[111] Case 161/84, *Pronuptia de Paris GmbH v Pronuptia de Paris Irmgard Schillgallis* EU:C:1986:41, para. 25.

[112] Guidelines, para. 199. Recommended and maximum RPM and selective distribution may also be covered by the VBER, see Section 5.C.v.

[113] Case 56/65, EU:C:1966:38 (see extract set out in Chap. 5).

[114] Cases 56 and 58/64, EU:C:1966:41 (see extract set out in Chap. 5). See also e.g. Case T-77/92, *Parker Pen v Commission* EU:T:1994:85, Case C-501/06 P, *GlaxoSmithKline Services Unlimited v Commission* EU:C:2009:610, para. 61, Case T-360/09, *E.ON Ruhrgas AG v Commission* EU:T:2012:332, and see also Cases C-403 and 429/08, *Football Association Premier League Ltd and Others v QC Leisure and Others and Karen Murphy v Media Protection Services Ltd (Murphy)* EU:C:2011:631, paras. 137–139 (and Chap. 12).

Article 101(1), clauses in a distribution agreement which go beyond this and result in the isolation of a national market, and/or in maintaining separate national markets, are liable to be found to have as their object the restriction of competition since they shelter the distributor from all intra-brand competition and lead to the division of national markets. In Chapter 5, it was seen that *Consten and Grundig* provides a clear example of the Court seeking to balance the EU policy of market integration with competition and efficiency.

As is the case for RPM, the rules governing market partitioning apply not only to agreements directly prohibiting dealers from selling in certain territories but to arrangements which indirectly do so through, for example, charging higher prices, using other pricing mechanisms (dual pricing or refusal or reduction of bonuses),[115] or guarantee systems, to deter export,[116] or by allowing exports only with the supplier's consent.[117]

Even if an export prohibition (or RPM) is not expressly incorporated into an agreement, it may be read into, and become part of, the agreement, via conduct if a concurrence of wills between the parties is established (for example, where a supplier's policy to prohibit export is explicitly or tacitly accepted by distributors following a refusal, or threat of a refusal, to supply the products, reductions in the volume of the product supplied, following receipt of a circular or an invoice which makes clear that export is prohibited).[118]

In *Pierre Fabre v Président de l'Autorité de la concurrence*,[119] the CJ held, extending the principles to the e-commerce context, that absolute restraints on online selling are also liable to restrict competition. Thus, as a requirement that a qualified pharmacist be present at a physical sales point operated as a *de facto* ban on internet selling which, in turn, considerably reduced the ability of a distributor to sell outside its territory, the provision was liable to restrict competition in that sector (see further the discussion of, and extract from, *Pierre Fabre* in Section 4.C.v). This emphasises the importance placed on online selling to 'the internal market in Europe because it broadens the market, improves the choices for customers, and generally speaking, enhances competition'.[120] Nonetheless, in *Coty*,[121]

[115] See e.g. COMP/28.282, *The Distillers Co Ltd* [1978] OJ L50/16, on appeal Case 30/78, *Distillers Co v Commission* EU:C:1980:186, COMP/30.228, *Distillers Co plc (Red Label)* [1983] OJ C245/3, COMP/32.390, *Newitt/Dunlop Slazenger International*, Case C-501/06 P, *GlaxoSmithKline* EU:C:2009:610, and COMP/35.918, *JCB* [2002] OJ L69/1, this aspect of the decision was upheld, Case T-67/01, *JCB Service v Commission* EU:T:2004:3, *aff'd* Case C-167/04 P, *JCB Service v Commission* EU:C:2006:594, COMP/36.623, 36.820, and 37.275, *Peugeot* [2005] OJ L173/49, *aff'd* (but fine reduced) Case T-450/05, *Peugeot v Commission* EU:T:2009:262 (discriminatory bonus system backed up by a threat to reduce supplies to exporting dealers). But see Section 5.C.v, especially n. 297 and text.

[116] COMP/1576, *Zanussi* 23 October 1978; Case 31/85, *ETA Fabriques d'Ébauches v DK Investments SA* EU:C:1985:494. Guarantees can be limited to products sold by an authorised distributor within a SDS, however, see Case C-376/92, *Metro v Cartier* EU:C:1994:5, paras. 32–34.

[117] Case T-77/92, *Parker Pen v Commission* EU:T:1994:85; Case 19/77, *Miller v Commission* EU:C:1978:19; COMP/37.975, *PO/Yamaha* 16 July 2003; AT.40428, *Guess* 17 December 2018; and *Voorne Koi v Oase*, NL:RBMNE:2014:6156, Utrecht District Court 3 December 2014.

[118] See Chap. 4 and, in particular, Case T-41/96, *Bayer AG v Commission* EU:T:2000:242, *aff'd* Cases C-2 and 3/01 P, EU:C:2004:2. See also COMP/35.679, *Novalliance/Systemform* [1997] OJ L47/11 an export ban was prohibited even though stipulated to be applicable only 'unless prohibited by law'; COMP/31.503, *Konica* [1988] OJ L78/34; Opinion of Van Gerven AG in Case C-277/87, *Sandoz Prodotti Farmaceutici SpA v Commission* EU:C:1989:363, COMP/35.733; *Volkswagen* [1998] OJ L124/60. See also the discussion of hardcore restraints prohibited by the VBER, Section 5.C.v.

[119] Case C-439/09, EU:C:2011:649.

[120] 'Interview with Dr. Alexander Italianer, Director-General for Competition, European Commission', *theantitrustsource*, April 2011, 1, 6; AT.40428, *Guess* 17 December 2018 (€40 million fine for geo-blocking, including through a prohibition of selling online without specific authorisation).

[121] Case C-230/16 EU:C:2017:941 and n. 237 and text. But see the settlement reached by the Bundeskartellamt (the German NCA) following its investigation into *Adidas*, Case B3 137/12, 27 June 2014 (English summary available at <www.bundeskartellamt.de/SharedDocs/Entscheidung/EN/Fallberichte/Kartellverbot/2014/B3-137-12.pdf?__blob=publicationFile&v=2>).

the CJ confirmed that a restraint which did not constitute an absolute prohibition on online selling, but which only prohibited certain forms of internet selling, in that case via a third party platform, might be compatible with Article 101(1) (see further Section 4.C).

These cases establish that even if economic theory may suggest that RPM and ATP may cause anti-competitive harm only in defined market circumstances (for example, where they are liable to facilitate collusion) and that pro-competitive rationales may exist for their use,[122] RPM and ATP are liable in principle to restrict competition by object. Further, that the legal and economic context of a case is unlikely to lead to a finding that the objective of the agreement is not to restrict competition.[123] Rather, a long line of cases indicates that EU authorities consider that such agreements may pose a high probability of negative effects on prices etc., or harm to competition through limiting important competition/rivalry between dealers and suppliers and, crucially, erecting private barriers to cross-border trade inimical to the internal market objective. Pleas that RPM or ATP have a pro-competitive or beneficial—not a restrictive—objective (for example, to enhance efficiency of the supply chain to the benefit of the parties and end customers[124]), have in contrast been rejected.[125]

The EU Courts have not therefore adopted a similar approach to the US Supreme Court which, relying on economic theory, overturned in three landmark cases, *Continental TV, Inc v GTE Sylvania*,[126] *State Oil v Khan*,[127] and *Leegin Creative Leather Products Inc v PSKS, Inc*,[128] previous rulings holding vertical customer and territorial restraints,[129] maximum RPM,[130] and minimum RPM[131] to be illegal per se. In these cases, the US Court held that as: (a) per se rules are appropriate only for restraints that always, or almost always, tend to restrict competition, have manifestly anti-competitive effects, and lack any redeeming virtue; and (b) the market impact of vertical intra-brand restrictions is complex because of their ability simultaneously to reduce intra-brand competition and to stimulate inter-brand competition and bring about distribution efficiencies, the competing effects resulting from such restraints should be analysed under the rule of reason. A claimant in the US must therefore demonstrate actual or likely anti-competitive effects of price and territorial restraints before a defendant is required to justify them.

In the EU, in contrast, there is concern that a move away from an assumption that ATP, RPM, and bans on online selling restrict competition under Article 101(1), might create a risk of false positives, especially given the budget limits constraining the activities of European Competition Network

[122] 'Theoretically, the only defensible position on vertical restraints seems to be the rule of reason. Most vertical restraints can increase or decrease welfare, depending on the environment. Legality or illegality per se thus seems unwarranted', J. Tirole, *The Theory of Industrial Organization* (MIT Press, 1988), 186 (although the author accepts that this conclusion puts too heavy a burden on antitrust authorities and recognises the need for economic theorists to develop classifications and criteria to facilitate a determination of when such restraints are liable to harm social welfare).

[123] See Chap. 5.

[124] Rather, the jurisprudence reflects an underlying presumption that RPM and parallel trade restrictions are a disproportionate means to achieve any aims alleged to be sought by the parties to the agreement. Thus in cases such as *Consten and Grundig* and *Distillers*, pleas that restrictions were required to enable the supplier to penetrate a new market have generally fallen on deaf ears, see nn. 115 and 335 and text. But see reference made in *Super Bock* n. 103 and text.

[125] Cases C-403 and 429/08, *Murphy* EU:C:2011:631, see also discussion in Chaps. 5, 12, and 16.

[126] 433 US 36 (1977). [127] 522 US 3 (1997).

[128] 551 US 887 (2007). For a fuller analysis of the case, see A. Jones, 'Resale Price Maintenance: A Debate About Competition Policy in Europe?' (2009) 5 *European Competition Journal* 479.

[129] *United States v Arnold, Schwinn & Co*, 388 US 365, 376 (1967).

[130] See *Keifer-Stewart Co v Joseph E. Seagram & Sons Inc*, 340 US 211 (1951) and *Albrecht v Herald Co*, 390 US 145 (1968).

[131] *Dr Miles Medical Co v John D Park & Sons Co*, 220 US 373 (1911).

(ECN) members.[132] The Commission (and NCAs[133]) has thus made it clear that, in absence of individually established efficiencies, these are likely to constitute serious infringements of the rules (likely to be held to restrict competition by object appreciably and unlikely to meet the Article 101(3) criteria (see Section 5)), which may attract fines, see for example in *VW*,[134] *Nintendo*,[135] *Yamaha*,[136] *Asus* (online RPM),[137] and *Guess* (geo-blocking).[138] The Guidelines do recognise, however, that severe restraints objectively necessary for the implementation of a particular vertical agreement 'for instance, to ensure compliance with a public ban on selling dangerous substances to certain customers for reasons of safety or health' may, exceptionally, fall outside the scope of Article 101(1).[139]

The Commission's wider concern about geo-blocking practices acting as barriers to cross-border online sellers has also been addressed by the adoption of Regulation 2018/302, the 'Geo-blocking Regulation'.[140] This Regulation targets a number of broad measures[141] that undermine online shopping, cross-border sales, and other forms of discrimination based on customers' nationality, place of residence or establishment, and which result in some customers being unable to buy goods and services from traders in a different Member State. It also prohibits a supplier from contractually prohibiting a retailer from responding to unsolicited customer requests, 'passive selling', in specified circumstances. Certain vertical restraints may therefore now be prohibited by the Geo-blocking Regulation as well as Article 101.[142] The Regulation forms part of a set of EU measures aimed at boosting e-commerce and cross-border online sales within the single market.

(iii) Other Object Restraints and Selective Distribution

The category of object restraints is not closed but includes any agreement whose content, context, and objective reveals in itself a sufficient degree of harm to competition. An important question therefore is what, if any, other vertical restraints might be considered to be restrictive by object.

[132] See also e.g. M.-L. Allain and C. Chambolle, 'Anti-competitive Effects of Resale-below-cost Laws', Working Papers hal-00367492_vl (2002), T. R. Overstreet, 'Resale Price Maintenance: Economic Theories and Empirical Evidence', Federal Trade Commission Bureau of Economics staff report (November 1983). See G. Shaffer, 'Anti-competitive Effects of RPM (Resale Price Maintenance) Agreements in Fragmented Markets', OFT report (February 2013).

[133] See e.g. Decision 19-D-14, *Bikeurope* 1 July 2019 (France), Decision 18-D-23, *Andreas Stihl* 24 October 2018 (France), and Case 50230, *Ping* 24 August 2017 (UK), *aff'd* Case 1279/1/12/17 *Ping Europe Ltd v CMA* [2018] CAT 13, [2020] EWCA Civ 13.

[134] COMP/35.733, *Volkswagen* [1998] OJ L124/60 (fines of €102 million (reduced to €90 million on appeal, Case T-62/98, *Volkswagen AG v Commission* EU:T:2000:180, *aff'd* Case C-338/00 P, *Volkswagen AG v Commission* EU:C:2003:473) in respect of a wide range of contractual practices designed to prevent distributors selling outside their contractual territory).

[135] COMP/35.706 and 36.321 [2003] OJ L255/33 (fines of €167.8 million on Nintendo and seven of its European distributors for colluding to prevent exports from low-priced to high-priced countries), *aff'd* (but fines reduced) Case T-12/03, *Itochu v Commission* EU:T:2009:130 and Case T-13/03, *Nintendo and Nintendo of Europe v Commission* EU:T:2009:131, Case C-260/09 P, *Activision Blizzard Germany GmbH v Commission* EU:C:2011:62. See also COMP/39.154, *Apple/iTunes* 18 March 2008.

[136] COMP/37.975, *Yamaha* 16 July 2003.

[137] AT.40465, *Asus* 24 July 2018, Commission Press Release IP/18/4601, n. 108 and text.

[138] AT.40428, 17 December 2018, see n. 236 and text.

[139] Guidelines, para. 180.

[140] Reg. 2018/302, on addressing unjustified geo-blocking and other forms of discrimination based on customers' nationality, place of residence or place of establishment within the internal market and amending Regs. (EC) No 2006/2004 and (EU) 2017/2394 and Dir. 2009/22/EC [2018] OJ L 60I/1.

[141] For example, blocking or limiting, through technological measures, a customer's access to a trader's online interface, redirecting customers from an online interface, or applying in certain circumstances different general conditions of access to goods or services.

[142] Reg. 2018/302, Art. 6 and recital 34.

In *Allianz Hungária Biztosító Zrt, Generali-Providencia Biztosító Zrt v Gazdasági Versenyhivatal*,[143] the CJ held that as vertical restrictions could have particularly significant restrictive potential, they had to be carefully examined to determine whether or not they were restrictive of competition by object.[144] This case involved a finding by the Hungarian competition authority, GVH, that a series of bilateral vertical agreements concluded annually between Hungarian insurance companies and car dealer/repairers relating to hourly rates for car repairs in the event of an accident (and linking that remuneration to the number and percentage of insurance contracts that the dealer sells for that company) had as their object the restriction of competition. Significant fines were imposed. Following judicial proceedings, the Hungarian Supreme Court referred the question of whether the contracts were restrictive of competition by object to the CJ.

The CJ held that a number of factors had to be taken into account in determining whether the agreements were by their very nature injurious to the proper functioning of normal competition, including whether the agreements: linked the dealers' remuneration and the insurance broker function; were designed to increase the market shares of Generali and Allianz; and were concluded on the basis of 'recommended prices' established in decisions taken by GÉMOSZ (the Hungarian Association of Automobile Dealers). The structure of the market should also be considered, along with the existence of alternative distribution methods, the market power of the parties, and whether Generali and Allianz had acted independently or in concert. The CJ also held that if decisions taken by GÉMOSZ during that period were found by the national court to restrict competition by object and that the insurance companies had voluntarily confirmed those decisions, the unlawfulness of those decisions would also vitiate an agreement concluded between one of the insurance companies and GÉMOSZ, which would be considered a restriction of competition by object. Although the Court identifies competition concerns, the broad approach adopted to identifying object restrictions is difficult to reconcile with later judgments emphasising the narrow nature of the object category and the limited role to be played by context in the process (see Chapter 5).

In *Pierre Fabre*, the CJ also held that as SDSs 'necessarily affect competition', they are to be considered, in the absence of objective justification, as restrictions by object.[145] This holding and SDSs are discussed more fully in Section 4.C.

B. ANALYSING THE RESTRICTIVE 'EFFECT' OF VERTICAL AGREEMENTS

(i) Introduction

Where an agreement does not have as its object the restriction of competition, it will not be prohibited under Article 101(1) unless it has an appreciable restrictive effect. The following sections explore the cases that consider how this analysis is conducted in relation to specific types of vertical restraint. The Article 101(3) Guidelines interpret this case law as providing that it must be established that the agreement affects:

- inter-brand competition, i.e. that it affects 'actual or potential competition to such an extent that on the relevant market negative effects on prices, output, innovation or the variety or quality of goods and services can be expected with a reasonable degree of probability';[146] or

[143] Case C-32/11, EU:C:2013:160. [144] Ibid., paras. 43–48.

[145] Case C-439/09, EU:C:2011:649, para. 39. For the view that the decision of the CJ to hold all SDSs to be restrictions by object is quite remarkable 'and probably a slip of the tongue. It is internally inconsistent because if one looks at the final holding of the Court, the restriction by object is only the ban on internet sales, not the use of selective distribution', see Monti, n. 3, 501.

[146] Article 101(3) Guidelines, para. 24. This could be because the agreement restricts actual or potential competition between the parties or between any one of the parties and third parties that could have existed absent the agreement, paras. 25–26.

- intra-brand competition—it restricts, without objective justification, distributors from competing with each other.[147]

Further that if, following these principles, the transaction is not restrictive of competition, restraints 'ancillary' to the main non-restrictive transaction also fall outside Article 101(1).[148]

Building on those principles, the Vertical Guidelines set out both general and specific guidance on the individual application of Article 101 to vertical agreements. They state that when assessing whether or not an agreement restricts competition by effect under Article 101(1), it must be determined whether the agreement affects actual or potential competition to such an extent that on the relevant market appreciable 'negative effects on prices, output, innovation, or the variety or quality of the goods or services can be expected with a reasonable degree of probability. . . . Appreciable anti-competitive effects are more likely to occur when at least one of the parties to the agreement has or obtains some degree of market power and the agreement contributes to the creation, maintenance or strengthening of that market power, or allows the parties to the agreement to exploit such market power.'[149]

The central inquiry thus focuses on the *market power* of the undertakings concerned:

Guidelines on Vertical Restraints

(278) . . . The following factors are particularly relevant to establish whether a vertical agreement brings about an appreciable restriction of competition within the meaning of Article 101(1) of the Treaty:

(a) the nature of the agreement;

(b) the market position of the parties;

(c) the market position of competitors (upstream and downstream);

(d) the market position of buyers of the contract goods or services;

(e) entry barriers;

(f) the level of the production or distribution chain that is affected;

(g) the nature of the product;

(h) the dynamics of the market.

(279) Other relevant factors may also be taken into account.

(280) The importance of individual factors may vary depending on the circumstances of the case. For instance, a high market share of the parties is usually a good indicator of market power. However, in the case of low entry barriers market power may be sufficiently constrained by actual or potential entry. It is therefore not possible to provide firm rules of general applicability on the importance of individual factors.

. . .

[147] Thus according to the Commission two counterfactuals may need to be used—one to determine whether the agreement restricts inter-brand competition (whether the agreement restricts actual or potential competition that would have existed without the agreement) and one to determine whether it restricts intra-brand competition (whether the agreement restricts actual or potential competition that would have existed in the absence of the contractual restraints), see Chap. 5.

[148] Article 101(3) Guidelines, paras. 28–31 and see Chap. 5. [149] Guidelines, para. 277.

(290) Other factors may also be relevant to the assessment. Those factors can include in particular:

(a) the presence of cumulative effects, deriving from the fact that the market is covered by similar vertical restraints imposed by other suppliers or buyers;

(b) whether the agreement is 'imposed' (namely, most of the restrictions or obligations apply only to one party to the agreement) or 'agreed' (both parties accept restrictions or obligations);

(c) the regulatory environment;

(d) behaviour that may indicate or facilitate collusion, such as price leadership, pre-announced price changes and price discussions, price rigidity in response to excess capacity, price discrimination and past collusive behaviour.

Other sections consider the case law, decisional practice, and guidance on the question of how Article 101(1) applies to specific types of vertical agreements or restraints—but do not always so obviously follow this framework. It has already been seen, however, that this complex assessment will ordinarily be circumvented where the parties' market shares do not exceed 30 per cent, since, absent object restraints (which closely parallel the VBER's category of hardcore restraints[150]), the VBER should apply.

(ii) Single Branding Agreements and *Delimitis*

One of the most important of all of the Court's judgments in the context of distribution agreements is *Delimitis v Henninger Bräu*,[151] in which the Court gave guidance to a national court on how to assess the compatibility of a beer-supply agreement with Article 101(1). It will be remembered (from Chapter 5) that the contract obliged the café proprietor to obtain certain of its beer requirements from the brewer, Henninger Bräu.

The CJ recognised that agreements such as this which oblige a buyer to obtain all, most, or a certain percentage or amount of its requirements from a named supplier frequently lead to efficiencies in distribution. A supplier is enabled to plan the number of sales it will make with greater precision, and distributors are encouraged actively to promote the supplier's product. Further, suppliers often confer reciprocal benefits (such as loans at below market rates, training, business and financial advice) on distributors who agree not to purchase a competitor's products. Obviously, the supplier will wish to ensure that these benefits are not used to assist sales of competitors' products. The CJ thus held that the object of the agreement was not to restrict competition.

Its effect on competition had to be assessed, however, since these non-compete or quantity-forcing agreements prohibit or deter distributors from handling competitors' products and may, together with networks of similar agreements, tie up outlets and preclude competitors (actual and potential) from gaining access to distributors (they have a direct impact on inter-brand competition by foreclosing the market to competing and potential suppliers). This worry is particularly acute in markets where access to the market is not easy on account of the existence of barriers to entry, such as planning restrictions or licensing requirements. They may also soften competition and facilitate collusion between suppliers (especially in case of cumulative use) or through a loss of in-store inter-brand competition.[152]

[150] Ibid., para. 179.

[151] Case C-234/89, *Delimitis v Henninger Bräu* EU:C:1991:91 and see also discussion and extract set out in Chap. 5.

[152] See Section 2.C.iii.

The CJ held that the effects were to be determined by, first, defining the relevant market and considering whether or not that market was foreclosed to other competitors or precluded expansion by existing competitors. If it was, secondly, it had to be determined whether or not the agreement in question restricted competition. It would only do so if the agreements concluded by that producer appreciably contributed to the foreclosure effect. It thus focused its inquiry on the important question whether or not the agreement, alone or in conjunction with a network of similar agreements, would lead to a restriction of inter-brand competition. It considered that only where the agreement contributed to the foreclosure of the market and to a restriction of inter-brand competition would it be found to restrict competition within the meaning of Article 101(1).

In a series of subsequent cases, the Commission dealt with single branding agreements notified to it for exemption; in some cases it found that such agreements did not infringe Article 101(1) at all,[153] in some cases it found that the agreements infringed Article 101(1) but met the Article 101(3) criteria,[154] and in others it found that the agreements infringed Article 101(1) and did not meet the Article 101(3) criteria.[155] In *Van den Bergh Foods v Commission*,[156] for example, the GC upheld a finding that freezer exclusivity operated by HB in Ireland infringed Article 101(1) and did not meet the criteria of Article 101(3). In respect to the analysis required under Article 101(1), the GC reiterated the need for a *Delimitis*-type analysis.[157] It found that the freezer exclusivity had the same effect as outlet exclusivity (the freezer exclusivity had prevented retailers from stocking competing ice-creams for which there was demand). The network of HB's agreements and their supply of exclusive freezer cabinets had 'a considerable dissuasive effect on retailers with regard to the installation of their own cabinet or that of another manufacturer and operate de facto as a tie on sales outlets that have only HB freezer cabinets'.[158] It thus concluded that it was 'clear from an examination of the entirety of the similar distribution agreements concluded on the relevant market, and other evidence of the economic and legal context of which those agreements form part, that the distribution agreements concluded by HB are liable to have an appreciable effect on competition for the purposes of Article [101(1)] of the Treaty and contribute significantly to a foreclosure of the market'.[159] The CJ also adopted a similar approach in *SIA 'Maxima Latvija' v Konkurences padome*.[160]

The Commission's approach in the Guidelines is consistent with the Court's case law.[161] Although many benefit from the VBER, the Commission stresses the central importance in the Article 101(1)

[153] See COMP/36.511, *Roberts/Greene King* 12 November 1998 (Greene King's network of agreements did not make a significant contribution to the foreclosure of the market of the distribution on beer in establishments selling alcoholic beverages for consumption on the premises in the UK, *aff'd* Case T-25/99, *Roberts v Commission* EU:T:2001:177) and, more remarkably, COMP/37.904, *Interbrew* 15 April 2003 (beer-supply agreements concluded by Interbrew, which had 56% of the Belgian Horeca market (Horeca (hotel/restaurant/catering) outlets are those that have concluded loan agreements or lease/sublease agreements with a brewer) did not, as amended, infringe Art. 101(1). Essentially the amended agreements gave Belgian Horeca outlets extended freedom to carry other beers not brewed by Interbrew as the non-compete obligations were limited to draught pils and, in the case of loan-tie agreements, could be terminated quite easily).

[154] See COMP/36.081, *Bass* [1999] OJ L186/1 and COMP/35.079, *Whitbread* [1999] OJ L88/26. But see the discussion of *Inntrepreneur Pub Co v Crehan* [2006] UKHL 38, in Chap. 14.

[155] See COMP/34.072, *Langnese-Iglo GmbH* [1993] OJ L183/19, especially paras. 94–95 and 101, *aff'd* Case T-7/93, *Langnese-Iglo GmbH v Commission* EU:T:1995:98 and Case C-279/95, EU:C:1998:447, and COMP/31.533 and 34.072, *Schöller Lebensmittel GmbH & Co KG* [1993] OJ L183/1, in which the Commission appeared to adopt an extremely narrow construction of the Court's judgment in Case C-234/89, *Delimitis v Henninger Bräu* EU:C:1991:91,

[156] Case T-65/98, EU:T:2003:281, *aff'd* Case C-552/03 P, *Unilever Bestfoods v Commission* EU:C:2006:607.

[157] Case T-65/98, *Van den Bergh* EU:T:2003:281, para. 83, *aff'd* Case C-552/03 P, *Unilever Bestfoods* EU:C:2006:607, paras. 84–85.

[158] Case T-65/98, *Van den Bergh* EU:T:2003:281, para. 98.

[159] Ibid., para. 118.

[160] Case C-345/14, EU:C:2015:784 and see Chap. 5.

[161] See also Case C-214/99, *Neste Markkinointi Oy v Yötuuli* EU:C:2000:679.

appraisal of single branding agreements of examining: the capacity of the obligation to result in anti-competitive foreclosure of competitors or potential competitors, especially taking account of the market position of the supplier and its competitors (and the latter's ability to compete on equal terms for each individual customer's entire demand), the scale of entry barriers and countervailing buyer power; and the level in the production and distribution chain.[162] A single or cumulative anti-competitive effect is not anticipated where the market share of the largest supplier is below 30 per cent and the market share of the five largest suppliers is below 50 per cent.[163]

(iii) Exclusive Distribution Agreements and *STM*

Exclusive distribution agreements, in which a manufacturer appoints a sole distributor for a particular area, have a number of positive effects and may consequently stimulate the competitive process. For example: efficiencies flow from the manufacturer's decision to deal only with one distributor in a particular territory; transaction costs are saved; customer feedback may be more easily obtained; and such an agreement may be essential to solve a free-rider problem and to encourage expenditure promoting and advertising the product. Suppliers thus 'often use exclusive distribution systems to incentivise distributors to make the financial and non-financial investments needed to develop the supplier's brand . . ., or to sell a new product . . ., or to incentivise distributors to focus their selling and promotional activities on a particular product. For the distributors, the protection provided by exclusivity may enable them to secure a certain volume of business and a margin that justifies their investment efforts.'[164]

The case law clearly recognises these benefits and that such agreements do not automatically infringe Article 101(1). In *STM*,[165] the CJ held that exclusive distribution agreements will not restrict competition if the appointment of the exclusive distributor is necessary to enable the manufacturer to penetrate a new market. The Court also held that in assessing the impact of the agreement on competition it was necessary to take into account the products at issue, the market position and importance of the parties, the existence (or not) of parallel networks of similar agreements, and the severity of the clauses intended to protect the exclusive dealership.

The Guidelines stress the importance under Article 101(1) of analysing the effect of these agreements on competition, and to assess their ability to reduce or soften competition or facilitate collusion. In particular, 'the market position of the supplier and its competitors is of major importance, as a loss of intra-brand competition will only be problematic if inter-brand competition is limited at the supplier or distributor level'.[166] The stronger the position of the supplier, the higher the likelihood that inter-brand competition is weak. Further, the stronger the position of the supplier's competitors, the more likely that any reduction in intra-brand competition will be outweighed by sufficient inter-brand competition. However, where there are a limited number of competitors with similar market positions, the greater the risk of collusion.[167] The Guidelines also note that when combined with single branding, exclusive dealing can make it more difficult for other suppliers to find alternative distributors.[168]

[162] Guidelines, paras. 299–312. See also e.g. Commission Press Release IP/17/97 <http://europa.eu/rapid/press-release_IP-17-97_en.htm> (closing of investigation into long-term exclusivity provisions between Audible and Apple following the parties' agreement to remove these obligations from their contracts).

[163] Ibid., para. 304. [164] Ibid., para. 118.

[165] Case 56/65, EU:C:1966:38, see extract set out in Chap. 5. Varying degrees of immunity from intra-brand competition can be granted on top of the grant of exclusivity for an area. If the agreement goes further and confers ATP, the agreement is likely to infringe Art. 101, whether or not the parties have market power and/or the ability to affect prices or output on the market, see Section 4.A.ii.

[166] Guidelines, para. 125. [167] Ibid., paras. 125–126.

[168] Ibid., para. 128.

(iv) Franchising Agreements and *Pronuptia de Paris*

The Commission describes franchise agreements in its Guidelines:

(165) Franchise agreements contain licences of IPRs relating, in particular, to trademarks or signs and know-how for the use and distribution of goods or services. In addition to the licence of IPRs, the franchisor usually provides the franchisee with commercial or technical assistance during the lifetime of the agreement. The licence and the assistance are integral components of the business method being franchised. The franchisor is in general paid a franchise fee by the franchisee for the use of the particular business method. Franchising may enable the franchisor to establish, with limited investments, a uniform network for the distribution of its products. In addition to the provision of the business method, franchise agreements usually contain a combination of various vertical restraints concerning the products being distributed, for instance selective distribution and/or non-compete obligations

Franchising arrangements may have a positive impact on competition on a market by assisting the entry of new competitors to a market and leading to an increase in inter-brand competition. They enable a franchisor to expand its reputation and network without engaging in substantial investment. A franchisee is also enabled to set up and to enter a market with the assistance of an entrepreneur whose business has already been tried and tested on the market.

In *Pronuptia de Paris GmbH v Pronuptia de Paris Irmgard Schillgallis*,[169] the CJ recognised that franchise agreements do not in themselves interfere with competition and accepted that two categories of clauses, essential to their successful operation, did not constitute restrictions of competition for the purposes of Article 101(1).

Case 161/84, *Pronuptia de Paris GmbH v Pronuptia de Paris Irmgard Schillgallis* EU:C:1986:41

Court of Justice

14. The compatibility of franchise agreements for the distribution of goods with Article [101(1)] cannot be assessed in abstracto but depends on the provisions contained in such agreements. . . .

15. In a system of distribution franchises of that kind an undertaking which has established itself as a distributor on a given market and thus developed certain business methods grants independent traders, for a fee, the right to establish themselves in other markets using its business name and the business methods which have made it successful. Rather than a method of distribution, it is a way for an undertaking to derive financial benefit from its expertise without investing its own capital. Moreover, the system gives traders who do not have the necessary experience access to methods which they could not have learned without considerable effort and allows them to benefit from the reputation of the franchisor's business name. Franchise agreements for the distribution of goods differ in that regard from dealerships or contracts which incorporate approved retailers into a selective distribution system, which do not involve the use of a single business name, the application of uniform business methods or the payment of royalties in return for the benefits granted. Such a system, which allows the franchisor to profit from his success, does not in itself interfere with competition. In order for the system to work two conditions must be met.

[169] Case 161/84, EU:C:1986:41.

> 16. First, the franchisor must be able to communicate his know-how to the franchisees and provide them with the necessary assistance in order to enable them to apply his methods, without running the risk that that know-how and assistance might benefit competitors, even indirectly. It follows that provisions which are essential in order to avoid that risk do not constitute restrictions on competition for the purposes of Article [101(1)]. That is also true of a clause prohibiting the franchisee, during the period of validity of the contract and for a reasonable period after its expiry, from opening a shop of the same or a similar nature in an area where he may compete with a member of the network. The same may be said of the franchisee's obligation not to transfer his shop to another party without the prior approval of the franchisor; that provision is intended to prevent competitors from indirectly benefiting from the know-how and assistance provided.
>
> 17. Secondly, the franchisor must be able to take the measures necessary for maintaining the identity and reputation of the network bearing his business name or symbol. It follows that provisions which establish the means of control necessary for that purpose do not constitute restrictions on competition for the purposes of Article [101(1)].

Because the franchisor had to be able: (a) to communicate its know-how to franchisees and to protect it from use by competitors; and (b) to maintain the identity and reputation of its network, the Court accepted that restraints on franchisees opening a shop of a similar nature during the period of the contract and for a reasonable period thereafter or selling the shop without the franchisor's consent might be essential to the contract and so fall outside Article 101(1). Further, clauses requiring the franchisee: to apply and to use the franchisor's business methods and know-how; to locate, lay out, and decorate the sales premises according to the franchisor's instructions; to gain the franchisor's approval prior to an assignment of the franchise; to sell only products supplied by the franchisor; and to gain the franchisor's approval for all advertising were unlikely to constitute restrictions.

The Court did not, however, totally embrace an economic approach to franchise agreements.[170] It would not accept that: (a) clauses effecting a division of territories between the franchisor and franchisees or between the franchisees *inter se*;[171] or that (b) clauses preventing price competition between them were essential to the operation of the franchise agreement. These are the types of clauses which in principle restrict competition by object. Justifications for their imposition are generally considered only when determining their compatibility with Article 101(3). Although, therefore, franchising agreements may not infringe Article 101(1), in many cases, they may incorporate clauses, in particular clauses involving market-sharing between the franchisor and franchisees or the franchisees *inter se*, which are liable to infringe Article 101(1). In such cases, assessment of the agreement will need to be completed under Article 101(3).[172]

(v) Online Sales and Online Advertising Restrictions

As e-commerce has developed, a number of different types of restraint on online selling have been incorporated in distribution agreements, including marketplace/platform bans, restrictions on the use of price comparison websites, online advertising restrictions (e.g. restricting use of manufacturers trademarks/brand names by retailers for online advertising or marketing purposes), or dual

[170] See also Chap. 5.

[171] This has created difficulties since many franchisees are not willing to make the requisite investment without such protection.

[172] See COMP/30.937, *Pronuptia* [1987] OJ L13/39, COMP/31.428–31.432, *Yves Rocher* [1987] OJ L8/49, COMP/32.358, *ServiceMaster* [1988] OJ L332/38, and COMP/31.697, *Charles Jourdan* [1989] OJ L35/31.

pricing provisions across sales channels (charging a retailer wholesale prices which differ depending on the sales channel that the retailer uses). The 2010 Guidelines provided limited guidance on how these should be assessed, and there are only a relatively small number of cases dealing with the compatibility of these arrangements with Article 101, most of which have arisen at the national level and been incorporated into SDSs.[173] Although prior to *Coty*[174] some NCAs treated agreements incorporating such prohibitions with suspicion,[175] since *Coty* it has been more broadly accepted that where such restraints do not constitute absolute prohibitions on online selling and using the internet as a means of marketing the contract goods, they may be compatible with Article 101, either because they do not infringe Article 101(1) at all[176] or because they satisfy the conditions of the VBER.[177] The 2022 Guidelines confirm that limitations (as opposed to prohibitions) on online selling, including dual pricing provisions: (a) can benefit from the VBER provided the agreement does not, directly or indirectly, have the object of preventing the effective use of the internet by the buyer to sell the products; and (b) even where the VBER does not apply, may not infringe Article 101(1), for example where incorporated in a SDS as a proportionate and appropriate means of preserving the quality and ensuring the proper use of the contract goods or services.[178]

(vi) Parity Obligations

Since the adoption of the 2010 VBER and Guidelines there has been considerable debate as to how APPAs, or MFNs, should be analysed under Article 101. For example, whether any are sufficiently deleterious to be treated as restrictive of competition by object, whether all, or some, benefit (or should benefit) from the VBER, or whether, given their potential for mixed effects—either to harm competition or to give rise to significant efficiencies (for example, by facilitating customer investment or market entry and/or reducing transaction costs)—individual effects analysis should be conducted.[179]

Despite this, no Commission decision has analysed a parity provision. In *E-books*,[180] the Commission was concerned about the distribution arrangements for e-books of five international publishers (together with Apple) which had been switched from a wholesale to an agency model and incorporated MFNs, relating to the price at which the publishers would sell their products on competing platforms. However, the compatibility with Article 101 of the individual vertical agency agreements (and the MFNs within them) alone did not directly arise in this case as the Commission

[173] But see the Commission's decision in AT.40428, *Guess*, 17 December 2018, n. 236 and text.

[174] Case C-230/16, EU:C:2017:941.

[175] For a discussion of these restraints and how they have been treated in the jurisprudence, see Expert report, n. 23.

[176] See e.g. Judgment 17/20787, *Caudalie* Paris Court of Appeal, 13 July 2018 (France). See also the treatment of the marketplace ban in Decision 18-D-23, *Andreas Stihl* 24 October 2018 (France) and see e.g. Case 3 U 250/16, *Plattformverbot bei Nahrungsergänzungsmitteln, Aloe2GO* (Higher Regional Court of Hamburg,) 22 March 2018.

[177] See e.g. *Nike European Operations Netherlands (NEON) v Action Sport* (Amsterdam Court of Appeal, 14 July 2020), <https://stek.com/en/amsterdam-court-of-appeal-coty-not-confined-to-luxury-products/> and Decision 20-D-20, *Dammann* 3 December 2020 (France) and Section 5.C.v.

[178] Guidelines, paras. 335–355 and Section 5.C.v.

[179] See a report published by the UK's Office of Fair Trading (OFT) and prepared by Laboratorio di Economia, Antitrust, Regolamentazione (LEAR), OFT 1438, 'Can "Fair" Prices be Unfair? A Review of Price Relationship Agreements' (September 2012), J. P. van der Veer, 'Antitrust Scrutiny of Most-favoured-customer Clauses: An Economic Analysis' (2013) 6 *JECLAP* 501, 503–504, OECD, 'Vertical Restraints for On-line Sales', DAF/COMP(2013)13, 145–150, <www.oecd.org/competition/VerticalRestraintsForOnlineSales2013.pdf>, papers and reports at <www.oecd.org/daf/competition/competition-cross-platform-parity.htm>, A. Fletcher and M. Hviid, 'Retail Price MFNs: Are they RPM "At Its Worst"', CCP Working Paper 14–5, and 'The Digitisation of European Cinemas', Commission Press Release IP/11/257.

[180] COMP/39.847, *E-books* [2012] OJ C73/17, see also Chap. 13 and the opinion of the Court of Appeals (2d Cir. 2015) in the US, *United States v Apple, Inc, and Others*, 30 June 2015 (for a criticism of the per se rule applied, see B. Klein, 'The Apple E-books Case: When is a Vertical Contract a Hub in a Hub-and-Spoke Conspiracy?' (2017) 13 *J of Competition Law and Economics* 423).

focused on a suspected concerted practice between the publishers and Apple to raise retail prices and the proceedings were ended when the parties gave commitments to the Commission. The theory of harm thus related to the coordination between the publishers and Apple rather than the individual use of MFNs in the vertical contracts. Nonetheless, the parties did commit to terminate existing agency agreements and to refrain from adopting price MFNs.

Parity clauses have, however, been analysed by NCAs and although treated with suspicion by some,[181] there have been disagreements as to the correct approach. For example, a number of NCAs[182] scrutinised the use of MFNs in contracts between hotels and online travel agents (OTAs, including Hotel Reservation Service (HRS), Booking.com and Expedia). Essentially, they related to the use of broad MFNs in the hotel online booking sector, obliging hotels to commit not to offer lower rates or better conditions/availability either itself, or on other platforms, to those offered on the OTA's platform. In 2013, the German NCA (the Bundeskartellamt, or Federal Cartel Office (FCO)) adopted a decision finding that HRS's MFNs infringed competition law (both German and EU);[183] the clauses restricted competition between the OTAs (preventing them from competing for the lowest commissions and best condition terms), made it more difficult for OTAs to enter the market and restricted competition between hotels, preventing them from competing for the best price of rooms. These anti-competitive effects were strengthened by the use of MFNs by the other major OTAs and the conditions of Article 101(3) were not met.[184] Although the FCO found at first glance that the free-riding argument raised to justify the clauses was persuasive, on closer scrutiny it did not find it to be supported by market data.

The FCO continued to pursue proceedings against Booking.com, even after other NCAs, including the French, Italian, and Swedish authorities, accepted commitments from Booking.com, coordinated within the forum of the ECN, to bring their proceedings against it to an end.[185] These latter commitments, allowing Booking.com to retain 'narrower' provisions—essentially permitting the hotels to give OTAs parity in respect of rates and conditions published by the hotels online, but eliminating availability parity and price/condition parity against other OTAs or through offline channels of hotels and allowing hotels to offer lower rates to, for example, loyal customers[186]—however proved controversial.[187]

[181] See e.g. decisions of UK NCA in Case CE/2596-03, *Tobacco* 15 April 2010 (holding that bilateral vertical agreements including 'parity and differential requirements' relating to competing linked brands, restricted competition by object), annulled on appeal, Cases 1160–1165/1/1/10 [2011] CAT 41, Case CE/9320-10, *Hotel Online Booking* 31 January 2014, Case CE/9692-12 *Amazon Retail* 1 November 2013, and comparethemarket.com, Case No. 50505, 19 November 2020, annulled on appeal, Case No. 1380/1/12/21 [2022] CAT 36.

[182] Including Austria, Belgium, Czech Republic, Denmark, France, Germany, Hungary, Ireland, Italy, Norway, Sweden, and the UK. But see the Commission's examination of Amazon's MFNs under Art. 102, discussed in Chap. 7.

[183] 20 December 2013, <www.bundeskartellamt.de/SharedDocs/Entscheidung/EN/Entscheidungen/Kartellverbot/B9-66-10.pdf%3F__blob%3DpublicationFile%26v%3D3>. This decision was upheld on appeal by the Higher Regional Court in Düsseldorf.

[184] It found that HRS's contractual terms could not be exempted under the Verticals Reg. (since the market share of the agent exceeded 30%) or individually under Art. 101(3). In particular, it was unclear how a fair share (of any established benefit) could be passed on to consumers since the hotels could not offer lower prices without offering them to all portals simultaneously.

[185] See E. N. Varona and A. Hernadez Canales, 'Online Hotel Booking', *CPI Antitrust Chronicle* 15 May 2015 and Report on the monitoring exercise carried out in the online hotel booking sector by EU competition authorities in 2016, <http://ec.europa.eu/competition/ecn/hotel_monitoring_report_en.pdf>. See also decision of the Czech NCA fining Booking.com 8 million Czech Crowns, reported in MLex 18 December 2018, <www.lexology.com/Commentary/Competition-Antitrust/Czech-Republic/Schoenherr-Attorneys-at-Law/Competition-office-fines-Bookingcom-033-million>.

[186] The NCAs hope that this will encourage competition between OTAs to compete for low commissions and encourage new entrants into the market.

[187] Not only did the FCO eventually prohibit these narrow MFNs, but in France the legislator intervened to render unenforceable contractual provisions that prohibit hotels from displaying better deals for rooms on their own websites, see the Macron Law (Law 2015-990) passed in France on 6 August 2015. Despite the close level of cooperation, the different approaches adopted created uncertainty and led to criticism of the Commission for declining to examine the case in June 2014.

The Commission has attempted in the 2022 regime to shed clearer light on the question of how APPAs should be analysed. The new regime provides that wider retail parity provisions imposed by OIS providers are more likely than other types of parity obligation to produce anti-competitive effects—through softening competition and facilitating collusion between OIS providers or foreclosing entry or expansion by new or smaller rivals. For this reason, agreements incorporating such restraints are excluded from benefiting from the VBER (see discussion of Article 5 in Section 5.C.vi[188]) and must be analysed individually to assess their anti-competitive effects and competing efficiencies under Article 101(1) and 101(3), respectively.[189]

Guidelines on Vertical Restraints

(361) For the assessment of this type of parity obligation, the following factors should be taken into account:

(a) the market position of the provider of online intermediation services that imposes the obligation and of its competitors;

(b) the share of buyers of the relevant online intermediation services that are covered by the obligations;

(c) the homing behaviour of the buyers of the online intermediation services and of end users (how many competing online intermediation services they use);

(d) the existence of barriers to entry to the relevant market for the supply of online intermediation services;

(e) the significance of the direct sales channels of buyers of the online intermediation services and the extent to which those buyers are able to remove their products from the platforms of the providers of online intermediation services (de-listing).

Although the Commission considers that narrow retail parity obligations are less problematic, as they do not prevent the offering of more favourable prices or conditions via other OISs, it recognises that they can still be anti-competitive, for example where the number of OIS providers is limited.[190] It also provides guidance on the appraisal of upstream parity and most favoured customer obligations.[191]

(vii) Tying

Although there have been relatively few cases which have dealt with tying under Article 101 (but see the discussion of tying and Article 102 in Chapter 7), paragraphs 389–397 of the Guidelines set out a framework for assessment. In particular, the Commission is concerned that tying may result in anti-competitive foreclosure on the tying and/or tied product markets. The Guidelines state that the main criteria for determining the effects of tying under Article 101 are: the market power of the supplier[192] (and its rivals[193]) on the tying market; entry barriers;[194] and the power of buyers on the market.[195]

[188] Contrast the position in the UK where post-Brexit wide retail parity obligations now constitute hardcore restrictions under the new UK block exemption, see Section 5.C.vi.

[189] Guidelines, para. 360. [190] Ibid., paras. 369–375. [191] Ibid., paras. 376–378.

[192] Ibid., para. 394. [193] Ibid., para. 395. [194] Ibid. [195] Ibid., para. 396.

(viii) Other Restraints

The Commission's Guidelines also provide specific guidance on the compatibility of exclusive supply (i.e. where one distributor only is appointed within the EU and where the main competition risk of such agreement is foreclosure of other buyers), upfront access payments, and category management agreements with Article 101(1) and Article 101(3).[196]

(ix) Effects Analysis—The Need to Develop a Clearer Framework?

Cases such as *Delimitis* support the view that, consistent with economic analysis, the Article 101(1) inquiry must focus on the important question whether or not the agreement would be likely to have an appreciable impact on the parameters of competition and allow the parties to exercise market power. The Court judgments dealing with intra-brand restraints and SDSs (see Section 4.C), however, attach greater weight to the importance of the structure of competition and undistorted competition in all market segments (including the distributor level) than to their impact on inter-brand competition (see also Chapter 5). These principles, derived from pre-modernisation cases, reflect a greater suspicion of restraints on rivalry between a supplier's dealers than on restraints between a supplier and its competitors, and considers the former to be restrictive of competition unless necessary: to facilitate the penetration of a new market; to encourage non-price competition between dealers; or to ensure the commercial success of a franchise agreement.

The approach adopted to vertical intra-brand restraints in the case law under Article 101(1) thus remains a relatively strict one, which is arguably out of line with the more economic approach developed in other areas of EU competition law and set out in the general framework set out in the Guidelines. Arguably, therefore, more still needs to be done to develop an approach, through the bringing of cases and reasoning which, in line with that conducted in analysis of vertical mergers, determines how:

- anti-competitive effects in terms of parameters of competition are to be identified under Article 101(1)—focusing on market power, a theory of harm, and proof of actual or likely anti-competitive effects (and departing from the objective necessity test set out in some cases); and
- pro-competitive effects identified under Article 101(3) are to be balanced against the anti-competitive effects identified under Article 101(1)—whether identified restraints are indispensable to achieve efficiencies which align incentives and stimulate inter-brand competition and which are likely to be passed on to consumers and offset the anti-competitive harm identified.

Such a step would place the emphasis in Article 101(1) analysis more squarely on the question of whether the conditions exist for either the exercise of market power by one of the parties to the agreement or for effective collusion (by suppliers or retailers) to be sustained, and whether the agreement in some way maintains, enhances, or facilitates the exercise of that market power.

C. SELECTIVE DISTRIBUTION AGREEMENTS

(i) The *Metro* Criteria

A supplier wishing to project a luxury or specific image for its goods and/or to ensure that sales are accompanied by the provision of specified services may decide to establish a SDS, selecting its retailers, perhaps by number or by reference to quality or location of the distributor. For example, it may wish

[196] Ibid., sections 8.2.2, 8.2.6, and 8.2.7, respectively.

to ensure that consumers purchasing its product receive a minimum level of pre-sales services and are fully informed about the product's qualities and capabilities. If such a system is to be effective both the supplier and the distributors will wish to ensure that non-authorised retailers, who will detract from the image they are attempting to create or which will free-ride on the pre-sales services provided, are not supplied. Although such arrangements may impact on *intra-brand* competition, they may thus be aimed at promoting inter-brand competition.

It has been seen, however, that in some cases the justifications for a SDS may not be as strong as the supplier suggests and that, especially where a supplier has a degree of market power or networks of similar agreements are operated (in cases of cumulative effect), the practice may reduce intra-brand competition and foreclose certain types of distributors, so softening competition, and/or facilitating collusion between suppliers or buyers.[197]

Since *Metro I*[198] the CJ has recognised that certain simple, qualitative SDSs may escape the Article 101(1) prohibition.

Case 26/76, *Metro-SB-Grossmärkte GmbH v Commission (Metro I)* EU:C:1977:167

SABA manufactured televisions, radios, and tape-recorders, which it distributed through a SDS, whereby only specialist dealers who met certain criteria sold the products. The Commission held that some aspects of the SDS were outside Article 101(1). Other provisions it held to be within Article 101(1) but it granted an exemption. Metro was a self-service dealer who SABA refused to admit to the network because it did not fulfil all the criteria. It appealed to the Court of Justice under Article 263 against the grant of the exemption to SABA.

Court of Justice

A Misuse of Powers

20. The requirement contained in . . . [Article 101] that competition shall not be distorted implies the existence on the market of workable competition, that is to say the degree of competition necessary to ensure the observance of the basic requirements and the attainment of the objectives of the Treaty, in particular the creation of a single market achieving conditions similar to those of a domestic market. In accordance with this requirement the nature and intensiveness of competition may vary to an extent dictated by the products or services in question and the economic structure of the relevant market sectors. In the sector covering the production of high quality and technically advanced consumer durables, where a relatively small number of large- and medium-scale producers offer a varied range of items which, or so consumers may consider, are readily interchangeable, the structure of the market does not preclude the existence of a variety of channels of distribution adapted to the peculiar characteristics of the various producers and to the requirements of the various categories of consumers. On this view the Commission was justified in recognising that selective distribution systems constituted, together with others, an aspect of competition which accords with Article [101(1)], provided that resellers are chosen on the basis of objective criteria of a qualitative nature relating to the technical qualifications of the reseller and his staff and the suitability of his trading premises and that such conditions are laid down uniformly for all potential resellers and are not applied in a discriminatory fashion.

[197] Ibid., para. 146 and Section 2.C.iii. [198] Case 26/76, EU:C:1977:167.

> 21. It is true that in such systems of distribution price competition is not generally emphasised either as an exclusive or indeed as a principal factor. This is particularly so when, as in the present case, access to the distribution network is subject to conditions exceeding the requirements of an appropriate distribution of the products. However, although price competition is so important that it can never be eliminated, it does not constitute the only effective form of competition or that to which absolute priority must in all circumstances be accorded. The powers conferred upon the Commission under Article [101(3)] show that the requirements for the maintenance of workable competition may be reconciled with the safeguarding of objectives of a different nature and that to this end certain restrictions on competition are permissible, provided that they are essential to the attainment of those objectives and that they do not result in the elimination of competition for a substantial part of the Common Market. For specialist wholesalers and retailers the desire to maintain a certain price level, which corresponds to the desire to preserve, in the interests of consumers, the possibility of the continued existence of this channel of distribution in conjunction with new methods of distribution based on a different type of competition policy, forms one of the objectives which may be pursued without necessarily falling under the prohibition contained in Article [101(1)], and, if it does fall thereunder, either wholly or in part, coming within the framework of Article [101(3)]. This argument is strengthened if, in addition, such conditions promote improved competition inasmuch as it relates to factors other than prices.

The judgment holds that certain restrictions in a SDS are not caught by Article 101(1) where necessary in pursuance of a desirable end and that, although limiting price competition, price competition does not necessarily constitute the only form of competition.[199] The Court, and subsequent case law,[200] also clarifies that such a reduction in price competition is acceptable under Article 101(1) only if certain conditions (explored further later) are satisfied:

(a) the characteristics or nature of the product in question necessitate a SDS;

(b) the distributors are chosen by reference to objective criteria of a qualitative nature which are set out uniformly and are not used arbitrarily to discriminate against certain retailers; and

(c) the criteria set out do not go beyond what is necessary for the product in question.[201]

In *Metro II*, the CJ confirmed that such agreements do not infringe Article 101(1), unless the market is tied up with a network of similar agreements, leading to excessive rigidity and no room for other methods of distribution.[202]

(ii) The Characteristics or the Nature of the Product

In *Metro I*,[203] the Court stated that the operation of a SDS was justified in 'the sector covering the production of high quality and technically advanced consumer durables'.[204] It is thus accepted that two categories of products justify a SDS: products which are sufficiently technically complex to justify a specialised distribution system[205] and luxury or branded products, where there is a need for the producer to preserve its brand image and to safeguard, in the mind of the consumer, the aura of exclusivity and prestige of the product has been assessed. In such cases, appropriate marketing and

[199] Ibid., para. 21. [200] See Case T-19/92, *Leclerc v Commission* EU:T:1996:190, para. 112.

[201] Case 31/80, *L'Oréal NV and L'Oréal SA v PVBA 'De Nieuwe AMCK'* EU:C:1980:289 and Case T-19/91, *Société d'Hygiène Dermatologique de Vichy v Commission* EU:T:1992:28. See COMP/30.299, *Grohe* [1985] OJ L19/17 (restrictions must be objectively necessary to protect the quality of the products in question).

[202] See Case 75/84, *Metro-SB-Grossmärkte GmbH v Commission (Metro II)* EU:C:1986:399.

[203] Case 26/76, EU:C:1977:167. [204] Ibid., para. 20

[205] Case 75/84, *Metro II* EU:C:1986:399.

a setting and presentation in line with the luxurious and exclusive nature and brand image of the product is essential.[206] Consequently, the following products have been found to justify such a system: televisions,[207] hi-fis,[208] cameras,[209] personal computers,[210] clocks and watches,[211] high-quality gold and silver products,[212] dinner services,[213] cars,[214] cosmetics, perfumes,[215] and products with an 'allure of luxury'.[216]

It also appears that 'selective distribution systems which are justified by the specific nature of the products or the requirements for their distribution may be established in other economic sectors'.[217] In *SA Binon & Cie v SA Agence et Messageries de la Presse*,[218] for example, it was accepted that newspapers and periodicals would constitute a suitable product for selective distribution, partly because of the limited shelf-life which each had. It may be more difficult to justify the use of a SDS for a product if a SDS is not operated in all jurisdictions in which the product is sold.

(iii) Qualitative Not Quantitative Criteria Applied Uniformly, and in a Non-discriminatory Manner

The Court in *Metro I* stated clearly that a SDS in which 'resellers are chosen on the basis of objective criteria of a qualitative nature relating to the technical qualifications of the reseller and his staff and the suitability of his trading premises and that such conditions are laid down uniformly for all potential resellers and are not applied in a discriminatory fashion'[219] would accord with Article 101. Any distributor satisfying the qualitative criteria should be supplied.

An immediate problem is to determine whether or not criteria are qualitative or quantitative in nature as qualitative restrictions inevitably lead to restrictions on the number of resellers selected. It is clear from *Metro I* itself that criteria relating to the technical qualification of the reseller and its staff, and the suitability of trading premises, are of a qualitative nature. Further, so are obligations precluding the sale of goods that would detract from the product's brand image[220] and requiring dealers to provide after-sales services.[221] In some cases, the Commission has found an obligation requiring a dealer to stock a wide or an entire range of products to be qualitative and in others it has found it to

[206] Case T-19/92, *Leclerc v Commission* EU:T:1996:190, para. 116.

[207] Case 75/84, *Metro II* EU:C:1986:399.

[208] COMP/29.420, *Grundig* [1985] OJ L233/1, renewed [1994] OJ L20/15.

[209] COMP/25.757, *Hasselblad* [1982] OJ L161/18, Case 86/82, *Hasselblad v Commission* EU:C:1984:65.

[210] COMP/30.849, *IBM* [1984] OJ L118/24.

[211] See Case T-712/14, *Confédération européenne des associations d'horlogers-répara.teurs (CEAHR) v Commission* EU:T:2017:748 (the nature of Swiss watches made a selective repair system necessary in order to preserve their quality, ensure their optimal use, prevent counterfeiting, and preserve the brand image and aura of exclusivity and prestige attached to those luxury products from the point of view of their consumers) and COMP/5715, *Junghans* [1977] OJ L30/10; cf. Case 31/85, *ETA Fabriques d'Ébauches v DK Investments SA* EU:C:1985:494.

[212] COMP/30.668, *Murat* [1983] OJ L348/20. [213] COMP/30.665, *Villeroy & Bosch* [1985] OJ L376/15.

[214] COMP/14.650, *BMW* [1975] OJ L29/1, but see COMP/30.299, *Grohe* [1985] OJ L19/17 (unclear whether plumbing fittings are technically advanced products that necessitate a SDS).

[215] COMP/33.542, *Parfums Givenchy* [1992] OJ L236/11, partially annulled Case T-88/92, *Groupement d'Achat Édouard Leclerc v Commission* EU:T:1996:192; COMP/33.242, *Yves Saint Laurent* [1992] OJ L12/24, partially annulled Case T-19/92, *Leclerc v Commission* EU:T:1996:190 (see also Commission Press Release IP/01/713 finding the *Yves Saint Laurent* SDS compatible with the VBER).

[216] Case C-230/16, *Coty* EU:C:2017:941. [217] Case T-19/92, *Leclerc v Commission* EU:T:1996:190, para. 113.

[218] Case 243/83, EU:C:1985:284, para. 32. [219] Case 26/76, EU:C:1977:167, para. 20.

[220] COMP/33.542, *Parfums Givenchy* [1992] OJ L236/11, Case T-88/92, *Leclerc v Commission* EU:T:1996:192.

[221] COMP/29.420, *Grundig* [1985] OJ L233/1, renewed [1994] OJ L20/15; COMP/30.665, *Villeroy & Bosch* [1985] OJ L376/15.

be quantitative; in such cases the classification appears to have turned upon the nature of the product involved.[222]

An obligation precluding members of the system from supplying unauthorised retailers does not infringe Article 101(1), since it is inherent in the SDS.[223] In contrast, provisions that protect approved network members from the competition of other retailers meeting the qualitative criteria will be quantitative, for example; a simple numerical limit placed on the number of distributors; clauses precluding cross-supplying between network members;[224] clauses restricting sales to specific types of stores;[225] or clauses requiring distributors to maintain specific amounts of stocks,[226] to promote the manufacturer's product, to stock an entire range of products,[227] or to have a minimum annual turnover.[228] Provisions setting out a difficult or lengthy procedure for retailers to join the network may also infringe Article 101(1).[229]

The *Metro* criteria will also not be satisfied if the supplier itself, acting in agreement with its distributors (and not unilaterally), refuses to supply those that meet the qualitative criteria. Thus suppliers (whether or not dominant) need to be careful which retailers they exclude from their SDS and refuse to deal with; the exclusion must be justified.[230]

(iv) The Criteria Must Not Go Beyond What is Necessary for the Product in Question

In *Metro I*,[231] the CJ held that there must be a relationship between the goods protected by the SDS and the restrictions imposed on distributors: the restrictions are permissible provided that they are essential to protect the 'quality' of the relevant product. Restrictions that go beyond this will infringe Article 101(1). In *Vichy v Commission*,[232] for example, the GC held that 'the requirement of the status of dispensing chemist, which is a pre-condition for admission to the distribution network for Vichy products, is certainly not necessary for the proper distribution of those [cosmetic] products'.[233] Rather, it was 'entirely unnecessary' and 'disproportionate'.[234]

In has been seen that although price competition is not emphasised in SDSs, the CJ has held that it cannot be eliminated; provisions directly or indirectly aimed at RPM or preventing approved retailers

[222] On requirements to stock a range contrast *Grundig* ibid. (requirement infringed Art. 101(1) but exempted under Art. 101(3)) and *Villeroy & Bosch* ibid (requirement did not infringe Art. 101(1)) and Guidelines, para. 187 (an obligation requiring distributors to sell a certain range of the products is purely of a qualitative nature).

[223] Nor does a provision precluding wholesalers from supplying private customers, Case 26/76, *Metro I* EU:C:1977:167, paras. 27 and 28.

[224] In e.g. COMP/25.757, *Hasselblad* [1982] OJ L161/18, Case 86/82, *Hasselblad v Commission* EU:C:1984:65, the supplier supplied only a few of those distributors which satisfied the criteria set out.

[225] Case T-19/92, *Leclerc v Commission* EU:T:1996:190 (it is not justifiable to have a provision precluding supermarkets or hypermarkets from becoming part of the network). See also Case T-19/91, *Société d'Hygiène Dermatologique de Vichy v Commission* EU:T:1992:28.

[226] Case 26/76, *Metro I* EU:C:1977:167. [227] COMP/29.420, *Grundig* [1994] OJ L20/15.

[228] See COMP/33.542, *Parfums Givenchy* [1992] OJ L236/11, partially annulled Case T-88/92, *Leclerc v Commission* EU:T:1996:192 and COMP/33.242, *Yves Saint Laurent* [1992] OJ L12/24, Case T-19/92, *Leclerc v Commission* EU:T:1996:190 (the GC annulled part of the decision which raised indirect obstacles to sale in supermarkets. The system was then modified to permit sales of perfume in multi-product sales points).

[229] Ibid.

[230] See Chap. 4. In Case T-24/90, *Automec v Commission (No. 2)* EU:T:1992:97, para. 51, the GC held that where a supplier is found to be operating a SDS in a discriminatory manner in breach of Art. 101(1), the Commission does not have power to order supply and to insist on contractual arrangements when other suitable means are available to ensure that the infringement is terminated, see Chap. 13. See also discussion of refusal to deal in Chap. 7.

[231] Case 26/76, EU:C:1977:167. [232] Case T-19/91, EU:T:1992:28. [233] Ibid., para. 69.

[234] Ibid., para. 69.

from selling to each other (bans on cross-suppliers) or to consumers in other Member States, for example through a ban on online selling (see discussion of *Pierre Fabre* in Section 4.C.v) will therefore be most unlikely to be considered necessary. As the Guidelines state, '[h]ardcore restrictions do not meet this proportionality test'.[235] In *Guess*,[236] for example, the Commission in a settlement decision fined Guess for incorporating a number of restraints in its distribution agreements enabling it to partition European markets through restricting authorised retailers engaging in online advertising, selling online without authorisation, selling to consumers outside the retailer's allocated territories, cross-selling to other authorised wholesalers/retailers, and independently setting retail price. Guess expressly acknowledged the facts and infringements in return for a 50 per cent reduction in its fine. In *Coty*,[237] however, the CJ confirmed that a SDS, permitting distributors to sell online through their own websites, but prohibiting (without discrimination) selling through third party marketplaces, such as amazon.de, would be compatible with Article 101(1) where designed, and proportionate to the objective of preserving the luxury image and prestige of the goods and preventing the deterioration of their online presentation. Such a prohibition 'enables the supplier of luxury goods to check that the goods will be sold online in an environment that corresponds to the qualitative conditions that it has agreed with its authorised distributors'.[238]

(v) Object or Effect Analysis?

The case law dealing with selective distribution adopts its own rather specific analysis to determine whether restraints are necessary to achieve its objectives and so whether such a system infringes Article 101(1). In *Pierre Fabre*,[239] the CJ interprets this line of cases as holding that if the *Metro I* criteria are not satisfied the agreement is restrictive by object.

Case C-439/09, *Pierre Fabre v Président de l'Autorité de la concurrence* EU:C:2011:649

Court of Justice

The classification of the restriction in the contested contractual clause as a restriction of competition by object

34. It must first of all be recalled that, to come within the prohibition laid down in Article 101(1) TFEU, an agreement must have 'as [its] object or effect the prevention, restriction or distortion of competition within the internal market'. It has, since the judgment in Case 56/65 *LTM* . . . been settled case-law that the alternative nature of that requirement, indicated by the conjunction 'or', leads, first, to the need to consider the precise purpose of the agreement, in the economic context in which it is to be applied. Where the anti-competitive object of the agreement is established it is not necessary to examine its effects on competition (see Joined Cases C-501/06 P, . . . *GlaxoSmithKline Services and Others v Commission and Others* . . . paragraph 55 and the case-law cited).

35. For the purposes of assessing whether the contractual clause at issue involves a restriction of competition 'by object', regard must be had to the content of the clause, the objectives it seeks to

[235] Guidelines, para. 150.

[236] AT.40428, 17 December 2018. See also e.g. Cases 228 and 229/82, *Ford-Werke AG and Ford of Europe Inc v Commission* EU:C:1984:80; Case 32/78, *BMW v Commission* EU:C:1979:191; COMP/24.055, *Kodak* [1970] OJ L142/24. Guarantees granted on sale in one Member State must be honoured by distributors in other Member States: Case 31/85, *ETA Fabriques d'Ébauches v DK Investments SA* EU:C:1985:494.

[237] Case C-230/16, EU:C:2017:941.

[238] Ibid., para. 47.

[239] Case C-439/09, EU:C:2011:649.

attain and the economic and legal context of which it forms a part (see *GlaxoSmithKline and Others v Commission and Others*, paragraph 58 and the case-law cited).

36. The selective distribution contracts at issue stipulate that sales of cosmetics and personal care products by the Avène, Klorane, Galénic and Ducray brands must be made in a physical space, the requirements for which are set out in detail, and that a qualified pharmacist must be present.

37. According to the referring court, the requirement that a qualified pharmacist must be present at a physical sales point de facto prohibits the authorised distributors from any form of internet selling.

38. As the Commission points out, by excluding de facto a method of marketing products that does not require the physical movement of the customer, the contractual clause considerably reduces the ability of an authorised distributor to sell the contractual products to customers outside its contractual territory or area of activity. It is therefore liable to restrict competition in that sector.

39. As regards agreements constituting a selective distribution system, the Court has already stated that such agreements necessarily affect competition in the common market (Case 107/82 *AEG-Telefunken v Commission* . . . paragraph 33). Such agreements are to be considered, in the absence of objective justification, as 'restrictions by object'.

40. However, it has always been recognised in the case-law of the Court that there are legitimate requirements, such as the maintenance of a specialist trade capable of providing specific services as regards high-quality and high-technology products, which may justify a reduction of price competition in favour of competition relating to factors other than price. Systems of selective distribution, in so far as they aim at the attainment of a legitimate goal capable of improving competition in relation to factors other than price, therefore constitute an element of competition which is in conformity with Article 101(1) TFEU (*AEG-Telefunken v Commission*, paragraph 33).

41. In that regard, the Court has already pointed out that the organisation of such a network is not prohibited by Article 101(1) TFEU, to the extent that resellers are chosen on the basis of objective criteria of a qualitative nature, laid down uniformly for all potential resellers and not applied in a discriminatory fashion, that the characteristics of the product in question necessitate such a network in order to preserve its quality and ensure its proper use and, finally, that the criteria laid down do not go beyond what is necessary (Case 26/76 *Metro* . . . paragraph 20, and Case 31/80 *L'Oréal* . . . paragraphs 15 and 16).

42. Although it is for the referring court to examine whether the contractual clause at issue prohibiting de facto all forms of internet selling can be justified by a legitimate aim, it is for the Court of Justice to provide it for this purpose with the points of interpretation of European Union law which enable it to reach a decision (see *L'Oréal*, paragraph 14).

43. It is undisputed that, under Pierre Fabre Dermo-Cosmétique's selective distribution system, resellers are chosen on the basis of objective criteria of a qualitative nature, which are laid down uniformly for all potential resellers. However, it must still be determined whether the restrictions of competition pursue legitimate aims in a proportionate manner in accordance with the considerations set out at paragraph 41 of the present judgment.

44. In that regard, it should be noted that the Court, in the light of the freedoms of movement, has not accepted arguments relating to the need to provide individual advice to the customer and to ensure his protection against the incorrect use of products, in the context of non-prescription medicines and contact lenses, to justify a ban on internet sales (see, to that effect, Deutscher Apothekerverband, paragraphs 106, 107 and 112, and Case C-108/09 *Ker-Optika* . . . paragraph 76).

45. Pierre Fabre Dermo-Cosmétique also refers to the need to maintain the prestigious image of the products at issue.

46. The aim of maintaining a prestigious image is not a legitimate aim for restricting competition and cannot therefore justify a finding that a contractual clause pursuing such an aim does not fall within Article 101(1) TFEU.

47. In the light of the foregoing considerations, the answer to the first part of the question referred for a preliminary ruling is that Article 101(1) TFEU must be interpreted as meaning that, in the context

of a selective distribution system, a contractual clause requiring sales of cosmetics and personal care products to be made in a physical space where a qualified pharmacist must be present, resulting in a ban on the use of the internet for those sales, amounts to a restriction by object within the meaning of that provision where, following an individual and specific examination of the content and objective of that contractual clause and the legal and economic context of which it forms a part, it is apparent that, having regard to the properties of the products at issue, that clause is not objectively justified.

The CJ thus states: (a) that SDSs necessarily affect competition and 'are to be considered, in the absence of objective justification, as "restrictions by object"'; but (b) that they may be in conformity with Article 101 and justified insofar as they aim at the attainment of legitimate goals (such as the maintenance of a specialist trade capable of providing specific services as regards high-quality or high-technology products) where 'resellers are chosen on the basis of objective criteria of a qualitative nature, laid down uniformly for all potential resellers and not applied in a discriminatory fashion, that the characteristics of the product in question necessitate such a network in order to preserve its quality and ensure its proper use and, finally, that the criteria laid down do not go beyond what is necessary'.[240]

Although the narrow finding of the CJ—that the contractual clause at issue (prohibiting all forms of internet selling) was incompatible with Article 101(1)—is consistent with earlier precedent dealing with object restraints, the broader wording suggesting that *all* SDSs are restrictive by object unless 'objectively justified' is more surprising. In treating the *Metro I* criteria as a mechanism for distinguishing between SDSs which are restrictive by object and those which are not, the CJ arguably displays a more sceptical tone towards selective distribution[241] and adopts an approach which is not easy to reconcile with the more traditional approach for identifying object restraints set out in cases such as *CB*. Further, if the *Metro* criteria were truly a mechanism for identifying restrictions of competition by object, one would expect a fuller effects analysis to be required in cases where a restriction of competition by object is not identified. The understanding, however, is that SDSs complying with the *Metro* criteria generally do not infringe Article 101(1), save where the market is tied up with a network of similar agreements.[242]

The CJ also does not clearly link its approach with that adopted in other case law (and discussed in Chapter 5) which establishes that restrictions of competition essential to, or inherent in, the pursuit of a legitimate objective or objectively necessary for the existence of the agreement fall outside the scope of Article 101(1).[243] The analysis adopted, rather, seems to serve as a mechanism for identifying restrictions of competition through a structured analysis which is, arguably, more reminiscent of that adopted in free movement rather than object or effect analysis in Article 101 cases.[244]

[240] Ibid., paras. 39–41 and see Monti, n. 3. [241] Monti, n. 3.

[242] See n. 202 and text. Further, although most object restraints do not benefit from a BER, many SDS are exempted by the VBER.

[243] But see the Opinion of Mazák AG in Case C-439/09, *Pierre Fabre* EU:C:2011:113, para. 35, who relies on Case C-309/99, *Wouters v Algemene Raad van de Nederlandse Order van Advocaten* EU:C:2002:98 for the view that the ban on internet selling would fall outside Art. 101(1) provided the limitations imposed were appropriate in the light of the legitimate objective (of a public law nature) sought and did not go beyond what was necessary. The Guidelines also take the view that agreements satisfying the *Metro* criteria fall outside the scope of Art. 101(1) but that agreements which do not satisfy the criteria or the terms of the block exemption need to be analysed to assess their possible anti-competitive effects, paras. 150–153.

[244] Monti, n. 3. The CJ relies on free movement cases (holding that the need to provide individual advice to a customer and to protect against incorrect use of products cannot justify a ban on internet sales of non-prescription medicines and contact lenses, in support of its conclusion that the aim of maintaining a prestigious brand is not a legitimate aim for restricting internet selling, Case C-108/09, *Ker-Optika* EU:C:2010:725, paras. 44–46).

Another difficulty is that some interpreted the judgment in *Pierre Fabre* as holding that the aim of maintaining a prestigious brand is not a legitimate aim for restricting competition within SDSs at all. In *Coty*,[245] however, the CJ reaffirmed that although SDSs[246] necessarily affect competition, they may be compatible with Article 101(1) where necessary to protect the allure and prestigious image of luxury goods and where an impairment of that aura of luxury is likely to affect the quality of those goods. In so doing, it emphasised that such a conclusion was not invalidated by *Pierre Fabre*, paragraph 46, which held only that the need to preserve a luxury image could not constitute a legitimate requirement for the purpose of justifying a comprehensive prohibition of the internet sale of those goods:[247] 'A selective distribution system designed, primarily, to preserve the luxury image of those goods is therefore compatible with Article 101(1) TFEU on condition that the criteria mentioned in paragraph 24 of the present judgment are met.'[248]

Finally, although the cases recognise that SDSs may enhance inter-brand competition,[249] some express concern about the over-regulatory limitations imposed.[250] Indeed, the case law has been criticised by some for ignoring the economic realities and effects of the arrangements and for engaging in 'unnecessary micro-management of the selective distribution relationship'.[251] For example, the requirement that the product should fall within a category that the Court has ruled should be able to benefit from such a system may not always be appropriate or relevant. Even if true that the need for a SDS has sometimes been exaggerated, a producer operating on a competitive market will be punished by consumers if they do not believe that the product in question merits the system. Further, the requirement that retailers should be selected by reference only to *qualitative* criteria makes no economic sense. If a retailer has to comply with stringent qualitative criteria this may involve considerable expense requiring a quantitative limit on the number of distributors. The requirement has also proved difficult to apply in practice.

The reality is, however, that, in practice, this complex analysis may often be sidestepped as many SDSs are exempted under Article 101(3)—in the past by the Commission accepting that an agreement incorporating quantitative restrictions meets the criteria of Article 101(3),[252] or, since 1999, through the more liberal VBER regime (irrespective of the nature of product or service at issue and even if quantitative limits are used).[253]

5. ARTICLE 101(3)

A. GENERAL

The complex assessment required to determine whether or not an agreement infringes Article 101(1) or individually meets the Article 101(3) criteria means that the VBER is of enormous importance in practice.

[245] Case C-230/16, EU:C:2017:941.

[246] Ibid. Under the terms of the SDS, Coty had to approve distributors' sales locations, which had to comply with environment and décor requirements, distributors were entitled to offer and sell the products on the internet, but, to preserve the luxury character of the products, only through a shop window of the authorised store (and not through a marketplace platform).

[247] Ibid., paras. 24–36. [248] Ibid., para. 29.

[249] Especially prior to 1999 when no block exemption existed for SDSs. [250] Hawk, n. 95, 985.

[251] Monti, n. 3, 492.

[252] See Case 26/76, *Metro I* EU:C:1977:167; COMP/29.420, *Grundig* [1985] OJ L233/1, renewed [1994] OJ L20/15; COMP/33.542, *Parfums Givenchy* [1992] OJ L236/11.

[253] See Case C-158/11, *Auto24 SARL v Jaguar Land Rover France SAS* EU:C:2012:351 and Section 5.C.

B. THE BLOCK EXEMPTIONS

Regulation 2790/1999, the first overarching BER for vertical agreements, replaced three 'old-style' BERs which applied to different categories of distribution agreement: Regulation 1983/83[254] (exclusive distribution agreements); Regulation 1984/83 (exclusive purchasing agreements (with special provisions for beer-supply and petrol agreements));[255] and Regulation 4087/88[256] (franchising agreements). These older BERs were influential in moulding the content of distribution agreements but had a number of problems. Not only did agreements not always fit neatly within one of these identified categories so stultifying the variety of distribution arrangements that suppliers sought to use (for example, there was no block exemption for selective distribution), but they significantly curtailed the parties' freedom of contract. Each BER applied only if it related to goods for resale and set out categories of clauses that were permissible (a white list)[257] and categories of clauses that were not (a black list of hardcore restraints). Any restriction on conduct not specifically exempted by the Regulation would compromise and risk the validity of the agreement.[258]

The 1999 VBER sought to avoid these problems by operating on the basis that all vertical agreements concluded between parties meeting stipulated market share thresholds are exempted so long as specified conditions are met, including, in particular, that the agreements do not incorporate identified hardcore restraints. Although the 2010 and 2022 regimes retained this scheme both introduced some important changes to, and clarifications on, the operation of the VBER.

C. THE VERTICAL BLOCK EXEMPTION REGULATION —REGULATION 2022/720

(i) The Background

The VBER provides an umbrella block exemption which applies to vertical agreements generally (but see discussion of motor vehicle distribution agreements in Section 5.D). Regulation 2022/720 came into force on 1 June 2022, replacing Regulation 330/2010, and applies until 31 May 2034.[259] The recitals set out the background to the Regulation and explain that vertical agreements 'can improve economic efficiency within a chain of production or distribution' and that the 'likelihood that such efficiency-enhancing effects will outweigh any anti-competitive effects due to restrictions contained in vertical agreements depends on the degree of market power of the parties to the agreement'.[260] It thus operates as a safe harbour for distribution agreements, whether for goods or services, which satisfy its market share thresholds and other provisions. The flowchart in Figure 11.2 outlines the working of the VBER.

[254] [1983] OJ L173/1.

[255] [1983] OJ L173/5. This and Reg. 1983/83 [1983] OJ L173/1 were the successors to Reg. 67/67 [1967] OJ 849/67 Spec. Ed. 10.

[256] [1988] OJ L359/46.

[257] They did not therefore apply to agreements relating to services or to intermediate goods that the distributor had to finish or prepare for resale. The VBER applies to goods (whether for resale or use by the distributor) and services.

[258] The impact of having a white list was that if the agreement contained any other clause there was a risk that the block exemption did not apply. In practice, therefore, parties would attempt to limit the restrictions on conduct and obligations imposed to the clauses explicitly permitted.

[259] VBER, Art. 11. [260] Ibid., recitals 6 and 7.

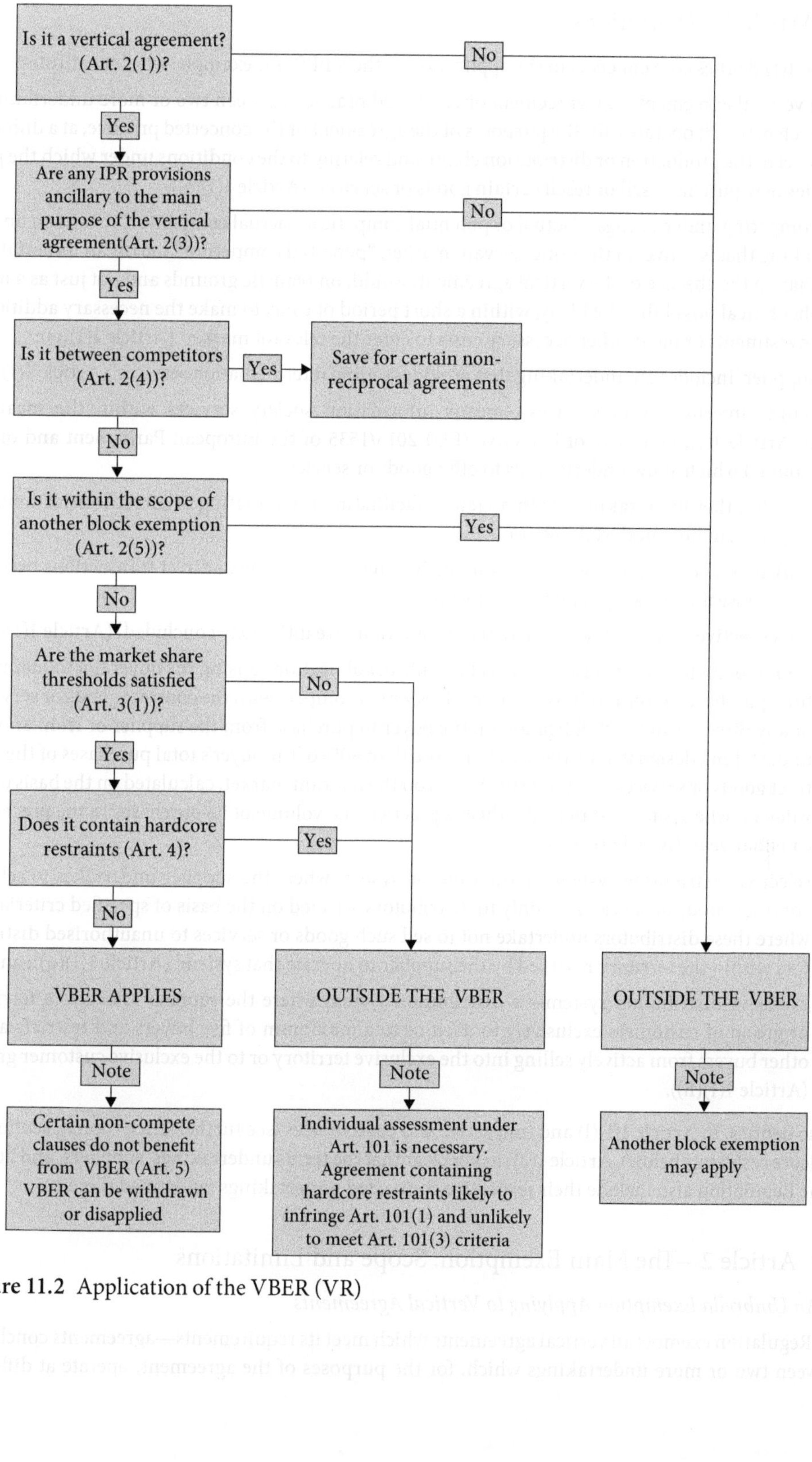

Figure 11.2 Application of the VBER (VR)

(ii) Article 1—Definitions

Article 1(1) defines core concepts to the application of the VBER, for example, what constitutes:

- a vertical agreement—'an agreement or concerted practice between two or more undertakings, each of which operates, for the purposes of the agreement or the concerted practice, at a different level of the production or distribution chain, and relating to the conditions under which the parties may purchase, sell or resell certain goods or services' (Article 1(1)(a));
- competing undertakings—'actual or potential competitor; "actual competitor" means an undertaking that is active on the same relevant market; "potential competitor" means an undertaking that, in the absence of the vertical agreement, would, on realistic grounds and not just as a mere theoretical possibility, be likely, within a short period of time, to make the necessary additional investments or incur other necessary costs to enter the relevant market' (Article 1(1)(c));
- supplier 'includes an undertaking that provides online intermediation services' (Article 1(1)(d));
- online intermediation services—'means information society services within the meaning of Article 1(1), point (b), of Directive (EU) 2015/1535 of the European Parliament and of the Council which allow undertakings to offer goods or services:

  (i) to other undertakings, with a view to facilitating the initiating of direct transactions between those undertakings, or

  (ii) to final consumers, with a view to facilitating the initiating of direct transactions between those undertakings and final consumers

  irrespective of whether and where the transactions are ultimately concluded' (Article 1(1)(e)).
- a non-compete obligation—'any direct or indirect obligation causing the buyer not to manufacture, purchase, sell or resell goods or services which compete with the contract goods or services, or any direct or indirect obligation on the buyer to purchase from the supplier or from another undertaking designated by the supplier more than 80% of the buyer's total purchases of the contract goods or services and their substitutes on the relevant market, calculated on the basis of the value or, where such is standard industry practice, the volume of its purchases in the preceding calendar year' (Article 1(1)(f));
- selective distribution system—'a distribution system where the supplier undertakes to sell the contract goods or services . . . only to distributors selected on the basis of specified criteria and where these distributors undertake not to sell such goods or services to unauthorised distributors within the territory reserved by the supplier to operate that system' (Article 1(1)(g)); and
- exclusive distribution system—'a distribution system where the supplier allocates a territory or group of customers exclusively to itself or to a maximum of five buyers and restricts all its other buyers from actively selling into the exclusive territory or to the exclusive customer group' (Article 1(1)(h)).

It also defines, in Article 1(1)(l) and (m), active and passive sales (see further discussion in section on hardcore restraints below). Article 1(2) makes clear that the terms undertakings, suppliers, and buyers in the Regulation also include their respective connected undertakings (as defined therein).

(iii) Article 2—The Main Exemption: Scope and Limitations

a. An Umbrella Exemption Applying to Vertical Agreements

The Regulation exempts all vertical agreements which meet its requirements—agreements concluded between two or more undertakings which, for the purposes of the agreement, operate at different levels of the production or distribution chain (for example, supplier, wholesaler, and retailer or a supplier of a raw material which the other uses as an input)[261]—relating to the conditions under which the parties 'may purchase, sell or resell certain goods or services', irrespective of whether they relate to final or intermediate goods and services.[262] It does not exempt agreements or restrictions or obligations that do not relate to the purchase, sale, or resale of goods or services, such as rent or leasing agreements or clauses preventing parties from carrying out independent R&D.[263]

b. *Vertical Agreements in the Online Platform Economy*

The 2022 Guidelines elaborate on how the VBER applies to vertical agreements in the online platform economy, 'including those entered into by providers of online intermediation services',[264] which are now much more prevalent than at the time of the 2010 VBER. The Guidelines recognise that although platforms 'enable new ways of doing business' they are not always easy 'to categorise using the concepts applied to vertical agreements in the brick and mortar environment'.[265]

As the Commission's view is that arrangements involving undertakings active in the online platform will generally fail to fulfil the requirements for constituting an 'agent' for competition law purposes,[266] an important question is how Article 101 applies to them. Where the vertical agreement relates to the provision of online intermediation services (Article 1(1)(e) VBER)—the undertaking facilitates the initiating of direct transactions between two other parties—a number of consequences follow:

Guidelines on Vertical Restraints

(67) . . . Pursuant to Article 1(1), point (d) of the Regulation, an undertaking that provides online intermediation services within the meaning of Article 1(1), point (e) of the Regulation is categorised as a supplier in respect of those services and an undertaking that offers or sells goods or services via online intermediation services is categorised as a buyer in respect of those online intermediation services, irrespective of whether it pays to use the online intermediation services. This has the following consequences for the application of [the VBER]:

(a) the undertaking that provides the online intermediation services cannot be categorised as a buyer within the meaning of Article 1(1), point (k) of the Regulation in respect of goods or services offered by third parties using those online intermediation services;

(b) for the purpose of applying the market share thresholds set out in Article 3(1) of the Regulation, the market share of the undertaking that provides the online intermediation services is calculated on the relevant market for the supply of those services. The scope of the relevant market depends on the facts of the case, in particular the degree of substitutability between online and offline intermediation services, between intermediation services used for different categories of goods or services and between intermediation services and direct sales channels;

(c) restrictions imposed by the undertaking that provides the online intermediation services on buyers of those services relating to the price at which, the territories to which, or the customers to whom the intermediated goods or services may be sold, including restrictions relating to online advertising and online selling, are subject to the provisions of Article 4 of the Regulation (hardcore restrictions).

[261] It does not, therefore, apply to an agreement between a supplier and two wholesalers.
[262] Guidelines, para. 59. [263] Ibid., para. 61. [264] Ibid., para. 60.
[265] Ibid., para. 62. [266] Ibid., para. 63 and Section 2.C.ii.c.

For example, pursuant to Article 4, point (a) of the Regulation, the exemption provided by Article 2(1) of the Regulation does not apply to an agreement under which a provider of online intermediation services imposes a fixed or minimum sale price for a transaction that it facilitates;

(d) pursuant to Article 5(1), point (d) of the Regulation, the exemption provided by Article 2(1) of the Regulation does not apply to across-platform retail parity obligations imposed by the undertaking that provides the online intermediation services on buyers of those services;

(e) pursuant to Article 2(6) of the Regulation, the exemption provided by Article 2(1) of the Regulation does not apply to agreements relating to the provision of online intermediation services where the provider of the services is a competing undertaking on the relevant market for the sale of the intermediated goods or services (hybrid function). As set out in section 4.4.4., such agreements must be assessed under the Horizontal Guidelines as regards possible collusive effects and under section 8 of these Guidelines as regards any vertical restraints.

In contrast, undertakings active in the online platform economy but which are not OIS providers may be categorised as either suppliers or buyers, for example suppliers of upstream input services or (re)sellers of goods or services downstream. This categorisation is important as it affects the definition of the relevant market for the purpose of applying the VBER market share thresholds as well as the question of whether a hardcore or excluded restraint has been incorporated into the agreement and so the question of whether the VBER applies.[267]

c. *Association of Retailers of Goods*

Article 2(2) provides that the VBER applies to vertical agreements concluded between an association of retailers[268] (no member of which, together with its connected undertakings, has a total turnover of more than €50 million) and its members or its supplier—i.e. cooperation between retailers in the area of purchasing and selling. Any horizontal agreement concluded between the members (such as an obligation on members to purchase from the association) must however be assessed first and separately for its compatibility with Article 101.

d. *Provisions Relating to the Assignment of Intellectual Property Rights*

The assignment of intellectual property rights (IPRs), such as trademarks, copyright, or know-how, may be essential to or enhance the effective performance of a vertical agreement. Article 2(3) provides that the VBER applies to such arrangements where five conditions are fulfilled:[269]

(a) the agreement is a vertical one and not, for example, an assignment of IPRs for the manufacture of goods or a pure licensing agreements;[270]

(b) the assignment or the licence of the IPRs must be made by the supplier to the buyer (and not vice versa);

(c) the IPR provisions are ancillary to the implementation of the vertical agreement and not its primary object;

[267] Ibid., para. 68.

[268] Retailers are distributors 'selling goods (and not services) to final consumers', ibid., paras. 69–70.

[269] See also ibid., para. 72.

[270] Ibid., para. 74. Reg. 772/2004 [2004] OJ L123/11, which applies to technology transfer agreements, may apply to such agreements; see Chap. 12. Para. 33 of the Guidelines sets out some examples of agreements which would not benefit from the VBER.

(d) the IPR provisions are directly related to the use, sale, or resale of goods or services by the buyer or its customers, for example where the licensing of a trademark or know-how is necessary for the marketing of a good;

(e) the clauses relating to the IPRs must not have the same object or effect as restrictions that are not exempted under the Regulation. For example, territorial exclusivity, which is prohibited by Article 4, cannot be circumvented by arrangements involving licensing or assignment of IPRs.[271]

These conditions are particularly relevant to franchise agreements which ordinarily involve the assignment or licensing of IPRs. Franchise agreements will ordinarily meet all five of the conditions set out in Article 2(3) as:

> the franchisor provides goods and/or services, in particular commercial or technical assistance services, to the franchisee. The IPRs help the franchisee to resell the products supplied by the franchisor or by a supplier designated by the franchisor, or to use these products and sell the resulting goods or services.[272]

Paragraph 86 of the Guidelines sets out the types of obligations related to IPRs which are generally considered necessary to protect the franchisor's IPRs and likely to benefit from the block exemption including obligations on the franchisee not to engage in a similar business, not to acquire financial interests in the capital of a competing undertaking, not to disclose know-how (not in the public domain) to third parties, to communicate to the franchisor experience gained in exploiting the franchise and to grant non-exclusive licences for the resulting know-how to the franchisor and other franchisees, to report and take action against infringements of licensed IPRs, not to use know-how other than for the exploitation of the franchise, and not to assign the rights and obligations without the franchisor's consent.

e. *Agreements Between Competing Undertakings*

The term vertical agreements encompasses agreements concluded between undertakings which, for the purposes of the agreement, operate at different levels of the production or distribution chain. However, the VBER prevents the block exemption from applying to agreements concluded between competing undertakings (actual or potential competitors)[273] even if operating for the purposes of the agreement at different levels of the production or distribution chain, *except* in the case of certain scenarios of 'dual distribution'—where the supplier of goods or services is also active downstream (on the basis that the potential negative impact of the agreement on the competitive relationship downstream is less important than the potential positive impact of the agreement). Article 2(4) provides:

> [The] exemption shall apply where competing undertakings enter into a non-reciprocal vertical agreement and one of the following applies:
>
> (a) the supplier is active at an upstream level as a manufacturer, importer, or wholesaler and at a downstream level as an importer, wholesaler, or retailer of goods, while the buyer is an importer, wholesaler, or retailer at the downstream level and not a competing undertaking at the upstream level where it buys the contract goods; or

[271] See also Cases 56 and 58/64, *Consten and Grundig* EU:C:1966:41. [272] Guidelines, para. 86.

[273] See definitions of vertical agreement and competing undertaking in Art. 1 and set out in Section 5.C.ii. See also Case C-331/21, *Autoridade da Concorrência and EDP* EU:C:2023:153, Opinion of Rantos AG, paras. 97–99.

(b) the supplier is a provider of services at several levels of trade, while the buyer provides its services at the retail level and is not a competing undertaking at the level of trade where it purchases the contract services.

Although during the review leading up to the 2022 VBER the Commission expressed concerns about the increased (since 2010) competitive risks raised by information exchanges in dual distribution scenarios,[274] in the end it has accepted that information exchange in dual distribution benefits from the VBER unless the exchange 'is either not directly related to the implementation of the vertical agreement or is not necessary to improve the production or distribution of the contract goods or services'.[275] Paragraph 99 of the Guidelines provides a non-exhaustive list of examples of information exchange that may be directly related to the implementation of the vertical agreement and necessary to improve the production of distribution of the goods or services, for example concerning technical or logistical information, the price at which the contract goods and services are sold to the buyer, recommended or maximum prices, marketing and promotion of the goods and services, and performance-related information (including aggregated information provided by the supplier to the buyer relating to the marketing and sales activities of other buyers of the contract goods or services, provided that this does not enable the buyer to identify the activities of particular competing buyers, as well as information relating to the volume or value of the buyer's sales of the contract goods or services relative to its sales of competing goods or services). In contrast, exchanges of information relating to future prices at which either the supplier or buyer intend to sell the products downstream, identified end-users of the contract goods or services, or to the buyer's own brand name are unlikely to be covered.[276]

The 2022 VBER also introduced Article 2(6), removing the benefit of the VBER for agreements 'relating to the provision of online intermediation services where the provider of the online intermediation services is a competing undertaking on the relevant market for the sale of the intermediated goods or services'.[277] Thus agreements concluded by hybrid online platforms, such as Amazon, frequently fall outside the scope of the VBER and have to be appraised individually for their compatibility with Article 101.

f. Agreements Falling Within the Scope of Another Block Exemption

Article 2(7) states that the VBER does not apply to vertical agreements the subject matter of which falls within the scope of another block exemption, unless otherwise provided for in such a regulation. For example, agreements potentially falling within the Technology Transfer Regulation[278] or concluded in connection with horizontal agreements that may potentially benefit from a block exemption[279] are excluded. The exclusion applies to types of agreements so, for example, a technology transfer agreement which does not meet the criteria of the technology transfer block exemption cannot be exempted by virtue of the VBER.

(iv) Article 3—The Market Share Cap

A feature introduced by Regulation 2790/1999, which was not used in previous BERs (which applied, unless withdrawn, whatever the market shares of the parties), was the introduction of a market share

[274] See further discussion of information exchanges in Chaps. 9 and 10.

[275] VBER, Art. 2(5) and see Expert report commissioned by the Commission on 'Information exchange in dual distribution' prepared by S. Pautke and J. M. Schultze, <https://ec.europa.eu/competition-policy/system/files/2022-02/kd0122032enn_VBER_dual_distribution_2.pdf>.

[276] Guidelines, para. 100. [277] See further ibid., paras. 104–109.

[278] Reg. 772/2004 [2004] OJ L123/11, see Chap. 12. [279] See Chap. 10.

cap of 30 per cent. Although the introduction of a market share test was criticised for introducing an element of uncertainty into a block exemption, a core purpose of which was to provide legal certainty, the objective of the threshold is to ensure that the VBER reflects its underlying economic objective and the fact that vertical restraints are unlikely to pose competition problems where inter-brand competition is strong and where imposed by a firm without significant market power.[280]

Since 2010, the market share cap has, recognising the potential competition problems arising from an increase in retailers' market power, been extended to include buyers. The VBER thus applies 'on condition that the market share held by the supplier does not exceed 30 % of the relevant market on which it sells the contract goods or services and the market share held by the buyer does not exceed 30 % of the relevant market on which it purchases the contract goods or services' (Article 3(1)). In a multi-party situation (for example, an agreement between a supplier, wholesaler, and retailer), the market shares of the supplier and the wholesaler (on the markets on which they sell the contract goods or services) and the market shares of the wholesaler and the retailer (on the market on which they purchase the goods or services) are relevant (Article 3(2)).

In addition to the Commission's general guidance on market definition, and the relevant jurisprudence, the Guidelines set out some specific guidance on market definition and market share calculation, focused on distribution cases.[281] Because of the inherent uncertainty which the market share test brings, it is important that the Guidelines recognise that even if the market share thresholds are (or may be) exceeded there is no presumption that the agreement either infringes Article 101(1) or does not satisfy the Article 101(3) criteria (unless the agreement contains object or hardcore restraints).[282] The Regulation itself provides in Article 8(d) for the situation where the agreement satisfies the market share thresholds initially but subsequently exceeds them (see later).

(v) Article 4—Hardcore Restrictions

a. *The VBER is Not Applicable to Agreements Containing Hardcore Restraints*

Vertical agreements cannot benefit from the VBER if they incorporate a hardcore restraint prohibited by Article 4. The insertion of just one of these clauses precludes the VBER from applying. Article 4 focuses on clauses, such as those imposing price or territorial restraints, which restrict intra-brand competition. It will be remembered that there has been concern that EU competition law has treated these types of restraint too harshly (especially when compared to the position that exists in the US). Nonetheless, in the reviews of the VBER and Guidelines the Commission has never proposed removing these restraints from the list of hardcore restraints. Indeed, as such a step would create a presumption of legality—which can only be withdrawn prospectively—for such restraints, it is considered that this would create a risk of exempting agreements with potential for serious anti-competitive effects. The Commission's view is that these restraints should in most cases be prohibited because of the harm they cause consumers.[283]

Article 4 Restrictions that remove the benefit of the block exemption—hardcore restrictions

The exemption provided for in Article 2 shall not apply to vertical agreements which, directly or indirectly, in isolation or in combination with other factors under the control of the parties, have as their object:

(a) the restriction of the buyer's ability to determine its sale price, without prejudice to the possibility of the supplier to impose a maximum sale price or recommend a sale price, provided that they do not

[280] This type of economic approach should arguably also be reflected more closely in the Art. 101(1) appraisal.
[281] See Chap. 1 and Guidelines, section 5. [282] Guidelines, para. 275. [283] Ibid., para. 177.

amount to a fixed or minimum sale price as a result of pressure from, or incentives offered by, any of the parties;

(b) where the supplier operates an exclusive distribution system, the restriction of the territory into which, or of the customers to whom, the exclusive distributor may actively or passively sell the contract goods or services, except:

  (i) the restriction of active sales by the exclusive distributor and its direct customers, into a territory or to a customer group reserved to the supplier or allocated by the supplier exclusively to a maximum of five other exclusive distributors;

  (ii) the restriction of active or passive sales by the exclusive distributor and its customers to unauthorised distributors located in a territory where the supplier operates a selective distribution system for the contract goods or services;

  (iii) the restriction of the exclusive distributor's place of establishment;

  (iv) the restriction of active or passive sales to end users by an exclusive distributor operating at the wholesale level of trade;

  (v) the restriction of the exclusive distributor's ability to actively or passively sell components, supplied for the purposes of incorporation, to customers who would use them to manufacture the same type of goods as those produced by the supplier;

(c) where the supplier operates a selective distribution system:

  (i) the restriction of the territory into which, or of the customers to whom, the members of the selective distribution system may actively or passively sell the contract goods or services, except:

    (1) the restriction of active sales by the members of the selective distribution system and their direct customers, into a territory or to a customer group reserved to the supplier or allocated by the supplier exclusively to a maximum of five exclusive distributors;

    (2) the restriction of active or passive sales by the members of the selective distribution system and their customers to unauthorised distributors located within the territory where the selective distribution system is operated

    (3) the restriction of the place of establishment of the members of the selective distribution system;

    (4) the restriction of active or passive sales to end users by members of the selective distribution system operating at the wholesale level of trade;

    (5) the restriction of the ability to actively or passively sell components, supplied for the purposes of incorporation, to customers who would use them to manufacture the same type of goods as those produced by the supplier;

  (ii) the restriction of cross-supplies between the members of the selective distribution system operating at the same or different levels of trade,

  (iii) the restriction of active or passive sales to end users by members of the selective distribution system operating at the retail level of trade, without prejudice to points (c)(i)(1) and (3);

(d) where the supplier operates neither an exclusive distribution system nor a selective distribution system, the restriction of the territory into which, or of the customers to whom, the buyer may actively or passively sell the contract goods or services, except:

  (i) the restriction of active sales by the buyer and its direct customers into a territory or to a customer group reserved to the supplier or allocated by the supplier exclusively to a maximum of five exclusive distributors;

  (ii) the restriction of active or passive sales by the buyer and its customers to unauthorised distributors located in a territory where the supplier operates a selective distribution system for the contract goods or services;

  (iii) the restriction of the buyer's place of establishment;

(iv) the restriction of active or passive sales to end users by a buyer operating at the wholesale level of trade;

(v) the restriction of the buyer's ability to actively or passively sell components, supplied for the purposes of incorporation, to customers who would use them to manufacture the same type of goods as those produced by the supplier;

(e) the prevention of the effective use of the internet by the buyer or its customers to sell the contract goods or services, as it restricts the territory into which or the customers to whom the contract goods or services may be sold within the meaning of points (b), (c) or (d), without prejudice to the possibility of imposing on the buyer:

(i) other restrictions of online sales; or

(ii) restrictions of online advertising that do not have the object of preventing the use of an entire online advertising channel

(f) the restriction, agreed between a supplier of components and a buyer who incorporates those components, of the supplier's ability to sell the components as spare parts to end users or to repairers, wholesalers or other service providers not entrusted by the buyer with the repair or servicing of its goods.

b. Article 4(a): Resale Price Maintenance

Article 4(a) prohibits clauses resulting, directly or indirectly, in the establishment of a fixed or minimum resale price or a fixed or minimum price level to be observed by the buyer. Recommended or maximum prices may be imposed so long as they do not amount to indirect means of achieving RPM.[284] Further, the imposition of a resale price in a fulfilment contract is not RPM.[285] Examples of price-fixing through indirect means and measures facilitating direct or indirect price-fixing are set out in paragraph 187 of the Guidelines and include: fixing the resale margin or maximum level of discount; making rebates etc dependent on observance of given price levels; imposing minimum advertised prices (MAPs); linking prescribed retail prices to competitors' resale prices; and threats, intimidation, penalties, refusal to deliver, or termination of dealers not observing given price levels. The Commission notes that both direct and indirect means of applying RPM may be more effective if combined with measures aimed at identifying price-cutters, such as through use of price monitoring software systems.

In paragraph 192 the Commission objects, where agency agreements fall within Article 101(1), to contractual provisions preventing or restricting the agent from sharing commission with the customer. Even if the principal sets the price, the agent should be 'free to reduce the effective price paid by the customer without reducing the income due to the principal'.[286] The Guidelines also clarify that an OIS provider cannot impose fixed or minimum sales prices for the products of goods and services of buyers of its services, in relation to the transactions it intermediates.[287]

c. Article 4(b)–(e): Territorial and Customer Restraints and Online Restraints

Broadly, Article 4(b)–(e) prohibits clauses that: (i) restrict the territory into which, or the customers to whom, the buyer party to the agreement or its customers may sell the contract goods or services subject to certain exceptions which depend on the type of distribution agreement—exclusive distribution, selective distribution, or other, 'free', distribution; (ii) restrict cross-supplies between members of a SDS; and (iii) prevent the effective use of the internet by the buyer or its customers to sell the contract goods or services. It covers both direct restrictions and indirect provisions that, in practice, induce a buyer not to sell to particular customers, for example: requiring the supplier's approval for

[284] Ibid., para. 188. [285] Ibid., para. 193. [286] Ibid., para. 192. [287] Ibid., para. 194.

such sales; refusing or reducing bonuses or discounts, or terminating (or threatening to terminate), reducing, or limiting supply to buyers selling to particular customers; charging higher prices for products to be sold to such customers (but see discussion of dual pricing later); or excluding products that are sold outside allocated territories from Union-wide guarantees.[288]

Ever since e-commerce has started to grow, an important issue has been the extent to which suppliers are allowed under the VBER to control, prevent, or limit sales by buyers over the internet (whether by 'click and brick'—brick and mortar stores which also sell over the internet—or 'pure players'—which sell only over the internet and do not have a brick and mortar store).[289] The 2022 VBER and Guidelines now seek to shed clearer light on these issues taking account of the rulings of the CJ in *Pierre Fabre*[290] and *Coty*[291] on this matter. In the former, the CJ held that a requirement that cosmetic products could be sold only at a premises with a pharmacist present at a physical sales point operated as a prohibition on passive selling and a hardcore restraint for the purposes of the previous VBER. The contractual clauses prohibited *de facto* internet selling which had as its object the restriction of passive sales to end-users wishing to purchase online and located outside the physical trading area of the retailer.[292] In contrast, in *Coty*[293] the CJ held that the previous VBER did not prohibit a provision prohibiting selling on the internet via third party platforms which operate in a discernible manner towards consumers; it did not constitute a restriction on the territory into which, or the customers to whom, authorised distributors could sell the luxury goods or a restriction on passive sales to end-users. Unlike in *Pierre Fabre*, the clause did not prohibit the use of the internet as a means of marketing the contract goods and platform customers could not be circumscribed from the group of online purchasers. Because distributors were able to advertise via the internet (e.g. using online search engines), customers were usually able to find the online offer through these means.

Seemingly drawing on these cases, Article 4(e) of the VBER prohibits the prevention of effective use of the internet by the buyer, and clarifies that this does not prevent other restrictions on online sales or restrictions on advertising that do not prevent the use of an entire online advertising channel. The 2022 Guidelines clarify that indirect means to prevent effective use of the internet may include: requiring buyers to block or reroute customers from different territories, to terminate transactions to customers with foreign credit card details, or to sell only from a physical space or in the physical presence of specialised personnel; prohibiting the buyer from using the supplier's trademarks or brand names online, from establishing or operating one or more online stores, or from using an entire online advertising channel, such as search engines or price comparison services.[294] However, restrictions relating to the use of particular online sales channels, such as online marketplaces, or the imposition of quality standards for online sales, can generally benefit from the VBER so long as not designed to prevent the effective use of the internet by buyers.

Online sale restrictions generally do not have such an object where the buyer remains free to operate its own online store and to advertise online. In such cases, the buyer is not prevented from making

[288] See the full list of examples in ibid., para. 204.

[289] Internet selling offers enormous potential benefits for both sellers and consumers (see n. 120 and text), enabling a distributor to target a broader range of customers than is possible through traditional sales methods as well as allowing it to provide 24-hour, and other, services not offered by traditional retailers. It may also intensify price competition, allowing internet sellers to pass on their lower costs to customers, to overcome geographic barriers, and to provide customers with a broader range of outlets. In some situations, however, internet sellers may be able to free-ride on the efforts of brick and mortar shops.

[290] Case C-439/09, EU:C:2011:649. [291] Case C-230/16, EU:C:2017:941.

[292] The Court rejected Pierre Fabre's argument that the ban on internet selling was simply equivalent to a prohibition on the retailer operating out of an unauthorised establishment.

[293] Case C-230/16, EU:C:2017:941. [294] Guidelines, para. 206.

> effective use of the internet to sell the contract goods or services. The following are examples of requirements relating to online sales that can benefit from the exemption provided by Article 2(1) of the Regulation:
>
> (a) requirements intended to ensure the quality or a particular appearance of the buyer's online store;
>
> (b) requirements regarding the display of the contract goods or services in the online store (such as the minimum number of items displayed, the way the supplier's trademarks or brands are displayed);
>
> (c) a direct or indirect ban on the use of online marketplaces;
>
> (d) a requirement that the buyer operates one or more brick and mortar shops or showrooms, for instance as a condition for becoming a member of the supplier's selective distribution system;
>
> (e) a requirement that the buyer sells a minimum absolute amount of the contract goods or services offline (in value or volume, but not as a proportion of its total sales) to ensure the efficient operation of its brick and mortar shop. This requirement can be the same for all buyers, or it can be set at a different level for each buyer, based on objective criteria, such as the buyer's size relative to other buyers, or its geographic location.[295]

A related question which has arisen is how dual pricing provisions affecting different offline and online sales channels (for example requiring a distributor to pay a higher price for products intended to be resold online than for ones sold offline in a brick and mortar store) should be assessed. Some EU cases have considered dual pricing affecting exports. These cases have prohibited such provisions where they have been found to have as their purpose the restriction of parallel trade or to form part of a strategy aimed at hindering all export sales.[296] Although not dealing specifically with dual pricing affecting different offline and online sales channels, the cases, read together with *Pierre Fabre* and *Coty*, provide support for the view that a dual pricing provision specifically designed to restrict online selling (and hence parallel trade) is liable in principle to restrict competition by object and will constitute a hardcore restraint. Where, however, the dual pricing provision does not operate as a *de facto* prohibition on online selling, for example where its purpose and effect is not to restrict parallel trade, or to prevent online selling, but to curb the risk of free-riding or to otherwise incentivise investment by retailers, neither a finding of restriction of competition by object nor a restriction of online selling would be warranted.

Although the 2010 Guidelines (see especially paragraphs 52(d) and 64) took a strict approach to dual pricing and the view that agreements incorporating such provisions generally infringe Article 101, the 2022 Guidelines now reflect the position set out above, stating that:

> [a] requirement that the buyer pays a different wholesale price for products sold online than for products sold offline (dual pricing) can benefit from the exemption . . ., as it may incentivise or reward an

[295] Ibid., para. 208.

[296] See e.g. Case C-501/06 P, *GlaxoSmithKline v Commission* EU:C:2009:610 (holding that an agreement requiring a (Spanish) wholesaler to pay a higher price for products to be exported than for sale domestically, and which was designed to restrict parallel trade, constituted a restriction of competition by object (the CJ however upheld the GC's finding that the Commission's decision in this case should be annulled as the Commission had not adequately discharged its burden of examining the Art. 101(3) arguments put forward by the parties and refuting them by means of substantiated evidence, see Chap. 5)), Case T-368/00, *General Motors Nederland v Commission* EU:T:2003:275 (upholding a Commission decision condemning a general strategy aimed at hindering all exports of the supplier's vehicle), *aff'd* Case C-551/03 P, EU:C:2006:229. See also Case C-338/00 P, *Volkswagen AG v Commission* EU:C:2003:473, paras. 44–45 (finding a differentiated bonus scheme (allowing for only 15% of sales made outside contract territory to be taken into account) to be incompatible with Art. 101(1)) and COMP/28.282, *The Distillers Co Ltd* [1978] OJ L50/16, *aff'd* Case 30/78, *Distillers Co v Commission* EU:C:1980:186.

appropriate level of investments in online or offline sales channels, provided that it does not have the object of restricting sales to particular territories or customers. . . . However, where the difference in the wholesale price has the object of preventing the effective use of the internet by the buyer to sell the contract goods or services to particular territories or customers, it is a hardcore restriction within the meaning of Article 4, point (e). . . . This would, in particular, be the case where the difference in the wholesale price makes selling online unprofitable or financially unsustainable, or where dual pricing is used to limit the quantity of products made available to the buyer for sale online. Conversely, dual pricing can benefit from the exemption . . . where the difference in the wholesale price is reasonably related to differences in the investments and costs incurred by the buyer to make sales in each channel. Similarly, the supplier may charge a different wholesale price for products that are to be sold through a combination of offline and online channels, where the price difference takes into account investments or costs related to that type of distribution.[297]

(1) Exclusive Distribution

With five exceptions, suppliers operating an exclusive distribution agreement—which since 2022 includes a distribution system where the supplier allocates a territory or group of customers either to itself, a single buyer, or a group of up to five buyers[298]—may not restrict the territory into which, or the customers to whom, a buyer can sell the products.

The first exception allows a supplier to restrict active (but not passive) sales by a buyer, or its direct customers, into an exclusive territory or to an exclusive consumer group exclusively allocated either to itself or to a maximum of five other distributors. This allows the supplier to protect the investment incentives of its exclusive distributors from active—but not passive—selling from all other buyers (but active and passive sales by these exclusive distributors within the exclusive territory or customer group cannot generally be restricted[299]).

Given the importance of the distinction between active and passive selling, Article 1(1)(l) and (m) define the terms and the 2022 Guidelines provide updated examples of how the line between them is to be drawn, especially in the online context.[300] The former involves actively targeting customers by visits, letters, emails, or targeted advertising and includes targeted price comparison tools or search advertising, or offering an online store with a language option (other than English) that is different from the languages commonly used in the seller's territory or with a top-level domain corresponding to a territory other than the one in which the seller is established. Passive sales in contrast (which cannot be prohibited in this context) means sales made in response to unsolicited requests from individual customers, including from an online store (even if it offers an English-language option), through the use of search engine optimisation, participation in public procurement, or responding to private tender invitations.[301]

The other exceptions allow restrictions on all selling to unauthorised dealers in a territory where the supplier operates a SDS (in the absence of such a provision, the SDS would obviously break down), a restriction on the distributor's place of establishment, a restriction on sales by wholesalers to end-users, and a restriction on sales of components for incorporation, to customers who would use them to manufacture a product which competes with that produced by the supplier.

(2) Selective Distribution

Exceptions also exist to the rule that suppliers may not restrict the territories into which, or the customers to whom, members of the SDS may actively or passively sell the contract goods. First,

[297] Guidelines, para. 209. [298] See Section 5.C.ii. [299] Guidelines, para. 122.
[300] Ibid., paras. 211–215. [301] Ibid.

members can be prohibited from actively selling into a territory reserved to the supplier or a maximum of five exclusive distributors. Further, members can be restricted from (actively or passively) selling to unauthorised distributors located in a SDS territory, and a restriction can be imposed on the distributor's place of establishment, on sales by wholesalers to end-users, and on sales of components for incorporation, to customers who would use them to manufacture a product which competes with that produced by the supplier.

Article 4(c)(ii) and (iii) also prohibit restrictions on cross-suppliers between members of the SDS network[302] and restrictions on sales to end-users by retail members of the SDS (unless in a territory reserved to the supplier or exclusive distributors and without prejudice to allowing a restriction of the place of establishment).[303] The supplier can, however, impose a location clause on its authorised distributors to prevent them from operating their business from different premises or from opening a new outlet in a different location (although it may require a buyer to operate one or more brick and mortar shops, establishment and use of an online store cannot be restricted).

The core difference to the assessment of SDSs conducted under Article 101(1), therefore, is that it is not necessary when applying the VBER to establish that the products concerned merit a SDS or that the members of the system are chosen only by reference to qualitative criteria—quantitative criteria may be used. The Guidelines make it clear that qualitative criteria should generally be set for both online and offline channels but (in a change of direction from the 2010 Guidelines) do not have to be equivalent, given the different characteristics of the channels. 'For example, a supplier may impose requirements to ensure quality standards for online sales, such as a requirement to set up and operate an online after-sales helpdesk; a requirement to cover the costs of customers returning purchased products, or the use of secure payment systems.'[304] The criteria must not, however, indirectly prevent the effective use of the internet by the buyer to sell the goods or services.

Although SDSs can be used in one territory and exclusive distribution in another, the VBER does not apply if combined in the same territory, for example where the supplier applies exclusive distribution at the wholesale level and SDSs at the retail level. Such an arrangement would involve the acceptance of hardcore restraints, contrary to Article 4(b) and (c).[305]

(3) *Free Distribution*

Restrictions on the territories into which, or the customers to whom, buyers can sell contract goods or services also constitute hardcore restraints in free distribution, subject to five exceptions.[306] These include restrictions on the buyer or its direct customers actively selling to territories allocated exclusively to other buyers or the supplier, restrictions on the buyer selling to unauthorised distributors in a territory where the supplier operates a SDS, imposition of a location clause on the buyer to restrict its place of establishment, restrictions on sales by wholesalers to end-users, and restrictions on sales of components for incorporation to customers who would use them to manufacture a product which competes with that produced by the supplier.[307]

[302] The members may not, therefore, be required to purchase products only from the supplier or a given source (although non-compete obligations are permissible so long as they are not excessive in time and are not targeted at specific suppliers), see ibid., para. 237 and discussion of Art. 5 of the VBER, Section 5.C.vi.

[303] In COMP/37.709, *B&W Loudspeakers* 24 June 2002, IP/02/916, the Commission objected to price restraints, restraints on cross-supplies between dealers, and restraints on distant selling via the internet in a notified SDS. Eventually, it granted a comfort letter after the parties agreed to remove these restraints.

[304] Guidelines, para. 235.

[305] Ibid., para. 236 (the supplier may, however, commit to supply only certain authorised distributors, for example in certain parts of the territory where the SDS is operated, or it may commit not to make any direct sales in that territory itself. It may also impose a location clause on its authorised distributors).

[306] Guidelines, paras. 238–239. [307] Ibid., paras. 240–244.

d. *Article 4(f): Restrictions on Sales of Spare Parts*

Where a manufacturer of components supplies a buyer, such as an original equipment manufacturer (OEM), with components which the latter incorporates into its products, the agreement may not prevent or restrict the component manufacturer from selling the parts to end-users, repairers, wholesalers, or service providers. Restrictions may, however, be placed on the supply of the spare parts to the repairers or service providers entrusted by the buyer with the repair or servicing of its products.[308]

(vi) Article 5—Excluded Restraints: Severable, Non-exempted Obligations

a. *Obligations Which are Excluded (Not Exempted) But Which May Be Severable*

In contrast to Article 4, Article 5 sets out a list of obligations which cannot be assumed with sufficient certainty to fulfil the conditions of Article 101(3)—and so are not covered by the VBER—but which do not necessarily prevent the VBER from applying. The agreement as a whole will only fail to satisfy the conditions of the VBER where the excluded restraint violates Article 101 and is *not* severable from the remaining provisions of the agreement.[309]

Article 5 Excluded restrictions

1. The exemption provided for in Article 2 shall not apply to the following obligations contained in vertical agreements:
   (a) any direct or indirect non-compete obligation, the duration of which is indefinite or exceeds five years;
   (b) any direct or indirect obligation causing the buyer, after termination of the agreement, not to manufacture, purchase, sell or resell goods or services;
   (c) any direct or indirect obligation causing the members of a selective distribution system not to sell the brands of particular competing suppliers;
   (d) any direct or indirect obligation causing a buyer of online intermediation services not to offer, sell or resell goods or services to end users under more favourable conditions via competing online intermediation services.
2. By way of derogation from paragraph 1, point (a), the time limitation of five years shall not apply where the contract goods or services are sold by the buyer from premises and land owned by the supplier or leased by the supplier from third parties not connected with the buyer, provided that the duration of the non-compete obligation does not exceed the period of occupancy of the premises and land by the buyer.
3. By way of derogation from paragraph 1, point (b), the exemption provided for in Article 2 shall apply to any direct or indirect obligation causing the buyer, after termination of the agreement, not to manufacture, purchase, sell or resell goods or services where the following conditions are fulfilled:
   (a) the obligation relates to goods or services which compete with the contract goods or services;
   (b) the obligation is limited to the premises and land from which the buyer has operated during the contract period;
   (c) the obligation is indispensable to protect know-how transferred by the supplier to the buyer;
   (d) the duration of the obligation is limited to a period of one year after termination of the agreement.

   Paragraph 1, point (b), shall be without prejudice to the possibility of imposing a restriction which is unlimited in time on the use and disclosure of know-how which has not entered the public domain.

308 Ibid., para. 245.

309 Whether or not the offending clauses can be severed is a question of national, not EU, law, see Chaps. 4 and 14.

b. *Article 5(1): Non-compete Obligations*

Article 5(1) provides that the exemption does not apply to non-compete obligations which are indefinite or in excess of five years.[310] An exception applies, however, where the buyer of the goods or services operates from premises owned by the supplier or leased by it from a third party not connected with the buyer (Article 5(2)). In this case, the non-compete obligation can be imposed for the duration of the buyer's occupancy of the land. It thus seems, for example, that brewers leasing premises to a publican will be able to impose a non-compete obligation for the entire duration of the lease. The reason for this latter exception is that 'it is generally unreasonable to expect a supplier to allow competing products to be sold from premises and land that it owns without its permission'.[311] But '[a]rtificial ownership constructions . . . intended to avoid the 5-year limitation, cannot benefit from this exception'.[312]

c. *Article 5(1)(b): Non-compete Obligations after the Termination of the Agreement*

Article 5(1)(b) states that the exemption does not apply to obligations imposed on the buyer which prevent it from manufacturing, purchasing, or selling or reselling goods or services after the termination of the agreement *unless*, as provided by Article 5(3), the prohibition: relates to competing goods or services; is limited to the premises and land from which the buyer has operated during the agreement; is indispensable to protect know-how[313] transferred by the supplier under the agreement; and is limited to a period of one year. A restriction which is unlimited in time may be possible, however, where essential to prevent the use or disclosure of know-how which has not entered the public domain (Article 5(3)).

d. *Article 5(1)(c): Non-compete Obligations and Selective Distribution Systems*

The block exemption covers the combination of selective distribution with a non-compete obligation, requiring authorised distributors not to resell competing brands. The exemption will not apply, however, where the supplier prevents distributors from buying products for resale from *specific* competing suppliers.

> The rationale for this exclusion is to avoid a situation whereby a number of suppliers using the same selective distribution outlets prevent one or more specific competitors from using those outlets to distribute their products. Such a scenario could lead to foreclosure of a competing supplier which would be a form of collective boycott.[314]

e. *Across-platform Retail Parity Obligations*

Although some competition authorities are wary of wide APPAs (in the UK, wide parity clause are treated as hardcore restraints[315]), the Commission decided not to include any APPAs in the list of hardcore restraints and only included across-platform retail parity obligations imposed by suppliers of online intermediation services in the list of excluded restraints, that is direct or indirect obligations which cause buyers of such services not to offer, sell, or resell goods or services to end-users under

[310] Under the 2010 VBER, the exclusion also applied if the arrangement was tacitly renewable. The current VBER now applies to non-compete obligations that are tacitly renewable, provided that the buyer can effectively renegotiate or terminate the agreement (the buyer is effectively allowed to switch at the end of a five-year period), Guidelines, para. 248.

[311] Ibid., para. 249. [312] Ibid. [313] VBER, Art. 1(1)(j).

[314] Guidelines, para. 252 and see COMP/33.542, *Parfums Givenchy* [1992] OJ L236/11.

[315] See the Competition Act 1998 (Vertical Agreements Block Exemption) Order 2022, art. 8(2)(f) and Section 4.B.vi.

more favourable conditions (including price, inventory, availability, or other terms or conditions) via competing online intermediation services. The exclusion applies whether the obligation results from a contractual clause or from other direct or indirect measures. 'For example, where the provider of online intermediation services makes the offering of better visibility for the buyer's goods or services on the provider's website or the application of a lower commission rate dependent on the buyer granting it parity of conditions relative to competing providers of such services, this amounts to an across-platform retail parity obligation.'[316] All other types of parity obligation[317] can benefit from the VBER.

(vii) Article 6—Withdrawal of the Block Exemption

The benefit of the block exemption can be withdrawn, pursuant to Article 29(1)(2) of Regulation 1/2003,[318] in relation to an agreement which, either in isolation or in conjunction with similar agreements, infringes Article 101. The Commission has the exclusive power to withdraw the benefit of the block exemption in respect of vertical agreements restricting competition on a relevant geographic market which is wider than the territory of a single Member State, but concurrent jurisdiction with designated NCAs[319] where the relevant geographic market constitutes the territory of a single Member State, or a part thereof.[320] Article 6(1) of the VBER clarifies that the Commission can withdraw the benefit of the VBER where it finds in a particular case that the agreement has effects, individually or in conjunction with similar agreements entered into by competing suppliers or buyers, which are incompatible with Article 101(3). 'The responsibility for an anti-competitive cumulative effect can only be attributed to those undertakings that make an appreciable contribution to it.'[321] 'Such effects may occur, for example, where the relevant market for the supply of online intermediation services is highly concentrated and competition between the providers of such services is restricted by the cumulative effect of parallel networks of similar agreements that restrict buyers of the online intermediation services from offering, selling or reselling goods or services to end users under more favourable conditions on their direct sales channels.'[322] Any withdrawal could not apply retrospectively, but would only have *ex nunc* effect, 'the exempted status of the agreements concerned remains unaffected for the period preceding the date on which the withdrawal becomes effective'.[323]

(viii) Article 7—Non-application of the Regulation

This provision allows the Commission to declare by regulation (applicable not to an individual undertaking but to all undertakings addressed) that the block exemption should not apply to agreements containing specified restraints in cases where more than 50 per cent of a relevant market is covered by networks of similar vertical restraints.[324] Any such regulation, fully restoring the application of Article 101 to the restraints and markets concerned,[325] must not take effect earlier than six months

[316] Guidelines, para. 253. [317] See nn. 26–27 and text and Section 4.B.vi. [318] See Chap. 5.

[319] NCAs 'may withdraw the benefit of this Regulation where the conditions of Article 29(2) of Regulation (EC) No 1/2003 are fulfilled', VBER, Art. 6(2).

[320] Guidelines, para. 264. [321] Ibid., para. 261. [322] VBER, Art. 6(1).

[323] Guidelines, para. 268. Although the withdrawal mechanism has not been used since 1999 and the modernised VBERs, the benefit of Reg. 1984/83 was withdrawn in COMP/34.072, *Langnese-Iglo GmbH* [1993] OJ L183/19, *aff'd* Case T-7/93, EU:T:1995:98.

[324] VBER, Art. 7, e.g. when parallel networks of SDS covering more than 50% of a market are liable to foreclose the market through use of selection criteria which are not required by the nature of relevant goods or which discriminate against certain forms of distribution of such goods or services, Guidelines, para. 270.

[325] Ibid., para. 271.

following its adoption[326] and does not affect the exempted status of the agreements concerned for the period preceding its coming into force.[327] When deciding whether to adopt a regulation the Commission will also consider whether withdrawal of the block exemption would be more appropriate. This will depend on the number of competing undertakings contributing to the cumulative effects and the number of affected geographic markets.[328]

Because the regulation must specify the scope of the regulation in relation both to the relevant product and geographic markets to which it applies and to the vertical restraints in respect of which the VBER will not apply, the regulation may not apply to all agreements concluded on an affected market. Rather:

> the Commission may modulate the scope of its regulation according to the competition concern which it intends to address. For instance, while all parallel networks of single-branding type arrangements may be taken into account when determining the 50 % market coverage ratio, the Commission may nevertheless restrict the scope of the [disapplication regulation] to non-compete obligations that exceed a certain duration. Thus, agreements of a shorter duration or of a less restrictive nature may be left unaffected, in view of the lesser degree of foreclosure attributable to such restraints. . . . Where appropriate, the Commission may also specify the level of market share level which, in the specific market context, may be regarded as insufficient for an individual undertaking to make a significant contribution to the cumulative effect.[329]

(ix) Articles 8, 9, and 10—Market Share, Turnover, and Transitional Provisions

Articles 8 and 9 contain provisions relating to the calculation of market share and turnover for the purposes of the Regulation. In particular, Article 8(d) makes provision to exempt agreements, for a period of two consecutive calendar years, which satisfy the 30 per cent threshold initially but subsequently rise above it. Article 10 provides that agreements already in force on 31 May 2022 and satisfying the provisions of Regulation 330/2010, but not Regulation 2022/720, shall not be prohibited from 1 June 2022 to 31 May 2023.

(x) Article 11—Commencement, Expiry, and Review

Article 11 provides that the block exemption entered into force on 1 June 2022[330] and expires on 31 May 2034.

D. THE MOTOR VEHICLE DISTRIBUTION BLOCK EXEMPTION

Until the end of May 2010, motor vehicle distribution agreements and agreements relating to repair, maintenance, and the supply of spare parts were not governed by the ordinary regime for vertical agreements but by Regulation 1400/02,[331] which recognised the special features of the motor vehicle sector and peculiar factors affecting it. Although many motor vehicle distribution agreements have now been brought within the ordinary verticals regime, a separate regime has been maintained for the supply of spare parts and repair and maintenance agreements, see Regulation 461/2010.[332]

326 Reg. 19/65, Art. 1a. 327 Guidelines, para. 274. 328 Ibid., para. 269. 329 Ibid., para. 272.

330 Except for the provision extending the application of the block exemption which has applied since 1 January 2000.

331 [2002] OJ L203/30. It entered into force in October 2002. In Case C-158/11, *Auto24 SARL v Jaguar Land Rover France SAS* EU:C:2012:351, the CJ gave a judgment which focused on the interpretation of specific provisions of Reg. 1400/2002 and the distinction set out therein between quantitative and qualitative selective distribution systems.

332 [2010] OJ L129/52.

Because the block exemption originally contained an expiry date of 31 May 2023, the Commission has had to consider whether this distinct regime should continue, should be amended to enable the industry to adapt to the green and digital transformations in the sector, or whether repair and maintenance agreements should also be brought within the scope of the ordinary verticals regime. In April 2023, however, the Commission published a Regulation prolonging the block exemption for five years (to 31 May 2028) and published updated Supplementary Guidelines.[333]

E. ARTICLE 101(3)—INDIVIDUAL ASSESSMENT

(i) Introduction

Where the parties cannot ensure that their agreement benefits from the VBER, and the risk of infringing Article 101(1) is real, it will be important to consider the application of Article 101(3).

(ii) 'Hardcore' Restraints

A supplier or distributor may perceive 'hardcore' restraints to be essential to the operation of a distribution agreement. The Commission has generally been unwilling, however, to accept that agreements incorporating such restraints meet the requirements of Article 101(3).[334] In *Grundig*,[335] for example, it was the clauses resulting in Consten being granted the exclusive right to sell Grundig's products in France which caused the Commission to find that the agreement both infringed Article 101(1) and did not meet the Article 101(3) criteria (it refused an exemption). Since then, the Commission has remained unreceptive to arguments that these types of clauses may produce efficiencies and satisfy the conditions of Article 101(1). For example, in 2003 in *Nintendo*,[336] the Commission relied on *Grundig* when it stated that agreements conferring ATP would not meet the criteria of Article 101(3) (the provisions were not indispensable to realise the potential benefits of the exclusive distribution system).[337]

Nonetheless, the EU Courts have always made it clear that any restrictive agreement is, in theory, capable of satisfying the criteria[338] so long as all four criteria are satisfied.[339] In Chapter 5, it is seen that in *GlaxoSmithKline Services Unlimited v Commission*,[340] the GC held that: the Commission's decision to refuse an exemption to a dual pricing system operated by Glaxo which prevented parallel trade was fundamentally flawed; and the Commission had not adequately discharged its duty under Article 101(3). Similarly, in *Binon*, the CJ indicated that the Commission might have to consider

[333] See Commission Reg. 2023/822 [2023] OJ L102 I/1 and Amendments to the Commission Notice—Supplementary guidelines on vertical restraints in agreements for the sale and repair of motor vehicles and for distribution of spare parts for motor vehicles [2023] OJ C133I/1 <https://competition-policy.ec.europa.eu/public-consultations/2022-motor-vehicle_en>.

[334] See COMP/35.733, *Volkswagen* [1998] OJ L124/60, on appeal Case T-62/98, *Volkswagen AG v Commission* EU:T:2000:180, the appeal to the CJ was dismissed, see Case C-338/00 P, *Volkswagen AG v Commission* EU:C:2003:473.

[335] COMP/3344, 23 September 1964. The result was that Grundig acquired Consten. See also e.g. COMP/28.282, *The Distillers Co Ltd* [1978] OJ L50/16, Case 30/78, *Distillers Co v Commission* EU:C:1980:186, and COMP/223, *Transocean Marine Paint Associations* [1967] OJ L163/10.

[336] COMP/35.706 and 36.321 [2003] OJ L255/33, *aff'd* Case T-12/03, *Itochu v Commission* EU:T:2009:130, and Case T-13/03, *Nintendo and Nintendo of Europe v Commission* EU:T:2009:131.

[337] 'Instead, in regard to the goods in question territories are hermetically sealed off, making interpenetrating of national markets impossible, thereby, bringing to nought economic integration' COMP/35.706 and COMP/36.321, ibid., para. 338.

[338] Case T-17/93, *Matra Hachette v Commission* EU:T:1994:89, para. 85, see Chap. 5.

[339] The requirements are cumulative, Case T-528/93, *Métropole Télévision SA v Commission* EU:T:1996:99, para. 93.

[340] Case T-168/01, EU:T:2006:265, *aff'd* Cases C-501, 513, 515, and 519/06 P, EU:C:2009:610, see Chap. 5.

whether or not an agreement, where a publisher fixed the prices of its newspapers and periodicals, fulfilled the requirements of Article 101(3).[341]

Case 243/83, *SA Binon & Cie v SA Agence et Messageries de la Presse* EU:C:1985:284

Court of Justice

44. It should be observed in the first place that provisions which fix the prices to be observed in contracts with third parties constitute, of themselves, a restriction on competition within the meaning of Article [101(1)]. . . .

45. In those circumstances, where an agreement which establishes a selective distribution system and which affects trade between Member States includes such a provision, an exemption from the prohibition contained in Article [101(1)] of the [EU] Treaty may only be granted by means of a decision adopted by the Commission in the conditions laid down by Article [101(3)].

46. If, in so far as the distribution of newspapers and periodicals is concerned, the fixing of the retail price by publishers constitutes the sole means of supporting the financial burden resulting from the taking back of unsold copies and if the latter practice constitutes the sole method by which a wide selection of newspapers and periodicals can be made available to readers, the Commission must take account of those factors when examining an agreement for the purposes of Article [101(3)].

In accordance with the case law, the Commission has been urged to ensure that the Guidelines reflect this position. Although the Commission still remains sceptical about the benefits of such restraints, and its starting position is that vertical agreements incorporating them are likely to fall within Article 101(1) and are unlikely to fulfil the conditions of Article 101(3),[342] it does recognise that the parties may demonstrate pro-competitive effects under Article 101(3) of the Treaty in an individual case.

For that purpose, the undertaking must substantiate that efficiencies are likely and that the efficiencies are likely to result from including the hardcore restriction in the agreement, as well as demonstrating that the other conditions of Article 101(3) of the Treaty are fulfilled. Where this is the case, the Commission will assess the negative impact on competition that is likely to result from including the hardcore restriction in the agreement before making a final assessment of whether the conditions of Article 101(3) of the Treaty are fulfilled.[343]

For example, the Commission recognises that RPM may lead to efficiencies, especially where supplier-driven, but that these must be substantiated with concrete evidence. Paragraph 197 of the Guidelines provides four examples of such efficiencies including when: (a) a manufacturer introduces a new product, and distributors need to be induced to better take into account the manufacturer's interest in promoting that product (and so long as there are no realistic and less restrictive alternative means of incentivising the distributors to promote the product, e.g. it is not feasible in practice to impose on all buyers effective promotion obligations by contract); (b) fixed resale prices are necessary to organise a coordinated short-term low price campaign (of two to six weeks in most cases), especially in a distribution system where the supplier applies a uniform distribution format, such as a franchise system; (c) a minimum resale price or MAP can be used to prevent a particular distributor from using the

[341] In neither case did the Court hold that the Art. 101(3) criteria were actually satisfied, however.

[342] Guidelines, para. 180. It applies a presumption against such agreements.

[343] Ibid., para. 181.

product of a supplier as a loss leader and damaging the brand image of the product and, over time, reducing overall demand for the product; and (d) the extra margin provided by RPM will allow retailers to provide additional pre-sales services, in particular in the case of complex products. If enough customers take advantage of such services in order to choose a product but subsequently purchase at a lower price with retailers that do not provide such services (and hence do not incur those costs), high-service retailers may reduce or stop providing pre-sales services, which enhance the demand for the supplier's product. 'The supplier must demonstrate that there is a risk of free riding at the distribution level, that fixed or minimum resale prices provide sufficient incentives for investments in pre-sale services and that there is no realistic and less restrictive alternative means of overcoming such free riding. In this situation, the likelihood that RPM will be considered as procompetitive is higher when competition between suppliers is fierce and the supplier has limited market power.'[344]

The Commission does therefore accept that hardcore restraints may sometimes satisfy the conditions of Article 101(3). Nonetheless, an extremely onerous burden rests on the parties who seek to demonstrate that efficiencies will result from including ATP or RPM in their agreement and to demonstrate also that the other conditions of Article 101(3) are fulfilled. Further, the limited examples provided in the Guidelines combined with the lack of jurisprudence on this issue[345] is likely to continue to make firms cautious about incorporating these restraints into their agreements.[346] Indeed, the Article 101(3) Guidelines[347] state that hardcore restraints are unlikely to create objective economic benefits, to benefit consumers, or to be indispensable to the attainment of any efficiencies created by the agreement.[348] The 2022 Guidelines also indicate that indispensability will present a problem to those seeking to rely on Article 101(3) to justify hardcore restraints, as they will need to demonstrate that no other restraint would be sufficient to achieve the efficiencies alleged. Paragraph 17 provides:

> There is a large degree of substitutability between the various vertical restraints, meaning that the same inefficiency problem can be addressed using different vertical restraints. For instance, it may be possible to achieve economies of scale in distribution by using exclusive distribution, selective distribution, quantity forcing or exclusive sourcing. However, the negative effects on competition may differ between the various vertical restraints. This is taken into account when indispensability is assessed under Article 101(3).

(iii) Other Restraints

In other cases, it is extremely important when drafting agreements to look at the jurisprudence and at both the Article 101(3) Guidelines and the Vertical Guidelines which set out how the Commission will enforce Article 101 in respect of individual agreements not covered by the block exemption.[349]

An example of a case in which a non-compete provision was found not to meet the criteria of Article 101(3) is *Van den Bergh Foods*.[350] In this case, the GC rejected the applicants' assertion that the Commission had erred in law in applying Article 101(3), in particular by wrongly concluding that the restrictive effects of its freezer exclusivity agreements outweighed the advantages flowing from the distribution efficiency they produced. The GC held that as the agreement did not satisfy the first

[344] Ibid., para. 197(d).

[345] But see the decision of the Australian Competition and Consumer Commission (ACCC) to grant authorisation to Tooltechnic to set minimum retail prices on Festool products until 31 December 2018, A91433 *Tooltechnic* 5 December 2014.

[346] It seems likely, however, that competition agencies do recognise that these provisions may sometimes be unproblematic and do not prioritise such cases for investigation.

[347] [2004] OJ C101/97. [348] See Chap. 5. [349] See, especially, Guidelines, section 8.2.

[350] Case T-65/98, EU:T:2003:281, *aff'd* Case C-552/03 P, *Unilever Bestfoods v Commission* EU:C:2006:607.

condition of Article 101(3), the Commission was entitled to refuse an exemption.[351] The advantages produced by the agreement were not objective ones but ensued to the parties to the agreement and strengthened HB's position on the market.[352]

In *Telenor/Canal+/Canal Digital*,[353] the European Commission approved complex contractual arrangements providing for the exclusive distribution by Canal Digital of pay-TV premium content channels and pay-per-view and near-video-on demand (PPV/NVOD) channels in the Nordic region.[354] The agreements also imposed non-compete obligations which, broadly, prohibited Canal Digital from owning, operating, or retailing any other pay-TV premium content or PPV/NVOD channels.

In order to gain approval for the agreements, the parties agreed to modify the agreements and: to mitigate foreclosure of potential entrants in the downstream DTH pay-TV market by reducing the duration and scope of Canal Digital's exclusivity; to alleviate foreclosure of potential entrants on the supply side in the upstream market for the wholesale supply of pay-TV by reducing the duration of the pay-TV non-compete obligations on Canal Digital; and to alleviate foreclosure of potential entrants on the supply side in the upstream market for the provision of transponder capacity for TV broadcasting by reducing non-compete obligations on Canal+.[355]

Although the Commission took the view that most of the clauses, even in their revised form, appreciably restricted competition within the meaning of Article 101(1)[356] and that the VBER did not apply,[357] it applied Article 101(3) of the Treaty,[358] finding that: (a) the modified exclusivity and non-compete provisions generated efficiencies and contributed to the improvement in distribution and the promotion of economic progress'; (b) consumers received a fair share of the benefits; and (c) the provisions were, for a strict limitation period, indispensable to attain the efficiencies (four years for

[351] The GC held that the review carried out in a case under the old notification and exemption system 'of the complex economic assessments undertaken by the Commission in the exercise of the discretion conferred on it by Article [101(3)] of the Treaty in relation to each of the four conditions laid down therein, must be limited to ascertaining whether the procedural rules have been complied with, whether proper reasons have been provided, whether the facts have been accurately stated and whether there has been any manifest error of appraisal or misuse of powers (see, to that effect, Cases T-39/92 and T-40/92, *CB and Europay v Commission* EU:T:1994:20, para. 109; Case T-17/93, *Matra Hachette v Commission* EU:T:1994:89, para,104; and Case T-29/92, *SPO and Others v Commission* EU:T:1995:34, para. 288). It is not for the [General Court] to substitute its own assessment for that of the Commission', Case T-65/98, *Van den Bergh Foods v Commission* EU:T:2003:281, para. 135. The judgment was *aff'd* Case C-552/03 P, *Unilever Bestfoods v Commission* EU:C:2006:607.

[352] Rather than improving distribution or promoting progress, the effect of the agreements was to strengthen the strong position of HB on the market.

[353] COMP/38.287, 29 December 2003.

[354] The notified agreements also related to the divestiture by Canal+ of its 50% shareholding in Canal Digital, previously jointly run with Telenor Broadband Services (TBS), and its acquisition by TBS. The distribution agreements related to the distribution by Canal Digital of Canal+ Nordic's pay-TV premium content channels and PPV/NVOD channels via direct-to-home (DTH) satellite platform, satellite master antenna television system networks (SMATV), and small cable networks in the Nordic region. Essentially, the agreements aimed to ensure continuity of the pay-TV content supply and distribution that had previously been secured within the vertically integrated company structure. Under the new arrangements there was a vertical relationship between the independent upstream supplier of pay-TV premium content, Canal+ Nordic, and an independent downstream DTH platform for the distribution of pay-TV to end consumers, Canal Digital.

[355] The parties also took steps to address horizontal cooperation concerns and to avoid foreclosure in related market segments.

[356] It granted negative clearance, however, to the clauses governing exclusive distribution by COMP/38.287, *Telenor/Canal+/Canal Digital* 29 December 2003, paras. 170–178.

[357] Both because the primary purpose of the exclusivity and non-compete arrangement was the use by the buyer of IPRs and because of Canal+'s strong market position, which exceeded the 30% threshold.

[358] COMP/38.287, *Telenor/Canal+/Canal Digital* 29 December 2003, para. 196.

the pay-TV channel exclusivity provisions and years in respect of the obligation on Telenor/Canal Digital not to own, operate, or distribute via DTH any other pay-TV premium content channels). The Commission concluded that the various contractual arrangements did not eliminate competition in the affected markets, that the cooperation for a limited period would maintain competition with the second satellite pay-TV distributor in the Nordic region, MTV/VIASAT, and preserve the possibility of market entry in the Nordic pay-TV segments in the mid- to long-term. It thus granted an exemption to the provisions found to infringe Article 101(1) for a five-year period.[359]

6. SUBCONTRACTING AGREEMENTS

Subcontracting agreements, under which a contractor entrusts the manufacture of goods or the supply of services to a subcontractor, are vertical in nature.[360] Goods or services in subcontracting agreements are provided, on the instructions of the contractor, to that contractor or, on its behalf, to a third party. The arrangement may also involve a licence of IPRs from the contractor to the subcontractor.

A Commission Notice concerning the assessment of certain subcontracting agreements in relation to Article 101(1) of the Treaty (the 'Subcontracting Notice') recognises that these agreements are frequently pro-competitive. It thus indicates that certain clauses in subcontracting agreements are unlikely to restrict competition and infringe Article 101(1). For example, a requirement that: (a) technology or equipment provided by the contractor (i) may not be used except for the purposes of the subcontracting agreement and (ii) may not be made available to third parties; and (b) goods or services resulting from such technology or equipment may be supplied only to the contractor or performed on his behalf, will fall outside Article 101(1) on condition that the technology or equipment provided is necessary to enable the subcontractor to manufacture the goods or supply the services or to carry out the work in accordance with the contractor's instructions.[361] Further, paragraph 3 provides that the following provisions are unlikely to violate Article 101(1): (a) an obligation that a specified 'trade mark, trade name or get-up'[362] provided under the contract be used by the subcontractor only as a means of identification in relation to the contract goods, services, or work; (b) an undertaking by either party not to reveal secret know-how (which has not become public knowledge) given by the other party during the negotiation and performance of the agreement; (c) an undertaking by the subcontractor not to make use, even after expiry of the agreement, of secret know-how (which has not become public knowledge) received during the currency of the agreement; and (d) an undertaking by the subcontractor to pass on to the contractor on a non-exclusive basis technical improvements or patentable inventions relating to improvements and/or new applications of the original invention, discovered during the currency of the agreement. However, other restrictions imposed on the subcontractor can fall within the scope of Article 101 of the Treaty, such as the obligation not to conduct or exploit the subcontractor's own R&D or not to produce in general for third parties.[363]

Where there is concern that the subcontracting agreements may violate Article 101(1), the agreement may be able to benefit from the VBER.[364] It has been seen in the previous discussion, however,

[359] The Commission took due account of Telenor's/Canal Digital's and Canal+ Nordic's legitimate interest in achieving a reasonable return on their investment in their pay-TV business so far.

[360] See Commission Notice of 18 December 1978 concerning its assessment of certain sub-contracting agreements in relation to Article [101(1)] (the Subcontracting Notice) [1979] OJ C1/2, para. 1.

[361] Subcontracting Notice, para. 2. [362] Ibid., para. 4. [363] Ibid., para. 3 and Guidelines, para. 47.

[364] Since the agreement is between undertakings which operate, for the purposes of the agreement, at different levels of the production or distribution chain, and the agreement relates to the conditions under which the parties may purchase, sell, or resell certain goods or services.

that this block exemption is not generally applicable if the agreement is between competitors or if the subject matter of the agreement falls within the scope of another block exemption. Further, it does not cover the licensing or assignment of IPRs unless they are assigned to the buyer, in this case, the *contractor.* In practice, therefore, although some subcontracting agreements may benefit from the VBER, such as agreements between non-competitors whereby the contractor provides only specifications to the subcontractor describing the goods or services to be supplied, many will in fact fall outside its scope. Nonetheless, where the primary object of the agreement is to enable the subcontractor to use licensed technology exclusively for the production of products for the contractor, the technology transfer block exemption may apply (see Chapter 12). Alternatively, if the agreement is between competitors, and if any provisions concerning the assignment or use of IPRs do not constitute the primary object of the agreement, the subcontracting agreement might constitute a specialisation agreement (capable of benefiting from the specialisation block exemption) or a production agreement, dealt with in the Commission's Horizontal Cooperation Guidelines (see Chapter 10).

7. ARTICLE 102 AND DISTRIBUTION

Where a party to a vertical agreement has a market share approaching 40 per cent, a finding of dominance within the meaning of Article 102 is possible. In such cases, it should additionally be considered whether certain provisions, such as clauses imposing unfair or discriminatory selling prices, single branding provisions, or tying provisions, may infringe Article 102.[365] Conduct that amounts to an abuse of a dominant position is unlikely to meet the criteria of Article 101(3).

8. CONCLUSIONS

1. The Verticals Guidelines and Regulation indicate that the Commission adopts an economic approach to vertical agreements.

2. A number of vertical agreements fall outside Article 101(1) where they do not appreciably effect trade or competition.

3. The VBER sets out a safe harbour for vertical agreements between undertakings whose market shares do not exceed the 30 per cent market share threshold and satisfy the other conditions of the Regulation. The benefit of the block exemption can only be withdrawn prospectively.

4. In contrast, agreements containing object or hardcore restraints are likely to infringe Article 101. Experience indicates that the presumption of illegality to these agreements is difficult to counter in practice. Indeed, the lack of clarity on the question of exactly when Article 101 does not apply to such practices means that businesses are wary about incorporating such provisions in their agreements, even if they perceive them to be helpful, or even indispensable, to the efficient distribution of their products or services. This uncertainty is compounded by the fact that (a) EU competition authorities continue to fine firms that incorporate such restraints or other restraints on online selling within their distribution agreements; but, in contrast, (b) there is little concrete jurisprudence dealing with the application of Article 101(3) to these types of restraints.

5. Although the Commission did not prioritise enforcement of Article 101 in relation to purely vertical agreements between 2005–2015, it has, since the launch of its e-commerce sector inquiry,[366]

[365] See Chap. 7. [366] E-commerce SWD Final Report, n. 10.

investigated a few cases involving online distribution. A number of NCAs (including in France and Germany) have also regularly investigated vertical agreements, focusing principally on object or hardcore restraints and restraints on online distribution. The 2022 VBER and Guidelines provide updated guidance on newer forms of distribution and vertical restraints, especially in the online context, and seek to ensure greater harmonisation of approach at the national level.

6. The centrality of the VBER, the focus on object restraints, and the Commission's methodology mean that the main centre of attention remains on a more mechanical application of the VBER safe harbour and the presumptions of illegality, rather than a detailed assessment of whether a vertical agreement restricts competition in the context in which it operates. Indeed, relatively little attention and modern case law considers how vertical agreements are to be appraised under the modernised antitrust framework.

7. Online selling, geo-blocking, and the role of platforms are also attracting the interest of a broader group of policy-makers and politicians. There is a growing view that competition law may not be able to deal with the multiplicity of issues arising and in the EU a number of measures, including the Geo-blocking Regulation, have already been adopted with the aim of boosting e-commerce and cross-border online sales within the single market. Chapter 16 discusses developments beyond competition law in the digital economy, especially the Digital Markets Act.

9. FURTHER READING

A. Chapters in Books

Jones, A., and de la Mano, M., 'Vertical Agreements under EU Competition Law: Proposals for Pushing Article 101 Analysis, and the Modernisation Process, to a Logical Conclusion' in D. Healey, M. Jacobs, and R. L. Smith (eds.), *Handbook of Research Methods and Models of Competition Law* (Edward Elgar, 2020)

B. Articles

Comanor, W. S., 'Vertical Price-fixing, Vertical Market Restraints, and the New Antitrust Policy' (1984–1985) 98 *Harvard LR* 983

Easterbrook, F. H., 'Vertical Arrangements and the Rule of Reason' (1984) 53 *Antitrust LJ* 135

Gyselen, L., 'Vertical Restraints in the Distribution Process: Strengths and Weaknesses of the Free Rider Rationale under EEC Competition Law' (1984) 21 *CMLRev* 647

Hawk, B. E., 'System Failure: Vertical Restraints and EC Competition Law' (1995) 32 *CMLRev* 973

Jones, A., 'Resale Price Maintenance: A Debate About Competition Policy in Europe' (2009) 5 *European Competition Journal* 479

Korah, V., 'Goodbye Red Label: Condemnation of Dual Pricing by Distillers' (1978) 3 *ELRev* 62

Monti, G., 'Restraints on Selective Distribution Agreements' (2013) 36 *World Competition* 489

Pitofsky, R., 'In Defense of Discounters: The No-frills Case for a Per Se Rule Against Vertical Price Fixing' (1983) 71 *Geo LJ* 1487

12

LICENSING AGREEMENTS AND OTHER AGREEMENTS INVOLVING INTELLECTUAL PROPERTY RIGHTS

1. CENTRAL ISSUES

1. Intellectual property rights (IPRs), such as patents, trademarks, copyrights, and designs, grant the holder of the right an exclusionary, and sometimes exclusive, right to the exploitation of an emanation of the human intellect. They are designed to provide an incentive for innovation and invention.
2. IPRs are still generally granted at the national level (although there are some EU rights).
3. The existence and exercise of IPRs (especially national rights) has sometimes created tension with the EU rules both on free movement and competition.
4. This chapter focuses on agreements involving IPRs, especially the compatibility of intellectual property (IP) licensing agreements with Article 101.
5. As with vertical agreements, the Commission's policy towards IP licensing agreements has been a tumultuous one. The policy has evolved from a permissive approach, to a more interventionist one, to the current approach, reflected in the block exemption for technology transfer agreements and accompanying Guidelines, which the Commission states is based on a consumer welfare objective.
6. The 2014 technology transfer block exemption (the TTBER) provides a safe harbour for bilateral technology transfer agreements broadly where: the parties do not exceed specified market share thresholds; and the agreement does not contain specified hardcore restraints.
7. Given particular difficulties involved in assessing relevant markets (and market shares) in the context of transfer technology agreements, the framework for individual Article 101 analysis set out in the Technology Transfer Guidelines is also of utmost importance. These Guidelines set out general principles concerning Article 101 and IPRs, explain the provisions and application of the TTBER, and the application of Article 101(1) and Article 101(3) to technology transfer agreements outside of the scope of the TTBER.
8. Trademark and copyright (except software copyright) licensing agreements are not covered by the technology transfer block exemption or Guidelines.

2. INTRODUCTION

A. GENERAL

Intellectual property rights (IPRs) grant the holder of the right an exclusionary, and sometimes exclusive, right to the exploitation of the product of the human intellect. They are recognised and protected in some way in all developed countries and encompass a broad spectrum of different rights. For example, they safeguard the creators of aesthetic and artistic works from having their creations distorted and purloined by others, they provide an incentive for invention and innovation by enabling those who develop new products and processes to reap the financial rewards of their efforts, and they allow those who develop brand names to exploit the reputation attached to the brand. The importance of IPRs in the modern commercial world is incontrovertible, but their interaction with EU law is complex. They raise problems not only for competition law but also for the free movement of goods and services and the operation of the internal market. This is because:

(a) Despite the introduction of some EU-wide rights[1] and growing international cooperation in relation to IP, IPRs are typically granted by national laws and enforced on a national basis, conferring protection within national territories. This inevitably leads to a potential conflict with the EU free movement provisions since simple reliance on a national right could be used as a mechanism to prevent importation of a good or service from another Member State.

(b) IPRs may erect barriers to entry to a market and thus affect the determination of whether an undertaking is in a dominant position for the purposes of Article 102. In addition, the exercise by a dominant undertaking of its IPRs may in exceptional circumstances constitute an abuse.[2]

(c) Transactions involving IPRs may fall within Article 101. Holders of IPRs often exploit their rights not by producing products or services exclusively themselves but, additionally or alternatively, by licensing others to use them (or assigning rights to them). The terms of such licences may restrict competition.

This chapter starts by looking at some of the different types of IPRs before outlining the relationship between IP and both EU competition law and the EU free movement rules. It focuses, however, on agreements involving IPRs, especially licensing agreements and their treatment under Article 101.

The application of Article 101 to IP licensing agreements has changed dramatically over the years and especially since the EU modernisation process. In particular, on 1 May 2004 a Technology Transfer Block Exemption, Regulation 772/2004 was adopted exempting certain 'technology transfer agreements' (patent, design, know-how, and/or software copyright licensing agreements) from Article 101(1).[3] It was accompanied by Technology Transfer Guidelines which explained in detail the Commission's approach to technology transfer agreements.[4] Following a review of the 2004 regime,

[1] See e.g. T. Aplin and J. Davis, *Intellectual Property Law: Text, Cases, and Materials* (4th edn, Oxford University Press, 2021), Chap. 1 and TFEU, Art. 118(1) (providing for the creation of EU intellectual property rights) and e.g. the EU Trade Mark Reg, Reg. 2017/1001, OJ [2017] L154/1; the European Patent Convention of 1973 (the EPC, which allows companies to obtain multiple national (rather than EU) patents from the European Patent Office on a single application); Regulations establishing a Unitary Patent, Reg. 1257/2012/EU [2012] OJ L361/1 and Reg. 1260/2012/EU [2012] OJ L361/89; and Agreement on a Unified Patent Court which will provide the legal basis for the European Unitary Patent System, see EU Council Press Releases 17824/12 and 6590/13 and <https://single-market-economy.ec.europa.eu/industry/strategy/intellectual-property/patent-protection-eu/unitary-patent-system_en> (the unitary patent system is was launched on 1 June 2023, initially in 17 countries). Some EU harmonisation has also occurred.

[2] See Chaps. 6 and 7.

[3] Reg. 772/2004 on technology transfer agreements [2004] OJ L123/11.

[4] Guidelines on the application of Article 81 of the EC Treaty to technology transfer agreements [2004] OJ C101/2.

a new Technology Transfer Block Exemption Regulation 316/2014[5] (TTBER) and accompanying Technology Transfer Guidelines[6] (the Guidelines) were adopted. The scheme of the 2004 regime was preserved although some significant changes were introduced. Section 3 of this chapter traces the development of EU competition policy to IP licensing agreements whilst Sections 4 and 5 examine the current TTBER, the Guidelines, and agreements involving intellectual property rights falling outside their scope. Section 6 outlines issues arising in cases involving IPRs under Article 102.

B. TYPES OF INTELLECTUAL PROPERTY RIGHTS

(i) The Nature of Intellectual Property Rights

IPRs give the holder an exclusionary, and sometimes exclusive, right to the exploitation of an emanation of the intellect. The nature of the right varies from one type of IP to another. IPRs vary in duration. Some arise only upon registration, while others arise from the act of creation itself. In the absence of harmonisation or harmonising measures, EU law does not regulate the conditions upon which national law grants IPRs,[7] although it may curtail their exercise.[8] This section very briefly outlines some of the main types of IPRs.[9]

(ii) Patents

Patents relate to inventions and relate to applied technology, not abstract ideas. The grant of a patent confers on the holder (the patentee), normally for a maximum period of 20 years,[10] a monopoly over a new and inventive product or process, and the right to prevent others from making, disposing of, using, or importing a product which is the subject of the patent or derived from it, or from using the patented process itself. Patents are granted in respect of the product or process disclosed in the specification when the patent is applied for, and on the expiry of the patent anyone may use the information contained in the specification.

(iii) Trademarks

A trademark is a mark or sign used to identify and differentiate a product or service. Registration of a trademark gives the holder an exclusive right to use it as such, although if it is a non-invented word it does not take the word out of general use, but only prevents its use by others as a trademark. Other parties remain free to offer competing goods and services under other marks and brand names. If renewal procedures are complied with trademark registration can continue indefinitely.

Marks and brand names which are not registered may also be protected by other means, for example through laws on passing-off or unfair competition.

[5] Reg. 316/2014 of 21 March 2014 on the application of Article 101(3) of the Treaty on the Functioning of the European Union to categories of technology transfer agreements (TTBER) [2014] OJ L93/17.

[6] Guidelines on the application of Article 101 of the Treaty on the Functioning of the European Union to technology transfer agreements (the Guidelines) [2014] OJ C89/3.

[7] See e.g. Case 144/81, *Keurkoop v Nancy Kean Gifts* EU:C:1982:289; Cases C-241–242/91 P, *RTE & ITP v Commission* EU:C:1995:98, para. 49.

[8] Through, e.g., the application of the free movement and competition laws.

[9] There are also, e.g., plant breeders' rights, given in respect of the creation of new plant varieties, which are similar to patents in that they confer a monopoly, see further e.g. W. Cornish, D. Llewelyn, and T. Aplin, *Intellectual Property: Patents, Copyright, Trade Marks and Allied Rights* (9th edn, Sweet & Maxwell, 2019).

[10] The maximum 20-year term is common throughout the EU, see the European Patent Convention, n. 1.

(iv) Copyright

Copyright protects 'works' such as literary, dramatic, musical, and artistic works, films, sound recordings, and broadcasts from unauthorised exploitation by third parties. Unlike a patent, copyright does not confer a monopoly because it prevents *copying*: if a third party independently comes up with the same melody or words, there will be no breach of copyright. Copyright does not depend on registration or formal procedures but arises automatically when the work is set down or recorded in some form. Copyright in the EU lasts for the lifetime of the author plus 70 years.[11]

There are greater differences between the laws of EU Member States in respect of copyright than there are with other forms of IP. Common law notions of copyright emphasise the right of the author to prevent others exploiting their work for commercial gain whereas the civil law emphasises the right of the creator of a work to be recognised as such and to be morally entitled to protect its integrity. UK copyright law covers performers' rights and similar rights, but in most EU countries there is a distinction drawn between the author and neighbouring rights (those accorded to sound recordings, broadcasts, and performers). In some jurisdictions, works created by the 'sweat of the brow', such as compilations of information, are accorded copyright protection, whereas civil law systems require a greater degree of creativity: this constituted a material difference in the Article 102 case on television listings, *Magill*.[12]

(v) Databases

Although Member States' copyright laws differed according to the extent of the protection that was afforded to databases and software, the 1996 Database Directive[13] now creates a *sui generis* right for their protection and the Software Directive[14] requires Member States to protect software by way of copyright as a literary work within the meaning of the Berne Convention.[15]

(vi) Designs

Under the Berne Convention[16] countries are free to choose the way in which they protect industrial designs, for example whether through registered rights and/or through rules governing unregistered rights. The 1998 Directive on the legal protection of designs,[17] a partial harmonisation measure, provides protection for registered designs for 25 years entitling the holder to prevent the making, offering, putting on the market, importing, exporting, and stocking of a product incorporating the design.

(vii) Know-how

Strictly speaking, know-how is not an IPR, but it often features in commercial transactions such as licensing arrangements to which Article 101 applies. Know-how is confidential, technical, commercially

[11] Under Dir. 2006/116/EC [2006] OJ L372/12, on the term of protection of copyright and certain related rights (amended by Dir. 2011/77/EU [2011] OJ L265/1). The EU's regulatory framework for copyright and neighbouring rights (*acquis*) is a set of 11 Directives and two Regulations, see https://digital-strategy.ec.europa.eu/en/policies/copyright-legislation.

[12] Cases C-241–242/91 P, *RTE & ITP v Commission* EU:C:1995:98; see Chap. 7 and the specific protection accorded to databases under Dir. 96/9/EC [1996] OJ L77/20, n. 13.

[13] Dir. 96/9/EC on the legal protection of databases [1996] OJ L77/20.

[14] Council Dir. 2009/24/EC on the legal protection of computer programs [2009] OJ L111/16.

[15] Software programs may also qualify for patent protection in all Member States.

[16] Berne Convention for the Protection of Literary and Artistic Works, 1886 (as subsequently revised).

[17] Dir. 98/71/EC [1998] OJ L289/28. See also Council Reg. 6/2002 on Community designs [2002] OJ L3/1.

valuable information which is not patented or registered in any way.[18] Know-how is defined for the purposes of the TTBER[19] and may be protected by contractual provisions and breach of confidence laws.

C. THE RELATIONSHIP BETWEEN INTELLECTUAL PROPERTY RIGHTS AND COMPETITION LAW

The relationship between IPRs and competition law has sometimes been an uneasy one.[20] The underlying issue of whether IPRs and competition law are fundamentally in conflict or whether they are different routes to the same central, economic goal(s) (especially the maximisation of consumer welfare) is controversial and explored in two extracts below from pieces written by Anderman and Kallaugher and Jones and Nazzini, respectively.

S. D. Anderman and J. Kallaugher, *Technology Transfer and the New EU Competition Rules: IP Licensing after Modernisation* (Oxford University Press, 2006)

B. Background—the Relationship between Competition Law and IP

1.11 The introduction of the new [EU] paradigm comes at a time when advocates of competition policy and proponents of intellectual property have reached an accommodation that recognises that both competition law and IPRs legislation constitute complementary components of a modern industrial policy. Although both policies pursue the common aim of improving innovation and consumer welfare each does so using rather different means. Intellectual property rights legislation such as patent, copyright and design rights laws offer intellectual property right holders a period of exclusive rights to exploit their property right as both a reward to the individual and as an incentive to the wider process of innovation and R&D investment. Trademarks perform a different function. Their exclusivity is meant to protect the consumer as well as to reward the originator. Modern competition policy attempts to keep markets innovative and competitive by maintaining effective competition. The means it uses to pursue this aim include maintaining access to markets and preventing 'foreclosure' or monopolisation of markets.

1.12 At first sight there may seem to be a potential clash in the methods used by the two systems of legal regulation to achieve their common aim. The concern to maintain access to markets appears to be implacably opposed to the concept of exclusive rights to make, use and sell a product. And indeed, there was a period when the misunderstanding of the economic effects of IPRs led EC competition law and policy to attempt to place overly strict limits on the exercise of IPRs, particularly in the field of patent licensing. Today, however, the interrelationship between the two systems of law is characterised more by its accommodations than by its conflict. These accommodations tend to occur most often as an incidental result of the ordinary doctrines of each system. Thus, intellectual property laws make a contribution to effective competition and maintaining access to market by devices within their own internal doctrine that strive to maintain a balance between 'initial' inventors and creators and 'follow-on' invention and creation. Good examples are the 'fair use' doctrine in copyright laws, the doctrine of 'non-obviousness' and the provision of compulsory licensing in patent law and interoperability imperatives

[18] Usually because it does not fulfil the necessary criteria for patentability, but sometimes the creator chooses not to patent in order to keep the information out of the public domain.

[19] TTBER, Art. 1(1)(i), see Section 4.

[20] As already seen in Chap. 7.

and decompilation rights in the computer program directive. On rare occasions, as in the [EU] database directive, the accommodation will be explicitly spelt out in the intellectual property law itself.

1.13 Within EC competition law the accommodation also tends to occur more owing to the incidental effect of the logic of the general doctrines of competition law rather that in the form of special treatment. When one looks at EC competition law the most obvious example of special treatment is the 'exceptional circumstances' test embedded within the abuse of refusal to supply under Article [102] . . .

1.14 This observation offers a good perspective for viewing the relationship between Article [101] and IP licensing under the new post-modernised legal framework. The accommodation with IPRs in the new Technology Transfer Block Exemption Regulation (TTBER) and Guidelines occurs almost entirely within the logic of the doctrines of competition law. Most of the accommodation takes place as an incidental benefit of the ordinary interpretation of Article [101] under the modernisation programme. In the Guidelines and Recitals there is evidence that the competition authorities have made a considerable effort to understand the nature of IPRs and their licensing. Thus, they acknowledge that the creation of IPRs often entails substantial investment and that it is often a risky endeavour. They state plainly that '[I]n order not to reduce dynamic competition and to maintain the incentive to innovate the innovator must not be unduly restricted in the exploitation of the IPR that turn out to be valuable'. In particular, they must be able to seek compensation for successful projects that takes failed projects into account. The Commission also acknowledges that technology licensing may require the licensee to make considerable sunk investment in the licensed technology and production assets necessary to exploit it. Moreover, the Guidelines have accepted that the great majority of licensing agreements are pro-competitive and compatible with Article [101].

1.15 This approach represents a conscious rejection of the argument that a special self-contained regime (like the old block exemptions) is necessary to satisfy the special requirements of IP licensing. As the Guidelines confidently proclaim '[in] assessing licensing agreements under Article [101], the existing analytical framework is sufficiently flexible to take due account of the dynamic aspects of technology licensing'. The new framework clearly harmonises the treatment of licensing agreements with that of other commercial agreements under Article [101] and, on the whole, this results in a reasonable treatment of IP licensing . . .

A. Jones and R. Nazzini, 'The Effect of Competition Law on Patent Remedies' in B. Biddle, J. L. Contreras, B. J. Love, and N. V. Siebrasse (eds.), *Patent Remedies and Complex Products: Toward a Global Consensus* (Cambridge University Press, 2019)

II. Objectives of Intellectual Property and Competition Law

It is often said that patent law (and intellectual property (IP) law more broadly) and competition law 'constitute complementary components of a modern industrial policy' which aim to improve innovation and consumer welfare. However, because of the different approaches they employ to achieve their objectives—the conferral of exclusive rights compared to the maintenance of effective competition—sometimes patent and competition law solutions to an identical issue appear to collide. Furthermore, even if it is recognised that they strive to achieve complementary goals, it does not mean that antitrust law should not sometimes constrain patent law, or vice versa; these distinct areas of law must be interpreted to accommodate each other.

Before examining those apparent collisions . . ., this part considers the ostensible tension between competition and patent law, focusing on the question of whether they are designed to achieve the same objectives—that is to improve welfare and to solve the same basic economic problem. Do they both aim to optimize the use of scarce resources in pursuit of providing the things that consumers want and need? If so, the systems should then work harmoniously together and yield to each other when required. Where exclusion or unrestrained exploitation is necessary for the creation and commercialization of a new technology, competition law should defer to patent law. In contrast where unconstrained exercise of IP rights goes beyond what is necessary for the creation and commercialization of a new technology and is detrimental to competition and efficiency, patent law should defer to competition law. With their unified goals, such trade-offs and concessions should be quite natural. In practice, however, things are not so simple and harmonious for a number of reasons.

First, although in some jurisdictions, including the U.S., there has been a growing consensus that competition law is 'technocratic' and built on the 'broad professional and policy consensus' that surrounds the basic microeconomic model of perfect competition, such an approach is by no means universal or without challenges. Further, there is no broad consensus on objectives on the patent side. Rather it is generally recognised that the patent system is a welfare enhancing, multi-purpose instrument serving a variety of objectives, including the provision of incentives to innovation and technology development, the promotion of technology dissemination and the coordination of 'the search for technological and market enhancement' (like prospects signal territories of interest to mine developers). Furthermore, despite broad accord that innovation is crucial to technological growth, some disagreement as to how to foster such growth exists. For example, it may be difficult to know how best to incentivize both innovation and follow-on innovation or improvements. Although conferral of patents may incentivize innovation, it is possible that in some circumstances rights conferred may be used to stifle competition that uses those patents and, consequently, subsequent innovation.

Secondly, in each field, agreement is lacking on how to achieve the objectives pursued. Even in jurisdictions where a competition consumer welfare goal is clearly pursued, there is still considerable scope for debate as to how to reflect that underpinning aim, and in particular how to balance competing economic factors and, for example, how allocative efficiency (for example, price equals marginal cost or price efficiency), productive efficiency (for example, cost optimization) and/or dynamic efficiency (for example, supply of improved and or new products/services) can be ensured. For example, a policy of ex post antitrust enforcement which prioritizes allocative efficiency over dynamic efficiency, would almost inevitably upset a patent policy that aimed ex ante to maximize innovators' rewards through extensive patent protection.

. . .

Thirdly, antitrust and patent laws involve different processes and are not enforced by common institutions. Rather, antitrust agencies and patent offices generally operate at arm's length from each other. This may create an initial disconnect that needs to be resolved ex post when competition enforcement action is taken in individual cases or where patent issues are litigated in the courts.

As a result of these factors, the interface between patent and competition law can be mired in an uneasy standoff. In an ideal world, there should not be such a disconnect. Rather a rational social planner should ensure wholesale consistency across policies in both fields and conflicts should not occur. Reality does not, however, match such an abstract model. The tension between antitrust and patent laws should not be exaggerated, however. Competition law is case specific. It is generally respectful of patent rights and only prohibits certain types of conduct, leaving patent owners free to behave as they see fit outside of its strictures. In particular, it generally only interferes with unilateral conduct of a patentee where that patentee is dominant or has a significant degree of market power. This point means that innovation-minded patent practitioners should not overreact to antitrust enforcement. Indeed coordination between competition law and patent law is, frequently, left to doctrinal tools and techniques that are designed to balance the laws on a case-by-case basis, such as:

a. Division of competences. Competition law application may recede in spheres that the legislature has previously covered with IP rights. The idea behind this doctrine is that there is a core of IP law that competition law cannot interfere with. For example, in the EU, the case law has accepted that

EU competition law cannot deprive the holder of an IP right of the specific subject matter of its IP right but can only regulate the exercise of the right.

b. An enhanced intervention threshold. Competition law frequently sets the bar particularly high for a finding of breach of its rules when an IP right is involved (the rules of engagement of antitrust liability are set higher than in non-IP rights cases). Put differently, antitrust law is only likely to interfere with the exercise of IP rights in 'exceptional circumstances.' Exceptionalism has been the approach ordinarily although the authorities in the EU have arguably been more willing to find that exceptional circumstances exist than their US counterparts. . . ..

c. Complementarity. Given their complementary goals, the ex post application of competition law generally takes into account the need to protect investment in a patented invention. Thus, competition law recognizes that dynamic efficiency, and in particular the need to preserve the incentives to innovate provided by patent and IP law, could, under certain circumstances, be a crucial factor in crafting a test to identify anticompetitive conduct or a valid business justification of conduct that would otherwise be held to be anti-competitive . . .

. . . .

e. Misrepresentation by a patentee. In some jurisdictions a relevant factor in determining whether antitrust liability should ensue, may be whether a patentee has made misrepresentations to an authority (such as a patent office), for example to acquire IP protection or otherwise to exclude a competitor.

These extracts note the tensions that exist between the two sets of laws, which is arguably being exacerbated by rapid innovation in the digital economy, significant expansion and widening of IP rights, and debate about the sustainability of the consumer welfare objective as an optimal standard for ensuring effective competition in markets.[21]

D. THE RELATIONSHIP BETWEEN INTELLECTUAL PROPERTY RIGHTS AND THE FREE MOVEMENT RULES

Perhaps surprisingly for a document purporting to lay down the foundations for a single market, the TFEU itself contains very little about IP. Article 345 TFEU, however, contains a general rule about property rights:

The Treaties shall in no way prejudice the rules in Member States governing the system of property ownership.

EU law therefore recognises the existence and ownership of rights given by national law. Nevertheless, this recognition potentially creates conflict with the principle of the internal market. Article 34 TFEU, the basic provision on the free movement of goods, states:

Quantitative restrictions on imports and all measures having equivalent effect shall, without prejudice to the following provisions, be prohibited between Member States.

[21] H. Schmidt, 'Competition Law and IP Rights: Not So Complementary: Time for Re-alignment of the Goals?' (2019) 42(4) *World Competition* 451.

However, if widgets made in France by F cannot be imported into Germany because they would infringe G's German patent, the market is divided along national lines. Not only that, but G may wish to use its German patent to prevent its *own* widgets, which it has manufactured in Poland, from being imported into Germany by a parallel importer. These simple examples illustrate that national IPRs can impede the free circulation of goods.

IPRs are dealt with in Article 36 TFEU, which provides a derogation from Article 34:

> The provisions of Articles 34 and 35 shall not preclude prohibitions or restrictions on imports, exports or goods in transit justified on grounds of public morality, public policy or public security; the protection of health and life of humans, animals or plants; the protection of national treasures possessing artistic, historic or archaeological value; or the protection of industrial and commercial property.[22] Such prohibitions or restrictions shall not, however, constitute a means of arbitrary discrimination or a disguised restriction on trade between Member States.

EU law therefore accepts that restrictions on free movement may be justified to protect national IPRs so long as they do not to constitute 'a means of arbitrary discrimination or a disguised restriction' on inter-State trade. This proviso has been used in a long line of cases to justify the imposition of many limitations on the exercise of national IPRs.[23] That case law is not dealt with further in this book,[24] but, broadly, has developed a number of interlinking concepts by which the Court has sought to reconcile the conflicting demands of the economic integration of the internal market and the protection of IPRs. In particular:

(a) it has drawn a dichotomy between the existence of IPRs and their exercise: the existence of rights is unaffected by the TFEU, but their exercise may be;[25]

(b) it developed the idea that there is a 'specific subject matter' of each kind of IPR, the protection of which is justified even if it leads to restrictions on inter-State trade: the exercise of IPRs which partitions the market will be allowed insofar as it is necessary to protect the 'specific subject matter' of that right;

(c) it has built up a jurisprudence on the 'exhaustion of rights'. Broadly, once a rights holder has consented to the marketing of the protected product within the EU (and EEA),[26] the rights encompassed in the 'specific subject matter' are exhausted and the holder cannot rely on national rights to prevent the movement of the goods between Member States.

[22] Although at first sight the phrase 'industrial and commercial' property does not appear to cover copyright, the CJ has clarified that it does: see Case 78/70, *Deutsche Grammophon v Metro* EU:C:1971:59, and Cases 55 and 57/80, *Musik-Vertrieb Membran v GEMA* EU:C:1981:10. 'Intellectual property' is the generic phrase now used both at EU and international level.

[23] Art. 56 is the basic provision which governs free movement of services and the principle in Art. 36 is applied to it by analogy. Restrictions on the movement of services may therefore also be justified by the need to protect IPRs, see Case 62/79, *Coditel v Ciné Vog Films (Coditel I)* EU:C:1980:84; Case 262/81, *Coditel v Ciné Vog Films (Coditel II)* EU:C:1982:334 and Cases C-403 and 429/08, *Premier League Ltd v QC Leisure* and *Murphy v Media Protection Services Ltd (Murphy)* EU:C:2011:631.

[24] But see e.g. Bellamy and Child (D. Bailey and L. John, eds.), *European Union Law of Competition* (8th edn, Oxford University Press, 2018), Chap. 9.

[25] The distinction between the existence and exercise of rights (introduced in Cases 56 and 58/64, *Consten and Grundig v Commission* EU:C:1966:41) is not convincing (a property right which exists but which cannot be exercised has no value, see Fennelly AG, para. 95 in Cases C-267 and 268/95, *Merck and Co Inc v Primecrown Ltd (Merck II)* EU:C:1996:468). Nonetheless the existence/exercise dichotomy has provided a flexible tool to enable the Court to develop policy in this area.

[26] The EEA (see Chap. 2) is the relevant area by virtue of Protocol 28 of the EEA Agreement, which provides for exhaustion throughout the EEA in accordance with the case law of the Court.

3. EXPLOITING INTELLECTUAL PROPERTY RIGHTS BY LICENSING

A. GENERAL

The owner of an IPR has a choice of ways in which to benefit from the right commercially; exploiting it itself or assigning or licensing it to a third party. The method chosen will depend on a number of factors. These include the resources available to the owner, the type of right concerned, the nature of the product and its life-cycle, manufacturing costs and complexity, the overall commercial strategy of the owner, local conditions in the territory in which the right is held, and taxation considerations. Some rights may be able to be carved up: for example, the owner of copyright in a book may deal separately with the rights to make a television programme of it, the rights to film it, the rights to serialise it in a newspaper, and the rights to make an audio tape or other recordings of it.

An *assignment*, whether gratuitous or by way of sale or swap, involves the outright transfer of the right to a third party. After transfer the original owner is excluded from using it without a licence from the new owner. Rights are commonly assigned with the transfer or takeover of a business to a new owner. In contrast, a *licence* involves the owner of an IPR conferring permission upon another party to exploit the owner's legally protected exclusive right. The advantages of licensing include:

(a) the owner (the licensor) has continuing control of the use of the rights (insofar as this is not limited by competition law);

(b) the ability to carve up the rights is normally greater;

(c) the owner can obtain a continuing revenue stream from the exploitation and can benefit from the licensees' successes;

(d) the owner can continue to exploit the right himself.

The TTBER treats certain assignments of patents, designs, know-how, and software copyright as licences where part of the risk associated with their exploitation remains with the assignor.

B. COMMERCIAL CONSIDERATIONS IN LICENCES

(i) General

A number of IPRs may be licensed together, for example patents, know-how, and trademarks in exchange for a financial return. The licensor may also wish to incorporate provisions in a licence agreement relating to, for example: safeguarding confidential information; ensuring quality control; supplying essential components or other goods to the licensee; ensuring (in the case of patents and know-how) that the licensor benefits from improvements made by the licensee; safeguarding the licensor from challenges by the licensee to the validity of the rights;[27] limiting what the licensee may do with the goods or services produced under the licence; ensuring that the licensee does not compete with the licensor; and providing for termination. Licensees will be concerned with the same issues but from the other side. In this section we look briefly at some of the terms commonly found in licensing agreements that may raise competition law concerns.

[27] With a patent, a licensee working it will be in the best position to identify the weaknesses in it.

(ii) Royalties

Payment by the licensee for the licence is by way of royalty obligations which may, for instance, take the form of lump sum payments, a percentage of the selling price, or a fixed amount for each product incorporating the licensed technology.[28] 'Running royalties' means royalties calculated on the basis of individual product sales. Where royalties are calculated on the basis of the licensee's products which incorporate the licensed technology the licensor may wish to stipulate that a minimum number are produced.

(iii) Territorial Restrictions on Production: Exclusive and Sole Licences

Licences can be exclusive, sole, or non-exclusive.

A licence is *exclusive* as regards a particular territory where it provides that the licensor will not grant further licences for that territory to other parties and will not itself exploit the licensed IPRs in the territory; *only* the licensee can exercise the licensed rights in the territory covered by the licence.

A *sole* licence is where the licensor undertakes not to grant other licences for the territory but remains free to exploit the rights there itself; the rights can only be exploited in the territory by the licensor and licensee.

A *non-exclusive* licence is where the licensor remains free to grant other licences if it wishes and to exploit the licence in the territory itself.

Licensees will frequently only be interested in taking a licence if they are granted some exclusivity (an exclusive or sole licence). For example, an undertaking may only be willing to take a licence if certain that, having invested large resources in tooling up to exploit the patented process, it will not face competition from other licensees (or even the licensor itself). Such licences may be of particular concern in the EU on account of the fact that they compartmentalise the single market (see further Section 3.C). The concern will be particularly acute where they are coupled (as they frequently are) with territorial sales restrictions.

(iv) Territorial Sales Restrictions and Customer Allocation

A licence may include restrictions as to where the licensor and/or licensee may sell (territorial restrictions) or to the customers or customer groups to whom they may sell (customer allocation). As with distribution agreements, sales restrictions can be on active or passive selling (soliciting sales or responding to unsolicited sales, respectively). Further restraints can be imposed directly or indirectly through, for example, quantity restrictions on output.

A licensee may be unwilling to take a licence unless protected not only from the licensor and/or other licensees *producing* in the same territory but also from them *selling* there. Such protection may be required to protect the investment required in order to tool up to exploit the licensed technology. In some cases, a licensee may desire absolute territorial protection (ATP) from sales by the licensor and other licensees in its territory. Similarly, the licensor may not be willing to disseminate its technology through licensing unless it can prevent the licensees selling their production in territories where it sells itself.

(v) Field of Use Restrictions

Where technology can be exploited in different ways (for example, a patented chemical may be used to produce both fertilisers and pesticides), field of use restrictions may allow a licensee only to exploit the technology for one or some of the uses. Such restrictions may be difficult to distinguish from, and have the same effect as, customer allocation.[29]

[28] Guidelines, 4.2.1. [29] Ibid., 4.2.4.

(vi) Tying and Bundling

Tying and bundling by a dominant undertakings is discussed in Chapter 7. In the context of the technology licensing:

> tying occurs when the licensor makes the licensing of one technology (the tying product) conditional upon the licensee taking a licence for another technology or purchasing a product from the licensor or someone designated by it (the tied product). Bundling occurs where two technologies or a technology and a product are only sold together as a bundle. In both cases, however, it is a condition that the products and technologies involved are distinct in the sense that there is distinct demand for each of the products and technologies forming part of the tie or the bundle. This is normally not the case where the technologies or products are by necessity linked in such a way that the licensed technology cannot be exploited without the tied product or both parts of the bundle cannot be exploited without the other . . . [30]

The licensor may use tying and bundling to exercise quality control over the licensee's output and maintain standards or ensure proper exploitation by ensuring that the licensee uses only certain inputs in its production process.

(vii) Non-compete Obligations

The licensor may wish to ensure that the licensee does not also use its own (or a third party's) technology to produce goods in competition with those produced under the licence. Limiting the licensee's ability to do this is one way of ensuring that the licensee produces a minimum amount under the licence and generates adequate royalties.

(viii) Non-challenge Clauses

The owner of a valid IPR can sue anyone who infringes its right. Although a licence entitles a licensee to use the technology or other matter protected by the IPR without infringing, it can only use the technology in accordance with the terms of the licence (including ordinarily the payment of royalties). Were the IPR not valid, however, the licensee would be able to produce without a licence, and free of its terms. As a licensee exploiting licensed technology is in a good position to detect anything which might render the IPR invalid (for example, that the subject matter of a patent is obvious in the light of prior art and therefore not novel), licensors often incorporate 'non-challenge clauses' into licences. These make it a breach of contract (actionable by damages) for the licensee to challenge the validity of the licensed IPR or even to challenge the validity of *any* of the licensor's IPRs. It should be noted, however, that it is not necessarily in the licensee's interest to establish the invalidity of an IPR because this may allow others to use the protected subject matter freely.

(ix) Improvements

While exploiting the licensed technology the licensee may well develop improvements or further know-how. These may be severable or non-severable. A severable improvement is one which can be exploited without infringing the licensed technology. Unless prevented by the terms of the licence therefore the licensee could continue using it after the licence has expired and/or could license or

[30] Ibid., para. 221.

assign it to third parties. Licensors, however, frequently seek exclusive access to the improvements and incorporate terms in the licence obliging the licensee to 'grant back' severable improvements. This may enable them to improve their own technology and 'feed-on' improvements made by one licensee to others.[31] However, competition law may be concerned to limit the terms of severable improvements clauses if they prevent third parties gaining access to the improvements and the licensee from becoming a stronger competitor. Non-severable improvements do not raise the same issues as they can be used only with the licensor's technology.

C. DEVELOPMENT OF COMPETITION POLICY TOWARDS LICENSING OF INTELLECTUAL PROPERTY

(i) Overview

The licensing of IPRs helps to disseminate new technology, brings new competitors on to the market, and increases the rewards for innovation. Its effects are generally pro-competitive and beneficial to consumer welfare. It can be argued that since a licence of IPRs allows a third party to exploit the rights, allowing it to do what would otherwise be unlawful, the grant of a licence opens up markets and does not restrict competition. It should not therefore infringe Article 101(1). However, because licence agreements commonly contain provisions which go beyond a bare permission for the licensee to exploit the right, such obligations require scrutiny to determine compatibility with competition law.

The Commission's policy on IP licensing agreements has developed and varied significantly over the years. Initially, a permissive approach was adopted but, gradually, the Commission's attitude hardened and a more interventionist approach was taken. The 2004 TTBER and Technology Transfer Guidelines, however, heralded the start of a modernised approach to these types of agreements based on a consumer welfare objective.

The Commission has, through the development of block exemptions and guidelines, played an influential role in the development of policy in this area, especially as there have been comparatively few Court decisions on licensing. The few judgments of the Court which have been given, however, are of importance and significance in the development not only of the law on licensing but also on the question of what amounts to a restriction of competition for the purposes of Article 101(1) more generally.[32]

(ii) The Evolution of the Commission's Policy Towards Licensing Agreements

The Commission's early attitude, illustrated by its 1962 Notice on patent licensing agreements (the so-called Christmas Message)[33] was that even exclusive patent licensing agreements did not fall within Article 101(1) so long as the restrictions did not go beyond the 'scope of the patent'.[34]

[31] The dynamics of feed-on arrangements disseminate technology are complex, however. If one licensee innovates and the others get the benefits while contributing little to the common knowledge, the first licensee may lose the incentive to innovate and will certainly not be keen to reveal its improvements, see e.g. Cornish, Llewelyn, and Aplin, n. 9.

[32] See Chap. 5.

[33] 24 December 1962 [1962–1963] JO 2922/62, withdrawn in 1984 [1984] OJ C220/14 (see also Reg. 17, Art. 4(2)(b), [1959–1962] OJ Spec. Ed.87, as amended by Council Reg. 1216/1999 [1999] OJ L148/5, which classed a narrow category of licensing agreements as non-notifiable).

[34] See further S. Anderman, *EC Competition Law and Intellectual Property Rights* (Clarendon Press, 1998), 53–54.

Later, however, the Commission's attitude shifted to the position that exclusive licences, unless de minimis, always fell within Article 101 and that many common non-territorial restraints also went beyond the scope of the patent and violated Article 101(1). This essentially meant that a patent (or other) licence which went beyond a simple right to exploit a patented invention against payment of royalties would violate Article 101(1) and require exemption.[35] Significant to this change in approach was the CJ's judgment in *Consten and Grundig*[36] finding that a trademark licence which had been used as a mechanism to create ATP for the distributor/licensee and to seal off the French market infringed Article 101 (see Chapter 5). By the time of this case, the Commission had become acutely conscious of the potential for exclusive licensing agreements to isolate markets. It was also haunted by the idea that if a licensor did not grant an *exclusive* licence it might give a *non-exclusive* one, allowing competition between different licensees in the same territory.

In the real world, however, licensees frequently demand an exclusive (or at least a sole) one. The commercial risk of a non-exclusive one is too great. The choice is often therefore between an exclusive licence and no licence, not between an exclusive and a non-exclusive one. The Commission was frequently criticised for considering matters with hindsight, *ex post*, rather than *ex ante*, as the parties would have done, when the transaction might well have looked risky. Nevertheless, throughout the 1970s the Commission held in a series of decisions that exclusive licences and many other restraints in licences restricted competition within the meaning of Article 101(1). Its approach to the latter is exemplified by *Windsurfing*.[37] In this case, Windsurfing International (WI) granted a number of non-exclusive licences of its German patent for windsurfing equipment to firms within the EU. Litigation was current in Germany over whether the patent covered both the rig and the board, but the Commission proceeded on the basis that it covered only the rig. The Commission found that a number of provisions relating to quality control, tying, licensed-by notices, non-challenge clauses,[38] and royalty calculation infringed Article 101(1).

(iii) The Case Law of the Court

Although in *Windsurfing* the CJ took a formalistic approach, upholding the bulk of the Commission's findings in relation to Article 101(1) and finding that the provisions went beyond the 'scope of the patent' and the 'specific subject matter of the patent',[39] the CJ never endorsed such a strict approach to exclusivity as that adopted by the Commission. This is illustrated by its important judgment in *Nungesser (Maize Seeds)*, the first judgment after *Consten and Grundig* in which it had to deal with an exclusive licence.

Case 258/78, *Nungesser v Commission* EU:C:1982:211

INRA, a French State research institute, developed new strains of hybrid maize seed of great importance in European agriculture. Acting through FRASEMA, a French company set up to deal with INRA's seed varieties, it gave Kurt Eisele (later Nungesser KG) the exclusive right to produce and distribute INRA varieties in Germany. INRA agreed with Eisele not to import its seed into Germany itself and to

[35] See e.g. the Commission's *IVth Report on Competition Policy* (1974), point 20.

[36] Cases 56 and 58/64, *Établissements Consten SA and Grundig-Verkaufs-GmbH v Commission* EU:C:1966:41. See discussion of case in Chap. 5.

[37] COMP/29.395, *Windsurfing International* [1982] OJ L229/1, Case 193/83, *Windsurfing International v Commission* EU:C:1986:75.

[38] The Commission took the view that non-challenge clauses restrict competition; it is in the public interest that invalid patents should be challenged.

[39] J. Venit, 'In the Wake of *Windsurfing*: Patent Licensing in the Common Market' [1986] *Fordham Corp L Inst* 517, 560–561.

prevent others from doing so. Eisele relied on the rights in Germany to prevent parallel importers from importing seed obtained from another source in France. One importer settled the action, but another complained to the Commission.

The Commission held that the exclusivity and territorial protection provisions were caught by Article 101(1) and could not be exempted. Eisele/Nungesser appealed.

Court of Justice

41. Th[e] synopsis of the German legislation shows that seeds certified and approved for marketing are subject to quality control on the part of the public authorities and that that control extends to the stability of the variety. However, breeders' rights are not intended to substitute for controls carried out by the competent authorities, controls carried out by the owner of those rights, but to confer on the owner a kind of protection, the nature and effects of which all derive from private law. From that point of view the legal position of a breeder of seeds is not different from that of the owner of patent or trade mark rights over a product subject to strict control by the public authorities, as is the case with pharmaceutical products

. . . .

43. It is therefore not correct to consider that breeder's rights are a species of commercial or industrial property right with characteristics of so special a nature as to require, in relation to the competition rules, a different treatment from other commercial or industrial property rights. That conclusion does not affect the need to take into consideration, for the purposes of the rules on competition, the specific nature of the products which form the subject-matter of breeders' rights.

. . .

48. The statement of reasons on which the decision is based refers to two sets of circumstances in order to justify the application of Article [101(1)] to the exclusive licence in question (II, No. 3). The accuracy of the facts thus stated has not been challenged.

49. The first set of circumstances is described as follows . . ..

> By licensing a single undertaking to exploit his breeders' rights in a given territory, the licensor deprives himself for the entire duration of the contract of the ability to issue licences to other undertakings in the same territory . . .
>
> By undertaking not to produce or market the product himself in the territory covered by the contract the licensor likewise eliminates himself, as well as FRASEMA and its members, as suppliers in that territory.

50. Corresponding to that part of the statement of reasons is Article 1(b) of the decision, which in its first and second indents declares the exclusive nature of the licence granted by the 1965 contract to be contrary to Article [101(1) TFEU] in so far as it imposes: An obligation upon INRA or those deriving rights through INRA to refrain from having the relevant seeds produced or sold by other licensees in Germany, and an obligation upon INRA or those deriving rights through INRA to refrain from producing or selling the relevant seeds in Germany themselves.

51. The second set of circumstances referred to in the decision is described as follows:

> The fact that third parties may not import the same seed [namely the seed under licence] from other [EU] countries into Germany, or export from Germany to other [EU] countries, leads to market sharing and deprives German farmers of any real room for negotiation since seed is supplied by one supplier and one supplier only.

52. That part of the statement of reasons is also reflected in Article 1 (b) of the decision, which in its third and fourth indents declares the exclusive nature of the licence granted by the 1965 contract to be contrary to Article [101(1) TFEU] in so far as it imposes:

An obligation upon INRA or those deriving rights through INRA to prevent third parties from exporting the relevant seeds to Germany without the licensee's authorization for use or sale there, and Mr Eisele's concurrent use of his exclusive contractual rights and his own breeder's rights to prevent all imports into Germany or exports to other Member States of the relevant seeds.

53. It should be observed that those two sets of considerations relate to two legal situations which are not necessarily identical. The first case concerns a so-called open exclusive licence or assignment and the exclusivity of the licence relates solely to the contractual relationship between the owner of the right and the licensee, whereby the owner merely undertakes not to grant other licences in respect of the same territory and not to compete himself with the licensee on that territory. On the other hand, the second case involves an exclusive licence or assignment with absolute territorial protection, under which the parties to the contact propose, as regards the products and the territory in question, to eliminate all competition from third parties, such as parallel importers or licensees for other territories.

54. That point having been clarified, it is necessary to examine whether, in the present case, the exclusive nature of the licence, in so far as it is an open licence, has the effect of preventing or distorting competition with the meaning of Article [101(1) TFEU].

55. In that respect the Government of the Federal Republic of Germany emphasized that the protection of agricultural innovations by means of breeders' rights constitutes a means of encouraging such innovations and the grant of exclusive rights for a limited period, is capable of providing a further incentive to innovative efforts.

From that it infers that a total prohibition of every exclusive licence, even an open one, would cause the interest of undertakings in licences to fall away, which would be prejudicial to the dissemination of knowledge and techniques in the Community.

56. The exclusive licence which forms the subject-matter of the contested decision concerns the cultivation and marketing of hybrid maize seeds which were developed by INRA after years of research and experimentation and were unknown to German farmers at the time when the co-operation between INRA and the applicants was taking shape. For that reason the concern shown by the interveners as regards the protection of new technology is justified.

57. In fact, in the case of a licence of breeders' rights over hybrid maize seeds newly developed in one Member State, an undertaking established in another Member State which was not certain that it would not encounter competition from other licensees for the territory granted to it, or from the owner of the right himself, might be deterred from accepting the risk of cultivating and marketing that product; such a result would be damaging to the dissemination of a new technology and would prejudice competition in the Community between the new product and similar existing products.

58. Having regard to the specific nature of the products in question, the Court concludes that in a case such as the present, the grant of an open exclusive licence, that is to say a licence which does not affect the position of third parties such as parallel importers and licensees for other territories, is not in itself incompatible with Article [101(1) TFEU].

59. Part B of the third submission is thus justified to the extent to which it concerns that aspect of the exclusive nature of the licence.

60. As regard to the position of third parties, the Commission in essence criticizes the parties to the contract for having extended the definition of exclusivity to importers who are not bound to the contract, in particular parallel importers . . ..

61. The Court has consistently held (cf . . .. *Consten and Grundig* . . .) that absolute territorial protection granted to a licensee in order to enable parallel imports to be controlled artificial maintenance of separate national markets, contrary to the Treaty

. . .

76. It must be remembered that under the terms of Article [101(3) TFEU] an exemption from the prohibition contained in Article [101(1) TFEU] may be granted in the case of any agreement between

> undertakings which contributes to improving the production or distribution of goods or to promoting technical progress, and which does not impose on the undertakings concerned restrictions which are not indispensable to the attainment of those objectives.
>
> 77. As it is a question of seeds intended to be used by a large number of farmers for the production of maize, which is an important product for human and animal foodstuffs, absolute territorial protection manifestly goes beyond what is indispensable for the improvement of production or distribution or the promotion of technical progress, as is demonstrated in particular in the present case by the prohibition, agreed to by both parties to the agreement of any parallel imports of INRA maize seeds into Germany even if those seeds were bred by INRA itself and marketed in France.
>
> 78. It follows that the absolute territorial protection conferred on the licensee, as established to exist by the contested decision, constituted a sufficient reason for refusing to grant an exemption under Article [101(3) TFEU]. It is therefore no longer necessary to examine the other grounds set out in the decision for refusing to grant such an exemption.

In this judgment, the CJ drew an important distinction between 'open' licences, pertaining only to the position between licensor and licensee (the licensor agrees not to grant further licences in the same territory and not to operate there itself) and 'closed' licences containing provisions which affect third parties and which create ATP (paragraph 53).[40] As far as open licences are concerned, the Court did not, as the Commission had done, conclude that the exclusivity provisions automatically infringed Article 101(1). Instead, the Court looked at the licence in its economic context: if the exclusivity provisions were necessary to induce the licensee to enter the transaction then competition was not restricted. Its realistic approach was limited, however. Clauses leading to the imposition of ATP were held without consideration of their possible economic justifications,[41] to separate national markets artificially and to be automatically caught by Article 101(1), and not to qualify for exemption under Article 101(3).

The principles in *Nungesser* have been found to apply to IPR licensing agreements other than those involving plant breeders' rights.[42] In particular, in *Premier League Ltd v QC Leisure* and *Murphy v Media Protection Services Ltd*[43] the Grand Chamber of the CJ distinguished, in the context of copyright licensing, between:

- a sole licence (granting the licensee an exclusive right to broadcast protected subject matter from a Member State)—which would not justify a finding that an agreement had an anti-competitive objective; and
- a licence aimed at partitioning national markets according to national borders—which was liable to frustrate the Treaty's objective of achieving the integration of those markets through the establishment of a single market and had to be regarded, in principle, as an agreement whose object is to restrict competition.

A licensing agreement conferring ATP will therefore be 'deemed to have as its object the restriction of competition, unless other circumstances falling within its economic and legal context justify the finding that such an agreement is not liable to impair competition'.[44] The EU Courts have

[40] For further discussion of the distinction between open and closed licences, see M. Siragusa, 'EEC Technology Transfers—A Private View' [1982] *Fordham Corp L Inst* 95, 116–118 and, e.g., COMP/31.302, *Boussois/Interpane* [1987] OJ L50/30.

[41] See further Chap. 5.

[42] The general applicability of *Nungesser* to such transactions is manifest from the Court's rationale for holding the open exclusive licence outside Art. 101(1) (i.e. the need to provide incentives for investment by the licensee).

[43] Cases C-403 and 429/08, EU:C:2011:631, para. 139.

[44] Ibid.

only found such justifications in two cases, *Erauw-Jacquéry v La Hesbignonne*[45] and *Coditel v SA Ciné Vog Films (Coditel II)*.[46] In both cases, the *nature* of the IPR appeared crucial. *Erauw-Jacquéry* concerned basic seed, which can lawfully be used to propagate further seed, as distinct from certified seed sold to produce crops. Plant breeders' rights in basic seeds are particularly vulnerable as they can easily be lost.[47]

Case 27/87, *Erauw-Jacquéry v La Hesbignonne* [1988] ECR 1919

The owner of plant breeders' rights licensed them to a cooperative on the terms that the cooperative could propagate basic seed and sell seed of the first or second generation but could not sell or export basic seed. The Court of Justice recognised the need for quality control and for assuring the proper handling of the basic seed by those allowed to propagate it. Advocate General Mischo likened the situation to one of a franchise, where the franchisor is justified in preventing its know-how benefiting competitors.

Court of Justice

8. In the first place the national court seeks to ascertain whether the provision prohibiting the holder of the licence for propagating basic seed from selling, assigning or exporting that seed falls within Article [101(1)].

9. The Commission and the breeder maintain that the provision prohibiting the sale and exportation of E2 basic seed, which is placed at the disposal of the growers only for the purposes of propagation, is not contrary to Article [101(1) TFEU]. Such a provision falls within the ambit of the plant breeder's rights.

10. In this respect, it must be pointed out that, as the Court acknowledged in its judgment of 8 June 1982 (in Case 258/78 *Nungesser v Commission* . . .), the development of the basic lines may involve considerable financial commitment. Consequently, a person who has made considerable efforts to develop varieties of basic seed which may be the subject-matter of plant breeders' rights must be allowed to protect himself against any improper handling of those varieties of seed. To that end, the breeder must be entitled to restrict propagation to the growers which he has selected as licensees. To that extent, the provision prohibiting the licensee from selling and exporting basic seed falls outside the prohibition contained in Article [101(1)].

11. Therefore, the answer to the first part of the question referred by the national court must be that a provision of an agreement concerning the propagation and sale of seed, in respect of which one of the parties is the holder or the agent of the holder of certain plant breeders' rights, which prohibits the licensee from selling and exporting the basic seed is compatible with Article [101(1) TFEU] in so far as it is necessary in order to enable the breeder to select the growers who are to be licensees.

The Court in this case stressed the need to protect the licensor's investment. The Court recognised the particularly fragile nature of basic seed (as compared with the certified seed at issue in *Nungesser*) and that in these special circumstances ATP did not infringe Article 101(1).[48]

In *Coditel II*, the CJ had to consider whether an exclusive licence (amounting in effect to ATP) infringed Article 101(1). In *Coditel v Ciné Vog Films (Coditel I)*,[49] the CJ held, in relation to the same facts

[45] Case 27/87, EU:C:1988:183. [46] Case 262/81, EU:C:1982:334.

[47] They were subject to cancellation if they ceased to be stable or uniform.

[48] The Commission emphasised the special nature of basic seeds, see *XVIIIth Report on Competition Policy* (1989), part 103; in COMP/35.280, *Sicasov* [1999] OJ L4/27, the Commission applied *Erauw-Jacquéry* to another licence of basic seed.

[49] Case 62/79, EU:C:1980:84.

(a Belgian cable company relaying in Belgium the transmission of a film (Chabrol's *Le Boucher*) shown in Germany for which Ciné Vog had exclusive distribution rights in Belgium), that copyright in film was not exhausted by the first showing of the film because the specific subject matter of the right was the entitlement of the owner to charge each time the film was shown. In the subsequent Article 101 proceedings, it also recognised the special nature of the rights concerned which were exploited through performance.

Case 262/81, *Coditel v SA Ciné Vog Films (Coditel II)* [1982] ECR 3381

Court of Justice

10. It should be noted, by way of a preliminary observation, that Article [36] permits prohibitions or restrictions on trade between Member States provided that they are justified on grounds, *inter alia*, of the protection of industrial and commercial property, a term which covers literary and artistic property, including copyright, whereas the main proceedings are concerned with the question of prohibitions or restrictions placed upon the free movement of services.

11. In this regard, as the Court held in its judgment of 18 March 1980 (*Coditel* . . .), the problems involved in the observance of a film producer's rights in relation to the requirements of the Treaty are not the same as those of which arise in connection with literary and artistic works the placing of which at the disposal of the public is inseparable from the circulation of the material form of the works, as in the case of books or records, whereas the film belongs to the category of literary and artistic works made available to the public by performances which may be infinitely repeated and the commercial exploitation of which comes under the movement of services, no matter whether the means whereby it is shown to the public be the cinema or television.

12. In the same judgment the Court further held that the right of the owner of the copyright in a film and his assigns to require fees for any showing of that film is part of the essential function of copyright.

13. The distinction, implicit in Article [36], between the existence of a right conferred by the legislation of a Member State in regard to the protection of artistic and intellectual property, which cannot be affected by the provisions of the Treaty, and the exercise of such right, which might constitute a disguised restriction on trade between Member States, also applies where that right is exercised in the context of the movement of services.

14. Just as it is conceivable that certain aspects of the manner in which the right is exercised may prove to be incompatible with Articles [56] and [57] it is equally conceivable that some aspects may prove to be incompatible with Article [101] where they serve to give effect to an agreement, decision or concerted practice which may have as its object or effect the prevention, restriction or distortion of competition within the common market.

15. However, the mere fact that the owner of the copyright in a film has granted to a sole licensee the exclusive right to exhibit that film in the territory of a Member State and, consequently, to prohibit, during a specified period, its showing by others, is not sufficient to justify the finding that such a contract must be regarded as the purpose, the means or the result of an agreement, decision or concerted practice prohibited by the Treaty.

16. The characteristics of the cinematographic industry and of its markets in the [EU], especially those relating to dubbing and subtitling for the benefit of different language groups, to the possibilities of television broadcasts, and to the system of financing cinematographic production in Europe serve to show that an exclusive exhibition licence is not, in itself, such as to prevent, restrict or distort competition.

17. Although copyright in a film and the right deriving from it, namely that of exhibiting the film, are not, therefore, as such subject to the prohibitions contained in Article [101], the exercise of those rights may, none the less, come within the said prohibitions where there are economic or legal circumstances

the effect of which is to restrict film distribution to an appreciable degree or to distort competition on the cinematographic market, regard being had to the specific characteristics of that market.

18. Since neither the question referred to the Court nor the file on the case provides any information in this respect, it is for the national court to make such inquiries as may be necessary.

19. It must therefore be stated that it is for national courts, where appropriate, to make such inquiries and in particular to establish whether or not the exercise of the exclusive right to exhibit a cinematographic film creates barriers which are artificial and unjustifiable in terms of the needs of the cinematographic industry, or the possibility of charging fees which exceed a fair return on investment, or an exclusivity the duration of which is disproportionate to those requirements, and whether or not, from a general point of view, such exercise within a given geographic area is such as to prevent, restrict or distort competition within the common market.

20. Accordingly, the answer to be given to the question referred to the Court must be that a contract whereby the owner of the copyright in a film grants an exclusive right to exhibit that film for a specific period in the territory of a Member State is not, as such, subject to the prohibitions contained in Article [101 TFEU]. It is, however, where appropriate, for the national court to ascertain whether, in a given case, the manner in which the exclusive right conferred by that contract is exercised is subject to a situation in the economic or legal sphere the object or effect of which is to prevent or restrict the distribution of films or to distort competition within the cinematographic market, regard being had to the specific characteristics of the market.

The Court therefore accepted that the exclusive right, which in this case precluded showing of the film by others during a specified period, was not *of itself* prohibited by Article 101(1), given the nature of the protected work and the characteristics of the film industry; in particular, the Court stressed that the essential function of the copyright in this case was to enable the owner of the copyright in a film and his assigns to require fees for any showing of that film. It did not, nevertheless, rule out the possibility that in certain circumstances the exercise of the exclusive right might have the effect of restricting competition. However, the criteria in the qualifications in paragraphs 17 and 19 of the judgment as to when exclusivity *will* infringe the prohibition (the exclusivity might create artificial and unjustifiable barriers to trade, lead to excessive prices, or be for an excessive duration) are imprecise and uncertain.[50]

Indeed, in *Premier League/Murphy*[51] the CJ, distinguishing *Coditel II*, declined to accept that prohibitions on parallel trade incorporated in licences to broadcast Premier League (PL) football matches fell outside Article 101(1). In this case, the Football Association Premier League Ltd (FAPL) licensed broadcasters the right to broadcast live PL football matches only in their licensed territory. Broadcasts are made by encrypted signals via satellite, and paying customers receive the broadcasts by use of a decoder card. Under the terms of the arrangements broadcasters outside the UK were prohibited from supplying their decoder cards for use in the UK. The proceedings in this case were brought by the FAPL against defendants alleged either to have supplied non-UK decoders in the UK or to have broadcast live PL football matches using a non-UK decoder.[52] One

[50] Para. 19 provides that a relevant factor is whether the rewards are excessive, although no indication is given of how the national court is to make such judgments in the context of the film industry.

[51] Cases C-403 and 429/08, *Murphy* EU:C:2011:631.

[52] See *The Football Association Premier League Ltd v QC Leisure* [2008] EWHC 44 (Ch), [2008] EWHC 1411 (Ch) and *Murphy v Media Protection Services Ltd* [2008] EWHC 1666 (Admin) (the latter case concerned criminal proceedings against the defendant for violation of the Copyright, Designs and Patents Act 1988, s. 297(1) (dishonestly receiving a programme included in a broadcasting service provided from a place in the UK with intent to avoid payment of any charge applicable to the reception of the programme)).

of the defences raised was that the territorial restraints preventing supply for use in the UK were in breach of Article 101. The claimants alleged, relying on *Coditel II*, that the restraints were compatible with EU law.

Following an Article 267 reference to it, the CJ drew an important distinction in its ruling between sole exclusive licences and licences which go further and restore divisions between national markets. Further, it went on to conclude that the FAPL licensing arrangements in this case did breach Article 101; they were restrictive of competition by object (the FAPL had not put forward any circumstances falling within the economic and legal context to justify a finding otherwise) and the clauses of the licence did not meet the Article 101(3) conditions. In so doing, it entrenched the traditional stance to ATP adopted in the jurisprudence since *Consten and Grundig*, and, following the analysis it had conducted in relation to the EU free movement provisions, cursorily dismissed arguments raised under Article 101(3) relating to the cultural and economic aspects of the IPRs underlying the broadcast rights. In so doing, the CJ referred back to the paragraphs where, earlier in its judgment, it had dealt with the question of whether national legislation conferring legal protection on the contractual restrictions on cross-border broadcasting infringed free movement provisions (Article 56 TFEU). In that section, the CJ held that as the legislation clearly constituted a restriction on the freedom to provide services, it was compatible with EU law only if it could be objectively justified by an overriding reason in the public interest; it had to be suitable for securing the attainment of that public interest objective and not go beyond what was necessary in order to attain it. It held, however, that the legislation in this case was not so justified, either by the need:

(a) to protect IPRs: the FAPL could not claim copyright in the PL matches themselves (sporting events were not 'works' within the meaning of the Copyright Directive, then Directive 2001/29/EC); and the protection of sporting events guaranteed only appropriate remuneration (a premium to guarantee absolute territorial exclusivity—which would result in artificial price differences between the partitioned national markets—went beyond what is necessary to ensure appropriate remuneration for the rights holders). The Court distinguished *Coditel I* as in that case the cable television broadcasting companies communicated a work to the public without having, in the Member State of the place of origin of that communication, an authorisation from the rights holders concerned and without having paid remuneration to them. In the case before it, the (non-UK) broadcasters carried out acts of communication to the public while having in the Member State of broadcast, which is the Member State of the place of origin of that communication, an authorisation from the rights holders concerned and by paying them remuneration—which, moreover, could take account of the actual and potential audience in the other Member States. In so ruling, the Court referred to the developments of EU law that had resulted, in particular, from the adoption of the Television without Frontiers Directive and the Satellite Broadcasting Directive which are intended to ensure the transition from national markets to a single programme production and distribution market;[53] or

(b) to encourage the public to attend football stadiums by prohibiting broadcasting in the UK within closed periods (Saturday afternoons). The CJ considered that even if this was a legitimate objective, the contractual restrictions were not a proportionate means for achieving it. Rather it could be achieved by incorporating contractual limitations in the licence agreements under which the broadcasters would be required not to broadcast during these closed periods.[54]

[53] Cases C-403 and 429/08, *Murphy* EU:C:2011:631, paras. 85–121.

[54] Ibid., paras. 122–125.

Cases C-403 and 429/08, *Premier League Ltd v QC Leisure* and *Murphy v Media Protection Services Ltd* EU:C:2011:631

Court of Justice

134. By Question 10 in Case C-403/08 and Question 8 in Case C-429/08, the referring courts ask, in essence, whether the clauses of an exclusive licence agreement concluded between a holder of intellectual property rights and a broadcaster constitute a restriction on competition prohibited by Article 101 TFEU where they oblige the broadcaster not to supply decoding devices giving access to that right holder's protected subject-matter outside the territory covered by the licence agreement concerned.

135. First of all, it should be recalled that an agreement falls within the prohibition laid down in Article 101(1) TFEU when it has as its object or effect the prevention, restriction or distortion of competition. The fact that the two criteria are alternatives means that it is appropriate, first and foremost, to determine whether just one of them is satisfied, here the criterion concerning the object of the agreement. It is only secondarily, when the analysis of the content of the agreement does not reveal a sufficient degree of impairment of competition, that the consequences of the agreement should be considered, and for it to be open to prohibition it is necessary to find that those factors are present which show that competition has in fact been prevented, restricted or distorted to an appreciable extent (see, to this effect, Case C-8/08 *T-Mobile Netherlands and Others* . . . paragraph 28, and Joined Cases C-501/06 P, C-513/06 P, C-515/06 P and C-519/06 P *GlaxoSmithKline Services and Others v Commission and Others* . . . paragraph 55).

136. In order to assess whether the object of an agreement is anti-competitive, regard must be had inter alia to the content of its provisions, the objectives it seeks to attain and the economic and legal context of which it forms a part (see, to this effect, *GlaxoSmithKline Services and Others* v *Commission and Others*, paragraph 58 and the case-law cited).

137. As regards licence agreements in respect of intellectual property rights, it is apparent from the Court's case-law that the mere fact that the right holder has granted to a sole licensee the exclusive right to broadcast protected subject-matter from a Member State, and consequently to prohibit its transmission by others, during a specified period is not sufficient to justify the finding that such an agreement has an anti-competitive object (see, to this effect, . . . *('Coditel II')* . . . paragraph 15).

138. That being so, and in accordance with Article 1(2)(b) of the Satellite Broadcasting Directive, a right holder may in principle grant to a sole licensee the exclusive right to broadcast protected subject-matter by satellite, during a specified period, from a single Member State of broadcast or from a number of Member States.

139. None the less, regarding the territorial limitations upon exercise of such a right, it is to be pointed out that, in accordance with the Court's case-law, an agreement which might tend to restore the divisions between national markets is liable to frustrate the Treaty's objective of achieving the integration of those markets through the establishment of a single market. Thus, agreements which are aimed at partitioning national markets according to national borders or make the interpenetration of national markets more difficult must be regarded, in principle, as agreements whose object is to restrict competition within the meaning of Article 101(1) TFEU (see, by analogy, in the field of medicinal products, Joined Cases C-468/06 to C-478/06 *Sot. Lélos kai Sia and Others* [2008] ECR I-7139, paragraph 65, and *GlaxoSmithKline Services and Others* v *Commission and Others*, paragraphs 59 and 61).

140. Since that case-law is fully applicable to the field of the cross-border provision of broadcasting services, as follows inter alia from paragraphs 118 to 121 of the present judgment, it must be held that, where a licence agreement is designed to prohibit or limit the cross-border provision of broadcasting services, it is deemed to have as its object the restriction of competition, unless other circumstances falling within its economic and legal context justify the finding that such an agreement is not liable to impair competition.

141. In the main proceedings, the actual grant of exclusive licences for the broadcasting of Premier League matches is not called into question. Those proceedings concern only the additional obligations designed to ensure compliance with the territorial limitations upon exploitation of those licences that are contained in the clauses of the contracts concluded between the right holders and the broadcasters concerned, namely the obligation on the broadcasters not to supply decoding devices enabling access to the protected subject-matter with a view to their use outside the territory covered by the licence agreement.

142. Such clauses prohibit the broadcasters from effecting any cross-border provision of services that relates to those matches, which enables each broadcaster to be granted absolute territorial exclusivity in the area covered by its licence and, thus, all competition between broadcasters in the field of those services to be eliminated.

143. Also, FAPL and others and MPS have not put forward any circumstance falling within the economic and legal context of such clauses that would justify the finding that, despite the considerations set out in the preceding paragraph, those clauses are not liable to impair competition and therefore do not have an anticompetitive object.

144. Accordingly, given that those clauses of exclusive licence agreements have an anticompetitive object, it is to be concluded that they constitute a prohibited restriction on competition for the purposes of Article 101(1) TFEU.

145. It should be added that while, in principle, Article 101(1) TFEU does not apply to agreements which fall within the categories specified in Article 101(3) TFEU, clauses of licence agreements such as the clauses at issue in the main proceedings do not meet the requirements laid down by the latter provision for reasons stated in paragraphs 105 to 124 of the present judgment and therefore the possibility of Article 101(1) TFEU being inapplicable does not arise.

146. In light of the foregoing, the answer to the questions referred is that the clauses of an exclusive licence agreement concluded between a holder of intellectual property rights and a broadcaster constitute a restriction on competition prohibited by Article 101 TFEU where they oblige the broadcaster not to supply decoding devices enabling access to that right holder's protected subject-matter with a view to their use outside the territory covered by that licence agreement.

(iv) Block Exemptions: 1996–2004

Although, prior to modernisation, the Commission was willing to exempt IP licensing agreements under Article 101(3),[55] generally on condition of modification of exclusivity clauses and other provisions found to be restrictions (such as tie-ins, non-challenge clauses, and grant backs of improvements), the broad, and rather uncertain, reach of Article 101(1) created a pressing need for some form of block exemption (given the inability of the Commission to grant many individual exemptions).[56] Despite the urgency, the path of the first block exemption was tortuous and contested and it was not adopted until 1984. Regulation 2349/84[57] applied to pure patent licensing agreements or to mixed patent and know-how licensing agreements where the patent was the predominant element. The second block exemption, Regulation 556/89,[58] applied to pure know-how licensing agreements and to mixed know-how and patent licensing agreements where know-how was the predominant element. The two Regulations were very similar: specifying the type of agreement covered and exempted and containing 'white lists' and 'black lists'.[59]

[55] See e.g. COMP/17.545, 6.964, 26.858, 18.673, and 17.448, *Re the Agreements of Davidson Rubber Co* [1972] OJ L143/31; COMP/5.400, *Burroughs/Deplanque* [1972] OJ L13/50; COMP/26.813, *Raymond/Nagoya* [1972] OJ L143/39; COMP/28.967, *Bronbemaling v Heidemaatschappij* [1975] OJ L249/27; COMP/26.949, *AOIP v Beyrard* [1976] OJ L6/8.

[56] See Chaps. 2–4. [57] [1984] OJ L219/15. [58] [1989] OJ L61/1. [59] See Chaps. 5 and 11.

Both Regulations were replaced in 1996 by a single block exemption, Regulation 240/96 on technology transfer agreements,[60] which encompassed any transaction in which the predominant element was the licensing of patents or know-how, but which also contained a (shortened) 'black list' of prohibited clauses and a (longer) 'white list'. On 1 May 2004, Regulation 772/2004 on technology transfer agreements[61] came into force which sought to avoid the formalistic, and 'straitjacketing' effect of the previous block exemptions and to bring it into line with the approach of the vertical, specialisation, and research and development (R&D) block exemptions and the modernisation proposals more generally.[62] The path to the adoption of this block exemption was not a smooth one. Comments on an Evaluation Report[63] and a draft regulation[64] were critical of a number of features of the proposed reform, in particular: the proposal to introduce market share thresholds (market definition (and share) being notoriously difficult to assess in many IP licensing situations) which were argued to be an inappropriate and arbitrary indicator of the real competitive situation in technology markets;[65] the proposal for different thresholds to apply depending on whether the agreement was between 'competitors' or 'non-competitors';[66] the reduction in legal certainty, and concomitant greater risk of *ex post* challenges to agreements by the Commission, national competition authorities (NCAs) or (more likely) before national courts; the more severe list of hardcore restrictions; and the introduction of a list of 'excluded' restrictions.[67]

The Commission accepted some, but not all, of these criticisms when adopting the 2004 Regulation and Guidelines.[68] Above all, it adhered to its decision to impose market share thresholds:

> The use of market share thresholds is mainly opposed because it is considered that market shares are of no relevance in high tech sectors, that the assessment of market shares throughout the life of the agreement decreases legal certainty and is costly and furthermore that relevant product and geographic markets are often difficult to define.
>
> Let me first recall that the TTBER applies to all sectors not just high tech ones. It is fair to state that most sectors are mature and that even sectors that are in such a state of flux are so usually only for a limited period. Therefore in most sectors, and that also means in most sectors where licensing takes place, market shares do matter. In addition, usually licensing concerns products that either will continue to compete with existing products or that will replace existing products. There are not many products which cater to a human need for which nothing existed before. Therefore market definition in case of licensing will not be markedly more difficult than market definition for most other agreements.[69]

60 [1996] OJ L31/2.

61 [2004] OJ L123/11.

62 Reg. 240/96 contained provisions (e.g., an opposition procedure) which would not have worked in a system without provision for the notification of agreements. The abolition of notification and exemption also meant that guidelines were desirable to assist undertakings make their own assessment of agreements outside the block exemption.

63 Published on the Commission's website on 19 July 2002.

64 Over 70 submissions were received see, e.g., speech of (then) Commissioner Mario Monti, 'The New EU Policy on Technology Transfer Agreements', Ecole des Mines, Paris, 16 January 2004.

65 See, e.g., the submission of the International Chamber of Commerce to the Commission, available on the Commission's website, but cf. Monti, ibid.

66 There was also concern that parties might start life as non-competitors but move into the competitor category during the lifetime of the agreement, with serious consequences for its validity.

67 For example, the territorial and customer restrictions were stricter.

68 Reg. 772/2004 [2004] OJ L123/11, Commission Guidelines on the application of Article 81 of the EC Treaty to technology transfer agreements [2004] OJ C101/2.

69 See Monti, n. 64.

Although following consultation[70] the 2004 block exemption and Guidelines were replaced in 2014, the general framework and scheme for analysing technology transfer agreements created in 2004 has, subject to some important refinements and changes to the detail, been preserved.[71] As the Regulation expires on 30 April 2026, the Commission launched an evaluation of the regime on 25 November 2022.

D. THE 2014 TTBER AND THE TECHNOLOGY TRANSFER GUIDELINES

(i) Methodology

The 2014 TTBER was adopted, with accompanying Guidelines, in March 2014 and came into force on 1 May 2014. Although the TTBER provides an important safe harbour for technology transfer agreements, the Guidelines go further, doing three things. First, they set out a framework of general principles concerning Article 101 and IPRs. Secondly, they explain the provisions and application of the TTBER. Thirdly, they explain the application of Article 101(1) and Article 101(3) to agreements outside the scope of the TTBER. This latter role is of utmost importance in the context of technology transfer agreements especially given the particular complexity involved in defining relevant markets in the context;[72] consequently, the Guidelines are the real centre piece. 'The central theme of the Guidelines is the need to identify competitive harm and to identify economic benefits that might outweigh those competitive harms in order to determine whether a licence agreement raised Article [101] issues . . . the . . . system demands a new type of legal and economic assessment of individual agreements.'[73]

As has been seen with the other block exemptions,[74] their existence turns the appraisal of the agreement under Article 101 on its head. It encourages undertakings to consider first whether their agreement falls (or can be made to fall) within their safe harbour even if they do not infringe Article 101(1). As the Guidelines explain:

> many licence agreements fall outside Article 101(1) of the Treaty, either because they do not restrict competition at all or because the restriction of competition is not appreciable. To the extent that such agreements would anyhow fall within the scope of the TTBER, there is no need to determine whether they are caught by Article 101(1).[75]

Only if there is uncertainty as to whether the technology transfer agreement falls within the TTBER is it necessary to consider the application of Articles 101(1) and 101(3).

In the next sections, the general principles applicable to IPRs and the framework for the assessment of technology transfer agreements set out in the Guidelines are considered. The provisions of the TTBER are then analysed prior to looking at how Article 101 applies to technology transfer agreements falling outside it.

[70] See IP/13/120.

[71] For a comprehensive discussion of the core changes between the two regimes see, e.g., S. Rabb, 'New EU Technology Transfer Block Exemption: A Note of Caution' (2014) 5 *JECLAP* 136 (the TTBER includes, e.g., changes in relation to agreements incorporating non-challenge/termination clauses, passive sales restrictions (protecting exclusive licensees) and grant backs of improvements meaning that in some ways it is less permissive than the 2004 regime, and the Guidelines contain, e.g., greater analysis of settlement agreements and patent pools).

[72] S. D. Anderman and J. Kallaugher, *Technology Transfer and the New EU Competition Rules: IP Licensing after Modernisation* (Oxford University Press, 2006), 1.16.

[73] Ibid., 1.19–1.20. [74] See Chaps. 10 and 11. [75] Guidelines, para. 42.

(ii) General Principles: Application of Article 101 to Intellectual Property Rights

The Commission sets out the general principles by which it approaches the application of Article 101 to IPRs in part 2 of the Guidelines. It considers the value of IPRs, the relationship of IPRs and competition law, and notes that IP licensing is generally pro-competitive and compatible with Article 101.

Guidelines on the application of Article 101 of the Treaty on the Functioning of the European Union to technology transfer agreements

2. General Principles

2.1. Article 101 of the Treaty and intellectual property rights

5. The aim of Article 101 of the Treaty as a whole is to protect competition on the market with a view to promoting consumer welfare and an efficient allocation of resources. . . .

6. Intellectual property laws confer exclusive rights on holders of patents, copyright, design rights, trademarks and other legally protected rights. The owner of intellectual property is entitled under intellectual property laws to prevent unauthorised use of its intellectual property and to exploit it, for example, by licensing it to third parties. Once a product incorporating an intellectual property right, with the exception of performance rights, has been put on the market inside the European Economic Area (EEA) by the holder or with its consent, the intellectual property right is exhausted in the sense that the holder can no longer use it to control the sale of the product (principle of Union exhaustion). The right holder has no right under intellectual property laws to prevent sales by licensees or buyers of such products incorporating the licensed technology. The principle of Union exhaustion is in line with the essential function of intellectual property rights, which is to grant the holder the right to exclude others from exploiting its intellectual property without its consent.

7. The fact that intellectual property laws grant exclusive rights of exploitation does not imply that intellectual property rights are immune from competition law intervention. Article 101 of the Treaty is in particular applicable to agreements whereby the holder licenses another undertaking to exploit its intellectual property rights. Nor does it imply that there is an inherent conflict between intellectual property rights and the Union competition rules. Indeed, both bodies of law share the same basic objective of promoting consumer welfare and an efficient allocation of resources. Innovation constitutes an essential and dynamic component of an open and competitive market economy. Intellectual property rights promote dynamic competition by encouraging undertakings to invest in developing new or improved products and processes. So does competition by putting pressure on undertakings to innovate. Therefore, both intellectual property rights and competition are necessary to promote innovation and ensure a competitive exploitation thereof.

8. In the assessment of licence agreements under Article 101 of the Treaty it must be kept in mind that the creation of intellectual property rights often entails substantial investment and that this is often a risky endeavour. In order not to reduce dynamic competition and to maintain the incentive to innovate, the innovator must not be unduly restricted in the exploitation of intellectual property rights that turn out to be valuable. For these reasons the innovator should be free to seek appropriate remuneration for successful projects that is sufficient to maintain investment incentives, taking failed projects into account. Technology rights licensing may also require the licensee to make significant sunk investments (that is to say, that upon leaving that particular field of activity the investment cannot be used by the licensee for other activities or sold other than at a significant loss) in the licensed technology and production assets necessary to exploit it. Article 101 cannot be applied without considering such ex ante investments made by the parties and the risks relating thereto. The risk facing the parties and the sunk investment that must be committed may thus lead to the agreement falling outside Article

101(1) or fulfilling the conditions of Article 101(3), as the case may be, for the period of time required to recoup the investment.

9. In assessing licensing agreements under Article 101 of the Treaty, the existing analytical framework is sufficiently flexible to take due account of the dynamic aspects of technology rights licensing. There is no presumption that intellectual property rights and licence agreements as such give rise to competition concerns. Most licence agreements do not restrict competition and create pro-competitive efficiencies. Indeed, licensing as such is pro-competitive as it leads to dissemination of technology and promotes innovation by the licensor and licensee(s). In addition, even licence agreements that do restrict competition may often give rise to pro-competitive efficiencies, which must be considered under Article 101(3) and balanced against the negative effects on competition. The great majority of licence agreements are therefore compatible with Article 101.

4. REGULATION 316/2014, THE TECHNOLOGY TRANSFER BLOCK EXEMPTION

A. GENERAL

The TTBER is both more flexible and stricter than the block exemptions that existed prior to 2004. In particular, it is more flexible as, like the other block exemptions adopted post-1999, it does not contain lists of 'white' or 'grey' clauses. All provisions which are not in the list of hardcore restrictions or the list of excluded restrictions are permitted. On the other hand, the incorporation of market share thresholds into the TTBER renders its application quite uncertain to many undertakings,[76] creating a risk that licensing agreements may be challenged for violation of Article 101.

B. THE SCHEME OF THE TTBER

The TTBER comprises 19 recitals and 11 Articles. Article 1 contains definitions of key terms, whilst Article 2 sets out the core exemption for bilateral technology transfer agreements which fall within it. Article 3 contains the market share thresholds, whilst Articles 4 and 5 contains lists of hardcore and excluded restrictions. As with the VBER, the presence of a hardcore restriction removes the entire agreement from the protection of the block exemption.[77] In contrast, excluded restraints are not exempted by the TTBER but do not automatically remove the remainder of the agreement from the protection of the block exemption.

Articles 6 and 7 deal with withdrawal and disapplication of the TTBER, Article 8 contains provisions about the calculation of the market share thresholds and provides for some marginal relief where market share increases during the lifetime of the agreement, and

Article 9 excludes the benefit of the TTBER to licensing agreements which fall within the scope of other block exemption regulations relating to R&D or specialisation agreements.

Article 10 contains transitional provisions (giving undertakings one year to transition to the new regime), whilst Article 11 provides that the TTBER enters into force on 1 May 2014 and expires on 30 April 2026.

[76] See Anderman and Kallaugher, nn. 72–73 and text.

[77] Pursuant to the judgment of the Court in Case C-234/89, *Delimitis* EU:C:1991:91.

C. PRINCIPAL FEATURES OF THE TTBER

Certain features of the TTBER, elaborated on in greater detail in the following sections, should be noted at the outset:

- it covers patent and know-how licensing and licences of computer software and of designs so long as certain market share thresholds are not exceeded;
- throughout the TTBER a distinction is drawn between agreements between competitors and agreements between non-competitors. The market share thresholds, the hardcore restrictions, and the excluded restrictions differ depending on whether the agreement is between competitors or non-competitors;
- in respect of some types of provisions the TTBER draws a distinction between reciprocal and non-reciprocal obligations;
- in applying the TTBER two markets need to be taken into account: the *technology* market (consisting of the licensed technology and its substitutes) and the *product or service* market (consisting of the market for the product or service incorporating the licensed technology).

D. SCOPE OF THE TTBER

(i) Agreements to Which the TTBER May Apply

a. *Article 2 TTBER*

Article 2 of the TTBER exempts from Article 101(1), for as long as the licensed technology rights have not expired, bilateral technology transfer agreements permitting the production of contract products. It also applies to provisions relating 'to the purchase of products by the licensee or which relate to the licensing or assignment of other intellectual property rights or know-how to the licensee, if, and to the extent that, those provisions are directly related to the production or sale of the contract products'.

b. *Bilateral Technology Transfer Agreement*

The definition of a technology transfer agreement is set out in Article 1(1)(c):

> 'technology transfer agreement' means:
>
> (i) a technology rights licensing agreement entered into between two undertakings for the purpose of the production of contract products by the licensee and/or its sub-contractor(s),
>
> (ii) an assignment of technology rights between two undertakings for the purpose of the production of contract products where part of the risk associated with the exploitation of the technology remains with the assignor;

The TTBER is thus limited to bilateral agreements (agreements between *two* undertakings).[78] When counting the parties to an agreement, however, each group of 'connected undertakings'[79] are counted as a single party. The two-party limitation does not prevent an agreement which affects third parties from falling within the TTBER however. For example, an agreement may require the licensee to impose obligations on resellers of the product produced under the licence.[80]

[78] Council Reg. 19/65 [1965–1966] OJ Spec. Ed. Series I, 35, the relevant enabling regulation, only empowers the Commission to block exempt bilateral technology transfer agreements.

[79] TTBER, Art. 1(2). See also the discussion of the single economic entity doctrine in Chap. 4.

[80] Guidelines, para. 55.

Article 1(1)(b) provides that 'technology rights' include know-how and/or patents, utility models, design rights, topographies of semiconductor products, supplementary protection certificates for medicinal products or other products for which such supplementary protection certificates may be obtained, plant breeders' certificates and software copyrights. Know-how is defined in Article 1(1)(i) as: a package of practical information, resulting from experience and testing, which is:

> (i) secret, that is to say, not generally known or easily accessible,
>
> (ii) substantial, that is to say, significant and useful for the production of the contract products, and
>
> (iii) identified, that is to say, described in a sufficiently comprehensive manner so as to make it possible to verify that it fulfils the criteria of secrecy and substantiality;

The meanings of 'secret', 'substantial', and 'identified' are further elaborated upon in the Guidelines.[81] A technology transfer agreement can therefore comprise:

- a pure patent licensing agreement;
- a pure know-how licensing agreement;
- a pure software copyright licence (but not other forms of copyright licensing or trademark licences);[82]
- a pure design licence;
- a 'mixed' agreement, by which two or more rights (patents, know-how, software copyright, designs) are licensed together (it is very common, for example, to license know-how together with a patent);
- provisions in technology transfer agreements relating to the licensing of other types of IP, such as trademarks and copyright, are covered only if, and to the extent that, they are directly related to the production or sale of the contract products (the rights serve to enable the licensee to better exploit the licensed technology rights).[83] The TTBER also covers licences which contain provisions about the purchase of goods provided those provisions are directly related to the production or sale of the contract products.[84]

The TTBER only covers agreements whereby technology is *transferred*, where technology 'flows from one undertaking to another',[85] i.e. normally where the licensor grants a licensee the right to use its technology to produce contract goods against the payment of royalties. It also covers a sub-licence by the licensee for the exploitation of the technology.[86]

c. The Agreement Must Concern the Production of Contract Products

The licensing agreement or assignment must be 'for the purpose of the production of contract products', that is to use the licensed technology to produce goods or services (the word 'goods' is hereafter used in this chapter to denote both goods and services unless the context otherwise requires). The TTBER does not therefore cover:[87]

- 'technology pools' whereby two or more parties agree to pool their respective technologies and license them as a package;[88]

[81] Ibid., para. 45.

[82] Ibid., para. 48 ('The Commission will, however, as a general rule apply the principles set out in the TTBER and these guidelines when assessing licensing of copyright for the production of contract products under Article 101 of the Treaty') and see Section 8.

[83] Ibid., para. 47 and, e.g., COMP/32.736, *Moosehead/Whitbread* decision [1990] OJ L100/32, n. 233 and text.

[84] Guidelines, para. 46. [85] Ibid., para. 51. [86] Ibid., para. 60. [87] Ibid., paras. 58–66.

[88] Ibid., para. 56. The Guidelines contain a lengthy section (4.4) on technology pools, see Section 5.F. Such agreements are unlikely to be 'bilateral' and the parties are unlikely to meet the market share thresholds of the TTBER.

- master-licensing agreements, the primary object of which is sub-licensing;
- agreements whose object is to enable the licensee to carry out further R&D (rather than produce goods or services);
- agreements whose primary object is the sale and purchase of products (rather than their production).[89]

On the other hand the TTBER *does* cover, for example, agreements:

- which are entered into to settle disputes over IPRs within the scope of the TTBER ('settlement' agreements), including cross-licensing;[90]
- which are subcontracting agreements whereby the technology is licensed in order for the licensee to produce certain products exclusively for the licensor;[91]
- whereby the licensee has to carry out development work before obtaining a product or process that can be commercially exploited, provided that a contract product has been identified and the primary purpose of the agreement is not R&D.[92]

(ii) Relationship with Other Block Exemptions

Specialisation, R&D, and vertical agreements may involve the transfer of technology between the contracting parties. Paragraphs 70–78 of the Guidelines deal with the interface of the TTBER with the specialisation, R&D, and vertical block exemptions. Broadly:[93]

- The specialisation block exemption,[94] not the TTBER, covers licensing in the context of a production joint venture (JV) (where the JV is licensed to exploit technology). It does not apply, however, to the situation where the JV engages in licensing technology to a third party. That amounts to a technology pool;
- The R&D block exemption,[95] and not the TTBER, covers licensing between parties and by parties to a joint entity in the context of an R&D agreement. Licensing of the fruits of the R&D to third parties might be covered by the TTBER, however.
- The block exemption on vertical restraints covers supply and distribution agreements. In Chapter 11, it was seen that the VBER covers vertical agreements involving licences of IP so long as certain conditions are met—including that the licence is ancillary to the vertical agreement and IPRs are assigned to the buyer (and not vice versa). Even though therefore the TTBER block exempts (within the safe harbour) a technology transfer agreement requiring a licensee to distribute the products in a particular way, vertical agreements are subject to the VBER and the Verticals Guidelines.[96]

E. SAFE HARBOUR: THE MARKET SHARE THRESHOLDS

(i) The Market Share Thresholds

The block exemption applies on condition that specified market share thresholds are not exceeded on affected technology and/or product markets. Where the parties are competitors (actual competitors

[89] Ibid., para. 61. [90] Ibid., para. 53. [91] Ibid., para. 64, see also Chap. 11. [92] Ibid., para. 65.
[93] Ibid., paras. 70–79. [94] See Chap. 10. [95] Ibid. [96] Guidelines, paras. 76–77.

or potential competitors on the product market(s) and/or actual competitors on the technology market[97]) the relevant market share is 20 per cent (Article 3(1)). Where the parties are non-competitors the relevant market is 30 per cent (Article 3(2)). With regard to competitors it is the *combined* market share which is relevant, but in the case of non-competitors it is the market share of *each* of the parties on the affected relevant technology and product markets that is relevant.

If the parties' market shares are below the thresholds at the time the agreement is entered into, but subsequently increase so that they exceed it, the TTBER will continue to apply for two consecutive calendar years following the year in which the relevant threshold is first exceeded.[98]

In order to determine whether the TTBER applies, it is therefore ordinarily necessary to identify the relevant markets, to calculate market shares, and to determine whether or not the parties are competitors.

(ii) Market Definition

The Guidelines provide guidance on specific issues which arise in the technology transfer context,[99] particularly as the relevant market means a combination of the relevant product or the technology market with the relevant geographic market.[100]

a. The Technology Market

The technology market is the licensed technology and any other technology that the licensees consider to be interchangeable with, or substitutable for, the technology by reason of the technologies' characteristics, their royalties, and their intended use.[101] Paragraph 22 of the Guidelines states that the objective is therefore to identify competing technologies to which licensees could switch in response to a small but permanent increase in prices (which in this context means the royalties) (the SSNIP test).[102] It also provides 'an alternative approach' to defining the technology market, which looks to the market for products incorporating the licensed technology (see also paragraph 25 of the Guidelines).

b. The Product Market

The relevant product market comprises products regarded as interchangeable with or substitutable for the contract products incorporating the licensed technology (whether an interim or final product market) by reason of the products' characteristics, price, and intended use.[103] Occasionally, it may be necessary to define an innovation market, in particular where the agreement affects innovation aimed at creating new products and R&D poles can be identified.[104]

(iii) Market Shares

a. Means of Calculation

Where it is available, market share is to be calculated on the basis of market sales value data. Otherwise 'other reliable market information' including market sales volume data may be used.[105]

[97] Ibid., para. 82. [98] TTBER, Art. 8(e). [99] Guidelines, para. 20. [100] TTBER, Art. 1(1)(m).
[101] Guidelines, para. 22. [102] See Chap. 1. [103] TTBER, Art. 1(1)(j) and Guidelines, para. 21.
[104] Guidelines, para. 26. [105] TTBER, Art. 8(a). The calculation is on the basis of the preceding year, Art. 8(b).

b. The Technology Market

The Guidelines suggest more than one method of calculating market shares on the technology market. One solution is to calculate the market shares by reference to the licensed technology and its substitutes. Market share can then be calculated on the basis of each technology's share of total licensing income from royalties. In practice, however, this test is hard to apply—especially as companies are unlikely to know the level of royalty income derived by their competitors. Article 8(d) thus provides that the market share can be defined with regard to the presence of the licensed technology on the relevant product market.

c. The Product Market

Market shares on the product market are assessed in the usual way, using sales data value if available.[106] The licensee's market share is the total sales of the licensee on the product market, i.e. products incorporating the licensor's technology and competing products. The licensor's sales (if any) on the product market must be included, but not those of other licensees.

(iv) The Distinction Between Competitors and Non-competitors

The provisions of the TTBER are based on the premise that agreements between competitors are likely to pose a greater risk to the competitive process than agreements between non-competitors.[107] Thus not only are the market share thresholds lower for agreements between competitors but a different, stricter set of hardcore restraints applies. Paragraph 28 of the Guidelines explains:

> In order to determine the competitive relationship between the parties it is necessary to examine whether the parties would have been actual or potential competitors in the absence of the agreement. If without the agreement the parties would not have been actual or potential competitors in any relevant market affected by the agreement they are deemed to be non-competitors.

Article 1(1)(n) of the TTBER defines competing undertakings as undertakings that compete on the relevant technology market and/or the relevant product market.

> 'competing undertakings' means undertakings which compete on the relevant market, that is to say:
>
> (i) competing undertakings on the relevant market where the technology rights are licensed, that is to say, undertakings which license out competing technology rights (actual competitors on the relevant market),
>
> (ii) competing undertakings on the relevant market where the contract products are sold, that is to say, undertakings which, in the absence of the technology transfer agreement, would both be active on the relevant market(s) on which the contract products are sold (actual competitors on the relevant market) or which, in the absence of the technology transfer agreement, would, on realistic grounds and not just as a mere theoretical possibility, in response to a small and permanent increase in relative prices, be likely to undertake, within a short period of time, the necessary additional investments or other necessary switching costs to enter the relevant market(s) (potential competitors on the relevant market);

It can be seen from this definition that as far as product markets are concerned, both actual and potential competitors are treated as competitors. As far as technology markets are concerned, however, only

[106] TTBER, Art. 8(a) and Guidelines, para. 92. [107] Guidelines, para. 31.

actual competitors are relevant. If the licensor and licensee are both active on the same technology or product market, without infringing each other's IPRs, they are actual competitors on the market. On technology markets the parties will be considered actual competitors if they are both licensing substitutable technologies or the licensee is already licensing out its technology and the licensor enters the technology market by granting a licence for a competing technology to the licensee.[108] The parties are potential competitors on the product market if, in the absence of the agreement and without infringing IPRs, they would be likely to undertake the necessary investments required to enter the market within a short period (one to two years) in response to a small but permanent increase in price.[109] Outside the safe harbour of the TTBER potential competitors on the technology market are taken into account.[110]

The reference in Article 1(1)(n) to parties being competing undertakings only where they are both active on the technology market or product market 'without infringing each other's [IPRs]' means that if there is a one-way (one party cannot exploit its technology without infringing the other's IPRs) or two-way (neither party can exploit its technology without infringing the other's IPRs) blocking situation, the parties will *not* be characterised as competitors.[111] The Commission is, however, alive to the fact that the parties will usually prefer to be classified as non-competitors and blocking claims have to be examined carefully.[112]

The Guidelines state that in cases of 'drastic innovation' parties should be classed as non-competitors even though they produce competing products. This will be the case where the licensed technology represents such a technological breakthrough that the licensee's technology becomes obsolete or uncompetitive (for example, the replacement of LP vinyl technology with CD technology).[113] Often, however, it will not be possible to draw this conclusion at the time the agreement is concluded. If it is *not* obvious at this time the parties will be classified as competitors initially but can be recognised as non-competitors later.[114]

It is extremely important when deciding whether the parties are competitors or non-competitors to remember that activities of their 'connected undertakings' must be taken into account.[115]

(v) Non-competitors Who Subsequently Become Competitors

What is the position if the parties are not competitors at the time the agreement is concluded but subsequently become competitors? Article 4(3) of the TTBER provides that the more liberal list of hardcore restrictions for agreements between non-competitors will apply during the full life of the agreement *unless* the agreement is subsequently amended 'in any material respect'. Where a material amendment occurs, including the conclusion of a new technology transfer agreement between the parties concerning competing technology rights, restraints previously block exempted may become hardcore restraints.[116] Paragraph 85 of the Guidelines explains, however, that the lower market share threshold will apply from the time that the parties become competitors:

> Where the parties become competitors within the meaning of Article 3(1) TTBER at a later point in time, for instance where the licensee was already present, before the licensing, on the relevant market where the contract products are sold and the licensor subsequently becomes an actual or potential supplier on the same relevant market, the 20% market share threshold will apply from the point in time

[108] Ibid., paras. 30 and 35. [109] Ibid., para. 27.
[110] See ibid., para. 81. This does not lead to the application of the hardcore list of restrictions relating to agreements between competitors.
[111] Ibid., para. 29. [112] Ibid., para. 33. [113] Ibid., para. 37. [114] Ibid. [115] See n. 79 and text.
[116] Guidelines, paras. 38–39.

when they became competitors. However, in that case the hardcore list relevant for agreements between non-competitors will continue to apply to the agreement unless the agreement is subsequently amended in any material respect (see Article 4(3) of the TTBER and point (39) of these guidelines).

This suggests that the benefit of the TTBER will be lost where parties become competitors and their combined market shares exceed the 20 per cent threshold and that the two-year transitional relief provided by Article 8(e) does not apply in these circumstances.

F. HARDCORE RESTRICTIONS

(i) General

The scheme of the TTBER is that, subject to Article 5, if a contractual restraint is not prohibited, it is permitted. The presence of a 'hardcore' restraint, defined in Article 4, prevents the block exemption from applying. As is the case in the context of vertical agreements, a restraint will be hardcore whether achieved directly or *indirectly*. Indeed, the Commission's view is that hardcore restraints are restrictive of competition by object and are most unlikely even *individually* to satisfy the Article 101(3) conditions.[117]

As already noted, there are two separate lists of hardcore restrictions: those applying to agreements between competitors (Article 4(1)) and those applying to agreements between non-competitors (Article 4(2)). In addition, the list of hardcore restraints in agreements between competitors may differ depending upon whether the agreement is reciprocal or non-reciprocal. These terms are defined in Article 1(1)(d) and (e) of the TTBER. Essentially, an agreement is reciprocal where the parties cross-license competing technologies or technologies which can be used for the production of competing products.

(ii) Agreements Between Competing Undertakings

The list of hardcore restraints applicable to agreements between competitors is set out in Article 4(1). It focuses, subject to specified exceptions, on agreements which directly or indirectly have as their object: price-fixing; limitations of output; allocation of markets or customers; restrictions on the licensee's ability to exploit its own technology; and provisions restraining either party from carrying out R&D unless indispensable to prevent disclosure of the licensed technology.

a. Article 4(1)(a)—Price Restrictions

Article 4(1)(a) targets agreements incorporating a 'restriction of a party's ability to determine its prices when selling products to third parties'. An obligation on the licensee to pay a certain minimum royalty does not in itself amount to price-fixing.[118] However, indirect price restraints, for example through disincentives to deviate from an agreed price level or through provisions for the royalty rate to increase if prices are reduced below a certain level, are prohibited.[119]

b. Article 4(1)(b)—Output Limitations

Article 4(1)(b) applies to a 'limitation of output, except limitations on the output of contract products imposed on the licensee in a non-reciprocal agreement or imposed on only one of the licensees in a

[117] Ibid., paras. 94–96. See generally on this point Chap. 5.

[118] A licensor is entitled to ensure that it obtains a certain minimum return for the licence.

[119] Guidelines, paras. 99–101.

reciprocal agreement'. This means, in effect, that reciprocal output restrictions and output restrictions on the licensor in respect of its own technology constitute hardcore restrictions.[120] Provisions which have the effect of output restrictions, such as disincentives to produce more than a certain amount, are also caught.[121]

c. *Article 4(1)(c)—Market or Customer Allocation*

Article 4(1)(c) seeks to reconcile the need to ensure that competitors are not able to share markets between themselves with an acceptance that in certain circumstances a licensee will require an exclusive or sole licence and protection from sales into its territory.[122] It targets the allocation of markets or customers unless one of four exceptions[123] applies.

(1) Article 4(1)(c)(i)

In a *non-reciprocal* licence, both licensor and licensee can be restricted from producing within an exclusively territory reserved for the other, or selling *actively* and *passively* into an exclusive territory or to the exclusive customer groups, reserved for the other.

(2) Article 4(1)(c)(ii)

In a *non-reciprocal* licence, the licensee can be prohibited from making *active* (but *not* passive) sales into exclusive territories or to customer groups allocated to another licensee (so long as that other licensee was not a competitor of the licensor when it was given its licence). If the licensees agree among themselves not to sell actively or passively into each other's territories or to customers this clearly goes beyond what is permitted and indeed amounts to market-sharing, which is prohibited by Article 101.[124]

(3) Article 4(1)(c)(iii)

This exception permits licensing where the licensee takes a licence in order to make products for its own use (known as captive use restrictions).[125] It enables the licensor to limit the licensee to making components to be incorporated into the licensee's own products and to prohibit it from selling them to others. The licensee must not, however, be restricted from selling the components as spare parts.

(4) Article 4(1)(c)(iv)

A non-reciprocal licence granted specifically to create an alternative source of supply for a customer may restrict the licensee to producing the contract products only for that customer (a 'second source' provision); the whole point of the agreement is to provide a particular customer with an alternative source of the products. It is possible, however, for more than one licensee to be given a licence in respect of the same customer (so the latter gets a third or even fourth source of supply).[126]

Table 12.1 summarises in tabular form permissible customer and territorial restraints in agreements between competitors.

[120] Ibid., para. 103. [121] Ibid.

[122] It considers that agreements between competitors sharing markets or customers (such as reciprocal exclusive licensing between competitors) have as their object the restriction of competition, ibid., para. 105.

[123] The 2014 TTBER reduced the list of these exceptions by merging them and so simplifying the list. The Commission considers that this has not led to any change in substance.

[124] Guidelines, para. 110. 'Active' and 'passive' sales have the same meaning as in respect of vertical agreements (see Chap. 11).

[125] Ibid., para. 111. [126] Ibid., para. 112.

Table 12.1 Table of permissible market or customer restraints in agreements between competitors under the TTBER

Restraint	Permitted in reciprocal agreement?	Permitted in non-reciprocal agreement?
Obligation on the licensor and/or licensee not to use technology to produce within one more exclusive territories reserved to the other	No	Yes, licensor can grant exclusive licence to produce and agree not to produce itself
Ban *active or passive* selling into territory/customer group, reserved to other (licensor or licensee)	No	Yes
Ban on *active* selling into territory of, or to the exclusive customer group reserved to, another licensee	No	Yes, as long as other licensee was not a competitor of the licensor at time the agreement was concluded
Ban on *passive* selling into territory of, or to exclusive customer group reserved to, another licensee	No	No
Captive use restriction	Yes, so long as can sell as spare parts	Yes, so long as can sell as spare parts
Second source provision (obligation on licensee to produce for a single customer)	No	Yes, if the licence was granted specifically to create a source of supply for that customer

Source: *Butterworths Competition Law* (LexisNexis, looseleaf), Division V, Chapter 3, para 575.

d. Article 4(1)(d)—Limitations on Technology Exploitation or R&D

Whether the agreement is reciprocal or non-reciprocal, the licensee cannot be restricted from exploiting its own technology rights and neither party to the agreement can be restricted from carrying out independent R&D unless indispensable to prevent the licensed know-how from being disclosed to third parties (in which case the restriction must be necessary and proportionate).[127] In addition, the licensee must not be prevented from exploiting its own technology.

(iii) Agreements Between Non-competing Undertakings

Where the parties are non-competitors they are allowed more leeway. The list of hardcore restraints is briefer and less limiting. In a similar way to the VBER, it focuses on restraints which directly or

[127] Ibid., para. 115.

indirectly fix or impose minimum resale prices or which, subject to specified exceptions, restrict the territory into which, or the customers to whom, the licensee may sell the contract product.

a. *Article 4(2)(a)—Price Restrictions*

Article 4(2)(a) provides that 'the restriction of a party's ability to determine its prices when selling products to third parties' constitutes a hardcore restraint, but 'without prejudice to the possibility of imposing a maximum sale price or recommending a sale price'. The prohibition of resale price maintenance (RPM) does not, therefore, unlike the hardcore competitor list, cover maximum or recommended prices so long as they do not really amount to fixed or minimum prices.

b. *Article 4(2)(b)—Passive Sales Restrictions Imposed on the Licensee*

This clause identifies, subject to five exceptions, the restriction of the territory into which, or of the customers to whom, the licensee may passively sell the contract products, as a hardcore restriction. This provision does not therefore blacklist any sales restrictions on the *licensor* or *active* sales restrictions on the *licensee* (but see discussion of Article 4(2)(c) later). The Commission explains:[128]

> The block exemption of restrictions on active selling is based on the assumption that such restrictions promote investments, non-price competition and improvements in the quality of services provided by the licensees by solving free rider problems and hold-up problems. In the case of restrictions of active sales between licensees' territories or customer groups, it is not necessary that the protected licensee has been granted an exclusive territory or an exclusive customer group. The block exemption also applies to active sales restrictions where more than one licensee has been appointed for a particular territory or customer group. Efficiency enhancing investment is likely to be promoted where a licensee can be sure that it will only face active sales competition from a limited number of licensees inside the territory and not also from licensees outside the territory.

(1) *Article 4(2)(b)(i)*

The first exception allows a restriction on passive sales into an exclusive territory or to an exclusive customer group reserved for the licensor. If the licensor could not prevent this it might not disseminate the technology through licensing in the first place:

> It is presumed that up to the market share threshold such restraints, where restrictive of competition, promote pro-competitive dissemination of technology and integration of such technology into the production assets of the licensee.[129]

The 2004 block exemption also permitted a restriction on passive sales into an exclusive territory or to an exclusive customer group reserved to another licensee. Although this is no longer block exempted, the Commission does recognise that such restraints may fall outside Article 101(1) altogether for a certain duration where objectively necessary for the licensee to penetrate a new market (for example, where licensees have to commit substantial investments in order to start up and develop a new market):

> In such circumstances, it is often the case that licensees would not enter into the licence agreement without protection for a certain period of time against (active and) passive sales into their territory or to

[128] Ibid., para. 120. [129] Ibid., para. 121.

> their customer groups by other licensees. Where substantial investments by the licensee are necessary to start up and develop a new market, restrictions of passive sales by other licensees into such a territory or to such a customer group fall outside Article 101(1) for the period necessary for the licensee to recoup those investments. In most cases a period of up to two years from the date on which the contract product was first put on the market in the exclusive territory by the licensee in question or sold to its exclusive customer group would be considered sufficient for the licensee to recoup the investments made. However, in an individual case a longer period of protection for the licensee might be necessary in order for the licensee to recoup the costs incurred.[130]

(2) Article 4(2)(b)(ii)

Article 4(2)(b)(ii) exempts captive use restrictions; 'an obligation to produce the contract products only for its own use provided that the licensee is not restricted in selling the contract products actively and passively as spare parts for its own products'.

(3) Article 4(2)(b)(iii)

Article 4(2)(b)(iii) exempts second source provisions; 'the obligation to produce the contract products only for a particular customer, where the licence was granted in order to create an alternative source of supply for that customer'.

(4) Article 4(2)(b)(iv)

This provision permits the maintenance of a distinction between wholesale and retail levels of trade, allowing 'the restriction of sales to end-users by a licensee operating at the wholesale level of trade'. The licensor can give the wholesale distribution function to a licensee and prohibit it from serving the end customers.

(5) Article 4(2)(b)(v)

As under the VBER,[131] this provision allows members of a selective distribution system to be restricted from selling to unauthorised distributors, thereby preserving the integrity of the system.

Table 12.2 provides in tabular form the passive sales restraints that may be imposed on licensees in a licence agreement between non-competitors.

c. Article 4(2)(c)—Active or Passive Sales Bans to End-users within Selective Distribution Systems

A licensee which operates at the retail level of a selective distribution system cannot be prevented from active or passive selling to any end-users without prejudice to the possibility of prohibiting a member of the system from operating out of an unauthorised place of establishment.

G. EXCLUDED RESTRICTIONS

(i) Introduction

Article 5 sets out the 'excluded restrictions'. These are restrictions which are not exempted by the TTBER but the inclusion of which does not automatically remove the protection of the TTBER from the remainder of the agreement. Individual assessment is required to determine whether the

130 See ibid., para. 126.

131 See Chap. 11.

Table 12.2 Table of permissible restraints in the context of agreements between non-competitors on the territory into which or the customer to whom the licensee can passively sell the contract product

Restraint	Permissible?
Passive sales into an exclusive territory or to an exclusive customer group reserved to the licensor	Yes
Captive use restriction	Yes, the licensee can be required to produce the product only for its own use provided he can sell as spare parts to customers or third parties performing after-sales services
Second source provision	Yes, an obligation on the licensee to produce the products only for a specified customer is permissible where the licence was granted to create an alternative source of supply
Sales to end-users	Yes, where the licensee operates at the wholesale level
Sales to unauthorised distributors within a selective distribution system	Yes, unless the licensee operates at the wholesale level, the licensee must be able to make sales (actively or passive) to end-users
Restriction on passive sales into an exclusive territory or to an exclusive customer group reserved to another licensee	Will not benefit from the block exemption but may be permitted for a period of up to two years if objectively necessary to penetrate a new market

Source: *Butterworths Competition Law* (LexisNexis, looseleaf), Division V, Chapter 3, para 591.

excluded restraints infringe Article 101 and, if they do, whether they can be severed from the rest of the agreement.

(ii) Article 5(1)(a): Improvements; Exclusive Grant Backs

Article 5(1)(a) deals with improvements made by the licensee to the licensed technology, excluding from the benefit of the TTBER 'any direct or indirect obligation on the licensee to grant an exclusive licence or to assign rights, in whole or in part, to the licensor or to a third party designated by the licensor in respect of its own improvements to, or its own new applications of, the licensed technology'. It thus excludes exclusive grant backs (even if the grant or assignment is compensated). The Commission explains the reason for excluding such provisions from the TTBER:[132]

> An obligation to grant the licensor an exclusive licence to improvements of the licensed technology or to assign such improvements to the licensor is likely to reduce the licensee's incentive to innovate since it hinders the licensee in exploiting the improvements, including by way of licensing to third parties.

[132] Guidelines, para. 129. The Commission changed its position to encourage follow-on improvements by the licensee and so encourages disruptive innovation by it.

Article 5 does not cover (so the TTBER does cover) *non-exclusive* grant back provisions even if they are non-reciprocal (i.e. only imposed on the licensee) and where the licensor is entitled to feed-on improvements to other licensees.

> A non-reciprocal grant back obligation may promote the dissemination of new technology by permitting the licensor to freely determine whether and to what extent to pass on its own improvements to its licensees. A feed-on clause may also promote the dissemination of technology, in particular when each licensee knows at the time of contracting that it will be on an equal footing with other licensees in terms of the technology on the basis of which it is producing.[133]

(iii) Article 5(1)(b): Non-challenge and Termination Clauses

Article 5(1)(b) excludes certain non-challenge clauses, 'any direct or indirect obligation on a party not to challenge the validity of intellectual property rights which the other party holds in the Union, without prejudice to the possibility, in the case of an exclusive licence, of providing for termination of the technology transfer agreement in the event that the licensee challenges the validity of any of the licensed technology rights'.

The general rule is thus that non-challenge clauses are excluded from the scope of the block exemption. As licensees are normally in the best position to determine whether or not an IPR is invalid the Commission considers that it is in the interest of undistorted competition and in accordance with the principles underlying the protection of IP, that invalid IPRs (which stifle innovation) should be eliminated.[134] The Guidelines thus state that such clauses require careful individual assessment under Article 101 to balance the incentives of the licensor and licensee and the public interest in eliminating obstacles to competition.[135]

An exception exists, however (so the TTBER does not exclude), for termination clauses which apply to challenges made by an exclusive licensee to the licensed technology. The Commission, in seeking to balance incentives to innovate against the public interest in removing invalid IPR rights from the register, considers that such clauses are 'usually less likely on balance to have anti-competitive effects':[136]

> Once the licence is granted, the licensor may find itself in a particular situation of dependency, as the licensee will be its only source of income as regards the licensed technology rights if royalties are dependent on production with the licensed technology rights, as may often be an efficient way to structure royalty payments. In this scenario, the incentives for innovation and for licensing out could be undermined if, for example, the licensor were to be locked into an agreement with an exclusive licensee which no longer makes significant efforts to develop, produce and market the product (to be) produced with the licensed technology rights . . .

(iv) Limitations on Technology Exploitation or R&D

Although restrictions on the licensee's ability to exploit its own technology rights or on either party's ability to carry out R&D (unless such latter restriction is indispensable to prevent the disclosure of the licensed know-how to third parties) are not hardcore restraints in agreements between

[133] Ibid., para. 131. [134] Ibid., para. 134. [135] Ibid., paras. 134–138.

[136] Ibid., para. 139. The 2004 TTBER permitted all terminate-on-challenge arrangements. Although the Commission proposed removing this exception entirely it accepted an intermediate position following consultation.

non-competitors, Article 5(2) provides that such restraints are excluded restraints and are not exempted by the TTBER.

H. WITHDRAWAL AND DISAPPLICATION OF THE BLOCK EXEMPTION

(i) Withdrawal

As with other block exemptions, the Commission has a general right to withdraw the benefit of the TTBER from any agreement which has effects which are incompatible with Article 101(3) (Article 29(1) of Regulation 1/2003) and the national authorities of the Member States have the right to withdraw it in relation to an agreement which has restrictive effects incompatible with Article 101(3) in the territory of their Member State (Article 29(2)). Article 6(1) of the TTBER states that withdrawal by the Commission may be appropriate in respect of technology transfer agreements where:

(a) access of third parties' technologies to the market is restricted, for instance by the cumulative effect of parallel networks of similar restrictive agreements prohibiting licensees from using third parties' technologies;

(b) access of potential licensees to the market is restricted, for instance by the cumulative effect of parallel networks of similar restrictive agreements prohibiting licensors from licensing to other licensees or because the only technology owner licensing out relevant technology rights concludes an exclusive license with a licensee who is already active on the product market on the basis of substitutable technology rights.

Withdrawal may only be made prospectively (it does not affect prior validity) and by way of an infringement decision (finding that the agreement infringes Article 101(1) *and* that it does not meet the conditions of Article 101(3)) or a decision making commitments binding on the undertakings concerned.[137]

(ii) Disapplication

As is the case in the VBER, Article 7 of the TTBER provides that the Commission may, by regulation, exclude from the scope of the TTBER parallel networks of similar agreements containing specified restraints, which cover more than 50 per cent of a relevant market.[138]

5. THE APPLICATION OF ARTICLE 101 TO AGREEMENTS INVOLVING INTELLECTUAL PROPERTY RIGHTS FALLING OUTSIDE THE TTBER

A. GENERAL PRINCIPLES

(i) Technology Transfer Agreements Outside the TTBER

Agreements may fall outside the TTBER because:

- they are not bilateral technology transfer agreements;
- they exceed the market share thresholds;
- they contain hardcore restrictions.

[137] See Chap. 13. [138] See Guidelines, paras. 149–155.

In addition, individual provisions may be outside the TTBER because they are excluded restrictions under Article 5.

As there is very little modern jurisprudence in this area, the Guidelines provide helpful guidance as to how Article 101 applies to agreements or provisions falling outside the TTBER. Although the principles applied in the TTBER and the Guidelines do not generally apply to agreements that do not constitute technology transfer agreements, the Guidelines indicate that these principles will apply by analogy to: technology transfer agreements to which more than two undertakings are party;[139] 'master licensing agreements';[140] and the licensing of copyright for the purposes of the production of contract products.[141] In the case of other licensing agreements, however, such as R&D subcontracting,[142] licensing of rental right and public performance rights protected by copyright,[143] and trademark licences,[144] guidance must be sought from other sources: the case law of the Court, the Commission's decisional practice, and the Commission's Article 101(3) Guidelines.

(ii) No Presumption of Illegality

The general framework for analysis of technology transfer agreements falling outside the TTBER is set out in paragraphs 156–159 of the Guidelines. A basic principle set out is that there is no presumption of illegality for agreements that fall outside the TTBER provided they do not contain hardcore restrictions. In particular, there is no presumption that Article 101(1) applies just because the market share thresholds are exceeded.[145]

(iii) The Second Safe Harbour

Further, the Commission accepts in paragraph 157 of the Guidelines that a technology transfer agreement, which does not contain hardcore restraints, is unlikely to infringe Article 101 where four or more independently controlled substitutable technologies exist in addition to those controlled by the parties, the 'second safe harbour':

> In order to promote predictability beyond the application of the TTBER and to confine detailed analysis to cases that are likely to present real competition concerns, the Commission takes the view that outside the area of hardcore restrictions Article 101 of the Treaty is unlikely to be infringed where there are four or more independently controlled technologies in addition to the technologies controlled by the parties to the agreement that may be substitutable for the licensed technology at a comparable cost to the user . . .

The fact that the agreement falls outside this safe harbour does not imply that the agreement is caught by Article 101(1) and, if so, that Article 101(3) is not satisfied. It merely creates a presumption that, in the stipulated circumstances, the agreement is not prohibited.[146] The basis for determining whether the technologies are sufficiently substitutable is discussed in paragraph 157 of the Guidelines.

[139] Ibid., para. 57. [140] Ibid., para. 60.

[141] Ibid., para. 48 (but not licensing of rental rights and public performance rights protected by copyright, in particular for films or music, which raise particular issues and may require assessment on the basis of other principles, para. 49 and see Section 8).

[142] Ibid., para. 66. [143] Ibid., para. 49. [144] Ibid., para. 50. [145] Ibid., paras. 9 and 156.

[146] Ibid., para. 158.

(iv) The Approach to the Analysis of Individual Agreements

The general approach to the application of Article 101 to technology transfer agreements is described in paragraphs 10–18 of the Guidelines.

The first question to be asked is, of course, whether or not an agreement falling within the scope of Article 101 has as its object or effect the restriction of competition. The Guidelines state, in line with the approach set out in the Article 101(3) Guidelines, that in applying Article 101(1) to technology transfer agreements it is concerned both with restrictions on inter-technology competition (competition between undertakings using different technologies) and restrictions on intra-technology competition (competition between undertakings using the same technology). This underpins their reliance upon *two* different 'counterfactuals', i.e. benchmarks against which the restriction of competition is measured,[147] asking both whether the licence agreement restricts actual or potential competition that would have existed without the contemplated agreement (paragraph 12(a))[148] *and* whether it restricts actual or potential competition that would have existed in the absence of the contractual restraint(s) (paragraph 12(b)[149]). The former focuses on inter-technology competition, by asking whether the agreement restricts competition between existing technologies by, for example, sales bans in cross-licensing agreements between undertakings holding competing technologies or non-compete obligations. The latter focuses on intra-technology competition, looking at the competitive situation arising from the agreement and comparing it with less restrictive alternatives. This EU concern with intra-technology restrictions (and intra-brand competition more generally) supports a relatively interventionist approach to technology transfer agreements under Article 101.

L. Peeperkorn, 'IP Licences and Competition Rules: Striking the Right Balance' (2003) 26 *World Competition* 527, 538–539

The proposed new block exemption regulation and guidelines maintain a stricter EU approach, stricter than the United States, towards intra-technology restrictions contained in agreements between non-competitors. The reasons for this divergence with the United States are threefold:

First, territorial restrictions are paid more attention in particular because of the additional market integration objective which EC competition policy has. Secondly, it reflects the higher importance EC competition policy attaches to intra-brand and intra-technology competition in general. It is considered important to protect intra-brand and intra-technology competition as a useful and sometimes essential

[147] See L. Peeperkorn, 'IP Licences and Competition Rules: Striking the Right Balance' (2003) 26 *World Competition* 527.

[148] 'If so, the agreement may be caught by Article 101(1). In making this assessment it is necessary to take into account competition between the parties and competition from third parties. For instance, where two undertakings established in different Member States cross licence competing technologies and undertake not to sell products in each other's home markets, (potential) competition that existed prior to the agreement is restricted. Similarly, where a licensor imposes obligations on its licensees not to use competing technologies and these obligations foreclose third party technologies, actual or potential competition that would have existed in the absence of the agreement is restricted.'

[149] 'If so, the agreement may be caught by Article 101(1). For instance, where a licensor restricts its licensees, who were not actual or potential competitors before the agreement, from competing with each other, (potential) competition that could have existed between the licensees in the absence of the restraints is restricted. Such restrictions include vertical price fixing and territorial or customer sales restrictions between licensees. However, certain restraints may in certain cases not be caught by Article 101(1) when the restraint is objectively necessary for the existence of an agreement of that type or that nature. Such exclusion of the application of Article 101(1) can only be made on the basis of objective factors external to the parties themselves and not the subjective views and characteristics of the parties. The question is not whether the parties in their particular situation would not have accepted to conclude a less restrictive agreement, but whether, given the nature of the agreement and the characteristics of the market, a less restrictive agreement would not have been concluded by undertakings in a similar setting. Claims that in the absence of a restraint the supplier would have resorted to vertical integration are not sufficient. Decisions on whether or not to vertically integrate depend on a broad range of complex economic factors, a number of which are internal to the undertaking concerned.'

complement to inter-brand competition. For instance, production costs of licensees and distribution costs of distributors make up a good deal of the end price of most products and competition between licensees or distributors may help to reduce these costs. It is also recognition of the fact that restraints are almost never only affecting intra-brand competition. There is no neat distinction between intra-brand and inter-brand restrictions. Reduced intra-brand competition may facilitate collusion and restrict inter-brand competition, especially in cases of cumulative use.

Thirdly, sales restrictions may be used to prevent arbitrage and support price discrimination between different markets, what economists call third degree price discrimination. This will in general lead to a loss of consumer welfare. While some consumers will pay a higher price and others will pay a lower price, collectively consumers will have to pay more to finance the extra profits obtained by the supplier (its motive to do price discrimination) and to cover the extra costs of supporting the price discrimination scheme and prevent arbitrage. Consumer welfare will also decline because of the loss of allocative efficiency because the marginal consumer in the high price market is willing to pay more than the marginal consumer in the low price market. Therefore consumer welfare will in general decline unless it can be clearly shown that otherwise the lower priced market would not be served at all and that therefore the price discrimination will lead to an undisputable increase of output. It is only in the latter case that consumer welfare may actually increase.

The Commission is concerned that a licensing agreement will lead to negative effects from:

(a) reduction of inter-technology competition between the companies operating on a technology market or on a market for products incorporating the technologies in question, including facilitation of collusion, both explicit and tacit;
(b) foreclosure of competitors by raising their costs, restricting their access to essential inputs or otherwise raising barriers to entry; and
(c) reduction of intra-technology competition between undertakings that produce products on the basis of the same technology.[150]

Agreements that restrict competition will be excepted from the Article 101(1) prohibition if they satisfy the Article 101(3) criteria. Although the Commission recognises in the Guidelines that even restrictive licence agreements will frequently produce pro-competitive effects in the form of efficiencies,[151] the Commission's general view is that hardcore restraints are most unlikely to satisfy the conditions of Article 101(3).[152]

The Guidelines also discuss factors which are particularly relevant to the application of Article 101 in individual cases, in particular:[153] the nature of the agreement; the market position of the parties, competitors, and buyers; entry barriers; and the maturity of the market. They also provide guidance on specific provisions.

B. PROVISIONS GENERALLY NOT RESTRICTIVE OF ARTICLE 101(1)

Paragraph 183 of the Guidelines sets out a list of obligations in licence agreements which are generally not restrictive of competition within the meaning of Article 101(1). These include:

(a) confidentiality obligations;
(b) obligations on licensees not to sub-license;

[150] Guidelines, para. 169. [151] Ibid., para. 174. [152] See Chap. 5. [153] Guidelines, para. 159.

(c) obligations not to use the licensed technology rights after the expiry of the agreement, provided that the licensed technology rights remain valid and in force;

(d) obligations to assist the licensor in enforcing the licensed intellectual property rights;

(e) obligations to pay minimum royalties or to produce a minimum quantity of products incorporating the licensed technology; and

(f) obligations to use the licensor's trademark or indicate the name of the licensor on the product.

C. LICENSING RESTRICTIONS

The Guidelines provide guidance for assessment of restrictions in licensing agreements,[154] such as royalty provisions,[155] exclusive and sole licences, sales restrictions, output restrictions, field of use restrictions,[156] captive use restrictions, tying and bundling provisions, non-challenge clauses, and improvements. They thus consider not only when they might constitute hardcore or excluded restraints under the TTBER, but how they should be analysed under Article 101 more generally (what are the likely antitrust concerns raised by each restraint and how can they be weighed against likely pro-competitive justifications).

D. SETTLEMENT AGREEMENTS

The TTBER covers settlement agreements involving a transfer of technology, designed to resolve disputes concerning the validity or scope of IP, insofar as they do not contain hardcore restrictions. Such agreements are common in patent-intensive industries, such as pharmaceuticals (where they are often concluded between the manufacturer of a patented (branded) drug and a generic provider of an equivalent drug). Such agreements may be beneficial, particularly where they put an end to infringements of valid patent rights without resorting to costly litigation. Outside the safe harbour, the general approach of the Commission is explained in the Guidelines:

> 234. Licensing of technology rights in settlement agreements may serve as a means of settling disputes or avoiding that one party exercises its intellectual property rights to prevent the other party from exploiting its own technology rights.
>
> 235. Settlement agreements in the context of technology disputes are, as in many other areas of commercial disputes, in principle a legitimate way to find a mutually acceptable compromise to a bona fide legal disagreement. The parties may prefer to discontinue the dispute or litigation because it proves to be too costly, time-consuming and/or uncertain as regards its outcome. Settlements can also save courts and/or competent administrative bodies effort in deciding on the matter and can therefore

[154] Ibid., 4.2.

[155] Royalty provisions, taking the form of a lump sum payment, a percentage of the selling price, or a fixed amount for each product incorporating licensed technology, are part and parcel of a licensing agreement and frequently fall outside Art. 101(1) and/or are block exempted where the TTBER market share thresholds are satisfied.

[156] Guidelines, 4.2.4 (field of use restrictions (in contrast to customer restrictions, restricting licensees from selling to specific identified customer groups which are hardcore restraints, Art. 4(1)(c) and Art. 4(2)(b)) are generally considered to be pro-competitive as they encourage the licensor to license its technology for applications that fall outside its main area of focus. Consequently, they are covered by the TTBER. Outside its scope, field of use restrictions are most likely to be problematic where incorporated in agreements between competitors and where they result in the licensee ceasing to be a competitive force outside the licensed field of use).

give rise to welfare enhancing benefits. On the other hand, it is in the general public interest to remove invalid intellectual property rights as an unmerited barrier to innovation and economic activity.

236. Licensing, including cross licensing, in the context of settlement agreements is generally not as such restrictive of competition since it allows the parties to exploit their technologies after the agreement is concluded. In cases where, in the absence of the licence, it is possible that the licensee could be excluded from the market, access to the technology at issue for the licensee by means of a settlement agreement is generally not caught by Article 101(1).

237. However, the individual terms and conditions of settlement agreements may be caught by Article 101(1). Licensing in the context of settlement agreements is treated in the same way as other licence agreements. In these cases, it is particularly necessary to assess whether the parties are potential or actual competitors.

Although the Commission recognises the importance and benefits of settlements, it is nonetheless concerned about pay-for restriction or pay-for-delay type settlement agreements (or 'reverse payments'),[157] which generally do not involve the transfer of technology, but are based on a value transfer from the originator or brand company in return for a limitation on the entry and/or expansion in the market of a generic company.[158] Where the payments exceed, or are based on, the profits the generic company would have made from entering the market, a concern is that it will increase the price of potentially life-saving drugs during the period of delayed generic entry.[159]

In July 2009, the Commission's inquiry into the pharmaceuticals sector[160] identified a number of competition concerns in the sector and a need for stronger enforcement of the competition rules, particularly in respect of patent settlements. In both its Preliminary and Final Reports,[161] the Commission indicated that patent settlement agreements concluded between originator and generic pharmaceutical companies might be restricting the ability of generic companies to market medicines or delaying entry into the markets;[162] just under half of the patent settlement agreements concluded in the EU, between January 2007 and July 2008, involved a limitation on generic entry (categorised as Type B settlements[163]) and just under half of those involved a value transfer from the originator to the generic company (Type B-II settlements) (in the form of a direct payment, a licence, a distribution agreement, or a side deal).[164]

Since then, the Commission has monitored patent settlements,[165] so increasing awareness of antitrust issues and reducing the number of problematic settlement agreements being concluded. Further,

[157] Reverse payments because ordinarily when a patent infringement case is settled it is the alleged infringer that pays the patentee (not the other way round).

[158] Guidelines, para. 238. If they do involve a licensing of technology rights, then they would need to be assessed under the TTBER. Where the parties are actual or potential competitors, the Commission will be particularly attentive to the risk of market sharing/allocation, para. 239.

[159] See S. Gallasch, 'Activating *Activas* in Europe—the Proposal for a "Structured Effects-based" Analysis for Pay-for-delay Settlements' (2016) 36 *Legal* Studies 683 and Study of the US Federal Trade Commission, 'Pay-for-delay: how drug company pay-offs cost consumers billions' (2010).

[160] <http//:ec.europa.eu/competition/sectors/pharmaceuticals/inquiry/communication_en.pdf>. See also 'Competition Enforcement in the Pharmaceutical Sector (2009–2017)', COM(2019) 17 final.

[161] Pharmaceutical Sector Inquiry, Preliminary Report, 28 November 2008, Final Report, 8 July 2009. The Inquiry was launched under Reg. 1/2003, Art. 17, see <http://ec.europa.eu/competition/sectors/pharmaceuticals/inquiry/index.html>.

[162] See Pharmaceutical Sector Inquiry, Preliminary Report, ibid., 2.4.

[163] The Commission divided settlement agreements into three categories: Types A, B-I, and B-II. Type A settlements allow a generic to enter the market.

[164] Of 207 settlement agreements concluded in at least one Member State between January 2007 and June 2008, 99 contained limitation on generic entry and 45 of those involved a value transfer from the originator company (IP/12/210, the Commission closed the investigation into the question of whether AstraZeneca and Nycomed had engaged in individual or joint action to delay new market entry).

[165] The last report was in 2018, 8th Monitoring Report, 9 March 2018.

recognising that settlements, particularly 'B-II' types, may eliminate potential competition, operate as market sharing arrangements, and share the resulting profits between the parties, to the detriment of consumers,[166] it has conducted a number of investigations into such agreements.[167] These have led to the adoption of four infringement decisions finding the agreements to restrict competition by object and imposing fines:

- in *Lundbeck*,[168] the Commission imposed fines on both an originator, Lundbeck (of €93.8 million), and producers of generic medicines (totalling €52.2 million), for delaying the market entry of cheaper generic products of Lundbeck's blockbuster antidepressant, citalopram. Under the agreements settling litigation related to process patents (Lundbeck's compound patent over the active pharmaceutical ingredient (API) of the drug had expired), the generic producers agreed not to enter the market in return for substantial payments and other inducements from Lundbeck. The Commission's decision, finding that the agreements restricted competition by object and did not satisfy the conditions of Article 101(3), was upheld on appeal;[169]
- in *Johnson & Johnson/Novartis (Fentanyl)*,[170] the Commission fined Johnson & Johnson and Novartis for deterring, through the conclusion of a co-promotion agreement, the entry of a new generic drug by Novartis's subsidiary;
- in *Servier/Périndopril*,[171] the Commission fined Servier and five generic producers for concluding settlements agreements containing non-challenge and non-competition provisions which, it concluded, restricted competition and excluded generic products from the market for its blockbuster blood-pressure control medicine (in this case Servier's patent on perindopril had expired but it retained secondary patents relating to processes and form). In contrast to its decision in *Lundbeck*, the Commission held that the agreement restricted competition both by object and effect,[172] found that an agreement by which Servier acquired alternative technology for the production of perindopril infringed Article 101, and held that Servier's conduct abused its dominant position. Although the findings on abuse were annulled on appeal (see Chapter 7), and the fines reduced, the GC upheld the findings that all the patent settlements in this case, except for one with Krka, were restrictive of competition by object;[173] and
- in *Teva/Cephalon: modafinil*,[174] the Commission fined Teva and Cephalon €60.5 million in relation to a 'pay-for-delay' patent settlement agreement by which Cephalon offered Teva a package of commercial side-deals and cash payments to delay its entry into the market.

[166] See e.g. F. A. S. Bokhari, 'What is the Price of Pay-To-Delay Deals?' (2013) 9 *J of Competition Law and Economics* 739.

[167] See e.g. IP/11/511, MEMO/08/734, IP/12/210, and N. Kroes, 'Five years of sector and antitrust inquiries', 3 December 2009.

[168] COMP/39.226, 9 June 2013.

[169] Case T-472/13, *H Lundbeck A/S v Commission* EU:T:2016:449 (affirming the Commission's finding that the benefits of the agreement alleged did not constitute appreciable objective advantages), Case C-591/16 P, EU:C:2021:243.

[170] COMP/39.685, 10 December 2013.

[171] COMP/39.612, *Périndopril (Servier)* 9 July 2014, IP14/799.

[172] Although the Commission concluded that the agreements restricted competition by object, for the sake of completeness it also analysed their likely restrictive effects.

[173] Case T-691/14, *Servier SAS v Commission* EU:T:2018:922, Cases C-176 and 201/19 P, judgment pending.

[174] COMP/39.686, 26 November 2020, IP/20/2220. Although this completes its final ongoing pay-for-delay investigation, the Commission remains vigilant and determined to enforce competition law to ensure patients and health systems and authorities in Member States can take full advantage of an innovative pharmaceutical industry, producing affordance and accessible medicines, IP/20/2220. The Commission has also launched a 'Pharmaceutical Strategy' (to improve access to innovative and affordable medicines by EU health systems), which is closely linked to its 'Intellectual Property Action Plan' (addressing challenges created by IP protection, including in relation to pharmaceutical products).

Similar cases have also arisen at the national level. For example, in *Paroxetine*,[175] the UK's Competition and Market Authority (CMA) found that settlement arrangements concluded between GlaxoSmithKline plc (GSK), Generics (UK), and others restricted competition by object (and effect), did not meet the conditions for exemption under Article 101(3), and so infringed Article 101 (and the UK equivalent).[176] The agreements were concluded after GSK's patent for the active ingredient of its originator medicine, Seroxat (an antidepressant), had expired, but following GSK obtaining a number of secondary process patents. During the course of appeal proceedings from this decision, the UK's Competition Appeal Tribunal (CAT)[177] referred a number of questions on these matters to the CJ, see *Generics (UK) Ltd v Competition and Markets Authority (Generics)*.[178]

Controversial and contested issues in these cases have included (from an Article 101 perspective) whether, and if so when, (a) generic producers can be said to be potential competitors of an originator and (b) such agreements are sufficiently deleterious that their precise purpose, or object, can be said to restrict competition.[179] Further, if they are not restrictive of competition by object, what factors should be relevant to determine their effects on competition under Article 101(1), and when might the agreement satisfy the conditions of Article 101(3).[180]

In *Lundbeck*, the Commission considered the agreements to be problematic because: (a) the generics were (at least) potential competitors that were seeking to enter the market—they had already made significant investments in preparation to enter the citalopram market—and (b) it was the reverse payment (involving a significant transfer of value), rather than fear of infringing valid patents, that was precluding market entry and protecting Lundbeck's position in the market. The Commission thus concluded, relying on *BIDS*,[181] that the agreements operated as market exclusion arrangements (a payment not to enter the market) and restricted competition by object; there was opportunity for market entry following the expiry of the API patent, Lundbeck's process patent was weak, entry would be likely to impact on drug prices, and evidence indicated that the parties' intention was to buy a certainty of no competition (instead of an uncertain patent situation) by way of rent sharing.

COMP/39.226, *Lundbeck* Decision of 19 June 2013

(661) In order to identify whether each agreement had the potential to restrict competition by its very nature, the analysis . . . will in particular take into account whether:

- the generic undertaking and the originator undertaking were at least potential competitors;
- the generic undertaking committed itself in the agreement to limit, for the duration of the agreement, its independent efforts to enter one or more EEA markets with generic product; and
- the agreement was related to a transfer of value from the originator undertaking which substantially reduced the incentives of the generic undertaking to independently pursue its efforts to enter one or more EEA markets with generic product.

175 Case CE/9531-11, 12 February 2016.

176 Ibid. The CMA also found that GSK has abused a dominant position and imposed financial penalties (see Chap. 7).

177 Case 1251/1/12/16 [2018] CAT 4. 178 Case C-307/18, EU:C:2020:52.

179 In the US the Supreme Court ruled in *Federal Trade Commission v Actavis, Inc*, 570 US 756 (2013) that, given their potential to lead to genuine adverse effects on competition, pay-for-delay settlements or reverse payment settlement arrangements are subject to scrutiny under the antitrust laws. Such arrangements are not to be treated as per se illegal or even presumptively invalid, however. Rather, the complexity and variability of the practices require a rule of reason inquiry.

180 See e.g. Gallasch, n. 159, L. Hancher and W. Sauter, 'A Dose of Competition: EU Antitrust Law in the Pharmaceuticals Sector' (2016) 4 *J of Antitrust Enforcement* 381, S. de Margerie, '"Pay-for-delay" Settlements: In Search of the Right Standard' (2013) 36 *World Competition* 85, F. Esposito and F. Montanaro, 'A Fistful of Euros: EU Competition Policy and Reverse Payments in the Pharmaceutical Industry' (2014) 10 *European Competition Journal* 499 and W. Choi, B. Den Uyl, and M. Hughes, 'Pay-For-Delay Practices in the Pharmaceutical Sector: *Lundbeck*, *Actavis*, and Others' (2014) 5 *JECLAP* 44.

181 COMP/39.226, 9 June 2013, especially, paras. 657–658.

(662) In the present case other important factors will also be taken into consideration, namely: the fact that the value which Lundbeck transferred took into consideration the turnover or the profit the generic undertaking expected if it had successfully entered the market; the fact that Lundbeck could not have obtained the limitations on entry through enforcement of its process patents, the obligations on the generic undertaking in the agreement going beyond the rights granted to holders of process patents; and the fact that the agreement contained no commitment from Lundbeck to refrain from infringement proceedings if the generic undertaking entered the market with generic citalopram after expiry of the agreement.

(663) In this case the Commission also analysed the parties' arguments on the existence of justifications for the agreements under Article 101(3) of the Treaty and found that the conditions of this provision were not met.

(664) The Commission has concluded that the agreements, containing transfers of value from Lundbeck which induced the generic undertakings in question not to pursue their independent efforts to enter the market, constituted infringements of Article 101 of the Treaty.

In *Servier*, the Commission reiterated the importance of the criteria identified in paragraphs 661 and 662 of its *Lundbeck* decision, in the determination of whether the content, objective, and legal and economic context of the patent settlement agreements concluded between Servier and the generic companies justified a conclusion that they restricted competition by object. In so doing, it rejected the parties' claims that the Commission's legal test was flawed, and that a presumption of legality should be applied to patent settlement agreements remaining within the scope of the patent even if accompanied by a value transfer, where: (a) the patent-in-suit has not been obtained by fraud; (b) the settled litigation was not fictitious or vexatious; and (c) settlement terms do not go beyond the exclusionary scope of the patents.

The complexity involved in assessing these identified criteria and conducting the required contextual analysis in these settlement cases has, however, led some to argue that neither economics nor experience justify a finding of a restrictive object in such cases rather than an intention to settle a genuine patent dispute.[182] Instead, because generics are only potential competitors with a *possibility* of entering a market and because any theory of harm is contingent on several assumptions—that entry would have been attempted and have succeeded in bringing down the market price—object classification may be considered to be inappropriate and might deter firms from concluding legitimate pro-competitive patent settlements, there being circumstances where pay-for-delay settlements may be the only viable form of settlement. This view has not been supported by the EU Courts, however, which have made it clear that although patent settlement agreements cannot be considered to restrict competition by object in all cases, they may do so in certain circumstances. Indeed, in both the *Lundbeck* and *Servier* appeals, the Commission's decisions finding certain patent settlement agreements to restrict competition by object were upheld. Together with the CJ's judgment in *Generics*, these judgments shed important light on the questions of: (a) how to determine whether originators and generics are potential competitors; (b) when patent settlement agreements may restrict competition by object; and, if not, (c) how restrictive effects are to be identified.

A vital, initial matter to be considered in assessing the competitive impact of a patent settlement is whether it constitutes a horizontal agreement—i.e. an agreement between competitors. In *Generics*,[183]

[182] See e.g. the US Supreme Court's Opinion in *Federal Trade Commission v Activas*, 570 US 136 (2013) and Choi, Den Uyl, and Hughes, n. 180.

[183] Case C-307/18, *Generics* EU:C:2020:52.

the Court held that a generic producer that is not present in a market may be a potential competitor of an originator in that market where there are real and concrete possibilities of the former entering the market sufficiently quickly and competing with the latter.[184] Further, that although hypothetical possibility of entry is not sufficient to demonstrate potential competition, entry (and successful entry) does not have to be demonstrated with certainty.[185] The existence of a process patent does not therefore mean that the parties cannot be potential competitors. On the contrary, because uncertainty as to the validity of patents covering medicines is a fundamental characteristic of the pharmaceutical sector, a genuine dispute between the parties about the validity of an originator's process patents (for an active ingredient that is in the public domain) and/or whether those patents have been infringed, may constitute evidence of the existence of a potential competitive relationship between the parties.[186] This is likely to be the case where the manufacturer of generic medicines has taken steps to enter the market,[187] has a firm intention and an inherent ability to enter the market, and if unsurmountable barriers to entry do not exist.[188] More generally, the Court noted that the conclusion of a market sharing agreement between undertakings operating at the same level in the production chain, but where some had no presence in the market concerned, constitutes a strong indication that a competitive relationship exists between those undertakings.[189]

Even if concluded between potential competitors, the CJ in *Generics* held that it must still be determined whether the agreement to restrain the generic's entry into the market is restrictive of competition by object. This may be the case, for example, if the dispute is entirely fictitious and the agreement is designed with the sole aim of disguising a market-sharing or market-exclusion agreement between the parties.[190] Where the dispute is genuine, however, and even where it involves a value transfer to the generic,[191] it must be determined whether the aim of the agreement is to share markets or whether it has 'any explanation other than the commercial interest of both the holder of the patent and the party allegedly infringing the patent not to engage in competition on the merits'.[192] In making such an assessment, relevant factors include the value of any transfer made under the agreement (pecuniary and non-pecuniary) and whether it is sufficiently significant[193] to encourage or incentivise the generic manufacturer to refrain from entering the market.[194] When it is sufficiently significant and not made in return for other goods or services, the agreement concerned must, in the absence of any other plausible justification,[195] be characterised as a 'restriction by object'.[196] Such a conclusion cannot be rebutted on the ground that the settlement agreement does not exceed the scope and the remaining period of validity of the patent nor on the ground that there is a genuine dispute about the ability of the patents to prevent market entry.[197] However, if pro-competitive effects are demonstrated, relevant, specifically related to the agreement concerned, and sufficiently significant, they will 'justify a reasonable doubt as to whether the settlement agreement concerned caused a sufficient degree of harm to competition, and, therefore, as to its anticompetitive object'.[198]

[184] Ibid., para. 36. See also Case C-591/16 P, *Lundbeck* EU:C:2021:243, para. 54. [185] Ibid., para. 38.

[186] Even where an interim injunction had been granted prohibiting a generic manufacturer's entry into the market (as the matter has not yet been decided).

[187] E.g. taking steps to obtain market authorisation, to ensure adequate stocks, and to challenge the process patents.

[188] Case C-307/18, *Generics* EU:C:2020:52, paras. 35–58 (the mere existence of a process patent cannot be regarded as an insurmountable barrier).

[189] Ibid., para. 55, relying on Case C-373/14 P, *Toshiba Corp v Commission* EU:C:2016:26, paras. 33–34.

[190] Ibid., para. 76. [191] Ibid., paras. 84–85. [192] Ibid., para. 87.

[193] And e.g. beyond sums to compensate the generic manufacturer for the costs of or disruption caused by the litigation, ibid., para. 86.

[194] Ibid., paras. 84–93. [195] Ibid., para. 89. [196] Ibid., para. 95. [197] Ibid., paras. 96–98.

[198] Ibid., para. 107. The Court considered that the factual situation raised by the referring court made it clear that the settlement agreements at issue gave rise to pro-competitive effects that were only minimal and uncertain.

These points were echoed by the CJ in *Lundbeck* when rejecting the complaint that the GC had erred in law in upholding the Commission's conclusion that the agreements had the object of restricting competition, in particular on the grounds that the agreements, when viewed in their economic and legal context, were not by their very nature harmful to competition, and were not comparable to market sharing agreements.

Case C-591/16 P, *H Lundbeck A/S v Commission* EU:C:2021:243

Court of Justice

110. As a preliminary point, it should be noted that Lundbeck's criticisms are of two kinds: the first, second and fourth parts of the first ground challenge the characterisation of the agreements at issue as 'restrictions by object', and the third part of that ground challenges the methodology used to arrive at that conclusion and, specifically, the failure of the General Court to examine the 'counterfactual scenario'.

. . .

112. As regards, in the first place, the first, second and fourth parts of the first ground, the Court of Justice has previously held, as the General Court pointed out in paragraph 343 of the judgment under appeal, that the concept of restriction of competition 'by object' must be interpreted strictly and can be applied only to some agreements between undertakings which reveal, in themselves and having regard to the content of their provisions, their objectives, and the economic and legal context of which they form part, a sufficient degree of harm to competition for the view to be taken that it is not necessary to assess their effects, since some forms of coordination between undertakings can be regarded, by their very nature, as being harmful to the proper functioning of normal competition (. . . *Generics (UK)* . . . paragraph 67 and the case-law cited).

113. With regard to similar settlement agreements that cover disputes over a process patent for the manufacture of an active ingredient that is in the public domain which have been concluded between a manufacturer of originator medicines and several manufacturers of generic medicines and have the effect of delaying the market entry of generic medicines in exchange for monetary or non-monetary transfers of value from the former to the latter, the Court of Justice has held that such agreements cannot be considered to be 'restrictions by object' in all cases for the purpose of Article 101(1) TFEU (. . . *Generics (UK)* . . . paragraphs 84 and 85).

114. However, such characterisation as a 'restriction by object' must be adopted when it is plain from the examination of the settlement agreement concerned that the transfers of value provided for by it cannot have any explanation other than the commercial interest of both the holder of the patent at issue and the party allegedly infringing the patent not to engage in competition on the merits, since agreements whereby competitors deliberately substitute practical cooperation between them for the risks of competition can clearly be characterised as 'restrictions by object' (see, to that effect, . . . *Generics (UK)* . . . paragraphs 83 and 87).

115. For the purpose of that examination, it is appropriate to assess on a case-by-case basis whether the net gain of the transfers of value from the manufacturer of originator medicines to the manufacturer of generic medicines was sufficiently significant actually to act as an incentive to the manufacturer of generic medicines to refrain from entering the market concerned and, consequently, not to compete on the merits with the manufacturer of originator medicines; however, there is no requirement that the net gain should necessarily be greater than the profits which that manufacturer of generic medicines would have made if it had been successful in the patent proceedings (see, to that effect, . . . *Generics (UK)* . . . paragraphs 93 and 94).

116. In the present case, it is apparent from the judgment under appeal that the effects of the agreements at issue were to keep the manufacturers of generic medicines outside the markets

concerned and to lead one of them—namely Merck (GUK)—to stop supplying a reseller operating on the Swedish market with the generic medicines concerned and to exit the UK market, as is apparent from paragraph 131 of the judgment under appeal.

117. In addition, paragraphs 361 to 363 and paragraph 366 of the judgment under appeal, which are not contested by Lundbeck in the context of its appeal, highlight, first, the fact that the parties to the agreements at issue were, prior to the conclusion of those agreements, in dispute over whether Lundbeck's new process patents were sufficiently strong to prevent the market entry of generic citalopram which means that those patents could not have constituted the decisive basis of the commitment by the manufacturers of generic medicines not to enter the market. Second, it is also apparent from those paragraphs that Lundbeck does not dispute that the amounts which it paid to those manufacturers could have been calculated by taking into consideration the profit or turnover which the latter expected to make during the term of the agreements at issue if they had entered the market. Third, those paragraphs also indicate that the evidence relating to the period preceding the conclusion of the agreements at issue shows that the manufacturers of generic medicines had made considerable efforts to prepare for their market entry and that they did not intend to desist from those efforts on account of Lundbeck's new process patents and, consequently, that it is principally the size of the reverse payments to the manufacturers of generic medicines which had induced them to accept the limitations governing their behaviour.

118. In the light of those findings of fact, and there being no need to determine whether the General Court was entitled to treat the agreements at issue, in paragraphs 435 and 476 of the judgment under appeal, as market exclusion agreements or even as market-sharing agreements, it concluded, without committing any error of law, that the agreements at issue should be characterised as 'restrictions by object' for the purpose of Article 101(1) TFEU, especially since Lundbeck has not in any way argued, in particular in its reply to the question to be answered in writing of 6 February 2020, that the transfers of value which are associated with the agreements at issue could be justified by the existence of possible consideration or proven and legitimate commitments by one or other of the manufacturers of generic medicines to refrain from taking action.

119. That conclusion cannot be called into question by the arguments put forward by Lundbeck.

120. First, in order to establish that the agreements at issue should not be characterised as 'restrictions by object', Lundbeck cannot validly rely on the fact that those agreements were limited to the scope of Lundbeck's new process patents, compliance with which that party is entitled to obtain.

121. While the conclusion by the holder of a patent with a party allegedly infringing that patent of a settlement agreement that does not exceed the scope and duration of remaining validity of that patent does constitute an expression of the intellectual property right of that holder, which permits that holder, inter alia, to oppose any infringement, the fact remains that that patent does not permit its holder to enter into contracts that are contrary to Article 101 TFEU (. . . *Generics (UK)* . . . paragraph 97).

122. As the General Court rightly found in paragraph 495 of the judgment under appeal, even if the agreements at issue also contained restrictions potentially falling within the scope of Lundbeck's new process patents, 'those agreements went beyond the specific subject matter of their intellectual property rights, which indeed included the right to oppose infringements, but not the right to conclude agreements by which actual or potential competitors were paid not to enter the market', which is confirmed, in essence, by paragraphs 117 and 118 of the present judgment.

123. Consequently, there is no basis for Lundbeck's attempt to rely on the fact that the agreements at issue are a legitimate expression of its intellectual property rights. In any event, such an allegation is based on the twofold assumption—which was not established at the time the agreements were concluded—that the validity of Lundbeck's new process patents cannot be called into question and that the manufacturers of generic medicines are infringing them (see, to that effect, . . . *Generics (UK)* . . . paragraph 88).

124. Second, nor can Lundbeck argue, in order to establish that the agreements at issue should not be characterised as 'restrictions by object', that those agreements pursued legitimate objectives since

their purpose was to protect Lundbeck's new process patents by recourse to a legitimate and commonplace means of dispute resolution, or that they were responding to an asymmetry of risk between manufacturers of originator medicines and manufacturers of generic medicines.

125. As regards, in the first place, the argument that the purpose of those agreements was to protect Lundbeck's new process patents by recourse to a legitimate and commonplace means of dispute resolution, it is sufficient to note that, as was stated previously in paragraph 121 of the present judgment and was correctly pointed out, in essence, by the General Court in paragraph 495 of the judgment under appeal, a patent does not permit its holder to enter into contracts that are contrary to Article 101 TFEU.

126. As regards, in the second place, the argument that the agreements at issue reflect the fact, referred to by the General Court in paragraph 378 of the judgment under appeal, that the damages to which manufacturers of originator medicines may be entitled in the event of the unlawful entry of generic medicines on the market are often substantially lower than the damage suffered by the former, it should be recalled that it is for public authorities and not private undertakings to ensure compliance with statutory requirements (judgment of 30 January 2020, *Generics (UK) and Others*, C-307/18, EU:C:2020:52, paragraph 88).

127. Thus, as the General Court rightly pointed out in paragraph 387 of the judgment under appeal, it is unacceptable for undertakings to attempt to mitigate the effects of legal rules which they consider excessively unfavourable by entering into restrictive arrangements intended to offset those disadvantages on the pretext that those rules have created an imbalance detrimental to them.

128. Consequently, the circumstances referred to by Lundbeck cannot legitimise an infringement of Article 101 TFEU, let alone a concerted practice which has been found to be sufficiently harmful to competition to be characterised as a 'restriction by object'.

129. Third, nor can Lundbeck argue, in order to establish that the agreements at issue should not be characterised as 'restrictions by object', that, at the time when the agreements at issue were concluded, there were doubts as to whether agreements such as the agreements at issue could be characterised as such, in particular in view of the lack of decision-making practice in relation to those agreements and the doubts arising, according to Lundbeck, from certain statements made by the Danish Competition Authority and the Commission.

130. As the General Court rightly pointed out in paragraphs 438 and 774 of the judgment under appeal, it is in no way necessary that the same type of agreement has already been censured by the Commission in order for such agreements to be considered to be restrictive of competition by object, and that remains the case even if they occur in a specific context, such as that of intellectual property rights.

131. In order for a given agreement to be characterised as a 'restriction by object', all that matters are the specific characteristics of that agreement (see, to that effect, judgment of 30 January 2020, *Generics (UK) and Others*, C-307/18, EU:C:2020:52, paragraphs 84 and 85) from which any particular harmfulness of that agreement for competition can be inferred, where necessary as a result of a detailed analysis of that agreement, its objectives and the economic and legal context of which it forms part.

132. Similarly, the adoption of contradictory positions—some of which are merely noted in reports—by the Commission and a national competition authority in respect of an agreement, such as those referred to in paragraphs 747 to 751 of the judgment under appeal, assuming that they are correct, cannot lead to the conclusion that that agreement cannot be characterised as a 'restriction by object' since it is in no way established that those positions are the result of an analysis such as that referred to in the previous paragraph.

133. Fourth, and finally, nor can Lundbeck rely, in order to establish that the agreements at issue should not be characterised as 'restrictions by object', on the fact that the agreements at issue did not contain any no-challenge clauses, unlike the agreements at issue in the case which gave rise to the judgment of 30 January 2020, *Generics (UK) and Others* (C-307/18, EU:C:2020:52), or the fact that

that judgment stressed the importance of taking into account the pro-competitive effects of the agreements at issue when deciding whether to characterise them as 'restrictions by object'.

134. In that regard, it was pointed out previously in paragraph 114 of the present judgment that, in the case of agreements such as the agreements at issue, it is necessary to determine whether, by those agreements, competitors deliberately substitute practical cooperation between them for the risks of competition, by assessing, in essence, whether the net gain of the transfers of value for which they provide can be explained only by the commercial interest of both the holder of the patent and the party allegedly infringing the patent not to engage in competition on the merits.

135. In paragraph 399 of the judgment under appeal, the General Court definitively found, first, that, even though the agreements at issue did not contain any no-challenge clause, the manufacturers of generic medicines had no incentive to challenge Lundbeck's new process patents after concluding the agreements at issue, since the reverse payments broadly correspond to the profits that those manufacturers expected to make if they had entered the market or to the damages which could have been paid to them if they had succeeded in litigation against Lundbeck, and, second, that even if those payments were of an amount less than the expected profits, they nevertheless constituted a certain and immediate profit, without those manufacturers having to take the risks that market entry would have entailed.

136. In the present case, such a finding is sufficient to establish that the agreements at issue are restrictive of competition by object, especially given that, in any event, Lundbeck does not in the appeal make mention of any pro-competitive effect associated with those agreements, and therefore does not satisfy the standard of proof required by the judgment of . . . *Generics (UK* . . . in particular in paragraph 107 of that judgment, in order to rebut characterisation of those agreements as 'restrictions by object' on the basis of reasonable doubts as to whether they caused a sufficient degree of harm to competition.

137. A mere unsubstantiated assertion concerning the pro-competitive effects of the agreements at issue is insufficient to rebut their characterisation as 'restrictions by object' (see, to that effect, . . . *Generics (UK)* . . . paragraph 110).

138. Although, in its action for annulment and, specifically, in the seventh plea in law relied on in support of that action, Lundbeck did indeed submit that the Commission made a manifest error of assessment by incorrectly assessing the efficiency gains of the agreements at issue in the context of the application of Article 101(3) TFEU, the fact remains that paragraphs 708 to 720 of the judgment under appeal, by which the General Court rejected that plea, have not been challenged in the present appeal, and that no reference has been made to the reasoning set out in those paragraphs in an effort to call into question the characterisation of those agreements as 'restrictions by object', particularly in the context of Lundbeck's reply to the question to be answered in writing of 6 February 2020.

139. In the second place, as regards the third part of the first ground of appeal directed against paragraphs 472 and 473 of the judgment under appeal, by which the General Court held, in essence, that it was not necessary to examine the 'counterfactual scenario' in order to characterise conduct as a 'restriction by object', it should be noted that that examination allows the effects of a concerted practice with regard to Article 101 TFEU to be assessed when the analysis of that practice does not reveal a sufficient degree of harm to competition to enable it to be characterised as a 'restriction by object' (. . . *Generics (UK)* . . . paragraphs 115 and 118 and the case-law cited).

140. Consequently, unless the clear distinction between the concept of 'restriction by object' and the concept of 'restriction by effect' arising from the wording itself of Article 101(1) TFEU (. . . *Generics (UK)* . . . paragraph 63) is to be held not to exist, an examination of the 'counterfactual scenario', the purpose of which is to make apparent the effects of a given concerted practice, cannot be required in order to characterise a concerted practice as a 'restriction by object'.

141. Therefore, and as the General Court rightly held in paragraph 472 of the judgment under appeal, in order to characterise such a practice as a 'restriction by object' it was only necessary to establish that that practice revealed a sufficient degree of harm to competition, in view of the content of the

> provisions involved in that practice, the objectives that that practice is intended to achieve and the economic and legal context of which it formed part; the Commission was not required, however, to examine the effects thereof.
>
> 142. Furthermore, contrary to what Lundbeck argued in its reply to the question to be answered in writing of 6 February 2020, the examination of the 'counterfactual scenario' is not required by paragraph 37 of the judgment . . . *Generics (UK)* . . .
>
> 143. Although, in that paragraph, the Court of Justice did indeed specify that, when the agreement at issue is one which has the effect of temporarily keeping an undertaking outside a market, it must be determined whether there would have existed, in the absence of that agreement, real and concrete possibilities for that undertaking to enter that market, it should be noted that that specific clarification concerned the assessment of the existence of a potential competitive relationship between the parties to an agreement such as those at issue in the case which gave rise to that judgment and not the characterisation of those agreements as a 'restriction by object'.

The judgments in this sphere thus stress the importance of 'context' in determining whether patent settlement agreements restrict competition by object. Even a patent settlement agreement involving reverse payments may not restrict competition by object where a restrictive purpose is not revealed and where another credible explanation for the agreement exists (other than the commercial interests of the parties not to compete).

Where the settlement agreement is not found to restrict competition by object, an analysis of its effects will be required to be determine if, assessed against a counterfactual situation in the absence of the agreement, competition was in fact prevented or restricted to an appreciable extent. In *Servier*, the GC did not uphold the Commission's finding that a patent settlement agreement made between Servier and Krka had the effect of restricting competition, because the counterfactual had not been adequately assessed.[199] In *Generics*, the CJ clarified that the purpose of the counterfactual is to establish the realistic possibilities with respect the generic manufacturer's conduct in the absence of the agreement at issue (taking account of the patent dispute).

> Accordingly, while that counterfactual cannot be unaffected by the chance of success of the manufacturer of generic medicines in the patent proceedings or again in relation to the probability of conclusion of a less restrictive agreement, those factors constitute, however only some factors among many to be taken into consideration in order to determine how the market will probably operate and be structure if the agreement concerned is not concluded. Consequently, in order to establish the existence of appreciable potential or real effects on competition of settlement agreements . . ., the referring court does not have to find either that the manufacturer of generic medicines who is a party to that agreement would probably have been successful in the patent proceedings, or that the parties to that agreement would probably have concluded a less restrictive settlement agreement.[200]

The Guidelines also contain guidance on settlement agreements whereby the parties cross-license each other and impose restrictions on the use of their technologies[201] and non-challenge clauses. Although cross-licensing provisions, which go beyond what is required to unblock blocking provisions may infringe Article 101(1), non-challenge clauses will frequently fall outside Article 101(1) since the whole point of the agreement is to settle disputes and avoid future ones.[202]

[199] Case T-684/14, *Krka v Commission* EU:T:2018:918.

[200] Case C-307/18, *Generics* EU:C:2020:52, paras. 120–121.

[201] Guidelines, paras. 240–241.

[202] Ibid., para. 242.

E. AGREEMENT BETWEEN A LICENSOR AND LICENSEE CONCERNING THE DISSEMINATION OF INFORMATION RELATING TO MARKETED PHARMACEUTICAL PRODUCTS

In *Hoffmann-La Roche and Novartis v Autorità Garante della Concorrenza e del Mercato (AGCM)*,[203] the CJ had to provide guidance to the Consiglio di Stato (Council of State, Italy) as to how to assess the compatibility with Article 101 of an agreement, or collusion, between a licensor and licensee designed to differentiate artificially between their two medicines—a cancer medicine (marketed by Roche) and an eye medicine (marketed by Novartis under licence from Roche).

The background to the case was that some doctors had been using the cheaper cancer medicine to treat eye conditions, even though the marketing authorisation for the cancer medicine did not specifically provide for such use ('off-label use'). The Italian competition authority (the AGCM) found that Roche and Novartis had, based on an alarmist interpretation of available data and exaggerating the perception of risks, communicated to authorities, doctors, and the public that the cancer medicine when used off-label was less safe than the eye medicine, and that this conduct, designed to reduce the competitive pressure on the eye medicine being caused by the cancer medicine, had as its object the restriction of competition.[204] On appeal from this decision, the Italian court referred several questions to the CJ.

In its judgment, the CJ affirmed that two medicines could compete with each other if used for the same therapeutic purpose (even if such use was not mentioned in the marketing authorisation), that the parties' conduct in this case could not be considered to be ancillary to the implementation of the licensing agreement, and that joint conduct communicating the risks associated with a product, pursued with the aim of reducing competitive pressure from the product in question, has as its object the restriction of competition. The Court stressed the strict interpretation given to the concept of a restriction of competition by object but stated that in the pharmaceuticals sector the impact of EU rules on pharmaceutical products was crucial in assessing the context of the agreement and identifying its purpose. It thus noted that responsibility for pharmacovigilance, including communication about the risks associated with a product, was the sole responsibility of the holder of the marketing authorisation and not that of another undertaking marketing a competing medicinal product. 'Accordingly, the fact that two undertakings collude with each other with a view to disseminating information specifically relating to the product marketed by only one of them might constitute evidence that the dissemination of information pursues objectives unrelated to pharmacovigilance.'[205]

The CJ also confirmed that the agreement could not benefit from the TTBER or Article 101(3) as the dissemination of misleading information in respect of a medicinal product could not be regarded as indispensable to the agreement.

F. TECHNOLOGY POOLS

The final part of the Guidelines deal at some length with agreements setting up technology pools,[206] 'arrangements whereby two or more parties assemble a package of technology which is licensed not only to contributors to the pool but also to third parties . . . the pool may allow licensees to operate on the market on the basis of a single licence'.[207] Technology pools are not covered by the TTBER (because the agreement establishing the pool does not allow the licensee to produce contract products) although

203 Case C-179/16, EU:C:2018:25. 204 Decision of 27 February 2014. It also imposed fines of €182.6 million.
205 Case C-179/16, EU:C:2018:25, para. 91. 206 Guidelines, 4.4.
207 Technology pools can be simple arrangements but may also be very elaborate, with the pooled technology entrusted to a separate entity, ibid., para. 244.

the TTBER may cover a licence granted by a technology pool to a third party when not a multi-party agreement.[208]

Technology pools often, but do not necessarily, support a *de jure* or *de facto* industry standard and may be pro-competitive; facilitating dissemination of technology through one-stop licensing of pooled technologies and reducing transaction costs and limiting cumulative royalties.[209] They can create competition concerns, however, for example where they involve licensing of substitute technologies (creating a risk of price-fixing or market-sharing) or when they support or establish an industry standard and result in a reduction of innovation by foreclosing alternative, competing technologies.[210]

The competitive risks have to be balanced against their efficiency-enhancing potential taking account of: the nature of the pooled technologies, and whether they are (a) complementary[211] or substitutes[212] and (b) essential[213] or non-essential;[214] and the institutional framework of the pool.[215] The Commission states:

> The way in which a technology pool is formed, organised and operated can reduce the risk of it having the object or effect of restricting competition and provide assurances to the effect that the arrangement is pro-competitive. In assessing the possible competitive risks and efficiencies, the Commission will, inter alia, take account of the transparency of the pool creation process; the selection and nature of the pooled technologies, including the extent to which independent experts are involved in the creation and operation of the pool and whether safeguards against exchange of sensitive information and independent dispute resolution mechanisms have been put in place.[216]

Further detail of how this assessment is to be conducted is explained in paragraphs 249–265 of the Guidelines. The Commission's 2014 Guidelines provide more extensive discussion of this than their predecessors. In addition, with the objective of encouraging the conclusion of pro-competitive pools, they provide a safe harbour for the creation of certain technology pools and subsequent licensing out by them.[217]

> The creation and operation of the pool, including the licensing out, generally falls outside Article 101(1) of the Treaty, irrespective of the market position of the parties, if all the following conditions are fulfilled:
>
> (a) participation in the pool creation process is open to all interested technology rights owners;
>
> (b) sufficient safeguards are adopted to ensure that only essential technologies (which therefore necessarily are also complements) are pooled;

[208] Ibid., para. 247. [209] Ibid., para. 245.

[210] Ibid., para. 246. See also e.g. IP/06/139 (the Commission announced that it had closed an investigation into the practices of Philips Electronics which had offered European manufacturers of CD-recordable discs a joint portfolio licence which included both its own CD-recordable disc patents and those of Sony and Taiyo Yuden. The Commission closed the investigation once Philips undertook to discontinue the joint patent portfolio licence in Europe and to offer revised individual licences limited to its own patents).

[211] Both technologies are required to produce the product or carry out the process in question (see Guidelines, para. 250).

[212] Either technology allows the holder to produce the product or carry out the process.

[213] There are no substitutes for the technology inside or outside the pool and the technology in question constitutes a necessary part of the package of technologies for the purposes of producing the product(s) or carrying out the process(es) to which the pool relates. The Guidelines provided greater clarity on this issue.

[214] Guidelines, paras. 252. Broadly, the creation of a pool composed of only essential complementary technologies is likely to fall outside Art. 101(1). In contrast, a pool of substitute technologies will constitute a price-fixing arrangement which violates Art. 101(1) and is unlikely to satisfy the conditions of Art. 101(3). A pool comprising non-essential substitute technologies may foreclose third party competing technologies, Guidelines, para. 255.

[215] Factors such as whether participation in the pool is open, whether experts are involved, how information exchange is dealt with, and how disputes should be resolved are relevant, Guidelines, paras. 256–260.

[216] Ibid., para. 248.

[217] Ibid., para. 261. Although they could be a helpful mechanism for dealing with licensing of SEPs, patent pools have not been used widely in the SEP context, see further Chap. 7.

(c) sufficient safeguards are adopted to ensure that exchange of sensitive information (such as pricing and output data) is restricted to what is necessary for the creation and operation of the pool;
(d) the pooled technologies are licensed into the pool on a non-exclusive basis;
(e) the pooled technologies are licensed out to all potential licensees on FRAND terms;
(f) the parties contributing technology to the pool and the licensees are free to challenge the validity and the essentiality of the pooled technologies, and;
(g) the parties contributing technology to the pool and the licensee remain free to develop competing products and technology.

Individual assessment will be required where the safe harbour does not apply. The Commission states that it applies four guiding principles when assessing individual restraints in licensing from the pool:[218]

In making its assessment of technology transfer agreements between the pool and its licensees the Commission will be guided by the following main principles:

(a) the stronger the market position of the pool the greater the risk of anti-competitive effects;
(b) the stronger the market position of the pool, the more likely that agreeing not to license to all potential licensees or to license on discriminatory terms will infringe Article 101;
(c) pools should not unduly foreclose third party technologies or limit the creation of alternative pools;
(d) the technology transfer agreements should not contain any of the hardcore restrictions listed in Article 4 of the TTBER (see section 3.4).

Where a technology pool compatible with Article 101 is created, provisions inherent in the establishment of the standard or pool, such as royalty provisions, also fall outside Article 101.[219] Where, however, the pool has a dominant position, closer scrutiny of the licensing provisions will be necessary and the Guidelines state, for example, that 'royalties and other licensing terms should be non-excessive and non-discriminatory and licences should be non-exclusive. These requirements are necessary to ensure that the pool is open and does not lead to foreclosure and other anti-competitive effects on down-stream markets.'[220] The Guidelines also seek to ensure that new technology is not foreclosed, for example by stating that restrictions on parties developing competing products or standards or on granting and obtaining licences outside the pool should not be incorporated.[221] They also provide that: grant back obligations should be non-exclusive and limited to essential or important developments; and pools should not be able to shield invalid patents through non-challenge and termination clauses between the pool and third parties.[222]

The Horizontal Cooperation Guidelines[223] contain separate guidance on the question of whether the agreement to establish an industry standard is compatible with Article 101—i.e. on standardisation agreements (agreements which 'have as their primary objective the definition of technical or quality requirements' for 'current or future products, production processes, value change due diligence processes, services or methods'[224]) and on the licensing of IPRs essential for technology used to implement a standard on fair, reasonable, and non-discriminatory (FRAND) terms, see Chapter 10.

[218] Ibid., para. 267 [219] Ibid., para. 268. [220] Ibid., para. 269. [221] Ibid., para. 270.
[222] Ibid., paras. 271–272. [223] Horizontal Cooperation Guidelines 17 July 2023.
[224] Ibid., para. 436.

6. TRADEMARK LICENCES

A. GENERAL

There is no block exemption which specifically covers trademark licences. In the discussion of the TTBER in Sections 4 and 5, however, it is seen that where the licence of a trademark is ancillary to a licence of patents, know-how, designs, or software the TTBER may apply. Further, where a trademark licence is directly related to the use, sale, or resale of goods or services (and does not constitute the primary object of the agreement) it may be ancillary to a vertical agreement, such as a franchising agreement and benefit from the VBER.[225] In other situations, the principles developed in these Guidelines do *not* apply by analogy[226] and guidance will need to be sought from relevant jurisprudence. The paucity (and age) of the cases that exist, however, mean that it is not easy to determine the principles that apply.

In *Consten and Grundig*,[227] it was held that an agreement seeking to confer ATP on the licensee of a trademark would infringe Article 101(1). Further, in the Commission's two formal decisions relating to trademark licences, *Campari*[228] and *Moosehead/Whitbread*,[229] it took a strict approach to exclusivity provisions and applied broadly the same principles to trademark licences as it did at the time in its decisions to patent and know-how licences. As the Commission's thinking has evolved considerably since this time, the reasoning in these cases, which support a formalistic approach to restraints on economic freedom, should be treated with some caution.

B. THE *CAMPARI* AND *MOOSEHEAD/WHITBREAD* DECISIONS

The *Campari* transaction[230] is difficult to classify but the trademark licence was a predominant element. The aperitifs Bitter Campari and Cordial Campari were made by mixing alcohol with a secret herbal concentrate. Campari-Milano set up a network of licensees to manufacture and sell its products in all EU countries except the UK and Ireland.[231] Under the agreements the licensees purchased the secret concentrate and colouring matter from the licensor and manufactured the drink in compliance with the licensor's instructions. The resulting bottles of aperitif were then sold under the licensor's Campari trademark. The licences were exclusive, prevented the licensees from manufacturing or handling competing products or pursuing an active sales policy outside their territory, banned exports outside the common market, and provided that only the original Italian product could be supplied to certain customers/outlets. There were also provisions about manufacture only at approved sites, confidentiality, advertising, and non-assignment. The Commission held that the following provisions were outside Article 101(1): the ban on exports outside the common market, as in the circumstances there was little chance of this indirectly affecting inter-Member State trade; the restriction of the licence to those plants capable of guaranteeing the quality of the product; the obligation to follow the licensor's manufacturing instructions and to buy secret raw materials from the licensor, as this was central to the product being of proper 'Campari' quality;[232] the confidentiality of

[225] Guidelines, para. 50 and Chap. 11. [226] Ibid., para. 50.

[227] Cases 56 and 58/64, EU:C:1966:41.

[228] COMP/171, 856, 172, 117, and 28.173, *Re the Agreement of Davide-Campari-Milano SpA* [1978] OJ L70/69.

[229] COMP/32.736, [1990] OJ L100/32.

[230] COMP/171, 856, 172, 117, and 28.173, *Re the Agreement of Davide-Campari-Milano SpA* [1978] OJ L70/69.

[231] The UK and Ireland were covered by a straightforward distribution agreement which fell within the block exemption then in force, Reg. 67/67 [1967] OJ Spec. Ed. 10.

[232] Certain other ingredients did not necessarily have to be bought from the licensor but had to be sourced on the basis of objective quality considerations.

the know-how; the minimum advertising commitments; and the prohibition on assignment. Other clauses, including the exclusivity and the active sales ban, were held to infringe Article 101(1). The Commission granted an exemption, however. The decision provides a good illustration of how the four criteria in Article 101(3) were applied.

Moosehead/Whitbread concerned a licence granted by the Canadian brewer Moosehead[233] to the British brewer Whitbread for the sole and exclusive right to produce and promote, market, and sell beer under the name 'Moosehead' in the UK using Moosehead's secret know-how. Moosehead gave Whitbread an exclusive licence of its UK trademark rights and agreed to provide it with all the relevant know-how (the know-how licence was non-exclusive) and to supply it with the necessary yeast. Whitbread agreed not to make active sales outside its territory, not to produce or promote any other beer identified as a Canadian beer, not to contest the ownership or validity of the trademark, to comply with Moosehead's directions in relation to the know-how, and to buy the yeast only from Moosehead or a designated third party.

The Commission held that the exclusivity provisions and the active sales ban in the trademark licence were caught by Article 101(1). It did not consider the non-challenge clause to the *ownership* of the mark was caught because no matter whose name it was registered in, other parties would be prevented from using it. A non-challenge clause in respect of validity, however, was another matter. The Commission held that whether such clauses may infringe Article 101(1) would depend on the circumstances, but in this case it did not. The Commission granted an exemption to the agreement, holding that the exclusivity provisions, active sales ban, and non-competition clauses met the Article 101(3) criteria, particularly in view of the amount of inter-brand competition on the UK beer market.

C. THE CURRENT POSITION

Although the Commission's decisions in *Campari* and *Moosehead* reflect the more formalistic approach to Article 101(1) it pursued prior to modernisation, they are useful in: (a) confirming that some types of clauses, such as non-challenge clauses, confidentiality provisions, and provisions dealing with quality control and manufacturing standards, may fall outside Article 101(1): and (b) setting out when provisions that may infringe Article 101(1) (such as exclusive licences, sales restraints, and non-compete provisions) are likely to satisfy the conditions of Article 101(3). It must not be forgotten, however, that the Commission (or a national court or NCA) analysing a case today would now be likely to adopt a more economic approach, in particular when applying Article 101(1). Although case law could be interpreted to support the Commission's view that exclusive licences, especially if accompanied by sales restraints, violate Article 101(1), it is likely that fuller analysis would now be required before it could be determined whether other provisions restrict competition within the meaning of Article 101(1).

7. TRADEMARK DELIMITATION AGREEMENTS

Trademark delimitation agreements are entered into in order to settle disputes.[234] They usually occur where one party opposes the other's application for, or use of, a mark on the ground that it is confusingly similar to one owned by the first party for similar products. The trademark delimitation

[233] COMP/32.736, *Moosehead/Whitbread* [1990] OJ L100/32.

[234] See n. 96 and text for settlement agreements potentially within the scope of the TTBER.

agreement may be adopted to settle protracted litigation. The CJ and Commission have made it clear that the provisions in such agreements may infringe Article 101(1)[235] in the same way as they might in any other agreement. The context in which the agreement is made does not therefore mean that it is immune from the application of Article 101(1). Delimitation agreements may restrict the class of products for which a party may use the mark, or the territories in which it may use the mark, or a party may accept a non-challenge obligation in relation to certain products or territories. In *BAT v Commission*,[236] the Court took a more liberal attitude to delimitation agreements than the Commission had done previously. The position now appears to be that an agreement will be outside Article 101(1) if there is a genuine risk of confusion between the parties, and it is not just a ploy for market-sharing, and if the agreement does not divide markets within the EU (at least if there is no less restrictive means of dealing with the dispute).[237]

8. COPYRIGHT (OTHER THAN SOFTWARE) LICENCES

A. GENERAL

Software licences are 'technology transfer agreements' and are thus governed by the TTBER and the accompanying Guidelines. Licences of other types of copyright, however, do not benefit from the TTBER, or the VBER, unless the licence is ancillary to a technology transfer or vertical agreement.[238] In discussing copyright licensing, the Technology Transfer Guidelines distinguish between the licensing of copyright for the production of contract products and other rights related to copyright on the other. The principles set out in the TTBER and the Guidelines will, as a general rule, be applied to the former.[239]

> . . . On the other hand, the licensing of rental rights and public performance rights protected by copyright, in particular for films or music, is considered to raise particular issues and it may not be warranted to assess such licensing on the basis of the principles developed in these guidelines. In the application of Article 101 the specificities of the work and the way in which it is exploited must be taken into account. The Commission will therefore not apply the TTBER and the present guidelines by way of analogy to the licensing of these other rights.[240]

B. BROADCASTING LICENCES AND PERFORMANCE COPYRIGHT

Other than on the issue of exclusive licences there is almost no jurisprudence in this area. It has been seen that although the CJ held in *Coditel II*[241] that an exclusive licence (amounting in effect to ATP) did not in itself infringe Article 101(1), the scope of this exception is uncertain. Indeed, in the *Premier League/Murphy*[242] cases the CJ held that exclusive broadcast licences did violate Article 101. In *Film Purchases by German Television Stations*,[243] the Commission also distinguished *Coditel II* in a case

[235] See Case 65/86, *Bayer AG and Maschinenfabrik Hennecke v Heinz Süllhöfer* EU:C:1988:448, concerning a non-challenge clause.

[236] Case 35/83, *BAT v Commission* EU:C:1985:32, the appeal from COMP/30.128, *Toltecs/Dorcet* [1982] OJ L379/19.

[237] See also COMP/27.879, *Sirdar/Phildar* [1975] OJ L125/27; *Hershey/Schiffers*, Commission Press Release IP/90/87; *Chiquita/Fyffes* IP(92)461.

[238] TTBER, Art. 1(1)(b). [239] Guidelines, para. 49. [240] Ibid., para. 50.

[241] Case 262/81, *Coditel II* EU:C:1982:334.

[242] Cases C-403 and 429/08, EU:C:2011:631, see Section 3.C.iii. [243] COMP/31.734, [1989] OJ L284/36.

involving an exclusive broadcasting licence of MGM/UA films granted to a group of German TV stations for 15 years with a further 'selection period' which preceded this.[244] The Commission held that the agreement was within Article 101(1) because of the number of films covered by the transaction[245] and the long duration of the arrangements which excluded third parties for a length of time which was described as 'disproportionate within the *Coditel II* judgment' and 'an artificial barrier to other undertakings'.[246] However, it exempted the agreement after provision was made for third party broadcasters in Germany to apply for licences to show the films at times which did not clash with those of the licensees. The Commission considered that the arrangements as a whole allowed more films to be shown to German audiences and to be dubbed into German.

Broadcast licences and licensing of digital content remains an issue of acute EU interest.[247] For example, the Commission investigated whether restrictions preventing cross-border access to online pay-TV services ('geo-blocking') or satellite pay-TV services incorporated in licensing agreements for audiovisual content, such as films, concluded between US film studios and EU pay-TV broadcasters (including Sky) infringe Article 101. During the course of the proceedings (and subsequently in its Commitments Decisions) the Commission indicated its concern that clauses preventing passive selling by broadcasters outside their allocated territories, and so granting absolute territorial exclusivity to them, in the absence of an objective justification, infringe Article 101 (the agreements restrict competition by object and do not meet the Article 101(3) criteria).[248] On the opening of the proceedings, the Competition Commissioner Margrethe Vestager stated:[249]

> European consumers want to watch the pay-TV channels of their choice regardless of where they live or travel in the EU. Our investigation shows that they cannot do this today, also because licensing agreements between the major film studios and Sky UK do not allow consumers in other EU countries to access Sky's UK and Irish pay-TV services, via satellite or online. We believe that this may be in breach of EU competition rules.

In the end, the proceedings were resolved after each of the investigated parties offered commitments.[250] In the first decision, the Commission accepted commitments from Paramount, essentially to abandon their geo-blocking practices and agreeing not to enforce existing clauses or to reintroduce them in film licensing contracts.[251] In an unsuccessful third party appeal challenging the decision, the GC held[252] (despite finding that the Commission was not required in a commitments decision to establish an infringement of Article 101(1) or to demonstrate the non-applicability of Article 101(3))

[244] In fact the Commission left open whether the transaction amounted to a licence 'in the legal and technical sense' or an assignment of rights for a limited period and to a limited extent. In either case, the Commission considered that there was a restriction of competition: ibid., para. 41.

[245] And the fact that many of the films were important or noteworthy or had 'particular mass appeal such as the James Bond films': ibid., para. 43.

[246] Ibid., para. 44.

[247] See e.g. <https://digital-strategy.ec.europa.eu/en/policies/copyright>.

[248] On 23 July 2015 the Commission sent a statement of objections to Sky UK and six major US film studios (Disney, NBC Universal, Paramount Pictures, Sony, Twentieth Century Fox, and Warner Bros) setting out the preliminary view that each of the six studios and Sky UK have agreed to prevent Sky UK from allowing EU consumers located elsewhere to access, via satellite or online, pay-TV services available in the UK and Ireland. On 22 April 2016 Paramount agreed to abandon its geo-blocking practices to end its part in the investigation.

[249] IP/15/4322. [250] COMP/40.023, *Cross-border access to pay TV*.

[251] See 26 July 2016, *aff'd* Case T-873/16, *Groupe Canal\+ v Commission*, EU:T:2018:904 (also rejecting the argument that the settlement would represent a threat to the French film industry and cultural diversity). In November and December 2018 Disney, Warner, NBC Universal, Sony Pictures, and Sky also offered similar commitments to address the Commission's competition concerns.

[252] Ibid.

that: although an exclusive copyright licence is in principle permitted, clauses conferring absolute territorial exclusivity on the broadcasters were object restrictions under Article 101 (given the absence of any justification in the legal or economic context—the distinction between active and passive sales applied in the digital context); and the restrictive clauses in this case went beyond what was necessary to protect the production and distribution of films and so did not satisfy Article 101(3).

The Commission's e-commerce sector inquiry[253] also examined licensing agreements for the online provision of audio-visual and music products, especially those incorporating geographic rights (relating to the geographic area in which the digital content provider may lawfully offer the product and commonly used in relation to premium products—such as sport, films, and fiction TV), territorial restrictions, or involving geo-blocking practices, barriers erected by companies to restrict access to online digital content services from other Member States. The Commission is especially concerned about geo-blocking and measures to counter it form an important part of its digital single market strategy.[254]

There is almost no other precedent which indicates how *other* provisions in performance copyright licences will be appraised under Article 101. In 2004, the Commission indicated that it might be suspicious of favoured nation clauses incorporated in such contracts. In a press release, it reported that it had closed an investigation into contracts concluded by certain of the major Hollywood studios.[255] These contracts, providing for the sale of their entire film production to European pay-TV broadcasters, had originally included most favoured nation clauses, giving the studios the right to enjoy the most favourable terms agreed between a pay-TV company and any one of them. The Commission considered that the cumulative effect of these clauses was an alignment of prices paid to the studios for the broadcasting rights. It closed its investigation into the contracts of six of the studios after they withdrew the clauses.

C. COLLECTIVE LICENSING OF COPYRIGHT

As with technology pooling, the collective licensing of copyright may frequently be pro-competitive and necessary to the operation of an agreement.[256] Generally a benign approach has been taken (under Article 102 and Article 101) to the conduct of collecting societies which manage authors' rights in the musical works which they have created, in particular by licensing categories of rights to commercial users on behalf of the societies' members.[257] Collecting societies exist because of the impracticality of performers, musicians, etc. individually giving permission for their work to be performed or collecting royalties. Performers' rights societies are usually organised on a national basis and often have a *de facto* monopoly. Their activities have often given rise to competition law problems under Article 102.[258] The Commission is concerned to address the issue of collecting societies as a whole and published a Communication on this in 2004.[259]

[253] See <http://ec.europa.eu/competition/antitrust/sector_inquiries_e_commerce.html> and Final Report, SWD (2017)154 final, COM(2017) 229 final.

[254] See e.g. Reg. 2017/1128 on portability of online content services throughout the EU and Reg. 2018/302 on addressing unjustified geo-blocking and other forms of discrimination based on customers' nationality, place of residence, or place of establishment within the internal market (see Chap. 11).

[255] IP/04/1314.

[256] See discussion in Chaps. 5 and 9 and, e.g., COMP/37.398, *Joint selling of the commercial rights of the UEFA Champions League* [2003] OJ L291/25.

[257] See e.g. Case T-224/95, *Tremblay v Commission* EU:T:1997:187, Case 395/87, *Ministère Public v Tournier* EU:C:1989:319.

[258] See Case C-177/16, *AKKA/LAA* EU:C:2017:689 and Case C-52/07, *Kanal 5 v STIM* EU:C:2008:703 (the CJ set out guidance on the question of when a copyright management organisation holding a dominant position might abuse that dominant position by engaging in excessive or discriminatory pricing practices).

[259] Communication from the Commission to the Council, European Parliament and ESC on the Management of Copyright and Related Rights in the Internal Market, COM(2004) 261 final. See also, e.g., the commitments adopted in relation to the Cannes Agreement, see IP/06/1311.

In *IFPI*,[260] the International Federation of the Phonic Industry notified a reciprocal agreement in the name of national collecting societies of music record companies designed to facilitate the grant of a multi-territorial licence which broadcasters could exploit *globally*, and not just nationally, by simulcasting sound recordings onto the global digital network of the internet. It enabled the creation of a new type of licence, ensured effective administration and protection of producers' rights in the face of global internet exploitation, and provided broadcasters with an alternative to obtaining a licence from the local society in every country in which their internet transmissions could be accessed. Although the agreement did involve some prices restrictions between the parties, the Commission concluded that the restrictions were indispensable to the agreement, would lead to substantial economic benefits, and would improve the distribution of music, which would benefit consumers.

In *CISAC*,[261] in contrast, the Commission was concerned about clauses in model contracts drawn up by the International Confederation of Societies of Authors and Composers (CISAC) and to be completed by contracting collecting societies. It declined, following market testing, to accept commitments offered by CISAC[262] and held that a number of clauses infringed Article 101(1) and that national territorial limitations (limiting the ability of each collecting society to offer services outside its domestic territory) resulted from a concerted practice which restricted competition between the collecting societies. On appeal, however, the GC[263] held that the Commission had not established, to the requisite legal standard, the existence of a concerted practice between the collecting societies to fix the national territorial limitations and had not put forward sufficient evidence to render implausible the collecting societies' explanation for their parallel conduct, based on the need to ensure the effectiveness of the fight against the unauthorised use of musical works. As no concerted practice was established the GC did not have to examine the argument put forward by CISAC that the national territorial limitations were not restrictive of competition but were necessary 'in order to avoid a race to the bottom with regard to royalties and to maintaining the existence of national one-stop-shops'.[264]

9. THE APPLICATION OF ARTICLE 102 TO INTELLECTUAL PROPERTY RIGHTS

There are two facets to the relationship between Article 102 and IPRs. First, there is the extent to which the ownership of IPRs puts the holder in a dominant position. Secondly, there is the question whether the holding, acquisition, or exploitation of IPRs can constitute an abuse of a dominant position and, if so, in what circumstances. Because it is impossible to divorce these questions about IPRs from the operation of Article 102 as a whole, the application of Article 102 to IPRs is dealt with in Chapters 6 and 7.

10. CONCLUSIONS

1. The TTBER and Guidelines seek to adopt an economic approach to IP licensing agreements. The TTBER sets out a presumption that technology transfer agreements which do not incorporate hardcore restraints and which are concluded between undertakings which do not exceed the market share thresholds are compatible with Article 101.

[260] COMP/38.014, OJ 107/46. [261] COMP/38.698, *CISAC* 16 July 2008. [262] Ibid.

[263] Case T-442/08, *International Confederation of Societies of Authors and Composers (CISAC) v Commission* EU:T:2013:188.

[264] Ibid., para. 183.

2. As with the approach to vertical agreements, the centrality of the TTBER means that the initial focus of attention is on whether or not a technology transfer agreement is compatible with Article 101(3).

3. In contrast with the position for vertical agreements, however, in practice it is likely to be much harder for firms to be sure about compliance with the provisions of the TTBER. Not only is it inherently more difficult to define technology markets but the hardcore and excluded restraints are more complex than those set out in the VBER.

4. The practical reality is, therefore, that in many situations parties to IP licensing or IP agreements may have to rely on self-assessment to determine their agreement's compatibility with Article 101. As there is relatively little decisional practice and case law in this sphere, the Technology Transfer Guidelines play a central role. These also provide important guidance on settlement agreements and technology pools. As trademark and copyright licences are generally not covered by the TTBER and Guidelines, recourse to general Article 101 principles will be necessary in such cases.

5. The Commission has fined a number of firms for concluding settlement agreements delaying the entry of generic products into pharmaceutical markets. These are likely to be especially problematic when concluded between potential competitors and when involving inducements to preclude generic entry.

11. FURTHER READING

A. Books

Anderman, S. D., and Kallaugher, J., *Technology Transfer and the New EU Competition Rules: IP Licensing after Modernisation* (Oxford University Press, 2006)

B. Articles

Aitman, D., and Jones A., 'Competition and Copyright: Has the Copyright Owner Lost Control?' [2003] *EIPR* 137

Anderman, S. D., 'EC Competition Law and Intellectual Property Rights in the New Economy' (2002) 47 *Ant Bull* 285

De Margerie, S., ' "Pay-for-delay" Settlements: In Search of the Right Standard' (2013) 36 *World Competition* 85

Gallasch, S., 'Activating *Activas* in Europe—the Proposal for a "Structured Effects-based" Analysis for Pay-for-delay Settlements' (2016) 36(4) *Legal Studies* 683

Peeperkorn, L., 'IP Licences and Competition Rules: Striking the Right Balance' (2003) 26 *World Competition* 527

Schmidt, H., 'Competition Law and IP Rights: Not So Complementary: Time for Re-alignment of the Goals?' (2019) 42(4) *World Competition* 451

13

PUBLIC ENFORCEMENT OF ARTICLE 101 AND ARTICLE 102 BY THE COMMISSION AND THE NATIONAL COMPETITION AUTHORITIES

1. CENTRAL ISSUES

1. The EU's primary method for enforcing Articles 101 and 102 is by a public enforcement system utilising both the Commission and competition authorities at Member State level. The enforcement of the Merger Control Regulation is discussed in Chapter 15.
2. The system for enforcing Articles 101 and 102 was fundamentally changed on 1 May 2004, when Regulation 1/2003 entered into force. This rendered Article 101(3) directly applicable, and 'decentralised' the enforcement of the antitrust provisions so that the Commission and the national competition authorities (NCAs) have parallel competence to apply the rules. The European Competition Network (ECN) is the network of NCAs and the Commission working in close cooperation with one another.
3. The Commission's own powers of enforcement are set out in Regulation 1/2003. The Commission combines investigative, prosecutorial, and adjudicative functions in one body.
4. Complaints about breaches of the competition rules play an important role. The Commission has no duty to pursue complaints but is obliged to make a formal rejection of them, which can be challenged before the EU Courts.
5. In investigating suspected breaches of the competition rules, the Commission may require information and may carry out, inter alia, unannounced inspections at the premises of undertakings, and at private homes.
6. The Commission may take a number of decisions, including decisions ordering terminations of infringements, imposing fines, or accepting commitments. It can impose behavioural or structural remedies. Commitments decisions were introduced by Regulation 1/2003 and are an important instrument for the Commission.
7. The Commission pursues an aggressive policy towards the detection and punishment of cartels. It operates a 'leniency policy', whereby participants in cartels are given immunity or a reduced penalty in exchange for providing the Commission with information. The Commission imposes heavy fines on undertakings found to have committed serious breaches of the competition rules. It has a direct settlement procedure to enable it to dispose more quickly of cartel cases where the undertakings admit liability.

8. Commission decisions in competition cases are subject to review by the EU Court. The extent of the compatibility of with the European Convention on Human Rights and the EU Charter of some aspects of the Commission's enforcement procedures, as well as the standard of judicial review applied by the Union Courts, is a matter of controversy.
9. Decentralisation and the parallel enforcement competence of the NCAs mean that there are complex procedures and arrangements within the ECN for matters such as allocating cases and sharing information. The enforcement powers of the NCAs have been augmented by the ECN+ Directive, which harmonised issues such as independence, resources, enforcement and fining powers, and national leniency programmes. Some Member States also have the power to enforce the EU competition rules through the use of criminal sanctions, particularly against cartel activity.
10. The principle of *ne bis in idem* (double jeopardy) applies to EU competition proceedings and has been considered in many cases. It requires facts that are materially identical and a duplication of enforcement proceedings.

2. INTRODUCTION

Public enforcement by the Commission and the competition authorities of the Member States (NCAs) is the primary method of enforcing the EU antitrust rules.[1] Council Regulation 1/2003,[2] which entered into force on 1 May 2004, is the linchpin of a 'modernised' EU enforcement regime. It grants expansive powers to the Commission, enabling it to investigate, determine, and sanction breaches of Articles 101 and 102. Within the Commission, these powers are exercised by a specific Directorate-General (or policy department), known as DG Comp. Regulation 1/2003 also 'decentralised' application of the competition rules away from the Commission solely, to make greater use of NCAs and national courts in the enforcement structure. This led, inter alia, to the establishment of the European Competition Network (ECN), which coordinates the work of the NCAs and the Commission who share competence to apply and enforce Articles 101 and 102. In tandem, human rights discourse—in particular, the right to a fair trial for defendants—has become more prominent in the context of EU competition enforcement, following the entry into force of the Charter of Fundamental Rights in 2009.

3. MODERNISATION AND ENFORCEMENT UNDER REGULATION 1/2003

The original enforcement regime in Europe was governed by Regulation 17/62.[3] It established what was in practice a highly centralised enforcement structure for the application of the competition rules. The key centralising influence was the fact that, although in theory Articles 101(1)

[1] For a detailed account of enforcement procedure, and practical considerations, reference should be had to practitioners' books. See e.g. L. Ortiz Blanco, *EU Competition Procedure* (4th edn, Oxford University Press, 2022); E. Rousseva (ed.), *EU Antitrust Procedure* (Oxford University Press, 2020); Bellamy and Child (D. Bailey and L. John, eds.), *European Union Law of Competition* (8th edn, Oxford University Press, 2018), Chaps. 13–16; J. Faull and A. Nikpay (eds.), *The EU Law of Competition* (3rd edn, Oxford University Press, 2014), Chaps 2 and 8.

[2] [2003] OJ L1/1.

[3] [1959–1962] OJ Spec. Ed. 87.

and 102 were directly effective, individual exemption under Article 101(3) lay within the 'sole power' of the Commission.[4] This meant that any presumptively restrictive agreement, which could not be brought within the protection of an applicable block exemption regulation,[5] had to be notified to the Commission for assessment and either 'negative clearance'[6] or the granting of an exemption under Article 101(3). Notification granted immunity from potential fines, and non-notification rendered any agreement in violation of Article 101(1) unenforceable before national courts, even if the conditions for exemption were otherwise met. This resulted, despite the cumbersome nature of the notification procedure, in an increasingly large and unwieldy number of agreements being notified; so many, in fact, that the Commission was unable to complete a formal assessment of the majority, and instead relied on an informal clearance mechanism, issuing what were known as 'comfort letters'.[7] This was considered to be far from satisfactory for many reasons, not least in terms of legal certainty.[8] With the anticipated accession of an additional ten new Member States on 1 May 2004, the existing problems with the notification system were likely to deteriorate. There was also a popular perception that the Commission alone had enforcement jurisdiction over the competition rules, which meant that undertakings preferred to complain to it rather than bring private proceedings before national courts, further cluttering the Commission's enforcement docket.

One potential solution to the logjam at Commission level was to extend the power to the NCAs to grant individual exemptions under Article 101(3). For years, the Commission had resisted this idea. In 1999, however, it adopted a White Paper exploring options for modernising the enforcement framework,[9] which proposed an even more radical change: namely, complete *abolishment* of the notification-and-exemption system. Article 101(3) would instead become directly applicable, and undertakings would self-assess the legitimacy of their arrangements. The White Paper also called for 'intensified *ex post* control', by which the Commission's powers of inquiry would be strengthened and it would be easier to lodge complaints.[10] The White Paper nonetheless recognised the importance of ensuring the uniform application of EU competition law, and proposed mechanisms and procedures to ensure continuing coherence and consistency.[11]

After extensive consultation, the Commission's proposals to decentralise the enforcement of the competition rules were accepted. The Council adopted Regulation 1/2003 in December 2002.[12] Its adoption was accompanied by various Notices which flesh out the bare bones. A major concern was to establish mechanisms for cooperation between the Commission and the NCAs, without which decentralisation could not work. The creation of the European Competition Network (ECN) has thus been of great importance. The changes made in 2004 shifted the focus of the Commission's enforcement. Since the enactment of Regulation 1/2003, the Commission has expended more of its resources on cartels and abuses of dominance rather than on vertical agreements or horizontal cooperation agreements.

The modernisation 'package', which took effect from 1 May 2004, comprises Regulation 1/2003 itself; an Implementing Regulation, adopted by the Commission; and several Commission Notices and

[4] Reg. 17, Art. 9(1). [5] This option remains available today: see Chap 5 for block exemptions generally.

[6] That is, a finding that the agreement did not infringement Art. 101(1) at all.

[7] According to the White Paper on modernisation of the rules implementing Arts. 85 and 86 [1999] OJ C132/1 (Modernisation White Paper), para. 34, 91% of cases were settled informally.

[8] For example, although assuring the parties that the Commission would not pursue the matter further, a comfort letter was not a decision which could be applied by national courts. [9] Modernisation White Paper.

[10] Ibid., para. 108.

[11] Coherence and consistency are not necessarily the same thing, see C. Townley, 'Which Goals Count in Article 101 TFEU?: Public Policy and its Discontents' [2011] *ECLR* 441, 446.

[12] [2003] OJ L1/1.

Guidelines. Regulation 1/2003 broadly addresses two matters. First, it renders Article 101(3) directly applicable and lays down the framework for cooperation between enforcers within the decentralised system. It effects the shift from *ex ante* to *ex post* control. Secondly, it provides for the powers and procedures of the Commission in the investigation of competition matters. Periodic reviews of the functioning of Regulation 1/2003 have indicated that it works well in practice,[13] although scope to strengthen the role and powers of the NCAs was identified.[14]

Regulation 773/2004,[15] the so-called Implementing Regulation, deals with the conduct of Commission proceedings in its application of the competition rules. It covers in more detail some of the matters provided for in Regulation 1/2003, such as the power to take statements, the handling of complaints, the exercise of the right to be heard,[16] and the right of 'access to the file'. The modernisation 'package' was augmented with various Commission Notices and Guidelines, which delimit the enforcement of the Commission's powers and the operation of the decentralised enforcement system. These are: the Commission Notice on cooperation within the network of competition authorities (NCA Cooperation Notice);[17] the Commission Notice on cooperation between the Commission and the courts of the EU Member States in the application of Articles 81 and 82 (the Cooperation Notice);[18] the Commission Notice on the handling of complaints;[19] the Commission Notice on informal guidance relating to novel questions concerning Articles 81 and 82 that arise in individual cases (Informal Guidance Notice);[20] the Guidelines on the effect on trade concept contained in Articles 81 and 82;[21] and the Guidelines on the application of Article 81(3).[22]

In 2011, the Commission published a Notice on 'Best Practices for the Conduct of Proceedings' (Best Practices), to give practical guidance on its procedures in respect of the enforcement of Articles 101 and 102.[23] The Notice seeks to 'increase understanding of the Commission's investigation process . . . and thereby enhance the efficiency of investigations and ensure a high degree of transparency and predictability'.[24] In *Google Android*, the GC described the Notice as 'capable of being raised against the Commission' by a defendant in an action for annulment.[25] The Commission has also issued a Staff Working Paper on 'Best Practices for the Submission of Economic Evidence'.[26] Since 2012, the Commission has published its internal manual on procedures (the 'Antitrust ManProc').[27]

[13] Communication from the Commission to the European Parliament and the Council, Report on the Functioning of Regulation 1/2003, COM(2009) 206 final; 'Ten Years of Antitrust Enforcement under Regulation 1/2003: Achievements and Future Perspectives', COM(2014) 453, accompanied by a Commission Staff Working Document, SWD (2014) 230 and SWD (2014) 231; and W. Wils, 'Regulation 1/2003: An Assessment After Twenty Years' (2023) 46 *World Competition* 3 (an informal retrospective by a current DG Comp official).

[14] See further Section 8.

[15] [2004] OJ L123/18, as amended by Commission Reg. 622/2008 [2008] OJ L171/3 on the conduct of settlement procedures in cartel cases, and by Reg. 2015/134 [2015] OJ L208/3.

[16] Reg. 773/2004 replaced Reg. 2842/98 [1998] OJ L354/18. [17] [2004] OJ C101/43.

[18] [2004] OJ C101/54, amended by [2015] OJ C256/4. [19] [2004] OJ C101/65.

[20] [2004] OJ C101/78, now amended by Commission Notice on informal guidance relating to novel or unresolved questions concerning Articles 101 and 102, C(2022) 6925 final.

[21] [2004] OJ C101/101. [22] [2004] OJ C101/96. [23] [2011] OJ C308/6.

[24] The Notice applies only to cases that were ongoing at the date of its publication, and to future ones: Best Practices, para. 6 and Case T-299/08, *Elf Aquitaine* EU:T:2011:217, para. 148.

[25] Case T-604/18, *Google Android* EU:T:2022:541, para. 979.

[26] See <http://ec.europa.eu/competition/antitrust/legislation/best_practices_submission_en.pdf>. It covers Arts. 101 and 102, and mergers.

[27] Most recently updated in November 2019, see <https://ec.europa.eu/competition/antitrust/antitrust_manproc_11_2019_en.pdf>. The Commission stresses that the ManProc constitutes internal guidance to staff and does not create or alter any rights or obligations under the competition rules.

In 2020, the European Court of Auditors (ECA)[28] published its first audit of the Commission's competition enforcement activities.[29] It reported that, 'overall the Commission made good use of its enforcement powers . . . and addressed competition concerns with its decisions'.[30] Yet it identified areas for improvement, including a need to be more proactive in initiating cases (rather than waiting for complaints or leniency applications), and the lengthiness of proceedings. The report also suggested that case allocation within the ECN could operate more effectively. The ECA did not discuss the adequacy of DG Comp's administrative budget and whether competition enforcement represents good value for money given its limited resources. This omission has been criticised in light of the 'hugely profitable' nature of DG Comp's activities if one factors in the contribution of fines to the overall EU budget.[31]

4. THE COMMISSION'S POWER TO ISSUE INFORMAL GUIDANCE

Although Regulation 1/2003 abolished the notification procedure, it recognised that, in some novel cases, guidance as to the compatibility of an agreement or practice may be necessary, whether to provide legal certainty[32] or to aid the consistent application of EU competition law.[33] Regulation 1/2003 allows the Commission to adopt decisions of 'inapplicability',[34] and envisages that 'informal guidance' may be issued to businesses in cases that 'give rise to genuine uncertainty because they present novel or unresolved questions' about the application of the EU competition rules.[35] A Commission Notice on the provision of such informal guidance was published as part of the modernisation package.[36] It established a demanding standard to be satisfied in the circumstances of any request, requiring in particular an absence of *any* available 'clarification' within the existing legal framework regarding the subject matter of the request.[37] Due to the strict criteria, the tool was never used,[38] as the Commission lacked sufficiently compelling requests from businesses.[39]

When the Covid-19 pandemic occurred, the Commission in April 2020 issued a Communication that set out general principles for the assessment of business cooperation to overcome the resulting supply chain challenges.[40] The Communication emphasised the 'major and unprecedented shock'[41] and the 'exceptional challenges'[42] faced by businesses, which meant that '[i]t may even be appropriate to provide undertakings with ad hoc feedback or comfort on the legality of specific cooperation initiatives'.[43] In tandem, the Commission issued a comfort letter to a trade association representing the pharmaceutical industry, which addressed coordination 'to increase production and to improve

[28] An independent EU institution, whose functions are to audit the effectiveness and efficiency of EU activity and to improve the management of its budget.

[29] European Court of Auditors, *The Commission's EU merger control and antitrust proceedings: a need to scale up market oversight* (2020), <www.eca.europa.eu/Lists/ECADocuments/SR20_24/SR_Competition_policy_EN.pdf>.

[30] Ibid., 4.

[31] C. Veljanovski, 'Auditor Says DG COMP Should "Scale Up" Its Enforcement—How?' (2021) 12 *JECLAP* 355, 356.

[32] See Reg. 1/2003, recital 38. [33] Ibid., recital 14. [34] Ibid., Art. 10. [35] Ibid., recital 38.

[36] Informal Guidance Notice [2004] OJ C101/78. [37] Ibid., para. 8.

[38] Commission Press Release, 'Competition: Commission adopts a more flexible antitrust Informal Guidance Notice; withdraws Antitrust COVID Temporary Framework', 3 October 2022, <https://ec.europa.eu/commission/presscorner/detail/en/ip_22_5887>.

[39] Commission Staff Working Paper on the functioning of Regulation 1/2003, SEC (2009) 574 final, para. 48.

[40] Communication from the Commission, 'Temporary Framework for assessing antitrust issues related to business cooperation in response to situations of urgency stemming from the current COVID-19 outbreak' [2020] C 116 I/7.

[41] Ibid., para. 1. [42] Ibid., para. 3. [43] Ibid., para. 7.

supply of urgently needed critical hospital medicines'.[44] A further comfort letter was issued in 2021, dealing with coordination between vaccine manufacturers to increase production capacity.[45] Having warmed up to informal guidance, the Commission has continued to do so outside the context of the pandemic. A comfort letter was issued to Gaia-X, the European cloud computing project sponsored by the German and French governments, in October 2021.[46] Following the finding of infringement in the *Car Emissions* cartel,[47] the Commission issued guidance to the convicted cartelists regarding permissible future coordination, which it made publicly available.[48]

In October 2022, the Commission withdrew the pandemic-related Communication and adopted a revised Informal Guidance Notice of general application.[49] The revised Notice relaxes the standard by which requests for guidance are assessed by the Commission. The Commission will have 'valid reasons to provide clarifications on the applicability of Articles 101 or 102' where two cumulative conditions are satisfied.[50] First, there must be 'no *sufficient* clarity in the existing Union legal framework'[51] and, secondly, issuing the guidance must 'provide added value with respect to legal certainty'.[52] The revised Notice nonetheless follows the approach of its (unused) predecessor in stating that the Commission will only issue guidance to the extent that this is consistent with its enforcement priorities.[53]

The decision to make greater use of informal guidance makes sense in the extraordinary circumstances of a global pandemic leading to extreme supply chain problems, but may sit less easily with the modernisation agenda if extended beyond this context.[54] It has been argued nonetheless that the development may provide a pragmatic solution to problems of legal uncertainty that arise, in particular, from the dearth of recent and relevant case law concerning the application of the Article 101(3) exception rule.[55] It is thus notable that the comfort letters issued to date address the permissible parameters of horizontal cooperation.

5. FUNDAMENTAL HUMAN RIGHTS AND COMPETITION ENFORCEMENT

The role of fundamental (human) rights in EU law generally was introduced in Chapter 2.[56] It was explained that EU law incorporates multiple sources of fundamental rights, in particular

[44] Commission, Letter of 8 April 2020, available at: <https://ec.europa.eu/competition/antitrust/medicines_for_europe_comfort_letter.pdf>.

[45] Commission, Letter of 25 March 2021, available at: <https://ec.europa.eu/competition/antitrust/comfort_letter_coronavirus_matchmaking_event_25032021.pdf>.

[46] 'Gaia-X Association Receives Guidance from European Commission's Directorate-General for Competition', 17 November 2021, <https://gaia-x.eu/news/latest-news/gaia-x-association-receives-guidance-from-european-commissions-directorate-general-for-competition/>.

[47] AT.40178, *Car Emissions* 8 July 2021.

[48] Commission, Letter of 8 July 2021, <https://ec.europa.eu/competition/antitrust/cases1/202146/AT_40178_8022302_3050_5.pdf>.

[49] Commission Notice on informal guidance relating to novel or unresolved questions concerning Articles 101 and 102 of the Treaty on the Functioning of the European Union that arise in individual cases (guidance letters), C(2022) 6925 final, 3 October 2022.

[50] Ibid., para. 7. [51] Ibid., para. 7(a) (emphasis added). [52] Ibid., para. 7(b). [53] Ibid., para. 6.

[54] S. Ünekbaş, 'The Resurrection of the Comfort Letter: Back to the Future?', Jean Monnet Network on EU Law Enforcement Working Paper Series No. 22/22, <https://jmn-eulen.nl/wp-content/uploads/sites/575/2022/05/WP-Series-No.-22-22-The-Resurrection-of-the-Comfort-Letter-Back-to-the-Future-Unekbas.pdf>.

[55] See e.g. J. Buhart and D. Henry, 'COVID-20: The Comfort Letter Is Dead. Long Live the Comfort Letter?' (2020) 43 *World Competition* 305, and suggesting a similar role for informal guidance in a pre-pandemic context, see D. Bailey, 'Reinvigorating the Role of Article 101(3) under Regulation 1/2003' (2016) 81 *Antitrust LJ* 111.

[56] Chap 2, Section 6.

the rights protected under the European Convention on Human Rights (ECHR)—to which the EU itself is not (yet) a signatory, but each of its Member States are—and the EU's Charter on Fundamental Rights. These statutory sources overlap, as Article 52 of the Charter provides that, where it contains rights corresponding to those in the ECHR, their meaning and scope shall be 'the same' as the latter.

Fundamental rights impose important and increasingly prominent constraints on the Commission's exercise of its competition enforcement powers. Recital 37 to Regulation 1/2003 states:

> This Regulation respects the fundamental rights and observes the principles recognised in particular by the Charter of Fundamental Rights of the European Union. Accordingly, this Regulation should be interpreted and applied with respect to those rights and principles.

The EU Courts have also emphasised the importance of ensuring that Commission enforcement proceedings respect the various 'rights of the defence' as a fundamental principle. The GC provided a summary of the applicable principles in its *Qualcomm* judgment, in which a Commission finding of infringement of Article 102 was quashed on the basis that the investigation failed to respect the defendant's rights of defence.

Case T-235/18, *Qualcomm Inc v European Commission* EU:T:2022:358

General Court

156. The rights of the defence are fundamental rights forming an integral part of the general principles of law whose observance the General Court and the Court of Justice ensure (. . . *Solvay v Commission* (C-109/10 P, EU:C:2011:686, paragraph 52)).

157. Observance of the rights of the defence is a general principle of EU law which applies where the authorities are minded to adopt a measure which will adversely affect an individual (. . . *Commission v United Parcel Service*, C-265/17 P, EU:C:2019:23, paragraph 28).

158. That general principle of EU law is enshrined in Article 41(2)(a) and (b) of the Charter of Fundamental Rights of the European Union (. . . *Deutsche Telekom v Commission*, C-152/19 P, EU:C:2021:238, paragraph 105).

159. In the context of competition law, observance of the rights of the defence means that any addressee of a decision finding that that addressee has committed an infringement of the competition rules must have been afforded the opportunity, during the administrative procedure, to make known its views on the truth and relevance of the facts and circumstances alleged as well as on the documents used by the Commission to support its claim that there has been such an infringement (. . . *Solvay v Commission*, C-109/10 P, EU:C:2011:686, paragraph 53, and . . . *Deutsche Telekom v Commission*, C-152/19 P, EU:C:2021:238, paragraph 106).

160. According to well-established case-law, the rights of the defence are infringed where it is possible that the outcome of the administrative procedure conducted by the Commission may have been different as a result of an error committed by it. An applicant undertaking establishes that there has been such infringement where it adequately demonstrates not that the Commission's decision would have been different in content, but rather that it would have been better able to ensure its defence had there been no procedural error (. . . *Thyssen Stahl v Commission*, C-194/99 P, EU:C:2003:527, paragraph 31, and . . . *Deutsche Telekom v Commission*, T-827/14, EU:T:2018:930, paragraph 129).

161. Such an assessment must be made in the light of the factual and legal circumstances of each case (. . . *Commission v RQ*, C-831/18 P, EU:C:2020:481, paragraph 107).

The EU Courts have recognised numerous distinct rights as being of relevance to enforcement of the competition rules. These include the basic right to a fair trial, the presumption of innocence, the protection of legitimate expectations, legal certainty, equal treatment, non-discrimination, privacy, non-retroactivity, proportionality, sound administration, the protection of confidential information, and the rule against double jeopardy. Many of these are now enshrined in the Charter.

Charter of Fundamental Rights [2012] OJ C 326/391

Article 7 Respect for private and family life

Everyone has the right to respect for his or her private and family life, home and communications.

. . .

Article 20 Equality before the law

Everyone is equal before the law.

. . .

Article 41 Right to good administration

1. Every person has the right to have his or her affairs handled impartially, fairly and within a reasonable time by the institutions, bodies, offices and agencies of the Union.
2. This right includes:
   (a) the right of every person to be heard, before any individual measure which would affect him or her adversely is taken;
   (b) the right of every person to have access to his or her file, while respecting the legitimate interests of confidentiality and of professional and business secrecy;
   (c) the obligation of the administration to give reasons for its decisions.
3. Every person has the right to have the Union make good any damage caused by its institutions or by its servants in the performance of their duties, in accordance with the general principles common to the laws of the Member States.
4. Every person may write to the institutions of the Union in one of the languages of the Treaties and must have an answer in the same language.

. . .

Article 47 Right to an effective remedy and to a fair trial

Everyone whose rights and freedoms guaranteed by the law of the Union are violated has the right to an effective remedy before a tribunal in compliance with the conditions laid down in this Article.

Everyone is entitled to a fair and public hearing within a reasonable time by an independent and impartial tribunal previously established by law. Everyone shall have the possibility of being advised, defended and represented.

Legal aid shall be made available to those who lack sufficient resources in so far as such aid is necessary to ensure effective access to justice.

Article 48 Presumption of innocence and right of defence

1. Everyone who has been charged shall be presumed innocent until proved guilty according to law.
2. Respect for the rights of the defence of anyone who has been charged shall be guaranteed.

. . .

Article 50 Right not to be tried or punished twice in criminal proceedings for the same criminal offence

No one shall be liable to be tried or punished again in criminal proceedings for an offence for which he or she has already been finally acquitted or convicted within the Union in accordance with the law.

The application of individual rights in respect of aspects of the enforcement of EU competition law is addressed in context throughout this chapter. Several overarching observations are useful at this juncture. The CJ has stated that the right to effective judicial protection laid down in Article 47 of the Charter secures in EU law the protection afforded by the wide-ranging Article 6 ECHR, which covers the right to a fair trial and due process. Effective judicial protection thus comprises various elements: in particular, the rights of the defence, the principle of equality of arms, the right of access to a tribunal, and the right to be advised, defended, and represented.[57]

Under Article 6 ECHR, however, certain rights are limited only to criminal and not to civil proceedings.[58] This potentially complicates the application of the ECHR-derived fair trial rights to the Commission's enforcement activities, as Article 23(5) of Regulation 1/2003[59] expressly states that decisions imposing fines 'shall not be of a criminal law nature'. Article 47, conversely, does not differentiate between criminal and civil cases, and of the main fundamental rights that are applicable to competition enforcement proceedings, it is only the prohibition on double jeopardy (*ne bis in idem*) that is expressly restricted to criminal offences.[60] In any event, it is generally accepted, applying the '*Engel*' criteria,[61] that the Commission's fining procedures in competition cases are 'criminal' in nature within the meaning of Article 6 ECHR.[62] This approach was essentially confirmed by the 2011 judgment of the European Court of Human Rights (ECtHR) in *Menarini*.[63]

That being the case, a further question arises as to whether the Commission's combined functions as investigator, prosecutor, and adjudicator in competition cases is compatible with the entitlement of defendants, under both Article 47 and Article 6 ECHR, to have their cases decided by an 'independent and impartial tribunal'.[64] Here, again, the distinctive approach to the notion of 'criminal' proceedings within the ECHR becomes relevant. The Strasbourg case law distinguishes between the

[57] Case C-199/11, *Europese Gemeenschap v Otis NV* EU:C:2012:684.

[58] Specifically, Art. 6(2) ECHR—the presumption of innocence—and Art. 6(3)—which enumerates various more precise rights of defence—apply only to individuals 'charged with a criminal offence'.

[59] Formerly Reg. 17, Art. 15(4).

[60] See Section 10.

[61] The notion of a 'criminal charge' is an autonomous concept within ECHR law. In *Engel v Netherlands*, App. nos. 5101/71 etc. (1976) 1 EHRR 647, the Strasbourg Court laid down three criteria to be considered when determining whether a charge should be considered criminal in nature: the classification of the offence under national law; the nature of the offence; and the nature and severity of the potential penalty.

[62] See e.g. Judge Vesterdorf, acting as AG in Cases T-1–4 and 6–15/89, *Rhône-Poulenc* EU:T:1991:38, 885; Léger AG in Case C-185/95 P, *Baustahlgewebe* EU:C:1998:37, para. 31 of the Opinion; Cases C-189/02 P etc., *Dansk Rørindustri* EU:C:2005:408, para. 202; Opinion in Case C-272/09 P, *KME Germany* EU:C:2011:63, para. 64; and Case T-799/17, *Scania* EU:T:2022:48, para. 110.

[63] *Menarini Diagnostics SRL v Italy*, App no. 43509/08, Judgment 27 September 2011, and see also *Société Bouygues Telecom v France*, App. no. 2324/08.

[64] See e.g. A. Andreangeli, 'Towards an EU Competition Court: "Article-6-Proofing" Antitrust Proceedings before the Commission?' (2007) 4 *World Competition* 595; I. Forrester, 'Due Process in EC Competition Case: A Distinguished Institution with Flawed Procedures' (2009) 34 *ELRev* 817; D. Slater, S. Thomas, and D. Waelbroeck, 'Competition Law Proceedings before the European Commission and the Right to a Fair Trial: No Need for Reform?' (2009) *European Competition Journal* 97; F. Castillo de la Torre, 'Evidence, Proof and Judicial Review in Cartel Cases' in C.-D. Ehlermann and M. Marquis (eds.), *European Competition Law Annual 2009: Evaluation of Evidence and its Judicial Review in Competition Cases* (Hart Publishing, 2011), 319; W. Wils, 'EU Antitrust Enforcement Powers and Procedural Rights and Guarantees: The Interplay between EU Law, National Law, the Charter of Fundamental Rights of the EU and the European Convention of Human Rights' (2011) 2 *World Competition* 189; and R. Nazzini, 'Administrative Enforcement, Judicial Review and Fundamental Rights in EU Competition Law: A Comparative Contextual-Functionalist Perspective' (2012) 49 *CMLRev* 971.

'hardcore' of criminal law and more minor offences, such as traffic offences and tax surcharges.[65] The criminal-head guarantees do not necessarily apply with their full stringency to the latter.[66] In particular, the right to a hearing before an impartial and independent tribunal does not preclude some minor 'non-core' criminal offences from being decided by administrative organs at the initial stage, provided that they are subject ultimately to judicial control,[67] before an independent and impartial adjudicator with full jurisdiction.[68]

Applying these principles, the Commission clearly does not qualify as a 'tribunal' under Article 6,[69] so that administrative proceedings before it cannot qualify as a hearing before an 'independent and impartial tribunal'. The question is whether the extent of the judicial review available before the Union Courts protects the right to a fair trial.[70] In *Menarini*,[71] the ECtHR considered the fining practices of the Italian competition authority, which utilises an equivalent enforcement framework to that of the Commission. It held that Italian competition fines are of a criminal nature for the purposes of Article 6 ECHR, but accepted that decisions imposing such fines could be taken by administrative authorities, provided that any decision was subject, subsequently, to full judicial review on matters of law and fact by independent courts with full jurisdiction. The Italian system satisfied these criteria.[72] In *Schindler*,[73] the CJ cited *Menarini* and, following the approach of the ECtHR as well as its own previous decision in *Chalkor*,[74] held that the levying of fines by the Commission was compatible with Article 6 ECHR and Article 47 of the Charter. It did so on the basis that the power of review by the Court under Article 263 TFEU, and its unlimited jurisdiction to review fines under Article 261 TFEU and Article 31 of Regulation 1/2003, were sufficient to fulfil the requirements of the principle of effective judicial protection.[75] This approach is not uncontroversial, particularly in light of the margin of discretion that the Court claims to grant to the Commission with respect to 'complex evaluations on economic matters'.[76] It is increasingly accepted, however, that this leeway is more apparent than actual in current practice.[77]

Perhaps unsurprisingly, there have also been calls to reform the competition enforcement structure at EU level in order to address these fair trial concerns more directly.[78] Some proposals, such

[65] *Jussila*, App. no. 73053/01 (2007) 45 EHRR 39, para. 43. [66] Ibid., para. 43.

[67] *Bendenoun*, App. no. 12547/86 (1994) 18 EHRR 54; *Jussila*, App. no. 73053/01 (2007) 45 EHRR 39, para. 43.

[68] *Le Compte*, App. no. 6878/75 (1983) 5 EHRR 183, para. 29.

[69] As held, e.g., in Cases 209–215 and 218/78, *Van Landewyck v Commission* EU:C:1980:248, para. 81.

[70] See e.g. Slater et al., n. 64; W. Wils, 'The Increased Level of Antitrust Fines, Judicial Review, and the European Convention on Human Rights' (2010) 33 *World Competition* 5; I. Forrester, 'Due Process in EC Competition Case: A Distinguished Institution with Flawed Procedures' (2009) 34 *ELRev* 817; A. Andreangeli, 'Towards an EU Competition Court: "Article-6-Proofing" Antitrust Proceedings before the Commission?' (2007) 4 *World Competition* 595.

[71] *Menarini Diagnostics SRL v Italy*, App. no. 43509/08, Judgment of 27 September 2011, and see also *Société Bouygues Telecom v France*, App. no. 2324/08.

[72] Although there was a powerful dissenting opinion by Judge Pinto de Albuquerque. For comments on *Menarini*, see P. Oliver, '*Diagnostics*—A Judgment Applying the European Convention of Human Rights to the Field of Competition' (2012) 3 *JECLAP* 163.

[73] Case C-501/11 P, *Schindler* EU:C:2013:522; repeated in Case C-295/12 P, *Telefónica* EU:C:2014:2062, paras. 51–57.

[74] Case C-386/10 P, *Chalkor* EU:C:2011:815; see also Case C-272/09 P, *KME* EU:C:2011:810.

[75] Case C-501/11 P, *Schindler* EU:C:2013:522, paras. 32–38.

[76] Case C-56/64, *Consten and Grundig* ECLI:EU:C:1966:41, para. 347.

[77] Commission, Note by the EU on the standard of review by courts in competition cases, Submission to OECD Roundtable, DAF/COMP/WP3/WD(2019)9, paras. 21–25.

[78] See e.g. Forrester, n. 70; B. Vesterdorf, 'Due Process Before the Commission of the European Union? Some Reflections Upon Reading the Commission Draft Paper on Best Practices in Antitrust Proceedings' (2010) 1 *CPI Antitrust Journal* April; D. Slater, S. Thomas, and D. Waelbroeck, 'Competition Law Proceedings before the European Commission and the Right to a Fair Trial: No Need for Reform?' (2009) *European Competition Journal* 97, 106; GCLC Working Paper 04/08; Andreangeli, n. 70; R. Nazzini, 'Administrative Enforcement, Judicial Review and Fundamental Rights in EU Competition Law: A Comparative Contextual-functionalist Perspective' (2012) 49 *CMLRev* 971. For a robust defence (mainly from those within the system), see F. Castillo de la Torre, 'Evidence, Proof and Judicial Review in Cartel Cases' (2009) 3 *World Competition* 505; P. Lowe, 'Cartels, Fines and Due Process' (2009) 2 *Global Competition Policy*; Wils, 'The Increased Level of Antitrust Fines, Judicial Review, and the European Convention on Human Rights', n. 70; A.-L. Sibony, 'Casenote on *KME v Commission*' (2012) 49 *CMLRev* 1977.

as strengthening the role of the Hearing Officer and separating the investigation, prosecution, and decision-making functions, could be achieved without any Treaty amendment. Others, such as having a separate 'competition court' as an independent first instance adjudicator, would be more radical.

6. ENFORCEMENT BY THE COMMISSION

A. INTRODUCTION

Despite the steps towards decentralisation, the Commission remains at the apex of the enforcement structure for EU competition law. In this capacity, it enjoys expansive powers to investigate and prosecute alleged breaches of Articles 101 and 102. In *Dansk Rørindustri*, the CJ said:[79]

> The supervisory task conferred on the Commission by Articles [101(1)] and [102] . . . not only includes the duty to investigate and punish individual infringements but also encompasses the duty to pursue a general policy designed to apply, in competition matters, the principles laid down by the Treaty and to guide the conduct of undertakings in the light of those principles.

The Commission may commence an investigation into alleged infringements on its own initiative or acting on a complaint.[80] In competition cases, the Commission plays the parts of law-maker, policeman, investigator, prosecutor, judge, and jury, subject only to review by the EU Courts. This situation, which has been widely criticised but is fiercely defended by the Commission,[81] was left unchanged by modernisation. Although the accumulation of functions in the Commission and the limited role of the EU Courts may raise fundamental rights concerns, the EU Courts have nonetheless approved the current situation.[82] The Commission has a margin of discretion to set priorities in enforcing the competition rules.[83] It has certain obligations when dealing with complaints, but otherwise can choose against whom, and when, to bring proceedings.[84]

There are two distinct stages to the Commission's administrative procedure.[85] The first is the preliminary investigation stage, covering the period up until the notification of the statement of objections (SO). This is a period of fact-finding intended 'to enable the Commission to gather all the

[79] Cases C-189, 202, 208, and 213/02 P, *Dansk Rørindustri A/S* EU:C:2005:408, para. 170, referring to Cases 100–103/80, *Musique Diffusion française SA v Commission (Pioneer)* EU:C:1983:158, para. 105; see also Case T-99/04, *AC-Treuhand* EU:T:2008:256, para. 163.

[80] This is clear from Reg. 1/2003, Art. 7, which gives the Commission power to take decisions when it has found an infringement; see also Best Practices, paras. 9–11. Many investigations in cartel cases are triggered by a leniency application.

[81] See A. Pera and M. Todino, 'Enforcement of EC Competition Rules: Need for a Reform?' [1996] *Fordham Corp Law Inst* 125, 144; F. Montag, 'The Case for Radical Reform of the Infringement Procedure under Regulation' [1998] *ECLR* 428; W. Wils, 'The Combination of the Investigative and Prosecutorial Function and the Adjudicative Function in EC Antitrust Enforcement: A Legal and Economic Analysis' (2004) 27 *World Competition* 201; I. Forrester, 'Due Process in EC Competition Case: A Distinguished Institution with Flawed Procedures' (2009) 34 *ELRev* 817; D. Slater, S. Thomas, and D. Waelbroeck, 'Competition Law Proceedings before the European Commission and the Right to a Fair Trial: No Need for Reform?' (2009) 5 *European Competition Journal* 97.

[82] In Cases T-548/08 etc., *Total SA* EU:T:2013:434 (on appeal Case C-597/13 P, EU:C:2015:613, judgment partially set aside on other grounds) the GC stated that the fact that the Commission is investigator, prosecutor, and decision-maker does not infringe the EU Charter.

[83] Case T-24/90, *Automec II* EU:T:1992:97.

[84] In Case T-219/99, *British Airways* EU:T:2003:343, for example, the GC dismissed the argument that the Commission had infringed the principle of non-discrimination by bringing an Art. 102 action only against British Airways but not other airlines.

[85] Case T-99/04, *AC-Treuhand* EU:T:2008:256.

relevant information confirming or not the existence of an infringement of the competition rules and to adopt an initial position on the course of the procedure and how it is to proceed'.[86] The second, 'inter partes' or 'adversarial' stage, covers the period from the notification of the SO to adoption of the final decision. The move from one stage to the other entails the 'initiation of proceedings'. The initiation of proceedings is a formal act by which the Commission indicates its intention to adopt a decision under Regulation 1/2003.[87] Under Article 11(6) of Regulation 1/2003, the initiation of proceedings by the Commission relieves the NCAs, temporarily, of their competence to apply Articles 101 and 102. National courts are not relieved of competence, but may not take a decision running counter to one adopted[88] or contemplated by the Commission.[89] It is not necessary for the Commission to initiate proceedings before rejecting a complaint.[90]

Article 2(3) of Regulation 773/2004 states that the Commission may exercise its powers of investigation before initiating proceedings. This is vital as, until the Commission has carried out its investigation, it may not be in a position to issue an SO.

B. COMPLAINTS

Enforcement cases come before the Commission through a variety of channels: after the conclusion of a sector inquiry under Article 17 of Regulation 1/2003;[91] on foot of information provided by an NCA;[92] pursuant to an application for immunity under the Leniency Notice in cartel cases;[93] or following a complaint submitted by third parties. Complainants play an important role in the enforcement process, both by drawing suspected breaches to the attention of the Commission and, potentially, through subsequent private enforcement in damages claims relating to the same violation.[94] The Commission is not *obliged* to pursue enforcement activity in respect of any specific complaint that it receives, and generally it wants to preserve its resources for cases in which a point of particular EU interest is raised. It may, therefore, decline to act on a complaint. Another risk of encouraging complaints is that, often, they are lodged by disgruntled entities losing out in the competitive process rather than by those suffering as a result of anti-competitive conduct infringing the competition rules.

Complaints can be made both to the Commission and to NCAs. An initial difficulty for potential complainants is to decide to whom they should complain: the Commission, one or more NCAs, or to all of these authorities. The Commission's Notice on the handling of complaints indicates that the complaint should be made to the 'authority most likely to be well placed to deal with their case'.[95] Case allocation between the Commission and NCAs is considered further in Section 8.C.

(i) Standing to Submit a Formal Complaint

There is a distinction between 'formal' complainants and undertakings or individuals who merely bring an issue to the attention of the Commission. Formal complainants benefit from certain procedural rights during the investigation process. To qualify as a formal complainant, it is necessary to demonstrate sufficient standing; Regulation 1/2003 provides that 'natural or legal persons who can

[86] Ibid., para. 47; see also Cases C-238, 244–245, 247, 250, 251–252, and 254/99 P, *Limburgse Vinyl Maatschappij* EU:C:2002:582, paras. 181–183; Case C-105/04 P, *Nederlandse Federatieve Vereniging voor de Groothandel op Elektrotechnisch Gebied* EU:C:2006:592, paras. 37–38.

[87] NCA Cooperation Notice [2004] OJ C101/54, para. 52. [88] Reg. 1/2003, Art. 16(1). [89] See Chap 14.

[90] Reg. 773/2004, Art. 2(4). [91] See Section 6.I. [92] See Section 8. [93] Section 6.H.

[94] See Chap 14.

[95] Commission Notice on the Handling of Complaints by the Commission under Articles 81 and 82 of the EC Treaty [2004] OJ C101/65, para. 21 (the Complaints Notice).

show a legitimate interest' and Member States (which are deemed to have a legitimate interest for all complaints they lodge) have standing to complain about breaches of the competition rules.[96]

Any applicant who is directly and adversely affected, or will be so affected, by the infringement will have standing. It has been held, for example, that an entity which has been excluded, or threatened with exclusion, from a distribution network;[97] which believes that it was negotiating with members of a cartel;[98] or which believes itself to be a victim of abusive behaviour by a dominant undertaking,[99] has a legitimate interest within the meaning of Article 3(2). The Complaints Notice provides further guidance, providing examples of entities which would have a legitimate interest such as consumer associations.

Commission Notice on the Handling of Complaints by the Commission under Article 101 and 102 of the EC Treaty [2004] OJ C101/65

36 . . . . [U]ndertakings (themselves or through associations that are entitled to represent their interests) can claim a legitimate interest where they are operating in the relevant market or where the conduct complained of is liable to directly and adversely affect their interests. This confirms the established practice of the Commission which has accepted that a legitimate interest can, for instance, be claimed by the parties to the agreement or practice which is the subject of the complaint, by competitors whose interests have allegedly been damaged by the behaviour complained of or by undertakings excluded from a distribution system.

37. Consumer associations can equally lodge complaints with the Commission.[100] The Commission moreover holds the view that individual consumers whose economic interests are directly and adversely affected insofar as they are the buyers of goods or services that are the object of an infringement can be in a position to show a legitimate interest.[101]

38. However, the Commission does not consider as a legitimate interest within the meaning of Article 7(2) the interest of persons or organizations that wish to come forward on general interest considerations without showing that they or their members are liable to be directly and adversely affected by the infringement (*pro bono publico*).

In *Österreichische Postsparkasse*,[102] the GC took a broad view of 'legitimate interest', extending the concept to any final consumer who could show that his or her economic interests had been harmed. The case involved the question of whether an Austrian political party could be said to have sufficient legitimate interest in a case concerning an alleged banking cartel, on the basis of its status as a *customer* of banking services. In concluding that it did have such a legitimate interest, the GC remarked that:

Competition law and competition policy . . . have an undeniable impact on the specific economic interests of final customers who purchase goods or services. Recognition that such customers—who show

[96] Art. 7(2). This is similar to the language previously used in Reg. 17, Art. 3.

[97] Case 210/81, *Demo-Studio Schmidt v Commission* EU:C:1983:277.

[98] See e.g. *Building and Construction Industry in the Netherlands* [1992] OJ L92/1 (a complaint about collusive tendering lodged by a local authority).

[99] See e.g. Cases 6 and 7/73, *Istituto Chemioterapico Italiano SpA and Commercial Solvents Corp v Commission* EU:C:1974:18; Case C-62/86, *AKZO Chemie BV v Commission* EU:C:1991:286, complaint lodged by ECS; see Chap 7, Sections 8 and 12.

[100] See e.g. Case T-37/92, *BEUC v Commission* EU:T:1994:54, para. 36.

[101] This point was raised in Cases T-213 and 214/01, *Österreichische Postsparkasse v Commission* EU:T:2006:151.

[102] Ibid.

> that they have suffered economic damage as a result of an agreement or conduct liable to restrict or distort competition—have a legitimate interest in seeking from the Commission a declaration that Articles [101 and 102] have been infringed contributes to the attainment of the objectives of competition law.[103]

An individual who does not have a legitimate interest even within the broad definition accepted in *Österreichische Postsparkasse*, or who does not want to make an official complaint, may draw the Commission's attention informally to market information which indicates a potential breach of the competition rules. The Commission is then free to commence proceedings on its own initiative if it considers it appropriate. The Commission also maintains an anonymous whistle-blower tool, which enables 'individuals who have knowledge of the existence or functioning of a cartel or other types of antitrust violations' to bring this information to the Commission's attention. The information is provided electronically, through an encrypted messaging system, which permits the Commission to confirm receipt and to ask clarifying questions, without requiring the whistle-blower to disclose their identity.[104]

(ii) The Complaints Procedure

A formal complaint must be submitted in compliance with Form C,[105] available on DG Comp's website. A complainant must provide information regarding itself, details and evidence of the alleged infringement, an explanation of the findings sought from the Commission, the grounds on which a legitimate interest is claimed, and details of any approach made to other competition authorities or lawsuits brought before a national court. In certain circumstances, the Commission may waive the need for submission of some of the comprehensive information and supporting documentation required.[106]

Once a complaint has been received, the Commission follows a three-stage procedure. First, it collects information from the complainant, gives an initial reaction to the case, and allows the complainant an opportunity to expand on its allegations.[107] Secondly, it investigates further to determine whether to initiate proceedings or to reject the complaint.[108] Before the Commission rejects a complaint, it must give the complainant an opportunity to make its views known on the Commission's provisional intention to reject, within a specified time limit.[109] This is known as an 'Article 7(1) letter'.[110] The complainant may also be provided with access to non-confidential documents on which the Commission has based its provisional assessment. Taking cognisance of the views of the complainant, the Commission, finally, initiates proceedings or rejects the complaint.[111]

(iii) Rejection of a Complaint

The Commission may after investigation consider that no breach of the competition rules has occurred.[112] Alternatively, it may consider that a breach might have occurred but that the case is of

[103] Cases T-213 and 214/01, *Österreichische Postsparkasse* EU:T:2006:151, para. 115.

[104] Commission Press Release, 'Antitrust: Commission introduces new anonymous whistleblower tool', 16 March 2017. The whistle-blower tool is accessed via the Commission's website, <https://competition-policy.ec.europa.eu/cartels/whistle-blower_en>.

[105] Reg. 773/2004 [2004] OJ L123/18, Art. 5, and Annex.

[106] Ibid., Art. 5(1).

[107] Complaints Notice, para. 55.

[108] Ibid., para. 56. The procedure prior to rejecting a complaint is set out in Best Practices, paras. 139–141.

[109] Reg. 773/2004 [2004] OJ L123/18, Art. 7(1).

[110] Ibid.

[111] Complaints Notice, para. 57.

[112] See e.g. Case T-751/15, *Contact Software* EU:T:2017:602, where the complainant's *own website* contradicted its claims regarding an alleged refusal to supply interoperability information. The GC confirmed that the Commission was entitled to reject the complaint on the basis of the low probability of successfully establishing an infringement.

insufficient Union interest to warrant the time and resources that would be required to investigate fully. It may also consider that another NCA within the ECN would be better placed to deal with the case. The Commission has a duty 'to examine carefully the facts and points of law brought to its notice by the complainant in order to decide whether they disclose conduct liable to distort competition in the [internal] market and affect trade between Member States'.[113] It does not, however, have a duty to proceed to a final decision on the alleged breach. This point was confirmed in *Automec II*,[114] where the GC held that the Commission may prioritise cases before it. As a public enforcer, it has a margin of discretion to set priorities in its enforcement activity. The rights conferred upon complainants do not, therefore, include a right to obtain a decision as regards the existence or otherwise of the alleged infringement.[115]

Case T-24/90, *Automec Srl v Commission (Automec II)* EU:T:1992:97

A complaint was lodged by Automec, in respect of the refusal by BMW to renew Automec's distributorship of BMW cars in Italy. Automec brought proceedings before the national courts to compel BMW to continue the contractual relationship, and it complained to the Commission claiming that BMW was obliged to supply it with vehicles and spare parts. The Commission informed Automec that it had no power to grant its application. Automec commenced review proceedings, challenging the Commission's refusal to pursue its case. The Commission subsequently sent Automec a letter rejecting the complaint, stating that there was insufficient Union interest to justify examining the facts. Automec brought further proceedings seeking annulment of the latter decision.

Note that the judgment refers to the precursor to Regulation 1/2003 (Regulations 17 and 99/63), but the points of law established remain equally applicable to the later regime.

General Court

71. The . . . question raised by this plea asks in substance what the Commission's obligations are when it receives [a complaint] from a natural or legal person.

72. . . . Regulations 17 and 99/63 confer procedural rights on persons who have lodged a complaint with the Commission, such as the right to be informed of the reasons for which the Commission intends to reject their complaint and the right to submit observations in this connection. Thus the [Union] legislature has imposed certain specified obligations upon the Commission. However, neither Regulation 17 nor Regulation 99/63 contain[s] express provisions relating to the action to be taken concerning the substance of a complaint and any obligations on the part of the Commission to carry out investigations.

73. In determining the Commission's obligations in this context, the first point to note is that the Commission is responsible for the implementation and orientation of [Union] competition policy (. . . Case C-234/89 *Delimitis* v. *Henninger Bräu AG* . . . at 991). For that reason, Article [105(1) TFEU] gave the Commission the task of ensuring that the principles laid down by Articles [101] and [102] were applied, and the provisions adopted pursuant to Article [103 TFEU] have conferred wide powers upon it.

74. The scope of the Commission's obligations in the field of competition law must be examined in the light of Article [105(1)], which, in this area, constitutes the specific expression of the general supervisory task entrusted to the Commission by Article [17(1) TEU]. However . . . that task does not mean that the Commission is bound to commence proceedings seeking to establish the existence of any infringement of [Union] law.

[113] Case T-575/93, *Koelman* EU:T:1996:1, para. 39. [114] Case T-24/90, EU:T:1992:97.

[115] Except where the subject matter of the complaint falls within the exclusive purview of the Commission, e.g. the withdrawal of a block exemption in an individual case, see Reg. 1/2003, Art. 29.

> 75. In that regard, . . . the rights conferred upon complainants by Regulations 17 and 99/63 do not include a right to obtain a decision, within the meaning of Article [288 TFEU], as regards the existence or otherwise of the alleged infringement . . .
>
> 76. As the Commission is under no obligation to rule on the existence or otherwise of an infringement it cannot be compelled to carry out an investigation, because such investigation could have no purpose other than to seek evidence of the existence or otherwise of an infringement, which it is not required to establish . . .
>
> 77. In that connection, . . . in the case of an authority entrusted with a public service task, the power to take all the organizational measures necessary for the performance of that task, including setting priorities within the limits prescribed by the law—where those priorities have not been determined by the legislature—is an inherent feature of administrative activity. This must be the case in particular where an authority has been entrusted with a supervisory and regulatory task as extensive and general as that which has been assigned to the Commission in the field of competition. Consequently, the fact that the Commission applies different degrees of priority to the cases submitted to it in the field of competition is compatible with the obligations imposed on it by [Union] law.
>
> . . .
>
> 79. However, although the Commission cannot be compelled to conduct an investigation, the procedural safeguards provided for by Article 3 of Regulation 17 and Article 6 of Regulation 99/63 oblige it nevertheless to examine carefully the factual and legal particulars brought to its notice by the complainant in order to decide whether they disclose conduct of such a kind as to distort competition in the [internal] market and affect trade between Member States (. . . *Demo-Studio Schmidt, CICCE* and *BAT and Reynolds*, cited above).

The GC furthermore confirmed that the question whether a case exhibits sufficient 'Union interest' constitutes a legitimate criterion by which the Commission may exercise its powers of case prioritisation, being consistent with its role as an administrative authority which must act in the public interest.[116]

The Commission's Complaints Notice sets out the criteria which it uses to assess whether a case has a Union interest.[117] The Commission does not regard any situation as excluded in principle from investigation, but will assess in each case how serious the alleged infringements are and how persistent their consequences. It must consider, in particular, the duration and the extent of the infringements complained of and their effect on competition in the Union. It may be necessary to balance the significance of the alleged breach as regards the functioning of the internal market, the probability of establishing the existence of the breach, and the scope of the investigation required. While the Commission's discretion does not depend on how advanced the investigation is, this forms part of the circumstances which the Commission may take into consideration. The Commission may decide that it is inappropriate to investigate a complaint where the undertakings concerned agree to change their conduct in such a way that it considers that there is no longer a sufficient Union interest to intervene, or where the practices in question have ceased. In the latter case, the Commission must consider whether anticompetitive effects persist, and whether the seriousness of the infringements or the persistence of their effects might nonetheless give the complaint a Union interest. Additionally, the Commission might reject a complaint on the ground that the complainant can bring an action before national courts.[118]

[116] Case T-24/90, *Automec II* EU:T:1992:97, paras. 85 and 86. [117] [2004] OJ C101/65, para. 44.

[118] The Commission applied these principles when rejecting a complaint about Athens airport, and was upheld on appeal: Case T-306/05, *Scippacercola* EU:T:2008:9 (COMP/38.469, *Athens International Airport*) upheld by order, Case C-159/08 P, EU:C:2009:188. See also Case T-60/05, *Union Française de l'Express v Commission (UFEX)* EU:T:2007:269 (Commission should consider seriousness of infringement even when terminated and without continuing anti-competitive effects); and Case T-74/11, *Omnis* EU:T:2013:283 (there is no obligatory or limited list of criteria the Commission must apply, it depends on the circumstances of the individual case).

It is clear from *Automec II*, however, that before rejecting a complaint, the Commission must: carefully examine the factual and legal particulars; set out the legal and factual considerations which led it to the conclusion of insufficient Union interest; and take account of the circumstances.[119] It must examine the complaint diligently and impartially in accordance with the principle of sound administration.[120] Sloppy errors in assessment even at this early stage, as in *CEAHR* where the Commission was held to have wrongly defined the relevant market,[121] may lead to annulment of the subsequent rejection decision by the EU Courts.

The Commission is entitled to reject a complaint on the grounds that an NCA is dealing, or has dealt, with the case.[122] This was explored in *easyJet*.[123] The airline lodged various complaints about charges at Schiphol airport with the Dutch competition authority. The NCA rejected all of these, having examined the charges under Article 102. The airline then complained to the Commission, again alleging breach of Article 102. The Commission rejected the complaint on the basis, inter alia, that it had been investigated by the NCA. The complainant appealed, claiming that because the complaint had been rejected, it had not been addressed. The GC held that a complaint has been dealt with for these purposes if an NCA has rejected it after a review carried out in the light of the EU competition rules.

Where the Commission decides not to act on a complaint, it must communicate this to the complainant, and allow it an opportunity to make its views known with an Article 7(1) letter. In conveying this information, the Commission is obliged to provide all relevant details of its intention to reject the complaint. In *Polskie Górnictwo Naftowe i Gazownictwo*, the Commission failed to state explicitly that it intended to rely upon the State action defence, an omission that meant it was held to have failed to fulfil its obligations to the complainant under Article 7(1) of Regulation 773/2004.[124] When this process is completed, the Commission must either initiate a procedure or reject the complaint under Article 7(2) of Regulation 773/2004.[125] Although the Commission is not required to proceed to a final decision on the permissibility of the impugned conduct, it must, if it opts not to investigate, formally reject the complaint by decision, stating reasons. This decision is subject to appeal before the GC.

(iv) Acting on a Complaint

If the Commission chooses to initiate proceedings, it does so by issuing an SO. It can take an infringement decision even if the complaint has been withdrawn in the meantime.[126] The Commission's fact-finding powers and the opening of a formal procedure are discussed in Sections 6.C and 6.D. A few points of importance are highlighted here. First, since the Commission is bound by a duty of confidentiality, the complainant should identify any business secrets or other confidential information which it does not wish the Commission to disclose. Secondly, if the Commission initiates proceedings and issues an SO relating to a matter in respect of which it has received a complaint, it must provide a non-confidential version to the complainant and give it an opportunity to make its views known.[127] Where appropriate, non-confidential versions of the replies to the SO can be given to the complainant, provided that business secrets are not disclosed and the suppliers of the information

[119] Case T-432/05, *EMC Development* EU:T:2010:189, paras. 59–60, appeal dismissed Case C-367/10 P, EU:C:2011:203.

[120] Case T-54/99, *max.mobil* EU:T:2002:20, paras. 56–57.

[121] Case T-427/08, *CEAHR* EU:T:2010:517.

[122] Reg. 1/2003, Art. 13.

[123] Case T-355/13, *easyJet* EU:T:2015:36.

[124] Case T-399/19 *Polskie Górnictwo Naftowe i Gazownictwo* EU:T:2022:44.

[125] Reg. 773/2004 [2004] OJ L123/18, Art. 7(2). See Case T-186/94, *Guérin Automobiles* EU:T:1995:114, para. 34, and Case T-64/89, *Automec I* [1990] ECR II-367.

[126] COMP/37.860, *Morgan Stanley/Visa International and Visa Europe*, on appeal Case T-461/07, EU:T:2011:181.

[127] This does not, however, apply in respect of the SO in the cartel settlement procedure, see Section 6.F.

have been consulted.[128] Thirdly, the complainant may be given the opportunity to make submissions at the oral hearing if it so requests.[129] Fourthly, if the Commission finds that an undertaking has infringed Article 101 or 102, it cannot compensate an entity which has suffered loss in consequence of breach.[130] Compensation must instead be pursued through private action in national courts, as discussed in Chapter 14.

(v) Judicial Review Proceedings

Where the Commission is in breach of an obligation to act it is in principle possible, under Article 265 TFEU, to bring proceedings in respect of its failure to act.[131] Before such proceedings can be brought, the Commission must be called upon to act and then fail to adopt a measure to which the complainant is legally entitled under EU law. Since a complainant cannot insist that the Commission should commence an investigation, it cannot bring proceedings under Article 265 alleging failure to do so. The complainant might, however, challenge a failure to issue an Article 7(1) letter within a reasonable time.[132] Because the Commission must formally reject a complaint, a complainant can also bring Article 265 proceedings where such a final decision has not been taken.

Once the Commission has formally rejected a complaint, the complainant may, if it wishes, challenge the validity of that decision under Article 263 TFEU.[133] If an individual has standing to complain to the Commission, it will have standing to institute proceedings where its complaint is rejected.[134] The formal rejection of a complaint is a reviewable act under Article 263.[135] The Commission's preliminary investigations cannot, however, be challenged. In some cases, it may be difficult to determine whether the Commission has given a final decision which is susceptible to review.[136]

C. THE INVESTIGATION STAGE OF THE ADMINISTRATIVE PROCEDURE: FACT-FINDING BY THE COMMISSION

(i) General

The Commission has extensive fact-finding powers under Articles 18–21 of Regulation 1/2003.[137] These enable the Commission to request and require the provision of information, to interview witnesses, and to conduct 'dawn raids' at business premises and other locations. These powers are not unconstrained, however, and the Commission's exercise of its fact-finding capabilities have frequently been challenged before the Union Courts, often on the grounds that the Commission has breached general principles of law or fundamental rights. The parties have no right to be heard before the investigatory stage, and the right to be heard does not apply fully until the SO has been issued. The principle of proportionality is of particular importance, insofar as measures adopted by the EU institutions cannot exceed what is appropriate and necessary to attain the legitimate objectives of the relevant

[128] Antitrust ManProc, Module 21, para. 17.

[129] Reg. 773/2004 [2004] OJ L123/18, Art. 6. Complaints Notice, paras. 64–67.

[130] Instead, the fine goes into the EU coffers.

[131] P. Craig and G. de Búrca, *EU Law: Text, Cases and Materials* (7th edn, Oxford University Press, 2020), Chap. 15.

[132] See Cases T-190/95 and T-45/96, *Sodima* EU:T:1999:318.

[133] In Case T-399/19 *Polskie Górnictwo Naftowe i Gazownictwo* EU:T:2022:44, a complainant succeeded in having the rejection of its complained overturned, on the basis both that the Commission failed to fulfil its obligations under Art. 7(1) of Reg. 773/2004, and that it committed a manifest error when assessing the prospects for an Art. 102 investigation on the facts.

[134] Case 26/76, *Metro SB-Grossmärkte* EU:C:1977:167, para. 13. [135] See Section 7.

[136] See e.g. Case T-37/92, *BEUC* EU:T:1994:54 and Case C-39/93 P, *SFEI* EU:C:1994:253.

[137] Arts. 18 and 20 of which correspond, respectively, to Arts. 11 and 14 of Reg. 17.

legislation. Where there is a choice between several appropriate measures, recourse must be had to the least onerous, and the disadvantages must not be disproportionate to the aims pursued.[138]

(ii) Article 18 Requests for Information

Under Article 18 of Regulation 1/2003, the Commission may request—and in certain instances, *demand*—that undertakings supply it with information. Article 18(1) provides that the Commission 'may, by simple request or by decision, require undertakings and associations of undertakings to provide all necessary information'. This includes requests for the disclosure of documents.[139] The difference between a 'simple request' and one made 'by decision' is the extent to which the receiving party is obliged to comply. An Article 18 request can be made at any time during a Commission investigation, and is not precluded, inter alia, by the Commission having already carried out an Article 20 inspection.[140]

Article 18(2) provides that a simple request for information must:

> state the legal basis and the purpose of the request, specify what information is required and fix the time-limit within which the information is to be provided, and the penalties provided for in Article 23 for supplying incorrect or misleading information.

There is no *duty* to comply, although the intentional or negligent provision of *incorrect* or *misleading* information can be fined under Article 23(1)(a) of Regulation 1/2003. A desire to cooperate and not to make the situation worse may be a spur to accuracy. The fact that, ultimately, the Commission can demand the information under Article 18(3) is another reason for complying with a simple request.

Where a request is made by decision under Article 18(3), recipients are legally obliged to provide the information specified, with fines and periodic penalty payments available for non-compliance pursuant to Articles 23 and 24 of Regulation 1/2003, respectively. A request by decision must state its legal basis and purpose, the information required, and the time limit. It must also warn of the possibility of fines for non-compliance, indicate or impose periodic penalties, and note that the decision is reviewable by the Court. The Commission's choice of an Article 18(3) decision rather than a simple request must be proportionate, meaning that the Commission must possess sufficiently serious evidence to justify its demand.

An Article 18(3) decision requires an adequate statement of reasons, in line with the overarching requirements of Article 296 TFEU. This was reiterated in the *Cement and Related Products* investigation, in which undertakings appealed against Article 18(3) decisions, inter alia on the ground that the Commission had not sufficiently set out the putative infringements under investigation.[141] Although initially upheld by the GC,[142] the CJ annulled the decisions on the basis that the statement of reasons was inadequate.[143]

[138] See e.g. Case C-331/88, *Fedesa* EU:C:1990:391, paras. 8 and 14; Case C-189/01, *Jippes* EU:C:2001:420, para. 81.

[139] Case 374/87, *Orkem* EU:C:1989:387, para. 14. [140] Ibid.

[141] Case T-292/11, *Cemex and Others* EU:T:2014:125; Case T-293/11, *Holcim (Deutschland) and Holcim* EU:T:2014:127; Case T-296/11, *Cementos Portland Valderrivas* EU:T:2014:121; Case T-297/11, *Buzzi Unicem* EU:T:2014:122; Case T-302/11, *HeidelbergCement* EU:T:2014:128; Case T-305/11, *Italmobiliare* EU:T:2014:126; Case T-306/11, *Schwenk Zement v Commission* EU:T:2014:123. The case concerned was COMP/39.520, *Cement and Related Products*.

[142] See e.g. Case T-302/11, *HeidelbergCement* EU:T:2014:128, para. 42; Case T-306/11, *Schwenk Zement* EU:T:2014:123, para. 37.

[143] Case C-247/14 P, *HeidelbergCement* EU:C:2016:149; Case C-248/14 P, *Schwenk Zement* EU:C:2016:150; Case C-267/14 P, *Buzzi Unicem* EU:C:2016:151; Case C-268/14 P, *Italmobiliare* EU:C:2016:152. For case analysis, see F. Carloni and G. Da Costa, 'Judgments in the *Cement* Case: Requirement for Greater Clarity, Specificity, and Justification for Information Requests from the Commission' (2016) 7 *JECLAP* 457.

Case C-247/14 P, *HeidelbergCement v Commission* EU:C:2016:149

Court of Justice

19. Th[e] obligation to state specific reasons is a fundamental requirement, designed not merely to show that the request for information is justified but also to enable the undertakings concerned to assess the scope of their duty to cooperate whilst at the same time safeguarding their rights of defence . . .

20. With respect to the obligation to state the 'purpose of the request', this relates to the Commission's obligation to indicate the subject of its investigation in its request, and therefore to identify the alleged infringement of competition rules (. . . *SEP* v *Commission*, C-36/92 P, . . . , paragraph 21).

21. In that regard, the Commission is not required to communicate to the addressee of a decision requesting information all the information at its disposal concerning the presumed infringements, or to make a precise legal analysis of those infringements, providing it clearly indicates the suspicions which it intends to investigate (. . . *Nexans and Nexans France* v *Commission*, C-37/13 P, . . . , paragraph 35 . . .).

22. That obligation may be explained, inter alia, by the fact that, as is apparent from Article 18(1) of Regulation No 1/2003 and recital 23 thereof, in order to carry out the duties assigned to it by that regulation, the Commission may, by simple request or by decision, require undertakings and associations of undertakings to provide 'all necessary information'.

23. As correctly noted by the General Court, . . . 'the Commission is entitled to require the disclosure only of information which may enable it to investigate presumed infringements which justify the conduct of the investigation and are set out in the request for information'.

24. Since the necessity of the information must be judged in relation to the purpose stated in the request for information, that purpose must be indicated with sufficient precision, otherwise it will be impossible to determine whether the information is necessary and the Court will be prevented from exercising judicial review (. . . *SEP* v *Commission*, C-36/92 P, . . . , paragraph 21).

25. The General Court also correctly held . . . that the adequacy of the statement of reasons of the decision at issue depends 'on whether or not the putative infringements that the Commission intends to investigate are defined in sufficiently clear terms'.

. . .

31. [The] statement of reasons [in the instant case] does not make it possible to determine with sufficient precision either the products to which the investigation relates or the suspicions of infringement justifying the adoption of that decision. It follows that that statement of reasons does not enable the undertaking in question to check whether the requested information is necessary for the purposes of the investigation or the European Union judicature to exercise its power of review.

The adequacy of a statement of reasons must be assessed with regard to its context as well as its wording and the relevant legal rules.[144] In the *Cement* investigation, the context included the fact that the decision was adopted more than two years after the first dawn raids, and after the Commission had already sent various other requests for information. The Commission therefore had enough information to present a more precise account of the suspected infringements.[145]

The concept of 'necessary information' must be interpreted by reference to the purposes for which the powers of investigation are conferred upon the Commission.[146] This is an application of the principles of proportionality and of protection against arbitrary and disproportionate intervention by

[144] Case T-302/11, *HeidelbergCement* EU:T:2014:128, para. 16.
[145] Ibid., para. 39.
[146] C-36/92 P, *SEP* EU:C:1994:205.

public authorities in the sphere of private activities.[147] The requirement for a correlation between the request for information and the presumed infringement is met if the request can be legitimately considered to be related, in the sense that the Commission may reasonably suppose that the document will help to determine whether the alleged infringement has occurred.[148] Although it is not easy to show that the Commission has exceeded its leeway in the information it has requested, the Commission cannot go on a 'fishing expedition'.[149]

In the *Cement* cases, undertakings also claimed that the requirement of 'necessity' was not met in respect of the excessive *quantity* of information requested.[150] On appeal, the GC admitted that the high volume of information requested imposed a heavy workload to answer, but held, nevertheless, that it was not disproportionate.[151] Taking a comparatively relaxed view of necessity, the GC said that the Commission need not have information establishing the existence of the infringement before sending the request; that it can request that the information be provided in a highly specific, detailed format;[152] and that it is not obliged to inform the undertakings what evidence it already possesses. However, the time limit must be adequate for the undertaking to provide its reply and to satisfy itself that it is supplying complete, correct, and not misleading information.[153] On appeal, Advocate General Wahl recommended the annulment of the decisions, inter alia on the grounds of lack of necessity and excessive burden.[154] As the CJ annulled the decisions due to the inadequacy of the statement of reasons, it did not directly address other issues. The Commission may justifiably claim that the GC's confirmation of its powers remains, but the position is unsatisfactory.

Intel[155] involved a claim that the Commission had failed to collect *sufficient* information, in that it had not obtained certain exculpatory documents that the defendant knew to be in the complainant's possession. The GC recognised that the principle of sound administration, enshrined in Article 41 of the Charter, required the Commission to examine all the relevant aspects of the individual case carefully and impartially. It was, however, in principle for the Commission to decide how it wished to conduct the investigation and to decide what documents it required.[156] The Commission was not obliged to ensure it had all potentially exculpatory evidence,[157] and had a margin of discretion in deciding whether to obtain documents requested by a defendant.[158] Nevertheless, in exceptional circumstances, there may an obligation to obtain documents at the

[147] Cases T-458/09 and 171/10, *Slovak Telecom* EU:T:2012:145, para. 81; Case T-296/11, *Cementos Portland Valderrivas* EU:T:2014:121, para. 39.

[148] Case C-36/92 P, *SEP* EU:C:1994:205, para. 21, approving Jacobs AG, para. 21; Cases T-458/09: 171/10, *Slovak Telecom* EU:T:2012:145, para. 40; and Case C-466/19 P, *Qualcomm* EU:C:2021:76, paras. 69–70.

[149] See Case C-94/00, *Roquette Frères* EU:C:2002:603, paras. 54–55; and Case T-296/11, *Cementos Portland Valderrivas* EU:T:2014:121, paras. 40–60.

[150] Case T-292/11, *Cemex and Others* EU:T:2014:125; Case T-293/11, *Holcim (Deutschland) and Holcim* EU:T:2014:127; Case T-297/11, *Buzzi Unicem* EU:T:2014:122; Case T-302/11, *HeidelbergCement* EU:T:2014128; Case T-305/11, *Italmobiliare* EU:T:2014:126; Case T-306/11, *Schwenk Zement* EU:T:014:123.

[151] Given the necessities of the inquiry and the extent of the claimed infringements; see e.g. Case T-296/11, *Cementos Portland Valderrivas* EU:T:2014:121, para. 89. A similar approach was taken in Case C-466/19 P, *Qualcomm* EU:C:2021:76, para. 109.

[152] Such as being broken down on the basis of 37 parameters, see Case T-296/11, *Cementos Portland Valderrivas* EU:T:2014:121, para. 87.

[153] Case T-306/11, *Schwenk* EU:T:014:123, para. 73. The GC held the two-week time limit to be 'disproportionate to say the least' (para. 92) and annulled the decision in respect of one set of questions. The Best Practices Notice, para. 38, says that the time limit is at least two weeks but will be set according to the length and complexity of the request. See also Case T-485/11, *Akzo Nobel* EU:T:2015:517.

[154] Opinion, EU:C:2015:694, 15 October 2015.

[155] Case T-286/09, *Intel* EU:T:2014:547; the point was not addressed on appeal in Case C-413/14 P, EU:C:2017:632.

[156] Ibid., para. 360. [157] Ibid., para. 361. [158] Ibid., para. 362.

request of the investigated undertaking. This would be where four cumulative conditions are fulfilled:[159]

- it is impossible for the defendant to obtain the documents itself or disclose them to the Commission;
- the relevant documents are identified as precisely as possible;
- the documents are probably of considerable importance to the undertaking's defence; and
- the volume of documents at issue must not be disproportionate to their importance in the context of the investigation.

Article 18(4) of Regulation 1/2003 provides that lawyers may supply information on behalf of their clients, although the client remains responsible if the information is incorrect, incomplete, or misleading. The Commission's guidance on 'Best Practices for the Submission of Economic Evidence'[160] explains the manner in which the Commission prefers undertakings to present economic and econometric evidence in reply to requests for quantitative data.

The Commission must send a copy of the request or decision to the NCA of the Member State whose territory is affected and/or in whose territory the seat of the undertaking concerned is situated.[161] By Article 18(6), the governments of the Member States and the NCAs must supply the Commission with all necessary information that it may request.

The questions of when undertakings may withhold documents from the Commission on the ground that they are legally privileged, and to what extent they can refuse to supply information on grounds of self-incrimination, are dealt with in Sections 6.C.vi and 6.C.vii.

(iii) Article 20 Inspections of Undertakings

a. General

Article 20(1) empowers the Commission to carry out 'all necessary inspections' of undertakings and associations of undertakings. This means investigations at the undertaking's physical business premises. Inspections are carried out by officials and 'other accompanying persons authorised by the Commission',[162] such as IT experts.

Again, Article 20 distinguishes between simple inspections and those ordered by decision of the Commission. Under Article 20(3), the Commission can conduct inspections simply by drafting a 'written authorisation' which must be produced at the time the inspection is carried out.[163] While the Commission is not obliged to give advance warning of any planned inspection to the undertaking concerned, it must give notice 'in good time before the inspection' to the NCA of the Member State in whose territory the inspection is conducted. So long as the Commission officials present only the Article 20(3) 'authorisation', an undertaking is under no legal obligation to submit to the inspection. Under Article 20(4), however, undertakings *must* submit to procedures ordered by a decision of the Commission.[164] The Commission cannot carry out inspections if the suspected agreement or concerted practice produces effects exclusively outside the internal market, as Articles 101 and 102 apply only to effects on inter-Member State trade. It can, however, examine documents relating to markets outside the EU in order to detect anti-competitive conduct which is liable to affect trade between Member States.[165]

[159] Ibid., paras. 375–382. [160] See n. 26. [161] Reg. 1/2003, Art. 18(5).

[162] Ibid., Art. 20(3), (5), and (6).

[163] This must contain the same or equivalent matters as required in respect of requests for information under Art. 18(2).

[164] Art. 20(4) decisions can be taken by the Commissioner responsible for competition as delegated by the College of Commissioners: Case 5/85, *AKZO* EU:C:1986:328; Cases 46/87 and 227/88, *Hoechst* EU:C:1989:337. The decision must contain the same or equivalent matters as required in respect of decisions under Art. 18(3).

[165] Case C-37/13 P, *Nexans France* EU:C:2014:2030, para. 40.

In a 'dawn raid', the officials arrive without warning, armed with an Article 20(4) decision. It is well established that the Commission is entitled to do so without first going through the Article 20(3) simple procedure.[166] There may be simultaneous surprise arrivals at undertakings across the EU where, for example, the Commission suspects the existence of a hardcore cartel.[167] The apparently draconian powers of the Commission have been justified as follows:[168]

> More often, the most serious cartels are . . . operated in conditions of strict secrecy. Communication between participants is kept to a minimum and knowledge of the arrangements confined to certain key employees. Meetings take place in safe countries or under the cover of a seemingly innocent trade association. There may even be emergency arrangements to shred documents and warn other participants . . . in the event of an investigation. Sometimes the cartel rules provide for members to deny all knowledge of documents or their contents even when these are found in the safe. In such circumstances resort to surprise must be a legitimate and essential precaution.

An Explanatory Note on the conduct of Article 20(4) inspections, setting out the Commission's understanding of its Article 20(4) powers, is published on DG Comp's website.[169]

Inspections, especially those conducted on foot of a decision taken under Article 20(4), raise questions about their compatibility with fundamental rights, in particular the right to respect for private and family life protected by Article 8 ECHR and Article 7 of the Charter. This concern was considered in the early case of *National Panasonic*,[170] where the CJ scrutinised the first unannounced dawn raid conducted by the Commission. The CJ roundly rejected arguments that Article 8 ECHR (and by analogy today, Article 7 of the Charter) entitled the defendant to advance notice of any planned inspection or granted it a right to be heard before any decision ordering an inspection was adopted. It emphasised the non-absolute nature of the protections granted by Article 8 ECHR, which permits deviation which 'is in accordance with the law and is necessary in a democratic society'.[171] It moreover recognised that the Commission's evidence-gathering powers are an essential aspect of its competition enforcement function, the exercise of which 'contributes to the maintenance of the system of competition intended by the Treaty which undertakings are absolutely bound to comply with'.[172] The CJ therefore concluded that an unannounced inspection authorised by a decision is not a breach of an undertaking's fundamental rights.

Article 20 does not require the Commission to obtain domestic judicial authorisation before adopting an inspection decision or carrying out the inspection. The lack of a need for such authorisation is held to be compatible with Article 8 ECHR, because the lawfulness of the inspection decision is subject to review by the Union Courts.[173] It is clear from the Strasbourg case law, however, that in the absence of prior judicial involvement, *ex post* judicial review must be stringent.[174] This was an issue in *Deutsche Bahn*,[175] in which the CJ upheld the GC's dismissal of the plea that the lack of prior judicial

[166] Case 136/79, *National Panasonic* EU:C:1980:169.

[167] The *Polypropylene Cartel* ([1986] OJ L230/1), for instance, involved ten simultaneous raids. The inspections may also be coordinated with inspections by competition authorities outside the EU.

[168] J. M. Joshua, 'The Element of Surprise' (1983) 8 *ELRev* 3, 5. The author was previously the Deputy Head of the Cartel Unit at DG Comp.

[169] See <http://ec.europa.eu/competition/antitrust/legislation/explanatory_note.pdf>.

[170] Case 136/79, *National Panasonic* EU:C:1980:169. [171] Ibid., para. 19. [172] Ibid., para. 20.

[173] Case C-583/13 P, *Deutsche Bahn* EU:C:2015:404, paras. 18–36; emphasising, as a matter of Convention jurisprudence, the importance of effective *ex post* judicial review in order to ensure compliance with Art. 8 ECHR, see *JanssenCilag SAS v France*, App. no. 33931/12, Judgment of 21 March 2017.

[174] See e.g. *Harju v Finland*, App. no. 56716/09, Judgment of 15 February 2011; *Delta Pekárny a.s. v The Czech Republic*, App. no. 97/11, Judgment of 2 October 2014.

[175] Case C-583/13 P, *Deutsche Bahn* EU:C:2015:404.

authorisation in EU law in respect of inspections could not be remedied by effective *ex post* review. It approved five categories of safeguards set out by the GC which form the framework for the inspection decision and against which the legality of the decision must be measured, namely: (a) the statement of reasons on which inspection decisions are based; (b) the limits imposed on the Commission during the conduct of inspections; (c) the impossibility for the Commission to carry out an inspection by force; (d) the intervention of national authorities; and (e) the existence of *ex post facto* remedies.[176] It held that the GC's detailed examination of the decision against that framework satisfied both the ECHR and EU law.

Case C-583/13 P, *Deutsche Bahn AG v Commission* EU:C:2015:404

Court of Justice

29. The detailed examination conducted by the General Court satisfies both the requirements of the ECtHR . . . and the letter of Regulation No 1/2003 and the Court of Justice's case-law.

30. On the one hand, it is apparent from Article 20(4) of Regulation No 1/2003 that the inspection decision must specify the subject-matter and purpose of the inspection, indicate the penalties incurred by the undertaking concerned and the undertaking's right to have the decision reviewed by the Court of Justice.

31. On the other hand, it is settled case-law that the Commission's powers of investigation are strictly defined, encompassing inter alia the exclusion of non-business documents from the scope of the investigation, the right to legal assistance, the preservation of the confidentiality of correspondence between legal counsel and clients, the obligation to state reasons for the inspection decision and the option of bringing proceedings before the EU courts (. . . *Roquette Frères*, . . . , paragraphs 44 to 50).

32. Moreover . . . the presence of a post-inspection judicial review is considered by the ECtHR as capable of offsetting the lack of prior judicial authorisation and thus capable of constituting a fundamental guarantee in order to ensure the compatibility of the inspection measure in question with Article 8 of the ECHR (see inter alia ECtHR, judgment in *Delta Pekárny a.s. v. the Czech Republic*, no. 97/11, paragraphs 83, 87 and 92, 2 October 2014).

33. That is precisely the case under the system put in place in the European Union, as Article 20(8) of Regulation No 1/2003 states expressly that the lawfulness of the Commission decision is to be subject to review by the Court of Justice.

34. The review provided for by the Treaties means that the European Union courts carry out an in-depth review of the law and of the facts on the basis of the evidence adduced by the applicant in support of the pleas in law put forward (. . . *Chalkor* v *Commission*, C-386/10 P, . . . , paragraph 62, and *CB* v *Commission*, paragraph 44).

35. It follows that the General Court was correct in holding that the fundamental right to the inviolability of private premises, as protected by Article 8 of the ECHR, is not disregarded by there being no prior judicial authorisation.

In *Deutsche Bahn*, the EU Courts were at pains to demonstrate the comprehensiveness of the judicial review of inspections, to show compliance with fundamental rights requirements.

There is one exception to the general rule that the Commission does not need to seek prior judicial authorisation at the domestic level: namely, where it anticipates or faces opposition to an inspection from the undertaking concerned, and so seeks 'necessary assistance . . . of the police or of an equivalent enforcement authority' of the Member State concerned under Article 20(6). While Member States

[176] Case T-289/11, *Deutsche Bahn* EU:T:2013:404, paras. 74–100.

are obliged to provide such help, they are nonetheless entitled to make the provision of assistance subject to 'authorisation from a judicial authority according to national rules'.[177] National courts are permitted to control the proportionality of the inspection decision, namely to assess whether 'the Commission decision is authentic and that the coercive measures envisaged are neither arbitrary nor excessive having regard to the subject matter of the inspection'.[178] National courts cannot, however, consider the lawfulness of the underlying decision, which is subject to review only by the Union Courts.[179]

Inspection decisions must be as precise as possible.[180] Inspections are intended to enable the Commission to gather documentary evidence to check the actual existence and scope of a given factual and legal situation about which *it already possesses certain information*. The Commission must therefore already possess 'certain information, constituting sufficiently serious indicia for it to suspect an infringement of the competition rules'.[181] Decisions must indicate the subject and objective of the inspection, in order to show that the intervention is proportional, to enable the undertaking to understand the scope of its duty to cooperate, and to preserve the rights of the defence.[182] However, the Commission is not required to communicate all the information at its disposal concerning the presumed infringements, or make a precise legal analysis of those infringements, providing that it clearly indicates the presumed facts under investigation.[183] So in *Nexans*,[184] an inspection decision covering suspected agreements and/or concerted practices which 'probably have a global reach' was held to be a sufficient delineation of its geographical scope.[185] The decision was annulled in part nonetheless, as the subject matter was described in a way that encompassed all electric cables, whereas the Commission had reasonable grounds for ordering an inspection only in respect of high-voltage underground and underwater cables.[186] In *Ceské dráhy*, a decision authorising a dawn raid at the premises of the Czech railway incumbent was annulled to the extent that it enabled the Commission to collect evidence outside the relatively narrow scope of its investigation into predatory pricing on the Prague–Ostrava rail route.[187]

The prohibition on fishing expeditions was reinforced in *Deutsche Bahn*. In *Dow Benelux*,[188] the CJ had held that if, during an inspection, the Commission 'happened to obtain' evidence of an infringement which related to matters outside the subject matter of the investigation, it was not barred from initiating an inquiry into those matters in reliance on that evidence. In *Deutsche Bahn*,[189] the CJ clarified that this applied only if the discovery of that evidence was purely fortuitous. It was otherwise where the Commission inspectors had been informed about a second complaint about the undertaking beforehand, and based further inspection decisions on the material relating to that second complaint which was found during the first inspection.

In *National Panasonic*, the CJ had accepted that the general EU law principle of proportionality also applies here, meaning that Commission decisions to order inspections must be proportionate

[177] Reg. 1/2003, Art. 20(7). [178] Ibid., Art. 20(8). [179] Ibid.

[180] Case C-94/00, *Roquette Frères* EU:C:2002:603, para. 83.

[181] Case T-249/17, *Casino* EU:T:2020:458, para. 165.

[182] Case C-37/13 P, *Nexans France* EU:C:2014:2030, para. 34; see also Cases 46/87 and 227/88, *Hoechst* EU:C:1989:337, para. 29.

[183] Case C-37/13 P, *Nexans France* EU:C:2014:2030, para. 35; Case C-94/00, *Roquette Frères* EU:C:2002:603, para. 82; Case 97/87, *Dow Chemical Ibérica* EU:C:1989:380, para. 46.

[184] Case C-37/13 P, *Nexans France* EU:C:2014:2030, *aff'g* Case T-135/09, *Nexans France* EU:T:2012:596

[185] Case C-37/13 P, *Nexans* EU:C:2014:2030, paras. 38–41.

[186] Case T-135/09, *Nexans* EU:T:2012:596, paras. 60–94.

[187] Case T-325/16, *České dráhy* EU:T:2018:368. This aspect of the GC's judgment was not in issue in the defendant's further appeal in Case C-538/18 P, *České dráhy* EU:C:2020:53.

[188] Case 85/87, *Dow Benelux* EU:C:1989:379. [189] Case C-583/13 P, *Deutsche Bahn* EU:C:2015:404.

to the legitimate objective pursued by an investigation.[190] This was not interpreted as a particularly demanding element, however, with the CJ requiring only that the decision to order inspections amount to 'an appropriate inquiry, having regard to the special features of the case'.[191] In *Ceské dráhy*, the CJ confirmed that, in principle, it is for the Commission to assess whether information is necessary for it to carry out its task of enforcing the competition rules. Therefore, even if it already has indications, or indeed evidence, relating to the existence of an infringement, the Commission can legitimately consider it necessary to make additional checks to enable it to better identify the nature and/or scope of the infringement at issue.[192] This means, inter alia, that where sufficiently serious evidence of a potential breach exists, the Commission is not required to evaluate potentially exculpatory evidence prior to adopting an Article 20(4) decision.[193] The latter, instead, can be invoked by defendants later in the Commission's administrative proceedings, or on appeal against any formal finding of breach.[194]

b. The Powers of the Inspectors

An undertaking must actively and fully cooperate with the inspection.[195] However, as discussed, this duty exists only in connection with its activities in the sectors in respect of which the Commission has reasonable grounds for suspecting an infringement.[196]

Unlike challenges to the *legality* of an inspection decision, which can be challenged immediately in separate proceedings, the EU Courts may review disputes over issues that arise *during* an inspection only as part of the review of any final Commission decision and not in a separate action, because they are only 'measures implementing the inspection decision'.[197] This can leave investigated undertakings in a difficult position. If they refuse to cooperate during the inspection, they are liable to be fined periodic penalty payments under Article 23(1)—a decision that at least could be challenged immediately—although the Commission may instead opt to punish the obstruction by increasing any fine imposed in the final infringement decision.

Digitalisation of business records increasingly poses distinct challenges for evidence-gathering by the Commission. The ease and speed at which digital records can be copied may create a proportionality problem; the use of personal electronic devices and data storage systems for work purposes may raise privacy issues; and the location of digital information may go beyond the physical scope of the inspection authorisation.[198] In *Prysmian*, the CJ confirmed that the Commission is empowered by Article 20(2)(b) to make copies of data stored digitally at business premises and to review these further back in Brussels.[199] The CJ justified this interpretation of the inspection power on two bases: the effectiveness of the investigation, and minimising disruption to the business activities of the investigated undertaking.[200] It is standard procedure for inspectors to request to block access to the email accounts of key personnel for the duration of the inspection. In *EPH*, the Commission fined an

[190] Case 136/79, *National Panasonic* EU:C:1980:169, paras. 28–30. [191] Ibid., para. 29.

[192] Case C-538/18 P, *České dráhy* EU:C:2020:53, para. 63. [193] Ibid., para. 64. [194] Ibid.

[195] Case 374/87, *Orkem* EU:C:1989:387, paras. 22 and 27.

[196] Case C-37/13 P, *Nexans* EU:C:2014:2030, para. 34.

[197] Case T-135/09, *Nexans France* EU:T:2012:596, para. 125. See also Case T-340/03, *France Télécom* EU:T:2007:22. A complaint about the conduct of the inspection may be made only by the inspected party, unless the procedural irregularity is likely to concern the other party directly: Case T-410/09, *Almanet* EU:T:2012:676. Arguing that the CJEU's position on this point is incompatible with ECHR jurisprudence, see A. Steene, '*Nexans, Deutsche Bahn* and the ECJ's Refusal to Follow ECHR Case Law on Dawn Raids' (2016) 7 *JECLAP* 180.

[198] OECD, *Digital Evidence Gathering in Cartel Investigations. Issues Note*, DAF/COMP/LACF(2020)2, para. 9.

[199] Case C-601/18 P, *Prysmian* EU:C:2020:751. [200] Ibid., para. 72.

undertaking for modifying the password to one account during the inspection and for diverting all emails away from some blocked accounts.[201]

Under Article 20(2), inspections involve the following powers:[202]

(1) The Power to Enter Any Premises, Land, and Means of Transport of Undertakings and Associations of Undertakings (Article 20(2)(a))

The extent of this power was established in *Hoechst*.[203] If the undertakings opt to cooperate, the Commission officials may have shown to them any documents they request, and may enter such premises they choose and have shown to them the contents of particular furniture. They are *not* entitled forcibly to enter premises or furniture, or to carry out searches without the undertaking's consent. If the undertaking does not submit to the investigation, Article 20(6) comes into play, and the Commission must rely on the assistance of the Member State.[204]

(2) The Power to Examine Books and Other Records Related to the Business, Irrespective of the Medium on Which They are Stored (Article 20(2)(b))

'Irrespective of the medium on which they are stored' encompasses all forms of information technology. The Commission's Explanatory Note elaborates details what IT tools the inspectors can use. In *EPH*, the Commission noted that 'paper-based evidence has become less important and most of the documents collected nowadays during inspections are extracted from e-mail accounts and electronic files'.[205] The duty to cooperate means that undertakings must do everything possible to assist the inspectors' access.

(3) The Power to Take or Obtain in Any Form Copies of or Extracts from Such Books or Records (Article 20(2)(c))

Nowadays, copies or extracts are usually taken in electronic format. Inspectors may search the 'IT-environment' (for example, servers, desktop computers, laptops, tablets, and other mobile devices) and all storage media, including external hard drives and cloud services of an undertaking. The Commission can also search private devices and media that are used for professional purposes when these are found on the premises.[206] At the end of the inspection, any collected data that is still to be searched is placed in a sealed envelope (or equivalent) and taken to Brussels or left with the undertaking for safe-keeping pending a further inspection visit.[207]

(4) The Power to Seal Any Business Premises and Books or Records for the Period and to the Extent Necessary for the Inspection (Article 20(2)(d))

To 'seal' business premises or other materials means to make these inaccessible to the undertaking concerned for the duration of inspection. This might, for instance, involve placing certain materials in a nominated room at the business premises during the course of a multi-day inspection, covering the entrance to prevent entry. The power to do so was expressly conferred on the Commission in

[201] COMP/39.793, *EPH*, IP/12/319; upheld on appeal, Case T-272/12, *Energetický a pru˚myslový* EU:T:2017:753.

[202] For the detail and practicalities of inspections, see the Commission's Explanatory Note, n. 169; C. Kerse and N. Khan (Khan ed.), *EU Antitrust Procedure* (6th edn, Sweet & Maxwell, 2012), 3.072–3.138; Faull and Nikpay, n. 1, 8.343–8.387.

[203] Cases 46/87 and 227/88, *Hoechst* EU:C:1989:337, paras. 31–32. [204] Ibid.

[205] *EPH*, Summary of decision [2012] OJ C316/8, para. 17. [206] Explanatory Note, para. 10.

[207] Ibid., paras. 14–18.

Regulation 1/2003, although previously the Commission affixed seals to premises when it thought it necessary. Premises should not normally be sealed for more than 72 hours.[208] Undertakings can be fined under Article 23(1)(e) for breaching seals. In *E.ON*, the Commission imposed a fine of €38 million for breaching a seal during an inspection, which had been affixed overnight to the door of a room in which the inspectors had placed documents.[209]

(5) The Power to Ask Any Representative or Member of Staff of the Undertaking or Association of Undertakings for Explanations on Facts or Documents Relating to the Subject Matter and Purpose of the Inspection and to Record the Answers

The Article 20(2)(e) power is a wide-ranging one, empowering inspectors to ask any representative or member of staff for explanations on facts and documents relating to the subject matter and purpose of the inspection. The answers can be recorded.[210] Article 23(1)(d) provides that the Commission may fine the undertaking up to 1 per cent of total turnover of the previous business year if, in response to a question asked in accordance with Article 20(2)(e), they: give an incorrect or misleading answer; fail to rectify within a time limit set by the Commission an incorrect, incomplete or misleading answer given by a member of staff; or fail or refuse to provide a complete answer on facts relating to the subject matter and purpose of an inspection ordered by a decision adopted pursuant to Article 20(4). 'They' refers to the undertaking, not to its individual members of staff. There are no powers under Regulation 1/2003 to impose fines on individuals.[211]

It is clear from *Nexans*[212] that questioning employees is an 'implementing measure'. It is not a separately reviewable act that can be challenged earlier than any challenge to the final infringement decision.

c. Legal Advice

Article 20 says nothing about an undertaking's right to have legal advisers present during the investigation. When conducting the unannounced investigation in *National Panasonic*,[213] the Commission was prepared to wait a short period for the undertakings' legal advisers, but subsequently proceeded in their absence. The CJ held that Panasonic's fundamental rights had not been infringed, although it did not expressly avert to the legal adviser point. The Explanatory Note on inspections[214] says that officials may enter the premises and occupy offices without waiting for the undertaking to consult its lawyer, and that it accepts only a short delay before proceeding. During any wait, the undertaking's management must ensure that business records remain as they were on the officials' arrival, and the officials must be allowed to enter and remain in the offices of their choice. In *Koninklijke Wegenbouw Stevin*, an undertaking's refusal to allow the inspection to begin before the arrival of its external lawyer was held to constitute a refusal to submit to the inspection.[215]

[208] Reg. 1/2003, recital 25.

[209] Commission Decision 30.1.2008, COMP/39.326; Case T-141/08, *E.ON Energie* EU:T:2010:516, *aff'd* Case C-89/11 P, *E.ON Energie* EU:C:2012:738. See also COMP/39.796, *Suez Environnement*, IP/11/632.

[210] Under Reg. 773/2004, Art. 4(2) a copy of any recording made must be made available to the undertaking subsequently.

[211] Explaining that this omission is a hangover from the schema of the ECSC Treaty, see W. Mölls, 'Why Does Regulation (EC) No 1/2003 Provide for the Imposition of Penalties Only on Undertakings?: A Historical Perspective' (2022) 45 *World Competition* 195.

[212] Case T-135/09, *Nexans France* EU:T:2012:596.

[213] Case 136/79, *National Panasonic* EU:C:1980:169.

[214] See n. 169, para. 6.

[215] Case T-357/06, *Koninklijke Wegenbouw Stevin* EU:T:2012:488 (the appeal, Case C-586/12 P, EU:C:2013:863, was on other grounds).

(iv) Inspections on Private Premises under Article 21

Regulation 1/2003 also gives the Commission power to conduct inspections at *private* premises.[216] In other words, dawn raids may be conducted at the homes (and within the private vehicles) of directors and employees. Article 21(1) states:

> If a reasonable suspicion exists that books or other records related to the business and to the subject-matter of the inspection, which may be relevant to prove a serious violation of Article [101] or Article [102] . . . are being kept in any other premises, land and means of transport, including the homes of directors, managers and other members of staff of the undertakings and associations of undertakings concerned, the Commission can by decision order an inspection to be conducted in such other premises, land and means of transport.

Recital 26 explains that the provision was introduced because, '[e]xperience has shown that there are cases where business records are kept in the homes of directors or other people working for an undertaking'. In particular, the Commission is determined that its efforts to crack hardcore cartels are not frustrated by individuals hiding incriminating evidence at home.[217] Unsurprisingly, the safeguards provided by Article 8 ECHR apply par excellence to Article 21. In particular, an inspection of private premises *requires* prior authorisation from the national judicial authority of the Member State concerned. The right of the national court to review the necessity for the inspection, however, is limited as in Article 20(8), so that the national judicial authority may not call into question the necessity or demand that it be provided with information in the Commission's file. In controlling that the Commission decision is authentic and that the measures envisaged are neither arbitrary nor excessive, the national court should have regard to 'the importance of the evidence sought' and 'the reasonable likelihood that business books and records relating to the subject matter of the inspection are kept in the premises for which the authorisation is requested'.[218] In the light of the jurisprudence of the ECtHR, there is doubt as to whether the limited functions of the national courts in respect of Article 21 inspections satisfy the requirements for prior judicial authorisation.[219] As in respect of Article 20, therefore, it is the possibility of effective *ex post* judicial review by the EU Courts which must satisfy Article 8.

There is no provision in Article 21 for sealing private premises, nor for questioning the person whose premises are being searched. Regulation 1/2003 does not impose penalties for opposing the inspection: there is no provision for the Commission to fine either the undertaking or individual concerned. The position as regards forcible entry, if provided for in national law, is the same as in respect of Article 20.[220] The first dawn raid on a private home under Article 21 was carried out in 2007 in connection with the *Marine Hoses cartel*.[221]

(v) The Power to Take Statements

Article 19 of Regulation 1/2003 gives the Commission the power to 'take statements', by which it can conduct formal interviews with natural or legal persons. Such persons could include, for example,

[216] An innovation in Reg. 1/2003, as Reg. 17 did not contain such a power.

[217] As occurred in e.g. *SAS/Maersk* [2001] OJ L265/15.

[218] Art. 21(3). See also Notice on cooperation between the Commission and the courts of the EU Member States [2004] OJ C101/54, para. 40.

[219] See Bellamy and Child, n. 1, 13.029; Kerse and Khan, n. 202, 3.142. [220] See Section 6.C.iii.

[221] COMP/39.406, 28 January 2009; IP/09/137 (decision partially annulled on appeal on the issue of economic continuity, Cases T-146/09 etc., *Parker ITR and Parker-Hannifin* EU:T:2013:258; judgment set aside by the CJ, Case C-434/13 P, *Commission v Parker Hannifin Manufacturing Srl* EU:C:2014:2456).

ex-employees, complainants, competitors, or employees of candidates for leniency.[222] Interviews can be conducted 'by any means including by telephone or electronic means'.[223] They can only be conducted for the purpose of collecting information relating to the subject matter of an investigation.[224] The fact that the interview is conducted by a high-ranking official from DG Comp, or even the Competition Commissioner, does not preclude it from being classified as an interview within the meaning of Article 19, where the purpose is indeed to collect information relating to the subject matter of an investigation.[225] Pursuant to Article 19(2), where an interview is conducted in the premises of an undertaking, the Commission must inform the competition authority of the Member State in whose territory the interview takes place, and if requested, permit officials of that authority to 'assist' in the interview process.

The power to take statements requires the consent of interviewees.[226] Prospective interviewees are free to refuse the Commission's invitation, and there is no sanction for doing so. The Commission is obliged, at the beginning of any interview, to 'recall its voluntary nature'.[227] During the interview, the person concerned can refuse to answer questions, can refuse to give reasons for the refusal, and need not provide documents. There are no penalties for giving incorrect or misleading information, in sharp contrast to Article 20(2)(e) (explanations on facts). Unsurprisingly, therefore, 'experience has shown that the absence of penalties for misleading or false replies may be a disincentive to provide correct and complete statements'.[228] Interviewees are entitled to be accompanied by lawyers and interviews may take place on or away from business premises. The Antitrust ManProc says that nobody can be prevented by their current or former employer from giving an interview, unless he or she acts on behalf of the undertaking.[229]

The Commission is obliged to make a record of all interviews held. This requirement is referenced somewhat obliquely in the Implementing Regulation,[230] but has been endorsed strongly by the Union Courts. In *Intel*, the Commission had sought to argue that a distinction should be drawn between formal interviews conducted according to the requirements of the Implementing Regulation, and informal interviews which could be conducted without a proper record.[231] The CJ instead held that Article 19(1) of Regulation 1/2003 provides the legal basis for *any* interview conducted by the Commission with a (legal or natural) person for the purpose of collecting information relating to the subject matter of a competition investigation.[232] This means, in particular, that 'if the Commission decides, with the consent of the person interviewed, to carry out such an interview on the basis of Article 19(1) of Regulation No 1/2003, it must record the interview in full, without prejudice to the fact that the Commission is free to decide on the type of recording'.[233] This requirement had not been satisfied during the *Intel* investigation in respect of an extended interview with a senior executive from one of Intel's most important customers. Nonetheless, the CJ held that this omission did not, in itself, vitiate the subsequent infringement decision, insofar as Intel had failed to establish that the Commission's non-compliance with Article 3 had deprived it of access to exculpatory evidence which might have been of use to its defence.[234]

[222] See the discussion in Faull and Nikpay, n. 1, 8.320. For the leniency policy, see Section 6.H.v.
[223] Reg. 773/2004, Art. 3(2). [224] Reg. 1/2003, Art. 19(1).
[225] Case T-604/18, *Google Android* EU:T:2022:541, paras. 916–920.
[226] Ibid. [227] Reg. 773/2004, Art. 3(1).
[228] Report on the Functioning of Reg. 1/2003, n. 13, para. 12; see also Faull and Nikpay, n. 1, 8.320.
[229] Antitrust ManProc (see n. 27), Module 8, para. 14.
[230] Reg. 773/2004, Art. 3(1), obliges the Commission to 'inform the person interviewed of its intention to make a record of the interview'. Art. 3(3) states '[t]he Commission may record the statements made by the persons interviewed in any form. A copy of any recording shall be made available to the person interviewed for approval.'
[231] Case C-413/14 P, paras. 86–87. The Commission had succeeded on this point before the GC: see Case T-286/09, *Intel* EU:T:2014:547, paras. 612–618.
[232] Case C-413/14 P, *Intel* EU:C:2017:632, para. 86. [233] Ibid., para. 90. [234] Ibid., paras. 96–103.

The opposite conclusion was reached in the *Qualcomm* judgment,[235] however, in which the defendant appealed against a decision finding that it had breached Article 102 on the basis of exclusivity payments.[236] Subsequent to receiving the decision, the defendant asked whether the Commission had held any interviews with third parties about which it, Qualcomm, had not been informed. Over the course of the following two years, the Commission, in piecemeal fashion, provided evidence of seven 'inadvertently' undisclosed meetings or conference calls with third parties, comprising both competitors and customers of the defendant. In some instances, the Commission was able retrospectively to provide only 'succinct notes' of the encounters; for others, it admitted a 'regrettable failure' to take *any* relevant notes. Following the approach in *Intel*, the GC confirmed that the legal basis provided by Article 19(1) 'refers to the simple fact of hearing a natural or legal person in order to gather information'.[237] The failure to take adequate notes of the seven belatedly disclosed meetings, and to include a record of those interviews in its case file, amounted to breach of its obligations under Article 19(1). The GC was unpersuaded, moreover, by the Commission's contention that it was 'plausible' that the information provided at those interviews was comparable to material to be found elsewhere in the case file, dismissing that argument as mere 'speculation' in the absence of any concrete evidence as to the actual content of the interviews. The upshot was that these procedural omissions breached Qualcomm's rights of defence, and thus merited annulment of the underlying infringement decision. This conclusion was reinforced by various errors in the Commission's substantive assessment of the Article 102 claim, as discussed in Chapter 7, Section 10.

The Commission also ran into difficulties in *Google Android*, where the GC agreed with the defendant that, of the 35 meetings conducted during the investigation, the notes of 32 of these were 'too late and too cursory to be capable of constituting the record of an interview in the sense prescribed by Article 19(1)'.[238] Despite this, the GC concluded that Google had sufficient access to alternative sources of information about the substance of the meetings,meaning that the Commission's procedural errors had not infringed Google's rights of defence.[239] Yet the GC could not resist providing the Commission with advice about how best to ensure respect for its obligations under Article 19 going forward.

> 933. In the future, it would be useful and appropriate for the record of each interview conducted by the Commission with a third party for the purpose of collecting information relating to the subject matter of an investigation to be made or approved at the time when that interview is held or shortly afterwards so as to be added to the file as quickly as possible to enable the person accused of an infringement, when the time comes, to acquaint himself or herself of it for the purpose of exercising the rights of the defence.

In *Les Mousquetaires*, the CJ confirmed that the holding in *Intel*, to the effect that the obligation to make a record applies to any interview conducted by the Commission to gather information within the scope of the subject matter of an investigation, also extends to interviews that are conducted *before* the investigation is formally opened. The upshot, in that case, was that several Commission decisions authorising inspections were annulled, on the basis that these were validated primarily on the basis of interview evidence that had not been properly recorded.[240]

[235] Case T-235/18 *Qualcomm* EU:T:2022:358.
[236] AT.40220, *Qualcomm (Exclusivity payments)* 24 January 2018.
[237] Case T-235/18, *Qualcomm* EU:T:2022:358, para. 184.
[238] Case T-604/18, *Google Android* EU:T:2022:541, para. 932.
[239] Ibid., para. 958.
[240] Case C-682/20 P, *Les Mousquetaires* EU:C:2023:170.

(vi) The Privilege Against Self-incrimination

The Commission's wide powers to carry out inspections and to ask for information raise the issue of whether EU law recognises a privilege against self-incrimination.[241] The position is that, while undertakings have a duty actively to cooperate with the Commission, this does not mean that an undertaking is required to incriminate itself by admitting to infringements of the competition rules. Yet the Commission may ask questions, or demand the production of documents, by means of which it can establish an infringement. This was first established in *Orkem*.

Case 374/87, *Orkem SA v Commission* EU:C:1989:387

The Commission was investigating alleged cartels in the thermoplastics industry. Using the equivalent of a request by decision under Article 18(3) of Regulation 1/2003, the Commission required the defendant undertaking to provide factual information about a meeting, but also information that clearly aimed at uncovering how cartels prices were agreed, implemented, and monitored. The undertaking challenged the decision, claiming that the Commission had infringed the general principle that no one may be compelled to give evidence against himself. The CJ held that neither the national laws, nor Article 6 ECHR, nor the International Covenant on Civil and Political Rights of 1966, could be interpreted as generating a distinct right for a legal person in a competition law investigation not to give evidence against itself. The CJ went on to consider, however, whether such a right might nonetheless be held to exist within the EU competition law sphere.

Court of Justice

32. It is necessary . . . to consider whether certain limitations on the Commission's powers of investigation are implied by the need to safeguard the rights of the defence which the Court has held to be [a] fundamental principle of the [Union] order (Case 322/102, *Michelin* v. *E.C. Commission*).

33. In that connection . . . whilst it is true that the rights of the defence must be observed in administrative procedures which may lead to the imposition of penalties, it is necessary to prevent those rights from being irremediably impaired during preliminary inquiry procedures which may be decisive in providing evidence of the unlawful nature of conduct engaged in by undertakings and for which they may be liable. Consequently, although certain rights of the defence relate only to contentious proceedings which follow the delivery of the statement of objections, other rights must be respected even during the preliminary inquiry.

34. Accordingly, whilst the Commission is entitled . . . to compel an undertaking to provide all necessary information concerning such facts as may be known to it and to disclose to it, if necessary, such documents relating thereto as are in its possession, even if the latter may be used to establish, against it or another undertaking, the existence of anti-competitive conduct, it may not, by means of a decision calling for information, undermine the rights of defence of the undertaking concerned.

35. Thus, the Commission may not compel an undertaking to provide it with answers which might involve an admission on its part of the existence of an infringement which it is incumbent upon the Commission to prove.

[241] For a general discussion of the privilege and its application in the competition law context, see A. MacCulloch, 'The Privilege Against Self-incrimination in Competition Investigations: Theoretical Foundations and Practical Implications' (2006) 26 *Legal Studies* 211.

On this basis, the CJ annulled the decision in respect of all the questions except the first relating to the cartel meeting. The Court drew a distinction between a right to compel the undertaking to provide factual information which can be used to establish a breach of the rules, and a right to compel it to admit to the breach. The Commission may exercise the former but not the latter right.[242]

Although the soundness of the distinction between admission of guilt and mere production of documents has been questioned,[243] this limited right against self-incrimination has been reiterated repeatedly by the Union Courts.[244] It is now replicated in the recitals to Regulation 1/2003.

Recital (23), Regulation 1/2003

The Commission should be empowered throughout the [Union] to require such information to be supplied as is necessary to detect any agreement, decision or concerted practice prohibited by [Article 101] or any abuse of a dominant position prohibited by [Article 102]. When complying with a decision of the Commission, undertakings cannot be forced to admit that they have committed an infringement, but they are in any event obliged to answer factual questions and to provide documents, even if this information may be used to establish against them or against another undertaking the existence of an infringement.

The question is thus, as the CJ put it subsequently in *Qualcomm*, whether the Commission's request for information or documents requires a defendant 'to undertake any assessment of such a kind as to lead them to admit that they acted in breach of [EU competition law]'.[245] Where this point is disputed between the Commission and a defendant undertaking, it falls to the Union Courts to determine whether the answer required of the undertaking 'is in fact equivalent to the admission of an infringement'.[246] Answers that are 'purely factual', however, 'cannot, as a rule, be regarded as capable of requiring the addressee to admit the existence of that infringement'.[247]

The Court had denied in *Orkem* that Article 6 ECHR included the right not to provide evidence against oneself.[248] A few years later in *Funke*, however, the ECtHR accepted that a person charged with a criminal offence within the meaning of Article 6(2) had the right 'to remain silent and not . . . contribute to incriminating himself'.[249] Reviewing the subsequent case law of the ECtHR, a Grand Chamber sitting of the CJ in *Consob* in 2021[250] noted that, although Article 6 makes no explicit reference to the right to silence, that right is a 'generally recognised international standard', which 'contributes to avoiding miscarriages of justice and to securing the aims of Article 6'.[251] It is clear that

[242] The privilege against self-incrimination is irrelevant to simple requests for information because there is no element of compulsion or sanction involved, see Case C-293/13 P, *Fresh del Monte Produce* EU:C:2015:416, paras. 193–199.

[243] See Opinion of Wahl AG in Case C-267/14 P, *Buzzi Unicem* EU:C:2015:696, in particular paras. 73–90. The CJ, however, declined to address his concerns in a judgment which overturned the GC on alternative grounds, see Case C-267/14 P, *Buzzi Unicem* EU:C:2016:151.

[244] See e.g. Case T-112/98, *Mannesmannröhren-Werke* EU:T:2001:61; Cases C-238/99 P etc., *Limburgse Vinyl Maatschappij* EU:C:2002:582; and Case C-301/04 P, *Commission v SGL Carbon* EU:C:2006:432.

[245] Case C-466/19 P *Qualcomm* EU:C:2021:76, para. 145. [246] Ibid. [247] Ibid.

[248] Case 374/87, *Orkem* EU:C:1989:387, para. 30.

[249] *Funke v France*, App. no. 10828/84 (1993) 16 EHRR 297, para. 44.

[250] Case C-481/19 *DB v Commissione Nazionale per le Società e la Borsa (Consob)* EU:C:2021:84. The case dealt primarily with EU secondary legislation relating to insider trading, but the CJ's analysis extended beyond the immediate factual context.

[251] Case C-481/19, *Consob* EU:C:2021:84, para. 38.

Article 6 does not provide an *absolute* right to silence:[252] in *Saunders v UK*,[253] for instance, the ECtHR found that the privilege against self-incrimination did not extend to material 'which has an existence independent of the will of the suspect such as . . . documents acquired pursuant to a warrant'.[254] Yet in *Consob*, the CJ articulated a comparatively broad right under Article 6, which at first glance extends beyond the parameters of the more limited *Orkem* principle:

> The right to silence cannot reasonably be confined to statements of admission of wrongdoing or to remarks which directly incriminate the person questioned, but rather also covers information on questions of fact which may subsequently be used in support of the prosecution and may thus have a bearing on the conviction or the penalty imposed on that person . . . [255]

Moreover, confirming the close relationship between EU and ECHR human rights law in this context,[256] the CJ accepted that equivalent protection is provided by Articles 47 and 48 of the Charter.[257]

Crucially, however, the Court drew a distinction between application of the right of silence to *natural* persons in criminal proceedings and to undertakings or associations of undertakings 'in proceedings seeking to establish an infringement of [the EU competition] rules'.[258] The full force of the right to silence applies only to natural persons 'charged' within the meaning of Article 48 of the Charter (presumption of innocence). Conversely, the CJ in *Consob* did not challenge the *Orkem* stipulation that *undertakings* may be compelled to hand over pre-existing documents that might nonetheless provide evidence of their guilt,[259] so long as they are not obliged to offer an 'admission' of guilt as such.[260] It has been queried whether, on the basis of the broad interpretation of the right to silence in *Consob*, the *Orkem* principle is indeed as 'Strasbourg-proof' as the CJ has insisted.[261] The judgment also raises interesting questions as to the application of the right to silence in cases where natural persons are prosecuted under the competition rules in their capacity as undertakings: should they be subject to the ECtHR case law or the *Orkem* principle in such circumstances?[262]

(vii) Legal Professional Privilege

a. *The Extent of Legal Professional Privilege*

Legal professional privilege (LPP) refers to the confidentiality attached to certain communications between a client and its lawyers.[263] The rationale for recognising that certain materials may be privileged, and thus immune from compulsory disclosure to a law enforcement agency such as the Commission when it acts in competition cases, was explained by Advocate General Kokott in the *Akzo Nobel* case.

[252] See further M. Berger, 'Self-incrimination and the European Court of Human Rights: Procedural Issues in the Enforcement of the Right to Silence' (2007) 5 *EHRLR* 514; M. Redmayne, 'Rethinking the Privilege Against Self-incrimination' (2007) 27 *OJLS* 209; N. Andrews, 'Privilege Against Self-incrimination in the Human Rights Era' (2007) 66 *CLJ* 47; A. Ashworth, 'Self-incrimination in European Human Rights Law—A Pregnant Pragmatism?' (2008–2009) 30 *Cardozo LR* 751; A. L.-T. Choo, *The Privilege Against Self-incrimination and Criminal Justice* (Hart Publishing, 2013).

[253] *Saunders v UK*, App. no. 19187/91 (1997) 23 EHRR 313.

[254] Ibid., para. 69. [255] Case C-481/19, *Consob* EU:C:2021:84, para. 40. [256] See Section 5.

[257] Case C-481/19, *Consob* EU:C:2021:84, para. 45. [258] Ibid., para. 46. [259] Ibid.

[260] Ibid., para. 47.

[261] M. Veenbrink, 'The Freedom from Self-Incrimination—A Strasbourg-Proof Approach? Cases C-466/19 P *Qualcomm* and C-481/19 P *DB v Consob*' (2021) 12 *JECLAP* 750, 751.

[262] Ibid.

[263] See generally C. Passmore and P. Boylan, 'Privilege in Competition Investigations' (2016) 15 *Comp Law* 5; and W. Wils, 'Legal Professional Privilege in EU Antitrust Enforcement: Law, Policy & Procedure' (2019) 42 *World Competition* 21.

Case C-550/07 P, *Akzo Nobel Chemicals Ltd and Akcros Chemicals Ltd v European Commission* EU:C:2010:229

Opinion of Advocate General Kokott

48. Legal professional privilege serves to protect communications between a client and a lawyer who is independent of that client. On the one hand, it is the essential corollary to the client's rights of defence (37) and, on the other hand, it is based on the specific role of the lawyer as 'collaborating in the interests of justice' and as being required to provide, in full independence, and in the overriding interests of justice, such legal assistance as the client needs.

49. Lawyers would be unable to carry out satisfactorily their task of advising, defending and representing their clients, who would in consequence be deprived of the rights conferred on them by Article 6 of the ECHR and by Articles 47 and 48 of the Charter of Fundamental Rights, if lawyers were obliged, in the context of judicial proceedings or the preparation for such proceedings, to cooperate with the authorities by passing them information obtained in the course of related legal consultations.

LPP is not addressed directly in the procedural framework that governs the application of the EU competition rules: neither Regulation 1/2003, nor Regulation 17 before it, mentions its availability (or lack therefore). Instead, a somewhat circumscribed category of privilege has been recognised in the case law of the Union Courts, the scope of which, as Advocate General Kokott herself noted, is 'fiercely disputed'.[264]

The first case considering the issue was *AM&S*, in which a UK-based undertaking argued that it was entitled to deny the Commission access to correspondence with its legal advisers that would have been privileged under English law. The problem arose in the context of several dawn raids conducted at the defendant's premises, during which it refused to disclose documents in respect of which it claimed LPP. Eventually, after meeting with the Commission in Brussels, AM&S provided all but one of the documents sought. It then immediately brought an action for annulment under Article 263, claiming that the Commission decision to require the material was void insofar as it required the disclosure of legally privileged documents. There were two main issues before the CJ: first, whether LPP applied in EU competition cases and, if so, whether it was a *Union* principle or a matter of recognising the rule in the Member State concerned; and secondly, if legal privilege was recognised, how should it be implemented, in procedural terms?

Case 155/79, *AM&S Ltd v Commission* EU:C:1982:157

Court of Justice

15. The purpose of Regulation 17 . . . is 'to ensure compliance with the prohibitions laid down in Article [101(1)] and in Article [102]' . . . . The regulation is thus intended to ensure that the aim stated in Article [3(1)(g) EC] is achieved. To that end it confers on the Commission wide powers of investigation and of obtaining information by providing in the eighth recital in its preamble that the Commission must be empowered, throughout the [internal] market, to require such information to be supplied and to undertake such investigations 'as are necessary' to bring to light infringements of Articles [101] and [102].

16. In Articles 11 and 14 of the regulation, therefore, it is provided that the Commission may obtain 'information' and undertake the 'necessary' investigations, for the purpose of proceedings in respect of infringements of the rules governing competition. Article 14(1) in particular empowers the Commission

[264] Opinion in Case C-550/07 P, *Akzo Nobel Chemicals Ltd and Akcros Chemicals Ltd* EU:C:2010:229, para. 50.

to require production of business records, that is to say, documents concerning the market activities of the undertaking, in particular as regards compliance with those rules. Written communications between lawyer and client fall, in so far as they have a bearing on such activities, within the category of documents referred to in Articles 11 and 14.

17. Furthermore since the documents which the Commission may demand are . . . those whose disclosure it considers 'necessary' in order that it may bring to light an infringement of the Treaty rules on competition, it is in principle for the Commission itself, and not the undertaking concerned or a third party, whether an expert or an arbitrator, to decide whether or not a document must be produced to it.

(b) Applicability of the protection of confidentiality in Community law

18. However, the above rules do not exclude the possibility of recognising, subject to certain conditions, that certain business records are of a confidential nature. [Union] law, which derives from not only the economic but also the legal interpenetration of the Member States, must take into account the principles and concepts common to the laws of those States concerning the observance of confidentiality, in particular, as regards certain communications between lawyer and client. That confidentiality serves the requirements, the importance of which is recognized in all of the Member States, that any person must be able, without constraint, to consult a lawyer whose profession entails the giving of independent legal advice to all those in need of it.

19. As far as the protection of written communications between lawyer and client is concerned, it is apparent from the legal systems of the Member States that, although the principle of such protection is generally recognised, its scope and the criteria for applying it vary, as has, indeed, been conceded both by the application and by the parties who have intervened in support of its conclusions.

20. Whilst in some of the Member States the protection against disclosure afforded to written communications between lawyer and client is based principally on a recognition of the very nature of the legal profession, inasmuch as it contributes towards the maintenance of the rule of law, in other Member States the same protection is justified by the more specific requirement (which, moreover, is also recognized in the first-mentioned States) that the rights of the defence must be respected.

21. Apart from these differences, however, there are to be found in the national laws of the Member States common criteria inasmuch as those law protect, in similar circumstances, the confidentiality of written communications between lawyer and client provided that, on the one hand, such communications are made for the purposes and in the interests of the client's rights of defence and, on the other hand, they emanate from independent lawyers, that is to say, lawyers who are not bound to the client by a relationship of employment.

22. Viewed in that context Regulation 17 must be interpreted as protecting, in its turn, the confidentiality of written communications between lawyer and client subject to those two conditions, and thus incorporating such elements of that protection as are common to the laws of the Member States.

23. As far as the first of those two conditions is concerned, in Regulation 17 itself. . .care is taken to ensure that the rights of the defence may be exercised to the full, and the protection of the confidentiality of written communications between lawyer and client is an essential corollary to those rights. In those circumstances, such protection must, if it is to be effective, be recognized as covering all written communications exchanged after the initiation of the administrative procedure under Regulation 17 which may lead to a decision on the application of Articles [101] and [102] or to a decision imposing a pecuniary sanction on the undertaking. It must also be possible to extend it to earlier written communications which have a relationship to the subject-matter of that procedure.

24. As regards the second condition, it should be stated that the requirement as to the position and status as an independent lawyer, which must be fulfilled by the legal adviser from whom the written communications which may be protected emanate, is based on a conception of the lawyer's role as collaborating in the administration of justice by the courts and as being required to provide, in full independence,

and in the overriding interests of that cause, such legal assistance as the client needs. The counterpart of that protection lies in the rules of professional ethics and discipline which are laid down and enforced in the general interest by institutions endowed with the requisite powers for that purpose. Such a conception reflects the legal traditions common to the Member States and is also to be found in [the] legal order of the [Union], as is demonstrated by Article 17 of the Protocols on the Statutes of the Court of Justice of the EEC and the EAEC [European Atomic Energy Community], and also by Article 20 of the Protocol on the Statute of the Court of Justice of the ECSC [European Coal and Steel Community].

25. Having regard to the principles of the Treaty concerning freedom of establishment and the freedom to provide services the protection thus afforded by [Union] law, in particular in the context of Regulation 17, to written communications between lawyer and client must apply without distinction to any lawyer entitled to practice his profession in one of the Member States, regardless of the Member State in which the client lives.

. . .

28. Finally, it should be remarked that the principle of confidentiality does not prevent a lawyer's client from disclosing the written communications between them if he considers that it is in his interests to do so.

The Court thus held that EU law recognises LPP. This judgment, holding that the Union legal order should recognise a principle contained in some form in nearly every Member State, is a famous example of the development of the jurisprudence on the general principles of law.[265] LPP in EU law is, however, a *Union* concept, which is subject to two conditions. The first is that the protected communications must be made for the purposes and in the interests of the clients' rights of defence. The Court interpreted this broadly in *AM&S*, and in practice it has not caused difficulty, as the Commission accepts that communications, made earlier than the initiation of proceedings but with a relationship to the subject matter of the proceedings, are covered. The second condition is that the communication must be with an independent lawyer entitled to practise in one of the Member States, not an in-house lawyer bound to the undertaking by an employment relationship.

The limitation of privilege to 'independent' lawyers is based on the role of the lawyer as collaborator in the administration of justice, and the fact that, in some Member States, different rules of professional discipline apply once a lawyer operates in an in-house employment relationship. In the lead-up to Regulation 1/2003, representations were made by in-house counsel in response to the Commission's White Paper, strongly arguing that privilege should be extended. Under the self-assessment system brought in by Regulation 1/2003, undertakings are more heavily reliant on legal advice, and the in-house lawyer community said that such an extension would promote effective compliance. They argued that all lawyers must act ethically as defined in the rules of professional ethics and discipline.[266] Regulation 1/2003, however, made no change to the position on LPP.

In *Akzo Nobel*, the issue was revisited. The defendant argued both that the concept of independence arising from *AM&S* had been misinterpreted to exclude in-house lawyers, and that the subsequent evolution of EU competition law required *AM&S* to be reconsidered. These arguments were rejected by the GC,[267] and on further appeal, by the CJ.[268] The CJ reaffirmed that, regardless of the weight of

[265] J. Temple Lang, 'The *AM & S* Judgment' in M. Hoskins and W. Robinson (eds.), *A True European—Essays for Judge David Edward* (Hart Publishing, 2004), Chap 12. See generally T. Tridimas, *The General Principles of EC Law* (2nd edn, Oxford University Press, 2006).

[266] Summary of observations on the White Paper on reform of Reg. 17, published by the Commission, 29 February 2000, para. 7.7.

[267] Cases T-125 and 253/03, *Akzo Nobel Chemicals* EU:T:2007:58.

[268] Case C-550/07 P, *Akzo Nobel Chemicals* EU:C:2010:512.

professional ethical obligations that an in-house lawyer may face, 'the position of an employee . . . by its very nature, does not allow [that lawyer] to ignore the commercial strategies pursued by his employer, and thereby affects his ability to exercise professional independence'.[269] These 'close ties' also meant that 'in-house lawyers are in a fundamentally different position from external lawyers, so that their respective circumstances are not comparable' for the purposes of applying the general EU law principle of equal treatment.[270] Moreover, in rejecting the argument that the more powerful array of enforcement powers granted to the Commission under Regulation 1/2003 merited strengthening rights of defence including the scope of LPP, the CJ instead countered that 'the detection of infringements of the competition rules is growing ever more difficult'[271] too, so that those powers should not be unduly curtailed by fundamental rights considerations.

The exclusion of in-house lawyers from LPP is a matter of great practical importance and remains contentious.[272] Neither the GC nor the CJ in *Akzo Nobel* dealt with the further limitation of LPP to lawyers entitled to practise in one of the Member States, although the issue has been prominent in the context of Brexit, as many UK-based competition lawyers sought to requalify in another Member State in order to retain the benefit of LPP in EU competition proceedings.[273]

b. Procedure in Claims of LPP

The procedure for dealing with claims of LPP is derived from the judgments of the CJ in *AM&S* and the GC in *Akzo Nobel*,[274] and set out in Best Practices, paragraphs 51–58. Ultimately, the determination as to whether a particular document is protected by LPP is a matter for the Court.

The undertaking claiming privilege must provide the inspectors with proof of that fact without revealing the contents of the document. If the inspectors are unconvinced, the Commission may take a decision under Article 20(4) of Regulation 1/2003 requiring the production of the document or further evidence of its status. Such a decision may be challenged under Article 263, with an application for interim measures under Articles 278 and 279 if appropriate. If the Commission officials cannot tell from a 'mere cursory look at the general layout, heading, title or other superficial features which would not reveal its content', whether a document is protected, and there is genuine doubt about its classification, the document is placed in a sealed envelope and taken to Brussels to await the outcome of any proceedings.[275] Disputes about LPP can be referred by the undertaking to the Hearing Officer.[276] If the matter remains unresolved even after the Hearing Officer's recommendation, the Commission can take a decision ordering the production of the document or the opening of the sealed envelope, which the undertaking can challenge before the GC.

The categorisation of particular documents into those protected by LPP and those not protected may be difficult. In *Hilti*,[277] a report made and circulated within the undertaking of the legal advice received from external legal counsel was granted privilege. On the other hand, in *John Deere*,[278] the

[269] Ibid., para. 47. [270] Ibid., para. 58. [271] Ibid., para. 84.

[272] See M. Frese, 'The Development of General Principles for EU Competition Law Enforcement—The Protection of Legal Professional Privilege' [2011] *ECLR* 196; G. di Frederico, 'Casenote' (2011) 48 *CMLRev* 581.

[273] In April 2019, for instance, it was reported that almost 3,000 solicitors originally qualified in England and Wales were now registered additionally at the Irish Bar: see Law Gazette, 'Brexit: England and Wales now accounts for one in seven "Irish" solicitors', 29 April 2019, <www.lawgazette.co.uk/law/brexit-england-and-wales-now-accounts-for-one-in-seven-irish-solicitors/5070102.article>.

[274] Cases T-125 and 253/03, *Akzo Nobel* EU:T:2007:58, paras. 79–90. This issue was not appealed to the CJ.

[275] Ibid., paras. 81–83; Best Practices, para. 54.

[276] Decision on the function and terms of reference of the hearing officer [2011] OJ L275/29, Art. 4(2)(a); W. Wils, 'The Role of the Hearing Officer in Competition Proceedings before the European Commission' (2012) 35 *World Competition* 431, 448–450; for the functions of the HO generally, see Section 6.D.iv.

[277] Case T-30/89, *Hilti* EU:T:1991:70. [278] [1985] OJ L35/58.

Commission examined advice from in-house lawyers and concluded that the undertaking was aware that it was infringing Article 101. It took this into account when imposing the fine. A preparatory document drawn up exclusively for the purpose of seeking advice from a lawyer in exercise of the rights of the defence may be covered by LPP.[279]

D. THE SECOND, *INTER PARTES* OR 'ADVERSARIAL', STAGE OF THE PROCEDURE

(i) General: The Rights of the Defence and the Right to be Heard

At the end of the investigative phase, the Commission may decide:

- to close the case;
- to proceed to a commitments decision if the parties offer commitments at that stage;[280] or
- to open a formal procedure, if it finds evidence of an infringement and no commitments are offered.

Before taking decisions under Regulation 1/2003 finding an infringement, taking interim measures, or imposing fines or periodic payments, the Commission must, by Article 27(1), grant defendant undertakings 'the opportunity of being heard on the matters to which the Commission has taken objection'.[281] Article 27(2) provides that 'the rights of defence of the parties concerned shall be fully respected in the proceedings', and they 'shall be entitled to have access to the Commission's file'.[282] The Commission may also hear other natural or legal persons. Article 27(4) provides for the hearing of interested third parties during the commitments decision procedure.[283]

The right to be heard in all proceedings initiated against a person which are liable to culminate in a measure adversely affecting that person is part of the rights of the defence, and thus a fundamental principle of EU law which must be guaranteed.[284] The right to a hearing means, in the first place, that parties must be told the case against them.[285] This is now embedded in Article 27(1), which provides that '[t]he Commission shall base its decisions only on objections on which the parties concerned have been able to comment'. The Commission satisfies this requirement by sending the undertakings a document called the statement of objections (SO). The undertakings may then make submissions in reply and are offered the opportunity of an oral hearing.[286] The relevant procedures are set out in Commission Regulation 773/2004.[287] If, at the end of the proceedings, the Commission finds that the competition rules have been infringed, it may adopt a decision under Article 7 or 8 of Regulation 1/2003 and may impose a penalty under Article 23.

[279] Cases T-125 and 253/03, *Akzo Nobel* EU:T:2007:58, para. 123.

[280] For commitments decisions, see Section 6.E.iii.

[281] There is no duty to give parties a hearing where the Commission is simply replacing a decision ruled invalid for procedural defects at the final, authentication stage with another which relies on the same evidence: see Cases C-238/99 P etc., *Limburgse Vinyl Maatschappij* EU:C:2002:582; Case C-109/10 P, *Solvay* EU:C:2011:686, para. 67. It is otherwise where the defects involved a failure to hear the parties in respect of the first decision, *Solvay*, paras. 68–71.

[282] For the application of this in an Art. 9 commitments decision, see Case C-441/07 P, *Commission v Alrosa* EU:C:2010:377.

[283] See Section 6.E.iii.

[284] Case C-32/95 P, *Commission v Lisrestal* EU:C:1996:402, para. 121 (a case on the European Social Fund).

[285] See Case 17/74, *Transocean Marine Paint Association (No. 2)* EU:C:1974:106; Cases C-68/94 and 30/95, *France & SCPA* EU:C:1998:148, para. 174.

[286] The right to know the case against them does not entitle undertakings to examine for themselves the witnesses heard by the Commission: Cases C-239/11 P etc., *Siemens* EU:C:2013:866, para. 319.

[287] [2004] OJ L123/18, which replaced Reg. 2842/98 [1998] OJ L354/18, which in turn replaced Reg. 99/63 [1963–1964] OJ Spec. Ed. 47.

Considerable problems arise over the content of the rights of defence, particularly where the right of undertakings to know the case against them conflicts with the Commission's duty to preserve the confidentiality of business secrets.

(ii) State of Play and Other Meetings

The Commission offers defendant undertakings the opportunity to attend 'State of Play' meetings with officials of DG Comp.[288] The meetings are not provided for in Regulation 1/2003 or in Regulation 773/2004, but have become an important part of Commission procedure. Best Practices says:[289]

> Throughout the procedure the Directorate-General for Competition endeavours to give, on its own initiative or upon request, parties subject to the proceedings ample opportunity for open and frank discussions—taking into account the stage of the investigation—and to make their points of view known.
>
> In this respect the Commission will offer State of Play meetings . . .

The meetings occur at the Commission's premises or, if appropriate, by telephone or virtually, and are normally chaired by senior DG Comp management.[290] Where several parties are being investigated, the Commission offers a separate bilateral meeting to each. The meetings are not offered to complainants except in certain circumstances,[291] or to third parties. Normally, State of Play meetings are offered: (a) shortly after the opening of proceedings; (b) at 'a sufficiently advanced stage in the investigation' where the parties can be given the opportunity to understand the Commission's preliminary views; and (c) if an SO is issued, after the addressees have replied or after the oral hearing. The timing of State of Play meetings is different under the commitments decision procedure.[292] In cartel cases, the undertakings are offered just one meeting, after the oral hearing.[293] The formalisation of State of Play meetings does not exclude the parties having discussions with the Commission on other occasions throughout the procedure.[294]

'Exceptionally', DG Comp may invite *all* the parties (and possibly the complainant and/or third parties) to a 'triangular' meeting[295] before any SO is issued. Senior officers of parties subject to proceedings can ask for a discussion of the case with the Director-General or Deputy Director-General of DG Comp, or even the Commissioner.[296]

(iii) The Statement of Objections

By Article 10(1) of Regulation 773/2004,[297] 'the Commission shall inform the parties in writing of the objections raised against them'. The basic principles regarding the issuance of the SO were summarised by the GC in the *Qualcomm* case.

[288] Best Practices, paras. 60–66; Antitrust ManProc, Module 10, paras. 21–27. [289] Best Practices, paras. 60–61.

[290] Ibid., para. 61. [291] Ibid., para. 65. [292] Ibid. [293] Ibid. [294] Ibid., para. 66.

[295] Ibid., paras. 67–69; Antitrust ManProc, Module 10, paras. 28–30. Held if DG Comp believes it is desirable to hear the views of all of them in a single meeting (e.g. if two or more opposing views on key data or evidence have been advanced).

[296] Best Practices, para. 70.

[297] [2004] OJ L123/18. See Best Practices, paras. 81–91; Kerse and Khan, n. 202, 4.011–4.027.

Case T-235/18, *Qualcomm Inc v European Commission* EU:T:2022:358

General Court

307. . . . Article 27(1) of Regulation 1/2003 envisages that the parties are to be sent a statement of objections. That statement must set out clearly all the essential elements on which the Commission is relying at that stage of the procedure (. . . *Panasonic v Commission*, C-608/15 P . . . EU:C:2016:538, paragraph 20).

308. However, that information may be given in summary form and the Commission decision by which it finds the existence of an infringement is not necessarily required to be a copy of the statement of objections, since that statement of objections is a preparatory document containing assessments of fact and of law which are purely provisional in nature. The Commission is required to hear the addressees of a statement of objections and, where relevant, to take account of any observations made in response to the objections upheld by amending its analysis specifically in order to respect their rights of defence (. . . *Panasonic v Commission*, C-608/15 P . . . EU:C:2016:538, paragraph 21).

309. Furthermore, the statement of objections is a procedural measure adopted preparatory to the decision which represents the culmination of the administrative procedure. Consequently, until a final decision has been adopted, the Commission may, in view, in particular, of the written or oral observations of the parties, abandon some or even all of the objections initially made against them and thus alter its position in their favour or, conversely, decide to add new complaints, provided that it affords the undertakings concerned the opportunity of making known their views in that respect (. . . *Microsoft v Commission*, T-167/08, EU:T:2012:323, paragraph 184).

310. Communication to the parties concerned of further objections is necessary only where the result of the investigations leads the Commission to take new facts into account against the undertakings or to alter materially the evidence for the contested infringements and not where the Commission fulfils its duty to abandon such objections as have, in the light of the replies to the statement of objections, been shown to be unfounded (. . . *Microsoft v Commission*, T-167/08, EU:T:2012:323, paragraph 191).

. . .

337. The statement of objections is inherently provisional and subject to amendments to be made by the Commission in its further assessment on the basis of the observations submitted to it by the parties and subsequent findings of fact. Because it is provisional, the statement of objections does not prevent the Commission from altering its standpoint in favour of the undertakings concerned and it is not obliged, in doing so, to explain any differences with respect to its provisional assessments as set out in that statement (. . . *Commission* v *United Parcel Service*, C-265/17 P, EU:C:2019:23, paragraph 36).

338. However, those considerations do not permit the inference that, subsequent to the statement of objections, the Commission may modify the scope of the objections in the light of which the undertaking concerned has presented an economic analysis, such as the critical margin analysis submitted by the applicant in the present case, without that modification being brought to the attention of that undertaking and allowing it to submit its comments in that regard, where necessary by adapting the economic analysis previously submitted. Such an interpretation would be contrary to the principle of observance of the rights of the defence and to Article 27(1) of Regulation 1/2003, which require that the undertaking concerned must have had the opportunity of making known effectively its view on the matters to which the Commission has taken objection (. . . *Commission* v *United Parcel Service*, C-265/17 P, EU:C:2019:23, paragraphs 31 and 37).

The SO sets out the facts as understood by the Commission, and a legal analysis explaining why it considers Article 101 or 102 to be infringed.[298] The SO also indicates what remedies, if any, the Commission envisages imposing, in sufficient detail to allow the addressees to defend themselves on the necessity and proportionality of the remedies,[299] which includes the factors which may affect the amount of the fine.[300] The SO must state the duration of the infringement.[301] The parties are invited to reply within a set time limit.[302] By Article 11(2) of Regulation 773/2004, Commission decisions can deal only with objections in respect of which the parties have been able to comment.[303] Accordingly, where the Commission's theory of harm evolves during the course of an investigation, it may be obliged to send a supplementary statement of objections (SSO) after the initial SO.[304] This is permissible so long as it gives the necessary time for the parties to comment.[305] The Commission cannot fine parties in the ultimate decision unless it has expressed an intention to do so in the SO.[306] An undertaking which does not challenge a matter of law or fact in the SO during the administrative procedure is not barred from later challenging it before the GC.[307]

In order for the parties to make their views known, the Commission must reveal the documents on which it intends to rely. The SO therefore indicates the addressee's right of access to the file, so that the addressee can see the evidence on which the Commission has based its case.[308] However, it is insufficient for the Commission to rely on items of evidence annexed to the SO which are not expressly referred to in the body of the SO, as that infringes the rights of the defence.[309] The addressees may then exercise their rights to inspect the file, at least insofar as the documents are 'accessible'.[310] The current practical arrangements for this are contained in the Commission's 2005 Notice on access to the file.[311]

The SO is not a reviewable act against which an action for annulment can be brought. It can be challenged only in an action brought against the act concluding the proceedings.[312] An *inadequate* SO amounts to a breach of an essential procedural requirement, and so is a ground for annulment under Article 263.

Due to its inherently provisional nature, the views set out by the Commission in the SO are not binding upon it.[313] The Commission is free to depart from the standpoint taken in the SO.[314] Findings of fact set out in the SO are not treated as established, and so the Commission is also free to depart from them in the final decision.[315] In *Qualcomm*, nonetheless, the Commission was held to have infringed the rights of defence where it failed to send a SSO after *abandoning* part of its original theory of harm, where this change in strategy left the defendant unable to comment meaningfully on the Commission's assessment of the economic impact of the impugned behaviour.[316] In *Google*

[298] See Antitrust ManProc, Module 11, 'Drafting of Statement of Objections'.

[299] Best Practices, para. 83.

[300] Ibid., para. 84.

[301] Cases 100–103/80, *Pioneer* EU:C:1983:158.

[302] Reg. 773/2004, Art. 10(2). The minimum time under Reg. 773/2004 is four weeks, but the period is usually two months and may be longer, see Best Practices, para. 100, Antitrust ManProc, Module 11, paras. 48–56.

[303] For instance, in Case C-699/19 P, *Quanta Storage* EU:C:2022:483, the CJ found breach of the rights of defence where the SO stated that the defendant had engaged in a single continuous infringement of Art. 101, whereas the infringement decision stated it had participated in 'several separate infringements'.

[304] A supplementary SO or 'letter of facts'. See Best Practices, paras. 109–111. A 'Letter of Facts' is sent where the new evidence merely corroborates previous evidence, rather than raising new objections.

[305] Case 107/82, *AEG-Telefunken* EU:C:1983:293; Cases T-305/94 etc., *Re the PVC Cartel II: Limburgse Vinyl Maatschappij NV* EU:T:1999:80, para. 497.

[306] See e.g. Cases T-25/95 etc., *Cimenteries CBR* EU:T:2000:77; and Cases C-395 and 396/96 P, *Compagnie Maritime Belge* EU:C:2000:132.

[307] Case C-407/08 P, *Knauf Gips* EU:C:2010:389, paras. 88–92.

[308] If the addressee accompanies its reply to the SO with other documents, the Commission can subsequently rely on them even though they were not referred to in the SO, Case T-11/89, *Shell* EU:T:1992:33.

[309] Case C-511/06 P, *Archer Daniels Midland* EU:C:2009:433, paras. 74–96.

[310] See Section 6.D.v.b.

[311] [2005] OJ C325/7.

[312] Case 60/81, *IBM* EU:C:1981:264.

[313] Case C-328/05 P, *SGL Carbon* EU:C:2007:277, para. 62.

[314] Cases 142 and 156/84, *British American Tobacco Co Ltd and R. J. Reynolds Industries Inc* EU:C:1987:490, para. 13.

[315] Case C-413/06 P, *Bertelsmann AG and Sony Corp of America v Commission (Impala)* EU:C:2008:392, paras. 63–67. See Chap 15.

[316] Case T-235/18, *Qualcomm* EU:T:2022:358, paras. 299–343.

Android, similarly, the GC condemned the Commission's choice to send several detailed 'letters of facts' following the SO, rather than a SSO, in circumstances where, 'in reality, the letters of facts substantially supplement[ed] the substance and scope of the objection . . . and therefore significantly alter[ed] the evidence of the contested infringements'.[317] The Commission breached Google's rights of defence by using the letters of facts as a means to avoid an oral hearing (which Google had initially declined). The underlying infringement was accordingly annulled,[318] without any need for Google to demonstrate that the contested decision would have been different had the oral hearing occurred.[319]

(iv) The Hearing Officer

In 1982 the Commission endeavoured to meet some of the criticisms of its position as investigator, prosecutor, and judge, and of a lack of objectivity in its decision-making process, by establishing the position of Hearing Officer (HO).[320] The rationale was to inject an element of disinterested objectivity into the Commission's decision-making processes. The HO is attached, for administrative purposes, to the Competition Commissioner but the principle is that he or she is 'independent'.[321] Originally, the HO's role was to preside over the oral hearing, but in 1994 it was extended to cover the whole of the Commission's administrative procedure. The role and functions are now governed by Commission Decision 2011/695,[322] and are explained in this chapter at the relevant points. Since 1994, the HO has jurisdiction in hearings under the Merger Regulation.[323]

(v) Access to the File

a. General

Access to the Commission's file on which the SO is based is an important element of the parties' rights to know the case against them. The right of access to the file was developed in the case law[324] and Commission practice.[325] It is now provided for in Article 27(2) of Regulation 1/2003, which gives 'the parties concerned' a right of access. It is expanded upon in Regulation 773/2004, which also provides

[317] Case T-604/18, *Google Android* EU:T:2022:541, para. 981.

[318] These were revenue-sharing agreements that the Commission had alleged amounted to exclusivity payments; this aspect of the decision was also annulled on substantive grounds, see Chap 7, Section 10.

[319] Case T-604/18, *Google Android* EU:T:2022:541, para. 998

[320] See Commission's *XIth Report on Competition Policy* (1981), paras. 26 and 27 and the *XIIth Report* (1982), paras. 36 and 37. See generally M. van der Woude, 'Hearing Officers and EC Antitrust Procedures; The Art of Making Subjective Procedures More Objective' (1996) 33 *CMLRev* 531; M. Albers and J. Jourdan, 'The Role of the Hearing Officers in EU Competition Proceedings: A Historical and Practical Perspective' (2011) 2 *JECLAP* 185; W. Wils, 'The Role of the Hearing Officer in Competition Proceedings before the European Commission' (2012) 35 *World Competition* 431.

[321] HO Terms of Reference, recitals 3–8 and Art. 2(2); 2001 Terms of Reference, recital 6 and Art. 2(2). It should be noted that the HO does not appear on the chart of the organisation of DG Comp on its website. There are currently two HOs.

[322] Decision of the President of the European Commission of 13 October 2011 on the function and terms of reference of the hearing officer in certain competition proceedings [2011] OJ L275/29 (the 'HO Terms of Reference'), replacing Commission Decision 2001/462/EC on the terms of reference of hearing officers in certain competition proceedings [2001] OJ L162/21.

[323] The EUMR, Reg. 139/2004 [2004] OJ L24/1. See the HO Terms of Reference, Art. 1(2).

[324] See Cases 56 and 58/64, *Consten and Grundig* EU:C:1966:41; Cases 43 and 63/82, *VBVB and VBBB* EU:C:1984:9; Case C-51/92 P, *Hercules Chemicals (Polypropylene)* EU:C:1999:357, paras. 75–76; Case C-185/95 P, *Baustahlgewebe* EU:C:1998:608, para. 89; Cases T-10–12 and 14–15/92, *Cimenteries* EU:T:1992:123, para. 38; Case T-30/91, *Solvay* EU:T:1995:115 and Case T-36/91, *ICI* EU:T:1995:118, *aff'd* Cases C-288 and 287/95 P, *Commission v Solvay* EU:C:2000:189; Cases T-305/94 etc., *Limburgse Vinyl Maatschappij* EU:T:1999:80; Cases C-204, 205, 211, 213, 217, and 219/00 P, *Aalborg Portland v Commission* EU:C:2004:6.

[325] Commission's *XXIInd Report on Competition Policy* (1982) parts 34 and 35.

for access by complainants whose complaint is to be rejected (Article 8). The practical arrangements are contained in the Notice on access to the file.[326]

Special provisions govern access to leniency corporate statements. The Commission's leniency procedure involves the undertakings concerned making 'corporate statements', i.e. presentations of their knowledge of the secret cartel and their role in it in return for immunity or leniency.[327] As we see in Chapter 14, the Damages Directive[328] is designed to facilitate damages actions, but the Commission still wishes to preserve the effectiveness of the leniency policy.[329] Addressees of SOs are given access to the leniency corporate statement of other participants in the alleged cartel as part of their rights of defence, but are strictly prohibited from using the information thereby gained for any purpose other than their defence in respect of Article 101 or Article 102 proceedings before the Commission, the EU Courts, or a national court in *directly* related proceedings.[330] Regulation 773/2004 was amended in the wake of the Damages Directive to provide this expressly. Settlement submissions made in the course of the cartel settlement procedure[331] are treated in respect of access to the file in the same way as leniency corporate statements.

The rules on allowing the parties access to the file reflect the principles originally set out in *Solvay*,[332] where the GC relied on the 'general principle of equality of arms' between the Commission and the undertakings being investigated. This means that the undertakings' knowledge of the file used in the proceedings should be the same as that of the Commission. Undertakings must have disclosed to them documents which tend to exonerate them (exculpatory documents), as well as those which tend to incriminate them (inculpatory documents). It is not for the Commission alone to decide what documents are useful to the defence. Breach of the principle laid down in *Solvay* does not lead automatically to annulment of the decision, however. It depends on whether the undertaking's ability to defend itself was prejudiced.[333] The undertaking need not show that, if it had had access to the non-disclosed documents, the Commission's decision would have been different, but only that those documents would have been useful in its defence.[334] The law was set out by the CJ in the final *Cement Cartel* appeals.

Cases C-204, 205, 211, 213, 217, and C-219/00 P, *Aalborg Portland A/S and Others v Commission* EU:C:2004:6

Court of Justice

68. A corollary of the principle of respect for the rights of the defence, the right of access to the file means that the Commission must give the undertaking concerned the opportunity to examine all the documents in the investigation file which may be relevant for its defence (see, to that effect, Case T-30/91, *Solvay* v. *Commission* . . . paragraph 101, and Case C-199/99 P *Corus UK* v. *Commission* . . . paragraphs 125 to 128). Those documents include both incriminating evidence and

[326] Commission Notice on the rules for access to the Commission file [2005] OJ C325/07 (replacing [1997] OJ C23/3), as amended by [2015] OJ C256/7 to take account of the Damages Dir. (see n. 328); see also the Antitrust ManProc, Module 12.

[327] See Reg. 773/2004, Art. 4a(2). For the leniency policy, see Section 6.H.v and Chap 9.

[328] Dir. 2014/104/EU on certain rules governing actions for damages under national law for infringements of the competition law provisions of the Member States and of the European Union [2014] OJ L349/1.

[329] On leniency more generally, see Section 6.H.v.

[330] Reg. 773/2004 [2004] OJ L123/18, Art. 16a, as amended by Reg. 2015/1348 [2015] OJ L208/3. Art. 16(a) is reinforced by amended para. 48 of the Access Notice and amended para. 34 of the Leniency Notice.

[331] See further Section 6.F and Chap 9.

[332] Case T-30/91, *Solvay* EU:T:1995:115 and Case T-36/91, *ICI* EU:T:1995:118, applied in Cases T-305/94 etc., *Limburgse Vinyl Maatschappij* EU:T:1999:80.

[333] See Cases C-238/99 P etc., *Limburgse Vinyl Maatschappij* EU:C:2002:582, paras. 315–328; Case C-51/92 P, *Hercules* EU:C:1999:357, paras. 75–101.

[334] Cases C-239/11 P etc., *Siemens* EU:C:2013:866, paras. 363–378.

exculpatory evidence, save where the business secrets of other undertakings, the internal documents of the Commission or other confidential information are involved (see Case 85/76, *Hoffmann-La Roche* v. *Commission* . . . paragraphs 9 and 11; Case C-51/92 P, *Hercules Chemicals* v. *Commission* . . . paragraph 75; and Joined Cases C-238/99 P, C-244/99 P, C-245/99 P, C-247/99 P, C-250/99 P to C-252/99 P and C-254/99 P, *Limburgse Vinyl Maatschappij and Others* v. *Commission* . . . paragraph 315).

69. It may be that the undertaking draws the Commission's attention to documents capable of providing a different economic explanation for the overall economic assessment carried out by the Commission, in particular those describing the relevant market and the importance and the conduct of the undertakings acting on that market (. . . *Solvay* v. *Commission*, cited above, paragraphs 76 and 77).

70. The European Court of Human Rights has nonetheless held that, just like observance of the other procedural safeguards enshrined in Article 6(1) of the ECHR, compliance with the adversarial principle relates only to judicial proceedings before a tribunal and that there is no general, abstract principle that the parties must in all instances have the opportunity to attend the interviews carried out or to receive copies of all the documents taken into account in the case of other persons (. . . Euro. Court H.R., *the Kerojärvi* v. *Finland* judgment of 19 July 1995, Series A No 322, § 42, and the *Mantovanelli* v. *France* judgment of 18 March 1997, Reports of Judgments and Decisions 1997-II, § 33).

71. The failure to communicate a document constitutes a breach of the rights of the defence only if the undertaking concerned shows, first, that the Commission relied on that document to support its objection concerning the existence of an infringement (. . . Case 322/101, *Michelin* v. *Commission* . . . paragraphs 7 and 9) and, second, that the objection could be proved only by reference to that document (see Case 107/102 *AEG* v. *Commission* . . . paragraphs 24 to 30, and *Solvay* v. *Commission*, cited above, paragraph 58).

72. If there were other documentary evidence of which the parties were aware during the administrative procedure that specifically supported the Commission's findings, the fact that an incriminating document not communicated to the person concerned was inadmissible as evidence would not affect the validity of the objections upheld in the contested decision (. . . *Musique Diffusion française and Others* v. *Commission*, cited above, paragraph 30, and *Solvay* v. *Commission*, cited above, paragraph 58).

73. It is thus for the undertaking concerned to show that the result at which the Commission arrived in its decision would have been different if a document which was not communicated to that undertaking and on which the Commission relied to make a finding of infringement against it had to be disallowed as evidence.

74. On the other hand, where an exculpatory document has not been communicated, the undertaking concerned must only establish that its non-disclosure was able to influence, to its disadvantage, the course of the proceedings and the content of the decision of the Commission (see *Solvay* v. *Commission*, paragraph 68).

75. It is sufficient for the undertaking to show that it would have been able to use the exculpatory documents in its defence (see *Hercules Chemicals* v. *Commission*, paragraph 101, and *Limburgse Vinyl Maatschappij and Others* v. *Commission*, paragraph 318), in the sense that, had it been able to rely on them during the administrative procedure, it would have been able to put forward evidence which did not agree with the findings made by the Commission at that stage and would therefore have been able to have some influence on the Commission's assessment in any decision it adopted, at least as regards the gravity and duration of the conduct of which it was accused and, accordingly, the level of the fine (. . . *Solvay* v. *Commission*, paragraph 98).

76. The possibility that a document which was not disclosed might have influenced the course of the proceedings and the content of the Commission's decision can be established only if a provisional examination of certain evidence shows that the documents not disclosed might—in the light of that evidence—have had a significance which ought not to have been disregarded (see *Solvay* v. *Commission*, paragraph 68).

77. In the context of that provisional analysis, it is for the [General Court] alone to assess the value which should be attached to the evidence produced to it (. . . C-19/95 P *San Marco* v *Commission* . . . paragraph 40) . . . . [I]ts assessment of the facts does not, provided the evidence is not distorted, constitute a question of law which is subject, as such, to review by the Court of Justice.

These principles were followed by the CJ in the appeal against the readopted *Solvay* soda-ash decisions. This resulted in annulment of the relevant infringement decision, where the Commission had failed to provide the defendant with access to 'whole sub-files which . . . could have contained essential documents relating to the procedure before the Commission which may have been relevant to Solvay's defence'.[335] The principles were also applied in *Intel*, where the GC held that the undertaking had no right of access to documents which the Commission had no duty to procure.[336]

b. Confidentiality

There is a fundamental tension between the right of the parties to know the case against them and the Commission's obligation to preserve confidentiality. A general duty of confidentiality is laid down in Article 339 TFEU:

> The members of the institutions of the Union, the members of committees, and the officials and other servants of the Union shall be required, even after their duties have ceased, not to disclose information of the kind covered by the obligation of professional secrecy, in particular information about undertakings, their business relations or their cost components.

Article 28 of Regulation 1/2003 on 'Professional Secrecy' provides that information collected pursuant to Articles 17–22 shall only be used for the purposes for which it is acquired. Article 28(2) addresses the matter of exchange of information within the network of competition authorities.[337] Article 30 provides that the publication of decisions shall 'have regard to the legitimate interest of undertakings in the protection of their business secrets'. Article 27(2) of Regulation 1/2003 states that the parties' right to have access to the Commission's file is 'subject to the legitimate interest of undertakings in the protection of their business secrets'.[338]

Confidentiality is a significant issue in competition proceedings, as the Commission may obtain highly sensitive information. 'Business secrets' comprise information about an undertaking's business activity, disclosure of which could result in serious harm to the undertaking.[339] 'Other confidential information' is information *other* than business secrets, disclosure of which would significantly harm a person or undertaking.[340] This includes matters which would identify 'whistle-blowers',[341] complainants, or other third parties who have a justified wish to remain anonymous. The Notice recognises that the EU Courts have acknowledged that it is legitimate to refuse to reveal letters from an undertaking's customers which might expose the writers to retaliatory measures.[342]

[335] Case C-109/10 P, *Solvay* EU:C:2011:686, para. 64. See also Case T-161/05, *Hoechst* EU:T:2009:366, paras. 160–166; Case T-53/03, *BPB* EU:T:2008:254, paras. 43–45; Case T-240/07, *Heineken* EU:T:2011:284, para. 256; Cases C-239/11 P etc., *Siemens* EU:C:2013:866.

[336] Case T-286/09, *Intel* EU:T:2014:547, para. 351.

[337] See Notice on cooperation within the Network of Competition Authorities (the NCA Cooperation Notice) [2004] OJ C101/54. 'Professional secrecy' is a Community law concept (NCA Cooperation Notice, para. 28(a)).

[338] See also Reg. 773/2004, Arts. 15(2) and 16(1).

[339] Access Notice, para. 18; Case T-353/94, *Postbank* EU:T:1996:119, para. 87. Examples given in the Notice are technical and/or financial information relating to an undertaking's know-how, methods of assessing costs, production secrets and processes, supply sources, quantities produced and sold, market shares, customer and distributor lists, marketing plans, cost and price structure, and sales strategy.

[340] Access Notice, para. 19.

[341] The Commission's notorious failure to conceal the identity of the whistle-blower Stanley Adams from Hoffmann-La Roche rendered the Commission liable to him in damages under Art. 340 (ex Art. 288(2), ex Art. 215(2)): Case 145/83, *Adams* EU:C:1985:323.

[342] Access Notice, para. 19. In Case C-310/93 P, *BPB Industries and British Gypsum* EU:C:1995:101 the CJ accepted that the Commission was entitled to keep such correspondence confidential because of the fear of retaliation from the dominant firm in an Art. 102 case. See also Case T-203/01, *Manufacture Française des Pneumatiques Michelin* EU:T:2003:250.

The basic principle is that the Commission cannot use to an undertaking's detriment facts or documents which cannot be disclosed to it, where the absence of disclosure adversely affects the undertaking's opportunity to be heard.[343] Article 16 of Regulation 773/2004 puts the onus on those providing information to the Commission to identify confidential material which they do not want disclosed and to provide a non-confidential version. The Notice sets out the practical arrangements for giving access to the file while preserving confidentiality.[344] The Notice clarifies that full access to the file is granted only to addressees of SOs, and that other parties (complainants and other parties involved in merger cases) have a separate, more limited, right of access to specific documents.

The Notice distinguishes between 'accessible' and 'non-accessible' documents. Both business secrets and confidential information are 'non-accessible'. The Commission's internal documents are 'non-accessible', as are those of the NCAs, correspondence between the Commission and the NCAs,[345] and correspondence between the NCAs *inter se* (insofar as this is in the Commission's file).[346] The rationale for protecting internal documents is that these are not, by their nature, either incriminating or exculpatory, and are not the sort of evidence on which the Commission can rely in its assessment.[347] The CJ confirmed in *EnBW Energie Baden-Württemberg*[348] that the Commission may apply a general presumption that the disclosure of internal documents would undermine both the protection of the commercial interests of the undertakings involved and the protection of the purpose of the Commission's investigations.

The Notice sets out the procedure for resolving confidentiality and access to non-accessible information claims. In essence, if the Commission and the undertakings or other parties cannot agree, the matter is dealt with by the Hearing Officer.[349] In Best Practices, the Commission sets out two practical possibilities for handling situations where otherwise undertakings would need to redact their submissions in relation to confidential information: a 'negotiated disclosure procedure'[350] and the 'data room' procedure.[351]

There are special provisions in respect of the protection of corporate statements made by applicants for leniency, discussed in Section 6.D.v.

c. Confidentiality and Complainants

It was held in *AKZO*[352] that business secrets are accorded 'very special protection', and cannot be disclosed to third parties who have lodged complaints, on the basis that, otherwise, competitors could obtain access to business secrets simply by lodging a complaint. In *AKZO*, the Commission had sent

343 Case 85/76, *Hoffmann-La Roche* EU:C:1979:36, para. 14.

344 Access Notice, paras. 35–43.

345 See Case T-623/13, *Unión de Almacenistas de Hierros de España* EU:T:2015:268.

346 Reg. 1/2003, Art. 27(2), and Reg. 773/2004, Art. 15(2).

347 Access Notice, para. 12. Examples of internal documents given in the Notice are drafts, opinions, memos, or notes from the Commission departments or other public authorities concerned.

348 Case C-365/12 P, *Commission v EnBW Energie Baden-Württemberg* EU:C:2014:112; see also Case T-611/15, *Edeka-Handelsgesellschaft Hessenring v Commission* EU:T:2018:63, extending this general presumption of confidentiality to the table of contents to the Commission's file.

349 Access Notice, paras. 42 and 47; HO Terms of Reference, Arts 7 and 8.

350 Whereby the party being granted access agrees bilaterally with interested parties to receive the entirety of the information they have provided to the Commission, including the confidential information rather than the redacted version. This involves the party granted access restricting its right to have access to the full file and the other party waiving confidentiality; Best Practices, para. 96.

351 By which part of the file, including confidential information, is gathered in a room at the Commission's premises to which limited access is given under the Commission's supervision under strict conditions; see Best Practices on the disclosure of information in data rooms in proceedings under Articles 101 and 102 TFEU and under the EU Merger Regulation, <http://ec.europa.eu/competition/mergers/legislation/disclosure_information_data_rooms_en.pdf>.

352 Case 53/85, *AKZO* EU:C:1986:256.

a copy of the SO and a number of documents in the annexes to the complainant, and the CJ's order to the Commission to recover the documents meant that ECS was unable to rely on them in national proceedings.

Complainants, therefore, cannot have the same access to the file as alleged infringers. The rights of third parties[353] are limited to the right to participate in the administrative procedure.[354] This is embodied in paragraphs 30–31 of the Notice on access to the file. However, a complainant who has been told of the intention to reject his or her complaint may request access to the documents on which the Commission based its provisional assessment, although (s)he cannot have access to the confidential information or business secrets of the firm complained about, or those of any third parties, which the Commission has acquired during its investigations.[355]

d. The Transparency Regulation

Under the Transparency Regulation, 1049/2001,[356] citizens of the Union, and any natural or legal person residing or having its registered office in a Member State, have a right of access to documents of the institutions, subject to the principles, conditions, and limits defined in the Regulation.[357] Exceptions to the right of access are set out in Article 4, and these derogations are strictly construed.[358] In principle, the Transparency Regulation covers documents prepared by the Commission in the exercise of its competition enforcement functions and, in a number of cases, the Commission's refusals to disclose such materials were overturned by the GC.[359] In *EnBW*,[360] however, the CJ held that the Commission is entitled to apply a general presumption that access to documents in its file would harm the protection of the commercial interests of the undertakings involved and the protection of the purpose of the investigation.[361] The general presumption may be rebutted by demonstrating that a specific document is not covered by the presumption, or that there is an overriding public interest in disclosure.[362] This is not satisfied by merely stating that disclosure was necessary to bring a claim for damages in a national court.[363] The presumption also applies to proceedings of NCAs.[364]

The requested documents in *EnBW* included leniency statements. As we see in Chapter 14, the Damages Directive, designed to facilitate damages actions,[365] has special provisions about disclosure of leniency corporate statements in national proceedings. Article 6(2), however, provides that nothing in the Directive affects access to documents under the Transparency Regulation.[366]

(vi) The Oral Hearing

The right to be heard is primarily exercised in writing, but Article 12 of Regulation 773/2004 gives the parties to whom an SO has been addressed the right to an oral hearing, if they request it in their

[353] Laid down in Reg. 1/2003, Art. 27.

[354] Case T-17/93, *Matra Hachette* EU:T:1994:89. [355] Reg. 773/2004, Art. 8.

[356] Reg. 1049/2001 [2001] OJ L145/43, adopted pursuant to the principle in what is now Art. 15(1) TFEU that Union institutions and bodies, etc., shall conduct their work as openly as possible.

[357] Transparency Reg., Art. 2(1).

[358] Case C-506/08 P, *Sweden v Commission* EU:C:2011:496, para. 75.

[359] See Case T-2/03, *Verein für Konsumenteninformation* EU:T:2005:125; Case T-437/08, *CDC Hydrogen Peroxide v Commission* EU:T:2011:752; Case T-181/10, *Reagens* EU:T:2014:139.

[360] Case C-365/12 P, *EnBW* EU:C:2014:112, overturning the GC's judgment, Case T-344/08, *EnBW Energie Baden-Württemberg v Commission* EU:T:2012:242.

[361] This was followed, e.g., in Cases T-534/11 P, *Schenker* EU:T:2014:854 and T-677/13, *AXA Versicherung* EU:T:2015:473.

[362] Case C-365/12 P, *EnBW* EU:C:2014:112, para. 117. [363] Ibid., para. 132.

[364] Case T-623/13, *Unión de Almacenistas de Hierros de España* EU:T:2015:268. [365] Dir. 2014/104/EU (see n. 328).

[366] See also recital 20 of the Directive, and Case T-677/13, *AXA* EU:T:2015:473, para. 135.

written submissions.[367] From the perspective of the average common lawyer, however, the oral hearing process is far removed from what one might think of as the undertaking having its 'day in court'. The oral hearing is not a formal trial, and is not heard in public.

Instead, it is controlled and supervised by the HO.[368] Third parties, such as complainants, may be heard in addition to the parties.[369] It may last anything from a day to two or three weeks, depending on the complexity of the case. Under Article 14(6) of Regulation 773/2004, parties 'may be heard separately', having regard to their legitimate interests in protecting their business secrets, etc. Article 14(6) does not create any absolute *right* to an *in camera* hearing, which remains within the discretion of the HO. In *SKW*, however, the CJ held that failure to grant an *in camera* hearing in circumstances where the defendant legitimately feared retaliation from other cartel participants amounted to breach of its rights of defence.[370] Article 14(5) of Regulation 773/2004 provides that the persons being heard may be 'assisted by' their lawyers.[371]

Article 14(8) of Regulation 773/2004 provides that the statements made at the hearing shall be recorded and the record made available to the persons who attended the hearing, regard being had to the protection of business secrets and confidential information. Business secrets and other confidential information are deleted.

The HO is not a judge. It is not the HO's function to determine issues of liability, but instead to make an interim report to the Competition Commissioner on the hearing and the conclusions to be drawn from it in respect of the right to be heard.[372] This report is not made available to the parties, who have no right to see or comment on it. The HO also makes a final report to be attached to the draft decision submitted to the College of Commissioners,[373] which is made known to the addressees of the decision and is published in the Official Journal together with the decision.[374] The limited nature of the HO's role is relevant to the question of the compatibility of competition procedure with Article 6(1) ECHR.

E. COMMISSION DECISIONS

(i) General

Regulation 1/2003 grants the Commission a variety of decision-making powers: encompassing both procedural decisions taken during an investigation, and final decisions finding infringement of the competition rules (or otherwise). Although the day-to-day business of enforcement is conducted by DG Comp, decisions are collegiate acts of the whole Commission.[375] When the Commission adopts

367 See Best Practices, paras. 106–108; Antitrust ManProc, Module 3.3. The Commission does not breach the right to be heard if it refuses a hearing when it does not receive a request within the stipulated time limits, Case T-286/09, *Intel* EU:T:2014:547, paras. 325–326.

368 HO Terms of Reference, Art. 10. See S. Durande and K. Williams, 'The Practical Impact of the Exercise of the Right to be Heard: A Special Focus on the Effect of Oral Hearings and the Role of the Hearing Officers' (2005) 2 *Competition Policy Newsletter* 22; W. Wils, 'The Oral Hearing in Competition Proceedings Before the European Commission' (2012) 35 *World Competition* 397.

369 Reg. 773/2004, Art. 13.

370 Case C-154/14 P, *SKW Stahl-Metallurgie* EU:C:2016:445, paras. 64–67, overturning the approach of the GC, in Case T-384/09, *SKW Stahl-Metallurgie* EU:T:2014:27. The CJ ultimately held that SKW had failed to establish that the procedural irregularity had affected the outcome of the case.

371 Not 'represented by', because it is necessary that someone from the undertaking itself (although that can be an in-house lawyer) is present to provide relevant information about the organisation, see Case 49/69, *BASF (Dyestuffs)* EU:C:1972:71. Persons 'invited to attend' may be represented by legal representatives, Reg. 773/2004, Art. 14(4).

372 HO Terms of Reference, Art. 13(1). 373 Ibid., Art. 14(1). 374 Ibid., Art. 16.

375 As emphasised by the GC in Cases T-25/95 etc., *Cimenteries* EU:T:2000:77, para. 721. Particular acts of management or administration can, however, be delegated to a single Commissioner.

an infringement decision, the Commissioner responsible for competition lays the draft before the College of Commissioners, which must adopt the measure.[376]

This section deals with the content of decisions other than the imposition of fines: fines are dealt with in Section 6.H.

(ii) Final Decisions: Infringement Decisions under Regulation 1/2003, Article 7

Perhaps the most natural outcome of an investigation into suspected anti-competitive practices is a finding of infringement of Article 101 and/or 102. Article 7 of Regulation 1/2003 provides as follows:

Finding and termination of infringement

1. Where the Commission, acting on a complaint or on its own initiative, finds that there is an infringement of Article [101] or of Article [102], it may by decision require the undertakings and associations of undertakings concerned to bring such infringement to an end. For this purpose, it may impose on them any behavioural or structural remedies which are proportionate to the infringement committed and necessary to bring the infringement effectively to an end. Structural remedies can only be imposed either where there is no equally effective behavioural remedy or where any equally effective behavioural remedy would be more burdensome for the undertaking concerned than the structural remedy. If the Commission has a legitimate interest in doing so, it may also find that an infringement has been committed in the past.
2. Those entitled to lodge a complaint for the purposes of paragraph 1 are natural or legal persons who can show a legitimate interest and Member States.

Rather curiously, the language of Article 7 is drafted primarily in terms of bringing ongoing violations of Article 101 or 102 to an end, with the Commission's power to find infringements of those provisions mentioned somewhat in passing. Article 7(1) thus states explicitly that a decision finding an infringement may order undertakings to bring that breach to an end where it has not already been terminated. These are referred to as 'cease and desist orders'.[377] The decision may also contain a 'like effects order', whereby the parties are prohibited from entering into similar arrangements.[378] Where there is more than one way of bringing an infringement effectively to an end, it is for the defendant to choose between the various options[379]—provided, of course, that its chosen approach is indeed effective. The Court established in *Cementhandelaren* that the Commission may also take a decision finding a past infringement after the breach has been terminated;[380] this power is now reflected in the final sentence of Article 7(1), where the Commission can demonstrate a 'legitimate interest in doing so'.

Article 7(1) further empowers the Commission, where appropriate, to require *positive* steps on the part of defendant undertakings in order to bring an established infringement to an end.[381]

[376] The failure of the College to adopt an authenticated version of the decision was one reason for the annulment of the *PVC* decision in Case C-137/92 P, *Commission v BASF and others* EU:C:1994:247.

[377] On the circumstances in which it may be appropriate to issue a 'cease and desist' order under Art. 7, see C. Ritter, 'How Far Can the Commission Go When Imposing Remedies for Antitrust Infringements?' (2016) 7 *JECLAP* 587.

[378] See Case T-410/03, *Hoechst* EU:T:2008:211, where the Commission decision prohibited future similar conduct, even though Hoechst had already left the relevant market.

[379] See e.g. Cases T-69/89, *RTE* EU:T:1991:39, para. 98, and T-167/08, *Microsoft* EU:T:2012:323, para. 95.

[380] Case 8/72, *Cementhandelaren* EU:C:1972:84; see also COMP/37.860, *Morgan Stanley/Visa International and Visa Europe*, upheld Case T-461/07, *Visa Europe and Visa International Service Association* EU:T:2011:181, where the infringement had ceased but the undertaking continued to deny wrongdoing.

[381] The power to adopt behavioural remedies was not addressed directly in the precursor to Art. 7, namely Art. 3 of Reg. 1/2003, although the CJ in *Commercial Solvents* held that such a power existed: see Cases 6 and 7/73, *Commercial Solvents* EU:C:1974:18, para. 45.

The purpose of such remedies is the 're-establishment of compliance with the rules infringed':[382] that is, to ensure that the defendant's behaviour going forward is in accordance with the requirements of Article 101 and/or 102. Such a remedy may be useful, for instance, in refusal to supply cases, where the dominant undertaking may be required to (re)commence supply or to share facilities.[383] The Commission might alternatively order an undertaking to amend its contractual terms or its pricing policies. Article 7(1) does not dictate or limit the type of behavioural remedies that may be imposed, but expressly states that any such remedies must be 'proportionate to the infringement committed and necessary to bring the infringement effectively to an end'.[384]

The key factor constraining the Commission's discretion under Article 7(1) is thus the proportionality of the behavioural remedies imposed. This proved to be a sticking point in the *Atlantic Container Line* cartel case,[385] where the infringement decision, inter alia, required the defendants to inform its customers that they were entitled to terminate or renegotiate the terms of contracts concluded within the context of the cartel.[386] The GC annulled the requirement on the basis that it went beyond what was required to end the infringement and thus to re-establish compliance with Article 101.[387] Similarly, in *Microsoft*,[388] the decision required Microsoft to appoint an independent monitoring trustee (IMT), which would be granted access to sensitive information regarding Microsoft's business activities. Microsoft was also required to bear all the costs of the appointment of the IMT. This part of the decision was annulled by the GC,[389] on the basis that the Commission was, in effect, compelling Microsoft to grant to the IMT powers which the Commission was not itself authorised to confer on third parties.

Article 7(1) of Regulation 1/2003 furthermore empowers the Commission to impose structural remedies in appropriate circumstances, again subject to a requirement of proportionality.[390] Notably, Article 7(1) expressly states a preference for behavioural over structural remedies, other things being equal, meaning that structural remedies can *only* be imposed where no behavioural remedy would be equally effective or where the behavioural remedy would be more burdensome. Recital 12 of Regulation 1/2003 states that changes to the structure of an undertaking would only be proportionate 'where there is a substantial risk of a lasting or repeated infringement that derives from the very structure of the undertaking'. On the one hand, the ability to impose structural remedies, i.e. to order divestment or break up companies, is a powerful weapon in the hands of a competition authority, and not one to be used lightly. On the other, as demonstrated by the preference for structural remedies in the merger control sphere, an effective structural remedy can not only provide a durable solution to a market failure, but also minimises the need for regulatory involvement going forward. This may, ultimately, prove to be less intrusive and thus more appealing for defendants.

The Commission makes limited use of its powers to impose behavioural or structural remedies under Article 7. This is probably, in part, because the demanding approach of the Union Courts to the proportionality criterion makes these powers rather inflexible in practice.[391] The Commission must

[382] See Cases C-241/91 P, *RTE and ITP* EU:C:1995:98, para. 93; and T-395/94, *Atlantic Container Line* EU:T:2002:49, para. 410.

[383] See Chap 7, Section 12.

[384] Noting this distinction, see F. Wagner-von Papp, 'Best and Even Better Practices in Commitment Procedures after *Alrosa*: The Dangers of Abandoning the "Struggle for Competition Law"' (2012) 49 *CMLRev* 929, 960.

[385] Case T-395/94, *Atlantic Container Line* EU:T:2002:49.

[386] *Trans-Atlantic Agreement* [1994] OJ L376/1, Art. 5.

[387] Case T-395/94, *Atlantic Container Line* EU:T:2002:49, para. 410.

[388] COMP/37.792, *Microsoft* 24 March 2004. [389] Case T-201/04, *Microsoft* EU:T:2007:289.

[390] The power to impose structural remedies was not addressed directly by Art. 3 of Reg. 17. A divestiture order was made in the context of the infringement decision in Case 6/72, *Continental Can* EU:C:1973:22, but because the decision was annulled on substantive grounds, the order was never enforced.

[391] Wagner-von Papp, n. 384, 960. Though see the proposed structural remedies in the *Google Adtech* investigation: Commission Press Release, 'Antitrust: Commission sends Statement of Objections to Google over abusive practices in online advertising technology', 14 June 2023.

demonstrate that any behavioural remedy imposed is the least restrictive alternative available, and additionally, in the case of structural remedies, that there are no suitable less restrictive behavioural options. There is also a question of monitoring and enforcing ongoing compliance of behavioural remedies in particular, a problem illustrated by the Commission's drawn-out efforts to secure compliance by Microsoft with the interoperability obligations imposed by the 2004 infringement decision.[392] The Commission may instead, as in *Google Shopping*,[393] choose to frame what are essentially positive obligations to change business behaviour in negative terms, that is, merely as a duty to ensure that the infringement is effectively terminated. The approach in *Google Shopping* is notable for two reasons. First, the Commission was remarkably prescriptive as to what 'ceasing and desisting' entailed in this context, outlining a series of principles to be respected in any remedy nominally voluntarily adopted by Google. Secondly, the Commission's reluctance to specify a precise remedy to be implemented to address its concerns is perhaps understandable in light of its failed efforts to agree adequate commitments with Google under the Article 9 procedure, prior to adoption of the Article 7 decision. Yet the significant disagreement that has followed the decision as to whether Google is complying with its obligation to terminate the violation, particularly the vocal disappointment of its rivals with respect to the changes accepted by the Commission, suggests that the choice to opt out of more prescriptive remedies may have been suboptimal.[394] The use of behavioural and/or structural remedies is more common in consensual enforcement proceedings, namely the commitment decision procedure and the increasingly popular informal settlement procedure under Article 7, both discussed below.

(iii) Final Decisions: Commitments Decisions under Regulation 1/2003, Article 9

a. General

Article 9 of Regulation 1/2003 provides an alternative case disposition mechanism that enables the Commission to adopt decisions whereby, without a finding of infringement, the case is concluded on the basis of binding commitments given by defendant undertakings about their future market behaviour.[395] This was a new power added by Regulation 1/2003. Previously the Commission could settle cases informally, but could not make the agreed commitments legally binding. Recital 13 of Regulation 1/2003 states that 'commitment decisions' are not suitable where the Commission intends to impose a fine, and consequently the Commission does not apply the Article 9 procedure to secret cartels that fall under the Leniency Notice,[396] or to other cases where the primary goal is to punish past behaviour.[397] However, Article 9 has been used in respect of what, if proved, would be serious

[392] Culminating in the case returning to the GC in Case T-167/08, *Microsoft* EU:T:2012:323, which found non-compliance by Microsoft with the obligations imposed in the original decision, and imposed a fine of €860,000 in response—a figure that eclipsed the fine of just under half a billion euro imposed for the original violation.

[393] AT.39740, *Google Search (Shopping)* 27 June 2017, paras. 697–705.

[394] For discussion of the substantive elements of the case, see Chap 7, Section 13.

[395] See generally J. Temple Lang, 'Commitment Decisions and Settlements with Antitrust Authorities and Private Parties Under European Antitrust Law' [2005] *Fordham Corp L Inst* 265; C. Cook, 'Commitment Decisions: The Law and Practice under Article 9' (2006) 29 *World Competition* 209; W. Wils, 'Settlements of EU Antitrust Investigations; Commitment Decisions under Article 9 of Regulation 1/2003' (2006) 29 *World Competition* 345; W. Wils, 'The Use of Settlements in Public Antitrust Enforcement: Objectives and Principles' (2008) 31 *World Competition* 335; W. Wils, 'Discretion and Prioritisation in Public Antitrust Enforcement' (2011) 34 *World Competition* 353; N. Dunne, 'Commitment Decisions in EU Competition Law' (2014) 10 *J of Competition Law and Economics* 399; A. Gautier and N. Petit, 'Optimal Enforcement of Competition Policy: The Commitments Procedure Under Uncertainty' (2018) 45 *European J of Law and Economics* 195; R. Stones, 'Commitment Decisions in EU Competition Enforcement: Policy Effectiveness v. the Formal Rule of Law' (2019) 38 *YEL* 361.

[396] Best Practices, para. 116. For the Leniency Notice see Section 6.H.v.

[397] 'To Commit or Not to Commit?' [2014] 3 *Competition Policy Brief* 1.

infringements of Article 102 where a heavy fine might have been expected.[398] Commitments may involve behavioural or structural obligations, and may go beyond what the Commission could impose in an Article 7 decision.[399] The Commission will not accept a mere commitment to comply with competition law in the future.[400] Behavioural commitments may additionally involve the defendant undertaking agreeing to appoint a monitoring trustee mechanism to ensure their implementation.[401]

Regulation 1/2003

Article 9

1. Where the Commission intends to adopt a decision requiring that an infringement be brought to an end and the undertakings concerned offer commitments to meet the concerns expressed to them by the Commission in its preliminary assessment, the Commission may by decision make those commitments binding on the undertakings. Such a decision may be adopted for a specified period and shall conclude that there are no longer grounds for action by the Commission.
2. The Commission may, upon request or on its own initiative, reopen the proceedings:
   (a) where there has been a material change in any of the facts on which the decision was based;
   (b) where the undertakings concerned act contrary to their commitments; or
   (c) where the decision was based on incomplete, incorrect or misleading information provided by the parties.

The power to take an Article 9 decision arises only where the Commission otherwise intends to adopt an Article 7 decision. It is not obliged to send an SO before taking a commitments decision, however, but is merely required to make a 'preliminary assessment' of its competition concerns. The procedure is explained in Best Practices.[402] If the parties under investigation wish to avoid an SO, they must offer commitments early on, and the Commission may then issue a preliminary assessment.[403] If the Commission is minded to accept the commitments offered by the defendant(s), on the basis that these meet its concerns, it 'market tests' these proposals in accordance with Article 27(4) of Regulation 1/2003. It does so by publishing the proposed commitments in the Official Journal and inviting third party comments.[404] Following the responses, the Commission may require amendments to the commitments,[405] or may drop the Article 9 procedure altogether and revert to Article 7.[406] If the commitments finally offered are acceptable, the Commission takes a formal decision under Article 9(1), thus making the defendant bound by them.

[398] For example, COMP/38.636, *Rambus*, IP/09/1897; COMP/39.530, *Microsoft (tying)*, IP/13/2013; COM/39.692, *IBM Maintenance Services*, IP/11/1539; AT.40394, *Aspen* 10 February 2021; see Chap 7.

[399] Case C-441/07 P, *Commission v Alrosa* EU:C:2010:377, para. 48.

[400] 'To Commit or Not to Commit?', n. 397.

[401] As in AT39654, *Reuters Instrument Codes (RICs)* 20 December 2012 and AT39530, *Microsoft (tying)* 6 March 2013.

[402] Best Practices, paras. 115–133.

[403] If an SO has already been sent, the SO fulfils the requirements of the Preliminary Assessment.

[404] Best Practices, paras. 129–133. It may also actively contact third parties, see Faull and Nikpay, n. 1, 2.134.

[405] As in AT39654, *Reuters Instrument Codes (RICs)* 20 December 2012, for instance.

[406] As happened in COMP/38.698, *CISAC*, on appeal Cases T-442/08 etc., *CISAC v Commission* EU:T:2013:188, and AT.39740 *Google Search (Shopping)* 27 June 2017.

Article 9(2) gives the Commission the power to reopen the proceedings in defined circumstances,[407] and a breach of an Article 9(1) decision may result in the Commission imposing a fine under Article 23(2)(c) of Regulation 1/2003. A fine of €561 million was imposed on Microsoft for breaching its commitments in respect of the browser choice screen following the *Microsoft (Tying II)* investigation.[408] The Commission, however, is not *obliged* to act against a breach of commitments. It has the same discretion in deciding whether to take such action as it has in respect of any alleged anti-competitive conduct.[409]

The scope for the defendant to appeal against an Article 9(1) decision to which it has voluntarily agreed is limited, and unlikely, although it could conceivably do so on procedural grounds.[410] Third parties with standing under Article 263 are more likely to appeal, as occurred in *Alrosa*[411] and *Groupe Canal+*.[412] Complainants dissatisfied with the outcome of the case may challenge the decision,[413] or complain that commitments have been breached.[414] Again, however, the chances of success are slim given the comparatively wide margin of discretion afforded to the Commission under Article 9.[415] A commitments decision does not preclude an NCA from taking proceedings against the undertaking after the Article 9 procedure is concluded.[416]

b. The Use of Article 9 Decisions

It quickly became apparent after Regulation 1/2003 came into force that commitments decisions would play a major role in the Commission's application of the competition rules. Outside hardcore cartels, where commitments decisions are unavailable, they became the predominant means of case disposition by the Commission.[417] Initially, the Commission used the procedure to dispose of a number of Article 101 cases that had been notified before May 2004.[418] It has since been used to deal with a wide range of Article 101 non-cartel cases including, inter alia, airline alliances,[419] non-compete obligations in joint ventures,[420] multilateral exchange fees,[421] and limitations of price competition in the e-books sector.[422]

The more striking use of Article 9, however, has been in respect of Article 102. Since 2007, a wide-ranging initiative against anti-competitive practices in the energy sector has seen numerous

[407] A material change in the facts; breach of the commitments; the decision was based on incomplete, incorrect, or misleading information supplied by the parties.

[408] COMP/39.530, *Microsoft*, IP/13/196.

[409] Case T-342/11, *CEEES* EU:T:2014:60.

[410] See Faull and Nikpay, n. 1, 2.143.

[411] Case C-441/07 P, *Commission v Alrosa* EU:C:2010:377.

[412] Case C-132/19 P, *Groupe Canal+* EU:C:2020:1007.

[413] As in Case T-76/14, *Morningstar* EU:T:2016:481 and Case T-616/18, *Polskie Górnictwo Naftowe i Gazownictwo* EU:T:2022:43.

[414] Case T-342/11, *CEEES* EU:T:2014:60; the appeal against the *Rambus* decision (COMP/38.636), Cases T-148 and 149/10, *SK Hynix v Commission* EU:T:2013:358, was withdrawn.

[415] As illustrated by *Alrosa*, the Commission is granted a wide margin of discretion under Art. 9.

[416] Case C-17/10, *Toshiba Corp* EU:C:2012:72, paras. 68–92; Case T-342/11, *CEEES* EU:T:2014:60, paras. 66–68.

[417] See [2015] 3 *Competition Policy Brief*, and statistics presented in W. Wils, 'Ten Years of Commitment Decisions under Article 9', n. 13.

[418] See e.g. COMP/37.214, *Deutsche Bundesliga* [2005] OJ L134/46 and COMP/38.173, *FA Premier League*, involving the collective selling of media rights to football matches; COMP/38.681, *Cannes Extension Agreement*, IP/06/1311, involving online music; and COMP/38.348, *Repsol* [2006] OJ L176/104, involving the fuel distribution system in Spain.

[419] COMP/*BA/AA/IB* [2010] OJ C278/14; COMP/39.595, *Air Canada/Continental Airlines/Lufthansa/United* [2013] OJ C201/7; COMP/39.964, *AF-KL/DL/AZ* [2015] OJ C212/5.

[420] COMP/39.736, *Siemens/Areva* [2012] OJ C280/8.

[421] COMP/39.398, *Visa MIF* [2014] OJ C147/7.

[422] COMP/39.847, *E-books* [2013] OJ C73/17 and [2013] OJ C378/25.

decisions.[423] Structural remedies have been secured in many cases.[424] Outside the energy sector, a number of high-profile and sometimes controversial Article 102 cases have been settled by commitments, as discussed in Chapter 7. These include cases premised upon excessive pricing,[425] refusals to deal,[426] and the abuse of standard-essential patents.[427]

Yet, Article 9 is not an inevitable instrument of case disposition by any means. Notably, in the telecommunications sector, the Commission has preferred to conclude its numerous Article 102 investigations through infringement decisions,[428] even in circumstances where the undertaking concerned had sought to provide commitments in lieu.[429] The somewhat notorious *Google Shopping* investigation, moreover, reverted to the Article 7 procedure after *three* sets of proposed commitments had been market-tested, but ultimately rejected by the Commission (and, perhaps not unrelatedly, after Margrethe Vestager succeeded Joaquín Almunia as Commissioner for Competition).[430] The GC, in its revised judgment in *CB* from 2016, emphasised the margin of discretion enjoyed by the Commission in choosing between the Article 7 and 9 procedures.[431] Where discussions with a view to a settlement under Article 9 precede an infringement decision, the Commission is not thereby precluded from deploying the full range of its ordinary powers under the latter (fines, a 'cease and desist' order, etc.),[432] nor do the proposed commitments discussed during the earlier stages predetermine the scope of any subsequent remedies imposed.[433] As the GC explained in *Google Shopping*:

> 633. . . . It is . . . apparent from the use of the verb 'may' in [Article 9], according to which, 'where . . . the undertakings concerned offer commitments to meet the concerns expressed to them by the Commission . . . , the Commission may by decision make those commitments binding', that the Commission is not obliged to pursue a commitments procedure on which it has embarked and that it may revert to a standard procedure for finding an infringement. The Commission is entitled to do so, for example, because it considers the commitments offered to be insufficient to resolve the competition issues identified, because the scope of the facts or of those issues is greater than initially determined or even because ultimately the Commission considers it more appropriate, for reasons of general competition policy, to make a finding of infringement that will, in some circumstances, be subject to judicial review.
>
> . . .
>
> 637. Although it is true that . . . recital 13 of Regulation No 1/2003 indicates that decisions accepting commitments are not appropriate where the Commission intends to impose a fine, the fact that, at a certain stage in the investigation of a possible infringement of Articles 101 and 102 TFEU, the Commission embarks on a commitments procedure merely represents a preliminary procedural option that is not definitive. Such a procedural choice cannot constitute a precise assurance that the Commission will not revert to the standard procedure for finding an infringement and that it will not impose a penalty . . .[434]

[423] COMP/39.386, *EDF—Long Term Electricity Contracts in France*; COMP/37.966, *Distrigaz* [2008] OJ C9/8; COMP/39.316, *GDF, Gas market in France* [2010] OJ C57/13; COMP/39.388, *German Electricity Wholesale Markets* and COMP/39.389, *German Electricity Balancing Markets (E.ON)* [2009] OJ C36/8; COMP/39.402, *RWE—Gas Foreclosure* [2009] OJ C133/9; COMP/39.351, *Swedish Interconnectors* [2010] OJ C142/28; COMP/39.317, *E.ON (Gas)* [2010] OJ C278/9; COMP/39.315, *ENI* 29 September 2010; COMP/39.727, *CEZ* [2013] OJ C251/4; *Bulgarian Energy Holding* COMP/39.767, 10 December 2015, IP/15/628; and AT.40335, *Romanian gas interconnectors* 6 March 2020. See further Chap 7.

[424] See *Distrigaz, RWE, E.ON (Gas), ENI*, and *CEZ* cited in the previous note.

[425] Including COMP/39.592, *Standard & Poor's* 15 November 2011, and AT.40394, *Aspen* 10 February 2021.

[426] COMP/C-3/39692 *IBM Maintenance Services* 13 December 2011.

[427] *Rambus*; COMP/39.985; and AT.39939 *Samsung* 29 April 2014.

[428] Including COMP/38.784, *Wanadoo España v Telefónica* 4 July 2007; COMP/39.525, *Telekomunikacja Polska* 22 June 2011; and AT.39523, *Slovak Telekom* 15 October 2014.

[429] See e.g. COMP/39.525, *Telekomunikacja Polska*, 22 June 2011, para. 6.

[430] AT.39740, *Google Search (Shopping)* 27 June 2017.

[431] Case T-491/07 RENV, *CB* EU:T:2016:379, para. 470.

[432] Ibid., para. 461.

[433] Ibid., para. 469.

[434] Case T-612/17, *Google Shopping* EU:T:2021:763.

c. *Proportionality and Article 9 Decisions*

We saw earlier that, under Article 7, the Commission's discretion is constrained by an exacting principle of proportionality, which requires it to be demonstrated that any behavioural or structural remedies *imposed* on undertakings are suitable and necessary to address the infringement identified. Under Article 9, conversely, the Commission has greater freedom to *accept* voluntarily-offered commitments which go beyond what can be considered strictly necessary to remedy the competition problem at issue. This point was established, not uncontentiously, in *Alrosa*. The case concerned an Article 9 decision concluded by the Commission with De Beers, at the time the world's largest diamond producer, under which De Beers agreed to phase out all purchases of rough diamonds from Alrosa, the second largest global producer.[435] The Commission had initially investigated the sales agreement under both Articles 101 and 102, and indeed market-tested joint commitments from De Beers and Alrosa to cap but not to cease all sales (to notably unfavourable responses). Alrosa was unhappy with the choice to exclude it from the final decision, and, considering itself seriously affected by the termination of its arrangements with De Beers, challenged that decision before the GC.

A sympathetic GC annulled the decision initially, on the grounds that it infringed the principle of proportionality.[436] The GC took the view that although commitments arise from an offer made by the parties and accepted by the Commission, that does not mean that the Commission is not the 'sole author' of the decision, which is binding *erga omnes*. The Commission, moreover, could not, the GC argued, take a decision under Article 9(1) that it could not also take as a final decision under Article 7(1). Since the principle of proportionality would have been infringed if this had been an Article 7(1) decision, as there were less onerous options available, so the principle of proportionality was equally infringed under Article 9(1).

On appeal, however, the CJ set aside the GC judgment.[437] The CJ clarified that the principle of proportionality applies to Article 9(1) commitment decisions differently from Article 7 decisions, imposing much less of a constraint on the Commission's enforcement discretion than in the case of infringement decisions.

Case C-441/07 P, *Commission v Alrosa* EU:C:2010:377

Court of Justice

35. [Article 9] is a new mechanism introduced by Regulation No 1/2003 which is intended to ensure that the competition rules laid down in the [EU] Treaty are applied effectively, by means of the adoption of decisions making commitments, proposed by the parties and considered appropriate by the Commission, binding in order to provide a more rapid solution to the competition problems identified by the Commission, instead of proceeding by making a formal finding of an infringement. More particularly, Article 9 of the regulation is based on considerations of procedural economy, and enables undertakings to participate fully in the procedure, by putting forward the solutions which appear to them to be the most appropriate and capable of addressing the Commission's concerns.

36. . . . [A]lthough Article 9, unlike Article 7 of Regulation No 1/2003, does not expressly refer to proportionality, the principle of proportionality, as a general principle of European Union law, is none the

[435] COMP/38.381, *DeBeers/Alrosa* [2006] OJ L205/24.

[436] Case T-170/06, *Alrosa* EU:T:2007:220.

[437] See M. Kellerbauer, 'Playground Instead of Playpen: The Court of Justice of the European Union's *Alrosa* Judgment on Article 9 of Regulation 1/2003' [2011] *ECLR* 1.

less a criterion for the lawfulness of any act of the institutions of the Union, including decisions taken by the Commission in its capacity of competition authority.

37. That being so, in the examination of acts of the Commission, whether in the context of Article 7 or of Article 9 of Regulation No 1/2003, the questions always arise, first, of the precise extent and limits of the obligations which flow from the observance of that principle and, second, of the limits of judicial review.

38. The specific characteristics of the mechanisms provided for in Articles 7 and 9 of Regulation No 1/2003 and the means of action available under each of those provisions are different, which means that the obligation on the Commission to ensure that the principle of proportionality is observed has a different extent and content, depending on whether it is considered in relation to the former or the latter article.

39. Article 7 of Regulation No 1/2003 expressly indicates the extent to which the principle of proportionality applies in situations covered by that article. In accordance with Article 7(1) of the regulation, the Commission may impose on the undertakings concerned any behavioural or structural remedies which are proportionate to the infringement committed and necessary to bring the infringement effectively to an end.

40. Article 9 of that regulation, by contrast, provides merely that in proceedings under that provision, as follows from recital 13 in the preamble to the regulation, the Commission is not required to make a finding of an infringement, its task being confined to examining, and possibly accepting, the commitments offered by the undertakings concerned in the light of the problems identified by it in its preliminary assessment and having regard to the aims pursued.

41. Application of the principle of proportionality by the Commission in the context of Article 9 of Regulation No 1/2003 is confined to verifying that the commitments in question address the concerns it expressed to the undertakings concerned and that they have not offered less onerous commitments that also address those concerns adequately. When carrying out that assessment, the Commission must, however, take into consideration the interests of third parties.

42. Judicial review for its part relates solely to whether the Commission's assessment is manifestly incorrect.

43. In the judgment under appeal, the General Court proceeded from the proposition that the application of the principle of proportionality has the same effect in relation to decisions taken under Article 7 of Regulation No 1/2003 as in relation to those taken under Article 9 of that regulation.

44. . . . [T]he General Court held that it would be contrary to the scheme of Regulation No 1/2003 for a decision which would, under Article 7(1) of the regulation, have to be regarded as disproportionate to the infringement that had been established to be taken by having recourse to the procedure laid down under Article 9(1) in the form of a commitment that is made binding.

45. That conclusion is not correct.

46. Those two provisions of Regulation No 1/2003 . . . pursue different objectives, one of them aiming to put an end to the infringement that has been found to exist and the other aiming to address the Commission's concerns following its preliminary assessment.

47. There is therefore no reason why the measure which could possibly be imposed in the context of Article 7 of Regulation No 1/2003 should have to serve as a reference for the purpose of assessing the extent of the commitments accepted under Article 9 of the regulation, or why anything going beyond that measure should automatically be regarded as disproportionate. Even though decisions adopted under each of those provisions are in either case subject to the principle of proportionality, the application of that principle none the less differs according to which of those provisions is concerned.

48. Undertakings which offer commitments on the basis of Article 9 of Regulation No 1/2003 consciously accept that the concessions they make may go beyond what the Commission could itself impose on them in a decision adopted under Article 7 of the regulation after a thorough examination. On

the other hand, the closure of the infringement proceedings brought against those undertakings allows them to avoid a finding of an infringement of competition law and a possible fine.

49. Moreover, the fact that the individual commitments offered by an undertaking have been made binding by the Commission does not mean that other undertakings are deprived of the possibility of protecting the rights they may have in connection with their relations with that undertaking.

50. It must therefore be concluded that . . . the General Court wrongly considered that the application of the principle of proportionality must be assessed, in the case of decisions taken under Article 9 of Regulation No 1/2003, by reference to the way in which it is assessed in connection with decisions taken under Article 7 of that regulation despite the different concepts underlying those two provisions.

Accordingly, under Article 9, the general EU law principle of proportionality requires only that the Commission satisfy itself that the commitments in question address its identified competition concerns and that the defendant undertaking has not offered less onerous commitments that also address those concerns adequately. The CJ went on to hold that, in finding that alternative less onerous solutions existed in this case, the GC had wrongly substituted its own assessment for that of the Commission.[438]

The diverging approaches of the GC and CJ in *Alrosa* evince notably different conceptions of the nature of commitments decisions. The GC took what has been called a 'public-law paradigm' view, whereby commitments decisions are part of an enforcement process 'epitomised by an authoritative, unilateral, top-down hierarchical command by the "State"'.[439] The CJ, however, saw them as having a 'contract-law' character, whereby they are the outcome of a negotiation and agreement between parties of similar bargaining power able to safeguard their own interests.[440] The CJ explicitly conceptualised the commitments offered by defendant undertakings as a sort of quid pro quo for avoiding the formal finding of infringement and the fine that would usually accompany an Article 7 decision.[441] The result of the CJ's conception of commitments decisions, it has been argued, is the marginalisation of judicial review and the sidelining of the principle of proportionality.[442] From this perspective, the CJ's judgment was an extreme example of the Court's willingness to defer to the Commission's discretion.

In articulating its deferential proportionality standard in paragraph 41 of *Alrosa*, the CJ nonetheless added a caveat: namely, that 'the Commission must . . . take into consideration the interests of third parties'. At first glance, based on the facts of *Alrosa* itself, this requirement appeared to have little bite. The commitments decision under appeal in that case had a detrimental impact on the business activities of the applicant, yet its interests were given little apparent weight by the CJ in its assessment. In *Groupe Canal+*,[443] however, the CJ accepted that the negative effects of an Article 9 decision were so harmful to third party interests as to merit the decision's annulment. The case represents the first occasion on which a commitments decision has been definitively annulled by the Union Courts.

[438] Case C-441/07 P, *Commission v Alrosa* EU:C:2010:377, paras. 59–68. [439] Wagner-von Papp, n. 384, 933.
[440] Ibid.
[441] Case C-441/07 P, *Commission v Alrosa* EU:C:2010:377, para. 48.
[442] See also F. Cengiz, 'Judicial Review and the Rule of Law in the EU Competition Law Regime after *Alrosa*' (2011) 7 *European Competition Journal* 127.
[443] Case C-132/19 P, *Groupe Canal+ v Commission* EU:C:2020:1007. The discussion here is based on N. Dunne, 'Challenging Competition Commitment Decisions: *Groupe Canal+*' (2021) 58 *CMLRev* 1229.

The *Groupe Canal+* challenge arose in the context of the Commission's *Cross Border Pay-TV* investigation, which addressed market segmentation practices allegedly in breach of Article 101. One of the defendants, Paramount, opted to settle under Article 9, committing to neither introduce nor enforce cross-border restrictions in its licensing arrangements with pay-TV broadcasters in the EEA.[444] Although Groupe Canal+'s relationship with Paramount had not been investigated directly by the Commission, the finalised commitments essentially invalidated the terms of its licensing agreement. As such, it was considered to have sufficient standing to challenge those commitments.[445] While the GC followed the logic of the *Alrosa* judgment and upheld the decision,[446] the CJ put greater emphasis on the previously underutilised caveat from paragraph 41 of *Alrosa*. It held that, 'when the Commission verifies commitments not from the perspective of whether they are appropriate to address its competition concerns, but also with regard to their effect on the interests of third parties, the principle of proportionality requires that those third parties' rights are not rendered meaningless'.[447] Since, in the CJ's view, Article 16(1) of Regulation 1/2003 effectively precluded national courts from enforcing the disputed restrictions within the licensing agreement between Groupe Canal+ and Paramount in light of the Commission's Article 9 decision,[448] the latter essentially emptied the contractual rights that Groupe Canal+ enjoyed under the agreement of all substance.[449] In the circumstances, the commitments 'rendered meaningless the contractual rights of third parties . . . and thereby infringed the principle of proportionality'.[450]

The CJ's interpretation of the Article 16(1) duty for national courts in respect of commitments decisions was pivotal to its approach in the case. Article 16(1) states:

> When national courts rule on agreements, decisions or practices under [Articles 101 or 102] which are already the subject of a Commission decision, they cannot take decisions running counter to the decision adopted by the Commission. They must also avoid giving decisions which would conflict with a decision contemplated by the Commission in proceedings it has initiated . . .

Commitments decisions are premised upon suspected breaches of Article 101 or 102, but do not constitute decisions 'adopted by the Commission' under these Articles for the purposes of the Article 16(1) duty. That is, national courts are not bound by the Commission's choice to opt against a formal finding of infringement and may find breaches of Article 101 or 102 arising the same facts.[451] In *Groupe Canal+*, however, the CJ drew an implicit distinction between the underlying theory of harm and the commitments actually agreed in a commitment decision. The latter are legally binding obligations, freely agreed by defendant undertakings, which must be recognised and respected by national courts adjudicating claims in the same subject area subsequently. The CJ thus answered in the affirmative the previously open question as to whether a national judicial measure requiring breach of Article 9 commitments would violate the Article 16(1) duty.[452]

More controversial, perhaps, is the assertion that Article 9 necessarily 'contemplates' a finding of infringement within the meaning of the second sentence of Article 16(1), and that this possibility persists even *after* an investigation is concluded by virtue of the provision for reopening proceedings in Article 9(2).[453] In such circumstances, the CJ found, national courts are not permitted, inter alia, to

[444] AT.40023, *Cross-border access to pay-TV (Paramount)* 26 July 2016.
[445] Case T-873/16, *Groupe Canal+* EU:T:2018:904, para. 25. [446] Ibid.
[447] Case C-132/19 P, *Groupe Canal+* EU:C:2020:1007, para. 106. [448] Ibid., paras. 107–115.
[449] Ibid., paras. 116–117. [450] Ibid., para. 127. [451] Ibid., para. 108, citing recital 13 of Reg. 1/2003.
[452] The point was raised but not definitively answered in the Commission Staff Working Paper accompanying the Report on the functioning of Reg. 1/2003, COM(2009)206 final, 29 April 2009, para. 107.
[453] Case C-132/19 P, *Groupe Canal+* EU:C:2020:1007, para. 113.

take 'negative' decisions finding an absence of infringement of Article 101 or 102 relating to the same facts.[454] The difficulty, however, is that Article 9(2) empowers the Commission to reopen an investigation for an array of reasons, including 'a material change in any of the facts on which the decision was based'. Yet markets are not static objects, so that, almost by definition, the 'summary and provisional' assessment contained in an Article 9 decision is vulnerable to obsolescence as the underpinning market dynamics change. A plain meaning reading of the *Groupe Canal+* judgment could thus suggest that national courts must continue to view concluded commitment decisions as potential impending infringement decisions, even years after the relevant investigation has concluded, though such an understanding seems absurd in practice. The CJ's approach also has the potential to create difficulties if and when commitment decisions are invoked as 'prima facie evidence' of breach in follow-on private damages claims,[455] a point considered in the next subsection.

d. *The Advantages and Disadvantages of Commitments Decisions*

Commitments decisions are an attractive option for the Commission. They enable speedy resolution of ongoing cases quickly while allowing the Commission to retain control over the outcome. The Commission identifies the advantages of Article 9 over Article 7 prohibition decisions as:[456]

- a *quicker impact on the market* and resolution of the competition concerns, a benefit that the Commission considers of particular importance in fast-moving markets or those in the process of liberalisation;
- *more effective remedies*: commitments are forward-looking, more finely tuned, and can go beyond what could have been imposed under Article 7;[457]
- *better and swifter implementation* of structural and behavioural measures: the fact that the undertakings design the commitments themselves 'facilitates their implementation', and the threat of fines for their violation 'provides companies with an incentive to implement them properly'.

For undertakings under investigation, the advantages include avoidance of the more burdensome Article 7 procedure, with its lengthy oral and written adversarial proceedings; input into the design of the remedy; and avoidance of fines and, potentially, of bad publicity. An attractive feature for defendants is that commitments decisions do not involve a formal finding of infringement, and therefore, in principle, do not facilitate follow-on actions as Article 7 decisions.[458] Undertakings in Article 9(1) proceedings do not have to admit guilt, and the Commission is explicitly precluded from making a finding of breach.[459] In *Gasorba*, however, the CJ was at pains to emphasise that an Article 9 decision 'does not certify that the practice, which was the subject of concern, complies with [the EU competition rules]',[460] nor can a defendant undertaking claim any legitimate expectation that it will be immune from future competition enforcement at the national level, whether public or private.[461] More contentiously, the CJ went on to suggest that the mere existence of a settlement under Article 9

[454] Ibid. Following the CJ judgment in Case C-375/09, *Tele2 Polska* EU:C:2011:270, paras. 19–30, NCAs are subject to a blanket prohibition on adopting 'negative' decisions. The policy justification for the narrow reading of Art. 5, Reg. 1/2003, in the *Tele2* case—namely the need to ensure the uniform application of the EU competition rules (para. 28)—would appear to be equally applicable to national courts, despite the more permissive wording of Art. 6, Reg. 1/2003.

[455] Case C-547/16, *Gasorba*, para. 29.

[456] [2015] 3 *Competition Policy Brief.*

[457] As emphasised by the CJ in Case C-441/07 P, *Commission v Alrosa* EU:C:2010:377, para. 48.

[458] See Chap 14.

[459] Reg. 1/2003, recital 13, states, 'Commitment decisions should find that there are no longer grounds for action by the Commission without concluding whether or not there has been or still is an infringement.'

[460] Case C-547/16, *Gasorba* EU:C:2017:891, para. 25.

[461] Ibid., para. 28.

might itself constitute evidence of an antitrust infringement, suggesting a sort of 'no-smoke-without-fire' rationale:

> 29. Nonetheless, national courts cannot overlook that type of decision. Such acts are, in any event, in the nature of a decision. In addition, both the principle of sincere cooperation laid down in Article 4(3) TEU and the objective of applying EU competition law effectively and uniformly require the national court to take into account the preliminary assessment carried out by the Commission and regard it as an indication, *if not prima facie evidence*, of the anti-competitive nature of the agreement at issue in the light of Article 101(1) TFEU.[462]

This approach raises a number of concerns. It seems directly contrary to the wording of Regulation 1/2003, and at odds with the contractual paradigm of commitments decisions endorsed by the CJ in *Alrosa*. Despite now constituting ostensible prima facie evidence of an infringement, the Commission's preliminary assessment is not made public, the summary provided in any finalised decision tends to be scant at best, and, most fundamentally, the Commission is not required to fully explain or prove its suspicion that the antitrust rules have been violated. From a wider competition policy perspective, to the extent that this expansive understanding of the legal implications of an Article 9 decision may facilitate follow-on damages claims,[463] it might even have the counter-productive effect of dissuading undertakings from entering into socially beneficial settlements with the Commission due to a fear of potentially unbounded future liabilities. The CJ in *Groupe Canal+* cited *Gasorba* approvingly but did not endorse the approach of paragraph 29 expressly (though the point was raised by both of the parties).[464]

Third parties may also be disadvantaged by Article 9 decisions, as shown in *Alrosa*.[465] Although Alrosa was able to mount a challenge under Article 263, the wide discretion left to the Commission by the CJ ensured that Alrosa was unable to overturn the decision. Regardless of what *Gasorba* might establish, the absence of a clear infringement decision is an impediment for would-be private damages claimants. Moreover, although complainants have a right to a decision on their complaint,[466] the wide discretion given to the Commission makes this of doubtful use. Third parties do, however, have the benefit of being able to participate more fully than under Article 7 because of the 'market-testing' stage.

It is also necessary to consider the effect of commitments decisions on the development of the law. The extensive use of Article 9 has shifted public enforcement from imposed infringement decisions to negotiated outcomes.[467] Although the Commission considers that it must base a commitments decision on a coherent theory of harm,[468] it can try out the application of Article 102 in novel situations without having to prove its case with extensive economic and legal analysis.[469] Absent an infringement decision, there is little chance of review by the EU Courts, and the resultant diminution in jurisprudence may not be in the public interest.[470] For example, the Commission proclaimed the

[462] Ibid., para. 29 (emphasis added).

[463] See e.g. C. Fratea, 'Commitment Decisions and Private Actions for Damages in EU Competition Law in Light of the *Gasorba* Judgment: A New Opening from the Court of Justice of the European Union?' (2018) 39 *ECLR* 501.

[464] Case C-132/19 P, *Groupe Canal+* EU:C:2020:1007.

[465] See generally E. Dean, 'The Effect of Article 9 Decisions on Contractual Relations between Undertakings' (2018) 39 *ECLR* 181.

[466] See Section 6.B.

[467] Although the Commission stresses that it does not enter a 'bargaining process' which allows undertakings to escape with insufficient commitments, see [2015] 3 *Competition Policy Brief*.

[468] Ibid. [469] For example, 'patent ambush' in *Rambus*, and 'strategic under-investment' in *ENI*.

[470] See Cengiz, n. 442; Wagner-von Papp, n. 384.

Microsoft internet browser commitments[471] as a great victory, but its case was never put to the test.[472] Had the Commission succeeded with its *Google* commitments, Article 102 would have been applied in a highly contentious way without the possibility of review.[473] The energy decisions, which have made extensive use of structural remedies, have been described as the Commission using Article 9 to pursue regulatory goals to further its liberalisation agenda,[474] again without going near the Courts. A member of the CJ has written, in a personal capacity, of a 'a growing and vocal disquiet within the EU competition law community concerning the European Commission's increasing recourse to commitment decisions', resulting in a 'paucity' of binding precedent:

> Perhaps the strongest criticism levied against the Commission's practice of adopting commitment decisions is that they fail to sufficiently elucidate the law in novel and complex competition cases. This is due to the lack of a formal finding of infringement . . . in commitment decisions coupled with the fact that they provide limited opportunities for the solution adopted to be challenged before the General Court and the Court of Justice. While a commitment decision may offer 'legal comfort' to its addressee and rapidly restore competition in a given instance, it may provide less clarity and thus legal certainty for other actors than infringement decisions, which provide a more effective legal road map . . . .
>
> [W]hile the paucity of precedent may be overstated [because of the incidence of preliminary references before the CJ], in my view, commitment decisions are a quick-fix solution the excessive recourse to which may become undesirable over time, particularly if they are not interspersed with infringement decisions or if the Court of Justice has not had the opportunity to rule on related competition law questions.[475]

(iv) Final Decisions: 'Consent Decrees' under Article 7?

The discussion thus far indicates a blunt binary choice for the Commission, between finding breach and imposing a fine (but rarely any other type of remedy) under Article 7, and entering into a cooperative settlement under Article 9 yet without the certainty of a formal statement of infringement. The quasi-'consent decree'[476] procedure first applied in the *ARA Foreclosure* case suggests a more nimble approach.[477] Under this procedure, which nominally occurs under paragraph 37 of the Commission's Fining Guidelines,[478] the Commission can settle cases under Article 7 with willing defendants. Such cases involve formal findings of infringement, thus aiming to address the concern about 'the paucity

[471] COMP/39.530, *Microsoft*, IP/10/216.

[472] See O. Vasquez Duque, 'Active Choice vs. Inertia? An Exploratory Assessment of the European Microsoft Case's Choice Screen' (2023) 19 *J of Competition Law and Economics* 60, suggesting that the remedy had little impact on consumer behaviour.

[473] See R. Nazzini, '*Google* and the (Ever-stretching) Boundaries of Article 102 TFEU' (2015) 6 *JECLAP* 301 and the discussion of the *Google Search (Shopping)* case in Chap 7, Section 13.

[474] Cengiz, n. 442, 138.

[475] M. Wathelet, Editorial, 'Commitment Decisions and the Paucity of Precedent' (2015) 6 *JECLAP* 553, 554.

[476] So described by H. Wollmann, '*ARA Foreclosure*: A Step Towards "Consent Decrees in EU Antitrust Proceedings"' (2017) 8 *JECLAP* 167. Consent decrees are settlement procedures used by the US antitrust authorities; although more often than not concluded without any formal finding of breach, consent decrees can nonetheless include both an admission of liability by the defendant and an agreement to pay penalty fines. See generally R. Epstein, *Antitrust Consent Decrees in Theory and Practice: Why Less is More* (AEI Press, Washington, 2007).

[477] AT39759, *ARA Foreclosure* 20 September 2016, discussed in Chap 7, Section 12.

[478] Which states: 'Although these Guidelines present the general methodology for the setting of fines, the particularities of a given case or the need to achieve deterrence in a particular case may justify departing from such methodology or from the limits specified in point 21.' See Guidelines on the method of setting fines imposed pursuant to Article 23(2) (a) of Regulation No 1/2003 [2006] OJ C210/2, para. 37.

of precedent'[479] that resulted from over-reliance on the Article 9 procedure. The defendant is incentivised to settle, nonetheless, by virtue of a discount on the fine imposed by the Commission.[480] Defendants must be 'willing to acknowledge their liability for an infringement (including the facts and their legal qualification)'.[481] In certain cases concluded under the procedure, defendants have also agreed to legally binding structural[482] or behavioural remedies,[483] or have provided the Commission with evidence of additional competition law breaches during the course of its investigation.[484] Since the procedure was first applied in 2016, the Commission has used it to conclude several Article 102 investigations,[485] and an extensive number of Article 101 cases involving vertical restraints.[486]

This model of case disposition might be praised as an effective compromise: between the need to encourage and facilitate cooperation and more constructive remedies, on the one hand, and the desirability of ensuring legal certainty and sufficiently deterrent penalties, on the other. The Commission's success in persuading defendants to settle has moreover belied any concerns that it may prove difficult to scale up, given that defendants have considerably fewer incentives than under Article 9.[487] Yet unlike the equivalent cartel settlement procedure, the non-cartel settlement procedure lacks a formal legal basis besides the somewhat unconvincing reference to paragraph 37, itself a notoriously 'vague' provision.[488] In 2018, to accompany the infringement decision in *Guess*, the Commission published a 'Fact Sheet' in order to 'explain[] the framework for this type of cooperation and how it can be applied in other antitrust cases'.[489] It emphasised, however, that 'each cooperation would need to be assessed on a case by case basis'.[490] Strictly speaking, the Commission remains bound in such cases by the strict proportionality requirement when imposing (or at least making legally binding) behavioural or structural remedies under Article 7. Yet unlike what typically follows where an Article 7 decision is disputed by the defendant, none of the cases concluded under this informal settlement procedure have been appealed to the GC to date. In practice, therefore, the improvised procedure only addresses concerns about the paucity of *Commission-level* competition law precedent. It does little to assuage broader concerns about the de-judicialisation of competition enforcement which results from the combined effects of cartel settlement, the Article 9 procedure, and now informal non-cartel settlement under Article 7.[491]

[479] See text accompanying n. 475.

[480] Discounts have ranged from 15% in AT.40134, *AB InBev beer trade restrictions* 13 May 2019, to 50% in AT.40428, *Guess* 17 December 2018.

[481] European Commission, *Fact Sheet. Cooperation—FAQ*, 17 December 2018, <https://ec.europa.eu/competition/publications/data/factsheet_guess.pdf>.

[482] As in AT39759, *ARA Foreclosure* 20 September 2016, where the defendant voluntarily proposed to divest part of its household collection infrastructure to one or more independent buyers.

[483] As in AT.40134, *AB InBev beer trade restrictions* 13 May 2019, where the defendant agreed to implement certain food-labelling practices for a period of five years to facilitate cross-border sales.

[484] As in AT.40428, *Guess* 17 December 2018, where the defendant informed the Commission about its prohibition on the use of Guess brand names and trademarks for the purposes of online search advertising.

[485] AT39759, *ARA Foreclosure* 20 September 2016 and AT.40134, *AB InBev beer trade restrictions* 13 May 2019.

[486] AT.40181, *Philips* 24 July 2018; AT.40182, *Pioneer* 24 July 2018; AT.40465, *ASUS* 24 July 2018; AT.40469, *Denon & Marantz* 24 July 2018; AT.40428, *Guess* 17 December 2018; AT.40436, *Ancillary Sports Merchandise (Nike)* 25 March 2019; AT.40432, *Sanrio* 9 July 2019; AT.40433 *Film merchandise (NBC Universal)* 30 January 2020; and AT.40529 *Melia (Holiday Pricing)* 21 February 2020. In the *Steam* gaming platform investigation, five video game publishers settled using the informal procedure, while the Commission pursued a standard infringement decision against the platform operator: AT.40413 *Focus Home*, AT.40414 *Koch Media*, AT.40420 *ZeniMax*, AT.40422 *Bandai Namco*, and AT.40424 *Capcom* 20 January 2021. See also Chap 11.

[487] See Wollmann, n. 476.

[488] See e.g. Case T-95/15, *Printeos* EU:T:2016:722, para. 48. [489] See n. 481. [490] Ibid.

[491] See N. Dunne, 'From Coercion to Cooperation: Settlement Within EU Competition Law' in D. Gerard and A. Komninos (eds.), *Remedies in EU Competition Law: Substance, Process and Policy* (Kluwer, 2020), <https://papers.ssrn.com/sol3/papers.cfm?abstract_id=3481419>.

This blurring of the line between cartel and non-cartel procedures is also seen in the context of the eLeniency online tool,[492] introduced by the Commission in March 2019, which also applies to defendants in non-cartel cases (for whom the formal leniency programme is unavailable).

(v) Final Decisions: Findings of Inapplicability

Under Article 10 of Regulation 1/2003, the Commission is permitted to take 'positive' decisions finding that Articles 101 and 102 are inapplicable to particular agreements or practices.

Regulation 1/2003

Article 10

Where the [Union] public interest relating to the application of Articles [101] and [102] so requires, the Commission, acting on its own initiative, may by decision find that Article [101] is not applicable to an agreement, a decision by an association of undertakings or a concerted practice, either because the conditions of Article [101(1)] are not fulfilled, or because the conditions of Article [101(3)] are satisfied.

The Commission may likewise make such a finding with reference to Article [102] of the Treaty.

Article 10 refers to such decisions being made when the 'public interest . . . so requires', and says that the Commission will act 'on its own initiative', making it clear that the decisions are not intended (at least primarily) for the benefit of the parties concerned. Recital 14 of Regulation 1/2003 says that inapplicability decisions will be adopted *in exceptional cases*, 'with a view to clarifying the law and ensuring its consistent application throughout the [Union], in particular with regard to new types of agreements or practices that have not been settled in the existing case-law and administrative practice'. Nevertheless, Article 10 decisions are clearly advantageous to the parties, as they are enforceable in national courts and give complete legal certainty. Further, Article 10 could in principle be used to pre-empt a decision by an NCA, since Article 11(6) of Regulation 1/2003 provides that, if the Commission initiates proceedings, NCAs are relieved of their competence to act under the same legal basis against the same practices.[493] As of April 2023, however, no Article 10 decisions had been adopted. The Commission has suggested that the lack of such decisions is because Article 10 was designed for truly exceptional cases, rather than as a replacement for the old notification system, and that the success of the ECN in promoting the coherent application of competition law makes its use to remove matters from the NCAs unnecessary.[494]

(vi) Procedural Decisions

As we have seen, the Commission, during an investigation, may take decisions about procedural matters. Information may be demanded by decision under Article 18(3) of Regulation 1/2003, and an

[492] See the Commission's website at <http://ec.europa.eu/competition/cartels/leniency/eleniency.html>.

[493] Notice on cooperation within the Network of Competition Authorities [2004] OJ C101/43, para. 51. And see also para. 54(d).

[494] Working Paper, paras. 112–114. Note, however, contrasting arguments that the Commission should make greater use of both comfort letters and the inapplicability procedure: R. Whish, 'Reflections on Regulation 1/2003, declarations of inapplicability and informal guidance' [2022] 2 *Concurrences* 106118, pp. 1–4.

inspection ordered under Article 20(4). Failure to comply can be penalised by fines.[495] The question of the confidentiality of documents is settled by a decision of the HO.[496]

(vii) Interim Measures

Article 8 of Regulation 1/2003 gives the Commission power to take decisions ordering interim measures.[497]

Regulation 1/2003

Article 8

1. In cases of urgency due to the risk of serious and irreparable damage to competition, the Commission, acting on its own initiative may by decision, on the basis of a prima facie finding of infringement, order interim measures.
2. A decision under paragraph 1 shall apply for a specified period of time and may be renewed in so far this is necessary and appropriate.

This was a new provision in Regulation 1/2003, although case law under Regulation 17 had recognised that the Commission possessed such powers implicitly.[498] The earlier jurisprudence established that certain conditions must be fulfilled before interim measures can be taken. *First*, there must be a prima facie infringement of the competition rules. *Secondly*, interim measures are only available in situations of proven urgency where there would otherwise be serious and irreparable damage to competition. Financial damage cannot, save in exceptional circumstances, be regarded as irreparable, unless the applicant can adduce evidence that would justify a prima facie finding that without the measures sought it would suffer losses that would threaten its survival. Damage may also be irreparable if without the measures there are likely to be developments on the market which will be very difficult, or impossible, to reverse. *Thirdly*, the measures must be of a temporary and conservatory nature only and restricted to what is required in a situation to preserve the status quo. That is, the measures have to accord with the principle of proportionality. *Fourthly*, the legitimate rights of the party on which the measures are being imposed must be observed and the 'essential guarantees' provided for by Regulation 1/2003, especially Article 27 on the right to be heard, must be maintained. *Finally*, the measures must be in a form which is subject to review by the EU Courts, i.e. a reasoned decision.

[495] See Section 6.H.

[496] The HO Terms of Reference, Decision 2011/695, Art. 8 [2010] OJ L275/29. The jurisdiction of the HO to take decisions in this respect means that the power to adopt a challengeable act has been delegated to a single official. Such delegation is permitted only where it does not involve a matter of principle: see Case T-450/93, *Lisrestal* EU:T:1994:290. Cf. the delegation of Reg. 1/2003, Art. 20(4) decisions to a single *Commissioner*: the validity of this in respect of Reg. 17, Art. 14(3) was confirmed in Case 53/85, *AKZO* EU:C:1986:256.

[497] On interim measures generally, see OECD, *Interim Measures in Antitrust Investigations* (2022), <www.oecd.org/daf/competition/interim-measures-in-antitrust-investigations-2022.pdf>.

[498] The power to take interim measures was first established in Case 792/79 R, *Camera Care* EU:C:1980:18; developed subsequently in Cases T-44/90, *La Cinq* EU:T:1992:5; 228–229/82 R, *Ford Werke* EU:C:1984:80; and T-184/01 R, *IMS Health* EU:T:2001:200, *aff'd* C-481/01 P (R), *NDC v IMS and Commission* EU:C:2002:223.

Several Commission decisions on refusal to supply under Article 102 involved interim decisions. In *Boosey & Hawkes*,[499] the interim measures ordered the dominant undertaking to maintain supplies to the complainant on the terms and conditions on which the parties had previously done business. In *Sealink/B&I*,[500] the port authority was ordered to return to its previous published timetable. By contrast, the Commission in *Sea Containers/Stena*[501] held that there was a prima facie case of abuse, but refused interim measures on the ground that there was insufficient urgency as the original complaint had been resolved. The most notorious case of interim measures was the decision ordering an undertaking to license its copyright in *NDC Health/IMS*.[502] The decision was suspended and ultimately withdrawn without a final decision being taken.[503]

In October 2019, the Commission issued its first interim measures in two decades, in the *Broadcom* case.[504] The case involved exclusive purchasing obligations in the semiconductor sector which allegedly breached Article 102.[505] The Commission was concerned, in light of the amount of time that would be necessary to conclude the case by an infringement decision under Article 7, that the practices would cause the exit or marginalisation of a critical mass of Broadcom's existing competitors in the meantime. The measures imposed under Article 8 prohibited Broadcom from applying or agreeing further 'exclusivity-inducing provisions' in its supply agreements with immediate effect.

The *Broadcom* decision is notable for several reasons. First, although premised merely on a prima facie infringement of Article 102, the 130-page decision contained an impressively detailed discussion of the problematic practices and their probable capacity to foreclose competition. This was all the more remarkable given that the Commission had begun informally investigating Broadcom's practices only a year earlier, opening a formal investigation in June 2019. Secondly, Broadcom vigorously disputed the Commission's allegations at the time of the interim measures decision, and lodged an appeal against it (subsequently withdrawn) before the GC.[506] Yet the fact that Broadcom was effectively precluded from applying its exclusivity-inducing provisions for the foreseeable future appears to have prompted it to change its tactics. Within a year, Broadcom chose instead to enter into a commitments decision with the Commission under Article 9, essentially agreeing 'voluntarily' to adhere to the same practices that had been imposed on it by the interim measures decision.[507] Finally, the case arguably reflects quite legitimate criticism about the length of time that the Commission can take to conclude investigations using the Article 7 infringement decision procedure, particularly complex investigations into alleged abuse of dominance.[508] These concerns have been especially prominent in the context of the digital economy, where there is a fear that the cumbersome nature of the Commission's enforcement procedures renders Article 102 an almost worthless tool to regulate large technology companies operating in fast-moving digital markets, as in *Broadcom*. This point is explored further in Chapter 16.

[499] *BBI/Boosey & Hawkes* [1987] OJ L286/36.

[500] IV/34.174, *Sealink/B&I Holyhead: Interim Measures* 11 June 1992; as in *Boosey & Hawkes*, the case did not go to final decision.

[501] [1994] OJ L15/8. [502] [2002] OJ L59/18.

[503] Case T-184/01 R, *IMS Health* EU:T:2001:200, *aff'd* Case C-481/01 P (R), *NDC Health v Commission* EU:C:2002:223. For the substantive issues in this case, see Chap 7, Section 12.

[504] AT.40608, *Broadcom* 16 October 2019. For discussion, see M. Kadar, 'The Use of Interim Measures and Commitments in the European Commission's Broadcom Case' (2021) 12 *JECLAP* 443.

[505] For discussion of the substantive aspects of the case, see Chap 7, Section 10.

[506] Order of the President of the General Court in Case T-876/19, *Broadcom* EU:T:2020:650.

[507] AT.40608, *Broadcom* 7 October 2020.

[508] On this aspect of the case, see D. Mantzari, 'Interim Measures in EU Competition Cases: Origins, Evolution, and Implications for Digital Markets' (2020) 11 *JECLAP* 487.

F. THE SETTLEMENT PROCEDURE IN CARTEL CASES

Since 2008 the Commission has offered a 'direct settlement' procedure for cartel cases. It was established by an amendment to Regulation 773/2004,[509] and is set out in the Notice on the conduct of settlement procedures (the Settlement Notice).[510] The aim of the settlement procedure is 'to simplify and speed up administrative procedures and to reduce the number of cases brought before the EU judicature, and thus to enable the Commission to handle more cases with the same resources'.[511] Leniency[512] and settlement can both be applied in the same case.

The procedure is for the Commission, on conclusion of its investigation, to decide whether the case is suitable for settlement.[513] If so, it invites the parties concerned to reach an agreement with it. It informs them of the evidence and tells them its conclusions as to duration, seriousness, liability, and the likely fine. The parties must then make a final settlement submission, in which they: acknowledge their liability 'in clear and unequivocal terms'; indicate the maximum fine they would accept under the procedure; confirm that they have been informed of the case against them and given sufficient opportunity to make their views known; confirm that they do not envisage requesting access to the file or to be heard orally again; and agree to accept an SO.[514] The SO reflects the settlement submissions. The Commission then proceeds, without further procedural steps, to adopt an Article 7 decision. Settlement submissions are protected from disclosure in the same way as leniency corporate statements.[515] Unsurprisingly, not every instance in which the Commission indicates a preliminary willingness to accept settlement submissions will culminate in a final decision under the procedure. The fact that the settlement procedure has been discontinued does not preclude the Commission from proceeding under the standard administrative procedure, nor is it considered to bias the Commission in any infringement decision adopted subsequently.[516]

According to paragraph 2 of the Settlement Notice, the procedure is not a negotiation, as the Commission 'does not negotiate the question of the existence of an infringement of [Union] law and the appropriate sanction . . .'. However, in *Timab* the GC said:

> The settlement procedure requires, by its very nature, an exchange of views between the parties. Accordingly, it is an inherent part of such a procedure that both the undertakings and the Commission should try to reach a common understanding of the situation . . . If, taking account of the simplified nature of the settlement procedure, the undertaking at issue and the Commission cannot agree on a common assessment of the situation, only the standard procedure remains.[517]

[509] Reg. 773/2004 as amended by Reg. 622/2008 [2008] OJ L171/3, further amended by Reg. 2015/1348 [2015] OJ L208/3, Art. 10a.

[510] Commission Notice on the conduct of settlement procedures [2008] OJ C167/1, as amended by [2015] OJ C256/2. See M. L. Tierno Centella, 'The New Settlement Procedure in Selected Cartel Cases' [2008] 3 *Competition Policy Newsletter* 30; J. Tyler, 'Act of Settlement' (2008) 3 *CLI* 79; J. Joshua, K. Hugmark, and I. Daems, 'What's the Deal? Navigating the European Commission's 2008 Settlement Notice' [2009] *European Antitrust Rev* 2; R. Gamble, '"Speaking (Formally) with the Enemy"—Cartel Settlements Evolve' [2011] *ECLR* 449.

[511] Case T-456/10, *Timab Industries* EU:T:2015:296, para. 60. [512] See Section 6.H.v.

[513] The parties have no *right* to settlement, see Case T-270/12, *Panalpina World Transport (Holding)* EU:T:2016:109, paras. 209–210; Case T-267/10, *Deutsche Bahn* EU:T:2016:110, para. 418. For a discussion of the exercise of the Commission's discretion, see Case T-265/12, *Schenker* EU:T:2016:111, paras. 390–438.

[514] Settlement Notice, para. 20. [515] By virtue of the Damages Dir., see Chap 14.

[516] Case T-762/14, *Koninklijke Philips* EU:T:2016:738, paras. 255–256.

[517] Case T-456/14/10, *Timab Industries* EU:T:2015:296, para. 117.

The advantages to the Commission are obvious: a saving of time, resources, and appeals to the EU Courts.[518] One advantage to the parties is that they receive a 10 per cent reduction (but only 10 per cent) on the fine that would otherwise have been imposed. They also are saved the trouble of protracted cartel proceedings, and may confine themselves to purely oral submissions. There are, however, disadvantages for settling parties. The procedure is totally in the control of the Commission, notwithstanding what the GC said in *Timab*. They lose certain rights of defence (the oral hearing and access to the file), and have to assess what fine they think the Commission will accept (albeit in the light of the Commission's indication). The admission of liability may form the basis for future third party actions.[519] In addition, the Commission can decide right up to the end to revert to the normal procedure. Despite these drawbacks, the procedure is popular among cartelists, and the majority of cartel cases are now dealt with under the settlement procedure. As of April 2023, 40 settlement decisions had been concluded under the procedure.[520]

Two related contentious issues have arisen in practice, however: the problem of so-called 'hybrid' settlements and the question of appeal to the Union Courts.

(i) Hybrid Settlements

Hybrid settlements involve investigations in which some but not all cartelists prosecuted are willing to cooperate. *Timab*[521] confirms that the Commission is entitled to pursue dual proceedings, i.e. in the context of the same investigation, it may legitimately deploy the settlement procedure to find infringement by those cartelists which opt for cooperation with its consequent reduction in fine, and the standard infringement procedure against undertakings which choose not to cooperate. On the facts on *Timab*, the defendant withdrew from the settlement procedure at a comparatively late stage, having already been informed that it could expect a fine in the region of €41–44 million. After subsequently choosing to dispute the facts, in particular the length of its participation, Timab ultimately received a fine of almost €60 million. Yet both the GC and CJ upheld the fine imposed, emphasising, in a manner not dissimilar to the Grand Chamber's strenuous defence of Article 9 settlements as a compromise in *Alrosa*, the defendant's own choice to opt out of the relative safety of the settlement procedure, thus subjecting itself to the full rigours of the standard infringement procedure.[522] Since the Commission in *Timab* had then applied, unimpeachably, the Leniency Notice and 2006 Fining Guidelines to determine the amount of the fine, the defendant could not claim to be unfairly disadvantaged.

In *Icap*,[523] however, the GC took a less benign view of hybrid settlement in circumstances where, in contrast to the situation in *Timab* where the findings of breach were simultaneous, the standard infringement decision was taken several years after that concluded under the settlement procedure. The earlier settlement decision, although not formally addressed to Icap, contained repeated references to its role as cartel facilitator. In this situation, the GC was persuaded by the defendant's argument that the hybrid procedure constituted a breach of the presumption of innocence.

[518] A survey of EU cartel investigations between 2000 and 2015 revealed a settlement-induced reduction in the number of appeals of about 53%: see M. Hellwig, K. Huschelrath, and U. Laitenberger, 'Settlements and Appeals in the European Commission's Cartel Cases: An Empirical Assessment' (2018) 52 *Rev of Industrial Organisation* 55. Moreover, the duration of cartel investigations concluded under the settlement procedure has reduced: see K. Huschelrath and U. Laitenberger, 'The Settlement Procedure in the European Commission's Cartel Cases: An Early Evaluation' (2017) 5 *J of Antitrust Enforcement* 458.

[519] See Chap 14.

[520] Commission Press Release, 'Antitrust: Commission fines styrene purchasers €157 million in cartel settlement', 29 November 2022.

[521] Case T-456/10, *Timab Industries* EU:T:2015:296, *aff'd* Case C-411/15 P, *Timab Industries* EU:C:2017:11.

[522] Case C-411/15 P, *Timab Industries* EU:C:2017:11, paras. 120–121.

[523] Case T-180/15, *Icap* EU:T:2017:795.

Case T-180/15 *Icap plc and others v Commission* EU:T:2017:795

General Court

256 . . . . [The presumption of innocence] constitutes a general principle of EU law, currently laid down in Article 48(1) of the Charter of Fundamental Rights, which applies to the procedures relating to infringements of the competition rules applicable to undertakings that may result in the imposition of fines or periodic penalty payments (. . . *E.ON Energie v Commission*, C-89/11 P, EU:C:2012:738, paragraphs 72 and 73 and the case-law cited).

257. The principle of the presumption of innocence implies that every person accused is presumed to be innocent until his guilt has been established according to law. It thus precludes any formal finding and even any allusion to the liability of an accused person for a particular infringement in a final decision unless that person has enjoyed all the usual guarantees accorded for the exercise of the rights of defence in the normal course of proceedings resulting in a decision on the merits of the case (. . . *Sumitomo Chemical and Sumika Fine Chemicals v Commission*, T-22/02 and T-23/02, EU:T:2005:349, paragraph 106; . . . *Pergan Hilfsstoffe für industrielle Prozesse v Commission*, T-474/04, EU:T:2007:306, paragraph 76, and . . . *Villeroy & Boch Austria v Commission*, T-373/10 and T-374/10, not published, EU:T:2013:455, paragraph 158).

258. In the present case, first, it should be noted that, in the part of the 2013 decision entitled 'Description of the events', the Commission specifies . . . how Icap 'facilitated' the infringements at issue imputed to the banks participating in the settlement procedure.

259. It must be stated that although those passages appear in the part of the 2013 decision setting out the facts and do not include as such a legal classification under Article 101(1) TFEU, they nonetheless reveal very clearly the Commission's position on Icap's participation in the unlawful conduct found with respect to the banks concerned . . .

260. Second, although recital 51 of the 2013 decision states that that decision does not make any finding as regards the legal qualification of, and Icap's liability for, its conduct, the fact remains that the Commission's position on the legal classification of Icap's conduct and the incurring of its liability of the six infringements at issue could easily be inferred from a reading of that decision.

. . .

262. Third, it should be pointed out that the 2013 decision constitutes a 'final decision' within the meaning of the case-law cited in paragraph 257 above.

263. In that regard, the parallel drawn by the Commission at the hearing between the expression of a view on the legality of Icap's conduct in the 2013 decision with the view that might appear in a statement of objections is irrelevant. In a statement of objections, the undertaking concerned is able to defend itself properly before the Commission adopts a final decision. Having decided not to participate in the settlement procedure, the applicants were not afforded an opportunity to make known their view before the adoption of that decision. Similarly, the possibility for the applicants to exercise their rights of defence in the action against the contested decision in no way detracts from the fact that, in a final decision prior to the contested decision, the Commission had already made a formal finding that Icap had participated in six infringements of Article 101 TFEU.

264. Lastly, fourth, that conclusion is not called in question by the Commission's line of argument alleging, in essence, that references to the participation of third persons may be necessary for the assessment of the guilt of those participating in a settlement procedure. The Commission observes that one of the objectives of the settlement procedure is to ensure greater rapidity and efficiency and infers from this that it would be contrary to the achievement of those objectives to allow a party which does not wish to enter into a settlement to delay the adoption of the settlement decision with regard to the other parties.

265. In that regard, it should be pointed out that, although the principle of presumption of innocence is enshrined in Article 48 of the Charter of Fundamental Rights, which, pursuant to Article 6 TEU, has

the same legal value as the Treaties, the origin of the settlement procedure is to be found in a regulation adopted by the Commission alone, on the basis of Article 33 of Regulation No 1/2003, namely Regulation No 622/2008, and that the procedure is optional for both the Commission and the undertakings concerned.

266. Accordingly, the requirements relating to compliance with the principle of presumption of innocence cannot be distorted by considerations linked to the safeguarding of the objectives of rapidity and efficiency of the settlement procedure, no matter how laudable those objectives may be. On the contrary, it is for the Commission to apply its settlement procedure in a manner that is compatible with the requirements of Article 48 of the Charter of Fundamental Rights.

267. It is true, as the Court noted in . . . *Timab Industries and CFPR v Commission* (T-456/10, EU:T:2015:296, paragraph 71), that where the settlement does not involve all the participants in an infringement, the Commission is entitled to adopt, on the one hand, following a simplified procedure, a decision addressed to the participants in the infringement who have decided to enter into a settlement and reflecting the commitment of each of them and, on the other hand, according to the standard procedure, a decision addressed to participants in the infringement who have decided not to enter into a settlement.

268. However, the implementation of such a 'hybrid' settlement procedure must be carried out in compliance with the presumption of innocence of the undertaking which has decided not to enter into a settlement. Accordingly, in circumstances where the Commission considers that it is not in a position to determine the liability of the undertakings participating in the settlement without also taking a view on the participation in the infringement of the undertaking which has decided not to enter into a settlement, it is for the Commission to take the necessary measures—including possible adoption on the same date of the decisions relating to all the undertakings concerned by the cartel, as it did in . . . *Timab Industries and CFPR v Commission* (T-456/10, EU:T:2015:296)—enabling that presumption of innocence to be safeguarded.

Although the judgment was appealed by the Commission, it did not challenge the GC's findings in this respect.[524] Nonetheless, from Icap's perspective, its victory was somewhat pyrrhic. Having conducted an in-depth review of the evidence against Icap presented by the Commission, and after concluding that this was defective in some instances but sufficient to sustain other allegations of cartel facilitation, the GC held that the breach of the presumption of innocence could have no further bearing on the outcome: the findings of infringement of Article 101 were either supported by the evidence in substance, or they were not.[525]

In the wake of the judgment, however, the prospects more generally for hybrid settlement were somewhat uncertain. The approach of the GC suggested that hybrid settlements were likely to raise fundamental rights concerns *unless* conducted in a simultaneous manner as in *Timab*.[526] This, inevitably, would restrict the discretion of the Commission under the settlement procedure, and could inhibit it from realising the goal of greater efficiency in cartel investigations, despite the fact that the GC had recognised this as a laudable objective.

The *Pometon* judgment has largely dispelled such concerns. It involved a cartel comprised of five undertakings, four of which opted to settle under the cartel settlement procedure. Two years later, the

[524] Case C-39/18 P, *Commission v Icap and Others* EU:C:2019:584, in which the CJ upheld the GC's finding that the Commission had erred in providing insufficient reasons in determining the amount of the fine.

[525] Ibid., paras. 269–279.

[526] For further discussion, see E. Aliende Rodriguez and R. Noorali, 'Case T-180/15 *Icap v Commission*: The Facilitator Doctrine and Other Cartel Concepts in Hybrid Settlements' (2018) 9 *JECLAP* 320.

Commission adopted a further infringement decision against the fifth defendant, Pometon, under the standard procedure. The initial settlement contained a footnote that stated explicitly that the question of Pometon's guilt was not addressed by that decision, and Pometon was mentioned only in the section describing the events of the cartel, and not in the sections considering the legal classification of those events. Nonetheless, Pometon challenged the decision against it on the basis that the Commission had attributed specific unlawful conduct to it in the settlement decision, which rendered the Commission itself unable to make an impartial assessment during the standard procedure. This argument was rejected by the GC,[527] whose findings on this point were upheld by the CJ.[528] The higher court reaffirmed the need for caution to ensure that hybrid settlements comply with the presumption of innocence. But it rejected the suggestion that non-simultaneous hybrid settlements are inherently unlawful: instead, a careful assessment of the wording of the earlier decision is required to ensure compliance with the presumption of innocence on the facts.

Case C-440/19 P, *Pometon SpA v European Commission* EU:C:2021:214

Court of Justice

62 . . . . [T]he principle of the presumption of innocence will be infringed if a judicial decision or a statement by a public official concerning a person charged with a criminal offence contains a clear declaration, in the absence of a final conviction that the person concerned has committed the crime in question. In that context, it should be underlined that the importance of the choice of words by the judicial authorities and of the particular circumstances in which they were made and of the nature and context of the proceedings at issue (. . . . 2019, *AH and Others (Presumption of innocence)*, C-377/18, EU:C:2019:670, paragraph 43, see also . . . *Karaman v. Germany*, CE:ECHR:2014:0227JUD001710310, paragraph 63).

63. Accordingly, in complex criminal proceedings involving several persons who cannot be tried together, references by the competent court to the participation of third persons, who may later be tried separately, may be indispensable for the assessment of the guilt of those who are on trial separately. However, if facts related to the involvement of third parties have to be introduced, the relevant court should avoid giving more information than necessary for the assessment of the legal responsibility of those persons who are accused in the trial before it. In addition, the reasoning of judicial decisions must be worded in such a way as to avoid a potential prejudgment about the guilt of the third parties concerned, capable of jeopardising the fair examination of the charges brought against them in the separate proceedings (. . . *AH and Others (Presumption of innocence)*, C-377/18, EU:C:2019:670, paragraph 44; see also . . . *Karaman v. Germany*, CE:ECHR:2014:0227JUD001710310, paragraphs 64 and 65).

64. . . . [T]he case-law relating to the presumption of innocence . . . is relevant, *mutatis mutandis*, where the Commission adopts, in relation to one and the same cartel, two decisions which have different addressees following two separate procedures, namely, first, a decision taken following a settlement procedure and addressed to the undertakings which have entered into a settlement agreement and, second, a decision taken at the end of an ordinary procedure and addressed to the other undertakings having participated in the cartel.

65. In such a case, described as a 'hybrid' procedure, which leads to the adoption of successive decisions, it may be objectively necessary for the Commission to address, in the decision terminating the settlement procedure, certain facts and behaviour concerning participants in the alleged cartel which are the subject of the standard procedure . . . [I]t is nevertheless for the Commission to ensure, in the decision concluding the settlement procedure, to preserve the presumption of innocence of

[527] Case T-433/16 *Pometon* EU:T:2019:201. [528] Case C-440/19 P, *Pometon* EU:C:2021:214.

> undertakings which have refused to enter into a settlement and which are the subject of an ordinary procedure.
>
> 66. In order to review the Commission's observance of the presumption of innocence, it is for the EU judicature to analyse a decision bringing the settlement procedure to an end and its reasoning as a whole and in the light of the particular circumstances in which that decision has been adopted. Any explicit reference, in certain parts of that decision, to the absence of guilt of the other participants to the alleged cartel would be devoid of sense if other parts of that decision were likely to be understood as a premature expression of their guilt (. . . *AH and Others (Presumption of innocence)*, C-377/18, EU:C:2019:670, paragraph 46).

The CJ approved the GC's approach of considering, first, whether the Commission had taken sufficient precautions in drafting the settlement decision in order to avoid a premature assessment of Pometon's guilt and, secondly, whether the existing references made to Pometon were necessary for the classification of liability of the addressees of that decision. The CJ concluded that, on the facts, the allusions to Pometon in the settlement decision did not violate the presumption of innocence.[529]

Pometon provides a welcome clarification that, even if non-simultaneous hybrid settlements are trickier to manoeuvre effectively and lawfully, they are by no means ruled out absolutely for the Commission.[530] This reduces the risk, inter alia, of the Commission 'being taken hostage' by the last cartelist to settle.[531] Yet, in a sense, by making everything hinge upon a close scrutiny of the specific wording of the settlement decision *ex post*, the CJ has merely kicked the can down the road. The Advocate General in *Pometon* had argued that:

> The settlement decision must, of course, be read holistically. Just because, for example, the occasional infelicitous word or phrase has been used in the document does not mean that this word or phrase should be seized upon as suggestive of pre-judgment by the decision-maker if, on a fair reading, the settlement decision as a whole does not lend itself to that interpretation.[532]

Yet conducting precisely such a holistic assessment, the Advocate General himself had arrived at quite a different conclusion to the CJ as to the compatibility of the settlement decision with the presumption of innocence.[533] The *Scania* judgment further illustrates the complexity of this exercise in practice.[534]

(ii) Appeal Against Decisions Taken under the Cartel Settlement Procedure

It is not only those defendants who have opted *against* settlement who may wish to appeal the bargain that has been struck. Having settled with the Commission in respect of the *EIRD* cartel, Société Générale subsequently appealed against the fine imposed on it, alleging violation of the principle of equal treatment. With proceedings before the GC still pending, the Commission proactively amended the original decision adopted under the settlement procedure, reducing Société Générale's

[529] Ibid., paras. 68–86.

[530] This point was further confirmed in Case T-799/17, *Scania* EU:T:2022:48, para. 104.

[531] M. Giangaspero, '*Pometon v Commission*: Reviving Staggered Hybrid Settlements?' (2020) 11 *JECLAP* 509, 511.

[532] Opinion in Case C-440/19 P, *Pometon* EU:C:2020:816, para. 73.

[533] 'I am of the view that the General Court could not properly have concluded . . . that the references to Pometon could not objectively lead to a suspicion that the Commission prejudged the guilt and liability of that undertaking in the cartel in question . . . ' (ibid., para. 81).

[534] Case T-799/17, *Scania* EU:T:2022:48, particularly paras. 107–63.

fine by more than €200 million.[535] *Printeos* saw the first successful appeal by a settling cartelist litigated to final judgment before the GC, on the basis that the Commission had failed to provide an adequate statement of reasons when applying different rates of reduction to the fines imposed on the settling undertakings.[536]

G. INFORMAL SETTLEMENTS

The Commission has sometimes not proceeded to a formal decision but terminated the matter informally. Under Regulation 17, notified agreements were usually dealt with by way of comfort letter rather than by formal decision.[537] Cases have also been terminated informally where the Commission and the parties have come to a settlement, usually if the companies had made sufficient concessions by way of undertakings given to the Commission. Several important cases were terminated in this way, including *IBM*,[538] *Microsoft*,[539] *Digital*,[540] and *Deutsche Telekom Tariffs*.[541] Settlements were frequently publicised, and often attained the status of precedent. There is nothing within Regulation 1/2003 that prevents informal settlements in future but, given the existence of the commitments procedure, any informal (i.e. non-legally binding) settlements going forward are likely to be rare.[542]

H. FINES AND PERIODIC PENALTY PAYMENTS

(i) General

Regulation 1/2003 empowers the Commission to take decisions to impose fines on undertakings and associations of undertakings, both for substantive infringements of the competition rules and for procedural infringements. The Commission may also impose periodic penalty payments, in order to compel undertakings to do what it requires by penalising defiance. Fines and penalties are levied on *undertakings*: Regulation 1/2003 does not impose liability on natural persons such as company directors and executives.[543]

The Commission's multiplicity of roles means that the prosecutor determines guilt and fixes the fine. However, Article 261 TFEU[544] provides that regulations 'may give the Court of Justice of the European Union unlimited jurisdiction with regard to the penalties provided'. Pursuant to this, Article 31 of Regulation 1/2003 states:

> The Court of Justice shall have unlimited jurisdiction to review decisions whereby the Commission has fixed a fine or periodic penalty payment. It may cancel, reduce or increase the fine or periodic penalty payment imposed.

The Union Courts' powers with respect to fines are considered later in this chapter.[545]

[535] Discussed by P. Zelenko and J. Marthan, 'Euro Interest Rate Derivatives: Reduction of Fine in the First-Ever Appeal Against a Settlement Decision' (2016) 7 *JECLAP* 525.

[536] Case T-95/15, *Printeos* EU:T:2016:722. The judgment was not appealed by the Commission.

[537] See Section 3. [538] [1984] 3 CMLR 147. [539] Commission Press Release IP/94/653.

[540] Commission Press Release IP/97/868.

[541] Commission's *XXVIIth Report on Competition Policy* (1997), part 77.

[542] J. Temple Lang, 'Commitment Decisions and Settlements with Antitrust Authorities and Private Parties under European Antitrust Law' [2005] *Fordham Corp L Inst* 265 (he suggests that informal settlements may still be used in 'small unimportant cases'). There were informal settlements in *OMV/Gazprom*, IP/05/195 in 2005, *E.ON Ruhrgas/Gazprom*, IP/05/710 in 2005, and *Philips CD-Recordable Discrimination Patent Licensing*, IP/06/139 in 2006. The Commission reached an informal settlement with Apple over iTunes in 2008, IP/08/22.

[543] See Mölls, n. 211. [544] Ex Art. 229. [545] See Section 7.

The limitation periods for the imposition of penalties provided for in Article 25 of Regulation 1/2003 are three years for procedural infringements and five years for all other infringements. Time runs from the day the infringement was committed or on the day it ended in the case of repeated or continuous infringements. Under Article 26, the time limit for enforcement is five years from the date of the decision.

(ii) Fines for Procedural Infringements

Article 23(1) of Regulation 1/2003 states:

> The Commission may by decision impose on undertakings and associations of undertakings fines not exceeding 1 per cent of the total turnover in the preceding business year where, intentionally or negligently:
>
> (a) they supply incorrect or misleading information in response to a request made pursuant to Article 17 or Article 18(2);
>
> (b) in response to a request made by decision adopted pursuant to Article 17 or Article 18(3), they supply incorrect, incomplete or misleading information or do not supply information within the required time-limit;
>
> (c) they produce the required books or other records related to the business in incomplete form during inspections under Article 20 or refuse to submit to inspections ordered by a decision adopted pursuant to Article 20(4);
>
> (d) in response to a question asked in accordance with Article 20(2)(e),
>
> — they give an incorrect or misleading answer,
>
> — they fail to rectify within a time-limit set by the Commission an incorrect, incomplete or misleading answer given by a member of staff, or
>
> — they fail or refuse to provide a complete answer on facts relating to the subject-matter and purpose of an inspection ordered by a decision adopted pursuant to Article 20(4);
>
> (e) seals affixed in accordance with Article 20(2)(d) by officials or other accompanying persons authorised by the Commission have been broken.

Under this provision the Commission can impose fines of up to 1 per cent of turnover for failure to cooperate with, or obstructing, its investigations under Articles 17,[546] 18, and 20 of Regulation 1/2003, or for supplying incorrect, incomplete, or misleading information.[547]

(iii) Periodic Penalty Payments

Periodic penalty payments may be imposed at a daily rate for defiance of the Commission. The maximum is 5 per cent of average daily turnover. Article 24 of Regulation 1/2003 states:

> 1. The Commission may, by decision, impose on undertakings or associations of undertakings periodic penalty payments not exceeding 5 per cent of the average daily turnover in the

[546] The provision which provides for investigations into sectors of the economy and types of agreements: see Section 6.I.

[547] See Section 6.C.

preceding business year per day and calculated from the date appointed by the decision, in order to compel them:

(a) to put an end to an infringement of Article [101] or Article [102], in accordance with a decision taken pursuant to Article 7;

(b) to comply with a decision ordering interim measures taken pursuant to Article 8;

(c) to comply with a commitment made binding by a decision pursuant to Article 9;

(d) to supply complete and correct information which it has requested by decision taken pursuant to Article 17 or Article 18(3);

(e) to submit to an inspection which it has ordered by decision taken pursuant to Article 20(4).

2. Where the undertakings or associations of undertakings have satisfied the obligation which the periodic penalty payment was intended to enforce, the Commission may fix the definitive amount of the periodic penalty payment at a figure lower than that which would arise under the original decision. Article 23(4) shall apply correspondingly.

Microsoft was the first undertaking to be fined for failure to comply with a decision. A long battle over its compliance with the 2004 decision which required it to disclose interoperability information on 'fair and reasonable terms'[548] ended in two decisions imposing penalty payments totalling almost €1.2 billion: one for failure to disclose the required level of information,[549] and the second for charging unreasonable royalties.[550] The GC approved the imposition of a fine but reduced it by €39 million.[551] Microsoft was also the first undertaking to be fined (€561 million) under Article 24(1)(c) for failing to comply with a commitments decision under Article 9.[552]

(iv) Fines for Substantive Infringements

a. Regulation 1/2003, Article 23(2)

Article 23(2) of Regulation 1/2003 provides for the imposition of fines for substantive infringements:

2. The Commission may by decision impose fines on undertakings and associations of undertakings where, either intentionally or negligently:

(a) they infringe Article [101] or Article [102]; or

(b) they contravene a decision ordering interim measures under Article 8; or

(c) they fail to comply with a commitment made binding by a decision pursuant to Article 9.

For each undertaking and association of undertakings participating in the infringement, the fine shall not exceed 10 per cent of its total turnover in the preceding business year.[553]

Where the infringement of an association relates to the activities of its members, the fine shall not exceed 10 per cent of the sum of the total turnover of each member active on the market affected by the infringement of the association.

[548] COMP/37.792, *Microsoft*, upheld on appeal Case T-201/04, *Microsoft* EU:T:2007:289, see Chap 7.
[549] Commission Decision of 12 July 2006, C(2006)4420.
[550] Commission Decision of 27 February 2008, C(2008) 764.
[551] Case T-167/08, *Microsoft* EU:T:2012:323.
[552] Commission Decision of 6 March 2013 in COMP/39.530, *Microsoft*, C(2013) 1210.
[553] The 'preceding business year' means the last full business year of each of the undertakings concerned at the date of adoption of the decision: Cases T-25/95 etc., *Cimenteries* EU:T:2000:77, para. 5009.

3. In fixing the amount of the fine, regard shall be had both to the gravity and to the duration of the infringement.

...

5. Decisions taken pursuant to paragraphs 1 and 2 shall not be of a criminal law nature.

There are four key elements. First, fines can only be imposed for intentional or negligent infringements. Secondly, the maximum fine is 10 per cent of turnover in the preceding business year[554] (although it does not specify what turnover is to be taken into account). Thirdly, in fixing the fine regard is to be had both to the *gravity* of the infringement and to its *duration*. Fourthly, fines are not criminal penalties.

The concept of the 'single continuous infringement' is discussed in Chapter 4.[555] Whether cartel participants, for example, are charged with a single continuous infringement or a series of separate infringements can impact upon the amount of the fine (the maximum applies to *each* infringement and the duration may be affected).[556]

b. *The Position of Trade Associations*

Article 23 of Regulation 1/2003 provides for fines to be imposed on associations of undertakings. Article 15 of Regulation 17 made no provision for joint and several liability, which could prevent the collection of fines.[557] Article 23(4) provides that, if the association is insolvent, it must call upon its members for contributions to the fine. If that does not produce the fine within the time limit imposed, the Commission may fine the members directly (up to 10 per cent of that undertaking's turnover) but only those which were implicated in the infringement.[558] The first fine on a professional body under this provision was imposed in *ONP*.[559]

c. *Intentional or Negligent Infringement*

Article 23(2) provides that the Commission may impose a fine only where the infringement was intentional or negligent. An undertaking can act only through human agency, however, and the intentions and negligence in issue are in effect those of its human directors and employees. EU competition law does not embrace theories of vicarious liability. Instead, the position is that an undertaking is responsible for the conduct of its directors and employees, and that it should have in place, and enforce, a compliance programme to prevent infractions.[560]

[554] In Case T-33/02, *Britannia Alloys and Chemicals* EU:T:2005:428, para. 50, the GC confirmed that the Commission was correct to use the undertaking's last 'full' business year.

[555] Section 3.B.v.

[556] See e.g. Case T-655/11, *FSL Holdings* EU:T:2015:383 where the GC reduced a fine because it held there was a single repeated infringement, not a single continuous infringement as the Commission had found in COMP/39.482, *Exotic Fruit (Bananas)* 12 October 2011.

[557] Commission's White Paper on Modernisation [1999] OJ C132/1, paras. 127–128, and see Cases T-213/95 and T-18/96, *SCK and FNK* EU:T:1997:157.

[558] See P. Callol, 'Mandatory Antitrust Liability under EU Competition Law of Trade Association Members in Case of Infringement by the Trade Association' [2015] *ECLR* 194.

[559] COMP/39.510, on appeal Case T-90/11, *Ordre National des Pharmaciens en France (ONP)* EU:T:2014:1049 the fine was reduced.

[560] See W. Wils, 'The Undertaking as Subject of EC Competition Law and the Imputation of Infringements to Natural or Legal Persons' (2000) 25 *ELRev* 99, 109–111. In Case C-338/00 P, *Volkswagen* EU:C:2003:473, paras. 94–98, the CJ rejected the argument that it was necessary for the Commission and GC to identify the persons who acted improperly and were therefore to be treated as responsible for the infringement.

'Intentional' means an intention to restrict competition, not an intention to infringe the rules. In *PVC Cartel II* the GC said:[561]

> For an infringement of the competition rules of the Treaty to be regarded as having been committed intentionally, it is not necessary for an undertaking to have been aware that it was infringing those rules; it is sufficient that it could not have been unaware that its conduct was aimed at restricting competition.

Even if the infringement is not characterised as intentional, it is likely to be held negligent. The EU Courts have never defined negligence for this purpose, but the Commission and the Courts expect experienced commercial entities to understand what they are doing.[562]

Since both intention and negligence incur liability to fines it may be unnecessary to decide whether an infringement is intentional or negligent, except that intentional infringements tend to attract heavier fines and that committing an infringement negligently is an attenuating circumstance under the Fining Guidelines. It is rare for undertakings to enter into cartels 'negligently'.[563] It is no defence that the undertaking acted on legal advice or on a previous NCA decision that held its conduct did not infringe the competition provisions, insofar as it could not be unaware of the anti-competitive nature of that conduct.[564] There are, however, rare instances where ignorance has led to non-imposition of a fine.[565]

d. *Novelty and Non-imposition of Fines*

The Commission has sometimes considered that an undertaking has not been negligent in its behaviour where the practice is condemned as an infringement of the competition rules for the first time.[566] No fine was imposed in *Clearstream*,[567] as the infringement had ended and there was no previous jurisprudence addressing the competition analysis of the relevant markets. The Commission instead adopted the decision principally in order to clarify the law 'at a moment when cross-border trade in securities is becoming more important'.[568] It refused the same latitude in *Intel*, however, where it said that the economic activity concerned did not raise similar controversial issues or novel or specific

[561] Cases T-305/94 etc., *Re the PVC Cartel II* EU:T:1999:80, para. 1111; see also Cases 100–103/80, *Pioneer* EU:C:1983:158, para. 221; Case T-65/89, *BPB Industries and British Gypsum* EU:T:1993:31, paras. 165–166; Case T-143/89, *Ferriere Nord* EU:T:1995:64, para. 41.

[562] See Case 27/76, *United Brands* EU:C:1978:22, paras. 298–301 where the Court said the undertaking had been 'engaged for a very long time in international and national trade, has special knowledge of antitrust laws and has already experienced their severity', and Case C-277/87, *Sandoz Prodotti Farmaceutici* EU:C:1989:363, where the company had 'export prohibited' printed on its invoices.

[563] See H. de Broca, 'The Commission Revises its Guidelines for Setting Fines in Antitrust Cases' (2006) 3 *Competition Policy Newsletter* 1.

[564] Case C-681/11, *Bundeswettbewerbsbehörde and Bundeskartellanwalt v Schenker & Co AG* EU:C:2013:404, paras. 33–43.

[565] See *Bayer Dental* [1990] OJ L351/46; *Stainless Steel* [1990] OJ L220/28; and the other cases discussed by L. Gyselen in 'The Commission's Fining Policy in Competition Cases—"Questo è il catalogo"' in P. Slot and A. McDonnell (eds.), *Procedure and Enforcement in EC and US Competition Law* (Sweet & Maxwell, 1993), 63–75.

[566] See e.g. *Vegetable Parchment* [1978] OJ L70/54. On the other hand, the arguable novelty of the developments in Art. 102 did not save United Brands (see n. 562), Hoffmann-La Roche in Case 85/76, EU:C:1979:36, Tetra Pak in Case C-333/94 P, *Tetra Pak II* EU:C:1996:436, or AstraZeneca in Case C-457/10 P, EU:C:2012:770, paras. 74–99. The Commission did not, however, impose a fine on Van den Bergh Foods when it held for the first time that freezer exclusivity was contrary to Art. 101 and an abuse under Art. 102: *Van den Bergh Foods Ltd* [1998] OJ L246/1, discussed in Chaps 7 and 11.

[567] COMP/38.096, *Clearstream* [2009] OJ C165/7, upheld Case T-301/04, *Clearstream* EU:T:2009:317.

[568] Commission Press Release IP/04/705.

circumstances.[569] No fine was imposed on Motorola in the first standard-essential patent decision under Article 102,[570] nor in *DSD*.[571] In the *Organic Peroxide Cartel* decision, the Commission imposed a merely symbolic fine on the first company fined under Article 101 for cartel facilitation.[572]

The *Google Shopping* decision,[573] which involved a €2.42 billion fine for self-preferencing, is a particularly contentious example.[574] On appeal, although denying that leveraging as such was an established abuse, the GC held that Google ought to have deduced that its behaviour violated Article 102 from the fact that it 'undermined equality of opportunity between the various economic operators'.[575] The GC also rejected the argument that the principle of equal treatment provided any entitlement to a reduction in fine to reflect novelty. This was because the previous decisions invoked by Google had 'concerned very different sectors and issues',[576] and thus involved insufficiently 'comparable situations'.[577] The Court did not acknowledge that this approach effectively rules out *any* application of the equal treatment principle in this context, insofar as the principle could only ever be invoked in situations that are so similar as to preclude any claim of novelty.

e. Development of the Commission's Fining Policy

There is remarkably little guidance in Regulation 1/2003 about the level at which the Commission should set fines. Article 23(2) merely establishes a ceiling that is unique to each undertaking, based on individual turnover. It makes references to gravity and duration, but not to the purpose of fines. The Commission has previously said that their purpose is twofold: 'to impose a pecuniary sanction on the undertaking for the infringement and prevent a repetition of the offence, and to make the prohibition in the Treaty more effective'.[578] The Commission's fining policy has developed over the years in its decisional practice and via two sets of Guidelines, the first issued in 1998,[579] and the second—currently in force—in 2006.[580]

The CJ has consistently held that the Commission is entitled to change its fining policy over time.[581] Undertakings can have no legitimate expectation that infringing behaviour will attract only a certain level of fine.

The Commission first imposed a fine in 1969 in the *Quinine Cartel*,[582] and, for the next ten years, the level of fines was 'relatively light'.[583] Change came in 1979 when the Commission indicated in *Pioneer* that it intended to reinforce the deterrent effect of fines by raising their general level in cases of serious infringements.[584] The undertakings appealed, and the CJ confirmed the legality of the Commission's policy and strategy.

[569] COMP/37.990, *Intel* 13 May 2009, para. 1768, upheld Case T-286/09, *Intel* EU:T:2014:547, paras. 219–220 (first use of the concept of a 'naked restriction').

[570] COMP/39.986, *Motorola*, IP/12/345.

[571] [2001] OJ L166/1, upheld Case T-151/01, *Der Grüne Punkt* EU:T:2007:154, and Case C-385/07 P, EU:C:2009:456.

[572] COMP/37.857, on appeal Case T-99/04, *AC-Treuhand* EU:T:2008:256.

[573] AT.39740, *Google Search (Shopping)* 27 June 2017.

[574] See e.g. M. Eben, 'Fining Google: A Missed Opportunity for Legal Certainty?' (2018) 14 *European Competition Journal* 129.

[575] Case T-612/17, *Google Shopping* EU:T:2021:763, para. 616.

[576] Ibid., para. 624. [577] Ibid., para. 622.

[578] Commission, *XIIIth Report on Competition Policy* (1983), para. 62.

[579] Guidelines on the method of setting fines imposed pursuant to Reg. No. 17, Art. 15(2) and Art. 65(5) of the ECSC Treaty [1998] OJ C9/3.

[580] Guidelines on the method of setting fines imposed pursuant to Art. 23(2)(a) of Reg. No. 1/2003 [2006] OJ C210/2.

[581] See Cases 100–103/80, *Pioneer* EU:C:1983:158; Cases C-189/02 P etc., *Dansk Rørindustri* EU:C:2005:408.

[582] [1969] OJ L192/5.

[583] Commission's *XIIIth Report on Competition Policy* (1983), para. 63.

[584] *Pioneer* [1980] OJ L60/21.

Cases 100–103/80, *Musique Diffusion française SA v Commission (Pioneer)* EU:C:1983:158

Court of Justice

106. It follows that, in assessing the gravity of an infringement for the purpose of fixing the amount of the fine, the Commission must take into consideration not only the particular circumstances of the case but also the context in which the infringement occurs and must ensure that its action has the necessary deterrent effect, especially as regards those types of infringement which are particularly harmful to the attainment of the objectives of the [Union].

107. From that point of view, the Commission was right to classify as very serious infringements prohibitions on exports and imports seeking artificially to maintain price differences between the markets of the various member-States. Such prohibitions jeopardize the freedom of intra-[Union] trade, which is a fundamental principle of the Treaty, and they prevent the attainment of one of its objectives, namely the creation of a single market.

108. It was also open to the Commission to have regard to the fact that practices of this nature, although they were established as being unlawful at the outset of [Union] competition policy, are still relatively frequent on account of the profit that certain of the undertakings concerned are able to derive from them and, consequently, it was open to the Commission to consider that it was appropriate to raise the level of fines so as to reinforce their deterrent effect.

109. For the same reasons, the fact that the Commission, in the past, imposed fines of a certain level for certain types of infringement does not mean that it is estopped from raising that level . . . if that is necessary to ensure the implementation of [Union] competition policy. On the contrary, the proper application of the [Union] competition rules requires that the Commission may at any time adjust the level of fines to the needs of that policy.

This confirmed that the Commission was justified in raising the level of fines and in using fines to deter other undertakings from infringing.

In setting the amount of the fine, the Commission considers several factors, depending on the nature of the infringement and the circumstances of the case, which may include the volume and value of the affected goods, as well as the size and economic power of the defendant undertaking.[585] In *Pioneer*, the Court established that 'turnover' means the *total* turnover of the undertaking or group.[586] When the defendant undertaking heads a group which constitutes an economic unit, the turnover of the group as a whole must be taken into account when calculating the 10 per cent upper limit.[587] The Commission does not have to prove that the undertakings form a single economic entity in the sense discussed in Chapter 4, as turnover for the purposes of Article 23(2) is a separate issue from whether each subsidiary determines its own conduct for the purposes of attributing liability.[588] The total turnover means total *worldwide* turnover.[589]

585 Cases C-100–103/80, *Musique Diffusion française* EU:C:1983:158, para. 121. See also Cases C-189/02 P etc., *Dansk Rørindustri* EU:C:2005:408, para. 243; Case C-397/03 P, *Archer Daniels Midland* EU:C:2006:328, para. 100; and Case C-580/12 P, *Guardian Industries* EU:C:2014:2363, para. 54.

586 Cases C-100–103/80, *Musique Diffusion française* EU:C:1983:158, para. 119.

587 Case C-58/12 P, *Groupe Gascogne SA v Commission* EU:C:2013:770, para. 52.

588 Ibid., para. 57.

589 The GC confirmed in Cases T-25/95 etc., *Cimenteries* EU:T:2000:77, paras. 5022–5023, that only total turnover gives an approximate indication of the undertaking's size and influence on the market. See also Case C-289/04 P, *Showa Denko v Commission* EU:C:2006:431, paras. 16–18, and the 2006 Fining Guidelines, para. 18.

Pioneer gave the Commission a wide discretion, allowing it to 'individualise' the fine to each infringing undertaking.[590] In 1992, the Commission announced that it would move closer to the maximum fines allowed under Regulation 17,[591] and that, whenever it could ascertain the level of ill-gotten gains from an infringement, the calculation of the fine would take this as its starting point.[592] Yet this fining policy was criticised for its lack of transparency. It was said that the Commission appeared to pluck figures from the air in what could only be described as a lottery, and that the increasingly high fines were based on no discernible methodology.[593] The debate about optimal fining policy also relates, inter alia, to the question whether certainty or uncertainty is more effective for deterrence. If undertakings know what infringements are likely to cost, will they engage in a cost–benefit analysis and, deciding that they will on balance gain or lose, then act accordingly?[594]

Decisions imposing fines can be challenged before the GC, on grounds, inter alia, of lack of adequate reasoning, lack of proportionality, and discrimination (the last being of particular relevance to the different treatment of cartel participants).[595]

f. The Adoption of the Commission's 1998 Guidelines on the Method of Setting Fines

Conscious of the criticisms of its fining policy, in 1998 the Commission published its first Guidelines on the method of setting fines.[596] These, in large part, reflected its previous practice and the rulings of the Court. The Guidelines built on the two criteria stipulated in Regulation 17, gravity and duration, on which it based the calculation of fines. The gravity of infringements was divided into 'minor', 'serious', and 'very serious', with indicative starting fines for each category. This figure was then increased according to the duration of the infringement. The gravity plus duration calculation gave the basic amount, which was increased for 'aggravating circumstances', and/or decreased for 'attenuating circumstances'.

In *Dansk Rørindustri*,[597] the CJ confirmed that the Commission was legally empowered to adopt fining Guidelines and had not exceeded its discretion in so doing. The criteria of gravity and duration were those referred to in Article 15(2) of Regulation 17 (now Regulation 1/2003, Article 23(2)) and the Guidelines were therefore in conformity with the overarching legal framework. The Commission was not *required* to calculate the fines on the basis of the turnover of the undertakings concerned, although it was permissible to take turnover into account in order to assess the gravity of the infringement. Echoing the *Pioneer* judgment, it said that the Commission could at any time adjust fining levels in the light of the needs of competition policy.[598] The Commission has wide discretionary

[590] The GC said in Case T-150/89, *Martinelli v Commission* EU:T:1995:70, para. 69, that the Commission could not be expected to apply a precise mathematical formula to fining calculations. And see also Case 322/81, *Michelin I* EU:C:1983:313, paras. 17–21; Case T-53/03, *BPB* EU:T:2008:254.

[591] Commission, *XXIst Competition Policy Report* (1992), para. 139.

[592] In Cases T-25/95 etc., *Cimenteries* EU:T:2000:77, paras. 4884–4885 the GC explained that this did not mean that the Commission had taken it upon itself to establish in every case the financial advantage obtained, but merely that it would take it into account where it could be assessed.

[593] See I. Van Bael, 'Fining à la Carte: The Lottery of EU Competition Law' [1995] *ECLR* 237.

[594] The GC has said that too much predictability in the fine is undesirable, see Case T-53/03, *BPB* EU:T:2008:254, para. 336. See also G. Becker, 'Crime and Punishment: An Economic Approach' (1968) 76 *J of Political Economy*; and W. Landes, 'Optimal Sanctions for Antitrust Violations' (1983) 50 *Univ Chic LR* 652.

[595] Art. 263(2) TFEU.

[596] Guidelines on the method of setting fines [1998] OJ C9/3.

[597] Cases C-189/02 P etc., *Dansk Rørindustri* EU:C:2005:408, the appeal from the judgments of the GC in the *Pre-Insulated Pipes Cartel* case.

[598] See also Case C-3/06 P, *Group Danone* EU:C:2007:88, para. 90.

powers in this field, and the changes in fining policy were reasonably foreseeable at the time of the infringements.[599] The CJ confirmed these principles in two *Archer Daniels Midland* judgments in 2006 and 2009.[600]

The *Dansk Rørindustri* judgment was also important in respect of the legal effect of the Guidelines on fines, and of other Notices. Although they are not binding legislation, the CJ held that by adopting the Guidelines, the Commission had imposed limits on its discretion.[601] Whilst not 'rules of law' which the administration must always observe, 'they nevertheless form rules of practice from which the administration may not depart in an individual case without giving reasons that are compatible with the principle of equal treatment'.[602] This principle is of significance for all Commission Notices regarding competition law. In practice, appeals from Commission decisions imposing cartel fines often involve detailed arguments about whether the Commission correctly followed the Fining Guidelines (and/or the Leniency Notice)[603] more than they involve arguments about whether there was an infringement in the first place.

g. *The 2006 Guidelines on the Method of Setting Fines*

While the 1998 Guidelines brought a more systematic approach to the calculation of fines, they contained many variables and many matters which required discretionary assessment by the Commission. The result was a flood of appeals against the calculation of the fines imposed, particularly in cartel cases. In 2006, the Commission adopted new Guidelines on the method of setting fines, in order to remedy perceived shortcomings in the 1998 methodology, to reflect the Commission's most recent practice, and to take on board recent case law.[604] The 2006 Guidelines follow a similar two-step methodology, in providing, first, for the calculation of a basic amount and, secondly, for an increase or decrease in the light of aggravating or attenuating circumstances.

Guidelines on the Method of Setting Fines Imposed Pursuant to Article 23(2)(A) of Regulation No. 1/2003 [2006] OJ C210/2

13. In determining the basic amount of the fine to be imposed, the Commission will take the value of the undertaking's sales of goods or services to which the infringement directly or indirectly . . . relates in the relevant geographic area within the EEA. It will normally take the sales made by the undertaking during the last full business year of its participation in the infringement (hereafter 'value of sales').

. . .

[599] This point is also relevant to the application of the 2006 Guidelines.

[600] Case C-397/03 P, *Archer Daniels Midland* EU:C:2006:328 (lysine (amino acid) cartel) and Case C-510/06 P, *Archer Daniels Midland* EU:C:2009:166 (sodium gluconate cartel).

[601] Cases C-189/02 P etc., *Dansk Rørindustri* EU:C:2005:408, paras. 209–211.

[602] Case C-397/03 P, *Archer Daniels Midland* EU:C:2006:328, para. 91.

[603] See Section 6.H.v.

[604] The Guidelines were amended because the Commission was dissatisfied in particular with the minor, serious, and very serious classification; accepted the criticisms of the lump sum base figures as vague and unsatisfactory; and wished to reinforce its policy with some more draconian elements. See Press Release, IP/06/857; de Broca, n. 563; Neelie Kroes, 'Delivering the crackdown: recent developments in the European Commission's campaign against cartels', SPEECH/06/595 (the Commissioner considered the effect of the 2006 Guidelines would be to increase the amount of fines by a factor of three); W. Wils, 'The European Commission's 2006 Guidelines on Antitrust Fines: A Legal and Economic Analysis' (2007) 30 *World Competition* 197. The Guidelines refer to the EEA rather than the EU because the competition rules apply to the whole EEA area.

B. Determination of the basic amount of the fine

19. The basic amount of the fine will be related to a proportion of the value of sales, depending on the degree of gravity of the infringement, multiplied by the number of years of infringement.

20. The assessment of gravity will be made on a case-by-case basis for all types of infringement, taking account of all the relevant circumstances of the case.

21. As a general rule, the proportion of the value of sales taken into account will be set at a level of up to 30 % of the value of sales.

22. In order to decide whether the proportion of the value of sales to be considered in a given case should be at the lower end or at the higher end of that scale, the Commission will have regard to a number of factors, such as the nature of the infringement, the combined market share of all the undertakings concerned, the geographic scope of the infringement and whether or not the infringement has been implemented.

23. Horizontal price-fixing, market-sharing and output-limitation agreements . . . which are usually secret, are, by their very nature, among the most harmful restrictions of competition. As a matter of policy, they will be heavily fined. Therefore, the proportion of the value of sales taken into account for such infringements will generally be set at the higher end of the scale.

24. In order to take fully into account the duration of the participation of each undertaking in the infringement, the amount determined on the basis of the value of sales (see points 20 to 23 above) will be multiplied by the number of years of participation in the infringement. Periods of less than six months will be counted as half a year; periods longer than six months but shorter than one year will be counted as a full year.

25. In addition, irrespective of the duration of the undertaking's participation in the infringement, the Commission will include in the basic amount a sum of between 15% and 25% of the value of sales as defined in Section A above in order to deter undertakings from even entering into horizontal price-fixing, market-sharing and output-limitation agreements. The Commission may also apply such an additional amount in the case of other infringements. For the purpose of deciding the proportion of the value of sales to be considered in a given case, the Commission will have regard to a number of factors, in particular those referred in point 22.

26. Where the value of sales by undertakings participating in the infringement is similar but not identical, the Commission may set for each of them an identical basic amount. Moreover, in determining the basic amount of the fine, the Commission will use rounded figures.

2. Adjustments to the basic amount

27. In setting the fine, the Commission may take into account circumstances that result in an increase or decrease in the basic amount as determined in Section 1 above. It will do so on the basis of an overall assessment which takes account of all the relevant circumstances.

A. Aggravating circumstances

28. The basic amount may be increased where the Commission finds that there are aggravating circumstances, such as:

— where an undertaking continues or repeats the same or a similar infringement after the Commission or a national competition authority has made a finding that the undertaking infringed [Article 101 or 102]: the basic amount will be increased by up to 100 % for each such infringement established;

— refusal to cooperate with or obstruction of the Commission in carrying out its investigations;

— role of leader in, or instigator of, the infringement; the Commission will also pay particular attention to any steps taken to coerce other undertakings to participate in the infringement and/or any retaliatory measures taken against other undertakings with a view to enforcing the practices constituting the infringement.

B. Mitigating circumstances

29. The basic amount may be reduced where the Commission finds that mitigating circumstances exist, such as:

— where the undertaking concerned provides evidence that it terminated the infringement as soon as the Commission intervened: this will not apply to secret agreements or practices (in particular, cartels);

— where the undertaking provides evidence that the infringement has been committed as a result of negligence;

— where the undertaking provides evidence that its involvement in the infringement is substantially limited and thus demonstrates that, during the period in which it was party to the offending agreement, it actually avoided applying it by adopting competitive conduct in the market: the mere fact that an undertaking participated in an infringement for a shorter duration than others will not be regarded as a mitigating circumstance since this will already be reflected in the basic amount;

— where the undertaking concerned has effectively cooperated with the Commission outside the scope of the Leniency Notice and beyond its legal obligation to do so;

— where the anti-competitive conduct of the undertaking has been authorized or encouraged by public authorities or by legislation.

C. Specific increase for deterrence

30. The Commission will pay particular attention to the need to ensure that fines have a sufficiently deterrent effect; to that end, it may increase the fine to be imposed on undertakings which have a particularly large turnover beyond the sales of goods or services to which the infringement relates.

31. The Commission will also take into account the need to increase the fine in order to exceed the amount of gains improperly made as a result of the infringement where it is possible to estimate that amount.

D. Legal maximum

32. The final amount of the fine shall not, in any event, exceed 10 % of the total turnover in the preceding business year of the undertaking or association of undertakings participating in the infringement, as laid down in Article 23(2) of Regulation No 1/2003.

. . .

F. Ability to pay

35. In exceptional cases, the Commission may, upon request, take account of the undertaking's inability to pay in a specific social and economic context. It will not base any reduction granted for this reason in the fine on the mere finding of an adverse or loss-making financial situation. A reduction could be granted solely on the basis of objective evidence that imposition of the fine as provided for in these Guidelines would irretrievably jeopardise the economic viability of the undertaking concerned and cause its assets to lose all their value.

Final Considerations

36. The Commission may, in certain cases, impose a symbolic fine. The justification for imposing such a fine should be given in its decision.

37. Although these Guidelines present the general methodology for the setting of fines, the particularities of a given case or the need to achieve deterrence in a particular case may justify departing from such methodology or from the limits specified in point 21.

Several aspects of the 2006 Guidelines are noteworthy. First, instead of specified categories of seriousness, the basic amount is calculated on a proportion of the value of sales, depending on the degree of gravity of the infringement. Unlike the 1998 Guidelines, the 2006 Guidelines do not provide for consideration of actual impact on the market if it can be measured, but the Commission is not precluded from taking it into account if it can provide 'specific, credible and adequate evidence'.[605]

Secondly, the calculation uses the value of the undertaking's sales of goods or services to which the infringement directly or indirectly relates in the relevant geographic area within the EEA.[606] As a general rule, the proportion of the value of the sales taken into account will be up to 30 per cent.[607] The value of the internal sales of vertically integrated undertakings should be taken into account as well as sales to independent third parties.[608] The Commission adopted the formula of value of sales multiplied by duration for the basic amount because it regards this as providing 'an appropriate proxy to reflect the economic importance of the infringement as well as the relative weight of each undertaking in the infringement'.[609] If, however, the purpose of the anti-competitive conduct is precisely to *decrease* the value of sales, for example in a purchase cartel to reduce the cost of inputs, then the Commission is likely to be justified in departing from this starting point in setting the basic amount.[610]

Thirdly, the amount determined by the value of sales is multiplied by the number of years of participation in the infringement.[611] Duration therefore plays a greater role in the determination of the basic amount than it did under the 1998 Guidelines. This provision alone would result in heavier fines than previously.

Fourthly, in the case of cartel offences, the Commission includes as part of the basic amount of the fine a further sum of 15–25 per cent of the value of the sales simply as a punishment for having entered into the arrangement: an 'entry fee'.[612] The purpose is to deter cartelists at the outset by making participation expensive even for a short time. The Commission may impose the entry fee in respect of other infringements too.

Finally, recidivism is heavily penalised, i.e. it is expensive to be a repeat offender. One aggravating circumstance is for an undertaking to continue or repeat the same or similar infringements after having been found by the Commission or an NCA to have infringed previously.[613] Recidivism has long been considered an aggravating feature, but in the 2006 Guidelines it is specifically provided that *each* subsequent infringement will increase ('uplift') the basic amount of the fine by up to 100 per cent. The 2006 Guidelines were applied in the *Calcium Carbide* cartel,[614] where the fine on

[605] Case T-286/09, *Intel* EU:T:2014:547, paras. 1624–1625.

[606] 2006 Guidelines, para. 13. 'Indirectly' encompasses situations such as horizontal price-fixing where the price of the product concerned then serves as a basis for the price of lower or higher quality products (para. 13 fn. 1). In the case of worldwide cartels, the Commission may take account of the value of sales in a relevant geographic area wider than the EEA (para. 18, relying on Cases T-236/01 etc., *Tokai Carbon* EU:T:2004:118, paras. 196–204 (*aff'd* Case C-289/04 P, *Showa Denko* EU:C:2006:431, paras. 16–18); Cases T-71, 74, 87, and 91/03, *Tokai Carbon* EU:T:2005:220, para. 186).

[607] 2006 Guidelines, para. 21. In para. 37 the Commission reserves the right to depart from this limit in a particular case. This may be necessary, for instance, where no turnover figures are available at all, see *Competition Policy Newsletter*, n. 563.

[608] Case C-580/12 P, *Guardian Industries* EU:C:2014:2363. [609] 2006 Guidelines, para. 6.

[610] See e.g. Case T-240/17, *Campine and Campine Recycling* EU:T:2019:778.

[611] 2006 Guidelines, para. 24. Less than six months counts as half a year, and six to 12 months counts as a full year.

[612] 2006 Guidelines, para. 25.

[613] 'Similar' means the same kind of infringement, such as price collusion in cartel cases (see e.g. COMP/38.638, *Butadiene Rubber and Emulsion Styrene Butadiene Rubber Cartel* [2008] OJ C7/11) or abusive loyalty-inducing discounts in the two *Michelin* cases, see Case T-203/01, *Manufacture Française des Pneumatiques Michelin v Commission (Michelin II)* EU:T:2003:250, paras. 283–288. The product or sector concerned is irrelevant. The infringements in *Michelin* were committed by two separate subsidiaries of the same parent. For recidivism in the context of EU antitrust enforcement generally, see W. Wils, 'Recidivism in EU Antitrust Enforcement—A Legal and Economic Analysis' (2012) 35 *World Competition* 5, and T. Eftychidou and F. Maiorano, 'Once Burned Twice Shy: What does Economics Say about Repeated Cartel Offences?' (2016) *JECLAP* 622.

[614] COMP/39.396 [2009] OJ C301/18, IP/09/1169.

Akzo Nobel would have been increased by 100 per cent for having been fined four times previously (!) had it not been granted immunity for whistle-blowing.[615]

It must be remembered that the final amount of the fine cannot exceed the 10 per cent of turnover in the preceding business year laid down in Article 23(2) of Regulation 1/2003.[616] The 'entry fee' and the uplift for recidivism potentially make cartel participation much more expensive than previously. In paragraph 30 of the 2006 Guidelines, the Commission says that it may increase fines on undertakings which have a particularly large turnover beyond the value of sales to which the infringement relates in order to provide sufficient deterrence. This continues the 'deterrence multiplier' practice developed in the application of the 1998 Guidelines and approved by the CJ.[617] Paragraph 31 says that the Commission may increase the fine in order to exceed the benefits of the infringement where it is possible to estimate them.[618]

Arguments that the Commission's discretion over fines infringes Article 7(1) ECHR[619] continue to be dismissed:

> ... [T]he fact that a law confers a discretion is not in itself inconsistent with the requirement of foreseeability, provided that the scope of the discretion and the manner of its exercise are indicated with sufficient clarity, having regard to the legitimate aim in question, to give the individual adequate protection against arbitrary interference.[620]

Although the thrust of the 2006 Guidelines is to increase the level of fines,[621] the application of the leniency policy and settlement procedure in cartel cases means that many infringers eventually pay nothing, and others have greatly decreased fines.[622] It has nonetheless been queried whether the significant uptick in the level of fines imposed by the Commission over the past couple of decades actually achieves its goal of deterrence, in the light of the prevalence of recidivism in many sectors. This, accordingly, raises the question of whether alternative sanctions, such as individual criminal penalties, should be contemplated to ensure the effective enforcement of EU competition law.[623]

h. Particular Issues in the Application of the Fining Guidelines

A detailed examination of the application of the Commission's fining policy is outside the scope of this book.[624] The following points should, nonetheless, be noted.

[615] Under the Leniency Notice, see Section 6.H.v. The fine on Degussa was increased by 50% for recidivism.

[616] And previously in Reg. 17, Art. 15(2). In the course of the calculation the Commission may exceed the 10%, so long as the final sum imposed on the undertaking is below it. The 10% does not therefore apply to the intermediate calculations: Cases C-189/02 P etc., *Dansk Rørindustri* EU:C:2005:408, paras. 277–278. Where the undertaking has committed a number of infringements the ceiling applies to each one separately; in Case C-564/08 P, *SGL Carbon* EU:C:2009:703 the undertaking claimed that the Commission had deliberately adopted four separate decisions for four separate infringements, thus evading the 10% cap. The CJ affirmed the GC's dismissal of this plea (Case T-68/04, *SGL Carbon* EU:T:2008:414).

[617] Case C-289/04 P, *Showa Denko* EU:C:2006:431, paras. 23–29. [618] 2006 Guidelines, para. 31.

[619] Which provides for non-retroactivity of criminal law and penalties. It follows that criminal offences and the relevant penalties must be clearly defined by law, so that the individual knows what acts and omissions make him criminally liable and what are the consequences.

[620] Case T-69/04, *Schunk* EU:T:2008:415, para. 33.

[621] 'These innovations are likely to increase average fines, particularly for long lasting infringements in large markets, where fines could well increase by a factor of three. I think all this will make potential cartelists think twice!', Neelie Kroes, 'Delivering on the crackdown: recent developments in the European Commission's campaign against cartels', SPEECH/06/595, 13 October 2006. For an analysis of the fines imposed on cartels from 2007 to 2011, see J. M. Connor, 'Cartel Fine Severity and the European Commission 2007–2011' [2011] *ECLR* 58.

[622] See Veljanovski, n. 31.

[623] D. Geradin and K. Sadrak, 'The EU Competition Law Fining System: A Quantitative Review of the Commission Decisions between 2000 and 2017', TILEC Discussion Paper DP 2017-018 (2017). See also Section 11.

[624] Interested readers are referred to the specialist practitioner texts, including Ortiz Blanco, n. 1, Chap 11; Kerse and Khan, n. 202, Chap 7; Bellamy and Child, n. 1, Chap 14.

(1) Deterrence

The major theme of the Commission fining policy, in accordance with the duty identified in *Pioneer*, is deterrence. This encompasses not only specific deterrence (by sanctioning the undertaking concerned) but also general deterrence (deterring other undertakings).[625] Deterrence may involve imposing separate penalties for each of a number of multiple breaches.[626] The large fines imposed on cartels are part of a deliberate policy to deter undertakings from entering into such arrangements, as explained in Chapter 9.[627]

(2) Aggravating Circumstances

The notion of aggravating circumstances 'describe[s] unlawful conduct or circumstances which render the infringement more harmful and which justify a particular ruling, resulting in an increase in the penalty imposed on the undertaking responsible'.[628] The list provided in paragraph 28 of the Guidelines (recidivism, refusal to cooperate with the Commission's investigation and being the leader or instigator of the infringement, or having taken coercive or retaliatory measures) is not exhaustive.[629] The issue of recidivism becomes a complex one if company restructuring and/or changes in ownership and control have taken place.[630] A fine may be increased for recidivism even if the previous infringement was in a different market, so long as the type of infringement is similar. Aggravation in the form of non-cooperation during an inspection is illustrated by *Professional Videotape*,[631] in which Sony's fine was increased by 30 per cent for failing to answer questions and for shredding documents during a dawn raid. There are frequent arguments played out in appeals to the GC about whether or not an undertaking played a leadership or instigation role.[632] In *Nintendo*,[633] the infringing agreement (to restrict parallel trade) was between a manufacturer and seven of its exclusive distributors. The manufacturer (Nintendo) was classified as the 'leader' and its fine increased accordingly. It argued that the leadership concept was relevant only in restrictive horizontal agreements, because in vertical agreements the role of manufacturer and leader merge. The GC rejected this and refused to limit the leadership concept to horizontal cartels. Although terminating an infringement when investigated is not a mitigating circumstance, continuing infringing conduct after the investigation has commenced *is* an aggravating circumstance.[634]

(3) Mitigating Circumstances

Undertakings commonly plead that they were merely 'passive' participants in cartels and therefore within the third indent of paragraph 29.[635] Paragraph 29 does not list as a mitigating factor the adoption of a compliance programme (that is, a set of measures put in place by an undertaking to ensure

[625] 2006 Guidelines, para. 4; Case C-511/11, *Versalis SpA* EU:C:2013:386, para. 94.

[626] Case T-446/05 P, *Amann & Söhne* EU:T:2010:165. [627] See Chap 9, Section 2.B.

[628] Case T-93/18, *International Skating Union v Commission* EU:T:2020:610, para. 152.

[629] Ibid., para. 151.

[630] This is similar to the problem which arises over liability for the infringement and for the fine, see Chap 4, Section 5.A; and see e.g. Case C-511/11, *Versalis* EU:C:2013:386.

[631] COMP/38.432. Sony's total fine was therefore over €47 million.

[632] See e.g. Case T-15/02, *BASF* EU:T:2006:74 (an appeal from the *Vitamins Cartel* decision [2003] OJ L6/1) in which the GC cancelled the 35% increase in the basic amount imposed on BASF for being a leader or instigator or leader of the cartel in respect of two vitamins (C and D3) as the Commission had not sufficiently established this. The refusal of leniency under the 1996 Notice on the ground that it was not available to the leader or instigator therefore had to be re-examined too, but the GC held that BASF still did not qualify.

[633] COMP/35.387, *PO Video Games* [2003] OJ L255/33, on appeal Case T-13/03, *Nintendo* EU:T:2009:131.

[634] See e.g. *PO Video Games*, where Nintendo got a 25% increase for this, upheld by the GC, Case T-13/03, *Nintendo v Commission* EU:T:2009:131.

[635] For a successful argument that limited participation merited a reduction in fine, see Case T-758/14 RENV, *Infineon Technologies* EU:T:2020:307, following annulment by the CJ (Case C-99/17 P, *Infineon Technologies* EU:C:2018:773) of an earlier rejection of the claim (Case T-758/14, *Infineon Technologies* EU:T:2016:737).

that none of its staff breach the competition rules thereby imposing liability on the undertaking). Before 1992 the Commission gave some fine reductions where the infringement was carried out in contravention of the undertaking's compliance programme, but its current practice is not to do so.[636] In *PO Video Games*, where Nintendo introduced a compliance programme *after* the infringement, the Commission said that, 'While the Commission does indeed welcome all steps taken by undertakings to raise awareness amongst their employees of existing competition rules, these initiatives cannot relieve the Commission of its duty to penalise their very serious infringement of competition rules.'[637] It is not a mitigating circumstance to cooperate with the Commission by producing information in response to an Article 18(2) request.[638]

In the *Calcium Carbide* cartel, one (Slovakian) company, NCZ, was fined an amount that nearly reached the maximum 10 per cent turnover ceiling despite pleading that its representatives at the meetings did not speak any foreign language fluently and so had to communicate through other cartel members, and that having emerged from a former Communist regime, its officers had no knowledge of competition law.[639]

(4) Ability to Pay

Paragraph 35 of the 2006 Guidelines reflects the case law of the CJ that the Commission is not *required* to take into account the undertaking's ability to pay the fine, but *may* do so. The plea of inability to pay has become more frequent since the financial crisis. Taking difficulty in paying into account, however, risks giving 'unjustified competitive advantages to undertakings least well adapted to the market conditions'.[640] The reference to 'specific social context' in paragraph 35 means the consequences which payment of a fine could have, in particular, by leading to an increase in unemployment or deterioration in the economic sectors upstream and downstream.[641] Faull and Nikpay say that 'this exceptional treatment of companies in financial distress may even be a necessity for guaranteeing the social acceptance of EU competition policy'.[642] The last sentence of paragraph 35, 'irretrievably jeopardise the economic viability and cause its assets to lose all their value . . . ' was considered in *Novácke Chemické Závody*. The GC confirmed that the mere fact that the fine might cause the bankruptcy of the undertaking concerned was not enough. Rather, it was a matter of looking at what would happen to the assets in such an event. If it was likely that the assets would not find a buyer, or be sold at a heavily reduced price, that could amount to losing all their value.[643] There is a concern to avoid an

[636] See e.g. Case T-53/06, *UPM-Kymmene* EU:T:2012:101, paras. 123–124. For the arguments around compliance programmes, see W. Wils, 'Antitrust Compliance Programmes and Optimal Antitrust Enforcement' (2013) 1 *J of Antitrust Enforcement* 52; D. Geradin, 'Antitrust Compliance Programmes and Optimal Antitrust Enforcement: A Reply to Wouter Wils' (2013) 1 *J of Antitrust Enforcement* 1; A. Riley and D. Sokol, 'Rethinking Compliance' (2015) 3 *J of Antitrust Enforcement* 31; and M. Carbonnel, 'Set Sail for the New World of Competition Law Compliance' (2019) 40 *ECLR* 76. The Commission provides further information for businesses about compliance on its website, <http://ec.europa.eu/competition/antitrust/compliance/index_en.html>.

[637] [2003] OJ L255/33, para. 451.

[638] Case C-294/13 P, *Commission v Fresh Del Monte Produce Inc* EU:C:2015:416, paras. 167–188, where the CJ overturned the GC's reduction of a fine for cooperation.

[639] COMP/39.396 [2009] OJ C301/18, appeal dismissed, Case T-352/09, *Novácke Chemické Závody* EU:T:2012: 673, para. 103.

[640] See Cases 96–102, 104, 105, 108, and 110/82, *IAZ International Belgium* EU:C:1983:310, paras. 54–55; Cases C-189/02 P etc., *Dansk Rørindustri* EU:C:2005:408, para. 327; Case C-308/04 P, *SGL Carbon AG v Commission* EU:C:2006:433, paras. 105–106.

[641] Case C-308/04 P, *SGL Carbon* EU:C:2006:433, para. 106. The CJ was interpreting the 1998 Guidelines.

[642] Faull and Nikpay, n. 1, 8.696.

[643] Case T-352/09, *Novácke Chemické Závody* EU:T:2012: 673, paras. 186–190.

undertaking leaving the market because of an inability to pay, leaving another firm dominant (especially if the latter has received immunity).[644]

The Commission gave reductions in, inter alia, *Animal Feed Phosphates*,[645] *Prestressing Steel*,[646] *Bathroom Fixtures and Fittings*,[647] *Retail Food Repackaging*,[648] and *Mushrooms*.[649] The large majority of undertakings who request a reduction on this basis do not receive one, however.[650] The Commission has published an Information Note on Inability to Pay, explaining its approach,[651] and in Best Practices sets out the information that an undertaking making the claim should provide.[652]

i. *General Principles of Law*

In imposing fines, as in all other aspects of competition procedure, the Commission must abide by the general principles of EU law. As well as non-retroactivity and legitimate expectation, the Commission must respect the principles of proportionality, equal treatment, and sound administration.[653] As far as proportionality is concerned, the CJ stated in *Pioneer* that the upper limit on fines (10 per cent of turnover) was intended to prevent fines from being disproportionate in relation to the size of the undertaking.[654] Equal treatment means that comparable situations must be treated in the same way and different situations treated differently, unless there is objective justification. Where a number of undertakings are involved in the same infringement—as a cartel—the Commission applies weightings to reflect the differing impact of the undertakings' conduct. This may involve grouping the undertakings concerned.[655] The CJ confirmed in *Dansk Rørindustri* that the Commission does not have to ensure that the final amounts of the fines resulting from its calculations reflect any distinctions between them in terms of their turnover.[656]

Appeals against fines on grounds of breach of the principles of proportionality and equal treatment are common. For example, in *Hoek Loos*,[657] the fine imposed on one undertaking in the *Industrial Gases Cartel* decision[658] amounted to nearly 50 per cent of the total fines imposed in that case. The undertaking claimed that this was disproportionate to its participation in the infringement or to its market share. The GC rejected this argument, saying that the final amount of a fine is not, in principle, an appropriate factor in assessing the possible lack of proportionality of the fine as regards the importance of the participants in the cartel. That final amount was set, inter alia, on the basis of various factors linked to the individual conduct of the undertaking in question, such as the duration of the infringement, the aggravating or attenuating circumstances, and the degree to which the undertaking cooperated.[659]

[644] See Case T-392/09, *I.garantovaná* EU:T:2012:674. [645] COMP/38.866, 20 July 2010.

[646] COMP/38.344, 25 July 2012, upheld in Case T-438/12, *Global Steel Wire v Commission* EU:T:2016:335.

[647] COMP/39.092, 23 June 2010, upheld on appeal by an undertaking which was not one of the five that received a reduction, Case T-376/10, *Mamoli Robinetteria* EU:T:2013:442, and Case C-619/13 P, EU:C:2017:50.

[648] COMP/39.563, 24 June 2015. [649] AT.39965, *Mushrooms* 25 June 2014.

[650] A study found that the Commission granted a reduction to 18.3% of undertakings who applied between 2001 and 2018: see I. G. Gabison, I. Kokkoris, and N. Pahari, 'Inability-to-Pay Fine Reductions in European' (2021) 44 *World Competition* 125.

[651] SEC(2010)737/2. [652] Best Practices, para. 88.

[653] For a case in which the principle of sound administration was breached, see Case T-410/03, *Hoechst* EU:T:2008:211, where the Commission was embroiled in negotiations with two undertakings at the same time under the Leniency Notice.

[654] Cases 100–103/80, *Pioneer* EU:C:1983:158, paras. 119–120; see Case T-33/02, *Britannia Alloys and Chemicals* EU:T:2005:428, para. 43.

[655] Case T-68/04, *SGL Carbon* EU:T:2008:414, *aff'd* Case C-564/08 P, *SGL Carbon* EU:C:2009:703.

[656] Cases C-189/02 P etc., *Dansk Rørindustri* EU:C:2005:408, para. 312.

[657] Case T-304/02, *Hoek Loos* EU:T:2006:184. [658] [2003] OJ L84/1.

[659] Case T-304/02, *Hoek Loos* EU:T:2006:184, para. 85.

On the other hand, in *Degussa*,[660] the GC held that the Commission was wrong to apply the same deterrence multiplier to the applicant as to another of the cartelists despite the difference in the size of the two undertakings. In *Guardian Industries*,[661] the CJ held that the Commission breached the principle of non-discrimination by not taking internal sales into account when calculating the value of sales, because it resulted in an undertaking which made sales only to third parties receiving a disproportionately large fine relative to other cartel members who were vertically integrated.

j. Liability for Fines

The consequences of the single economic entity doctrine for the liability of parent companies for infringements by subsidiaries and the problems where an undertaking responsible for an infringement no longer exists (or no longer exists in an identical form) are discussed in Chapter 4.

k. The Payment and Collection of Fines

The payment of fines is enforceable pursuant to Article 299 TFEU, which provides that enforcement of decisions of the Council or Commission which impose a pecuniary obligation on persons other than States shall be governed by the rules of civil procedure in the State in the territory of which it is carried out. Member States must designate a relevant national authority for enforcement purposes. Fines are normally expressed in euros. Decisions normally give the undertakings concerned three months in which to pay the fine, and state that interest becomes payable after the specified time.[662] A challenge to the decision before the GC does not operate to suspend the payment of the fine, but the Commission usually agrees to defer enforcement pending the outcome of the appeal if the undertakings agree to pay interest and provide a bank guarantee. The question of whether fines are tax deductible arose in the Article 267 reference, *XBV*. While not expressly ruling on the tax deductibility of fines, the CJ has clearly disapproved of this notion, it, saying that it might significantly reduce the effectiveness of the Commission decision.[663] Any fines collected are paid into the general EU budget.[664]

(v) The Leniency Policy in Cartel Cases

a. General

In Chapter 9 we discuss cartels and the problems in detecting them and in proving them to the standard required by the EU Courts, particularly where oligopolistic industries are concerned. The leniency policy (or 'programme') is the Commission's major weapon in the fight against cartels.[665]

[660] Case T-279/02, EU:T:2006:103. Degussa's further appeal against the fine was rejected, Case C-266/06 P, *Evonik Degussa* EU:C:2008:295.

[661] Case C-580/12 P, *Guardian Industries* EU:C:2014:2363. This approach was extended in Case C-231/14 P, *InnoLux* EU:C:2015:451 to internal sales to subsidiaries located outside the EEA, where the finished products were subsequently sold to third parties within the EEA. For analysis of the Commission's approach to setting fines for vertically integrated cartelists, see M. Martyniszyn, 'How High (and Far) Can You Go? On Setting Fines in Cartel Cases involving Vertically-integrated Undertakings and Foreign Sales' (2016) 37 *ECLR* 99, and P. Bentley and D. Henry, 'Calculating the Cartel Fine: A Question of Jurisdiction or a Question of Economic Importance?' (2016) 39 *World Competition* 431.

[662] The payment of interest was approved by the CJ in Case 107/82, *AEG-Telefunken* EU:C:1983:293; see also the GC in Case T-275/94, *CB* EU:T:1995:141. In Case C-564/08 P, *SGL Carbon* EU:C:2009:703, the CJ confirmed that the Commission could set a higher rate of interest than the market rate applicable to ordinary borrowers.

[663] Case C-429/07, *Inspecteur van de Belastingdienst* EU:C:2009:359, para. 39. The case was the first occasion on which the Commission intervened in national proceedings.

[664] See the Commission's website at <https://competition-policy.ec.europa.eu/index/fines_en>.

[665] See Chap 9, Section 3.B.

Although it has the inspection powers described previously in this chapter, obtaining direct evidence of a cartel is easier if participants can be induced to turn informer. This was demonstrated in *Cartonboard* in 1994, when one of the ringleaders 'spontaneously admitted' the infringement and provided detailed evidence to the Commission, receiving in return a greatly reduced fine.[666] In 1996, the Commission published a Leniency Notice which put this practice on a systematic footing.[667] It provided that, where cartel participants gave information to the Commission and cooperated with any ensuing investigation, they could expect a reduction in the fine which would otherwise be imposed, or even no fine at all.[668] It did not, however, *guarantee* full immunity to the first participant to come forward, in contrast to the equivalent US and Canadian policies.[669]

The Commission published an amended Notice in 2002,[670] which, amongst other improvements, guaranteed immunity to the first undertaking to submit evidence which met certain criteria, if the undertaking itself fulfilled certain conditions. Some problems remained, but the increased certainty it offered, in particular the guaranteed immunity, made it a successful tool in the fight against cartels.[671] Guaranteed immunity sets the scene for a 'race to the Commission's door', as there can be only one grant of full immunity per cartel. The CJ thus describes the objective of the programme as 'speeding up the dismantling of cartels'.[672]

The 2002 Notice was replaced by the current one in 2006.[673] The 2006 Notice (the Notice) is consistent with the ECN Model Leniency Programme (MLP) adopted to deal with divergences between national leniency policies.[674] Explicit legislative provision for the leniency policy was provided for the first time when Regulation 773/2004 was amended in 2015.[675] The Commission cannot depart in an individual case from the rules of practice set out in the Notice without giving reasons compatible with the principle of equal treatment.[676] The leniency policy does not bind the Member States,[677] although the ECN+ Directive requires the adoption of harmonised leniency programmes at national level.[678] The EU leniency policy does not provide for what is known as 'Amnesty Plus' (or 'Leniency Plus'), whereby an applicant for leniency in respect of one cartel is further rewarded if it reveals another cartel in the course of the proceedings.[679]

666 [1994] OJ L243/1, para. 171. See the discussion in the GC judgments in the appeals from the decision, e.g. Case T-319/94, *Fiskeby Board* EU:T:1998:95, paras. 86–104.

667 Commission Notice on the non-imposition or reduction of fines in cartel cases [1996] OJ C204/14.

668 The Leniency Notices only apply in cartel cases, Case T-13/03, *Nintendo* EU:T:2009:131.

669 Conversely, the US policy only grants full immunity, whereas reductions of fines are dealt with under a plea-bargaining process.

670 Commission Notice on immunity from fines and reduction of fines in cartel cases [2002] OJ C45/3. For comments on the Notice, see e.g. N. Levy and R. O'Donoghue, 'The EU Leniency Programme Comes of Age' (2004) 92 *World Competition* 75–99.

671 See B. van Barlingen and M. Barennes, 'The European Commission's 2002 Leniency Notice in Practice' (2005) 3 *Competition Policy Newsletter* 6.

672 Case C-563/19 P, *Recylex* EU:C:2021:428, para. 59.

673 Commission Notice on immunity from fines and reduction of fines in cartel cases [2006] OJ C298/11; Commission Press Release, IP/06/1705.

674 See at <http://ec.europa.eu/competition/ecn/mlp_revised_2012_en.pdf>. There is no EU-wide system of leniency, and an application for leniency to the Commission does not count as an application to an NCA, see Case C-428/14, *DHL Express Italy srl and DHL Global Forwarding (Italy)* EU:C:2016:27, discussed in Section 8.

675 Reg. 2015/1348 [2015] OJ L208/3, Art. 1 inserted a new Art. 4a into Reg. 773/2004.

676 Case C-510/11 P, *Kone Oyj* EU:C:2013:696, para. 29.

677 Case C-557/12, *Kone v ÖBB-Infrastruktur* EU:C:2014:1317, para. 36.

678 See Section 8.

679 See D. McElwee, 'Should the European Commission adopt "Amnesty Plus" in its Fight Against Hardcore Cartels?' [2004] *ECLR* 558; M. Fullarton and A. Singh, 'Amnesty Plus: The Way Forward for EU Leniency Policy?' [2016] *ECLR* 193; and M. Martyniszyn, 'Leniency (Amnesty Plus): A Building Block or a Trojan Horse' (2015) 3 *J of Antitrust Enforcement* 391.

Regulation 773/2004 [2004] OJ L123/18

Article 4a The Commission's Leniency Programme

1. The Commission may set the requirements and cooperation conditions under which it may reward undertakings that are or have been party to secret cartels, for their cooperation in disclosing the cartel and facilitating the establishment of an infringement, with immunity from fines or a reduction in fines which would otherwise be imposed under Article 23(2) of Regulation (EC) No 1/2003 (the Commission leniency programme).

   Immunity from fines may be granted to the undertaking that is the first to submit evidence which in the Commission's view would enable it to carry out a targeted inspection or find an infringement of Article 101 of the Treaty in connection with the alleged cartel. A reduction in fines may be granted to undertakings which provide the Commission with evidence of the alleged infringement which represents significant added value with respect to the evidence already in the Commission's possession.

   The Commission will only grant immunity from or a reduction of the fine under its leniency programme if, at the end of the administrative proceedings, the undertaking has met the requirements and cooperation conditions set out in the leniency programme. Those may cover, among others, the type of information and evidence the undertakings are required to submit and the further cooperation expected from the undertakings during the administrative proceedings.

The Commission website explains how to apply for leniency and gives practical information.[680] The Commission has launched an eLeniency online system.[681] This provides leniency applicants with an alternative means by which to submit corporate statements, emulating the legal protections offered by the oral procedure. Access to the eLeniency portal extends to undertakings that wish to provide evidence of participation in non-cartel infringements.[682]

The application of the Notice allows the Commission considerable discretion on crucial matters, such as what amounts to sufficient evidence and information to attract full immunity, or what qualifies as 'significant added value' to merit a reduction in fine. This discretion is, however, subject to an in-depth review of the law and the facts by the GC.[683]

b. Immunity

Full immunity from fines is guaranteed to the first undertaking to submit evidence sufficient for the Commission either to mount a targeted Article 20(4) inspection or to enable the Commission to find an infringement, if certain other conditions are fulfilled.

Commission Notice on Immunity from Fines and Reduction of Fines in Cartel Cases [2006] OJ C298/17

II. Immunity from Fines

A. Requirements to qualify for immunity from fines

(8) The Commission will grant immunity from any fine which would otherwise have been imposed to an undertaking disclosing its participation in an alleged cartel affecting the Community if that undertaking is the first to submit information and evidence which in the Commission's view will enable it to:

[680] See <http://ec.europa.eu/competition/cartels/leniency/leniency.html>.

[681] See <https://competition-policy.ec.europa.eu/cartels/leniency/eleniency_en>.

[682] Ibid.

[683] See e.g. Case C-510/11 P, *Kone* EU:C:2013:696; Case C-455/11 P, *Solvay* EU:C:2013:796.

(a) carry out a targeted inspection in connection with the alleged cartel . . . or

(b) find an infringement of Article [101] in connection with the alleged cartel.

(9) For the Commission to be able to carry out a targeted inspection within the meaning of point (8)(a), the undertaking must provide the Commission with the information and evidence listed below, to the extent that this, in the Commission's view, would not jeopardize the inspections:

(a) A corporate statement . . . which includes, in so far as it is known to the applicant at the time of submission:

- A detailed description of the alleged cartel arrangement, including for instance its aims, activities and functioning; the product or service concerned, the geographic scope, the duration of and the estimated market volumes affected by the alleged cartel; the specific dates, locations, content of and participants in alleged cartel contacts, and all relevant explanations in connection with the pieces of evidence provided in support of the application.
- The name and address of the legal entity submitting the immunity application as well as the names and addresses of all the other undertakings that participate(d) in the alleged cartel;
- The names, positions, office locations and, where necessary, home addresses of all individuals who, to the applicant's knowledge, are or have been involved in the alleged cartel, including those individuals which have been involved on the applicant's behalf;
- Information on which other competition authorities, inside or outside the EU, have been approached or are intended to be approached in relation to the alleged cartel; and

(b) Other evidence relating to the alleged cartel in possession of the applicant or available to it at the time of the submission, including in particular any evidence contemporaneous to the infringement.

(10) Immunity pursuant to point (8)(a) will not be granted if, at the time of the submission, the Commission had already sufficient evidence to adopt a decision to carry out an inspection in connection with the alleged cartel or had already carried out such an inspection.

(11) Immunity pursuant to point (8)(b) will only be granted on the cumulative conditions that the Commission did not have, at the time of the submission, sufficient evidence to find an infringement of Article [101] in connection with the alleged cartel and that no undertaking had been granted conditional immunity from fines under point (8)(a) in connection with the alleged cartel. In order to qualify, an undertaking must be the first to provide contemporaneous, incriminating evidence of the alleged cartel as well as a corporate statement containing the kind of information specified in point (9)(a), which would enable the Commission to find an infringement of Article [101].

(12) In addition to the conditions set out in points (8)(a), (9) and (10) or in points (8)(b) and 11, all the following conditions must be met in any case to qualify for any immunity from a fine:

(a) The undertaking cooperates genuinely, fully, on a continuous basis and expeditiously from the time it submits its application throughout the Commission's administrative procedure. This includes:

- providing the Commission promptly with all relevant information and evidence relating to the alleged cartel that comes into its possession or is available to it;
- remaining at the Commission's disposal to answer promptly to any request that may contribute to the establishment of the facts;
- making current (and, if possible, former) employees and directors available for interviews with the Commission;
- not destroying, falsifying or concealing relevant information or evidence relating to the alleged cartel; and
- not disclosing the fact or any of the content of its application before the Commission has issued a statement of objections in the case, unless otherwise agreed;

(b) The undertaking ended its involvement in the alleged cartel immediately following its application, except for what would, in the Commission's view, be reasonably necessary to preserve the integrity of the inspections;

(c) When contemplating making its application to the Commission, the undertaking must not have destroyed, falsified or concealed evidence of the alleged cartel nor disclosed the fact or any of the content of its contemplated application, except to other competition authorities.

(13) An undertaking which took steps to coerce other undertakings to join the cartel or to remain in it is not eligible for immunity from fines. It may still qualify for a reduction of fines if it fulfils the relevant requirements and meets all the conditions therefor.

The applicant for immunity is required to make a corporate statement containing the matters set out in paragraph 9. To receive full immunity, an applicant must provide information and evidence which enables the Commission to carry out a targeted inspection or to find an Article 101 infringement. 'Targeted' inspection means that the Commission can carry out a more focused Article 20 inspection with precise 'insider' information 'as to, for instance, what to look for and where in terms of evidence'.[684] The problem for undertakings contemplating immunity applications is that, at the time of the submission, the Commission must not *already* have sufficient evidence to carry out the inspection or find an infringement, and the undertaking concerned must be the first participant to provide this material. The threshold for evidence required under paragraph 8(a) is lower than under paragraph 8(b) (contemporaneous and incriminating—a high standard) in order to encourage undertakings to come forward early.

Paragraph 12 sets out what is required of the applicant in terms of *ongoing* participation in the Commission's investigation: namely, full, continuous, and expeditious cooperation with the Commission. In addition, the undertaking must end its involvement in the cartel. In *Deltafina*, the defendant applied for immunity but subsequently informed its fellow cartelists that it had confessed to the Commission, before the Commission had mounted inspections at their premises. The CJ upheld the Commission's decision to withdraw the conditional immunity insofar as Deltafina had failed to cooperate continuously and expeditiously, as such cooperation included refraining from taking steps which could undermine the Commission's ability to investigate and/or find the infringement.[685]

The third indent of paragraph 12 (making employees and directors available for interview) refers to Article 19 of Regulation 1/2003.[686] The Commission recognises that these individuals may not be keen to talk in the light of the criminal proceedings for cartel participation in some Member States.[687] It considers, however, that the provisions in Article 12 on the exchange of information within the ECN[688] provide a sufficient safeguard.[689] The information the undertaking must provide in its corporate statement—the confession which the leniency applicant has to make to the Commission—has to include, where necessary and as far as the applicant knows them, the home addresses of implicated individuals. This reflects the powers of the Commission under Article 21 of Regulation 1/2003 to carry out inspections at private premises.

It is possible to make a formal application in 'hypothetical terms'.[690] The purpose is 'to allow companies to ascertain whether the evidence in their possession would meet the immunity threshold

[684] MEMO/06/469, 7 December 2006. The quality of the applicant's submission is judged *ex ante*, and not in the light of what happens at the inspection.

[685] COMP/38.281, *Italian Raw Tobacco*, para. 432; upheld in Case C-578/11 P, *Deltafina* EU:C:2014:1742.

[686] See Section 6.C. [687] See Section 11. [688] See the discussion of Art. 12, in Section 8.

[689] MEMO/06/469. [690] 2006 Notice, para. 16(b).

before disclosing their identity or the infringement'.[691] It does so, in principle, by providing copies of the actual evidence available to it, albeit in anonymised form.[692]

In addition, the 2006 Notice introduced a 'marker' system, whereby an undertaking may reserve its place in the queue for immunity (but not for fine reduction) by making an application which gives limited information. The objective of the marker process is to enable the Commission 'to ascertain whether it already has a previous immunity application for the same cartel and ensure that the company is seriously engaged to provide the evidence',[693] and so certain minimum information specified in the Notice must be provided. If the marker is granted, the applicant is then given a period of time, set at the Commission's discretion,[694] to 'perfect' the application by providing the additional evidence required.

Commission Notice on Immunity from Fines and Reduction of Fines in Cartel Cases [2006] OJ C298/17

(15) The Commission services may grant a marker protecting an immunity applicant's place in the queue for a period to be specified on a case-by-case basis in order to allow for the gathering of the necessary information and evidence. To be eligible to secure a marker, the applicant must provide the Commission with information concerning its name and address, the parties to the alleged cartel, the affected products(s) and territory(-ies), the estimated duration of the alleged cartel and the nature of the cartel conduct. The applicant should also inform the Commission on other past or possible future leniency applications to other authorities in relation to the alleged cartel and justify its request for a marker. Where a marker is granted, the Commission services determine the period within which the applicant has to perfect the marker by submitting the information and evidence required to meet the relevant threshold for immunity. Undertakings which have been granted a marker cannot perfect it by making a formal application in hypothetical terms. If the applicant perfects the marker within the period set by the Commission services, the information and evidence provided will be deemed to have been submitted on the date when the marker was granted.

The 2006 Notice makes clear that applying for a marker and making a formal application in hypothetical terms are distinct options for applicants.

c. *Reductions in the Fine*

Undertakings which do not meet the criteria for immunity can get a reduction of the fine. How great a reduction depends on their position in the queue: the first gets 30–50 per cent, the second 20–30 per cent, and subsequent applicants up to 20 per cent. This reflects the underlying aim of the Notice 'to encourage undertakings to cooperate as quickly and effectively as possible with the Commission in its investigative work'.[695] To receive a reduction, applicants are required to produce information of 'significant added value',[696] and to comply with the same cooperation stipulations set out in paragraph 12. The further down the queue an undertaking is, the more difficult it is to produce information of 'significant added value'. There is no 'marker' system in respect of reductions.

[691] MEMO/06/469. [692] Ibid. [693] Ibid.

[694] Ibid., the length of time provided 'will need to be decided based on the circumstances of each case'.

[695] Case C-563/19 P, *Recylex* EU:C:2021:428, para. 59.

[696] For what amounts to 'significant added value', and disagreement between the GC and Commission on this matter, see e.g. Case T-186/06, *Solvay* EU:T:2011:276, upheld Case C-455/11 P, *Solvay SA* EU:C:2013:796; Case T-154/09, *Manuli Rubber Industries* EU:T:2013:260; Case T-406/09, *Donau Chemie* EU:T:2014:254.

Commission Notice on Immunity from Fines and Reduction of Fines in Cartel Cases [2006] OJ C298/17

III. Reduction of a Fine

A. Requirements to qualify for reduction of a fine

(23) Undertakings disclosing their participation in an alleged cartel affecting the Community that do not meet the conditions under section II above may be eligible to benefit from a reduction of any fine that would otherwise have been imposed.

(24) In order to qualify, an undertaking must provide the Commission with evidence of the alleged infringement which represents significant added value with respect to the evidence already in the Commission's possession and must meet the cumulative conditions set out in points 12(a) to 12(c) above.

(25) The concept of 'added value' refers to the extent to which the evidence provided strengthens, by its very nature and/or its level of detail, the Commission's ability to prove the alleged cartel. In this assessment, the Commission will generally consider written evidence originating from the period of time to which the facts pertain to have a greater value than evidence subsequently established. Incriminating evidence directly relevant to the facts in question will generally be considered to have a greater value than that with only indirect relevance. Similarly, the degree of corroboration from other sources required for the evidence submitted to be relied upon against undertakings involved in the case will have an impact on the value of that evidence, so that compelling evidence will be attributed a greater value than evidence such as statements which require corroboration if contested.

(26) The Commission will determine in any final decision adopted at the end of the administrative procedure the level of reduction an undertaking will benefit from, relative to the fine which would otherwise be imposed. For the:

— first undertaking to provide significant added value: a reduction of 30–50%,

— second undertaking to provide significant added value: a reduction of 20–30%,

— subsequent undertakings that provide significant added value: a reduction of up to 20%.

In order to determine the level of reduction within each of these bands, the Commission will take into account the time at which the evidence fulfilling the condition in point (24) was submitted and the extent to which it represents added value.

d. Corporate Statements and Civil Litigation

As the Commission points out in the Notice,[697] nothing in the leniency programme can protect an undertaking in a damages action brought by injured third parties. This is an important consideration, as claimants can rely on Commission decisions before national courts.[698] It is possible that an increase in private damages actions in national courts may serve as a disincentive to undertakings to take advantage of the leniency programme. Such damages actions have been facilitated by the Damages Directive,[699] but, as explained in respect of access to the file,[700] the Commission does not want private litigation to discourage leniency applicants. Provisions in the Damages Directive,[701] and in the

[697] 2006 Notice, para. 31. [698] See discussion in Chap 14.

[699] See Chap 14. [700] Section 6.D.v.

[701] Dir. 2014/104/EU on certain rules governing actions for damages under national law for infringements of the competition law provisions of the Member States and of the European Union [2014] OJ L349/1, Art. 6(6).

amended Regulation 773/2004, the amended Notice on access to the file, and the amended Leniency Notice itself, protect leniency corporate statements from being used in national proceedings.

In order to protect statements from possible discovery actions, the Commission has for some time allowed leniency applicants to make oral corporate statements,[702] of which only the Commission retains a transcript. This procedure was formalised in the 2006 Notice. The leniency applicant may make oral corporate statements at the Commission's premises which the Commission will record and transcribe, and which the applicant then listens to and checks.[703] The rationale is that if the transcript is part of the Commission's file, and access is limited to addressees of an SO in the same case under strict conditions,[704] and the applicant does not retain a copy, third parties cannot use discovery procedures to obtain it.

In *AKZO Nobel*, however, the GC approved the Commission policy of publishing less heavily redacted versions of its cartel decisions.[705] This increases the amount of useful information (much of it derived from leniency statements) that damages claimants can derive from the published decision and may decrease the attractiveness of leniency for undertakings.[706]

e. *The Future of the Leniency Programme: Prospects and Alternatives?*

Although the leniency programme remains, at least in principle, the cornerstone of anti-cartel enforcement,[707] it faces several challenges. On the one hand, there is increasing awareness that overreliance on leniency as the predominant means of cartel detection may lead to under-enforcement, particularly against active cartels.[708] On the other hand, it has been argued that the Commission's single-minded efforts to enhance private enforcement have precipitated a significant fall in the number of leniency applications made to both the Commission and NCAs.[709] The measures to harmonise leniency programmes across the Member States contained within the ECN+ Directive suggest that policy-makers at EU level remain persuaded of the benefits of a robust and comprehensive EU-wide framework for leniency in cartel cases.[710] As discussed in Section 8.C.iii, however, the Directive does not overcome the basic problem of the absence of a 'one-stop-shop' for leniency applications across the EU. Yet, going forward, the current dominant role afforded to leniency programmes is likely to be supplemented by additional detection mechanisms, including proactive screening of markets

[702] In Cases T-236/01 etc., *Tokai Carbon* EU:T:2004:118 and Case T-15/02, *BASF* EU:T:2006:74, the GC confirmed that statements could be made to the Commission orally.

[703] 2006 Notice, para. 32. The Commission published new guidance 'Delivering Oral Statements at DG Competition' in October 2013, <http://ec.europa.eu/competition/cartels/leniency/oral_statements_procedure_en.pdf>. Only the description of the alleged cartel can be provided orally; other information such as product and market description, general market information, and publicly available information must be submitted in writing.

[704] Because of the rights of the defence: see Commission Notice on the rules for access to the Commission file [2005] OJ C325/7, see Section 6.D.v.

[705] Case T-345/12, *Akzo Nobel* EU:T:2015:50; see A. Kafetzopoulos, 'European Commission Policy on Publication of Cartel Decisions: The Latest Victory of Damage Claimants Against Leniency Applicants' [2015] *ECLR* 295.

[706] See C. Swaak and R. Wessling, 'Reconsidering the Leniency Option: If Not First In, Good Reasons to Stay Out' [2015] *ECLR* 346, who argue that the degree of exposure makes it less attractive in particular for undertakings who will merely qualify for a reduction, which may be small.

[707] A fairly positive assessment is W. Wils, 'The Use of Leniency in EU Cartel Enforcement: An Assessment after Twenty Years' (2016) 39 *World Competition* 327.

[708] See e.g. A. Stephan and A. Nikpay, 'Leniency Decision-Making from a Corporate Perspective: Complex Realities' in C. Beaton-Wells and C. Tran (eds.), *Anti-Cartel Enforcement in a Contemporary Age: The Leniency Religion* (Hart Publishing, 2015); also, suggesting that recidivist firms 'learn to play the leniency game' to their own advantage, see C. Marvao, 'The EU Leniency Programme and Recidivism' (2016) 48 *Rev of Industrial Organization* 1.

[709] J. Ysewyn and S. Kahmann, 'The Decline and Fall of the Leniency Programme in Europe' [2018] 1 *Concurrences* 44–59.

[710] See Section 8.C.

through use of economic tools,[711] and greater efforts to encourage individual whistle-blowers to come forward with evidence of a cartel within their organisation.[712]

I. SECTOR INQUIRIES

As explained in Chapter 9,[713] Article 17 of Regulation 1/2003 empowers the Commission to conduct general inquiries into a sector of the economy. To this end the Commission has the powers to require information and carry out inspections contained in Articles 18, 19, and 20 (but not 21),[714] and to request the NCAs to carry out investigations under Article 22. It may impose fines and penalties under Articles 23 and 24 (for example, to sanction the provision of incorrect information).

7. PROCEEDINGS BEFORE THE COURT OF JUSTICE OF THE EUROPEAN UNION

A. JUDICIAL REVIEW

(i) General

Commission competition decisions can be challenged in an action for annulment under Article 263 TFEU.[715] Since 1989, annulment actions are heard first by the GC, with appeal on points of law to the CJ. Although these actions are colloquially called 'appeals', they are in fact reviews of legality, i.e. judicial review proceedings. They do not entail a rehearing. The question of the intensity of the review in which the GC engages when reviewing Commission competition decisions is a central issue. Under Article 261 TFEU,[716] the CJEU has 'unlimited jurisdiction' in respect of fines and penalties imposed in competition cases.

The review process before the GC is often protracted.[717] In cartel cases, there may be numerous parties who appeal to the GC, all claiming slightly different defects in the details of the Commission's procedure. There may then be an appeal to the CJ. By the end, the argument may be about events which occurred decades earlier.[718]

[711] See e.g. J. Harrington, 'Behavioral Screening and the Detection of Cartels' in C. Ehlermann and I. Anatasiu (eds.), *European Competition Law Annual 2006* (Hart Publishing, 2007); C. Lorenz, 'Screening Markets for Cartel Detection: Collusive Markers in the CFD Cartel-audit' (2008) 26 *European J of Law and Economics* 213; and U. Laitenberger and K. Hüschelrath, 'The Adoption of Screening Tools by Competition Authorities' (2011) 2 *CPI Antitrust Chronicle* September.

[712] The Commission in March 2017 adopted an anonymous whistle-blowing tool, utilising an encrypted messaging system that enables two-way communications between the Commission and would-be whistle-blowers: Commission Press Release, 'Antitrust: Commission introduces new anonymous whistleblower tool', 16 March 2017. In 2019, the EU adopted a Directive to provide additional protections to whistle-blowers who disclose breaches of EU law, including the competition rules: see Dir. (EU) 2019/1937 of the European Parliament and of the Council of 23 October 2019 on the protection of persons who report breaches of Union law [2019] OJ L305/17.

[713] Chap 9, Section 4.C.

[714] The first dawn raids under Art. 20 in a sector inquiry were conducted when the pharmaceutical sector inquiry was launched, IP/08/49, 16 January 2008.

[715] Ex Art. 230 EC. [716] Ex Art. 229 EC.

[717] The expedited procedure for cases of urgency (currently Rules of Procedure of the General Court [2015] OJ L105/45, Arts. 151–155) is usually inapplicable to this kind of appeal.

[718] The limitation period laid down in Reg. 1/2003, Art. 25, runs only from the day the infringement ceases. In *Cement Cartel*, for example, the Commission commenced its investigations in 1989, and adopted the decision in 1994, [1994] OJ L343/1. It found infringements going back to January 1983. The GC judgment was delivered in 2000 (Cases T-25/95 etc., *Cimenteries* EU:T:2000:77) and the CJ judgment in January 2004 (Cases C-204/00 P etc., *Aalborg Portland* EU:C:2004:6).

(ii) Article 263 TFEU

Article 263 states:

> The Court of Justice of the European Union shall review the legality of legislative acts, of acts of the Council, of the Commission and of the European Central Bank, other than recommendations and opinions, and of acts of the European Parliament and of the European Council intended to produce legal effects vis-à-vis third parties. It shall also review the legality of acts of bodies, offices or agencies of the Union intended to produce legal effects vis-à-vis third parties.
>
> It shall for this purpose have jurisdiction in actions brought by a Member State, the European Parliament, the Council or the Commission on grounds of lack of competence, infringement of an essential procedural requirement, infringement of the Treaties or of any rule of law relating to their application, or misuse of powers.
>
> . . .
>
> Any natural or legal person may, under the conditions laid down in the first and second paragraphs, institute proceedings against an act addressed to that person or which is of direct and individual concern to them, and against a regulatory act which is of direct concern to them and does not entail implementing measures.
>
> . . .

The principal issues which arise in competition cases are:

- Does the natural or legal person wishing to make the challenge have standing to do so?
- Is there a challengeable act?
- Are there grounds for annulling the act?

There is a time limit of two months from publication or notification for bringing an action, which is strictly applied.[719]

(iii) *Locus Standi*—Who Can Bring an Action?

Under Article 263(4), natural and legal persons have limited standing, meaning that they are able only to challenge a decision actually addressed to them, an act which is of direct and individual concern to them, or a regulatory act of direct concern to them which does not entail implementing measures.[720]

The test formulated for 'individual concern' is restrictive, and generally makes it difficult for individuals to gain standing.[721] It has, however, been more generously applied in competition cases. The CJ first allowed standing to a non-addressee of a decision in *Metro I*,[722] in respect of a party who had complained under Article 3(2)(b) of Regulation 17.[723] In *Metro II*,[724] it widened the 'complainant' category to cover a party who had not *formally* complained, but who had taken part in the Commission's proceedings and had been recognised by the Commission as having a 'legitimate interest'. The applicant in both *Metro* cases was a retailer who was excluded by the provisions of an exempted selective

[719] Art. 263(6).

[720] Art. 263(4) appears not to have changed the situation under the corresponding provision in the EC Treaty, Art. 230(4) whereby a person could only challenge a decision which was of 'direct and individual concern' to it although in the form of a regulation or a decision addressed to *another* person. Legislation is not a 'regulatory act' within Art. 263(4): Case C-583/11 P, *Inuit Tapiiritt Kanatami* EU:C:2013:625.

[721] It is whether the decision 'affects them by reason of certain attributes which are peculiar to them or by reason of circumstances in which they are differentiated from all other persons and by virtue of these factors distinguishes them individually just as in the case of the person addressed', Case 25/62, *Plaumann* EU:C:1963:17.

[722] Case 26/76, *Metro I* EU:C:1977:167.

[723] Now Reg. 1/2003, Art. 7(2).

[724] Case 75/84, *Metro II* EU:C:1986:399.

distribution system from distributing the supplier's products. In *Métropole*,[725] Antena 3 was refused membership of the European Broadcasting Union (EBU) before the Commission adopted a decision exempting the EBU's rules. Antena 3 brought an annulment action. It had not submitted observations.[726] The GC held that taking part in the administrative proceedings was not a prerequisite for standing under Article 263(4), and that its application to join the EBU distinguished Antena 3 as if it were an addressee of the decision.

On the other hand, in *Kruidvat*[727] the Commission denied standing to a retailer who wished to challenge the Article 101(3) exemption of Givenchy's selective distribution network. It had taken no part in the Commission proceedings, had not complained to the Commission, had not applied to become a member of Givenchy's network, and did not wish to be one. It was simply a competitor of Givenchy's authorised distributors. The GC agreed with the Commission's view that to grant Kruidvat standing would be to 'allow a practically limitless number of actions from unforeseeable sources to be brought', and said that individual concern could not be established on the basis that the legality of the decision might affect indirectly related national proceedings. Although there are no individual exemption decisions under Regulation 1/2003, it is possible that a third party might wish to challenge a 'finding of inapplicability' decision under Article 10, if and when one is adopted.[728]

In *Alrosa*, a non-addressee was allowed to challenge an Article 9 commitments decision.[729] Alrosa was directly and individually concerned by the decision: it was adopted at the conclusion of proceedings in which Alrosa had participated; it expressly referred to Alrosa; it was aimed at ending the long-standing trading relationship between Alrosa and the addressee; it was liable to have an appreciable effect on Alrosa's competitive position; and it produced direct and immediate effects on Alrosa's legal situation.

As far as representative bodies are concerned, the GC granted *locus standi* to the International Confederation of Societies of Authors and Composers in *CISAC*. The body was not an addressee of the decision, but had been an addressee of the SO, and the GC accepted that the decision was of direct and individual concern to it.[730]

(iv) Which Acts Can be Challenged?

In addition to formal decisions, other 'acts' taken by the Commission in the course of its procedures can be challenged. The basic principle, laid down in *ERTA*,[731] is that Article 263 covers 'all measures adopted by the institutions which are intended to have legal force'. This was applied in *IBM*[732] where an undertaking wished to challenge the SO. The CJ said:

> 9. Any measure the legal effects of which are binding on, and capable of affecting the interests of, the applicant by bringing about a distinct change in his legal position is an act or decision which may be the object of an action under Article [263] for a declaration that it is void.

[725] Cases T-528, 542, 543, and 546/93, *Métropole Télévision* EU:T:1996:99.
[726] Following the publication of the Reg. 17, Art. 19(3) notice.
[727] Case T-87/92, *BVBA Kruidvat* EU:T:1996:191.
[728] See Section 6.E.v.
[729] Case T-170/06, *Alrosa* EU:T:2007:220, paras. 39–41; the judgment was set aside on appeal, Case C-441/07 P, *Alrosa* EU:C:2010:377, but the CJ did not deny Alrosa's right to standing (para. 90). For discussion, see Section 6.E.iii.
[730] Case T-442/08, *CISAC* EU:T:2013:188.
[731] Case 22/70, *Commission v Council, Re ERTA* EU:C:1971:32.
[732] Case 60/81, *IBM* EU:C:1981:264.

The test is: does the act change the applicant's legal position? The SO does not do so; it is merely a preparatory act and any irregularity can be addressed in a challenge to the act which concludes the proceedings. Although decisions authorising Article 20 inspections can be challenged, the *conduct* of an inspection may only be challenged in proceedings against any ensuing infringement decision, since the conduct amounts only to 'implementing measures'.[733]

Decisions imposing interim measures can be challenged.[734] Where complaints are concerned, 'Article 7' letters cannot be challenged but the final rejection of the complaint can be, even if it is only in the form of a letter.

(v) The Grounds of Review

a. General

Article 263 provides four grounds of challenge, although they overlap and are in a sense all really encompassed in the third one, namely, infringement of the Treaties or of any rule of law relating to their application. Applicants often frame their cases in general terms. Most of the grounds can be considered only if they are raised by the applicant.[735] Infringement of an essential procedural requirement is, however, a matter of public policy that must be raised by the Court of its own motion if it is not raised by the applicant,[736] and so is lack of competence.[737] The fourth ground, misuse of powers, has never succeeded in a competition case.[738]

b. Lack of Competence

Lack of competence covers: a lack of competence of the Union to act at all, on the basis that no Treaty provision empowers it to do so; a lack of competence of the institutions to act under a particular empowering provision (incorrect legal basis); and a lack of competence of the particular institution or official to take the challenged act.

In the competition field, the best example of the first situation is challenges made to the extraterritorial application of the competition rules. Undertakings outside the Union have argued that the EU rules could not be applied to them because they were outside the jurisdiction. These challenges have not hitherto succeeded.[739]

The second situation is exemplified in the challenges brought by Member States to directives adopted by the Commission on the basis of Article 106(3), discussed in Chapter 8.[740] In *British Airways*,[741] the GC dismissed the undertaking's claim that the Commission had no competence to apply Regulation 17 to practices in the market for air travel agency services as it should have used

[733] See Case T-135/09, *Nexans France* EU:T:2012:596. A challenge may be made to a fining decision under Art. 23(1) in respect of the undertaking's non-cooperation with the allegedly improper conduct of the inspection.

[734] As in respect of the *IMS* decision, Case T-184/01 R, *IMS Health* EU:T:2001:200 (President of the GC), confirmed Case C-481/01 P (R), *NDC Health* EU:C:2002:223 (President of the CJ).

[735] Case C-272/09 P, *KME* EU:C:2011:810.

[736] Case C-272/09 P, *KME Germany* EU:C:2011:810, para. 101. Cf. Case C-122/16, *British Airways* EU:C:2017:861, one of the appeals in the *Airfreight* cartel, in which the CJ upheld the decision of the GC (in Case T-48/11, EU:T:2015:988) to annul the decision against British Airways only in part despite the existence of an essential procedural defect, on the basis that the defendant's own application at first instance had sought only partial annulment in the circumstances.

[737] Cases T-79/89 etc., EU:T:1992:26 , para. 31.

[738] Although it has been pleaded: see e.g. Case 5/85, *AKZO Chemie* EU:C:1986:328; Case T-5/93, *Roger Tremblay* EU:T:1995:12.

[739] See Chap. 17. [740] Chap 8, Section 8.C. [741] Case T-219/99, *British Airways* EU:T:2003:343.

Regulation 3975/87 on the air transport sector.[742] A number of cases additionally arose from the expiry of the ECSC Treaty in 2002.[743]

The third situation has arisen in competition cases where parties have alleged that the power to take decisions was unlawfully delegated. The delegation to the Commissioner responsible for competition of the power to take decisions ordering 'dawn raid' inspections was unsuccessfully challenged in *AKZO*,[744] and the delegation of the signing of documents such as SOs has similarly been upheld.[745] A challenge to the adoption of a final decision finding an infringement by a single Commissioner was nonetheless successful in the first *PVC Cartel* case, where an appeal premised both on grounds of competence and infringement of an essential procedural requirement grounds succeeded spectacularly.[746] The appointment of the monitoring trustee in the *Microsoft* decision was annulled because the Commission lacked authority to impose such measures.[747] British Airways claimed that the Commission lacked competence to adopt the *Virgin/BA* decision in July 1999[748] as, all the members of the Commission having resigned en bloc in March 1999, they had authority only to deal with current business pending their replacement in September. The GC held that the Commissioners could exercise their normal powers until their resignations took effect on the date of their actual replacement.[749]

c. *Infringement of an Essential Procedural Requirement*

Infringement of an essential procedural requirement covers situations where a measure has been passed without complying with the legislative process laid down by the Treaties,[750] or with the rules of procedure of the relevant institution,[751] or with a general principle of law concerned with procedure,[752] or where the measure does not contain an adequate statement of reasons.

The GC annuls acts only for breach of an *essential* procedural requirement, and what amounts to such is a matter for the Court. A requirement is essential if the failure to observe it might have affected the final outcome of the act. On this basis, the wrongful revelation of confidential material to the complainant in *AKZO*[753] was not a ground for annulling the Commission decision. In *Riva Fire*,[754] the failure of the Commission to reissue an SO when readopting, under Regulation 1/2003, a decision initially taken under the now-expired ECSC Treaty, did not constitute breach of an essential procedural requirement, insofar as annulment of the earlier decision did not affect the validity of the measures preparatory to it. Yet the readopted decision was annulled nonetheless, as the Commission had failed to conduct the oral hearing of June 2002 in the presence of representatives of the Member

[742] [1987] OJ L374/1.

[743] The *Reinforcing Bars Cartel* decision, COMP/37.956, was annulled since the Commission had adopted it under Art. 65(1) ECSC post the expiry, Cases T-27/03 etc., *SP* EU:T:2007:317. See Chap 2. See also Case T-405/06, *Arcelor Mittal* EU:T:2009:90, *aff'd* Case C-201/09 P, *Arcelor Mittal* EU:C:2011:190. However, the GC upheld the readopted *Alloy Surcharge* decision of 20 December 2006 in which the Commission used Reg. 1/2003 in respect of an infringement of Art. 65(1): Case T-24/07, *ThyssenKrupp* EU:T:2009:236, *aff'd* Case C-352/09 P, *ThyssenKrupp* EU:C:2011:191.

[744] Case 5/85, *AKZO* EU:C:1986:328.

[745] See Case 48/69, *ICI v Commission (Dyestuffs)* EU:C:1972:70.

[746] Cases T-79/89 etc., *BASF* EU:T:1992:26, on appeal Case C-137/92 P, *Commission v BASF* EU:C:1994:247: see Section 8.A.

[747] Case T-201/04, *Microsoft* EU:T:2007:289. [748] [2000] OJ L30/1.

[749] Case T-219/99, *British Airways* EU:T:2003:343, paras. 55–57.

[750] As where Parliament is not consulted: Case 138/79, *Roquette Frères* EU:C:1980:249.

[751] Case 68/86, *UK v Council* EU:C:1988:85; note the application of this in the *PVC Cartel* case: Case C-137/92 P, *Commission v BASF* EU:C:1994:247.

[752] Such as the *audi alteram partem* rule giving parties a right to a hearing: Case 17/74, *Transocean Marine Paint* EU:C:1974:106.

[753] Case 53/85, *AKZO* EU:C:1986:256. [754] Case C-89/15 P, *Riva Fire* EU:C:2017:713.

States, a duty not contained in the ECSC Treaty yet treated as an essential procedural requirement under Regulation 1/2003.[755]

An adequate statement of reasons is an essential procedural requirement. The statement of reasons 'must be appropriate to the measure at issue and must disclose clearly and unequivocally the reasoning followed by the institution which adopted that measure in such a way as to enable the persons concerned to ascertain the reasons for it and to enable the competent court to review its legality'.[756] The adequacy of a statement of reasons depends 'on all the circumstances of each case, in particular, the content of the measure in question, the nature of the reasons given and the interest which the addressees of the measure, or other parties to whom it is of direct and individual concern, may have in obtaining explanations'.[757] In competition cases, where the Commission has a wide margin of appreciation and power of appraisal, the reasoning is of fundamental importance because, in reviewing the decision, the Court must be able to establish whether the factual and legal matters upon which the exercise of the power of appraisal depended were present and whether the Commission has dealt properly with the parties' arguments.[758] The GC annulled the *Air Freight* cartel decision[759] because the decision was vitiated by contradictions between the statement of reasons (grounds) and the operative part and within the grounds themselves.[760]

Challenges to competition decisions frequently plead procedural defects as grounds for annulment. The GC annulled the *Soda-ash* decisions,[761] for example, on grounds that insufficient access to the Commission's file prejudiced the parties' right to be heard. A significant part of the *TACA* decision was similarly annulled,[762] because the Commission had relied on an interpretation of several inculpatory documents upon which the undertakings had been given no opportunity to comment.[763]

Arguably, the most notorious example of annulment on procedural grounds (and of lack of competence) is the *PVC I* case. There the GC found differences (going beyond corrections of grammar and syntax) in both the statement of reasons and the operative part of the decision, between the version adopted by the College of Commissioners at its relevant meeting and the version notified to the undertakings concerned. The Commission was unable to produce an authenticated version of the decision as adopted by the College. A draft in only three languages was available at the meeting, and the Competition Commissioner was authorised to adopt the measure in the other official Union languages, including those of undertakings to which the decision was addressed. Further, the Competition Commissioner whose signature appeared on the decision notified to all the addressees had left office some days before the notified version was finalised. The GC considered these procedural defects, including the breach of the principle of collegiate responsibility, so serious that it did not merely annul the decision, it declared it *non-existent*.[764] On appeal, the CJ held that the flaws were not so fundamental as to render the act non-existent, but nonetheless annulled it.[765]

[755] Ibid., para. 47. The requirement to hold an oral hearing to which the competition authorities of the Member States are invited is contained in Art. 14(3) of Reg. 1/2003.

[756] Case C-247/14 P, *HeidelbergCement* EU:C:2016:149, para. 16.

[757] Ibid.

[758] In the *Net Book Agreement* case, the CJ annulled a decision because the Commission had not adequately dealt with the evidence one party put forward about the benefits of RPM accepted by the UK courts, Case C-360/92 P, *Publishers' Association* EU:C:1995:6 setting aside the GC judgment, Case T-66/89, *Publishers' Association* EU:T:1992:84.

[759] COMP/39.258, 9 November 2010.

[760] Cases T-9/11 etc., *Air Canada* EU:T:2015:994. The confusion concerned whether the Commission was finding a single continuous infringement or four separate single and continuous infringements.

[761] Cases T-30/91 etc., *Solvay SA (No. 2)* EU:T:1995:115; the readopted decisions were also annulled for lack of access to the file, Case C-109/10 P, *Solvay* EU:C:2011:686.

[762] [1999] OJ L95/1.

[763] Cases T-191 and 212–214/98, *Atlantic Container Line* EU:T:2003:245.

[764] Cases T-79/89 etc., *BASF* EU:T:1992:26.

[765] Case C-137/92 P, *Commission v BASF* EU:C:1994:247.

d. Infringement of the Treaties or Any Rule of Law Relating to Their Application

This ground is wide enough to cover the other three grounds as well. 'The Treaties' means the TEU and TFEU together with the Protocols, Acts of Accession, the Charter of Fundamental Rights, and any future amending Treaties. 'Any rule of law relating to their application' covers all the other binding provisions of the Union legal order, including the general principles of law and human rights developed in the Court's jurisprudence (many of which are now embedded in the Charter) and provisions of international law, particularly principles of customary international law and agreements the EU itself has concluded. It also covers the duty of the Commission to follow any Notices or other measure to which it has committed itself, such as the Fining Guidelines and the Leniency Notice. Review under Article 263 entails ensuring that the Commission has properly interpreted the law.

The GC will annul a decision where the Commission has committed an error of law or failed to abide by general principles such as proportionality, equality, non-discrimination, legitimate expectation, the presumption of innocence, or legal certainty.[766] This ground also covers the Court finding that the evidence invoked or the facts established by the Commission do not support its findings. An example of the latter arose in *Servier*, where the Commission had found violations of Articles 101 and 102 arising from a complex mesh of practices designed to protect Servier's market position for blood pressure medication. Without commenting on the theory of harm, the GC annulled the finding of breach of Article 102, on the basis that, having incorrectly defined the relevant market, the Commission had failed in its first fundamental task of establishing dominance.[767] In such circumstances, the GC must look at the facts[768] (as it did in impressive detail in *Servier*), not to rehear the case, but rather to see whether the factual basis of the Commission decision was correct or sufficient and that the burden of proof was discharged. It annuls decisions where it finds that the Commission drew the wrong conclusions from the facts. The CJ said in *Kone* that the fact that the Court's analysis in an action for annulment had neither the object nor effect of replacing a full investigation in the context of an administrative procedure was inherent in the notion of a review of legality.[769]

(vi) Appeals Against Penalties: Article 261 TFEU

The Commission has a wide discretion in setting fines under Articles 23 and 24 of Regulation 1/2003.[770] It also has a discretion in respect of many matters in the Leniency Notice,[771] such as whether the conditions of paragraph 8 are met, whether information provided represents 'significant added value', or whether an undertaking coerced others. Article 31 of Regulation 1/2003 gives the Court 'unlimited jurisdiction to review decisions whereby the Commission has fixed a fine or periodic penalty payment'. This is pursuant to Article 261 TFEU,[772] which provides that regulations may give the Court unlimited jurisdiction with regard to penalties provided for in such regulations. The action under Article 261 cannot be used to circumvent the time limits laid down in Article 263 as it not an autonomous remedy, but is instead part of the Court's Article 263 jurisdiction.[773]

766 Legal certainty was cited in the *PVC I* judgments (Cases T-79/89 etc., *BASF* EU:T:1992:26, on appeal Case C-137/92 P, *Commission v BASF* EU:C:1994:247) as being infringed when the Commission did not follow its own rules of procedure and could not produce the authenticated decision.

767 Case T-691/14, *Servier* EU:T:2018:922, pending appeal in Case C-176/19 P.

768 It can play an active role by ordering measures of inquiry such as experts' reports. GC Rules of Procedure, 2015, Arts. 91–100.

769 Case C-510/11 P, *Kone Oyj* EU:C:2013:696, para. 26. 770 See Sections 6.H.ii–6.H.iv.

771 See Section 6.H.v. 772 Ex Art. 229 EC.

773 Case T-252/03, *Fédération nationale de l'industrie et des commerces en gros des viandes (FNICGV) v Commission* EU:T:2004:326.

The distinction between the Court's powers under Articles 261 and 263 is that, under the former, the Court has *full jurisdiction*. It may change the Commission's decision, by cancelling, increasing, or reducing the fine (but not imposing one where the Commission did not). Although the EU Courts are not bound by the Fining Guidelines,[774] they may derive guidance from them when exercising the unlimited jurisdiction.[775] This is particularly relevant when the Courts are dealing with a fine imposed on one of several cartel participants, as exercise of this jurisdiction must not result in discrimination between the participants.[776] Under Article 263, however, the Court is limited to reviewing the legality of the decision and annulling all or part of it on the grounds laid down in the Article but cannot substitute its own judgment for that of the Commission. In *Galp*, the CJ emphasised that 'unlimited jurisdiction' in Article 261 relates only to penalties.[777] As with Article 263 itself, appeals against penalties go to the GC, with an appeal to the CJ. Where the CJ disagrees with the GC on a point of law the CJ can exercise the unlimited jurisdiction and adjust the fine confirmed, reduced, or increased by the GC, accordingly.[778]

Conventionally, the GC was tolerant of the Commission's general approach to fining to a degree that was criticised.[779] The CJ approved the change to higher fines for the sake of deterrence in *Pioneer*[780] and did not object to the higher level of fines imposed since. The GC will reduce or quash the fine, however, when it takes a different view to the Commission of such matters as the duration of an infringement[781] or of an undertaking's level of involvement in an infringement.[782] The Guidelines create legitimate expectations and the GC examines whether the Commission exercised its discretion in accordance with the methodology set out in the Guidelines and whether any departure is supported by sufficient legal reasoning (which must be compatible with the principle of equal treatment).[783]

Many of the fiercest arguments before the GC are about immunity or reductions which the Commission has accorded under the Leniency Notice. In the *Graphite Electrodes* appeal, the GC *increased* the fine on an undertaking which, having been granted leniency for cooperation, then disputed the facts before the GC.[784] In *BASF (Choline Chloride cartel)*, the applicant's successful argument that the global and European cartel arrangements in which it was implicated could not be considered a 'single and continuous infringement' of Article 101(1) resulted in it losing the benefit of the leniency policy, with the result that its fine was increased by its victory.[785]

In an Article 263 review, the Commission cannot rely on evidence that was not in the decision.

[774] Case C-70/12 P, *Quin Barlo* EU:C:2013:351, para. 45.

[775] Case C-603/13 P, *Galp* EU:C:2016:38, para. 80.

[776] See C-441/11 P, *Verhuizingen Coppens* EU:C:2012:778, para. 80.

[777] '[T]he unlimited jurisdiction enjoyed by the General Court on the basis of Article 31 of Regulation No 1/2003 concerns solely the assessment by that Court of the fine imposed by the Commission, to the exclusion of any alteration of the constituent elements of the infringement lawfully determined by the Commission in the decision under examination by the General Court': Case C-603/13 P, *Galp* EU:C:2016:38, paras. 76–77. For commentary, see P. Martinez-Lage, '*Galp Energia España*: Limitations on the General Court's Unlimited Jurisdiction to Review Decisions Imposing Fines' (2016) 7 *JECLAP* 608.

[778] See Case C-603/13 P, *Galp* EU:C:2016:38, where the fine was reduced by the GC and then again by the CJ.

[779] See e.g. I. Forrester, 'A Bush in Need of Pruning: The Luxuriant Growth of "Light Judicial Review"' in C.-D. Ehlermann and M. Marquis (eds.), *European Competition Law Annual 2009: Evaluation of Evidence and its Judicial Review in Competition Cases* (Hart Publishing, 2011).

[780] Cases 100–103/80, *Pioneer* EU:C:1983:158.

[781] See e.g. the GC judgment in the *Cement Cartel* cases, Cases T-25/95 etc., *Cimenteries* EU:T:2000:77.

[782] Ibid.

[783] See e.g. Case C-70/12 P, *Quin Barlo* EU:C:2013:351, para. 53; Case T-116/04, *Wieland-Werke AG v Commission* EU:T:2009:140, paras. 29–33.

[784] Cases T-236/01 etc., *Tokai Carbon* EU:T:2004:118.

[785] Cases T-101 and 111/05, *BASF v Commission* EU:T:2007:380, paras. 212–213.

(vii) Burden of Proof, Standard of Proof, and Standard of Review

The burden of proof is discussed in Chapter 4, Section 3 (Article 101) and Chapter 7, Section 5 (Article 102). The EU Courts require that the Commission produces 'sufficiently precise and coherent proof' to support its case.[786] The meaning of that was explained by the GC in *Intel*.

Case T-286/09, *Intel v Commission* EU:T:2014:547

General Court

62. According to Article 2 of Regulation No 1/2003, in any proceedings for the application of Article [102], the burden of proving an infringement of that article rests on the party or the authority alleging the infringement, namely, in the present case, the Commission. Furthermore, according to well settled case-law, any doubt in the mind of the Court must operate to the advantage of the undertaking to which the decision finding an infringement was addressed. The Court cannot therefore conclude that the Commission has established the infringement at issue to the requisite legal standard if it still entertains any doubts on that point, in particular in proceedings for annulment of a decision imposing a fine (Joined Cases T-67/00, T-68/00, T-71/00 and T-78/00 *JFE Engineering and Others* v *Commission* . . . , paragraph 177, and Case T-112/07 *Hitachi and Others* v *Commission* . . . , paragraph 58).

63. In the latter situation, it is necessary to take account of the principle of the presumption of innocence resulting in particular from Article 6(2) of the European Convention for the Protection of Human Rights and Fundamental Freedoms (ECHR), signed in Rome on 4 November 1950, and from Article 47 of the Charter of Fundamental Rights of the European Union. Given the nature of the infringements in question and the nature and degree of severity of the ensuing penalties, the principle of the presumption of innocence applies in particular to the procedures relating to infringements of the competition rules applicable to undertakings that may result in the imposition of fines or periodic penalty payments (Case C-199/92 P *Hüls* v *Commission* . . . , paragraphs 149 and 150; and Case C-235/92 P *Montecatini* v *Commission* . . . , paragraphs 175 and 176; *JFE*, . . . paragraph 178).

64. Although the Commission must produce sufficiently precise and consistent evidence to support the firm conviction that the alleged infringement took place, it is important to emphasise that it is not necessary for every item of evidence produced by the Commission to satisfy those criteria in relation to every aspect of the infringement. It is sufficient if the body of evidence relied on by the institution, viewed as a whole, meets that requirement, as held by the case-law concerning the implementation of Article [101] (see, to that effect Joined Cases C-238/99 P, C-244/99 P, C-245/99 P, C-247/99 P, C-250/99 P to C-252/99 P and C-254/99 P *Limburgse Vinyl Maatschappij and Others* v *Commission*, paragraphs 513 to 523). That principle applies also in cases concerning the implementation of Article [102] (Case T-321/05 *AstraZeneca* v *Commission* . . . , paragraph 477).

The GC thus distinguished between two situations. The first is where the Commission finds an infringement on the basis that the established facts cannot be explained by anything other than anti-competitive behaviour, where the decision will be annulled if the undertakings can show another plausible explanation.[787] The second is where the Commission relies on evidence which in principle is sufficient to demonstrate existence of the infringement, when it is for the undertaking to call into question the probative values of that evidence.[788]

[786] See e.g. Cases 29 and 30/83, *CRAM and Rheinzink v Commission* EU:C:1984:130, para. 20; Cases C-89/85 etc., *A. Ahlström Oy v Commission (Wood Pulp II)* EU:C:1993:120, para. 127; Case T-201/04, *Microsoft* EU:T:2007:289, para. 564.

[787] See e.g. Cases C-89/85 etc., *Wood Pulp II* EU:C:1993:120.

[788] See e.g. Case T-286/09, *Intel* EU:T:2014:547, paras. 65–67.

Continental Can was an early case where the decision was annulled because there the Commission had failed to establish why a particular type of container constituted a relevant market. This meant that there was no basis for its finding of dominance and the application of Article 102.[789] In *Wood Pulp II*,[790] the Court appointed experts to produce a report on parallelism of prices in the wood pulp industry, whether the documents relied on by the Commission justified their conclusions on pricing, and whether there was a distinction between the documents gathered before and after the SO. A second experts' report into the structure and characteristics of the market was commissioned. These reports, particularly the finding that the market was oligopolistic, were crucial to the Court's judgment, and it (largely) annulled the infringement decision.

The GC was established principally to relieve the CJ of dealing with complex issues of fact. Thus, in many early cases, the Court conducted an assiduous examination of the factual basis of the competition decision under appeal.[791] However, it became established that the GC undertook only a limited review of what are termed matters of 'complex economic assessment' in which the Commission has a 'margin of appreciation'. The CJ stated in *Aalborg* that '[E]xamination by the [Union] judicature of the complex economic assessments made by the Commission must necessarily be confined to verifying whether the rules on procedure and on the statement of reasons have been complied with, whether the facts have been accurately stated and whether there has been any manifest error of appraisal or misuse of powers'.[792] *Microsoft*, discussed in Chapter 7, is a prime example of the GC wrestling with the inherent problems of engaging in only a limited review. The GC explained that its role where 'complex' economic *and technical* appraisals were concerned was 'necessarily limited to checking whether the relevant rules on procedure and on stating reasons have been complied with, whether the facts have been accurately stated and whether there has been any manifest error of assessment or a misuse of powers' and that the Commission's appraisals were 'in principle subject to only limited review by the Court'.[793] Yet it nevertheless examined the facts in detail:

> . . . while the [Union] Courts recognise that the Commission has a margin of appreciation in economic or technical matters, that does not mean that they must decline to review the Commission's interpretation of economic or technical data. The [Union] Courts must not only establish whether the evidence put forward is factually accurate, reliable and consistent but must also determine whether that evidence contains all the relevant data that must be taken into consideration in appraising a complex situation and whether it is capable of substantiating the conclusions drawn from it . . . [794]

There are also matters which do not necessarily involve complex economic assessments but where the Commission has a margin of discretion. These include application of the Fining Guidelines and the Leniency Notice, the decision to accept commitments,[795] and rejection of complaints.

[789] Case 6/72, *Continental Can* EU:C:1973:22.

[790] Cases C-89/85 etc., *Wood Pulp II* EU:C:1993:120; see Chap 9.

[791] Including, for instance, in *Wood Pulp II*, Cases T-68/89 etc., *Società Italiana Vetro* EU:T:1992:38, Cases T-528/93 etc., *Métropole Télévision* EU:T:1996:99, and Cases T-374–375, 384, and 388/94, *European Night Services* EU:T:1998:198.

[792] Cases C-204/00 P etc., *Aalborg Portland* EU:C:2004:6, echoing Case 42/84, *Remia v Commission* EU:C:1985:327. Reference is often made to the Commission's 'discretion' or 'margin of discretion' in this respect, but it has been cogently argued that it is a 'margin of appreciation' rather than discretion, in that discretion involves choosing the standards according to which power is exercised or a decision made while a margin of appreciation involves weighing up the evidence and assessing whether a given standard is reached, see O. Odudu, 'Article 101(3), Discretion and Direct Effect' [2002] *ECLR* 17; D. Bailey, 'Scope of Judicial Review Under Article 101 EC' (2004) 41 *CMLRev* 1327. Nevertheless the EU Courts use the terms interchangeably.

[793] Case T-201/04, *Microsoft* EU:T:2007:289, paras. 87 and 88. [794] Ibid., para. 89.

[795] See Case C-441/07 P, *Alrosa* EU:C:2010:377 (nn. 282 and 729), discussed in Section 6.E.iii, where the CJ overturned the GC for excessive interference with the Commission's discretion in respect of a commitments decision.

Limiting the role of judicial review to 'manifest errors of appraisal' in situations of complex economic (and technical) assessments and in other situations where the Commission has a 'margin of discretion' raises difficulties.[796] The pervasive problem is the Commission's multifaceted role and the extent to which enforcement procedures are compliant with Article 6(1) ECHR and Article 47 of the Charter as a result.[797] The Commission is not a tribunal within Article 6, as its decisions are those of an administrative authority.[798] Nevertheless, the GC has held itself to be an independent and impartial court, established in order to improve the judicial protection of individuals by making a close inspection of complex facts.[799] Accordingly, it has been held that the requirements of Article 6(1) are satisfied by the right of the parties to challenge Commission decisions in that Court. In the appeals against the *Copper Plumbing Tubes* cartel decisions,[800] the defendants challenged directly the compatibility of the EU enforcement system with fundamental rights. In its judgments in *KME*[801] and *Chalkor*,[802] the CJ said that the EU system of review by the GC under Article 263 and Article 261 provided effective judicial protection which satisfied Article 47. However, the CJ did not refer to a 'manifest error of appraisal'. Instead, it talked of the 'in-depth review' which the GC conducts. The *Copper Tubes* judgments were followed by similar ones in the appeals from the *Elevators and Escalators* decision,[803] *Schindler*,[804] *Otis*,[805] and *Kone*.[806] What 'in-depth review' entails is summarised in the GC's *Google Android* judgment.

Case T-604/18, *Google and Alphabet v Commission (Google Android)* EU:T:2022:541

General Court

In-depth review of all the relevant evidence

74. As regards the review of legality provided for in Article 263 TFEU, it should be noted that the scope of that review extends to all the elements of Commission decisions relating to proceedings applying Articles 101 and 102 TFEU which are subject to in-depth review by the General Court, in law and in fact, in the light of the pleas raised by the applicant and taking into account all the relevant evidence submitted by the latter (. . . *Infineon Technologies* v *Commission*, C-99/17 P, EU:C:2018:773, paragraph 48 . . .).

75. In that regard, in so far as the contested decision imposes a fine and a periodic penalty payment for an infringement of competition law, the Courts of the European Union must, inter alia, establish not only whether the evidence relied on by the Commission is factually accurate, reliable and consistent but also whether that evidence contains all the information which must be taken into account in order to

[796] Moreover, it has been pointed out that the extension of this in *Microsoft* to 'technical matters' exacerbates the matter: Forrester, n. 779.

[797] See Section 5.

[798] Cases 209–215 and 218/78, *Van Landewyck* EU:C:1980:248, para. 81; Cases 100–103/80, *Pioneer* EU:C:1983:158, para. 7; Case T-11/89, *Shell* EU:T:1992:33, para. 39.

[799] Case T-348/94, *Española* EU:T:1998:102, paras. 57–63; Cases T-25/95 etc., *Cimenteries* EU:T:2000:77, paras. 718–719.

[800] COMP/38.069, 3 September 2004.

[801] Case C-272/09 P, *KME Germany* EU:C:2011:810, and Case C-389/10 P, *KME Germany* EU:C:2011:816.

[802] Case C-386/10 P, *Chalkor* EU:C:2011:815.

[803] COMP/38.823, 2 February 2007.

[804] Case C-501/11 P, *Schindler Holdings* EU:C:2013:522.

[805] Case C-199/11 P, *Otis and Others* EU:C:2012:684.

[806] Case C-510/11 P, *Kone Oyj* EU:C:2013:696. See also the EFTA Court judgment, Case E-15/10, *Posten Norge v EFTA Surveillance Authority*, 18 April 2012. J. Temple Lang, 'Judicial Review of Competition Decisions under the European Convention on Human Rights and the Importance of the EFTA Court: The *Norway Post* Judgment' (2012) 37 *ELRev* 464, considered the Court's statements in that case to be clearer than the judgments of the CJ in the *Copper Plumbing Tubes* cases, and broader in their implications.

assess whether the circumstances constituting the infringement exist, and whether that evidence substantiates the Commission's interpretation of it in the contested decision (. . . *Chalkor* v *Commission*, C-386/10 P, EU:C:2011:815, paragraph 54 . . .).

76. Unlike, for example, a prospective analysis of the kind required for the examination of a proposed concentration, which makes it necessary to predict events which are more or less likely to occur in future if a decision prohibiting the planned concentration or laying down the conditions for it is not adopted, it is usually a matter for the Commission, when penalising an abuse of a dominant position, to examine past events, for which there is generally a variety of evidence available that makes it possible to understand the causes and to assess the effects on effective competition (. . . *Commission* v *Tetra Laval*, C-12/03 P, EU:C:2005:87, paragraph 42).

77. In such a situation, it is for the Commission to prove not only the existence of the abuse but also its duration. More particularly, the Commission must prove the infringement which it has found and adduce evidence capable of demonstrating to the requisite legal standard the existence of the circumstances constituting the infringement (. . . *Romana Tabacchi* v *Commission*, T-11/06, EU:T:2011:560, paragraph 129 and . . . *Trafilerie Meridionali* v *Commission*, T-422/10, EU:T:2015:512, paragraph 88 . . .).

78. In this respect, any doubt in the mind of the Court must operate to the advantage of the undertaking to which the decision finding the infringement was addressed. The Court cannot therefore conclude that the Commission has established the infringement at issue to the requisite legal standard if it still entertains any doubts on that point, in particular in proceedings for annulment or variation of a decision imposing a fine (. . . *Romana Tabacchi* v *Commission*, T-11/06, EU:T:2011:560, paragraph 129 and . . . *Trafilerie Meridionali* v *Commission*, T-422/10, EU:T:2015:512, paragraph 88 . . .).

79. In particular, where the Commission finds an infringement of the competition rules on the basis that the facts established cannot be explained other than by the existence of anti-competitive behaviour, the Court will find it necessary to annul the decision in question if the undertaking concerned puts forward arguments which cast the facts established by the Commission in a different light and which thus allow another plausible explanation of the facts to be substituted for the one adopted by the Commission in concluding that there has been an infringement. In such a case, the Commission cannot be regarded as having furnished proof of the existence of an infringement of competition law (. . . *Compagnie royale asturienne des mines and Rheinzink* v *Commission*, 29/83 and 30/83, EU:C:1984:130, paragraph 16, and . . . *Ahlström Osakeyhtiö and Others* v *Commission*, C-89/85 . . . EU:C:1993:120, paragraphs 126 and 127).

80. Where there is any doubt as to the existence of circumstances constituting the infringement, it is necessary to take account of the principle of the presumption of innocence, which is one of the fundamental rights protected in the EU legal order and which has been affirmed by Article 48(1) of the Charter of Fundamental Rights of the European Union. Given the nature of the infringements in question and the nature and degree of severity of the ensuing penalties, the principle of the presumption of innocence applies in particular to the procedures relating to infringements of the competition rules applicable to undertakings that may result in the imposition of fines or periodic penalty payments. It is accordingly necessary for the Commission to produce sufficiently precise and consistent evidence to support the firm conviction that the alleged infringement took place (. . . *Romana Tabacchi* v *Commission*, T-11/06, EU:T:2011:560, paragraph 129 and . . . *Trafilerie Meridionali* v *Commission*, T-422/10, EU:T:2015:512, paragraph 88 . . .).

81. Nevertheless, although the Commission must produce sufficiently precise and consistent evidence to support the firm conviction that the infringement took place, it must be pointed out that it is not necessary for every item of evidence produced by the Commission to satisfy those criteria in relation to every aspect of the infringement. It is sufficient if the body of evidence relied on by the Commission, viewed as a whole, meets that requirement (. . . *Commission* v *Keramag Keramische Werke and Others*, C-613/13 P, EU:C:2017:49, paragraph 52 . . .).

(viii) Annulment

Article 264 TFEU states that, if the action is well founded, 'the Court of Justice of the European Union shall declare the act concerned to be void'. The finding of defects in a decision does not necessarily lead to annulment of the whole if the defects relate only to ancillary components which do not alter the substance of the decision: if the defective parts can be severed the rest of the decision will stand.[807] Any parts that are not annulled definitively form part of the Union legal structure and continue to produce legal effects. Thus, in *Compagnie Maritime Belge* for example, annulling the fine for procedural reasons did not affect the legality of the rest of the decision finding the infringement.[808] In *Verhuizingen Coppens*, the CJ overruled the GC for wrongly annulling the *International Removal Service* decision in respect of Coppens entirely instead of partially.[809]

A decision finding an infringement of the competition rules addressed to a number of undertakings (as is common in cartel cases) is in effect a bundle of individual decisions. The decision can therefore be annulled only as regards the addressees who have successfully challenged it. Twenty-eight of the 36 addressees of the *Wood Pulp* decision[810] brought an action for annulment. The CJ annulled or reduced the fines imposed on the appellants.[811] The CJ upheld the Commission's refusal to refund the other addressees: they had not challenged the decision within the two-month time limit and it continued to be valid and binding on them.[812] In *CISAC*,[813] 21 of the addressees brought a successful action for annulment on the grounds of insufficient evidence of a concerted practice. One undertaking brought an appeal on different grounds, which failed, and the GC did not allow it to adopt at the hearing stage the other appellants' submissions.[814]

The EU Courts cannot substitute their own decision for that of the Commission. So, in *European Night Services*,[815] the GC refused to annul the conditions which the Commission had attached to the Article 101(3) exemption, but instead annulled the decision completely.

Article 266 TFEU says:

> The institution or institutions whose act has been declared void or whose failure to act has been declared contrary to the Treaties shall be required to take the necessary measures to comply with the judgment of the Court of Justice of the European Union.

This covers repayment of any fine already paid, including default interest. The rate of interest payable is the ECB refinancing rate, which must be returned to the successful appellant regardless of whether the Commission itself has received that rate in the interim.[816] Where the fine is partially reduced,

[807] Case C-441/11 P, *Commission v Verhuizingen Coppens* EU:C:2012:778, paras. 36–38; Case C-603/13 P, *Galp Energía España* EU:C:2016:38, para. 86.

[808] Case T-276/04, *Compagnie Maritime Belge* EU:T:2008:237. The original fines on the shipping lines were annulled because the Commission had announced an intention to fine only the conference, not the individual shipping lines, Cases C-395 and 396/96 P, *Compagnie Maritime Belge* EU:C:2000:132.

[809] Case C-441/11 P, *Verhuizingen Coppens* EU:C:2012:778.

[810] [1985] OJ L85/1.

[811] Cases C-89/85 etc., *Ahlström Oy v Commission (Wood Pulp II)* EU:C:1993:120.

[812] Case C-310/97 P, *Commission v AssiDomän* EU:C:1999:407.

[813] Case T-442/08, *CISAC v Commission* EU:T:2013:188.

[814] Case T-451/08, *Föreningen Svenska Tonsättares Internationella Musikbyrå u.p.a. (Stim) v Commission* EU:T:2013:189.

[815] Cases T-374–375, 384, and 388/94, *European Night Services* EU:T:1998:198.

[816] This point was established in Case C-301/19 P, *Commission v Printeos* EU:C:2021:39, where the CJ held that the Commission could not escape its obligation to pay default interest at the ECB refinancing rate even where it had actually invested the fine in a fund during the appeals process, which had performed negatively during that period. Applying this principle in Case T-610/19, *Deutsche Telekom* EU:T:2022:15, the GC held that the successful appellant was entitled to compensation of the relevant amount under Art. 268 TFEU.

the relevant proportion and interest must likewise be repaid.[817] Where decisions are annulled for procedural defects the Commission often readopts them. The Commission responded to the final annulment of the *PVC I* decision[818] by adopting a new one six weeks later. The undertakings again appealed, inter alia on the grounds that this breached the principle of double jeopardy, *ne bis in idem*, and that the Commission had denied them the right to be heard by not sending a new SO and holding new hearings. The CJ held that *ne bis in idem* did not apply when the annulment was only on procedural grounds, and that, given that the Court had not found any defects in the preparatory stages of the Commission's procedure, there was no need to repeat those stages. A right to be heard was necessary only in respect of matters which were not in the original decision.[819] The Commission's practice is, consequently, to readopt decisions annulled for procedural reasons, and the triumph of those who win on procedural grounds can be short-lived.[820]

(ix) Appeals from the General Court to the Court of Justice

An appeal lies from the GC to the CJ on a point of law.[821] This means that the appeal is limited to the grounds of lack of competence of the GC, a breach of procedure before it adversely affecting the interests of the applicant, or the infringement of EU law by the GC.[822] An error of law includes the legal characterisation of facts by the GC and the legal conclusions it draws from them.[823] The appellant must state the errors of law alleged to have been made by the GC.[824] It is insufficient for it simply to repeat the arguments it raised before the GC,[825] and it may not adduce new arguments. The CJ will not entertain arguments whereby the appellant is really trying to argue about the facts found in the original decision rather than identify errors committed by the GC. In several cases, the CJ has been highly critical of appeals where it has struggled to identify the grounds.[826] The CJ has explained the respective roles of the CJ and the GC on many occasions. The following is an extract from *Siemens*.[827]

Cases C-239, 489, and 498/11 P, *Siemens AG and others v Commission* EU:C:2013:866

Court of Justice

38. First of all, it must be borne in mind that, in an appeal, the Court of Justice has no jurisdiction to establish the facts or, in principle, to examine the evidence which the General Court accepted in support of those facts. Provided that the evidence has been properly obtained and the general principles of law and the rules of procedure in relation to the burden of proof and the taking of evidence have been observed, it is for the General Court alone to assess the value which should be attached to the evidence produced to it. Save where the evidence adduced before the General Court has been distorted, the appraisal therefore does not constitute a point of law which is subject to review by the

[817] Case T-53/03, *BPB v Commission* EU:T:2008:254.
[818] Case C-137/92 P, *Commission v BASF* EU:C:1994:247.
[819] Cases C-238/99 P etc., *Limburgse Vinyl Maatschappij (PVC II)* EU:C:2002:582, paras. 59–76.
[820] For two further examples of decisions readopted after annulments for procedural reasons, see COMP/38.907, *Steel Beams* [2008] OJ C235/4, and COMP/39.234, *Alloy Surcharge* 20 December 2006.
[821] Art. 256 TFEU. [822] Art. 58 of the Statute of the Court of Justice.
[823] Case C-67/13 P, *CB* EU:C:2014:2204, para. 41. The CJ set aside the GC's judgment because it had, inter alia, failed to carry out a sufficiently in-depth review, showed defective reasoning, and misinterpreted and misapplied Art. 101(1).
[824] See Case C-295/12 P, *Telefónica* EU:C:2014:2062.
[825] Case C-19/95 P, *San Marco* EU:C:1996:331.
[826] For instance, Case C-295/12 P, *Telefónica* EU:C:2014:2062, paras. 30–31.
[827] The appeals in the *Gas Insulated Switchgear* cartel, COMP/38.899, 24 January 2007, upheld on appeal.

Court of Justice (Joined Cases C-403/04 P and C-405/04 P *Sumitomo Metal Industries and Nippon Steel* v *Commission* . . . , paragraph 38 and the case-law cited).

39. The jurisdiction of the Court of Justice to review the findings of fact by the General Court therefore extends, inter alia, to the substantive inaccuracy of those findings as apparent from the documents in the file, the distortion of the evidence, the legal characterisation of that evidence and the question whether the rules relating to the burden of proof and the taking of evidence have been observed (*Sumitomo Metal Industries and Nippon Steel* v *Commission*, paragraph 39 and the case-law cited).

40. By contrast, contrary to what Siemens maintains, the Court's power of review in the context of an appeal cannot extend to the alleged infringement of purported principles derived from experience, such as those claimed by Siemens, concerning, inter alia, established knowledge relating to the functioning of the memory and the psychology of witnesses, or the fact that individuals from an undertaking involved in the cartel may themselves have an interest in maximising the unlawful conduct of competitors and minimising their own liability.

41. Review of an infringement of that nature requires a factual assessment which is fundamentally different from the marginal review which the Court carries out when an appellant complains, in a sufficiently detailed manner, that the General Court distorted the evidence.

42. It should be pointed out that, according to settled case-law, the distortion must be obvious from the documents in the Court's file, without there being any need to carry out a new assessment of the facts and the evidence (see, inter alia, Case C-260/09 P *Activision Blizzard Germany* v *Commission* . . . , paragraph 53 and the case-law cited).

. . .

44. Next, it should be borne in mind that the review carried out by the Court in order to assess a ground of appeal alleging the distortion of evidence is restricted to ascertaining that, in relying on that evidence to make a finding that an undertaking participated in a cartel, the General Court did not manifestly exceed the limits of a reasonable assessment of that evidence. The task of the Court of Justice is not, therefore, to assess independently whether the Commission has established such participation to the requisite legal standard and thus discharged the burden of proof necessary to show that the rules of competition law were infringed, but to determine whether, in finding that that was actually so, the General Court misconstrued the evidence in a manner manifestly at odds with its wording (see, to that effect, *Activision Blizzard Germany* v *Commission*, paragraph 57).

The correction of a manifest error by the GC was made in *Aalborg*.[828] The GC had included within the calculation of the fine to be imposed on one of the participants in the cement cartel the turnover of its Belgian subsidiary. However, at the time of the infringement, the undertaking concerned had not yet assumed control of the Belgian company. This was apparent from the *Cement Cartel* decision itself.[829] The CJ reduced the fine by nearly €3 million as it considered it had the necessary evidence to give judgment. It did so under Article 61 of the Statute of the Court of Justice, which provides that, if an appeal is well founded, the CJ must quash the GC's decision and either refer the matter back to the GC or, 'where the state of proceedings so permits', itself give final judgment. The effect of this was nicely illustrated by CJ's judgment in *PVC Cartel II*. It held that the GC had wrongly refused to consider, on procedural grounds, Montedison's plea that its right of access to the file had been infringed, and its plea about the Commission's power to fine in the circumstances of the case.[830] The

[828] Cases C-204/00 P etc., *Aalborg Portland* EU:C:2004:6. [829] [1994] OJ L343/1.

[830] The peculiarities of the proceedings against the PVC cartel, which resulted in a first annulled decision being replaced by a second one, are described in Section 7.A.

CJ therefore partially annulled the GC's decision. However, it decided that this was a case in which it could give final judgment itself. It therefore considered Montedison's pleas and rejected them, leaving Montedison in the same position as it was after the GC judgment.[831]

Errors of law do not lead to the setting aside of a judgment where it is upheld on other grounds.[832]

In a number of cases, applicants have claimed that proceedings before the GC were of such an excessive length that their right to a fair trial within a reasonable period under Article 6(1) ECHR and (now) Article 47 of the Charter was infringed. The CJ considers the length of the proceedings in the light of the complexity of the case.[833] If the CJ concludes that the delay was unreasonable but did not prejudice the outcome of the case, the judgment is not set aside. Rather, the remedy is for the appellant to bring an action for damages before the GC (differently constituted if the GC itself was responsible for the delay).[834] In this matter, the CJ has changed its previous approach, which was to reduce the fine in such cases.[835] The drawn-out saga of the *Industrial Bags* cartel, however, demonstrates the practical difficulties of succeeding on the basis of non-contractual liability against unjustified delay.[836] The revised Rules of Procedure of the GC which entered into force in 2015[837] were intended to strengthen the Court's capacity to deal with cases in a reasonable time in accordance with Article 47.

Where appeals against judgments of the GC on fines are concerned, the CJ has held that it is for the GC to examine how the Commission assessed the gravity of the infringement and to decide whether the fine should be changed. The CJ will not substitute its own assessment for that of the GC. It stated in *Ferriere Nord*:[838]

> 31. . . . [I]t is not for this Court, when ruling on questions of law in the context of an appeal, to substitute, on grounds of fairness, its own assessment for that of the [GC] exercising its unlimited jurisdiction to rule on the amount of fines imposed on undertakings for infringements of [Union] law . . . In contrast, the Court of Justice does have jurisdiction to consider whether the [GC] has responded to a sufficient legal standard to all the arguments raised by the appellant with a view to having the fine abolished or reduced.

[831] Cases C-238/99 P etc., *Limburgse Vinyl Maatschappij* EU:C:2002:582, paras. 355–379, 416–428, and 647–698.

[832] As in, e.g., Case C-501/06 P, *GlaxoSmithKline* EU:C:2009:610; Case C-113/07 P, *SELEX Systemi Integrati* EU:C:2009:191. For instances where the GC judgment was set aside completely, see Case C-310/97 P, *AssiDomän Kraft Products* EU:C:1999:407; Case C-441/07 P, *Alrosa* EU:C:2010:377; and Case C-132/19 P, *Groupe Canal+* EU:C:2020:1007.

[833] E.g. Case C-185/95 P, *Baustahlgewebe* EU:C:1998:608; Case C-194/99 P, *Thyssen Stahl* EU:C:2003:527; Cases C-403 and 405/04 P, *Sumitomo Metal Industries* EU:C:2007:52.

[834] Case C-40/12 P, *Gascogne Sack Deutschland* EU:C:2013:768, paras. 86–90; Case C-50/12 P, *Kendrion* EU:C:2013:771, paras. 91–95; Case C-58/12 P, *Groupe Gascogne* EU:C:2013:770, paras. 80–84; Case C-295/12 P, *Telefónica* EU:C:2014:2062, paras. 66–67; Case C-603/13 P, *Galp* EU:C:2016:38, paras. 55–58. The length of the proceedings in *Galp* was almost five years and nine months, including a period of over four years, without any procedural acts, between the end of the written procedure and the hearing. See generally L. Bressers, 'Damages for Delay: The EU Held Liable for Harm Caused by "Unjustified Inactivity" in General Court Proceedings' (2017) 8 *JECLAP* 492.

[835] In Case C-185/95 P, *Baustahlgewebe* EU:C:1998:608, the CJ reduced the fine of three million ECUs by 50,000 ECUs.

[836] The underlying infringement decision—Commission Decision C(2005) 4634 in COMP/F/38.354, *Industrial bags*—was taken in November 2005, and appealed within the two-month window under Art. 263 TFEU. The GC, however, did not rule on the appeal until 2011 (Cases T-72/06 etc., *Groupe Gascogne*), upheld subsequently by the CJ in 2013 (Cases C-40/12 P etc., *Groupe Gascogne*). The defendants then sued the EU for compensation for damage allegedly suffered as a result of the length of the proceedings before the GC and were successful at first instance (Cases T-577/14 etc., *Gascogne Sack Deutschland*). On subsequent appeal (Case C-138/17 P, *European Union v Gascogne Sack Deutschland*), however, the CJ annulled the compensation awarded to the extent that it covered material damage in the form of bank guarantee costs for the duration of the appeal, on the dubious ground that, having themselves opted to provide a bank guarantee in lieu of upfront payment of fines, the defendants had broken the causal link between the delay and the damage incurred.

[837] [2015] OJ L105/1.

[838] Case C-219/95, *Ferriere Nord* EU:C:1997:375; see also Case C-310/93 P, *BPB Industries and British Gypsum* EU:C:1995:101, para. 34; Case C-185/95 P, *Baustahlgewebe* EU:C:1998:608, paras. 128–129; Case C-359/01 P, *British Sugar* EU:C:2004:255, paras. 47–48; Cases C-189/02 P etc., *Dansk Rørindustri* EU:C:2005:408, paras. 244–246 and 302.

(x) Interim Measures by the Court under Article 278 TFEU

Bringing an Article 263 action for annulment does not automatically suspend the contested act. However, Article 278 TFEU states:

> Actions brought before the Court of Justice of the European Union shall not have suspensory effect. The Court may, however, if it considers that circumstances so require, order that application of the contested act be suspended.

Article 279 TFEU similarly provides that in any cases before it, the Court may prescribe any necessary measures. The President of the GC normally hears applications for suspension.[839] His or her decision may be appealed to the CJ.

In order for a decision to be suspended, the applicants must show that the main action is admissible and that suspension is urgently needed to prevent them suffering irreparable damage which could not be remedied in the event of their winning the main action. On this basis suspension was ordered, inter alia, in *United Brands*,[840] *Magill*,[841] *Net Book Agreement*,[842] *Adalat*,[843] *Atlantic Container Line*,[844] *Van den Bergh*,[845] and *IMS*.[846] In *Facebook*, the President of the GC suspended part of a request for information made under Article 18(3) of Regulation 1/2003, in circumstances where, the defendant argued, it would otherwise be obliged to hand over large quantities of sensitive personal data in breach, inter alia, of data protection obligations.[847] The Commission's intention to publish a revised 'non-confidential version' of a final decision was suspended in *Akzo Nobel*.[848] Suspension was refused in *Microsoft*, however, on the grounds that the undertaking had failed to show the likelihood of serious and irreparable damage.[849]

The President balances the harm to the applicant from non-suspension (foreseeable with a sufficient degree of probability)[850] with any harm which will be suffered by other parties if the suspension is granted. In *Adalat*, the President considered that as a result of the order the applicant, Bayer, might be obliged to lower the prices of the drug in issue, risking major and irrecoverable losses of profit, and that there was a risk that the pharmaceutical base of one subsidiary 'might be deprived of its economic basis, resulting in the dismissal of many employees'. He considered this would be disproportionate in relation to the interests of wholesalers in Spain and France in increasing their exports.[851] Moreover, he was concerned that the Commission's interpretation of the law (i.e. its view of what constitutes an 'agreement' for the purposes of Article 101) was questionable (as, indeed it proved to be).[852]

The suspension in *IMS* was of an interim decision. Again, as with *Adalat*, the President of the GC was concerned about the legal basis of the Commission's decision (the compulsory licensing of a

[839] For the procedure before the GC, see GC Rules of Procedure (2015), Arts. 156–161.

[840] Case 27/76 R, *United Brands* EU:C:1978:22. [841] Cases 76–77 and 91/89 R, *RTE* EU:C:1989:192.

[842] Case 56/89 R, *Publishers' Association* EU:C:1989:238.

[843] Case T-41/96 R, *Bayer* EU:T:1996:68.

[844] Case C-149/95 P (R), *Commission v Atlantic Container Line* EU:C:1995:257.

[845] Case T-65/98 R, *Van den Bergh Foods* EU:T:1998:155.

[846] Case T-184/01 R, *NDC Health* EU:T:2001:200 (President of the GC), Case C-481/01 P (R), *IMS Health* EU:C:2002:223 (President of the CJ).

[847] Order in Case T-452/20 R, *Facebook Ireland* EU:T:2020:516 (President of the GC). In Case T-452/20 *Meta Platforms* EU:T:2023:276, however, the GC dismissed the underlying challenge on substantive grounds.

[848] Case T-345/12 R, *Akzo Nobel* EU:T:2012:605; the publication was finally allowed by the GC in Case T-345/12, *Akzo Nobel* EU:T:2015:50.

[849] Case T-201/04 R, *Microsoft* EU:T:2007:289. [850] Case C-280/93 R, *Commission v Germany* EU:C:1993:270.

[851] EU:T:1996:68, paras. 59–60.

[852] The Commission's decision was annulled in Case T-41/96, *Bayer v Commission* EU:T:2000:242, confirmed by the CJ, Cases C-2 and 3/01 P, *Bundesverband der Arzneimittel-Importeure EV and the Commission v Bayer AG* EU:C:2004:2.

copyright).[853] The GC may suspend the obligation to give a bank guarantee ensuring payment of the fine but this is done only exceptionally.[854] The GC (and on appeal, the CJ) refused to do so in respect of one of the shipping lines fined in *TACA*.[855]

B. ACTIONS FOR DAMAGES UNDER ARTICLE 340 TFEU

Article 340 TFEU provides for damages for non-contractual liability:

> In the case of non-contractual liability, the Union shall, in accordance with the general principles common to the laws of the Member States, make good any damage caused by its institutions or by its servants in the performance of their duties.

This raises the possibility that, where a decision of the Commission is overturned by the EU Courts, the undertakings concerned may be able to sue the Commission for any damage caused to it by the defective decision. Actions under Article 340 are notoriously difficult for plaintiffs to win.[856] The Union institution must have committed a sufficiently serious breach of a superior rule of law intended to confer rights on individuals, the test being whether the institution manifestly and gravely disregarded the limits on its discretion.[857] These conditions were not fulfilled in *Holcim*, for instance, where the GC excused the Commission on the grounds, inter alia, of the difficulties it had faced in the case.[858] Stanley Adams, however, did succeed in a damages claim under Article 340 when the Commission's negligent breach of confidentiality in revealing his identity to Hoffmann-La Roche led to his imprisonment in Switzerland.[859]

As explained in Section 7.A.ix, the CJ considers that an action for damages is the proper remedy for unreasonable delays in proceedings before the GC.

8. ENFORCEMENT BY THE NATIONAL COMPETITION AUTHORITIES WITHIN THE EUROPEAN COMPETITION NETWORK

A. GENERAL

The NCAs have, since 1 May 2004, played a more significant role in the enforcement of the EU competition rules.[860] Regulation 1/2003 creates a system of parallel competences, in which Articles 101 and 102 are enforced by a network of competition authorities through the ECN, as well as by national courts.[861] The basic powers of the NCAs are set out in Article 5 of Regulation 1/2003,

[853] The suspension was confirmed by the President of the CJ. Case C-481/01 P (R), *NDC Health* EU:C:2002:223. The decision was withdrawn and a final decision not adopted, Chap 7, Section 12.

[854] See Case T-295/94 R, *Buchmann* EU:T:1998:88.

[855] Case C-364/99 P (R), *DSR-Senator Lines* EU:C:1999:609.

[856] See Craig and de Búrca, n.131, Chap 16.

[857] Case C-352/98 P, *Bergaderm and Goupil* EU:C:2000:361.

[858] Case T-28/03, *Holcim* EU:T:2005:139, *aff'd* by the CJ, Case C-282/05 P, *Holcim* EU:C:2007:226. See also Case T-834/17, *UPS v Commission* EU:T:2022:84.

[859] Case 53/84, *Stanley Adams* EU:C:1985:449.

[860] See also Chap 2.

[861] The individual websites of each NCA are accessible through a link from the Commission's website, <http://ec.europa.eu/competition/ecn/competition_authorities.html>.

while Chapter IV makes provision for cooperation between the NCAs and the Commission. A Commission Notice on cooperation within the Network of Competition Authorities (the NCA Cooperation Notice) further elaborated upon the latter.[862] This bare-bones framework has now been augmented by adoption of the ECN+ Directive,[863] which seeks to bolster the work of the NCAs in a number of dimensions.[864] The impetus for the Directive was a Commission report, *Ten Years of Antitrust Enforcement under Regulation 1/2003*, which offered a largely positive assessment of the decentralised regime, but concluded that greater harmonisation was required to strengthen both the institutional position and enforcement powers of NCAs.[865] The proposed legislation was touted as a means to realise the 'untapped potential for more effective enforcement of the EU competition rules by NCAs'.[866] The stated aim of the Directive, which Member States were required to transpose by February 2021, is 'to ensure that national competition authorities have the necessary guarantees of independence, resources, and enforcement and fining powers to be able to effectively apply Article 101 and 102' going forward.[867] The harmonised powers to be guaranteed to NCAs are clearly modelled on those possessed by the Commission, thus raising the question of whether the Commission's own enforcement framework should always be viewed as 'best practice' in this context.

Regulation 1/2003 leaves the Member State to determine which national body enforces the competition rules and the mechanisms for investigating infringements and enforcing decisions that apply. It does not demand any particular arrangement, so long as an NCA is designated[868] and there is compliance with the provisions of the Regulation. Article 35 of Regulation 1/2003 provides that the designated authorities may include courts. The ECN+ Directive imposes requirements of independence for NCAs,[869] which encompasses freedom from both political and private external influences,[870] and of sufficient resources, including 'a sufficient number of qualified staff and sufficient financial, technical and technological resources that are necessary for the effective performance of their duties'.[871]

[862] Commission Notice on cooperation within the Network of Competition Authorities [2004] OJ C101/43.

[863] Dir. (EU) 2019/1 of the European Parliament and of the Council of 11 December 2018 to empower the competition authorities of the Member States to be more effective enforcers and to ensure the proper functioning of the internal market [2019] OJ C11/3 (the ECN+ Dir.).

[864] For commentary on the ECN+ Dir., see A. Sinclair, 'Proposal for a Directive to Empower National Competition Authorities to be More Effective Enforcers' (2017) 8 *JECLAP* 625; M Botta, 'The Draft on the Powers of National Competition Authorities: The Glass Half Empty and Half Full' (2017) 38 *ECLR* 470; and W. Wils, 'Competition Authorities: Towards More Independence and Prioritisation?—The European Commission's "ECN+" Proposal for a Directive to empower the competition authorities of the Member States to be more effective enforcers' [2017] 4 *Concurrences* 84881, pp. 60–80. An insightful survey of the challenges faced by NCAs more generally is provided in A. Ezrachi and W. Kovacic, 'Journal of Antitrust Enforcement Agency Effectiveness Study' (2016) 4 *J of Antitrust Enforcement* 229.

[865] Communication from the Commission to the European Parliament and the Council, Ten Years of Antitrust Enforcement under Regulation 1/2003: Achievements and Future Perspectives, COM(2014) 453.

[866] Proposal for a Directive of the European Parliament and of the Council to empower the competition authorities of the member States to be more effective enforcers and to ensure the proper functioning of the internal market, COM(2017) 142 final, p. 2.

[867] ECN+ Dir., Art. 1(1).

[868] Reg. 1/2003, Art. 35.

[869] Arguing that the ECN+ Dir. results in stronger guarantees of the independence of NCAs than exist at EU level for the Commission, see R. Perea Molleda, 'The ECN+ Directive and the Next Steps for Independence in Competition Law Enforcement' (2021) 12 *JECLAP* 167.

[870] ECN+ Dir., Art. 4. See also discussion of Case T-791/19, *Sped-Pro* EU:T:2022:67, Section 8.C.i.

[871] ECN+ Dir., Art. 5.

B. ENFORCEMENT POWERS OF THE NATIONAL COMPETITION AUTHORITIES

The enforcement powers of the NCAs are provided within Article 5 of Regulation 1/2003, now supplemented by the provisions of the ECN+ Directive.

Regulation 1/2003

Article 5 Powers of the competition authorities of the Member States

The competition authorities for the Member States shall have the power to apply Articles [101 and 102 TFEU] in individual cases. For the purpose, acting on their own initiative or on a complaint, they may take the following decisions:

— requiring that an infringement be brought to an end,

— ordering interim measures,

— accepting commitments,

— imposing fines, periodic penalty payments or any other penalty provided for in their national law.

Where on the basis of the information in their possession the conditions for prohibition are not met they may likewise decide that there are no grounds for action on their part.

Article 5, accordingly, specifies the baseline powers that NCAs must possess when enforcing the antitrust rules. Beyond the formal power to find violations of Article 101 or 102, NCAs can issue 'cease and desist' orders, impose fines or interim measures, or accept commitments in lieu. NCAs *cannot*, however, take a non-infringement decision, even in circumstances where they consider that the requirements for Article 101 or 102 are not satisfied on the facts. This limitation stems from the final sentence of Article 5, as interpreted by the CJ in *Tele2 Polska*[872] and confirmed in *Schenker*,[873] which states merely that NCAs may decide that there are no grounds for action in a particular instance.[874] The CJ in *Schenker* further established that NCAs should only exceptionally refrain from imposing a fine where an undertaking has intentionally or negligently infringed Article 101(1) (such as where a national leniency programme is applied).[875]

The ECN+ Directive significantly augments and elaborates upon these enforcement powers, covering the application of Articles 101 and 102 *and* the parallel application of national competition law to the same case.[876] The Directive, first, largely replicates the information-gathering powers of the Commission provided by Chapter V of Regulation 1/2003. Thus, NCAs must be empowered to conduct unannounced inspections (i.e. dawn raids) at business premises,[877] and at other premises including private homes;[878] they must be able to issue requests for information;[879] and to require individuals to attend interview.[880] Where NCAs find infringement of Article 101 or 102, they must have essentially the same enforcement powers as the Commission under Article 7 of Regulation 1/2003,

[872] Case C-375/09, *Tele2 Polska* EU:C:2011:270; for commentary, see S. Brammer, 'Casenote on *Tele2 Polska*' (2012) 49 *CMLRev* 1163.

[873] Case C-681/11, *Bundeswettbewerbsbehörde and Bundeskartellanwalt v Schenker & Co AG* EU:C:2013:404, para. 42.

[874] Pursuant to the ECN+ Dir., Art. 10(2), NCAs must inform the Commission where they close an investigation on the basis that there are no grounds to continue.

[875] Case C-681/11, *Bundeswettbewerbsbehörde and Bundeskartellanwalt v Schenker & Co AG* EU:C:2013:404, para. 40.

[876] ECN+ Dir., Art. 1(2). [877] Ibid., Art. 6. [878] Ibid., Art. 7. [879] Ibid., Art. 8. [880] Ibid., Art. 9.

including the ability to impose behavioural or structural remedies, and to take decisions finding infringements committed in the past.[881] The Directive is particularly prescriptive in terms of the circumstances in which NCAs may impose, and the methodology by which they must calculate, fines and periodic penalty payments,[882] once again largely replicating the powers and the practice of the Commission. Articles 11 and 12 of the ECN+ Directive mirror Articles 8 and 9 of Regulation 1/2003, respectively, elaborating the circumstances in which NCAs may impose interim measures or accept commitments in lieu of a finding of infringement. Chapter VI of the Directive, which aims at harmonisation of national leniency programmes for secret cartels, is considered further in Section 8.C.iii.

C. DIVISION OF WORK

(i) Case Allocation—Which Authority is Well Placed to Deal with a Case?

Chapter IV of Regulation 1/2003 deals with cooperation, including cooperation between the Commission and NCAs. Further, a Joint Statement of the Council and the European Commission on the Functioning of the Network of Competition Authorities (the Joint Statement)[883] sets out the main principles governing the ECN, whilst the Commission's NCA Cooperation Notice provides fuller and more specific detail of cooperation and division of work. Article 101 and 102 cases can be dealt with by:

- a single NCA (possibly with the assistance of others);
- several NCAs acting in parallel; or
- the Commission.[884]

The basic principles are that a case should be dealt with by the authority best placed to deal with it and able to restore or maintain competition in the market, and that cases should be allocated according to a predictable process and as soon as possible.[885] The allocation principles are set out with examples in the NCA Cooperation Notice.[886]

In order for an authority to be well placed, there must be a material link between the infringement and the territory of the authority (the conduct has substantial direct actual or foreseeable effects in the territory), the authority must be able to bring the entire infringement effectively to an end (either on its own or in parallel with another authority), and the authority must be able to gather the evidence required (whether or not with the assistance of another authority). Where two or more NCAs are well placed to act, then one NCA only should act where the action of one would be sufficient to bring the entire infringement to an end. If it would not, then two or more NCAs should act. The authorities should coordinate their action and where possible designate a lead authority for the case.[887] The guidance in the NCA Cooperation Notice is relatively limited and does not deal with what is to happen in the event of a dispute as to which NCA should act and/or which NCA should take the lead in an investigation.

The Commission is likely to be best placed to deal with an agreement or practice where: it affects competition in three or more Member States; the conduct is linked with other Union provisions

[881] Ibid., Art.10.

[882] Ibid., Arts. 13–16 and 29. For a critique of the approach, see S. Thomas and M. Duenas, 'The Draft Provisions on Antitrust Fines in the Commission's ECN+ Proposal' (2018) 16 *Zeitschrift für Wettbewerbsrecht* 1.

[883] Joint Statement of the European Council and the European Commission on the functioning of the network of competition authorities, 10 December 2002, <http://ec.europa.eu/competition/ecn/joint_statement_en.pdf>.

[884] NCA Cooperation Notice [2004] OJ C101/43, para. 5.

[885] Joint Statement, paras. 11–14. [886] Ibid., paras. 8–15. [887] Ibid., para. 18.

which may be exclusively or more effectively applied by the Commission; or the Union interest requires it (to develop competition policy or to ensure effective enforcement).[888]

The determination as to which authority deals with the case may be of critical importance to the undertakings investigated, the complainant (if any), and the authorities themselves, to the extent that, even after modernisation, different authorities continue to take rather different views of certain substantive issues. Although Regulation 1/2003 has made provision for the handling of certain matters within the ECN, problems remain.[889] The 'offbeat'[890] *Sped-Pro* judgment adds another factor into the mix.[891] Here, the GC held that, for an NCA to be considered well placed to address a complaint, it may be necessary to examine whether that authority has sufficient independence from domestic political pressure to act in a manner that is compatible with the rule of law. This is because, as the GC explained, 'for the purposes of application of Articles 101 and 102 TFEU, cooperation between the Commission, the competition authorities of the Member States and the national courts is based on the principles of mutual recognition, mutual trust and loyal cooperation, which oblige each of those authorities and courts to consider, except in exceptional circumstances, that all the other authorities and courts respect EU law and, in particular, the fundamental rights recognised by that law'.[892] Although mutual trust is generally assumed with the EU framework, it must be examined to the extent that the issue is genuinely called into question.[893]

In order to ensure that allocation takes place as quickly as possible, and normally within a period of two months,[894] Article 11(3) of Regulation 1/2003 imposes an obligation on NCAs to inform the Commission and other NCAs 'before or without delay after commencing the first formal investigative measure'. Further, the Commission is obliged to transmit copies of documents to the NCAs that it has collected pursuant to its powers of investigation under Regulation 1/2003. Once a case has been allocated, it should not ordinarily be reallocated unless the known facts change materially during the proceedings.[895] Article 13 of Regulation 1/2003 specifically provides that an authority (the Commission or an NCA) may suspend proceedings or reject a case that is being, or has been, dealt with by another competition authority.[896] This provision was applied in *easyJet*, where the Commission rejected a complaint on the grounds that an NCA had already dealt the matter.[897] In *Trajektna Iuka Split*, where the applicant complained to both an NCA and the Commission in tandem, the GC confirmed that the Commission does not function as an appellate body for complaints already assessed by NCAs, but rather, that review of such domestic decisions is reserved for national courts.[898] Moreover, given that the applicant had submitted its complaint to the NCA, it could not subsequently argue that that NCA

[888] Ibid., para. 19.

[889] See e.g. R. Nazzini, *Concurrent Proceedings in Competition Law* (Oxford University Press, 2004); S. Brammer, 'Concurrent Jurisdiction under Regulation 1/2003 and the Issue of Case Allocation' (2005) 42 *CMLRev* 1383; A. Andreangeli, 'The Impact of the Modernisation Regulation on the Guarantees of Due Process in Competition Proceedings' (2006) 31 *ELRev* 342.

[890] D. Pérez de Lamo, 'Mutual Trust and Rule-of-law Considerations in EU Competition Law: The General Court Extends the "L.M. Doctrine" to Cooperation Between Competition Authorities (*Sped-Pro*, T-791/19)' *Kluwer Competition Law Blog*, 1 March 2022, <http://competitionlawblog.kluwercompetitionlaw.com/2022/03/01/mutual-trust-and-rule-of-law-considerations-in-eu-competition-law-the-general-court-extends-the-l-m-doctrine-to-cooperation-between-competition-authorities-sped-pro-t-791-19/>.

[891] Case T-791/19, *Sped-Pro* EU:T:2022:67. [892] Ibid., para. 88.

[893] On the facts of *Sped-Pro*, the complainant wished to have its complaint (against a Polish State-operated company) considered by the Commission, rather than the Polish competition authority, which the complainant argued was susceptible to political pressure.

[894] Cooperation Notice [2004] OJ C101/43, para. 18. [895] Ibid., para. 19.

[896] The Commission can also reject a complaint which lacks Union interest or which fails to substantiate an allegation, see Section 6.C. National provisions may also provide an alternative basis for suspending a complaint.

[897] Case T-355/13, *easyJet* EU:T:2015:36.

[898] Case T-70/15, *Trajektna luka Split* EU:T:2016:592, para. 34.

was not 'well placed' to assess its case within the meaning of the ECN case allocation procedure: 'It is not for the Commission to approve or disapprove of the procedural choice made by the applicant.'[899]

(ii) Transfer of Information and Other Assistance

Where an authority suspends national proceedings or rejects a complaint on the grounds that it is being dealt with by another authority, that authority is permitted to transfer information, including confidential information, to the authority which is dealing with the case. Article 12(1) of Regulation 1/2003 enables the Commission and the NCAs to provide one another with and use in evidence 'any matter of fact or of law, including confidential information'.[900] In *FSL Holdings*, the CJ approved the transmission to the Commission from the Italian customs and finance police of evidence of a cartel, found during inspections in the course of a national tax investigation, as compatible with Article 12.[901]

In order to protect the interests of individuals and undertakings, safeguards exist against the use and exchange of this information. In particular, the competition authorities are bound by an obligation of professional secrecy, the information transferred can be used only for the purposes of applying Article 101 or 102 (and, in certain circumstances, national competition law) and in respect of the subject matter for which it was collected,[902] and the information can only be used to impose sanctions on *natural* persons where the law of the transmitting authority foresees sanctions of a similar kind in relation to the infringement, or the information has been collected in a way that affords the person the same level of protection of rights provided for under the rules of the receiving authorities. Thus, by Article 12(3), an NCA which may not impose sanctions on individuals, may not transfer information to an NCA which may, unless: (a) the information was collected in a way which respects the rights of defence afforded to the individuals by the rules of the receiving authority (but custodial sanctions can be imposed only where both the transmitting and the receiving authority can impose such a sanction); or (b) the receiving authority does not use the information in proceedings against an individual but only in proceedings against an undertaking. The safeguards are explained more fully in paragraph 28 of the NCA Cooperation Notice.

It has been argued that, despite these provisions, doubts remain as to how well the rights of the defence are safeguarded by the exchange of information provided for by Article 12(1).[903] There is a particular problem in the divergence between the Member States' legal systems in the protection given to certain classes of information, such as that covered by legal professional privilege.[904] This could result in an NCA using information it would have been unable to collect under the rules of its own jurisdiction.[905] The Commission's 2009 Report on the Functioning of Regulation 1/2003[906] suggested that the provisions in Article12(3) about information and criminal sanctions are 'too far-reaching and an obstacle to efficient enforcement' and might appropriately be re-examined.[907]

[899] Ibid., para. 42.
[900] The information must have been collected in a legal manner by the transmitting authority.
[901] Case C-469/15 P, *FSL Holdings* EU:C:2017:308, paras. 32–50.
[902] Reg. 1/2003, Art. 12(2).
[903] A. Andreangeli, 'The Impact of the Modernisation Regulation on the Guarantees of Due Process in Competition Proceedings' (2006) 31 *ELRev* 342.
[904] For the position on legal professional privilege in EU law, see Section 6.C.vii.
[905] Andreangeli, n. 903, 354–356; B. Vesterdorf, 'Legal Professional Privilege and the Privilege Against Self-incrimination in EC Law: Recent Developments and Current Issues' [2004] *Fordham Corp L Inst* 19.
[906] COM(2009) 206 final.
[907] Ibid., para. 27, see also the Staff Working Paper on the functioning of Regulation 1/2003, SEC (2009) 574 final, paras. 244–245.

The ECN+ Directive makes provision for 'mutual assistance' between NCAs, in particular in the context of dawn raids conducted by one authority on behalf of another,[908] the notification of documents issued by one authority to undertakings located in the territory of another,[909] and the enforcement of decisions imposing fines or periodic penalty payments.[910]

(iii) Leniency Applications

Both in Chapter 9 and in Section 6.H.v of this chapter, the centrality of leniency regimes in the fight against cartels has been stressed, and the Commission's leniency regime discussed. Prompted in part by the ECN+ Directive, all Member States today operate leniency programmes at national level. Because there is no EU-wide system, however, 'an application for leniency to a given authority is not to be considered as an application for leniency to any other authority'.[911] An undertaking contemplating a leniency application therefore has to consider making an application to *all* authorities which have competence to apply Article 101 in the territory affected by the infringement and have leniency policies, and which are may be considered to be well placed to deal with the infringement. In view of the importance of timing in leniency applications, it is usually advisable to make simultaneous applications. An authority considering opening an investigation as a result of a leniency application has a duty to inform other members of the ECN.[912] Information submitted to the network in this way may not, however, be used by the receiving authorities as a basis for starting an investigation on their own behalf. Further, information will, generally,[913] only be transmitted pursuant to Article 12 with the consent of the leniency applicant.[914]

Given the Commission's belief that leniency plays an important part in the fight against cartels, the inability for firms to file a single 'EU' leniency application was a notable omission from the NCA Cooperation Notice.[915] In order to alleviate this perceived gap, the ECN considered various options for centralisation.[916] First, a system of mutual recognition could have been established, by which immunity or a reduction of fines granted by one authority would be recognised by all other members of the ECN. Secondly, a fully centralised 'one-stop shop' could have been established, by which all leniency applications would be made to the Commission: if the case was later allocated to an NCA (or NCAs) the leniency application would go with the allocation. Thirdly, the ECN considered a system analogous to the regime established by the Merger Regulation,[917] whereby jurisdictional criteria would be developed for allocating cases between authorities and the applicants would approach those which would be dealing with their case. All these ideas presented difficulties in practice, however, and were rejected.

Instead, the ECN turned to (soft) harmonisation, in the form of its Model Leniency Programme (MLP), the aim of which was to produce a model setting out the minimum standards with which all ECN policies should be aligned.[918] Early indications were that adoption of the MLP had encouraged Member States to introduce and/or develop their own leniency policies, but that significant divergences remained.[919] Moreover, the MLP has had a less than sympathetic reception before the CJ. Although the problems regarding the operation of national leniency programmes which followed

[908] ECN+ Dir., Art. 24. [909] Ibid., Art. 25. [910] Ibid., Art. 26.
[911] NCA Cooperation Notice, para. 37. [912] Reg. 1/2003, Art. 11.
[913] But see NCA Cooperation Notice, para. 41 for exceptions to this. [914] Ibid., paras. 39–42.
[915] See C. Gauer and M. Jaspers, 'Designing a European Solution for a "One Stop Leniency Shop"' [2006] *ECLR* 685.
[916] Ibid. [917] Reg. 139/2004 [2004] OJ L24/1, see Chap 15.
[918] Or, in the case of Member States without a leniency programme, adopted and then aligned.
[919] European Commission, *ECN Model Leniency Programme: Report on Assessment of the State of Convergence* (2009), <http://ec.europa.eu/competition/ecn/model_leniency_programme.pdf>.

from the judgment in *Pfleiderer*[920] have now been addressed by the Damages Directive,[921] discussed in Chapter 14, the CJ in *Pfleiderer* nonetheless held that neither the NCA Cooperation Notice, the Leniency Notice, nor the MLP were binding on the courts and tribunals of Member States.[922] A further blow was dealt in *DHL*.[923] Here, the CJ ruled that the MLP was not binding on NCAs and that there was no legal link between an application submitted to the Commission and the 'summary application' to an NCA in line with the provisions of the MLP. The NCA is not required to assess the summary application in the light of the application to the Commission, nor is it required to contact the Commission in order to obtain information on the purpose and results of the Commission procedure. This is because the Commission's leniency programme and those of the Member States coexist and each of the programmes is autonomous. The judgment has been criticised, both for its questionable assumption that preserving an almost radical degree of uncertainty with respect to the process of applying for leniency is most appropriate to ensure the effectiveness of public anti-cartel enforcement, and for its clear prioritisation of the latter principle over the rights of defence of leniency applicants.[924]

The ECN+ Directive provides for the strengthening of leniency policies throughout the EU through the (hard) harmonisation of national leniency regimes, although it does not address the more fundamental problems posed by an absence of centralisation. The Directive requires each Member State to put in place a leniency programme specifically with respect to the detection of 'secret cartels', and dictates the broad contours of what this must entail.[925] The provisions of the Directive transpose, in essence, the main principles of the MLP, which in turn mirror the leniency programme applied by the Commission. Accordingly, each national leniency programme must provide for full immunity from fines for undertakings which disclose their participation in a secret cartel and provide information sufficient to enable the NCA to carry out dawn raids or find an infringement;[926] and a reduction of fines for undertakings which disclose their participation and provide evidence of 'significant added value' to the investigation.[927] It must be possible for leniency statements to be provided in a variety of forms, including orally;[928] and national leniency programmes must encompass both a marker system[929] and the possibility of submitting summary applications.[930]

D. CONSISTENT APPLICATION OF ARTICLES 101 AND 102

(i) General

It has been explained that, despite the creation of a network of authorities, the Commission has sought to retain its central role 'as the guardian of the Treaty', having 'the ultimate but not the sole responsibility for developing policy and safeguarding consistency when it comes to the application of [EU] competition law'.[931]

[920] Case C-360/09, *Pfleiderer* EU:C:2011:389; confirmed in Case C-536/11, *Donau Chemie* EU:C:2013:366.

[921] Dir. 2014/104/EU, see n. 328, and Chap 14.

[922] Case C-360/09, *Pfleiderer* EU:C:2011:389, paras. 21–22.

[923] Case C-428/14, *DHL Express* EU:C:2016:27; for case commentary, see E. Lachnit, 'Apply at Your Own Risk. The Difficulties with Multi-jurisdictional Leniency Applications' (2016) 23 *Maastricht Journal* 4.

[924] See C. Volpin, 'Protecting the Effectiveness of Leniency Programmes: Applying for Leniency is a Leap in the Dark: *DHL Express*' (2017) 54 *CMLRev* 1179.

[925] ECN+ Dir., Chap. VI. [926] Ibid., Art. 17. [927] Ibid., Art. 18.

[928] Ibid., Art. 20. [929] Ibid., Art. 21. [930] Ibid., Art. 22.

[931] NCA Cooperation Notice, para. 43.

(ii) Mechanism of Cooperation

Article 11 of Regulation 1/2003 deals with cooperation between the Commission and the competition authorities of the Member States, providing that the NCAs and Commission should apply the EU competition rules in 'close cooperation'.[932] It therefore provides for the Commission and NCAs respectively to inform each other when acting under Article 101 or 102,[933] and for the early allocation of cases. Article 11(4) also provides for the NCAs to inform the Commission[934] 30 days prior to the adoption of a decision applying Article 101 or 102 and requiring that the infringement be brought to an end.[935] The Commission may then make written observations on the case before the adoption of the decision by the NCA, or may decide itself to initiate proceedings. Article 11(6) of Regulation 1/2003 establishes that the initiation of proceedings by the Commission relieves the NCAs of their competence to apply Articles 101 and 102. 'This means that once the Commission has opened proceedings, NCAs cannot act under the same legal basis against the same agreement(s) or practice(s) by the same undertaking(s) on the same relevant geographic and product market.'[936] The existence of Article 11(6) is thus a powerful weapon in the hands of the Commission, and gives it considerable leverage over an NCA when it disapproves of the decision it is about to adopt. The Commission deals with the full consequence of its Article 11(6) power in its Cooperation Notice. The Notice indicates that it will only rarely initiate proceedings where a case has initially been allocated to another NCA. A defendant undertaking does not have any right, under Article 11(6), to require the Commission to exercise its power of pre-emption in order to remove an investigation from an NCA.[937]

9. THE RELATIONSHIP BETWEEN EU AND NATIONAL COMPETITION LAW

Articles 101 and 102 and the domestic competition rules of the Member States can be applied concurrently. The applicability of Articles 101 and 102 does not preclude the application of national competition provisions.[938] The fact that the rules may apply concurrently obviously leads to the possibility that their joint application may not always achieve the same outcome. Important questions which have arisen therefore are whether an NCA or national court could, for example: (a) authorise an agreement or practice prohibited by Article 101 or 102; or (b) condemn conduct which is not prohibited by EU law (for example, because an agreement does not infringe Article 101(1) or meets the criteria of Article 101(3)).

In the context of the EUMR, the allocation of jurisdiction over mergers between the EU and national authorities is defined by the Regulation itself.[939] In contrast, Regulation 17 did not deal with

[932] Reg. 1/2003, Art. 11(1).

[933] In 2022, NCAs informed the Commission of 148 new case investigations, and 78 envisaged decisions (Commission's *Report on Competition Policy 2022*, COM(2023) 184 final, p.26).

[934] The information may also be shared with the NCAs, Reg. 1/2003, Art. 11(4).

[935] Art. 11(5) states that the NCAs may consult the Commission on any case involving the application of Union law. This may be useful, e.g., where the NCA wishes to adopt a decision rejecting a complaint or closing a procedure.

[936] NCA Cooperation Notice, para. 51.

[937] Order of the GC in Case T-19/21, *Amazon* EU:T:2021:730, upheld on appeal in Case C-815/21 P, *Amazon* EU:C:2023:308. Here, the Commission opened a formal investigation into various alleged abuses of dominance by the defendant, but carved out Amazon's activities in Italy from the scope of the EU-level probe, as these issues were already being investigated by the NCA. The GC held that Amazon was not entitled to require the Commission to take over the entire investigation.

[938] Case 14/68, *Walt Wilhelm v Bundeskartellamt* EU:C:1969:4.

[939] See Chap 15.

this situation. Rather, case law developed which provided, in accordance with the principle of supremacy[940] and Article 10 EC (now Article 4 TEU),[941] that national law could be applied so long as its application did not 'prejudice the full and uniform application of [Union] law or the effects of measures taken or to be taken to implement it'.[942] The case law made it clear that a national authority could not authorise an agreement or conduct prohibited by Union law,[943] but was less clear as to whether, and if so when, national rules could be used to prohibit an agreement authorised at the Union level. The position is now dealt with in Article 3 of Regulation 1/2003.

Regulation 1/2003

Article 3 Relationship between Articles [101] and [102] of the Treaty and national competition laws

1. Where the competition authorities of the Member States or national courts apply national competition law to agreements, decisions by associations of undertakings or concerted practices within the meaning of Article [101(1)] which may affect trade between Member States within the meaning of that provision, they shall also apply Article [101] to such agreements, decisions or concerted practices. Where the competition authorities of the Member States or national courts apply national competition law to any abuse prohibited by Article [102], they shall also apply [Article 102].
2. The application of national competition law may not lead to the prohibition of agreements, decisions by associations of undertakings or concerted practices which may affect trade between Member States but which do not restrict competition within the meaning of Article [101(1)], or which fulfil the conditions of Article [101(3)] or which are covered by a Regulation for the application of Article [101(3)]. Member States shall not under this Regulation be precluded from adopting and applying on their territory stricter national laws which prohibit or sanction unilateral conduct engaged in by undertakings.
3. Without prejudice to general principles and other provisions of [Union] law, paragraphs 1 and 2 do not apply when the competition authorities and the courts of the Member States apply national merger control laws nor do they preclude the application of provisions of national law that predominantly pursue an objective different from that pursued by Articles [101 and 102].

Article 3(1) accordingly provides that where an NCA or national court applies national competition law to conduct which constitutes an agreement, decision, or concerted practice within the meaning of Article 101 or an abuse prohibited by Article 102, which affects trade between Member States,[944] it *shall* also apply Article 101 or Article 102.[945] National authorities are obliged when applying national law to agreements and abusive conduct that affect trade between Member States to also apply EU law. We mentioned Article 11(6) of Regulation 1/2003 in Section 8.D.ii. In *Toshiba*,[946] the CJ held that the combined effect of that provision with Article 3(1) is that the Commission's initiation of proceedings deprives NCAs of their competence to apply Articles 101 and 102 and national competition laws until the Commission proceedings are concluded.

[940] Case 6/64, *Costa v ENEL* EU:C:1964:66. [941] See Chap 8, Section 3.
[942] Case 14/68, *Walt Wilhelm v Bundeskartellamt* EU:C:1969:4, para. 9.
[943] Ibid. The fact that an agreement had been authorised at the national level did not preclude the Commission from subsequently finding that the agreement in fact infringes Art. 101: see Case C-360/92 P, *Publishers' Association v Commission* EU:C:1995:6.
[944] For the meaning of an effect on trade between Member States, see Chap 4, Section 5.E and Chap 6, Section 5.E.
[945] Reg. 1/2003, Art. 3(1).
[946] In Case C-17/10, *Toshiba v Úřad pro ochranu hospodářské soutěže* EU:C:2012:72.

In order to provide a level playing field,[947] Article 3(2) deals with the relationship between EU and national law and, specifically, with when national authorities may apply stricter national laws to agreements or conduct. The position differs depending upon whether Article 101 or Article 102 applies. If an agreement is authorised by Article 101, either because it does not restrict competition within the meaning of Article 101(1), it fulfils the criteria of Article 101(3), or satisfies the conditions of a block exemption, it cannot be prohibited by national law. The national authorities are, however, free to apply national competition laws which are stricter than Article 102 to unilateral conduct. They may therefore prohibit or impose sanctions on unilateral conduct engaged in by undertakings which does not constitute an abuse of a dominant position.[948] The Digital Markets Act[949] qualifies this freedom, however, insofar as it precludes the application of national competition rules prohibiting forms of unilateral conduct *other than* abuses of dominant positions, which are applied to gatekeeper undertakings within the meaning of that regulation and which cover the same ground as the obligations imposed by the DMA.[950]

Article 3(2) does not address the position where conduct is prohibited by Article 101 or Article 102. However, the principle of supremacy of Union law means that such an agreement or conduct cannot be permitted under national law.

Article 3(3) makes it clear that neither Article 3(1) nor Article 3(2) applies where the authority wishes to apply national merger control rules or national provisions that predominantly pursue a different objective to agreements or conduct. An NCA applying national merger rules to an acquisition or joint venture which is not a concentration with a Union dimension (or which has a Union dimension but has been referred back to the NCA) does not have to apply Article 101 or Article 102. Further, the Regulation does not preclude the implementation of more onerous 'national legislation, which protects other legitimate interests provided that such legislation is compatible with general principles and other provisions of [Union] law'.[951] This means that regulators applying sectoral powers which pursue a predominantly different objective to Articles 101 and 102, are not obliged to apply Article 101 or Article 102. To the extent that they are applying national competition rules or sectoral powers pursuing the same objective, however, they must apply Articles 101 and 102 and comply with Article 3(2).

10. *NE BIS IN IDEM* (DOUBLE JEOPARDY)

The principle of *ne bis in idem* (double jeopardy) means that a party cannot be prosecuted, tried, and convicted twice for the same (criminal) behaviour.[952] It is enshrined in Article 50 of the EU Charter of Fundamental Rights and is a fundamental principle of Union law.[953] Although Article 50

[947] Reg. 1/2003, recital 8.

[948] Perhaps the most notable applicable of this power was the decision of the Bundeskartellamt in its *Facebook Germany* investigation (discussed in Chap 16, Section 5.B.ii), to proceed solely on the basis of the German rule prohibiting 'abuse of market power' and not Art. 102 in parallel, on the basis that 'only the case-law of the highest German court has been established which can take into account constitutional or other legal principles (in this case data protection) in assessing abusive practices of a dominant company'. See Bundeskartellamt, 'Bundeskartellamt prohibits Facebook from combining user data from different sources. Background information on the Bundeskartellamt's Facebook proceeding', 7 February 2019, <www.bundeskartellamt.de/SharedDocs/Publikation/EN/Pressemitteilungen/2019/07_02_2019_Facebook_FAQs.pdf?__blob=publicationFile&v=6>.

[949] Reg. (EU) 2022/1925 of the European Parliament and of the Council of 14 September 2022 on contestable and fair markets in the digital sector and amending Directives (EU) 2019/1937 and (EU) 2020/1828 (DMA) [2022] OJ L265/1.

[950] Ibid., Art. 1(6)(b).

[951] Reg. 1/2003, recital 9.

[952] For the issue of whether competition proceedings are civil or criminal, see Section 5.

[953] Cases 18 and 35/65, *Gutmann v Commission* EU:C:1966:24; Commission Green Paper, 'On Conflicts of Jurisdiction and the Principle of *ne bis in idem* in Criminal Proceedings', COM(2005) 696 final; M. Wasmeier and N. Thwaites, 'The Development of *ne bis in idem* into a Transnational Fundamental Right in EU Law: Comments on Recent Developments' (2006) 31 *ELRev* 565; R. Nazzini, 'Fundamental Rights beyond Legal Positivism: Rethinking the *Ne Bis in Idem* Principle in EU Competition Law' (2014) 2 *J of Antitrust Enforcement* 225; A. Andreangeli, *EU Competition Enforcement and Human Rights* (Edward Elgar, 2008), 207–212.

is the only fair trial right within the Charter that is expressly restricted to criminal offences,[954] it is generally accepted that the Commission's fining procedures in competition cases are 'criminal' in nature,[955] an approach essentially confirmed by the ECtHR in *Menarini*.[956] Whether domestic proceedings under Article 101 or 102 or which are brought under an alternative regulatory framework are criminal in nature must be determined by reference to the particular circumstances,[957] applying the '*Engel*' criteria.[958]

In respect of competition cases, the principle of *ne bis in idem* precludes an undertaking from being found guilty or proceedings being brought against it a second time on the grounds of anti-competitive conduct in respect of which it has been penalised or declared not liable by a previous unappealable decision.[959] It was explained in Section 7.A.viii that the *ne bis in idem* principle is not engaged where decisions are annulled for procedural reasons and subsequently readopted.[960] The Commission's hierarchically superior role within the EU competition enforcement system[961] makes it unlikely that an NCA or national court would seek to find a violation of Article 101 or 102 in circumstances where the Commission has already done so.[962] Double jeopardy concerns can nonetheless arise in a variety of circumstances within the EU competition framework: for instance, where competition law is applied to behaviour that has already been punished under a sector-specific regulatory regime; where two NCAs prosecute the same behaviour; or where the Commission prosecutes behaviour that has been the subject of enforcement activity at national level.

Under the test formulated in *Aalborg Portland*,[963] the CJ previously applied a different standard in competition cases than it did in other areas of EU law. This hinged on the idea of *idem crimen*, and meant that the *ne bis in idem* principle was engaged only where it could be demonstrated that the two legal regimes sought to protect the same legal asset, and not merely that the same offender was being prosecuted for the same behaviour.[964] Accordingly, it was necessary to establish that three conditions were fulfilled under the *Aalborg Portland* test: identity of the facts, unity of the offender, and unity of the legal interest protected.[965] The benefit of this approach, as Advocate General Bokek explained in *bpost*, is that it allows behaviour that harms 'different protected legal or social interests' to be prosecuted from those distinct standpoints in tandem.[966] Yet the distortion within the fabric of EU law that was created by having a competition-specific standard troubled many Advocates General,[967] and the notion of 'unity of legal interest' was elusive.

[954] See Section 5. [955] See case law cited in n. 62.

[956] *Menarini Diagnostics SRL v Italy*, App no. 43509/08, Judgment of 27 September 2011, and see also *Société Bouygues Telecom v France*, App. no. 2324/08.

[957] Case C-117/20 *bpost* EU:C:2022:202, paras. 25–26. [958] See n. 61.

[959] Cases C-238/99 P etc., *Limburgse Vinyl Maatschappij* EU:C:2002:582, para. 59. [960] Ibid.

[961] Including the facts that it can temporarily exclude enforcement activity by NCAs by opening a formal investigation under Art. 11(6) of Reg. 1/2003, and that Art. 16 of Reg. 1/2003 precludes both NCAs and national courts from taking decisions that would run counter to a Commission decision applying Art. 101 or 102. See also Case C-857/19, *Slovak Telekom v Protimonopolný úrad Slovenskej republiky* EU:C:2021:139, which emphasises that an NCA *cannot* take an infringement decision during the period it is relieved of its competences under Art. 11(6).

[962] The situation is more complicated where the Commission has adopted a commitments decision under Art. 9 of Reg. 1/2003: see discussion in Section 6.E.iii.d.

[963] Cases C-204/00 P etc., *Aalborg Portland* EU:C:2004:6.

[964] P. van Cleynenbreugel, '*BPost* and *Nordzucker*: Searching for the Essence of Ne Bis in Idem in European Union Law' (2022) 18 *EuConst* 357, 359.

[965] Cases C-204/00 P etc., *Aalborg Portland* EU:C:2004:6, para. 338; Case C-17/10, *Toshiba v Úřad pro ochranu hospodářské soutěže* EU:C:2012:72, para. 97.

[966] Opinion in Case 117/20, *bPost v Autorité belge de la concurrence* EU:C:2021:680, para. 126.

[967] See Opinion of Kokott AG in Case C-17/10, *Toshiba Corp v Úřad pro ochranu hospodářské soutěže* EU:C:2011:552, paras. 120–122 and Opinion of Wahl AG in Case C-617/17 *Powszechny Zakład Ubezpieczeń na Życie S.A. w Warszawie v Prezes Urzędu Ochrony Konkurencji I Konsumentów* EU:C:2018:976, paras. 18–49.

Two preliminary rulings delivered by the Grand Chamber in March 2022 offered an opportunity to clarify the rules. In *bpost*,[968] the defendant was the incumbent postal services provider in Belgium. It was fined under domestic postal regulation for imposing discriminatory tariffs, although that finding was later overturned on appeal. Subsequently, the NCA prosecuted the same behaviour as an abuse of dominance contrary to Article 102. The question referred by the national court was whether the *ne bis in idem* principle (which the court labelled the 'non' *bis in idem* principle) meant that the former proceeding precluded the latter. In *Nordzucker*,[969] the defendant was prosecuted concurrently by the Austrian and German competition authorities under Article 101 and its domestic equivalents for participation in a cartel that affected both Member States. Each NCA restricted the focus of its investigation to the defendant's activities on the relevant domestic market. The infringement decision of the German competition authority, however, made reference to a telephone conversation which had discussed the Austrian market. This led the first instance Austrian court subsequently to dismiss the competition authority's action against the defendant, on the basis that it had already been penalised for the behaviour in another Member State. Again, the question before the CJ was the extent to which the *ne bis in idem* principle precludes the application of competition law in that instance.

The CJ took an equivalent approach in both cases. Heeding the advice of its various Advocates General, it declared that 'the scope of the protection conferred by Article 50 of the Charter cannot vary from one Member State to another'.[970] Instead of its prior approach premised on *idem crimen*, it adopted a looser standard premised on *idem factum*, focused on the identify of facts between the two proceedings. Nonetheless, on the facts of the *bpost* case, the different legal interests protected by the two regimes was potentially relevant insofar as this might justify an exception to the general rule against double jeopardy. The point is explained in the extract below.

Case C-117/20, *bpost SA v Autorité belge de la concurrence* EU:C:2022:202

Court of Justice

28. The application of the *non bis in idem* principle is subject to a twofold condition, namely, first, that there must be a prior final decision (the 'bis' condition) and, secondly, that the prior decision and the subsequent proceedings or decisions must concern the same facts (the 'idem' condition).

The 'bis' condition

29. As regards the 'bis' condition, in order for a judicial decision to be regarded as having given a final ruling on the facts subject to a second set of proceedings, that decision must not only have become final but must also have been taken after a determination has been made as to the merits of the case (. . . *M*, C-398/12, EU:C:2014:1057, paragraphs 28 and 30).

. . .

The 'idem' condition

31. As regards the 'idem' condition, it follows from the very wording of Article 50 of the Charter that that provision prohibits the same person from being tried or punished in criminal proceedings more than once for the same offence.

. . .

[968] Case C-117/20, *bpost* EU:C:2022:202.
[969] Case C-151/20, *Bundeswettbewerbsbehörde v Nordzucker* EU:C:2022:203.
[970] Case C-117/20, *bpost* EU:C:2022:202, para. 34, and Case C-151/20, *Nordzucker* EU:C:2022:203, para. 39.

33. . . . [T]he relevant criterion for the purposes of assessing the existence of the same offence is identity of the material facts, understood as the existence of a set of concrete circumstances which are inextricably linked together and which have resulted in the final acquittal or conviction of the person concerned. Therefore, Article 50 of the Charter prohibits the imposition, with respect to identical facts, of several criminal penalties as a result of different proceedings brought for those purposes (. . . *Menci*, C-524/15, EU:C:2018:197, paragraph 35, and . . . *Garlsson Real Estate and Others*, C-537/16, EU:C:2018:193, paragraph 37 and the case-law cited).

34. Moreover, . . . the legal classification under national law of the facts and the legal interest protected are not relevant for the purposes of establishing the existence of the same offence, in so far as the scope of the protection conferred by Article 50 of the Charter cannot vary from one Member State to another (. . . *Menci*, C-524/15, EU:C:2018:197, paragraph 36, and . . . *Garlsson Real Estate and Others*, C-537/16, EU:C:2018:193, paragraph 38).

35. The same is true of the application of the non bis in idem principle laid down in Article 50 of the Charter in the field of EU competition law, inasmuch as . . . the scope of the protection conferred by that provision cannot, unless otherwise provided by EU law, vary from one field of EU law to another.

36. In that regard, . . . the 'idem' condition requires the material facts to be identical. By contrast, the non bis in idem principle is not intended to be applied where the facts in question are not identical but merely similar.

37. Identity of the material facts must be understood to mean a set of concrete circumstances stemming from events which are, in essence, the same, in that they involve the same perpetrator and are inextricably linked together in time and space (. . . *Sergey Zolotukhin v. Russia*, CE:ECHR:2009:0210JUD001493903, § 83 and 84, and . . . *Pirttimäki v. Finland*, CE:ECHR:2014:0520JUD003523211, § 49 to 52).

38. In the present case, it is for the referring court to determine whether the facts in respect of which the two sets of proceedings were initiated under sectoral rules and competition law, respectively, are identical. To that end, it is for that court to examine the facts taken into account in each of those proceedings, as well as the infringement period alleged.

39. Should the referring court consider that the facts which are the subject of the two sets of proceedings at issue in the main action are identical, that duplication would constitute a limitation of the fundamental right guaranteed by Article 50 of the Charter.

Justification for a possible limitation of the fundamental right guaranteed by Article 50 of the Charter.

40. A limitation of the fundamental right guaranteed by Article 50 of the Charter may be justified on the basis of Article 52(1) thereof (. . . *Spasic*, C-129/14 PPU, EU:C:2014:586, paragraphs 55 and 56, and . . . *Menci*, C-524/15, EU:C:2018:197, paragraph 40).

41. In accordance with the first sentence of Article 52(1) of the Charter, any limitation on the exercise of the rights and freedoms recognised by the Charter must be provided for by law and respect the essence of those rights and freedoms. According to the second sentence of Article 52(1) thereof, subject to the principle of proportionality, limitations on those rights and freedoms may be made only if they are necessary and genuinely meet objectives of general interest recognised by the European Union or the need to protect the rights and freedoms of others.

. . .

43. Such a possibility of a duplication of proceedings and penalties respects the essence of Article 50 of the Charter, provided that the national legislation does not allow for proceedings and penalties in respect of the same facts on the basis of the same offence or in pursuit of the same objective, but provides only for the possibility of a duplication of proceedings and penalties under different legislation.

. . .

48. As regards compliance with the principle of proportionality, it requires that the duplication of proceedings and penalties provided for by the national legislation does not exceed what is appropriate and

necessary in order to attain the objectives legitimately pursued by that legislation, its being understood that, when there is a choice between several appropriate measures, recourse must be had to the least onerous and the disadvantages caused must not be disproportionate to the aims pursued (. . . *Menci*, C-524/15, EU:C:2018:197, paragraph 46 and the case-law cited).

49. In that regard, it must be stated that public authorities can legitimately choose complementary legal responses to certain conduct that is harmful to society through different procedures forming a coherent whole so as to address different aspects of the social problem involved, provided that the accumulated legal responses do not represent an excessive burden for the individual concerned (. . . *A and B v. Norway*, CE:ECHR:2016:1115JUD002413011, § 121 and 132). Consequently, the fact that two sets of proceedings are pursuing distinct objectives of general interest which it is legitimate to protect cumulatively can be taken into account, in an analysis of the proportionality of the duplication of proceedings and penalties, as a factor that would justify that duplication, provided that those proceedings are complementary and that the additional burden which that duplication represents can accordingly be justified by the two objectives pursued.

50. National rules which provide for the possible duplication of proceedings and penalties under sectoral rules and competition law are capable of achieving the objective of general interest of ensuring that each of the two sets of legislation concerned is applied effectively, since they are pursuing . . . distinct legitimate objectives . . . On that basis, it will be for the referring court to assess . . . whether the duplication of penalties of a criminal nature can be justified, in the dispute in the main proceedings, by the fact that the proceedings initiated by those authorities pursue complementary aims relating to different aspects of the same unlawful conduct (. . . *Menci*, C-524/15, EU:C:2018:197, paragraph 44).

51. With regard to the strict necessity of such duplication of proceedings and penalties, it is necessary to assess whether there are clear and precise rules making it possible to predict which acts or omissions are liable to be subject to a duplication of proceedings and penalties, and also to predict that there will be coordination between the different authorities, whether the two sets of proceedings have been conducted in a manner that is sufficiently coordinated and within a proximate timeframe and whether any penalty that may have been imposed in the proceedings that were first in time was taken into account in the assessment of the second penalty, meaning that the resulting burden, for the persons concerned, of such duplication is limited to what is strictly necessary and the overall penalties imposed correspond to the seriousness of the offences committed (. . . *Menci*, C-524/15, EU:C:2018:197, paragraphs 49, 52, 53, 55 and 58, and . . . *A and B v. Norway*, CE:ECHR:2016:1115JUD002413011, § 130 to 132).

52 Admittedly, . . . a full assessment of necessity as described in the preceding paragraph and, consequently, the overall analysis of the question as to whether the duplication of proceedings can be justified under Article 52(1) of the Charter, can only be undertaken in full ex post, given the nature of some of the factors to be taken into account.

53 However, the protection derived from the twofold condition governing the application of the *non bis in idem* principle, . . . subject to the possible justification under Article 52(1) of the Charter of a limitation of the rights that may flow from that principle in a specific case, respects the essence of Article 50 of the Charter . . . [R]eliance on such justification requires that it be established that the duplication of the proceedings in question was strictly necessary, taking account in that context, in essence, of the existence of a sufficiently close connection in substance and time between the two sets of proceedings involved (*Menci*, C-524/15, EU:C:2018:197, paragraph 61, and . . . *A and B v. Norway*, CE:ECHR:2016:1115JUD002413011, § 130). Accordingly, any justification for a duplication of penalties is subject to conditions which, when satisfied, are intended in particular to limit, albeit without calling into question the existence of 'bis' as such, the functionally distinct character of the proceedings in question and therefore the actual impact on the persons concerned of the fact that those proceedings against them are brought cumulatively.

The outcome in *bpost* was that the CJ gave a strong steer that, to the extent that the facts that comprised both the regulatory proceedings and the abuse of dominance investigation were 'identical' (and not merely 'similar'), then this duplication of proceedings constituted a prima facie infringement of the right to be protected from double jeopardy, as provided by Article 50 of the Charter. Nonetheless, the CJ accepted that this limitation was potentially justifiable, holding that 'public authorities can legitimately choose complementary legal responses to certain conduct that is harmful to society through different procedures forming a coherent whole'.[971] The CJ indicated certain factors that would support a conclusion that the duplication was legitimate: namely, that the duplication represented a proportionate response to the diverse public interest objectives pursued; that there were 'clear and precise rules' that allowed an *ex ante* determination of when duplication might arise; and that there was sufficient 'coordination' between the two prosecuting authorities, with respect to the time frame and penalties imposed.

In *Nordzucker*, the CJ reiterated that the crux of the principle is the identity of the material facts, 'understood as the existence of a set of concrete circumstances which are inextricably linked together and which have resulted in the final acquittal or conviction of the person concerned'.[972] This would preclude, inter alia, an NCA in one Member State taking subsequent proceedings against behaviour that had already been sanctioned in an infringement decision by an NCA in another Member State. Yet the 'mere fact' that certain conduct was referenced in the initial infringement decision, as on the facts of *Nordzucker*, was 'insufficient to support the inference that that factual element gave rise to the proceedings or was found by that authority to be one of the constituent elements of that infringement'.[973] Instead, questions of *ne bis in idem* would arise only to the extent that the earlier decision involved a reasoned legal assessment of the conduct, and sought to penalise it.[974] This itself was a factual question, which would have to be determined by reference to the circumstances.

Where two competition authorities penalise behaviour under the same antitrust provision but with respect to different relevant *markets*, no issue of *ne bis in idem* arises. This is because behaviour occurring on different markets does not satisfy the *idem* requirement, namely identical material facts.[975] This is also the case where the *same* NCA penalises conduct simultaneously under Article 101/102 and the equivalent provision of national competition law.[976] In this instance, it is because that principle 'specifically targets the *repetition* of proceedings concerning the same material act which have been concluded by a final decision'.[977] NCAs are, nonetheless, required to ensure that the cumulative fines imposed are proportionate to the nature of the infringement.[978]

Questions of potential double jeopardy have arisen on various occasions in the context of the Commission's enforcement activity. In *Archer Daniels Midland*,[979] the CJ held that the Commission was justified in refusing to take into account when setting the fine for a cartel violation that the undertaking had already been sanctioned in the US for participation in the same (worldwide) cartel, at least where it had not been proved that the actions complained of were identical. In *Showa Denko*, the CJ explained that, in applying competition law, the Commission is protecting specific Union interests, that the objective of deterrence which the Commission is entitled to pursue when setting the fine is to ensure compliance with the competition rules, and that consequently 'when assessing the deterrent

[971] Case C-117/20, *bpost* EU:C:2022:202, para. 49.

[972] Case C-151/20, *Nordzucker* EU:C:2022:203, para. 38; the same formulation was used in Case C-117/20, *bpost* EU:C:2022:202, para. 33.

[973] Ibid., para. 44. [974] Ibid., para. 45.

[975] Case C-857/19, *Slovak Telekom v Protimonopolný úrad Slovenskej republiky* EU:C:2021:139.

[976] Case C-617/19, *Powszechny Zakład Ubezpieczeń na Życie S.A. v Prezes Urzędu Ochrony Konkurencji i Konsumentów* EU:C:2019:283.

[977] Ibid., para. 32 (emphasis added). [978] Ibid., para. 38.

[979] Case C-397/03 P, *Archer Daniels Midland* EU:C:2006:328, paras. 46–53.

nature of a fine to be imposed for infringement of those rules, the Commission is not required to take into account any penalties imposed on an undertaking for infringement of the competition rules of non-member States'.[980] Where behaviour has already been addressed by another competition authority within the ECN, the Commission typically carves out this conduct from the scope of any investigation that it pursues subsequently. This occurred in *Aspen*,[981] which concerned alleged excessive pricing in the EEA excepting Italy, as the same practices had already been the subject of an infringement decision under Article 102 taken by the Italian competition authority.[982] In *Telekomunikacja Polska*, the Commission took the view that the fact that precisely the same behaviour had been fined previously by a sector-specific regulator did not preclude it from imposing a fine for breach of Article 102, because the legal interest protected was different.[983] The analysis of this question following *bpost* would probably take a different form, although it is not obvious that the ultimate legal conclusion would differ. In any event, in *Telekomunikacja Polska*, the Commission subtracted the (admittedly paltry) fines levied by the Polish telecommunications regulator from the fine it imposed.[984]

11. CRIMINALISATION AND SANCTIONS AGAINST INDIVIDUALS

EU competition law does not impose criminal liability or any type of sanction on natural persons, i.e. it does not punish individuals. The conduct of employees, directors, and officers by which an undertaking infringes the competition rules results in fines for the undertaking and not in penalties for those individuals.[985]

As we saw in Chapter 9, there is, however, a global trend for criminalising some forms of 'hardcore' cartel conduct. An increasing number of jurisdictions impose criminal liability on individuals for cartel behaviour. The most notorious is the US, where the Sherman Act may be enforced by the DOJ through both civil and criminal processes.[986] For the most part, only clear intentional violations, mostly cases of explicit price-fixing or bid-rigging, are the subject of criminal proceedings,[987] but prosecutions are pursued as a matter of determined and aggressive policy which includes custodial prison sentences.[988] The principal argument in favour of criminalisation is that it has a deterrent effect way beyond that produced by sanctions against undertakings.[989] There is evidence that the possibility of prison leads some international cartels to 'carve out' the US, i.e. to collude in respect of the rest of the world but not the US.[990] However, there is also a great deal of debate about how real such deterrence actually is. In order

980 Case C-289/04 P, *Showa Denko v Commission* EU:C:2006:431, para. 61.

981 AT.40394, *Aspen* 12 February 2021.

982 Ibid., fn. 4. See Decision of Autorità Garante della Concorrenza e del Mercato in Case A-480, *Incremento Prezzo Farmaci Aspen* 29 September 2016.

983 See e.g. COMP/39.525, *Telekomunikacja Polska* 22 June 2011, paras. 136–139.

984 Ibid., para. 920.

985 See the discussion of fines, in Section 6.H. Where individuals give misleading or incorrect information in the course of an inspection under Art. 20, for instance, the fine for the procedural offence is levied on the undertaking. Although the Commission now has power to conduct an inspection on the homes of individuals under Art. 21, it is still only the undertaking that is responsible for what is found there.

986 The Federal Trade Commission has no criminal jurisdiction.

987 H. Hovenkamp, *Federal Antitrust Policy: The Law of Competition and its Practice* (4th edn, West, 2011), 643.

988 Statistics on the use of criminal sanctions in antitrust cases are available on the US Department of Justice's website, <www.justice.gov/atr/criminal-enforcement-fine-and-jail-charts>.

989 See G. Werden, S. Hammond, and B. Barnett, 'Deterrence and Detection of Cartels: Using all the Tools and Sanctions', DOJ Speech, 1 March 2012, <www.justice.gov/atr/public/speeches/283738.pdf>.

990 M. Bloom, 'Immunity/Leniency/Financial Incentives/Plea Bargaining', 11th EUI Competition Law and Policy Workshop, 2006; applications for immunity under the DOJ leniency programme are usually accompanied by leniency applications from the individuals implicated.

to deter, there has to be knowledge of the sanction and a likelihood of detection and punishment. These factors are not always present in the cartel context. Furthermore, in democratic societies there needs to be acceptance of cartel conduct as criminal behaviour,[991] and there are practical difficulties in many jurisdictions in formulating an offence in terms which fit into the criminal law system. All these matters, and others, have produced a large body of literature on the subject of criminalisation.[992]

A number of EU Member States provide for the criminalisation of behaviour that constitutes a breach of Article 101 and sometimes Article 102.[993] The problems of criminalisation in practice were demonstrated in the UK (albeit no longer a Member State), where the Enterprise Act 2002 originally created a statutory criminal offence for individuals who 'dishonestly' engaged in price-fixing, market-sharing, and bid-rigging arrangements. Individuals are liable to a sentence of up to five years' imprisonment and/or a substantial fine. The standard for 'dishonesty' was that laid down in the normal criminal law, however, and there were concerns about how readily a jury might be persuaded that cartel behaviour is indeed *dishonest*. Prosecutions under the Act proved very difficult to bring, and the UK Government subsequently removed the dishonesty requirement and replaced it with statutory exclusions and defences.[994] In the 'Tyrie Letter', the then Chairman of the UK's Competition and Markets Authority (CMA) suggested that the criminal enforcement powers of the CMA might instead 'sit more naturally with an agency that routinely brings criminal prosecutions, such as the Serious Fraud Office'.[995] It has been argued that disqualification orders against company directors may provide a more effective route to securing compliance with competition rules than criminal sanctions.[996]

Liability on individuals for breach of the EU competition rules could only be imposed across the EU by a harmonisation measure which would entail each Member State making it an offence within its jurisdiction. Such a measure would need to go through the Council, meaning that EU-wide individual liability is not an imminent prospect. In the meantime, the disparity between members of the ECN in matters of individual liability can lead to difficulties.[997]

[991] For empirical work suggesting that this may not always be the case even in jurisdictions which adopt cartel criminalisation, see C. Beaton-Wells and C. Parker, 'Justifying Criminal Sanctions for Cartel Conduct: A Hard Case' (2013) 1 *J of Antitrust Enforcement* 198, and A. Stephan, 'An Empirical Evaluation of the Normative Justifications for Cartel Criminalisation' (2017) 37 *Legal Studies* 621.

[992] See e.g. K. Cseres, M. Schinkel, and F. Vogelaar (eds.), *Criminalization of Competition Law Enforcement: Economic and Legal Implications for the EU Member States* (Edward Elgar, 2006); C. Beaton-Wells and A. Ezrachi (eds.), *Criminalising Cartels: Critical Studies of an International Regulatory Movement* (Hart Publishing, 2011); C. Harding, 'A Pathology of Business Cartels: Original Sin or the Child of Regulation?' (2010) 1 *NJECL* 44; A. Stephan, 'Survey of Public Attitudes to Price-fixing and Cartel Enforcement in Britain' (2008) 5 *Competition Law Review* 123; P. Whelan, 'A Principled Argument for Personal Criminal Sanctions as Punishment under EC Cartel Law' (2007) 30 *World Competition* 197; I. Lianos and I. Kokorris (eds.), *The Reform of Competition Law: Towards an Optimal Enforcement System* (Kluwer International, 2010); P. Grodecki and S. Maxwell, 'Alternative Approaches to Sentencing in Cartel Cases: The European Union, Ireland and the United States' (2013) 9 *European Law Journal* 341; P. Whelan, *The Criminalization of European Antitrust Enforcement: Theoretical, Legal, and Practical Challenges* (Oxford University Press, 2014); A. Jones and R. Williams, 'The UK Response to the Global Effort Against Cartels: Is Criminalization Really the Solution' (2014) 2 *J of Antitrust Enforcement* 100; A. Stephan, 'Four Key Challenges to the Successful Criminalization of Cartel Law' (2014) 2 *J of Antitrust Enforcement* 333.

[993] In Ireland, for instance, the Competition Act, 2002, creates separate offences of violating Art. 101(1) and the domestic equivalent (s. 6) and Art. 102 and the domestic equivalent (s. 7).

[994] See Enterprise Act 2002, ss. 188A–188B, as amended by the Enterprise and Regulatory Reform Act 2013.

[995] Letter of Lord Tyrie to the Secretary of State for Business, Energy and Industrial Strategy, 21 February 2019, <https://assets.publishing.service.gov.uk/government/uploads/system/uploads/attachment_data/file/781151/Letter_from_Andrew_Tyrie_to_the_Secretary_of_State_BEIS.pdf>.

[996] See A. Khan, 'Rethinking Sanctions for Breaching Competition Law: Is Director Disqualification the Answer?' (2012) 35 *World Competition* 77; and J. Galloway, 'Securing the Legitimacy of Individual Sanctions in UK Competition Law' (2017) 40 *World Competition* 121.

[997] See B. Perrin, 'Challenges Facing the EU Network of Competition Authorities: Insights from a Comparative Criminal Law Perspective' (2006) 31 *ELRev* 540.

12. CONCLUSIONS

1. Regulation 1/2003 made fundamental changes to the way that Articles 101 and 102 are enforced, with the principal objective of strengthening enforcement of those rules. The changes have had significant effects on the Commission, NCAs, and undertakings. The operation of the ECN has so far been highly successful, but the judgment in *Tele2 Polska* underlined the fact that NCAs are junior partners to the Commission.

2. The Commission gained new powers under Regulation 1/2003 to facilitate its task of detecting and punishing breaches of Articles 101 and 102. It pursues an increasingly aggressive policy, particularly towards cartels, with draconian fines. Its actions against cartels are heavily dependent on the leniency policy and the settlement procedure allows the Commission to save time and resources.

3. The Commission's extensive use of the commitments decision procedure in Article 9, of the settlement procedure in cartel cases, and of informal settlements under Article 7 in non-cartel cases, has changed the nature of the Commission's enforcement strategy. Top-down enforcement has been largely replaced by negotiated outcomes. This is advantageous to the Commission and may be convenient for the parties, but commitments decisions in particular are prejudicial to the development of the law, as what may be novel and controversial points of law, and remedies which would be impossible under Article 7, are removed from review by the EU Courts.

4. The extensive powers of the Commission in competition cases and the (limited) role of the EU Courts are questionable in the light of the human rights guarantees provided in the EU's own legal order, and in the ECHR which it reflects and to which the EU is, under the Treaty of Lisbon, committed to acceding. The CJ has approved the enforcement system as compliant with the Charter, and changed the terms in which the intensity of the GC's review is described, but it has not put an end to criticisms of the system. The question remains as to whether the investigation and prosecutorial functions of the Commission should be separated from adjudication.

5. The ECN+ Directive has sought to improve both the institutional position and enforcement powers of the NCAs. The harmonised powers that must be guaranteed to NCAs are mirrored on those possessed by the Commission, suggesting that the latter functions as a (now mandatory) model for 'best practice' in public enforcement of the EU competition rules. The continuing absence of a centralised regime for cartel leniency applications remains a notable omission, particularly in the light of concerns that the growing importance of private damages claims may be having a negative knock-on effect on public leniency programmes.

13. FURTHER READING

A. Books

AMATO, G., *Antitrust and the Bounds of Power* (Hart Publishing, 1997), Chap 8

ANDERSSON, H., *Dawn Raids under Challenge: Due Process Aspects on the European Commission's Dawn Raid Practices* (Hart Publishing, 2018)

ANDREANGELI, A., *EU Competition Enforcement and Human Rights* (Edward Elgar, 2008)

BEATON-WELLS, C., and EZRACHI, A. (eds.), *Criminalising Cartels: Critical Studies of an International Regulatory Movement* (Hart Publishing, 2011)

BEATON-WELLS, C., and TRAN, C., *Anti-cartel Enforcement in a Contemporary Age: Leniency Religion* (Hart Publishing, 2015)

CASTILLO DE LA TORRE, F., AND GIPPINI FOURNIER, E., *Evidence, Proof and Judicial Review in EU Competition Law* (Edward Elgar, 2017)

Ehlermann, C.-D., and Atanasiu, I. (eds.), *European Competition Law Annual 2000: The Modernisation of EC Antitrust Policy* (Hart Publishing, 2001)

Ehlermann, C.-D., and Atanasiu, M. (eds.), *European Competition Law Annual 2001: Effective Enforcement of EC Antitrust Law* (Hart Publishing, 2003)

Ehlermann, C.-D., and Marquis, M. (eds.), *European Competition Law Annual 2008: Antitrust Settlements Under EC Competition Law* (Hart Publishing, 2010)

Ehlermann, C.-D., and Marquis, M. (eds.), *European Competition Law Annual 2009: The Evaluation of Evidence and its Judicial Review in Competition Cases* (Hart Publishing, 2011)

Faull, J., and Nikpay, A., *The EU Law of Competition* (3rd edn, Oxford University Press, 2014), Chap. 2 and Chap 8, 8.95–8.725

Frese, M., *Sanctions in EU Competition Law: Principles and Practice* (Hart Publishing, 2016)

Kalintiri, A., *Evidence Standards in EU Competition Enforcement: The EU Approach* (Hart Publishing, 2019)

Kerse, C., and Khan, N. (Khan ed.), *EU Antitrust Procedure* (6th edn, Sweet & Maxwell, 2012)

Lianos, I., and Geradin, D. (eds.), *Handbook on European Competition Law (Enforcement and Procedure)* (Edward Elgar, 2013)

Merola, M., and Derenne, J., *The Role of the Court of Justice of the European Union in Competition Law Cases* (Bruylant, 2012)

Nazzini, R., *Concurrent Proceedings in Competition Law* (Oxford University Press, 2004)

Nazzini, R., *Competition Enforcement and Procedure* (Oxford University Press, 2016)

Nihoul, P., and Skoczy, T. (eds.), *Procedural Fairness in Competition Proceedings* (Edward Elgar, 2015)

Ortiz Blanco, L., *EU Competition Procedure* (4th edn, Oxford University Press, 2022)

Simonsson, I., *Legitimacy in EU Cartel Control* (Hart Publishing, 2010)

Sokol, D. D., and Guzman, A. T. (eds.), *Antitrust Procedural Fairness* (Oxford University Press, 2019)

Van Bael, I., *Due Process in EU Competition Proceedings* (Kluwer, 2011)

Van den Bergh, R. J., *Comparative Competition Law and Economics* (Edward Elgar Publishing, 2017), Chap 8.

Wardhaugh, B., *Cartels, Markets and Crime: A Normative Justification for Criminalization of Economic Collusion* (Cambridge University Press, 2014)

Wesseling, R., *The Modernisation of EC Antitrust Law* (Hart Publishing, 2000)

Whelan, P., The Criminalization of European Antitrust Enforcement: Theoretical, Legal, and Practical Challenges (Oxford University Press, 2014)

B. Chapters in Books

Forrester, I., 'A Bush in Need of Pruning: The Luxuriant Growth of "Light Judicial Review"' in C.-D. Ehlermann and M. Marquis (eds.), *European Competition Law Annual 2009: The Evaluation of Evidence and its Judicial Review in Competition Cases* (Hart Publishing, 2010)

Lianos, I., 'Is the Availability of "Appropriate" Remedies a Limit to Competition Law Liability under Article 102 TFEU? The Mischiefs of "Discretionary Remedialism" in Competition Law' in F. Etro and I. Kokkoris (eds.), *Competition Law and the Enforcement of Article 102* (Oxford University Press, 2010), Chap 10

PACE, L. F., and SEIDEL, K., 'The Drafting and Role of Regulation 17: A Hard-Fought Compromise' in K. K. Patel and H. Schweitzer (eds.), *The Historical Foundations of EU Competition Law* (Oxford University Press, 2013)

WAGNER-VON PAPP, F., 'Remedies, Sanctions and Commitments' in P. Akman, O. Brook, and K. Stylianou (eds.), *Research Handbook on Abuse of Dominance and Monopolization* (Edward Elgar, 2023)

C. Articles

ALBERS, M., and JOURDAN, J., 'The Role of Hearing Officers in EU Competition Proceedings: A Historical and Practical Perspective' (2011) 2 *JECLAP* 185

AMORY, B. E., and DESMEDT, Y. N., 'The European Ombudsman's First Scrutiny of the EC Commission in Antitrust Matters' [2009] *ECLR* 205

ANDREANGELI, A., 'The Impact of the Modernisation Regulation on the Guarantees of Due Process in Competition Proceedings' (2006) 31 *ELRev* 342

ANDREANGELI, A., 'Towards an EU Competition Court: "Article-6-Proofing" Antitrust Proceedings before the Commission?' (2007) 4 *World Competition* 595

BAILEY, D., 'Scope of Judicial Review Under Article 101 EC' (2004) 41 *CMLRev* 1327

BEATON-WELLS, C., and PARKER, C., 'Justifying Criminal Sanctions for Cartel Conduct: A Hard Case' (2013) 1 *J of Antitrust Enforcement* 198

BILLIET, P., 'How Lenient is the EC Leniency Policy? A Matter of Certainty and Predictability' [2009] *ECLR* 14

BRAMMER, S., 'Concurrent Jurisdiction under Regulation 1/2003 and the Issue of Case Allocation' (2005) 42 *CMLRev* 1383

BRONKERS. M., and VALLERY, A., 'No Longer Presumed Guilty: The Impact of Fundamental Rights on Certain Dogmas of EU Competition Law' (2011) 43 *World Competition* 535

CASTILLO DE LA TORRE, F., 'Evidence, Proof and Judicial Review in Cartel Cases' (2009) 32 *World Competition* 505

CENGIZ, F., 'Multi-level Governance in Competition Policy: The European Competition Network' (2010) 35 *ELRev* 660

CENGIZ, F., 'Judicial Review and the Rule of Law in the EU Competition Law Regime after *Alrosa*' (2011) 7 *European Competition Journal* 127

CONNOR, J. M., 'Cartel Fine Severity and the European Commission 2007–2011' [2011] *ECLR* 58

DEKEYSER, K., and GAUER, C., 'The New Enforcement System for Articles 101 and 102 and the Rights of Defence' [2004] *Fordham Corp L Inst* 549

DUNNE, N., 'Commitment Decisions in EU Competition Law' (2014) 10 *J of Competition Law and Economics* 399

EZRACHI, A., AND KOVACIC, W., 'Journal of Antitrust Enforcement Agency Effectiveness Study' (2016) 4 *J of Antitrust Enforcement* 229

FAURE, M., AND WEBER, F., 'The Diversity of the EU Approach to Law Enforcement—Towards a Coherent Model Inspired by a Law and Economics Approach' (2017) 18 *German LJ* 823

Forrester, I., 'Due Process in EC Competition Case: A Distinguished Institution with Flawed Procedures' (2009) 34 *ELRev* 817

Forrester, I., 'A Challenge for Europe's Judges: The Review of Fines in Competition Cases' (2011) 36 *ELRev* 185

Gauer, C., and Jaspers, M., 'Designing a European Solution for a "One Stop Leniency Shop"' [2006] *ECLR* 685

Gautier, A., and Petit, N., 'Optimal Enforcement of Competition Policy: The Commitments Procedure Under Uncertainty' (2018) 45 *European J of Law and Economics* 195

Geradin, D., 'Breaking the EU Antitrust Enforcement Deadlock: Re-empowering the Courts?' (2011) 36 *ELRev* 457

Geradin, D., 'Antitrust Compliance Programmes and Optimal Antitrust Enforcement: A Reply to Wouter Wils' (2013) 1 *J of Antitrust Enforcement* 1

Geradin, D., and Henry, D., 'EC Fining for Competition Law Violations: An Empirical Study of the Commission's Decisional Practice and the Community Courts' Judgments' (2005) 1 *European Competition Journal* 401

Geradin, D., and Mattioli, E., 'The Transactionalization of EU Competition Law: A Positive Development?' (2017) 8 *J of Competition Law and Economics* 634

Grodecki, P., and Maxwell, S., 'Alternative Approaches to Sentencing in Cartel Cases: The European Union, Ireland and the United States' (2013) 9 *European Law Journal* 341

ter Haar, M., 'Obstruction of Investigation in EU Competition Law: Issues and Developments in the European Commission's Approach' (2013) 2 *World Competition* 247

Heimler, A., and Mehta, K., 'Violations of Antitrust Provisions: The Optimal Level of Fines for Achieving Deterrence' (2012) 35 *World Competition* 103

Hellwig, M., and Huschelrath, K., 'Cartel Cases and the Cartel Enforcement Process in the European Union 2001–2015: A Quantitative Assessment' (2017) 62 *Ant Bull* 400

Holles, B., 'The Hearing Officer: Thirty Years Protecting the Right to Be Heard' (2013) 36 *World Competition* 5

Ioannidou, M., '"Responsive" Remodeling of Competition Law Enforcement' (2020) 40 *OJLS* 848

Joshua, J., 'The Element of Surprise' (1983) 8 *ELRev* 3

Kalintiri, A., 'What's in a Name? The Marginal Standard of Review of "Complex Economic Assessments" in EU Competition Enforcement' (2016) 53 *CMLRev* 1283

Kalintiri, A., 'Revising Parental Liability in EU Competition Law' (2018) 43 *ELRev* 145

Katsoulacos, Y., and Ulph, D., 'Optimal Enforcement Structures for Competition Policy: Implications of Judicial Reviews and of Internal Error Correction Mechanisms' (2011) 7 *European Competition Journal* 71

Kellerbauer, M., 'Playground Instead of Playpen: The Court of Justice of the European Union's *Alrosa* Judgment on Article 9 of Regulation 1/2003' [2011] *ECLR* 1

Khan, A., 'Rethinking Sanctions for Breaching Competition Law: Is Director Disqualification the Answer?' (2012) 35 *World Competition* 77

Levy, N., and O'Donoghue, R., 'The EU Leniency Programme Comes of Age' (2004) 27 *World Competition* 75

Melícias, M. J., '*Did They Do It?* The Interplay Between the Standard of Proof and the Presumption of Innocence in EU Cartel Investigations' (2012) 35 *World Competition* 471

MONTAG, F., 'The Case for Radical Reform of the Infringement Procedure under Regulation 17' [1996] *ECLR* 428

NAZZINI, R., 'Administrative Enforcement, Judicial Review and Fundamental Rights in EU Competition Law: A Comparative Contextual-Functionalist Perspective' (2012) 49 *CMLRev* 971

NAZZINI, R., 'Fundamental Rights Beyond Legal Positivism: Rethinking the *Ne Bis In Idem* Principle in EU Competition Law' (2014) 2 *J of Antitrust Enforcement* 225

PETIT, N., and RATO, M., 'From Hard to Soft Enforcement of EC Competition Law—A Bestiary of "Sunshine" Enforcement Instruments', 2008 <http://ssrn.com/abstract=1270109>

PREK, M., and LEFÈVRE, S., 'Competition Litigation Before the General Court: Quality if not Quantity' (2016) 53 *CMLRev* 65

RILEY, A., 'EC Antitrust Modernisation: The Commission Does Very Nicely—Thank You! Part One: Regulation 1 and the Notification Burden' [2003] *ECLR* 604

RILEY, A., 'EC Antitrust Modernisation: The Commission Does Very Nicely—Thank You! Part Two: Between the Idea and the Reality: Decentralisation under Regulation 1' [2003] *ECLR* 657

RILEY, A., and SOKOL, D., 'Rethinking Compliance' (2015) 3 *J of Antitrust Enforcement* 31

RITTER, C., 'How Far Can the Commission Go When Imposing Remedies for Antitrust Infringements?' (2016) 7 *JECLAP* 587

RODGER, B., 'The Commission White Paper on Modernisation of the Rules Implementing Articles 101 and 102 of the EC Treaty' (1999) 24 *ELRev* 653

SLATER, D., THOMAS, S., and WAELBROECK, D., 'Competition Law Proceedings Before the European Commission and the Right to a Fair Trial: No Need for Reform?' (2009) 5 *European Competition Journal* 97

STEPHAN, A., 'An Empirical Assessment of the European Leniency Notice' (2009) 5 *J of Competition Law and Economics* 537

STEPHAN, A., 'Four Key Challenges to the Successful Criminalization of Cartel Law' (2014) 2 *J of Antitrust Enforcement* 333

STONES, R., 'Commitment Decisions in EU Competition Enforcement: Policy Effectiveness v. the Formal Rule of Law' (2019) 38 *YEL* 361

SWAAK, C., and WESSLING, R., 'Reconsidering the Leniency Option: If Not First In, Good Reasons to Stay Out' [2015] *ECLR* 346

TEMPLE LANG, J., 'Commitment Decisions and Settlements with Antitrust Authorities and Private Parties Under European Antitrust Law' [2005] *Fordham Corp L Inst* 265

TEMPLE LANG, J., 'Judicial Review of Competition Decisions under the European Convention on Human Rights and the Importance of the EFTA Court: The *Norway Post* Judgment' (2012) 37 *ELRev* 464

TEMPLE LANG, J., 'The Strengths and Weaknesses of the DG Competition Manual of Procedure' (2013) 1 *J of Antitrust Enforcement* 132

VARONA, E. N., 'The Combination of the Investigative and Prosecutorial Function and the Adjudicative Function in EC Antitrust Enforcement: A Legal and Economic Analysis' (2004) 27 *World Competition* 201

VARONA, E. N., and DURÁTEZ, H. G., 'Interim Measures in Competition Cases Before the European Commission and the Courts' [2002] *ECLR* 512

VESTERDORF, B., 'Legal Professional Privilege and the Privilege Against Self-incrimination in EC Law: Recent Developments and Current Issues' [2004] *Fordham Corp L Inst* 107

VESTERDORF, B., 'The Court of Justice and Unlimited Jurisdiction: What Does It Mean in Practice?' (2009) 2 *Global Competition Policy* (June)

WAGNER-VON PAPP, F., 'Best and Even Better Practices in Commitment Procedures After *Alrosa*: The Dangers of Abandoning the "Struggle for Competition Law"' (2012) 49 *CMLRev* 929

WALSH, D. J., 'Carrots and Sticks—Leniency and Fines in EC Cartel Cases' [2009] *ECLR* 30

WASMEIER, M., and THWAITES, N., 'The Development of *Ne Bis in Idem* into a Transnational Fundamental Right in EU Law: Comments on Recent Developments' (2006) 31 *ELRev* 565

WATHELET, M., 'Commitment Decisions and the Paucity of Precedent' (2015) 6 *JECLAP* 553

WESSELING, R., 'A Principled Argument for Personal Criminal Sanctions as Punishment under EC Cartel Law' (2007) 30 *World Competition* 197

WESSELING, R., and VAN DER WOUDE, M., 'The Lawfulness and Acceptability of Enforcement of European Cartel Law' (2012) 35 *World Competition* 569

WHELAN, P., 'Legal Certainty and Cartel Criminalisation within the EU Member States' (2012) 71 *CLJ* 677

WHELAN, P., 'Cartel Criminalization and the Challenge of "Moral Wrongfulness"' (2013) 33 *OJLS* 535

WHELAN, P., 'Cartel Criminalisation and Due Process: The Challenge Imposing Criminal Sanctions Alongside Administrative Sanctions within the EU' (2013) 64 *Northern Ireland Legal Quarterly* 143

WILS, W., 'Self-incrimination in EC Antitrust Enforcement: A Legal and Economic Analysis' (2003) 26 *World Competition* 567

WILS, W., 'The Principle of *Ne Bis in Idem* in EC Antitrust Enforcement: A Legal and Economic Analysis' (2003) 26 *World Competition* 131

WILS, W., 'The European Commission's 2006 Guidelines on Antitrust Fines: A Legal and Economic Analysis' (2007) 30 *World Competition* 197

WILS, W., 'The Increased Level of Antitrust Fines, Judicial Review, and the European Convention on Human Rights' (2010) 33 *World Competition* 5

WILS, W., 'Discretion and Prioritisation in Public Antitrust Enforcement' (2011) 34 *World Competition* 353

WILS, W., 'Recidivism in EU Antitrust Enforcement: A Legal and Economic Analysis' (2012) 35 *World Competition* 5

WILS, W., 'The Oral Hearing in Competition Proceedings Before the European Commission' (2012) 35 *World Competition* 397

WILS, W., 'The Role of the Hearing Officer in Competition Proceedings Before the European Commission' (2012) 35 *World Competition* 431

WILS, W., 'Antitrust Compliance Programmes and Optimal Antitrust Enforcement' (2013) 1 *J of Antitrust Enforcement* 52

WILS, W., 'The Use of Leniency in EU Cartel Enforcement: An Assessment after Twenty Years' (2016) 39 *World Competition* 327

WILS, W., 'Private Enforcement of EU Antitrust Law and its Relationship with Public Enforcement: Past, Present and Future' (2017) 40 *World Competition* 3

YSEWYN, J., and KAHMANN, S., 'The Decline and Fall of the Leniency Programme in Europe' [2018] 1 *Concurrences* 44

14

PRIVATE ENFORCEMENT OF ARTICLES 101 AND 102

1. CENTRAL ISSUES

1. In Chapter 13, it is seen that the Commission and the national competition authorities (NCAs) play a crucial role in detecting, halting, deterring, and punishing violations of EU competition law.
2. This chapter focuses on private enforcement, which may supplement public enforcement by helping to ensure infringements of the rules are brought to an end, violations are deterred, and that the law is developed and clarified. It can also achieve corrective justice by allowing victims to obtain compensation.
3. Prior to the adoption of the Damages Directive (Directive 2014/104/EU) in November 2014, no EU legislation specifically addressed private rights of action for breach of Articles 101 and 102. In a series of judgments, however, the EU Courts made it clear that EU law requires national courts to:
    (a) apply directly effective provisions of EU law, including Articles 101 and 102;
    (b) ensure that their decisions do not run counter to those adopted by the Commission;
    (c) render provisions in an agreement that contravene Article 101 (and it seems Article 102) void and unenforceable;
    (d) ensure effective judicial protection of rights conferred by Articles 101 and 102 and that effective remedies are available to protect them. In particular, damages, entailing full compensation, must, in principle, be available to those that have suffered loss in consequence of a breach of Article 101 or 102. Further, in certain circumstances injunctions must be available to protect putative EU rights; and
    (e) ensure effective judicial protection by making sure that national rules governing such actions (i) are not less favourable than those relating to similar claims of a domestic nature and (ii) do not make it virtually impossible or excessively difficult to exercise the right that the national courts are obliged to protect (the principles of equivalence and effectiveness).
4. The Commission became concerned that the autonomy still conferred on national systems, and the obstacles to litigation existing in a number of Member States, meant that insufficient amounts of antitrust litigation were being brought by private individuals before national

courts in the EU, especially actions for damages.

5. Following extensive consultation and debate, the Damages Directive was adopted. The Directive is designed to ensure full compensation for all antitrust victims, to create a level playing field across the Member States through partial harmonisation of national laws governing such claims, and to ensure the effective coordination of public and private enforcement. All Member States have now transposed it into their national laws.

6. The Directive is supplemented by a Recommendation of non-binding principles for collective redress mechanisms for the Member States, a practical guide on the quantification of harm for damages to assist national courts, and guidelines on the passing-on of overcharges.

7. Private actions are becoming more routine. Indeed, it is now common, especially in cartel cases, for those harmed by competition law infringements to bring 'follow-on' actions for damages following a Commission or NCA decision finding a breach. Further, a stand-alone action (where the claimant has to prove the breach) may provide quicker relief for an applicant than that which can be provided by a competition authority or the only relief, if no public enforcement takes place.

2. INTRODUCTION

In order for the objectives of a competition law system to be achieved, effective enforcement of the rules must take place. Without it, the meaning of the law will not be developed and elucidated, breaches of the rules will not be halted, punished, or deterred, and victims of violations will not be compensated;[1] 'deterrence, compensation, and remediation'[2] will not be ensured. A critical issue to be determined when designing or developing a competition law system is therefore how effective enforcement mechanisms can be established.

Chapter 13 examines public enforcement through the European competition network (the Commission and the national competition authorities (NCAs)). Public enforcers, however, have limited resources, which they may prioritise and concentrate predominantly on ensuring that violations causing significant harm to consumer welfare are brought to an end and deterred. Accordingly, they are not able to root out and prevent all violations of the rules or to ensure compensation for victims.[3] Civil enforcement of the rules, through claims made by private litigants in the national courts and tribunals of the individual Member States (the national courts), may consequently also play a role in ensuring effective enforcement of competition law and redress. This chapter concentrates on

[1] W. Wils, 'The Relationship Between Public Antitrust Enforcement and Private Actions for Damages' (2009) 32 *World Competition* 3. See also N. Dunne, 'The Role of Private Enforcement within EU Competition Law' (2013–2014) 16 *Cambridge Yearbook of European Legal Studies* 143 (conceptualising competition law as rules to correct public wrongs, private wrongs, or market failures).

[2] See A. I. Gavil, 'Designing Private Rights of Action for Competition Policy Systems: The Role of Interdependence and the Advantages of a Sequential Approach' in P. Lowe and M. Marquis (eds.), *European Competition Law Annual 2011: Integrating Public and Private Enforcement Competition Law—Implications for Courts and Agencies* (Hart Publishing, 2014) (remediation provides means for halting offensive conduct and perhaps correcting for its adverse competitive effects, as with equitable and injunctive relief) and A. Komninos, 'Private Enforcement in the EU with Emphasis on Damages Actions' in I. Lianos and D. Geradin (eds.), *Handbook on European Competition Law: Enforcement and Procedure* (Edward Elgar, 2013).

[3] It may be possible to settle a case subject to a commitment to compensate victims, see e.g. OFT Press Release 88/06, 'Independent Schools agree settlement', 19 May 2006, Wils, n. 1, 12; Gavil, n. 2, 6.

private enforcement of the rules by those specifically affected by a competition law violation in the EU and considers what its principal function is, or should be, how it has been encouraged and facilitated in the EU, and how it is balanced with public enforcement.

The chapter commences in Section 3 by examining the way in which private antitrust litigation may contribute to effective enforcement of competition law and the core function, or functions, it may fulfil. In particular, it scrutinises the private enforcement system in the US where the legislature made a conscious policy choice, reflected in the antitrust laws, to encourage private litigants to participate in their enforcement.[4] It is seen that over time, and combined with other elements of, and developments in, the US system, the net result of this choice has been that, uniquely in the world, a vast majority of antitrust enforcement in the US (approximately 90 per cent of cases[5]) has traditionally emanated from private litigation rather than public enforcement. Such actions have been argued by some to play a crucial function, decentralising decision-taking, democratising antitrust policy, affirming the rule of law, deterring violations, and ensuring that victims obtain compensation. The system encouraged such high volumes of litigation, however, that a series of steps have been taken to limit and curtail litigation and to ensure that some of its perceived excesses are moderated;[6] in particular, to ensure that unmeritorious litigation is not encouraged which may have the potential to chill pro-competitive behaviour and so undermine the objectives of the antitrust laws.[7] There is now concern that some of these steps have contributed to the undue narrowing of the scope of the US antitrust laws and, consequently, their failure to protect competition adequately.[8]

Section 4 then examines the EU system, the obligations that EU law imposes on national courts, the different factors that have operated over time as barriers to private litigation in the EU Member States, and the package of measures that has been adopted to overcome these obstacles. In this section, it is seen that the Treaty contains no specific provision governing private rights of action following a violation of the EU competition law rules. Further, although private proceedings in the national courts have long been possible by virtue of the fact that Articles 101 and 102 have direct effect, and a key objective of Regulation 1/2003[9] was to allow a more decentralised enforcement system to emerge with the national courts (and NCAs) participating more actively within it, a number of factors initially combined to preclude private actions from developing evenly across the EU. Even though, therefore, litigation grew rapidly in some Member States, particularly the UK, the Netherlands, and Germany,[10] significant barriers to private antitrust actions existed in others.

For many years the Commission took the view that this EU situation was unsatisfactory and that more needed to be done, whilst avoiding the types of problems experienced in the US, to stimulate and harmonise national rules governing private enforcement which could then contribute to promoting

[4] See now especially Clayton Act 1914, s. 4 (superseding and expanding provisions set out in the Sherman Act 1890) and s. 16 and Section 3.

[5] See e.g. H. J. Hovenkamp, 'Quantification of Harm in Private Antitrust Actions in the United States', University of Iowa Legal Studies Research Paper, <https://papers.ssrn.com/sol3/papers.cfm?abstract_id=1758751>, Report for the European Commission, 'Making antitrust damages actions more effective in the EU: welfare impact and potential scenarios', DG COMP/2006/A3/012D, 28 and D. Crane, *The Institutional Structure of Antitrust Enforcement* (Oxford University Press, 2011), 163. It is difficult to get completely precise statistics relating to the ratio of private to public enforcement however (e.g. because many separate private action cases may be filed in relation to the same case before consolidation, there may be over-counting of private actions. In contrast, as many public cases may be resolved before a case is filed, there may be under-counting of government actions).

[6] '[T]he conventional wisdom in the international competition community [is] that U.S.-style private enforcement has been a disaster', R. H. Lande, 'The Proposed Damages Directive: The Real Lessons from the United States' (2014) 2 *CPI Antitrust Chronicle* 1, 1.

[7] But see, e.g., Lande, ibid. and Section 3. [8] See Chap. 1. [9] See n. 60 and text.

[10] See e.g. M. Kuijpers, S. Tuinenga, S. Wisking, K. Dietzel, S. Campbell, and A. Fritzsche, 'Actions for Damages in the Netherlands, the United Kingdom, and Germany' (2015) 6 *JECLAP* 129.

a culture of competition: 'The overall enforcement of the EU competition rules is best guaranteed through complementary public and private enforcement.'[11] After extensive debate and discussion as to whether, and if so how, to develop a European approach to private enforcement,[12] the Commission adopted a package of measures on private antitrust actions including:

- a Directive on certain rules governing actions for damages under national law for infringements of the competition law provisions of the Member States and of the EU (the Damages Directive). Following the publication of a draft Directive[13] in 2013, the final Directive was signed into law on 26 November 2014.[14] It had to be transposed into national law by 27 December 2016[15] and has now been transposed by all Member States (the Commission is in the process of examining whether the national rules implement the Directive completely and correctly);[16]
- a Recommendation of non-binding principles for collective redress mechanisms for Member States (although an EU Directive on consumer redress (allowing consumer organisations to bring damages actions and strengthening collective redress mechanisms across the EU) came into force on 24 December 2020, allowing qualified representatives to bring collective actions and seek injunctive relief or redress on behalf of EU consumer groups harmed by conduct in breach of specific EU consumer protection laws, it does not cover actions in respect of competition law);[17] and
- a practical guide on the quantification of harm for damages to assist national courts.[18]

[11] Commission, 'Proposal for a Directive of the European Parliament and the Council on certain rules governing actions for damages under national law for infringements of the Competition law provisions of the Member States and the European Union', COM(2013) 404 final, Explanatory Memorandum 1.2.

[12] They focus on damages actions (but see n. 17), see especially: a study prepared for DG Comp by Ashurst on damages actions before national courts of the then 25 Member States, D. Waelbroeck, D. Slater, and G. Even-Shoshan, 'Ashurst Study on the conditions of claims for damages in case of infringement of EC competition rules: Comparative Report' (2004) (The Ashurst Report); Commission, 'Green Paper on Damages Actions for Breach of the EC Antitrust Rules', COM(2005) 672 final, Commission, 'Staff Working Paper, Annex to the Green Paper on Damages Actions for Breach of the EC Antitrust Rules', SEC(2005) 1732; and Commission, 'White Paper on Damages Actions for Breach of the EC Antitrust Rules', COM(2008) 165 final.

[13] Commission Proposal, n. 11.

[14] Dir. 2014/104/EU on certain rules governing actions for damages under national law for infringements of the competition law provisions of the Member States and of the European Union [2014] OJ L349/1. The Digital Markets Act (DMA) also provides for enforcement by national authorities, including national courts, recitals 42 and 92 and Art. 39, see Chap. 16.

[15] Ibid., Art. 21. It also contains provisions stating the conditions for the temporal application of its substantive and non-substantive provisions, see Art. 22, see Case C-267/20, *Volvo and DAF Trucks* EU:C:2022:494, para. 35, Case C-57/21, *RegioJet as* EU:C:2023:6, and Case C-312/21, *Tráficos Manuel Ferrer SL v Daimler AG* EU:C:2023:99 (holding, respectively, that the rules relating to disclosure and estimation of harm in the Damages Dir. are procedural, not substantive, provisions). For a discussion of the extent to which the provisions of the Directive may be applicable retroactively, to proceedings prior to entry into force of the implementing legislation, or where not implemented, or incorrectly implemented, by the deadline for implementation, see P. Kirst, 'The Temporal Scope of the Damages Directive: A Comparative Analysis of the Applicability of the New Rules on Competition Infringements in Europe' (2020) 16(1) *European Competition Journal* 97 and P. Kirst, 'Skanska, Cogeco and Otis: Harmonisation Through the Back Door?' (2020) 41(5) *ECLR* 245.

[16] See nn. 202 and 203 and text, although some of the Member States implemented it late.

[17] Dir. (EU) 2020/1828 of the European Parliament and the Council on representative actions for the protection of the collective interests of consumers [2020] OJ L409/1, and repealing Dir. 2009/22/EC, COM(2018) 184 final, SWD(2018) 98 final and Commission Recommendation 2013/396/EU of 11 June 2013. Although the Commission originally intended to incorporate provisions on collective redress within the Damages Dir., this proposal caused controversy, especially in the European Parliament.

[18] Commission, 'Staff Working Document—Practical Guide on Quantifying Harm in Actions for Damages Based on Breaches of Article 101 or 102 of the Treaty on the Functioning of the European Union', SWD(2013) 205.

The Commission has also published complementary quantification guidance on the passing-on of overcharges.[19]

Section 5 concludes that although the package of reforms constitutes a courageous and innovative step to draw private litigants throughout the EU into the enforcement process, without encouraging unmeritorious actions and over-enforcement of the rules, it still remains to be seen whether it will be sufficient to boost and facilitate private damages actions evenly across the EU. Not only does the Directive not institute a completely harmonised framework, leaving a number of potential obstacles to national actions and areas of legal ambiguity outstanding, but some of the Directive's provisions introduce considerable complexities into national proceedings. Further, as scope for divergences between national rules remains, such differences are likely to continue to affect where litigants choose to commence their actions and to result in forum-shopping.

3. THE ROLE OF PRIVATE ANTITRUST LITIGATION, ITS RELATIONSHIP WITH PUBLIC ENFORCEMENT, AND THE EXPERIENCE IN THE US

Private civil actions provide a mechanism for achieving corrective justice by allowing compensation of victims. They thus have an important 'compensation function'—to compensate those harmed by the competition law infringement. Further, private enforcement (for example, in the form of actions for damages, restitution, and/or an injunction) may provide the springboard for the law to be developed, relieve enforcement pressure on public enforcement agencies, fill public enforcement gaps,[20] and result in violations of the rules being brought to an end and/or deterred (through exposing those in violation to liability for damages). Indeed, if violations are sufficiently deterred, the need for actions for compensation will be reduced. Private litigation may, like public enforcement, thus serve a variety of important functions, including remediation and 'deterrent' functions—to deter the violation of the competition rules and to punish the perpetrators;[21] it is interdependent with and complementary to public enforcement requiring public and private enforcement to be combined harmoniously.[22]

If private enforcement is to play a meaningful part in the enforcement process, however, important issues to be resolved include what the primary function of private enforcement should be—for example, should it be deterrence[23] of public wrongs that distort competition and harm society as a whole, or compensation of specific victims harmed by an antitrust infringement and whose private rights have been infringed—and how can the optimal balance between private and public enforcement be achieved? These factors may influence the shape of the rules which govern it.

[19] Guidelines for national courts on how to estimate the share of overcharge which was passed on to the indirect purchaser [2019] OJ C267/4.

[20] S. Weber Waller, 'Towards a Constructive Public–Private Partnership to Enforce Competition Law' (2006) 29 *World Competition* 367.

[21] See A. P. Komninos, 'Public and Private Antitrust Enforcement in Europe: Complement? Overlap?' (2006) 3 *Competition Law Review* 1, 9; R. Nazzini, and A. Nikpay, 'Private Actions in EC Competition Law' (2008) 4 *Competition Policy International* 107, 109.

[22] OECD (2011), 12; A. Komninos, *EC Private Antitrust Enforcement: Decentralised Application of the EC Competition Law by National Courts* (Hart Publishing, 2008), 9; R. Van den Bergh, 'Private Enforcement of European Competition Law and the Persisting Collective Action Problem' (2013) 20 *Maastricht J of European and Comparative Law* 12, 15; S. Campbell and T. Feunteun, 'Designing a Balanced System: Damages, Deterrence, Leniency and Litigants' Rights—A Claimant's Perspective' in Lowe and Marquis, n. 2, 27, 28–29; W. Kovacic, 'Private Rights of Action and the Enforcement of Public Competition Laws' in C. Baudenbacher (ed.), *Current Developments in European and International Competition Law: 17th St Gallen International Competition Law Forum ICF 2010* (Helbing & Lichtenhahn, 2011), 421.

[23] G. Becker and G. Stigler, 'Law Enforcement, Malfeasance and Compensation of Enforcers' (1974) 3 *J of Legal Studies* 1, 14. See also G. Becker, 'Crime and Punishment: An Economic Approach' (1968) 76 *J of Political Economy 169.*

In the US, private enforcement seems to have been designed to compensate victims but also, specifically, to act as a deterrent. Indeed, the Clayton Act[24] encourages private enforcement of the antitrust laws by providing, for: treble damages for those injured by reason of anything forbidden in the antitrust laws;[25] injunctive relief against threatened loss or damage by a violation;[26] the use of judgments entered against the defendant as prima facie evidence against that defendant;[27] clear limitation periods;[28] and successful plaintiffs (claimants) to recover costs, including reasonable attorney's fees, contrary to the ordinary rule in the US that each party bears its own attorney fees and costs.[29]

Although these provisions were not sufficient on their own to trigger large volumes of private antitrust litigation, different individual features of the US system have combined and developed sequentially[30] to allow such actions to play a significant role in the enforcement process. In the 1960s and 1970s, private litigation began to burgeon. Partly, this growth reflected the development of an interventionist antitrust policy between the 1940s and 1960s, underpinned by a scepticism about the ability of firms and the markets to provide a successful economic outcome and a mistrust of big business and concentrated markets.[31] Especially during the Warren Court era, the Supreme Court[32] adopted broad interpretations of the antitrust statutes (for example, making wide use of per se rules and applying lenient procedural, substantive, and evidential burdens of proof[33]), which made it relatively easy for plaintiffs to win cases.[34] This position, combined with the fact that:[35]

- wide-ranging pre-trial discovery powers exist in the US, which assist the collection of relevant and essential evidence;
- federal rules allow for consolidation of antitrust claims and for the bringing of opt-out class actions;[36]
- lawyers regularly accept antitrust cases on a contingency fee (no win, no fee) basis;
- most antitrust cases are tried by jury[37] (so conferring an element of 'unpredictability' to antitrust trials); and
- defendants, as joint tortfeasors, are jointly and severally liable for any damage caused with no right to contribution from co-defendants;[38]

meant that private litigation was able to flourish.

In 1968 and 1977, the Supreme Court also handed down two important judgments, *Hanover Shoe Inc v United Shoe Machine Corp*[39] and *Illinois Brick Co v Illinois*,[40] which facilitated private litigation and clearly seemed to elevate the remediation and deterrent functions served by private enforcement

[24] See n. 4 and text. [25] Clayton Act 1914, s. 4. [26] Ibid., s. 16. [27] Ibid., s. 5(a).

[28] The ordinary limitation period of four years also gets suspended during government enforcement proceedings, ibid., ss. 4B and 5(i).

[29] Ibid., s. 5(a). [30] See e.g. Gavil, n. 2.

[31] See e.g. E. Levi, 'The Antitrust Laws and Monopoly' (1974) 14 *Univ Chic LR* 153, C. Kaysen and D. Turner, *Antitrust Policy* (Harvard University Press, 1959).

[32] At this time the Chief Justice was Earl Warren (1953–1969).

[33] For example, courts have applied lesser burdens of proof as to the amount of damages in antitrust cases, e.g. *Zenith Radio Corp v Hazeltine Research*, 395 US 100 (1969).

[34] H. Hovenkamp, *The Antitrust Enterprise: Principle and Execution* (Harvard University Press, 2005), 1.

[35] See Gavil, n. 2 (explaining that 'the field of *complex litigation*' did not develop until mid-century).

[36] So permitting small claimants to spread costs and aggregate similar claims, making them easier and more economical to bring, see Federal Rules of Civil Procedure (FRCP), Rule 23 (defining the standards for bringing class actions).

[37] Criminal antitrust proceedings always involve trial by jury (US Const., Fifth Amendment) and both the plaintiff and the defendant can demand a jury trial in civil cases (US Const., Seventh Amendment).

[38] *Texas Industries v Radcliff Materials, Inc*, 451 US 630 (1981).

[39] *Hanover Shoe Inc v United Shoe Machine Corp*, 392 US 481 (1968).

[40] *Illinois Brick Co v Illinois*, 431 US 720 (1977).

higher than its 'compensation function'. These cases hold that: the possibility that a claimant might have recouped some of an anti-competitive overcharge by passing it on to its customers is *not* relevant in the assessment of antitrust damages cases;[41] and claims brought by *indirect* purchasers, who may have been harmed by an overcharge being passed on to them by a direct purchaser, should generally be refused[42] (indirect purchaser actions are however possible in a number of states under state law[43]). Although these principles might be criticised on the grounds that they may deny compensation to the real victims of the anti-competitive activity and allow direct purchasers to collect a windfall, they do concentrate antitrust claims in the hands of those most likely to sue, simplify damages litigation by allowing extremely difficult issues of remoteness and tracing of injury to be sidestepped, and reduce the process costs of litigation.[44]

By enlisting in these ways, the help of those most directly affected by anti-competitive conduct in the enforcement of the law, numerous antitrust cases have been privately litigated, providing the platform for some of the most significant principles of antitrust law to be developed, the rapid evolution of the law, the offsetting of periods of lax government enforcement, and disputes between private parties to be resolved privately (without drawing public agencies within them).[45]

It is well known, nonetheless, that the virtues of the US private enforcement system are not universally extolled and that its benefits have been hotly debated. Widespread concern has been articulated that features of the system have encouraged overinvestment in private litigation (motivated by private profit rather than public-interest considerations), over-enforcement, and over-deterrence[46] and that, especially in the 1960s to 1970s and in relation to class actions, damages actions got 'out of control'[47]—the system became prone to error and encouraged weak claims to be brought and settled by defendants eager to avoid protracted and expensive litigation. In addition, there has been concern that private actions might actually undermine public enforcement and deterrence, by discouraging leniency applications.

Although not all might agree with these, or all of these, criticisms, they have led to a dramatic recalibration of the US system. Not only has the legislator stepped in in order to diminish the disincentive of submitting amnesty (leniency) applications, by de-trebling antitrust damages and removing joint and several liability for corporations that participate in the amnesty programme and

[41] Otherwise such claims would become excessively complicated, private actions would be deterred, and a wrongdoer in breach would be able to retain his unlawful profits and the fruits of his own illegality. See also A. Jones and D. Beard, 'Co-contractors, Damages and Article 81: The ECJ Finally Speaks' [2002] *ECLR* 246.

[42] If the fact that loss has been passed on by the purchaser may not be taken into account *defensively* in a claim between the seller and the purchaser, it should not be open to an indirect purchaser to use the passing-on principle *offensively* in damages proceedings. The court set out three exceptions to this position. The scope of the direct purchaser rule arose again before the Supreme Court in *Apple Inc v Pepper*, 587 US __, 130 S.Ct. 1514 (2019) (purchasers of apps for iPhones through Apple's App Store were direct purchasers from Apple).

[43] Such rules are not pre-empted by federal law, *California v ARC Corp*, 490 US 93 (1989).

[44] In practice it is complex to determine who bore the cost of an overcharge and whether it has been shifted from direct to indirect purchasers, see e.g. P. Caro De Sousa, 'EU and National Approaches to Passing On and Causation in Competition Damages Cases: A Doctrine in Search of Balance' (2018) 55 *CMLRev* 1751. In addition, from the defendant's perspective, they preclude a multiplicity of claims and the risks of duplicate recovery from arising, but see n. 43 and text. But contrast the position now adopted in Dir. 2014/104/EU, see Section 4.D.v.

[45] An important issue which has arisen is whether claimants that have suffered loss in consequence of a cartel operated worldwide or internationally can pursue a US class action in respect of cartelised products purchased from the companies but delivered outside the US, that is encompassing claimants whose case does *not* arise from the *US effect* of the anti-competitive conduct. In *F. Hoffmann-La Roche Ltd v Empagran SA*, 542 US 155 (2004) the Supreme Court held they may *not* do so in respect of injuries flowing exclusively from foreign effects of allegedly anti-competitive global conduct, where the foreign effects are independent of, and not intertwined with, the US effects, see further Chap. 17.

[46] W. Landes and R. Posner, 'The Private Enforcement of Law' (1975) 4 *J of Legal Studies* 1.

[47] See further, n. 195 and text.

cooperate with claimants,[48] but the Supreme Court has expressed concerns about the 'coercive'[49] elements of the antitrust system, the risk of false positives they create, and has handed down a series of opinions which, collectively, limit the types of antitrust claim that can successfully be brought and appreciably raise the bar for antitrust claimants.[50] The courts have thus been supportive of efforts to safeguard against antitrust claims having a chilling effect on competition through the use of evidential, procedural, and substantive rules.[51] The developments relating to procedure have, in particular, made it easier for antitrust defendants to escape a full antitrust trial either on the basis that the complaint fails to state a claim upon which relief can be granted[52] or following discovery on the basis that 'there is no genuine issue as to any material fact' so that 'the moving party is entitled to judgment as a matter of law'.[53] Further, and crucially, there seems little doubt that the perceived 'excesses' of the treble damages system have been one factor influencing the Supreme Court in its post-1977 reining in of the substantive reach of the antitrust laws, which has made it more difficult for private plaintiffs not only to bring antitrust actions but to 'win' them.[54] The Supreme Court has repeatedly expressed fear that enforcement should not be permitted to 'chill the very conduct the antitrust laws are designed to protect'[55] and this concern has influenced its efforts to:

> scale back the application of the U.S. antitrust laws. The consequence of getting it wrong—or false positives—is much greater when a firm is exposed to treble, rather than single, damages for its alleged wrongdoing . . . These combination of factors has led our Supreme Court to craft increasingly tough liability rules for antitrust offences and increasingly high hurdles for plaintiffs to move beyond the pleadings stage or to survive summary judgment or a directed verdict to get to a jury. The concern is not just that juries will get it wrong, but that the fear of false positives will chill business behaviour that may benefit consumers.[56]

It has been seen in Chapter 1 that there is now widespread concern in the US that the pendulum has swung too far; rules are so rigorous and provide so little certainty that meritorious litigation is being discouraged[57] and that the risks of false negatives have been ignored.[58] The Biden administration has consequently sought to recalibrate the system.

[48] The Antitrust Criminal Penalty Enhancement and Reform Act 2004.

[49] See e.g. *Bell Atlantic Corp v Twombly*, 550 US 544, 557 (2007) and F. H. Easterbrook, 'Discovery as Abuse' (1989) 69 *Boston Univ LR* 635.

[50] Gavil, n. 2.

[51] See e.g. ibid.; *Brunswick Corp v Pueblo Bowl-O-Mat, Inc*, 429 US 477 (1977); *Monsanto Co v Spray-Rite Service Corp*, 465 US 752 (1984); *Matsushita Electric Industrial Co v Zenith Radio Corp*, 475 US 574 (1986); *Daubert v Merrell Dow Pharmaceuticals, Inc*, 509 US 579 (1993); *Verizon Communications Inc v Law Offices of Curtis V. Trinko LLP*, 540 US 398 (2004); *Bell Atlantic Corp v Twombly* 550 US 554, 557 (2007); *Leegin Creative Leather Products Inc v PSKS, Inc*, 551 US 877 (2007).

[52] A FRCP 12(b)(6) motion results in the dismissal of claims that do not allege the facts necessary to sustain a cause of action. It requires 'a short and plain statement of the claim showing that the pleader is entitled to relief', FRCP 8(a)(2).

[53] FRCP 56(c).

[54] W. Kolasky, 'Different Roads' (2008) 11 *Global Competition Review* 17, 17.

[55] *Matsushita Electric v Zenith Radio Corp*, 475 US 574, 594 (1986); *Monsanto Co v Spray-Rite Service Corp*, 465 US 752, 762–764 (1984).

[56] Kolasky, n. 54, 19.

[57] Indeed, following an important study of 60 private US antitrust cases (R. H. Lande and J. P. Davis, 'Benefits from Private Antitrust Enforcement: An Analysis of Forty Cases' (2008) 42 *Univ San Francisco LR* 879, and J. P. Davis and R. H. Lande, 'Toward an Empirical and Theoretical Assessment of Private Antitrust Enforcement (2013) 36 *Seattle Univ LR* 1269) Davis and Lande published a paper rejecting some of the more anecdotal and unsubstantiated concerns about private enforcement, and concluding that the private actions studied demonstrated that they had played an important role both in compensating victims and deterring violations, J. P. Davis and R. H. Lande, 'Defying Conventional Wisdom: The Case for Private Enforcement' (2013) 48 *Georgia LR* 1. See also R. H. Lande and J. P. Davis, 'Comparative Deterrence from Private Enforcement and Criminal Enforcements of the US Antitrust Laws' (2011) *Brigham Young Univ LR* 315, but see G. J. Werden, S. D. Hammond, and B. A. Bartlett, 'Deterrence and Detection of Cartels: Using All The Tools and Sanctions' (2011) 56 *Ant Bull* 207 and R. H. Lande and J. P. Davis, 'The Extraordinary Deterrence of Private Antitrust Enforcement: A Reply to Werden, Hammond and Barnett' (2013) 58 *Ant Bull* 173.

[58] Gavil, n. 2, 7–8.

The long experience of the US provides some important lessons for other jurisdictions. Not only does it illustrate how private actions can play an important role in the enforcement process and in ensuring that its compensatory, remediation, and/or deterrence functions are achieved, but it illustrates that a number of pitfalls exist. Further, that in developing a system of private enforcement a number of issues should be addressed, including how to: (a) craft rules in a way that will achieve, and balance, the competing objectives pursued, and which will minimise error costs; and (b) ensure that it does not undermine public enforcement.

Because of the close connection between private and public enforcement, many public enforcement agencies take a keen interest in the development of private enforcement. It has already been seen that, in the EU, it has been the Commission that has spearheaded the campaign to encourage greater private enforcement of the EU antitrust laws, whilst at the same time stressing that it should not adversely impact on public enforcement. The Commission has been facilitated in this task by its unique and unusual position of having separate and central roles within the EU legal order both as a competition enforcement agency and as the EU institution which ordinarily formulates legislative proposals (including those to promote the effective application of competition law).

4. PRIVATE ENFORCEMENT IN THE EU

A. OVERVIEW: EFFECTIVE JUDICIAL PROTECTION AND THE PRINCIPLE OF NATIONAL PROCEDURAL AUTONOMY

The EEC Treaty, the EC Treaty, and the TFEU have all been silent on the question of whether private rights of action for damages or injunctions must follow from a violation of the EU competition law rules; until the Damages Directive was adopted in 2014, no EU legislation specifically addressed private rights of action. Rather, prior to the Directive such rights derived only from the jurisprudence of the CJ,[59] which developed in a piecemeal fashion.[60]

Nonetheless, since 1974 it has been clear that private actions are possible by virtue of the fact that Articles 101 and 102 have direct effect (see *Belgische Radio en Televisie v SV SABAM*[61]). Further, in a series of subsequent cases the CJ has established that national courts[62] must provide effective judicial protection of the rights that individuals derive from directly effective provisions of EU law, and give them precedence over conflicting principles of national law.[63] These principles, combined with Article 3 of Regulation 1/2003,[64] mean that national courts, like NCAs: have an obligation to apply EU law in combination with national law to conduct which affects trade between Member States; cannot apply national law to authorise conduct prohibited by EU law; can only apply national competition law more

[59] Which are now affirmed in Reg. 1/2003 on the implementation of the rules on competition laid down in [Arts. 101 and 102 TFEU] (Reg. 1/2003) [2003] OJ L1/1 (providing that national courts must have the power to apply Arts. 101 and 102 and for cooperation between the national courts and the Commission and consistency in interpretation of the provisions by all decision-takers).

[60] Until 2004 it was difficult for national courts to play a meaningful part in the enforcement of Art. 101 because Reg. 17 of 1962 [1959–1962] OJ Sp. Ed. 87, conferred the exclusive right on the Commission to rule on the compatibility of an individual agreement with Art. 101(3), see Chaps. 2 and 4.

[61] Case 127/73, EU:C:1974:25, para. 16 ('As the prohibitions of Articles [101(1) and 102] tend by their very nature to produce direct effects in relations between individuals, these articles create direct rights in respect of the individuals concerned with the national courts must safeguard').

[62] See also now Reg. 1/2003, Art. 3(1).

[63] See Case 14/68, *Walt Wilhelm v Bundeskartellamt* EU:C:1969:4, para. 9.

[64] [2003] OJ L1/1.

strictly in the circumstances specified by Regulation 1/2003; and must ensure effective remedies are available to protect EU rights derived from EU law.

Until the implementation of the Damages Directive, litigation involving vindication or protection of EU competition law rights before a national court was governed by the principle of 'national procedural autonomy':

> in the absence of Community rules on this subject, it is for the domestic legal system of each Member State to designate the courts having jurisdiction and to determine the procedural conditions governing actions at law intended to ensure the protection of rights which citizens have from the direct effect of [EU] law.[65]

Under this principle, the protection given to EU rights is dependent on national procedural, evidential, and substantive rules, subject to the national courts' duty of sincere cooperation to ensure the availability of adequate remedies sufficient to guarantee real and *effective* judicial protection for those EU rights and to comply with the principles of equivalence and effectiveness—national rules: (a) must not be less favourable than those relating to similar claims of a domestic nature (the principle of equivalence); and (b) must not make it virtually impossible or excessively difficult to exercise the rights that the national courts are obliged to protect (the principle of effectiveness).[66] Although these obligations leave a national court freedom to determine how best to protect EU rights,[67] in some cases it may require a court to grant one of two or more possible remedies[68] or even a specific remedy to rectify a specific wrong.[69] For example, the CJ has held that a Member State is obliged, in defined circumstances, to compensate individuals who have been injured by its breach of EU law (*Francovich v Italy*)[70] and to repay charges it has levied in breach of EU law.[71] National courts are not required to grant *new* remedies,[72] but this obligation means that national rules may have to be adapted or extended to ensure that a remedy is available where required by EU law. National defences and procedural limitations to such a claim apply insofar as they comply with the principles of equivalence and effectiveness (the *acquis communautaire*).

In the context of Articles 101 and 102, these principles combined to require national courts to ensure that:

(a) they apply Articles 101 and 102 as interpreted by the EU Courts;

(b) they do not take decisions that run counter to those adopted by the Commission (see Section 4.B);

(c) individual *clauses* in an agreement affected by the Article 101(1)—and Article 102—prohibition are held to be void (see Section 4.C);

(d) interim relief is available where necessary to protect putative EU rights (see Section 4.D);

(e) full compensation is, in principle, available to those that have suffered loss in consequence of a breach of Article 101 or 102 (see Section 4.D);

(f) defences and limitations to such rights/actions are only applied insofar as the principles of equivalence and effectiveness are respected (see Section 4.D).

[65] Case 33/76, *Rewe-Zentralfinanz eG and Rewe-Zentral AG v Landwirtschaftskammer für das Saarland* EU:C:1976:188.

[66] See Case 14/83, *Von Colson and Kamann v Land Nordrhein-Westfalen* EU:C:1984:153, especially para. 23 and Case 33/76, *Rewe-Zentralfinanz*, ibid., para. 5.

[67] Case 34/67, *Lück v Hauptzollamt Köln* EU:C:1968:24.

[68] See Case C-271/91, *Marshall v Southampton and South-West Hampshire Area Health Authority (Teaching) (No. 2)* EU:C:1993:335.

[69] See e.g. Case 199/82, *Amministrazione delle Finanze dello Stato v San Giorgio SpA* EU:C:1983:318 (the applicant's right to restitution is a 'consequence of and an adjunct to' the rights conferred on that individual by EU law).

[70] See Cases C-6 and 9/90, EU:C:1991:428.

[71] See e.g. Case C-242/95, *GT-Link A/S v De Danske Statsbaner (DSB)* EU:C:1997:376.

[72] Case 158/80, *Rewe-Handelsgesellschaft Nord mbH v Hauptzollamt Kiel* EU:C:1981:163.

Further constraints on the autonomy of national systems have now also come into place following implementation by the Member States of the Damages Directive (see Section 4.D). As, however, the Directive does not harmonise *all* aspects of national law governing private claims the principle of national procedural autonomy continues to have importance in relation to the matters falling outside its scope. The continuing differences between the national regimes mean that private litigants still seek to select the Member State which they consider to be the most favourable in which to bring proceedings (forum shopping). Indeed, the Brussels Regulation, Regulation 1215/2012 on jurisdiction and the recognition and enforcement of judgment in civil and commercial matters,[73] does provide leeway on this matter. Although the general rule is that proceedings should be heard in the State where the defendant is domiciled (Article 4), other jurisdictional gateways exist so, for example, tortious claims can also be heard in the Member State where the harm occurred (where the causal act took place or where the damage occurred, Article 7(2)) or in a jurisdiction where an 'anchor' defendant is domiciled and being sued (where the claims are so closely connected that it is expedient to hear and determine them together, so avoiding the risk of irreconcilable judgments resulting from the same proceedings, Article 8(1)[74]).

B. UNIFORM AND CONCURRENT APPLICATION OF ARTICLES 101 AND 102

(i) Cooperation Between the Commission and National Courts

A concern that follows from decentralised enforcement of Articles 101 and 102, is that the Commission, the individual NCAs, and national courts respectively may adopt inconsistent interpretations and applications of the rules. When applying Articles 101 and 102, the national courts are bound to interpret those provisions in accordance with that adopted by the CJ and to respect the principle of primacy of EU law. Article 267 provides an important mechanism for national courts uncertain about the interpretation of EU law.

Further, the CJ has held that the duty of cooperation requires the Commission to assist national courts in their application of EU law and vice versa.[75] Both Regulation 1/2003 itself and the Commission's Notice on cooperation with courts of the EU Member States in the application of [Articles 101 and 102 TFEU] (the Cooperation Notice)[76] explain how that cooperation may manifest itself. In particular, Article 15 of Regulation 1/2003 provides that the national courts might request the Commission to provide information or an opinion on the application of the EU competition rules

[73] [2012] OJ L351/1 (replacing Reg. 44/2001 [2001] OJ L12/1), see G. Van Calster, 'The EU Rules on Jurisdiction for and the Law Applicable to, Follow-on and Stand-alone Damages Following Competition Infringement' (2020) 11(3)–(4) *JECLAP* 175. A number of EU and national judgments deal with the question of its interpretation, see e.g. Case C-59/19, *Wikingerhof GmbH & Co KG v Booking.com* EU:C:2020:950, Case C-451/18, *Tibor-Trans Fuvarozó és Kereskedelmi Kft v DAF Trucks NV*, judgment of 29 July 2019, EU:C:2019:635, Case C-27/17, *AB 'flyLAL-Lithuanian Airlines' v 'Starptautiskā lidosta "Rīga"' VAS, 'Air Baltic Corporation' AS* EU:C:2018:533, Case C-618/15, *Concurrence Sàrl v Samsung Electronics France SAS and Amazon Services Europe Sàrl* EU:C:2016:976, Case C-352/13, *Cartel Damage Claims (CDC) Hydrogen Peroxide SA v Akzo Nobel NV v Akzo Nobel NV* EU:C:2015:335, Case C-451/18, *Tibor-Trans Fuvarozó és Kereskedelmi Kft v DAF Trucks NV* EU:C:2019:635, *Provimi v Aventis* [2003] EWHC 961 (Comm), and *Cooper Tire & Rubber v Shell Chemicals* [2009] EWHC 2609 (Comm), [2010] EWCA Civ 864. (The Lugano Convention (signed by the EU, Iceland, Norway, Denmark, and Switzerland) contains rules based on the Brussels Reg.). Rome II, Reg. 864/2007 on the Law Applicable to Non-contractual Obligations [2007] OJ L199/40, determines which substantive rules apply.

[74] See *CDC* ibid.

[75] See e.g. Case 234/89, *Delimitis v Henninger Bräu* EU:C:1991:91, para. 53.

[76] [2004] OJ C101.

and that the Commission may, where 'the coherent application of Article [101] or Article [102] so requires', submit written observations to the national courts and also, with their permission, make oral observations (it may act as amicus curiae to the national courts).[77] Any opinion so provided is published but does not have binding effect on the courts (although it may have persuasive impact).[78]

Regulation 1/2003 also provides how the national courts must assist the Commission in the fulfilment of its tasks. In addition to providing the Commission and NCAs with the documents necessary for preparing written or oral observations to the courts, Member States must forward to the Commission 'a copy of any written judgment of national courts deciding on the application of Articles [101] or Article [102]' without delay.[79] The Commission publishes these judgments on its website according to the Member State of origin.[80]

(ii) Judgments Contrary to Decisions of the Commission

Article 11(6), which relieves NCAs of their competence to apply Articles 101 and 102 following initiation of proceedings by the Commission, does not apply to national courts. Nonetheless, the CJ has held that the duty of cooperation set out in EU law requires a national court to follow a Commission decision dealing with the same parties and the same agreement in the same Member State.[81] Further, in order to ensure a uniform application of Articles 101 and 102, Article 16 of Regulation 1/2003 provides that the national courts must not adopt decisions contrary to a previous Commission decision and must avoid giving decisions that would conflict with a decision contemplated by the Commission. The fact that the Commission has initiated public proceedings in relation to an infringement does not, however, mean that national courts are required to stay damages proceedings brought before them in relation to the same infringements.[82]

Regulation 1/2003 does not deal with the impact of decisions of NCAs within the European Competition Network on national courts. Although the Commission proposed that NCAs' decisions should be given similar effect to its decisions, the final Damages Directive provides that Member States only have to ensure that domestic competition law infringement decisions are binding in that jurisdiction. In *ZA etc v Repsol Comercial de Productos Petolíferos SA*[83] the CJ also held that a finding

[77] Reg. 1/2003, Art. 15(3) (NCAs are also entitled to submit written observations to the national courts of their Member State and oral observations with permission).

[78] The opinions issued are available at <https://ec.europa.eu/competition-policy/antitrust/national-courts/requests-information-or-opinion_en>. See e.g. Case C-429/07, *Inspecteur van de Belastingdienst v X BV* EU:C:2009:359 (the CJ upheld the Commission's ability to intercede under Art. 15(3) in national proceedings where the outcome of the dispute was capable of impairing the effectiveness of the penalty it had imposed).

[79] Art. 15(2).

[80] See the National Court Cases Database, <http://ec.europa.eu/competition/elojade/antitrust/nationalcourts/>.

[81] See e.g. Case C-344/98, *Masterfoods v HB Ice Cream Ltd* EU:C:2000:689 and Case 234/89, *Delimitis v Henninger Bräu* EU:C:1991:91.

[82] Case C-57/21, *RegioJet as* EU:C:2023:6, paras. 62–67 (they may also be able to order disclosure of documents in an ongoing action even if the national court has stayed the proceedings while awaiting the end of the Commission's proceedings, see further Section 4.D.v.c). See also Case C-199/11, *European Commission v Otis* EU:C:2012:684 (confirming that the rule applies when national courts are hearing damages actions), and Cooperation Notice, n. 76, paras. 11–13. See also Case C-547/16, *Gasprba v Repsol* EU:C:2017:891 (preliminary assessments carried out by the Commission may provide an indication, if not prima facie evidence, of an infringement). For a narrow interpretation of the duty of sincere cooperation, see *Inntrepreneur Pub Co v Crehan* [2006] UKHL 38 where the UK's House of Lords (now Supreme Court) (following clarification by the CJ of an EU right to damages in competition cases, see Section 4.D.ii and text), concluded that the beer tie agreement did not infringe Art. 101 despite the Commission finding that similar agreement concluded by other UK brewers foreclosed the UK market for the distribution of beer in on-licensed premises and violated Art. 101(1), e.g. COMP/35.079, *Whitbread* [1999] OJ L88/26, *aff'd* Case T-13/99, *Shaw v Commission* EU:T:2002:209, COMP/36.081, *Bass* [1999] OJ L186/1, and COMP/35.992, *Scottish and Newcastle* [1999] OJ L186/28.

[83] Case C-25/21, EU:C:2023:298, see also Commission Proposal, n. 11, Art. 9, and see n. 188 and text.

of an infringement by an NCA (which has become final following appeals), must be deemed to be established both in the context of an action by an applicant for a declaration of nullity and an action for damages brought before the courts in that same Member State until proof to the contrary is established by the defendant (thereby shifting the burden of proof established in Article 2 of Regulation 1/2003).

Where the Commission has initiated proceedings but not determined a case, a national court must not, therefore, adopt a decision that might conflict with that which will be adopted by the Commission. The Commission will provide the national court with information as to whether it has initiated proceedings, the progress of proceedings, and the likelihood of a decision. Unless the national court cannot doubt the Commission's contemplated decision or the Commission has already decided on a similar case, it should ordinarily stay the proceedings before it.[84] Where this occurs the Commission will endeavour to give the case priority. Where the Commission has already decided on the case, however, the Commission's decision is binding on the national court, without prejudice to the interpretation of EU law by the CJ.[85] If the national court does not agree with the decision of the Commission it must either await the outcome of an appeal, if any, from its decision, or refer the question to the CJ for a preliminary ruling.[86] Where the national court does stay proceedings in the context of parallel or consecutive proceedings, it should consider whether it should impose interim measures in order to safeguard the interests of the parties involved.[87]

C. THE ENFORCEABILITY OF AGREEMENTS INFRINGING ARTICLE 101 OR 102

In Chapter 4, it was seen that although Article 101 provides that agreements or decisions prohibited by Article 101(1) are void,[88] the nullity provided for in Article 101(2) in fact applies only to individual clauses in the agreement affected by the Article 101(1) prohibition.[89] The agreement as a whole is void only where those clauses are not severable from the remaining terms of the agreement.[90]

In *Manfredi v Lloyd Adriatico Assicurazioni SpA*, the CJ clarified that the invalidity of the agreement (or affected clauses) is absolute—the agreement has no effect as between the contracting parties and cannot be invoked against third parties.[91] As an agreement infringes Article 101 only if all of the elements of Article 101(1) are satisfied and the four conditions of Article 101(3) are not met, it is possible that, as events change over a period of time, an agreement that does not infringe Article 101(1) will subsequently be found to do so, and vice versa. Suppose, for example, a small, local undertaking concludes an agreement which does not infringe Article 101(1) on account of its minor importance (the undertaking has an extremely small share of the market). Suppose further, that that undertaking is subsequently taken over by a larger undertaking so that the agreement now does have

[84] See e.g. Case 234/89, *Delimitis v Henninger Bräu* EU:C:1991:91, paras. 43–55. See *AAH Pharmaceuticals Ltd and Others v Pfizer Ltd and UniChem Ltd* [2007] EWHC 565 (Ch).

[85] Case 314/85, *Foto-Frost v Hauptzollamt Lübeck-Ost* EU:C:1987:452, paras. 12–20.

[86] Ibid., para. 12.

[87] Case C-344/98, *Masterfoods v HB Ice Cream Ltd* EU:C:2000:689, para. 58.

[88] A plea that an agreement infringed Art. 101 and was void caused acute difficulties in the cases that arose prior to 2004 under the old Reg. 17 system on account of the national courts' inability to apply Art. 101(3) to individual cases, see Case 234/89, *Delimitis v Henninger Bräu* EU:C:1991:91.

[89] Case 56/65, *Société La Technique Minière v Maschinenbau Ulm GmbH* EU:C:1966:38, 250. See also Case C-25/21, *ZA etc v Repsol Comercial de Productos Petolíferos SA* EU:C:2023:298.

[90] Ibid. and Case 319/82, *Société de Vente de Ciments et Bétons de l'Est SA v Kerpen & Kerpen GmbH & Co KG* EU:C:1983:374, see Chap. 4.

[91] See Cases C-295–298/04, EU:C:2006:461, para. 57.

an appreciable effect on competition and trade, does not meet the conditions of a block exemption, and does not fulfil the conditions of Article 101(3). The agreement that previously fell outside Article 101(1) (and was valid) now becomes subject to its prohibition (and void). The reverse may also occur: an agreement which is initially void may become valid (and possibly void again) as the agreement falls within and without the Article 101(1) prohibition.[92]

Although the effect of Article 101(2) has been spelt out by the CJ, the question of whether the prohibited clauses can actually be severed from the remaining provisions in the contract is a matter for national law.[93] In some jurisdictions, it may also be the case that, in addition to being void, offending provisions are *illegal*. The compatibility of the plea of illegality with EU law is discussed in greater detail in Section 4.D.

A further question which arises is whether contracts concluded in implementation, or in consequence, of an illegal agreement might be vitiated, for example a contract for sale at prices inflated in consequence of a cartel agreement entered into by the seller or sales contracts made in consequence of an invalid beer tie. In certain circumstances, EU law makes it clear that a contract confirming an illegal contract is also in violation of Article 101.[94] Otherwise, it seems it is for national law,[95] subject to the principles of equivalence and effectiveness, to determine whether or not a contract concluded with a third party on the basis of a void agreement should also be tainted by the illegality and 'regarded as springing from or founded on the agreement rendered illegal'.[96]

Although Article 102 contains no declaration of nullity equivalent to that set out in Article 101,[97] it implicitly prohibits many contracts and contractual terms. It appears, therefore, that Article 102 also renders a contract, or severable terms of a contract, affected by its prohibition void[98] or, at the very least, unenforceable.[99]

D. REMEDIES: INJUNCTIONS AND DAMAGES

(i) An EU Right to an Injunction

For many years a lack of clarity surrounded the question of what *exact* rights Articles 101 and 102 conferred upon individuals and what remedies had to be available to protect them. In *R v Secretary*

[92] See e.g. the English case of *Passmore v Morland plc* [1999] 3 All ER 1005.

[93] Case C-25/21, *ZA etc v Repsol Comercial de Productos Petolíferos SA* EU:C:2023:298. This means that the enforceability of a contract will vary depending on which Member State's rules are applicable and will not necessarily be uniform throughout the EU.

[94] See e.g. discussion of Case C-32/11, *Allianz Hungária Biztosító Zrt, Generali-Providencia Biztosító Zrt v Gazdasági Versenyhivatal* EU:C:2013:160 in Chap. 11.

[95] Case 319/82, *Société de Vente de Ciments et Bétons de l'Est SA v Kerpen & Kerpen GmbH & Co KG* EU:C:1983:374.

[96] *Courage v Crehan* [2004] EWCA Civ 637. See also, e.g., the view of the Swedish Supreme Court in *Boliden Mineral AB v Birka*, OCL 057 (SE 2004) and C. Cauffman, 'The Impact of Voidness from Infringement of Article 101 TFEU on Related Contracts' (2012) 8 *European Competition Journal* 95.

[97] This omission is not surprising since it focuses on a broader range of abusive conduct, see Chaps. 5 and 7.

[98] See e.g. the view of the High Court of England and Wales in *English Welsh & Scottish Railway Ltd v E.ON UK plc* [2007] EWHC 599 (Comm) (contractual provision and contract (if exclusionary term not severable) offending Art. 102 is illegal and void), the Swedish Court of Appeal, *Scandinavian Airlines System (SAS) v Swedish Board of Aviation* (unreported), U. Bernitz, 'The Arlanda Terminal 2 Case: Substantial Damages Awarded on the Basis of Article 82 TEC' [2004] 1 *Comp Law* 195, and R. Whish, 'The Enforcement of EC Competition Law in the Domestic Courts of the Member States' in J. Lonbay (ed.), *Frontiers of Competition Law* (Wiley, 1994), Chap. 5. In many cases an agreement concluded by a dominant undertaking which incorporates a contractual clause infringing Art. 102 is likely also to infringe Art. 101(1).

[99] See e.g. *Gibbs Mew plc v Gemmell* [1999] 1 EGLR 43.

of State for Transport, ex parte Factortame Ltd,[100] however, the CJ made it clear that a national court must ensure that interim measures are available where necessary to protect putative EU rights:[101]

> 19. In accordance with the case-law of the Court, it is for the national courts, in application of the principle of cooperation laid down in Article [10] of the [EC] Treaty, to ensure the legal protection which persons derive from the direct effect of provisions of Community law . . .
>
> 20. The Court has also held that any provision of a national legal system and any legislative, administrative or judicial practice which might impair the effectiveness of Community law by withholding from the national court having jurisdiction to apply such law the power to do everything necessary at the moment of its application to set aside national legislative provisions which might prevent, even temporarily, Community rules from having full force and effect are incompatible with those requirements, which are the very essence of Community law.. . .
>
> 21. . . . [T]he full effectiveness of Community law would be just as much impaired if a rule of national law could prevent a court seized of a dispute governed by Community law from granting interim relief in order to ensure the full effectiveness of the judgment to be given on the existence of the rights claimed under Community law. It follows that a court which in those circumstances would grant interim relief, if it were not for a rule of national law, is obliged to set aside that rule.

It was not until 2001, in *Courage Ltd v Crehan*, however, that the question of whether damages were required to protect rights derived under Articles 101 and 102 was finally resolved.

(ii) Development of an EU Right to Damages

The EU right to damages for loss suffered in consequence of a breach of EU competition law was finally decided following an Article 267 reference of questions to the CJ by the English Court of Appeal, made in the course of its hearing of conjoined appeals in the case of *Courage Ltd v Crehan*.[102] The case concerned two leases of public houses that had been concluded between Inntrepreneur Estates (CPC) Ltd (owned equally by Grand Metropolitan plc and Courage Ltd) and Mr Crehan and which required Mr Crehan to purchase minimum quantities of various beers for resale at the leased premises from Courage, and no other person. The proceedings involved an action brought by the brewers for the recovery of £15,266, alleged to be the price of beers sold and delivered to Mr Crehan. By way of defence Crehan alleged, amongst other things, that the beer tie in the lease was in breach of Article 101. He counterclaimed for damages and/or restitution. The case thus raised the compatibility of the beer ties and the leases with Article 101 and the impact of any such incompatibility on the claims and counterclaims made by the parties.

Courage Ltd v Crehan was one of a series of similar cases that had arisen before the English courts, involving proceedings for damages on account of a brewer's breach of statutory duty[103] or recovery

[100] Case 213/89, EU:C:1990:257.

[101] An individual suffering in consequence of a breach of the competition rules might request an injunction, final or interim (pending resolution of the final dispute), to prevent the undertaking or undertakings committing a breach of the rules in future. The availability of an interim injunction will be of particular importance to an undertaking which believes that it is being driven out of the market by, e.g., exclusionary conduct infringing Art. 102.

[102] [1999] EuLR 834, see also n. 82.

[103] They therefore claimed the difference between the contract price of the beer and its market value and other consequential loss, see e.g. *Gibbs Mew plc v Gemmell* [1998] EuLR 588 and *Trent Taverns v Sykes* [1999] EuLR 492.

of payments made pursuant to the void contract (the restitutionary claim).[104] By the time the *Crehan* case reached the Court of Appeal, authority established, for a variety of reasons, that the claims must fail,[105] including because the claims were based on an illegal act. The English courts have generally refused to assist a claimant whose action is founded on an illegal act: *ex turpi causa non oritur actio*[106] and to allow a party to a prohibited contract either to enforce that contract or to bring any other action based upon it: *in pari delicto potior est conditio defendentis*.[107] Although the Court of Appeal in *Courage Ltd v Crehan* agreed that English law would not afford a remedy of damages to a party to an agreement prohibited by Article 101,[108] it recognised that there might be sound policy arguments in favour of accepting that a party to a prohibited agreement has a right to sue for damages[109] and that a party in a case such as that before it might have rights protected by EU law and which supersede any principle of English law denying the right. The Court of Appeal thus made a reference to the CJ essentially asking whether EU law required a national court to provide a remedy of damages to claimants injured by a breach of Article 101, even if it was a party to the prohibited contract.[110] The CJ replied as follows.

Case C-453/99, *Courage Ltd v Crehan* EU:C:2001:465

Court of Justice

19. It should be borne in mind, first of all, that the Treaty has created its own legal order, which is integrated into the legal systems of the Member States and which their courts are bound to apply. The subjects of that legal order are not only the Member States but also their nationals. Just as it imposes burdens on individuals, Community law is also intended to give rise to rights which become part of their legal assets. Those rights arise not only where they are expressly granted by the Treaty but also by virtue of obligations which the Treaty imposes in a clearly defined manner both on individuals and on the Member States and the Community institutions (see the judgments in Case 26/62, *Van Gend en Loos* [1963] ECR 1, Case 6/64, *Costa* . . . and Joined Cases C-6/90 and C-9/90, *Francovich and Others* . . . , para. 31).

20. Secondly, according to Article 3(g) of the EC Treaty (now, after amendment, Art. 3(1)(g) EC), Article [101 TFEU] constitutes a fundamental provision which is essential for the accomplishment of the tasks entrusted to the Community and, in particular, for the functioning of the internal market (judgment in Case C-126/97, *Eco Swiss* [1999] ECR I-3055, para. 36).

21. Indeed, the importance of such a provision led the framers of the Treaty to provide expressly, in Article [101(2) TFEU], that any agreements or decisions prohibited pursuant to that article are to be automatically void (judgment in *Eco Swiss*, cited para. 36).

[104] In many cases the restitutionary claims were eventually abandoned, see e.g. A. Jones, *Restitution and EC Law* (LLP, 2000), Chap. 6 and A. Jones and B. Sufrin, *EC Competition Law: Text, Cases, and Materials* (Oxford University Press, 2001), Chap. 15, 991–1002.

[105] See *Inntrepreneur Estates (CPC) plc v Milne*, unreported, 30 July 1993, *Matthew Brown plc v Campbell* [1998] EuLR 530.

[106] 'No court will lend its aid to a man who founds his action upon an immoral or illegal act.'

[107] 'Where both parties are equally wrongful the position of the defendant is stronger', *Holman v Johnson* (1775) 1 Cowp 341, 343. The rule is a principle not of justice but of policy which discourages all contracts that are contrary to public policy. 'For an agreement to be illegal it need not be in breach of the criminal law', *Gibbs Mew plc v Gemmell* [1999] 1 EGLR 43, 49, [1998] EuLR 588.

[108] *Courage Ltd v Crehan* [1999] EuLR 834.

[109] Referring to the US Supreme Court's opinion in *Perma Life Mufflers Inc v International Parts Corp*, 392 US 134 (1968) (the illegality defence did not bar an action brought by a party to an anti-competitive agreement that was in an economically weaker position and not equally at fault (*in pari delicto*)—private suits important to antitrust enforcement and furthering the public policy in favour of competition).

[110] On the right to claim damages for a violation of the EEA agreement competition law provisions, see Case E-6/17, *Fjarskipti hf v Síminn hf* 18 May 2018.

22. That principle of automatic nullity can be relied on by anyone, and the courts are bound by it once the conditions for the application of Article [101(1)] are met and so long as the agreement concerned does not justify the grant of an exemption under Article [101(3) TFEU] (on the latter point, see, *inter alia*, Case 10/69, *Portelange* [1969] ECR 309, para. 10). Since the nullity referred to in Article [101(2)] is absolute, an agreement which is null and void by virtue of this provision has no effect as between the contracting parties and cannot be set up against third parties (see the judgment in Case 22/71, *Béguelin* [1971] ECR 949, para. 29). Moreover, it is capable of having a bearing on all the effects, either past or future, of the agreement or decision concerned (see the judgment in Case 48/72, *Brasserie de Haecht II* [1973] ECR 77, para. 26).

23. Thirdly, it should be borne in mind that the Court has held that Article [101(1) TFEU] and Article [102] produce direct effects in relations between individuals and create rights for the individuals concerned which the national courts must safeguard (judgments in Case, 127/73 *BRT and SABAM* [1974] ECR 51, para. 16, (*BRT I*) and Case C-282/95 P, *Guérin Automobiles v Commission* [1997] ECR I-1503, para. 39).

24. It follows from the foregoing considerations that any individual can rely on a breach of Article [101(1) TFEU] before a national court even where he is a party to a contract that is liable to restrict or distort competition within the meaning of that provision.

25. As regards the possibility of seeking compensation for loss caused by a contract or by conduct liable to restrict or distort competition, it should be remembered from the outset that, in accordance with settled case-law, the national courts whose task it is to apply the provisions of Community law in areas within their jurisdiction must ensure that those rules take full effect and must protect the rights which they confer on individuals (see, *inter alia*, the judgments in Case 106/77, *Simmenthal* . . . , para. 16, and in Case C-213/89, *Factortame* . . . , para. 19).

26. The full effectiveness of Article [101 TFEU] and, in particular, the practical effect of the prohibition laid down in Article [101(1)] would be put at risk if it were not open to any individual to claim damages for loss caused to him by a contract or by conduct liable to restrict or distort competition.

27. Indeed, the existence of such a right strengthens the working of the Community competition rules and discourages agreements or practices, which are frequently covert, which are liable to restrict or distort competition. From that point of view, actions for damages before the national courts can make a significant contribution to the maintenance of effective competition in the Community.

28. There should not therefore be any absolute bar to such an action being brought by a party to a contract which would be held to violate the competition rules.

29. However, in the absence of Community rules governing the matter, it is for the domestic legal system of each Member State to designate the courts and tribunals having jurisdiction and to lay down the detailed procedural rules governing actions for safeguarding rights which individuals derive directly from Community law, provided that such rules are not less favourable than those governing similar domestic actions (principle of equivalence) and that they do not render practically impossible or excessively difficult the exercise of rights conferred by Community law (principle of effectiveness) (see Case C-261/95 *Palmisani* . . . , para. 27).

30. In that regard, the Court has held that Community law does not prevent national courts from taking steps to ensure that the protection of the rights guaranteed by Community law does not entail the unjust enrichment of those who enjoy them (see, in particular, Case 238/78, *Ireks-Arkady v Council and Commission* . . . , para. 14, Case 68/79, *Just* . . . , para. 26, and Joined Cases C-441/98 and C-442/98, *Michaïlidis* . . . , para. 31).

31. Similarly, provided that the principles of equivalence and effectiveness are respected (see *Palmisani*, cited above, para. 27), Community law does not preclude national law from denying a party who is found to bear significant responsibility for the distortion of competition the right to obtain damages from the other contracting party. Under a principle which is recognised in most of the legal systems of the Member States and which the Court has applied in the past (see Case 39/72, *Commission v Italy* . . . , para. 10), a litigant should not profit from his own unlawful conduct, where this is proven.

32. In that regard, the matters to be taken into account by the competent national court include the economic and legal context in which the parties find themselves and, as the United Kingdom Government rightly points out, the respective bargaining power and conduct of the two parties to the contract.

33. In particular, it is for the national court to ascertain whether the party who claims to have suffered loss through concluding a contract that is liable to restrict or distort competition found himself in a markedly weaker position than the other party, such as seriously to compromise or even eliminate his freedom to negotiate the terms of the contract and his capacity to avoid the loss or reduce its extent, in particular by availing himself in good time of all the legal remedies available to him.

34. Referring to the judgments in Case 23/67, *Brasserie de Haecht*... and Case C-234/89, *Delimitis*..., paras. 14–26, the Commission and the United Kingdom Government also rightly point out that a contract might prove to be contrary to Article [101(1) TFEU] for the sole reason that it is part of a network of similar contracts which have a cumulative effect on competition. In such a case, the party contracting with the person controlling the network cannot bear significant responsibility for the breach of Article [101], particularly where in practice the terms of the contract were imposed on him by the party controlling the network.

35. Contrary to the submission of Courage, making a distinction as to the extent of the parties' liability does not conflict with the case-law of the Court to the effect that it does not matter, for the purposes of the application of Article [101 TFEU], whether the parties to an agreement are on an equal footing as regards their economic position and function (see, *inter alia*, Joined Cases 56/64 and 58/64, *Consten and Grundig v Commission* . . .). That case-law concerns the conditions for application of Article [101 TFEU] while the questions put before the Court in the present case concern certain consequences in civil law of a breach of that provision.

36. Having regard to all the foregoing considerations, the questions referred are to be answered as follows:

— a party to a contract liable to restrict or distort competition within the meaning of Article [101 TFEU] can rely on the breach of that article to obtain relief from the other contracting party;

— Article [101 TFEU] precludes a rule of national law under which a party to a contract liable to restrict or distort competition within the meaning of that provision is barred from claiming damages for loss caused by performance of that contract on the sole ground that the claimant is a party to that contract;

— Community law does not preclude a rule of national law barring a party to a contract liable to restrict or distort competition from relying on his own unlawful actions to obtain damages where it is established that that party bears significant responsibility for the distortion of competition.

The Court thus stressed the new legal order created by the EU, the rights the Treaty provisions confer on individuals, the centrality of the competition rules to the EU project, and the direct effect of Article 101(1). The judgment establishes that: (a) Article 101 confers rights on individuals, even parties to a contract in breach; and (b) any breach of Article 101 is sufficiently serious to trigger an EU right to damages, so creating a new 'Euro-tort'[111] along the lines of *Francovich*.[112] Individuals must, in principle, be entitled to claim damages for loss caused by an agreement or conduct that restricts competition. Whatever the position normally, a right to claim damages to compensate breaches of both Article 101 and Article 102 must be available under national law.[113] It thus underlines the obligation

[111] N. Dunne, 'Antitrust and the Making of European Tort Law' (2015) 36 *OJLS* 1, 3.

[112] See Cases C-6 and 9/90, EU:C:1991:428 and n. 70 and text.

[113] Although the Court did not specifically deal with Art. 102 it referred to the need to compensate those who have suffered loss caused to them by a contract *or* by conduct liable to restrict or distort competition.

of national courts to ensure that EU rules take full effect and to protect the EU rights those provisions conferred on individuals[114] and highlights the importance of private actions to the enforcement of EU law.[115] The Court also concludes that there should be no absolute bar to a damages claim, even to one brought by a party to a contract violating the competition rules. Insofar as a national principle of illegality provides an absolute bar to a claim for damages commenced under Article 101, it is therefore undoubtedly incompatible with EU law. It might be compatible, however, where it respects the EU principles of equivalence and effectiveness; for example, where a right to obtain damages is denied to a contracting party found to bear *significant responsibility* for the distortion of competition.[116]

In *Manfredi v Lloyd Adriatico Assicurazioni SpA*,[117] the CJ reiterated that the practical effect of the Article 101(1) prohibition would be put at risk if it were not open to any individual to claim damages for loss caused to him by a contract or by conduct liable to restrict or distort competition. 'It follows that any individual can claim compensation for the harm suffered where there is a causal relationship between that harm and an agreement or practice prohibited under Article [101].'[118]

In this case, the Court was also asked whether Article 101 had to be interpreted as requiring national courts to award 'punitive' damages, greater than the advantage obtained by the offending operator, thereby deterring the adoption of prohibited agreements.[119] The CJ stressed that the right to claim damages was designed to strengthen the working of the EU competition rules and to discourage prohibited agreements but that the question of whether to award punitive damages was, in the absence of EU rules governing the matter,[120] for the domestic legal system of each Member State to determine, provided that the principles of equivalence and effectiveness are observed. It thus stated that:

(a) it must be possible to award punitive damages if such damages may be awarded pursuant to similar actions founded on domestic law. However, EU law did not prevent national courts from taking steps to ensure that protection of EU rights does not entail unjust enrichment of those who enjoy them; and

(b) the right to seek compensation must include compensation not only for actual loss but also for loss of profit plus interest.[121]

The CJ has also confirmed that any individual (whether or not a customer or supplier of a cartelist),[122] and the EU itself,[123] can bring a damages claim, that the full effectiveness of Article 102 would be put at risk if it were not open to any individual to claim damages for loss caused by abusive conduct of a dominant firm,[124] and that damages claims are not necessarily restricted to claimants in a vertical chain with the defendant (for example, a direct or indirect purchaser from the defendant), so long as it can be established that the loss caused to the claimant resulted in consequence of the infringing

[114] Case C-453/99, EU:C:2001:465, para. 26. [115] Ibid., para. 27.

[116] Ibid., para. 31. In these circumstances the principle of EU law that a litigant should not profit from his own unlawful conduct would be respected, Case 39/72, *Commission v Italy* EU:C:1973:13, para. 10. On remission of the case to the English court, this factor led Park J and the Court of Appeal to hold that the tenant's claim could not be barred by the principle of illegality or significant responsibility, but see discussion of the case in n. 82 and text.

[117] Cases C-295–298/04, EU:C:2006:461, para. 60. [118] Ibid., para. 61.

[119] Ibid., paras. 83–100. In the UK, contrast *Devenish Nutrition Ltd v Sanofi Aventis SA* [2007] EWHC 2394 (Ch) (exemplary damages not available where the Commission has imposed a fine in relation to the same offence), *aff'd* [2008] EWCA Civ 10 with Case 1178/5/7/11, *2 Travel Group plc (in liquidation) v Cardiff City Transport Services Ltd* [2012] CAT 19 (exemplary damages awarded). See also Case 1166/5/10, *Albion Water Ltd v Dwr Cymru Cyfyngedig* [2013] CAT 6.

[120] But see now Dir. 2014/104/EU, Art. 3(3), n. 177 and text.

[121] The Commission recognises in its Notice on cooperation with the national courts the particular difficulties that may arise in consequence of the fact that there is no harmonisation of procedures in the Member States, see the Cooperation Notice, n. 76, paras. 9–10.

[122] Case C-435/18, *Otis GmbH v Land Oberosterreich* EU:C:2019:1069.

[123] See Case C-199/11, *Europese Gemeenschap v Otis NV* EU:C:2012:684.

[124] Case C-637/17, *Cogeco Communications* EU:C:2019:263.

conduct. In *Kone AG v ÖBB-Infrastruktur AG*,[125] the claimant alleged before an Austrian court that it had been harmed by the market-sharing cartel at issue in the elevators and escalators market which had enabled suppliers (which were not themselves in the cartel) to raise their prices. Austrian law did not, however, permit such a claim, because the alleged loss resulted from an independent business decision of the non-cartelist.

The CJ concluded that the full effectiveness of Article 101 would be put at risk if it were not open to any individual to claim damages for loss caused to him by infringing conduct. A claimant was thus entitled to claim compensation for the harm suffered where a causal link with an agreement or practice prohibited under Article 101 could be established. Because market price was one of the main factors taken into consideration by an undertaking when determining the price at which it will offer its goods or services, it could not be ruled out that a competing undertaking, outside the cartel in question, might choose to set the price of its offer at an amount higher than it would have chosen in the absence of that cartel where the cartel resulted in artificially high prices for particular goods. The victim of such 'umbrella pricing' should consequently be able to obtain compensation for such loss from the members of a cartel, 'where it is established that the cartel at issue was, in the circumstances of the case and, in particular, the specific aspects of the relevant market, liable to have the effect of umbrella pricing being applied by third parties acting independently, and that those circumstances and specific aspects could not be ignored by the members of that cartel'.[126]

(iii) The Principle of National Procedural Autonomy—the Difficulties

Prior to the Damages Directive, the principle of national procedural autonomy conferred considerable latitude on the national systems and the national courts. The protection given to EU rights was consequently heavily dependent on the procedural, evidential, and substantive rules governing civil litigation applicable in each individual Member State and how EU law—in particular, the principles of equivalence and effectiveness—constrained their operation.[127]

This meant that opacity surrounded a multiplicity of questions arising at the national level, including how national claims should be framed (and whether fault should or can be a constituent element of the cause of action), how causation can be established and damages calculated, whether national courts are required to award 'punitive' damages and whether other national rules governing the claim comply with EU law, and, especially, the principle of effectiveness; for example, rules relating to standing, remoteness, illegality, a passing-on defence, or setting out limitation periods.

It has been seen that the CJ ruled on some of these issues, including on the compatibility of the English principle of illegality and the availability of punitive damages with the EU principle of effectiveness.[128] In *Manfredi v Lloyd Adriatico Assicurazioni SpA*,[129] the CJ was also asked for guidance on the question of whether a national limitation period was compatible with EU law. The relevant limitation period in that case began to run from the day on which that prohibited agreement or practice was adopted. The CJ held that a national rule governing limitation could make it practically impossible to

[125] Case C-557/12, EU:C:2014:1317. See also e.g. F. Maier-Rigaud, 'Umbrella Effects and the Ubiquity of Damage Resulting from Competition Law Violations' (2014) 5 *JECLAP* 247.

[126] Case C-557/12, EU:C:2014:1317, para. 34.

[127] See obstacles identified by the Commission in its Green Paper, n. 12 and n. 159 and text. As many national cases settle it is not easy to draw a picture of how national courts resolve these issues, K Coates, 'Cartels and Follow On Damages Actions', Competition Law Lecture Series, Lincoln's Inn, 24 November 2014.

[128] For example, in Case C-453/99, *Courage Ltd v Crehan* EU:C:2001:465, para. 31, the CJ held that although the illegality of the agreement cannot operate as a general bar to claims brought between parties to a contract concluded in breach of Art. 101(1), it can do so where the claimant co-contractor can be said to bear 'significant responsibility' for the breach, see n. 116 and text. See also Case C-295–298/04, *Manfredi* EU:C:2006:461.

[129] Cases C-295–298/04, EU:C:2006:461. See also Case C-637/17, *Cogeco Communications* EU:C:2019:263.

exercise the right to seek compensation for the harm caused by that prohibited agreement or practice, particularly if it imposed a short limitation period which is not capable of being suspended. It noted that in the case of continuous or repeated infringement, it was possible in these circumstances that the limitation period would expire even before the infringement was brought to an end. The principles of equivalence and effectiveness thus require national rules which render nugatory the right to compensation, to be struck down, or disapplied.[130] This position created a number of difficulties.

First, even in areas where the CJ had ruled, scope for variations in national rules and different determinations of whether a specific national rule (for example, a limitation period or a rule of illegality) was compliant with EU law remained.

Secondly, where no specific ruling existed, the compatibility of certain national rules with EU law remained in doubt and, in particular, dependent on the core goals underpinning the EU principle of effectiveness stressed in the CJ's *Crehan* and *Manfredi* judgments. For instance, the CJ never ruled on the question of whether EU law demanded that *indirect purchasers* should have standing to bring antitrust proceedings and/or whether defendants should be able to raise a passing-on defence. Some argued that the principal purpose of the effectiveness principle was the attainment of corrective justice[131]—with deterrence operating merely as a socially beneficial by-product of such actions[132]—, so suggesting that indirect purchasers should have standing and a passing-on defence should be allowed (the approach now taken in the Damages Directive[133]).[134]

P. Nebbia, 'Damages Actions for the Infringement of EC Competition Law: Compensation or Deterrence?' (2008) 33 *ELRev*, 23, 35–36

Which principle of 'effectiveness' for *Courage*?

It is here submitted that the notion of 'effectiveness' on which the *Crehan* decision relies is that of 'effective judicial protection', rather than 'effective enforcement'. First and foremost, *Crehan* is commonly considered as the logical extension of the same principle that generated *Francovich* and *Brasserie du Pêcheur*. As noted at the outset, the Commission acknowledges that: '[T]he existence of a Community law remedy of damages against individuals for breach of Articles [101 and 102 TFEU] follows from the same principles [as those that give rise] to such a remedy against Member States for breaches of other provisions of Community law. This principle is, as discussed above, predominantly based on 'effective judicial protection'.

Secondly, the wording of the *Crehan* decision is very similar to that of *Brasserie du Pêcheur*: After highlighting that 'Community law is intended to give rise to rights which become part of [individual] legal assets', the [CJ] reaffirms the principle that: '[T]he full effectiveness of [Article 101] of the Treaty would be put at risk if it were not open to any individual to claim damages for loss caused to him by a contract or conduct liable to restrict or distort competition.'

The subsequent paragraph is then devoted to the 'enforcement' argument, and acknowledges the contribution that such a right would give 'to the maintenance of effective competition in the Community'. This argument, however, seems to be used to reinforce, rather than to establish, the basis of liability.

[130] Case C-536/11, *Bundeswettbewerbsbehörde v Donau Chemie* EU:C:2013:366, para. 32.

[131] P. Nebbia, 'Damages Actions for the Infringement of EC Competition Law: Compensation or Deterrence?' (2008) 33 *ELRev* 23, 28, 35–36.

[132] K. Roach and M. J. Trebilcock, 'Private Enforcement of Competition Laws' (1996) 34 *Osgoode Hall LJ* 461, 496.

[133] See n. 178 and text.

[134] Wils, n. 1, 12–13, also supports as a 'separate-tasks approach', relying on the 2008 White Paper on Damages, n. 12. In its 2005 Green Paper, n. 12, 2.7, however, the Commission stated that damages actions and public enforcement serve the same deterrence objective.

This emerges more clearly in the *Manfredi* decision. In that case, the [CJ] affirmed more explicitly than in *Crehan* the existence of a Community-based right to compensation for the infringement of antitrust law but, in so doing, only echoed the part of the *Crehan* judgment that dealt with judicial protection . . . :

> '[I]t should be recalled that the full effectiveness of Article [101] and, in particular, the practical effect of the prohibition laid down in Article [101(1)] would be put at risk if it were not open to any individual to claim damages for loss caused to him by a contract or by conduct liable to restrict or distort competition (*Courage and Crehan* . . . para. 26).'

The 'enforcement' argument can only be found much later, where the CJ deals with the question of whether punitive damages should be awarded.

If the reasoning here developed is correct, it is clear that the [EU] context is remarkably different from that of the United States: the primary aim of private enforcement should be compensation, and any measure proposed to enhance its operation should take this priority into account. In this respect, the conclusions drawn here have significant practical implications as different views on which objective should be prioritised may imply quite different (but not necessarily conflicting) policy agendas.

Others, however, such as Nazzini, argue that private enforcement is principally a tool to increase enforcement and to bring to an end and deter violations, which might suggest a different impact on national law, including those governing indirect purchaser claims and the passing-on defence.[135]

R. Nazzini, 'The Objective of Private Remedies in EU Competition Law' (2011) 4 *Global Competition Litigation Review* 131, 139–140

(iii) The case law on the right to damages for breach of art. 101 or 102 TFEU

When the court was required to address the core question of whether those who have been harmed by a breach of art.101(1) TFEU have a right to damages, the enforcement rationale becomes more evident.

In *Crehan*, the Court of Justice was called upon to decide whether the English law rule *ex turpi causa non oritur actio* was incompatible with EU law in so far as it prevented a party to an agreement prohibited by art.101(1) TFEU from recovering damages from the other party. The court said that the full effectiveness of art.101 of the Treaty and, in particular, the practical effect of the prohibition laid down in art.101(1) would be put at risk if it were not open to any individual to claim damages for loss caused to him by a contract or by conduct liable to restrict or distort competition. The court added that the existence of such a right strengthens the working of the EU competition rules and discourages anti-competitive agreements or practices. Finally, the court said that actions for damages before the national courts can make a significant contribution to the maintenance of effective competition in the European Union. The enforcement rationale could not be more clearly articulated.

In the subsequent case of *Manfredi*, the court repeated almost verbatim paras. 26 and 27 of the *Crehan* case. The court was ruling on whether art.101 TFEU must be interpreted as requiring national

[135] R. Nazzini, 'The Objective of Private Remedies in EU Competition Law' (2011) 4 *Global Competition Litigation Review* 131, 139–140. See also Jones and Beard, n. 41, 253–255 and Opinion of Wahl AG in Case C-724/17, *Skanska Industrial Solutions* EU:C:2019:100 (emphasising the importance of deterrence and stating that 'the rationale of a right to claim compensation for harm caused by an infringement of EU competition law was in *Kone* firmly tied to deterrence', para. 44).

courts to award punitive damages, greater than the advantage obtained by the defendant, thereby deterring agreements or concerted practices prohibited under that article. The question explicitly linked the award of punitive damages to deterrence. It was, therefore, important for the court to make it clear that the fact that EU law does not require the award of punitive damages does not mean that the right to damages for loss caused by a breach of art.101 or 102 TFEU is any less important in ensuring the effectiveness of EU competition law.

Although strictly not required to do so, the court went on to determine the content of the right in the light of its function of ensuring the full effectiveness of EU competition law. The court considered that the effectiveness of EU competition law and the right to seek compensation required that the claimant be entitled to 'full compensation', including actual loss, loss of profit and interest, but leaving the award of punitive damages to national law subject to the principle of equivalence. In determining the damages recoverable, the court relied both on the principle of effectiveness and on the right to seek compensation. In doing so, the court applied a test similar to that set out in *Brasserie du Pêcheur SA and Factortame*, whereby the remedies available for the protection of the right are determined according to both the requirement of full effectiveness of EU law and the requirement of effective judicial protection.

Applying the three-stage framework proposed in this chapter, it would appear that, in the first stage, the EU right to damages for breach of art.101 or 102 TFEU is recognised based entirely upon the enforcement rationale. In the second stage, the principle of full effectiveness of EU law applies, in conjunction with the principle of effective judicial protection, to determine the content of the right. Finally, in the third stage, under the doctrine of procedural autonomy, the principles of full effectiveness of EU law and effective judicial protection apply to assess whether national rules on remedies and procedure are compatible with EU law. . . .

Some appear to argue that the objective of the EU law right to damages for breach of the competition provisions is compensation and not the effectiveness of the regime. However, it is necessary to distinguish between the content of the right, on the one hand, and its legal basis and function, on the other. The discussion so far has demonstrated that full compensation as the content of the right is consistent with the objective of ensuring the effective enforcement of EU competition law. Furthermore, the competition law cases of *Crehan* and *Manfredi* clearly articulate in unambiguous language an enforcement rationale for the conferral of the right to damages.

Thirdly, it was unclear to what extent EU law could require Member States more positively, or proactively, to facilitate damages claims and to put in place measures or reform institutions in a way which would ensure an effective enforcement framework.[136] In particular, the existence, or not, of specialist competition law tribunals or courts, the speed of litigation and individual national rules governing access to information and evidence, litigation costs, funding and cost rules, follow-on actions, mechanisms for collective redress, and remedies for final consumers are all factors which may dramatically affect the culture of competition in each Member State and the feasibility of successfully launching private litigation there. Thus, even if, for example, the CJ had made it clear that EU law demands that indirect purchasers should be able to seek compensation before a national court, such a right might be worthless in a State where the national tools are inadequate to allow that right to be effectively exercised—perhaps because procedural mechanisms do not allow for actions to be grouped together collectively or for relevant evidence to be uncovered, collected, or

[136] See Dunne, n. 1.

appropriately processed and assessed. In some jurisdictions, individuals may simply be less litigious than in others.[137]

Arguably, it was a range of these features of the national litigation systems that was deterring or constraining EU private claimants in some Member States, including:

- the cost and risk of litigation, especially where claimants had not suffered much loss individually and where class or other consolidated actions and contingency fees were not available[138] or where national cost rules provided disincentives to litigation (for example, where claimants were obliged to pay the defendant's legal costs if unsuccessful);[139]
- the difficulty claimants faced in some Member States in gathering the requisite evidence under national disclosure rules;[140]
- uncertainty over the weight to be given to decisions of NCAs;
- the fact that some national courts have limited experience dealing with antitrust arguments and may not, consequently, be the most appropriate or understanding forum for the hearing.[141]

Finally, a matter of specific contention became the strained relationship between public and private enforcement. In particular, tensions arose between the need to ensure, on the one hand, the effectiveness of the right to compensation available to victims of anti-competitive practices and, on the other, the effectiveness of the leniency programme, which constitutes a key tool for the Commission in its fight against cartels and, consequently, to public enforcement.

Litigants have frequently sought access to documents held on the Commission's file, including leniency evidence, under disclosure rules (as well as separately through seeking access to a competition agency's file or by filing a claim under EU transparency rules, see Chapter 13[142]). Although the Commission, supported by some NCAs and Advocate General Mazák, has taken the view that access should *not* be granted to self-incriminating statements voluntarily provided by leniency applicants as this could substantially reduce the attractiveness of the leniency programme and, in turn, the effective enforcement of Article 101,[143] in *Pfleiderer* the CJ favoured a more balanced approach and

[137] For a discussion of the position in the Member States on many of these issues, see B. Rodger (ed.), *Competition Law: Comparative Private Enforcement and Collective Redress Across the EU* (Wolters Kluwer, 2014), especially Chap. 2. For the view that individuals in Lithuania are less litigious because, historically, the clutches of the Soviet Union precluded the Lithuanian legal system from development, see J. Malinauskaite, 'Private Enforcement of Competition Law in Lithuania: A Story of Underdevelopment' (2013) 3 *Global Competition LR* 123, 133.

[138] Only 0.4% of the 1,268 antitrust judgments decided between 1999–2012 identified in Rodger, n. 137, 162 were aggregated/class consumer cases. Class actions may not only facilitate relief for certain victims but may produce external benefits for society as a whole, W. B. Rubenstein, 'Why Enable Litigation? A Positive Externalities Theory of the Small Claims Class Action', Public Law and Legal Theory Research Paper Series, UCLA School of Law, No. 06–10, <www.ssrn.com/abstract=890303>.

[139] See e.g. J. Peysner, 'Costs and Financing in Private Third Party Competition Damages Actions' (2006) 3 *Competition Law Review* 97. In Case C-312/21, *Tráficos Manuel Ferrer SL v Daimler AG* EU:C:2023:99, the CJ confirmed that Art. 101, read in conjunction with the Directive, did not preclude a national rule of civil procedure under which, in the event that the claim is upheld in part, costs are to be borne by each party and each party bears half of the common costs, except in cases of wrongful conduct, paras. 34–49.

[140] Disclosure although recognised in some Member States, did not exist in many civil law systems. National courts may ask the Commission to transmit to them information in its possession or its opinion on questions concerning the application of the EU competition law rules, see Reg. 1/2003, Art. 15(1).

[141] See e.g. Gavil. n. 2 and Malinauskaite, n. 137, 133.

[142] See Reg. 1049/2001 regarding public access to European Parliament, Council and Commission documents (Transparency Reg.) [2001] OJ L145/43, Case T-2/03, *Verein für Konsumenteninformation* EU:T:2005:125, Case T-437/08, *CDC Hydrogen Peroxide v Commission* EU:T:2011:752, and Ombudsman Decision 3699/2006/ELB, 2010.

[143] Case C-360/09, *Pfleiderer AG v Bundeskartellamt* EU:C:2011:782, Mazák AG, paras. 38–42. In his view an interference with the injured parties' right to an effective remedy and a fair trial was justified by the legitimate aim of ensuring the effective enforcement of Art. 101 by NCAs and ultimately private litigants' possibility of obtaining an effective remedy.

held that a national court had, in deciding whether to grant access to leniency documents, to weigh, according to national law and taking into account all the relevant factors in the case,[144] the respective interests of the leniency applicant (to have voluntarily submitted corporate statements protected) and the claimant (to have access to documents which would facilitate the claim).[145]

Further, in *Bundeswettbewerbsbehörde v Donau Chemie*,[146] the CJ held that an Austrian law which prohibited disclosure to third parties of court files on public law competition proceedings, unless all parties to the proceedings agreed, was not compatible with the principle of effectiveness and so conflicted with EU law. '[I]n competition law . . . any rule that is rigid, either by providing for absolute refusal to grant access . . . or for granting access as a matter of course . . . is liable to undermine the effective application of . . . Article 101'.[147] Although both of these cases stressed that the national court should have the opportunity to consider the issues on a case-by-case basis weighing the competing interests, in *EnBW*[148] the Court did, in the context of proceedings relating to the Transparency Regulation, recognise that access should be required only in cases of absolutely necessity where relevant evidence was not available from alternative mechanisms. In addition, the Damages Directive now makes it clear that national courts will not be able to give access to leniency statements (or settlement submissions) under national disclosure rules.[149]

(iv) A Need for Clarification and Harmonisation: The EU Package and Damages Directive

The previous discussion establishes that although EU law established that damages must in principle be available to compensate breaches of Articles 101 and 102, national rules retained significant impact on the likelihood of a claim's success or failure. This led to forum shopping and private actions being clustered in jurisdictions where national systems governing private litigation were perceived to be most favourable.

In 2005, the Commission expressed its view that as '[s]ignificant obstacles exist in the different Member States to the effective operation of damages actions for infringement of Community antitrust law'[150] the system of damages presented 'a picture of "total underdevelopment" '.[151] Further, even though private enforcement had steadily been increasing, from approximately 54 decided judgments within the EU in 1999 to 146 in 2011,[152] the Commission concluded that 'most victims of infringements of the EU competition rules in practice do not obtain compensation for the harm suffered';[153] victims only commenced private actions in 25 per cent of cases where antitrust infringement decisions had been adopted by the Commission.

Although not all agreed that steps were necessary to stimulate private enforcement,[154] or that EU measures were required, desirable, and/or practicable,[155] the Commission reflected deeply on the

[144] Case C-360/09, *Pfleiderer* EU:C:2011:389, para. 31. [145] Ibid., para. 30.

[146] Case C-536/11, EU:C:2013:366.

[147] Case C-536/11, *Bundeswettbewerbsbehörde v Donau Chemie* EU:C:2013:366, para. 31.

[148] Case C-365/12 P, *Commission v EnBW Energie Baden-Württemberg AG* EU:C:2014:112. [149] See n. 185.

[150] COM/2005/0672/final, 1.2. [151] Green Paper, n. 12, 1.2. This view was based on the Ashurst Report, n. 12.

[152] See Rodger, n. 137, 87. Only 31% of all the cases analysed were damages claims.

[153] Commission Proposal, n. 11, Explanatory Memorandum, 1.2 and ibid.

[154] See e.g. W. Wils, 'Should Private Antitrust Enforcement be Encouraged?' (2003) 26 *World Competition* 473 (but see now Wils, n. 1, 3), F. Jacobs, 'Civil Enforcement of EEC Antitrust Law' (1984) 82 *Mich LR* 1364, Dunne, n. 111, and S. Peyer, 'Private Antitrust Litigation in Germany from 2005 to 2007: Empirical Evidence' (2012) 8 *J of Competition Law and Economics* 331.

[155] Although final judgments are relatively low, these do not take account of the numerous cases that are settled, see e.g. speech by Coates, n. 127 ('Many of these cases settle. I was talking to an economist a few months ago who had advised on—he thought approximately—50 damages calculations. Not one of the cases went to final judgment').

question of whether measures could, and should, be adopted to amend and/or harmonise national procedural and substantive rules governing damages claims further, for example on costs, access to evidence, limitation periods, standing, class or representative actions, fault, and/or defences, such as the passing-on defence.

In its 2005 Green Paper on Damages actions for breach of the EC antitrust rules,[156] and an accompanying Commission Staff Working Paper,[157] the Commission thus sought: (a) 'to identify the main obstacles to a more efficient system of damages claims and to set out different options for further reflection and possible action to improve both follow-on actions (for example, cases in which the civil action is brought after a competition authority has found an infringement) and stand-alone actions (that is to say, actions which do not follow on from a prior finding by a competition authority of an infringement of competition law)';[158] and (b) to invite a discussion on obstacles identified and options formulated for overcoming them and allowing a competition culture to develop. Following the receipt of comments, it published further proposals in its White Paper on Damages actions (to be read together with a Commission Staff Working Document and an Impact Assessment Report)[159] recommending a broad range of measures aimed to ensure that all victims of anti-competitive behaviour are able to obtain full compensation (but not punitive or multiple damages) for harm suffered but that unmeritorious claims are not encouraged.[160] It recognised, however, that '[i]mproving compensatory justice would . . . inherently also produce beneficial effects in terms of deterrence of future infringements and greater compliance with [EU] antitrust rules. Safeguarding undistorted competition is an integral part of the internal market and important for implementing the Lisbon strategy. A competition culture contributes to better allocation of resources, greater economic efficiency, increased innovation and lower prices.'[161] It thus concluded that EU instruments *were* requisite to overcome barriers to litigation and to stimulate and harmonise damages actions,[162] and to balance it with public enforcement. In its view, the new measures adopted 'will democratise enforcement and empower the victims of antitrust infringements to receive effective compensation . . . '[163]

In considering what EU measures should be enacted, the Commission had a tortuous path to navigate, both politically and legally.[164] Not only did it have to convince the Parliament[165] and the Council that EU legislation was required which encroaches on national litigation systems and entrenched principles developed within them,[166] but it had to reflect on an array of factors when considering what those measure should look like and what they should cover. In addition to considering how to overcome national obstacles to litigation, it has thus had to consider: what legislative proposals

[156] COM/2005/0672/final.

[157] Commission Staff Working Paper, Annex to the Green Paper, n. 12.

[158] Green Paper, n. 12, 1.3.

[159] COM(2008) 165 final, SEC(2008)404, and SEC(2008)405, available at <http://ec.europa.eu/competition/antitrust/actionsdamages/documents.html>.

[160] SEC(2008)404, paras. 2, 12, and 16. [161] COM(2008) 165 final.

[162] See Section 2. The Commission has not proposed specific measures to stimulate other sorts of private enforcement actions.

[163] Speech J. Almunia, 'Looking back at five years of competition enforcement in the EU', Global Antitrust Enforcement Symposium, Washington DC, 10 September 2014.

[164] See e.g. Dunne, n. 111.

[165] A first Directive proposed by the Commission in 2009 was based on Art. 103 TFEU and would have excluded the Parliament from the legislative procedure. In the end, the Directive was adopted under Arts. 103 and 114, so requiring use of the co-decision procedure.

[166] In some Member States, e.g. Germany, there has been resistance to the introduction of disclosure rules on the basis that litigation proceeds on the basis that it is for the claimant to prove its case, see A. Howard, 'Too Little, Too Late? The European Commission's Legislative Proposals on Anti-trust Damages Actions' (2013) 4 *JECLAP* 455, 460 (the extent of compromises in the Directive and timid selection of procedural issues is linked to political concerns regarding the sanctity of national procedural autonomy, ibid. 464).

would realistically be accepted, how it should balance the potential deterrent, compensatory, and other functions of private actions; how it should balance private and public enforcement; whether it should adopt a more holistic, all-encompassing, or a more gradual, sequential approach; and how to encompass lessons emerging from the US experience and to safeguard against an unleashing of some of the excesses connected with the litigation culture developed there.[167] It has therefore had to exercise caution to ensure that, in seeking to bolster and encourage private enforcement in the EU, rules are not made so claimant friendly that the system encourages undeserving claims to be commenced (creating the risk of false positives).[168] Were that to occur, courts might become inclined to adopt narrow constructions of substantive and procedural rules making it harder for public enforcement agencies,[169] as well as private litigants, to establish violations.

An examination of the package of EU measures illustrates how the Commission and the legislature sought to resolve the issues and to alter private enforcement in the Member States (see also Table 14.1). A first (obvious) point is that the Commission took the view that legislation governing damages action was required to clarify and harmonise certain issues (only, minimum harmonisation). Although some matters have been dealt with primarily through soft recommendations and guidance, others (many relating to procedural change) have been dealt with through harmonising legislation, the Damages Directive.

(v) The Provisions of the Damages Directive

a. The Core Objectives: Full Compensation for All Victims of Antitrust Infringements, Levelling the Playing Field Throughout the EU, and Coordination of Public and Private Enforcement

Article 1 explains that the Directive 'sets out certain rules necessary to ensure that anyone who has suffered harm caused by an infringement of Article 101 or 102 of the Treaty or of national competition law, can effectively exercise the right to full compensation for that harm', and which are designed to foster undistorted competition in the internal market, to ensure equivalent protection for those who have suffered antitrust harm throughout the EU, and to coordinate public and private enforcement. In *AD v PACCAR*,[170] the CJ stressed the important role of the Directive in ensuring full compliance with Articles 101 and 102, preventing infringements (and remedying not only the direct damage to victims but also the indirect harm to the structure and operation of the market), and facilitating enforcement by private litigants, whilst balancing the legitimate interests of all parties and third parties concerned. These objectives are to be achieved through the Directive's provisions. Some important definitions are set out in Article 4.

b. The Compensatory Approach

In line with the approach advocated in the White Paper, the Directive has generally embraced the compensatory approach, reflecting the Commission's articulated view that public and private enforcement should pursue different, albeit complementary, objectives and that *all* victims of antitrust violations, including small and medium-sized enterprises (SMEs) and consumers, should be able to

[167] See e.g. the responses to the Commission's Green Paper, n. 12.

[168] A choice may have to be made as to whether false positives or negatives are worse. For the view that the new regime is not likely to encourage new claims, see S. Peyer, 'Compensation and the Damages Directive' (2016) 12(1) *European Competition Journal* 87.

[169] See e.g. W. E. Kovacic, *Private Participation in the Enforcement of Public Competition Laws* (15 May 2003), <www.ftc.gov/public-statements/2003/05/private-participation-enforcement-public-competition-laws>.

[170] Case C-163/21, *AD v PACCAR Inc* EU:C:2022:863, paras. 54–69. See also Case C-25/21, *ZA etc v Repsol Comercial de Productos Petolíferos SA* EU:C:2023:298, paras. 31–32 (confirming that actions for declarations of nullity (and other types of action) do not fall within the scope of the Directive).

obtain damages. Consequently, Article 3 mandates national courts to ensure that *any* natural or legal person who has suffered harm caused by a competition law infringement is able to claim and to obtain full compensation—for actual loss and for loss of profit, plus the payment of interest.[171] The Directive establishes a rebuttable evidential presumption of harm (but no specific amount of harm) in cartel (but not other) cases[172] and empowers national courts to estimate the amount of harm in cases where precise quantification of damages (which involves estimating the price that would have occurred absent the breach) is impossible or excessively difficult.[173] The Commission's practical guide on the quantification of harm for damages is designed to assist national courts in this sphere by setting out potential methods of assessment.[174] When implementing the legislation, three Member States have introduced rebuttable presumptions that cartels cause an overcharge of a specific amount—10 per cent (Hungary and Latvia) and 20 per cent (Romania).[175] In other Member States, victims will have to provide evidence of the quantity of harm.[176]

Article 3 also specifies that such actions shall *not* lead to overcompensation, for example by means of punitive or multiple damages.[177]

Directive 2014/104/EU (the Damages Directive)

Article 3 Right to full compensation

1. Member States shall ensure that any natural or legal person who has suffered harm caused by an infringement of competition law is able to claim and to obtain full compensation for that harm.
2. Full compensation shall place a person who has suffered harm in the position in which that person would have been had the infringement of competition law not been committed. It shall therefore cover the right to compensation for actual loss and for loss of profit, plus the payment of interest.
3. Full compensation under this Directive shall not lead to overcompensation, whether by means of punitive, multiple or other types of damages.

[171] Dir. 2014/104/EU, Art. 3(2). The basis is tortious—to ensure that the compensation puts the person who suffered harm in the position that it would have been had the infringement of competition law not been committed, ibid. See also Case C-312/21, *Tráficos Manuel Ferrer SL v Daimler AG* EU:C:2023:99.

[172] Ibid., Art. 17(2), pushing the burden onto the defendant to rebut the presumption by providing evidence to establish there was in fact no overcharge. See also Art. 17(3) (NCAs shall on request assist national courts with respect to the determination of quantum of damages). Some NCAs are now going out of their way to provide evidence of effects and quantum of harm in their cartel decisions and, consequently, to facilitate private enforcement, see B. Veronese, 'European Public and Private Antitrust Enforcement: It Takes Two to Tango' (2014) 5 *JECLAP* 563.

[173] Ibid., Art. 17(1), Case C-312/21, *Tráficos Manuel Ferrer SL v Daimler AG* EU:C:2023:99, paras. 50–65 (considering the question of when evidence disclosed by the parties affects the possibility for a national court to estimate harm under Art. 17(1)) and see J.-F. *Laborde*, 'Cartel Damages Claims in Europe: How Courts Have Assessed Overcharges' (2021) 3 *Concurrences* 3-2021; (2018 ed.), Concurrences Rev. 2 (Feb. 2019); and *Concurrences* Rev. 36 (Feb. 2017). The Directive also incorporates provisions on consensual dispute resolution. Economics is consequently bound to play an ever-increasing role in private enforcement cases, Veronese, n. 172, and E. Clark and R. Sanders, 'Navigating the Quantum Minefield in Cartel Damages Cases' (2015) 6 *JECLAP* 153.

[174] SWD(2013) 205, n. 18. See also, e.g., an external study prepared for the Commission, Oxera, 'Quantifying antitrust damages. Towards non-binding guidance for courts. Study prepared for the European Commission' (Publications Office of the European Union, 2010); and Commission, 'Draft Guidance Paper—Quantifying Harm in Actions for Damages based on Breaches of Article 101 or 102 of the Treaty on the Functioning of the European Union' (June 2011), <http://ec.europa.eu/competition/consultations/2011_actions_damages/draft_guidance_paper_en.pdf>.

[175] See Commission Staff Working Document on the implementation of Directive 2014/104/EU, SWD(2020) 338.

[176] See P. van Wijk and F. Weber, 'The Abstract Presumption of Harm in the Damages Directive: Overconcern or Overcompensation (2021) 18(1) *European Competition Journal* 204.

[177] Contrast the approach of the CJ in *Manfredi* nn. 119–121 and text.

Articles 12 and 14 clarify that indirect, as well as direct, purchasers can sue (and indeed in some cases overcharges are presumed to be passed on to them by direct purchasers, see especially Article 14(2)). Article 13 requires, in line with the principle that overcompensation must not ensue, national courts to ensure the passing-on defence is available to defendants; the burden of proof, however, is on the defendant to establish passing-on has occurred. These provisions, which will demand rigorous analysis to determine where the loss falls and the appropriate level of damages, widen the pool of claimants beyond those permitted under federal antitrust rules in the US. Recognising the complexity that is likely to follow for national courts in applying a passing-on defence, the Directive provides that '[t]he Commission shall issue guidelines for national courts on how to estimate the share of the overcharge which was passed on to the indirect purchaser' and these were published in 2019.[178]

Chapter IV The Passing-on of Overcharges

Article 12 Passing-on of overcharges and the right to full compensation

1. To ensure the full effectiveness of the right to full compensation as laid down in Article 3, Member States shall ensure that, in accordance with the rules laid down in this Chapter, compensation of harm can be claimed by anyone who suffered it, irrespective of whether they are direct or indirect purchasers from an infringer, and that compensation of harm exceeding that caused by the infringement of competition law to the claimant, as well as the absence of liability of the infringer, are avoided.
2. In order to avoid overcompensation, Member States shall lay down procedural rules appropriate to ensure that compensation for actual loss at any level of the supply chain does not exceed the overcharge harm suffered at that level.
3. This Chapter shall be without prejudice to the right of an injured party to claim and obtain compensation for loss of profits due to a full or partial passing-on of the overcharge.
4. Member States shall ensure that the rules laid down in this Chapter apply accordingly where the infringement of competition law relates to a supply to the infringer.
5. Member States shall ensure that the national courts have the power to estimate, in accordance with national procedures, the share of any overcharge that was passed on.

Article 13 Passing-on defence

Member States shall ensure that the defendant in an action for damages can invoke as a defence against a claim for damages the fact that the claimant passed on the whole or part of the overcharge resulting from the infringement of competition law. The burden of proving that the overcharge was passed on shall be on the defendant, who may reasonably require disclosure from the claimant or from third parties.

Article 14 Indirect purchasers

1. Member States shall ensure that, where in an action for damages the existence of a claim for damages or the amount of compensation to be awarded depends on whether, or to what degree, an overcharge was passed on to the claimant, taking into account the commercial practice that price

[178] See Art. 16 and Guidelines for national courts on how to estimate the share of overcharge which was passed on to the indirect purchaser [2019] OJ C267/4, n. 19 and text.

increases are passed on down the supply chain, the burden of proving the existence and scope of such a passing-on shall rest with the claimant, who may reasonably require disclosure from the defendant or from third parties.

2. In the situation referred to in paragraph 1, the indirect purchaser shall be deemed to have proven that a passing-on to that indirect purchaser occurred where that indirect purchaser has shown that:
   (a) the defendant has committed an infringement of competition law;
   (b) the infringement of competition law has resulted in an overcharge for the direct purchaser of the defendant; and
   (c) the indirect purchaser has purchased the goods or services that were the object of the infringement of competition law, or has purchased goods or services derived from or containing them.

   This paragraph shall not apply where the defendant can demonstrate credibly to the satisfaction of the court that the overcharge was not, or was not entirely, passed on to the indirect purchaser.

c. Disclosure

The Directive has sought to tackle some (but not all) of the practical difficulties which have been confronting victims of EU antitrust infringements, to encourage damages actions and to establish certain minimum standards for litigation throughout the EU. In Article 5, it addresses the problem of information asymmetry and that disclosure is not widely available in some Member States by providing that, subject to certain conditions, national courts must be able to order a defendant (or claimant) to disclose relevant evidence under its control where a request is accompanied by a reasoned justification sufficient to support its plausibility.[179] The interpretation of the Directive's disclosure provisions was considered by the CJ in its judgments in *AD v PACCAR*[180] and *RegioJet as*.[181] In *PACCAR*, the CJ held that to ensure the achievement of the Directive's objectives, disclosure of relevant evidence covers evidence that the party to whom the request to disclose evidence is addressed must create *ex novo* (e.g. by compiling or classifying information, knowledge, or data in its possession). It stressed, however, that disclosure of evidence should be restricted by the national court to what is relevant, necessary, and proportionate (taking into account the legitimate interests and fundamental rights of that party); it should not impose a disproportionate burden on that party. In so ruling, the Court emphasised, relying on the Directive's recitals (14 and 15), the important aim of the Directive to correct information asymmetries between the parties and to ensure the disclosure of evidence necessary to support a claim for damages.[182] In *RegioJet*, the CJ held that a national court may, subject to the requirements of the Directive, order disclosure in an action for damages occurring simultaneously with public proceedings, so long as the disclosure of evidence does not unduly interfere with the competition authority's ongoing investigation. National courts 'are therefore called upon to carry out a thorough examination of the request submitted to them as regards the relevance of the evidence

[179] It also provides for disclosure from third parties and competition agencies.

[180] Case C-163/21, *AD v PACCAR Inc* EU:2022: C:863. In this case, the applicants had purchased trucks from manufacturers found by the Commission to have participated in the trucks cartel, AT/39.824, *Trucks* 19 July 2016. They sought evidence from the defendants to facilitate the quantification of the artificial price increase, and to compare prices before, during, and after the cartel period, ibid., para. 20.

[181] Case C-57/21, *RegioJet as* EU:C:2023:6.

[182] Case C-163/21, EU:2022:C:863, paras. 61–69, and e.g. the approach to proportionality of Roth J in the English High Court in *National Grid Electricity Transmission Plc v ABB Ltd* [2012] EWHC 869 (Ch). The defendants argued that as some of the documents had to be drawn up, such an obligation entailed an excessive and disproportionate burden on them, going beyond a mere order to disclose evidence, ibid., para. 21.

requested, the link between that evidence and the claim for damages submitted, whether that evidence is sufficiently precise and as regards its proportionality'.[183]

National courts must also protect confidential information and give full effect to legal professional privilege. In order to ensure that such actions do not disrupt public enforcement, however, Articles 6 and 7 of the Directive provides for more limited access to material in the files of competition authorities and, overriding the case law of the CJ,[184] limits national rules governing disclosure by providing an *absolute bar* on the disclosure of leniency statements and settlement submissions.[185]

Article 5 Disclosure of evidence

1. Member States shall ensure that in proceedings relating to an action for damages in the Union upon request of a claimant who has presented a reasoned justification containing reasonably available facts and evidence sufficient to support the plausibility of its claim for damages, national courts are able to order the defendant or a third party to disclose relevant evidence which lies in their control, subject to the conditions set out in this Chapter. Member States shall ensure that national courts are able, upon request of the defendant, to order the claimant or a third party to disclose relevant evidence. This paragraph is without prejudice to the rights and obligations of national courts under Regulation (EC) No 1206/2001.
2. Member States shall ensure that national courts are able to order the disclosure of specified items of evidence or relevant categories of evidence circumscribed as precisely and as narrowly as possible on the basis of reasonably available facts in the reasoned justification.
3. Member States shall ensure that national courts limit the disclosure of evidence to that which is proportionate. In determining whether any disclosure requested by a party is proportionate, national courts shall consider the legitimate interests of all parties and third parties concerned. They shall, in particular, consider:
   (a) the extent to which the claim or defence is supported by available facts and evidence justifying the request to disclose evidence;
   (b) the scope and cost of disclosure, especially for any third parties concerned, including preventing non-specific searches for information which is unlikely to be of relevance for the parties in the procedure;
   (c) whether the evidence the disclosure of which is sought contains confidential information, especially concerning any third parties, and what arrangements are in place for protecting such confidential information.

[183] Case C-57/21, para. 72. Where the national proceedings have been stayed owing to a Commission investigation, the Court must ensure that that disclosure, which must follow a request that is sufficiently circumscribed and substantiated, is necessary and proportionate for the purpose of pursuing the action, ibid., paras. 77–78. The judgment also deals with the question of when, pursuant to Damages Dir. Art. 6, restrictions can be imposed on the disclosure of information prepared for the proceedings of a competition authority and information submitted for those purposes.

[184] In both Case C-360/09, *Pfleiderer* EU:C:2011:389, paras. 23–24 and Case C-536/11, *Donau Chemie* EU:C:2013:366, paras. 25–27 the CJ recognised that national courts could only apply, subject to EU law and particularly the principle of effectiveness, their national rules on the right of access to documents, if no binding regulation under EU law on the subject applied. For the position under the Transparency Reg., see Chap. 13.

[185] Dir. 2014/104/EU, Art. 6(6). In some US cases, a claimant's request for discovery of documents held by the Commission, including leniency applicants, has been denied to maintain confidentiality, see e.g. *In re Rubber Chemicals Antitrust Litigation*, 486 F. Supp 2d 1078 (ND Cal. 2007), but contrast *FTC v Qualcomm Inc* (N.D. Cal. 17 January 2017), see I. Vandenborre, T. Goetz, and A. Kafetzopoulos, 'Access to the EU Commission's File or Decision for Purposes of Damages Claims, and Confidentiality of Information under European Competition Law' (2018) 9(1) *JECLAP* 655.

4. Member States shall ensure that national courts have the power to order the disclosure of evidence containing confidential information where they consider it relevant to the action for damages. Member States shall ensure that, when ordering the disclosure of such information, national courts have at their disposal effective measures to protect such information.
5. The interest of undertakings to avoid actions for damages following an infringement of competition law shall not constitute an interest that warrants protection.
6. Member States shall ensure that national courts give full effect to applicable legal professional privilege under Union or national law when ordering the disclosure of evidence.
7. Member States shall ensure that those from whom disclosure is sought are provided with an opportunity to be heard before a national court orders disclosure under this Article.
8. Without prejudice to paragraphs 4 and 7 and to Article 6, this Article shall not prevent Member States from maintaining or introducing rules which would lead to wider disclosure of evidence.

Article 6 Disclosure of evidence included in the file of a competition authority

1. Member States shall ensure that, for the purpose of actions for damages, where national courts order the disclosure of evidence included in the file of a competition authority, this Article applies in addition to Article 5.
2. This Article is without prejudice to the rules and practices on public access to documents under Regulation (EC) No 1049/2001.
3. This Article is without prejudice to the rules and practices under Union or national law on the protection of internal documents of competition authorities and of correspondence between competition authorities.
4. When assessing, in accordance with Article 5(3), the proportionality of an order to disclose information, national courts shall, in addition, consider the following:
   (a) whether the request has been formulated specifically with regard to the nature, subject-matter or contents of documents submitted to a competition authority or held in the file thereof, rather than by a non-specific application concerning documents submitted to a competition authority,
   (b) whether the party requesting disclosure is doing so in relation to an action for damages before a national court; and
   (c) in relation to paragraphs 5 and 10, or upon request of a competition authority pursuant to paragraph 11, the need to safeguard the effectiveness of the public enforcement of competition law.
5. National courts may order the disclosure of the following categories of evidence only after a competition authority, by adopting a decision or otherwise, has closed its proceedings:
   (a) information that was prepared by a natural or legal person specifically for the proceedings of a competition authority;
   (b) information that the competition authority has drawn up and sent to the parties in the course of its proceedings; and
   (c) settlement submissions that have been withdrawn.
6. Member States shall ensure that, for the purpose of actions for damages, national courts cannot at any time order a party or a third party to disclose any of the following categories of evidence:
   (a) leniency statements; and
   (b) settlement submissions.
7. A claimant may present a reasoned request that a national court access the evidence referred to in points (a) or (b) of paragraph 6 for the sole purpose of ensuring that their contents correspond to

the definitions in points (16) and (18) of Article 2. In that assessment, national courts may request assistance only from the competent competition authority. The authors of the evidence in question may also have the possibility to be heard. In no case shall the national court permit other parties or third parties access to that evidence.

8. If only parts of the evidence requested are covered by paragraph 6, the remaining parts thereof shall, depending on the category under which they fall, be released in accordance with the relevant paragraphs of this Article.
9. The disclosure of evidence in the file of a competition authority that does not fall into any of the categories listed in this Article may be ordered in actions for damages at any time, without prejudice to this Article.
10. Member States shall ensure that national courts request the disclosure from a competition authority of evidence included in its file only where no party or third party is reasonably able to provide that evidence.
11. To the extent that a competition authority is willing to state its views on the proportionality of disclosure requests, it may, acting on its own initiative, submit observations to the national court before which a disclosure order is sought.

Article 7 Limits on the use of evidence obtained solely through access to the file of a competition authority

1. Member States shall ensure that evidence in the categories listed in Article 6(6) which is obtained by a natural or legal person solely through access to the file of a competition authority is either deemed to be inadmissible in actions for damages or is otherwise protected under the applicable national rules to ensure the full effect of the limits on the disclosure of evidence set out in Article 6.
2. Member States shall ensure that, until a competition authority has closed its proceedings by adopting a decision or otherwise, evidence in the categories listed in Article 6(5) which is obtained by a natural or legal person solely through access to the file of that competition authority is either deemed to be inadmissible in actions for damages or is otherwise protected under the applicable national rules to ensure the full effect of the limits on the disclosure of evidence set out in Article 6.
3. Member States shall ensure that evidence which is obtained by a natural or legal person solely through access to the file of a competition authority and which does not fall under paragraph 1 or 2, can be used in an action for damages only by that person or by a natural or legal person that succeeded to that person's rights, including a person that acquired that person's claim.

d. Follow-on Actions, Limitation, and Joint and Several Liability

The Directive also clarifies that:

- as is the case for Commission findings,[186] the finding of an infringement by an NCA or a review court should be irrefutably established for the purposes of damages claims based on it before a national court in that State (so in these follow-on actions a claimant will have to establish only causation, loss, and the quantum of damages,[187] not the existence of the breach);[188]

[186] See nn. 81–82 and text.

[187] Although, of course, these may be formidable obstacles to overcome.

[188] Dir. 2014/104/EU, Art. 9 (NCA decisions did not previously have any binding effect in a majority of States). The Commission's original proposal that decisions of NCAs were to constitute full proof before civil courts that an infringement occurred provoked considerable debate and was not adopted in the final Directive, see n. 83 (although such decisions may be presented before the national courts of another Member State as at least prima facie evidence of a competition law infringement).

- national limitation periods must not be less than five years and cannot commence to run before the infringement has ceased and the claimant knows, or can reasonably be expected to know, of it. Further, to ensure effective interaction between public and private enforcement, the limitation period must be suspended or interrupted until public enforcement proceedings are final (when the decision cannot be, or can no longer be, appealed by ordinary means[189]) or terminated.[190] Claimants must therefore have a reasonable time within which to seek compensation; and
- undertakings responsible for an infringement through joint behaviour should be jointly and severally liable for it.[191] Thus, in principle, any infringer may potentially be liable for the entire loss caused by the breach; each must however be able to seek contributions from joint infringers reflecting their relative responsibility for the harm.[192] Exceptions apply for certain SMEs (which are not ringleaders, repeat offenders, or firms that have coerced others into infringements) and full immunity recipients. Such firms are generally liable only for the damage to their direct and indirect purchasers. Settling defendants also benefit from an exemption from joint and several liability and limitations on contribution.[193]

e. *Consensual Dispute Resolution*

The Directive also incorporates provisions relating to, and designed to incentivise, consensual dispute resolution, such as the suspension of limitation periods during the period.[194]

f. *The Impact of the Directive*

The Commission has been keen to ensure that unmeritorious antitrust claims are not encouraged, so avoiding the 'toxic cocktail' of provisions alleged to exist in the US (consisting of, in particular, class actions, contingency fee arrangements, favourable attorneys' fees rules, treble damages, broad discovery, jury trials, and the rule of joint and several liability, with no right of contribution).[195] Although an innovative package, it has been questioned whether the reforms are sufficient to achieve the Commission's objective of increasing, and harmonising, private damages actions across the EU or whether more still needs to be done to overcome the impediments to litigation, to reduce its cost for claimants, and to increase the likelihood of reward.[196] Indeed, some problems remain.

First, because the Commission has not adopted a holistic approach, attempting to introduce a completely harmonised framework,[197] a number of not insignificant obstacles to national actions and areas

[189] Ibid., Art. 2.

[190] Ibid., Art. 10 (this means in practice that proceedings may commence many years after an infringement has ended).

[191] Ibid., Art. 11. See C. Koenig, 'Making Contribution Work: The Liability of Privileged and Non-privileged Injurers in EU Competition Law' (2018) 14(1) *European Competition Journal* 110.

[192] Principles governing relative responsibility for infringements are thus governed by national laws of the Member States governing contribution, see M. J. Frese, 'Civil Liability for Single and Continuous Infringements' (2018) 41(2) *World Competition* 179, 193.

[193] Dir. 2014/104/EU, Art. 19 and see e.g. O. Bodnar, M. Fremerey, H.-T. Normann, and J. Schad, 'The Effects of Private Damage Claims on Cartel Activity: Experimental Evidence' (2021) *J of Law, Economics, and Organization*, 7 August 2021 (private damages action can make cartels more stable, but that these negative effects can be avoided by providing immunity applicants with protection from damages).

[194] Ibid., Arts. 18 and 19. Art. 18(3) provides that a competition authority may consider compensation paid as a consensual settlement prior to its decision imposing a fine to be a mitigating factor.

[195] See e.g. Gavil, n. 2.

[196] For the view that they have not, see Peyer, n. 168.

[197] Howard, n. 166, 456 ('At first glance, the proposed Directive appears to be a random selection of minimum procedural requirements that lack coherence or structure. This is not a blueprint set of procedural rules that govern damages actions from start to finish'). Although the Directive is based on both Arts. 103 and 114 TFEU, n. 165 (to ensure that the differences in the liability regimes applicable in the Member States do not negatively affect both competition and the proper functioning of the internal market), arguably it simply provides a guarantee that a minimum set of rules will govern actions across the EU rather than providing a set of harmonised rules.

of legal ambiguity appear to remain. For example, the Directive does not contain provisions dealing with some important factors which might impact on the success of a national claim, for example: which courts should hear antitrust damages actions; the substantive grounds and conditions of liability—whether the type of liability should be based on tort, the extent to which fault or negligence should be required as a basis for negligence, and whether parent companies or managers can or must be held liable for the conduct of their subsidiaries (in both *Skanska Industrial Solutions* and *Sumal*, however, the CJ confirmed that the determination of which entity is liable to pay damages is governed by EU law and that it is the undertaking—an autonomous concept of EU law—which is liable);[198] admissibility of economic evidence; causation; remoteness; quantification of damages (dealt with only in the form of a non-binding practical guide); funding or cost rules; rules governing admissibility of expert evidence; motions to dismiss; summary judgment; or the availability of class actions or collective redress. Indeed, a core concern in relation to the latter is that the Recommendation[199] 'soft law', on collective redress, based on the 'opt-in' principle (under which claimant parties are formed through directly expressed consent of their members), will be insufficient to bolster the position of final consumers and SMEs in mass-harm situations;[200] classes will encompass only a small percentage of antitrust victims.[201]

A number of issues thus continue to be governed by national law, subject to their compliance with the principles of effectiveness and equivalence (see Table 14.1).

Table 14.1 The impact of the Damages Directive on private antitrust actions in the EU Member States

	The position prior to the implementation of the Damages Directive	**The position once the Damages Directive is implemented**
Statutory provision governing private rights of action?	No statutory provision but principles developed by the CJ. Essentially EU right to compensation/injunction governed by national law *subject to it being compatible with EU principles of equivalence and effectiveness (in particular rules must not render exercise of rights practically impossible or excessively difficult)*	Directive: requires Member States to set out rules necessary to ensure that anyone who has suffered harm caused by a competition law infringement can obtain full compensation (Art. 1). Directive does not deal with who is liable, under what conditions, the basis of the claim, or with the right to an injunction

[198] Case C-724/17, *Vantaan kaupunki v Skanska Industrial Solutions Oy* EU:C:2019:204 (preliminary ruling from the Korkein oikeus (Supreme Court, Finland)) confirming that the concept of undertaking includes the principle of economic continuity and consequently that where all the shares in companies which participated in the cartel were subsequently acquired by other companies, which dissolved the former companies and continued their commercial activities, the acquiring companies may be held liable (noting that although national law determines which entity is jointly and severally liable for harm caused (Dir. 2014/104/EU, Art. 11(1)), this applies not to the definition of entities liable but to the attribution of liability between those entities) and Case C-882/19, *Sumal, SL v Mercedes Benz Trucks España, SL* EU:C:2021:800. See also Chap. 4, B. J. Rodger, M. Sousa Ferro, and F. Marcos, 'A Comparative View of the Implementation of the EU Antitrust Damages Directive in Sixteen Member States', Working Paper IE Law School AJ8-243-I (2018) and C. Koenig, 'Comparing Parent Company Liability in EU and US Competition Law' (2018) 41(1) *World Competition* 69.

[199] But see n. 17 and text.

[200] The Commission had considered including an opt-out class procedure in the Damages Dir. but it became apparent that this proposal would be unlikely to be accepted by the Parliament, see e.g. Dunne, n. 111, G. Barling, 'Collective Redress for Breach of Competition Law—A Case for Reform?' [2011] *Comp Law* 5, A. Andreangeli, *Private Enforcement of Antitrust: Regulating Corporate Behaviour through Collective Claims in the EU and the US* (Edward Elgar, 2014), and M. Ioannidou, *Consumer Involvement in Private EU Competition Law Enforcement* (Oxford University Press, 2016).

[201] See Lande, n. 6, 6 (recovery in the EU will also be severely limited if lawyers are not allowed to receive contingency fees; 'the vast majority of consumer-victims and small business-victims' may therefore 'continue to be uncompensated').

Table 14.1 *Continued*

	The position prior to the implementation of the Damages Directive	The position once the Damages Directive is implemented
Right to compensation: Compensatory principle? Punitive or multiple damages?	EU right to damages governed by national law *subject to EU principles of equivalence and effectiveness* (punitive damages must be available if available in equivalent situations under national law, *Manfredi*)	Full compensation for actual loss and loss of profit, plus interest. Full compensation shall not lead to over compensation whether by means of, e.g., punitive or multiple damages (Art. 3)
Standing and remoteness	Governed by national law *subject to EU principles of equivalence and effectiveness*	Compensation for any person that has suffered harm but no provision as to how rules of remoteness to be applied
Passing-on and indirect purchasers	Governed by national law *subject to EU principles of equivalence and effectiveness*	Indirect purchaser actions expressly permitted and passing-on defence mandated (Arts. 12 and 14)
Application of illegality defence, *in pari delicto* doctrine	Governed by national law but principle of effectiveness requires damages for loss caused by an infringement unless claimant bears significant responsibility for the breach (*Crehan*)	
Follow-on cases: weight of public law finding	Commission decisions binding but impact of NCA decisions governed by national law (Reg. 1/2003, Art. 16)	Commission decisions binding and decisions of NCA or review court binding on national courts in that Member State (Art. 9)
Causation, harm, and quantification	Governed by national law *subject to EU principles of equivalence and effectiveness*	Evidential presumption of harm in cartel cases—national courts to estimate harm (Art. 17)
Limitation periods	Governed by national law *subject to EU principles of equivalence and effectiveness*—litigation in some Member States (see e.g. Manfredi), *especially as to when limitation periods start to run*	Limitation periods must not be less than 5 years—stipulation of when periods can start to run (Art. 10)
Availability of class actions	Governed by national law *subject to EU principles of equivalence and effectiveness—but Recommendation for Member States to adopt opt-in class actions*	
Legal costs	Governed by national law *subject to EU principles of equivalence and effectiveness*—some Member States apply loser pays principle (see *Tráficos Manuel Ferrer SL v Daimler AG*)	

	The position prior to the implementation of the Damages Directive	The position once the Damages Directive is implemented
Disclosure of evidence	Governed by national law—disclosure not widely available in civil systems although recognised by common law systems (e.g. UK/Ireland)	Subject to some exceptions, provision for disclosure of evidence supported by plausible claim (Art. 5)
Impact on leniency	National court must balance competing interests of claimant and defendant when deciding when to order disclosure of leniency documents—no absolute rule against or in favour of disclosure permitted	Absolute bar on disclosure of leniency documents and settlement decisions (Art. 6)
Joint and several liability	Governed by national law *subject to EU principles of equivalence and effectiveness*	Joint and several liability for co-infringers with exceptions for certain SMEs and leniency applicants
Admissibility of expert evidence	Governed by national law *subject to EU principles of equivalence and effectiveness*	
Motions to dismiss and summary judgment	Governed by national law *subject to EU principles of equivalence and effectiveness*	

Secondly, even in some areas where harmonising rules have been adopted, scope for divergence remains, which will affect the incentive to sue and place of action.[202] Not only do discrepancies in implementation exist (and perhaps even some infringements of the duty to transpose the Directive faithfully),[203] but some Member States provide more favourable rules. In addition, it seems likely that pre-existing heterogeneity between legal orders on issues such as calculation of compensation and interest and access to evidence, are likely to linger.[204] For example, traditional national approaches to disclosure are liable to result in the adoption of varying interpretations of the Directive's requirements relating to the plausibility and proportionality of a request for disclosure. Further as the Directive does not deal with cost rules, including those which govern who bears the cost of disclosure, and leaves Member States the opportunity to introduce more favourable national rules, some Member States have sought to encourage private actions, for example by adopting more generous rules relating to disclosure, limitation periods, and class actions.[205] The existence of national differences is therefore likely to continue to affect where litigants choose to commence their actions.

[202] E.g., although Dir. 2004/48/EC of the European Parliament and of the Council of 29 April 2004 on the enforcement of intellectual property rights [2004] OJ L157/70 provides effective means of enforcement of intellectual property rights, principally through private litigation and requires Member States to ensure minimum procedural standards, evidence indicates that the concepts within the Directive have been subject to different interpretation at the national level, see Dunne, n. 111, 11.

[203] See Rodger, Sousa Ferro, and Marcos, n. 198. [204] Ibid.

[205] E.g., the UK Government, when still a Member State, introduced changes to competition legislation in 2015 designed to facilitate private litigation, see the Consumer Rights Act 2015. See also Case C-312/21, *Tráficos Manuel Ferrer SL v Daimler AG* EU:C:2023:99, n. 139.

Thirdly, the working of a number of the Directive's provisions introduce considerable complexities into national proceedings, for example as the intricate rules applicable to limitation, joint and several liability, and passing-on. In particular, recognition of the passing-on defence (requiring account to be taken of the over-charge, the pass-on, and volume effects)[206] raises acute challenges for national courts, which have tended to rely on legal, rather than economic, approaches to assessing damage suffered in competition cases[207] and has a negative effect on direct purchasers' incentives to bring legal actions, both by decreasing the expected reward from litigation or settlement and by increasing the legal costs of litigation. This will be problematic if indirect purchaser actions remain rare.[208]

These types of concerns led some initially to conclude that the Directive fails its very own objectives; most of the provisions do not encourage victims to seek compensation and the Directive does not deal with some of the most crucial factors impacting on antitrust litigation—legal costs, cost shifting, and claim aggregation.[209]

(vi) Litigation post-Directive

It appears that private actions are now beginning to play an even greater part in the EU enforcement framework in some EU Member States at least.[210] For example, studies conducted of cartel damages claims in EU Member States (and Norway, Switzerland, and the UK) between 2017 and 2021 indicate that private actions are growing, and report numerous cases, for example in Spain (following the Spanish paper envelopes cartel and the Commission's *Trucks* decision) and in Finland (related to the Finish asphalt cartel).[211] Indeed, the 2021 study uncovers, despite a drop-off and delay to proceedings during the Covid pandemic, 299 cases 'from 14 countries: Germany (177 cases), France (52 cases), Spain (25 cases), Hungary (8 cases), Italy and the Netherlands (6 cases each), Belgium (5 cases), Austria, Finland and Greece (4 cases each), Denmark (3 cases), Poland and the United Kingdom (2 cases each), and Portugal (1 case)' (representing 472 relevant judgments),[212] significantly more than the 46 judgments identified in a study prepared for the Commission in 2009. These figures also do not account for a number of cases settled in the UK, Czech Republic, Lithuania, Norway, Romania, Slovakia, and Sweden.

[206] See e.g. De Sousa, n. 44, F. Weber, 'Tackling Pass-on in Cartel Cases: A Comparative Analysis of the Interplay Between Damages Law and Economic Insights' (2020) 16(2)–(3) *European Competition Journal* 570, and U. Jaremba and L. Lalikova, 'Effectiveness of Private Enforcement of European Competition Law in Case of Passing-on of Overcharges: Implementation of Antitrust Damages Directive in Germany, France, and Ireland' (2018) 9(4) *JECLAP* 266.

[207] See De Sousa, n. 44 (noting that national courts have treated passing-on as falling within the scope of national doctrine regarding the calculation of damages—a natural consequence of damages being a type of tort law damages that remain a matter of national competence—and considering whether such approaches are compatible with the Directive).

[208] See Peyer, n. 168.

[209] Ibid and e.g. Rodger, Sousa Ferro, and Marcos, n. 198 (noting that most rapporteurs were unclear about the extent to which implementation of the Directive would make a radical difference to private enforcement practice in their States).

[210] See A. Biondi, G. Muscolo, and R. Nazzini (eds.), *After the Damages Directive: Policy and Practice in the EU Member States and the United Kingdom* (Wolters Kluwer, 2022). See also H. W. Friederiszick, L. Gratz, and M, Rauber, 'The Impact of EU Cartel Policy Reforms on the Timing of Settlements in Private Follow-on Damages Disputes—An Empirical Assessment of Cases from 2001 to 2015' (2020) 8 *J of Antitrust Enforcement* 1.

[211] See Laborde (2021), (2019), (2017), n. 173 ('In the 30 European countries covered, 299 cartel damages actions have been identified. They include 58 cases in which damages were awarded, 93 cases in which liability was established, and 134 cases that resulted in dismissals. Fourteen cases are also pending, often after a judgment was quashed' (2021), para. 15). But see also Biondi, Muscolo, and Nazzini, n. 210, suggesting it is still too early to assess the impact on the Dir. (and noting the difficulty of getting formal statistics relating to private enforcement), different pictures in the different Member States and that not insignificant barriers to litigation remain in some.

[212] Laborde, ibid., paras. 16–17.

In addition, it appears that national courts are referring an increasing number of questions relating to damages actions for infringements of Article 101 or 102 and the working of the Directive to the CJ and the CJ has now delivered a number of judgments relating to such proceedings.[213]

5. CONCLUSIONS

1. The Commission's modernisation programme was designed to allow the Commission to refocus its scarce resources and to encourage greater enforcement of the rules at the national level. The Commission has not only sought to enlist the aid of NCAs in the enforcement of the rules, but has been eager that private actions should be used more frequently to bolster public enforcement and ensure compensation of antitrust victims. Both the Commission and a number of Member States have taken steps to encourage private enforcement, particularly damages actions.

2. Although the EU Courts made it clear that national courts must ensure effective judicial protection of rights conferred by Articles 101 and 102, litigants in competition cases faced a number of hurdles to their claims. The Damages Directive and package is designed to overcome a number of these impediments and to stimulate private litigation throughout the EU.

3. Although in some respects the Damages Directive goes further than US federal antitrust law (expanding to umbrella and indirect purchaser claims), it has been designed to ensure that it does not encourage unmeritorious claims.[214] The Directive provides for full—but not over—compensation, seeks to avoid fishing exercises by restricting disclosure to scenarios where a request for evidence is plausible, provides for joint and several liability but with some limits and no bar on a right to contribution, and does not deal with attorney fees, jury trials, or class actions (the latter being dealt with only by a Recommendation). Although one concern could be that as substantive EU antitrust laws are interpreted more broadly than their US counterparts in some areas, such as vertical restraints and unilateral conduct, there is a danger that greater volumes of private action will create a risk of false positives, the EU package does not provide huge additional incentives to the launch of these types of claim. Rather, many of its more detailed provisions focus on measures designed to stimulate actions in cartel damages cases; indeed, its provisions seem likely to have greatest impact in follow-on cases. Further, it could be argued that these are areas where litigation *should* be encouraged, as few competition agencies have sufficient resources to dedicate towards enforcement in these spheres.

4. A greater concern may thus be whether the reforms have done enough to overcome the impediments to litigation and to achieve the Commission's objectives of increasing, and harmonising, private damages actions across the EU. Although some of the provisions arguably detract from these objectives,[215] evidence indicates that private litigation is growing.

5. The Commission and the EU legislature have taken a bold step in the journey towards encouraging damages claims throughout the EU and the development of a coherent EU system governing them. Indeed, it arguably constitutes the 'most complete vertical example of European tort law to date'.[216] The EU legislature has worked hard to avoid the pitfalls experienced in the US and the new

[213] See Commission SWD, n. 175, and e.g. Case C-882/19, *Sumal, SL v Mercedes Benz Trucks España, SL* EU:C:2021:800, Case C-724/17, *Skanska Industrial Solutions* EU:C:2019:204, Case C-637/17, *Cogeco Communications* EU:C:2019:263, Case C-163/21, *AD v PACCAR* EU:C:2022:863, Case C-57/21, *RegioJet as* EU:C:2023:6, Case C-312/21, *Tráficos Manuel Ferrer SL v Daimler AG* EU:C:2023:99, and Case C-25/21, *ZA etc v Repsol Comercial de Productos Petolíferos SA* EU:C:2023:298.

[214] See e.g. Gavil, n. 2 and n. 195 and text.

[215] See e.g., Peyer n. 168 and see n. 209 and text. Howard, n. 166, 456 ('At first glance, the proposed Directive appears to be a random selection of minimum procedural requirements that lack coherence or structure. This is not a blueprint set of procedural rules that govern damages actions from start to finish').

[216] Dunne, n. 111, 19 (although the author notes that completeness is not exactly a characteristic of European tort law as such).

framework lays the foundations for the law in this area to develop sequentially as the EU and national courts interpret and assess the full implications of the provisions in cases arising before them.

6. FURTHER READING

A. Books

ANDREANGELI, A., *Private Enforcement of Antitrust: Regulating Corporate Behaviour through Collective Claims in the EU and the US* (Edward Elgar, 2014)

BERGSTRÖM, M., IACOVIDES, M., and STRAND, M. (eds.), *Harmonising EU Competition Litigation: The New Directive and Beyond* (Hart Publishing, 2016)

BIONDI, A., MUSCOLO, G., and NAZZINI, R. (eds.), *After the Damages Directive: Policy and Practice in the EU Member States and the United Kingdom* (Wolters Kluwer, 2022)

IOANNIDOU, M., *Consumer Involvement in Private EU Competition Law Enforcement* (Oxford University Press, 2016)

PARCU, P. L., MONTI G., and BOTTA, M. (eds.), *Private Enforcement of EU Competition Law* (Edward Elgar, 2018)

RODGER, B. (ed.), *Competition Law: Comparative Private Enforcement and Collective Redress Across the EU* (Wolters Kluwer, 2014)

B. Articles

DUNNE, N., 'The Role of Private Enforcement within EU Competition Law' (2013–2014) 16 *Cambridge Yearbook of European Legal Studies* 143

DUNNE, N., 'Antitrust and the Making of European Tort Law' (2015) 36 *OJLS* 1

JACOBS, F. G., 'Civil Enforcement of EEC Antitrust Law' (1984) 82 *Mich LR* 1364

JONES, A., and BEARD, D., 'Co-contractors, Damages and Article 81: The ECJ Finally Speaks' [2002] *ECLR* 246

ODUDU, O., 'Developing Private Enforcement in the EU: Lessons from the Roberts Court' (2008) 53 *Ant Bull* 873

PEYER S., 'Compensation and the Damages Directive' (2016) 12 *European Competition Journal* 87

RODGER, B., 'Why Not Court? A Study of Follow-on Actions in the UK' (2013) 1 *J of Antitrust Enforcement* 104

RODGER, B. J., SOUSA FERRO, M., and MARCOS, F., 'A Comparative View of the Implementation of the EU Antitrust Damages Directive in Sixteen Member States', Working Paper IE Law School AJ8-243-I (2018)

WILS, W., 'Should Private Antitrust Enforcement be Encouraged?' (2003) 26 *World Competition* 473

WILS, W., 'The Relationship Between Public Antitrust Enforcement and Private Actions for Damages' (2009) 32 *World Competition* 3

15

MERGERS

1. CENTRAL ISSUES

1. In 1989, the Council adopted a European Merger Control Regulation (EUMR) to regulate changes in market structure in the EU. The Regulation came into force in 1990, but was amended in 1997 before being amended again and consolidated into a new regulation in 2004, Regulation 139/2004.
2. Prior to the EUMR coming into force in 1990, the Commission had to rely on its power to apply Articles 102 and 101 to control mergers in the EU.
3. The 2004 EUMR declares incompatible with the internal market 'concentrations' which would significantly impede effective competition in the internal market or a substantial part of it, in particular as a result of the creation or strengthening of a dominant position.
4. A 'concentration' occurs where two or more undertakings on a market 'merge', where there is a change of 'control' over an undertaking, or where a full-function joint venture is created.
5. In principle, the EUMR applies to concentrations with a 'Community dimension' (or an 'EU' dimension). The concept of EU dimension aims to ensure that mergers creating structural changes, which impact beyond the national borders of a Member State, are appraised by the Commission under the EUMR. It is a quantitative test based on the turnovers of the undertakings concerned.
6. The general scheme of the EUMR is that:
   (a) concentrations with an EU dimension are appraised exclusively by the Commission under the provisions of the EUMR (they benefit from a 'one-stop shop');
   (b) concentrations without an EU dimension are appraised exclusively at the national level.

   Exceptions to this position exist, however. Indeed, a case referral system allows for the transfer of cases involving concentrations (or aspects of cases) between the Commission and national authorities in defined circumstances.
7. Concentrations with an EU dimension must ordinarily be notified to the Commission for appraisal prior to completion and are generally suspended pending investigation under the tight statutory timetable set out in the EUMR.
8. Merging parties may be motivated by the desire to increase efficiency. Nonetheless, horizontal mergers (between actual or potential competitors) reduce the number of players on the market, increase the market

share of the post-merger firm, and may significantly impede effective competition on a market by enabling the post-merger firm to exercise market power either individually (through unilateral, or non-coordinated, effects), or collectively, through collusion or coordination with other firms operating on the market (coordinated effects).

9. Non-horizontal mergers are less likely to cause competition concerns and provide significant scope for efficiencies. A concern, however, is that where one of the parties to such a merger has market power in at least one market, vertical and conglomerate mergers may harm competition through:
   (a) foreclosure of a distinct upstream, downstream, or related market; or
   (b) changing the structure of competition on a market in such a way that the firms operating on it are likely to coordinate their behaviour.

10. Merger analysis requires assessment of factors which are likely to counteract the merged firm's ability to exercise market power, such as countervailing buyer power or new entry. Efficiencies achieved by the merger may also offset any anti-competitive consequences. Where one of the merging parties is failing, the merger may not be the cause of any anti-competitive harm arising on the market.

11. Current controversial issues include whether merger control is sufficiently rigorous, and whether the approach to substantive appraisal of mergers under the EUMR needs to be amended in any way, for example to enable public interest (or non-competition) factors to be taken into account in the appraisal, such as the impact of a concentration on jobs, equality, sustainability, democracy, industrial policy, or national security.

2. INTRODUCTION

A. WHAT IS A MERGER?

A merger is generally defined as occurring where two or more formerly independent entities unite. A number of different transactions and agreements concluded by undertakings could result in a unification of independent undertakings' decision-making process. Every jurisdiction needs, therefore, to adopt a definition of what constitutes a merger for the purposes of their merger control legislation. The European Union Merger Regulation (the EUMR)[1] applies to 'concentrations'. Broadly, there is a concentration where two or more previously independent undertakings merge their businesses, where there is a change in control of an undertaking (sole or joint control of an undertaking being *acquired* by another undertaking or undertakings), or where a full-function joint venture (JV) is created.[2]

B. THE PURPOSES OF MERGER CONTROL

The purpose of merger control is to regulate changes in market structure and to determine whether two or more commercial companies should be permitted to merge, combine, or consolidate their businesses into one. It has been seen that the EU competition authorities scrutinise agreements concluded

[1] Reg. 139/2004 [2004] OJ L24/1 (the EUMR).

[2] EUMR, Art. 3, discussed in Section 3.A.

between independent undertakings closely for their compatibility with Article 101.[3] Mergers naturally create a more permanent and lasting change on the market than agreements.[4] It might be expected, therefore, that many mergers, especially horizontal mergers, would be forbidden. However, mergers also offer significant efficiency opportunities and give the owner of a business the opportunity to sell it and to realise capital profits from it.

> The reasons for not making mergers unlawful per se or for not even coming anywhere near such a rule are plain. Widespread prohibition of mergers would impose serious, if not intolerable, burdens upon owners of businesses who wished to liquidate their holdings for irreproachable personal reasons. Moreover, economic welfare is significantly served by maintaining a good market for capital assets . . . Most importantly, a policy of free transferability of capital assets tends to put them in the hands of those who will use them to their utmost economic advantage, thus tending to maximize society's total output of goods and services.
>
> Growth by merger . . . will often yield substantial economies of scale—in production, research, distribution, cost of capital and management. Entry by merger . . . may stimulate improved economic performance in an industry characterized by oligopolistic lethargy and inefficiency. Finally, acquisition of diversified lines of business, by stabilizing profits, may minimize the risk of business failure and bankruptcy.[5]

The task of the competition authorities is consequently generally to identify and to prohibit (or impose conditions on) those mergers which significantly impede, or substantially lessen, effective competition on a market. A contested and topical issue is whether, and if so when, public interest (or non-competition) factors should also be relevant to the assessment of a merger and, if so, how they should be balanced with the competition law assessment.

(i) A Damaging Effect on Competition

A core concern is that a merger will allow the merging parties to achieve or to strengthen their market power.

> In horizontal mergers, and especially in the massive consolidations that took place [in the US] around the turn of the [20th] century, the desire to achieve or strengthen monopoly power played a prominent role. Some 1887–1904 consolidations gained monopoly power by creating firms that dominated their industries. Others fell short of dominance, but transformed market structures sufficiently to curb the tendencies toward price competition toward which sellers gravitated in the rapidly changing market conditions of the time. As Thomas Edison remarked to a reporter concerning reasons for the formation of the General Electric Company in 1892:
>
> Recently there has been sharp rivalry between [Thomson-Houston and Edison General Electric], and prices have been cut so that there has been little profit in the manufacture of electrical machinery for anybody. The consolidation of the companies . . . will do away with competition which has become so sharp that the product of the factories has been worth little more than ordinary hardware.
>
> Those were days when businesspeople were not yet intimidated by the wrath of trustbusters or public opinion. Now they are more circumspect, and evidence of monopoly-creating intent is harder to find.[6]

[3] See especially Chap. 9.

[4] See e.g. K. Hüschelrath and F. Smuda, 'Do Cartel Breakdowns Induce Mergers? Evidence From EC Cartel Cases' (2013) 9(2) *European Competition Journal* 407.

[5] D. Turner, 'Conglomerate Mergers and Section 7 of the Clayton Act' (1965) 78 *Harvard LR* 1313, 1317.

[6] F. M. Scherer and D. Ross, *Industrial Market Structure and Economic Performance* (3rd edn, Houghton Mifflin, 1990), 160.

a. *Horizontal Mergers*

A horizontal merger is one which occurs between undertakings operating at the same level of the economy. Such mergers generally have two important implications for the market on which the merging firms operate: (a) there is one less player than before; and (b) the new firm has a larger market share than either of the merging parties had before the merger.[7] These developments may raise competition concerns where they allow the merging parties to acquire individual market power which might be exploited at the expense of customers and protected by anti-competitive behaviour (unilateral or non-coordinated effects). Alternatively, it may lead to a substantial increase in the concentration of a particular industry and enable the merging parties to raise prices and restrict output, by explicit or tacit collusion with the other firms operating on the market (coordinated effects). The discussion in this chapter also records the rising concern about so-called 'killer acquisitions' of potential competitors—companies purchasing start-ups or developers of innovative or more sustainable products[8] (especially in the digital economy, agrochemical, or pharmaceutical industries) in order to shut them down or to neutralise the competitive threat that they create (incumbent firms may find it more profitable to acquire potential rivals than to compete against them).[9]

b. *Vertical Mergers*

A vertical merger is one concluded between firms at different levels of production in the economy. The motive for vertical mergers may be to achieve efficiencies and/or to obtain a secure supply of a raw material or a secure outlet for the sale of products. They may, however, raise competition concerns, especially in concentrated markets. A predominant fear is that where the merging firms have market power at one or more vertical level, vertical mergers may 'foreclose' the market or a source of supply to competitors. For example, a merger between a manufacturer of a product and a supplier of an essential component for that product (backward integration) may have severe implications for competing manufacturers. The foreclosure effect will be acute where there are few or no other suppliers of the essential components. Similarly, the acquisition by a manufacturer of a distributor (forward integration) could make it more difficult for competitors to gain access to distributors. A vertical merger may also increase price transparency or facilitate collusion between firms operating on the market.

c. *Conglomerate Mergers*

Conglomerate mergers are concentrations which have no horizontal or vertical effect. As such mergers do not result in horizontal overlaps or vertical effects, they do not obviously raise competition problems. Rather they are frequently motivated by innocuous objectives from a competition perspective,

[7] H. Hovenkamp, *Federal Antitrust Policy: The Law of Competition and its Practice* (6th edn, West, 2020), 12.1b.

[8] See DG Comp, [2021] 1 *Competition Policy Brief* and DG Comp [2021] 3 *Competition Policy Brief* (Special Issue, Young Experts' Views on Greening of Competition Policy).

[9] See e.g. N. L. Rose and C. Shapiro, 'What Next for the Horizontal Merger Guidelines?' (2022) 36(2) *Antitrust* Spring 4, 8, M. Walker, 'Competition Policy and Digital Platforms: Six Uncontroversial Propositions' (2020) 16(1) *European Competition Journal* 1, keynote speech of J. Tirole, at Commissioner Vestager's 'Shaping Competition Policy in the Era of Digitalization' Conference, 19 January 2019, report commissioned by the UK's competition authority by LEAR, 'Ex post-Assessment of Merger Control Decisions in Digital Markets', 3 June 2019 (stating that between 2008 and 2018, Google, Facebook, and Amazon acquired 168, 71, and 60 companies, respectively and noting that most of the acquisitions were of young firms (median age was 2.5 years for Facebook), and of firms producing complementary products), C. Cunningham, F. Ederer, and S. Ma, 'Killer Acquisitions' (2021) 129 *J of Political Economy* 649 (estimating that 5.3–7.4% of acquisitions in the pharmaceutical industry to be killer acquisitions and that acquired drug projects are less likely to be developed when they overlap with the acquirer's existing product portfolio), K. A. Bryan and E. Hovenkamp, 'Antitrust Limits on Startup Acquisitions' (2020) 56 *Review of Industrial Organization* 615, and discussion of EUMR, Art. 22 (in Section 3.D.iii) and n. 528 and text.

such as the need for risk reduction. An undertaking may, for example, wish to expand into another market where it is operating in a declining or cyclical industry or simply to spread risk. However, where post-merger a firm will have market power in one market there may be a fear that it will use this power to foreclose competition in a neighbouring or related market, for example by engaging in tying or by predating in that market.[10] This may be more likely where the relevant markets are closely related and the merged undertakings will be able to offer a portfolio of products.

Alternatively, conglomeracy could lead to a growing consolidation of, or increase in, private power (especially in the digital economy) or loss of potential competition. For example, a merger of firms operating in different product or geographic markets may eliminate the threat of the parties entering each other's markets. In the EU, although the elimination of a potential competitor is identified as a horizontal issue,[11] the Commission has also displayed concerns about purely conglomerate mergers.

d. *Efficiency*

Mergers, and the markets for corporate control, may provide the opportunity for efficiencies to be realised and discipline the management of companies. 'Not only do mergers provide the opportunity for management innovation, the purchase of weak firms, and the movement of capacity from declining to growth sectors, but they may allow the merging firms to engage in consolidation, to increase productivity, and to deliver technological innovation and efficiencies',[12] including marketing efficiencies, pooling research and development (R&D) skills, complementarities, economies of scale, and scope.

Therefore, even where a merger harms competition the parties may claim that that harm is offset by the economic growth which will be promoted, through raising the efficiency of resources, total factor productivity, by enabling undertakings to increase efficient levels of manufacture, R&D, and distribution more rapidly and more cheaply than they could by internal growth.

e. *Failing Undertakings*

A merger may also provide an escape route for a failing or flailing company. In these circumstances, the possibility of selling the business to another may mean that assets are kept in production or not downsized, that creditors, owners, and employees are protected from the adverse consequences of the undertaking's failure, and/or that stability is preserved in a critical industry sector (for example, the financial sector).

(ii) Evolving Policy Towards Mergers

Concern is more frequently being expressed that, in the past at least, a number of competition agencies (particularly the US federal agencies) have been too lax, ineffective, or insufficiently rigorous in exercising merger control especially with respect to mergers in the digital economy and in high profit-margin industries.[13] Further, that as a result, markets have become too concentrated, competition

[10] See Chap. 7.

[11] Guidelines on the assessment of horizontal mergers under the Council Regulation on the control of concentrations between undertakings (the HMG) [2004] OJ C31/5, para. 59 ('A merger with a potential competitor can generate horizontal anti-competitive effects . . . if the potential competitor significantly constrains the behaviour of the firms active in the market'), but see n. 529 and text.

[12] A. Jones and J. Davies, 'Merger Control and the Public Interest: Balancing EU and National Law in the Protectionist Debate' (2015) 10 *European Competition Journal* 453.

[13] See e.g. President Biden's Executive Order, 9 July 2021, T. Philippon, *The Great Reversal—How America Gave up on Free Markets* (The Belknap Press, 2019), P. C. Carstensen and R. H. Lande, 'The Merger Incipiency Doctrine and the Importance of "Redundant" Competitors' [2018] *Wisconsin LR* 783, J. Kwoka, *Mergers, Merger Control, and Remedies* (MIT Press, 2015), but see M. Vita and D. F. Osinski, 'John Kwoka's Mergers, Merger Control, and Remedies: A Critical Review' (2018) 82(1) *Antitrust LJ* 361 and n. 26.

has declined in many industries,[14] a small number of enormous, digital platforms have emerged with entrenched positions,[15] and too many problematic mergers (including in already very concentrated markets) have been allowed both from a consumer welfare and a broader public interest perspective[16]—competition authorities have been overly concerned about the risk of incorrect intervention (Type I errors), at the expense of the risk of incorrect clearance (Type II errors).[17] Indeed, Mike Walker, Chief Economic Advisor at the Competition and Markets Authority (the UK's competition authority), has stated that '[i]t is very hard to avoid the conclusion that competition authorities have under-enforced with respect to tech mergers'.[18]

In addition, concern has grown that many mergers in fact fail to realise the efficiencies and innovation promised or predicted and, consequently, the increase in value for shareholders.[19] A report commissioned by the Commission concluded that even if mergers do sometimes create efficiencies there seemed to be 'no empirical support for a general presumption' that they do so.[20]

Although not all agree with all of the criticisms, the vigorous debate on these issues has led to broad discussion across jurisdictions as to whether current merger appraisal techniques—which in the EU and US had begun to converge—have got it right or whether a more interventionist approach, or tightening of merger enforcement, is required. This has led some to call, in relation to certain deals at least, for the use of structural presumptions or presumptions of illegality and a lowering of the standard of proof, or shifting the burden of proof onto firms to demonstrate the efficiencies.[21] The debate has also been reignited as to whether, and if so when, broader public interest or political economy factors should be taken into account in the appraisal of mergers.

(iii) Public Interest Concerns

In recent years, concerns about the impact of mergers on a wider set of broadly identified public interest factors have been proliferating. Numerous jurisdictions (including many EU Member States)

[14] See e.g. DG Comp [2021] 2 *Competition Policy Brief* ('Data on the five largest European countries' last two decades show increasing average industry concentration, and an increasing share of high concentration industries. Aggregate profitability estimates also show an increasing trend'), J. De Loecker, J. Eeckhout, and G. Unger, 'The Rise of Market Power and the Macrooeconomic Implications' (2020) 135(2) *Quarterly Journal of Economics* 561.

[15] Partly at least due to the larger number of mergers they completed, see e.g. LEAR report, n. 9.

[16] See e.g. speech of T. Valletti, then Chief Competition Economist, DG Comp, 'Concentration Trends in Europe', December 2017, Rose and Shapiro, n. 9, H. Hovenkamp and C. Shapiro, 'Horizontal Mergers, Market Structure, and Burdens of Proof' (2018) 27 *Yale LJ* 1996, J. Padilla, 'Should Profit Margins Play a More Decisive Role in Horizontal Merger Control?' (2018) 9(4) *JECLAP* 260, T. Valletti and H. Zenger, 'Should Profit Margins Play a More Decisive Role in Horizontal Merger Control? A Rejoinder to Jorge Padilla' (2018) 9(5) *JECLAP* 336, J. Padilla, 'Should Profit Margins Play a More Decisive Role in Horizontal Merger Control? A Reply to Valletti and Zenger' (2018) 9(6) *JECLAP* 379,

[17] E. Argentesi, P. Buccirossi, E. Calvano, T. Duso, A. Marrazzo, and S. Nava, 'Merger Policy in Digital Markets: An Ex Post Assessment', available at <https://papers.ssrn.com/sol3/papers.cfm?abstract_id=3501501>.

[18] Walker, n. 9 (noting the Furman Review's finding that between 2008–18 Google, Amazon, Facebook, and Microsoft made over 300 acquisitions but none of them were blocked). See also a joint statement by the UK, German, and Australian competition authorities proposing more rigorous merger control, available at <www.gov.uk/government/publications/joint-statement-by-the-competition-and-markets-authority-bundeskartellamt-and-australian-competition-and-consumer-commission-on-merger-control/joint-statement-on-merger-control-enforcement>. The US authorities also launched a review of their merger guidelines in 2022, see <www.regulations.gov/document/FTC-2022-0003-0001>.

[19] See e.g. M. Monti, SPEECH/02/252, 'Review of the EC Merger Regulation—Roadmap for the Reform Project', Speech to British Chamber of Commerce, Brussels, 4 June 2002, S. A. Christofferson, S. McNich, and D. L. Sias, 'Where Mergers Go Wrong', *McKinsey Quarterly* 1 May 2004 (buyers routinely overvalue the synergies to be had from acquisitions), and J. Kwoka, *Controlling Mergers and Market Power* (Competition Policy International, 2020).

[20] See L.-H. Röller, J. Stennek, and F. Verboven, 'Efficiency Gains From Mergers', European Economy, no. 5/2001, Brussels, speech by Monti, ibid., B. A. Blonigen and J. R. Pierce, 'Evidence for the Effects of Mergers on Market Power and Efficiency', Finance and Economics Discussion Series 2016–082.

[21] See further nn. 24–26 and text.

have merger control regimes that incorporate a public interest component, whether as part of the regular merger control process or separately.[22] Public interest concerns may include, for example:

a. *Fear of Big Business*

Some commentators believe that conglomeracy, or mergers that would create large businesses, have implications for the freedom of society more generally. It is feared that too great an economic concentration is anti-democratic and restricts individual freedom and enterprise or may adversely affect the distribution of wealth.[23]

As noted in Chapter 1, it has been argued that one of the goals of competition laws should be the diffusion of economic power and the protection of individual freedom.

> Private power can cross economic boundaries and poses the threat of an 'extra market' power which can change the rules of the game in favour of the dominant corporations. In such a situation, where relationships between firms and their socio-economic environment constitute a mixture of market and non-market bonds, the authorities aim at the dispersion of private power. Even if this entails some loss of economic efficiency, such a choice would not necessarily be irrational, because such costs may be outweighed by social or political advantages.[24]

This 'big is bad' sentiment has re-emerged in recent years, especially following the 2008 financial and economic crisis, leading some, including members of the Neo-Brandeis School in the US, leading players in the Biden administration in the US,[25] to call for stricter and more effective merger control enforcement, a broad category of mergers to be presumptively unlawful and for account to be taken of their impact not only on efficiency but also on income inequality, wages, employment, political power, and democracy.[26] The Biden administration has consequently been concerned to deconcentrate the economy, and to diffuse the political power of very large firms which they believe threatens democracy. Others, however, vigorously contend that a return to populist antitrust would 'send antitrust enforcement careening backwards in time toward a regime that harmed consumers and propped up inefficient corporations'.[27] A further related question which has arisen is whether care should be taken to ensure that no firm is allowed to become so large that it is 'too big to fail' and, if so, whether merger rules should play any role in enforcing such a policy.[28]

[22] For a review of 39 identified regimes with public interest components (including Austria, Belgium, Cyprus, France, Germany, Greece, Hungary, Ireland, the Netherlands, Poland, Portugal, Slovenia, Spain, and Sweden), see J. Mellott and R. Ciric, 'Public Interest in Merger Control: The Law of the Land' (2020) 65(2) *Ant Bull* 208. See also more generally Chap. 1 and DG Comp [2021] 3 *Competition Policy Brief* (Special Issue, Young Experts' Views on Greening of Competition Policy), especially pp. 14–20.

[23] A. Cairncross et al., *Economic Policy for the European Community* (Macmillan, 1974).

[24] A. P. Jacquemin and H. W. de Jong, *European Industrial Organisation* (Macmillan, 1997), 198–199.

[25] E.g. President Biden appointed Lina Khan as Chair of the Federal Trade Commission (FTC), Tim Wu as a special assistant to the president with responsibility for Technology and Competition Policy, and Jonathan Kanter as Assistant Attorney General of the Department of Justice Antitrust Division.

[26] See discussion of the 'neo-Brandeis' movement in T. Wu, *The Curse of Bigness: Antitrust in the New Gilded Age* (Columbia Global Reports, 2018), Chap. 1 and e.g. 'The next capitalist revolution; Competition' and other articles in *The Economist*, November 2018, M. S. Gal and T. K. Cheng, 'Aggregate Concentration: A Study of Competition Law Solutions' (2016) 4 *J of Antitrust Enforcement* 282.

[27] J. D. Wright, E. Dorsey, J. Rybnicek, and J. Klick, 'Requiem for a Paradox: The Dubious Rise and Inevitable Fall of Hipster Antitrust' [2019] *Arizona State LJ* 3.

[28] See e.g. J. T. Rosch, 'Implications of the Financial Meltdown for the FTC', Speech at the New York Bar Association Annual Dinner, New York, 29 January 2009.

b. National or European Champions

The desire to increase the scale of national and European companies may be a goal of a jurisdiction's industrial policy. The ability to restructure or to create national or European champions may, for example, mean that the parties can, in combination, survive and compete more effectively on international markets, contribute to technical and economic progress, and/or facilitate cross-border trade. This may be considered especially important where firms compete with (non-EU) State-owned or State-subsidised entities. In December 2018, representatives of 19 Member States called for EU competition law to be updated to facilitate the emergence of European industrial giants capable of fighting fierce competition from the US and China and in 2019, following the Commission's controversial prohibition of a merger between Siemens and Alstom, the French and German Governments circulated a manifesto[29] calling for merger reform and a right of appeal to the Council which should be able to override Commission decisions.[30]

Commissioner Vestager, however, like Competition Commissioners before her, has to date been clear that Europe only needs champions which 'are not coddled favourites, freed from the need to compete within Europe. The champions we need are the ones that can fight their way to the top of a competitive market in Europe—and go on to do the same across the world.'[31] In her view, no reform of EU merger rules is required. Champions should be built, not by undermining competition—which would lead to consumers paying more for less choice and less innovative products, but by competing on the merits on a level playing field. To create a more level competitive playing field between EU and non-EU undertakings, however, the EU introduced at the end of 2022 'foreign subsidy' control rules. The Foreign Subsidies Regulation[32] allows the Commission to investigate financial contributions granted by, or attributable to, public authorities of a non-EU country which selectively benefit companies engaging in economic activity in the EU and to redress their distortive effects. In outline, the Regulation includes, amongst other things, mandatory notification of participation in large public procurement procedures in the EU and certain merger transactions (concentrations) involving parties that have received financial contributions from non EU governments. In relation to the latter, the rules apply where a financial contribution of more than €50 million has been made and where the acquired company, one of the merging parties, or the joint venture generates a turnover of at least €500 million.[33] Such concentrations cannot be completed pending the Commission's review and until cleared (whether conditionally or unconditionally) by the Commission.

[29] 'Manifesto for a European industrial policy fit for the 21st Century', 19 February 2018 (later joined by Poland).

[30] M.8677, 6 February 2019, see n. 730 and text. In January 2019, Commissioner Katainen (then Commission Vice President) indicated that he would be open to consider tweaks to update (but not change entirely) competition law in order to cope with strong competition from US and Chinese firms, see <www.competitionpolicyinternational.com/eu-ec-vice-president-open-to-tweaks-to-competition-policy/>.

[31] See M. Vestager, speeches, 'Hitting the sweet spot in antitrust enforcement', 25 September 2018 and 'The Champions Europe Needs', 9 January 2019.

[32] Reg. (EU) 2022/2560 of the European Parliament and of the Council of 14 December 2022 on foreign subsidies distorting the internal market [2022] OJ L330/1. The Reg. entered into force on 12 January 2023, and applies from 12 July 2023 with notification requirements taking effect from 12 October 2023. A concern has been that recipients of foreign subsidies have an unfair advantage in acquiring companies or obtaining public procurement contracts in the EU, to the detriment of fair competition. The merger review investigates whether the financial contribution distorts the internal market.

[33] See <https://competition-policy.ec.europa.eu/international/foreign-subsidies_en> and the Commission's White Paper on levelling the playing field as regards foreign subsidies, 17 June 2020, COM(2020) 253 final.

c. *Special Sectors and Foreign Control*

Cross-border mergers, through foreign direct investment (FDI),[34] have been facilitated by technological change, global competition, and the liberalisation of markets.[35] FDI has played a key role in the process of global economic integration and has been 'positively correlated with growth'.[36] For developed countries, 'the limited evidence available indicates fairly consistently that the productivity of domestically owned firms is positively related to the presence of foreign firms'[37] and 'that FDI triggers technology spillovers, assists human capital formation, contributes to international trade integration, helps create a more competitive business environment and enhances enterprise development'.[38] Cross-border mergers may also facilitate EU market integration. '[E]xternal growth by means of mergers and acquisitions can be a means of quickly realizing potential cost savings and integration gains offered by the internal market.'[39] In general, in merger control the Commission has been guided by the principle of competitive and ownership neutrality—it applies the merger control rules in the same way irrespective of the nationality or ownership of the company (when appraising mergers involving a State-owned enterprise (SOE), however, other SOEs owned by the same government may be treated as part of the same economic unit[40]).

A question arising nonetheless, is whether tighter control should be exercised over, and a broader range of factors taken into account in relation to, mergers which occur in particularly sensitive sectors. For example, interests of democracy may suggest the preservation of the 'plurality of the press' or national security may suggest that the ownership of certain industries, such as oil and defence equipment or other critical infrastructure, should not pass overseas. In recent years, as global protectionism and concerns about the globalised free market have risen, there have been numerous instances, both within and outside the EU, in which the impact of a proposed merger on a Member State's interest has provoked debate. In particular, popular backlash against foreign control of key

[34] A company may invest in another country either by merging, setting up a joint venture (JV) with, or acquiring control over or a shareholding in, a business already registered in that country, or by setting up its own business or subsidiary there (greenfield investment).

[35] See Almunia, SPEECH/13/360, 'The evolutionary pressure of globalisation on competition control', ICN 12th annual conference, Warsaw, 24 April 2013 (FDI 'passed from 6.5% of world GDP in 1980 to over 30% before the onset of this long [financial and economic] crisis').

[36] IMF Working Paper, Middle Eastern Department, WP/Ol/175, 'Determinants of, and the Relation between, Foreign Direct Investment and Growth: A Summary of the Recent Literature', Prepared by Ewe-Ghee Lim, November 2001; OECD, *Economic and Other Impacts of Foreign Corporate Takeovers in OECD Countries* (2007), 68–70 (cross-border openness may also contribute to national security and regional or international stabilisation). See also e.g. A. Nourry and N. Jung, 'Protectionism in the Age of Austerity—A Further Unlevelling of the Playing Field' (2012) 8 *Competition Policy International* 1.

[37] Ibid. For a discussion of some of the benefits which have resulted in the UK from high amounts of inward and outward FDI, see speech of A. Chisholm, 'Public interest and competition-based merger control: An agency perspective on the lessons from evolution of the current regime', Fordham Competition Law Institute Annual Conference, 12 September 2014, 8–9.

[38] Given the appropriate host-country policies and a basic level of development, OECD, *Foreign Direct Investment for Development: Maximising Benefits and Minimising Costs* (2002) (concluding that the macroeconomic benefits of inward FDI in most cases outweigh the costs).

[39] European Commission, 'Competition and Integration: Community Merger Policy' (1994) 57 *European Economy* vii.

[40] See e.g. M.7962, *ChemChina.Syngenta* 5 April 2017 and A. Svetlicinii, 'Consolidation of the State-owned Enterprises in China: A Missed Opportunity for the EU Merger Control?' (2022) 13(1) *JECLAP* 17 and discussion of the single economic unit concept in Chap. 4. This approach would mean, however that certain SOE-to-SOE mergers fall outside the scope of the EUMR where they do not constitute a merger between independent economic units, but see e.g. M.9626, *PKN Orlen/Energa* 31 March 2020. See also discussion of the Foreign Subsidies Reg. n. 32 and text.

national businesses has sometimes led national governments to take steps to protect industry and sparked differences in opinion as to how the benefits and costs of the respective transactions should be assessed and a clash between proponents of the principle of an open market economy and proponents of greater protectionism and economic patriotism.[41]

Some Member States have become increasingly sensitive about capital flows in and out of their States, the costs and benefits of inward FDI (both from within and outside the EU), and the impact of mergers on certain public policy factors. Accordingly, a growing number of States have introduced or intensified[42] public interest or foreign investment rules which allow competition agencies, politicians, or other institutions to assess the impact of takeovers[43] on national security, businesses perceived to be of national strategic importance, critical infrastructure, technological capabilities, jobs, and exports. This has led to an increased politicisation of, and increased regulatory hurdles to, mergers globally.

Until 2020, review of FDI on public security grounds in the EU occurred only at the national level (and when compatible with EU law). The EU has, however, now created a framework for screening FDI (from third countries) that affects security and public order in the EU.[44] Although it provides for EU-wide cooperation and information sharing between the Commission and Member States, the ability to block an investment remains with the Member State(s) (approximately half of which already have national security mechanisms) where the investment is implemented.

d. *Unemployment*

Mergers may mean asset-stripping, profits to shareholders, rationalisation, and loss of jobs.[45] Mergers which occur in depressed regions or in areas in which unemployment is already high may, therefore, cause concern and lead to pressure on politicians to intervene.

e. *Data*

An increasing concern in the information economy is the impact of transactions on personal data and the extent to which the aggregation, use, or protection, of such data by digital technology businesses should be a relevant factor impacting on, or subsumed within, substantive merger assessment.[46] Indeed, a merger may provide the best and fastest way of acquiring a high volume of varied and valuable data and building digital capabilities. The acquisition of a data-advantage may thus be

[41] See e.g. Pfizer's proposed acquisition of AstraZeneca discussed in Jones and Davies, n. 12 and S. Mariotti, 'Competition Policy in the new wave of global protectionism. Prospects for preserving a fdi-friendly institutional environment' [2023] *J of Industrial and Business Economics*.

[42] See n. 22 and text. Some jurisdictions also lowered thresholds allowing them to capture even smaller transactions and minority transactions.

[43] Although economic theory is neutral as to the form FDI takes, governments tend to be more welcoming of FDI through greenfield investment (see n. 34) and more suspicious of FDI through foreign mergers, OECD, n. 36, 70–71.

[44] See Reg. (EU) 2019/452 of the European Parliament and of the Council establishing a framework for screening of foreign direct investments into the European Union [2019] OJ L791/1 and <https://trade.ec.europa.eu/access-to-markets/en/content/investment>.

[45] In the US, the federal authorities during the Biden administration have challenged mergers on the basis of perceived harm to workers, see e.g. Penguin Random House's acquisition of Simon & Schuster.

[46] See nn. 518–520 and text, Chap. 1 and e.g. F. Costa-Cabral and O. Lynskey, 'The Internal and External Constraints of Data Protection on Competition Law in the EU', LSE Law, Society and Economy Working Papers 25/2015 and D. Sokol and R. E. Comerford, 'Does Antitrust Have a Role to Play in Regulating Big Data?' in R. D. Blair and D. Sokol (eds.), *Cambridge Handbook of Antitrust, Intellectual Property and High Tech* (Cambridge University Press, 2016).

a motivation for mergers in businesses where firms rely on personal data as a key input, in particular in 'two-sided markets; companies offer consumers free services with the aim of acquiring valuable personal data to assist advertisers to better target them with behavioral ads'.[47]

f. Sustainability

The debate discussed in previous Chapters surrounding the question of how competition, sustainability, and environmental policies interact, is also of acute relevance to merger control. Important issues include how to incorporate arguments relating to green efficiencies in a merger review and how to prevent acquisitions designed to neutralise greener competitors.

C. THE HISTORY OF THE EUROPEAN MERGER CONTROL REGULATION

(i) The Initial Lacuna and the Drive for Merger Control at the EU Level

The original EEC Treaty, unlike the ECSC Treaty, did not contain any specific provision for controlling mergers.[48] The Commission recognised this lacuna and the crucial need for rules specifically focused on mergers from early on[49] and adopted its first legislative proposal for a merger control regulation in 1973.[50] Any regulation on merger control had, however, to be passed unanimously by the Council[51] and, for a long time, there was no consensus amongst the Member States as to: whether EU merger control was necessary at all; whether power to control changes in industrial structure in their territories should be ceded to the Commission; and/or what substantive criteria should be used to appraise mergers and, in particular, whether only the effects on competition should be relevant, or whether social and industrial policy considerations should also be taken into account. There were, therefore, two major sticking points:

(a) jurisdiction—whether, and if so at what point, control should be relinquished by the Member States to the Commission and what the relationship between EU and national law should be; and
(b) appraisal criteria—should factors other than competition be taken into account in the substantive assessment?[52]

(ii) The Catalysts for the EUMR

Frustrated by the lack of a specific merger control provision, the Commission sought not only to persuade the Council to enact such a measure but applied its existing tools to control mergers. It utilised Articles 102 and, subsequently, 101 TFEU to prevent takeovers and acquisitions of shareholdings in other undertakings.

[47] M. Stucke and A. Grunes, 'Debunking the Myths Over Big Data and Antitrust' (2015) 5 *CPI Antitrust Chronicle* 1.

[48] Likely explanations include that: the ECSC was a *traité-loi* whilst the EEC was a *traité-cadre* (a framework document, to be fleshed out by implementing legislation) and it was easier to agree on a rule which would affect only specific industries perceived to be of vital importance given their political and military significance, see Art. 66(7) of the ECSC Treaty and S. Bulmer, 'Institutions and Policy Change: The Case of Merger Control' (1994) 72 *Public Administration* 423, 427–428. It may also have been considered that the objectives set out in EEC Treaty, Art. 2 (of economic expansion) might be achieved by concentrating economic power rather than prohibiting mergers.

[49] See Memorandum on the Concentration of Enterprises in the Common Market, EEC Competition Series Study No. 3 and, e.g., C. Overbury, 'Politics or Policy? The Demystification of EC Merger Control' [1992] *Fordham Corp L Inst* 561.

[50] A series of draft regulations was proposed and rejected by the Council between 1973 and 1989: see [1973] OJ C92/1, [1982] OJ C36/3, [1984] OJ C51/8, [1988] OJ C130/4, [1989] OJ C22/141.

[51] The legal basis for the EUMR is Arts. 103 and 352 TFEU.

[52] See also nn. 13, 19, and 21 and text.

In Chapter 7, it is seen that in *Europemballage Corp and Continental Can Co Inc v Commission*[53] the CJ upheld the Commission's view that Article 102 could be used to prevent a dominant undertaking from abusing its dominant position by acquiring a competitor and thereby strengthening its dominant position (see further the discussion of *Towercast v Autorité de la Concurrence* in Section 3.E.ii). Article 102 proved to be a reasonably effective weapon against mergers, but its use is limited by the fact that the acquiring company must have a dominant position before Article 102 can apply; it may not therefore catch all problematic mergers, including where two or more undertakings merge to create a dominant position.[54]

Although Article 101 does not appear to be particularly suitable for controlling mergers[55] (as it strikes at agreements, it might be artificial to try and deal with many types of mergers under its provisions, for example hostile takeovers), the Commission did apply it to merger situations. In *BAT and Reynolds v Commission*,[56] the CJ confirmed that Article 101 might apply to the acquisition by an undertaking of a minority shareholding in another. The difficulties raised, and the ambiguities left unresolved, by the judgment 'were fully exploited by the Commission and the resulting uncertainty was used skilfully . . . to persuade Member States to return to the negotiating table on a new draft of a merger control regulation . . .'[57]

The internal market programme also led to industry calls for EU merger control. Business restructuring, and EU-wide mergers, was a natural result of the programme in the lead-up to 1992.[58] Firms called for a level playing field and to have to comply with only *one* set of merger rules.

A combination of Commission support, pressure from industry, the internal market programme, and increasing numbers of mergers led to the eventual realisation that a system of European merger control was inevitable.

(iii) The Original Merger Control Regulation—Council Regulation (EEC) 4064/89

The original Merger Control Regulation was adopted by the Council of Ministers on 21 December 1989[59] and came into force on 21 September 1990. It set out jurisdictional, procedural, and substantive rules. The procedural requirements were fleshed out by Regulation 447/98[60] and numerous Commission Notices set out guidance on how the Commission interpreted various aspects of the regulations.

The Commission constantly keeps the working and operation of the Regulation, especially its jurisdictional thresholds, under review.[61] Although the Regulation was reviewed[62] and then amended by Council Regulation 1310/97,[63] in 2001 the Commission embarked on a more comprehensive review of

[53] Case 6/72, *Europemballage Corp and Continental Can Co Inc v Commission* EU:C:1973:22.

[54] Case C-449/21, EU:C:2023:207. '[O]nly the strengthening of dominant positions and not their creation can be controlled under Art. [102]': Case T-102/96, *Gencor Ltd v Commission* EU:T:1999:65, para. 155; and see Case 6/72, ibid., para. 26.

[55] See Commission's Memorandum on the Concentration of Enterprises in the Common Market, EEC Competition Series Study No. 3 (published in 1966), para. 58.

[56] Cases 142 and 156/84, EU:C:1987:490, paras. 36–39.

[57] C. J. Cook and C. S. Kerse, *EC Merger Control* (5th edn, Sweet & Maxwell, 2009), 1-003. Soon after this judgment the green light was given to the Commission to put forward another proposal for a merger regulation.

[58] L. Tsoukalis, *The New European Economy Revisited* (2nd edn, Oxford University Press, 1993), 103 (115 mergers in 1982–1983, 492 by 1988–1989, and 622 in 1989–1990).

[59] Council Reg. (EEC) 4064/89 of 21 December 1989 on the control of concentrations between undertakings [1989] OJ L395/1.

[60] Commission Reg. 447/98 [1998] OJ L61/1 (replacing Reg. 2367/90).

[61] It had an obligation to report to the Council on the jurisdictional thresholds, the old EUMR, Art. 1(4), see the Report to the Council on the application of the Merger Regulation Thresholds, COM(2000) 399 final.

[62] Community Merger Control, COM(96) 19 final.

[63] Council Reg. 1310/97 of 30 June 1997 [1997] OJ L180/1 (it, e.g., introduced an additional (lower) jurisdictional threshold, and changed the rules dealing with JVs).

the Regulation, publishing a Green Paper[64] and mooting wide-ranging changes to its substantive and procedural provisions as well as jurisdictional ones. This led, following consultation, to a proposal for a package of measures reforming the provisions and working of the EUMR and an entire new consolidated merger regulation.[65]

(iv) The Current Merger Control Regulation, Council Regulation (EC) 139/2004

Following intensive debate, political agreement on the new text of the EUMR was reached leading to the adoption of the current, recast, EUMR,[66] Regulation 139/2004. Essentially, it incorporates elements of the original 1989 Regulation and amendments introduced in both 1997 and 2004. The 2004 Regulation is, like its predecessor, supplemented by an implementing regulation[67] and a number of Commission Notices which provide guidance as to the interpretation of its various provisions. The following Notices are of particular importance:[68]

(a) Commission Consolidated Jurisdictional Notice[69] (the 'Jurisdictional Notice', replacing and consolidating into a single Notice previous Notices on the concept of a concentration, undertakings concerned, the calculation of turnover, and on the concept of full function joint ventures);
(b) Notice on simplified procedure for the treatment of certain concentrations;[70]
(c) Notice on remedies;[71]
(d) Notice on restrictions directly related and necessary to concentrations;[72]
(e) Notices on the appraisal of both horizontal and non-horizontal mergers;[73]
(f) Commission Notices on Case Referral in respect of concentrations and the referral mechanism under Article 22;[74]
(g) Notice on access to the file.[75]

The Commission has also published Best Practice Guidelines on the conduct of EUMR proceedings, Economic Evidence (how best to present economic and empirical evidence),[76] and model texts for divestiture commitments and trustee mandates.[77]

[64] 2001 Green Paper on the Review of Council Regulation (EEC) No. 4064/89, COM(2001) 745/6 final.

[65] COM(2002) 711 final, OJ [2003] C20/4.

[66] In the interest of legal certainty, the Commission recast the Regulation, adopting a single legislative text to make the desired amendments, see the Inter-institutional agreement of 28 November 2001 on a more structured use of recasting technique for legal acts [2002] OJ C77/1.

[67] A new Implementing Reg. was adopted on 20 April 2023 (entering into force on 1 September 2023), Reg. 2023/914, [2023] OJ L119/22, replacing and repealing Reg. 802/2004.

[68] The Commission's Notice on market definition is also crucial, see Chap. 3 and Section 5.D.

[69] [2008] OJ C95/1, replacing Notices on: the concept of concentration [1998] OJ C66/5; on the concept of undertakings concerned [1998] OJ C66/14; on calculation of turnover [1998] OJ C66/25; and on the concept of full-function joint ventures [1998] OJ C66/1.

[70] See Commission Notice of 20 April 2023 on a simplified procedure for treatment of certain concentrations under Council Regulation (EC) No. 139/2004 (Notice on Simplified Procedure), C(2023) 2401 final, replacing a notice of 5 December 2013, [2013] OJ C366/5 and adopted following consultation in May 2022, , see <https://ec.europa.eu/info/law/better-regulation/have-your-say/initiatives/12957-Merger-control-in-the-EU-further-simplification-of-procedures_en>.

[71] [2008] OJ C267/1. [72] [2005] OJ C56/24. [73] [2004] OJ C31/5 and [2008] OJ C265/6.

[74] [2005] OJ C56/2 and Commission Guidance on the application of the referral mechanism set out in Article 22 of the Merger Regulation to certain categories of cases, 26 March 2021, C(2021) 1959 final.

[75] [2005] OJ C325/7. See also decision on the terms of reference of Hearing Officers [2001] L162/21, Chap. 13.

[76] 17 October 2011. See also OECD Best Practice Roundtable, *Economic Evidence in Merger Analysis*, DAF/COMP(2011) 23.

[77] Available with the other legislation on DG Comp's website at: <http://ec.europa.eu/competition/mergers/legislation/legislation.html>.

(v) Subsequent Review

The EUMR provides for mandatory review of the jurisdictional thresholds and provisions dealing with the pre-notification reasoned submissions,[78] and the Commission monitors the working of the rules more generally.

A concern of the Commission has been to ensure that the regulatory burden imposed by the Regulation is not excessive or disproportionate. In 2013, it launched a review[79] leading to changes to the simplified procedure[80] for non-problematic mergers; in 2014, it published a White Paper,[81] consulting on ideas for, for example, improving the jurisdictional provisions (to deal with enforcement gaps, including in relation to acquisitions of non-controlling minority interests and start-ups with low turnover), ensuring the effectiveness and smoothness of the case referral system, simplifying procedures further, and fostering coherence of, and convergence between, merger rules in the EU; and, in 2016, it consulted on the 'Evaluation of the procedural and jurisdictional aspects of EU Merger control' the findings of which it summarised in March 2021.[82] In view of the latter , the Commission adopted a new communication on the use of Article 22 of the EUMR as a referral mechanism from Member States to the Commission[83] and launched a consultation on how it could further improve simplification procedures. The latter resulted in the introduction in 2023 of changes to the simplification procedures (a new Notice on Simplified Procedure), the adoption of a new Implementing Regulation, and Forms CO, RS, and RM, and a Communication on the transmission of documents.[84]

There has been some debate as to whether changes to the substantive provisions of the EUMR are required to allow a broader range of factors, beyond consumer welfare, to be taken into account in the Commission's appraisal.[85] The Commission's view, however, appears to be that the Regulation is working well and that with the simplification steps, closing of jurisdictional gaps, and consideration of how to accommodate sustainability considerations within the EUMR review, other more wide-ranging changes are not required.[86]

All of these issues are discussed further in the following sections.

D. SCHEME OF THE EUROPEAN UNION MERGER REGULATIONS

The EUMR applies to concentrations with a 'Community'—an EU—dimension. The concept of an EU dimension allocates responsibility over concentrations between the Commission and the Member States and imposes an external limit on merger transactions caught within its jurisdiction. Broadly, with certain limited (but important) exceptions, concentrations that do not have an EU dimension

[78] EUMR, Art. 1(4).

[79] See IP/13/584, Commission Staff Working Document, Towards more effective EU merger control.

[80] See Sections 3.B.i and 4.A.

[81] White Paper, Towards more effective EU merger control, COM/2014/0449 final (see also accompanying Staff Working Document and Impact Assessment, <http://ec.europa.eu/competition/mergers/publications_en.html>).

[82] See Commission Staff Working Document, 'Evaluation of procedural and jurisdictional aspects of EU merger control', SWD(2021) 66 final.

[83] See <https://ec.europa.eu/competition/consultations/2021_merger_control/guidance_article_22_referrals.pdf> and Section 3.D.iii.

[84] See Commission further cuts red tape for merging firms businesses, IP/23/2357 and Sections 3.B.i and 4.A

[85] See e.g. n. 29 text.

[86] See e.g. Speech by K. Dekeyser, Acting Director of Policy and Strategy at DG Competition, Breugel conference in Brussels,11 December 2018.

are assessed under any applicable national competition legislation (no EU competition law applies), whilst concentrations with an EU dimension are assessed by the Commission under the provisions of the EUMR and benefit from a 'one-stop shop'. A case referral system applies, however, allowing cases to be transferred between the EU and national authorities in defined circumstances.

Concentrations with an EU dimension must be notified to the Commission and must, in general, be suspended until the Commission's final decision either clearing (conditionally or unconditionally) or prohibiting the merger. The Commission's decision must be taken within tight timetables.[87] There is a right of appeal from Commission decisions[88] to the GC and a further appeal, on a point of law, to the CJ. Despite recognition of a need for speed in merger cases, the expedited appeals procedure applies only in exceptional cases.[89]

The basic scheme of the EUMR is illustrated in Fig. 15.1. Section 3 deals more fully with the EUMR's jurisdictional provisions. Section 4 considers procedure whilst Section 5 examines substantive appraisal of EU mergers. Sections 6, 7, and 8 deal respectively with merger statistics, judicial review, and international issues, whilst Section 9 sets out some conclusions.

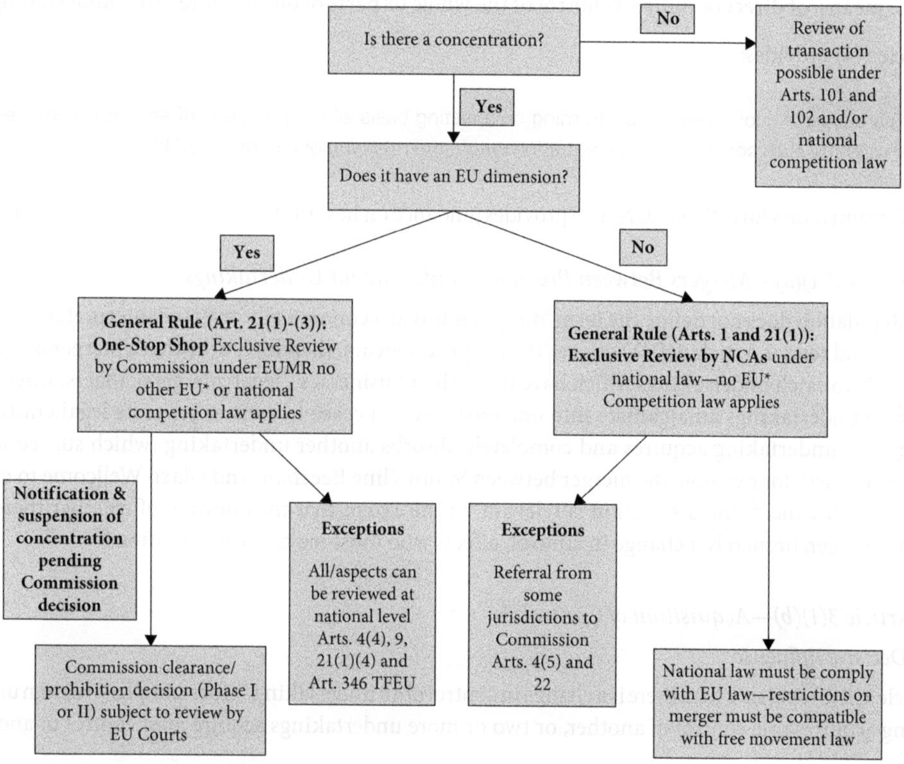

Figure 15.1 Scheme of the EUMR

* NB the residual application of Arts. 101 and 102, see Section 3.E.

87 Delays in review should not hamper the flexibility of undertakings seeking to engage in industrial restructuring.
88 But not a decision by the Commission to open Phase II proceedings, see n. 319.
89 See Section 7 and Chap. 13.

3. JURISDICTION

A. CONCENTRATIONS

(i) Definition

The EUMR applies to concentrations. The concept targets operations resulting in 'a lasting change in the control of the undertakings concerned and therefore in the structure of the market'.[90] Article 3 of the EUMR defines concentration.

Article 3(1) provides:

> A concentration shall be deemed to arise where a change of control on a lasting basis results from:
>
> (a) the merger of two or more previously independent undertakings or parts of undertakings, or
>
> (b) the acquisition, by one or more persons already controlling at least one undertaking, or by one or more undertakings whether by purchase of securities or assets, by contract or by any other means, of direct or indirect control of the whole or parts of one or more other undertakings.

Article 3(4) provides:

> The creation of a joint venture performing on a lasting basis all the functions of an autonomous economic entity shall constitute a concentration within the meaning of paragraph 3(1)(b).

The Commission's Jurisdictional Notice provides guidance on how the Commission interprets Article 3.[91]

a. *Article 3(1)(a)—Mergers Between Previously Independent Undertakings*

The Regulation does not define the term 'merge'. A broad, economically oriented interpretation of the term would render Article 3(1)(b) otiose. The purpose appears, therefore, to be that a merger is defined narrowly to catch undertakings which have fused their businesses ('legal' mergers), that is, where two or more undertakings amalgamate into one business and cease to exist as separate legal entities or where one undertaking acquires and completely absorbs another undertaking (which subsequently ceases to exist), for example the merger between SmithKline Beecham and Glaxo Wellcome to create GlaxoSmithKline.[92] The distinction is relevant, to the extent that the question of whether there has been a merger, or merely a change in control, affects who must make the notification.[93]

b. *Article 3(1)(b)—Acquisition of Control*

(1) Decisive Influence

Article 3(1)(b) applies where there is a change in control of an undertaking,[94] for example: where an undertaking acquires sole control of another, or two or more undertakings acquire *joint* control of another.

[90] EUMR, recital 20.

[91] The Commission Consolidated Jurisdictional Notice [2008] OJ C95/1 (the Jurisdictional Notice).

[92] See Jurisdictional Notice, para. 9. Para. 10 of the Notice states that a merger may also occur where, in the absence of a legal merger, the combining of the activities of previously independent undertakings results in the creation of a single economic unit.

[93] See Section 4.

[94] It does not matter whether control is acquired in one, two, or more stages or by means of one or more transactions, provided the end result constitutes a single concentration. Thus a concentration may be deemed to arise where a number of formally distinct legal transactions are interdependent so that none of them would be carried out without the others and the result consists in conferring on one or more undertakings direct or indirect economic control over the activities of another, see Case T-282/02, *Cementbouw Handel & Industrie BV v Commission* EU:T:2006:64, paras. 104–109.

Article 3(2) clarifies that the Regulation is intended to catch transactions which lead to an undertaking or undertakings acquiring the ability to exercise *decisive influence* over another—the ability to control the strategic commercial behaviour of the undertakings concerned (acquired through the acquisition of property rights, assets, shareholders' agreements, or resulting from economic dependence):[95]

> Control shall be constituted by rights, contracts or any other means which, either separately or in combination and having regard to the considerations of fact or law involved, confer the possibility of exercising decisive influence on an undertaking, in particular by:
>
> (a) ownership or the right to use all or part of the assets of an undertaking;
>
> (b) rights or contracts which confer decisive influence on the composition, voting or decisions of the organs of an undertaking.

(2) *Sole Control*

Sole control is acquired if one undertaking alone can exercise decisive influence over another undertaking. It can be acquired both, where the one undertaking enjoys the power to determine strategic commercial decisions of the other, and where a shareholder is able to veto strategic decisions in an undertaking but does not have the power to impose such decisions (negative sole control). It can be acquired on a *de jure* or *de facto* basis.

Sole control, or decisive influence, is ordinarily acquired on a legal basis through an acquisition of more than 50 per cent of the share capital and with it, more than 50 per cent of the voting rights of another undertaking.[96] However, it will always be necessary to look at other factors. Even an undertaking with more than 50 per cent of the share capital will not acquire sole control if, for example, it does not have control of a majority of the voting rights or where a supermajority of voting rights is required for strategic decisions. In such circumstances, the acquisition of a simple majority may lead to a scenario of negative or joint control.[97]

Sole control may also be gained where a share of considerably less than 50 per cent is acquired (a minority shareholding).[98] For example, it may be acquired on: a legal basis where special rights are attached to the preferential shareholding (a majority of the voting rights are nonetheless conferred on the shareholder or the shareholder has power to appoint more than half of the management team); a *de facto* basis where the remainder of the shares are widely dispersed,[99] the shareholder is likely to get a majority of votes at a shareholders meeting,[100] or an agreement confers an option to purchase shares in the near future.[101] The analysis in each case is fact-specific and it is important to consider a number of factors, including all shareholdings, special rights, and veto rights attached to the shareholding or set out in a management or shareholding agreement. In *Yara/Kemira GrowHow*,[102] for example, the Commission considered that the acquisition of 30.05 per cent of the shares in GrowHow constituted

[95] Jurisdictional Notice, para. 16.

[96] Ibid., paras. 18–34 (it can also be acquired on a contractual basis or through the acquisition of assets).

[97] Ibid., para. 56. See M.17, *MBB/Aerospatiale* 25 February 1991 (Aerospatiale and MBB had joint control of a joint venture formed to carry out their helicopter businesses. Although Aerospatiale received 60% of equity (and MBB only 40%), all strategic decisions for the JV required unanimous consent of both partners).

[98] Ibid., para. 57, M.258, *CCIE/GTE* 25 September 1992 and M.4994, *Electrabel/CNR* 29 April 2008, *aff'd* Case T-332/09, *Electrabel v Commission* EU:T:2012:672 (Electrabel's holding of 49.94% of CNR's capital and 47.92% of its voting right amounts to sole control), Case C-84/13P, EU:C:2014:2040.

[99] See e.g. M.25, *Arjomari/Wiggins Teape* 10 December 1990 (39% shareholding conferred sole control since no other entity had more than a 4% shareholding).

[100] See e.g. M.343, *Société Générale de Belgique/Générale de Banque* 3 August 1993 and Case T-332/09, *Electrabel v Commission* EU:T:2012:672, *aff'd* Case C-84/13 P, EU:C:2014:2040.

[101] Case T-2/93, *Air France v Commission* EU:T:1994:55 and Jurisdictional Notice, paras. 59–60.

[102] M.4730, 21 September 2007.

an acquisition of control. In practice, based on attendance at the last three AGMs, Yara would have been able to control a majority of votes at a shareholders meeting.

Negative sole control exists where a sole shareholder has enough voting rights to veto all strategic decisions.[103] Such a shareholder does not have joint control as, although it can block strategic decisions, no other shareholder enjoys the same level of influence and the shareholder does not necessarily have to cooperate with other shareholders in determining the strategic behaviour of the controlled undertaking.[104] Decisive influence and hence control results from the ability of the shareholder to produce a deadlock situation.

In *Ryanair/Aer Lingus*,[105] the Commission concluded that Ryanair's acquisition of a 25 per cent stake in Aer Lingus did *not* constitute acquisition of control. Although it prohibited the proposed merger (a hostile public bid by Ryanair for the remaining entire share capital of Aer Lingus), the Commission concluded it could not require Ryanair to divest this non-controlling stake it had already acquired. The GC upheld the Commission's decision that Ryanair's shareholding did not confer control or amount to partial implementation of a concentration.[106]

Although in the end the UK competition authority required Ryanair to sell most of its stake using powers conferred by UK law,[107] the Commission has reflected on the questions of whether: (a) its inability to review acquisitions of non-controlling minority shareholdings (especially those held in a rival)—which could allow the owner to have an influence over the conduct of a rival—constitutes a serious lacuna or gap in its powers to regulate transactions which have potential to cause significant harm to competition (through unilateral or coordinated effects);[108] and (b) Article 8(4) should be amended to allow it to 'require the dissolution of partially implemented transactions declared incompatible with the internal market in line with the scope of the suspension obligation . . .'[109] The Commission, believing that Articles 101 and 102 do not provide suitable alternatives, proposed a targeted transparency system in its White Paper.[110] Nonetheless, and mindful of negative responses to its proposal, it recognises that it will be a challenge to design a system of control without imposing an unnecessary and disproportionate regulatory burden and cost on companies and competition agencies. Indeed, Commissioner Vestager made it clear that such a system would require time to design correctly and that '[t]here is no need to rush. What counts is that the new rules—when they are introduced—work well and are proportionate to the problem'.[111] There is also a concern, especially in the US, that cross- or common ownership—where a shareholder, for example an institutional investor or investment fund, holds shares in a number of rival companies, may harm or soften competition, especially in oligopolistic markets, and so should be subject to review.[112]

[103] Jurisdictional Notice, paras. 54 and 57.

[104] Ibid., para. 54.

[105] M.4439, 27 June 2007. For a discussion of this case and the legal issues raised by the repeated attempts of Ryanair to acquire Aer Lingus, see M. Furse, 'Testing the Limits: *Ryanair/Aer Lingus* and the Boundaries of Merger Control' (2016) 12 *European Competition Journal* 462.

[106] Case T-411/07, *Aer Lingus Group v Commission* EU:T:2010:281.

[107] See Case No. 1219/4/8/13, *Ryanair Holdings v CMA* [2014] CAT 3, *aff'd* [2015] EWCA Civ 83. Merger control rules in Austria and Germany, as in the UK, allow investigation of acquisitions of non-controlling minority interests.

[108] See Commission's White Paper, n. 81, M.4153, *Toshiba/Westinghouse* 19 September 2006 and e.g. OFT 1218, *Minority Interests in Competitors: A Research Report prepared by DotEcon Ltd*, March 2010 and A. Ezrachi and D. Gilo, 'EC Competition Law and the Regulation of Passive Investments Among Competitors' (2006) 26 *OJLS* 327.

[109] Commission Staff Working Document, Towards more effective EU merger control, 20 June 2013, 21–22.

[110] See n. 81 and e.g. M. Gassler, 'Non-controlling Minority Shareholdings and EU Merger Control' (2018) 41 *World Competition* 3.

[111] See speech by Commissioner Vestager, 'Thoughts on merger reform and market definition', 12 March 2015.

[112] See e.g. J. Azar, M. C. Schmalz, and I. Tecu, 'Anticompetitive Effects of Common Ownership' (2018) 73 *J of Finance* 1513, E. Elhauge, 'Horizontal Shareholdings' (2016) 129 *Harvard LR* 1267, Speech of M. Vestager, 'A Market that Works for Consumers', March 2018, but see Blackrock's letter to the FTC at <www.blackrock.com/corporate/literature/publication/ftc-hearing-8-competition-consumer-protection-21st-century-011419.pdf> and A. J. Burnside and A. Kidane, 'Common Ownership: And EU Perspective' (2020) 8 *J of Antitrust Enforcement* 456.

(3) *Joint Control*

The Commission explains joint control, where two or more undertakings have the possibility of exercising decisive influence over another, in its Jurisdictional Notice.[113]

Jurisdictional Notice [2008] OJ C95/1

62. Joint control exists where two or more undertakings or persons have the possibility of exercising decisive influence over another undertaking. Decisive influence in this sense normally means the power to block actions which determine the strategic commercial behaviour of an undertaking. Unlike sole control, which confers upon a specific shareholder the power to determine the strategic decisions in an undertaking, joint control is characterized by the possibility of a deadlock situation resulting from the power of two or more parent companies to reject proposed strategic decisions. It follows, therefore, that these shareholders must reach a common understanding in determining the commercial policy of the joint venture and that they are required to cooperate.

63. As in the case of sole control, the acquisition of joint control can also be established on a *de jure* or *de facto* basis. There is joint control if the shareholders (the parent companies) must reach agreement on major decisions concerning the controlled undertaking (the joint venture).

Joint control may thus be acquired where two parents hold the voting rights equally and also in the absence of equality (for example, where minority shareholders have additional rights which allow them to veto decisions which are essential for the strategic commercial behaviour of the joint venture). It is necessary to consider not only the size of the undertakings' shareholdings but also factors such as the voting rights attached to the shareholdings and shareholder and management agreements, veto rights, and the ability of two or more undertakings to jointly exercise the majority of voting rights.[114]

(4) *Changes in the Quality of Control*

The EUMR applies to operations leading to a change in the quality of control[115] catching transactions leading to: a change from sole to joint control; a change in joint control (by the entrance of a new shareholder, by replacement of an existing shareholder, or possibly by a reduction in the number of jointly controlling shareholders); or a change from joint to sole control. It thus covers: (a) an entrance of one or more new controlling shareholders irrespective of whether or not they replace existing controlling shareholders; and (b) a reduction of the number of controlling shareholders (although the simplified procedure is likely to apply where a party is to acquire sole control of an undertaking over which it already has joint control).[116] Acquisition of joint control of a pre-existing JV is, however, like the creation of a JV, only caught if the JV acts as an autonomous economic entity on the market.[117]

[113] See also, in particular, the GC's judgment in Case T-282/02, *Cementbouw Handel & Industrie BV v Commission* EU:T:2006:64.

[114] Jurisdictional Notice, paras. 64–82.

[115] Ibid., paras. 83–90 and, e.g., M.23, *ICI/Tioxide* 28 November 1990.

[116] Notice on Simplified Procedure, para. 5(e), see Jurisdictional Notice, para. 84.

[117] Case C-248/16, *Austria Asphalt v Bundeskartellanwalt* EU:C:2017:643 (ensuring that established and newly created JVs are treated in the same way; non-full function JVs are not capable of having an effect on the structure of the market and should not therefore be included within the ambit of the EUMR, paras. 22–24).

(ii) Joint Ventures

a. Introduction

The creation of a separate JV is dealt with under the EUMR only where it amounts to a 'concentration'. Where it does constitute a concentration with an EU dimension it will, like other concentrations, generally benefit from a '*one-stop shop*' appraisal by the Commission under the EUMR (national competition rules do not apply).[118] In contrast, if the JV falls to be assessed under Article 101, the application of national law (subject to Article 3 of Regulation 1/2003) is not precluded and an authorisation decision is most unlikely (self-assessment is generally required). Further, the JV agreement is valid only insofar as the agreement satisfies the conditions of Article 101 both at the time the agreement is concluded and in the future.[119]

The differences in treatment of JVs under the EUMR and Article 101 respectively, have led the Commission to make several changes to its approach over the years. Not only has it sought to ameliorate the way in which it deals with JVs under Article 101,[120] but in 1998 the definition of JV set out in the EUMR was expanded to bring more JVs within its scope.

b. 'Full-function' Joint Ventures

Article 3(4)[121] provides that the creation of a JV constitutes a concentration only if the JV (a greenfield JV or a JV with assets) is jointly controlled by two or more undertakings and it is 'full-function'. The full-functionality criterion, which also applies where joint control of an existing undertaking with market presence is acquired[122] (there is a move from sole to joint control) or a new JV partner is added or replaces an existing one, requires that the JV is formed on a lasting basis to carry out the functions of an autonomous economic entity—it is autonomous from an operational point of view and has sufficient resources to operate independently on a market.[123] It must have 'a management dedicated to its day-to day operations and access to sufficient resources including finance, staff, and assets (tangible and intangible) in order to conduct on a lasting basis its business activities within the area provided for in the joint-venture agreement'.[124] It will not be full-function if it simply takes over one specific function for its parents, for example distribution or sale of its parent companies' products.[125]

Another relevant factor in the determination of full-functionality may be whether the parent companies make sales or purchases to or from the JV. Where sales are made to the parent companies, the main issue to be determined is whether, regardless of these sales, the JV can play an active role on the market and be considered economically autonomous from an operational viewpoint.[126] Further, a JV is unlikely to be full-function where it operates like a joint sales agency purchasing from its parents and adding little value to the products or services concerned.[127]

The Jurisdictional Notice also states that the fact that the agreement contains a clause providing for the dissolution of the JV, for example on its failure or on disagreement between the parents, does not mean that the JV has not been established on a lasting basis (rather, it may speak in favour of it as there will be little incentive to seek dissolution). In addition, a JV created for a finite period but long enough to affect the structure of the market will also be established on a lasting basis, but one established for a short finite period will not.

[118] See Section 3.C. [119] See Chap. 10. [120] Ibid.

[121] Old EUMR, Art. 3(2).

[122] See Case C-248/16, *Austria Asphalt v Bundeskartellanwalt* EU:C:2017:643 (cf. Jurisdictional Notice, para. 91) and, e.g., L. Rudolf, '*Austria Asphalt*: Only Full-function Joint Ventures Subject to Review under EUMR' (2018) 9 *JECLAP* 107.

[123] Jurisdictional Notice, paras. 91–109. [124] Ibid., para. 94. [125] Ibid., paras. 95–96.

[126] Ibid., paras. 98–100. [127] Ibid., para. 97.

The Notice, at paragraphs 106–109, provides that enlargement of the scope of the JV's activities may constitute a concentration requiring notification, in particular where it entails the acquisition of the whole or part of another undertaking from the parents that would, considered in isolation, qualify as a concentration.

(1) The Relevance of Coordination of Competitive Behaviour

The original EUMR provided that a JV which has as its object or effect the coordination of the competitive behaviour of undertakings which remain independent could not constitute a concentration. Although this complex *negative* condition was removed from the jurisdictional test in 1997, the issue is still of relevance to the *substantive* appraisal. JVs are appraised in the same way as other concentrations, but their coordinative aspects are assessed additionally in accordance with the criteria set out in Article 101 TFEU.[128]

(iii) Article 3(5) and Warehousing Arrangements

Article 3(5) of the EUMR sets out several circumstances in which a concentration shall be deemed not to arise. These deal with shares held by financial institutions on a temporary basis, the acquisition of control by liquidators or other administrators, and operations carried out by financial holding companies.[129] An important issue is whether, and if so when, the exception for shares held by financial interests can apply to temporary shareholdings acquired in warehousing structures (where an ultimate purchaser seeking to acquire another does so through a third party, interim purchaser, which holds the shares on a temporary basis). The Commission's view, set out in the Jurisdictional Notice, is that such structures do not benefit from the exemption if the interim transaction forms part of a broader, single concentration,[130] that is, where:

> an undertaking is 'parked' with an interim buyer, often a bank, on the basis of an agreement on the future onward sale of the business to an ultimate acquirer. The interim buyer generally acquires shares 'on behalf' of the ultimate acquirer, which often bears the major part of the economic risks and may also be granted specific rights. In such circumstances, the first transaction is only undertaken to facilitate the second transaction and the first buyer is directly linked to the ultimate acquirer . . . no other ultimate acquirer is involved, the target business remains unchanged, and the sequence of transactions is initiated alone by the sole ultimate acquirer. . . . [T]he Commission will examine the acquisition of control by the ultimate acquirer, as provided for in the agreements entered into by the parties. The Commission will consider the transaction by which the interim buyer acquires control in such circumstances as the first step of a single concentration comprising the lasting acquisition of control by the ultimate buyer.[131]

Where the interim buyer's purchase forms part of the concentration with the ultimate acquirer, the EUMR's notification and suspensory provisions are triggered.

Prior to the publication of the Jurisdictional Notice, however, in *Lagardère/Natexis/VUP*,[132] the Commission applied Article 3(5)(a) to a scenario in which Lagardère, the ultimate buyer, agreed to take the assets out of the hands of VUP and parked the shares with a bank prior to obtaining clearance for the transaction. Had the bank's acquisition formed part of the concentration between Lagardère

[128] EUMR, Art. 2(4)(5), discussed in Section 5.H.
[129] Jurisdictional Notice, paras. 110–118. [130] Ibid., para. 114.
[131] Ibid., para. 35. This approach was confirmed in Case T-609/19, *Canon Inc v Commission* EU:T:2022:299.
[132] M.2978, 7 January 2004.

and VUP there would have been a breach of the stand-still obligation. Éditions Odile, one of the competing bidders for VUP, brought an appeal before the GC and CJ. Neither the GC nor the CJ had to decide the warehousing point directly as it did not affect the legality of the Commission's clearance decision (this issue affected only the question of whether the suspensory obligation had been breached and whether the parties could have been fined).[133] Although the GC[134] indicated that Lagardère had not acquired control at the time of the bank's interim acquisition, as it could not exercise control over the target at this time, the CJ made it clear that these statements had not been necessary to the ruling but had merely 'been made for the sake of completeness'.[135] If the temporary and ultimate acquisitions of the shares do not form part of the same concentration, then, unless Article 3(5) applies, the interim transaction will constitute a separate concentration.

(iv) Abandonment of a Concentration

If the Commission initiates Phase II proceedings following notification of a concentration to it, it must close the proceeding by means of a decision adopted under Article 8 of the EUMR 'unless the undertakings concerned have demonstrated to the satisfaction of the Commission that they have abandoned the concentration'.[136] In *MCI WorldCom/Sprint*,[137] for example, the Commission issued a decision prohibiting a concentration even though the parties stated that they had abandoned the merger. On appeal, however, the GC annulled the Commission's decision, holding that the Commission had exceeded its powers by adopting a prohibition decision when the notifying parties had formally withdrawn their notification and informed it of the abandonment of the concentration in the form envisaged in the notification.

Where the Commission indicates that it is likely to prohibit a merger the parties sometimes prefer to abandon it rather than to receive a prohibition decision.[138] The Commission's Jurisdictional Notice now sets out guidance as to how the parties may demonstrate that the transaction has been abandoned. General guidance, set out in paragraphs 119–120, is followed by specific guidance on the type of proof that is required depending upon whether the original concentration takes the form of a binding agreement, a good faith intention to conclude an agreement, a public announcement of a public bid or of the intention to make a public bid, or an implemented concentration.

B. EU DIMENSION

(i) A Bright-line Jurisdictional Test and Simplified Procedure

The concept of an EU dimension is designed to catch concentrations which create significant structural changes having an impact beyond the national borders of any one Member State.[139] Broadly, whether or not a merger has an EU dimension is assessed by reference to the *turnover* of the parties

[133] Cases C-551, 553, and 554/10, *Éditions Odile Jacob v Commission* EU:C:2013:809, paras. 34–38.

[134] See Case T-279/04, *Éditions Odile Jacob v Commission* EU:T:2010:384 on appeal, Cases C-551/10 etc., ibid., paras. 34–38.

[135] Cases C-551/10 etc., ibid., para. 40.

[136] EUMR, Art. 6(1)(c).

[137] M.1741, 28 June 2000, on appeal Case T-310/00, *MCI v Commission* EU:T:2004:275.

[138] See e.g. M.9162, *Fincantieri/Chantiers de l'Atlantique* (withdrawn), M.9637 *IAG/Air Europa* (withdrawn), M.9097, *Boeing/Embraer* (withdrawn), M.9547 *Johnson & Johnson/Tachosil* (withdrawn), M.8907 *Aperam/VDM* (withdrawn), M.7419, *TeliaSonera/Telenor/JV* (withdrawn) and speech of Commissioner Vestager, 'Competition in Telecoms Markets', 42nd Conference on International Antitrust Law and Policy, Fordham University, 2 October 2015.

[139] EUMR, recital 8.

involved.[140] Since the notification to the Commission of such concentrations is compulsory, the jurisdictional test incorporated within the EUMR is intended to be a bright-line test which can be applied relatively simply, objectively, and easily (although inevitably some complexities arise in practice).[141]

The corollary of having a relatively bright-line test based on turnover is that:[142] jurisdiction over EU mergers is not always in fact allocated appropriately as between the Commission and the Member States; certain problematic concentrations may not meet the thresholds; and concentrations between undertakings which obviously will not raise competition problems may be brought within the regulation and subject to mandatory notification (the impact on competition being relevant only to the substantive assessment).[143] In order to deal with these limitations, the Commission has sought:[144]

- to ensure that flexible mechanisms exist for referral of cases as between the Commission and national competition authorities (NCAs) where appropriate;
- to put in place mechanisms which allow for scrutiny of deals involving acquisitions of a high value, which do not meet the turnover thresholds; and
- to reduce inconvenience and cost by introducing, and honing, a simplified procedure for the treatment of concentrations that do not raise competition concerns.[145] In such cases, it is possible to submit a short-form notification,[146] which may be followed by a short-form decision. In 2013[147] and 2023,[148] this procedure was extended to a greater category of 'non-problematic' mergers and the information requirements were reduced/streamlined.

(ii) Article 1(2)

The primary test is that set out in Article 1(2). Only if this test is *not* satisfied is it necessary for an undertaking to consider whether or not the thresholds set out in Article 1(3) are satisfied.

[140] 'Turnover is used as a proxy for the economic resources being combined in a concentration, and is allocated geographically in order to reflect the geographic distribution of those resources', Jurisdictional Notice, para. 124.

[141] In some States, jurisdiction may be determined by reference to the market shares of parties, which can be more complex to determine.

[142] It also catches some mergers between non-EU undertakings whose business is principally carried on outside the EU, see Section 8 and, e.g., M.9343, *Daewoo Shipbuilding and Marine Engineering (DMSE)/Hyundai Heavy Industries(HHI)*13 January 2022 (although the undertakings involved in this transaction are foreign shipbuilders, located outside the EEA, the EUMR applies provided the parties are active in Europe and the transaction has an impact within the EEA. In this case the transaction was notified on the basis of the geographical allocation of turnover and the relevant market was a worldwide one, with a significant part of demand in the market originating from the EEA. Consequently, the transaction was likely to affect competition in the EEA, see DG Comp [2022] 2 *Competition Merger Brief* 10).

[143] For the view that because more than half of the mergers notified do not give rise to competition concerns at the EU level, alternative jurisdictional delimitations should be considered, see M. Broberg, 'Improving the EU Merger Regulation's Delimitation of Jurisdiction: Re-defining the Notion of Union Dimension' (2014) 5 *JECLAP* 261.

[144] See further Sections 3.C and D and 4.

[145] See n. 70.

[146] See Short Form for the notification of a concentration pursuant to Reg. 139/2004, attached to the Implementing Reg.

[147] Following the 2013 changes, Commissioner Vestager noted that it led to around 10% of cases moving from the normal to the simplified procedure, see speech by Commissioner Vestager, n. 111.

[148] See Section 2.C.v.

Article 1

1. Without prejudice to Article 4(5) and Article 22, this Regulation shall apply to all concentrations with a Community dimension as defined in this Article.
2. A concentration has a Community dimension where:
   (a) the combined aggregate worldwide turnover of all the undertakings concerned is more than EUR 5,000 million; and
   (b) the aggregate Community-wide turnover of each of at least two of the undertakings concerned is more than EUR 250 million

   unless each of the undertakings concerned achieves more than two-thirds of its aggregate Community-wide turnover within one and the same Member State.

This test looks to the combined worldwide turnover of the undertakings concerned and the EU-wide turnover of at least two of the undertakings involved in the concentration. Even where the thresholds are met, jurisdiction is denied if the *proviso* applies—if each of the undertakings concerned achieves more than two-thirds of its EU turnover within one and the same Member State. Although the purpose of the proviso is to exclude concentrations the effects of which are felt primarily in one Member State, the Commission has had some concerns about its operation, as it can mean that consolidations between large national players escape scrutiny under EU rules even if they produce effects on competition across the EU.[149] No change to this rule is currently envisaged, however.

(iii) Article 1(3) of the EUMR

The Commission would have preferred (and has proposed) lower thresholds than those set out in Article 1(2). The compromise reached was to add Article 1(3).[150] This provides that a concentration which satisfies lower worldwide and EU-wide turnovers than those set out in Article 1(2) may be caught if two additional criteria are satisfied. Broadly, these aim to catch concentrations where the undertakings concerned, jointly and individually, have a minimum level of activities in three or more Member States and which are therefore likely to be subject to the merger rules of those three or more Member States.[151] Article 1(3) also contains a proviso excluding concentrations where two-thirds of the EU-wide turnover of all of the undertakings involved is achieved in one and the same Member State.

[149] E.g. in the energy sector, see Commission Report to Council on the functioning of Regulation 139/2004, COM(2009) 281 final, para. 16, Green Paper on Community Merger Control, COM(96) 19 final, para. 48. The two-thirds rule can also mean that competing bids for a company are assessed under different regimes, see e.g.: Gas Natural's (Spain's largest gas operator) bid for Spanish electricity operator, Endesa did not have an EU dimension because of the two-thirds rule (Endesa's appeal against the Commission's refusal to take jurisdiction was rejected, Case T-417/05, *Endesa v Commission* EU:T:2006:219) whilst E.ON's and ENEL/Acciona's bids did, see M.4110 and M.4685 and discussion of cases at n. 233 and text.

[150] Introduced by Council Reg. 1310/97. The original EUMR anticipated a review, and a lowering, of the thresholds by the end of 1993 but this did not occur for fear of opposition from a number of Member States.

[151] Reg. 1310/97 [1997] OJ L180/1, Art. 1(1)(a) and (b).

Article 1(3)

A concentration that does not meet the thresholds laid down in paragraph 2 has a Community dimension where:

(a) the combined aggregate worldwide turnover of all the undertakings concerned is more than EUR 2 500 million;

(b) in each of at least three Member States, the combined aggregate turnover of all the undertakings concerned is more than EUR 100 million;

(c) in each of at least three Member States included for the purpose of point (b), the aggregate turnover of each of at least two of the undertakings concerned is more than EUR 25 million; and

(d) the aggregate Community-wide turnover of each of at least two of the undertakings concerned is more than EUR 100 million

unless each of the undertakings concerned achieves more than two-thirds of its aggregate Community-wide turnover within one and the same Member State.

(iv) Concentrations, Undertakings Concerned, and Calculation of Worldwide and Community-wide Turnover

In order to apply the Article 1(2) and (3) tests, it is first necessary to identify the number of concentrations involved. In simple cases, such as the acquisition of B by A, there will usually be only one. In more complex cases, such as the division of an existing JV company between its parents, there may be more than one concentration.[152] Once the appropriate concentration(s) is identified it is necessary to determine (a) the undertakings concerned and (b) their turnover (world and Community-wide). The meaning of 'undertakings concerned' and 'turnover' has been clarified in the Jurisdictional Notice.

The Notice seeks, guided by prior cases, to identify undertakings concerned in most typical situations. Paragraphs 134–153 provide detailed analysis of who the undertakings concerned are in acquisition of control cases.

Once the undertakings concerned have been identified their turnover must be calculated. Article 5(1) defines turnover as 'the amount derived by the undertakings concerned in the previous financial year from the sale of products and provision of services falling within the undertaking's ordinary activities' (i.e. net sales—ordinarily assessed from audited accounts from the last financial year).[153] Article 5(2) provides that where the concentration consists of an acquisition of part or parts, of one or more undertakings (such as a subsidiary or a division), only the turnover of the relevant parts which are the subject of the concentration shall be taken into account with regard to the seller or sellers.[154] Article 5(3) sets out special turnover rules which apply, for example, to credit and financial institutions and insurance undertakings. Article 5(4) provides (subject to Article 5(2)) that turnover is calculated by reference not only to those undertakings concerned but also to the turnover of all those

[152] See e.g. M.197, *Solvay/LaPorte* [1992] OJ C165/26 (notification of the division of a JV, between the parties. The Commission concluded that this was two separate concentrations. The Solvay concentration had an EU dimension but the Laporte concentration did not).

[153] Jurisdictional Notice, paras. 157–174. The reliance on turnover in the previous financial year may mean that some transactions in industries heavily impacted by the Covid-19 pandemic, may have fallen below the thresholds.

[154] Acquisitions of parts between the same persons or undertakings in a series of transactions within a two-year period are treated as one and the same concentration, EUMR, Art. 5(2).

entities which they control or by which they are controlled, and to other connected undertakings. The operation of Article 5(4) is explained in the Jurisdictional Notice.

Jurisdictional Notice [2008] OJ C95/1

177. Article 5(4) of the Merger Regulation provides the following:

Without prejudice to paragraph 2 [acquisition of parts], the aggregate turnover of an undertaking concerned within the meaning of Article 1(2) and (3) shall be calculated by adding together the respective turnovers of the following:

(a) the undertakings concerned;

(b) those undertakings in which the undertaking concerned directly or indirectly;

- (i) owns more than half the capital of business assets, or
- (ii) has the power to exercise more than half the voting rights, or
- (iii) has the power to appoint more than half the members of the supervisory board, the administrative board or bodies legally representing the undertakings, or
- (iv) has the right to manage the undertaking's affairs;

(c) those undertaking which have in an undertaking concerned the rights or powers listed in (b);

(d) those undertakings in which an undertaking as referred to in (c) has the rights or powers listed in (b);

(e) those undertakings in which two or more undertakings as referred to in (a) to (d) jointly have the rights or powers listed in (b).

An undertaking which has in another undertaking the rights and powers mentioned in Article 5(4) (b) will be referred to as the 'parent' of the latter in the present section of the Notice dealing with the calculation of turnover, whereas the latter is referred to as 'subsidiary' of the former. In short, Article 5(4) therefore provides that the turnover of the undertaking concerned by the concentration (point (a)) should include its subsidiaries (point (b)), its parent companies (point (c)), the other subsidiaries of its parent undertakings (point (d)) and any other subsidiary jointly held by two or more of the undertakings identified under (a)–(d) (point (e)).

Note that with the aim of providing greater legal certainty, the definition of control in Article 5(4) is different from, and more tightly defined than, the definition of control set out in Article 3(2).[155] In general, the whole turnover of undertakings identified in Article 5 is taken into account. However, for JVs between two or more undertakings concerned, turnover of the JVs is apportioned equally amongst the undertakings concerned.[156] Further, in practice, the Commission allocates turnover for JVs between undertakings concerned and third parties on a per capita basis according to the number of undertakings exercising joint control.[157]

a. Examples

The following examples seek to clarify how Article 5 applies to identify the undertakings whose turnover is taken into account for the purposes of calculating EU dimension.

[155] No harmonisation of approach has been made, see 2001 Green Paper on the Review of Council Regulation (EEC) No. 4064/89, COM(2001) 745/6 final.

[156] EUMR, Art. 5(5)(b).

[157] Jurisdictional Notice, para. 187.

(1) Group A

A is a wholly owned subsidiary of W. A has two wholly owned subsidiaries, X and Y. Y and a third party, TP, jointly control Z.

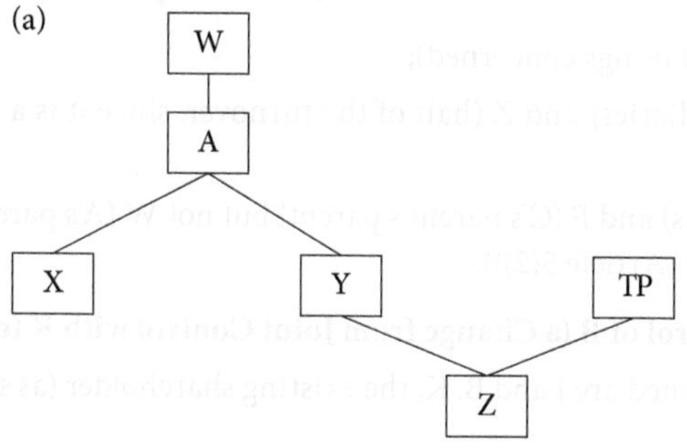

(2) Group B

B is company jointly owned by J and K. K has a wholly owned subsidiary L. B has a wholly owned subsidiary, M.

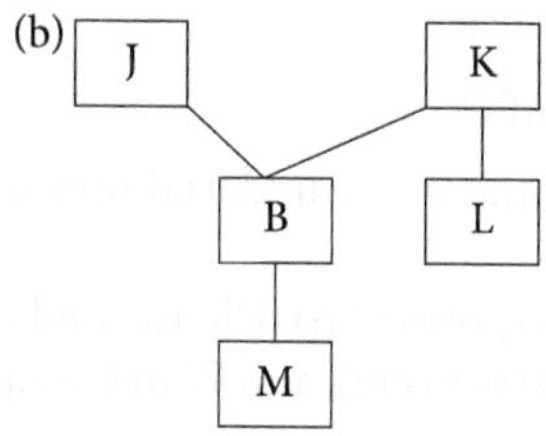

(3) Group C

C is a company jointly controlled by D and E. E is a wholly owned subsidiary of F.

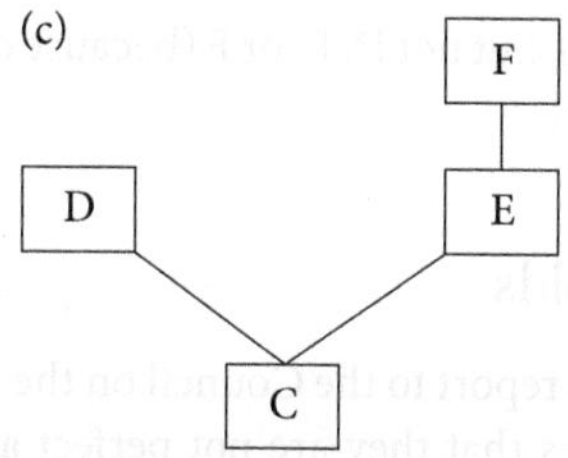

1. A Acquires B

The undertakings concerned are A and B.

The aggregate turnover for the purposes of Article 1(2) and (3) is calculated by adding together the respective turnovers of A, X, Y, Z (50 per cent), and W in Group A and B and M (in Group B) That is:

a. A and B (the undertakings concerned);
b. X, Y, and M (subsidiaries) and Z (half of the turnover, since it is a company jointly controlled with a third party);
c. W (A's parent) but not J and K (B's parents, because only an acquisition of part of seller (Article 5(2)).

2. C Acquires Sole Control of A

The undertakings concerned are the acquiring undertakings, C, and the target company, A. The aggregate turnover for the purposes of Article 1(2) and (3) is calculated by adding together the respective turnovers of C, D, E, and F in Group C and A, X, Y, and Z (50 per cent) in Group A. That is:

a. C and A (the undertakings concerned);

b. X and Y (the subsidiaries) and Z (half of the turnover, since it is a company jointly controlled with a third party);

c. D and E (C's parents) and F (C's parent's parent) but not W (A's parent because only an acquisition of part of seller (Article 5(2))).

3. J Acquires Sole Control of B (a Change from Joint Control with K to Sole Control by J)

The undertakings concerned are J and B. K, the existing shareholder (as seller) is not an undertaking concerned.

The aggregate turnover for the purposes of Article 1(2) and (3) is calculated by adding together the respective turnovers of J, B, and M. That is:

a. J and B (the undertakings concerned);

b. M (B's subsidiary). To avoid double counting the turnover of J has to be calculated without the turnover of the JV, B.[158]

4. A and B Acquire joint Control of C

The undertakings concerned are A and B (the undertakings acquiring joint control) and C (the pre-existing acquired undertaking).

The aggregate turnover for the purposes of Article 1(2) and (3) is calculated by adding together the respective turnovers of A, X, Y, Z (50 per cent), and W in Group A; B, J, K, and L in Group B; and C in Group C. That is:

a. A, B, and C (the undertakings concerned);

b. X, Y, and M (the subsidiaries) and Z (half of the turnover, since it is a company jointly controlled with a third party);

c. W, J, and K (A and B's parents), but not D, E, or F (because only acquisition of part (Article 5(2)));

d. L (a subsidiary of B's parent K).

(v) Rethinking the Thresholds

Periodically, the Commission must report to the Council on the operation of the jurisdictional thresholds.[159] The Commission recognises that they are not perfect and, amongst other difficulties, that a number of transactions with significant cross-border effects are not caught by them.[160] Although it has mooted change,[161] to date it has opted, instead of amending the EUMR itself, to focus on ensuring that there are requisite mechanisms in place to ensure concentrations can be scrutinised appropriately, for

[158] The turnover of B's parents is not included. K's turnover is excluded because it is an acquisition of part and to avoid double counting the turnover of the JV has to be taken without the turnover of the acquiring shareholder, J.

[159] The old EUMR, Art. 1(4).

[160] See e.g. the Report to the Council on the application of the Merger Regulation Thresholds, COM(2000) 399 final.

[161] Green Paper on the Review of Council Regulation (EEC) No. 4064/89, COM(2001) 745/6 final, paras. 24–28.

example by transfer of cases between the Commission and NCAs.[162] It has also considered how to deal with the fact that the current jurisdictional thresholds do not allow it to review acquisitions of minority interests[163] or transactions where a target does not have a large turnover but the transaction value is high. The latter problem has been most acute in relation to acquisitions of targets in digital and pharmaceutical industries, for example where a target is a start-up and/or has limited turnover which does not reflect the transaction's importance given the valuable data, large consumer or user base involved, or the innovative new drug or product being developed which has not yet been marketed. The issue may also arise where an incumbent company with a strong market position, but which does not pursue environmentally friendly business strategies, seeks to acquire an undertaking active in 'green' innovation.[164]

To deal with the low turnover-high transaction value difficulty, some states (including Germany and Austria[165]) have introduced jurisdictional thresholds based on transaction value. The Commission is concerned, however, that a similar approach at the EU level might capture too many unproblematic transactions, leading to a disproportionate increase in administrative burden and cost.[166] Consequently, it has decided for now to rely on Member States, or parties, referring problematic mergers to it.[167] This approach has been used not only where mergers are caught by national merger control rules (this occurred in *Facebook/WhatsApp* where the parties themselves made a reasoned submission requesting the Commission to take jurisdiction because the concentration was notifiable in three or more Member States (Article 4(5)[168])), but also where Member States do not have jurisdiction (see discussion of *Illumina/Grail*[169] in Section 3.D). Article 14 of the Digital Markets Act[170] also requires 'gatekeepers' to inform the Commission, prior to implementation, of any intended concentration where the merging entities or the target provide core platform services, provide other services in the digital sector, or enable the collection of data, irrespective of whether it is notifiable under the EUMR or under national merger rules (see further Chapter 16). Although no formal 'notification' of the transaction is required, the information provided will alert EU authorities of the transaction and facilitate the triggering of available merger control provisions. A further question which has arisen is whether Article 102 can be used to bridge this regulatory gap, a matter considered in Section 3.E.[171]

C. CONCENTRATIONS WITH AN EU DIMENSION: A ONE-STOP SHOP?

(i) Exclusive Competence of the Commission under the EUMR

Article 21(1)–(3) provides:

> 1. This Regulation alone shall apply to concentrations as defined in Article 3, and Council Regulations (EC) No 1/2003, (EEC) No 1017/68, (EEC) No 4056/86 and (EEC) No 3597/87[172] shall not apply,

[162] See e.g. Commission Report to Council on the Functioning of Regulation 139/2004, COM(2009) 281 final.

[163] See nn. 108–110 and text.

[164] DG Comp [2021] 1 *Competition Policy Brief*.

[165] See Act against Restraints of Competition 2013 and Cartel Act 2005 respectively. This is the approach utilised in the US. Some other Member States have mechanisms for calling in mergers which fall below the jurisdictional thresholds.

[166] See also 2019 Report on Competition in the Digital Era, n. 24.

[167] See discussion of Art. 22, Section 3.D.iii. See also discussion of use of Art. 102 TFEU in Section 3.E.

[168] M.7217, *Facebook/WhatsApp* 3 October 2014. See discussion of Art. 4(5), Section 4.B.iii.

[169] M.10188, on appeal Case T-227/21, *Illumina v Commission* EU:T:2022:447.

[170] [2022] OJ L265/1 (applying from 2 May 2023, Art. 54).

[171] See, in particular, discussion of Case C-449/21, *Towercast v Autorité de la Concurrence* EU:C:2023:207 in Section 3.E.ii.

[172] Reg. 3597/87 has essentially been repealed by Reg. 411/2004 [2004] OJ L68/1.

except in relation to joint ventures that do not have a Community dimension and which have as their object or effect the coordination of competitive behaviour of undertakings that remain independent.

2. Subject to review by the Court of Justice, the Commission shall have sole jurisdiction to take the decisions provided for in this Regulation.
3. No Member State shall apply its national legislation on competition to any concentration that has a Community dimension . . .

Article 21 encompasses the 'one-stop shop' principle. The general rule is that the EUMR, and no other EU or national competition law, applies to concentrations with an EU dimension and the Commission has sole jurisdiction over such transactions. Further it sets out the general rule (combined with Article 1) that no EU competition law applies to concentrations without an EU dimension.

(ii) Case Referrals

The financial criteria relevant to the assessment of an EU dimension generally serve as effective proxies for identifying transactions with an EU dimension. The EUMR jurisdictional mechanism is, however, flexible, allowing cases to be referred to or from the Member States,[173] consistently with the principles of subsidiarity and one-stop shop appraisal for EU mergers.[174] The EUMR[175] thus provides (as described in more detail below) for circumstances in which, at the initiative, or invitation, of the Commission, the Member State, or the parties:

- a concentration with an EU dimension, or aspects of it, may be referred to a national authority for assessment under its domestic law;
- a concentration without an EU dimension may be referred to the Commission.[176]

The Commission's Notice on Case Referral in respect of concentrations (the 'Notice on case referral')[177] describes the rationale underlying the system, provides practical guidance on its operation and best practices on cooperation and dialogue between the Commission and NCAs.

Commission Notice on Case Referral in respect of concentrations [2005] OJ C56/2

Guiding principles

8. The system of merger control established by the Merger Regulation, including the mechanism for re-attributing cases between the Commission and Member States contained therein, is consistent with the principle of subsidiarity enshrined in the EC Treaty. Decisions taken with regard to the referral of cases should accordingly take due account of all aspects of the application of the principle of subsidiarity in this context, in particular the suitability of a concentration being examined by the authority more appropriate for carrying out the investigation, the benefits inherent in a 'one-stop shop' system, and the importance of legal certainty with regard to jurisdiction. These factors are inter-linked and the

[173] Commission Notice on Case Referral in respect of concentrations (Notice on case referral) [2005] OJ C56/2, para. 3.
[174] Ibid., para. 5.
[175] See also, e.g., Art. 346 TFEU, n. 219 and text.
[176] And/or in which Arts. 101 and 102 can be applied to a concentration by the Commission itself or by a national court or NCA.
[177] [2005] OJ C56/2. See also 'Best Practices on Cooperation between the EU National Competition Authorities', <http://ec.europa.eu/competition/ecn/nca_best_practices_merger_review_en.pdf>.

respective weight placed upon each of them will depend upon the specificities of a particular case. Above all, in considering whether or not to exercise their discretion to make or accede to a referral, the Commission and Member States should bear in mind the need to ensure effective protection of competition in all markets affected by the transaction.

More appropriate authority

9. In principle, jurisdiction should only be re-attributed to another competition agency in circumstances where the latter is the more appropriate for dealing with a merger, having regard to the specific characteristics of the case as well as the tools and expertise available to the agency. Particular regard should be had to the likely locus of any impact on competition resulting from the merger. Regard may also be had to the implications, in terms of administrative effort, of any contemplated referral.

10. The case for re-attributing jurisdiction is likely to be more compelling where it appears that a particular transaction may have a significant impact on competition and thus may deserve careful scrutiny.

One-stop shop

11. Decisions on the referral of cases should also have regard to the benefits inherent in a 'one-stop shop' system, which is at the core of the Merger Regulation. The provision of a one-stop shop is beneficial to competition authorities and businesses alike. The handling of a merger by a single competition agency normally increases administrative efficiency, avoiding duplication and fragmentation of enforcement effort as well as potentially incoherent treatment (regarding investigation, assessment and possible remedies) by multiple authorities. It normally also brings advantages to businesses, in particular to merging firms, by reducing the costs and burdens arising from multiple filing obligations and by eliminating the risk of conflicting decisions resulting from the concurrent assessment of the same transaction by a number of competition authorities under diverse legal regimes.

12. Fragmentation of cases through referral should therefore be avoided where possible, unless it appears that multiple authorities would be in a better position to ensure that competition in all markets affected by the transaction is effectively protected. Accordingly, while postal referrals are possible under Articles 4(4) and 9, it would normally be appropriate for the whole of a case (or at least all connected parts thereof) to be dealt with by a single authority.[178]

Legal certainty

13. Due account should also be taken of the importance of legal certainty regarding jurisdiction over a particular concentration, from the perspective of all concerned. Accordingly, referral should normally only be made when there is a compelling reason for departing from 'original jurisdiction' over the case in question, particularly at the post-notification stage. Similarly, if a referral has been made prior to notification, a post-notification referral in the same case should be avoided to the greatest extent possible.

14. The importance of legal certainty should also be borne in mind with regard to the legal criteria for referral, and particularly—given the tight deadlines—at the pre-notification stage. Accordingly, prefiling referrals should in principle be confined to those cases where it is relatively straightforward to establish, from the outset, the scope of the geographic market and/or the existence of a possible competitive impact, so as to be able to promptly decide upon such requests.

[178] See e.g. M.2389, *Shell/DEA* 20 December 2001 and M.2533, *BP/E.ON* 20 December 2001 (referral to Germany of all of the markets for downstream oil products, 6 December 2001, but retention by the Commission of the parts of the cases involving upstream markets) and M.2706, *P&O Princess/Carnival* 24 July 2002 (Commission did not refer part of the case to the UK, because it wished to avoid a fragmentation of the case, see IP/02/552).

Concentrations with an EU dimension, or aspects of such a concentration, may be dealt with by an NCA pursuant to Article 9 or Article 21(4) of the EUMR, Article 346 TFEU, or following a reasoned submission by a party to a concentration (Article 4(4)).

(iii) Article 9—Distinct Markets

a. Objective of Article 9

Article 21(3), paragraph 2 states that the prohibition on a Member State applying its national competition legislation to a concentration with an EU dimension is 'without prejudice to any Member State's power to carry out any enquiries necessary for the application of Articles 4(4), 9(2) or after referral, pursuant to Article 9(3) first subparagraph, indent (b), or Article 9(5), to take the measures strictly necessary for the application of Article 9(8)'.

Article 9 of the EUMR was included at the particular insistence of Germany (hence it is sometimes referred to as the 'German clause'), which feared that local or regional issues might not be sufficiently addressed by the Commission.[179] Article 9 provides for the referral, at the request of a national authority, of a merger, or aspects of it (i.e. total or partial referrals), to that authority where the concentration threatens competition in a 'distinct' market in that authority's State.

The Notice on case referral recognises that the objective of Article 9 is to ensure, subject to the principle of the one-stop shop and legal certainty, that an NCA should deal with a case when it is in the best position to do so.[180]

b. The Article 9 Procedure

Council Regulation (EC) No. 139/2004 of 20 January 2004 on the Control of Concentrations between Undertakings [2004] OJ L24/1

Article 9

1. The Commission may, by means of a decision notified without delay to the undertakings concerned and the competent authorities of the other Member States, refer a notified concentration to the competent authorities of the Member State concerned in the following circumstances.
2. Within 15 working days of the date of receipt of the copy of the notification, a Member State, on its own initiative or upon the invitation of the Commission, may inform the Commission, which shall inform the undertakings concerned, that:
   (a) a concentration threatens to affect significantly competition in a market within that Member State, which presents all the characteristics of a distinct market, or
   (b) a concentration affects competition in a market within that Member State, which presents all the characteristics of a distinct market and which does not constitute a substantial part of the common market.

[179] EUMR, Art. 2 only permits the Commission to take action against concentrations which would impede competition in 'the common market or in a substantial part of it'.

[180] Notice on case referral, paras. 9–13 and 37 and EUMR, recital 11.

3. If the Commission considers that, having regard to the market for the products or services in question and the geographical reference market within the meaning of paragraph 7, there is such a distinct market and that such a threat exists, either:
   (a) it shall itself deal with the case in accordance with this Regulation, or
   (b) it shall refer the whole or part of the case to the competent authorities of the Member State concerned with a view to the application of that State's national competition law.

   If, however, the Commission considers that such a distinct market or threat does not exist, it shall adopt a decision to that effect which it shall address to the Member State concerned, and shall itself deal with the case in accordance with the Regulation.

   In cases where a Member State informs the Commission pursuant to paragraph 2(b) that a concentration affects competition in a distinct market within its territory that does not form a substantial part of the common market, the Commission shall refer the whole or part of the case relating to the distinct market concerned, if it considers that such a distinct market is affected.

Article 9 is not triggered unless a Member State makes a request, either on its own initiative or on the invitation of the Commission, for a reference back within 15 working days (WDs) of receipt of the copy of the notification from the Commission.

Where the Commission receives a request from a Member State in accordance with Article 9(2)(a), the Commission must determine whether the requesting State has prima facie demonstrated that (a) a distinct market exists[181] and (b) the concentration threatens to affect significantly competition within that Member State. Even where these conditions are satisfied, the Commission has a discretion to deal with the case itself rather than making a (total or partial[182]) referral.[183] It is only in Article 9(2)(b)[184] cases where the Member State has provided preliminary evidence establishing that the concentration affects competition in a distinct market which does not constitute a substantial part of the internal market (markets with a narrow geographic scope)[185] that the Commission *must* refer the whole or part of the case relating to the distinct market.

Except in Article 9(2)(b) cases, the Commission is thus the arbiter of whether or not the matter should be referred to the Member State. Nonetheless, the Commission and NCAs work together to ensure that their respective competences are applied in close cooperation, 'using efficient arrangements for information-sharing and consultation, with a view to ensuring that a case is dealt with by the most appropriate authority, in the light of the principle of subsidiarity and with a view to ensuring that multiple notifications of a given concentration are avoided to the greatest extent possible'.[186] This means that a partial or full referral back is made in a vast majority of cases.[187]

[181] Whether a distinct market exists is determined with regard to the market for the products or services in question and, in particular, the geographical reference market; an area 'in which the undertakings concerned are involved in the supply and demand of products or services, in which the conditions of competition are sufficiently homogeneous and which can be distinguished from neighbouring areas because, in particular, conditions of competition are appreciably different in those areas', Art. 9(7) EUMR.

[182] See M.180, *Steetley plc/Tarmac* discussed in n. 197 and accompanying text.

[183] EUMR, Art. 9(3). Notice on case referral [2005] OJ C56/2, para. 37.

[184] Notice on case referral, ibid., paras. 38–41.

[185] It is thus a relatively narrow provision. The first Art. 9(2)(b) reference made was M.2446, *Govia/Connex South Central* 20 July 2001. See also M.2730, *Connex/DNVBVG* 24 April 2001 and M.3130, *Arla Foods/Express Dairies* 10 June 2003.

[186] EUMR, recital 14.

[187] At the end of October 2022, only 15 out of 130 requests had been refused, see <https://competition-policy.ec.europa.eu/mergers/statistics_en>.

c. A Reference Back

The Commission's decision to refer, or not, must generally be taken within 35 WDs of notification, or 65 WDs where Phase II proceedings have been initiated.[188] If the Commission does make a reference to the national authority that authority must decide the case 'without undue delay' and, in any event, must inform the undertakings concerned of the result of the preliminary competition assessment and what further action it proposes to take within 45 WDs of the Commission's referral (or national notification if requested).[189]

Insofar as a reference is made, the Commission delegates power to investigate to the Member State which may only take 'measures strictly necessary to safeguard or restore effective competition on the market concerned'.[190]

d. Examples of Article 9 Decisions

Although a reference back under Article 9 is not guaranteed,[191] it is likely to result in a full or partial referral back where, for example, it raises specific issues in a Member State[192] or regional[193] or local[194] markets. In *ProSiebenSat.1/RTL/JV*,[195] the Commission partially referred back aspects of the concentration to *two* authorities—the German and Austrian agencies—who it considered were well placed to investigate the impact of the transaction in their respective national markets.

In many cases, a decision to make a reference to a national authority may cause concern to the notifying parties as the reference is unlikely to be requested unless the concentration is considered to pose particular risks for the distinct national market affected.[196]

The first case in which the Commission agreed to make a reference back was *Steetley plc/Tarmac*.[197] In this case, competing bids had been made for Steetley plc by Tarmac and Redland. The Tarmac bid, which had an EU dimension (the Redland bid fell to be assessed in the UK), would have pooled the building materials activities of the undertakings and conferred very high market shares on the merged entity for bricks and clay tiles in some regions of England. The Commission accepted that the concentration would lead to particular local problems in the market for the manufacture and sale of bricks and the manufacture of clay tiles,[198] and that the economic implications in relation to these products were substantially limited to the UK. The Commission issued a decision referring these

[188] EUMR, Arts. 9(4) and 10(1). See M.330, *McCormick/CPC/Ostmann* 29 October 1993.

[189] Ibid., Art. 9(6). [190] Ibid., Art. 9(8).

[191] See e.g. M.165, *Alcatel/AEG Kabel* 18 December 1991; M.238, *Siemens/Philips* (subsequently abandoned); M.7000, *Liberty Global/Ziggo* 25 June 2014; and M.7018, *Telefónica Deutschland/E-Plus* 30 January 2014.

[192] See e.g. M.5996, *Thomas Cook/CGL and Midland* 6 January 2011.

[193] See e.g. M.3373, *Accor/Barrière/Colony* 4 June 2004 and M.3905, *Tesco/Carrefour* 22 December 2005.

[194] See e.g. M.2533, *BP/E.ON* 6 September 2001 and M.2730, *Connex/DNVBVG* 24 April 2001.

[195] M.5881, 24 September 2010.

[196] See M.2044, *Interbrew/Bass* [2000] OJ C293/11, in the UK, Interbrew SA and Bass plc: *A report on the acquisition by Interbrew SA of the brewing interests of Bass plc* (Cm. 5014, 2001) (recommendation that the transaction should be prohibited, but permitted subject to conditions following judicial review, *Interbrew SA and Interbrew UK Holdings Ltd v Competition Commission and Secretary of State for Trade and Industry* [2001] EWHC Admin 367), M. 3905, *Tesco/Carrefour* 22 December 2005 (approved by the Commission but Slovakian acquisitions prohibited following an Art. 9(2)(b) referral of part). But see M.460, *Holdercim/Cedest* [1994] OJ C211/5 (the French authorities cleared aspects of a concentration which had been referred to it under Art. 9), M.3130, *Express Dairies/Arla Foods* 10 June 2003 (cleared by the UK authorities: DTI Press Release, 15 October 2003), and discussion of *SEB/Moulinex*, n. 200 and accompanying text.

[197] M.180, 12 February 1992. A number of Art. 9 referrals have involved the building or construction industries, see also e.g. M.4298, *Aggregate Industries/Foster Yeoman* 6 September 2006.

[198] The Commission also considered the fact that a competing bid was being assessed at the domestic level.

aspects of the merger back to the UK and a decision finding that the remaining aspects of the concentration were compatible with the internal market.[199]

An Article 9 case which illustrates the difficulties that can result from dual scrutiny in derogation of the one-stop shop principle is *SEB/Moulinex*.[200] In this case, SEB proposed to purchase Moulinex, which was in the midst of bankruptcy proceedings. Both companies were French and operated in the small household electrical appliances business. The Commission appraised the concentration insofar as it affected 14 countries,[201] but made a partial reference to the French authorities (under Article 9(2)(a)) as the primary effects of the merger were to be felt in France. Although the Commission cleared the merger subject to commitments (rejecting the failing firm defence[202]), the French authorities went on to unconditionally clear it, applying its 'failing firm' defence, even though the combined entity would achieve an average of 60–70 per cent market share on segments of the French small electrical household appliances market[203] Eventually, however, the French administrative court (Conseil d'État)[204] annulled the French authorities' authorisation, holding that the failing firm conditions had not in fact been fulfilled.

Two competitors of the merging parties, BaByliss and Royal Philips, challenged both the Commission's appraisal of the aspects of the transaction it considered (which was successful), and its decision to refer the concentration to the national authority (unsuccessful).[205] In relation to the latter, the GC held that it was not at liberty to rule on the compatibility of the French authority's decision with the Commission's approval decision (or with EU law), *only* on whether the Commission was entitled to refer the concentration to the French authorities, i.e. whether the conditions of Article 9(2)(a) were satisfied and, if so, whether the Commission had properly exercised its discretion. The fact that the referral fragmented the examination of the concentration and interfered with the one-stop shop principle did not affect the conclusion since 'a fragmented assessment undermining the "one-stop shop" principle is inherent in the referral procedure'.[206]

The Commission has to exercise its discretion carefully, if it is not to rob the one-stop shop principle of its substance and add to the length and cost of the review unnecessarily;[207] and the GC has made it clear that such references should only be made in exceptional circumstances.[208] In a series of cases, the Commission has made it clear that it will be reluctant to make references back in the telecommunications sector, given the importance of the sector to development of competition in the EU and its experience in assessing such mergers.[209]

(iv) Article 4(4) Request for Referral to a National Competition Authority

Article 4(4) (discussed in Section 4) allows notifying parties, instead of notifying a concentration with an EU dimension to the Commission, to make a reasoned submission that a concentration may

[199] M.180, 12 February 1992. [200] M.2621, IP/02/22.

[201] Ibid., annulled on appeal Case T-119/02, *Royal Philips Electronics v Commission* EU:T:2003:101 (insofar as it had cleared the concentration without commitments in five Member States). The Commission subsequently reopened the case and again cleared it unconditionally.

[202] Ibid. For a discussion of the failing firm defence, see Section 5.E.vii. The next application for an Art. 9 reference by the French authorities was rejected, see M.2978, *Lagardère/Natexis/VUP*, IP/03/808.

[203] Despite the objectives of Art. 9 (to allow Member States to look at mergers where the effects are likely to be particularly acute in the national market), the French authority approved the concentration unconditionally whilst the Commission did so only after commitments had been offered, Case T-119/02, *Royal Philips Electronics v Commission* EU:T:2003:101, para. 345.

[204] No. 249627, 6 February 2004. [205] Case T-119/02, *Royal Philips Electronics v Commission* EU:T:2003:101.

[206] Ibid., para. 355. See also Cases T-346 and 347/02, *Cableuropa v Commission* EU:T:2003:256.

[207] [2005] OJ C56/2. [208] Case T-119/02, *Royal Philips Electronics v Commission* EU:T:2003:101.

[209] The Commission rejected Germany's request to review the merger between Telefónica and E-Plus, see M.7018, *Telefónica Deutschland/E-Plus* 30 January 2014.

significantly affect competition in a distinct market in a Member State and should be examined in whole or in part by that Member State. In contrast with an Article 9 request, it is thus lodged *by* the parties themselves and *prior* to notification.

(v) Article 21(4)—Legitimate Interests

Article 21(4) recognises that there are some matters which are so sensitive to the national interest that the Member States should be entitled to retain control over them. Under Article 21(4), a Member State may take steps to protect 'legitimate interests' not protected under the EUMR itself:

> Notwithstanding paragraphs 2 and 3, Member States may take appropriate measures to protect legitimate interests other than those taken into consideration by this Regulation and compatible with the general principles and other provisions of EU law.
>
> Public security, plurality of the media and prudential rules shall be regarded as legitimate interests within the meaning of the first subparagraph.
>
> Any other public interest must be communicated to the Commission by the Member State concerned and shall be recognised by the Commission after an assessment of its compatibility with the general principles and other provisions of EU law before the measures referred to above may be taken. The Commission shall inform the Member State concerned of its decision within 25 working days of that communication.

Indeed, Member States are becoming increasingly sensitive about these issues, and some are becoming more willing to nurture national champions and to protect them from foreign takeovers.[210] A few important points about Article 21(4) should be noted.

First, to date, it has only been used defensively—to enable a Member State to protect its legitimate interests by scrutinising, and, if necessary, *prohibiting* mergers which raise concerns other than purely competition ones (even if cleared under the EUMR). It does not seem to allow a Member State, as it can where the EUMR does not apply,[211] to authorise a merger on public interest grounds (even if it is problematic from a competition perspective,[212] see also the discussion of *Siemens/Alstom*[213]).

Secondly, in cases of uncertainty as to whether one of the recognised legitimate interests set out in Article 21(4) applies, whether such measures conform with EU law,[214] or where a Member State wishes to act to protect any other public interest, the Member State must notify it to the Commission.[215] The Commission may thus consider whether the narrow criteria of Article 21(4) are satisfied. The interest to be protected, if not a recognised interest, must be a 'public' interest which is not protected by the EUMR itself (it is not a 'competition' interest). In addition, the measures taken must be compatible with EU law, particularly the rules on freedom of establishment and free movement of capital rules (Articles 49 and 63 TFEU). These provisions impose substantial constraints on the ability of a Member State to impose 'restrictions' on free movement (the capital provisions apply to restrictions on movement not only between Member States but also between Member States and third

[210] For a discussion on the position in Hungary and Poland, see e.g. M. Bernatt, *Populism and Antitrust. The Illiberal Influence of Populist Government on the Competition Law System* (Cambridge University Press, 2022).

[211] See Section 3.D. [212] This seems consistent with principle of supremacy of EU law, see Jones and Davies, n. 12.

[213] M.8677, *Siemens/Alstom* 6 February 2019, n. 496 and text.

[214] See e.g. M.1616, *BSCH/A.Champalimaud* [1999] OJ C306/37, para. 66.

[215] EUMR, Art. 21(4) and M.1616, ibid.

countries),[216] for example through prohibiting, submitting to conditions, or prejudicing, investments through shareholding, mergers, and acquisitions. Such measures are incompatible with EU law unless the Member State can show that the measure is both: (a) justifiable, either on the basis of one of the specific Treaty-based exceptions or the Court-recognised justifications—the overriding requirements of public interest; and (b) proportionate.[217]

An inextricable and important link thus exists between 'legitimate interests', within the meaning of Article 21(4), and the exceptions and justifications that apply to the free movement of capital and freedom of establishment rules. If the national rules 'restrict' free movement of capital and/or freedom of establishment and do not fall within one of the exceptions or justifications to those rules, it will not be permitted under Article 21(4). The legitimate interest pursued must therefore constitute a valid public interest justification within the meaning of those rules. The close link between the concept of legitimate interest under Article 21(4) and the free movement provisions is reinforced by the fact that the recognised interests (public security, plurality of the media, and prudential rules) are concepts whose specific meaning have been developed under free movement law.

In a number of cases, the Commission has accepted that Member States may take action to: protect defence policy or military security[218] (the Member States also have a general right, set out in Article 346 TFEU, to act to protect national security[219]); maintain diversified sources of information, plurality of opinion, and a multiplicity of views in media markets;[220] or safeguard 'prudential rules' (aiming to ensure, for example, capital adequacy requirements (solvency) and the good repute and honesty of those running the company concerned).[221] In *Newspaper Publishing*,[222] for example, although the proposed acquisition of Newspaper Publishing plc (publisher of the *Independent*) by Promotora de Informaciones SA, Editoriale l'Espresson SpA, and Mirror Group Newspapers plc fell within the scope of the EUMR, the UK was able to take steps to protect its legitimate interests, in this case the plurality of the media.[223] Any measures adopted by the UK authorities had, however, to be objectively the least restrictive to achieve the end pursued (to comply with the EU principle of

216 Uniquely amongst the four freedoms the capital rules have applied to restrictions on flows between EU and third countries, albeit subject to a less liberalised framework, see also n. 22 and text.

217 See Jones and Davies, n. 12.

218 See e.g. M.1858, *Thomson CSF/Racal (II)* 15 June 2000 (impacting on defence electronics markets), M.336, *IBM France/CGI* 19 May 1993 (involving IT businesses, including hardware, software, and services), M.3418, *General Dynamics/Alvis* 26 May 2004 (involving British armoured combat vehicles), M.3720, *BAE Systems/AMS* 14 March 2005 (involving defence and commercial aerospace systems and BAE's communications and avionics business), and M.4561, *GE/Smiths Aerospace* 23 April 2007 (involving Smiths Group's aerospace division).

219 EUMR, recital 19 makes it clear that the Regulation (and in particular Art. 21(4)) does not affect a Member State's ability to act under Art. 346 TFEU. A list of arms referred to by Art. 346 TFEU was adopted by the Council (Decision 255/58). When acting under Art. 346 TFEU, Member States, instead of acting in addition to the Commission under the EUMR (as is the case under EUMR, Art. 21(4)), have generally instructed firms not to notify the exclusively military aspects of the deal to the Commission at all, see e.g. M.528, *British Aerospace/VSEL* 24 November 1994 and M.529, *GEC/VSEL* 7 December 1994. If the Commission considers that a Member State is making improper use of these powers it may take the matter directly before the Court under Art. 348 TFEU.

220 See e.g. M.423, *Newspaper Publishing* 14 March 1984 and M.5932, *NewsCorp/BSkyB* 21 December 2010, paras. 304–309.

221 See the Commission's Notes on Council Regulation (EEC) 4064/89 (prudential interests should be understood to cover, e.g. measures to ensure the good repute of individuals managing such undertakings, the honesty of transactions, and the rules of solvency) and M.1724, *BSCH/A.Champalimaud* 20 July 1999, para. 36 (EU harmonising provisions should also be taken into account to determine the EU notion of prudential interest which should include interests protected by harmonising Directives).

222 M.423, 14 March 1984.

223 A number of States consider that media ownership may require a different approach from that ordinarily applicable in domestic competition law.

proportionality). In *Thomson CSF/Racal (II)*,[224] the UK authorities also stated an intention to consider the public security aspects of a concentration impacting on 'defence electronics' markets under Article 21(4) and in *Sun Alliance/Royal Insurance*[225] the Commission accepted that the UK authorities could apply UK insurance legislation to the transaction.

By analogy with the free movement rules, it also seems that public security would encompass proportionate measures to counter a genuine and sufficiently serious threat to the security of supplies of a product or service which is of fundamental importance for the existence of, or survival of those in, that Member State (such as oil, gas, water, electricity, telecommunications)[226] or of vital or essential interest for the population's health.[227] In *Lyonnaise des Eaux SA/Northumbrian Water Group*,[228] for example, the Commission accepted that the regulation of the UK water industry constituted a legitimate interest. In accepting the legitimate interests of the UK, however, the Commission stressed that the UK authorities should not, in their scrutiny of the concentration, take account of factors properly falling for assessment by the Commission.[229]

Thirdly, although, to ensure the *effet utile* of the EUMR, non-recognised interests must be notified to the Commission, in some cases Members States have not complied with the notification and the stand-still obligation in circumstances where the Commission believes that the conditions of Article 21(4) are not satisfied. An important ruling therefore is *Portuguese Republic v Commission*,[230] where the Court confirmed that, even if no communication is made by the Member State to the Commission, the Commission is still entitled to adopt a decision under Article 21 assessing whether measures taken by a Member State are compatible with Article 21(4) and requiring a Member State to withdraw measures which it finds are not. Otherwise, Member States could easily avoid the scrutiny of the Commission and national measures could irretrievably prejudice a merger with an EU dimension.[231]

In practice, therefore, where the Commission believes that a Member State has violated the exclusivity provisions of the EUMR, it communicates this preliminary view to the Member State and gives it a chance to respond, before issuing an Article 21 decision.[232] For example, it contested the Spanish authorities' actions in relation to competing bids for Spanish electricity operator, Endesa. In that case, the Commission had cleared E.ON's and ENEL/Acciona's respective bids under the EUMR[233] (a third bid (which was supported by the Spanish Government) by Spanish Gas Natural, did not have an EU dimension and was appraised by the Spanish competition authorities). Nonetheless, the Spanish authorities imposed conditions on the approved transactions under regulatory powers. In its Article 21

[224] M.1858, 15 June 2000. See also e.g. M.4561, *GE/Smiths Group* 23 April 2007 where the Commission approved GE's proposed acquisition of Smiths Group's aerospace division. The UK Secretary of State intervened under EUMR, Art. 21(4), but eventually accepted undertakings from the parties rather than referring it to the UK's Competition Commission.

[225] M.759 [1996] OJ C225/12. [226] See Case 72/83, *Campus Oil* EU:C:1984:256.

[227] See the Commission's Notes on Council Regulation (EEC) 4064/89, n. 221. An important issue is also likely to be whether 'sustainability' is a legitimate interest for the purposes of Art. 21(4).

[228] M.567 [1996] OJ C11/3 (as the UK water authority sought to maintain competitive pressures on water suppliers (enjoying a monopoly in the provision of local or regional services) by making comparisons of, for example, the relative operating and capital costs of the different water enterprises, a sufficient number of independent providers had to be maintained.) Contrast M.1346, *EDF/London Electricity* 27 January 1999.

[229] M.567, ibid. [230] Case C-42/01, *Portuguese Republic v Commission* EU:C:2004:379.

[231] Ibid., para. 55.

[232] 'Our line is clear: if interference by any Member State—is not justified by a legitimate public interest, the Commission will continue to condemn such national measures': SPEECH/07/301, N. Kroes, 'European competition policy facing a renaissance of protectionism–which strategy for the future?', Speech to the St Gallen International Competition Law Forum, 11 May 2007.

[233] Cases M.4110 and M.4197, *E.ON/Endesa* 25 April 2006, 26 September, and 20 December 2006, Case T-200/06, *Iberdrola v Commission* (appeal withdrawn) and M.4685, *ENEL/Acciona/Endesa* 5 July 2007.

EUMR decisions,[234] the Commission found that the actions were not justified by a need to protect the security of supply risks alleged and were contrary to the capital and establishment provisions and required Spain to withdraw them without delay. Public security could be relied on only if there were a genuine and sufficiently serious threat to a fundamental interest of society, such as ensuring a minimum level of energy supplies in the event of a crisis. As the measures were not withdrawn, the Commission eventually brought enforcement proceedings against Spain under Article 258 TFEU (the general Treaty mechanism empowering the Commission to bring proceedings against Member States infringing EU law). The Court confirmed that, by not withdrawing conditions to the E.ON merger, Spain had failed to fulfil its Treaty obligations.[235]

In *BSCH/A.Champalimaud*,[236] the Commission also found that Portugal had improperly applied Article 21(4) of the EUMR to a transaction in the insurance sector. The Portuguese Minister of Finance relied on measures restricting a foreign firm from acquiring in excess of 20 per cent of domestic insurance firms to prohibit a proposed concentration with an EU dimension between Banco Santander Central Hispano (BSCH), a Spanish banking group, and Champalimaud (which was ultimately cleared by the Commission). The Portuguese authorities had not communicated any public interest to the Commission but in press statements had stated that they had acted to protect national interests and strategic sectors for the national economy. The Commission considered that the Government should have notified its actions to it and that the protection of national interests and strategic sectors for the national economy could not constitute a legitimate interest within the meaning of Article 21(4). Further, it entertained considerable doubt as to whether the actions were really based on prudential rules rather than constituting a discriminatory measure designed to prevent the opening of the financial services sector to non-nationals. The Commission thus ordered the Republic of Portugal to suspend the measures adopted and to notify them to it as required. In the end, the Portuguese authorities agreed to the modified arrangements which were also cleared by the Commission under the EUMR.[237]

Similarly, the Commission concluded that a decision by Hungary to veto, under emergency FDI legislation introduced during the Covid-19 pandemic, the acquisition (approved by the Commission[238]) of Hungarian subsidiaries of the AEGON Group by Vienna Insurance Group infringed Article 21.[239] The Commission had reasonable doubts that the veto was genuinely aimed at protecting Hungary's legitimate interests or that the transaction posed a threat to a fundamental interest of society, given that VIG and AEGON were well-established EU insurance companies.

Although there have been a number of cases in which Member State have successfully relied on recognised interests to scrutinise a merger for its impact on non-competition factors, recognition of other legitimate interests has been rare. This is important, especially since several Member States have revamped and expanded their foreign investment review laws. The new EU Regulation governing FDI provides for cooperation between Member States in screening investments, but only in relation to those coming from non-EU Member States.[240]

[234] See *E.ON/Endesa*, n. 233, and *ENEL/Acciona/Endesa*, n. 233.

[235] Case C-196/07, *Commission v Spain* EU:C:2008:146 and see n. 232. Eventually the ENEL/Acciona bid did prevail.

[236] See Cases M.1616, M.1680, and M.1724, *BSCH/A.Champalimaud (1999)*, IP/99/669, IP/99/772, IP/99/774 and IP/99/818, IP/00/296 (withdrawing the EUMR, Art. 21 proceedings).

[237] See also e.g. *Cimpor*, C(2000)3543 final (challenge to the actions of Portugal, in relation to a proposed acquisition of Portuguese cement business, Cimpor, a former State-owned entity) and M.3894, *Unicredito/HVB*, IP/05/1299 (infringement of Art. 21 by Poland in relation to a merger which had been cleared by the Commission but in which the Polish Treasury Minister intervened in order to protect the 'privatisation' process of Polish banks and to ensure the de-monopolisation of, and the protection of competition in, the financial and banking services, M.4125, IP/06/277).

[238] M.10494, 12 August 2021.

[239] M.10494, 21 February 2022.

[240] See n. 44 and text.

D. CONCENTRATIONS WITHOUT AN EU DIMENSION

(i) National Law Applies

Article 21(1) provides that the EUMR alone applies to 'concentrations' and disapplies Regulation 1/2003 and the other implementing regulations that confer power on the Commission and NCAs to implement Articles 101 and 102. The general principle is thus that national competition law *only* applies to concentrations which do not have an EU dimension.[241]

The application of national merger rules must, however, be compatible with EU law more generally, and must not impose restrictions on freedom of establishment and free movement of capital unless justifiable and proportionate (see the discussion in the previous section on Article 21(4)).[242] The free movement rules are, however, triggered only by restrictions and do not, therefore, appear to preclude a Member State from, for example, exercising regulatory *approval* of mergers between domestic companies on public interest grounds (as is permitted in a number of Member States), even if the application of such rules might result in the creation of a national champion at the expense of competition and the interest of consumer welfare within the EU. Indeed, there is some concern that in some cases Member States have applied national law to permit mergers without an EU dimension (most likely because of the two-thirds rules) which are liable to harm competition throughout the EU and that this is a growing risk in the current climate.

For example, the German Government's decision to overrule the decision of the German NCA and authorise a merger between energy companies *E.ON/Ruhrgas*[243] and hence the creation of a national champion, caused considerable consternation. Further, during the 2008 financial crisis, the UK Government stepped in to support and permit a merger which did not have an EU dimension between Lloyds TSB and HBOS.[244] Controversially, the Government considered that the public interest in the stability of the UK financial system outweighed the concerns of the competition agency that the merger might substantially lessen competition in relation to banking services and the provision of mortgages in the UK.

(ii) Joint Ventures

Article 21(1) itself makes it clear that there is an exception, for full-function JVs with coordinative aspects, to the general position that no EU competition law applies to concentrations which do not have an EU dimension.[245]

(iii) Article 22, Referrals to the Commission

a. Background

Article 22, known as the 'Dutch clause',[246] also derogates from the general rule that concentrations without an EU dimension may be appraised only at the national level. The Article provides a mechanism by which one or more Member States may request the Commission to examine a concentration which does not have

[241] The prohibition, in Art. 21(3), on a Member State applying its national legislation on competition applies only where the concentration has an EU dimension. But see discussion in Section 3.E on the residual role of Arts. 101 and 102 TFEU.

[242] See Jones and Davies, n. 12. [243] E.On eventually acquired Ruhras in 2003.

[244] 31 October 2008, see OFT, *Anticipated acquisition by Lloyds TSB plc of HBOS plc Report to the Secretary of State for Business Enterprise and Regulatory Reform* (2008).

[245] See Chap. 10. [246] The clause having been inserted at the request of the Dutch.

an EU dimension but affects trade between Member States and where it has been prima facie established that the concentration significantly affects competition within the territory of the requesting State.[247]

Article 22 was originally included to enable Member States without merger control rules to refer troublesome concentrations, from a competition perspective, to the Commission.[248] As most Member States now have merger control rules,[249] for a number of years it has principally been used as a corrective mechanism for cases in which a Member State or States have jurisdiction but the Commission is better placed to review the cross-border effects and where the transaction presents a real risk of negative effects on competition and trade between Member States[250] (*Promatech SpA/Sulzer AG*[251] was the first case of a joint referral to the Commission made by the authorities of Spain, Italy, the UK, Germany, France, Portugal, and Austria and a number of joint referrals have been made subsequently, see, for example, *GEES/Unison*,[252] *GE/AGFA NDT*,[253] *Omya/Huber*,[254] *Caterpillar/MWM*,[255] *Sara Lee (Insecticides* and *Airfresheners)*,[256] and *Apple/Shazam*[257]).

In March 2021, however, the Commission issued guidance recommending that Article 22 also be used to fill the jurisdictional gap that exists at the EU level in relation to acquisitions of start-ups (with low turnover).[258] The guidance states that the mechanism should be used by Member States, even if they do not have jurisdiction, to refer concentrations to the Commission where the legal criteria of Article 22 are satisfied and where the turnover of one of the parties does not reflect its competitive potential and, consequently, the loss to competition or innovation, or access to key inputs, which is threatened by the transaction. Further, that when considering whether to accept a referral in situations where the transaction is not notifiable under the laws of the referring Member States, the Commission will take account of the value of the transaction (the consideration to be paid for the target). Article 22 has already been used to make references in these circumstances, for example in *Illumina/Grail*[259] (request from France, joined by Belgium, Greece, Iceland, the Netherlands, and Norway in circumstances where the proposed transaction did not meet EU thresholds and was not notified in any Member State).[260] The Commission considered the referral to be appropriate given

[247] Art. 22(1), Notice on case referral, paras. 42–45.

[248] Indeed three of the first four Art. 22 references were made by Member States which did not have merger control rules and all three of these concentrations were prohibited by the Commission, see M.553, *RTL/Veronica/Endemol* [1996] OJ L294/14 (*aff'd* Case T-221/95, *Endemol Entertainment Holding BV v Commission* EU:T:1999:85), M.784, *Kesko/Tuko* [1997] OJ L174/47 (request by the Finnish NCA. The Commission prohibited the concentration and, as the acquisition had already taken place, ordered Kesko to divest itself of the Tuko business, *aff'd* Case T-22/99, *Kesko Oy v Commission* EU:T:2000:47), and M.890, *Blokker/Toys 'R' Us* [1998] OJ L316/1. The fourth was made by Belgium which wished the Commission to intervene in the *British Airways/Dan Air* merger (M.278, 17 February 1993, cleared unconditionally). The Belgian authorities did not have jurisdiction to preclude a merger between two UK companies.

[249] Only Luxembourg does not have merger control rules.

[250] Notice on case referral, para. 45.

[251] M.2698, IP/02/1140.

[252] M.2738, *GEES/Unison*, IP/02/578 (referral requests from the authorities of Germany, France, Spain, Italy, the UK, and Greece—the merger was cleared by the Commission on 14 April 2002).

[253] M.3136, IP/03/1666 (Art. 6 clearance subject to conditions and obligations).

[254] M.3796, IP/06/1017.

[255] M.6106, 26 January 2011 (full referral), 19 October 2011.

[256] Cases M.5969, 9 May 2011 and M.5828, 31 March and 17 June 2010. As the Commission has cleared a number of these unconditionally it has been speculated that the Commission may be accepting these requests too readily, see e.g. G. Drauz, S. Mavroghenis, and S. Ashall, 'Recent Developments in EU Merger Control' (2012) 3 *JECLAP* 52, 65.

[257] M.8788, 6 September 2018.

[258] On 12 December 2022, the Commission also published some Frequently Asked Questions and Answers on the application of Art. 22 EUMR. Some Member States, including Germany, have indicated that they would not refer a case to the Commission if they did not have jurisdiction over the merger.

[259] M.10188.

[260] See also discussion of Case C-449/21, *Towercast v Autorité de la Concurrence* EU:C:2023:207 in Section 3.E.ii. An Art. 22 request was also made in M.10262, *Facebook (Meta)/Kustomer* although in this case the request was made by Austria, which had jurisdiction, and joined by Belgium, Bulgaria, France, Iceland, Ireland, Italy, the Netherlands, Portugal, and Romania, see also n. 266.

that the proposed transaction affected trade within the single market, threatened to significantly affect competition within the territory of the referring Member States, and that Grail's competitive significance was not reflected in its turnover. Although the parties challenged the use of the Article 22 procedure in these circumstances, the GC upheld the Commission's competence confirming that the Commission's jurisdiction over concentrations derives not only from turnover thresholds but also from the EUMR referral mechanisms (which are necessary to ensure effective control of mergers which may have a significant effect on competition in the EU).[261]

Despite the Commission's attempts to ensure that the guidance provides a degree of predictability as to when references should be made and accepted, the approach has created disquiet: increased uncertainty for firms when concluding merger transactions; concern that the carefully crafted jurisdictional rules set out in the EUMR and national merger control systems have been undermined; and complaints that a transaction value jurisdictional threshold or informal voluntary notification system has been introduced through the back door. A particular problem is that, given the broad category of transactions potentially affected, and that NCAs are able to make referrals to the Commission up to 15 WDs from the date on which the concentration was notified, or otherwise made known,[262] to it, there is little clarity as to when the risk of a referral will end, and so when the concentration can be safely completed.

b. The Article 22 Procedure

A Member State making an Article 22 request, on its own initiative or at the invitation of the Commission, must do so within 15 WDs of the date on which the concentration was notified, or otherwise made known, to it. The procedure does not, therefore, prevent the parties from having to make national notifications (and perhaps multiple ones) prior to the request or requests being made.[263]

Where a request is made by a Member State under Article 22, the Commission must inform the competent authorities of all the Member States and the undertakings concerned of the request without delay. At this time all applicable national time limits are suspended and, to the extent that the concentration has not been implemented, the suspensory provisions in Article 7 apply.[264] Once such a notice is received, the other Member States have 15 WDs to decide if they would like to join the initial request. If a Member State decides not to join the request and informs the Commission the suspension of its national time limit ends.

Within 25 WDs of informing the Member States and undertakings of the initial request, the Commission may decide to examine the concentration (if it does not adopt a decision within this time period it is deemed to have accepted the request). If it does accept the request the referring Member States retain no control over the Commission's investigation[265] and they may no longer apply their national competition rules (jurisdiction ceases). The Commission may require notification from the parties. If so, the time periods set out in Article 10 run as usual from the date of notification. Where notification is not required the time periods run from the WD after the Commission informs the undertakings that it has decided to examine the concentration. Although the Commission is empowered to proceed as if the merger itself had an EU dimension, the transaction may also be

[261] Case T-227/21, *Illumina v Commission* EU:T:2022:447, paras. 83–185, Cases C-611 and 625/22 P, judgment pending.

[262] Case T-227/21, ibid. (it is made known when the Member State has enough information, actively transmitted to it, to make an assessment of whether the criteria for referral are met, para. 204).

[263] But see Art. 4(5) (enabling parties to make a reasoned submission to the Commission *prior* to notification at the national level), discussed in Section 4.B.

[264] See Section 4.C.

[265] Case T-221/95, *Endemol Entertainment Holding BV v Commission* EU:T:1999:85, para. 42.

scrutinised at the national level by Member States that did not join in the referral.[266] With the aim of better implementing the one-stop shop principle, the 2004 EUMR sought to simplify and clarify the Article 22 procedure (and to deal with its procedural and operational weaknesses).[267]

(iv) Article 4(5), Request for a Referral to the Commission

Article 4(5) (discussed in Section 4) provides a mechanism for parties to a concentration which does not have an EU dimension and which is capable of being reviewed under the national competition laws of at least three Member States, to request that the Commission should examine the concentration *prior* to national notification.

E. A RESIDUAL ROLE FOR ARTICLES 101 AND 102 OF THE TREATY

(i) The Relevance of Articles 101 and 102 TFEU

It has been seen that prior to the enactment of the EUMR the Commission used both Articles 102 and 101 to conduct *ex-post* reviews of transactions which would now amount to a 'concentration'. Further, that subject to certain provisos and exceptions, the general rule is that the EUMR alone should apply to concentrations which have an EU dimension and that national law alone should apply to concentrations which do not. The purpose is to exclude the possible application of Article 101 or Article 102 to concentrations altogether.

The difficulty is that the EUMR disapplies only the implementing legislation, which delegates responsibility for the enforcement of the rules to the Commission. It cannot disapply Articles 101 and 102, Treaty provisions.

(ii) The Commission, National Competition Authorities, and National Courts

A question which thus arises is whether the Commission, an NCA, or a national court (in the context of private litigation) could apply Articles 101 and 102 to a concentration.[268]

Article 105 authorises the Commission to investigate a breach of Article 101 or Article 102 on its own initiative or at the request of a Member State. Although the Commission has never made use of Article 105 in this way, it could in theory do so,[269] albeit without powers conferred on it by Regulation 1/2003.

Article 104 authorises the competition authorities of the Member States to act when no implementing legislation applies.[270] Where a concentration has an EU dimension it had been understood that, since the parties are obliged to notify such concentrations to the Commission, the jurisdiction of the Member States is denied.[271] It was less clear, however, whether jurisdiction exists in relation

[266] See e.g. M/10626, *Meta/Kustomer* (a referral by Austria was joined by nine other Member States, but the transaction was also reviewed in Germany which did not join the referral).

[267] See 2001 Green Paper on the Review of Council Regulation (EEC) No. 4064/89, COM(2001) 745/6 final, 25–26 and EUMR, recital 12.

[268] These provisions are discussed in Chap. 2.

[269] If the concentration does have an EU dimension it will in any event be examining the transaction under the provisions of the EUMR.

[270] The competent national authorities' power to apply Arts. 101 and 102 TFEU by Reg. 1/2003, Art. 5 is disapplied.

[271] See the Opinion of Kokott AG in Case C-449/21, *Towercast v Autorité de la Concurrence* EU:C:2022:777, although the CJ was less clear as to whether Art. 102 could be applied to a concentration with an EU dimension, see nn. 273–274 and text and Chap. 7, Section 14.F.

to a concentration that does not have an EU dimension, as then, generally, neither the provisions of the EUMR nor those of Regulation 1/2003 apply.[272] In *Towercast v Autorité de la Concurrence*,[273] the CJ had an opportunity to shed light on these matters. In this case, an applicant sought annulment of the French NCA's decision refusing to examine an acquisition by TDF of a competitor company for its compatibility with Article 102. Although the transaction constituted a concentration, it did not have an EU dimension, it had not been reviewed by the French NCA under French merger control rules (it fell below French turnover thresholds), and had not been referred to the Commission under Article 22 of the EUMR. The French Cour d'appel de Paris asked the CJ whether, in these circumstances, Article 21(1) of the EUMR had to be interpreted as precluding an NCA from regarding the concentration as an abuse of a dominant position in a national market. In March 2023, the CJ issued a judgment, agreeing with its Advocate General that Article 21(1) did not preclude the NCA, using its own procedural rules, from applying Article 102 to a concentration involving a dominant undertaking, which falls below the EUMR, and national merger control, jurisdictional thresholds, and where an Article 22 EUMR referral has not been made. In these circumstances, Article 102 may apply to the transaction if the degree of dominance reached by that undertaking would substantially impede competition, and where only undertakings whose behaviour depends on the dominant firm remain in the market.[274] In so ruling, the CJ stressed Article 102's importance as a provision of primary, directly effective EU law (but without making crystal clear whether, and if so when, Article 102 could be applied where the transaction had already been reviewed under EU, or national, merger rules or what remedies, structural or behavioural, should be applied in the event of a finding of an Article 102 infringement). It also reiterated that Article 102 creates rights for individuals which national courts must protect and declined to limit the temporal effect of its ruling.

Case C-449/21, *Towercast v Autorité de la Concurrence* EU:C:2023:207

Court of Justice

Consideration of the question referred

30 By its question, the referring court asks whether Article 21(1) of Regulation No 139/2004 is to be interpreted as precluding a national competition authority from regarding a concentration of undertakings which has no Community dimension within the meaning of Article 1 thereof, is below the thresholds for mandatory *ex ante* control laid down in national law, and has not been referred to the Commission under Article 22 of that regulation, as constituting an abuse of a dominant position prohibited under Article 102 TFEU, in the light of the structure of competition on a market which is national in scope.

31 According to settled case-law, the interpretation of a provision of EU law requires account to be taken not only of its wording, but also of the context in which it occurs, as well as the objectives and purpose pursued by the act of which it forms part. The legislative history of a provision of EU law may also reveal elements that are relevant to its interpretation (judgment of 25 June 2020, *A and Others (Wind turbines at Aalter and Nevele)*, C-24/19, EU:C:2020:503, paragraph 37 and the case-law cited).

[272] Consequently, it might appear that both Arts. 101 and 102, which are directly effective, could be applied.

[273] Case C-449/21, EU:C:2023:207, see also EU:C:2022:777 (Opinion of Kokott AG). Similar issues have also arisen in Belgium, Italy, and Luxembourg, see G. Mingsar, 'Bridging the "Regulatory Gap" in EU Merger Control with Towercast (C-449/21)—A Comparison Between the Member States', 16 November 2022 and after the *Towercast* judgment the Belgian competition authority opened an ex officio investigation into an alleged abuse of dominance by Proximus, in the context of its takeover of edpenet, see Press Release 10/2021, 22 March 2023.

[274] EU:C:2023:207, para. 52 and see Section 2.C.ii and Chap. 7, Section 14.F.

32 First of all, as regards the wording of Article 21(1) of Regulation No 139/2004, it is apparent from that wording that that regulation 'alone [is to] apply to concentrations as defined in Article 3' thereof, to which Regulation No 1/2003 is not, in principle, applicable.

33 Article 21(1) of Regulation No 139/2004 is therefore intended to govern the scope of that regulation with regard to the examination of concentration operations in relation to the scope of other pieces of secondary EU legislation concerning competition.

34 By contrast, the examination of the wording of that provision does not answer the question of whether the provisions of primary law, and, in particular, Article 102 TFEU, remain applicable to a concentration of undertakings, within the meaning of Article 3 of Regulation No 139/2004, in particular in a situation, such as the situation at issue in the main proceedings, where the concentration concerned, first, has not met the thresholds for control laid down by EU and national law and, second, has not been referred to the Commission under Article 22 of that regulation, with the result that no *ex ante* control under the law on concentrations has been carried out.

35 Next, as regards the legislative history of Article 21(1) of that regulation, that provision, which reproduces *mutatis mutandis* the substance of Article 22 of Regulation No 4064/89 that was previously applicable, reflects the intention of the EU legislature, alluded to in the seventh recital of Regulation No 4064/89, to specify that the other regulations implementing competition law cease, in principle, to be applicable to all concentrations, that is to say, both to those constituting an abuse of a dominant position and to those which give the undertakings concerned the power to hinder effective competition in the internal market.

36 Lastly, as regards the objectives and general scheme of Regulation No 139/2004, it should be pointed out that, as is stated in recital 5 thereof, that regulation seeks to ensure that corporate reorganisations, particularly in the form of concentrations, do not result in lasting damage to competition. EU law must therefore include provisions governing those concentrations which may significantly impede effective competition in the internal market or in a substantial part of it. The EU legislature intended, in that regard, to make clear that Regulation No 139/2004 is the only procedural instrument applicable to the prior and centralised examination of concentrations which, as is stated in recital 6 thereof, must permit effective control of all concentrations in terms of their effect on the structure of competition (see, to that effect, judgments of 7 September 2017, *Austria Asphalt*, C-248/16, EU:C:2017:643, paragraph 21, and of 31 May 2018, *Ernst & Young*, C-633/16, EU:C:2018:371, paragraph 41).

37 Although that regulation, under the 'one-stop shop' system introduced thereby, is a specific procedural instrument intended to apply exclusively to concentrations of undertakings involving significant structural changes, the impact of which on the market goes beyond the national borders of any one Member State, as is apparent from recital 8 of that regulation, it cannot, however, be inferred from this that the legislature intended to render the control carried out at national level on a concentration operation in the light of Article 102 TFEU devoid of purpose.

38 Thus, it is stated in recital 7 of Regulation No 139/2004 that 'Articles [101 and 102 TFEU], while applicable, . . . are not sufficient to control all operations which may prove to be incompatible with the system of undistorted competition envisaged in the Treaty'.

39 It is apparent from that last statement that, far from depriving the competent authorities of the Member States of the possibility of applying the Treaty provisions on competition to concentrations, as defined in Article 3 of Regulation No 139/2004, that regulation forms part of a legislative whole intended to implement Articles 101 and 102 TFEU and to establish a system of control ensuring that competition is not distorted in the internal market of the European Union (judgments of 7 September 2017, *Austria Asphalt*, C-248/16, EU:C:2017:643, paragraph 31, and of 31 May 2018, *Ernst & Young*, C-633/16, EU:C:2018:371, paragraph 55).

40 In addition, it should be borne in mind that, in order to close gaps in the system of protection against distortions of competition which may result from corporate reorganisations, that regulation was adopted on the basis of Article 83 EC (now Article 103 TFEU), which concerns the regulations or

directives that may be adopted in order to give effect to the principles set out in Articles 101 and 102 TFEU, and of Article 308 EC (now Article 352 TFEU), under which the Union may give itself the additional powers of action necessary for the attainment of its objectives. Although the functioning and general scheme of the protection afforded by EU law against possible distortions of competition arising from concentration operations support the proposition that, for reasons of legal certainty, the mechanism for the prior control of concentrations as defined in Article 3 of Regulation No 139/2004 must be applied as a matter of priority, that cannot, however, preclude the possibility for a competition authority to capture a concentration operation under Article 102 TFEU under certain conditions.

41 It thus follows from the scheme of Regulation No 139/2004 that, although that regulation introduces an *ex ante* control for concentration operations with a Community dimension, it does not preclude an *ex post* control of concentration operations that do not meet that threshold. While it is true that Article 3 of that regulation sets out a substantive definition of a concentration of undertakings without reference to the thresholds mentioned in that regulation, the regulation must be read in the light of its context, and in particular of Article 1 and recitals 7 and 9 thereof. It follows from this, first, that that regulation applies only to concentrations with a Community dimension and, second, that it is accepted that certain concentrations may both escape an *ex ante* control and be subject to an *ex post* control.

42 The interpretation put forward in the present case by the Competition Authority, Tivana and TDF, as well as by the French and Netherlands Governments, ultimately amounts to ruling out the direct applicability of a provision of primary law by reason of the adoption of a piece of secondary legislation covering certain types of conduct of undertakings on the market.

43 In that regard, it must be borne in mind that, under Article 102 TFEU, any abuse by one or more undertakings of a dominant position within the internal market or in a substantial part of it is to be prohibited as incompatible with the internal market in so far as it may affect trade between Member States.

44 It is well established that that article is a provision having direct effect and that its application is not conditional on the prior adoption of a procedural regulation. That article creates rights for individuals which national courts must protect (see, to that effect, judgment of 14 March 2019, *Skanska Industrial Solutions and Others*, C-724/17, EU:C:2019:204, paragraph 24 and the case-law cited).

45 In that connection, it is also important to clarify that no exemption may be granted, in any manner whatsoever, in respect of abuse of a dominant position; such abuse is simply prohibited by the Treaty. It is for the competent national authorities or the Commission, as the case may be, to act on that prohibition within the limits of their powers (judgment of 11 April 1989, *Saeed Flugreisen and Silver Line Reisebüro*, 66/86, EU:C:1989:140, paragraph 32).

46 The Court has held that the list of practices and types of conduct contained in Article 102 TFEU is not exhaustive, so that the list of abusive practices contained in that provision does not exhaust the methods of abusing a dominant position prohibited by EU law (see, to that effect, judgments of 21 February 1973, *Europemballage and Continental Can* v *Commission*, 6/72, EU:C:1973:22, paragraph 26, and of 17 February 2011, *TeliaSonera Sverige*, C-52/09, EU:C:2011:83, paragraph 26).

47 As has been stated by the Commission, the inapplicability of Regulation No 1/2003, and in particular of Article 5 thereof, which concerns the power of the competition authorities of the Member States to apply Articles 101 and 102 TFEU to the concentration operations defined in Article 3 of Regulation No 139/2004, cannot result in national competition authorities being prohibited from applying Article 102 TFEU to concentrations.

48 Notwithstanding the principle, set out in Article 21(1) thereof, that Regulation No 139/2004 is the only regulation applicable to concentration operations, it is the procedural law of the Member States that is applicable to concentrations with a non-Community dimension.

49 It is true that the application, in the judgment of 21 February 1973, *Europemballage and Continental Can* v *Commission* (6/72, EU:C:1973:22), of Article 86 of the EEC Treaty (thereafter

Article 82 EC, now Article 102 TFEU) in the specific context of concentration operations was used and perceived as a means of overcoming the absence in the EEC Treaty of any express provision for the control of those operations. That said, with the entry into force of autonomous provisions on the control of concentrations, as now laid down in Regulation No 139/2004, recourse to the procedural rules relating to the implementation of Articles 81 and 82 EC (now Articles 101 and 102 TFEU), set out initially by Regulation No 17 and subsequently by Regulation No 1/2003, has become devoid of purpose.

50 Thus, Regulation No 139/2004 cannot preclude a concentration operation with a non-Community dimension, such as the operation at issue in the main proceedings, from being subject to a control by the national competition authorities and by the national courts, on the basis of the direct effect of Article 102 TFEU, having recourse to their own procedural rules.

51 The prohibition laid down in Article 102 TFEU is sufficiently clear, precise and unconditional, with the result that there is no need for a rule of secondary law expressly prescribing or authorising its application by the national authorities and courts.

52 It follows that a concentration operation which does not meet the respective thresholds for prior control laid down by Regulation No 139/2004 and by the applicable national law may be subject to Article 102 TFEU where the conditions laid down in that article for establishing the existence of an abuse of a dominant position are satisfied. In particular, it is for the authority in question to verify that a purchaser who is in a dominant position on a given market and who has acquired control of another undertaking on that market has, by that conduct, substantially impeded competition on that market. In that regard, the mere finding that an undertaking's position has been strengthened is not sufficient for a finding of abuse, since it must be established that the degree of dominance thus reached would substantially impede competition, that is to say, that only undertakings whose behaviour depends on the dominant undertaking would remain in the market (see, to that effect, judgments of 21 February 1973, *Europemballage and Continental Can* v *Commission*, 6/72, EU:C:1973:22, paragraph 26, and of 16 March 2000, *Compagnie maritime belge transports and Others* v *Commission*, C-395/96 P and C-396/96 P, EU:C:2000:132, paragraph 113).

53 In the light of all the foregoing considerations, the answer to the question referred is that Article 21(1) of Regulation No 139/2004 must be interpreted as not precluding the competition authority of a Member State from regarding a concentration of undertakings which has no Community dimension within the meaning of Article 1 thereof, is below the thresholds for mandatory *ex ante* control laid down in national law, and has not been referred to the Commission under Article 22 of that regulation, as constituting an abuse of a dominant position prohibited under Article 102 TFEU, in the light of the structure of competition on a market which is national in scope.

4. PROCEDURE

A. NOTIFICATION

To ensure effective control, the EUMR requires the concentrations with an EU dimension[275] to be notified within the time period set out in Article 4.

[275] The Commission must publish the fact of notification taking account of the legitimate interest of the undertakings in the protection of their business secrets and is bound by a general duty of confidentiality, see EUMR, Arts. 4(3) and 17(2) and Chap. 13.

Article 4

1. Concentrations with a Community dimension . . . shall be notified to the Commission prior to their implementation and following the conclusion of the agreement, the announcement of the public bid, or the acquisition of a controlling interest.

   Notification may also be made where the undertakings concerned demonstrate to the Commission a good faith intention to conclude an agreement or, in the case of a public bid, where they have publicly announced an intention to make such a bid, provided that the intended agreement or bid would result in a concentration with a Community dimension.

Parties may therefore notify any time prior to the implementation of an agreement, public bid, or acquisition of a controlling interest even where an agreement or public bid has not actually been made—provided that it can be demonstrated 'that their plan for that proposed concentration is sufficiently concrete, for example on the basis of an agreement in principle, a memorandum of understanding, or a letter of intent signed by all undertakings concerned, or, in the case of a public bid, where they have publicly announced an intention to make such a bid'.[276]

Which parties to the concentration are obliged to notify is dependent on the type of transaction. Broadly, joint notification must be made by the merging parties in true merger cases or by those acquiring control in other cases.[277] The Implementing Regulation[278] and Form CO set out how notification should be made and the information and documents which must be furnished to the Commission (a simplified procedure for certain concentrations that do not raise competition concerns applies, in which case a Short Form, also attached to the implementing regulation, is used[279]).

Form CO is not a form but a pattern, divided into sections, which prescribes how the information requested must be presented. A large amount of information is required (to enable the Commission to comply with the tight deadlines imposed on it), including a description of the concentration, information about the parties, details of the concentration, information about ownership and control, supporting documentation (which includes information bringing about the concentration and also copies of all analyses, reports, studies, surveys, and any comparable documents submitted to, or prepared by or for, any member(s) of the board of directors for the purposes of assessing or analysing the concentration with respect to market shares, competition condition, competitors, the rationale of the concentration, potential for sales growth),[280] information on market definitions and affected markets, overall market context and efficiencies, and cooperative effects of a JV.

It can be seen from this description that notification is costly and time-consuming to complete. Failure to recognise the time and effort involved in the notification could thus disrupt the completion of the deal. Further, if all the requisite information is not supplied the notification will be 'incomplete' and could lead to the parties having to renotify.[281] Pre-notification discussions with the Commission

[276] EUMR, recital 34. The relevant date for establishing jurisdiction (the date of the conclusion of a binding legal agreement, the announcement of the public bid, the acquisition of a controlling interest, or the date of filing, whichever date is earlier) is crucial to the calculation of turnover, Jurisdictional Notice, paras. 154–156.

[277] EUMR, Art. 4(2). [278] C(2023) 2400 final, Art. 3(1). [279] See Section 4.A.

[280] Form CO, s. 5(4). These internal documents (e.g. reports or presentations) are viewed by competition authorities, including the Commission, as crucial probative evidence relating to the nature of competition in the parties' markets, the rationale for the deal, and its likely impact. They may be problematic therefore if they do not support, or even undermine, the parties' arguments. The Commission is experimenting with technology-assisted review, to facilitate the identification of relevant documents using search algorithms.

[281] The tight time limits do not start to run until notification is complete.

are always possible and in practice tend to be extensive and play 'an important part of the whole review process',[282] allowing the Commission to start to acquire preliminary market information. Pre-notification discussions may minimise the possibility of an incomplete notification and may lead to a reduction in the amount of information that the parties are required to provide. The Commission's Best Practices Guidelines provide guidance on pre-notification contacts and the preparation of a draft and final Form CO.

In *Gencor/Lonrho*,[283] the Commission took the view that the parties' notification of the concentration to it meant that they had submitted to the EU jurisdiction.[284]

B. REASONED SUBMISSIONS

(i) Background

It has been explained that there has been a consistent concern that the simple turnover thresholds set out in Article 1(2) and (3) do not correctly divide jurisdiction between the Commission and NCAs in all cases. The EUMR thus provides flexible mechanisms for the transfer of such cases between the Commission and the national authorities and, since 2004, has enabled the parties to provide input into the determination of jurisdiction through the submission of reasoned submissions to the Commission *prior* to notification at the EU or national level (as relevant). Such submissions are made on Form RS, attached to the implementing regulation. The Commission's Notice on case referral[285] provides guidance on the system and practical guidance relating to its working.

The procedure may also enable the parties to speed up the reference procedure and may preclude the need for a notification to an authority which is simply going to refer the case to another.

(ii) Article 4(4), Request for Referral to a National Competition Authority

Article 4(4) provides that where a concentration has an EU dimension the notifying parties may, prior to notification to the Commission, make a reasoned submission that a concentration may significantly affect competition in a distinct market in a Member State and should be examined in whole or in part by that Member State. Where such a submission is made the Commission must inform the relevant Member State without delay (usually within three WDs) and that State has a period of 15 WDs to express agreement or disagreement with the request to refer the case.

Unless the Member State disagrees the Commission has a period of 25 WDs from receiving the reasoned submission to determine whether or not to refer the case.[286] In deciding whether or not to make a reference, the Commission considers guiding principles[287] and in particular whether the national authority (or authorities), taking account of the likely locus of the competitive effects, is the most appropriate authority for dealing with the case.[288]

Where the Commission decides to refer the whole of the case *no* notification to the Commission is required and national competition law applies, subject to the conditions set out in Article 9.[289]

[282] DG Comp, 'Best Practices on the conduct of EC merger control proceedings', para. 5.

[283] M.619 [1997] OJ L11/42. [284] See discussion in Section 8, and Chap. 17.

[286] A decision to refer is deemed if it fails to adopt a decision within this time period.

[287] [2005] OJ C56/2, paras. 8–14. [288] Ibid., paras. 19–23.

[289] See EUMR, Art. 9(6)–(9). Although Art. 4(4) requests may occur where the parties anticipate that an Art. 9 request will be made by a Member State, the Commission recognises that it is a problem that the parties essentially have to 'self-incriminate' themselves by claiming that the transaction may significantly affect competition in a market, see White Paper, n. 81, para. 75.

(iii) Article 4(5), Request for a Referral to the Commission

Article 4(5) provides that parties to a concentration which does not have an EU dimension, and which is capable of being reviewed under the national competition laws of at least three Member States, may, prior to national notification, make a reasoned submission that the concentration should be examined by the Commission. The parties may not implement the concentration while the Commission is considering it under Article 4(5). The Commission must transmit such submissions to the Member States without delay. The Member States then have a period of 15 WDs to express their disagreement with the procedure. The procedure is terminated if one Member State disagrees. Where, however, no Member State disagrees the concentration is deemed to have an EU dimension. It becomes notifiable to the Commission and *no* Member State is permitted to apply its national competition law to the concentration.

The advantage of the Article 4(5) procedure is apparent: if no Member State objects the parties may be saved multiple notifications and the transaction may be deemed to have an EU dimension. The risks are also obvious: if just one Member State objects the procedure is terminated. This would mean that the parties may, having already made a reasoned submission, then have to make multiple notifications to the national authorities (and still risk the possibility that some of the Member States may then make an Article 22 reference to the Commission, making a notification necessary).[290] In order to minimise this risk and to encourage the use of Article 4(5), the Commission's Notice on case referral[291] provides guidance on the question of when the Commission is likely to be considered the most appropriate authority for dealing with the case.[292]

C. SUSPENSION

Article 7(1) provides that a concentration with an EU dimension, or to be examined by the Commission pursuant to Article 4(5), is not to be implemented 'either before its notification or until it has been declared compatible with the internal market pursuant to a decision under Articles 6(1)(b), 8(1) or 8(2), or on the basis of a presumption according to Article 10(6)'. The suspensory obligation prohibits 'gun jumping', closing a transaction and actually acquiring control, or engaging in actions which contribute to the change or acquisition of control over a target,[293] prior to notification or implementing a notified transaction prior to obtaining clearance. Exchanges of strategic information between the transaction parties prior to clearance may also constitute a form of implementation, and gun-jumping.[294] As a general rule therefore parties must be careful not to take steps towards implementation of the merger *and* not to engage in information-sharing or other conduct which might infringe the competition law rules before clearance has been obtained, for example, through: coordinating their commercial activities; integrating business expertise; coordinating price, production, or research strategies; and/or engaging in joint marketing or advertising.[295]

[290] See e.g. M.6502, *London Stock Exchange/LCH Clearnet Group* 14 July 2012.

[291] [2005] OJ C56/2.

[292] Ibid., paras. 25–32. Given that vetoes by the Member States have been rare in practice, the Commission has proposed modification of Art. 4(5) to facilitate its use, White Paper, n. 81, 4.2.1.

[293] Case C-633/16, *Ernst & Young P/S v Konkurrencerådet* EU:C:2018:371 (it was a question of fact whether the termination of a cooperation agreement with a third party could be regarded as bringing about the implementation of a concentration).

[294] See Case T-425/18, *Altice Europe NV v Commission* EU:T:2021:607.

[295] Such actions may not only breach the EUMR but also constitute a violation of Art. 101 TFEU, see e.g. M.4734, *Ineos/Kerling* 30 January 2008 (suspected infringement of the stand-still obligation investigated through unannounced inspections), see e.g. F. Depoortere and S. Lelart, 'The Standstill Obligation in the ECMR' [2010] *World Competition* 103.

The Commission may permit derogations from this suspensory effect following a request (and has occasionally used this power to allow rescue operations requiring quick closure during a financial or economic crisis)[296] and Article 7(2) provides an automatic derogation for public bids[297] 'or a series of transactions in securities including those convertible into other securities admitted to trading on a market such as a stock exchange, by which control is acquired from various sellers, provided that'[298] (a) the concentration is notified to the Commission without delay and (b) the acquirer does not exercise its voting rights or does so only to maintain the full value of its investments (based on an express derogation by the Commission). Persons intentionally or negligently breaching these provisions, by failing to notify a concentration (in accordance with Articles 4 and 22(3)) prior to implementation and/or by implementing a concentration in breach of Article 7, can be fined by the Commission, (up to 10 per cent of the aggregate turnover of the undertakings concerned, see Article 14(2)(a)(b) EUMR). The validity of any transaction closed in breach is dependent upon a clearance decision of the Commission.[299]

The Commission first imposed a fine of ECU 33,000 (at this time the amount of the fine could not exceed ECU 50,000)[300] on an undertaking, Samsung, which had failed to notify a concentration, its acquisition of control over an American firm, AST Research Inc, in due time.[301] In subsequent cases, however, fines have been larger.[302] Indeed, in both *Electrabel*[303] and *Marine Harvest*,[304] the Commission imposed fines of €20 million for gun-jumping. In the latter case, the Commission, upheld on appeal,[305] found that Marine Harvest, a salmon farmer and processor, had acquired, through the purchase of a 48.5 per cent stake, *de facto* sole control over its rival Morpol without prior EUMR authorisation and that the exception to notification provided for by Article 7(2) of the EUMR did not apply. The Commission concluded that the €20 million fine for both failing to notify *and* breaching the suspensory provision[306] reflected: (a) the serious nature of the breach both generally (given the importance of the stand-still obligation to ensuring permanent and irreparable damage is not done to effective competition) and specifically in this case (given the serious competition problems raised by the case which combined two of the largest farmers and primary processors of Scottish salmon);[307] and (b) mitigating factors, including that Marine Harvest had not exercised its voting rights in Morpol and had informed the Commission through pre-notification contacts shortly after closing the transaction.

[296] EUMR, Art. 7(3), see e.g. M.4956, *STX/Aker Yards* 5 May 2008, M.5363, *Santander/Bradford & Bingley Assets* 17 December 2008, M.7184, M.9287, *Connect Airways/Flybe* 9 December 2020, M.8869, *Ryanair/Laudamotion* 4 October 2018, and M.8633, *Lufthansa/Air Berlin assets* 22 November 2017 (refused, M.5969, *SCJ/Sara Lee* 9 May 2011).

[297] See e.g. M.2283, *Schneider/Legrand* 10 October 2001 (Schneider made a public exchange offer in respect of the shares held in Legrand and acquired 98.7% of the shares in Legrand prior to the Commission's final decision prohibiting the merger and ordering the separation of Schneider and Legrand (see EUMR, Art. 8(4), (5) in Section 4.E)). The Commission's decision was annulled on appeal, Case T-310/01, *Schneider Electric SA v Commission* EU:T:2002:254 and Schneider subsequently brought proceedings against the Commission in respect of its loss, see Section 7.

[298] See e.g. M.4730, *Yara/Kemira GrowHow* 21 September 2007.

[299] EUMR, Art. 7(4).

[300] The fines that can be imposed were significantly increased by Reg. 139/2004.

[301] M.920, *Samsung/AST* [1999] OJ L225/1.

[302] See e.g. M.969, *AP Moller* [1999] OJ L183/29.

[303] Electrabel acquired control over Compagnie Nationale du Rhône (France's second largest electricity producer) in 2003 without notification, MEMO/09/267, Case T-332/09, *Electrabel v Commission* EU:T:2012:672 (dismissing Electrabel's appeal), *aff'd* Case C-84/13 P, EU:C:2014:2040.

[304] M.7184, IP/14/862 (in the end the merger was cleared conditionally).

[305] Case T-704/14, *Marine Harvest ASA v Commission* EU:T:2017:753, Case C-10/18 P, EU:C:2020:149. See M. Kadar, '*Case T-704/14—Marine Harvest v Commission*: On "Gun Jumping" and Public Bids' (2018) 9 *JECLAP* 239.

[306] The GC, ibid., held that the Commission correctly penalised Marine Harvest for infringement of both the failure to notify and suspensory provisions (even if one infringement necessarily entails the other) and that this did not amount to double punishments infringing the *ne bis in idem* principle, paras. 305–357.

[307] The Commission only authorised the transaction subject to conditions, M.6850, IP/13/896.

The Commission also imposed a fine of €125 million on Altice for early implementation (reduced to €118.275 million on appeal)[308] and of €28 million on Canon[309] for partial implementation of a deal. In 2021, the Commission adopted interim measures to restore and maintain competition following Illumina's breach of the stand-still obligation in its acquisition of Grail.[310]

D. PHASE I INVESTIGATION

The Commission must examine notifications as soon as they are received.[311] The time limits for initiating proceedings and decisions are set out in Article 10.[312] Where the Commission fails to adopt a decision within the prescribed periods the concentration 'shall be deemed to have been declared to be compatible with the common market' (Article 10(6)).

Phase I decisions must generally be taken within 25 WDs following receipt of complete notification. The period is extended to 35 WDs in Article 9 cases or cases where commitments designed to render the concentration compatible with the internal market are offered[313] (so long as the commitments are offered within 20 WDs of notification).[314] Details of notification must be published in the Official Journal in order to give third parties the opportunity to react.[315]

At the end of the 25- or 35-WD period the Commission must adopt a decision under Article 6. This may take one of several forms.

(i) Article 6(1)(a)

Where the notified transaction does not in fact fall within the EUMR at all, it does not amount to a concentration with an EU dimension, the Commission may issue a decision to that effect. Such decisions are understandably rare in practice (less than 1 per cent of all notifications).[316]

(ii) Article 6(1)(b)

The Commission may declare the notified concentration to be compatible with the internal market either unconditionally or conditionally (subject to the acceptance of commitments by the parties[317]). Clearance decisions are deemed to cover restrictions incorporated in the transaction which are directly related and necessary to the implementation of the concentration.[318]

(iii) Article 6(1)(c)

Where the Commission has serious doubts about the concentration's compatibility with the internal market it must issue a decision to that effect and initiate proceedings launching a second-phase investigation. In-depth reviews occur in only a very small percentage of notified cases (see further Section 6).

[308] M.7933, *Altice/PT Portugal* 24 April 2018, *aff'd* Case T-425/18, *Altice Europe NV v Commission* EU:T:2021:607 (but reducing the fine) (fine for acquiring the right to exercise control, and actually exercising control, over PT Portugal). The decision makes clear that any pre-closing undertakings incorporated in a merger transaction must be monitored carefully, including purchaser consent rights which must be limited to what is necessary to preserve the value of the target prior to closing.

[309] M.8179, *Canon/Toshiba Medical Systems Corporation* 27 June 2019, *aff'd* Case T-609/19, *Canon Inc. v Commission*,EU:T:2022:299.

[310] M.10188, *Illumina/Grail* 29 October 2021, on appeal Case T-755/21, *Illumina v Commission*, judgment pending.

[311] EUMR, Art. 6(1). [312] For further information on their operation, see the Implementing Reg. 2023/914, Chap. III.

[313] EUMR, Art. 10(1). [314] Implementing Reg., Art. 19(1). [315] EUMR, Art. 4(3).

[316] See <https://competition-policy.ec.europa.eu/mergers/statistics_en>.

[317] EUMR, Art. 6(2), see discussion of commitments in Section 5.J. [318] See Section 5.I.

Where such proceedings are launched then, without prejudice to Article 9, unless the undertakings can demonstrate to the satisfaction of the Commission that they have abandoned their concentration, the proceedings must be closed by virtue of a final decision under Article 8 decision. An Article 6(1)(c) decision initiating proceedings is not an appealable decision.[319]

E. PHASE II

The Commission has a period of 90 WDs from the day following the initiation of proceedings to make its assessment in Phase II proceedings.[320] This time period can be extended by 15 WDs where commitments are offered by the parties *after* the 54th WD (commitments must generally be offered within 65 WDs).[321] Further, it is possible that the period can be extended up to a total of 20 WDs either by the parties or at the request of the Commission with the consent of the parties.[322] This means that in complex cases the time period may be extended to a maximum of 125 WDs. Occasionally, however, the time periods may be expanded even beyond this statutory timetable if the Commission 'stops the clock' on account of the parties' failure to respond to requests for information by a stipulated time period.[323] Indeed, in *DSME/HHI*[324] the clock was stopped three times (the final one lasting for 16 months), meaning that the Phase II investigated took over two years to complete. Again, if no decision is taken within the prescribed period the concentration is deemed to be compatible with the internal market.[325]

At the end of the proceedings the Commission may under Article 8 of the EUMR either:[326]

(a) declare the concentration to be compatible with the common market;

(b) declare that the concentration, following modification and/or subject to commitments, is compatible with the common market;[327]

(c) declare the concentration to be *incompatible* with the common market.[328]

In Article 8(1) and (2) cases, the clearance decision is deemed to cover restrictions related and necessary to the concentration.[329] Where the concentration is prohibited and the parties have already completed the transaction, the Commission has comprehensive powers, including the power to take interim measures or to take restorative measures.[330] These powers can also be exercised where a concentration is implemented in breach of a condition or obligation.

[319] See Case C-188/06 P, *Schneider Electric SA v Commission* EU:C:2007:158 (upholding the GC's view that a challenge to a decision opening a Phase II merger investigation was inadmissible since the decision was not a challengeable act but an intermediary act, to assist the Commission in reaching a final decision. The parties had therefore to wait to contest the final decision of the Commission determining the outcome of the case (in fact the parties abandoned the merger)) and Case T-902/16, *HeidelbergCement v Commission* EU:T:2017:846.

[320] EUMR, Art. 10(3). [321] Implementing Reg., Art. 19(2). [322] EUMR, Art. 10(3), second para.

[323] See e.g. M.2282, *Schneider/Legrand*, IP/01/408 (the Commission stopped the clock on account of the failure of the parties to respond to 322 questions within 12 calendar days (five WD)), *aff'd* Case T-310/01, *Schneider Electric SA v Commission* EU:T:2002:254, para. 100 (a request for information was reasonable given the circumstances of the case and the requirement for speed which characterises the overall scheme of the EUMR). See also e.g. Case T-145/06, *Omya v Commission* EU:T:2009:27 and e.g. M.7095, *SOCAR/DESFA*.

[324] M. 9343, 13 January 2022 (prohibited). [325] EUMR, Art. 10(6).

[326] It may revoke decisions which are based on incorrect information, EUMR, Art. 8(6).

[327] EUMR, Art. 8(2). Commitments are discussed in Section 5.J.

[328] EUMR, Art. 8(3). [329] See Section 5.I.

[330] EUMR, Art. 8(4) and (5), see e.g. M.2416, *Tetra Laval/Sidel* 30 October 2001, M.2283, *Schneider/Legrand* 10 October 2001 and 30 January 2002, M.890, *Blokker/Toys 'R' Us* 26 June 1997, M.784, *Kesko/Tuko* 19 February 1997 and M.10188, *Illumina/Grail* 29 October 2021, n. 310 and text.

F. CONDUCT OF MERGER INVESTIGATIONS

When making its assessment, within the short periods stipulated, the Commission has power under Articles 11 and 13 of the EUMR to obtain information from the parties, or third parties (such as customers, suppliers, or competitors), by means of a request, either by a simple request or decision,[331] or by an inspection (including unannounced on-the-spot investigations).[332] Third parties play an important role in the merger proceedings. The investigation is ordinarily conducted in the form of requests for information to customers, suppliers, or competitors but may also be addressed to the notifying parties. It may also seek the views of these parties orally, for example through minuted calls. The Commission's powers of investigation were extended by the current Regulation to bring them more closely into line with the Commission's corresponding powers under Regulation 1/2003.

The Commission has power under Articles 14 and 15 to impose both fines, not exceeding 1 per cent of the aggregate turnover of the undertakings concerned, and periodic penalty payments for a number of offences, such as intentionally or negligently failing to respond to an Article 11 letter or supplying incorrect or misleading information in a notification or following a request for information[333] (they can be imposed not only on merger parties but also third parties).[334] For example: in *BP/Erdölchemie*,[335] the Commission imposed a fine of €35,000 on Deutsche BP for having omitted to identify important information in its Form CO (at the time, however, the maximum fine was €50,000); in *Facebook*,[336] the Commission imposed fines of €110 million for providing misleading information to the Commission in relation to its acquisition of WhatsApp (but held that its decision did not impact on its decision to authorise the merger); in *GE/LM Wind*,[337] the Commission imposed a fine of €52 million on General Electric for providing incorrect information during the investigation; and in *Merck/Sigma-Aldrich*,[338] a fine of €7.5 million was imposed on Sigma-Aldrich for providing incorrect or misleading information during the investigation which may have had a bearing on the commitments offered. A decision adopted on the basis of incorrect information for which one of the undertakings is responsible may be revoked.[339]

State of play meetings are generally held during this process with the objective of contributing to the quality and efficiency of the decision-making process and of ensuring transparency and communication between DG Comp and the parties. If Phase II proceedings are initiated there are usually state of play meetings at five different points in the procedure. Occasionally, voluntary 'triangular' meetings involving the parties and third parties are held.

In the course of Phase II investigations, a statement of objections (SO) may be served on the notifying parties. This lets the parties know the Commission's objections to the concentration.[340] Parties then have an opportunity to respond to the statement in writing by a specified date (the Commission is not obliged to take account of comments received after that date);[341] they have a right of access to the file[342] and to attend and speak at the oral hearing, which, unless waived, is conducted by the Hearing Officer in full independence.[343] Further, other involved parties[344]

[331] EUMR, Art. 11.

[332] Ibid., Arts. 12 and 13, see M.4734, *Ineos/Kerling* 30 January 2008. The power to carry out dawn raids is equivalent to those set out in Reg. 1/2003 [2003] OJ L1/1, discussed in Chap. 13. The power is rarely used in practice given the tight time periods for review set out in the EUMR.

[333] EUMR, Art. 14(1), COMP/29.895, *Telos* [1982] OJ L58/19.

[334] In M.1634, *Mitsubishi Heavy Industries (Articles 11 and 14 proc)* 14 July 2000 a fine was imposed on Mitsubishi for failure to supply information on the *Kvaerner/Ahlström* joint venture.

[335] M.2624 [2004] OJ L91/40.

[336] M.8228, 17 May 2017.

[337] M. 8436, 21 January 2020.

[338] M.8181, 3 May 2021.

[339] EUMR, Arts. 6(3) and 8(6).

[340] Ibid., Art. 18(1) and (2).

[341] Ibid., Art. 18(3), Implementing Reg., Chap. IV.

[342] Ibid., Art. 18(3), Implementing Reg., Chap. V.

[343] Implementing Reg., Arts. 14 and 15.

[344] Parties to the transaction other than the notifying parties.

and third parties, including customers, suppliers, competitors, members of the administrative or management bodies of the undertakings concerned or the recognised representative of their employees, and consumer associations where the proposed concentration concerns products or services used by end consumers,[345] may have a right to receive the SO (with confidential information redacted), to respond to it, to have access to the file,[346] to attend the oral hearing, and to speak at it. If disputes arise in the course of this procedure, the issue can be raised with the Hearing Officer.

The Court takes the procedural obligations of the Commission, in particular respecting rights of defence, very seriously. In both *Schneider Electric SA v Commission*[347] and *United Parcel Service (UPS) v Commission*,[348] Commission decisions were annulled on account of procedural irregularities committed. In the former, the GC found that the SO had not adequately stated the Commission's case against the parties. The SO identified only horizontal effects, whilst the final decision took account of the conglomerate effects of the merger. The GC held that the SO had to state objections in a sufficiently precise way to enable the parties to rebut the case against them and/or to devise or present remedies capable of saving the merger.[349] In the latter, the CJ affirmed the GC's finding that the Commission should have communicated a final version of an econometric analysis model, on which it based its objections, to the applicant before adopting its decision. It stressed in paragraph 56 that failure to disclose an econometric model is cause for annulment if 'there was even a slight chance' that the notifying party could have better defended itself if disclosure had been made. Rights of defence thus require the parties to be able to make known effectively their views on the accuracy and relevance of factors that the Commission intends to base its decision on.[350]

Concentrations are initially investigated and appraised by merger units within DG Comp. In Phase II investigations, an independent 'panel' is appointed with the task of scrutinising the case team's conclusions with a fresh pair of eyes at key points of the inquiry (devil's advocate process).[351] This step was added to deal with the criticism that the case team was often convinced of its own arguments at the end of Phase I, and that this affected the outcome of the second-phase investigations. The Advisory Committee on Concentrations must be consulted before a final decision is taken.[352] The final decision is made by the College of Commissioners[353] save, where delegated,[354] where it is adopted by a single Commissioner (usually the Competition Commissioner) or the Director-General (e.g. in simplified cases).

[345] See e.g. Implementing Reg., Art. 11(1)(b)(c). See also on the rights of third parties, Cases C-68/94 and 30/95, *France v Commission, Société Commerciale des Potasses et de l'Azote (SCPA) v Commission* EU:C:1998:148.

[346] Third parties may also seek access to Commission documents using the Transparency Reg., see Cases C-404/10 P, *Commission v Éditions Odile Jacob* and C-477/10 P, *Commission v Agrofert Holding* EU:C:2012:393 and Chap. 13.

[347] Case T-310/01, EU:T:2002:254.

[348] Case T-194/13, *United Parcel Service v Commission* EU:T:2017:742, *aff'd* Case C-265/17 P, EU:C:2019:23. See also discussion of the subsequent claims for damages launched by Schneider and UPS against the Commission in Section 7.

[349] In Case T-5/02, *Tetra Laval v Commission* EU:T:2002:264 (GC rejected Tetra Laval's arguments that the Commission had failed to respect Tetra's rights to access to the file).

[350] Case C-265/17 P, *United Parcel Service v Commission* EU:C:2019:23, para. 31.

[351] See M. Monti, SPEECH/02/545, 'Merger Control in the European Union: a radical reform', European Commission/International Bar Association, Brussels, 7 November 2002. Representatives from the staff of the Chief Competition Economist participated in this panel.

[352] It must also be consulted, for example, before a decision imposing a fine or penalty or ordering divestment is taken.

[353] See further Section 5.G.

[354] Phase I decisions are usually delegated.

G. SUMMARY

Figure 15.2 sets out an outline summary of the EUMR's merger procedure provisions.

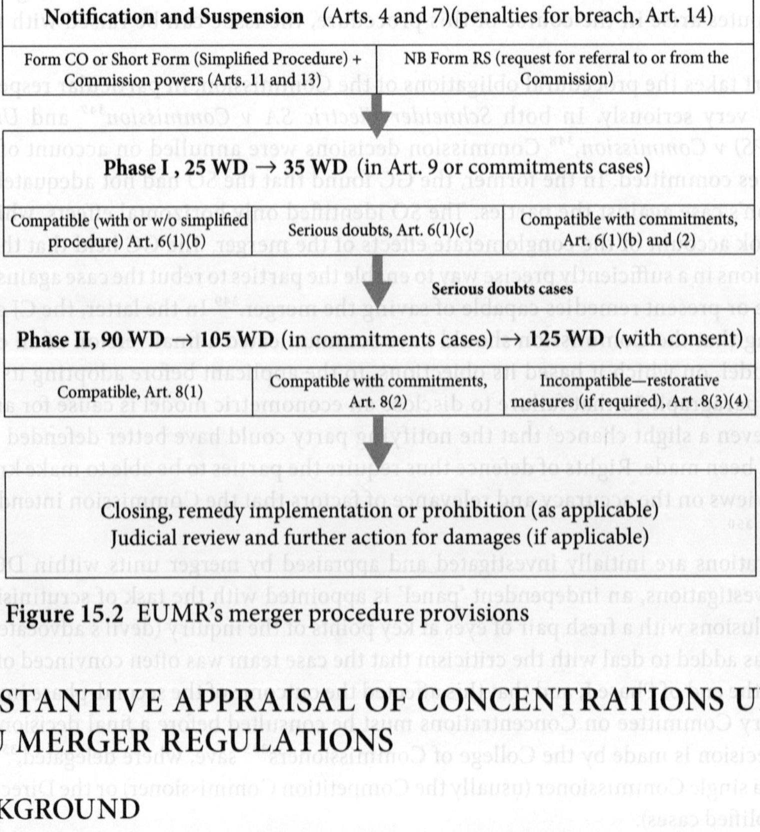

Figure 15.2 EUMR's merger procedure provisions

5. SUBSTANTIVE APPRAISAL OF CONCENTRATIONS UNDER THE EU MERGER REGULATIONS

A. BACKGROUND

The *original* EUMR[355] adopted a 'dominance' test for substantive appraisal, providing in Article 2(3) that:

> A concentration which creates or strengthens a dominant position as a result of which effective competition would be significantly impeded in the common market or in a substantial part of it shall be declared incompatible with the common market.

In its 2001 Green Paper,[356] however, the Commission launched a debate as to whether there should be a move to the 'substantial lessening of competition' (SLC) test. Both procedural and substantive arguments arguably favoured such reform. The gist of the procedural argument was that alignment of the test with the SLC test used in a number of jurisdictions, including the US,[357] would lead to greater

[355] The substantive test was not amended by Reg. 1310/97 [1997] OJ L180/1.

[356] 2001 Green Paper on the Review of Council Regulation (EEC) No. 4064/89, COM(2001) 745/6 final, especially paras. 160–167.

[357] The test is also used, e.g., in Canada, Australia, the UK, and Ireland.

international convergence in the application of merger rules (switching to such a test would, however, create inconsistency in the EU where many Member and acceding States had modelled their merger rules on the dominance test).

The substantive reasons advanced hinged on the relative flexibility of the SLC test, in particular when dealing with mergers in concentrated markets. Although it had been established that the old EUMR applied not only to mergers leading to the creation or strengthening of a dominant position held by a single undertaking, but to mergers leading to the creation or strengthening of a collective dominant position (that is, a dominant position held by the merging parties and another or other undertakings operating on the market, mergers resulting in *coordinated effects*),[358] it was argued[359] that, nonetheless, the dominance test was not broad enough to capture and prevent all problematic mergers occurring on a concentrated market. For example, a merger between the second and third largest competitors on a market with only three players might not lead to the creation of a single dominant position, it might not lead to the coordination of the competitive behaviour of the firms remaining on the market, but it might substantially lessen competition and lead to higher prices on the market (through *unilateral effects*) by eliminating the rivalry between the merging firms and the competitive constraint that they had exercised both on each other and on the market leader. It was thus contended that the EUMR had a 'blind spot' or gap, which arguably created difficulties for the Commission in the *Airtours* case discussed later.[360]

An example given of this gap situation was the US 'baby food' case.[361] In this case Heinz, the third largest producer of baby food in the US, wished to acquire Milnot Holding Corp, whose subsidiary, Beech-Nut, was the second largest producer of baby food in the US. Following the merger, the parties would have acquired around 33 per cent of the relevant market, whilst Gerber would have retained 65 per cent of the prepared baby food market. The merger would not have given the merging parties a 'dominant' position, but was scrutinised to determine whether it might have led either to coordinated effects on the market (e.g. tacit coordination of prices by the merged entity and Gerber) or to a substantial lessening of competition on the market since the merging parties competed vigorously to be chosen as the number two supplier in supermarkets and in innovation in product development and differentiation. Although the challenge to this merger led to its eventual abandonment, it was argued that, had the same facts arisen in the EU, the EU authorities would have been powerless to prevent the merger unless collective dominance (or coordinated effects) could be established.

Although the Commission indicated in its Green Paper that it thought this so-called 'gap' was more hypothetical than real, it launched a debate which raged until the last moments before the text for the new EUMR was finally agreed.[362]

[358] See also the discussion of collective dominance in Chap. 9.

[359] See e.g. J. Vickers, 'Competition Economics and Policy' [2003] *ECLR* 95, and Z. Biro and M. Parker, 'A New EC Merger Test? Dominance v Substantial Lessening of Competition' [2002] 1 *Comp Law* 157.

[360] M.1524, *Airtours/First Choice* [2000] OJ L93/1, annulled on appeal, Case T-342/99, *Airtours v Commission* EU:T:2002:146, see discussion especially n. 565 and text. See also J. Vickers, 'How to reform the EC merger test', Speech at the EC/IBA merger control conference, Brussels, 9 November 2004.

[361] *FTC v HJ Heinz Co*, 246 F.3d 708 (DC Cir. 2001), 116 F. Supp.2d 190 (2000).

[362] E.g. the UK, Irish, and Swedish delegations were in favour of the SLC test (see submissions to the Commission's 2001 Green Paper, available on DG Comp's website) whilst the German delegation favoured retention of the dominance test (see also, e.g., submissions of Italy, the Netherlands, and the European Parliament). Some Member States (e.g. Portugal and Denmark) favoured a retention of the dominance test, but with a clarification of how the test applied on oligopolistic markets whilst France and Spain supported a dual test combining features of the SLC and dominance tests.

B. REFORM AND THE NEW SUBSTANTIVE TEST

Given the need for unanimous agreement in the Council, the end result of the reform process was a classic, yet ingenious, European 'compromise' designed to meet the arguments of those in both the SLC and dominance camps. The substantive test *was* altered but the SLC test was *not* adopted. The decision was made to utilise, but reorganise, the wording of the original EUMR. Article 2(3) of the current Regulation states:

> A concentration which would significantly impede effective competition in the common market or in a substantial part of it, in particular as a result of the creation or strengthening of a dominant position, shall be declared incompatible with the common market.

The 'SIEC' test is thus broader than the old test. A merger may be prohibited even if it does not create or strengthen a dominant position if it would lead to a significant impediment to effective competition (SIEC). By referring to the creation or strengthening of a dominant position, however, the EUMR preserved previous decisional practice and case law of the CJ. Horizontal Merger Guidelines (HMG)[363] were also adopted with the objective of clearly and comprehensively articulating the analytical approach under the new test.

The twin objectives, of broadening the test whilst at the same time preserving the case law on the meaning of dominance, are explained in recitals 25 and 26 of the EUMR. In particular, recital 25 clarifies that the substantive test is designed to catch mergers that will result in non-coordinated effects on an oligopolistic market even though a position of single or collective dominance may not be established.

The test was thus designed to enable the Commission 'to move away from an excessively structuralist analysis in merger control towards a more effects based one and to close a gap with respect to cases leading to unilateral effects in a non-collusive oligopoly',[364] to bring the standard for substantive assessment more closely into line with that adopted under Article 101, and to focus the assessment on the likely impact of the merger in the main market competition parameters (price, output, innovation).[365] The substantive test set out in Article 2 of the EUMR must therefore be seen in the light of these goals as well as the broader spirit and scheme of the competition law system which is designed to prohibit conduct insofar as it proves incompatible with the system of undistorted competition in the internal market.[366] In interpreting and applying the EUMR, it is necessary to ensure that a fair balance is drawn between the rights of the parties involved and the broader interest of society and consumers in effective and undistorted competition.

Article 2(1) sets out the criteria to be used in appraising concentrations.

> Concentrations within the scope of this Regulation shall be appraised in accordance with the objectives of this Regulation and the following provisions with a view to establishing whether or not they are compatible with the common market.

[363] [2004] OJ C31/5, para. 5. The Non-Horizontal Merger Guidelines were adopted subsequently.

[364] Speech of then Deputy Director-General (Mergers) at DG Comp, Carles Esteva Mosso, 'The Contribution of Merger Control to the Definition of Harm to Competition', GCLC Conference, Brussels, February 2016.

[365] Ibid.

[366] See discussion of Cases C-68/94 and 30/95, *France v Commission, Société Commerciale des Potasses et de l'Azote (SCPA) v Commission* EU:C:1998:148, n. 569 and text.

> In making this appraisal, the Commission shall take into account:
>
> (a) the need to maintain and develop effective competition within the common market in view of, among other things, the structure of all the markets concerned and the actual or potential competition from undertakings located either within or outwith the Community;
> (b) the market position of the undertakings concerned and their economic and financial power, the alternatives available to suppliers and users, their access to supplies or markets, any legal or other barriers to entry, supply and demand trends for the relevant goods and services, the interests of the intermediate and ultimate consumers, and the development of technical and economic progress provided that it is to consumers' advantage and does not form an obstacle to competition.

Article 2(4) and (5) set out an additional test applying the criteria of Article 101 to the aspects of a full-function JV that may appreciably restrict competition between undertakings that remain independent. Section 5 examines how the Commission applies the substantive test.

C. BURDEN AND STANDARD OF PROOF

(i) Burden on Proof

The burden is on the Commission to establish that the merger is *either* compatible *or* incompatible with the internal market.[367] No presumption of compatibility or incompatibility with the common market applies. A positive case for either must be made.[368]

In assessing the competitive effects of a concentration, the Commission must consider not only the adverse effect of the merger on effective competition but also evidence relating to efficiencies adduced by the parties (see Section 5.E.vii). An important issue is whether the legal burden relating to efficiencies is on the Commission or shifts, as it does under Articles 101 and 102, to the parties. As most of the evidence relating to efficiencies rests with the parties,[369] the Commission's Guidelines indicate that the parties bear both the legal and evidential burden relating to efficiencies—it is for them to demonstrate that the claimed efficiencies are merger-specific, are likely to be realised, and the extent to which they will counteract any adverse effects of the merger.[370] Endorsing this approach, the GC has held that it is for the merging parties to demonstrate efficiencies that are likely to counteract any adverse effects that might otherwise result from the merger.[371]

In conducting the assessment, the merger must be assessed in the context of the position that would exist were the merger not to be completed (the counterfactual)—a causal link between completion of the merger and the competitive harm must be demonstrated.

> 9. In assessing the competitive effects of a merger, the Commission compares the competitive conditions that would result from the notified merger with the conditions that would have prevailed without the merger. In most cases, the competitive conditions existing at the time of the merger constitute the relevant comparison for evaluating the effects of a merger. However, in some circumstances, the Commission may take into account future changes to the market that can reasonably

[367] EUMR, Arts. 6 and 8 and Case C-413/06 P, *Bertelsmann and Sony Corp v Commission* EU:C:2008, para. 52
[368] Case C-413/06 ibid., paras. 46, 48.
[369] Case T-342/07, *Ryanair*, paras. 386–444. Case T-87/05, *EDP* EU:T:2005:333.
[370] HMG, para. 87 and see Section 5.E.vii.
[371] See e.g. Case T-175/12, *Deutsche Börse v Commission* EU:T:2015:14.

> be predicted. It may, in particular, take account of the likely entry or exit of firms if the merger did not take place when considering what constitutes the relevant comparison.[372]

Although mergers are normally assessed against the competitive conditions existing at the time of the merger, assessing the counterfactual may be more complex in some scenarios, for example where entry or exit from the markets is likely or where two mergers take place close together in time in the same industry or relevant market. In this latter situation, the Commission now seems to favour assessing the first merger without regard to the second but the second taking account of the first (giving priority to the transaction notified first).[373] In *Western Digital/Viviti*,[374] the Commission applied this first come, first served rule assessing that transaction taking into account the *Seagate/Samsung*[375] merger (also affecting the market for hard disk drives) which had been notified one day earlier.[376]

(ii) Standard of Proof

Article 2(1) EUMR provides that the Commission must appraise any notified concentration with a view to establishing whether or not it is compatible with the internal market. It is thus obliged to assess, ordinarily using a prospective analysis, whether the concentration would (or would not), lead to a situation in which effective competition in the relevant market is significantly impeded. (The sections below discuss the legal tests to be satisfied, and relevant factors to be taken into account, to demonstrate if a merger would, or would not, lead to a SIEC.) Because the EUMR specifically provides that a concentration must be declared either compatible or incompatible with the internal market, the case law makes it clear that there is no presumption that a merger is either compatible or incompatible and that the standard of proof required to prove the Commission's case is the same whether or not it clears or prohibits a merger.[377] In *Bertelsmann and Sony* the CJ stressed that the prospective analysis required by the EUMR made it necessary for the Commission to examine how a merger might alter the factors determining the state of competition, and so whether it would give rise to a SIEC, by envisaging 'various chains of cause and effect' with a view to ascertaining which of them 'is the most likely'.[378]

> 46 Thus, as the Court has, in substance, already held, the prospective analysis called for in relation to the control of concentrations, which consists of an examination of how a concentration might alter the factors determining the state of competition on a given market in order to establish whether it would give rise to a significant impediment to effective competition, makes it necessary to envisage various

[372] HMG, para. 9. See also discussion of the failing firm defence in Section 5.E.viii.

[373] See J. Almunia, SPEECH 11/561, 'Policy Objectives in Merger Control', 8 September 2011. But compare, e.g., Cases M.2533, *BP/E.ON* 20 December 2011 and M.2389, *Shell/DEA* 20 December 2011 with Cases M.4601, *KarstadtQuelle/MyTravel* 4 May 2007 and M.4600, *TUI/First Choice* 4 June 2007 (in the latter the first filing was assessed independently from the second) and see generally G. Drauz, S. Mavroghenis, and S. Ashall, 'Recent Developments in EU Merger Control' (2012) 3 *JECLAP* 52, 72–75 (the Commission initially favoured the combined approach but is now more inclined to adopt the priority rule approach).

[374] M.6203, *Western Digital Ireland/Viviti Technologies* 23 November 2011.

[375] M.6214, 19 October 2011.

[376] The proposed transaction would, after the Seagate/Samsung merger, reduce the number of suppliers in the market to three, and in some markets to two.

[377] See Case C-413/06 P, *Bertelsmann and Sony Corp v Commission* EU:C:2008:392, paras. 46–48, Kokott AG, EU:C:2007:790, paras. 208–211.

[378] See *Bertelsmann and Sony Corp* ibid., para. 47, Case C-12/03 P, *Commission v Tetra Laval BV* EU:C:2005:87, para. 43, Case T-87/05, *EDP v Commission* EU:T:2005:333, para. 6.

> chains of cause and effect with a view to ascertaining which of them is the most likely (see, to that effect, Case C-12/03 P *Commission* v *Tetra Laval* [2005] ECR I-987, paragraph 43).
>
> 48 Contrary to what the appellants submit, it cannot therefore be inferred from the Regulation that there is a general presumption that a notified concentration is compatible with, or incompatible with, the common market.
>
> 49 That interpretation of the Regulation is not invalidated by Article 10(6), which provides that a notified concentration is to be deemed compatible with the common market where the Commission has not taken a decision on the compatibility of that concentration within the prescribed period. That provision is a specific expression of the need for speed, which characterises the general scheme of the Regulation and which requires the Commission to comply with strict time-limits for the adoption of the final decision (see, in that regard, Case C-202/06 P *Cementbouw Handel & Industrie* v *Commission* [2007] ECR I-0000, paragraph 39). It is, however, an exception to the general scheme of the Regulation, which is laid down in particular in Articles 6(1) and 8(1), according to which the Commission is to rule expressly on the concentrations which are notified to it.
>
> 50 Furthermore, it is true that, as is apparent from the Court's case-law, the decisions of the Commission as to the compatibility of concentrations with the common market must be supported by a sufficiently cogent and consistent body of evidence (see, to that effect, Joined Cases C-68/94 and C-30/95 *France and Others* v *Commission* [1998] ECR I-1375, *'Kali & Salz'*, paragraph 228) and that in the context of the analysis of a 'conglomerate-type' concentration the quality of the evidence produced by the Commission in order to establish that it is necessary to adopt a decision declaring the concentration incompatible with the common market is particularly important (see *Commission* v *Tetra Laval*, paragraph 44).

Albeit expressed in a fairly open-textured way, the Court thus appears to require the Commission to prove, supported by a sufficiently consistent and cogent body of evidence, that a SIEC is more likely than not, an approach which is consistent with the EUMR requirement that either compatibility or incompatibility with the internal market must be established (otherwise a swathe of mergers might be left which cannot be cleared or prohibited). Because merger review in the EU is ordinarily an *ex ante* one, anti-competitive effects will generally need to be demonstrated through indirect or circumstantial evidence, meeting the cogent and consistent requirement set out by the Court. Although in *CK Telecoms*[379] the GC suggested that where a SIEC is inferred from a body of evidence and indicia, and is based on several theories of harm, the Commission is required to produce sufficient evidence to demonstrate a *strong probability* of the existence of a SIEC (a stricter standard of proof than 'more likely than not', or a 'balance of probabilities', but less strict than 'beyond all reasonable doubt'),[380] this is not entirely easy to reconcile with the approach of the CJ in *Sony* and would, arguably, also weaken the Commission's ability to carry out its policy functions[381] and create too high a risk of clearing anti-competitive mergers. It is not entirely surprising, therefore, that in the course of the appeal, AG Kokott considered the correct standard to correspond to the balance of probabilities, and that as the GC's judgment imposed too high a standard, it was vitiated by an error or law.[382] Indeed, some argue that, given the prospective nature of merger analysis, even a balance of probabilities standard is too

[379] Case T-399/16, EU:T:2020:217, on appeal C-376/20 P, *Commission v CK Telecoms*, judgment pending.

[380] Ibid., para. 118, relying on the opinions of Tizzano AG and Jääskinen AG in Cases C-12/03 P, *Tetra Laval v Commission* EU:C:2004:318, para. 74 and C-559/12 P, *France v Commission* EU:C:2013:76, para. 35 respectively, but disagreeing with Kokott AG, n. 377.

[381] See Kokott AG in Case C-413/06 P, *Bertelsmann and Sony Corp v Commission* EU:C:2007:790, para. 210 also noting that a higher standard would be difficult to reconcile with the Commission's margin of appreciation.

[382] C-376/20 P, *Commission v CK Telecoms* EU:C:2022:817.

high, at least in certain circumstances, for example where a strong incumbent purchases a potential entrant or start-up in a market and the concern is about future unilateral effects—where unilateral effects will only occur 'probabilistically'.[383] In these circumstances, merger control should arguably be able to prevent acquisitions of a firm which has a reasonable prospect of competing with the acquiring firm in the future (it is credibly developing a new product that significantly threatens the acquirer's profits) even if such future competition cannot be shown to be more likely than not.[384]

The cases make it clear, nonetheless, that the GC will rigorously review the Commission's decisions and that, although recognising the Commission's margin of discretion with regard to economic matters, it will consider whether the evidence relied upon by the Commission is correct, reliable, convincing, and consistent, and is capable of substantiating the conclusions it has drawn—i.e. whether the reasoning and evidence relied upon provide a proper factual basis for the conclusions and all the information which must be taken into account in order to assess a complex situation.[385] The Commission consequently has an acute burden to fulfil and must demonstrate how a concentration might, in the future, alter the factors determining the state of competition on a market. If the Commission does not meet it, the GC will annul its decision.[386]

It appears that the standard of proof does not change with the complexity of the theory of competitive harm.[387] The complexity of the theory is, however, inevitably a relevant factor when assessing the plausibility of the various consequences that the merger might have, especially where those effects may only take effect in a longer time frame.[388] The more uncertain the theory, the more demanding the EU Courts will be when examining the Commission's evidence.[389]

Case C-12/03 P, *Tetra Laval BV v Commission* [2005] ECR I-98739

Court of Justice

39. Whilst the Court recognises that the Commission has a margin of discretion with regard to economic matters that does not mean that the Community Courts must refrain from reviewing the Commission's interpretation of the information of an economic nature. Not only must the Community Courts, *inter alia*, establish whether the evidence relied on is factually accurate, reliable and consistent but also whether that evidence contains all the information which must be taken into account in order to assess a complex situation and whether it is capable of substantiating the conclusions drawn from it. Such a review is all the more necessary in the case of a prospective analysis required when examining a planned merger with conglomerate effect.

40. Thus, the [GC] was right to find . . ., that the Commission's analysis of a merger producing a conglomerate effect is subject to requirements similar to those defined by the Court with regard to the creation

[383] Rose and Shapiro, n. 9.

[384] See e.g. ibid., 9 ('Harm to competition does not require that successful introduction of the new product be highly likely, much less certain').

[385] See further Chap. 13. The tight time constraints that the Commission is operating under is, however, relevant to the assessment of the appraisal conducted, see e.g. Case T-151/05, *Nederlandse Vakbond Varkenshouders v Commission* EU:T:2009:144 (the Commission cannot be expected to verify the accuracy to the last detail of all the information it receives in the course of Phase I proceedings).

[386] See Case T-342/99, *Airtours v Commission* EU:T:2002:146; Case T-310/01, *Schneider Electric SA v Commission* EU:T:2002:254; and Case T-5/02, *Tetra Laval v Commission* EU:T:2002:264.

[387] See also C-376/20 P, *Commission v CK Telecoms* EU:C:2022:817 (Kokott AG).

[388] Case C-413/06 P, *Bertelsmann and Sony Corp v Commission* EU:C:2008:392, para. 51.

[389] But see n. 384 and text.

of a situation of collective dominance and that it calls for a close examination of the circumstances which are relevant for an assessment of that effect on the conditions of competition on the reference market.

41. Although the [GC] stated, in paragraph 155, that proof of anti-competitive conglomerate effects of a merger of the kind notified calls for a precise examination, supported by convincing evidence, of the circumstances which allegedly produce those effects, it by no means added a condition relating to the requisite standard of proof but merely drew attention to the essential function of evidence, which is to establish convincingly the merits of an argument or, as in the present case, of a decision on a merger.

42. A prospective analysis of the kind necessary in merger control must be carried out with great care since it does not entail the examination of past events—for which often many items of evidence are available which make it possible to understand the causes—or of current events, but rather a prediction of events which are more or less likely to occur in future if a decision prohibiting the planned concentration or laying down the conditions for it is not adopted.

43. Thus, the prospective analysis consists of an examination of how a concentration might alter the factors determining the state of competition on a given market in order to establish whether it would give rise to a serious impediment to effective competition. Such an analysis makes it necessary to envisage various chains of cause and effect with a view to ascertaining which of them are the most likely.

44. The analysis of a 'conglomerate-type' concentration is a prospective analysis in which, first, the consideration of a lengthy period of time in the future and, secondly, the leveraging necessary to give rise to a significant impediment to effective competition mean that the chains of cause and effect are dimly discernible, uncertain and difficult to establish. That being so, the quality of the evidence produced by the Commission in order to establish that it is necessary to adopt a decision declaring the concentration incompatible with the common market is particularly important, since that evidence must support the Commission's conclusion that, if such a decision were not adopted, the economic development envisaged by it would be plausible.

D. A SIGNIFICANT IMPEDIMENT TO EFFECTIVE COMPETITION

(i) General and definition

Although the EUMR does not define a SIEC, case law has elucidated its meaning and, in accordance with recital 28 of the EUMR, the Commission has published Horizontal and Non-Horizontal Merger Guidelines[390] clarifying and explaining how it conducts its appraisal within a sound economic framework. Although the Commission is bound by its guidelines (insofar as they do not depart from the TFEU or the EUMR), they describe an analytical approach to be followed and do not provide a mechanical checklist requiring application of all the mentioned factors in each and every case.[391] Further although a useful point of reference, they do not bind the EU Courts.[392]

These sources make it clear that the EUMR aims to preserve effective competition on a market, and to deliver benefits to consumers in the form of low prices, high-quality products, a wide selection of goods and services, and innovation and, consequently, to prevent mergers that would deprive

[390] Available on DG Comp's website. The Commission commissioned and published on its website an *ex post* review of Merger Control Decisions, prepared by LEAR.

[391] Case T-282/06, *Sun Chemical Group v Commission* EU:T:2007:203, para. 56.

[392] Case T-399/16, *CK Telecoms v Commission* EU:T:2020:217, para. 100, Case C-376/20 P, judgment pending (if the judgment is upheld on appeal, some aspects of the Guidelines may require rewriting or updating to reflect the Court's interpretation of the SIEC test).

customers of these benefits by significantly increasing the market power of firms.[393] 'By "increased market power" is meant the ability of one or more firms to profitably increase prices, reduce output, choice or quality of goods and services, diminish innovation, or otherwise influence the parameters of competition.'[394] This could result from unilateral (non-coordinated) or coordinated effects which result from the merger and which are not offset by countervailing factors or efficiencies.

One important, preliminary question arising is how the 'significance' of any identified impediment to effective competition is to be appraised. The concept may have been introduced to exclude increases in market power, or price effects, which are too small to matter,[395] but it is open to different interpretations (from large, to not insignificant, to worthy of consideration), which may require different approaches in distinct contexts. Although in *CK Telecoms*[396] the GC held that the Commission is required to demonstrate that any adverse price effects identified would be significant (but is not obliged to set out a *de minimis* safe harbour), it did not provide clarification on how this is to be accomplished.[397] In the course of the appeal, Advocate General Kokott took the view that the GC was not entitled to criticise the Commission for having failed to establish that the possible price increases were, on the basis of comparisons in other cases, significant, as it failed to explain the comparability of the situations at issue.[398]

(ii) Market Power and Market Definition

Because merger assessment focuses on the question of whether the merger will increase the market power of firms—whether on the seller or buyer side, market definition has traditionally played an important role; in particular, as a mechanism for obtaining meaningful information regarding market power and how competition operates on the relevant market. 'The main purpose of market definition is to identify in a systematic way the immediate competitive constraints facing the merged entity.'[399]

Although market definition is not 'an end in itself but a tool to identify situations where there might be competition concerns',[400] and it is increasingly being questioned whether it is required at all in certain merger cases (see the discussion of pricing pressure indices later[401]), the CJ has held that:

> a proper definition of the relevant market is a necessary precondition for any assessment of the effect of a concentration on competition.[402]

[393] This inevitably involves a comparison of the existing competitive conditions with the conditions that will exist post-merger.

[394] HMG, para. 8. See also paras. 1 and 4 ('The creation or the strengthening of a dominant position is a primary form of such competitive harm' and provides 'an important indication as to the standard of competitive harm that is applicable when determining whether a concentration is likely to impede effective competition to a significant degree').

[395] See e.g. G. Monti, 'EU Merger Control After *CK Telecoms UK Investments v Commission*' (2020) 43(4) *World Competition* 447, 450.

[396] Case T-399/16, EU:T:2020:217, paras. 274–276, Case C-376/20 P, judgment pending.

[397] But see its approach to the importance of the competitive force and closeness of competition discussion in Section 5.E.iii.

[398] C-376/20 P, *Commission v CK Telecoms* EU:C:2022:817, para. 146.

[399] HMG, para. 10.

[400] M. Monti, 'Market Definition as a Cornerstone of EU Competition Policy', Speech at Workshop on Market Definition, Helsinki Fair Centre, 5 October 2001.

[401] Section 5.E.ii. See also, e.g., the UK's CMA129, Merger Assessment Guidelines, 18 March 2021, which downgrade the importance of market definition in merger cases, focusing more closely on how the merger will impact on rivalry and competitive constraints.

[402] Cases C-68/94 and 30/95, *France v Commission, Société Commerciale des Potasses et de l'Azote (SCPA) v Commission* EU:C:1998:148, para. 143. In some Phase I clearance decisions, however, the Commission does not need to make a final determination of the relevant market because it will not affect the outcome of the case whichever way the market is defined, see e.g. M.232, *PepsiCo/General Mills* [1992] OJ C228/6 and M.833, *The Coca-Cola Co/Carlsberg A/S* [1998] OJ L145/41.

The complexities of market definition are discussed in Chapter 3, including the importance of the SSNIP test,[403] the review and updating of the Notice on the definition of the relevant market, and the particular difficulties of market definition in the digital economy, especially those involving multi-sided platforms and eco-systems, and in situations where competition is driven not by price but by innovation or non-price factors (including the production of more sustainable products[404]).

There is, however, now a significant number of merger (and Article 102[405]) decisions which may provide useful indications of how market definition might be approached in particular spheres.[406] Nonetheless, as noted by Mosso, then Deputy Director-General for Mergers in DG Comp,[407] caution needs to be exercised with past precedents as market definition needs to be approached differently in merger and Article 101/102 cases respectively, and must be freshly addressed in each case in accordance with the facts of the case and evolving market circumstances.[408]

In many cases, the merging parties are likely to prefer a broad product and geographic[409] market in which their market shares are lower. On some occasions, however, a narrower product market definition may work to the parties' advantage, since this could result in a finding that there is no, or less, significant horizontal overlap in their products.[410]

The extent of the geographic market may be crucial, for example, where the merger might create a national or EU champion.[411] A drawing of a 'worldwide' market may be possible in the case of highly technical products involving significant R&D and large capital and manufacturing costs[412] or where a product is very valuable, internationally traded, and relatively cheap to transport. In *Gencor/Lonrho*,[413] for example, the Commission identified worldwide markets for various metal products, including platinum, which were traded on a global basis at publicly quoted prices. Further, in *Aérospatiale/Alenia/de Havilland*[414] the Commission concluded that the geographic market for

[403] Since the practical problem presented by the *cellophane fallacy* (especially relevant in Art. 102 cases) does not ordinarily apply.

[404] See DG Comp [2021] 1 *Competition Policy Brief*.

[405] In M.2416, *Tetra Laval/Sidel* 30 October 2001, e.g., the market definition adopted in Case C-333/94 P, *Tetra Pak II* EU:C:1996:436, was followed.

[406] Although merger cases are grouped on DG Comp's website by reference to an industry NACE code, Nomenclature générale des Activités économiques dans les Communautés Européennes, at time of notification, market definition may follow different directions from here. The Commission may take account of consumer preferences for sustainable products when defining relevant markets, see DG Comp [2021] 1 *Competition Policy Brief* and [2021] 4 *Competition Merger Brief* 13 and Case M.10047, *Schwarz Group/Suez Waste Management Companies* 17 December 2021.

[407] Mosso, n. 364, 4–5.

[408] Cases T-125 and 127/97, *Coca-Cola v Commission* EU:T:2000:84 (as market definitions change with market circumstances, a previous market definition finding is not binding upon the Commission). See P. McGeown and A. Barthélemy, 'Recent Developments in EU Merger Control' (2015) 6 *JECLAP* 440, 440.

[409] Even if a more narrowly drawn geographic market will not result in horizontal overlaps, the Commission may be prepared to characterise a merger between parties present on the same product market but in neighbouring geographic product markets as having horizontal effects in consequence of their being 'potential' competitors.

[410] See e.g. M.1578, *Sanitec/Sphinx* [2000] OJ L294/1, M.7284 *Siemens/John Wood/Rolls-Royce Combined ADGT Business/RWG* 4 August 2014 and M.7259, *Carphone Warehouse/Dixons* 25 June 2014.

[411] This was an important issue in relation to M.8677, *Siemens/Alstom* 7 February 2019, n. 496 and text.

[412] See e.g. M.269, *Shell/Montecatini* [1994] OJ L332/48.

[413] M.619 [1997] OJ L11/30.

[414] M.53 [1991] OJ L334/42. See also M.877, *Boeing/McDonnell Douglas* [1997] OJ L336/16. A worldwide market was also found in M.9343, *DSME/HHI* 13 January 2022.

the commuter aircraft[415] was worldwide, excluding China and Eastern Europe. There were no tangible barriers to the importation of these aircraft into the EU and the costs of transportation were negligible.[416]

E. COMPETITIVE ASSESSMENT OF HORIZONTAL MERGERS

(i) Introduction and Overview

Mergers between undertakings that are competitors, or potential competitors, on the same market may, by eliminating a competitive restraint on the market, lead to the firms' gaining or enhancing their market power. Form CO thus requires the parties to provide data in relation to affected markets where 'two or more of the parties to the concentration are engaged in business activities in the same relevant market and where the concentration will lead to a combined market share of 20% or more'.[417]

The HMG clarify that the following factors are relevant to the assessment: the market shares of the parties and concentration thresholds;[418] the likelihood of anti-competitive effects on the market, through non-coordinated or coordinated effects;[419] and whether countervailing factors, including buyer power, new entry, or efficiencies would counteract potentially harmful effects identified.[420] A concentration may be permitted where any anti-competitive effects result from the failure of a firm, rather than the merger.[421]

(ii) Market Shares, Concentration Levels, and GUPPI

The Commission's HMG explain that: 'Market shares and concentration levels provide useful first indications of the market structure and of the competitive importance of both the merging parties and their competitors.'[422]

The Commission states that where the market share of the undertakings concerned does not exceed 25 per cent the merger is not liable to impede effective competition and is presumed to be compatible with the internal market. Further, the Notice on simplified procedure applies if the parties' combined market share is less than 20 per cent or if the merger leads only to a small incremental increase in market share.[423] Conversely, a market share of over 50 per cent may in itself be evidence of the existence of a dominant market position.[424] The Commission accepts, however, that high market shares cannot necessarily be equated with market power, for example where the merged entity is met by

[415] The Commission relied on the evidence of customers and competitors to conclude that there was not just one market for all aircraft of between 20 and 70 seats but three separate turbo-prop commuter aircraft markets for commuters with 20–39 seats, 40–59 seats, and 60+ seats, each of which attracted different categories of buyers.

[416] M.53, *Aérospatiale/Alenia/de Havilland* [1991] OJ L334/42, para. 20.

[417] Form CO, s. 6.3. [418] HMG, part III. [419] Ibid., part IV.

[420] Ibid., parts V–VII. [421] Ibid., part VIII. [422] Ibid., para. 14.

[423] Notice on simplified procedure, para. 5(d)(i). In 2023, the Commission introduced a flexibility clause in the notice to allow the Commission to treat mergers under the simplified procedure at the request of the notifying parties where the combined market share of the parties is below 25%, para. 8.

[424] HMG, paras. 17–18 and see, e.g., M.6166, *Deutsche Börse/NYSE Euronext* 1 February 2012, *aff'd* Case T-175/12, *Deutsche Börse v Commission* EU:T:2015:148. See also later discussion of market shares and entry analysis and Case C-62/86, *AKZO Chemie BV v Commission* EU:C:1991:286, para. 60 (in the context of an Art. 102 case, the CJ reiterated that: 'very large shares are in themselves, and save in exceptional circumstances, evidence of the existence of a dominant position . . . That is the situation where there is a market share of 50%', see Chap. 6).

rigorous competition from an active competitor on the market,[425] where the increase in market share is insignificant or market shares are declining,[426] where they will be counteracted by buyer power[427] or new entry,[428] or market shares are volatile.[429]

The Commission also considers that the overall concentration level in a market, may provide an indication of the competitive situation, the market structure, and of the competitive importance of the merging parties and their competitors.[430] For example, the Herfindahl–Hirschman index (the HHI) seeks to identify the concentration of a particular market by using numerical distinctions[431] which reflect both concentration levels on the market generally and the degree to which larger firms are dominant in the market. It operates by adding together the squares of the market shares of each of the undertakings operating in the market.[432] The degree of concentration on the market is assessed by reference to the sum of those market shares (it thus gives greater weight proportionately to the market shares of the larger firms).

Like market shares, the HHI is used as an initial indicator of the absence of competition concerns, but 'do not give rise to a presumption of either the existence or the absence of such concerns'.[433] The Guidelines state that the Commission is *unlikely* to identify competition concerns in a market:[434]

- with a post-merger HHI below 1,000;
- with a post-merger HHI between 1,000 and 2,000, where the change in the HHI (the delta) is below 250;
- with a post-merger HHI above 2,000, where the delta is below 150;

except where special circumstances exist, for example: one of the firms is a potential entrant or an important innovator; one of the firms is a maverick likely to disrupt coordinated conduct; one of the firms has a pre-merger market share of 50 per cent or more; cross-shareholdings exist between the market participants; or there is evidence of past coordination or facilitating practices on the market.

425 See e.g. M.68, *Tetra Pak/Alfa Laval* [1991] OJ L290/35, 38–39; M.12, *Varta/Bosch* [1991] OJ L320/26 (the merged entity held 44% of the German battery market but a competitor, with only 5–10% of the market would provide strong competition on account of its reputation and resources); M.4, *Renault/Volvo* [1990] OJ C281/2 (Renault would acquire 54% of the French market but Mercedes, which had only 18%, had the reputation and resources to be able to exercise sufficient competitive restraint on Renault); and M.4533, *SCA/P&G* 5 September 2007 (European facial tissue business) (market shares of 80–90% would not enable the merged entity to exercise market power because of vigorous competition from private labels). However, some competitors may not provide effective competition and may be unlikely to do so in the future: M.190, *Nestlé/Perrier* [1992] OJ L356/1.

426 See e.g. McGeown and Barthélemy, n. 408, 444.

427 See e.g. M.1225, *Enso/Stora* [1999] OJ L254/9 and M.4617, *Nutreco/BASF* 25 September 2007. Mergers can also lead to increases in buyer power, see R. Inderst and N. Mazzarotto, 'Can the SIEC Test be Used to Assess Effects from Buyer Power' (2017) 8 *JECLAP* 185.

428 M.42, *Alcatel/Telettra* [1991] OJ L122/48 and see Section 5.E.v.

429 See e.g. Case T-79/12, *Cisco Systems Inc v Commission* EU:T:2013:635, n. 437 and text, M.354, *American Cyanamid/Shell* [1993] OJ C273/6 ('an analysis focusing on market shares alone is not particularly probative in a dynamic and R&D-intensive industry') and M.7217, *Facebook/WhatsApp* 3 October 2014.

430 HMG, paras. 14–21.

431 The HHI has some serious limitations, see S. Bishop and M. Walker, *The Economics of EC Competition Law: Concepts, Application and Measurement* (3rd edn, Sweet & Maxwell, 2010), 3-016–3-019.

432 'Although it is best to include all firms in the calculation, lack of information about very small firms may not be important because such firms do not affect the HHI significantly.' HMG, para. 16.

433 Ibid., para. 21. The view could be taken, however, that structural presumptions should be applied, especially against mergers reducing the number of players on the market to below 5, see e.g. Kwoka, n. 19, Chap. 4.

434 HMG, paras. 19–21.

In *Sun Chemical Group v Commission*,[435] the GC had to consider the importance of these preliminary tools to the robustness of a Commission decision authorising a merger between Apollo and Akzo Nobel (the first and second players in the market). The appellants argued that the Commission had failed (a) to draw the right conclusions from the fact that the merger would result in a combined market share of 40–50 per cent (indicative of dominance) and (b) to consider concentration levels which would have indicated real concern. The GC held that the analysis of market shares did not in itself show the existence of dominance.[436] Further, that the Commission's failure to make an HHI calculation did not affect the finding on dominance (even if, as the applicants alleged, the calculation indicated that the effects of the merger exceeded the Commission's stipulated thresholds). Exceeding the HHI thresholds did not give rise to a presumption of competition concerns. On the contrary, market shares and concentration levels, whilst providing useful first indications, did not have to be assessed in every decision.

In *Cisco Systems Inc v Commission*,[437] the GC similarly rejected the claimant's action seeking an annulment of the Commission's decision clearing the *Microsoft/Skype* merger on the grounds that the combination of a very high market share and HHI concentration degree (of 7,340) provided, at the very least, a 'strong indicia of the existence of competition concerns warranting additional scrutiny'.[438] Again the Court stressed that these factors provided only a starting point in the assessment; 'market shares may only be used as indicia of competition concerns . . . .'[439] The Court noted that in this case the markets shares were very unstable, particularly as the sector (consumer communications) was a recent and fast-growing one, characterised by short innovation cycles in which 'large market shares may turn out to be ephemeral. In such a dynamic context, high market shares are not necessarily indicative of market power and, therefore, of lasting damage to competition which Regulation No 139/2004 seeks to prevent.'[440] The GC also referred to a number of features of the market which meant that the market shares and concentration ratio could not be said to be 'indicative of a degree of market power which would enable the new entity to significantly impede effective competition in the internal market'.[441]

Some competition agencies now supplement or substitute traditional analysis based on market definition, market shares, and concentration measures with other, arguably more meaningful, tools, such as pricing pressure indices (PPIs)—especially for mergers in differentiated product markets where the competitive effect depends more upon the closeness of competition between the merging parties than on market shares—and merger simulation,[442] based on oligopoly models.[443] 'Upward pricing pressure' (UPP) seeks to measure the incentives of the merged firm to increase the price of its products post-merger and is calculated on the basis of diversion ratios and price/cost margins.[444] For example, the US Horizontal Merger Guidelines (which are currently under review) state:[445]

> In some cases, where sufficient information is available, the Agencies assess the value of diverted sales, which can serve as an indicator of upward pricing pressure [UPP] on the first product resulting from the merger. Diagnosing unilateral price effects based on the value of diverted sales need not rely

[435] Case T-282/06, EU:T:2007:203. [436] Ibid., paras. 133–142. [437] Case T-79/12, EU:T:2013:635.

[438] Ibid., para. 56. [439] Ibid., para. 65. It held that the same is true for concentration ratios.

[440] Ibid., para. 69. [441] Ibid., para. 74. [442] See e.g. n. 478 and text.

[443] See e.g. OECD Roundtable on Market Definition, Discussion paper, DAF/COMP(2012) 13, and Chap. 3.

[444] See e.g. J. Farrell and C. Shapiro, 'Antitrust Evaluation of Horizontal Mergers: An Economic Alternative to Market Definition' (2010) 10 *B.E. J of Theoretical Economics* (Policies perspectives) and A. Oldale and J. Padilla, 'EU Merger Assessment of Upward Pricing Pressure: Making Sense of UPP, GUPPI and the Like' (2013) 4 *JECLAP* 375.

[445] US DOJ and FTC, Horizontal Merger Guidelines, 19 August 2010 (2010 Guidelines), 6.1.

on market definition or the calculation of market shares and concentration. The Agencies rely much more on the value of diverted sales than on the level of the HHI for diagnosing unilateral price effects in markets with differentiated products. If the value of diverted sales is proportionately small, significant unilateral price effects are unlikely.

As this approach does not take account of efficiencies or other factors that would create downward pricing pressure,[446] it is generally described as the 'gross upward pricing pressure index', or GUPPI.

Although the Commission still considers traditional assessment based on market shares, etc. to provide an 'important and strong' first indication of market power in many markets (such as mature, basic industries in which firms produce relatively homogenous products)[447] and does not refer to UPP or GUPPI in its guidelines, analysis of UPP does form an integral part of its 'quantitative merger assessment' in some cases (see, for example, *Hutchison 3G Austria/Orange Austria*,[448] *Telefónica Deutschland/E-Plus*,[449] *Hutchison 3G UK/Telefónica Ireland*[450] and *Hutchison 3G UK/Telefónica UK*).[451] Indeed, in horizontal unilateral effects cases the Commission now routinely takes account of UPP through assessing diversion ratios and the profit margins of firms when determining the closeness of competition between the merging firms and assessing incentives to increase prices post-merger. Further in *EssilorLuxottica/GrandVision*,[452] the Commission for the first time used such indices to assess vertical incentives to raise prices (vGUPPI).

In *CK Telekom*,[453] the GC accepted that indicators of upward pressures on prices may be useful as a 'first' screen, but found that they did not provide 'credible forecasts of price increases of simulations of mergers'.[454] A difficulty is that horizontal mergers will, in addition to increasing concentration, likely result in gross upward pricing pressure. The GC stressed that to have greater probative value, the quantitative analysis would need to be more elaborate, taking account not only of the likely reaction of competitors (based on a GUPPI analysis), but also the significance of the price increase and, controversially, 'standard' efficiencies (resulting from the integration of production and distribution processes).[455] Because, however, quantitative analysis generally forms just one piece of evidence relied on by the Commission to predict likely unilateral anti-competitive effects, the suggestion that it should take account of 'standard', but undemonstrated, efficiencies in its assessment has been argued to misunderstand the scheme of the EUMR and the nature of the analysis and has been contested on appeal.[456] In the course of the appeal, Advocate General Kokott considered that the GC had erred in law in requiring the Commission to include standard efficiencies in its UPP analysis as these were not, as the law currently stands, recognised by the EUMR or the Guidelines. Rather the law envisaged the Commission only had to take account of substantiated and likely efficiencies.[457]

[446] It is not a means for assessing entry, buyer power, or efficiencies etc.

[447] M.6471, *Outokumpu/Inoxum* 7 November 2012, paras. 315 and 360.

[448] M.6497, 12 December 2012, see n. 506 and text.

[449] M.7018, 2 July 2014, see n. 507 and text. [450] M.6992, see n. 508 and text.

[451] M.7612, 11 May 2016 (prohibited), annulled Case T-399/19, *CK Telecoms v Commission* EU:T:2020:217, Case C-376/20 P, judgment pending. See L. Wiethaus and R. Nitsche, 'Upward Pricing Pressure Analysis: Critical Issues in Recent Applications' (2015) 6 *JECLAP* 48 and G. Drauz, P. McGeown, and B. Record, 'Recent Developments in EU Merger Control' (2013) 4 *JECLAP* 146, 153. See also n. 468 and text, and e.g. S. Thomas, 'Close Competitors in Merger Review' (2013) 4 *JECLAP* 391 ('[a]lthough the analysis of closeness of competition is an important enhancement of substantive merger appraisal, it is not appropriate to waive market definition as such').

[452] M.9569, 23 March 2021 and see DG Comp [2021] 3 *Competition Merger Brief* 9.

[453] Case T-399/16, EU:T:2020:217, Case C-376/20 P, judgment pending.

[454] Ibid., para. 256. [455] Ibid., paras. 258–279. [456] Case C-376/20 P (fourth ground of appeal).

[457] C-376/20 P, *Commission v CK Telecoms* EU:C:2022:817, paras. 150–158.

(iii) Non-coordinated Anti-competitive Effects

The most frequent category of concerns investigated by the Commission is non-coordinated effects in horizontal merger cases, whether alone or in parallel with other theories of harm.[458] Where a merger removes important competitive constraints on the merging firms those firms may acquire greater market power. The merged entity may then be able to increase price or reduce quality, choice, or innovation irrespective of the response of its competitors.[459] Such market power may be acquired where it creates or strengthens a (single) dominant firm, a concept familiar from the Court's case law under Article 102.[460] Non-coordinated effects may also arise outside this classic scenario where the merger occurs on an oligopolistic market.[461] In *CK Telecoms*,[462] the GC, for the first time, ruled on the legal test to be applied in this latter situation. In particular, it stated:

> 90 . . . Article 2(3) of Regulation No 139/2004 must be interpreted as allowing the Commission to prohibit, in certain circumstances, on oligopolistic markets concentrations which, although not giving rise to the creation or strengthening of an individual or collective dominant position, are liable to affect the competitive conditions on the market to an extent equivalent to that attributable to such positions, by conferring on the merged entity the power to enable it to determine, by itself, the parameters of competition and, in particular, to become a price maker instead of remaining a price taker.
>
> . . .
>
> 96 Thus, Article 2(3) of Regulation No 139/2004 must be interpreted in the light of recital 25 thereof, which lays down two cumulative conditions in order that non-coordinated effects arising from a concentration may, under certain circumstances, result in a significant impediment to effective competition: the concentration must involve (i) 'the elimination of important competitive constraints that the merging parties had exerted upon each other' and (ii) 'a reduction of competitive pressure on the remaining competitors'.

Although the GC's goal of increasing legal certainty in this sphere is important, a question to be decided on appeal is whether these statements, combined with the other limiting principles imposed in the judgment on unilateral effects analysis,[463] construe Article 2(3) too narrowly and in a way which is out of tune with the EUMR's objectives and the standard economics it seeks to reflect. For example, some have argued that by requiring the merged entity to act, like a dominant firm, as a price-maker, the GC reintroduced the more formalistic dominance approach back into the EUMR and limited the Regulation's ability to reach the non-collusive oligopoly gap cases the 2004 SIEC test was specifically designed to reach. Further, by demanding proof of a reduction in competitive pressure on remaining

[458] See e.g. P. Werner, S. Clerckx, and H. de la Barre, 'Commission Expansionism in EU Merger Control—Fact and Fiction' (2018) 9 *JECLAP* 133 and T. Buettner, 'Closeness of Competition from an Economic Perspective' (2016) 7 *JECLAP* 690.

[459] If other firms on the market follow, then the anti-competitive effects will be felt throughout the market. In contrast with coordinated effects cases, however, the ability of the merged entity to increase price is not dependent upon the reaction of other undertakings in the market. A SIEC may also arise where the concentration impacts on the buyer side of the market, 'both suppliers and buyers can have market power', HMG, paras. 8 and 61 and see Case M.9409, *Aurubis/Metallo* 4 May 2020. However, assessment of buyer power requires a careful analysis of the impact of the merger on upstream and downstream markets as buyer power may generate consumer benefits through the passing on of lower prices to consumers, see also Chaps. 9 and 10.

[460] In practice, however, merger decisions dealing with unilateral market power post-2004 may be articulated without reference to the dominance concept.

[461] HMG, para. 25 (and see Sections 5.A and 5.B).

[462] Case T-399/16, EU:T:2020:217, Case C-376/20 P, judgment pending.

[463] See further discussion of the case at nn. 471 and 516 and text.

competitors, the GC added an additional requirement beyond proof that the merged entity will be able to raise prices unilaterally as a result of the elimination of important competitive constraints that they exercised on each other. The GC thus arguably raised the bar for proving unilateral effects in oligopolistic markets at a time when concern about concentration in markets, especially oligopolistic ones, is mounting.[464] In the appeal proceedings, however, Advocate General Kokott took the view that the GC had adopted a contradictory approach and erred in law by adopting a formalistic and reductionist reading of the SIEC test and by limiting the concept to the two cumulative conditions set out in recital 25 and treating them as both cumulative and exhaustive. Such an approach would prevent the Commission from taking account of factors relevant to the appraisal and analysis. In so doing, however, the Advocate General offered little guidance on the key elements of non-coordinated effects and how they are to be interpreted.[465]

The Guidelines set out a non-exhaustive list of factors that the Commission considers may influence its decision as to whether significant non-coordinated anti-competitive effects are likely to result from the merger:

a. The Market Shares Held by the Merging Firms and the Closeness of Competition Between Them

The larger the combined, and increase in, market shares, the more likely it is that the merger will lead to a significant increase in market power.[466] As, however, market shares are just one factor in a dominance or unilateral effects assessment, the HMG recognise that a high market share will not constitute 'decisive proof that the merged group will hold market power';[467] assessment of other factors, including the nature of the product and industry and the closeness of competition between the mergers, is also vital.

24. A merger may significantly impede effective competition in a market by removing important competitive constraints on one or more sellers, who consequently have increased market power. The most direct effect of the merger will be the loss of competition between the merging firms. For example, if prior to the merger one of the merging firms had raised its price, it would have lost some sales to the other merging firm. The merger removes this particular constraint. Non-merging firms in the same market can also benefit from the reduction of competitive pressure that results from the merger, since the merging firms' price increase may switch some demand to the rival firms, which, in turn, may find it profitable to increase their prices. The reduction in these competitive constraints could lead to significant price increases in the relevant market.

Where products are differentiated on a market, some will be closer substitutes for each other than others. Mergers 'between producers offering products which a substantial number of customers regard as their first and second choices could generate a significant price increase'.[468] The competition between firms may also be more intense the more proximately located the competitors.

464 See Section 5.2.B.ii. 465 C-376/20 P, *Commission v CK Telecoms* EU:C:2022:817, paras. 73–80.

466 See HMG, paras. 27–30 and e.g. M.6663, *Ryanair/Aer Lingus* 27 February 2013 (discussed from n. 480 and text), M.4404, *Universal/BMG* 22 May 2007; M.4523, *Travelport/Worldspan* 21 August 2007; M.4381, *JCI/FIAMM* 10 May 2007; and M.4734, *INEOS/Kerling* 30 January 2008.

467 HMG, para. 27. 468 Ibid., para. 28.

S. Bishop and M. Walker, *The Economics of EC Competition Law: Concepts, Application and Measurement* (3rd edn, Sweet & Maxwell, 2010)

Mergers involving differentiated products

7.026 Potential variations in the 'closeness' of competition between competing firms that arises from product or geographical differentiation raises a number of additional complications in applying the traditional approach to assessing whether a merger gives rise to unilateral effects . . . [I]t is often argued that defining the relevant market is much more problematic in industries characterized by a high degree of differentiation, But . . . the Hypothetical Monopolist Test is well-suited to addressing such issues. This implies that any additional complications that arise in industries with highly differentiated goods and services relate to the interpretation that can be drawn from market shares rather than the definition of the relevant market. Interpreting market shares in highly differentiated industries is rendered more difficult since the very essence of competition between differentiated products implies that consumers do not consider all products to be equally substitutable. In consequence, products do not all impose the same strength of competitive constraint on each other. Where this is the case, market shares provide a poor proxy for discriminating 'close' competitors and 'not so close' competitors.

A competitor will be said to be, loosely speaking, 'close' if following a relative price increase a significant proportion of the resulting lost sales would be gained by that competitor. The concept of 'closeness of competition' when a merger concerns highly differentiated products can be thought of in terms of product characteristics and geographical location. For example, a premium ice cream, say, is likely to face 'closer' competition from another supplier of a premium ice cream brand than from a supplier of an own-label product. Similarly, when transportation costs are important, a supplier is likely to face 'closer' competition from suppliers located nearby than from those located far away.

The concept of 'closeness' of competition is illustrated in the following example. Suppose there are four firms, A, B, C, and D, each with sales of 100. Suppose that if A raises its price by 5 per cent, it will lose 20 per cent of its sales, which makes the price rise unprofitable. These sales would be diverted to the other three firms as shown in Table 7.2. This table shows that 15 consumers divert from A to B, three divert to C and two divert to D. In this sense, B is a closer competitor to A than either C or D; the extent to which consumers would divert from A to B is understated by B's market share. If A and B were to merge, then an increase in the post-merger price of products supplied by A would lead to the combined firm, AB, losing only five units of sales. In consequence, increasing the price of A by 5 per cent is more likely to be profitable than a merger between A and D, where the same increase in the price of products supplied by A would lead to the loss of 18 units of sale.

Table 7.2 An illustration of Unilateral Effects

Firm	Sales at current prices	Sales if A raises price 5 per cent
A	100	80
B	100	115
C	100	103
D	100	102
AB	200	195

This example illustrates that the degree to which a merger in a differentiated product market might result in a unilateral price increase depends on the relative 'closeness' of the merging firms to one another. Based on market shares alone, B, C and D all appear to be providing an equally strong competitive constraint on A. However, examination of the diversion of sales from A to these firms shows that in this hypothetical example, B provides a much stronger pre-merger competitive constraint on A than either C or D since most of A's lost sales went to B, indicating that A and B are in some sense particularly 'close' competitors.

However, it is important to understand that the concept of closeness of competition cannot be divorced entirely from an assessment of market shares. In the above example, B is said to represent a particularly close competitor because the proportion of sales lost to B exceeds that predicted by market share alone; on the basis of market shares, we would predict that six to seven units would be diverted to B whereas in reality the number of units diverted (in the hypothetical example) would be 15. Assessing whether a merger will result in a reduction in the effectiveness of competition therefore requires an assessment of whether market shares provide a good proxy for the degree of pre-merger competitive constraint or whether they understate or overstate the importance of that competitive constraint. In the case where market shares understate the competitive constraint, we can properly consider two firms to be 'close' competitors.

When assessing closeness of competition, it is important that the source of that closeness is clearly articulated and closely examined. All too often, it is asserted that two firms are particularly close competitors without reference being made to the alleged source of that closeness. Assessing whether two firms represent particularly close competitors is an empirical question and cannot (or should not) be determined solely with reference to physical or geographical attributes of the firms concerned. For example, consider a straight road on which four petrol stations are located. On one level, it might appear intuitive that the petrol stations adjacent to one another provide 'closer' competitive constraints than no-adjacent petrol stations. But that is not necessarily the case. If all potential consumers drive past all of these four petrol stations on their way to work from home then all the petrol stations could be equally close. Similarly, the fact that two firms have more similar offerings than some other competitors cannot by itself be determinative that they represent particularly close competitors.

In some cases, the closeness of competition between the merging parties may consequently be more important than their market shares. The Commission will thus seek to obtain both qualitative and quantitative evidence on the degree of substitutability through diversion ratios or estimates of cross-price elasticity, which may be based on internal documents, survey evidence (questionnaires sent to customers and competitors of the merging parties), customer switching patterns, bid data, critical loss or shock analysis, or merger simulation. Measurement is therefore generally dependent on the availability of data.[469] Difficult issues, however, are exactly what are the best tools to assess closeness of competition, and what degree of closeness is required for the transaction to be problematic. Indeed, mounting concern has been articulated that the Commission too easily finds firms to be close competitors in oligopolistic markets[470] and that limiting principles to the concept need to be identified. Although in *CK Telecoms*[471] the GC held that the Commission is required to establish that the parties are 'particularly close'[472] competitors, it did not provide guidance as to what precisely it meant by this and its relationship to the question of whether the closeness of competition between the firms means

[469] Where reliable quantitative measures of the degree of substitutability are not available, a market share-based analysis (which is often correlated with diversion ratios) may remain important, Buettner, n. 458.

[470] See e.g. W. Berg and S. Real, 'How Close Is Too Close? A Critical Review of the European Commission's Assessment of Closeness of Competition' (2016) 7 *JECLAP* 442.

[471] Case T-399/16, EU:T:2020:217, Case C-376/20 P, judgment pending.

[472] Ibid., para. 247.

that a merger between them would be able to generate significant price effects. On appeal, Advocate General Kokott took the view that the EUMR did not require the parties to the concentration to be particularly close—rather, this requirement was based on the excessive standard of proof which the GC had imposed on the Commission—and that the GC had erred in law in holding the Commission's analysis of the closeness of competition to be flawed, but the ruling from the CJ is awaited.[473]

On markets where the parties are found not to be close competitors, see for example *Carphone Warehouse/Dixons*,[474] a finding of anti-competitive effects is unlikely, even perhaps if the merging parties have significant combined markets shares. In contrast, a merger between firms which produces products with a high degree of substitutability (where they are close competitors, even if not the closest competitors) is more likely to produce anti-competitive consequences and either be prohibited or cleared only subject to commitments. In *Volvo/Scania*,[475] the Commission, in assessing the effect of Volvo's acquisition of a controlling stake in Scania, was influenced by the fact that in various markets Volvo and Scania (active on the heavy trucks markets) had similar market positions and that their products were each other's closest substitutes. The loss of competition between them would significantly increase the merged entity's advantage over its competitors. In *Schwarz Group/Suez Waste Management Companies*,[476] the Commission took account of Dutch customers' preference for disposing of waste in the least environmentally harmful manner when assessing the closeness of competition between Dutch and German suppliers of lightweight packaging sorting services.

In *GE/Instrumentarium*,[477] the Commission was concerned about the proposed acquisition by GE Medical Equipment of a Finnish-based company, Instrumentarium, which was a leading manufacturer of hospital equipment. The merger would bring together two of the four leading players in Europe in patient monitors, markets characterised by differentiated products with competition taking place through tenders. In particular, the Commission considered that the merger would lead to the merged entity acquiring high market shares in a number of national EU markets for perioperative monitors, used by anaesthesiologists to monitor patients during operations. The Commission conducted a series of statistical analyses and relied on bidding data and win-loss analysis[478] to establish that the parties were particularly close competitors, at least on some markets, so that the merger would significantly increase their market power.[479] Analysis showed that each of the parties was likely to charge a lower price where the other took part in the bidding contest. In the end, the concentration was cleared subject to a package of remedies designed to remove the horizontal overlaps in the perioperative monitoring market.

The closeness of competition between the merging parties was an important factor in the Commission's first decision[480] prohibiting Ryanair's hostile takeover bid for Aer Lingus.[481] This was a

[473] C-376/20 P, *Commission v CK Telecoms* EU:C:2022:817, paras. 123–125.

[474] M.7259, 25 June 2014, the Commission accepted that the businesses were not close competitors, partly because they operated very different business models.

[475] M.1672 [2001] OJ L143/74, see especially paras. 31–70 and 107 (the geographical scope of the market was crucial in this case. If, as the parties alleged, the market was an EU or EEA market, the parties' market shares would have been diluted since they did not have such a significant presence on markets outside four Nordic countries and Ireland. The Commission concluded that for these five countries the relevant geographic markets were still national in scope).

[476] Case M.10047, 17 December 2021, see also n. 406.

[477] M.3083 [2004] OJ L109/1.

[478] The analysis considered the closeness of competition between the merging parties by analysing the ranking of the other party in contracts won by one of them. The Commission also conducted economic analysis of bids in M.7278, *GE/Alstom* 8 September 2015.

[479] M.3083, *GE/Instrumentarium* IP/03/1193, para. 131 ff. But contrast e.g. M.3765, *Amer/Salomon* 12 October 2005.

[480] The transaction was notified three times, see M.4439, 27 June 2007 (prohibited), M.5434 (withdrawn in January 2009), and M.6663, 27 February 2013 (prohibited).

[481] M.4439, 27 June 2007; Case T-342/07, *Ryanair v Commission* EU:T:2010:280; Case T-411/07, *Aer Lingus v Commission* EU:T:2010:281 (both appeals were dismissed). The Commission also prohibited a subsequent attempt by Ryanair to take over Aer Lingus in 2013, M.6663, *Ryanair/Aer Lingus* 27 February 2013; and see A. Witt, 'From *Airtours* to *Ryanair*: Is the More Economic Approach to EU Merger Law Really About More Economics?' (2012) 49 *CMLRev* 217.

controversial case, not only because it was the first merger prohibition since 2004 but also because it was the first time that the Commission has prohibited a merger between airlines.[482]

In assessing the competitive effects, the Commission found not only that the parties would have had very high combined market shares on a large number of routes, as they would acquire a monopoly position on 22 of the routes and more than 60 per cent market share on 13 more routes,[483] but that the merger would eliminate competition between the two closest competitors on the routes and that barriers to entry into the markets were high. Ryanair argued that it and Aer Lingus were not close competitors. In particular, Ryanair argued that it targeted customers whose alternative was not to fly with another airline but rather not to fly at all[484] and that unlike Aer Lingus, a 'mid-frills' operator,[485] it was a 'no-frills' operator.

The Commission rejected these arguments finding that Aer Lingus had become increasingly similar to Ryanair[486] and sought to compete with the no-frills airlines.[487] Both airlines flew point-to-point,[488] i.e. directly between individual airports, rather than on a hub-and-spoke model where traffic flows through a central hub,[489] operated out of, and were based at, Dublin airport[490] and had a combined share of about 80 per cent of all scheduled European traffic to and from Dublin. Each party also closely monitored the other's marketing campaigns and price changes and constrained each other's behaviour.[491] The Commission corroborated its findings by a price regression analysis, and a specifically designed passenger survey.[492]

The Commission thus found the parties to be each other's closest actual competitor[493] and that the merger would eliminate competition on these routes and give the merged entity significantly increased market power. Consequently, it could be predicated that, post-merger, both carriers would have an incentive to set higher fares (or reduce the number of flights) for Aer Lingus; if Aer Lingus customers were lost, many would be captured by Ryanair. Further, the merger would take away incentives to increase quality and to innovate.[494]

[482] See IP/07/893, see also M.5830, *Olympic Air/Aegean Airlines I* 26 January 2011, n. 615 and text. Contrast e.g. M.5335, *Lufthansa/SN Airholding (Brussels Airline)* 14 April 2010, M.5747, *Iberia/British Airways* 14 July 2010, and M.6447, *IAG/bmi* 30 March 2012 (cleared subject to commitments to give up airport slots) and for a review of a number of airline mergers, see e.g. G. Drauz, T. Chellingsworth, and H. Hyrkas, 'Recent Developments in EC Merger Control' (2010) 1 *JECLAP* 12, 14–17.

[483] M.4439, *Ryanair/Aer Lingus* 27 June 2007, para. 342.

[484] Ibid., paras. 52, 53, 432, and 433 (consequently its pricing was not constrained by other airlines but rather by the price sensitivity of its passengers).

[485] Ibid., para. 353 (e.g. flying to more centrally located airports).

[486] The Commission noted that there was a range of airlines offering different levels of service so that at one end of the spectrum would be 'full-service' airlines offering, e.g., seat reservation, online check-in, last-minute bookings, customer loyalty schemes, free baggage handling, business lounges, free drinks and food on board, etc., and at the other end of the spectrum would be the 'no-frills' airlines offering a rudimentary level of service encompassing few, if any, of the above, ibid., para. 49.

[487] E.g. Aer Lingus had adopted its marketing slogan ('Low Fares—Way Better'). This slogan appeared to constitute a direct response to Ryanair's slogan: 'The Low Fares Airline', ibid., para. 367, Case T-342/07, EU:T:2010:280, paras. 92–93.

[488] M.4439, 27 June 2007, paras. 47–48.

[489] In contrast to previous airline cases decided by the Commission which involved network carriers operating at different airports in different countries, see e.g. M.3940, *Lufthansa/Eurowings* 22 December 2005, M.3280, *Air France/KLM* 11 February 2002, *aff'd* Case T-177/04, *easyJet v Commission* EU:T:2006:187.

[490] Where they concentrate their operations and the point from where a majority of their flights begin and end. It is also the place of: overnighting aircraft; maintenance, customer care, and ground-handling services; stand-by planes; and where staff are based, M.4439, 27 June 2007, paras. 404–407.

[491] Ibid., para. 434 ff.

[492] A price regression analysis is a specific tool for understanding the relationship between two or more variables, see e.g. M. de la Mano, E. Pesaresi, and O. Stehman, 'Econometric and survey evidence in the competitive assessment of the Ryanair-Aer Lingus merger' (2007) 3 *Competition Policy Newsletter* 73, M.4439, 27 June 2007.

[493] Ibid., para. 431.

[494] Ibid., para. 492. The Commission was also concerned about the impact the merger would have on potential competition. As the airlines were the main carriers operating on routes to/from Dublin, the merger would eliminate the most likely entrant on routes out of that airport currently served by only one of them.

The Commission has blocked a number of other mergers on the basis of a non-coordinated effects theory. (although they constitute a very small fraction of those notified). For example, it prohibited mergers between: *Deutsche Börse/NYSE Euronext*[495] which would have led to parties acquiring extremely high market shares in a number of exchange-traded financial derivatives markets (e.g. bonds); *Siemens/Alstom*[496] which would have brought together two of the largest suppliers for certain railway and metro signalling systems and rolling stock in the EU so creating a market leader in some signalling markets and a dominant player in very high-speed trains, resulting in higher prices and reduced choice and innovation to the detriment of EU consumers; and *Daewoo Shipbuilding and Marine Engineering (DSME)/Hyundai Heavy Industries (HHI)*,[497] which would have created a dominant position in the worldwide market for the construction of large liquified natural gas carriers (LLNGC).[498] In the latter case, the Commission placed emphasis on the fact that the LLNGC were highly sophisticated, expensive, and differentiated vessels, and that the merger would result in the parties acquiring a significant market share (of at least 60 per cent, in itself consistent with dominance). The merged entity would also have had a significant share of total capacity to build the vessels and there was only one other large competitor in the market, which would not have been sufficient, or have enough capacity, to act as a credible constraint on the new company. The market was also characterised by very high barriers to entry and expansion.

In *UPS/TNT Express*,[499] a so-called gap case, the Commission prohibited the merger having found that the parties were close competitors, it would have created a stronger number two player in the express delivery services market (behind DHL), and would result in UPP which was not offset by efficiency benefits. As the decision was annulled on appeal on procedural grounds, the substantive arguments in this case were not considered.[500]

The Commission has also closely scrutinised mergers increasing concentration, and bringing together close competitors in mobile telecoms markets, especially where they may eliminate a new or maverick player from the market. In *T-Mobile/tele.ring*,[501] the Commission assessed a merger between the second (T-Mobile Austria) and fourth (tele.ring) players in the Austrian mobile telephony services market. Post-merger, Mobilkom would remain the market leader so that, despite an increase in market shares, the merged entity would remain the number two player on the market. The Commission was nonetheless concerned about the removal of tele.ring from the already concentrated market. Although it did not explicitly rely on the particular closeness of competition between the merging parties, it did consider that tele.ring had exerted significant competitive pressure on both Mobilkom and T-Mobile and that its removal from the market would result in non-coordinated

[495] M.6166, 1 February 2012, *aff'd* Case T-175/12, *Deutsche Börse v Commission* EU:T:2015:148. The Commission rejected the parties' claim that extensive efficiencies would outweigh the negative effects of the merger, see especially n. 641 and text.

[496] M.8677, 7 February 2019, see nn. 730–736 and text. An important disputed issue was whether Chinese manufacturers of high-speed trains were potential competitors. The Commission concluded that there was insufficient evidence to demonstrate their competitive threat.

[497] M.9343, 13 January 2022. This was the first prohibition since June 2019, and of the von der Leyen Commission, see <https://app.parr-global.com/intelligence/view/intelcms-txxvgc>.

[498] M.9343, 13 January 2022, The Commission, following a very lengthy Phase II review, blocked the merger between the two South Korean shipbuilders as no formal remedies were offered to address the concerns, see also DG Comp [2022] 2 *Competition Merger Brief*, pp. 10–11 (noting that the vessels involved are an essential element in the supply chain of LNG and therefore contribute to the diversification of Europe's source of energy, improving energy security).

[499] M.6570, 30 January 2013.

[500] Case T-194/13, *United Parcel Service v Commission* EU:T:2017:742, *aff'd* Case C-265/17 P, EU:C:2019:23, see n. 348 and text. Following the prohibition, FedEx acquired TNT.

[501] M.3916, 26 April 2006.

effects.[502] In particular, tele.ring was a relatively new entrant to the market which had quickly gained market share through vibrant competitive practices and low prices;[503] it was an aggressive and innovative competitor.[504] The Commission thus approved the merger only after specific remedies designed to strengthen the position of smaller players on the market were agreed.[505] Subsequently, the Commission has investigated a number of other mergers in, for example, the Austrian,[506] German,[507] Irish,[508] Danish,[509] Italian,[510] Dutch,[511] and UK[512] mobile telecoms markets (considering in each case that the geographical markets are national).

The Commission has reviewed each of these telecom mergers on a case-by-case basis assessing each in the context of the national market in which it operates and stressing that there is no magic 'acceptable' number of mobile network operators in a given country. The Commission is nonetheless concerned that, based on past experience, four to three or three to two mergers in this sphere will lead to lower investment and higher prices. Consequently, in several cases structural remedies have been required before clearance, as the Commission was not convinced that the alleged innovation and efficiencies resulting from the transaction were merger-specific or likely to be passed on to consumers. Rather it has taken the view that companies usually have strongest incentives to invest and innovate in competitive markets.[513]

In *Hutchison 3G UK/Telefónica UK*,[514] the Commission refused to accept commitments and prohibited a four-three merger based on concerns about non-coordinated effects on the oligopolistic

[502] The s. 6(1)(c) document raised concerns about both coordinated and non-coordinated effects but the former was not pursued in the final decision.

[503] The Commission described tele.ring as a 'maverick', normally a more important issue in coordinated effects cases, see Section 5.E.iv and HMG, para. 42.

[504] For the view that 'the Commission appears to be exploring alternative ways of describing and assessing closeness of competition', including by describing 'one or more of the merging parties as "particularly aggressive or innovative" ', see McGeown and Barthélemy, n. 408, 448.

[505] The merging parties agreed to divest UMTS frequencies and mobile telephony sites off to smaller players, such as Hutchison 3G. These commitments were designed to enable Hutchison 3G to expand its Austrian network without being dependent on its current national roaming agreement with Mobilkom.

[506] M.6497, *Hutchison 3G Austria/Orange Austria* 12 December 2012 (merger reducing the number of players on the Austrian market from four to three was cleared subject to commitments. The Commission declined to make a reference back to the Austrian authorities under Art. 9). See subsequent *ex post* evaluation of the impact of the merger, <www.bwb.gv.at/fileadmin/user_upload/PDFs/BWB2016-re-Ex-post_evaluation_of_the_mobile_telecommunications_market.pdf> and <www.rtr.at/TKP/aktuelles/publikationen/publikationen/Analysis_merger_H3G_Orange.de.html>.

[507] M.7018, *Telefónica Deutschland/E-Plus* 2 July 2014.

[508] M.6992, *Hutchison 3G UK/Telefónica Ireland* 28 May 2014 (the Commission was worried that the merger, which would reduce the number of mobile network operators in Ireland from four to three, would eliminate the newest and an aggressive or innovative competitor from the market. In the end the merger was cleared subject to commitments).

[509] M.7419, *TeliaSonera/Telenor/JV* (withdrawn). The parties abandoned this merger, which would have created the largest mobile network operator in Denmark and a highly concentrated market structure (the merged entity and TDC would have had around 80% of the market), when it became clear that the Commission was likely to reject the remedies offered by the parties and prohibit it. The Commission was concerned that the merger would have both anti-competitive unilateral effects and coordinated effects and was not clear how these would be offset by greater investment, see speech of Vestager, n. 138.

[510] M.7758, *Hutchison 3G Italy/Wind/JV* 1 September 2016.

[511] M.8792, *T-Mobile NL/Tele2 NL* 27 November 2018.

[512] M.7612, *Hutchison 3G UK/Telefónica UK* 11 May 2016 (prohibited), annulled Case T-399/19, *CK Telecoms v Commission* EU:T:2020:217, Case C-376/20 P, judgment pending.

[513] See Vestager, n. 111 (citing a lack of compelling evidence that would support the existence of a trade-off between competition and investment. Rather, research seems to suggest that a reduction of the number of players from four to three in a national mobile market in the EU can lead to higher prices for consumers, without leading to more investment per subscriber) and discussion of efficiencies in 5.E.vii.

[514] M.7612, 11 May 2016, annulled Case T-399/19, *CK Telecoms v Commission* EU:T:2020:217.

retail (mobile retail services) and wholesale (mobile network) markets. However, in a robust and extremely critical judgment the GC, in *CK Telecoms v Commission*,[515] annulled this decision on several grounds, including that the Commission had not adequately demonstrated that the parties were particularly close competitors in the retail mobile telephone market or exerted important competitive constraints on each other. Although the judgment of the CJ is pending in this case, the Advocate General considered that the GC had made errors of law and proposed to the CJ that it should set aside the GC's judgment and refer the case back to it.[516]

In many of the cases discussed in the previous section, the emphasis has been on the impact of the reduction of competition on price (or output). In some markets, however, the primary concern may be the impact of the transaction on the quality of the products/services offered (including privacy protection), consumer choice, innovation, or potential or dynamic competition (especially in pharmaceutical and agrochemical sectors and in the digital economy) post-merger. These non-price, quality, pipeline, and innovation competition effects are especially difficult to assess.[517]

In the information economy, for example, consumers may especially value privacy and security as a form of non-price competition,[518] and the level of data protection offered to them. In *Microsoft/LinkedIn*,[519] the Commission was concerned that the transaction might lead to the foreclosure of professional social networks (PSNs) competing with LinkedIn which might, amongst other things, offer greater privacy protection. The Commission considered privacy protection to be relevant to the competition assessment if seen as a significant factor of quality by consumers, and an important parameter of competition between PSNs. In the end, the merger was cleared subject to commitments.

Mergers may also give rise to concern that acquisitions of control over large volumes of data will increase the market power of the merging entities and increase barriers to entry and expansion to potential and existing competitors[520] or eliminate competition between them on the basis of the data that each party held pre-merger. In *Microsoft/LinkedIn*, the Commission considered, but did not find, competition concerns resulting either from the possible post-merger combination of data held by the parties (in relation to online advertising) or from a lack of third party access to data held by them (vertical effects). In relation to the former, it held:

> (180) In the case at hand, however, the Transaction does not give rise to this type of concerns in relation to online advertising. First, Microsoft and LinkedIn do not make available their data to third parties for advertising purposes, with very limited exceptions. Second, the combination of their respective datasets does not appear to result in raising the barriers to entry/expansion for other players in this space, as there will continue to be a large amount of internet user data that are valuable for advertising purposes and that are not within Microsoft's exclusive control. Third, the Parties are small market players and compete with each other only to a very limited extent in online advertising and its possible segments.

[515] Ibid., para. 249. [516] Case T-399/16, EU:T:2020:217, Case C-376/20 P, judgment pending.

[517] See e.g. Stucke and Grunes, n. 47, 5, J. Kwoka and S. Kilpatrick, 'Nonprice Effects of Mergers: Issues and Evidence' (2018) 63(2) *Ant Bull* 169, I. Kokorris and T. Valletti, 'Innovation Considerations in Horizontal Merger Control' (2020) 16(2) *J of Competition Law and Economics* 220. See also, e.g., Costa-Cabral and Lynskey, n. 46.

[518] See Chap. 1, Stucke and Grunes, n. 47 and, e.g., M.7217, *Facebook/WhatsApp* 3 October 2014.

[519] See also e.g. M.4731, *Google/DoubleClick* 11 March 2008 and *Facebook/WhatsApp*, ibid.

[520] See e.g. M.9660, *Google/Fitbit* 17 December 2020 (clearance subject to commitments), *Google/DoubleClick* and *Facebook/WhatsApp*, ibid. (assessing the impact of big data mergers in online advertising markets) and B. Holles de Peyer, 'EU Merger Control and Big Data' (2018) 13 *J of Competition Law and Economics* 767.

Mergers may also reduce innovation, by lessening the pressure on the parties, and the ability of rivals, to innovate or by removing a potential competitor or start-up in the early stage of its life-cycle—so eliminating a firm which has the potential to introduce new or increased competition. This may imply a loss of future or dynamic competition between the merging firms. In such cases, important issues may be whether either firm would have been likely to enter, expand, innovate, or invest absent the merger.

An innovation theory of harm—that a merger will reduce incentives to continue with, or initiate, development of new products—was raised in *Dow/Du Pont*,[521] a merger in the agrochemicals industry. In this case, the Commission focused on the impact of the transaction on, not only crop protection and petrochemical products, but also, on innovation competition in crop protection. A core concern, bolstered in part by the parties' internal documents which revealed a planned reduction in R&D, was thus that the transaction would impact negatively on innovation rivalry in herbicide, insecticide, and fungicide, and lead to the discontinuation, delay, or redirection of overlapping lines of research, the production of pipeline products, and the development of new active ingredients. In the end, the transaction was cleared, but only subject to significant divestiture commitments, which included most of Du Pont's global crop protection business and its R&D organisation. The Commission's willingness to conclude, or presume, that mergers between innovators will in many cases harm innovation through reduced competitive pressure has been controversial, with many contending that such mergers may enhance R&D through the creation of merger synergies and efficiencies[522] and that a careful case-by-case analysis is required.[523]

Acquisitions of start-ups may also 'have significant adverse effects on market structure, competition, and the diffusion of innovations',[524] for example where start-ups are acquired by highly dominant incumbents, and the acquired technology could plausibly have an appreciable impact on competition if used exclusively by the acquirer, or the acquirer has an established pattern of buying promising start-ups and declining to license rivals.[525] A concern is that, given the challenges of assessing mergers in this context, competition agencies may, in the past, have too readily waved through acquisitions of start-ups in the digital economy that have potentially resulted in a loss of competition.[526] Indeed, a core difficulty is to develop tools which will allow an agency to identify problematic acquisitions, to identify a counterfactual and predict the markets evolution, and to mount a viable antitrust challenge, especially where the target is not yet a fully-fledged rival of the purchaser. In such cases, the static effects of the merger may be benign, requiring a dynamic perspective to be taken.[527]

Some, including the former Chief Economist of DG Comp, have argued that, in cases involving targets that have not yet monetised their ideas, the burden of proof should be reversed, and the onus put on the merging parties to establish the efficiencies arising from the transaction.[528] The 2019 Report on

[521] M.7932, 12 October 2017. See also M.8523, *BD/Bard*, M.8401, *J&J/Actelion*, M.7275, *Novartis/Glaxosmithkline Oncology Business*, and M.9461, *Abbvie/Allergan*.

[522] See Werner, Clerckx, and de la Barre, n. 458, 141–142 and J. Padilla, 'Revisiting the Horizontal Mergers and Innovation Policy Debate' (2019) 10(7) *JECLAP* 463.

[523] See e.g. V. Denicoló and M. Polo 'The innovation theory of Harm: An appraisal', IEFE Working Paper No. 103 (2018).

[524] Bryan and Hovenkamp, n. 9. 615. [525] Ibid. [526] See e.g. Argentisi et al, n. 17.

[527] See e.g. the approach of the UK's competition agency in CMA129, n. 401, section 5.

[528] See Valletti, n. 16 and Tirole, n. 9 ('First, we need to reconsider our burden of proof in antitrust decisions. This is a delicate matter. Consider the acquisition of WhatsApp and Instagram by Facebook. They were social networks, just like Facebook. They could have become Facebook competitors. But is there any evidence for that? Not really, as this is just a guess on what the future would have looked at in the absence of acquisition. The suppression of competition in the absence of data is hard to prove. My guess is that we should err on the side of competition, while recognizing that we will make mistakes in the process.'). See also discussion of standard of proof in Section 5.C.ii.

Competition Policy for the Digital Era,[529] in contrast, proposed modifications of existing substantive theories of harm, and a heightened degree of control of acquisitions of small start-ups, in cases where a dominant platform and/or ecosystem, which benefits from strong positive network effects and data access, acquires a target with a low turnover but a high future market potential.[530] The Report suggests that this can also be done through developing a test which analyses such acquisitions as a possible defensive strategy against partial user defection, and developing a test for appraising them as 'conglomerate' mergers where uncertainty exists as to whether the target is truly an actual or potential competitor (with horizontal effects).

J. Crémer, Y.-A. de Montjoye, and H. Schweitzer, *Report on Competition Policy for the Digital Era*, European Commission, 4 April 2019, 11

While the EUMR's 'significant impediment to effective competition' test remains a sound basis for assessing mergers in the digital economy, we believe that there is a need to revisit the substantive theories of harm to properly assess certain specific cases. This concerns specifically cases where a dominant platform and/or ecosystem which benefits from strong positive network effects and data access, which act as a significant barrier to entry, acquires a target with a currently low turnover but a large and/or fastgrowing user base and a high future market potential. In such cases, competition law should be particularly concerned about protecting the ability of competitors to enter markets, as competition in the market is typically reduced and competitive threats will typically come from the fringe. Buying up promising start-ups that offer fringe products or services may therefore result in early elimination of potential competitive threats. In this setting, the competitive risk resulting from an acquisition is not limited—as in traditional 'conglomerate' theories of harm—to the foreclosure of rivals' access to inputs. It extends to the strengthening of the platform's (or ecosystem's) dominance, because the acquisition can: (i) intensify the loyalty of those users that consider the new services as complements to services already offered by the platform/ecosystem; and (ii) help retain other users for which the new services might be partial substitutes to the ones already available. Therefore, we think that the best way to handle these acquisitions is to inject some 'horizontal' elements into the 'conglomerate' theories of harm and try to answer the following questions:

(i) Does the acquirer benefit from barriers to entry linked to network effects or use of data?

(ii) Is the target a potential or actual competitive constraint within the technological/users space or ecosystem?

(iii) Does its elimination increase market power within this space notably through increased barriers to entry?

(iv) If so, is the merger justified by efficiencies?

The test proposed here would imply a heightened degree of control of acquisitions of small start-ups by dominant platforms and/or ecosystems, to be analysed as a possible strategy against partial user defection from the ecosystem. Where an acquisition is plausibly part of such a strategy, the notifying parties should bear the burden of showing that the adverse effects on competition are offset by merger-specific efficiencies. This theory of harm does not create a presumption against the legality of such mergers. However, it takes due account of new business strategies and the competitive risks they raise, and should help to minimise 'false negatives' in a setting where the costs of systematic false negatives are particularly high.

[529] J. Crémer, Y.-A. de Montjoye, and H. Schweitzer, European Commission, 4 April 2019, 11.

[530] See also e.g. Argentisi et al, n. 17 suggesting that the social costs of wrong clearances may be higher in digital markets, especially because the structure of such markets are concentrated with high barriers to entry.

b. The Ability of Customers to Switch

Customers unable to switch, for example because of the limited availability of alternative suppliers or significant switching costs, are particularly vulnerable to price rises.[531] In contrast, where customers are able to switch, any attempt by the merging parties to raise price would be likely to be counteracted. In *Votorantim/Fischer*,[532] for example, the Commission cleared a concentration between two global orange juice producers. A number of other suppliers existed and customers could easily switch between them.

c. The Likelihood That Competitors Will Increase Supply

If competitors (of the merged parties) cannot increase output (or do not have the incentive to do so), it may be easier for the merging firms to restrict output themselves and to benefit from price rises:[533]

> When market conditions are such that the competitors of the merging parties are unlikely to increase their supply substantially if prices increase, the merging firms may have an incentive to reduce output below the combined premerger levels, thereby raising market prices. The merger increases the incentive to reduce output by giving the merged firm a larger base of sales on which to enjoy the higher margins resulting from an increase in prices induced by the output reduction.[534]

Conversely, where rivals have the capability to expand output and sufficient spare capacity to do so, the Commission is unlikely to find that the merger will create or strengthen a dominant position or otherwise significantly impede effective competition.[535]

In merger cases, especially those involving homogeneous products where buyers' preferences are primarily dictated by price, it is therefore important to assess competitors' ability to increase output in response to a price rise, and their incentives to do so.[536] Ability might be limited by capacity constraints, the cost of increasing capacity, or 'barriers to expansion'. Such barriers may originate from the merging firms themselves,[537] for example as a result of their controlling or influencing the supply of essential inputs, access to distribution channels, and access to intellectual property rights (IPRs) or data, or where the merged entity would have the ability and incentive to raise costs or decrease the quality of services provided to rivals in markets where interoperability between different infrastructures or platforms is important (e.g., in energy, telecommunications, and communications industries).[538]

In *MCI Worldcom/Sprint*,[539] the Commission prohibited a proposed merger of two global communications companies, MCI Worldcom Inc and Sprint Corp. It considered that the combination of the merged firms' extensive networks and customer base would create such a powerful force that both competitors and customers would have been dependent upon them to obtain universal internet connectivity. In particular, it would create a:

> super-tier provider of global internet connectivity. strong position due to its absolute and relative size compared to its competitors. Given the size of the merged entity, it will be able to control the prices of

[531] HMG, para. 31 and see, e.g., M.4381, *JCI/FIAMM* 10 May 2007. [532] M.5907, 4 May 2011.

[533] See e.g. M.4525, *Kronospan/Constantia* 19 July 2007. [534] HMG, para. 32.

[535] Ibid., para. 33. See e.g. M.7230, *Bakaert/Pirelli Steel Tyre Cord Business* 30 July 2014.

[536] The inability of competitors to expand capacity is most likely to be problematic where products are homogenous, but it may also be important when suppliers produce differentiated products, HMG, para. 35.

[537] Ibid., para. 36.

[538] The fact that such behaviour might constitute an abuse of a dominant position is one factor that must be taken into account, see nn. 675–680 and following text.

[539] M.1741, 28 June 2000, annulled, Case T-310/00, *MCI v Commission* EU:T:2004:275.

> its competitors and customers. It will also be in a position to control technical developments. The combined entity will be able to sustain such behaviour due to its capacity to discipline the market notably through the threat of selective degradation of its competitors internet connectivity offering . . . and also through its essential ability to determine and agree any new technical development to enable advance internet services . . .[540]

In *GE/Instrumentarium*,[541] the Commission also feared that the parties would be able to foreclose other perioperative monitor suppliers from the market by making its anaesthesia machines incompatible with rival monitors. This would, of course, have made it difficult for the competitors to respond to an increase in price by increasing capacity.

In addition to considering evidence of competitors' ability to expand output, the Commission will also assess whether competitors would have the incentive to expand output sufficiently, that is to say whether they would find it profitable to expand output in response to a likely price increase by the merged entity. In *INEOS/Solvay JV*,[542] for example, the Commission considered that as, post-merger, three firms would hold more than 80–90% of sales, the market would be highly concentrated so that a price increase from the newly created JV would shift some demand to competitors and reduce the competitive pressure on those competitors.

> (1024) When faced with an increase in demand following a price increase by the JV, therefore, the Notifying Parties' competitors would generally respond by increasing their price and expanding production or redirecting their output into [North Western Europe], or possibly both. Reactions by rivals of the merging parties in a concentrated market can therefore generally be expected not to be sufficiently strong to make a price increase unprofitable for the JV.
>
> (1025) This prediction remains applicable also in the presence of spare capacity pre-Transaction. In particular, in an oligopolistic market, competitors do not necessarily have an incentive to expand output up to the full capacity utilization, as it can often happen that the profit maximizing level of output is below maximum capacity. Even in markets which are characterised by levels of spare capacity at the industry level such as in this case, therefore, a merger which leads to a substantial consolidation of production capacities can be expected to lead to significant non-coordinated effects, as described at Paragraph 24 of the Horizontal Merger Guidelines.
>
> (1026) Thus, in a mature, concentrated market where the degree of product homogeneity is very high . . . reactions by rivals of the merging parties even in the presence of spare capacity can generally be expected not to be sufficiently strong to make a price increase unprofitable for the JV.
>
> (1027) In this case, therefore, non-merging parties . . . can most likely be expected to benefit from the reduction of competitive pressure between INEOS and Solvay, which will result from the Transaction. Those rivals are therefore expected to refrain from making full use of their spare capacity, when available, to expand output so as to offset a price increase by the JV post-Transaction. Conversely, they would likely expand output to some extent and increase their prices.
>
> (1028) . . . [T]he Notifying Parties' competitors will have no incentive, as well as no ability, to expand output sufficiently so as to offset a likely price increase by the JV post-Transaction . . .[543]

540 M.1741, *MCI Worldcom/Sprint* 28 June 2000, para. 146.
541 M.3083, IP/03/1193.
542 M.6905, 8 May 2014. See also M.6471, *Outokumpu/Inoxum* 7 November 2012.
543 Ibid.

d. The Competitive Force Eliminated by the Merger

The merger is more likely to cause concern where it involves a firm that is likely to change the competitive dynamics of a market more than its market share suggests, e.g. if the merger involves a new entrant or an important innovator in the market.[544]

In *Boeing/McDonnell Douglas*,[545] the Commission was concerned that the merger would strengthen Boeing's already dominant position in the markets for large commercial aircraft and for narrow-body and wide-body aircraft. Although McDonnell Douglas's market share had been declining, responses from airlines indicated that its competitive influence had been greater than that reflected in its market share. Its participation in the competitive process and influence on competition was of significant importance leading, it appeared, to a reduction of over 7 per cent in the realised price. In the end, the Commission cleared the merger subject to the parties complying with specified commitments.

In *Danone/Numico*,[546] the Commission examined a merger between two major players on the French, Belgian, and Dutch markets for baby milk, meals, snacks, cereals, and drinks. In the French infant milk market, for example, the parties were close competitors and owned a high number of must-have brands. Numico had played an important role in making the market competitive, keeping prices down, and introducing innovative products. The Commission considered that the merger would lead to the removal of a strong competitive constraint on prices. In the end, the merger was cleared at the end of Phase I, subject to a commitment to divest the Numico baby milk business in France and a package of other remedies.

The question of whether one of the merging parties constitutes an independent competitive force and the weight attached to such a finding needs to be approached with care, however. In *CK Telecoms*,[547] the GC held that the elimination of an important competitive force is not in itself enough to demonstrate an elimination of important competitive constraints or a SIEC. It also held that, in an oligopolistic market, an important competitive force should be shown to exert competitive pressure by standing out from its competitors in terms of impact on competition.[548] In the course of the appeal to the CJ, however, Advocate General Kokott took the view that the concept of important competitive force should not be interpreted in such a restrictive manner. 'On the contrary, such an interpretation would risk underestimating from the outset the competitive forces present within an already concentrated oligopolistic market. Even though the adjective "important" implies that the competitive behaviour of the undertaking concerned on the market should be *substantial*, that is to say such as to "change the competitive dynamics in a significant, anticompetitive way" extending beyond the undertaking's significance in terms of market shares or similar measures, it cannot be interpreted as requiring that undertaking to be "competing particularly aggressively in terms of prices".'[549]

(iv) Coordinated Anti-competitive Effects—Collective or Joint Dominance

The HMG deal separately with the question of how mergers leading to 'coordinated effects' or the creation or strengthening of a 'collective dominant position' can be identified.

544 HMG, paras. 37–38 and see discussion of the mobile mergers, nn. 501–512 and text.
545 M.877 [1997] OJ L336/16.
546 M.4842, 31 October 2007.
547 Case T-399/16, EU:T:2020:217, Case C-376/20 P, judgment pending.
548 Ibid., paras. 171–174.
549 C-376/20 P, *Commission v CK Telecoms* EU:C:2022:817, para. 110.

Horizontal Merger Guidelines

39. In some markets the structure may be such that firms would consider it possible, economically rational, and hence preferable, to adopt on a sustainable basis a course of action on the market aimed at selling at increased prices. A merger in a concentrated market may significantly impede effective competition, through the creation or the strengthening of a collective dominant position, because it increases the likelihood that firms are able to coordinate their behaviour in this way and raise prices, even without entering into an agreement or resorting to a concerted practice within the meaning of Article [101] TFEU. A merger may also make coordination easier, more stable or more effective for firms, that were already coordinating before the merger, either by making the coordination more robust or by permitting firms to coordinate on even higher prices.

40. Coordination may take various forms. In some markets, the most likely coordination may involve keeping prices above the competitive level. In other markets, coordination may aim at limiting production or the amount of new capacity brought to the market. Firms may also coordinate by dividing the market, for instance by geographic area or other customer characteristics, or by allocating contracts in bidding markets.

In concentrated markets, the Commission thus examines mergers to determine whether or not they will make coordination more likely to emerge in markets through the creation or strengthening of a collectively held dominant position. The Guidelines state that coordination is more likely to emerge in markets where it is relatively simple for the firms to reach a common understanding on terms of coordination and:

- the coordinating firms are able to monitor whether the terms of coordination are being adhered to;
- there is some form of credible deterrent mechanism to ensure discipline; and
- the reaction of outsiders, customers, or competitors will not jeopardise the results expected from the coordination.[550]

These conditions derive from case law developed under the old EUMR on the meaning of a collective dominant position, and in particular the GC's judgment in *Airtours*.

a. Background

It was seen in Chapter 9 that Article 101 prohibits explicit, but not tacit, collusion, but that explicit collusion is hard to detect. Further, that Article 102 provides less than an ideal tool for controlling tacit collusion. Given these difficulties, it is critical that the EUMR should be able to *prevent* mergers that might lead to collusion (whether explicit or tacit) on a market.[551]

The old EUMR only allowed the Commission to prohibit mergers leading to the creation or strengthening of a dominant position. An important question was thus whether its scope was broad enough to prevent mergers which would lead to the creation or strengthening of a dominant position held collectively[552] by two or more independent entities united together by 'economic links'.

[550] HMG, para. 41. See also discussion of explicit and tacit collusion in Chap. 9.

[551] See Commission's *XVIth Report on Competition Policy* (1986), 285.

[552] Cases T-68 and 77–78/89, *Società Italiana Vetro (SIV) v Commission* EU:T:1992:38, see Chap. 9.

Even though the old EUMR provided *no* textual support for such an approach,[553] the Commission took the view that it did,[554] a view subsequently affirmed in a series of judgments of the EU Courts.

The CJ first clarified, interpreting the original EUMR in accordance with 'its purpose and general structure',[555] that 'collective dominant positions do not fall outside the scope of the Regulation'[556] in *France v Commission.*[557] In this case, the Commission had concluded that the merger led to the creation of a market-leading duopoly in the EU (except Germany) market for potash enjoyed by: Kali und Salz (K+S)/MdK (the merging parties) and Société Commerciale des Potasses et de l'Azote (SCPA) but cleared it, subject to commitments which affected not only the merging parties, but also SCPA. On the facts, the CJ annulled the Commission's decision, finding that it had not established that the concentration would in fact give rise to a collective dominant position on the market.[558] Nonetheless, it confirmed that the EUMR precluded mergers leading to the creation or strengthening of a dominant position and that the key to collective dominance was the parties' ability to adopt a common policy on the market and to act independently of their competitors, customers, and consumers.

In *France v Commission*, the CJ did not (as in *Flat Glass*[559]) expressly state whether a collective dominant position could be held by parties other than those with contractual or other links between them (non-oligopolistic collective dominance). However, the judgments of *Gencor Ltd v Commission*,[560] *Airtours plc v Commission*,[561] and *Impala*,[562] spelled out that a collective dominant position could be held by members of a 'tight oligopoly' (oligopolistic collective dominance), and that the EUMR prohibited mergers which might result in explicit or tacit collusion (coordinated effects) on the market.

Gencor[563] concerned a decision by two companies, Gencor Ltd (a South African company) and Lonrho Plc (a UK company), to merge their business activities in the platinum group metal (PGM) sector. Although the platinum businesses were both based in South Africa (and the South African Competition Board did not consider that the operation gave rise to competition policy concerns under South African law), the Commission nevertheless issued a decision prohibiting it. It considered that the merger would create a duopoly between the merged entity and Anglo American Corporation of South Africa Ltd (AAC), which, through its associated company, Amplats, was the remaining competitor on the market. Further, the anti-competitive effects of that duopoly would be felt on the relevant markets within the EU and EEA.[564] No contractual or other structural links existed between the parties.

[553] Although Art. 102 refers to a dominant position held by 'one or more' undertakings, the old EUMR simply referred to concentrations which lead to the creation or strengthening of *a* dominant position, see the arguments raised in Case T-102/96, *Gencor Ltd v Commission* EU:T:1999:65, report for the hearing, paras. 110–127 and D. Ridyard, 'Economic Analysis of Single Firm and Oligopolistic Dominance' [1994] *ECLR* 255, 258.

[554] It introduced the concept in M.165, *Alcatel/AEG Kabel* [1992] OJ C6/23 but nonetheless cleared the merger. In M.190, *Nestlé/Perrier* [1992] OJ L356/1 the Commission first took commitments as a condition for clearing a concentration (between Nestlé and Perrier) which it considered would 'create a duopolistic dominant position which would significantly impede [the] effective competition position on the French bottled water market'.

[555] In so doing, the CJ stressed that a textual and historical examination of the Regulation was not conclusive. Rather, an interpretation in accordance with its underlying objective (to prevent mergers which would prove incompatible with the system of undistorted competition envisaged by the Treaty) precluded a narrow interpretation which would deprive the Regulation of its intended effect, Cases C-68/94 and 30/95, *France v Commission, Société Commerciale des Potasses et de l'Azote (SCPA) v Commission* EU:C:1998:148, paras. 165–177.

[556] Ibid., para. 178. [557] Ibid.

[558] This was the first case in which the CJ annulled a Commission decision under the EUMR. Following the annulment, the Commission re-examined the concentration and cleared it in Phase I proceedings.

[559] Cases T-68 and 77–78/89, *Società Italiana Vetro (SIV) v Commission* EU:T:1992:38.

[560] Case T-102/96, *Gencor Ltd v Commission* EU:T:1999:65. [561] Case T-342/99, EU:T:2002:146.

[562] Case T-464/04, EU:T:2006:216, Case C-413/06 P, *Bertelsmann and Sony Corp v Commission* EU:C:2008:392.

[563] Case T-102/96, *Gencor Ltd v Commission* EU:T:1999:65. [564] See also Section 8 and Chap. 17.

The applicant sought annulment of the Commission's decision. After reiterating that 'collective dominant positions do not fall outside the scope of the Regulation' the Court rejected the applicant's claim that, in order for a finding of collective dominance to be made, formal 'structural' links had to exist between the undertakings involved.

Case T-102/96, *Gencor Ltd v Commission* [1999] ECR II-753

General Court

273. In its judgment in the *Flat Glass* case, the Court referred to links of a structural nature only by way of example and did not lay down that such links must exist in order for a finding of collective dominance to be made.

274. It merely stated . . . that there is nothing, in principle to prevent two or more independent economic entities from being united by economic links in a specific market and, by virtue of that fact, from together holding a dominant position *vis-à-vis* the other operators on the same market.

. . .

276. Furthermore, there is no reason whatsoever in legal or economic terms to exclude from the notion of economic links the relationship of interdependence existing between the parties to a tight oligopoly within which, in a market with the appropriate characteristics, in particular in terms of market concentration, transparency and product homogeneity, those parties are in a position to anticipate one another's behaviour and are therefore strongly encouraged to align their conduct in the market, in particular in such a way as to maximise their joint profits by restricting production with a view to increasing prices. In such a context, each trader is aware that highly competitive action on its part designed to increase its market share (for example a price cut) would provoke identical action by the others, so that it would derive no benefit from its initiative. All the traders would thus be affected by the reduction in price levels.

277. That conclusion is all the more pertinent with regard to the control of concentrations, whose objective is to prevent anti-competitive market structures from arising or being strengthened. Those structures may result from the existence of economic links in the strict sense argued by the applicant or from market structures of an oligopolistic kind where each undertaking may become aware of common interests and, in particular, cause prices to increase without having to enter into an agreement or resort to a concerted practice.

278. In the [present] case, therefore, the applicant's ground of challenge alleging that the Commission failed to establish the existence of structural links is misplaced.

279. The Commission was entitled to conclude, relying on the envisaged alteration in the structure of the market and on the similarity of the costs of Amplats and [Implats/LPD], that the proposed transaction would create a collective dominant position and lead in actual fact to a duopoly constituted by those two undertakings.

The case is illuminating. By referring to *Flat Glass* when considering the links required between undertakings before a finding of collective dominance can be made, the Court clearly envisages that collective dominance has the same meaning under both Article 102 and the EUMR.[565]

In addition, the Court establishes that the contractual links given as examples of economic links in *Flat Glass* are not necessary to support a finding of collective dominance. Although the Court does not fully explain the difference between the 'structural' and 'economic links' it refers to, it is clear that

[565] See Chaps. 6 and 9.

the market structure itself (the relationship of interdependence existing between parties to a tight oligopoly) suffices.

In *Airtours/First Choice*,[566] the Commission adopted a controversial decision prohibiting the acquisition by Airtours of First Choice. It held that the concentration would lead to the creation or strengthening of a collective dominant position on the UK short-haul foreign package holiday (FPH) market. The dominant position would be held by Airtours/First Choice (32 per cent), Thomson (27 per cent), and Thomas Cook (20 per cent). The remainder of the market was highly fragmented, and this meant that no effective restraint on the competitive conduct of the larger players would be exercised.

In reaching its decision, the Commission appeared to expand the concept of collective dominance. Paragraph 54 of its decision provided that it was not necessarily essential to show that the parties would adopt a common policy on the market. Rather, it appeared to take the view that the ability to engage in explicit or tacit coordination is not essential. It was sufficient that each individual undertaking operating on the oligopolistic market had sufficient market power to enable it to act independently (arguably therefore this was a 'gap' case). Nonetheless, the Commission did consider that tacit coordination between the parties would occur, but in relation to output or capacity on the market, not price.

On appeal the GC annulled the Commission's decision in a judgment that was highly critical of the Commission's economic reasoning. It held that the Commission's analysis had not been based on cogent evidence and that the decision was vitiated by a series of errors of assessment as to factors fundamental to any assessment of whether a collective dominant position might be created. Building upon the judgments in *France v Commission* and *Gencor v Commission*, it set out the conditions necessary for a finding of a collective dominant position.

Case T-342/99, *Airtours plc v Commission* [2002] ECR II-2585

General Court

62. As the applicant has argued and as the Commission has accepted in its pleadings, three conditions are necessary for a finding of collective dominance as defined:

— first, each member of the dominant oligopoly must have the ability to know how the other members are behaving in order to monitor whether or not they are adopting the common policy. As the Commission specifically acknowledges, it is not enough for each member of the dominant oligopoly to be aware that interdependent market conduct is profitable for all of them but each member must also have a means of knowing whether the other operators are adopting the same strategy and whether they are maintaining it. There must, therefore, be sufficient market transparency for all members of the dominant oligopoly to be aware, sufficiently precisely and quickly, of the way in which the other members' market conduct is evolving;

— second, the situation of tacit coordination must be sustainable over time, that is to say, there must be an incentive not to depart from the common policy on the market. As the Commission observes, it is only if all the members of the dominant oligopoly maintain the parallel conduct that all can benefit. The notion of retaliation in respect of conduct deviating from the common policy is thus inherent in this condition. In this instance, the parties concur that, for a situation of collective dominance to be viable, there must be adequate deterrents to ensure that there is a long-term incentive in not departing from the common policy, which means that each member of the dominant

[566] M.1524, *Airtours/First Choice* [2000] OJ L93/1, annulled, Case T-342/99, *Airtours v Commission* EU:T:2002:146.

oligopoly must be aware that highly competitive action on its part designed to increase its market share would provoke identical action by the others, so that it would derive no benefit from its initiative (see, to that effect, *Gencor v Commission*, paragraph 276);

— third, to prove the existence of a collective dominant position to the requisite legal standard, the Commission must also establish that the foreseeable reaction of current and future competitors, as well as of consumers, would not jeopardise the results expected from the common policy.

The GC thus requires proof of three criteria in collective dominance cases, which are now echoed by the Commission in paragraph 41 of the HMG and were reiterated by the GC in *Independent Music Publishers and Labels Association (Impala) v Commission*:[567]

- sufficient market transparency to enable each member of the dominant oligopoly to know how the other members are behaving and to monitor whether or not they are adopting a common policy;
- the ability to sustain the situation of tacit coordination over time, i.e. the existence of deterrents to ensure that there is a long-term incentive not to depart from the common policy; and
- the common policies must not be at risk from the foreseeable reaction of competitors or consumers.

Although on appeal the CJ expressed the collective dominance test in slightly different terms, the wording is not inconsistent with the test adopted by the GC. Both formulations accord with the economists' views of the conditions required for coordinated effects (i.e. the ability of firms to reach a tacit understanding as to which parameters of competition they will moderate, the ability of firms to sustain any tacit understanding (monitoring adherence to and deviations from the tacit understanding and punishing deviations), and immunity from destabilising reactions from firms outside the coordinating group).[568] The CJ stresses however that a too mechanical approach should not be adopted; rather a more rounded approach to the theory of harm is required.

Case C-413/06 *P Bertelsmann and Sony Corp v Commission* [2008] ECR I-4951

Court of Justice

120. In the case of an alleged creation or strengthening of a collective dominant position, the Commission is obliged to assess, using a prospective analysis of the reference market, whether the concentration which has been referred to it will lead to a situation in which effective competition in the relevant market is significantly impeded by the undertakings which are parties to the concentration and one or more other undertakings which together, in particular because of correlative factors which exist between them, are able to adopt a common policy on the market (see *Kali & Salz*, paragraph 221) in order to profit from a situation of collective economic strength, without actual or potential competitors, let alone customers or consumers, being able to react effectively.

121. Such correlative factors include, in particular, the relationship of interdependence existing between the parties to a tight oligopoly within which, on a market with the appropriate characteristics, in

[567] Case T-464/04, EU:T:2006:216, para. 254. [568] Bishop and Walker, n. 431, 7.049–7.053.

particular in terms of market concentration, transparency and product homogeneity, those parties are in a position to anticipate one another's behaviour and are therefore strongly encouraged to align their conduct on the market in such a way as to maximise their joint profits by increasing prices, reducing output, the choice or quality of goods and services, diminishing innovation or otherwise influencing parameters of competition. In such a context, each operator is aware that highly competitive action on its part would provoke a reaction on the part of the others, so that it would derive no benefit from its initiative.

122. A collective dominant position significantly impeding effective competition in the common market or a substantial part of it may thus arise as the result of a concentration where, in view of the actual characteristics of the relevant market and of the alteration to those characteristics that the concentration would entail, the latter would make each member of the oligopoly in question, as it becomes aware of common interests, consider it possible, economically rational, and hence preferable, to adopt on a lasting basis a common policy on the market with the aim of selling at above competitive prices, without having to enter into an agreement or resort to a concerted practice within the meaning of Article [101] and without any actual or potential competitors, let alone customers or consumers, being able to react effectively.

123. Such tacit coordination is more likely to emerge if competitors can easily arrive at a common perception as to how the coordination should work, and, in particular, of the parameters that lend themselves to being a focal point of the proposed coordination. Unless they can form a shared tacit understanding of the terms of the coordination, competitors might resort to practices that are prohibited by Article [101] in order to be able to adopt a common policy on the market. Moreover, having regard to the temptation which may exist for each participant in a tacit coordination to depart from it in order to increase its short-term profit, it is necessary to determine whether such coordination is sustainable. In that regard, the coordinating undertakings must be able to monitor to a sufficient degree whether the terms of the coordination are being adhered to. There must therefore be sufficient market transparency for each undertaking concerned to be aware, sufficiently precisely and quickly, of the way in which the market conduct of each of the other participants in the coordination is evolving. Furthermore, discipline requires that there be some form of credible deterrent mechanism that can come into play if deviation is detected. In addition, the reactions of outsiders, such as current or future competitors, and also the reactions of customers, should not be such as to jeopardise the results expected from the coordination.

124. The conditions laid down by the [GC] in paragraph 62 of its judgment in *Airtours v Commission*, which that court concluded, in paragraph 254 of the judgment under appeal, should be applied in the dispute before it, are not incompatible with the criteria set out in the preceding paragraph of this judgment.

125. In applying those criteria, it is necessary to avoid a mechanical approach involving the separate verification of each of those criteria taken in isolation, while taking no account of the overall economic mechanism of a hypothetical tacit coordination.

126. In that regard, the assessment of, for example, the transparency of a particular market should not be undertaken in an isolated and abstract manner, but should be carried out using the mechanism of a hypothetical tacit coordination as a basis. It is only if such a hypothesis is taken into account that it is possible to ascertain whether any elements of transparency that may exist on a market are, in fact, capable of facilitating the reaching of a common understanding on the terms of coordination and/or of allowing the competitors concerned to monitor sufficiently whether the terms of such a common policy are being adhered to. In that last respect, it is necessary, in order to analyse the sustainability of a purported tacit coordination, to take into account the monitoring mechanisms that may be available to the participants in the alleged tacit coordination in order to ascertain whether, as a result of those mechanisms, they are in a position to be aware, sufficiently precisely and quickly, of the way in which the market conduct of each of the other participants in that coordination is evolving.

b. *Establishing Coordinated Effects (or Collective Dominance)*

The Commission has an onerous burden to discharge to establish that a collective dominant position has been created or strengthened and that coordinated effects on a market would result. In both *France v Commission*[569] and *Airtours plc v Commission*,[570] the CJ and GC respectively annulled the Commission's decision on the ground that this burden had not been discharged. The Commission's finding of collective dominance, or coordinated effects, must therefore be rigorously supported by evidence, beyond that relating to market shares. Subsequently, the Commission cleared a number of mergers, even where the number of players on the market would reduce from four to three[571] or from three to two,[572] where no coordinated (or unilateral) effects seemed likely. In 2014, the Commission concluded in *Holcim/Cemex West*[573] and *Cemex/Holcim Assets*[574] that, despite preliminary concerns about coordination in cement markets in parts of Germany, Spain, and Belgium, the mergers were unlikely to make potential coordination easier, more stable, or more effective. The Commission nonetheless remains concerned about coordinated effects and has not shied away from pursuing this theory, for example in *AB InBev/SAB Miller*[575] and *Hutchison 3G Italy/WIND/JV*.[576]

In *Gencor/Lonrho*, the Commission carefully set out the factors in that case supporting its finding that a collective dominant position would be created on the platinum market. For example, it stated at paragraph 141 of its decision:

> 141. (a) on the demand side, there is moderate growth, inelastic demand and insignificant countervailing buyer power. Buyers are therefore highly vulnerable to a potential abuse;
>
> (b) the supply side is highly concentrated with high market transparency for a homogenous product, mature production technology, high entry barriers (including high sunk costs) and suppliers with financial links and multi-market contacts. These supply side characteristics make it easy for suppliers to engage in parallel behaviour and provide them with incentives to do so, without any countervailing checks from the demand side.

On appeal,[577] the GC affirmed that these factors had been correctly relied upon. Although the relevant factors may vary from market to market, this reliance on a checklist of factors was 'based upon the standard "textbook" characteristics which are thought to facilitate tacit collusion in a market'.[578]

In its HMG, the Commission devotes 13 paragraphs[579] to the market features that are likely: (a) to enable the firms to reach terms of coordination; (b) to monitor deviation; (c) to provide a deterrent mechanism; and (d) to prevent outsiders jeopardising the outcome of the expected coordination.

[569] Cases C-68/94 and 30/95, *France v Commission, Société Commerciale des Potasses et de l'Azote (SCPA) v Commission* EU:C:1998:148, paras. 179–250 (finding that the Commission had not shown to the necessary legal standard that the concentration would give rise to a collective dominant position. In particular, a market share of 60% (which would be held by K\+S/MdK and SCPA after the concentration, they had 23% and 37% shares respectively) did not of itself point conclusively to the existence of a collective dominant position of the undertakings. Further, the structural links between K\+S and SCPA were not as tight or as binding as the Commission had sought to make out, and the Commission had not succeeded in showing that there was no effective competitive counterweight to the grouping allegedly formed by K\+S/MdK and SCPA).

[570] Case T-342/99, EU:T:2002:146.

[571] See e.g. M.4523, *Worldspan/Travelport* 21 August 2007, M.4601, *KarstadtQuelle/MyTravel* 4 May 2007.

[572] See e.g. M.4662, *BSG/Universe* 4 December 2007 and M.4600, *TUI/First Choice* 4 June 2007. See also nn. 501–509 and text.

[573] M.7009, 5 June 2014. [574] M.7054, 9 September 2014. [575] M.7881, 24 May 2016.

[576] M.7758, 1 September 2016. [577] Case T-102/96, *Gencor Ltd v Commission* EU:T:1999:65.

[578] The Lexecon *Competition Memo* of November 1999. See Chap. 9. [579] HMG, paras. 45–57.

In *AB InBev/SABMiller*,[580] the Commission carefully referred to the factors that would lead to tacit coordination between the merged entity, a merger between the world's largest and second largest brewers, and other leading international brewers (such as Heineken and Carlsberg) in the tightly oligopolistic market in the EU. In some countries, there was already evidence of coordinated follow-the-leader pricing and a reduction in the number of competitors, and increased multimarket contacts, would increase the likelihood of tact price coordination occurring. The deal was saved only by a commitment to divest virtually the entire beer business of SABMiller in the EU. In *Hutchison 3G Italy/WIND/JV*,[581] the Commission, applying the *Airtours* criteria, also considered that the merger would be likely to increase the incentive and ability for the market players to coordinate behaviour by reducing the number of mobile network operators on the market from four to three, increasing market share symmetry, and removing a smaller competitor with a track record of aggressive pricing (which was corroborated by the parties' internal documents). On account of the high degree of market transparency, deviations from coordination could be easily detected and deterred and the parties engaged in a number of practices which would be likely to facilitate coordination, such as information exchange, signalling, and maintaining close contact. The transaction was cleared only subject to commitments to divest sufficient assets to allow a new operator to enter the market. These cases indicate that structural remedies are likely to be required to meet tacit collusion concerns.

Given the difficulties involved in proving collective dominance or the likelihood of coordinated effects, an interesting twist of events was the GC's judgment in *Independent Music Publishers and Labels Association (Impala) v Commission*[582] in which it annulled a Commission decision unconditionally *clearing* a merger between two of the five music majors, Sony and BMG.[583] In its decision, the Commission, despite indicating otherwise in its SO, made a dramatic U-turn, concluding that the five to four merger would not lead either to the strengthening or the creation of a collective dominant position in the physical or digital recorded music markets.[584] With regard to the physical recorded music market, for example, the Commission found that there was no strengthening of a dominant position as the market was not characterised by features facilitating coordinated behaviour. Not only was there no evidence of parallel pricing, but the Commission considered that the market was not transparent, the heterogeneity of the products made coordination unlikely, and there was no evidence of past cheating or retaliation against deviations from a collusive strategy.

The GC annulled the Commission's decision on the grounds that the Commission's reasoning was inadequate and contained manifest errors of assessment. It concluded that the Commission had failed to contain a sufficient statement of reasons for its finding that the market was not conducive to collective dominance.

In its assessment of whether a position of collective dominance existed, the Commission had focused on the question of whether the *Airtours* conditions existed. The GC indicated that in the case of a strengthening of an *existing* dominant position, the Commission, instead of proving the *Airtours* criteria in the traditional way through recourse to theoretical analysis, could have established

[580] M.7881, 24 May 2016. [581] M.7758, 1 September 2016.

[582] Case T-464/04, EU:T:2006:216 and Case C-413/06 P, *Bertelsmann and Sony Corp v Commission* EU:C:2008:392.

[583] M.3333, 3 October 2007. The Commission therefore had to reconsider the merger and, after a very thorough investigation, again cleared the transaction in 2007. Although Impala recommenced proceedings before the GC (Case T-229/08, *Impala v Commission*) these proceedings were abandoned when Sony purchased Bertelsmann's share of the joint venture, M.5272, *Sony/SonyBMG* 15 September 2008.

[584] M.3333, ibid.

satisfaction of the *Airtours* criteria by reference to 'indicia and items of evidence relating to the signs, manifestations and phenomena inherent in the presence of a collective dominant position'.[585]

Case T-464/04, *Independent Music Publishers and Labels Association (Impala) v Commission* [2006] ECR II-2289

General Court

250. The determination of the existence of a collective dominant position must be supported by a series of elements of established facts, past or present, which show that there is a significant impediment of competition on the market owing to the power acquired by certain undertakings to adopt together the same course of conduct on that market, to a significant extent, independently of their competitors, their customers and consumers.

251. It follows that, in the context of the assessment of the existence of a collective dominant position, although the three conditions defined by the [GC] in [Case T-342/99] *Airtours v Commission* [[2002] ECR II-2585], which were inferred from a theoretical analysis of the concept of a collective dominant position, are indeed also necessary, they may, however, in the appropriate circumstances, be established indirectly on the basis of what may be a very mixed series of indicia and items of evidence relating to the signs, manifestations and phenomena inherent in the presence of a collective dominant position.

252. Thus, in particular, close alignment of prices over a long period, especially if they are above a competitive level, together with other factors typical of a collective dominant position, might, in the absence of an alternative reasonable explanation, suffice to demonstrate the existence of a collective dominant position, even where there is no firm direct evidence of strong market transparency, as such transparency may be presumed in such circumstances.

253. It follows that, in the present case, the alignment of prices, both gross and net, over the last six years, even though the products are not the same (each disc having a different content), and also the fact that they were maintained at such a stable level, and at a level seen as high in spite of a significant fall in demand, together with other factors (power of the undertakings in an oligopoly situation, stability of market shares, etc.), as established by the Commission in the [contested decision], might, in the absence of an alternative explanation, suggest, or constitute an indication, that the alignment of prices is not the result of the normal play of effective competition and that the market is sufficiently transparent in that it allowed tacit price coordination.

The GC thus suggested that when assessing whether a collective dominant position already exists, it may be possible, or necessary, for the Commission, instead of relying on prospective analysis of the probable development of the market or theoretical analysis, to determine, using past or present facts, that a number of undertakings have power to adopt the same course of conduct.

On appeal, the CJ reversed the judgment of the GC (and remitted the case back to it)[586] but did not overrule this statement. Rather, it stated that 'the investigation of a pre-existing collective dominant position based on a series of elements normally considered to be indicative of the presence of the likelihood of tacit coordination between competitors cannot therefore be considered to be objectionable

[585] Case T-464/04, *Impala v Commission* EU:T:2006:216, para. 251. The GC also quashed the Commission's finding that the merger would not lead to the *creation* of a collective dominant position on the basis that the examinations carried out by the Commission were too 'succinct' and 'superficial' to satisfy its obligation to carry out a prospective analysis, see paras. 525–528.

[586] Broadly on the grounds that the Commission's reasoning was, on the facts of the case and in the light of tight time constraints under which the Commission had to act, adequate.

of itself. However . . . it is essential that such an investigation be carried out with care and, above all, that it should adopt an approach based on the analysis of such plausible coordination strategies as may exist in the circumstances.'[587]

(v) Countervailing Buyer Power

Customers with countervailing buyer power may also exercise a competitive constraint over the parties post-merger.[588] Such a buyer may have the incentive[589] to credibly threaten to find an alternative source of supply, perhaps by changing supplier, vertically integrating, or persuading/sponsoring new entry, were the supplier to increase price.[590] In such cases, the countervailing buyer power may neutralise the market power of the parties.[591] It is only in a relatively few cases that the defence has been decisive. Rather, fairly exceptional market conditions have to be satisfied for the countervailing buyer power to tilt the balance.[592]

In *Enso/Stora*,[593] the Commission considered that even though the merging parties would acquire a share of 60 per cent in the market for liquid packaging board the merger would not be problematic since they would face a very concentrated buying situation. In particular, Tetra Pak purchased 60 per cent of the packaging board and would be likely to set up an alternative source of supply if the new entity sought to exploit its market power.

Countervailing purchaser power was also relevant in *Alcatel/Telettra*.[594] In this case, the Commission cleared a merger which gave the parties market shares of 83 per cent. The Commission considered that Telefónica, the only purchaser, would be able to exert a downward pressure on prices.[595] Further, the Commission's initiative to erode barriers to cross-border trade in this sphere meant that Telefónica would seek products elsewhere if the concentration sought to charge excessive prices (high market shares in a market are unlikely to be significant in an opening market).

(vi) Entry Analysis and Barriers to Entry and Expansion

The Commission will not be concerned with a horizontal merger if the parties' decision to raise prices or reduce quality, variety, or innovation will be frustrated by new entry into the market.

> For entry to be considered a sufficient competitive constraint on the merging parties, it must be shown to be likely, timely and sufficient to deter or defeat any potential anti-competitive effects of the merger.[596]

[587] Case C-413/06 P, *Bertelsmann and Sony Corp v Commission* EU:C:2008:392, para. 129. See also M.6458, *Universal/ EMI Music* 21 September 2102 (clearance, subject to commitments of a merger which would reduce the number of major players on the wholesale market for digital music by record companies from four to three).

[588] Although buyer power may be relevant where the merger will create or strengthen buyer power in a way which will lead to a SIEC, its consideration as 'countervailing' buyer power is more common, see e.g. A. Ezrachi and M. Ioannidou, 'Buyer Power in European Union Merger Control' [2014] *European Competition Journal* 69.

[589] It may not if, for example, it can pass on the price increases to its customers, see e.g. M.1225, *Enso/Stora* [1999] OJ L254/9, para. 91.

[590] Ibid., para. 65.

[591] M.833, *The Coca-Cola Co/Carlsberg A/S* [1998] OJ L145/41.

[592] See Ezrachi and Ioannidou, n. 588.

[593] M.1225 [1999] OJ L254/9. See also, e.g., M.4057, *Körsnäs/AssiDomän Cartonboard* 12 May 2006, especially paras. 57–64 and M.1630, *Air Liquide/BOC* [2004] OJ L92/1.

[594] M.42 [1991] OJ L122/48. See also, e.g., M.3732, *Procter & Gamble/Gillette* 15 July 2005.

[595] See also M.4, *Renault/Volvo* [1990] OJ C281/2 where the Commission found that large fleet buyers would exercise downward pressure on truck and bus prices.

[596] HMG, para. 68 and Chap. 3.

Clear evidence that a position of market strength will only be temporary and will be quickly eroded because of a high probability of strong and timely market entry will thus lead to a finding that the concentration is compatible with the internal market.[597] In *HP/Compaq*,[598] for example, the Commission cleared a merger in which the parties would gain market shares of between 85 and 95 per cent on the basis that timely and sufficient new entry was likely.

The Commission may also take account of constraining competition from manufacturers operating outside the geographic market.[599] The Commission will therefore consider a great variety of factors in its assessment of barriers to entry, such as whether: legal or regulatory barriers to entry exist;[600] the ownership of patents, other IPRs, or data[601] operate as a barrier to entry into a market, particularly in technology markets[602] (in *Tetra Pak/Alfa Laval*[603] the Commission relied on a number of factors, including Tetra Pak's ownership of patents, to conclude that new entry was not likely in the market for aseptic carton packaging machines[604]); and/or other technical factors will inhibit entry. In *The Coca-Cola Co/Carlsberg*,[605] for example, the Commission considered that new entry into the carbonated soft drinks markets (CSDs)[606] in Denmark and Sweden was not likely on account of severe barriers to entry which included access to brands, access to a distribution network, access to shelf space, the need for a sales and service network, brand image, customer loyalty, and (sunk) advertising costs.[607]

Factors such as the evolution of the market (entry is less likely to be profitable in a mature market than a dynamic one), scale economies, and network effects are also relevant.[608] In making the assessment, the Commission considers only potential competitors which are likely to enter the market within a relatively short time frame (although 'timeliness' is dependent upon the characteristics or dynamics of the market, entry must generally occur within two years)[609] and whether market entry will be on a sufficient scale to deter or defeat the anti-competitive effects of the merger.[610]

In *Aérospatiale/Alenia/de Havilland*,[611] the Commission held that countervailing factors would not prevent the anti-competitive effects that would result from the parties acquiring very large shares on the commuter aircraft market generally. The high risks involved in entering the market on account of the high sunk costs that would be required and the maturity of the market reduced the likelihood of new entry.[612] Further any new entry into the commuter aircraft market was likely to occur only after a period of time and too late to catch an expected period of high demand.

In *Ryanair/Aer Lingus*, the Commission also concluded that significant barriers to entry meant that new entry was most unlikely. In particular, other airlines did not have a large base in Dublin, and they faced significant entry costs and capacity constraints in terms of obtaining slots at Dublin

[597] See e.g. M.477, *Mercedes-Benz/Kässbohrer* [1995] OJ L211/1; cf. M.774, *Saint Gobain/Wacker-Chemie/NOM* [1997] OJ L247/1.

[598] M.2609, 31 January 2002. [599] M.315, *Mannesmann/Vallourec/Ilva* [1994] OJ L102/15.

[600] See e.g. M.1430, *Vodafone/Airtouch* 21 May 1999 (the need for a licence to provide mobile telephony communications services).

[601] See e.g. M.4854, *TomTom/Tele Atlas* 14 May 2008.

[602] See e.g. M.269, *Shell/Montecatini* [1994] OJ L332/48, para. 32. [603] M.68 [1991] OJ L290/35, point 3.4.

[604] See also Chap. 6. [605] M.833 [1998] OJ L145/41.

[606] Although the Commission considered that the market could be defined more narrowly, to include different flavours of CSDs, the exact definition did not affect the outcome of this case, ibid., para. 43.

[607] M.833, *The Coca-Cola Co/Carlsberg* [1998] OJ L145/41, paras. 72–75 (it was very unlikely that anyone other than the existing international brand owners would be able to launch a new international CSD).

[608] HMG, para. 73. [609] Ibid., para. 74. This was an important issue in M.8677, *Siemens/Alstom*, n. 496.

[610] Ibid., para. 75 and, e.g., M.1157, *Skanska/Scancem* [1999] OJ L183/1, para. 184.

[611] M.53 [1991] OJ L334/42, para. 53. [612] Ridyard, n. 553, 256.

and destination airports. Further, Ryanair had a reputation of reacting aggressively against new entrants.[613] This view was reinforced by the fact that easyJet, another major low-cost carrier present in Europe, had tried and failed to enter routes in competition with Ryanair.[614] In *Olympic Air/Aegean Airlines I*,[615] the Commission also considered that new entry was not likely, even if slots were available at Athens airport.

(vii) Efficiencies

a. *An Efficiency Defence*

It was unclear whether the wording of the original EUMR left scope for a form of efficiency defence.[616] Further, some commentators complained that early Commission decisions were more reflective of an 'efficiency offence', a fear that mergers which would enable the parties to achieve significant economies of scale or scope may be more likely to result in a finding of incompatibility given the parties' greater advantages over their nearest competitors.[617] For example, in some cases involving conglomerate mergers, the Commission accepted that efficiencies resulting from a merger would enable the merging parties to lower their prices and so damage competitors.[618]

It was argued, however, that, as in the US,[619] the EUMR should admit an 'efficiency defence', allowing a concentration which increased concentration and market power to be redeemed where it resulted in significant, offsetting cost savings and economies of scale. The rationale for such a defence is based on Williamson's model,[620] which illustrates the welfare trade-offs that result from a merger which increases market power (leading to allocative inefficiency and decreasing social welfare), but at the same time creates efficiencies reducing costs (improving social welfare). These trade-offs suggest that a merger should be permitted where it creates a net positive effect or efficiency gain—where consumer (and deadweight) loss is offset by a greater gain in cost or resource savings (which are spread across the entire output).

Although the importance of Williamson's conclusions remains, and the model has been refined in several ways,[621] some difficulties arise.[622] In particular, it treats all efficiency gains in the same way

[613] Ryanair had a history of responding to third parties attempting to run services in competition with them by starting aggressive fare wars until the third party withdrew from the route, M.4439, *Ryanair/Aer Lingus* 27 June 2007, para. 515, *aff'd* Case T-342/07, EU:T:2010:280, para. 286.

[614] M.4439, ibid., para. 514.

[615] M.5830, 26 January 2011, the merger was eventually cleared, however, see n. 651 and text.

[616] Although Art. 2(1)(b) allows for 'technical and economic progress' to be taken into account 'provided it is to consumers' advantage and does not form an obstacle to competition', it was queried if this could be established if the consumer would have to pay supra-competitive prices post-merger, see e.g. A. Jacquemin, 'Mergers and European Policy' in P. H. Admiral (ed.), *Merger and Competition Policy in the European Community* (Blackwell, 1990), 36.

[617] In M.53, *Aérospatiale-Alenia/de Havilland* [1991] OJ L334/42, e.g. the parties claimed that efficiency gains that arose from the merger appeared to have 'merely strengthened the Commission's view that the merged group would enjoy benefits that would be out of the reach of its competitors. If anything, the "efficiency defence" seems in this case to have reduced the chances of clearance for the deal', Ridyard, n. 553, 256–257.

[618] See discussion of M.2220, *GE/Honeywell* 3 July 2001, *aff'd* Cases T-209 and 210/01, *Honeywell v Commission* and *General Electric Co v Commission* EU:T:2005:455 and EU:T:2005:456 in Section 5.F.iv. But see refutation of Mario Monti, then Commissioner for Competition, 'Antitrust in the US and Europe: A History of Convergence', SPEECH/01/540, General Counsel Roundtable American Bar Association, Washington DC, 14 November 2001.

[619] While the Supreme Court itself has never recognised an efficiency defence to a prima facie unlawful merger, both the US DOJ and FTC, 2010 Guidelines, n. 445, §10 (the onus of proving qualifying efficiencies rests on the parties) and several of the Circuits accept it.

[620] O. Williamson, 'Economics as an Antitrust Defence: The Welfare Tradeoffs' (1968) 58 *Am Econ Rev* 23.

[621] See e.g. G. Bet and R. D. Blair, 'Williamson's Welfare Trade-Off Around the World' (2019) 55 *Review of Industrial Organization* 515.

[622] Hovenkamp, n. 7, 12.2b1.

no matter who gets the benefit; a merger which has an overall efficient effect (increasing total welfare) may sometimes still lead to an increase in price for consumers (e.g. where the benefits accrue to the merging parties or to out-of-market citizens).[623] In most jurisdictions, however, a consumer—rather than a social—welfare objective is pursued, suggesting that merger efficiencies must be sufficient to reverse harm to affected consumers, for example by ensuring that post-merger prices do not exceed pre-merger ones.

Another acute difficulty lies in the practical application of the defence. Not only can it be difficult to provide adequate evidence to determine the scope of the future efficiencies and that they cannot be obtained by means other than the merger, but courts (and competition agencies) may not always have the information they require to make the necessary measurements and analysis.[624]

b. The Horizontal Merger Guidelines

In view of the uncertain position towards efficiencies in the original EUMR, the Regulation was, following consultation,[625] amended to clarify that it 'is possible that the efficiencies brought forward by the concentration counteract the effects on competition, and in particular the potential harm to consumers, that it might otherwise have and that, as a consequence, the concentration would not significantly impede effective competition, in particular as a result of the creation or strengthening of a dominant position' (recital 29). The Commission also deals with efficiencies in its HMG.[626]

The Guidelines recognise that, in making its substantive appraisal, the Commission takes account of the development of technical and economic progress,[627] and that 'efficiencies generated by the merger are likely to enhance the ability and incentive of the merged entity to act pro-competitively for the benefit of consumers, thereby counteracting the adverse effects on competition which the merger might otherwise have'.[628] The burden is on the parties to establish the efficiency defence.[629] The Commission will thus only take account of substantiated efficiencies which: (a) benefit consumers; (b) are merger specific;[630] and (c) are verifiable.[631] Thus:

> efficiencies brought about by a merger may counteract its possible anti-competitive effects and thus not lead to a SIEC—in a very similar way to an agreement or practice meeting the test of Article 101(3) TFEU . . .

In both instances:

- the restriction of competition according to Article 101(1) must be necessary to obtain them, or respectively, the efficiencies must be 'merger-specific';
- the restriction of competition must allow 'consumers a fair share of the resulting benefit', or respectively, the efficiencies resulting from the merger must be 'passed on to consumers';

[623] See e.g. Bet and Blair, n. 621.
[624] Some suggest that even if the comparison *could* be made, it *should* not. Huge cost savings would be necessary to offset any associated price increases, see e.g. Scherer and Ross, n. 6, 174 (statistical evidence supporting the hypotheses that profitability and efficiency increase following mergers is at best weak).
[625] 2001 Green Paper on the Review of Council Regulation (EEC) No. 4064/89, COM(2001) 745/6 final. Most respondents considered that, as part of a sound economics-based merger control policy, the Commission should take account of efficiencies in its analysis of the overall effects likely to be produced by a proposed merger.
[626] [2004] OJ C31/5. Form CO also has a section on efficiency gains.
[627] HMG, para. 76.
[628] Ibid., para. 77.
[629] Case T-175/12, *Deutsche Börse v Commission* EU:T:2015:148 and Section 5.C.
[630] Ibid., para. 85.
[631] Ibid., paras. 77–88. See discussion of mergers in the telecoms market, n. 513 and text.

- finally, while under Article 101(3) a restriction of competition may not afford the parties 'the possibility of eliminating competition in respect of a substantial part of the products in question', the HMG state that a merger resulting in a near-monopoly is unlikely to product efficiencies large enough to exclude a SIEC.[632]

(1) Benefit to Consumers

Consumers should not be worse off as a result of the merger. The merger must thus bring timely efficiencies that will result, for example, in lower prices (perhaps through reduction in variable or marginal costs) or in new, improved, or more sustainable products or services (for example, from efficiency gains in the sphere of R&D). In the context of coordinated effects, efficiencies may lead to incentives to increase production and reduce output and disincentives to coordinate behaviour.

The greater the market power acquired by the undertakings the more difficult it will be to show that benefits will result which will be passed on to consumers. Further, the Commission states that the efficiencies should in principle benefit consumers in the market where the competition problems arise, a potential difficulty where sustainability arguments are raised.[633]

(2) Merger Specificity

Paragraph 85 of the HMG explains the requirement of merger specificity.

> Efficiencies are relevant to the competitive assessment when they are a direct consequence of the notified merger and cannot be achieved to a similar extent by less anti-competitive alternatives. In these circumstances, the efficiencies are deemed to be caused by the merger and thus, merger specific. It is for the parties to provide in due time all the relevant information necessary to demonstrate that there are no less anti-competitive, realistic and attainable alternatives of a non-concentrative nature (e.g., a licensing agreement, or a cooperative joint venture) or of a concentrative nature (e.g., a concentrative joint venture, or a differently structured merger) than the notified merger which preserve the claimed efficiencies. The Commission only considers alternatives that are reasonably practical in the business situation faced by the merging parties having regard to established business practices in the industry concerned.

(3) Verifiability

The parties must be able to verify the efficiencies so that 'the Commission can be reasonably certain that the efficiencies are likely to materialize, and be substantial enough to counteract a merger's potential harm to consumers'.[634] The Commission states that the parties should quantify the efficiencies where possible or otherwise identify the positive impact on consumers.

[632] Mosso, n. 364 (in each, the burden of proof is on the parties (see Section 5.C)—the same is true for the objective justification of otherwise abusive conduct).

[633] See by analogy the discussion of the treatment of sustainability benefits under Art. 101(3) in Chaps. 5 and 10.

[634] HMG, para. 85. See e.g. D. Gerard, 'Merger Control Policy: How to Give Meaningful Consideration to Efficiency Claims?' (2003) 40 *CMLRev* 1367.

(4) Cases

Although efficiencies have not yet been given as a decisive factor for a merger clearance,[635] they were given as one of them in *Körsnäs/AssiDomän Cartonboard*.[636] In this case, the Commission accepted that synergies resulting from the merger between two of the three main players active in the worldwide market for the production of liquid carton packaging board were likely to be passed on to consumers. The Commission also considered, however, that countervailing buyer power as well as competition from EnsoStora,[637] suppliers outside the EU, and suppliers of other board materials, were likely to constrain the behaviour of the merged parties.

In both *UPS/TNT Express*[638] and *Ryanair/Aer Lingus*,[639] the Commission also carefully scrutinised efficiencies submitted by the parties. In *UPS/TNT*, a large volume of economic evidence addressed efficiencies, the substantial cost savings it was alleged would arise in management, administration, ground transportation, and the air network, and whether they would outweigh likely negative effects on pricing. The Commission recognised a number of them but prohibited the merger because it considered that they would not outweigh the price increases likely to result from it; in particular, it was unlikely that any alleged cost savings (mainly relating in this case to fixed not variable costs) would be passed through to consumers. As the decision was annulled on procedural grounds, the EU Courts did not have to deal with the substantive assessment of efficiencies. They did, however, stress the importance of the Commission disclosing the final version of an econometric model on which it relied in relation to net effects, if there was even a slight chance that its disclosure would have better enabled UPS to defend itself.[640]

In *Ryanair/Aer Lingus*, the Commission rejected the argument that offsetting efficiencies would be brought about by the merger. Rather, it found that the efficiencies that would result from a reduction of Aer Lingus's operating costs constituted more of a general assertion than a verifiable claim and were not merger-specific (since it appeared that they could be generated by Aer Lingus simply applying Ryanair's business plan). Further, given that the Commission had established that the merged entity would face little, if any, competition on a number of routes and that many of the claimed efficiencies related to fixed costs, the Commission considered there to be little incentive for any cost savings made to be passed on to consumers—the efficiencies were of insufficient benefit to consumers to outweigh a merger to monopoly on some routes.[641] The GC upheld the Commission's decision and rejected Ryanair's allegation that the Commission had set the bar to establish efficiencies too high. The conclusion reached in this case lends support to the view set out in paragraph 84 of the HMG that

[635] See e.g. B. Buehler and G. Federico, 'Recent Developments in the Assessment of Efficiencies of EU Mergers' (2016) 2 *Competition Law & Policy Debate* and D. Cardwell. 'The Role of the Efficiency Defence in EU Merger Control Proceedings Following *UPS/TNT, FedEx/TNT* and *UPS v Commission*' (2017) 8 *JECLAP* 551.

[636] M.4057, 12 May 2006, especially paras. 57–64. See also e.g. M.3732, *Procter & Gamble/Gillette* 15 July 2005; M.3664, *Repsol Butano/Shell Gas* 2 March 2005; and M.4000, *Inco/Falconbridge* 4 July 2006 (the parties' efficiencies claims were rejected).

[637] See n. 584 and accompanying text.

[638] M.6570, 30 January 2013, annulled on appeal, Case T-194/13, *United Parcel Service v Commission* EU:T:2017:742, *aff'd* Case C-265/17 P, EU:C:2019:23, see n. 348 and text. In M.7630, *FedEx/TNT Express* 8 January 2016 the Commission was sympathetic to the parties' efficiencies arguments although they did not play the decisive role in that case, especially as the parties were found not to be close competitors. See also e.g. M.6360, *Nynas/Shell/Harburg Refinery Assets* 2 September 2013 and M.6166, *Deutsche Börse/NYSE Euronext* 1 February 2012, *aff'd* Case T-175/12, *Deutsche Börse v Commission* EU:T:2015:148.

[639] M.4439, *Ryanair/Aer Lingus* 27 June 2007, *aff'd* Case T-342/07, *Ryanair v Commission* EU:T:2010:280, para. 443.

[640] See also n. 348 and text.

[641] M.4439, *Ryanair/Aer Lingus* 27 June 2007, para. 1151, *aff'd* Case T-342/07, *Ryanair v Commission* EU:T:2010:280, para. 443. See also Case T-175/12, *Deutsche Börse v Commission* EU:T:2015:148 (stressing the need for the parties to demonstrate that customers will benefit from the efficiencies).

it is highly unlikely that a merger leading to a market position approaching monopoly can be declared compatible with the internal market on the ground that the efficiency gains would be sufficient to counteract its potential anti-competitive effects.[642]

(viii) The Failing Firm Defence or Rescue Mergers

The failing firm defence, well established in US antitrust practice,[643] provides an escape route for a merger involving a firm facing an otherwise inevitable liquidation. In the US, it appears to have been adopted historically to ensure the protection of the creditors, owners, and/or employees of small businesses; it was therefore concerned not with efficiency but with distributive justice. Nonetheless, a narrowly applied failing company could be efficient if it enables a failing firm and its creditors to avoid the high administrative costs of bankruptcy and keeps on the market productive assets that would otherwise likely be taken out of production.[644]

In the EU, a failing firm defence was first recognised in *Kali und Salz/MdK/Treuhand*[645] which raised the question whether or not an undertaking with large market shares could combine activities with its only, or main, failing competitor. It has been seen that the case concerned the combination of the potash and rock-salt activities of K\+S and MdK. Although the Commission found that the concentration would acquire enormous shares on the potash market in Germany and the magnesium products market of 98 per cent and 100 per cent respectively, it concluded that it was not the merger that was the cause of the deterioration in the competitive structure. Even if the merger was prohibited, the acquiring undertaking would inevitably achieve or reinforce its dominant position to the same extent. The French Government challenged the decision but the CJ upheld it, confirming that if a concentration is not the cause of the significant impediment to competition it must be declared compatible with the internal market.[646]

Cases C-68/94 and C-30/95, *France v Commission, Société Commerciale des Potasses et de l'Azote (SCPA) v Commission* EU:C:1998:148

Court of Justice

111. It appears from point 71 of the contested decision that, in the Commission's opinion, a concentration which would normally be considered as leading to the creation or reinforcement of a dominant position on the part of the acquiring undertaking may be regarded as not being the cause of it if, even in the event of the concentration being prohibited, that undertaking would inevitably achieve or

[642] See also M.6166, *Deutsche Börse/NYSE Euronext* 1 February 2012 and Mosso, n. 364.

[643] US DOJ and FTC, 2010 Guidelines, n. 445, §11 (the Guidelines are, however, in the process of being revised). See also OECD, 'Failing Firm Defence' (2009), available at <www.oecd.org/daf/competition/mergers/45810821.pdf> and M. Lopez-Galdos, 'Comparing the US & the EU Failing Firm Defense: Reflections from an Economic Perspective' (2016) 28 *Loyola Consumer LR* 297.

[644] 2010 Guidelines ibid., para. 12.9, 545.

[645] M.308 [1994] OJ L186/30; on appeal Cases C-68/94 and C-30/95, *France v Commission, Société Commerciale des Potasses et de l'Azote (SCPA) v Commission* EU:C:1998:148. The Commission had rejected the defence in M.53, *Aérospatiale/Alenia/de Havilland* [1991] OJ L334/42. See G. Monti and E. Rousseva, 'Failing Firms in the Framework of the EC Merger Regulation' (1999) 24 *ELRev* 38.

[646] Cases C-68/94 and C-30/95, *France v Commission, Société Commerciale des Potasses et de l'Azote (SCPA) v Commission* EU:C:1998:148, para. 110.

reinforce a dominant position. Point 71 goes on to state that, as a general matter, a concentration is not the cause of the deterioration of the competitive structure if it is clear that:

— the acquired undertaking would in the near future be forced out of the market if not taken over by another undertaking,

— the acquiring undertaking would gain the market share of the acquired undertaking if it were forced out of the market,

— there is no less anti-competitive alternative purchase.

112. It must be observed, first of all, that the fact that the conditions set by the Commission for concluding that there was no causal link between the concentration and the deterioration of the competitive structure do not entirely coincide with the conditions applied in connection with the United States 'failing company defence' is not in itself a ground of invalidity of the contested decision. Solely the fact that the conditions set by the Commission were not capable of excluding the possibility that a concentration might be the cause of the deterioration in the competitive structure of the market could constitute a ground of invalidity of the decision.

113. In the present case, the French Government disputes the relevance of the criterion that it must be verified that the acquiring undertaking would in any event obtain the acquired undertaking's share of the market if the latter were to be forced out of the market.

114. However, in the absence of that criterion, a concentration could, provided the other criteria were satisfied, be considered as not being the cause of the deterioration of the competitive structure of the market even though it appeared that, in the event of the concentration not proceeding, the acquiring undertaking would not gain the entire market share of the acquired undertaking. Thus, it would be possible to deny the existence of a causal link between the concentration and the deterioration of the competitive structure of the market even though the competitive structure of the market would deteriorate to a lesser extent if the concentration did not proceed.

115. The introduction of that criterion is intended to ensure that the existence of a causal link between the concentration and the deterioration of the competitive structure of the market can be excluded only if the competitive structure resulting from the concentration would deteriorate in similar fashion even if the concentration did not proceed.

116. The criterion of absorption of market shares, although not considered by the Commission as sufficient in itself to preclude any adverse effect of the concentration on competition, therefore helps to ensure the neutral effects of the concentration as regards the deterioration of the competitive structure of the market. This is consistent with the concept of causal connection set out in Article 2(2) of the Regulation.

117. As to the criticism of the Commission that it failed to show that if the concentration did not proceed MdK would inevitably have been forced out of the market, it should be observed that the Commission stated in point 73 of the contested decision that, even though MdK had been restructured by 1 January 1993, that undertaking continued to make considerable losses in the first six months of the year. According to the Commission, MdK's serious economic situation was essentially a result of its obsolete operating structure and the crisis in sales attributable primarily to the collapse of markets in eastern Europe. MdK also lacked an efficient distribution system (see points 74 and 75 of the contested decision).

118. In point 76 of the contested decision, the Commission observed that MdK had been able to continue operating until now only because Treuhand had consistently covered its losses. The Commission added, however, that Treuhand could not cover MdK's losses in the long term from public aid, since that was in any case incompatible with the Treaty provisions on State aid.

119. In the light of the foregoing, the Commission cannot be criticised for finding that MdK was no longer economically viable and for considering that it was probable that, on its own, MdK would continue to accumulate losses even if Treuhand provided the funds envisaged for restructuring purposes in the proposed concentration.

120. In those circumstances, the Commission's forecast that MdK was highly likely to close down in the near future if it were not taken over by a private undertaking cannot be regarded as unsupported by a consistent body of evidence.

121. Finally, with respect to the condition concerning the absence of an alternative, less anti-competitive method of acquiring MdK, it should be noted that the French Government's complaint is that the Commission, because of the lack of transparency in the tendering procedure, failed to show that that condition was in fact satisfied.

122. Suffice it to note that the French Government has merely observed that the MdK trade unions pointed to a lack of transparency in the tendering procedure, without providing any details as to what constituted the alleged lack of transparency.

123. In the absence of any details of that complaint, it cannot be upheld.

124. It follows from the foregoing that the absence of a causal link between the concentration and the deterioration of the competitive structure of the German market has not been effectively called into question. Accordingly, it must be held that, so far as that market is concerned, the concentration appears to satisfy the criterion referred to in Article 2(2) of the Regulation, and could thus be declared compatible with the common market without being amended. Consequently, contrary to the French Government's assertion, it is not possible without contradicting that premise to require the Commission, with respect to the German market, to attach any condition whatever to its declaration of the concentration's compatibility.

Since *Kali and Salz* the Commission has been prepared to apply the failing firm defence or the concept of the 'rescue merger' more broadly. The defence has been pleaded in a number of cases[647] and was developed in *BASF/Pantochim/Eurodiol*.[648] This concentration was likely to lead to the acquisition of high market shares on certain base chemical markets. In applying the failing firm defence the Commission stressed that the approach taken by the CJ in its *Kali and Salz* judgment was wider than the criteria set out in the Commission's own decision in that case. The key requirement for a merger to be regarded as a rescue merger was that the competitive structure resulting from the concentration would deteriorate in a similar fashion even if the concentration did not proceed, i.e. even if the concentration was prohibited. Thus the essential conditions are that the undertaking to be acquired can be regarded as a 'failing firm' and that the merger will not be the *cause* of the deterioration of the competitive structure. The Commission does not therefore require that the acquiring company would inevitably acquire the entire market share of the acquired undertaking if it were forced out of the market, but only that the acquired company's assets would inevitably exit the market were the firm not taken over.

The approach is followed in the HMG.

Guidelines on the Assessment of Horizontal Mergers under the Council Regulation on the Control of Concentrations between Undertakings [2004] OJ C31/5

VIII. Failing firm

89. The Commission may decide that an otherwise problematic merger is nevertheless compatible with the common market if one of the merging parties is a failing firm. The basic requirement is that the deterioration of the competitive structure that follows the merger cannot be said to be caused by

[647] It has been rejected in a number of cases, see, e.g., M.774, *Saint-Gobain/Wacker-Chemie-NOM* [1997] OJ L247/1.

[648] COMP/M.2314, IP/01/984. See also M.2876, *Newscorp/Telepiù*, IP/03/478 and I. Kokkoris, 'Failing Firm Defence in the European Union: A Panacea for Mergers?' [2006] *ECLR* 494.

the merger. This will arise where the competitive structure of the market would deteriorate to at least the same extent in the absence of the merger.

90. The Commission considers the following three criteria to be especially relevant for the application of a 'failing firm defence'. First, the allegedly failing firm would in the near future be forced out of the market because of financial difficulties if not taken over by another undertaking. Second, there is no less anti-competitive alternative purchase than the notified merger. Third, in the absence of a merger, the assets of the failing firm would inevitably exit the market.

91. It is for the notifying parties to provide in due time all the relevant information necessary to demonstrate that the deterioration of the competitive structure that follows the merger is not caused by the merger.

The criteria set by the Commission in the cases and guidelines are high and have, in spite of financial, health, and economic crises, only been met in relatively few cases, for example *Aegean/Olympic II*[649] and *Nynas/Shell Harburg Refinery Assets*.[650] In *Aegean/Olympic II*, the Commission, despite having prohibited the merger a couple of years before (because it would lead to a merger with Aegean's closest competitor and a monopoly on several domestic routes),[651] approved the merger unconditionally, accepting that Olympic was failing and would be forced to leave the market. The ongoing Greek crisis meant that demand for domestic air travel was continuing to drop significantly. Further, no less anti-competitive purchase was credible. As, absent the merger, Olympic's assets were likely to leave the market completely, the merger would have no additional adverse effect on competition.

In *Nynas/Shell*, the Commission approved Nynas's acquisition of Shell's Harburg refinery assets finding that, absent the merger, the refinery (producing naphthenic base and process and transformer oils) was likely to be closed. Such a closure would reduce production capacity and increase prices in the EEA.

The Commission has not ruled out the possibility of the defence applying where only part of the firm is failing. It appears, however, that the defence, and lack of causality between the merger and the adverse effect on competition, will be much harder to establish in such cases.[652]

F. COMPETITIVE ASSESSMENT OF NON-HORIZONTAL MERGERS

(i) The Non-Horizontal Merger Guidelines

The Commission's merger decisions have also reflected concerns with significant impediments to effective competition resulting from vertical, and/or conglomerate, mergers.

Some of these decisions, in particular those adopted in *GE/Honeywell*[653] and *Tetra Laval/Sidel*,[654] have been extremely controversial. In 2007, however, the Commission adopted[655] Non-Horizontal

[649] M.6796, 9 October 2013, see e.g. A. Komninos and J. Jeram, 'Changing Mind in Changed Circumstances: *Aegean/Olympic II* and the Failing Firm Defence' (2014) 5 *JECLAP* 605.

[650] M.6360, 2 September 2013.

[651] M.5830, 26 January 2011, Case T-202/11 *Aeroporia Aigaiou Aeroporiki v Commission* (proceedings discontinued).

[652] See M.1221, *Rewe/Meinl* [1999] OJ L274/1 and M.2876, *Newscorp/Telepiù*, IP/03/478, I. Kokkoris and R. Olivares-Caminal, *Antitrust Law Amidst Financial Crises* (Cambridge University Press, 2010), 109, E. F. Clark and C. E. Foss, 'When the Failing Firm Defence Fails' (2012) 3 *JECLAP* 317 and Lopez-Galdos, n. 643.

[653] M.2220, *General Electric/Honeywell* 3 July 2001, *aff'd* Cases T-209 and 210/01, *Honeywell Intl v Commission* EU:T:2005:455 and EU:T:2005:456.

[654] M.2416, 30 October 2001, annulled on appeal Case T-5/02 [2002] ECR II-4381, *aff'd* Case C-12/03 P, EU:C:2005:87.

[655] Following a public consultation on the draft guidelines (see IP/07/178). See also Report for DG Competition, European Commission prepared by Jeffrey Church (University of Calgary, Canada), September 2004, *The Impact of Vertical and Conglomerate Mergers on Competition*, <https://publications.europa.eu/en/publication-detail/-/publication/d95d239c-2844-4c95-80a4-2181e85e8329>.

Merger Guidelines (NHMG), designed to provide clear and predictable guidance to companies as to how it will analyse the impact of non-horizontal mergers on competition. These Guidelines aim to complement the Commission's guidance on horizontal mergers and, no doubt, to meet the challenges, standards, and demands required of it by EU Courts in non-horizontal merger cases.

The NHMG accept that non-horizontal mergers are generally less likely to lead to a SIEC than horizontal mergers. Not only do vertical and conglomerate mergers not entail the loss of direct competition between the merging parties in the same relevant market but it is recognised that they provide substantial scope for efficiencies, particularly through the integration of complementary activities and the reduction of transaction costs.[656]

Non-Horizontal Merger Guidelines

12. First, unlike horizontal mergers, vertical or conglomerate mergers do not entail the loss of direct competition between the merging firms in the same relevant market. As a result, the main source of anti-competitive effect in horizontal mergers is absent from vertical and conglomerate mergers.

13. Second, vertical and conglomerate mergers provide substantial scope for efficiencies. A characteristic of vertical mergers and certain conglomerate mergers is that the activities and/or the products of the companies involved are complementary to each other. The integration of complementary activities or products within a single firm may produce significant efficiencies and be pro-competitive. In vertical relationships for instance, as a result of the complementarity, a decrease in mark-ups downstream will lead to higher demand also upstream. A part of the benefit of this increase in demand will accrue to the upstream suppliers. An integrated firm will take this benefit into account. Vertical integration may thus provide an increased incentive to seek to decrease prices and increase output because the integrated firm can capture a larger fraction of the benefits. This is often referred to as the 'internalisation of double mark-ups'. Similarly, other efforts to increase sales at one level (e.g. improve service or stepping up innovation) may provide a greater reward for an integrated firm that will take into account the benefits accruing at other levels.

14. Integration may also decrease transaction costs and allow for a better co-ordination in terms of product design, the organisation of the production process, and the way in which the products are sold. Similarly, mergers which involve products belonging to a range or portfolio of products that are generally sold to the same set of customers (be they complementary products or not) may give rise to customer benefits such as one-stop shopping.

The Commission is nonetheless still concerned that both types of mergers may lead to a SIEC on a market by giving rise to non-coordinated effects (principally through foreclosure) and/or coordinated effects (through changing the nature of competition so the firms are significantly more likely to coordinate and raise prices). The Commission makes it clear in its Guidelines, heeding perhaps the criticism it faced following its decision in *GE/Honeywell*, that it focuses on the effects of the merger on the customers to which the merged entity and its competitors are selling. 'Consequently, the fact that a merger affects competitors is not in itself a problem. It is the impact on effective competition that matters, not the mere impact on competitors at some level of the supply chain. In particular, the fact that a rival may be harmed because a merger creates efficiencies cannot in itself give rise to competition concerns.'[657]

[656] NHMG, paras. 11–13. [657] Ibid., paras. 16 and 27.

(ii) Market Shares and Concentration Levels

The Commission considers that non-horizontal mergers pose no threat to effective competition unless the merged entity has a significant degree of market power in at least one of the markets affected by the merger. Market shares and concentration levels provide useful *first indications* of market power (a significant degree of market power is a necessary, but not sufficient, condition for competitive harm). The NHMG state that the Commission is unlikely to have concerns with non-horizontal mergers where the market share post-merger of the new entity in each of the markets concerned is below 30 per cent[658] and the post-merger HHI is below 2,000.[659] Indeed, the simplified procedure applies where the market share of the new entity in each of the markets concerned is less than 30 per cent.[660]

(iii) Assessment of Vertical Mergers

A number of cases illustrate the Commission's concern about vertical mergers.[661] *AOL/Time Warner*,[662] for example, concerned a merger between Time Warner, a media and entertainment company, and AOL, the leading internet access provider in the US. The merger would create the first internet vertically integrated content provider and would be able to distribute Time Warner content (music, news, and films) through AOL's internet distribution network. AOL would also have access to Bertelsmann content in consequence of a JV it had with the latter in Europe. The Commission was concerned that AOL would be able to dominate the emerging market for internet music delivery online through its becoming the gatekeeper to the nascent market. In the end, the Commission cleared the merger subject to a 'remedy package' which essentially required AOL to sever its links with Bertelsmann. This would leave Europe's largest media company free to compete and prevent the merged entity from dominating the market.

Indeed, the Commission now often reviews vertical mergers closely, especially those raising concerns about access to data, IPR, or technology access.[663] In *Illumina/Grail*,[664] the Commission prohibited a proposed acquisition which it feared would reduce competition and innovation in the emerging market for the development and commercialisation of cancer-detection tests based on sequencing technologies—techniques which could emerge as a game changer in the fight against the disease. The merger would bring together two US-based companies, Illumina, a leading supplier of next-generation sequencing (NGS) systems for genetic and genomic analysis, and Grail, a customer of

[658] This percentage accords with the market share threshold included in the Verticals Block Exemption, see Chap. 11.

[659] The Commission will extensively investigate such cases only where 'special circumstances' exist: (a) the merger involves a company that is likely to expand in the near future; (b) there are significant cross-shareholdings or cross-directorships among market participants; (c) one of the merging parties is a firm which is likely to disrupt coordinated conduct; or (d) where indications of prior or ongoing facilitating practices are present, NHMG, paras. 25–26.

[660] Notice on Simplified Procedure, 5(d)(ii). In 2023, this was expanded to incorporate a flexibility clause allowing the Commission to review certain concentrations under the simplified procedure at the request of the notifying parties (e.g. where the individual or combined market shares of the parties to the concentration are lower than 35% or do not exceed 50% in one market and 10% in the other market).

[661] See e.g. M.3440, *EDP/ENI/GDP* (*aff'd* Case T-87/05, *EDP v Commission* EU:T:2005:333), M.3696, *E.ON/MOL*, M.10702, *KPS/Real Alloy* 10 October 2022, M.10792, *Philip Morris/ Swedish Match* 25 October 2022, and M.9569 *EssilorLuxottica/GrandVision* 23 March 2023.

[662] M.1845, *Time Warner/AOL*, IP/00/1145. See also e.g. M.4504, *SFR/Télé2 France*.

[663] See e.g. M.9987, *NVIDIA/Arm* (transaction abandoned), M.9564, *LSEG/Refinitiv* (cleared subject to commitments) 22 October 2021, M.10262, *Facebook(Meta)/Kustomer* (cleared subject to commitments, including non-discriminatory, free access to APIs for its messaging channels, and to improvements made to those channels) 13 October 2022.

[664] M.10188, 6 September 2022.

Illumina which develops cancer-detection tests relying on NGS systems. The Commission's principal concern was that giving Illumina's leading position in NGS systems—critical inputs for the development and commercialisation of NGS-based cancer-detection tests—Illumina would, post-merger, have the ability and incentive to engage in foreclosure strategies (by preventing or hindering access to Illumina's technology) which would increase barriers to Grail's competitors in the development of NGS-based cancer-detection tests space, so hampering innovation, reducing the choice, innovative features, and performance of products available to patients, doctors, and health systems.

In *Google/Fitbit*,[665] the Commission also investigated whether a transaction combining Google's and Fitbit's complementary activities[666] would: (a) allow Google to acquire access to a vast amount of data making it difficult for rivals to compete in the ad tech space (e.g. in the markets for online search advertising and online display advertising); (b) restrict players in the digital healthcare market's access to Fitbit's web application programming interface, so preventing them from providing services to Fitbit users and getting access to their data; and (c) put competing manufacturers of wrist-worn devices at a disadvantage by degrading their interoperability with Android smartphones. Eventually, the transaction was cleared after the Commission accepted a complex remedy package designed to allay its concerns, including a ten-year commitment by Google not to use Fitbit data for its Google Ad business, and to ensure interoperability of other wrist-worn health and fitness devices with Android devices. Although the Commission investigated privacy concerns for users, and whether they would be able to track what their health data would be used for, it concluded that as Google would have to comply with the provisions and principles of the GDPR, these concerns were not 'within the remit of merger control and there are regulatory tools better placed to address them'.

a. Non-coordinated Effects: Foreclosure

With regard to the danger of non-coordinated effects, the focus is on foreclosure:[667] whether actual or potential rivals' access to supplies or markets is materially hampered or eliminated as a result of the merger, thereby reducing those companies' ability to compete and so allowing the merging parties—and possibly some of its competitors as well—profitably to increase the price charged to consumers. This may result from:

(a) input foreclosure—where the merger will restrict access to an important input raising downstream rivals' costs; and/or

(b) customer foreclosure—where vertical integration forecloses upstream rivals by foreclosing their access to a sufficient customer base.

[665] M.9660, 17 December 2020. Conglomerate concerns also arose in several markets but in the end were resolved through behavioural remedies.

[666] Google, a multinational technology company, is active in a wide range of product areas including online advertising technology, internet search, cloud computing, software, and hardware. Amongst other products and services, Google develops licensable operating systems for smartphones and smartwatches, as well as applications, such as a health and fitness application. The company also offers IT and information/research services for the healthcare industry. Fitbit, a US company, is active in the development, manufacturing, and distribution of wearable devices (both smartwatches and fitness trackers) and connected sales in the health and wellness sector. Fitbit is also active in the supply of related software and services.

[667] The Commission is also concerned that non-coordinated effects may occur where the merged entity may, by vertically integrating, gain access to commercially sensitive information regarding the upstream or downstream activities of rivals and that the merger may also put competitors at a competitive disadvantage, thereby dissuading them from entering or expanding in the market, NHMG, para. 78.

In each case, the Commission assesses: the *ability* of the merging parties to foreclose access to inputs or customers; the *incentive* to do so; and the overall *likely effect* on competition (taking into account efficiencies that benefit consumers, are merger-specific and verifiable, where they 'are likely to enhance the ability and incentive of the merged entity to act pro-competitively for the benefit of consumers, thereby counteracting the adverse effects on competition which the merger might otherwise have'.[668] These three factors are closely intertwined and are generally considered together.

In *Philip Morris/Swedish Match*,[669] the Commission was concerned that a merger between two suppliers of tobacco and nicotine products would lead to foreclosure effects in Sweden, where Swedish Match held, through a subsidiary SMD Logistics, a *de facto* monopoly in the distribution of tobacco and nicotine products. The transaction was cleared, however, following a commitment to divest SMD Logistics.

In the context of input foreclosure, it seems unlikely that these conditions will be satisfied unless the input is sufficiently important, the firm has market power in the upstream market, the foreclosure will be profitable to the merged entity, and foreclosure will result in a SIEC in the downstream market (through, for example, increasing costs of downstream rivals and raising barriers to entry to potential competitors). In *TomTom/Tele Atlas*,[670] for example, the Commission cleared an acquisition by TomTom, a Personal Navigation Device (PND) manufacturer with a leading position, of Tele Atlas (one of two producers of navigable digital maps, an essential input for PND manufacturers). Although the Commission had been concerned that the duopoly in the upstream market for navigable digital maps, combined with TomTom's strong position on the market for PNDs, would lead to a SIEC, following an in-depth examination it concluded that the merged entity would not have the ability to increase the costs of other PND manufacturers for navigable digital maps or to limit their access to these maps. Its ability to restrict access to digital maps for others would be limited by the presence of an upstream competitor, Navteq. Further, it found that the merged company would have no incentive to restrict access to digital maps because the sales of digital maps lost by Tele Atlas would not be compensated by additional sales of PNDs.

In *EssilorLuxottica/GrandVision*,[671] in contrast, the Commission was concerned about input foreclosure in the optical industry when a worldwide leader in the supply of optical products (EssilorLuxottica), with an unparalleled brand portfolio and a wide retail operation, sought to acquire the largest optical retailer in the EEA, GrandVision. The Commission reviewed three interlinked effects on the retail market: the merger's horizontal impact on the retail market; its vertical foreclosure effects; and the 'diagonal' aspects of the agreement (which meant that post-merger a lost sale by GrandVision following a price increase, would be recaptured by the earning of additional upstream margins). The merger was cleared only following a commitment to divest a large number of retail stores in Belgium, Italy, and the Netherlands.

The ability or incentive to foreclose may also be affected by legislation or regulation.[672] These were discussed in both *Google/Motorola*[673] and *Lenovo/Motorola Mobility*.[674] In the former, the

[668] E.g., internalisation of double mark-ups; improved coordination of the production and distribution process; and alignment of incentives for investments in new products, new production processes, and marketing, NHMG, paras. 55–57. Ability to foreclose is likely to arise where the merger involves an important input for the downstream product and the merged firm has market power in the upstream market or where the downstream merging party is an important customer in the downstream market and there are significant economies of scale or scope in the input market.

[669] M.10792, 25 October 2022.

[670] M.4854, 14 May 2008. The Commission also investigated the proposed acquisition of Tele Atlas's main competitor, Navteq, by Nokia, M.4942, 2 July 2008 (notified shortly after TomTom/Tele Atlas).

[671] M.9569, 23 March 2021 and see DG Comp [2021] 3 *Competition Merger Brief* 9

[672] See e.g. M.7268, *CSAV/HGV/Kühne Maritime/Hapag-Lloyd AG* 11 September 2014.

[673] M.6381, 13 February 2012. [674] M.7202, 26 June 2014.

Commission considered that Google's open-source Android OS, one of the most popular mobile operating systems (OS), and a number of Motorola's 'standard essential' patents (SEPs)[675] were key inputs in smart mobile devices (Motorola, being a leading player in the development of smart phones and tablets). Ultimately, however, the merger was cleared unconditionally in Phase I proceedings. With regard to the SEPs, the Commission did not consider that the merger would significantly change the current position and was also influenced by Google's 'legally binding' and 'irrevocable' letter to standard-setting organisations to honour Motorola's pre-existing commitment to license them on fair, reasonable, and non-discriminatory (FRAND) terms. Further, it did not consider that Google would have the incentive to prevent Motorola's competitors from using its OS as that would stifle the spread of its other services. In the latter, it considered that Lenovo's ability to foreclose access to SEPs would be constrained by FRAND commitments which bound it, its inability to enforce an injunction against a willing licensee, and the fact that it had widely licensed SEPs in the past.

The Commission will also consider countervailing factors (such as buyer power and potential competition) and assess efficiencies resulting from the merger (such as the internalisation of double mark-ups, better coordination of the production and distribution process, and alignment of parties' incentives).

b. *Incentives to Foreclose and Article 102 TFEU*

In considering incentives to foreclose, the Commission is required, in both vertical and conglomerate effects cases, to take into account the possibility that the foreclosing conduct might be illegal (under Article 102 TFEU). The question of the extent to which the existence of Article 102 can be expected to affect the incentive of the merged entity to engage in a course of conduct in breach of it (i.e. is the merger appraisal affected by the fact that foreclosure of the downstream, upstream, or related market would, or might, constitute an abuse of a dominant position?) arose in *GE/Honeywell*[676] and *Tetra Laval/Sidel*[677] (both of which involved potential vertical *and* conglomerate effects).

In *Tetra Laval*, the GC[678] stressed the importance of the Commission basing its analysis of the likelihood of anti-competitive behaviour in the future on sufficiently convincing, plausible, and cogent evidence. It held that it could not be assumed that a dominant firm would automatically commit abuses of a dominant position and that its conduct would not be constrained by the existence of the competition rules. Rather, it was also required to assess whether, despite the prohibition, it was nonetheless likely that the entity would act in a way which would constitute an abuse or whether the illegal nature of the conduct and/or the risk of detection would make such a strategy unlikely.

On appeal, the Commission alleged that such a burden would be impossible to comply with in practice. The CJ[679] appeared to agree, finding that although the Commission must make some assessment of the Article 102 position, the extent of the obligation imposed by the GC was excessive. It would run counter to the purpose of the merger rules to require the Commission to examine in every merger case the extent to which the incentives to adopt anti-competitive conduct would be reduced or

[675] For a discussion of anti-competitive conduct in the context of standard-setting organisations, see also Chaps. 7 and 12.

[676] M.2220, 3 July 2001, *aff'd* Cases T-209 and 210/01, *Honeywell v Commission* EU:T:2005:455 and EU:T:2005:456. With regard to the vertical effects, however, the GC considered that the Commission had committed a manifest error of assessment and had failed to prove that the practices would in fact create or strengthen a dominant position. In particular, the Commission had been concerned that the merged entity would have an incentive not to supply engine starters to rival manufacturers of jet engines.

[677] M.2416, 30 October 2001, annulled on appeal Case T-5/02, EU:T:2002:264, *aff'd* Case C-12/03 P, EU:C:2005:87.

[678] Case T-5/02, ibid., especially para. 159.

[679] Case C-12/03 P, *Tetra Laval v Commission* EU:C:2005:87.

eliminated as a result of the unlawfulness of the conduct in question, the likelihood of its detection, the action taken by the competent authorities, both at EU and national level, and the financial penalties which could ensue. Such an investigation would require too speculative an assessment about how Article 102 would apply to hypothetical future events.[680]

Case C-12/03 P, *Commission v Tetra Laval BV* [2005] ECR I-987

Court of Justice

74. Since the view is taken in the contested decision that adoption of the conduct referred to recital 364 in that decision is an essential step in leveraging, the [GC] was right to hold that the likelihood of its adoption must be examined comprehensively, that is to say, taking account, as stated in paragraph 159 of the judgment under appeal, both of the incentives to adopt such conduct and the factors liable to reduce, or even eliminate, those incentives, including the possibility that the conduct is unlawful.

75. However, it would run counter to the Regulation's purpose of prevention to require the Commission, as was held in the last sentence in paragraph 159 of the judgment under appeal, to examine, for each proposed merger, the extent to which the incentives to adopt anti-competitive conduct would be reduced, or even eliminated, as a result of the unlawfulness of the conduct in question, the likelihood of its detection, the action taken by the competent authorities, both at Community and national level, and the financial penalties which could ensue.

76. An assessment such as that required by the [GC] would make it necessary to carry out an exhaustive and detailed examination of the rules of the various legal orders which might be applicable and of the enforcement policy practised in them. Moreover, if it is to be relevant, such an assessment calls for a high probability of the occurrence of the acts envisaged as capable of giving rise to objections on the ground that they are part of anti-competitive conduct.

77. It follows that, at the stage of assessing a proposed merger, an assessment intended to establish whether an infringement of Article [102 TFEU] is likely and to ascertain that it will be penalised in several legal orders would be too speculative and would not allow the Commission to base its assessment on all of the relevant facts with a view to establishing whether they support an economic scenario in which a development such as leveraging will occur.

78. Consequently, the [GC] erred in law in rejecting the Commission's conclusions as to the adoption by the merged entity of anti-competitive conduct capable of resulting in leveraging on the sole ground that the Commission had, when assessing the likelihood that such conduct might be adopted, failed to take account of the unlawfulness of that conduct and, consequently, of the likelihood of its detection, of action by the competent authorities, both at Community and national level, and of the financial penalties which might ensue. Nevertheless, since the judgment under appeal is also based on the failure to take account of the commitments offered by Tetra, it is necessary to continue the examination of the second ground of appeal.

79. With respect to the argument that the [GC] departed from the approach taken by it in the Gencor judgment, it must be held that, contrary to what the Commission claims, the [GC] did not depart from the position taken by it in paragraph 94 of that judgment, namely that there will be a significant impediment to effective competition if there is a lasting alteration of the structure of the relevant markets as a result of a concentration having the direct and immediate effect of creating conditions in which abusive conduct is possible and economically rational.

80. The situation in the Gencor case was entirely different from that addressed in the contested decision. As is clear from paragraph 91 of the judgment in that case, the concentration would have led to

[680] It also held that the Commission was required to take account of behavioural undertakings that would prevent that conduct, see discussion of remedies in Section 5.J.

the creation of a dominant duopoly in the platinum and rhodium markets, as a result of which effective competition would have been significantly impeded in the common market.

81. It was therefore the concentration which would have given rise to a lasting alteration of the structure of the relevant markets in that case and thus would have made abuses possible and economically rational.

82. In the present case, it is true that the notified merger was capable of slightly altering the structure of the market for carton inasmuch as the merged entity could strengthen the dominant position which Tetra had held for some time on that market and which, moreover, had been the subject of a Commission decision pursuant to Article [102 TFEU]. However, it was not effective competition on the carton market which the Commission intended to protect by prohibiting the merger but competition on the market for PET equipment, in particular that for low and high capacity SBM machines used for sensitive products.

83. The structure of that market would not have been immediately and directly affected by the notified merger but it could have been so affected only as a result of leveraging and, in particular, abusive conduct by the merged entity on the carton market.

84. It follows from the above considerations that the situation examined in the Gencor case is not sufficiently comparable to that on which the [GC] ruled by the judgment under appeal for that court to have been able to draw any useful inferences from it. The structure of the market on which the Commission intended, by the contested decision, to preserve effective competition was, in the Gencor case, directly altered by the merger whereas, in the present case, it could be altered only by leveraging.

85. With respect to consideration of the behavioural commitments offered by Tetra, the [GC] was right to hold, in paragraph 161 of the judgment under appeal, that the fact that Tetra had, in the present case, offered commitments relating to its future conduct was a factor which the Commission had to take into account when assessing the likelihood that the merged entity would act in such a way as to make it possible to create a dominant position on one or more of the relevant markets for PET equipment.

The inquiry demanded by the CJ thus appears to be a pragmatic one, proportionate to the fact that the Commission is investigating a merger under constrained time limits. Indeed, in *General Electric v Commission* the GC suggests that a summary, not detailed, analysis of this issue is required.[681] The GC does not, however, address the concern raised by the CJ in *Tetra Laval* that this issue should not have an adverse impact on the EUMR's preventative function.

Case T-210/01, *General Electric Co v Commission* [2005] ECR II-5575

General Court

73. It follows from the foregoing that the Commission must, in principle, take into account the potentially unlawful, and thus sanctionable, nature of certain conduct as a factor which might diminish, or even eliminate, incentives for an undertaking to engage in particular conduct. That appraisal does not, however, require an exhaustive and detailed examination of the rules of the various legal orders which might be applicable and of the enforcement policy practised within them, given that an assessment intended to establish whether an infringement is likely and to ascertain that it will be penalised in several legal orders would be too speculative.

[681] See also Case T-209/01, *Honeywell v Commission* EU:T:2005:455.

> 74. Thus, where the Commission, without undertaking a specific and detailed investigation into the matter, can identify the unlawful nature of the conduct in question, in the light of Article [102] or of other provisions of Community law which it is competent to enforce, it is its responsibility to make a finding to that effect and take account of it in its assessment of the likelihood that the merged entity will engage in such conduct (see, to that effect, *Commission* v *Tetra Laval*, paragraph 60 above, paragraph 74).
>
> 75. It follows that, although the Commission is entitled to take as its basis a summary analysis, based on the evidence available to it at the time when it adopts its merger-control decision, of the lawfulness of the conduct in question and of the likelihood that it will be punished, it must none the less, in the course of its appraisal, identify the conduct foreseen and, where appropriate, evaluate and take into account the possible deterrent effect represented by the fact that the conduct would be clearly, or highly probably, unlawful under Community law.

The Commission seeks to synthesise the obligations imposed on it in these cases in its NHMG when it states:

> 46. In addition, when the adoption of a specific course of conduct by the merged entity is an essential step in foreclosure, the Commission examines both the incentives to adopt such conduct and the factors liable to reduce, or even eliminate, those incentives, including the possibility that the conduct is unlawful. Conduct may be unlawful inter alia because of competition rules or sector-specific rules at the EU or national levels. This appraisal, however, does not require an exhaustive and detailed examination of the rules of the various legal orders which might be applicable and of the enforcement policy practised within them. Moreover, the illegality of a conduct may be likely to provide significant disincentives for the merged entity to engage in such conduct only in certain circumstances. In particular, the Commission will consider, on the basis of a summary analysis: (i) the likelihood that this conduct would be clearly, or highly probably, unlawful under EU law, (ii) the likelihood that this illegal conduct could be detected, and (iii) the penalties which could be imposed.

c. Other Non-coordinated Effects and Coordinated Effects in Vertical Mergers

The Commission has not ordinarily been concerned with vertical mergers which have no foreclosure effects. However, the NHMG state that vertical mergers may also cause concern where the merged entity gains access to commercially sensitive information regarding the upstream or downstream activities of rivals, or where vertical integration changes the nature of competition in such a way that firms that previously were not coordinating their behaviour are significantly more likely to coordinate and raise prices or otherwise harm competition. A vertical merger may also make coordination easier, more stable, or more effective for firms which were coordinating prior to a merger. For example, a vertical merger may, by reducing the number of effective competitors in a market, make it easier for the firms concerned to reach a common understanding on the terms of coordination. It may also increase the level of market transparency between firms (for example, through access to sensitive information on rivals or by making it easier to monitor pricing) and reduce the scope for outsiders to destabilise the coordination by increasing barriers to enter the market.

In *J&J/Pfizer*,[682] the Commission had concerns about non-coordinated effects that would result from the acquisition of Pfizer's Consumer Healthcare (PCH) division by Johnson & Johnson (J&J).

[682] M.4314, 11 December 2006.

Through the proposed transaction, J&J would acquire PCH's Nicorette business. As a result, J&J would own a leading Nicotine Replacement Therapy (NRT) patch brand (PCH's Nicorette) and would be the sole supplier of nicotine patches to its principal downstream competitor, GSK. The Commission considered that there was a risk that this vertical relationship would give the merged entity the ability and incentive to foreclose GSK from the market for nicotine patches/NRT products by making it harder for it to obtain supplies under similar prices and conditions as would be available absent the merger. This would advantage the merged entity's Nicorette business and lead to harm to consumers (a risk of input foreclosure). Further, there was a risk that the merged entity would gain access to confidential information about GSK which it could use post-merger to the benefit of the acquired Nicorette business. In order to resolve the vertical concerns, J&J offered to divest part of its international nicotine patch manufacturing business. It also agreed to transfer relevant supply agreements, trademarks, and technology and to provide manufacturing capacities and technical assistance to the purchaser until the latter became fully operational. The proposed remedies would therefore structurally eliminate the vertical relationship.

(iv) Assessment of Conglomerate Mergers

Despite the adoption of some controversial decisions on conglomerate effects, the Commission confirms in its NHMG that the majority of conglomerate mergers will not lead to any competition problems. In certain cases, however, where the companies are active in closely related markets (for example, complementary products or products belonging to a range of products purchased by the same set of customers for the same use)[683] harm may arise. As in its assessment of vertical effects, the Commission considers both the possible anti-competitive effects arising from conglomerate mergers and the possible pro-competitive effects stemming from substantiated efficiencies.

a. *GE/Honeywell and Tetra Laval/Sidel*

The approach taken in the Guidelines is, no doubt, an attempt to meet the challenges set by the EU Courts in appeals from the Commission's decisions in *GE/Honeywell*[684] and *Tetra Laval/Sidel*[685] respectively. In both cases, the Commission prohibited mergers, principally on account of their conglomerate effects, and on the basis that the mergers would create incentives for the merged firms to leverage market power between related markets. In both cases the Courts were extremely critical of the Commission's analysis. The Commission's right to intervene in mergers resulting in conglomerate effects was, however, upheld.

In *GE/Honeywell*,[686] the Commission prohibited the proposed acquisition of Honeywell Inc by General Electric Co even though it had been cleared by the US antitrust authorities.[687] Essentially, the Commission was concerned that the $42 billion merger would, by enabling the merged entity to leverage its market power by engaging in bundling or strategic price cuts, strengthen GE's already dominant position in the markets for jet engines for large commercial aircraft and regional aircraft

[683] NHMG, paras. 90–91.

[684] M.2220, 3 July 2001, *aff'd* Cases T-209 and 210/01, EU:T:2005:455 and EU:T:2005:456.

[685] M.2416, 30 October 2001, annulled on appeal Case T-5/02, EU:T:2002:264, *aff'd* Case C-12/03 P, EU:C:2005:87. See also M.794, *Coca-Cola Enterprises/Amalgamated Beverages* [1997] OJ L218/15; M.833, *The Coca-Cola Co/Carlsberg A/S* [1998] OJ L145/41; M.938, *Guinness/Grand Metropolitan* [1998] OJ L288/24.

[686] M.2220, 3 July 2001, *aff'd* Cases T-209 and 210/01, EU:T:2005:455 and EU:T:2005:456. See e.g. G. Drauz, 'Unbundling *GE/Honeywell*' [2003] *ECLR* 115.

[687] See e.g. F. D. Platt Majoras, '*GE-Honeywell*: The US Decision', Remarks before the Antitrust Law Section, State Bar of Georgia, 29 November 2001. For the extraterritorial aspects of this decision, see Chap. 17.

and create a dominant position in avionics, non-avionics, and corporate jet engines (Honeywell was the leading supplier of these products).[688] The anticipated outcome of the bundling or strategic price costs was that, although prices would reduce in the short term, the pricing policy would drive competitors from the market so that, eventually, prices could be expected to rise and product quality and service would reduce.[689] The speculative nature of this prediction triggered a 'firestorm of criticism', particularly in the US, 'not just from the US antitrust authorities, senior [US] administration officials, but also from the business community generally and from leading economists, antitrust legal scholars, and editorial writers'.[690]

The criticism centred on the notion that the EU authorities had prohibited a merger which was to lead to a reduction in prices and increase in output. The anti-competitive effect would only result if the other competitors could not match the merged firm's offerings. This view was supported at the time in the US, where the authorities went out of their way to stress that they would not prohibit a merger which would make a firm more efficient, because of fears that it might force competitors from a market: antitrust laws 'protect competition, not competitors'. In their view, a competition authority should be very cautious about adopting a merger policy that sacrificed short-term efficiencies in the name of maintaining competition.[691]

In the appeal from the Commission's decision, the GC[692] upheld the Commission's decision but *only* on the basis that its analysis of horizontal effects (the creation of a monopoly in the market for engines for large regional jets) provided a sufficient basis to prohibit the merger. With regard to the leveraging theory, the Court considered that the Commission had made a manifest error of assessment and had failed to provide evidence to substantiate its claim that bundling between engines and avionics/non-avionics was possible or feasible. The Commission had not established that the merged entity had an economic incentive to bundle and consequently it had the burden of putting forward other evidence to suggest that the merged entity would make the strategic decision to sacrifice profits in the short term with a view of reaping larger profits in the future. This could be done, for example, through economic studies or the production of internal documents showing that GE's directors had that objective on the launch of their bid for Honeywell.[693]

Case T-210/01, *General Electric Co v Commission* [2005] ECR II-5575

General Court

399. The Commission stated in essence in the contested decision that, following the merger, the merged entity would have the ability, unlike its competitors, to offer its customers packages for large commercial aircraft, large regional aircraft and corporate aircraft, encompassing both engines and avionics and non-avionics products. It also held that such behaviour would clearly be in the commercial interests of the merged entity and would thus probably be engaged in after the merger had taken

[688] It was also concerned that the aircraft financing arm of GE, GECAS, would specify Honeywell equipment in its aircraft purchases.

[689] See D. Giotakos, L. Petit, G. Garnier, and P. De Luyck, '*General Electric/Honeywell*—An Insight into the Commission's Investigation and Decision' (2001) 3 *Competition Policy Newsletter* 5.

[690] See W. J. Kolasky, 'Conglomerate Mergers and Range Effects: It's a Long Way from Chicago to Brussels', Address before George Mason University Symposium Washington DC, 9 November 2001.

[691] See Kolasky, ibid. See also the disagreement over the *Oracle/Sun Microsystems* case in which the DOJ published a press release backing the merger on the same date that the Commission launched Phase II proceedings.

[692] Cases T-209 and 210/01, *Honeywell v Commission* and *General Electric v Commission* EU:T:2005:455 and EU:T:2005:456, see D. Howarth, 'The Court of First Instance in *GE/Honeywell*' [2006] *ECLR* 485.

[693] Case T-210/01, EU:T:2005:456, para. 466.

place (recitals 350 to 404, 412 to 416, 432 to 434, 443 and 444 and 445 to 458). As a consequence, a dominant position would have been created for Honeywell on the markets for avionics and non-avionics products and GE's dominant positions would have been strengthened, particularly on the market for large commercial jet aircraft engines (recital 458 of the contested decision).

400. The Commission's case is based on the fact that jet engines, on the one hand, and avionics and non-avionics products, on the other, are complementary, since all these products are indispensable in the construction of an aircraft. The final customer, the operator of the aircraft, must therefore purchase all of them, directly or indirectly, from their manufacturer. The Commission held in the contested decision that on the whole the customers are essentially the same for all those products and that the latter could therefore be bundled. The Commission also observes that the applicant's group is financially very strong, both compared with its main competitors on the engines markets and with its competitors on the markets for avionics and non-avionics products (see, as regards the latter, recitals 302 to 304, 323 and 324 of the contested decision; see also recital 398 et seq.). The merged entity would thus be in a position to reduce its profit margins on avionics and non-avionics products with a view to increasing its market share and making larger profits in the future.

401. It should be noted, as a preliminary point, that the way it is predicted that the merged entity will behave in the future is a vital aspect of the Commission's analysis of bundling in the present case. It follows from the fact that the applicant had no presence on the markets for avionics and non-avionics products prior to the merger, together with the fact that Honeywell had no presence on the market for large commercial jet aircraft engines before the merger, that the merger would have had no horizontal anti-competitive effect on those markets. Thus, the merger would, prima facie, have had no effect whatsoever on those markets.

402. Moreover, in so far as the Commission predicts, at recitals 443 and 444 of the contested decision, that bundling will have an impact on the market for engines for corporate jet aircraft, it should be noted that the applicant's pre-merger share of that market was only [10–20]%, in terms of the installed base, whilst Honeywell's was [40–50]%, and only [0–10]%, in terms of the installed base on those aircraft still in production, as compared with Honeywell's [40–50]% share (recital 88 of the contested decision). In those circumstances, even if it were shown that the merged entity would bundle those engines with avionics and non-avionics products after the merger, there would be no causal link between the merger and the bundled offers, except in the small minority of cases in which the engine was a product of the former GE. Moreover, it is not suggested in the contested decision that either of the parties to the merger manufactures engines for small regional aircraft. It follows that any bundling which might be engaged in by the merged entity on the market for regional aircraft would in any event concern only large regional aircraft.

403. The Commission held in the contested decision that each avionics product for regional and corporate aircraft constitutes a market in itself and that there is a market for each non-avionics product for all types of aircraft, including large commercial aircraft. Accordingly, its reasoning with regard to the creation, by means of bundling, of dominant positions on the markets for the different avionics products cannot be accepted in relation to the markets for each of the various avionics products for corporate and regional aircraft. Indeed, on the assumption that it actually becomes a reality after the transaction, any bundling attributable to the merger will affect only one segment of those markets, the large regional aircraft segment. In the same way, the Commission's reasoning is undermined (albeit to a lesser degree) in relation to non-avionics products, for which the Commission defined an individual market for each specific product, irrespective of the size and other features of the aircraft equipped.

404. It is therefore, in principle, in the sector for large commercial aircraft, for which the Commission has defined distinct markets both for jet engines and for each avionics product, that the Commission's case on bundling could conceivably be sustained.

405. In relation to the possible impact of the merger on (i) the markets for jet engines for large commercial aircraft and large regional aircraft, (ii) those for avionics products for large commercial aircraft

and (iii) those for non-avionics products, the Court must determine whether the Commission has established that the merged entity would not only have the capability to engage in the bundling practices described in the contested decision but also, on the basis of convincing evidence, that it would have been likely to engage in those practices after the merger and that, in consequence, a dominant position would have been created or strengthened on one or more of the relevant markets in the relatively near future (*Tetra Laval* v *Commission*, paragraph 58 above, paragraphs 146 to 162).

Notwithstanding the general controversy the Commission's decision in *GE/Honeywell* provoked, in *Tetra Laval/Sidel*[694] the Commission prohibited another merger which it considered would enable the merged entity to leverage its market power in one market into another. This case concerned a public bid by Tetra Laval SA for shares in Sidel SA. Tetra, part of the Tetra Pak company, is the world market leader in the area of liquid food carton packaging. In contrast, Sidel is involved in the production of packaging equipment and systems and is a worldwide leader for the production and supply of stretch blow moulding (SBM) machines, used in the production of polyethlylene terephthalate (PET) plastic bottles. The Commission considered that the merger would strengthen Tetra's dominant position in the market for aseptic carton packaging machines and cartons and create a dominant position in the market for PET packaging equipment. The Commission made findings of horizontal and vertical effects and held that the merger would enable the merged entity to exploit its dominant position on the carton markets by leveraging into the market for PET packaging equipment in order to dominate it. The Commission set out its reasons for concluding that the market structure was particularly conducive to leverage effects at paragraph 359 of its decision.

- There would be a common pool of customers requiring both carton and PET packaging systems to package sensitive liquids.
- Tetra has a particularly strong dominant position in aseptic carton packaging with more than 80–90 per cent of the market and a dependent customer base.
- Tetra/Sidel would start from a strong, leading, position in PET packaging systems and in particular SBM machines with a market share in the region of 60–70 per cent.
- Tetra/Sidel would have the ability to target selectively specific customers or specific customer groups as the structure of the market enables price discrimination.
- Tetra/Sidel would have a strong economic incentive to engage in leveraging practices. As carton and PET are technical substitutes, when a customer switches to PET he/she is a lost customer on the carton side of the business either because he/she partially switched *from* carton or because he/she did not switch some of the production *to* carton from other packaging materials. This creates an added incentive to capture the customer on the PET side of the business to recover the loss. Therefore, by leveraging its current market position in carton, Tetra/Sidel would not only enhance its market share on the PET side but defend or compensate its possible loss on the carton side.
- Competitors of Tetra/Sidel in both the carton and the PET equipment markets would be much smaller, with the largest competitor having no more than 10–20 per cent share in the market for carton packaging machines or SBM machines.

[694] M.2416, 30 October 2001. See also M.2283, *Schneider/Legrand* 10 October 2001, annulled as the Commission had not identified its conglomeracy concerns in the SO, see n. 794, Case T-310/01, *Schneider Electric SA v Commission* EU:T:2002:254.

The Commission considered that the leveraging would foreclose competitors from the rest of the SBM machine market and turn Sidel's leading position on the market into a dominant one. On appeal, the GC annulled the Commission's decision, finding the pleas alleging lack of horizontal, vertical, and conglomerate anti-competitive effects were well founded.[695] The GC's judgment was upheld by the CJ on appeal.[696] The GC devoted more than half of its judgment to the plea that the Commission had failed to establish foreseeable conglomerate effects,[697] concluding that the decision did not establish that the merger would give rise to significant anti-competitive conglomerate effects to the requisite legal standard.[698]

The GC accepted that the EUMR can apply to merger transactions having horizontal, vertical, or conglomerate effects so long as the conditions set out in Article 2(3) are met[699] and drew a distinction between mergers where the conglomerate effects would be structural (arising directly from the economic structure created)[700] and those where they might be behavioural, in the sense that they arise only if the new entity created engages in certain commercial practices.[701] *Tetra Laval* was of the latter type. It was therefore necessary to determine whether the merger would have anti-competitive effects by, in all likelihood, allowing the new entity to obtain, in the relatively near future, a dominant position on a market in which one of the parties held a leading position, as a result of leveraging from a market in which the other party was already dominant.[702] In a case involving prospective analysis of conglomerate effects, the Commission must establish that competition will be significantly impeded in the near future:[703] the parties must have both the ability and the incentive to leverage, and the consequences of leveraging must be particularly plausible and must in all likelihood occur in the very near future.

The judgment stressed the importance of the Commission basing its analysis of the likelihood of leveraging, and of the consequences of such leveraging, on sufficiently convincing, plausible, and cogent evidence.

Case T-5/02, *Tetra Laval BV v Commission* [2002] ECR II-4381

General Court

146. It should be observed, first, that the Regulation, particularly at Article 2(2) and (3), does not draw any distinction between, on the one hand, merger transactions having horizontal and vertical effects and, on the other hand, those having a conglomerate effect. It follows that, without distinction between those types of transactions, a merger can be prohibited only if the two conditions laid down in Article 2(3) are met (see paragraph 120 above). Consequently, a merger having a conglomerate effect must, like any other merger (see paragraph 120 above), be authorised by the Commission if it is not established that it creates or strengthens a dominant position in the common market or in a substantial part of it and that, as a result, effective competition will be significantly impeded.

. . .

[695] Case T-5/02, EU:T:2002:264, *aff'd* Case C-12/03 P, EU:C:2005:87. When the Commission re-examined the merger, it cleared it subject to a commitment that Tetra Laval license the new technology for making PET bottles to third parties.

[696] Case C-12/03 P, EU:C:2005:87.

[697] Case T-5/02, EU:T:2002:264, paras. 142–336.

[698] Ibid., para. 226. In the end the Commission cleared the merger, M.2416, 13 January 2003.

[699] Ibid., paras. 146–152.

[700] I.e. where the new entity would immediately and automatically create a second dominant position which the new entity could abuse.

[701] Case T-5/02, EU:T:2002:264, para. 147.

[702] Ibid., para. 148.

[703] Ibid., para. 153.

> 155. The Commission's analysis of a merger producing a conglomerate effect is conditioned by requirements similar to those defined by the Court with regard to the creation of a situation of collective dominance (*Kali & Salz*, paragraph 222; and *Airtours v Commission*, paragraph 63). Thus the Commission's analysis of a merger transaction which is expected to have an anti-competitive conglomerate effect calls for a particularly close examination of the circumstances which are relevant for an assessment of that effect on the conditions of competition in the reference market. As the Court has already held, where the Commission takes the view that a merger should be prohibited because it will create or strengthen a dominant position within a foreseeable period, it is incumbent upon it to produce convincing evidence thereof (*Airtours v Commission*, paragraph 63). Since the effects of a conglomerate-type merger are generally considered to be neutral, or even beneficial, for competition on the markets concerned, as is recognised in the present case by the economic writings cited in the analyses annexed to the parties' written pleadings, the proof of anti-competitive conglomerate effects of such a merger calls for a precise examination, supported by convincing evidence, of the circumstances which allegedly produce those effects (see, by analogy, *Airtours v Commission*, paragraph 63).

The CJ rejected the Commission's appeal in its entirety. Although it did find that the GC had in some respects erred in the law, it held that these errors did not call into question the judgment insofar as it annulled the Commission's decision.[704] In its judgment, the CJ stressed that the prospective analysis required in merger control had to be carried out with great care: it required an analysis not of past events but of a prediction of the future, making it necessary to envisage various chains of cause and effect with a view to ascertaining which of them was most likely. The quality of evidence relied upon by the Commission in such circumstances is particularly important.[705]

Despite the difficulties inherent in this analysis, the Commission has continued to raise conglomerate effects theories of harm in a number of cases and, arguably, these may be becoming of increasing relevance in the digital economy. It has, nonetheless, often been willing to accept commitments to counter the harms identified.[706] In *Microsoft/LinkedIn*,[707] the Commission was concerned that the merged entity would have the ability and incentive to tie Microsoft Windows and Office customers to LinkedIn PSN (professional social network).[708] It cleared the transaction subject to commitments: relating to (but not prohibiting) pre-installing LinkedIn on Windows PCs and its integration into Office; ensuring LinkedIn can be removed if pre-installed; and ensuring the existing levels of interoperability with Office for rival PSNs is maintained. Similarly, in *Qualcomm/NXP*[709] the Commission accepted commitments to allay its concerns about a merger between Qualcomm, a producer of cellular baseband chips for mobile telephones (allowing smart phones to connect to cellular networks), and NXP, a supplier of semi-conductors for smart phones (used for secure payment transactions on smart phones), and a developer of leading technology (MIFARE), used as a ticketing and fare collection platform by many EEA transport authorities. In addition to concerns that the combination of the

[704] Case C-12/03 P, EU:C:2005:87. See Tizzano AG, para. 123 ('the [GC] correctly found that, just as the Commission had assessed the economic incentives for engaging in such conduct, so it ought to have taken into consideration the possible disincentives in that respect of the unlawful nature of the conduct in question . . . or of the commitments into which that company had offered to enter').

[705] See Section 7.

[706] See e.g. C. Cook, V. Novak, and S. Frisch, 'Recent Developments in EU Merger Remedies' (2018) 9 *JECLAP* 403.

[707] M.8124, 20 January 2017. See also e.g. M.7822, *Dentsply/Sirona* 25 February 2016.

[708] See the discussion of AT.39530 *Microsoft (Tying)* 16 December 2009 in Chap. 7.

[709] M.8306, 27 March 2018. See also M.8394, *Essilor/Luxottica* 1 March 2018 (cleared unconditionally following a Phase II investigation) and M.9660, 17 December 2020, n. 665 and text.

companies' considerable IP portfolios would allow them to charge significantly higher royalties for their patents, the Commission considered that the new entity would have the ability and the incentive to foreclosure rivals' access to MIFARE technology and degrade interoperability between their and their rivals' products. Amongst other things, the commitments were designed to ensure that, for eight years, licences of MIFARE technology and trademarks would be offered on terms at least as advantageous as prior to the merger and that the same level of interoperability would be provided.

b. Non-coordinated Effects—Foreclosure

In its Guidelines, the Commission states that its analysis of non-coordinated effects focuses on the possibility of foreclosure:[710] the possibility that the merger will confer on the merged entity the ability and incentive to leverage a strong market position from one market to another by means of tying or bundling or other exclusionary practices.[711] The Commission will examine intertwined factors to determine whether the merged firm would have the ability to foreclose its rivals (which is unlikely unless, for example, one of the products is viewed by many customers as particularly important and there is a common pool of customers for the individual products concerned), whether it would have the economic incentive to do so (which is dependent on the profitability of the strategy and the extent to which the incentive is reduced or eliminated by, for example, the possibility that the conduct is unlawful), and whether a foreclosure strategy would have a significant detrimental effect on competition thereby causing harm to consumers.

The NHMG express concern that bundling or tying may reduce sales by single-component rivals by affecting their ability or incentive to compete and allowing the merged entity subsequently to acquire market power (in the market for the tied or bundled good) and/or maintain market power (in the market for the tying or leveraging good). The effect on competition is assessed in the light of substantiated efficiencies, for example lowering margins on the sale of complementary goods,[712] and costs savings in the form of economies of scope.[713] In *Google/DoubleClick*,[714] the Commission investigated but ruled out various foreclosure scenarios that might have resulted from the acquisition by Google (a leading player in search advertising and a major provider of online advertising space and intermediation services for online advertisements) of DoubleClick, the leading supplier of ad serving technology.

c. Portfolio Power and Foreclosure

Prior to the adoption of the NHMG, in *Guinness/Grand Metropolitan*[715] the Commission had to examine a concentration which had an impact on certain separate spirits markets. Although there was some horizontal overlap in the relevant markets in which the parties operated, the merger also led to an extension of the complementary products and range of spirits offered. The Commission displayed concern about 'portfolio power'.

[710] NHMG, paras. 93–118.

[711] The Commission accepts that tying and bundling as such are common practices that often have no anti-competitive consequences, ibid., para. 92.

[712] The Cournot effect, i.e. the merged firm has an incentive to lower margin on one product to boost sales of a complementary product.

[713] The Guidelines state, however, that '[s]uch economies of scope . . . are necessary but not sufficient to provide an efficiency justification for bundling or tying. Indeed, benefits from economies of scope frequently can be realized without any need for technical or contractual bundling', NHMG, para. 118.

[714] M.4371. See e.g. J. Brockhoff, B. Jehanno, V. Pozzato, C. Buhr, P. Eberl, and P. Papandropoulos, '*Google/DoubleClick*: The First Test for the Commission's Non-Horizontal Merger Guidelines' (2008) 2 *Competition Policy Newsletter* 53.

[715] M.938 [1998] OJ L288/24.

M.938, *Guinness/Grand Metropolitan* [1998] OJ L228/24

Commission

40. The holder of a portfolio of leading spirit brands may enjoy a number of advantages. In particular, his position in relation to his customers is stronger since he is able to provide a range of products and will account for a greater proportion of their business, he will have greater flexibility to structure his prices, promotions and discounts, he will have greater potential for tying, and he will be able to realize economies of scale and scope in his sales and marketing activities, Finally, the implicit (or explicit) threat of a refusal to supply is more potent.

41. The strength of these advantages, and their potential effect on the competitive structure of the market, depends on a number of factors, including whether the holder of the portfolio has the brand leader or one or more leading brands in a particular market; the market shares of the various brands, particularly in relation to the shares of competitors; the relative importance of the individual markets in which the parties have significant shares and brands across the range of product markets in which the portfolio is held; and/or the number of markets in which the portfolio holder has a brand leader or leading brand.

The Commission concluded that the merger in that case would have portfolio effects. The effect was particularly acute on the Greek market where the merged entity would have a dominant position in the gin, brandy, and rum markets and where it would be able to supply the leading brands, with the exception of vodka. Through portfolio effects the dominant position in these markets would be reinforced.[716] This decision received criticism not for its adoption of the concept of portfolio power but for failing to identify with sufficient clarity what is wrong with an undertaking's acquisition of a wider portfolio of products. For example, some paragraphs, including paragraph 40, of the Commission's decision indicate that the Commission objected to the economies of scale and scope offered to the parties from the increased range of products that the merger allowed.[717] Such benefits would, however, not harm but benefit consumers and intervention on these grounds would give the Commission a broad discretion. An objection to portfolio power on the ground that it would give the merged entity greater power to tie products is less controversial.[718]

The Guidelines clarify that the fact that the merged entity will have a broad range or portfolio of products does not, as such, raise competition concerns but that this factor may be relevant when determining whether the merged entity will have the ability to foreclose the market. In such circumstances, customers may have a strong incentive to save transaction costs by buying the range of products from a single source rather than from many.

In *Nestlé/Gerber*,[719] the Commission unconditionally cleared Nestlé's acquisition of Novartis's Gerber baby food business. Although the activities of the parties overlapped in several segments of manufactured baby food (baby meals, drinks, and cereals) in some Member States, the Commission found these did not give rise to competitive concerns. In the course of its investigation, the Commission also considered possible portfolio effects in the context of the relative strength of competitors' brands and their portfolios (in some markets, Nestlé would become a full-range supplier of baby foods with strong brands in other food markets), in particular whether Nestlé would be able to use its portfolio

[716] Ibid., paras. 90–118. The Commission permitted the merger only once the parties agreed to end the distribution arrangements for Bacardi rum in Greece even though the merger did not increase the parties' market shares on this market.

[717] Ibid., para. 40.

[718] See e.g. Bishop and Walker, n. 431, 8.030–8.032.

[719] M.4688, 27 July 2007.

power to prevent new entry or to impede the expansion of existing 'single-brand' competitors (by, for example, limiting the access of competitors to distribution channels and reducing their shelf space).

In assessing conglomerate effects, the Commission drew a distinction between a 'pure portfolio effect' (an incentive on customers to buy the range of products from a single source rather than from many suppliers because it entails efficiencies) and a strategic use of portfolio and financial leverage, such as product bundling, targeted discounts, and discriminatory across-the-board promotions.[720] The Commission considered that the former, although conferring a competitive advantage on suppliers, is not necessarily regarded as anti-competitive. It clarified that conglomerate effects result in a significant impediment to effective competition when the merged entity decides to condition its sales in a particular and strategic way in order to disadvantage its competitors or potential entrants. On the facts, the Commission found no evidence that Nestlé would have the opportunity or incentive, post-merger, to adopt an anti-competitive bundling strategy. The Commission was also concerned about possible bundling and technical tying of security products and services (made by McAfee) with Intel's central processing units and chipsets in *Intel/McAfee*.[721] In the end, however, the merger was cleared in Phase I proceedings after commitments were offered to allay the Commission's concerns. The Commission also rejected concerns about tying in *Microsoft/Skype*.[722]

d. Coordinated Effects

The NHMG state that conglomerate mergers may, in certain circumstances, facilitate anti-competitive coordination in markets, for example by reducing the number of effective competitors, where foreclosed rivals choose not to contest the situation of coordination and/or by increasing the scope and effectiveness of a disciplining mechanism by increasing the extent and importance of multi-market competition.

> 119. Conglomerate mergers may in certain circumstances facilitate anticompetitive co-ordination in markets, even in the absence of an agreement or a concerted practice within the meaning of Article [101 TFEU]. The framework set out in Section IV of the Notice on Horizontal Mergers also applies in this context. In particular, co-ordination is more likely to emerge in markets where it is fairly easy to identify the terms of co-ordination and where such co-ordination is sustainable.
>
> 120. One way in which a conglomerate merger may influence the likelihood of a coordinated outcome in a given market is by reducing the number of effective competitors to such an extent that tacit coordination becomes a real possibility. Also when rivals are not excluded from the market, they may find themselves in a more vulnerable situation. As a result, foreclosed rivals may choose not to contest the situation of co-ordination, but may prefer instead to live under the shelter of the increased price level.
>
> 121. Further, a conglomerate merger may increase the extent and importance of multi-market competition. Competitive interaction on several markets may increase the scope and effectiveness of disciplining mechanisms in ensuring that the terms of co-ordination are being adhered to.

G. INDUSTRIAL, SOCIAL, AND OTHER POLICY

(i) General

An important question is whether non-competition factors can, should be, or are/have been taken into account when appraising mergers under Article 2. Could, for example, the fact that a merger is advantageous from a sustainability, industrial, or social policy perspective be relied on as a basis

[720] Ibid., para. 35. [721] M.5984, 26 January 2011.

[722] M.6281, 7 October 2001, Case T-79/12, *Cisco Systems Inc v Commission* EU:T:2013:635.

for clearing an otherwise problematic merger? Alternatively, could non-competition factors (such as the impact on national security, employment, or equality) be relied upon to prohibit a merger that is otherwise unproblematic from a competition perspective?

(ii) Other Policies as a Countervailing Factor

Industrial policy could support industrial restructuring where it is necessary for the undertakings to compete in a global market, to encourage cross-border concentration, to encourage technical progress, or to protect certain industries or employment, even where a concentration might lead to a SIEC. In the run-up to the adoption of the original EUMR, some Member States feared that EU industrial policy, aimed at safeguarding and ensuring 'the competitiveness of European industry', might be permitted to support the creation of a Euro champion in circumstances where that Euro champion would be dominant.

At first sight, Article 2 of the EUMR does not appear to permit non-competition factors, other than sustainability factors impacting on the choice and quality of products and services, to be taken into account as part of the appraisal process;[723] it permits technical and economic progress to be taken into account but only 'provided that it is to the consumers' advantage and does not form an obstacle to competition'. Recital 23 of the EUMR does, however, state that the Commission must place its appraisal within the general framework of the fundamental objectives of the Treaties and some Member States support a broader approach.[724] Further, the final decision to clear or prohibit a concentration following a Phase II merger investigation is made by the College of Commissioners[725] and not simply by the Commissioner responsible for competition.[726] This means that in controversial or politically charged cases, lobbying of the Commissioners frequently takes place. Indeed, DG Comp has often come under pressure both from businesses and politicians to relax the application of the competition rules and to subordinate pro-market policies to industrial and other policies supportive of struggling businesses.

Nonetheless, it does not appear that an industrial or other EU policy, or lobbying, has, in recent years at least,[727] affected the final outcome of Commission merger decisions. Competition Commissioners have been clear that crises or recessions are not excuses 'to relax the rules'. Since 2008, it has, therefore,

[723] Subject to a teleological interpretation being given to the provision, see Chaps. 2 and 4. At the time of the adoption of the original EUMR the then Competition Commissioner Leon Brittan was adamant that the Regulation should give primacy to the competition criterion. For an empirical analysis concluding that a dataset of mergers notified between 1990–2014 reveals no evidence that the Commission has systematically used its authority for protectionist ends (to intervene more frequently or extensively in relation to acquisitions of EU firms by non-EU firms), see A. Badford, R. J. Jackson, and J. Zytnick, 'Is EU Merger Control Used for Protectionism? An Empirical Analysis' (2018) 15 *J of Empirical Legal Studies* 165.

[724] See n. 30 and text. Recital 13 to the original EUMR also stated that the appraisal should be made within the general framework of the fundamental objectives referred to in Art. 2 of the EC Treaty, including the strengthening of the EU's economic and social cohesion, see also Case T-12/93, *Comité Central d'Enterprise de la Société Anonyme Vittel v Commission* EU:T:1995:78, paras. 38–40.

[725] See e.g. W. Sauter, *Competition Law and Industrial Policy in the EU* (Clarendon Press, 1997), 140.

[726] See Chap. 2.

[727] In M.315, *Mannesmann/Vallourec/Ilva* [1994] OJ L102/1, e.g., it appears that the College of Commissioners authorised a merger which DG Comp wished to prohibit on the ground that it would lead to the creation of a collective dominant position on the West European market for seamless steel tubes. The case was strongly supported by the Commissioner responsible for industry. It is believed that the College of Commissioners was deadlocked so that, since the Commission had not voted to prohibit the merger, the decision was rewritten to avoid clearance by default (which would have occurred had the Commissioners failed to deliver a formal decision in time). The fear that this type of thing could happen has led in the past to a call for an independent European Cartel Office to be created, which would be seen to operate independently and free from political constraints, see also Chap. 13.

so far been 'business as usual in cartels, mergers and antitrust'.[728] Thus, although some high-profile cases, such as the merger between NYSE Euronext and Deutsche Börse,[729] and Siemens' proposed acquisition of Alstom,[730] which might have created a European or national[731] champion, have caused public clashes between advocates of industrial policy and supporters of a competition policy based strictly on competition factors alone, in most cases the Commission has resolutely opposed mergers which are not to the consumers' advantage or which form an obstacle to competition. It adheres to the view that EU rules allow firms to search for the best scale and size to compete globally, but ensures that they face sufficient competition to secure performance in international markets.[732] Its decisions to block the mergers in *MSG/Media Services GmbH*,[733] *Volvo/Scania*,[734] and *Siemens/Alstom*[735] were controversial. In practice, therefore, the College of Commissioners ordinarily accepts the decisions prepared by DG Comp overseen by the Commissioner for Competition. Although then President of the Commission, Jean-Claude Juncker, defended the Commission's approach under the merger rules in *Siemens/Alstom*, stressing that although the EU wanted strong companies that can compete globally, competition had to be maintained, the case led France and Germany to call for reform of merger law.[736]

(iii) Other Policies Where the Concentration Does Not Significantly Impede Effective Competition

A concentration which does not significantly impede effective competition must be declared compatible with the internal market. Even though it is possible that things could change, Competition Commissioners have, to date, worked hard to send the message that industrial and other

[728] N. Kroes, SPEECH/09/152, 'Competition, the crisis and the road to recovery', 30 March 2009, <http://ec.europa.eu/competition/speeches/index_2009.html> and see n. 31 and text.

[729] M.6166, 1 February 2012 (prohibited), *aff'd* Case T-175/12, *Deutsche Börse v Commission* EU:T:2015:148.

[730] M.8677, *Siemens/Alstom* 6 February 2019. Prior to the prohibition there was huge debate about the impact of a prohibition on the development of EU industry and its ability to compete globally. E.g. French and German ministers supported the transaction economically and politically, but the Commission also received complaints and negative comments from customers, competitors, industry associations, trade unions, and several NCAs, see Open Letter of 20 December 2018 to the Commission from UK, Belgian, Spanish, and Dutch competition authorities expressing the view that the remedies offered by the parties did not solve the significant competition concerns raised by the merger, <https://assets.publishing.service.gov.uk/government/uploads/system/uploads/attachment_data/file/767087/Siemens_Alstom_-_open_letter_to_COM.pdf>. In addition, prior to its decision in M.7018, *Telefónica Deutschland/E-Plus* 2 July 2014, Angela Merkel and Jean-Claude Juncker (now President of the Commission) expressed their view that the Commission should make it easier for telecom operators to merge so that they can compete more effectively in international markets.

[731] See, e.g., IP/04/501, 'The Commission puts industry centre stage and reinforces competitiveness in an enlarged European Union', M.469, *MSG Media Service GmbH* 9 November 1994, M.1672, *Volvo/Scania* [2001] OJ L143/74, M.53, *Aérospatiale-Alenia/de Havilland* [1991] OJ L334/42 (it seems that although the French and Italian Governments, the (then) Commissioner for Industry, Martin Bangemann, and the then President of the Commission, Jacques Delors, supported the concentration, others, including the then Competition Commissioner, Sir Leon Brittan, opposed it, believing that it would lead to the creation of a dominant position. The Commission's decision to prohibit the merger was controversial).

[732] See Section 2.B. [733] M.469, 9 November 1994. [734] M.1672 [2001] OJ L143/74.

[735] M.8677, 7 February 2019.

[736] See 'EU Industry Days 2019', 5 February 2019 (even though the Commission structure under Commission President Juncker, emphasised cooperation and coordination between the Commissioners). Note, however, that in 2012 then Commission President Barroso asked Commissioner Almunia to give early advance notice of cases with a dimension going beyond the scope of competition policy which might impact on other EU policies, see minutes of the 2022nd meeting of the Commission, PV(2012)2022 final.

'non-competition' criteria do not prevail in their EU merger decisions.[737] Further, it has been seen that although Member States may preclude an EU concentration where necessary to protect their 'legitimate interests' or 'essential interests of security', the Commission polices the exercise of such powers carefully and tackles 'nationalistic' or 'protectionist' measures by Member States that breach EU law by bringing proceedings against them.[738] Nonetheless, it is clear that concern about FDI is mounting in the Member States, especially about acquisitions by non-EU SOEs, or other non-EU companies, of corporations in strategic or sensitive sectors.[739] As a result, the number and range of public interest and foreign investment rules in the Member States[740] has been expanding and some Member States pushed for EU rules to provide protection from unfair competition and reciprocity in trade and investment. The EU framework for screening FDI that affects security and public order in the EU has applied since 11 October 2020.[741] It has also been seen that to ensure fair competition, the EU has adopted rules on foreign subsidies, requiring notification to the Commission of certain concentrations involving foreign undertakings which have received non-EU subsidies.[742]

H. ARTICLE 2(4), (5), JOINT VENTURES

The review of JVs[743] under the EUMR[744] is potentially bipartite. It is first necessary to determine whether the creation of the JV itself leads to a SIEC. Secondly, it is necessary to determine whether the JV will lead to the coordination of the competitive behaviour of undertakings which remain independent on any market, in particular, an upstream or downstream market or in the market of the JV itself. If it may lead to the coordination of the independent undertakings' behaviour Article 2(4) and (5) of the EUMR provides that these coordinative aspects of the JV will be appraised in accordance with criteria set out in Article 101:

> 4. To the extent that the creation of a joint venture constituting a concentration pursuant to Article 3 has as its object or effect the co-ordination of the competitive behaviour of undertakings that remain independent, such co-ordination shall be appraised in accordance with the criteria of Article [101(1)] and (3) [TFEU], with a view to establishing whether or not the operation is compatible with the common market.

[737] EUMR, Art. 2(2). Some concern has been expressed that the Commission's willingness to adopt an expansive approach to the concept of an undertaking and single economic unit in the context of State-owned enterprises heightens the risk of EU merger review and distorts merger assessment involving, for example, Chinese companies, see e.g. A. Zhang, 'The Single Entity Theory: An Antitrust Time-bomb for Chinese State-owned Enterprises' (2012) 8 *J of Competition Law and Economics* 805. The Commission has stressed, however, that it applies the same criteria to all transactions, wherever the inward investment originates from, see speech by then Commissioner Almunia, SPEECH/11/561, 'Policy Objectives in Merger Control', Fordham Competition Conference, New York, 8 September 2011. The EUMR affords no grounds for applying less favourable rules, and for retaliating against, companies of third countries that discriminate against EU companies in their own merger control or foreign investment legislation (see EUMR, Art. 24, n. 856 and text).

[738] See discussion of EUMR, Art. 21(4) and especially e.g. n. 232 and text.

[739] See Section 2.B.ii and iii. [740] See n. 22 and text. [741] See n. 44 and text. [742] See nn. 32–33 and text.

[743] From 1998 to April 2002, Art. 2(4) cases were designated as 'JV' cases and were often handled outside the then Merger Task Force. Since April 2002 they have been designated and have been handled like other merger cases within the merger network.

[744] All jointly controlled full-function JVs established on a lasting basis which have an EU dimension fall for assessment under the EUMR.

> 5. In making this appraisal, the Commission shall take into account in particular:
>   — whether two or more parent companies retain, to a significant extent, activities in the same market as the joint venture or in a market which is downstream or upstream from that of the joint venture or in a neighbouring market closely related to this market,
>   — whether the co-ordination which is the direct consequence of the creation of the joint venture affords the undertakings concerned the possibility of eliminating competition in respect of a substantial part of the products or services in question.

These provisions thus require the Commission to consider whether two or more parent companies retain significant activities in the same market as the JV or in downstream, upstream, or neighbouring markets (the identification of candidate markets), and whether any coordination which is the direct consequence of the creation of the JV affords the undertakings concerned the possibility of eliminating competition in respect of a substantial part of the products or services in question. There must therefore be a causal link between the setting up of the JV and the appreciable restriction of competition on the market.[745]

There is no specific Commission guidance on the application of Article 2(4) and (5) to JV cases although decisional practice and the guidance on the application of Article 101 to horizontal co-operation agreements[746] are helpful. The Commission's decisions under the EUMR have been welcomed for displaying an economically realistic approach to the Article 101 assessment required.[747] In *Telia/Telenor/Schibsted*,[748] for example, the parties notified a JV for the provision of various internet services. The Commission considered that the parents remained active on two markets in which coordinated behaviour might be possible. In particular, both Telia and Telenor remained present on the market to provide 'dial-up' internet access. Although the parents already had joint market shares of between 35 per cent and 65 per cent of the market it was concluded that coordinated behaviour between the parents was not likely. These market shares were not significant on the growing market for dial-up internet access in Sweden. The market was characterised by high growth, low barriers to entry, and low switching costs. On the other market, the website production market, the parent companies and the JV had less than 10 per cent of the market. Any coordination on such a market would not amount to appreciable restriction of competition.[749]

Nonetheless, the Commission has, in some cases, dealt with coordination concerns. In *Fujitsu/Siemens*,[750] for example, the parties' agreement to create a JV to develop, manufacture, distribute, market, and sell desktop computers did not have a significant impact on competition. The Commission was worried, however, about the effect that the merger would have on the parents' activities in a number of upstream and downstream markets. In particular, the structure of the 'financial workstation'[751] market made coordination between the parents in financial workstations likely. The parties, however, proposed a remedy to resolve the problem identified and the Commission cleared the concentration subject to conditions and obligations.

The methodology adopted by the Commission seems to be to consider (a) whether or not the creation of the JV has the object of coordinating the behaviour of the parents; and (b) if it does not, whether or not this is its effect. In making this latter determination, the Commission identifies candidate markets, considers whether coordination is likely on those markets, and whether the coordination would appreciably restrict competition. The Commission did not consider Article 101(3) elements in *Fujitsu/Siemens* as the parties proposed remedies to address the Article 101(1) problems identified.

[745] See e.g. JV.2, *ENEL/DT/FT* [1999] OJ C178/15. [746] See Chap. 10. [747] See Chaps. 5 and 10.
[748] JV.1 [1999] OJ C178/15. [749] See Chaps. 4 and 13. [750] Case IV/JV.22 [1999] OJ C318/15.
[751] ATMs and cash dispensers.

I. RESTRICTIONS DIRECTLY RELATED AND NECESSARY TO THE CONCENTRATION

Ancillary restraints are clauses which are vital to the particular concentration as, in their absence, the transaction would not take place. For example, it is usually a condition of a sale of a business that the vendor covenants not to compete with the business for a period of time. Otherwise the goodwill of the business may be rendered valueless.[752] Similarly, in JVs the parents may agree to license IPRs to the JV and perhaps not to compete with the JV. The EUMR makes it clear that restrictions directly related and necessary to the implementation of the concentration ('ancillary restraints') may be cleared along with the concentration.[753] To the extent that the restrictions are ancillary, the EUMR alone applies to them.[754] By contrast, Articles 101 and 102 remain applicable to restrictions that cannot be considered to be ancillary.

Prior to 2001 the Commission used to clear ancillary restraints in its decision to clear the concentration as a whole. In 2001, however, the Commission issued a Notice regarding restrictions directly related and necessary to concentrations[755] making it clear that it did not intend to assess such restrictions in its merger decisions any longer, and tightening its interpretation of ancillary restraints. Although the GC held in *Lagardère SCA* and *Canal\+SA v Commission*[756] that the practice of not assessing the restraints in individual cases was not consistent with the Commission's obligations under the original EUMR, the wording of the EUMR was altered to legitimise this practice.[757]

The Commission's Notice[758] is consequently of critical importance since it provides guidance as to when ancillary restraints are automatically covered by the Commission's clearance decisions.[759] It sets out both general principles[760] and principles applicable to commonly encountered restrictions in cases of acquisitions,[761] and JV cases.[762]

With regard to restrictions agreed in relation to the transfer of an undertaking the Commission states, for example, that non-competition obligations on the vendor are generally justified for periods of up to two or three years (three, where both goodwill and know-how are included in the transfer).[763] Non-competition clauses are not considered necessary when the transfer is limited to physical assets or to exclusive industrial and commercial property rights.[764] Any non-competition clause should ordinarily be limited to the products and services forming the economic activity of the undertaking transferred and the geographical area in which the vendor offered them.[765] Licences of patents, similar rights, or know-how, and purchase and supply obligations, may also be considered necessary to the implementation of the concentration.[766]

In the context of JV agreements, the Commission considers that non-competition obligations between the parent undertakings and a JV may be ancillary to the concentration for the lifetime of the JV where the obligations correspond to the products, services, and territories covered by the JV

[752] See also, e.g., the discussion of ancillary restraints in Chap. 5. [753] EUMR, Art. 8(2). See also Art. 6(1).
[754] EUMR, Art. 21(1). [755] [2001] OJ C188/5. [756] Case T-251/00, EU:T:2002:278.
[757] EUMR, Arts. 6(1)(b) and 8(1) and (2) and recital 21 (providing that the Commission's clearance decisions (under both Phase I and Phase II) 'shall be deemed to cover' ancillary restraint). The Commission believes that this makes it clear that the legislator does not require it to assess and individually address ancillary restraints.
[758] Notice of Ancillary Restraints [2005] OJ C56/24.
[759] If the Notice does not provide guidance on a particular restraint and there is no other guidance to be found, the parties may apply to the Commission for individual assessment of a case which presents 'novel and unresolved questions giving rise to genuine uncertainty', ibid., paras. 3–6 (and EUMR, recital 21).
[760] Ibid., part II. [761] Ibid., part III. [762] Ibid., part IV.
[763] Ibid., para. 20. The Commission evaluates non-solicitation and confidentiality clauses in the same way as non-competition clauses, para. 26.
[764] Ibid., para. 21. [765] Ibid., paras. 22–23. [766] Ibid., paras. 27–35.

agreement or its by-laws.[767] Further, it may be legitimate for the parents to grant IP licences to the JV (whether granted exclusively, for a period of time, or whether a field of use restriction is incorporated), for licences to be granted by the JV to one of the parents, for cross-licences to be granted, or for purchase and supply agreements to be concluded by the parent undertakings and the JV. Licence agreements between the parents are not ancillary to the implementation of the JV.[768]

J. COMMITMENTS OR REMEDIES

(i) Legal Basis and Time Periods

The discussion in the previous sections illustrates that in some cases the parties may propose modifications to the original concentration plan and offer commitments to the Commission in order to allow it to clear the transaction. It is crucial, however, that the commitments offered are full and effective and satisfy the Commission that the remedies are sufficient to restore the conditions of effective competition on a permanent basis;[769] if not, ultimately the transaction may be prohibited.[770]

The EUMR makes it clear that the Commission 'may attach to its decision . . . conditions and obligations intended to ensure that the undertakings concerned comply with the commitments they have entered into vis-à-vis the Commission with a view to rendering the concentration compatible with the common market'[771] in both Phase I, prior to initiation of proceedings, and in Phase II proceedings. Commitments must be offered (on Form RM) within specified timetables; 20 WDs of notification in Phase I proceedings and within 65 WDs of the initiation of Phase II proceedings.[772] Any such offer extends the time period for examining the concentration by 10 WD (in Phase I) and 15 WD (in Phase II).[773] In very complex cases, a further extension of up to 20 WDs may be agreed in Phase II. As the time periods are extremely tight, the possibility of offering commitments should be considered very early on in the procedure and, generally, prior to notification.[774]

If offered in Phase I, the commitments will have to be sufficient to rule out any of the Commission's 'serious doubts' within the meaning of Article 6(1)(c).[775] Plainly, the Commission has significant bargaining power at this first stage of the proceedings, and the parties may have to be prepared to give up more at this juncture if they wish to avoid second-phase proceedings. Nonetheless a significant number of cases are resolved through Phase I commitments each year.[776] In Phase II cases, it is for the Commission to communicate its competition concerns, for the parties to formulate appropriate

767 Ibid., para. 36. 768 Ibid., paras. 42–43.

769 The Commission does not, otherwise, have power to authorise a concentration which has been found to be incompatible with the internal market.

770 Remedies were proposed but ultimately deemed insufficient (leading to the prohibition of the merger) in e.g. M.6166, *Deutsche Börse/NYSE Euronext* 1 February 2012, *aff'd* Case T-175/12, *Deutsche Börse v Commission* EU:T:2015:14 and M.7612, *Hutchison 3G UK/Telefónica UK* 11 May 2016 (prohibited), annulled Case T-399/19, *CK Telecoms v Commission* EU:T:2020:217, Case C-376/20 P, judgment pending.

771 EUMR, Arts. 6(2) and 8(2).

772 Implementing Reg., Art. 19(1) and (2).

773 Only if offered after the 54th WD.

774 See e.g. M.7881, *AbInbev/SAB Miller* 24 May 2016 where significant divestments were made before notification. The case was then conditionally cleared in Phase I.

775 See e.g. M.9110, *Amerra/Mubadala/Nireus/Selonda* 15 February 2019 where the Commission accepted commitments to divest fish farms, packaging facilities, and hatchers (to be chosen from a menu of assets) and to provide access to their genetic improvement programme.

776 More Phase I commitments decisions have been taken than the number of Phase II proceedings launched, see <https://competition-policy.ec.europa.eu/mergers/statistics_en>.

remedies proposals (the Commission cannot impose them), and for the Commission, if it wants to reject the commitments, to demonstrate that the remedies offered do not resolve the competition concerns identified and that the concentration, as modified, still would lead to a SIEC. It is not, therefore, for the parties to prove that their commitments eliminate the competition concerns identified (although they must provide the relevant information necessary for the assessment); the Commission is obliged to examine a concentration as modified by the commitments validly proposed by the parties to the concentration and can declare the concentration incompatible with the internal market only where those commitments are insufficient to prevent that transaction from significantly impeding effective competition.[777] The parties' ability to influence the outcome of the decision is, therefore, significant. In cases raising serious competition problems, however, the commitments may have to substantially modify the terms and conditions of the transaction.

The Commission tests the commitments submitted by taking them to the market. Indeed, the Regulation specifically provides that transparency must be maintained and that Member States and interested third parties should be consulted.[778] Third parties, competitors, suppliers, and customers are, therefore, heavily involved in the process.

In *Oracle/SunMicrosystems*,[779] the Commission cleared a transaction subject, not to formal commitments, but taking account of public announcements of a series of pledges made by Oracle to customers, users, and developers.

(ii) The Commission's Notice on Remedies Acceptable under the EUMR

In 2008, the Commission replaced a 2001 Notice[780] with a revised Notice on remedies.[781] 'The notice sets out the general principles applicable to remedies acceptable to the Commission, the main types of commitments that may be accepted . . . the specific requirements which proposals of commitments need to fulfil in both phases of the procedure, and the main requirements for the implementation of commitments.'[782]

(iii) Types of Commitments

Commitments may relate to the *structure* of the concentration or to the *behaviour* of the parties. A structural remedy ordinarily requires divestiture of the activities of an existing viable business that can operate on a stand-alone basis. Alternatively, a behavioural commitment might be sufficient to facilitate rivalry or restore effective competition, for example to terminate exclusive agreements or to grant competitors access to infrastructure, platforms, key technology, production, or R&D facilities, or to license IPRs.

777 See e.g. Case T-87/05, *EDP v Commission* EU:T:2005:333, paras. 63–69. See also review of Commission's prohibition decision and rejection of commitments in Case T-251/19, *Wieland-Werke AG v Commission* EU:T:2022:296.

778 EUMR, recital 30. See also Cases C-68/94 and C-30/95, *France v Commission, Société Commerciale des Potasses et de l'Azote (SCPA) v Commission* EU:C:1998:148.

779 M.5529, 21 January 2010, Case T-292/10, *Monty Program AB* (appeal withdrawn). See D. Zimmer, 'The Merger Between Oracle and Sun: European Commission in Line with DoJ' (2010) 1(4) *JECLAP* 315 and the discussion of *Google/Motorola*, n. 673 and text.

780 [2001] OJ C6/3. See also the Commission's 2005 Merger Remedies Study, available at <http://ec.europa.eu/competition/mergers/legislation/remedies_study.pdf>.

781 Remedies Notice [2008] OJ C267/1. See also e.g. ICN Merger Working Group's Merger Remedies Guide (2016).

782 Remedies Notice, para. 3.

In practice, a structural solution, such as a commitment to sell a subsidiary, may be preferable, since it may prevent (and could be the only solution to prevent[783]) the SIEC arising and it does not require medium- or long-term monitoring measures.[784] Further, behavioural remedies may be difficult to control and enforce.[785] Although either are acceptable so long as they ensure the effective competitive structure of the market and 'are capable of rendering the notified transaction compatible with the common market',[786] the Commission is concerned that a number of behavioural remedies evaluated have been insufficient. It adopts a stringent approach towards remedies, generally preferring clear-cut divestitures, and identification of suitable upfront buyers, where possible, or ancillary commitments designed to strengthen a purchaser's ability to compete (especially to deal with horizontal effects[787]). Although some NCAs[788] have urged the Commission to show more flexibility, and to pay greater attention to the relevance of behavioural remedies, between 2015 and 2019 approximately two-thirds of the Commission's conditional approvals involved purely structural remedies.[789] Behavioural remedies may, however, be particularly appropriate to address non-horizontal concerns, especially conglomerate effects and may be backed up by mechanisms to ensure effectiveness, for example arbitration clauses, conferral of powers on monitoring trustees, and penalties for non-compliance.[790] Remedies designed to deal with innovation-related concerns are also becoming increasingly prominent.[791]

In some situations, no remedy may be adequate to deal with the adverse effects identified or may be so complex that the Commission cannot determine with the required degree of certainty that effective competition will be restored.[792] In *Deutsche Börse/NYSE Euronext*,[793] for example, not only was the Commission concerned about the sufficiency of the remedies proposed, but it was concerned about their workability and effectiveness. Although in *Schneider/Legrand*,[794] the Commission rejected remedies submitted by the parties twice, the second time on the ground that they were too complex and did not address the Commission's concerns, on appeal, the GC considered that the Commission had not clearly identified its concerns with the transaction in its SO. Consequently, the parties had been unable to put forward proposals for divestiture capable of rendering the concentration compatible with the internal market. The effect of the Commission's irregularities was particularly serious as the Commission had made it clear that remedies were the only means of preventing the concentration falling under Article 2(3) of the Regulation and being declared incompatible. The decision was thus vitiated by the infringement of the rights of defence and annulled.[795]

[783] See M.469, *MSG Media Service GmbH* [1994] OJ L364/1, para. 99.

[784] Case T-102/96, *Gencor Ltd v Commission* EU:T:1999:65, para. 319.

[785] See M.490, *Nordic Satellite Distribution* [1990] OJ L53/21 where the Commission rejected the undertakings offered by the parties on these grounds.

[786] Case T-102/96, *Gencor Ltd v Commission* EU:T:1999:65, para. 318. See also Case C-12/03 P, *Tetra Laval BV v Commission* EU:C:2005:87, paras. 85–89.

[787] See e.g. n. 529 and text.

[788] Joint Letter of French, German and Polish Ministries of the Economy, 4 July 2019, see. C. Cook, S. Frisch, and V. Novak, 'Recent Developments in EU Merger Remedies' (2020) 11(5)–(6) *JECLAP* 309.

[789] See e.g. Cook, Frisch, and Novak, ibid. and in (2021) 12(10) *JECLAP* 772 (making up 63% in 2020).

[790] See e.g. C. Cook, V. Novak, and S. Frisch, 'Recent Developments in EU Merger Remedies' (2018) 9 *JECLAP* 403, (2017) 8 *JECLAP* 341, and (2016) 7 *JECLAP* 349.

[791] Ibid.

[792] See e.g. M.7612, *Hutchison 3G UK/Telefónica UK* 11 May 2016 (prohibited).

[793] M.6166, 1 February 2012, *aff'd* Case T-175/12, *Deutsche Börse v Commission* EU:T:2015:148.

[794] M.2283, 10 October 2001.

[795] Case T-310/01, *Schneider Electric SA v Commission* EU:T:2002:254, paras. 421–463.

(iv) Divestiture

The most effective means of restoring effective competition is through divestiture of a subsidiary or production facilities and the creation of a new competitive entity or the strengthening of existing competitors.[796] The divestiture gives a new or existing competitor the possibility of gaining access to the market. In such cases, the Commission will wish to ensure that the activities, consisting of a viable business which can operate on a stand-alone basis and compete effectively with the merged entity on a lasting basis, are divested to a suitable purchaser within a specified time period. Increasingly, instead of a standard remedy permitting completion prior to a sale, the Commission is requiring parties to find an approved buyer prior to completion of the notified operation (an upfront buyer or fix-it-first (where a buyer is identified, and a binding agreement is concluded prior to the Commission's clearance decision)).[797] The sale of the entity may itself amount to a notifiable concentration.

Usually, tight deadlines are set within which the divestiture must occur, and the commitments will set out specific details and procedures relating to the Commission's oversight of the divestiture, in particular, approval of the trustee and approval of the purchaser and purchase agreement.[798]

The Commission sometimes accepts alternative remedies packages, accepting an equally effective alternative in case the preferred divestiture option proves difficult to complete. The Commission explains alternative divestiture commitments and 'crown jewels' in its Remedies Notice:

1.4 Alternative Divestiture commitments: Crown Jewels

In certain cases, the implementation of the parties' preferred divestiture option (of a viable business solving the competition concerns) might be uncertain in view, for example, of third parties' pre-emption rights or uncertainty as to the transferability of key contracts, intellectual property rights, or the uncertainty of finding a suitable purchaser. Nevertheless, the parties may consider that they would be able to divest this business to a suitable purchaser within a very short time period. In such circumstances, the Commission cannot take the risk that, in the end, effective competition will not be maintained. Accordingly, the Commission will only accept such divestiture commitments under the following conditions: (a) absent the uncertainty, the first divestiture proposed in the commitments would consist of a viable business, and (b) the parties will have to propose a second alternative divestiture which the parties will be obliged to implement if they are not able to implement the first commitment within the given time frame for the first divestiture. Such an alternative commitment normally has to be a 'crown jewel', i.e. it should be as least as good as the first proposed divestiture in terms of creating a viable competitor once implemented, it should not involve any uncertainties as to its implementation and it should be capable of being implemented quickly in order to avoid that the overall implementation period exceeds what would normally be regarded as acceptable in the conditions of the market in question. In order to limit the risks in the interim period, it is indispensable that interim preservation and holding separate measures apply to all assets included in both divestiture alternatives. Furthermore, the commitment has to establish clear criteria and a strict timetable as to how and when the alternative divestiture obligation will become effective and the Commission will require shorter periods for its implementation.

If there is uncertainty as to the implementation of the divestiture due to third party rights or as to finding a suitable purchaser crown jewel commitments and up-front buyers as discussed below in paragraphs 54 address the same concerns, and the parties may therefore choose between both structures.

[796] Remedies Notice, para. 22, see e.g. M.6471, *Outokumpu/Inoxum* 7 November 2012, M.6503, *La Poste/Swiss Post/JV* 4 July 2012, M.7881, *AB InBev/SAB Miller* 24 May 2016, and M.7744, *Heidelberg Cement/Italcementi* 26 May 2016.

[797] See Remedies Notice, paras. 53–57.

[798] Ibid., part IV deals with requirements for the implementation of commitments. See also the Best Practice Guidelines: The Commission's Model Texts for Divestiture Commitments and the Trustee Mandate under the EC Merger Regulation which provide standard model texts for divestiture commitments and for trustee mandates.

Divestiture commitments may also be used for removing links between the parties and competitors where these links contribute to competitive concerns raised by the merger.[799]

(v) Other Remedies: Access Remedies, Behavioural Commitments, and 'Remedy Packages'

A general distinction can be made between divestitures, other structural remedies, such as granting access to key infrastructure or inputs on non-discriminatory terms, and commitments relating to the future behaviour of the merged entity. Divestiture commitments are the best way to eliminate competition concerns resulting from horizontal overlaps, and may also be the best means of resolving problems resulting from vertical or conglomerate concerns. Other structural commitments may be suitable to resolve all types of concerns if those remedies are equivalent to divestitures in their effects, as explained in more detail later. Commitments relating to the future behaviour of the merged entity may be acceptable only exceptionally. In particular, commitments in the form of undertakings not to raise prices, to reduce product ranges, or to remove brands, etc., will generally not eliminate competition concerns resulting from horizontal overlaps. In any case, those types of remedies can only be accepted if their workability is fully ensured by effective implementation and monitoring in line with the considerations set out in paragraphs 13–14, 66, and 69 of the Remedies Notice, and if they do not risk leading to distorting effects on competition.

Other commitments, such as access remedies and change of long-term exclusive contracts, may also be offered and accepted.[800] These are often aimed at opening the market to competitors, through giving access to infrastructure[801] or key technology. The parties may also have to make commitments as to 'interoperability'. In *GE/Instrumentarium*,[802] for example, the Commission was concerned about the effect of the merger in the perioperative monitors market and also that the parties could take steps to ensure that competitors' critical care and patient monitors could not interoperate with their anaesthesia equipment. GE adopted a package of measures, divestiture of a company, and a series of supply agreements with its acquirer, to deal with the horizontal overlaps and to ensure the emergence of an effective competitor to the merged entity on the perioperative monitors market. It also undertook to provide the electrical and mechanical interface for third parties' patient monitors to be able to interconnect with its own anaesthesia equipment. In *Google/Fitbit*,[803] the Commission accepted an extremely long and complex package of commitments to deal with its range of concerns, including commitments relating to the separation of, and limitations on Google's use of, data collected from wrist-worn devices and other Fitbit devices, access, and interoperability obligations.

In the Remedies Notice, the Commission states, 'non-structural types of remedies, such as promises by the parties to abstain from certain commercial behaviour (e.g. bundling products), will generally not eliminate the competition concerns resulting from horizontal overlaps. In any case, it may be difficult to achieve the required degree of effectiveness of such a remedy due to the absence of effective monitoring of its implementation . . . Therefore, the Commission may examine other types of non-divesture remedies, such as behavioural promises, only exceptionally in specific circumstances, such as in respect of competition concerns arising in conglomerate structures.'[804]

[799] See e.g. M.492, *VEBA/Degussa* [1994] OJ C303/5; M.3653 and M.1845, *Time Warner/AOL* 11 October 2000.

[800] M.877, *Boeing/McDonnell Douglas* [1997] OJ L336/16. Further, the Commission also required Boeing to make some of its IPRs available, through licences, to competitors. These types of remedies may be particularly relevant in telecommunications and media cases.

[801] See e.g. JV.37, *BSkyB/Kirch* 21 March 2000.

[802] M.3083, IP/03/1193.

[803] M.9660, 17 December 2020.

[804] Remedies Notice, para. 69.

Behavioural commitments have sometimes been offered to deal with problems arising in coordinated effects or conglomerate cases. In *Kali und Salz/MdK/Treuhand*,[805] for example, the parties to the concentration offered to sever links with its main competitor, SCPA (which were considered to facilitate anti-competitive behaviour on the oligopolistic market).[806] Further, in both *GE/Honeywell*[807] and *Tetra Laval/Sidel*[808] the parties offered commitments to abstain from certain commercial behaviour (for example, bundling products) to deal with the Commission's concerns. In the latter cases, the Commission rejected the commitments on the grounds that they were pure promises and would involve excessive monitoring. In the *GE/Honeywell* appeals,[809] the GC did not need to rule on the correctness of the Commission's actions in this regard as it considered that its competition assessment of the conglomerate effects contained manifest errors of assessments. In *Commission v Tetra Laval BV*,[810] however, the CJ held that as the Commission had rejected the commitments as a matter of principle, the GC had been correct to find that the promises should have been taken into account when assessing the likelihood that the merged entity would act in a particular way. In *Intel/McAfee*,[811] in contrast, the Commission accepted a range of behavioural remedies to deal with its concerns both about bundling and technical tying in a conglomerate merger case and foreclosure of competing security solution providers.

(vi) Other Cases

The broad range of packages accepted often requires the parties to be 'inventive' and to propose remedy packages which will resolve the competition problems identified by the Commission. In some cases, the Commission has accepted alternative remedies packages. For example, in *Nestlé/Ralston Purina*[812] the Commission was concerned about the impact of the concentration in the Spanish markets for dry dog food, dry cat food, and snacks and treats for cats and in the Italian and Greek markets for dry cat food. With regard to Spain, the party undertook to divest itself of its 'Friskies' brand, through the grant of exclusive licences for a substantial period and to divest itself of a Spanish production plant or, if not implemented within a specified time period, alternatively, to remove the overlap in Spain by divesting itself of Ralston Purina's 50 per cent shareholding in the JV, Gallina Blanca Purina.

In some cases, a concentration has been saved by a third party to the transaction. In *Alcatel/Telettra*,[813] for example, the Spanish telecommunications company, Telefónica, agreed to sell its interests in the parties to the concentration in order to persuade the Commission that the undertakings' potential market power would be counteracted by the countervailing exercise of monopolistic demand.

[805] M.308 [1994] OJ L186/30; on appeal Cases C-68/94 and C-30/95, *France v Commission, Société Commerciale des Potasses et de l'Azote (SCPA) v Commission* EU:C:1998:148.

[806] Their imposition was one of the factors which caused SCPA and France to challenge, successfully, the legitimacy of the Commission's decision.

[807] M.2220, 3 July 2001.

[808] M.2416, 30 October 2001, annulled on appeal Case T-5/02, EU:T:2002:264, *aff'd* Case C-12/03 P, EU:C:2005:87.

[809] Cases T-209 and 210/01, *Honeywell v Commission* and *General Electric Co v Commission* EU:T:2005:455 and EU:T:2005:456.

[810] Case C-12/03 P, EU:C:2005:87, paras. 85–89.

[811] M.5984, 26 January 2011.

[812] M.2337, IP/01/1136.

[813] M.42, *Alcatel/Telettra* [1991] OJ L122/48.

(vii) Breach of a Condition or Obligations

Commitments consist of both 'conditions' and 'obligations'. The Commission may take a decision prohibiting the concentration where it finds that it has been implemented in contravention of a condition attached to a decision.[814] Further, it may revoke a decision where the undertakings concerned commit a breach of an obligation, relating to the steps necessary to implement the commitment, attached to the decision.[815] In addition, the Commission may impose fines of up to 10 per cent of the aggregate turnover of the undertakings concerned that have failed to comply with conditions or obligations imposed, and periodic penalty payments for delay caused by failure to comply with an obligation.[816] In 2019, the Commission for the first time charged a company, Telefónica Deutschland, with breaching a commitment;[817]in this case a promise to offer wholesale 4G services to all interested parties at best prices and under benchmark conditions. Subsequently, in *Aleris/Novelis*[818] the Commission dealt with Novelis' failure to complete divestiture commitments, offered to address the Commission's competition concerns, within specified deadlines by adopting provisional interim measures to preserve competition pursuant to Article 8(5) EUMR. Further, even after the completion of the divestments, the Commission took the view that final measures, including non-reacquisition and non-solicitation measures, were necessary to ensure that the sale remained effective (Article 8(4)(b) EUMR).

(viii) Modification and Waiver of Commitments

In some exceptional cases, the Commission has been prepared to modify or waive certain commitments which had been attached to a clearance decision.[819]

6. EUMR STATISTICS

DG Comp publishes statistics setting out what happens to merger notifications.[820] These provide interesting information on, for example, the number of notifications, the number of referrals, Phase II proceedings, Phase I and II clearances, and prohibitions. They suggest that although the Commission does enforce EU merger rules rigorously, the intervention rate is relatively low compared to the number of notified mergers. For example, out of 8,816 notifications (between September 1990 and 31 March 2023):

- 7,863 cases (including 4,631 under the simplified procedure) in Phase I, and 63 cases in Phase II, were cleared unconditionally;
- 298 Phase II proceedings were initiated;
- 241 cases were withdrawn (in Phase I or II proceedings);[821]
- 349 cases in Phase I, and 144 in Phase II, were cleared in conjunction with commitments;
- 32 transactions were prohibited.

[814] EUMR, Art. 8(7). [815] Ibid., Arts. 6(3) and 8(6). [816] Ibid., Arts. 14(2)(d) and 15(1)(c).

[817] M.9003, *Telefónica Deutschland/E-Plus* 22 February 2019 (concerning M.7018, *Telefónica Deutschland/E-Plus* 30 January 2014).

[818] M.9076, IP/21/687.

[819] See M.950, *Hoffmann-La Roche/Boehringer Mannheim* 3 May 2011 and M.8947, *NIDEC/ Whirlpool (Embraco)* 15 May 2020 (the Commission partially waived commitments).

[820] <https://competition-policy.ec.europa.eu/mergers/statistics_en>.

[821] Some cases were also referred to national authorities under EUMR referral mechanisms.

7. JUDICIAL REVIEW AND OTHER PROCEEDINGS

The EUMR itself provides the CJ with unlimited jurisdiction to review penalties imposed by the Commission and to cancel, reduce, or increase any such fine imposed.[822] The ordinary provisions in the TFEU also authorise the review of institutions' acts and failure to act. A party to a concentration may, therefore, institute proceedings against a final merger decision under Article 263 TFEU.[823] Further, third parties (such as a competitor of the merging parties[824] or a third party affected by commitments given)[825] may appeal if it can be established that the decision (for example, a conditional or unconditional clearance decision[826] or an Article 9 reference decision[827]) 'is of direct and individual concern' to them.[828]

It has been seen in this chapter that many appeals have been brought in merger cases and that even though the GC consistently stresses that, when reviewing the Commission's decisions, it takes account of the wide discretion that the Regulation imposes upon the Commission and the complex economic assessments required,[829] it has shown itself to be rigorous in its review and, where necessary, has been prepared to annul the Commission's decisions. Where a Commission decision is annulled, in whole or in part, the Commission has to examine the concentration 'afresh' in the light of current market conditions.[830]

The appeals procedure is discussed more fully in Chapter 13. An acute difficulty with the system in the merger context is that although the Commission has to proceed within very tight time limits under the EUMR, proceedings before the EU Courts may take several years so placing the Commission in a powerful position.[831] Although since 2001[832] an expedited procedure has been available before the GC, it only applies in cases (not limited to competition cases) capable of being resolved by abbreviated written procedures and a full oral procedure. The procedure, which ordinarily takes between nine

[822] EUMR, Art. 16.

[823] Most likely a prohibition decision, see e.g. Case C-188/06 P, *Schneider Electric SA v Commission* EU:C:2007:158.

[824] See e.g. Case T-2/93, *Air France v Commission* EU:T:1994:55; Case T-119/02, *Royal Philips Electronics v Commission* EU:T:2003:101; Case T-177/04, *easyJet Airline Co Ltd v Commission* EU:T:2006:187; and Case T-394/15, *KPN BV v Commission* EU:T:2017:756 (the GC annulled the Commission's decision clearing Liberty Global's acquisition of sole control over Ziggo NV on the basis that it failed to provide sufficient reasons for one part of its decision).

[825] See Cases C-68/94 and C-30/95, *France v Commission, Société Commerciale des Potasses et de l'Azote (SCPA) v Commission* EU:C:1998:148, paras. 173–175. See also Case T-464/04, *Independent Music Publishers and Labels Association (Impala) v Commission* EU:T:2006:216; Case C-413/06 P, *Bertelsmann and Sony Corp v Commission* EU:C:2008:392; Case T-79/12, *Cisco Systems Inc v Commission* EU:T:2013:635.

[826] Ibid.

[827] See e.g. Case T-119/02, *Royal Philips Electronics v Commission* EU:T:2003:101.

[828] No direct and individual concern was established in, e.g., Case T-350/03, *Wirtschaftskammer Kärnten and best connect Ampere Strompool v Commission* [2006] ECR II-68; Case T-96/92 R, *CCE de la Société générale des grandes sources and others v Commission* EU:T:1995:77. Proceedings have also been brought by employees and shareholders of one of the undertakings concerned, see e.g. Case T-83/92, *Zunis Holding v Commission* EU:T:1993:93.

[829] See e.g. Cases C-68/94 and C-30/95, *France v Commission, Société Commerciale des Potasses et de l'Azote (SCPA) v Commission* EU:C:1998:148, paras. 223–224; and Case T-221/95, *Endemol Entertainment Holding BV v Commission* EU:T:1999:85.

[830] EUMR, Art. 10(5). This requires the parties to put in a new notification, a supplement to the original notification, or a certification stating that there are no changes, before the ordinary Phase I time procedure runs. In the second investigation into the *Tetra Laval/Sidel* merger, M.2416, 13 January 2003, the merger was eventually cleared subject to commitments. Following a launch of a further Phase II investigation in the *Schneider* case, however, the merger was eventually abandoned.

[831] It may encourage the undertakings involved to give commitments to persuade the Commission to authorise the merger. Further, the parties will have to observe a prohibition or commitments imposed until the Commission's decision is suspended or annulled.

[832] The GC modified its rules of procedure, see [2000] OJ L322/4.

and 12 months, was used, for example, in the *Philips*,[833] *Schneider*,[834] *Tetra Laval*,[835] and *Impala*[836] appeals.[837]

In *My Travel* (previously *Airtours*), *Schneider*, and *UPS*, claimants launched damages proceedings against the Commission in respect of the loss suffered in consequence of the wrongful prohibition of their proposed acquisitions (under Article 340(2) TFEU, dealing with the non-contractual liability of the EU).[838] Both My Travel's and UPS's claims were dismissed[839] and although the GC in *Schneider v Commission* awarded Schneider damages in respect of two of the categories of loss claimed (having found that some of the Commission's failures had manifestly and gravely disregarded the limit on its discretion), the CJ set aside the judgment insofar as it ordered the Commission to make good the loss claimed as a result of the reduction in the sale price of Legrand. It significantly reduced the sum awarded, holding that the Commission was only liable to pay compensation to cover costs incurred in respect of the resumed merger control procedure. The sum of €50,000 eventually awarded was significantly less than the €1.6 billion originally claimed.

8. INTERNATIONAL ISSUES

A. COOPERATION WITH OTHER COMPETITION AUTHORITIES

Mergers which have to be notified in two or more jurisdictions create complexities for merging parties. Each of these jurisdictions is likely to have differing jurisdictional, procedural, or substantive rules, leading to coordination and timing problems and the prospects of different outcomes being reached by the different authorities. Although competition agencies across the world seek to cooperate with each other when conducting reviews, in some cases 'divergences' may be inevitable, given different legal and market contexts.[840]

B. THE LONG ARM OF THE EUMR

The quantitative jurisdictional tests incorporated within the EUMR look not to the effect of the concentration on inter-State trade or on competition but to the size of the undertakings involved. This means that they may encompass: mergers between non-EU undertakings even though the undertakings' business is principally carried on outside the EU and/or the merger is completed outside the EU;

[833] Case T-119/02, EU:T:2003:101. See also e.g. Case T-87/05, *EDP v Commission* EU:T:2005:333.

[834] Case T-310/01, EU:T:2002:254. [835] Case T-5/02, EU:T:2002:264.

[836] Case T-464/04, EU:T:2006:216, Case C-413/06 P, *Bertelsmann and Sony Corp v Commission* EU:C:2008:392. Although this case was run under the expedited procedure, judgment was not handed down until 19 months after the Commission's decision had passed. The GC was critical of the way that Impala had handled the case, having requested the expedited procedure, and this fact was reflected in the costs order it made, see paras. 544–554.

[837] Schneider agreed to cut back its case so that the expedited procedure could be used. In both *Schneider* and *Tetra Laval* the GC gave judgment within a period of about a year from the Commission's decision.

[838] Case T-212/03, *MyTravel v Commission* EU:T:2008:315, Case T-351/03, *Schneider v Commission* EU:T:2007:212, Case C-440/07 P, EU:C:2009:459, and Case T-834/17, *United Parcel Service v Commission* EU:T:2022:84 (UPS sought €1.7 billion damages), see D. Arts, '"Schneider" and the Non-contractual Liability of the European Community in the Field of Merger Control' (2010) 1(1) *JECLAP* 27.

[839] In *UPS*, ibid., although the GC found that the Commission had committed a serious breach of EU law, it found that there was no causal link between the infringement and the damages claimed—UPS did not provide evidence that the Commission would have cleared the case if it had followed the correct procedure.

[840] See further Chap. 13.

a JV set up by non-EU parents even though it has no activities in the EU;[841] a transaction which has no or little impact on competition within the EU; and even if the transaction has been cleared in another jurisdiction. As there is no exemption for mergers occurring outside the EU or any requirement that any of the undertakings involved is established or has substantial operations in the EU,[842] the Commission's scrutiny of some mergers has been extremely politically sensitive in nature.

In 1997, for example, the Commission considered a merger announced in December 1996 between Boeing and McDonnell Douglas, neither of which had facilities or assets in the EU.[843] The merger was instigated with the encouragement of the US authorities (the Clinton administration) and was not challenged by the US FTC in July 1997.[844] Although the Commission had concerns about the merger, in the end, a political storm was saved by Boeing's offer of acceptable commitments to the Commission. In *Gencor/Lonrho*,[845] however, the Commission prohibited a concentration concluded between a South African (Gencor) and a UK (Lonrho) company, merging business activities based in South Africa, even though the South African Competition Board did not consider that the operation gave rise to competition concerns under South African law. Similarly, in *GE/Honeywell*,[846] the Commission prohibited a merger which had been permitted by the US authorities.

It can be seen from these examples that a number of important issues arise in the application of the EUMR. The first is to what extent the Commission has *jurisdiction* to apply the EUMR extraterritorially to concentrations between foreign entities. The second relates to whether the provisions of the EUMR can be enforced against merging parties and third parties located outside the EU.[847] The third relates to comity and what steps have been taken to cooperate with the competition authorities of other States involved in the investigation of the same case, to exchange information where possible, and to avoid conflicting decisions. This has become an increasingly important issue as the number of jurisdictions around the world with merger control regimes has grown and as parties to international merger transactions more frequently have to make multi-jurisdictional filings. The Commission now often cooperates, through formal and more informal arrangements, successfully with other agencies, particularly the US ones, to coordinate their merger reviews, insofar as is possible, and to ensure consistency in remedies where required. In *Deutsche Börse/NYSE Euronext*[848] and *Intel/McAfee*[849] for example, the Commission cooperated closely with the US DOJ and FTC respectively, in *UPS/TNT Express*[850] it cooperated closely with both the US and Canadian authorities

[841] If the parent companies, or other connected undertakings within the group, satisfy the worldwide and EU-wide turnover thresholds, the JV transaction will have an EU dimension even if the JV created is not established in the EU, does not have activities in or make sales into the EU, and it is not foreseeable that the JV will produce any direct and substantial effects in the EU. These transactions are likely to be dealt with under the simplified procedure however.

[842] In earlier EUMR drafts it was a requirement that at least one of the undertakings was established in the EU and had substantial operations in one of the Member States: see [1973] OJ C92/1, Art. 1(1), [1982] OJ C36/3, [1988] OJ C130/4.

[843] M.877 [1997] OJ L336/16. The extraterritorial aspects of this case are discussed in greater detail in Chap. 16.

[844] See US FTC Press Releases of 1 July 1997: 'FTC Allows Merger of the Boeing Company and McDonnell Douglas Corporation', 23 September 1997.

[845] M.619 [1997] OJ L11/30.

[846] M.2220, 3 July 2001, *aff'd* Cases T-209 and 210/01, EU:T:2005:455 and EU:T:2005:456.

[847] Neither the EUMR itself nor the implementing regulation explicitly deal with the limits of enforcement jurisdiction. Rather, the provisions apply broadly. Further, the Commission has in practice used the powers to request information from parties and even third parties located outside the EU and to prohibit, or to clear subject to compliance with conditions or obligations, transactions between non-EU firms. See Chap. 17.

[848] M.6166, 1 February 2012, *aff'd* Case T-175/12, *Deutsche Börse v Commission* EU:T:2015:148.

[849] M. 5984, *Intel/McAfee* 26 January 2011 and see revised best practices for US–EU cooperation in merger investigations (14 October 2011). See also, ICN Practical Guide to International Enforcement Cooperation in Mergers available at <www.internationalcompetitionnetwork.org/working-groups/merger>.

[850] M.6570, 30 January 2013.

and in *Thermo-Fisher/Life Technologies*[851] and *GE/Alstom*[852] it cooperated with a large number of agencies across the globe.

In *Gencor Ltd v Commission*[853] the GC had to deal with an argument which raised the right of the Commission to assert jurisdiction over the JV which Gencor alleged had no activities within the EU, was not implemented within the EU,[854] and did not have an immediate, direct, and substantial effect within the EU. The GC upheld the legality of the Commission's prohibition decision, ruling that the Commission's assertion of jurisdiction was not inconsistent with the EUMR, other EU case law, or the rules of public international law.[855] Indeed, the GC made it clear that even where there is doubt about the legality of the assertion of jurisdiction under the EUMR, compulsory notification of such transactions is justifiable, as the Commission must be in a position to assess whether or not a transaction falls within its purview.[856] These issues, and this aspect of the GC's judgment in *Gencor*, are discussed in Chapter 17.

C. RECIPROCITY

Article 24 of the EUMR makes provision for the Member States to inform the Commission 'of any general difficulties encountered by their undertakings with concentrations ... in a non-member country'. Further it provides for the Commission to draw up reports on this issue.

Where it appears that certain non-Member States do not permit or otherwise make it difficult for EU undertakings to carry out mergers in circumstances in which undertakings from that State would be permitted to carry out a merger in the EU, 'the Commission may submit proposals to the Council for an appropriate mandate for negotiation with a view to obtaining comparable treatment for EU undertakings'.[857]

9. CONCLUSIONS

1. In the relatively short period since the EUMR first came into force, the Commission has developed an effective and well-respected system of merger control.

2. The Commission has not shied away from adopting decisions involving complex and difficult analysis within the stringent time periods prescribed by the EUMR. The rigorous economic approach adopted routinely in merger cases, impacted on, and encouraged the development and modernisation of the Commission's analysis under Articles 101 and 102.

3. The Commission regularly reviews the operation and working of the EUMR, considering how to improve procedures and substantive analysis as well as tackling the complex jurisdictional problems that the EUMR provokes.

[851] M.6944, 26 November 2013. [852] M.7278, 8 September 2015.

[853] Case T-102/96, *Gencor Ltd v Commission* EU:T:1999:65.

[854] Arguably, as the structural changes in *Gencor* were not implemented within the EU, the implementation test expounded in *Wood Pulp* had not been satisfied. For the view that both cases endorse the effects doctrine, see Mosso, n. 364, 7 (see Chap. 17).

[855] Further, that the principles of non-interference or proportionality did not require the Commission to refrain from exercising jurisdiction where another authority had authorised but not required the transaction.

[856] The parties may be spared the inconvenience of a full notification in this situation as the short-form notification and simplified procedure is likely to apply, see Sections 3.B.i and 4.A.

[857] EUMR, Art. 24(3). See also the measures being adopted on FDI to ensure reciprocity, n. 44 and text.

4. The challenge for the Commission remains to conduct the rigorous analysis demanded of it by the GC, within the tight time periods set out in the EUMR.

5. A current debate is whether the EUMR allows the Commission to tackle all problematic mergers, especially in pharmaceutical and digital industries, and/or whether new approaches, tools, or a broader substantive review is required, possibly admitting consideration of public policy factors. Some public policy factors are taken into account by a number of Member States in the context of merger, public security, or foreign investment review. The exercise of these powers must be compatible with EU law. Regulation 2019/452 sets out an EU framework for the screening of FDI affecting security and public order in the EU and for EU-wide cooperation in this matter and Regulation 2022/2560 creates a system of foreign subsidy control.

10. FURTHER READING

A. Books

Lindsay, A., and Berridge, A., *The EU Merger Regulation: Substantive Issues* (5th edn, Sweet & Maxwell, 2017)

B. Articles

Brittan, L., 'The Law and Policy of Merger Control in the EEC' (1990) 15 *ELRev* 351

Deutscher, E., 'Prometheus Bound? The Uncertain Future of the Unilateral Effects Analysis in EU Merger Control after CK Telecoms' (2022) 18(2) *J of Competition Law and Economics* 323

Mezzanotte, F. E., 'Direct versus Indirect Proof of the *Airtours* Criterion in *Impala*' (2009) 31 *World Competition* 253

Röller, L. H., and de la Mano, M., 'The Impact of the New Substantive Test in European Merger Control' (2006) 2 *European Competition Journal* 9

Witt, A., 'From *Airtours* to *Ryanair*: Is the More Economic Approach to EU Merger Law Really About More Economics?' (2012) 49 *CMLRev* 217

16

EU COMPETITION LAW AND POLICY IN THE DIGITAL ECONOMY

1. CENTRAL ISSUES

1. The term 'digital economy' refers to a range of market circumstances where digital technologies play a central role. From a competition policy perspective, the term is often applied more narrowly to focus specifically on the activities of digital platforms.

2. Although the digital economy includes numerous different technologies and economic activities, digital markets typically exhibit many of the same competition dynamics, which are relevant to the application of competition law. These include extreme returns to scale, market multi-sidedness and network externalities, and the central role of data.

3. Many digital markets are prone to 'tipping', whereby the market coalesces around a single, ultra-dominant provider. While competition 'for the market' occurs initially, once the market has tipped, the successful platform is largely insulated from competition for the foreseeable future.

4. Given the distinctive features of digital markets, it is disputed as to whether the ordinary competition rules can be applied to address digital competition problems. The Commission has applied Articles 101 and 102 to competition problems in the digital economy in the past. Its efforts under the EU Merger Control Regulation have arguably been less successful.

5. There are several obstacles to applying competition law effectively in the digital context. Market definition and the assessment of market power are more complex. The concepts of agreement and concerted practice struggle to encapsulate algorithmic collusion.

6. Because of the new models of business and services provided in the digital economy, it is often necessary to develop new theories of antitrust harm to address anti-competitive behaviour.

7. The speed of intervention and the effectiveness of conventional competition law remedies has also been criticised.

8. The perceived difficulties of applying ordinary competition law effectively resulted in worldwide efforts to supplement the existing frameworks with sector-specific rules for large digital actors. In the EU, this has culminated in the Digital Markets Act (DMA).

9. The DMA regulates the activities of 'gatekeepers' that provide 'core platform services'. Where an undertaking is designated as a gatekeeper for the purposes of the DMA, it becomes subject to a series of obligations relating to data usage, access,

and portability; distribution channels; advertising; leveraging; device and platform neutrality; and interoperability. Certain obligations are 'self-executing' whereas others are 'susceptible of being further specified' by the Commission. Undertakings have a positive duty to comply with all of the obligations imposed by the DMA, including taking steps to demonstrate their ongoing compliance to the Commission.

10. The Commission is the sole enforcer of the DMA. It has the power to take decisions finding non-compliance and systematic non-compliance, to impose fines and behavioural and structural remedies, and to accept commitments.

11. National authorities have a very limited enforcement role under the DMA, a position that has been criticised. Private enforcement is foreseen but not facilitated by the DMA.

12. The DMA states that its obligations are 'complementary to, but different from' Articles 101 and 102 and equivalent national competition rules. There is, however, considerable overlap between the scope of application of the DMA and Article 102 in particular.

2. INTRODUCTION

The digital economy has been the focal point for some of the most contentious competition policy debates and the most ambitious enforcement efforts in the EU and beyond in recent years. As explained in Chapter 1, the term digital economy refers to an expansive range of market circumstances where digital technologies play a central role, involving in particular the use of the internet to conduct business.[1] From a competition policy perspective, the term is sometimes applied more narrowly to focus specifically on the activities of digital platforms.[2] Digital markets function as an increasingly critical component of the overall economy, as a result of the continuous introduction of new digital products and business models, alongside the digital transformation of established business activities. In 2015, the EU published its Digital Single Market Strategy, with three key pillars: to improve access for consumers and businesses to online goods and services; to create the right conditions for digital networks and services to flourish; and to maximise the growth potential of the digital economy in Europe.[3] In addition to efforts in areas as diverse as data protection, telecommunications regulation, cyber security, digital inclusion, and the much-touted New Green Deal, this heightened focus is discernible in the area of EU competition law and policy. The Commission and national competition authorities (NCAs) have aggressively enforced the competition rules in digital markets, especially against the 'Big Tech' giants, also known as 'GAFAM'.[4] Yet the challenges of keeping digital markets open and competitive—and *fair*—have prompted a lively debate about the adequacy of the current competition rules, and the extent to which these might need to be revised or extended to provide suitable digital market supervision. At EU level, this has culminated in sector-specific legislation, the Digital Markets Act, which aims to ensure 'contestable and fair markets in the digital sector'.[5]

[1] See Chap. 1, Section 12.

[2] See e.g. J. Crémer, Y.-A. de Montjoye, and H. Schweitzer, *Competition Policy for the Digital Era* (2019), <https://ec.europa.eu/competition/publications/reports/kd0419345enn.pdf>, hereafter 'Commission Digital Report', 19–24, where the terms 'digital economy' and 'platform economy' are treated essentially as synonyms. On the definition of digital platforms generally, see European Commission, 'Communication on Online Platforms and the Digital Single Market—Opportunities and Challenges for Europe', COM(2016) 288 final, 2–3.

[3] European Commission, 'A Digital Single Market Strategy for Europe', COM(2015) 192 final, 6 May 2015.

[4] Which stands for Google, Apple, Facebook, Amazon, and Microsoft.

[5] See Section 6.C.

This chapter explores the issues for competition law and policy that have been generated by the inexorable emergence of the digital economy. It begins by considering the recurrent dynamics of digital economy markets. These arguably increase the need for antitrust scrutiny, yet at the same time complicate the task of applying the established rules. Drawing on examples from across the preceding chapters, we survey enforcement practice to date, which demonstrates that the EU competition rules have proven reasonably adept at addressing anti-competitive behaviour by digital actors. Nonetheless, there are perceived gaps and undesirable limitations within the existing framework. The question of how best to regulate competition in the digital economy, whether using competition law or other legal instruments, returns us to the topic of the optimal goals of competition law, introduced in Chapter 1.

3. COMPETITION DYNAMICS IN THE DIGITAL ECONOMY

The 'digital economy' is an umbrella term, which refers to a wide spectrum of different economic activities and technologies.[6] Previous editions of this book used the equally broad term 'new economy' to describe the same phenomenon, a phrase which captures the novel, dynamic nature of the business activities in many digital markets.[7] Despite the heterogeneity of the business models and services provided, digital markets often exhibit many of the same competition dynamics, which are relevant to the application of competition law. This section discusses some of the more salient features from a competition perspective. Not every digital market exhibits every element to the same extent; but it is this bundle of characteristics, taken as a whole, which has informed the policy perception that the digital economy merits special scrutiny from a competition law perspective, and may indeed require the rules to be adapted or supplemented to meet the concerns that arise.[8]

The distinctive characteristics of digital markets have been discussed at length in numerous reports on digital competition policy published by competition agencies and other institutions in recent years.[9] These include, most notably for our purposes, the expert report on *Competition Policy for the Digital Era*, prepared for the European Commission and published in 2019 (hereafter 'Commission Digital Report').[10] The Commission Digital Report identified three key characteristics that informed its assessment of the extent to which competition law can address the challenges of digital markets: very high returns to scale, network effects,[11] and the role of data.

First, digital markets often feature what the Commission Digital Report referred to as 'extreme' returns to scale, namely where the cost of production of digital products is much less than proportional to the number of customers served. Scale economies, as a general phenomenon, provide incumbents with a competitive advantage, as it is typically much cheaper to increase existing production than for new entrants to bring competing products on stream. In the digital context, however, scale returns

[6] F. Lancieri and P. Morita Sakowski, 'Competition in Digital Markets: A Review of Expert Reports' (2021) 26 *Stanford J of Law, Business & Finance* 65, 74–75.

[7] See also R. Posner, 'Antitrust in the New Economy', University of Chicago John Olin Law & Economics Working Paper No.106 (2000).

[8] Explaining how the growth of digital technologies may affect standard economic models, see A. Goldfarb and C. Tucker, 'Digital Economics' (2019) 57 *J of Economic Literature* 3.

[9] Including 'Unlocking Digital Competition. Report of the Digital Expert Competition Panel', March 2019 (UK); ACCC, 'Digital Platforms inquiry. Final Report', 26 July 2019 (Australia); and 'A New Competition Framework for the Digital Economy'. Report by the Commission 'Competition Law 4.0', 9 September 2019 (Germany). A useful summary is Lancieri and Sakowski, n. 6.

[10] See n. 2.

[11] The Commission Digital Report used the phrases network effects and network externalities interchangeably, and did not consider negative network externalities (i.e. congestion).

may be *so* immense as to make competition wholly unrealistic. The Commission Digital Report explains this in the following terms:

> With increasing returns to scale, competition between two firms producing the same product will not allow them to cover their costs. Indeed, were they to cover their (total) costs, they would have to price above the cost of serving an additional consumer (the marginal cost) and each of them would find it profitable to lower their price to steal the other's clients. As a consequence, no firm, unless armed with a much superior and cheaper technology, would want to enter a market dominated by an incumbent, even when this incumbent is making large profits.[12]

These very substantial returns to scale also, according to the Commission Digital Report, explain the preponderance of free services in digital sectors. Since consumers are attracted to a zero-price, high returns to scale create significant incentives for firms to distribute their products at zero-price, generating their income instead on advertising.[13] Zero-prices are not a competition problem in themselves, although it is something of a contemporary cliché that 'if you're not paying for a product, you *are* the product' (e.g. through the extraction of sensitive personal data). Yet the zero-price model initially posed difficulties to the application of competition law in digital markets, insofar as conventional approaches to market definition and identifying harm are linked to the ability to raise prices.[14]

The second key characteristic identified by the Commission Digital Report is the pervasiveness of network effects: whereby 'the usefulness for each user of using a technology or a service increases as the number of users increases'.[15] Network effects are closely associated with the concept of market multi-sidedness.[16] A multi-sided market is one that involves two or more interrelated sources of demand. A digital platform exhibits multi-sidedness when it connects at least two different and well-identified groups of users.[17] For instance, an online search engine satisfies the demands of individual users who want answers to their search queries, and of advertisers who wish to reach consumers with certain characteristics. The Commission Digital Report nonetheless notes that although multi-sidedness is a characteristic of many if not most digital platform activities, it is not a *necessary* element, citing the messaging system WhatsApp as an example of an entity subject to network effects but falling outside the multi-sided paradigm.[18]

Network externalities undoubtedly can generate benefits for users and enhance consumer welfare from this perspective: simply put, a product may become more valuable to a consumer merely by virtue of the fact that an increasing number of *other* consumers also use that product, i.e. are part of the same network. From a competition policy perspective, positive network externalities may imply that concentration is desirable, or at least it is the most efficient market structure.[19] This is because, other things being equal, a larger platform that services (and thus connects) a greater number of users provides a more valuable product to those users.[20] Moreover, even if a new technologically or otherwise superior product emerges, the presence of network externalities poses a barrier to switching by consumers. There is, in short, a coordination problem: users overall would be better off switching, but have little incentive to do so individually, because this entails giving up the benefits of the network.[21]

[12] Commission Digital Report, 20. [13] Ibid.

[14] Arguing persuasively that zero-price markets are markets susceptible to antitrust regulation nonetheless, see J. Newman, 'Antitrust in Zero-Price Markets: Foundations' (2015) 164 *U Pa LR* 149. See also discussion of zero-price products in the context of market definition under Art. 102 in Chap. 6, Section 8.A.vi.

[15] Commission Digital Report, 20. [16] See Chap. 3. [17] Commission Digital Report, 21.

[18] Ibid. [19] Ibid., 23. [20] Ibid., 22. [21] Ibid.

Multi-sidedness is also relevant from a competition policy perspective insofar as interventions which affect competition on one side of a market can have knock-on effects in others. This might, for instance, affect the antitrust assessment of allegedly predatory prices, where low or even zero-prices on one side of the market are funded by profits earned on another related side.[22] The Commission Digital Report notes that '[i]t is perfectly natural and can be pro-competitive for a platform to subsidise one side of the market when its presence on the platform is very valuable to the other side'.[23] Conversely, self-preferencing—i.e. 'giving preferential treatment to one's own products or services when they are in competition with products and services provided by other entities using the platform'[24]—is a well-recognised competition concern in the digital context.

The third characteristic discussed by the Commission Digital Report is the central role of data.[25] Digitisation enables companies to collect, store, and use large quantities of data, which facilitates, inter alia, the effective monetisation of existing products and business models and the development of innovative new ones. Because data is often obtained as a by-product of the day-to-day operation of a platform, incumbents with access to a steady stream of new data may have a competitive advantage. Yet the Commission Digital Report emphasised that, in reality, data is a complex phenomenon, raising equally complicated questions about the extent to which it impacts upon competition and, in turn, whether it should be regulated by competition law.[26] Data encompasses various types—volunteered, observed, inferred[27]—which can be put to many uses by digital actors.[28] Yet raw data, in itself, is of limited use; rather, it is the algorithms that process the data which turn it into something that can impact the operation of markets. The use of *personal* data is further regulated (and constrained) by data protection rules—in the EU, the primary instrument being the General Data Protection Regulation (GDPR).[29]

These characteristics of digital markets, together, tend to lead to 'tipping' in the digital sector, whereby the market coalesces around a single, ultra-dominant provider.[30] Markets that are prone to tipping are not impervious to competition, but it tends to be frontloaded, in the form of competition 'for the market' initially.[31] Once the market tips, the successful platform is largely insulated from competition for the foreseeable future, due to e.g. the economic unviability of challenging an incumbent profiting from significant scale economies, the difficulties of persuading consumers to switch where this entails giving up the benefits of network effects, the technical infeasibility of developing competing products without access to relevant user data, etc. Displacing a leading digital platform is not impossible—Facebook overtaking MySpace in the late 2000s is a much-cited example—but it can be practically very difficult, thus enabling the successful incumbent to enjoy significant market power in the interim.[32]

[22] See e.g. A. Fletcher, 'Predatory Pricing in Two-sided Markets: A Brief Comment' (2007) 3 *Competition Policy International* 221, and generally, M. Katz and J. Sallet, 'Multisided Platforms and Antitrust Enforcement' (2018) 127 *Yale LJ* 2142.

[23] Commission Digital Report, 22. [24] Ibid., 7.

[25] Ibid., 24. See also I. Graef, 'Market Definition and Market Power in Data: The Case of Online Platforms' (2015) 38 *World Competition* 473; and H. Shelanski, 'Information, Innovation and Competition Policy for the Internet' (2013) 161 *U Pa LR* 1663, 1678–1680.

[26] Commission Digital Report, 24–29. [27] Ibid., 24–25.

[28] The Commission Digital Report, 25, cites four categories: non-anonymous use of individual-level data, anonymous use of individual level data, aggregated data, and contextual data.

[29] Reg. (EU) 2016/679 of the European Parliament and of the Council of 27 April 2016 on the protection of natural persons with regard to the processing of personal data and on the free movement of such data, and repealing Dir. 95/46/EC [2016] OJ L119/1.

[30] Lancieri and Morita-Sakowski, n. 6, 75. [31] Ibid.

[32] Arguing, conversely, that consumer-facing digital platforms do not face winner-takes-all competition, but rather must compete on the merits or else use exclusionary practices to maintain their market share, see H. Hovenkamp, 'Antitrust and Platform Monopoly' (2021) *Yale LJ* 1952.

There is a further aspect of the digital economy that is discussed relatively little in competition policy reports but is arguably implicit in the apparent consensus that such markets require greater intervention. This is the fact that many of these sectors are chronically under-regulated at present, not merely from a competition perspective, but in broader economic and social policy terms too. This is, in part, because of the innovativeness of the services provided or business models utilised: regulation has simply failed to keep up with these new practices. It is also, arguably, partly because of a policy choice for regulatory restraint in the dynamic context of the digital economy, where policy-makers can be reluctant to intervene for fear of diminishing innovation. Less benignly, however, the explanation may be that certain digital business models exist precisely to escape conventional regulation as it applies to more analogue actors, including in areas like taxation, labour rights, public hire vehicle regulation, and tourist accommodation laws. Furthermore, the growth of the digital economy has exacerbated problems like fake news, hate speech, and efforts at election meddling, with limited legal consequences for digital platforms that facilitate or tolerate such practices. This stunning absence of regulation has arguably heightened calls for intervention on an antitrust basis, as the most immediate way that the EU can 'do something' within its limited powers in the digital sphere.[33]

4. EU COMPETITION LAW ENFORCEMENT IN THE DIGITAL SPHERE

The distinctive characteristics of the digital economy increase the likelihood that durable positions of significant market power will arise; they also complicate competition law analysis, as features like market multi-sidedness, zero-price products, and the centrality of data challenge our conventional approaches to understanding market dynamics and harms. Yet an advantage of the open-textured nature of the competition rules is that this apparent ambiguity incorporates a large degree of flexibility. Articles 101 and 102 have been described as 'magic boxes, capable of expanding their contents'[34] to address new forms of corporate misbehaviour. Accordingly, it has long been argued that, despite the particularities of the digital economy, the competition rules are sufficiently 'supple' to adapt.[35] This was, similarly, the conclusion of the experts who produced the Commission Digital Report. In the extract below, they explain their view that competition law remains the most appropriate vehicle by which to pursue well-functioning competitive digital markets—even if certain tweaks to the existing framework, both procedural and substantive, are likely to be required.

J. Crémer, Y.-A. de Montjoye, and H. Schweitzer, *Competition Policy for the Digital Era* (2019), 39

Despite the differences between the economics of the digital sector and those of other sectors of the economy, it is widely accepted, and we concur, that vigorous competition continues to be the best way to serve the interests of consumers and the economy as a whole. The goal of competition policy as set out in Protocol No. 27 on the internal market and competition annexed to the Treaty on the Functioning

[33] The phrase comes from an interview with Commissioner Vestager in *The Observer*, 'Interview with Margrethe Vestager: "We are doing this because people are angry"', 17 September 2018.

[34] G Amato, *Antitrust and the Bounds of Power: The Dilemma of Liberal Democracy in the History of the Market* (Hart Publishing, 1997), 43.

[35] Posner, n. 7, 2.

> of the EU remains valid in the digital era, namely the goal to establish and protect 'a system ensuring that competition is not distorted'.
>
> Over the last 60 years, EU competition rules have provided a solid basis for protecting competition in a broad variety of market settings. Competition law doctrine has evolved and reacted to the varying challenges on a case-by-case basis. This evolutionary method has allowed competition law enforcers to react to changing circumstances based on the solid empirical evidence of real-life cases. At the same time, the stable core of EU competition rules has prevented EU competition policy from following fashions. We are convinced that the basic framework of competition law, as embedded in Articles 101 and 102 of the TFEU, continues to provide a sound and sufficiently flexible basis for protecting competition in the digital era. However, the challenges stemming from the rise of the Internet, the 'new economy' and, today, the digital economy do require an adaptation of the way this basic framework is applied. The specificities of platforms, digital ecosystems and the data economy require adaptation and refinement of established concepts, doctrines and methodologies, and competition law enforcement itself.

The argument that the EU competition rules are sufficiently broadly-framed to regulate digital competition problems is borne out by the simple fact that, for several decades, these rules have been applied to do precisely that.[36] This section provides a short overview of enforcement activity in the digital economy to date; it should be read alongside the more extensive discussions of the relevant cases in the preceding chapters.

Article 102, unsurprisingly, is the area where the most prominent cases attacking the market power of Big Tech giants have arisen. The *IBM* case, which commenced in the late 1970s, has been described as Europe's 'first big antitrust case'.[37] It required the Commission to get to grips with the then-nascent and evolving markets for mainframe computers and peripheral equipment. While the case ended in an informal settlement, its terms were not unimportant: IBM committed to providing interoperability information,[38] thus prefiguring the remedy in *Microsoft*[39] and indeed many of the obligations under the Digital Markets Act.[40]

The *Microsoft* case itself represented a crucial milestone in the adaptation of EU competition law to the particularities of the digital economy. It involved an infringement decision against a super-dominant, US-based technology firm, and a then record-breaking fine. The theories of harm deployed—tying and refusal to supply—were well established in traditional case law. Yet, in each instance, the Commission was obliged to adapt and essentially re-engineer the applicable legal standard to provide a meaningful benchmark in a market context far from the worlds of nail guns and newspaper delivery.[41] The *Microsoft* decision and subsequent GC judgment have their critics, but the holding and the reasoning therein have stood the test of time. What proved more problematic was the

[36] For further discussion, see V. Robertson, 'Antitrust Law and Digital Market. A Guide to the European Competition Law Experience in the Digital Economy' in H. Kurz, M. Schütz, R. Strohmaier, and S. Zilian (eds.), *The Routledge Handbook of Smart Technologies: An Economic and Social Perspective* (Routledge, 2022), Chap. 21; A. Kontosakou, 'European Antitrust Enforcement in the Digital Era: How It Started, How It's Going, and the Risks Lying Ahead' (2022) 67 *Ant Bull* 522.

[37] A. Van Laer, 'The European Lilliputians Attacking IBM: Balancing Innovation and Competition in the European Commission's First Big Antitrust Case (1973–1984)' (2020) 62 *Business History* 837.

[38] [1984] 3 CMLR 147.

[39] COMP/37.792, *Microsoft* 24 March 2004; essentially upheld on appeal in Case T-201/04, *Microsoft v Commission* EU:T:2007:289.

[40] See discussion in Section 6.

[41] Notably, adding a foreclosure requirement in the context of tying, while modifying the *Bronner* criteria to catch behaviour that prevents 'technical development' in the context of refusal to deal. See Chap. 7, Sections 11 and 12.

implementation of the subsequent remedy,[42] which has fuelled a perception that competition law may not be so nimble when it comes to actually *fixing* digital competition problems.

As the digital economy has expanded, so too has the number of cases pursued by the Commission against large digital actors across a variety of market segments. The trio of infringement decisions against Google from 2017–2019—*Shopping*, *Android*, and *AdSense*—is the most high-profile strand of activity. The cases cover sectors as diverse as online search engines and comparison-shopping services,[43] mobile operating systems and software applications used in smartphones,[44] and advertising services offered to online publishers.[45] What connects these disparate activities is Google's core business model as an 'attention broker',[46] selling eyeballs to advertisers. The markets concerned are marked by many of the apparently challenging features discussed in the preceding section, including multi-sidedness and network effects, zero-price products, and the role of data as a barrier to entry and critical driver of competitive success. Yet these were not insurmountable obstacles to the articulation of plausible theories of harm, whether reflecting established categories of abusive behaviour—tying,[47] exclusive dealing[48]—or more novel types like self-preferencing.[49] Indeed, in *Google Shopping* the GC was more convinced than the Commission that placement within Google's general search results could be 'indispensable' within the meaning of the demanding *Bronner* criteria, once factors like high upfront investment, scale economies, and network effects were considered.[50] Once again, record-breaking fines were imposed in these decisions, and thus far, the Commission's efforts have largely survived appeal before the GC.[51]

The *Google* decisions appear to have opened the floodgates for enforcement against Big Tech at EU level. In late 2022, the Commission entered into a commitments decision with Amazon addressing various alleged self-preferencing practices relating to its online retail marketplace.[52] The *Amazon Marketplace* and *Buy Box* investigations moreover come half a decade after that undertaking agreed commitments to end abusive practices with respect to its e-book sales policies.[53] As described in Chapter 7, at the time of writing the Commission has further complaints ongoing against Google,[54] Apple,[55] and Meta (Facebook).[56] Though beyond the focus of this textbook, several of the larger national

[42] Resulting in two Commission decisions finding non-compliance, Decision of 12 July 2006, C(2006)4420 and Decision of 27 February 2008, C(2008) 764. See also Chap. 13.

[43] AT.39740, *Google Search (Shopping)* 27 June 2017.

[44] AT.40099, *Google Android* 18 July 2018.

[45] AT.40411 *Google Search (AdSense)* 20 March 2019.

[46] Involving 'the resale of human attention. It is to attract attention by offering something to the public (entertainment, news, free services, and so on), and then reselling that attention to advertisers for cash.' See T. Wu, 'Blind Spot: The Attention Economy and the Law' (2019) 82 *Antitrust LJ* 771, 772.

[47] In *Android*; see discussion in Chap. 7, Section 11.

[48] In both *Android* (though this finding did not survive appeal before the GC) and *AdSense*; see discussion in Chap. 7, Section 10.

[49] In *Shopping*; see discussion in Chap. 7, Section 13.

[50] Case T-612/17, *Google Shopping* EU:T:2021:763, paras. 224–227.

[51] Ibid. and Case T-604/18, *Google Android* EU:T:2022:541.

[52] AT.40462, *Amazon Marketplace* and AT.40703, *Amazon Buy Box* 20 December 2022. See discussion in Chap. 7, Section 13.C.

[53] AT.40153 *E-book MFNs and related matters (Amazon)* 4 May 2017. See discussion in Chap. 7, Section 16.B.

[54] Commission Press Release, 'Antitrust: Commission sends Statement of Objections to Google over abusive practices in online advertising technology', 14 June 2023, and J. Masson, 'Google Confirms EU Play Store Investigation', *Global Competition Review*, 28 October 2022, <https://globalcompetitionreview.com/article/google-confirms-eu-play-store-investigation>. Note, however, that in December 2022 the Commission closed an investigation into possible anti-competitive collusive conduct by Google and Facebook in the area of online display advertising (Case AT.40774, *Google-Meta (Open Bidding) agreement*).

[55] Commission Press Release, 'Antitrust: Commission sends Statement of Objections to Apple over practices regarding Apple Pay', 2 May 2022, and Commission Press Release, 'Antitrust: Commission sends Statement of Objections to Apple clarifying concerns over App Store rules for music streaming providers', 28 February 2023.

[56] Commission Press Release, 'Antitrust: Commission sends Statement of Objections to Meta over abusive practices benefiting Facebook Marketplace', 19 December 2022.

competition authorities have also been active in applying domestic and EU competition rules against the tech giants.[57]

Outside the immediate context of the largest tech platforms, the Commission has considerable experience applying Article 102 in sectors adjacent to or forming part of the physical infrastructure of the digital economy. These include numerous cases in the semiconductor industry[58] and involving standard-essential patents.[59]

Under Article 101, the Commission has focused on restrictive practices in the e-commerce sphere. This aligns with the objective of the Digital Single Market Strategy to improve access for consumers and businesses to online goods and services.[60] In 2017, the Commission's E-Commerce Sector Inquiry provided evidence of the growing use of vertical restraints by manufacturers to constrain the vigorous retail-level competition enabled by online selling.[61] The Commission responded, inter alia, by updating the Vertical Block Exemption Regulation (VBER) and Vertical Guidelines to better reflect distribution practices online.[62] It also pursued various infringement decisions against manufacturers that use obviously problematic vertical restraints. These can be grouped broadly into two categories: resale price maintenance (RPM)[63] and barriers to cross-border sales.[64]

What is most remarkable about these decisions is the orthodoxy of the Commission's approach to assessment of the practices, despite the digital context. Both categories of restraints were treated as 'by object' restrictions contrary to Article 101(1), with the Commission relying upon much earlier and fairly formalistic case law to support its conclusion of, essentially, per se illegality. Notably, the Commission failed to conduct the context-specific assessment of the restraints that would appear to be required in light of judgment like *Cartes Bancaires*[65] and *Maxima Latvija*.[66] Had it done so, it may be questionable whether the practices, particularly RPM, could be found to rise to the level of inherent harmfulness from a competition perspective, so as to merit 'by object' prohibition. On the one hand, it is clear that the digital context may exacerbate the restrictive impact of these practices, thus justifying their continued regulation. The widespread use of price-setting algorithms by online retailers, for instance, can greatly enhance the effectiveness of RPM in maintaining elevated retail prices.[67] On the other, the justifications given by small and medium-sized producers for using vertical restraints online may be more compelling, particularly in order to counter the considerable market power of the largest online sales platforms.[68] The latter concern arguably persuaded the CJ in its *Coty* judgment,

[57] National level enforcement is also discussed in Robertson, n. 36.

[58] COMP/37.990, *Intel* 13 May 2009 (although overturned on appeal in Case T-286/09 RENV, *Intel Corp v Commission* EU:T:2022:19); AT.40220, *Qualcomm (Exclusivity payments)* 24 January 2018 (also overturned on appeal in Case T-235/18, *Qualcomm Inc* EU:T:2022:358); AT.39711, *Qualcomm (Predation)* 18 July 2019; and AT.40608, *Broadcom* 7 October 2020.

[59] See COMP/38.636, *Rambus* 9 December 2009, COMP/39.939, *Samsung* 29 April 2014, and COMP/39.985, *Motorola* 29 April 2014.

[60] See n. 3.

[61] European Commission, 'Final report on the E-commerce Sector Inquiry', COM(2017) 229 final, 10 May 2017.

[62] See Chap. 11.

[63] AT.40181, *Philips*, AT.40182, *Pioneer*, AT.40465, *ASUS*, AT.40469, *Denon & Marantz* 24 July 2018, and AT.40428, *Guess* 17 December 2018.

[64] AT.40436, *Ancillary Sports Merchandise (Nike)* 25 March 2019, AT.40432, *Sanrio* 9 July 2019, AT.40413 *Focus Home*, AT.40414 *Koch Media*, AT.40420 *ZeniMax*, AT.40422, *Bandai Namco*, and AT.40424, *Capcom* 20 January 2021.

[65] Case C-67/13 P, *CB* EU:C:2014:2204.

[66] Case C-345/14, *Maxima Latvija* EU:C:2015:784.

[67] Both because manufacturers may use software-monitoring tools to scrutinise online pricing, thus enabling the detection of lower-than-permitted retail prices both more rapidly and more systematically (*Asus*, para. 27), and because the widespread use of price-setting algorithms by online retailers potentially reinforces the restrictive effect of individual RPM practices, preventing 'online price erosion', and resulting in a market-wide softening of price competition (*Pioneer*, paras. 134–139).

[68] See e.g. Oxera, 'Why vertical restraints? New evidence from a business survey', *Oxera Agenda*, April 2016 <www.oxera.com/wp-content/uploads/2018/07/Why-vertical-restraints-New-evidence-from-a-business-survey-1.pdf-1.pdf>.

where the Court accepted that manufacturers may have a legitimate interest in constraining (though not necessarily outright prohibiting[69]) online sales.[70]

Another e-commerce issue that has seen considerable scrutiny under Article 101, albeit not at EU level, is the treatment of 'most favoured nations' (MFN) or parity clauses, particularly their use by online intermediation services platforms.[71] The *Booking.com* investigation divided NCAs across the EU, with most concluding that narrow MFNs[72] are permissible but that wide MFNs[73] could breach Article 101(1).[74] Germany's Bundeskartellamt, however, held that both wide and narrow clauses are prohibited.[75] Parity clauses that 'caus[e] a buyer of online intermediation services not to offer, sell or resell goods or services to end users under more favourable conditions via competing online intermediation services' are listed in Article 5(1)(d) of the revised VBER as a new category of excluded restrictions, namely one which cannot be exempted under the Regulation and instead requires a case-by-case assessment under Article 101.

Finally, the *Eturas* judgment,[76] a preliminary reference stemming from enforcement activity of the Lithuanian competition authority, confirms the capacity of Article 101 to prohibit hub and spoke cartels administered by an online intermediation services provider. The key question is whether the requisite element of coordination can be established through sufficient 'objective and consistent' evidence.[77] The risk that parallel vertical restraints may disguise more malign horizontal coordination was also a concern in the Commission's *Ebooks* investigation, which was ultimately settled on the basis of binding commitments from Apple and leading book publishers.[78]

Arguably, EU-level competition law enforcement has seen least success in the area of merger control. Big Tech's strategy of growth through acquisitions, but also of stifling future competition by removing potential rivals from the marketplace at an early stage, is infamous. Yet the Commission has intervened against only three acquisitions by 'GAFAM' to date,[79] and have never prohibited such a transaction. There is a strong perception that by failing to intervene against various critical acquisitions by today's Big Tech giants, the merger control framework in Europe and beyond has allowed

[69] Contrast Case C-439/09, *Pierre Fabre Dermo-Cosmétique* EU:C:2011:649.

[70] Case C-230/16, *Coty Germany* EU:C:2017:941. [71] See Chap. 11.

[72] A narrow MFN 'links the price and terms quoted on an online platform, to those available directly on the upstream supplier's website, ensuring that the former will not be less attractive than the latter': see A. Ezrachi, 'The Competitive Effects of Parity Clauses on Online Commerce' (2015) 11 *European Competition Journal* 488, 489.

[73] A wide MFN 'provides for similar protection on a wider scale, aiming to ensure that the price and terms quoted through the platform in question will not be higher than the price available directly on the upstream supplier's website or on any other platform': ibid.

[74] In April 2015, the NCAs of France, Italy, and Sweden jointly accepted commitments from Booking.com to this effect: see Autorité de la concurrence Press Release, '21 April 2015: Online hotel booking sector', <www.autoritedelaconcurrence.fr/en/communiques-de-presse/21-april-2015-online-hotel-booking-sector>.

[75] Bundeskartellamt, *Booking.com*, B 9-121/13, Decision of 23 December 2015. This decision was initially overturn on first appeal, but subsequently upheld by the Federal Supreme Court: see A. Deuschle, 'Good Night, "Most Favoured Nations" Clauses!', *D'Kart Antitrust Blog*, 19 May 2021, <www.d-kart.de/en/blog/2021/05/19/good-night-bestpreisklauseln/>.

[76] Case C-74/14, *'Eturas' UAB and Others v Lietuvos Respublikos konkurencijos taryba* EU:C:2016:42.

[77] Ibid., para. 37.

[78] AT.39847, *Ebooks* 12 December 2012 and 25 July 2013.

[79] As at June 2023. These were M.8124, *Microsoft/LinkedIn* 6 December 2016, M.9660, *Google/Fitbit* 17 December 2020, and M.10646, *Microsoft/Activision Blizzard* 15 May 2023, each of which were permitted subject to remedies.

the consolidation of very significant positions of market power that now require regulation through antitrust intervention.[80] There are at least two reasons for this lack of success.

First, the turnover thresholds applied to grant jurisdiction under the EUMR are peculiarly ill-suited to catch many transactions occurring in the digital sphere. Here, target companies often have little or no current turnover yet have a sticker price that runs to billions of euro. The Commission has occasionally been able to obtain jurisdiction at the behest of the merging parties[81] or following a referral from NCAs,[82] and it continues to rely upon essentially informal methods of obtaining jurisdiction under its Article 22 guidance issued in 2021.[83] It is arguably unsatisfactory that the regulation of such highly consequential transactions remains in effect discretionary. Yet the Commission Digital Report resisted calls to supplement the jurisdictional provisions of the EUMR in the digital context, cautioning about the enhanced transactions costs this would entail, and advising of the need to gather evidence of the effectiveness of any proposed alternatives.[84]

Secondly, the substantive assessment standard deployed under the EUMR—the significant impediment to effective competition (SIEC) test—focuses primarily on the competitive relationship between the merging parties at the time of the transaction, and on existing or sufficiently imminent competitive constraints.[85] It thus may fail to catch mergers where the principal concern is that future market changes *may* render one of the parties to the transaction a rather more important competitive presence, or that the transaction is intended to prevent the target from realising its potential (but by no means guaranteed) status as a future competitor of its new owner. Competition authorities worldwide, including the Commission, are now placing greater emphasis on potential competition in their assessment of digital mergers.[86] But it is not unfair to say that, by permitting mergers like *Google/DoubleClick*[87] and *Facebook/WhatsApp*[88] previously, the Commission appears to have significantly underestimated the extent to which these acquisitions would bolster the purchaser's market power.

A further issue is that the SIEC standard focuses exclusively on *competition* in the internal market. It can reflect parallel public interest concerns like data privacy only to the extent that these are conceptualised in antitrust-relevant terms like quality, choice, or innovation.[89] The *Google/Fitbit* merger is a notorious example of this limitation. Critics argued strongly that the transaction should be prohibited, insofar as 'the combination of Fitbit's health data with Google's other data creates unique opportunities for discrimination and exploitation of consumers in healthcare, health insurance and other sensitive

[80] Critiquing the Commission's efforts to date in this regard, see e.g. J. van den Boom and P. Samranchit, 'Digital Ecosystem Mergers in Big Tech—A Theory of Long-run Harm with Applications' (2022) 13 *JECLAP* 365 and H. Schmidt, 'Merger Regulation in the Digital Economy and the Forgotten Goal of Innovation' The updated reference is (2023) 11 *J of Antitrust Enforcement* i102. Noting, however, the comparative absence of empirical evidence (and attempting to provide some), see P. Affeldt and R. Kesler, 'Big Tech Acquisitions—Towards Empirical Evidence' (2021) 12 *JECLAP* 471. An interesting retrospective analysis of digital merger assessment by the UK's Competition and Markets Authority, alongside a consideration of what could have been done differently, is Lear, 'Ex-post Assessment of Merger Control Decisions in Digital Markets', 9 May 2019, <www.learlab.com/wp-content/uploads/2019/06/CMA_past_digital_mergers_GOV.UK_version-1.pdf>.

[81] As in COMP/M.721, *Facebook/WhatsApp* 3 October 2014.

[82] As in M.8788, *Apple/Shazam* 6 September 2018.

[83] Commission Guidance on the application of the referral mechanism set out in Article 22 of the Merger Regulation to certain categories of cases, C(2021) 1959 final, 26 March 2021. See discussion in Chap. 15.

[84] Commission Digital Report, 115–116.

[85] See Chap. 15.

[86] See OECD, 'Potential Competition' (2012), <www.oecd.org/daf/competition/the-concept-of-potential-competition.htm>.

[87] COMP/M.4731, *Google/DoubleClick* 11 March 2008. [88] See n. 81.

[89] An approach first adopted in M.8124, *Microsoft/LinkedIn* 6 December 2016.

areas, with major implications for privacy too'.[90] While specific data protection rules regulate the latter, these 'have known limitations', and in any event it was argued that competition authorities 'cannot just look away hoping that privacy regulators will pick up the ball'.[91] These concerns did not persuade the Commission, which permitted the transaction with behavioural remedies that focused on ensuring post-merger competition in advertising markets and on interoperability between wearable health devices and smartphones.[92] On the data privacy point, the Commission was blunt: 'such concerns are not within the remit of merger control and there are regulatory tools better placed to address them'.[93]

Finally, the growth of the digital economy impacts not just the *sort of cases* that are coming across the Commission's competition docket, but also the *process* of enforcement. Chapter 13 discussed ways in which digitalisation is both facilitating and potentially complicating public enforcement, from the use of eLeniency tools to the complexity of dealing with seized digital evidence. A more nascent development, but one of potentially great importance in future, is 'computational antitrust'. This involves the development of computational methods to enable the automation of enforcement, in order 'to maintain and improve antitrust agencies' ability to detect, analyse, and remedy anti-competitive practices'.[94] It remains, for all competition agencies today, a work in progress.[95]

5. ENFORCEMENT CHALLENGES IN DIGITAL MARKETS

The preceding discussion illustrated the extent to which the digital economy can be regulated under the conventional EU competition law framework. Yet, although enforcement is clearly possible, it faces challenges that may delay or inhibit effective application of the competition rules in this context.[96]

A. SCOPE OF APPLICATION OF THE EU COMPETITION RULES

A first problem is the scope of the EU rules, which are not always well calibrated to catch harmful behaviour arising in the digital sphere. We saw a first example in the realm of merger control, where the turnover-focused basis of jurisdiction under the EUMR fails to capture many high-value and highly consequential transactions involving target companies with limited turnover. An equally

[90] M. Bourreau et al., 'Google/Fitbit will monetise health data and harm consumers', CEPR Policy Insight No. 107, September 2020, 1, <https://cepr.org/system/files/2022-08/PolicyInsight107.pdf>.

[91] Ibid., 3.

[92] M.9660, *Google/Fitbit* 17 December 2020. For discussion of the remedies, see S. Vande Walle, 'Clearance: The European Commission Clears the Acquisition of a Maker of Fitness Trackers and Smartwatches by a Major Online Platform, Subject to Long-lasting Behavioural Remedies (*Fitbit/Google*)' (2021) 3 *Concurrences* Art. No. 101736, 123–126.

[93] European Commission Press Release, 'Mergers: Commission clears acquisition of Fitbit by Google, subject to conditions', 17 December 2020.

[94] T. Schrepel, 'Computational Antitrust: An Introduction and Research Agenda' (2021) *Stanford Computational Antitrust*, <https://papers.ssrn.com/sol3/papers.cfm?abstract_id=3766960>. See also J. Amthauer, J. Fleiß, F. Guggi, and V. Robertson, 'Ready or Not? A Systematic Review of Case Studies Using Data-Driven Approaches to Detect Real-World Antitrust Violations', Graz Law Working Paper No. 19-2022 (2022), <https://papers.ssrn.com/sol3/papers.cfm?abstract_id=4304371>.

[95] Information on research projects and the efforts of different NCAs can be found on the website of the Stanford Computational Antitrust project, <https://law.stanford.edu/codex-the-stanford-center-for-legal-informatics/computational-antitrust/>.

[96] See, generally, H. Hovenkamp, 'Antitrust Presumptions for Digital Platforms', University of Pennsylvania, Institute for Law & Econ Research Paper No. 22-42 (2022), <https://papers.ssrn.com/sol3/papers.cfm?abstract_id=4224554>.

acute concern is the need to establish a dominant position in a relevant market to trigger the application of Article 102.[97] This is not, as the many recent investigations against 'GAFAM' demonstrate, an insurmountable obstacle to enforcement. Yet there are several potential difficulties.

(i) Market Definition

The first difficulty relates to the preliminary task of market definition, which the Union Courts have consistently confirmed is a necessary prerequisite to finding dominance within the meaning of Article 102.[98] Yet, if market definition is an inexact science in more analogue contexts, it is particularly complicated in the digital economy.[99] The traditional approach is premised upon identifying the products and suppliers that impose competitive constraints on would-be dominant undertakings, meaning that price increases by the latter result in increased demand for the former.[100] Yet where market multisidedness and network externalities exist, measuring prices and demand is more difficult.[101] This is further complicated by the widespread presence of zero-price products in the digital economy, which makes the conventional SSNIP test[102] rather meaningless.[103] The GC has instead approved the use of a 'small but significant non-transitory decrease in quality' (SSNDQ) test,[104] but there are concerns about the extent to which this approach can be operationalised in practice.[105]

Digital markets are also marked by continuous development and evolution. This results in 'fluid, quickly-changing relationships of substitutability and possibly partial overlaps of varying significance between different services, sometimes combined with practices of multi-homing and/or changing perceptions of consumer needs'.[106] There may be a need to define innovation markets, focusing on the dynamic nature of competition.[107]

Finally, many commentators argue that the conventional 'relevant market' concept is less appropriate or useful in the digital context. Instead, at least in certain segments, 'firms compete to draw consumers into more or less comprehensive ecosystems'.[108] While the concept of a digital ecosystem is still evolving, it can be defined broadly as: 'communities of collaborating firms that collectively produce goods, services, or solutions, that coevolve their products under an aligned vision and that must deal with either unique or supermodular complementarities that are non-generic, requiring the creation of a specific structure of relationships and alignment to create value'.[109] From a competition policy perspective, it is necessary to consider *inter*-ecosystem competition (substitutability between multi-product ecosystems), *horizontal intra*-ecosystem competition (between firms offering rivalrous, potentially substitute offerings within the same ecosystem), and *vertical intra*-ecosystem

[97] See Chap. 6, Sections 7–9. [98] See Chap. 6, Section 8.

[99] See e.g. J. Franck and M. Peitz, 'Market Definition in the Platform Economy' (2021) 23 *CYELS* 91; M. Eben and V. Robertson, 'Digital Market Definition in the European Union, United States, and Brazil: Past, Present, and Future' (2021) 18 *J of Competition Law and Economics* 417; R. Smith and A. Duke, 'Platform Businesses and Market Definition' (2020) 17 *European Competition Journal* 93.

[100] See Chap. 3. [101] Commission Digital Report, 42–43.

[102] Which requires regulators to consider the likely impact on demand of a 'small but significant non-transitory increase in price': see Chap. 3, Section 4.E.

[103] Commission Digital Report, 44–45. [104] Case T-604/18, *Google Android* EU:T:2022:541, paras. 176–177.

[105] OECD, 'Quality Considerations in Digital Zero-Price Markets' (2018), <www.oecd.org/daf/competition/quality-considerations-in-the-zero-price-economy.htm>.

[106] Commission Digital Report, 47.

[107] P. Alexiadis and A. de Streel, 'Designing an EU Intervention Standard for Digital Platforms', EUI Working Papers RSCAS 2020/14 (2020), 27–28.

[108] Commission Digital Report, 47.

[109] M. Jacobides and I. Lianos, 'Ecosystems and Competition Law in Theory and Practice' (2021) 30 *Industrial and Corporate Change* 1199, 1200–1201.

competition (typically referring to restraints that may be imposed by the orchestrator of the ecosystem on other suppliers operating within the platform).[110]

The ecosystem concept was considered and endorsed by the GC in the *Android* judgment. In the extract below, the GC explains how the established 'relevant market' requirement under Article 102 can be adapted to reflect the existence of a wider digital ecosystem, 'which brings together several categories of supplier, customer and consumer and causes them to interact within a platform'.[111] The judgment emphasises, however, the fact-specific, detailed nature of the inquiry required in such cases, and does not shy away from acknowledging the complexity of this exercise. Accordingly, even if ecosystem competition can be accommodated within the framework of Article 102 analysis, it makes the preliminary task of identifying existing and potential future competitive constraints that much more complicated in practice.

Case T-604/18, *Google and Alphabet v Commission (Google Android)* EU:T:2022:541

General Court

109. In that regard, it must be pointed out that the purpose of determining the relevant market and the dominant position held on that market by the undertaking concerned is not only to define the fact and extent of internal competitive constraints specific to that market, but also to verify that there are no external competitive constraints from products, services or territories other than those which form part of the relevant market under consideration.

110. In general terms, it is necessary for the Commission to identify and define the boundaries within which the undertakings compete in order to determine whether the undertaking concerned can, to an appreciable extent, act independently of the constraints imposed by effective competition.

111. As the Court of Justice has previously pointed out, the interchangeability and substitutability of products or services are naturally dynamic, in that a new supply may alter the conception of the products or services considered to be interchangeable with a product or service already present on the market or as substitutable for that product or a service and, in that way, justify a new definition of the parameters of the relevant market (. . . Generics (UK) and Others, C-307/18, EU:C:2020:52, paragraph 130).

112. Such a finding presupposes, however, that there is a sufficient degree of interchangeability between the products or services which form part of the relevant market and those envisaged to meet the demand on that market. That would be the case if the alternative provider was in a position to respond to demand within a short period of time with sufficient strength to constitute a serious counterbalance to the power held by the undertaking concerned on the relevant market (. . . Generics (UK) and Others, C-307/18, EU:C:2020:52, paragraphs 132 and 133).

113. Although, in certain circumstances, it may therefore be appropriate to examine the external constraint that an alternative supply might represent, it is also necessary to take account of the specific features inherent in certain situations, in particular in the case of several interlocking markets.

114. Although the principles set out above remain valid for the purpose of defining a clear and transparent analytical framework for the concepts of relevant market and dominance, their application sometimes calls for a more detailed examination, going beyond mere segmentation into markets, in order better to assess the competitive constraints prevailing on those markets and the position of economic strength enjoyed by the undertaking concerned.

115. That is particularly so in the case of markets which, as in the present case, fall within the digital economy, where traditional parameters such as the price of products or services or the market share of

[110] Ibid., 1201. [111] *Android*, para. 116.

> the undertaking concerned may be less important than in traditional markets, compared to other variables such as innovation, access to data, multi-sidedness, user behaviour or network effects.
>
> 116. Thus, in a digital 'ecosystem', which brings together several categories of supplier, customer and consumer and causes them to interact within a platform, the products or services which form part of the relevant markets that make up that ecosystem may overlap or be connected to each other on the basis of their horizontal or vertical complementarity. Taken together, the relevant markets may also have a global dimension in the light of the system that brings its components together and of any competitive constraints within that system or from other systems.
>
> 117. Identifying the conditions of competition relevant to the assessment of the position of economic strength enjoyed by the undertaking concerned may therefore require multi-level or multi-directional examination in order to determine the fact and extent of the various competitive constraints that may be exerted on that undertaking.

The implications of this were seen in the *Android* case itself,[112] where the GC held that the competition constraint imposed on Google's Play Store by Apple's App Store could not be dissociated from the competition constraint imposed on the Android ecosystem by the Apple ecosystem more broadly. Yet the recognition of the ecosystem concept in *Android* offers little guidance as to how it arises in practice, or the implications for antitrust liability in such circumstances, with respect to either inter- or intra-platform competition. The Commission's decision with regard to tying in *Android*, upheld on appeal by the GC, has been criticised precisely on the basis that it failed to understand how the impugned practices related to the operation of the Android ecosystem, and how this informed competition with other ecosystems like Apple's.[113] The draft revised Market Definition Notice attempts to provide further assistance.[114] Yet in line with the non-prescriptive approach of the latter, it merely concludes that the relevant principles to assess a particular ecosystem might be those relating to aftermarkets, or for others the principles relating to bundles, and for yet still others some alternative unspecified framework entirely.[115]

(ii) Market Power Assessment

Once a plausible 'relevant market' is identified, then the task of assessing market power begins. Again, in the digital context, this is more difficult to do in a convincing fashion.[116] As the Commission Digital Report explains, market multi-sidedness makes market share figures an even more imperfect proxy for market power.[117] Network effects may generate significant power on one side of a platform, even if

[112] Discussed in Chap. 6, Section 8.a.i.

[113] P. Siciliani, 'On the Law and Economics of the *Android* Case' (2020) 10 *JECLAP* 638.

[114] Commission Press Release, 'Competition: Commission seeks feedback on draft revised Market Definition Notice', 8 November 2022, <https://ec.europa.eu/commission/presscorner/detail/en/ip_22_6528>, which provides access to the text, paras. 99–103.

[115] Ibid., para. 103.

[116] See e.g. E. Calvano and M. Polo, 'Market Power, Competition and Innovation in Digital Markets: A Survey' (2021) 54 *Information Economics and Policy* 100853; D. Moss, 'Toward a Coherent Approach to Market Power in the Digital Sector: Complexity, Growth through Acquisition, and Remedies' (2022) 67 *Ant Bull* 536. Arguing for a different way of conceptualising harmful power in this context, see A. Gerbrandy and P. Phoa, 'The Power of Big Tech Corporations as Modern Bigness and a Vocabulary for Shaping Competition Law as Counter-power' in M. Bennett, H. Brouwer, and R. Claassen (eds.), *Wealth and Power* (Routledge, 2022).

[117] Commission Digital Report, 48–49.

the related side remains fiercely competitive.[118] Market dominance may, alternatively or additionally, hinge on access to or control over large quantities of commercially valuable data.[119] The Commission Digital Report argues that, 'in digital markets there is no single parameter that would enable competition authorities to measure market power, or to declare that a firm is dominant, even as a rough approximation'.[120]

Things get even more complicated if one moves away from the concept of market power as such, and instead focuses on what has variously been described as 'platform power',[121] 'intermediation power',[122] 'strategic market status',[123] or 'gatekeeper' power.[124] These notions all reflect the broader function of digital platforms as 'market makers [that] play a pivotal role in the digital ecosystem as a result of factors such as their size, business model and connection capacity'.[125] From this perspective, the pivotal characteristics from a regulatory perspective are *connectivity* (insofar as the platform controls access to certain markets, services, customer groups, or even data) and *dependence* (on the part of consumers *and* other businesses).[126] These features can arise even where an undertaking's market share, however measured, falls significantly below the 40 per cent threshold[127] beneath which the Commission considers that dominance is 'not likely' to arise.[128] The question is thus if and how the existing dominance concept can be adapted to accommodate the overlapping but not quite contiguous concerns generated by gatekeeper power, or whether instead we need a parallel set of regulatory rules to address this issue, as considered later in Section 6.

(iii) Concepts of 'Agreement' and 'Concerted Practice'

Although the debate about the suitability of the existing competition framework to regulate the digital economy has focused on unilateral conduct, a prominent concern has arisen with respect to coordination: namely, the extent to which Article 101 might apply to algorithmic collusion. Where undertakings deliberately coordinate their use of price-setting algorithms in order to fix prices, the underlying behaviour easily comes within the scope of the prohibition on anti-competitive agreements and concerted practices under Article 101(1).[129] If, however, a number of pricing algorithms 'learn' organically to engage in collusive behaviour, the position is more complicated. The problem is that absent any positive direction from the undertakings concerned, such behaviour may benefit from the lacuna for conscious parallelism,[130] thus falling outside the regulatory ambit

[118] Ibid., 49.

[119] Ibid. See also J. Eeckhout and L. Veldkamp, 'Data and Market Power', CEPR Discussion Paper No. DP17272 (2022), <https://papers.ssrn.com/sol3/papers.cfm?abstract_id=4121456>.

[120] Ibid., 50.

[121] O. Lynskey, 'Regulating "Platform Power"', LSE Law, Society and Economy Working Papers 1/2017, 9.

[122] Commission Digital Report, 49.

[123] 'Unlocking Digital Competition. Report of the Digital Expert Competition Panel', March 2019, particularly paras. 2.25–2.27.

[124] I. Graef, 'Differentiated Treatment in Platform-to-Business Relations: EU Competition Law and Economic Dependence' (2019) 38 *YEL* 448, 486.

[125] Lynskey, n. 121, 9.

[126] N. Dunne, 'Platforms as Regulators' (2021) 9 *J of Antitrust Enforcement* 244, 261.

[127] Commission Digital Report, 69–70.

[128] Guidance on the Commission's enforcement priorities in applying Article 82 of the EC Treaty to abusive exclusionary conduct by dominant undertakings [2009] OJ C 45/7, para. 14.

[129] As in Case 50223, *Online sales of posters and frames*, Decision of the UK Competition and Markets Authority of 12 August 2016 (applying domestic law but following EU case law to inform the concepts of agreement and concerted practice, see paras. 5.9–5.16).

[130] Case C-89/85, *Ahlström Osakeyhtiö ('Wood pulp')* EU:C:1993:120.

of Article 101.[131] The urgency of this problem from a competition policy perspective is disputed,[132] but there is evidence that pricing algorithms *can* learn to collude organically, even if there is little evidence to date that this is arising in practice.[133]

B. NOVEL OR CONTROVERSIAL THEORIES OF HARM

A second problem in digital markets is the need to apply novel or more controversial theories of harm to capture the problematic behaviour under scrutiny. On the one hand, this is unremarkable, given the innovative nature of competition (and thus potentially anti-competitive behaviour) within the digital economy. On the other, it raises concerns about legal certainty and fairness, even for large digital actors, and about the extent to which these theories of harm adhere to the underlying objectives of the EU competition framework. From the competition enforcer's perspective, there may be a greater likelihood of being overturned on appeal, a possibility that is detrimental not just because it can leave harmful behaviour unregulated, but also because it may damage the reputation and morale of an agency.

Below we consider three prominent issues of this sort that have either arisen in practice in the digital context or have been flagged as likely concerns in the literature. Notably, each of these practices are also reflected, to some extent, in the obligations imposed on gatekeeper platforms under the Digital Markets Act, discussed later.

(i) Self-preferencing

Self-preferencing was described in Chapter 7 as the preeminent theory of harm applied in contemporary competition enforcement against Big Tech platforms.[134] It is a form of leveraging, which the Commission in *Google Shopping* described as 'a well-established, independent, form of abuse falling outside the scope of competition on the merits'.[135] The GC rejected the breadth of this claim,[136] but was prepared to accept that, in the circumstances, the Commission provided sufficient evidence that Google's conduct departed from 'normal' competition. Controversially, the Court invoked the general principle of equal treatment to justify its holding that 'certain differences in treatment may be considered contrary to Article 102 TFEU when what is at issue are favouring practices established by operators in a dominant position in the internet sector'.[137] The frequency with which self-preferencing

[131] See e.g. A. Ezrachi and M. Stucke, *Virtual Competition* (Harvard University Press, 2016), Chap. 2; OECD, 'Algorithms and Collusion' (2017), <www.oecd.org/competition/algorithms-and-collusion.htm>; M. Gal, 'Algorithms as Illegal Agreements' (2019) 34 *Berkeley Technology LJ* 67; and G. Colangelo, 'Artificial Intelligence and Anticompetitive Collusion: From the "Meeting of Minds" Towards the "Meeting of Algorithms"?', TTLF Stanford Law School Working Paper No. 74 (2021).

[132] See e.g. A. Ittoo and N. Petit, 'Algorithmic Pricing Agents and Tacit Collusion: A Technological Perspective' in H. Jacquemin and A. de Streel (eds.), *L'intelligence artificielle et le droit* (Larcier, 2017); T. Schrepel, 'The Fundamental Unimportance of Algorithmic Collusion for Antitrust Law', *JOLT Digest*, 7 February 2020, <https://jolt.law.harvard.edu/digest/the-fundamental-unimportance-of-algorithmic-collusion-for-antitrust-law>; and C. Veljanovski, 'Pricing Algorithms as Collusive Devices' (2020), <https://papers.ssrn.com/sol3/papers.cfm?abstract_id=3644360>.

[133] E. Calvano, G. Calzolari, V. Denicolò, and S. Pastorello, 'Artificial Intelligence, Algorithmic Pricing and Collusion', CEPR Discussion Paper No. DP13405 (2019); P. Siciliani, 'Tackling Algorithmic-facilitated Tacit Collusion in a Proportionate Way' (2019) 10 *JECLAP* 31; F. Beneke and M. Mackenrodt, 'Remedies for Algorithmic Tacit Collusion' (2021) 9 *J of Antitrust Enforcement* 152; M. Gal, 'Limiting Algorithmic Collusion' (2023) *Berkeley Technology LR* forthcoming.

[134] See Chap. 7, Section 13. [135] AT.39740, *Google Search (Shopping)* 27 June 2017, para. 649.

[136] Case T-612/17, *Google Shopping* EU:T:2021:763, paras. 162–163.

[137] Ibid., para. 180. For discussion of the extent to which the *Google Shopping* judgment establishes a *general* principle of equal treatment under Art. 102, see Chap. 7, Section 13.B.

concerns arise in digital markets is directly connected to the multi-sided nature of digital platform activities, which give platforms both the opportunity and incentive to discriminate in favour of their own business activities at the expense of rival users of the platform. Yet the fundamental objection to conceptualising this conduct as an antitrust abuse is that self-preferencing is an innate characteristic of any self-maximising firm: think, for instance, of the vertically integrated firm that purchases inputs only from its upstream subsidiary, or that distributes its products downstream only through its integrated distribution wing. Self-preferencing is thus a theory of harm that pushes the boundary of Article 102 liability, by blurring the line between exclusion and non-discrimination.[138]

(ii) Non-compliance with Data Protection Obligations

The GDPR imposes an EU-wide regime that constrains what 'controllers' and 'processors' of personal data may do with that information. In contradistinction with, say, the EU telecommunications liberalisation regime, EU data protection law is not concerned primarily with maintaining a competitive market. This means that non-compliance may generate difficulties for the undertaking concerned under data privacy rules, but should not, in principle, have antitrust implications.[139] This was the approach taken by the CJ in *Asnef-Equifax*, where it held that 'any possible issues relating to the sensitivity of personal data are not, as such, a matter for competition law'.[140] We saw earlier that the Commission in the *Google/Fitbit* merger similarly insisted that such concerns do not fall within the remit of EU merger control.[141]

Nonetheless, it has been suggested that non-compliance with data protection obligations may violate Article 102, under a theory of harm that combines elements of both excessive pricing and the imposition of unfair contractual conditions. The leading case is an investigation by the German competition authority (Bundeskartellamt) into the data privacy policies of the online social network, Facebook. The thrust of the concern was consumer exploitation: namely, 'an abusive imposition of unfair conditions',[142] whereby poorly informed users were forced or manipulated into surrendering excessive quantities of personal data while using Facebook services. Central to the theory of harm was the fact that Facebook had failed to comply with its obligations under data protection law, which was treated essentially as a proxy for the parameters of 'normal' competition in data-intensive markets. In 2019, following a formal finding of 'abuse of market power based on the extent of collecting, using and merging data in a [Facebook] user account', the Bundeskartellamt imposed 'far-reaching restrictions' on Facebook's ability to collect and combine consumer data without adequate consent.[143] Significantly, however, it confined its findings to the relevant provisions of the German law on abuse of market power, arguably implicitly recognising that Article 102 does not (yet) treat violations of data protection law as abusive.[144] The decision was overturned on first appeal, but was reinstated by

[138] C. Bergqvist, 'Google and the Search for a Theory of Harm' (2018) 39 *ECLR* 149.

[139] For an overview of the relationship between EU data protection and competition laws, see F. Costa-Cabral and O. Lynskey, 'Family Ties: The Intersection Between Data Protection and Competition in EU Law' (2017) 54 *CMLRev* 11.

[140] Case C-238/05, *Asnef-Equifax* EU:C:2006:734, para. 63.

[141] See n. 92.

[142] Bundeskartellamt Press Release, 'Bundeskartellamt initiates proceeding against Facebook on suspicion of having abused its market power by infringing data protection rules', 2 March 2016. On consumer exploitation through data collection more generally, see A. Ezrachi and V. Robertson, 'Competition, Market Power and Third-party Tracking' (2019) 42 *World Competition* 5.

[143] Bundeskartellamt Press Release, 'Bundeskartellamt prohibits Facebook from combining user data from different sources. Background information on the Bundeskartellamt's Facebook proceeding', 7 February 2019, <www.bundeskartellamt.de/SharedDocs/Publikation/EN/Pressemitteilungen/2019/07_02_2019_Facebook_FAQs.pdf?__blob=publicationFile&v=6>.

[144] Ibid.

the Federal Court of Justice, which emphasised the denial of consumer choice as the key indicator of harm in the circumstances.[145] The case was also the subject of a preliminary reference to the CJ, which has focused on data protection rather than competition law aspects.[146]

The *Facebook* case illustrates clearly that zero-price services are not necessarily cost-less: in essence, the argument is that users inadvertently give up too much valuable personal data as the *quid pro quo* for use of this ostensibly free service. The investigation might thus be conceived of as an instance of excessive pricing in the digital age—although commentators disagree as to whether such an extension makes sense as a matter of competition law or policy.[147] Although the Bundeskartellamt additionally suggested that the behaviour may have knock-on *exclusionary* effects in the social network and targeted advertising markets,[148] it has been persuasively argued that the latter claims are tenuous and unrealistic.[149]

What the case illustrates most clearly are the weaknesses within the decentralised supervisory framework for data protection enforcement in the EU.[150] Facebook's activities are primarily regulated by the Irish data protection supervisor, but enforcement by the Irish authority was slow, to a point where it has been suggested that the innovative theory of harm was motivated primarily by a desperate need to plug a regulatory gap which could not be filled by the relevant sector-specific regulators in Germany.[151] One can sympathise with a Member State that considers that vital welfare interests of its citizens remain unprotected. Yet it is a more difficult question whether competition law should essentially be deployed to fill in gaps in the wider regulatory fabric of the digital economy. Similar objections have been raised to the application of competition law to address hate speech or fake news online, in the absence of adequate alternative regulation.[152]

[145] See Bundeskartellamt Press Release No. 080/2020, 'Federal Court of Justice provisionally confirms allegation of Facebook abusing dominant position', 23 June 2020, <www.bundeskartellamt.de/SharedDocs/Publikation/EN/Press emitteilungen/2020/23_06_2020_BGH_Facebook.pdf?__blob=publicationFile&v>. For discussion of the conflicting rulings, see A. Witt, 'Excessive Data Collection as a Form of Anticompetitive Conduct—The German Facebook Case' (2021) 66 *Ant Bull* 276, and R. Scheele, 'Facebook: From Data Privacy to a Concept of Abuse by Restriction of Choice' (2021) 12 *JECLAP* 34.

[146] Case C-252/21, *Facebook Inc and Others v Bundeskartellamt*, pending.

[147] Compare the generally favourable attitudes of M. Volmar and K. Helmdach, 'Protecting Consumers and their Data through Competition Law? Rethinking Abuse of Dominance in Light of the Federal Cartel Officer's Facebook Investigation' (2018) 14 *European Competition Journal* 195; M. Botta and K. Wiedemann, 'EU Competition Law Enforcement Vis-à-Vis Exploitative Conducts in the Data Economy—Exploring the Terra Incognita', Max Planck Institute for Innovation & Competition Research Paper No. 18-08 (2018); and G. Schneider, 'Testing Art. 102 TFEU in the Digital Marketplace: Insights from the Bundeskartellamt's Investigation against Facebook' (2018) 9 *JECLAP* 213, with the more sceptical perspectives of G. Colangelo and M. Maggiolino, 'Data Accumulation and the Privacy–Antitrust Interface: Insights from the Facebook Case' (2018) 8 *International Data Privacy Law* 224, and R. Van den Bergh and F. Weber, 'The German Facebook Saga: Abuse of Dominance or Abuse of Competition Law? (2021) 44 *World Competition* 29.

[148] 'In the authority's assessment, Facebook's conduct represents above all a so-called exploitative abuse. Dominant companies may not use exploitative practices to the detriment of the opposite side of the market, i.e. in this case the consumers who use Facebook. This applies above all if the exploitative practice also impedes competitors that are not able to amass such a treasure trove of data': Bundeskartellamt Press Release, n. 143.

[149] Colangelo and Maggiolino, n. 147.

[150] For further discussion of this aspect of the case, see N. Dunne, 'The Role of Regulation in EU Competition Law Assessment' (2021) 44 *World Competition* 287.

[151] R. Podszun, 'Facebook: Next Stop Europe', *D'Kart Blog*, 25 March 2021, <www.d-kart.de/en/blog/2021/03/25/facebook-next-stop-europe/>.

[152] N. Petit, *Big Tech and the Digital Economy: The Moligopoly Scenario* (Oxford University Press, 2020), Chap. 6.

(iii) Refusal to Supply 'Big Data'

Chapter 7 described the evolving case law on refusal to supply, encompassing access to both tangible and intangible assets. Arguably, the next frontier for refusal to supply case law under Article 102 is the possibility of treating access to valuable consumer data as a type of essential facility, thus generating an antitrust duty to supply. Section 3 highlighted the centrality of consumer data as a crucial input in digital markets. The question of whether access to data might be considered 'indispensable' in the antitrust sense, however, is much disputed.[153] It is clear that data *as such* cannot constitute a relevant product market, insofar as many diverse kinds and sources of data exist, which are substitutable to a greater or lesser extent.[154] All data is not equal, moreover, as different types of data may be more or less costly to collect, or their relevance may expire at a faster or slower rate (referred to as 'timeliness'). Access to data is also conditioned by other legal and institutional factors including, for personal data, the GDPR.[155]

The conventional objection to conceptualising data as an 'essential facility' is that data collection is a non-rivalrous activity: the fact that commercially valuable data is held by one (dominant) undertaking does not, generally, preclude rival firms from collecting equivalent data from alternative sources.[156] Critics also argue that claims for mandatory access effectively sanction free-riding, and query the utility of data transfers as such as opposed to the innovative—and proprietary—uses made of it by successful digital platforms. Colangelo and Maggiolino identify various practical problems for imposing a mandatory duty to supply data. These include the almost metaphysical question of what data, precisely, from a large and unknown 'Big Data' set must be provided, and whether, if timeliness is an issue, dominant firms might be subject to an ongoing obligation to update the data supplied.[157]

In practice, however, it may simply be impossible for a firm to obtain the sorts of data necessary to build a successful online platform without operating within that marketplace, creating a 'chicken and egg' problem which may tip access to consumer data into the category of indispensability.[158] In *Google Shopping*, the Commission treated Google's substantial data collection advantages as a barrier to entry reinforcing its dominant market position.[159] The Commission Digital Report goes further, explicitly arguing that a duty to grant access to data may arise under Article 102. Although it rejected a strict application of the *Bronner* test, it nonetheless advocated that 'indispensability' should operate as the central criterion by which to determine whether an antitrust duty to supply data arises.[160] While the GDPR provides a right of data portability for the benefit of 'data subjects',[161] this is not equivalent to an antitrust duty to deal (though could potentially provide a conduit by which to harmonise

[153] A comprehensive treatment is I. Graef, *EU Competition Law, Data Protection and Online Platforms: Data as Essential Facility* (Kluwer Law International, 2016); see also M. Gal and N. Elkin-Koren, 'Algorithmic Consumers' (2017) 30 *Harvard J of Law and Technology* 309 and on a sceptical note, C. Tucker, 'Digital Data, Platforms and the Usual [Antitrust] Suspects: Network Effects, Switching Costs, Essential Facility', 31 January 2019, <https://papers.ssrn.com/sol3/papers.cfm?abstract_id=3326385>.

[154] N. Schepp and A. Wambach, 'On Big Data and Its Relevance for Market Power Assessment' (2016) 7 *JECLAP* 120, 121. This point is also emphasised in the Commission Digital Report, 74.

[155] Commission Digital Report, 73. [156] Schepp and Wambach, n. 154, 123.

[157] G. Colangelo and M. Maggiolino, 'Big Data as Misleading Facilities' (2017) 13 *European Competition Journal* 249.

[158] See e.g. I. Graef, *EU Competition Law, Data Protection and Online Platforms: Data as Essential Facility* (Wolters Kluwer, 2016); and B. Lundquist, 'Standardization for the Digital Economy—The Issue of Interoperability and Access under Competition Law', Faculty of Law, Stockholm University Research Paper No. 10 (2017).

[159] AT39740, *Google Search (Shopping)* 27 June 2017. [160] Commission Digital Report, 98–105.

[161] GDPR, Art. 20.

approaches under competition and data protection laws going forward).[162] The Commission Digital Report concluded:

> Very likely, mandated data access will therefore, in the end, be a sector-specific regime, subject to some sort of regulation and regulatory oversight. Nonetheless, competition law can specify the general preconditions and give a more fundamental, pro-competitive orientation to the regulatory regimes that are likely to arise.[163]

C. SPEED OF INTERVENTION

A third problem when applying competition law in the digital economy is the speed (or perceived lack thereof) of intervention, particularly for cases occurring under Articles 101 and 102.[164] There are two interlinked aspects to this concern. On the one hand, a direct result of the complexity described in Section 3 is that digital economy investigations can take a long time.[165] Typically, the competition authority needs to acquaint itself as best it can with unfamiliar industry dynamics; it must engage in a detailed and time-consuming analysis to define the relevant market(s) and assess market power; and it may have to build a novel theory of harm that is sufficiently robust to survive the almost inevitable appeal against its finding. The seven-year lag between the first complaints in the *Google Shopping* investigation and the ultimate infringement decision is often cited as evidence of how drawn-out such proceedings can be[166]—although the quarter-century of enforcement activity in the more peripherally digital *Intel* case is perhaps the more striking and absurd example.[167]

On the other hand, it has been argued, it is precisely in the context of the rapidly moving digital economy that timely and effective enforcement is needed most acutely.[168] The propensity of digital markets to 'tip' into positions of sustained and entrenched market power makes early intervention vital in order to keep markets open and competitive. Perhaps counter-intuitively, this leads to the argument that more prescriptive closely tailored, sector-specific regulation may be more appropriate here.

A consequence of the 'need for speed' when it comes to antitrust (or antitrust-inspired) intervention in digital markets is that enforcers are being urged to make greater use of interim measures while investigations are ongoing.[169] Chapter 13 discussed the *Broadcom* case, in which the Commission exercised its power to impose interim measures for the first time in two decades, in a case involving exclusive dealing in the semiconductor industry.[170] Yet the evidence suggests that, '[a]lthough there may be good reasons to consider the *possibility* of using [interim measures] more often in cases involving

[162] See O. Lynskey, 'Aligning Data Protection Rights with Competition Law Remedies? The GDPR Right to Data Portability' (2017) 42 *ELRev* 793; and S. Lucchini, J. Moscianese, I. de Angelis, and F. Di Benedetto, 'Online Digital Services and Competition Law: Why Competition Authorities Should be More Concerned About Portability Rather Than About Privacy' (2018) 9 *JECLAP* 563.

[163] Commission Digital Report, 109.

[164] The Commission's ability to intervene under the EUMR is disciplined by the time limits for intervention set out in that Regulation: see Chap. 15.

[165] Commission Digital Report, 52. See also OECD, 'Ex ante regulation of digital markets. OECD Competition Committee Discussion Paper' (2021), <www.oecd.org/daf/competition/ex-ante-regulation-and-competition-in-digital-markets.htm>, 11–12.

[166] See Chap. 7, Section 13.

[167] See Chap. 7, Section 10.

[168] See e.g. P. Marsden and R. Podszun, 'Restoring Balance to Digital Competition—Sensible Rules, Effective Enforcement', Report for Konrad-Adenauer-Stiftung (2020).

[169] See discussion in OECD, 'Interim Measures in Antitrust Investigations' (2022), <www.oecd.org/daf/competition/interim-measures-in-antitrust-investigations.htm>.

[170] AT.40608, *Broadcom* 16 October 2019. See Chap. 13, Section 6.E.vii.

the digital economy, this does not mean that *deciding* in favour of [interim measures] should be automatic'.[171] Instead, a careful case-by-case assessment is required beforehand.

D. EFFECTIVENESS OF REMEDIES IMPOSED

Finally, there are concerns about the effectiveness of the remedies that have been imposed following competition law interventions in digital markets: described as 'a range of fixes whose efficacy was mixed, at best'.[172] A related aspect is the need to monitor the implementation of any remedies imposed, albeit a problem that is not unique to the digital economy.[173] In the EU, the half-baked nature of the remedies imposed in certain digital cases is a result, at least in part, of the Commission's reluctance to use its coercive power to impose behavioural or structural remedies under Article 7 of Regulation 1/2003. It typically prefers instead to impose fines and generic obligations to ensure compliance going forward.[174] Less prescriptive remedies are less likely to be overturned by the Union Courts on appeal, a lesson the Commission learned in the *Microsoft* case when its innovative monitoring trustee requirement was annulled on the basis that it exceeded the scope of the Commission's own jurisdiction.[175] Such remedies are also, however, less likely to achieve the policy objective sought than more 'radical' alternatives.[176]

The limited efficacy of the remedies imposed may also stem from a lack of joined-up thinking between the theory of harm pursued in an investigation and the case disposition sought.[177] The *Google Shopping* decision, once again, provides a useful example.[178] Here, the Commission proceeded to an infringement decision only after it had repeatedly tried and failed to agree effective commitments under Article 9 with the defendant. Having reverted to the Article 7 procedure, the infringement decision nominally required the defendant to 'cease and desist' from the proscribed behaviour in future. Yet this merely kicked the can down the road, insofar as the vexed and previously unanswered question of *how* Google should remedy the abuse immediately presented itself again. More than half a decade after the infringement decision, it remained unresolved.[179]

6. BEYOND COMPETITION 'LAW'?

The discussion in the preceding sections makes two points clear. First, competition law is largely applicable and more or less able to address competition problems that arise in the digital economy. But, secondly, it is neither optimally calibrated nor especially nimble when it comes to regulating novel forms of 'bad' behaviour in fast-moving digital markets. There is thus a widely held perception that 'competition law achieves too little too late' in the digital sphere.[180] The question of how

[171] J. Caminade, A. Chapsal, and J. Penglase, 'Interim Measures in Antitrust Investigations: An Economic Analysis' (2021) 17 *J of Competition Law and Economics* 437, 454 (emphasis in original).

[172] F. Lancieri and C. Pereira Neto, 'Designing Remedies for Digital Markets: The Interplay Between Antitrust and Regulation' (2022) 18 *J of Competition Law and Economics* 613, 614. See also OECD Discussion Paper, n. 165, 11–12.

[173] It is, for instance, a recurrent objection to certain theories of harm under Art. 102, including refusal to supply and excessive pricing cases.

[174] See Chap. 13, Section 6.E. [175] Case T-201/04, *Microsoft* EU:T:2007:289.

[176] Considering the case for more radical remedial intervention in digital markets, see M. Gal and N. Petit, 'Radical Restorative Remedies for Digital Markets' (2021) 36 *Berkeley Technology LJ* 617.

[177] Lancieri and Pereira Neto, n. 172. [178] See Chap. 13, Section 6.E.ii.

[179] See N. Lomas, 'Google antitrust complainants call for EU to shutter its Shopping Ads Units', *TechCrunch*, 18 October 2022, <https://techcrunch.com/2022/10/18/eu-antitrust-complaint-google-shopping-units/>.

[180] R. Podszun, P. Bongartz, and S. Langenstein, 'The Digital Markets Act: Moving from Competition Law to Regulation for Large Gatekeepers' (2021) 10 *European Consumer and Market Law* 60, 60.

best to address competition problems in the digital economy coincides with wider debates about the adequacy of contemporary competition law, in particular the question whether we should ditch the 'more economic approach' and embrace a more aggressive attitude to competition interventions.[181] In the digital context, this has translated in several jurisdictions into the adoption of sector-specific legislation which introduces more interventionist and ambitious rules specifically to regulate the competitive activities of large digital platforms. The extent to which these new regimes can be considered as examples of competition 'law' is disputed, however, a point considered in the last part of this section.

A. ENHANCED REGULATION OF THE DIGITAL ECONOMY—A GLOBAL PREOCCUPATION?

Section 3 described the proliferation of policy reports that highlighted some of the limitations of the existing competition regime in digital economy markets. These were followed, in many jurisdictions, by substantive legal changes designed to implement at least some of the policy recommendations. Germany, for instance, introduced in January 2021 an ambitious amendment to its domestic competition Act, the §19a tool.[182] This is aimed specifically at very large digital firms that are held by the national competition authority, the Bundeskartellamt, to be of 'paramount significance for competition across markets'. Following such a finding, the Bundeskartellamt is empowered to prohibit the firm concerned from engaging in any or all of seven specified practices, including self-preferencing, denial of interoperability, or data portability, and the use of data to raise barriers to entry. The §19a tool thus enables the *ex ante* regulation of large digital platforms, in order to 'shut the stable door before the horse has bolted' in competition terms.[183] It also attempts to address concerns about the drawn-out nature of enforcement proceedings in digital markets, by providing for a truncated review only by the higher Federal Court of Justice. The §19a tool, which has some similarity to the DMA, has been described as 'a testing ground for digital platform regulation', which will enable other policy-makers to 'watch and learn from the wanted and unwanted effects of the Bundeskartellamt's future §19a interventions'.[184]

In the UK—no longer a Member State but whose competition rules remain heavily modelled on the EU framework—a new Digital Markets Unit (DMU) has been established within the UK's Competition and Markets Authority.[185] This was first proposed by the expert Furman Report, which foresaw the DMU's role as being to 'design and implement pro-competition rules' for digital markets, through 'a co-operative approach, working with platforms, other businesses and other stakeholders'.[186] It is anticipated[187] that the DMU will focus on regulating large digital firms with 'strategic market status' (SMS), defined as 'substantial and entrenched market power in at least one activity, providing [the firm] with a strategic position'.[188] Such firms will be subject to an enforceable code

[181] See Chap. 1.

[182] The discussion in this paragraph is based on J. Franck and M. Peitz, 'Digital Platforms and the New 19a Tool in the German Competition Act' (2021) 12 *JECLAP* 513.

[183] Bundeskartellamt, 'Amendment of the German Act against Restraints of Competition', 19 January 2021, <www.bundeskartellamt.de/SharedDocs/Meldung/EN/Pressemitteilungen/2021/19_01_2021_GWB%20Novelle.html>.

[184] Franck and Peitz, n. 182, 526.

[185] For discussion of the origins and anticipated parameters of the DMU, see N. Dunne, 'Pro-competition Regulation in the Digital Economy: The United Kingdom's Digital Markets Unit' (2022) 67 *Ant Bull* 341.

[186] 'Unlocking Digital Competition', n. 9, para. 2.6.

[187] The Digital Markets, Competition and Consumers Bill was first published on 25 April 2023.

[188] 'A new pro-competition regime for digital markets', CP 489, July 2021, para. 50.

of conduct, which aims to promote the values of fair trading, open choices, and trust and transparency in digital markets.[189] Although a number of specific obligations likely to apply to firms with SMS have been identified, each code of conduct will be tailored to the business activities of individual regulated firms. The DMU will additionally be able to adopt 'pro-competitive interventions', namely 'measures which aim to open up markets to greater competition,[190] where this is necessary "to tackle the sources and effects" of an SMS firm's market power'.[191] Mandatory notification of mergers involving firms with SMS status is also anticipated, in a departure from the UK's otherwise voluntary regime.[192]

Enhanced regulation of digital competition is on the agenda beyond Europe. In February 2021, Australia introduced a binding news media bargaining code.[193] This formally aims to address perceived power imbalances between digital platforms like Google and Facebook and domestic news businesses, although critics argued that it is intended primarily to advance the vested interests of the latter.[194] In the US, a series of (largely bipartisan) bills were introduced in Congress in June 2021, which aimed primarily to enhance regulation of the tech industry.[195] These would, if enacted, inter alia prohibit online self-preferencing[196] and certain digital mergers,[197] enhance data portability,[198] and, most contentiously, require divestment by vertically integrated platforms in order to avoid 'conflicts of interest' in the provision of intermediation services.[199] The proposals followed a 'scathing'[200] report on competition in digital markets issued by the House Judiciary Committee in 2020,[201] and the Biden administration's appointment of prominent critics of Big Tech to leadership roles within the federal antitrust enforcement agencies.[202] Though the prospects for the various bills are decidedly mixed, these legislative efforts indicate a remarkable turnaround from the hands-off approach of US antitrust enforcers to intervention in digital markets that was evident in the earlier years of the 'new' economy.

B. DEVELOPMENTS AT EU LEVEL: P2B REGULATION, 'NEW COMPETITION TOOL' AND THE DIGITAL SERVICES ACT PACKAGE

As the discussion in Section 4 illustrated, competition authorities in Europe, both at Member State and at EU level, have historically been less reluctant to intervene in digital markets than their counterparts in the US. The adequacy of the EU competition rules to address the perceived problems of the digital economy has similarly been questioned, nonetheless. An early effort at enhanced supervision was contained in the Platform-to-Business (P2B) Regulation, which was proposed in 2018[203] and entered into

[189] Ibid., para. 83. [190] Ibid., para. 102. [191] Ibid., para. 104. [192] Ibid., para. 174.

[193] Treasury Laws Amendment (News Media and Digital Platforms Mandatory Bargaining Code) Act 2021.

[194] 'Media bargaining code will entrench Murdoch empire's dominance: Rudd', *Sydney Morning Herald*, 19 February 2021.

[195] Additionally, two more generally applicable bills would raise merger filing fees to generate greater funds for antitrust enforcement (Merger Filing Fee Modernization Act) and enhance the discretion of state antitrust enforcers (State Antitrust Enforcement Venue Act).

[196] American Choice and Innovation Online Act. [197] Platform Competition and Opportunity Act.

[198] Augmenting Compatibility and Competition by Enabling Service Switching Act.

[199] Ending Platform Monopolies Act.

[200] 'Lawmakers, Taking Aim at Big Tech, Push Sweeping Overhaul of Antitrust', *New York Times*, 12 June 2021.

[201] Subcommittee on Antitrust, Commercial and Administrative Law of the Committee on the Judiciary, *Investigation of Competition in Digital Markets. Majority Staff Report and Recommendations* (2020).

[202] S. Ghaffary, 'Biden stacks his administration with yet another tech foe', *Vox.com*, 20 July 2021, <www.vox.com/recode/22585851/jonathen-kanter-biden-google-facebook-tech-antitrust-department-justice-tim-wu-lina-khan-apple>.

[203] Proposal for a Regulation of the European Parliament and of the Council on promoting fairness and transparency for business users of online intermediation services, COM(2018) 238 final, 26 April 2018.

force in July 2020.[204] The P2B Regulation aimed at 'promoting fairness and transparency' by imposing obligations on providers of online intermediation services specifically in respect of interactions with business users.[205] These focused, primarily, on the terms and conditions offered, including clarity in respect of ranking criteria, differentiated treatment, mandated access to data, and restrictions or termination of service. The P2B Regulation applies, horizontally, to *all* providers of online intermediation services, thereby sidestepping any requirement of dominance and the thorny question of what that concept entails in the digital sphere. The trade-off, however, is a weak enforcement framework, focused primarily on encouraging voluntary compliance by providers and on facilitating private enforcement by business users.[206] The P2B Regulation thus frames the question of 'fair' treatment in the platform environment as a matter of private law, rather than one to be viewed primarily through the lens of competition law. Yet fears about the inadequacy of the P2B Regulation, particularly with respect to the supervision of large gatekeeper platforms, meant that even before it entered into force, the Commission mooted the possibility of its revision and extension: first, to specifically regulate or proscribe certain emerging problematic business practices, and, secondly, to strengthen the oversight and enforcement mechanisms.[207]

When a new European Commission took office for a five-year term in 2019, it set as one of its key priorities to develop 'a Europe fit for the digital age'.[208] In a move that cannot have been inadvertent, the accompanying portfolio was handed to Margrete Vestager, who was also renewed for a second term as Competition Commissioner and promoted to Executive Vice-President. The Commission's February 2020 Communication on 'Shaping Europe's Digital Future' identified 'a fair and competitive economy' as one of three undergirding principles.[209] This was to be achieved, inter alia, through a 'review of the fitness of EU competition rules for the digital age' alongside the possible enactment of 'ex ante rules to ensure that markets characterised by large platforms with significant network effects acting as gatekeepers, remain fair and contestable for innovators, businesses, and new market entrants'.[210]

This culminated, in June 2020, in the announcement of two public consultations on possible additions to the existing competition framework. The first comprised a 'new competition tool' (NCT), which would aim 'to deal with structural competition problems across markets which cannot be tackled or addressed in the most effective manner on the basis of the current competition rules'.[211] The proposal resembled the UK's market investigation regime (MIR), which empowers the NCA to conduct in-depth examination of markets that may not be working well and to impose necessary and

[204] Reg. 2019/1150 on promoting fairness and transparency for business users of online intermediation services [2019] OJ L186/57, hereafter 'P2B Regulation'.

[205] Defined, under the P2B Regulation, Art. 2(1), as any private individual or legal person, 'which, through online intermediation services offers goods or services to consumers for purposes relating to its trade, business, craft or profession'.

[206] Including the mandatory establishment of internal complaint-handling systems by providers (P2B Regulation, Art. 11), and provision for external mediation of private disputes where these cannot be resolved internally (Art. 12).

[207] A possibility explored in Commission, 'Inception Impact Assessment: Digital Services Act package: Ex ante regulatory instrument for large online platforms with significant network effects acting as gate-keepers in the European Union's internal market', Ares(2020)2877647, 2 June 2020.

[208] See the Commission's website, 'The European Commission's Priorities 2019–24', <https://ec.europa.eu/info/strategy/priorities-2019-2024_en>.

[209] Commission Communication, 'Shaping Europe's Digital Future' (2020). The two other pillars are 'technology that works for people' and 'an open, democratic and sustainable society'.

[210] Ibid.

[211] Commission Press Release, 'Antitrust: Commission consults stakeholders on a possible new competition tool', 2 June 2020.

appropriate remedies where market features generate an adverse effect on competition.[212] Individual 'bad behaviour' is therefore not the trigger for intervention under the MIR, distinguishing the mechanism from individualised enforcement under Article 102. The NCT proposal, similarly, dispensed with the need to establish abusive conduct; and the consultation suggested abandoning dominance as the threshold for action.[213] Although the proposed NCT was nominally of general application, the sorts of structural market problems that were anticipated to come within its ambit—including network effects, consumer lock-in, data accumulation, and tacit collusion through algorithms[214]—tend to arise with greatest frequency and urgency within the digital economy.[215] The underlying rationale for its adoption, therefore, was a perceived need for a more 'flexible' regulatory tool that enabled the Commission to address ostensible markets failures within the platform economy, unconstrained by the limitations of the existing jurisprudence.[216] In this regard, the NCT proposal diverged from the Commission Digital Report, which had offered a more upbeat assessment of the prospects for progressive development of the *existing* competition rules to meet the challenges of digital markets.[217]

The second consultation launched in June 2020 was for a digital services package. This would comprise two strands: liability rules for the provision of digital services across the EU, and of specific relevance to the overlap with competition law, rules for ensuring 'the level playing field in European digital markets, where currently a few large online platforms act as gatekeepers'.[218] This culminated, in December 2020, in formal proposals for pieces of legislation for both strands.[219] The Digital Services Act is intended to update the liability rules first introduced in the E-Commerce Directive,[220] while the Digital Markets Act aims to ensure 'fair and contestable markets in the digital sector'.[221] Notably, the December 2020 package did not include formal legislative efforts to advance the NCT, which had met with a 'lukewarm' response at the public consultation stage, and has been essentially rolled into the DMA instead.[222]

[212] Governed by Part 4 of the Enterprise Act 2002. For discussion of how the MIR works in practice, and the extent to which this might translate to the EU context, see A. Fletcher, 'Market Investigations for Digital Platforms: Panacea or Complement?' (2021) 12 *JECLAP* 44.

[213] The impact assessment for the NCT proposal outlines four options, two of which hinged on dominance, and two on 'market structure-based' concerns: see Commission, 'Inception Impact Assessment: New Competition Tool ("NCT")', Ares(2020)2877634, 2 June 2020.

[214] Ibid. [215] As discussed in Commission Digital Report, Chap. 2.

[216] A. Lamadrid, 'Can This Be the New Normal? 10 Questions on the Proposed New Competition Tool', *Chillin' Competition Blog*, 11 June 2020, <https://chillingcompetition.com/2020/06/11/can-this-be-the-new-normal-10-questions-on-the-proposed-new-competition-tool/>. See also 'Inception Impact Assessment', n. 207, which situates the proposal within the context of the challenges to conventional competition law posed by the emergence of the digital economy, while acknowledging that similar problems may arise outside the digital sphere.

[217] See n. 213.

[218] Commission Press Release, 'Commission launches consultation to seek views on Digital Services Act package', 2 June 2020.

[219] For discussion of the two strands and their interrelationship, see M. Eifert, A. Metzger, H. Schweitzer, and G. Wagner, 'Taming the Giants: The DMA/DSA Package' (2021) 58 *CMLRev* 987.

[220] Reg. (EU) 2022/2065 of the European Parliament and of the Council of 19 October 2022 on a Single Market for Digital Services and amending Dir. 2000/31/EC (Digital Services Act) [2022] OJ L277/1.

[221] Reg. (EU) 2022/1925 of the European Parliament and of the Council of 14 September 2022 on contestable and fair markets in the digital sector and amending Dirs. (EU) 2019/1937 and (EU) 2020/1828 (Digital Markets Act) [2022] OJ L265/1.

[222] M. Cini and P. Czulno, 'Digital Single Market and the EU Competition Regime: An Explanation of Policy Change' (2022) 44 *J of European Integration* 41, 45. Criticising the decision to opt for 'rigid and static' rules in the DMA rather than a more flexible market investigation tool, see J. Davies, V. Meunier, and A. Stenimachitis, 'A Missed Opportunity: The European Union's New Powers over Digital Platforms' (2022) 67 *Ant Bull* 504.

C. DIGITAL MARKETS ACT

Following a legislative process involving the European Parliament and the Council,[223] the Digital Markets Act (DMA) was signed into law on 14 September 2022. It takes the shape of a Regulation,[224] and aims at the activities of large digital 'gatekeepers' that provide 'core platform services'. The rationale for focusing regulatory attention on this subset of digital actors is explained in the introductory recitals. In doing so, the Regulation invokes many of the distinctive characteristics of digital markets discussed at the outset of this chapter.

Regulation (EU) 2022/1925 of the European Parliament and of the Council of 14 September 2022 on contestable and fair markets in the digital sector and amending Directives (EU) 2019/1937 and (EU) 2020/1828 (Digital Markets Act) [2022] OJ L265/1

(1) Digital services in general and online platforms in particular play an increasingly important role in the economy, in particular in the internal market, by enabling businesses to reach users throughout the Union, by facilitating cross-border trade and by opening entirely new business opportunities to a large number of companies in the Union to the benefit of consumers in the Union.

(2) At the same time, among those digital services, core platform services feature a number of characteristics that can be exploited by the undertakings providing them. An example of such characteristics of core platform services is extreme scale economies, which often result from nearly zero marginal costs to add business users or end users. Other such characteristics of core platform services are very strong network effects, an ability to connect many business users with many end users through the multisidedness of these services, a significant degree of dependence of both business users and end users, lock-in effects, a lack of multi-homing for the same purpose by end users, vertical integration, and data driven-advantages. All these characteristics, combined with unfair practices by undertakings providing the core platform services, can have the effect of substantially undermining the contestability of the core platform services, as well as impacting the fairness of the commercial relationship between undertakings providing such services and their business users and end users. In practice, this leads to rapid and potentially far-reaching decreases in business users' and end users' choice, and therefore can confer on the provider of those services the position of a so-called gatekeeper. At the same time, it should be recognised that services which act in a non-commercial purpose capacity such as collaborative projects should not be considered as core platform services for the purpose of this Regulation.

(3) A small number of large undertakings providing core platform services have emerged with considerable economic power that could qualify them to be designated as gatekeepers pursuant to this Regulation. Typically, they feature an ability to connect many business users with many end users through their services, which, in turn, enables them to leverage their advantages, such as their access to large amounts of data, from one area of activity to another. Some of those undertakings exercise control over whole platform ecosystems in the digital economy and are structurally extremely difficult to challenge or contest by existing or new market operators, irrespective of how innovative and efficient those market operators may be. Contestability is reduced in particular due to the existence of very high barriers to entry or exit, including high investment costs, which cannot, or not easily, be recuperated in case of exit, and the absence of, or reduced access to, some key inputs in the digital economy, such as data. As a result, the likelihood increases that the underlying markets do not function well, or will soon fail to function well.

[223] The DMA was enacted under Art. 114 TFEU, which utilises the 'ordinary legislative procedure' under Art. 294 TFEU, requiring co-decision-making between the Council and Parliament.

[224] Art. 288 TFEU: 'A regulation shall have general application. It shall be binding in its entirety and directly applicable in all Member States.'

(4) The combination of those features of gatekeeper is likely to lead, in many cases, to serious imbalances in bargaining power and, consequently, to unfair practices and conditions for business users, as well as for end users of core platform services provided by gatekeepers, to the detriment of prices, quality, fair competition, choice and innovation in the digital sector.

Designation as a gatekeeper triggers the application of a series of prescriptive obligations, that serve to constrain the market behaviour of gatekeepers going forward. Despite vigorous requests from some NCAs to be given a greater role, enforcement of the DMA is essentially centralised in the European Commission, including stringent sanctions for breach. The key questions in terms of the application of the DMA are thus: the process of designation as a gatekeeper; the *ex ante* regulation rules that apply once gatekeeper status has been recognised; the legal framework that exists for enforcing those rules against gatekeepers; and the relationship between the obligations imposed under the DMA and the ordinary EU competition rules.

(i) Designation as a 'Gatekeeper' Providing 'Core Market Services'

The *ex ante* rules contained in the DMA apply only to the activities of 'gatekeepers' that provide 'core platform services' (CPSs). By restricting application of the DMA to certain activities of only a handful of the largest online platforms, the aim is to minimise the risk of regulatory overkill.[225] Both of the key underpinning concepts, which are not existing terms within the EU legal framework, are defined within the DMA. The definition of a gatekeeper is set out in Article 3, which provides as follows:

Designation of gatekeepers

1. An undertaking shall be designated as a gatekeeper if:
   (a) it has a significant impact on the internal market;
   (b) it provides a core platform service which is an important gateway for business users to reach end users; and
   (c) it enjoys an entrenched and durable position, in its operations, or it is foreseeable that it will enjoy such a position in the near future.
2. An undertaking shall be presumed to satisfy the respective requirements in paragraph 1:
   (a) as regards paragraph 1, point (a), where it achieves an annual Union turnover equal to or above EUR 7,5 billion in each of the last three financial years, or where its average market capitalisation or its equivalent fair market value amounted to at least EUR 75 billion in the last financial year, and it provides the same core platform service in at least three Member States;
   (b) as regards paragraph 1, point (b), where it provides a core platform service that in the last financial year has at least 45 million monthly active end users established or located in the Union and at least 10 000 yearly active business users established in the Union, identified and calculated in accordance with the methodology and indicators set out in the Annex;
   (c) as regards paragraph 1, point (c), where the thresholds in point (b) of this paragraph were met in each of the last three financial years.

. . .

[225] G. Crawford, J. Crémer, D. Dinielli, A. Fletcher, P. Heidhues, M. Schnitzer, F. Scott Morton, and K. Seim, 'Fairness and Contestability in the Digital Markets Act', Digital Regulation Project Policy Discussion Paper No. 3 (6 July 2021), 4.

Recital 5 of the DMA states explicitly that the gatekeeper concept is intended to cover actors 'that are not necessarily dominant in competition-law terms'. Instead, the definition in Article 3 focuses on three elements that may, but do not inevitably, coincide with the notion of significant market power: the 'significant impact' of the gatekeeper's activities across the internal market, the fact that it provides a specified CPS matching large numbers of business users to consumers, and the long-standing—'entrenched and durable'—nature of its position. These criteria are qualitative in nature, and, like the approach of the German and UK digital regimes, the DMA makes provision in Article 3(8) for the Commission to designate an undertaking as a gatekeeper after a thorough market investigation.[226] Yet Article 3(2) also adopts a quantitative approach to designation, with a presumption that an undertaking which satisfies certain criteria, as to turnover or market capitalisation and number of monthly and yearly users, holds gatekeeper status. An undertaking may challenge this presumption, but it bears the burden of providing 'sufficiently substantiated arguments manifestly calling into question' the soundness of the Article 3(2) presumption.[227] The DMA states expressly that such challenges are likely to succeed only 'exceptionally'.[228]

An expansive list of CPSs is provided in Article 2(2). It encompasses: online intermediation services; online search engines; online social networking services; video-sharing platform services; number-independent interpersonal communications services; operating systems; web browsers; virtual assistants; cloud computing services; and online advertising services, including any advertising networks, advertising exchanges, and any other advertising intermediation services, provided by an undertaking that provides any of the other enumerated core platform services. The recitals to the DMA suggest two interlinked reasons for the inclusion of an activity on the list: the fact that certain services have 'the capacity to affect a large number of end users and businesses',[229] and that this furthermore creates a 'more frequent and pronounced' risk of weak contestability and unfair practicing arising in those sectors.[230] The DMA foresees the possibility of adding 'additional services within the digital sector' to the specified list of CPSs in future, although this can be achieved only after a market investigation by the Commission, and requires a formal amendment to the DMA to be passed by the Parliament and Council.[231]

The requirements of the designation process are set out in the DMA, and will be specified further in an Implementing regulation.[232] Where an undertaking meets the quantitative criteria so as to engage the presumption of gatekeeper status, 'it shall notify the Commission thereof without delay and in any event within 2 months after those thresholds are met and provide it with the relevant information' to confirm that the thresholds are satisfied.[233] The Commission is then obliged to designate the undertaking as a gatekeeper within 45 working days.[234] Failure to notify the Commission and/or provide the required information entitles the Commission to designate the undertaking as a gatekeeper without its involvement, 'based on information available to the Commission'.[235] As noted, the Commission may also designate as a gatekeeper any undertaking that satisfies the qualitative Article 3(1) criteria but not the quantitative Article 3(2) criteria, but may only do so after a context-specific market investigation.[236] Because undertakings are designated as gatekeepers with respect to discrete CPSs, any designation decision must list the relevant services provided by that undertaking to which the status attaches.[237] Moreover, because of 'the very rapidly changing and complex technological nature of core

[226] Conducted under DMA, Art. 17. [227] DMA, Art. 3(5). [228] Ibid. [229] Ibid., recital (14).
[230] Ibid., recital (13). [231] Ibid., Art. 19.
[232] Commission Press Release, 'Digital Markets Act: rules for digital gatekeepers to ensure open markets enter into force', 31 October 2022, <https://ec.europa.eu/commission/presscorner/detail/en/IP_22_6423>.
[233] DMA, Art. 3(3). [234] Ibid., Art. 3(4). [235] Ibid., Art. 3(3). [236] Ibid., Art. 3(8).
[237] Ibid., Art. 3(9).

platform services',[238] the Commission is obliged to keep any individual designation under regular review, and to reassess 'at least every 3 years . . . whether the gatekeepers continue to satisfy the requirements laid down in Article 3(1)'.[239] Based on the outcome of that review, the Commission may confirm or conversely repeal its original designation decision, or amend it to include more or fewer CPSs.[240]

(ii) Obligations Applying to Gatekeepers

The DMA is not a 'no-fault' monopolisation statute, meaning that being a gatekeeper is not outlawed as such.[241] Instead, designation triggers application of a prescriptive series of obligations, set out in Articles 5–7, which apply with respect to each CPS provided by the gatekeeper listed in the designation decision. Unlike the approach of the recently enacted German and UK regimes, the requirements imposed are not tailored to the specific business activities of and/or risks posed by an undertaking, but apply as a blanket set of restrictions to all its designated services: 'a uniform, one-size-fits-all code of conduct'.[242]

While the initial legislative proposal had asserted that the DMA would be targeted at 'the most salient incidences of unfair practices and weak contestability'[243] in digital markets, dozens of discrete and quite distinct restrictions are included across Articles 5–7. These are united by two overarching themes, namely that each aims to protect contestability and/or fairness with respect to the relevant CPS. Contestability is defined as 'the ability of undertakings to effectively overcome barriers to entry and expansion and challenge the gatekeeper on the merits of their products and services'.[244] Unfairness refers to 'an imbalance between the rights and obligations of business users where the gatekeeper obtains a disproportionate advantage'.[245] A fair outcome is thus one where market participants 'have the ability to adequately capture the benefits resulting from their innovative or other efforts'.[246] The recitals to the DMA note that these objectives are 'intertwined', in the sense that problems that stem from unfair practices or a lack of contestability are potentially mutually reinforcing.[247] The result is that a particular obligation specified in Articles 5–7 may address both objectives.[248]

Article 5 contains the unambiguous 'obligations for gatekeepers'. These, according to the initial legislative proposal, are intended to be 'self-executing'[249] in the sense that designated gatekeepers are bound directly and unequivocally by the obligations contained in Article 5(2)–(10). Article 6 provides an additional set of obligations that are 'susceptible of being further specified'. In respect of the latter, Article 8 makes provision for 'possible dialogue'[250] between the Commission and designated undertakings, whereby a gatekeeper 'may request the Commission to engage in a process to determine whether the measures that that gatekeeper intends to implement or has implemented to ensure compliance . . . are effective in achieving the objective of the relevant obligation in the specific circumstances of the gatekeeper'.[251] The Commission is not obliged to enter into such a dialogue, although in exercising its discretion it is bound by the principles of equal treatment, proportionality, and good administration.[252] If it chooses to formally specify compliance measures, these are binding on the gatekeeper concerned, meaning that non-compliance with the prescribed measures can be the subject of a non-compliance decision subsequently.[253]

[238] Ibid., recital (30). [239] Ibid., Art. 4(2). [240] Ibid.

[241] Exploring this possibility in the digital context, see M. Lao, 'No-fault Digital Platform Monopolization' (2020) 61 *William & Mary LR* 755.

[242] Eifert et al., n. 219, 1003. Comparing the approach of all three regimes, see A. Witt, 'Platform Regulation in Europe—*Per Se* Rules to the Rescue?' (2022) 18 *J of Competition Law and Economics* 670.

[243] Commission, Proposal for a Regulation of the European Parliament and of the Council on contestable and fair markets in the digital sector (Digital Markets Act), COM(2020) 842 final, 15 December 2020, 2.

[244] DMA, recital 32. [245] Ibid., recital 33. [246] Ibid. [247] Ibid., recital 34. [248] Ibid.

[249] DMA Proposal, n. 243, 13. [250] Ibid. [251] DMA, Art. 8(3). [252] Ibid.

[253] Ibid., Arts. 8(2) and 29(1)(b).

The obligations contained in Articles 5 and 6 address a broad range of business practices that could potentially be utilised, unfairly or in an anti-competitive manner, by large digital actors. These include data usage, access, and portability; distribution channels; advertising; leveraging; device and platform neutrality; and interoperability. The enumerated practices have either formed the basis of previous antitrust investigations brought by the Commission or an NCA, or have been identified in one or more digital competition reports as presenting problems from an antitrust policy perspective.[254] These include the misuse of personal data, as in the *German Facebook*[255] case (Article 5(2)); the use of 'most favoured nation' clauses, as in the *Amazon E-Books*[256] case (Article 5(3)); the tying of two or more core platform services provided by a gatekeeper, as in the *Google Android*[257] case (Article 5(8)); the misuse of confidential business data, as in the *Amazon Marketplace*[258] case (Article 6(2)); and self-preferential ranking of search results, as in the *Google Shopping*[259] case (Article 6(5)). Several of the obligations relate to practices that have been held to raise barriers to entry in digital markets, such as pre-installation of software applications[260] (Article 6(3)), and the need to access data generated by end-users of online search engines[261] (Article 6(11)). Importantly, however, the obligations specified in Articles 5 and 6 represent a repudiation of the effects-based approach that was adopted in the various decisions that provided their inspiration.[262] Accordingly, gatekeepers can be held to be non-compliant with their obligations under the DMA simply be engaging in the proscribed practices, without the need to demonstrate even a capacity to foreclose effective competition as a result. Moreover, there is no possibility for regulated gatekeepers to justify their behaviour, either by reference to countervailing efficiencies or on the basis that it generates predominantly positive effects on competition.[263]

Article 7 imposes obligations with respect to interoperability on gatekeepers that offer 'number-independent interpersonal communications services', such as those provided by the WhatsApp, Telegram, or Facebook Messenger applications. While such services were listed as CPSs in the original legislative proposal, the obligations in Article 7 were added only midway through the legislative process. Article 7 requires gatekeepers that are designated with respect to such services, to make the 'basic functionalities' of their services interoperable with the number-independent interpersonal communications services of other providers, 'by providing the necessary technical interfaces or similar solutions that facilitate interoperability, upon request, and free of charge'.[264] Gatekeepers benefit from an extended timetable to provide this information, the full extent of which must be disclosed only within four years of the designation decision.[265] The interoperability obligations imposed by Article 7 are also susceptible to further specification under Article 8, although the Commission again has discretion as to whether it engages with gatekeepers.[266]

The default position under the DMA is that all obligations apply in respect of each designated CPS across the board. There are, however, a number of limited exceptions to this position. First, where a gatekeeper is designated on the basis that it is likely to enjoy an entrenched and durable position in the near future but does not yet do so, only a subset of obligations are potentially applicable,[267] and these must be identified explicitly by the Commission in the designation decision.[268] Secondly, a gatekeeper

[254] In particular, Table 2 of the Commission's Staff Working Document issued alongside the initial legislative proposal provides a detailed list of 'concrete examples/evidence' for each proposed obligation: see Impact Assessment Report Accompanying the Proposal for a Regulation of the European Parliament and of the Council on contestable and fair markets in the digital sector (Digital Markets Act), COM(2020) 842 final.

[255] See n. 146. [256] See n. 52. [257] See n. 44. [258] See n. 52. [259] See n. 50.

[260] An issue in COMP/37.792, *Microsoft* 24 March 2004 and AT.40099, *Google Android* 18 July 2018.

[261] An issue in AT.39740, *Google Search (Shopping)* 27 June 2017.

[262] On the effects-based approach to Art. 102, see Chap. 7, Section 3.F. [263] Eifert et al., n. 219, 1004.

[264] DMA, Art. 7(1). [265] Ibid., Art. 7(2). [266] Ibid., Art. 8(3).

[267] Namely, the obligations contained in Art. 5(3)–(6), and Art. 6(4), (7), (9), (10), and 13). [268] DMA, Art. 17(4).

may seek to have a specific obligation suspended temporarily,[269] on the basis that its application otherwise 'would endanger, due to exceptional circumstances beyond the gatekeeper's control, the economic viability of its operation in the Union'.[270] Article 9(1) emphasises that such a suspension is likely to be granted only 'exceptionally', and must be limited 'to the extent and duration necessary to address such threat to the gatekeeper's viability'. Finally, Article 10 contains a rather curious power to exempt a gatekeeper, 'in whole or part',[271] from any specific obligation contained in Articles 5–7, on 'grounds of public health or public security'.[272] This basis for exemption was referred to as 'overriding reasons of public interest' in the original legislative proposal,[273] and echoes the express grounds for derogation from the free movement rules to be found in the Treaty on the Functioning of the European Union.[274]

Article 12 enables the Commission to 'supplement' the obligations in Articles 5 and 6 with additional requirements targeted at emerging practices that may harm contestability or be deemed unfair. Before doing so, the Commission must examine the impugned practices by way of a market investigation under Article 19.[275] The anticipated direction of travel, notably, is one-way only: despite Article 12 being titled '*updating* obligations for gatekeepers', there does not appear to be scope to remove obligations that, for instance, subsequently prove to be unnecessary in practice, or that are rendered obsolete by market or technological developments. The Commission may, additionally, supplement the interoperability obligations contained in Article 7, 'by specifying the manner in which those obligations are to be performed in order to ensure effective compliance'.[276] In this context, there does appear to be greater potential to deregulate in future, however, as the Commission is empowered to add to *or remove* items from the list of 'basic functionalities' provided by Article 7(2).[277]

Finally, gatekeepers have an obligation to inform the Commission of any intended concentration within the meaning of Article 3 of the EUMR, in advance of its implementation, 'where the merging entities or the target of concentration provide core platform services or any other services in the digital sector or enable the collection of data'.[278] This obligation is without prejudice to any parallel notification requirements under EU or national merger control rules.[279] The Commission is required to pass this information on to any competent Member State authorities, which may then choose to use their power to refer the merger for review by the Commission under Article 22 of the EUMR.

(iii) Enforcement Framework of the DMA

The obligations imposed on gatekeepers are, as noted, intended to be largely self-executing.[280] The DMA provides for what is essentially a six-month grace period following a designation decision to allow the gatekeeper to get its affairs in order, after which it 'shall comply' with the requirements contained in Articles 5–7.[281] Gatekeepers thereafter have a duty to 'ensure and demonstrate compliance'.[282] Measures implemented to secure compliance must be 'effective in achieving the objectives of [the DMA] and of the relevant obligation'.[283] This includes the establishment of a so-called 'compliance function' within the gatekeeper but independent of its operational activities, to be composed of one or more 'compliance officers'.[284] The role of the compliance function is 'to monitor the compliance of the gatekeeper',[285] an objective that entails inter alia supervising the business activities of the undertaking, liaising with its management, and cooperating with the Commission in respect of the gatekeeper's obligations under the DMA.[286] These obligations include providing the Commission

[269] Where exemption is granted, the Commission is required to review its suspension decision at least once a year: ibid., Art. 9(2).

[270] Ibid., Art. 9(1). [271] Ibid., Art. 10(1). [272] Ibid., Art. 10(3). [273] DMA Proposal, n. 243, 42.

[274] Specifically, Arts. 36, 45, and 52 TFEU. [275] DMA, Art. 12(1). [276] Ibid., Art. 12(4).

[277] Ibid., Art. 12(3). Again, this can occur only after a market investigation. [278] Ibid., Art. 14. [279] Ibid.

[280] See n. 249. [281] DMA, Art. 3(10). [282] Ibid., Art. 8(1). [283] Ibid. [284] Ibid., Art. 28(1).

[285] Ibid., Art. 28(2). [286] Ibid., Art. 28(5).

with an annual report, 'describing in a detailed and transparent manner the measures [the gatekeeper] has implemented to ensure compliance'.[287] Providers of core platform services are also subject to a series of 'anti-circumvention' measures, which prohibit strategic behaviour intended to evade the quantitative thresholds in Article 3(2), to undermine effective compliance, or to degrade the conditions or quality of services that it provides to any users which have exercised rights or choices generated by the obligations in Articles 5–7.[288]

Yet despite the utopian vision of a strict yet self-enforcing regulatory regime, it is anticipated that compliance is likely to prove tricky with respect to many aspects of the DMA.[289] What happens if and when non-compliance arises proved to be a contentious question during the passage of the DMA, with several Member States pushing for an enhanced role for national authorities in enforcing the rules.[290] Ultimately, however, enforcement remains heavily centralised in the Commission, which is described as 'sole enforcer of this Regulation' within the text of the DMA.[291] Enforcement powers are to be shared between the Directorates-General for Competition (DG Comp) and for communications networks, content, and technology (DG Connect).[292]

The duty of gatekeepers to ensure effective compliance with their DMA obligations is matched by a concomitant duty on the Commission to 'take the necessary actions' to monitor such implementation and compliance efforts.[293] The Commission is empowered, inter alia, to investigate and make formal findings of non-compliance with respect to any of the obligations in Articles 5–7, or with previously specified measures for compliance with Articles 6 and 7. In such cases, where intentional or negligent breach is demonstrated, the Commission can impose fines of up to 10 per cent of the gatekeeper's total worldwide turnover in the preceding year, which is the same maximum level that can be imposed for violations under Regulation 1/2003 and the EUMR.[294] Periodic penalty payments are also available in order to compel adherence to non-compliance and other decisions taken by the Commission under the DMA.[295]

In cases of 'systematic non-compliance', the Commission is authorised, following a market investigation, to impose 'any behavioural or structural remedies which are proportionate and necessary to ensure effective compliance'.[296] Since systematic non-compliance is 'deemed' to have occurred where the Commission has issued at least three non-compliance decisions against a gatekeeper in relation to any of its designated CPSs within the preceding eight years,[297] the purpose of the market investigation would appear to be primarily to enable the Commission to identify effective remedies. Subsequent non-compliance with behavioural or structural remedies also attracts fines of up to 10 per cent of worldwide turnover,[298] with provision for fines of up to 20 per cent for recidivism (i.e. where a gatekeeper has been subject to two non-compliance decisions with respect to the same obligation in respect of the same CPS within an eight-year period).[299]

Similar to the Article 9 procedure under Regulation 1/2003, a gatekeeper may choose to offer commitments to the Commission to conclude an investigation into systematic non-compliance, in lieu of

[287] Ibid., Art. 11(1). [288] Ibid., Art. 13.

[289] See e.g. P. Akman, 'Regulating Competition in Digital Platform Markets: A Critical Assessment of the Framework and Approach of the EU Digital Markets Act' (2022) 47 *ELRev* 85.

[290] See joint statement of France, Germany, and the Netherland ('Friends of an effective Digital Market Act'), *Strengthening the Digital Markets Act and its Enforcement* (May 2021), <www.bmwk.de/Redaktion/DE/Downloads/M-O/non-paper-friends-of-an-effective-digital-markets-act.pdf?__blob=publicationFile&v=4>.

[291] DMA, Art. 38(7).

[292] 'Sneak peek: how the Commission will enforce the DSA & DMA', Blog of Commissioner Thierry Breton, 5 July 2022, <https://ec.europa.eu/commission/presscorner/detail/en/STATEMENT_22_4327>.

[293] DMA, Art. 26(1). [294] See DMA, Art. 30(1)(a), Reg. 1/2003, Art. 23(2), and EUMR, Art. 14(2).

[295] DMA, Art. 31. [296] Ibid., Art. 18(1). [297] Ibid., Art. 18(3). [298] Ibid., Art. 30(1)(c).

[299] Ibid., Art. 30(2).

behavioural or structural remedies. Such commitments may be made binding by the Commission, which shall then 'declare that there are no further grounds for action'.[300] Non-compliance with legally binding commitments can similarly attract a fine of up to 10 per cent of turnover.[301]

In order to carry out its enforcement functions under the DMA, the Commission has a broad range of information-gathering powers, equivalent to those provided under Chapter V of Regulation 1/2003.[302] These include the powers to request information, to carry out interviews with natural or legal persons, and to conduct inspections at business premises. 'In cases of urgency', during the course of an investigation with a view to a possible adoption of a non-compliance decision, the Commission can adopt interim measures, premised upon a prima facie finding of infringement of Article 5, 6, or 7.[303] Breach of interim measures is a fineable offence.[304]

Formal decisions taken by the Commission under the DMA can be challenged before the Union Courts under Article 263 TFEU.[305] Article 45 of the DMA reiterates the Court of Justice's unlimited jurisdiction to review decisions by which the Commission has imposed fines or periodic penalty payments, as provided by Article 261 TFEU.

It was noted earlier that the highly centralised enforcement structure of the DMA was challenged, unsuccessfully, by a number of influential Member States during the passage of the legislation.[306] This approach also sits uncomfortably with the overtly decentralised framework for enforcing Articles 101 and 102 under Regulation 1/2003.[307] Nonetheless, with the Commission as sole enforcer of the DMA with respect to the tasks both of designating gatekeepers and of enforcing the obligations imposed, there is limited scope for Member State involvement in the regulatory process. Article 41 makes provision for individual Member States to request the Commission to open a market investigation into suspected systematic non-compliance,[308] or, where the request comes from three or more Member States, to open a market investigation with a view to designating a new gatekeeper[309] or to making additions to the list of CPSs or obligations imposed.[310] Unsurprisingly, Member States cannot require the Commission to action any such request, though it is obliged to 'examine whether there are reasonable grounds to open a market investigation'.[311]

Any 'competent authority' of a Member State is itself permitted, under Article 38(7), to 'conduct an investigation into a case of possible non-compliance with Articles 5, 6 or 7 . . . on its territory'. Crucially, any such investigation may occur only within the context of enforcement proceedings taking place under Article 101 or 102, or under national competition rules regulating anti-competitive coordination, mergers or 'other forms of unilateral conduct insofar as they are applied to undertakings other than gatekeepers or amount to the imposition of further obligations on gatekeepers'.[312] National authorities are not authorised formally to find non-compliance with obligations imposed under the DMA. Accordingly, to the extent that an investigation into 'possible non-compliance' occurs at national level, it appears to be relevant only insofar as breach of a DMA-imposed obligation may influence the national authority's assessment of whether the EU-level or domestic competition rules have been infringed.[313]

The fact that DMA-imposed obligations can be treated as indisputable features of a market aligns with the fact that, as an EU Regulation, the DMA is directly applicable in all Member States.[314] Accordingly, even if the Commission is the 'sole' agency with direct regulatory powers under the

300 Ibid., Art. 25(1). 301 Ibid., Art. 30(1)(e). 302 Ibid., Art. 30(1)(e). 303 Ibid., Art. 24.
304 Ibid., Art. 30(1)(d).
305 This would include decisions taken pursuant to Arts. 3, 4, 8(2), 9, 10, 16–20, 24, and 25(1).
306 See n. 290. 307 See discussion in Chap. 13, Section 9. 308 DMA, Art. 41(2). 309 Ibid., Art. 41(1).
310 Ibid., Art. 41(3). 311 Ibid., Art. 41(5). 312 Ibid., Art. 1(6).
313 Along the lines of the CJ's argument in Case C-165/19 P, *Slovak Telekom* EU:C:2021:239, para. 57, that 'a regulatory obligation can be relevant for the assessment of abusive conduct'.
314 The need to secure direct effect for the obligations imposed was cited in the legislative proposal as one reason why use of a Regulation, as opposed to another legislative instrument, was necessary in the circumstances: see DMA Proposal, n. 243, 6.

DMA, it creates obligations with direct effect at the national level, which can be invoked in domestic proceedings.[315] On the other hand, national authorities are explicitly prohibited from taking decisions 'which run counter to a decision adopted by the Commission' under the DMA.[316] There is, moreover, a duty of 'close cooperation and coordinat[ion]' between Member States and the Commission, 'to ensure coherent, effective and complementary enforcement of available legal instruments applied to gatekeepers'.[317]

National authorities also have several more procedural roles under the DMA. The Commission is empowered to 'consult national authorities where appropriate' on any issue relating to the DMA.[318] The Commission 'may ask' NCAs 'to support any of its market investigations',[319] although the latter are not apparently obliged to give such assistance. By contrast, Article 21(5) *requires* 'competent authorities of the Member States' to provide the Commission, at its request, 'with all necessary information in their possession to carry out the duties assigned to it' by the DMA. National official may play a role in interviews[320] and inspections[321] conducted in the national territory, and in monitoring compliance with, inter alia, the Article 5–7 obligations, measures specified under Article 6 or 7, behavioural or structural remedies imposed, or commitments accepted in lieu.[322] Third parties are empowered to provide national authorities with information regarding behaviour by gatekeepers falling within the scope of the DMA, which, should the authority 'determine' to potentially raise 'an issue of non-compliance', must be passed on to the Commission.[323]

Finally, the DMA says comparatively little about private enforcement. As explained, the Regulation is directly applicable, and the text anticipates that 'proceedings for the application of this Regulation' are likely to arise before national courts.[324] Article 39 makes provision for national courts to request information from the Commission, for the Commission to provide written and oral observations to national courts '[w]here the coherent application of this Regulation so requires', and for national judgments applying the DMA to be transmitted to the Commission in a timely fashion. Article 42 confirms that Directive 2020/1828,[325] which requires Member States to put in place collective redress mechanisms for consumer cases, 'shall apply to the representative actions brought against infringements by gatekeepers of provisions of this Regulation that harm or may harm the collective interests of consumers'. Beyond this, however, enforcement by private parties would appear to be regulated by the general principles that govern the protection of directly effective EU law rights at the national level.[326] This omission has been described as a 'missed opportunity',[327] insofar as effective enforcement of the DMA obligations now hinges primarily on the Commission's efforts, and concomitantly, on its resources and resolve. The counterview, however, is that greater private enforcement risks fragmentation of the new regime.[328]

[315] See e.g. DMA, Art. 39(1), which refers expressly to 'proceedings for the application of this Regulation' that may be taking place before national courts.

[316] Ibid., Art. 1(7). [317] Ibid., Art. 37(1). [318] Ibid., Art. 37(2). [319] Ibid., Art. 38(6).

[320] Ibid., Art. 22. [321] Ibid., Art. 23. [322] Ibid., Art. 26(2). [323] Ibid., Art. 27.

[324] Ibid., Art. 39(1).

[325] Dir. (EU) 2020/1828 of the European Parliament and of the Council of 25 November 2020 on representative actions for the protection of the collective interests of consumers and repealing Dir. 2009/22/EC [2020] OJ L409/1.

[326] See P. Craig and G. de Búrca, *EU Law: Text, Cases, and Materials* (7th edn, Oxford University Press, 2020), Chap. 9.

[327] R. Podszun, 'Private Enforcement and Gatekeeper Regulation: Strengthening the Rights of Private Parties in the Digital Markets Act' (2022) 13 *JECLAP* 254, 263.

[328] A. Komninos, 'The Digital Markets Act and Private Enforcement: Proposals for an Optimal System of Enforcement' in N. Charbit and S. Gachot (eds.), *Eleanor M. Fox Liber Amicorum. Antitrust Ambassador to the World* (Concurrences, 2021).

(iv) The Nature of the Obligations under the DMA

Finally, we come to perhaps the most interesting question that arises when discussing the DMA within a textbook that focuses on EU competition law: to what extent can and should the obligations that it contains be viewed as a category of sector-specific competition law, or instead as a rather different regulatory instrument? In its recitals, the DMA is quite firm on this point: although the EU competition rules and the obligations imposed on gatekeepers under the DMA are complementary in nature, they are distinct forms of regulation. This is both because of the rather different structure of analysis under Articles 101 and 102 TFEU when compared with the DMA, and because of the different aims pursued by each field of law.

(5) . . . [M]arket processes are often incapable of ensuring fair economic outcomes with regard to core platform services. Although Articles 101 and 102 of the Treaty on the Functioning of the European Union (TFEU) apply to the conduct of gatekeepers, the scope of those provisions is limited to certain instances of market power, for example dominance on specific markets and of anti-competitive behaviour, and enforcement occurs ex post and requires an extensive investigation of often very complex facts on a case by case basis. Moreover, existing Union law does not address, or does not address effectively, the challenges to the effective functioning of the internal market posed by the conduct of gatekeepers that are not necessarily dominant in competition-law terms.

. . .

(10) . . . [S]ince this Regulation aims to complement the enforcement of competition law, it should apply without prejudice to Articles 101 and 102 TFEU, to the corresponding national competition rules and to other national competition rules regarding unilateral conduct that are based on an individualised assessment of market positions and behaviour, including its actual or potential effects and the precise scope of the prohibited behaviour, and which provide for the possibility of undertakings to make efficiency and objective justification arguments for the behaviour in question, and to national rules concerning merger control. However, the application of those rules should not affect the obligations imposed on gatekeepers under this Regulation and their uniform and effective application in the internal market.

(11) Articles 101 and 102 TFEU and the corresponding national competition rules concerning anticompetitive multilateral and unilateral conduct as well as merger control have as their objective the protection of undistorted competition on the market. This Regulation pursues an objective that is complementary to, but different from that of protecting undistorted competition on any given market, as defined in competition-law terms, which is to ensure that markets where gatekeepers are present are and remain contestable and fair, independently from the actual, potential or presumed effects of the conduct of a given gatekeeper covered by this Regulation on competition on a given market. This Regulation therefore aims to protect a different legal interest from that protected by those rules and it should apply without prejudice to their application.

Let us consider these claims in turn. First, it is indisputable that the obligations under the DMA cover much of the same ground as Article 102 with respect to large digital platforms. Under the quantitative thresholds set out in Article 3, only about ten entities are likely to qualify for gatekeeper status.[329] Many of these, most obviously the five Big Tech firms known as GAFAM, have already been found

[329] Discussing the likely implications of different quantitative thresholds, see Commission Impact Assessment, n. 254, paras. 148–149.

to hold dominance in a relevant CPS market for the purposes of Article 102 or are currently subject to an antitrust investigation on this basis.[330] While the DMA explicitly states that dominance 'in competition-law terms' in not the relevant benchmark,[331] the elements set out in both the quantitative and qualitative criteria overlap considerably with those that would support a finding of dominance within the meaning of the Article 102 jurisprudence. The obligations then imposed by Articles 5 and 6, furthermore, mostly have their origins in theories of harm pursued in competition enforcement cases.[332] Accordingly, the DMA seeks to prevent gatekeeper undertakings, *ex ante*, from engaging in behaviour that would, in many instances, also amount to an abuse of dominance if assessed *ex post* under Article 102. It is in this sense that one can understand its characterisation as a form of sector-specific competition law, albeit applied prospectively to address the particular challenges posed by the activities of very large digital actors.[333]

On the other hand, it is not merely the *ex ante* versus *ex post* distinction which differentiates the approach of the DMA from ordinary Article 102 assessment. Particularly where the Article 3 quantitative thresholds are presumptively satisfied, regulation under the DMA takes effect entirely without reference to 'the actual, potential or presumed effects of the conduct ... on competition on a given market'.[334] We saw, in Chapter 7, that the GC in *Google Shopping* suggested that 'a practice cannot be categorised as abuse of a dominant position unless it is demonstrated that there is an anticompetitive effect, or at the very least a potential anticompetitive effect'.[335] This question is assessed, in Article 102 cases, by reference to the factual circumstances of the case. The approach of the DMA removes not only the need for such an assessment, but also the possibility of justifying superficially restrictive conduct by reference to its *inability* to harm competition, an important aspect of substantive Article 102 analysis as emphasised by the Grand Chamber in *Intel*.[336] It is for this reason, namely the very different approach to identifying proscribed conduct and the basis on which it is prohibited, that some commentators strongly resist the depiction of the DMA as competition law as such.[337] Instead, as Eifert et al. put it, the obligations imposed by the DMA 'do not react to a specified harm, but to special features of digital markets, thereby covering settings that would lie at or outside the boundaries of competition law; they are supposed to function proactively and ensure a (more) level playing field'.[338]

There is a further question of whether, even if we accept that the DMA is distinct from the ordinary competition rules, the Regulation more broadly represents an instrument of competition policy.[339] Again, the DMA expressly differentiates itself in terms of the objectives that it pursues: whereas competition law aims, in its understanding, at the 'protection of undistorted competition on the market',

[330] See discussion in Section 4. [331] DMA, recital 5. [332] See n. 254.

[333] A perspective endorsed, e.g., by N. Petit, 'The Proposed Digital Markets Act (DMA): A Legal and Policy Review' (2021) 12 *JECLAP* 529; E. Deutscher, 'Reshaping Digital Competition: The New Platform Regulations and the Future of Modern Antitrust' (2022) 67 *Ant Bull* 302 (albeit he argues that the DMA represents a 'paradigm adjustment' of contemporary competition law); and to an extent by P. Larouche and A. de Streel, 'The European Digital Markets Act: A Revolution Grounded on Traditions' (2021) 12 *JECLAP* 542 (who argue, 545, that the DMA is akin to a 'lost child of competition law') and G. Colangelo, 'The European Digital Markets Act and Antitrust Enforcement: A Liaison Dangereuse' (2022) 47 *ELRev* 597.

[334] DMA, recital (11). [335] Case T-612/17, *Google Shopping* EU:T:2021:763, para. 438.

[336] See Chap. 7, Section 10.

[337] See e.g. P. Ibáñez Colomo, 'The Draft Digital Markets Act: A Legal and Institutional Analysis' (2021) 12 *JECLAP* 561 (highlighting the extent to which both the aims and analytical structure of the DMA diverge from conventional competition law); H. Schweitzer, 'The Art to Make Gatekeeper Positions Contestable and the Challenge to Know What is Fair: A Discussion of the Digital Markets Act Proposal' (2021) 3 *Zeitschrift für Europäisches Privatrecht* 503 (arguing that the structure of the DMA must be distinguished from competition *law* even if it pursues objectives that are related broadly to competition *policy*); and Podszun et al., n. 180.

[338] Eifert et al., n. 219, 1004. [339] Eifert et al., ibid, argue that the DMA has 'obvious competition policy roots'.

the Regulation instead seeks to ensure markets that are 'contestable and fair'.[340] It is difficult, however, to maintain a rigid separation between these objectives.[341] In *Google Shopping*, the GC argued that undistorted competition is essentially a synonym for fair competition;[342] while the definition of contestability provided by the DMA[343] would appear to be wholly consistent with the notion of 'competition as such'.[344] The contention that the two regimes protect separate 'legal interests' is thus unconvincing.[345]

The issue is of practical relevance insofar as it serves (at least in principle) to condition the interrelationship between the DMA and EU-level and national competition laws going forward. It was explained in Chapter 13 that, although EU law recognises the *ne bis in idem* principle, the concurrent application of competition law and sectoral regulation to the same facts may be justifiable where it represents a proportionate departure from Article 50 of the Charter which pursues a legitimate public interest objective.[346] Accordingly, the enactment of the DMA is without prejudice to EU-level and national competition laws on the basis that the latter pursue different interests, meaning that concurrent application is not ruled out *a priori*. The DMA nonetheless takes precedence in certain situations relating to the regulation of unilateral conduct by gatekeepers, and Member States are precluded from imposing sector regulation in the same circumstances. The general principles guiding the interrelationship between the DMA, competition laws, and other domestic digital regulation is set out in Article 1 of the DMA.

Subject matter and scope

. . .

5. In order to avoid the fragmentation of the internal market, Member States shall not impose further obligations on gatekeepers by way of laws, regulations or administrative measures for the purpose of ensuring contestable and fair markets. Nothing in this Regulation precludes Member States from imposing obligations on undertakings, including undertakings providing core platform services, for matters falling outside the scope of this Regulation, provided that those obligations are compatible with Union law and do not result from the fact that the relevant undertakings have the status of a gatekeeper within the meaning of this Regulation.
6. This Regulation is without prejudice to the application of Articles 101 and 102 TFEU. It is also without prejudice to the application of:
   (a) national competition rules prohibiting anti-competitive agreements, decisions by associations of undertakings, concerted practices and abuses of dominant positions;
   (b) national competition rules prohibiting other forms of unilateral conduct insofar as they are applied to undertakings other than gatekeepers or amount to the imposition of further obligations on gatekeepers; and
   (c) Council Regulation (EC) No 139/2004 (23) and national rules concerning merger control.
7. National authorities shall not take decisions which run counter to a decision adopted by the Commission under this Regulation. The Commission and Member States shall work in close cooperation and coordinate their enforcement actions on the basis of the principles established in Articles 37 and 38.

[340] DMA, recital (11). [341] Petit, n. 333, 531, thus argues that the DMA is 'underspecified'.
[342] Case T-612/17, *Google Shopping* EU:T:2021:763, paras. 433–434. [343] See n. 244.
[344] See e.g. Case C-501/06 P, *GlaxoSmithKline* EU:C:2009:610, para. 63.
[345] As asserted in DMA, recital (11).
[346] See Case C-117/20, *bpost* EU:C:2022:202, discussed in detail in Chap. 13, Section 11.

Since secondary legislation cannot override the primary Treaty rules,[347] it is unsurprising that Article 1(6) states without qualification that the DMA is without prejudice to the application of Articles 101 and 102. As the DMA and Article 102 tread much the same regulatory ground, this raises the possibility that the same behaviour may fall under and potentially even be sanctioned under both regimes.[348] Regrettably, the DMA provides relatively little in terms of concrete mechanisms for co-ordination of concurrent enforcement under the Regulation and the EU competition rules,[349] besides a basic prohibition on national authorities and courts 'tak[ing] decisions which run counter to a decision adopted by the Commission under this regulation'.[350] Similarly, national competition laws are largely unaffected by the DMA, apart from rules that address 'other forms of unilateral conduct' besides abuses of dominance, which are superseded to the extent that the provisions apply to gatekeepers and regulate the behaviour covered by Articles 5–7 of the DMA.[351] Because Member States are also precluded from imposing sector-specific regulation on gatekeepers that seeks to secure contestable and fair markets,[352] it is unclear whether, for instance, Germany's §19a framework is entirely compatible with the DMA.[353]

(v) Comment

The DMA entered into force on 2 May 2023,[354] which started the clock on the two-month timeframe within which undertakings that satisfy the quantitative criteria for gatekeeper status must notify the Commission.[355] Yet the advisability of the DMA as an instrument of regulatory policy remains a much-debated question. Many observers would query whether the underlying case for sector-specific regulation in the digital sector was ever established concretely, though that battle is now definitively lost in practice, at least for the time being. Moreover, with its neat (albeit lengthy) list of proscribed and required practices, the DMA may understate the complexity of achieving competitive outcomes in practice in digital markets.[356] Concerns regarding the quantitative approach to gatekeeper designation, the irrelevance of anti-competitive effects (or lack thereof) to the question of compliance with the mandatory obligations, and the absence of any efficiency defence within the DMA have also been noted. And within just a short period after its enactment, other pressing concerns have emerged in the digital sphere—for instance, AI—that fall largely outside its scope.

[347] An explicit ground of review under the Art. 263 TFEU action for annulment is 'infringement of the Treaties'. For an example of secondary legislation being struck down as incompatible with the underlying Treaty requirements, see e.g. Cases C-293/12 etc., *Digital Rights Ireland* EU:C:2014:238.

[348] EU law does not preclude the application of the competition rules to behaviour that has already been subject to *ex ante* regulation; in fact, breach of the latter may form part of the theory of harm supporting a finding of abusive or restrictive conduct under the latter, see Case C-165/19 P, *Slovak Telekom* EU:C:2021:239 and discussion in Chap. 7, Section 12.

[349] Highlighting the ensuing possibility of tension and even conflict between the regimes, see C. Fernández, 'A New Kid on the Block: How Will Competition Law Get along with the DMA?' (2021) 12 *JECLAP* 271.

[350] DMA, Arts. 1(7) and 39(5). [351] Ibid., Art. 1(6)(b). [352] Ibid., Art. 1(5).

[353] See e.g. L. Kabelka, 'DMA: Germany the test bench for complementarity with competition authorities', *Euractiv.com*, 12 April 2022, <www.euractiv.com/section/digital/news/dma-application-could-lead-to-legal-uncertainty-in-germany/>.

[354] DMA, Art. 54. [355] Ibid., Art. 3(3).

[356] Expressing concern with respect to the theories of harm behind the *Shopping* and *Android* cases, respectively, see P. Marsden, 'Google Shopping for the Empress's New Clothes—When a Remedy Isn't a Remedy (and How to Fix it)' (2020) 11 *JECLAP* 553, 560, and T. Thomes and T. Weck, 'The *Google Android* case and the DMA—Lessons Learned?' (2022) 43 *ECLR* 52.

Given the proliferation of digital regulatory regimes elsewhere alongside the EU's efforts, we arguably have the makings of a natural experiment informing whether and how best to regulate these markets. The comparative ease and enthusiasm with which the DMA was passed by EU legislators is notable, despite the vaunted lobbying power of Big Tech.[357] Yet the proof of this ambitious regulatory 'leap of faith' will be in its outcomes: both as to whether the new regime proves nimble enough to meet the challenges of the fast-moving digital economy, and whether the deliberate and categorical decision to jettison a 'more economic approach' in this highly dynamic context is advisable.

7. CONCLUSIONS

1. The optimal role of competition law in the digital economy has dominated policy debates and enforcement activity in the EU in recent years. Critics of Big Tech are concerned that very large technology firms have, inter alia, entrenched their dominance, exploited consumers, and stifled innovation. Many of the competition concerns identified also reflect the fact that there is an absence of effective regulation more generally in digital markets. The application of competition law in digital markets in the EU also has a political dimension, as it is connected to the EU's Digital Single Market strategy.

2. It has been argued that certain features of digital markets make competition problems (in particular entrenched positions of dominance) more likely to arise, but also more difficult to accommodate within the established competition law assessment framework. These include extreme economies of scale and scope, market multi-sidedness and network effects, and the pivotal role of data in developing and monetising many digital markets. Yet the Commission's competition enforcement activity in the digital sphere demonstrates that there are no insurmountable obstacles to either developing coherent theories of harm or defending these successfully on appeal before the Union Courts.

3. Aspects of the conventional competition law framework arguably work less well, however. The relevant market concept which is the cornerstone of EU competition enforcement is less meaningful in the context of ecosystem competition. An understanding of market power premised upon the ability to raise price to supra-competitive levels does not work well for zero-price products. Moreover, market power in a competition law sense does not map precisely onto the notion of platform power, which reflects the strategic importance of large platforms within an ecosystem. Competition enforcement can be too slow in fast-moving digital markets, and it can be difficult to devise effective remedies.

4. Although well-established types of anti-competitive conduct arise in digital markets (including tying, exclusive dealing, or resale price maintenance), it may be necessary to develop new theories of antitrust liability. Self-preferencing addresses discriminatory leveraging by dominant online platforms. Breach of data protection rules was a key element of the *Facebook* case in Germany. Data may be deemed an indispensable input in the context of a refusal to supply claim. It is yet unclear whether price-fixing engaged in by self-learning pricing algorithms could be prosecuted as a cartel between the undertakings which each use that technology.

5. The difficulties of applying competition law in digital markets have led to calls in many jurisdictions for sector-specific digital regulation. In the EU, the Digital Markets Act (DMA) was enacted in 2022. It aims to ensure contestable and fair markets in the digital sector. To do so, it imposes a series

[357] Noting the 'surprising' enthusiasm of both Member States and parliamentarians for the Commission's initial legislative proposal, see T. Käseberg, 'The DMA—Taking Stock and Looking Ahead' (2022) 13 *JECLAP* 1, 1. Exploring the political drivers of regulatory change in this context, see Cini and Czulno, n. 222.

of *ex ante* obligations on certain very large digital undertakings which have been designated as 'gatekeepers'. Gatekeepers are designated with respect to the provision of various 'core platform services'. While many undertakings that are likely to qualify as gatekeepers also hold a 'dominant position' under Article 102, the DMA states explicitly that the concepts do not coincide exactly.

6. The obligations imposed under the DMA are numerous, wide-ranging, and highly prescriptive. Many have their origins in theories of harm developed in competition cases. However, the DMA applies without regard to the *effects* of the conduct, meaning that a gatekeeper cannot avoid liability under the DMA by claiming that its behaviour lacks the capacity to foreclose competition. The DMA has thus been criticised for its potential over-inclusiveness, and a risk that it will prevent digital firms from engaging in innovative and welfare-enhancing market practices.

7. The DMA is enforced solely by the Commission. This aspect of the Regulation was criticised during the legislative process by certain Member States, who wanted NCAs to have a greater role in enforcement. It remains to be seen whether the Commission will have sufficient resources to enforce the DMA obligations effectively.

8. FURTHER READING

A. Books

Baker, J., *The Antitrust Paradigm* (Harvard University Press, 2019)

Belleflamme, P. and Peitz, M., *The Economics of Platforms. Concepts and Strategy* (Cambridge University Press, 2021)

Ducci, F., *Natural Monopolies in Digital Platform Markets* (Cambridge University Press, 2020)

Ezrachi, A., and Stucke, M., *Virtual Competition* (Harvard University Press, 2016)

Graef, I., *EU Competition Law, Data Protection and Online Platforms: Data as Essential Facility* (Kluwer, 2016)

Klobuchar, A., *Antitrust: Taking on Monopoly Power from the Gilded Age to the Digital Age* (Random House, 2021)

O'Donoghue, R. and Padilla, J., *The Law and Economics of Article* 102 (3rd edn, Hart Publishing, 2020), Chap. 17

Petit, N., *Big Tech and the Digital Economy: The Moligopoly Scenario* (Oxford University Press, 2020)

Robertson, V., *Competition Law's Innovation Factor* (Hart Publishing, 2020)

Schrepel, T., *Blockchain + Antitrust* (Edward Elgar, 2021)

B. Chapters in Books

Gerbrandy, A., 'Revisiting the Concept of Power in the Digital Era' in O. Andryichuk (ed.), *Antitrust and the Bounds of Power—25 Years On* (Hart Publishing, 2023)

Lovdahl Gormsen, L., 'Competition Law and the Digital Economy in the UK and Beyond' in B. Rodger, P. Whelan, and A. MacCulloch (eds.), *The UK Competition Regime: A Twenty-Year Retrospective* (Oxford University Press, 2021)

Pardolesi, R., 'Digital Antitrust and Private Powers: The (Uneasy) Case of Marketplace Platforms' in O. Andryichuk (ed.), *Antitrust and the Bounds of Power—25 Years On* (Hart Publishing, 2023)

C. Articles

Akman, P., 'A Web of Paradoxes: Empirical Evidence on Online Platform Users and Implications for Competition and Regulation in Digital Markets' (2022) 16(2) *Virginia Law & Business Review* 217

Alexiadis, P., and de Streel, A., 'Designing an EU Intervention Standard for Digital Platforms', EUI Working Papers RSCAS 2020/14 (2020)

Andreangeli, A., 'The Digital Markets Act and the Enforcement of EU Competition Law: Some Implications for the Application of Articles 101 and 102 TFEU in Digital Markets' (2022) 43 *ECLR* 496

Andriychuk, O., 'Shifting the Digital Paradigm: Towards a *Sui Generis* Competition Policy' (2022) 46 *Computer Law & Security Review* 105733

Athey, S., and Scott Morton, F., 'Platform Annexation' (2022) 84 *Antitrust LJ* 677

Costa Cabral, F., and Lysnkey, O., 'Family Ties: The Intersection between Data Protection and Competition in EU Law' (2017) 54 *CMLRev* 11

Coyle, D., 'Practical Competition Policy Implications of Digital Platforms' (2019) 82 *Antitrust LJ* 835

Cremer, J., Dinielli, D., Heidhues, P., Kimmelman, G., Monti, G., Podszun, R., Schnitzer, M., Scott Morton, F., and de Streel, A., 'Enforcing the Digital Markets Act: Institutional Choices, Compliance, and Antitrust' (2023) *J of Antitrust Enforcement* (forthcoming)

Deutscher, E., 'Reshaping Digital Competition: The New Platform Regulations and the Future of Modern Antitrust' (2022) 67 *Ant Bull* 302

Ducci, F., 'Procedural Implications of Market Definition in Platform Cases' (2019) 7 *J of Antitrust Enforcement* 419

Economides, N., and Lianos, I., 'Restrictions on Privacy and Exploitation in the Digital Economy: A Market Failure Perspective' (2021) 17 *J of Competition Law and Economics* 765

Evans, D., 'Basic Principles for the Design of Antitrust Analysis for Multisided Platforms' (2019) 7 *J of Antitrust Enforcement* 319

Gal, M., 'Limiting Algorithmic Coordination' (2023) 38 *Berkeley Technology LJ* forthcoming

Gal, M., and Petit, N., 'Radical Restorative Remedies for Digital Markets' (2021) 36 *Berkeley Technology LJ* 617

Geradin, D., and Dimitrios, K., 'Strengthening Effective Antitrust Enforcement in Digital Platform Markets' (2022) 18 *European Competition Journal* 356

Goldfarb, A., and Tucker, C., 'Digital Economics' (2019) 57 *J of Economic Literature.* 3

Graef, I., 'Market Definition and Market Power in Data: The Case of Online Platforms' (2015) 38 *World Competition* 473

Graef, I., 'Differentiated Treatment in Platform-to-Business Relations: EU Competition Law and Economic Dependence' (2019) 38 *YEL* 448

Jenny, F., 'Changing the Way We Think: Competition, Platforms and Ecosystems' (2021) 9 *J of Antitrust Enforcement* 1

Krämer, J., and Schnurr, S., 'Big Data and Digital Markets Contestability: Theory of Harm and Data Access Remedies' (2022) 18 *J of Competition Law and Economics* 255

Kuenzler, A., 'Competition Law Enforcement on Digital Markets—Lessons from Recent EU Case Law' (2019) 7 *J of Antitrust Enforcement* 249

Lancieri, F., 'Digital Protectionism? Antitrust, Data Protection, and the EU/US Transatlantic Rift' (2019) 7 *J of Antitrust Enforcement* 27

Lancieri, F., and Pereira Neto, C., 'Designing Remedies for Digital Markets: The Interplay Between Antitrust and Regulation' (2022) 18 *J of Competition Law and Economics* 613

Lancieri, F., and Sakowski, P., 'Competition in Digital Markets: A Review of Expert Reports' (2021) 26 *Stanford J of Law, Business & Finance* 65

Lianos, I., 'Competition Law for the Digital Era: A Complex Systems' Perspective', UCL Centre for Law, Economics and Society Research Paper 6/2019

Mandrescu, D., 'Abusive Pricing Practices by Online Platforms: A Framework Review of Article 102 TFEU for Future Cases' (2022) 10 *J of Antitrust Enforcement* 469

Robertson, V., 'Antitrust, Big Tech, and Democracy: A Research Agenda' (2022) 67 *Ant Bull* 589

Sauter, W., 'A Duty of Care to Prevent Online Exploitation of Consumers? Digital Dominance and Special Responsibility in EU Competition Law' (2020) 8 *J of Antitrust Enforcement* 406

Vezzoso, S., 'The Dawn of Pro-competition Data Regulation for Gatekeepers in the EU' (2021) 17 *European Competition Journal* 391

Witt, A., 'Platform Regulation in Europe—*Per Se* Rules to the Rescue?' (2022) 18 *J of Competition Law and Economics* 670

17

INTERNATIONAL ASPECTS

1. CENTRAL ISSUES

1. In a globalised marketplace, the effects of anti-competitive conduct can be felt far from where they originate and mergers frequently involve undertakings from different jurisdictions or multinational companies that operate worldwide. Very many States now have competition law regimes but although trade and competition are global, competition laws remain national (or supranational in the case of the EU).
2. It was the US which first developed concepts to deal with jurisdictional problems in competition law. It formulated the 'effects doctrine' whereby US antitrust laws apply to conduct which has a direct, substantial, and reasonably foreseeable effect in the US.
3. The US is an attractive jurisdiction to foreign plaintiffs. Damages actions for competition injury are more common in the US than in Europe and many aspects of US litigation are plaintiff friendly. Recent US cases, however, have limited the use of the US courts by foreign plaintiffs.
4. The EU's single economic entity doctrine brings many foreign companies within its jurisdiction. The EU has also formulated the 'implementation' doctrine and has adopted a 'qualified effects' doctrine. The Merger Regulation takes jurisdiction over undertakings anywhere in the world on the basis of their turnover in the EU.
5. The EU has entered into a number of agreements, including dedicated bilateral co-operation agreements on competition, with other States.
6. Plans for international competition regimes or rules, for instance within the WTO, have not progressed. However, there is a great deal of international co-operation between competition agencies from around the world, in particular through the International Competition Network (ICN).

2. INTRODUCTION

It is difficult, if not impossible, to isolate the geographical effects of transactions which take place on the global market. Companies such as Microsoft or Google have a dominant position throughout the world. Consumers anywhere can be injured by global conspiracies to fix prices or rig markets and multinational mergers can affect many jurisdictions. However, although trade and competition are global, competition laws remain national (or supranational in the case of the EU). Attempts to counteract this problem include the use of existing international law doctrines or the development of new ones, the conclusion of bilateral and multilateral international arrangements, and dealing with competition policy within the framework of existing international mechanisms, or establishing new ones.

In this chapter, we look first at the question of extraterritoriality in international law; secondly at competition law and extraterritoriality in respect of the EU and the US; thirdly at bilateral agreements entered into by the EU; and lastly at the 'internationalisation' of competition law and the moves which have been made towards dealing with competition issues on a global footing to match the global operations of undertakings on world markets.

3. INTERNATIONAL LAW

States taking jurisdiction outside their own territory is known as *extraterritoriality*.[1] International law traditionally distinguishes between two types of jurisdiction. *Subject-matter* (or *prescriptive* or *legislative*) jurisdiction is the right of States to make their laws applicable to persons, territory, or situations. *Enforcement* jurisdiction is the capacity to take executive action to enforce compliance with those laws.

The two undoubted bases for jurisdiction in international law are nationality and territory.[2] The *nationality* principle gives a State jurisdiction over its nationals, including companies incorporated under its laws. The *territoriality* principle has two aspects. *Subjective territoriality* gives a State jurisdiction over acts which originated within its territory even if they were completed abroad. *Objective territoriality* gives a State jurisdiction over acts which originated abroad but were completed, at least partially, within that State's territory. Objective territoriality was in effect recognised by the Permanent Court of International Justice (PCIJ) in the *Lotus* case.[3] Further possible principles of jurisdiction are the passive personality principle, by which States claim jurisdiction over aliens who have committed acts abroad harmful to their nationals, and the protective or security principle[4] by which they claim jurisdiction over aliens for acts committed abroad which harm the security of the State.

The application of the objective territoriality principle in competition law is controversial. Objective territoriality was developed in respect of physical actions (the weapon fired across the frontier scenario), not economic activities. Most States make murder a criminal offence but even in States with

[1] There is an enormous literature on jurisdiction in international law, of which the question of jurisdiction in competition law is but a small part. See e.g. M. Akehurst, 'Jurisdiction in International Law' (1972–1973) 46 *BYIL* 145; F. A. Mann, 'The Doctrine of International Jurisdiction Revisited After Twenty Years' (1984) 156 *RdC* 9; F. A. Mann, 'The Doctrine of Jurisdiction in International Law' (1964) 111 *RdC* 3; D. W. Bowett, 'Jurisdiction: Changing Problems of Authority over Activities and Resources' (1982) 53 *BYIL* 1; A. Mills, 'Rethinking Jurisdiction in International Law' (2014) 84 *BYIL* 187; J. Crawford, *Brownlie's Principles of Public International Law* (9th edn, Oxford University Press, 2019), Chap. 21; R. Jennings and A. Watts (eds.), *Oppenheim's International Law, Vol. 1* (9th edn, Oxford University Press, 2008), 72–478; C. Ryngaert, *Jurisdiction in International Law* (2nd edn, Oxford University Press, 2015); M. Shaw, *International Law* (9th edn, Cambridge University Press, 2021), Chap. 12. With particular reference to antitrust law, see K. M. Meessen, 'Antitrust Jurisdiction under Customary International Law' (1984) 78 *AJIL* 783; P. J. Slot and E. Grabandt, 'Extraterritoriality and Jurisdiction' (1986) 23 *CMLRev* 545; P. M. Roth, 'Reasonable Extraterritoriality: Correcting the "Balance of Interests" ' (1992) 41 *ICLQ* 245.

[2] See e.g. *Brownlie's Principles of Public International Law*, n. 1; *Oppenheim's International Law*, n. 1; Akehurst, n. 1, 177.

[3] (1927) PCIJ Ser. A, No. 10, 23. See the discussion of *Lotus* in J. Griffin, 'Reactions to US Assertions of Extraterritorial Jurisdiction' [1998] *ECLR* 64, 68.

[4] See the *Cutting* case (1886), in J. B. Moore, *Digest of International Law, Vol. II* (US Government Printing Office, 1906). A further principle, not relevant here, is the universality principle, where jurisdiction is taken over aliens as a matter of international public policy for crimes such as piracy or aircraft hijacking.

competition law regimes the objectives of the laws may vary, or the authorities' application of them in a specific situation may differ. For example, the EU and US authorities have differed over some transactions despite the close cooperation between the two jurisdictions in competition matters and the existence of similar laws. Moreover, if States try to apply their competition laws extraterritorially undertakings may find themselves subject to a number of competing and irreconcilable actions, there may be conflict between national authorities, and States may feel their sovereignty to be infringed.

It may not be enough for a State to merely take subject-matter jurisdiction. It may also need enforcement jurisdiction whereby its authorities can conduct investigations, collect evidence, serve proceedings, and recover penalties abroad. The distinction between subject-matter and enforcement jurisdiction was explored by the Advocates General in the EU cases, *Dyestuffs*[5] and *Wood Pulp I*.[6] They considered that the mere imposition of a pecuniary sanction is a matter of subject-matter jurisdiction, enforcement jurisdiction being involved only when steps are taken for its recovery, because only then is the State taking coercive measures in the territory of a foreign sovereign. A number of international instruments provide for cooperation between jurisdictions, in particular with regard to the recognition and enforcement of judgments,[7] and the taking of evidence abroad,[8] but the extraterritorial enforcement of a State's competition law is highly contentious.

The question then arises as to whether the US 'effects doctrine', discussed in Section 4, is in conformity with the principle of objective territoriality in international law or is an illegitimate extension of it which is inconsistent with the principle of the sovereignty of nations. The US view is that it does comply with international law. Many States have adopted some form of the effects doctrine. It has now been confirmed that the 'qualified effects' doctrine applies in EU law[9] and, as we see in Section 5, the EU Courts have been careful to state that the principles they have crafted are in accordance with international law.

4. US LAW

A. GENERAL

The extraterritorial reach of the Sherman Act 1890 became an issue before the EEC even existed.[10] The 'effects doctrine' propounded in the US courts has provided the central concept around which the discussion of extraterritoriality in competition law is conducted. The extraterritorial application of US antitrust law has long been contentious, not just as a matter of principle but because of the features of US antitrust litigation. These include, for example, the recovery of 'treble damages' for breaches of the antitrust laws,[11] far-ranging pre-trial discovery, and 'opt-out' class actions.[12] In recent years, the attractions to litigants of pursuing in US courts competition law claims with only an indirect connection to the US have led to much debate about the jurisdiction of US courts.[13]

[5] Opinion of Mayras AG in Case 48/69, *ICI v Commission (Dyestuffs)* EU:C:1972:32, 695.

[6] Opinion of Darmon AG in Cases 89, 104, 114, 116, 117, and 125–9/85, *A. Ahlström Oy v Commission* EU:C:1988:258 (*Wood Pulp I*), paras. 19–32 and 47–58.

[7] See the Hague Convention on the Recognition and Enforcement of Judgments on Civil and Commercial Matters, 1971.

[8] The Hague Convention on the Taking of Evidence Abroad in Civil or Commercial Matters, 1970.

[9] Case C-413/14 P, *Intel Corp v Commission* EU:C:2017:632.

[10] See R. Y. Jennings, 'Extraterritorial Jurisdiction and the United States Antitrust Laws' (1957) 33 *BYIL* 146.

[11] Clayton Act, 15 USC s. 15. [12] See Chap. 14, Section 3.

[13] See *F. Hoffmann-La Roche Ltd v Empagran*, Section 4.D, p. 1256.

Two particular points about US law should be noted. First, there is a multiplicity of actors in US antitrust law and different courts of equal authority can come to different conclusions on the same issues which may sometimes render it difficult to make general statements about US law.[14] Secondly, extraterritoriality in antitrust law is but one aspect of the long arm of US law.[15]

B. THE EFFECTS DOCTRINE

At first the US courts were diffident about applying the Sherman Act[16] extraterritorially. In the *American Banana* case,[17] Justice Oliver Wendell Holmes said in the Supreme Court that 'the general and almost universal rule is that the character of an act as lawful or unlawful must be determined wholly by the law of the country where the act is done'. Later cases retreated from this self-denying ordinance,[18] and in *Alcoa*,[19] which concerned a cartel of aluminium producers based in Switzerland which fixed production quotas to boost prices, Judge Learned Hand laid down in 1945 what is known as the 'effects doctrine'. He said that the Sherman Act *did* apply to agreements concluded outside the US which were intended to affect US imports and did actually affect them:

> . . . it is settled law that any State may impose liabilities, even upon persons not within its allegiance, for conduct outside its borders which has consequences within its borders which the State reprehends; and these liabilities other States will ordinarily recognise.[20]

In 1982, the Foreign Trade Antitrust Improvements Act (FTAIA) amended the Sherman Act. The FTAIA stipulates that as regards foreign commerce other than import commerce the antitrust laws will not apply unless the conduct has a *direct, substantial, and reasonably foreseeable* effect on US commerce or on US exports and such effect gives rise to a claim under the Sherman Act or FTC Acts. In other words, the FTAIA exempts export transactions from the Sherman Act unless they injure the US economy. This provision has inevitably come to be seen as a statutory formulation of the effects doctrine. In *Hartford Fire Insurance*, Justice Souter, delivering the majority opinion of the Supreme Court, held that 'it is well established by now that the Sherman Act applies to foreign conduct that was meant to produce and did in fact produce some substantial effect in the United States'.[21] He looked to the FTAIA formulation as expressing the effects doctrine.

The US courts also apply the principle of international comity, which plays a 'central role in US foreign relations law'.[22] 'Comity' means living peacefully with other nations in mutual respect and accommodating their interests or, as one authority puts it, the 'rules of politeness, convenience and

[14] See the varying views of the different Circuits which culminated in the *Empagran* case, see Section 4.D, p. 1256.

[15] See, e.g., legislation such as the Iran–Libya Sanctions Act 1996, later the Iran Sanctions Act 2006, and the Iran Freedom and Counter-Proliferation Act 2012, the Alien Tort Statute 1789 (now 1948), and the CLOUD Act 2018 compelling US-based technology companies to provide to the federal authorities data stored on servers outside the US as well as on US soil. The Supreme Court has reaffirmed the principle that there is a presumption against extraterritoriality in that '[w]hen a statute gives no indication of an extraterritorial application, it has none', *Morrison v National Australia Bank Ltd*, 130 S.Ct 2869 (2010) (concerning the Securities and Exchange Act 1934); see also *EEOC v Arabian American Oil Co*, 499 US 244 (1991).

[16] 15 USC, 2 July 1890.

[17] *American Banana Co v United Fruit Co*, 213 US 347, 356, 29 S.Ct 511, 512 (1909).

[18] See *United States v Sisal Sales Corp*, 274 US 268, 47 S.Ct 592 (1927). The *American Banana* case has been limited to its facts and read in a limited way.

[19] *United States v Aluminum Co of America*, 148 F.2d 416 (2d Cir. 1945).

[20] Ibid., 444. See further M. Winerman and W. Kovacic, 'Learned Hand, *Alcoa*, and the Reluctant Application of the Sherman Act' (2013) 79 *Antitrust LJ* 295, <http://ssrn.com/abstract=2417338>.

[21] *Hartford Fire Insurance Co v California*, 509 US 764, 796, 113 S.Ct 2891 (1993).

[22] W. S. Dodge, 'International Comity in American Law' (2015) 115(8) *Columbia LR* 2071, 2071.

goodwill observed by States in their mutual intercourse without being legally bound by them'.[23] Comity was defined by the US Supreme Court in *Hilton v Guyot* in 1895 as 'the recognition which one nation allows within its territory to the legislative, executive or judicial acts of another nation, having due regard both to international duty and convenience, and to the rights of its own citizens or of other persons who are under the protection of its laws'.[24] In *Timberlane*,[25] the Ninth Circuit Court of Appeals recognised the effects doctrine as laid down in *Alcoa*, but considered that its application had to be balanced against the interests of international comity. Judge Choy said that the question which needed to be asked was 'whether the interests of and links to the United States, including the magnitude of the effect on American commerce, are sufficiently strong, *vis-à-vis* those of other nations, to justify an assertion of extra-territorial authority'.[26] He said that the following should be taken into account: the degree of conflict with foreign law or policy, the nationality or allegiance of the parties and the locations or principal places of business of corporations, the extent to which enforcement by either State can be expected to achieve compliance, the relative significance of effects on the United States as compared with those elsewhere, the extent to which there is explicit purpose to harm or affect American commerce, the foreseeability of such effect, and the relative importance to the violations charged of conduct within the United States as compared with conduct abroad. The criteria were expanded in *Mannington Mills*.[27]

Timberlane and *Mannington Mills* do not deny jurisdiction to the US courts in the interests of comity, but hold that it should not be exercised where the interests of the US in asserting jurisdiction are outweighed by the interests of comity.[28]

In *Hartford Fire Insurance*,[29] the Supreme Court recognised the claims of comity, but took a robust approach to applying the effects doctrine. Justice Souter held that the court should first decide whether it had jurisdiction. Then it could be determined whether jurisdiction should be declined on comity grounds. In this case, there was no reason to decline it. He took the view that although the UK *allowed* the impugned conduct (a collective insurance boycott), it did not *compel* it.[30] There was therefore no conflict between British and American policy, and no reason for comity concerns to override the effects doctrine. The problem is, however, that if international comity is only to prevent the US taking jurisdiction in such narrowly drawn conflict situations it will rarely prevail.[31] Justice Scalia dissented in *Hartford Fire Insurance*. He considered that comity is an integral part of determining whether the court has jurisdiction in the first place, rather than something to be taken into account when deciding whether to *exercise* jurisdiction.[32]

[23] *Oppenheim's International Law*, n. 1, Vol. 1, 34; see J. R. Paul, 'Comity in International Law' (1991) 32 *Harvard Int'l LJ* 1.
[24] *Hilton v Guyot*, 159 U.S. 113, 164 (1895).
[25] *Timberlane Lumber Co v Bank of America*, 549 F.2d 597 (9th Cir. 1976). [26] Ibid.
[27] *Accord Mannington Mills Inc v Congoleum Corp*, 595 F.2d 1287 (3d Cir. 1979).
[28] Such a balancing act had earlier been advocated by Kingman Brewster, who called it a 'jurisdictional rule of reason' in *Antitrust and American Business Abroad* (McGraw-Hill, 1958).
[29] *Hartford Fire Insurance Co v California*, 509 US 764, 113 S.Ct 2891 (1993).
[30] The 'foreign sovereign compulsion defence' therefore did not apply. The US also recognises 'foreign sovereign immunity' (the Act of State defence) whereby foreign governments have immunity in the courts, although usually only for commercial activities (see the Foreign Sovereign Immunities Act 1976).
[31] When dealing with internal inconsistencies between federal antitrust law and the laws of US states, it is accepted that immunity from the former may sometimes arise as a consequence of the latter, even where the individual or undertaking concerned could comply with both, see A. Robertson and M. Demetriou, ' "But That Was in Another Country . . .": The Extraterritorial Application of US Antitrust Laws in the US Supreme Court' (1994) 43 *ICLQ* 417, 421–422. The issue of another jurisdiction which merely permits rather than compels is demonstrated by the EU merger case, Case T-102/96, *Gencor Ltd v Commission*, EU:T:1999:65 discussed at Section 5.D, p. 1264.
[32] See also the minority opinion by Judge Adams in *Mannington Mills*, 595 F.2d 1287 (3d Cir. 1979). And see F. A. Mann, 'The Doctrine of International Jurisdiction Revisited After Twenty Years' (1984) 186 *RdC* 9, who considers that if a court has jurisdiction it must exercise it. If, on the other hand, international law says it has no jurisdiction that is the end of the matter. One cannot, however, have a court which has a discretion whether or not to exercise its own jurisdiction.

In respect of 'public' enforcement, the DOJ and FTC have jointly issued the *Antitrust Enforcement Guidelines for International Operations*.[33] These explain, inter alia, that 'in determining whether to investigate or bring an action, or to seek particular remedies in a given case, the Agencies take into account whether significant interests of any foreign sovereign would be affected'.[34] The Guidelines discuss a number of factors[35] and illustrative examples that will be considered when making the decision. Once the decision is made, however, this represents 'a determination that the importance of antitrust enforcement outweighs any relevant foreign policy concerns'.[36]

C. ENFORCEMENT AND THE REACTIONS OF OTHER STATES

Problems arise where the US wishes to take enforcement action extraterritorially. In *United States v ICI Ltd*,[37] a US court ordered, on the grounds of infringement of the Sherman Act, the cancellation of agreements between ICI and Du Pont by which Du Pont assigned to ICI certain patents which were to be registered in the UK. ICI was ordered to reassign the patents to Du Pont. ICI, however, had already contracted to license the patents to a UK company which sued in the English courts to enforce its contractual rights. Danckwerts J granted a decree of specific performance, saying that the US judge 'was applying an enactment of Congress, which has no application to the United Kingdom'.[38]

US pre-trial discovery confers wide-ranging powers on US plaintiffs wishing to search abroad for evidence of antitrust violations. In *Rio Tinto Zinc*,[39] letters rogatory from a US court requested the High Court of England and Wales to require directors and employees of a British company to give oral evidence before an examiner in London and to require the company to produce certain documents. The House of Lords held that the request fell within the exceptions to the obligation to assist in requests for discovery by foreign courts contained in the Evidence (Proceedings in Other Jurisdictions) Act 1975, and consequently refused discovery. The UK subsequently passed the Protection of Trading Interest Act 1980 to 'block' the enforcement of any foreign international trade laws, but in reality largely directed at US antitrust laws. Other countries, including Canada, Australia, and France have enacted similar blocking statutes.[40]

Violation of s. 1 of the Sherman Act is a criminal offence.[41] However, executives can escape US jails by lurking in countries which will not extradite to the US for antitrust offences. In *Norris*,[42] the UK courts refused to extradite to the US for the antitrust offence as at the time participation in a cartel was not criminal in UK law[43] but did extradite in respect of the charge of obstruction of justice, which was.[44]

[33] January 2017, replacing the 1995 Guidelines, <www.justice.gov/atr/internationalguidelines/download>.
[34] *International Operations Guidelines*, para. 4.1.
[35] Para. 4.1. The list is very similar to that in *Timberlane*, 549 F.2d 597 (9th Cir. 1976).
[36] Para.4.1, *International Operations Guidelines*.
[37] 105 F. Supp. 215 (1952). [38] *British Nylon Spinners Ltd v ICI Ltd* [1955] Ch 37.
[39] *Rio Tinto Zinc Corp v Westinghouse Electric Corp* [1978] AC 547.
[40] See generally A. V. Lowe, *Extraterritorial Jurisdiction* (Grotius Publications, 1983).
[41] For the criminalisation of cartel arrangements generally, see Chap. 13, Section 11.
[42] *Norris v Government of the United States of America* [2008] UKHL 16, see Chap. 13, Section 11.
[43] The 'cartel' offence, introduced into UK law by the Enterprise Act 2002, s. 188, is extraditable but not retrospectively so. The argument that price-fixing was an offence of conspiracy to defraud at common law, failed in the House of Lords as 'aggravating circumstances' had not been shown, *Norris v Government of the United States of America* [2008] UKHL 16.
[44] *Norris v Government of the United States of America* [2010] UKSC 9.

D. FOREIGN PLAINTIFFS IN US COURTS

In Chapter 14 we saw that private litigation of antitrust cases is far more common in US courts than it is in the EU and discussed the features of the US system which make it more attractive for plaintiffs in the US to bring actions.[45]

Overseas litigants often look with envy at the sight of US plaintiffs winning large damages awards in US courts, sometimes in respect of international cartels which had effects in numerous countries. Overseas victims of international cartels therefore started litigating in US courts in respect of harm suffered outside the US. At first these actions seemed unlikely to succeed because of the FTAIA's stipulation that as regards foreign commerce the antitrust laws will not apply unless the conduct has a direct, substantial, and reasonably foreseeable effect on US commerce.[46] However, various US Courts of Appeals differed in their reactions to claims over harm overseas. The matter went to the Supreme Court in *F. Hoffmann-La Roche Ltd v Empagran*.[47]

The first argument in *Empagran* was about the statutory construction of the FTAIA in the light of international comity. The second was about its construction in the light of its legislative history. The issue was whether the US could or should act as a kind of world policeman, welcoming litigants from all over the world who have been injured abroad by cartels which have also caused injury inside the US. In *Empagran*, the plaintiffs were, inter alia, Ukrainian, Ecuadorean, and Panamanian buyers, while the defendant sellers were German and Swiss. One argument for the US courts taking jurisdiction was that global cartels do not really 'take place' in any particular territory. When foreign purchasers contract with a multinational corporation the contract could be sourced anywhere, and there is no reason why a party's ability to recover should depend on how the multinational structures its transactions. Further it is argued that global cartels do harm US consumers, because in a globalised world there is no such thing as domestic price-fixing: the important thing to do is to deter cartel behaviour by making it too expensive. The DOJ argued in its amicus curiae brief to the Supreme Court in *Empagran* that, in particular, the taking of jurisdiction by US courts would undermine the DOJ's leniency programme by expanding the scope of the cartelists' potential civil liability, and would undermine cooperation with other competition authorities.

The Supreme Court held that the FTAIA excluded foreign plaintiffs from seeking damages in the US where the harm flowed exclusively from the foreign effects of the conduct which infringed the Sherman Act. It considered the question of comity. Several foreign governments submitted briefs to the Supreme Court arguing against the US courts taking jurisdiction, and the Supreme Court gave these considerable weight.

***F. Hoffmann-La Roche Ltd v Empagran SA*, 542 US 155 (2004), 14 June 2004**

Opinion of the Supreme Court

Justice Breyer

IV

. . . The price-fixing conduct significantly and adversely affects both customers outside the United States and customers within the United States, but the adverse foreign effect is independent of any adverse domestic effect. In these circumstances, we find that the FTAIA exception does not apply (and thus the Sherman Act does not apply) for two main reasons. *First*, this Court ordinarily construes

[45] Chap. 14, Section 3.

[46] See the discussion of the FTAIA in the UK High Court in *Granville Technology Group Ltd v Infineon Technologies AG* [2020] EWHC 415 (Comm), paras. 100–101.

[47] 542 US 155 (2004).

ambiguous statutes to avoid unreasonable interference with the sovereign authority of other nations . . . This rule of construction reflects principles of customary international law—law that (we must assume) Congress ordinarily seeks to follow . . .

This rule of statutory construction cautions courts to assume that legislators take account of the legitimate sovereign interests of other nations when they write American laws. It thereby helps the potentially conflicting laws of different nations work together in harmony—a harmony particularly needed in today's highly interdependent commercial world.

No one denies that America's antitrust laws, when applied to foreign conduct, can interfere with a foreign nation's ability independently to regulate its own commercial affairs. But our courts have long held that application of our antitrust laws to foreign anti-competitive conduct is nonetheless reasonable, and hence consistent with principles of prescriptive comity, insofar as they reflect a legislative effort to redress domestic antitrust injury that foreign anti-competitive conduct has caused. . . . But why is it reasonable to apply those laws to foreign conduct insofar as that conduct causes independent foreign harm and that foreign harm alone gives rise to the plaintiff's claim? Like the former case, application of those laws creates a serious risk of interference with a foreign nation's ability independently to regulate its own commercial affairs. But, unlike the former case, the justification for that interference seems insubstantial. See Restatement §403(2) (determining reasonableness on basis of such factors as connections with regulating nation, harm to that nation's interests, extent to which other nations regulate, and the potential for conflict). Why should American law supplant, for example, Canada's or Great Britain's or Japan's own determination about how best to protect Canadian or British or Japanese customers from anti-competitive conduct engaged in significant part by Canadian or British or Japanese or other foreign companies?

We recognize that principles of comity provide Congress greater leeway when it seeks to control through legislation the actions of American companies, see Restatement §402; and some of the anti-competitive price-fixing conduct alleged here took place in America. But the higher foreign prices of which the foreign plaintiffs here complain are not the consequence of any domestic anti-competitive conduct that Congress sought to forbid, for Congress did not seek to forbid any such conduct insofar as it is here relevant, i.e., insofar as it is intertwined with foreign conduct that causes independent foreign harm. Rather Congress sought to release domestic (and foreign) anti-competitive conduct from Sherman Act constraints when that conduct causes foreign harm. Congress, of course, did make an exception where that conduct also causes domestic harm. See House Report 13 (concerns about American firms' participation in international cartels addressed through 'domestic injury' exception). But any independent domestic harm the foreign conduct causes here has, by definition, little or nothing to do with the matter.

We thus repeat the basic question: Why is it reasonable to apply this law to conduct that is significantly foreign insofar as that conduct causes independent foreign harm and that foreign harm alone gives rise to the plaintiff's claim? We can find no good answer to the question . . .

. . .

Respondents reply that many nations have adopted antitrust laws similar to our own, to the point where the practical likelihood of interference with the relevant interests of other nations is minimal. Leaving price fixing to the side, however, this Court has found to the contrary. See, e.g., *Hartford Fire*, 509 U.S. at 797–799 (noting that the alleged conduct in the London reinsurance market, while illegal under United States antitrust laws, was assumed to be perfectly consistent with British law and policy); . . .

Regardless, even where nations agree about primary conduct, say price fixing, they disagree dramatically about appropriate remedies. The application, for example, of American private treble-damages remedies to anti-competitive conduct taking place abroad has generated considerable controversy . . . And several foreign nations have filed briefs here arguing that to apply our remedies would unjustifiably permit their citizens to bypass their own less generous remedial schemes, thereby upsetting a balance of competing considerations that their own domestic antitrust laws embody . . .

These briefs add that a decision permitting independently injured foreign plaintiffs to pursue private treble-damages remedies would undermine foreign nations' own antitrust enforcement policies by diminishing foreign firms' incentive to cooperate with antitrust authorities in return for prosecutorial amnesty . . . Respondents alternatively argue that comity does not demand an interpretation of the FTAIA that would exclude independent foreign injury cases across the board. Rather, courts can take (and sometimes have taken) account of comity considerations case by case, abstaining where comity considerations so dictate. Cf., e.g., *Hartford Fire* . . .; *United States* v. *Nippon Paper Industries Co.*, . . .; *Mannington Mills, Inc* v. *Congoleum Corp*, . . .

In our view, however, this approach is too complex to prove workable. The Sherman Act covers many different kinds of anti-competitive agreements. Courts would have to examine how foreign law, compared with American law, treats not only price fixing but also, say, information-sharing agreements, patent-licensing price conditions, territorial product resale limitations, and various forms of joint venture, in respect to both primary conduct and remedy. The legally and economically technical nature of that enterprise means lengthier proceedings, appeals, and more proceedings—to the point where procedural costs and delays could themselves threaten interference with a foreign nation's ability to maintain the integrity of its own antitrust enforcement system. Even in this relatively simple price-fixing case, for example, competing briefs tell us (1) that potential treble-damage liability would help enforce widespread anti-price-fixing norms (through added deterrence) and (2) the opposite, namely that such liability would hinder antitrust enforcement (by reducing incentives to enter amnesty programs) . . . How could a court seriously interested in resolving so empirical a matter—a matter potentially related to impact on foreign interests—do so simply and expeditiously?

We conclude that principles of prescriptive comity counsel against the Court of Appeals' interpretation of the FTAIA. Where foreign anti-competitive conduct plays a significant role and where foreign injury is independent of domestic effects, Congress might have hoped that America's antitrust laws, so fundamental a component of our own economic system, would commend themselves to other nations as well. But, if America's antitrust policies could not win their own way in the international marketplace for such ideas, Congress, we must assume, would not have tried to impose them, in an act of legal imperialism, through legislative fiat.

The Supreme Court then considered the legislative history of the FTAIA and concluded that its 'language and history suggest that Congress designed the FTAIA to clarify, perhaps to limit, but not to expand in any significant way, the Sherman Act's scope as applied to foreign commerce'.[48]

The Supreme Court based its judgment on the assumption that the foreign effects of the cartel were independent of its effects in the US. It left open the question of what would be the position if the foreign and domestic effects could be shown to be intertwined, for example if the prices abroad would have been lower had it not been for the effects in the US. However, *Re Monosodium Glutamate Antitrust Litigation* upheld a ruling excluding foreign plaintiffs from bringing a class action against manufacturers involved in a cartel. The court said that 'the domestic effects of the price fixing scheme—increased US prices—were not the direct cause of the appellants' injuries. Rather it was the foreign effects of the price fixing scheme—increased prices abroad'.[49] The court set a high standard of proof for any effect on US commerce and rejected claims that a worldwide conspiracy in which prices must be inflated in every market (to avoid arbitrage) could satisfy the standard.

[48] On remand, the DC Circuit ruled for the defendants, *Empagran SA v F.Hoffmann-La Roche Ltd* 417 F.3d 1267 (DC Cir. 2005).

[49] 477 F.3d 535 (8th Cir. 2007).

The Seventh Circuit Court of Appeals considered *Empagran* and comity in *Motorola Mobility v AU Optronics*,[50] which arose out of a price-fixing cartel that took place in Taiwan whereby Korean and Taiwanese manufacturers conspired to fix the prices of liquid crystal display panels (LCDs).[51] Motorola sued the LCD panel manufacturers in the US courts for damages in respect of the small percentage of cartelised LCDs it had imported into the US and itself incorporated into mobile phones, and also in respect of the much larger number bought by its foreign subsidiaries and incorporated by them in mobile phones abroad which they had then imported into the US for resale by the parent company. The court held that the claim on behalf of the foreign subsidiaries did not meet the direct, substantial, and foreseeable test. The immediate victims were the foreign subsidiaries, not Motorola. The FTAIA requires that the effect of the anti-competitive conduct on domestic US commerce should give rise to an 'antitrust cause of action'. Here it did not do so because in US law the rule in *Illinois Brick* denies redress to indirect purchasers.[52] The court referred again to the undesirability of the US trying to police the world: 'are we to *presume* the inadequacy of the antitrust laws of our foreign allies? Would such a presumption be consistent with international comity, or more concretely with good relations with allied nations in a world in turmoil?'[53] In fact, some commentators outside the US are disappointed by the stance of the US courts in these cases, viewing it as a failure to confront the realities of global value chains and international conspiracies in the twenty-first century.[54]

E. THE EFFECTS DOCTRINE AND FOREIGN CONDUCT AFFECTING EXPORTS

The FTAIA provides that the Sherman Act only applies to export commerce where the conduct has a direct, substantial, and reasonably foreseeable effect on US commerce. If US exports are injured by being denied access to foreign markets there may be a disadvantageous effect on commerce inside the US. Although the US agencies consider that they do in theory have jurisdiction over conduct abroad which affects exports,[55] they do not usually take action against it.[56] The practical enforcement problems are very great.

5. EU LAW

A. GENERAL

Articles 101 and 102 are silent on whether or not they apply extraterritorially. From the outset, the Commission tried to apply an effects test in order to take subject-matter jurisdiction. The Court did not approve this. At first, the development of the single economic entity doctrine[57] avoided the need to

[50] *Motorola Mobility v AU Optronics*, 775 F.3d 816 (2015). See further *The Antitrust Counselor*, Vol. 84, 2014 (published by the ABA). The Supreme Court refused to hear the appeal, 15 June 2015.

[51] It was the subject of a European Commission cartel decision, COMP/39.309, *LCD* 8 December 2010.

[52] See Chap. 14, Section 3.

[53] *Motorola Mobility v AU Optronics*, 775 F.3d 816, 825 (2015). In *US v Hsi Hsiung* 778 F.3d 738 (9th Cir. 2015), however, the effects of the cartel were enough to found a criminal conviction.

[54] See e.g. D. M. Davis, 'Extraterritoriality and Competition Law Jurisdiction' in D. Gerard and I. Lianos (eds.), *Reconciling Efficiency and Equity: A Global Challenge for Competition Policy* (Cambridge University Press, 2019), 385.

[55] Antitrust Enforcement Guidelines for International Operations, para. 3.2.

[56] But see *United States v Pilkington* (1994–1992) 70 *Trade Cases* 482, which concerned the terms in a technology licence. By a consent decree the defendant agreed not to enforce the terms against US firms.

[57] See Chap. 4, Section A.vii.

confront the issue but in *Wood Pulp I*[58] the single economic entity doctrine could not be applied and the CJ formulated the 'implementation' doctrine. The 'qualified effects' doctrine was finally adopted by the CJ in its *Intel* judgment in 2017.[59] Many matters in respect of its application remain to be resolved, however, particularly in respect of private damages actions.

The Merger Regulation, the EUMR,[60] contains a jurisdiction threshold which may catch concentrations between undertakings based outside the EU, as we saw in Chapter 15.[61] As the antitrust and merger cases reference each other we discuss the cases in chronological order in this section. Enforcement jurisdiction in respect of Articles 101 and 102 is dealt with in Section F of this chapter.

B. THE SINGLE ECONOMIC ENTITY DOCTRINE

The question whether there is an effects doctrine in what was then EEC law was raised in the *Dyestuffs* case.[62] The Commission found a cartel among aniline dyes producers. The participants included ICI, a company incorporated and having its headquarters in the UK which was not at the time a member of the EEC. It was found to have engaged in concerted practices contrary to Article 101(1) by virtue of the instructions it had given to its Belgian subsidiary, and was fined 50,000 units of account.[63] In the Decision, the Commission asserted jurisdiction over ICI on the basis of 'effects':

> Under Article [101(1)] . . . all agreements between undertakings, all decisions by associations of undertakings and all concerted practices which may affect trade between Member States and the object or effect of which is to prevent, restrict or distort competition within the Common Market shall be prohibited as incompatible with the Common Market. The competition rules of the Treaty are, consequently, applicable to all restrictions of competition which produce within the Common Market effects set out in Article [101(1)]. There is therefore no need to examine whether the undertakings which are the cause of these restrictions of competition have their seat within or outside the Community.[64]

On appeal, ICI claimed that the Commission had no power to apply the competition rules to an undertaking established outside the EEC. In reply, the Commission relied both on an elaboration of the effects point and on the claim that, although the subsidiaries within the Community had separate legal personality in law, in reality they were merely carrying out the parent's orders and so appeared 'as mere extensions of ICI in the Common Market'.[65]

Advocate General Mayras recommended upholding the Decision on the basis of the effects doctrine.[66] Having reviewed the national laws of the Member States, the international law arguments, and US law he said that the conditions necessary for taking extraterritorial jurisdiction were that the agreement or concerted practice must create a *direct and immediate* restriction of competition, that the effect must be *reasonably foreseeable*, and that the effect on the territory must be *substantial*.

[58] Cases 89/85 etc, *A. Ahlström Oy v Commission* EU:C:1988:447.

[59] Case C-413/14 P, *Intel Corp v Commission* EU:C:2017:632. [60] Council Reg. 139/2004 [2004] L24/1.

[61] See Chap. 15, Section 8.

[62] Case 48/69, *ICI v Commission (Dyestuffs)* EU:C:1972:70. Earlier, in Case 22/71, *Béguelin Import Co v GL Import Export* EU:C:1971:13 the CJ considered the distribution arrangements of a Japanese manufacturer with its French distributor which compartmentalised the common market on national lines. As one of the parties to the agreement was clearly within the Community, and in the context of the case the imposition of a penalty on the Japanese undertaking did not arise, jurisdiction could be asserted without the question of extraterritorially being addressed.

[63] *Re the Cartel in Aniline Dyes* [1969] OJ L195/11. [64] Ibid., para. 28.

[65] Case 48/69, *ICI v Commission (Dyestuffs)* EU:C:1972:70.

[66] Case 48/69, *Dyestuffs*, Opinion, EU:C:1972:32.

The Advocate General justified the adoption of what amounted to an effects doctrine on grounds both of principle and pragmatism.[67]

As already mentioned in Section 3, he drew a distinction between subject-matter and enforcement jurisdiction.[68] He accepted that the decision taken by the Commission might not be capable of *enforcement*, as taking coercive measures, or measures of inquiry, investigation, or supervision in the territory another State would inevitably infringe the internal sovereignty of that State.[69]

The CJ's judgment did not take up the Advocate General's espousal of an effects doctrine. Instead it upheld the Commission's decision on the basis of nationality by applying what has become known as the single economic entity doctrine. It is explained in Chapter 3 howt EU law has developed this doctrine, by which parents and subsidiaries are considered to be one undertaking for the purposes of the application of the competition rules. In *Dyestuffs*, the Court relied on this concept to impute the conduct of the subsidiary to the parent and uphold the finding of jurisdiction.

Case 48/69, *ICI v Commission (Dyestuffs)* EU:C:1972:70

Court of Justice

130. By making use of its power to control its subsidiaries established in the Community, the applicant was able to ensure that its decision was implemented on that market.

131. The applicant objects that this conduct is to be imputed to its subsidiaries and not to itself.

132. The fact that a subsidiary has separate legal personality is not sufficient to exclude the possibility of imputing its conduct to the parent company.

133. Such may be the case in particular where the subsidiary, although having separate legal personality, does not decide independently upon its own conduct on the market, but carries out, in all material respects, the instructions given to it by the parent company.

134. Where a subsidiary does not enjoy real autonomy in determining its course of action in the market, the prohibitions set out in Article [101(1)] may be considered inapplicable in the relationship between it and the parent company with which it forms one economic unit.

135. In view of the unity of the group thus formed, the actions of the subsidiaries may in certain circumstances be attributed to the parent company.

136. It is well-known that at the time the applicant held all or at any rate the majority of the shares in those subsidiaries.

137. The applicant was able to exercise decisive influence over the policy of the subsidiaries as regards selling prices in the Common Market and in fact used this power upon the occasion of the three price increases in question.

The CJ therefore held that the subsidiary did not have 'real autonomy' but acted on its parent's instructions, so that the infringing conduct in the EEC could be treated as having been committed by the subsidiary as an agent of the parent.[70]

In *Dyestuffs*, the CJ neither approved nor disapproved the Advocate General's views on the effects doctrine but its silence encouraged the Commission's belief that Community law did recognise the doctrine.

[67] See in particular EU:C:1972:32, 696. [68] See Section 3, p. 1252.

[69] Case 48/69, *Dyestuffs* EU:C:1972:32, 695.

[70] F. A. Mann argued that the facts of the case did not support this conclusion: '*Dyestuffs* Case in the Court of Justice of the European Communities' (1973) 22 *ICLQ* 35 and 'Responsibility of Parent Companies for Foreign Subsidiaries' in C. Olmstead (ed.), *Extra-territorial Application of Laws and Responses Thereto* (ESC Publishing, 1984), 156.

C. THE IMPLEMENTATION DOCTRINE

In *Wood Pulp I*,[71] the CJ pronounced the 'implementation' doctrine.

The Commission found a price-fixing cartel in the wood pulp industry.[72] All 43 producers and trade associations concerned had their registered offices outside the EEC and not all of them had branches, subsidiaries, agencies, or other establishments within the Community. Many of the addressees appealed on the ground that the Commission had no jurisdiction to apply EC competition rules to them.[73]

Advocate General Darmon surveyed the relevant international and US law and the scholarly literature and concluded that the Community was entitled to take, and should take, jurisdiction in this case on the basis of the effects doctrine, which was not contrary to international law:

> 57. . . . [T]here is no rule of international law which is capable of being relied upon against the criterion of the direct, substantial and foreseeable effect. Nor does the concept of international comity, in view of its uncertain scope, militate against the criterion either.
>
> 58. In the absence of any such prohibitive rule and in the light of widespread State practice, I would therefore propose that in view of its appropriateness to the field of competition, it be adopted as a criterion for the jurisdiction of the Community.[74]

The CJ, however, couched its judgment in different terms.

> **Cases 89, 104, 114, 116, 117, and 125–129/85, *A. Ahlström Oy v Commission* EU:C:1988:447**
>
> **Court of Justice**
>
> 12. It should be noted that the main sources of supply of wood pulp are outside the Community, in Canada, the United States, Sweden and Finland and that the market therefore has global dimensions. Where wood pulp producers established in those countries sell directly to purchasers established in the Community and engage in price competition in order to win orders from those customers, that constitutes competition within the Common Market.
>
> 13. It follows that where those producers concert on the prices to be charged to their customers in the Community and put that concertation into effect by selling at prices which are actually coordinated, they are taking part in concertation which has the object and effect of restricting competition within the Common Market within the meaning of Article [101].
>
> 14. Accordingly, it must be concluded that by applying the competition rules in the Treaty in the circumstances of this case to undertakings whose registered offices are situated outside the Community, the Commission has not made an incorrect assessment of the territorial scope of Article [101].
>
> 15. The applicants have submitted that the decision is incompatible with public international law on the grounds that the application of the competition rules in this case was founded exclusively on the economic repercussions within the Common Market of conduct restricting competition which [was] adopted outside the Community.
>
> 16. It should be observed that an infringement of Article [101], such as the conclusion of an agreement which has had the effect of restricting competition within the Common Market, consists of

[71] Cases 89, 104, 114, 116, 117, and 125–9/85, *A. Ahlström Oy v Commission* EU:C:1988:447 (*Wood Pulp I*).
[72] *Woodpulp* [1985] OJ L85/1, see Chap. 9.
[73] For the appeal on the concerted practices issue, see Cases C-89, 104, 114, 116, 117, and 125–129/85, *A. Ahlström Osakeyhtiö v Commission (Wood Pulp II)* EU:C:1993:120, and Chaps. 4 and 9.
[74] EU:C:1988:258.

conduct made up of two elements, the formation of the agreement, decision or concerted practice and the implementation thereof. If the applicability of prohibitions laid down under competition law were made to depend on the place where the agreement, decision or concerted practice was formed, the result would obviously be to give undertakings an easy means of evading those prohibitions. The decisive factor is therefore the place where it is implemented.

17. The producers in this case implemented their pricing agreement within the Common Market. It is immaterial in that respect whether or not they had recourse to subsidiaries, agents, sub-agents, or branches within the Community in order to make their contacts with purchasers within the Community.

18. Accordingly the Community's jurisdiction to apply its competition rules to such conduct is covered by the territoriality principle as universally recognized in public international law.

19. As regards the argument based on the infringement of the principle of non-interference, it should be pointed out that the applicants who are members of KEA have referred to a rule according to which where two States have jurisdiction to lay down and enforce rules and the effect of those rules is that a person finds himself subject to contradictory orders as to the conduct he must adopt, each State is obliged to exercise its jurisdiction with moderation. The applicants have concluded that by disregarding that rule in applying its competition rules the Community has infringed the principle of non-interference.

20. There is no need to enquire into the existence in international law of such a rule since it suffices to observe that the conditions for its application are in any event not satisfied. There is not, in this case, any contradiction between the conduct required by the United States and that required by the Community since the Webb–Pomerene Act[75] merely exempts the conclusion of export cartels from the application of United States antitrust laws but does not require such cartels to be concluded.

. . .

22. As regards the argument relating to disregard of international comity, it suffices to observe that it amounts to calling in question the Community's jurisdiction to apply its competition rules to conduct such as that found to exist in this case and that, as such, that argument has already been rejected.

23. Accordingly it must be concluded that the Commission's decision is not contrary to Article [101] or to the rules of public international law relied on by the applicants.

Given the terms in which the Commission decision, the arguments before the Court, and the Advocate General's Opinion had been couched, the avoidance of specific reference to the effects doctrine was clearly deliberate.

It will be noted that the Court dealt first, in paragraphs 11–14, with whether or not the Commission infringed *the Treaty* by applying the competition rules to the individual undertakings.[76] The Court held that the Commission had correctly assessed the territorial scope of Article 101. Secondly, paragraphs 15–18 consider whether the Commission had infringed *international* law. The CJ held that the taking of jurisdiction was covered by the 'universally recognized' territoriality principle (paragraph 18). Thirdly, paragraphs 19–22 reject the argument based on a possible 'non-interference' principle by saying that the US legislation did not *require* export cartels to be entered into, but merely tolerated them.[77]

In paragraph 16, the Court divided the infringing conduct into two elements, the formation of the agreement and its implementation. The place of formation was irrelevant: the decisive factor was

[75] The Webb–Pomerene Act 1918 is a US statute which allows American exporters to act together in export markets in ways which would otherwise violate the Sherman Act.

[76] The decision was annulled in respect of one trade association as the CJ held that it had not played a separate role in the implementation of the price-fixing agreements: EU:C:1988:447, paras. 24–28.

[77] This is the same position as that reached by the Supreme Court in *Hartford Fire* in respect of UK law. See Section 4.B, p. 1254.

where it was 'implemented'. The crucial question is what is meant by 'implementation'. As the CJ said in paragraph 17 that it was immaterial whether or not the producers used subsidiaries, agents, sub-agents, or branches inside the Community, 'implementation' must cover direct sales to EU purchasers and not depend on the sellers establishing some form of marketing organisation within the EU. Jurisdiction is taken simply because of sale into the EU.[78] This was confirmed in both *Gencor*[79] and *Intel*.[80] The preponderant view is that 'implementation' does not cover negative behaviour such as agreements concluded outside the EU by which undertakings agree not to sell within the EU, or agree not to purchase from EU producers.[81] Such conduct would fall, rather, within the effects doctrine. In his Opinion in *Intel*,[82] Advocate General Wahl doubted that the conduct in that case, consisting of the agreements between a US and a Chinese company concerning sales of CPUs manufactured and sold outside the EU for incorporation into computers manufactured in China, was 'implemented' in the EU.

D. THE QUALIFIED EFFECTS DOCTRINE

(i) The Meaning of 'Qualified' Effects

The form of effects doctrine discussed, and now accepted, as a basis for extraterritorial jurisdiction in EU law is called the 'qualified effects' doctrine (or test). The word 'qualified' denotes that in order to ground jurisdiction in any particular case the effects produced in the EU must satisfy certain conditions, i.e. be immediate, substantial, and foreseeable.

(ii) The *Gencor* Case

Although, as we have seen earlier, the Commission and various Advocates General have consistently argued for a qualified effects test, the first time one of the EU Courts accepted it was in the judgment of the GC in the merger case, *Gencor*.[83]

a. *The Terms of the Merger Regulation*

As explained in Chapter 15, the EU Merger Regulation (EUMR)[84] provides that the Commission has sole jurisdiction[85] over concentrations with an 'EU dimension'.[86] The meaning of this is set out in Article 1.

Article 1 does not expressly say anything about where the undertakings concerned are incorporated, or carry on business, or whether the undertakings must have assets in the EU. The criteria relate only to a worldwide turnover figure and a much smaller EU-wide turnover figure. Article 5, which

[78] For the argument that this is not justified in international law, see e.g. W. Van Gerven, 'EC Jurisdiction in Antitrust Matters: The *Wood Pulp* Judgment' [1989] *Fordham Corp L Inst* 451.

[79] Case T-102/96, *Gencor* EU:T:1999:65, para. 87; see the following extract.

[80] Case T-286/09, *Intel* EU:T:2014:547, para. 241.

[81] See e.g. Griffin, n. 3; Van Gerven, n. 78. Van Gerven's view is also that any attempt to encompass such conduct within 'implementation' would be contrary to international law as there would not be a sufficiently close link to support jurisdiction.

[82] Case C-413/14 P, *Intel Corp v Commission* EU:C:2016:788, paras. 3081–3313.

[83] Case T-102/96, *Gencor* EU:T:1999:65.

[84] Reg. 139/2004 [2004] OJ L24/1 (replacing Reg. 4064/89 [1989] OJ L395/1). For the EUMR generally, see Chap. 15.

[85] Subject to certain exceptions, discussed in Chap. 15, such as Art. 9 which allows for concentrations to be referred back to national authorities.

[86] For a full analysis of the 'Union dimension', see M. Broberg, *The European Commission's Jurisdiction to Scrutinise Mergers* (4th edn, Wolters Kluwer, 2013).

deals with the calculation of turnover, says that '[t]urnover in the [Union] or in a Member State, shall comprise products sold and services provided to undertakings or consumers, in the [Union] or in that Member State as the case may be'.[87] The EU dimension test made it inevitable that undertakings established abroad would be drawn into the net of EU merger control by involvement in transactions with EU undertakings. The Union dimension threshold can, however, also catch transactions which involve *only* undertakings located outside the EU with few assets inside it, and transactions which have minimal impact inside the EU. The broad jurisdiction is unlikely to cause great problems in most cases, in that the concentration concerned will clearly not be incompatible with the internal market under the test in Article 2 of the EUMR.[88] Even so, non-EU undertakings may object to the Commission's jurisdiction, and the obligation to notify.

b. *The* Gencor *Judgment*

In *Gencor/Lonrho*, the Commission prohibited a merger in the South African mining industry, on the ground that it would create a position of duopolistic dominance.[89]

The facts of the case are given in Chapter 15.[90] To recap, it concerned a proposed merger between the platinum and rhodium mining interests of two companies incorporated in South Africa. All the production was in South Africa. The proposed merger was notified to the South African authorities, which found no competition problems.[91] The merger had a Community dimension because of the worldwide and Community-wide turnover of the merging companies. The Commission was concerned that the merger would reduce the major players on the market from three to two, creating a duopoly. It found the merger to be incompatible with the common market on account of the anti-competitive effects which the creation of the dominant duopoly position would have on *sales* of the products in the Community.[92]

One party, Gencor, contested the assumption of jurisdiction before the GC.[93] It argued[94] that the EUMR applies only if the activities forming the subject matter of the concentration are located within the Community. The location of the concentration was South Africa, as would be the place of implementation if the *Wood Pulp* test was applied, not the EEC. Moreover, even if the test for jurisdiction *was* whether the merger had an immediate and substantial effect on competition within the EEC, that test was not satisfied either: 'the Commission cannot claim jurisdiction in respect of a concentration on the basis of future and hypothetical behaviour in which undertakings in the relevant market might engage and which might or might not fall within its purview under the Treaty'.[95] The GC, however, upheld the Commission's decision.

[87] Merger Reg., Art. 5(1), second para. The main reason for the original Merger Reg. not directly addressing the jurisdiction issue seems to be that the Council Working Group was dealing with the details of the Regulation at the time *Wood Pulp I* was before the CJ. In the light of that, express references to jurisdiction were deleted from the final version, see C. J. Cook and C. S. Kerse, *EC Merger Control* (3rd edn, Sweet & Maxwell, 2000), 11–12.

[88] And will receive Art. 6(1) clearance within a month, see Chap. 15, Section 4.

[89] M.619 [1997] OJ L11/30.

[90] Chap. 15, Section 5.D.

[91] The South African Government told the Commission that it would not contest the Commission's policy, but that it considered that two equally matched competitors (as Anglo-American and Gencor/Lonrho would be) were preferable to the prevailing situation of one dominant firm (Anglo-American), *Gencor/Lonrho* [1997] OJ L11/30, para. 19.

[92] See M.619 [1997] OJ L11/30, para. 206.

[93] Once the Commission had blocked the merger there was no possibility of the transaction going ahead, since under the agreement between the parties it was a condition precedent that clearance from the Commission should be obtained by a certain date. The entire purchase agreement had therefore lapsed. Nevertheless, the GC held that the action for annulment was still admissible since the applicant had an interest in having the legality of the decision addressed to it examined by the Community judicature: Case T-102/96, *Gencor* EU:T:1999:65, paras. 40–46.

[94] Case T-102/96, *Gencor Ltd v Commission* [1999] ECR II-753, paras. 48–63.

[95] Ibid., para. 61.

Case T-102/96, *Gencor Ltd v Commission* EU:T:1999:65

General Court

81. The applicant's arguments to the effect that the legal bases for the Regulation and the wording of its preamble and substantive provisions preclude its application to the concentration at issue cannot be accepted.

82. The legal bases for the Regulation, namely Articles [103 and 352 TFEU], and more particularly the provisions to which they are intended to give effect, that is to say Articles 3(g) [EC] and [101 and 102 TFEU], as well as the first to fifth, ninth and eleventh recitals in the preamble to the Regulation, merely point to the need to ensure that competition is not distorted in the common market, in particular by concentrations which result in the creation or strengthening of a dominant position. They in no way exclude from the Regulation's field of application concentrations which, while relating to mining and/or production activities outside the Community, have the effect of creating or strengthening a dominant position as a result of which effective competition in the common market is significantly impeded.

83. In particular, the applicant's view cannot be founded on the closing words of the 11th recital in the preamble to the Regulation.

84. That recital states that 'a concentration with a Community dimension exists . . . where the concentrations are effected by undertakings which do not have their principal fields of activities in the Community but which have substantial operations there'.

85. By that reference, in general terms, to the concept of substantial operations, the Regulation does not, for the purpose of defining its territorial scope, ascribe greater importance to production operations than to sales operations. On the contrary, by setting quantitative thresholds in Article 1 which are based on the worldwide and Community turnover of the undertakings concerned, it rather ascribes greater importance to sales operations within the common market as a factor linking the concentration to the Community. It is common ground that Gencor and Lonrho each carry out significant sales in the Community (valued in excess of ECU 250 million).

86. Nor is it borne out by either the 30th recital in the preamble to the Regulation or Article 24 thereof that the criterion based on the location of production activities is well founded. Far from laying down a criterion for defining the territorial scope of the Regulation, Article 24 merely regulates the procedures to be followed in order to deal with situations in which non-member countries do not grant Community undertakings treatment comparable to that accorded by the Community to undertakings from those non-member countries in relation to the control of concentrations.

87. The applicant cannot, by reference to the judgment in *Wood Pulp*, rely on the criterion as to the implementation of an agreement to support its interpretation of the territorial scope of the Regulation. Far from supporting the applicant's view, that criterion for assessing the link between an agreement and Community territory in fact precludes it. According to *Wood Pulp*, the criterion as to the implementation of an agreement is satisfied by mere sale within the Community, irrespective of the location of the sources of supply and the production plant. It is not disputed that Gencor and Lonrho carried out sales in the Community before the concentration and would have continued to do so thereafter.

88. Accordingly, the Commission did not err in its assessment of the territorial scope of the Regulation by applying it in this case to a proposed concentration notified by undertakings whose registered offices and mining and production operations are outside the Community.

2. Compatibility of the contested decision with public international law

. . .

90. Application of the Regulation is justified under public international law when it is foreseeable that a proposed concentration will have an immediate and substantial effect in the Community.

91. In that regard, the concentration would, according to the contested decision, have led to the creation of a dominant duopoly on the part of Amplats and Implats/LPD in the platinum and rhodium markets, as a result of which effective competition would have been significantly impeded in the common market within the meaning of Article 2(3) of the Regulation.

92. It is therefore necessary to verify whether the three criteria of immediate, substantial and foreseeable effect are satisfied in this case.

It can be seen from this extract that in paragraph 87 the GC returned to the *Wood Pulp* judgment and confirmed that the criterion of the implementation of an agreement is satisfied by mere sale in the Community. In paragraphs 90–111, the GC considered whether the decision was in accordance with public international law. It concluded that it was. In paragraph 90, the GC says, in words redolent of the effects doctrine, that the application of the EUMR is justified in international law 'when it is foreseeable that a proposed concentration will have an immediate and substantial effect in the Community'. The GC did not, therefore, straightforwardly adopt the effects doctrine, but rather examined whether taking jurisdiction on grounds of implementation in this case conformed to the criteria which it identified as required by international law. However, in *Intel*,[96] the GC said that *Gencor* 'relied solely on the qualified effects'.[97]

The *Gencor* judgment went on to consider whether the conditions identified in paragraph 90 required to make the taking of jurisdiction justified in international law—an immediate, substantial, and foreseeable effect—were satisfied. It concluded that they were, since it was foreseeable that the merger would result in a dominant duopoly on the world market with all the competition problems to which that was likely to give rise.[98] *Gencor* is a striking demonstration of the implications of extraterritoriality. The EC forbade a merger involving producer undertakings in a non-Member State because of the sales of the product (less than a quarter of the worldwide total) in the Community. The GC examined the matter in the light of the principles of non-interference and proportionality (paragraphs 102–108 of the judgment) but concluded that there was no conflict with the interests of South Africa because South Africa did not require the transaction to take place. There is no conflict of jurisdiction between a State which prohibits something and a State which allows it (rather than requires it). The difficulty with this is that merger control invariably operates only to forbid certain concentrations, not to require them, and the prohibiting jurisdiction will always trump the other. However, in *Gencor* the transaction was likely to have a more serious impact on the economy of South Africa than on consumers in the EC.[99]

(iii) The *InnoLux* Case

Chronologically the *InnoLux*[100] case came between the GC *Intel* judgment[101] and the CJ judgment,[102] but it is convenient to consider it here.

InnoLux concerned the calculation of the fine imposed on the appellant undertaking for its participation in the worldwide *LCD Panels* cartel.[103] For the purpose of calculating the value of sales under

[96] See Section 5.D.iv.b. [97] Case 286/09, *Intel* EU:T:2014:547, para. 240.

[98] EU:T:1999:65, paras. 93–101. For a discussion of the substantive aspects of the case in the context of horizontal mergers which lead to positions of collective dominance, see Chap. 15, Section 5.D.iii.d.

[99] See E. Fox, 'The Merger Regulation and its Territorial Reach' [1999] *ECLR* 334, for a critique of *Gencor* on these grounds.

[100] Case C-231/14 P, *InnoLux Corp v Commission* EU:C:2015:451.

[101] Case T-286/09, *Intel v Commission* EU:T:2014:547. [102] Case C-413/14 P, *Intel Corp v Commission* EU:C:2017:632.

[103] COMP/39.309, 8 December 2010. The US cases, *US v Hui Hsiung* and *Motorola Mobility* (n. 53), see Section 4.D, arose from the same cartel.

paragraph 13 of the Fining Guidelines,[104] the Commission took into account the value of sales in the EEA of 'transformed products', i.e. products into which the vertically integrated cartelist had incorporated the cartelised product in China and Taiwan. The GC upheld this,[105] but Advocate General Wathelet[106] considered that the 'only justification for the Commission's having jurisdiction with regard to the sales at issue must arise in this case from application of the "qualified effects" test' because indirect sales could not constitute implementation.[107] He did not consider that the Commission had produced sufficient evidence of such effects.

The CJ, however, did not address the extraterritorial issue. It did not mention qualified effects or the arguments of the Advocate General. It noted that according to *Wood Pulp I* there was no question about its jurisdiction over the LCD cartel itself. It treated the case as simply being about the amount of the fine and said that the vertically integrated participants in a cartel could not, 'solely because they incorporated the goods the subject of the infringement into the finished products outside the EEA, expect to have excluded from the calculation of the fine the proportion of the value of their sales of those finished products in the EEA that are capable of being regarded as corresponding to the value of the goods the subject of the infringement'.[108]

(iv) The *Intel* Case

a. *The Commission Decision*

The substance of *Intel* is discussed in Chapter 7. It is seen there that the abuses found by the Commission were exclusivity rebates and so-called 'naked restrictions' whereby Intel, a US company, paid computer manufacturers to delay or cancel the marketing of products containing their competitor's (AMD) x86CPUs. One of the manufacturers was the Chinese company Lenovo which purchased Intel's CPUs outside the EEA and incorporated them into its computers outside the EEA.

b. Intel *in the General Court*

On appeal Intel, inter alia, challenged the EU's jurisdiction over the Lenovo transactions on the grounds that they all took place outside the EEA and that very few of the affected computers would have been sold in the EEA.

Case T-286/09, *Intel v Commission* EU:T:2014:547

General Court

231. First of all, it should be noted that, in the case-law of the Court of Justice and the General Court, two approaches have been followed in order to establish that the Commission's jurisdiction is justified under the rules of public international law.

232. The first approach is based on the principle of territoriality. That approach was followed in Joined Cases 89/85 [etc.] *Ahlström Osakeyhtiö and Others* v *Commission*, '*Woodpulp*'). In paragraph 16 of that judgment, the Court held that it was necessary to distinguish two elements of conduct, namely

[104] See Chap. 13, Section 6.H. [105] Case T-91/11, *InnoLux v Commission* EU:T:2014:92.

[106] Case C-231/14 P, EU:C:2015:292, para. 44.

[107] Ibid., para. 46. Wahl AG giving his Opinion in Case C-413/14 P, *Intel Corp v Commission* EU:C:2016:788, para. 292, did not agree with Wathelet AG about indirect sales and implementation, see p. 1270.

[108] Case C-231/14 P, *InnoLux v Commission*, para. 55; see S. S. H. Chan, '*InnoLux Corp v Commission*: Establishment of the Effects Doctrine in Extraterritoriality of EU Competition Law?' [2015] *ECLR* 463.

the formation of the agreement, decision or concerted practice and the implementation thereof. If the applicability of prohibitions laid down under competition law were made to depend on the place where the agreement, decision or concerted practice was formed, the result would obviously be to give undertakings an easy means of evading those prohibitions. The Court therefore held that the decisive factor is the place where it is implemented.

233. The second approach is based on the qualified effects of the practices in the European Union. That approach was followed in Case T-102/96 *Gencor* v *Commission* '*Gencor*'. In paragraph 90 of that judgment, the Court held that application of Council Regulation (EEC) No 4064/89 . . . on the control of concentrations between undertakings . . ., is justified under public international law when it is foreseeable that a proposed concentration will have an immediate and substantial effect in the European Union.

234. By submitting that where trade with third countries is involved, even where implementation of the practices at issue takes place within the European Union, the Commission must also prove the existence of immediate, substantial, direct and foreseeable effects within the European Union, the applicant's reasoning amounts to an assertion that implementation and qualified effects in the European Union are cumulative conditions.

235. The Commission stated, at the hearing, that, in the present case, its jurisdiction was justified, first, under the doctrine of implementation of the practices at issue in the EEA, which was followed in *Woodpulp*, paragraph 232 above, and, second, under the effects doctrine, which was followed in *Gencor*, paragraph 233 above.

236. In that regard, the Court would point out that demonstrating the implementation of the practices at issue in the EEA or demonstrating qualified effects are alternative and not cumulative approaches for the purposes of establishing that the Commission's jurisdiction is justified under the rules of public international law.

237. In *Woodpulp*, paragraph 232 above, the Court of Justice relied solely on the implementation of the conduct at issue in the territory of the European Union.

238. The applicant may not rely on the fact that Advocate General Darmon stated, in point 82 of his Opinion in *Woodpulp*, paragraph 232 above, that it would be for the Court 'to ascertain whether the effects of the conduct alleged by the Commission were substantial, direct and foreseeable in order to determine whether the Commission was right in exercising jurisdiction over the applicants'. The Advocate General proposed that the Court should rely on the effects of the conduct at issue in the territory of the European Union in order to establish the Commission's jurisdiction. The Court did not follow the Advocate General's proposal and relied on the implementation of the agreement in the European Union. It therefore follows from the judgment of the Court in that case that, where the Commission's jurisdiction can be established on the basis of the implementation of the conduct at issue in the European Union, it is not necessary to examine whether there were any effects in order to establish the Commission's jurisdiction.

239. The applicant relies in that context also on *Gencor*, paragraph 233 above.

240. However, in *Gencor*, paragraph 233 above (paragraphs 89 to 101), the General Court relied solely on the qualified effects in order to establish that the Commission's jurisdiction was justified under the rules of public international law.

241. It is indeed true that, in paragraph 87 of that judgment, the Court observed that, according to *Woodpulp*, paragraph 232 above, the criterion as to the implementation of an agreement is satisfied by mere sale within the European Union. However, paragraph 87 forms part of the reasoning of the Court by which the latter held that Regulation No 4064/89 did not, for the purpose of defining its territorial scope, ascribe greater importance to production operations than to sales operations (*Gencor*, paragraph 233 above, paragraphs 85 to 88). In that context, the Court rejected an argument of the applicant based on *Woodpulp*, paragraph 232 above, by holding that, according to that judgment, the criterion as to the implementation of an agreement is satisfied by mere sales. The Court therefore rejected the

applicant's argument that it follows from *Woodpulp*, paragraph 232 above, that greater importance is ascribed to production activities than to sales activities.

242. Next, the Court examined, in paragraphs 89 to 101 of *Gencor*, paragraph 233 above, whether the application of Regulation No 4064/89 in that case was consistent with public international law. In that context, the Court confined itself to examining whether the criteria of immediate, substantial and foreseeable effect were satisfied.

243. It therefore follows from *Gencor*, paragraph 233 above, that, in order to justify the Commission's jurisdiction according to the rules of public international law, it is sufficient that the criteria of immediate, substantial and foreseeable effect in the European Union be satisfied.

244. It follows from the foregoing that, in order to justify the Commission's jurisdiction under public international law, it is sufficient to establish either the qualified effects of the practice in the European Union or that it was implemented in the European Union.

The GC then proceeded to examine whether on the facts the effects were indeed substantial, immediate,[109] and foreseeable.[110] The main issue was substantiality, as the effects were not just foreseeable but intended, and the fact that Intel itself did not sell into the EEA did not make the effects of Intel's conduct indirect because it did directly concern its customers' sales.[111] On substantiality the GC said that it is not necessary for the EEA to be more affected than other regions in the world, and that the EEA constitutes a significant part of the world market.[112] The effects do not have to be actual, so that the Commission can act to prevent a threat to the effective competition structure.[113] Moreover, weakening Intel's sole significant competitor at the worldwide level was capable of having repercussions on the competitive structure of the common market.[114] Another element in proving substantiality was the treatment of Intel's various abuses as 'a single continuous infringement' rather than as a number of separate abuses.[115]

In this judgment, therefore, the GC identified two alternative bases on which the Commission can take jurisdiction: implementation and qualified effects, both of which are justified under international law (paragraph 236), so that is sufficient to establish either the qualified effects of the practice in the EU or that it was implemented in the EU (paragraph 244). If qualified effects are established it is not necessary to also establish that the conduct was implemented in the EU although 'for the sake of completeness' the GC did do that.[116] Conversely, where jurisdiction can be established on the basis of implementation it is unnecessary to examine if there are any effects.[117]

c. *The* Intel *Case in the Court of Justice*

Intel appealed to the CJ from the GC on a number of grounds, including the jurisdiction issue. Advocate General Wahl thoroughly analysed the jurisdiction issue.[118] Although he approved both the implementation and qualified effects doctrines, he considered that neither justified taking jurisdiction here. Intel's abuse could not be characterised as having been implemented, executed, or put into effect in the internal market, and the effects were hypothetical, speculative, and unsubstantiated rather than immediate, substantial, and foreseeable.[119]

[109] The GC seems to use 'immediate' and 'direct' synonymously, although in para. 234 it mentions both together.
[110] Case 286/09, *Intel* EU:T:2014:547, paras. 259–296. [111] Ibid., para. 279. [112] Ibid., paras. 261–262.
[113] Ibid., para. 251. [114] Ibid., para. 275. [115] Ibid., paras. 267–272. [116] Ibid., paras. 297–314.
[117] Case T-286/09, *Intel v Commission* EU:T:2014:547, para. 238.
[118] Case C-413/14 P, *Intel Corp v Commission* EU:C:2016:788, paras. 280–327.
[119] Ibid., paras. 313 and 324.

The Grand Chamber of the CJ did not follow the Advocate General. It held that the qualified effects test could serve as a basis for jurisdiction and that the conditions for its application were fulfilled. It did not examine the application of the implementation test.[120]

Case C-413/14 P, *Intel Corporation v Commission* EU:C:2017:632

Court of Justice

40. The General Court, in paragraph 244 of the judgment under appeal, held that the Commission's jurisdiction under public international law to find and punish conduct adopted outside the European Union may be established on the basis of either the implementation test or the qualified effects test, before assessing the Commission's jurisdiction in the present case in the light of the qualified effects test and then, in the alternative, in the light of the implementation test.

41. In that context, it is appropriate to examine, in the first place, the argument put forward by Intel and ACT that the General Court wrongly accepted that the qualified effects test may serve as a basis for the Commission's jurisdiction.

42. In that respect, it must be borne in mind that, as the Advocate General noted in point 288 of his Opinion, the EU competition rules set out in Articles 101 and 102 TFEU are intended to prevent collective or unilateral conduct of undertakings limiting competition within the internal market. While Article 101 TFEU prohibits agreements and practices which have as their object or effect the prevention, restriction or distortion of competition 'within the internal market', Article 102 TFEU prohibits the abuse of a dominant position 'within the internal market or in a substantial part of it'.

43. Thus, the Court has held, as regards the application of Article 101 TFEU, that the fact that an undertaking participating in an agreement is situated in a third country does not prevent the application of that provision if that agreement is operative on the territory of the internal market (judgment of 25 November 1971, *Béguelin Import*, 22/71, . . ., paragraph 11).

44. Moreover, it must be noted that, in order to justify the application of the implementation test, the Court has emphasised that if the applicability of prohibitions laid down under competition law were made to depend on the place where the agreement, decision or concerted practice was formed, the result would obviously be to give undertakings an easy means of evading those prohibitions (see, by analogy, judgment of 27 September 1988, *Ahlström Osakeyhtiö and Others* v *Commission*, 89/85, . . ., paragraph 16).

45. The qualified effects test pursues the same objective, namely preventing conduct which, while not adopted within the EU, has anticompetitive effects liable to have an impact on the EU market.

46. The argument put forward by Intel, supported by ACT, that the qualified effects test cannot serve as a basis for the Commission's jurisdiction is therefore incorrect.

The Court then briefly examined the GC's finding of foreseeable, immediate, and substantial effects. It said that in order to determine whether the conditions were fulfilled, the conduct had to be viewed as a whole. It said that the GC had rightly held that it is sufficient to take account of the probable effects of conduct on competition in order for the foreseeability criterion to be satisfied.[121] As Intel's conduct vis-à-vis Lenovo formed part of an overall strategy to ensure that no Lenovo notebook equipped with its rival's CPU would be available on the market, the GC did not err in finding that it was capable of producing an immediate effect in the EEA.[122] The GC was also right in holding the effects to be substantial by considering the conduct as a whole and as part of an overall strategy.[123]

[120] Because the GC had considered it only for the sake of completeness, EU:C:2017:632, paras. 62–63.

[121] EU:C:2017:632, para. 51. [122] Ibid., para. 52. [123] Ibid., paras. 54–58.

Thus, after 45 years of pushing by the Commission and recommendations by Advocates General the CJ finally and unequivocally embraced the qualified effects doctrine as a basis for jurisdiction in EU law. It did so in the most anti-climactic manner possible. There was no extensive discussion or analysis. Just a one-sentence paragraph it which it said that the argument that the qualified effects test could not serve as a basis for jurisdiction was incorrect. The only explanation was that the qualified effects test serves the same objective as the implementation test.

In looking at the 'foreseeable, immediate and substantial' criteria, the CJ was undemanding. The GC had upheld a Commission decision in which conduct that was engaged in outside the EU and might indirectly prevent a fairly negligible number of products from being marketed in the EU was found to satisfy the conditions. The CJ, contrary to the advice of the Advocate General, just nodded that through. Now that the qualified effects doctrine is established as part of EU law the focus should turn to the question of whether it should be applied more stringently.[124]

The qualified effects test was applied again in the *International Skating Union* case, the facts of which are given in Chapter 2.[125] One of the grounds of the appeal by the ISU against the Commission decision that its Eligibility Rules infringed Article 101(1) by object was that the Dubai Grand Prix was not taking place within the EEA and that the ISU's actions were therefore outside the territorial scope of Article 101(1). The GC held that the decision was not really aimed at the Dubai event, and that the Commission had merely used that as an illustration of what was wrong with the ISU rules. However, the GC cited *Intel* and said that the qualified effects conditions were, in any case, satisfied here:

> . . . it must be held that, in view in particular of the severe and disproportionate penalties provided for in the event of the participation of skaters in events not authorised by the applicant and the absence of objective, transparent, non-discriminatory and verifiable authorisation criteria, the applicant's eligibility rules prevent skaters from offering their services to organisers of international speed skating events not authorised by the applicant and, therefore, prevent those organisers from using their services for competing events within or outside the EEA. Consequently, the eligibility rules are capable of producing immediate, substantial and foreseeable effects in the territory of the European Union within the meaning of the case-law referred to in paragraph 125 above. Accordingly, the Commission was entitled in the present case to adopt the contested decision and that decision was not adopted in breach of the territorial scope of Article 101 TFEU.[126]

E. JURISDICTION AND PRIVATE LITIGATION

We discuss private enforcement of EU competition law in Chapter 14. The issue of the territorial scope of Articles 101 and 102 arises in respect of private actions as well as of public enforcement and the question is whether the same jurisdiction principles apply in public and private actions.[127] The Advocate General in *Intel* expressly limited his consideration of jurisdiction to public enforcement.[128]

The problem is illustrated by actions in the UK courts for damages in respect of the associated *LCD* and *CRT* cartels.[129] The Commission found that prices of CDs and CRTs were fixed by a manufacturers' cartel in East Asia. The cartelised products were sold to manufacturers of TVs and monitors in

[124] See further P. Huizing, 'The ECJ Finally Accepts the Qualified Effects Test: Now Was That So Hard?' [2018] *ECLR* 24.

[125] Case T-93/18, *International Skating Union v Commission* EU:T:2020:610, on appeal, Case C-124/21 P, judgment pending, see Chap. 2, Section 7.F.

[126] Ibid., para.129.

[127] See in the US, *US v Hui Hsiung*, 778 F.3d. 738 (9th Cir. 2015) and *Motorola Mobility v AU Optronics*, 775 F.3d 816 (2015), noted in Section 4.D, n. 53, where criminal enforcement and private actions have been treated differently.

[128] Case C-413/14 P, *Intel Corp v Commission* EU:C:2016:788, para. 287.

[129] COMP/39.309, *LCD*, 8 December 2010; AT/39.437, *TV and Computer Monitor Tubes—CRT*, 5 December 2012.

Asia and the finished products were then exported, inter alia into the EEA. *iiyama*, a Japanese television and computer monitor distributor bought the finished products and sold them via intra-group transfers to its European subsidiaries. It claimed damages arising from the purchase of products sold at an unlawful overcharge. In the High Court, its claims were contested on the grounds that as the cartelised components were first sold to third party entities outside the EEA any loss by iiyama was outside the territorial scope of Article 101. The Court of Appeal refused to strike out or summarily dismiss the claim on the jurisdiction ground.[130] Having examined the EU authorities, and on the basis of *Intel*, the court said that it could not exclude the possibility that there were qualified effects in the EEA. The court was referred to the US *Motorola* case but said that although the qualified effects doctrine originated in the US it was by no means certain that the test would be applied the same way under EU law.[131]

F. ENFORCEMENT JURISDICTION

In many cases, problems of enforcement jurisdiction against non-EU undertakings may be avoided by the single economic entity doctrine. Requests and demands for information under Regulation 1/2003, Article 18 may be addressed to the branch or subsidiary of a non-EU undertaking which is situated within the EU and final decisions may be served on and enforced against EU subsidiaries, as was done in *Dyestuffs*.[132]

It appears that a statement of objections (SO) may be served on a branch or subsidiary within the EU.[133] However, it is sufficient for the purposes of EU law for the Commission to send the SO in a registered letter by post direct to the non-EU undertaking's address outside the EU. The CJ merely requires that the undertaking receives the SO in circumstances which enable it to take cognisance of the case against it.[134]

Matters are more difficult where the Commission cannot rely on the single economic entity doctrine. There appears to be no objection to sending an Article 18(2) request for information to an undertaking outside the EU as it does not entail any element of compulsion but it is otherwise with an Article 18(3) demand by decision and the better view is that the Commission cannot do this,[135] although it is permissible for the Commission to require information from an undertaking in a Member State pertaining to a period before that Member State acceded to the EU.[136] It is generally thought inconceivable that the Commission could mount an Article 20 or 21 inspection outside the EU although it might ask the competition authorities in a non-Member State for help in its investigation. If a trade association has a presence in the EU it cannot resist an Article 20 inspection on the grounds that some of its members are outside the EU.[137] As with an SO, a final decision may be served

[130] *iiyama v Samsung* [2018] EWCA Civ 220.

[131] Ibid., para. 105. The case was referred to the Competition Appeal Tribunal but was withdrawn by consent in March 2020 (Case 1333/5/7/19(T)). See also *Granville Technology Group Ltd v Infineon Technologies AG* [2020] EWHC 415 (Comm), paras. 94–108.

[132] Case 48/69, *Dyestuffs* EU:C:1972:70.

[133] C. Kerse and N. Khan (Khan ed.), *EU Antitrust Procedure* (6th edn, Sweet & Maxwell, 2012), 4-023.

[134] Case 52/69, *Geigy v Commission* EU:C:1972:73 (one of the *Dyestuffs* cases). The SO was sent to Geigy's address in Switzerland. Geigy returned it arguing that this infringed both Swiss and public international law and thus vitiated the proceedings. The CJ rejected this.

[135] Art. 18(5) provides for a copy of both an Art. 18(2) request and an Art.18(3) decision to be forwarded to the NCA of the Member State in which the undertaking's seat is situated, which would be impossible in the case of a non-EU undertaking, but this would not necessarily affect the possibility of using Art. 18(2) given the lack of coercion.

[136] Cases T-458/09 and T-171/10, *Slovak Telecom v Commission* EU:T:2012:145, para. 134.

[137] *Ukwal* [1992] OJ L121/45.

directly on a non-EU undertaking and it is sufficient that the undertaking receives it and can take cognisance of it, even if it returns it without reading it.[138] Whilst decisions imposing fines can be sent to undertakings outside the EU[139] they cannot be enforced unless the undertaking has assets inside the EU which can be seized.

6. INTERNATIONAL COOPERATION

A. GENERAL

International agreements provide at least a partial solution to some of the problems of the application and enforcement of competition laws in the globalised economy. Agreements in place at present are mainly bilateral ones between major trading partners, but there are also some multilateral regional trading arrangements which contain competition provisions.[140]

National competition agencies often cooperate with each other closely. In its 2014 Competition Report, the Commission stated that it currently worked with agencies outside the EU in 64 per cent of its abuse of dominance cases, 58 per cent of its complex merger investigations, and 78 per cent of cartel decisions. In merger cases, where the Commission normally tries to establish contact with the relevant other authorities as soon as it becomes aware that approval will also be required in other jurisdictions, it is standard practice for the Commission to ask the parties for a confidentiality waiver, to allow the agencies to exchange information. The parties are normally happy to agree in order to smooth the path of the transaction.[141]

Broadly, the EU enters into two types of bilateral agreements. 'Dedicated' agreements are those dealing solely with competition. The others are those where the provisions on competition are part of a wider agreement on trade.[142]

B. EU BILATERAL AGREEMENTS

(i) EU–US Cooperation

a. The 1991 and 1998 Cooperation Agreements

In 1991, the Commission concluded an agreement with the US authorities on cooperation over the enforcement of their competition laws.[143]

[138] Case 6/72, *Europemballage Corp and Continental Can Co Inc v Commission* EU:C:1973:22.

[139] As happened in, e.g., *Wood Pulp* [1985] OJ L85/1.

[140] See C. Noonan, *The Emerging Principles of International Competition Law* (Oxford University Press, 2008), 13.2.3.

[141] See J. Faull and A. Nikpay (eds.), *The EU Law of Competition* (3rd edn, Oxford University Press, 2014), 5.318–5.330. See in particular the relationship with the US agencies, Section B.

[142] See the tables at <https://competition-policy.ec.europa.eu/international/bilateral-relations_en>. There are special arrangements for countries that are candidates for Accession.

[143] Agreement between the Government of the US and the Commission of the European Communities regarding the application of their Competition Laws, 23 September 1991. The Commission's authority to enter into the agreement was challenged by France, supported by Spain and the Netherlands, and the CJ found that the Commission did not have the power to conclude (as distinct from negotiate) agreements with foreign countries, Case C-327/91, *France v Commission* EU:C:1994:305. The agreement was finally approved by a joint decision of the Council and Commission in 1995, [1995] OJ L95/47. For a reflection on the state of cooperation with the US in 2021, see Executive Vice-President Vestager's speech at the Fordham International Conference, 1 October 2021, <https://ec.europa.eu/commission/commissioners/2019–2024/vestager/announcements/evp-margrethe-vestagers-speech-fordham-international-antitrust-law-and-policy-conference-new-york-1_en>.

The Agreement provides for: the reciprocal notification of cases under investigation by either authority, where they may affect the important interests of the other party (Article II); exchanges of information and periodic meetings between competition officials from each country (Article III); and rendering each other assistance and coordinating their enforcement activities (Article IV). Article V is the 'positive comity' Article, providing the possibility for one authority to request the other to take enforcement action, and Article VI provides for 'traditional' or 'negative' comity, i.e. for each authority to take into account the important interests of the other in the course of its enforcement activities.

The Competition Commissioner said that this amounted to 'a commitment by the EU and the USA to cooperate with respect to antitrust enforcement, and not to act unilaterally and extraterritorially unless the avenues provided by comity have been exhausted'.[144]

The parties strengthened the positive comity provisions by the 1998 EU–US Positive Comity Agreement.[145] This spells out more clearly the circumstances in which a request for positive comity will be made and the manner in which such requests should be treated (Article III). Article IV provides for investigations by the requesting party to be deferred or suspended in reliance on the requested party's enforcement. The effect of the 1998 Agreement is to create a presumption that 'when anti-competitive activities occur in the whole or in a substantial part of the territory of one of the parties and affect the interests of the other party, the latter will normally defer or suspend its enforcement activities in favour of' the former, particularly when these anti-competitive activities do not have a direct, substantial, and reasonably foreseeable impact on consumers in the territory of the party deferring or suspending its activities.[146]

The 1998 Agreement represents a commitment on the part of the EU and the US to cooperate with respect to antitrust enforcement in certain situations, rather than to seek to apply their antitrust laws extraterritorially.

b. *The Application of the Agreements*

The EU and US authorities consider that their cooperation has made a positive contribution to competition law enforcement. The authorities have a close relationship. The 1991 procedures worked particularly successfully, for example, in respect of the investigation into Microsoft in 1994.[147] One drawback in the operation of the agreement is that Articles VII of the 1991 Agreement and V of the 1998 Agreement provide for the maintenance of the confidentiality of information acquired by the authorities in the course of their investigations. Further, Articles IX and VII respectively provide that nothing in the Agreements is to be interpreted in a manner which is inconsistent with the parties' existing laws. This limits the information which the authorities may exchange although, as already mentioned, in merger cases particularly the parties normally agree to confidentiality waivers. In the 1994 Microsoft investigation, the undertaking was happy to have the US and EU investigations combined as it was easier for the company to deal with the two authorities together, so it agreed to waive its rights to confidentiality and to allow information exchanges between the Commission and the DOJ. The EU's 2013 cooperation agreement with Switzerland was innovative in enabling the competition authorities to exchange information.

144 Commission's *XXVIIth Report on Competition Policy* (1998), foreword, 5.
145 [1998] OJ L173/28. 146 Commission's *XXVIIIth Report on Competition Policy* (1998), 315.
147 Although because of the case brought by France (see n. 143) the agreement was not officially in force.

The existence of the EU–US cooperation agreement did not prevent the 1997 dispute over the *Boeing/McDonnell Douglas* merger[148] or the *GE/Honeywell* row.[149] In *Boeing/McDonnell Douglas*, for instance, the authorities did consult each other. In accordance with the provisions of the Agreement, the Commission and the FTC carried out the necessary notifications and consultations, and the Commission took into account the US concerns over its defence interests. In the end, however, as the Director General recognised, '[p]rocedures of notification and consultation and the principles of traditional and positive comity allow us to bring our respective approaches closer in cases of common interest but there exist[s] no mechanism for resolving conflicts in cases of substantial divergence of analysis'.[150] Nevertheless, cases of conflict between the EU and US are rare.

c. *Merger Best Practices*

As the EU merger rules do not allow for the deferral or suspension of action which the 1998 Agreement envisages, the EU merger rules are not within it.[151] However, the EU and US have established a merger working group which has adopted a set of 'Best Practices' on cooperation in merger investigations where the same transaction is being investigated in both jurisdictions.[152] When adopting the 2002 Merger Best Practices the authorities recognised that 'cooperation is most effective when the investigation timetables of the reviewing agencies run more or less in parallel'. The 2011 Best Practices[153] state that 'cooperation between DG Competition and the US agencies is beneficial not only for the agencies, but also for merging parties and third parties, as it increases the efficiency of the respective investigations, reduces the burden on merging parties and third parties, and increases the overall transparency of the merger review process'.[154] Best Practices encourages undertakings to allow the EU and US agencies to exchange information which they have submitted during the course of an investigation and to allow joint EU/US interviews. The document identifies key points at which consultations between the agencies are likely to be particularly useful and says that consultations between senior officials in the respective agencies may be appropriate at any time.

d. *Joint Technology Competition Policy Dialogue*

In June 2021, the Commission President and President Biden launched the EU–US Trade and Technology Council, to serve as a forum for the EU and US to coordinate approaches to key global trade, economic, and technology issues.[155] Pursuant to this, in December 2021 the Commission, the FTC, and the DOJ Antitrust Division[156] launched the Joint Technology Competition Policy Dialogue

[148] M.877 [1997] OJ L336/16, see Chap. 15, Section 8.A. See further A. Bavasso, 'Boeing/McDonnell Douglas: Did the Commission Fly Too High?' [1998] *ECLR* 243; A. Schaub, 'International Co-operation in Antitrust Matters: Making the Point in the Wake of the Boeing/MDD Proceedings' (1998) 1 *Competition Policy Newsletter* 2, 3–4; B. Bishop, 'Editorial, The Boeing/McDonnell Douglas Merger' [1997] *ECLR* 417; A. Kaczorowska, 'International Competition Law in the Context of Global Capitalism' [2000] *ECLR* 117, 118. A. Burnside, 'GE, Honey I Sank the Merger' [2002] *ECLR* 107; D. Giotakos, L. Petit, G. Garnier, and P. De Luyck, '*GE/Honeywell*—An Insight into the Commission's Investigation and Decision' (2001) 3 *Competition Policy Newsletter* 5.

[149] M.2220 upheld by the GC, Case T-210/01, *General Electric v Commission* EU:T:2005:456, see Chap. 15; see A. Burnside, 'GE, Honey I Sank the Merger' [2002] *ECLR* 107; D. Giotakos, L. Petit, G. Garnier, and P. De Luyck, '*GE/Honeywell*—An Insight into the Commission's Investigation and Decision' (2001) 3 *Competition Policy Newsletter* 5.

[150] Schaub, n. 148.

[151] Art. II(4)(a).

[152] 2002, revised in 2011, <http://ec.europa.eu/competition/mergers/legislation/international_cooperation.html>.

[153] See <http://ec.europa.eu/competition/mergers/legislation/best_practices_2011_en.pdf>.

[154] Ibid., para. 1.2.

[155] IP/21/2990, <https://ec.europa.eu/commission/presscorner/detail/en/ip_21_2990>.

[156] For the US antitrust institutions, see Chap. 1 Section 8.

(TCPD) to develop common approaches and strengthen cooperation on competition policy and enforcement in the technology sector.[157] The TCPD held its second meeting in October 2022.[158]

(ii) Other Dedicated Bilateral Competition Cooperation Agreements

Encouraged by the success of its agreement with the US, the EU entered into a similar agreement with Canada in 1999. It has subsequently entered into dedicated agreements with a number of States: Japan (2003), Morocco (2004), Brazil (2009), Korea (2009), Russia (2011), India (2013), Switzerland (2014), South Africa (2016), and Mexico (2018).

In respect of China, an agreement on a EU–China competition policy dialogue was reached in 2004. After a number of other steps[159] a Memorandum of Understanding on a dialogue in the area of State aid control and what in China is called the 'Fair Competition Review System', together with new Terms of Reference for the dialogue, were agreed in April 2019 between DG Comp and the current Chinese agency, the State Administration for Market Regulation.[160] The Terms of Reference are the basis for two sets of Practical Guidance agreed at the same time, one on merger cooperation and the other on cooperation in investigating antitrust cases.

(iii) Other Bilateral Cooperation Arrangements

The EU enters into bilateral trade and development agreements with many countries, including developing countries and/or those with economies in transition. It is usual for these to contain competition provisions and/or (where relevant) to provide for the adoption by the other party of competition rules. There are certain groups of agreements containing similar provisions, such as agreements with candidate countries or countries of the Western Balkans (Stabilization and Association Agreements and Euro-Mediterranean Agreements) establishing an association with countries of the southern Mediterranean.

The African Caribbean and Pacific (ACP) agreement (the Cotonou Agreement) between the EU and over 70 ACP countries, replaced the Lomé Agreement. It came into force in 2003 for 20 years. It contained provisions on political cooperation, trade links, and development assistance and also a provision on competition, Article 45. In 2022, its replacement was held up by Hungary's objections to the migration provisions and transitional provisions extended it to June 2023.[161]

In some cases, there are competition provisions in trade arrangements despite there also being dedicated competition agreements. This is so, for example, in respect of the EU–Canada Comprehensive and Economic Trade Agreement, 2017[162] and the EU–Japan Economic Partnership Agreement of 2019.[163]

In respect of the UK, there are references to competition in the UK Withdrawal Agreement 2021[164] and provisions on cooperation in competition law in the Trade and Cooperation Agreement 2020.[165] Article 361 of the latter contains a provision on exchanging information to the extent their laws allow.

The texts of all bilateral agreements are available on the Commission's website.[166]

[157] IP/21/6671, <https://ec.europa.eu/commission/presscorner/detail/en/IP_21_6671>.

[158] IP/22/6167, <https://ec.europa.eu/commission/presscorner/detail/en/ip_22_6167>.

[159] Including Practical Guidance for Merger Cooperation in 2015, and a Memorandum of Understanding in 2017.

[160] The aim of both the State aid control regime and Fair Competition Review System are stated in the Memorandum to be 'to prevent public policies from distorting and restricting competition while maintaining fair market competition and promoting a unified market'. See <https://competition-policy.ec.europa.eu/system/files/2021-06/China-EU_memorandum-of-understanding_2019_en.pdf>.

[161] Decision 1/2022 of the ACP–EU Committee of Ambassadors [2022] OJ L176/88.

[162] Chap. 17; <http://ec.europa.eu/trade/policy/in-focus/ceta/ceta-chapter-by-chapter/>.

[163] Chap. 11, which refers to the 2003 Agreement, see <http://trade.ec.europa.eu/doclib/docs/2018/august/tradoc_157228.pdf#page=333>.

[164] [2019] OJ C 384/1.

[165] [2021] L149/10.

[166] <http://ec.europa.eu/competition/international/bilateral/>.

C. MULTILATERAL COOPERATION

(i) General

There are now well over a hundred countries in the world with some form of competition laws—the International Competition Network (ICN) has 140 members from 130 jurisdictions. Many countries have adopted competition laws under pressure from, or under the influence of, the EU, often as a result of bilateral trade agreements.[167] US law has been influential but it is the EU system which is the more commonly copied. This is not only because of pressure from the EU but because other countries prefer to adopt a public enforcement system rather than the US litigation model which is the product of a particular and singular legal system. One distinguished American commentator considers that the EU model has 'trumped' the US as the model for the world because it resonates with developing and transitional countries as it deals with the emergence from statism and with the development of a single market while displaying qualities such as openness, transparency, and non-discrimination. Moreover, the ECN provides a model of how regional cooperation in competition policy can work.[168]

There is a continuing discourse about the suitable form and content of competition laws for developing and transitional economies and the way in which both the substantive and procedural rules need to take account of local political and cultural conditions.[169] The US adherence to the Chicago School principle of efficiency has not been widely adopted by other countries and it has been shown that the EU, with its more nuanced and multifaceted approach, has been more influential.[170] Many competition laws have explicit socio-political goals, are expressly put at the service of industrial policies, or are given specific public interest tasks. For example, South Africa's competition law has six purposes, one of which is 'to promote the greater spread of ownership, in particular to increase the ownership stakes of historically disadvantaged persons';[171] and China's competition law is stated to be enacted for the purpose, inter alia, of 'promoting the healthy development of the socialist market economy'.[172] However, most systems of competition law include the three core elements of provisions on restrictive agreements, dominant firms/monopolies, and mergers.[173] There is considerable convergence on restrictive agreements (with universal hostility to cartels), less on mergers, and much less on dominant firms, where some systems are greatly concerned with excessive pricing and many take issue with unilateral conduct at significantly lower market share levels than does the EU. The idea of an international competition law regime, therefore, although much discussed, is not currently any type of possibility. There are, however, initiatives within various international fora aimed at formulating mechanisms for increasing cooperation over competition laws and avoiding conflicts. These have led to more convergence on procedural and institutional matters and are briefly described here.

[167] International bodies such as the IMF have also played a role, on occasion making loans conditional on the adoption of competition rules (e.g. Indonesia).

[168] Professor Eleanor Fox speaking at the EU Competition Forum, 2 February 2012.

[169] See Gerard and Lianos, n. 54; for an interesting discussion of the relationship between Islam and competition law and policy, for example, see M. Dabbah, *Competition Law and Policy in the Middle East* (Cambridge University Press, 2007), Chap. 2.

[170] A. Bradford, A. Chilton, C. Megaw, and N. Sokol, 'Competition Law Gone Global: Introducing the Comparative Competition Law and Enforcement Datasets' (2019) 16(2) *J of Empirical Legal Studies* 411; A. Bradford, A. S. Chilton, and F. M. Lancieri, 'The Chicago School's Limited Influence on International Antitrust' (2020) 87(2) *U Chic LR* 297.

[171] Competition Act no. 89 of 1998, s. 2(f).

[172] Anti-Monopoly Law, Art. 1. And see the further examples on national provisions given in A. Ezrachi, 'Sponge' (2017) 5 *J of Antitrust Enforcement* 49, 56–59.

[173] See B. Hawk, *Antitrust and Competition Laws* (Juris, 2020), Chap. 5.

(ii) UNCTAD

The United Nations' Set of Multilaterally Agreed Equitable Principles and Rules for the Control of Restrictive Business Practices were adopted in 1980 under the auspices of UNCTAD[174] but provide only a voluntary, non-binding Code.

(iii) OECD

In 1967, the OECD (Organisation for Economic Co-operation and Development) adopted a Recommendation that its member countries should cooperate with each other in the enforcement of their national competition laws.[175] This provides: for one country to notify another when the latter's important interests are affected by the former's investigation or enforcement; for countries to share information and to consult; for them to coordinate parallel investigations; for countries to assist one another in obtaining information inside each other's territory; and for countries to consider dealing with anti-competitive behaviour affecting their interests but occurring in another country's territory by requesting the latter's authorities to take action (positive comity). The bilateral agreements described in Section 6.B reflect these provisions but the 1991 EC–US Agreement was the first to include the 'positive comity' principle. In May 1998, the OECD Committee of Competition Law and Policy adopted a recommendation on hardcore cartels, aimed at strengthening the effectiveness and efficiency of the member countries' enforcement of their competition laws against such cartels.[176] In 2006, the OECD issued a report, 'Competition Law and Policy in the EU'.[177] The Commission cooperates closely with the competition authorities of other OECD member countries based on the 1995 OECD recommendation. There is a direct link from the Commission website to the OECD Competition Committee.[178] The Competition Committee holds regular Roundtable meetings to which the Commission contributes and its submissions to the Working Parties are available on the website.[179] A Roundtable was held in 2017 on the 'Extraterritorial Reach of Competition Remedies' and in 2022 it held an event on market power in the digital economy. The OECD 'soft law' instruments are both effective and influential.

(iv) The WTO

When the WTO was being negotiated in 1993 a Draft International Antitrust Code was drawn up by a group of experts at the Max Planck Institute. This would have established an international antitrust regime.[180] The parties to the WTO did not agree to its adoption, however, and no agreement on international competition law was annexed to the WTO Charter. Promoted by the EU, the matter was later taken up at the First Ministerial Conference of the parties to the WTO in Singapore in 1996 and a Working Group on Trade and Competition Policy was set up in 1997. From 1997 to 2004 there were strenuous efforts to adopt some type of competition framework within the WTO but these collapsed

[174] The United Nations Conference on Trade and Development.

[175] Amended, inter alia, in 1995: OECD Doc. C(95)130/FINAL.

[176] OECD C(98)35/final, 25 March 1998.

[177] Available on the Commission's website, <http://ec.europa.eu/competition/international/multilateral/oecd.html>, and on the OECD website, <www.oecd.org/dataoecd/7/41/35908641.pdf>.

[178] <www.oecd.org/competition>.

[179] <http://ec.europa.eu/competition/international/multilateral/oecd_submissions.html>.

[180] For the details, see C. Cocuzza and M. Montini, 'International Antitrust Co-operation in a Global Economy' [1998] *ECLR* 156, 160–161; E. U. Petersmann, 'International Competition Rules for Governments and for Private Business' (1996) 30 *J of World Trade* 5.

at the Fifth Ministerial Conference at Cancun in 2003.[181] There were complex reasons for this.[182] The agricultural subsidies offered by the EU and the US Government to their home producers were a cause of dissension and some developing countries had become unhappy with 'free trade' as a remedy for the world's ills. The WTO, like the World Bank, was seen in many quarters as part of the problem, not the remedy. In 2004, the General Council of the WTO abandoned any attempt to work on a set of antitrust rules.[183] It appears that this was partly due to the fears of the smaller or developing nations that the rules would be based on those of the US or EU and would interfere with their industrial policy or socio-political goals, but the marked reluctance of the US, worried about the dilution of its system and unwilling to subordinate it to an international body, was also a factor.[184]

(v) The International Competition Network

While attempts to establish a competition regime in the WTO ran into difficulties, competition authorities from around the world quietly got on with establishing procedures and mechanisms through which they cooperate. In October 2001, the International Competition Network was established, with the EU as a founder member.[185] The impetus came from the US ICPAC report (International Competition Policy Advisory Committee) in 2000.[186] According to its website,[187] the 'ICN's mission is to advocate the adoption of superior standards and procedures in competition policy around the world, formulate proposals for procedural and substantive convergence, and seek to facilitate effective international cooperation to the benefit of member agencies, consumers and economies worldwide'.

The ICN has proved a useful and productive organisation. It has five active working groups including the Merger Working Group, which has adopted 'guiding principles and recommended practices' which competition authorities should abide by when analysing mergers across several jurisdictions; and the Cartels Working Group, which organises annual cartel workshops and has produced a number of reports on anti-cartel policy and a cartel enforcement manual, including a template for ICN member agencies to set out their rules governing cartel enforcement.[188]

This 'soft law' harmonisation is highly effective and the ICN is a particularly valuable resource for competition agencies from developing countries and those which have only recently adopted competition laws. It is open to national and multinational organisations responsible for the enforcement of competition law. However, the competition authority of China has never been a member (despite its bilateral agreement with the European Commission[189]) and in March 2022 the ICN entered the political arena when the chair suspended the Russian authority, the Federal Antimonopoly Service, from participation.

[181] See F. Jenny, 'WTO Core Principles and Trade/Competition, Policies' [2003] *Fordham Corp L Inst* 703.

[182] See F. Jenny, 'Competition Trade and Development Before and After Cancun' [2003] *Fordham Corp L Inst* 631. And see W. Pape, 'Socio-cultural Differences and International Competition Law' (1999) 5 *European Law Journal* 438 for the argument that it is essential to take account of socio-cultural divergences in any set of competition rules which are adopted at an international level.

[183] Doha Work Programme Decision, 1 August 2004.

[184] See E. Elhauge and D. Geradin, *Global Competition Law and Economics* (2nd edn, Hart Publishing, 2011) 1242–1247, for a discussion of this.

[185] P. Lugard and D. Anderson, (eds.), *The International Competition Network at Twenty* (Concurrences, 2022).

[186] US DOJ: available at <www.justice.gov/atr/final-report>.

[187] <www.internationalcompetitionnetwork.org>.

[188] The others are Agency Effectiveness, Advocacy, and Unilateral Conduct.

[189] See Section 6.B.ii.

7. CONCLUSIONS

1. Traditional concepts of extraterritorial jurisdiction are being reinterpreted to deal with globalised trade, more multinational companies, longer and more complex supply chains, and the fact that unilateral behaviour, international cartels, and international mergers have consequences which resound throughout the world. In the absence of an international competition law regime, national (or in the case of the EU, supranational) competition authorities (or courts) must find a way of protecting their jurisdiction from the anti-competitive effects of conduct and transactions originating outside their territory while remaining within the bounds of international law.

2. Some form of the effects doctrine, an offshoot of the objective territoriality principle for subject-matter (prescriptive) jurisdiction, has been adopted by many States. The effects doctrine was originally developed by the US and is now generally called the 'qualified effects' doctrine (or test), whereby a State takes jurisdiction over conduct originating outside its territory if it has effects within it which meet certain criteria.

3. An effects doctrine should be tempered by some form of 'comity', meaning that the State applying its law extraterritorially is sensitive to, and accommodating of, the interests of other States.

4. The US is an attractive jurisdiction in which to bring private damages actions for losses stemming from the activities of international cartels. The US Supreme Court is wary of the US acting as a world policeman and reluctant to impinge on the jurisdiction of other States with their own developed and fully functioning systems of competition law by too easily allowing foreign plaintiffs to sue in US courts.

5. In the EU, the CJ has unequivocally adopted the 'qualified effects' doctrine but the requirement that the effects must be foreseeable, immediate, and substantial, and the application of these conditions is likely to give rise to difficulty in specific cases.

6. Ideas for international competition regimes are unrealistic and overambitious and are not currently being pursued. The consequence of this is that powerful global corporations are only dealt with by separate, national authorities.

7. Bilateral agreements and friendly and cooperative relations between enforcers can work well. Much has been done to establish an international consensus on procedures. The most productive best way forward at present is through soft law instruments.

8. Competition laws are a global phenomenon. It is crucial to recognise the international dimensions of competition law and to see the EU system in a global perspective.

8. FURTHER READING

A. Books

COOK, P., FABELLA, R. V., and LEE, C. (eds.), *Competitive Advantage and Competition Policy in Developing Countries* (Edward Elgar, 2007)

CRAWFORD, J., *Brownlie's Principles of Public International Law* (9th edn, Oxford University Press, 2019), Chap. 21

DABBAH, M., *The Internationalisation of Antitrust Policy* (Cambridge University Press, 2003)

DABBAH, M., *Competition Law and Policy in the Middle East* (Cambridge University Press, 2007)

DABBAH, M., *International and Comparative Competition Law* (Cambridge University Press, 2010)

ELHAUGE, E., and GERADIN, D., *Global Competition Law and Economics* (2nd edn, Hart Publishing, 2011)

EPSTEIN, R., and GREVE, M. (eds.), *Competition Laws in Conflict: Antitrust Jurisdiction in a Global Economy* (AEI Press, 2004)

FURSE, M., *Antitrust Law in China, Korea and Vietnam* (Oxford University Press, 2009)

GAL, M., *Competition Policy for Small Market Economies* (Harvard University Press, 2003)

GERARD, D., and LIANOS, I. (eds.), *Reconciling Efficiency and Equity: A Global Challenge for Competition Policy* (Cambridge University Press, 2019)

GERBER, D., *Global Competition: Law, Markets, and Globalization* (Oxford University Press, 2010)

GUZMAN, A., (ed.), *Cooperation, Comity, and Competition Policy* (Oxford University Press, 2010)

HIGGINS, R., *Problems and Process: International Law and How We Use It* (Clarendon Press, 1994)

JENNINGS, R. Y., and WATTS, A. (eds.), *Oppenheim's International Law* (9th edn, Longman, 1992)

JONES, C. A., and MATSUSHITA, M., (eds.), *Competition Policy in the Global Trading System* (Kluwer, 2002)

KENNEDY, K., *Competition Law and the World Trade Organization: The Limits of Multilateralism* (Sweet & Maxwell, 2001)

LUGARD, P., and ANDERSON, D. (eds.), *The International Competition Network at Twenty* (Concurrences, 2022)

NOONAN, C., *The Emerging Principles of International Competition Law* (Oxford University Press, 2008)

OLMSTEAD C. (ed.), *Extra-territorial Application of Laws and Responses Thereto* (ESC Publishing, 1984), 156

PAPADOPOULOS, A., *The International Dimension of EU Competition Law and Policy* (Cambridge University Press, 2010)

RYNGAERT, C., *Jurisdiction in International Law* (Oxford University Press, 2008)

STIGLITZ, J., *Globalization and its Discontents Revisited* (Penguin, 2017)

ZÄCH, R., and HEINEMANN, A. (eds.), *The Development of Competition Law Global Perspectives* (Edward Elgar, 2010)

ZANETTIN, B., *Cooperation Between Antitrust Agencies at the International Level* (Hart Publishing, 2002)

B. Chapters in Books

SWAN, A. C., 'The Hartford Insurance Company Case; Antitrust in the Global Economy' in J. Bhandari and A. Sykes (eds.), *Economic Dimensions in International Law* (Cambridge University Press, 1997)

WOOD, D. P., 'The Trade Effects of Domestic Antitrust Enforcement' in J. Bhandari and A. Sykes (eds.), *Economic Dimensions in International Law* (Cambridge University Press, 1997)

C. Articles

AKEHURST, M., 'Jurisdiction in International Law' (1972–1973) 46 *BYIL* 145

BAVASSO, A., 'Boeing/McDonnell Douglas: Did the Commission Fly Too High?' [1998] *ECLR* 243

BISHOP, B., 'Editorial, The Boeing/McDonnell Douglas Merger' [1997] *ECLR* 417

Blockx, J. 'Competition Law in an Era of Deglobalization' [2022] 4 *Concurrences*

Botteman, Y., and Patsa, A., 'The Jurisdictional Reach of EU Anti-cartel Rules: Unmuddling the Limits' (2012) 8 *European Competition Journal* 365

Bowett, D. W., 'Jurisdiction: Changing Problems of Authority over Activities and Resources' (1982) 53 *BYIL* 1

Bradford, A., Chilton, A. S., and Lancieri, F. M., 'The Chicago School's Limited Influence on International Antitrust' (2020) 87(2) *U Chic LR* 297

Bradford, A., Chilton, A., Megaw, C., and Sokol, N., 'Competition Law Gone Global: Introducing the Comparative Competition Law and Enforcement Datasets' (2019) 16(2) *J of Empirical Legal Studies* 411

Burnside, A., 'GE, Honey I Sank the Merger' [2002] *ECLR* 107

Cocuzza, C., and Montini, M., 'International Antitrust Co-operation in a Global Economy' [1998] *ECLR* 156

Collins, L., 'Blocking and Clawback Statutes' [1986] *JBL* 372

Davidow, J., and Shapiro, C., 'The Feasibility and Worth of a WTO Competition Agreement' (2003) 37 *J of World Trade* 49

Ezrachi, A., 'Sponge' (2017) 5 *J of Antitrust Enforcement* 49

First, H., 'Digital Platforms and Competition Policy in Developing Countries' [2021] 2 *Concurrences* 1

Di Frederico, G., 'The New Anti-monopoly Law in China from a European Perspective' (2009) 32 *World Competition* 249

Durand, B., Font Galarza, A., and Mehta, K., 'The Interface Between Competition Policy and International Trade Liberalisation. Looking into the Future: Applying a New Virtual Anti-trust Standard' (2004) 27 *World Competition* 3

Fox, E., 'Towards World Antitrust and Market Access' (1997) 91 *AJIL* 1

Fox, E., 'The Merger Regulation and its Territorial Reach' [1999] *ECLR* 334

E. Fox, 'Remedies and the Courage of Convictions in a Globalized World: How Globalization Corrupts Relief' (2005) 80 *Tulane LR* 571

Gal, M., 'Antitrust in a Globalized Economy: The Unique Enforcement Challenges Faced by Small and Developing Jurisdictions' (2009) 33 *Fordham Int'l LJ* 1

Gal, M., 'Regional Competition Law Agreements: An Important Step for Antitrust Enforcement' (2010) 60 *U Toronto LJ* 239

Gerven, W. Van, 'EC Jurisdiction in Antitrust Matters: The *Wood Pulp* Judgment' [1989] *Fordham Corp L Inst* 451

Gerven, Y. Van, and Hoet, L., '*Gencor*: Some Notes on Transnational Competition Law Issues' (2001) 28 *LIEI* 195

Grewlich, A. S., 'Globalisation and Conflict in Competition Law' (2001) 24 *World Competition* 367

Griffin, J., 'Reactions to U.S. Assertions of Extraterritorial Jurisdiction' [1998] *ECLR* 64

Guzman, A., 'The Case for International Antitrust' (2004) 22 *Berkeley J of Int'l Law* 355

Hoffet, F., and Brei, G., 'The First and Second Generation Competition Enforcement Co-operation Treaty: Free Flow of Information Between Switzerland and the EU?' [2014] *ECLR* 157

Huizing, P., 'The ECJ Finally Accepts the Qualified Effects Test: Now Was That So Hard?' [2018] *ECLR* 24

JENNINGS, R. Y., 'Extraterritorial Jurisdiction and the United States Antitrust Laws' (1957) 33 *BYIL* 146

JENNY, F., 'Competition, Trade and Development Before and After Cancun' [2003] *Fordham Corp L Inst* 631

JENNY, F., 'Competition Law and Policy: Global Governance Issues' (2003) 26 *World Competition* 609

KACZOROWSKA, A., 'International Competition Law in the Context of Global Capitalism' [2000] *ECLR* 117

KEYTE, J., JENNY, F., and FOX, E.., 'Buckle Up: The Global Future of Antitrust Enforcement and Regulation' (Spring 2021) 35(2) *ABA Antitrust Magazine* 32

LANGE, D. F. G., and SANDAGE, J. B., 'The *Wood Pulp* Decision' (1989) 26 *CMLRev* 137

LIANOS, I., 'The Contribution of the United Nations to the Emergence of Global Antitrust Law' (2007) 15 *Tulane J of International and Comparative Law* 145

LIPSKY, JR., A. B., 'Competition and the WTO: Beyond Cancun' [2003] *Fordham Corp L Inst* 657

MANN, F. A., 'The Doctrine of Jurisdiction in International Law' (1964) 111 *RdC* 1

MANN, F. A., 'Casenote' (1973) 22 *ICLQ* 35

MANN, F. A., 'The Doctrine of International Jurisdiction Revisited After Twenty Years' (1984) 186 *RdC* 9

MEESSEN, K. M., 'Antitrust Jurisdiction under Customary International Law' (1984) 78 *AJIL* 783

MITCHELL, A. D., 'Broadening the Vision of Trade Liberalisation' (2001) 24 *World Competition* 367

MURRAY, S., 'With a Little Help from My Friends: How a US Judicial International Comity Balancing Test Can Foster Global Antitrust Private Redress' (2017) 41 *Fordham Int'l LJ* 227

PAPE, W., 'Socio-cultural Differences and International Competition Law' (1999) 5 *European Law Journal* 438

PARISI, J., 'Enforcement Co-operation Among Antitrust Authorities' [1999] *ECLR* 133

PETERSMANN, E. U., 'International Competition Rules for Governments and for Private Business' (1996) 30 *J of World Trade Law* 5

PETERSMANN, E. U., 'WTO Core Principles and Trade/Competition' [2003] *Fordham Corp L Inst* 669

PITOFSKY, R., 'Competition Policy in a Global Economy' (1999) 3 *JIEL* 403

REYNOLDS, R. M., SICILIAN, J., and WELLMAN, P. S., 'The Extraterritorial Application of the US Antitrust Laws to Criminal Conspiracies' [1998] *ECLR* 151

RITZENHOFF, L., 'Indirect Effect: Fine Calculation, Territorial Jurisdiction, and Double Jeopardy' (2015) 6 *JECLAP* 691

ROBERTSON, A., and DEMETRIOU, M., '"But That Was in Another Country": The Extraterritorial Application of US Antitrust Laws in the US Supreme Court' (1994) 43 *ICLQ* 417

ROTH, P. M., 'Reasonable Extraterritoriality: Correcting the "Balance of Interests"' (1992) 41 *ICLQ* 245

SLOT P. J., and GRABANDI, E., 'Extraterritoriality and Jurisdiction' (1986) 23 *CMLRev* 545

TAY, A., and WILLMAN, G., 'Why (No) Global Competition Policy is a Tough Choice' (2005) *Quarterly Rev of Economics and Finance* 312

TORREMANS, P., 'Extraterritorial Application of EC and US Competition Law' (1996) 21 *ELRev* 280

VANDERGRIFT, S., and LUCAS, J., 'The *GE/Honeywell* Saga? Ehh, What's Up Doc? A Comparative Approach Between US and EU Merger Control Proceedings Almost 15 Years Later' [2014] *ECLR* 172

WHELAN, P., 'Resisting the Long Arm of Criminal Antitrust Laws: *Norris v. US*' (2009) 72 *MLR* 272

WOOD, D. P., 'Soft Harmonization Among Competition Laws: Track Record and Prospects' (2003) 48 *Ant Bull* 305

INDEX

Tables and figures are indicated by an italic *t* and *f* following the page number.

A

I

J

T